Table of Contents

THE OLD TESTAMENT

THE NEW TESTAMENT

PRESENTED TO:

Helen

BY:

Mum & Dad

ON THIS DAY OF:

Christmas 2009

Letter from the Editors

Dear Reader:

Do you feel overwhelmed by the many roles you've been called to play in life? Whether you're single, married, or single again, you probably juggle a combination of many different daily duties. Husbands, kids, employers, and family members, not to mention church and community commitments, are common things that vie for our attention.

So how do you find time in the midst of it all to work on the role God created just for you? How do you become the someone God wants you to be in every area of your multifaceted life?

We can't clear your calendar or simplify your to-do list, and we know your quiet moments are few. But we pray that this devotional Bible will help you connect with God and will renew your heart as you spend time in the Scriptures.

Becoming: The Devotional Bible for Women addresses every issue women face in the twenty-first century, and the easy-to-read text of the New Century Version (NCV) ensures that you'll understand what the Bible has to say about the situations and decisions you're dealing with today. Along with both the Old and New Testaments, this Bible is packed with these supplemental materials:

- ***In-depth introductions to each Bible book***
  These introductions will fill you in on all the historical facts, but we've also packed these intros with lots of personal information on the author and original audience. Even if you're already familiar with the Bible, witnessing the real emotions of real people will help you read with fresh eyes.
- ***Stirring biographical narratives on fascinating women in the Bible***
  These character profiles take a look at fifty of the most well-known and influential women of the Bible. Through their mistakes and triumphs, you will find yourself identifying with these women in a whole new way. You may even be surprised to see a bit of yourself in their stories.
- ***365 daily devotionals drawing from the most beloved passages of Scripture***
  Connecting biblical teachings with contemporary life, these devotionals feature insightful writings from some of today's leading women in Christian discipleship. These readings will connect with your heart and your mind, pointing the way to becoming God's woman for today.
- ***Topical devotional studies written for women by women in today's culture***
  With questions to get you thinking and numerous passages for further investigation, these studies will help you dig deeper to find out what the Bible has to say about issues like beauty, weakness, divorce, parenting, and more!
- ***Topical index listing themes presented throughout the Bible***
  If you've ever wondered what the Bible has to say about a particular subject, but you've been unsure where to find what you need, this topical index will get you headed in the right direction. Our handy reference lists all of the daily devotionals, topical studies, and character profiles to provide quick answers to your questions.

Our deepest desire is to help you connect your faith with your daily life. We pray that through reading God's Word, you will be renewed in your spirit and more confident of who you are becoming in Christ.

THE EDITORS

P.S. If you'd like to find out more about connecting your faith and life, visit this great Web site where other people are learning more about who they are becoming in Christ—www.myfaithandlife.com!

Meet the Contributors

The following women contributed to *Becoming: The Devotional Bible for Women*:

Lisa Harper has been lauded as a master storyteller whose writing and speaking overflows with colorful characters and anecdotes bridging Bible times with today. Formerly the director of women's ministry at Focus on the Family, Lisa has authored several books including, *Holding Out for a Hero* and *What Every Girl Wants.* She lives near Nashville, Tennessee, where she's enrolled in seminary, actively pursuing a Masters of Biblical Studies . . . when she's not riding her Harley!

Lou M. Taylor is the president of Tri Star Sports and Entertainment Group, a business management firm that sows truth into the lives of the rich and famous. Lou delivers biblical truths that impact her clients' character, career, and finances—and influence pop culture because of it. It is truly an adventure being *in* the world but not *of* it. She has been married seventeen years to Rob Taylor, Pastor of Calvary Chapel in Brentwood, Tennessee.

Lisa West Tchividjian began her journey with God as a young child. She received her degree in elementary education and now enjoys teaching Bible studies for women, writing, and public speaking. Lisa is happily married to Stephan Tchividjian (eldest grandchild of Billy and Ruth Graham) who runs a private consulting firm. They enjoy co-teaching marriage retreats, serving on several boards of non-profit organizations, and raising their family of four children together.

Angela Thomas is an ordinary woman who is passionately pursuing God, even in the midst of long days of writing, traveling, and packing sack lunches for her four children. She's been honored to walk alongside women of all ages and walks of life through her best-selling books and speaking engagements. Angela would tell you that her heart's desire is to remain surrendered over the altar of God, becoming the woman he has always dreamed of.

Donna VanLiere is the *New York Times* and *USA Today* best-selling author of *The Christmas Hope* series. She loves to write stories and found writing about the women of the Bible extremely rewarding saying, "Whoever said the Bible is boring has never really read it!" Married with two children, Donna also enjoys acting and travels with Women of Faith as their dramatist.

Joy Williams is a young woman committed to living a life of loving others and God with a relevant, honest, and vulnerable spirit. She has a heart for people and for music and has traveled around the world with songs she's written for the last five years. She's a California girl who grew up surfing and sipping coffee with friends, and she now resides with her husband in Franklin, Tennessee.

We would like to offer special thanks to Angela Thomas for the creative shaping and content direction she offered to help us tailor this Bible's supplemental materials to best address the most pressing and common issues modern women are facing today.

Introduction

The story is told that many years ago, Art Linkletter saw a small boy scrawling wildly on a sheet of paper. "What are you drawing?" Linkletter asked.

"I'm drawing a picture of God."

"You can't do that, because nobody knows what God looks like."

"They will when I'm finished," the boy confidently replied.

As senseless as this story is, many of us have based our life beliefs on foundations no more solid than the young boy's drawing. It is no surprise that life's difficulties expose the lack of meaning in our lives and the inadequacy of our sources for answers to the questions of our hearts.

Let's face it, we all have questions in life. When you lay your head down on the pillow at night, what are the questions that you ask? When you're alone in the dark, do you find life's really hard questions running through your mind? *How can I find peace and true contentment? What is the purpose of life? Why am I here? Where have I come from, and where am I going? Is there a God, and if so, what is he like? Can I know God personally? Is there a source of ultimate truth for me to live by?*

Many of those questions relate to our faith and our own search for truth. For instance, who has not asked the question, "Why does God allow unthinkable acts of terrorism?" Or, "When my world seems to be falling apart around me, who can I trust?" Or, "What do I do with my fears?"

Throughout our lives, we all face a litany of questions that trouble our souls for answers grounded in the truth. *Can I mend a broken relationship? How far is too far when I'm dating? How can I cope with disappointment? Will my marriage survive hard times? Can I be forgiven for my sins? How do I nourish my child's heart? What is prayer? Is death really the end? What do I do with my spiritual doubts?*

So where do we find the answers? Must we end our days with the same questions staring us in the face? Can our questions be answered, and can we find the peace we are seeking?

We answer that with a resounding "Yes!" In your hands you hold what reveals the *real answers*—God's Word. The Bible is *the* most important book and the single most popular book ever written. Within its pages God speaks with divine instruction to multiple generations of people who faced the same life issues and questions that you face today. He reveals himself through his Word and presents the absolute truth that provides the only reliable answers to all of life's ultimate questions. It dares tackle those questions honestly and openly and offers counsel for our problems, comfort for our sorrows, guidance for our confusion, inspiration for our needs, and hope for our despair.

What Is the Bible About?

The Bible cannot be considered just a "crutch" that you can turn to when the pressures of life overwhelm you. It is a supernatural book that has survived and thrived through centuries of being scoffed at, ridiculed, and banned. Kings have branded it as illegal, and countless lives have been martyred because they had the courage to stand by its truths. For the millions and millions of people who have tested its answers to life's questions and found them true, there is only one conclusion—the Bible is God's book. Every word is inspired by him and reveals something very important about him. From these pages we hear the voice of God.

In reality, the Bible is a library of books. It contains sixty-six different books, which together tell the story of God's wonderful love for people. It teaches us how to live the way God wants us to live. The Bible reveals the truth about God, explains the origin of humankind, offers the only way to salvation and eternal life in Jesus Christ, and does not sidestep the ancient problem of sin and suffering. It's a book you'll want to read and study over and over again.

Who is the Bible for? Most of the books in the Old Testament were written for the Jewish people (also called Israelites). They were the nation God chose to be a part of bringing his Son into the world.

Books in the New Testament were written to many others. Sometimes the names of the books give you a clue. For instance, Paul wrote Romans to the Christians who live in Rome. He wrote Ephesians to the Christians at Ephesus. Other New Testament books were addressed to all of Christ's followers. These books were passed around from church to church for everyone to read and hear.

But wait! The Bible was written for you, too. Just as it told the Christians in the first century how to live for God, it tells the same to you, too. God's Word, the Bible, is a personal guide for everyone who wants to follow God. It's God's love letter just for you.

The Old Testament

The first section of the Bible begins with how God created the world. It tells the story of God's love for his people from the beginning until just before he sent his Son into the world. There are thirty-nine books in the Old Testament section of the Bible. We can divide them into even smaller sections and categorize them according to the specific purposes each book has.

Books of Law

The first five books of the Old Testament—Genesis, Exodus, Leviticus, Numbers, and Deuteronomy—are sometimes called the "Pentateuch," which simply means "five books." The Jews called these five books the "Torah." They are called Books of Law because they contain the many laws God gave to the Jewish people to keep them pure and holy. It was very important for them to stay pure because God would someday send his Son, Jesus, to us through this group of people. These were special laws for God's special people, and they reveal to us the extent of God's holiness. The Books of Law begin with the creation of the world and end with the people of Israel ready to enter the land God had promised to them.

Books of History

The next twelve books of the Old Testament—Joshua, Judges, Ruth, 1-2 Samuel, 1-2 Kings, 1-2 Chronicles, Ezra, Nehemiah, and Esther—tell the history of God's chosen people. This part of the story begins with Joshua. He was God's chosen leader who brought the Israelites into the Promised Land. These books tell the stories of the kings (such as Saul and David and Solomon), and what happened when they obeyed God and when they didn't. These books also tell how God allowed the Israelites to be captured by other nations when they disobeyed God. Finally, the books tell how the Jewish people returned to God and their Promised Land.

Books of Poetry

These five books of the Old Testament—Job, Psalms, Proverbs, Ecclesiastes, and Song of Songs—are beautiful words of prayer and praise to God, as well as wise sayings. They were written by people who loved God very much. The poems and songs were used by the Jewish people during their feasts and festivals. They were used to celebrate God's goodness to them, and they were also used to praise and honor God. Today many of our songs of praise and prayer contain the words found in the Books of Poetry.

Books of Prophecy

The last seventeen books of the Old Testament—Isaiah, Jeremiah, Lamentations, Ezekiel, Daniel, Hosea, Joel, Amos, Obadiah, Jonah, Micah, Nahum, Habakkuk, Zephaniah, Haggai, Zechariah, and Malachi—are about God's special messengers, or "prophets." The books of prophecy are God's important messages to his chosen people, Israel. The prophets were sent to remind the people about God's laws and how they were to live. There are five long books of prophecy by the "major" prophets. "Major" only means that their books are longer, not more important. The books that are called the major prophets are Isaiah, Jeremiah, Lamentations, Ezekiel, and Daniel. The other twelve books of prophecy are shorter, and thus called "minor" prophets.

The New Testament

The second major section of the Bible begins with the birth of Jesus Christ, the Son of God. It tells us about Jesus' life and teachings, how he was killed and buried, and how he rose from the dead and ascended to heaven. The New Testament tells us about God's church. It also tells us that Jesus will come back someday. There are twenty-seven books in the New Testament. They also can be divided into smaller sections.

The Gospels

The first four books of the New Testament—Matthew, Mark, Luke, and John—are called the Gospels. The word *gospel* means "good news." The Gospels contain God's good news of the story of his Son, Jesus Christ, and reveal in all his truth and beauty what Jesus said and did. These narratives are not just filled with information about Christ; they are truly fascinating. The Gospels tell about Jesus' birth, teachings, death, burial, and coming back to life. It is the greatest story *ever* told. Even though the Gospels have the same story to tell us, each tells the story in a slightly different way.

History of the Church

The fifth book of the New Testament is the Acts of the Apostles. This book provides a historical account of the tremendous spread and growth of the early church despite fierce persecution. It begins with Jesus telling his followers to go and teach the whole world about him, after which Jesus went to heaven. His followers began teaching everyone in Jerusalem about Jesus. Then they traveled to other places and started churches by telling the story of Jesus to everyone they met. In the Book of Acts, we read about the preaching of Paul. He preached in Jerusalem, all around Asia Minor and Greece, and as far as Rome, the capital of the Roman Empire. The church that began in those pages of the Book of Acts is still alive and growing today!

The Letters

The next twenty-one books of the New Testament—Romans, 1-2 Corinthians, Galatians, Ephesians, Philippians, Colossians, 1-2 Thessalonians, 1-2 Timothy, Titus, Philemon, Hebrews, James, 1-2 Peter,

1-2-3 John, and Jude—are actually letters or "epistles." Thirteen of these letters were written by the apostle Paul. The full meaning of Jesus' birth, life, death, and resurrection are explained in these letters from the apostles. They were written because some believers were confused about Jesus. Sometimes they didn't understand what Jesus had taught about living as God wants his people to live. The teachings God gives through these letters have been changing lives for almost two thousand years.

The Book of Prophecy

The last book of the Bible—Revelation—is a book with a special message, a vision of Christ's glorious return to the earth in the end times. It was written to Christians who were facing great danger. The apostle John had a wonderful message. He told the Christians that the world should expect hard times and trouble. But he also told them that they would be the winners at the end! Revelation tells Christians not to lose hope because they will share in the final victory with Jesus at the end of time.

The Greatest Story Ever Told

Clearly, the great theme of the Bible is the person of Jesus Christ and his work of salvation for humankind. Christianity is rooted in the person of Jesus, and the best reason for believing that Christianity is true is Jesus. Throughout the Old Testament, the promises of his coming and his work are prophesied and graphically portrayed in numerous types and symbols. We can look at how God has made himself known in many ways—through the Jewish people, through the events of history, through the shape and form of the universe itself, and through visions and personal encounters with him. But he has most supremely made himself known in and through Jesus Christ. Through the incarnation of Christ, God has intervened decisively and directly in the world he created.

Until recent decades the question "Who is Jesus?" was not such a prevalent issue. Jesus was precisely who the Bible said he was: Jesus was not only a man, but he was God himself, who had come down from the glory of heaven to walk on this earth and show us what God is like. He lived an exemplary life, performed the signs and miracles that the Gospels said he did, taught what the New Testament said he taught, called together a group of followers and was crucified, giving his life as a ransom for many. He was resurrected three days later, continued to teach his followers, and then ascended into heaven back to God. He will come again to wrap up history and to usher in the full reign of God over all of his creation.

Concerning the historical Jesus of Nazareth, John Stott wrote in his book *Basic Christianity:* "The person and work of Christ are the rock upon which the Christian religion is built. Take Christ from Christianity, and . . . there is practically nothing left. Christ is the center of Christianity; all else is circumference."

Today, however, many people would have us believe that Jesus was merely a social reformer, who came to change society and free those people who were bound by injustice and oppression. Others say he came to show us his acts of love so that we might know how we should live. Some people will tell you that he was simply a misguided religious figure with no relevance for today.

But none of these things alone are adequate to explain the Jesus Christ pictured clearly in the New Testament. In unmistakable language, it is pronounced that Jesus was God himself in human form. He is the one and only Son of God who came to earth to reveal the nature of God to people and save them from their fatal state as sinners—Jesus took on himself the punishment for all the wrong things people do when he died on the cross. God demonstrated beyond all doubt that Jesus is the divine Savior and Lord by raising him from the dead. "The Good News is about God's Son, Jesus Christ our Lord. As a man, he was born from the family of David. But through the Spirit of holiness he was declared to be God's Son with great power by rising from the dead" (Romans 1:3–4).

What About the Resurrection of Jesus Christ?

The truth of Christianity lies in the resurrection of Jesus Christ from the grave. The question is not whether he was a good teacher or a prophet, but did he rise from the dead? The apostle Paul was perfectly clear about its importance: "If Christ has not been raised, then your faith has nothing to it; you are still guilty of your sins" (1 Corinthians 15:17). In his book *The Day Death Died*, Michael Green stated that Christianity "maintains that in Jesus, God broke into our world. His whole life was a demonstration of what God is like. And when men crucified him through envy and hatred on the first Good Friday, God raised him from the dead on Easter day, vindicating his claims, his teaching, his life, and his sacrificial death. That is, and always has been, the Christian claim. So if you want to examine the truth of Christianity, and whether or not you can credit the answers it gives to the problems of our world, it is to the resurrection you should turn."

Jesus' own words, "I am the way, and the truth, and the life. The only way to the Father is through me" (John 14:6), leave no room for doubt concerning his understanding of himself and the work he came to do on this earth. He also said, "I am the resurrection and the life. Those who believe in me will have life even if they die. And everyone who lives and believes in me will never die" (John 11:25–26). The resurrection is clearly the event in human history that boldly demonstrates the existence of God and his intentions for the salvation of people on earth. What makes the Christian faith unique is that it is founded on this unique historical event. No other religion can make such a claim.

In God's power, those first-century followers of Christ turned the world upside down and the world has never been the same. All of history bears testimony to this fact that the early Christians turned the world for the better, and human dignity, decency, and honor followed wherever Christianity spread. Virtually every significant social movement in Western civilization—from the abolition of slavery to child labor laws—owes its origin to the influence of Jesus Christ.

So Why the NCV?

The New Century Version is one of the easiest translations of the Bible to understand. It accurately communicates the messages found in the original languages of biblical manuscripts, using the kind of terms you use every day. It uses contemporary phrases, word pictures, and expressions, and replaces vague and overly religious language with down-to-earth vocabulary. The end result is a fresh, straightforward, and strong translation of God's truth and it is something you can connect with in your daily life. You'll find it easier to experience God's Word as it truly is—absolutely clear, powerfully alive, and completely life-changing.

This may be the greatest opportunity you will ever find to read and understand the Bible and to come to a personal understanding of God's plan for your life. The Bible, it should be remembered, is not an end in itself, but it is a means to the end of knowing God and doing his will. Through his Word we hear his voice and come to understand his mind.

So we challenge you to read the NCV. Anyone who will take the time can see and understand what God has given us in his Word and how it applies to us today. It may be the most important and life-changing step you will ever take.

How Do I Read the Bible?

The Bible is such a big book that it scares a lot of people. They think they don't know how to read it, where to start reading, or when to read. The amazing thing about the Bible is that it really doesn't matter how you read it, when you read it, or where you start reading.

Right before the first book of the Bible there's the Table of Contents that lists all the books of the Bible and the pages they start on. Let's say you want to find the Book of Luke. The Table of Contents tells you the starting page for Luke, and you'll find the page numbers for this Bible at the top of the pages. If you are looking for a specific passage, such as Luke 10:41, the number "10" tells you the chapter and "41" the verse. So open to the page number for Luke, and then follow the headings at top of the pages to find Luke 10. Scan down the page, and you're there. Once you get the hang of it, it's simple.

You can read the Bible anytime, anywhere, for any reason. You can start in the Old Testament, or you can start in the New Testament. And you can read the same Bible stories again and again, and they never get old. How you read does not matter as much as getting started right away and reading from God's Word often.

If you're looking for suggestions on where to start, we'd like to offer you a very basic six-week program that will introduce you to some of the most important passages of the Bible. This will be easy for you to accomplish, and you'll find it a great help in capturing an overall understanding of what the Bible is all about. As you might guess, we begin with the life and ministry of God's Son, Jesus Christ.

The Life of Jesus Christ—Weeks 1 and 2

Day 1	Luke 1	The events leading up to the birth of Jesus
Day 2	John 1:1–18	Who Jesus is
Day 3	Luke 2	The fullest account of Jesus' birth and childhood
Day 4	Matthew 4	The temptation of Jesus and beginning of ministry
Day 5	Matthew 5—6	The heart of what Jesus taught
Day 6	John 3	Salvation by God's grace alone
Day 7	John 5	The authority of Jesus to heal and work miracles
Day 8	Matthew 13	Stories of God's kingdom
Day 9	John 11	The power of Jesus over death
Day 10	John 15	What it means to be a follower of Christ
Day 11	John 17	Jesus' prayer for his followers
Day 12	Matthew 26—27	The betrayal, arrest, and crucifixion of Jesus
Day 13	John 20	The fullest account of Jesus' resurrection
Day 14	Luke 24	The resurrection and ascension of Jesus

The Life of the Early Church—Weeks 3 and 4

Day 1	Acts 2	The birth of the first church
Day 2	Acts 9	The conversion and calling of Saul
Day 3	Acts 16	The Good News is taken to Europe

Day 4	Acts 26	Paul's legal defense of the Christian faith
Day 5	Romans 3	The message of being made right with God by faith
Day 6	Romans 7	Our personal fight against sin
Day 7	Romans 8	What it means to be free from sin's power
Day 8	Romans 12	Always give your life to God in service
Day 9	1 Corinthians 13	Christianity is defined by love
Day 10	1 Corinthians 15	The power of the resurrection life
Day 11	Galatians 5	Our freedom in Christ through the Holy Spirit
Day 12	Ephesians 6	Our equipment for daily spiritual battles
Day 13	Philippians 2	How we are to live our lives
Day 14	Hebrews 11	What faith is and what it does

Great Stories of the Old Testament—Weeks 5 and 6

Day 1	Genesis 1—2	The creation of the world and humankind
Day 2	Genesis 3	The beginning of sin
Day 3	Genesis 15	God's agreement with Abraham and his family
Day 4	Genesis 41	Joseph is made ruler over Egypt
Day 5	Exodus 3—4	Moses is called by God to deliver his people
Day 6	Exodus 20	God gives the Ten Commandments
Day 7	Joshua 1	God's command to take over the Promised Land
Day 8	1 Samuel 17	David and Goliath
Day 9	1 Kings 8	King Solomon's Temple is dedicated
Day 10	1 Kings 18	The prophet Elijah confronts the prophets of Baal
Day 11	2 Kings 25	The fall of Jerusalem and captivity of Judah
Day 12	Daniel 2	Daniel's remarkable rise to power in Babylon
Day 13	Ezra 3	The rebuilding of the Temple in Jerusalem
Day 14	Isaiah 53	Isaiah's amazing description of the coming Messiah

This, of course, is only an introduction to the Bible. We recommend that you read the Bible daily and pray that God will show you his truth for your life. As you respond to what God is saying to you, you'll be amazed at the changes that will happen in your life. We trust that you will be blessed with a relationship with God that will satisfy the deepest longings of your heart and soul.

Topical Index

Eternal Life

Evangelism

Faith

Character Profiles

Topical Studies

Preface

God intended for everyone to be able to read and understand his Word. The Old Testament is written in Hebrew, the language of the people of Israel. Through the use of vivid stories based on real events and beautiful poetry, it appeals to the minds and hearts of the educated and the uneducated. The New Testament was first written in the simple Greek of everyday life, not in the Latin of Roman courts or the classical Greek of the academies. Even Jesus, the Master Teacher, taught spiritual principles by comparing them to such familiar terms as pearls, seeds, rocks, trees, and sheep. Likewise, the New Century Version translates the Scriptures in familiar, everyday words of our times.

The New Century Version is a translation of God's Word from the original Hebrew and Greek languages. A previous edition of the complete New Century Version, the International Children's Bible, was published in 1986.

A Trustworthy Translation

Two basic premises guided the translation process of the New Century Version. The first concern was that the translation be faithful to the manuscripts in the original languages. A team composed of the World Bible Translation Center and fifty additional, highly qualified and experienced Bible scholars and translators was assembled. The team included people with translation experience on such accepted versions as the New International Version, the New American Standard Bible, and the New King James Version. The most recent scholarship and the best available Hebrew and Greek texts were used, principally the third edition of the United Bible Societies' Greek text and the latest edition of the *Biblia Hebraica*, along with the Septuagint.

A Clear Translation

The second concern was to make the language clear enough for anyone to read the Bible and understand it. In maintaining clear language, several guidelines were followed. Vocabulary choice has been based upon *The Living Word Vocabulary* by Dr. Edgar Dale and Dr. Joseph O'Rourke (Worldbook-Childcraft International, 1981), which is the standard used by the editors of *The World Book Encyclopedia* to determine appropriate vocabulary. For difficult words that have no simpler synonyms, footnotes and references are provided. Footnotes appear at the bottom of the page and are indicated in the text by an *n* (for "note").

The New Century Version aids understanding by putting concepts into natural terms. Modern measurements and geographical locations have been used as much as possible. For instance, terms such as "shekels," "cubits," "omer," and "hin" have been converted to modern equivalents of weights and measures. Where geographical references are identical, the modern name has been used, such as the "Mediterranean Sea" instead of "Great Sea" or "Western Sea." Also, to minimize confusion, the most familiar name for a place is used consistently instead of using variant names for the same place. "Lake Galilee" is used throughout the text rather than its variant forms, "Sea of Kinnereth," "Lake Gennesaret," and "Sea of Tiberias."

Ancient customs are often unfamiliar to modern readers. Customs such as shaving a man's beard to shame him or walking between the halves of a dead animal to seal an agreement are meaningless to most people today. So these are clarified either in the text or in a footnote.

Since *meanings* of words change with time, care has been taken to avoid potential misunderstandings. Frequently in the Old Testament God tells his people to "devote" something to him, as when he tells the Israelites to devote Jericho and everything in it to him. While we might understand this to mean he is telling them to keep it safe and holy, the exact opposite is true. He is telling them to destroy it totally as an offering to him. The New Century Version communicates the idea clearly by translating "devoted" in these situations as "destroyed as an offering to the LORD."

Rhetorical questions in many instances have been stated according to their implied answer. The psalmist's question "What god is so great as our God?" has been stated more directly as "No god is as great as our God."

Figures of speech have been translated according to their meanings. For instance, the expression "the Virgin Daughter of Zion," which is frequently used in the Old Testament, is simply translated "the people of Jerusalem."

Idiomatic expressions of the biblical languages are translated to communicate the same meaning to today's reader that would have been understood by the original audience. For example, the Hebrew idiom "he rested with his fathers" is translated by its meaning—"he died."

Obscure terms have been clarified. In the Old Testament God frequently condemns the people for their "high places" and "Asherah poles." The New Century Version translates these according to their meanings, which would have been understood by the Hebrews. "High places" is translated "places where gods were worshiped," and "Asherah poles" is translated "Asherah idols."

Gender language has been rendered in keeping with the principles of meaning-based translation. In the interest of providing the best rendering of the original Hebrew and Greek texts in contemporary English, appropriate gender terms are used whenever it is possible to do so without hindering clarity or accuracy. Masculine terms are used when the meaning of the original has to do with males, including references to deity and to male cultural situations such as the military and the priesthood. Feminine terms are used when the meaning of the original has to do with females. When the meaning of the original has to do with both males and females, nongendered terms are used. (In such cases, the masculine resumptive pronoun has sometimes been preferred to changing person or number.)

The divine name YHWH, *the tetragrammaton*, has been indicated in the New Century Version by putting "LORD," and sometimes "GOD," in capital letters, following the tradition of other English versions. This is to distinguish it from *Adonai*, another Hebrew word that is translated "Lord."

Proper English style has been maintained while clarifying concepts and communication. The beauty of the Hebrew parallelism in poetry and the wordplays have been retained, and the images of the ancient languages have been captured in equivalent English images wherever possible.

Study Aids

Other features to enhance understanding of the text include subject headings throughout the text to identify speakers and topics and footnotes offering additional information on selected verses.

Our Prayer

It is with great humility and prayerfulness that this Bible is presented. We acknowledge the infallibility of God's Word, as well as our own human frailty. We pray that God has worked through us as his vessels so that we all might better learn his truth for ourselves and that it might richly grow in our lives. It is to his glory that this Bible is given.

THE PUBLISHER

Prayers

Prayer of Salvation

Dear Lord, thank you for your abundant grace and rich mercies. I know that I am a sinner and that I can never be perfect. Please forgive me for my sins and come into my life. I believe that you are the Lord and Father of all. I believe that your Son, Jesus Christ, died on the cross for my sins, was resurrected from the dead, and lives today with you in heaven. Lord, be the center of my life. I give you my heart, and I give you my life. All that I am and all that I ever will be is yours. Amen.

*If you have just prayed the **Prayer of Salvation,** we would love to hear from you. Please log on to www.myfaithandlife.com and click on "Share Your Story." Welcome to the family of God!*

Prayer of Dedication and Discipline

Dear Lord, today I pray that you will open my ears, my eyes, and my heart to what you want to teach me. I want to know you, Father. As I open your Word today, please teach me something new about who you are and about how I can love you more. I pray that you will take my life and mold me into the woman you want me to be. Lord, give me discipline to be a woman who lives by and in your love. Please grant me understanding, wisdom, patience, and humility. I give this day and our time together to you—please meet me where I am and speak to my heart. In your holy name, Amen.

Time of Reflection

We encourage you to use this next section to list praises and prayer requests or to reflect on what you hope to learn from your time with God as you read through this devotional Bible.

Old Testament

Genesis

From a Greek word meaning "beginning" or "generation"

Person Holding the Pen God Wrote With: It's generally agreed that *Moses* wrote the first five books of the Old Testament. Collectively, they were the first inspired body of Scripture. These five volumes are often called the "Pentateuch," referring to their total number, or the "Torah," because they include the laws God gave Israel.

When the Text Was Written: Between 1445 and 1405 B.C.

Spiritual Posture of the Original Recipients: This divine story linking *eternity past* with *eternity present* was first heard by the Israelites around 1405 B.C. before they were led by Joshua, Moses' successor, into the land God had promised to Abraham, Isaac, and Jacob. They were a relatively young "theocracy" (a community of people governed by God himself) in the throes of spiritual adolescence.

Storyline Synopsis: Genesis reveals history at a fast and furious pace. Remarkably, the book covers more time (from Creation to 1804 B.C.) than the rest of the Bible combined! The author records the beginning of time and space (chapter 1), the origin of humanity (chapter 2), the initial rebellion of man against God (chapter 3), the genealogy of Adam and Eve's descendents (chapters 3—11), God's blessing of Abraham as the father of his chosen people and the establishment of Israel as a theocracy (chapters 11—25), the formation of Israel's twelve tribes (Gen. 29:31—30:24; 35:16–20), and other colorful details in the story of God and man. Keep in mind that the Bible is a "progressive revelation"; in other words, the full story of God's sovereign plan to redeem mankind through Jesus' birth, death, and resurrection isn't clear until the New Testament.

A Moment Worth Discussing: In chapter 15, Abraham is depressed because he and his wife Sarah don't have any kids—and parenthood seems unlikely at their advanced age. But God says, "Cheer up because you're going to have a houseful of children!" Abraham believes him . . . at first. But when doubt creeps in, God makes a dramatic agreement with Abraham to reinforce his faithfulness to him. Discuss how this Old Testament symbolism points to Jesus shedding his blood in the New Testament.

Interesting (But Likely to Be Overlooked) Character: *Benjamin,* the baby brother of Joseph (Gen. 35:16–19), the "colorful coated" guy, is a fascinating individual. He carried the heavy burden of the hopes of his father, Jacob, who assumed that his first favorite son (Joseph) was dead. Talk about pressure!

The Beginning of the World

1 In the beginning God created the sky
and the earth. [2]The earth was empty and
had no form. Darkness covered the ocean,
and God's Spirit was moving over the water.
[3]Then God said, "Let there be light," and
there was light. [4]God saw that the light was
good, so he divided the light from the
darkness. [5]God named the light "day" and
the darkness "night." Evening passed, and
morning came. This was the first day.
[6]Then God said, "Let there be something
to divide the water in two." [7]So God made
the air and placed some of the water above
the air and some below it. [8]God named the
air "sky." Evening passed, and morning
came. This was the second day.
[9]Then God said, "Let the water under the
sky be gathered together so the dry land
will appear." And it happened. [10]God
named the dry land "earth" and the water
that was gathered together "seas." God saw
that this was good.
[11]Then God said, "Let the earth produce
plants—some to make grain for seeds and
others to make fruits with seeds in them.
Every seed will produce more of its own
kind of plant." And it happened. [12]The
earth produced plants with grain for seeds
and trees that made fruits with seeds in
them. Each seed grew its own kind of plant.
God saw that all this was good. [13]Evening
passed, and morning came. This was the
third day.
[14]Then God said, "Let there be lights in
the sky to separate day from night. These
lights will be used for signs, seasons, days,
and years. [15]They will be in the sky to give
light to the earth." And it happened.
[16]So God made the two large lights. He
made the brighter light to rule the day and
made the smaller light to rule the night. He
also made the stars. [17]God put all these in the
sky to shine on the earth, [18]to rule over the
day and over the night, and to separate
the light from the darkness. God saw that all
these things were good. [19]Evening passed,
and morning came. This was the fourth day.
[20]Then God said, "Let the water be filled
with living things, and let birds fly in the
air above the earth."
[21]So God created the large sea animals
and every living thing that moves in the sea.
The sea is filled with these living things,
with each one producing more of its own
kind. He also made every bird that flies, and
each bird produced more of its own kind.
God saw that this was good. [22]God blessed
them and said, "Have many young ones so
that you may grow in number. Fill the water
of the seas, and let the birds grow in
number on the earth." [23]Evening passed, and
morning came. This was the fifth day.
[24]Then God said, "Let the earth be filled
with animals, each producing more of its
own kind. Let there be tame animals and
small crawling animals and wild animals,
and let each produce more of its kind." And
it happened.
[25]So God made the wild animals, the
tame animals, and all the small crawling
animals to produce more of their own kind.
God saw that this was good.
[26]Then God said, "Let us make human
beings in our image and likeness. And let
them rule over the fish in the sea and the
birds in the sky, over the tame animals, over
all the earth, and over all the small crawling
animals on the earth."
[27]So God created human beings in his
image. In the image of God he created them.
He created them male and female. [28]God
blessed them and said, "Have many children
and grow in number. Fill the earth and be
its master. Rule over the fish in the sea and
over the birds in the sky and over every
living thing that moves on the earth."
[29]God said, "Look, I have given you all the
plants that have grain for seeds and all the
trees whose fruits have seeds in them. They
will be food for you. [30]I have given all the
green plants as food for every wild animal,
every bird of the air, and every small
crawling animal." And it happened. [31]God
looked at everything he had made, and it
was very good. Evening passed, and
morning came. This was the sixth day.

The Seventh Day—Rest

2 So the sky, the earth, and all that filled
them were finished. [2]By the seventh day
God finished the work he had been doing, so
he rested from all his work. [3]God blessed the
seventh day and made it a holy day, because
on that day he rested from all the work he
had done in creating the world.

devotion 1

GENESIS 1:27

I ENJOY BEING A GIRL

So many times through the years, I have been frustrated with my "girlieness." I've mentally kicked myself for being emotional or hormonal or spending so long searching for beautiful. Even as a grown-up woman, I still get my tender heart broken all the time. I cry over little things, and I am inclined to feel loneliness very deeply. I really do prefer the chick flicks where the girl gets rescued and falls madly in love with the soldier who saves the world in the nick of time. And doggone it, I'll probably live the rest of my life holding out for hope, believing that the girlie desires of my heart and the dreams in my head are still completely possible.

I've learned that every time I try to pretend not to be girlie, I end up hurting all the more. Every time I try to "take it like a man" or work like a man or think like a man, I end up in a huge mess. More crying. More alone than ever. Feeling completely unknown and unseen. I get hurt because I have tried to deny the very wiring inside of me. The fact is, I *am* a woman. Created feminine. Made to feel deeply and long for beauty all because of God's amazing design.

From the very beginning, you and I were created female. We were intended to interact and feel and become from the depth of our exquisite feminine soul. There is nothing to hide. Gender neutral is ridiculous. To be feminine is to reflect back to God his image in your creation.

The First People

4This is the story of the creation of the sky
and the earth. When the LORD God first
made the earth and the sky, 5there were still
no plants on the earth. Nothing was growing
in the fields because the LORD God had not
yet made it rain on the land. And there was
no person to care for the ground, 6but a mist
would rise up from the earth and water all
the ground.
7Then the LORD God took dust from the
ground and formed a man from it. He
breathed the breath of life into the man's
nose, and the man became a living person.
8Then the LORD God planted a garden in the
east, in a place called Eden, and put the man
he had formed into it. 9The LORD God caused
every beautiful tree and every tree that was
good for food to grow out of the ground. In
the middle of the garden, God put the tree
that gives life and also the tree that gives the
knowledge of good and evil.
10A river flowed through Eden and
watered the garden. From there the river
branched out to become four rivers. 11The
first river, named Pishon, flows around the
whole land of Havilah, where there is gold.
12The gold of that land is excellent. Bdellium
and onyx[n] are also found there. 13The second
river, named Gihon, flows around the whole
land of Cush. 14The third river, named Tigris,
flows out of Assyria toward the east. The
fourth river is the Euphrates.
15The LORD God put the man in the garden
of Eden to care for it and work it. 16The LORD
God commanded him, "You may eat the fruit
from any tree in the garden, 17but you must
not eat the fruit from the tree which gives

2:12 bdellium and onyx Bdellium is an expensive, sweet-smelling resin like myrrh, and onyx is a gem.

Eve

GENESIS 3

Eve sits at the river's edge, watching two giraffes lift their mouths to a branch of emerald leaves. A hippo emerges from the depths, spraying her with water. Eve giggles at the spectacle. She strolls through the trees, admiring their limbs that are heavy with succulent fruit. As she peels an orange, its juice runs down her hand. A playful lion cub licks her fingers clean. Life couldn't possibly be better.

"Did God really say that you must not eat fruit from any tree in the garden?"

Taken aback, she turns. She hadn't seen the snake approaching, but she assures him they can eat from the trees. "But God told us, 'You must not eat fruit from the tree that is in the middle of the garden. You must not even touch it, or you will die.'"

The serpent slithers closer. "You will not die. God knows that if you eat the fruit from that tree, you will learn about good and evil and you will be like God!"

Her gaze falls on the tree. *Why didn't God tell us that? Doesn't he want us to be like him?* She turns to question the snake, but the creature is gone.

The tree is more beautiful than all the others; its fruit is dazzling, ripe, and within reach. *Maybe the snake's right,* she reasons as she takes a bite.

Satan's words are few, but he says enough to cause Eve to doubt God's word. In what area is Satan causing you to question God?

the knowledge of good and evil. If you ever
eat fruit from that tree, you will die!"

The First Woman

18 Then the LORD God said, "It is not good
for the man to be alone. I will make a helper
who is right for him."
19 From the ground God formed every wild
animal and every bird in the sky, and he
brought them to the man so the man could
name them. Whatever the man called each
living thing, that became its name. 20 The man
gave names to all the tame animals, to the
birds in the sky, and to all the wild animals.
But Adam[n] did not find a helper that was
right for him. 21 So the LORD God caused the
man to sleep very deeply, and while he was
asleep, God removed one of the man's ribs.
Then God closed up the man's skin at the
place where he took the rib. 22 The LORD God
used the rib from the man to make a woman,
and then he brought the woman to the man.
23 And the man said,

"Now, this is someone whose bones came
from my bones,
whose body came from my body.
I will call her 'woman,'
because she was taken out of man."

24 So a man will leave his father and
mother and be united with his wife, and the
two will become one body.
25 The man and his wife were naked, but
they were not ashamed.

The Beginning of Sin

3 Now the snake was the most clever of all
the wild animals the LORD God had
made. One day the snake said to the woman,
"Did God really say that you must not eat
fruit from any tree in the garden?"
2 The woman answered the snake, "We
may eat fruit from the trees in the garden.
3 But God told us, 'You must not eat fruit
from the tree that is in the middle of the
garden. You must not even touch it, or you
will die.'"
4 But the snake said to the woman, "You
will not die. 5 God knows that if you eat the
fruit from that tree, you will learn about
good and evil and you will be like God!"
6 The woman saw that the tree was
beautiful, that its fruit was good to eat, and

2:20 Adam This is the name of the first man. It also means "humans," including men and women.

that it would make her wise. So she took
some of its fruit and ate it. She also gave
some of the fruit to her husband who was
with her, and he ate it.
7Then, it was as if their eyes were opened.
They realized they were naked, so they
sewed fig leaves together and made
something to cover themselves.
8Then they heard the LORD God walking
in the garden during the cool part of the day,
and the man and his wife hid from the LORD
God among the trees in the garden. 9But the
LORD God called to the man and said, "Where
are you?"
10The man answered, "I heard you
walking in the garden, and I was afraid
because I was naked, so I hid."
11God asked, "Who told you that you were
naked? Did you eat fruit from the tree from
which I commanded you not to eat?"
12The man said, "You gave this woman to
me and she gave me fruit from the tree, so I
ate it."
13Then the LORD God said to the
woman, "How could you have done such a
thing?"
She answered, "The snake tricked me, so I
ate the fruit."
14The LORD God said to the snake,

"Because you did this,
a curse will be put on you.
You will be cursed as no other animal,
tame or wild, will ever be.
You will crawl on your stomach,
and you will eat dust all the days of
your life.
15I will make you and the woman
enemies to each other.
Your descendants and her descendants
will be enemies.
One of her descendants will crush your
head,
and you will bite his heel."

16Then God said to the woman,

"I will cause you to have much trouble
when you are pregnant,
and when you give birth to children,
you will have great pain.
You will greatly desire your husband,
but he will rule over you."

17Then God said to the man, "You listened
to what your wife said, and you ate fruit
from the tree from which I commanded you
not to eat.

"So I will put a curse on the ground,
and you will have to work very hard for
your food.
In pain you will eat its food
all the days of your life.
18The ground will produce thorns and
weeds for you,
and you will eat the plants of the field.
19You will sweat and work hard for your
food.
Later you will return to the ground,
because you were taken from it.
You are dust,
and when you die, you will return to
the dust."

20The man named his wife Eve,[n] because
she was the mother of all the living.
21The LORD God made clothes from
animal skins for the man and his wife and
dressed them. 22Then the LORD God said,
"Humans have become like one of us; they
know good and evil. We must keep them
from eating some of the fruit from the tree
of life, or they will live forever." 23So the
LORD God forced Adam out of the garden
of Eden to work the ground from which he
was taken. 24After God forced humans out
of the garden, he placed angels and a
sword of fire that flashed around in every
direction on its eastern border. This kept
people from getting to the tree of life.

The First Family

4 Adam had sexual relations with his wife
Eve, and she became pregnant and gave
birth to Cain.[n] Eve said, "With the LORD's help,
I have given birth to a man." 2After that, Eve
gave birth to Cain's brother Abel. Abel took
care of flocks, and Cain became a farmer.
3Later, Cain brought some food from the
ground as a gift to God. 4Abel brought the
best parts from some of the firstborn of his
flock. The LORD accepted Abel and his gift,
5but he did not accept Cain and his gift. So
Cain became very angry and felt rejected.
6The LORD asked Cain, "Why are you
angry? Why do you look so unhappy? 7If you
do things well, I will accept you, but if you do
not do them well, sin is ready to attack you.
Sin wants you, but you must rule over it."

3:20 Eve This name sounds like the Hebrew word meaning "alive."
4:1 Cain This name sounds like the Hebrew word for "I have given birth."

devotion 2

GENESIS 3:8–9

WHERE DO YOU HIDE?

All the outward signs seemed normal in the garden that day. Everything was beautiful and bright, with the Lord himself strolling in the cool of the day. Of course, normal is relative—just try to find Adam and Eve. What are *they* doing? Hiding out, checking out, and waiting in fear.

Here's the question, though: where do you go to hide from God? For Adam and Eve, it was among the trees.

So often as we struggle with our sin today, our first reaction is still to hide. When sin is left alone in our hearts or our minds, it causes us to retreat from those who love us most. We flee from the body of Christ, or most frightful of all, flee from the presence of the only One who can make us whole again. The enemy desires to keep us isolated, but God wants us to know he is here, right now, walking in the cool of the day *with* us (1 John 1:9).

Where do you try to hide? Do you keep busy so you don't have to think about the guilt you feel? Do you paint on a smile to hide the brokenness of your thoughts? No matter where you try to hide, the truth is this: you are with a loving God (Ps. 73:23). This very minute, why don't you extend your hands, worship him, and allow the Lord to pour forgiveness over your heart and mind. Walk boldly in the garden with the Father.

8Cain said to his brother Abel, "Let's go out into the field." While they were out in the field, Cain attacked his brother Abel and killed him.

9Later, the LORD said to Cain, "Where is your brother Abel?"

Cain answered, "I don't know. Is it my job to take care of my brother?"

10Then the LORD said, "What have you done? Your brother's blood is crying out to
me from the ground. 11And now you will be cursed in your work with the ground, the same ground where your brother's blood fell
and where your hands killed him. 12You will work the ground, but it will not grow good crops for you anymore, and you will wander around on the earth."

13Then Cain said to the LORD, "This punishment is more than I can stand!
14Today you have forced me to stop working the ground, and now I must hide from you. I must wander around on the earth, and anyone who meets me can kill me."

15The LORD said to Cain, "No! If anyone kills you, I will punish that person seven times more." Then the LORD put a mark on Cain warning anyone who met him not to kill him.

Cain's Family

16So Cain went away from the LORD and
lived in the land of Nod,[n] east of Eden. 17He
had sexual relations with his wife, and she became pregnant and gave birth to Enoch. At that time Cain was building a city, which
he named after his son Enoch. 18Enoch had a son named Irad, Irad had a son named Mehujael, Mehujael had a son named Methushael, and Methushael had a son named Lamech.

19Lamech married two women, Adah and
Zillah. 20Adah gave birth to Jabal, who became the first person to live in tents and
raise cattle. 21Jabal's brother was Jubal, the first person to play the harp and flute.
22Zillah gave birth to Tubal-Cain, who made

4:16 Nod This name sounds like the Hebrew word for "wander."

tools out of bronze and iron. The sister of
Tubal-Cain was Naamah.

23 Lamech said to his wives:

"Adah and Zillah, hear my voice!
You wives of Lamech, listen to what I say.
I killed a man for wounding me,
a young man for hitting me.
24 If Cain's killer is punished seven times,
then Lamech's killer will be punished seventy-seven times."

Adam and Eve Have a New Son

25 Adam had sexual relations with his wife
Eve again, and she gave birth to a son. She
named him Seth[n] and said, "God has given
me another child. He will take the place of
Abel, who was killed by Cain." 26 Seth also
had a son, and they named him Enosh. At
that time people began to pray to the LORD.

Adam's Family History

5 This is the family history of Adam. When
God created human beings, he made
them in his own likeness. 2 He created them
male and female, and on that day he
blessed them and named them human
beings.

3 When Adam was 130 years old, he
became the father of another son in his
likeness and image, and Adam named him
Seth. 4 After Seth was born, Adam lived 800
years and had other sons and daughters. 5 So
Adam lived a total of 930 years, and then he
died.

6 When Seth was 105 years old, he had a
son named Enosh. 7 After Enosh was born,
Seth lived 807 years and had other sons and
daughters. 8 So Seth lived a total of 912 years,
and then he died.

9 When Enosh was 90 years old, he had a
son named Kenan. 10 After Kenan was born,
Enosh lived 815 years and had other sons
and daughters. 11 So Enosh lived a total of
905 years, and then he died.

12 When Kenan was 70 years old, he had a
son named Mahalalel. 13 After Mahalalel was
born, Kenan lived 840 years and had other
sons and daughters. 14 So Kenan lived a total
of 910 years, and then he died.

15 When Mahalalel was 65 years old, he
had a son named Jared. 16 After Jared was
born, Mahalalel lived 830 years and had
other sons and daughters. 17 So Mahalalel
lived a total of 895 years, and then he died.

18 When Jared was 162 years old, he had a
son named Enoch. 19 After Enoch was born,
Jared lived 800 years and had other sons and
daughters. 20 So Jared lived a total of 962
years, and then he died.

21 When Enoch was 65 years old, he had a
son named Methuselah. 22 After Methuselah
was born, Enoch walked with God 300 years
more and had other sons and daughters. 23 So
Enoch lived a total of 365 years. 24 Enoch
walked with God; one day Enoch could not
be found, because God took him.

25 When Methuselah was 187 years old, he
had a son named Lamech. 26 After Lamech
was born, Methuselah lived 782 years and
had other sons and daughters. 27 So
Methuselah lived a total of 969 years, and
then he died.

28 When Lamech was 182, he had a son.
29 Lamech named his son Noah[n] and said, "He
will comfort us in our work, which comes
from the ground the LORD has cursed."
30 After Noah was born, Lamech lived 595
years and had other sons and daughters. 31 So
Lamech lived a total of 777 years, and then
he died.

32 After Noah was 500 years old, he became
the father of Shem, Ham, and Japheth.

The Human Race Becomes Evil

6 The number of people on earth began to
grow, and daughters were born to them.
2 When the sons of God saw that these girls
were beautiful, they married any of them
they chose. 3 The LORD said, "My Spirit will
not remain in human beings forever,
because they are flesh. They will live only
120 years."

4 The Nephilim were on the earth in those
days and also later. That was when the sons
of God had sexual relations with the
daughters of human beings. These women
gave birth to children, who became famous
and were the mighty warriors of long ago.

5 The LORD saw that the human beings on
the earth were very wicked and that
everything they thought about was evil. 6 He
was sorry he had made human beings on the
earth, and his heart was filled with pain. 7 So

4:25 Seth This name sounds like the Hebrew word for "to give."
5:29 Noah This name sounds like the Hebrew word for "rest."

devotion 3

GENESIS 6:8

SEEING THE UNSEEN

When my son was just two-and-a-half years old, he had a violent case of the flu. One night, exhausted, I cradled him in my arms in bed watching the same Mickey Mouse cartoon for the tenth time and feeding him ice chips. He looked at me with those big eyes and said, "Mommy, pray Jesus make me well." We prayed together. Five minutes later, he was sick again. After we cleaned him up, he looked at me and said, "Now Jesus make me well." My heart sank. He was sick several more times, and after each episode, he would say, "Now Jesus make me well."

I was a little upset with God as I walked out of the room. "Lord," I prayed, "don't you see his faith? Couldn't you please just answer this one little prayer of a two-year-old?"

The Lord spoke to my heart and said, "Don't you understand? Faith is believing what you do not see." I went back to my son's room and found him sound asleep. He slept through the night and was well in the morning.

Noah pleased God with his faith. He spent 120 years building a boat for a flood he could not see. What is it in your life that God is using to build your faith? Know that God hears your prayers and has an answer for each and every one. But it's faith that pleases God. So put a smile on the face of God today—have faith for something you do not see.

the LORD said, "I will destroy all human
beings that I made on the earth. And I will
destroy every animal and everything that
crawls on the earth and the birds of the air,
because I am sorry I have made them." 8But
Noah pleased the LORD.

Noah and the Great Flood

9This is the family history of Noah. Noah
was a good man, the most innocent man of
his time, and he walked with God. 10He had
three sons: Shem, Ham, and Japheth.

11People on earth did what God said was
evil, and violence was everywhere. 12When
God saw that everyone on the earth did only
evil, 13he said to Noah, "Because people have
made the earth full of violence, I will destroy
all of them from the earth. 14Build a boat of
cypress wood for yourself. Make rooms in it
and cover it inside and outside with tar.
15This is how big I want you to build the
boat: four hundred fifty feet long,
seventy-five feet wide, and forty-five feet
high. 16Make an opening around the top of
the boat that is eighteen inches high from
the edge of the roof down. Put a door in the
side of the boat. Make an upper, middle, and
lower deck in it. 17I will bring a flood of
water on the earth to destroy all living
things that live under the sky, including
everything that has the breath of life.
Everything on the earth will die. 18But I will
make an agreement with you—you, your
sons, your wife, and your sons' wives will all
go into the boat. 19Also, you must bring into
the boat two of every living thing, male and
female. Keep them alive with you. 20Two of
every kind of bird, animal, and crawling
thing will come to you to be kept alive.
21Also gather some of every kind of food and
store it on the boat as food for you and the
animals."

22Noah did everything that God
commanded him.

The Flood Begins

7 Then the LORD said to Noah, "I have seen
that you are the best person among the

people of this time, so you and your family
can go into the boat. 2Take with you seven
pairs, each male with its female, of every
kind of clean animal, and take one pair, each
male with its female, of every kind of
unclean animal. 3Take seven pairs of all the
birds of the sky, each male with its female.
This will allow all these animals to continue
living on the earth after the flood. 4Seven
days from now I will send rain on the earth.
It will rain forty days and forty nights, and I
will wipe off from the earth every living
thing that I have made."

5Noah did everything the LORD
commanded him.

6Noah was six hundred years old when
the flood came. 7He and his wife and his
sons and their wives went into the boat to
escape the waters of the flood. 8The clean
animals, the unclean animals, the birds, and
everything that crawls on the ground 9came
to Noah. They went into the boat in groups
of two, male and female, just as God had
commanded Noah. 10Seven days later the
flood started.

11When Noah was six hundred years old,
the flood started. On the seventeenth day of
the second month of that year the
underground springs split open, and the
clouds in the sky poured out rain. 12The rain
fell on the earth for forty days and forty
nights.

13On that same day Noah and his wife, his
sons Shem, Ham, and Japheth, and their
wives went into the boat. 14They had every
kind of wild and tame animal, every kind of
animal that crawls on the earth, and every
kind of bird. 15Every creature that had the
breath of life came to Noah in the boat in
groups of two. 16One male and one female of
every living thing came, just as God had
commanded Noah. Then the LORD closed the
door behind them.

17Water flooded the earth for forty days,
and as it rose it lifted the boat off the ground.
18The water continued to rise, and the boat
floated on it above the earth. 19The water
rose so much that even the highest
mountains under the sky were covered by it.
20It continued to rise until it was more than
twenty feet above the mountains.

21All living things that moved on the
earth died. This included all the birds, tame
animals, wild animals, and creatures that
swarm on the earth, as well as all human
beings. 22So everything on dry land that had
the breath of life in it died. 23God destroyed
from the earth every living thing that was
on the land—every man, animal, crawling
thing, and bird of the sky. All that was left
was Noah and what was with him in the
boat. 24And the waters continued to cover
the earth for one hundred fifty days.

The Flood Ends

8 But God remembered Noah and all
the wild and tame animals with him in
the boat. He made a wind blow over the
earth, and the water went down. 2The
underground springs stopped flowing, and
the clouds in the sky stopped pouring down
rain. 3-4The water that covered the earth
began to go down. After one hundred fifty
days it had gone down so much that the boat
touched land again. It came to rest on one of
the mountains of Ararat[n] on the seventeenth
day of the seventh month. 5The water
continued to go down so that by the first day
of the tenth month the tops of the
mountains could be seen.

6Forty days later Noah opened the
window he had made in the boat, and 7he
sent out a raven. It flew here and there until
the water had dried up from the earth. 8Then
Noah sent out a dove to find out if the water
had dried up from the ground. 9The dove
could not find a place to land because water
still covered the earth, so it came back to the
boat. Noah reached out his hand and took
the bird and brought it back into the boat.

10After seven days Noah again sent out the
dove from the boat, 11and that evening it
came back to him with a fresh olive leaf in
its mouth. Then Noah knew that the ground
was almost dry. 12Seven days later he sent
the dove out again, but this time it did not
come back.

13When Noah was six hundred and one
years old, in the first day of the first month
of that year, the water was dried up from the
land. Noah removed the covering of the boat
and saw that the land was dry. 14By the
twenty-seventh day of the second month the
land was completely dry.

8:3–4 Ararat The ancient land of Urartu, an area in Eastern Turkey.

[15]Then God said to Noah, [16]"You and your
wife, your sons, and their wives should go
out of the boat. [17]Bring every animal out of
the boat with you—the birds, animals, and
everything that crawls on the earth. Let
them have many young ones so that they
might grow in number."
[18]So Noah went out with his sons, his
wife, and his sons' wives. [19]Every animal,
everything that crawls on the earth, and
every bird went out of the boat by families.
[20]Then Noah built an altar to the LORD. He
took some of all the clean birds and animals,
and he burned them on the altar as offerings
to God. [21]The LORD was pleased with these
sacrifices and said to himself, "I will never
again curse the ground because of human
beings. Their thoughts are evil even when
they are young, but I will never again
destroy every living thing on the earth as I
did this time.

[22]"As long as the earth continues,
planting and harvest,
cold and hot,
summer and winter,
day and night
will not stop."

The New Beginning

9 Then God blessed Noah and his sons and
said to them, "Have many children; grow
in number and fill the earth. [2]Every animal
on earth, every bird in the sky, every animal
that crawls on the ground, and every fish in
the sea will respect and fear you. I have
given them to you.
[3]"Everything that moves, everything that
is alive, is yours for food. Earlier I gave you
the green plants, but now I give you
everything for food. [4]But you must not eat
meat that still has blood in it, because blood
gives life. [5]I will demand blood for life. I will
demand the life of any animal that kills a
person, and I will demand the life of anyone
who takes another person's life.

[6]"Whoever kills a human being
will be killed by a human being,
because God made humans
in his own image.

[7]"As for you, Noah, I want you and your
family to have many children, to grow in
number on the earth, and to become
many."
[8]Then God said to Noah and his sons,
[9]"Now I am making my agreement with you
and your people who will live after you,
[10]and with every living thing that is with
you—the birds, the tame and the wild
animals, and with everything that came out
of the boat with you—with every living
thing on earth. [11]I make this agreement with
you: I will never again destroy all living
things by a flood. A flood will never again
destroy the earth."
[12]And God said, "This is the sign of the
agreement between me and you and every
living creature that is with you. [13]I am
putting my rainbow in the clouds as the sign
of the agreement between me and the earth.
[14]When I bring clouds over the earth and a
rainbow appears in them, [15]I will remember
my agreement between me and you and
every living thing. Floods will never again
destroy all life on the earth. [16]When the
rainbow appears in the clouds, I will see it
and I will remember the agreement that
continues forever between me and every
living thing on the earth."
[17]So God said to Noah, "The rainbow is a
sign of the agreement that I made with all
living things on earth."

Noah and His Sons

[18]The sons of Noah who came out of the
boat with him were Shem, Ham, and
Japheth. (Ham was the father of Canaan.)
[19]These three men were Noah's sons, and all
the people on earth came from these three
sons.
[20]Noah became a farmer and planted a
vineyard. [21]When he drank wine made from
his grapes, he became drunk and lay naked
in his tent. [22]Ham, the father of Canaan,
looked at his naked father and told his
brothers outside. [23]Then Shem and Japheth
got a coat and, carrying it on both their
shoulders, they walked backwards into the
tent and covered their father. They turned
their faces away so that they did not see
their father's nakedness.
[24]Noah was sleeping because of the wine.
When he woke up and learned what his
youngest son, Ham, had done to him, [25]he
said,

"May there be a curse on Canaan!
May he be the lowest slave to his
brothers."

[26]Noah also said,

devotion 4

GENESIS 9:13–15

CHASING A RAINBOW

As a child, do you remember the excitement that would well up inside of you when you spotted a rainbow in the sky? If you were like me, chasing those brilliant rays was a spring and summertime hobby . . . running in worn sneakers with hair up in a ponytail just aching to find the rainbow's mysterious starting point. There was beauty and "magic" in those arched colors in the sky.

Little did I know back then that this was more than a Technicolor parade above me—it was a promise. Our Creator uses beautifully bold strokes to remind not only us, but himself, of the agreement he made with humanity. The infinite God made a promise *to us* even though we have not always been faithful in keeping our promises to him.

Over the years, I have wandered away many times from the Lord like a child chasing a rainbow. But I know that his commitment to me never wanes. And unlike the rainbows he creates that fade into the blue, our God is not so illusive.

Your life may be accompanied by many clouds of frustrating gray and a sour mist of uncertainty. The waters of stress or sadness may seem to be rising to a new watermark each day. While God did not say you wouldn't ever have a flood of overwhelming circumstances in your life, he has promised this: he will never let the water of your circumstances overcome you.

Take heart in knowing that the God of all creation wants to give you hope today.

"May the LORD, the God of Shem, be
praised!
May Canaan be Shem's slave.
27May God give more land to Japheth.
May Japheth live in Shem's tents,
and may Canaan be their slave."
28After the flood Noah lived 350 years.
29He lived a total of 950 years, and then he
died.

Nations Grow and Spread

10 This is the family history of Shem,
Ham, and Japheth, the sons of Noah.
After the flood these three men had sons.

Japheth's Sons

2The sons of Japheth were Gomer, Magog,
Madai, Javan, Tubal, Meshech, and Tiras.
3The sons of Gomer were Ashkenaz,
Riphath, and Togarmah.
4The sons of Javan were Elishah, Tarshish,
Kittim,[n] and Rodanim. 5Those who lived in
the lands around the Mediterranean Sea
came from these sons of Japheth. All the
families grew and became different nations,
each nation with its own land and its own
language.

Ham's Sons

6The sons of Ham were Cush, Mizraim,[n]
Put, and Canaan.
7The sons of Cush were Seba, Havilah,
Sabtah, Raamah, and Sabteca.
The sons of Raamah were Sheba and
Dedan.
8Cush also had a descendant named
Nimrod, who became a very powerful man
on earth. 9He was a great hunter before the
LORD, which is why people say someone is
"like Nimrod, a great hunter before the LORD."

10:4 Kittim His descendants were the people of Cyprus.
10:6 Mizraim This is another name for Egypt.

10At first Nimrod's kingdom covered Babylon,
Erech, Akkad, and Calneh in the land of
Babylonia. 11From there he went to Assyria,
where he built the cities of Nineveh,
Rehoboth Ir, and Calah. 12He also built Resen,
the great city between Nineveh and Calah.
13Mizraim was the father of the Ludites,
Anamites, Lehabites, Naphtuhites,
14Pathrusites, Casluhites, and the people of
Crete. (The Philistines came from the
Casluhites.)
15Canaan was the father of Sidon, his first
son, and of Heth. 16He was also the father of
the Jebusites, Amorites, Girgashites,
17Hivites, Arkites, Sinites, 18Arvadites,
Zemarites, and Hamathites. The families of
the Canaanites scattered. 19Their land
reached from Sidon to Gerar as far as Gaza,
and then to Sodom, Gomorrah, Admah, and
Zeboiim, as far as Lasha.
20All these people were the sons of Ham,
and all these families had their own
languages, their own lands, and their own
nations.

Shem's Sons

21Shem, Japheth's older brother, also had
sons. One of his descendants was the father
of all the sons of Eber.
22The sons of Shem were Elam, Asshur,
Arphaxad, Lud, and Aram.
23The sons of Aram were Uz, Hul, Gether,
and Meshech.
24Arphaxad was the father of Shelah, who
was the father of Eber. 25Eber was the father
of two sons—one named Peleg,[n] because the
earth was divided during his life, and the
other was named Joktan.
26Joktan was the father of Almodad,
Sheleph, Hazarmaveth, Jerah, 27Hadoram,
Uzal, Diklah, 28Obal, Abimael, Sheba,
29Ophir, Havilah, and Jobab. All these people
were the sons of Joktan. 30They lived in the
area between Mesha and Sephar in the hill
country in the East.
31These are the people from the family of
Shem, arranged by families, languages,
countries, and nations.
32This is the list of the families from the
sons of Noah, arranged according to their
nations. From these families came all the
nations who spread across the earth after the
flood.

The Languages Confused

11 At this time the whole world spoke
one language, and everyone used the
same words. 2As people moved from the east,
they found a plain in the land of Babylonia
and settled there.
3They said to each other, "Let's make
bricks and bake them to make them hard."
So they used bricks instead of stones, and tar
instead of mortar. 4Then they said to each
other, "Let's build a city and a tower for
ourselves, whose top will reach high into the
sky. We will become famous. Then we will
not be scattered over all the earth."
5The LORD came down to see the city and
the tower that the people had built. 6The
LORD said, "Now, these people are united, all
speaking the same language. This is only the
beginning of what they will do. They will be
able to do anything they want. 7Come, let us
go down and confuse their language so they
will not be able to understand each other."
8So the LORD scattered them from there
over all the earth, and they stopped building
the city. 9The place is called Babel[n] since that
is where the LORD confused the language of
the whole world. So the LORD caused them to
spread out from there over the whole world.

The Story of Shem's Family

10This is the family history of Shem. Two
years after the flood, when Shem was 100
years old, his son Arphaxad was born. 11After
that, Shem lived 500 years and had other
sons and daughters.
12When Arphaxad was 35 years old, his
son Shelah was born. 13After that, Arphaxad
lived 403 years and had other sons and
daughters.
14When Shelah was 30 years old, his son
Eber was born. 15After that, Shelah lived 403
years and had other sons and daughters.
16When Eber was 34 years old, his son
Peleg was born. 17After that, Eber lived 430
years and had other sons and daughters.
18When Peleg was 30 years old, his son
Reu was born. 19After that, Peleg lived 209
years and had other sons and daughters.
20When Reu was 32 years old, his son
Serug was born. 21After that, Reu lived 207
years and had other sons and daughters.
22When Serug was 30 years old, his son

10:25 Peleg This name sounds like the Hebrew word for "divided."
11:9 Babel This name sounds like the Hebrew word for "confused."

Nahor was born. 23After that, Serug lived 200
years and had other sons and daughters.
24When Nahor was 29 years old, his son
Terah was born. 25After that, Nahor lived 119
years and had other sons and daughters.
26After Terah was 70 years old, his sons
Abram, Nahor, and Haran were born.

The Story of Terah's Family

27This is the family history of Terah. Terah
was the father of Abram, Nahor, and Haran.
Haran was the father of Lot. 28While his
father, Terah, was still alive, Haran died in Ur
in Babylonia, where he was born. 29Abram
and Nahor both married. Abram's wife was
named Sarai, and Nahor's wife was named
Milcah. She was the daughter of Haran, who
was the father of both Milcah and Iscah.
30Sarai was not able to have children.
31Terah took his son Abram, his grandson
Lot (Haran's son), and his daughter-in-law
Sarai (Abram's wife) and moved out of Ur of
Babylonia. They had planned to go to the
land of Canaan, but when they reached the
city of Haran, they settled there.
32Terah lived to be 205 years old, and then
he died in Haran.

God Calls Abram

12 The LORD said to Abram, "Leave your
country, your relatives, and your
father's family, and go to the land I will show
you.
2I will make you a great nation,
and I will bless you.
I will make you famous,
and you will be a blessing to others.
3I will bless those who bless you,
and I will place a curse on those who
harm you.
And all the people on earth
will be blessed through you."
4So Abram left Haran as the LORD had told
him, and Lot went with him. At this time
Abram was 75 years old. 5He took his wife
Sarai, his nephew Lot, and everything they
owned, as well as all the servants they had
gotten in Haran. They set out from Haran,
planning to go to the land of Canaan, and in
time they arrived there.
6Abram traveled through that land as far
as the great tree of Moreh at Shechem. The
Canaanites were living in the land at that
time. 7The LORD appeared to Abram and said,
"I will give this land to your descendants." So

devotion 5

GENESIS 11:4–7

WHO'S THE BIG DEAL?

Not long ago, someone told me that our job as believers is to make a big deal out of God every day. I love that. But I often forget. I want everything about my life to glorify God, but sometimes I get turned around. Sometimes it seems my goals, my reputation, and my dreams are at stake. Many days, I get busy building my own tower, figuring out new and improved ways for it to reach higher into the sky and make me famous.

This day our job is to make God famous. When I remember this, every single part of my day falls into place. How will I make God famous to my kids today? Will they learn to seek his presence because of his presence in me? Will they be able to recognize godliness because they have witnessed godliness in me? I am a very important representation of his character to them. Will they adore him or turn from the Father because I failed to make him the big deal? How will I make God famous to my neighbors and co-workers?

Just remembering my calling gives me clarity and realigns my priorities in those relationships. If it's not about me, then I am able to love with God's pure love and forgive according to the lavish forgiveness he has already given to me.

So make a big deal out of God today. The tower of your life is for his glory.

Make him famous everywhere you go and with everyone he sends your way.

Abram built an altar there to the LORD, who had appeared to him. 8Then he traveled from Shechem to the mountain east of Bethel and set up his tent there. Bethel was to the west, and Ai was to the east. There Abram built another altar to the LORD and worshiped him. 9After this, he traveled on toward southern Canaan.

Abram Goes to Egypt

10At this time there was not much food in the land, so Abram went down to Egypt to live because there was so little food. 11Just before they arrived in Egypt, he said to his wife Sarai, "I know you are a very beautiful woman. 12When the Egyptians see you, they will say, 'This woman is his wife.' Then they will kill me but let you live. 13Tell them you are my sister so that things will go well with me and I may be allowed to live because of you."

14When Abram came to Egypt, the Egyptians saw that Sarai was very beautiful. 15The Egyptian officers saw her and told the king of Egypt how beautiful she was. They took her to the king's palace, and 16the king was kind to Abram because he thought Abram was her brother. He gave Abram sheep, cattle, male and female donkeys, male and female servants, and camels.

17But the LORD sent terrible diseases on the king and all the people in his house because of Abram's wife Sarai. 18So the king sent for Abram and said, "What have you done to me? Why didn't you tell me Sarai was your wife? 19Why did you say, 'She is my sister' so that I made her my wife? Now, here is your wife. Take her and leave!" 20Then the king commanded his men to make Abram leave Egypt; so Abram and his wife left with everything they owned.

Abram and Lot Separate

13 So Abram, his wife, and Lot left Egypt, taking everything they owned, and traveled to southern Canaan. 2Abram was very rich in cattle, silver, and gold.

3He left southern Canaan and went back to Bethel where he had camped before, between Bethel and Ai, 4and where he had built an altar. So he worshiped the LORD there.

5During this time Lot was traveling with Abram, and Lot also had flocks, herds, and tents. 6Abram and Lot had so many animals that the land could not support both of them together, 7so Abram's herdsmen and Lot's herdsmen began to argue. The Canaanites and the Perizzites were living in the land at this time.

8Abram said to Lot, "There should be no arguing between you and me, or between your herdsmen and mine, because we are brothers. 9We should separate. The whole land is there in front of you. If you go to the left, I will go to the right. If you go to the right, I will go to the left."

10Lot looked all around and saw the whole Jordan Valley and that there was much water there. It was like the LORD's garden, like the land of Egypt in the direction of Zoar. (This was before the LORD destroyed Sodom and Gomorrah.) 11So Lot chose to move east and live in the Jordan Valley. In this way Abram and Lot separated. 12Abram lived in the land of Canaan, but Lot lived among the cities in the Jordan Valley, very near to Sodom. 13Now the people of Sodom were very evil and were always sinning against the LORD.

14After Lot left, the LORD said to Abram, "Look all around you—to the north and south and east and west. 15All this land that you see I will give to you and your descendants forever. 16I will make your descendants as many as the dust of the earth. If anyone could count the dust on the earth, he could count your people. 17Get up! Walk through all this land because I am now giving it to you."

18So Abram moved his tents and went to live near the great trees of Mamre at the city of Hebron. There he built an altar to the LORD.

Lot Is Captured

14 Now Amraphel was king of Babylonia, Arioch was king of Ellasar, Kedorlaomer was king of Elam, and Tidal was king of Goiim. 2All these kings went to war against several other kings: Bera king of Sodom, Birsha king of Gomorrah, Shinab king of Admah, Shemeber king of Zeboiim, and the king of Bela. (Bela is also called Zoar.)

3These kings who were attacked united their armies in the Valley of Siddim (now the Dead Sea). 4They had served Kedorlaomer for twelve years, but in the thirteenth year, they all turned against him. 5Then in the

devotion 6

GENESIS 12:1

I WILL SHOW YOU!

Most of us are quite content to just stay quietly in our own land in the experience we know. As we walk with the Lord, though, we will sometimes be called to a different "land." It happened to Abram. Everything he had known was in his first homeland. It was where he traveled and lived. It was where he raised his family and walked with the Lord. But the Lord asked him to leave everything familiar.

I had lived in southern Florida for twelve years when the Lord called my husband to be a senior pastor in a new land. In Florida, our land was bordered by white beaches, blue waters, and giant palm trees. Our church family was amazing, and both of our businesses were rockin'!

Our *new* land was locked in by other land. Our church body grew out of a two-year home Bible study, and I had to start my business all over again. Still, when the call came, we recognized his voice saying, "Go to the land I will show you" (Gen. 12:1).

What happens in your heart when the Lord calls you to a new job or a new church body or any other new land? When we can't quite see the destination, it requires a great faith to trust God's leading. If you are hearing the still, small voice of the Lord today telling you to go to the land he will show you, then you must go. Don't hesitate another moment!

fourteenth year, Kedorlaomer and the kings
with him came and defeated the Rephaites
in Ashteroth Karnaim, the Zuzites in Ham,
and the Emites in Shaveh Kiriathaim. 6They
also defeated the Horites in the mountains of
Edom to El Paran (near the desert). 7Then
they turned back and went to En Mishpat
(that is, Kadesh). They defeated all the
Amalekites, as well as the Amorites who
lived in Hazazon Tamar.
8At that time the kings of Sodom,
Gomorrah, Admah, Zeboiim, and Bela went
out to fight in the Valley of Siddim. (Bela is
called Zoar.) 9They fought against
Kedorlaomer king of Elam, Tidal king of
Goiim, Amraphel king of Babylonia, and
Arioch king of Ellasar—four kings fighting
against five. 10There were many tar pits in
the Valley of Siddim. When the kings of
Sodom and Gomorrah and their armies ran
away, some of the soldiers fell into the tar
pits, but the others ran away to the
mountains.
11Now Kedorlaomer and his armies took
everything the people of Sodom and
Gomorrah owned, including their food.
12They took Lot, Abram's nephew who was
living in Sodom, and everything he owned.
Then they left. 13One of the men who was
not captured went to Abram, the Hebrew,
and told him what had happened. At that
time Abram was camped near the great trees
of Mamre the Amorite. Mamre was a brother
of Eshcol and Aner, and they had all made an
agreement to help Abram.

Abram Rescues Lot

14When Abram learned that Lot had been
captured, he called out his 318 trained men
who had been born in his camp. He led the
men and chased the enemy all the way to
the town of Dan. 15That night he divided his
men into groups, and they made a surprise
attack against the enemy. They chased them
all the way to Hobah, north of Damascus.
16Then Abram brought back everything the
enemy had stolen, the women and the other
people, and Lot, and everything Lot owned.

Sarai, or Sarah

GENESIS 16

Sarai runs a finger over the wrinkles on her hands. There's no glossing over this truth: she is old—and getting older every day. The promise God made to Abram about children has not been fulfilled, and her aching body tells her time is running out. Some days she doubts she has the strength and energy to make it through a taxing pregnancy, let alone run after a little one.

Abram sits, washing the dust off his feet. Should she tell him what she's been thinking?

"Abram?" He turns. As she kneels in front of him, he searches her eyes. They are overflowing with the pain of one desperately longing to be a mother. Emotion rises to her throat and breaks as she speaks, "I want a child."

He reminds her of the Lord's promise: "You will have a son of your own," Abram says. "It's what the Lord said."

She shakes her head, grasping his hands between hers. *God has not kept his promise,* she reasons to herself, *and now something must be done.* "Look, the Lord has not allowed me to have children, so have sexual relations with my slave girl. If she has a child, maybe I can have my own family through her."

Abram studies her face. She is determined. He agrees and she kisses his hands. She will finally have a child!

God didn't need Sarai's help to accomplish his plan. He wanted her obedience. Are you impatient with God and trying to "help" him with your life?

17After defeating Kedorlaomer and the
kings who were with him, Abram went
home. As he was returning, the king of
Sodom came out to meet him in the Valley
of Shaveh (now called King's Valley).
18Melchizedek king of Salem brought out
bread and wine. He was a priest for God
Most High 19and blessed Abram, saying,
"Abram, may you be blessed by God Most
High,
the God who made heaven and earth.
20And we praise God Most High,
who has helped you to defeat your
enemies."
Then Abram gave Melchizedek a tenth of
everything he had brought back from the
battle.
21The king of Sodom said to Abram, "You
may keep all these things for yourself. Just
give me my people who were captured."
22But Abram said to the king of Sodom, "I
make a promise to the LORD, the God Most
High, who made heaven and earth. 23I
promise that I will not keep anything that is
yours. I will not keep even a thread or a
sandal strap so that you cannot say, 'I made
Abram rich.' 24I will keep nothing but the
food my young men have eaten. But give
Aner, Eshcol, and Mamre their share of what
we won, because they went with me into
battle."

God's Agreement with Abram

15 After these things happened, the LORD
spoke his word to Abram in a vision:
"Abram, don't be afraid. I will defend you,
and I will give you a great reward."
2But Abram said, "Lord GOD, what can you
give me? I have no son, so my slave Eliezer
from Damascus will get everything I own
after I die." 3Abram said, "Look, you have
given me no son, so a slave born in my house
will inherit everything I have."
4Then the LORD spoke his word to Abram:
"He will not be the one to inherit what you
have. You will have a son of your own who
will inherit what you have."
5Then God led Abram outside and said,
"Look at the sky. There are so many stars you
cannot count them. Your descendants also
will be too many to count."
6Abram believed the LORD. And the LORD
accepted Abram's faith, and that faith made
him right with God.

7God said to Abram, "I am the LORD who
led you out of Ur of Babylonia so that I could
give you this land to own."

8But Abram said, "Lord GOD, how can I be
sure that I will own this land?"

9The LORD said to Abram, "Bring me a
three-year-old cow, a three-year-old goat, a
three-year-old male sheep, a dove, and a
young pigeon."

10Abram brought them all to God. Then
Abram killed the animals and cut each of
them into two pieces, laying each half
opposite the other half. But he did not cut
the birds in half. 11Later, large birds flew
down to eat the animals, but Abram chased
them away.

12As the sun was going down, Abram fell
into a deep sleep. While he was asleep, a
very terrible darkness came. 13Then the
LORD said to Abram, "You can be sure that
your descendants will be strangers and
travel in a land they don't own. The people
there will make them slaves and be cruel
to them for four hundred years. 14But I will
punish the nation where they are slaves.
Then your descendants will leave that
land, taking great wealth with them. 15And
you, Abram, will die in peace and will be
buried at an old age. 16After your great-
great-grandchildren are born, your people
will come to this land again. It will take
that long, because I am not yet going to
punish the Amorites for their evil
behavior."

17After the sun went down, it was very
dark. Suddenly a smoking firepot and a
blazing torch passed between the halves of
the dead animals.[n] 18So on that day the LORD
made an agreement with Abram and said, "I
will give to your descendants the land
between the river of Egypt and the great
river Euphrates. 19This is the land of the
Kenites, Kenizzites, Kadmonites, 20Hittites,
Perizzites, Rephaites, 21Amorites, Canaanites,
Girgashites, and Jebusites."

Ishmael Is Born

16 Sarai, Abram's wife, had no children,
but she had a slave girl from Egypt
named Hagar. 2Sarai said to Abram, "Look,
the LORD has not allowed me to have
children, so have sexual relations with my
slave girl. If she has a child, maybe I can
have my own family through her."

Abram did what Sarai said. 3It was after he
had lived ten years in Canaan that Sarai gave
Hagar to her husband Abram. (Hagar was
her slave girl from Egypt.)

4Abram had sexual relations with
Hagar, and she became pregnant. When
Hagar learned she was pregnant, she began
to treat her mistress Sarai badly. 5Then
Sarai said to Abram, "This is your fault. I
gave my slave girl to you, and when she
became pregnant, she began to treat me
badly. Let the LORD decide who is right—
you or me."

6But Abram said to Sarai, "You are Hagar's
mistress. Do anything you want to her."
Then Sarai was hard on Hagar, and Hagar
ran away.

7The angel of the LORD found Hagar beside
a spring of water in the desert, by the road to
Shur. 8The angel said, "Hagar, Sarai's slave
girl, where have you come from? Where are
you going?"

Hagar answered, "I am running away from
my mistress Sarai."

9The angel of the LORD said to her, "Go
home to your mistress and obey her." 10The
angel also said, "I will give you so many
descendants they cannot be counted."

11The angel added,

"You are now pregnant,
  and you will have a son.
You will name him Ishmael,[n]
  because the LORD has heard your
    cries.
12Ishmael will be like a wild donkey.
  He will be against everyone,
  and everyone will be against him.
He will attack all his brothers."

13The slave girl gave a name to the LORD
who spoke to her: "You are 'God who sees
me,' " because she said to herself, "Have I
really seen God who sees me?" 14So the well
there, between Kadesh and Bered, was called
Beer Lahai Roi.[n]

15Hagar gave birth to a son for Abram, and
Abram named him Ishmael. 16Abram was
eighty-six years old when Hagar gave birth
to Ishmael.

15:17 passed . . . animals This showed that God sealed the agreement between himself and Abram. **16:11 Ishmael** The Hebrew words for "Ishmael" and "has heard" sound similar. **16:14 Beer Lahai Roi** This means "the well of the Living One who sees me."

devotion 7

GENESIS 16:7–9

WHAT DOES OBEDIENCE DO?

Hagar was a pregnant runaway slave girl with nowhere to go. She had to be amazed that the one true God even noticed she was gone, much less came *looking* for her. Hagar called on the Lord, the *God who sees*. She realized that God saw her heart as well as her circumstances and that he loved her. And yet God told her to go back to the very situation she was trying to escape from. Knowing that God understood gave Hagar the courage to obey.

My husband came to me one day and told me he believed God had asked him if he was willing to be a youth pastor for the rest of his life. "What did you say?" I asked a bit fearfully.

"I said yes," he answered.

It upset me. We had been in youth ministry for eight years, and we loved working with the teenagers, but I had always thought God had other plans for our lives. My husband's salary was on the low end, and we had three small children, which meant that I couldn't work. On top of that, we were carrying a good bit of debt. Was I willing? As I wrestled with God over it, I began to realize that God understood our situation in every dimension. The real question was whether I was willing to be obedient to God's will for our lives. Hagar obeyed God and thirteen years later God freed her from slavery. Her obedience resulted in blessing. Obedience always does.

Proof of the Agreement

17 When Abram was ninety-nine years
old, the LORD appeared to him and
said, "I am God Almighty. Obey me and do
what is right. 2 I will make an agreement
between us, and I will make you the
ancestor of many people."
3 Then Abram bowed facedown on the
ground. God said to him, 4 "I am making my
agreement with you: I will make you the
father of many nations. 5 I am changing your
name from Abram[n] to Abraham[n] because I
am making you a father of many nations. 6 I
will give you many descendants. New
nations will be born from you, and kings
will come from you. 7 And I will make an
agreement between me and you and all your
descendants from now on: I will be your God
and the God of all your descendants. 8 You
live in the land of Canaan now as a stranger,
but I will give you and your descendants all
this land forever. And I will be the God of
your descendants."
9 Then God said to Abraham, "You and
your descendants must keep this agreement
from now on. 10 This is my agreement with
you and all your descendants, which you
must obey: Every male among you must be
circumcised. 11 Cut away your foreskin to
show that you are prepared to follow the
agreement between me and you. 12 From
now on when a baby boy is eight days old,
you will circumcise him. This includes any
boy born among your people or any who is
your slave, who is not one of your
descendants. 13 Circumcise every baby boy
whether he is born in your family or bought
as a slave. Your bodies will be marked to

17:5 Abram This name means "honored father."
17:5 Abraham The end of the Hebrew word for "Abraham" sounds like the beginning of the Hebrew word for "many."

show that you are part of my agreement that
lasts forever. 14Any male who is not
circumcised will be cut off from his people,
because he has broken my agreement."

Isaac—the Promised Son

15God said to Abraham, "I will change the
name of Sarai,[n] your wife, to Sarah.[n] 16I will
bless her and give her a son, and you will be
the father. She will be the mother of many
nations. Kings of nations will come from
her."
17Abraham bowed facedown on the
ground and laughed. He said to himself,
"Can a man have a child when he is a
hundred years old? Can Sarah give birth to a
child when she is ninety?" 18Then Abraham
said to God, "Please let Ishmael be the son
you promised."
19God said, "No, Sarah your wife will have
a son, and you will name him Isaac.[n] I will
make my agreement with him to be an
agreement that continues forever with all
his descendants.
20"As for Ishmael, I have heard you. I will
bless him and give him many descendants.
And I will cause their numbers to grow
greatly. He will be the father of twelve great
leaders, and I will make him into a great
nation. 21But I will make my agreement with
Isaac, the son whom Sarah will have at this
same time next year." 22After God finished
talking with Abraham, God rose and left
him.
23Then Abraham gathered Ishmael, all the
males born in his camp, and the slaves he
had bought. So that day Abraham
circumcised every man and boy in his camp
as God had told him to do. 24Abraham was
ninety-nine years old when he was
circumcised. 25And Ishmael, his son, was
thirteen years old when he was circumcised.
26Abraham and his son were circumcised on
the same day. 27Also on that day all the men
in Abraham's camp were circumcised,
including all those born in his camp and all
the slaves he had bought from other nations.

The Three Visitors

18 Later, the LORD again appeared to
Abraham near the great trees of
Mamre. Abraham was sitting at the entrance
of his tent during the hottest part of the day.
2He looked up and saw three men standing
near him. When Abraham saw them, he ran
from his tent to meet them. He bowed
facedown on the ground before them 3and
said, "Sir, if you think well of me, please stay
awhile with me, your servant. 4I will bring
some water so all of you can wash your feet.
You may rest under the tree, 5and I will get
some bread for you so you can regain your
strength. Then you may continue your
journey."
The three men said, "That is fine. Do as
you said."
6Abraham hurried to the tent where Sarah
was and said to her, "Hurry, prepare twenty
quarts of fine flour, and make it into loaves
of bread." 7Then Abraham ran to his herd
and took one of his best calves. He gave it to
a servant, who hurried to kill it and to
prepare it for food. 8Abraham gave the three
men the calf that had been cooked and milk
curds and milk. While they ate, he stood
under the tree near them.
9The men asked Abraham, "Where is your
wife Sarah?"
"There, in the tent," said Abraham.
10Then the LORD said, "I will certainly
return to you about this time a year from
now. At that time your wife Sarah will have
a son."
Sarah was listening at the entrance of the
tent which was behind him. 11Abraham and
Sarah were very old. Since Sarah was past
the age when women normally have
children, 12she laughed to herself, "My
husband and I are too old to have a baby."
13Then the LORD said to Abraham, "Why
did Sarah laugh? Why did she say, 'I am too
old to have a baby'? 14Is anything too hard
for the LORD? No! I will return to you at the
right time a year from now, and Sarah will
have a son."
15Sarah was afraid, so she lied and said, "I
didn't laugh."
But the LORD said, "No. You did laugh."
16Then the men got up to leave and
started out toward Sodom. Abraham walked
along with them a short time to send them
on their way.

17:15 Sarai An Aramaic name meaning "princess." **17:15 Sarah** A Hebrew name meaning "princess."
17:19 Isaac The Hebrew words for "he laughed" (v. 17) and "Isaac" sound the same.

devotion 8

GENESIS 18:14

CAN DOESN'T MEAN *WILL*

Nothing is too hard for God. I believe that with everything in me. He is Savior, King, Lord Almighty, and the Maker of heaven and earth, for goodness' sake. No person or thing even comes remotely close to him. Certainly, he can do anything.

But sometimes I get this turned around. Sometimes I find myself thinking that because he can, then he will or he should. Of course God *can* give my brother and his wife the baby they long for. I am absolutely sure that he *can* remove my girlfriend's cancer. But just because he *can* do something doesn't mean that thing is his will or his timing.

There is nothing in our lives too hard for God. That truth gives me great peace. There is no difficulty or heartache that he cannot overcome. What matters for our hearts is the pursuit of his will and his timing. We are called to grow and desire the mind of Christ, waiting in his presence until our desires have become like his, until our hearts can discern his pleasure. What great rejoicing there will be at the very moment your desire intersects the "right time" of his divine will.

What seems too hard for you today? Prayerfully lay that on the altar of God and whisper, *Lord, it's too big for me, but nothing is too hard for you. I trust you. You are faithful. I will wait in your presence for your right time. Amen.*

Abraham's Bargain with God

17The LORD said, "Should I tell Abraham
what I am going to do now? 18Abraham's
children will certainly become a great and
powerful nation, and all nations on earth
will be blessed through him. 19I have chosen
him so he would command his children and
his descendants to live the way the LORD
wants them to, to live right and be fair. Then
I, the LORD, will give Abraham what I
promised him."

20Then the LORD said, "I have heard many
complaints against the people of Sodom and
Gomorrah. They are very evil. 21I will go
down and see if they are as bad as I have
heard. If not, I will know."

22So the men turned and went toward
Sodom, but Abraham stood there before the
LORD. 23Then Abraham approached him and
asked, "Do you plan to destroy the good
people along with the evil ones? 24What if
there are fifty good people in that city? Will
you still destroy it? Surely you will save the
city for the fifty good people living there.
25Surely you will not destroy the good
people along with the evil ones; then they
would be treated the same. You are the judge
of all the earth. Won't you do what is right?"

26The LORD said, "If I find fifty good people
in the city of Sodom, I will save the whole
city because of them."

27Then Abraham said, "Though I am only
dust and ashes, I have been brave to speak to
the Lord. 28What if there are only forty-five
good people in the city? Will you destroy the
whole city for the lack of five good people?"

The LORD said, "If I find forty-five there, I
will not destroy the city."

29Again Abraham said to him, "If you find
only forty good people there, will you
destroy the city?"

The LORD said, "If I find forty, I will not
destroy it."

30Then Abraham said, "Lord, please don't
be angry with me, but let me ask you this. If
you find only thirty good people in the city,
will you destroy it?"

He said, "If I find thirty good people there,
I will not destroy the city."

31 Then Abraham said, "I have been brave
to speak to the Lord. But what if there are
twenty good people in the city?"

He answered, "If I find twenty there, I will
not destroy the city."

32 Then Abraham said, "Lord, please don't
be angry with me, but let me bother you this
one last time. What if you find ten there?"

He said, "If I find ten there, I will not
destroy it."

33 When the LORD finished speaking to
Abraham, he left, and Abraham returned
home.

Lot Leaves Sodom

19 The two angels came to Sodom in the
evening as Lot was sitting near the
city gate. When he saw them, he got up and
went to them and bowed facedown on the
ground. 2 Lot said, "Sirs, please come to my
house and spend the night. There you can
wash your feet, and then tomorrow you may
continue your journey."

The angels answered, "No, we will spend
the night in the city's public square."

3 But Lot begged them to come, so they
agreed and went to his house. Then Lot
prepared a meal for them. He baked bread
without yeast, and they ate it.

4 Before bedtime, men both young and old
and from every part of Sodom surrounded
Lot's house. 5 They called to Lot, "Where are
the two men who came to you tonight?
Bring them out to us so we can have sexual
relations with them."

6 Lot went outside to them, closing the
door behind him. 7 He said, "No, my brothers!
Do not do this evil thing. 8 Look! I have two
daughters who have never slept with a man.
I will give them to you, and you may do
anything you want with them. But please
don't do anything to these men. They have
come to my house, and I must protect them."

9 The men around the house answered,
"Move out of the way!" Then they said to
each other, "This man Lot came to our city as
a stranger, and now he wants to tell us what
to do!" They said to Lot, "We will do worse
things to you than to them." They started
pushing him back and were ready to break
down the door.

10 But the two men staying with Lot
opened the door, pulled him back inside the
house, and then closed the door. 11 They
struck those outside the door with blindness,
so the men, both young and old, could not
find the door.

12 The two men said to Lot, "Do you have
any other relatives in this city? Do you have
any sons-in-law, sons, daughters, or any
other relatives? If you do, tell them to leave
now, 13 because we are about to destroy this
city. The LORD has heard of all the evil that is
here, so he has sent us to destroy it."

14 So Lot went out and said to his future
sons-in-law who were pledged to marry his
daughters, "Hurry and leave this city! The
LORD is about to destroy it!" But they thought
Lot was joking.

15 At dawn the next morning, the angels
begged Lot to hurry. They said, "Go! Take
your wife and your two daughters with you
so you will not be destroyed when the city is
punished."

16 But Lot delayed. So the two men took
the hands of Lot, his wife, and his two
daughters and led them safely out of the city.
So the LORD was merciful to Lot and his
family. 17 After they brought them out of the
city, one of the men said, "Run for your lives!
Don't look back or stop anywhere in the
valley. Run to the mountains, or you will be
destroyed."

18 But Lot said to one of them, "Sir, please
don't force me to go so far! 19 You have been
merciful and kind to me and have saved my
life. But I can't run to the mountains. The
disaster will catch me, and I will die. 20 Look,
that little town over there is not too far
away. Let me run there. It's really just a little
town, and I'll be safe there."

21 The angel said to Lot, "Very well, I will
allow you to do this also. I will not destroy
that town. 22 But run there fast, because I
cannot destroy Sodom until you are safely in
that town." (That town is named Zoar,[n]
because it is little.)

Sodom and Gomorrah Are Destroyed

23 The sun had already come up when Lot
entered Zoar. 24 The LORD sent a rain of
burning sulfur down from the sky on Sodom
and Gomorrah 25 and destroyed those cities.
He also destroyed the whole Jordan Valley,

19:22 Zoar This name sounds like the Hebrew word for "little."

everyone living in the cities, and even all the
plants.
[26]At that point Lot's wife looked back.
When she did, she became a pillar of salt.
[27]Early the next morning, Abraham got up
and went to the place where he had stood
before the LORD. [28]He looked down toward
Sodom and Gomorrah and all the Jordan
Valley and saw smoke rising from the land,
like smoke from a furnace.
[29]God destroyed the cities in the valley,
but he remembered what Abraham had
asked. So God saved Lot's life, but he
destroyed the city where Lot had lived.

Lot and His Daughters

[30]Lot was afraid to continue living in Zoar,
so he and his two daughters went to live in
the mountains in a cave. [31]One day the older
daughter said to the younger, "Our father is
old. Everywhere on the earth women and
men marry, but there are no men around
here for us to marry. [32]Let's get our father
drunk and have sexual relations with him.
We can use him to have children and
continue our family."
[33]That night the two girls got their father
drunk, and the older daughter went and had
sexual relations with him. But Lot did not
know when she lay down or when she got up.
[34]The next day the older daughter said to
the younger, "Last night I had sexual
relations with my father. Let's get him drunk
again tonight so you can go and have sexual
relations with him, too. In this way we can
use our father to have children to continue
our family." [35]So that night they got their
father drunk again, and the younger
daughter went and had sexual relations with
him. Again, Lot did not know when she lay
down or when she got up.
[36]So both of Lot's daughters became
pregnant by their father. [37]The older
daughter gave birth to a son and named him
Moab. He is the ancestor of all the Moabite
people who are still living today. [38]The
younger daughter also gave birth to a son
and named him Ben-Ammi. He is the father
of all the Ammonite people who are still
living today.

Abraham Tricks Abimelech

20 Abraham left Hebron and traveled to
southern Canaan where he stayed
awhile between Kadesh and Shur. When he
moved to Gerar, [2]he told people that his wife
Sarah was his sister. Abimelech king of
Gerar heard this, so he sent some servants to
take her. [3]But one night God spoke to
Abimelech in a dream and said, "You will
die. The woman you took is married."
[4]But Abimelech had not gone near Sarah,
so he said, "Lord, would you destroy an
innocent nation? [5]Abraham himself told me,
'This woman is my sister,' and she also said,
'He is my brother.' I am innocent. I did not
know I was doing anything wrong."
[6]Then God said to Abimelech in the
dream, "Yes, I know you did not realize what
you were doing. So I did not allow you to sin
against me and touch her. [7]Give Abraham
his wife back. He is a prophet. He will pray
for you, and you will not die. But if you do
not give Sarah back, you and all your family
will surely die."
[8]So early the next morning, Abimelech
called all his officers and told them
everything that had happened in the dream.
They were very afraid. [9]Then Abimelech
called Abraham to him and said, "What have
you done to us? What wrong did I do against
you? Why did you bring this trouble to my
kingdom? You should not have done these
things to me. [10]What were you thinking that
caused you to do this?"
[11]Then Abraham answered, "I thought no
one in this place respected God and that
someone would kill me to get Sarah. [12]And it
is true that she is my sister. She is the
daughter of my father, but she is not the
daughter of my mother. [13]When God told
me to leave my father's house and wander in
many different places, I told Sarah, 'You
must do a special favor for me. Everywhere
we go tell people I am your brother.' "
[14]Then Abimelech gave Abraham some
sheep, cattle, and male and female slaves. He
also gave Sarah, Abraham's wife, back to him
[15]and said, "Look around you at my land. You
may live anywhere you want."
[16]Abimelech said to Sarah, "I gave your
brother Abraham twenty-five pounds of
silver to make up for any wrong that people
may think about you. I want everyone to
know that you are innocent."
[17]Then Abraham prayed to God, and God
healed Abimelech, his wife, and his servant
girls so they could have children. [18]The LORD

had kept all the women in Abimelech's house from having children as a punishment on Abimelech for taking Abraham's wife Sarah.

A Baby for Sarah

21 The LORD cared for Sarah as he had said and did for her what he had promised. [2]Sarah became pregnant and gave birth to a son for Abraham in his old age. Everything happened at the time God had said it would. [3]Abraham named his son Isaac, the son Sarah gave birth to. [4]He circumcised Isaac when he was eight days old as God had commanded.

[5]Abraham was one hundred years old when his son Isaac was born. [6]And Sarah said, "God has made me laugh.[n] Everyone who hears about this will laugh with me. [7]No one thought that I would be able to have Abraham's child, but even though Abraham is old I have given him a son."

Hagar and Ishmael Leave

[8]Isaac grew, and when he became old enough to eat food, Abraham gave a great feast. [9]But Sarah saw Ishmael making fun of Isaac. (Ishmael was the son of Abraham by Hagar, Sarah's Egyptian slave.) [10]So Sarah said to Abraham, "Throw out this slave woman and her son. Her son should not inherit anything; my son Isaac should receive it all."

[11]This troubled Abraham very much because Ishmael was also his son. [12]But God said to Abraham, "Don't be troubled about the boy and the slave woman. Do whatever Sarah tells you. The descendants I promised you will be from Isaac. [13]I will also make the descendants of Ishmael into a great nation because he is your son, too."

[14]Early the next morning Abraham took some food and a leather bag full of water. He gave them to Hagar and sent her away. Carrying these things and her son, Hagar went and wandered in the desert of Beersheba.

[15]Later, when all the water was gone from the bag, Hagar put her son under a bush. [16]Then she went away a short distance and sat down. She thought, "My son will die, and I cannot watch this happen." She sat there and began to cry.

[17]God heard the boy crying, and God's angel called to Hagar from heaven. He said, "What is wrong, Hagar? Don't be afraid! God has heard the boy crying there. [18]Help him up and take him by the hand. I will make his descendants into a great nation."

[19]Then God showed Hagar a well of water. So she went to the well and filled her bag with water and gave the boy a drink.

[20]God was with the boy as he grew up. Ishmael lived in the desert and became an archer. [21]He lived in the Desert of Paran, and his mother found a wife for him in Egypt.

Abraham's Bargain with Abimelech

[22]Then Abimelech came with Phicol, the commander of his army, and said to Abraham, "God is with you in everything you do. [23]So make a promise to me here before God that you will be fair with me and my children and my descendants. Be kind to me and to this land where you have lived as a stranger—as kind as I have been to you."

[24]And Abraham said, "I promise." [25]Then Abraham complained to Abimelech about Abimelech's servants who had seized a well of water.

[26]But Abimelech said, "I don't know who did this. You never told me about this before today."

[27]Then Abraham gave Abimelech some sheep and cattle, and they made an agreement. [28]Abraham also put seven female lambs in front of Abimelech.

[29]Abimelech asked Abraham, "Why did you put these seven female lambs by themselves?"

[30]Abraham answered, "Accept these lambs from me to prove that you believe I dug this well."

[31]So that place was called Beersheba[n] because they made a promise to each other there.

[32]After Abraham and Abimelech made the agreement at Beersheba, Abimelech and Phicol, the commander of his army, went back to the land of the Philistines.

[33]Abraham planted a tamarisk tree at Beersheba and prayed to the LORD, the God who lives forever. [34]And Abraham lived as a

21:6 laugh The Hebrew words for "he laughed" and "Isaac" sound the same.
21:31 Beersheba This name means "well of the promise" or "well of seven."

stranger in the land of the Philistines for a
long time.

God Tests Abraham

22 After these things God tested
Abraham's faith. God said to him,
"Abraham!"
And he answered, "Here I am."
2 Then God said, "Take your only son,
Isaac, the son you love, and go to the land of
Moriah. Kill him there and offer him as a
whole burnt offering on one of the
mountains I will tell you about."
3 Abraham got up early in the morning and
saddled his donkey. He took Isaac and two
servants with him. After he cut the wood for
the sacrifice, they went to the place God had
told them to go. 4 On the third day Abraham
looked up and saw the place in the distance.
5 He said to his servants, "Stay here with the
donkey. My son and I will go over there and
worship, and then we will come back to you."
6 Abraham took the wood for the sacrifice
and gave it to his son to carry, but he himself
took the knife and the fire. So he and his son
went on together.
7 Isaac said to his father Abraham,
"Father!"
Abraham answered, "Yes, my son."
Isaac said, "We have the fire and the wood,
but where is the lamb we will burn as a
sacrifice?"
8 Abraham answered, "God will give us the
lamb for the sacrifice, my son."
So Abraham and his son went on together
9 and came to the place God had told him
about. Abraham built an altar there. He laid
the wood on it and then tied up his son Isaac
and laid him on the wood on the altar.
10 Then Abraham took his knife and was
about to kill his son.
11 But the angel of the LORD called to
him from heaven and said, "Abraham!
Abraham!"
Abraham answered, "Yes."
12 The angel said, "Don't kill your son or
hurt him in any way. Now I can see that you
trust God and that you have not kept your
son, your only son, from me."
13 Then Abraham looked up and saw a
male sheep caught in a bush by its horns. So
Abraham went and took the sheep and

devotion 9

GENESIS 22:2, 8–10

SURRENDER

Surrender and obedience go hand in hand. Almost every time I realize I am being called to obey God, there is a holy surrender that needs to happen in my life, an act or a decision that requires righteous submission on my part. And almost every time I have to surrender, something or someone precious to me is involved.

For me, surrender feels like a free fall in the dark. I feel alone. I can't see where I'm going. I don't know how far I'll fall, but I am trusting in the dark that the strong arms of God will save me.

When Abraham laid his son on the altar, I cannot imagine the grief that must have overcome him. Surely he felt like he was falling in the dark, acting in obedience but praying for some other way. *Any* other way. Then God stepped in. His big, strong, faithful arms came to save the ones that he loved.

Nothing has changed with God since Abraham's day. There are times he will ask you to die to a dream or a relationship or even something that seems good and holy so that he can be glorified for his faithfulness. To act in obedience when God calls you to surrender is a spiritual act of worship. When you make the hard choice to lay your life on his altar, he has promised to be faithful to come. When he calls you to obedience, will you surrender?

killed it. He offered it as a whole burnt
offering to God, and his son was saved.
14So Abraham named that place The LORD
Provides. Even today people say, "On the
mountain of the LORD it will be provided."
15The angel of the LORD called to Abraham
from heaven a second time 16and said, "The
LORD says, 'Because you did not keep back
your son, your only son, from me, I make
you this promise by my own name: 17I will
surely bless you and give you many
descendants. They will be as many as the
stars in the sky and the sand on the seashore,
and they will capture the cities of their
enemies. 18Through your descendants all the
nations on the earth will be blessed, because
you obeyed me.' "
19Then Abraham returned to his servants.
They all traveled back to Beersheba, and
Abraham stayed there.
20After these things happened, someone
told Abraham: "Your brother Nahor and his
wife Milcah have children now. 21The first
son is Uz, and the second is Buz. The third
son is Kemuel (the father of Aram). 22Then
there are Kesed, Hazo, Pildash, Jidlaph, and
Bethuel." 23Bethuel became the father of
Rebekah. Milcah was the mother of these
eight sons, and Nahor, Abraham's brother,
was the father. 24Also Nahor had four other
sons by his slave woman Reumah. Their
names were Tebah, Gaham, Tahash, and
Maacah.

Sarah Dies

23 Sarah lived to be one hundred twenty-
seven years old. 2She died in Kiriath
Arba (that is, Hebron) in the land of Canaan.
Abraham was very sad and cried because of
her. 3After a while he got up from the side of
his wife's body and went to talk to the
Hittites. He said, 4"I am only a stranger and a
foreigner here. Sell me some of your land so
that I can bury my dead wife."
5The Hittites answered Abraham, 6"Sir,
you are a great leader among us. You may
have the best place we have to bury your
dead. You may have any of our burying
places that you want, and none of us will
stop you from burying your dead wife."
7Abraham rose and bowed to the people
of the land, the Hittites. 8He said to them, "If
you truly want to help me bury my dead
wife here, speak to Ephron, the son of Zohar
for me. 9Ask him to sell me the cave of
Machpelah at the edge of his field. I will pay
him the full price. You can be the witnesses
that I am buying it as a burial place."
10Ephron was sitting among the Hittites at
the city gate. He answered Abraham, 11"No,
sir. I will give you the land and the cave that
is in it, with these people as witnesses. Bury
your dead wife."
12Then Abraham bowed down before the
Hittites. 13He said to Ephron before all the
people, "Please let me pay you the full price
for the field. Accept my money, and I will
bury my dead there."
14Ephron answered Abraham, 15"Sir, the
land is worth ten pounds of silver, but I
won't argue with you over the price. Take
the land, and bury your dead wife."
16Abraham agreed and paid Ephron in
front of the Hittite witnesses. He weighed
out the full price, ten pounds of silver, and
they counted the weight as the traders
normally did.
17-18So Ephron's field in Machpelah, east of
Mamre, was sold. Abraham became the
owner of the field, the cave in it, and all the
trees that were in the field. The sale was
made at the city gate, with the Hittites as
witnesses. 19After this, Abraham buried his
wife Sarah in the cave in the field of
Machpelah, near Mamre. (Mamre was later
called Hebron in the land of Canaan.) 20So
Abraham bought the field and the cave in it
from the Hittites to use as a burying place.

A Wife for Isaac

24 Abraham was now very old, and the
LORD had blessed him in every way.
2Abraham said to his oldest servant, who
was in charge of everything he owned, "Put
your hand under my leg.[n] 3Make a promise
to me before the LORD, the God of heaven
and earth. Don't get a wife for my son from
the Canaanite girls who live around here.
4Instead, go back to my country, to the land of
my relatives, and get a wife for my son Isaac."
5The servant said to him, "What if this
woman does not want to return with me to
this land? Then, should I take your son with
me back to your homeland?"

24:2 Put . . . leg This showed that a person would keep the promise.

6Abraham said to him, "No! Don't take my son back there. 7The LORD, the God of heaven, brought me from the home of my father and the land of my relatives. And he promised me, 'I will give this land to your descendants.' The LORD will send his angel before you to help you get a wife for my son there. 8If the girl won't come back with you, you will be free from this promise. But you must not take my son back there." 9So the servant put his hand under his master's leg and made a promise to Abraham about this.

10The servant took ten of Abraham's camels and left, carrying with him many different kinds of beautiful gifts. He went to Northwest Mesopotamia to Nahor's city. 11In the evening, when the women come out to get water, he made the camels kneel down at the well outside the city.

12The servant said, "LORD, God of my master Abraham, allow me to find a wife for his son today. Please show this kindness to my master Abraham. 13Here I am, standing by the spring, and the girls from the city are coming out to get water. 14I will say to one of them, 'Please put your jar down so I can drink.' Then let her say, 'Drink, and I will also give water to your camels.' If that happens, I will know she is the right one for your servant Isaac and that you have shown kindness to my master."

15Before the servant had finished praying, Rebekah, the daughter of Bethuel, came out of the city. (Bethuel was the son of Milcah and Nahor, Abraham's brother.) Rebekah was carrying her water jar on her shoulder. 16She was very pretty, a virgin; she had never had sexual relations with a man. She went down to the spring and filled her jar, then came back up. 17The servant ran to her and said, "Please give me a little water from your jar."

18Rebekah said, "Drink, sir." She quickly lowered the jar from her shoulder and gave him a drink. 19After he finished drinking, Rebekah said, "I will also pour some water for your camels." 20So she quickly poured all the water from her jar into the drinking trough for the camels. Then she kept running to the well until she had given all the camels enough to drink.

21The servant quietly watched her. He wanted to be sure the LORD had made his trip successful. 22After the camels had finished drinking, he gave Rebekah a gold ring weighing one-fifth of an ounce and two gold arm bracelets weighing about four ounces each. 23He asked, "Who is your father? Is there a place in his house for me and my men to spend the night?"

24Rebekah answered, "My father is Bethuel, the son of Milcah and Nahor." 25Then she said, "And, yes, we have straw for your camels and a place for you to spend the night."

26The servant bowed and worshiped the LORD 27and said, "Blessed is the LORD, the God of my master Abraham. The LORD has been kind and truthful to him and has led me to my master's relatives."

28Then Rebekah ran and told her mother's family about all these things. 29She had a brother named Laban, who ran out to Abraham's servant, who was still at the spring. 30Laban had heard what she had said and had seen the ring and the bracelets on his sister's arms. So he ran out to the well, and there was the man standing by the camels at the spring. 31Laban said, "Sir, you are welcome to come in; you don't have to stand outside. I have prepared the house for you and also a place for your camels."

32So Abraham's servant went into the house. After Laban unloaded the camels and gave them straw and food, he gave water to Abraham's servant so he and the men with him could wash their feet. 33Then Laban gave the servant food, but the servant said, "I will not eat until I have told you why I came."

So Laban said, "Then tell us."

34He said, "I am Abraham's servant. 35The LORD has greatly blessed my master in everything, and he has become a rich man. The LORD has given him many flocks of sheep, herds of cattle, silver and gold, male and female servants, camels, and horses. 36Sarah, my master's wife, gave birth to a son when she was old, and my master has given everything he owns to that son. 37My master had me make a promise to him and said, 'Don't get a wife for my son from the Canaanite girls who live around here. 38Instead, you must go to my father's people and to my family. There you must get a wife for my son.' 39I said to my master, 'What if the woman will not come back with me?' 40But he said, 'I serve the LORD, who will send

his angel with you and will help you. You
will get a wife for my son from my family
and my father's people. 41Then you will be
free from the promise. But if they will not
give you a wife for my son, you will be free
from this promise.'

42"Today I came to this spring. I said,
'LORD, God of my master Abraham, please
make my trip successful. 43I am standing by
this spring. I will wait for a young woman to
come out to get water, and I will say, "Please
give me water from your jar to drink."
44Then let her say, "Drink this water, and I
will also get water for your camels." By this I
will know the LORD has chosen her for my
master's son.'

45"Before I finished my silent prayer,
Rebekah came out of the city with her water
jar on her shoulder. She went down to the
spring and got water. I said to her, 'Please
give me a drink.' 46She quickly lowered the
jar from her shoulder and said, 'Drink this. I
will also get water for your camels.' So I
drank, and she gave water to my camels too.
47When I asked her, 'Who is your father?'
she answered, 'My father is Bethuel son of
Milcah and Nahor.' Then I put the ring in
her nose and the bracelets on her arms, 48and
I bowed my head and thanked the LORD. I
praised the LORD, the God of my master
Abraham, because he led me on the right
road to get the granddaughter of my master's
brother for his son. 49Now, tell me, will you
be kind and truthful to my master? And if
not, tell me so. Then I will know what I
should do."

50Laban and Bethuel answered, "This is
clearly from the LORD, and we cannot change
what must happen. 51Rebekah is yours. Take
her and go. Let her marry your master's son
as the LORD has commanded."

52When Abraham's servant heard these
words, he bowed facedown on the ground
before the LORD. 53Then he gave Rebekah
gold and silver jewelry and clothes. He also
gave expensive gifts to her brother and
mother. 54The servant and the men with him
ate and drank and spent the night there.
When they got up the next morning, the
servant said, "Now let me go back to my
master."

55Rebekah's mother and her brother said,
"Let Rebekah stay with us at least ten days.
After that she may go."

56But the servant said to them, "Do
not make me wait, because the LORD has
made my trip successful. Now let me go
back to my master."

57Rebekah's brother and mother said, "We
will call Rebekah and ask her what she
wants to do." 58They called her and asked
her, "Do you want to go with this man
now?"

She said, "Yes, I do."

59So they allowed Rebekah and her nurse
to go with Abraham's servant and his men.
60They blessed Rebekah and said,

"Our sister, may you be the mother of
thousands of people,
and may your descendants capture the
cities of their enemies."

61Then Rebekah and her servant girls got
on the camels and followed the servant and
his men. So the servant took Rebekah and
left.

62At this time Isaac had left Beer Lahai Roi
and was living in southern Canaan. 63One
evening when he went out to the field to
think, he looked up and saw camels coming.
64Rebekah also looked and saw Isaac. Then
she jumped down from the camel 65and
asked the servant, "Who is that man walking
in the field to meet us?"

The servant answered, "That is my
master." So Rebekah covered her face with
her veil.

66The servant told Isaac everything that
had happened. 67Then Isaac brought
Rebekah into the tent of Sarah, his mother,
and she became his wife. Isaac loved her
very much, and so he was comforted after
his mother's death.

Abraham's Family

25 Abraham married again, and his new
wife was Keturah. 2She gave birth to
Zimran, Jokshan, Medan, Midian, Ishbak,
and Shuah. 3Jokshan was the father of
Sheba and Dedan. Dedan's descendants
were the people of Assyria, Letush, and
Leum. 4The sons of Midian were Ephah,
Epher, Hanoch, Abida, and Eldaah. All these
were descendants of Keturah. 5Abraham left
everything he owned to Isaac. 6But before
Abraham died, he did give gifts to the sons of
his other wives, then sent them to the East
to be away from Isaac.

7Abraham lived to be one hundred

devotion 10

GENESIS 24:48

SINGLE AND NOT LOVING IT

Abraham wished for a wife for his son Isaac. Abraham didn't want just any woman for his son; he wanted the woman that the Lord had chosen. He sent the oldest servant in his house to find her, a servant who sought God's divine intervention. Notice Abraham's confidence. He sent out his servant and told him that the Lord would help him find the right girl for his son (Gen. 24:7). In other words, he knew the Lord cared about this concern.

The Lord cares about your desires as well, and he knows what is important to you in a mate. He knows about all the secret chambers that you keep closed while you wait for the right someone to unlock them. Not only does he care but he also wants you to know there is an appointed time and place where he will unlock the vision and present his gift to you.

It is that appointed time that you anticipate while you wait on God. Abraham's servant prayed specifically, even down to the words the virgin would speak. He wasn't asking for just the right time, but the *appointed* time.

Even as you pray, God is already at work. If you are single and not loving it, be specific and seek the Lord for his intervention and his appointed time to be fulfilled. When your wedding day comes, you too will bow your head and worship the Lord for the blessing he has given to you in your husband.

seventy-five years old. [8]He breathed his last
breath and died at an old age, after a long
and satisfying life. [9]His sons Isaac and
Ishmael buried him in the cave of
Machpelah in the field of Ephron east of
Mamre. (Ephron was the son of Zohar the
Hittite.) [10]So Abraham was buried with his
wife Sarah in the same field that he had
bought from the Hittites. [11]After Abraham
died, God blessed his son Isaac. Isaac was
now living at Beer Lahai Roi.

[12]This is the family history of Ishmael,
Abraham's son. (Hagar, Sarah's Egyptian
servant, was Ishmael's mother.) [13]These are
the names of Ishmael's sons in the order
they were born: Nebaioth, the first son, then
Kedar, Adbeel, Mibsam, [14]Mishma, Dumah,
Massa, [15]Hadad, Tema, Jetur, Naphish, and
Kedemah. [16]These were Ishmael's sons, and
these are the names of the tribal leaders
listed according to their settlements and
camps. [17]Ishmael lived one hundred
thirty-seven years and then breathed his last
breath and died. [18]His descendants lived
from Havilah to Shur, which is east of Egypt
stretching toward Assyria. They often
attacked the descendants of his brothers.

Isaac's Family

[19]This is the family history of Isaac.
Abraham had a son named Isaac. [20]When
Isaac was forty years old, he married Rebekah,
who came from Northwest Mesopotamia. She
was Bethuel's daughter and the sister of
Laban the Aramean. [21]Isaac's wife could not
have children, so Isaac prayed to the LORD for
her. The LORD heard Isaac's prayer, and
Rebekah became pregnant.

[22]While she was pregnant, the babies
struggled inside her. She asked, "Why is this
happening to me?" Then she went to get an
answer from the LORD.

[23]The LORD said to her,

"Two nations are in your body,
and two groups of people will be taken
from you.

One group will be stronger than the other,
and the older will serve the younger."
24When the time came, Rebekah gave
birth to twins. 25The first baby was born red.
Since his skin was like a hairy robe, he was
named Esau.[n] 26When the second baby was
born, he was holding on to Esau's heel, so
that baby was named Jacob.[n] Isaac was sixty
years old when they were born.
27When the boys grew up, Esau became a
skilled hunter. He loved to be out in the
fields. But Jacob was a quiet man and stayed
among the tents. 28Isaac loved Esau because
he hunted the wild animals that Isaac
enjoyed eating. But Rebekah loved Jacob.
29One day Jacob was boiling a pot of
vegetable soup. Esau came in from hunting
in the fields, weak from hunger. 30So Esau
said to Jacob, "Let me eat some of that red
soup, because I am weak with hunger." (That
is why people call him Edom.[n])
31But Jacob said, "You must sell me your
rights as the firstborn son."[n]
32Esau said, "I am almost dead from
hunger. If I die, all of my father's wealth will
not help me."
33But Jacob said, "First, promise me that
you will give it to me." So Esau made a
promise to Jacob and sold his part of their
father's wealth to Jacob. 34Then Jacob gave
Esau bread and vegetable soup, and he ate
and drank, and then left. So Esau showed
how little he cared about his rights as the
firstborn son.

Isaac Lies to Abimelech

26 Now there was a time of hunger in
the land, besides the time of hunger
that happened during Abraham's life. So
Isaac went to the town of Gerar to see
Abimelech king of the Philistines. 2The LORD
appeared to Isaac and said, "Don't go down
to Egypt, but live in the land where I tell you
to live. 3Stay in this land, and I will be with
you and bless you. I will give you and your
descendants all these lands, and I will keep
the oath I made to Abraham your father. 4I
will give you many descendants, as hard to
count as the stars in the sky, and I will give
them all these lands. Through your
descendants all the nations on the earth will
be blessed. 5I will do this because your father
Abraham obeyed me. He did what I said and
obeyed my commands, my teachings, and
my rules."
6So Isaac stayed in Gerar. 7His wife
Rebekah was very beautiful, and the men of
that place asked Isaac about her. Isaac said,
"She is my sister," because he was afraid to
tell them she was his wife. He thought they
might kill him so they could have her.
8Isaac lived there a long time. One day as
Abimelech king of the Philistines looked out
his window, he saw Isaac holding his wife
Rebekah tenderly. 9Abimelech called for
Isaac and said, "This woman is your wife.
Why did you say she was your sister?"
Isaac said to him, "I was afraid you would
kill me so you could have her."
10Abimelech said, "What have you done to
us? One of our men might have had sexual
relations with your wife. Then we would
have been guilty of a great sin."
11So Abimelech warned everyone,
"Anyone who touches this man or his wife
will be put to death."

Isaac Becomes Rich

12Isaac planted seed in that land, and that
year he gathered a great harvest. The LORD
blessed him very much, 13and he became
rich. He gathered more wealth until he
became a very rich man. 14He had so many
slaves and flocks and herds that the
Philistines envied him. 15So they stopped up
all the wells the servants of Isaac's father
Abraham had dug. (They had dug them
when Abraham was alive.) The Philistines
filled those wells with dirt. 16And Abimelech
said to Isaac, "Leave our country because you
have become much more powerful than we
are."
17So Isaac left that place and camped in
the Valley of Gerar and lived there. 18Long
before this time Abraham had dug many
wells, but after he died, the Philistines filled
them with dirt. So Isaac dug those wells
again and gave them the same names his
father had given them. 19Isaac's servants dug
a well in the valley, from which a spring of
water flowed. 20But the herdsmen of Gerar
argued with them and said, "This water is

25:25 Esau This name may mean "hairy." **25:26 Jacob** This name sounds like the Hebrew word for "heel." "Grabbing someone's heel" is a Hebrew saying for tricking someone. **25:30 Edom** This name sounds like the Hebrew word for "red." **25:31 rights . . . son** Usually the firstborn son had a high rank in the family. The firstborn son usually became the new head of the family.

Rebekah

GENESIS 27

Rebekah's faith was strong—so strong that she left her father and mother for a man she'd never met named Isaac. She was beautiful and courageous but couldn't bear children for twenty years. When she finally discovered there were two babies in her womb, she was overjoyed. Her thoughts turned to praise: *God has blessed me indeed!*

During the delivery, the second child grasped the heel of the baby boy coming out first, as if he were vying for position ahead of his brother. Jacob was the second born—but he was first in Rebekah's heart.

Years later when Isaac called Esau, his firstborn, to bless him, Rebekah hatched a scheme to deceive her near-blind husband. She covered Jacob's hands and neck with goatskins so he would feel hairy like his brother. She dressed him in Esau's clothes and held her breath as Isaac's aged hands reached out for his son. The old man was fooled, and Jacob received the choicest blessing.

When Esau discovered the deed, he begged Isaac for his blessing—but after it had been given, the benediction could not be withdrawn. Rebekah had not anticipated Esau's anger or the vow to kill his twin brother. With a heavy heart and tears streaming down her face, she sent her beloved son away, never to see him again or discover how God would use him.

Our motivations are often wrong, but God's faithfulness endures. Despite what we do, he will fulfill his promises.

ours." So Isaac named that well Argue
because they argued with him. 21 Then his
servants dug another well. When the people
also argued about it, Isaac named that well
Fight. 22 He moved from there and dug
another well. No one argued about this one,
so he named it Room Enough. Isaac said,
"Now the LORD has made room for us, and
we will be successful in this land."

23 From there Isaac went to Beersheba.
24 The LORD appeared to him that night and
said, "I am the God of your father Abraham.
Don't be afraid, because I am with you. I will
bless you and give you many descendants
because of my servant Abraham." 25 So Isaac
built an altar and worshiped the LORD there.
He also made a camp there, and his servants
dug a well.

26 Abimelech came from Gerar to see Isaac.
He brought with him Ahuzzath, who
advised him, and Phicol, the commander of
his army. 27 Isaac asked them, "Why have you
come to see me? You were my enemy and
forced me to leave your country."

28 They answered, "Now we know that the
LORD is with you. Let us swear an oath to
each other. Let us make an agreement with
you 29 that since we did not hurt you, you
will not hurt us. We were good to you and
sent you away in peace. Now the LORD has
blessed you."

30 So Isaac prepared food for them, and
they all ate and drank. 31 Early the next
morning the men swore an oath to each
other. Then Isaac sent them away, and they
left in peace.

32 That day Isaac's servants came and told
him about the well they had dug, saying,
"We found water in that well." 33 So Isaac
named it Shibah[n] and that city is called
Beersheba even now.

34 When Esau was forty years old, he
married two Hittite women—Judith
daughter of Beeri and Basemath daughter of
Elon. 35 These women brought much sorrow
to Isaac and Rebekah.

Jacob Tricks Isaac

27 When Isaac was old, his eyesight was
poor, so he could not see clearly. One
day he called his older son Esau to him and
said, "Son."

Esau answered, "Here I am."

26:33 Shibah This name sounds like the Hebrew words for "seven" and "promise."

2 Isaac said, "I am old and don't know
when I might die. 3 So take your bow and
arrows and go hunting in the field for an
animal for me to eat. 4 When you prepare the
tasty food that I love, bring it to me, and I
will eat. Then I will bless you before I die."
5 So Esau went out in the field to hunt.

Rebekah was listening as Isaac said this to
his son Esau. 6 She said to her son Jacob,
"Listen, I heard your father saying to your
brother Esau, 7 'Kill an animal and prepare
some tasty food for me to eat. Then I will
bless you in the presence of the LORD before I
die.' 8 So obey me, my son, and do what I tell
you. 9 Go out to our goats and bring me two
of the best young ones. I will prepare them
just the way your father likes them. 10 Then
you will take the food to your father, and he
will bless you before he dies."

11 But Jacob said to his mother Rebekah,
"My brother Esau is a hairy man, and I am
smooth! 12 If my father touches me, he will
know I am not Esau. Then he will not bless
me but will place a curse on me because I
tried to trick him."

13 So Rebekah said to him, "If your father
puts a curse on you, I will accept the blame.
Just do what I said. Go get the goats for me."

14 So Jacob went out and got two goats and
brought them to his mother, and she cooked
them in the special way Isaac enjoyed. 15 She
took the best clothes of her older son Esau
that were in the house and put them on the
younger son Jacob. 16 She also took the skins
of the goats and put them on Jacob's hands
and neck. 17 Then she gave Jacob the tasty
food and the bread she had made.

18 Jacob went in to his father and said,
"Father."

And his father said, "Yes, my son. Who are
you?"

19 Jacob said to him, "I am Esau, your first
son. I have done what you told me. Now sit
up and eat some meat of the animal I hunted
for you. Then bless me."

20 But Isaac asked his son, "How did you
find and kill the animal so quickly?"

Jacob answered, "Because the LORD your
God helped me to find it."

21 Then Isaac said to Jacob, "Come near so I
can touch you, my son. Then I will know if
you are really my son Esau."

22 So Jacob came near to Isaac his father.
Isaac touched him and said, "Your voice
sounds like Jacob's voice, but your hands are
hairy like the hands of Esau." 23 Isaac did not
know it was Jacob, because his hands were
hairy like Esau's hands, so Isaac blessed him.
24 Isaac asked, "Are you really my son Esau?"

Jacob answered, "Yes, I am."

25 Then Isaac said, "Bring me the food, and
I will eat it and bless you." So Jacob gave him
the food, and he ate. Jacob gave him wine,
and he drank. 26 Then Isaac said to him, "My
son, come near and kiss me." 27 So Jacob went
to his father and kissed him. When Isaac
smelled Esau's clothes, he blessed him and
said,

"The smell of my son
  is like the smell of the field
  that the LORD has blessed.
28 May God give you plenty of rain
  and good soil
  so that you will have plenty of grain
    and new wine.
29 May nations serve you
  and peoples bow down to you.
May you be master over your brothers,
  and may your mother's sons bow down
    to you.
May everyone who curses you be cursed,
  and may everyone who blesses you be
    blessed."

30 Isaac finished blessing Jacob. Then, just
as Jacob left his father Isaac, Esau came in
from hunting. 31 He also prepared some tasty
food and brought it to his father. He said,
"Father, rise and eat the food that your son
killed for you and then bless me."

32 Isaac asked, "Who are you?"

He answered, "I am your son—your
firstborn son—Esau."

33 Then Isaac trembled greatly and said,
"Then who was it that hunted the animals
and brought me food before you came? I ate
it, and I blessed him, and it is too late now to
take back my blessing."

34 When Esau heard the words of his father,
he let out a loud and bitter cry. He said to his
father, "Bless me—me, too, my father!"

35 But Isaac said, "Your brother came and
tricked me. He has taken your blessing."

36 Esau said, "Jacob[n] is the right name for
him. He has tricked me these two times. He

27:36 Jacob This name sounds like the Hebrew word for "heel." "Grabbing someone's heel" is a Hebrew saying for tricking someone.

took away my share of everything you own,
and now he has taken away my blessing."
Then Esau asked, "Haven't you saved a
blessing for me?"

37Isaac answered, "I gave Jacob the power
to be master over you, and all his brothers
will be his servants. And I kept him strong
with grain and new wine. There is nothing
left to give you, my son."

38But Esau continued, "Do you have only
one blessing, Father? Bless me, too, Father!"
Then Esau began to cry out loud.

39Isaac said to him,

"You will live far away from the best land,
far from the rain.
40You will live by using your sword,
and you will be a slave to your brother.
But when you struggle,
you will break free from him."

41After that Esau hated Jacob because of
the blessing from Isaac. He thought to
himself, "My father will soon die, and I will
be sad for him. Then I will kill Jacob."

42Rebekah heard about Esau's plan to kill
Jacob. So she sent for Jacob and said to him,
"Listen, your brother Esau is comforting
himself by planning to kill you. 43So, my
son, do what I say. My brother Laban is
living in Haran. Go to him at once! 44Stay
with him for a while, until your brother is
not so angry. 45In time, your brother will not
be angry, and he will forget what you did to
him. Then I will send a servant to bring you
back. I don't want to lose both of my sons on
the same day."

46Then Rebekah said to Isaac, "I am tired
of Hittite women. If Jacob marries one of
these Hittite women here in this land, I
want to die."

Jacob Searches for a Wife

28 Isaac called Jacob and blessed him
and commanded him, "You must
not marry a Canaanite woman. 2Go to the
house of Bethuel, your mother's father, in
Northwest Mesopotamia. Laban, your
mother's brother, lives there. Marry one of
his daughters. 3May God Almighty bless you
and give you many children, and may you
become a group of many peoples. 4May he
give you and your descendants the blessing
of Abraham so that you may own the land
where you are now living as a stranger, the
land God gave to Abraham." 5So Isaac sent
Jacob to Northwest Mesopotamia, to Laban
the brother of Rebekah. Bethuel the Aramean
was the father of Laban and Rebekah, and
Rebekah was the mother of Jacob and Esau.

6Esau learned that Isaac had blessed Jacob
and sent him to Northwest Mesopotamia to
find a wife there. He also learned that Isaac
had commanded Jacob not to marry a
Canaanite woman 7and that Jacob had
obeyed his father and mother and had gone
to Northwest Mesopotamia. 8So Esau saw
that his father Isaac did not want his sons to
marry Canaanite women. 9Now Esau already
had wives, but he went to Ishmael son of
Abraham, and he married Mahalath,
Ishmael's daughter. Mahalath was the sister
of Nebaioth.

Jacob's Dream at Bethel

10Jacob left Beersheba and set out for
Haran. 11When he came to a place, he spent
the night there because the sun had set. He
found a stone and laid his head on it to go to
sleep. 12Jacob dreamed that there was a ladder
resting on the earth and reaching up into
heaven, and he saw angels of God going up
and coming down the ladder. 13Then Jacob
saw the LORD standing above the ladder, and
he said, "I am the LORD, the God of Abraham
your grandfather, and the God of Isaac. I will
give you and your descendants the land on
which you are now sleeping. 14Your
descendants will be as many as the dust of the
earth. They will spread west and east, north
and south, and all the families of the earth
will be blessed through you and your
descendants. 15I am with you and will protect
you everywhere you go and will bring you
back to this land. I will not leave you until I
have done what I have promised you."

16Then Jacob woke from his sleep and
said, "Surely the LORD is in this place, but I
did not know it." 17He was afraid and said,
"This place frightens me! It is surely the
house of God and the gate of heaven."

18Jacob rose early in the morning and took
the stone he had slept on and set it up on its
end. Then he poured olive oil on the top of
it. 19At first, the name of that city was Luz,
but Jacob named it Bethel.[n]

28:19 Bethel This name means "house of God."

20Then Jacob made a promise. He said, "I
want God to be with me and to protect me
on this journey. I want him to give me food
to eat and clothes to wear 21so I will be able
to return in peace to my father's house. If the
LORD does these things, he will be my God.
22This stone which I have set up on its end
will be the house of God. And I will give God
one-tenth of all he gives me."

Jacob Arrives in Northwest Mesopotamia

29 Then Jacob continued his journey and
came to the land of the people of the
East. 2He looked and saw a well in the field
and three flocks of sheep lying nearby,
because they drank water from this well. A
large stone covered the mouth of the well.
3When all the flocks would gather there, the
shepherds would roll the stone away from
the well and water the sheep. Then they
would put the stone back in its place.
4Jacob said to the shepherds there, "My
brothers, where are you from?"
They answered, "We are from Haran."
5Then Jacob asked, "Do you know Laban,
grandson of Nahor?"
They answered, "We know him."
6Then Jacob asked, "How is he?"
They answered, "He is well. Look, his
daughter Rachel is coming now with his
sheep."
7Jacob said, "But look, it is still the middle
of the day. It is not time for the sheep to be
gathered for the night, so give them water
and let them go back into the pasture."
8But they said, "We cannot do that until
all the flocks are gathered. Then we will roll
away the stone from the mouth of the well
and water the sheep."
9While Jacob was talking with the
shepherds, Rachel came with her father's
sheep, because it was her job to care for
the sheep. 10When Jacob saw Laban's
daughter Rachel and Laban's sheep, he went
to the well and rolled the stone from its
mouth and watered Laban's sheep. Now
Laban was the brother of Rebekah, Jacob's
mother. 11Then Jacob kissed Rachel and cried.
12He told her that he was from her father's
family and that he was the son of Rebekah.
So Rachel ran home and told her father.
13When Laban heard the news about his
sister's son Jacob, he ran to meet him. Laban
hugged him and kissed him and brought
him to his house, where Jacob told Laban
everything that had happened.
14Then Laban said, "You are my own flesh
and blood."

Jacob Is Tricked

Jacob stayed there a month. 15Then Laban
said to Jacob, "You are my relative, but it is
not right for you to work for me without
pay. What would you like me to pay you?"
16Now Laban had two daughters. The
older was Leah, and the younger was Rachel.
17Leah had weak eyes, but Rachel was very
beautiful. 18Jacob loved Rachel, so he said to
Laban, "Let me marry your younger
daughter Rachel. If you will, I will work
seven years for you."
19Laban said, "It would be better for her to
marry you than someone else, so stay here
with me." 20So Jacob worked for Laban seven
years so he could marry Rachel. But they
seemed like just a few days to him because
he loved Rachel very much.
21After seven years Jacob said to Laban,
"Give me Rachel so that I may marry her.
The time I promised to work for you is over."
22So Laban gave a feast for all the people
there. 23That evening he brought his
daughter Leah to Jacob, and they had sexual
relations. 24(Laban gave his slave girl Zilpah
to his daughter to be her servant.) 25In the
morning when Jacob saw that he had had
sexual relations with Leah, he said to Laban,
"What have you done to me? I worked hard
for you so that I could marry Rachel! Why
did you trick me?"
26Laban said, "In our country we do not
allow the younger daughter to marry before
the older daughter. 27But complete the full
week of the marriage ceremony with Leah,
and I will give you Rachel to marry also. But
you must serve me another seven years."
28So Jacob did this, and when he had
completed the week with Leah, Laban gave
him his daughter Rachel as a wife. 29(Laban
gave his slave girl Bilhah to his daughter
Rachel to be her servant.) 30So Jacob had
sexual relations with Rachel also, and Jacob
loved Rachel more than Leah. Jacob worked
for Laban for another seven years.

Jacob's Family Grows

31When the LORD saw that Jacob loved
Rachel more than Leah, he made it possible

Leah

GENESIS 29

Leah watches from a distance. Her younger sister Rachel has always been more beautiful and outgoing. Though Leah is Jacob's first wife, he is talking with Rachel whom he married seven years later. The conversation is effortless between them, and Jacob's laugh is easy.

Leah turns away, tears filling her eyes. She knows Jacob loves Rachel more than her. The only reason he married Leah was because her father deceived him; Jacob thought he was marrying Rachel. She still remembers the look of disappointment and dread when she took off her veil and revealed the harsh truth. "Why can't he love me, Lord?" she whispers. "Why can't he love me like he loves Rachel?"

A pang of nausea doubles her over. She has been sick for more than a week with a queasiness that overtakes her without warning. She lifts her head and places a hand on her stomach with sudden realization: *There is a child! The Lord has seen my misery and has given me a child!* Joy fills her heart because Leah knows she is loved. She is loved by her Creator who thinks she is beautiful and worthy. She watches Jacob and Rachel, no longer consumed with jealousy. As she puts a hand to her belly, she smiles.

Leah became the mother of Jacob's first four sons and his daughter. David's royal line traces back to her son Judah—a line that would eventually include Jesus. Do you feel unloved or unworthy? God loves you, and he will use you in a mighty way!

for Leah to have children, but not Rachel.
32Leah became pregnant and gave birth to a
son. She named him Reuben,[n] because she
said, "The LORD has seen my troubles. Surely
now my husband will love me."
33Leah became pregnant again and gave
birth to another son. She named him
Simeon[n] and said, "The LORD has heard that I
am not loved, so he has given me this son."
34Leah became pregnant again and gave
birth to another son. She named him Levi[n]
and said, "Now, surely my husband will be
close to me, because I have given him three
sons."
35Then Leah gave birth to another son.
She named him Judah,[n] because she said,
"Now I will praise the LORD." Then Leah
stopped having children.

30 When Rachel saw that she was not
having children for Jacob, she envied
her sister Leah. She said to Jacob, "Give me
children, or I'll die!" 2Jacob became angry
with her and said, "Can I do what only God
can do? He is the one who has kept you
from having children."
3Then Rachel said, "Here is my slave girl
Bilhah. Have sexual relations with her so she
can give birth to a child for me. Then I can
have my own family through her."
4So Rachel gave Bilhah, her slave girl, to
Jacob as a wife, and he had sexual relations
with her. 5She became pregnant and gave
Jacob a son. 6Rachel said, "God has judged
me innocent. He has listened to my prayer
and has given me a son," so she named him
Dan.[n]
7Bilhah became pregnant again and gave
Jacob a second son. 8Rachel said, "I have
struggled hard with my sister, and I have
won." So she named that son Naphtali.[n]
9Leah saw that she had stopped having
children, so she gave her slave girl Zilpah to
Jacob as a wife. 10When Zilpah had a son,
11Leah said, "I am lucky," so she named him
Gad.[n] 12Zilpah gave birth to another son,
13and Leah said, "I am very happy! Now
women will call me happy," so she named
him Asher.[n]

29:32 Reuben This name sounds like the Hebrew word for "he has seen my troubles." **29:33 Simeon** This name sounds like the Hebrew word for "has heard." **29:34 Levi** This name sounds like the Hebrew word for "be close to." **29:35 Judah** This name sounds like the Hebrew word for "praise." **30:6 Dan** This name means "he has judged." **30:8 Naphtali** This name sounds like the Hebrew word for "my struggle." **30:11 Gad** This name may mean "lucky." **30:13 Asher** This name may mean "happy."

devotion 11

GENESIS 29:31–35

FINDING CONTENTMENT

When the Lord saw that Jacob loved Rachel more than Leah, he made it possible for Leah to have children, but not Rachel. The story of Leah and Rachel is a heartbreaker. Many of us have sisters we've competed with, and all of us have heartbreak stories of loving a man who didn't love us back. But can you imagine being married to your sister's husband and knowing that he only loved her? How would you find contentment and peace in that kind of home?

The story of Leah and Rachel is actually a much bigger story than two women struggling for the affections of one man. While these women were struggling, they were also becoming the mothers of all the tribes of Israel. Our Lord himself was a descendant of Leah. God used these women in an incredible way, but he also understood their situation was a difficult one.

I love the progression of Leah's perspective as she is blessed with children. With her first child, she has hope and says, "Surely now my husband will love me." With her second, you can hear her discouragement: "The Lord has heard that I am not loved, so he has given me this son." After her third son, she gives up on love: "Now, surely my husband will be close to me." But her fourth son brings a totally different response: "Now I will praise the Lord." Leah's situation never changed, but she did. Even in an incredibly difficult situation, she found contentment in the Lord.

14During the wheat harvest Reuben went
into the field and found some mandrake[n]
plants and brought them to his mother Leah.
But Rachel said to Leah, "Please give me
some of your son's mandrakes."
15Leah answered, "You have already taken
away my husband, and now you are trying
to take away my son's mandrakes."

But Rachel answered, "If you will give me
your son's mandrakes, you may sleep with
Jacob tonight."
16When Jacob came in from the field that
night, Leah went out to meet him. She said,
"You will have sexual relations with me
tonight because I have paid for you with my
son's mandrakes." So Jacob slept with her
that night.
17Then God answered Leah's prayer, and
she became pregnant again. She gave birth
to a fifth son 18and said, "God has given me
what I paid for, because I gave my slave girl
to my husband." So Leah named her son
Issachar.[n]
19Leah became pregnant again and gave
birth to a sixth son. 20She said, "God has
given me a fine gift. Now surely Jacob will
honor me, because I have given him six
sons," so she named him Zebulun.[n] 21Later
Leah gave birth to a daughter and named her
Dinah.
22Then God remembered Rachel and
answered her prayer, making it possible
for her to have children. 23When she
became pregnant and gave birth to a son,
she said, "God has taken away my shame,"
24and she named him Joseph.[n] Rachel said,
"I wish the LORD would give me another
son."

30:14 mandrake A plant which was believed to cause a woman to become pregnant. **30:18 Issachar** This name sounds like the Hebrew word for "paid for." **30:20 Zebulun** This name sounds like the Hebrew word for "honor." **30:24 Joseph** This name sounds like the Hebrew word for "he adds."

Jacob Tricks Laban

25 After the birth of Joseph, Jacob said to
Laban, "Now let me go to my own home and
country. 26 Give me my wives and my
children and let me go. I have earned them
by working for you, and you know that I
have served you well."
27 Laban said to him, "If I have pleased you,
please stay. I know the LORD has blessed me
because of you. 28 Tell me what I should pay
you, and I will give it to you."
29 Jacob answered, "You know that I have
worked hard for you, and your flocks have
grown while I cared for them. 30 When I
came, you had little, but now you have
much. Every time I did something for you,
the LORD blessed you. But when will I be able
to do something for my own family?"
31 Laban asked, "Then what should I give
you?"
Jacob answered, "I don't want you to give
me anything. Just do this one thing, and I
will come back and take care of your flocks.
32 Today let me go through all your flocks. I
will take every speckled or spotted sheep,
every black lamb, and every spotted or
speckled goat. That will be my pay. 33 In the
future you can easily see if I am honest.
When you come to look at my flocks, if I
have any goat that isn't speckled or spotted
or any lamb that isn't black, you will know I
stole it."
34 Laban answered, "Agreed! We will do
what you ask." 35 But that day Laban took
away all the male goats that had streaks or
spots, all the speckled and spotted female
goats (all those that had white on them), and
all the black sheep. He told his sons to watch
over them. 36 Then he took these animals to a
place that was three days' journey away
from Jacob. Jacob took care of all the flocks
that were left.
37 So Jacob cut green branches from
poplar, almond, and plane trees and peeled
off some of the bark so that the branches had
white stripes on them. 38 He put the branches
in front of the flocks at the watering places.
When the animals came to drink, they also
mated there, 39 so the flocks mated in front of
the branches. Then the young that were
born were streaked, speckled, or spotted.
40 Jacob separated the young animals from
the others, and he made them face the
streaked and dark animals in Laban's flock.
Jacob kept his animals separate from
Laban's. 41 When the stronger animals in the
flock were mating, Jacob put the branches
before their eyes so they would mate near
the branches. 42 But when the weaker
animals mated, Jacob did not put the
branches there. So the animals born from
the weaker animals were Laban's, and those
born from the stronger animals were Jacob's.
43 In this way Jacob became very rich. He had
large flocks, many male and female servants,
camels, and donkeys.

Jacob Runs Away

31 One day Jacob heard Laban's sons
talking. They said, "Jacob has taken
everything our father owned, and in this
way he has become rich." 2 Then Jacob
noticed that Laban was not as friendly as he
had been before. 3 The LORD said to Jacob, "Go
back to the land where your ancestors lived,
and I will be with you."
4 So Jacob told Rachel and Leah to meet
him in the field where he kept his flocks.
5 He said to them, "I have seen that your
father is not as friendly with me as he used
to be, but the God of my father has been
with me. 6 You both know that I have worked
as hard as I could for your father, 7 but he
cheated me and changed my pay ten times.
But God has not allowed your father to harm
me. 8 When Laban said, 'You can have all the
speckled animals as your pay,' all the
animals gave birth to speckled young ones.
But when he said, 'You can have all the
streaked animals as your pay,' all the flocks
gave birth to streaked babies. 9 So God has
taken the animals away from your father
and has given them to me.
10 "I had a dream during the season when
the flocks were mating. I saw that the only
male goats who were mating were streaked,
speckled, or spotted. 11 The angel of God
spoke to me in that dream and said, 'Jacob!' I
answered, 'Yes!' 12 The angel said, 'Look! Only
the streaked, speckled, or spotted male goats
are mating. I have seen all the wrong things
Laban has been doing to you. 13 I am the God
who appeared to you at Bethel, where you
poured olive oil on the stone you set up on
end and where you made a promise to me.
Now I want you to leave here and go back to
the land where you were born.' "
14 Rachel and Leah answered Jacob, "Our

father has nothing to give us when he dies.
15He has treated us like strangers. He sold us
to you, and then he spent all of the money
you paid for us. 16God took all this wealth
from our father, and now it belongs to us
and our children. So do whatever God has
told you to do."
17So Jacob put his children and his wives
on camels, 18and they began their journey
back to Isaac, his father, in the land of
Canaan. All the flocks of animals that Jacob
owned walked ahead of them. He carried
everything with him that he had gotten
while he lived in Northwest Mesopotamia.
19While Laban was gone to cut the wool
from his sheep, Rachel stole the idols that
belonged to him. 20And Jacob tricked Laban
the Aramean by not telling him he was
leaving. 21Jacob and his family left quickly,
crossed the Euphrates River, and traveled
toward the mountains of Gilead.
22Three days later Laban learned that
Jacob had run away, 23so he gathered his
relatives and began to chase him. After seven
days Laban found him in the mountains of
Gilead. 24That night God came to Laban the
Aramean in a dream and said, "Be careful! Do
not say anything to Jacob, good or bad."

The Search for the Stolen Idols

25So Laban caught up with Jacob. Now
Jacob had made his camp in the mountains,
so Laban and his relatives set up their camp
in the mountains of Gilead. 26Laban said to
Jacob, "What have you done? You cheated
me and took my daughters as if you had
captured them in a war. 27Why did you run
away secretly and trick me? Why didn't you
tell me? Then I could have sent you away
with joy and singing and with the music of
tambourines and harps. 28You did not even
let me kiss my grandchildren and my
daughters good-bye. You were very foolish to
do this! 29I have the power to harm you, but
last night the God of your father spoke to me
and warned me not to say anything to you,
good or bad. 30I know you want to go back to
your home, but why did you steal my idols?"
31Jacob answered Laban, "I left without
telling you, because I was afraid you would
take your daughters away from me. 32If you
find anyone here who has taken your idols,
that person will be killed! Your relatives will
be my witnesses. You may look for anything
that belongs to you and take anything that is
yours." (Now Jacob did not know that Rachel
had stolen Laban's idols.)
33So Laban looked in Jacob's tent, in Leah's
tent, and in the tent where the two slave
women stayed, but he did not find his idols.
When he left Leah's tent, he went into
Rachel's tent. 34Rachel had hidden the idols
inside her camel's saddle and was sitting on
them. Although Laban looked through the
whole tent, he did not find them.
35Rachel said to her father, "Father, don't
be angry with me. I am not able to stand up
before you because I am having my monthly
period." So Laban looked through the camp,
but he did not find his idols.
36Then Jacob became very angry and said,
"What wrong have I done? What law have I
broken to cause you to chase me? 37You have
looked through everything I own, but you
have found nothing that belongs to you. If
you have found anything, show it to
everyone. Put it in front of your relatives and
my relatives, and let them decide which one
of us is right. 38I have worked for you now
for twenty years. During all that time none
of the lambs and kids died during birth, and
I have not eaten any of the male sheep from
your flocks. 39Any time an animal was killed
by wild beasts, I did not bring it to you, but
made up for the loss myself. You made me
pay for any animal that was stolen during
the day or night. 40In the daytime the sun
took away my strength, and at night I was
cold and could not sleep. 41I worked like a
slave for you for twenty years—the first
fourteen to get your two daughters and the
last six to earn your flocks. During that time
you changed my pay ten times. 42But the
God of my father, the God of Abraham and
the God of Isaac, was with me. Otherwise,
you would have sent me away with nothing.
But he saw the trouble I had and the hard
work I did, and last night he corrected you."

Jacob and Laban's Agreement

43Laban said to Jacob, "These girls are my
daughters. Their children belong to me, and
these flocks are mine. Everything you see
here belongs to me, but I can do nothing to
keep my daughters and their children. 44Let
us make an agreement, and let us set up a
pile of stones to remind us of it."
45So Jacob took a large rock and set it up

on its end. 46He told his relatives to gather
rocks, so they took the rocks and piled them
up; then they ate beside the pile. 47Laban
named that place in his language A Pile to
Remind Us, and Jacob gave the place the
same name in Hebrew.
48Laban said to Jacob, "This pile of rocks
will remind us of the agreement between
us." That is why the place was called A Pile
to Remind Us. 49It was also called Mizpah,[n]
because Laban said, "Let the LORD watch over
us while we are separated from each other.
50Remember that God is our witness even if
no one else is around us. He will know if you
harm my daughters or marry other women.
51Here is the pile of rocks that I have put
between us and here is the rock I set up on
end. 52This pile of rocks and this rock set on
end will remind us of our agreement. I will
never go past this pile to hurt you, and you
must never come to my side of them to hurt
me. 53Let the God of Abraham, who is the
God of Nahor and the God of their ancestors,
punish either of us if we break this
agreement."
So Jacob made a promise in the name of
the God whom his father Isaac worshiped.
54Then Jacob killed an animal and offered it
as a sacrifice on the mountain, and he
invited his relatives to share in the meal.
After they finished eating, they spent the
night on the mountain. 55Early the next
morning Laban kissed his grandchildren and
his daughters and blessed them, and then he
left to return home.

Jacob Meets Esau

32 When Jacob also went his way, the
angels of God met him. 2When he
saw them, he said, "This is the camp of God!"
So he named that place Mahanaim.[n]
3Jacob's brother Esau was living in the
area called Seir in the country of Edom.
Jacob sent messengers to Esau, 4telling them,
"Give this message to my master Esau: 'This
is what Jacob, your servant, says: I have lived
with Laban and have remained there until
now. 5I have cattle, donkeys, flocks, and male
and female servants. I send this message to
you and ask you to accept us.' "
6The messengers returned to Jacob and
said, "We went to your brother Esau. He is
coming to meet you and has four hundred
men with him."
7Then Jacob was very afraid and worried.
He divided the people who were with him
and all the flocks, herds, and camels into two
camps. 8Jacob thought, "Esau might come
and destroy one camp, but the other camp
can run away and be saved."
9Then Jacob said, "God of my father
Abraham! God of my father Isaac! LORD, you
told me to return to my country and my
family. You said that you would treat me
well. 10I am not worthy of the kindness and
continual goodness you have shown me. The
first time I traveled across the Jordan River, I
had only my walking stick, but now I own
enough to have two camps. 11Please save me
from my brother Esau. I am afraid he will
come and kill all of us, even the mothers
with the children. 12You said to me, 'I will
treat you well and will make your children
as many as the sand of the seashore. There
will be too many to count.' "
13Jacob stayed there for the night and
prepared a gift for Esau from what he had
with him: 14two hundred female goats and
twenty male goats, two hundred female
sheep and twenty male sheep, 15thirty female
camels and their young, forty cows and ten
bulls, twenty female donkeys, and ten male
donkeys. 16Jacob gave each separate flock of
animals to one of his servants and said to
them, "Go ahead of me and keep some space
between each herd." 17Jacob gave them their
orders. To the servant with the first group of
animals he said, "My brother Esau will come
to you and ask, 'Whose servant are you?
Where are you going and whose animals are
these?' 18Then you will answer, 'They belong
to your servant Jacob. He sent them as a gift
to you, my master Esau, and he also is
coming behind us.' "
19Jacob ordered the second servant, the
third servant, and all the other servants to do
the same thing. He said, "Say the same thing
to Esau when you meet him. 20Say, 'Your
servant Jacob is coming behind us.' " Jacob
thought, "If I send these gifts ahead of me,
maybe Esau will forgive me. Then when I
see him, perhaps he will accept me." 21So
Jacob sent the gifts to Esau, but he himself
stayed that night in the camp.

31:49 Mizpah This name sounds like the Hebrew word for "watch."
32:2 Mahanaim This name means "two camps."

devotion 12

GENESIS 31:50

GOD IS OUR WITNESS

Laban's words to Jacob are also applicable to our day and age. Laban wanted Jacob to remember that even if he never knew if Jacob mistreated Rachel or Leah, God Almighty would know. This agreement between them wasn't something Jacob would have taken lightly, and we shouldn't take our commitments lightly either.

When I was a teenager, I remember making a promise to a good friend of mine. It was nothing of consequence now that years have gone by, but it was something she told me in confidence that I've kept safe all these years. To be honest, she has moved away, so perhaps if I told that juicy bit of gossip to some old friends of ours, she might not even know about it. But it's not my secret to tell. Even if she never knew, God would be completely aware that I'd broken my word.

Perhaps like Jacob and Laban, you've made a vow with someone over the years. If God was your witness, and he was, then don't be tempted to break it. As long as it's not something harmful to the person or someone else, remember that God wants you to keep your vow. A promise is something you should honor, no matter how many years have gone by. Before you make a commitment—whether it is in marriage, friendship, or another relationship—remember you're making that promise before God. Pray that you'll be the kind of friend, wife, or mother who is always trustworthy.

Jacob Wrestles with God

22 During the night Jacob rose and crossed
the Jabbok River at the crossing, taking with
him his two wives, his two slave girls, and
his eleven sons. 23 He sent his family and
everything he had across the river. 24 So Jacob
was alone, and a man came and wrestled
with him until the sun came up. 25 When the
man saw he could not defeat Jacob, he struck
Jacob's hip and put it out of joint. 26 Then he
said to Jacob, "Let me go. The sun is coming
up."

But Jacob said, "I will let you go if you will
bless me."

27 The man said to him, "What is your
name?"

And he answered, "Jacob."

28 Then the man said, "Your name will no
longer be Jacob. Your name will now be
Israel,[n] because you have wrestled with God
and with people, and you have won."

29 Then Jacob asked him, "Please tell me
your name."

But the man said, "Why do you ask my
name?" Then he blessed Jacob there.

30 So Jacob named that place Peniel,[n]
saying, "I have seen God face to face, but my
life was saved." 31 Then the sun rose as he
was leaving that place, and Jacob was
limping because of his leg. 32 So even today
the people of Israel do not eat the muscle
that is on the hip joint of animals, because
Jacob was touched there.

Jacob Shows His Bravery

33 Jacob looked up and saw Esau
coming, and with him were four
hundred men. So Jacob divided his children
among Leah, Rachel, and the two slave girls.
2 Jacob put the slave girls with their children
first, then Leah and her children behind
them, and Rachel and Joseph last. 3 Jacob

32:28 Israel This name means "he wrestles with God."
32:30 Peniel This name means "the face of God."

himself went out in front of them and
bowed down flat on the ground seven times
as he was walking toward his brother.
4But Esau ran to meet Jacob and put his
arms around him and hugged him. Then
Esau kissed him, and they both cried. 5When
Esau looked up and saw the women and
children, he asked, "Who are these people
with you?"
Jacob answered, "These are the children
God has given me. God has been good to me,
your servant."
6Then the two slave girls and their
children came up to Esau and bowed down
flat on the earth before him. 7Leah and her
children also came up to Esau and also
bowed down flat on the earth. Last of all,
Joseph and Rachel came up to Esau, and
they, too, bowed down flat before him.
8Esau said, "I saw many herds as I was
coming here. Why did you bring them?"
Jacob answered, "They were to please you,
my master."
9But Esau said, "I already have enough, my
brother. Keep what you have."
10Jacob said, "No! Please! If I have pleased
you, then accept the gift I give you. I am very
happy to see your face again. It is like seeing
the face of God, because you have accepted
me. 11So I beg you to accept the gift I give
you. God has been very good to me, and I
have more than I need." And because Jacob
begged, Esau accepted the gift.
12Then Esau said, "Let us be going. I will
travel with you."
13But Jacob said to him, "My master, you
know that the children are weak. And I must
be careful with my flocks and their young
ones. If I force them to go too far in one day,
all the animals will die. 14So, my master, you
go on ahead of me, your servant. I will
follow you slowly and let the animals and
the children set the speed at which we
travel. I will meet you, my master, in Edom."
15So Esau said, "Then let me leave some of
my people with you."
"No, thank you," said Jacob. "I only want
to please you, my master." 16So that day Esau
started back to Edom. 17But Jacob went to
Succoth, where he built a house for himself
and shelters for his animals. That is why the
place was named Succoth.[n]

18Jacob left Northwest Mesopotamia and
arrived safely at the city of Shechem in the
land of Canaan. There he camped east of the
city. 19He bought a part of the field where he
had camped from the sons of Hamor father
of Shechem for one hundred pieces of silver.
20He built an altar there and named it after
God, the God of Israel.

Dinah Is Attacked

34 At this time Dinah, the daughter of
Leah and Jacob, went out to visit the
women of the land. 2When Shechem son of
Hamor the Hivite, the ruler of the land, saw
her, he took her and forced her to have
sexual relations with him. 3Shechem fell in
love with Dinah, and he spoke kindly to her.
4He told his father, Hamor, "Please get this
girl for me so I can marry her."
5Jacob learned how Shechem had
disgraced his daughter, but since his sons
were out in the field with the cattle, Jacob
said nothing until they came home. 6While
he waited, Hamor father of Shechem went to
talk with Jacob.
7When Jacob's sons heard what had
happened, they came in from the field. They
were very angry that Shechem had done
such a wicked thing to Israel. It was wrong
for him to have sexual relations with Jacob's
daughter; a thing like this should not be
done.
8But Hamor talked to Dinah's brothers
and said, "My son Shechem is deeply in love
with Dinah. Please let him marry her. 9Marry
our people. Give your women to our men as
wives and take our women for your men as
wives. 10You can live in the same land with
us. You will be free to own land and to trade
here."
11Shechem also talked to Jacob and to
Dinah's brothers and said, "Please accept my
offer. I will give anything you ask. 12Ask as
much as you want for the payment for the
bride, and I will give it to you. Just let me
marry Dinah."
13Jacob's sons answered Shechem and his
father with lies, because Shechem had
disgraced their sister Dinah. 14The brothers
said to them, "We cannot allow you to
marry our sister, because you are not
circumcised. That would be a disgrace to us.

33:17 Succoth This name means "shelters."

[15]But we will allow you to marry her if you
do this one thing: Every man in your town
must be circumcised like us. [16]Then your
men can marry our women, and our men
can marry your women, and we will live in
your land and become one people. [17]If you
refuse to be circumcised, we will take Dinah
and leave."

[18]What they asked seemed fair to Hamor
and Shechem. [19]So Shechem quickly went to
be circumcised because he loved Jacob's
daughter.

Now Shechem was the most respected
man in his family. [20]So Hamor and Shechem
went to the gate of their city and spoke to
the men of their city, saying, [21]"These people
want to be friends with us. So let them live
in our land and trade here. There is enough
land for all of us. Let us marry their women,
and we can let them marry our women.
[22]But we must agree to one thing: All our
men must be circumcised as they are. Then
they will agree to live in our land, and we
will be one people. [23]If we do this, their
cattle and their animals will belong to us.
Let us do what they say, and they will stay in
our land." [24]All the people who had come to
the city gate heard this. They agreed with
Hamor and Shechem, and every man was
circumcised.

[25]Three days later the men who were
circumcised were still in pain. Two of Jacob's
sons, Simeon and Levi (Dinah's brothers),
took their swords and made a surprise attack
on the city, killing all the men there. [26]They
killed Hamor and his son Shechem and then
took Dinah out of Shechem's house and left.
[27]Jacob's sons came upon the dead bodies
and stole everything that was in the city, to
pay them back for what Shechem had done
to their sister. [28]So the brothers took the
flocks, herds, and donkeys, and everything in
the city and in the fields. [29]They took every
valuable thing the people owned, even their
wives and children and everything in the
houses.

[30]Then Jacob said to Simeon and Levi,
"You have caused me a lot of trouble. Now
the Canaanites and the Perizzites who live in
the land will hate me. Since there are only a
few of us, if they join together to attack us,
my people and I will be destroyed."

[31]But the brothers said, "We will not allow
our sister to be treated like a prostitute."

Jacob in Bethel

35 God said to Jacob, "Go to the city of
Bethel and live there. Make an altar to
the God who appeared to you there when you
were running away from your brother Esau."

[2]So Jacob said to his family and to all who
were with him, "Put away the foreign gods
you have, and make yourselves clean, and
change your clothes. [3]We will leave here and
go to Bethel. There I will build an altar to
God, who has helped me during my time of
trouble. He has been with me everywhere I
have gone." [4]So they gave Jacob all the
foreign gods they had, and the earrings they
were wearing, and he hid them under the
great tree near the town of Shechem. [5]Then
Jacob and his sons left there. But God caused
the people in the nearby cities to be afraid,
so they did not follow them. [6]And Jacob and
all the people who were with him went to
Luz, which is now called Bethel, in the land
of Canaan. [7]There Jacob built an altar and
named the place Bethel, after God, because
God had appeared to him there when he was
running from his brother.

[8]Deborah, Rebekah's nurse, died and was
buried under the oak tree at Bethel, so they
named that place Oak of Crying.

Jacob's New Name

[9]When Jacob came back from Northwest
Mesopotamia, God appeared to him again
and blessed him. [10]God said to him, "Your
name is Jacob, but you will not be called
Jacob any longer. Your new name will be
Israel." So he called him Israel. [11]God said to
him, "I am God Almighty. Have many
children and grow in number as a nation.
You will be the ancestor of many nations
and kings. [12]The same land I gave to
Abraham and Isaac I will give to you and
your descendants." [13]Then God left him.
[14]Jacob set up a stone on edge in that place
where God had talked to him, and he poured
a drink offering and olive oil on it to make it
special for God. [15]And Jacob named the place
Bethel.

Rachel Dies Giving Birth

[16]Jacob and his group left Bethel. Before
they came to Ephrath, Rachel began giving
birth to her baby, [17]but she was having much
trouble. When Rachel's nurse saw this, she

said, "Don't be afraid, Rachel. You are giving birth to another son." [18]Rachel gave birth to the son, but she herself died. As she lay dying, she named the boy Son of My Suffering, but Jacob called him Benjamin.[n]

[19]Rachel was buried on the road to Ephrath, a district of Bethlehem, [20]and Jacob set up a rock on her grave to honor her. That rock is still there. [21]Then Israel[n] continued his journey and camped just south of Migdal Eder.

[22]While Israel was there, Reuben had sexual relations with Israel's slave woman Bilhah, and Israel heard about it.

The Family of Israel

Jacob had twelve sons. [23]He had six sons by his wife Leah: Reuben, his first son, then Simeon, Levi, Judah, Issachar, and Zebulun.

[24]He had two sons by his wife Rachel: Joseph and Benjamin.

[25]He had two sons by Rachel's slave girl Bilhah: Dan and Naphtali.

[26]And he had two sons by Leah's slave girl Zilpah: Gad and Asher.

These are Jacob's sons who were born in Northwest Mesopotamia.

[27]Jacob went to his father Isaac at Mamre near Hebron, where Abraham and Isaac had lived. [28]Isaac lived one hundred eighty years. [29]So Isaac breathed his last breath and died when he was very old, and his sons Esau and Jacob buried him.

Esau's Family

36 This is the family history of Esau (also called Edom). [2]Esau married women from the land of Canaan: Adah daughter of Elon the Hittite; and Oholibamah daughter of Anah, the son of Zibeon the Hivite; [3]and Basemath, Ishmael's daughter, the sister of Nebaioth.

[4]Adah gave birth to Eliphaz for Esau. Basemath gave him Reuel, [5]and Oholibamah gave him Jeush, Jalam, and Korah. These were Esau's sons who were born in the land of Canaan.

[6]Esau took his wives, his sons, his daughters, and all the people who lived with him, his herds and other animals, and all the belongings he had gotten in Canaan, and he went to a land away from his brother Jacob. [7]Esau and Jacob's belongings were becoming too many for them to live in the same land. The land where they had lived could not support both of them, because they had too many herds. [8]So Esau lived in the mountains of Edom. (Esau is also named Edom.)

[9]This is the family history of Esau. He is the ancestor of the Edomites, who live in the mountains of Edom.

[10]Esau's sons were Eliphaz, son of Adah and Esau, and Reuel, son of Basemath and Esau.

[11]Eliphaz had five sons: Teman, Omar, Zepho, Gatam, and Kenaz. [12]Eliphaz also had a slave woman named Timna, and Timna and Eliphaz gave birth to Amalek. These were Esau's grandsons by his wife Adah.

[13]Reuel had four sons: Nahath, Zerah, Shammah, and Mizzah. These were Esau's grandsons by his wife Basemath.

[14]Esau's third wife was Oholibamah the daughter of Anah. (Anah was the son of Zibeon.) Esau and Oholibamah gave birth to Jeush, Jalam, and Korah.

[15]These were the leaders that came from Esau: Esau's first son was Eliphaz. From him came these leaders: Teman, Omar, Zepho, Kenaz, [16]Korah, Gatam, and Amalek. These were the leaders that came from Eliphaz in the land of Edom. They were the grandsons of Adah.

[17]Esau's son Reuel was the father of these leaders: Nahath, Zerah, Shammah, and Mizzah. These were the leaders that came from Reuel in the land of Edom. They were the grandsons of Esau's wife Basemath.

[18]Esau's wife Oholibamah gave birth to these leaders: Jeush, Jalam, and Korah. These are the leaders that came from Esau's wife Oholibamah the daughter of Anah. [19]These were the sons of Esau (also called Edom), and these were their leaders.

[20]These were the sons of Seir the Horite, who were living in the land: Lotan, Shobal, Zibeon, Anah, [21]Dishon, Ezer, and Dishan. These sons of Seir were the leaders of the Horites in Edom.

[22]The sons of Lotan were Hori and Homam. (Timna was Lotan's sister.)

[23]The sons of Shobal were Alvan, Manahath, Ebal, Shepho, and Onam.

[24]The sons of Zibeon were Aiah and Anah.

35:18 Benjamin This name means "right-hand son" or "favorite son."
35:21 Israel Also called Jacob.

Anah is the man who found the hot springs
in the desert while he was caring for his
father's donkeys.
25The children of Anah were Dishon and
Oholibamah daughter of Anah.
26The sons of Dishon were Hemdan,
Eshban, Ithran, and Keran.
27The sons of Ezer were Bilhan, Zaavan,
and Akan.
28The sons of Dishan were Uz and Aran.
29These were the names of the Horite
leaders: Lotan, Shobal, Zibeon, Anah,
30Dishon, Ezer, and Dishan.
These men were the leaders of the Horite
families who lived in the land of Edom.
31These are the kings who ruled in the land
of Edom before the Israelites ever had a king:
32Bela son of Beor was the king of Edom.
He came from the city of Dinhabah.
33When Bela died, Jobab son of Zerah
became king. Jobab was from Bozrah.
34When Jobab died, Husham became king.
He was from the land of the Temanites.
35When Husham died, Hadad son of
Bedad, who had defeated Midian in the
country of Moab, became king. Hadad was
from the city of Avith.
36When Hadad died, Samlah became king.
He was from Masrekah.
37When Samlah died, Shaul became king.
He was from Rehoboth on the Euphrates
River.
38When Shaul died, Baal-Hanan son of
Acbor became king.
39When Baal-Hanan son of Acbor died,
Hadad became king. He was from the city of
Pau. His wife's name was Mehetabel
daughter of Matred, who was the daughter
of Me-Zahab.
40These Edomite leaders, listed by their
families and regions, came from Esau. Their
names were Timna, Alvah, Jetheth,
41Oholibamah, Elah, Pinon, 42Kenaz, Teman,
Mibzar, 43Magdiel, and Iram. They were the
leaders of Edom. (Esau was the father of the
Edomites.) The area where each of these
families lived was named after that family.

Joseph the Dreamer

37 Jacob lived in the land of Canaan,
where his father had lived. 2This is
the family history of Jacob:
Joseph was a young man, seventeen years
old. He and his brothers, the sons of Bilhah
and Zilpah, his father's wives, cared for the
flocks. Joseph gave his father bad reports
about his brothers. 3Since Joseph was born
when his father Israel[n] was old, Israel loved
him more than his other sons. He made
Joseph a special robe with long sleeves.
4When Joseph's brothers saw that their
father loved him more than he loved them,
they hated their brother and could not speak
to him politely.
5One time Joseph had a dream, and when
he told his brothers about it, they hated him
even more. 6Joseph said, "Listen to the dream
I had. 7We were in the field tying bundles of
wheat together. My bundle stood up, and
your bundles of wheat gathered around it
and bowed down to it."
8His brothers said, "Do you really think
you will be king over us? Do you truly think
you will rule over us?" His brothers hated
him even more because of his dreams and
what he had said.
9Then Joseph had another dream, and he
told his brothers about it also. He said,
"Listen, I had another dream. I saw the sun,
moon, and eleven stars bowing down to me."
10Joseph also told his father about this
dream, but his father scolded him, saying,
"What kind of dream is this? Do you really
believe that your mother, your brothers, and
I will bow down to you?" 11Joseph's brothers
were jealous of him, but his father thought
about what all these things could mean.
12One day Joseph's brothers went to
Shechem to graze their father's flocks.
13Israel said to Joseph, "Go to Shechem
where your brothers are grazing the flocks."
Joseph answered, "I will go."
14His father said, "Go and see if your
brothers and the flocks are all right. Then
come back and tell me." So Joseph's father
sent him from the Valley of Hebron.
When Joseph came to Shechem, 15a man
found him wandering in the field and asked
him, "What are you looking for?"
16Joseph answered, "I am looking for my
brothers. Can you tell me where they are
grazing the flocks?"
17The man said, "They have already gone.
I heard them say they were going to

37:3 Israel Also called Jacob.

Dothan." So Joseph went to look for his
brothers and found them in Dothan.

Joseph Sold into Slavery

18Joseph's brothers saw him coming from
far away. Before he reached them, they made
a plan to kill him. 19They said to each other,
"Here comes that dreamer. 20Let's kill him
and throw his body into one of the wells. We
can tell our father that a wild animal killed
him. Then we will see what will become of
his dreams."

21But Reuben heard their plan and saved
Joseph, saying, "Let's not kill him. 22Don't
spill any blood. Throw him into this well
here in the desert, but don't hurt him!"
Reuben planned to save Joseph later and
send him back to his father. 23So when
Joseph came to his brothers, they pulled off
his robe with long sleeves 24and threw him
into the well. It was empty, and there was no
water in it.

25While Joseph was in the well, the
brothers sat down to eat. When they looked
up, they saw a group of Ishmaelites traveling
from Gilead to Egypt. Their camels were
carrying spices, balm, and myrrh.

26Then Judah said to his brothers, "What
will we gain if we kill our brother and hide
his death? 27Let's sell him to these
Ishmaelites. Then we will not be guilty of
killing our own brother. After all, he is our
brother, our own flesh and blood." And the
other brothers agreed. 28So when the
Midianite traders came by, the brothers took
Joseph out of the well and sold him to the
Ishmaelites for eight ounces of silver. And
the Ishmaelites took him to Egypt.

29When Reuben came back to the well
and Joseph was not there, he tore his clothes
to show he was upset. 30Then he went back
to his brothers and said, "The boy is not
there! What shall I do?" 31The brothers killed
a goat and dipped Joseph's robe in its blood.
32Then they brought the long-sleeved robe to
their father and said, "We found this robe.
Look it over carefully and see if it is your
son's robe."

33Jacob looked it over and said, "It is my
son's robe! Some savage animal has eaten
him. My son Joseph has been torn to pieces!"
34Then Jacob tore his clothes and put on
rough cloth to show that he was upset, and
he continued to be sad about his son for a
long time. 35All of his sons and daughters
tried to comfort him, but he could not be
comforted. He said, "I will be sad about my
son until the day I die." So Jacob cried for his
son Joseph.

36Meanwhile the Midianites who had
bought Joseph had taken him to Egypt. There
they sold him to Potiphar, an officer to the
king of Egypt and captain of the palace guard.

Judah and Tamar

38 About that time, Judah left his
brothers and went to stay with a man
named Hirah in the town of Adullam.
2There Judah met a Canaanite girl, the
daughter of a man named Shua, and married
her. Judah had sexual relations with her,
3and she became pregnant and gave birth to
a son, whom Judah named Er. 4Later she
gave birth to another son and named him
Onan. 5Still later she had another son and
named him Shelah. She was at Kezib when
this third son was born.

6Judah chose a girl named Tamar to be the
wife of his first son Er. 7But Er, Judah's oldest
son, did what the LORD said was evil, so the
LORD killed him. 8Then Judah said to Er's
brother Onan, "Go and have sexual relations
with your dead brother's wife.[n] It is your
duty to provide children for your brother in
this way."

9But Onan knew that the children would
not belong to him, so when he was supposed
to have sexual relations with Tamar he did
not complete the sex act. This made it
impossible for Tamar to become pregnant
and for Er to have descendants. 10The LORD
was displeased by this wicked thing Onan
had done, so the LORD killed Onan also.
11Then Judah said to his daughter-in-law
Tamar, "Go back to live in your father's
house, and don't marry until my young son
Shelah grows up." Judah was afraid that
Shelah also would die like his brothers. So
Tamar returned to her father's home.

12After a long time Judah's wife, the
daughter of Shua, died. After Judah had
gotten over his sorrow, he went to Timnah

38:8 Go . . . wife It was a custom in Israel that if a man died without children, one of his brothers would marry the widow. If a child was born, it would be considered the dead man's child.

devotion 13

GENESIS 37:28

HEARTACHE, THE TEACHER

Have you ever felt like the people who should love you just sold you to the Ishmaelites for eight pieces of silver? Ever spent any time in a well of despair? Ever had people you know plot your ruin? Sometimes God allows persecution and heartache, especially when he has something bigger in mind.

They say that character is acquired in pain. I wish it were not so. I wish you could sit beside the beach on vacation and get character. Or it would be nice to read about character and then have some. That's just not the way God works.

Inside the well of betrayal, God can give you a tender heart. Through a desert of loneliness, God can teach you how to love. Underneath heavy burdens, God can show you how to surrender. Great women and men have allowed their deepest life pain to become God's greatest instrument.

My never-before-married girlfriend fell in love with a man who had been through an awful divorce. She says that he knows how to love so much better than she does. He forgives and forgets much more quickly. Her husband decided to let brokenness be his teacher. He became a man of great character because of his pain.

What is your deepest pain? Where have you felt abandoned or betrayed? You can take comfort in reading the rest of Joseph's story. It didn't end in despair—he became the ruler of Egypt. What if God wants to use your heartache to prepare you for a big life you cannot yet see?

to his men who were cutting the wool from
his sheep. His friend Hirah from Adullam
went with him. 13 Tamar learned that Judah,
her father-in-law, was going to Timnah to
cut the wool from his sheep. 14 So she took
off the clothes that showed she was a widow
and covered her face with a veil to hide who
she was. Then she sat down by the gate of
Enaim on the road to Timnah. She did this
because Judah's younger son Shelah had
grown up, but Judah had not made plans for
her to marry him.

15 When Judah saw her, he thought she
was a prostitute, because she had covered
her face with a veil. 16 So Judah went to her
and said, "Let me have sexual relations with
you." He did not know that she was Tamar,
his daughter-in-law.

She asked, "What will you give me if I let
you have sexual relations with me?"

17 Judah answered, "I will send you a
young goat from my flock."

She answered, "First give me something to
keep as a deposit until you send the goat."

18 Judah asked, "What do you want me to
give you as a deposit?"

Tamar answered, "Give me your seal and
its cord,[n] and give me your walking stick." So
Judah gave these things to her. Then Judah
and Tamar had sexual relations, and Tamar
became pregnant. 19 When Tamar went
home, she took off the veil that covered her
face and put on the clothes that showed she
was a widow.

20 Judah sent his friend Hirah with the
young goat to find the woman and get back

38:18 seal . . . cord A seal was used like a rubber stamp, and people ran a string through it to tie around the neck. They wrote a contract, folded it, put wax or clay on the contract, and pressed the seal onto it as a signature.

his seal and the walking stick he had given
her, but Hirah could not find her. 21He asked
some of the people at the town of Enaim,
"Where is the prostitute who was here by
the road?"
They answered, "There has never been a
prostitute here."
22So he went back to Judah and said, "I
could not find the woman, and the people
who lived there said, 'There has never been a
prostitute here.' "
23Judah said, "Let her keep the things. I
don't want people to laugh at us. I sent her
the goat as I promised, but you could not
find her."
24About three months later someone told
Judah, "Tamar, your daughter-in-law, is
guilty of acting like a prostitute, and now
she is pregnant."
Then Judah said, "Bring her out and let
her be burned to death."
25When the people went to bring Tamar
out, she sent a message to her father-in-law
that said, "The man who owns these things
has made me pregnant. Look at this seal and
its cord and this walking stick, and tell me
whose they are."
26Judah recognized them and said, "She is
more in the right than I. She did this because
I did not give her to my son Shelah as I
promised." And Judah did not have sexual
relations with her again.
27When the time came for Tamar to give
birth, there were twins in her body. 28While
she was giving birth, one baby put his hand
out. The nurse tied a red string on his hand
and said, "This baby came out first." 29But he
pulled his hand back in, so the other baby
was born first. The nurse said, "So you are
able to break out first," and they named him
Perez.[n] 30After this, the baby with the red
string on his hand was born, and they
named him Zerah.

Joseph Is Sold to Potiphar

39 Now Joseph had been taken down to
Egypt. An Egyptian named Potiphar
was an officer to the king of Egypt and the
captain of the palace guard. He bought
Joseph from the Ishmaelites who had
brought him down there. 2The LORD was
with Joseph, and he became a successful
man. He lived in the house of his master,
Potiphar the Egyptian.
3Potiphar saw that the LORD was with
Joseph and that the LORD made Joseph
successful in everything he did. 4So Potiphar
was very happy with Joseph and allowed
him to be his personal servant. He put
Joseph in charge of the house, trusting him
with everything he owned. 5When Joseph
was put in charge of the house and
everything Potiphar owned, the LORD blessed
the people in Potiphar's house because of
Joseph. And the LORD blessed everything that
belonged to Potiphar, both in the house and
in the field. 6So Potiphar left Joseph in
charge of everything he owned and was not
concerned about anything except the food
he ate.

Joseph Is Put into Prison

Now Joseph was well built and handsome.
7After some time the wife of Joseph's master
began to desire Joseph, and one day she said
to him, "Have sexual relations with me."
8But Joseph refused and said to her, "My
master trusts me with everything in his
house. He has put me in charge of
everything he owns. 9There is no one in his
house greater than I. He has not kept
anything from me except you, because you
are his wife. How can I do such an evil
thing? It is a sin against God."
10The woman talked to Joseph every day,
but he refused to have sexual relations with
her or even spend time with her.
11One day Joseph went into the house to
do his work as usual and was the only man
in the house at that time. 12His master's wife
grabbed his coat and said to him, "Come and
have sexual relations with me." But Joseph
left his coat in her hand and ran out of the
house.
13When she saw that Joseph had left his
coat in her hands and had run outside, 14she
called to the servants in her house and said,
"Look! This Hebrew slave was brought here
to shame us. He came in and tried to have
sexual relations with me, but I screamed.
15My scream scared him and he ran away,
but he left his coat with me." 16She kept his
coat until her husband came home, 17and
she told him the same story. She said, "This

38:29 Perez This name means "breaking out."

Hebrew slave you brought here came in to
shame me! 18When he came near me, I
screamed. He ran away, but he left his coat."
19When Joseph's master heard what his
wife said Joseph had done, he became very
angry. 20So Potiphar arrested Joseph and put
him into the prison where the king's
prisoners were put. And Joseph stayed there
in the prison.
21But the LORD was with Joseph and
showed him kindness and caused the prison
warden to like Joseph. 22The prison warden
chose Joseph to take care of all the prisoners,
and he was responsible for whatever was
done in the prison. 23The warden paid no
attention to anything that was in Joseph's
care because the LORD was with Joseph and
made him successful in everything he did.

Joseph Interprets Two Dreams

40 After these things happened, two of
the king's officers displeased the
king—the man who served wine to the king
and the king's baker. 2The king became
angry with his officer who served him wine
and his baker, 3so he put them in the prison
of the captain of the guard, the same prison
where Joseph was kept. 4The captain of the
guard put the two prisoners in Joseph's care,
and they stayed in prison for some time.
5One night both the king's officer who
served him wine and the baker had a dream.
Each had his own dream with its own
meaning. 6When Joseph came to them the
next morning, he saw they were worried.
7He asked the king's officers who were with
him, "Why do you look so unhappy today?"
8The two men answered, "We both had
dreams last night, but no one can explain
their meaning to us."
Joseph said to them, "God is the only One
who can explain the meaning of dreams. Tell
me your dreams."
9So the man who served wine to the king
told Joseph his dream. He said, "I dreamed I
saw a vine, and 10on the vine were three
branches. I watched the branches bud and
blossom, and then the grapes ripened. 11I
was holding the king's cup, so I took the
grapes and squeezed the juice into the cup.
Then I gave it to the king."
12Then Joseph said, "I will explain the
dream to you. The three branches stand for
three days. 13Before the end of three days the
king will free you, and he will allow you to
return to your work. You will serve the king
his wine just as you did before. 14But when
you are free, remember me. Be kind to me,
and tell the king about me so I can get out of
this prison. 15I was taken by force from the
land of the Hebrews, and I have done
nothing here to deserve being put in prison."
16The baker saw that Joseph's explanation
of the dream was good, so he said to him, "I
also had a dream. I dreamed there were three
bread baskets on my head. 17In the top
basket were all kinds of baked food for the
king, but the birds were eating this food out
of the basket on my head."
18Joseph answered, "I will tell you what
the dream means. The three baskets stand
for three days. 19Before the end of three days,
the king will cut off your head! He will hang
your body on a pole, and the birds will eat
your flesh."
20Three days later, on his birthday, the
king gave a feast for all his officers. In front
of his officers, he released from prison the
chief officer who served his wine and the
chief baker. 21The king gave his chief officer
who served wine his old position, and once
again he put the king's cup of wine into the
king's hand. 22But the king hanged the baker
on a pole. Everything happened just as
Joseph had said it would, 23but the officer
who served wine did not remember Joseph.
He forgot all about him.

The King's Dreams

41 Two years later the king dreamed he
was standing on the bank of the Nile
River. 2He saw seven fat and beautiful cows
come up out of the river, and they stood
there, eating the grass. 3Then seven more
cows came up out of the river, but they were
thin and ugly. They stood beside the seven
beautiful cows on the bank of the Nile. 4The
seven thin and ugly cows ate the seven
beautiful fat cows. Then the king woke up.
5The king slept again and dreamed a second
time. In his dream he saw seven full and
good heads of grain growing on one stalk.
6After that, seven more heads of grain sprang
up, but they were thin and burned by the
hot east wind. 7The thin heads of grain ate
the seven full and good heads. Then the king
woke up again, and he realized it was only a
dream. 8The next morning the king was

Potiphar's Wife

GENESIS 39

She has noticed Joseph before. He's younger and more handsome than the other slaves, with a strong back and chiseled, bronzed limbs. Perhaps his youth or muscular frame is why her husband, Potiphar, put him in charge of their household.

Each day her mind races with thoughts of being alone with him. She approaches him from behind, moving her hands up his back. Joseph turns to see his master's wife. "Have sexual relations with me," she says, coiling her hand around his arm.

He pulls his arm from her clutch. "My master trusts me with everything in his house. He has not kept anything from me except you. How can I do such an evil thing? It is a sin against God."

Day after day she follows him, brushing up against him as he works. "Come to my quarters," she whispers. Again he refuses and tends to his work.

He has made a fool of her one too many times. When he is alone in the house with her again, she presses into his back. "Come and have sexual relations with me." Joseph tries to flee, but she grabs his coat. He runs from the palace without it.

Failing again to seduce him and fearing what he will tell her husband, she concocts her story. She'll say that he tried to rape her. No one will make her feel undesirable or look foolish again. No one. Especially not a common slave.

Saying yes to God's authority makes it easier to say no to temptation.

troubled about these dreams, so he sent for
all the magicians and wise men of Egypt.
The king told them his dreams, but no one
could explain their meaning to him.
9Then the chief officer who served wine
to the king said to him, "Now I remember
something I promised to do, but I forgot
about it. 10There was a time when you
were angry with the baker and me, and
you put us in prison in the house of the
captain of the guard. 11In prison we each
had a dream on the same night, and each
dream had a different meaning. 12A young
Hebrew man, a servant of the captain of
the guard, was in the prison with us.
When we told him our dreams, he
explained their meanings to us. He told
each man the meaning of his dream, and
13things happened exactly as he said they
would: I was given back my old position,
and the baker was hanged."
14So the king called for Joseph. The guards
quickly brought him out of the prison, and
he shaved, put on clean clothes, and went
before the king.
15The king said to Joseph, "I have had a
dream, but no one can explain its meaning
to me. I have heard that you can explain a
dream when someone tells it to you."
16Joseph answered the king, "I am not able
to explain the meaning of dreams, but God
will do this for the king."
17Then the king said to Joseph, "In my
dream I was standing on the bank of the Nile
River. 18I saw seven fat and beautiful cows
that came up out of the river and ate the
grass. 19Then I saw seven more cows come
out of the river that were thin and lean and
ugly—the worst looking cows I have seen in
all the land of Egypt. 20And these thin and
ugly cows ate the first seven fat cows, 21but
after they had eaten the seven cows, no one
could tell they had eaten them. They looked
just as thin and ugly as they did in the
beginning. Then I woke up.
22"I had another dream. I saw seven full
and good heads of grain growing on one
stalk. 23Then seven more heads of grain
sprang up after them, but these heads were
thin and ugly and were burned by the hot
east wind. 24Then the thin heads ate the
seven good heads. I told this dream to the
magicians, but no one could explain its
meaning to me."

Joseph Tells the Dreams' Meaning

25 Then Joseph said to the king, "Both of
these dreams mean the same thing. God is
telling you what he is about to do. 26 The
seven good cows stand for seven years, and
the seven good heads of grain stand for
seven years. Both dreams mean the same
thing. 27 The seven thin and ugly cows
stand for seven years, and the seven thin
heads of grain burned by the hot east wind
stand for seven years of hunger. 28 This will
happen as I told you. God is showing the
king what he is about to do. 29 You will
have seven years of good crops and plenty
to eat in all the land of Egypt. 30 But after
those seven years, there will come seven
years of hunger, and all the food that grew
in the land of Egypt will be forgotten. The
time of hunger will eat up the land.
31 People will forget what it was like to have
plenty of food, because the hunger that
follows will be so great. 32 You had two
dreams which mean the same thing. This
shows that God has firmly decided that
this will happen, and he will make it
happen soon.

33 "So let the king choose a man who is
very wise and understanding and set him
over the land of Egypt. 34 And let the king
also appoint officers over the land, who
should take one-fifth of all the food that is
grown during the seven good years. 35 They
should gather all the food that is produced
during the good years that are coming, and
under the king's authority they should store
the grain in the cities and guard it. 36 That
food should be saved to use during the seven
years of hunger that will come on the land of
Egypt. Then the people in Egypt will not die
during the seven years of hunger."

Joseph Is Made Ruler over Egypt

37 This seemed like a very good idea to the
king, and all his officers agreed. 38 And the
king asked them, "Can we find a better man
than Joseph to take this job? God's spirit is
truly in him!"

39 So the king said to Joseph, "God has
shown you all this. There is no one as wise
and understanding as you are, so 40 I will put
you in charge of my palace. All the people
will obey your orders, and only I will be
greater than you."

41 Then the king said to Joseph, "Look! I
have put you in charge of all the land of
Egypt." 42 Then the king took off from his
own finger his ring with the royal seal on
it, and he put it on Joseph's finger. He gave
Joseph fine linen clothes to wear, and he
put a gold chain around Joseph's neck.
43 The king had Joseph ride in the second
royal chariot, and people walked ahead of
his chariot calling, "Bow down!" By doing
these things, the king put Joseph in charge
of all of Egypt.

44 The king said to him, "I am the king, and
I say that no one in all the land of Egypt may
lift a hand or a foot without your
permission." 45 The king gave Joseph the
name Zaphenath-Paneah. He also gave
Joseph a wife named Asenath, who was the
daughter of Potiphera, priest of On. So
Joseph traveled through all the land of
Egypt.

46 Joseph was thirty years old when he
began serving the king of Egypt. And he
left the king's court and traveled through
all the land of Egypt. 47 During the seven
good years, the crops in the land grew well.
48 And Joseph gathered all the food
produced in Egypt during those seven
years of good crops and stored the food in
the cities. In every city he stored grain that
had been grown in the fields around that
city. 49 Joseph stored much grain, as much
as the sand of the seashore—so much that
he could not measure it.

50 Joseph's wife was Asenath daughter of
Potiphera, the priest of On. Before the years
of hunger came, Joseph and Asenath had
two sons. 51 Joseph named the first son
Manasseh[n] and said, "God has made me
forget all the troubles I have had and all my
father's family." 52 Joseph named the second
son Ephraim[n] and said, "God has given me
children in the land of my troubles."

53 The seven years of good crops came to
an end in the land of Egypt. 54 Then the seven
years of hunger began, just as Joseph had
said. In all the lands people had nothing to
eat, but in Egypt there was food. 55 The time
of hunger became terrible in all of Egypt,

41:51 Manasseh This name sounds like the Hebrew word for "made me forget."
41:52 Ephraim This name sounds like the Hebrew word for "given me children."

devotion 14

GENESIS 41:38–40

FAVOR WITH THE KING

Joseph was a boy who overcame adverse circumstances to become a man that the Lord's favor rested on. God had given Joseph everything he needed to interpret dreams and govern the affairs of the land of Egypt, not to mention Pharaoh's personal household. Pharaoh was impressed with Joseph's interpretation and advice. Joseph said to store up during the years of plenty so that Egypt could survive during the years of famine. Even though Pharaoh was not a man who sought the Lord, he knew that Joseph's interpretation was true and wise, reflecting the favor of the Lord!

When the Spirit of the Lord lives in you, you are equipped to operate in full discernment and wisdom. Since the Holy Spirit never leaves you or forsakes you, he is ever present to give you understanding. When you need insight or favor in some regard, express your requests to the One who has given you that power. I do not believe there is a woman alive that does not want to be considered wise. Not only do I want to be considered wise, I want to live that way as well (Prov. 31:25). If you remember the opening of the story, young Joseph had been betrayed by just about everyone he knew, but he never questioned God's presence in the midst of harsh circumstances.

Draw your heart close to the Lord, and seek his wisdom first in everything. It is alive and real, and you will see the very Spirit of God at work in your life.

and the people cried to the king for food. He
said to all the Egyptians, "Go to Joseph and
do whatever he tells you."
56The hunger was everywhere in that part
of the world. And Joseph opened the
storehouses and sold grain to the people of
Egypt, because the time of hunger became
terrible in Egypt. 57And all the people in that
part of the world came to Joseph in Egypt to
buy grain because the hunger was terrible
everywhere in that part of the world.

The Dreams Come True

42 Jacob learned that there was grain in
Egypt, so he said to his sons, "Why are
you just sitting here looking at one another?
2I have heard that there is grain in Egypt. Go
down there and buy grain for us to eat, so
that we will live and not die."
3So ten of Joseph's brothers went down
to buy grain from Egypt. 4But Jacob did not
send Benjamin, Joseph's brother, with
them, because he was afraid that
something terrible might happen to him.
5Along with many other people, the sons
of Israel[n] went to Egypt to buy grain,
because the people in the land of Canaan
were also hungry.
6Now Joseph was governor over Egypt.
He was the one who sold the grain to people
who came to buy it. So Joseph's brothers
came to him and bowed facedown on the
ground before him. 7When Joseph saw his
brothers, he knew who they were, but he
acted as if he didn't know them. He asked
unkindly, "Where do you come from?"
They answered, "We have come from the
land of Canaan to buy food."
8Joseph knew they were his brothers, but
they did not know who he was. 9And Joseph
remembered his dreams about his brothers
bowing to him. He said to them, "You are

42:5 Israel Also called Jacob.

spies! You came to learn where the nation is
weak!"
10But his brothers said to him, "No, my
master. We come as your servants just to buy
food. 11We are all sons of the same father.
We are honest men, not spies."
12Then Joseph said to them, "No! You have
come to learn where this nation is weak!"
13And they said, "We are ten of twelve
brothers, sons of the same father, and we live
in the land of Canaan. Our youngest brother
is there with our father right now, and our
other brother is gone."
14But Joseph said to them, "I can see I was
right! You are spies! 15But I will give you a
way to prove you are telling the truth. As
surely as the king lives, you will not leave
this place until your youngest brother comes
here. 16One of you must go and get your
brother. The rest of you will stay here in
prison. We will see if you are telling the
truth. If not, as surely as the king lives, you
are spies." 17Then Joseph put them all in
prison for three days.
18On the third day Joseph said to them, "I
am a God-fearing man. Do this and I will let
you live: 19If you are honest men, let one of
your brothers stay here in prison while the
rest of you go and carry grain back to feed
your hungry families. 20Then bring your
youngest brother back here to me. If you do
this, I will know you are telling the truth,
and you will not die."
The brothers agreed to this. 21They said to
each other, "We are being punished for what
we did to our brother. We saw his trouble,
and he begged us to save him, but we refused
to listen. That is why we are in this trouble
now."
22Then Reuben said to them, "I told you
not to harm the boy, but you refused to
listen to me. So now we are being punished
for what we did to him."
23When Joseph talked to his brothers, he
used an interpreter, so they did not know that
Joseph understood what they were saying.
24Then Joseph left them and cried. After a
short time he went back and spoke to them.
He took Simeon and tied him up while the
other brothers watched. 25Joseph told his
servants to fill his brothers' bags with grain
and to put the money the brothers had paid
for the grain back in their bags. The servants
were also to give them what they would need
for their trip back home. And the servants did
this.
26So the brothers put the grain on their
donkeys and left. 27When they stopped for
the night, one of the brothers opened his
sack to get food for his donkey. Then he saw
his money in the top of the sack. 28He said to
the other brothers, "The money I paid for the
grain has been put back. Here it is in my
sack!"
The brothers were very frightened. They
said to each other, "What has God done to
us?"

The Brothers Return to Jacob

29The brothers went to their father Jacob in
the land of Canaan and told him everything
that had happened. 30They said, "The master
of that land spoke unkindly to us. He accused
us of spying on his country, 31but we told him
that we were honest men, not spies. 32We told
him that we were ten of twelve brothers—
sons of one father. We said that one of our
brothers was gone and that our youngest
brother was with our father in Canaan.
33"Then the master of the land said to us,
'Here is a way I can know you are honest
men: Leave one of your brothers with me,
and take grain to feed your hungry families,
and go. 34And bring your youngest brother
to me so I will know you are not spies but
honest men. Then I will give you back your
brother whom you leave with me, and you
can move about freely in our land.' "
35As the brothers emptied their sacks,
each of them found his money in his sack.
When they and their father saw it, they were
afraid.
36Their father Jacob said to them, "You are
robbing me of all my children. Joseph is
gone, Simeon is gone, and now you want to
take Benjamin away, too. Everything is
against me."
37Then Reuben said to his father, "You
may put my two sons to death if I don't bring
Benjamin back to you. Trust him to my care,
and I will bring him back to you."
38But Jacob said, "I will not allow
Benjamin to go with you. His brother is
dead, and he is the only son left from my
wife Rachel. I am afraid something terrible
might happen to him during the trip to
Egypt. Then I would be sad until the day I
die."

The Brothers Go Back to Egypt

43 Still no food grew in the land of Canaan. 2When Jacob's family had eaten all the grain they had brought from Egypt, Jacob said to them, "Go to Egypt again and buy a little more grain for us to eat."

3But Judah said to Jacob, "The governor of that country strongly warned us, 'If you don't bring your brother back with you, you will not be allowed to see me.' 4If you will send Benjamin with us, we will go down and buy food for you. 5But if you refuse to send Benjamin, we will not go. The governor of that country warned us that we would not see him if we didn't bring Benjamin with us."

6Israel[n] said, "Why did you tell the man you had another brother? You have caused me a lot of trouble."

7The brothers answered, "He questioned us carefully about ourselves and our family. He asked us, 'Is your father still alive? Do you have another brother?' We just answered his questions. How could we know he would ask us to bring our other brother to him?"

8Then Judah said to his father Jacob, "Send Benjamin with me, and we will go at once so that we, you, and our children may live and not die. 9I will guarantee you that he will be safe, and I will be personally responsible for him. If I don't bring him back to you, you can blame me all my life. 10If we had not wasted all this time, we could have already made two trips."

11Then their father Jacob said to them, "If it has to be that way, then do this: Take some of the best foods in our land in your packs. Give them to the man as a gift: some balm, some honey, spices, myrrh, pistachio nuts, and almonds. 12Take twice as much money with you this time, and take back the money that was returned to you in your sacks last time. Maybe it was a mistake. 13And take Benjamin with you. Now leave and go to the man. 14I pray that God Almighty will cause the governor to be merciful to you and that he will allow Simeon and Benjamin to come back with you. If I am robbed of my children, then I am robbed of them!"

15So the brothers took the gifts. They also took twice as much money as they had taken the first time, and they took Benjamin. They hurried down to Egypt and stood before Joseph.

16When Joseph saw Benjamin with them, he said to the servant in charge of his house, "Bring those men into my house. Kill an animal and prepare a meal. Those men will eat with me today at noon." 17The servant did as Joseph told him and brought the men to Joseph's house.

18The brothers were afraid when they were brought to Joseph's house and thought, "We were brought here because of the money that was put in our sacks on the first trip. He wants to attack us, make us slaves, and take our donkeys." 19So the brothers went to the servant in charge of Joseph's house and spoke to him at the door of the house. 20They said, "Master, we came here once before to buy food. 21While we were going home, we stopped for the night and when we opened our sacks each of us found all his money in his sack. We brought that money with us to give it back to you. 22And we have brought more money to pay for the food we want to buy this time. We don't know who put that money in our sacks."

23But the servant answered, "It's all right. Don't be afraid. Your God, the God of your father, must have put the money in your sacks. I got the money you paid me for the grain last time." Then the servant brought Simeon out to them.

24The servant led the men into Joseph's house and gave them water, and they washed their feet. Then he gave their donkeys food to eat. 25The men prepared their gift to give to Joseph when he arrived at noon, because they had heard they were going to eat with him there.

26When Joseph came home, the brothers gave him the gift they had brought into the house and bowed down to the ground in front of him. 27Joseph asked them how they were doing. He said, "How is your aged father you told me about? Is he still alive?"

28The brothers answered, "Your servant, our father, is well. He is still alive." And they bowed low before Joseph to show him respect.

29When Joseph saw his brother Benjamin, who had the same mother as he, Joseph

43:6 Israel Also called Jacob.

asked, "Is this your youngest brother you
told me about?" Then he said to Benjamin,
"God be good to you, my son!" 30 Then Joseph
hurried off because he had to hold back the
tears when he saw his brother Benjamin. So
Joseph went into his room and cried there.
31 Then he washed his face and came out. He
controlled himself and said, "Serve the
meal."

32 So they served Joseph at one table, his
brothers at another table, and the Egyptians
who ate with him at another table. This was
because Egyptians did not like Hebrews and
never ate with them. 33 Joseph's brothers
were seated in front of him in order of their
ages, from oldest to youngest. They looked at
each other because they were so amazed.
34 Food from Joseph's table was taken to
them, but Benjamin was given five times
more food than the others. Joseph's brothers
ate and drank freely with him.

Joseph Sets a Trap

44 Then Joseph gave a command to the
servant in charge of his house. He
said, "Fill the men's sacks with as much
grain as they can carry, and put each man's
money into his sack with the grain. 2 Put my
silver cup in the sack of the youngest
brother, along with his money for the grain."
The servant did what Joseph told him.

3 At dawn the brothers were sent away
with their donkeys. 4 They were not far from
the city when Joseph said to the servant in
charge of his house, "Go after the men.
When you catch up with them, say, 'Why
have you paid back evil for good? 5 The cup
you have stolen is the one my master uses
for drinking and for explaining dreams. You
have done a very wicked thing!' "

6 So the servant caught up with the
brothers and said to them what Joseph had
told him to say.

7 But the brothers said to the servant,
"Why do you say these things? We would
not do anything like that! 8 We brought back
to you from the land of Canaan the money
we found in our sacks. So surely we would
not steal silver or gold from your master's
house. 9 If you find that silver cup in the sack
of one of us, then let him die, and we will be
your slaves."

10 The servant said, "We will do as you say,
but only the man who has taken the cup
will become my slave. The rest of you may
go free."

11 Then every brother quickly lowered his
sack to the ground and opened it. 12 The
servant searched the sacks, going from the
oldest brother to the youngest, and found
the cup in Benjamin's sack. 13 The brothers
tore their clothes to show they were afraid.
Then they put their sacks back on the
donkeys and returned to the city.

14 When Judah and his brothers went back
to Joseph's house, Joseph was still there, so
the brothers bowed facedown on the ground
before him. 15 Joseph said to them, "What
have you done? Didn't you know that a man
like me can learn things by signs and
dreams?"

16 Judah said, "Master, what can we say?
And how can we show we are not guilty?
God has uncovered our guilt, so all of us will
be your slaves, not just Benjamin."

17 But Joseph said, "I will not make you all
slaves! Only the man who stole the cup will
be my slave. The rest of you may go back
safely to your father."

18 Then Judah went to Joseph and said,
"Master, please let me speak plainly to you,
and please don't be angry with me. I know
that you are as powerful as the king of Egypt
himself. 19 When we were here before, you
asked us, 'Do you have a father or a brother?'
20 And we answered you, 'We have an old
father. And we have a younger brother, who
was born when our father was old. This
youngest son's brother is dead, so he is the
only one of his mother's children left alive,
and our father loves him very much.' 21 Then
you said to us, 'Bring that brother to me. I
want to see him.' 22 And we said to you, 'That
young boy cannot leave his father, because if
he leaves him, his father would die.' 23 But
you said to us, 'If you don't bring your
youngest brother, you will not be allowed to
see me again.' 24 So we went back to our
father and told him what you had said.

25 "Later, our father said, 'Go again and buy
us a little more food.' 26 We said to our father,
'We cannot go without our youngest
brother. Without our youngest brother, we
will not be allowed to see the governor.'
27 Then my father said to us, 'You know that
my wife Rachel gave me two sons. 28 When
one son left me, I thought, "Surely he has
been torn apart by a wild animal," and I

haven't seen him since. 29Now you want to
take this son away from me also. But
something terrible might happen to him,
and I would be miserable until the day I die.'
30Now what will happen if we go home to
our father without our youngest brother? He
is so important in our father's life that
31when our father sees the young boy is not
with us, he will die. And it will be our fault.
We will cause the great sorrow that kills our
father.

32"I gave my father a guarantee that the
young boy would be safe. I said to my father,
'If I don't bring him back to you, you can
blame me all my life.' 33So now, please allow
me to stay here and be your slave, and let the
young boy go back home with his brothers.
34I cannot go back to my father if the boy is
not with me. I couldn't stand to see my
father that sad."

Joseph Reveals Who He Is

45 Joseph could not control himself in
front of his servants any longer, so he
cried out, "Have everyone leave me." When
only the brothers were left with Joseph, he
told them who he was. 2Joseph cried so
loudly that the Egyptians heard him, and the
people in the king's palace heard about it. 3He
said to his brothers, "I am Joseph. Is my father
still alive?" But the brothers could not answer
him, because they were very afraid of him.

4So Joseph said to them, "Come close to
me." When the brothers came close to him,
he said to them, "I am your brother Joseph,
whom you sold as a slave to go to Egypt.
5Now don't be worried or angry with
yourselves because you sold me here. God
sent me here ahead of you to save people's
lives. 6No food has grown on the land for
two years now, and there will be five more
years without planting or harvest. 7So God
sent me here ahead of you to make sure you
have some descendants left on earth and to
keep you alive in an amazing way. 8So it was
not you who sent me here, but God. God has
made me the highest officer of the king of
Egypt. I am in charge of his palace, and I am
the master of all the land of Egypt.

9"So leave quickly and go to my father.
Tell him, 'Your son Joseph says: God has
made me master over all Egypt. Come down
to me quickly. 10Live in the land of Goshen
where you will be near me. Your children,

devotion 15

GENESIS 45:10–15

WHO BETTER THAN FAMILY?

My family is very close. My husband says, "When my wife's family comes into town, our lives stop. We have to eat every meal together and plan each day around their schedules." We love being together. So you can imagine my heartbreak when my older brother decided he didn't want to be part of our family for a variety of reasons. At first I was just angry and didn't want anything to do with him anyway. Then I began to feel grief as if he were dead. Finally, I realized that I needed to forgive him, but I didn't know if I could. It doesn't matter who is right and who is wrong, God commands us to forgive one another, just as he forgives us. Slowly, painfully, I began the process of forgiveness, but it was only through the Lord's gentle working in my heart.

Joseph's forgiveness was complete. He promised to care for the very brothers who had sold him into slavery. He did not wield his power over them or make them pay for their actions. He hugged them, kissed them, and talked with them. He loved them for who they were, his brothers. But most of all, Joseph did not blame them. He gave his feelings of blame over to God and showed his family how God had been in control from the very beginning. Family brings out the best and worst in us. But often God uses family in our lives to teach us how to forgive.

your grandchildren, your flocks and herds,
and all that you have will also be near me.
11I will care for you during the next five
years of hunger so that you and your family
and all that you have will not starve.'
12"Now you can see for yourselves, and so
can my brother Benjamin, that the one
speaking to you is really Joseph. 13So tell my
father about how powerful I have become in
Egypt. Tell him about everything you have
seen. Now hurry and bring him back to me."
14Then Joseph hugged his brother Benjamin
and cried, and Benjamin cried also. 15And
Joseph kissed all his brothers and cried as he
hugged them. After this, his brothers talked
with him.
16When the king of Egypt and his officers
learned that Joseph's brothers had come,
they were very happy. 17So the king said to
Joseph, "Tell your brothers to load their
animals and go back to the land of Canaan
18and bring their father and their families
back here to me. I will give them the best
land in Egypt, and they will eat the best food
we have here. 19Tell them to take some
wagons from Egypt for their children and
their wives and to bring their father back
also. 20Tell them not to worry about bringing
any of their things with them, because we
will give them the best of what we have in
Egypt."
21So the sons of Israel did this. Joseph gave
them wagons as the king had ordered and
food for their trip. 22He gave each brother a
change of clothes, but he gave Benjamin five
changes of clothes and about seven and
one-half pounds of silver. 23Joseph also sent
his father ten donkeys loaded with the best
things from Egypt and ten female donkeys
loaded with grain, bread, and other food for
his father on his trip back. 24Then Joseph told
his brothers to go. As they were leaving, he
said to them, "Don't quarrel on the way
home."
25So the brothers left Egypt and went to
their father Jacob in the land of Canaan.
26They told him, "Joseph is still alive and is
the ruler over all the land of Egypt." Their
father was shocked and did not believe them.
27But when the brothers told him everything
Joseph had said, and when Jacob saw the
wagons Joseph had sent to carry him back to
Egypt, he felt better. 28Israel[n] said, "Now I
believe you. My son Joseph is still alive, and I
will go and see him before I die."

Jacob Goes to Egypt

46 So Israel[n] took all he had and started
his trip. He went to Beersheba, where
he offered sacrifices to the God of his father
Isaac. 2During the night God spoke to Israel
in a vision and said, "Jacob, Jacob."
And Jacob answered, "Here I am."
3Then God said, "I am God, the God of
your father. Don't be afraid to go to Egypt,
because I will make your descendants a
great nation there. 4I will go to Egypt with
you, and I will bring you out of Egypt
again. Joseph's own hands will close your
eyes when you die."
5Then Jacob left Beersheba. The sons of
Israel loaded their father, their children, and
their wives in the wagons the king of Egypt
had sent. 6They also took their farm animals
and everything they had gotten in Canaan.
So Jacob went to Egypt with all his
descendants— 7his sons and grandsons, his
daughters and granddaughters. He took all
his family to Egypt with him.

Jacob's Family

8Now these are the names of the children
of Israel who went into Egypt (Jacob and his
descendants).
Reuben was Jacob's first son. 9Reuben's
sons were Hanoch, Pallu, Hezron, and Carmi.
10Simeon's sons were Jemuel, Jamin,
Ohad, Jakin, Zohar, and Shaul (Simeon's son
by a Canaanite woman).
11Levi's sons were Gershon, Kohath, and
Merari.
12Judah's sons were Er, Onan, Shelah,
Perez, and Zerah (but Er and Onan had died
in the land of Canaan). Perez's sons were
Hezron and Hamul.
13Issachar's sons were Tola, Puah, Jashub,
and Shimron.
14Zebulun's sons were Sered, Elon, and
Jahleel.
15These are the sons of Leah and Jacob
born in Northwest Mesopotamia, in addition
to his daughter Dinah. There were
thirty-three persons in this part of Jacob's
family.

45:28; 46:1 Israel Also called Jacob.

16Gad's sons were Zephon, Haggi, Shuni,
Ezbon, Eri, Arodi, and Areli.
17Asher's sons were Imnah, Ishvah, Ishvi,
and Beriah, and their sister was Serah.
Beriah's sons were Heber and Malkiel.
18These are Jacob's sons by Zilpah, the
slave girl whom Laban gave to his daughter
Leah. There were sixteen persons in this part
of Jacob's family.
19The sons of Jacob's wife Rachel were
Joseph and Benjamin. 20In Egypt, Joseph
became the father of Manasseh and Ephraim
by his wife Asenath, the daughter of
Potiphera, priest of On.
21Benjamin's sons were Bela, Beker,
Ashbel, Gera, Naaman, Ehi, Rosh, Muppim,
Huppim, and Ard.
22These are the sons of Jacob by his wife
Rachel. There were fourteen persons in this
part of Jacob's family.
23Dan's son was Hushim.
24Naphtali's sons were Jahziel, Guni, Jezer,
and Shillem.
25These are Jacob's sons by Bilhah, the
slave girl whom Laban gave to his daughter
Rachel. There were seven persons in this part
of Jacob's family.
26So the total number of Jacob's direct
descendants who went to Egypt was
sixty-six, not counting the wives of Jacob's
sons. 27Joseph had two sons born in Egypt, so
the total number in the family of Jacob in
Egypt was seventy.

Jacob Arrives in Egypt

28Jacob sent Judah ahead of him to see
Joseph in Goshen. When Jacob and his
people came into the land of Goshen,
29Joseph prepared his chariot and went to
meet his father Israel in Goshen. As soon as
Joseph saw his father, he hugged him, and
cried there for a long time.
30Then Israel said to Joseph, "Now I am
ready to die, because I have seen your face
and I know you are still alive."
31Joseph said to his brothers and his
father's family, "I will go and tell the king
you are here. I will say, 'My brothers and my
father's family have left the land of Canaan
and have come here to me. 32They are
shepherds and take care of farm animals,
and they have brought their flocks and their
herds and everything they own with them.'
33When the king calls you, he will ask,
'What work do you do?' 34This is what you
should tell him: 'We, your servants, have
taken care of farm animals all our lives. Our
ancestors did the same thing.' Then the king
will allow you to settle in the land of
Goshen, away from the Egyptians, because
they don't like to be near shepherds."

Jacob Settles in Goshen

47 Joseph went in to the king and said,
"My father and my brothers have
arrived from Canaan with their flocks and
herds and everything they own. They are
now in the land of Goshen." 2Joseph chose
five of his brothers to introduce to the king.
3The king said to the brothers, "What
work do you do?"

And they said to him, "We, your servants,
are shepherds, just as our ancestors were."
4They said to the king, "We have come to
live in this land, because there is no grass in
the land of Canaan for our animals to eat,
and the hunger is terrible there. So please
allow us to live in the land of Goshen."
5Then the king said to Joseph, "Your father
and your brothers have come to you, 6and
you may choose any place in Egypt for them
to live. Give your father and your brothers
the best land; let them live in the land of
Goshen. And if any of them are skilled
shepherds, put them in charge of my sheep
and cattle."
7Then Joseph brought in his father Jacob
and introduced him to the king, and Jacob
blessed the king.
8Then the king said to Jacob, "How old are
you?"
9Jacob said to him, "My life has been spent
wandering from place to place. It has been
short and filled with trouble—only one
hundred thirty years. My ancestors lived
much longer than I." 10Then Jacob blessed
the king and left.
11Joseph obeyed the king and gave his
father and brothers the best land in Egypt,
near the city of Rameses. 12And Joseph gave
his father, his brothers, and everyone who
lived with them the food they needed.

Joseph Buys Land for the King

13The hunger became worse, and since
there was no food anywhere in the land,
Egypt and Canaan became very poor.
14Joseph collected all the money that was to

be found in Egypt and Canaan. People paid
for the grain they were buying, and he
brought that money to the king's palace.
15After some time, when the people in Egypt
and Canaan had no money left, they went to
Joseph and said, "Please give us food. Our
money is gone, and if we don't eat, we will
die here in front of you."

16Joseph answered, "Since you have no
money, give me your farm animals, and I
will give you food in return." 17So people
brought their farm animals to Joseph, and he
gave them food in exchange for their horses,
sheep, goats, cattle, and donkeys. And he
kept them alive by trading food for their
farm animals that year.

18The next year the people came to Joseph
and said, "You know we have no money left,
and all our animals belong to you. We have
nothing left except our bodies and our land.
19Surely both we and our land will die here
in front of you. Buy us and our land in
exchange for food, and we will be slaves to
the king, together with our land. Give us
seed to plant so that we will live and not die,
and the land will not become a desert."

20So Joseph bought all the land in Egypt
for the king. Every Egyptian sold Joseph his
field, because the hunger was very great. So
the land became the king's, 21and Joseph
made the people slaves from one end of
Egypt to the other. 22The only land he did
not buy was the land the priests owned.
They did not need to sell their land because
the king paid them for their work. So they
had money to buy food.

23Joseph said to the people, "Now I have
bought you and your land for the king, so I
will give you seed and you can plant your
fields. 24At harvest time you must give one-
fifth to the king. You may keep four-fifths for
yourselves to use as seed for the field and as
food for yourselves, your families, and your
children."

25The people said, "You have saved our
lives. If you like, we will become slaves of
the king."

26So Joseph made a law in Egypt, which
continues today: One-fifth of everything
from the land belongs to the king. The only
land the king did not get was the priests'
land.

"Don't Bury Me in Egypt"

27The Israelites continued to live in the
land of Goshen in Egypt. There they got
possessions and had many children and
grew in number.

28Jacob[n] lived in Egypt seventeen years, so
he lived to be one hundred forty-seven years
old. 29When Israel knew he soon would die,
he called his son Joseph to him and said to
him, "If you love me, put your hand under
my leg.[n] Promise me you will not bury me in
Egypt. 30When I die, carry me out of Egypt,
and bury me where my ancestors are
buried."

Joseph answered, "I will do as you say."

31Then Jacob said, "Promise me." And
Joseph promised him that he would do this.
Then Israel worshiped as he leaned on the
top of his walking stick.

Blessings for Manasseh and Ephraim

48 Some time later Joseph learned that
his father was very sick, so he took his
two sons Manasseh and Ephraim and went to
his father. 2When Joseph arrived, someone
told Jacob,[n] "Your son Joseph has come to see
you." Jacob was weak, so he used all his
strength and sat up on his bed.

3Then Jacob said to Joseph, "God Almighty
appeared to me at Luz in the land of Canaan
and blessed me there. 4He said to me, 'I will
give you many children. I will make you the
father of many peoples, and I will give your
descendants this land forever.' 5Your two
sons, who were born here in Egypt before I
came, will be counted as my own sons.
Ephraim and Manasseh will be my sons just
as Reuben and Simeon are my sons. 6But if
you have other children, they will be your
own, and their land will be part of the land
given to Ephraim and Manasseh. 7When I
came from Northwest Mesopotamia, Rachel
died in the land of Canaan, as we were
traveling toward Ephrath. This made me very
sad, and I buried her there beside the road to
Ephrath." (Today Ephrath is Bethlehem.)

8Then Israel saw Joseph's sons and said,
"Who are these boys?"

9Joseph said to his father, "They are my
sons that God has given me here in Egypt."

Israel said, "Bring your sons to me so I may
bless them."

47:28; 48:2 Jacob Also called Israel.
47:29 put . . . leg This showed that a person would keep a promise.

10At this time Israel's eyesight was bad
because he was old. So Joseph brought the
boys close to him, and Israel kissed the
boys and put his arms around them. 11He
said to Joseph, "I thought I would never see
you alive again, and now God has let me
see you and also your children." 12Then
Joseph moved his sons off Israel's lap and
bowed facedown to the ground. 13He put
Ephraim on his right side and Manasseh on
his left. (So Ephraim was near Israel's left
hand, and Manasseh was near Israel's right
hand.) Joseph brought the boys close to
Israel. 14But Israel crossed his arms and put
his right hand on the head of Ephraim,
who was younger. He put his left hand on
the head of Manasseh, the firstborn son.
15And Israel blessed Joseph and said,

"My ancestors Abraham and Isaac served
our God,
and like a shepherd God has led me all
my life.
16He was the Angel who saved me from all
my troubles.
Now I pray that he will bless these boys.
May my name be known through these
boys,
and may the names of my ancestors
Abraham and Isaac be known
through them.
May they have many descendants
on the earth."

17When Joseph saw that his father put his
right hand on Ephraim's head, he didn't like
it. So he took hold of his father's hand,
wanting to move it from Ephraim's head to
Manasseh's head. 18Joseph said to his father,
"You are doing it wrong, Father. Manasseh is
the firstborn son. Put your right hand on his
head."
19But his father refused and said, "I know,
my son, I know. Manasseh will be great and
have many descendants. But his younger
brother will be greater, and his descendants
will be enough to make a nation."
20So Israel blessed them that day and said,

"When a blessing is given in Israel, they
will say:
'May God make you like Ephraim and
Manasseh.' "

In this way he made Ephraim greater than
Manasseh.
21Then Israel said to Joseph, "Look at me; I
am about to die. But God will be with you
and will take you back to the land of your
fathers. 22I have given you something that I
did not give your brothers—the land of
Shechem that I took from the Amorite
people with my sword and my bow."

Jacob Blesses His Sons

49 Then Jacob called his sons to him. He
said, "Come here to me, and I will tell
you what will happen to you in the future.

2"Come together and listen, sons of Jacob.
Listen to Israel, your father."

3"Reuben, my first son, you are my
strength.
Your birth showed I could be a father.
You have the highest position among my
sons,
and you are the most powerful.
4But you are uncontrolled like water,
so you will no longer lead your
brothers.
This is because you got into your father's
bed
and shamed me by having sexual
relations with my slave girl.

5"Simeon and Levi are brothers
who used their swords to do violence.
6I will not join their secret talks,
and I will not meet with them to plan
evil.
They killed men because they were angry,
and they crippled oxen just for fun.
7May their anger be cursed, because it is too
violent.
May their violence be cursed, because it
is too cruel.
I will divide them up among the tribes of
Jacob
and scatter them through all the tribes
of Israel.

8"Judah, your brothers will praise you.
You will grab your enemies by the neck,
and your brothers will bow down to
you.
9Judah is like a young lion.
You have returned from killing, my son.
Like a lion, he stretches out and lies down
to rest,
and no one is brave enough to wake
him.
10Kings will come from Judah's family;
someone from Judah will always be on
the throne.

Judah will rule until Shiloh comes,
and the nations will obey him.
11He ties his donkey to a grapevine,
his young donkey to the best branch.
He can afford to use wine to wash his clothes
and the best wine to wash his robes.
12His eyes are dark like the color of wine,
and his teeth are as white as the color of milk.

13"Zebulun will live near the sea.
His shore will be a safe place for ships,
and his land will reach as far as Sidon.

14"Issachar is like a strong donkey
who lies down while carrying his load.
15When he sees his resting place is good
and how pleasant his land is,
he will put his back to the load
and become a slave.

16"Dan will rule his own people
like the other tribes in Israel.
17Dan will be like a snake by the side of the road,
a dangerous snake lying near the path.
That snake bites a horse's leg,
and the rider is thrown off backward.

18"LORD, I wait for your salvation.

19"Robbers will attack Gad,
but he will defeat them and drive them away.

20"Asher's land will grow much good food;
he will grow food fit for a king.

21"Naphtali is like a female deer that runs free,
that has beautiful fawns.

22"Joseph is like a grapevine that produces much fruit,
a healthy vine watered by a spring,
whose branches grow over the wall.
23Archers attack him violently
and shoot at him angrily,
24but he aims his bow well.
His arms are made strong.
He gets his power from the Mighty God of Jacob
and his strength from the Shepherd, the Rock of Israel.
25Your father's God helps you.
God Almighty blesses you.
He blesses you with rain from above,
with water from springs below,
with many babies born to your wives,
and many young ones born to your animals.
26The blessings of your father are greater
than the blessings of the oldest mountains,
greater than the good things of the long-lasting hills.
May these blessings rest on the head of Joseph,
on the forehead of the one who was separated from his brothers.

27"Benjamin is like a hungry wolf.
In the morning he eats what he has caught,
and in the evening he divides what he has taken."

28These are the twelve tribes of Israel, and
this is what their father said to them. He gave
each son the blessing that was right for him.
29Then Israel gave them a command and
said, "I am about to die. Bury me with my
ancestors in the cave in the field of Ephron
the Hittite. 30That cave is in the field of
Machpelah east of Mamre in the land of
Canaan. Abraham bought the field and cave
from Ephron the Hittite for a burying place.
31Abraham and Sarah his wife are buried
there. Isaac and Rebekah his wife are buried
there, and I buried my wife Leah there. 32The
field and the cave in it were bought from the
Hittite people." 33After Jacob finished talking
to his sons, he lay down. He put his feet back
on the bed, took his last breath, and died.

Jacob's Burial

50 When Jacob died, Joseph hugged his
father and cried over him and kissed
him. 2He commanded the doctors who
served him to prepare his father's body, so
the doctors prepared Jacob's body to be
buried. 3It took the doctors forty days to
prepare his body (the usual time it took).
And the Egyptians had a time of sorrow for
Jacob that lasted seventy days.

4When this time of sorrow had ended,
Joseph spoke to the king's officers and said,
"If you think well of me, please tell this to
the king: 5'When my father was near death, I
made a promise to him that I would bury
him in a cave in the land of Canaan, in a

burial place that he cut out for himself. So please let me go and bury my father, and then I will return.'"

[6]The king answered, "Keep your promise. Go and bury your father."

[7]So Joseph went to bury his father. All the king's officers, the elders of his court, and all the elders of Egypt went with Joseph.
[8]Everyone who lived with Joseph and his brothers went with him, as well as everyone who lived with his father. They left only their children, their flocks, and their herds in the land of Goshen. [9]They went with Joseph in chariots and on horses. It was a very large group.

[10]When they came to the threshing floor of Atad, near the Jordan River, they cried loudly and bitterly for his father. Joseph's time of sorrow continued for seven days.
[11]The people that lived in Canaan saw the sadness at the threshing floor of Atad and said, "Those Egyptians are showing great sorrow!" So now that place is named Sorrow of the Egyptians.

[12]So Jacob's sons did as their father commanded. [13]They carried his body to the land of Canaan and buried it in the cave in the field of Machpelah near Mamre. Abraham had bought this cave and field from Ephron the Hittite to use as a burial place. [14]After Joseph buried his father, he returned to Egypt, along with his brothers and everyone who had gone with him to bury his father.

The Brothers Fear Joseph

[15]After Jacob died, Joseph's brothers said, "What if Joseph is still angry with us? We did many wrong things to him. What if he plans to pay us back?" [16]So they sent a message to Joseph that said, "Your father gave this command before he died. [17]He said to us, 'You have done wrong and have sinned and done evil to Joseph. Tell Joseph to forgive you, his brothers.' So now, Joseph, we beg you to forgive our wrong. We are the servants of the God of your father." When Joseph received the message, he cried.

devotion 16

GENESIS 50:19–21

FORGIVING THE UNFORGIVABLE

The story of Joseph is one of my favorites. While it is a story filled with neon shades of betrayal and triumph, what touches my heart is something far more subtle—forgiveness.

I have often wondered how I would respond in the face of all that Joseph had to endure. As a young man, he was shackled and sold by his own jealous brothers! Were there sleepless nights when he cried tears of bitterness, anger, or fear? Did he dream about revenge . . . or a loving reunion?

Joseph did not let the wrongs of his brothers stop him on his journey of trusting God. He discovered he would never be freed from pain—inflicted or self-induced—until he found forgiveness in the Lord. Years later, in the midst of a prime opportunity to exact revenge, he chose grace over justice. Forgiveness over retribution. God had softened his heart enough to leave the consequences up to heaven.

Many of us know all too well that family is where the deepest wounds can be inflicted. Yet holding grudges found no place or purpose in Joseph's life. He knew that God could turn even the darkest choices into something much richer than Satan's anemic plans.

What have you done with the pain in your own life? The Lord is able to take away the slavery of your suffering and offer you something that is more beautiful and long lasting: freedom in forgiveness.

It is yours for the taking through him.

[18]And his brothers went to him and bowed
low before him and said, "We are your slaves."
[19]Then Joseph said to them, "Don't be
afraid. Can I do what only God can do? [20]You
meant to hurt me, but God turned your evil
into good to save the lives of many people,
which is being done. [21]So don't be afraid. I
will take care of you and your children." So
Joseph comforted his brothers and spoke
kind words to them.
[22]Joseph continued to live in Egypt with
all his father's family. He died when he was
one hundred ten years old. [23]During Joseph's
life Ephraim had children and
grandchildren, and Joseph's son Manasseh
had a son named Makir. Joseph accepted
Makir's children as his own.

The Death of Joseph

[24]Joseph said to his brothers, "I am about
to die, but God will take care of you. He will
lead you out of this land to the land he
promised to Abraham, Isaac, and Jacob."
[25]Then Joseph had the sons of Israel make a
promise. He said, "Promise me that you will
carry my bones with you out of Egypt."
[26]Joseph died when he was one hundred
ten years old. Doctors prepared his body for
burial, and then they put him in a coffin in
Egypt.

Exodus

From a Greek word meaning "the way out," this word refers to the Israelites' deliverance from slavery in Egypt. The original Hebrew title includes a word meaning "and" or "now," suggesting this book is the sequel to Genesis.

Person Holding the Pen God Wrote With: It's generally agreed that *Moses* wrote this book, as indicated in Exodus 24:4.

When the Text Was Written: Between 1445 and 1405 B.C.

Spiritual Posture of the Original Recipients: God's people were no doubt relieved to be *hearing* this story of liberation, rather than having to *live it* all over again.

Storyline Synopsis: While Genesis provides the "once upon a time" of Scripture, Exodus records the Jews' first real experiences with persecution, which was meted out through cruel Egyptian despots (chapter 1). But the narrative grows hopeful with the miraculous birth of Moses, the man God ordained to rescue his people. We learn that Moses is uniquely prepared for leadership (chapter 2) and see his "Are-you-sure-you've-got-the-right-guy?" response to the marching orders God issued through a flaming topiary (chapter 3). The rest of the book describes Israel's dramatic escape from the clutches of Pharaoh (chapters 7—14), their journey to Mount Sinai (chapters 15—18), the first handwritten "instruction book on life"—known as the Ten Commandments—given to Moses by God (chapters 19—31), the golden bovine that infuriated both God and Moses (chapters 32—33), and the second list of rules God dictated to Moses after he broke—literally—the first ones (chapters 34—40).

A Moment Worth Discussing: God advertised his bond with the Israelites and provided them with direction via a supernatural "blimp" in the wilderness—a cloud that led by day and morphed into a ball of fire at night (Ex. 13:17–22). He didn't attempt to conceal his relationship with the Israelites—he displayed it in full glory in the sky. God's explicit directions and undisguised affection for his people is a concurrent and comforting theme throughout Exodus.

Interesting (But Likely to Be Overlooked) Character: *Aaron*, Moses' older brother, always seems to be in his sibling's shadow. Despite his golden calf gaffe, God chose him as the first high priest of Israel, and his descendants followed in his footsteps (Ex. 28:1–4).

Jacob's Family Grows Strong

1 When Jacob[n] went to Egypt, he took his sons, and each son took his own family with him. These are the names of the sons of Israel: [2]Reuben, Simeon, Levi, Judah, [3]Issachar, Zebulun, Benjamin, [4]Dan, Naphtali, Gad, and Asher. [5]There was a total of seventy people who were descendants of Jacob. Jacob's son Joseph was already in Egypt.

[6]Some time later, Joseph and his brothers died, along with all the people who had lived at that same time. [7]But the people of Israel had many children, and their number grew greatly. They became very strong, and the country of Egypt was filled with them.

Trouble for the People of Israel

[8]Then a new king began to rule Egypt, who did not know who Joseph was. [9]This king said to his people, "Look! The people of Israel are too many and too strong for us to handle! [10]If we don't make plans against them, the number of their people will grow even more. Then if there is a war, they might join our enemies and fight us and escape from the country!"

[11]So the Egyptians made life hard for the Israelites. They put slave masters over them, who forced the Israelites to build the cities Pithom and Rameses as supply centers for the king. [12]But the harder the Egyptians forced the Israelites to work, the more the Israelites grew in number and spread out. So the Egyptians became very afraid of them [13]and demanded even more of them. [14]They made their lives bitter. They forced the Israelites to work hard to make bricks and mortar and to do all kinds of work in the fields. The Egyptians were not merciful to them in all their painful work.

[15]Two Hebrew nurses, named Shiphrah and Puah, helped the Israelite women give birth to their babies. The king of Egypt said to the nurses, [16]"When you are helping the Hebrew women give birth to their babies, watch! If the baby is a girl, let her live, but if it is a boy, kill him!" [17]But the nurses feared God, so they did not do as the king told them; they let all the boy babies live. [18]Then the king of Egypt sent for the nurses and said, "Why did you do this? Why did you let the boys live?"

[19]The nurses said to him, "The Hebrew women are much stronger than the Egyptian women. They give birth to their babies before we can get there." [20]God was good to the nurses. And the Hebrew people continued to grow in number, so they became even stronger. [21]Because the nurses feared God, he gave them families of their own.

[22]So the king commanded all his people, "Every time a boy is born to the Hebrews, you must throw him into the Nile River, but let all the girl babies live."

Baby Moses

2 Now a man from the family of Levi married a woman who was also from the family of Levi. [2]She became pregnant and gave birth to a son. When she saw how wonderful the baby was, she hid him for three months. [3]But after three months she was not able to hide the baby any longer, so she got a basket made of reeds and covered it with tar so that it would float. She put the baby in the basket. Then she put the basket among the tall stalks of grass at the edge of the Nile River. [4]The baby's sister stood a short distance away to see what would happen to him.

[5]Then the daughter of the king of Egypt came to the river to take a bath, and her servant girls were walking beside the river. When she saw the basket in the tall grass, she sent her slave girl to get it. [6]The king's daughter opened the basket and saw the baby boy. He was crying, so she felt sorry for him and said, "This is one of the Hebrew babies."

[7]Then the baby's sister asked the king's daughter, "Would you like me to go and find a Hebrew woman to nurse the baby for you?"

[8]The king's daughter said, "Go!" So the girl went and got the baby's own mother.

[9]The king's daughter said to the woman, "Take this baby and nurse him for me, and I will pay you." So the woman took her baby and nursed him. [10]When the child grew older, the woman took him to the king's daughter, and she adopted the baby as her

1:1 Jacob Also called Israel.

Jochebed

EXODUS 2

Jochebed cradles her son in her arms, examining his fingers, toes, and the eyes that strain to focus on her. He is a fine, beautiful child. She feels his breath against her neck and her heart pounds; she knows that if anyone discovers his birth, he will be taken from her. The order has come down from Pharaoh himself: every male Hebrew child must be thrown into the Nile.

She holds him tighter. Prayers rise with every breath she takes. She nurses him for three months, but as the child grows, he becomes more active. It is now difficult to conceal him as his cries grow louder. Her heart aches—she knows she must give up the child, and this is a sacrifice too hard to bear. Who will take care of him? Protect him? She perceives the answer with her spirit: *I will*, the Lord tells her.

She has seen Pharaoh's daughter bathing in the Nile many times. If the princess could see how beautiful Moses is, maybe she would raise him in the palace. Jochebed covers a basket with tar so it will float and makes a bed inside for her son. She clings to him and whispers yet another prayer. She kisses every part of his body—then kisses each part again. With extraordinary faith, she sets the basket into the river, releasing him into God's hands.

It takes faith to release our children, career, spouse, singleness, dreams, etc. into God's hands. What do you need to release?

own son. The king's daughter named him
Moses,[n] because she had pulled him out of
the water.

Moses Tries to Help

11 Moses grew and became a man. One day
he visited his people and saw that they were
forced to work very hard. He saw an
Egyptian beating a Hebrew man, one of
Moses' own people. 12 Moses looked all
around and saw that no one was watching,
so he killed the Egyptian and hid his body in
the sand.

13 The next day Moses returned and saw
two Hebrew men fighting each other. He
said to the one that was in the wrong, "Why
are you hitting one of your own people?"

14 The man answered, "Who made you our
ruler and judge? Are you going to kill me as
you killed the Egyptian?"

Moses was afraid and thought, "Now
everyone knows what I did."

15 When the king heard what Moses had
done, he tried to kill him. But Moses ran
away from the king and went to live in the
land of Midian. There he sat down near a
well.

Moses in Midian

16 There was a priest in Midian who had
seven daughters. His daughters went to that
well to get water to fill the water troughs for
their father's flock. 17 Some shepherds came
and chased the girls away, but Moses
defended the girls and watered their flock.

18 When they went back to their father
Reuel,[n] he asked them, "Why have you come
home early today?"

19 The girls answered, "The shepherds
chased us away, but an Egyptian defended
us. He got water for us and watered our
flock."

20 He asked his daughters, "Where is this
man? Why did you leave him? Invite him to
eat with us."

21 Moses agreed to stay with Jethro, and he
gave his daughter Zipporah to Moses to be
his wife. 22 Zipporah gave birth to a son.
Moses named him Gershom,[n] because Moses
was a stranger in a land that was not his
own.

2:10 Moses The name "Moses" sounds like the Hebrew word for "to pull out." **2:18 Reuel** He was also called Jethro.
2:22 Gershom This name sounds like the Hebrew word meaning "a stranger there."

23After a long time, the king of Egypt died.
The people of Israel groaned, because they
were forced to work very hard. When they
cried for help, God heard them. 24God heard
their cries, and he remembered the
agreement he had made with Abraham,
Isaac, and Jacob. 25He saw the troubles of the
people of Israel, and he was concerned about
them.

The Burning Bush

3 One day Moses was taking care of Jethro's
flock. (Jethro was the priest of Midian
and also Moses' father-in-law.) When Moses
led the flock to the west side of the desert, he
came to Sinai, the mountain of God. 2There
the angel of the LORD appeared to him in
flames of fire coming out of a bush. Moses
saw that the bush was on fire, but it was not
burning up. 3So he said, "I will go closer to
this strange thing. How can a bush continue
burning without burning up?"

4When the LORD saw Moses was coming
to look at the bush, God called to him from
the bush, "Moses, Moses!"

And Moses said, "Here I am."

5Then God said, "Do not come any closer.
Take off your sandals, because you are
standing on holy ground. 6I am the God of
your ancestors—the God of Abraham, the
God of Isaac, and the God of Jacob." Moses
covered his face because he was afraid to
look at God.

7The LORD said, "I have seen the troubles
my people have suffered in Egypt, and I have
heard their cries when the Egyptian slave
masters hurt them. I am concerned about
their pain, 8and I have come down to save
them from the Egyptians. I will bring them
out of that land and lead them to a good land
with lots of room—a fertile land. It is the
land of the Canaanites, Hittites, Amorites,
Perizzites, Hivites, and Jebusites. 9I have
heard the cries of the people of Israel, and I
have seen the way the Egyptians have made
life hard for them. 10So now I am sending
you to the king of Egypt. Go! Bring my
people, the Israelites, out of Egypt!"

11But Moses said to God, "I am not a great
man! How can I go to the king and lead the
Israelites out of Egypt?"

12God said, "I will be with you. This will
be the proof that I am sending you: After you
lead the people out of Egypt, all of you will
worship me on this mountain."

13Moses said to God, "When I go to the
Israelites, I will say to them, 'The God of
your ancestors sent me to you.' What if the
people say, 'What is his name?' What should
I tell them?"

14Then God said to Moses, "I AM WHO I AM."[n]
When you go to the people of Israel, tell
them, 'I AM sent me to you.'"

15God also said to Moses, "This is what
you should tell the people: 'The LORD is the
God of your ancestors—the God of
Abraham, the God of Isaac, and the God of
Jacob. He sent me to you.' This will always
be my name, by which people from now on
will know me.

16"Go and gather the elders and tell them
this: 'The LORD, the God of your ancestors
Abraham, Isaac, and Jacob, has appeared to
me. He said, I care about you, and I have seen
what has happened to you in Egypt. 17I
promised I would take you out of your
troubles in Egypt. I will lead you to the land
of the Canaanites, Hittites, Amorites,
Perizzites, Hivites, and Jebusites—a fertile
land.'

18"The elders will listen to you. And then
you and the elders of Israel will go to the
king of Egypt and tell him, 'The LORD, the
God of the Hebrews, appeared to us. Let us
travel three days into the desert to offer
sacrifices to the LORD our God.'

19"But I know that the king of Egypt will
not let you go. Only a great power will
force him to let you go, 20so I will use my
great power against Egypt. I will strike
Egypt with all the miracles that will
happen in that land. After I do that, he will
let you go. 21I will cause the Egyptians to
think well of the Israelites. So when you
leave, they will give gifts to your people.
22Each woman should ask her Egyptian
neighbor and any Egyptian woman living
in her house for gifts—silver, gold, and
clothing. You should put those gifts on
your children when you leave Egypt. In
this way you will take with you the riches
of the Egyptians."

3:14 I . . . I AM The Hebrew words are like the name "Yahweh." This Hebrew name for God, usually called "LORD," shows that God always lives and is always with his people.

devotion 17

EXODUS 3:11-12

SOMEONE LIKE ME

Not only am I not great—I am also prone to cowardice instead of courage. I don't do so well with confrontation. I get tongue-tied and nervous and forget my words. And then there's my worth. I haven't ever felt worthy of God's goodness to me, and I'm always sure he could find someone more qualified to send.

And yet I still hear God calling me. He is moving in my heart and stirring my mind toward his will. I remind him that I am not great, and he continues to call me anyway. He asks me to be brave in raising my children. But I am a single mom, and I am not brave. *I will be with you.* And he sends me, with all my flaws, to speak to people in his name. *I will be with you.* He knows I'm confident one day and a pitiful mess the next. *I will be with you.*

Do you hear God calling you out? Do you hear him asking you to use every one of your gifts for his glory? Like mine, does your heart whisper, "But I am not great"?

Listen to God and trust that he will be with you. When a woman like you (or like me) does anything powerful or strong or brave, everyone can see that you are being led by the hand of God. And then they will see God and worship the One who has been with you and before you and protecting you all along.

Proof for Moses

4 Then Moses answered, "What if the
people of Israel do not believe me or
listen to me? What if they say, 'The LORD did
not appear to you'?"
2The LORD said to him, "What is that in
your hand?"
Moses answered, "It is my walking stick."
3The LORD said, "Throw it on the ground."
So Moses threw it on the ground, and it
became a snake. Moses ran from the snake,
4but the LORD said to him, "Reach out and
grab the snake by its tail." When Moses
reached out and took hold of the snake, it
again became a stick in his hand. 5The LORD
said, "This is so that the Israelites will
believe that the LORD appeared to you. I am
the God of their ancestors, the God of
Abraham, the God of Isaac, and the God of
Jacob."
6Then the LORD said to Moses, "Put your
hand inside your coat." So Moses put his
hand inside his coat. When he took it out, it
was white with a skin disease.
7Then he said, "Now put your hand inside
your coat again." So Moses put his hand
inside his coat again. When he took it out,
his hand was healthy again, like the rest of
his skin.
8Then the LORD said, "If the people do not
believe you or pay attention to the first
miracle, they may believe you when you
show them this second miracle. 9After these
two miracles, if they still do not believe or
listen to you, take some water from the Nile
River and pour it on the dry ground. The
water will become blood when it touches
the ground."
10But Moses said to the LORD, "Please, Lord,
I have never been a skilled speaker. Even
now, after talking to you, I cannot speak
well. I speak slowly and can't find the best
words."
11Then the LORD said to him, "Who made
a person's mouth? And who makes someone
deaf or not able to speak? Or who gives a
person sight or blindness? It is I, the LORD.
12Now go! I will help you speak, and I will
teach you what to say."

[13]But Moses said, "Please, Lord, send
someone else."
[14]The LORD became angry with Moses and
said, "Your brother Aaron, from the family of
Levi, is a skilled speaker. He is already
coming to meet you, and he will be happy
when he sees you. [15]You will speak to Aaron
and tell him what to say. I will help both of
you to speak and will teach you what to do.
[16]Aaron will speak to the people for you. You
will tell him what God says, and he will
speak for you. [17]Take your walking stick
with you, and use it to do the miracles."

Moses Returns to Egypt

[18]Moses went back to Jethro, his father-in-
law, and said to him, "Let me go back to my
people in Egypt. I want to see if they are still
alive."
Jethro said to Moses, "Go! I wish you well."
[19]While Moses was still in Midian, the
LORD said to him, "Go back to Egypt, because
the men who wanted to kill you are dead
now."
[20]So Moses took his wife and his sons, put
them on a donkey, and started back to
Egypt. He took with him the walking stick
of God.
[21]The LORD said to Moses, "When you get
back to Egypt, do all the miracles I have
given you the power to do. Show them to
the king of Egypt. But I will make the king
very stubborn, and he will not let the people
go. [22]Then say to the king, 'This is what the
LORD says: Israel is my firstborn son. [23]I told
you to let my son go so he may worship me.
But you refused to let Israel go, so I will kill
your firstborn son.' "
[24]As Moses was on his way to Egypt, he
stopped at a resting place for the night. The
LORD met him there and tried to kill him.
[25]But Zipporah took a flint knife and
circumcised her son. Taking the skin, she
touched Moses' feet with it and said to him,
"You are a bridegroom of blood to me." [26]She
said, "You are a bridegroom of blood,"
because she had to circumcise her son. So
the LORD let Moses alone.
[27]Meanwhile the LORD said to Aaron, "Go
out into the desert to meet Moses." When
Aaron went, he met Moses at Sinai, the
mountain of God, and kissed him. [28]Moses
told Aaron everything the LORD had said to
him when he sent him to Egypt. He also told
him about the miracles which the LORD had
commanded him to do.
[29]Moses and Aaron gathered all the elders
of the Israelites, [30]and Aaron told them
everything that the LORD had told Moses.
Then Moses did the miracles for all the
people to see, [31]and the Israelites believed.
When they heard that the LORD was
concerned about them and had seen their
troubles, they bowed down and worshiped
him.

Moses and Aaron Before the King

5 After Moses and Aaron talked to the
people, they went to the king of Egypt
and said, "This is what the LORD, the God of
Israel, says: 'Let my people go so they may
hold a feast for me in the desert.' "
[2]But the king of Egypt said, "Who is the
LORD? Why should I obey him and let Israel
go? I do not know the LORD, and I will not let
Israel go."
[3]Then Aaron and Moses said, "The God of
the Hebrews has met with us. Now let us
travel three days into the desert to offer
sacrifices to the LORD our God. If we don't do
this, he may kill us with a disease or in war."
[4]But the king said to them, "Moses and
Aaron, why are you taking the people away
from their work? Go back to your jobs!
[5]There are very many Hebrews, and now you
want them to quit working!"
[6]That same day the king gave a command
to the slave masters and foremen. [7]He said,
"Don't give the people straw to make bricks
as you used to do. Let them gather their own
straw. [8]But they must still make the same
number of bricks as they did before. Do not
accept fewer. They have become lazy, and
that is why they are asking me, 'Let us go to
offer sacrifices to our God.' [9]Make these
people work harder and keep them busy;
then they will not have time to listen to the
lies of Moses."
[10]So the slave masters and foremen went
to the Israelites and said, "This is what the
king says: I will no longer give you straw.
[11]Go and get your own straw wherever you
can find it. But you must make as many
bricks as you made before." [12]So the people
went everywhere in Egypt looking for dry
stalks to use for straw. [13]The slave masters
kept forcing the people to work harder. They
said, "You must make just as many bricks as

you did when you were given straw." 14The
king's slave masters had made the Israelite
foremen responsible for the work the people
did. The Egyptian slave masters beat these
men and asked them, "Why aren't you
making as many bricks as you made in the
past?"
15Then the Israelite foremen went to the
king and complained, "Why are you treating
us, your servants, this way? 16You give us no
straw, but we are commanded to make
bricks. Our slave masters beat us, but it is
your own people's fault."
17The king answered, "You are lazy! You
don't want to work! That is why you ask to
leave here and make sacrifices to the LORD.
18Now, go back to work! We will not give
you any straw, but you must make just as
many bricks as you did before."
19The Israelite foremen knew they were in
trouble, because the king had told them,
"You must make just as many bricks each
day as you did before." 20As they were
leaving the meeting with the king, they met
Moses and Aaron, who were waiting for
them. 21So they said to Moses and Aaron,
"May the LORD punish you. You caused the
king and his officers to hate us. You have
given them an excuse to kill us."

Moses Complains to God

22Then Moses returned to the LORD and
said, "Lord, why have you brought this
trouble on your people? Is this why you sent
me here? 23I went to the king and said what
you told me to say, but ever since that time
he has made the people suffer. And you have
done nothing to save them."
6 Then the LORD said to Moses, "Now you
will see what I will do to the king of
Egypt. I will use my great power against
him, and he will let my people go. Because of
my power, he will force them out of his
country."
2Then God said to Moses, "I am the LORD.
3I appeared to Abraham, Isaac, and Jacob by
the name God Almighty, but they did not
know me by my name, the LORD. 4I also
made my agreement with them to give them
the land of Canaan. They lived in that land,
but it was not their own. 5Now I have heard
the cries of the Israelites, whom the
Egyptians are treating as slaves, and I
remember my agreement. 6So tell the people
of Israel that I say to them, 'I am the LORD. I
will save you from the hard work the
Egyptians force you to do. I will make you
free, so you will not be slaves to the
Egyptians. I will free you by my great
power, and I will punish the Egyptians
terribly. 7I will make you my own people,
and I will be your God. You will know that
I am the LORD your God, the One who saves
you from the hard work the Egyptians force
you to do. 8I will lead you to the land that
I promised to Abraham, Isaac, and Jacob,
and I will give you that land to own. I am
the LORD.'"
9So Moses told this to the Israelites, but
they would not listen to him. They were
discouraged, and their slavery was hard.
10Then the LORD said to Moses, 11"Go tell
the king of Egypt that he must let the
Israelites leave his land."
12But Moses answered, "The Israelites will
not listen to me, so surely the king will not
listen to me either. I am not a good speaker."
13But the LORD spoke to Moses and Aaron
and gave them orders about the Israelites
and the king of Egypt. He commanded them
to lead the Israelites out of Egypt.

Families of Israel

14These are the leaders of the families of
Israel:

Israel's first son, Reuben, had four sons:
Hanoch, Pallu, Hezron, and Carmi. These are
the family groups of Reuben.
15Simeon's sons were Jemuel, Jamin,
Ohad, Jakin, Zohar, and Shaul, the son of a
Canaanite woman. These are the family
groups of Simeon.
16Levi lived one hundred thirty-seven
years. These are the names of his sons
according to their family history: Gershon,
Kohath, and Merari.
17Gershon had two sons, Libni and
Shimei, with their families.
18Kohath lived one hundred thirty-three
years. The sons of Kohath were Amram,
Izhar, Hebron, and Uzziel.
19The sons of Merari were Mahli and
Mushi.

These are the family groups of Levi,
according to their family history.
20Amram married his father's sister
Jochebed, who gave birth to Aaron and

devotion 18

EXODUS 6:6–7

THE GOD OF "I WILL"

God told Moses that he would provide for him in every way:

"I will bring you out from under the burdens."

"I will rescue you."

"I will redeem you."

"I will take you."

"I will be your God."

God is clear about the fact that he does not desire for anyone or anything else to take credit for the deliverance that comes only from his hand. Do you need to be rescued from whatever has a hold on some part (or all) of your life? Your freedom lies in the "I will" of the Lord.

Read through the promises God made to Moses, and insert your name in the blanks: "I am the Lord, and I will deliver you, ________, from your burdens. I will rescue you, and I will redeem you. I will take you, and I will be your God. Yes, I am the Lord your God who brings you out from under your heavy burdens, so leave them here with me today, ________. You will never again return to bondage."

Thank you, Father! "I will" forever in my heart trust you and rely on your deliverance and provision.

Moses. Amram lived one hundred
thirty-seven years.
21Izhar's sons were Korah, Nepheg, and
Zicri.
22Uzziel's sons were Mishael, Elzaphan,
and Sithri.
23Aaron married Elisheba, the daughter of
Amminadab and the sister of Nahshon.
Elisheba gave birth to Nadab, Abihu, Eleazar,
and Ithamar.
24The sons of Korah were Assir, Elkanah,
and Abiasaph. These are the family groups of
the Korahites.
25Eleazar son of Aaron married a daughter
of Putiel, and she gave birth to Phinehas.
These are the leaders of the family groups
of the Levites.
26This was the Aaron and Moses to whom
the LORD said, "Lead the people of Israel out
of Egypt by their divisions." 27Aaron and
Moses are the ones who talked to the king of
Egypt and told him to let the Israelites leave
Egypt.

God Repeats His Call to Moses

28The LORD spoke to Moses in the land of
Egypt 29and said, "I am the LORD. Tell the
king of Egypt everything I tell you."
30But Moses answered, "I am not a good
speaker. The king will not listen to me."
7 The LORD said to Moses, "I have made
you like God to the king of Egypt, and
your brother Aaron will be like a prophet for
you. 2Tell Aaron your brother everything
that I command you, and let him tell the
king of Egypt to let the Israelites leave his
country. 3But I will make the king
stubborn. I will do many miracles in
Egypt, 4but he will still refuse to listen. So
then I will punish Egypt terribly, and I
will lead my divisions, my people the
Israelites, out of that land. 5I will punish
Egypt with my power, and I will bring the
Israelites out of that land. Then they will
know I am the LORD."
6Moses and Aaron did just as the LORD had
commanded them. 7Moses was eighty years

old and Aaron was eighty-three when they
spoke to the king.

Aaron's Walking Stick Becomes a Snake

8The LORD said to Moses and Aaron,
9"Moses, when the king asks you to do a
miracle, tell Aaron to throw his walking
stick down in front of the king, and it will
become a snake."

10So Moses and Aaron went to the king as
the LORD had commanded. Aaron threw his
walking stick down in front of the king and
his officers, and it became a snake.

11So the king called in his wise men and
his magicians, and with their tricks the
Egyptian magicians were able to do the same
thing. 12They threw their walking sticks on
the ground, and their sticks became snakes.
But Aaron's stick swallowed theirs. 13Still
the king was stubborn and refused to listen
to Moses and Aaron, just as the LORD had
said.

The Water Becomes Blood

14Then the LORD said to Moses, "The king
is being stubborn and refuses to let the
people go. 15In the morning the king will go
out to the Nile River. Go meet him by the
edge of the river, and take with you the
walking stick that became a snake. 16Tell
him: The LORD, the God of the Hebrews, sent
me to you. He said, 'Let my people go
worship me in the desert.' Until now you
have not listened. 17This is what the LORD
says: 'This is how you will know that I am
the LORD. I will strike the water of the Nile
River with this stick in my hand, and the
water will change into blood. 18Then the fish
in the Nile will die, and the river will begin
to stink. The Egyptians will not be able to
drink the water from the Nile.' "

19The LORD said to Moses, "Tell Aaron:
'Take the walking stick in your hand and
stretch your hand over the rivers, canals,
ponds, and pools in Egypt.' The water will
become blood everywhere in Egypt, both in
wooden buckets and in stone jars."

20So Moses and Aaron did just as the LORD
had commanded. In front of the king and his
officers, Aaron raised his walking stick and
struck the water in the Nile River. So all the
water in the Nile changed into blood. 21The
fish in the Nile died, and the river began to
stink, so the Egyptians could not drink water
from it. Blood was everywhere in the land of
Egypt.

22Using their tricks, the magicians of
Egypt did the same thing. So the king was
stubborn and refused to listen to Moses and
Aaron, just as the LORD had said. 23The king
turned and went into his palace and ignored
what Moses and Aaron had done. 24The
Egyptians could not drink the water from
the Nile, so all of them dug along the bank of
the river, looking for water to drink.

The Frogs

25Seven days passed after the LORD
changed the Nile River.

8 Then the LORD told Moses, "Go to the
king of Egypt and tell him, 'This is what
the LORD says: Let my people go to worship
me. 2If you refuse, I will punish Egypt with
frogs. 3The Nile River will be filled with
frogs. They will come up into your palace,
into your bedroom, on your bed, into the
houses of your officers, and onto your
people. They will come into your ovens
and into your baking pans. 4The frogs will
jump all over you, your people, and your
officers.' "

5Then the LORD said to Moses, "Tell Aaron
to hold his walking stick in his hand over
the rivers, canals, and ponds. Make frogs
come up out of the water onto the land of
Egypt."

6So Aaron held his hand over all the
waters of Egypt, and the frogs came up out of
the water and covered the land of Egypt.
7The magicians used their tricks to do the
same thing, so even more frogs came up
onto the land of Egypt.

8The king called for Moses and Aaron
and said, "Pray to the LORD to take the frogs
away from me and my people. I will let
your people go to offer sacrifices to the
LORD."

9Moses said to the king, "Please set the
time when I should pray for you, your
people, and your officers. Then the frogs will
leave you and your houses and will remain
only in the Nile."

10The king answered, "Tomorrow."

Moses said, "What you want will happen.
By this you will know that there is no one
like the LORD our God. 11The frogs will leave
you, your houses, your officers, and your
people. They will remain only in the Nile."

12After Moses and Aaron left the king,
Moses asked the LORD about the frogs he had
sent to the king. 13And the LORD did as Moses
asked. The frogs died in the houses, in the
yards, and in the fields. 14The Egyptians put
them in piles, and the whole country began
to stink. 15But when the king saw that they
were free of the frogs, he became stubborn
again. He did not listen to Moses and Aaron,
just as the LORD had said.

The Gnats

16Then the LORD said to Moses, "Tell Aaron
to raise his walking stick and strike the dust
on the ground. Then everywhere in Egypt
the dust will change into gnats." 17They did
this, and when Aaron raised the walking
stick that was in his hand and struck the dust
on the ground, everywhere in Egypt the dust
changed into gnats. The gnats got on the
people and animals. 18Using their tricks, the
magicians tried to do the same thing, but
they could not make the dust change into
gnats. The gnats remained on the people and
animals. 19So the magicians told the king
that the power of God had done this. But the
king was stubborn and refused to listen to
them, just as the LORD had said.

The Flies

20The LORD told Moses, "Get up early in
the morning, and meet the king of Egypt as
he goes out to the river. Tell him, 'This is
what the LORD says: Let my people go so they
can worship me. 21If you don't let them go, I
will send swarms of flies into your houses.
The flies will be on you, your officers, and
your people. The houses of Egypt will be full
of flies, and they will be all over the ground,
too. 22But I will not treat the Israelites the
same as the Egyptian people. There will not
be any flies in the land of Goshen, where my
people live. By this you will know that I, the
LORD, am in this land. 23I will treat my
people differently from your people. This
miracle will happen tomorrow.' "

24So the LORD did as he had said, and great
swarms of flies came into the king's palace
and his officers' houses. All over Egypt flies
were ruining the land. 25The king called for
Moses and Aaron and told them, "Offer
sacrifices to your God here in this country."

26But Moses said, "It wouldn't be right to
do that, because the Egyptians hate the
sacrifices we offer to the LORD our God. If
they see us offering sacrifices they hate, they
will throw stones at us and kill us. 27Let us
make a three-day journey into the desert. We
must offer sacrifices to the LORD our God
there, as the LORD told us to do."

28The king said, "I will let you go so that
you may offer sacrifices to the LORD your
God in the desert, but you must not go very
far away. Now go and pray for me."

29Moses said, "I will leave and pray to the
LORD, and he will take the flies away from
you, your officers, and your people
tomorrow. But do not try to trick us again.
Do not stop the people from going to offer
sacrifices to the LORD."

30So Moses left the king and prayed to the
LORD, 31and the LORD did as he asked. He
removed the flies from the king, his officers,
and his people so that not one fly was left.
32But the king became stubborn again and
did not let the people go.

The Disease on the Farm Animals

9 Then the LORD told Moses, "Go to the
king of Egypt and tell him, 'This is what
the LORD, the God of the Hebrews, says: Let
my people go to worship me. 2If you refuse
to let them go and continue to hold them,
3the LORD will punish you. He will send a
terrible disease on your farm animals that
are in the fields. He will cause your horses,
donkeys, camels, cattle, goats, and sheep to
become sick. 4But the LORD will treat Israel's
animals differently from the animals of
Egypt. None of the animals that belong to
the Israelites will die. 5The LORD has set
tomorrow as the time he will do this in the
land.' " 6The next day the LORD did as he
promised. All the farm animals in Egypt
died, but none of the animals belonging to
Israelites died. 7The king sent people to see
what had happened to the animals of Israel,
and they found that not one of them had
died. But the king was still stubborn and did
not let the people go.

The Boils

8The LORD said to Moses and Aaron, "Fill
your hands with ashes from a furnace.
Moses, throw the ashes into the air in front
of the king of Egypt. 9The ashes will spread
like dust through all the land of Egypt. They
will cause boils to break out and become

sores on the skin of people and animals
everywhere in the land."
[10]So Moses and Aaron took ashes from a
furnace and went and stood before the king.
Moses threw ashes into the air, which caused
boils to break out and become sores on
people and animals. [11]The magicians could
not stand before Moses, because all the
Egyptians had boils, even the magicians.
[12]But the LORD made the king stubborn, so
he refused to listen to Moses and Aaron, just
as the LORD had said.

The Hail

[13]Then the LORD said to Moses, "Get up
early in the morning and go to the king of
Egypt. Tell him, 'This is what the LORD, the
God of the Hebrews, says: Let my people go
to worship me. [14]If you don't, this time I will
punish you, your officers, and your people,
with all my power. Then you will know
there is no one in the whole land like me.
[15]By now I could have used my power and
caused a terrible disease that would have
destroyed you and your people from the
earth. [16]But I have let you live for this
reason: to show you my power so that my
name will be talked about in all the earth.
[17]You are still against my people and do not
want to let them go. [18]So at this time
tomorrow, I will send a terrible hailstorm,
the worst in Egypt since it became a nation.
[19]Now send for your animals and whatever
you have in the fields, and bring them into a
safe place. The hail will fall on every person
or animal that is still in the fields. If they
have not been brought in, they will die.' "
[20]Some of the king's officers respected the
word of the LORD and hurried to bring their
slaves and animals inside. [21]But others
ignored the LORD's message and left their
slaves and animals in the fields.
[22]The LORD told Moses, "Raise your hand
toward the sky. Then the hail will start
falling in all the land of Egypt. It will fall on
people, animals, and on everything that
grows in the fields of Egypt." [23]When Moses
raised his walking stick toward the sky, the
LORD sent thunder and hail, and lightning
flashed down to the earth. So he caused hail
to fall upon the land of Egypt. [24]There was
hail, and lightning flashed as it hailed—the
worst hailstorm in Egypt since it had
become a nation. [25]The hail destroyed all the
people and animals that were in the fields in
all the land of Egypt. It also destroyed
everything that grew in the fields and broke
all the trees in the fields. [26]The only place it
did not hail was in the land of Goshen,
where the Israelites lived.
[27]The king sent for Moses and Aaron and
told them, "This time I have sinned. The
LORD is in the right, and I and my people are
in the wrong. [28]Pray to the LORD. We have
had enough of God's thunder and hail. I will
let you go; you do not have to stay here any
longer."
[29]Moses told the king, "When I leave the
city, I will raise my hands to the LORD in
prayer, and the thunder and hail will stop.
Then you will know that the earth belongs
to the LORD. [30]But I know that you and your
officers do not yet fear the LORD God."
[31]The flax was in bloom, and the barley
had ripened, so these crops were destroyed.
[32]But both wheat crops ripen later, so they
were not destroyed.
[33]Moses left the king and went outside the
city. He raised his hands to the LORD, and the
thunder and hail stopped. The rain also
stopped falling to the ground. [34]When the
king saw that the rain, hail, and thunder had
stopped, he sinned again, and he and his
officers became stubborn. [35]So the king
became stubborn and refused to let the
Israelites go, just as the LORD had said
through Moses.

The Locusts

10 The LORD said to Moses, "Go to
the king of Egypt. I have made him
and his officers stubborn so I could show
them my powerful miracles. [2]I also did
this so you could tell your children and
your grandchildren how I was hard on the
Egyptians. Tell them about the miracles I did
among them so that all of you will know
that I am the LORD."
[3]So Moses and Aaron went to the king and
told him, "This is what the LORD, the God of
the Hebrews, says: 'How long will you refuse
to be sorry for what you have done? Let my
people go to worship me. [4]If you refuse to let
my people go, tomorrow I will bring locusts
into your country. [5]They will cover the land
so that no one will be able to see the ground.
They will eat anything that was left from the
hailstorm and the leaves from every tree
growing in the field. [6]They will fill your

devotion 19

EXODUS 9:15–16

GOD'S WILL—WILL YOU?

Several years ago, my husband began to feel the Lord tugging on his heart to start his own business. We prayed and prayed for God to show us his will for our lives. We had been down this road before, and our business eventually went under. It was a difficult and painful experience—one I did not want to go through again. As we went through the decision process, I waffled back and forth about what to do. I finally concluded that God wanted us to step out and do this regardless of whether our business succeeded or failed.

You see, we too often want God's will for our lives if it means we will succeed and have all our prayers answered the way we think they should be answered. We are quick to say that God is in control when things are good, but quicker to say God has abandoned us when things are bad. The truth is that God is in control through the good and the bad. God allowed the Egyptians, Israel's captors, to live during the days of Moses so that he could reveal himself to the rest of the world. The king of Egypt thought he was in total control of his life (and everyone else's), but we know better.

There will be times when God fills your life with good, positive things. But when those times come that are difficult or painful, know that God is still in control. And remember that someday it will all make sense.

palaces and all your officers' houses, as well
as the houses of all the Egyptians. There will
be more locusts than your fathers or
ancestors have ever seen—more than there
have been since people began living in
Egypt.'" Then Moses turned and walked
away from the king.
7The king's officers asked him, "How long
will this man make trouble for us? Let the
Israelites go to worship the LORD their God.
Don't you know that Egypt is ruined?"
8So Moses and Aaron were brought back
to the king. He said to them, "Go and
worship the LORD your God. But tell me, just
who is going?"
9Moses answered, "We will go with our
young and old people, our sons and
daughters, and our flocks and herds, because
we are going to have a feast to honor the
LORD."
10The king said to them, "The LORD will
really have to be with you if ever I let you
and all of your children leave Egypt. See, you
are planning something evil! 11No! Only the
men may go and worship the LORD, which is
what you have been asking for." Then the
king forced Moses and Aaron out of his
palace.
12The LORD told Moses, "Raise your hand
over the land of Egypt, and the locusts will
come. They will spread all over the land of
Egypt and will eat all the plants the hail did
not destroy."
13So Moses raised his walking stick over
the land of Egypt, and the LORD caused a
strong wind to blow from the east. It blew
across the land all that day and night, and
when morning came, the east wind had
brought the locusts. 14Swarms of locusts
covered all the land of Egypt and settled
everywhere. There were more locusts than
ever before or after, 15and they covered the
whole land so that it was black. They ate
everything that was left after the hail—
every plant in the field and all the fruit on
the trees. Nothing green was left on any tree
or plant anywhere in Egypt.
16The king quickly called for Moses and

Aaron. He said, "I have sinned against the
LORD your God and against you. 17Now
forgive my sin this time. Pray to the LORD
your God, and ask him to stop this
punishment that kills."
18Moses left the king and prayed to the
LORD. 19So the LORD changed the wind. He
made a very strong wind blow from the
west, and it blew the locusts away into the
Red Sea. Not one locust was left anywhere in
Egypt. 20But the LORD caused the king to be
stubborn again, and he did not let the
Israelites go.

The Darkness

21Then the LORD told Moses, "Raise your
hand toward the sky, and darkness will cover
the land of Egypt. It will be so dark you will
be able to feel it." 22Moses raised his hand
toward the sky, and total darkness was
everywhere in Egypt for three days. 23No one
could see anyone else, and no one could go
anywhere for three days. But the Israelites
had light where they lived.
24Again the king of Egypt called for Moses.
He said, "All of you may go and worship the
LORD. You may take your women and
children with you, but you must leave your
flocks and herds here."
25Moses said, "You must let us have
animals to use as sacrifices and burnt
offerings, because we have to offer them to
the LORD our God. 26So we must take our
animals with us; not a hoof will be left
behind. We have to use some of the animals
to worship the LORD our God. We won't
know exactly what we will need to worship
the LORD until we get there."
27But the LORD made the king stubborn
again, so he refused to let them go. 28Then he
told Moses, "Get out of here, and don't come
again! The next time you see me, you will
die."
29Then Moses told the king, "I'll do what
you say. I will not come to see you again."

The Death of the Firstborn

11 Now the LORD had told Moses, "I have
one more way to punish the king and
the people of Egypt. After this, the king will
send all of you away from Egypt. When he
does, he will force you to leave completely.
2Tell the men and women of Israel to ask
their neighbors for things made of silver and
gold." 3The LORD had caused the Egyptians to
respect the Israelites, and both the king's
officers and the Egyptian people considered
Moses to be a great man.
4So Moses said to the king, "This is what
the LORD says: 'About midnight tonight I will
go through all Egypt. 5Every firstborn son in
the land of Egypt will die—from the
firstborn son of the king, who sits on his
throne, to the firstborn of the slave girl
grinding grain. Also the firstborn farm
animals will die. 6There will be loud outcries
everywhere in Egypt, worse than any time
before or after this. 7But not even a dog will
bark at the Israelites or their animals.' Then
you will know that the LORD treats Israel
differently from Egypt. 8All your officers will
come to me. They will bow facedown to the
ground before me and say, 'Leave and take all
your people with you.' After that, I will
leave." Then Moses very angrily left the king.
9The LORD had told Moses, "The king will
not listen to you and Aaron so that I may do
many miracles in the land of Egypt." 10Moses
and Aaron did all these great miracles in
front of the king. But the LORD made him
stubborn, and the king would not let the
Israelites leave his country.

The First Passover

12 The LORD spoke to Moses and Aaron
in the land of Egypt: 2"This month
will be the beginning of months, the first
month of the year for you. 3Tell the whole
community of Israel that on the tenth day of
this month each man must get one lamb for
the people in his house. 4If there are not
enough people in his house to eat a whole
lamb, he must share it with his closest
neighbor, considering the number of people.
There must be enough lamb for everyone to
eat. 5The lamb must be a one-year-old male
that has nothing wrong with it. This animal
can be either a young sheep or a young
goat. 6Take care of the animals until the
fourteenth day of the month. On that day all
the people of the community of Israel will
kill them in the evening before dark. 7The
people must take some of the blood and put
it on the sides and tops of the doorframes of
the houses where they eat the lambs. 8On
this night they must roast the lamb over a
fire. They must eat it with bitter herbs and
bread made without yeast. 9Do not eat the

lamb raw or boiled in water. Roast the whole
lamb over a fire—with its head, legs, and
inner organs. 10You must not leave any of it
until morning, but if any of it is left over
until morning, you must burn it with fire.

11"This is the way you must eat it: You
must be fully dressed as if you were going on
a trip. You must have your sandals on and
your walking stick in your hand. You must
eat it in a hurry; this is the LORD's Passover.

12"That night I will go through the land of
Egypt and kill all the firstborn animals and
people in the land of Egypt. I will also
punish all the gods of Egypt. I am the LORD.
13But the blood will be a sign on the houses
where you are. When I see the blood, I will
pass over you. Nothing terrible will hurt you
when I punish the land of Egypt.

14"You are always to remember this day
and celebrate it with a feast to the LORD. Your
descendants are to honor the LORD with this
feast from now on. 15For this feast you must
eat bread made without yeast for seven days.
On the first day, you are to remove all the
yeast from your houses. No one should eat
any yeast for the full seven days of the feast,
or that person will be cut off from Israel.
16You are to have holy meetings on the first
and last days of the feast. You must not do
any work on these days; the only work you
may do is to prepare your meals. 17You must
celebrate the Feast of Unleavened Bread,
because on this very day I brought your
divisions of people out of Egypt. So all of
your descendants must celebrate this day.
This is a law that will last from now on. 18In
the first month of the year you are to eat
bread made without yeast, from the evening
of the fourteenth day until the evening of
the twenty-first day. 19For seven days there
must not be any yeast in your houses.
Anybody who eats yeast during this time,
either an Israelite or non-Israelite, must be
cut off from the community of Israel.
20During this feast you must not eat
anything made with yeast. You must eat
only bread made without yeast wherever
you live."

21Then Moses called all the elders of Israel
together and told them, "Get the animals for
your families and kill the lamb for the
Passover. 22Take a branch of the hyssop
plant, dip it into the bowl filled with blood,
and then wipe the blood on the sides and
tops of the doorframes. No one may leave
that house until morning. 23When the LORD
goes through Egypt to kill the Egyptians, he
will see the blood on the sides and tops of
the doorframes, and he will pass over that
house. He will not let the one who brings
death come into your houses and kill you.

24"You must keep this command as a law
for you and your descendants from now on.
25Do this when you go to the land the LORD
has promised to give you. 26When your
children ask you, 'Why are we doing these
things?' 27you will say, 'This is the Passover
sacrifice to honor the LORD. When we were
in Egypt, the LORD passed over the houses of
Israel, and when he killed the Egyptians, he
saved our homes.' " Then the people bowed
down and worshiped the LORD. 28They did
just as the LORD commanded Moses and
Aaron.

29At midnight the LORD killed all the
firstborn sons in the land of Egypt—from
the firstborn of the king who sat on the
throne to the firstborn of the prisoner in jail.
Also, all the firstborn farm animals died.
30The king, his officers, and all the Egyptians
got up during the night because someone
had died in every house. So there was a loud
outcry everywhere in Egypt.

Israel Leaves Egypt

31During the night the king called for
Moses and Aaron and said, "Get up and leave
my people. You and your people may do as
you have asked; go and worship the LORD.
32Take all of your flocks and herds as you
have asked, and go. And also bless me." 33The
Egyptians also asked the Israelites to hurry
and leave, saying, "If you don't leave, we will
all die!"

34So the people took their dough before
the yeast was added. They wrapped the
bowls for making dough in clothing and
carried them on their shoulders. 35The
Israelites did what Moses told them to do
and asked their Egyptian neighbors for
things made of silver and gold and for
clothing. 36The LORD caused the Egyptians
to think well of them, and the Egyptians
gave the people everything they asked
for. So the Israelites took rich gifts from
them.

37The Israelites traveled from Rameses to
Succoth. There were about six hundred

thousand men walking, not including the
women and children. [38]Many other people
who were not Israelites went with them, as
well as a large number of sheep, goats, and
cattle. [39]The Israelites used the dough they
had brought out of Egypt to bake loaves of
bread without yeast. The dough had no yeast
in it, because they had been rushed out of
Egypt and had no time to get food ready for
their trip.
[40]The people of Israel had lived in Egypt
for four hundred thirty years; [41]on the very
day the four hundred thirty years ended, the
LORD's divisions of people left Egypt. [42]That
night the LORD kept watch to bring them out
of Egypt, and so on this same night the
Israelites are to keep watch to honor the
LORD from now on.
[43]The LORD told Moses and Aaron, "Here
are the rules for Passover: No foreigner is to
eat the Passover. [44]If someone buys a slave
and circumcises him, the slave may eat the
Passover. [45]But neither a person who lives for
a short time in your country nor a hired
worker may eat it.
[46]"The meal must be eaten inside a house;
take none of the meat outside the house.
Don't break any of the bones. [47]The whole
community of Israel must take part in this
feast. [48]A foreigner who lives with you may
share in the LORD's Passover if all the males
in his house become circumcised. Then,
since he will be like a citizen of Israel, he
may share in the meal. But a man who is
not circumcised may not eat the Passover
meal. [49]The same rules apply to an Israelite
born in the country or to a foreigner living
there."
[50]So all the Israelites did just as the LORD
had commanded Moses and Aaron. [51]On that
same day the LORD led the Israelites out of
Egypt by their divisions.

The Law of the Firstborn

13 Then the LORD said to Moses, [2]"Give
every firstborn male to me. Every

devotion 20

EXODUS 13:21–22

FOLLOWING HIS TRAIL

When I was growing up in Michigan, my dad and I would take walks together in the wintertime. I can remember feeling like a bubble-wrapped package inside my hat, earmuffs, layers of scarves, and long underwear my mom would hurriedly place on my wriggling body before I raced out the door. I wanted to lead the way . . . my father could follow *me*. But I learned quickly. I was too small, not to mention that I did not know my way. Within minutes, Dad always came to the rescue, and I would follow behind in the big, snowy footprints that he had laid out before me.

It is still true today. Though I've left behind the Michigan winters with dad-daughter walks in the woods, I still carry with me the lesson that life is best lived when following after the footsteps of my heavenly Father.

We may not have the fortunate privilege of clouded pillars or scorching fire in the sky as the Israelites once did, but we have something greater than that: Christ within us, guiding us along the stormy, snowy trails we walk each day.

Take comfort in the fact that you are never alone in the journey. Your heavenly Father will map out the steps to follow when you ask. We were not meant to walk through this life alone. And though you probably won't see the signs the Israelites saw, you can rely on the Holy Spirit within you as you journey through this life with him.

firstborn male among the Israelites belongs to me, whether human or animal."

3Moses said to the people, "Remember this day, the day you left Egypt. You were slaves in that land, but the LORD with his great power brought you out of it. You must not eat bread made with yeast. 4Today, in the month of Abib, you are leaving Egypt. 5The LORD will lead you to the land of the Canaanites, Hittites, Amorites, Hivites, and Jebusites. This is the land he promised your ancestors he would give you, a fertile land. There you must celebrate this feast during the first month of every year. 6For seven days you must eat bread made without yeast, and on the seventh day there will be a feast to honor the LORD. 7So for seven days you must not eat any bread made with yeast. There must be no bread made with yeast anywhere in your land. 8On that day you should tell your son: 'We are having this feast because of what the LORD did for me when I came out of Egypt.' 9This feast will help you remember, like a mark on your hand or a reminder on your forehead. This feast will remind you to speak the LORD's teachings, because the LORD used his great power to bring you out of Egypt. 10So celebrate this feast every year at the right time.

11"And when the LORD takes you into the land of the Canaanites, the land he promised to give you and your ancestors, 12you must give him every firstborn male. Also every firstborn male animal must be given to the LORD. 13Buy back every firstborn donkey by offering a lamb. But if you don't want to buy the donkey back, then break its neck. You must buy back from the LORD every firstborn of your sons.

14"From now on when your son asks you, 'What does this mean?' you will answer, 'With his great power, the LORD brought us out from Egypt, the land where we were slaves. 15The king of Egypt was stubborn and refused to let us leave. But the LORD killed every firstborn male in Egypt, both human and animal. That is why I sacrifice every firstborn male animal to the LORD, and that is why I buy back each of my firstborn sons from the LORD.' 16This feast is like a mark on your hand and a reminder on your forehead to help you remember that the LORD brought us out of Egypt with his great power."

The Way Out of Egypt

17When the king sent the people out of Egypt, God did not lead them on the road through the Philistine country, though that was the shortest way. God said, "If they have to fight, they might change their minds and go back to Egypt." 18So God led them through the desert toward the Red Sea. The Israelites were dressed for fighting when they left the land of Egypt.

19Moses carried the bones of Joseph with him, because before Joseph died, he had made the Israelites promise to do this. He had said, "When God saves you, remember to carry my bones with you out of Egypt."

20The Israelites left Succoth and camped at Etham, on the edge of the desert. 21The LORD showed them the way; during the day he went ahead of them in a pillar of cloud, and during the night he was in a pillar of fire to give them light. In this way they could travel during the day or night. 22The pillar of cloud was always with them during the day, and the pillar of fire was always with them at night.

14 Then the LORD said to Moses, 2"Tell the Israelites to turn back to Pi Hahiroth and to camp between Migdol and the Red Sea. Camp across from Baal Zephon, on the shore of the sea. 3The king will think, 'The Israelites are lost, trapped by the desert.' 4I will make the king stubborn again so he will chase after them, but I will defeat the king and his army. This will bring honor to me, and the Egyptians will know that I am the LORD." The Israelites did just as they were told.

The King Chases the Israelites

5When the king of Egypt was told that the Israelites had left, he and his officers changed their minds about them. They said, "What have we done? We have let the Israelites leave. We have lost our slaves!" 6So the king prepared his war chariot and took his army with him. 7He took six hundred of his best chariots, together with all the other chariots of Egypt, each with an officer in it. 8The LORD made the king of Egypt stubborn, so he chased the Israelites, who were leaving victoriously. 9The Egyptians—with all the king's horses, chariot drivers, and army—chased the

Israelites. They caught up with them while
they were camped by the Red Sea, near Pi
Hahiroth and Baal Zephon.
10When the Israelites saw the king and his
army coming after them, they were very
frightened and cried to the LORD for help.
11They said to Moses, "What have you done
to us? Why did you bring us out of Egypt to
die in the desert? There were plenty of
graves for us in Egypt. 12We told you in
Egypt, 'Let us alone; we will stay and serve
the Egyptians.' Now we will die in the
desert."
13But Moses answered, "Don't be afraid!
Stand still and you will see the LORD save
you today. You will never see these
Egyptians again after today. 14You only need
to remain calm; the LORD will fight for you."
15Then the LORD said to Moses, "Why are
you crying out to me? Command the
Israelites to start moving. 16Raise your
walking stick and hold it over the sea so that
the sea will split and the people can cross it
on dry land. 17I will make the Egyptians
stubborn so they will chase the Israelites,
but I will be honored when I defeat the king
and all of his chariot drivers and chariots.
18When I defeat the king, his chariot drivers,
and chariots, the Egyptians will know that I
am the LORD."
19Now the angel of God that usually
traveled in front of Israel's army moved
behind them. Also, the pillar of cloud moved
from in front of the people and stood behind
them. 20So the cloud came between the
Egyptians and the Israelites. This made it
dark for the Egyptians but gave light to the
Israelites. So the cloud kept the two armies
apart all night.
21Then Moses held his hand over the sea.
All that night the LORD drove back the sea
with a strong east wind, making the sea
become dry ground. The water was split,
22and the Israelites went through the sea on
dry land, with a wall of water on their right
and on their left.
23Then all the king's horses, chariots, and
chariot drivers followed them into the sea.
24When morning came, the LORD looked
down from the pillar of cloud and fire at the
Egyptian army and made them panic. 25He
kept the wheels of the chariots from turning,
making it hard to drive the chariots. The
Egyptians shouted, "Let's get away from the

devotion 21

EXODUS 14:13

STAND UP

I was babbling and crying, and my girlfriends were trying to make out my story in between sobs. There was attack from every area of my life. Ridiculous persecution. Complete exhaustion. I didn't know what to do or where to hide, and I was absolutely ruining our fun lunch by losing it in the restaurant. I had heard God prompt me, "Get over your pride, and ask these women to pray for you." I poured it all out.

Then with great authority, my friend said, "Stand up," and I obeyed. She took me by the hands, looked me squarely in the eyes, and commanded me, in the name of Jesus, to stand. She said, "You have done everything you can do. You have prayed and asked for help and walked with integrity. Now stand. Do not be afraid. It is time for you to stand still and watch. The Lord is coming to save you." Then she prayed the most bold prayer I've ever heard. And we were done. I had my orders. I could rest. It was time just to stand.

Have you done everything you know to do? Have you prayed and cried and asked for wise counsel? Have you turned left and then right, but you cannot find your way out? Then stand. If you have sought the Lord, you do not have to be afraid. Just stand and open your eyes so that you don't miss seeing the Lord when he comes to save you.

Israelites! The LORD is fighting for them and
against Egypt."
26Then the LORD told Moses, "Hold your
hand over the sea so that the water will
come back over the Egyptians, their chariots,
and chariot drivers." 27So Moses raised his
hand over the sea, and at dawn the sea
returned to its place. The Egyptians tried to
run from it, but the LORD swept them away
into the sea. 28The water returned, covering
the chariots, chariot drivers, and all the
king's army that had followed the Israelites
into the sea. Not one of them survived.
29But the Israelites crossed the sea on dry
land, with a wall of water on their right and
on their left. 30So that day the LORD saved the
Israelites from the Egyptians, and the
Israelites saw the Egyptians lying dead on
the seashore. 31When the Israelites saw the
great power the LORD had used against the
Egyptians, they feared the LORD, and they
trusted him and his servant Moses.

The Song of Moses

15 Then Moses and the Israelites sang
this song to the LORD:

"I will sing to the LORD,
because he is worthy of great honor.
He has thrown the horse and its rider
into the sea.
2The LORD gives me strength and makes
me sing;
he has saved me.
He is my God,
and I will praise him.
He is the God of my ancestors,
and I will honor him.
3The LORD is a warrior;
the LORD is his name.
4The chariots and soldiers of the king of
Egypt
he has thrown into the sea.
The king's best officers
are drowned in the Red Sea.
5The deep waters covered them,
and they sank to the bottom like a rock.
6Your right hand, LORD,
is amazingly strong.
LORD, your right hand
broke the enemy to pieces.
7In your great victory
you destroyed those who were against
you.
Your anger destroyed them,
like fire burning straw.
8Just a blast of your breath,
and the waters piled up.
The moving water stood like a wall;
the deep waters became solid in the
middle of the sea.

9"The enemy bragged,
'I'll chase them and catch them.
I'll take all their riches;
I'll take all I want.
I'll pull out my sword,
and my hand will destroy them.'
10But you blew on them with your breath
and covered them with the sea.
They sank like lead
in the raging water.

11"Are there any gods like you, LORD?
There are no gods like you.
You are wonderfully holy,
amazingly powerful,
a worker of miracles.
12You reached out with your right hand,
and the earth swallowed our enemies.
13You keep your loving promise
and lead the people you have saved.
With your strength you will guide them
to your holy place.

14"The other nations will hear this and
tremble with fear;
terror will take hold of the Philistines.
15The leaders of the tribes of Edom will be
very frightened;
the powerful men of Moab will shake
with fear;
the people of Canaan will lose all their
courage.
16Terror and horror will fall on them.
When they see your strength,
they will be as still as a rock.
They will be still until your people pass
by, LORD.
They will be still until the people you
have taken as your own pass by.
17You will lead your people and place them
on your very own mountain,
the place that you, LORD, made for yourself
to live,
the temple, Lord, that your hands have
made.
18The LORD will be king forever!"
19The horses, chariot drivers, and chariots

of the king of Egypt went into the sea, and
the LORD covered them with water from the
sea. But the Israelites walked through the sea
on dry land. 20Then Aaron's sister Miriam, a
prophetess, took a tambourine in her hand.
All the women followed her, playing
tambourines and dancing. 21Miriam told
them:

"Sing to the LORD,
because he is worthy of great honor;
he has thrown the horse and its rider
into the sea."

Bitter Water Becomes Good

22Moses led the Israelites away from the
Red Sea into the Desert of Shur. They
traveled for three days in the desert but
found no water. 23Then they came to Marah,
where there was water, but they could not
drink it because it was too bitter. (That is
why the place was named Marah.[n]) 24The
people grumbled to Moses and asked, "What
will we drink?"

25So Moses cried out to the LORD, and the
LORD showed him a tree. When Moses threw
the tree into the water, the water became
good to drink.

There the LORD gave the people a rule and
a law to live by, and there he tested their
loyalty to him. 26He said, "You must obey the
LORD your God and do what he says is right.
If you obey all his commands and keep his
rules, I will not bring on you any of the
sicknesses I brought on the Egyptians. I am
the LORD who heals you."

27Then the people traveled to Elim, where
there were twelve springs of water and
seventy palm trees. So the people camped
there near the water.

The People Demand Food

16 The whole Israelite community left
Elim and came to the Desert of Sin,
which was between Elim and Sinai; they
arrived there on the fifteenth day of the
second month after they had left Egypt.
2Then the whole Israelite community
grumbled to Moses and Aaron in the desert.
3They said to them, "It would have been
better if the LORD had killed us in the land of
Egypt. There we had meat to eat and all the
food we wanted. But you have brought us
into this desert to starve us to death."

4Then the LORD said to Moses, "I will cause
food to fall like rain from the sky for all of
you. Every day the people must go out and
gather what they need for that day. I want to
see if the people will do what I teach them.
5On the sixth day of each week, they are to
gather twice as much as they gather on other
days. Then they are to prepare it."

6So Moses and Aaron said to all the
Israelites: "This evening you will know that
the LORD is the one who brought you out of
Egypt. 7Tomorrow morning you will see the
glory of the LORD, because he has heard you
grumble against him. We are nothing, so
you are not grumbling against us, but
against the LORD." 8And Moses said, "Each
evening the LORD will give you meat to eat,
and every morning he will give you all the
bread you want, because he has heard you
grumble against him. You are not grumbling
against Aaron and me, because we are
nothing; you are grumbling against the
LORD."

9Then Moses said to Aaron, "Speak to the
whole community of the Israelites, and say
to them, 'Meet together in the presence of
the LORD, because he has heard your
grumblings.' "

10While Aaron was speaking to the whole
community of the Israelites, they looked
toward the desert. There the glory of the
LORD appeared in a cloud.

11The LORD said to Moses, 12"I have heard
the grumblings of the people of Israel. So tell
them, 'At twilight you will eat meat, and
every morning you will eat all the bread you
want. Then you will know I am the LORD
your God.' "

13That evening quail came and covered
the camp, and in the morning dew lay
around the camp. 14When the dew was gone,
thin flakes like frost were on the desert
ground. 15When the Israelites saw it, they
asked each other, "What is it?" because they
did not know what it was.

So Moses told them, "This is the bread the
LORD has given you to eat. 16The LORD has
commanded, 'Each one of you must gather
what he needs, about two quarts for every
person in your family.' "

17So the people of Israel did this; some
people gathered much, and some gathered

15:23 Marah This name means "bitter."

devotion 22

EXODUS 16:8

WHO'S MANNING THE COMPLAINT DEPARTMENT?

"I have a complaint!" Just hearing that statement immediately bugs me. When someone notices what's wrong or missing instead of what's organized and right, I struggle not to come unglued. Why, when the report card has all As and Bs and one D, do we give quick notice to the D over all the accomplished As and Bs?

The Lord refers to a few things as mysteries, and I am convinced one of those mysteries has to be the children of Israel. The Israelites must have designed the complaint department. They saw the sea stand up, Pharaoh's army destroyed, bitter water turned sweet, and yet they complained. When I read this passage of Scripture, I can't help but think to myself, *Are they crazy? Come on people, the sea stood up!*

Sadly, I wonder if I had walked with them, would I have been in the thick of it? Maybe I would have been the grievance secretary: "Thank you for your complaint today. I will make note of it and see if we can cause some division. Please come again." Would I have stared longingly at my empty pot that once roasted beef, or would I have gathered the manna and worshiped the hand that made it?

Purpose in your heart today—if you see something out of place, put it back. If you hear an unkind word, counter it with a compliment. If you feel unappreciated, remember Jesus loves you. And he is not manning the complaint department!

little. 18Then they measured it. The person
who gathered more did not have too much,
nor did the person who gathered less have
too little. Each person gathered just as much
as he needed.
19Moses said to them, "Don't keep any of it
to eat the next day." 20But some of the people
did not listen to Moses and kept part of it to
eat the next morning. It became full of
worms and began to stink, so Moses was
angry with those people.
21Every morning each person gathered as
much food as he needed, but when the sun
became hot, it melted away.
22On the sixth day the people gathered
twice as much food—four quarts for every
person. When all the leaders of the
community came and told this to Moses,
23he said to them, "This is what the LORD
commanded, because tomorrow is the
Sabbath, the LORD's holy day of rest. Bake
what you want to bake, and boil what you
want to boil today. Save the rest of the food
until tomorrow morning."
24So the people saved it until the next
morning, as Moses had commanded, and
none of it began to stink or have worms in it.
25Moses told the people, "Eat the food you
gathered yesterday. Today is a Sabbath, the
LORD's day of rest; you will not find any out
in the field today. 26You should gather the
food for six days, but the seventh day is a
Sabbath day. On that day there will not be
any food on the ground."
27On the seventh day some of the
people went out to gather food, but they
couldn't find any. 28Then the LORD said to
Moses, "How long will you people refuse
to obey my commands and teachings?
29Look, the LORD has made the Sabbath a
day of rest for you. So on the sixth day he
will give you enough food for two days,
but on the seventh day each of you must
stay where you are. Do not go anywhere."

[30]So the people rested on the seventh
day.
[31]The people of Israel called the food
manna. It was like small white seeds and
tasted like wafers made with honey.
[32]Then Moses said, "The LORD said, 'Save
two quarts of this food for your descendants.
Then they can see the food I gave you to eat
in the desert when I brought you out of
Egypt.' "
[33]Moses told Aaron, "Take a jar and fill it
with two quarts of manna. Then place it
before the LORD, and save it for your
descendants." [34]So Aaron did what the LORD
had commanded Moses. He put the jar of
manna in front of the Agreement to keep it
safe. [35]The Israelites ate manna for forty
years, until they came to the land where
they settled—the edge of the land of Canaan.
[36]The measure they used for the manna was
two quarts, or one-tenth of an ephah.[n]

Water from a Rock

17 The whole Israelite community left
the Desert of Sin and traveled from
place to place, as the LORD commanded. They
camped at Rephidim, but there was no water
there for the people to drink. [2]So they
quarreled with Moses and said, "Give us
water to drink."

Moses said to them, "Why do you quarrel
with me? Why are you testing the LORD?"
[3]But the people were very thirsty for
water, so they grumbled against Moses. They
said, "Why did you bring us out of Egypt?
Was it to kill us, our children, and our farm
animals with thirst?"
[4]So Moses cried to the LORD, "What can I
do with these people? They are almost ready
to stone me to death."
[5]The LORD said to Moses, "Go ahead of the
people, and take some of the elders of Israel
with you. Carry with you the walking stick
that you used to strike the Nile River. Now
go! [6]I will stand in front of you on a rock at
Mount Sinai. Hit that rock with the stick,
and water will come out of it so that the
people can drink." Moses did these things as
the elders of Israel watched. [7]He named that
place Massah,[n] because the Israelites tested
the LORD when they asked, "Is the LORD with
us or not?" He also named it Meribah,[n]
because they quarreled.

The Amalekites Fight Israel

[8]At Rephidim the Amalekites came and
fought the Israelites. [9]So Moses said to
Joshua, "Choose some men and go and fight
the Amalekites. Tomorrow I will stand on
the top of the hill, holding the walking stick
of God in my hands."
[10]Joshua obeyed Moses and went to fight
the Amalekites, while Moses, Aaron, and
Hur went to the top of the hill. [11]As long as
Moses held his hands up, the Israelites
would win the fight, but when Moses put his
hands down, the Amalekites would win.
[12]Later, when Moses' arms became tired, the
men put a large rock under him, and he sat
on it. Then Aaron and Hur held up Moses'
hands—Aaron on one side and Hur on the
other. They kept his hands steady until the
sun went down. [13]So Joshua defeated the
Amalekites in this battle.
[14]Then the LORD said to Moses, "Write
about this battle in a book so people will
remember. And be sure to tell Joshua,
because I will completely destroy the
Amalekites from the earth."
[15]Then Moses built an altar and named it
The LORD Is My Banner. [16]Moses said, "I lifted
my hands toward the LORD's throne. The
LORD will fight against the Amalekites
forever."

Jethro Visits Moses

18 Jethro, Moses' father-in-law, was the
priest of Midian. He heard about
everything that God had done for Moses and
his people, the Israelites, and how the LORD
had led the Israelites out of Egypt. [2]Now
Moses had sent his wife Zipporah to Jethro,
his father-in-law, [3]along with his two sons.
The first son was named Gershom,[n] because
when he was born, Moses said, "I am a
stranger in a foreign country." [4]The other son
was named Eliezer,[n] because when he was
born, Moses said, "The God of my father is my
help. He saved me from the king of Egypt."
[5]So Jethro, Moses' father-in-law, took
Moses' wife and his two sons and went to
Moses. He was camped in the desert near the

16:36 ephah An ephah was a measure that equaled twenty quarts. **17:7 Massah** This name is the Hebrew word for "testing." **17:7 Meribah** This name is the Hebrew word for "quarrel." **18:3 Gershom** This name sounds like the Hebrew word for "a stranger there." **18:4 Eliezer** This name sounds like the Hebrew words "My God is my help."

mountain of God. 6Jethro had sent a message
ahead to Moses that said, "I, Jethro, your
father-in-law, am coming to you with your
wife and her two sons."
7So Moses went out to meet his father-in-
law and bowed down and kissed him. After
the two men asked about each other's
health, they went into Moses' tent. 8Moses
told his father-in-law everything the LORD
had done to the king and the Egyptians to
help Israel. He told about all the problems
they had faced along the way and how the
LORD had saved them.
9Jethro was very happy to hear all the
good things the LORD had done for Israel
when he had saved them from the
Egyptians. 10He said, "Praise the LORD. He has
saved you from the Egyptians and their king,
and he has saved the people from the power
of the Egyptians. 11Now I know the LORD is
greater than all gods, because he did this to
those who looked down on Israel." 12Then
Jethro, Moses' father-in-law, gave a whole
burnt offering and other sacrifices to God.
Aaron and all the elders of Israel came to
Moses' father-in-law to eat the holy meal
together before God.
13The next day Moses solved
disagreements among the people, and the
people stood around him from morning
until night. 14When Moses' father-in-law saw
all that Moses was doing for the people, he
asked, "What is all this you are doing for the
people? Why are you the only one to solve
disagreements? All the people are standing
around you from morning until night!"
15Then Moses said to his father-in-law, "It
is because the people come to me for God's
help in solving their disagreements. 16When
people have a disagreement, they come to
me, and I decide who is right. I tell them
God's laws and teachings."
17Moses' father-in-law said to him, "You
are not doing this right. 18You and the people
who come to you will get too tired. This is
too much work for you; you can't do it by
yourself. 19Now listen to me, and I will give
you some advice. I want God to be with you.
You must speak to God for the people and
tell him about their disagreements. 20Warn
them about the laws and teachings, and
teach them the right way to live and what
they should do. 21But choose some capable
men from among the people—men who
respect God, who can be trusted, and who
will not change their decisions for money.
Make these men officers over the people, to
rule over groups of thousands, hundreds,
fifties, and tens. 22Let these officers solve the
disagreements among the people all the
time. They can bring the hard cases to you,
but they can decide the simple cases
themselves. That will make it easier for you,
because they will share the work with you.
23If you do this as God commands you, then
you will be able to do your job, and all the
people will go home with their
disagreements solved."
24So Moses listened to his father-in-law
and did everything he said. 25He chose
capable men from all the Israelites and made
them leaders over the people; they were
officers over groups of thousands, hundreds,
fifties, and tens. 26These officers solved
disagreements among the people all the
time. They brought the hard cases to Moses,
but they decided the simple cases
themselves.
27So Moses sent his father-in-law on his
way, and Jethro went back to his own home.

Israel Camps at Sinai

19 Exactly three months after the
Israelites had left Egypt, they reached
the Desert of Sinai. 2When they left
Rephidim, they came to the Desert of Sinai
and camped in the desert in front of the
mountain. 3Then Moses went up on the
mountain to God. The LORD called to him
from the mountain and said, "Say this to the
family of Jacob, and tell the people of Israel:
4'Every one of you has seen what I did to the
people of Egypt. You saw how I carried you
out of Egypt, as if on eagle's wings. And I
brought you here to me. 5So now if you obey
me and keep my agreement, you will be my
own possession, chosen from all nations.
Even though the whole earth is mine, 6you
will be my kingdom of priests and a holy
nation.' You must tell the Israelites these
words."
7So Moses went down and called the
elders of the people together. He told them
all the words the LORD had commanded him
to say. 8All the people answered together,
"We will do everything he has said." Then
Moses took their answer back to the LORD.
9And the LORD said to Moses, "I will come
to you in a thick cloud and speak to you. The

people will hear me speaking with you and
will always trust you." Then Moses told the
LORD what the people had said.

10The LORD said to Moses, "Go to the
people and have them spend today and
tomorrow preparing themselves. They must
wash their clothes 11and be ready by the day
after tomorrow. On that day I, the LORD, will
come down on Mount Sinai, and all the
people will see me. 12But you must set a
limit around the mountain that the people
are not to cross. Tell them not to go up on
the mountain and not to touch the foot of it.
Anyone who touches the mountain must be
put to death 13with stones or shot with
arrows. No one is allowed to touch him.
Whether it is a person or an animal, he will
not live. But the trumpet will make a long
blast, and only then may the people go up
on the mountain."

14After Moses went down from the
mountain to the people, he made them
prepare themselves for service to God, and
they washed their clothes. 15Then Moses said
to the people, "Be ready in three days. Do not
have sexual relations during this time."

16On the morning of the third day, there
was thunder and lightning with a thick
cloud on the mountain. There was a very
loud blast from a trumpet, and all the people
in the camp trembled. 17Then Moses led the
people out of the camp to meet God, and
they stood at the foot of the mountain.
18Mount Sinai was covered with smoke,
because the LORD came down on it in fire.
The smoke rose from the mountain like
smoke from a furnace, and the whole
mountain shook wildly. 19The sound from
the trumpet became louder. Then Moses
spoke, and the voice of God answered him.

20When the LORD came down on top of
Mount Sinai, he called Moses to come up to
the top of the mountain, and Moses went up.
21The LORD said to Moses, "Go down and
warn the people that they must not force
their way through to see me. If they do,
many of them will die. 22Even the priests,
who may come near me, must first prepare
themselves. If they don't, I, the LORD, will
punish them."

23Moses told the LORD, "The people cannot
come up on Mount Sinai, because you
yourself told us, 'Set a limit around the
mountain, and set it apart as holy.' "

24The LORD said to him, "Go down and
bring Aaron up with you, but don't allow the
priests or the people to force their way
through. They must not come up to the
LORD, or I will punish them."

25So Moses went down to the people and
told them these things.

The Ten Commandments

20 Then God spoke all these words:
2"I am the LORD your God, who
brought you out of the land of Egypt where
you were slaves.

3"You must not have any other gods
except me.

4"You must not make for yourselves an
idol that looks like anything in the sky
above or on the earth below or in the water
below the land. 5You must not worship or
serve any idol, because I, the LORD your God,
am a jealous God. If you hate me, I will
punish your children, and even your
grandchildren and great-grandchildren. 6But
I show kindness to thousands who love me
and obey my commands.

7"You must not use the name of the LORD
your God thoughtlessly; the LORD will
punish anyone who misuses his name.

8"Remember to keep the Sabbath holy.
9Work and get everything done during six
days each week, 10but the seventh day is a
day of rest to honor the LORD your God. On
that day no one may do any work: not you,
your son or daughter, your male or female
slaves, your animals, or the foreigners living
in your cities. 11The reason is that in six days
the LORD made everything—the sky, the
earth, the sea, and everything in them. On
the seventh day he rested. So the LORD
blessed the Sabbath day and made it holy.

12"Honor your father and your mother so
that you will live a long time in the land that
the LORD your God is going to give you.

13"You must not murder anyone.

14"You must not be guilty of adultery.

15"You must not steal.

16"You must not tell lies about your
neighbor.

17"You must not want to take your
neighbor's house. You must not want his
wife or his male or female slaves, or his ox or
his donkey, or anything that belongs to your
neighbor."

18When the people heard the thunder and

devotion 23

EXODUS 20:3

TOOLS OR IDOLS?

Allen Emery, a wealthy businessman who was a dear friend of ours, wrote a book called *Turtle on a Fencepost*. In this book, he talked about everything in our lives being either a tool or an idol. He told about how after buying a new Mercedes Benz, one of the teenage boys from a Bible study he was hosting asked if he could take the car out for a quick test drive. Allen knew he had a choice to make. He could make his new car a tool to reach a teenager or an idol in his own life. He handed the boy the car keys.

You see, everything in your life is either a tool or an idol, and it doesn't make any difference how much money you make. Mr. Emery drove a Mercedes, but a Volkswagen Beetle can be an idol just as easily. Do you have idols in your life? Is your home open to a neighbor even when the beds aren't made? Do you offer rides to others who are without a car? Are you giving your money to those in need even if you don't get a tax write-off? God has asked us to have nothing in our lives that is more important than him. As you learn to understand the heart of God, you will want to use the things of this world to share the love of God with others. Turn the idols in your life into tools to further God's kingdom. He is a God worth sacrificing for.

the trumpet, and when they saw the
lightning and the smoke rising from the
mountain, they shook with fear and stood
far away from the mountain. 19Then they
said to Moses, "Speak to us yourself, and we
will listen. But don't let God speak to us, or
we will die."
20Then Moses said to the people, "Don't be
afraid, because God has come to test you. He
wants you to respect him so you will not
sin."
21The people stood far away from the
mountain while Moses went near the dark
cloud where God was. 22Then the LORD told
Moses to say these things to the Israelites:
"You yourselves have seen that I talked with
you from heaven. 23You must not use gold or
silver to make idols for yourselves; do not
worship these gods in addition to me.
24"Make an altar of dirt for me, and
sacrifice on it your whole burnt offerings
and fellowship offerings, your sheep and
your cattle. Worship me in every place that I
choose, and I will come and bless you. 25If
you use stones to make an altar for me, don't
use stones that you have shaped with tools.
When you use any tools on them, you make
them unsuitable for use in worship. 26And
you must not go up to my altar on steps, or
people will be able to see under your
clothes."

Laws for Living

21 Then God said to Moses, "These are
the laws for living that you will give
to the Israelites:
2"If you buy a Hebrew slave, he will serve
you for six years. In the seventh year you are
to set him free, and he will have to pay
nothing. 3If he is not married when he
becomes your slave, he must leave without a
wife. But if he is married when he becomes
your slave, he may take his wife with him.
4If the slave's master gives him a wife, and
she gives birth to sons or daughters, the
woman and her children will belong to the
master. When the slave is set free, only he
may leave.
5"But if the slave says, 'I love my master,
my wife and my children, and I don't want to

go free,’ 6then the slave’s master must take
him to God. The master is to take him to a
door or doorframe and punch a hole through
the slave’s ear using a sharp tool. Then the
slave will serve that master all his life.
7“If a man sells his daughter as a slave, the
rules for setting her free are different from
the rules for setting the male slaves free. 8If
the master wanted to marry her but then
decided he was not pleased with her, he
must let one of her close relatives buy her
back. He has no right to sell her to
foreigners, because he has treated her
unfairly. 9If the man who bought her
promises to let the woman marry his son, he
must treat her as a daughter. 10If the man
who bought her marries another woman, he
must not keep his first wife from having
food or clothing or sexual relations. 11If he
does not give her these three things, she may
go free, and she owes him no money.

Laws About Injuries

12“Anyone who hits a person and kills him
must be put to death. 13But if a person kills
someone accidentally, God allowed that to
happen, so the person must go to a place I
will choose. 14But if someone plans and
murders another person on purpose, put
him to death, even if he has run to my altar
for safety.
15“Anyone who hits his father or his
mother must be put to death.
16“Anyone who kidnaps someone and
either sells him as a slave or still has him
when he is caught must be put to death.
17“Anyone who says cruel things to his
father or mother must be put to death.
18“If two men argue, and one hits the
other with a rock or with his fist, the one
who is hurt but not killed might have to stay
in bed. 19Later if he is able to get up and walk
around outside with his walking stick, the
one who hit him is not to be punished. But
he must pay the injured man for the loss of
his time, and he must support the injured
man until he is completely healed.
20“If a man beats his male or female slave
with a stick, and the slave dies on the spot,
the owner must be punished. 21But if the
slave gets well after a day or two, the owner
will not be punished since the slave belongs
to him.
22“Suppose two men are fighting and hit a
pregnant woman, causing the baby to come
out. If there is no further injury, the man
who caused the accident must pay money—
whatever amount the woman’s husband says
and the court allows. 23But if there is further
injury, then the punishment that must be
paid is life for life, 24eye for eye, tooth for
tooth, hand for hand, foot for foot, 25burn for
burn, wound for wound, and bruise for
bruise.
26“If a man hits his male or female slave in
the eye, and the eye is blinded, the man is to
free the slave to pay for the eye. 27If a master
knocks out a tooth of his male or female
slave, the man is to free the slave to pay for
the tooth.
28“If a man’s bull kills a man or woman,
you must kill that bull by throwing stones at
it, and you should not eat the bull. But the
owner of the bull is not guilty. 29However,
suppose the bull has hurt people in the past
and the owner, though warned, did not keep
it in a pen. Then if it kills a man or woman,
the bull must be stoned to death, and the
owner must also be put to death. 30But if the
family of the dead person accepts money, the
one who owned the bull may buy back his
life, but he must pay whatever is demanded.
31Use this same law if the bull kills a
person’s son or daughter. 32If the bull kills a
male or female slave, the owner must pay
the master the price for a new slave, or
twelve ounces of silver, and the bull must
also be stoned to death.
33“If a man takes the cover off a pit, or digs
a pit and does not cover it, and another
man’s ox or donkey comes and falls into it,
34the owner of the pit must pay the owner of
the animal for the loss. The dead animal will
belong to the one who pays.
35“If a man’s bull kills another man’s bull,
they must sell the bull that is alive. Both
men will get half of the money and half of
the bull that was killed. 36But if a person’s
bull has hurt other animals in the past and
the owner did not keep it in a pen, that
owner must pay bull for bull, and the dead
animal is his.

Property Laws

22 “If a man steals a bull or a sheep and
kills or sells it, he must pay back five
bulls for the one bull he stole and four sheep
for the one sheep he stole.

2-4 “The robber who is caught must pay
back what he stole. If he owns nothing, he
must be sold as a slave to pay for what he
stole. If the stolen animal is found alive with
the robber, he must give the owner two
animals for every animal he stole, whether it
was a bull, donkey, or sheep.

“If a thief is killed while breaking into a
house at night, the one who killed him is not
guilty of murder. But if this happens during
the day, he is guilty of murder.

5 “If a man lets his farm animal graze in his
field or vineyard, and it wanders into
another man’s field or vineyard, the owner of
the animal must pay back the loss from the
best of his crop.

6 “Suppose a man starts a fire that spreads
through the thornbushes to his neighbor’s
field. If the fire burns his neighbor’s growing
grain or grain that has been stacked, or if it
burns his whole field, the person who
started the fire must pay for what was
burned.

7 “Suppose a man gives his neighbor
money or other things to keep for him and
those things are stolen from the neighbor’s
house. If the thief is caught, he must pay
back twice as much as he stole. 8 But if the
thief is never found, the owner of the house
must make a promise before God that he has
not stolen his neighbor’s things.

9 “Suppose two men disagree about who
owns something—whether ox, donkey,
sheep, clothing, or something else that is
lost. If each says, ‘This is mine,’ each man
must bring his case to God. God’s judges will
decide who is guilty, and that person must
pay the other man twice as much as the
object is worth.

10 “Suppose a man asks his neighbor to
keep his donkey, ox, sheep, or some other
animal for him, and that animal dies, gets
hurt, or is taken away, without anyone
seeing what happened. 11 That neighbor
must promise before the LORD that he did
not harm or kill the other man’s animal, and
the owner of the animal must accept his
promise made before God. The neighbor
does not have to pay the owner for the
animal. 12 But if the animal was stolen from
the neighbor, he must pay the owner for it.
13 If wild animals killed it, the neighbor must
bring the body as proof, and he will not have
to pay for the animal that was killed.

14 “If a man borrows an animal from his
neighbor, and it gets hurt or dies while the
owner is not there, the one who borrowed it
must pay the owner for the animal. 15 But if
the owner is with the animal, the one who
borrowed it does not have to pay. If the
animal was rented, the rental price covers
the loss.

Laws and Relationships

16 “Suppose a man finds a woman who is
not pledged to be married and has never had
sexual relations with a man. If he tricks her
into having sexual relations with him, he
must give her family the payment to marry
her, and she will become his wife. 17 But if
her father refuses to allow his daughter to
marry him, the man must still give the usual
payment for a bride who has never had
sexual relations.

18 “Put to death any woman who does evil
magic.

19 “Put to death anyone who has sexual
relations with an animal.

20 “Destroy completely any person who
makes a sacrifice to any god except the LORD.

21 “Do not cheat or hurt a foreigner,
because you were foreigners in the land of
Egypt.

22 “Do not cheat a widow or an orphan. 23 If
you do, and they cry out to me for help, I
certainly will hear their cry. 24 And I will be
very angry and kill you in war. Then your
wives will become widows, and your
children will become orphans.

25 “If you lend money to one of my people
who is poor, do not treat him as a
moneylender would. Charge him nothing
for using your money. 26 If your neighbor
gives you his coat as a promise for the
money he owes you, you must give it back
to him by sunset, 27 because it is the only
cover to keep his body warm. He has
nothing else to sleep in. If he cries out to
me for help, I will listen, because I am
merciful.

28 “You must not speak against God or
curse a leader of your people.

29 “Do not hold back your offering from
the first of your harvest and the first wine
that you make. Also, you must give me your
firstborn sons. 30 You must do the same with
your bulls and your sheep. Let the firstborn
males stay with their mothers for seven

days, and on the eighth day you must give them to me.

31 "You are to be my holy people. You must not eat the meat of any animal that has been killed by wild animals. Instead, give it to the dogs.

Laws About Fairness

23 "You must not tell lies. If you are a witness in court, don't help a wicked person by telling lies.

2 "You must not do wrong just because everyone else is doing it. If you are a witness in court, you must not ruin a fair trial. You must not tell lies just because everyone else is. 3 If a poor person is in court, you must not take his side just because he is poor.

4 "If you see your enemy's ox or donkey wandering away, you must return it to him. 5 If you see that your enemy's donkey has fallen because its load is too heavy, do not leave it there. You must help your enemy get the donkey back on its feet.

6 "You must not be unfair to a poor person when he is in court. 7 You must not lie when you accuse someone in court. Never allow an innocent or honest person to be put to death as punishment, because I will not treat guilty people as if they were innocent.

8 "You must not accept money from a person who wants you to lie in court, because such money will not let you see what is right. Such money makes good people tell lies.

9 "You must not mistreat a foreigner. You know how it feels to be a foreigner, because you were foreigners in Egypt.

Laws for the Sabbath

10 "For six years you are to plant and harvest crops on your land. 11 Then during the seventh year, do not plow or plant your land. If any food grows there, allow the poor people to have it, and let the wild animals eat what is left. You should do the same with your vineyards and your orchards of olive trees.

12 "You should work six days a week, but on the seventh day you must rest. This lets your ox and your donkey rest, and it also lets the slave born in your house and the foreigner be refreshed.

13 "Be sure to do all that I have said to you. You must not even say the names of other gods; those names must not come out of your mouth.

Three Yearly Feasts

14 "Three times each year you must hold a feast to honor me. 15 You must celebrate the Feast of Unleavened Bread in the way I commanded you. For seven days you must eat bread that is made without yeast at the set time during the month of Abib, the month when you came out of Egypt. No one is to come to worship me without bringing an offering.

16 "You must celebrate the Feast of Weeks. Offer to God the first things you harvest from the crops you planted in your fields.

"You must celebrate the Feast of Shelters in the fall, when you gather all the crops from your fields.

17 "So three times during every year all your males must come to worship the LORD God.

18 "You must not offer animal blood along with anything that has yeast in it.

"You must not save any of the fat from the sacrifice for the next day.

19 "You must bring the best of the firstfruits of your land to the Holy Tent[n] of the LORD your God.

"You must not cook a young goat in its mother's milk.

God Will Help Israel

20 "I am sending an angel ahead of you, who will protect you as you travel. He will lead you to the place I have prepared. 21 Pay attention to the angel and obey him. Do not turn against him; he will not forgive such turning against him because my power is in him. 22 If you listen carefully to all he says and do everything that I tell you, I will be an enemy to your enemies. I will fight all who fight against you. 23 My angel will go ahead of you and take you into the land of the Amorites, Hittites, Perizzites, Canaanites, Hivites, and Jebusites, and I will destroy them.

24 "You must not bow down to their gods or worship them. You must not live the way those people live. You must destroy their

23:19 Holy Tent Literally, "house of the LORD your God." See Exodus 25:9.

devotion 24

EXODUS 23:1

THE *GIFT* OF GAB?

Sometimes rumors fly around like monarch butterflies in spring gardens: "I don't mean to gossip, but . . ." And it's not just a contemporary problem. When Moses laid out God's laws for the Israelites (when the Ten Commandments were brand spanking new), he talked about the importance of telling the truth.

We women have to be particularly careful about this—we love to talk! And why not? We're pretty good at it. On average, a woman will speak up to three times more words a day than a man. With so many words flitting about in the air, we need to take stock of our conversations.

For instance, if I were to collect your day's words in my butterfly net, how many of them would be true, positive, and enriching? How many would be shifty, sharp, or rotting? Believe me, being an initial pessimist to almost everything I encounter, this has been a sobering life lesson for me. But I have discovered that as I ask God for his love of truth and goodness, I've found my critical thoughts weeded out.

What are you growing in the corners of your mind? What kinds of words are you chasing in your garden? Words can be as fragrant and beautiful as your favorite gardenia or as deadly as poison. Choose your words wisely. Before you speak, temper yourself with reality and honesty. God wants you to use this feminine gift of gab in ways that enrich your life and the lives of those living in the garden around you.

idols, breaking into pieces the stone pillars
they use in worship. 25If you worship the
LORD your God, I will bless your bread and
your water. I will take away sickness from
you. 26None of your women will have her
baby die before it is born, and all women
will have children. I will allow you to live
long lives.
27"I will make your enemies afraid of me.
I will confuse any people you fight against,
and I will make all your enemies run away
from you. 28I will send terror ahead of you
that will force the Hivites, Canaanites, and
Hittites out of your way. 29But I will not
force all those people out in only one year. If
I did, the land would become a desert and
the wild animals would become too many
for you. 30Instead, I will force those people
out slowly, until there are enough of you to
take over the land.
31"I will give you the land from the Red
Sea to the Mediterranean Sea, and from the
desert to the Euphrates River. I will give you
power over the people who now live in the
land, and you will force them out ahead of
you. 32You must not make an agreement
with those people or with their gods. 33You
must not let them live in your land, or they
will make you sin against me. If you worship
their gods, you will be caught in a trap."

God and Israel Make Their Agreement

24 The LORD told Moses, "You, Aaron,
Nadab, Abihu, and seventy of the
elders of Israel must come up to me and
worship me from a distance. 2Then Moses
alone must come near me; the others must
not come near. The rest of the people must
not come up the mountain with Moses."
3Moses told the people all the LORD's
words and laws for living. Then all of the
people answered out loud together, "We will
do all the things the LORD has said." 4So
Moses wrote down all the words of the LORD.

And he got up early the next morning and
built an altar near the bottom of the
mountain. He set up twelve stones, one
stone for each of the twelve tribes of Israel.
5Then Moses sent young Israelite men to
offer whole burnt offerings and to sacrifice
young bulls as fellowship offerings to the
LORD. 6Moses put half of the blood of these
animals in bowls, and he sprinkled the other
half of the blood on the altar. 7Then he took
the Book of the Agreement and read it so the
people could hear him. And they said, "We
will do everything that the LORD has said; we
will obey."

8Then Moses took the blood from the
bowls and sprinkled it on the people,
saying, "This is the blood that begins the
Agreement, the Agreement which the LORD
has made with you about all these words."

9Moses, Aaron, Nadab, Abihu, and seventy
of the elders of Israel went up the mountain
10and saw the God of Israel. Under his feet
was a surface that looked as if it were paved
with blue sapphire stones, and it was as clear
as the sky! 11These leaders of the Israelites
saw God, but God did not destroy them.
Then they ate and drank together.

God Promises Moses the Stone Tablets

12The LORD said to Moses, "Come up the
mountain to me. Wait there, and I will give
you two stone tablets. On these are the
teachings and the commands I have written
to instruct the people."

13So Moses and his helper Joshua set out,
and Moses went up to Sinai, the mountain of
God. 14Moses said to the elders, "Wait here for
us until we come back to you. Aaron and Hur
are with you, and anyone who has a
disagreement with others can take it to
them."

Moses Meets with God

15When Moses went up on the mountain,
the cloud covered it. 16The glory of the LORD
came down on Mount Sinai, and the cloud
covered it for six days. On the seventh day
the LORD called to Moses from inside the
cloud. 17To the Israelites the glory of the
LORD looked like a fire burning on top of the
mountain. 18Then Moses went into the
cloud and went higher up the mountain. He
was on the mountain for forty days and forty
nights.

Gifts for the Lord

25 The LORD said to Moses, 2"Tell the
Israelites to bring me gifts. Receive for
me the gifts each person wants to give.
3These are the gifts that you should receive
from them: gold, silver, bronze; 4blue,
purple, and red thread; fine linen, goat hair,
5sheepskins that are dyed red; fine leather;
acacia wood; 6olive oil to burn in the lamps;
spices for sweet-smelling incense, and the
special olive oil poured on a person's head to
make him a priest; 7onyx stones, and other
jewels to be put on the holy vest and the
chest covering.

8"The people must build a holy place for
me so that I can live among them. 9Build
this Holy Tent and everything in it by the
plan I will show you.

The Ark of the Agreement

10"Use acacia wood and build an Ark forty-
five inches long, twenty-seven inches wide,
and twenty-seven inches high. 11Cover the
Ark inside and out with pure gold, and put a
gold strip all around it. 12Make four gold
rings for the Ark and attach them to its four
feet, two rings on each side. 13Then make
poles from acacia wood and cover them with
gold. 14Put the poles through the rings on the
sides of the Ark, and use these poles to carry
it. 15These poles must always stay in the
rings of the Ark. Do not take them out.
16Then put in the Ark the Agreement which
I will make with you.

17"Then make a lid of pure gold for the
Ark; this is the mercy seat. Make it forty-five
inches long and twenty-seven inches wide.
18Then hammer gold to make two creatures
with wings, and put one on each end of the
lid. 19Attach one creature on one end of the
lid and the other creature on the other end.
Make them to be one piece with the lid at
the ends. 20The creatures' wings should be
spread upward, covering the lid, and the
creatures are to face each other across the
lid. 21Put this lid on top of the Ark, and put
in the Ark the Agreement which I will make
with you. 22I will meet with you there, above
the lid between the two winged creatures on
the Ark of the Agreement. There I will give
you all my commands for the Israelites.

The Table

23"Make a table out of acacia wood,
thirty-six inches long, eighteen inches wide,

devotion 25

EXODUS 25:8

AM I HOLY INSIDE?

During the time of Moses and long before the time of Jesus, God told his followers to build a Holy Tent, a kind of portable temple that would serve as God's headquarters. This structure would become the holy place where God would live, and he would also meet with the Israelites there. After the life and work of Jesus, the Holy Tent was no longer needed because Jesus' death made a way for God to come and live inside the holy place of your heart and mine. I want God's full presence inside of me more than anything, so one of my spiritual assignments is keeping my heart holy. I want to make sure that my heart is a place where God would want to fully abide, a place he would desire to hang out, a place ready to receive his guidance and move at his will.

Keeping a holy place inside of me seems impossible at first. But God has promised that he is the One who can make us holy. We are responsible for asking to be clean, but he will make it so. We are supposed to make choices with holiness in mind, to stay away from activities that will tarnish the holy place inside of us, and to pursue a life that will embrace the powerful presence of God's Holy Spirit.

As God looks at your life and considers the condition of your heart today, will he find a holy place waiting inside of you?

and twenty-seven inches high. 24Cover it
with pure gold, and put a gold strip around
it. 25Make a frame three inches high that
stands up all around the edge, and put a gold
strip around it. 26Then make four gold rings.
Attach them to the four corners of the table
where the four legs are. 27Put the rings close
to the frame around the top of the table,
because they will hold the poles for carrying
it. 28Make the poles out of acacia wood, cover
them with gold, and carry the table with
these poles. 29Make the plates and bowls for
the table, as well as the jars and cups, out of
pure gold. They will be used for pouring out
the drink offerings. 30On this table put the
bread that shows you are in my presence so
that it is always there in front of me.

The Lampstand

31"Hammer pure gold to make a
lampstand. Its base, stand, flower-like cups,
buds, and petals must all be joined together
in one piece. 32The lampstand must have six
branches going out from its sides—three on
one side and three on the other. 33Each
branch must have three cups shaped like
almond flowers on it. Each cup must have a
bud and a petal. Each of the six branches
going out from the lampstand must be the
same. 34And there must be four more cups
made like almond flowers on the lampstand
itself. These cups must also have buds and
petals. 35Put a bud under each pair of
branches that goes out from the lampstand.
Each of the six branches going out from the
lampstand must be the same. 36The branches,
buds, and lampstand must be made of one
piece, hammered out of pure gold.

37"Then make seven small oil lamps and
put them on the lampstand so that they give
light to the area in front of it. 38The wick
trimmers and trays must be made of pure
gold. 39Use seventy-five pounds of pure gold
to make the lampstand and everything with
it. 40Be very careful to make them by the
plan I showed you on the mountain.

The Holy Tent

26 "Make for the Holy Tent ten curtains
of fine linen and blue, purple, and red

thread. Have a skilled craftsman sew designs
of creatures with wings on the pieces of
cloth. 2Make each curtain the same size—
forty-two feet long and six feet wide. 3Sew
five curtains together for one set, and sew
the other curtains together for the second
set. 4Make loops of blue cloth on the edge of
the end curtain of one set, and do the same
for the end curtain of the other set. 5Make
fifty loops on the end curtain of the first set
and fifty loops on the end curtain of the
second set. These loops must be opposite
each other. 6And make fifty gold hooks to
join the two sets of curtains so that the Holy
Tent is one piece.

7"Then make another tent that will cover
the Holy Tent, using eleven curtains made
from goat hair. 8All these curtains must be
the same size—forty-five feet long and six
feet wide. 9Sew five of the curtains together
into one set. Then sew the other six curtains
together into the second set. Fold the sixth
curtain double over the front of the Tent.
10Make fifty loops down the edge of the end
curtain of one set, and do the same for the
end curtain of the other set. 11Then make
fifty bronze hooks and put them in the loops
to join the tent together so that the covering
is one piece. 12Let the extra half piece of
cloth hang over the back of the Holy Tent.
13There will be eighteen inches hanging over
the sides of the Holy Tent, to protect it.
14Make a covering for the Holy Tent from
sheepskins colored red, and over that make a
covering from fine leather.

15"Use acacia wood to make upright
frames for the Holy Tent. 16Each frame must
be fifteen feet long and twenty-seven inches
wide, 17with two pegs side by side. Every
frame must be made the same way. 18Make
twenty frames for the south side of the Holy
Tent. 19Each frame must have two silver
bases to go under it, a peg fitting into each
base. You must make forty silver bases for
the frames. 20Make twenty more frames for
the north side of the Holy Tent 21and forty
silver bases for them—two bases for each
frame. 22You must make six frames for the
rear or west end of the Holy Tent 23and two
frames for each corner at the rear. 24The two
frames are to be doubled at the bottom and
joined at the top with a metal ring. Both
corner frames must be made this way. 25So
there will be a total of eight frames at the
rear of the Tent, and there will be sixteen
silver bases—two bases under each frame.

26"Make crossbars of acacia wood to
connect the upright frames of the Holy Tent.
Make five crossbars to hold the frames
together on one side 27and five to hold the
frames together on the other side. Also make
five crossbars to hold the frames together on
the west end, at the rear. 28The middle
crossbar is to be set halfway up the frames,
and it is to run along the entire length of
each side and rear. 29Make gold rings on the
sides of the frames to hold the crossbars, and
cover the frames and the crossbars with gold.
30Set up the Holy Tent by the plan shown to
you on the mountain.

31"Make a curtain of fine linen and blue,
purple, and red thread, and have a skilled
craftsman sew designs of creatures with
wings on it. 32Hang the curtain by gold
hooks on four posts of acacia wood that are
covered with gold, and set them in four
silver bases. 33Hang the curtain from the
hooks in the roof, and put the Ark of the
Agreement containing the two stone tablets
behind it. This curtain will separate the Holy
Place from the Most Holy Place. 34Put the lid
on the Ark of the Agreement in the Most
Holy Place.

35"Outside the curtain, put the table on
the north side of the Holy Tent. Put the
lampstand on the south side of the Holy
Tent across from the table.

The Entrance of the Holy Tent

36"Then, for the entrance of the Tent,
make a curtain with fine linen and blue,
purple, and red thread. Someone who can
sew well is to sew designs on it. 37Make five
posts of acacia wood covered with gold.
Make gold hooks for them on which to hang
the curtain, and make five bronze bases for
them.

The Altar for Burnt Offerings

27 "Make an altar of acacia wood, four
and one-half feet high. It should be
square—seven and one-half feet long and
seven and one-half feet wide. 2Make each of
the four corners of the altar stick out like a
horn, in such a way that the corners with
their horns are all one piece. Then cover the
whole altar with bronze.

3"Use bronze to make all the tools and

dishes that will be used on the altar: the pots
to remove the ashes, the shovels, the bowls
for sprinkling blood, the meat forks, and the
pans for carrying the burning wood.
4"Make a large bronze screen to hold the
burning wood, and put a bronze ring at each
of the four corners of it. 5Put the screen
inside the altar, under its rim, halfway up
from the bottom.
6"Make poles of acacia wood for the altar,
and cover them with bronze. 7Put the poles
through the rings on both sides of the altar
to carry it. 8Make the altar out of boards and
leave the inside hollow. Make it as you were
shown on the mountain.

The Courtyard of the Holy Tent

9"Make a wall of curtains to form a
courtyard around the Holy Tent. The south
side should have a wall of fine linen curtains
one hundred fifty feet long. 10Hang the
curtains with silver hooks and bands on
twenty bronze posts with twenty bronze
bases. 11The north side must also be one
hundred fifty feet long. Hang its curtains on
silver hooks and bands on twenty bronze
posts with twenty bronze bases.
12"The west end of the courtyard must
have a wall of curtains seventy-five feet long,
with ten posts and ten bases on that wall.
13The east end of the courtyard must also be
seventy-five feet long. 14On one side of the
entry, there is to be a wall of curtains
twenty-two and one-half feet long, held up
by three posts on three bases. 15On the other
side of the entry, there is also to be a wall of
curtains twenty-two and one-half feet long,
held up by three posts on three bases.
16"The entry to the courtyard is to be a
curtain thirty feet wide, made of fine linen
with blue, purple, and red thread. Someone
who can sew well is to sew designs on it. It is
to be held up by four posts on four bases.
17All the posts around the courtyard must
have silver bands and hooks and bronze
bases. 18The courtyard must be one hundred
fifty feet long and seventy-five feet wide,
with a wall of curtains around it seven and
one-half feet high, made of fine linen. The
bases in which the posts are set must be
bronze. 19All the things used in the Holy
Tent and all the tent pegs for the Holy Tent
and the wall around the courtyard must be
made of bronze.

Oil for the Lamp

20"Command the people of Israel to bring
you pure olive oil, made from pressed olives,
to keep the lamps on the lampstand
burning. 21Aaron and his sons must keep the
lamps burning before the LORD from evening
till morning. This will be in the Meeting
Tent, outside the curtain which is in front of
the Ark. The Israelites and their descendants
must obey this rule from now on.

Clothes for the Priests

28 "Tell your brother Aaron to come to
you, along with his sons Nadab, Abihu,
Eleazar, and Ithamar. Separate them from the
other Israelites to serve me as priests. 2Make
holy clothes for your brother Aaron to give
him honor and beauty. 3Tell all the skilled
craftsmen to whom I have given wisdom to
make special clothes for Aaron—clothes to
show that he belongs to me so that he may
serve me as a priest. 4These are the clothes
they must make: a chest covering, a holy vest,
an outer robe, a woven inner robe, a turban,
and a cloth belt. The craftsmen must make
these holy clothes for your brother Aaron and
his sons. Then they may serve me as priests.
5The craftsmen must use gold and blue,
purple and red thread, and fine linen.

The Holy Vest

6"Use gold and blue, purple and red
thread, and fine linen to make the holy vest;
skilled craftsmen are to make it. 7At each top
corner of this holy vest there will be a pair of
shoulder straps tied together over each
shoulder.
8"The craftsmen will very carefully weave
a belt on the holy vest that is made with the
same materials—gold and blue, purple and
red thread, and fine linen.
9"Take two onyx stones and write the
names of the twelve sons of Israel on them,
10six on one stone and six on the other.
Write the names in order, from the oldest
son to the youngest. 11Carve the names of
the sons of Israel on these stones in the same
way a person carves words and designs on a
seal. Put gold around the stones to hold
them on the holy vest. 12Then put the two
stones on the two straps of the holy vest as
reminders of the twelve sons of Israel. Aaron
is to wear their names on his shoulders in
the presence of the LORD as reminders of the

sons of Israel. 13Make two gold pieces to hold
the stones 14and two chains of pure gold,
twisted together like a rope. Attach the chains
to the two gold pieces that hold the stones.

The Chest Covering

15"Make a chest covering to help in
making decisions. The craftsmen should
make it as they made the holy vest, using
gold and blue, purple and red thread, and
fine linen. 16The chest covering must be
square—nine inches long and nine inches
wide—and folded double to make a pocket.
17Put four rows of beautiful gems on the
chest covering: The first row must have a
ruby, topaz, and yellow quartz; 18the second
must have turquoise, a sapphire, and an
emerald; 19the third must have a jacinth, an
agate, and an amethyst; 20the fourth must
have a chrysolite, an onyx, and a jasper. Put
gold around these jewels to attach them to
the chest covering. 21There must be twelve
jewels on the chest covering—one jewel for
each of the names of the sons of Israel. Carve
the name of one of the twelve tribes on each
of the stones as you would carve a seal.

22"Make chains of pure gold, twisted
together like rope, for the chest covering.
23Make two gold rings and put them on the
two upper corners of the chest covering.
24Attach the two gold chains to the two rings
at the upper corners of the chest covering.
25Attach the other ends of the two chains to
the two gold pieces on the shoulder straps in
the front of the holy vest.

26"Make two gold rings and put them at
the two lower corners of the chest covering,
on the inside edge next to the holy vest.
27Make two more gold rings and attach them
to the bottom of the shoulder straps in the
front of the holy vest. Put them close to the
seam above the woven belt of the holy vest.
28Join the rings of the chest covering to the
rings of the holy vest with blue ribbon,
connecting it to the woven belt so the chest
covering will not swing out from the holy
vest.

29"When Aaron enters the Holy Place, he
will wear the names of the sons of Israel over
his heart, on the chest covering that helps in
making decisions. This will be a continual
reminder before the LORD. 30And put the
Urim and Thummim inside the chest
covering so that they will be on Aaron's
heart when he goes before the LORD. They
will help in making decisions for the
Israelites. So Aaron will always carry them
with him when he is before the LORD.

31"Make the outer robe to be worn under
the holy vest, using only blue cloth. 32Make
a hole in the center for Aaron's head, with a
woven collar around the hole so it will not
tear. 33Make balls like pomegranates of blue,
purple, and red thread, and hang them
around the bottom of the outer robe with
gold bells between them. 34All around the
bottom of the outer robe there should be a
gold bell and a pomegranate ball, a gold bell
and a pomegranate ball. 35Aaron must wear
this robe when he serves as priest. The
ringing of the bells will be heard when he
enters and leaves the Holy Place before the
LORD so that Aaron will not die.

36"Make a strip of pure gold and carve
these words on it as you would carve a seal:
'Holy to the LORD.' 37Use blue ribbon to tie it
to the turban; put it on the front of the
turban. 38Aaron must wear this on his
forehead. In this way, he will be blamed if
anything is wrong with the gifts of the
Israelites. Aaron must always wear this on
his head so the LORD will accept the gifts of
the people.

39"Make the woven inner robe of fine
linen, and make the turban of fine linen also.
Make the cloth belt with designs sewn on it.
40Also make woven inner robes, cloth belts,
and headbands for Aaron's sons, to give
them honor and beauty. 41Put these clothes
on your brother Aaron and his sons, and
pour olive oil on their heads to appoint
them as priests. Make them belong to me so
they may serve me as priests.

42"Make for them linen underclothes to
cover them from the waist to the upper parts
of the legs. 43Aaron and his sons must wear
these underclothes when they enter the
Meeting Tent and anytime they come near
the altar to serve as priests in the Holy Place.
If they do not wear these clothes, they will
be guilty of wrong, and they will die. This
will be a law that will last from now on for
Aaron and all his descendants.

Appointing the Priests

29 "This is what you must do to appoint
Aaron and his sons to serve me as
priests. Take one young bull and two male

devotion 26

EXODUS 28:36

IF THE CROWN FITS . . .

The Lord instructed Aaron to make an engraving on a pure gold plate that would read, "Holy to the Lord." This circular plate resembled a flower or a petal and could be fastened like a crown to a person's head using a ribbon. It was a perpetual reminder to all that read its inscription that holiness was due the Lord.

Crowns are pretty obvious, both to the onlookers and to the wearer. Many a beauty queen has walked down the runway struggling to balance her crown without it crashing to the floor. If the Lord asked you to place this same holiness crown on your head, could you wear it all day without any conflict of conscience? Would your life match its message? How many times would you have to ask the Lord to look away for just a minute while you gently untied the ribbon and let the crown slip into your hand? Would it be while you were driving the car? At work behind a closed door? In the mall while you were shopping? At home talking on the phone?

Today, you don't see a bunch of Christians running around with crowns on their heads, but God still wants you to live as a woman called to be separate and set apart for his purpose. And he still wants his words to dwell in your heart (Ps. 119:11). So place his Word at the top of your heart as a reminder that God deserves and requires holiness.

sheep that have nothing wrong with them.
2Use fine wheat flour without yeast to make
bread, cakes mixed with olive oil, and wafers
brushed with olive oil. 3Put these in one
basket, and bring them along with the bull
and two male sheep. 4Bring Aaron and his
sons to the entrance of the Meeting Tent and
wash them with water. 5Take the clothes and
dress Aaron in the inner robe and the outer
robe of the holy vest. Then put on him the
holy vest and the chest covering, and tie the
holy vest on him with its skillfully woven
belt. 6Put the turban on his head, and put the
holy crown on the turban. 7Take the special
olive oil and pour it on his head to make
him a priest.
8"Then bring his sons and put the inner
robes on them. 9Put the headbands on their
heads, and tie cloth belts around their
waists. Aaron and his descendants will be
priests in Israel, according to a rule that will
continue from now on. This is how you
will appoint Aaron and his sons as priests.
10"Bring the bull to the front of the
Meeting Tent, and Aaron and his sons must
put their hands on the bull's head. 11Then
kill the bull before the LORD at the entrance
to the Meeting Tent. 12Use your finger to put
some of the bull's blood on the corners of
the altar, and then pour the blood that is left
at the bottom of the altar. 13Take all the fat
that covers the inner organs, as well as the
best part of the liver, both kidneys, and the
fat around them, and burn them on the altar.
14Take the bull's meat, skin, and intestines,
and burn them outside the camp. This is an
offering to take away sin.
15"Take one of the male sheep, and have
Aaron and his sons put their hands on its
head. 16Kill it, and take its blood and sprinkle
it on all four sides of the altar. 17Then cut it
into pieces and wash its inner organs and its
legs, putting them with its head and its other
pieces. 18Burn the whole sheep on the altar;
it is a burnt offering made by fire to the
LORD. Its smell is pleasing to the LORD.
19"Take the other male sheep, and have
Aaron and his sons put their hands on its

head. 20Kill it and take some of its blood. Put the blood on the bottom of the right ears of Aaron and his sons and on the thumbs of their right hands and on the big toes of their right feet. Then sprinkle the rest of the blood against all four sides of the altar. 21Take some of the blood from the altar, and mix it with the special oil used in appointing priests. Sprinkle this on Aaron and his clothes and on his sons and their clothes. This will show that Aaron and his sons and their clothes are given to my service.

22"Then take the fat from the male sheep, the fat tail, and the fat that covers the inner organs. In addition, take the best part of the liver, both kidneys, and the fat around them, and the right thigh. (This is the male sheep to be used in appointing priests.)

23"Then take the basket of bread that you made without yeast, which you put before the LORD. From it take a loaf of bread, a cake made with olive oil, and a wafer. 24Put all of these in the hands of Aaron and his sons, and tell them to present them as an offering to the LORD. 25Then take them from their hands and burn them on the altar with the whole burnt offering. This is an offering made by fire to the LORD; its smell is pleasing to the LORD. 26Then take the breast of the male sheep used to appoint Aaron as priest, and present it before the LORD as an offering. This part of the animal will be your share. 27Set aside the breast and the thigh of the sheep that were used to appoint Aaron and his sons as priests. These parts belong to them. 28They are to be the regular share which the Israelites will always give to Aaron and his sons. It is the gift the Israelites must give to the LORD from their fellowship offerings.

29"The holy clothes made for Aaron will belong to his descendants so that they can wear these clothes when they are appointed as priests. 30Aaron's son, who will become high priest after Aaron, will come to the Meeting Tent to serve in the Holy Place. He is to wear these clothes for seven days.

31"Take the male sheep used to appoint priests and boil its meat in a place that is holy. 32Then at the entrance of the Meeting Tent, Aaron and his sons must eat the meat of the sheep and the bread that is in the basket. 33They should eat these offerings that were used to remove their sins and to make them holy when they were made priests. But no one else is to eat them, because they are holy things. 34If any of the meat from that sheep or any of the bread is left the next morning, it must be burned. It must not be eaten, because it is holy.

35"Do all these things that I commanded you to do to Aaron and his sons, and spend seven days appointing them. 36Each day you are to offer a bull to remove the sins of Aaron and his sons so they will be given for service to the LORD. Make the altar ready for service to the LORD, and pour oil on it to make it holy. 37Spend seven days making the altar ready for service to God and making it holy. Then the altar will become very holy, and anything that touches it must be holy.

The Daily Sacrifices

38"Every day from now on, offer on the altar two lambs that are one year old. 39Offer one lamb in the morning and the other in the evening before dark. 40In the morning, when you offer the first lamb, offer also two quarts of fine flour mixed with one quart of oil from pressed olives. Pour out a quart of wine as a drink offering. 41Offer the second lamb in the evening with the same grain offering and drink offering as you did in the morning. This is an offering made by fire to the LORD, and its smell is pleasing to him.

42"You must burn these things as an offering to the LORD every day, from now on, at the entrance of the Meeting Tent before the LORD. When you make the offering, I, the LORD, will meet you there and speak to you. 43I will meet with the people of Israel there, and that place will be holy because of my glory.

44"So I will make the Meeting Tent and the altar holy; I will also make Aaron and his sons holy so they may serve me as priests. 45I will live with the people of Israel and be their God. 46And they will know that I am the LORD their God who led them out of Egypt so that I could live with them. I am the LORD their God.

The Altar for Burning Incense

30 "Make an altar out of acacia wood for burning incense. 2Make it square—eighteen inches long and eighteen inches wide—and make it thirty-six inches high. The corners that stick out like horns must be one piece with the altar. 3Cover its top, its sides, and its corners with pure gold, and put a gold strip all around the altar. 4Make two gold rings beneath the gold strip on opposite sides of the altar, and slide poles through them to carry the altar. 5Make the poles from acacia wood and cover them with gold. 6Put the altar of incense in front of the curtain that is near the Ark of the Agreement, in front of the lid that covers that Ark. There I will meet with you.

7"Aaron must burn sweet-smelling incense on the altar every morning when he comes to take care of the oil lamps. 8He must burn incense again in the evening when he lights the lamps, so incense will burn before the LORD every day from now on. 9Do not use this altar for offering any other incense, or burnt offering, or any kind of grain offering, or drink offering. 10Once a year Aaron must make the altar ready for service to God by putting blood on its corners—the blood of the animal offered to remove sins. He is to do this once a year from now on. This altar belongs completely to the LORD's service."

The Tax for the Meeting Tent

11The LORD said to Moses, 12"When you count the people of Israel, every person must buy back his life from the LORD so that no terrible things will happen to the people when you number them. 13Every person who is counted must pay one-fifth of an ounce of silver. (This is set by using one-half of the Holy Place measure, which weighs two-fifths of an ounce.) This amount is a gift to the LORD. 14Every person who is counted and is twenty years old or older must give this amount to the LORD. 15A rich person must not give more than one-fifth of an ounce, and a poor person must not give less. You are paying this to the LORD to buy back your lives. 16Gather from the people of Israel this money paid to buy back their lives, and spend it on things for the service in the Meeting Tent. This payment will remind the LORD that the Israelites' lives have been bought back."

The Bronze Bowl

17The LORD said to Moses, 18"Make a bronze bowl, on a bronze stand, for washing. Put the bowl and stand between the Meeting Tent and the altar, and put water in the bowl. 19Aaron and his sons must wash their hands and feet with the water from this bowl. 20Each time they enter the Meeting Tent they must wash with water so they will not die. Whenever they approach the altar to serve as priests and offer a sacrifice to the LORD by fire, 21they must wash their hands and their feet so they will not die. This is a rule which Aaron and his descendants are to keep from now on."

Oil for Appointing

22Then the LORD said to Moses, 23"Take the finest spices: twelve pounds of liquid myrrh, half that amount (that is, six pounds) of sweet-smelling cinnamon, six pounds of sweet-smelling cane, 24and twelve pounds of cassia. Weigh all these by the Holy Place measure. Also take four quarts of olive oil, 25and mix all these things like a perfume to make a holy olive oil. This special oil must be put on people and things to make them ready for service to God. 26Put this oil on the Meeting Tent and the Ark of the Agreement, 27on the table and all its dishes, on the lampstand and all its tools, and on the incense altar. 28Also, put the oil on the altar for burnt offerings and on all its tools, as well as on the bowl and the stand under the bowl. 29You will prepare all these things for service to God, and they will be very holy. Anything that touches these things must be holy.

30"Put the oil on Aaron and his sons to give them for service to me, that they may serve me as priests. 31Tell the Israelites, 'This is to be my holy olive oil from now on. It is to be put on people and things to make them ready for service to God. 32Do not pour it on the bodies of ordinary people, and do not make perfume the same way you make this oil. It is holy, and you must treat it as holy. 33If anyone makes perfume like it or puts it on someone who is not a priest, that person must be cut off from his people.'"

Incense

34Then the LORD said to Moses, "Take these sweet-smelling spices: resin, onycha, galbanum, and pure frankincense. Be sure that you have equal amounts of each. 35Make incense as a person who makes perfume would do. Add salt to it to keep it pure and holy. 36Beat some of the incense

into a fine powder, and put it in front of the
Ark of the Agreement in the Meeting Tent,
where I will meet with you. You must use
this incense powder only for its very special
purpose. 37Do not make incense for
yourselves the same way you make this
incense. Treat it as holy to the LORD.
38Whoever makes incense like this to use as
perfume must be cut off from his people."

Bezalel and Oholiab Help

31 Then the LORD said to Moses, 2"See, I
have chosen Bezalel son of Uri from
the tribe of Judah. (Uri was the son of Hur.) 3I
have filled Bezalel with the Spirit of God and
have given him the skill, ability, and
knowledge to do all kinds of work. 4He is
able to design pieces to be made from gold,
silver, and bronze, 5to cut jewels and put
them in metal, to carve wood, and to do all
kinds of work. 6I have also chosen Oholiab
son of Ahisamach from the tribe of Dan to
work with Bezalel. I have given skills to all
the craftsmen, and they will be able to make
all these things I have commanded you: 7the
Meeting Tent, the Ark of the Agreement, the
lid that covers the Ark, and everything in the
Tent. 8This includes the table and everything
on it, the pure gold lampstand and
everything with it, the altar of incense, 9the
altar for burnt offerings and everything used
with it, and the bowl and the stand under it.
10They will make the woven clothes and the
holy clothes for Aaron and the clothes for
his sons to wear when they serve as priests.
11They will also make the special olive oil
used in appointing people and things to the
service of the LORD, and the sweet-smelling
incense for the Holy Place.

"These workers will make all these things
just as I have commanded you."

The Day of Rest

12Then the LORD said to Moses, 13"Tell the
Israelites, 'You must keep the rules about my
Sabbaths, because they will be a sign
between you and me from now on. In this
way you will know that I, the LORD, make
you holy.

14" 'Make the Sabbath a holy day. If
anyone treats the Sabbath like any other day,
that person must be put to death; anyone

devotion 27

EXODUS 31:13–14

SO WHAT ABOUT DAY #7?

God gave us the Ten Commandments for two reasons: to bring order to a chaotic world and to teach us how to live a holy life. Some of God's laws are easier to follow than others. Not killing and not stealing are commands that most of us have no trouble keeping. Coveting only makes us miserable. Obeying parents keeps children from becoming selfish adults. Each one of the Ten in some way keeps our lives from spinning out of control. So what about keeping the Sabbath? How does that commandment teach us to be holy or bring order to our lives?

In Mark 2:23-28, Jesus told the Pharisees that the Sabbath was made for man, not man for the Sabbath. The Sabbath was designed for man to rest from his work just as God rested from Creation. We live in a culture that never stops. We rarely have quiet time in our lives. It seems there is always something to distract us. Our homes are filled with television, our cars are filled with the radio, and our free time is spent on the computer. God made us and he knows that we need time to rest and refocus on a weekly basis. Keeping the Sabbath sets us apart from the rest of the world. When we faithfully take that day each week to rest and spend time with the Lord, others notice. So honor God with your Sabbath. It will become your favorite day of the week.

who works on the Sabbath day must be cut
off from his people. 15There are six days for
working, but the seventh day is a day of rest,
a day holy for the LORD. Anyone who works
during the Sabbath day must be put to
death. 16The Israelites must remember the
Sabbath day as an agreement between them
and me that will continue from now on.
17The Sabbath day will be a sign between me
and the Israelites forever, because in six days
I, the LORD, made the sky and the earth. On
the seventh day I did not work; I rested.' "
18When the LORD finished speaking to
Moses on Mount Sinai, he gave him the two
stone tablets with the Agreement written on
them, written by the finger of God.

The People Make a Gold Calf

32 The people saw that a long time had
passed and Moses had not come down
from the mountain. So they gathered around
Aaron and said, "Moses led us out of Egypt,
but we don't know what has happened to
him. Make us gods who will lead us."
2Aaron said to the people, "Take off the
gold earrings that your wives, sons, and
daughters are wearing, and bring them to
me." 3So all the people took their gold
earrings and brought them to Aaron. 4He
took the gold from the people and formed it
with a tool and made a statue of a calf. Then
the people said, "Israel, these are your gods
who brought you out of the land of Egypt!"
5When Aaron saw all this, he built an
altar before the calf and announced,
"Tomorrow there will be a special feast to
honor the LORD." 6The people got up early
the next morning and offered whole burnt
offerings and fellowship offerings. They sat
down to eat and drink, and then they got up
and sinned sexually.
7Then the LORD said to Moses, "Go down
from this mountain, because your people,
the people you brought out of the land of
Egypt, have ruined themselves. 8They have
quickly turned away from the things I
commanded them to do. They have made for
themselves a calf covered with gold, and
they have worshiped it and offered sacrifices
to it. They have said, 'Israel, these are your
gods who brought you out of Egypt.' "
9The LORD said to Moses, "I have seen
these people, and I know that they are very
stubborn. 10So now do not stop me. I am so
angry with them that I am going to destroy
them. Then I will make you and your
descendants a great nation."
11But Moses begged the LORD his God and
said, "LORD, don't let your anger destroy your
people, whom you brought out of Egypt
with your great power and strength. 12Don't
let the people of Egypt say, 'The LORD
brought the Israelites out of Egypt for an evil
purpose. He planned to kill them in the
mountains and destroy them from the earth.'
So stop being angry, and don't destroy your
people. 13Remember the men who served
you—Abraham, Isaac, and Israel. You
promised with an oath to them and said, 'I
will make your descendants as many as the
stars in the sky. I will give your descendants
all this land that I have promised them, and
it will be theirs forever.' " 14So the LORD
changed his mind and did not destroy the
people as he had said he might.
15Then Moses went down the mountain,
and in his hands he had the two stone
tablets with the Agreement on them. The
commands were written on both sides of
each stone, front and back. 16God himself
had made the tablets, and God himself had
written the commands on the tablets.
17When Joshua heard the sound of the
people shouting, he said to Moses, "It sounds
like war down in the camp."
18Moses answered:
"It is not a shout of victory;
it is not a cry of defeat.
It is the sound of singing that I hear."
19When Moses came close to the camp, he
saw the gold calf and the dancing, and he
became very angry. He threw down the stone
tablets that he was carrying and broke them
at the bottom of the mountain. 20Then he
took the calf that the people had made and
melted it in the fire. He ground it into
powder. Then he threw the powder into the
water and forced the Israelites to drink it.
21Moses said to Aaron, "What did these
people do to you? Why did you cause them
to do such a terrible sin?"
22Aaron answered, "Don't be angry, master.
You know that these people are always ready
to do wrong. 23The people said to me, 'Moses
led us out of Egypt, but we don't know what
has happened to him. Make us gods who
will lead us.' 24So I told the people, 'Take off
your gold jewelry.' When they gave me the

gold, I threw it into the fire and out came
this calf!"
25Moses saw that the people were acting
wildly. Aaron had let them get out of control
and become fools in front of their enemies.
26So Moses stood at the entrance to the camp
and said, "Let anyone who wants to follow
the LORD come to me." And all the people
from the family of Levi gathered around
Moses.
27Then Moses said to them, "The LORD,
the God of Israel, says this: 'Every man must
put on his sword and go through the camp
from one end to the other. Each man must
kill his brother, his friend, and his
neighbor.' " 28The people from the family of
Levi obeyed Moses, and that day about three
thousand of the Israelites died. 29Then
Moses said, "Today you have been given for
service to the LORD. You were willing to kill
your own sons and brothers, and God has
blessed you for this."
30The next day Moses told the people,
"You have done a terrible sin. But now I will
go up to the LORD. Maybe I can do something
so your sins will be removed." 31So Moses
went back to the LORD and said, "How
terribly these people have sinned! They have
made for themselves gods from gold. 32Now,
please forgive them of this sin. If you will
not, then erase my name from the book in
which you have written the names of your
people."
33But the LORD told Moses, "I will erase
from my book the names of the people who
sin against me. 34So now, go. Lead the people
where I have told you, and my angel will
lead you. When the time comes to punish, I
will punish them for their sin."
35So the LORD caused terrible things to
happen to the people because of what they
did with the calf Aaron had made.

33 Then the LORD said to Moses, "You
and the people you brought out of
Egypt must leave this place. Go to the land
that I promised with an oath to give to
Abraham, Isaac, and Jacob when I said, 'I will
give that land to your descendants.' 2I will
send an angel to lead you, and I will force
these people out of the land: the Canaanites,
Amorites, Hittites, Perizzites, Hivites, and
Jebusites. 3Go up to a fertile land. But I will
not go with you, because I might destroy
you on the way, since you are such a
stubborn people."
4When the people heard this bad news,
they became very sad, and none of them put
on jewelry. 5This was because the LORD had
said to Moses, "Tell the Israelites, 'You are a
stubborn people. If I were to go with you
even for a moment, I would destroy you. So
take off all your jewelry, and I will decide
what to do with you.' " 6So the people of
Israel took off their jewelry at Mount Sinai.

The Meeting Tent

7Moses used to take a tent and set it up a
long way outside the camp; he called it the
"Meeting Tent." Anyone who wanted to ask
the LORD about something would go to the
Meeting Tent outside the camp. 8Whenever
Moses went out to the Tent, all the people
would rise and stand at the entrances of
their tents, watching him until he entered
the Meeting Tent. 9When Moses went into
the Tent, the pillar of cloud would always
come down and stay at the entrance of the
Tent while the LORD spoke with Moses.
10Whenever the people saw the pillar of
cloud at the entrance of the Tent, they stood
and worshiped, each person at the entrance
of his own tent.
11The LORD spoke to Moses face to face as
a man speaks with his friend. Then Moses
would return to the camp, but Moses' young
helper, Joshua son of Nun, did not leave the
Tent.
12Moses said to the LORD, "You have told
me to lead these people, but you did not say
whom you would send with me. You have
said to me, 'I know you very well, and I am
pleased with you.' 13If I have truly pleased
you, show me your plans so that I may know
you and continue to please you. Remember
that this nation is your people."
14The LORD answered, "I myself will go
with you, and I will give you victory."
15Then Moses said to him, "If you yourself
don't go with us, then don't send us away
from this place. 16If you don't go with us, no
one will know that you are pleased with me
and with your people. These people and I
will be no different from any other people
on earth."
17Then the LORD said to Moses, "I will do
what you ask, because I know you very well,
and I am pleased with you."

Moses Sees God's Glory

18 Then Moses said, "Now, please show me
your glory."
19 The LORD answered, "I will cause all my
goodness to pass in front of you, and I will
announce my name, the LORD, so you can
hear it. I will show kindness to anyone to
whom I want to show kindness, and I will
show mercy to anyone to whom I want to
show mercy. 20 But you cannot see my face,
because no one can see me and live.
21 "There is a place near me where you
may stand on a rock. 22 When my glory
passes that place, I will put you in a large
crack in the rock and cover you with my
hand until I have passed by. 23 Then I will
take away my hand, and you will see my
back. But my face must not be seen."

Moses Gets New Stone Tablets

34 The LORD said to Moses, "Cut two
more stone tablets like the first two,
and I will write the same words on them
that were on the first two stones which you
broke. 2 Be ready tomorrow morning, and
then come up on Mount Sinai. Stand before
me there on the top of the mountain. 3 No
one may come with you or even be seen any
place on the mountain. Not even the flocks
or herds may eat grass near that mountain."
4 So Moses cut two stone tablets like the
first ones. Then early the next morning he
went up Mount Sinai, just as the LORD had
commanded him, carrying the two stone
tablets with him. 5 Then the LORD came
down in the cloud and stood there with
Moses, and the LORD called out his name:
the LORD.
6 The LORD passed in front of Moses and
said, "I am the LORD. The LORD is a God who
shows mercy, who is kind, who doesn't
become angry quickly, who has great love
and faithfulness 7 and is kind to thousands of
people. The LORD forgives people for evil, for
sin, and for turning against him, but he does
not forget to punish guilty people. He will
punish not only the guilty people, but also
their children, their grandchildren, their

devotion 28

EXODUS 34:6–7

IF THOSE CARDS COULD TALK

When I was a child, my family was addicted to card games, especially Uno. Mom, Dad, Sara, and I would sit eagerly after dinner, elbows on the table, leaning into the cards as they were dealt. The others played so fluidly, so easily. But my fat, stubby fingers could barely hold all the cards in place. And grasping all the rules of the game proved even more difficult. I lost every time.

There was one game in particular that taught me more than I bargained for. Just after the hand had been dealt, the phone rang and Dad ran for it. Mom decided to check the apple crisp while he did that. Sara scuttled for a bathroom break. And there I was, all alone . . . with everybody's cards left defenseless on the mahogany wood like sugar coated morsels of power. I leapt at the chance to sneak a peak, and I thoroughly snatched the win once my family arrived back to their posts.

The thrill of victory was short-lived, however. My father realized I had cheated, and it was time for "correction." His grasp on my arm was gentle, but his stern blue eyes blazed with love and discipline through his thick glasses. He reminded me that lying would not be tolerated. My dad also told me that he forgave and loved me. And because of that love, he was choosing to discipline me.

My father showed me a glimpse into the heart of God. I was guilty but he forgave me. And all this from a game of Uno . . .

great-grandchildren, and their great-great-
grandchildren."
8Then Moses quickly bowed to the ground
and worshiped. 9He said, "Lord, if you are
pleased with me, please go with us. I know
that these are stubborn people, but forgive
our evil and our sin. Take us as your own
people."
10Then the LORD said, "I am making this
agreement with you. I will do miracles in
front of all your people—things that have
never before been done for any other nation
on earth—and the people with you will see
my work. I, the LORD, will do wonderful
things for you. 11Obey the things I command
you today, and I will force out the Amorites,
Canaanites, Hittites, Perizzites, Hivites, and
Jebusites ahead of you. 12Be careful that you
don't make an agreement with the people
who live in the land where you are going,
because it will bring you trouble. 13Destroy
their altars, break their stone pillars, and cut
down their Asherah idols. 14Don't worship
any other god, because I, the LORD, the
Jealous One, am a jealous God.
15"Be careful that you don't make an
agreement with the people who live in that
land. When they worship their gods, they
will invite you to join them. Then you will
eat their sacrifices. 16If you choose some of
their daughters as wives for your sons and
those daughters worship gods, they will lead
your sons to do the same thing.
17"Do not make gods of melted metal.
18"Celebrate the Feast of Unleavened
Bread. For seven days you must eat bread
made without yeast as I commanded you. Do
this during the month I have chosen, the
month of Abib, because in that month you
came out of Egypt.
19"The firstborn of every mother belongs
to me, including every firstborn male
animal that is born in your flocks and
herds. 20You may buy back a donkey by
paying for it with a lamb, but if you don't
want to buy back a donkey, you must break
its neck. You must buy back all your
firstborn sons.
"No one is to come before me without a
gift.
21"You must work for six days, but on the
seventh day you must rest—even during the
planting season and the harvest season.
22"Celebrate the Feast of Weeks when you
gather the first grain of the wheat harvest.
And celebrate the Feast of Shelters in the
fall.
23"Three times each year all your males
must come before the Lord GOD, the God of
Israel. 24I will force out nations ahead of you
and expand the borders of your land. You
will go before the LORD your God three times
each year, and at that time no one will try to
take your land from you.
25"Do not offer the blood of a sacrifice to
me with anything containing yeast, and do
not leave any of the sacrifice of the Feast of
Passover until the next morning.
26"Bring the best first crops that you
harvest from your ground to the Tent of the
LORD your God.
"You must not cook a young goat in its
mother's milk."
27Then the LORD said to Moses, "Write
down these words, because with these words
I have made an agreement with you and
Israel."
28Moses stayed there with the LORD forty
days and forty nights, and during that time
he did not eat food or drink water. And
Moses wrote the words of the Agreement—
the Ten Commandments—on the stone
tablets.

The Face of Moses Shines

29Then Moses came down from Mount
Sinai, carrying the two stone tablets of the
Agreement in his hands. But he did not
know that his face was shining because he
had talked with the LORD. 30When Aaron
and all the people of Israel saw that Moses'
face was shining, they were afraid to go near
him. 31But Moses called to them, so Aaron
and all the leaders of the people returned to
Moses, and he talked with them. 32After that,
all the people of Israel came near him, and
he gave them all the commands that the
LORD had given him on Mount Sinai.
33When Moses finished speaking to the
people, he put a covering over his face.
34Anytime Moses went before the LORD to
speak with him, Moses took off the covering
until he came out. Then Moses would come
out and tell the Israelites what the LORD had
commanded. 35They would see that Moses'
face was shining. So he would cover his face
again until the next time he went in to speak
with the LORD.

Rules About the Sabbath

35 Moses gathered all the Israelite
community together and said to
them, "These are the things the LORD has
commanded you to do. 2You are to work for
six days, but the seventh day will be a holy
day, a Sabbath of rest to honor the LORD.
Anyone who works on that day must be put
to death. 3On the Sabbath day you must not
light a fire in any of your houses."

4Moses said to all the Israelites, "This is
what the LORD has commanded: 5From what
you have, take an offering for the LORD. Let
everyone who is willing bring this offering
to the LORD: gold, silver, bronze, 6blue,
purple, and red thread, and fine linen, goat
hair 7and male sheepskins that are colored
red. They may also bring fine leather, acacia
wood, 8olive oil for the lamps, spices for the
special olive oil used for appointing priests
and for the sweet-smelling incense, 9onyx
stones, and other jewels to be put on the
holy vest and chest covering of the priests.

10"Let all the skilled workers come and
make everything the LORD commanded:
11the Holy Tent, its outer tent and its
covering, the hooks, frames, crossbars, posts,
and bases; 12the Ark of the Agreement, its
poles, lid, and the curtain in front of it; 13the
table, and its poles, all the things that go
with the table, and the bread that shows we
are in God's presence; 14the lampstand for
the light and all the things that go with it,
the lamps, and olive oil for the light; 15the
altar of incense and its poles, the special oil
and the sweet-smelling incense, the curtain
for the entrance of the Meeting Tent; 16the
altar of burnt offering and its bronze screen,
its poles and all its tools, the bronze bowl
and its base; 17the curtains around the
courtyard, their posts and bases, and the
curtain at the entry to the courtyard; 18the
pegs of the Holy Tent and of the courtyard
and their ropes; 19the special clothes that the
priest will wear in the Holy Place. These are
the holy clothes for Aaron the priest and his
sons to wear when they serve as priests."

20Then all the people of Israel went away
from Moses. 21Everyone who wanted to give
came and brought a gift to the LORD for
making the Meeting Tent, all the things in
the Tent, and the special clothes. 22All the
men and women who wanted to give
brought gold jewelry of all kinds—pins,
earrings, rings, and bracelets. They all
presented their gold to the LORD. 23Everyone
who had blue, purple, and red thread, and
fine linen, and anyone who had goat hair or
male sheepskins colored red or fine leather
brought them to the LORD. 24Everyone who
could give silver or bronze brought that as a
gift to the LORD, and everyone who had
acacia wood to be used in the work brought
it. 25Every skilled woman used her hands to
make the blue, purple, and red thread, and
fine linen, and they brought what they had
made. 26All the women who were skilled and
wanted to help made thread of the goat hair.
27The leaders brought onyx stones and other
jewels to put on the holy vest and chest
covering for the priest. 28They also brought
spices and olive oil for the sweet-smelling
incense, the special oil, and the oil to burn in
the lamps. 29All the men and women of
Israel who wanted to help brought gifts to
the LORD for all the work the LORD had
commanded Moses and the people to do.

30Then Moses said to the Israelites, "Look,
the LORD has chosen Bezalel son of Uri the
son of Hur, from the tribe of Judah. 31The
LORD has filled Bezalel with the Spirit of God
and has given him the skill, ability, and
knowledge to do all kinds of work. 32He is
able to design pieces to be made of gold,
silver, and bronze, 33to cut stones and jewels
and put them in metal, to carve wood, and to
do all kinds of work. 34Also, the LORD has
given Bezalel and Oholiab, the son of
Ahisamach from the tribe of Dan, the ability
to teach others. 35The LORD has given them
the skill to do all kinds of work. They are
able to cut designs in metal and stone.
They can plan and sew designs in the fine
linen with the blue, purple, and red thread.
And they are also able to weave things.

36 So Bezalel, Oholiab, and every skilled
person will do the work the LORD has
commanded, because he gave them the
wisdom and understanding to do all the
skilled work needed to build the Holy Tent."

2Then Moses called Bezalel, Oholiab, and
all the other skilled people to whom the
LORD had given skills, and they came because
they wanted to help with the work. 3They
received from Moses everything the people
of Israel had brought as gifts to build the

devotion 29

EXODUS 35:31

THE RIGHT WOMAN FOR THE RIGHT JOB

Bezalel could design and carve and weave. He had exactly the right gifts for the huge, Holy Tent construction project. And all of his gifts were given by the Spirit of God. Bezalel was a tent-building hero because his gifts were a precise fit for the tasks he had been given.

I think one of the best things that can happen to a woman is when her God-given gifts are matched with the right assignment. I can't tell you how many times I have beaten my head against the wall because I took my gifts and tried to complete the same assignment as my girlfriend. My gifts won't work for her assignment. It's so incredibly frustrating trying to make my square-peg gifts fit someone else's round-hole calling.

But every once in a while, I'll get really honest about who I am and what I'm good at. Then I pray to see clearly the very thing I'm called to do and—Bingo!—I'm in my sweet spot. I am being led by the Spirit, knocking every ball out of the park.

One of the worst things you can do is look over at anyone else and try to do what she's doing. It's a setup. You'll always fail in the comparison. And you'll waste a lot of time in the wrong direction. What skills and abilities and knowledge has the Spirit of God given to you? Applaud your girlfriend and start operating in your own strengths with your own assignment.

Holy Tent. The people continued to bring
gifts each morning because they wanted to.
[4]So all the skilled workers left the work they
were doing on the Holy Tent, [5]and they said
to Moses, "The people are bringing more
than we need to do the work the LORD
commanded."

[6]Then Moses sent this command
throughout the camp: "No man or woman
should make anything else as a gift for the
Holy Tent." So the people were kept from
giving more, [7]because what they had was
already more than enough to do all the
work.

The Holy Tent

[8]Then the skilled workers made the Holy
Tent. They made the ten curtains of blue,
purple, and red cloth, and they sewed
designs of creatures with wings on the
curtains. [9]Each curtain was the same size—
forty-two feet long and six feet wide. [10]Five
of the curtains were fastened together to
make one set, and the other five were
fastened together to make another set.
[11]Then they made loops of blue cloth along
the edge of the end curtain on the first set of
five, and they did the same thing with the
other set of five. [12]There were fifty loops on
one curtain and fifty loops on the other
curtain, with the loops opposite each other.
[13]They made fifty gold hooks to join the two
curtains together so that the Holy Tent was
joined together as one piece.

[14]Then the workers made another tent of
eleven curtains made of goat hair, to put
over the Holy Tent. [15]All eleven curtains
were the same size—forty-five feet long and
six feet wide. [16]The workers sewed five
curtains together into one set and six
together into another set. [17]They made fifty
loops along the edge of the outside curtain of
one set and fifty loops along the edge of the
outside curtain of the other set. [18]Then they
made fifty bronze rings to join the two sets
of cloth together and make the tent one

piece. [19]They made two more coverings for
the outer tent—one made of male
sheepskins colored red and the other made
of fine leather.

[20]Then they made upright frames of
acacia wood for the Holy Tent. [21]Each frame
was fifteen feet tall and twenty-seven inches
wide, [22]and there were two pegs side by side
on each one. Every frame of the Holy Tent
was made this same way. [23]They made
twenty frames for the south side of the Tent,
[24]and they made forty silver bases that went
under the twenty frames. There were two
bases for every frame—one for each peg of
each frame. [25]They also made twenty frames
for the north side of the Holy Tent [26]and
forty silver bases—two to go under each
frame. [27]They made six frames for the rear or
west end of the Holy Tent [28]and two frames
for the corners at the rear of the Holy Tent.
[29]These two frames were doubled at the
bottom and joined at the top with a metal
ring. They did this for each of these corners.
[30]So there were eight frames and sixteen
silver bases—two bases under each frame.

[31]Then they made crossbars of acacia
wood to connect the upright frames of the
Holy Tent. Five crossbars held the frames
together on one side of the Tent, [32]and five
held the frames together on the other side.
Also, five crossbars held the frames together
on the west end, at the rear of the Tent.
[33]They made the middle crossbar run along
the entire length of each side and rear of the
Tent. It was set halfway up the frames.
[34]They made gold rings on the sides of the
frames to hold the crossbars, and they
covered the frames and the crossbars with
gold.

[35]Then they made the curtain of blue,
purple, and red thread, and fine linen. A
skilled craftsman sewed designs of creatures
with wings on it. [36]They made four posts of
acacia wood for it and covered them with
gold. Then they made gold hooks for the
posts, as well as four silver bases in which to
set the posts. [37]For the entrance to the Tent,
they made a curtain of blue, purple, and red
thread, and fine linen. A person who sewed
well sewed designs on it. [38]Then they made
five posts and hooks for it. They covered the
tops of the posts and their bands with gold,
and they made five bronze bases for the
posts.

The Ark of the Agreement

37 Bezalel made the Ark of acacia wood;
it was forty-five inches long, twenty-
seven inches wide, and twenty-seven inches
high. [2]He covered it, both inside and out,
with pure gold, and he put a gold strip
around it. [3]He made four gold rings for it and
attached them to its four feet, with two rings
on each side. [4]Then he made poles of acacia
wood and covered them with gold. [5]He put
the poles through the rings on each side of
the Ark to carry it. [6]Then he made a lid of
pure gold that was forty-five inches long and
twenty-seven inches wide. [7]Then Bezalel
hammered gold to make two creatures with
wings and attached them to each end of the
lid. [8]He made one creature on one end of the
lid and the other creature on the other end.
He attached them to the lid so that it would
be one piece. [9]The creatures' wings were
spread upward, covering the lid, and the
creatures faced each other across the lid.

The Table

[10]Then he made the table of acacia wood;
it was thirty-six inches long, eighteen inches
wide, and twenty-seven inches high. [11]He
covered it with pure gold and put a gold
strip around it. [12]He made a frame three
inches high that stood up all around the
edge, and he put a gold strip around it.
[13]Then he made four gold rings for the table
and attached them to the four corners of the
table where the four legs were. [14]The rings
were put close to the frame around the top
of the table, because they held the poles for
carrying it. [15]The poles for carrying the table
were made of acacia wood and were covered
with gold. [16]He made of pure gold all the
things that were used on the table: the
plates, bowls, cups, and jars used for pouring
the drink offerings.

The Lampstand

[17]Then he made the lampstand of pure
gold, hammering out its base and stand. Its
flower-like cups, buds, and petals were
joined together in one piece with the base
and stand. [18]Six branches went out from the
sides of the lampstand—three on one side
and three on the other. [19]Each branch had
three cups shaped like almond flowers, and
each cup had a bud and a petal. Each of the

six branches going out from the lampstand
was the same. 20There were four more cups
shaped like almond flowers on the
lampstand itself, each with its buds and
petals. 21Three pairs of branches went out
from the lampstand. A bud was under the
place where each pair was attached to the
lampstand. Each of the six branches going
out from the lampstand was the same. 22The
buds, branches, and lampstand were all one
piece of pure, hammered gold. 23He made
seven pure gold lamps for this lampstand,
and he made pure gold wick trimmers and
trays. 24He used about seventy-five pounds of
pure gold to make the lampstand and all the
things that go with it.

The Altar for Burning Incense

25Then he made the altar of incense out of
acacia wood. It was square—eighteen inches
long and eighteen inches wide—and it was
thirty-six inches high. Each corner that
stuck out like a horn was joined into one
piece with the altar. 26He covered the top
and all the sides and the corners with pure
gold, and he put gold trim around the altar.
27He made two gold rings and put them
below the trim on opposite sides of the altar;
these rings held the poles for carrying it.
28He made the poles of acacia wood and
covered them with gold.

29Then he made the holy olive oil for
appointing the priests and the pure, sweet-
smelling incense. He made them like a
person who mixes perfumes.

The Altar for Burnt Offerings

38 Then he built the altar for burnt
offerings out of acacia wood. The altar
was square—seven and one-half feet long
and seven and one-half feet wide—and it
was four and one-half feet high. 2He made
each corner stick out like a horn so that the
horns and the altar were joined together in
one piece. Then he covered the altar with
bronze. 3He made all the tools of bronze to
use on the altar: the pots, shovels, bowls for
sprinkling blood, meat forks, and pans for
carrying the fire. 4He made a large bronze
screen to hold the burning wood for the altar
and put it inside the altar, under its rim,
halfway up from the bottom. 5He made
bronze rings to hold the poles for carrying
the altar, and he put them at the four corners
of the screen. 6Then he made poles of acacia
wood and covered them with bronze. 7He
put the poles through the rings on both sides
of the altar, to carry it. He made the altar of
boards and left the inside hollow.

The Bronze Bowl

8He made the bronze bowl for washing,
and he built it on a bronze stand. He used
the bronze from mirrors that belonged to the
women who served at the entrance to the
Meeting Tent.

The Courtyard of the Holy Tent

9Then he made a wall of curtains to form
a courtyard around the Holy Tent. On the
south side the curtains were one hundred
fifty feet long and were made of fine linen.
10The curtains hung on silver hooks and
bands, placed on twenty bronze posts with
twenty bronze bases. 11On the north side the
wall of curtains was also one hundred fifty
feet long, and it hung on silver hooks and
bands on twenty posts with twenty bronze
bases.

12On the west side of the courtyard, the
wall of curtains was seventy-five feet long. It
was held up by silver hooks and bands on
ten posts with ten bases. 13The east side was
also seventy-five feet long. 14On one side of
the entry there was a wall of curtains
twenty-two and one-half feet long, held up
by three posts and three bases. 15On the
other side of the entry there was also a wall
of curtains twenty-two and one-half feet
long, held up by three posts and three bases.
16All the curtains around the courtyard were
made of fine linen. 17The bases for the posts
were made of bronze. The hooks and the
bands on the posts were made of silver, and
the tops of the posts were covered with
silver also. All the posts in the courtyard had
silver bands.

18The curtain for the entry of the
courtyard was made of blue, purple, and red
thread, and fine linen, sewn by a person who
could sew well. The curtain was thirty feet
long and seven and one-half feet high, the
same height as the curtains around the
courtyard. 19It was held up by four posts and
four bronze bases. The hooks and bands on
the posts were made of silver, and the tops
on the posts were covered with silver. 20All
the tent pegs for the Holy Tent and for the

curtains around the courtyard were made of
bronze.
21This is a list of the materials used to
make the Holy Tent, where the Agreement
was kept. Moses ordered the Levites to make
this list, and Ithamar son of Aaron was in
charge of keeping it. 22Bezalel son of Uri, the
son of Hur of the tribe of Judah, made
everything the LORD commanded Moses.
23Oholiab son of Ahisamach of the tribe of
Dan helped him. He could cut designs into
metal and stone; he was a designer and also
skilled at sewing the blue, purple, and red
thread, and fine linen.
24The total amount of gold used to build
the Holy Tent was presented to the LORD. It
weighed over 2,000 pounds, as set by the
Holy Place measure.
25The silver was given by the members of
the community who were counted. It
weighed 7,550 pounds, as set by the Holy
Place measure. 26All the men twenty years
old or older were counted. There were
603,550 men, and each man had to pay one-
fifth of an ounce of silver, as set by the Holy
Place measure. 27Of this silver, 7,500 pounds
were used to make the one hundred bases
for the Holy Tent and for the curtain—
75 pounds of silver in each base. 28They used
50 pounds of silver to make the hooks for
the posts and to cover the tops of the posts
and to make the bands on them.
29The bronze which was presented to the
LORD weighed about 5,000 pounds. 30They
used the bronze to make the bases at the
entrance of the Meeting Tent, to make the
altar and the bronze screen, and to make all
the tools for the altar. 31This bronze was also
used to make bases for the wall of curtains
around the courtyard and bases for curtains
at the entry to the courtyard, as well as to
make the tent pegs for the Holy Tent and the
curtains that surrounded the courtyard.

Clothes for the Priests

39 They used blue, purple, and red
thread to make woven clothes for the
priests to wear when they served in the Holy
Place. They made the holy clothes for Aaron
as the LORD had commanded Moses.
2They made the holy vest of gold, and
blue, purple, and red thread, and fine linen.
3They hammered the gold into sheets and
then cut it into long, thin strips. They
worked the gold into the blue, purple, and
red thread, and fine linen. This was done by
skilled craftsmen. 4They made the shoulder
straps for the holy vest, which were attached
to the top corners of the vest and tied
together over each shoulder. 5The skillfully
woven belt was made in the same way; it
was joined to the holy vest as one piece. It
was made of gold, and blue, purple, and red
thread, and fine linen, the way the LORD
commanded Moses.
6They put gold around the onyx stones
and then wrote the names of the sons of
Israel on these gems, as a person carves
words and designs on a seal. 7Then they
attached the gems on the shoulder straps of
the holy vest, as reminders of the twelve
sons of Israel. This was done just as the LORD
had commanded Moses.
8The skilled craftsmen made the chest
covering like the holy vest; it was made of
gold, and blue, purple, and red thread, and
fine linen. 9The chest covering was square—
nine inches long and nine inches wide—and
it was folded double to make a pocket.
10Then they put four rows of beautiful
jewels on it: In the first row there was a ruby,
a topaz, and a yellow quartz; 11in the second
there was a turquoise, a sapphire, and an
emerald; 12in the third there was a jacinth,
an agate, and an amethyst; 13in the fourth
there was a chrysolite, an onyx, and a jasper.
Gold was put around these jewels to attach
them to the chest covering, 14and the names
of the sons of Israel were carved on these
twelve jewels as a person carves a seal. Each
jewel had the name of one of the twelve
tribes of Israel.
15They made chains of pure gold, twisted
together like a rope, for the chest covering.
16The workers made two gold pieces and two
gold rings. They put the two gold rings on
the two upper corners of the chest covering.
17Then they put two gold chains in the two
rings at the ends of the chest covering, 18and
they fastened the other two ends of the
chains to the two gold pieces. They attached
these gold pieces to the two shoulder straps
in the front of the holy vest. 19They made
two gold rings and put them at the lower
corners of the chest covering on the inside
edge next to the holy vest. 20They made two
more gold rings on the bottom of the
shoulder straps in front of the holy vest, near

the seam, just above the woven belt of the holy vest. 21They used a blue ribbon and tied the rings of the chest covering to the rings of the holy vest, connecting it to the woven belt. In this way the chest covering would not swing out from the holy vest. They did all these things the way the LORD commanded.

22Then they made the outer robe to be worn under the holy vest. It was woven only of blue cloth. 23They made a hole in the center of the outer robe, with a woven collar sewn around it so it would not tear. 24Then they made balls like pomegranates of blue, purple, and red thread, and fine linen and hung them around the bottom of the outer robe. 25They also made bells of pure gold and hung these around the bottom of the outer robe between the balls. 26So around the bottom of the outer robe there was a bell and a pomegranate ball, a bell and a pomegranate ball. The priest wore this outer robe when he served as priest, just as the LORD had commanded Moses.

27They wove inner robes of fine linen for Aaron and his sons, 28and they made turbans, headbands, and underclothes of fine linen. 29Then they made the cloth belt of fine linen, and blue, purple, and red thread, and designs were sewn onto it, just as the LORD had commanded Moses.

30They made a strip of pure gold, which is the holy crown, and carved these words in the gold, as one might carve on a seal: "Holy to the LORD." 31Then they tied this flat piece to the turban with a blue ribbon, as the LORD had commanded Moses.

32So all the work on the Meeting Tent was finished. The Israelites did everything just as the LORD had commanded Moses. 33Then they brought the Holy Tent to Moses: the Tent and all its furniture, hooks, frames, crossbars, posts, and bases; 34the covering made of male sheepskins colored red, the covering made of fine leather, and the curtain that covered the entrance to the Most Holy Place; 35the Ark of the Agreement, its poles and lid; 36the table, all its containers, and the bread that showed they were in God's presence; 37the pure gold lampstand with its lamps in a row, all its tools, and the olive oil for the light; 38the gold altar, the special olive oil used for appointing priests, the sweet-smelling incense, and the curtain that covered the entrance to the Tent; 39the bronze altar and its screen, its poles and all its tools, the bowl and its stand; 40the curtains for the courtyard with their posts and bases, the curtain that covered the entry to the courtyard, the cords, pegs, and all the things in the Meeting Tent. 41They brought the clothes for the priests to wear when they served in the Holy Tent—the holy clothes for Aaron the priest and the clothes for his sons, which they wore when they served as priests.

42The Israelites had done all this work just as the LORD had commanded Moses. 43Moses looked closely at all the work and saw they had done it just as the LORD had commanded. So Moses blessed them.

Setting Up the Holy Tent

40 Then the LORD said to Moses: 2"On the first day of the first month, set up the Holy Tent, which is the Meeting Tent. 3Put the Ark of the Agreement in it and hang the curtain in front of the Ark. 4Bring in the table and arrange everything on the table that should be there. Then bring in the lampstand and set up its lamps. 5Put the gold altar for burning incense in front of the Ark of the Agreement, and put the curtain at the entrance to the Holy Tent.

6"Put the altar of burnt offerings in front of the entrance of the Holy Tent, the Meeting Tent. 7Put the bowl between the Meeting Tent and the altar, and put water in it. 8Set up the courtyard around the Holy Tent, and put the curtain at the entry to the courtyard.

9"Use the special olive oil and pour it on the Holy Tent and everything in it, in order to give the Tent and all that is in it for service to the LORD. They will be holy. 10Pour the special oil on the altar for burnt offerings and on all its tools. Give the altar for service to God, and it will be very holy. 11Then pour the special olive oil on the bowl and the base under it so that they will be given for service to God.

12"Bring Aaron and his sons to the entrance of the Meeting Tent, and wash them with water. 13Then put the holy clothes on Aaron. Pour the special oil on him, and give him for service to God so that he may serve me as a priest. 14Bring Aaron's sons and put the inner robes on them. 15Pour

the special oil on them in the same way that
you appointed their father as priest so that
they may also serve me as priests. Pouring
oil on them will make them a family of
priests, they and their descendants from now
on." 16 Moses did everything that the LORD
commanded him.

17 So the Holy Tent was set up on the first
day of the first month during the second
year after they left Egypt. 18 When Moses set
up the Holy Tent, he put the bases in place,
and he put the frames on the bases. Next he
put the crossbars through the rings of the
frames and set up the posts. 19 After that,
Moses spread the cloth over the Holy Tent
and put the covering over it, just as the LORD
commanded.

20 Moses put the stone tablets that had the
Agreement written on them into the Ark. He
put the poles through the rings of the Ark
and put the lid on it. 21 Next he brought the
Ark into the Tent and hung the curtain to
cover the Ark, just as the LORD commanded
him.

22 Moses put the table in the Meeting Tent
on the north side of the Holy Tent in front
of the curtain. 23 Then he put the bread on
the table before the LORD, just as the LORD
commanded him. 24 Moses put the
lampstand in the Meeting Tent on the south
side of the Holy Tent across from the table.
25 Then he put the lamps on the lampstand
before the LORD, just as the LORD
commanded him.

26 Moses put the gold altar for burning
incense in the Meeting Tent in front of the
curtain. 27 Then he burned sweet-smelling
incense on it, just as the LORD commanded
him. 28 Then he hung the curtain at the
entrance to the Holy Tent.

29 He put the altar for burnt offerings at
the entrance to the Holy Tent, the Meeting
Tent, and offered a whole burnt offering and
grain offerings on it, just as the LORD
commanded him. 30 Moses put the bowl
between the Meeting Tent and the altar for
burnt offerings, and he put water in it for
washing. 31 Moses, Aaron, and Aaron's sons
used this water to wash their hands and feet.
32 They washed themselves every time they

devotion 30

EXODUS 40:34–35

MANAGING THE DETAILS

The children of Israel were journeymen following the signs of the Lord on a continual basis. When the cloud was present over the Holy Tent, the Israelites stayed put, but they knew it was time to continue when it was taken up. This was a definite sign from the Lord—clear direction from the Spirit of God.

That same Spirit lives today in each heart that receives Christ. Since we are the temple of the Holy Spirit, we too should wait on his direction. As women, we face a special danger when it comes to conducting our lives in our own strength. You know why? Because we are capable multitaskers that can accomplish much. The result of those abilities can lead to walking through an entire day without consulting our Father even once. One of my favorite sayings is, "Just because you can doesn't mean you should." Whew! Can you relate to that?

Purpose in your heart to seek God in all that comes your way today. He wants to be your one and only God—of your details, of your heart, of your conversation, of your financial decisions. He wants to be the guide of your life. If you do not see the clear direction of the Lord guiding you, be patient and trust him. Know that he is at work and wants you to be still during this season (Ps. 46:10). There is no greater joy than seeing the hand of the Lord at work in the details of your life.

entered the Meeting Tent and every time
they went near the altar for burnt offerings,
just as the LORD commanded Moses.

33Then Moses set up the courtyard around
the Holy Tent and the altar, and he put up
the curtain at the entry to the courtyard. So
Moses finished the work.

The Cloud over the Holy Tent

34Then the cloud covered the Meeting
Tent, and the glory of the LORD filled the
Holy Tent. 35Moses could not enter the
Meeting Tent, because the cloud had settled
on it, and the glory of the LORD filled the
Holy Tent.

36When the cloud rose from the Holy
Tent, the Israelites would begin to travel,
37but as long as the cloud stayed on the Holy
Tent, they did not travel. They stayed in that
place until the cloud rose. 38So the cloud of
the LORD was over the Holy Tent during the
day, and there was a fire in the cloud at
night. So all the Israelites could see the cloud
while they traveled.

Leviticus

From the Latin Vulgate meaning "matters of the Levites"
(The Latin Vulgate was the first common translation from the original Hebrew and Aramaic texts. It was the standard version of the Bible used by Roman Catholics for over a millennium, and its text was used in translating the King James Version of the Bible.)

Person Holding the Pen God Wrote With: It's generally agreed that *Moses* is the author, as confirmed in Leviticus 27:34.

When the Text Was Written: Between 1445 and 1405 B.C.

Spiritual Posture of the Original Recipients: God's people, the Israelites, were still camping out at the foot of Mount Sinai, probably in a state of awe after witnessing Jehovah's glory fill the Holy Tent (Ex. 40:34).

Storyline Synopsis: Leviticus opens just after the Holy Tent (God's transient "desert dwelling place," which preceded the permanent Temple in Jerusalem) was built and furnished. This detailed book of rules and regulations spells out the responsibilities of the priests to facilitate worship in the Holy Tent, as well as the responsibilities of the people to be faithful to God's Law. The first seventeen chapters are all about redemption—*the way to God*—while the last ten chapters deal with restoration—*our walk with God*. The resounding theme of all twenty-seven chapters is God's absolute *holiness*.

A Moment Worth Discussing: Chapter 25 describes a *Year of Jubilee*, which God decreed was to take place once every fifty years (verses 8–17). During those twelve months, anyone held in bondage was to be released, whether that bondage involved credit card debt or an orange jumpsuit! It was God's merciful provision for people who'd fallen on hard times to have the opportunity to get back on their feet. It was a divinely innovative and effective strategy for keeping inflation in check. Discuss the ramifications—both positive and negative—if such a Year of Jubilee were in practice in modern civilization.

Interesting (But Likely to Be Overlooked) Character: Leviticus 19:14 describes a law against mistreating a *deaf* or *blind* person. While societies throughout history have often marginalized and even abused the physically disabled, God has always shown compassion for the weak.

The Burnt Offering

1 The LORD called to Moses and spoke to
him from the Meeting Tent, saying, 2"Tell
the people of Israel: 'When you bring an
offering to the LORD, bring as your offering
an animal from the herd or flock.
3" 'If the offering is a whole burnt offering
from the herd, it must be a male that has
nothing wrong with it. The person must take
the animal to the entrance of the Meeting
Tent so that the LORD will accept the offering.
4He must put his hand on the animal's head,
and the LORD will accept it to remove the
person's sin so he will belong to God. 5He
must kill the young bull before the LORD, and
Aaron's sons, the priests, must bring its blood
and sprinkle it on all sides of the altar at the
entrance to the Meeting Tent. 6After that he
will skin the animal and cut it into pieces.
7The priests, when they have put wood and
fire on the altar, 8are to lay the head, the fat,
and other pieces on the wood that is on the
fire of the altar. 9The animal's inner organs
and legs must be washed with water. Then
the priest must burn all the animal's parts on
the altar. It is a whole burnt offering, an
offering made by fire, and its smell is
pleasing to the LORD.
10" 'If the burnt offering is a sheep or a
goat from the flock, it must be a male that
has nothing wrong with it. 11The person
must kill the animal on the north side of the
altar before the LORD, and Aaron's sons, the
priests, must sprinkle its blood on all sides of
the altar. 12The person must cut the animal
into pieces, and the priest must lay them,
with the head and fat, on the wood that is on
the fire of the altar. 13The person must wash
the animal's inner organs and legs with
water, and then the priest must burn all its
parts on the altar. It is a whole burnt
offering, an offering made by fire, and its
smell is pleasing to the LORD.
14" 'If the whole burnt offering for the
LORD is a bird, it must be a dove or a young
pigeon. 15The priest will bring it to the altar
and pull off its head, which he will burn on
the altar; the bird's blood must be drained
out on the side of the altar. 16The priest
must remove the bird's crop[n] and its
contents and throw them on the east side of
the altar, where the ashes are. 17Then he
must tear the bird open by its wings
without dividing it into two parts. He must
burn the bird on the altar, on the wood
which is on the fire. It is a whole burnt
offering, an offering made by fire, and its
smell is pleasing to the LORD.

The Grain Offering

2 " 'When anyone offers a grain offering to
the LORD, it must be made from fine
flour. The person must pour oil on it, put
incense on it, 2and then take it to Aaron's
sons, the priests. The priest must take a
handful of the fine flour and oil and all the
incense, and burn it on the altar as a
memorial portion. It is an offering made by
fire, and its smell is pleasing to the LORD.
3The rest of the grain offering will belong to
Aaron and the priests; it is a most holy part
of the offerings made by fire to the LORD.
4" 'If you bring a grain offering that was
baked in the oven, it must be made from fine
flour. It may be loaves made without yeast
and mixed with oil, or it may be wafers
made without yeast that have oil poured
over them. 5If your grain offering is cooked
on a griddle, it must be made, without yeast,
of fine flour mixed with oil. 6Crumble it and
pour oil over it; it is a grain offering. 7If your
grain offering is cooked in a pan, it must be
made from fine flour and oil. 8Bring the
grain offering made of these things to the
LORD. Give it to the priest, and he will take it
to the altar. 9He will take out the memorial
portion from the grain offering and burn it
on the altar, as an offering made by fire. Its
smell is pleasing to the LORD. 10The rest of
the grain offering belongs to Aaron and the
priests. It is a most holy part of the offerings
made to the LORD by fire.
11" 'Every grain offering you bring to the
LORD must be made without yeast, because
you must not burn any yeast or honey in an
offering made by fire to the LORD. 12You may
bring yeast and honey to the LORD as an
offering from the first harvest, but they must
not be burned on the altar as a pleasing
smell. 13You must also put salt on all your
grain offerings. Salt stands for your

1:16 crop A small bag inside a bird's throat. When a bird eats, its food goes into this part first. There, the food is made soft before it goes into the stomach.

devotion 31

LEVITICUS 1:4

WHAT WOULD YOU SACRIFICE?

In the Old Testament, animal sacrifices were essential for the removal of sin. That's a foreign concept today, but sacrifices were commonplace in Old Testament times. The problem was that sin separated the Israelites from God. Our God is holy, and he cannot have communion with sin. So God provided a way to atone for sin and have a relationship with his children. As a permanent solution to our sin problem, Christ came to earth and sacrificed his life. Once we accept his forgiveness, we belong to the Lord. Isn't that an amazing thought? The God of the universe, the Holy of Holies, the Beginning and the End, wants me to be a part of his family.

My husband and I have recently become foster parents. We are currently waiting for our first foster child to be placed in our home. It doesn't matter whether it's a boy or a girl, black or white, sick or healthy, this child will belong to us for a season in his or her life. And I can't wait. I already love and feel protective of this little one. God feels the same way about you.

We sometimes see sin as inevitable rather than something that breaks the heart of a Father who really loves us. It's important to remember that God wants to be a part of your life so much that he allowed the sacrifice of his only Son to have a relationship with you.

agreement with God that will last forever; do
not leave it out of your grain offering. You
must add salt to all your offerings.
14" 'If you bring a grain offering from the
first harvest to the LORD, bring crushed heads
of new grain roasted in the fire. 15Put oil and
incense on it; it is a grain offering. 16The
priest will burn the memorial portion of the
crushed grain and oil, with the incense on it.
It is an offering by fire to the LORD.

The Fellowship Offering

3 " 'If a person's fellowship offering to the
LORD is from the herd, it may be a male
or female, but it must have nothing wrong
with it. 2The person must put his hand on
the animal's head and kill it at the entrance
to the Meeting Tent. Then Aaron's sons, the
priests, must sprinkle the blood on all sides
of the altar. 3From the fellowship offering he
must make a sacrifice by fire to the LORD. He
must offer the fat of the animal's inner
organs (both the fat that is in them and that
covers them), 4both kidneys with the fat that
is on them near the lower back muscle, and
the best part of the liver, which he will
remove with the kidneys. 5Then the priests
will burn these parts on the altar, on the
whole burnt offering that is on the wood of
the fire. It is an offering made by fire, and its
smell is pleasing to the LORD.
6" 'If a person's fellowship offering to the
LORD is a lamb or a goat, it may be a male or
female, but it must have nothing wrong
with it. 7If he offers a lamb, he must bring it
before the LORD 8and put his hand on its
head. Then he must kill the animal in front
of the Meeting Tent, and the priests must
sprinkle its blood on all sides of the altar.
9From the fellowship offering the person
must make a sacrifice by fire to the LORD. He
must bring the fat, the whole fat tail cut off
close to the backbone, the fat of the inner
organs (both the fat that is in them and that
covers them), 10both kidneys with the fat
that is on them, near the lower back muscle,
and the best part of the liver, which he will
remove with the kidneys. 11Then the priest

will burn these parts on the altar as food; it will be an offering made by fire to the LORD.

12“ ‘If a person’s offering is a goat, he must offer it before the LORD 13and put his hand on its head. Then he must kill it in front of the Meeting Tent, and the priests must sprinkle its blood on all sides of the altar. 14From this offering the person must make a sacrifice by fire to the LORD. He must offer all the fat of the goat’s inner organs (both the fat that is in them and that covers them), 15both kidneys with the fat that is on them near the lower back muscle, and the best part of the liver, which he will remove with the kidneys. 16The priest will burn these parts on the altar as food. It is an offering made by fire, and its smell is pleasing to the LORD. All the fat belongs to the LORD.

17“ ‘This law will continue for people from now on, wherever you live: You must not eat any fat or blood.’ ”

The Sin Offering

4 The LORD said to Moses, 2“Tell the people of Israel this: ‘When a person sins by accident and does some things the LORD has commanded not to be done, that person must do these things:

3“ ‘If the appointed priest sins so that he brings guilt on the people, then he must offer a young bull to the LORD, one that has nothing wrong with it, as a sin offering for the sin he has done. 4He will bring the bull to the entrance of the Meeting Tent in front of the LORD, put his hand on its head, and kill it before the LORD. 5Then the appointed priest must bring some of the bull’s blood into the Meeting Tent. 6The priest is to dip his finger into the blood and sprinkle it seven times before the LORD in front of the curtain of the Most Holy Place. 7The priest must also put some of the blood on the corners of the altar of incense that stands before the LORD in the Meeting Tent. The rest of the blood he must pour out at the bottom of the altar of burnt offering, which is at the entrance of the Meeting Tent. 8He must remove all the fat from the bull of the sin offering—the fat on and around the inner organs, 9both kidneys with the fat that is on them near the lower back muscle, and the best part of the liver which he will remove with the kidneys. 10(He must do this in the same way the fat is removed from the bull of the fellowship offering.) Then the priest must burn the animal parts on the altar of burnt offering. 11But the priest must carry off the skin of the bull and all its meat, along with the rest of the bull—its head, legs, intestines, and other inner organs. 12He must take it outside the camp to the special clean place where the ashes are poured out. He must burn it on a wood fire on the pile of ashes.

13“ ‘If the whole nation of Israel sins accidentally without knowing it and does something the LORD has commanded not to be done, they are guilty. 14When they learn about the sin they have done, they must offer a young bull as a sin offering and bring it before the Meeting Tent. 15The elders of the group of people must put their hands on the bull’s head before the LORD, and it must be killed before the LORD. 16Then the appointed priest must bring some of the bull’s blood into the Meeting Tent. 17Dipping his finger in the blood, he must sprinkle it seven times before the LORD in front of the curtain. 18Then he must put some of the blood on the corners of the altar that is before the LORD in the Meeting Tent. The priest must pour out the rest of the blood at the bottom of the altar of burnt offering, which is at the entrance to the Meeting Tent. 19He must remove all the fat from the animal and burn it on the altar; 20he will do the same thing with this bull that he did with the first bull of the sin offering. In this way the priest removes the sins of the people so they will belong to the LORD and be forgiven. 21Then the priest must carry the bull outside the camp and burn it, just as he did with the first bull. This is the sin offering for the whole community.

22“ ‘If a ruler sins by accident and does something the LORD his God has commanded must not be done, he is guilty. 23When he learns about his sin, he must bring a male goat that has nothing wrong with it as his offering. 24The ruler must put his hand on the goat’s head and kill it in the place where they kill the whole burnt offering before the LORD; it is a sin offering. 25The priest must take some of the blood of the sin offering on his finger and put it on the corners of the altar of burnt offering. He must pour out the rest of the blood at the bottom of the altar of burnt offering. 26He

must burn all the goat's fat on the altar in
the same way he burns the fat of the
fellowship offerings. In this way the priest
removes the ruler's sin so he belongs to the
LORD, and the LORD will forgive him.
27" 'If any person in the community sins
by accident and does something which the
LORD has commanded must not be done, he
is guilty. 28When the person learns about his
sin, he must bring a female goat that has
nothing wrong with it as an offering for his
sin. 29He must put his hand on the animal's
head and kill it at the place of the whole
burnt offering. 30Then the priest must take
some of the goat's blood on his finger and
put it on the corners of the altar of burnt
offering. He must pour out the rest of the
goat's blood at the bottom of the altar.
31Then the priest must remove all the goat's
fat in the same way the fat is removed from
the fellowship offerings. He must burn it on
the altar as a smell pleasing to the LORD. In
this way the priest will remove that person's
sin so he will belong to the LORD, and the
LORD will forgive him.
32" 'If this person brings a lamb as his
offering for sin, he must bring a female that
has nothing wrong with it. 33He must put
his hand on the animal's head and kill it as a
sin offering in the place where the whole
burnt offering is killed. 34The priest must
take some of the blood from the sin offering
on his finger and put it on the corners of the
altar of burnt offering. He must pour out the
rest of the lamb's blood at the bottom of the
altar. 35Then the priest must remove all the
lamb's fat in the same way that the lamb's
fat is removed from the fellowship offerings.
He must burn the pieces on the altar on top
of the offerings made by fire for the LORD. In
this way the priest will remove that person's
sins so he will belong to the LORD, and the
LORD will forgive him.

Special Types of Accidental Sins

5 " 'If a person is ordered to tell in court
what he has seen or what he knows and
he does not tell the court, he is guilty of sin.
2" 'Or someone might touch something
unclean, such as the dead body of an
unclean wild animal or an unclean farm
animal or an unclean crawling animal. Even
if he does not know that he touched it, he
will still be unclean and guilty of sin.
3" 'Someone might touch human
uncleanness—anything that makes
someone unclean—and not know it. But
when he learns about it, he will be guilty.
4" 'Or someone might make a promise
before the LORD without thinking. It might
be a promise to do something bad or
something good; it might be about anything.
Even if he forgets about it, when he
remembers, he will be guilty.
5" 'When anyone is guilty of any of these
things, he must tell how he sinned. 6He
must bring an offering to the LORD as a
penalty for sin; it must be a female lamb or
goat from the flock. The priest will perform
the acts to remove that person's sin so he
will belong to the LORD.
7" 'But if the person cannot afford a lamb,
he must bring two doves or two young
pigeons to the LORD as the penalty for his sin.
One bird must be for a sin offering, and the
other must be for a whole burnt offering. 8He
must bring them to the priest, who will first
offer the one for the sin offering. He will pull
the bird's head from its neck, but he will not
pull it completely off. 9He must sprinkle the
blood from the sin offering on the side of the
altar, and then he must pour the rest of the
blood at the bottom of the altar; it is a sin
offering. 10Then the priest must offer the
second bird as a whole burnt offering, as the
law says. In this way the priest will remove
the person's sin so he will belong to the
LORD, and the LORD will forgive him.
11" 'If the person cannot afford two doves
or two pigeons, he must bring about two
quarts of fine flour as an offering for sin. He
must not put oil or incense on the flour,
because it is a sin offering. 12He must bring
the flour to the priest. The priest will take a
handful of the flour as a memorial offering
and burn it on the altar on top of the
offerings made by fire to the LORD; it is a sin
offering. 13In this way the priest will remove
the person's sins so he will belong to the
LORD, and the LORD will forgive him. What is
left of the sin offering belongs to the priest,
like the grain offering.' "

The Penalty Offering

14The LORD said to Moses, 15"If a person
accidentally sins and does something against
the holy things of the LORD, he must bring
from the flock a male sheep that has nothing

devotion 32

LEVITICUS 5:5

BE A *LIVING* SACRIFICE

If you were to read Leviticus 5, you'd read about the animal sacrifices the Israelites were required to make. That was before Jesus came, and thankfully we don't have to sacrifice animals anymore in order to be forgiven—Jesus paid the ultimate blood sacrifice for us. Now we only need to confess our sins and accept cleansing forgiveness through him. What a relief!

However, as I was reading Leviticus today, I was reminded that no matter what day and age we are living in, it's apparent that God still wants us to be holy before him. Sure, we don't need to slaughter a lamb. In fact, I have to admit that even if God asked me to make a blood sacrifice, I'd first have trouble locating an animal, and then I'd have a very difficult time performing the sacrifice. It would, in reality, be an incredible undertaking.

Do you see what a wonderful gift God has given us through Jesus? Presenting his very Son as a sacrifice is evidence of how vastly he loves his children. Have you confessed your sins before God and accepted his grace in your life? Do you have a stain on your heart that needs forgiveness? Are you a Christian but have been so busy that you sometimes forget to confess your sins to the Lord? I want to encourage you to confess your sins to him today; be a living sacrifice and experience the freedom and abundant life that only Jesus can give.

wrong with it. This will be his penalty
offering to the LORD. Its value in silver must
be correct as set by the Holy Place measure.
It is a penalty offering. 16That person must
pay for the sin he did against the holy thing,
adding one-fifth to its value. Then he must
give it all to the priest. In this way the priest
will remove the person's sin so he will
belong to the LORD, by using the male sheep
as the penalty offering. And the LORD will
forgive the person.
17"If a person sins and does something the
LORD has commanded not to be done, even if
he does not know it, he is still guilty. He is
responsible for his sin. 18He must bring the
priest a male sheep from the flock, one that
has nothing wrong with it and that is worth
the correct amount. It will be a penalty
offering. Though the person sinned without
knowing it, with this offering the priest will
remove the sin so the person will belong to
the LORD, and the LORD will forgive him.
19The person is guilty of doing wrong, so he
must give the penalty offering to the LORD."

6 The LORD said to Moses, 2"A person might
sin against the LORD by doing one of
these sins: He might lie about what
happened to something he was taking care
of for someone else, or he might lie about a
promise he made. He might steal something
or cheat someone. 3He might find something
that had been lost and then lie about it. He
might make a promise before the LORD about
something and not mean it, or he might do
some other sin. 4If he does any of these
things, he is guilty of sin. He must bring
back whatever he stole or whatever he took
by cheating. He must bring back the thing
he took care of for someone else. He must
bring back what he found and lied about
5or what he made a false promise about. He
must pay the full price plus an extra one-
fifth of the value of what he took. He must
give the money to the true owner on the day

he brings his penalty offering. 6He must bring his penalty to the priest—a male sheep from the flock, one that does not have anything wrong with it and that is worth the correct amount. It will be a penalty offering to the LORD. 7Then the priest will perform the acts to remove that person's sin so he will belong to the LORD, and the LORD will forgive him for the sins that made him guilty."

The Whole Burnt Offering

8The LORD said to Moses, 9"Give this command to Aaron and the priests: 'These are the teachings about the whole burnt offering: The burnt offering must stay on the altar all night until morning, and the altar's fire must be kept burning. 10The priest must put on his linen robe and linen underclothes next to his body. Then he will remove the ashes from the burnt offering on the altar and put them beside the altar. 11Then he must take off those clothes and put on others and carry the ashes outside the camp to a special clean place. 12But the fire must be kept burning on the altar; it must not be allowed to go out. The priest must put more firewood on the altar every morning, place the whole burnt offering on the fire, and burn the fat of the fellowship offerings. 13The fire must be kept burning on the altar all the time; it must not go out.

The Grain Offering

14" 'These are the teachings about the grain offering: The priests must bring it to the LORD in front of the altar. 15The priest must take a handful of fine flour, with the oil and all of the incense on it, and burn the grain offering on the altar as a memorial offering to the LORD. Its smell is pleasing to him. 16Aaron and the priests may eat what is left, but it must be eaten without yeast in a holy place. They must eat it in the courtyard of the Meeting Tent. 17It must not be cooked with yeast. I have given it as their share of the offerings made to me by fire; it is most holy, like the sin offering and the penalty offering. 18Any male descendant of Aaron may eat it as his share of the offerings made to the LORD by fire, and this will continue from now on. Whatever touches these offerings shall become holy.' "

19The LORD said to Moses, 20"This is the offering Aaron and the priests must bring to the LORD on the day they appoint Aaron as high priest: They must bring two quarts of fine flour for a continual grain offering, half of it in the morning and half in the evening. 21The fine flour must be mixed with oil and cooked on a griddle. Bring it when it is well mixed. Present the grain offering that is broken into pieces, and it will be a smell that is pleasing to the LORD. 22One of the priests appointed to take Aaron's place as high priest must make the grain offering. It is a rule forever that the grain offering must be completely burned to the LORD. 23Every grain offering made by a priest must be completely burned; it must not be eaten."

The Sin Offering

24The LORD said to Moses, 25"Tell Aaron and the priests: 'These are the teachings about the sin offering: The sin offering must be killed in front of the LORD in the same place the whole burnt offering is killed; it is most holy. 26The priest who offers the sin offering must eat it in a holy place, in the courtyard of the Meeting Tent. 27Whatever touches the meat of the sin offering must be holy, and if the blood is sprinkled on any clothes, you must wash them in a holy place. 28The clay pot the meat is cooked in must be broken, or if a bronze pot is used, it must be scrubbed and rinsed with water. 29Any male in a priest's family may eat the offering; it is most holy. 30But if the blood of the sin offering is taken into the Meeting Tent and used to remove sin in the Holy Place, that sin offering must be burned with fire. It must not be eaten.

The Penalty Offering

7 " 'These are the teachings about the penalty offering, which is most holy: 2The penalty offering must be killed where the whole burnt offering is killed. Then the priest must sprinkle its blood on all sides of the altar. 3He must offer all the fat from the penalty offering—the fat tail, the fat that covers the inner organs, 4both kidneys with the fat that is on them near the lower back muscle, and the best part of the liver, which is to be removed with the kidneys. 5The priest must burn all these things on the altar as an offering made by fire to the LORD. It is a

penalty offering. 6 Any male in a priest's family may eat it. It is most holy, so it must be eaten in a holy place.

7 " 'The penalty offering is like the sin offering in that the teachings are the same for both. The priest who offers the sacrifice to remove sins will get the meat for food. 8 The priest who offers the burnt offering may also have the skin from it. 9 Every grain offering that is baked in an oven, cooked on a griddle, or baked in a dish belongs to the priest who offers it. 10 Every grain offering, either dry or mixed with oil, belongs to the priests, and all priests will share alike.

The Fellowship Offering

11 " 'These are the teachings about the fellowship offering a person may offer to the LORD: 12 If he brings the fellowship offering to show his thanks, he should also bring loaves of bread made without yeast that are mixed with oil, wafers made without yeast that have oil poured over them, and loaves of fine flour that are mixed with oil. 13 He must also offer loaves of bread made with yeast along with his fellowship offering, which he gives to show thanks. 14 One of each kind of offering will be for the LORD; it will be given to the priest who sprinkles the blood of the fellowship offering. 15 When the fellowship offering is given to thank the LORD, the meat from it must be eaten the same day it is offered; none of it must be left until morning.

16 " 'If a person brings a fellowship offering just to give a gift to God or because of a special promise to him, the sacrifice should be eaten the same day he offers it. If there is any left, it may be eaten the next day. 17 If any meat from this sacrifice is left on the third day, it must be burned up. 18 Any meat of the fellowship offering eaten on the third day will not be accepted, nor will the sacrifice count for the person who offered it. It will become unclean, and anyone who eats the meat will be guilty of sin.

19 " 'People must not eat meat that touches anything unclean; they must burn this meat with fire. Anyone who is clean may eat other meat. 20 But if anyone is unclean and eats the meat from the fellowship offering that belongs to the LORD, he must be cut off from his people.

21 " 'If anyone touches something unclean—uncleanness that comes from people, from an animal, or from some hated thing—touching it will make him unclean. If he then eats meat from the fellowship offering that belongs to the LORD, he must be cut off from his people.' "

22 The LORD said to Moses, 23 "Tell the people of Israel: 'You must not eat any of the fat from cattle, sheep, or goats. 24 If an animal is found dead or torn by wild animals, you may use its fat for other things, but you must not eat it. 25 If someone eats fat from an animal offering made by fire to the LORD, he must be cut off from his people. 26 No matter where you live, you must not eat blood from any bird or animal. 27 Anyone who eats blood must be cut off from his people.' "

The Priests' Share

28 The LORD said to Moses, 29 "Tell the people of Israel: 'If someone brings a fellowship offering to the LORD, he must give part of it as his sacrifice to the LORD. 30 He must carry that part of the gift in his own hands as an offering made by fire to the LORD. He must bring the fat and the breast of the animal to the priest, to be presented to the LORD as the priests' share. 31 Then the priest must burn the fat on the altar, but the breast of the animal will belong to Aaron and the priests. 32 You must also give the right thigh from the fellowship offering to the priest as a gift; 33 it will belong to the priest who offers the blood and fat of the fellowship offering. 34 I have taken the breast and the thigh from the fellowship offerings of the Israelites, and I have given these parts to Aaron and the priests as their share for all time from the Israelites.' "

35 This is the portion that belongs to Aaron and his sons from the offerings made by fire to the LORD. They were given this share on the day they were presented to the LORD as priests. 36 On the day the LORD appointed the priests, he commanded Israel to give this share to them, and it is to be given to the priests as their share from now on.

37 These are the teachings about the whole burnt offering, the grain offering, the sin offering, the penalty offering, the offering for the appointment of priests, and the fellowship offering. 38 The LORD gave these teachings to Moses on Mount Sinai on the day he commanded the Israelites to bring

their offerings to the LORD in the Sinai
Desert.

Aaron and His Sons Appointed

8 The LORD said to Moses, 2“Bring Aaron
and his sons and their clothes, the
special olive oil used in appointing people
and things to the service of the LORD, the
bull of the sin offering and the two male
sheep, and the basket of bread made without
yeast. 3Then gather the people together at
the entrance to the Meeting Tent.” 4Moses
did as the LORD commanded him, and the
people met together at the entrance to the
Meeting Tent.

5Then Moses spoke to the people and said,
“This is what the LORD has commanded to be
done.” 6Bringing Aaron and his sons forward,
Moses washed them with water. 7He put the
inner robe on Aaron and tied the cloth belt
around him. Then Moses put the outer robe
on him and placed the holy vest on him. He
tied the skillfully woven belt around him so
that the holy vest was tied to Aaron. 8Then
Moses put the chest covering on him and
put the Urim and the Thummim in the chest
covering. 9He also put the turban on Aaron’s
head. He put the strip of gold, the holy
crown, on the front of the turban, as the
LORD commanded him to do.

10Then Moses put the special oil on the
Holy Tent and everything in it, making them
holy for the LORD. 11He sprinkled some oil on
the altar seven times, sprinkling the altar
and all its tools and the large bowl and its
base. In this way he made them holy for the
LORD. 12He poured some of the special oil on
Aaron’s head to make Aaron holy for the
LORD. 13Then Moses brought Aaron’s sons
forward. He put the inner robes on them,
tied cloth belts around them, and put
headbands on them, as the LORD had
commanded him.

14Then Moses brought the bull for the sin
offering, and Aaron and his sons put their
hands on its head. 15Moses killed the bull,
took the blood, and with his finger put some
of it on all the corners of the altar, to make it
pure. Then he poured out the rest of the
blood at the bottom of the altar. In this way
he made it holy and ready for service to God.
16Moses took all the fat from the inner
organs of the bull, the best part of the liver,
and both kidneys with the fat that is on
them, and he burned them on the altar. 17But
he took the bull’s skin, its meat, and its
intestines and burned them in a fire outside
the camp, as the LORD had commanded him.

18Next Moses brought the male sheep of
the burnt offering, and Aaron and his sons
put their hands on its head. 19Then Moses
killed it and sprinkled the blood on all sides
of the altar. 20He cut the male sheep into
pieces and burned the head, the pieces, and
the fat. 21He washed the inner organs and legs
with water and burned the whole sheep on
the altar as a burnt offering made by fire to
the LORD; its smell was pleasing to the LORD.
Moses did these things as the LORD had
commanded him.

22Then Moses brought the other male
sheep, the one used in appointing Aaron and
his sons as priests, and Aaron and his sons
put their hands on its head. 23Then Moses
killed the sheep and put some of its blood on
the bottom of Aaron’s right ear, some on the
thumb of Aaron’s right hand, and some on
the big toe of his right foot. 24Then Moses
brought Aaron’s sons close to the altar. He
put some of the blood on the bottom of their
right ears, some on the thumbs of their right
hands, and some on the big toes of their
right feet. Then he sprinkled blood on all
sides of the altar. 25He took the fat, the fat
tail, all the fat on the inner organs, the best
part of the liver, both kidneys with their fat,
and the right thigh. 26From the basket of
bread made without yeast that is put before
the LORD each day, Moses took a loaf of
bread, a loaf made with oil, and a wafer. He
put these pieces of bread on the fat and right
thigh of the male sheep. 27All these things he
put in the hands of Aaron and his sons and
presented them as an offering before the
LORD. 28Then Moses took them from their
hands and burned them on the altar on top
of the burnt offering. So this was the offering
for appointing Aaron and his sons as priests.
It was an offering made by fire to the LORD,
and its smell was pleasing to him. 29Moses
also took the breast and presented it as an
offering before the LORD. It was Moses’ share
of the male sheep used in appointing the
priests, as the LORD had commanded him.

30Moses took some of the special oil and
some of the blood which was on the altar, and
he sprinkled them on Aaron and Aaron’s
clothes and on Aaron’s sons and their clothes.

In this way Moses made Aaron, his clothes, his sons, and their clothes holy for the LORD.

31Then Moses said to Aaron and his sons, "I gave you a command, saying, 'Aaron and his sons will eat these things.' So take the meat and basket of bread from the offering for appointing priests. Boil the meat at the door of the Meeting Tent, and eat it there with the bread. 32If any of the meat or bread is left, burn it. 33The time of appointing will last seven days; you must not go outside the entrance of the Meeting Tent until that time is up. Stay there until the time of your appointing is finished. 34The LORD commanded the things that were done today to remove your sins so you will belong to him. 35You must stay at the entrance of the Meeting Tent day and night for seven days. If you don't obey the LORD's commands, you will die. The LORD has given me these commands."

36So Aaron and his sons did everything the LORD had commanded through Moses.

Aaron and His Sons Offer Sacrifices

9 On the eighth day after the time of appointing, Moses called for Aaron and his sons and for the elders of Israel. 2He said to Aaron, "Take a bull calf and a male sheep that have nothing wrong with them, and offer them to the LORD. The calf will be a sin offering, and the male sheep will be a whole burnt offering. 3Tell the people of Israel, 'Take a male goat for a sin offering and a calf and a lamb for a whole burnt offering; each must be one year old, and it must have nothing wrong with it. 4Also take a bull and a male sheep for fellowship offerings, along with a grain offering mixed with oil. Offer all these things to the LORD, because the LORD will appear to you today.' "

5So all the people came to the front of the Meeting Tent, bringing the things Moses had commanded them to bring, and they stood before the LORD. 6Moses said, "You have done what the LORD commanded, so you will see the LORD's glory."

7Then Moses told Aaron, "Go to the altar and offer sin offerings and whole burnt offerings. Do this to remove your sins and the people's sins so you will belong to God. Offer the sacrifices for the people and perform the acts to remove their sins for them so they will belong to the LORD, as the LORD has commanded."

8So Aaron went to the altar and killed the bull calf as a sin offering for himself. 9Then his sons brought the blood to him, and he dipped his finger in the blood and put it on the corners of the altar. He poured out the rest of the blood at the bottom of the altar. 10Aaron took the fat, the kidneys, and the best part of the liver from the sin offering and burned them on the altar, in the way the LORD had commanded Moses. 11The meat and skin he burned outside the camp.

12Then Aaron killed the animal for the whole burnt offering. His sons brought the blood to him, and he sprinkled it on all sides of the altar. 13As they gave him the pieces and head of the burnt offering, Aaron burned them on the altar. 14He also washed the inner organs and the legs of the burnt offering and burned them on top of the burnt offering on the altar.

15Then Aaron brought the offering that was for the people. He took the goat of the people's sin offering and killed it and offered it for the sin offering, just as he had done the first sin offering.

16Then Aaron brought the whole burnt offering and offered it in the way that the LORD had commanded. 17He also brought the grain offering to the altar. He took a handful of the grain and burned it on the altar, in addition to the morning's burnt offering.

18Aaron also killed the bull and the male sheep as the fellowship offerings for the people. His sons brought him the blood, and he sprinkled it on all sides of the altar. 19Aaron's sons also brought to Aaron the fat of the bull and the male sheep—the fat tail, the fat covering the inner organs, the kidneys, and the best part of the liver. 20Aaron's sons put them on the breasts of the bull and the sheep. Then Aaron burned these fat parts on the altar. 21He presented the breasts and the right thigh before the LORD as the priests' share of the offering, as Moses had commanded.

22Then Aaron lifted his hands toward the people and blessed them. When he had finished offering the sin offering, the burnt offering, and the fellowship offering, he stepped down from the altar.

23Moses and Aaron went into the Meeting Tent. Then they came out and blessed the

people, and the LORD's glory came to all the
people. 24Fire came out from the LORD and
burned up the burnt offering and fat on the
altar. When the people saw this, they
shouted with joy and bowed facedown on
the ground.

God Destroys Nadab and Abihu

10 Aaron's sons Nadab and Abihu took
their pans for burning incense, put
fire in them, and added incense; but they did
not use the special fire Moses had
commanded them to use in the presence of
the LORD. 2So fire came down from the LORD
and destroyed Nadab and Abihu, and they
died in front of the LORD. 3Then Moses said
to Aaron, "This is what the LORD was
speaking about when he said,

'I must be respected as holy
by those who come near me;
before all the people
I must be given honor.' "

So Aaron did not say anything about the
death of his sons.

4Aaron's uncle Uzziel had two sons named
Mishael and Elzaphan. Moses said to them,
"Come here and pick up your cousins'
bodies. Carry them outside the camp away
from the front of the Holy Place." 5So
Mishael and Elzaphan obeyed Moses and
carried the bodies of Nadab and Abihu, still
clothed in the special priest's inner robes,
outside the camp.

6Then Moses said to Aaron and his other
sons, Eleazar and Ithamar, "Don't show
sadness by tearing your clothes or leaving
your hair uncombed. If you do, you will die,
and the LORD will be angry with all the
people. All the people of Israel, your
relatives, may cry loudly about the LORD
burning Nadab and Abihu, 7but you must
not even leave the Meeting Tent. If you go
out of the entrance, you will die, because the
LORD has appointed you to his service." So
Aaron, Eleazar, and Ithamar obeyed Moses.

8Then the LORD said to Aaron, 9"You and
your sons must not drink wine or beer when
you go into the Meeting Tent. If you do, you
will die. This law will continue from now
on. 10You must keep what is holy separate

devotion 33

LEVITICUS 10:1–2

DO YOU THINK HE MEANT IT?

I don't know if you've thought about it lately, but God is serious about his instructions. The consequences for disobedience are a whole lot more severe than a little ruler tap on the hand or some time-out in the corner for bad behavior.

God is the creator, and by virtue of his unparalleled position as almighty and sovereign, he has also decided how his created should behave and interact. When he told the ancient priests to "use the special fire," he meant *use the special fire*. He didn't mean the other fire, not the fire you made yourself, but the very fire God commanded and nothing else.

In the same way, there are some very specific living commandments in Scripture. And God is not kidding. He's not even hinting. He is the creator commanding the created. Don't steal from people. Don't have sex before you're married. Don't lie. Don't align yourself with fools. And that's just the beginning—God has given us so much wisdom that will keep us from the awful consequences of choosing any "fire" we'd like.

Maybe you've been choosing your own fire instead of God's fire. Here's what I know for sure: the consequences of your disobedience are coming. They always do. But some people just won't learn. They keep choosing the other fire over and over, and others just sit back and watch as the years go by and their lives are destroyed.

Hey, I know it sounds simplistic, but the next time God says "special fire," I'd go with that one.

from what is not holy; you must keep what
is clean separate from what is unclean. 11 You
must teach the people all the laws that the
LORD gave to them through Moses."
12 Moses said to Aaron and his remaining
sons, Eleazar and Ithamar, "Eat the part of
the grain offering that is left from the
sacrifices offered by fire to the LORD, but do
not add yeast to it. Eat it near the altar
because it is most holy. 13 You must eat it in a
holy place, because this part of the offerings
made by fire to the LORD belongs to you and
your sons. I have been commanded to tell
you this.
14 "Also, you and your sons and daughters
may eat the breast and thigh of the
fellowship offering that was presented to the
LORD. You must eat them in a clean place;
they are your share of the fellowship
offerings given by the Israelites. 15 The
people must bring the fat from their animals
that was part of the offering made by fire,
and they must present it to the LORD along
with the thigh and the breast of the
fellowship offering. They will be the regular
share of the offerings for you and your
children, as the LORD has commanded."
16 Moses looked for the goat of the sin
offering, but it had already been burned up.
So he became very angry with Eleazar and
Ithamar, Aaron's remaining sons. He said,
17 "Why didn't you eat that goat in a holy
place? It is most holy, and the LORD gave it to
you to take away the guilt of the people, to
remove their sins so they will belong to the
LORD. 18 You didn't bring the goat's blood
inside the Holy Place. You were supposed to
eat the goat in a holy place, as I
commanded!"
19 But Aaron said to Moses, "Today they
brought their sin offering and burnt offering
before the LORD, but these terrible things
have still happened to me! Do you think the
LORD would be any happier if I ate the sin
offering today?" 20 When Moses heard this,
he was satisfied.

Rules About What May Be Eaten

11 The LORD said to Moses and Aaron,
2 "Tell the Israelites this: 'These are the
land animals you may eat: 3 You may eat any
animal that has split hoofs completely
divided and that chews the cud.
4 " 'Some animals only chew the cud or
only have split hoofs, and you must not eat
them. The camel chews the cud but does not
have a split hoof; it is unclean for you. 5 The
rock badger chews the cud but does not have
a split hoof; it is unclean for you. 6 The rabbit
chews the cud but does not have a split hoof;
it is unclean for you. 7 Now the pig has a split
hoof that is completely divided, but it does
not chew the cud; it is unclean for you. 8 You
must not eat the meat from these animals or
even touch their dead bodies; they are
unclean for you.
9 " 'Of the animals that live in the sea or in
a river, if the animal has fins and scales, you
may eat it. 10 But whatever lives in the sea or
in a river and does not have fins and scales—
including the things that fill the water and
all other things that live in it—you should
hate. 11 You must not eat any meat from them
or even touch their dead bodies, because you
should hate them. 12 You must hate any
animal in the water that does not have fins
and scales.
13 " 'Also, these are the birds you are to hate.
They are hateful and should not be eaten.
You must not eat eagles, vultures, black
vultures, 14 kites, any kind of falcon, 15 any
kind of raven, 16 horned owls, screech owls,
sea gulls, any kind of hawk, 17 little owls,
cormorants, great owls, 18 white owls, desert
owls, ospreys, 19 storks, any kind of heron,
hoopoes, or bats.
20 " 'Don't eat insects that have wings and
walk on all four feet; they also are to be
hated.
21 " 'But you may eat certain insects that
have wings and walk on four feet. You may
eat those that have legs with joints above
their feet so they can jump. 22 These are the
insects you may eat: all kinds of locusts,
winged locusts, crickets, and grasshoppers.
23 But all other insects that have wings and
walk on four feet you are to hate. 24 Those
insects will make you unclean, and anyone
who touches the dead body of one of these
insects will become unclean until evening.
25 Anyone who picks up one of these dead
insects must wash his clothes and be
unclean until evening.
26 " 'Some animals have split hoofs, but the
hoofs are not completely divided; others do
not chew the cud. They are unclean for you,
and anyone who touches the dead body of
one of these animals will become unclean.

27Of all the animals that walk on four feet,
the animals that walk on their paws are
unclean for you. Anyone who touches the
dead body of one of these animals will
become unclean until evening. 28Anyone
who picks up their dead bodies must wash
his clothes and be unclean until evening;
these animals are unclean for you.

29" 'These crawling animals are unclean for
you: moles, rats, all kinds of great lizards,
30geckos, crocodiles, lizards, sand reptiles,
and chameleons. 31These crawling animals
are unclean for you; anyone who touches
their dead bodies will be unclean until
evening.

32" 'If an unclean animal dies and falls on
something, that item will also become
unclean. This includes anything made from
wood, cloth, leather, or rough cloth,
regardless of its use. Whatever the animal
falls on must be washed with water and be
unclean until evening; then it will become
clean again. 33If the dead, unclean animal
falls into a clay bowl, anything in the bowl
will become unclean, and you must break
the bowl. 34If water from the unclean clay
bowl gets on any food, that food will become
unclean. 35If any dead, unclean animal falls
on something, it becomes unclean. If it is a
clay oven or a clay baking pan, it must be
broken into pieces. These things will be
unclean; they are unclean for you.

36" 'A spring or well that collects water
will stay clean, but anyone who touches
the dead body of any unclean animal will
become unclean. 37If a dead, unclean
animal falls on a seed to be planted, that
seed is still clean. 38But if you put water on
some seeds and a dead, unclean animal
falls on them, they are unclean for you.

39" 'Also, if an animal which you use for
food dies, anyone who touches its body will
be unclean until evening. 40Anyone who eats
meat from this animal's dead body must
wash his clothes and be unclean until
evening. Anyone who picks up the animal's
dead body must wash his clothes and be
unclean until evening.

41" 'Every animal that crawls on the ground
is to be hated; it must not be eaten. 42You
must not eat any of the animals that crawl on
the ground, including those that crawl on
their stomachs, that walk on all four feet, or
on many feet. They are to be hated. 43Do not
make yourself unclean by these animals; you
must not become unclean by them. 44I am
the LORD your God. Keep yourselves holy for
me because I am holy. Don't make yourselves
unclean with any of these crawling animals.
45I am the LORD who brought you out of
Egypt to be your God; you must be holy
because I am holy.

46" 'These are the teachings about all of
the cattle, birds, and other animals on earth,
as well as the animals in the sea and those
that crawl on the ground. 47These teachings
help people know the difference between
unclean animals and clean animals; they
help people know which animals may be
eaten and which ones must not be eaten.' "

Rules for New Mothers

12 The LORD said to Moses, 2"Tell the
people of Israel this: 'If a woman gives
birth to a son, she will become unclean for
seven days, as she is unclean during her
monthly period. 3On the eighth day the boy
must be circumcised. 4Then it will be thirty-
three days before she becomes clean from
her loss of blood. She must not touch
anything that is holy or enter the Holy Tent
until her time of cleansing is finished. 5But if
she gives birth to a daughter, the mother
will be unclean for two weeks, as she is
unclean during her monthly period. It will
be sixty-six days before she becomes clean
from her loss of blood.

6" 'After she has a son or daughter and her
days of cleansing are over, the new mother
must bring certain sacrifices to the Meeting
Tent. She must give the priest at the
entrance a year-old lamb for a burnt offering
and a dove or young pigeon for a sin
offering. 7He will offer them before the LORD
to make her clean so she will belong to the
LORD again; then she will be clean from her
loss of blood. These are the teachings for a
woman who gives birth to a boy or girl.

8" 'If she cannot afford a lamb, she is to
bring two doves or two young pigeons, one
for a burnt offering and one for a sin
offering. In this way the priest will make her
clean so she will belong to the LORD again,
and she will be clean.' "

Rules About Skin Diseases

13 The LORD said to Moses and Aaron,
2"Someone might have on his skin a

swelling or a rash or a bright spot. If the sore looks like a harmful skin disease, the person must be brought to Aaron the priest or to one of Aaron's sons, the priests. 3The priest must look at the sore on the person's skin. If the hair in the sore has become white, and the sore seems deeper than the person's skin, it is a harmful skin disease. When he has finished looking at the person, the priest must announce that the person is unclean.

4"If there is a white spot on a person's skin, but the spot does not seem deeper than the skin, and if the hair from the spot has not turned white, the priest must separate that person from other people for seven days. 5On the seventh day the priest must look at the person again. If he sees that the sore has not changed and it has not spread on the skin, the priest must keep the person separated for seven more days. 6On the seventh day the priest must look at the person again. If the sore has faded and has not spread on the skin, the priest must announce that the person is clean. The sore is only a rash. The person must wash his clothes, and he will become clean again.

7"But if the rash spreads again after the priest has announced him clean, the person must come again to the priest. 8The priest must look at him, and if the rash has spread on the skin, the priest must announce that the person is unclean; it is a harmful skin disease.

9"If a person has a harmful skin disease, he must be brought to the priest, 10and the priest must look at him. If there is a white swelling in the skin, and the hair has become white, and the skin looks raw in the swelling, 11it is a harmful skin disease. It is one he has had for a long time. The priest must announce that the person is unclean. He will not need to separate that person from other people, because everyone already knows that the person is unclean.

12"If the skin disease spreads all over a person's body, covering his skin from his head to his feet, as far as the priest can see, the priest must look at the person's whole body. 13If the priest sees that the disease covers the whole body and has turned all of the person's skin white, he must announce that the person is clean.

14"But when the person has an open sore, he is unclean. 15When the priest sees the open sore, he must announce that the person is unclean. The open sore is not clean; it is a harmful skin disease. 16If the open sore becomes white again, the person must come to the priest. 17The priest must look at him, and if the sores have become white, the priest must announce that the person with the sores is clean. Then he will be clean.

18"Someone may have a boil on his skin that is healed. 19If in the place where the boil was, there is a white swelling or a bright red spot, this place on the skin must be shown to the priest. 20And the priest must look at it. If the spot seems deeper than the skin and the hair on it has become white, the priest must announce that the person is unclean. The spot is a harmful skin disease that has broken out from inside the boil. 21But if the priest looks at the spot and there are no white hairs in it and the spot is not deeper than the skin and it has faded, the priest must separate the person from other people for seven days. 22If the spot spreads on the skin, the priest must announce that the person is unclean; it is a disease that will spread. 23But if the bright spot does not spread or change, it is only the scar from the old boil. Then the priest must announce that the person is clean.

24"When a person gets a burn on his skin, if the open sore becomes white or red, 25the priest must look at it. If the white spot seems deeper than the skin and the hair at that spot has become white, it is a harmful skin disease. The disease has broken out in the burn, and the priest must announce that the person is unclean. It is a harmful skin disease. 26But if the priest looks at the spot and there is no white hair in the bright spot, and the spot is no deeper than the skin and has faded, the priest must separate the person from other people for seven days. 27On the seventh day the priest must look at him again. If the spot has spread on the skin, the priest must announce that the person is unclean. It is a harmful skin disease. 28But if the bright spot has not spread on the skin but has faded, it is the swelling from the burn. The priest must announce that the person is clean, because the spot is only a scar from the burn.

29"When a man or a woman gets a sore on the scalp or on the chin, 30a priest must look

at the sore. If it seems deeper than the skin
and the hair around it is thin and yellow, the
priest must announce that the person is
unclean. It is an itch, a harmful skin disease
of the head or chin. 31But if the priest looks
at it and it does not seem deeper than the
skin and there is no black hair in it, the
priest must separate the person from other
people for seven days. 32On the seventh day
the priest must look at the sore. If it has not
spread, and there are no yellow hairs
growing in it, and the sore does not seem
deeper than the skin, 33the person must
shave himself, but he must not shave the
sore place. The priest must separate that
person from other people for seven more
days. 34On the seventh day the priest must
look at the sore. If it has not spread on the
skin and it does not seem deeper than the
skin, the priest must announce that the
person is clean. So the person must wash his
clothes and become clean. 35But if the sore
spreads on the skin after the person has
become clean, 36the priest must look at him
again. If the sore has spread on the skin, the
priest doesn't need to look for the yellowish
hair; the person is unclean. 37But if the priest
thinks the sore has stopped spreading, and
black hair is growing in it, the sore has
healed. The person is clean, and the priest
must announce that he is clean.

38"When a man or a woman has white
spots on the skin, 39a priest must look at
them. If the spots on the skin are dull white,
the disease is only a harmless rash. That
person is clean.

40"When anyone loses hair from his head
and is bald, he is clean. 41If he loses hair from
the front of his head and has a bald forehead,
he is clean. 42But if there is a red-white sore
on his bald head or forehead, it is a skin
disease breaking out in those places. 43A
priest must look at that person. If the
swelling of the sore on his bald head or
forehead is red-white, like a skin disease that
spreads, 44that person has a skin disease. He
is unclean. The priest must announce that
the person is unclean because of the sore on
his head.

45"If a person has a skin disease that
spreads, he must warn other people by
shouting, 'Unclean, unclean!' His clothes
must be torn at the seams, he must let his
hair stay uncombed, and he must cover his
mouth. 46That person will be unclean the
whole time he has the disease; he is
unclean. He must live alone outside the
camp.

Rules About Mildew

47"Clothing might have mildew on it. It
might be clothing made of linen or wool
48(either woven or knitted), or of leather, or
something made from leather. 49If the
mildew in the clothing, leather, or woven or
knitted material is green or red, it is a
spreading mildew. It must be shown to the
priest. 50The priest must look at the mildew,
and he must put that piece of clothing in a
separate place for seven days. 51On the
seventh day he must look at the mildew
again. If the mildew has spread on the cloth
(either woven or knitted) or the leather, no
matter what the leather was used for, it is a
mildew that destroys; it is unclean. 52The
priest must burn the clothing. It does not
matter if it is woven or knitted, wool or
linen, or made of leather, because the
mildew is spreading. It must be burned.

53"If the priest sees that the mildew has
not spread in the cloth (either knitted or
woven) or leather, 54he must order the
people to wash that piece of leather or
cloth. Then he must separate the clothing
for seven more days. 55After the piece with
the mildew has been washed, the priest
must look at it again. If the mildew still
looks the same, the piece is unclean, even
if the mildew has not spread. You must
burn it in fire; it does not matter if the
mildew is on one side or the other.

56"But when the priest looks at that piece
of leather or cloth, the mildew might have
faded after the piece has been washed. Then
the priest must tear the mildew out of the
piece of leather or cloth (either woven or
knitted). 57But if the mildew comes back to
that piece of leather or cloth (either woven
or knitted), the mildew is spreading. And
whatever has the mildew must be burned
with fire. 58When the cloth (either woven or
knitted) or the leather is washed and the
mildew is gone, it must be washed again;
then it will be clean.

59"These are the teachings about mildew
on pieces of cloth (either woven or knitted)
or leather, to decide if they are clean or
unclean."

devotion 34

LEVITICUS 13:58

THE CHAMBERS OF YOUR HEART

How does the Levitical law describe the process of washing something clean? You wash it until the stain has disappeared, and then you wash it a second time. While laundry is not my favorite chore, the concept of washing something twice is very real to me since most of my laundry runs through the washer at least that many times. Why? Simply because I forgot it was in there in the first place! At times our hearts can be like a washing machine full of all sorts of things that need to be cleaned, and yes, sometimes twice.

As women, God has given us amazing hearts. Our hearts have many chambers: love, compassion, sexiness, nurture, wisdom, and even bravery. The chamber that causes us the most internal struggle is the one where we hide our sin—not from the Father (for he knows our hearts), but from the world. We try to put up a perfect front, and it is this part of the heart and the things that we hold onto that we must allow the Lord to wash away—our sin and hurts.

Your sin is washed in the blood of the Lamb. What does that mean? If there is a place in your heart where you are still hiding sin, go to the Lord now and ask him to wash you clean. Enjoy a holy washing in the secret chambers that only you and the Lord know about, and ask the Holy Spirit to minister his truth to your heart.

Rules for Cleansing from Skin Diseases

14 The LORD said to Moses, 2"These are
the teachings for the time at which
people who had a harmful skin disease are
made clean.

"The person shall be brought to the priest,
3and the priest must go outside the camp
and look at the one who had the skin
disease. If the skin disease is healed, 4the
priest will command that two living, clean
birds, a piece of cedar wood, a piece of red
string, and a hyssop plant be brought for
cleansing the person with the skin disease.

5"The priest must order one bird to be
killed in a clay bowl containing fresh water.
6Then he will take the living bird, the piece
of cedar wood, the red string, and the hyssop;
all these he will dip into the blood of the
bird that was killed over the fresh water.
7The priest will sprinkle the blood seven
times on the person being cleansed from the
skin disease. He must announce that the
person is clean and then go to an open field
and let the living bird go free.

8"The person to be cleansed must wash his
clothes, shave off all his hair, and bathe in
water. Then he will be clean and may go into
the camp, though he must stay outside his
tent for the first seven days. 9On the seventh
day he must shave off all his hair—the hair
from his head, his beard, his eyebrows, and
the rest of his hair. He must wash his clothes
and bathe his body in water, and he will be
clean.

10"On the eighth day the person who had
the skin disease must take two male lambs
that have nothing wrong with them and a
year-old female lamb that has nothing
wrong with it. He must also take six quarts
of fine flour mixed with oil for a grain
offering and two-thirds of a pint of olive oil.
11The priest who is to announce that the
person is clean must bring him and his
sacrifices before the LORD at the entrance of
the Meeting Tent. 12The priest will take one
of the male lambs and offer it with the olive
oil as a penalty offering; he will present
them before the LORD as an offering. 13Then

he will kill the male lamb in the holy place,
where the sin offering and the whole burnt
offering are killed. The penalty offering is
like the sin offering—it belongs to the priest
and it is most holy.
14"The priest will take some of the blood
of the penalty offering and put it on the
bottom of the right ear of the person to be
made clean. He will also put some of it on
the thumb of the person's right hand and on
the big toe of the person's right foot. 15Then
the priest will take some of the oil and pour
it into his own left hand. 16He will dip a
finger of his right hand into the oil that is in
his left hand, and with his finger he will
sprinkle some of the oil seven times before
the LORD. 17The priest will put some oil from
his hand on the bottom of the right ear of
the person to be made clean, some on the
thumb of the person's right hand, and some
on the big toe of the person's right foot. The
oil will go on these places on top of the
blood for the penalty offering. 18He will put
the rest of the oil that is in his left hand on
the head of the person to be made clean. In
this way the priest will make that person
clean so he can belong to the LORD again.
19"Next the priest will offer the sin
offering to make that person clean so he can
belong to the LORD again. After this the
priest will kill the animal for the whole
burnt offering, 20and he will offer the burnt
offering and grain offering on the altar. In
this way he will make that person clean so
he can belong to the LORD again.
21"But if the person is poor and unable to
afford these offerings, he must take one male
lamb for a penalty offering. It will be
presented to the LORD to make him clean so
he can belong to the LORD again. The person
must also take two quarts of fine flour mixed
with oil for a grain offering. He must also
take two-thirds of a pint of olive oil 22and
two doves or two young pigeons, which he
can afford. One bird is for a sin offering and
the other for a whole burnt offering. 23On
the eighth day the person will bring them
for his cleansing to the priest at the entrance
of the Meeting Tent, before the LORD. 24The
priest will take the lamb for the penalty
offering and the oil, and he will present
them as an offering before the LORD. 25Then
he will kill the lamb of the penalty offering,
take some of its blood, and put it on the
bottom of the right ear of the person to be
made clean. The priest will put some of this
blood on the thumb of the person's right
hand and some on the big toe of the person's
right foot. 26He will also pour some of the oil
into his own left hand. 27Then with a finger
of his right hand, he will sprinkle some of
the oil from his left hand seven times before
the LORD. 28The priest will take some of the
oil from his hand and put it on the bottom of
the right ear of the person to be made clean.
He will also put some of it on the thumb of
the person's right hand and some on the big
toe of the person's right foot. The oil will go
on these places on top of the blood from the
penalty offering. 29The priest must put the
rest of the oil that is in his hand on the head
of the person to be made clean, to make him
clean so he can belong to the LORD again.
30Then the priest will offer one of the doves
or young pigeons, which the person can
afford. 31He must offer one of the birds for a
sin offering and the other for a whole burnt
offering, along with the grain offering. In
this way the priest will make the person
clean so he can belong to the LORD again; he
will become clean.
32"These are the teachings for making a
person clean after he has had a skin disease,
if he cannot afford the regular sacrifices for
becoming clean."

Rules for Cleaning Mildew

33The LORD also said to Moses and Aaron,
34"I am giving the land of Canaan to your
people. When they enter that land, if I cause
mildew to grow in someone's house in that
land, 35the owner of that house must come
and tell the priest. He should say, 'I have seen
something like mildew in my house.' 36Then
the priest must order the people to empty
the house before he goes in to look at the
mildew. This is so he will not have to say
that everything in the house is unclean.
After this, the priest will go in to look at it.
37He will look at the mildew, and if the
mildew on the walls of the house is green or
red and goes into the wall's surface, 38he
must go out and close up the house for seven
days. 39On the seventh day the priest must
come back and check the house. If the
mildew has spread on the walls of the house,
40the priest must order the people to tear out

the stones with the mildew on them. They
should throw them away, at a certain
unclean place outside the city. 41 Then the
priest must have all the inside of the house
scraped. The people must throw away the
plaster they scraped off the walls, at a certain
unclean place outside the city. 42 Then the
owner must put new stones in the walls, and
he must cover the walls with new clay
plaster.

43 "Suppose a person has taken away the
old stones and plaster and put in new stones
and plaster. If mildew again appears in his
house, 44 the priest must come back and
check the house again. If the mildew has
spread in the house, it is a mildew that
destroys things; the house is unclean. 45 Then
the owner must tear down the house,
remove all its stones, plaster, and wood, and
take them to the unclean place outside the
city. 46 Anyone who goes into that house
while it is closed up will be unclean until
evening. 47 Anyone who eats in that house or
lies down there must wash his clothes.

48 "Suppose after new stones and plaster
have been put in a house, the priest checks it
again and the mildew has not spread. Then
the priest will announce that the house is
clean, because the mildew is gone.

49 "Then, to make the house clean, the
priest must take two birds, a piece of cedar
wood, a piece of red string, and a hyssop
plant. 50 He will kill one bird in a clay bowl
containing fresh water. 51 Then he will take
the bird that is still alive, the cedar wood,
the hyssop, and the red string, and he will
dip them into the blood of the bird that was
killed over the fresh water. The priest will
sprinkle the blood on the house seven times.
52 He will use the bird's blood, the fresh
water, the live bird, the cedar wood, the
hyssop, and the red string to make the house
clean. 53 He will then go to an open field
outside the city and let the living bird go
free. This is how the priest makes the house
clean and ready for service to the LORD."

54 These are the teachings about any kind
of skin disease, 55 mildew on pieces of cloth
or in a house, 56 swellings, rashes, or bright
spots on the skin; 57 they help people decide
when things are unclean and when they are
clean. These are the teachings about all these
kinds of diseases.

Rules About a Person's Body

15 The LORD also said to Moses and
Aaron, 2 "Say to the people of Israel:
'When a fluid comes from a person's body,
the fluid is unclean. 3 It doesn't matter if the
fluid flows freely or if it is blocked from
flowing; the fluid will make him unclean.
This is the way the fluid makes him unclean:

4 " 'If the person who discharges the body
fluid lies on a bed, that bed becomes
unclean, and everything he sits on becomes
unclean. 5 Anyone who touches his bed must
wash his clothes and bathe in water, and the
person will be unclean until evening.
6 Whoever sits on something that the person
who discharges the fluid sat on must wash
his clothes and bathe in water; he will be
unclean until evening. 7 Anyone who
touches the person who discharges the body
fluid must wash his clothes and bathe in
water; he will be unclean until evening.

8 " 'If the person who discharges the body
fluid spits on someone who is clean, that
person must wash his clothes and bathe in
water; he will be unclean until evening.
9 Everything on which the person who is
unclean sits when riding will become
unclean. 10 Anyone who touches something
that was under him will be unclean until
evening. And anyone who carries these
things must wash his clothes and bathe in
water; he will be unclean until evening.

11 " 'If the person who discharges a body
fluid has not washed his hands in water and
touches another person, that person must
wash his clothes and bathe in water; he will
be unclean until evening.

12 " 'If a person who discharges a body
fluid touches a clay bowl, that bowl must be
broken. If he touches a wooden bowl, that
bowl must be washed in water.

13 " 'When a person who discharges a body
fluid is made clean, he must count seven
days for himself for his cleansing. He must
wash his clothes and bathe his body in fresh
water, and he will be clean. 14 On the eighth
day he must take two doves or two young
pigeons before the LORD at the entrance of
the Meeting Tent. He will give the two birds
to the priest. 15 The priest will offer the birds,
one for a sin offering and the other for a burnt
offering. And the priest will make that person
clean so he can belong to the LORD again.

16“ ‘If semen[n] goes out from a man, he
must bathe in water; he will be unclean
until evening. 17If the fluid gets on any
clothing or leather, it must be washed with
water; it will be unclean until evening.
18“ ‘If a man has sexual relations with a
woman and semen comes out, both people
must bathe in water; they will be unclean
until evening.

Rules About a Woman's Body

19“ ‘When a woman has her monthly
period, she is unclean for seven days; anyone
who touches her will be unclean until
evening. 20Anything she lies on during this
time will be unclean, and everything she sits
on during this time will be unclean.
21Anyone who touches her bed must wash
his clothes and bathe in water; that person
will be unclean until evening. 22Anyone who
touches something she has sat on must wash
his clothes and bathe in water; that person
will be unclean until evening. 23It does not
matter if the person touched the woman's
bed or something she sat on; he will be
unclean until evening.
24“ ‘If a man has sexual relations with a
woman and her monthly period touches
him, he will be unclean for seven days; every
bed he lies on will be unclean.
25“ ‘If a woman has a loss of blood for
many days and it is not during her regular
monthly period, or if she continues to have a
loss of blood after her regular period, she
will be unclean, as she is during her
monthly period. She will be unclean for as
long as she continues to bleed. 26Any bed she
lies on during all the time of her bleeding
will be like her bed during her regular
monthly period. Everything she sits on will
be unclean, as during her regular monthly
period.
27“ ‘Whoever touches those things will be
unclean and must wash his clothes and
bathe in water; he will be unclean until
evening. 28When the woman becomes clean
from her bleeding, she must wait seven days,
and after this she will be clean. 29Then on
the eighth day she must take two doves or
two young pigeons and bring them to the
priest at the entrance of the Meeting Tent.
30The priest must offer one bird for a sin
offering and the other for a whole burnt
offering. In this way the priest will make her
clean so she can belong to the LORD again.
31“ ‘So you must warn the people of Israel
to stay separated from things that make
them unclean. If you don't warn the people,
they might make my Holy Tent unclean, and
then they would have to die!’ ”
32These are the teachings for the person
who discharges a body fluid and for the man
who becomes unclean from semen[n] coming
out of his body. 33These are the teachings for
the woman who becomes unclean from her
monthly period, for a man or woman who
has a discharge, and for a man who becomes
unclean by having sexual relations with a
woman who is unclean.

The Day of Cleansing

16 Now two of Aaron's sons had died
while offering incense to the LORD, and
after that time the LORD spoke to Moses. 2The
LORD said to him, “Tell your brother Aaron
that there are times when he cannot go
behind the curtain into the Most Holy Place
where the Ark is. If he goes in when I appear
in a cloud over the lid on the Ark, he will die.
3“This is how Aaron may enter the Most
Holy Place: Before he enters, he must offer a
bull for a sin offering and a male sheep for a
whole burnt offering. 4He must put on the
holy linen inner robe, with the linen
underclothes next to his body. His belt will
be the cloth belt, and he will wear the linen
turban. These are holy clothes, so he must
bathe his body in water before he puts
them on.
5“Aaron must take from the people of
Israel two male goats for a sin offering and
one male sheep for a burnt offering. 6Then
he will offer the bull for the sin offering for
himself to remove sins from him and his
family so they will belong to the LORD.
7“Next Aaron will take the two goats and
bring them before the LORD at the entrance
to the Meeting Tent. 8He will throw lots for
the two goats—one will be for the LORD and
the other for the goat that removes sin.
9Then Aaron will take the goat that was
chosen for the LORD by throwing the lot, and
he will offer it as a sin offering. 10The other
goat, which was chosen by lot to remove the

15:16, 32 semen A man's body fluid by which he can make a woman pregnant.

sin, must be brought alive before the LORD. The priest will use it to perform the acts that remove Israel's sin so they will belong to the LORD. Then this goat will be sent out into the desert as a goat that removes sin.

11"Then Aaron will offer the bull as a sin offering for himself, to remove the sins from him and his family so they will belong to the LORD; he will kill the bull for the sin offering for himself. 12Then he must take a pan full of burning coals from the altar before the LORD and two handfuls of sweet incense that has been ground into powder. He must bring it into the room behind the curtain. 13He must put the incense on the fire before the LORD so that the cloud of incense will cover the lid on the Ark. Then when Aaron comes in, he will not die. 14Also, he must take some of the blood from the bull and sprinkle it with his finger on the front of the lid; with his finger he will sprinkle the blood seven times in front of the lid.

15"Then Aaron must kill the goat of the sin offering for the people and bring its blood into the room behind the curtain. He must do with the goat's blood as he did with the bull's blood, sprinkling it on the lid and in front of the lid. 16Because the people of Israel have been unclean, Aaron will perform the acts to make the Most Holy Place ready for service to the LORD. Then it will be clean from the sins and crimes of the Israelites. He must also do this for the Meeting Tent, because it stays in the middle of unclean people. 17When Aaron makes the Most Holy Place ready for service to the LORD, no one is allowed in the Meeting Tent until he comes out. So Aaron will perform the acts to remove sins from himself, his family, and all the people of Israel, so they will belong to the LORD. 18Afterward he will go out to the altar that is before the LORD and will make it ready for service to the LORD. Aaron will take some of the bull's blood and some of the goat's blood and put it on the corners of the altar on all sides. 19Then, with his finger, he will sprinkle some of the blood on the altar seven times to make the altar holy for the LORD and clean from all the sins of the Israelites.

20"When Aaron has finished making the Most Holy Place, the Meeting Tent, and the altar ready for service to the LORD, he will offer the living goat. 21He will put both his hands on the head of the living goat, and he will confess over it all the sins and crimes of Israel. In this way Aaron will put the people's sins on the goat's head. Then he will send the goat away into the desert, and a man who has been appointed will lead the goat away. 22So the goat will carry on itself all the people's sins to a lonely place in the desert. The man who leads the goat will let it loose there.

23"Then Aaron will enter the Meeting Tent and take off the linen clothes he had put on before he went into the Most Holy Place; he must leave these clothes there. 24He will bathe his body in water in a holy place and put on his regular clothes. Then he will come out and offer the whole burnt offering for himself and for the people, to remove sins from himself and the people so they will belong to the LORD. 25Then he will burn the fat of the sin offering on the altar.

26"The person who led the goat, the goat to remove sins, into the desert must wash his clothes and bathe his body in water. After that, he may come back into the camp.

27"The bull and the goat for the sin offerings, whose blood was brought into the Most Holy Place to make it ready for service to the LORD, must be taken outside the camp; the animals' skins, bodies, and intestines will be burned in the fire. 28Then the one who burns them must wash his clothes and bathe his body in water. After that, he may come back into the camp.

29"This law will always continue for you: On the tenth day of the seventh month, you must deny yourself and you must not do any work. The travelers or foreigners living with you must not work either. 30It is on this day that the priests will make you clean so you will belong to the LORD again. All your sins will be removed. 31This is a very important day of rest for you, and you must deny yourselves. This law will continue forever.

32"The priest appointed to take his father's place, on whom the oil was poured, will perform the acts for making things ready for service to the LORD. He must put on the holy linen clothes 33and make the Most Holy Place, the Meeting Tent, and the altar ready for service to the LORD. He must also remove the sins of the priests and all the people of Israel so they will belong to the LORD. 34That

law for removing the sins of the Israelites so
they will belong to the LORD will continue
forever. You will do these things once a year."
So they did the things the LORD had
commanded Moses.

Offering Sacrifices

17 The LORD said to Moses, 2"Speak to
Aaron, his sons, and all the people of
Israel. Tell them: 'This is what the LORD has
commanded. 3If an Israelite kills an ox, a
lamb, or a goat either inside the camp or
outside it, 4when he should have brought
the animal to the entrance of the Meeting
Tent as a gift to the LORD in front of the
LORD's Holy Tent, he is guilty of killing. He
has killed, and he must be cut off from the
people. 5This rule is so people will bring
their sacrifices, which they have been
sacrificing in the open fields, to the LORD.
They must bring those animals to the LORD
at the entrance of the Meeting Tent; they
must bring them to the priest and offer them
as fellowship offerings. 6Then the priest will
sprinkle the blood from those animals on
the LORD's altar near the entrance of the
Meeting Tent. And he will burn the fat from
those animals on the altar, as a smell
pleasing to the LORD. 7They must not offer
any more sacrifices to their goat idols, which
they have chased like prostitutes. These
rules will continue for people from now on.'
8"Tell the people this: 'If any citizen of
Israel or foreigner living with you offers a
burnt offering or sacrifice, 9that person must
take his sacrifice to the entrance of the
Meeting Tent to offer it to the LORD. If he
does not do this, he must be cut off from the
people.
10" 'I will be against any citizen of Israel or
foreigner living with you who eats blood. I
will cut off that person from the people.
11This is because the life of the body is in the
blood, and I have given you rules for pouring
that blood on the altar to remove your sins
so you will belong to the LORD. It is the blood
that removes the sins, because it is life. 12So I
tell the people of Israel this: "None of you
may eat blood, and no foreigner living
among you may eat blood."
13" 'If any citizen of Israel or foreigner
living among you catches a wild animal or

devotion 35

LEVITICUS 17:11

LET'S TALK ABOUT LIFE

Life is precious to God. He breathed life into man when he created him. He gave eternal life to man when he saved him. John 10:10 tells us that Jesus came into the world to give us "life in all its fullness." Sin brings death, which is the opposite of life. God never intended man to experience sin or death, but he did give man a free will and man chose sin. God was not willing to leave man in his sin. He had a plan to save man and give him back eternal life, but in order to do that, one life had to be sacrificed for the payment of sin.

Enter the Son of God. He was the one person who lived on earth without sin. His blood was pure, perfect, and undefiled. God sent his Son, Jesus, to earth to be the perfect sacrifice to redeem all mankind. 1 John 1:7 says, "Then the blood of Jesus, God's Son, cleanses us from every sin." The shedding of Jesus' blood is what provides forgiveness and eternal life.

Life is precious. The thing we often miss is that our eternal life starts now. God has saved you for a reason. He has a purpose for your life. Someday we will live with God in heaven, but today we have work to do on earth. Ask yourself if you are accomplishing the purpose God has given you. If your answer is no, then ask God to show you how to change that.

bird that can be eaten, that person must
pour the blood on the ground and cover it
with dirt. 14If blood is still in the meat, the
animal's life is still in it. So I give this
command to the people of Israel: "Don't eat
meat that still has blood in it, because the
animal's life is in its blood. Anyone who eats
blood must be cut off."
15" 'If a person, either a citizen or a
foreigner, eats an animal that died by itself
or was killed by another animal, he must
wash his clothes and bathe in water. He will
be unclean until evening; then he will be
clean. 16If he does not wash his clothes and
bathe his body, he will be guilty of sin.' "

Rules About Sexual Relations

18 The LORD said to Moses, 2"Tell the
people of Israel: 'I am the LORD your
God. 3In the past you lived in Egypt, but you
must not do what was done in that country.
And you must not do as they do in the land
of Canaan, where I am bringing you. Do not
follow their customs. 4You must obey my
rules and follow them. I am the LORD your
God. 5Obey my laws and rules; a person who
obeys them will live because of them. I am
the LORD.
6" 'You must never have sexual relations
with your close relatives. I am the LORD.
7" 'You must not shame your father by
having sexual relations with your mother.
She is your mother; do not have sexual
relations with her. 8You must not have
sexual relations with your father's wife; that
would shame your father.
9" 'You must not have sexual relations
with your sister, either the daughter of your
father or your mother. It doesn't matter if she
was born in your house or somewhere else.
10" 'You must not have sexual relations
with your son's daughter or your daughter's
daughter; that would bring shame on you.
11" 'If your father and his wife have a
daughter, she is your sister. You must not
have sexual relations with her.
12" 'You must not have sexual relations
with your father's sister; she is your father's
close relative. 13You must not have sexual
relations with your mother's sister; she is
your mother's close relative. 14You must not
have sexual relations with the wife of your
father's brother, because this would shame
him. She is your aunt.
15" 'You must not have sexual relations
with your daughter-in-law; she is your son's
wife. Do not have sexual relations with her.
16" 'You must not have sexual relations
with your brother's wife. That would shame
your brother.
17" 'You must not have sexual relations
with both a woman and her daughter. And
do not have sexual relations with this
woman's granddaughter, either the daughter
of her son or her daughter; they are her close
relatives. It is evil to do this.
18" 'While your wife is still living, you
must not take her sister as another wife. Do
not have sexual relations with her.
19" 'You must not go near a woman to have
sexual relations with her during her
monthly period, when she is unclean.
20" 'You must not have sexual relations
with your neighbor's wife and make yourself
unclean with her.
21" 'You must not give any of your
children to be sacrificed to Molech, because
this would show that you do not respect
your God. I am the LORD.
22" 'You must not have sexual relations
with a man as you would a woman. That is a
hateful sin.
23" 'You must not have sexual relations
with an animal and make yourself unclean
with it. Also a woman must not have sexual
relations with an animal; it is not natural.
24" 'Don't make yourself unclean by any of
these wrong things. I am forcing nations out
of their countries because they did these
sins, and I am giving their land to you. 25The
land has become unclean, and I punished it
for its sins, so the land is throwing out those
people who live there.
26" 'You must obey my laws and rules, and
you must not do any of these hateful sins.
These rules are for the citizens of Israel and
for the people who live with you. 27The
people who lived in the land before you did
all these hateful things and made the land
unclean. 28If you do these things, you will
also make the land unclean, and it will
throw you out as it threw out the nations
before you. 29Anyone who does these hateful
sins must be cut off from the people. 30Keep
my command not to do these hateful sins
that were done by the people who lived in the
land before you. Don't make yourself unclean
by doing them. I am the LORD your God.' "

Other Laws

19 The LORD said to Moses, 2“Tell all the
people of Israel: ‘I am the LORD your
God. You must be holy because I am holy.
3“ ‘You must respect your mother and
father, and you must keep my Sabbaths. I am
the LORD your God.
4“ ‘Do not worship idols or make statues
of gods for yourselves. I am the LORD your
God.
5“ ‘When you sacrifice a fellowship
offering to the LORD, offer it in such a way
that will be accepted. 6You may eat it the
same day you offer it or on the next day.
But if any is left on the third day, you must
burn it up. 7If any of it is eaten on the
third day, it is unclean, and it will not be
accepted. 8Anyone who eats it then will be
guilty of sin, because he did not respect
the holy things that belong to the LORD. He
must be cut off from the people.
9“ ‘When you harvest your crops on your
land, do not harvest all the way to the
corners of your fields. If grain falls onto the
ground, don't gather it up. 10Don't pick all
the grapes in your vineyards, and don't pick
up the grapes that fall to the ground. You
must leave those things for poor people and
for people traveling through your country. I
am the LORD your God.
11“ ‘You must not steal. You must not cheat
people, and you must not lie to each other.
12You must not make a false promise by my
name, or you will show that you don't
respect your God. I am the LORD.
13“ ‘You must not cheat your neighbor or
rob him. You must not keep a hired worker's
salary all night until morning. 14You must
not curse a deaf person or put something in
front of a blind person to make him fall. But
you must respect your God. I am the LORD.
15“ ‘Be fair in your judging. You must not
show special favor to poor people or great
people, but be fair when you judge your
neighbor. 16You must not spread false
stories against other people, and you must
not do anything that would put your
neighbor's life in danger. I am the LORD.
17“ ‘You must not hate your fellow citizen
in your heart. If your neighbor does
something wrong, tell him about it, or you
will be partly to blame. 18Forget about the
wrong things people do to you, and do not
try to get even. Love your neighbor as you
love yourself. I am the LORD.
19“ ‘Obey my laws. You must not mate two
different kinds of cattle or sow your field
with two different kinds of seed. You must
not wear clothing made from two different
kinds of material mixed together.
20“ ‘If a man has sexual relations with a
slave girl of another man, but this slave girl
has not been bought or given her freedom,
there must be punishment. But they are not
to be put to death, because the woman was
not free. 21The man must bring a male sheep
as his penalty offering to the LORD at the
entrance to the Meeting Tent. 22The priest
will offer the sheep as a penalty offering
before the LORD for the man's sin, to remove
the sins of the man so he will belong to the
LORD. Then he will be forgiven for his sin.
23“ ‘In the future, when you enter your
country, you will plant many kinds of trees
for food. After planting a tree, wait three
years before using its fruit. 24In the fourth
year the fruit from the tree will be the
LORD's, a holy offering of praise to him.
25Then in the fifth year, you may eat the
fruit from the tree. The tree will then
produce more fruit for you. I am the LORD
your God.
26“ ‘You must not eat anything with the
blood in it.
“ ‘You must not try to tell the future by
signs or black magic.
27“ ‘You must not cut the hair on the sides
of your heads or cut the edges of your beard.
28You must not cut your body to show
sadness for someone who died or put tattoo
marks on yourselves. I am the LORD.
29“ ‘Do not dishonor your daughter by
making her become a prostitute. If you do
this, the country will be filled with all kinds
of sin.
30“ ‘Obey the laws about Sabbaths, and
respect my Most Holy Place. I am the LORD.
31“ ‘Do not go to mediums or fortune-
tellers for advice, or you will become
unclean. I am the LORD your God.
32“ ‘Show respect to old people; stand up
in their presence. Show respect also to your
God. I am the LORD.
33“ ‘Do not mistreat foreigners living in
your country, 34but treat them just as you
treat your own citizens. Love foreigners as
you love yourselves, because you were

foreigners one time in Egypt. I am the LORD
your God.
35“ ‘Do not cheat when you measure the
length or weight or amount of something.
36Your weights and balances should weigh
correctly, with your weighing baskets the
right size and your jars holding the right
amount of liquid. I am the LORD your God. I
brought you out of the land of Egypt.
37“ ‘Remember all my laws and rules, and
obey them. I am the LORD.’ ”

Warnings About Various Sins

20 The LORD said to Moses, 2“You must
also tell the people of Israel these
things: ‘If a person in your country gives
one of his children to Molech, that person
must be killed. It doesn’t matter if he is a
citizen or a foreigner living in Israel; you
must throw stones at him and kill him. 3I
will be against him and cut him off from
his people, because he gave his children to
Molech. He showed that he did not respect
my holy name, and he made my Holy Place
unclean. 4The people of the community
might ignore that person and not kill the
one who gave his children to Molech. 5But I
will be against him and his family, and I
will cut him off from his people. I will do
this to anyone who follows him in being
unfaithful to me by worshiping Molech.
6“ ‘I will be against anyone who goes to
mediums and fortune-tellers for advice,
because that person is being unfaithful to
me. So I will cut him off from his people.
7“ ‘Be my holy people. Be holy because I
am the LORD your God. 8Remember and obey
my laws. I am the LORD, and I have made you
holy.
9“ ‘Anyone who curses his father or
mother must be put to death. He has cursed
his father or mother, so he has brought his
own death on himself.

Punishments for Sexual Sins

10“ ‘If a man has sexual relations with his
neighbor’s wife, both the man and the
woman are guilty of adultery and must be

devotion 36

LEVITICUS 20:6

COOKIES FOR THE BUDDHA

I can’t tell you how many times I have heard about Christian women who secretly consult a psychic or a fortune-teller or tarot cards for the answers to their questions and insight for the future. Of course, it’s only occasionally (wink, wink), when they need a backup or aren’t hearing what they want to hear from God.

I realize desperate women do desperate things, but many times we are willing to look everywhere except right into the heart of God for a solution. God is very clear here. To consult a medium or a fortune-teller is to be unfaithful to him. Our God is a jealous God. He wants you to respect that he is the only One with the future in his hands. He is the only source who can give divine direction and guidance. He alone can answer prayers or give comfort to a fretting heart.

I went into a store the other day where the owners obviously turn to a little Buddha statue for direction. I walked past some burning incense and saw that beside the statue were some cookies offered there. A trade-off. Cookies for the Buddha in exchange for some guidance for the day.

That’s what misguided people do. They call 1-900 psychic numbers. They have their palms read. They lay cookies beside a plastic statue. Each one is an act of unfaithfulness to the only God who can answer.

Renew your faithfulness to God. Praise him as Lord of all and the keeper of truth.

put to death. 11If a man has sexual relations
with his father's wife, he has shamed his
father, and both the man and his father's
wife must be put to death. They have
brought it on themselves.
12" 'If a man has sexual relations with his
daughter-in-law, both of them must be put to
death. What they have done is not natural.
They have brought their own deaths on
themselves.
13" 'If a man has sexual relations with
another man as a man does with a woman,
these two men have done a hateful sin. They
must be put to death. They have brought it
on themselves.
14" 'If a man has sexual relations with both
a woman and her mother, this is evil. The
people must burn that man and the two
women in fire so that your people will not
be evil.
15" 'If a man has sexual relations with an
animal, he must be put to death. You must
also kill the animal. 16If a woman approaches
an animal and has sexual relations with it,
you must kill the woman and the animal.
They must be put to death. They have
brought it on themselves.
17" 'It is shameful for a brother to marry
his sister, the daughter of either his father or
his mother, and to have sexual relations
with her. In front of everyone they must
both be cut off from their people. The man
has shamed his sister, and he is guilty of sin.
18" 'If a man has sexual relations with a
woman during her monthly period, both the
woman and the man must be cut off from
their people. They sinned because they
showed the source of her blood.
19" 'Do not have sexual relations with your
mother's sister or your father's sister,
because that would shame a close relative.
Both of you are guilty of this sin.
20" 'If a man has sexual relations with his
uncle's wife, he has shamed his uncle. That
man and his uncle's wife will die without
children; they are guilty of sin.
21" 'It is unclean for a man to marry his
brother's wife. That man has shamed his
brother, and they will have no children.
22" 'Remember all my laws and rules, and
obey them. I am leading you to your own
land, and if you obey my laws and rules, that
land will not throw you out. 23I am forcing
out ahead of you the people who live there.
Because they did all these sins, I have hated
them. Do not live the way those people
lived.
24" 'I have told you that you will get their
land, which I will give to you as your very
own; it is a fertile land. I am the LORD your
God, and I have set you apart from other
people and made you my own. 25So you
must treat clean animals and birds
differently from unclean animals and birds.
Do not make yourselves unclean by any of
these unclean birds or animals or things that
crawl on the ground, which I have made
unclean for you. 26So you must be holy to
me because I, the LORD, am holy, and I have
set you apart from other people to be my
own.
27" 'A man or woman who is a medium or
a fortune-teller must be put to death. You
must stone them to death; they have
brought it on themselves.' "

How Priests Must Behave

21 The LORD said to Moses, "Tell these
things to Aaron's sons, the priests: 'A
priest must not make himself unclean by
touching a dead person. 2But if the dead
person was one of his close relatives, he may
touch him. The priest may make himself
unclean if the dead person is his mother or
father, son or daughter, brother or 3unmarried
sister who is close to him because she has no
husband. The priest may make himself
unclean for her if she dies. 4But a priest must
not make himself unclean if the dead person
was only related to him by marriage.
5" 'Priests must not shave their heads, or
shave off the edges of their beards, or cut
their bodies. 6They must be holy to their
God and show respect for God's name,
because they present the offerings made by
fire to the LORD, which is the food of their
God. So they must be holy.
7" 'A priest must not marry an unclean
prostitute or a divorced woman, because he
is holy to his God. 8Treat him as holy,
because he offers up the food of your God.
Think of him as holy; I am the LORD who
makes you holy, and I am holy.
9" 'If a priest's daughter makes herself
unclean by becoming a prostitute, she
shames her father. She must be burned with
fire.
10" 'The high priest, who was chosen from

among his brothers, had the special olive oil poured on his head. He was also appointed to wear the priestly clothes. So he must not show his sadness by letting his hair go uncombed or tearing his clothes. 11He must not go into a house where there is a dead body. He must not make himself unclean, even if it is for his own father or mother. 12The high priest must not go out of the Holy Place, because if he does and becomes unclean, he will make God's Holy Place unclean. The special oil used in appointing priests was poured on his head to separate him from the rest of the people. I am the LORD.

13" 'The high priest must marry a woman who is a virgin. 14He must not marry a widow, a divorced woman, or a prostitute. He must marry a virgin from his own people 15so the people will respect his children as his own. I am the LORD. I have set the high priest apart for his special job.' "

16The LORD said to Moses, 17"Tell Aaron: 'If any of your descendants have something wrong with them, they must never come near to offer the special food of their God. 18Anyone who has something wrong with him must not come near: blind men, crippled men, men with damaged faces, deformed men, 19men with a crippled foot or hand, 20hunchbacks, dwarfs, men who have something wrong with their eyes, men who have an itching disease or a skin disease, or men who have damaged sex glands.

21" 'If one of Aaron's descendants has something wrong with him, he cannot come near to make the offerings made by fire to the LORD. He has something wrong with him; he cannot offer the food of his God. 22He may eat the most holy food and also the holy food. 23But he may not go through the curtain into the Most Holy Place, and he may not go near the altar, because he has something wrong with him. He must not make my Holy Place unfit. I am the LORD who makes these places holy.' "

24So Moses told these things to Aaron, Aaron's sons, and all the people of Israel.

22 The LORD said to Moses, 2"Tell Aaron and his sons: 'The people of Israel will give offerings to me. These offerings are holy, and they are mine, so you must respect them to show that you respect my holy name. I am the LORD.' 3Say to them: 'If any one of your descendants from now on is unclean and comes near the offerings that the Israelites made holy for me, that person must be cut off from appearing before me. I am the LORD.

4" 'If one of Aaron's descendants has a harmful skin disease, or if he discharges a body fluid, he cannot eat the holy offerings until he becomes clean. He could also become unclean from touching a dead body, from his own semen,[n] 5from touching any unclean crawling animal, or from touching an unclean person (no matter what made the person unclean). 6Anyone who touches those things will become unclean until evening. That person must not eat the holy offerings unless he washes with water. 7He will be clean only after the sun goes down. Then he may eat the holy offerings; the offerings are his food.

8" 'If a priest finds an animal that died by itself or that was killed by some other animal, he must not eat it. If he does, he will become unclean. I am the LORD.

9" 'If the priests keep all the rules I have given, they will not become guilty; if they are careful, they will not die. I am the LORD who has made them holy. 10Only people in a priest's family may eat the holy offering. A visitor staying with the priest or a hired worker must not eat it. 11But if the priest buys a slave with his own money, that slave may eat the holy offerings; slaves who were born in his house may also eat his food. 12If a priest's daughter marries a person who is not a priest, she must not eat any of the holy offerings. 13But if the priest's daughter becomes widowed or divorced, with no children to support her, and if she goes back to her father's house where she lived as a child, she may eat some of her father's food. But only people from a priest's family may eat this food.

14" 'If someone eats some of the holy offering by mistake, that person must pay back the priest for that holy food, adding another one-fifth of the price of that food.

15" 'When the Israelites give their holy offerings to the LORD, the priest must not

22:4 semen A man's body fluid by which he can make a woman pregnant.

treat these holy things as though they were
not holy. 16 The priests must not allow those
who are not priests to eat the holy offerings.
If they do, they cause the ones who eat the
holy offerings to become guilty, and they
will have to pay for it. I am the LORD, who
makes them holy.' "

17 The LORD said to Moses, 18 "Tell Aaron
and his sons and all the people of Israel: 'A
citizen of Israel or a foreigner living in Israel
might want to bring a whole burnt offering,
either for some special promise he has made
or for a special gift he wants to give to the
LORD. 19 If he does, he must bring a male
animal that has nothing wrong with it—a
bull, a sheep, or a goat—so it might be
accepted for him. 20 He must not bring an
animal that has something wrong with it, or
it will not be accepted for him.

21 " 'If someone brings a fellowship
offering to the LORD, either as payment for a
special promise the person has made or as a
special gift the person wants to give the
LORD, it might be from the herd or from the
flock. But it must be healthy, with nothing
wrong with it, so that it will be accepted.
22 You must not offer to the LORD any animal
that is blind, that has broken bones or is
crippled, that has running sores or any sort
of skin disease. You must not offer any
animals like these on the altar as an offering
by fire to the LORD.

23 " 'If an ox or lamb is smaller than
normal or is not perfectly formed, you may
give it as a special gift to the LORD; it will be
accepted. But it will not be accepted as
payment for a special promise you have
made.

24 " 'If an animal has bruised, crushed, torn,
or cut sex glands, you must not offer it to the
LORD. You must not do this in your own land,
25 and you must not take such animals from
foreigners as sacrifices to the LORD. Because
the animals have been hurt in some way and
have something wrong with them, they will
not be accepted for you.' "

26 The LORD said to Moses, 27 "When an ox, a
sheep, or a goat is born, it must stay seven
days with its mother. But from the eighth
day on, this animal will be accepted as a
sacrifice by fire to the LORD. 28 But you must
not kill the animal and its mother on the
same day, either an ox or a sheep.

29 "If you want to offer some special
offering of thanks to the LORD, you must do
it in a way that pleases him. 30 You must eat
the whole animal that same day and not
leave any of the meat for the next morning. I
am the LORD.

31 "Remember my commands and obey
them; I am the LORD. 32 Show respect for my
holy name. You Israelites must remember
that I am holy; I am the LORD, who has made
you holy. 33 I brought you out of Egypt to be
your God. I am the LORD."

Special Holidays

23 The LORD said to Moses, 2 "Tell the
people of Israel: 'You will announce
the LORD's appointed feasts as holy meetings.
These are my special feasts.

The Sabbath

3 " 'There are six days for you to work, but
the seventh day will be a special day of rest.
It is a day for a holy meeting; you must not
do any work. It is a Sabbath to the LORD in all
your homes.

The Passover and Unleavened Bread

4 " 'These are the LORD's appointed feasts,
the holy meetings, which you will announce
at the times set for them. 5 The LORD's
Passover is on the fourteenth day of the first
month, beginning at twilight. 6 The Feast of
Unleavened Bread begins on the fifteenth
day of the same month. You will eat bread
made without yeast for seven days. 7 On the
first day of this feast you will have a holy
meeting, and you must not do any work.
8 For seven days you will bring an offering
made by fire to the LORD. There will be a
holy meeting on the seventh day, and on
that day you must not do any regular
work.' "

The First of the Harvest

9 The LORD said to Moses, 10 "Tell the people
of Israel: 'You will enter the land I will give
you and gather its harvest. At that time you
must bring the first bundle of grain from
your harvest to the priest. 11 The priest will
present the bundle before the LORD, and it
will be accepted for you; he will present the
bundle on the day after the Sabbath.

12 " 'On the day when you present the
bundle of grain, offer a male lamb, one year
old, that has nothing wrong with it, as a

devotion 37

LEVITICUS 22:32

CASUAL DAY?

We live casually these days. We dress down and *kind of* obey the laws and turn our work in a little late just to get by. Many of our professional formalities are gone forever and that's OK. A lot of the old structure in our society is crumbling underneath all the pressures and demands of our day-to-day lives. A carryout dinner instead of a homemade meal can relieve a lot of stress at the end of a crazy day. We've become casual because, in many ways, it makes life easier.

But we cannot become casual about God. God expects us to remember that he is holy and that he has been our deliverer. He is the Lord of heaven and earth. His gracious mercy is the only means by which we will ever be made holy.

What if in this moment, you remembered the holiness of God and prayed something like this: *Father God, you are holy. You are my creator and my protector and my redeemer. I bow my life before you today in reverence for who you are. I worship you in these moments because you have always been holy, and you are without even a shadow of change. I honor you because your holiness is consistent and true and pure. I want to show my respect with my life. Lord, please forgive me. Make me clean. Restore my heart. Give strength to my feebleness. Heal these wounds and make me holy for your glory and your renown. Amen.*

burnt offering to the LORD.
13You must also
offer a grain offering—four quarts of fine
flour mixed with olive oil as an offering
made by fire to the LORD; its smell will be
pleasing to him. You must also offer a quart
of wine as a drink offering.
14Until the day
you bring your offering to your God, do not
eat any new grain, roasted grain, or bread
made from new grain. This law will always
continue for people from now on, wherever
you live.

The Feast of Weeks

15" 'Count seven full weeks from the
morning after the Sabbath. (This is the
Sabbath that you bring the bundle of grain to
present as an offering.)
16On the fiftieth day,
the first day after the seventh week, you will
bring a new grain offering to the LORD.
17On
that day bring two loaves of bread from your
homes to be presented as an offering. Use
yeast and four quarts of flour to make those
loaves of bread; they will be your gift to the
LORD from the first wheat of your harvest.

18" 'Offer with the bread one young bull,
two male sheep, and seven male lambs that
are one year old and have nothing wrong
with them. Offer them with their grain
offerings and drink offerings, as a burnt
offering to the LORD. They will be an offering
made by fire, and the smell will be pleasing
to the LORD.
19You must also offer one male
goat for a sin offering and two male, one-
year-old lambs as a fellowship offering.
20" 'The priest will present the two lambs
as an offering before the LORD, along with
the bread from the first wheat of the harvest.
They are holy to the LORD, and they will
belong to the priest.
21On that same day you
will call a holy meeting; you must not do
any work that day. This law will continue for
you from now on, wherever you live.
22" 'When you harvest your crops on your
land, do not harvest all the way to the
corners of your field. If grain falls onto the
ground, don't gather it up. Leave it for poor
people and foreigners in your country. I am
the LORD your God.' "

The Feast of Trumpets

23Again the LORD said to Moses, 24"Tell the people of Israel: 'On the first day of the seventh month you must have a special day of rest, a holy meeting, when you blow the trumpet for a special time of remembering. 25Do not do any work, and bring an offering made by fire to the LORD.' "

The Day of Cleansing

26The LORD said to Moses, 27"The Day of Cleansing will be on the tenth day of the seventh month. There will be a holy meeting, and you will deny yourselves and bring an offering made by fire to the LORD. 28Do not do any work on that day, because it is the Day of Cleansing. On that day the priests will go before the LORD and perform the acts to make you clean from sin so you will belong to the LORD.

29"Anyone who refuses to give up food on this day must be cut off from the people. 30If anyone works on this day, I will destroy that person from among the people. 31You must not do any work at all; this law will continue for people from now on wherever you live. 32It will be a special day of rest for you, and you must deny yourselves. You will start this special day of rest on the evening after the ninth day of the month, and it will continue from that evening until the next evening."

The Feast of Shelters

33Again the LORD said to Moses, 34"Tell the people of Israel: 'On the fifteenth day of the seventh month is the Feast of Shelters. This feast to the LORD will continue for seven days. 35There will be a holy meeting on the first day; do not do any work. 36You will bring an offering made by fire to the LORD each day for seven days. On the eighth day you will have another holy meeting, and you will bring an offering made by fire to the LORD. This will be a holy meeting; do not do any work.

37(" 'These are the LORD's special feasts, when there will be holy meetings and when you bring offerings made by fire to the LORD. You will bring whole burnt offerings, grain offerings, sacrifices, and drink offerings—each at the right time. 38These offerings are in addition to those for the LORD's Sabbath days, in addition to offerings you give as payment for special promises, and in addition to special offerings you want to give to the LORD.)

39" 'So on the fifteenth day of the seventh month, after you have gathered in the crops of the land, celebrate the LORD's festival for seven days. You must rest on the first day and the eighth day. 40On the first day you will take good fruit from the fruit trees, as well as branches from palm trees, poplars, and other leafy trees. You will celebrate before the LORD your God for seven days. 41Celebrate this festival to the LORD for seven days each year. This law will continue from now on; you will celebrate it in the seventh month. 42Live in shelters for seven days. All the people born in Israel must live in shelters 43so that all your descendants will know I made Israel live in shelters during the time I brought them out of Egypt. I am the LORD your God.' "

44So Moses told the people of Israel about all of the LORD's appointed feast days.

The Lampstand and the Holy Bread

24 The LORD said to Moses, 2"Command the people of Israel to bring you pure oil from crushed olives. That oil is for the lamps so that these lamps may never go out. 3Aaron will keep the lamps burning in the Meeting Tent from evening until morning before the LORD; this is in front of the curtain of the Ark of the Agreement. This law will continue from now on. 4Aaron must always keep the lamps burning on the lampstands of pure gold before the LORD.

5"Take fine flour and bake twelve loaves of bread with it, using four quarts of flour for each loaf. 6Put them in two rows on the golden table before the LORD, six loaves in each row. 7Put pure incense on each row as the memorial portion to take the place of the bread. It is an offering made by fire to the LORD. 8Every Sabbath day Aaron will put the bread in order before the LORD, as an agreement with the people of Israel that will continue forever. 9That bread will belong to Aaron and his sons. They will eat it in a holy place, because it is a most holy part of the offerings made by fire to the LORD. That bread is their share forever."

The Man Who Cursed God

10Now there was a son of an Israelite woman and an Egyptian father who was

walking among the Israelites. A fight broke
out in the camp between him and an
Israelite. 11The son of the Israelite woman
began cursing and speaking against the
LORD, so the people took him to Moses. (The
mother's name was Shelomith, the daughter
of Dibri from the family of Dan.) 12The
people held him as a prisoner while they
waited for the LORD's command to be made
clear to them.

13Then the LORD said to Moses, 14"Take the
one who spoke against me outside the camp.
Then all the people who heard him must put
their hands on his head, and all the people
must throw stones at him and kill him.
15Tell the people of Israel this: 'If anyone
curses his God, he is guilty of sin. 16Anyone
who speaks against the LORD must be put to
death; all the people must kill him by
throwing stones at him. Foreigners must be
punished just like the people born in Israel;
if they speak against the LORD, they must be
put to death.

17" 'Whoever kills another person must be
put to death. 18Whoever kills an animal that
belongs to another person must give that
person another animal to take its place.
19And whoever causes an injury to a
neighbor must receive the same kind of
injury in return: 20Broken bone for broken
bone, eye for eye, tooth for tooth. Anyone
who injures another person must be injured
in the same way in return. 21Whoever kills
another person's animal must give that
person another animal to take its place. But
whoever kills another person must be put to
death.

22" 'The law will be the same for the
foreigner as for those from your own
country. I am the LORD your God.' "

23Then Moses spoke to the people of
Israel, and they took the person who had
cursed outside the camp and killed him by
throwing stones at him. So the people of
Israel did as the LORD had commanded
Moses.

The Time of Rest for the Land

25 The LORD said to Moses at Mount
Sinai, 2"Tell the people of Israel this:
'When you enter the land I will give you, let
it have a special time of rest, to honor the
LORD. 3You may plant seed in your field for
six years, and you may trim your vineyards
for six years and bring in their fruits. 4But
during the seventh year, you must let the
land rest. This will be a special time to honor
the LORD. You must not plant seed in your
field or trim your vineyards. 5You must not
cut the crops that grow by themselves after
harvest, or gather the grapes from your vines
that are not trimmed. The land will have a
year of rest.

6" 'You may eat whatever the land
produces during that year of rest. It will be
food for your men and women servants, for
your hired workers, and for the foreigners
living in your country. 7It will also be food
for your cattle and the wild animals of your
land. Whatever the land produces may be
eaten.

The Year of Jubilee

8" 'Count off seven groups of seven years,
or forty-nine years. During that time there
will be seven years of rest for the land. 9On
the Day of Cleansing, you must blow the
horn of a male sheep; this will be on the
tenth day of the seventh month. You must
blow the horn through the whole country.
10Make the fiftieth year a special year, and
announce freedom for all the people living
in your country. This time will be called
Jubilee.[n] You will each go back to your own
property, each to your own family and
family group. 11The fiftieth year will be a
special time for you to celebrate. Don't plant
seeds, or harvest the crops that grow by
themselves, or gather grapes from the vines
that are not trimmed. 12That year is Jubilee;
it will be a holy time for you. You may eat
only the crops that come from the field. 13In
the year of Jubilee you each must go back to
your own property.

14" 'If you sell your land to your neighbor,
or if you buy land from your neighbor, don't
cheat each other. 15If you want to buy your
neighbor's land, count the number of years
since the last Jubilee, and use that number to
decide the right price. If your neighbor sells
the land to you, count the number of years
left for harvesting crops, and use that
number to decide the right price. 16If there
are many years, the price will be high. But if

25:10 Jubilee This word comes from the Hebrew word for a horn of a male sheep.

there are only a few years, lower the price,
because your neighbor is really selling only
a few crops to you. 17You must not cheat
each other, but you must respect your God. I
am the LORD your God.
18" 'Remember my laws and rules, and
obey them so that you will live safely in the
land. 19The land will give good crops to you,
and you will eat as much as you want and
live safely in the land.
20" 'But you might ask, "If we don't plant
seeds or gather crops, what will we eat the
seventh year?" 21I will send you such a great
blessing during the sixth year that the land
will produce enough crops for three years.
22When you plant in the eighth year, you
will still be eating from the old crop; you
will eat the old crop until the harvest of the
ninth year.

Property Laws

23" 'The land really belongs to me, so you
can't sell it for all time. You are only
foreigners and travelers living for a while on
my land. 24People might sell their land, but it
must always be possible for the family to get
its land back. 25If a person in your country
becomes very poor and sells some land, then
close relatives must come and buy it back.
26If there is not a close relative to buy the
land back, but if the person makes enough
money to be able to buy it back, 27the years
must be counted since the land was sold.
That number must be used to decide how
much the first owner should pay back the
one who bought it. Then the land will
belong to the first owner again. 28But if there
is not enough money to buy it back, the one
who bought it will keep it until the year of
Jubilee. During that celebration, the land
will go back to the first owner's family.
29" 'If someone sells a home in a walled
city, for a full year after it is sold, the person
has the right to buy it back. 30But if the
owner does not buy back the house before a
full year is over, it will belong to the one
who bought it and to his future sons. The
house will not go back to the first owner at
Jubilee. 31But houses in small towns without
walls are like open country; they can be
bought back, and they must be returned to
their first owner at Jubilee.
32" 'The Levites may always buy back their
houses in the cities that belong to them. 33If
someone buys a house from a Levite, that
house in the Levites' city will again belong
to the Levites in the Jubilee. This is because
houses in Levite cities belong to the people
of Levi; the Israelites gave these cities to
them. 34Also the fields and pastures around
the Levites' cities cannot be sold, because
those fields belong to the Levites forever.

Rules for Slave Owners

35" 'If anyone from your country becomes
too poor to support himself, help him to live
among you as you would a stranger or
foreigner. 36Do not charge him any interest
on money you loan to him, but respect your
God; let the poor live among you. 37Don't
lend him money for interest, and don't try to
make a profit from the food he buys. 38I am
the LORD your God, who brought you out of
the land of Egypt to give the land of Canaan
to you and to become your God.
39" 'If anyone from your country becomes
very poor and sells himself as a slave to you,
you must not make him work like a slave.
40He will be like a hired worker and a visitor
with you until the year of Jubilee. 41Then he
may leave you, take his children, and go
back to his family and the land of his
ancestors. 42This is because the Israelites are
my servants, and I brought them out of
slavery in Egypt. They must not become
slaves again. 43You must not rule this person
cruelly, but you must respect your God.
44" 'Your men and women slaves must
come from other nations around you; from
them you may buy slaves. 45Also you may
buy as slaves children from the families of
foreigners living in your land. These child
slaves will belong to you, 46and you may
even pass them on to your children after you
die; you can make them slaves forever. But
you must not rule cruelly over your own
people, the Israelites.
47" 'Suppose a foreigner or visitor among
you becomes rich. If someone in your country
becomes so poor that he has to sell himself as
a slave to the foreigner living among you or to
a member of the foreigner's family, 48the poor
person has the right to be bought back and
become free. One of his relatives may buy
him back: 49His uncle, his uncle's son, or any
one of his close relatives may buy him back.
Or, if he gets enough money, he may pay the
money to free himself.

50“ ‘He and the one who bought him must
count the time from when he sold himself
up to the next year of Jubilee. Use that
number to decide the price, because the
person really only hired himself out for a
certain number of years. 51If there are still
many years before the year of Jubilee, the
person must pay back a large part of the
price. 52If there are only a few years left until
Jubilee, the person must pay a small part of
the first price. 53But he will live like a hired
person with the foreigner every year; don't
let the foreigner rule cruelly over him.

54“ ‘Even if no one buys him back, at the
year of Jubilee, he and his children will
become free. 55This is because the people of
Israel are servants to me. They are my
servants, whom I brought out of Egypt. I am
the LORD your God.

Rewards for Obeying God

26 “ ‘Don't make idols for yourselves or
set up statues or memorials. Don't put
stone statues in your land to bow down to,
because I am the LORD your God.

2“ ‘Remember my Sabbaths, and respect
my Holy Place. I am the LORD.

3“ ‘If you remember my laws and
commands and obey them, 4I will give you
rains at the right season; the land will
produce crops, and the trees of the field will
produce their fruit. 5Your threshing will
continue until the grape harvest, and your
grape harvest will continue until it is time to
plant. Then you will have plenty to eat and
live safely in your land. 6I will give peace to
your country; you will lie down in peace,
and no one will make you afraid. I will keep
harmful animals out of your country, and
armies will not pass through it.

7“ ‘You will chase your enemies and defeat
them, killing them with your sword. 8Five of
you will chase a hundred men; a hundred of
you will chase ten thousand men. You will
defeat your enemies and kill them with your
sword.

9“ ‘Then I will show kindness to you and
let you have many children; I will keep my
agreement with you. 10You will have enough
crops to last for more than a year. When you
harvest the new crops, you will have to
throw out the old ones to make room for
them. 11Also I will place my Holy Tent
among you, and I will not turn away from
you. 12I will walk with you and be your God,
and you will be my people. 13I am the LORD
your God, who brought you out of Egypt,
where you were slaves. I broke the heavy
weights that were on your shoulders and let
you walk proudly again.

Punishment for Not Obeying God

14“ ‘But if you do not obey me and keep all
my commands, 15and if you turn away from
my rules and hate my laws, refusing to obey
all my commands, you have broken our
agreement. 16As a result, I will do this to you:
I will cause terrible things to happen to you.
I will cause you to have disease and fever
that will destroy your eyes and slowly kill
you. You will not have success when you
plant your seed, and your enemy will eat
your crops. 17I will be against you, and your
enemies will defeat you. These people who
hate you will rule over you, and you will run
away even when no one is chasing you.

18“ ‘If after all this you still do not obey
me, I will punish you seven times more for
your sins. 19I will break your great pride, and
I will make the sky like iron and the earth
like bronze.[n] 20You will work hard, but it will
not help. Your land will not grow any crops,
and your trees will not give their fruit.

21“ ‘If you still turn against me and refuse
to obey me, I will beat you seven times
harder. The more you sin, the more you will
be punished. 22I will send wild animals to
attack you, and they will take your children
away from you and destroy your cattle. They
will make you so few in number the roads
will be empty.

23“ ‘If you don't learn your lesson after all
these things, and if you still turn against me,
24I will also turn against you. I will punish
you seven more times for your sins. 25You
broke my agreement, and I will punish you. I
will bring armies against you, and if you go
into your cities for safety, I will cause
diseases to spread among you so that your
enemy will defeat you. 26There will be very
little bread to eat; ten women will be able to
cook all your bread in one oven. They will
measure each piece of bread, and you will
eat, but you will still be hungry.

26:19 sky . . . bronze This means the sky will give no rain and the earth will produce no crops.

devotion 38

LEVITICUS 26:6, 11–13

DO NOT BE AFRAID

Fear can be so paralyzing that at times it makes you think that your heart will just break in two. I know when fear leads my life and covers my mind, I become disabled and unable to accomplish anything. Most of the time, I find that the things I fear most never really come to pass. Have you ever heard that saying, "My life is full of great tragedies, most of which have never occurred"? My dear friend, know that fear is the weapon that Satan uses to poison us. It makes our bodies and our hearts sick with worry, and anytime sick and worry are present, peace and joy are absent.

Jesus wants you to know that you can trust him as the Great Shepherd. In Psalm 23, David paints a beautiful picture of God making us lie down in green pastures. Without total trust in the shepherd, the sheep will not lie down in the pasture for fear of being attacked. Jesus is your Shepherd, and you are his sheep. He loves you and wants to see you lie down in green pastures of his love.

The Lord's promise is that no matter where you are today, he is walking with you. Tonight you will lie down, and fear will not overtake you. You will not be a slave to anyone or anything because you are precious in his sight because of his love for you. That is a promise that only he can fulfill in your life.

27" 'If you still refuse to listen to me and
still turn against me, 28I will show my great
anger; I will punish you seven more times
for your sins. 29You will eat the bodies of
your sons and daughters. 30I will destroy
your places where gods are worshiped and
cut down your incense altars. I will pile your
dead bodies on the lifeless forms of your
idols. I will hate you. 31I will destroy your
cities and make your holy places empty, and
I will not smell the pleasing smell of your
offerings. 32I will make the land empty so
that your enemies who come to live in it will
be shocked at it. 33I will scatter you among
the nations, and I will pull out my sword
and destroy you. Your land will become
empty, your cities a waste. 34When you are
taken to your enemy's country, your land
will finally get its rest. It will enjoy its time
of rest all the time it lies empty. 35During the
time the land is empty, it will have the rest
you should have given it while you lived
in it.

36" 'Those of you who are left alive will
lose their courage in the land of their
enemies. They will be frightened by the
sound of a leaf being blown by the wind.
They will run as if someone were chasing
them with a sword, and they will fall even
when no one is chasing them. 37They will
fall over each other, as if someone were
chasing them with a sword, even though no
one is chasing them. You will not be strong
enough to stand up against your enemies.
38You will die among other nations and
disappear in your enemies' countries. 39So
those who are left alive will rot away in their
enemies' countries because of their sins.
They will also rot away because of their
ancestors' sins.

There Is Always Hope

40" 'But maybe the people will confess
their sins and the sins of their ancestors;
maybe they will admit they turned against
me and sinned against me, 41which made

me turn against them and send them into
the land of their enemies. If these
disobedient people are sorry for what they
did and accept punishment for their sin, 42I
will remember my agreement with Jacob,
my agreement with Isaac, and my agreement
with Abraham, and I will remember the
land. 43The land will be left empty by its
people, and it will enjoy its time of rest as it
lies bare without them. Then those who are
left alive will accept the punishment for
their sins. They will learn that they were
punished because they hated my laws and
refused to obey my rules. 44But even though
this is true, I will not turn away from them
when they are in the land of their enemies. I
will not hate them so much that I
completely destroy them and break my
agreement with them, because I am the LORD
their God. 45For their good I will remember
the agreement with their ancestors, whom I
brought out of the land of Egypt so I could
become their God; the other nations saw
these things. I am the LORD.' "

46These are the laws, rules, and teachings
the LORD made between himself and the
Israelites through Moses at Mount Sinai.

Promises Are Important

27 The LORD said to Moses, 2"Speak to
the people of Israel and tell them: 'If
someone makes a special promise to give a
person as a servant to the LORD by paying a
price that is the same value as that person,
3the price for a man twenty to sixty years
old is about one and one-fourth pounds of
silver. (You must use the measure as set by
the Holy Place.) 4The price for a woman
twenty to sixty years old is about twelve
ounces of silver. 5The price for a man five to
twenty years old is about eight ounces of
silver; for a woman it is about four ounces
of silver. 6The price for a baby boy one
month to five years old is about two ounces
of silver; for a baby girl the price is about
one and one-half ounces of silver. 7The price
for a man sixty years old or older is about
six ounces of silver; for a woman it is about
four ounces of silver.

8" 'If anyone is too poor to pay the price,
bring him to the priest, and the priest will
set the price. The priest will decide how
much money the person making the vow
can afford to pay.

Gifts to the Lord

9" 'Some animals may be used as sacrifices
to the LORD. If someone promises to bring
one of these to the LORD, it will become holy.
10That person must not try to put another
animal in its place or exchange it, a good
animal for a bad one, or a bad animal for a
good one. If this happens, both animals will
become holy.

11" 'Unclean animals cannot be offered as
sacrifices to the LORD, and if someone brings
one of them to the LORD, that animal must be
brought to the priest. 12The priest will decide
a price for the animal, according to whether it
is good or bad; as the priest decides, that is the
price for the animal. 13If the person wants to
buy back the animal, an additional one-fifth
must be added to the price.

Value of a House

14" 'If a person gives a house as holy to the
LORD, the priest must decide its value,
according to whether the house is good or
bad; as the priest decides, that is the price for
the house. 15But if the person who gives the
house wants to buy it back, an additional
one-fifth must be added to the price. Then
the house will belong to that person again.

Value of Land

16" 'If a person gives some family property
to the LORD, the value of the fields will
depend on how much seed is needed to plant
them. It will cost about one and one-fourth
pounds of silver for each six bushels of
barley seed needed. 17If the person gives a
field at the year of Jubilee, its value will stay
at what the priest has decided. 18But if the
person gives the field after the Jubilee, the
priest must decide the exact price by
counting the number of years to the next
year of Jubilee. Then he will subtract that
number from its value. 19If the person who
gave the field wants to buy it back, one-fifth
must be added to that price, and the field
will belong to the first owner again.

20" 'If the person does not buy back the
field, or if it is sold to someone else, the first
person cannot ever buy it back. 21When the
land is released at the year of Jubilee, it will
become holy to the LORD, like land specially
given to him. It will become the property of
the priests.

22“ ‘If someone gives to the LORD a field he
has bought, which is not a part of his family
land, 23the priest must count the years to the
next Jubilee. He must decide the price for the
land, and the price must be paid on that day.
Then that land will be holy to the LORD. 24At
the year of Jubilee, the land will go back to its
first owner, to the family who sold the land.
25“ ‘You must use the measure as set by
the Holy Place in paying these prices; it
weighs two-fifths of an ounce.

Value of Animals

26“ ‘If an animal is the first one born to its
parent, it already belongs to the LORD, so
people may not give it again. If it is a cow or
a sheep, it is the LORD’s. 27If the animal is
unclean, the person must buy it back for the
price set by the priest, and the person must
add one-fifth to that price. If it is not bought
back, the priest must sell it for the price he
had decided.
28“ ‘There is a special kind of gift that
people set apart to give to the LORD; it may
be a person, animal, or field from the family
property. That gift cannot be bought back or
sold. Every special kind of gift is most holy
to the LORD.
29“ ‘If anyone is given for the purpose of
being destroyed, he cannot be bought back;
he must be put to death.
30“ ‘One-tenth of all crops belongs to the
LORD, including the crops from fields and the
fruit from trees. That one-tenth is holy to the
LORD. 31If a person wants to get back that
tenth, one-fifth must be added to its price.
32“ ‘The priest will take every tenth
animal from a person’s herd or flock, and it
will be holy to the LORD. 33The owner should
not pick out the good animals from the bad
or exchange one animal for another. If that
happens, both animals will become holy;
they cannot be bought back.’ ”
34These are the commands the LORD gave
to Moses at Mount Sinai for the people of
Israel.

Numbers

Refers to the ancient Jewish census that took place on two occasions in this book (chapters 1—4, 26)

Person Holding the Pen God Wrote With: It's generally agreed that *Moses* authored this book, which is affirmed by Numbers 33:2 and 36:13.

When the Text Was Written: Between 1445 and 1405 B.C.

Spiritual Posture of the Original Recipients: Since Numbers covers the time period when God's people were wandering in the wilderness, the Israelites were often whining about their feet and the food. They even had the nerve to imply that if he *really* loved them, God would've allowed them to stay in Egypt.

Storyline Synopsis: These thirty-six chapters describe events that happened during the Israelite's divine desert ramblings. Their journey from Egypt to the land God promised them involved three mountains: Mount Sinai, Mount Hor, and Mount Nebo. God prepared them for the long trip at Mount Sinai (chapters 1—9); they walked, mostly in circles, for almost thirty-nine years in the Wilderness of Paran near Mount Hor (chapters 10—21); and they finally arrived at the gate of their destination on Mount Nebo (chapters 22—36). Their forty-year odyssey saw the death of one generation and the rise of another—they started out with 603,550 male sojourners over the age of twenty (Num. 1:46) and ended up with 601,730 different guys (26:51). These two censuses counted only the men who met the qualifications for military service. This was a vital number to keep in mind, given Israel's propensity for being picked on by other nations.

A Moment Worth Discussing: Chapter 21 reads like a Stephen King novel: the Israelites had become such impatient grumblers that they began to question Jehovah's goodness, so God sent serpents to literally bite them back in line. The inflammation caused by these poisonous snakes also caused the Israelite's hearts to swell with remorse. They confessed their sins to Moses and begged him to ask God to remove the slithery curse. God answered Moses' request with a very unique "prayer pole" that solved the problem (Num. 21:4–9; see also John 3:14–15).

Interesting (But Likely to Be Overlooked) Characters: The *daughters of Zelophehad* did what would cause most women to wince today: they married their first cousins (Num. 36:8–12). However, their behavior actually epitomized obedience to God, maintaining each tribe's individual inheritance.

The People of Israel Are Counted

1 The LORD spoke to Moses in the Meeting
Tent in the Desert of Sinai. This was on
the first day of the second month in the
second year after the Israelites left Egypt. He
said to Moses: 2"You and Aaron must count
all the people of Israel by families and family
groups, listing the name of each man. 3You
and Aaron must count every man twenty
years old or older who will serve in the army
of Israel, and list them by their divisions.
4One man from each tribe, the leader of his
family, will help you. 5These are the names
of the men who will help you:

from the tribe of Reuben—Elizur son of Shedeur;
6from the tribe of Simeon—Shelumiel son of Zurishaddai;
7from the tribe of Judah—Nahshon son of Amminadab;
8from the tribe of Issachar—Nethanel son of Zuar;
9from the tribe of Zebulun—Eliab son of Helon;
10from the tribe of Ephraim son of Joseph—Elishama son of Ammihud;
from the tribe of Manasseh son of Joseph—Gamaliel son of Pedahzur;
11from the tribe of Benjamin—Abidan son of Gideoni;
12from the tribe of Dan—Ahiezer son of Ammishaddai;
13from the tribe of Asher—Pagiel son of Ocran;
14from the tribe of Gad—Eliasaph son of Deuel;
15from the tribe of Naphtali—Ahira son of Enan."

16These were the men chosen from the
people to be leaders of their tribes, the heads
of Israel's family groups.

17Moses and Aaron took these men who
had been picked 18and called all the people
of Israel together on the first day of the
second month. Then the people were listed
by their families and family groups, and all
the men who were twenty years old or older
were listed by name. 19Moses did exactly
what the LORD had commanded and listed
the people while they were in the Desert of
Sinai.

20The tribe of Reuben, the first son born to
Israel, was counted; all the men twenty years
old or older who were able to serve in the
army were listed by name with their families
and family groups. 21The tribe of Reuben
totaled 46,500 men.

22The tribe of Simeon was counted; all the
men twenty years old or older who were
able to serve in the army were listed by
name with their families and family groups.
23The tribe of Simeon totaled 59,300 men.

24The tribe of Gad was counted; all the
men twenty years old or older who were
able to serve in the army were listed by
name with their families and family groups.
25The tribe of Gad totaled 45,650 men.

26The tribe of Judah was counted; all the
men twenty years old or older who were
able to serve in the army were listed by
name with their families and family groups.
27The tribe of Judah totaled 74,600 men.

28The tribe of Issachar was counted; all
the men twenty years old or older who were
able to serve in the army were listed by
name with their families and family groups.
29The tribe of Issachar totaled 54,400 men.

30The tribe of Zebulun was counted; all
the men twenty years old or older who were
able to serve in the army were listed by
name with their families and family groups.
31The tribe of Zebulun totaled 57,400 men.

32The tribe of Ephraim, a son of Joseph,
was counted; all the men twenty years old or
older who were able to serve in the army
were listed by name with their families and
family groups. 33The tribe of Ephraim
totaled 40,500 men.

34The tribe of Manasseh, also a son of
Joseph, was counted; all the men twenty
years old or older who were able to serve in
the army were listed by name with their
families and family groups. 35The tribe of
Manasseh totaled 32,200 men.

36The tribe of Benjamin was counted; all
the men twenty years old or older who were
able to serve in the army were listed by
name with their families and family groups.
37The tribe of Benjamin totaled 35,400 men.

38The tribe of Dan was counted; all the
men twenty years old or older who were
able to serve in the army were listed by
name with their families and family groups.
39The tribe of Dan totaled 62,700 men.

40The tribe of Asher was counted; all the
men twenty years old or older who were

able to serve in the army were listed by
name with their families and family groups.
41The tribe of Asher totaled 41,500 men.
42The tribe of Naphtali was counted; all
the men twenty years old or older who were
able to serve in the army were listed by
name with their families and family groups.
43The tribe of Naphtali totaled 53,400 men.
44Moses, Aaron, and the twelve leaders of
Israel, one from each of the families, counted
these men. 45Every man of Israel twenty years
old or older who was able to serve in the
army was counted and listed with his family.
46The total number of men was 603,550.
47The families from the tribe of Levi were
not listed with the others, because 48the
LORD had told Moses: 49"Do not count the
tribe of Levi or include them with the other
Israelites. 50Instead put the Levites in charge
of the Holy Tent of the Agreement and
everything that is with it. They must carry
the Holy Tent and everything in it, and they
must take care of it and make their camp
around it. 51Any time the Holy Tent is
moved, the Levites must take it down, and
any time it is set up, the Levites must do it.
Anyone else who goes near the Holy Tent
will be put to death. 52The Israelites will
make their camps in separate divisions, each
family near its flag. 53But the Levites must
make their camp around the Holy Tent of
the Agreement so that I will not be angry
with the Israelites. The Levites will take care
of the Holy Tent of the Agreement."
54So the Israelites did everything just as
the LORD commanded Moses.

The Camp Arrangement

2 The LORD said to Moses and Aaron: 2"The
Israelites should make their camps
around the Meeting Tent, but they should
not camp too close to it. They should camp
under their family flag and banners."
3The camp of Judah will be on the east
side, where the sun rises, and they will camp
by divisions there under their flag. The
leader of the people of Judah is Nahshon son
of Amminadab. 4There are 74,600 men in his
division.
5Next to them the tribe of Issachar will
camp. The leader of the people of Issachar is
Nethanel son of Zuar. 6There are 54,400 men
in his division.
7Next is the tribe of Zebulun. The leader
of the people of Zebulun is Eliab son of
Helon. 8There are 57,400 men in his division.
9There are a total of 186,400 men in the
camps of Judah and its neighbors, in all their
divisions. They will be the first to march out
of camp.
10The divisions of the camp of Reuben will
be on the south side, where they will camp
under their flag. The leader of the people of
Reuben is Elizur son of Shedeur. 11There are
46,500 men in his division.
12Next to them the tribe of Simeon will
camp. The leader of the people of Simeon is
Shelumiel son of Zurishaddai. 13There are
59,300 men in his division.
14Next is the tribe of Gad. The leader of
the people of Gad is Eliasaph son of Deuel.
15There are 45,650 men in his division.
16There are a total of 151,450 men in the
camps of Reuben and its neighbors, in all
their divisions. They will be the second
group to march out of camp.
17When the Levites march out with the
Meeting Tent, they will be in the middle of
the other camps. The tribes will march out
in the same order as they camp, each in its
place under its flag.
18The divisions of the camp of Ephraim
will be on the west side, where they will
camp under their flag. The leader of the
people of Ephraim is Elishama son of
Ammihud. 19There are 40,500 men in his
division.
20Next to them the tribe of Manasseh will
camp. The leader of the people of Manasseh
is Gamaliel son of Pedahzur. 21There are
32,200 men in his division.
22Next is the tribe of Benjamin. The leader
of the people of Benjamin is Abidan son of
Gideoni. 23There are 35,400 men in his
division.
24There are a total of 108,100 men in the
camps of Ephraim and its neighbors, in all
their divisions. They will be the third group
to march out of camp.
25The divisions of the camp of Dan will be
on the north side, where they will camp
under their flag. The leader of the people of
Dan is Ahiezer son of Ammishaddai. 26There
are 62,700 men in his division.
27Next to them the tribe of Asher will
camp. The leader of the people of Asher is
Pagiel son of Ocran. 28There are 41,500 men
in his division.

29Next is the tribe of Naphtali. The leader of the people of Naphtali is Ahira son of Enan. 30There are 53,400 men in his division.

31There are 157,600 men in the camps of Dan and its neighbors. They will be the last to march out of camp, and they will travel under their own flag.

32These are the Israelites who were counted by families. The total number of Israelites in the camps, counted by divisions, is 603,550. 33Moses obeyed the LORD and did not count the Levites among the other people of Israel.

34So the Israelites obeyed everything the LORD commanded Moses. They camped under their flags and marched out by families and family groups.

Aaron's Family, the Priests

3 This is the family history of Aaron and Moses at the time the LORD talked to Moses on Mount Sinai.

2Aaron had four sons: Nadab, the oldest, Abihu, Eleazar, and Ithamar. 3These were the names of Aaron's sons, who were appointed to serve as priests. 4But Nadab and Abihu died in the presence of the LORD when they offered the wrong kind of fire before the LORD in the Desert of Sinai. They had no sons. So Eleazar and Ithamar served as priests during the lifetime of their father Aaron.

5The LORD said to Moses, 6"Bring the tribe of Levi and present them to Aaron the priest to help him. 7They will help him and all the Israelites at the Meeting Tent, doing the work in the Holy Tent. 8The Levites must take care of everything in the Meeting Tent and serve the people of Israel by doing the work in the Holy Tent. 9Give the Levites to Aaron and his sons; of all the Israelites, the Levites are given completely to him. 10Appoint Aaron and his sons to serve as priests, but anyone else who comes near the holy things must be put to death."

11The LORD also said to Moses, 12"I am choosing the Levites from all the Israelites to take the place of all the firstborn children of Israel. The Levites will be mine, 13because the firstborn are mine. When you were in Egypt, I killed all the firstborn children of the Egyptians and took all the firstborn of Israel to be mine, both animals and children. They are mine. I am the LORD."

14The LORD again said to Moses in the Desert of Sinai, 15"Count the Levites by families and family groups. Count every male one month old or older." 16So Moses obeyed the LORD and counted them all.

17Levi had three sons, whose names were Gershon, Kohath, and Merari.

18The Gershonite family groups were Libni and Shimei.

19The Kohathite family groups were Amram, Izhar, Hebron, and Uzziel.

20The Merarite family groups were Mahli and Mushi.

These were the family groups of the Levites.

21The family groups of Libni and Shimei belonged to Gershon; they were the Gershonite family groups. 22The number that was counted was 7,500 males one month old or older. 23The Gershonite family groups camped on the west side, behind the Holy Tent. 24The leader of the families of Gershon was Eliasaph son of Lael. 25In the Meeting Tent the Gershonites were in charge of the Holy Tent, its covering, the curtain at the entrance to the Meeting Tent, 26the curtains in the courtyard, the curtain at the entry to the courtyard around the Holy Tent and the altar, the ropes, and all the work connected with these items.

27The family groups of Amram, Izhar, Hebron, and Uzziel belonged to Kohath; they were the Kohathite family groups. 28They had 8,600 males one month old or older, and they were responsible for taking care of the Holy Place. 29The Kohathite family groups camped south of the Holy Tent. 30The leader of the Kohathite families was Elizaphan son of Uzziel. 31They were responsible for the Ark, the table, the lampstand, the altars, the tools of the Holy Place which they were to use, the curtain, and all the work connected with these items. 32The main leader of the Levites was Eleazar son of Aaron, the priest, who was in charge of all those responsible for the Holy Place.

33The family groups of Mahli and Mushi belonged to Merari; they were the Merarite family groups. 34The number that was counted was 6,200 males one month old or older. 35The leader of the Merari families was Zuriel son of Abihail, and they were to camp north of the Holy Tent. 36The Merarites were

devotion 39

NUMBERS 3:10

HOLINESS MEETS UNHOLINESS

Our God is a holy God. It is because of his holiness that he is faithful, trustworthy, loving, just, and merciful. However, his holiness also keeps him from having a relationship with anyone who is sinful.

Man was created perfect but was given a free will to obey God or not to obey, and when man chose sin, he separated himself from God. Still (and this is the great part), God wasn't willing to let man go. That's why, in the ancient Hebrew world, God established the role of the high priest to come before him and offer sacrifices for the sins of the people. The high priest became a mediator between God and man, providing a way for a relationship to happen.

Look up Hebrews 4:14-16. Jesus is now our high priest and sits at the right hand of God the Father interceding for us. We no longer need an earthly high priest because Jesus took away the sins of the world when he died on the cross. The amazing thing is that Jesus understands our weaknesses because he lived on earth as a man. He was tempted just like we are, and yet he did not sin. Sometimes when I find myself being tempted, I avoid talking to the Lord about it because I'm embarrassed. Yet Jesus understands what I'm experiencing and wants me to come to his throne and receive mercy. So let us go to him boldly and receive the understanding and grace that we so desperately need.

responsible for the frames of the Holy Tent,
the braces, the posts, the bases, and all the
work connected with these items. 37They
were also responsible for the posts in the
courtyard around the Holy Tent and their
bases, tent pegs, and ropes.

38Moses, Aaron, and his sons camped east
of the Holy Tent, toward the sunrise, in front
of the Meeting Tent. They were responsible
for the Holy Place for the Israelites. Anyone
else who came near the Holy Place was to be
put to death.

39Moses and Aaron counted the Levite
men by their families, as the LORD
commanded, and there were 22,000 males
one month old or older.

Levites Take the Place of the Firstborn Sons

40The LORD said to Moses, "Count all the
firstborn sons in Israel one month old or
older, and list their names. 41Take the Levites
for me instead of the firstborn sons of Israel;
take the animals of the Levites instead of the
firstborn animals from the rest of Israel. I am
the LORD."

42So Moses did what the LORD
commanded and counted all the firstborn
sons of the Israelites. 43When he listed all
the firstborn sons one month old or older,
there were 22,273 names.

44The LORD also said to Moses, 45"Take
the Levites instead of all the firstborn
sons of the Israelites, and take the animals
of the Levites instead of the animals of the
other people. The Levites are mine. I am
the LORD. 46Since there are 273 more
firstborn sons than Levites, 47collect two
ounces of silver for each of the 273 sons.
Use the measure as set by the Holy Place,
which is two-fifths of an ounce. 48Give the
silver to Aaron and his sons as the
payment for the 273 Israelites."

49So Moses collected the money for the
people the Levites could not replace. 50From
the firstborn of the Israelites, he collected
thirty-five pounds of silver, using the

measure set by the Holy Place. 51Moses
obeyed the command of the LORD and gave
the silver to Aaron and his sons.

The Jobs of the Kohath Family

4 The LORD said to Moses and Aaron,
2"Count the Kohathites among the
Levites by family groups and families.
3Count the men from thirty to fifty years old,
all who come to serve in the Meeting Tent.
4"The Kohathites are responsible for the
most holy things in the Meeting Tent.
5When the Israelites are ready to move,
Aaron and his sons must go into the Holy
Tent, take down the curtain, and cover the
Ark of the Agreement with it. 6Over this
they must put a covering made from fine
leather, then spread the solid blue cloth over
that, and put the poles in place.
7"Then they must spread a blue cloth over
the table for the bread that shows a person is
in God's presence. They must put the plates,
pans, bowls, and the jars for drink offerings
on the table; they must leave the bread that
is always there on the table. 8Then they
must put a red cloth over all of these things,
cover everything with fine leather, and put
the poles in place.
9"With a blue cloth they must cover the
lampstand, its lamps, its wick trimmers, its
trays, and all the jars for the oil used in the
lamps. 10Then they must wrap everything in
fine leather and put all these things on a
frame for carrying them.
11"They must spread a blue cloth over the
gold altar, cover it with fine leather, and put
the poles in place.
12"They must gather all the things used for
serving in the Holy Place and wrap them in a
blue cloth. Then they must cover that with
fine leather and put these things on a frame
for carrying them.
13"They must clean the ashes off the
bronze altar and spread a purple cloth over
it. 14They must gather all the things used for
serving at the altar—the pans for carrying
the fire, the meat forks, the shovels, and the
bowls—and put them on the bronze altar.
Then they must spread a covering of fine
leather over it and put the poles in place.
15"When the Israelites are ready to move,
and when Aaron and his sons have covered
the holy furniture and all the holy things,
the Kohathites may go in and carry them
away. In this way they won't touch the holy
things and die. It is the Kohathites' job to
carry the things that are in the Meeting Tent.
16"Eleazar son of Aaron, the priest, will be
responsible for the Holy Tent and for
everything in it, for all the holy things it has:
the oil for the lamp, the sweet-smelling
incense, the continual grain offering, and the
oil used to appoint priests and things to the
LORD's service."
17The LORD said to Moses and Aaron,
18"Don't let the Kohathites be cut off from
the Levites. 19Do this for the Kohathites so
that they may go near the Most Holy Place
and not die: Aaron and his sons must go in
and show each Kohathite what to do and
what to carry. 20The Kohathites must not
enter and look at the holy things, even for a
second, or they will die."

The Jobs of the Gershon Family

21The LORD said to Moses, 22"Count the
Gershonites by families and family groups.
23Count the men from thirty to fifty years
old, all who have a job to do in the Meeting
Tent.
24"This is what the Gershonite family
groups must do and what they must carry.
25They must carry the curtains of the Holy
Tent, the Meeting Tent, its covering, and its
outer covering made from fine leather. They
must also carry the curtains for the entrance
to the Meeting Tent, 26the curtains of the
courtyard that go around the Holy Tent and
the altar, the curtain for the entry to the
courtyard, the ropes, and all the things used
with the curtains. They must do everything
connected with these things. 27Aaron and his
sons are in charge of what the Gershonites
do or carry; you tell them what they are
responsible for carrying. 28This is the work
of the Gershonite family group at the
Meeting Tent. Ithamar son of Aaron, the
priest, will direct their work.

The Jobs of the Merari Family

29"Count the Merarite families and family
groups. 30Count the men from thirty to fifty
years old, all who work at the Meeting Tent.
31It is their job to carry the following as they
serve in the Meeting Tent: the frames of the
Holy Tent, the crossbars, the posts, and bases,
32in addition to the posts that go around the
courtyard, their bases, tent pegs, ropes, and

everything that is used with the poles
around the courtyard. Tell each man exactly
what to carry. 33 This is the work the Merarite
family group will do for the Meeting Tent.
Ithamar son of Aaron, the priest, will direct
their work."

The Levite Families

34 Moses, Aaron, and the leaders of Israel
counted the Kohathites by families and
family groups, 35 the men from thirty to fifty
years old who were to work at the Meeting
Tent. 36 There were 2,750 men in the family
groups. 37 This was the total of the Kohath
family groups who worked at the Meeting
Tent, whom Moses and Aaron counted as the
LORD had commanded Moses.

38 Also, the Gershonites were counted by
families and family groups, 39 the men from
thirty to fifty years old who were given work
at the Meeting Tent. 40 The families and
family groups had 2,630 men. 41 This was the
total of the Gershon family groups who
worked at the Meeting Tent, whom Moses
and Aaron counted as the LORD had
commanded.

42 Also, the men in the families and family
groups of the Merari family were counted,
43 the men from thirty to fifty years old who
were to work at the Meeting Tent. 44 The
family groups had 3,200 men. 45 This was the
total of the Merari family groups, whom
Moses and Aaron counted as the LORD had
commanded Moses.

46 So Moses, Aaron, and the leaders of
Israel counted all the Levites by families and
family groups. 47 They counted the men from
thirty to fifty who were given work at the
Meeting Tent and who carried the Tent.
48 The total number of these men was 8,580.
49 Each man was counted as the LORD had
commanded Moses; each man was given his
work and told what to carry as the LORD had
commanded Moses.

Rules About Cleanliness

5 The LORD said to Moses, 2 "Command the
Israelites to send away from camp
anyone with a harmful skin disease. Send
away anyone who gives off body fluid or
who has become unclean by touching a dead
body. 3 Send both men and women outside
the camp so that they won't spread the
disease there, where I am living among you."
4 So Israel obeyed the LORD's command and
sent those people outside the camp. They did
just as the LORD had told Moses.

Paying for Doing Wrong

5 The LORD said to Moses, 6 "Tell the
Israelites: 'When a man or woman does
something wrong to another person, that is
really sinning against the LORD. That person
is guilty 7 and must admit the wrong that has
been done. The person must fully pay for the
wrong that has been done, adding one-fifth
to it, and giving it to the person who was
wronged. 8 But if that person is dead and does
not have any close relatives to receive the
payment, the one who did wrong owes the
LORD and must pay the priest. In addition,
the priest must sacrifice a male sheep to
remove the wrong so that the person will
belong to the LORD. 9 When an Israelite
brings a holy gift, it should be given to the
priest. 10 No one has to give these holy gifts,
but if someone does give them, they belong
to the priest.' "

Suspicious Husbands

11 Then the LORD said to Moses, 12 "Tell the
Israelites: 'A man's wife might be unfaithful
to him 13 and have sexual relations with
another man. Her sin might be kept hidden
from her husband so that he does not know
about the wrong she did. Perhaps no one saw
it, and she wasn't caught. 14 But if her
husband has feelings of jealousy and
suspects she has sinned—whether she has or
not— 15 he should take her to the priest. The
husband must also take an offering for her of
two quarts of barley flour. He must not pour
oil or incense on it, because this is a grain
offering for jealousy, an offering of
remembrance. It is to find out if she is guilty.

16 " 'The priest will bring in the woman
and make her stand before the LORD. 17 He
will take some holy water in a clay jar, and
he will put some dirt from the floor of the
Holy Tent into the water. 18 The priest will
make the woman stand before the LORD, and
he will loosen her hair. He will hand her the
offering of remembrance, the grain offering
for jealousy; he will hold the bitter water
that brings a curse. 19 The priest will make
her take an oath and ask her, "Has another
man had sexual relations with you? Have
you been unfaithful to your husband? If you

haven't, this bitter water that brings a curse
won't hurt you. 20But if you have been
unfaithful to your husband and have had
sexual relations with a man besides him"—
21the priest will then put on her the curse
that the oath will bring—"the LORD will
make the people curse and reject you. He
will make your stomach get big, and he will
make your body unable to give birth to
another baby. 22This water that brings a
curse will go inside you and make your body
unable to give birth to another baby."

" 'The woman must say, "I agree."

23" 'The priest should write these curses
on a scroll, wash the words off into the bitter
water, 24and make the woman drink the
bitter water that brings a curse. If she is
guilty, the water will make her sick. 25Then
the priest will take the grain offering for
jealousy from her. He will present it before
the LORD and bring it to the altar. 26He will
take a handful of the grain, which is a
memorial offering, and burn it on the altar.
After that he will make the woman drink
the water 27to see if she is not pure and if she
has sinned against her husband. When it
goes into her, if her stomach gets big and she
is not able to have another baby, her people
will reject her. 28But if the woman has not
sinned, she is pure. She is not guilty, and she
will be able to have babies.

29" 'So this is the teaching about jealousy.
This is what to do when a woman does
wrong and is unfaithful while she is married
to her husband. 30It also should be done if
the man gets jealous because he suspects his
wife. The priest will have her stand before
the LORD, and he will do all these things, just
as the teaching commands. 31In this way the
husband can be proven correct, and the
woman will suffer if she has done wrong.' "

Rules for the Nazirites

6 The LORD said to Moses, 2"Tell the
Israelites: 'If men or women want to
promise to belong to the LORD in a special
way, they will be called Nazirites. 3During
this time, they must not drink wine or beer,
or vinegar made from wine or beer. They
must not even drink grape juice or eat
grapes or raisins. 4While they are Nazirites,
they must not eat anything that comes from
the grapevine, even the seeds or the skin.

5" 'During the time they have promised to
belong to the LORD, they must not cut their
hair. They must be holy until this special
time is over. They must let their hair grow
long. 6During their special time of belonging
to the LORD, Nazirites must not go near a
dead body. 7Even if their own father, mother,
brother, or sister dies, they must not touch
them, or they will become unclean. They
must still keep their promise to belong to
God in a special way. 8While they are
Nazirites, they belong to the LORD in a
special way.

9" 'If they are next to someone who dies
suddenly, their hair, which was part of their
promise, has been made unclean. So they
must shave their head seven days later to be
clean. 10Then on the eighth day, they must
bring two doves or two young pigeons to the
priest at the entrance to the Meeting Tent.
11The priest will offer one as a sin offering
and the other as a burnt offering. This
removes sin so they will belong to the LORD.
(They had sinned because they were near a
dead body.) That same day they will again
promise to let their hair grow 12and give
themselves to the LORD for another special
time. They must bring a male lamb a year
old as a penalty offering. The days of the
special time before don't count, because they
became unclean during their first special
time.

13" 'This is the teaching for the Nazirites.
When the promised time is over, they must
go to the entrance of the Meeting Tent 14and
give their offerings to the LORD. They must
offer a year-old male lamb that has nothing
wrong with it, as a burnt offering, a year-old
female lamb that has nothing wrong with it,
as a sin offering, and a male sheep that has
nothing wrong with it, for a fellowship
offering. 15They must also bring the grain
offerings and drink offerings that go with
them. And they must bring a basket of bread
made without yeast, loaves made with fine
flour mixed with oil, and wafers made
without yeast spread with oil.

16" 'The priest will give these offerings to
the LORD and make the sin offering and the
burnt offering. 17Then he will kill the male
sheep as a fellowship offering to the LORD;
along with it, he will present the basket of
bread made without yeast, the grain offering,
and the drink offering.

18" 'The Nazirites must go to the entrance

of the Meeting Tent and shave off their hair
that they grew for their promise. The hair
will be put in the fire that is under the
sacrifice of the fellowship offering.
19“ ‘After the Nazirites cut off their hair,
the priest will give them a boiled shoulder
from the male sheep. From the basket he
will also give a loaf and a wafer, both made
without yeast. 20Then the priest will present
them to the LORD. They are holy and belong
to the priest. Also, he is to present the breast
and the thigh from the male sheep. After
that, the Nazirites may drink wine.
21“ ‘This is the teaching for the Nazirites
who make a promise. Everyone who makes
the Nazirite promise must give all of these
gifts to the LORD. If they promised to do
more, they must keep their promise,
according to the teaching of the Nazirites.’ ”

The Priests' Blessings

22The LORD said to Moses, 23“Tell Aaron
and his sons, ‘This is how you should bless
the Israelites. Say to them:
24“May the LORD bless you and keep you.
25May the LORD show you his kindness
and have mercy on you.
26May the LORD watch over you
and give you peace.” ’
27“So Aaron and his sons will bless the
Israelites with my name, and I will bless
them.”

The Holy Tent

7 When Moses finished setting up the
Holy Tent, he gave it for service to the
LORD by pouring olive oil on the Tent and on
everything used in it. He also poured oil on
the altar and all its tools to prepare them for
service to the LORD. 2Then the leaders of
Israel made offerings. These were the heads
of the families, the leaders of each tribe who
counted the people. 3They brought to the
LORD six covered carts and twelve oxen—
each leader giving an ox, and every two
leaders giving a cart. They brought these to
the Holy Tent.
4The LORD said to Moses, 5“Accept these
gifts from the leaders and use them in the
work of the Meeting Tent. Give them to the
Levites as they need them.”
6So Moses accepted the carts and the oxen
and gave them to the Levites. 7He gave two
carts and four oxen to the Gershonites,
which they needed for their work. 8Then
Moses gave four carts and eight oxen to the
Merarites, which they needed for their work.
Ithamar son of Aaron, the priest, directed the
work of all of them. 9Moses did not give any
oxen or carts to the Kohathites, because their
job was to carry the holy things on their
shoulders.
10When the oil was poured on the altar,
the leaders brought their offerings to it to
give it to the LORD's service; they presented
them in front of the altar. 11The LORD told
Moses, “Each day one leader must bring his
gift to make the altar ready for service to me.”
12-83Each of the twelve leaders brought
these gifts. Each leader brought one silver
plate that weighed about three and one-
fourth pounds, and one silver bowl that
weighed about one and three-fourths pounds.
These weights were set by the Holy Place
measure. The bowl and the plate were filled
with fine flour mixed with oil for a grain
offering. Each leader also brought a large gold
dish that weighed about four ounces and was
filled with incense.
In addition, each of the leaders brought
one young bull, one male sheep, and one
male lamb a year old for a burnt offering;
one male goat for a sin offering; and two
oxen, five male sheep, five male goats, and
five male lambs a year old for a fellowship
offering.
On the first day Nahshon son of
Amminadab brought his gifts. He was the
leader of the tribe of Judah.
On the second day Nethanel son of Zuar
brought his gifts. He was the leader of the
tribe of Issachar.
On the third day Eliab son of Helon
brought his gifts. He was the leader of the
tribe of Zebulun.
On the fourth day Elizur son of Shedeur
brought his gifts. He was the leader of the
tribe of Reuben.
On the fifth day Shelumiel son of
Zurishaddai brought his gifts. He was the
leader of the tribe of Simeon.
On the sixth day Eliasaph son of Deuel
brought his gifts. He was the leader of the
tribe of Gad.
On the seventh day Elishama son of
Ammihud brought his gifts. He was the
leader of the tribe of Ephraim.
On the eighth day Gamaliel son of

devotion 40

NUMBERS 6:24–26

YOU PICK: BLESSINGS OR CURSES?

We live in a life-or-death culture. Almost everywhere we look, the world is speaking death. The media messages we receive are often disheartening and discouraging. And so many of us walk around with paralyzing wounds from the hurtful words that have been spoken to us.

You and I have a choice. We can choose to speak a blessing instead of a curse. We can choose to call on the strong name of our Lord for his life-giving perspective. Aaron, the first high priest in the Old Testament, was entrusted with encouraging words to speak to God's people. And God made a promise that his people would indeed receive the blessings Aaron pronounced over them.

Sometimes it takes every Holy Spirit resource you have to speak helpful words instead of harmful words. But really, in the end, what good does it do to speak judgment and curses? People have been beaten down and attacked. They carry such heavy burdens. Almost everyone I know is so very tired and low on emotional resources. What if we left the condemnation to God and began speaking his mercy, his peace, and his kindness?

Wouldn't it be cool to live out and give out the promised blessings of God? The world is full of chaos. The wounded are empty and dying without hope. But what if people came into your presence and received blessings instead of curses? What if they came to know of the Lord's mercy because he honored the words of your blessing?

Pedahzur brought his gifts. He was the leader of the tribe of Manasseh.

On the ninth day Abidan son of Gideoni brought his gifts. He was the leader of the tribe of Benjamin.

On the tenth day Ahiezer son of Ammishaddai brought his gifts. He was the leader of the tribe of Dan.

On the eleventh day Pagiel son of Ocran brought his gifts. He was the leader of the tribe of Asher.

On the twelfth day Ahira son of Enan brought his gifts. He was the leader of the tribe of Naphtali.

84So these were the gifts from the Israelite leaders when oil was poured on the altar and it was given for service to the LORD: twelve silver plates, twelve silver bowls, and twelve gold dishes. 85Each silver plate weighed about three and one-fourth pounds, and each bowl weighed about one and three-fourths pounds. All the silver plates and silver bowls together weighed about sixty pounds according to a weight set by the Holy Place measure. 86The twelve gold dishes filled with incense weighed four ounces each, according to the weight set by the Holy Place measure. Together the gold dishes weighed about three pounds. 87The total number of animals for the burnt offering was twelve bulls, twelve male sheep, and twelve male lambs a year old. There was also a grain offering, and there were twelve male goats for a sin offering. 88The total number of animals for the fellowship offering was twenty-four bulls, sixty male sheep, sixty male goats, and sixty male lambs a year old. All these offerings were for giving the altar to the service of the LORD after the oil had been poured on it.

89When Moses went into the Meeting Tent to speak with the LORD, he heard the LORD speaking to him. The voice was coming

from between the two gold creatures with
wings that were above the lid of the Ark of
the Agreement. In this way the LORD spoke
with him.

The Lampstand

8 The LORD said to Moses, 2"Speak to Aaron
and tell him, 'Put the seven lamps where
they can light the area in front of the
lampstand.'"

3Aaron did this, putting the lamps so they
lighted the area in front of the lampstand; he
obeyed the command the LORD gave Moses.
4The lampstand was made from hammered
gold, from its base to the flowers. It was
made exactly the way the LORD had showed
Moses.

The Levites Are Given to God

5The LORD said to Moses, 6"Take the
Levites away from the other Israelites and
make them clean. 7This is what you should
do to make them clean: Sprinkle the
cleansing water on them, and have them
shave their bodies and wash their clothes so
they will be clean. 8They must take a young
bull and the grain offering of flour mixed
with oil that goes with it. Then take a second
young bull for a sin offering. 9Bring the
Levites to the front of the Meeting Tent, and
gather all the Israelites around. 10When you
bring the Levites before the LORD, the
Israelites should put their hands on them.[n]
11Aaron will present the Levites before the
LORD as an offering presented from the
Israelites. Then the Levites will be ready to
do the work of the LORD.

12"The Levites will put their hands on the
bulls' heads—one bull will be a sin offering
to the LORD, and the other will be a burnt
offering, to remove the sins of the Levites so
they will belong to the LORD. 13Make the
Levites stand in front of Aaron and his sons
and present the Levites as an offering to the
LORD. 14In this way you must set apart the
Levites from the other Israelites; the Levites
will be mine.

15"Make the Levites pure, and present
them as an offering so that they may come
to work at the Meeting Tent. 16They will be
given completely to me from the Israelites; I
have taken them for myself instead of the
firstborn of every Israelite woman. 17All the
firstborn in Israel—people or animals—are
mine. When I killed all the firstborn in
Egypt, I set the firstborn in Israel aside for
myself. 18But I have taken the Levites instead
of all the firstborn in Israel. 19From all the
Israelites I have given the Levites to Aaron
and his sons so that they may serve the
Israelites at the Meeting Tent. They will help
remove the Israelites' sins so they will
belong to the LORD and so that no disaster
will strike the Israelites when they approach
the Holy Place."

20So Moses, Aaron, and all the Israelites
obeyed and did with the Levites what the
LORD commanded Moses. 21The Levites made
themselves clean and washed their clothes.
Then Aaron presented them as an offering to
the LORD. He also removed their sins so they
would be pure. 22After that, the Levites came
to the Meeting Tent to work, and Aaron and
his sons told them what to do. They did with
the Levites what the LORD commanded
Moses.

23The LORD said to Moses, 24"This
command is for the Levites. Everyone
twenty-five years old or older must come to
the Meeting Tent, because they all have jobs
to do there. 25At the age of fifty, they must
retire from their jobs and not work again.
26They may help their fellow Levites with
their work at the Meeting Tent, but they
must not do the work themselves. This is the
way you are to give the Levites their jobs."

The Passover Is Celebrated

9 The LORD spoke to Moses in the Desert of
Sinai in the first month of the second year
after the Israelites left Egypt. He said, 2"Tell
the Israelites to celebrate the Passover at the
appointed time. 3That appointed time is the
fourteenth day of this month at twilight; they
must obey all the rules about it."

4So Moses told the Israelites to celebrate
the Passover, 5and they did; it was in the
Desert of Sinai at twilight on the fourteenth
day of the first month. The Israelites did
everything just as the LORD commanded
Moses.

6But some of the people could not
celebrate the Passover on that day because
they were unclean from touching a dead

8:10 put . . . them This showed that the people had a part in giving the Levites their special work.

beauty

I was reading a magazine the other day that highlighted a "before" and "after" picture of a prominent movie star. While I already thought this celebrity was stunning in form and figure in the "before" picture to the left, the "after" shot on the right was the actual cover of the magazine after computerized "alterations" had been made on her body. I was amazed—and not in a good way! She looked void of all personality and sparkle without the laugh lines or freckles that were the visual history of her life.

Is this what beauty has been reduced to—to be "enhanced" with air-brushed slim thighs and porcelain-perfect complexions? There must be more to beauty than what I see these days. The more I live, the more I realize we must fight for true beauty—the loveliness from within. Sure, we could lose ten pounds or dye our hair, but that is merely accessorizing.

The stuff of allure originates from none other than the very One who created us in the first place. Beauty radiates from the heart first. There is an inward sense of self only God can give, no matter the condition of the externals. God furiously fashioned our entire beings . . . external and internal. Who are we to complain to the Creator about how we look?

Let's stop putting the magnifying glass up to the moody trap of outward beauty. A heart that is soft and kind through Christ, a soul that can throw her head back and laugh at her "flaws" instead of obsessing over them, a mind set on knowing others and being known by her Father—this is beauty! This is the exquisite charm that his beauty alone can bring.

THINK ABOUT IT: What does inward beauty mean to you?
What physical areas do you judge yourself harshly on and thus detract from your confidence in how God has made you?

DIG DEEPER: Psalm 139:14–16 (God created you), Jeremiah 1:5 (you are called), Romans 10:15 (the beauty of our ministry), and 1 Peter 3:1–6 (inward beauty)

weakness

My least favorite passage in all of Scripture is 2 Timothy 3:6. I've felt that way since the day I realized God was talking about me. The passage talks about a woman who is weak-willed. The bully of fear has brought a whole heap of ungodliness and consequences into her life. She's unable to stand in strength and is a real spiritual pansy. One commentator even calls this woman "unstable and needy." Yuck. I have been the weak-willed woman.

When you are a weak-willed, silly woman of fear, that weakness can manifest itself in a multitude of ways. I believe the Holy Spirit will speak to you if this passage holds any truth in your life, but here are some of the characteristics of a weak-willed woman, just to get you thinking. She's . . .

- Consumed with worry and fear.
- Self-absorbed and obsessed with the opinions of others.
- Either beaten down or loud and brash.
- Filled with no personal ambition, yet wants to control.
- Unsure of her hope in glory.
- Empty and turns to everyone but God.
- Harboring grudges.
- A gossip.
- Obsessively indulgent in secret.
- Easily hurt or offended.
- Filled with some spiritual knowledge but no spiritual power.
- Critical in spirit.

The weak-willed woman is easy prey for the enemy. She cowers when he bullies and taunts her with lies. The weak-willed woman eventually hides out, afraid to stand for anything or do what is right. Spiritually hesitant, she watches everyone else live while she's stuck inside her own weakness.

According to the Word of God, the fear that bullies the weak-willed woman cannot live in the same room as perfect love. Jesus will come to rescue the woman that he loves. He can take a silly, scared woman and make her brave.

THINK ABOUT IT: Have you ever lived like a weak-willed woman?
How did that weakness manifest itself in your life?
What does a woman look like when perfect love chases away the bully of fear?

DIG DEEPER: Isaiah 61:1–3 (God's call and redemption), 2 Timothy 3:1–7 (weak women), and 1 John 4:16–18 (God's love erases fear)

loved

The apostle John emphasized his close connection with the Messiah throughout his Gospel account. He even referred to himself as "the follower Jesus loved," not once or twice, but five times! I used to think his language was a bit braggadocios, that the way he described himself was akin to arrogance. I could just picture the other followers listening to him and exchanging sideways glances that echoed loudly their "Oh brother, here he goes again!" sentiments.

But then I read one little, seemingly insignificant verse that clarified John's confidence: "Peter turned and saw that the follower Jesus loved was walking behind them. (This was the follower who had leaned against Jesus at the supper and had said, 'Lord, who will turn against you?')" (John 21:20).

John wrote this book at the end of his life, probably about fifty years after this event we often refer to as the "Last Supper" (John 13:23). Much had happened since that symbolic meal. John had experienced Jesus' crucifixion and resurrection (John 19—21). He'd been awestruck when a tornado-like wind blew through a Pentecost party and turned out to be the Holy Spirit (Acts 2:1–4). He'd watched a middle-aged crippled man do cartwheels after being healed through the power of Jesus' name (Acts 3:1–10). He'd also been mocked, jailed, and beaten for the sake of his Savior.

Half a century crammed full of activity had passed since John literally leaned against the Lamb of God . . . but he never forgot the embrace. He'd been held by the very God who holds the moon and stars in his mighty hand, and the intimacy of that moment lingered in his mind and heart for the rest of his life. It seared his soul with a sense of belonging. It literally shaped the way this sensitive follower defined himself. John wasn't arrogant; he was simply secure in the fact that Jesus loved him.

THINK ABOUT IT: When was the last time you metaphorically leaned on Jesus? How does being adored by Jesus affect the way you define yourself?

DIG DEEPER: Isaiah 43:1–4 (deliverance) and John 15:1–17 (love)

divorce

In my twenties, life seemed to be all about weddings and baby showers. As I entered my thirties, I thought it would be all about settling in and enjoying the relationships that my husband and I had cultivated. I never imagined that one of the most precious friendships we had was about to unravel. Divorce happens. I had already seen it happen in the church, but it had never affected our hearts and personal lives so deeply until it happened to our best friends. Even now, it's hard to reconcile the fact that there aren't going to be any more pictures of us skiing together, no more Christmas mornings cooking breakfast in our PJs, no more motorcycle rides, no more dinners filled with laughter. From here on out, it would be only the three musketeers, not the four. After a particularly difficult day of ministering to our friend's heart, my husband said, "Now you know why God hates divorce. It destroys everything that is good."

My friend's husband had walked with the Lord for eighteen years, ministering the truth of God's love and counseling in the Word. Wasn't he also doing all of that for his wife? What about our part in it? How could we have been so blind? This was not just some couple coming into the pastor's office for counseling—these were our best friends. In Malachi 2:16 the Lord says he hates divorce and cautions the men of Israel not to break their trust. There is no freedom when you purposely break the trust of a marriage covenant. If you are headed down this road, don't do it! Do everything you can to make things right in your spirit and with each other; God is able to restore even the most broken parts of a marriage.

THINK ABOUT IT: Is your first response to conflict one that wants to withdraw yourself from the circumstance and/or the other person? Have you been breaking your trust with God because your personal circumstances seem to be all-consuming?

DIG DEEPER: Matthew 5:23–24 (reconciliation), Matthew 19:6 (unity), and Romans 12:1–2 (transformation)

body. So they went to Moses and Aaron that
day and 7said to Moses, "We are unclean
because of touching a dead body. But why
should we be kept from offering gifts to the
LORD at this appointed time? Why can't we
join the other Israelites?"
8Moses said to them, "Wait, and I will find
out what the LORD says about you."
9Then the LORD said to Moses, 10"Tell the
Israelites this: 'If you or your descendants
become unclean because of a dead body, or if
you are away on a trip during the Passover,
you must still celebrate the LORD's Passover.
11But celebrate it at twilight on the
fourteenth day of the second month. Eat the
lamb with bitter herbs and bread made
without yeast. 12Don't leave any of it until
the next morning or break any of its bones.
When you celebrate the Passover, follow all
the rules. 13Anyone who is clean and is not
away on a trip but does not eat the Passover
must be cut off from the people. That person
did not give an offering to the LORD at the
appointed time and must be punished for
the sin.
14" 'Foreigners among you may celebrate
the LORD's Passover, but they must follow all
the rules. You must have the same rules for
foreigners as you have for yourselves.' "

The Cloud Above the Tent

15On the day the Holy Tent, the Tent of the
Agreement, was set up, a cloud covered it.
From dusk until dawn the cloud above the
Tent looked like fire. 16The cloud stayed
above the Tent, and at night it looked like
fire. 17When the cloud moved from its place
over the Tent, the Israelites moved, and
wherever the cloud stopped, the Israelites
camped. 18So the Israelites moved at the
LORD's command, and they camped at his
command. While the cloud stayed over the
Tent, they remained camped. 19Sometimes
the cloud stayed over the Tent for a long
time, but the Israelites obeyed the LORD and
did not move. 20Sometimes the cloud was

devotion 41

NUMBERS 9:23

READY . . . SET . . . GO!

God has promised to lead us. He will tell us when to stay put and when it's time to get going. Obedience is moving when God says, "Okay . . . now!"—and then waiting until he speaks again. My biggest life lessons have come during the in-between waiting parts—camping out in God's presence, listening and seeking, waiting until I have received the next moving instructions.

From the longing for romantic love to the desire to use and improve our spiritual gifts, God gives us many desires that require a determined wait. But the journey of your desires is not a wild and random rocket ride. God has orchestrated a plan outlining each step and its timing. Going the distance with God requires patience and discernment.

More than the goal or the desire itself, what matters most is how you wait for God's next command. Will you wait with a seeking heart? Will you pursue contentment and peace? Will you surrender, laying down your internal striving, and worship God instead of fretting?

The mature woman knows how to wait on God. She has learned through tears, disappointment, and even rejection that sometimes it's just not your turn. That doesn't mean that it won't ever be. Or that you're not qualified. Or that you've gone completely the wrong way. It's just not yet.

This day, search your heart. Lay every worry on the altar of God's faithfulness. Decide that you will wait with the strength God gives until you hear his next command.

over it only a few days. At the LORD's command the people camped, and at his command they moved. 21Sometimes the cloud stayed only from dusk until dawn; when the cloud lifted the next morning, the people moved. When the cloud lifted, day or night, the people moved. 22The cloud might stay over the Tent for two days, a month, or a year. As long as it stayed, the people camped, but when it lifted, they moved. 23At the LORD's command the people camped, and at his command they moved. They obeyed the LORD's order that he commanded through Moses.

The Silver Trumpets

10 The LORD said to Moses, 2"Make two trumpets of hammered silver, and use them to call the people together and to march out of camp. 3When both trumpets are blown, the people should gather before you at the entrance to the Meeting Tent. 4If you blow only one trumpet, the leaders, the heads of the family groups of Israel, should meet before you. 5When you loudly blow the trumpets, the tribes camping on the east should move. 6When you loudly blow them again, the tribes camping on the south should move; the loud sound will tell them to move. 7When you want to gather the people, blow the trumpets, but don't blow them as loudly.

8"Aaron's sons, the priests, should blow the trumpets. This is a law for you and your descendants from now on. 9When you are fighting an enemy who attacks you in your own land, blow the trumpets loudly. The LORD your God will take notice of you and will save you from your enemies. 10Also blow your trumpets at happy times and during your feasts and at New Moon festivals. Blow them over your burnt offerings and fellowship offerings, because they will help you remember your God. I am the LORD your God."

The Israelites Move Camp

11The cloud lifted from the Tent of the Agreement on the twentieth day of the second month of the second year. 12So the Israelites moved from the Desert of Sinai and continued until the cloud stopped in the Desert of Paran. 13This was their first time to move, and they did it as the LORD had commanded Moses.

14The divisions from the camp of Judah moved first under their flag. Nahshon son of Amminadab was the commander. 15Nethanel son of Zuar was over the division of the tribe of Issachar. 16Eliab son of Helon was over the division of the tribe of Zebulun. 17Then the Holy Tent was taken down, and the Gershonites and Merarites, who carried it, moved next.

18Then came the divisions from the camp of Reuben under their flag, and Elizur son of Shedeur was the commander. 19Shelumiel son of Zurishaddai was over the division of the tribe of Simeon. 20Eliasaph son of Deuel was over the division of the tribe of Gad. 21Then came the Kohathites, who carried the holy things; the Holy Tent was to be set up before they arrived.

22Next came the divisions from the camp of Ephraim under their flag, and Elishama son of Ammihud was the commander. 23Gamaliel son of Pedahzur was over the division of the tribe of Manasseh, 24and Abidan son of Gideoni was over the division of the tribe of Benjamin.

25The last ones were the rear guard for all the tribes. These were the divisions from the camp of Dan under their flag, and Ahiezer son of Ammishaddai was the commander. 26Pagiel son of Ocran was over the division of the tribe of Asher; 27Ahira son of Enan was over the division of the tribe of Naphtali. 28This was the order the Israelite divisions marched in when they moved.

29Hobab was the son of Reuel the Midianite,[n] who was Moses' father-in-law. Moses said to Hobab, "We are moving to the land the LORD promised to give us. Come with us and we will be good to you, because the LORD has promised good things to Israel."

30But Hobab answered, "No, I will not go. I will go back to my own land where I was born."

31But Moses said, "Please don't leave us. You know where we can camp in the desert, and you can be our guide. 32Come with us. We will share with you all the good things the LORD gives us." 33So they left the mountain of the LORD and traveled for three

10:29 Reuel the Midianite Also called Jethro.

days. The Ark of the LORD's Agreement went
in front of the people for those three days, as
they looked for a place to camp. 34The LORD's
cloud was over them during the day when
they left their camp.

35When the Ark left the camp, Moses said,

"Rise up, LORD!
Scatter your enemies:
make those who hate you run from
you."

36And when the Ark was set down, Moses
said,

"Return, LORD,
to the thousands of people of Israel."

Fire from the Lord

11 Now the people complained to the
LORD about their troubles, and when
he heard them, he became angry. Then fire
from the LORD burned among the people at
the edge of the camp. 2The people cried out
to Moses, and when he prayed to the LORD,
the fire stopped burning. 3So that place was
called Taberah,[n] because the LORD's fire had
burned among them.

Seventy Elders Help Moses

4Some troublemakers among them
wanted better food, and soon all the
Israelites began complaining. They said, "We
want meat! 5We remember the fish we ate
for free in Egypt. We also had cucumbers,
melons, leeks, onions, and garlic. 6But now
we have lost our appetite; we never see
anything but this manna!"

7The manna was like small white seeds.
8The people would go to gather it, and then
grind it in handmills, or crush it between
stones. After they cooked it in a pot or made
cakes with it, it tasted like bread baked with
olive oil. 9When the dew fell on the camp
each night, so did the manna.

10Moses heard every family crying as they
stood in the entrances of their tents. Then
the LORD became very angry, and Moses got
upset. 11He asked the LORD, "Why have you
brought me, your servant, this trouble?
What have I done wrong that you made me
responsible for all these people? 12I am not
the father of all these people, and I didn't
give birth to them. So why do you make me
carry them to the land you promised to our
ancestors? Must I carry them in my arms as a
nurse carries a baby? 13Where can I get meat
for all these people? They keep crying to me,
'We want meat!' 14I can't take care of all
these people alone. It is too much for me. 15If
you are going to continue doing this to me,
then kill me now. If you care about me, put
me to death, and then I won't have any more
troubles."

16The LORD said to Moses, "Bring me
seventy of Israel's elders, men that you know
are leaders among the people. Bring them to
the Meeting Tent, and have them stand there
with you. 17I will come down and speak
with you there. I will take some of the Spirit
that is in you, and I will give it to them. They
will help you care for the people so that you
will not have to care for them alone.

18"Tell the people this: 'Make yourselves
holy for tomorrow, and you will eat meat.
You cried to the LORD, "We want meat! We
were better off in Egypt!" So now the LORD
will give you meat to eat. 19You will eat it
not for just one, two, five, ten, or even
twenty days, 20but you will eat that meat for
a whole month. You will eat it until it comes
out your nose, and you will grow to hate it.
This is because you have rejected the LORD,
who is with you. You have cried to him,
saying, "Why did we ever leave Egypt?"' "

21Moses said, "LORD, here are six hundred
thousand people standing around me, and
you say, 'I will give them enough meat to eat
for a month!' 22If we killed all the flocks and
herds, that would not be enough. If we
caught all the fish in the sea, that would not
be enough."

23But the LORD said to Moses, "Do you
think I'm weak? Now you will see if I can do
what I say."

24So Moses went out to the people and
told them what the LORD had said. He
gathered seventy of the elders together and
had them stand around the Tent. 25Then the
LORD came down in the cloud and spoke to
Moses. The LORD took some of the Spirit
Moses had, and he gave it to the seventy
leaders. With the Spirit in them, they
prophesied, but just that one time.

26Two men named Eldad and Medad were
also listed as leaders, but they did not go to
the Tent. They stayed in the camp, but the

11:3 Taberah This name means "burning."

devotion 42

NUMBERS 11:13–17

A LITTLE WISDOM GOES A LONG WAY

At some time or another for all of us, the pressures of our responsibilities begin to cave in on our lives. Juggling the tasks of being a dutiful employee, domestic goddess, hospitality extraordinaire, fantastic lover, supportive wife, and everything in between can bring us to our knees in angst. We reach a ledge somewhere and cry out, "I cannot make another decision, solve another problem, or even make sense of my own thoughts. I'm out of energy, and my strength is gone!" I find myself seeking the Lord for the smallest clue that I am not totally out of my mind, that he is near and cares about the well-being of my heart, the details of my life, my stress, and my troubles.

When Moses felt overwhelmed with his responsibilities, the Lord acknowledged his pain. God didn't say, "Get up and take it like a man!" Instead, he offered a solution—godly wisdom. Think about women you know who walk closely in tune with the Spirit of the Lord. Who can come alongside you to encourage you in the things of the Spirit, hold you accountable, and love you even in your times of trouble? I only take counsel from women who are surrendered to the Holy Spirit. Why would you receive counsel from any other source? Today if you feel small under the large load you are carrying, pray and ask the Father to show you who is walking with the Spirit that he can use to encourage your soul.

Spirit was also given to them, and they
prophesied in the camp. 27A young man ran
to Moses and said, "Eldad and Medad are
prophesying in the camp."

28Joshua son of Nun said, "Moses, my
master, stop them!" (Ever since he was a
young boy, Joshua had been Moses'
assistant.)

29But Moses answered, "Are you jealous for
me? I wish all the LORD's people could
prophesy. I wish the LORD would give his
Spirit to all of them!" 30Then Moses and the
leaders of Israel went back to the camp.

The Lord Sends Quail

31The LORD sent a strong wind from the
sea, and it blew quail into the area all
around the camp. The quail were about
three feet deep on the ground, and there
were quail a day's walk in any direction.
32The people went out and gathered quail
all that day, that night, and the next day.
Everyone gathered at least sixty bushels,
and they spread them around the camp.
33But the LORD became very angry, and he
gave the people a terrible sickness that
came while the meat was still in their
mouths. 34So the people named that place
Kibroth Hattaavah,[n] because there they
buried those who wanted other food.

35From Kibroth Hattaavah the people
went to stay at Hazeroth.

Miriam and Aaron Speak Against Moses

12 Miriam and Aaron began to talk
against Moses because of his Cushite
wife (he had married a Cushite). 2They said,
"Is Moses the only one the LORD speaks
through? Doesn't he also speak through us?"
And the LORD heard this.

3(Now Moses was very humble. He was
the least proud person on earth.)

4So the LORD suddenly spoke to Moses,
Aaron, and Miriam and said, "All three of
you come to the Meeting Tent." So they
went. 5The LORD came down in a pillar of

11:34 Kibroth Hattaavah This name in Hebrew means "graves of wanting."

cloud and stood at the entrance to the Tent.
He called to Aaron and Miriam, and they
both came near. 6He said, "Listen to my
words:

When prophets are among you,
I, the LORD, will show myself to them
in visions;
I will speak to them in dreams.
7But this is not true with my servant
Moses.
I trust him to lead all my people.
8I speak face to face with him—
clearly, not with hidden meanings.
He has even seen the form of the
LORD.
You should be afraid
to speak against my servant Moses."

9The LORD was very angry with them, and
he left.
10When the cloud lifted from the Tent and
Aaron turned toward Miriam, she was as
white as snow; she had a skin disease.
11Aaron said to Moses, "Please, my master,
forgive us for our foolish sin. 12Don't let her
be like a baby who is born dead. (Sometimes
a baby is born with half of its flesh eaten
away.)"
13So Moses cried out to the LORD, "God,
please heal her!"
14The LORD answered Moses, "If her father
had spit in her face, she would have been
shamed for seven days, so put her outside
the camp for seven days. After that, she may
come back." 15So Miriam was put outside of
the camp for seven days, and the people did
not move on until she came back.
16After that, the people left Hazeroth and
camped in the Desert of Paran.

The Spies Explore Canaan

13 The LORD said to Moses, 2"Send men
to explore the land of Canaan, which I
will give to the Israelites. Send one leader
from each tribe."
3So Moses obeyed the LORD's command
and sent the Israelite leaders out from the
Desert of Paran. 4These are their names: from
the tribe of Reuben, Shammua son of Zaccur;
5from the tribe of Simeon, Shaphat son of
Hori; 6from the tribe of Judah, Caleb son of
Jephunneh; 7from the tribe of Issachar, Igal
son of Joseph; 8from the tribe of Ephraim,
Hoshea son of Nun; 9from the tribe of
Benjamin, Palti son of Raphu; 10from the
tribe of Zebulun, Gaddiel son of Sodi; 11from
the tribe of Manasseh (a tribe of Joseph),
Gaddi son of Susi; 12from the tribe of Dan,
Ammiel son of Gemalli; 13from the tribe of
Asher, Sethur son of Michael; 14from the
tribe of Naphtali, Nahbi son of Vophsi;
15from the tribe of Gad, Geuel son of Maki.
16These are the names of the men Moses
sent to explore the land. (Moses gave Hoshea
son of Nun the new name Joshua.)
17Moses sent them to explore Canaan and
said, "Go through southern Canaan and then
into the mountains. 18See what the land
looks like. Are the people who live there
strong or weak? Are there a few or many?
19What kind of land do they live in? Is it
good or bad? What about the towns they live
in—are they open like camps, or do they
have walls? 20What about the soil? Is it
fertile or poor? Are there trees there? Try to
bring back some of the fruit from that land."
(It was the season for the first grapes.)
21So they went up and explored the land,
from the Desert of Zin all the way to Rehob
by Lebo Hamath. 22They went through the
southern area to Hebron, where Ahiman,
Sheshai, and Talmai, the descendants of
Anak lived. (The city of Hebron had been
built seven years before Zoan in Egypt.) 23In
the Valley of Eshcol, they cut off a branch of
a grapevine that had one bunch of grapes on
it and carried that branch on a pole between
two of them. They also got some
pomegranates and figs. 24That place was
called the Valley of Eshcol,[n] because the
Israelites cut off the bunch of grapes there.
25After forty days of exploring the land, the
men returned to the camp.
26They came back to Moses and Aaron
and all the Israelites at Kadesh, in the Desert
of Paran. The men reported to them and
showed everybody the fruit from the land.
27They told Moses, "We went to the land
where you sent us, and it is a fertile land!
Here is some of its fruit. 28But the people
who live there are strong. Their cities are
walled and very large. We even saw some
Anakites there. 29The Amalekites live in the
southern area; the Hittites, Jebusites, and
Amorites live in the mountains; and the

13:24 Eshcol This name in Hebrew means "bunch."

Miriam

NUMBERS 12

Miriam gently removes the layers of cloth she has wound around her arm. She stares at the white dangling pieces; they will fall to the ground if she doesn't cover the rotting flesh. She carefully winds the cloth back around her arm and leans her head against the wall. For seven days she must stay here outside the camp, away from the worship, laughter, and friends. "Oh Lord, forgive me. I am a fool."

In a moment of jealousy, she had spoken against her brother Moses. "Is Moses the only one the Lord speaks through?" she and her brother Aaron had asked. "Doesn't he also speak through us?"

Tears sting her eyes as she remembers her words. She *had* been chosen by God to lead with Moses and Aaron. Why did she lash out against Moses, God's chosen leader for their nation? Adding shame to her misery, it was Moses who cried out to God in her defense. But God carried out her punishment. She cocks her head—music is coming from the camp. Oh, how she longs to fellowship and worship with her people! "I am your servant, Lord," she says, letting tears stream down her face.

Miriam rebelled against Moses' authority (and ultimately God's authority) and had to deal with the consequences of her sin. Her shame brought her closer to God, and she became a respected leader among the Israelites. God's discipline either brings us closer to him or farther away. The choice is ours.

Canaanites live near the sea and along the
Jordan River."
30Then Caleb told the people near Moses
to be quiet, and he said, "We should certainly
go up and take the land for ourselves. We
can certainly do it."
31But the men who had gone with him
said, "We can't attack those people; they are
stronger than we are." 32And those men gave
the Israelites a bad report about the land
they explored, saying, "The land that we
explored is too large to conquer. All the
people we saw are very tall. 33We saw the
Nephilim people there. (The Anakites come
from the Nephilim people.) We felt like
grasshoppers, and we looked like
grasshoppers to them."

The People Complain Again

14 That night all the people in the camp
began crying loudly. 2All the Israelites
complained against Moses and Aaron, and
all the people said to them, "We wish we had
died in Egypt or in this desert. 3Why is the
LORD bringing us to this land to be killed
with swords? Our wives and children will be
taken away. We would be better off going
back to Egypt." 4They said to each other,
"Let's choose a leader and go back to Egypt."
5Then Moses and Aaron bowed facedown
in front of all the Israezlites gathered there.
6Joshua son of Nun and Caleb son of
Jephunneh, who had explored the land, tore
their clothes. 7They said to all of the
Israelites, "The land we explored is very
good. 8If the LORD is pleased with us, he will
lead us into that land and give us that fertile
land. 9Don't turn against the LORD! Don't be
afraid of the people in that land! We will
chew them up. They have no protection, but
the LORD is with us. So don't be afraid of
them."
10Then all the people talked about killing
them with stones. But the glory of the LORD
appeared at the Meeting Tent to all the
Israelites. 11The LORD said to Moses, "How
long will these people ignore me? How long
will they not believe me in spite of the
miracles I have done among them? 12I will
give them a terrible sickness and get rid of
them. But I will make you into a great nation
that will be stronger than they are."
13Then Moses said to the LORD, "The
Egyptians will hear about it! You brought

devotion 43

NUMBERS 14:3–4

"I'M FREAKING MYSELF OUT!"

My three daughters sat on the dock behind our house one night playing a game. The wind was still as the canal water quietly lapped the seawall. Suddenly, a large fish burst through the water beside the dock sending my girls into screams of panic. The littlest one, who was three years old at the time, came running into the house ahead of the others, her red hair flying. She was yelling at the top of her voice, "I'm freaking myself out! I'm freaking myself out! I'm freaking myself *out*!"

This was the picture of the Israelites. God himself had already told them that he would give them the land of Canaan. Yet when they saw fortified cities with men as big as giants guarding the gates, they ran back to camp yelling, "I'm freaking out!" Their fear quickly turned to doubt that God was capable of doing what he had said he would do.

What in your life brings that kind of fear? Cancer sends fear through my spirit. I had melanoma six years ago and faced a doctor who told me that I needed surgery or I could die. I remember sitting in the car with my husband after my appointment with tears streaming down my face saying, "Emotionally I'm falling apart, but somehow in my spirit, I have a peace that I'm going to be fine." And I was. God turned my fear into faith, and whatever fear you're facing, you can trust God to do the same for you.

these people from there by your great power,
[14]and the Egyptians will tell this to those
who live in this land. They have already
heard about you, LORD. They know that you
are with your people and that you were seen
face to face. They know that your cloud stays
over your people and that you lead your
people with that cloud during the day and
with fire at night. [15]If you put these people
to death all at once, the nations who have
heard about your power will say, [16]'The LORD
was not able to bring them into the land he
promised them. So he killed them in the
desert.'

[17]"So show your strength now, Lord. Do
what you said: [18]'The LORD doesn't become
angry quickly, but he has great love. He
forgives sin and law breaking. But the LORD
never forgets to punish guilty people. When
parents sin, he will also punish their
children, their grandchildren, their great-
grandchildren, and their great-great-
grandchildren.' [19]By your great love, forgive
these people's sin, just as you have forgiven
them from the time they left Egypt until
now."

[20]The LORD answered, "I have forgiven
them as you asked. [21]But, as surely as I live
and as surely as my glory fills the whole
earth, I make this promise: [22]All these people
saw my glory and the miracles I did in Egypt
and in the desert, but they disobeyed me and
tested me ten times. [23]So not one of them
will see the land I promised to their
ancestors. No one who rejected me will see
that land. [24]But my servant Caleb thinks
differently and follows me completely. So I
will bring him into the land he has already
seen, and his children will own that land.
[25]Since the Amalekites and the Canaanites
are living in the valleys, leave tomorrow and
follow the desert road toward the Red Sea."

The Lord Punishes the People

[26]The LORD said to Moses and Aaron,
[27]"How long will these evil people complain
about me? I have heard the grumbling and
complaining of these Israelites. [28]So tell

them, 'This is what the LORD says. I heard what you said, and as surely as I live, I will do those very things to you: 29You will die in this desert. Every one of you who is twenty years old or older and who was counted with the people—all of you who complained against me—will die. 30Not one of you will enter the land where I promised you would live; only Caleb son of Jephunneh and Joshua son of Nun will go in. 31You said that your children would be taken away, but I will bring them into the land to enjoy what you refused. 32As for you, you will die in this desert. 33Your children will be shepherds here for forty years. Because you were not loyal, they will suffer until you lie dead in the desert. 34For forty years you will suffer for your sins—a year for each of the forty days you explored the land. You will know me as your enemy.' 35I, the LORD, have spoken, and I will certainly do these things to all these evil people who have come together against me. So they will all die here in this desert."

36The men Moses had sent to explore the land had returned and spread complaints among all the people. They had given a bad report about the land. 37The men who gave a very bad report died; the LORD killed them with a terrible sickness. 38Only two of the men who explored the land did not die—Joshua son of Nun and Caleb son of Jephunneh.

39When Moses told these things to all the Israelites, they were very sad. 40Early the next morning they started to go toward the top of the mountains, saying, "We have sinned. We will go where the LORD told us."

41But Moses said, "Why are you disobeying the LORD's command? You will not win! 42Don't go, because the LORD is not with you and you will be beaten by your enemies. 43You will run into the Amalekites and Canaanites, who will kill you with swords. You have turned away from the LORD, so the LORD will not be with you."

44But they were proud. They went toward the top of the mountains, but Moses and the Ark of the Agreement with the LORD did not leave the camp. 45The Amalekites and the Canaanites who lived in those mountains came down and attacked the Israelites and beat them back all the way to Hormah.

Rules About Sacrifices

15 The LORD said to Moses, 2"Speak to the Israelites and say to them, 'When you enter the land that I am giving you as a home, 3give the LORD offerings made by fire. These may be from your herds or flocks, as a smell pleasing to the LORD. These may be burnt offerings or sacrifices for special promises, or as gifts to him, or as festival offerings. 4The one who brings the offering shall also give the LORD a grain offering. It should be two quarts of fine flour mixed with one quart of olive oil. 5Each time you offer a lamb as a burnt offering or sacrifice, also prepare a quart of wine as a drink offering.

6" 'If you are giving a male sheep, also prepare a grain offering of four quarts of fine flour mixed with one and one-fourth quarts of olive oil. 7Also prepare one and one-fourth quarts of wine as a drink offering. Its smell will be pleasing to the LORD.

8" 'If you prepare a young bull as a burnt offering or sacrifice, whether it is for a special promise or a fellowship offering to the LORD, 9bring a grain offering with the bull. It should be six quarts of fine flour mixed with two quarts of olive oil. 10Also bring two quarts of wine as a drink offering. This offering is made by fire, and its smell will be pleasing to the LORD. 11Prepare each bull or male sheep, lamb or young goat this way. 12Do this for every one of the animals you bring.

13" 'All citizens must do these things in this way, and the smell of their offerings by fire will be pleasing to the LORD. 14From now on if foreigners who live among you want to make offerings by fire so the smell will be pleasing to the LORD, they must offer them the same way you do. 15The law is the same for you and for foreigners, and it will be from now on; you and the foreigners are alike before the LORD. 16The teachings and rules are the same for you and for the foreigners among you.' "

17The LORD said to Moses, 18"Tell the Israelites: 'You are going to another land, where I am taking you. 19When you eat the food there, offer part of it to the LORD. 20Offer a loaf of bread from the first of your grain, which will be your offering from the threshing floor. 21From now on offer to the LORD the first part of your grain.

22“ ‘Now what if you forget to obey any of
these commands the LORD gave Moses?
23These are the LORD’s commands given to
you through Moses, which began the day the
LORD gave them to you and will continue
from now on. 24If the people forget to obey
one of these commands, all the people must
offer a young bull as a burnt offering, a smell
pleasing to the LORD. By law you must also
give the grain offering and the drink offering
with it, and you must bring a male goat as a
sin offering.
25“ ‘The priest will remove that sin for all
the Israelites so they will belong to the LORD.
They are forgiven, because they didn’t know
they were sinning. For the wrong they did
they brought offerings to the LORD, an
offering by fire and a sin offering. 26So all of
the people of Israel and the foreigners living
among them will be forgiven. No one meant
to do wrong.
27“ ‘If just one person sins without
meaning to, a year-old female goat must
be brought for a sin offering. 28The priest
will remove the sin of the person who
sinned accidentally. He will remove it
before the LORD, and the person will be
forgiven. 29The same teaching is for
everyone who sins accidentally—for those
born Israelites and for foreigners living
among you.
30“ ‘But anyone who sins on purpose is
against the LORD and must be cut off from
the people, whether it is someone born
among you or a foreigner. 31That person has
turned against the LORD’s word and has not
obeyed his commands. Such a person must
surely be cut off from the others. He is
guilty.’ ”

A Man Worked on the Sabbath

32When the Israelites were still in the
desert, they found a man gathering wood on
the Sabbath day. 33Those who found him
gathering wood brought him to Moses and
Aaron and all the people. 34They held the
man under guard, because they did not
know what to do with him. 35Then the LORD
said to Moses, “The man must surely die. All
the people must kill him by throwing
stones at him outside the camp.” 36So all the
people took him outside the camp and
stoned him to death, as the LORD
commanded Moses.

The Tassels

37The LORD said to Moses, 38“Speak to the
Israelites and tell them this: ‘Tie several
pieces of thread together and attach them to
the corners of your clothes. Put a blue thread
in each one of these tassels. Wear them from
now on. 39You will have these tassels to look
at to remind you of all the LORD’s commands.
Then you will obey them and not be disloyal
by following what your bodies and eyes
want. 40Then you will remember to obey all
my commands, and you will be God’s holy
people. 41I am the LORD your God, who
brought you out of Egypt to be your God. I
am the LORD your God.’ ”

Korah, Dathan, Abiram, and On

16 Korah, Dathan, Abiram, and On
turned against Moses. (Korah was the
son of Izhar, the son of Kohath, the son of
Levi; Dathan and Abiram were brothers, the
sons of Eliab; and On was the son of Peleth;
Dathan, Abiram, and On were from the tribe
of Reuben.) 2These men gathered two
hundred fifty other Israelite men, well-
known leaders chosen by the community,
and challenged Moses. 3They came as a
group to speak to Moses and Aaron and said,
“You have gone too far. All the people are
holy, every one of them, and the LORD is
among them. So why do you put yourselves
above all the people of the LORD?”
4When Moses heard this, he bowed
facedown. 5Then he said to Korah and all his
followers: “Tomorrow morning the LORD will
show who belongs to him. He will bring the
one who is holy near to him; he will bring to
himself the person he chooses. 6So Korah,
you and all your followers do this: Get some
pans for burning incense. 7Tomorrow put
fire and incense in them and take them
before the LORD. He will choose the man
who is holy. You Levites have gone too far.”
8Moses also said to Korah, “Listen, you
Levites. 9The God of Israel has separated you
from the rest of the Israelites. He brought
you near to himself to do the work in the
LORD’s Holy Tent and to stand before all the
Israelites and serve them. Isn’t that enough?
10He has brought you and all your fellow
Levites near to himself, yet now you want to
be priests. 11You and your followers have
joined together against the LORD. Your
complaint is not against Aaron.”

[12]Then Moses called Dathan and Abiram,
the sons of Eliab, but they said, "We will not
come! [13]You have brought us out of a fertile
land to this desert to kill us, and now you
want to order us around. [14]You haven't
brought us into a fertile land; you haven't
given us any land with fields and vineyards.
Will you put out the eyes of these men? No!
We will not come!"

[15]Then Moses became very angry and said
to the LORD, "Don't accept their gifts. I have
not taken anything from them, not even a
donkey, and I have not done wrong to any of
them."

[16]Then Moses said to Korah, "You and all
your followers must stand before the LORD
tomorrow. And Aaron will stand there
with you and them. [17]Each of you must
take your pan and put incense in it;
present these two hundred fifty pans
before the LORD. You and Aaron must also
present your pans." [18]So each man got his
pan and put burning incense in it and
stood with Moses and Aaron at the
entrance to the Meeting Tent. [19]Korah
gathered all his followers who were
against Moses and Aaron, and they stood at
the entrance to the Meeting Tent. Then the
glory of the LORD appeared to everyone.

[20]The LORD said to Moses and Aaron,
[21]"Move away from these men so I can
destroy them quickly."

[22]But Moses and Aaron bowed facedown
and cried out, "God, you are the God over the
spirits of all people. Please don't be angry
with this whole group. Only one man has
really sinned."

[23]Then the LORD said to Moses, [24]"Tell
everyone to move away from the tents of
Korah, Dathan, and Abiram."

[25]Moses stood and went to Dathan and
Abiram; the elders of Israel followed him.
[26]Moses warned the people, "Move away
from the tents of these evil men! Don't touch
anything of theirs, or you will be destroyed
because of their sins." [27]So they moved away
from the tents of Korah, Dathan, and
Abiram. Dathan and Abiram were standing
outside their tents with their wives,
children, and little babies.

[28]Then Moses said, "Now you will know
that the LORD has sent me to do all these
things; it was not my idea. [29]If these men die
a normal death—the way men usually die—
then the LORD did not really send me. [30]But if
the LORD does something new, you will
know they have insulted the LORD. The
ground will open and swallow them. They
will be buried alive and will go to the place
of the dead, and everything that belongs to
them will go with them."

[31]When Moses finished saying these
things, the ground under the men split open.
[32]The earth opened and swallowed them and
all their families. All Korah's men and
everything they owned went down. [33]They
were buried alive, going to the place of the
dead, and everything they owned went with
them. Then the earth covered them. They
died and were gone from the community.
[34]The people of Israel around them heard
their screams and ran away, saying, "The
earth will swallow us, too!"

[35]Then a fire came down from the LORD
and destroyed the two hundred fifty men
who had presented the incense.

[36]The LORD said to Moses, [37]"Tell Eleazar
son of Aaron, the priest, to take all the
incense pans out of the fire. Have him
scatter the coals a long distance away. But
the incense pans are still holy. [38]Take the
pans of these men who sinned and lost their
lives, and hammer them into flat sheets that
will be used to cover the altar. They are
holy, because they were presented to the
LORD, and they will be a sign to the
Israelites."

[39]So Eleazar the priest gathered all the
bronze pans that had been brought by the
men who were burned up. He had the pans
hammered into flat sheets to put on the
altar, [40]as the LORD had commanded him
through Moses. These sheets were to remind
the Israelites that only descendants of Aaron
should burn incense before the LORD.
Anyone else would die like Korah and his
followers.

Aaron Saves the People

[41]The next day all the Israelites
complained against Moses and Aaron and
said, "You have killed the LORD's people."

[42]When the people gathered to complain
against Moses and Aaron, they turned
toward the Meeting Tent, and the cloud
covered it. The glory of the LORD appeared.
[43]Then Moses and Aaron went in front of the
Meeting Tent.

44The LORD said to Moses, 45"Move away from these people so I can destroy them quickly." So Moses and Aaron bowed facedown.

46Then Moses said to Aaron, "Get your pan, and put fire from the altar and incense in it. Hurry to the people and remove their sin. The LORD is angry with them; the sickness has already started." 47So Aaron did as Moses said. He ran to the middle of the people, where the sickness had already started among them. So Aaron offered the incense to remove their sin. 48He stood between the dead and the living, and the sickness stopped there. 49But 14,700 people died from that sickness, in addition to those who died because of Korah. 50Then Aaron went back to Moses at the entrance to the Meeting Tent. The terrible sickness had been stopped.

Aaron's Walking Stick Buds

17 The LORD said to Moses, 2"Speak to the people of Israel and get twelve walking sticks from them—one from the leader of each tribe. Write the name of each man on his stick, and 3on the stick from Levi, write Aaron's name. There must be one stick for the head of each tribe. 4Put them in the Meeting Tent in front of the Ark of the Agreement, where I meet with you. 5I will choose one man whose walking stick will begin to grow leaves; in this way I will stop the Israelites from always complaining against you."

6So Moses spoke to the Israelites. Each of the twelve leaders gave him a walking stick—one from each tribe—and Aaron's walking stick was among them. 7Moses put them before the LORD in the Tent of the Agreement.

8The next day, when Moses entered the Tent, he saw that Aaron's stick (which stood for the family of Levi) had grown leaves. It had even budded, blossomed, and produced almonds. 9So Moses brought out to the Israelites all the walking sticks from the LORD's presence. They all looked, and each man took back his stick.

10Then the LORD said to Moses, "Put Aaron's walking stick back in front of the Ark of the Agreement. It will remind these people who are always turning against me to stop their complaining against me so they won't die." 11So Moses obeyed what the LORD commanded him.

12The people of Israel said to Moses, "We are going to die! We are destroyed. We are all destroyed! 13Anyone who even comes near the Holy Tent of the LORD will die. Will we all die?"

The Work of the Priests and Levites

18 The LORD said to Aaron, "You, your sons, and your family are now responsible for any wrongs done against the Holy Place; you and your sons are responsible for any wrongs done against the priests. 2Bring with you your fellow Levites from your tribe, and they will help you and your sons serve in the Tent of the Agreement. 3They are under your control, to do all the work that needs to be done in the Tent. But they must not go near the things in the Holy Place or near the altar. If they do, both you and they will die. 4They will join you in taking care of the Meeting Tent. They must do the work at the Tent, and no one else may come near you.

5"You must take care of the Holy Place and the altar so that I won't become angry with the Israelites again. 6I myself chose your fellow Levites from among the Israelites as a gift given for you to the LORD, to work at the Meeting Tent. 7But only you and your sons may serve as priests. Only you may serve at the altar or go behind the curtain. I am giving you this gift of serving as a priest, and anyone else who comes near the Holy Place will be put to death."

8Then the LORD said to Aaron, "I myself make you responsible for the offerings given to me. All the holy offerings that the Israelites give to me, I give to you and your sons as your share, your continual portion. 9Your share of the holy offerings is that part which is not burned. When the people bring me gifts as most holy offerings, whether they are grain or sin or penalty offerings, they will be set apart for you and your sons. 10You must eat the offering in a most holy place. Any male may eat it, but you must respect it as holy.

11"I also give you the offerings the Israelites present to me. I give these to you and your sons and daughters as your continual share. Anyone in your family who is clean may eat it.

12"And I give you all the best olive oil and

all the best new wine and grain. This is what the Israelites give to me, the LORD, from the first crops they harvest. 13When they bring to the LORD all the first things they harvest, they will be yours. Anyone in your family who is clean may eat these things.

14"Everything in Israel that is given to the LORD is yours. 15The first one born to any family, whether people or animals, will be offered to the LORD. And that will be yours. But you must make a payment for every firstborn child and every firstborn animal that is unclean. 16When they are one month old, you must make a payment for them of two ounces of silver, as set by the Holy Place measure.

17"But you must not make a payment for the firstborn ox or sheep or goat. Those animals are holy. Sprinkle their blood on the altar and burn their fat as an offering made by fire. The smell is pleasing to the LORD. 18But the meat will be yours, just as the breast that is presented and the right thigh will be yours. 19Anything the Israelites present as holy gifts I, the LORD, give to you, your sons and daughters as your continual portion. This is a lasting agreement of salt[n] before the LORD for you and your children forever."

20The LORD also said to Aaron, "You will not inherit any of the land, and you will not own any land among the other people. I will be yours. Out of all the Israelites, only you will inherit me.

21"When the people of Israel give me a tenth of what they make, I will give that tenth to the Levites. This is their payment for the work they do serving at the Meeting Tent. 22But the other Israelites must never go near the Meeting Tent, or they will die for their sin. 23Only the Levites should work in the Meeting Tent and be responsible for any sins against it. This is a rule from now on. The Levites will not inherit any land among the other Israelites, 24but when the Israelites give a tenth of everything they make to me, I will give that tenth to the Levites as a reward. That is why I said about the Levites: 'They will not inherit any land among the Israelites.' "

25The LORD said to Moses, 26"Speak to the Levites and tell them: 'You will receive a tenth of everything the Israelites make, which I will give to you. But you must give a tenth of that back to the LORD. 27I will accept your offering just as much as I accept the offerings from others, who give new grain or new wine. 28In this way you will present an offering to the LORD as the other Israelites do. When you receive a tenth from the Israelites, you will give a tenth of that to Aaron, the priest, as the LORD's share. 29Choose the best and holiest part from what you are given as the portion you must give to the LORD.'

30"Say to the Levites: 'When you present the best, it will be accepted as much as the grain and wine from the other people. 31You and your families may eat all that is left anywhere, because it is your pay for your work in the Meeting Tent. 32And if you always give the best part to the LORD, you will never be guilty. If you do not sin against the holy offerings of the Israelites, you will not die.' "

The Offering for Cleansing

19 The LORD said to Moses and Aaron, 2"These are the teachings that the LORD commanded. Tell the Israelites to get a young red cow that does not have anything wrong with it and that has never been worked. 3Give the cow to Eleazar the priest; he will take it outside the camp and kill it. 4Then Eleazar the priest must put some of its blood on his finger and sprinkle it seven times toward the front of the Meeting Tent. 5The whole cow must be burned while he watches; the skin, the meat, the blood, and the intestines must all be burned. 6Then the priest must take a cedar stick, a hyssop branch, and a red string and throw them onto the burning cow. 7After the priest has washed himself and his clothes with water, he may come back into the camp, but he will be unclean until evening. 8The man who burns the cow must wash himself and his clothes in water; he will be unclean until evening.

9"Then someone who is clean will collect the ashes from the cow and put them in a clean place outside the camp. The Israelites will keep these ashes to use in the cleansing water, in a special ceremony to cleanse away

18:19 agreement of salt The meaning is not clear, but Leviticus 2:13 says, "Salt stands for your agreement with God that will last forever."

devotion 44

NUMBERS 18:29

WHO GETS YOUR BEST?

I recently heard someone say, "Save your best for your family." I love that. What a great perspective. But as a believer, I decided those words need a little revision. What if I save my best for my Lord, and then because he gets the best of me, my family will get a double blessing? They will get a woman who loves them like crazy and is drawing her strength from her Savior.

I realize the world is clamoring. The alarm goes off too early. The days are always full. There is work and family, church and community. Some days it seems like your best gets used up before you can even turn around twice, so giving your best and purest to God must be intentional or it might never happen.

But here's the hard part. No one around us really cares if you or I live intentionally. Nobody in my house checks in with me to see if I loved God or cared for my soul today. Worrying about whether I'm giving my best to God is not on their list. In fact, sometimes it feels like everyone is getting in the way of it. That's the point—no one will choose intentionally for you or for me. We have to wake up and keep choosing for ourselves.

We must decide that the best and holiest of our lives belongs to God. He should get the beginning of our day, a pure heart throughout, and all his due glory at the end.

sin. 10The man who collected the cow's
ashes must wash his clothes and be unclean
until evening. This is a lasting rule for the
Israelites and for the foreigners among them.
11"Those who touch a dead person's body
will be unclean for seven days. 12They
must wash themselves with the cleansing
water on the third day and on the seventh
day; then they will be clean. But if they do
not wash themselves on the third day and
the seventh day, they cannot be clean. 13If
those who touch a dead person's body stay
unclean and go to the LORD's Holy Tent, it
becomes unclean; they must be cut off
from Israel. If the cleansing water is not
sprinkled on them, they are unclean and
will stay unclean.
14"This is the teaching about someone
who dies in a tent: Anyone in the tent or
anyone who enters it will be unclean for
seven days. 15And every open jar or pot
without a cover becomes unclean. 16If
anyone is outside and touches someone who
was killed by a sword or who died a natural
death, or if anyone touches a human bone or
a grave, that person will be unclean for
seven days.
17"So you must use the ashes from the
burnt offering to make that person clean
again. Pour fresh water over the ashes into a
jar. 18A clean person must take a hyssop
branch and dip it into the water, and then he
must sprinkle it over the tent and all its
objects. He must also sprinkle the people
who were there, as well as anyone who
touched a bone, or the body of someone who
was killed, or a dead person, or a grave. 19The
person who is clean must sprinkle this water
on the unclean people on the third day and
on the seventh day. On the seventh day they
will become clean. They must wash their
clothes and take a bath, and they will be
clean that evening. 20If any who are unclean
do not become clean, they must be cut off
from the community. Since they were not
sprinkled with the cleansing water, they stay
unclean, and they could make the LORD's
Holy Tent unclean. 21This is a lasting rule.

Those who sprinkle the cleansing water
must also wash their clothes, and anyone
who touches the water will be unclean until
evening. 22Anything an unclean person
touches becomes unclean, and whoever
touches it will be unclean until evening."

Moses Disobeys God

20 In the first month all the people of
Israel arrived at the Desert of Zin, and
they stayed at Kadesh. There Miriam died
and was buried. 2There was no water for the
people, so they came together against Moses
and Aaron. 3They argued with Moses and
said, "We should have died in front of the
LORD as our brothers did. 4Why did you bring
the LORD's people into this desert? Are we and
our animals to die here? 5Why did you bring
us from Egypt to this terrible place? It has no
grain, figs, grapevines, or pomegranates, and
there's no water to drink!"
6So Moses and Aaron left the people and
went to the entrance of the Meeting Tent.
There they bowed facedown, and the glory
of the LORD appeared to them. 7The LORD said
to Moses, 8"Take your walking stick, and you
and your brother Aaron should gather the
people. Speak to that rock in front of them
so that its water will flow from it. When you
bring the water out from that rock, give it to
the people and their animals."
9So Moses took the stick from in front of
the LORD, as he had said. 10Moses and Aaron
gathered the people in front of the rock, and
Moses said, "Now listen to me, you who turn
against God! Do you want us to bring water
out of this rock?" 11Then Moses lifted his
hand and hit the rock twice with his stick.
Water began pouring out, and the people
and their animals drank it.
12But the LORD said to Moses and Aaron,
"Because you did not believe me, and
because you did not honor me as holy
before the people, you will not lead them
into the land I will give them."
13These are the waters of Meribah,[n] where
the Israelites argued with the LORD and
where he showed them he was holy.

Edom Will Not Let Israel Pass

14From Kadesh, Moses sent messengers to
the king of Edom. He said, "Your brothers,
the Israelites, say to you: You know about all
the troubles we have had, 15how our
ancestors went down into Egypt and we
lived there for many years. The people of
Egypt were cruel to us and our ancestors,
16but when we cried out to the LORD, he
heard us and sent us an angel to bring us out
of Egypt.
"Now we are here at Kadesh, a town on
the edge of your land. 17Please let us pass
through your country. We will not touch
any fields of grain or vineyards, and will not
drink water from the wells. We will travel
only along the king's road, not turning right
or left until we have passed through your
country."
18But the king of Edom answered: "You
may not pass through here. If you try, I will
come and meet you with swords."
19The Israelites answered: "We will go
along the main road, and if we or our
animals drink any of your water, we will pay
for it. We only want to walk through. That's
all."
20But he answered: "You may not pass
through here."
Then the Edomites went out to meet the
Israelites with a large and powerful army.
21The Edomites refused to let them pass
through their country, so the Israelites
turned back.

Aaron Dies

22All the Israelites moved from Kadesh
to Mount Hor, 23near the border of Edom.
There the LORD said to Moses and Aaron,
24"Aaron will die. He will not enter the land
that I'm giving to the Israelites, because
you both acted against my command at the
waters of Meribah. 25Take Aaron and his
son Eleazar up on Mount Hor, 26and take
off Aaron's special clothes and put them on
his son Eleazar. Aaron will die there; he
will join his ancestors."
27Moses obeyed the LORD's command.
They climbed up Mount Hor, and all the
people saw them go. 28Moses took off
Aaron's clothes and put them on Aaron's son
Eleazar. Then Aaron died there on top of the
mountain. Moses and Eleazar came back
down the mountain, 29and when all the
people learned that Aaron was dead,

20:13 Meribah This name in Hebrew means "argument."

everyone in Israel cried for him for thirty days.

War with the Canaanites

21 The Canaanite king of Arad lived in the southern area. When he heard that the Israelites were coming on the road to Atharim, he attacked them and captured some of them. 2Then the Israelites made this promise to the LORD: "If you will help us defeat these people, we will completely destroy their cities." 3The LORD listened to the Israelites, and he let them defeat the Canaanites. The Israelites completely destroyed the Canaanites and their cities, so the place was named Hormah.[n]

The Bronze Snake

4The Israelites left Mount Hor and went on the road toward the Red Sea, in order to go around the country of Edom. But the people became impatient on the way 5and grumbled at God and Moses. They said, "Why did you bring us out of Egypt to die in this desert? There is no bread and no water, and we hate this terrible food!"

6So the LORD sent them poisonous snakes; they bit the people, and many of the Israelites died. 7The people came to Moses and said, "We sinned when we grumbled at you and the LORD. Pray that the LORD will take away these snakes." So Moses prayed for the people.

8The LORD said to Moses, "Make a bronze snake, and put it on a pole. When anyone who is bitten looks at it, that person will live." 9So Moses made a bronze snake and put it on a pole. Then when a snake bit anyone, that person looked at the bronze snake and lived.

The Journey to Moab

10The Israelites went and camped at Oboth. 11They went from Oboth to Iye Abarim, in the desert east of Moab. 12From there they went and camped in the Zered Valley. 13From there they went and camped across the Arnon, in the desert just inside the Amorite country. The Arnon is the border between the Moabites and the Amorites. 14That is why the Book of the Wars of the LORD says:

"... and Waheb in Suphah, and the
ravines,
the Arnon, 15and the slopes of the
ravines
that lead to the settlement of Ar.
These places are at the border of Moab."

16The Israelites went from there to Beer; a well is there where the LORD said to Moses, "Gather the people and I will give them water."

17Then the Israelites sang this song:

"Pour out water, well!
Sing about it.
18Princes dug this well.
Important men made it.
With their scepters and poles,
they dug it."

The people went from the desert to Mattanah. 19From Mattanah they went to Nahaliel and on to Bamoth. 20From Bamoth they went to the valley of Moab where the top of Mount Pisgah looks over the desert.

Israel Kills Sihon and Og

21The Israelites sent messengers to Sihon, king of the Amorites, saying, 22"Let us pass through your country. We will not go through any fields of grain or vineyards, or drink water from the wells. We will travel only along the king's road until we have passed through your country."

23But King Sihon would not let the Israelites pass through his country. He gathered his whole army together, and they marched out to meet Israel in the desert. At Jahaz they fought the Israelites. 24Israel killed the king and captured his land from the Arnon River to the Jabbok River. They took the land as far as the Ammonite border, which was strongly defended. 25Israel captured all the Amorite cities and lived in them, taking Heshbon and all the towns around it. 26Heshbon was the city where Sihon, the Amorite king, lived. In the past he had fought with the king of Moab and had taken all the land as far as the Arnon.

27That is why the poets say:

"Come to Heshbon
and rebuild it;
rebuild Sihon's city.
28A fire began in Heshbon;
flames came from Sihon's city.

21:3 Hormah This name in Hebrew means "completely destroyed."

devotion 45

NUMBERS 21:7-9

YOU NEED A SNAKE, A POLE, AND A LITTLE FAITH

God considers negative attitudes and a complaining heart a serious condition of your soul. The children of Israel complained in secret and then brought charges against Moses *and* the Lord. Their complaints? They felt the Lord had led them into the desert with little food or water, and they detested the provision of manna that he provided. The Lord knew every step they were taking, and he was meeting their needs all along the way. He had purposed for them to go to a promised land—yet they complained.

The path of life can have its discouraging moments, but the Lord is there. His plan is to get us from one place to another, though it is a journey that requires courage and faith. It is also a journey that brings healing if we let it. Have you ever witnessed the condition of someone who is constantly complaining or challenging the Lord simply because things do not turn out the way they expected? I liken that type of person to someone who is full of venom. They sow discord. They are sickly in their faith, and they destroy relationships.

The Lord had Moses erect a pole with a bronze serpent upon it. Anytime someone was bitten, they could look upon the pole, be healed from the bite, and remember that God was their provider and healer. That pole and serpent are still the universal mark for healing today. God hasn't changed either—he is still your healer and provider forever.

It destroyed Ar in Moab,
and it burned the Arnon highlands.
29 How terrible for you, Moab!
The people of Chemosh are ruined.
His sons ran away
and his daughters were captured
by Sihon, king of the Amorites.
30 But we defeated those Amorites.
We ruined their towns from Heshbon
to Dibon,
and we destroyed them as far as
Nophah, near Medeba."

31 So Israel lived in the land of the
Amorites.
32 After Moses sent spies to the town of
Jazer, they captured the towns around it,
forcing out the Amorites who lived there.
33 Then the Israelites went up the road
toward Bashan. Og king of Bashan and his
whole army marched out to meet the
Israelites, and they fought at Edrei.
34 The LORD said to Moses, "Don't be afraid
of him. I will hand him, his whole army, and
his land over to you. Do to him what you did
to Sihon, the Amorite king who lived in
Heshbon."
35 So the Israelites killed Og and his sons
and all his army; no one was left alive. And
they took his land.

Balak Sends for Balaam

22 Then the people of Israel went to the
plains of Moab, and they camped near
the Jordan River across from Jericho.
2 Balak son of Zippor saw everything the
Israelites had done to the Amorites. 3 And
Moab was scared of so many Israelites; truly,
Moab was terrified by them.
4 The Moabites said to the elders of
Midian, "These people will take everything
around us like an ox eating grass."
Balak son of Zippor was the king of
Moab at this time. 5 He sent messengers to
Balaam son of Beor at Pethor, near the
Euphrates River in his native land. Balak
said, "A nation has come out of Egypt that
covers the land. They have camped next to
me, 6 and they are too powerful for me. So

come and put a curse on them. Maybe then
I can defeat them and make them leave the
area. I know that if you bless someone, the
blessings happen, and if you put a curse on
someone, it happens."
7The elders of Moab and Midian went
with payment in their hands. When they
found Balaam, they told him what Balak had
said.
8Balaam said to them, "Stay here for the
night, and I will tell you what the LORD tells
me." So the Moabite leaders stayed with him.
9God came to Balaam and asked, "Who are
these men with you?"
10Balaam said to God, "The king of Moab,
Balak son of Zippor, sent them to me with
this message: 11'A nation has come out of
Egypt that covers the land. So come and put
a curse on them, and maybe I can fight them
and force them out of my land.' "
12But God said to Balaam, "Do not go with
them. Don't put a curse on those people,
because I have blessed them."
13The next morning Balaam awoke and
said to Balak's leaders, "Go back to your own
country; the LORD has refused to let me go
with you."
14So the Moabite leaders went back to
Balak and said, "Balaam refused to come
with us."
15So Balak sent other leaders—this time
there were more of them, and they were
more important. 16They went to Balaam and
said, "Balak son of Zippor says this: Please
don't let anything stop you from coming to
me. 17I will pay you very well, and I will do
what you say. Come and put a curse on these
people for me."
18But Balaam answered Balak's servants,
"King Balak could give me his palace full of
silver and gold, but I cannot disobey the
LORD my God in anything, great or small.
19You stay here tonight as the other men did,
and I will find out what more the LORD tells
me."
20That night God came to Balaam and
said, "These men have come to ask you to go
with them. Go, but only do what I tell you."

Balaam's Donkey Speaks

21Balaam got up the next morning and put
a saddle on his donkey. Then he went with
the Moabite leaders. 22But God became angry
because Balaam went, so the angel of the
LORD stood in the road to stop Balaam.
Balaam was riding his donkey, and he had
two servants with him. 23When the donkey
saw the angel of the LORD standing in the
road with a sword in his hand, the donkey
left the road and went into the field. Balaam
hit the donkey to force her back on the road.
24Later, the angel of the LORD stood on a
narrow path between two vineyards, with
walls on both sides. 25Again the donkey
saw the angel of the LORD, and she walked
close to one wall, crushing Balaam's foot
against it. So he hit her again.
26The angel of the LORD went ahead again
and stood at a narrow place, too narrow to
turn left or right. 27When the donkey saw
the angel of the LORD, she lay down under
Balaam. This made him so angry that he hit
her with his stick. 28Then the LORD made the
donkey talk, and she said to Balaam, "What
have I done to make you hit me three
times?"
29Balaam answered the donkey, "You have
made me look foolish! I wish I had a sword
in my hand! I would kill you right now!"
30But the donkey said to Balaam, "I am
your very own donkey, which you have
ridden for years. Have I ever done this to you
before?"
"No," Balaam said.
31Then the LORD let Balaam see the angel
of the LORD, who was standing in the road
with his sword drawn. Then Balaam bowed
facedown on the ground.
32The angel of the LORD asked Balaam,
"Why have you hit your donkey three
times? I have stood here to stop you, because
what you are doing is wrong. 33The donkey
saw me and turned away from me three
times. If she had not turned away, I would
have killed you by now, but I would have let
her live."
34Then Balaam said to the angel of the
LORD, "I have sinned; I did not know you
were standing in the road to stop me. If I am
wrong, I will go back."
35The angel of the LORD said to Balaam,
"Go with these men, but say only what I tell
you." So Balaam went with Balak's leaders.
36When Balak heard that Balaam was
coming, he went out to meet him at Ar in
Moab, which was beside the Arnon, at the
edge of his country. 37Balak said to Balaam, "I
had asked you before to come quickly. Why

didn't you come to me? I am able to reward
you well."

[38]But Balaam answered, "I have come to
you now, but I can't say just anything. I can
only say what God tells me to say."

[39]Then Balaam went with Balak to Kiriath
Huzoth. [40]Balak offered cattle and sheep as a
sacrifice and gave some meat to Balaam and
the leaders with him.

[41]The next morning Balak took Balaam to
Bamoth Baal; from there he could see the
edge of the Israelite camp.

Balaam's First Message

23 Balaam said to Balak, "Build me seven
altars here, and prepare seven bulls
and seven male sheep for me." [2]Balak did
what Balaam asked, and they offered a bull
and a male sheep on each of the altars.

[3]Then Balaam said to Balak, "Stay here
beside your burnt offering and I will go. If
the LORD comes to me, I will tell you
whatever he shows me." Then Balaam went
to a higher place.

[4]God came to Balaam there, and Balaam
said to him, "I have prepared seven altars,
and I have offered a bull and a male sheep on
each altar."

[5]The LORD told Balaam what he should
say. Then the LORD said, "Go back to Balak
and give him this message."

[6]So Balaam went back to Balak. Balak and
all the leaders of Moab were still standing
beside his burnt offering [7]when Balaam gave
them this message:

"Balak brought me here from Aram;
 the king of Moab brought me from the
  eastern mountains.
Balak said, 'Come, put a curse on the
  people of Jacob for me.
 Come, call down evil on the people of
  Israel.'
[8]But God has not cursed them,
 so I cannot curse them.
The LORD has not called down evil on
  them,
 so I cannot call down evil on them.
[9]I see them from the top of the mountains;
 I see them from the hills.
I see a people who live alone,
 who think they are different from other
  nations.
[10]No one can number the many people of
  Jacob,
 and no one can count a fourth of Israel.
Let me die like good men,
 and let me end up like them!"

[11]Balak said to Balaam, "What have you
done to me? I brought you here to curse my
enemies, but you have only blessed them!"

[12]But Balaam answered, "I must say what
the LORD tells me to say."

Balaam's Second Message

[13]Then Balak said to him, "Come with me
to another place, where you can also see the
people. But you can only see part of them,
not all of them. Curse them for me from
there." [14]So Balak took Balaam to the field of
Zophim, on top of Mount Pisgah. There Balak
built seven altars and offered a bull and a
male sheep on each altar.

[15]So Balaam said to Balak, "Stay here by
your burnt offering, and I will meet with
God over there."

[16]So the LORD came to Balaam and told
him what to say. Then he said, "Go back to
Balak and say such and such."

[17]So Balaam went to Balak, where he and
the leaders of Moab were standing beside his
burnt offering. Balak asked him, "What did
the LORD say?"

[18]Then Balaam gave this message:

"Stand up, Balak, and listen.
 Hear me, son of Zippor.
[19]God is not a human being, and he will not
  lie.
 He is not a human, and he does not
  change his mind.
What he says he will do, he does.
 What he promises, he makes come
  true.
[20]He told me to bless them,
 so I cannot change the blessing.
[21]He has found no wrong in the people of
  Jacob;
 he saw no fault in Israel.
The LORD their God is with them,
 and they praise their King.
[22]God brought them out of Egypt;
 they are as strong as a wild ox.
[23]No tricks will work on the people of
  Jacob,
 and no magic will work against Israel.
People now say about them,
 'Look what God has done for Israel!'
[24]The people rise up like a lioness;
 they get up like a lion.
Lions don't rest until they have eaten,

devotion 46

NUMBERS 23:19

KNOWING WHO TO TRUST

When my oldest was a year old, he loved to play in the dirt of a potted plant in our family room. One day I walked into the room to find him sitting by the plant with dirt all around him. I said, "What are you doing?" He looked at me, turned to our cat that was sitting beside him, and said, "No-no, Kitty!" Here he was, only a year old, and he was lying to me. It is part of human nature to lie.

God is not capable of lying. It's not part of his nature. If he says he will do something, it will be done. He is totally reliable, dependable, and faithful. That makes the Word of God priceless to us as believers. Every word in the Bible is true. We can believe it, stand on it, and know that God will do what he says he will do.

My husband and I went to Israel with our church several years ago. As we drove through Jerusalem, someone was playing music in the tape deck of the tour bus. The words "I believe in the Word of God," from a song by Steven Curtis Chapman, rang through the bus as we passed by the many sites of the Bible. I just couldn't help but think, "It's all true." Every road, every garden, every mountain that Scripture talked about was right there before my eyes. The Bible is true, and God will do what he says he will do.

until they have drunk their enemies'
blood."

25Then Balak said to Balaam, "You haven't
cursed these people, so at least don't bless
them!"

26Balaam answered Balak, "I told you
before that I can only do what the LORD tells
me."

Balaam's Third Message

27Then Balak said to Balaam, "Come, I will
take you to another place. Maybe God will
be pleased to let you curse them from there."
28So Balak took Balaam to the top of Peor,
the mountain that looks over the desert.

29Balaam told Balak, "Build me seven
altars here and prepare for me seven bulls
and seven male sheep." 30Balak did what
Balaam asked, and he offered a bull and a
male sheep on each altar.

24 Balaam saw that the LORD wanted to
bless Israel, so he did not try to use
any magic but looked toward the desert.
2When Balaam saw the Israelites camped in
their tribes, the Spirit of God took control of
him, 3and he gave this message:

"This is the message of Balaam son of
Beor,
the message of a man who sees clearly;
4this is the message of a man who hears
the words of God.
I see a vision from the Almighty,
and my eyes are open as I fall before
him.
5Your tents are beautiful, people of Jacob!
So are your homes, Israel!
6Your tents spread out like valleys,
like gardens beside a river.
They are like spices planted by the LORD,
like cedar trees growing by the water.
7Israel's water buckets will always be full,
and their crops will have plenty of
water.
Their king will be greater than Agag;
their kingdom will be very great.
8God brought them out of Egypt;
they are as strong as a wild ox.
They will defeat their enemies

and break their enemies' bones;
they will shoot them with arrows.
9 Like a lion, they lie waiting to attack;
like a lioness, no one would be brave
enough to wake them.
Anyone who blesses you will be blessed,
and anyone who curses you will be
cursed."

10 Then Balak was angry with Balaam,
and he pounded his fist. He said to Balaam,
"I called you here to curse my enemies, but
you have continued to bless them three
times. 11 Now go home! I said I would pay
you well, but the LORD has made you lose
your reward."

12 Balaam said to Balak, "When you sent
messengers to me, I told them, 13 'Balak could
give me his palace filled with silver and gold,
but I still cannot go against the LORD's
commands. I could not do anything, good or
bad, on my own, but I must say what the
LORD says.' 14 Now I am going back to my
own people, but I will tell you what these
people will do to your people in the future."

Balaam's Final Message

15 Then Balaam gave this message:
"This is the message of Balaam son of
Beor,
the message of a man who sees clearly;
16 this is the message of a man who hears
the words of God.
I know well the Most High God.
I see a vision from the Almighty,
and my eyes are open as I fall before
him.
17 I see someone who will come someday,
someone who will come, but not
soon.
A star will come from Jacob;
a ruler will rise from Israel.
He will crush the heads of the Moabites
and smash the skulls of the sons of
Sheth.
18 Edom will be conquered;
his enemy Edom will be conquered,
but Israel will grow wealthy.
19 A ruler will come from the descendants of
Jacob
and will destroy those left in the city."

20 Then Balaam saw Amalek and gave this
message:
"Amalek was the most important nation,
but Amalek will be destroyed at last."

21 Then Balaam saw the Kenites and gave
this message:
"Your home is safe,
like a nest on a cliff.
22 But you Kenites will be burned up;
Assyria will keep you captive."
23 Then Balaam gave this message:
"No one can live when God does this.
24 Ships will sail from the shores of
Cyprus
and defeat Assyria and Eber,
but they will also be destroyed."

25 Then Balaam got up and returned home,
and Balak also went on his way.

Israel Worships Baal at Peor

25 While the people of Israel were still
camped at Acacia, the men began
sinning sexually with Moabite women. 2 The
women invited them to their sacrifices to
their gods, and the Israelites ate food there
and worshiped these gods. 3 So the Israelites
began to worship Baal of Peor, and the LORD
was very angry with them.

4 The LORD said to Moses, "Get all the
leaders of the people and kill them in open
daylight in the presence of the LORD. Then
the LORD will not be angry with the people
of Israel."

5 So Moses said to Israel's judges, "Each of
you must put to death your people who have
become worshipers of Baal of Peor."

6 Moses and the Israelites were gathered at
the entrance to the Meeting Tent, crying
there. Then an Israelite man brought a
Midianite woman to his brothers in plain
sight of Moses and all the people. 7 Phinehas
son of Eleazar, the son of Aaron, the priest,
saw this, so he left the meeting and got his
spear. 8 He followed the Israelite into his tent
and drove his spear through both the
Israelite man and the Midianite woman.
Then the terrible sickness among the
Israelites stopped.

9 This sickness had killed twenty-four
thousand people.

10 The LORD said to Moses, 11 "Phinehas son
of Eleazar, the son of Aaron, the priest, has
saved the Israelites from my anger. He hates
sin as much as I do. Since he tried to save my
honor among them, I will not kill them. 12 So
tell Phinehas that I am making my peace
agreement with him. 13 He and his
descendants will always be priests, because

devotion 47

NUMBERS 25:1–3

WHO *ISN'T* TEMPTED?

We still have the same temptations we read about in the book of Numbers, except they can come disguised. They come in the form of magazines, movies, and even racy novels. Sex itself is almost a god in our world. And does the true God get as angry with our generation's obsession as he did with the Israelites? I think I hear a resounding yes.

But as women, are we tempted by "those things"? While it's sometimes hard to admit that we can be tempted by things that many men are constantly assailed with in our culture every single day, there's no doubt that we are also in danger of being ensnared by lustful temptations. Whether we are single or married, we need to be aware that we are all just one step away from facing temptation. We should do whatever we can to avoid even the very confrontation of promiscuity, but it can surface when we least expect it.

I hope that as you think about these verses, you'll be convinced to look out for temptation. Be aware of the message you might be sending *and* receiving as you go to work and even church. Impurity, even if it's only in our minds, can have devastating consequences. Save your desire for your husband or future husband. Taking a stand for purity doesn't only need to be for teens. It's never too late to guard your mind and heart so you can remain pure before your mate—and most of all, before God.

he had great concern for the honor of his
God. He removed the sins of the Israelites so
they would belong to God."
14The Israelite man who was killed with
the Midianite woman was named Zimri son
of Salu. He was the leader of a family in the
tribe of Simeon. 15And the name of the
Midianite woman who was put to death was
Cozbi daughter of Zur, who was the chief of
a Midianite family.
16The LORD said to Moses, 17"The
Midianites are your enemies, and you should
kill them. 18They have already made you
their enemies, because they tricked you at
Peor and because of their sister Cozbi, the
daughter of a Midianite leader. She was the
woman who was killed when the sickness
came because the people sinned at Peor."

The People Are Counted

26 After the great sickness, the LORD said
to Moses and Eleazar son of Aaron,
the priest, 2"Count all the people of Israel by
families. Count all the men who are twenty
years old or older who will serve in the army
of Israel." 3Moses and Eleazar the priest
spoke to the people on the plains of Moab
near the Jordan River, across from Jericho.
They said, 4"Count the men twenty years old
or older, as the LORD commanded Moses."
Here are the Israelites who came out of
Egypt:
5The tribe of Reuben, the first son born to
Israel, was counted. From Hanoch came the
Hanochite family group; from Pallu came
the Palluite family group; 6from Hezron
came the Hezronite family group; from
Carmi came the Carmite family group.
7These were the family groups of Reuben,
and the total number of men was 43,730.
8The son of Pallu was Eliab, 9and Eliab's
sons were Nemuel, Dathan, and Abiram.
Dathan and Abiram were the leaders who
turned against Moses and Aaron and

followed Korah when he turned against the
LORD. 10The earth opened up and swallowed
them and Korah; they died at the same time
the fire burned up the 250 men. This was a
warning, 11but the children of Korah did not
die.
12These were the family groups in the
tribe of Simeon: From Nemuel came the
Nemuelite family group; from Jamin came
the Jaminite family group; from Jakin
came the Jakinite family group; 13from
Zerah came the Zerahite family group;
from Shaul came the Shaulite family
group. 14These were the family groups of
Simeon, and the total number of men was
22,200.
15These were the family groups in the
tribe of Gad: From Zephon came the
Zephonite family group; from Haggi came the
Haggite family group; from Shuni came the
Shunite family group; 16from Ozni came
the Oznite family group; from Eri came the
Erite family group; 17from Arodi came the
Arodite family group; from Areli came
the Arelite family group. 18These were the
family groups of Gad, and the total number
of men was 40,500.
19Two of Judah's sons, Er and Onan, died
in Canaan.
20These were the family groups in the
tribe of Judah: From Shelah came the
Shelanite family group; from Perez came the
Perezite family group; from Zerah came
the Zerahite family group. 21These were
the family groups from Perez: From Hezron
came the Hezronite family group; from
Hamul came the Hamulite family group.
22These were the family groups of Judah,
and the total number of men was 76,500.
23These were the family groups in the
tribe of Issachar: From Tola came the Tolaite
family group; from Puah came the Puite
family group; 24from Jashub came the
Jashubite family group; from Shimron came
the Shimronite family group. 25These were
the family groups of Issachar, and the total
number of men was 64,300.
26These were the family groups in the
tribe of Zebulun: From Sered came the
Seredite family group; from Elon came the
Elonite family group; from Jahleel came the
Jahleelite family group. 27These were the
family groups of Zebulun, and the total
number of men was 60,500.
28These were the family groups of Joseph
through Manasseh and Ephraim.
29These were the family groups of
Manasseh: From Makir came the Makirite
family group (Makir was the father of
Gilead); from Gilead came the Gileadite
family group. 30These were the family
groups that came from Gilead: From Iezer
came the Iezerite family group; from Helek
came the Helekite family group; 31from
Asriel came the Asrielite family group;
from Shechem came the Shechemite
family group; 32from Shemida came the
Shemidaite family group; from Hepher
came the Hepherite family group.
33(Zelophehad son of Hepher had no sons;
he had only daughters, and their names
were Mahlah, Noah, Hoglah, Milcah, and
Tirzah.) 34These were the family groups of
Manasseh, and the total number of men
was 52,700.
35These were the family groups in the
tribe of Ephraim: From Shuthelah came the
Shuthelahite family group; from Beker came
the Bekerite family group; from Tahan came
the Tahanite family group. 36This was the
family group from Shuthelah: From Eran
came the Eranite family group. 37These were
the family groups of Ephraim, and the total
number of men was 32,500. These are the
family groups that came from Joseph.
38These were the family groups in the
tribe of Benjamin: From Bela came the
Belaite family group; from Ashbel came the
Ashbelite family group; from Ahiram came
the Ahiramite family group; 39from
Shupham came the Shuphamite family
group; from Hupham came the Huphamite
family group. 40These were the family
groups from Bela through Ard and Naaman:
From Ard came the Ardite family group;
from Naaman came the Naamite family
group. 41These were the family groups of
Benjamin, and the total number of men was
45,600.
42This was the family group in the tribe of
Dan: From Shuham came the Shuhamite
family group. That was the family of Dan,
43and the total number of men in the
Shuhamite family group of Dan was 64,400.
44These were the family groups in the
tribe of Asher: From Imnah came the
Imnite family group; from Ishvi came the
Ishvite family group; from Beriah came the

Beriite family group. 45These were the
family groups that came from Beriah: From
Heber came the Heberite family group;
from Malkiel came the Malkielite family
group. 46(Asher also had a daughter named
Serah.) 47These were the family groups of
Asher, and the total number of men was
53,400.

48These were the family groups in the
tribe of Naphtali: From Jahzeel came the
Jahzeelite family group; from Guni came
the Gunite family group; 49from Jezer
came the Jezerite family group; from
Shillem came the Shillemite family group.
50These were the family groups of
Naphtali, and the total number of men
was 45,400.

51So the total number of the men of Israel
was 601,730.

52The LORD said to Moses, 53"Divide the
land among these people by the number of
names. 54A large tribe will get more land,
and a small tribe will get less land; the
amount of land each tribe gets will depend
on the number of its people. 55Divide the
land by drawing lots, and the land each tribe
gets will be named for that tribe. 56Divide
the land between large and small groups by
drawing lots."

57The tribe of Levi was also counted.
These were the family groups of Levi: From
Gershon came the Gershonite family group;
from Kohath came the Kohathite family
group; from Merari came the Merarite
family group. 58These also were Levite
family groups: the Libnite family group, the
Hebronite family group, the Mahlite family
group, the Mushite family group, and the
Korahite family group. (Kohath was the
ancestor of Amram, 59whose wife was
named Jochebed. She was from the tribe of
Levi and she was born in Egypt. She and
Amram had two sons, Aaron and Moses, and
their sister Miriam. 60Aaron was the father of
Nadab, Abihu, Eleazar, and Ithamar. 61But
Nadab and Abihu died because they made an
offering before the LORD with the wrong
kind of fire.)

62The total number of male Levites one
month old or older was 23,000. But these
men were not counted with the other
Israelites, because they were not given any
of the land among the other Israelites.

63Moses and Eleazar the priest counted all
these people. They counted the Israelites on
the plains of Moab across the Jordan River
from Jericho. 64Moses and Aaron the priest
had counted the Israelites in the Desert of
Sinai, but no one Moses counted on the
plains of Moab was in the first counting.
65The LORD had told the Israelites they
would all die in the desert, and the only two
left were Caleb son of Jephunneh and Joshua
son of Nun.

Zelophehad's Daughters

27 Then the daughters of Zelophehad
came near. Zelophehad was the son of
Hepher, the son of Gilead, the son of Makir,
the son of Manasseh. Zelophehad's
daughters belonged to the family groups of
Manasseh son of Joseph. The daughters'
names were Mahlah, Noah, Hoglah, Milcah,
and Tirzah. 2They went to the entrance of
the Meeting Tent and stood before Moses,
Eleazar the priest, the leaders, and all the
people. They said, 3"Our father died in the
desert. He was not one of Korah's followers
who came together against the LORD, but he
died because of his own sin, and he had no
sons. 4Our father's name will die out because
he had no sons. Give us property among our
father's relatives."

5So Moses brought their case to the LORD,
6and the LORD said to him, 7"The daughters
of Zelophehad are right; they should
certainly get what their father owned. Give
them property among their father's relatives.

8"Tell the Israelites, 'If a man dies and has
no son, then everything he owned should go
to his daughter. 9If he has no daughter, then
everything he owned should go to his
brothers. 10If he has no brothers, then
everything he owned should go to his
father's brothers. 11And if his father had no
brothers, then everything he owned should
go to the nearest relative in his family group.
This should be a rule among the people of
Israel, as the LORD has given this command
to Moses.' "

Joshua Is the New Leader

12Then the LORD said to Moses, "Climb this
mountain in the Abarim Mountains, and
look at the land I have given to the Israelites.
13After you have seen it, you will die and join
your ancestors as your brother Aaron did,
14because you both acted against my
command in the Desert of Zin. You did not

honor me as holy before the people at the
waters of Meribah." (This was at Meribah in
Kadesh in the Desert of Zin.)
15Moses said to the LORD, 16"The LORD is
the God of the spirits of all people. May he
choose a leader for these people, 17who will
go in and out before them. He must lead
them out like sheep and bring them in; the
LORD's people must not be like sheep
without a shepherd."
18So the LORD said to Moses, "Take Joshua
son of Nun, because my Spirit is in him. Put
your hand on him, 19and have him stand
before Eleazar the priest and all the people.
Then give him his orders as they watch.
20Let him share your honor so that all the
Israelites will obey him. 21He must stand
before Eleazar the priest, and Eleazar will get
advice from the LORD by using the Urim. At
his command all the Israelites will go out,
and at his command they will all come in."
22Moses did what the LORD told him. He
took Joshua and had him stand before
Eleazar the priest and all the people, 23and he
put his hands on him and gave him orders,
just as the LORD had told him.

Daily Offerings

28 The LORD said to Moses, 2"Give this
command to the Israelites. Tell them:
'Bring me food offerings made by fire, for a
smell that is pleasing to me, and be sure to
bring them at the right time.' 3Say to them,
'These are the offerings you must bring to
the LORD: two male lambs, a year old, as a
burnt offering each day. They must have
nothing wrong with them. 4Offer one lamb
in the morning and the other lamb at
twilight. 5Also bring a grain offering of two
quarts of fine flour, mixed with one quart of
oil from pressed olives. 6This is the daily
burnt offering which began at Mount Sinai;
its smell is pleasing to the LORD. 7Offer one
quart of wine with each lamb as a drink
offering; pour it out to the LORD at the Holy
Place. 8Offer the second lamb at twilight. As
in the morning, also give a grain offering
and a drink offering. This offering is made by
fire, and its smell is pleasing to the LORD.

Sabbath Offerings

9" 'On the Sabbath day you must give two
male lambs, a year old, that have nothing
wrong with them. Also give a drink offering
and a grain offering; the grain offering must
be four quarts of fine flour mixed with olive
oil. 10This is the burnt offering for every
Sabbath, in addition to the daily burnt
offering and drink offering.

Monthly Offerings

11" 'On the first day of each month bring a
burnt offering to the LORD. This will be two
young bulls, one male sheep, and seven male
lambs a year old, and they must have
nothing wrong with them. 12Give a grain
offering with each bull of six quarts of fine
flour mixed with olive oil. Also give a grain
offering with the male sheep. It must be four
quarts of fine flour mixed with olive oil.
13And give a grain offering with each lamb
of two quarts of fine flour mixed with olive
oil. This is a burnt offering, and its smell is
pleasing to the LORD. 14The drink offering
with each bull will be two quarts of wine,
with the male sheep it will be one and one-
third quarts, and with each lamb it will be
one quart of wine. This is the burnt offering
that must be offered each month of the year.
15Besides the daily burnt offerings and drink
offerings, bring a sin offering of one goat to
the LORD.

The Passover

16" 'The LORD's Passover will be on the
fourteenth day of the first month. 17The Feast
of Unleavened Bread begins on the fifteenth
day of that month. For seven days, you may
eat only bread made without yeast. 18Have a
holy meeting on the first day of the festival,
and don't work that day. 19Bring to the LORD
an offering made by fire, a burnt offering of
two young bulls, one male sheep, and seven
male lambs a year old. They must have
nothing wrong with them. 20With each bull
give a grain offering of six quarts of fine flour
mixed with olive oil. With the male sheep it
must be four quarts of fine flour mixed with
oil. 21With each of the seven lambs, it must
be two quarts of fine flour mixed with oil.
22Bring one goat as a sin offering, to remove
your sins so you will belong to God. 23Bring
these offerings in addition to the burnt
offerings you give every morning. 24So bring
food for the offering made by fire each day
for seven days, for a smell that is pleasing to
the LORD. Do it in addition to the daily burnt
offering and its drink offering. 25On the

seventh day have a holy meeting, and don't
work that day.

The Feast of Weeks

26“ 'On the day of firstfruits when you
bring new grain to the LORD during the Feast
of Weeks, have a holy meeting. Don't work
that day. 27Bring this burnt offering to the
LORD: two young bulls, one male sheep, and
seven male lambs a year old. This smell is
pleasing to the LORD. 28Also, with each bull
give a grain offering of six quarts of fine
flour mixed with oil. With the male sheep, it
must be four quarts of flour, 29and with each
of the seven lambs offer two quarts of flour.
30Offer one male goat to remove your sins so
you will belong to God. 31Bring these
offerings and their drink offerings in
addition to the daily burnt offering and its
grain offering. The animals must have
nothing wrong with them.

The Feast of Trumpets

29 “ 'Have a holy meeting on the first day
of the seventh month, and don't work
on that day. That is the day you blow the
trumpets. 2Bring these burnt offerings as a
smell pleasing to the LORD: one young bull,
one male sheep, and seven male lambs a year
old. They must have nothing wrong with
them. 3With the bull give a grain offering of
six quarts of fine flour mixed with oil. With
the male sheep offer four quarts, 4and with
each of the seven lambs offer two quarts.
5Offer one male goat for a sin offering to
remove your sins so you will belong to God.
6These offerings are in addition to the
monthly and daily burnt offerings. Their
grain offerings and drink offerings must be
done as you have been told. These offerings
are made by fire to the LORD, and their smell
is pleasing to him.

The Day of Cleansing

7“ 'Have a holy meeting on the tenth day
of the seventh month. On that day do not
eat and do not work. 8Bring these burnt
offerings as a smell pleasing to the LORD:
one young bull, one male sheep, and seven
male lambs a year old. They must have
nothing wrong with them. 9With the bull
give a grain offering of six quarts of fine

devotion 48

NUMBERS 28–30

BEAUTIFUL AND BROKEN

My relationship with Jesus began with my dreams of becoming a mature, faithful follower. I wanted to shine so brightly that God would really be proud of me. I wanted to be a woman whose life would become an offering to God, a woman who would please God with her sacrifice and service. I wanted to be a perfect Jesus-girl.

I look back now and shake my head, but not in regret. I wince at my lack of understanding. I did not understand the heart of God. I didn't realize that forgiveness would be an ongoing process for this earthly pilgrim. I didn't think that brokenness was acceptable to God. I didn't know that because of his compassionate heart, God would mercifully accept the offering of my brokenness and pain.

Jesus wants you to know that when you are broken, shivering, alone, or afraid, with nothing left and nowhere to go, you can turn in his direction and lay yourself at the foot of his love. You can lay your broken offering on his altar. He will come and carry you into his presence. He will hold you with the warmth of his embrace and cover you with the blanket of his kingdom inheritance.

He asks for the offering of your life. He already knows it won't be perfect because it's just you, the woman who has needed a Savior all along. Thankfully, he is the One who has promised to provide the grace to cover the offering you bring and make it beautiful.

flour mixed with oil. With the male sheep
it must be four quarts, [10]and with each of
the seven lambs it must be two quarts.
[11]Offer one male goat as a sin offering. This
will be in addition to the sin offering
which removes your sins, the daily burnt
offering with its grain offering, and the
drink offerings.

The Feast of Shelters

[12]" 'Have a holy meeting on the fifteenth
day of the seventh month, and do not work
on that day. Celebrate a festival to the LORD
for seven days. [13]Bring these burnt offerings,
made by fire, as a smell pleasing to the LORD:
thirteen young bulls, two male sheep, and
fourteen male lambs a year old. They must
have nothing wrong with them. [14]With each
of the thirteen bulls offer a grain offering of
six quarts of fine flour mixed with oil. With
each of the two male sheep it must be four
quarts, [15]and with each of the fourteen
lambs it must be two quarts. [16]Offer one
male goat as a sin offering in addition to the
daily burnt offering with its grain and drink
offerings.

[17]" 'On the second day of this festival give
an offering of twelve bulls, two male sheep,
and fourteen male lambs a year old. They
must have nothing wrong with them.
[18]Bring the grain and drink offerings for the
bulls, sheep, and lambs, according to the
number required. [19]Offer one male goat as a
sin offering, in addition to the daily burnt
offering with its grain and drink offerings.

[20]" 'On the third day offer eleven bulls,
two male sheep, and fourteen male lambs a
year old. They must have nothing wrong
with them. [21]Bring the grain and drink
offerings for the bulls, sheep, and lambs,
according to the number required. [22]Offer
one male goat as a sin offering, in addition to
the daily burnt offering with its grain and
drink offerings.

[23]" 'On the fourth day offer ten bulls, two
male sheep, and fourteen male lambs a year
old. They must have nothing wrong with
them. [24]Bring the grain and drink offerings
for the bulls, sheep, and lambs, according to
the number required. [25]Offer one male goat
as a sin offering, in addition to the daily
burnt offering with its grain and drink
offerings.

[26]" 'On the fifth day offer nine bulls, two
male sheep, and fourteen male lambs a year
old. They must have nothing wrong with
them. [27]Bring the grain and drink offerings
for the bulls, sheep, and lambs, according to
the number required. [28]Offer one male goat
as a sin offering, in addition to the daily
burnt offering with its grain and drink
offerings.

[29]" 'On the sixth day offer eight bulls, two
male sheep, and fourteen male lambs a year
old. They must have nothing wrong with
them. [30]Bring the grain and drink offerings
for the bulls, sheep, and lambs, according to
the number required. [31]Offer one male goat
as a sin offering, in addition to the daily
burnt offering with its grain and drink
offerings.

[32]" 'On the seventh day offer seven bulls,
two male sheep, and fourteen male lambs a
year old. They must have nothing wrong
with them. [33]Bring the grain and drink
offerings for the bulls, sheep, and lambs,
according to the number required. [34]Offer
one male goat as a sin offering, in addition to
the daily burnt offering with its grain and
drink offerings.

[35]" 'On the eighth day have a closing
meeting, and do not work on that day.
[36]Bring an offering made by fire, a burnt
offering, as a smell pleasing to the LORD.
Offer one bull, one male sheep, and seven
male lambs a year old. They must have
nothing wrong with them. [37]Bring the grain
and drink offerings for the bull, the male
sheep, and the lambs, according to the
number required. [38]Offer one male goat as a
sin offering, in addition to the daily burnt
offering with its grain and drink offerings.

[39]" 'At your festivals you should bring
these to the LORD: your burnt offerings, grain
offerings, drink offerings and fellowship
offerings. These are in addition to other
promised offerings and special gifts you
want to give to the LORD.' "

[40]Moses told the Israelites everything the
LORD had commanded him.

Rules About Special Promises

30 Moses spoke with the leaders of the
Israelite tribes. He told them these
commands from the LORD.

[2]"If a man makes a promise to the LORD or
says he will do something special, he must
keep his promise. He must do what he said.

3If a young woman still living at home
makes a promise to the LORD or pledges to do
something special, 4and if her father hears
about the promise or pledge and says
nothing, she must do what she promised.
She must keep her pledge. 5But if her father
hears about the promise or pledge and does
not allow it, then the promise or pledge does
not have to be kept. Her father would not
allow it, so the LORD will free her from her
promise.

6"If a woman makes a pledge or a careless
promise and then gets married, 7and if her
husband hears about it and says nothing, she
must keep her promise or the pledge she
made. 8But if her husband hears about it and
does not allow it, he cancels her pledge or
the careless promise she made. The LORD will
free her from keeping it.

9"If a widow or divorced woman makes a
promise, she must do whatever she
promised.

10"If a woman makes a promise or pledge
while she is married, 11and if her husband
hears about it but says nothing and does not
stop her, she must keep her promise or
pledge. 12But if her husband hears about it
and cancels it, she does not have to do what
she said. Her husband has canceled it, so the
LORD will free her from it. 13A woman's
husband may make her keep or cancel any
promise or pledge she has made. 14If he says
nothing to her about it for several days, she
must keep her promises. If he hears about
them and says nothing, she must keep her
promises. 15But if he cancels them long after
he heard about them, he is responsible if she
breaks her promise."

16These are commands that the LORD gave
to Moses for husbands and wives, and for
fathers with daughters living at home.

Israel Attacks the Midianites

31 The LORD spoke to Moses and said,
2"Pay back the Midianites for what
they did to the Israelites; after that you will
die."

3So Moses said to the people, "Get some
men ready for war. The LORD will use them
to pay back the Midianites. 4Send to war a
thousand men from each of the tribes of
Israel." 5So twelve thousand men got ready
for war, a thousand men from each tribe.
6Moses sent those men to war; Phinehas son
of Eleazar the priest was with them. He took
with him the holy things and the trumpets
for giving the alarm. 7They fought the
Midianites as the LORD had commanded
Moses, and they killed every Midianite man.
8Among those they killed were Evi, Rekem,
Zur, Hur, and Reba, who were the five kings
of Midian. They also killed Balaam son of
Beor with a sword.

9The Israelites captured the Midianite
women and children, and they took all their
flocks, herds, and goods. 10They burned all
the Midianite towns where they had settled
and all their camps, 11but they took all the
people and animals and goods. 12Then they
brought the captives, the animals, and the
goods back to Moses and Eleazar the priest
and all the Israelites. Their camp was on the
plains of Moab near the Jordan River, across
from Jericho.

13Moses, Eleazar the priest, and all the
leaders of the people went outside the camp
to meet them. 14Moses was angry with the
army officers, the commanders over a
thousand men, and those over a hundred
men, who returned from war.

15He asked them, "Why did you let the
women live? 16They were the ones who
followed Balaam's advice and turned the
Israelites from the LORD at Peor. Then a
terrible sickness struck the LORD's people.
17Kill all the Midianite boys, and kill all the
Midianite women who have had sexual
relations. 18But save for yourselves the girls
who have not had sexual relations with a
man.

19"All you men who killed anyone or
touched a dead body must stay outside the
camp for seven days. On the third and
seventh days you and your captives must
make yourselves clean. 20You must clean all
your clothes and anything made of leather,
goat hair, or wood."

21Then Eleazar the priest said to the
soldiers who had gone to war, "These are the
teachings that the LORD gave to Moses: 22Put
any gold, silver, bronze, iron, tin, or lead—
23anything that will not burn—into the fire,
and then it will be clean. But also purify
those things with the cleansing water. Then
they will be clean. If something cannot stand
the fire, wash it with the water. 24On the
seventh day wash your clothes, and you will
be clean. After that you may come into the
camp."

Dividing the Goods

25 The LORD said to Moses, 26 "You, Eleazar
the priest, and the leaders of the family
groups should take a count of the goods, the
men, and the animals that were taken.
27 Then divide those possessions between the
soldiers who went to war and the rest of the
people. 28 From the soldiers who went to war,
take a tax for the LORD of one item out of
every five hundred. This includes people,
cattle, donkeys, or sheep. 29 Take it from the
soldiers' half, and give it to Eleazar the priest
as the LORD's share. 30 And from the people's
half, take one item out of every fifty. This
includes people, cattle, donkeys, sheep, or
other animals. Give that to the Levites, who
take care of the LORD's Holy Tent." 31 So
Moses and Eleazar did as the LORD
commanded Moses.

32 There remained from what the soldiers
had taken 675,000 sheep, 33 72,000 cattle,
34 61,000 donkeys, 35 and 32,000 women who
had not had sexual relations with a man.
36 The soldiers who went to war got 337,500
sheep, 37 and they gave 675 of them to the
LORD. 38 They got 36,000 cattle, and they gave
72 of them to the LORD. 39 They got 30,500
donkeys, and they gave 61 of them to the
LORD. 40 They got 16,000 people, and they
gave 32 of them to the LORD. 41 Moses gave
the LORD's share to Eleazar the priest, as the
LORD had commanded him.

42 Moses separated the people's half from
the soldiers' half. 43 The people got 337,500
sheep, 44 36,000 cattle, 45 30,500 donkeys,
46 and 16,000 people. 47 From the people's half
Moses took one item out of every fifty for
the LORD. This included the animals and the
people. Then he gave them to the Levites,
who took care of the LORD's Holy Tent. This
was what the LORD had commanded Moses.

48 Then the officers of the army, the
commanders of a thousand men and
commanders of a hundred men, came to
Moses. 49 They told Moses, "We, your
servants, have counted our soldiers under
our command, and not one of them is
missing. 50 So we have brought the LORD a
gift of the gold things that each of us found:
arm bands, bracelets, signet rings, earrings,
and necklaces. These are to remove our sins
so we will belong to the LORD."

51 So Moses and Eleazar the priest took the
gold from them, which had been made into
all kinds of objects. 52 The commanders of a
thousand men and the commanders of a
hundred men gave the LORD the gold, and all
of it together weighed about 420 pounds;
53 each soldier had taken something for
himself. 54 Moses and Eleazar the priest took
the gold from the commanders of a
thousand men and the commanders of a
hundred men. Then they put it in the
Meeting Tent as a memorial before the LORD
for the people of Israel.

The Tribes East of the Jordan

32 The people of Reuben and Gad had
large flocks and herds. When they
saw that the lands of Jazer and Gilead were
good for the animals, 2 they came to Moses,
Eleazar the priest, and the leaders of the
people. 3-4 They said, "We, your servants, have
flocks and herds. The LORD has captured for
the Israelites a land that is good for
animals—the land around Ataroth, Dibon,
Jazer, Nimrah, Heshbon, Elealeh, Sebam,
Nebo, and Beon. 5 If it pleases you, we would
like this land to be given to us. Don't make
us cross the Jordan River."

6 Moses told the people of Gad and
Reuben, "Shall your brothers go to war while
you stay behind? 7 You will discourage the
Israelites from going over to the land the
LORD has given them. 8 Your ancestors did the
same thing. I sent them from Kadesh Barnea
to look at the land. 9 They went as far as the
Valley of Eshcol, and when they saw the
land, they discouraged the Israelites from
going into the land the LORD had given them.
10 The LORD became very angry that day and
made this promise: 11 'None of the people
who came from Egypt and who are twenty
years old or older will see the land that I
promised to Abraham, Isaac, and Jacob.
These people have not followed me
completely. 12 Only Caleb son of Jephunneh
the Kenizzite and Joshua son of Nun
followed the LORD completely.'

13 "The LORD was angry with Israel, so he
made them wander in the desert for forty
years. Finally all the people who had sinned
against the LORD died, 14 and now you are
acting just like your ancestors! You sinful
people are making the LORD even more
angry with Israel. 15 If you quit following
him, it will add to their stay in the desert,
and you will destroy all these people."

[16]Then the Reubenites and Gadites came up to Moses and said, "We will build pens for our animals and cities for our children here. [17]Then our children will be in strong, walled cities, safe from the people who live in this land. Then we will prepare for war. We will help the other Israelites get their land, [18]and we will not return home until every Israelite has received his land. [19]We won't take any of the land west of the Jordan River; our part of the land is east of the Jordan."

[20]So Moses told them, "You must do these things. You must go before the LORD into battle [21]and cross the Jordan River armed, until the LORD forces out the enemy. [22]After the LORD helps us take the land, you may return home. You will have done your duty to the LORD and Israel, and you may have this land as your own.

[23]"But if you don't do these things, you will be sinning against the LORD; know for sure that you will be punished for your sin. [24]Build cities for your children and pens for your animals, but then you must do what you promised."

[25]The Gadites and Reubenites said to Moses, "We are your servants, and we will do what you, our master, command. [26]Our children, wives, and all our cattle will stay in the cities of Gilead, [27]but we, your servants, will prepare for battle. We will go over and fight for the LORD, as you, our master, have said."

[28]So Moses gave orders about them to Eleazar the priest, to Joshua son of Nun, and to the leaders of the tribes of Israel. [29]Moses said to them, "If the Gadites and Reubenites prepare for battle and cross the Jordan River with you, to go before the LORD and help you take the land, give them the land of Gilead for their own. [30]But if they do not go over armed, they will not receive it; their land will be in Canaan with you."

[31]The Gadites and Reubenites answered, "We are your servants, and we will do as the LORD said. [32]We will cross over into Canaan and go before the LORD ready for battle. But our land will be east of the Jordan River."

[33]So Moses gave that land to the tribes of Gad, Reuben, and East Manasseh. (Manasseh was Joseph's son.) That land had been the kingdom of Sihon, king of the Amorites, and the kingdom of Og, king of Bashan, as well as all the cities and the land around them.

[34]The Gadites rebuilt the cities of Dibon, Ataroth, Aroer, [35]Atroth Shophan, Jazer, Jogbehah, [36]Beth Nimrah, and Beth Haran. These were strong, walled cities. And they built sheep pens.

[37]The Reubenites rebuilt Heshbon, Elealeh, Kiriathaim, [38]Nebo, Baal Meon, and Sibmah. They renamed Nebo and Baal Meon when they rebuilt them.

[39]The descendants of Makir son of Manasseh went and captured Gilead and forced out the Amorites who were there. [40]So Moses gave Gilead to the family of Makir son of Manasseh, and they settled there. [41]Jair son of Manasseh went out and captured the small towns there, and he called them the Towns of Jair. [42]Nobah went and captured Kenath and the small towns around it; then he named it Nobah after himself.

Israel's Journey from Egypt

33 These are the places the Israelites went as Moses and Aaron led them out of Egypt in divisions. [2]At the LORD's command Moses recorded the places they went, and these are the places they went.

[3]On the fifteenth day of the first month, the day after the Passover, the Israelites left Rameses and marched out boldly in front of all the Egyptians. [4]The Egyptians were burying their firstborn sons, whom the LORD had killed; the LORD showed that the gods of Egypt were false.

[5]The Israelites left Rameses and camped at Succoth.

[6]They left Succoth and camped at Etham, at the edge of the desert.

[7]They left Etham and went back to Pi Hahiroth, to the east of Baal Zephon, and camped near Migdol.

[8]They left Pi Hahiroth and walked through the sea into the desert. After going three days through the Desert of Etham, they camped at Marah.

[9]They left Marah and went to Elim; there were twelve springs of water and seventy palm trees where they camped.

[10]They left Elim and camped near the Red Sea.

[11]They left the Red Sea and camped in the Desert of Sin.

12They left the Desert of Sin and camped
at Dophkah.
13They left Dophkah and camped at
Alush.
14They left Alush and camped at
Rephidim, where the people had no water to
drink.
15They left Rephidim and camped in the
Desert of Sinai.
16They left the Desert of Sinai and camped
at Kibroth Hattaavah.
17They left Kibroth Hattaavah and
camped at Hazeroth.
18They left Hazeroth and camped at
Rithmah.
19They left Rithmah and camped at
Rimmon Perez.
20They left Rimmon Perez and camped at
Libnah.
21They left Libnah and camped at Rissah.
22They left Rissah and camped at
Kehelathah.
23They left Kehelathah and camped at
Mount Shepher.
24They left Mount Shepher and camped at
Haradah.
25They left Haradah and camped at
Makheloth.
26They left Makheloth and camped at
Tahath.
27They left Tahath and camped at Terah.
28They left Terah and camped at
Mithcah.
29They left Mithcah and camped at
Hashmonah.
30They left Hashmonah and camped at
Moseroth.
31They left Moseroth and camped at Bene
Jaakan.
32They left Bene Jaakan and camped at
Hor Haggidgad.
33They left Hor Haggidgad and camped at
Jotbathah.
34They left Jotbathah and camped at
Abronah.
35They left Abronah and camped at Ezion
Geber.
36They left Ezion Geber and camped at
Kadesh in the Desert of Zin.
37They left Kadesh and camped at Mount
Hor, on the border of Edom. 38Aaron the
priest obeyed the LORD and went up Mount
Hor. There he died on the first day of the
fifth month in the fortieth year after the
Israelites left Egypt. 39Aaron was 123 years
old when he died on Mount Hor.
40The Canaanite king of Arad, who lived
in the southern area of Canaan, heard that
the Israelites were coming.
41The people left Mount Hor and camped
at Zalmonah.
42They left Zalmonah and camped at
Punon.
43They left Punon and camped at Oboth.
44They left Oboth and camped at Iye
Abarim, on the border of Moab.
45They left Iye Abarim and camped at
Dibon Gad.
46They left Dibon Gad and camped at
Almon Diblathaim.
47They left Almon Diblathaim and
camped in the mountains of Abarim, near
Nebo.
48They left the mountains of Abarim and
camped on the plains of Moab near the
Jordan River across from Jericho. 49They
camped along the Jordan on the plains of
Moab, and their camp went from Beth
Jeshimoth to Abel Acacia.
50On the plains of Moab by the Jordan
River across from Jericho, the LORD spoke to
Moses. He said, 51"Speak to the Israelites and
tell them, 'When you cross the Jordan River
and go into Canaan, 52force out all the
people who live there. Destroy all of their
carved statues and metal idols. Wreck all of
their places of worship. 53Take over the land
and settle there, because I have given this
land to you to own. 54Throw lots to divide
up the land by family groups, giving larger
portions to larger family groups and smaller
portions to smaller family groups. The land
will be given as the lots decide; each tribe
will get its own land.
55" 'But if you don't force those people out
of the land, they will bring you trouble. They
will be like sharp hooks in your eyes and
thorns in your sides. They will bring trouble
to the land where you live. 56Then I will
punish you as I had planned to punish
them.' "

The Borders of Canaan

34 The LORD said to Moses, 2"Give this
command to the people of Israel: 'You
will soon enter Canaan and it will be yours.
These shall be the borders: 3On the south
you will get part of the Desert of Zin near the

border of Edom. On the east side your
southern border will start at the south end of
the Dead Sea, 4cross south of Scorpion Pass,
and go through the Desert of Zin and south
of Kadesh Barnea. Then it will go to Hazar
Addar and over to Azmon. 5From Azmon it
will go to the brook of Egypt, and it will end
at the Mediterranean Sea.

6" 'Your western border will be the
Mediterranean Sea.

7" 'Your northern border will begin at the
Mediterranean Sea and go to Mount Hor.
8From Mount Hor it will go to Lebo Hamath,
and on to Zedad. 9Then the border will go to
Ziphron, and it will end at Hazar Enan. This
will be your northern border.

10" 'Your eastern border will begin at Hazar
Enan and go to Shepham. 11From Shepham
the border will go east of Ain to Riblah and
along the hills east of Lake Galilee. 12Then
the border will go down along the Jordan
River and end at the Dead Sea.

" 'These are the borders around your
country.' "

13So Moses gave this command to the
Israelites: "This is the land you will receive.
Throw lots to divide it among the nine and
one-half tribes, because the LORD
commanded that it should be theirs. 14The
tribes of Reuben, Gad, and East Manasseh
have already received their land. 15These two
and one-half tribes received land east of the
Jordan River, across from Jericho."

16Then the LORD said to Moses, 17"These are
the men who will divide the land: Eleazar the
priest and Joshua son of Nun. 18Also take one
leader from each tribe to help divide the land.
19These are the names of the leaders: from
the tribe of Judah, Caleb son of Jephunneh;
20from the tribe of Simeon, Shemuel son of
Ammihud; 21from the tribe of Benjamin,
Elidad son of Kislon; 22from the tribe of Dan,
Bukki son of Jogli; 23from the tribe of
Manasseh son of Joseph, Hanniel son of
Ephod; 24from the tribe of Ephraim son of
Joseph, Kemuel son of Shiphtan; 25from the
tribe of Zebulun, Elizaphan son of Parnach;
26from the tribe of Issachar, Paltiel son of
Azzan; 27from the tribe of Asher, Ahihud son
of Shelomi; 28from the tribe of Naphtali,
Pedahel son of Ammihud."

29The LORD commanded these men to
divide the land of Canaan among the
Israelites.

The Levites' Towns

35 The LORD spoke to Moses on the plains
of Moab across from Jericho by the
Jordan River. He said, 2"Command the
Israelites to give the Levites cities to live in
from the land they receive. Also give the
Levites the pastureland around these cities.
3Then the Levites will have cities where they
may live and pastureland for their cattle,
flocks, and other animals. 4The pastureland
you give the Levites will extend fifteen
hundred feet from the city wall. 5Also
measure three thousand feet in each
direction outside the city wall—three
thousand feet east of the city, three thousand
feet south of the city, three thousand feet
west of the city, and three thousand feet
north of the city, with the city in the center.
This will be pastureland for the Levites' cities.

Cities of Safety

6"Six of the cities you give the Levites will
be cities of safety. A person who accidentally
kills someone may run to one of those cities
for safety. You must also give forty-two other
cities to the Levites; 7give the Levites a total
of forty-eight cities and their pastures. 8The
larger tribes of Israel must give more cities,
and the smaller tribes must give fewer cities.
Each tribe must give some of its cities to the
Levites, but the number of cities they give
will depend on the size of their land."

9Then the LORD said to Moses, 10"Tell the
Israelites these things: 'When you cross the
Jordan River and go into Canaan, 11you must
choose cities to be cities of safety, so that a
person who accidentally kills someone may
run to them for safety. 12There the person
will be safe from the dead person's relative
who has the duty of punishing the killer. He
will not die before he receives a fair trial in
court. 13The six cities you give will be cities
of safety. 14Give three cities east of the Jordan
River and three cities in Canaan as cities of
safety. 15These six cities will be places of
safety for citizens of Israel, as well as for
foreigners and other people living with you.
Any of these people who accidentally kills
someone may run to one of these cities.

16" 'Anyone who uses an iron weapon to
kill someone is a murderer. He must be put
to death. 17Anyone who takes a rock and
kills a person with it is a murderer. He must

be put to death. [18]Anyone who picks up a
piece of wood and kills someone with it is a
murderer. He must be put to death. [19]A
relative of the dead person must put the
murderer to death; when they meet, the
relative must kill the murderer. [20]A person
might shove someone or throw something
at someone and cause death. [21]Or a person
might hit someone with his hand and cause
death. If it were done from hate, the person
is a murderer and must be put to death. A
relative of the dead person must kill the
murderer when they meet.

[22]" 'But a person might suddenly shove
someone, and not from hatred. Or a person
might accidentally throw something and hit
someone. [23]Or a person might drop a rock on
someone he couldn't see and kill that person.
There was no plan to hurt anyone and no
hatred for the one who was killed. [24]If that
happens, the community must judge
between the relative of the dead person and
the killer, according to these rules. [25]They
must protect the killer from the dead
person's relative, sending the killer back to
the original city of safety, to stay there until
the high priest dies (the high priest had the
holy oil poured on him).

[26]" 'Such a person must never go outside
the limits of the city of safety. [27]If a relative
of the dead person finds the killer outside
the city, the relative may kill that person and
not be guilty of murder. [28]The killer must
stay in the city of safety until the high priest
dies. After the high priest dies, the killer may
go home.

[29]" 'These laws are for you from now on,
wherever you live.

[30]" 'If anyone kills a person, the murderer
may be put to death only if there are
witnesses. No one may be put to death with
only one witness.

[31]" 'Don't take money to spare the life of a
murderer who should be put to death. A
murderer must be put to death.

[32]" 'If someone has run to a city of safety,
don't take money to let the person go back
home before the high priest dies.

devotion 49

NUMBERS 36:6–8

WHOSE HAND YOU HOLD

Have you ever noticed that none of life's circumstances are missing from the Scriptures? That is especially true when it comes to understanding God's heart for marriage and relationships. When you profess Christ as your Savior, you commit your life and your body to the truth of the Word that you are holding in your hands today. One of the Bible's truths is that you should not enter into a dating, marriage, or business partnership with those who do not believe.

Walking in these types of relationships with unbelievers will certainly bring about very painful experiences. One of my dearest friends married a man who is not a believer. She remembers her wedding day, standing at the altar, and hearing the Holy Spirit telling her not to marry him. He is a good man with all the qualities any woman would want, but he is not a believer. Their nineteen years of marriage have been full of heartache because of this difference. Her children, now teenagers, are very aware of the absence of their father in their upbringing and even their social lives.

In the book of Amos, we are charged with a question: can two walk together if they do not agree? The answer is, of course not! If you are cultivating any of these relationships right now in your life and cannot get past that one question, then STOP! The Lord has something amazing for you! He wants your most intimate relationships built with two Christ-centered hearts, not just one.

33" 'Don't let murder spoil your land. The
only way to remove the sin of killing an
innocent person is for the murderer to be
put to death. 34I am the LORD, and I live
among the Israelites. I live in that land with
you, so do not spoil it with murder.' "

Land for Zelophehad's Daughters

36 The leaders of Gilead's family group
went to talk to Moses and the
leaders of the families of Israel. (Gilead was
the son of Makir, the son of Manasseh, the
son of Joseph.) 2They said, "The LORD
commanded you, our master, to give the
land to the Israelites by throwing lots, and
the LORD commanded you to give the land
of Zelophehad, our brother, to his
daughters. 3But if his daughters marry men
from other tribes of Israel, then that land
will leave our family, and the people of the
other tribes will get that land. So we will
lose some of our land. 4When the time of
Jubilee comes for the Israelites, their
land will go to the tribes of the people
they marry; their land will be taken away
from us, the land we received from our
fathers."
5Then Moses gave the Israelites this
command from the LORD: "These men from
the tribe of Joseph are right. 6This is the
LORD's command to Zelophehad's daughters:
You may marry anyone you wish, as long as
the person is from your own tribe. 7In this
way the Israelites' land will not pass from
tribe to tribe, and each Israelite will keep
the land in the tribe that belonged to his
ancestors. 8A woman who inherits her
father's land may marry, but she must
marry someone from her own tribe. In this
way every Israelite will keep the land that
belonged to his ancestors. 9The land must
not pass from tribe to tribe, and each
Israelite tribe will keep the land it received
from its ancestors."
10Zelophehad's daughters obeyed the
LORD's command to Moses.
11So Zelophehad's daughters—Mahlah,
Tirzah, Hoglah, Milcah, and Noah—married
their cousins, their father's relatives. 12Their
husbands were from the tribe of Manasseh
son of Joseph, so their land stayed in their
father's family group and tribe.
13These were the laws and commands that
the LORD gave to the Israelites through
Moses on the plains of Moab by the Jordan
River, across from Jericho.

Deuteronomy

A Greek translation of the Hebrew words meaning "copy of the law" or "second law"
This is the last book of the Pentateuch.

Person Holding the Pen God Wrote With: It's generally agreed that *Moses* authored this book, as indicated in Deuteronomy 1:1, 5 and 31:9, 22, and 24.

When the Text Was Written: Between 1445 and 1405 B.C.

Spiritual Posture of the Original Recipients: Like Leviticus, the events in Deuteronomy took place in one location. The entire nation of Israel was camped out near the Jordan River, almost forty years after escaping from Egypt. They were most likely physically and emotionally exhausted, yet looking forward to the final push into Canaan.

Storyline Synopsis: Because of his disobedience at Meribah in Numbers 20, Moses was forbidden to enter the land God had promised the Israelites. So in the final weeks of Moses' life, the beloved boss of Israel passes the mantle of authority on to his protégé, Joshua. Moses clears his throat to get everyone's attention, and he bellows three good-bye speeches to the people he has led and loved for forty years. His first monologue recounts God's faithfulness throughout their journey (Deut. 1—4:43). His second address reiterates the laws God personally dictated to him on Mount Sinai (4:44—26). And his last lecture explains the life and death consequences that come with obedience or rebellion to God's divine agreement. It also contains a moving charge for the Israelites to obey God and a formal baton pass to Joshua (chapters 27—31). Then Moses looks toward the heavens, sings praises to the Creator, blesses each tribe individually, and finally dies (chapters 32—34).

A Moment Worth Discussing: For anyone who's grieved the fact that poor Moses didn't get to set foot in the land flowing with milk and honey after putting up with the whiney Israelites for all those years, take heart! Go ahead and thumb to Matthew 17 where Jesus is transfigured with dazzling white light from God. Now look at who's standing right next to the Messiah. This New Testament event took place on top of a mountain with an incredible view—from a peak that was right smack dab in the *middle* of the land God had promised his chosen people! Discuss God's sovereign mercy that's apparent in Moses' eventual visit to Canaan.

Interesting (But Likely to Be Overlooked) Character: *Joseph,* who had to endure the bullying and betrayal of his brothers but whose faith in God never wavered (Gen. 37—50), is remembered and rewarded through this blessing of material wealth and military power for his descendants (Deut. 33:13–17).

Moses Talks to the Israelites

1 This is the message Moses gave to all the
people of Israel in the desert east of the
Jordan River. They were in the desert area
near Suph, between Paran and the towns of
Tophel, Laban, Hazeroth, and Dizahab.
2(The trip from Mount Sinai to Kadesh
Barnea on the Mount Seir road takes eleven
days.) 3Forty years after the Israelites had left
Egypt, on the first day of the eleventh
month, Moses told the people of Israel
everything the LORD had commanded him to
tell them. 4This was after the LORD had
defeated Sihon and Og. Sihon was king of
the Amorite people and lived in Heshbon.
Og was king of Bashan and lived in
Ashteroth and Edrei.
5Now the Israelites were east of the Jordan
River in the land of Moab, and there Moses
began to explain what God had commanded.
He said:
6The LORD our God spoke to us at Mount
Sinai and said, "You have stayed long enough
at this mountain. 7Get ready, and go to the
mountain country of the Amorites, and to all
the places around there—the Jordan Valley,
the mountains, the western hills, the
southern area, the seacoast, the land of
Canaan, and Lebanon. Go as far as the great
river, the Euphrates. 8See, I have given you
this land, so go in and take it for yourselves.
The LORD promised it to your ancestors—
Abraham, Isaac, and Jacob and their
descendants."

Moses Appoints Leaders

9At that time I said, "I am not able to take
care of you by myself. 10The LORD your God
has made you grow in number so that there
are as many of you as there are stars in the
sky. 11I pray that the LORD, the God of your
ancestors, will give you a thousand times
more people and do all the wonderful things
he promised. 12But I cannot take care of your
problems, your troubles, and your
arguments by myself. 13So choose some men
from each tribe—wise men who have
understanding and experience—and I will
make them leaders over you."
14And you said, "That's a good thing to
do."
15So I took the wise and experienced
leaders of your tribes, and I made them your
leaders. I appointed commanders over a
thousand people, over a hundred people,
over fifty people, and over ten people and
made them officers over your tribes. 16Then I
told your leaders, "Listen to the arguments
between your people. Judge fairly between
two Israelites or between an Israelite and a
foreigner. 17When you judge, be fair to
everyone; don't act as if one person is more
important than another, and don't be afraid
of anyone, because your decision comes
from God. Bring the hard cases to me, and I
will judge them." 18At that time I told you
everything you must do.

Spies Enter the Land

19Then, as the LORD our God commanded
us, we left Mount Sinai and went toward the
mountain country of the Amorite people.
We went through that large and terrible
desert you saw, and then we came to
Kadesh Barnea. 20I said to you, "You have
now come to the mountain country of the
Amorites, to the land the LORD our God will
give us. 21Look, here it is! Go up and take it.
The LORD, the God of your ancestors, told
you to do this, so don't be afraid and don't
worry."
22Then all of you came to me and said,
"Let's send men before us to spy out the land.
They can come back and tell us about the
way we should go and the cities we will
find."
23I thought that was a good idea, so I
chose twelve of your men, one for each tribe.
24They left and went up to the mountains,
and when they came to the Valley of Eshcol
they explored it. 25They took some of the
fruit from that land and brought it down to
us, saying, "It is a good land that the LORD
our God is giving us."

Israel Refuses to Enter

26But you refused to go. You would not
obey the command of the LORD your God,
27but grumbled in your tents, saying, "The
LORD hates us. He brought us out of Egypt
just to give us to the Amorites, who will
destroy us. 28Where can we go now? The
spies we sent have made us afraid, because
they said, 'The people there are stronger and
taller than we are. The cities are big, with
walls up to the sky. And we saw the Anakites
there!' "

29Then I said to you, "Don't be frightened;
don't be afraid of those people. 30The LORD
your God will go ahead of you and fight for
you as he did in Egypt; you saw him do it.
31And in the desert you saw how the LORD
your God carried you, like one carries a
child. And he has brought you safely all the
way to this place."
32But you still did not trust the LORD your
God, even though 33he had always gone
before you to find places for you to camp. In
a fire at night and in a cloud during the day,
he showed you which way to go.
34When the LORD heard what you said, he
was angry and made an oath, saying, 35"I
promised a good land to your ancestors, but
none of you evil people will see it. 36Only
Caleb son of Jephunneh will see it. I will give
him and his descendants the land he walked
on, because he followed the LORD
completely."
37Because of you, the LORD was also angry
with me and said, "You won't enter the land
either, 38but your assistant, Joshua son of
Nun, will enter it. Encourage him, because
he will lead Israel to take the land for their
own.
39"Your little children that you said would
be captured, who do not know right from
wrong at this time, will go into the land. I
will give the land to them, and they will take
it for their own. 40But you must turn around
and follow the desert road toward the Red
Sea."
41Then you said to me, "We have sinned
against the LORD, but now we will go up and
fight, as the LORD our God commanded us."
Then all of you put on weapons, thinking it
would be easy to go into the mountains.
42But the LORD said to me, "Tell the people,
'You must not go up there and fight. I will
not be with you, and your enemies will
defeat you.' "
43So I told you, but you would not listen.
You would not obey the LORD's command.
You were proud, so you went on up into the
mountains, 44and the Amorites who lived in
those mountains came out and fought you.
They chased you like bees and defeated you
from Edom to Hormah. 45So you came back
and cried before the LORD, but the LORD did
not listen to you; he refused to pay attention
to you. 46So you stayed in Kadesh a long
time.

Israel Wanders in the Desert

2 Then we turned around, and we traveled
on the desert road toward the Red Sea, as
the LORD had told me to do. We traveled
through the mountains of Edom for many
days.
2Then the LORD said to me, 3"You have
traveled through these mountains long
enough. Turn north 4and give the people this
command: 'You will soon go through the
land that belongs to your relatives, the
descendants of Esau who live in Edom. They
will be afraid of you, but be very careful. 5Do
not go to war against them. I will not give
you any of their land—not even a foot of it,
because I have given the mountains of Edom
to Esau as his own. 6You must pay them in
silver for any food you eat or water you
drink.' "
7The LORD your God has blessed
everything you have done; he has protected
you while you traveled through this great
desert. The LORD your God has been with
you for the past forty years, and you have
had everything you needed.
8So we passed by our relatives, the
descendants of Esau who lived in Edom. We
turned off the Jordan Valley road that
comes from the towns of Elath and Ezion
Geber and traveled along the desert road to
Moab.

The Land of Ar

9Then the LORD said to me, "Don't bother
the people of Moab. Don't go to war against
them, because I will not give you any of
their land as your own; I have given Ar to
the descendants of Lot as their own." 10(The
Emites, who lived in Ar before, were strong
people, and there were many of them. They
were very tall, like the Anakites. 11The
Emites were thought to be Rephaites, like
the Anakites, but the Moabite people called
them Emites. 12The Horites also lived in
Edom before, but the descendants of Esau
forced them out and destroyed them, taking
their place as Israel did in the land the LORD
gave them as their own.)
13And the LORD said to me, "Now get up
and cross the Zered Valley." So we crossed
the valley. 14It had been thirty-eight years
from the time we left Kadesh Barnea until
we crossed the Zered Valley. By then, all the
fighting men from that time had died, as the

LORD had promised would happen. 15The LORD continued to work against them to remove them from the camp until they were all dead.

16When the last of those fighting men had died, 17the LORD said to me, 18"Today you will pass by Ar, on the border of Moab. 19When you come near the people of Ammon, don't bother them or go to war against them, because I will not give you any of their land as your own. I have given it to the descendants of Lot for their own."

20(That land was also thought to be a land of the Rephaites, because those people used to live there, but the Ammonites called them Zamzummites. 21They were strong people, and there were many of them; they were very tall, like the Anakites. The LORD destroyed the Zamzummites, and the Ammonites forced them out of the land and took their place. 22The LORD did the same thing for the descendants of Esau, who lived in Edom, when he destroyed the Horites. The Edomites forced them out of the land and took their place, and they live there to this day. 23The Cretan people came from Crete and destroyed the Avvites, who lived in towns all the way to Gaza; the Cretans destroyed them and took their place.)

Fighting the Amorites

24The LORD said, "Get up and cross the Arnon Ravine. See, I am giving you the power to defeat Sihon the Amorite, king of Heshbon, and I am giving you his land. So fight against him and begin taking his land. 25Today I will begin to make all the people in the world afraid of you. When they hear reports about you, they will shake with fear, and they will be terrified of you."

26I sent messengers from the desert of Kedemoth to Sihon king of Heshbon. They offered him peace, saying, 27"If you let us pass through your country, we will stay on the road and not turn right or left. 28We will pay you in silver for any food we eat or water we drink. We only want to walk through your country. 29The descendants of Esau in Edom let us go through their land, and so did the Moabites in Ar. We want to cross the Jordan River into the land the LORD our God has given us." 30But Sihon king of Heshbon would not let us pass, because the LORD your God had made him stubborn. The LORD wanted you to defeat Sihon, and now this has happened.

31The LORD said to me, "See, I have begun to give Sihon and his country to you. Begin taking the land as your own."

32Then Sihon and all his army came out and fought us at Jahaz, 33but the LORD our God gave Sihon to us. We defeated him, his sons, and all his army. 34We captured all his cities at that time and completely destroyed them, as well as the men, women, and children. We left no one alive. 35But we kept the cattle and valuable things from the cities for ourselves. 36We defeated Aroer on the edge of the Arnon Ravine, and we defeated the town in the ravine, and even as far as Gilead. No town was too strong for us; the LORD our God gave us all of them. 37But you did not go near the land of the Ammonites, on the shores of the Jabbok River, or the towns in the mountains, as the LORD our God had commanded.

The Battle at Bashan

3 When we turned and went up the road toward Bashan, Og king of Bashan and all his army came out to fight us at Edrei. 2The LORD said to me, "Don't be afraid of Og, because I will hand him, his whole army, and his land over to you. Do to him what you did to Sihon king of the Amorites, who ruled in Heshbon."

3So the LORD our God gave us Og king of Bashan and all his army; we defeated them and left no one alive. 4Then we captured all of Og's cities, all sixty of them, and took the whole area of Argob, Og's kingdom in Bashan. 5All these were strong cities, with high walls and gates with bars. And there were also many small towns with no walls. 6We completely destroyed them, just like the cities of Sihon king of Heshbon. We killed all the men, women, and children, 7but we kept all the cattle and valuable things from the cities for ourselves.

8So at that time we took the land east of the Jordan River, from the Arnon Ravine to Mount Hermon, from these two Amorite kings. 9(Hermon is called Sirion by the Sidonian people, but the Amorites call it Senir.) 10We captured all the cities on the high plain and all of Gilead, and we took all of Bashan as far as Salecah and Edrei, towns in Og's kingdom of Bashan. 11(Only Og king

of Bashan was left of the few Rephaites. His
bed was made of iron, and it was more than
thirteen feet long and six feet wide! It is still
in the Ammonite city of Rabbah.)

The Land Is Divided

12At that time we took this land to be our
own. I gave the people of Reuben and Gad
the land from Aroer by the Arnon Ravine, as
well as half of the mountain country of
Gilead and the cities in it. 13To the people of
East Manasseh I gave the rest of Gilead and
all of Bashan, the kingdom of Og. (The area
of Argob in Bashan was called the land of the
Rephaites. 14Jair, a descendant of Manasseh,
took the whole area of Argob, all the way to
the border of the Geshurites and Ma-
acathites. So that land was named for Jair,
and even today Bashan is called the Towns of
Jair.) 15I gave Gilead to Makir. 16I gave the
Reubenites and the Gadites the land that
begins at Gilead and goes from the Arnon
Ravine (the middle of the Arnon is the
border) to the Jabbok River, which is the
Ammonite border. 17The border on the west
was the Jordan River in the Jordan Valley,
and it goes from Lake Galilee to the Dead Sea
west of Mount Pisgah.

18At that time I gave you this command:
"The LORD your God has given you this land
as your own. Now your fighting men must
take their weapons, and you must lead the
other Israelites across the river. 19Your wives,
your young children, and your cattle may
stay here. I know you have many cattle, and
they may stay here in the cities I have given
you, 20until the LORD also gives your Israelite
relatives a place to rest. They will receive the
land the LORD your God has given them on
the other side of the Jordan River. After that,
you may each return to the land I have given
you."

21Then I gave this command to Joshua:
"You have seen for yourself all that the LORD
your God has done to these two kings. The
LORD will do the same thing to all the
kingdoms where you are going. 22Don't be
afraid of them, because the LORD your God
will fight for you."

Moses Cannot Enter the Land

23Then I begged the LORD: 24"Lord GOD,
you have begun to show me, your servant,
how great you are. You have great strength,
and no other god in heaven or on earth can
do the powerful things you do. There is no
other god like you. 25Please let me cross the
Jordan River so that I may see the good land
by the Jordan. I want to see the beautiful
mountains and Lebanon."

26But the LORD was angry with me because
of you, and he would not listen to me. The
LORD said to me, "That's enough. Don't talk
to me anymore about it. 27Climb to the top
of Mount Pisgah and look west, north, south,
and east. You can look at the land, but you
will not cross the Jordan River. 28Appoint
Joshua and help him be brave and strong. He
will lead the people across the river and give
them the land that they are to inherit, but
you can only look at it." 29So we stayed in
the valley opposite Beth Peor.

Moses Tells Israel to Obey

4 Now, Israel, listen to the laws and
commands I will teach you. Obey them
so that you will live and so that you will go
over and take the land the LORD, the God of
your ancestors, is giving to you. 2Don't add to
these commands, and don't leave anything
out, but obey the commands of the LORD
your God that I give you.

3You have seen for yourselves what the
LORD did at Baal Peor, how the LORD your
God destroyed everyone among you who
followed Baal in Peor. 4But all of you who
continued following the LORD your God are
still alive today.

5Look, I have taught you the laws and
rules the LORD my God commanded me.
Now you can obey the laws in the land you
are entering, in the land you will take. 6Obey
these laws carefully, in order to show the
other nations that you have wisdom and
understanding. When they hear about these
laws, they will say, "This great nation of
Israel is wise and understanding." 7No other
nation is as great as we are. Their gods do not
come near them, but the LORD our God
comes near when we pray to him. 8And no
other nation has such good teachings and
commands as those I am giving to you today.

9But be careful! Watch out and don't forget
the things you have seen. Don't forget them
as long as you live, but teach them to your
children and grandchildren. 10Remember the
day you stood before the LORD your God at
Mount Sinai. He said to me, "Bring the

people together so I can tell them what I
have to say. Then they will respect me as
long as they live in the land, and they will
teach these things to their children."
11 When you came and stood at the bottom
of the mountain, it blazed with fire that
reached to the sky, and black clouds made it
very dark. 12 The LORD spoke to you from the
fire. You heard the sound of words, but you
did not see him; there was only a voice.
13 The LORD told you about his Agreement,
the Ten Commandments. He told you to
obey them, and he wrote them on two stone
tablets. 14 Then the LORD commanded me to
teach you the laws and rules that you must
obey in the land you will take when you
cross the Jordan River.

Laws About Idols

15 Since the LORD spoke to you from the
fire at Mount Sinai, but you did not see him,
watch yourselves carefully! 16 Don't sin by
making idols of any kind, and don't make
statues—of men or women, 17 of animals on
earth or birds that fly in the air, 18 of anything
that crawls on the ground, or of fish in the
water below. 19 When you look up at the sky,
you see the sun, moon, and stars, and
everything in the sky. But don't bow down
and worship them, because the LORD your
God has made these things for all people
everywhere. 20 But the LORD brought you out
of Egypt, which tested you like a furnace for
melting iron, and he made you his very own
people, as you are now.

21 The LORD was angry with me because of
you, and he swore that I would not cross the
Jordan River to go into the good land the
LORD your God is giving you as your own.
22 I will die here in this land and not cross the
Jordan, but you will soon go across and take
that good land. 23 Be careful. Don't forget the
Agreement of the LORD your God that he
made with you, and don't make any idols for
yourselves, as the LORD your God has
commanded you not to do. 24 The LORD your
God is a jealous God, like a fire that burns
things up.

25 Even after you have lived in the land a
long time and have had children and
grandchildren, don't do evil things. Don't
make any kind of idol, and don't do what the
LORD your God says is evil, because that will
make him angry. 26 If you do, I ask heaven
and earth to speak against you this day that
you will quickly be removed from this land
that you are crossing the Jordan River to
take. You will not live there long after that,
but you will be completely destroyed. 27 The
LORD will scatter you among the other
nations. Only a few of you will be left alive,
and those few will be in other nations where
the LORD will send you. 28 There you will
worship gods made by people, gods made of
wood and stone, that cannot see, hear, eat, or
smell. 29 But even there you can look for the
LORD your God, and you will find him if you
look for him with your whole being. 30 It will
be hard when all these things happen to you.
But after that you will come back to the LORD
your God and obey him, 31 because the LORD
your God is a merciful God. He will not leave
you or destroy you. He will not forget the
Agreement with your ancestors, which he
swore to them.

The Lord Is Great

32 Nothing like this has ever happened
before! Look at the past, long before you
were even born. Go all the way back to when
God made humans on the earth, and look
from one end of heaven to the other.
Nothing like this has ever been heard of!
33 No other people have ever heard God
speak from a fire and have still lived. But you
have. 34 No other god has ever taken for
himself one nation out of another. But the
LORD your God did this for you in Egypt,
right before your own eyes. He did it with
tests, signs, miracles, war, and great sights,
by his great power and strength.

35 He showed you things so you would
know that the LORD is God, and there is no
other God besides him. 36 He spoke to you
from heaven to teach you. He showed you
his great fire on earth, and you heard him
speak from the fire. 37 Because the LORD loved
your ancestors, he chose you, their
descendants, and he brought you out of
Egypt himself by his great strength. 38 He
forced nations out of their land ahead of you,
nations that were bigger and stronger than
you were. The LORD did this so he could
bring you into their land and give it to you
as your own, and this land is yours today.

39 Know and believe today that the LORD is
God. He is God in heaven above and on the
earth below. There is no other god! 40 Obey

devotion 50

DEUTERONOMY 4:29

EVEN THERE

Moses promised his people that if they searched for God in their new land, "even there" they would find him. Where is "even there"? For the Israelites, it was a foreign land with foreign customs and foreign gods.

I recently spent time in New York City. If you love big cities, this is the one to visit. Just walk through Times Square, with billboards larger than life and the all-encompassing lights, sounds, and smells. You can't help but feel as though the world is screaming for your attention. It's so easy to get caught up in the thrill of it all. The Broadway plays, the shopping, the food, the celebrities! *Even there*, can you look for God?

The Word says that if you look for God "with your whole being," you will find him. We can't look for God occasionally. We can't watch a preacher on TV once in a while or pick up our Bibles when our lives seem to be coming apart. Look for him with your whole being. That means actively looking. Attend church *and* get involved. Be in the Word of God, read it every day, *and* apply it to your life. Say a blessing at mealtime *and* spend time on your knees. Are you searching for God with your whole being? We may live in the world, but our hearts need to be looking for God in the midst of it. If you do, wherever you are, you will find him even there.

his laws and commands that I am giving you
today so that things will go well for you and
your children. Then you will live a long time
in the land that the LORD your God is giving
to you forever.

Cities of Safety

41 Moses chose three cities east of the
Jordan River, 42 where a person who
accidentally killed someone could go. If the
person was not killed because of hatred, the
murderer's life could be saved by running to
one of these cities. 43 These were the cities:
Bezer in the desert high plain was for the
Reubenites; Ramoth in Gilead was for the
Gadites; and Golan in Bashan was for
the Manassites.

The Laws Moses Gave

44 These are the teachings Moses gave to
the people of Israel. 45 They are the rules,
commands, and laws he gave them when
they came out of Egypt. 46 They were in the
valley near Beth Peor, east of the Jordan
River, in the land of Sihon. Sihon king of the
Amorites ruled in Heshbon and was defeated
by Moses and the Israelites as they came out
of Egypt. 47 The Israelites took his land and
the land of Og king of Bashan, the two
Amorite kings east of the Jordan River.
48 This land went from Aroer, on the edge of
the Arnon Ravine, to Mount Hermon. 49 It
included all the Jordan Valley east of the
Jordan River, and it went as far as the Dead
Sea below Mount Pisgah.

The Ten Commandments

5 Moses called all the people of Israel
together and said: Listen, Israel, to the
commands and laws I am giving you today.
Learn them and obey them carefully. 2 The
LORD our God made an Agreement with us at
Mount Sinai. 3 He did not make this
Agreement with our ancestors, but he made
it with us, with all of us who are alive here
today. 4 The LORD spoke to you face to face
from the fire on the mountain. 5 (At that time
I stood between you and the LORD in order to

tell you what the LORD said; you were afraid
of the fire, so you would not go up on the
mountain.) The LORD said:
6 "I am the LORD your God; I brought you
out of the land of Egypt where you were
slaves.
7 "You must not have any other gods
except me.
8 "You must not make for yourselves any
idols or anything to worship that looks like
something in the sky above or on the earth
below or in the water below the land. 9 You
must not worship or serve any idol, because
I, the LORD your God, am a jealous God. If
people sin against me and hate me, I will
punish their children, even their
grandchildren and great-grandchildren. 10 But
I will be very kind for a thousand lifetimes
to those who love me and obey my
commands.
11 "You must not use the name of the LORD
your God thoughtlessly, because the LORD
will punish anyone who uses his name in
this way.
12 "Keep the Sabbath as a holy day, as the
LORD your God has commanded you. 13 You
may work and get everything done during
six days each week, 14 but the seventh day is a
day of rest to honor the LORD your God. On
that day no one may do any work: not you,
your son or daughter, your male or female
slaves, your ox, your donkey, or any of your
animals, or the foreigners living in your
cities. That way your servants may rest as
you do. 15 Remember that you were slaves in
Egypt and that the LORD your God brought
you out of there by his great power and
strength. So the LORD your God has
commanded you to rest on the Sabbath day.
16 "Honor your father and your mother as
the LORD your God has commanded you.
Then you will live a long time, and things
will go well for you in the land that the LORD
your God is going to give you.
17 "You must not murder anyone.
18 "You must not be guilty of adultery.
19 "You must not steal.
20 "You must not tell lies about your
neighbor.
21 "You must not want to take your
neighbor's wife. You must not want to take
your neighbor's house or land, his male or
female slaves, his ox or his donkey, or
anything that belongs to your neighbor."
22 The LORD spoke these commands to all
of you on the mountain in a loud voice out
of the fire, the cloud, and the deep darkness;
he did not say anything else. Then he wrote
them on two stone tablets, and he gave them
to me.
23 When you heard the voice from the
darkness, as the mountain was blazing with
fire, all the leaders of your tribes and your
elders came to me. 24 And you said, "The LORD
our God has shown us his glory and majesty,
and we have heard his voice from the fire.
Today we have seen that a person can live
even if God speaks to him. 25 But now, we
will die! This great fire will burn us up, and
we will die if we hear the LORD our God
speak anymore. 26 No human being has ever
heard the living God speaking from a fire
and still lived, but we have. 27 Moses, you go
near and listen to everything the LORD our
God says. Then you tell us what the LORD our
God tells you, and we will listen and obey."
28 The LORD heard what you said to me,
and he said to me, "I have heard what the
people said to you. Everything they said was
good. 29 I wish their hearts would always
respect me and that they would always obey
my commands so that things would go well
for them and their children forever!
30 "Go and tell the people to return to their
tents, 31 but you stay here with me so that I
may give you all the commands, rules, and
laws that you must teach the people to obey
in the land I am giving them as their own."
32 So be careful to do what the LORD your
God has commanded you, and follow the
commands exactly. 33 Live the way the LORD
your God has commanded you so that you
may live and have what is good and have a
long life in the land you will take.

The Command to Love God

6 These are the commands, rules, and laws
that the LORD your God told me to teach
you to obey in the land you are crossing the
Jordan River to take. 2 You, your children, and
your grandchildren must respect the LORD
your God as long as you live. Obey all his
rules and commands I give you so that you
will live a long time. 3 Listen, Israel, and
carefully obey these laws. Then all will go
well for you, and you will become a great
nation in a fertile land, just as the LORD, the
God of your ancestors, has promised you.

4Listen, people of Israel! The LORD our God
is the only LORD. 5Love the LORD your God
with all your heart, all your soul, and all
your strength. 6Always remember these
commands I give you today. 7Teach them to
your children, and talk about them when
you sit at home and walk along the road,
when you lie down and when you get up.
8Write them down and tie them to your
hands as a sign. Tie them on your forehead
to remind you, 9and write them on your
doors and gates.

10The LORD your God will bring you into
the land he promised to your ancestors, to
Abraham, Isaac, and Jacob, and he will give it
to you. The land has large, growing cities
you did not build, 11houses full of good
things you did not buy, wells you did not dig,
and vineyards and olive trees you did not
plant. You will eat as much as you want.
12But be careful! Do not forget the LORD, who
brought you out of the land of Egypt where
you were slaves.

13Respect the LORD your God. You must
worship him and make your promises only
in his name. 14Do not worship other gods as
the people around you do, 15because the
LORD your God is a jealous God. He is present
with you, and if you worship other gods, he
will become angry with you and destroy you
from the earth. 16Do not test the LORD your
God as you did at Massah. 17Be sure to obey
the commands of the LORD your God and the
rules and laws he has given you. 18Do what
the LORD says is good and right so that things
will go well for you. Then you may go in and
take the good land the LORD promised to
your ancestors. 19He will force all your
enemies out as you go in, as the LORD has
said.

20In the future when your children ask
you, "What is the meaning of the laws,
commands, and rules the LORD our God gave
us?" 21tell them, "We were slaves to the king
of Egypt, but the LORD brought us out of
Egypt by his great power. 22The LORD showed
us great and terrible signs and miracles,
which he did to Egypt, the king, and his
whole family. 23The LORD brought us out of
Egypt to lead us here and to give us the land

devotion 51

DEUTERONOMY 6:5–9

SATURATED

My mom videotaped a conversation with me when I was two. If you played the tape now, you'd see me in a pink Onesie with strawberry jam plastered on my face, and you'd hear my mom's voice from behind the camera asking questions like, "Who is Jesus?" "Does he love you?" "How much does he love you?" "What did God make that you see around you right now?" And from my high chair came answers that only a toddler could compose about the love and creativity of our Maker.

There were many nights my parents read Scripture aloud around the dinner table, prayed, or took time out to talk "life." Though I didn't realize it at the time, my parents were following the words of Deuteronomy 6:7 by saturating my life in everyday ways with the loving truth of the Lord. I have yet to become a mom, but when I do, I pray I'll be able to pepper my children's days with the reality of who God truly is.

I hope you will also be inspired to take the words of this passage to your own heart. If you are a mom, be encouraged to talk to your children constantly about their heavenly Father. If you are an aunt, grandmother, or friend, you also have a unique opportunity to practice the words of Deuteronomy 6. Whatever your adult role, you can talk with the children in your life about God any time. Everything is a potential lesson about God's great love.

he promised our ancestors. [24]The LORD ordered us to obey all these commands and to respect the LORD our God so that we will always do well and stay alive, as we are today. [25]The right thing for us to do is this: Obey all these rules in the presence of the LORD our God, as he has commanded."

You Are God's People

7 The LORD your God will bring you into the land that you are entering and that you will have as your own. As you go in, he will force out these nations: the Hittites, Girgashites, Amorites, Canaanites, Perizzites, Hivites, and Jebusites—seven nations that are stronger than you. [2]The LORD your God will hand these nations over to you, and when you defeat them, you must destroy them completely. Do not make a peace treaty with them or show them any mercy. [3]Do not marry any of them, or let your daughters marry their sons, or let your sons marry their daughters. [4]If you do, those people will turn your children away from me, to begin serving other gods. Then the LORD will be very angry with you, and he will quickly destroy you. [5]This is what you must do to those people: Tear down their altars, smash their holy stone pillars, cut down their Asherah idols, and burn their idols in the fire. [6]You are holy people who belong to the LORD your God. He has chosen you from all the people on earth to be his very own.

[7]The LORD did not care for you and choose you because there were many of you—you are the smallest nation of all. [8]But the LORD chose you because he loved you, and he kept his promise to your ancestors. So he brought you out of Egypt by his great power and freed you from the land of slavery, from the power of the king of Egypt. [9]So know that the LORD your God is God, the faithful God. He will keep his agreement of love for a thousand lifetimes for people who love him and obey his commands. [10]But he will pay back those people who hate him. He will destroy them, and he will not be slow to pay back those who hate him. [11]So be careful to obey the commands, rules, and laws I give you today.

[12]If you pay attention to these laws and obey them carefully, the LORD your God will keep his agreement and show his love to you, as he promised your ancestors. [13]He will love and bless you. He will make the number of your people grow; he will bless you with children. He will bless your fields with good crops and will give you grain, new wine, and oil. He will bless your herds with calves and your flocks with lambs in the land he promised your ancestors he would give you. [14]You will be blessed more than any other people. Every husband and wife will have children, and all your cattle will have calves. [15]The LORD will take away all disease from you; you will not have the terrible diseases that were in Egypt, but he will give them to all the people who hate you. [16]You must destroy all the people the LORD your God hands over to you. Do not feel sorry for them, and do not worship their gods, or they will trap you.

[17]You might say to yourselves, "Because these nations are stronger than we are, we can't force them out." [18]But don't be afraid of them. Remember what the LORD your God did to all of Egypt and its king. [19]You saw for yourselves the troubles, signs, and miracles he did, how the LORD's great power and strength brought you out of Egypt. The LORD your God will do the same thing to all the nations you now fear. [20]The LORD your God will also send terror among them so that even those who are alive and hiding from you will die. [21]Don't be afraid of them, because the LORD your God is with you; he is a great God and people are afraid of him. [22]When the LORD your God forces those nations out of the land, he will do it little by little ahead of you. You won't be able to destroy them all at once; otherwise, the wild animals will grow too many in number. [23]But the LORD your God will hand those nations over to you, confusing them until they are destroyed. [24]The LORD will help you defeat their kings, and the world will forget who they were. No one will be able to stop you; you will destroy them all. [25]Burn up their idols in the fire. Do not wish for the silver and gold they have, and don't take it for yourselves, or you will be trapped by it. The LORD your God hates it. [26]Do not bring one of those hateful things into your house, or you will be completely destroyed along with it. Hate and reject those things; they must be completely destroyed.

devotion 52

DEUTERONOMY 7:7–9

NO WALLFLOWERS

Here is what I'm learning about God. There are no faceless women standing around the edge of the room with him. He did not bring you to this life just to shove you into a corner and tell you to have a great time watching. You have been chosen. You have been set apart. You were made for bright lights, and you do not have to shuffle around in the shadows hoping that one day it'll be your turn.

You are not just one of the crowd. God sees you. He walks across the room, looks directly at you, and from the depth of his "thousand lifetimes" love, calls you beautiful. You are not a wanna-be to him. No matter how dark your life might seem right now, you are not hidden from the Lord.

He will bring you out of every Egypt you walk through. He will set you free. Because he is faithful, God will keep the agreement of his love. The Lord of heaven and earth has vowed to keep his promises to you. He's coming to your rescue.

Over and over throughout Scripture, we watch the God of the universe rescue those who belong to him. He sends plagues and then comes as cloud and fire. He shuts the mouths of lions and opens the mouth of a whale. He breaks the chains of captives. He calls the dead to come out of their graves. He rolls away the stone. He saves any who would call him Lord. Our God is a rescuing God.

Because of his love, you have been chosen. And whatever your Egypt, God promises he will be your deliverer.

Remember the Lord

8 Carefully obey every command I give
you today. Then you will live and grow
in number, and you will enter and take the
land the LORD promised your ancestors.
2Remember how the LORD your God has led
you in the desert for these forty years, taking
away your pride and testing you, because he
wanted to know what was in your heart. He
wanted to know if you would obey his
commands. 3He took away your pride when
he let you get hungry, and then he fed you
with manna, which neither you nor your
ancestors had ever seen. This was to teach
you that a person does not live on bread
alone, but by everything the LORD says.
4During these forty years, your clothes did
not wear out, and your feet did not swell.
5Know in your heart that the LORD your God
corrects you as a parent corrects a child.

6Obey the commands of the LORD your
God, living as he has commanded you and
respecting him. 7The LORD your God is
bringing you into a good land, a land with
rivers and pools of water, with springs that
flow in the valleys and hills, 8a land that has
wheat and barley, vines, fig trees,
pomegranates, olive oil, and honey. 9It is a
land where you will have plenty of food,
where you will have everything you need,
where the rocks are iron, and where you can
dig copper out of the hills.

10When you have all you want to eat,
then praise the LORD your God for giving
you a good land. 11Be careful not to forget
the LORD your God so that you fail to obey
his commands, laws, and rules that I am
giving to you today. 12When you eat all you
want and build nice houses and live in
them, 13when your herds and flocks grow
large and your silver and gold increase,

when you have more of everything, [14]then
your heart will become proud. You will
forget the LORD your God, who brought you
out of the land of Egypt, where you were
slaves. [15]He led you through the large and
terrible desert that was dry and had no
water, and that had poisonous snakes and
stinging insects. He gave you water from a
solid rock [16]and manna to eat in the desert.
Manna was something your ancestors had
never seen. He did this to take away your
pride and to test you, so things would go
well for you in the end. [17]You might say to
yourself, "I am rich because of my own
power and strength," [18]but remember the
LORD your God! It is he who gives you the
power to become rich, keeping the
agreement he promised to your ancestors,
as it is today.
[19]If you ever forget the LORD your God and
follow other gods and worship them and
bow down to them, I warn you today that
you will be destroyed. [20]Just as the LORD
destroyed the other nations for you, you can
be destroyed if you do not obey the LORD
your God.

The Lord Will Be with Israel

9 Listen, Israel. You will soon cross the
Jordan River to go in and force out
nations that are bigger and stronger than
you. They have large cities with walls up to
the sky. [2]The people there are Anakites, who
are strong and tall. You know about them,
and you have heard it said: "No one can stop
the Anakites." [3]But today remember that the
LORD your God goes in before you to destroy
them like a fire that burns things up. He will
defeat them ahead of you, and you will force
them out and destroy them quickly, just as
the LORD has said.
[4]After the LORD your God has forced those
nations out ahead of you, don't say to
yourself, "The LORD brought me here to take
this land because I am so good." No! It is
because these nations are evil that the LORD
will force them out ahead of you. [5]You are
going in to take the land, not because you
are good and honest, but because these
nations are evil. That is why the LORD your
God will force them out ahead of you, to
keep his promise to your ancestors, to

devotion 53

DEUTERONOMY 8:2–3

BREAD ALONE? WHAT ABOUT CAKE?

Man does not live by bread alone? Of course we need bread! We need food! We need water! Occasionally we need chocolate cake! Now we may not need those great black boots we just saw in the window, but food and water we need! These bodies are made of flesh and bones, and without the tangible nourishment of food and water, we are doomed to become withered, weak little bodies that ultimately would just fade away.

Our bodies respond in various ways when hunger sets in, like headaches, irritability, and a growling stomach. Few of us can go more than a few hours without eating, much less a day. And none of us would consider eating or drinking only once in a seven-day week! Yet many of us only feed on the Word or draw from the living well on Sunday mornings. How will we stay spiritually strong if we only eat or drink of the Word once in a while?

The Lord is speaking to you today through Moses' words to the Israelites. He's encouraging you that he is the bread and wellspring of your life. He does not want you to be without physical provision, nor does he want you to skip your spiritual meals. The Word is purposed to give you nourishment for your soul, strength to accomplish your tasks, and wisdom to judge between right and wrong. Do not miss an opportunity to feast on the goodness of the Lord, and remember that dessert comes after the meal!

Abraham, Isaac, and Jacob. 6The LORD your
God is giving you this good land to take as
your own. But know this: It is not because
you are good; you are a stubborn people.

Remember the Lord's Anger

7Remember this and do not forget it: You
made the LORD your God angry in the desert.
You would not obey the LORD from the day
you left Egypt until you arrived here. 8At
Mount Sinai you made the LORD angry—
angry enough to destroy you. 9When I went
up on the mountain to receive the stone
tablets, the tablets with the Agreement the
LORD had made with you, I stayed on the
mountain for forty days and forty nights; I
did not eat bread or drink water. 10The LORD
gave me two stone tablets, which God had
written on with his own finger. On them
were all the commands that the LORD gave to
you on the mountain out of the fire, on the
day you were gathered there.

11When the forty days and forty nights
were over, the LORD gave me the two stone
tablets, the tablets with the Agreement on
them. 12Then the LORD told me, "Get up and
go down quickly from here, because the
people you brought out from Egypt are
ruining themselves. They have quickly
turned away from what I commanded and
have made an idol for themselves."

13The LORD said to me, "I have watched
these people, and they are very stubborn!
14Get away so that I may destroy them and
make the whole world forget who they are.
Then I will make another nation from you
that will be bigger and stronger than they
are."

15So I turned and came down the
mountain that was burning with fire, and
the two stone tablets with the Agreement
were in my hands. 16When I looked, I saw
you had sinned against the LORD your God
and had made an idol in the shape of a calf.
You had quickly turned away from what the
LORD had told you to do. 17So I took the two
stone tablets and threw them down,
breaking them into pieces right in front of
you.

18Then I again bowed facedown on the
ground before the LORD for forty days and
forty nights; I did not eat bread or drink
water. You had sinned by doing what the
LORD said was evil, and you made him angry.
19I was afraid of the LORD's anger and rage,
because he was angry enough with you to
destroy you, but the LORD listened to me
again. 20And the LORD was angry enough
with Aaron to destroy him, but then I prayed
for Aaron, too. 21I took that sinful calf idol
you had made and burned it in the fire. I
crushed it into a powder like dust and threw
the dust into a stream that flowed down the
mountain.

22You also made the LORD angry at Taberah, Massah, and Kibroth Hattaavah.

23Then the LORD sent you away from
Kadesh Barnea and said, "Go up and take the
land I have given you." But you rejected the
command of the LORD your God. You did not
trust him or obey him. 24You have refused
to obey the LORD as long as I have known
you.

25The LORD had said he would destroy you,
so I threw myself down in front of him for
those forty days and forty nights. 26I prayed
to the LORD and said, "Lord GOD, do not
destroy your people, your own people,
whom you freed and brought out of Egypt
by your great power and strength.
27Remember your servants Abraham, Isaac,
and Jacob. Don't look at how stubborn these
people are, and don't look at their sin and
evil. 28Otherwise, Egypt will say, 'It was
because the LORD was not able to take his
people into the land he promised them, and
it was because he hated them that he took
them into the desert to kill them.' 29But they
are your people, LORD, your own people,
whom you brought out of Egypt with your
great power and strength."

New Stone Tablets

10 At that time the LORD said to me, "Cut
two stone tablets like the first ones
and come up to me on the mountain. Also
make a wooden Ark. 2I will write on the
tablets the same words that were on the first
tablets, which you broke, and you will put
the new tablets in the Ark."

3So I made the Ark out of acacia wood,
and I cut out two stone tablets like the
first ones. Then I went up on the mountain
with the two tablets in my hands. 4The
LORD wrote the same things on these
tablets he had written before—the Ten
Commandments that he had told you on the
mountain from the fire, on the day you were

gathered there. And the LORD gave them to
me. [5]Then I turned and came down the
mountain; I put the tablets in the Ark I had
made, as the LORD had commanded, and they
are still there.

[6](The people of Israel went from the wells
of the Jaakanites to Moserah. Aaron died
there and was buried; his son Eleazar
became priest in his place. [7]From Moserah
they went to Gudgodah, and from Gudgodah
they went to Jotbathah, a place with streams
of water. [8]At that time the LORD chose the
tribe of Levi to carry the Ark of the
Agreement with the LORD. They were to
serve the LORD and to bless the people in his
name, which they still do today. [9]That is
why the Levites did not receive any land of
their own; instead, they received the LORD
himself as their gift, as the LORD your God
told them.)

[10]I stayed on the mountain forty days and
forty nights just like the first time, and the
LORD listened to me this time also. He did
not want to destroy you. [11]The LORD said to
me, "Go and lead the people so that they will
go in and take the land I promised their
ancestors."

What the Lord Wants You to Do

[12]Now, Israel, this is what the LORD your
God wants you to do: Respect the LORD your
God, and do what he has told you to do. Love
him. Serve the LORD your God with your
whole being, [13]and obey the LORD's
commands and laws that I am giving you
today for your own good.

[14]The LORD owns the world and everything
in it—the heavens, even the highest heavens,
are his. [15]But the LORD cared for and loved
your ancestors, and he chose you, their
descendants, over all the other nations, just
as it is today. [16]Give yourselves completely to
serving him, and do not be stubborn any
longer. [17]The LORD your God is God of all
gods and Lord of all lords. He is the great God,
who is strong and wonderful. He does not
take sides, and he will not be talked into
doing evil. [18]He helps orphans and widows,
and he loves foreigners and gives them food
and clothes. [19]You also must love foreigners,
because you were foreigners in Egypt.
[20]Respect the LORD your God and serve him.
Be loyal to him and make your promises in
his name. [21]He is the one you should praise;
he is your God, who has done great and

devotion 54

DEUTERONOMY 10:18

MY FRIEND BERTHA

She sits at the post office most of the day, never bothering anyone or anything as she watches the world go by. Her clothes are tattered, and she always has her basket of worldly possessions nearby. The first time I spoke to her, she simply asked for a ride to the bus stop. I loaded her bags into the back of my minivan and drove her down the street. Her name is Bertha, and she is a believer with no family living nearby. She stole my heart that day. I bought her a few things over the next couple of months—an electric skillet, a meal, a new outfit—but mostly we just became friends.

God loves the foreigner. So who is the foreigner of our day? I believe it is the outcast, the outsider, the one that just doesn't seem to fit in. We see them every day, though sometimes they are more obvious than other times. The real question is whether or not we take the time to notice them. I feared befriending Bertha because I didn't know where it would lead. Would I find myself being manipulated or hurt by her? Would I be able to help her? The bottom line was that God just wanted me to love her. Is there someone out there, a foreigner, who God wants you to reach out to today? Ask him. I thought I could bless Bertha with my friendship, but in the end, she was the one who blessed me.

wonderful things for you, which you have
seen with your own eyes. [22]There were only
seventy of your ancestors when they went
down to Egypt, and now the LORD your God
has made you as many as the stars in the sky.

Great Things Israel Saw

11 Love the LORD your God and always
obey his orders, rules, laws, and
commands. [2]Remember today it was not
your children who saw and felt the
correction of the LORD your God. They did
not see his majesty, his power, his strength,
[3]or his signs and the things he did in Egypt
to the king and his whole country. [4]They did
not see what he did to the Egyptian army, its
horses and chariots, when he drowned them
in the Red Sea as they were chasing you. The
LORD ruined them forever. [5]They did not see
what he did for you in the desert until you
arrived here. [6]They did not see what he did
to Dathan and Abiram, the sons of Eliab the
Reubenite, when the ground opened up and
swallowed them, their families, their tents,
and everyone who stood with them in Israel.
[7]It was you who saw all these great things
the LORD has done.

[8]So obey all the commands I am giving
you today so that you will be strong and can
go in and take the land you are going to take
as your own. [9]Then you will live a long time
in the land that the LORD promised to give to
your ancestors and their descendants, a
fertile land. [10]The land you are going to take
is not like Egypt, where you were. There you
had to plant your seed and water it, like a
vegetable garden, by using your feet. [11]But
the land that you will soon cross the Jordan
River to take is a land of hills and valleys, a
land that drinks rain from heaven. [12]It is a
land the LORD your God cares for. His eyes
are on it continually, and he watches it from
the beginning of the year to the end.

[13]If you carefully obey the commands I
am giving you today and love the LORD your
God and serve him with your whole being,
[14]then he will send rain on your land at the
right time, in the fall and spring, and you
will be able to gather your grain, new wine,
and oil. [15]He will put grass in the fields for
your cattle, and you will have plenty to eat.

[16]Be careful, or you will be fooled and will
turn away to serve and worship other gods.
[17]If you do, the LORD will become angry with
you and will shut the heavens so it will not
rain. Then the land will not grow crops, and
you will soon die in the good land the LORD
is giving you. [18]Remember my words with
your whole being. Write them down and tie
them to your hands as a sign; tie them on
your foreheads to remind you. [19]Teach them
well to your children, talking about them
when you sit at home and walk along the
road, when you lie down and when you get
up. [20]Write them on your doors and gates
[21]so that both you and your children will
live a long time in the land the LORD
promised your ancestors, as long as the skies
are above the earth.

[22]If you are careful to obey every
command I am giving you to follow, and
love the LORD your God, and do what he has
told you to do, and are loyal to him, [23]then
the LORD will force all those nations out of
the land ahead of you, and you will take the
land from nations that are bigger and
stronger than you. [24]Everywhere you step
will be yours. Your land will go from the
desert to Lebanon and from the Euphrates
River to the Mediterranean Sea. [25]No one
will be able to stop you. The LORD your God
will do what he promised and will make the
people afraid everywhere you go.

[26]See, today I am letting you choose a
blessing or a curse. [27]You will be blessed if
you obey the commands of the LORD your
God that I am giving you today. [28]But you
will be cursed if you disobey the commands
of the LORD your God. So do not disobey the
commands I am giving you today, and do not
worship other gods you do not know.
[29]When the LORD your God brings you into
the land you will take as your own, you are
to announce the blessings from Mount
Gerizim and the curses from Mount Ebal.
[30](These mountains are on the other side of
the Jordan River, to the west, toward the
sunset. They are near the great trees of
Moreh in the land of the Canaanites who
live in the Jordan Valley opposite Gilgal.)
[31]You will soon cross the Jordan River to
enter and take the land the LORD your God is
giving you. When you take it over and live
there, [32]be careful to obey all the commands
and laws I am giving you today.

The Place for Worship

12 These are the commands and laws
you must carefully obey in the land

the LORD, the God of your ancestors, is giving
you. Obey them as long as you live in the
land. 2 When you inherit the lands of these
nations, you must completely destroy all the
places where they serve their gods, on high
mountains and hills and under every green
tree. 3 Tear down their altars, smash their
holy stone pillars, and burn their Asherah
idols in the fire. Cut down their idols and
destroy their names from those places.

4 Don't worship the LORD your God that
way, 5 but look for the place the LORD your
God will choose—a place among your tribes
where he is to be worshiped. Go there, 6 and
bring to that place your burnt offerings and
sacrifices; bring a tenth of what you gain and
your special gifts; bring what you have
promised and the special gifts you want to
give the LORD, and bring the first animals
born to your herds and flocks.

7 There you will be together with the LORD
your God. There you and your families will
eat, and you will enjoy all the good things
for which you have worked, because the
LORD your God has blessed you.

8 Do not worship the way we have been
doing today, each person doing what he
thinks is right. 9 You have not yet come to a
resting place, to the land the LORD your God
will give you as your own. 10 But soon you
will cross the Jordan River to live in the land
the LORD your God is giving you as your
own, where he will give you rest from all
your enemies and you will live in safety.
11 Then the LORD your God will choose a
place where he is to be worshiped. To that
place you must bring everything I tell you:
your burnt offerings and sacrifices, your
offerings of a tenth of what you gain, your
special gifts, and all your best things you
promised to the LORD. 12 There rejoice before
the LORD your God. Everyone should rejoice:
you, your sons and daughters, your male and
female servants, and the Levites from your
towns who have no land of their own. 13 Be
careful that you don't sacrifice your burnt
offerings just anywhere you please. 14 Offer
them only in the place the LORD will choose.
He will choose a place in one of your tribes,
and there you must do everything I am
commanding you.

15 But you may kill your animals in any of
your towns and eat as much of the meat as
you want, as if it were a deer or a gazelle; this
is the blessing the LORD your God is giving
you. Anyone, clean or unclean, may eat this
meat, 16 but do not eat the blood. Pour it out
on the ground like water. 17 Do not eat in
your own towns what belongs to the LORD:
one-tenth of your grain, new wine, or oil; the
first animals born to your herds or flocks;
whatever you have promised to give; the
special gifts you want to give to the LORD, or
any other gifts. 18 Eat these things when you
are together with the LORD your God, in the
place the LORD your God chooses to be
worshiped. Everyone must do this: you, your
sons and daughters, your male and female
servants, and the Levites from your towns.
Rejoice in the LORD your God's presence
about the things you have worked for. 19 Be
careful not to forget the Levites as long as
you live in the land.

20 When the LORD your God enlarges your
country as he has promised, and you want
some meat so you say, "I want some meat,"
you may eat as much meat as you want. 21 If
the LORD your God chooses a place where he
is to be worshiped that is too far away from
you, you may kill animals from your herds
and flocks, which the LORD has given to you.
I have commanded that you may do this.
You may eat as much of them as you want in
your own towns, 22 as you would eat gazelle
or deer meat. Both clean and unclean people
may eat this meat, 23 but be sure you don't eat
the blood, because the life is in the blood.
Don't eat the life with the meat. 24 Don't eat
the blood, but pour it out on the ground like
water. 25 If you don't eat it, things will go well
for you and your children, because you will
be doing what the LORD says is right.

26 Take your holy things and the things
you have promised to give, and go to the
place the LORD will choose. 27 Present your
burnt offerings on the altar of the LORD your
God, both the meat and the blood. The blood
of your sacrifices should be poured beside
the altar of the LORD your God, but you may
eat the meat. 28 Be careful to obey all the
rules I am giving you so that things will
always go well for you and your children,
and you will be doing what the LORD your
God says is good and right.

29 You will enter the land and take it away
from the nations that the LORD your God will
destroy ahead of you. When you force them
out and live in their land, 30 they will be

destroyed for you, but be careful not to be trapped by asking about their gods. Don't say, "How do these nations worship? I will do the same." 31 Don't worship the LORD your God that way, because the LORD hates the evil ways they worship their gods. They even burn their sons and daughters as sacrifices to their gods!

32 Be sure to do everything I have commanded you. Do not add anything to it, and do not take anything away from it.

False Prophets

13 Prophets or those who tell the future with dreams might come to you and say they will show you a miracle or a sign. 2 The miracle or sign might even happen, and then they might say, "Let's serve other gods" (gods you have not known) "and let's worship them." 3 But you must not listen to those prophets or dreamers. The LORD your God is testing you, to find out if you love him with your whole being. 4 Serve only the LORD your God. Respect him, keep his commands, and obey him. Serve him and be loyal to him. 5 The prophets or dreamers must be killed, because they said you should turn against the LORD your God, who brought you out of Egypt and saved you from the land where you were slaves. They tried to turn you from doing what the LORD your God commanded you to do. You must get rid of the evil among you.

6 Someone might try to lead you to serve other gods—it might be your brother, your son or daughter, the wife you love, or a close friend. The person might say, "Let's go and worship other gods." (These are gods that neither you nor your ancestors have known, 7 gods of the people who live around you, either nearby or far away, from one end of the land to the other.) 8 Do not give in to such people. Do not listen or feel sorry for them, and do not let them go free or protect them. 9 You must put them to death. You must be the first one to start to kill them, and then everyone else must join in. 10 You must throw stones at them until they die, because they tried to turn you away from the LORD your God, who brought you out of the land of Egypt, where you were slaves. 11 Then everyone in Israel will hear about this and be afraid, and no one among you will ever do such an evil thing again.

Cities to Destroy

12 The LORD your God is giving you cities in which to live, and you might hear something about one of them. Someone might say 13 that evil people have moved in among you. And they might lead the people of that city away from God, saying, "Let's go and worship other gods." (These are gods you have not known.) 14 Then you must ask about it, looking into the matter and checking carefully whether it is true. If it is proved that a hateful thing has happened among you, 15 you must kill with a sword everyone who lives in that city. Destroy the city completely and kill everyone in it, as well as the animals, with a sword. 16 Gather up everything those people owned, and put it in the middle of the city square. Then completely burn the city and everything they owned as a burnt offering to the LORD your God. That city should never be rebuilt; let it be ruined forever. 17 Don't keep for yourselves any of the things found in that city, so the LORD will not be angry anymore. He will give you mercy and feel sorry for you, and he will make your nation grow larger, as he promised to your ancestors. 18 You will have obeyed the LORD your God by keeping all his commands that I am giving to you today, and you will be doing what the LORD says is right.

God's Special People

14 You are the children of the LORD your God. When someone dies, do not cut yourselves or shave your heads to show your sadness. 2 You are holy people, who belong to the LORD your God. He has chosen you from all the people on earth to be his very own.

3 Do not eat anything the LORD hates. 4 These are the animals you may eat: oxen, sheep, goats, 5 deer, gazelle, roe deer, wild goats, ibex, antelope, and mountain sheep. 6 You may eat any animal that has a split hoof and chews the cud, 7 but you may not eat camels, rabbits, or rock badgers. These animals chew the cud, but they do not have split hoofs, so they are unclean for you. 8 Pigs are also unclean for you; they have split hoofs, but they do not chew the cud. Do not eat their meat or touch their dead bodies.

9 There are many things that live in the

devotion 55

DEUTERONOMY 14:2

THE PICTURE OF HOLINESS

I don't feel like holy people. I certainly don't look like holy people. And if you took a glance at my résumé, you'd be certain—no way, she is not holy people. But God says that if I belong to him, he has made me holy. Amazing, isn't it? It's also a little overwhelming and so completely undeserved. And yet every time God says something, it's always true.

God lives inside of holy people. They are imperfect people made holy by a perfect God's love. The holiness is the Lord's, given as a lavish gift from the depths of his love. Our job is to protect the holiness he has given.

Here's what I know from both personal experience and observation. A clean life and a clear conscience allow us to operate in holiness. If your conscience is not clear, you spend a lot of emotional energy trying to cover things up. The murky conscience requires a great deal of mental power for inner wrangling and rationalizing. This burdened conscience keeps you shackled to a wall of guilt, and it never lets you get very far in life. It will keep you from holiness.

You belong to God. It is a privilege to live inside his blessing and to be made holy. Are you clean today? Is your conscience clear? God chose you and me. That is amazing. And he is the only One who can make you clean. Amazing again. Ask him to make it so and consider it done.

water. You may eat anything that has fins
and scales, [10]but do not eat anything that
does not have fins and scales. It is unclean
for you.
[11]You may eat any clean bird. [12]But do not
eat these birds: eagles, vultures, black
vultures, [13]red kites, falcons, any kind of kite,
[14]any kind of raven, [15]horned owls, screech
owls, sea gulls, any kind of hawk, [16]little
owls, great owls, white owls, [17]desert owls,
ospreys, cormorants, [18]storks, any kind of
heron, the hoopoes, or bats.
[19]All insects with wings are unclean for
you; do not eat them. [20]Other things with
wings are clean, and you may eat them.
[21]Do not eat anything you find that is
already dead. You may give it to a foreigner
living in your town, and he may eat it, or
you may sell it to a foreigner. But you are
holy people, who belong to the LORD your
God.

Do not cook a baby goat in its mother's milk.

Giving One-Tenth

[22]Be sure to save one-tenth of all your
crops each year. [23]Take it to the place the
LORD your God will choose where he is to be
worshiped. There, where you will be together
with the LORD, eat the tenth of your grain,
new wine, and oil, and eat the animals born
first to your herds and flocks. Do this so that
you will learn to respect the LORD your God
always. [24]But if the place the LORD will
choose to be worshiped is too far away and
he has blessed you so much you cannot carry
a tenth, [25]exchange your one-tenth for silver.
Then take the silver with you to the place the
LORD your God shall choose. [26]Use the silver
to buy anything you wish—cattle, sheep,
wine, beer, or anything you wish. Then you
and your family will eat and celebrate there
before the LORD your God. [27]Do not forget the
Levites in your town, because they have no
land of their own among you.
[28]At the end of every third year, everyone
should bring one-tenth of that year's crop

and store it in your towns. 29This is for the
Levites so they may eat and be full. (They
have no land of their own among you.) It is
also for strangers, orphans, and widows who
live in your towns so that all of them may
eat and be full. Then the LORD your God will
bless you and all the work you do.

The Special Seventh Year

15 At the end of every seven years, you
must tell those who owe you
anything that they do not have to pay you
back. 2This is how you must do it: Everyone
who has loaned money must cancel the loan
and not make a neighbor or relative pay it
back. This is the LORD's time for canceling
what people owe. 3You may make a
foreigner pay what is owed to you, but you
must not collect what another Israelite owes
you. 4But there should be no poor people
among you, because the LORD your God will
richly bless you in the land he is giving you
as your own. 5He will bless you if you obey
the LORD your God completely, but you must
be careful to obey all the commands I am
giving you today. 6The LORD your God will
bless you as he promised, and you will lend
to other nations, but you will not need to
borrow from them. You will rule over many
nations, but none will rule over you.

7If there are poor among you, in one of
the towns of the land the LORD your God is
giving you, do not be selfish or greedy
toward them. 8But give freely to them, and
freely lend them whatever they need.
9Beware of evil thoughts. Don't think, "The
seventh year is near, the year to cancel what
people owe." You might be mean to the
needy and not give them anything. Then
they will complain to the LORD about you,
and he will find you guilty of sin. 10Give
freely to the poor person, and do not wish
that you didn't have to give. The LORD your
God will bless your work and everything
you touch. 11There will always be poor
people in the land, so I command you to give
freely to your neighbors and to the poor and
needy in your land.

Letting Slaves Go Free

12If one of your own people sells himself
to you as a slave, whether it is a Hebrew man
or woman, that person will serve you for six
years. But in the seventh year you must let
the slave go free. 13When you let slaves go,
don't send them away without anything.
14Give them some of your flock, your grain,
and your wine, giving to them as the LORD
has given to you. 15Remember that you were
slaves in Egypt, and the LORD your God saved
you. That is why I am commanding this to
you today.

16But if your slave says to you, "I don't
want to leave you," because he loves you and
your family and has a good life with you,
17stick an awl[n] through his ear into the door;
he will be your slave for life. Also do this to a
female slave.

18Do not think of it as a hard thing when
you let your slaves go free. After all, they
served you six years and did twice the work
of a hired person. The LORD your God will
bless you in everything you do.

Rules About Firstborn Animals

19Save all the first male animals born to
your herds and flocks. They are for the
LORD your God. Do not work the first calf
born to your oxen, and do not cut off the
wool from the first lamb born to your sheep.
20Each year you and your family are to eat
these animals in the presence of the LORD
your God, in the place he will choose to be
worshiped. 21If an animal is crippled or blind
or has something else wrong, do not sacrifice
it to the LORD your God. 22But you may eat
that animal in your own town. Both clean
and unclean people may eat it, as they
would eat a gazelle or a deer. 23But don't eat
its blood; pour it out on the ground like
water.

The Passover

16 Celebrate the Passover of the LORD
your God during the month of Abib,
because it was during Abib that he brought
you out of Egypt at night. 2As the sacrifice
for the Passover to the LORD your God, offer
an animal from your flock or herd at the
place the LORD will choose to be worshiped.
3Do not eat it with bread made with yeast.
But for seven days eat bread made without
yeast, the bread of suffering, because you left
Egypt in a hurry. So all your life you will

15:17 awl A tool like a big needle with a handle at one end.

remember the time you left Egypt. 4There
must be no yeast anywhere in your land for
seven days. Offer the sacrifice on the evening
of the first day, and eat all the meat before
morning; do not leave it overnight.
5Do not offer the Passover sacrifice in just
any town the LORD your God gives you, 6but
offer it in the place he will choose to be
worshiped. Offer it in the evening as the sun
goes down, which is when you left Egypt.
7Roast the meat and eat it at the place the
LORD your God will choose. The next
morning go back to your tents. 8Eat bread
made without yeast for six days. On the
seventh day have a special meeting for the
LORD your God, and do not work that day.

The Feast of Weeks

9Count seven weeks from the time you
begin to harvest the grain, 10and then
celebrate the Feast of Weeks for the LORD
your God. Bring an offering as a special gift
to him, giving to him just as he has blessed
you. 11Rejoice before the LORD your God at
the place he will choose to be worshiped.
Everybody should rejoice: you, your sons and
daughters, your male and female servants,
the Levites in your town, the strangers,
orphans, and widows living among you.
12Remember that you were slaves in Egypt,
and carefully obey all these laws.

The Feast of Shelters

13Celebrate the Feast of Shelters for seven
days, after you have gathered your harvest
from the threshing floor and winepress.
14Everybody should rejoice at your Feast:
you, your sons and daughters, your male and
female servants, the Levites, strangers,
orphans, and widows who live in your
towns. 15Celebrate the Feast to the LORD your
God for seven days at the place he will
choose, because the LORD your God will bless
all your harvest and all the work you do, and
you will be completely happy.
16All your men must come before the
LORD three times a year to the place he will
choose. They must come at these times: the
Feast of Unleavened Bread, the Feast of
Weeks, and the Feast of Shelters. No man
should come before the LORD without a gift.
17Each of you must bring a gift that will
show how much the LORD your God has
blessed you.

Judges for the People

18Appoint judges and officers for your
tribes in every town the LORD your God is
giving you; they must judge the people
fairly. 19Do not judge unfairly or take sides.
Do not let people pay you to make wrong
decisions, because that kind of payment
makes wise people seem blind, and it
changes the words of good people. 20Always
do what is right so that you will live and
always have the land the LORD your God is
giving you.

God Hates Idols

21Do not set up a wooden Asherah idol
next to the altar you build for the LORD your
God, 22and do not set up holy stone pillars.
The LORD your God hates them.

17 If an ox or sheep has something wrong
with it, do not offer it as a sacrifice to
the LORD your God. He would hate that.
2A man or woman in one of the towns
the LORD gave you might be found doing
something evil and breaking the
Agreement. 3That person may have served
other gods and bowed down to them or to
the sun or moon or stars of the sky, which
I have commanded should not be done. 4If
someone has told you about it, you must
look into the matter carefully. If it is true
that such a hateful thing has happened in
Israel, 5take the man or woman who has
done the evil thing to the city gates and
throw stones at that person until he dies.
6There must be two or three witnesses
that it is true before the person is put to
death; if there is only one witness, the
person should not be put to death. 7The
witnesses must be the first to throw stones
at the person, and then everyone else
will follow. You must get rid of the evil
among you.

Courts of Law

8Some cases that come before you, such as
murder, quarreling, or attack, may be too
difficult to judge. Take these cases to the
place the LORD your God will choose. 9Go to
the priests who are Levites and to the judge
who is on duty at that time. Ask them about
the case, and they will decide. 10You must
follow the decision they give you at the
place the LORD your God will choose. Be

careful to do everything they tell you.
11Follow the teachings they give you, and do
whatever they decide, exactly as they tell
you. 12The person who does not show
respect for the judge or priest who is there
serving the LORD your God must be put to
death. You must get rid of that evil from
Israel. 13Then everyone will hear about this
and will be afraid, and they will not show
disrespect anymore.

Choosing a King

14When you enter the land the LORD your
God is giving you, taking it as your own and
living in it, you will say, "Let's appoint a king
over us like the nations all around us." 15Be
sure to appoint over you the king the LORD
your God chooses. He must be one of your
own people. Do not appoint as your king a
foreigner who is not a fellow Israelite. 16The
king must not have too many horses for
himself, and he must not send people to
Egypt to get more horses, because the LORD
has told you, "Don't return that way again."
17The king must not have many wives, or his
heart will be led away from God. He must
not have too much silver and gold.
18When he becomes king, he should write
a copy of the teachings on a scroll for
himself, a copy taken from the priests and
Levites. 19He should keep it with him all the
time and read from it every day of his life.
Then he will learn to respect the LORD his
God, and he will obey all the teachings and
commands. 20He should not think he is
better than his fellow Israelites, and he must
not stop obeying the law in any way so that
he and his descendants may rule the
kingdom for a long time.

Shares for Priests and Levites

18 The priests are from the tribe of Levi,
and that tribe will not receive a share
of the land with the Israelites. They will eat
the offerings made to the LORD by fire, which
is their share. 2They will not inherit any of
the land like their brothers, but they will
inherit the LORD himself, as he has promised
them.
3When you offer a bull or sheep as a
sacrifice, you must share with the priests,
giving them the shoulder, the cheeks, and
the inner organs. 4Give them the first of your
grain, new wine, and oil, as well as the first
wool you cut from your sheep. 5The LORD
your God has chosen the priests and their
descendants out of all your tribes to stand
and serve the LORD always.
6If a Levite moves from one of your towns
anywhere in Israel where he lives and comes
to the place the LORD will choose, because he
wants to serve the LORD there, 7he may serve
the LORD his God. He will be like his fellow
Levites who serve there before the LORD.
8They all will have an equal share of the
food. That is separate from what he has
received from the sale of family possessions.

Do Not Follow Other Nations

9When you enter the land the LORD your
God is giving you, don't learn to do the
hateful things the other nations do. 10Don't
let anyone among you offer a son or
daughter as a sacrifice in the fire. Don't let
anyone use magic or witchcraft, or try to
explain the meaning of signs. 11Don't let
anyone try to control others with magic, and
don't let them be mediums or try to talk
with the spirits of dead people. 12The LORD
hates anyone who does these things. Because
the other nations do these things, the LORD
your God will force them out of the land
ahead of you. 13But you must be innocent in
the presence of the LORD your God.

The Lord's Special Prophet

14The nations you will force out listen to
people who use magic and witchcraft, but
the LORD your God will not let you do those
things. 15The LORD your God will give you a
prophet like me, who is one of your own
people. Listen to him. 16This is what you
asked the LORD your God to do when you
were gathered at Mount Sinai. You said,
"Don't make us listen to the voice of the
LORD our God again, and don't make us look
at this terrible fire anymore, or we will die."
17So the LORD said to me, "What they have
said is good. 18So I will give them a prophet
like you, who is one of their own people. I
will tell him what to say, and he will tell
them everything I command. 19This prophet
will speak for me; anyone who does not
listen when he speaks will answer to me.
20But if a prophet says something I did not
tell him to say as though he were speaking
for me, or if a prophet speaks in the name of
other gods, that prophet must be killed."
21You might be thinking, "How can we

know if a message is not from the LORD?"
22If what a prophet says in the name of the
LORD does not happen, it is not the LORD's
message. That prophet was speaking his
own ideas. Don't be afraid of him.

Cities of Safety

19 When the LORD your God gives you
land that belongs to the other nations,
nations that he will destroy, you will force
them out and live in their cities and houses.
2Then choose three cities in the middle of
the land the LORD your God is giving you as
your own. 3Build roads to these cities, and
divide the land the LORD is giving you into
three parts so that someone who kills
another person may run to these cities.
4This is the rule for someone who kills
another person and runs to one of these
cities in order to save his life. But the person
must have killed a neighbor without
meaning to, not out of hatred. 5For example,
suppose someone goes into the forest with a
neighbor to cut wood and swings an ax to
cut down a tree. If the ax head flies off the
handle, hitting and killing the neighbor, the
one who killed him may run to one of these
cities to save his life. 6Otherwise, the dead
person's relative who has the duty of
punishing a murderer might be angry and
chase him. If the city is far away, the relative
might catch and kill the person, even
though he should not be killed because
there was no intent to kill his neighbor.
7This is why I command you to choose these
three cities.
8-9Carefully obey all these laws I'm giving
you today. Love the LORD your God, and
always do what he wants you to do. Then
the LORD your God will enlarge your land as
he promised your ancestors, giving you the
whole land he promised to them. After that,
choose three more cities of safety 10so that
innocent people will not be killed in your
land, the land that the LORD your God is
giving you as your own. By doing this you
will not be guilty of allowing the death of
innocent people.
11But if a person hates his neighbor and,
after hiding and waiting, attacks and kills
him and then runs to one of these cities for
safety, 12the elders of his own city should
send for the murderer. They should bring the
person back from the city of safety and hand
him over to the relative who has the duty of
punishing the murderer. 13Show no mercy.
You must remove from Israel the guilt of
murdering innocent people so that things
will go well for you.
14Do not move the stone that marks the
border of your neighbor's land, which
people long ago set in place. It marks what
you inherit in the land the LORD your God is
giving you as your own.

Rules About Witnesses

15One witness is not enough to accuse a
person of a crime or sin. A case must be
proved by two or three witnesses.
16If a witness lies and accuses a person of a
crime, 17the two people who are arguing
must stand in the presence of the LORD
before the priests and judges who are on
duty. 18The judges must check the matter
carefully. The witness who is a liar, lying
about a fellow Israelite, 19must be punished.
He must be punished in the same way the
other person would have been punished.
You must get rid of the evil among you.
20The rest of the people will hear about this
and be afraid, and no one among you will
ever do such an evil thing again. 21Show no
mercy. A life must be paid for a life, an eye
for an eye, a tooth for a tooth, a hand for a
hand, a foot for a foot.

Laws for War

20 When you go to war against your
enemies and you see horses and
chariots and an army that is bigger than
yours, don't be afraid of them. The LORD your
God, who brought you out of Egypt, will be
with you. 2The priest must come and speak
to the army before you go into battle. 3He
will say, "Listen, Israel! Today you are going
into battle against your enemies. Don't lose
your courage or be afraid. Don't panic or be
frightened, 4because the LORD your God goes
with you, to fight for you against your
enemies and to save you."
5The officers should say to the army, "Has
anyone built a new house but not given it to
God? He may go home, because he might die
in battle and someone else would get to give
his house to God. 6Has anyone planted a
vineyard and not begun to enjoy it? He may
go home, because he might die in battle and
someone else would enjoy his vineyard.

devotion 56

DEUTERONOMY 20:1–4

YOUR LAST HOPE

Don't be afraid of circumstances that cause you pain. Don't fear those who want to overtake you or the sea that blocks your way. Do not look back or run and hide. Stand still—and watch God show up in all his glory. When your world caves in, when the lights go out, when devastating news arrives, when fools rush in, when you have done everything you can and find yourself crushed by the weight of doing—right there is where God wants you to stop. Stand before the only hope you have and wait.

Do you trust God? I mean really? I tell God that I trust him, but I wish I lived more in the power of that truth. One day I believe that I am strong, only to feel my trust bending under the strain of gusting winds the next day.

God knows that life can throw us up against a wall with no options and that the pain can be intense, but he stands vigil over us like a pillar of cloud and fire. We are beautiful to him, and his eye is continually upon us.

He will be our strength and refuge while we wait in the dark. He will hold us as a Father holds his wounded child. He delights to fight our battles. He wants to rescue us from the ever-encroaching rings of fire. He wants to do what we cannot even imagine. He wants us to know that he is the only hope we'll ever have and the only hope we'll ever need.

7Is any man engaged to a woman and not yet
married to her? He may go home, because he
might die in battle and someone else would
marry her." 8Then the officers should also
say, "Is anyone here afraid? Has anyone lost
his courage? He may go home so that he will
not cause others to lose their courage, too."
9When the officers finish speaking to the
army, they should appoint commanders to
lead it.
10When you march up to attack a city,
first make them an offer of peace. 11If they
accept your offer and open their gates to
you, all the people of that city will become
your slaves and work for you. 12But if they
do not make peace with you and fight you
in battle, you should surround that city.
13The LORD your God will give it to you.
Then kill all the men with your swords,
14and you may take everything else in the
city for yourselves. Take the women,
children, and animals, and you may use
these things the LORD your God gives you
from your enemies. 15Do this to all the cities
that are far away, that do not belong to the
nations nearby.
16But leave nothing alive in the cities of
the land the LORD your God is giving you.
17Completely destroy these people: the
Hittites, Amorites, Canaanites, Perizzites,
Hivites, and Jebusites, as the LORD your God
has commanded. 18Otherwise, they will
teach you what they do for their gods, and if
you do these hateful things, you will sin
against the LORD your God.
19If you surround and attack a city for a
long time, trying to capture it, do not destroy
its trees with an ax. You can eat the fruit
from the trees, but do not cut them down.
These trees are not the enemy, so don't make
war against them. 20But you may cut down
trees that you know are not fruit trees and
use them to build devices to attack the city
walls, until the city is captured.

A Person Found Murdered

21 Suppose someone is found murdered,
lying in a field in the land the LORD

your God is giving you as your own, and no
one knows who killed the person. 2Your
elders and judges should go to where the
body was found, and they should measure
how far it is to the nearby cities. 3The elders
of the city nearest the body must take a
young cow that has never worked or worn a
yoke, 4and they must lead her down to a
valley that has never been plowed or planted,
with a stream flowing through it. There they
must break the young cow's neck. 5The
priests, the sons of Levi, should come
forward, because they have been chosen by
the LORD your God to serve him and to give
blessings in the LORD's name. They are the
ones who decide cases of quarreling and
attacks. 6Then all the elders of the city
nearest the murdered person should wash
their hands over the young cow whose neck
was broken in the valley. 7They should
declare: "We did not kill this person, and we
did not see it happen. 8LORD, remove this sin
from your people Israel, whom you have
saved. Don't blame your people, the Israelites,
for the murder of this innocent person." And
so the murder will be paid for. 9Then you will
have removed from yourselves the guilt of
murdering an innocent person, because you
will be doing what the LORD says is right.

Captive Women as Wives

10When you go to war against your
enemies, the LORD will help you defeat them
so that you will take them captive. 11If you
see a beautiful woman among the captives
and are attracted to her, you may take her as
your wife. 12Bring her into your home, where
she must shave her head and cut her nails
13and change the clothes she was wearing
when you captured her. After she has lived
in your house and cried for her parents for a
month, you may marry her. You will be her
husband, and she will be your wife. 14But if
you are not pleased with her, you must let
her go anywhere she wants. You must not
sell her for money or make her a slave,
because you have taken away her honor.

The Oldest Son

15A man might have two wives, one he
loves and one he doesn't. Both wives might
have sons by him. If the older son belongs to
the wife he does not love, 16when that man
wills his property to his sons he must not
give the son of the wife he loves what
belongs to the older son, the son of the
wife he does not love. 17He must agree to
give the older son two shares of everything
he owns, even though the older son is from
the wife he does not love. That son was
the first to prove his father could have
children, so he has the rights that belong
to the older son.

Sons Who Refuse to Obey

18If someone has a son who is stubborn,
who turns against his father and mother and
doesn't obey them or listen when they
correct him, 19his parents must take him to
the elders at the city gate. 20They will say to
the elders, "Our son is stubborn and turns
against us. He will not obey us. He eats too
much, and he is always drunk." 21Then all
the men in his town must throw stones at
him until he dies. Get rid of the evil among
you, because then all the people of Israel will
hear about this and be afraid.

Other Laws

22If someone is guilty of a sin worthy of
death, he must be put to death and his body
displayed on a tree. 23But don't leave his body
hanging on the tree overnight; be sure to
bury him that same day, because anyone
whose body is displayed on a tree is cursed
by God. You must not ruin the land the LORD
your God is giving you as your own.

22 If you see your fellow Israelite's ox or
sheep wandering away, don't ignore it.
Take it back to its owner. 2If the owner
does not live close to you, or if you do not
know who the owner is, take the animal
home with you. Keep it until the owner
comes looking for it; then give it back.
3Do the same thing if you find a donkey or
coat or anything someone lost. Don't just
ignore it.

4If you see your fellow Israelite's donkey
or ox fallen on the road, don't ignore it. Help
the owner get it up.

5A woman must not wear men's clothes,
and a man must not wear women's clothes.
The LORD your God hates anyone who
does that.

6If you find a bird's nest by the road,
either in a tree or on the ground, and the
mother bird is sitting on the young birds or
eggs, do not take the mother bird with the

devotion 57

DEUTERONOMY 21:22–23

GUILTY AS CHARGED

The heart of our Savior is that while we were still sinners, he was willing to die for our sin. I know I need atonement for my sin. You need atonement for your sin as well, and all the people I know need atonement for their sin. If what Moses described as a "sin worthy of death" was part of the law of the land today, I can assure you I would not be present to share this devotion. Unfortunately, I am one of those people who have committed a sin worthy of death, so my body would be hanging on a tree. Instead, because of God's grace, I am a testimony of restoration and forgiveness and would not dare to imply that the work of the Cross was somehow unnecessary. It was God's gift, whether I consider myself worthy of it or not.

Have you committed a sin worthy of death in your life? You can be free through Jesus and the profession of your heart (Ps. 32:5). Do not let your heart condemn you. If you continue to struggle in condemnation, you are saying that Jesus' death on the cross was not enough. Do not let the truth of his forgiveness escape you. Hold on to it, cling to it, and make sure your heart knows that the full price has been paid and the work has already been completed. God has given you a fresh start, and he loves you with all his heart.

young birds. [7]You may take the young birds,
but you must let the mother bird go free.
Then things will go well for you, and you
will live a long time.
[8]When you build a new house, build a
low wall around the edge of the roof[n] so you
will not be guilty if someone falls off the
roof.
[9]Don't plant two different kinds of seeds
in your vineyard. Otherwise, both crops will
be ruined.
[10]Don't plow with an ox and a donkey tied
together.
[11]Don't wear clothes made of wool and
linen woven together.
[12]Tie several pieces of thread together;
then put these tassels on the four corners of
your coat.

Marriage Laws

[13]If a man marries a girl and has sexual
relations with her but then decides he does
not like her, [14]he might talk badly about her
and give her a bad name. He might say, "I
married this woman, but when I had sexual
relations with her, I did not find that she was
a virgin." [15]Then the girl's parents must
bring proof that she was a virgin to the
elders at the city gate. [16]The girl's father will
say to the elders, "I gave my daughter to this
man to be his wife, but now he does not
want her. [17]This man has told lies about my
daughter. He has said, 'I did not find your
daughter to be a virgin,' but here is the proof
that my daughter was a virgin." Then her
parents are to show the sheet to the elders of
the city, [18]and the elders must take the man
and punish him. [19]They must make him pay
about two and one-half pounds of silver to
the girl's father, because the man has given
an Israelite virgin a bad name. The girl will
continue to be the man's wife, and he may
not divorce her as long as he lives.
[20]But if the things the husband said about

22:8 roof In Bible times houses were built with flat roofs. The roof was used for drying things such as flax and fruit. And it was used as an extra room, as a place for worship, and as a cool place to sleep in the summer.

his wife are true, and there is no proof that she was a virgin, [21]the girl must be brought to the door of her father's house. Then the men of the town must put her to death by throwing stones at her. She has done a disgraceful thing in Israel by having sexual relations before she was married. You must get rid of the evil among you.

[22]If a man is found having sexual relations with another man's wife, both the woman and the man who had sexual relations with her must die. Get rid of this evil from Israel.

[23]If a man meets a virgin in a city and has sexual relations with her, but she is engaged to another man, [24]you must take both of them to the city gate and put them to death by throwing stones at them. Kill the girl, because she was in a city and did not scream for help. And kill the man for having sexual relations with another man's wife. You must get rid of the evil among you.

[25]But if a man meets an engaged girl out in the country and forces her to have sexual relations with him, only the man who had sexual relations with her must be put to death. [26]Don't do anything to the girl, because she has not done a sin worthy of death. This is like the person who attacks and murders a neighbor; [27]the man found the engaged girl in the country and she screamed, but no one was there to save her.

[28]If a man meets a virgin who is not engaged to be married and forces her to have sexual relations with him and people find out about it, [29]the man must pay the girl's father about one and one-fourth pounds of silver. He must also marry the girl, because he has dishonored her, and he may never divorce her for as long as he lives.

[30]A man must not marry his father's wife; he must not dishonor his father in this way.

The Lord's People

23 No man who has had part of his sex organ cut off may come into the meeting to worship the LORD.

[2]No one born to parents who were forbidden by law to marry may come into the meeting to worship the LORD. The descendants for ten generations may not come in either.

[3]No Ammonite or Moabite may come into the meeting to worship the LORD, and none of their descendants for ten generations may come in. [4]This is because the Ammonites and Moabites did not give you bread and water when you came out of Egypt. And they hired Balaam son of Beor, from Pethor in Northwest Mesopotamia, to put a curse on you. [5]But the LORD your God would not listen to Balaam. He turned the curse into a blessing for you, because the LORD your God loves you. [6]Don't wish for their peace or success as long as you live.

[7]Don't hate Edomites; they are your close relatives. Don't hate Egyptians, because you were foreigners in their country. [8]The great-grandchildren of these two peoples may come into the meeting to worship the LORD.

Keeping the Camp Clean

[9]When you are camped in time of war, keep away from unclean things. [10]If a man becomes unclean during the night, he must go outside the camp and not come back. [11]But when evening comes, he must wash himself, and at sunset he may come back into the camp.

[12]Choose a place outside the camp where people may go to relieve themselves. [13]Carry a tent peg with you, and when you relieve yourself, dig a hole and cover up your dung. [14]The LORD your God moves around through your camp to protect you and to defeat your enemies for you, so the camp must be holy. He must not see anything unclean among you so that he will not leave you.

Other Laws

[15]If an escaped slave comes to you, do not hand over the slave to his master. [16]Let the slave live with you anywhere he likes, in any town he chooses. Do not mistreat him.

[17]No Israelite man or woman must ever become a temple prostitute. [18]Do not bring a male or female prostitute's pay to the Temple of the LORD your God to pay what you have promised to the LORD, because the LORD your God hates prostitution.

[19]If you loan your fellow Israelites money or food or anything else, don't make them pay back more than you loaned them. [20]You may charge foreigners, but not fellow Israelites. Then the LORD your God will bless everything you do in the land you are entering to take as your own.

[21]If you make a promise to give something to the LORD your God, do not be slow to pay

it, because the LORD your God demands it from you. Do not be guilty of sin. [22]But if you do not make the promise, you will not be guilty. [23]You must do whatever you say you will do, because you chose to make the promise to the LORD your God.

[24]If you go into your neighbor's vineyard, you may eat as many grapes as you wish, but do not put any grapes into your basket. [25]If you go into your neighbor's grainfield, you may pick grain with your hands, but you must not cut down your neighbor's grain with your sickle.

24 A man might marry a woman but later decide she doesn't please him because he has found something bad about her. He writes out divorce papers for her, gives them to her, and sends her away from his house. [2]After she leaves his house, she goes and marries another man, [3]but her second husband does not like her either. So he writes out divorce papers for her, gives them to her, and sends her away from his house. Or the second husband might die. [4]In either case, her first husband who divorced her must not marry her again, because she has become unclean. The LORD would hate this. Don't bring this sin into the land the LORD your God is giving you as your own.

[5]A man who has just married must not be sent to war or be given any other duty. He should be free to stay home for a year to make his new wife happy.

[6]If someone owes you something, do not take his two stones for grinding grain—not even the upper one—in place of what he owes, because this is how the person makes a living.

[7]If someone kidnaps a fellow Israelite, either to make him a slave or sell him, the kidnapper must be killed. You must get rid of the evil among you.

[8]Be careful when someone has a skin disease. Do exactly what the priests, the Levites, teach you, being careful to do what I have commanded them. [9]Remember what the LORD your God did to Miriam on your way out of Egypt.

[10]When you make a loan to your neighbors, don't go into their homes to get something in place of it. [11]Stay outside and let them go in and get what they promised you. [12]If a poor person gives you a coat to show he will pay the loan back, don't keep it overnight. [13]Give the coat back at sunset, because your neighbor needs that coat to sleep in, and he will be grateful to you. And the LORD your God will see that you have done a good thing.

[14]Don't cheat hired servants who are poor and needy, whether they are fellow Israelites or foreigners living in one of your towns. [15]Pay them each day before sunset, because they are poor and need the money. Otherwise, they may complain to the LORD about you, and you will be guilty of sin.

[16]Parents must not be put to death if their children do wrong, and children must not be put to death if their parents do wrong. Each person must die for his own sin.

[17]Do not be unfair to a foreigner or an orphan. Don't take a widow's coat to make sure she pays you back. [18]Remember that you were slaves in Egypt, and the LORD your God saved you from there. That is why I am commanding you to do this.

[19]When you are gathering your harvest in the field and leave behind a bundle of grain, don't go back and get it. Leave it there for foreigners, orphans, and widows so that the LORD your God can bless everything you do. [20]When you beat your olive trees to knock the olives off, don't beat the trees a second time. Leave what is left for foreigners, orphans, and widows. [21]When you harvest the grapes in your vineyard, don't pick the vines a second time. Leave what is left for foreigners, orphans, and widows. [22]Remember that you were slaves in Egypt; that is why I am commanding you to do this.

25 If two people have an argument and go to court, the judges will decide the case. They will declare one person right and the other guilty. [2]If the guilty person has to be punished with a beating, the judge will make that person lie down and be beaten in front of him. The number of lashes should match the crime. [3]But don't hit a person more than forty times, because more than that would disgrace him before others.

[4]When an ox is working in the grain, do not cover its mouth to keep it from eating.

[5]If two brothers are living together, and one of them dies without having a son, his

widow must not marry someone outside her
husband's family. Her husband's brother
must marry her, which is his duty to her as a
brother-in-law. 6The first son she has counts
as the son of the dead brother so that his
name will not be forgotten in Israel.
7But if a man does not want to marry his
brother's widow, she should go to the elders
at the town gate. She should say, "My
brother-in-law will not carry on his brother's
name in Israel. He refuses to do his duty for
me."
8Then the elders of the town must call for
the man and talk to him. But if he is
stubborn and says, "I don't want to marry
her," 9the woman must go up to him in front
of the elders. She must take off one of his
sandals and spit in his face and say, "This is
for the man who won't continue his
brother's family!" 10Then that man's family
shall be known in Israel as the Family of the
Unsandaled.
11If two men are fighting and one man's
wife comes to save her husband from his
attacker, grabbing the attacker by his sex
organs, 12you must cut off her hand. Show
her no mercy.
13Don't carry two sets of weights with you,
one heavy and one light. 14Don't have two
different sets of measures in your house, one
large and one small. 15You must have true
and honest weights and measures so that
you will live a long time in the land the LORD
your God is giving you. 16The LORD your God
hates anyone who is dishonest and uses
dishonest measures.
17Remember what the Amalekites did to
you when you came out of Egypt. 18When
you were tired and worn out, they met you
on the road and attacked all those lagging
behind. They were not afraid of God.
19When the LORD your God gives you rest
from all the enemies around you in the land
he is giving you as your own, you shall
destroy any memory of the Amalekites on
the earth. Do not forget!

The First Harvest

26 When you go into the land the LORD
your God is giving you as your own,
to take it over and live in it, 2you must take
some of the first harvest of crops that grow
from the land the LORD your God is giving
you. Put the food in a basket and go to the
place where the LORD your God will choose
to be worshiped. 3Say to the priest on duty at
that time, "Today I declare before the LORD
your God that I have come into the land the
LORD promised our ancestors that he would
give us." 4The priest will take your basket
and set it down in front of the altar of the
LORD your God. 5Then you shall announce
before the LORD your God: "My father was a
wandering Aramean. He went down to
Egypt with only a few people, but they
became a great, powerful, and large nation
there. 6But the Egyptians were cruel to us,
making us suffer and work very hard. 7So we
prayed to the LORD, the God of our ancestors,
and he heard us. When he saw our trouble,
hard work, and suffering, 8the LORD brought
us out of Egypt with his great power and
strength, using great terrors, signs, and
miracles. 9Then he brought us to this place
and gave us this fertile land. 10Now I bring
part of the first harvest from this land that
you, LORD, have given me." Place the basket
before the LORD your God and bow down
before him. 11Then you and the Levites and
foreigners among you should rejoice,
because the LORD your God has given good
things to you and your family.
12Bring a tenth of all your harvest the
third year (the year to give a tenth of your
harvest). Give it to the Levites, foreigners,
orphans, and widows so that they may eat in
your towns and be full. 13Then say to the
LORD your God, "I have taken out of my
house the part of my harvest that belongs to
God, and I have given it to the Levites,
foreigners, orphans, and widows. I have done
everything you commanded me; I have not
broken your commands, and I have not
forgotten any of them. 14I have not eaten any
of the holy part while I was in sorrow. I have
not removed any of it while I was unclean,
and I have not offered it for dead people. I
have obeyed you, the LORD my God, and have
done everything you commanded me. 15So
look down from heaven, your holy home.
Bless your people Israel and bless the land
you have given us, which you promised to
our ancestors—a fertile land."

Obey the Lord's Commands

16Today the LORD your God commands
you to obey all these rules and laws; be
careful to obey them with your whole being.

[17]Today you have said that the LORD is your
God, and you have promised to do what he
wants you to do—to keep his rules,
commands, and laws. You have said you will
obey him. [18]And today the LORD has said that
you are his very own people, as he has
promised you. But you must obey his
commands. [19]He will make you greater than
all the other nations he made. He will give
you praise, fame, and honor, and you will be
a holy people to the LORD your God, as he
has said.

The Law Written on Stones

27 Then Moses, along with the elders of
Israel, commanded the people, saying,
"Keep all the commands I have given you
today. [2]Soon you will cross the Jordan River
to go into the land the LORD your God is
giving you. On that day set up some large
stones and cover them with plaster. [3]When
you cross over, write all the words of these
teachings on them. Then you may enter the
land the LORD your God is giving you, a
fertile land, just as the LORD, the God of your
ancestors, promised. [4]After you have crossed
the Jordan River, set up these stones on
Mount Ebal, as I command you today, and
cover them with plaster. [5]Build an altar of
stones there to the LORD your God, but don't
use any iron tool to cut the stones; [6]build the
altar of the LORD your God with stones from
the field. Offer burnt offerings on it to the
LORD your God, [7]and offer fellowship
offerings there, and eat them and rejoice
before the LORD your God. [8]Then write
clearly all the words of these teachings on
the stones."

Curses of the Law

[9]Then Moses and the Levites who were
priests spoke to all Israel and said, "Be quiet,
Israel. Listen! Today you have become the
people of the LORD your God. [10]Obey the
LORD your God, and keep his commands and
laws that I give you today."

[11]That day Moses also gave the people this
command:

[12]When you cross the Jordan River, these
tribes must stand on Mount Gerizim to bless
the people: Simeon, Levi, Judah, Issachar,
Joseph and Benjamin. [13]And these tribes
must stand on Mount Ebal to announce the
curses: Reuben, Gad, Asher, Zebulun, Dan,
and Naphtali.

[14]The Levites will say to all the people of
Israel in a loud voice:

[15]"Anyone will be cursed who makes an

devotion 58

DEUTERONOMY 26:17-18

WHAT IT'S ALL ABOUT

You call yourself a Christian, but does your life look any different than your next-door neighbor's? How do we live a life that pleases God? God has given us an instruction manual, and you are holding it in your hand right now. He has a purpose for your life, but the only way you will ever find it is by reading his Word. The Scriptures were written to change the heart of man, not just to give us a list of dos and don'ts. Read 2 Timothy 3:16-17. It says that Scripture is used for four things—to teach, to show people what is wrong in their lives, to correct, and to teach us how to live right. I often pray, "Lord, show me what I'm doing wrong!" That's exactly what the Word is meant to do.

In fact, verse 17 says, "Using the Scriptures, the person who serves God will be capable, having all that is needed to do every good work." Are you looking for purpose in your life today? You have more capabilities than you could possibly imagine. You also have all that is needed to do what God has called you to do. Trust him to finish what he has started in your life. Spend time in the Word every day, and ask God to teach you, to show you, and to correct you. Finding God's purpose for your life is what an abundant life is all about.

idol or statue and secretly sets it up, because
the LORD hates the idols people make."
Then all the people will say, "Amen!"
16"Anyone will be cursed who dishonors
his father or mother."
Then all the people will say, "Amen!"
17"Anyone will be cursed who moves the
stone that marks a neighbor's border."
Then all the people will say, "Amen!"
18"Anyone will be cursed who sends a
blind person down the wrong road."
Then all the people will say, "Amen!"
19"Anyone will be cursed who is unfair to
foreigners, orphans, or widows."
Then all the people will say, "Amen!"
20"A man will be cursed who has sexual
relations with his father's wife, because it is
a dishonor to his father."
Then all the people will say, "Amen!"
21"Anyone will be cursed who has sexual
relations with an animal."
Then all the people will say, "Amen!"
22"A man will be cursed who has sexual
relations with his sister, whether she is
his father's daughter or his mother's
daughter."
Then all the people will say, "Amen!"
23"A man will be cursed who has sexual
relations with his mother-in-law."
Then all the people will say, "Amen!"
24"Anyone will be cursed who kills a
neighbor secretly."
Then all the people will say, "Amen!"
25"Anyone will be cursed who takes
money to murder an innocent person."
Then all the people will say, "Amen!"
26"Anyone will be cursed who does not
agree with the words of these teachings and
does not obey them."
Then all the people will say, "Amen!"

Blessings for Obeying

28 You must completely obey the LORD
your God, and you must carefully
follow all his commands I am giving you
today. Then the LORD your God will make
you greater than any other nation on earth.
2Obey the LORD your God so that all these
blessings will come and stay with you:
3You will be blessed in the city and
blessed in the country.
4Your children will be blessed, as well as
your crops; your herds will be blessed with
calves and your flocks with lambs.
5Your basket and your kitchen will be
blessed.
6You will be blessed when you come in
and when you go out.
7The LORD will help you defeat the
enemies that come to fight you. They will
attack you from one direction, but they will
run from you in seven directions.
8The LORD your God will bless you with
full barns, and he will bless everything you
do. He will bless the land he is giving you.
9The LORD will make you his holy people,
as he promised. But you must obey his
commands and do what he wants you to do.
10Then everyone on earth will see that you
are the LORD's people, and they will be afraid
of you. 11The LORD will make you rich: You
will have many children, your animals will
have many young, and your land will give
good crops. It is the land that the LORD
promised your ancestors he would give to
you.
12The LORD will open up his heavenly
storehouse so that the skies send rain on
your land at the right time, and he will bless
everything you do. You will lend to other
nations, but you will not need to borrow
from them. 13The LORD will make you like
the head and not like the tail; you will be on
top and not on bottom. But you must obey
the commands of the LORD your God that I
am giving you today, being careful to keep
them. 14Do not disobey anything I
command you today. Do exactly as I
command, and do not follow other gods or
serve them.

Curses for Disobeying

15But if you do not obey the LORD your
God and carefully follow all his commands
and laws I am giving you today, all these
curses will come upon you and stay:
16You will be cursed in the city and cursed
in the country.
17Your basket and your kitchen will be
cursed.
18Your children will be cursed, as well as
your crops; the calves of your herds and the
lambs of your flocks will be cursed.
19You will be cursed when you go in and
when you go out.
20The LORD will send you curses,
confusion, and punishment in everything
you do. You will be destroyed and suddenly

ruined because you did wrong when you left
him. 21 The LORD will give you terrible
diseases and destroy you from the land you
are going to take. 22 The LORD will punish
you with disease, fever, swelling, heat, lack
of rain, plant diseases, and mildew until you
die. 23 The sky above will be like bronze, and
the ground below will be like iron.[n] 24 The
LORD will turn the rain into dust and sand,
which will fall from the skies until you are
destroyed.

25 The LORD will help your enemies defeat
you. You will attack them from one
direction, but you will run from them in
seven directions. And you will become a
thing of horror among all the kingdoms on
earth. 26 Your dead bodies will be food for all
the birds and wild animals, and there will be
no one to scare them away. 27 The LORD will
punish you with boils like those the
Egyptians had. You will have bad growths,
sores, and itches that can't be cured. 28 The
LORD will give you madness, blindness, and a
confused mind. 29 You will have to feel
around in the daylight like a blind person.
You will fail in everything you do. People
will hurt you and steal from you every day,
and no one will save you.

30 You will be engaged to a woman, but
another man will force her to have sexual
relations with him. You will build a house,
but you will not live in it. You will plant a
vineyard, but you will not get its grapes.
31 Your ox will be killed before your eyes, but
you will not eat any of it. Your donkey will
be taken away from you, and it will not be
brought back. Your sheep will be given to
your enemies, and no one will save you.
32 Your sons and daughters will be given to
another nation, and you will grow tired
looking for them every day, but there will be
nothing you can do. 33 People you don't know
will eat the crops your land and hard work
have produced. You will be mistreated and
abused all your life. 34 The things you see will
cause you to go mad. 35 The LORD will give
you sore boils on your knees and legs that
cannot be cured, and they will go from the
soles of your feet to the tops of your heads.

36 The LORD will send you and your king
away to a nation neither you nor your
ancestors know, where you will serve other
gods made of wood and stone. 37 You will
become a hated thing to the nations where
the LORD sends you; they will laugh at you
and make fun of you.

38 You will plant much seed in your field,
but your harvest will be small, because
locusts will eat the crop. 39 You will plant
vineyards and work hard in them, but you
will not pick the grapes or drink the wine,
because the worms will eat them. 40 You will
have olive trees in all your land, but you will
not get any olive oil, because the olives will
drop off the trees. 41 You will have sons and
daughters, but you will not be able to keep
them, because they will be taken captive.
42 Locusts will destroy all your trees and
crops.

43 The foreigners who live among you will
get stronger and stronger, and you will get
weaker and weaker. 44 Foreigners will lend
money to you, but you will not be able to
lend to them. They will be like the head, and
you will be like the tail.

45 All these curses will come upon you.
They will chase you and catch you and
destroy you, because you did not obey the
LORD your God and keep the commands and
laws he gave you. 46 The curses will be signs
and miracles to you and your descendants
forever. 47 You had plenty of everything, but
you did not serve the LORD your God with
joy and a pure heart, 48 so you will serve the
enemies the LORD sends against you. You will
be hungry, thirsty, naked, and poor, and the
LORD will put a load on you until he has
destroyed you.

The Curse of an Enemy Nation

49 The LORD will bring a nation against you
from far away, from the end of the world,
and it will swoop down like an eagle. You
won't understand their language, 50 and they
will look mean. They will not respect old
people or feel sorry for the young. 51 They
will eat the calves from your herds and the
harvest of your field, and you will be
destroyed. They will not leave you any grain,
new wine or oil, or any calves from your
herds or lambs from your flocks. You will be
ruined. 52 That nation will surround and
attack all your cities. You trust in your high,
strong walls, but they will fall down. That

28:23 sky . . . iron This means the sky will give no rain and the earth will produce no crops.

nation will surround all your cities
everywhere in the land the LORD your God is
giving you.
[53]Your enemy will surround you. Those
people will make you starve so that you will
eat your own babies, the bodies of the sons
and daughters the LORD your God gave you.
[54]Even the most gentle and kind man among
you will become cruel to his brother, his
wife whom he loves, and his children who
are still alive. [55]He will not even give them
any of the flesh of his children he is eating,
because it will be all he has left. Your enemy
will surround you and make you starve in all
your cities. [56]The most gentle and kind
woman among you, so gentle and kind she
would hardly even walk on the ground, will
be cruel to her husband whom she loves and
to her son and daughter. [57]She will give birth
to a baby, but she will plan to eat the baby
and what comes after the birth itself. She
will eat them secretly while the enemy
surrounds the city. Those people will make
you starve in all your cities.
[58]Be careful to obey everything in these
teachings that are written in this book. You
must respect the glorious and wonderful
name of the LORD your God, [59]or the LORD
will give terrible diseases to you and your
descendants. You will have long and serious
diseases, and long and miserable sicknesses.
[60]He will give you all the diseases of Egypt
that you dread, and the diseases will stay
with you. [61]The LORD will also give you
every disease and sickness not written in
this Book of the Teachings, until you are
destroyed. [62]You people may have
outnumbered the stars, but only a few of you
will be left, because you did not obey the
LORD your God. [63]Just as the LORD was once
happy with you and gave you good things
and made you grow in number, so then the
LORD will be happy to ruin and destroy you,
and you will be removed from the land you
are entering to take as your own.
[64]Then the LORD will scatter you among
the nations—from one end of the earth to
the other. There you will serve other gods of
wood and stone, gods that neither you nor
your ancestors have known. [65]You will have
no rest among those nations and no place
that is yours. The LORD will make your mind
worried, your sight weak, and your soul sad.
[66]You will live with danger and be afraid
night and day. You will not be sure that you
will live. [67]In the morning you will say, "I
wish it were evening," and in the evening
you will say, "I wish it were morning." Terror
will be in your heart, and the things you
have seen will scare you. [68]The LORD will
send you back to Egypt in ships, even
though I, Moses, said you would never go
back to Egypt. And there you will try to sell
yourselves as slaves to your enemies, but no
one will buy you.

The Agreement in Moab

29 The LORD commanded Moses to make
an agreement with the Israelites in
Moab in addition to the agreement he had
made with them at Mount Sinai. These are
the words of that agreement.
[2]Moses called all the Israelites together
and said to them:
You have seen everything the LORD did
before your own eyes to the king of Egypt
and to the king's leaders and to the whole
country. [3]With your own eyes you saw
the great troubles, signs, and miracles. [4]But
to this day the LORD has not given you a
mind that understands; you don't really
understand what you see with your eyes or
hear with your ears. [5]I led you through the
desert for forty years, and during that time
neither your clothes nor sandals wore out.
[6]You ate no bread and drank no wine or beer.
This was so you would understand that I am
the LORD your God.
[7]When you came to this place, Sihon king
of Heshbon and Og king of Bashan came out
to fight us, but we defeated them. [8]We
captured their land and gave it to the tribes
of Reuben, Gad, and East Manasseh to be
their own.
[9]You must carefully obey everything in
this agreement so that you will succeed in
everything you do. [10]Today you are all
standing here before the LORD your God—
your leaders and important men, your
elders, officers, and all the other men of
Israel, [11]your wives and children and the
foreigners who live among you, who chop
your wood and carry your water. [12]You are
all here to enter into an agreement and a
promise with the LORD your God, an
agreement the LORD your God is making
with you today. [13]This will make you today
his own people. He will be your God, as he

told you and as he promised your ancestors
Abraham, Isaac, and Jacob. [14]But I am not
just making this agreement and its promises
with you [15]who are standing here before the
LORD your God today, but also with those
who are not here today.
[16]You know how we lived in Egypt and
how we passed through the countries when
we came here. [17]You saw their hateful idols
made of wood, stone, silver, and gold. [18]Make
sure no man, woman, family group, or tribe
among you leaves the LORD our God to go
and serve the gods of those nations. They
would be to you like a plant that grows
bitter, poisonous fruit.
[19]These are the kind of people who hear
these curses but bless themselves, thinking,
"We will be safe even though we continue
doing what we want to do." Those people
may destroy all of your land, both wet and
dry. [20]The LORD will not forgive them. His
anger will be like a burning fire against
those people, and all the curses written in
this book will come on them. The LORD will
destroy any memory of them on the earth.
[21]He will separate them from all the tribes of
Israel for punishment. All the curses of the
Agreement that are written in this Book of
the Teachings will happen to them.
[22]Your children who will come after you,
as well as foreigners from faraway lands, will
see the disasters that come to this land and
the diseases the LORD will send on it. They
will say, [23]"The land is nothing but burning
cinders and salt. Nothing is planted, nothing
grows, and nothing blooms. It is like Sodom
and Gomorrah, and Admah and Zeboiim,
which the LORD destroyed because he was
very angry." [24]All the other nations will ask,
"Why has the LORD done this to the land?
Why is he so angry?"
[25]And the answer will be, "It is because the
people broke the Agreement of the LORD, the
God of their ancestors, which he made with
them when he brought them out of Egypt.
[26]They went and served other gods and
bowed down to gods they did not even
know. The LORD did not allow that, [27]so he
became very angry at the land and brought
all the curses on it that are written in this

devotion 59

DEUTERONOMY 30:11-14

ON THE ONE HAND . . .

Every single day, you and I have a choice. Will you choose life or death today? Will you choose blessings or curses? Will you decide to pursue things that bring life to your spirit, or will you walk in the shadows where death abides?

God clearly marks the way. He outlines the consequences and the blessings and then says, "Now you can choose." God leads but he will not force you. He guides but he will not push. Sometimes choosing God is the loneliest place on earth. Sometimes it makes you feel weird and alienated to go God's way because most everyone else has decided not to. But the truth remains—you alone can choose how you will live. Choosing life means you love God and obey him. And you stay huddled up inside his arms of wisdom and protection. You consider his wisdom before your decisions. You surrender your selfishness. You remember that he is your provider, your Savior. Your next breath comes because of his grace, and so you live gratefully. You have eyes to see where he is working. You have a heart to run toward his promptings. You feel dependent and desperate for him to show up and thankful every time he does.

Do you want the life he dreamed of when he dreamed of you? Do you want to live underneath the promise of his blessing? All of heaven and earth will be the witnesses, and the choice to live is yours.

book. 28Since the LORD became angry and furious with them, he took them out of their land and put them in another land where they are today."

29There are some things the LORD our God has kept secret, but there are some things he has let us know. These things belong to us and our children forever so that we will do everything in these teachings.

The Israelites Will Return

30 When all these blessings and curses I have described happen to you, and the LORD your God has sent you away to other nations, think about these things. 2Then you and your children will return to the LORD your God, and you will obey him with your whole being in everything I am commanding you today. 3Then the LORD your God will give you back your freedom. He will feel sorry for you, and he will bring you back again from the nations where he scattered you. 4He may send you to the ends of the earth, but he will gather you and bring you back from there, 5back to the land that belonged to your ancestors. It will be yours. He will give you success, and there will be more of you than there were of your ancestors. 6The LORD your God will prepare you and your descendants to love him with your whole being so that you will live. 7The LORD your God will put all these curses on your enemies, who hate you and are cruel to you. 8And you will again obey the LORD, keeping all his commands that I give you today. 9The LORD your God will make you successful in everything you do. You will have many children, your cattle will have many calves, and your fields will produce good crops, because the LORD will again be happy with you, just as he was with your ancestors. 10But you must obey the LORD your God by keeping all his commands and rules that are written in this Book of the Teachings. You must return to the LORD your God with your whole being.

Choose Life or Death

11This command I give you today is not too hard for you; it is not beyond what you can do. 12It is not up in heaven. You do not have to ask, "Who will go up to heaven and get it for us so we can obey it and keep it?" 13It is not on the other side of the sea. You do not have to ask, "Who will go across the sea and get it? Who will tell it to us so we can keep it?" 14No, the word is very near you. It is in your mouth and in your heart so you may obey it.

15Look, today I offer you life and success, death and destruction. 16I command you today to love the LORD your God, to do what he wants you to do, and to keep his commands, his rules, and his laws. Then you will live and grow in number, and the LORD your God will bless you in the land you are entering to take as your own.

17But if you turn away from the LORD and do not obey him, if you are led to bow and serve other gods, 18I tell you today that you will surely be destroyed. And you will not live long in the land you are crossing the Jordan River to enter and take as your own.

19Today I ask heaven and earth to be witnesses. I am offering you life or death, blessings or curses. Now, choose life! Then you and your children may live. 20To choose life is to love the LORD your God, obey him, and stay close to him. He is your life, and he will let you live many years in the land, the land he promised to give your ancestors Abraham, Isaac, and Jacob.

Joshua Takes Moses' Place

31 Then Moses went and spoke these words to all the Israelites: 2"I am now one hundred twenty years old, and I cannot lead you anymore. The LORD told me I would not cross the Jordan River; 3the LORD your God will lead you across himself. He will destroy those nations for you, and you will take over their land. Joshua will also lead you across, as the LORD has said. 4The LORD will do to those nations what he did to Sihon and Og, the kings of the Amorites, when he destroyed them and their land. 5The LORD will give those nations to you; do to them everything I told you. 6Be strong and brave. Don't be afraid of them and don't be frightened, because the LORD your God will go with you. He will not leave you or forget you."

7Then Moses called Joshua and said to him in front of the people, "Be strong and brave, because you will lead these people into the land the LORD promised to give their ancestors, and help them take it as their own. 8The LORD himself will go before you.

He will be with you; he will not leave you or
forget you. Don't be afraid and don't worry."

Moses Writes the Teachings

9So Moses wrote down these teachings
and gave them to the priests and all the
elders of Israel. (The priests are the sons of
Levi, who carry the Ark of the Agreement
with the LORD.) 10-11Then Moses commanded
them: "Read these teachings for all Israel to
hear at the end of every seven years, which is
the year to cancel what people owe. Do it
during the Feast of Shelters, when all the
Israelites will come to appear before the
LORD your God and stand at the place he will
choose. 12Gather all the people: the men,
women, children, and foreigners living in
your towns so that they can listen and learn
to respect the LORD your God and carefully
obey everything in this law. 13Since their
children do not know this law, they must
hear it. They must learn to respect the LORD
your God for as long as they live in the land
you are crossing the Jordan River to take for
your own."

The Lord Calls Moses and Joshua

14The LORD said to Moses, "Soon you will
die. Get Joshua and come to the Meeting
Tent so that I may command him." So Moses
and Joshua went to the Meeting Tent.
15The LORD appeared at the Meeting Tent
in a cloud; the cloud stood over the entrance
of the Tent. 16And the LORD said to Moses,
"You will soon die. Then these people will
not be loyal to me but will worship the
foreign gods of the land they are entering.
They will leave me, breaking the Agreement
I made with them. 17Then I will become very
angry at them, and I will leave them. I will
turn away from them, and they will be
destroyed. Many terrible things will happen
to them. Then they will say, 'It is because
God is not with us that these terrible things
are happening.' 18I will surely turn away
from them then, because they have done
wrong and have turned to other gods.
19"Now write down this song and teach it
to the Israelites. Then have them sing it,
because it will be my witness against them.
20When I bring them into the land I

devotion 60

DEUTERONOMY 31:8

HOW'S YOUR MEMORY?

You'd think that I could remember not to worry. I should know better by now. God says all through Scripture that he is with us and that we don't have to worry. But sometimes I forget. Before I realize what's happened, my stomach hurts and my head aches and I can literally feel the worry.

I worry because I have kids who keep outgrowing their jeans. I worry because my friend needs more blood work because her enzymes came back outside of the normal range. I worry because I have known pain, and I fear knowing pain again. I worry about rejection and what I cannot see and my lack of courage. I am just a human being, and so many times God has to remind me not to worry.

One thought that gives me rest is that God is not mad about my worry. He doesn't want us to worry, but he obviously knew it came with our humanity. He tells us not to worry because he is very aware of our natural inclination toward anxiety. He knows that we need to be reminded of truths we have already learned. He knows that weariness can set in, hearts can give up, and the spirit can become fretful and poor.

Maybe you already know of God's promise. But maybe today you just need to be reminded. The Lord God has you. He is with you. He has not forgotten you. Let your heart be at rest.

promised to their ancestors, a fertile land,
they will eat as much as they want and get
fat. Then they will turn to other gods and
serve them. They will reject me and break
my Agreement. 21 Then when many troubles
and terrible things happen to them, this
song will testify against them, because the
song will not be forgotten by their
descendants. I know what they plan to do,
even before I take them into the land I
promised them." 22 So Moses wrote down the
song that day, and he taught it to the
Israelites.

23 Then the LORD gave this command to
Joshua son of Nun: "Be strong and brave,
because you will lead the people of Israel to
the land I promised them, and I will be with
you."

24 After Moses finished writing all the
words of the teachings in a book, 25 he gave a
command to the Levites, who carried the Ark
of the Agreement with the LORD. 26 He said,
"Take this Book of the Teachings and put it
beside the Ark of the Agreement with the
LORD your God. It must stay there as a
witness against you. 27 I know how stubborn
and disobedient you are. You have disobeyed
the LORD while I am alive and with you, and
you will disobey even more after I die!
28 Gather all the elders of your tribes and all
your officers to me so that I may say these
things for them to hear, and so that I may
ask heaven and earth to testify against them.
29 I know that after I die you will become
completely evil. You will turn away from
the commands I have given you. Terrible
things will happen to you in the future when
you do what the LORD says is evil, and you
will make him angry with the idols you
have made."

Moses' Song

30 And Moses spoke this whole song for all
the people of Israel to hear:

32 Hear, heavens, and I will speak.
Listen, earth, to what I say.
2 My teaching will drop like rain;
my words will fall like dew.
They will be like showers on the grass;
they will pour down like rain on young plants.
3 I will announce the name of the LORD.
Praise God because he is great!
4 He is like a rock; what he does is perfect,
and he is always fair.
He is a faithful God who does no wrong,
who is right and fair.

5 They have done evil against him.
To their shame they are no longer his children;
they are an evil and lying people.
6 This is not the way to repay the LORD,
you foolish and unwise people.
He is your Father and Maker,
who made you and formed you.

7 Remember the old days.
Think of the years already passed.
Ask your father and he will tell you;
ask your elders and they will inform you.
8 God Most High gave the nations their lands,
dividing up the human race.
He set up borders for the people
and even numbered the Israelites.
9 The LORD took his people as his share,
the people of Jacob as his very own.

10 He found them in a desert,
a windy, empty land.
He surrounded them and brought them up,
guarding them as those he loved very much.
11 He was like an eagle building its nest
that flutters over its young.
It spreads its wings to catch them
and carries them on its feathers.
12 The LORD alone led them,
and there was no foreign god helping him.
13 The LORD brought them to the heights of the land
and fed them the fruit of the fields.
He gave them honey from the rocks,
bringing oil from the solid rock.
14 There were milk curds from the cows and milk from the flock;
there were fat sheep and goats.
There were sheep and goats from Bashan
and the best of the wheat.
You drank the juice of grapes.

15 Israel grew fat and kicked;
they were fat and full and firm.

They left the God who made them
and rejected the Rock who saved them.
16They made God jealous with foreign gods
and angry with hateful idols.
17They made sacrifices to demons, not God,
to gods they had never known,
new gods from nearby,
gods your ancestors did not fear.
18You left God who is the Rock, your
Father,
and you forgot the God who gave you
birth.

19The LORD saw this and rejected them;
his sons and daughters had made him
angry.
20He said, "I will turn away from them
and see what will happen to them.
They are evil people,
unfaithful children.
21They used things that are not gods to
make me jealous
and worthless idols to make me angry.
So I will use those who are not a nation to
make them jealous;
I will use a nation that does not
understand to make them angry.
22My anger has started a fire
that burns down to the place of the
dead.
It will burn up the ground and its crops,
and it will set fire to the base of the
mountains.

23"I will pile troubles upon them
and shoot my arrows at them.
24They will be starved and sick,
destroyed by terrible diseases.
I will send them vicious animals
and gliding, poisonous snakes.
25In the streets the sword will kill;
in their homes there will be terror.
Young men and women will die,
and so will babies and gray-haired men.
26I will scatter them as I said,
and no one will remember them.
27But I didn't want their enemy to brag;
their enemy might misunderstand
and say, 'We have won!
The LORD has done none of this.' "

28Israel has no sense;
they do not understand.
29I wish they were wise and understood
this;
I wish they could see what will happen
to them.
30One person cannot chase a thousand
people,
and two people cannot fight ten
thousand
unless their Rock has sold them,
unless the LORD has given them up.
31The rock of these people is not like our
Rock;
our enemies agree to that.
32Their vine comes from Sodom,
and their fields are like Gomorrah.
Their grapes are full of poison;
their bunches of grapes are bitter.
33Their wine is like snake poison,
like the deadly poison of cobras.

34"I have been saving this,
and I have it locked in my storehouses.
35I will punish those who do wrong; I will
repay them.
Soon their foot will slip,
because their day of trouble is near,
and their punishment will come
quickly."
36The LORD will defend his people
and have mercy on his servants.
He will see that their strength is gone,
that nobody is left, slaves or free.
37Then he will say, "Where are their
gods?
Where is the rock they trusted?
38Who ate the fat from their sacrifices,
and who drank the wine of their drink
offerings?
Let those gods come to help you!
Let them protect you!

39"Now you will see that I am the one God!
There is no god but me.
I send life and death;
I can hurt, and I can heal.
No one can escape from me.
40I raise my hand toward heaven and make
this promise:
As surely as I live forever,
41I will sharpen my flashing sword,
and I will take it in my hand to judge.
I will punish my enemies
and pay back those who hate me.
42My arrows will be covered with their
blood;
my sword will eat their flesh.

The blood will flow from those who are
killed and the captives.
The heads of the enemy leaders will be
cut off."

43Be happy, nations, with his people,
because he will repay you for the blood
of his servants.
He will punish his enemies,
and he will remove the sin of his land
and people.

44Moses came with Joshua son of Nun,
and they spoke all the words of this song for
the people to hear. 45When Moses finished
speaking these words to all Israel, 46he said
to them: "Pay careful attention to all the
words I have said to you today, and
command your children to obey carefully
everything in these teachings. 47These
should not be unimportant words for you,
but rather they mean life for you! By these
words you will live a long time in the land
you are crossing the Jordan River to take as
your own."

Moses Goes Up to Mount Nebo

48The LORD spoke to Moses again that
same day and said, 49"Go up the Abarim
Mountains, to Mount Nebo in the country of
Moab, across from Jericho. Look at the land
of Canaan that I am giving to the Israelites
as their own. 50On that mountain that you
climb, you will die and join your ancestors,
just as your brother Aaron died on Mount
Hor and joined his ancestors. 51You both
sinned against me at the waters of Meribah
Kadesh in the Desert of Zin, and you did not
honor me as holy there among the Israelites.
52So now you will only look at the land from
far away. You will not enter the land I am
giving the people of Israel."

Moses Blesses the People

33 Moses, the man of God, gave this
blessing to the Israelites before he
died. 2He said:
"The LORD came from Mount Sinai
and rose like the sun from Edom;
he showed his greatness from Mount
Paran.
He came with thousands of angels
from the southern mountains.
3The LORD surely loves his people
and takes care of all those who belong
to him.
They bow down at his feet,
and they are taught by him.
4Moses gave us the teachings
that belong to the people of Jacob.
5The LORD became king of Israel
when the leaders of the people
gathered,
when the tribes of Israel came together.

6"Let the people of Reuben live and not die,
but let the people be few."

7Moses said this about the people of Judah:
"LORD, listen to Judah's prayer;
bring them back to their people.
They defend themselves with their hands.
Help them fight their enemies!"

8Moses said this about the people of Levi:
"LORD, your Thummim and Urim belong
to Levi, whom you love.
LORD, you tested him at Massah
and argued with him at the waters of
Meribah.
9He said about his father and mother,
'I don't care about them.'
He did not treat his brothers as favorites
or give special favors to his children,
but he protected your word
and guarded your agreement.
10He teaches your laws to the people of
Jacob
and your teachings to the people of
Israel.
He burns incense before you
and makes whole burnt offerings on
your altar.
11LORD, make them strong;
be pleased with the work they do.
Defeat those who attack them,
and don't let their enemies rise up
again."

12Moses said this about the people of
Benjamin:
"The LORD's loved ones will lie down in
safety,
because he protects them all day long.
The ones he loves rest with him."

13Moses said this about the people of
Joseph:
"May the LORD bless their land with
wonderful dew from heaven,
with water from the springs below,
14with the best fruits that the sun brings,

and with the best fruits that the moon
brings.
15Let the old mountains give the finest
crops,
and let the everlasting hills give the
best fruits.
16Let the full earth give the best fruits,
and let the LORD who lived in the
burning bush be pleased.
May these blessings rest on the head of
Joseph,
on the forehead of the one who was
blessed among his brothers.
17Joseph has the majesty of a firstborn bull;
he is as strong as a wild ox.
He will stab other nations,
even those nations far away.
These are the ten thousands of Ephraim,
and these are the thousands of
Manasseh."

18Moses said this about the people of
Zebulun:
"Be happy when you go out, Zebulun,
and be happy in your tents, Issachar.
19They will call the people to the mountain,
and there they will offer the right
sacrifices.
They will do well from all that is in the
sea,
and they will do well from the treasures
hidden in the sand on the shore."

20Moses said this about the people of
Gad:
"Praise God who gives Gad more land!
Gad lives there like a lion,
who tears off arms and heads.
21They chose the best land for themselves.
They received a large share, like that
given to an officer.
When the leaders of the people gathered,
the people of Gad did what the LORD
said was right,
and they judged Israel fairly."

22Moses said this about the people of
Dan:
"Dan is like a lion's cub,
who jumps out of Bashan."

23Moses said this about the people of
Naphtali:

devotion 61

DEUTERONOMY 33:26–27

WOULD YOU RATHER FIGHT . . . OR WIN?

Is there something or someone that has you scared right now? Is your heart so consumed with fear that you are feeling paralyzed and unable to function? Is your enemy known or unknown? There are so many variables to the seen and the unseen world, but one thing is for certain—God knows all things. There is not one plot devised that he is unaware of. If someone is trying to ruin your reputation, spread gossip, or purposely wage war on your family, believe me, he is aware and ready to defend you.

Rest in the Lord. Don't move out in your own strength or defend yourself with explanations or further gossip. If you do, you'll miss out on the opportunity of watching God valiantly ride into the clouds of your circumstances and dispel the evil. If you want to be a spiritual giant, allow his hands alone to hold you up. For a moment, close your eyes and picture yourself mounted up on the most beautiful thundering cloud you have ever seen, and there sitting next to you is the Lord himself. The two of you ride onto the battlefield side by side. You do not see the faces of your enemies; only their backs are visible as they retreat as fast as they can. Wow! The next time you are tempted to take the battle into your own hands, return to this scripture and remember you really don't have to just imagine it—it's already the reality of your life.

"Naphtali enjoys special kindnesses,
and they are full of the LORD's
blessings.
Take as your own the west and south."

24 Moses said this about the people of
Asher:
"Asher is the most blessed of the sons;
let him be his brothers' favorite.
Let him bathe his feet in olive oil.
25 Your gates will have locks of iron and
bronze,
and you will be strong as long as you
live.

26 "There is no one like the God of Israel,
who rides through the skies to help
you,
who rides on the clouds in his majesty.
27 The everlasting God is your place of
safety,
and his arms will hold you up forever.
He will force your enemy out ahead of
you,
saying, 'Destroy the enemy!'
28 The people of Israel will lie down in
safety.
Jacob's spring is theirs alone.
Theirs is a land full of grain and new
wine,
where the skies drop their dew.
29 Israel, you are blessed!
No one else is like you,
because you are a people saved by the
LORD.
He is your shield and helper,
your glorious sword.
Your enemies will be afraid of you,
and you will walk all over their holy
places."

Moses Dies

34 Then Moses climbed Mount Nebo
from the plains of Moab to the top of
Mount Pisgah, across from Jericho. From
there the LORD showed him all the land from
Gilead to Dan, 2 all of Naphtali and the lands
of Ephraim and Manasseh, all the land of
Judah as far as the Mediterranean Sea, 3 as
well as the southern desert and the whole
Valley of Jericho up to Zoar. (Jericho is called
the city of palm trees.) 4 Then the LORD said
to Moses, "This is the land I promised to
Abraham, Isaac, and Jacob when I said to
them, 'I will give this land to your
descendants.' I have let you look at it, Moses,
but you will not cross over there."
5 Then Moses, the servant of the LORD, died
there in Moab, as the LORD had said. 6 He
buried Moses in Moab in the valley opposite
Beth Peor, but even today no one knows
where his grave is. 7 Moses was one hundred
twenty years old when he died. His eyes
were not weak, and he was still strong. 8 The
Israelites cried for Moses for thirty days,
staying in the plains of Moab until the time
of sadness was over.
9 Joshua son of Nun was then filled with
wisdom, because Moses had put his hands
on him. So the Israelites listened to Joshua,
and they did what the LORD had commanded
Moses.
10 There has never been another prophet
in Israel like Moses. The LORD knew Moses
face to face 11 and sent him to do signs and
miracles in Egypt—to the king, to all his
officers, and to the whole land of Egypt.
12 Moses had great power, and he did great
and wonderful things for all the Israelites to
see.

Joshua

Meaning "Jehovah saves" or "the Lord is salvation"
This is the first of twelve historical books in the Old Testament, which chronicle the adventures of God's often-unfaithful people.

Person Holding the Pen God Wrote With: Although he doesn't brag about this literary feat, *Joshua* is the most probable author. He was Moses' right-hand man and the most able person to assume the mantle of leadership after Moses died. God himself presided over Joshua's swearing-in ceremony (Josh. 1:1–2)!

When the Text Was Written: In light of the events recorded, this book was likely written between 1405 and 1385 B.C.

Spiritual Posture of the Original Recipients: The Israelites had been wandering in the desert for about forty years by now, so they were no doubt stinky and sweaty. But they were walking faster and with more purpose at this point because they could see the light at the end of the tunnel. For the most part, they were following God's directions—via Joshua—because God's promises were now within their grasp.

Storyline Synopsis: God had promised the Israelites a land of milk and honey, and after an excruciatingly long, hot, difficult road trip, they finally reached their divine destination! Joshua begins with a sort of training camp (Josh. 1—6), goes off-course with a spiritual train wreck (7—10:28), inches toward the thrill of victory (10:29—12), then celebrates and divides the spoils of success (13—21). Finally, Joshua and his "team" sit back, take stock, and thank God for giving them the ability to triumph over their enemies.

A Moment Worth Discussing: Chapter 3 tells a story that is very similar to the dramatic Red Sea event that occurred when the Israelites were hightailing it out of Egypt with Pharaoh's army in hot pursuit. Israel responds to this second water-crossing miracle in chapter 4 with an unforgettable rock ceremony. Discuss the example the Israelites have given us as a means to "remember God's goodness" with our own friends and family.

Interesting (But Likely to Be Overlooked) Character: *Achan*, Carmi's shoplifting son, was a real stinker. His greed for shiny Babylonian baubles prompted him to disobey God and undermine Joshua. His deception resulted in an unnecessary military defeat and the loss of Israeli troops. This bad decision eventually led to his court-martial and capital punishment (Josh. 7:1–26).

God's Command to Joshua

1 After Moses, the servant of the LORD, died,
the LORD spoke to Joshua son of Nun,
Moses' assistant. 2The LORD said, "My servant
Moses is dead. Now you and all these people
go across the Jordan River into the land I am
giving to the Israelites. 3I promised Moses I
would give you this land, so I will give you
every place you go in the land. 4All the land
from the desert in the south to Lebanon in
the north will be yours. All the land from
the great river, the Euphrates, in the east,
to the Mediterranean Sea in the west will be
yours, too, including the land of the Hittites.
5No one will be able to defeat you all your
life. Just as I was with Moses, so I will be
with you. I will not leave you or forget you.
6"Joshua, be strong and brave! You must
lead these people so they can take the land
that I promised their fathers I would give
them. 7Be strong and brave. Be sure to obey
all the teachings my servant Moses gave you.
If you follow them exactly, you will be
successful in everything you do. 8Always
remember what is written in the Book of the
Teachings. Study it day and night to be sure
to obey everything that is written there. If
you do this, you will be wise and successful
in everything. 9Remember that I
commanded you to be strong and brave.
Don't be afraid, because the LORD your God
will be with you everywhere you go."

Joshua's Orders to the People

10Then Joshua gave orders to the officers
of the people: 11"Go through the camp and
tell the people, 'Get your supplies ready.
Three days from now you will cross the
Jordan River and take the land the LORD your
God is giving you.' "
12Then Joshua said to the people of
Reuben, Gad, and East Manasseh,
13"Remember what Moses, the servant of the
LORD, told you. He said the LORD your God
would give you rest and would give you this
land. 14Now the LORD has given you this land
east of the Jordan River. Your wives, children,
and animals may stay here, but your fighting
men must dress for war and cross the Jordan
River ahead of your brothers to help them.

devotion 62

JOSHUA 1:9

NEVER EVER ALONE

Sometimes parenting terrifies me. Yet just as Joshua led the Israelites, I am leading my children. That nagging question of "What if?" crosses my mind on a regular basis. God tells us—no, commands us—to be strong and brave. My children need to see me as strong, not weak. They need to see me as willing to face the next challenge, not anxious and unsure of myself. The problem is that I don't feel strong or brave most of the time. The Lord knows this about me. That's why he says he will be with me everywhere I go. I cannot do it without him.

A friend of mine, in the middle of a divorce from her husband, tucked her little girl into bed one night. The little girl was scared. "Mommy, what's going to happen to us now?" she asked. My friend really didn't know what tomorrow would hold for them, but she knew that what her little girl needed more than anything else was for her to be strong and brave. "Well," she answered, "that's for me to figure out, sweetie. Your job is to worry about playing and cleaning up your room tomorrow; my job is to take care of the rest. But remember, God will always take care of us. That's a promise."

Take a deep breath and determine in your heart to be strong as you face life's challenges today. And remember, God will be with you everywhere you go.

Rahab

JOSHUA 2

Rahab's heart races as she whisks the two Israelites through her home and up onto the roof to hide them. Why did they come to her house? Surely they know she is a harlot. Her words come in short, whispered breaths that are barely heard over the pounding inside her chest: "Everyone living in this land is terribly afraid of you."

She knows their God is powerful, and Rahab must save her family. She looks into the eyes of the foreigners, searching for a sign. She believes they are good men. "Promise me before the Lord that you will show kindness to my family just as I showed kindness to you. Save us from death." They agree and she waits. And waits.

When the Israelite army draws close, people huddle terrified in their homes. "We must run," her father says.

"No!" Rahab insists. "The men of God have promised me."

On the seventh day, Rahab holds her family close and watches as the army of Israel marches around the city blowing their trumpets. The noise is disturbing, but Rahab clings to the promise of the men and their God. As the army marches around a seventh time, shouts ring through her ears. Her house shakes as dwellings on either side of her crumble to the ground.

It was a small seed of belief that changed Rahab's life. The lineage of Jesus is traced back through her. God will take your faith and use it for his glory!

15The LORD has given you a place to rest and
will do the same for your brothers. But you
must help them until they take the land the
LORD their God is giving them. Then you
may return to your own land east of the
Jordan River, the land that Moses, the
servant of the LORD, gave you."
16Then the people answered Joshua,
"Anything you command us to do, we will
do. Any place you send us, we will go. 17Just
as we fully obeyed Moses, we will obey you.
We ask only that the LORD your God be with
you just as he was with Moses. 18Whoever
refuses to obey your commands or turns
against you will be put to death. Just be
strong and brave!"

Spies Sent to Jericho

2 Joshua son of Nun secretly sent out two
spies from Acacia and said to them, "Go
and look at the land, particularly at the city
of Jericho."
So the men went to Jericho and stayed at
the house of a prostitute named Rahab.
2Someone told the king of Jericho, "Some
men from Israel have come here tonight to
spy out the land."
3So the king of Jericho sent this message
to Rahab: "Bring out the men who came to
you and entered your house. They have
come to spy out our whole land."
4But the woman had hidden the two men.
She said, "They did come here, but I didn't
know where they came from. 5In the
evening, when it was time to close the city
gate, they left. I don't know where they went,
but if you go quickly, maybe you can catch
them." 6(The woman had taken the men up
to the roof[n] and had hidden them there
under stalks of flax that she had spread out.)
7So the king's men went out looking for the
spies on the road that leads to the crossings
of the Jordan River. The city gate was closed
just after the king's men left the city.
8Before the spies went to sleep for the
night, Rahab went up to the roof. 9She said
to them, "I know the LORD has given this
land to your people. You frighten us very
much. Everyone living in this land is terribly
afraid of you 10because we have heard how

2:6 roof In Bible times houses were built with flat roofs. The roof was used for drying things such as flax and fruit. And it was used as an extra room, as a place for worship, and as a cool place to sleep in the summer.

the LORD dried up the Red Sea when you
came out of Egypt. We have heard how you
destroyed Sihon and Og, two Amorite kings
who lived east of the Jordan. 11 When we
heard this, we were very frightened. Now
our men are afraid to fight you because the
LORD your God rules the heavens above and
the earth below! 12 So now, promise me
before the LORD that you will show kindness
to my family just as I showed kindness to
you. Give me some proof that you will do
this. 13 Allow my father, mother, brothers,
sisters, and all of their families to live. Save
us from death."

14 The men agreed and said, "It will be our
lives for your lives if you don't tell anyone
what we are doing. When the LORD gives us
the land, we will be kind and true to you."

15 The house Rahab lived in was built on
the city wall, so she used a rope to let the
men down through a window. 16 She said to
them, "Go into the hills so the king's men
will not find you. Hide there for three days.
After the king's men return, you may go on
your way."

17 The men said to her, "You must do as we
say. If not, we cannot be responsible for
keeping this oath you have made us swear.
18 When we return to this land, you must tie
this red rope in the window through which
you let us down. Bring your father, mother,
brothers, and all your family into your
house. 19 If anyone leaves your house and is
killed, it is his own fault. We cannot be
responsible for him. If anyone in your house
is hurt, we will be responsible. 20 But if you
tell anyone about this, we will be free from
the oath you made us swear."

21 Rahab answered, "I agree to this." So she
sent them away, and they left. Then she tied
the red rope in the window.

22 The men left and went into the hills
where they stayed for three days. The king's
men looked for them all along the road, but
after three days, they returned to the city
without finding them. 23 Then the two men
started back. They left the hills and crossed
the river and came to Joshua son of Nun and
told him everything that had happened to
them. 24 They said, "The LORD surely has
given us all of the land. All the people in
that land are terribly afraid of us."

Crossing the Jordan

3 Early the next morning Joshua and all
the Israelites left Acacia. They traveled to
the Jordan River and camped there before
crossing it. 2 After three days the officers went
through the camp 3 and gave orders to the
people: "When you see the priests and
Levites carrying the Ark of the Agreement
with the LORD your God, leave where you
are and follow it. 4 That way you will
know which way to go since you have never
been here before. But do not follow too
closely. Stay about a thousand yards behind
the Ark."

5 Then Joshua told the people, "Make
yourselves holy, because tomorrow the LORD
will do amazing things among you."

6 Joshua said to the priests, "Take the Ark
of the Agreement and go ahead of the
people." So the priests lifted the Ark and
carried it ahead of the people.

7 Then the LORD said to Joshua, "Today I
will begin to make you great in the opinion
of all the Israelites so the people will know I
am with you just as I was with Moses. 8 Tell
the priests who carry the Ark of the
Agreement to go to the edge of the Jordan
River and stand in the water."

9 Then Joshua said to the Israelites, "Come
here and listen to the words of the LORD your
God. 10 Here is proof that the living God is
with you and that he will force out the
Canaanites, Hittites, Hivites, Perizzites,
Girgashites, Amorites, and Jebusites. 11 The
Ark of the Agreement with the Lord of the
whole world will go ahead of you into the
Jordan River. 12 Now choose twelve men
from among you, one from each of the
twelve tribes of Israel. 13 The priests will
carry the Ark of the LORD, the Master of the
whole world, into the Jordan ahead of you.
When they step into the water, it will stop.
The river will stop flowing and will stand up
in a heap."

14 So the people left the place where they
had camped, and they followed the priests
who carried the Ark of the Agreement across
the Jordan River. 15 During harvest the Jordan
overflows its banks. When the priests
carrying the Ark came to the edge of the
river and stepped into the water, 16 the water
upstream stopped flowing. It stood up in a

devotion 63

JOSHUA 3:15–16

WHAT'S *YOUR* NEXT STEP?

You might recall an old song some of us learned in Sunday school: "Trust and obey, for there's no other way, to be happy in Jesus, but to trust and obey." When children sing those words, they express their excitement about following God's rules, but we all know that children usually spend a large part of their growing up years questioning and disobeying their parents.

As the Lord guided the Israelites to the land he had promised them, they repeatedly questioned and disobeyed him, too. Because of that, they lost their way for forty years. You might say the Israelites were in their "growing up" years, but like a loving parent, God continued to help them find their way.

When God foretold through Joshua that the waters of the Jordan River would dry up if the people followed his instructions, it might have sounded outlandish to the Israelites. After all, it was flood season. Still, they obeyed and the moment the feet of the priests touched the water, it piled up in a great heap far enough away that the nation was able to cross the Jordan.

It must have been a wonderful feeling for the Israelites to experience God's grace through yet another miracle after they'd been disobedient in the past. While we have all ventured away from our Lord at some point or lost our way, you can experience his grace today by trusting him to lead you in the journey he has planned for your life.

heap a great distance away at Adam, a town near Zarethan. The water flowing down to the Sea of Arabah (the Dead Sea) was completely cut off. So the people crossed the river near Jericho.
17 The priests carried the Ark of the Agreement with the LORD to the middle of the river and stood there on dry ground. They waited there while all the people of Israel walked across the Jordan River on dry land.

Rocks to Remind the People

4 After all the people had finished crossing the Jordan, the LORD said to Joshua,
2 "Choose twelve men from among the people, one from each tribe.
3 Tell them to get twelve rocks from the middle of the river, from where the priests stood. Carry the rocks and put them down where you stay tonight."
4 So Joshua chose one man from each tribe. Then he called the twelve men together
5 and said to them, "Go out into the river where the Ark of the LORD your God is. Each of you bring back one rock, one for each tribe of Israel, and carry it on your shoulder.
6 They will be a sign among you. In the future your children will ask you, 'What do these rocks mean?'
7 Tell them the water stopped flowing in the Jordan when the Ark of the Agreement with the LORD crossed the river. These rocks will always remind the Israelites of this."
8 So the Israelites obeyed Joshua and carried twelve rocks from the middle of the Jordan River, one rock for each of the twelve tribes of Israel, just as the LORD had commanded Joshua. They carried the rocks with them and put them down where they made their camp.
9 Joshua also put twelve rocks in the middle of the Jordan River where the priests had stood while carrying the Ark of the Agreement. These rocks are still there today.
10 The priests carrying the Ark continued

standing in the middle of the river until
everything was done that the LORD had
commanded Joshua to tell the people, just as
Moses had told Joshua. The people hurried
across the river. 11After they finished
crossing the river, the priests carried the Ark
of the LORD to the other side as the people
watched. 12The men from the tribes of
Reuben, Gad, and East Manasseh obeyed
what Moses had told them. They were
dressed for war, and they crossed the river
ahead of the other people. 13About forty
thousand soldiers prepared for war
passed before the LORD as they marched
across the river, going toward the plains
of Jericho.

14That day the LORD made Joshua great in
the opinion of all the Israelites. They
respected Joshua all his life, just as they had
respected Moses.

15Then the LORD said to Joshua,
16"Command the priests to bring the Ark of
the Agreement out of the river."

17So Joshua commanded the priests,
"Come up out of the Jordan."

18Then the priests carried the Ark of the
Agreement with the LORD out of the river. As
soon as their feet touched dry land, the water
began flowing again. The river again
overflowed its banks, just as it had before
they crossed.

19The people crossed the Jordan on the
tenth day of the first month and camped at
Gilgal, east of Jericho. 20They carried with
them the twelve rocks taken from the
Jordan, and Joshua set them up at Gilgal.
21Then he spoke to the Israelites: "In the
future your children will ask you, 'What do
these rocks mean?' 22Tell them, 'Israel
crossed the Jordan River on dry land. 23The
LORD your God caused the water to stop
flowing until you finished crossing it, just as
the LORD did to the Red Sea. He stopped the
water until we crossed it. 24The LORD did this
so all people would know he has great
power and so you would always respect the
LORD your God.' "

5 All the kings of the Amorites west of the
Jordan and the Canaanite kings living by
the Mediterranean Sea heard that the LORD
dried up the Jordan River until the Israelites
had crossed it. After that they were scared
and too afraid to face the Israelites.

The Israelites Are Circumcised

2At that time the LORD said to Joshua,
"Make knives from flint stones and
circumcise the Israelites." 3So Joshua made
knives from flint stones and circumcised the
Israelites at Gibeath Haaraloth.

4This is why Joshua circumcised the men:
After the Israelites left Egypt, all the men old
enough to serve in the army died in the
desert on the way out of Egypt. 5The men
who had come out of Egypt had been
circumcised, but none of those who were
born in the desert on the trip from Egypt had
been circumcised. 6The Israelites had moved
about in the desert for forty years. During
that time all the fighting men who had left
Egypt had died because they had not obeyed
the LORD. So the LORD swore they would not
see the land he had promised their ancestors
to give them, a fertile land. 7Their sons took
their places. But none of the sons born on
the trip from Egypt had been circumcised, so
Joshua circumcised them. 8After all the
Israelites had been circumcised, they stayed
in camp until they were healed.

9Then the LORD said to Joshua, "As slaves
in Egypt you were ashamed, but today I have
removed that shame." So Joshua named that
place Gilgal, which it is still named today.

10The people of Israel were camped at
Gilgal on the plains of Jericho. It was there,
on the evening of the fourteenth day of the
month, they celebrated the Passover Feast.
11The day after the Passover, the people ate
food grown on that land: bread made
without yeast and roasted grain. 12The day
they ate this food, the manna stopped
coming. The Israelites no longer got the
manna from heaven. They ate the food
grown in the land of Canaan that year.

13Joshua was near Jericho when he looked
up and saw a man standing in front of him
with a sword in his hand. Joshua went to
him and asked, "Are you a friend or an
enemy?"

14The man answered, "I am neither. I have
come as the commander of the LORD's army."

Then Joshua bowed facedown on the
ground and asked, "Does my master have a
command for me, his servant?"

15The commander of the LORD's army
answered, "Take off your sandals, because
the place where you are standing is holy." So
Joshua did.

The Fall of Jericho

6 The people of Jericho were afraid
because the Israelites were near. They
closed the city gates and guarded them. No
one went into the city, and no one came out.
2 Then the LORD said to Joshua, "Look, I
have given you Jericho, its king, and all its
fighting men. 3 March around the city with
your army once a day for six days. 4 Have
seven priests carry trumpets made from
horns of male sheep and have them march
in front of the Ark. On the seventh day
march around the city seven times and have
the priests blow the trumpets as they march.
5 They will make one long blast on the
trumpets. When you hear that sound, have
all the people give a loud shout. Then the
walls of the city will fall so the people can go
straight into the city."
6 So Joshua son of Nun called the priests
together and said to them, "Carry the Ark of
the Agreement. Tell seven priests to carry
trumpets and march in front of it." 7 Then
Joshua ordered the people, "Now go! March
around the city. The soldiers with weapons
should march in front of the Ark of the
Agreement with the LORD."
8 When Joshua finished speaking to the
people, the seven priests began marching
before the LORD. They carried the seven
trumpets and blew them as they marched.
The priests carrying the Ark of the
Agreement with the LORD followed them.
9 Soldiers with weapons marched in front of
the priests, and armed men walked behind
the Ark. The priests were blowing their
trumpets. 10 But Joshua had told the people
not to give a war cry. He said, "Don't shout.
Don't say a word until the day I tell you.
Then shout." 11 So Joshua had the Ark of the
LORD carried around the city one time. Then
they went back to camp for the night.
12 Early the next morning Joshua got up,
and the priests carried the Ark of the LORD
again. 13 The seven priests carried the seven
trumpets and marched in front of the Ark of

devotion 64

JOSHUA 6:2–5

THE WALLS ARE GOD'S BUSINESS

What is your Jericho? A financial burden too big to overcome? An all-consuming desire to be loved with a healthy, manly love? The heartache of a difficult, unrelenting relationship? Or maybe your soul is empty—desperately dry and asleep, without passion or purpose. When the walls are too high for you to see over and the enemy is too fierce for you to get through on your own, you are facing a Jericho.

What we have to remember when we are standing in front of an impossible circumstance is that God's promise to Joshua still holds true for you and me. God promised to be with Joshua and go before him, and God always keeps his promises.

Here is what we can learn from God's man. God gave instructions and Joshua obeyed with great faith. It could've seemed a little ridiculous—walking around a fortified city, blowing trumpets, shouting—but Joshua trusted and the walls came down. God will take care of the walls; your job is to live in obedience to his instructions by faith, trusting his ways.

For the single woman, that might mean really keeping your body pure until marriage. For the financially burdened, it might mean tithing. For the empty heart, the instruction might mean praying and seeking the presence of God anyway. Take your Jericho to the Lord. Ask him for marching instructions. Then by faith watch what God will do because of your willingness to obey.

the LORD, blowing their trumpets. Soldiers with weapons marched in front of them, and other soldiers walked behind the Ark of the LORD. All this time the priests were blowing their trumpets. 14So on the second day they marched around the city one time and then went back to camp. They did this every day for six days.

15On the seventh day they got up at dawn and marched around the city, just as they had on the days before. But on that day they marched around the city seven times. 16The seventh time around the priests blew their trumpets. Then Joshua gave the command: "Now, shout! The LORD has given you this city! 17The city and everything in it are to be destroyed as an offering to the LORD. Only Rahab the prostitute and everyone in her house should remain alive. They must not be killed, because Rahab hid the two spies we sent out. 18Don't take any of the things that are to be destroyed as an offering to the LORD. If you take them and bring them into our camp, you yourselves will be destroyed, and you will bring trouble to all of Israel. 19All the silver and gold and things made from bronze and iron belong to the LORD and must be saved for him."

20When the priests blew the trumpets, the people shouted. At the sound of the trumpets and the people's shout, the walls fell, and everyone ran straight into the city. So the Israelites defeated that city. 21They completely destroyed with the sword every living thing in the city—men and women, young and old, cattle, sheep, and donkeys.

22Joshua said to the two men who had spied out the land, "Go into the prostitute's house. Bring her out and bring out those who are with her, because of the promise you made to her." 23So the two men went into the house and brought out Rahab, her father, mother, brothers, and all those with her. They put all of her family in a safe place outside the camp of Israel.

24Then Israel burned the whole city and everything in it, but they did not burn the things made from silver, gold, bronze, and iron. These were saved for the LORD. 25Joshua saved Rahab the prostitute, her family, and all who were with her, because Rahab had helped the men he had sent to spy out Jericho. Rahab still lives among the Israelites today.

26Then Joshua made this oath:

"Anyone who tries to rebuild this city of
    Jericho
  will be cursed by the LORD.
The one who lays the foundation of this
    city
  will lose his oldest son,
and the one who sets up the gates
  will lose his youngest son."

27So the LORD was with Joshua, and Joshua became famous through all the land.

The Sin of Achan

7 But the Israelites did not obey the LORD. There was a man from the tribe of Judah named Achan. (He was the son of Carmi and grandson of Zabdi, who was the son of Zerah.) Because Achan kept some of the things that were to be given to the LORD, the LORD became very angry at the Israelites.

2Joshua sent some men from Jericho to Ai, which was near Beth Aven, east of Bethel. He told them, "Go to Ai and spy out the area." So the men went to spy on Ai.

3Later they came back to Joshua and said, "There are only a few people in Ai, so we will not need all our people to defeat them. Send only two or three thousand men to fight. There is no need to send all of our people." 4So about three thousand men went up to Ai, but the people of Ai beat them badly. 5The people of Ai killed about thirty-six Israelites and then chased the rest from the city gate all the way down to the canyon, killing them as they went down the hill. When the Israelites saw this, they lost their courage.

6Then Joshua tore his clothes in sorrow. He bowed facedown on the ground before the Ark of the LORD and stayed there until evening. The leaders of Israel did the same thing. They also threw dirt on their heads to show their sorrow. 7Then Joshua said, "Lord GOD, you brought our people across the Jordan River. Why did you bring us this far and then let the Amorites destroy us? We would have been happy to stay on the other side of the Jordan. 8Lord, there is nothing I can say now. Israel has been beaten by the enemy. 9The Canaanites and all the other people in this country will hear about this and will surround and kill us all! Then what will you do for your own great name?"

10The LORD said to Joshua, "Stand up!

Why are you down on your face? [11]The
Israelites have sinned; they have broken the
agreement I commanded them to obey. They
took some of the things I commanded them
to destroy. They have stolen and lied and
have taken those things for themselves.
[12]That is why the Israelites cannot face their
enemies. They turn away from the fight and
run, because I have commanded that they be
destroyed. I will not help you anymore
unless you destroy everything as I
commanded you.

[13]"Now go! Make the people holy. Tell
them, 'Set yourselves apart to the LORD for
tomorrow. The LORD, the God of Israel, says
some of you are keeping things he
commanded you to destroy. You will never
defeat your enemies until you throw away
those things.

[14]" 'Tomorrow morning you must be
present with your tribes. The LORD will
choose one tribe to stand alone before him.
Then the LORD will choose one family group
from that tribe to stand before him. Then the
LORD will choose one family from that
family group to stand before him, person by
person. [15]The one who is keeping what
should have been destroyed will himself be
destroyed by fire. Everything he owns will be
destroyed with him. He has broken the
agreement with the LORD and has done a
disgraceful thing among the people of
Israel!' "

[16]Early the next morning Joshua led all of
Israel to present themselves in their tribes,
and the LORD chose the tribe of Judah. [17]So
the family groups of Judah presented
themselves, and the LORD then chose the
family group of Zerah. When all the families
of Zerah presented themselves, the family of
Zabdi was chosen. [18]And Joshua told all the
men in that family to present themselves.
The LORD chose Achan son of Carmi. (Carmi
was the son of Zabdi, who was the son of
Zerah.)

[19]Then Joshua said to Achan, "My son, tell
the truth. Confess to the LORD, the God of
Israel. Tell me what you did, and don't try to
hide anything from me."

[20]Achan answered, "It is true! I have
sinned against the LORD, the God of Israel.
This is what I did: [21]Among the things I saw
was a beautiful coat from Babylonia and
about five pounds of silver and more than
one and one-fourth pounds of gold. I wanted
these things very much for myself, so I took
them. You will find them buried in the
ground under my tent, with the silver
underneath."

[22]So Joshua sent men who ran to the tent
and found the things hidden there, with the
silver. [23]The men brought them out of the
tent, took them to Joshua and all the
Israelites, and spread them out on the
ground before the LORD. [24]Then Joshua and
all the people led Achan son of Zerah to the
Valley of Trouble. They also took the silver,
the coat, the gold, Achan's sons, daughters,
cattle, donkeys, sheep, tent, and everything
he owned. [25]Joshua said, "I don't know why
you caused so much trouble for us, but now
the LORD will bring trouble to you." Then all
the people threw stones at Achan and his
family until they died. Then the people
burned them. [26]They piled rocks over
Achan's body, and they are still there today.
That is why it is called the Valley of Trouble.
After this the LORD was no longer angry.

Ai Is Destroyed

8 Then the LORD said to Joshua, "Don't be
afraid or give up. Lead all your fighting
men to Ai. I will help you defeat the king of
Ai, his people, his city, and his land. [2]You
will do to Ai and its king what you did to
Jericho and its king. Only this time you may
take all the wealth and keep it for
yourselves. Now tell some of your soldiers to
set up an ambush behind the city."

[3]So Joshua led his whole army toward Ai.
Then he chose thirty thousand of his best
fighting men and sent them out at night.
[4]Joshua gave them these orders: "Listen
carefully. You must set up an ambush behind
the city. Don't go far from it, but continue to
watch and be ready. [5]I and the men who are
with me will march toward the city, and the
men in the city will come out to fight us,
just as they did before. Then we will turn
and run away from them. [6]They will chase
us away from the city, thinking we are
running away from them as we did before.
When we run away, [7]come out from your
ambush and take the city. The LORD your
God will give you the power to win. [8]After
you take the city, burn it. See to it! You have
your orders."

[9]Then Joshua sent them to wait in

ambush between Bethel and Ai, to the west
of Ai. But Joshua stayed the night with his
people.
10Early the next morning Joshua gathered
his men together. He and the older leaders
of Israel led them up to Ai. 11All of the
soldiers who were with Joshua marched up
to Ai and stopped in front of the city and
made camp north of it. There was a valley
between them and the city. 12Then Joshua
chose about five thousand men and set
them in ambush in the area west of the city
between Bethel and Ai. 13So the people took
their positions; the main camp was north
of the city, and the other men were hiding
to the west. That night Joshua went down
into the valley.
14Now when the king of Ai saw the army
of Israel, he and his people got up early the
next morning and hurried out to fight them.
They went out to a place east of the city, but
the king did not know soldiers were waiting
in ambush behind the city. 15Joshua and all
the men of Israel let the army of Ai push
them back. Then they ran toward the desert.
16The men in Ai were called to chase Joshua
and his men, so they left the city and went
after them. 17All the men of Ai and Bethel
chased the army of Israel. The city was left
open; not a man stayed to protect it.
18Then the LORD said to Joshua, "Hold
your spear toward Ai, because I will give you
that city." So Joshua held his spear toward
the city of Ai. 19When the Israelites who
were in ambush saw this, they quickly came
out of their hiding place and hurried toward
the city. They entered the city, took control
of it, and quickly set it on fire.
20When the men of Ai looked back, they
saw smoke rising from their city. At the
same time the Israelites stopped running
and turned against the men of Ai, who could
not escape in any direction. 21When Joshua
and all his men saw that the army had taken
control of the city and saw the smoke rising
from it, they stopped running and turned to
fight the men of Ai. 22The men who were in
ambush also came out of the city to help
with the fight. So the men of Ai were caught
between the armies of Israel. None of the
enemy escaped. The Israelites fought until
not one of the men of Ai was left alive,
except 23the king of Ai, and they brought
him to Joshua.

A Review of the Fighting

24During the fighting the army of Israel
chased the men of Ai into the fields and
desert and killed all of them. Then they went
back to Ai and killed everyone there. 25All
the people of Ai died that day, twelve
thousand men and women. 26Joshua had
held his spear toward Ai, as a sign to destroy
the city, and did not draw it back until all the
people of Ai were destroyed. 27The people of
Israel kept for themselves the animals and
the other things the people of Ai had owned,
as the LORD had commanded Joshua to do.
28Then Joshua burned the city of Ai and
made it a pile of ruins. And it is still like that
today. 29Joshua hanged the king of Ai on a
tree and left him there until evening. At
sunset Joshua told his men to take the king's
body down from the tree and to throw it
down at the city gate. Then they covered it
with a pile of rocks, which is still there
today.
30Joshua built an altar for the LORD, the
God of Israel, on Mount Ebal, as 31Moses, the
LORD's servant, had commanded. Joshua
built the altar as it was explained in the
Book of the Teachings of Moses. It was made
from uncut stones; no tool was ever used on
them. On that altar the Israelites offered
burnt offerings to the LORD and fellowship
offerings. 32There Joshua wrote the
teachings of Moses on stones for all the
people of Israel to see. 33The elders, officers,
judges, and all the Israelites were there;
Israelites and non-Israelites were all
standing around the Ark of the Agreement
with the LORD in front of the priests, the
Levites who had carried the Ark. Half of the
people stood in front of Mount Ebal, and half
stood in front of Mount Gerizim. This was
the way the LORD's servant Moses had earlier
commanded the people to be blessed.
34Then Joshua read all the words of the
teachings, the blessings and the curses,
exactly as they were written in the Book of
the Teachings. 35All the Israelites were
gathered together—men, women, and
children—along with the non-Israelites who
lived among them. Joshua read every
command that Moses had given.

The Gibeonite Trickery

9 All the kings west of the Jordan River
heard about these things: the kings of the

Hittites, Amorites, Canaanites, Perizzites,
Hivites, and Jebusites. They lived in the
mountains and on the western hills and
along the whole Mediterranean Sea coast.
2So all these kings gathered to fight Joshua
and the Israelites.
3When the people of Gibeon heard how
Joshua had defeated Jericho and Ai, 4they
decided to trick the Israelites. They gathered
old sacks and old leather wine bags that
were cracked and mended, and they put
them on the backs of their donkeys. 5They
put old sandals on their feet and wore old
clothes, and they took some dry, moldy
bread. 6Then they went to Joshua in the
camp near Gilgal.
The men said to Joshua and the Israelites,
"We have traveled from a faraway country.
Make a peace agreement with us."
7The Israelites said to these Hivites,
"Maybe you live near us. How can we make a
peace agreement with you?"
8The Hivites said to Joshua, "We are your
servants."
But Joshua asked, "Who are you? Where
do you come from?"
9The men answered, "We are your
servants who have come from a far country,
because we heard of the fame of the LORD
your God. We heard about what he has done
and everything he did in Egypt. 10We heard
that he defeated the two kings of the
Amorites from the east side of the Jordan
River—Sihon king of Heshbon and Og king
of Bashan who ruled in Ashtaroth. 11So our
elders and our people said to us, 'Take food
for your journey and go and meet the
Israelites. Tell them, "We are your servants.
Make a peace agreement with us." '
12"Look at our bread. On the day we left
home to come to you it was warm and fresh,
but now it is dry and moldy. 13Look at our
leather wine bags. They were new and filled
with wine, but now they are cracked and old.
Our clothes and sandals are worn out from
the long journey."
14The men of Israel tasted the bread, but
they did not ask the LORD what to do. 15So
Joshua agreed to make peace with the
Gibeonites and to let them live. And the
leaders of the Israelites swore an oath to
keep the agreement.

devotion 65

JOSHUA 9:1–14

IS WHAT YOU SEE *REALLY* WHAT YOU GET?

Not all things are as they seem to be. The outward appearance of the people in our lives really can have very little relevance to what resides in their hearts. When someone has purposed to deceive you, they will make sure you see only what they want you to see. They will present themselves in a manner that seems to be acceptable, and they will make sure they are prepared for you to question them. They will be just like the Gibeonites, who presented themselves to Joshua after an allegedly long journey.

It is a sad reality to acknowledge that some people will try to get to know you or manipulate circumstances to get close to you for all the wrong reasons. In my line of work, many of my clients are famous. I find that there are times that people enter into my life with the sole purpose of trying to meet or be a part of my client's lives. This concerned me a great deal early in my career, but I learned to trust the leading of the Holy Spirit very quickly. God gives you discernment for a reason, and when you are being introduced to new relationships, pray and ask the Holy Spirit to pour that discernment all over you. Listen to that still, small voice, and walk out those relationships with care and caution for a season. My husband's grandmother has a great saying: "Patience is the weapon that forces deception to reveal itself." Be patient.

16Three days after they had made the
agreement, the Israelites learned that the
Gibeonites lived nearby. 17So the Israelites
went to where they lived and on the third
day came to their cities: Gibeon, Kephirah,
Beeroth, and Kiriath Jearim. 18But the
Israelites did not attack those cities, because
they had made a promise to them before the
LORD, the God of Israel.

All the Israelites grumbled against the
leaders. 19But the leaders answered, "We have
given our promise before the LORD, the God
of Israel, so we cannot attack them now.
20This is what we must do. We must let
them live. Otherwise, God's anger will be
against us for breaking the oath we swore to
them. 21So let them live, but they will cut
wood and carry water for our people." So the
leaders kept their promise to them.

22Joshua called for the Gibeonites and
asked, "Why did you lie to us? Your land was
near our camp, but you told us you were
from a far country. 23Now, you will be placed
under a curse to be our slaves. You will have
to cut wood and carry water for the house of
my God."

24The Gibeonites answered Joshua, "We
lied to you because we were afraid you
would kill us. We heard that the LORD your
God commanded his servant Moses to give
you all of this land and to kill all the people
who lived in it. That is why we did this.
25Now you can decide what to do with us,
whatever you think is right."

26So Joshua saved their lives by not
allowing the Israelites to kill them, 27but he
made the Gibeonites slaves. They cut wood
and carried water for the Israelites, and they
did it for the altar of the LORD—wherever he
chose it to be. They are still doing this today.

The Sun Stands Still

10 At this time Adoni-Zedek king of
Jerusalem heard that Joshua had
defeated Ai and completely destroyed it, as
he had also done to Jericho and its king. The
king also learned that the Gibeonites had
made a peace agreement with Israel and that
they lived nearby. 2Adoni-Zedek and his
people were very afraid because of this.
Gibeon was not a little town like Ai; it was a
large city, as big as a city that had a king,
and all its men were good fighters. 3So
Adoni-Zedek king of Jerusalem sent a
message to Hoham king of Hebron, Piram
king of Jarmuth, Japhia king of Lachish, and
Debir king of Eglon. He begged them,
4"Come with me and help me attack Gibeon,
which has made a peace agreement with
Joshua and the Israelites."

5Then these five Amorite kings—the
kings of Jerusalem, Hebron, Jarmuth,
Lachish, and Eglon—gathered their armies,
went to Gibeon, surrounded it, and
attacked it.

6The Gibeonites sent this message to
Joshua in his camp at Gilgal: "Don't let us,
your servants, be destroyed. Come quickly
and help us! Save us! All the Amorite kings
from the mountains have joined their armies
and are fighting against us."

7So Joshua marched out of Gilgal with his
whole army, including his best fighting men.
8The LORD said to Joshua, "Don't be afraid of
those armies, because I will hand them over
to you. None of them will be able to stand
against you."

9Joshua and his army marched all night
from Gilgal for a surprise attack. 10The LORD
confused those armies when Israel attacked,
so Israel defeated them in a great victory at
Gibeon. They chased them along the road
going up to Beth Horon and killed men all
the way to Azekah and Makkedah. 11As they
chased the enemy down the Beth Horon Pass
to Azekah, the LORD threw large hailstones
on them from the sky and killed them. More
people were killed by the hailstones than by
the Israelites' swords.

12On the day that the LORD gave up the
Amorites to the Israelites, Joshua stood
before all the people of Israel and said to the
LORD:

"Sun, stand still over Gibeon.
Moon, stand still over the Valley of
Aijalon."
13So the sun stood still,
and the moon stopped
until the people defeated their enemies.

These words are written in the Book of
Jashar.

The sun stopped in the middle of the sky
and waited to go down for a full day. 14That
has never happened at any time before that
day or since. That was the day the LORD
listened to a human being. Truly the LORD
was fighting for Israel!

15After this, Joshua and his army went
back to the camp at Gilgal.

[16]During the fight the five kings ran away
and hid in a cave near Makkedah, [17]but
someone found them hiding in the cave at
Makkedah and told Joshua. [18]So he said,
"Cover the opening of the cave with large
rocks. Put some men there to guard it, [19]but
don't stay there yourselves. Continue
chasing the enemy and attacking them from
behind. Don't let them get to their cities,
because the LORD your God will hand them
over to you."

[20]So Joshua and the Israelites killed the
enemy, but a few were able to get back to
their strong, walled cities. [21]After the
fighting, Joshua's men came back safely to
him at Makkedah. No one was brave enough
to say a word against the Israelites.

[22]Joshua said, "Move the rocks that are
covering the opening of the cave and bring
those five kings out to me." [23]So Joshua's
men brought the five kings out of the cave—
the kings of Jerusalem, Hebron, Jarmuth,
Lachish, and Eglon. [24]When they brought
the five kings out to Joshua, he called for all
his men. He said to the commanders of his
army, "Come here! Put your feet on the necks
of these kings." So they came close and put
their feet on their necks.

[25]Joshua said to his men, "Be strong and
brave! Don't be afraid, because I will show
you what the LORD will do to the enemies
you will fight in the future." [26]Then Joshua
killed the five kings and hung their bodies
on five trees, where he left them until
evening.

[27]At sunset Joshua told his men to take the
bodies down from the trees. Then they
threw them into the same cave where they
had been hiding and covered the opening of
the cave with large rocks, which are still
there today.

[28]That day Joshua defeated Makkedah. He
killed the king and completely destroyed all
the people in that city as an offering to the
LORD; no one was left alive. He did the same
thing to the king of Makkedah that he had
done to the king of Jericho.

Defeating Southern Cities

[29]Joshua and all the Israelites traveled
from Makkedah to Libnah and attacked it.
[30]The LORD handed over the city and its king.
They killed every person in the city; no one
was left alive. And they did the same thing
to that king that they had done to the king
of Jericho.

[31]Then Joshua and all the Israelites left
Libnah and went to Lachish, which they
surrounded and attacked. [32]The LORD handed
over Lachish on the second day. The
Israelites killed everyone in that city just as
they had done to Libnah. [33]During this same
time Horam king of Gezer came to help
Lachish, but Joshua also defeated him and
his army; no one was left alive.

[34]Then Joshua and all the Israelites went
from Lachish to Eglon. They surrounded
Eglon, attacked it, and [35]captured it the same
day. They killed all its people and
completely destroyed everything in it as an
offering to the LORD, just as they had done to
Lachish.

[36]Then Joshua and the Israelites went
from Eglon to Hebron and attacked it,
[37]capturing it and all the little towns near it.
The Israelites killed everyone in Hebron; no
one was left alive there. Just as they had
done to Eglon, they completely destroyed
the city and all its people as an offering to
the LORD.

[38]Then Joshua and the Israelites went
back to Debir and attacked it. [39]They
captured that city, its king, and all the little
towns near it, completely destroying
everyone in Debir as an offering to the LORD;
no one was left alive there. Israel did to
Debir and its king just as they had done to
Libnah and its king, just as they had done to
Hebron.

[40]So Joshua defeated all the kings of the
cities of these areas: the mountains,
southern Canaan, the western hills, and the
slopes. The LORD, the God of Israel, had told
Joshua to completely destroy all the people
as an offering to the LORD, so he left no one
alive in those places. [41]Joshua captured all
the cities from Kadesh Barnea to Gaza, and
from Goshen to Gibeon. [42]He captured all
these cities and their kings on one trip,
because the LORD, the God of Israel, was
fighting for Israel.

[43]Then Joshua and all the Israelites
returned to their camp at Gilgal.

Defeating Northern Kings

11 When Jabin king of Hazor heard
about all that had happened, he sent
messages to Jobab king of Madon, to the

king of Shimron, and to the king of Acshaph.
2He sent messages to the kings in the
northern mountains and also to the kings in
the Jordan Valley south of Lake Galilee and
in the western hills. He sent a message to the
king of Naphoth Dor in the west 3and to the
kings of the Canaanites in the east and in the
west. He sent messages to the Amorites,
Hittites, Perizzites, and Jebusites in the
mountains. Jabin also sent one to the
Hivites, who lived below Mount Hermon in
the area of Mizpah. 4So the armies of all
these kings came together with their horses
and chariots. There were as many soldiers as
grains of sand on the seashore.

5All of these kings met together at the
waters of Merom, joined their armies
together into one camp, and made plans to
fight against the Israelites.

6Then the LORD said to Joshua, "Don't be
afraid of them, because at this time
tomorrow I will give them to you. You will
cripple their horses and burn all their
chariots."

7So Joshua and his whole army surprised
the enemy by attacking them at the waters
of Merom. 8The LORD handed them over to
Israel. They chased them to Greater Sidon,
Misrephoth Maim, and the Valley of Mizpah
in the east. Israel fought until none of the
enemy was left alive. 9Joshua did what the
LORD said to do; he crippled their horses and
burned their chariots.

10Then Joshua went back and captured
the city of Hazor and killed its king. (Hazor
had been the leader of all the kingdoms that
fought against Israel.) 11Israel killed
everyone in Hazor, completely destroying
them; no one was left alive. Then they
burned Hazor itself.

12Joshua captured all of these cities, killed
all of their kings, and completely destroyed
everything in these cities. He did this just as
Moses, the servant of the LORD, had
commanded. 13But the Israelites did not
burn any cities that were built on their
mounds, except Hazor; only that city was
burned by Joshua. 14The people of Israel
kept for themselves everything they found
in the cities, including all the animals. But
they killed all the people there; they left no
one alive. 15Long ago the LORD had
commanded his servant Moses to do this,
and then Moses had commanded Joshua to
do it. Joshua did everything the LORD had
commanded Moses.

16So Joshua defeated all the people in the
land. He had control of the mountains and
the area of southern Canaan, all the areas of
Goshen, the western hills, and the Jordan
Valley. He controlled the mountains of Israel
and all the hills near them. 17Joshua
controlled all the land from Mount Halak
near Edom to Baal Gad in the Valley of
Lebanon, below Mount Hermon. Joshua also
captured all the kings in the land and killed
them. 18He fought against them for many
years. 19The people of only one city in all the
land had made a peace agreement with
Israel—the Hivites living in Gibeon. All the
other cities were defeated in war. 20The LORD
made those people stubborn so they would
fight against Israel and he could completely
destroy them without mercy. This is what
the LORD had commanded Moses to do.

21Now Joshua fought the Anakites who
lived in the mountains of Hebron, Debir,
Anab, Judah, and Israel, and he completely
destroyed them and their towns. 22There
were no Anakites left living in the land of
the Israelites and only a few were left in
Gaza, Gath, and Ashdod. 23Joshua took
control of all the land of Israel as the LORD
had told Moses to do long ago. He gave the
land to Israel, because he had promised it to
them. Then Joshua divided the land among
the tribes of Israel, and there was peace in
the land.

Kings Defeated by Israel

12 The Israelites took control of the land
east of the Jordan River from the
Arnon Ravine to Mount Hermon and all the
land along the eastern side of the Jordan
Valley. These lands belonged to the kings
whom the Israelites defeated.

2Sihon king of the Amorites lived in the
city of Heshbon and ruled the land from
Aroer at the Arnon Ravine to the Jabbok
River. His land started in the middle of the
ravine, which was their border with the
Ammonites. Sihon ruled over half the land
of Gilead 3and over the eastern side of the
Jordan Valley from Lake Galilee to the Dead
Sea. And he ruled from Beth Jeshimoth
south to the slopes of Pisgah.

4Og king of Bashan was one of the last
of the Rephaites. He ruled the land in

Ashtaroth and Edrei. 5He ruled over Mount
Hermon, Salecah, and all the area of Bashan
up to where the people of Geshur and
Maacah lived. Og also ruled half the land of
Gilead up to the border of Sihon king of
Heshbon.
6The LORD's servant Moses and the
Israelites defeated all these kings, and Moses
gave that land to the tribes of Reuben and
Gad and to East Manasseh as their own.
7Joshua and the Israelites also defeated
kings in the land west of the Jordan River. He
gave the people the land and divided it
among the twelve tribes to be their own. It
was between Baal Gad in the Valley of
Lebanon and Mount Halak near Edom. 8This
included the mountains, the western hills,
the Jordan Valley, the slopes, the desert, and
southern Canaan. This was the land where
the Hittites, Amorites, Canaanites, Perizzites,
Hivites, and Jebusites had lived. The
Israelites defeated the king of each of the
following cities: 9Jericho, Ai (near Bethel),
10Jerusalem, Hebron, 11Jarmuth, Lachish,
12Eglon, Gezer, 13Debir, Geder, 14Hormah,
Arad, 15Libnah, Adullam, 16Makkedah,
Bethel, 17Tappuah, Hepher, 18Aphek,
Lasharon, 19Madon, Hazor, 20Shimron
Meron, Acshaph, 21Taanach, Megiddo,
22Kedesh, Jokneam in Carmel, 23Dor (in
Naphoth Dor), Goyim in Gilgal, and
24Tirzah.

The total number of kings was thirty-one.

Land Still to Be Taken

13 When Joshua was very old, the LORD
said to him, "Joshua, you have grown
old, but there is still much land for you to
take. 2This is what is left: the regions of
Geshur and of the Philistines; 3the area from
the Shihor River at the border of Egypt to
Ekron in the north, which belongs to the
Canaanites; the five Philistine leaders at
Gaza, Ashdod, Ashkelon, Gath, and Ekron;
the Avvites, 4who live south of the
Canaanite land; 5the Gebalites, and the area
of Lebanon east of Baal Gad below Mount
Hermon to Lebo Hamath.
6"The Sidonians are living in the hill
country from Lebanon to Misrephoth Maim,
but I will force all of them out ahead of the
Israelites. Be sure to remember this land
when you divide the land among the
Israelites, as I told you.
7"Now divide the land among the nine
tribes and West Manasseh."

Dividing the Land

8East Manasseh and the tribes of Reuben
and Gad had received their land. The LORD's
servant Moses had given them the land east
of the Jordan River. 9Their land started at
Aroer at the Arnon Ravine and continued to
the town in the middle of the ravine, and it
included the whole plain from Medeba to
Dibon. 10All the towns ruled by Sihon king
of the Amorites, who ruled in the city of
Heshbon, were in that land. The land
continued to the area where the Ammonites
lived. 11Gilead was also there, as well as the
area where the people of Geshur and
Maacah lived, and all of Mount Hermon and
Bashan as far as Salecah. 12All the kingdom
of Og king of Bashan was in the land. Og was
one of the last of the Rephaites, and in the
past he ruled in Ashtaroth and Edrei. Moses
had defeated them and had taken their land.
13Because the Israelites did not force out the
people of Geshur and Maacah, they still live
among the Israelites today.
14The tribe of Levi was the only one that
did not get any land. Instead, they were
given all the burned sacrifices made to the
LORD, the God of Israel, as he had promised
them.
15Moses had given each family group
from the tribe of Reuben some land: 16Theirs
was the land from Aroer near the Arnon
Ravine to the town of Medeba, including the
whole plain and the town in the middle of
the ravine; 17Heshbon and all the towns on
the plain: Dibon, Bamoth Baal, and Beth Baal
Meon, 18Jahaz, Kedemoth, Mephaath,
19Kiriathaim, Sibmah, Zereth Shahar on the
hill in the valley, 20Beth Peor, the hills of
Pisgah, and Beth Jeshimoth. 21So that land
included all the towns on the plain and all
the area that Sihon king of the Amorites had
ruled from the town of Heshbon. Moses had
defeated him along with the leaders of the
Midianites, including Evi, Rekem, Zur, Hur,
and Reba. All these leaders fought together
with Sihon and lived in that country. 22The
Israelites killed many people during the
fighting, including Balaam of Beor, who tried
to use magic to tell the future. 23The land
given to Reuben stopped at the shore of the
Jordan River. So the land given to the family

groups of Reuben included all these towns
and their villages that were listed.
24This is the land Moses gave to the tribe
of Gad, to all its family groups: 25the land of
Jazer and all the towns of Gilead; half the
land of the Ammonites that went as far as
Aroer near Rabbah; 26the area from Heshbon
to Ramath Mizpah and Betonim; the area
from Mahanaim to the land of Debir; 27in
the valley, Beth Haram, Beth Nimrah,
Succoth, and Zaphon, the other land Sihon
king of Heshbon had ruled east of the Jordan
River and continuing to the end of Lake
Galilee. 28All this land went to the family
groups of Gad, including all these towns and
their villages.

29This is the land Moses had given to East
Manasseh. Half of all the family groups in
the tribe of Manasseh were given this land:
30The land started at Mahanaim and
included all of Bashan and the land ruled
by Og king of Bashan; all the towns of Jair
in Bashan, sixty cities in all; 31half of
Gilead, Ashtaroth, and Edrei, the cities
where Og king of Bashan had ruled. All this
went to the family of Makir son of
Manasseh, and half of all his sons were
given this land.

32Moses had given this land to these tribes
on the plains of Moab across the Jordan
River east of Jericho. 33But Moses had given
no land to the tribe of Levi because the LORD,
the God of Israel, promised that he himself
would be the gift for the Levites.

14 Eleazar the priest, Joshua son of Nun,
and the leaders of all the tribes of
Israel decided what land to give to the
people in the land of Canaan. 2The LORD had
commanded Moses long ago how he wanted
the people to choose their land. The people
of the nine-and-a-half tribes threw lots to
decide which land they would receive.
3Moses had already given the two-and-a-half
tribes their land east of the Jordan River. But
the tribe of Levi was not given any land like
the others. 4The sons of Joseph had divided
into two tribes—Manasseh and Ephraim.
The tribe of Levi was not given any land. It
was given only some towns in which to
live and pastures for its animals. 5The LORD
had told Moses how to give the land to the
tribes of Israel, and the Israelites divided
the land.

Caleb's Land

6One day some men from the tribe of
Judah went to Joshua at Gilgal. Among them
was Caleb son of Jephunneh the Kenizzite.
He said to Joshua, "You remember what the
LORD said at Kadesh Barnea when he was
speaking to the prophet Moses about you
and me. 7Moses, the LORD's servant, sent me
to look at the land where we were going. I
was forty years old then. When I came back,
I told Moses what I thought about the land.
8The other men who went with me
frightened the people, but I fully believed
the LORD would allow us to take the land.
9So that day Moses promised me, 'The land
where you went will become your land, and
your children will own it forever. I will give
you that land because you fully believed in
the LORD, my God.'

10"Now then, the LORD has kept his
promise. He has kept me alive for forty-five
years from the time he said this to Moses
during the time we all wandered in the
desert. Now here I am, eighty-five years old.
11I am still as strong today as I was the day
Moses sent me out, and I am just as ready to
fight now as I was then. 12So give me the
mountain country the LORD promised me
that day long ago. Back then you heard that
the Anakite people lived there and the cities
were large and well protected. But now with
the LORD helping me, I will force them out,
just as the LORD said."

13Joshua blessed Caleb son of Jephunneh
and gave him the city of Hebron as his own.
14Hebron still belongs to the family of Caleb
son of Jephunneh the Kenizzite because he
had faith and obeyed the LORD, the God of
Israel. 15(In the past it was called Kiriath
Arba, named for Arba, the greatest man
among the Anakites.)

After this there was peace in the land.

Land for Judah

15 The land that was given to the tribe of
Judah was divided among all the family
groups. It went all the way to the Desert of
Zin in the far south, at the border of Edom.

2The southern border of Judah's land
started at the south end of the Dead Sea 3and
went south of Scorpion Pass to Zin. From
there it passed to the south of Kadesh
Barnea and continued past Hezron to Addar.
From Addar it turned and went to Karka.

devotion 66

JOSHUA 14:6-15

EVERYBODY NEEDS A CALEB

How often well-meaning Christians frighten us out of doing what God has called us to do. A year ago, my husband and I decided to become foster parents. We have four children of our own but felt led as a family to reach out to these little orphans. When I shared with people that we were going to foster, inevitably most replied, "I could never do that because I wouldn't be able to give them back." And each time I heard this, I felt fear creeping into my heart that I was setting my family up for heartbreak. I contemplated giving up the whole idea of foster parenting several times.

However there were "Calebs" in our lives who, as Joshua 14:8 says, fully believed that the Lord would allow us to take the land. Those friends and family were priceless in our journey toward following God's will. We have now fostered three little girls, and I can't even describe what a joy it has been. Those girls have blessed our family and deepened our walk with the Lord more than you could imagine. I'm so glad I didn't let my fears keep my family and me from receiving this blessing. I want to be a Caleb in the lives of others. I want to encourage others to step out in faith and do something radical for God. What kind of a spy are you for God? Do you frighten others or encourage them to take the land the Lord has promised?

4It continued to Azmon, the brook of Egypt,
and then to the Mediterranean Sea. This was
the southern border.
5The eastern border was the shore of the
Dead Sea, as far as the mouth of the Jordan
River.
The northern border started at the bay of
the sea at the mouth of the Jordan River.
6Then it went to Beth Hoglah and continued
north of Beth Arabah to the stone of Bohan
son of Reuben. 7Then the northern border
went through the Valley of Achor to Debir
where it turned toward the north and went
to Gilgal. Gilgal is across from the road that
goes through Adummim Pass, on the south
side of the ravine. The border continued to
the waters of En Shemesh and stopped at En
Rogel. 8Then it went through the Valley of
Ben Hinnom, next to the southern side of
the Jebusite city (which is called Jerusalem).
There the border went to the top of the hill
on the west side of Hinnom Valley, at the
northern end of the Valley of Giants. 9From
there it went to the spring of the waters of
Nephtoah and then it went to the cities near
Mount Ephron. There it turned and went
toward Baalah, which is called Kiriath
Jearim. 10At Baalah the border turned west
and went toward Mount Seir. It continued
along the north side of Mount Jearim (also
called Kesalon) and came to Beth Shemesh.
From there it went past Timnah 11to the hill
north of Ekron. Then it turned toward
Shikkeron and went past Mount Baalah and
continued on to Jabneel, ending at the sea.
12The Mediterranean Sea was the western
border. Inside these borders lived the family
groups of Judah.
13The LORD had commanded Joshua to
give Caleb son of Jephunneh part of the land
in Judah, so he gave Caleb the town of
Kiriath Arba, also called Hebron. (Arba was
the father of Anak.) 14Caleb forced out the
three Anakite families living in Hebron:
Sheshai, Ahiman, and Talmai, the
descendants of Anak. 15Then he left there
and went to fight against the people living
in Debir. (In the past Debir had been called

Kiriath Sepher.) 16 Caleb said, "I will give
Acsah, my daughter, as a wife to the man
who attacks and captures the city of Kiriath
Sepher." 17 Othniel son of Kenaz, Caleb's
brother, captured the city, so Caleb gave his
daughter Acsah to Othniel to be his wife.
18 When Acsah came to Othniel, she told him
to ask her father for a field.

So Acsah went to her father. When she
got down from her donkey, Caleb asked her,
"What do you want?"

19 Acsah answered, "Do me a special favor.
Since you have given me land in southern
Canaan, also give me springs of water." So
Caleb gave her the upper and lower springs.

20 The tribe of Judah got the land God had
promised them. Each family group got part
of the land.

21 The tribe of Judah got all these towns in
the southern part of Canaan near the border
of Edom: Kabzeel, Eder, Jagur, 22 Kinah,
Dimonah, Adadah, 23 Kedesh, Hazor, Ithnan,
24 Ziph, Telem, Bealoth, 25 Hazor Hadattah,
Kerioth Hezron (also called Hazor), 26 Amam,
Shema, Moladah, 27 Hazar Gaddah, Heshmon,
Beth Pelet, 28 Hazar Shual, Beersheba,
Biziothiah, 29 Baalah, Iim, Ezem, 30 Eltolad,
Kesil, Hormah, 31 Ziklag, Madmannah,
Sansannah, 32 Lebaoth, Shilhim, Ain, and
Rimmon. There were twenty-nine towns and
their villages.

33 The tribe of Judah got these towns in the
western hills: Eshtaol, Zorah, Ashnah,
34 Zanoah, En Gannim, Tappuah, Enam,
35 Jarmuth, Adullam, Socoh, Azekah,
36 Shaaraim, Adithaim, and Gederah (also
called Gederothaim). There were fourteen
towns and their villages.

37 Judah was also given these towns in the
western hills: Zenan, Hadashah, Migdal Gad,
38 Dilean, Mizpah, Joktheel, 39 Lachish,
Bozkath, Eglon, 40 Cabbon, Lahmas, Kitlish,
41 Gederoth, Beth Dagon, Naamah, and
Makkedah. There were sixteen towns and
their villages.

42 Judah was also given these towns in the
western hills: Libnah, Ether, Ashan, 43 Iphtah,
Ashnah, Nezib, 44 Keilah, Aczib, and
Mareshah. There were nine towns and their
villages.

45 The tribe of Judah was also given these
towns: Ekron and all the small towns and
villages near it; 46 the area west of Ekron and
all the villages and small towns near
Ashdod; 47 Ashdod and the small towns and
villages around it; the villages and small
towns around Gaza as far as the brook of
Egypt and along the coast of the
Mediterranean Sea.

48 The tribe of Judah was also given these
towns in the mountains: Shamir, Jattir,
Socoh, 49 Dannah, Kiriath Sannah (also called
Debir), 50 Anab, Eshtemoh, Anim, 51 Goshen,
Holon, and Giloh. There were eleven towns
and their villages.

52 They were also given these towns in the
mountains: Arab, Dumah, Eshan, 53 Janim,
Beth Tappuah, Aphekah, 54 Humtah, Kiriath
Arba (also called Hebron), and Zior. There
were nine towns and their villages.

55 Judah was also given these towns in the
mountains: Maon, Carmel, Ziph, Juttah,
56 Jezreel, Jokdeam, Zanoah, 57 Kain, Gibeah,
and Timnah. There were ten towns and their
villages.

58 They were also given these towns in the
mountains: Halhul, Beth Zur, Gedor,
59 Maarath, Beth Anoth, and Eltekon. There
were six towns and their villages.

60 The people of Judah were also given the
two towns of Rabbah and Kiriath Baal (also
called Kiriath Jearim) and their villages.

61 Judah was given these towns in the
desert: Beth Arabah, Middin, Secacah,
62 Nibshan, the City of Salt, and En Gedi.
There were six towns and all their villages.

63 The army of Judah was not able to force
out the Jebusites living in Jerusalem, so the
Jebusites still live among the people of Judah
to this day.

Land for Ephraim and Manasseh

16 This is the land the tribe of Joseph
received. It started at the Jordan River
near Jericho and continued to the waters of
Jericho, just east of the city. The border went
up from Jericho to the mountains of Bethel.
2 Then it continued from Bethel (also called
Luz) to the Arkite border at Ataroth. 3 From
there it went west to the border of the
Japhletites and continued to the area of the
Lower Beth Horon. Then it went to Gezer
and ended at the sea.

4 So Manasseh and Ephraim, sons of
Joseph, received their land.

5 This is the land that was given to the
family groups of Ephraim: Their border
started at Ataroth Addar in the east, went to

Upper Beth Horon, 6and then to the sea.
From Micmethath it turned eastward toward
Taanath Shiloh and continued eastward to
Janoah. 7Then it went down from Janoah to
Ataroth and to Naarah. It continued until it
touched Jericho and stopped at the Jordan
River. 8The border went from Tappuah west
to Kanah Ravine and ended at the sea. This
is all the land that was given to each family
group in the tribe of the Ephraimites.
9Many of the towns were actually within
Manasseh's borders, but the people of
Ephraim got those towns and their villages.
10The Ephraimites could not force the
Canaanites to leave Gezer, so the Canaanites
still live among the Ephraimites today, but
they became slaves of the Ephraimites.

17 Then land was given to the tribe of
Manasseh, Joseph's first son.
Manasseh's first son was Makir, the father of
Gilead. Makir was a great soldier, so the
lands of Gilead and Bashan were given to his
family. 2Land was also given to the other
family groups of Manasseh—Abiezer, Helek,
Asriel, Shechem, Hepher, and Shemida.
These were all the other sons of Manasseh
son of Joseph.

3Zelophehad was the son of Hepher, who
was the son of Gilead, who was the son of
Makir, who was the son of Manasseh.
Zelophehad had no sons, but he had five
daughters, named Mahlah, Noah, Hoglah,
Milcah, and Tirzah. 4They went to Eleazar
the priest and to Joshua son of Nun and all
the leaders. They said, "The LORD told Moses
to give us land like the men received." So
Eleazar obeyed the LORD and gave the
daughters some land, just like the brothers
of their father. 5So the tribe of Manasseh had
ten sections of land west of the Jordan River
and two more sections, Gilead and Bashan,
on the east side of the Jordan River. 6The
daughters of Manasseh received land just as
the sons did. Gilead was given to the rest of
the families of Manasseh.

7The lands of Manasseh were in the area
between Asher and Micmethath, near
Shechem. The border went south to the En
Tappuah area, 8which belonged to
Manasseh, except for the town of Tappuah. It
was along the border of Manasseh's land and
belonged to the sons of Ephraim. 9The
border of Manasseh continued south to
Kanah Ravine. The cities in this area of
Manasseh belonged to Ephraim. Manasseh's
border was on the north side of the ravine
and went to the sea. 10The land to the south
belonged to Ephraim, and the land to the
north belonged to Manasseh. The
Mediterranean Sea was the western border.
The border touched Asher's land on the
north and Issachar's land on the east.

11In the areas of Issachar and Asher, the
people of Manasseh owned these towns: Beth
Shan and its small towns; Ibleam and its
small towns; the people who lived in Dor and
its small towns; the people in Naphoth Dor
and its small towns; the people who lived in
Taanach and its small towns; the people in
Megiddo and its small towns. 12Manasseh
was not able to defeat those cities, so the
Canaanites continued to live there. 13When
the Israelites grew strong, they forced the
Canaanites to work for them, although they
did not force them to leave the land.

14The people from the tribes of Joseph
said to Joshua, "You gave us only one area of
land, but we are many people. Why did you
give us only one part of all the land the LORD
gave his people?"

15And Joshua answered them, "If you have
too many people, go up to the forest and
make a place for yourselves to live there in
the land of the Perizzites and the Rephaites.
The mountain country of Ephraim is too
small for you."

16The people of Joseph said, "It is true. The
mountain country of Ephraim is not enough
for us, but the land where the Canaanites
live is dangerous. They are skilled fighters.
They have powerful weapons in Beth Shan
and all the small towns in that area, and they
are also in the Valley of Jezreel."

17Then Joshua said to the people of
Joseph—to Ephraim and Manasseh, "There
are many of you, and you have great power.
You should be given more than one share of
land. 18You also will have the mountain
country. It is a forest, but you can cut down
the trees and make it a good place to live.
You will own all of it because you will
force the Canaanites to leave the land even
though they have powerful weapons and are
strong."

The Rest of the Land Divided

18 All of the Israelites gathered together
at Shiloh where they set up the

Meeting Tent. The land was now under their
control. 2But there were still seven tribes of
Israel that had not yet received their land.
3So Joshua said to the Israelites: "Why do
you wait so long to take your land? The
LORD, the God of your ancestors, has given
this land to you. 4Choose three men from
each tribe, and I will send them out to study
the land. They will describe in writing the
land their tribe wants as its share, and then
they will come back to me. 5They will divide
the land into seven parts. The people of
Judah will keep their land in the south, and
the people of Joseph will keep their land in
the north. 6You should describe the seven
parts of land in writing and bring what you
have written to me. Then I will throw lots in
the presence of the LORD our God. 7But the
Levites do not get any part of these lands,
because they are priests, and their work is to
serve the LORD. Gad, Reuben, and East
Manasseh have received the land promised
to them, which is east of the Jordan River.
Moses, the servant of the LORD, gave it to
them."
8So the men who were chosen to map the
land started out. Joshua told them, "Go and
study the land and describe it in writing.
Then come back to me, and I will throw lots
in the presence of the LORD here in Shiloh."
9So the men left and went into the land.
They described in a scroll each town in the
seven parts of the land. Then they came back
to Joshua, who was still at the camp at
Shiloh. 10There Joshua threw lots in the
presence of the LORD to choose the lands that
should be given to each tribe.

Land for Benjamin

11The first part of the land was given to
the tribe of Benjamin. Each family group
received some land between the land of
Judah and the land of Joseph. This is the land
chosen for Benjamin: 12The northern border
started at the Jordan River and went along
the northern edge of Jericho, and then it
went west into the mountains. That
boundary continued until it was just east of
Beth Aven. 13From there it went south to Luz
(also called Bethel) and then down to
Ataroth Addar, which is on the hill south of
Lower Beth Horon.
14At the hill to the south of Beth Horon,
the border turned and went south near the
western side of the hill. It went to Kiriath
Baal (also called Kiriath Jearim), a town
where people of Judah lived. This was the
western border.
15The southern border started near Kiriath
Jearim and went west to the waters of
Nephtoah. 16Then it went down to the
bottom of the hill, which was near the Valley
of Ben Hinnom, on the north side of the
Valley of Rephaim. The border continued
down the Hinnom Valley just south of the
Jebusite city to En Rogel. 17There it turned
north and went to En Shemesh. It continued
to Geliloth near the Adummim Pass. Then it
went down to the great Stone of Bohan son
of Reuben. 18The border continued to the
northern part of Beth Arabah and went
down into the Jordan Valley. 19From there it
went to the northern part of Beth Hoglah
and ended at the north shore of the Dead
Sea, where the Jordan River flows into the
sea. This was the southern border.
20The Jordan River was the border on the
eastern side. So this was the land given to
the family groups of Benjamin with the
borders on all sides.
21The family groups of Benjamin received
these cities: Jericho, Beth Hoglah, Emek
Keziz, 22Beth Arabah, Zemaraim, Bethel,
23Avvim, Parah, Ophrah, 24Kephar Ammoni,
Ophni, and Geba. There were twelve towns
and all their villages.
25The tribe of Benjamin also received
Gibeon, Ramah, Beeroth, 26Mizpah,
Kephirah, Mozah, 27Rekem, Irpeel, Taralah,
28Zelah, Haeleph, the Jebusite city
(Jerusalem), Gibeah, and Kiriath. There were
fourteen towns and their villages. All these
areas are the lands the family groups of
Benjamin were given.

Land for Simeon

19 The second part of the land was given
to the tribe of Simeon. Each family
group received some of the land inside the
area of Judah. 2They received Beersheba (also
called Sheba), Moladah, 3Hazar Shual, Balah,
Ezem, 4Eltolad, Bethul, Hormah, 5Ziklag,
Beth Marcaboth, Hazar Susah, 6Beth
Lebaoth, and Sharuhen. There were thirteen
towns and their villages.
7They received the towns of Ain, Rimmon,
Ether, and Ashan, four towns and their
villages. 8They also received all the very small

areas with people living in them as far as Baalath Beer (this is the same as Ramah in southern Canaan). So these were the lands given to the family groups in the tribe of Simeon. 9The land of the Simeonites was taken from part of the land of Judah. Since Judah had much more land than they needed, the Simeonites received part of their land.

Land for Zebulun

10The third part of the land was given to the tribe of Zebulun. Each family group of Zebulun received some of the land. The border of Zebulun went as far as Sarid. 11Then it went west to Maralah and came near Dabbesheth and then near Jokneam. 12Then it turned to the east. It went from Sarid to the area of Kisloth Tabor and on to Daberath and to Japhia. 13It continued eastward to Gath Hepher and Eth Kazin, ending at Rimmon. There the border turned and went toward Neah. 14At Neah it turned again and went to the north to Hannathon and continued to the Valley of Iphtah El. 15Inside this border were the cities of Kattath, Nahalal, Shimron, Idalah, and Bethlehem. There were twelve towns and their villages.

16So these are the towns and the villages that were given to the family groups of Zebulun.

Land for Issachar

17The fourth part of the land was given to the tribe of Issachar. Each family group of Issachar received some of the land. 18Their land included Jezreel, Kesulloth, Shunem, 19Hapharaim, Shion, Anaharath, 20Rabbith, Kishion, Ebez, 21Remeth, En Gannim, En Haddah, and Beth Pazzez.

22The border of their land touched the area called Tabor, Shahazumah, and Beth Shemesh and stopped at the Jordan River. There were sixteen towns and their villages.

23These cities and towns were part of the land that was given to the family groups of Issachar.

Land for Asher

24The fifth part of the land was given to the tribe of Asher. Each family group of Asher received some of the land. 25Their land included Helkath, Hali, Beten, Acshaph, 26Allammelech, Amad, and Mishal.

The western border touched Mount Carmel and Shihor Libnath. 27Then it turned east and went to Beth Dagon, touching Zebulun and the Valley of Iphtah El. Then it went north of Beth Emek and Neiel and passed north to Cabul. 28From there it went to Abdon, Rehob, Hammon, and Kanah and continued to Greater Sidon. 29Then the border went back south toward Ramah and continued to the strong, walled city of Tyre. There it turned and went toward Hosah, ending at the sea. This was in the area of Aczib, 30Ummah, Aphek, and Rehob. There were twenty-two towns and their villages.

31These cities and their villages were part of the land that was given to the family groups of Asher.

Land for Naphtali

32The sixth part of the land was given to the tribe of Naphtali. Each family group of Naphtali received some of the land. 33The border of their land started at the large tree in Zaanannim, which is near Heleph. Then it went through Adami Nekeb and Jabneel, as far as Lakkum, and ended at the Jordan River. 34Then it went to the west through Aznoth Tabor and stopped at Hukkok. It went to the area of Zebulun on the south, Asher on the west, and Judah, at the Jordan River, on the east. 35The strong, walled cities inside these borders were called Ziddim, Zer, Hammath, Rakkath, Kinnereth, 36Adamah, Ramah, Hazor, 37Kedesh, Edrei, En Hazor, 38Iron, Migdal El, Horem, Beth Anath, and Beth Shemesh. There were nineteen towns and all their villages.

39The towns and the villages around them were in the land that was given to the family groups of Naphtali.

Land for Dan

40The seventh part of the land was given to the tribe of Dan. Each family group of Dan received some of the land. 41Their land included Zorah, Eshtaol, Ir Shemesh, 42Shaalabbin, Aijalon, Ithlah, 43Elon, Timnah, Ekron, 44Eltekeh, Gibbethon, Baalath, 45Jehud, Bene Berak, Gath Rimmon, 46Me Jarkon, Rakkon, and the area near Joppa.

47(But the Danites had trouble taking their land. They went and fought against Leshem, defeated it, and killed the people who lived

there. So the Danites moved into the town of
Leshem and changed its name to Dan,
because he was the father of their tribe.)
48 All of these towns and villages were given
to the family groups of Dan.

Land for Joshua

49 After the leaders finished dividing the
land and giving it to the different tribes, the
Israelites gave Joshua son of Nun his land
also. 50 They gave Joshua the town he asked
for, Timnath Serah in the mountains of
Ephraim, just as the LORD commanded. He
built up the town and lived there.

51 So these lands were given to the
different tribes of Israel. Eleazar the priest,
Joshua son of Nun, and the leaders of each
tribe divided up the land by lots at Shiloh.
They met in the presence of the LORD at the
entrance to the Meeting Tent. Now they
were finished dividing the land.

Cities of Safety

20 Then the LORD said to Joshua: 2 "Tell
the Israelites to choose the special
cities of safety, as I had Moses command you
to do. 3 If a person kills someone accidentally
and without meaning to kill him, that
person may go to a city of safety to hide.
There the killer will be safe from the relative
who has the duty of punishing a murderer.

4 "When the killer runs to one of those
cities, he must stop at the entrance gate,
stand there, and tell the leaders of the people
what happened. Then that person will be
allowed to enter the city and will be given a
place to live among them. 5 But if the one
who is chasing him follows him to that city,
the leaders of the city must not hand over
the killer. It was an accident. He did not hate
him beforehand or kill him on purpose.
6 The killer must stay in the city until a court
comes to a decision and until the high
priest dies. Then he may go back home to
the town from which he ran away."

7 So the Israelites chose these cities to be
cities of safety: Kedesh in Galilee in the
mountains of Naphtali; Shechem in the
mountains of Ephraim; Kiriath Arba (also
called Hebron) in the mountains of Judah;
8 Bezer on the east side of the Jordan River
near Jericho in the desert in the land of
Reuben; Ramoth in Gilead in the land of Gad;
and Golan in Bashan in the land of Manasseh.
9 Any Israelite or anyone living among them
who killed someone accidentally was to be
allowed to run to one of these cities of safety.
There he would not be killed, before he was
judged, by the relative who had the duty of
punishing a murderer.

Towns for the Levites

21 The heads of the Levite families went
to talk to Eleazar the priest, to Joshua
son of Nun, and to the heads of the families
of all the tribes of Israel. 2 At Shiloh in the
land of Canaan, the heads of the Levite
families said to them, "The LORD commanded
Moses that you give us towns where we may
live and pastures for our animals." 3 So the
Israelites obeyed this command of the LORD
and gave the Levite people these towns and
pastures for their own land: 4 The Kohath
family groups were part of the tribe of Levi.
Some of the Levites in the Kohath family
groups were from the family of Aaron the
priest. To these Levites were given thirteen
towns in the areas of Judah, Simeon, and
Benjamin. 5 The other family groups of
Kohath were given ten towns in the areas of
Ephraim, Dan, and West Manasseh.

6 The people from the Gershon family
groups were given thirteen towns in the
land of Issachar, Asher, Naphtali, and the
East Manasseh in Bashan.

7 The family groups of Merari were given
twelve towns in the areas of Reuben, Gad,
and Zebulun.

8 So the Israelites gave the Levites these
towns and the pastures around them, just as
the LORD had commanded Moses.

9 These are the names of the towns that
came from the lands of Judah and Simeon.
10 The first choice of towns was given to the
Kohath family groups of the Levites. 11 They
gave them Kiriath Arba, also called Hebron,
and all its pastures in the mountains of
Judah. (Arba was the father of Anak.) 12 But
the fields and the villages around Kiriath
Arba had been given to Caleb son of
Jephunneh.

13 So they gave the city of Hebron to the
descendants of Aaron (Hebron was a city of
safety). They also gave them the towns of
Libnah, 14 Jattir, Eshtemoa, 15 Holon, Debir,
16 Ain, Juttah, and Beth Shemesh, and all the
pastures around them. Nine towns were
given from these two tribes.

devotion 67

JOSHUA 21:43–45

NEVER TOO LATE

If you think there's anything you've done in your life that can possibly keep you from God's promises, then you need to learn from the Israelites. After all their failures, the Israelites did receive the land promised to their ancestors. In fact, each and every promise God made them came true. Think about it. Only the kind, forgiving, and true God would give his children such an enormous gift even after they'd disobeyed him so often in the past. Isn't it comforting to know that God never breaks a promise? Even if we've strayed from him, like the Israelites, we can still depend on him to come through for us.

While it's true that sooner is better than later, it's never too late to call out to God and choose to follow him. No matter what we've done in our lives; even if we've put God last in everything we've done, it's never too late to turn things around. Do you feel like God has forgotten you? Do you feel like you're all alone and that he's turned his back on you? Perhaps there are days when you feel totally unlovable and unforgivable. When you feel that way, be encouraged by the story of the Israelites. Call out to the Lord and know you're going to make it. There is peace to be had. He will save you from the enemies of despair and self-doubt and lead you to a better land, just as he did the Israelites.

17 They also gave the people of Aaron
these cities that belonged to the tribe of
Benjamin: Gibeon, Geba, 18 Anathoth, and
Almon. They gave them these four towns
and the pastures around them.
19 So these thirteen towns with their
pastures were given to the priests, who were
from the family of Aaron.
20 The other Kohathite family groups of
the Levites were given these towns from the
tribe of Ephraim: 21 Shechem in the
mountains of Ephraim (which was a city of
safety), Gezer, 22 Kibzaim, and Beth Horon.
There were four towns and their pastures.
23 The tribe of Dan gave them Eltekeh,
Gibbethon, 24 Aijalon, and Gath Rimmon.
There were four towns and their pastures.
25 West Manasseh gave them Taanach and
Gath Rimmon and the pastures around these
two towns.
26 So these ten towns and the pastures
around them were given to the rest of the
Kohathite family groups.
27 The Gershonite family groups of the
Levite tribe were given these towns: East
Manasseh gave them Golan in Bashan,
which was a city of safety, and Be Eshtarah,
and the pastures around these two towns.
28 The tribe of Issachar gave them Kishion,
Daberath, 29 Jarmuth, and En Gannim, and
the pastures around these four towns.
30 The tribe of Asher gave them Mishal,
Abdon, 31 Helkath, and Rehob, and the
pastures around these four towns.
32 The tribe of Naphtali gave them Kedesh
in Galilee (a city of safety), Hammoth Dor,
and Kartan, and the pastures around these
three towns.
33 So the Gershonite family groups
received thirteen towns and the pastures
around them.
34 The Merarite family groups (the rest of
the Levites) were given these towns: The
tribe of Zebulun gave them Jokneam, Kartah,
35 Dimnah, and Nahalal, and the pastures
around these four towns.
36 The tribe of Reuben gave them Bezer,
Jahaz, 37 Kedemoth, and Mephaath, along
with the pastures around these four towns.
38 The tribe of Gad gave them Ramoth in

Gilead (a city of safety), Mahanaim,
39Heshbon, and Jazer, and the pastures
around these four towns.
40So the total number of towns given to
the Merarite family groups was twelve.
41A total of forty-eight towns with their
pastures in the land of Israel were given to
the Levites. 42Each town had pastures
around it.
43So the LORD gave the people all the land
he had promised their ancestors. The people
took the land and lived there. 44The LORD
gave them peace on all sides, as he had
promised their ancestors. None of their
enemies defeated them; the LORD handed all
their enemies over to them. 45He kept every
promise he had made to the Israelites; each
one came true.

Three Tribes Go Home

22 Then Joshua called a meeting of all
the people from the tribes of Reuben,
Gad, and East Manasseh. 2He said to them,
"You have done everything Moses, the LORD's
servant, told you to do. You have also obeyed
all my commands. 3For a long time you have
supported the other Israelites. You have been
careful to obey the commands the LORD your
God gave you. 4The LORD your God promised
to give the Israelites peace, and he has kept
his promise. Now you may go back to your
homes, to the land that Moses, the LORD's
servant, gave you, on the east side of the
Jordan River. 5But be careful to obey the
teachings and laws Moses, the LORD's
servant, gave you: to love the LORD your God
and obey his commands, to continue to
follow him and serve him the very best you
can."
6Then Joshua said good-bye to them, and
they left and went away to their homes.
7Moses had given the land of Bashan to East
Manasseh. Joshua gave land on the west side
of the Jordan River to West Manasseh. And
he sent them to their homes and he blessed
them. 8He said, "Go back to your homes and
your riches. You have many animals, silver,
gold, bronze, and iron, and many beautiful
clothes. Also, you have taken many things
from your enemies that you should divide
among yourselves."
9So the people from the tribes of Reuben,
Gad, and East Manasseh left the other
Israelites at Shiloh in Canaan and went back
to Gilead. It was their own land, given to
them by Moses as the LORD had commanded.
10The people of Reuben, Gad, and East
Manasseh went to Geliloth, near the Jordan
River in the land of Canaan. There they built
a beautiful altar. 11The other Israelites still at
Shiloh heard about the altar these three
tribes built at the border of Canaan at
Geliloth, near the Jordan River on Israel's
side. 12All the Israelites became very angry at
these three tribes, so they met together and
decided to fight them.
13The Israelites sent Phinehas son of
Eleazar the priest to Gilead to talk to the
people of Reuben, Gad, and East Manasseh.
14They also sent one leader from each of the
ten tribes at Shiloh. Each of them was a
leader of his family group of Israelites.
15These leaders went to Gilead to talk to
the people of Reuben, Gad, and East
Manasseh. They said: 16"All the Israelites ask
you: 'Why did you turn against the God of
Israel by building an altar for yourselves?
You know that this is against God's law.
17Remember what happened at Peor? We
still suffer today because of that sin, for
which God made many Israelites very sick.
18And now are you turning against the LORD
and refusing to follow him?
" 'If you don't stop what you're doing
today, the LORD will be angry with everyone
in Israel tomorrow. 19If your land is unclean,
come over into our land where the LORD's
Tent is. Share it with us. But don't turn
against the LORD and us by building another
altar for the LORD our God. 20Remember how
Achan son of Zerah refused to obey the
command about what must be completely
destroyed. That one man broke God's law, but
all the Israelites were punished. Achan died
because of his sin, but others also died.' "
21The people from Reuben, Gad, and East
Manasseh answered, 22"The LORD is God of
gods! The LORD is God of gods! God knows,
and we want you to know also. If we have
done something wrong, you may kill us. 23If
we broke God's law, we ask the LORD himself
to punish us. We did not build this altar to
offer burnt offerings or grain and fellowship
offerings.
24"We did not build it for that reason. We
feared that someday your people would not
accept us as part of your nation. Then they
might say, 'You cannot worship the LORD, the

God of Israel. 25The LORD made the Jordan
River a border between us and you people of
Reuben and Gad. You cannot worship the
LORD.' So we feared that your children might
make our children stop worshiping the
LORD.

26"That is why we decided to build this
altar. But it is not for burnt offerings and
sacrifices. 27This altar is proof to you and us
and to all our children who will come after
us that we worship the LORD with our whole
burnt offerings, grain, and fellowship
offerings. This was so your children would
not say to our children, 'You are not the
LORD's.'

28"In the future if your children say that,
our children can say, 'See the altar made by
our ancestors. It is exactly like the LORD's
altar, but we do not use it for sacrifices. It
shows that we are part of Israel.'

29"Truly, we don't want to be against the
LORD or to stop following him by building an
altar for burnt offerings, grain offerings, or
sacrifices. We know the only true altar to the
LORD our God is in front of the Holy Tent."

30When Phinehas the priest and the ten
leaders heard the people of Reuben, Gad, and
East Manasseh, they were pleased. 31So
Phinehas, son of Eleazar the priest, said,
"Now we know the LORD is with us and that
you didn't turn against him. Now the
Israelites will not be punished by the LORD."

32Then Phinehas and the leaders left the
people of Reuben and Gad in Gilead and
went back to Canaan where they told the
Israelites what had happened. 33They were
pleased and thanked God. So they decided
not to fight the people of Reuben and Gad
and destroy those lands.

34And the people of Reuben and Gad
named the altar Proof That We Believe the
LORD Is God.

The Last Words of Joshua

23 The LORD gave Israel peace from their
enemies around them. Many years
passed, and Joshua grew very old. 2He called
a meeting of all the elders, heads of families,
judges, and officers of Israel. He said, "I am
now very old. 3You have seen what the
LORD has done to our enemies to help us.
The LORD your God fought for you.
4Remember that your people have been
given their land between the Jordan River
and the Mediterranean Sea in the west, the
land I promised to give you. 5The LORD your
God will force out the people living there.
The LORD will push them out ahead of you.
And you will own the land, as he has
promised you.

6"Be strong. You must be careful to obey
everything commanded in the Book of the
Teachings of Moses. Do not stray from it
either from the left or the right. 7Don't
become friends with the people living
among us who are not Israelites. Don't say
the names of their gods or make anyone
swear by them. Don't serve or worship them.
8You must continue to follow the LORD your
God, as you have done in the past.

9"The LORD has forced many great and
powerful nations to leave ahead of you. No
nation has been able to defeat you. 10With
his help, one Israelite could defeat a
thousand, because the LORD your God fights
for you, as he promised to do. 11So you must
be careful to love the LORD your God.

12"If you turn away from the way of the
LORD and become friends with these people
who are not part of Israel and marry them,
13the LORD your God will not help you defeat
your enemies. They will be like traps for
you, like whips on your back and thorns
in your eyes, and none of you will be left
in this good land the LORD your God has
given you.

14"It's almost time for me to die. You know
and fully believe that the LORD has done
great things for you. You know that he has
not failed to keep any of his promises.
15Every good promise that the LORD your
God made has come true, and in the same
way, his other promises will come true. He
promised that evil will come to you and
that he will destroy you from this good
land that he gave you. 16This will happen if
you don't keep your agreement with the
LORD your God. If you go and serve other
gods and worship them, the LORD will
become very angry with you. Then none of
you will be left in this good land he has
given you."

24 Joshua gathered all the tribes of Israel
together at Shechem. He called the
elders, heads of families, judges, and officers
of Israel to stand before God.

2Then Joshua said to all the people,
"Here's what the LORD, the God of Israel, says

to you: 'A long time ago your ancestors lived
on the other side of the Euphrates River.
Terah, the father of Abraham and Nahor,
worshiped other gods. 3But I, the LORD, took
your ancestor Abraham from the other side
of the river and led him through the land of
Canaan. And I gave him many children,
including his son Isaac. 4I gave Isaac two
sons named Jacob and Esau. I gave the land
around the mountains of Edom to Esau, but
Jacob and his sons went down to Egypt.
5Then I sent Moses and Aaron to Egypt,
where I brought many disasters on the
Egyptians. Afterwards I brought you out.
6When I brought your ancestors out of
Egypt, they came to the Red Sea, and the
Egyptians chased them with chariots and
men on horses. 7So the people called out to
the LORD. And I brought darkness between
you and the Egyptians and made the sea to
cover them. You yourselves saw what I did to
the army of Egypt. After that, you lived in
the desert for a long time.

8" 'Then I brought you to the land of the
Amorites, east of the Jordan River. They
fought against you, but I handed them over
to you. I destroyed them before you, and you
took control of that land. 9But the king of
Moab, Balak son of Zippor, prepared to fight
against the Israelites. The king sent for
Balaam son of Beor to curse you, 10but I
refused to listen to Balaam. So he asked for
good things to happen to you! I saved you
and brought you out of his power.

11" 'Then you crossed the Jordan River and
came to Jericho, where the people of Jericho
fought against you. Also, the Amorites,
Perizzites, Canaanites, Hittites, Girgashites,
Hivites, and Jebusites fought against you.
But I handed them over to you. 12I sent terror
ahead of you to force out two Amorite kings.
You took the land without using swords and
bows. 13I gave you that land where you did
not have to work. I gave you cities that you
did not have to build. And now you live in
that land and in those cities, and you eat
from vineyards and olive trees that you did
not plant.' "

14Then Joshua said to the people, "Now
respect the LORD and serve him fully and
sincerely. Throw away the gods that your
ancestors worshiped on the other side of the
Euphrates River and in Egypt. Serve the
LORD. 15But if you don't want to serve the

devotion 68

JOSHUA 24:14–15

THE SAFEST PLACE I KNOW

Will you choose to serve God? If so, you will certainly be in the minority. Your friends might think you're weird. You'll probably have to go it alone some days. Even some of the folks at church are still trying to decide if they are really going to serve God.

You know that you can serve anything you like. You can serve yourself or your money or your kids or your hobby. You can spend years wandering around all over the world, looking for spiritual enlightenment. You can worship haute couture or immoral sex. God will let you do whatever you'd like, but he has clearly called you to choose him.

Have you ever made the decision to surrender each piece of yourself to God? Have you decided to make your heart a haven for the Spirit of God? Have you taken spiritual inventory of your relationships and the people who speak into your heart? What about your secret life? Are you clean? Are you serving God in private? Have you determined that no matter what it takes or where it leads, you and your family will serve the Lord?

God honors that kind of life. Joshua made the decision to serve God no matter what and God blessed him. God will also honor that choice in your life. It's a scary thing to live outside the covering of God's direction and protection. It's the safest place in all the world to choose God and live underneath the blessing of his unfailing love.

LORD, you must choose for yourselves today whom you will serve. You may serve the gods that your ancestors worshiped when they lived on the other side of the Euphrates River, or you may serve the gods of the Amorites who lived in this land. As for me and my family, we will serve the LORD."

[16]Then the people answered, "We will never stop following the LORD to serve other gods! [17]It was the LORD our God who brought our ancestors out of Egypt. We were slaves in that land, but the LORD did great things for us there. He brought us out and protected us while we traveled through other lands. [18]Then he forced out all the people living in these lands, even the Amorites. So we will serve the LORD, because he is our God."

[19]Then Joshua said, "You are not able to serve the LORD, because he is a holy God and a jealous God. If you turn against him and sin, he will not forgive you. [20]If you leave the LORD and serve other gods, he will send you great trouble. The LORD may have been good to you, but if you turn against him, he will destroy you."

[21]But the people said to Joshua, "No! We will serve the LORD."

[22]Then Joshua said, "You are your own witnesses that you have chosen to serve the LORD."

The people said, "Yes, we are."

[23]Then Joshua said, "Now throw away the gods that you have. Love the LORD, the God of Israel, with all your heart."

[24]Then the people said to Joshua, "We will serve the LORD our God, and we will obey him."

[25]On that day at Shechem Joshua made an agreement for the people. He made rules and laws for them to follow. [26]Joshua wrote these things in the Book of the Teachings of God. Then he took a large stone and set it up under the oak tree near the LORD's Holy Tent.

[27]Joshua said to all the people, "See this stone! It will remind you of what we did today. It was here the LORD spoke to us today. It will remind you of what happened so you will not turn against your God."

Joshua Dies

[28]Then Joshua sent the people back to their land.

[29]After that, Joshua son of Nun died at the age of one hundred ten. [30]They buried him in his own land at Timnath Serah, in the mountains of Ephraim, north of Mount Gaash.

[31]The Israelites served the LORD during the lifetime of Joshua and during the lifetimes of the elders who lived after Joshua who had seen what the LORD had done for Israel.

Joseph Comes Home

[32]When the Israelites left Egypt, they carried the bones of Joseph with them. They buried them at Shechem, in the land Jacob had bought for a hundred pieces of silver from the sons of Hamor (Hamor was the father of Shechem). This land now belonged to Joseph's children.

[33]And Eleazar son of Aaron died and was buried at Gibeah in the mountains of Ephraim, which had been given to Eleazar's son Phinehas.

Judges

Refers to the system of government God gave to the Israelites during this period of history

Person Holding the Pen God Wrote With: Technically the author is anonymous, although Jewish tradition holds that the prophet *Samuel* was the narrator God used.

When the Text Was Written: Since these events were recorded before Israel had a king (Judg. 17:6; 18:1; 21:25), the book of Judges was certainly written before Saul's coronation around 1043 B.C. And since the Jebusites were still the bullies in charge of Jerusalem (1:21), this story was put to paper prior to when King David conquered the holy city in 1004 B.C.

Spiritual Posture of the Original Recipients: There was no king on the throne in Israel, the Word of God was not being taught in the land, and everyone did what was right in his or her own eyes—a recipe for disaster! It was a season of spiritual disobedience and anarchy.

Storyline Synopsis: This book picks up where Joshua left off. God's people have entered the land he promised their ancestors, and just when you think they're going to settle down and show some spiritual maturity, the bottom drops out! Instead of living lives of humble gratitude to Jehovah, who rescued them from Egypt and kept them from harm in the desert, they forget his faithfulness. They pointedly ignore his commands and begin to frolic with pagan idols and cavort with people not belonging to God. The Israelites act like ungrateful, spoiled children.

A Moment Worth Discussing: Deborah's story in chapters 4—5 is a bright spot in this torrid journal of rebellion and debauchery. It's especially refreshing to read about a godly female leader in a period when women weren't even supposed to study Scripture, much less star in the role of God's chosen mouthpiece. Deborah's bravery outshines even that of the military brass in her day!

Interesting (But Likely to Be Overlooked) Character: *Jael,* another courageous chick, whose innovative use of a tent stake (Judg. 4:17–22) has been heralded by oppressed women throughout history. Her bravery makes you want to shout, "You go girl!" Her feat is memorialized in Deborah's victory song (5:24–27).

Judah Fights the Canaanites

1 After Joshua died, the Israelites asked the LORD, "Who will be first to go and fight for us against the Canaanites?"

2 The LORD said to them, "The tribe of Judah will go. I have handed the land over to them."

3 The men of Judah said to the men of Simeon, their relatives, "Come and help us fight the Canaanites for our land. If you do, we will go and help you fight for your land." So the men of Simeon went with them.

4 When Judah attacked, the LORD handed over the Canaanites and the Perizzites to them, and they defeated ten thousand men at the city of Bezek. 5 There they found Adoni-Bezek, the ruler of the city, and fought him. The men of Judah defeated the Canaanites and the Perizzites, 6 but Adoni-Bezek ran away. The men of Judah chased him, and when they caught him, they cut off his thumbs and big toes.

7 Adoni-Bezek said, "Seventy kings whose thumbs and big toes had been cut off used to eat scraps that fell from my table. Now God has paid me back for what I did to them." The men of Judah took Adoni-Bezek to Jerusalem, and he died there.

8 Then the men of Judah fought against Jerusalem and captured it. They attacked with their swords and burned the city.

9 Later, they went down to fight the Canaanites who lived in the mountains, in the dry country to the south, and in the western hills. 10 The men of Judah went to fight against the Canaanites in the city of Hebron (which used to be called Kiriath Arba). And they defeated Sheshai, Ahiman, and Talmai.

Caleb and His Daughter

11 Then they left there and went to fight against the people living in Debir. (In the past Debir had been called Kiriath Sepher.) 12 Before attacking the city, Caleb said, "I will give Acsah, my daughter, as a wife to the man who attacks and captures the city of Kiriath Sepher." 13 Othniel son of Kenaz, Caleb's younger brother, captured the city, so Caleb gave his daughter Acsah to Othniel to be his wife. 14 When Acsah came to Othniel, she told him to ask her father for a field. When she got down from her donkey, Caleb asked her, "What do you want?"

15 Acsah answered him, "Do me a special favor. Since you have given me land in southern Canaan, also give me springs of water." So Caleb gave her the upper and lower springs.

Fights with the Canaanites

16 The Kenite people, who were from the family of Moses' father-in-law, left Jericho, the city of palm trees. They went with the men of Judah to the Desert of Judah to live with them there in southern Judah near the city of Arad.

17 The men of Judah and the men of Simeon, their relatives, defeated the Canaanites who lived in Zephath. They completely destroyed the city, so they called it Hormah.[n] 18 The men of Judah captured Gaza, Ashkelon, Ekron, and the lands around them.

19 The LORD was with the men of Judah. They took the land in the mountains, but they could not force out the people living on the plain, because they had iron chariots. 20 As Moses had promised, Hebron was given to Caleb, and Caleb forced out the three sons of Anak. 21 But the people of Benjamin could not make the Jebusite people leave Jerusalem. Since that time the Jebusites have lived with the Benjaminites in Jerusalem.

22 The men of Joseph went to fight against the city of Bethel, and the LORD was with them. 23 They sent some spies to Bethel (which used to be called Luz). 24 The spies saw a man coming out of the city and said to him, "Show us a way into the city, and we will be kind to you." 25 So the man showed them the way into the city. The men of Joseph attacked with swords the people in Bethel, but they let the man and his family go free. 26 He went to the land where the Hittites lived and built a city. He named it Luz, which it is called even today.

27 There were Canaanites living in the cities of Beth Shan, Taanach, Dor, Ibleam, Megiddo, and the small towns around them. The people of Manasseh did not force those people out of their towns, because the Canaanites were determined to stay there. 28 Later, the Israelites

1:17 Hormah Hormah sounds like the Hebrew word meaning "to destroy completely."

grew strong and forced the Canaanites to
work as slaves, but they did not make all the
Canaanites leave their land. 29The people of
Ephraim did not force out all of the
Canaanites living in Gezer. So the Canaanites
continued to live in Gezer with the people of
Ephraim. 30The people of Zebulun did not
force out the Canaanites living in the cities of
Kitron and Nahalol. They stayed and lived
with the people of Zebulun, but Zebulun
made them work as slaves.

31The people of Asher did not force the
Canaanites from the cities of Acco, Sidon,
Ahlab, Aczib, Helbah, Aphek, and Rehob.
32Since the people of Asher did not force
them out, the Canaanites continued to live
with them. 33The people of Naphtali did not
force out the people of the cities of Beth
Shemesh and Beth Anath. So they continued
to live with the Canaanites in those cities,
and the Canaanites worked as slaves. 34The
Amorites forced the Danites back into the
mountains and would not let them come
down to live in the plain. 35The Amorites
were determined to stay in Mount Heres,
Aijalon, and Shaalbim. But when the
Israelites grew stronger, they made the
Amorites work as slaves. 36The land of the
Amorites was from Scorpion Pass to Sela and
beyond.

The Angel of the Lord at Bokim

2 The angel of the LORD went up from
Gilgal to Bokim and said, "I brought you
up from Egypt and led you to the land I
promised to give your ancestors. I said, 'I will
never break my agreement with you. 2But
you must not make an agreement with the
people who live in this land. You must
destroy their altars.' But you did not obey
me. How could you do this? 3Now I tell you,
'I will not force out the people in this land.
They will be your enemies, and their gods
will be a trap for you.' "

4After the angel gave Israel this message
from the LORD, they cried loudly. 5So they
named the place Bokim.[n] There they offered
sacrifices to the LORD.

Joshua Dies

6Then Joshua sent the people back to their
land. 7The people served the LORD during the
lifetime of Joshua and during the lifetimes of
the elders who lived after Joshua and who
had seen what great things the LORD had
done for Israel. 8Joshua son of Nun, the
servant of the LORD, died at the age of one
hundred ten. 9They buried him in his own
land at Timnath Serah in the mountains of
Ephraim, north of Mount Gaash.

The People Disobey

10After those people had died, their
children grew up and did not know the LORD
or what he had done for Israel. 11So they did
what the LORD said was wrong, and they
worshiped the Baal idols. 12They quit
following the LORD, the God of their
ancestors who had brought them out of
Egypt. They began to worship the gods of
the people who lived around them, and that
made the LORD angry. 13The Israelites quit
following the LORD and worshiped Baal and
Ashtoreth. 14The LORD was angry with the
people of Israel, so he handed them over to
robbers who took their possessions. He let
their enemies who lived around them defeat
them; they could not protect themselves.
15When the Israelites went out to fight, they
always lost, because the LORD was not with
them. The LORD had sworn to them this
would happen. So the Israelites suffered very
much.

God Chooses Judges

16Then the LORD chose leaders called
judges,[n] who saved the Israelites from the
robbers. 17But the Israelites did not listen to
their judges. They were not faithful to God
but worshiped other gods instead. Their
ancestors had obeyed the LORD's commands,
but they quickly turned away and did not
obey. 18When their enemies hurt them, the
Israelites cried for help. So the LORD felt
sorry for them and sent judges to save them
from their enemies. The LORD was with those
judges all their lives. 19But when the judges
died, the Israelites again sinned and
worshiped other gods. They became worse
than their ancestors. The Israelites were very
stubborn and refused to change their evil
ways.

20So the LORD became angry with the
Israelites. He said, "These people have

2:5 Bokim This name means "crying." **2:16 judges** They were not judges in courts of law, but leaders of the people in times of emergency.

Deborah

JUDGES 4

She summons him and Barak rushes at once to her tent. Deborah is a prophetess, judge, and the leader of Israel. She is wise and just in settling disputes. "The Lord, the God of Israel, commands you," she tells him.

Barak listens to her words. He is to lead an army of men to Mount Tabor. He is thoughtful and slow to respond: "I will go if you will go with me, but if you won't go with me, I won't go." He understands that God speaks through this woman and that she will be given wisdom and direction for the battle at hand. He will fight and she will prophesy. He will band together a strong military army, and she will be the spiritual warrior! Together they will make a formidable team. She rises and assures him that she will go.

"Get up!" Deborah says to Barak one day. "Today is the day the Lord will hand over Sisera. The Lord has already cleared the way for you." They know their foe is mighty and many in numbers, much greater than their ten thousand men. But without hesitation, Barak leads his men. The Lord has spoken through Deborah and given them a victory celebration even before they fight the battle!

Deborah listened for the voice of God and shared his words with others. She trusted him implicitly, so much so that Barak knew he must take her with him into battle. Do others see your unwavering trust in God?

broken the agreement I made with their ancestors. They have not listened to me. 21I will no longer defeat the nations who were left when Joshua died. 22I will use them to test Israel, to see if Israel will keep the LORD's commands as their ancestors did." 23In the past the LORD had permitted those nations to stay in the land. He did not quickly force them out or help Joshua's army defeat them.

3 These are the nations the LORD did not force to leave. He wanted to test the Israelites who had not fought in the wars of Canaan. 2(The only reason the LORD left those nations in the land was to teach the descendants of the Israelites who had not fought in those wars how to fight.) 3These are the nations: the five rulers of the Philistines, all the Canaanites, the people of Sidon, and the Hivites who lived in the Lebanon mountains from Mount Baal Hermon to Lebo Hamath. 4Those nations were in the land to test the Israelites—to see if they would obey the commands the LORD had given to their ancestors by Moses.

5The people of Israel lived with the Canaanites, Hittites, Amorites, Perizzites, Hivites, and Jebusites. 6The Israelites began to marry the daughters of those people, and they allowed their daughters to marry the sons of those people. Israel also served their gods.

Othniel, the First Judge

7The Israelites did what the LORD said was wrong. They forgot about the LORD their God and served the idols of Baal and Asherah. 8So the LORD was angry with Israel and allowed Cushan-Rishathaim king of Northwest Mesopotamia to rule over the Israelites for eight years. 9When Israel cried to the LORD, the LORD sent someone to save them. Othniel son of Kenaz, Caleb's younger brother, saved the Israelites. 10The Spirit of the LORD entered Othniel, and he became Israel's judge. When he went to war, the LORD handed over to him Cushan-Rishathaim king of Northwest Mesopotamia. 11So the land was at peace for forty years. Then Othniel son of Kenaz died.

Ehud, the Judge

12Again the people of Israel did what the LORD said was wrong. So the LORD gave Eglon

king of Moab power to defeat Israel because
of the evil Israel did. 13Eglon got the
Ammonites and the Amalekites to join him.
Then he attacked Israel and took Jericho, the
city of palm trees. 14So the people of Israel
were ruled by Eglon king of Moab for
eighteen years.

15When the people cried to the LORD, he
sent someone to save them. He was Ehud,
son of Gera from the people of Benjamin,
who was left-handed. Israel sent Ehud to
give Eglon king of Moab the payment he
demanded. 16Ehud made himself a sword
with two edges, about eighteen inches long,
and he tied it to his right hip under his
clothes. 17Ehud gave Eglon king of Moab the
payment he demanded. Now Eglon was a
very fat man. 18After he had given Eglon the
payment, Ehud sent away the people who
had carried it. 19When he passed the statues
near Gilgal, he turned around and said to
Eglon, "I have a secret message for you, King
Eglon."

The king said, "Be quiet!" Then he sent all
of his servants out of the room. 20Ehud went
to King Eglon, as he was sitting alone in the
room above his summer palace.

Ehud said, "I have a message from God for
you." As the king stood up from his chair,
21Ehud reached with his left hand and took
out the sword that was tied to his right hip.
Then he stabbed the sword deep into the
king's belly! 22Even the handle sank in, and
the blade came out his back. The king's fat
covered the whole sword, so Ehud left the
sword in Eglon. 23Then he went out of the
room and closed and locked the doors
behind him.

24When the servants returned just after
Ehud left, they found the doors to the room
locked. So they thought the king was
relieving himself. 25They waited for a long
time. Finally they became worried because
he still had not opened the doors. So they got
the key and unlocked them and saw their
king lying dead on the floor!

26While the servants were waiting, Ehud
had escaped. He passed by the statues and
went to Seirah. 27When he reached the
mountains of Ephraim he blew the trumpet.
The people of Israel heard it and went down
from the hills with Ehud leading them.

28He said to them, "Follow me! The LORD
has helped you to defeat your enemies, the
Moabites." So Israel followed Ehud and
captured the crossings of the Jordan River.
They did not allow the Moabites to cross the
Jordan River. 29Israel killed about ten
thousand strong and able men from Moab;
not one escaped. 30So that day Moab was
forced to be under the rule of Israel, and
there was peace in the land for eighty years.

Shamgar, the Judge

31After Ehud, Shamgar son of Anath saved
Israel. Shamgar killed six hundred
Philistines with a sharp stick used to guide
oxen.

Deborah, the Woman Judge

4 After Ehud died, the Israelites again did
what the LORD said was wrong. 2So he let
Jabin, a king of Canaan who ruled in the city
of Hazor, defeat Israel. Sisera, who lived in
Harosheth Haggoyim, was the commander
of Jabin's army. 3Because he had nine
hundred iron chariots and was very cruel to
the people of Israel for twenty years, they
cried to the LORD for help.

4A prophetess named Deborah, the wife of
Lappidoth, was judge of Israel at that time.
5Deborah would sit under the Palm Tree of
Deborah, which was between the cities of
Ramah and Bethel, in the mountains of
Ephraim. And the people of Israel would
come to her to settle their arguments.

6Deborah sent a message to Barak son of
Abinoam. Barak lived in the city of Kedesh,
which is in the area of Naphtali. Deborah
said to Barak, "The LORD, the God of Israel,
commands you: 'Go and gather ten thousand
men of Naphtali and Zebulun and lead them
to Mount Tabor. 7I will make Sisera, the
commander of Jabin's army, and his chariots,
and his army meet you at the Kishon River. I
will hand Sisera over to you.' "

8Then Barak said to Deborah, "I will go if
you will go with me, but if you won't go
with me, I won't go."

9"Of course I will go with you," Deborah
answered, "but you will not get credit for the
victory. The LORD will let a woman defeat
Sisera." So Deborah went with Barak to
Kedesh. 10At Kedesh, Barak called the people
of Zebulun and Naphtali together. From
them, he gathered ten thousand men to
follow him, and Deborah went with him
also.

devotion 69

JUDGES 4:4–10

HOMEMAKER AND SOLDIER?

If ever there were a woman in the Bible I would like to resemble, it would be Deborah. Deborah's stellar reputation was known all throughout Israel, and the list of her qualities included power, wisdom, and fair judgment. Deborah not only had trust in her Lord but she also sought the Lord with everything she had. She took her responsibilities of judging the matters of Israel as a privilege and wanted to make sure only the counsel of the Lord would be rendered. Even Barak would not go into battle without her. He did not need her physical strength, but her spiritual strength.

The thing I love most about Deborah is that she was married. Although she was judge of Israel, she still had wifely duties to fulfill and a man that needed her as a companion and desired her as a lover. We can be strong and wise women with leadership skills that are powerful, yet submissive in spirit to the Lord and especially our husbands. When my husband goes into battle to win souls for Christ, I want to make sure he knows that I am right there with him—not ahead of him that he needs to catch up, not behind him that I would drag him down, but right in step with him. We might not be riding a horse to Mount Tabor like Deborah, but we are in the battle, and I think it would benefit us all to be trained by her example.

[11]Now Heber the Kenite had left the other
Kenites, the descendants of Hobab, Moses'
brother-in-law. Heber had put up his tent by
the great tree in Zaanannim, near Kedesh.
[12]When Sisera was told that Barak son of
Abinoam had gone to Mount Tabor, [13]Sisera
gathered his nine hundred iron chariots and
all the men with him, from Harosheth
Haggoyim to the Kishon River.
[14]Then Deborah said to Barak, "Get up!
Today is the day the LORD will hand over
Sisera. The LORD has already cleared the way
for you." So Barak led ten thousand men
down Mount Tabor. [15]As Barak approached,
the LORD confused Sisera and his army and
chariots. The LORD defeated them with the
sword, but Sisera left his chariot and ran away
on foot. [16]Barak and his men chased Sisera's
chariots and army to Harosheth Haggoyim.
With their swords they killed all of Sisera's
men; not one of them was left alive.
[17]But Sisera himself ran away to the tent
where Jael lived. She was the wife of Heber,
one of the Kenite family groups. Heber's
family was at peace with Jabin king of Hazor.
[18]Jael went out to meet Sisera and said to
him, "Come into my tent, master! Come in.
Don't be afraid." So Sisera went into Jael's
tent, and she covered him with a rug.
[19]Sisera said to Jael, "I am thirsty. Please
give me some water to drink." So she opened
a leather bag of milk and gave him a drink.
Then she covered him up.
[20]He said to her, "Go stand at the entrance
to the tent. If anyone comes and asks you, 'Is
anyone here?' say, 'No.' "
[21]But Jael, the wife of Heber, took a tent
peg and a hammer and quietly went to
Sisera. Since he was very tired, he was in a
deep sleep. She hammered the tent peg
through the side of Sisera's head and into the
ground. And so Sisera died.
[22]At that very moment Barak came by
Jael's tent, chasing Sisera. Jael went out to
meet him and said, "Come. I will show you
the man you are looking for." So Barak
entered her tent, and there Sisera lay dead,
with the tent peg in his head.

23On that day God defeated Jabin king of
Canaan in the sight of Israel.
24Israel became stronger and stronger
against Jabin king of Canaan until finally
they destroyed him.

The Song of Deborah

5 On that day Deborah and Barak son of Abinoam sang this song:

2"The leaders led Israel.
The people volunteered to go to battle.
Praise the LORD!
3Listen, kings.
Pay attention, rulers!
I myself will sing to the LORD.
I will make music to the LORD, the God of Israel.

4"LORD, when you came from Edom,
when you marched from the land of Edom,
the earth shook,
the skies rained,
and the clouds dropped water.
5The mountains shook before the LORD, the God of Mount Sinai,
before the LORD, the God of Israel!

6"In the days of Shamgar son of Anath,
in the days of Jael, the main roads were empty.
Travelers went on the back roads.
7There were no warriors in Israel
until I, Deborah, arose,
until I arose to be a mother to Israel.
8At that time they chose to follow new gods.
Because of this, enemies fought us at our city gates.
No one could find a shield or a spear
among the forty thousand people of Israel.
9My heart is with the commanders of Israel.
They volunteered freely from among the people.
Praise the LORD!

10"You who ride on white donkeys
and sit on saddle blankets,
and you who walk along the road, listen!
11Listen to the sound of the singers
at the watering holes.
There they tell about the victories of the LORD,
the victories of the LORD's warriors in Israel.
Then the LORD's people went down to the city gates.

12"Wake up, wake up, Deborah!
Wake up, wake up, sing a song!
Get up, Barak!
Go capture your enemies, son of Abinoam!

13"Then those who were left came down to the important leaders.
The LORD's people came down to me with strong men.
14They came from Ephraim in the mountains of Amalek.
Benjamin was among the people who followed you.
From the family group of Makir, the commanders came down.
And from Zebulun came those who lead.
15The princes of Issachar were with Deborah.
The people of Issachar were loyal to Barak
and followed him into the valley.
The Reubenites thought hard
about what they would do.
16Why did you stay by the sheepfold?
Was it to hear the music played for your sheep?
The Reubenites thought hard
about what they would do.
17The people of Gilead stayed east of the Jordan River.
People of Dan, why did you stay by the ships?
The people of Asher stayed at the seashore,
at their safe harbors.
18But the people of Zebulun risked their lives,
as did the people of Naphtali on the battlefield.

19"The kings came, and they fought.
At that time the kings of Canaan fought
at Taanach, by the waters of Megiddo.
But they took away no silver or possessions of Israel.
20The stars fought from heaven;
from their paths, they fought Sisera.

[21]The Kishon River swept Sisera's men away,
that old river, the Kishon River.
March on, my soul, with strength!
[22]Then the horses' hoofs beat the ground.
Galloping, galloping go Sisera's mighty horses.
[23]'May the town of Meroz be cursed,' said the angel of the LORD.
'Bitterly curse its people,
because they did not come to help the LORD.
They did not fight the strong enemy.'

[24]"May Jael, the wife of Heber the Kenite,
be blessed above all women who live in tents.
[25]Sisera asked for water,
but Jael gave him milk.
In a bowl fit for a ruler,
she brought him cream.
[26]Jael reached out and took the tent peg.
Her right hand reached for the workman's hammer.
She hit Sisera! She smashed his head!
She crushed and pierced the side of his head!
[27]At Jael's feet he sank.
He fell, and he lay there.
At her feet he sank. He fell.
Where Sisera sank, there he fell, dead!

[28]"Sisera's mother looked out through the window.
She looked through the curtains and cried out,
'Why is Sisera's chariot so late in coming?
Why are sounds of his chariots' horses delayed?'
[29]The wisest of her servant ladies answer her,
and Sisera's mother says to herself,
[30]'Surely they are robbing the people they defeated!
Surely they are dividing those things among themselves!
Each soldier is given a girl or two.
Maybe Sisera is taking pieces of dyed cloth.
Maybe they are even taking
pieces of dyed, embroidered cloth for the necks of the victors!'

[31]"Let all your enemies die this way, LORD!
But let all the people who love you
be as strong as the rising sun!"

Then there was peace in the land for forty
years.

The Midianites Attack Israel

6 Again the Israelites did what the LORD
said was wrong. So for seven years the
LORD handed them over to Midian. [2]Because
the Midianites were very powerful and were
cruel to Israel, the Israelites made hiding
places in the mountains, in caves, and in
safe places. [3]Whenever the Israelites planted
crops, the Midianites, Amalekites, and other
peoples from the east would come and
attack them. [4]They camped in the land and
destroyed the crops that the Israelites had
planted as far away as Gaza. They left
nothing for Israel to eat, and no sheep,
cattle, or donkeys. [5]The Midianites came
with their tents and their animals like
swarms of locusts to ruin the land. There
were so many people and camels they could
not be counted. [6]Israel became very poor
because of the Midianites, so they cried out
to the LORD.

[7]When the Israelites cried out to the LORD
against the Midianites, [8]the LORD sent a
prophet to them. He said, "This is what the
LORD, the God of Israel, says: I brought you
out of Egypt, the land of slavery. [9]I saved you
from the Egyptians and from all those who
were against you. I forced the Canaanites out
of their land and gave it to you. [10]Then I said
to you, 'I am the LORD your God. Live in the
land of the Amorites, but do not worship
their gods.' But you did not obey me."

The Angel of the Lord Visits Gideon

[11]The angel of the LORD came and sat
down under the oak tree at Ophrah that
belonged to Joash, one of the Abiezrite
people. Gideon, Joash's son, was separating
some wheat from the chaff in a winepress to
keep the wheat from the Midianites. [12]The
angel of the LORD appeared to Gideon and
said, "The LORD is with you, mighty warrior!"

[13]Then Gideon said, "Sir, if the LORD is
with us, why are we having so much
trouble? Where are the miracles our
ancestors told us he did when the LORD
brought them out of Egypt? But now he has
left us and has handed us over to the
Midianites."

[14]The LORD turned to Gideon and said, "Go
with your strength and save Israel from the

Midianites. I am the one who is sending
you."

15But Gideon answered, "Lord, how can I
save Israel? My family group is the weakest
in Manasseh, and I am the least important
member of my family."

16The LORD answered him, "I will be with
you. It will seem as if the Midianites you are
fighting are only one man."

17Then Gideon said to the LORD, "If you are
pleased with me, give me proof that it is
really you talking with me. 18Please wait
here until I come back to you. Let me bring
my offering and set it in front of you."

And the LORD said, "I will wait until you
return."

19So Gideon went in and cooked a young
goat, and with twenty quarts of flour, made
bread without yeast. Then he put the meat
into a basket and the broth into a pot. He
brought them out and gave them to the
angel under the oak tree.

20The angel of God said to Gideon, "Put
the meat and the bread without yeast on
that rock over there. Then pour the broth on
them." And Gideon did as he was told. 21The
angel of the LORD touched the meat and the
bread with the end of the stick that was in
his hand. Then fire jumped up from the rock
and completely burned up the meat and the
bread! And the angel of the LORD
disappeared! 22Then Gideon understood he
had been talking to the angel of the LORD. So
Gideon cried out, "Lord GOD! I have seen the
angel of the LORD face to face!"

23But the LORD said to Gideon, "Calm
down! Don't be afraid! You will not die!"

24So Gideon built an altar there to
worship the LORD and named it The LORD Is
Peace. It still stands at Ophrah, where the
Abiezrites live.

Gideon Tears Down the Altar of Baal

25That same night the LORD said to
Gideon, "Take the bull that belongs to your
father and a second bull seven years old. Pull
down your father's altar to Baal, and cut
down the Asherah idol beside it. 26Then
build an altar to the LORD your God with its
stones in the right order on this high

devotion 70

JUDGES 6:23–24

PEACE? ARE YOU KIDDING?

The story of Gideon is such an encouragement because Gideon says exactly what most of us would have wanted to say in the same situation. The angel of the Lord comes to him and says, "The Lord is with you, mighty warrior" (Judg. 6:12).

Watch how Gideon answers: "If the Lord is with us, why are we having so much trouble?" (6:13). He sounds a bit frustrated, doesn't he? Then the angel of the Lord says, "Go with your strength and save Israel" (6:14).

I love Gideon's response. You can almost hear the panic in his voice as he starts telling God that he's chosen the wrong man for this job. Gideon considers himself the weakest member of his family, which is the weakest family in the tribe of Manasseh. The fact is, that is probably why God chose him in the first place.

But Gideon is still in denial, so he basically asks God for a miracle: "Give me proof that it is really you talking with me" (6:17). And once God gives him that proof, he begins to panic again. I love the Lord's words to Gideon at this point: "Calm down! Don't be afraid!" (6:23). With those words, the peace of God comes over Gideon like he has never experienced before. "The Lord Is Peace," Gideon says (6:24).

What in your life brings that feeling of panic? God wants to replace your panic with peace. Spend time in prayer today asking God for this gift that he truly wants to give you.

ground. Kill and burn a second bull on this
altar, using the wood from the Asherah idol."
27So Gideon got ten of his servants and did
what the LORD had told him to do. But
Gideon was afraid that his family and the
men of the city might see him, so he did it at
night, not in the daytime.
28When the men of the city got up the
next morning, they saw that the altar for
Baal had been destroyed and that the
Asherah idol beside it had been cut down!
They also saw the altar Gideon had built and
the second bull that had been sacrificed on
it. 29The men of the city asked each other,
"Who did this?"
After they asked many questions, someone
told them, "Gideon son of Joash did this."
30So they said to Joash, "Bring your son
out. He has pulled down the altar of Baal and
cut down the Asherah idol beside it. He must
die!"
31But Joash said to the angry crowd around
him, "Are you going to take Baal's side? Are
you going to defend him? Anyone who takes
Baal's side will be killed by morning! If Baal is
a god, let him fight for himself. It's his altar
that has been pulled down." 32So on that day
Gideon got the name Jerub-Baal, which
means "let Baal fight against him," because
Gideon pulled down Baal's altar.

Gideon Defeats Midian

33All the Midianites, the Amalekites, and
other peoples from the east joined together
and came across the Jordan River and
camped in the Valley of Jezreel. 34But the
Spirit of the LORD entered Gideon, and he
blew a trumpet to call the Abiezrites to
follow him. 35He sent messengers to all of
Manasseh, calling them to follow him. He
also sent messengers to the people of Asher,
Zebulun, and Naphtali. So they also went up
to meet Gideon and his men.
36Then Gideon said to God, "You said you
would help me save Israel. 37I will put some
wool on the threshing floor. If there is dew
only on the wool but all of the ground is dry,
then I will know that you will use me to
save Israel, as you said." 38And that is just
what happened. When Gideon got up early
the next morning and squeezed the wool, he
got a full bowl of water from it.
39Then Gideon said to God, "Don't be
angry with me if I ask just one more thing.
Please let me make one more test. Let
only the wool be dry while the ground
around it gets wet with dew." 40That night
God did that very thing. Just the wool was
dry, but the ground around it was wet with
dew.

7 Early in the morning Jerub-Baal (also
called Gideon) and all his men set up
their camp at the spring of Harod. The
Midianites were camped north of them in
the valley at the bottom of the hill called
Moreh. 2Then the LORD said to Gideon, "You
have too many men to defeat the Midianites.
I don't want the Israelites to brag that they
saved themselves. 3So now, announce to the
people, 'Anyone who is afraid may leave
Mount Gilead and go back home.' " So
twenty-two thousand men returned home,
but ten thousand remained.
4Then the LORD said to Gideon, "There are
still too many men. Take the men down to
the water, and I will test them for you there.
If I say, 'This man will go with you, he will
go. But if I say, 'That one will not go with
you,' he will not go."
5So Gideon led the men down to the
water. There the LORD said to him, "Separate
them into those who drink water by lapping
it up like a dog and those who bend down to
drink." 6There were three hundred men who
used their hands to bring water to their
mouths, lapping it as a dog does. All the rest
got down on their knees to drink.
7Then the LORD said to Gideon, "Using the
three hundred men who lapped the water, I
will save you and hand Midian over to you.
Let all the others go home." 8So Gideon sent
the rest of Israel to their homes. But he kept
three hundred men and took the jars and the
trumpets of those who left.
Now the camp of Midian was in the
valley below Gideon. 9That night the LORD
said to Gideon, "Get up. Go down and
attack the camp of the Midianites, because I
will give them to you. 10But if you are afraid
to go down, take your servant Purah with
you. 11When you come to the camp of
Midian, you will hear what they are saying.
Then you will not be afraid to attack the
camp."

Gideon Is Encouraged

So Gideon and his servant Purah went
down to the edge of the enemy camp. 12The

Midianites, the Amalekites, and all the
peoples from the east were camped in that
valley. There were so many of them they
seemed like locusts. Their camels could not
be counted because they were as many as
the grains of sand on the seashore!
13When Gideon came to the enemy camp,
he heard a man telling his friend about a
dream. He was saying, "I dreamed that a loaf
of barley bread rolled into the camp of
Midian. It hit the tent so hard that the tent
turned over and fell flat!"
14The man's friend said, "Your dream is
about the sword of Gideon son of Joash, a
man of Israel. God will hand Midian and the
whole army over to him!"
15When Gideon heard about the dream
and what it meant, he worshiped God. Then
Gideon went back to the camp of Israel and
called out to them, "Get up! The LORD has
handed the army of Midian over to you!"
16Gideon divided the three hundred men
into three groups. He gave each man a
trumpet and an empty jar with a burning
torch inside.
17Gideon told the men, "Watch me and do
what I do. When I get to the edge of the
camp, do what I do. 18Surround the enemy
camp. When I and everyone with me blow
our trumpets, you blow your trumpets, too.
Then shout, 'For the LORD and for Gideon!' "

Midian Is Defeated

19So Gideon and the one hundred men
with him came to the edge of the enemy
camp just after they had changed guards. It
was during the middle watch of the night.
Then Gideon and his men blew their
trumpets and smashed their jars. 20All three
groups of Gideon's men blew their trumpets
and smashed their jars. They held the
torches in their left hands and the trumpets
in their right hands. Then they shouted, "A
sword for the LORD and for Gideon!" 21Each
of Gideon's men stayed in his place around
the camp, but the Midianites began shouting
and running to escape.
22When Gideon's three hundred men
blew their trumpets, the LORD made all the
Midianites fight each other with their
swords! The enemy army ran away to the
city of Beth Shittah toward Zererah. They
ran as far as the border of Abel Meholah,
near the city of Tabbath. 23Then men of
Israel from Naphtali, Asher, and all of
Manasseh were called out to chase the
Midianites. 24Gideon sent messengers
through all the mountains of Ephraim,
saying, "Come down and attack the
Midianites. Take control of the Jordan River
as far as Beth Barah before the Midianites
can get to it."

So they called out all the men of Ephraim,
who took control of the Jordan River as far as
Beth Barah. 25The men of Ephraim captured
two princes of Midian named Oreb and
Zeeb. They killed Oreb at the rock of Oreb
and Zeeb at the winepress of Zeeb, and
they continued chasing the Midianites.
They brought the heads of Oreb and Zeeb
to Gideon, who was east of the Jordan
River.

8 The men of Ephraim asked Gideon, "Why
did you treat us this way? Why didn't
you call us when you went to fight against
Midian?" They argued angrily with Gideon.
2But he answered them, "I have not done
as well as you! The small part you did was
better than all that my people of Abiezer did.
3God let you capture Oreb and Zeeb, the
princes of Midian. How can I compare what
I did with what you did?" When the men of
Ephraim heard Gideon's answer, they were
not as angry anymore.

Gideon Captures Two Kings

4When Gideon and his three hundred
men came to the Jordan River, they were
tired, but they chased the enemy across to
the other side. 5Gideon said to the men of
Succoth, "Please give my soldiers some
bread because they are very tired. I am
chasing Zebah and Zalmunna, the kings of
Midian."
6But the leaders of Succoth said, "Why
should we give your soldiers bread? You
haven't caught Zebah and Zalmunna yet."
7Then Gideon said, "The LORD will
surrender Zebah and Zalmunna to me. After
that, I will whip your skin with thorns and
briers from the desert."
8Gideon left Succoth and went to the city
of Peniel and asked them for food. But the
people of Peniel gave him the same answer
as the people of Succoth. 9So Gideon said to
the men of Peniel, "After I win the victory, I
will return and pull down this tower."
10Zebah and Zalmunna and their army

were in the city of Karkor. About fifteen
thousand men were left of the armies of the
peoples of the east. Already one hundred
twenty thousand soldiers had been killed.
11Gideon went up the road of those who live
in tents east of Nobah and Jogbehah, and he
attacked the enemy army when they did not
expect it. 12Zebah and Zalmunna, the kings
of Midian, ran away, but Gideon chased and
captured them and frightened away their
army.

13Then Gideon son of Joash returned from
the battle by the Pass of Heres. 14Gideon
captured a young man from Succoth and
asked him some questions. So the young
man wrote down for Gideon the names of
seventy-seven officers and elders of Succoth.

Gideon Punishes Succoth

15When Gideon came to Succoth, he said
to the people of that city, "Here are Zebah
and Zalmunna. You made fun of me by
saying, 'Why should we give bread to your
tired men? You have not caught Zebah and
Zalmunna yet.' " 16So Gideon took the elders
of the city and punished them with thorns
and briers from the desert. 17He also pulled
down the tower of Peniel and killed the
people in that city.

18Gideon asked Zebah and Zalmunna,
"What were the men like that you killed on
Mount Tabor?"

They answered, "They were like you. Each
one of them looked like a prince."

19Gideon said, "Those were my brothers,
my mother's sons. As surely as the LORD lives,
I would not kill you if you had spared them."
20Then Gideon said to Jether, his oldest son,
"Kill them." But Jether was only a boy and
was afraid, so he did not take out his sword.

21Then Zebah and Zalmunna said to
Gideon, "Come on. Kill us yourself. As the
saying goes, 'It takes a man to do a man's
job.' " So Gideon got up and killed Zebah and
Zalmunna and took the decorations off their
camels' necks.

Gideon Makes an Idol

22The people of Israel said to Gideon, "You
saved us from the Midianites. Now, we want
you and your son and your grandson to rule
over us."

23But Gideon told them, "The LORD will be
your ruler. I will not rule over you, nor will
my son rule over you." 24He said, "I want you
to do this one thing for me. I want each of
you to give me a gold earring from the
things you took in the fighting." (The
Ishmaelites[n] wore gold earrings.)

25They said, "We will gladly give you what
you want." So they spread out a coat, and
everyone threw down an earring from what
he had taken. 26The gold earrings weighed
about forty-three pounds. This did not count
the decorations, necklaces, and purple robes
worn by the kings of Midian, nor the chains
from the camels' necks. 27Gideon used the
gold to make a holy vest, which he put in his
hometown of Ophrah. But all the Israelites
were unfaithful to God and worshiped it, so
it became a trap for Gideon and his family.

The Death of Gideon

28So Midian was under the rule of Israel;
they did not cause trouble anymore. And the
land had peace for forty years, as long as
Gideon was alive.

29Gideon[n] son of Joash went to his home
to live. 30He had seventy sons of his own,
because he had many wives. 31He had a slave
woman who lived in Shechem, and he had a
son by her, whom he named Abimelech. 32So
Gideon son of Joash died at a good old age.
He was buried in the tomb of Joash, his
father, in Ophrah, where the Abiezrites live.

33As soon as Gideon died, the people of
Israel were again unfaithful to God and
followed the Baals. They made Baal-Berith
their god. 34The Israelites did not remember
the LORD their God, who had saved them
from all their enemies living all around
them. 35And they were not kind to the
family of Jerub-Baal, also called Gideon, for
all the good he had done for Israel.

Abimelech Becomes King

9 Abimelech son of Gideon went to his
uncles in the city of Shechem. He said to
his uncles and all of his mother's family
group, 2"Ask the leaders of Shechem, 'Is it
better for the seventy sons of Gideon to rule
over you or for one man to rule?' Remember,
I am your relative."

3Abimelech's uncles spoke to all the

8:24 Ishmaelites Another name for the Midianites. See Genesis 37:25–28. **8:29 Gideon** Also called Jerub-Baal.

leaders of Shechem about this. And they
decided to follow Abimelech, because they
said, "He is our relative." 4 So the leaders of
Shechem gave Abimelech about one and
three-quarter pounds of silver from the
temple of the god Baal-Berith. Abimelech
used the silver to hire some worthless,
reckless men, who followed him wherever
he went. 5 He went to Ophrah, the
hometown of his father, and murdered his
seventy brothers, the sons of Gideon. He
killed them all on one stone. But Gideon's
youngest son, Jotham, hid from Abimelech
and escaped. 6 Then all of the leaders of
Shechem and Beth Millo gathered beside the
great tree standing in Shechem. There they
made Abimelech their king.

Jotham's Story

7 When Jotham heard this, he went and
stood on the top of Mount Gerizim. He
shouted to the people: "Listen to me, you
leaders of Shechem, so that God will listen to
you! 8 One day the trees decided to appoint a
king to rule over them. They said to the olive
tree, 'You be king over us!'
9 "But the olive tree said, 'Men and gods are
honored by my oil. Should I stop making it
and go and sway over the other trees?'
10 "Then the trees said to the fig tree,
'Come and be king over us!'
11 "But the fig tree answered, 'Should I stop
making my sweet and good fruit and go and
sway over the other trees?'
12 "Then the trees said to the vine, 'Come
and be king over us!'
13 "But the vine answered, 'My new wine
makes men and gods happy. Should I stop
making it and go and sway over the trees?'
14 "Then all the trees said to the thornbush,
'Come and be king over us.'
15 "But the thornbush said to the trees, 'If
you really want to appoint me king over
you, come and find shelter in my shade! But
if not, let fire come out of the thornbush and
burn up the cedars of Lebanon!'
16 "Now, were you completely honest and
sincere when you made Abimelech king?
Have you been fair to Gideon[n] and his
family? Have you treated Gideon as you
should? 17 Remember, my father fought for
you and risked his life to save you from the
power of the Midianites. 18 But now you have
turned against my father's family and have
killed his seventy sons on one stone. You
have made Abimelech, the son of my father's
slave girl, king over the leaders of Shechem
just because he is your relative! 19 So then, if
you have been honest and sincere to Gideon
and his family today, be happy with
Abimelech as your king. And may he be
happy with you! 20 But if not, may fire come
out of Abimelech and completely burn you
leaders of Shechem and Beth Millo! Also
may fire come out of the leaders of Shechem
and Beth Millo and burn up Abimelech!"
21 Then Jotham ran away and escaped to
the city of Beer. He lived there because he
was afraid of his brother Abimelech.

Abimelech Fights Against Shechem

22 Abimelech ruled Israel for three years.
23 Then God sent an evil spirit to make
trouble between Abimelech and the leaders
of Shechem so that the leaders of Shechem
turned against him. 24 Abimelech had killed
Gideon's[n] seventy sons, his own brothers,
and the leaders of Shechem had helped him.
So God sent the evil spirit to punish them.
25 The leaders of Shechem were against
Abimelech then. They put men on the
hilltops in ambush who robbed everyone
going by. And Abimelech was told.
26 A man named Gaal son of Ebed and his
brothers moved into Shechem, and the
leaders of Shechem trusted him. 27 They
went out to the vineyards to pick grapes, and
they squeezed the grapes. Then they had
a feast in the temple of their god, where
they ate and drank and cursed Abimelech.
28 Gaal son of Ebed said, "We are the men of
Shechem. Who is Abimelech that we should
serve him? Isn't he one of Gideon's sons, and
isn't Zebul his officer? We should serve the
men of Hamor, Shechem's father. Why
should we serve Abimelech? 29 If you made
me commander of these people, I would get
rid of Abimelech. I would say to him, 'Get
your army ready and come out to battle.' "
30 Now when Zebul, the ruler of Shechem,
heard what Gaal son of Ebed said, he was
very angry. 31 He sent secret messengers to
Abimelech, saying, "Gaal son of Ebed and
Gaal's brothers have come to Shechem, and

9:16, 24 Gideon Also called Jerub-Baal.

they are turning the city against you! 32 You and your men should get up during the night and hide in the fields outside the city. 33 As soon as the sun comes up in the morning, attack the city. When Gaal and his men come out to fight you, do what you can to them."

34 So Abimelech and all his soldiers got up during the night and hid near Shechem in four groups. 35 Gaal son of Ebed went out and was standing at the entrance to the city gate. As he was standing there, Abimelech and his soldiers came out of their hiding places.

36 When Gaal saw the soldiers, he said to Zebul, "Look! There are people coming down from the mountains!"

But Zebul said, "You are seeing the shadows of the mountains. The shadows just look like people."

37 But again Gaal said, "Look, there are people coming down from the center of the land, and there is a group coming from the fortune-tellers' tree!"

38 Zebul said to Gaal, "Where is your bragging now? You said, 'Who is Abimelech that we should serve him?' You made fun of these men. Now go out and fight them."

39 So Gaal led the men of Shechem out to fight Abimelech. 40 Abimelech and his men chased them, and many of Gaal's men were killed before they could get back to the city gate. 41 While Abimelech stayed at Arumah, Zebul forced Gaal and his brothers to leave Shechem.

42 The next day the people of Shechem went out to the fields. When Abimelech was told about it, 43 he separated his men into three groups and hid them in the fields. When he saw the people coming out of the city, he jumped up and attacked them. 44 Abimelech and his group ran to the entrance gate to the city. The other two groups ran out to the people in the fields and struck them down. 45 Abimelech and his men fought the city of Shechem all day until they captured it and killed its people. Then he tore it down and threw salt[n] over the ruins.

The Tower of Shechem Burns

46 When the leaders who were in the Tower of Shechem heard what had happened to Shechem, they gathered in the safest room of the temple of El Berith. 47 Abimelech heard that all the leaders of the Tower of Shechem had gathered there. 48 So he and all his men went up Mount Zalmon, near Shechem. Abimelech took an ax and cut some branches and put them on his shoulders. He said to all those with him, "Hurry! Do what I have done!" 49 So all those men cut branches and followed Abimelech and piled them against the safest room of the temple. Then they set them on fire and burned the people inside. So all the people who were at the Tower of Shechem also died—about a thousand men and women.

Abimelech's Death

50 Then Abimelech went to the city of Thebez. He surrounded the city, attacked it, and captured it. 51 But inside the city was a strong tower, so all the men, women, and leaders of that city ran to the tower. When they got inside, they locked the door behind them. Then they climbed up to the roof of the tower. 52 Abimelech came to the tower to attack it. He approached the door of the tower to set it on fire, 53 but as he came near, a woman dropped a grinding stone on his head, crushing his skull.

54 He quickly called to the officer who carried his armor and said, "Take out your sword and kill me. I don't want people to say, 'A woman killed Abimelech.'" So the officer stabbed Abimelech, and he died. 55 When the people of Israel saw Abimelech was dead, they all returned home.

56 In that way God punished Abimelech for all the evil he had done to his father by killing his seventy brothers. 57 God also punished the men of Shechem for the evil they had done. So the curse spoken by Jotham, the youngest son of Gideon,[n] came true.

Tola, the Judge

10 After Abimelech died, another judge came to save Israel. He was Tola son of Puah, the son of Dodo. Tola was from the people of Issachar and lived in the city of Shamir in the mountains of Ephraim. 2 Tola was a judge for Israel for twenty-three years. Then he died and was buried in Shamir.

9:45 salt The salt would keep crops from growing there. **9:57 Gideon** Also called Jerub-Baal.

Jair, the Judge

3After Tola died, Jair from the region of
Gilead became judge. He was a judge for
Israel for twenty-two years. 4Jair had thirty
sons, who rode thirty donkeys. These thirty
sons controlled thirty towns in Gilead,
which are called the Towns of Jair to this
day. 5Jair died and was buried in the city of
Kamon.

The Ammonites Trouble Israel

6Again the Israelites did what the LORD
said was wrong. They worshiped Baal and
Ashtoreth, the gods of Aram, Sidon, Moab,
and Ammon, and the gods of the Philistines.
The Israelites left the LORD and stopped
serving him. 7So the LORD was angry with
them and handed them over to the
Philistines and the Ammonites. 8In the same
year those people destroyed the Israelites
who lived east of the Jordan River in the
region of Gilead, where the Amorites lived.
So the Israelites suffered for eighteen years.
9The Ammonites then crossed the Jordan
River to fight the people of Judah, Benjamin,
and Ephraim, causing much trouble to the
people of Israel. 10So the Israelites cried out
to the LORD, "We have sinned against you.
We left our God and worshiped the Baal
idols."

11The LORD answered the Israelites,
"When the Egyptians, Amorites,
Ammonites, Philistines, 12Sidonians,
Amalekites, and Maonites were cruel to you,
you cried out to me, and I saved you. 13But
now you have left me again and have
worshiped other gods. So I refuse to save you
again. 14You have chosen those gods. So go
call to them for help. Let them save you
when you are in trouble."

15But the people of Israel said to the LORD,
"We have sinned. Do to us whatever you
want, but please save us today!" 16Then the
Israelites threw away the foreign gods
among them, and they worshiped the LORD
again. So he felt sorry for them when he saw
their suffering.

17The Ammonites gathered for war and
camped in Gilead. The Israelites gathered
and camped at Mizpah. 18The leaders of the
people of Gilead said, "Who will lead us to
attack the Ammonites? He will become the
head of all those who live in Gilead."

Jephthah Is Chosen as Leader

11 Jephthah was a strong soldier from
Gilead. His father was named Gilead,
and his mother was a prostitute. 2Gilead's
wife had several sons. When they grew up,
they forced Jephthah to leave his home,
saying to him, "You will not get any of our
father's property, because you are the son of
another woman." 3So Jephthah ran away
from his brothers and lived in the land of
Tob. There some worthless men began to
follow him.

4After a time the Ammonites fought
against Israel. 5When the Ammonites made
war against Israel, the elders of Gilead went
to Jephthah to bring him back from Tob.
6They said to him, "Come and lead our army
so we can fight the Ammonites."

7But Jephthah said to them, "Didn't you
hate me? You forced me to leave my father's
house. Why are you coming to me now that
you are in trouble?"

8The elders of Gilead said to Jephthah, "It
is because of those troubles that we come to
you now. Please come with us and fight
against the Ammonites. You will be the ruler
over everyone who lives in Gilead."

9Then Jephthah answered, "If you take me
back to Gilead to fight the Ammonites and
the LORD helps me win, I will be your ruler."

10The elders of Gilead said to him, "The
LORD is listening to everything we are saying.
We promise to do all that you tell us to do."
11So Jephthah went with the elders of Gilead,
and the people made him their leader and
commander of their army. Jephthah repeated
all of his words in front of the LORD at
Mizpah.

Jephthah Sends Messengers to the Ammonite King

12Jephthah sent messengers to the king of
the Ammonites, asking, "What have you got
against Israel? Why have you come to attack
our land?"

13The king of the Ammonites answered
the messengers of Jephthah, "We are fighting
Israel because you took our land when you
came up from Egypt. You took our land from
the Arnon River to the Jabbok River to the
Jordan River. Now give our land back to us
peacefully."

14Jephthah sent the messengers to the
Ammonite king again. 15They said:

"This is what Jephthah says: Israel did not
take the land of the people of Moab or
Ammon. 16When the Israelites came out of
Egypt, they went into the desert to the Red
Sea and then to Kadesh. 17Israel sent
messengers to the king of Edom, saying, 'Let
the people of Israel go across your land.' But
the king of Edom refused. We sent the same
message to the king of Moab, but he also
refused. So the Israelites stayed at Kadesh.
18"Then the Israelites went into the desert
around the borders of the lands of Edom and
Moab. Israel went east of the land of Moab
and camped on the other side of the Arnon
River, the border of Moab. They did not cross
it to go into the land of Moab.
19"Then Israel sent messengers to Sihon
king of the Amorites, king of the city of
Heshbon, asking, 'Let the people of Israel
pass through your land to go to our land.'
20But Sihon did not trust the Israelites to
cross his land. So he gathered all of his
people and camped at Jahaz and fought with
Israel.
21"But the LORD, the God of Israel, handed
Sihon and his army over to Israel. All the
land of the Amorites became the property of
Israel. 22So Israel took all the land of the
Amorites from the Arnon River to the
Jabbok River, from the desert to the Jordan
River.
23"It was the LORD, the God of Israel, who
forced out the Amorites ahead of the people
of Israel. So do you think you can make
them leave? 24Take the land that your god
Chemosh has given you. We will live in the
land the LORD our God has given us!
25"Are you any better than Balak son of
Zippor, king of Moab? Did he ever quarrel or
fight with the people of Israel? 26For three
hundred years the Israelites have lived in
Heshbon and Aroer and the towns around
them and in all the cities along the Arnon
River. Why have you not taken these cities
back in all that time? 27I have not sinned
against you, but you are sinning against me
by making war on me. May the LORD, the
Judge, decide whether the Israelites or the
Ammonites are right."
28But the king of the Ammonites ignored
this message from Jephthah.

Jephthah's Promise

29Then the Spirit of the LORD entered
Jephthah. Jephthah passed through Gilead
and Manasseh and the city of Mizpah in
Gilead to the land of the Ammonites.
30Jephthah made a promise to the LORD,
saying, "If you will hand over the
Ammonites to me, 31I will give you as a
burnt offering the first thing that comes out
of my house to meet me when I return from
the victory. It will be the LORD's."
32Then Jephthah went over to fight the
Ammonites, and the LORD handed them over
to him. 33In a great defeat Jephthah struck
them down from the city of Aroer to the area
of Minnith, and twenty cities as far as the
city of Abel Keramim. So the Ammonites
were defeated by the Israelites.
34When Jephthah returned to his home in
Mizpah, his daughter was the first one to
come out to meet him, playing a tambourine
and dancing. She was his only child; he had
no other sons or daughters. 35When
Jephthah saw his daughter, he tore his
clothes to show his sorrow. He said, "My
daughter! You have made me so sad because
I made a promise to the LORD, and I cannot
break it!"
36Then his daughter said, "Father, you
made a promise to the LORD. So do to me just
what you promised, because the LORD helped
you defeat your enemies, the Ammonites."
37She also said, "But let me do one thing. Let
me be alone for two months to go to the
mountains. Since I will never marry, let me
and my friends go and cry together."
38Jephthah said, "Go." So he sent her away
for two months. She and her friends stayed
in the mountains and cried for her because
she would never marry. 39After two months
she returned to her father, and Jephthah did
to her what he had promised. Jephthah's
daughter never had a husband.

From this came a custom in Israel that
40every year the young women of Israel
would go out for four days to remember the
daughter of Jephthah from Gilead.

Jephthah and Ephraim

12 The men of Ephraim called all their
soldiers together and crossed the river
to the town of Zaphon. They said to
Jephthah, "Why didn't you call us to help
you fight the Ammonites? We will burn
your house down with you in it."
2Jephthah answered them, "My people
and I fought a great battle against the

Ammonites. I called you, but you didn't come to help me. 3When I saw that you would not help me, I risked my own life and went against the Ammonites. The LORD handed them over to me. So why have you come to fight against me today?"

4Then Jephthah called the men of Gilead together and fought the men of Ephraim. The men of Gilead struck them down because the Ephraimites had said, "You men of Gilead are nothing but deserters from Ephraim—living between Ephraim and Manasseh." 5The men of Gilead captured the crossings of the Jordan River that led to the country of Ephraim. A person from Ephraim trying to escape would say, "Let me cross the river." Then the men of Gilead would ask him, "Are you from Ephraim?" If he replied no, 6they would say to him, "Say the word 'Shibboleth.' " The men of Ephraim could not say that word correctly. So if the person from Ephraim said, "Sibboleth," the men of Gilead would kill him at the crossing. So forty-two thousand people from Ephraim were killed at that time.

7Jephthah was a judge for Israel for six years. Then Jephthah, the man from Gilead, died and was buried in a town in Gilead.

Ibzan, the Judge

8After Jephthah died, Ibzan from Bethlehem was a judge for Israel. 9He had thirty sons and thirty daughters. He let his daughters marry men who were not in his family group, and he brought thirty women who were not in his tribe to be wives for his sons. Ibzan judged Israel for seven years. 10Then he died and was buried in Bethlehem.

Elon, the Judge

11After Ibzan died, Elon from the tribe of Zebulun was a judge for Israel. He judged Israel for ten years. 12Then Elon, the man of Zebulun, died and was buried in the city of Aijalon in the land of Zebulun.

Abdon, the Judge

13After Elon died, Abdon son of Hillel from the city of Pirathon was a judge for Israel. 14He had forty sons and thirty grandsons, who rode on seventy donkeys. He judged Israel for eight years. 15Then Abdon son of Hillel died and was buried in Pirathon in the land of Ephraim, in the mountains where the Amalekites lived.

The Birth of Samson

13 Again the people of Israel did what the LORD said was wrong. So he handed them over to the Philistines for forty years.

2There was a man named Manoah from the tribe of Dan, who lived in the city of Zorah. He had a wife, but she could not have children. 3The angel of the LORD appeared to Manoah's wife and said, "You have not been able to have children, but you will become pregnant and give birth to a son. 4Be careful not to drink wine or beer or eat anything that is unclean, 5because you will become pregnant and have a son. You must never cut his hair, because he will be a Nazirite, given to God from birth. He will begin to save Israel from the power of the Philistines."

6Then Manoah's wife went to him and told him what had happened. She said, "A man from God came to me. He looked like an angel from God; his appearance was frightening. I didn't ask him where he was from, and he didn't tell me his name. 7But he said to me, 'You will become pregnant and will have a son. Don't drink wine or beer or eat anything that is unclean, because the boy will be a Nazirite to God from his birth until the day of his death.' "

8Then Manoah prayed to the LORD: "Lord, I beg you to let the man of God come to us again. Let him teach us what we should do for the boy who will be born to us."

9God heard Manoah's prayer, and the angel of God came to Manoah's wife again while she was sitting in the field. But her husband Manoah was not with her. 10So she ran to tell him, "He is here! The man who appeared to me the other day is here!"

11Manoah got up and followed his wife. When he came to the man, he said, "Are you the man who spoke to my wife?"

The man said, "I am."

12So Manoah asked, "When what you say happens, what kind of life should the boy live? What should he do?"

13The angel of the LORD said, "Your wife must be careful to do everything I told her to do. 14She must not eat anything that grows on a grapevine, or drink any wine or beer, or

eat anything that is unclean. She must do
everything I have commanded her."
15Manoah said to the angel of the LORD,
"We would like you to stay awhile so we can
cook a young goat for you."
16The angel of the LORD answered, "Even if
I stay awhile, I would not eat your food. But
if you want to prepare something, offer a
burnt offering to the LORD." (Manoah did not
understand that the man was really the
angel of the LORD.)
17Then Manoah asked the angel of the
LORD, "What is your name? Then we will
honor you when what you have said really
happens."
18The angel of the LORD said, "Why do you
ask my name? It is too amazing for you to
understand." 19So Manoah sacrificed a young
goat on a rock and offered some grain as a
gift to the LORD. Then an amazing thing
happened as Manoah and his wife watched.
20The flames went up to the sky from the
altar. As the fire burned, the angel of the
LORD went up to heaven in the flame. When
Manoah and his wife saw that, they bowed
facedown on the ground. 21The angel of the
LORD did not appear to them again. Then
Manoah understood that the man was really
the angel of the LORD. 22Manoah said, "We
have seen God, so we will surely die."
23But his wife said to him, "If the LORD
wanted to kill us, he would not have
accepted our burnt offering or grain offering.
He would not have shown us all these things
or told us all this."
24So the woman gave birth to a boy and
named him Samson. He grew, and the LORD
blessed him. 25The Spirit of the LORD began
to work in Samson while he was in the city
of Mahaneh Dan, between the cities of Zorah
and Eshtaol.

Samson's First Marriage

14 Samson went down to the city of
Timnah where he saw a Philistine
woman. 2When he returned home, he said
to his father and mother, "I saw a Philistine
woman in Timnah. I want you to get her for
me so I can marry her."
3His father and mother answered, "Surely

devotion 71

JUDGES 13:3, 12–14, 23–25

SO YOU WANNA BE FREE, DO YOU?

The Philistines had oppressed the Israelites for forty years. When God decided it was time to begin their deliverance, he chose a man named Samson to free his people from the Philistines' hold. An angel announced Samson's miraculous birth to a woman who previously couldn't have children. (I love it when God does that.) Because his parents followed God's instructions, Samson was born and grew up under the blessing of the Lord, filled and led by his Spirit.

You too have been chosen by God. You belong to him, and he desires your whole heart. Maybe you have wandered like the Israelites, or maybe your heart has grown weary and cold. Or maybe you're in bondage to sin or sadness or guilt.

You might think the only way you'll ever be free is a miracle. God does those. You might not have any idea what to do or how to find your way out. God gives instructions. Maybe you've never been able to see God or hear his voice or know his will. When he speaks to you, you'll know it's him, just as Samson's parents did. Make sure that you worship and bow your life before the only One who can set you free.

God will not leave you in bondage—even bondage you have chosen. His love is too great and his mercy too deep. Lift up your eyes and see when he comes. Just as he did for the Israelites through Samson, God will send strength and freedom just for you.

there is a woman from Israel you can marry.
Do you have to marry a woman from the
Philistines, who are not circumcised?"
But Samson said, "Get that woman for me!
She is the one I want!" 4(Samson's parents
did not know that the LORD wanted this to
happen because he was looking for a way to
challenge the Philistines, who were ruling
over Israel at this time.) 5Samson went down
with his father and mother to Timnah, as far
as the vineyard near there. Suddenly, a
young lion came roaring toward Samson!
6The Spirit of the LORD entered Samson with
great power, and he tore the lion apart with
his bare hands. For him it was as easy as
tearing apart a young goat. But Samson did
not tell his father or mother what he had
done. 7Then he went down to the city and
talked to the Philistine woman, and he liked
her.

8Several days later Samson went back to
marry her. On his way he went over to look
at the body of the dead lion and found a
swarm of bees and honey in it. 9Samson got
some of the honey with his hands and
walked along eating it. When he came to his
parents, he gave some to them. They ate it,
too, but Samson did not tell them he had
taken the honey from the body of the dead
lion.

10Samson's father went down to see the
Philistine woman. And Samson gave a feast,
as was the custom for the bridegroom.
11When the people saw him, they sent thirty
friends to be with him.

Samson's Riddle

12Samson said to them, "Let me tell you a
riddle. Try to find the answer during the
seven days of the feast. If you can, I will give
you thirty linen shirts and thirty changes of
clothes. 13But if you can't, you must give me
thirty linen shirts and thirty changes of
clothes."

So they said, "Tell us your riddle so we can
hear it."

14Samson said,
"Out of the eater comes something to eat.
Out of the strong comes something
sweet."
After three days, they had not found the
answer.

15On the fourth[n] day they said to Samson's
wife, "Did you invite us here to make us
poor? Trick your husband into telling us the
answer to the riddle. If you don't, we will
burn you and everyone in your father's
house."

16So Samson's wife went to him, crying,
and said, "You hate me! You don't really love
me! You told my people a riddle, but you
won't tell me the answer."

Samson said, "I haven't even told my
father or mother. Why should I tell you?"

17Samson's wife cried for the rest of the
seven days of the feast. So he finally gave her
the answer on the seventh day, because she
kept bothering him. Then she told her
people the answer to the riddle.

18Before sunset on the seventh day of the
feast, the Philistine men had the answer.
They came to Samson and said,
"What is sweeter than honey?
What is stronger than a lion?"
Then Samson said to them,
"If you had not plowed with my young
cow,
you would not have solved my riddle!"
19Then the Spirit of the LORD entered
Samson and gave him great power. Samson
went down to the city of Ashkelon and
killed thirty of its men and took all that they
had and gave the clothes to the men who
had answered his riddle. Then he went to his
father's house very angry. 20And Samson's
wife was given to his best man.

Samson Troubles the Philistines

15 At the time of the wheat harvest,
Samson went to visit his wife, taking
a young goat with him. He said, "I'm going
to my wife's room," but her father would not
let him go in.

2He said to Samson, "I thought you really
hated your wife, so I gave her to your best
man. Her younger sister is more beautiful.
Take her instead."

3But Samson said to them, "This time no
one will blame me for hurting you
Philistines!" 4So Samson went out and
caught three hundred foxes. He took two
foxes at a time, tied their tails together, and
then tied a torch to the tails of each pair of
foxes. 5After he lit the torches, he let the

14:15 fourth The Hebrew word is "seventh." Some old translations say "fourth," which fits the order of events better.

Delilah

JUDGES 16

Delilah knows the power she holds in her embrace, in the scent of her perfume, in her kiss. Her body is supple and full, and her voice can make a man weak as she whispers his name. She is charming, beautiful, and cunning, able to make men do as she requests.

When Samson saw her smile, it made his heart drop, and he knew he had to have her. When they are together, Samson is lost in her arms, tangled in a sin that he cannot break away from. Delilah is well aware of the conquest she has made when Samson lies in her arms. He is the strongest man in the land, a powerful leader, and handsome beyond words. She is giddy with the power she feels when she is able to seduce him with just a look. He is putty in her hands.

Word spreads that Samson lies often in Delilah's bed, and the Philistine rulers offer her money if she can reveal where his strength lies. She closes her door, ponders what they have offered her, and smiles. What seduction! Yet another chance to wield her power through conquest! "So easy," she says, making plans for the money she will earn. "So, so easy!"

Women have a great deal of influence—positive or negative—over men's thoughts and actions, depending on the way we speak, dress, and conduct ourselves. Do you act in such a way that seduces the world for selfish gain or draws it closer to Jesus?

foxes loose in the grainfields of the
Philistines so that he burned up their
standing grain, the piles of grain, their
vineyards, and their olive trees.
6 The Philistines asked, "Who did this?"
Someone told them, "Samson, the son-in-
law of the man from Timnah, did because
his father-in-law gave his wife to his best
man."
So the Philistines burned Samson's wife
and her father to death. 7 Then Samson said
to the Philistines, "Since you did this, I won't
stop until I pay you back!" 8 Samson attacked
the Philistines and killed many of them.
Then he went down and stayed in a cave in
the rock of Etam.
9 The Philistines went up and camped in
the land of Judah, near a place named Lehi.
10 The men of Judah asked them, "Why have
you come here to fight us?"
They answered, "We have come to make
Samson our prisoner, to pay him back for
what he did to our people."
11 Then three thousand men of Judah
went to the cave in the rock of Etam and
said to Samson, "What have you done to us?
Don't you know that the Philistines rule
over us?"
Samson answered, "I only paid them back
for what they did to me."
12 Then they said to him, "We have come
to tie you up and to hand you over to the
Philistines."
Samson said to them, "Promise me you
will not hurt me yourselves."
13 The men from Judah said, "We agree. We
will just tie you up and give you to the
Philistines. We will not kill you." So they
tied Samson with two new ropes and led
him up from the cave in the rock. 14 When
Samson came to the place named Lehi, the
Philistines came to meet him, shouting for
joy. Then the Spirit of the LORD entered
Samson and gave him great power. The
ropes on him weakened like burned strings
and fell off his hands! 15 Samson found the
jawbone of a dead donkey, took it, and killed
a thousand men with it!
16 Then Samson said,
"With a donkey's jawbone
I made donkeys out of them.
With a donkey's jawbone
I killed a thousand men!"
17 When he finished speaking, he threw

away the jawbone. So that place was named
Ramath Lehi.[n]
18Samson was very thirsty, so he cried out
to the LORD, "You gave me, your servant, this
great victory. Do I have to die of thirst now?
Do I have to be captured by people who are
not circumcised?" 19Then God opened up a
hole in the ground at Lehi, and water came
out. When Samson drank, he felt better; he
felt strong again. So he named that spring
Caller's Spring, which is still in Lehi.
20Samson judged Israel for twenty years in
the days of the Philistines.

Samson Goes to the City of Gaza

16 One day Samson went to Gaza and
saw a prostitute there. He went in to
spend the night with her. 2When the people
of Gaza heard, "Samson has come here!" they
surrounded the place and waited for him
near the city gate all night. They whispered
to each other, "When dawn comes, we will
kill Samson!"
3But Samson only stayed with the
prostitute until midnight. Then he got up
and took hold of the doors and the two posts
of the city gate and tore them loose, along
with the bar. He put them on his shoulders
and carried them to the top of the hill that
faces the city of Hebron.

Samson and Delilah

4After this, Samson fell in love with a
woman named Delilah, who lived in the
Valley of Sorek. 5The Philistine rulers went
to Delilah and said, "Find out what makes
Samson so strong. Trick him into telling you
how we can overpower him and capture
him and tie him up. If you do this, each one
of us will give you twenty-eight pounds of
silver."
6So Delilah said to Samson, "Tell me why
you are so strong. How can someone tie you
up and capture you?"
7Samson answered, "Someone would have
to tie me up with seven new bowstrings that
have not been dried. Then I would be as
weak as any other man."
8The Philistine rulers brought Delilah
seven new bowstrings that had not been
dried, and she tied Samson with them.
9Some men were hiding in another room.
Delilah said to him, "Samson, the Philistines
are here!" But Samson broke the bowstrings
like pieces of burned string. So the
Philistines did not find out the secret of
Samson's strength.
10Then Delilah said to Samson, "You made
a fool of me. You lied to me. Now tell me
how someone can tie you up."
11Samson said, "They would have to tie
me with new ropes that have not been used
before. Then I would become as weak as any
other man."
12So Delilah took new ropes and tied
Samson. Some men were hiding in another
room. She called out to him, "Samson, the
Philistines are here!" But he broke the ropes
as easily as if they were threads.
13Then Delilah said to Samson, "Again you
have made a fool of me. You lied to me. Tell
me how someone can tie you up."
He said, "Using the loom,[n] weave the
seven braids of my hair into the cloth, and
tighten it with a pin. Then I will be as weak
as any other man."
While Samson slept, Delilah wove the
seven braids of his hair into the cloth.
14Then she fastened it with a pin.
Again she said to him, "Samson, the
Philistines are here!" Samson woke up and
pulled out the pin and the loom with the
cloth.
15Then Delilah said to him, "How can you
say, 'I love you,' when you don't even trust
me? This is the third time you have made a
fool of me. You haven't told me the secret of
your great strength." 16She kept bothering
Samson about his secret day after day until
he felt he was going to die!
17So he told her everything. He said, "I
have never had my hair cut, because I have
been set apart to God as a Nazirite since I
was born. If someone shaved my head, I
would lose my strength and be as weak as
any other man."
18When Delilah saw that he had told her
everything sincerely, she sent a message to
the Philistine rulers. She said, "Come back
one more time, because he has told me
everything." So the Philistine rulers came
back to Delilah and brought the silver with
them. 19Delilah got Samson to sleep, lying in
her lap. Then she called in a man to shave off

15:17 Ramath Lehi This name means "Jawbone Hill." **16:13 loom** A machine for making cloth from thread.

the seven braids of Samson's hair. In this way she began to make him weak, and his strength left him.

20 Then she said, "Samson, the Philistines are here!"

He woke up and thought, "I'll leave as I did before and shake myself free." But he did not know that the LORD had left him.

21 Then the Philistines captured Samson and tore out his eyes. They took him down to Gaza, where they put bronze chains on him and made him grind grain in the prison. 22 But his hair began to grow again.

Samson Dies

23 The Philistine rulers gathered to celebrate and to offer a great sacrifice to their god Dagon. They said, "Our god has handed Samson our enemy over to us." 24 When the people saw him, they praised their god, saying,

"This man destroyed our country.
He killed many of us!
But our god handed over
our enemy to us."

25 While the people were enjoying the celebration, they said, "Bring Samson out to perform for us." So they brought Samson from the prison, and he performed for them. They made him stand between the pillars. 26 Samson said to the servant holding his hand, "Let me feel the pillars that hold up the temple so I can lean against them." 27 Now the temple was full of men and women. All the Philistine rulers were there, and about three thousand men and women were on the roof[n] watching Samson perform. 28 Then Samson prayed to the LORD, "Lord GOD, remember me. God, please give me strength one more time so I can pay these Philistines back for putting out my two eyes!" 29 Then Samson turned to the two center pillars that supported the whole temple. He braced himself between the two pillars, with his right hand on one and his left hand on the other. 30 Samson said, "Let me die with these Philistines!" Then he pushed as hard as he could, causing the temple to fall on the rulers and all the people in it. So Samson killed more of the Philistines when he died than when he was alive.

31 Samson's brothers and his whole family went down to get his body. They brought him back and buried him in the tomb of Manoah, his father, between the cities of Zorah and Eshtaol. Samson was a judge for the people of Israel for twenty years.

Micah's Idols

17 There was a man named Micah who lived in the mountains of Ephraim. 2 He said to his mother, "I heard you speak a curse about the twenty-eight pounds of silver that were taken from you. I have the silver with me; I took it."

His mother said, "The LORD bless you, my son!"

3 Micah gave the twenty-eight pounds of silver to his mother. Then she said, "I will give this silver to the LORD. I will have my son make an idol and a statue. So I will give the silver back to you."

4 When he gave the silver back to his mother, she took about five pounds and gave it to a silversmith. With it he made an idol and a statue, which stood in Micah's house. 5 Micah had a special holy place, and he made a holy vest and some household idols. Then Micah chose one of his sons to be his priest. 6 At that time Israel did not have a king, so everyone did what seemed right.

7 There was a young man who was a Levite[n] from the city of Bethlehem in Judah who was from the people of Judah. 8 He left Bethlehem to look for another place to live, and on his way he came to Micah's house in the mountains of Ephraim. 9 Micah asked him, "Where are you from?"

He answered, "I'm a Levite from Bethlehem in Judah. I'm looking for a place to live."

10 Micah said to him, "Live with me and be my father and my priest. I will give you four ounces of silver each year and clothes and food." So the Levite went in. 11 He agreed to live with Micah and became like one of Micah's own sons. 12 Micah made him a priest, and he lived in Micah's house. 13 Then Micah said, "Now I know the LORD will be good to me, because I have a Levite as my priest."

16:27 roof In Bible times houses were built with flat roofs. The roof was used for drying things such as flax and fruit. And it was used as an extra room, as a place for worship, and as a cool place to sleep in the summer. **17:7 Levite** The Levites were the only ones God had appointed as priests.

devotion 72

JUDGES 16:28

COMING TO OUR SENSES

Samson's story always amazes me. He was chosen by God and used by God, but he was also immoral and prone to follow the path of sensuality. Ultimately, the consequences of his disobedience made him a blind slave to the Philistines.

I imagine that all the time he spent in chains grinding grain in the Philistine prison gave Samson some time to remember where he had come from and to whom he belonged. I believe he remembered what it felt like to be led by the Spirit of God, and his heart grieved when he realized God's Spirit and power had left him. Samson had been sent by God to kill Philistines and deliver the Israelites from their oppression, yet he found himself a slave to them as well.

But God's favor is everlasting. He lets us suffer the consequences of our choices, but he also lets us come to our senses. Samson asked one last time for God's anointing. God allowed a blind and chained Samson to come to his senses and return to his purpose.

Maybe today you are suffering from the consequences of your choices. Maybe you feel blind and bound to your mistakes. God still lets the ones who belong to him come to their senses. You can pray the same way Samson did: "Lord God, remember me. God, please give me strength." And every time you pray according to his will and for his glory, God will be faithful to hear and to come.

Dan's Family Captures Laish

18 At that time Israel did not have a king.
And at that time the tribe of Dan was
still looking for a land where they could live,
a land of their own. The Danites had not yet
been given their own land among the tribes
of Israel. 2So, from their family groups, they
chose five soldiers from the cities of Zorah
and Eshtaol to spy out and explore the land.
They were told, "Go, explore the land."

They came to the mountains of Ephraim,
to Micah's house, where they spent the
night. 3When they came near Micah's house,
they recognized the voice of the young
Levite.[n] So they stopped there and asked
him, "Who brought you here? What are you
doing here? Why are you here?"

4He told them what Micah had done for
him, saying, "He hired me. I am his priest."

5They said to him, "Please ask God if our
journey will be successful."

6The priest said to them, "Go in peace. The
LORD is pleased with your journey."

7So the five men left. When they came to
the city of Laish, they saw that the people
there lived in safety, like the people of Sidon.
They thought they were safe and had plenty
of everything. They lived a long way from
the Sidonians and had no dealings with
anyone else.

8When the five men returned to Zorah
and Eshtaol, their relatives asked them,
"What did you find?"

9They answered, "We have seen the land,
and it is very good. We should attack them.
Aren't you going to do something? Don't
wait! Let's go and take that land! 10When
you go, you will see there is plenty of land—
plenty of everything! The people are not
expecting an attack. Surely God has handed
that land over to us!"

11So six hundred Danites left Zorah and

18:3 Levite The Levites were the only ones God had appointed as priests.

Eshtaol ready for war. [12]On their way they
set up camp near the city of Kiriath Jearim
in Judah. That is why the place west of
Kiriath Jearim is named Mahaneh Dan[n] to
this day. [13]From there they traveled on to the
mountains of Ephraim. Then they came to
Micah's house.

[14]The five men who had explored the land
around Laish said to their relatives, "Do you
know in one of these houses there are a holy
vest, household gods, an idol, and a statue?
You know what to do." [15]So they stopped at
the Levite's house, which was also Micah's
house, and greeted the Levite. [16]The six
hundred Danites stood at the entrance gate,
wearing their weapons of war. [17]The five
spies went into the house and took the idol,
the holy vest, the household idols, and the
statue. The priest and the six hundred men
armed for war stood by the entrance gate.

[18]When the spies went into Micah's house
and took the image, the holy vest, the
household idols, and the statue, the priest
asked them, "What are you doing?"

[19]They answered, "Be quiet! Don't say a
word. Come with us and be our father and
priest. Is it better for you to be a priest for
one man's house or for a tribe and family
group in Israel?" [20]This made the priest
happy. So he took the holy vest, the
household idols, and the idol and went with
the Danites. [21]They left Micah's house,
putting their little children, their animals,
and everything they owned in front of them.

[22]When they had gone a little way from
Micah's house, the men who lived near
Micah were called out and caught up with
them. [23]The men with Micah shouted at the
Danites, who turned around and said to
Micah, "What's the matter with you? Why
have you been called out to fight?"

[24]Micah answered, "You took my gods
that I made and my priest. What do I have
left? How can you ask me, 'What's the
matter?' "

[25]The Danites answered, "You should not
argue with us. Some of our angry men might
attack you, killing you and your family."
[26]Then the Danites went on their way.
Micah knew they were too strong for him, so
he turned and went back home.

[27]Then the Danites took what Micah had
made and his priest and went on to Laish.
They attacked those peaceful people and
killed them with their swords and then
burned the city. [28]There was no one to save
the people of Laish. They lived too far from
Sidon, and they had no dealings with anyone
else. Laish was in a valley near Beth Rehob.

The people of Dan rebuilt the city and
lived there. [29]They changed the name of
Laish to Dan, naming it for their ancestor
Dan, one of the sons of Israel.

[30]The people of Dan set up the idols in the
city of Dan. Jonathan son of Gershom,
Moses' son, and his sons served as priests for
the tribe of Dan until the land was captured.
[31]The people of Dan set up the idols Micah
had made as long as the Holy Tent of God
was in Shiloh.

A Levite and His Servant

19 At that time Israel did not have a king.
There was a Levite who lived in the
faraway mountains of Ephraim. He had
taken a slave woman from the city of
Bethlehem in the land of Judah to live with
him, [2]but she was unfaithful to him. She left
him and went back to her father's house in
Bethlehem in Judah and stayed there for four
months. [3]Then her husband went to ask her
to come back to him, taking with him his
servant and two donkeys. When the Levite
came to her father's house, she invited him
to come in, and her father was happy to see
him. [4]The father-in-law, the young woman's
father, asked him to stay. So he stayed for
three days and ate, drank, and slept there.

[5]On the fourth day they got up early in
the morning. The Levite was getting ready to
leave, but the woman's father said to his son-
in-law, "Refresh yourself by eating
something. Then go." [6]So the two men sat
down to eat and drink together. After that,
the father said to him, "Please stay tonight.
Relax and enjoy yourself." [7]When the man
got up to go, his father-in-law asked him to
stay. So he stayed again that night. [8]On the
fifth day the man got up early in the
morning to leave. The woman's father said,
"Refresh yourself. Wait until this afternoon."
So the two men ate together.

[9]When the Levite, his slave woman, and
his servant got up to leave, the father-in-law,

18:12 Mahaneh Dan This name means "the camp of Dan."

the young woman's father, said, "It's almost
night. The day is almost gone. Spend the
night here and enjoy yourself. Tomorrow
morning you can get up early and go home."
10But the Levite did not want to stay another
night. So he took his two saddled donkeys
and his slave woman and traveled toward
the city of Jebus (also called Jerusalem).

11As the day was almost over, they came
near Jebus. So the servant said to his master,
"Let's stop at this city of the Jebusites, and
spend the night here."

12But his master said, "No. We won't go
inside a foreign city. Those people are not
Israelites. We will go on to the city of
Gibeah." 13He said, "Come on. Let's try to
make it to Gibeah or Ramah so we can spend
the night in one of those cities." 14So they
went on. The sun went down as they came
near Gibeah, which belongs to the tribe of
Benjamin. 15They stopped there to spend the
night. They came to the public square of the
city and sat down, but no one invited them
home to spend the night.

16Finally, in the evening an old man came
in from his work in the fields. His home was
in the mountains of Ephraim, but now he
was living in Gibeah. (The people of Gibeah
were from the tribe of Benjamin.) 17He saw
the traveler in the public square and asked,
"Where are you going? Where did you come
from?"

18The Levite answered, "We are traveling
from Bethlehem in Judah to my home in the
mountains of Ephraim. I have been to
Bethlehem in Judah, but now I am going to
the Holy Tent of the LORD. No one has
invited me to stay in his house. 19We already
have straw and food for our donkeys and
bread and wine for me, the young woman,
and my servant. We don't need anything."

20The old man said, "You are welcome to
stay at my house. Let me give you anything
you need, but don't spend the night in the
public square." 21So the old man took the
Levite into his house, and he fed their
donkeys. They washed their feet and had
something to eat and drink.

22While they were enjoying themselves,
some wicked men of the city surrounded the
house and beat on the door. They shouted to
the old man who owned the house, "Bring
out the man who came to your house. We
want to have sexual relations with him."

23The owner of the house went outside
and said to them, "No, my friends. Don't be
so evil. This man is a guest in my house.
Don't do this terrible thing! 24Look, here are
my daughter, who has never had sexual
relations before, and the man's slave woman.
I will bring them out to you now. Do
anything you want with them, but don't do
such a terrible thing to this man."

25But the men would not listen to him. So
the Levite took his slave woman and sent
her outside to them. They forced her to have
sexual relations with them, and they abused
her all night long. Then, at dawn, they let
her go. 26She came back to the house where
her master was staying and fell down at the
door and lay there until daylight.

27In the morning when the Levite got up,
he opened the door of the house and went
outside to go on his way. But his slave
woman was lying at the doorway of the
house, with her hands on the doorsill. 28The
Levite said to her, "Get up; let's go." But she
did not answer. So he put her on his donkey
and went home.

29When the Levite got home, he took a
knife and cut his slave woman into twelve
parts, limb by limb. Then he sent a part to
each area of Israel. 30Everyone who saw this
said, "Nothing like this has ever happened
before, not since the people of Israel came
out of Egypt. Think about it. Tell us what to
do."

The War Between Israel and Benjamin

20 So all the Israelites from Dan to
Beersheba,[n] including the land of
Gilead, joined together before the LORD in
the city of Mizpah. 2The leaders of all the
tribes of Israel took their places in the
meeting of the people of God. There were
400,000 soldiers with swords. 3(The people of
Benjamin heard that the Israelites had gone
up to Mizpah.) Then the Israelites said to the
Levite, "Tell us how this evil thing happened."

4So the husband of the murdered woman
answered, "My slave woman and I came to
Gibeah in Benjamin to spend the night.
5During the night the men of Gibeah came
after me. They surrounded the house and

20:1 Dan . . . Beersheba Dan was the city farthest north in Israel. Beersheba was the city farthest south. So this means all the people of Israel.

wanted to kill me. They forced my slave
woman to have sexual relations and she
died. 6I took her and cut her into parts and
sent one part to each area of Israel because
the people of Benjamin did this wicked and
terrible thing in Israel. 7Now, all you
Israelites, speak up. What is your
decision?"

8Then all the people stood up at the same
time, saying, "None of us will go home. Not
one of us will go back to his house! 9Now
this is what we will do to Gibeah. We will
throw lots. 10That way we will choose ten
men from every hundred men from all the
tribes of Israel, and we will choose a
hundred men from every thousand, and a
thousand men from every ten thousand.
These will find supplies for the army. Then
the army will go to the city of Gibeah of
Benjamin to repay them for the terrible
thing they have done in Israel." 11So all the
men of Israel were united and gathered
against the city.

12The tribes of Israel sent men throughout
the tribe of Benjamin demanding, "What is
this evil thing some of your men have done?
13Hand over the wicked men in Gibeah so
that we can put them to death. We must
remove this evil from Israel."

But the Benjaminites would not listen to
their fellow Israelites. 14The Benjaminites left
their own cities and met at Gibeah to fight
the Israelites. 15In only one day the
Benjaminites got 26,000 soldiers together
who were trained with swords. They also had
700 chosen men from Gibeah. 16Seven
hundred of these trained soldiers were left-
handed, each of whom could sling a stone at a
hair and not miss!

17The Israelites, except for the
Benjaminites, gathered 400,000 soldiers with
swords.

18The Israelites went up to the city of
Bethel and asked God, "Which tribe shall be
first to attack the Benjaminites?"

The LORD answered, "Judah shall go first."

19The next morning the Israelites got up
and made a camp near Gibeah. 20The men of
Israel went out to fight the Benjaminites and
took their battle position at Gibeah. 21Then
the Benjaminites came out of Gibeah and
killed 22,000 Israelites during the battle that
day. 22-23The Israelites went before the LORD
and cried until evening. They asked the
LORD, "Shall we go to fight our relatives, the
Benjaminites, again?"

The LORD answered, "Go up and fight
them." The men of Israel encouraged each
other. So they took the same battle positions
they had taken the first day.

24The Israelites came to fight the
Benjaminites the second day. 25The
Benjaminites came out of Gibeah to attack
the Israelites. This time, the Benjaminites
killed 18,000 Israelites, all of whom carried
swords.

26Then the Israelites went up to Bethel.
There they sat down and cried to the LORD
and fasted all day until evening. They also
brought burnt offerings and fellowship
offerings to the LORD. 27The Israelites asked
the LORD a question. (In those days the Ark of
the Agreement with God was there at Bethel.
28A priest named Phinehas son of Eleazar, the
son of Aaron, served before the Ark of the
Agreement.) They asked, "Shall we go to fight
our relatives, the Benjaminites, again, or shall
we stop fighting?"

The LORD answered, "Go, because
tomorrow I will hand them over to you."

29Then the Israelites set up ambushes all
around Gibeah. 30They went to fight against
the Benjaminites at Gibeah on the third day,
getting into position for battle as they had
done before. 31When the Benjaminites came
out to fight them, the Israelites backed up
and led the Benjaminites away from the city.
The Benjaminites began to kill some of the
Israelites as they had done before. About
thirty Israelites were killed—some in the
fields and some on the roads leading to
Bethel and to Gibeah.

32The Benjaminites said, "We are winning
as before!"

But the Israelites said, "Let's run. Let's
trick them into going farther away from
their city and onto the roads."

33All the Israelites moved from their
places and got into battle positions at a place
named Baal Tamar. Then the Israelites ran
out from their hiding places west of Gibeah.
34Ten thousand of the best trained soldiers
from all of Israel attacked Gibeah. The battle
was very hard. The Benjaminites did not
know disaster was about to come to them.
35The LORD used the Israelites to defeat the
Benjaminites. On that day the Israelites
killed 25,100 Benjaminites, all armed with

swords. 36Then the Benjaminites saw that
they were defeated.
The Israelites had moved back because
they were depending on the surprise attack
they had set up near Gibeah. 37The men in
hiding rushed into Gibeah, spread out, and
killed everyone in the city with their swords.
38Now the Israelites had set up a signal with
the men in hiding. The men in the surprise
attack were to send up a cloud of smoke
from the city. 39Then the army of Israel
turned around in the battle.
The Benjaminites had killed about thirty
Israelites. They were saying, "We are winning,
as in the first battle!" 40But then a cloud of
smoke began to rise from the city. The
Benjaminites turned around and saw that the
whole city was going up in smoke. 41Then the
Israelites turned and began to fight. The
Benjaminites were terrified because they
knew that disaster was coming to them. 42So
the Benjaminites ran away from the Israelites
toward the desert, but they could not escape
the battle. And the Israelites who came out of
the cities killed them. 43They surrounded the
Benjaminites and chased them and caught
them in the area east of Gibeah. 44So 18,000
brave Benjaminite fighters were killed. 45The
Benjaminites ran toward the desert to the
rock of Rimmon, but the Israelites killed
5,000 Benjaminites along the roads. They
chased them as far as Gidom and killed 2,000
more Benjaminites there.
46On that day 25,000 Benjaminites were
killed, all of whom had fought bravely
with swords. 47But 600 Benjaminites ran
to the rock of Rimmon in the desert,
where they stayed for four months. 48Then
the Israelites went back to the land of
Benjamin and killed the people in every city
and also the animals and everything they
could find. And they burned every city they
found.

Wives for the Men of Benjamin

21 At Mizpah the men of Israel had
sworn, "Not one of us will let his
daughter marry a man from the tribe of
Benjamin."
2The people went to the city of Bethel and
sat before God until evening, crying loudly.
3They said, "LORD, God of Israel, why has this
terrible thing happened to us so that one
tribe of Israel is missing today?"

devotion 73

JUDGES 21:25

HAVE YOU BEEN TO THE WHITE HOUSE?

On a recent tour of the White House, I was amazed with how many details of the Christian faith make up the White House decor. There were pictures, Bibles, statues, and foreign gifts that spanned hundreds of years. It was obvious that the whole world knew that the United States loved God. What touched me the most was the prayer John Adams had engraved into the fireplace of the formal dining room: "I pray Heaven to bestow the best of Blessings on this House and all that shall hereafter inhabit it. May none but honest and wise Men ever rule under this roof."

The founders of this country were wise men who knew that in order to be great leaders, they had to lead with the Word of the Lord as their guide. Just as the founders of this country sought the Lord for wisdom and understanding, we too are charged with that same responsibility for our families, friends, and employers. It does not matter what laws are legislated, what kings or presidents do, or what pop culture sets as a standard. It is never permissible for us to do what is right in our own eyes. If you are seeking God for wisdom and direction, ask the Holy Spirit this very minute to direct you to the answer in his Word. A prayer carved in a mantle is a sweet reminder that we are honest and wise women who guide our households with the Word of our heavenly King.

4 Early the next day the people built an
altar and put burnt offerings and fellowship
offerings to God on it.
5 Then the Israelites asked, "Did any tribe
of Israel not come here to meet with us in
the presence of the LORD?" They asked this
question because they had sworn that
anyone who did not meet with them at
Mizpah would be killed.
6 The Israelites felt sorry for their relatives,
the Benjaminites. They said, "Today one tribe
has been cut off from Israel. 7 We swore
before the LORD that we would not allow our
daughters to marry a Benjaminite. How can
we make sure that the remaining men of
Benjamin will have wives?" 8 Then they
asked, "Which one of the tribes of Israel did
not come here to Mizpah?" They found that
no one from the city of Jabesh Gilead had
come. 9 The people of Israel counted
everyone, but there was no one from Jabesh
Gilead.
10 So the whole group of Israelites sent
twelve thousand soldiers to Jabesh Gilead to
kill the people with their swords, even the
women and children.
11 "This is what you must do: Kill every
man in Jabesh Gilead and every married
woman." 12 The soldiers found four hundred
young unmarried women in Jabesh Gilead,
so they brought them to the camp at Shiloh
in Canaan.
13 Then the whole group of Israelites sent a
message to the men of Benjamin, who were
at the rock of Rimmon, offering to make
peace with them. 14 So the men of Benjamin
came back at that time. The Israelites gave
them the women from Jabesh Gilead who
had not been killed, but there were not
enough women.
15 The people of Israel felt sorry for the
Benjaminites because the LORD had
separated the tribes of Israel. 16 The elders of
the Israelites said, "The women of Benjamin
have been killed. Where can we get wives
for the men of Benjamin who are still alive?
17 These men must have children to continue
their families so a tribe in Israel will not die
out. 18 But we cannot allow our daughters to
marry them, because we swore, 'Anyone who
gives a wife to a man of Benjamin is cursed.'
19 We have an idea! There is a yearly festival
of the LORD at Shiloh, which is north of the
city of Bethel, east of the road that goes from
Bethel to Shechem, and south of the city of
Lebonah."
20 So the elders told the men of Benjamin,
"Go and hide in the vineyards. 21 Watch for
the young women from Shiloh to come out
to join the dancing. Then run out from the
vineyards and take one of the young Shiloh
women and return to the land of Benjamin.
22 If their fathers or brothers come to us and
complain, we will say: 'Be kind to the men of
Benjamin. We did not get wives for
Benjamin during the war, and you did not
give the women to the men from Benjamin.
So you are not guilty.' "
23 So that is what the Benjaminites did.
While the young women were dancing, each
man caught one of them, took her away, and
married her. Then they went back to the
land God had given them and rebuilt their
cities and lived there.
24 Then the Israelites went home to their
own tribes and family groups, to their own
land that God had given them.
25 In those days Israel did not have a king.
All the people did whatever seemed right in
their own eyes.

Ruth

This book is one of only two in the entire Bible named after a woman (the other is Esther). Ruth's name might have come from an ancient Hebrew or Moabite word meaning "friendship."

Person Holding the Pen God Wrote With: The author is theoretically anonymous, although Jewish tradition holds that *Samuel* wrote this story. This is certainly plausible since King David is mentioned in the text (Ruth 4:17, 22); thus, Samuel likely lived during the time period when these events took place.

When the Text Was Written: It was probably penned sometime during King David's reign, which lasted from 1011–971 B.C.

Spiritual Posture of the Original Recipients: This romantic adventure takes place during the tumultuous period when judges ruled the land. Just as in the book of Judges, there was no king in Israel, the Word of God was not being taught, and everyone did what was right in his or her own eyes. In other words, God's people were in spiritual chaos—which makes this tender tale read like a rose among thorns!

Storyline Synopsis: The drama unfolds with a cash-strapped family packing up their U-Haul in Bethlehem and moving to Moab—aka "Sin City." But they'll return to the little town of Bethlehem for a three-hankie ending! Along the way, women become widows, faithfulness is personified, and the most eligible bachelor named Boaz saves the day! The book of Ruth records a beautiful, historical love story. More importantly, it points to the greater story of how God will redeem his people.

A Moment Worth Discussing: When Boaz returns home from a business trip to find a pretty young woman gathering grain in one of his fields, his eyes widen, a grin splits his face, and he elbows his foreman in the ribs while asking, "Who in the world is she?" (Ruth 2:5). This is basically the Old Testament equivalent of *hubba hubba!*

Interesting (But Likely to Be Overlooked) Character: *Obed,* Ruth and Boaz's little boy (Ruth 4:17–22) has an *amazing* genealogy. It winds through ancient history, generation to generation, all the way to another baby boy's birth in the same small town of Bethlehem. (Want a hint? The other baby's name is Jesus.)

Naomi and Ruth

RUTH

Naomi watches with joy as the couple exchange vows. The bride, Ruth, has stood by Naomi through her darkest days. When her husband and two sons died, Naomi was left with nothing except her daughters-in-law, both Moabite women. Orpah and Ruth were grieved when Naomi said she was leaving; both women cried. Orpah made the choice to return home to her own people. Ruth, however, clung to her mother-in-law. "Where you go, I will go. Where you live, I will live. Your people will be my people, and your God will be my God." Naomi put her hand on Ruth's face. Why would this young widow choose friendship with an old woman?

Although a foreigner in a new land, Ruth's reputation for taking care of her mother-in-law endeared her to many, especially Boaz. Naomi smiles at the way God rewarded Ruth's loyalty when she gleaned barley in Boaz's fields. He noticed her and discovered she was a woman of worth. "All the people in our town know you are a good woman," Boaz said to her one day. He watched over Ruth, making sure his workers left extra barley stalks for her. He was an answer to her prayer.

Naomi's heart swells when she recounts the ways God has guided her and Ruth to this day of celebration. It was a long journey, but now, by God's grace, there is joy.

Naomi and Ruth are examples of commitment, trust, and loyalty to each other and God. Are you a friend of this kind?

The Story of a Girl from Moab

1 Long ago when the judges[n] ruled Israel,
there was a shortage of food in the land.
2 So a man named Elimelech left the town of
Bethlehem in Judah to live in the country of
Moab with his wife and his two sons. His
wife was named Naomi, and his two sons
were named Mahlon and Kilion. They were
Ephrathahites from Bethlehem in Judah.
When they came to Moab, they settled there.
3 Then Naomi's husband, Elimelech, died,
and she was left with her two sons. 4 These
sons married women from Moab. One was
named Orpah, and the other was named
Ruth. Naomi and her sons had lived in Moab
about ten years 5 when Mahlon and Kilion
also died. So Naomi was left alone without
her husband or her two sons.
6 While Naomi was in Moab, she heard
that the LORD had come to help his people
and had given them food again. So she and
her daughters-in-law got ready to leave Moab
and return home. 7 Naomi and her daughters-
in-law left the place where they had lived
and started back to the land of Judah. 8 But
Naomi said to her two daughters-in-law, "Go
back home, each of you to your own
mother's house. May the LORD be as kind to
you as you have been to me and my sons
who are now dead. 9 May the LORD give you
another happy home and a new husband."
When Naomi kissed the women good-bye,
they began to cry out loud. 10 They said to
her, "No, we want to go with you to your
people."
11 But Naomi said, "My daughters, return to
your own homes. Why do you want to go
with me? I cannot give birth to more sons to
give you new husbands; 12 go back, my
daughters, to your own homes. I am too old
to have another husband. Even if I told
myself, 'I still have hope' and had another
husband tonight, and even if I had more
sons, 13 should you wait until they were
grown into men? Should you live for so
many years without husbands? Don't do
that, my daughters. My life is much too sad
for you to share, because the LORD has been
against me!"
14 The women cried together out loud
again. Then Orpah kissed her mother-in-law

1:1 judges They were not judges in courts of law, but leaders of the people in times of emergency.

devotion 74

RUTH 1:16

HOW DO YOU CHOOSE?

Ruth was willing to leave everything behind to follow God. Remember, this meant her home, her family, her friends, and the only life she had ever known. Ruth had met God through her mother-in-law, and she was not willing to give up on God or Naomi, her godly influence, for anything. What is it that you need to leave behind to follow God? Jesus said to take up your cross daily and follow him. But what does that mean in your day-to-day life? Are you so busy keeping up with a husband, the children, the house, the errands, and the bills that you don't have the time to follow after God?

We need to learn how to say no to the world and yes to God. We can't follow God if we don't have time to even have a devotional life. How easy it is to get caught up in the rat race of life. Our children have to play every sport, we have to go to every party we're invited to, and we have to volunteer for everything we're asked to do because of what others might think. The question is, what is God thinking when he looks upon your life? Have you made him the first priority? Are you willing to leave behind certain things in order to follow his will? Following after God may not always be easy, but it will always be rewarding. Ruth had a tough choice to make—and so do you.

Naomi good-bye, but Ruth held on to her
tightly.
15Naomi said to Ruth, "Look, your sister-
in-law is going back to her own people and
her own gods. Go back with her."

Ruth Stays with Naomi

16But Ruth said, "Don't beg me to leave
you or to stop following you. Where you go,
I will go. Where you live, I will live. Your
people will be my people, and your God will
be my God. 17And where you die, I will die,
and there I will be buried. I ask the LORD to
punish me terribly if I do not keep this
promise: Not even death will separate us."
18When Naomi saw that Ruth had firmly
made up her mind to go with her, she
stopped arguing with her. 19So Naomi and
Ruth went on until they came to the town of
Bethlehem. When they entered Bethlehem,
all the people became very excited. The
women of the town said, "Is this really
Naomi?"
20Naomi answered the people, "Don't call
me Naomi.[n] Call me Mara,[n] because the
Almighty has made my life very sad.
21When I left, I had all I wanted, but now,
the LORD has brought me home with
nothing. Why should you call me Naomi
when the LORD has spoken against me and
the Almighty has given me so much
trouble?"
22So Naomi and her daughter-in-law Ruth,
the Moabite, returned from Moab and
arrived at Bethlehem at the beginning of the
barley harvest.

Ruth Meets Boaz

2 Now Naomi had a rich relative named
Boaz, from Elimelech's family.
2One day Ruth, the Moabite, said to
Naomi, "I am going to the fields. Maybe
someone will be kind enough to let me
gather the grain he leaves behind."
Naomi said, "Go, my daughter."
3So Ruth went to the fields and gathered

1:20 Naomi This name means "happy" or "pleasant." **1:20 Mara** This name means "bitter" or "sad."

the grain that the workers cutting the grain
had left behind. It just so happened that the
field belonged to Boaz, from Elimelech's
family.
4 Soon Boaz came from Bethlehem and
greeted his workers, "The LORD be with you!"
And the workers answered, "May the LORD
bless you!"
5 Then Boaz asked his servant in charge of
the workers, "Whose girl is that?"
6 The servant answered, "She is the young
Moabite woman who came back with
Naomi from the country of Moab. 7 She said,
'Please let me follow the workers cutting
grain and gather what they leave behind.'
She came and has remained here, from
morning until just now. She has stopped
only a few moments to rest in the shelter."
8 Then Boaz said to Ruth, "Listen, my
daughter. Don't go to gather grain for
yourself in another field. Don't even leave
this field at all, but continue following
closely behind my women workers. 9 Watch
to see into which fields they go to cut grain
and follow them. I have warned the young
men not to bother you. When you are
thirsty, you may go and drink from the water
jugs that the young men have filled."
10 Then Ruth bowed low with her face to
the ground and said to him, "I am not an
Israelite. Why have you been so kind to
notice me?"
11 Boaz answered her, "I know about all the
help you have given your mother-in-law
after your husband died. You left your father
and mother and your own country to come
to a nation where you did not know anyone.
12 May the LORD reward you for all you have
done. May your wages be paid in full by the
LORD, the God of Israel, under whose wings
you have come for shelter."
13 Then Ruth said, "I hope I can continue
to please you, sir. You have said kind and
encouraging words to me, your servant,
though I am not one of your servants."
14 At mealtime Boaz told Ruth, "Come here.
Eat some of our bread and dip it in our
sauce."
So Ruth sat down beside the workers. Boaz
handed her some roasted grain, and she ate
until she was full; she even had some food
left over. 15 When Ruth rose and went back
to work, Boaz commanded his workers, "Let
her gather even around the piles of cut grain.
Don't tell her to go away. 16 In fact, drop some
full heads of grain for her from what you
have in your hands, and let her gather them.
Don't tell her to stop."
17 So Ruth gathered grain in the field until
evening. Then she separated the grain from
the chaff, and there was about one-half
bushel of barley. 18 Ruth carried the grain
into town, and her mother-in-law saw how
much she had gathered. Ruth also took out
the food that was left over from lunch and
gave it to Naomi.
19 Naomi asked her, "Where did you gather
all this grain today? Where did you work?
Blessed be whoever noticed you!"
Ruth told her mother-in-law whose field
she had worked in. She said, "The man I
worked with today is named Boaz."
20 Naomi told her daughter-in-law, "The
LORD bless him! He continues to be kind to
us—both the living and the dead!" Then
Naomi told Ruth, "Boaz is one of our close
relatives,[n] one who should take care of us."
21 Then Ruth, the Moabite, said, "Boaz also
told me, 'Keep close to my workers until
they have finished my whole harvest.' "
22 But Naomi said to her daughter-in-law
Ruth, "It is better for you to continue
working with his women workers. If you
work in another field, someone might hurt
you." 23 So Ruth continued working closely
with the workers of Boaz, gathering grain
until the barley harvest and the wheat
harvest were finished. And she continued to
live with Naomi, her mother-in-law.

Naomi's Plan

3 Then Naomi, Ruth's mother-in-law, said
to her, "My daughter, I must find a
suitable home for you, one that will be good
for you. 2 Now Boaz, whose young women
you worked with, is our close relative.[n]
Tonight he will be working at the threshing
floor. 3 Wash yourself, put on perfume,
change your clothes, and go down to the
threshing floor. But don't let him know
you're there until he has finished his dinner.
4 Watch him so you will know where he lies

2:20; 3:2 close relatives In Bible times the closest relative could marry a widow without children so she could have children. He would care for this family, but they and their property would not belong to him. They would belong to the dead husband.

down to sleep. When he lies down, go and
lift the cover off his feet[n] and lie down. He
will tell you what you should do."
5Then Ruth answered, "I will do
everything you say."
6So Ruth went down to the threshing
floor and did all her mother-in-law told her
to do. 7After his evening meal, Boaz felt good
and went to sleep lying beside the pile of
grain. Ruth went to him quietly and lifted
the cover from his feet and lay down.
8About midnight Boaz was startled and
rolled over. There was a woman lying near
his feet! 9Boaz asked, "Who are you?"
She said, "I am Ruth, your servant girl.
Spread your cover over me, because you are
a relative who is supposed to take care of
me."[n]
10Then Boaz said, "The LORD bless you, my
daughter. This act of kindness is greater than
the kindness you showed to Naomi in the
beginning. You didn't look for a young man
to marry, either rich or poor. 11Now, my
daughter, don't be afraid. I will do everything
you ask, because all the people in our town
know you are a good woman. 12It is true that
I am a relative who is to take care of you, but
you have a closer relative than I. 13Stay here
tonight, and in the morning we will see if he
will take care of you. If he decides to take
care of you, that is fine. But if he refuses, I
will take care of you myself, as surely as the
LORD lives. So stay here until morning."
14So Ruth stayed near his feet until
morning but got up while it was still too
dark to recognize anyone. Boaz thought,
"People in town must not know that the
woman came here to the threshing floor."
15So Boaz said to Ruth, "Bring me your shawl
and hold it open."
So Ruth held her shawl open, and Boaz
poured six portions of barley into it. Boaz
then put it on her head and went back to the
city.
16When Ruth went back to her mother-in-
law, Naomi asked, "How did you do, my
daughter?"
Ruth told Naomi everything that Boaz did
for her. 17She said, "Boaz gave me these six
portions of barley, saying, 'You must not go
home without a gift for your mother-in-law.' "
18Naomi answered, "Ruth, my daughter,
wait here until you see what happens. Boaz
will not rest until he has finished doing
what he should do today."

Boaz Marries Ruth

4 Boaz went to the city gate and sat there
until the close relative he had mentioned
passed by. Boaz called to him, "Come here,
friend, and sit down." So the man came over
and sat down. 2Boaz gathered ten of the
elders of the city and told them, "Sit down
here!" So they sat down.
3Then Boaz said to the close relative,
"Naomi, who has come back from the
country of Moab, wants to sell the piece of
land that belonged to our relative Elimelech.
4So I decided to tell you about it: If you want
to buy back the land, then buy it in front of
the people who are sitting here and in front
of the elders of my people. But if you don't
want to buy it, tell me, because you are the
only one who can buy it, and I am next after
you."
The close relative answered, "I will buy
back the land."
5Then Boaz explained, "When you buy
the land from Naomi, you must also marry
Ruth, the Moabite, the dead man's wife. That
way, the land will stay in the dead man's
name."
6The close relative answered, "I can't buy
back the land. If I did, I might harm what I
can pass on to my own sons. I cannot buy
the land back, so buy it yourself."
7Long ago in Israel when people traded or
bought back something, one person took off
his sandal and gave it to the other person.
This was the proof of ownership in Israel.
8So the close relative said to Boaz, "Buy
the land yourself," and he took off his sandal.
9Then Boaz said to the elders and to all the
people, "You are witnesses today. I am
buying from Naomi everything that
belonged to Elimelech and Kilion and
Mahlon. 10I am also taking Ruth, the
Moabite who was the wife of Mahlon, as my
wife. I am doing this so her dead husband's
property will stay in his name and his name
will not be separated from his family and his
hometown. You are witnesses today."
11So all the people and elders who were at
the city gate said, "We are witnesses. May the

3:4 lift . . . feet This showed Ruth was asking him to be her husband. **3:9 Spread . . . me** By this, Ruth was asking Boaz to marry her.

LORD make this woman, who is coming into
your home, like Rachel and Leah, who had
many children and built up the people of
Israel. May you become powerful in the
district of Ephrathah and famous in
Bethlehem. [12]As Tamar gave birth to Judah's
son Perez,[n] may the LORD give you many
children through Ruth. May your family be
great like his."

[13]So Boaz took Ruth home as his wife and
had sexual relations with her. The LORD let
her become pregnant, and she gave birth to a
son. [14]The women told Naomi, "Praise the
LORD who gave you this grandson. May he
become famous in Israel. [15]He will give you
new life and will take care of you in your old
age because of your daughter-in-law who
loves you. She is better for you than seven
sons, because she has given birth to your
grandson."

[16]Naomi took the boy, held him in her
arms, and cared for him. [17]The neighbors
gave the boy his name, saying, "This boy was
born for Naomi." They named him Obed.
Obed was the father of Jesse, and Jesse was
the father of David.

[18]This is the family history of Perez, the
father of Hezron. [19]Hezron was the father of
Ram, who was the father of Amminadab.
[20]Amminadab was the father of Nahshon,
who was the father of Salmon. [21]Salmon was
the father of Boaz, who was the father of
Obed. [22]Obed was the father of Jesse, and
Jesse was the father of David.

4:12 Perez One of Boaz's ancestors.

1 Samuel

Earliest translations of 1 and 2 Samuel actually lumped them together as one book simply called "Samuel," a Hebrew name that means "God hears."

Person Holding the Pen God Wrote With: The author is officially anonymous, although some people assume *Samuel* recorded both 1 and 2 Samuel as an autobiography. This, however, is not possible because Samuel's death is recorded in this volume (1 Sam. 25:1).

When the Text Was Written: This book was penned after the breakup of the original kingdom of Israel in 931 B.C., but almost assuredly before the Babylonian captivity ended from 560–540 B.C. (which is sort of like saying "bigger than a bread box but smaller than the Empire State building").

Spiritual Posture of the Original Recipients: The twelve tribes of Israel, which basically functioned as separate entities when the nation first settled in Canaan, have now morphed into a more united people group under the inaugural monarchy of Saul. But while they've progressed socially, they're still prone to drift about spiritually—much like their literal wanderings in the desert.

Storyline Synopsis: Once upon a time there was an infertile woman named Hannah who cried out to God for a child of her own. God answered her prayers in the form of a bouncing baby boy named Samuel, who matured under the tutelage of a priest named Eli into the first divinely appointed judge of God's people. Samuel's biggest career challenge was facilitating the process of finding a human king for Israel, which he did with a sad face since the Israelites' desire for a flesh and blood monarch was a reflection of their tenuous trust in God. Samuel sighed when they cast their votes for a brawny guy named Saul, who turned out to be a jealous caricature of a king. But before his death, dear old Samuel got to anoint *God's* choice for the next King of Israel—a skinny shepherd boy named David.

A Moment Worth Discussing: Abigail is a plucky woman whose commitment to Jehovah leads to wise actions that catapult her from a horrible marriage with a nasty buffoon named Nabal (who dies, probably as a result of his own gluttony) into a whistles-and-bells romance with King David. Her true tale (1 Sam. 25) reads like a Cinderella story! And her behavior with both Nabal and David is a godly example for all women, whether you're *happily* married, *unhappily* married, or *not yet* married.

Interesting (But Likely to Be Overlooked) Character: *Peninnah* (1 Sam. 1), who ties with Queen Jezebel (1 Kin. 18—19) for the "Most Obnoxious Woman in the Entire Old Testament" award.

Hannah

1 SAMUEL 1

Hannah's heart breaks as she prays. How long has she asked for a child? Tears spill over as she mutters a prayer from the depths of her soul. "Lord All-Powerful, remember me and don't forget me. If you will give me a son, I will give him back to you all his life."

Her husband, Elkanah, was a good man, but he couldn't understand her desire for a child. "Why are you sad?" he had asked. "Don't I mean more to you than ten sons?" Of course she loved her husband, but her desire to be a mother was set in her heart long before she met Elkanah. His wife Peninnah had many children and teased Hannah for having none—how deeply those words cut Hannah!

Each year they all traveled to Shiloh to pray, worship, and offer sacrifices. It was there that Hannah would plead again with the Lord for a son. Eli watched as she prayed—he thought she was drunk. "No, sir," Hannah says, troubled at his accusation. "I was telling the Lord about all my problems. I have been praying because I have many troubles and am very sad." She doesn't tell him why she is crying or praying, but he is kind in his response. "Go! May the God of Israel give you what you asked of him." And he does!

When all seemed hopeless, Hannah persevered in prayer. Are you patient as you pray for a specific need or desire, or do you give up?

Samuel's Birth

1 There was a man named Elkanah son of
Jeroham from Ramathaim in the
mountains of Ephraim. Elkanah was from
the family of Zuph. (Jeroham was Elihu's
son. Elihu was Tohu's son, and Tohu was the
son of Zuph from the family group of
Ephraim.) 2 Elkanah had two wives named
Hannah and Peninnah. Peninnah had
children, but Hannah had none.
3 Every year Elkanah left his town of
Ramah and went up to Shiloh to worship
the LORD All-Powerful and to offer sacrifices
to him. Shiloh was where Hophni and
Phinehas, the sons of Eli, served as priests of
the LORD. 4 When Elkanah offered sacrifices,
he always gave a share of the meat to his
wife Peninnah and to her sons and
daughters. 5 But Elkanah always gave a
special share of the meat to Hannah, because
he loved Hannah and because the LORD had
kept her from having children. 6 Peninnah
would tease Hannah and upset her, because
the LORD had made her unable to have
children. 7 This happened every year when
they went up to the house of the LORD at
Shiloh. Peninnah would upset Hannah until
Hannah would cry and not eat anything.
8 Her husband Elkanah would say to her,
"Hannah, why are you crying and why won't
you eat? Why are you sad? Don't I mean
more to you than ten sons?"
9 Once, after they had eaten their meal in
Shiloh, Hannah got up. Now Eli the priest
was sitting on a chair near the entrance to
the LORD's house. 10 Hannah was so sad that
she cried and prayed to the LORD. 11 She made
a promise, saying, "LORD All-Powerful, see
how sad I am. Remember me and don't
forget me. If you will give me a son, I will
give him back to you all his life, and no one
will ever cut his hair with a razor."[n]
12 While Hannah kept praying, Eli
watched her mouth. 13 She was praying in
her heart so her lips moved, but her voice
was not heard. Eli thought she was drunk
14 and said to her, "Stop getting drunk! Throw
away your wine!"
15 Hannah answered, "No, sir, I have not
drunk any wine or beer. I am a deeply
troubled woman, and I was telling the LORD

1:11 cut . . . razor People who made special promises not to cut their hair or to drink wine or beer were called Nazirites. These people gave a specific time in their lives, or sometimes their entire lives, to the Lord. See Numbers 6:1–5.

about all my problems. 16 Don't think I am an
evil woman. I have been praying because I
have many troubles and am very sad."
17 Eli answered, "Go! I wish you well. May
the God of Israel give you what you asked of
him."
18 Hannah said, "May I always please you."
When she left and ate something, she was
not sad anymore.
19 Early the next morning Elkanah's family
got up and worshiped the LORD. Then they
went back home to Ramah. Elkanah had
sexual relations with his wife Hannah, and
the LORD remembered her. 20 So Hannah
became pregnant, and in time she gave birth
to a son. She named him Samuel,[n] saying,
"His name is Samuel because I asked the
LORD for him."

Hannah Gives Samuel to God

21 Every year Elkanah went with his whole
family to Shiloh to offer sacrifices and to
keep the promise he had made to God. 22 But
one time Hannah did not go with him. She
told him, "When the boy is old enough to
eat solid food, I will take him to Shiloh.
Then I will give him to the LORD, and he will
always live there."
23 Elkanah, Hannah's husband, said to her,
"Do what you think is best. You may stay
home until the boy is old enough to eat. May
the LORD do what you have said." So Hannah
stayed at home to nurse her son until he was
old enough to eat.
24 When Samuel was old enough to eat,
Hannah took him to the house of the LORD
at Shiloh, along with a three-year-old bull,
one-half bushel of flour, and a leather bag
filled with wine. 25 After they had killed the
bull for the sacrifice, Hannah brought Samuel
to Eli. 26 She said to Eli, "As surely as you live,
sir, I am the same woman who stood near you
praying to the LORD. 27 I prayed for this child,
and the LORD answered my prayer and gave
him to me. 28 Now I give him back to the
LORD. He will belong to the LORD all his life."
And he worshiped the LORD there.

Hannah Gives Thanks

2 Hannah prayed:
"The LORD has filled my heart with joy;
I feel very strong in the LORD.
I can laugh at my enemies;
I am glad because you have helped me!
2 "There is no one holy like the LORD.
There is no God but you;
there is no Rock like our God.
3 "Don't continue bragging,
don't speak proud words.
The LORD is a God who knows everything,
and he judges what people do.
4 "The bows of warriors break,
but weak people become strong.
5 Those who once had plenty of food now
must work for food,
but people who were hungry are
hungry no more.
The woman who could not have children
now has seven,
but the woman who had many children
now is sad.
6 "The LORD sends death,
and he brings to life.
He sends people to the grave,
and he raises them to life again.
7 The LORD makes some people poor,
and others he makes rich.
He makes some people humble,
and others he makes great.
8 The LORD raises the poor up from the dust,
and he lifts the needy from the ashes.
He lets the poor sit with princes
and receive a throne of honor.
"The foundations of the earth belong to
the LORD,
and the LORD set the world upon them.
9 He protects those who are loyal to him,
but evil people will be silenced in
darkness.
Power is not the key to success.
10 The LORD destroys his enemies;
he will thunder in heaven against
them.
The LORD will judge all the earth.
He will give power to his king
and make his appointed king strong."

Eli's Evil Sons

11 Then Elkanah went home to Ramah, but
the boy continued to serve the LORD under
Eli the priest.
12 Now Eli's sons were evil men; they did

1:20 Samuel This name sounds like the Hebrew word for "God heard."

not care about the LORD. 13This is what the priests would normally do to the people: Every time someone brought a sacrifice, the meat would be cooked in a pot. The priest's servant would then come carrying a fork that had three prongs. 14He would plunge the fork into the pot or the kettle. Whatever the fork brought out of the pot belonged to the priest. But this is how they treated all the Israelites who came to Shiloh to offer sacrifices. 15Even before the fat was burned, the priest's servant would come to the person offering sacrifices and say, "Give the priest some meat to roast. He won't accept boiled meat from you, only raw meat."

16If the one who offered the sacrifice said, "Let the fat be burned up first as usual, and then take anything you want," the priest's servant would answer, "No, give me the meat now. If you don't, I'll take it by force."

17The LORD saw that the sin of the servants was very great because they did not show respect for the offerings made to the LORD.

Samuel Grows Up

18But Samuel obeyed the LORD. As a boy he wore a linen holy vest. 19Every year Samuel's mother made a little coat for him and took it to him when she went with her husband to Shiloh for the sacrifice. 20When Eli blessed Elkanah and his wife, he would say, "May the LORD repay you with children through Hannah to take the place of the boy Hannah prayed for and gave back to the LORD." Then Elkanah and Hannah would go home. 21The LORD was kind to Hannah, so she became the mother of three sons and two daughters. And the boy Samuel grew up serving the LORD.

22Now Eli was very old. He heard about everything his sons were doing to all the Israelites and how his sons had sexual relations with the women who served at the entrance to the Meeting Tent. 23Eli said to his sons, "Why do you do these evil things that the people tell me about? 24No, my sons. The LORD's people are spreading a bad report about you. 25If you sin against someone, God can help you. But if you sin against the LORD himself, no one can help you!" But Eli's sons would not listen to him, because the LORD had decided to put them to death.

26The boy Samuel grew physically. He pleased the LORD and the people.

27A man of God came to Eli and said, "This is what the LORD says: 'I clearly showed myself to the family of your ancestor Aaron when they were slaves to the king of Egypt. 28I chose them from all the tribes of Israel to be my priests. I wanted them to go up to my altar, to burn incense, and to wear the holy vest. I also let the family of your ancestor have part of all the offerings sacrificed by the Israelites. 29So why don't you respect the sacrifices and gifts? You honor your sons more than me. You grow fat on the best parts of the meat the Israelites bring to me.'

30"So the LORD, the God of Israel, says: 'I promised that your family and your ancestor's family would serve me always.' But now the LORD says: 'This must stop! I will honor those who honor me, but I will dishonor those who ignore me. 31The time is coming when I will destroy the descendants of both you and your ancestors. No man will grow old in your family. 32You will see trouble in my house. No matter what good things happen to Israel, there will never be an old man in your family. 33I will not totally cut off your family from my altar. But your eyes will cry and your heart be sad, because all your descendants will die.

34" 'I will give you a sign. Both your sons, Hophni and Phinehas, will die on the same day. 35I will choose a loyal priest for myself who will listen to me and do what I want. I will make his family continue, and he will always serve before my appointed king. 36Then everyone left in your family will come and bow down before him. They will beg for a little money or a little food and say, "Please give me a job as priest so I can have food to eat." ' "

God Calls Samuel

3 The boy Samuel served the LORD under Eli. In those days the LORD did not speak directly to people very often; there were very few visions.

2Eli's eyes were so weak he was almost blind. One night he was lying in bed. 3Samuel was also in bed in the LORD's house, where the Ark of the Agreement was. God's lamp was still burning.

4Then the LORD called Samuel, and Samuel answered, "I am here!" 5He ran to Eli and said, "I am here. You called me."

But Eli said, "I didn't call you. Go back to bed." So Samuel went back to bed.

6The LORD called again, "Samuel!"
Samuel again went to Eli and said, "I am
here. You called me."
Again Eli said, "I didn't call you. Go back
to bed."
7Samuel did not yet know the LORD, and
the LORD had not spoken directly to him yet.
8The LORD called Samuel for the third
time. Samuel got up and went to Eli and
said, "I am here. You called me."
Then Eli realized the LORD was calling the
boy. 9So he told Samuel, "Go to bed. If he
calls you again, say, 'Speak, LORD. I am your
servant and I am listening.'" So Samuel went
and lay down in bed.
10The LORD came and stood there and
called as he had before, "Samuel, Samuel!"
Samuel said, "Speak, LORD. I am your
servant and I am listening."
11The LORD said to Samuel, "Watch, I am
going to do something in Israel that will
shock those who hear about it. 12At that time
I will do to Eli and his family everything I
promised, from beginning to end. 13I told Eli
I would punish his family always, because
he knew his sons were evil. They acted
without honor, but he did not stop them.
14So I swore to Eli's family, 'Your guilt will
never be removed by sacrifice or offering.'"
15Samuel lay down until morning. Then
he opened the doors of the house of the
LORD. He was afraid to tell Eli about the
vision, 16but Eli called to him, "Samuel, my
son!"
Samuel answered, "I am here."
17Eli asked, "What did the LORD say to
you? Don't hide it from me. May God punish
you terribly if you hide from me anything he
said to you." 18So Samuel told Eli everything
and did not hide anything from him. Then
Eli said, "He is the LORD. Let him do what he
thinks is best."
19The LORD was with Samuel as he grew
up; he did not let any of Samuel's messages
fail to come true. 20Then all Israel, from Dan
to Beersheba,[n] knew Samuel was a true
prophet of the LORD. 21And the LORD
continued to show himself at Shiloh, and
he showed himself to Samuel through his
word.

4 So, news about Samuel spread through
all of Israel.

3:20 Dan to Beersheba Dan was the city farthest north in Israel, and Beersheba was the city farthest south. So this means all the people of Israel.

devotion 75

1 SAMUEL 3:10

WHO'S CALLING?

Have you heard God call your name as Samuel did? Or have you been too busy tuning in to the other people in your life to hear God's message for you? As women these days, we can get so engaged in our tasks that we don't have time to think about how we can serve God in our lives. Be assured that every person has a calling from the Lord. To find out what it is, we need to make sure we're serving God first in everything that we do. Perhaps you are meant to be successful in a huge way that brings glory to God, but then again, maybe his primary task for you today is standing right there in front of you with a dirty, tear-stained face and a scuffed knee. What a huge calling!

Whether we are called to take care of our children, accept a new job, or travel to India to spread the Good News of Jesus, we need to listen for God's calling. What is his purpose for your life? Is he trying to tell you something? I want to encourage you to follow Samuel's example and choose to be God's servant in everything you do. God calls us to different tasks at different times in our lives. If you dream of doing something grand, maybe God is whispering to you, but don't overlook the fact that you are meant to serve God in small ways everyday along the way.

The Philistines Capture the Ark of the Agreement

At that time the Israelites went out to
fight the Philistines. The Israelites camped at
Ebenezer and the Philistines at Aphek. 2The
Philistines went to meet the Israelites in
battle. And as the battle spread, they
defeated the Israelites, killing about four
thousand soldiers on the battlefield. 3When
some Israelite soldiers went back to their
camp, the elders of Israel asked, "Why did
the LORD let the Philistines defeat us? Let's
bring the Ark of the Agreement with the
LORD here from Shiloh and take it with us
into battle. Then God will save us from our
enemies."

4So the people sent men to Shiloh. They
brought back the Ark of the Agreement with
the LORD All-Powerful, who sits between the
gold creatures with wings. Eli's two sons,
Hophni and Phinehas, were there with the
Ark.

5When the Ark of the Agreement with the
LORD came into the camp, all the Israelites
gave a great shout of joy that made the
ground shake. 6When the Philistines heard
Israel's shout, they asked, "What's all this
shouting in the Hebrew camp?"

Then the Philistines found out that the
Ark of the LORD had come into the Hebrew
camp. 7They were afraid and said, "A god has
come into the Hebrew camp! We're in
trouble! This has never happened before!
8How terrible it will be for us! Who can save
us from these powerful gods? They are the
ones who struck the Egyptians with all
kinds of disasters in the desert. 9Be brave,
Philistines! Fight like men! In the past they
were our slaves. So fight like men, or we will
become their slaves."

10So the Philistines fought hard and
defeated the Israelites, and every Israelite
soldier ran away to his own home. It was a
great defeat for Israel, because thirty
thousand Israelite soldiers were killed. 11The
Ark of God was taken by the Philistines, and
Eli's two sons, Hophni and Phinehas, died.

12That same day a man from the tribe of
Benjamin ran from the battle. He tore his
clothes and put dust on his head to show his
great sadness. 13When he arrived in Shiloh,
Eli was by the side of the road. He was sitting
there in a chair, watching, because he was
worried about the Ark of God. When the
Benjaminite entered Shiloh, he told the bad
news. Then all the people in town cried
loudly. 14Eli heard the crying and asked,
"What's all this noise?"

The Benjaminite ran to Eli and told him
what had happened. 15Eli was now ninety-
eight years old, and he was blind. 16The
Benjaminite told him, "I have come from the
battle. I ran all the way here today."

Eli asked, "What happened, my son?"

17The Benjaminite answered, "Israel ran
away from the Philistines, and the Israelite
army has lost many soldiers. Your two sons
are both dead, and the Philistines have taken
the Ark of God."

18When he mentioned the Ark of God, Eli
fell backward off his chair. He fell beside the
gate, broke his neck, and died, because he
was old and fat. He had led Israel for forty
years.

The Glory Is Gone

19Eli's daughter-in-law, the wife of
Phinehas, was pregnant and was about to
give birth. When she heard the news that
the Ark of God had been taken and that Eli,
her father-in-law, and Phinehas, her
husband, were both dead, she began to give
birth to her child. The child was born, but
the mother had much trouble in giving
birth. 20As she was dying, the women who
helped her said, "Don't worry! You've given
birth to a son!" But she did not answer or pay
attention. 21She named the baby Ichabod,[n]
saying, "Israel's glory is gone." She said this
because the Ark of God had been taken and
her father-in-law and husband were dead.
22She said, "Israel's glory is gone, because the
Ark of God has been taken away."

Trouble for the Philistines

5 After the Philistines had captured the
Ark of God, they took it from Ebenezer
to Ashdod. 2They carried it into Dagon's
temple and put it next to Dagon. 3When the
people of Ashdod rose early the next
morning, they found that Dagon had fallen
on his face on the ground before the Ark of
the LORD. So they put Dagon back in his
place. 4The next morning when they rose,
they again found Dagon fallen on the

4:21 Ichabod This name means "no glory."

ground before the Ark of the LORD. His head and hands had broken off and were lying in the doorway. Only his body was still in one piece. 5So, even today, Dagon's priests and others who enter his temple at Ashdod refuse to step on the doorsill.

6The LORD was hard on the people of Ashdod and their neighbors. He caused them to suffer and gave them growths on their skin. 7When the people of Ashdod saw what was happening, they said, "The Ark of the God of Israel can't stay with us. God is punishing us and Dagon our god." 8The people of Ashdod called all five Philistine kings together and asked them, "What should we do with the Ark of the God of Israel?"

The rulers answered, "Move the Ark of the God of Israel to Gath." So the Philistines moved it to Gath.

9But after they moved it to Gath, there was a great panic. The LORD was hard on that city also, and he gave both old and young people in Gath growths on their skin. 10Then the Philistines sent the Ark of God to Ekron.

But when it came into Ekron, the people of Ekron yelled, "Why are you bringing the Ark of the God of Israel to our city? Do you want to kill us and our people?" 11So they called all the kings of the Philistines together and said, "Send the Ark of the God of Israel back to its place before it kills us and our people!" All the people in the city were struck with terror because God was so hard on them there. 12The people who did not die were troubled with growths on their skin. So the people of Ekron cried loudly to heaven.

The Ark of God Is Sent Home

6 The Philistines kept the Ark of God in their land seven months. 2Then they called for their priests and magicians and said, "What should we do with the Ark of the LORD? Tell us how to send it back home!"

3The priests and magicians answered, "If you send back the Ark of the God of Israel, don't send it back empty. You must give a penalty offering. If you are then healed, you will know that it was because of the Ark that you had such trouble."

4The Philistines asked, "What kind of penalty offering should we send to Israel's God?"

They answered, "Make five gold models of the growths on your skin and five gold models of rats. The number of models must match the number of Philistine kings, because the same sickness has come on you and your kings. 5Make models of the growths and the rats that are ruining the country, and give honor to Israel's God. Then maybe he will stop being so hard on you, your gods, and your land. 6Don't be stubborn like the king of Egypt and the Egyptians. After God punished them terribly, they let the Israelites leave Egypt.

7"You must build a new cart and get two cows that have just had calves. These must be cows that have never had yokes on their necks. Hitch the cows to the cart, and take the calves home, away from their mothers. 8Put the Ark of the LORD on the cart and the gold models for the penalty offering in a box beside the Ark. Then send the cart straight on its way. 9Watch the cart. If it goes toward Beth Shemesh in Israel's own land, the LORD has given us this great sickness. But if it doesn't, we will know that Israel's God has not punished us. Our sickness just happened by chance."

10The Philistines did what the priests and magicians said. They took two cows that had just had calves and hitched them to the cart, but they kept their calves at home. 11They put the Ark of the LORD and the box with the gold rats and models of growths on the cart. 12Then the cows went straight toward Beth Shemesh. They stayed on the road, mooing all the way, and did not turn right or left. The Philistine kings followed the cows as far as the border of Beth Shemesh.

13Now the people of Beth Shemesh were harvesting their wheat in the valley. When they looked up and saw the Ark of the LORD, they were very happy. 14The cart came to the field belonging to Joshua of Beth Shemesh and stopped near a large rock. The people of Beth Shemesh chopped up the wood of the cart. Then they sacrificed the cows as burnt offerings to the LORD. 15The Levites took down the Ark of the LORD and the box that had the gold models, and they put both on the large rock. That day the people of Beth Shemesh offered whole burnt offerings and made sacrifices to the LORD. 16After the five Philistine kings saw this, they went back to Ekron the same day.

17 The Philistines had sent these gold models of the growths as penalty offerings to the LORD. They sent one model for each Philistine town: Ashdod, Gaza, Ashkelon, Gath, and Ekron. 18 And the Philistines also sent gold models of rats. The number of rats matched the number of towns belonging to the Philistine kings, including both strong, walled cities and country villages. The large rock on which they put the Ark of the LORD is still there in the field of Joshua of Beth Shemesh.

19 But some of the men of Beth Shemesh looked into the Ark of the LORD. So God killed seventy of them. The people of Beth Shemesh cried because the LORD had struck them down. 20 They said, "Who can stand before the LORD, this holy God? Whom will he strike next?"

21 Then they sent messengers to the people of Kiriath Jearim, saying, "The Philistines have brought back the Ark of the LORD. Come down and take it to your city."

7 The men of Kiriath Jearim came and took the Ark of the LORD to Abinadab's house on a hill. There they made Abinadab's son Eleazar holy for the LORD so he could guard the Ark of the LORD.

The Lord Saves the Israelites

2 The Ark stayed at Kiriath Jearim a long time—twenty years in all. And the people of Israel began to follow the LORD again. 3 Samuel spoke to the whole group of Israel, saying, "If you're turning back to the LORD with all your hearts, you must remove your foreign gods and your idols of Ashtoreth. You must give yourselves fully to the LORD and serve only him. Then he will save you from the Philistines."

4 So the Israelites put away their idols of Baal and Ashtoreth, and they served only the LORD.

5 Samuel said, "All Israel must meet at Mizpah, and I will pray to the LORD for you." 6 So the Israelites met together at Mizpah. They drew water from the ground and poured it out before the LORD and fasted that day. They confessed, "We have sinned against the LORD." And Samuel served as judge of Israel at Mizpah.

7 The Philistines heard the Israelites were meeting at Mizpah, so the Philistine kings came up to attack them. When the Israelites heard they were coming, they were afraid. 8 They said to Samuel, "Don't stop praying to the LORD our God for us! Ask him to save us from the Philistines!" 9 Then Samuel took a baby lamb and offered it to the LORD as a whole burnt offering. He called to the LORD for Israel's sake, and the LORD answered him.

10 While Samuel was burning the offering, the Philistines came near to attack Israel. But the LORD thundered against them with loud thunder. They were so frightened they became confused. So the Israelites defeated the Philistines in battle. 11 The men of Israel ran out of Mizpah and chased the Philistines almost to Beth Car, killing the Philistines along the way.

Peace Comes to Israel

12 After this happened Samuel took a stone and set it up between Mizpah and Shen. He named the stone Ebenezer,[n] saying, "The LORD has helped us to this point." 13 So the Philistines were defeated and did not enter the Israelites' land again.

The LORD was against the Philistines all Samuel's life. 14 Earlier the Philistines had taken towns from the Israelites, but the Israelites won them back, from Ekron to Gath. They also took back from the Philistines the lands near these towns. There was peace also between Israel and the Amorites.

15 Samuel continued as judge of Israel all his life. 16 Every year he went from Bethel to Gilgal to Mizpah and judged the Israelites in all these towns. 17 But Samuel always went back to Ramah, where his home was. There he judged Israel and built an altar to the LORD.

Israel Asks for a King

8 When Samuel was old, he made his sons judges for Israel. 2 His first son was named Joel, and his second son was named Abijah. Joel and Abijah were judges in Beersheba. 3 But Samuel's sons did not live as he did. They tried to get money dishonestly, and they accepted money secretly to make wrong judgments.

7:12 Ebenezer This name means "stone of help."

4 So all the elders came together and met Samuel at Ramah. 5 They said to him, "You're old, and your sons don't live as you do. Give us a king to rule over us like all the other nations."

6 When the elders said that, Samuel was not pleased. He prayed to the LORD, 7 and the LORD told Samuel, "Listen to whatever the people say to you. They have not rejected you. They have rejected me from being their king. 8 They are doing as they have always done. When I took them out of Egypt, they left me and served other gods. They are doing the same to you. 9 Now listen to the people, but warn them what the king who rules over them will do."

10 So Samuel told those who had asked him for a king what the LORD had said. 11 Samuel said, "If you have a king ruling over you, this is what he will do: He will take your sons and make them serve with his chariots and his horses, and they will run in front of the king's chariot. 12 The king will make some of your sons commanders over thousands or over fifties. He will make some of your other sons plow his ground and reap his harvest. He will take others to make weapons of war and equipment for his chariots. 13 He will take your daughters to make perfume and cook and bake for him. 14 He will take your best fields, vineyards, and olive groves and give them to his servants. 15 He will take one-tenth of your grain and grapes and give it to his officers and servants. 16 He will take your male and female servants, your best cattle, and your donkeys and use them all for his own work. 17 He will take one-tenth of your flocks, and you yourselves will become his slaves. 18 When that time comes, you will cry out because of the king you chose. But the LORD will not answer you then."

19 But the people would not listen to Samuel. They said, "No! We want a king to rule over us. 20 Then we will be the same as all the other nations. Our king will judge for us and go with us and fight our battles."

21 After Samuel heard all that the people said, he repeated their words to the LORD. 22 The LORD answered, "You must listen to them. Give them a king."

devotion 76

1 SAMUEL 8:1–22

CAREFUL WHAT YOU WISH FOR

The Israelites came to Samuel in his old age and asked for a king. They begged for someone to rule over them so they could be like other nations. They rejected God as their king because they wanted someone they could see and touch—an earthly king like their neighbors had. Samuel said there would be consequences for their refusal to follow God's plan. And shortly after Saul ascended the throne, many of Samuel's predictions came true. The people had to sacrifice many good things in order to have what they thought they wanted.

The very same thing can happen to you and me. We can look around and decide that we want what others have, resolving that we clearly deserve a house like that or a car like that or a husband like that. We can beg and cry and plead and stomp, manipulating and conniving until we have our way. Having a nice house or a great husband are not bad things. But not waiting for God's plan or timing is, and always has been, foolishness.

When God gives the car, the vacation, or another desire of your heart, it becomes a gift to be shared and enjoyed. But when you have schemed your way into your desire, the heart grows prideful and haughty. The consequences are piled on and suffering is inevitable.

What is the desire of your heart? God wants to hear. He wants to answer. Will you wait for his goodness instead of getting ahead of his timing?

Then Samuel told the people of Israel, "Go
back to your towns."

Saul Looks for His Father's Donkeys

9 Kish, son of Abiel from the tribe of
Benjamin, was an important man. (Abiel
was the son of Zeror, who was the son of
Becorath, who was the son of Aphiah of
Benjamin.) [2]Kish had a son named Saul, who
was a fine young man. There was no Israelite
better than he. Saul stood a head taller than
any other man in Israel.
[3]Now the donkeys of Saul's father, Kish,
were lost. So Kish said to Saul, his son, "Take
one of the servants, and go and look for the
donkeys." [4]Saul went through the
mountains of Ephraim and the land of
Shalisha, but he and the servant could not
find the donkeys. They went into the land of
Shaalim, but the donkeys were not there.
They went through the land of Benjamin,
but they still did not find them. [5]When they
arrived in the area of Zuph, Saul said to his
servant, "Let's go back or my father will stop
thinking about the donkeys and will start
worrying about us."
[6]But the servant answered, "A man of God
is in this town. People respect him because
everything he says comes true. Let's go into
the town now. Maybe he can tell us
something about the journey we have
taken."
[7]Saul said to his servant, "If we go into the
town, what can we give him? The food in
our bags is gone. We have no gift to give
him. Do we have anything?"
[8]Again the servant answered Saul. "Look, I
have one-tenth of an ounce of silver. Give it
to the man of God. Then he will tell us about
our journey." [9](In the past, if someone in
Israel wanted to ask something from God, he
would say, "Let's go to the seer." We call the
person a prophet today, but in the past he
was called a seer.)
[10]Saul said to his servant, "That's a good
idea. Come, let's go." So they went toward
the town where the man of God was.
[11]As Saul and the servant were going up
the hill to the town, they met some young
women coming out to get water. Saul and
the servant asked them, "Is the seer here?"
[12]The young women answered, "Yes, he's
here. He's ahead of you. Hurry now. He has
just come to our town today, because the
people will offer a sacrifice at the place of
worship. [13]As soon as you enter the town,
you will find him before he goes up to the
place of worship to eat. The people will not
begin eating until the seer comes, because he
must bless the sacrifice. After that, the guests
will eat. Go now, and you should find him."

Saul Meets Samuel

[14]Saul and the servant went up to the
town. Just as they entered it, they saw
Samuel coming toward them on his way up
to the place of worship.
[15]The day before Saul came, the LORD had
told Samuel: [16]"About this time tomorrow I
will send you a man from the land of
Benjamin. Appoint him to lead my people
Israel. He will save my people from the
Philistines. I have seen the suffering of my
people, and I have listened to their cry."
[17]When Samuel first saw Saul, the LORD
said to Samuel, "This is the man I told you
about. He will organize my people."
[18]Saul approached Samuel at the gate and
said, "Please tell me where the seer's house is."
[19]Samuel answered, "I am the seer. Go
with me to the place of worship. Today you
and your servant are to eat with me.
Tomorrow morning I will answer all your
questions and send you home. [20]Don't worry
about the donkeys you lost three days ago,
because they have been found. Soon all the
wealth of Israel will belong to you and your
family."
[21]Saul answered, "But I am from the tribe
of Benjamin, the smallest tribe in Israel. And
my family group is the smallest in the tribe
of Benjamin. Why are you saying such
things?"
[22]Then Samuel took Saul and his servant
into a large room and gave them a choice
place at the table. About thirty guests were
there. [23]Samuel said to the cook, "Bring the
meat I gave you, the portion I told you to set
aside."
[24]So the cook took the thigh and put it on
the table in front of Saul. Samuel said, "This
is the meat saved for you. Eat it, because it
was set aside for you for this special time. As
I said, 'I had invited the people.' " So Saul ate
with Samuel that day.
[25]After they finished eating, they came
down from the place of worship and went to
the town. Then Samuel talked with Saul on

the roof[n] of his house. 26At dawn they got up, and Samuel called to Saul on the roof. He said, "Get up, and I will send you on your way." So Saul got up and went out of the house with Samuel. 27As Saul, his servant, and Samuel were getting near the edge of the city, Samuel said to Saul, "Tell the servant to go on ahead of us, but you stay, because I have a message from God for you."

Samuel Appoints Saul

10 Samuel took a jar of olive oil and poured it on Saul's head. He kissed Saul and said, "The LORD has appointed you to lead his people. 2After you leave me today, you will meet two men near Rachel's tomb on the border of Benjamin at Zelzah. They will say to you, 'The donkeys you were looking for have been found. But now your father has stopped thinking about his donkeys and is worrying about you. He is asking, "What will I do about my son?" '

3"Then you will go on until you reach the big tree at Tabor. Three men on their way to worship God at Bethel will meet you there. One man will be carrying three goats. Another will be carrying three loaves of bread. And the third will have a leather bag full of wine. 4They will greet you and offer you two loaves of bread, which you must accept. 5Then you will go to Gibeah of God, where a Philistine camp is. When you approach this town, a group of prophets will come down from the place of worship. They will be playing harps, tambourines, flutes, and lyres, and they will be prophesying. 6Then the Spirit of the LORD will rush upon you with power. You will prophesy with these prophets, and you will be changed into a different man. 7After these signs happen, do whatever you find to do, because God will help you.

8"Go ahead of me to Gilgal. I will come down to you to offer whole burnt offerings and fellowship offerings. But you must wait seven days. Then I will come and tell you what to do."

Saul Made King

9When Saul turned to leave Samuel, God changed Saul's heart. All these signs came true that day. 10When Saul and his servant arrived at Gibeah, Saul met a group of prophets. The Spirit of God rushed upon him, and he prophesied with the prophets. 11When people who had known Saul before saw him prophesying with the prophets, they asked each other, "What has happened to Kish's son? Is even Saul one of the prophets?"

12A man who lived there said, "Who is the father of these prophets?" So this became a famous saying: "Is even Saul one of the prophets?" 13When Saul finished prophesying, he entered the place of worship.

14Saul's uncle asked him and his servant, "Where have you been?"

Saul said, "We were looking for the donkeys. When we couldn't find them, we went to talk to Samuel."

15Saul's uncle asked, "Please tell me. What did Samuel say to you?"

16Saul answered, "He told us the donkeys had already been found." But Saul did not tell his uncle what Samuel had said about his becoming king.

17Samuel called all the people of Israel to meet with the LORD at Mizpah. 18He said, "This is what the LORD, the God of Israel, says: 'I led Israel out of Egypt. I saved you from Egypt's control and from other kingdoms that were troubling you.' 19But now you have rejected your God. He saves you from all your troubles and problems, but you said, 'No! We want a king to rule over us.' Now come, stand before the LORD in your tribes and family groups."

20When Samuel gathered all the tribes of Israel, the tribe of Benjamin was picked. 21Samuel had them pass by in family groups, and Matri's family was picked. Then he had each man of Matri's family pass by, and Saul son of Kish was picked. But when they looked for Saul, they could not find him. 22They asked the LORD, "Has Saul come here yet?"

The LORD said, "Yes. He's hiding behind the baggage."

23So they ran and brought him out. When Saul stood among the people, he was a head taller than anyone else. 24Then Samuel said

9:25 roof In Bible times houses were built with flat roofs. The roof was used for drying things such as flax and fruit. And it was used as an extra room, as a place for worship, and as a cool place to sleep in the summer. See Deuteronomy 22:8.

to the people, "See the man the LORD has
chosen. There is no one like him among all
the people."

Then the people shouted, "Long live the
king!"

25Samuel explained the rights and duties
of the king and then wrote them in a book
and put it before the LORD. Then he told the
people to go to their homes.

26Saul also went to his home in Gibeah.
God touched the hearts of certain brave men
who went along with him. 27But some
troublemakers said, "How can this man save
us?" They disapproved of Saul and refused to
bring gifts to him. But Saul kept quiet.

Nahash Troubles Jabesh Gilead

11 About a month later Nahash the
Ammonite and his army surrounded
the city of Jabesh in Gilead. All the people of
Jabesh said to Nahash, "Make a treaty with
us, and we will serve you."

2But he answered, "I will make a treaty
with you only if I'm allowed to poke out the
right eye of each of you. Then all Israel will
be ashamed!"

3The elders of Jabesh said to Nahash, "Give
us seven days to send messengers through
all Israel. If no one comes to help us, we will
give ourselves up to you."

4When the messengers came to Gibeah
where Saul lived and told the people the
news, they cried loudly. 5Saul was coming
home from plowing the fields with his oxen
when he heard the people crying. He asked,
"What's wrong with the people that they are
crying?" Then they told Saul what the
messengers from Jabesh had said. 6When
Saul heard their words, God's Spirit rushed
upon him with power, and he became very
angry. 7So he took a pair of oxen and cut
them into pieces. Then he gave the pieces of
the oxen to messengers and ordered them to
carry them through all the land of Israel.

The messengers said, "This is what will
happen to the oxen of anyone who does not
follow Saul and Samuel." So the people
became very afraid of the LORD. They all
came together as if they were one person.
8Saul gathered the people together at Bezek.
There were three hundred thousand men
from Israel and thirty thousand men from
Judah.

9They said to the messengers who had
come, "Tell the people at Jabesh Gilead this:
'Before the day warms up tomorrow, you
will be saved.'" So the messengers went and
reported this to the people at Jabesh, and
they were very happy. 10The people said to
Nahash the Ammonite, "Tomorrow we will
come out to meet you. Then you can do
anything you want to us."

11The next morning Saul divided his
soldiers into three groups. At dawn they
entered the Ammonite camp and defeated
them before the heat of the day. The
Ammonites who escaped were scattered; no
two of them were still together.

12Then the people said to Samuel, "Who
didn't want Saul as king? Bring them here
and we will kill them!"

13But Saul said, "No! No one will be put to
death today. Today the LORD has saved
Israel!"

14Then Samuel said to the people, "Come,
let's go to Gilgal. There we will again
promise to obey the king." 15So all the
people went to Gilgal, and there, before the
LORD, the people made Saul king. They
offered fellowship offerings to the LORD, and
Saul and all the Israelites had a great
celebration.

Samuel's Farewell Speech

12 Samuel said to all Israel, "I have done
everything you wanted me to do and
have put a king over you. 2Now you have a
king to lead you. I am old and gray, and my
sons are here with you. I have been your
leader since I was young. 3Here I am. If I
have done anything wrong, you must testify
against me before the LORD and his
appointed king. Did I steal anyone's ox or
donkey? Did I hurt or cheat anyone? Did I
ever secretly accept money to pretend not to
see something wrong? If I did any of these
things, I will make it right."

4The Israelites answered, "You have not
cheated us, or hurt us, or taken anything
unfairly from anyone."

5Samuel said to them, "The LORD is a
witness to what you have said. His
appointed king is also a witness today that
you did not find anything wrong in me."

"He is our witness," they said.

6Then Samuel said to the people, "It is the
LORD who chose Moses and Aaron and
brought your ancestors out of Egypt. 7Now,

stand there, and I will remind you of all the good things the LORD did for you and your ancestors.

8"After Jacob entered Egypt, his descendants cried to the LORD for help. So the LORD sent Moses and Aaron, who took your ancestors out of Egypt and brought them to live in this place.

9"But they forgot the LORD their God. So he handed them over as slaves to Sisera, the commander of the army of Hazor, and as slaves to the Philistines and the king of Moab. They all fought against your ancestors. 10Then your ancestors cried to the LORD and said, 'We have sinned. We have left the LORD and served the Baals and the Ashtoreths. But now save us from our enemies, and we will serve you.' 11So the LORD sent Gideon,[n] Barak, Jephthah, and Samuel. He saved you from your enemies around you, and you lived in safety. 12But when you saw Nahash king of the Ammonites coming against you, you said, 'No! We want a king to rule over us!'—even though the LORD your God was your king. 13Now here is the king you chose, the one you asked for. The LORD has put him over you. 14You must honor the LORD and serve him. You must obey his word and not turn against his commands. Both you and the king ruling over you must follow the LORD your God. If you do, it will be well with you. 15But if you don't obey the LORD, and if you turn against his commands, he will be against you. He will do to you what he did to your ancestors.

16"Now stand still and see the great thing the LORD will do before your eyes. 17It is now the time of the wheat harvest.[n] I will pray for the LORD to send thunder and rain. Then you will know what an evil thing you did against the LORD when you asked for a king."

18Then Samuel prayed to the LORD, and that same day the LORD sent thunder and rain. So the people were very afraid of the LORD and Samuel. 19They said to Samuel, "Pray to the LORD your God for us, your servants! Don't let us die! We've added to all our sins the evil of asking for a king."

20Samuel answered, "Don't be afraid. It's true that you did wrong, but don't turn away from the LORD. Serve the LORD with all your heart. 21Idols are of no use, so don't worship them. They can't help you or save you. They are useless! 22For his own sake, the LORD won't leave his people. Instead, he was pleased to make you his own people. 23I will surely not stop praying for you, because that would be sinning against the LORD. I will teach you what is good and right. 24You must honor the LORD and truly serve him with all your heart. Remember the wonderful things he did for you! 25But if you are stubborn and do evil, he will sweep you and your king away."

13 Saul was thirty years old when he became king, and he was king over Israel forty-two years.[n] 2Saul chose three thousand men from Israel. Two thousand men stayed with him at Micmash in the mountains of Bethel, and one thousand men stayed with Jonathan at Gibeah in Benjamin. Saul sent the other men in the army back home.

3Jonathan attacked the Philistine camp in Geba, and the other Philistines heard about it. Saul said, "Let the Hebrews hear what happened." So he told the men to blow trumpets through all the land of Israel. 4All the Israelites heard the news. The men said, "Saul has defeated the Philistine camp. Now the Philistines will really hate us!" Then the Israelites were called to join Saul at Gilgal.

5The Philistines gathered to fight Israel with three thousand[n] chariots and six thousand men to ride in them. Their soldiers were as many as the grains of sand on the seashore. The Philistines went and camped at Micmash, which is east of Beth Aven. 6When the Israelites saw that they were in trouble, they went to hide in caves and bushes, among the rocks, and in pits and wells. 7Some Hebrews even went across the Jordan River to the land of Gad and Gilead.

But Saul stayed at Gilgal, and all the men in his army were shaking with fear. 8Saul waited seven days, because Samuel had said he would meet him then. But Samuel did not come to Gilgal, and the soldiers began to leave.

9So Saul said, "Bring me the whole burnt

12:11 Gideon Also called Jerub-Baal. **12:17 time . . . harvest** This was a dry time in the summer when no rains fell.
13:1 Saul . . . years This is how the verse is worded in some early Greek copies. The Hebrew is not clear here.
13:5 three thousand Some Greek copies say three thousand. The Hebrew copies say thirty thousand.

devotion 77

1 SAMUEL 12:23–24

WHAT DOES GOD COLLECT?

Prayer time with the Lord is a sacred communion. The Lord cherishes our prayers so much that he has golden bowls full of the prayers of his saints—that means you and me (Rev. 5:8). Our prayers to God come from our hearts, hearts that offer praises to him, hearts that seek him for counsel, and hearts that desire him as comfort. Prayers are what our heavenly Father deems worthy of collection, the desires and needs of the hearts he gave us. What are your praises today, what are your needs, and what are your desires? Who or what will you lean on to fulfill the work of your heart? The Lord wants you! All of you!

Yes, he has put friends, counselors, and pastors in our lives to train, support, and encourage us, but be careful—God wants to be your first confidant. We have to caution ourselves not to replace our prayer lives and communication with the Lord with phone calls or meetings with friends.

I had a girlfriend once tell me that her daughter withheld many of the details of her life from her, and that part of their relationship caused my friend a great deal of heartache. Who wants to give birth to, nurture, and provide for a child and then have communication cut off? You can understand the pain that would cause, and God feels the same way about us. Treat God as your best friend and most trusted ally. Turn to him first in all of life's circumstances.

offering and the fellowship offerings." Then
Saul offered the whole burnt offering. [10]Just
as he finished, Samuel arrived, and Saul
went to greet him.
[11]Samuel asked, "What have you done?"
Saul answered, "I saw the soldiers leaving
me, and you were not here when you said
you would be. The Philistines were
gathering at Micmash. [12]Then I thought,
'The Philistines will come against me at
Gilgal, and I haven't asked for the LORD's
approval.' So I forced myself to offer the
whole burnt offering."
[13]Samuel said, "You acted foolishly! You
haven't obeyed the command of the LORD
your God. If you had obeyed him, the LORD
would have made your kingdom continue in
Israel always, [14]but now your kingdom will
not continue. The LORD has looked for the
kind of man he wants. He has appointed him
to rule his people, because you haven't
obeyed his command."
[15]Then Samuel left Gilgal and went to
Gibeah in Benjamin. Saul counted the men
who were still with him, and there were
about six hundred.

Hard Times for Israel

[16]Saul and his son Jonathan and the
soldiers with him stayed in Gibeah in the
land of Benjamin. The Philistines made their
camp at Micmash. [17]Three groups went out
from the Philistine camp to make raids. One
group went on the Ophrah road in the land
of Shual. [18]The second group went on the
Beth Horon road. The third group went on
the border road that overlooks the Valley of
Zeboim toward the desert.
[19]The whole land of Israel had no
blacksmith because the Philistines had said,
"The Hebrews might make swords and
spears." [20]So all the Israelites had to go down
to the Philistines to have their plows, hoes,
axes, and sickles sharpened. [21]The Philistine

blacksmiths charged about one-fourth of an
ounce of silver for sharpening plows and
hoes. And they charged one-eighth of an
ounce of silver for sharpening picks, axes,
and the sticks used to guide oxen.
22 So when the battle came, the soldiers
with Saul and Jonathan had no swords or
spears. Only Saul and his son Jonathan had
them.

Israel Defeats the Philistines

23 A group from the Philistine army had
gone out to the pass at Micmash.
14 One day Jonathan, Saul's son, said to
the officer who carried his armor,
"Come, let's go over to the Philistine camp
on the other side." But Jonathan did not tell
his father.
2 Saul was sitting under a pomegranate
tree at the threshing floor near Gibeah. He
had about six hundred men with him. 3 One
man was Ahijah who was wearing the holy
vest. (Ahijah was a son of Ichabod's brother
Ahitub. Ichabod was the son of Phinehas, the
son of Eli, the LORD's priest in Shiloh.) No
one knew Jonathan had left.
4 There was a steep slope on each side of
the pass that Jonathan planned to go
through to reach the Philistine camp. The
cliff on one side was named Bozez, and
the cliff on the other side was named Seneh.
5 One cliff faced north toward Micmash. The
other faced south toward Geba.
6 Jonathan said to his officer who carried
his armor, "Come. Let's go to the camp of
those men who are not circumcised. Maybe
the LORD will help us. The LORD can give us
victory if we have many people, or just a
few."
7 The officer who carried Jonathan's armor
said to him, "Do whatever you think is best.
Go ahead. I'm with you."
8 Jonathan said, "Then come. We will cross
over to the Philistines and let them see us.
9 If they say to us, 'Stay there until we come
to you,' we will stay where we are. We
won't go up to them. 10 But if they say, 'Come
up to us,' we will climb up, and the LORD
will let us defeat them. This will be the sign
for us."
11 When both Jonathan and his officer let
the Philistines see them, the Philistines said,
"Look! The Hebrews are crawling out of the
holes they were hiding in!" 12 The Philistines
in the camp shouted to Jonathan and his
officer, "Come up to us. We'll teach you a
lesson!"
Jonathan said to his officer, "Climb up
behind me, because the LORD has given the
Philistines to Israel!" 13 So Jonathan climbed
up, using his hands and feet, and his officer
climbed just behind him. Jonathan struck
down the Philistines as he went, and his
officer killed them as he followed behind
him. 14 In that first fight Jonathan and his
officer killed about twenty Philistines over a
half acre of ground.
15 All the Philistine soldiers panicked—
those in the camp and those in the raiding
party. The ground itself shook! God had
caused the panic.
16 Saul's guards were at Gibeah in the land
of Benjamin when they saw the Philistine
soldiers running in every direction. 17 Saul
said to his army, "Check to see who has left
our camp." When they checked, they
learned that Jonathan and his officer were
gone.
18 So Saul said to Ahijah the priest, "Bring
the Ark of God." (At that time it was with the
Israelites.) 19 While Saul was talking to the
priest, the confusion in the Philistine camp
was growing. Then Saul said to Ahijah, "Put
your hand down!"
20 Then Saul gathered his army and
entered the battle. They found the
Philistines confused, striking each other
with their swords! 21 Earlier, there were
Hebrews who had served the Philistines and
had stayed in their camp, but now they
joined the Israelites with Saul and Jonathan.
22 When all the Israelites hidden in the
mountains of Ephraim heard that the
Philistine soldiers were running away, they
also joined the battle and chased the
Philistines. 23 So the LORD saved the Israelites
that day, and the battle moved on past Beth
Aven.

Saul Makes Another Mistake

24 The men of Israel were miserable that
day because Saul had made an oath for all of
them. He had said, "No one should eat food
before evening and before I finish defeating
my enemies. If he does, he will be cursed!" So
no Israelite soldier ate food.
25 Now the army went into the woods,
where there was some honey on the ground.

26 They came upon some honey, but no one
took any because they were afraid of the
oath. 27 Jonathan had not heard the oath Saul
had put on the army, so he dipped the end of
his stick into the honey and lifted some out
and ate it. Then he felt better. 28 Then one of
the soldiers told Jonathan, "Your father made
an oath for all the soldiers. He said any man
who eats today will be cursed! That's why
they are so weak."

29 Jonathan said, "My father has made
trouble for the land! See how much better I
feel after just tasting a little of this honey!
30 It would have been much better for the
men to eat the food they took from their
enemies today. We could have killed many
more Philistines!"

31 That day the Israelites defeated the
Philistines from Micmash to Aijalon. After
that, they were very tired. 32 They had taken
sheep, cattle, and calves from the Philistines.
Now they were so hungry they killed the
animals on the ground and ate them,
without draining the blood from them!
33 Someone said to Saul, "Look! The men are
sinning against the LORD. They're eating
meat without draining the blood from it!"

Saul said, "You have sinned! Roll a large
stone over here now!" 34 Then he said, "Go to
the men and tell them that each person
must bring his ox and sheep to me and kill it
here and eat it. Don't sin against the LORD by
eating meat without draining the blood
from it."

That night everyone brought his animals
and killed them there. 35 Then Saul built an
altar to the LORD. It was the first altar he had
built to the LORD.

36 Saul said, "Let's go after the Philistines
tonight and rob them. We won't let any of
them live!"

The men answered, "Do whatever you
think is best."

But the priest said, "Let's ask God."

37 So Saul asked God, "Should I chase the
Philistines? Will you let us defeat them?" But
God did not answer Saul at that time. 38 Then
Saul said to all the leaders of his army,
"Come here. Let's find out what sin has been
done today. 39 As surely as the LORD lives who
has saved Israel, even if my son Jonathan did
the sin, he must die." But no one in the army
spoke.

40 Then Saul said to all the Israelites, "You
stand on this side. I and my son Jonathan
will stand on the other side."

The men answered, "Do whatever you
think is best."

41 Then Saul prayed to the LORD, the God
of Israel, "Give me the right answer."

And Saul and Jonathan were picked; the
other men went free. 42 Saul said, "Now let us
discover if it is I or Jonathan my son who is
guilty." And Jonathan was picked.

43 Saul said to Jonathan, "Tell me what you
have done."

So Jonathan told Saul, "I only tasted a
little honey from the end of my stick. And
must I die now?"

44 Saul said, "Jonathan, if you don't die,
may God punish me terribly."

45 But the soldiers said to Saul, "Must
Jonathan die? Never! He is responsible for
saving Israel today! As surely as the LORD
lives, not even a hair of his head will fall to
the ground! Today Jonathan fought against
the Philistines with God's help!" So the army
saved Jonathan, and he did not die.

46 Then Saul stopped chasing the
Philistines, and they went back to their own
land.

Saul Fights Israel's Enemies

47 When Saul became king over Israel, he
fought against Israel's enemies all around.
He fought Moab, the Ammonites, Edom, the
king of Zobah, and the Philistines.
Everywhere Saul went he defeated Israel's
enemies. 48 He fought bravely and defeated
the Amalekites. He saved the Israelites from
their enemies who had robbed them.

49 Saul's sons were Jonathan, Ishvi, and
Malki-Shua. His older daughter was named
Merab, and his younger daughter was
named Michal. 50 Saul's wife was Ahinoam
daughter of Ahimaaz. The commander of his
army was Abner son of Ner, Saul's uncle.
51 Saul's father Kish and Abner's father Ner
were sons of Abiel.

52 All Saul's life he fought hard against the
Philistines. When he saw strong or brave
men, he took them into his army.

Saul Rejected as King

15 Samuel said to Saul, "The LORD sent
me to appoint you king over Israel.
Now listen to his message. 2 This is what the
LORD All-Powerful says: 'When the Israelites

came out of Egypt, the Amalekites tried to
stop them from going to Canaan. So I will
punish them. 3 Now go, attack the
Amalekites and destroy everything they
own as an offering to the LORD. Don't let
anything live. Put to death men and women,
children and small babies, cattle and sheep,
camels and donkeys.' "
4 So Saul called the army together at
Telaim. There were two hundred thousand
foot soldiers and ten thousand men from
Judah. 5 Then Saul went to the city of
Amalek and set up an ambush in the ravine.
6 He said to the Kenites, "Go away. Leave the
Amalekites so that I won't destroy you with
them, because you showed kindness to the
Israelites when they came out of Egypt." So
the Kenites moved away from the
Amalekites.
7 Then Saul defeated the Amalekites. He
fought them all the way from Havilah to
Shur, at the border of Egypt. 8 He took King
Agag of the Amalekites alive, but he killed
all of Agag's army with the sword. 9 Saul and
the army let Agag live, along with the best
sheep, fat cattle, and lambs. They let every
good animal live, because they did not want
to destroy them. But when they found an
animal that was weak or useless, they
killed it.
10 Then the LORD spoke his word to
Samuel: 11 "I am sorry I made Saul king,
because he has stopped following me and
has not obeyed my commands." Samuel
was upset, and he cried out to the LORD all
night long.
12 Early the next morning Samuel got up
and went to meet Saul. But the people told
Samuel, "Saul has gone to Carmel, where he
has put up a monument in his own honor.
Now he has gone down to Gilgal."
13 When Samuel came to Saul, Saul said,
"May the LORD bless you! I have obeyed the
LORD's commands."
14 But Samuel said, "Then why do I hear
cattle mooing and sheep bleating?"
15 Saul answered, "The soldiers took them
from the Amalekites. They saved the best
sheep and cattle to offer as sacrifices to the
LORD your God, but we destroyed all the
other animals."

devotion 78

1 SAMUEL 15:22

SAME OLD SAME OLD

Sacrifice was a routine for the people of Israel. It was like going to Sunday school—a checkmark on the list of to-dos for the week. You show up, you do what is expected, and you go home. But did you really please God while you were there?

How much of what we do in our Christian life has become routine rather than from a heart that is fully engaged? How many Christians play the part on Sunday but go back to living a godless life on Monday morning? Who are we fooling? Do we really think God is impressed with our offering of two hours on Sunday morning?

God says that it is better to obey his voice than to play the part of being a Christian. He wants us to live out our Christianity every day of the week. He sees the hearts of everyone, and he knows when your walk with him has become routine. God wants us to listen to his voice so we can keep our walk with him fresh and growing. We need to be in the Word to hear his voice. His Word will change us and make us more and more like Christ. We will become obedient to the voice of God, and we won't even realize we're doing it. Examine your life today to see if your relationship with God has become routine. Ask God to speak to you through his Word, and see how you will please him when you do.

[16]Samuel said to Saul, "Stop! Let me tell
you what the LORD said to me last night."
Saul answered, "Tell me."
[17]Samuel said, "Once you didn't think
much of yourself, but now you have become
the leader of the tribes of Israel. The LORD
appointed you to be king over Israel. [18]And
he sent you on a mission. He said, 'Go and
destroy those evil people, the Amalekites.
Make war on them until all of them are
dead.' [19]Why didn't you obey the LORD? Why
did you take the best things? Why did you
do what the LORD said was wrong?"
[20]Saul said, "But I did obey the LORD. I did
what the LORD told me to do. I destroyed all
the Amalekites, and I brought back Agag
their king. [21]The soldiers took the best sheep
and cattle to sacrifice to the LORD your God
at Gilgal."
[22]But Samuel answered,

"What pleases the LORD more:
burnt offerings and sacrifices
or obedience to his voice?
It is better to obey than to sacrifice.
It is better to listen to God than to offer
the fat of sheep.
[23]Disobedience is as bad as the sin of
sorcery.
Pride is as bad as the sin of worshiping
idols.
You have rejected the LORD's command.
Now he rejects you as king."

[24]Then Saul said to Samuel, "I have
sinned. I didn't obey the LORD's commands
and your words. I was afraid of the people,
and I did what they said. [25]Now, I beg you,
forgive my sin. Come back with me so I may
worship the LORD."
[26]But Samuel said to Saul, "I won't go back
with you. You rejected the LORD's command,
and now he rejects you as king of Israel."
[27]As Samuel turned to leave, Saul caught
his robe, and it tore. [28]Samuel said to him,
"The LORD has torn the kingdom of Israel
from you today and has given it to one of
your neighbors who is better than you. [29]The
LORD is the Eternal One of Israel. He does not
lie or change his mind. He is not a human
being, so he does not change his mind."
[30]Saul answered, "I have sinned. But
please honor me in front of the elders of my
people and in front of the Israelites. Come
back with me so that I can worship the LORD
your God." [31]So Samuel went back with Saul,
and Saul worshiped the LORD.
[32]Then Samuel said, "Bring me King Agag
of the Amalekites."
Agag came to Samuel in chains, but Agag
thought, "Surely the threat of death has
passed."
[33]Samuel said to him, "Your sword made
other mothers lose their children. Now your
mother will have no children." And Samuel
cut Agag to pieces before the LORD at Gilgal.
[34]Then Samuel left and went to Ramah,
but Saul went up to his home in Gibeah.
[35]And Samuel never saw Saul again the rest
of his life, but he was sad for Saul. And the
LORD was very sorry he had made Saul king
of Israel.

Samuel Goes to Bethlehem

16 The LORD said to Samuel, "How long
will you continue to feel sorry for
Saul? I have rejected him as king of Israel.
Fill your container with olive oil and go. I
am sending you to Jesse who lives in
Bethlehem, because I have chosen one of his
sons to be king."
[2]But Samuel said, "If I go, Saul will hear
the news and will try to kill me."
The LORD said, "Take a young calf with
you. Say, 'I have come to offer a sacrifice to
the LORD.' [3]Invite Jesse to the sacrifice. Then I
will tell you what to do. You must appoint
the one I show you."
[4]Samuel did what the LORD told him to do.
When he arrived at Bethlehem, the elders of
Bethlehem shook with fear. They met him
and asked, "Are you coming in peace?"
[5]Samuel answered, "Yes, I come in peace. I
have come to make a sacrifice to the LORD.
Set yourselves apart to the LORD and come to
the sacrifice with me." Then he set Jesse and
his sons apart to the LORD, and he invited
them to come to the sacrifice.
[6]When they arrived, Samuel saw Eliab, and
he thought, "Surely the LORD has appointed
this person standing here before him."
[7]But the LORD said to Samuel, "Don't look
at how handsome Eliab is or how tall he is,
because I have not chosen him. God does not
see the same way people see. People look at
the outside of a person, but the LORD looks at
the heart."
[8]Then Jesse called Abinadab and told him
to pass by Samuel. But Samuel said, "The

LORD has not chosen this man either." 9Then
Jesse had Shammah pass by. But Samuel said,
"No, the LORD has not chosen this one."
10Jesse had seven of his sons pass by Samuel.
But Samuel said to him, "The LORD has not
chosen any of these."
11Then he asked Jesse, "Are these all the
sons you have?"

Jesse answered, "I still have the youngest son. He is out taking care of the sheep."

Samuel said, "Send for him. We will not sit down to eat until he arrives."

12So Jesse sent and had his youngest son
brought in. He was a fine boy, tanned, and
handsome.

The LORD said to Samuel, "Go, appoint him, because he is the one."

13So Samuel took the container of olive oil
and poured it on Jesse's youngest son to
appoint him in front of his brothers. From
that day on, the LORD's Spirit worked in
David. Samuel then went back to Ramah.

David Serves Saul

14But the LORD's Spirit had left Saul, and an
evil spirit from the LORD troubled him.
15Saul's servants said to him, "See, an evil
spirit from God is troubling you. 16Give us
the command to look for someone who can
play the harp. When the evil spirit from God
troubles you, he will play, and you will feel
better."
17So Saul said to his servants, "Find
someone who can play well and bring him
to me."
18One of the servants said, "I have seen a
son of Jesse of Bethlehem play the harp. He
is brave and courageous. He is a good
speaker and handsome, and the LORD is with
him."
19Then Saul sent messengers to Jesse,
saying, "Send me your son David, who is
with the sheep." 20So Jesse loaded a donkey
with bread, a leather bag full of wine, and a
young goat, and he sent them with his son
David to Saul.
21When David came to Saul, he began to
serve him. Saul liked David and made him
the officer who carried his armor. 22Saul sent
a message to Jesse, saying, "Let David stay
and serve me because I like him."
23When the evil spirit from God troubled

devotion 79

1 SAMUEL 16:7

MEASURING UP?

Have you ever told a little girl how adorable she is, only for her to answer, "I know"? It makes us chuckle, and many a mom has probably worried her unabashed daughter will grow up to be conceited. In reality, the opposite may be true. When the little girl hits puberty, her mom might wonder what happened to all that self-confidence.

Teens are not the only ones who struggle with self-esteem issues. We'd also do well to listen to God's standard for value where people are concerned, but it can be difficult to control our insecurities. For example, we all know someone who seems to have it all—she never gains a pound, never has a blemish on her skin, has a perfect career, never yells at her kids, and has an extremely supportive husband. Doesn't she ever mess up? Well yes, but do you think we're going to notice when we're playing the comparison game?

If we fall into the trap of comparing ourselves, young girls will see and may follow suit. God wants them to know—and he wants us to know as well—that he doesn't look at the outside, but at the inside. What do our hearts look like? Are we focused on making our hearts more beautiful? Let's get inspired to work on a part of ourselves that we really can change—the part that really matters. Let's not let the world of fashion, perfection, and diets define us; let's be beautiful in the eyes of the Lord.

Saul, David would take his harp and play. Then the evil spirit would leave him, and Saul would feel better.

David and Goliath

17 The Philistines gathered their armies for war. They met at Socoh in Judah and camped at Ephes Dammim between Socoh and Azekah. [2]Saul and the Israelites gathered in the Valley of Elah and camped there and took their positions to fight the Philistines. [3]The Philistines controlled one hill while the Israelites controlled another. The valley was between them.

[4]The Philistines had a champion fighter from Gath named Goliath. He was about nine feet, four inches tall. He came out of the Philistine camp [5]with a bronze helmet on his head and a coat of bronze armor that weighed about one hundred twenty-five pounds. [6]He wore bronze protectors on his legs, and he had a bronze spear on his back. [7]The wooden part of his larger spear was like a weaver's rod, and its blade weighed about fifteen pounds. The officer who carried his shield walked in front of him.

[8]Goliath stood and shouted to the Israelite soldiers, "Why have you taken positions for battle? I am a Philistine, and you are Saul's servants! Choose a man and send him to fight me. [9]If he can fight and kill me, we will be your servants. But if I can kill him, you will be our servants." [10]Then he said, "Today I stand and dare the army of Israel! Send one of your men to fight me!" [11]When Saul and the Israelites heard the Philistine's words, they were very scared.

[12]Now David was the son of Jesse, an Ephrathite from Bethlehem in Judah. Jesse had eight sons. In Saul's time Jesse was an old man. [13]His three oldest sons followed Saul to the war. The first son was Eliab, the second was Abinadab, and the third was Shammah. [14]David was the youngest. Jesse's three oldest sons followed Saul, [15]but David went back and forth from Saul to Bethlehem, where he took care of his father's sheep.

[16]For forty days the Philistine came out every morning and evening and stood before the Israelite army.

[17]Jesse said to his son David, "Take this half bushel of cooked grain and ten loaves of bread to your brothers in the camp. [18]Also take ten pieces of cheese to the commander and to your brothers. See how your brothers are and bring back some proof to show me that they are all right. [19]Your brothers are with Saul and the army in the Valley of Elah, fighting against the Philistines."

[20]Early in the morning David left the sheep with another shepherd. He took the food and left as Jesse had told him. When David arrived at the camp, the army was going out to their battle positions, shouting their war cry. [21]The Israelites and Philistines were lining up their men to face each other in battle.

[22]David left the food with the man who kept the supplies and ran to the battle line to talk to his brothers. [23]While he was talking with them, Goliath, the Philistine champion from Gath, came out. He shouted things against Israel as usual, and David heard him. [24]When the Israelites saw Goliath, they were very much afraid and ran away.

[25]They said, "Look at this man! He keeps coming out to challenge Israel. The king will give much money to whoever kills him. He will also let whoever kills him marry his daughter. And his father's family will not have to pay taxes in Israel."

[26]David asked the men who stood near him, "What will be done to reward the man who kills this Philistine and takes away the shame from Israel? Who does this uncircumcised Philistine think he is? Does he think he can speak against the armies of the living God?"

[27]The Israelites told David what would be done for the man who would kill Goliath.

[28]When David's oldest brother Eliab heard David talking with the soldiers, he was angry with David. He asked David, "Why did you come here? Who's taking care of those few sheep of yours in the desert? I know you are proud and wicked at heart. You came down here just to watch the battle."

[29]David asked, "Now what have I done wrong? Can't I even talk?" [30]When he turned to other people and asked the same questions, they gave him the same answer as before. [31]Yet what David said was told to Saul, and he sent for David.

[32]David said to Saul, "Don't let anyone be discouraged. I, your servant, will go and fight this Philistine!"

[33]Saul answered, "You can't go out against

this Philistine and fight him. You're only a
boy. Goliath has been a warrior since he was
a young man."

34But David said to Saul, "I, your servant,
have been keeping my father's sheep. When
a lion or bear came and took a sheep from
the flock, 35I would chase it. I would attack it
and save the sheep from its mouth. When it
attacked me, I caught it by its fur and hit it
and killed it. 36I, your servant, have killed
both a lion and a bear! This uncircumcised
Philistine will be like them, because he has
spoken against the armies of the living God.
37The LORD who saved me from a lion and a
bear will save me from this Philistine."

Saul said to David, "Go, and may the LORD
be with you." 38Saul put his own clothes on
David. He put a bronze helmet on his head
and dressed him in armor. 39David put on
Saul's sword and tried to walk around, but
he was not used to all the armor Saul had
put on him.

He said to Saul, "I can't go in this, because
I'm not used to it." Then David took it all
off. 40He took his stick in his hand and
chose five smooth stones from a stream. He
put them in his shepherd's bag and grabbed
his sling. Then he went to meet the
Philistine.

41At the same time, the Philistine was
coming closer to David. The man who held
his shield walked in front of him. 42When
Goliath looked at David and saw that he was
only a boy, tanned and handsome, he looked
down on David with disgust. 43He said, "Do
you think I am a dog, that you come at me
with a stick?" He used his gods' names to
curse David. 44He said to David, "Come here.
I'll feed your body to the birds of the air and
the wild animals!"

45But David said to him, "You come to me
using a sword and two spears. But I come to
you in the name of the LORD All-Powerful,
the God of the armies of Israel! You have
spoken against him. 46Today the LORD will
hand you over to me, and I'll kill you and cut
off your head. Today I'll feed the bodies of
the Philistine soldiers to the birds of the air
and the wild animals. Then all the world
will know there is a God in Israel!
47Everyone gathered here will know the
LORD does not need swords or spears to save
people. The battle belongs to him, and he
will hand you over to us."

48As Goliath came near to attack him,
David ran quickly to meet him. 49He took a
stone from his bag, put it into his sling, and
slung it. The stone hit the Philistine and
went deep into his forehead, and Goliath fell
facedown on the ground.

50So David defeated the Philistine with
only a sling and a stone. He hit him and
killed him. He did not even have a sword in
his hand. 51Then David ran and stood beside
him. He took Goliath's sword out of its
holder and killed him by cutting off his
head.

When the Philistines saw that their
champion was dead, they turned and ran.
52The men of Israel and Judah shouted and
chased the Philistines all the way to the
entrance of the city of Gath and to the gates
of Ekron.

The Philistines' bodies lay on the
Shaaraim road as far as Gath and Ekron.
53The Israelites returned after chasing the
Philistines and robbed their camp. 54David
took Goliath's head to Jerusalem and put
Goliath's weapons in his own tent.

55When Saul saw David go out to meet
Goliath, Saul asked Abner, commander of
the army, "Abner, who is that young man's
father?"

Abner answered, "As surely as you live,
my king, I don't know."

56The king said, "Find out whose son
he is."

57When David came back from killing
Goliath, Abner brought him to Saul. David
was still holding Goliath's head.

58Saul asked him, "Young man, who is
your father?"

David answered, "I am the son of your
servant Jesse of Bethlehem."

Saul Fears David

18 When David finished talking with
Saul, Jonathan felt very close to
David. He loved David as much as he loved
himself. 2Saul kept David with him from
that day on and did not let him go home to
his father's house. 3Jonathan made an
agreement with David, because he loved
David as much as himself. 4He took off his
coat and gave it to David, along with his
armor, including his sword, bow, and belt.

5Saul sent David to fight in different
battles, and David was very successful. Then

Saul put David over the soldiers, which
pleased Saul's officers and all the other
people.
6After David had killed the Philistine, he
and the men returned home. Women came
out from all the towns of Israel to meet King
Saul. They sang songs of joy, danced, and
played tambourines and stringed
instruments. 7As they played, they sang,

"Saul has killed thousands of his enemies,
but David has killed tens of thousands."

8The women's song upset Saul, and he
became very angry. He thought, "The
women say David has killed tens of
thousands, but they say I have killed only
thousands. The only thing left for him to
have is the kingdom!" 9So Saul watched
David closely from then on, because he was
jealous.
10The next day an evil spirit from God
rushed upon Saul, and he prophesied in his
house. David was playing the harp as he
usually did, but Saul had a spear in his hand.
11He threw the spear, thinking, "I'll pin
David to the wall." But David escaped from
him twice.
12The LORD was with David but had left
Saul. So Saul was afraid of David. 13He sent
David away and made him commander of a
thousand soldiers. So David led them in
battle. 14He had great success in everything
he did because the LORD was with him.
15When Saul saw that David was very
successful, he feared David even more. 16But
all the people of Israel and Judah loved
David because he led them well in battle.

Saul's Daughter Marries David

17Saul said to David, "Here is my older
daughter Merab. I will let you marry her. All
I ask is that you remain brave and fight the
LORD's battles." Saul thought, "I won't have to
kill David. The Philistines will do that."
18But David answered Saul, saying, "Who
am I? My family is not important enough for
me to become the king's son-in-law." 19So,
when the time came for Saul's daughter
Merab to marry David, Saul gave her instead
to Adriel of Meholah.
20Now Saul's other daughter, Michal,
loved David. When they told Saul, he was
pleased. 21He thought, "I will let her marry
David. Then she will be a trap for him, and
the Philistines will defeat him." So Saul said
to David a second time, "You may become
my son-in-law."
22And Saul ordered his servants to talk
with David in private and say, "Look, the
king likes you. His servants love you. You
should be his son-in-law."
23Saul's servants said these words to
David, but David answered, "Do you think it
is easy to become the king's son-in-law? I am
poor and unimportant."
24When Saul's servants told him what
David had said, 25Saul said, "Tell David, 'The
king doesn't want money for the bride. All
he wants is a hundred Philistine foreskins to
get even with his enemies.'" Saul planned to
let the Philistines kill David.
26When Saul's servants told this to David,
he was pleased to become the king's son-in-
law. 27So he and his men went out and killed
two hundred Philistines. David brought all
their foreskins to Saul so he could be the
king's son-in-law. Then Saul gave him his
daughter Michal for his wife. 28Saul saw that
the LORD was with David and that his
daughter Michal loved David. 29So he grew
even more afraid of David, and he was
David's enemy all his life.
30The Philistine commanders continued
to go out to fight the Israelites, but every
time, David was more skillful than Saul's
officers. So he became famous.

Saul Tries to Kill David

19 Saul told his son Jonathan and all his
servants to kill David, but Jonathan
liked David very much. 2So he warned David,
"My father Saul is looking for a chance to kill
you. Watch out in the morning. Hide in a
secret place. 3I will go out and stand with my
father in the field where you are hiding, and
I'll talk to him about you. Then I'll let you
know what I find out."
4When Jonathan talked to Saul his father,
he said good things about David. Jonathan
said, "The king should do no wrong to your
servant David since he has done nothing
wrong to you. What he has done has helped
you greatly. 5David risked his life when he
killed Goliath the Philistine, and the LORD
won a great victory for all Israel. You saw it
and were happy. Why would you do wrong
against David? He's innocent. There's no
reason to kill him!"
6Saul listened to Jonathan and then made

this promise: "As surely as the LORD lives,
David won't be put to death."
7So Jonathan called to David and told him
everything that had been said. He brought
David to Saul, and David was with Saul as
before.
8When war broke out again, David went
out to fight the Philistines. He defeated
them, and they ran away from him.
9But once again an evil spirit from the
LORD rushed upon Saul as he was sitting in
his house with his spear in his hand. David
was playing the harp. 10Saul tried to pin
David to the wall with his spear, but David
jumped out of the way. So Saul's spear went
into the wall, and David ran away that
night.
11Saul sent messengers to David's house to
watch it and to kill him in the morning. But
Michal, David's wife, warned him, saying,
"Tonight you must run for your life. If you
don't, you will be dead in the morning." 12So
she let David down out of a window, and he
ran away and escaped. 13Then Michal took
an idol, laid it on the bed, covered it with
clothes, and put goats' hair at its head.
14Saul sent messengers to take David
prisoner, but Michal said, "He is sick."
15Saul sent them back to see David,
saying, "Bring him to me on his bed so I can
kill him."
16When the messengers entered David's
house, they found just an idol on the bed
with goats' hair on its head.
17Saul said to Michal, "Why did you trick
me this way? You let my enemy go so he
could run away!"
Michal answered Saul, "David told me if I
did not help him escape, he would kill me."
18After David had escaped from Saul, he
went to Samuel at Ramah and told him
everything Saul had done to him. Then
David and Samuel went to Naioth and
stayed there. 19Saul heard that David was in
Naioth at Ramah. 20So he sent messengers to
capture him. But they met a group of
prophets prophesying, with Samuel
standing there leading them. So the Spirit of
God entered Saul's men, and they also
prophesied.
21When Saul heard the news, he sent
more messengers, but they also prophesied.
Then he sent messengers a third time, but
they also prophesied. 22Finally, Saul himself
went to Ramah, to the well at Secu. He
asked, "Where are Samuel and David?"
The people answered, "In Naioth at
Ramah."
23When Saul went to Naioth at Ramah,
the Spirit of God also rushed upon him. And
he walked on, prophesying until he came to
Naioth at Ramah. 24He took off his robes and
prophesied in front of Samuel. He lay that
way all day and all night. That is why people
ask, "Is even Saul one of the prophets?"

Jonathan Helps David

20 Then David ran away from Naioth in
Ramah. He went to Jonathan and
asked, "What have I done? What is my
crime? How did I sin against your father?
Why is he trying to kill me?"
2Jonathan answered, "No! You won't die!
See, my father doesn't do anything great or
small without first telling me. Why would
he keep this from me? It's not true!"
3But David took an oath, saying, "Your
father knows very well that you like me. He
says to himself, 'Jonathan must not know
about it, or he will tell David.' As surely as
the LORD lives and as you live, I am only a
step away from death!"
4Jonathan said to David, "I'll do anything
you want me to do."
5So David said, "Look, tomorrow is the
New Moon festival. I am supposed to eat
with the king, but let me hide in the field
until the third evening. 6If your father
notices I am gone, tell him, 'David begged
me to let him go to his hometown of
Bethlehem. Every year at this time his family
group offers a sacrifice.' 7If your father says,
'Fine,' I am safe. But if he becomes angry, you
will know that he wants to hurt me.
8Jonathan, be loyal to me, your servant. You
have made an agreement with me before the
LORD. If I am guilty, you may kill me
yourself! Why hand me over to your father?"
9Jonathan answered, "No, never! If I learn
that my father plans to hurt you, I will warn
you!"
10David asked, "Who will let me know if
your father answers you unkindly?"
11Then Jonathan said, "Come, let's go out
into the field." So the two of them went out
into the field.
12Jonathan said to David, "I promise this
before the LORD, the God of Israel: At this

same time the day after tomorrow, I will find out how my father feels. If he feels good toward you, I will send word to you and let you know. 13But if my father plans to hurt you, I will let you know and send you away safely. May the LORD punish me terribly if I don't do this. And may the LORD be with you as he has been with my father. 14But show me the kindness of the LORD as long as I live so that I may not die. 15You must never stop showing your kindness to my family, even when the LORD has destroyed all your enemies from the earth."

16So Jonathan made an agreement with David. He said, "May the LORD hold David's enemies responsible." 17And Jonathan asked David to repeat his promise of love for him, because he loved David as much as he loved himself.

18Jonathan said to David, "Tomorrow is the New Moon festival. Your seat will be empty, so my father will miss you. 19On the third day go to the place where you hid when this trouble began. Wait by the rock Ezel. 20On the third day I will shoot three arrows to the side of the rock as if I am shooting at a target. 21Then I will send a boy to find the arrows. If I say to him, 'The arrows are near you; bring them here,' you may come out of hiding. You are safe. As the LORD lives, there is no danger. 22But if I say to the boy, 'Look, the arrows are beyond you,' you must go, because the LORD is sending you away. 23Remember what we talked about. The LORD is a witness between you and me forever."

24So David hid in the field. When the New Moon festival came, the king sat down to eat. 25He sat where he always sat, near the wall. Jonathan sat across from him, and Abner sat next to Saul, but David's place was empty. 26That day Saul said nothing. He thought, "Maybe something has happened to David so that he is unclean." 27But the next day was the second day of the month, and David's place was still empty. So Saul said to Jonathan, "Why hasn't the son of Jesse come to the feast yesterday or today?"

28Jonathan answered, "David begged me to let him go to Bethlehem. 29He said, 'Let me go, because our family has a sacrifice in the town, and my brother has ordered me to be there. Now if I am your friend, please let me go to see my brothers.' That is why he has not come to the king's table."

30Then Saul became very angry with Jonathan. He said, "You son of a wicked, worthless woman! I know you are on the side of David son of Jesse! You bring shame on yourself and on your mother who gave birth to you. 31As long as Jesse's son lives, you will never be king or have a kingdom. Now send for David and bring him to me. He must die!"

32Jonathan asked his father, "Why should David be killed? What wrong has he done?" 33Then Saul threw his spear at Jonathan, trying to kill him. So Jonathan knew that his father really wanted to kill David. 34Jonathan was very angry and left the table. That second day of the month he refused to eat. He was ashamed of his father and upset over David.

35The next morning Jonathan went out to the field to meet David as they had agreed. He had a young boy with him. 36Jonathan said to the boy, "Run and find the arrows I shoot." When he ran, Jonathan shot an arrow beyond him. 37The boy ran to the place where Jonathan's arrow fell, but Jonathan called, "The arrow is beyond you!" 38Then he shouted, "Hurry! Go quickly! Don't stop!" The boy picked up the arrow and brought it back to his master. 39(The boy knew nothing about what this meant; only Jonathan and David knew.) 40Then Jonathan gave his weapons to the boy and told him, "Go back to town."

41When the boy left, David came out from the south side of the rock. He bowed facedown on the ground before Jonathan three times. Then David and Jonathan kissed each other and cried together, but David cried the most.

42Jonathan said to David, "Go in peace. We have promised by the LORD that we will be friends. We said, 'The LORD will be a witness between you and me, and between our descendants always.' " Then David left, and Jonathan went back to town.

David Goes to See Ahimelech

21 David went to Nob to see Ahimelech the priest. Ahimelech shook with fear when he saw David, and he asked, "Why are you alone? Why is no one with you?"

2David answered him, "The king gave me a special order. He told me, 'No one must know what I am sending you to do or what I

told you to do.' I told my men where to meet
me. 3Now, what food do you have with you?
Give me five loaves of bread or anything you
find."

4The priest said to David, "I don't have any
plain bread here, but I do have some holy
bread.[n] You may eat it if your men have kept
themselves from women."

5David answered, "No women have been
near us for days. My men always keep
themselves holy, even when we do ordinary
work. And this is especially true when the
work is holy."

6So the priest gave David the holy bread
from the presence of God because there was
no other. Each day the holy bread was
replaced with hot bread.

7One of Saul's servants happened to be
there that day. He had been held there before
the LORD. He was Doeg the Edomite, the
chief of Saul's shepherds.

8David asked Ahimelech, "Do you have a
spear or sword here? The king's business was
very important, so I left without my sword
or any other weapon."

9The priest answered, "The sword of
Goliath the Philistine, the one you killed in
the Valley of Elah, is here. It is wrapped in a
cloth behind the holy vest. If you want it,
you may take it. There's no other sword here
but that one."

David said, "There is no other sword like
it. Give it to me."

David Goes to Gath

10That day David ran away from Saul and
went to Achish king of Gath. 11But the
servants of Achish said to him, "This is
David, the king of the Israelites. He's the
man they dance and sing about, saying:

'Saul has killed thousands of his enemies,
but David has killed tens of thousands.' "

12David paid attention to these words and
was very much afraid of Achish king of
Gath. 13So he pretended to be crazy in front
of Achish and his servants. While he was
with them, he acted like a madman and
clawed on the doors of the gate and let spit
run down his beard.

14Achish said to his servants, "Look at the
man! He's crazy! Why do you bring him to
me? 15I have enough madmen. I don't need
you to bring him here to act like this in front
of me! Don't let him in my house!"

David at Adullam and Mizpah

22 David left Gath and escaped to the
cave of Adullam. When his brothers
and other relatives heard that he was there,
they went to see him. 2Everyone who was in
trouble, or who owed money, or who was
unsatisfied gathered around David, and he
became their leader. About four hundred
men were with him.

3From there David went to Mizpah in
Moab and spoke to the king of Moab. He
said, "Please let my father and mother come
and stay with you until I learn what God is
going to do for me." 4So he left them with
the king of Moab, and they stayed with him
as long as David was hiding in the
stronghold.

5But the prophet Gad said to David, "Don't
stay in the stronghold. Go to the land of
Judah." So David left and went to the forest
of Hereth.

Saul Destroys Ahimelech's Family

6Saul heard that David and his men had
been seen. Saul was sitting under the
tamarisk tree on the hill at Gibeah, and all
his officers were standing around him. He
had a spear in his hand. 7Saul said to them,
"Listen, men of Benjamin! Do you think the
son of Jesse will give all of you fields and
vineyards? Will David make you
commanders over thousands of men or
hundreds of men? 8You have all made plans
against me! No one tells me when my son
makes an agreement with the son of Jesse!
No one cares about me! No one tells me
when my son has encouraged my servant to
ambush me this very day!"

9Doeg the Edomite, who was standing
there with Saul's officers, said, "I saw the son
of Jesse. He came to see Ahimelech son of
Ahitub at Nob. 10Ahimelech prayed to the
LORD for David and gave him food and gave
him the sword of Goliath the Philistine."

11Then the king sent for the priest
Ahimelech son of Ahitub and for all of
Ahimelech's relatives who were priests at
Nob. And they all came to the king. 12Saul

21:4 holy bread This was the bread that showed the people were in the presence of God. Normally only the priests ate this bread.

said to Ahimelech, "Listen now, son of
Ahitub."
Ahimelech answered, "Yes, master."
13Saul said, "Why are you and Jesse's son
against me? You gave him bread and a
sword! You prayed to God for him. David has
turned against me and is waiting to attack
me even now!"
14Ahimelech answered, "You have no
other servant who is as loyal as David, your
own son-in-law and captain of your
bodyguards. Everyone in your house respects
him. 15That was not the first time I prayed to
God for David. Don't blame me or any of my
relatives. I, your servant, know nothing
about what is going on."
16But the king said, "Ahimelech, you and
all your relatives must die!" 17Then he told
the guards at his side, "Go and kill the priests
of the LORD, because they are on David's side.
They knew he was running away, but they
didn't tell me."
But the king's officers refused to kill the
priests of the LORD.
18Then the king ordered Doeg, "Go and
kill the priests." So Doeg the Edomite went
and killed the priests. That day he killed
eighty-five men who wore the linen holy
vest. 19He also killed the people of Nob, the
city of the priests. With the sword he killed
men, women, children, babies, cattle,
donkeys, and sheep.
20But Abiathar, a son of Ahimelech, who
was the son of Ahitub, escaped. He ran away
and joined David. 21He told David that Saul
had killed the LORD's priests. 22Then David
told him, "Doeg the Edomite was there at
Nob that day. I knew he would surely tell
Saul. So I am responsible for the death of all
your father's family. 23Stay with me. Don't be
afraid. The man who wants to kill you also
wants to kill me. You will be safe with me."

David Saves the People of Keilah

23 Someone told David, "Look, the
Philistines are fighting against Keilah
and stealing grain from the threshing floors."
2David asked the LORD, "Should I go and
fight these Philistines?"
The LORD answered him, "Go. Attack
them, and save Keilah."
3But David's men said to him, "We're afraid
here in Judah. We will be more afraid if we go
to Keilah where the Philistine army is."
4David again asked the LORD, and the LORD
answered, "Go down to Keilah. I will help
you defeat the Philistines." 5So David and his
men went to Keilah and fought the
Philistines and took their cattle. David killed
many Philistines and saved the people of
Keilah. 6(Now Abiathar son of Ahimelech
had brought the holy vest with him when he
came to David at Keilah.)

Saul Chases David

7Someone told Saul that David was now
at Keilah. Saul said, "God has handed David
over to me! He has trapped himself, because
he has entered a town with gates and bars."
8Saul called all his army together for battle,
and they prepared to go down to Keilah to
attack David and his men.
9David learned Saul was making evil plans
against him. So he said to Abiathar the
priest, "Bring the holy vest." 10David prayed,
"LORD, God of Israel, I have heard that Saul
plans to come to Keilah to destroy the town
because of me. 11Will the leaders of Keilah
hand me over to Saul? Will Saul come down
to Keilah, as I heard? LORD, God of Israel, tell
me, your servant!"
The LORD answered, "Saul will come
down."
12Again David asked, "Will the leaders of
Keilah hand me and my men over to Saul?"
The LORD answered, "They will."
13So David and his six hundred men left
Keilah and kept moving from place to place.
When Saul found out that David had
escaped from Keilah, he did not go there.
14David stayed in the desert hideouts and
in the hills of the Desert of Ziph. Every day
Saul looked for David, but the LORD did not
surrender David to him.
15While David was at Horesh in the
Desert of Ziph, he learned that Saul was
coming to kill him. 16But Saul's son Jonathan
went to David at Horesh and strengthened
his faith in God. 17Jonathan told him, "Don't
be afraid, because my father won't touch
you. You will be king of Israel, and I will be
second to you. Even my father Saul knows
this." 18The two of them made an agreement
before the LORD. Then Jonathan went home,
but David stayed at Horesh.
19The people from Ziph went to Saul at
Gibeah and told him, "David is hiding in our
land. He's at the hideouts of Horesh, on the

devotion 80

1 SAMUEL 23:15–18

WITH SOMEONE TO RUN BESIDE ME

Today has been very lonely. I felt misunderstood at every turn. Every place in my home shouted to me of family management failure. I lay on my face this morning and rambled before the Lord. I am sure he smiled as his weary daughter came into his presence and then wouldn't sit still. I put a frozen lasagna in the oven tonight and heard my "super mom" voice whisper that my children deserve better.

I wallowed in the frustration of my inadequacy until the Lord led me to call a friend—a woman who has permission to walk around in my soul. She listened. She agreed with me. She picked up my burden and stood under it with me. She gracefully led me to the mercy of Jesus. Her words held me with their love. With my burden shared, I was stronger. With my tears dried, I could see clearly. With someone to run beside, my pace quickened and my energy returned. They say you pace yourself according to who you run beside. I am so grateful to pace beside a woman who is running headlong into the arms of God.

We have been wired by our Creator with a deep need for friendships—the kind that David and Jonathan experienced where burdens are shared and joys are doubled. Women can care for each other with the profound ability that comes from affinity and experience, from understanding and familiarity. It is the kinship of sisterhood; it is one of God's gifts for a woman's soul.

hill of Hakilah, south of Jeshimon. 20Now,
our king, come down anytime you want. It's
our duty to hand David over to you."
21Saul answered, "The LORD bless you for
helping me. 22Go and learn more about him.
Find out where he is staying and who has
seen him there. I have heard that he is clever.
23Find all the hiding places he uses, and
come back and tell me everything. Then I'll
go with you. If David is in the area, I will
track him down among all the families in
Judah."
24So they went back to Ziph ahead of Saul.
Now David and his men were in the Desert
of Maon[n] in the desert area south of
Jeshimon. 25Saul and his men went to look
for David, but David heard about it and went
down to a rock and stayed in the Desert of
Maon. When Saul heard that, he followed
David into the Desert of Maon.
26Saul was going along one side of the
mountain, and David and his men were on
the other side. They were hurrying to get
away from Saul, because Saul and his men
were closing in on them. 27But a messenger
came to Saul, saying, "Come quickly! The
Philistines are attacking our land!" 28So Saul
stopped chasing David and went to challenge
the Philistines. That is why people call this
place Rock of Parting. 29David also left the
Desert of Maon and stayed in the hideouts of
En Gedi.

David Shames Saul

24 After Saul returned from chasing the
Philistines, he was told, "David is in
the Desert of En Gedi." 2So he took three
thousand chosen men from all Israel and
began looking for David and his men near
the Rocks of the Wild Goats.
3Saul came to the sheep pens beside the
road. A cave was there, and he went in to

23:24 Maon Some early Greek copies say "Maon." The Hebrew copies say "Paran."

relieve himself. Now David and his men were hiding far back in the cave. [4]The men said to David, "Today is the day the LORD spoke of when he said, 'I will give your enemy over to you. Do anything you want with him.' "

Then David crept up to Saul and quietly cut off a corner of Saul's robe. [5]Later David felt guilty because he had cut off a corner of Saul's robe. [6]He said to his men, "May the LORD keep me from doing such a thing to my master! Saul is the LORD's appointed king. I should not do anything against him, because he is the LORD's appointed king!" [7]David used these words to stop his men; he did not let them attack Saul. Then Saul left the cave and went his way.

[8]When David came out of the cave, he shouted to Saul, "My master and king!" Saul looked back, and David bowed facedown on the ground. [9]He said to Saul, "Why do you listen when people say, 'David wants to harm you'? [10]You have seen something with your own eyes today. The LORD put you in my power in the cave. They said I should kill you, but I was merciful. I said, 'I won't harm my master, because he is the LORD's appointed king.' [11]My father, look at this piece of your robe in my hand! I cut off the corner of your robe, but I didn't kill you. Now understand and know I am not planning any evil against you. I did nothing wrong to you, but you are hunting me to kill me. [12]May the LORD judge between us, and may he punish you for the wrong you have done to me! But I am not against you. [13]There is an old saying: 'Evil things come from evil people.' But I am not against you. [14]Whom is the king of Israel coming out against? Whom are you chasing? It's as if you are chasing a dead dog or a flea. [15]May the LORD be our judge and decide between you and me. May he support me and show that I am right. May he save me from you!"

[16]When David finished saying these words, Saul asked, "Is that your voice, David my son?" And he cried loudly. [17]He said, "You are a better man than I am. You have been good to me, but I have done wrong to you. [18]You told me what good things you did. The LORD handed me over to you, but you did not kill me. [19]People don't normally let an enemy get away like this, do they? May the LORD reward you because you were good to me today. [20]I know you will surely be king, and you will rule the kingdom of Israel. [21]Now swear to me by the LORD that you will not kill my descendants and that you won't wipe out my name from my father's family."

[22]So David made the promise to Saul. Then Saul went back home, and David and his men went up to their hideout.

Nabal Insults David

25 Now Samuel died, and all the Israelites met and had a time of sadness for him. Then they buried him at his home in Ramah.

David moved to the Desert of Maon.[n] [2]A man in Maon who had land at Carmel was very rich. He had three thousand sheep and a thousand goats. He was cutting the wool off his sheep at Carmel. [3]His name was Nabal, and he was a descendant of Caleb. His wife was named Abigail. She was wise and beautiful, but Nabal was cruel and mean.

[4]While David was in the desert, he heard that Nabal was cutting the wool from his sheep. [5]So he sent ten young men and told them, "Go to Nabal at Carmel, and greet him for me. [6]Say to Nabal, 'May you and your family and all who belong to you have good health! [7]I have heard that you are cutting the wool from your sheep. When your shepherds were with us, we did not harm them. All the time your shepherds were at Carmel, we stole nothing from them. [8]Ask your servants, and they will tell you. We come at a happy time, so be kind to my young men. Please give anything you can find for them and for your son David.' "

[9]When David's men arrived, they gave the message to Nabal, but Nabal insulted them. [10]He answered them, "Who is David? Who is this son of Jesse? Many slaves are running away from their masters today! [11]I have bread and water, and I have meat that I killed for my servants who cut the wool. But I won't give it to men I don't know."

[12]David's men went back and told him all Nabal had said. [13]Then David said to them, "Put on your swords!" So they put on their swords, and David put on his also. About four hundred men went with David, but two hundred men stayed with the supplies.

25:1 Maon Some early Greek copies say "Maon." The Hebrew copies say "Paran."

devotion 81

1 SAMUEL 24:15

GOD WILL DO THE DEALING

First Samuel 24 is such an amazing account of David's faithfulness to the Lord. Even though Saul was seeking David's life for no other reason than his own fear and vanity, David was faithful to spare Saul. While David and his men were hiding in the cave, David would not permit anyone to attack Saul because he was God's anointed king. It was God's responsibility to deal with him. When the confrontation finally took place between David and Saul, David once again proved why he was a man after God's own heart. Although he had every opportunity to take poor Saul's life, all he took was the corner of his robe.

In the New Testament, the Lord says we are not to repay evil with evil (1 Pet. 3:9). Even though David had every right to defend himself physically from Saul, he knew to do so would be a sin. That judgment is reserved for God alone. Let God judge between you and those who come against you. I could not begin to share how many stories and testimonies I know where people have been purposely wicked and plotted in secret only to have the Lord expose every single one of them and even render judgment. If someone is plotting against you, rest assured that there will come a time when you can offer up a prayer of thanksgiving because the Lord saved you in his timing and in his way with his hand alone.

14One of Nabal's servants said to Abigail,
Nabal's wife, "David sent messengers from
the desert to greet our master, but Nabal
insulted them. 15These men were very
good to us. They did not harm us. They
stole nothing from us during all the time
we were out in the field with them.
16Night and day they protected us. They
were like a wall around us while we were
with them caring for the sheep. 17Now
think about it, and decide what you can
do. Terrible trouble is coming to our
master and all his family. Nabal is such a
wicked man that no one can even talk to
him."
18Abigail hurried. She took two hundred
loaves of bread, two leather bags full of wine,
five cooked sheep, a bushel of cooked grain,
a hundred cakes of raisins, and two hundred
cakes of pressed figs and put all these on
donkeys. 19Then she told her servants, "Go
on. I'll follow you." But she did not tell her
husband.
20Abigail rode her donkey and came down
toward the mountain hideout. There she
met David and his men coming down
toward her.
21David had just said, "It's been useless! I
watched over Nabal's property in the desert.
I made sure none of his sheep was missing. I
did good to him, but he has paid me back
with evil. 22May God punish my enemies
even more. I will not leave one of Nabal's
men alive until morning."
23When Abigail saw David, she quickly
got off her donkey and bowed facedown on
the ground before him. 24She fell at David's
feet and said, "My master, let the blame be on
me! Please let me talk to you. Listen to what
I say. 25My master, don't pay attention to this
worthless man Nabal. He is like his name.
His name means 'fool,' and he is truly a fool.
But I, your servant, didn't see the men you
sent. 26The LORD has kept you from killing
and punishing anyone. As surely as the LORD
lives and as surely as you live, may your
enemies become like Nabal! 27I have brought
a gift to you for the men who follow
you.28Please forgive my wrong. The LORD
will certainly let your family have many

Abigail

1 SAMUEL 25

Abigail was busy preparing the evening meal when a servant rushed through the door. The poor man was out of breath and rested his hands on his knees. "What is it?" Abigail demanded, stepping toward him.

"Nabal," the man answered breathlessly. Abigail's jaw tightened as her anger rose. What had her foolish husband done this time? Her blood raced as the servant explained how Nabal's shepherds had been in the fields near David's army but were never harmed. Neither David nor his men ever touched them or stole anything from them. Now, David was asking for help for his men, but Nabal refused, even insulting David. "Terrible trouble is coming to our master and all his family," the servant said. "Nabal is such a wicked man that no one can even talk to him."

Abigail knew there wasn't much time to protect her family. She gathered and prepared food for hundreds but did not tell her husband. Riding a donkey through a mountain passage, she met David and his men. Immediately, she bowed before him, asking forgiveness for the wrong done to him. David listened as she pleaded with him not to act out of vengeance. "God will throw away your enemies' lives," she said, then looked up at him and waited.

"May you be blessed for your wisdom," David said. "Go home in peace. I will do what you have asked."

Wisdom and discernment are gifts God gives for guidance. Ask and he will give them to you.

kings, because you fight his battles. As long
as you live, may you do nothing bad.
29Someone might chase you to kill you, but
the LORD your God will keep you alive. He
will throw away your enemies' lives as he
would throw a stone from a sling. 30The
LORD will keep all his promises of good
things for you. He will make you leader over
Israel. 31Then you won't feel guilty or
troubled because you killed innocent people
and punished them. Please remember me
when the LORD brings you success."

32David answered Abigail, "Praise the
LORD, the God of Israel, who sent you to meet
me. 33May you be blessed for your wisdom.
You have kept me from killing or punishing
people today. 34As surely as the LORD, the
God of Israel, lives, he has kept me from
hurting you. If you hadn't come quickly to
meet me, not one of Nabal's men would have
lived until morning."

35Then David accepted Abigail's gifts. He
told her, "Go home in peace. I have heard
your words, and I will do what you have
asked."

Nabal's Death

36When Abigail went back to Nabal, he
was in the house, eating like a king. He was
very drunk and in a good mood. So she told
him nothing until the next morning. 37In
the morning when he was not drunk, his
wife told him everything. His heart stopped,
and he became like stone. 38About ten days
later the LORD struck Nabal and he died.

39When David heard that Nabal was dead,
he said, "Praise the LORD! Nabal insulted me,
but the LORD has supported me! He has kept
me from doing wrong. The LORD has
punished Nabal for his wrong."

Then David sent a message to Abigail,
asking her to be his wife. 40His servants went
to Carmel and said to Abigail, "David sent us
to take you so you can become his wife."

41Abigail bowed facedown on the ground
and said, "I am your servant. I'm ready to
serve you and to wash the feet of my
master's servants." 42Abigail quickly got on a
donkey and went with David's messengers,
with her five maids following her. And she
became David's wife.

43David also had married Ahinoam of
Jezreel. So they were both David's wives.
44Saul's daughter Michal was also David's

wife, but Saul had given her to Paltiel son of
Laish, who was from Gallim.

David Shames Saul Again

26 The people of Ziph went to Saul at
Gibeah and said to him, "David is
hiding on the hill of Hakilah opposite
Jeshimon."
2So Saul went down to the Desert of Ziph
with three thousand chosen men of Israel to
look for David there. 3Saul made his camp
beside the road on the hill of Hakilah
opposite Jeshimon, but David stayed in the
desert. When he heard Saul had followed
him, 4he sent out spies and learned for
certain that Saul had come to Hakilah.
5Then David went to the place where Saul
had camped. He saw where Saul and Abner
son of Ner, the commander of Saul's army,
were sleeping. Saul was sleeping in the
middle of the camp with all the army
around him.
6David asked Ahimelech the Hittite and
Abishai son of Zeruiah, Joab's brother, "Who
will go down into Saul's camp with me?"
Abishai answered, "I'll go with you."
7So that night David and Abishai went
into Saul's camp. Saul was asleep in the
middle of the camp with his spear stuck in
the ground near his head. Abner and the
army were sleeping around Saul. 8Abishai
said to David, "Today God has handed your
enemy over to you. Let me pin Saul to the
ground with my spear. I'll only have to do it
once. I won't need to hit him twice."
9But David said to Abishai, "Don't kill
Saul! No one can harm the LORD's appointed
king and still be innocent! 10As surely as the
LORD lives, the LORD himself will punish
Saul. Maybe Saul will die naturally, or
maybe he will go into battle and be killed.
11But may the LORD keep me from harming
his appointed king! Take the spear and water
jug that are near Saul's head. Then let's go."
12So David took the spear and water jug
that were near Saul's head, and they left. No
one saw them or knew about it or woke up,
because the LORD had put them sound asleep.
13David crossed over to the other side of
the hill and stood on top of the mountain far
from Saul's camp. They were a long way
away from each other. 14David shouted to
the army and to Abner son of Ner, "Won't
you answer me, Abner?"
Abner answered, "Who is calling for the
king? Who are you?"
15David said, "You're the greatest man in
Israel. Isn't that true? Why didn't you guard
your master the king? Someone came into
your camp to kill your master the king!
16You have not done well. As surely as the
LORD lives, you and your men should die.
You haven't guarded your master, the LORD's
appointed king. Look! Where are the king's
spear and water jug that were near his
head?"
17Saul knew David's voice. He said, "Is that
your voice, David my son?"
David answered, "Yes, it is, my master and
king." 18David also said, "Why are you
chasing me, my master? What wrong have I
done? What evil am I guilty of? 19My master
and king, listen to me. If the LORD made you
angry with me, let him accept an offering.
But if people did it, may the LORD curse
them! They have made me leave the land the
LORD gave me. They have told me, 'Go and
serve other gods.' 20Now don't let me die far
away from the LORD's presence. The king of
Israel has come out looking for a flea! You're
just hunting a bird in the mountains!"
21Then Saul said, "I have sinned. Come
back, David my son. Today you respected my
life, so I will not try to hurt you. I have been
very stupid and foolish."
22David answered, "Here is your spear. Let
one of your young men come here and get it.
23The LORD rewards us for the things we do
right and for our loyalty to him. The LORD
handed you over to me today, but I wouldn't
harm the LORD's appointed king. 24As I
respected your life today, may the LORD also
respect my life and save me from all
trouble."
25Then Saul said to David, "You are
blessed, my son David. You will do great
things and succeed."
So David went on his way, and Saul went
back home.

David Lives with the Philistines

27 But David thought to himself, "Saul
will catch me someday. The best thing
I can do is escape to the land of the
Philistines. Then he will give up looking for
me in Israel, and I can get away from him."
2So David and his six hundred men left
Israel and went to Achish son of Maoch,

king of Gath. 3David, his men, and their
families made their home in Gath with
Achish. David had his two wives with him—
Ahinoam of Jezreel and Abigail of Carmel,
the widow of Nabal. 4When Saul heard that
David had run away to Gath, he stopped
looking for him.

5Then David said to Achish, "If you are
pleased with me, give me a place in one of
the country towns where I can live. I don't
need to live in the royal city with you."

6That day Achish gave David the town of
Ziklag, and Ziklag has belonged to the kings
of Judah ever since. 7David lived in the
Philistine land a year and four months.

8David and his men raided the people of
Geshur, Girzi, and Amalek. (These people
had lived for a long time in the land that
reached to Shur and Egypt.) 9When David
fought them, he killed all the men and
women and took their sheep, cattle,
donkeys, camels, and clothes. Then he
returned to Achish.

10Achish would ask David, "Where did
you go raiding today?" And David would tell
him that he had gone to the southern part of
Judah, or Jerahmeel, or to the land of the
Kenites. 11David never brought a man or
woman alive to Gath. He thought, "If we
bring people alive, they may tell Achish,
'This is what David really did.' " David did
this all the time he lived in the Philistine
land. 12So Achish trusted David and said to
himself, "David's own people, the Israelites,
now hate him very much. He will serve me
forever."

Saul and the Medium of Endor

28 Later, the Philistines gathered their
armies to fight against Israel. Achish
said to David, "You understand that you and
your men must join my army."

2David answered, "You will see for
yourself what I, your servant, can do!"

Achish said, "Fine, I'll make you my
permanent bodyguard."

3Now Samuel was dead, and all the
Israelites had shown their sadness for him.
They had buried Samuel in his hometown of
Ramah.

And Saul had forced out the mediums and
fortune-tellers from the land.

4The Philistines came together and made
camp at Shunem. Saul gathered all the
Israelites and made camp at Gilboa. 5When
he saw the Philistine army, he was afraid,
and his heart pounded with fear. 6He prayed
to the LORD, but the LORD did not answer him
through dreams, Urim, or prophets. 7Then
Saul said to his servants, "Find me a woman
who is a medium so I may go and ask her
what will happen."

His servants answered, "There is a
medium in Endor."

8Then Saul put on other clothes to
disguise himself, and at night he and two of
his men went to see the woman. Saul said to
her, "Talk to a spirit for me. Bring up the
person I name."

9But the woman said to him, "Surely you
know what Saul has done. He has forced the
mediums and fortune-tellers from the land.
You are trying to trap me and get me killed."

10Saul made a promise to the woman in
the name of the LORD. He said, "As surely as
the LORD lives, you won't be punished for
this."

11The woman asked, "Whom do you want
me to bring up?"

He answered, "Bring up Samuel."

12When the woman saw Samuel, she
screamed. She said, "Why have you tricked
me? You are Saul!"

13The king said to the woman, "Don't be
afraid! What do you see?"

The woman said, "I see a spirit coming up
out of the ground."

14Saul asked, "What does he look like?"

The woman answered, "An old man
wearing a coat is coming up."

Then Saul knew it was Samuel, and he
bowed facedown on the ground.

15Samuel asked Saul, "Why have you
disturbed me by bringing me up?"

Saul said, "I am greatly troubled. The
Philistines are fighting against me, and God
has left me. He won't answer me anymore,
either by prophets or in dreams. That's why I
called for you. Tell me what to do."

16Samuel said, "The LORD has left you and
has become your enemy. So why do you call
on me? 17He has done what he said he would
do—the things he said through me. He has
torn the kingdom out of your hands and
given it to one of your neighbors, David.
18You did not obey the LORD; you did not
show the Amalekites how angry he was
with them. That's why he has done this to

devotion 82

1 SAMUEL 28:6–7

TIRED OF WAITING?

Saul prayed to the Lord, but he was not willing to wait for an answer. He felt like God was ignoring him, so he decided to find his answer through other means. He disguised himself and went out under the cover of night to meet with the medium in Endor. Saul's impatience led him right into the hands of Satan. How often we allow our impatience to get us into situations we later regret. We try to take things into our own hands rather than wait on the Lord's answer.

In our culture, patience is not something that is appreciated. Actually, it is usually considered a weakness. Yet sometimes patience has some value we overlook. When you ask God to open a door for you or give you an answer, do you expect an immediate response? Do you force the door open without God's approval as Saul did, or are you willing to wait on the Lord? In my life, patience has kept me from embarrassing situations. It has also kept me from committing to things that I later realized I did not want to be a part of. When someone pressures you that if you don't do something right now or you'll lose the chance of a lifetime—that's your first warning that deception may be in the air. Take time to go to the Lord for each decision you make. Time is your friend, and patience will reveal God's will in each decision you face.

you today. 19The LORD will hand over both
Israel and you to the Philistines. Tomorrow
you and your sons will be with me. The LORD
will hand over the army of Israel to the
Philistines."
20Saul quickly fell flat on the ground and
was afraid of what Samuel had said. He was
also very weak because he had eaten
nothing all that day and night.
21Then the woman came to Saul and saw
that he was really frightened. She said,
"Look, I, your servant, have obeyed you. I
have risked my life and done what you told
me to do. 22Now please listen to me. Let me
give you some food so you may eat and have
enough strength to go on your way."
23But Saul refused, saying, "I won't eat."
His servants joined the woman in asking
him to eat, and he listened to them. So he
got up from the ground and sat on the bed.
24At the house the woman had a fat calf,
which she quickly killed. She took some
flour and mixed dough with her hands. Then
she baked some bread without yeast. 25She
put the food before them, and they ate. That
same night they got up and left.

David Goes Back to Ziklag

29 The Philistines gathered all their
soldiers at Aphek. Israel camped by
the spring at Jezreel. 2The Philistine kings
were marching with their groups of a
hundred and a thousand men. David and his
men were marching behind Achish. 3The
Philistine commanders asked, "What are
these Hebrews doing here?"
Achish told them, "This is David. He
served Saul king of Israel, but he has been
with me for over a year now. I have found
nothing wrong in David since the time he
left Saul."
4But the Philistine commanders were
angry with Achish and said, "Send David back
to the city you gave him. He cannot go with
us into battle. If he does, we'll have an enemy
in our own camp. He could please his king by
killing our own men. 5David is the one the
Israelites dance and sing about, saying:

'Saul has killed thousands of his enemies,
but David has killed tens of thousands.' "
[6]So Achish called David and said to him,
"As surely as the LORD lives, you are loyal. I
would be pleased to have you serve in my
army. Since the day you came to me, I have
found no wrong in you. But the other kings
don't trust you. [7]Go back in peace. Don't do
anything to displease the Philistine kings."
[8]David asked, "What wrong have I done?
What evil have you found in me from the
day I came to you until now? Why can't I go
fight your enemies, my lord and king?"
[9]Achish answered, "I know you are as
good as an angel from God. But the Philistine
commanders have said, 'David must not go
with us into battle.' [10]Early in the morning
you and your master's servants should leave.
Get up as soon as it is light and go."
[11]So David and his men got up early in the
morning and went back to the country of
the Philistines. And the Philistines went up
to Jezreel.

David's War with the Amalekites

30 On the third day, when David and his
men arrived at Ziklag, he found that
the Amalekites had raided southern Judah
and Ziklag, attacking Ziklag and burning it.
[2]They captured the women and everyone,
young and old, but they had not killed
anyone. They had only taken them away.
[3]When David and his men came to Ziklag,
they found the town had been burned and
their wives, sons, and daughters had been
taken as prisoners. [4]Then David and his
army cried loudly until they were too weak
to cry anymore. [5]David's two wives had also
been taken—Ahinoam of Jezreel and Abigail
the widow of Nabal from Carmel. [6]The men
in the army were threatening to kill David
with stones, which greatly upset David. Each
man was sad and angry because his sons and
daughters had been captured, but David
found strength in the LORD his God. [7]David
said to Abiathar the priest, "Bring me the
holy vest."
[8]Then David asked the LORD, "Should I
chase the people who took our families?
Will I catch them?"
The LORD answered, "Chase them. You will
catch them, and you will succeed in saving
your families."
[9]David and the six hundred men with him
came to the Besor Ravine, where some of the
men stayed. [10]David and four hundred men
kept up the chase. The other two hundred
men stayed behind because they were too
tired to cross the ravine.
[11]They found an Egyptian in a field and
brought him to David. They gave the
Egyptian some water to drink and some food
to eat. [12]And they gave him a piece of a fig
cake and two clusters of raisins. Then he felt
better, because he had not eaten any food or
drunk any water for three days and nights.
[13]David asked him, "Who is your master?
Where do you come from?"
He answered, "I'm an Egyptian, the slave
of an Amalekite. Three days ago my master
left me, because I was sick. [14]We had raided
the southern area of the Kerethites, the land
of Judah, and the southern area of Caleb. We
burned Ziklag, as well."
[15]David asked him, "Can you lead me to
the people who took our families?"
He answered, "Yes, if you promise me
before God that you won't kill me or give me
back to my master. Then I will take you to
them."
[16]So the Egyptian led David to the
Amalekites. They were lying around on the
ground, eating and drinking and celebrating
with the things they had taken from the
land of the Philistines and from Judah.
[17]David fought them from sunset until the
evening of the next day. None of them
escaped, except four hundred young men
who rode off on their camels. [18]David got his
two wives back and everything the
Amalekites had taken. [19]Nothing was
missing. David brought back everyone,
young and old, sons and daughters. He
recovered the valuable things and
everything the Amalekites had taken.
[20]David took all the sheep and cattle, and his
men made these animals go in front, saying,
"They are David's prize."
[21]Then David came to the two hundred
men who had been too tired to follow him,
who had stayed at the Besor Ravine. They
came out to meet David and the people with
him. When he came near, David greeted the
men at the ravine.
[22]But the evil men and troublemakers
among those who followed David said,
"Since these two hundred men didn't go
with us, we shouldn't give them any of the

things we recovered. Just let each man take
his wife and children and go."
23David answered, "No, my brothers. Don't
do that after what the LORD has given us. He
has protected us and given us the enemy
who attacked us. 24Who will listen to what
you say? The share will be the same for the
one who stayed with the supplies as for the
one who went into battle. All will share
alike." 25David made this an order and rule
for Israel, which continues even today.

26When David arrived in Ziklag, he sent
some of the things he had taken from the
Amalekites to his friends, the leaders of
Judah. He said, "Here is a present for you
from the things we took from the LORD's
enemies."

27David also sent some things to the
leaders in Bethel, Ramoth in the southern
part of Judah, Jattir, 28Aroer, Siphmoth,
Eshtemoa, 29Racal, the cities of the
Jerahmeelites and the Kenites, 30Hormah,
Bor Ashan, Athach, 31Hebron, and to the
people in all the other places where he and
his men had been.

The Death of Saul

31 The Philistines fought against Israel,
and the Israelites ran away from them.
Many Israelites were killed on Mount
Gilboa. 2The Philistines fought hard against
Saul and his sons, killing his sons Jonathan,
Abinadab, and Malki-Shua. 3The fighting
was heavy around Saul. The archers shot
him, and he was badly wounded. 4He said to
the officer who carried his armor, "Pull out
your sword and kill me. Then those
uncircumcised men won't make fun of me
and kill me." But Saul's officer refused,
because he was afraid. So Saul took his own
sword and threw himself on it. 5When the
officer saw that Saul was dead, he threw
himself on his own sword, and he died with
Saul. 6So Saul, his three sons, and the officer
who carried his armor died together that day.

7When the Israelites who lived across the
Jezreel Valley and those who lived across
the Jordan River saw how the Israelite army
had run away, and that Saul and his sons
were dead, they left their cities and ran away.
Then the Philistines came and lived there.

8The next day when the Philistines came
to take all the valuable things from the
dead soldiers, they found Saul and his three
sons dead on Mount Gilboa. 9They cut off
Saul's head and took off his armor. Then
they sent messengers through all the land of
the Philistines to tell the news in the
temple of their idols and to their people.
10They put Saul's armor in the temple of the
Ashtoreths and hung his body on the wall
of Beth Shan.

11When the people living in Jabesh Gilead
heard what the Philistines had done to Saul,
12the brave men of Jabesh marched all night
and came to Beth Shan. They removed the
bodies of Saul and his sons from the wall of
Beth Shan and brought them to Jabesh.
There they burned the bodies. 13They took
their bones and buried them under the
tamarisk tree in Jabesh. Then the people of
Jabesh fasted for seven days.

2 Samuel

Person Holding the Pen God Wrote With: Author is unknown (see explanation under 1 Sam.).

When the Text Was Written: This book was penned sometime during the almost four-hundred-year span between 931 B.C. and 540 B.C. Some scholars argue a more specific "pre-exilic" time span between 931 and 722 B.C. (prior to Israel's Babylonian exile).

Spiritual Posture of the Original Recipients: As in 1 Samuel, the twelve tribes of Israel, functioning as separate entities when they first settled in Canaan, have become somewhat united under the monarchy of Saul. However, they're still wandering spiritually.

Storyline Synopsis: Second Samuel records the poignant story of David, a shepherd boy who became one of the most prolific kings in history. The book begins with David ascending the throne after King Saul's death. Saul had become so jealous of David that he tried to murder him on several occasions, but because Saul was also Jonathan's dad (David's best friend)—and God's "anointed"—David still grieved at his funeral. The rest of this historical journal reveals the highs and lows of David's monarchy, concluding with the twilight of his kingly career. An apt title for all twenty-four chapters could be "One Imperfect Man After God's Own Heart."

A Moment Worth Discussing: *Mephibosheth*, one of Jonathan's sons, was crippled as a toddler during the frenzy following Saul's defeat when his nurse dropped him on the fancy marble floor of the palace (2 Sam. 4:4). He hobbled through a life of obscurity, dependant on the kindness of others until David—now the popular and powerful King of Israel—remembered the promise he'd made to "Bo's" daddy, Jonathan, and beckoned Mephibosheth back to Jerusalem (chapter 9). David's generosity toward the undeserving, lame grandson of the man who tried to kill him is a wonderful illustration of the way God extends grace toward us.

Interesting (But Likely to Be Overlooked) Character: King David encountered a nut named *Shimei*—somehow related to Saul—who slung gravel at him and his "secret service guys" (2 Sam. 16:5–8). It's a tribute to David's character that he didn't let his security guards knock Shimei's block off. Instead, David chose to ignore the rock throwing (16:9–14), and in the end, David's patience paid off (19:16–20).

David Learns About Saul's Death

1 Now Saul was dead. After David had
defeated the Amalekites, he returned to
Ziklag and stayed there two days. 2On the
third day a young man from Saul's camp
came to Ziklag. To show his sadness, his
clothes were torn and he had dirt on his
head. He came and bowed facedown on the
ground before David.
3David asked him, "Where did you come
from?"

The man answered, "I escaped from the Israelite camp."

4David asked him, "What happened?
Please tell me!"

The man answered, "The people have run away from the battle, and many of them have fallen and are dead. Saul and his son Jonathan are dead also."

5David asked him, "How do you know
Saul and his son Jonathan are dead?"
6The young man answered, "I happened
to be on Mount Gilboa. There I saw Saul
leaning on his spear. The Philistine chariots
and the men riding in them were coming
closer to Saul. 7When he looked back and
saw me, he called to me. I answered him,
'Here I am!'
8"Then Saul asked me, 'Who are you?'

"I told him, 'I am an Amalekite.'

9"Then Saul said to me, 'Please come here
and kill me. I am badly hurt and am almost
dead already.'
10"So I went over and killed him. He had
been hurt so badly I knew he couldn't live.
Then I took the crown from his head and the
bracelet from his arm, and I have brought
them here to you, my master."
11Then David tore his clothes to show his
sorrow, and all the men with him did also.
12They were very sad and cried and fasted
until evening. They cried for Saul and his
son Jonathan and for all the people of the
LORD and for all the Israelites who had died
in the battle.

David Orders the Amalekite Killed

13David asked the young man who
brought the report, "Where are you from?"

The young man answered, "I am the son of a foreigner, an Amalekite."

14David asked him, "Why were you not
afraid to kill the LORD's appointed king?"

devotion 83

2 SAMUEL 1:12

NO WAY AROUND

What's the difficult thing about grief and mourning? We want someone to take it away or something to numb it away, but no one or nothing can. The self-help books say that mourning is healthy. Psychologists reason that it's necessary. I am learning that whether we are ancient Israelites grieving for a king or modern people grieving a myriad of losses, the only way to the other side is *through*. The difficulty is that the only path is poorly marked, fraught with potholes, sharp turns, and steep, harrowing cliffs on either side. And it's always dark when we're grieving—a deep, dark night of the soul.

Eventually we just have to give it up and give in to mourning the emptiness of knowing that we cannot recover our lost lives or lost loves or lost dreams. Ultimately we have to look straight into our agony and stop avoiding it. We have to hold up our sorrow, remember what was, accept what's gone, and cry until the ocean of our pain is empty.

When you are grieving, your head says that God is far away, but God is actually closer than ever . . . even as close as your breath. This day, if your soul aches and your heart mourns, please know that you are not alone. You are being held and healed by the unfailing love of God. Decide to believe what your head cannot conceive and trust in God's abiding love, even through your darkest night of grief.

15Then David called one of his men and told him, "Go! Kill the Amalekite!" So the Israelite killed him. 16David had said to the Amalekite, "You are responsible for your own death. You confessed by saying, 'I have killed the LORD's appointed king.' "

David's Song About Saul and Jonathan

17David sang a funeral song about Saul and his son Jonathan, 18and he ordered that the people of Judah be taught this song. It is called "The Bow," and it is written in the Book of Jashar:

19"Israel, your leaders have been killed on the hills.
How the mighty have fallen in battle!
20Don't tell it in Gath.
Don't announce it in the streets of Ashkelon.
If you do, the Philistine women will be happy.
The daughters of the Philistines will rejoice.

21"May there be no dew or rain on the mountains of Gilboa,
and may their fields produce no grain,
because there the mighty warrior's shield was dishonored.
Saul's shield will no longer be rubbed with oil.
22Jonathan's bow did not fail
to kill many soldiers.
Saul's sword did not fail
to wound many strong men.

23"We loved Saul and Jonathan
and enjoyed them while they lived.
They are together even in death.
They were faster than eagles.
They were stronger than lions.

24"You daughters of Israel, cry for Saul.
Saul clothed you with red dresses
and put gold decorations on them.

25"How the mighty have fallen in battle!
Jonathan is dead on Gilboa's hills.
26I cry for you, my brother Jonathan.
I enjoyed your friendship so much.
Your love to me was wonderful,
better than the love of women.

27"How the mighty have fallen!
The weapons of war are gone."

David Is Made King of Judah

2 Later, David prayed to the LORD, saying, "Should I go up to any of the cities of Judah?"

The LORD said to David, "Go."

David asked, "Where should I go?"

The LORD answered, "To Hebron."

2So David went up to Hebron with his
two wives: Ahinoam from Jezreel and
Abigail, the widow of Nabal from Carmel.
3David also brought his men and their
families, and they all made their homes in
the cities of Hebron. 4Then the men of Judah
came to Hebron and appointed David king
over Judah.

They told David that the men of Jabesh
Gilead had buried Saul. 5So David sent
messengers to the men of Jabesh Gilead and
said to them, "The LORD bless you. You have
shown loyalty to your master Saul by burying
him. 6May the LORD now be loyal and true to
you. I will also treat you well because you
have done this. 7Now be strong and brave.
Saul your master is dead, and the people of
Judah have appointed me their king."

War Between Judah and Israel

8Abner son of Ner was the commander
of Saul's army. Abner took Saul's son
Ish-Bosheth to Mahanaim 9and made him
king of Gilead, Ashuri, Jezreel, Ephraim,
Benjamin, and all Israel. 10Saul's son
Ish-Bosheth was forty years old when he
became king over Israel, and he ruled two
years. But the people of Judah followed
David. 11David was king in Hebron for seven
years and six months.

12Abner son of Ner and the servants of
Ish-Bosheth son of Saul left Mahanaim and
went to Gibeon. 13Joab son of Zeruiah and
David's men also went there and met Abner
and Ish-Bosheth's men at the pool of Gibeon.
Abner's group sat on one side of the pool;
Joab's group sat on the other.

14Abner said to Joab, "Let the young men
have a contest here."

Joab said, "Yes, let them have a contest."

15Then the men got up and were
counted—twelve from the people of
Benjamin for Ish-Bosheth son of Saul, and
twelve from David's men. 16Each man
grabbed the one opposite him by the head
and stabbed him in the side with a knife. So

the men fell down together. For that reason,
that place in Gibeon is called the Field of
Knives. 17That day there was a terrible battle,
and David's men defeated Abner and the
Israelites.

Abner Kills Asahel

18Zeruiah's three sons, Joab, Abishai, and
Asahel, were there. Now Asahel was a fast
runner, as fast as a deer in the field. 19Asahel
chased Abner, going straight toward him.
20Abner looked back and asked, "Is that you,
Asahel?"

Asahel said, "Yes, it is."

21Then Abner said to Asahel, "Turn to
your right or left and catch one of the young
men and take his armor." But Asahel refused
to stop chasing him.

22Abner again said to Asahel, "Stop
chasing me! If you don't stop, I'll have to kill
you! Then I won't be able to face your
brother Joab again!"

23But Asahel refused to stop chasing
Abner. So using the back end of his spear,
Abner stabbed Asahel in the stomach, and
the spear came out of his back. Asahel died
right there, and everyone stopped when they
came to the place where Asahel's body lay.

24But Joab and Abishai continued chasing
Abner. As the sun was going down, they
arrived at the hill of Ammah, near Giah on
the way to the desert near Gibeon. 25The
men of Benjamin came to Abner, and all
stood together at the top of the hill.
26Abner shouted to Joab, "Must the sword
kill forever? Surely you must know this will
only end in sadness! Tell the people to stop
chasing their own brothers!"

27Then Joab said, "As surely as God lives, if
you had not said anything, the people would
have chased their brothers until morning."
28Then Joab blew a trumpet, and his people
stopped chasing the Israelites. They did not
fight them anymore.

29Abner and his men marched all night
through the Jordan Valley. They crossed the
Jordan River, and after marching all day,
arrived at Mahanaim.

30After he had stopped chasing Abner,
Joab came back and gathered the people
together. Asahel and nineteen of David's
men were missing. 31But David's men had
killed three hundred sixty Benjaminites who
had followed Abner. 32David's men took
Asahel and buried him in the tomb of his
father at Bethlehem. Then Joab and his men
marched all night. The sun came up as they
reached Hebron.

3

There was a long war between the
people who supported Saul's family and
those who supported David's family. The
supporters of David's family became
stronger and stronger, but the supporters
of Saul's family became weaker and
weaker.

David's Sons

2Sons were born to David at Hebron. The
first was Amnon, whose mother was
Ahinoam from Jezreel. 3The second son was
Kileab, whose mother was Abigail, the
widow of Nabal from Carmel. The third son
was Absalom, whose mother was Maacah
daughter of Talmai, the king of Geshur. 4The
fourth son was Adonijah, whose mother was
Haggith. The fifth son was Shephatiah,
whose mother was Abital. 5The sixth son
was Ithream, whose mother was Eglah,
David's wife. These sons were born to David
at Hebron.

Abner Joins David

6During the war between the supporters
of Saul's family and the supporters of
David's family, Abner made himself a
main leader among the supporters of
Saul.

7Saul once had a slave woman named
Rizpah, who was the daughter of Aiah.
Ish-Bosheth said to Abner, "Why did you
have sexual relations with my father's slave
woman?"

8Abner was very angry because of what
Ish-Bosheth said, and he replied, "I have been
loyal to Saul and his family and friends! I
didn't hand you over to David. I am not a
traitor working for Judah! But now you are
saying I did something wrong with this
woman! 9May God help me if I don't join
David! I will make sure that what the LORD
promised does happen! 10I will take the
kingdom from the family of Saul and make
David king of Israel and Judah, from Dan to
Beersheba!"[n]

3:10 Dan to Beersheba Dan was the city farthest north in Israel, and Beersheba was the city farthest south. So this means all the people of Israel.

11 Ish-Bosheth couldn't say anything to
Abner, because he was afraid of him.
12 Then Abner sent messengers to ask
David, "Who is going to rule the land? Make
an agreement with me, and I will help you
unite all Israel."
13 David answered, "Good! I will make an
agreement with you, but I ask you one thing.
I will not meet with you unless you bring
Saul's daughter Michal to me." 14 Then David
sent messengers to Saul's son Ish-Bosheth,
saying, "Give me my wife Michal. She was
promised to me, and I killed a hundred
Philistines to get her."
15 So Ish-Bosheth sent men to take Michal
from her husband Paltiel son of Laish.
16 Michal's husband went with her, crying as
he followed her to Bahurim. But Abner said
to Paltiel, "Go back home." So he went home.
17 Abner sent this message to the elders of
Israel: "You have been wanting to make
David your king. 18 Now do it! The LORD said
of David, 'Through my servant David, I will
save my people Israel from the Philistines
and all their enemies.' "
19 Abner also said these things to the
people of Benjamin. He then went to Hebron
to tell David what the Benjaminites and
Israel wanted to do. 20 Abner came with
twenty men to David at Hebron. There
David prepared a feast for them. 21 Abner said
to David, "My master and king, I will go and
bring all the Israelites to you. Then they will
make an agreement with you so you will
rule over all Israel as you wanted." So David
let Abner go, and he left in peace.

Abner's Death

22 Just then Joab and David's men came
from a battle, bringing many valuable things
they had taken from the enemy. David had
let Abner leave in peace, so he was not with
David at Hebron. 23 When Joab and all his
army arrived at Hebron, the army said to
Joab, "Abner son of Ner came to King David,
and David let him leave in peace."
24 Joab came to the king and said, "What
have you done? Abner came to you. Why did
you let him go? Now he's gone. 25 You know
Abner son of Ner! He came to trick you! He
came to learn about everything you are
doing!"
26 After Joab left David, he sent messengers
after Abner, and they brought him back
from the well of Sirah. But David did not
know this. 27 When Abner arrived at Hebron,
Joab took him aside into the gateway. He
acted as though he wanted to talk with
Abner in private, but Joab stabbed him in
the stomach, and Abner died. Abner had
killed Joab's brother Asahel, so Joab killed
Abner to pay him back.
28 Later when David heard the news, he
said, "My kingdom and I are innocent
forever of the death of Abner son of Ner. The
LORD knows this. 29 Joab and his family are
responsible for this. May his family always
have someone with sores or with a skin
disease. May they always have someone who
must lean on a crutch. May some of his
family be killed in war. May they always
have someone without food to eat."
30 (Joab and his brother Abishai killed
Abner, because he had killed their brother
Asahel in the battle at Gibeon.)
31 Then David said to Joab and to all the
people with Joab, "Tear your clothes and put
on rough cloth to show how sad you are. Cry
for Abner." King David himself followed the
body of Abner. 32 They buried Abner in
Hebron, and David and all the people cried
at Abner's grave.
33 King David sang this funeral song for
Abner.

"Did Abner die like a fool?
34 His hands were not tied.
His feet were not in chains.
He fell at the hands of evil men."

Then all the people cried again for Abner.
35 They came to encourage David to eat while
it was still day. But he made a promise,
saying, "May God punish me terribly if I eat
bread or anything else before the sun sets!"
36 All the people saw what happened, and
they agreed with what the king was doing,
just as they agreed with everything he did.
37 That day all the people of Judah and Israel
understood that David did not order the
killing of Abner son of Ner.
38 David said to his officers, "You know
that a great man died today in Israel. 39 Even
though I am the appointed king, I feel
empty. These sons of Zeruiah are too much
for me. May the LORD give them the
punishment they should have."

Ish-Bosheth's Death

4 When Ish-Bosheth son of Saul heard that
Abner had died at Hebron, he was

shocked and all Israel became frightened.
2Two men who were captains in Saul's army
came to Ish-Bosheth. One was named
Baanah, and the other was named Recab.
They were the sons of Rimmon of Beeroth,
who was a Benjaminite. (The town Beeroth
belonged to the tribe of Benjamin. 3The
people of Beeroth ran away to Gittaim, and
they still live there as foreigners today.)
4(Saul's son Jonathan had a son named
Mephibosheth, who was crippled in both
feet. He was five years old when the news
came from Jezreel that Saul and Jonathan
were dead. Mephibosheth's nurse had picked
him up and run away. But as she hurried to
leave, she dropped him, and now he was
lame.)
5Recab and Baanah, sons of Rimmon from
Beeroth, went to Ish-Bosheth's house in
the afternoon while he was taking a nap.
6-7They went into the middle of the house
as if to get some wheat. Ish-Bosheth was
lying on his bed in his bedroom. Then Recab
and Baanah stabbed him in the stomach,
killed him, cut off his head, and took it with
them. They escaped and traveled all night
through the Jordan Valley. 8When they
arrived at Hebron, they gave his head to
David and said to the king, "Here is the head
of Ish-Bosheth son of Saul, your enemy. He
tried to kill you! Today the LORD has paid
back Saul and his family for what they did
to you!"
9David answered Recab and his brother
Baanah, the sons of Rimmon of Beeroth, "As
surely as the LORD lives, he has saved me
from all trouble! 10Once a man thought he
was bringing me good news. When he told
me, 'Saul is dead!' I seized him and killed
him at Ziklag. That was the reward I gave
him for his news! 11So even more I must put
you evil men to death because you have
killed an innocent man on his own bed in
his own house!"
12So David commanded his men to kill
Recab and Baanah. They cut off the hands
and feet of Recab and Baanah and hung
them over the pool of Hebron. Then they
took Ish-Bosheth's head and buried it in
Abner's tomb at Hebron.

David Is Made King of Israel

5 Then all the tribes of Israel came to
David at Hebron and said to him, "Look,
we are your own family. 2Even when Saul
was king, you were the one who led Israel in
battle. The LORD said to you, 'You will be a
shepherd for my people Israel. You will be
their leader.' "
3So all the elders of Israel came to King
David at Hebron, and he made an agreement
with them in Hebron in the presence of the
LORD. Then they poured oil on David to
make him king over Israel.
4David was thirty years old when he
became king, and he ruled forty years. 5He
was king over Judah in Hebron for seven
years and six months, and he was king
over all Israel and Judah in Jerusalem for
thirty-three years.
6When the king and his men went to
Jerusalem to attack the Jebusites who
lived there, the Jebusites said to David,
"You can't get inside our city. Even the
blind and the crippled can stop you." They
thought David could not enter their city.
7But David did take the city of Jerusalem
with its strong walls, and it became the City
of David.
8That day David said to his men, "To
defeat the Jebusites you must go through the
water tunnel. Then you can reach those
'crippled' and 'blind' enemies. This is why
people say, 'The blind and the crippled may
not enter the palace.' "
9So David lived in the strong, walled city
and called it the City of David. David built
more buildings around it, beginning where
the land was filled in. He also built more
buildings inside the city. 10He became
stronger and stronger, because the LORD God
All-Powerful was with him.
11Hiram king of the city of Tyre sent
messengers to David, along with cedar logs,
carpenters, and stonecutters. They built a
palace for David. 12Then David knew that
the LORD really had made him king of Israel
and that the LORD had made his kingdom
great because the LORD loved his people
Israel.
13After he came from Hebron, David took
for himself more slave women and wives in
Jerusalem. More sons and daughters were
born to David. 14These are the names of the
sons born to David in Jerusalem: Shammua,
Shobab, Nathan, Solomon, 15Ibhar, Elishua,
Nepheg, Japhia, 16Elishama, Eliada, and
Eliphelet.

Michal

2 SAMUEL 6

People have filled the streets to welcome King David who is bringing the Ark of the Agreement back to Jerusalem. David and the Israelites laugh and dance and play instruments in worship. The noise is deafening. When had Jerusalem last seen such a celebration?

David's wife Michal watches from a window in her quarters and can feel the hairs rising on the back of her neck. She tightens her jaw as anger swells. Her husband is wearing nothing more than a linen vest—his actions are not worthy of the King of Israel. *Where is his dignity? He is as lowly and common as the rest of them, romping around like a goat.*

Michal had loved David once. She wanted to marry him and was thrilled when her father, King Saul, agreed. David made her heart leap when he looked at her; she would have done anything for him—and she did, hiding him from her father when he wanted David killed. Her love had been strong and deep and endless.

But then there were the years of separation. Bitterness crept in and her heart grew cold toward David and the God he served. Watching him now, she despises David as he winds his way through the crowded streets, laughing and singing. She won't worship; she feels nothing for David or his God. She turns from the window and walks away.

Worship begins in the heart. The walls we build hinder our love for each other and our worship for God.

David Defeats the Philistines

17 When the Philistines heard that David
had been made king over Israel, all the
Philistines went to look for him. But when
David heard the news, he went down to the
stronghold. 18 The Philistines came and
camped in the Valley of Rephaim. 19 David
asked the LORD, "Should I attack the
Philistines? Will you hand them over to
me?"

The LORD said to David, "Go! I will
certainly hand them over to you."

20 So David went to Baal Perazim and
defeated the Philistines there. David said,
"Like a flood of water, the LORD has broken
through my enemies in front of me." So
David named the place Baal Perazim.[n] 21 The
Philistines left their idols behind at Baal
Perazim, so David and his men carried them
away.

22 Once again the Philistines came and
camped at the Valley of Rephaim. 23 When
David prayed to the LORD, he answered,
"Don't attack the Philistines from the front.
Instead, go around and attack them in front
of the balsam trees. 24 When you hear the
sound of marching in the tops of the balsam
trees, act quickly. I, the LORD, will have gone
ahead of you to defeat the Philistine army."
25 So David did what the LORD commanded.
He defeated the Philistines and chased them
all the way from Gibeon to Gezer.

The Ark Is Brought to Jerusalem

6 David again gathered all the chosen men
of Israel—thirty thousand of them.
2 Then he and all his people went to Baalah
in Judah[n] to bring back the Ark of God. The
Ark is called by the Name, the name of the
LORD All-Powerful, whose throne is between
the gold creatures with wings. 3 They put the
Ark of God on a new cart and brought it out
of Abinadab's house on the hill. Uzzah and
Ahio, sons of Abinadab, led the new cart
4 which had the Ark of God on it. Ahio was
walking in front of it. 5 David and all the
Israelites were celebrating in the presence of
the LORD. They were playing wooden instruments: lyres, harps, tambourines, rattles, and
cymbals.

6 When David's men came to the
threshing floor of Nacon, the oxen stumbled.

5:20 Baal Perazim This name means "the Lord breaks through." **6:2 Baalah in Judah** Another name for Kiriath Jearim.

devotion 84

2 SAMUEL 5:10–12

WHAT'S YOUR PURPOSE ON EARTH?

David entered into his divine purpose as the King of Israel. God gave him strengths, blessings, and favor to do something beyond himself: to lead a nation for God's glory. God was glorified because David operated in his God-given passion and callings.

Somewhere inside of you there is at least a thread of passion and purpose, a divine thread put there by God. It defines who you are and is a part of the reason you were created. Do you sense the yearning for purpose in your spirit? Do you long to find the thread that has been woven through your life?

Some people go through their whole lives and never really come to realize God's purpose for them. That's scary. I don't want to hear God say, "You had incredible potential, but you buried the talent I gave you. I gave you gifts that you never unwrapped."

Keep in mind that we must care for our souls and walk with our Savior if we want to hear his voice and know his will. From a spiritual distance, we become hard of hearing. We cannot discern or decide how the Lord is leading. We cannot distinguish his voice from everyone else's. We cannot identify the strengths and gifts he has put together in our personalities. Just like David, we have to stay connected with God to clearly see the passions he is building into our lives. God will be glorified when we enter into the strength of our divine purpose.

So Uzzah reached out to steady the Ark of
God. 7The LORD was angry with Uzzah and
killed him because of what he did. So Uzzah
died there beside the Ark of God. 8David was
angry because the LORD had killed Uzzah.
Now that place is called the Punishment of
Uzzah.

9David was afraid of the LORD that day, and
he said, "How can the Ark of the LORD come
to me now?" 10So David would not move the
Ark of the LORD to be with him in Jerusalem.
Instead, he took it to the house of
Obed-Edom, a man from Gath. 11The Ark of
the LORD stayed in Obed-Edom's house for
three months, and the LORD blessed Obed-
Edom and all his family.

12The people told David, "The LORD has
blessed the family of Obed-Edom and all that
belongs to him, because the Ark of God is
there." So David went and brought it up
from Obed-Edom's house to Jerusalem with
joy. 13When the men carrying the Ark of the
LORD had walked six steps, David sacrificed a
bull and a fat calf. 14Then David danced with
all his might before the LORD. He had on a
holy linen vest. 15David and all the Israelites
shouted with joy and blew the trumpets as
they brought the Ark of the LORD to the city.

16As the Ark of the LORD came into the
city, Saul's daughter Michal looked out the
window. When she saw David jumping and
dancing in the presence of the LORD, she
hated him.

17David put up a tent for the Ark of the
LORD, and then the Israelites put it in its
place inside the tent. David offered whole
burnt offerings and fellowship offerings
before the LORD. 18When David finished
offering the whole burnt offerings and the
fellowship offerings, he blessed the people in
the name of the LORD All-Powerful. 19David
gave a loaf of bread, a cake of dates, and a

cake of raisins to every Israelite, both men
and women. Then all the people went home.
20David went back to bless the people in
his home, but Saul's daughter Michal came
out to meet him. She said, "With what honor
the king of Israel acted today! You took off
your clothes in front of the servant girls of
your officers like one who takes off his
clothes without shame!"
21Then David said to Michal, "I did it in
the presence of the LORD. The LORD chose me,
not your father or anyone from Saul's family.
The LORD appointed me to be over Israel. So I
will celebrate in the presence of the LORD.
22Maybe I will lose even more honor, and
maybe I will be brought down in my own
opinion, but the girls you talk about will
honor me!"
23And Saul's daughter Michal had no
children to the day she died.

David Wants to Build a Temple

7 King David was living in his palace, and
the LORD had given him peace from all
his enemies around him. 2Then David said
to Nathan the prophet, "Look, I am living in
a palace made of cedar wood, but the Ark of
God is in a tent!"
3Nathan said to the king, "Go and do what
you really want to do, because the LORD is
with you."
4But that night the LORD spoke his word to
Nathan, 5"Go and tell my servant David,
'This is what the LORD says: Will you build a
house for me to live in? 6From the time I
brought the Israelites out of Egypt until now
I have not lived in a house. I have been
moving around all this time with a tent as
my home. 7As I have moved with the
Israelites, I have never said to the tribes,
whom I commanded to take care of my
people Israel, "Why haven't you built me a
house of cedar?"'
8"You must tell my servant David, 'This is
what the LORD All-Powerful says: I took you
from the pasture and from tending the sheep
and made you leader of my people Israel. 9I
have been with you everywhere you have
gone and have defeated your enemies for
you. I will make you as famous as any of the
great people on the earth. 10Also I will
choose a place for my people Israel, and I
will plant them so they can live in their own
homes. They will not be bothered anymore.
Wicked people will no longer bother them
as they have in the past 11when I chose
judges for my people Israel. But I will give
you peace from all your enemies. I also tell
you that I will make your descendants kings
of Israel after you.
12" 'When you die and join your ancestors,
I will make one of your sons the next king,
and I will set up his kingdom. 13He will
build a house for me, and I will let his
kingdom rule always. 14I will be his father,
and he will be my son. When he sins, I will
use other people to punish him. They will be
my whips. 15I took away my love from Saul,
whom I removed before you, but I will never
stop loving your son. 16But your family and
your kingdom will continue always before
me. Your throne will last forever.' "
17Nathan told David everything God had
said in this vision.

David Prays to God

18Then King David went in and sat in
front of the LORD. David said, "Lord GOD, who
am I? What is my family? Why did you
bring me to this point? 19But even this is not
enough for you, Lord GOD. You have also
made promises about my future family. This
is extraordinary, Lord GOD.
20"What more can I say to you, Lord GOD,
since you know me, your servant, so well!
21You have done this great thing because you
said you would and because you wanted to,
and you have let me know about it. 22This is
why you are great, Lord GOD! There is no one
like you. There is no God except you. We
have heard all this ourselves! 23There is no
nation like your people Israel. They are the
only people on earth that God chose to be
his own. You made your name well known.
You did great and wonderful miracles for
them. You went ahead of them and forced
other nations and their gods out of the land.
You freed your people from slavery in Egypt.
24You made the people of Israel your very
own people forever, and, LORD, you are their
God.
25"Now, LORD God, keep the promise
forever that you made about my family and
me, your servant. Do what you have said.
26Then you will be honored always, and
people will say, 'The LORD All-Powerful is
God over Israel!' And the family of your
servant David will continue before you.

27“LORD All-Powerful, the God of Israel,
you have said to me, ‘I will make your family
great.’ So I, your servant, am brave enough to
pray to you. 28Lord GOD, you are God, and
your words are true. And you have promised
these good things to me, your servant.
29Please, bless my family. Let it continue
before you always. Lord GOD, you have said
so. With your blessing let my family always
be blessed.”

David Wins Many Wars

8 Later, David defeated the Philistines,
conquered them, and took the city of
Metheg Ammah.

2He also defeated the people of Moab. He
made them lie on the ground, and then he
used a rope to measure them. Those who
were measured within two rope lengths
were killed, but those who were within the
next rope length were allowed to live. So the
people of Moab became servants of David
and gave him the payment he demanded.

3David also defeated Hadadezer son of
Rehob, king of Zobah, as he went to take
control again at the Euphrates River. 4David
captured one thousand chariots, seven
thousand men who rode in chariots, and
twenty thousand foot soldiers. He crippled
all but a hundred of the chariot horses.

5Arameans from Damascus came to help
Hadadezer king of Zobah, but David killed
twenty-two thousand of them. 6Then David
put groups of soldiers in Damascus in Aram.
The Arameans became David’s servants and
gave him the payment he demanded. The
LORD gave David victory everywhere he
went.

7David took the shields of gold that had
belonged to Hadadezer’s officers and
brought them to Jerusalem. 8David also took
many things made of bronze from Tebah and
Berothai, which had been cities under
Hadadezer’s control.

9Toi king of Hamath heard that David had
defeated all the army of Hadadezer. 10So Toi
sent his son Joram to greet and congratulate
King David for defeating Hadadezer.
(Hadadezer had been at war with Toi.) Joram
brought items made of silver, gold, and
bronze. 11King David gave them to the LORD,
along with the silver and gold he had taken
from the other nations he had defeated.
12These nations were Edom, Moab, Ammon,
Philistia, and Amalek. David also gave the
LORD what he had taken from Hadadezer son
of Rehob, king of Zobah.

13David was famous after he returned
from defeating eighteen thousand Arameans
in the Valley of Salt. 14He put groups of
soldiers all over Edom, and all the Edomites
became his servants. The LORD gave David
victory everywhere he went.

15David was king over all Israel, and he did
what was fair and right for all his people.
16Joab son of Zeruiah was commander over
the army. Jehoshaphat son of Ahilud was the
recorder. 17Zadok son of Ahitub and
Abiathar son of Ahimelech were priests.
Seraiah was the royal secretary. 18Benaiah
son of Jehoiada was over the Kerethites and
Pelethites.[n] And David’s sons were priests.

David Helps Saul’s Family

9 David asked, “Is anyone still left in Saul’s
family? I want to show kindness to that
person for Jonathan’s sake!”

2Now there was a servant named Ziba
from Saul’s family. So David’s servants called
Ziba to him. King David said to him, “Are
you Ziba?”

He answered, “Yes, I am your servant.”

3The king asked, “Is anyone left in Saul’s
family? I want to show God’s kindness to
that person.”

Ziba answered the king, “Jonathan has a
son still living who is crippled in both feet.”

4The king asked Ziba, “Where is this son?”

Ziba answered, “He is at the house of
Makir son of Ammiel in Lo Debar.”

5Then King David had servants bring
Jonathan’s son from the house of Makir son
of Ammiel in Lo Debar. 6Mephibosheth,
Jonathan’s son, came before David and
bowed facedown on the floor.

David said, “Mephibosheth!”

Mephibosheth said, “I am your servant.”

7David said to him, “Don’t be afraid. I will
be kind to you for your father Jonathan’s
sake. I will give you back all the land of your
grandfather Saul, and you will always eat at
my table.”

8Mephibosheth bowed to David again
and said, “You are being very kind to me,

8:18 Kerethites and Pelethites These were probably special units of the army that were responsible for the king’s safety, a kind of palace guard.

your servant! And I am no better than a
dead dog!"
9Then King David called Saul's servant
Ziba. David said to him, "I have given your
master's grandson everything that belonged
to Saul and his family. 10You, your sons, and
your servants will farm the land and harvest
the crops. Then your family will have food
to eat. But Mephibosheth, your master's
grandson, will always eat at my table."
(Now Ziba had fifteen sons and twenty
servants.) 11Ziba said to King David, "I, your
servant, will do everything my master, the
king, commands me."
So Mephibosheth ate at David's table
as if he were one of the king's sons.
12Mephibosheth had a young son named
Mica. Everyone in Ziba's family became
Mephibosheth's servants. 13Mephibosheth
lived in Jerusalem, because he always ate at
the king's table. And he was crippled in
both feet.

War with the Ammonites and Arameans

10 When Nahash king of the
Ammonites died, his son Hanun
became king after him. 2David said, "Nahash
was loyal to me, so I will be loyal to his son
Hanun." So David sent his messengers to
comfort Hanun about his father's death.
David's officers went to the land of the
Ammonites. 3But the Ammonite leaders said
to Hanun, their master, "Do you think David
wants to honor your father by sending men
to comfort you? No! David sent them to
study the city and spy it out and capture it!"
4So Hanun arrested David's officers. To
shame them he shaved off half their beards
and cut off their clothes at the hips. Then he
sent them away.
5When the people told David, he sent
messengers to meet his officers because they
were very ashamed. King David said, "Stay in
Jericho until your beards have grown back.
Then come home."
6The Ammonites knew that they had
insulted David. So they hired twenty
thousand Aramean foot soldiers from Beth
Rehob and Zobah. They also hired the king
of Maacah with a thousand men and twelve
thousand men from Tob.
7When David heard about this, he sent
Joab with the whole army. 8The Ammonites
came out and prepared for battle at the city
gate. The Arameans from Zobah and Rehob
and the men from Tob and Maacah were out
in the field by themselves.
9Joab saw that there were enemies both in
front of him and behind him. So he chose
some of the best soldiers of Israel and sent
them out to fight the Arameans. 10Joab put
the rest of the army under the command of
Abishai, his brother. Then he sent them out
to fight the Ammonites. 11Joab said to
Abishai, "If the Arameans are too strong for
me, you must help me. Or, if the Ammonites
are too strong for you, I will help you. 12Be
strong. We must fight bravely for our people
and the cities of our God. The LORD will do
what he thinks is right."
13Then Joab and the army with him went
to attack the Arameans, and the Arameans
ran away. 14When the Ammonites saw that
the Arameans were running away, they
also ran away from Abishai and went back
to their city. So Joab returned from the
battle with the Ammonites and came to
Jerusalem.
15When the Arameans saw that Israel had
defeated them, they came together into one
big army. 16Hadadezer sent messengers to
bring the Arameans from east of the
Euphrates River, and they went to Helam.
Their leader was Shobach, the commander
of Hadadezer's army.
17When David heard about this, he
gathered all the Israelites together. They
crossed over the Jordan River and went to
Helam. There the Arameans prepared for
battle and attacked him. 18But the Arameans
ran away from the Israelites. David killed
seven hundred Aramean chariot drivers and
forty thousand Aramean horsemen. He also
killed Shobach, the commander of the
Aramean army.
19When the kings who served Hadadezer
saw that the Israelites had defeated them,
they made peace with the Israelites and
served them. And the Arameans were afraid
to help the Ammonites again.

David Sins with Bathsheba

11 In the spring, when the kings
normally went out to war, David sent
out Joab, his servants, and all the Israelites.
They destroyed the Ammonites and attacked
the city of Rabbah. But David stayed in
Jerusalem. 2One evening David got up from

devotion 85

2 SAMUEL 10:12

TIRED OF UNPACKING BOXES?

Being strong can get exhausting. We wear ourselves out emotionally, mentally, and certainly physically. At lunch today, my girlfriend asked Gracie, a little girl that is wise beyond her four years, "Gracie, tell me what life's all about." To which Gracie replied without missing a millisecond of a beat, "Work is life." Her mother quickly chimed in to explain that she had instructed Gracie to unpack the boxes in her new room. Gracie quickly expressed her frustration with her work project, and her mom responded, "Tough. That's life." After an hour had passed, Gracie marched herself back into the living room and announced to her mom, "That's it. I don't want to do life anymore."

Gracie is four and I am forty, and I find myself doing the same thing—marching right into my prayer time with the Lord and telling him, "That's it. I am not doing life anymore!" If you feel like God keeps sending you boxes to be unpacked, you are right. He wants you to be his hands and feet in the lives he puts in your path. He wants to send you the hurting, the betrayed, the sinful, and the repentant. And sometimes, he sends a box that is meant to bless you. That is why we keep pressing on to fight the good fight and to restore all those who are boxed up in their sin and hopelessness. Don't quit on life. Be strong in the Lord, and he will use you to help unpack the boxes.

his bed and walked around on the roof[n] of
his palace. While he was on the roof, he saw
a woman bathing. She was very beautiful.
3So David sent his servants to find out who
she was. A servant answered, "That woman
is Bathsheba daughter of Eliam. She is the
wife of Uriah the Hittite." 4So David sent
messengers to bring Bathsheba to him.
When she came to him, he had sexual
relations with her. (Now Bathsheba had
purified herself from her monthly period.)
Then she went back to her house. 5But
Bathsheba became pregnant and sent word
to David, saying, "I am pregnant."

6So David sent a message to Joab: "Send
Uriah the Hittite to me." And Joab sent Uriah
to David. 7When Uriah came to him, David
asked him how Joab was, how the soldiers
were, and how the war was going. 8Then
David said to Uriah, "Go home and rest."

So Uriah left the palace, and the king sent
a gift to him. 9But Uriah did not go home.
Instead, he slept outside the door of the
palace as all the king's officers did.

10The officers told David, "Uriah did not
go home."

Then David said to Uriah, "You came from
a long trip. Why didn't you go home?"

11Uriah said to him, "The Ark and the
soldiers of Israel and Judah are staying in
tents. My master Joab and his officers are
camping out in the fields. It isn't right for me
to go home to eat and drink and have sexual
relations with my wife!"

12David said to Uriah, "Stay here today.
Tomorrow I'll send you back to the battle."
So Uriah stayed in Jerusalem that day and
the next. 13Then David called Uriah to come
to see him, so Uriah ate and drank with
David. David made Uriah drunk, but he still
did not go home. That evening Uriah again
slept with the king's officers.

11:2 roof In Bible times houses were built with flat roofs. The roof was used for drying things such as flax and fruit. And it was used as an extra room, as a place for worship, and as a cool place to sleep in the summer.

Bathsheba

2 SAMUEL 11

A servant slips Bathsheba's robe from her shoulders, and raven hair falls over her creamy skin. The king's palace overlooks her roof, and she can see that he is home this evening. It is spring, a time when King David and his men are normally at war, but he has stayed behind in Jerusalem. Perhaps he'll be walking on his roof again. She turns toward the king's palace and sweeps her hair so it hangs down her back.

King David gets up from his bed and walks to his roof as he has done so many nights before. He stops at the sight. *Who is that?* She steps into the bath, but David can't stop watching. The vision is too lovely.

Soon a messenger calls her to the king, and though she is married, Bathsheba does not protest. She is willing to see him. Their eyes meet and the passion cannot be denied. She is beautiful and he is the King of Israel!

He dismisses his servants for the evening. Their time together is unbridled and powerful—something David had nearly forgotten in his loveless marriage. Bathsheba makes him feel alive and special and worthy of attention. She wraps her arms around his neck and smiles. Who knew that one simple bath could lead to this? *I did,* she thinks, kissing him. *And so did he.*

Sin quickly escalates. A thought in the mind can take us to a place we never thought we were capable of going.

[14]The next morning David wrote a letter
to Joab and sent it by Uriah. [15]In the letter
David wrote, "Put Uriah on the front lines
where the fighting is worst and leave him
there alone. Let him be killed in battle."
[16]Joab watched the city and saw where its
strongest defenders were and put Uriah there.
[17]When the men of the city came out to fight
against Joab, some of David's men were killed.
And Uriah the Hittite was one of them.
[18]Then Joab sent David a complete
account of the war. [19]Joab told the messenger,
"Tell King David what happened in the war.
[20]After you finish, the king may be angry
and ask, 'Why did you go so near the city
to fight? Didn't you know they would
shoot arrows from the city wall? [21]Do you
remember who killed Abimelech son of
Jerub-Besheth?[n] It was a woman on the city
wall. She threw a large stone for grinding
grain on Abimelech and killed him there in
Thebez. Why did you go so near the wall?' If
King David asks that, tell him, 'Your servant
Uriah the Hittite also died.' "
[22]The messenger left and went to David
and told him everything Joab had told him
to say. [23]The messenger told David, "The
men of Ammon were winning. They came
out and attacked us in the field, but we
fought them back to the city gate. [24]The
archers on the city wall shot at your
servants, and some of your men were killed.
Your servant Uriah the Hittite also died."
[25]David said to the messenger, "Say this to
Joab: 'Don't be upset about this. The sword
kills everyone the same. Make a stronger
attack against the city and capture it.'
Encourage Joab with these words."
[26]When Bathsheba heard that her
husband was dead, she cried for him. [27]After
she finished her time of sadness, David sent
servants to bring her to his house. She
became David's wife and gave birth to his
son, but the LORD did not like what David
had done.

David's Son Dies

12 The LORD sent Nathan to David.
When he came to David, he said,
"There were two men in a city. One was rich,
but the other was poor. [2]The rich man had
many sheep and cattle. [3]But the poor man

11:21 Jerub-Besheth Another name for Gideon.

had nothing except one little female lamb he
had bought. The poor man fed the lamb, and
it grew up with him and his children. It
shared his food and drank from his cup and
slept in his arms. The lamb was like a
daughter to him.
4“Then a traveler stopped to visit the rich
man. The rich man wanted to feed the
traveler, but he didn't want to take one of his
own sheep or cattle. Instead, he took the
lamb from the poor man and cooked it for
his visitor.”
5David became very angry at the rich man.
He said to Nathan, “As surely as the LORD
lives, the man who did this should die! 6He
must pay for the lamb four times for doing
such a thing. He had no mercy!”
7Then Nathan said to David, “You are the
man! This is what the LORD, the God of Israel,
says: ‘I appointed you king of Israel and
saved you from Saul. 8I gave you his
kingdom and his wives. And I made you
king of Israel and Judah. And if that had not
been enough, I would have given you even
more. 9So why did you ignore the LORD's
command? Why did you do what he says is
wrong? You killed Uriah the Hittite with the
sword of the Ammonites and took his wife
to be your wife! 10Now there will always be
people in your family who will die by a
sword, because you did not respect me; you
took the wife of Uriah the Hittite for
yourself!’
11“This is what the LORD says: ‘I am
bringing trouble to you from your own
family. While you watch, I will take your
wives from you and give them to someone
who is very close to you. He will have sexual
relations with your wives, and everyone will
know it. 12You had sexual relations with
Bathsheba in secret, but I will do this so all
the people of Israel can see it.’ ”
13Then David said to Nathan, “I have
sinned against the LORD.”
Nathan answered, “The LORD has taken
away your sin. You will not die. 14But what
you did caused the LORD's enemies to lose all
respect for him. For this reason the son who
was born to you will die.”
15Then Nathan went home. And the LORD
caused the son of David and Bathsheba,
Uriah's widow, to be very sick. 16David
prayed to God for the baby. David fasted and
went into his house and stayed there, lying
on the ground all night. 17The elders of
David's family came to him and tried to pull
him up from the ground, but he refused to
get up or to eat food with them.
18On the seventh day the baby died.
David's servants were afraid to tell him that
the baby was dead. They said, “Look, we tried
to talk to David while the baby was alive,
but he refused to listen to us. If we tell him
the baby is dead, he may do something
awful.”
19When David saw his servants
whispering, he knew that the baby was dead.
So he asked them, “Is the baby dead?”
They answered, “Yes, he is dead.”
20Then David got up from the floor,
washed himself, put lotions on, and changed
his clothes. Then he went into the LORD's
house to worship. After that, he went home
and asked for something to eat. His servants
gave him some food, and he ate.
21David's servants said to him, “Why are
you doing this? When the baby was still
alive, you fasted and you cried. Now that the
baby is dead, you get up and eat food.”
22David said, “While the baby was still
alive, I fasted, and I cried. I thought, ‘Who
knows? Maybe the LORD will feel sorry for
me and let the baby live.’ 23But now that the
baby is dead, why should I fast? I can't bring
him back to life. Someday I will go to him,
but he cannot come back to me.”
24Then David comforted Bathsheba his
wife. He slept with her and had sexual
relations with her. She became pregnant
again and had another son, whom David
named Solomon. The LORD loved Solomon.
25The LORD sent word through Nathan the
prophet to name the baby Jedidiah,[n] because
the LORD loved the child.

David Captures Rabbah

26Joab fought against Rabbah, a royal city
of the Ammonites, and he was about to
capture it. 27Joab sent messengers to David
and said, “I have fought against Rabbah and
have captured its water supply. 28Now bring
the other soldiers together and attack this
city. Capture it before I capture it myself and
it is called by my name!”

12:25 Jedidiah This name means “loved by the LORD.”

Tamar

2 SAMUEL 13

It wasn't love; it was lust. Amnon's sin took root in his mind, and he shared it with a cousin. Together, they plotted a way for Amnon to have sexual relations with his half-sister Tamar. The plan included deceiving their father, David.

Amnon lay in bed, pretending to be ill, when beautiful, young Tamar brought him food. He could no longer control his urges and grabbed her hands. Frightened, Tamar screamed. "No, brother! Don't force me! Don't do this shameful thing! I could never get rid of my shame!"

Her tears and her cries fell on deaf ears. He was stronger and overpowered her, forcing her to do something she never thought possible. Tamar begged for mercy from this violent act, but her pleas were meaningless. When he was finished, Amnon despised Tamar and threw her from his chambers.

Broken and used, Tamar gasped for breath. She threw ashes on her head and tore the beautiful robe the virgin daughters of the king wore. She was no longer a virgin, no longer worthy to be given in marriage by the king. Her grief was unbearable, and her mind struggled to comprehend. *How could he do this? How could he take so much from me? How can I live with this shame?* She felt so alone. In one brief moment her world had turned upside down.

Violence against you is not your fault. God longs for you to be free of the guilt, shame, and pain you've experienced.

29 So David gathered all the army and went to Rabbah and fought against it and captured it. 30 David took the crown off their king's head and had it placed on his own head. That gold crown weighed about seventy-five pounds, and it had valuable gems in it. And David took many valuable things from the city. 31 He also brought out the people of the city and forced them to work with saws, iron picks, and axes. He also made them build with bricks. David did this to all the Ammonite cities. Then David and all his army returned to Jerusalem.

Amnon and Tamar

13 David had a son named Absalom and a son named Amnon. Absalom had a beautiful sister named Tamar, and Amnon loved her. 2 Tamar was a virgin. Amnon made himself sick just thinking about her, because he could not find any chance to be alone with her.

3 Amnon had a friend named Jonadab son of Shimeah, David's brother. Jonadab was a very clever man. 4 He asked Amnon, "Son of the king, why do you look so sad day after day? Tell me what's wrong!"

Amnon told him, "I love Tamar, the sister of my half-brother Absalom."

5 Jonadab said to Amnon, "Go to bed and act as if you are sick. Then your father will come to see you. Tell him, 'Please let my sister Tamar come in and give me food to eat. Let her make the food in front of me so I can watch and eat it from her hand.' "

6 So Amnon went to bed and acted sick. When King David came in to see him, Amnon said to him, "Please let my sister Tamar come in. Let her make two of her special cakes for me while I watch. Then I will eat them from her hands."

7 David sent for Tamar in the palace, saying, "Go to your brother Amnon's house and make some food for him." 8 So Tamar went to her brother Amnon's house, and he was in bed. Tamar took some dough and pressed it together with her hands. She made some special cakes while Amnon watched. Then she baked them. 9 Next she took the pan and served him, but he refused to eat.

He said to his servants, "All of you, leave me alone!" So they all left him alone. 10 Amnon said to Tamar, "Bring the food into the bedroom so I may eat from your hand."

Tamar took the cakes she had made and
brought them to her brother Amnon in the
bedroom. 11She went to him so he could eat
from her hands, but Amnon grabbed her. He
said, "Sister, come and have sexual relations
with me."

12Tamar said to him, "No, brother! Don't
force me! This should never be done in
Israel! Don't do this shameful thing! 13I could
never get rid of my shame! And you will be
like the shameful fools in Israel! Please talk
with the king, and he will let you marry me."

14But Amnon refused to listen to her. He
was stronger than she was, so he forced her
to have sexual relations with him. 15After
that, Amnon hated Tamar. He hated her
more than he had loved her before. Amnon
said to her, "Get up and leave!"

16Tamar said to him, "No! Sending me
away would be worse than what you've
already done!"

But he refused to listen to her. 17He called
his young servant back in and said, "Get this
woman out of here and away from me! Lock
the door after her." 18So his servant led her
out of the room and bolted the door after
her.

Tamar was wearing a special robe with
long sleeves, because the king's virgin
daughters wore this kind of robe. 19To show
how upset she was, Tamar put ashes on her
head and tore her special robe and put her
hand on her head. Then she went away,
crying loudly.

20Absalom, Tamar's brother, said to her,
"Has Amnon, your brother, forced you to
have sexual relations with him? For now,
sister, be quiet. He is your half-brother. Don't
let this upset you so much!" So Tamar lived
in her brother Absalom's house and was sad
and lonely.

21When King David heard the news, he
was very angry. 22Absalom did not say a
word, good or bad, to Amnon. But he hated
Amnon for disgracing his sister Tamar.

Absalom's Revenge

23Two years later Absalom had some men
come to Baal Hazor, near Ephraim, to cut the
wool from his sheep. Absalom invited all the
king's sons to come also. 24Absalom went to
the king and said, "I have men coming to cut
the wool. Please come with your officers and
join me."

25King David said to Absalom, "No, my
son. We won't all go, because it would be too
much trouble for you." Although Absalom
begged David, he would not go, but he did
give his blessing.

26Absalom said, "If you don't want to
come, then please let my brother Amnon
come with us."

King David asked, "Why should he go
with you?"

27Absalom kept begging David until he let
Amnon and all the king's sons go with
Absalom.

28Then Absalom instructed his servants,
"Watch Amnon. When he is drunk, I will tell
you, 'Kill Amnon.' Right then, kill him! Don't
be afraid, because I have commanded you! Be
strong and brave!" 29So Absalom's young
men killed Amnon as Absalom commanded,
but all of David's other sons got on their
mules and escaped.

30While the king's sons were on their way,
the news came to David, "Absalom has killed
all of the king's sons! Not one of them is left
alive!" 31King David tore his clothes and lay
on the ground to show his sadness. All his
servants standing nearby tore their clothes
also.

32Jonadab son of Shimeah, David's
brother, said to David, "Don't think all the
young men, your sons, are killed. No, only
Amnon is dead! Absalom has planned this
ever since Amnon forced his sister Tamar to
have sexual relations with him. 33My master
and king, don't think that all of the king's
sons are dead. Only Amnon is dead!"

34In the meantime Absalom had run
away.

A guard standing on the city wall saw
many people coming from the other side of
the hill. 35So Jonadab said to King David,
"Look, I was right! The king's sons are
coming!"

36As soon as Jonadab had said this, the
king's sons arrived, crying loudly. David and
all his servants began crying also. 37David
cried for his son every day.

But Absalom ran away to Talmai[n] son of
Ammihud, the king of Geshur. 38After
Absalom ran away to Geshur, he stayed

13:37 Talmai He was Absalom's grandfather.

there for three years. 39When King David got over Amnon's death, he missed Absalom greatly.

Joab Sends a Wise Woman to David

14 Joab son of Zeruiah knew that King David missed Absalom very much. 2So Joab sent messengers to Tekoa to bring a wise woman from there. He said to her, "Pretend to be very sad. Put on funeral clothes and don't put lotion on yourself. Act like a woman who has been crying many days for someone who died. 3Then go to the king and say these words." Then Joab told her what to say.

4So the woman from Tekoa spoke to the king. She bowed facedown on the ground to show respect and said, "My king, help me!"

5King David asked her, "What is the matter?"

The woman said, "I am a widow; my husband is dead. 6I had two sons. They were out in the field fighting, and no one was there to stop them. So one son killed the other son. 7Now all the family group is against me. They said to me, 'Bring the son who killed his brother so we may kill him for killing his brother. That way we will also get rid of the one who would receive what belonged to his father.' My son is like the last spark of a fire. He is all I have left. If they kill him, my husband's name and property will be gone from the earth."

8Then the king said to the woman, "Go home. I will take care of this for you."

9The woman of Tekoa said to him, "Let the blame be on me and my father's family. My master and king, you and your throne are innocent."

10King David said, "Bring me anyone who says anything bad to you. Then he won't bother you again."

11The woman said, "Please promise in the name of the LORD your God. Then my relative who has the duty of punishing a murderer won't add to the destruction by killing my son."

David said, "As surely as the LORD lives, no one will hurt your son. Not one hair from his head will fall to the ground."

12The woman said, "Let me say something to you, my master and king."

The king said, "Speak."

13Then the woman said, "Why have you decided this way against the people of God? When you judge this way, you show that you are guilty for not bringing back your son who was forced to leave home. 14We will all die someday. We're like water spilled on the ground; no one can gather it back. But God doesn't take away life. Instead, he plans ways that those who have been sent away will not have to stay away from him! 15My master and king, I came to say this to you because the people have made me afraid! I thought, 'Let me talk to the king. Maybe he will do what I ask. 16Maybe he will listen. Perhaps he will save me from those who want to keep both me and my son from getting what God gave us.'

17"Now I say, 'May the words of my master the king give me rest. Like an angel of God, you know what is good and what is bad. May the LORD your God be with you!' "

18Then King David said, "Do not hide the truth. Answer me one question."

The woman said, "My master the king, please ask your question."

19The king said, "Did Joab tell you to say all these things?"

The woman answered, "As you live, my master the king, no one could avoid that question. You are right. Your servant Joab did tell me to say these things. 20Joab did it so you would see things differently. My master, you are wise like an angel of God who knows everything that happens on earth."

Absalom Returns to Jerusalem

21The king said to Joab, "Look, I will do what I promised. Bring back the young man Absalom."

22Joab bowed facedown on the ground and blessed the king. Then he said, "Today I know you are pleased with me, because you have done what I asked."

23Then Joab got up and went to Geshur and brought Absalom back to Jerusalem. 24But King David said, "Absalom must go to his own house. He may not come to see me." So Absalom went to his own house and did not go to see the king.

25Absalom was greatly praised for his handsome appearance. No man in Israel was as handsome as he. No blemish was on him from his head to his foot. 26At the end of every year, Absalom would cut his hair, because it became too heavy. When he

devotion 86

2 SAMUEL 14:25–26

THE WEIGHT OF A VAIN MAN'S LOCKS

Absalom was so proud of his hair that he weighed it. It seems like such a ridiculous thing to do. Yet we often do the same thing. We spend hundreds of dollars on our hair, nails, makeup, and fashion accessories. Where do we draw the line? Absalom was greatly praised for his appearance. Was it his downfall? He did eventually try to steal the throne from his father, King David. He did create a lot of dissension in the kingdom. And, believe it or not, his hair brought about his death in the end.

So maybe you'll never weigh your hair, but is it possible that you think too much about your appearance? Could it be your downfall? My son attended the MTV Music Awards this year. I don't usually watch MTV, but with my oldest child being there, I did. I couldn't help but think of Absalom as I watched it. The money spent on the appearances of the stars was the highlight of the evening. The sad thing is that so many lives are destroyed by that world of fame and fortune. The world watches and dreams of being a star. The reality is that the stars are not any happier than the rest of the world.

Is it wrong to care about appearance? No. God created us in his image; he created us to care. But when we have to weigh our hair to feel good about ourselves, maybe we have crossed the line.

weighed it, it would weigh about five
pounds by the royal measure.
27Absalom had three sons and one
daughter. His daughter's name was also
Tamar, and she was a beautiful woman.
28Absalom lived in Jerusalem for two full
years without seeing King David. 29Then
Absalom sent for Joab so he could send him
to the king, but Joab would not come.
Absalom sent a message a second time, but
Joab still refused to come. 30Then Absalom
said to his servants, "Look, Joab's field is next
to mine, and he has barley growing there. Go
burn it." So Absalom's servants set fire to
Joab's field.
31Then Joab went to Absalom's house and
said to him, "Why did your servants burn
my field?"
32Absalom said to Joab, "I sent a message
to you, asking you to come here. I wanted to
send you to the king to ask him why he
brought me home from Geshur. It would
have been better for me to stay there! Now
let me see the king. If I have sinned, he can
put me to death!"
33So Joab went to the king and told him
Absalom's words. Then the king called for
Absalom. Absalom came and bowed
facedown on the ground before the king, and
the king kissed him.

Absalom Plans to Take David's Kingdom

15 After this, Absalom got a chariot and
horses for himself and fifty men to
run before him. 2Absalom would get up
early and stand near the city gate.[n] Anyone
who had a problem for the king to settle
would come here. When someone came,
Absalom would call out and say, "What city
are you from?"
The person would answer, "I'm from one
of the tribes of Israel."
3Then Absalom would say, "Look, your
claims are right, but the king has no one to

15:2 city gate People came here to conduct business. Public meetings and court cases were also held here.

listen to you." 4Absalom would also say, "I
wish someone would make me judge in this
land! Then people with problems could come
to me, and I could help them get justice."
5People would come near Absalom to bow
to him. When they did, Absalom would
reach out his hand and take hold of them
and kiss them. 6Absalom did that to all the
Israelites who came to King David for
decisions. In this way, Absalom stole the
hearts of all Israel.
7After four years Absalom said to King
David, "Please let me go to Hebron. I want to
carry out my promise that I made to the
LORD 8while I was living in Geshur in Aram.
I said, 'If the LORD takes me back to
Jerusalem, I will worship him in Hebron.' "
9The king said, "Go in peace."
So Absalom went to Hebron. 10But he sent
secret messengers through all the tribes of
Israel. They told the people, "When you hear
the trumpets, say this: 'Absalom is the king
at Hebron!' "
11Absalom had invited two hundred men
to go with him. So they went from Jerusalem
with him, but they didn't know what he was
planning. 12While Absalom was offering
sacrifices, he sent for Ahithophel, one of the
people who advised David, to come from his
hometown of Giloh. So Absalom's plans
were working very well. More and more
people began to support him.
13A messenger came to David, saying, "The
Israelites are giving their loyalty to
Absalom."
14Then David said to all his officers who
were with him in Jerusalem, "We must leave
quickly! If we don't, we won't be able to get
away from Absalom. We must hurry before
he catches us and destroys us and kills the
people of Jerusalem."
15The king's officers said to him, "We will
do anything you say."
16The king set out with everyone in his
house, but he left ten slave women to take
care of the palace. 17The king left with all his
people following him, and they stopped at a
house far away. 18All the king's servants
passed by him—the Kerethites and
Pelethites,[n] all those from Gath, and the six
hundred men who had followed him.
19The king said to Ittai, a man from Gath,
"Why are you also going with us? Turn back
and stay with King Absalom because you are
a foreigner. This is not your homeland. 20You
joined me only a short time ago. Should I
make you wander with us when I don't even
know where I'm going? Turn back and take
your brothers with you. May kindness and
loyalty be shown to you."
21But Ittai said to the king, "As surely as
the LORD lives and as you live, I will stay
with you, whether it means life or death."
22David said to Ittai, "Go, march on." So
Ittai from Gath and all his people with their
children marched on. 23All the people cried
loudly as everyone passed by. King David
crossed the Kidron Valley, and then all the
people went on to the desert. 24Zadok and all
the Levites with him carried the Ark of the
Agreement with God. They set it down, and
Abiathar offered sacrifices until all the
people had left the city.
25The king said to Zadok, "Take the Ark of
God back into the city. If the LORD is pleased
with me, he will bring me back and will let
me see both it and Jerusalem again. 26But if
the LORD says he is not pleased with me, I am
ready. He can do what he wants with me."
27The king also said to Zadok the priest,
"Aren't you a seer? Go back to the city in
peace and take your son Ahimaaz and
Abiathar's son Jonathan with you. 28I will
wait near the crossings into the desert until I
hear from you." 29So Zadok and Abiathar
took the Ark of God back to Jerusalem and
stayed there.
30David went up the Mount of Olives,
crying as he went. He covered his head and
went barefoot. All the people with David
covered their heads also and cried as they
went. 31Someone told David, "Ahithophel is
one of the people with Absalom who made
secret plans against you."
So David prayed, "LORD, please make
Ahithophel's advice foolish."
32When David reached the top of the
mountain where people used to worship
God, Hushai the Arkite came to meet him.
Hushai's coat was torn, and there was dirt on
his head to show how sad he was. 33David
said to Hushai, "If you go with me, you will
be just one more person for me to take care
of. 34But if you return to the city, you can

15:18 Kerethites and Pelethites These were probably special units of the army that were responsible for the king's safety, a kind of palace guard.

make Ahithophel's advice useless. Tell
Absalom, 'I am your servant, my king. In the
past I served your father, but now I will serve
you.' 35The priests Zadok and Abiathar will
be with you. Tell them everything you hear
in the royal palace. 36Zadok's son Ahimaaz
and Abiathar's son Jonathan are with them.
Send them to tell me everything you hear."
37So David's friend Hushai entered Jerusalem
just as Absalom arrived.

Ziba Meets David

16 When David had passed a short way
over the top of the Mount of Olives,
Ziba, Mephibosheth's servant, met him. Ziba
had a row of donkeys loaded with two
hundred loaves of bread, one hundred cakes
of raisins, one hundred cakes of figs, and
leather bags full of wine. 2The king asked
Ziba, "What are these things for?"

Ziba answered, "The donkeys are for your
family to ride. The bread and cakes of figs are
for the servants to eat. And the wine is for
anyone to drink who might become weak in
the desert."

3The king asked, "Where is
Mephibosheth?"

Ziba answered him, "Mephibosheth is
staying in Jerusalem because he thinks,
'Today the Israelites will give my father's
kingdom back to me!' "

4Then the king said to Ziba, "All right.
Everything that belonged to Mephibosheth, I
now give to you!"

Ziba said, "I bow to you. I hope I will
always be able to please you."

Shimei Curses David

5As King David came to Bahurim, a man
came out and cursed him. He was from
Saul's family group, and his name was
Shimei son of Gera. 6He threw stones at
David and his officers, but the people and
soldiers gathered all around David. 7Shimei
cursed David, saying, "Get out, get out, you
murderer, you troublemaker. 8The LORD is
punishing you for the people in Saul's
family you killed! You took Saul's place as
king, but now the LORD has given the
kingdom to your son Absalom! Now you are
ruined because you are a murderer!"

9Abishai son of Zeruiah said to the king,
"Why should this dead dog curse you, the
king? Let me go over and cut off his head!"

10But the king answered, "This does not
concern you, sons of Zeruiah! If he is cursing
me because the LORD told him to, who can
question him?"

11David also said to Abishai and all his
officers, "My own son is trying to kill me!
This man is a Benjaminite and has more
right to kill me! Leave him alone, and let
him curse me because the LORD told him to
do this. 12Maybe the LORD will see my misery
and repay me with something good for
Shimei's curses today!"

13So David and his men went on down the
road, but Shimei followed on the nearby
hillside. He kept cursing David and throwing
stones and dirt at him. 14When the king and
all his people arrived at the Jordan, they
were very tired, so they rested there.

15Meanwhile, Absalom, Ahithophel, and
all the Israelites arrived at Jerusalem.
16David's friend Hushai the Arkite came to
Absalom and said to him, "Long live the
king! Long live the king!"

17Absalom asked, "Why are you not loyal
to your friend David? Why didn't you leave
Jerusalem with your friend?"

18Hushai said, "I belong to the one chosen
by the LORD and by these people and
everyone in Israel. I will stay with you. 19In
the past I served your father. So whom
should I serve now? David's son! I will serve
you as I served him."

Ahithophel's Advice

20Absalom said to Ahithophel, "Tell us
what we should do."

21Ahithophel said, "Your father left behind
some of his slave women to take care of the
palace. Have sexual relations with them.
Then all Israel will hear that your father is
your enemy, and all your people will be
encouraged to give you more support." 22So
they put up a tent for Absalom on the roof[n]
of the palace where everyone in Israel could
see it. And Absalom had sexual relations
with his father's slave women.

23At that time people thought
Ahithophel's advice was as reliable as God's

16:22 roof In Bible times houses were built with flat roofs. The roof was used for drying things such as flax and fruit. And it was used as an extra room, as a place for worship, and as a cool place to sleep in the summer.

own word. Both David and Absalom thought it was that reliable.

17 Ahithophel said to Absalom, "Let me choose twelve thousand men and chase David tonight. 2I'll catch him while he is tired and weak, and I'll frighten him so all his people will run away. But I'll kill only King David. 3Then I'll bring everyone back to you. If the man you are looking for is dead, everyone else will return safely." 4This plan seemed good to Absalom and to all the leaders of Israel.

5But Absalom said, "Now call Hushai the Arkite, so I can hear what he says." 6When Hushai came to Absalom, Absalom said to him, "This is the plan Ahithophel gave. Should we follow it? If not, tell us."

7Hushai said to Absalom, "Ahithophel's advice is not good this time." 8Hushai added, "You know your father and his men are strong. They are as angry as a bear that is robbed of its cubs. Your father is a skilled fighter. He won't stay all night with the army. 9He is probably already hiding in a cave or some other place. If the first attack fails, people will hear the news and think, 'Absalom's followers are losing!' 10Then even the men who are as brave as lions will be frightened, because all the Israelites know your father is a fighter. They know his men are brave!

11"This is what I suggest: Gather all the Israelites from Dan to Beersheba.[n] There will be as many people as grains of sand by the sea. Then you yourself must go into the battle. 12We will go to David wherever he is hiding. We will fall on him as dew falls on the ground. We will kill him and all of his men so that no one will be left alive. 13If David escapes into a city, all the Israelites will bring ropes to that city and pull it into the valley. Not a stone will be left!"

14Absalom and all the Israelites said, "The advice of Hushai the Arkite is better than that of Ahithophel." (The LORD had planned to destroy the good advice of Ahithophel so the LORD could bring disaster on Absalom.)

15Hushai told Zadok and Abiathar, the priests, what Ahithophel had suggested to Absalom and the elders of Israel. He also reported to them what he himself had suggested. Hushai said, 16"Quickly! Send a message to David. Tell him not to stay tonight at the crossings into the desert but to cross over the Jordan River at once. If he crosses the river, he and all his people won't be destroyed."

17Jonathan and Ahimaaz were waiting at En Rogel. They did not want to be seen going into the city, so a servant girl would go out to them and give them messages. Then Jonathan and Ahimaaz would go and tell King David.

18But a boy saw Jonathan and Ahimaaz and told Absalom. So Jonathan and Ahimaaz left quickly and went to a man's house in Bahurim. He had a well in his courtyard, and they climbed down into it. 19The man's wife spread a sheet over the opening of the well and covered it with grain. No one could tell that anyone was hiding there.

20Absalom's servants came to the woman at the house and asked, "Where are Ahimaaz and Jonathan?"

She said to them, "They have already crossed the brook."

Absalom's servants then went to look for Jonathan and Ahimaaz, but they could not find them. So they went back to Jerusalem.

21After Absalom's servants left, Jonathan and Ahimaaz climbed out of the well and went to tell King David. They said, "Hurry, cross over the river! Ahithophel has said these things against you!" 22So David and all his people crossed the Jordan River. By dawn, everyone had crossed the Jordan.

23When Ahithophel saw that the Israelites did not accept his advice, he saddled his donkey and went to his hometown. He left orders for his family and property, and then he hanged himself. He died and was buried in his father's tomb.

War Between David and Absalom

24David arrived at Mahanaim. And Absalom and all his Israelites crossed over the Jordan River. 25Absalom had made Amasa captain of the army instead of Joab. Amasa was the son of a man named Jether the Ishmaelite. Amasa's mother was Abigail daughter of Nahash and sister of Zeruiah, Joab's mother. 26Absalom and the Israelites camped in the land of Gilead.

17:11 Dan to Beersheba Dan was the city farthest north in Israel, and Beersheba was the city farthest south. So this means all the people of Israel.

[27]Shobi, Makir, and Barzillai were at
Mahanaim when David arrived. Shobi son of
Nahash was from the Ammonite town of
Rabbah. Makir son of Ammiel was from Lo
Debar, and Barzillai was from Rogelim in
Gilead. [28]They brought beds, bowls, clay
pots, wheat, barley, flour, roasted grain,
beans, small peas, [29]honey, milk curds,
sheep, and cheese made from cows' milk for
David and his people. They said, "The people
are hungry and tired and thirsty in the
desert."

18 David counted his men and placed
over them commanders of thousands
and commanders of hundreds. [2]He sent the
troops out in three groups. Joab commanded
one-third of the men. Joab's brother Abishai
son of Zeruiah commanded another third.
And Ittai from Gath commanded the last
third. King David said to them, "I will also go
with you."

[3]But the men said, "You must not go with
us! If we run away in the battle, Absalom's
men won't care. Even if half of us are killed,
Absalom's men won't care. But you're worth
ten thousand of us! You can help us most by
staying in the city."

[4]The king said to his people, "I will do
what you think is best." So the king stood at
the side of the gate as the army went out in
groups of a hundred and a thousand.

[5]The king commanded Joab, Abishai, and
Ittai, "Be gentle with young Absalom for my
sake." Everyone heard the king's orders to
the commanders about Absalom.

[6]David's army went out into the field
against Absalom's Israelites, and they fought
in the forest of Ephraim. [7]There David's
army defeated the Israelites. Many died that
day—twenty thousand men. [8]The battle
spread through all the country, but that day
more men died in the forest than in the
fighting.

Absalom Dies

[9]Then Absalom happened to meet David's
troops. As Absalom was riding his mule, it
went under the thick branches of a large
oak tree. Absalom's head got caught in the
tree, and his mule ran out from under him.
So Absalom was left hanging above the
ground.

[10]When one of the men saw it happen, he
told Joab, "I saw Absalom hanging in an oak
tree!"

[11]Joab said to him, "You saw him? Why
didn't you kill him and let him fall to the
ground? I would have given you a belt and
four ounces of silver!"

[12]The man answered, "I wouldn't touch
the king's son even if you gave me twenty-
five pounds of silver. We heard the king
command you, Abishai, and Ittai, 'Be careful
not to hurt young Absalom.' [13]If I had killed
him, the king would have found out, and
you would not have protected me!"

[14]Joab said, "I won't waste time here with
you!" Absalom was still alive in the oak tree,
so Joab took three spears and stabbed him in
the heart. [15]Ten young men who carried
Joab's armor also gathered around Absalom
and struck him and killed him.

[16]Then Joab blew the trumpet, so the
troops stopped chasing the Israelites. [17]Then
Joab's men took Absalom's body and threw it
into a large pit in the forest and filled the pit
with many stones. All the Israelites ran away
to their homes.

[18]When Absalom was alive, he had set up
a pillar for himself in the King's Valley. He
said, "I have no son to keep my name alive."
So he named the pillar after himself, and it is
called Absalom's Monument even today.

[19]Ahimaaz son of Zadok said to Joab, "Let
me run and take the news to King David. I'll
tell him the LORD has saved him from his
enemies."

[20]Joab answered Ahimaaz, "No, you are
not the one to take the news today. You may
do it another time, but do not take it today,
because the king's son is dead."

[21]Then Joab said to a man from Cush, "Go,
tell the king what you have seen." The
Cushite bowed to Joab and ran to tell David.

[22]But Ahimaaz son of Zadok begged Joab
again, "No matter what happens, please let
me go along with the Cushite!"

Joab said, "Son, why do you want to carry
the news? You won't get any reward."

[23]Ahimaaz answered, "No matter what
happens, I will run."

So Joab said to Ahimaaz, "Run!" Then
Ahimaaz ran by way of the Jordan Valley and
passed the Cushite.

[24]David was sitting between the inner and
outer gates of the city. The watchman went
up to the roof of the gate by the walls, and as

he looked up, he saw a man running alone.
25He shouted the news to the king.
The king said, "If he is alone, he is
bringing good news!"
The man came nearer and nearer to the
city. 26Then the watchman saw another man
running, and he called to the gatekeeper,
"Look! Another man is running alone!"
The king said, "He is also bringing good
news!"
27The watchman said, "I think the first
man runs like Ahimaaz son of Zadok."
The king said, "Ahimaaz is a good man. He
must be bringing good news!"
28Then Ahimaaz called a greeting to the
king. He bowed facedown on the ground
before the king and said, "Praise the LORD
your God! The LORD has defeated those who
were against you, my king."
29The king asked, "Is young Absalom all
right?"
Ahimaaz answered, "When Joab sent me, I
saw some great excitement, but I don't know
what it was."
30The king said, "Step over here and wait."
So Ahimaaz stepped aside and stood there.
31Then the Cushite arrived. He said,
"Master and king, hear the good news! Today
the LORD has punished those who were
against you!"
32The king asked the Cushite, "Is young
Absalom all right?"
The Cushite answered, "May your
enemies and all who come to hurt you be
like that young man!"
33Then the king was very upset, and he
went to the room over the city gate and
cried. As he went, he cried out, "My son
Absalom, my son Absalom! I wish I had died
and not you. Absalom, my son, my son!"

Joab Scolds David

19 People told Joab, "Look, the king is sad
and crying because of Absalom."
2David's army had won the battle that day.
But it became a very sad day for all the
people, because they heard that the king was
very sad for his son. 3The people came into
the city quietly that day. They were like an
army that had been defeated in battle and
had run away. 4The king covered his face
and cried loudly, "My son Absalom!
Absalom, my son, my son!"
5Joab went into the king's house and said,
"Today you have shamed all your men. They
saved your life and the lives of your sons,
daughters, wives, and slave women. 6You
have shamed them because you love those
who hate you, and you hate those who love
you. Today you have made it clear that your
commanders and men mean nothing to you.
What if Absalom had lived and all of us
were dead? I can see you would be pleased.
7Now go out and encourage your servants. I
swear by the LORD that if you don't go out, no
man will be left with you by tonight! That
will be worse than all the troubles you have
had from your youth until today."
8So the king went to the city gate.[n] When
the news spread that the king was at the
gate, everyone came to see him.

David Goes Back to Jerusalem

All the Israelites who had followed
Absalom had run away to their homes.
9People in all the tribes of Israel began to
argue, saying, "The king saved us from the
Philistines and our other enemies, but he left
the country because of Absalom. 10We
appointed Absalom to rule us, but now he
has died in battle. We should make David
the king again."
11King David sent a message to Zadok and
Abiathar, the priests, that said, "Speak to the
elders of Judah. Say, 'Even in my house I have
heard what all the Israelites are saying. So
why are you the last tribe to bring the king
back to his palace? 12You are my brothers, my
own family. Why are you the last tribe to
bring back the king?' 13And say to Amasa,
'You are part of my own family. May God
punish me terribly if I don't make you
commander of the army in Joab's place!' "
14David touched the hearts of all the
people of Judah at once. They sent a message
to the king that said, "Return with all your
men." 15Then the king returned as far as the
Jordan River. The men of Judah came to
Gilgal to meet him and to bring him across
the Jordan.
16Shimei son of Gera, a Benjaminite who
lived in Bahurim, hurried down with the
men of Judah to meet King David. 17With
Shimei came a thousand Benjaminites. Ziba,
the servant from Saul's family, also came,

19:8 city gate People came here to conduct business. Public meetings and court cases were also held here.

bringing his fifteen sons and twenty servants
with him. They all hurried to the Jordan
River to meet the king. 18The people went
across the Jordan to help bring the king's
family back to Judah and to do whatever the
king wanted. As the king was crossing the
river, Shimei son of Gera came to him and
bowed facedown on the ground in front of
the king. 19He said to the king, "My master,
don't hold me guilty. Don't remember the
wrong I did when you left Jerusalem! Don't
hold it against me. 20I know I have sinned.
That is why I am the first person from
Joseph's family to come down and meet you
today, my master and king!"
21But Abishai son of Zeruiah said, "Shimei
should die because he cursed you, the LORD's
appointed king!"
22David said, "This does not concern you,
sons of Zeruiah! Today you're against me! No
one will be put to death in Israel today.
Today I know I am king over Israel!" 23Then
the king promised Shimei, "You won't die."
24Mephibosheth, Saul's grandson, also went
down to meet King David. Mephibosheth
had not cared for his feet, cut his beard, or
washed his clothes from the time the king
had left Jerusalem until he returned safely.
25When Mephibosheth came from
Jerusalem to meet the king, the king asked
him, "Mephibosheth, why didn't you go with
me?"
26He answered, "My master, my servant
Ziba tricked me! I said to Ziba, 'I am crippled,
so saddle a donkey. Then I will ride it so I
can go with the king.' 27But he lied about me
to you. You, my master and king, are like an
angel from God. Do what you think is good.
28You could have killed all my grandfather's
family. Instead, you put me with those
people who eat at your own table. So I don't
have a right to ask anything more from the
king!"
29The king said to him, "Don't say
anything more. I have decided that you and
Ziba will divide the land."
30Mephibosheth said to the king, "Let Ziba
take all the land now that my master the
king has arrived safely home."
31Barzillai of Gilead came down from
Rogelim to cross the Jordan River with the
king. 32Barzillai was a very old man, eighty

devotion 87

2 SAMUEL 19:33

RESPECTING YOUR ELDERS?

King David extended an invitation to a man named Barzillai to travel all the way to Jerusalem with him. David also offered to give Barzillai anything he needed. What strikes me about this is that not only did David extend an offer to a friend, but to a very elderly friend. Barzillai was, by his own admission, already showing signs of a weakening body due to his age. He might not have even made it to Jerusalem had he accepted the king's offer. It's also interesting that King David allowed Barzillai to decide what he wanted to do with the rest of his life. By doing so, David illustrated that he had high regard for his elderly companion.

I have a friend who is a Physical Therapist's Assistant and cares for many aging patients. In order to earn their trust in her abilities, she says she must first approach them as the younger person that she is. She calls them ma'am and sir and treats them as if they're her grandparents. When they see her respect, they open up and begin to let her help ease their aching muscles. Her attitude with them is the kind we all ought to have around those who are in their twilight years. Let's think about how we treat elderly people when we see them at church, in our communities, and in our families. Do we speak to them like they are children? Or do we treat them as the experienced and wise souls they have become?

years old. He had taken care of the king
when David was staying at Mahanaim,
because Barzillai was a very rich man.
33David said to Barzillai, "Cross the river
with me. Come with me to Jerusalem, and I
will take care of you."
34But Barzillai answered the king, "Do you
know how old I am? Do you think I can go
with you to Jerusalem? 35I am eighty years
old! I am too old to taste what I eat or drink. I
am too old to hear the voices of men and
women singers. Why should you be
bothered with me? 36I am not worthy of a
reward from you, but I will cross the Jordan
River with you. 37Then let me go back so I
may die in my own city near the grave of my
father and mother. But here is Kimham, your
servant. Let him go with you, my master and
king. Do with him whatever you want."
38The king answered, "Kimham will go
with me. I will do for him anything you
wish, and I will do anything for you that you
wish." 39The king kissed Barzillai and blessed
him. Then Barzillai returned home, and the
king and all the people crossed the Jordan.
40When the king crossed over to Gilgal,
Kimham went with him. All the troops of
Judah and half the troops of Israel led David
across the river.
41Soon all the Israelites came to the king
and said to him, "Why did our relatives, the
people of Judah, steal you away? Why did
they bring you and your family across the
Jordan River with your men?"
42All the people of Judah answered the
Israelites, "We did this because the king is
our close relative. Why are you angry about
it? We have not eaten food at the king's
expense or taken anything for ourselves!"
43The Israelites answered the people of
Judah, "We have ten tribes in the kingdom,
so we have more right to David than you do!
But you ignored us! We were the first ones to
talk about bringing our king back!"

But the people of Judah spoke even more
unkindly than the people of Israel.

Sheba Leads Israel Away from David

20 It happened that a troublemaker
named Sheba son of Bicri from the
tribe of Benjamin was there. He blew the
trumpet and said:

"We have no share in David!
We have no part in the son of Jesse!
People of Israel, let's go home!"

2So all the Israelites left David and
followed Sheba son of Bicri. But the people
of Judah stayed with their king all the way
from the Jordan River to Jerusalem.
3David came back to his palace in
Jerusalem. He had left ten of his slave
women there to take care of the palace. Now
he put them in a locked house. He gave them
food, but he did not have sexual relations
with them. So they lived like widows until
they died.
4The king said to Amasa, "Tell the men of
Judah to meet with me in three days, and
you must also be here." 5So Amasa went to
call the men of Judah together, but he took
more time than the king had said.
6David said to Abishai, "Sheba son of Bicri
is more dangerous to us than Absalom was.
Take my men and chase him before he finds
walled cities and escapes from us." 7So Joab's
men, the Kerethites and the Pelethites,[n] and
all the soldiers went with Abishai. They
went out from Jerusalem to chase Sheba son
of Bicri.
8When Joab and the army came to the
great rock at Gibeon, Amasa came out to
meet them. Joab was wearing his uniform,
and at his waist he wore a belt that held his
sword in its case. As Joab stepped forward,
his sword fell out of its case. 9Joab asked
Amasa, "Brother, is everything all right with
you?" Then with his right hand he took
Amasa by the beard to kiss him. 10Amasa
was not watching the sword in Joab's hand.
So Joab pushed the sword into Amasa's
stomach, causing Amasa's insides to spill
onto the ground. Joab did not have to stab
Amasa again; he was already dead. Then Joab
and his brother Abishai continued to chase
Sheba son of Bicri.
11One of Joab's young men stood by
Amasa's body and said, "Everyone who is for
Joab and David should follow Joab!"
12Amasa lay in the middle of the road,
covered with his own blood. When the
young man saw that everyone was stopping
to look at the body, he dragged it from the
road, laid it in a field, and put a cloth over it.
13After Amasa's body was taken off the road,

20:7 Kerethites and Pelethites These were probably special units of the army that were responsible for the king's safety, a kind of palace guard.

all the men followed Joab to chase Sheba
son of Bicri.
[14]Sheba went through all the tribes of
Israel to Abel Beth Maacah. All the Berites
also came together and followed him. [15]So
Joab and his men came to Abel Beth Maacah
and surrounded it. They piled dirt up against
the city wall, and they began hacking at the
walls to bring them down.
[16]But a wise woman shouted out from the
city, "Listen! Listen! Tell Joab to come here. I
want to talk to him!"
[17]So Joab came near her. She asked him,
"Are you Joab?"

He answered, "Yes, I am."

Then she said, "Listen to what I say."

Joab said, "I'm listening."

[18]Then the woman said, "In the past people
would say, 'Ask for advice at Abel,' and the
problem would be solved. [19]I am one of the
peaceful, loyal people of Israel. You are trying
to destroy an important city of Israel. Why
must you destroy what belongs to the LORD?"
[20]Joab answered, "I would prefer not to
destroy or ruin anything! [21]That is not what
I want. But there is a man here from the
mountains of Ephraim, who is named Sheba
son of Bicri. He has turned against King
David. If you bring him to me, I will leave
the city alone."

The woman said to Joab, "His head will be
thrown over the wall to you."

[22]Then the woman spoke very wisely to
all the people of the city. They cut off the
head of Sheba son of Bicri and threw it over
the wall to Joab. So he blew the trumpet, and
the army left the city. Every man returned
home, and Joab went back to the king in
Jerusalem.
[23]Joab was commander of all the army of
Israel. Benaiah son of Jehoiada led the
Kerethites and Pelethites. [24]Adoniram was in
charge of the men who were forced to do
hard work. Jehoshaphat son of Ahilud was
the recorder. [25]Sheba was the royal secretary.
Zadok and Abiathar were the priests, [26]and
Ira the Jairite was David's priest.

The Gibeonites Punish Saul's Family

21 During the time David was king, there
was a shortage of food that lasted for
three years. So David prayed to the LORD.

The LORD answered, "Saul and his family
of murderers are the reason for this shortage,
because he killed the Gibeonites." [2](Now the
Gibeonites were not Israelites; they were a
group of Amorites who were left alive. The
Israelites had promised not to hurt the
Gibeonites, but Saul had tried to kill them,
because he was eager to help the people of
Israel and Judah.)

King David called the Gibeonites
together and spoke to them. [3]He asked,
"What can I do for you? How can I make up
for the harm done so you can bless the
LORD's people?"
[4]The Gibeonites said to David, "We cannot
demand silver or gold from Saul or his
family. And we don't have the right to kill
anyone in Israel."

Then David asked, "What do you want me
to do for you?"
[5]The Gibeonites said, "Saul made plans
against us and tried to destroy all our people
who are left in the land of Israel. [6]So bring
seven of his sons to us. Then we will kill
them and hang them on stakes in the
presence of the LORD at Gibeah, the
hometown of Saul, the LORD's chosen king."

The king said, "I will give them to you."
[7]But the king protected Mephibosheth, the
son of Jonathan, the son of Saul, because of
the promise he had made to Jonathan in the
LORD's name. [8]The king did take Armoni and
Mephibosheth,[n] sons of Rizpah and Saul.
(Rizpah was the daughter of Aiah.) And the
king took the five sons of Saul's daughter
Merab. (Adriel son of Barzillai the
Meholathite was the father of Merab's five
sons.) [9]David gave these seven sons to the
Gibeonites. Then the Gibeonites killed them
and hung them on stakes on a hill in the
presence of the LORD. All seven sons died
together. They were put to death during the
first days of the harvest season at the
beginning of barley harvest.
[10]Aiah's daughter Rizpah took the rough
cloth that was worn to show sadness and put
it on a rock for herself. She stayed there from
the beginning of the harvest until the rain
fell on her sons' bodies. During the day she
did not let the birds of the sky touch her
sons' bodies, and during the night she did
not let the wild animals touch them.

21:8 Mephibosheth This is not Jonathan's son but another man with the same name.

Rizpah

2 SAMUEL 21

Rizpah stood on the hill in Israel, moaning and beating her chest, as the seven men were strung up on stakes for execution. Her body convulsed with sorrow, but her cries could not save her two sons, condemned to die for crimes committed against the Gibeonites by their father, Saul. She fell to her knees, weeping and screaming. All that she loved in this life was gone. As one of Saul's concubines, she was nothing, a nobody—but her sons loved her, and they meant the world to her.

Although there is a law requiring burial by sunset, the bodies of these "criminals" are left to rot on the hillside. Despite being urged to leave, Rizpah draws close to the bloodied bodies of her precious sons. She will not leave. She cannot leave. Not while their bodies remain unburied. She spreads sackcloth on a rock and begins her vigil.

Day after day, month after month, she shoos away the birds and beats back the dogs. She will not hide her grief behind closed doors. Instead, she displays her anguish in public, giving meaning to the death of her sons. For four months she grieves while guarding their remains. Upon hearing of her devotion, King David orders that the bodies of the men be buried. Rizpah's vigil comes to an end and she returns home.

Despite our circumstances, God asks that we be faithful and leave everything else to him. God knows our needs and will provide for them in his time.

11 People told David what Aiah's daughter
Rizpah, Saul's slave woman, was doing.
12 Then David took the bones of Saul and
Jonathan from the men of Jabesh Gilead.
(The Philistines had hung the bodies of Saul
and Jonathan in the public square of Beth
Shan after they had killed Saul at Gilboa.
Later the men of Jabesh Gilead had secretly
taken them from there.) 13 David brought
the bones of Saul and his son Jonathan from
Gilead. Then the people gathered the bodies
of Saul's seven sons who were hanged on
stakes. 14 The people buried the bones of
Saul and his son Jonathan at Zela in
Benjamin in the tomb of Saul's father Kish.
The people did everything the king
commanded.
Then God answered the prayers for the
land.

Wars with the Philistines

15 Again there was war between the
Philistines and Israel. David and his men
went out to fight the Philistines, but David
became tired. 16 Ishbi-Benob, one of the sons
of Rapha, had a bronze spearhead weighing
about seven and one-half pounds and a new
sword. He planned to kill David, 17 but
Abishai son of Zeruiah killed the Philistine
and saved David's life.
Then David's men made a promise to him,
saying, "Never again will you go out with us
to battle. If you were killed, Israel would lose
its greatest leader."
18 Later, at Gob, there was another battle
with the Philistines. Sibbecai the Hushathite
killed Saph, another one of the sons of
Rapha.
19 Later, there was another battle at Gob
with the Philistines. Elhanan son of
Jaare-Oregim from Bethlehem killed
Goliath[n] from Gath. His spear was as large as
a weaver's rod.
20 At Gath another battle took place. A
huge man was there; he had six fingers on
each hand and six toes on each foot—
twenty-four fingers and toes in all. This man
also was one of the sons of Rapha. 21 When
he challenged Israel, Jonathan son of
Shimeah, David's brother, killed him.
22 These four sons of Rapha from Gath
were killed by David and his men.

21:19 Goliath In 1 Chronicles 20:5 he is called Lahmi, brother of Goliath.

David's Song of Praise

22 David sang this song to the LORD when the LORD saved him from Saul and all his other enemies. 2He said:

"The LORD is my rock, my fortress, my
Savior.
3My God is my rock.
I can run to him for safety.
He is my shield and my saving strength,
my defender and my place of safety.
The LORD saves me from those who
want to harm me.
4I will call to the LORD, who is worthy of
praise,
and I will be saved from my enemies.

5"The waves of death came around me;
the deadly rivers overwhelmed me.
6The ropes of death wrapped around me.
The traps of death were before me.
7In my trouble I called to the LORD;
I cried out to my God.
From his temple he heard my voice;
my call for help reached his ears.

8"The earth trembled and shook.
The foundations of heaven began to
shake.
They trembled because the LORD was
angry.
9Smoke came out of his nose,
and burning fire came out of his mouth.
Burning coals went before him.
10He tore open the sky and came down
with dark clouds under his feet.
11He rode a creature with wings and flew.
He raced on the wings of the wind.
12He made darkness his shelter,
surrounded by fog and clouds.
13Out of the brightness of his presence
came flashes of lightning.
14The LORD thundered from heaven;
the Most High raised his voice.
15He shot his arrows and scattered his
enemies.
His bolts of lightning confused them
with fear.
16The LORD spoke strongly.
The wind blew from his nose.
Then the valleys of the sea appeared,
and the foundations of the earth were
seen.

17"The LORD reached down from above and
took me;
he pulled me from the deep water.
18He saved me from my powerful enemies,
from those who hated me, because they
were too strong for me.
19They attacked me at my time of trouble,
but the LORD supported me.
20He took me to a safe place.
Because he delights in me, he saved me.

21"The LORD spared me because I did what
was right.
Because I have not done evil, he has
rewarded me.
22I have followed the ways of the LORD;
I have not done evil by turning from
my God.
23I remember all his laws
and have not broken his rules.
24I am innocent before him;
I have kept myself from doing evil.
25The LORD rewarded me because I did what
was right,
because I did what the LORD said was
right.

26"LORD, you are loyal to those who are
loyal,
and you are good to those who are
good.
27You are pure to those who are pure,
but you are against those who are evil.
28You save the humble,
but you bring down those who are
proud.
29LORD, you give light to my lamp.
The LORD brightens the darkness
around me.
30With your help I can attack an army.
With God's help I can jump over a wall.

31"The ways of God are without fault;
the LORD's words are pure.
He is a shield to those who trust him.
32Who is God? Only the LORD.
Who is the Rock? Only our God.
33God is my protection.
He makes my way free from fault.
34He makes me like a deer that does not
stumble;
he helps me stand on the steep
mountains.
35He trains my hands for battle
so my arms can bend a bronze bow.
36You protect me with your saving shield.
You have stooped to make me great.

37You give me a better way to live,
so I live as you want me to.
38I chased my enemies and destroyed them.
I did not quit till they were destroyed.
39I destroyed and crushed them
so they couldn't rise up again.
They fell beneath my feet.
40You gave me strength in battle.
You made my enemies bow before me.
41You made my enemies turn back,
and I destroyed those who hated me.
42They called for help,
but no one came to save them.
They called to the LORD,
but he did not answer them.
43I beat my enemies into pieces,
like dust on the ground.
I poured them out and walked on them
like mud in the streets.

44"You saved me when my people
attacked me.
You kept me as the leader of nations.
People I never knew serve me.
45Foreigners obey me.
As soon as they hear me, they obey me.
46They all become afraid
and tremble in their hiding places.

47"The LORD lives!
May my Rock be praised!
Praise God, the Rock, who saves me!
48God gives me victory over my enemies
and brings people under my rule.
49He frees me from my enemies.
"You set me over those who hate me.
You saved me from violent people.
50So I will praise you, LORD, among the
nations.
I will sing praises to your name.
51The LORD gives great victories to his king.
He is loyal to his appointed king,
to David and his descendants forever."

David's Last Words

23 These are the last words of David.
This is the message of David son of
Jesse.
The man made great by the Most High
God speaks.
He is the appointed king of the God of
Jacob;
he is the sweet singer of Israel:

2"The LORD's Spirit spoke through me,
and his word was on my tongue.
3The God of Israel spoke;
the Rock of Israel said to me:
'Whoever rules fairly over people,
who rules with respect for God,
4is like the morning light at dawn,
like a morning without clouds.
He is like sunshine after a rain
that makes the grass sprout from the
ground.'

5"This is how God has cared for my family.
God made a lasting agreement with me,
right and sure in every way.
He will accomplish my salvation
and satisfy all my desires.

6"But all evil people will be thrown away
like thorns
that cannot be held in a hand.
7No one can touch them
except with a tool of iron or wood.
They will be thrown in the fire and
burned where they lie."

David's Army

8These are the names of David's warriors:
Josheb-Basshebeth, the Tahkemonite, was
head of the Three.[n] He killed eight hundred
men at one time.
9Next was Eleazar son of Dodai the
Ahohite. Eleazar was one of the three
soldiers who were with David when they
challenged the Philistines. The Philistines
were gathered for battle, and the Israelites
drew back. 10But Eleazar stayed where he
was and fought the Philistines until he was
so tired his hand stuck to his sword. The
LORD gave a great victory for the Israelites
that day. The troops came back after Eleazar
had won the battle, but only to take
weapons and armor from the enemy.
11Next there was Shammah son of Agee
the Hararite. The Philistines came together
to fight in a vegetable field. Israel's troops
ran away from the Philistines, 12but
Shammah stood in the middle of the field
and fought for it and killed the Philistines.
And the LORD gave a great victory.
13Once, three of the Thirty, David's chief
soldiers, came down to him at the cave of
Adullam during harvest. The Philistine

23:8 Three These were David's most powerful soldiers. See 1 Chronicles 11:11.

devotion 88

2 SAMUEL 23:10–12

WE WIN!

A woman came to church for the first time. She heard the truth about Jesus and met with the pastor. The woman decided to trust Jesus as her Savior. The pastor wanted to meet with the woman in a week, but he told her to get a Bible and begin reading in the meantime. The next day the brand-new believer came running into the pastor's office. "Preacher, I bought a Bible like you said, and I've been reading it all day. I couldn't wait a week. I just had to come talk to you."

Curious about what was so urgent, the pastor asked, "What did you read?"

"Well, I didn't know where to begin, so when it flipped open to the book of Revelation, I started there."

The pastor felt a little uneasy. This woman who had never been to church in her life began reading the Bible in one of the most difficult books to understand. "What did you learn?" the pastor hesitantly inquired.

"We win!" the woman exclaimed. "At the end, we win!"

The pastor smiled. "You're exactly right. We do win."

King David had thirty powerful warriors, but what mattered more than their strength or experience was that the Lord was with them. Some seasons of life require you to be a powerful warrior. Some days will feel like a fight. But the Lord will bring ultimate and eternal victory to those who fight in his trenches. If the Lord is with you, he promises a victory. We win!

army had camped in the Valley of Rephaim.
14At that time David was in the stronghold,
and some of the Philistines were in
Bethlehem.
15David had a strong desire for some
water. He said, "Oh, I wish someone would
get me water from the well near the city gate
of Bethlehem!" 16So the three warriors broke
through the Philistine army and took water
from the well near the city gate of
Bethlehem. Then they brought it to David,
but he refused to drink it. He poured it out
before the LORD, 17saying, "May the LORD
keep me from drinking this water! It would
be like drinking the blood of the men who
risked their lives!" So David refused to drink
it. These were the brave things that the three
warriors did.
18Abishai, brother of Joab son of Zeruiah,
was captain of the Three. Abishai fought
three hundred soldiers with his spear and
killed them. He became as famous as the
Three 19and was more honored than the
Three. He became their commander even
though he was not one of them.
20Benaiah son of Jehoiada was a brave
fighter from Kabzeel who did mighty
things. He killed two of the best warriors
from Moab. He also went down into a pit
and killed a lion on a snowy day. 21Benaiah
killed a large Egyptian who had a spear in
his hand. Benaiah had a club, but he
grabbed the spear from the Egyptian's
hand and killed him with his own spear.
22These were the things Benaiah son of
Jehoiada did. He was as famous as the Three.
23He received more honor than the Thirty,
but he did not become a member of the
Three. David made him leader of his
bodyguards.

The Thirty Chief Soldiers

24The following men were among the
Thirty:
Asahel brother of Joab;
Elhanan son of Dodo from Bethlehem;
25Shammah the Harodite;
Elika the Harodite;
26Helez the Paltite;
Ira son of Ikkesh from Tekoa;
27Abiezer the Anathothite;
Mebunnai the Hushathite;
28Zalmon the Ahohite;
Maharai the Netophathite;
29Heled son of Baanah the Netophathite;
Ithai son of Ribai from Gibeah in
Benjamin;
30Benaiah the Pirathonite;
Hiddai from the ravines of Gaash;
31Abi-Albon the Arbathite;
Azmaveth the Barhumite;
32Eliahba the Shaalbonite;
the sons of Jashen;
Jonathan 33son of Shammah the
Hararite;
Ahiam son of Sharar the Hararite;
34Eliphelet son of Ahasbai the Maacathite;
Eliam son of Ahithophel the Gilonite;
35Hezro the Carmelite;
Paarai the Arbite;
36Igal son of Nathan of Zobah;
the son of Hagri;
37Zelek the Ammonite;
Naharai the Beerothite, who carried the
armor of Joab son of Zeruiah;
38Ira the Ithrite;
Gareb the Ithrite,
39and Uriah the Hittite.
There were thirty-seven in all.

David Counts His Army

24 The LORD was angry with Israel again,
and he caused David to turn against
the Israelites. He said, "Go, count the people
of Israel and Judah."
2So King David said to Joab, the
commander of the army, "Go through all the
tribes of Israel, from Dan to Beersheba,[n] and
count the people. Then I will know how
many there are."
3But Joab said to the king, "May the LORD
your God give you a hundred times more
people, and may my master the king live to
see this happen. Why do you want to do
this?"
4But the king commanded Joab and the
commanders of the army, so they left the
king to count the Israelites.
5After crossing the Jordan River, they
camped near Aroer on the south side of the
city in the ravine. They went through Gad
and on to Jazer. 6Then they went to Gilead
and the land of Tahtim Hodshi and to Dan
Jaan and around to Sidon. 7They went to the
strong, walled city of Tyre and to all the
cities of the Hivites and Canaanites. Finally,
they went to southern Judah, to Beersheba.
8After nine months and twenty days, they
had gone through all the land. Then they
came back to Jerusalem.
9Joab gave the list of the people to the
king. There were eight hundred thousand
men in Israel who could use the sword and
five hundred thousand men in Judah.
10David felt ashamed after he had counted
the people. He said to the LORD, "I have
sinned greatly by what I have done. LORD, I
beg you to forgive me, your servant, because
I have been very foolish."
11When David got up in the morning, the
LORD spoke his word to Gad, who was a
prophet and David's seer. 12The LORD told
Gad, "Go and tell David, 'This is what the
LORD says: I offer you three choices. Choose
one of them and I will do it to you.' "
13So Gad went to David and said to him,
"Should three years of hunger come to you
and your land? Or should your enemies
chase you for three months? Or should there
be three days of disease in your land? Think
about it. Then decide which of these things I
should tell the LORD who sent me."
14David said to Gad, "I am in great trouble.
Let the LORD punish us, because the LORD is
very merciful. Don't let my punishment
come from human beings!"
15So the LORD sent a terrible disease on
Israel. It began in the morning and
continued until the chosen time to stop.
From Dan to Beersheba seventy thousand
people died. 16When the angel raised his
arm toward Jerusalem to destroy it, the LORD
felt very sorry about the terrible things that
had happened. He said to the angel who was
destroying the people, "That is enough! Put

24:2 Dan to Beersheba Dan was the city farthest north in Israel, and Beersheba was the city farthest south. So this means all the people of Israel.

down your arm!" The angel of the LORD was
then by the threshing floor of Araunah the
Jebusite.
[17]When David saw the angel that killed
the people, he said to the LORD, "I am the one
who sinned and did wrong. These people
only followed me like sheep. They did
nothing wrong. Please punish me and my
family."
[18]That day Gad came to David and said,
"Go and build an altar to the LORD on the
threshing floor of Araunah the Jebusite."
[19]So David did what Gad told him to do, just
as the LORD commanded.
[20]Araunah looked and saw the king and
his servants coming to him. So he went out
and bowed facedown on the ground before
the king. [21]He said, "Why has my master the
king come to me?"

David answered, "To buy the threshing
floor from you so I can build an altar to
the LORD. Then the terrible disease will
stop."
[22]Araunah said to David, "My master and
king, you may take anything you want for a
sacrifice. Here are some oxen for the whole
burnt offering and the threshing boards and
the yokes for the wood. [23]My king, I give
everything to you." Araunah also said to the
king, "May the LORD your God be pleased
with you."
[24]But the king answered Araunah, "No, I
will pay you for the land. I won't offer to the
LORD my God burnt offerings that cost me
nothing."

So David bought the threshing floor and
the oxen for one and one-fourth pounds of
silver. [25]He built an altar to the LORD there
and offered whole burnt offerings and
fellowship offerings. Then the LORD
answered his prayer for the country, and the
disease in Israel stopped.

1 Kings

Much like 1 and 2 Samuel, 1 and 2 Kings were originally one book that was simply entitled "Kings" in the earliest texts.

Person Holding the Pen God Wrote With: The author's identity is unknown. Jewish rabbis argued that Jeremiah wrote 1 Kings, but that's unlikely since the last events recorded take place in Babylon and Jeremiah never visited that pagan place!

When the Text Was Written: Between 561 and 538 B.C.

Spiritual Posture of the Original Recipients: The Israelites are in a position of "faith flux." As usual, they're exhibiting signs of spiritual attention deficit disorder and wavering in their commitment to God and his laws.

Storyline Synopsis: First Kings lives up to its title by chronicling the exploits of the "first kings" of Israel. This monarch lineup begins with David and Bathsheba's wise son, Solomon, who became king after lots of colorful skirmishes with his brothers (chapters 1—2). He was the third and final ruler of a united kingdom (following Saul and David), and the first half of this book details his rise and fall. The highlight of Solomon's résumé was the construction of the Temple, which was the earthly residence of Jehovah as first envisioned by his dad (chapters 5—6). Solomon's shame was his lack of discipline with women—specifically foreign, *pagan* women. The second half of this book records the crumbling of the united nation of Israel, which was exacerbated by some very bad kings (chapters 12—22).

A Moment Worth Discussing: The contest on Mount Carmel (chapter 18) is a riveting display of good versus evil. It pits one of Jehovah's prophets in a white hat, Elijah, against a whole bunch of wicked false prophets representing a fake god named "Baal." God's sovereign power and authority is revealed in the outcome of this winner-takes-all duel. But the best part of the story takes place right after the dramatic victory when Elijah wilts and whines under a tree—in spite of the fact that Jehovah had just rescued him from being decapitated! God's merciful response to this tired man's spiritual amnesia should bring comfort to us all (chapter 19).

Interesting (But Likely to Be Overlooked) Character: *Omri*, who was evil King Ahab's dad (1 Kin. 16:21–28), gives credence to the saying that "the apple doesn't fall far from the tree."

Adonijah Tries to Become King

1 At this time King David was very old, and
although his servants covered him with
blankets, he could not keep warm. 2They
said to him, "We will look for a young
woman to care for you. She will lie close to
you and keep you warm." 3After searching
everywhere in Israel for a beautiful young
woman, they found a girl named Abishag
from Shunam and brought her to the king.
4The girl was very beautiful, and she cared
for the king and served him. But the king did
not have sexual relations with her.
5Adonijah was the son of King David and
Haggith, and he was very proud. "I will be
the king," he said. So he got chariots and
horses for himself and fifty men for his
personal bodyguard. 6Now David had never
interfered with Adonijah by questioning
what he did. Born next after Absalom,
Adonijah was a very handsome man.
7Adonijah spoke with Joab son of Zeruiah
and Abiathar the priest, and they agreed to
help him. 8But Zadok the priest, Benaiah son
of Jehoiada, Nathan the prophet, Shimei, Rei,
and King David's special guard did not join
Adonijah.
9Then Adonijah killed some sheep, cows,
and fat calves for sacrifices at the Stone of
Zoheleth near the spring of Rogel. He invited
all his brothers, the other sons of King
David, to come, as well as all the men of
Judah. 10But Adonijah did not invite Nathan
the prophet, Benaiah, his father's special
guard, or his brother Solomon.
11When Nathan heard about this, he went
to Bathsheba, Solomon's mother. "Have you
heard that Adonijah, Haggith's son, has made
himself king?" Nathan asked. "Our real king,
David, does not know it. 12I strongly advise
you to save yourself and your sons. 13Go to
King David and tell him, 'My master and
king, you promised that my son Solomon
would be king and would rule on your
throne after you. Why then has Adonijah
become king?' 14While you are still talking
to the king, I will come in and tell him that
what you have said about Adonijah is true."
15So Bathsheba went in to see the aged
king in his bedroom, where Abishag, the girl
from Shunam, was caring for him.
16Bathsheba bowed and knelt before the
king. He asked, "What do you want?"
17She answered, "My master, you made a
promise to me in the name of the LORD your
God. You said, 'Your son Solomon will
become king after me, and he will rule on
my throne.' 18But now, unknown to you,
Adonijah has become king. 19He has killed
many cows, fat calves, and sheep for
sacrifices. And he has invited all your sons,
as well as Abiathar the priest and Joab the
commander of the army, but he did not
invite Solomon, who serves you. 20My
master and king, all the Israelites are
watching you, waiting for you to decide who
will be king after you. 21As soon as you die,
Solomon and I will be treated as criminals."
22While Bathsheba was still talking with
the king, Nathan the prophet arrived. 23The
servants told the king, "Nathan the prophet
is here." So Nathan went to the king and
bowed facedown on the ground before him.
24Nathan said, "My master and king, have
you said that Adonijah will be the king after
you and that he will rule on your throne?
25Today he has sacrificed many cows, fat
calves, and sheep, and he has invited all your
other sons, the commanders of the army, and
Abiathar the priest. Right now they are
eating and drinking with him. They are
saying, 'Long live King Adonijah!' 26But he
did not invite me, your own servant, or
Zadok the priest, or Benaiah son of Jehoiada,
or your son Solomon. 27Did you do this?
Since we are your servants, why didn't you
tell us who should be king after you?"

David Makes Solomon King

28Then the king said, "Tell Bathsheba to
come in!" So she came in and stood before
the king.
29Then the king made this promise, "The
LORD has saved me from all trouble. As
surely as he lives, 30I will do today what I
have promised you in the name of the LORD,
the God of Israel. I promised that your son
Solomon would be king after me and rule on
my throne in my place."
31Then Bathsheba bowed facedown on the
ground and knelt before the king and said,
"Long live my master King David!"
32Then King David said, "Tell Zadok the
priest, Nathan the prophet, and Benaiah son
of Jehoiada to come in." When they came
before the king, 33he said to them, "Take my
servants with you and put my son Solomon
on my own mule. Take him down to the

spring called Gihon. 34There Zadok the
priest and Nathan the prophet should pour
olive oil on him and make him king over
Israel. Blow the trumpet and shout, 'Long
live King Solomon!' 35Then come back up
here with him. He will sit on my throne and
rule in my place, because he is the one I have
chosen to be the ruler over Israel and Judah."

36Benaiah son of Jehoiada answered the
king, "Amen! This is what the LORD, the God
of my master, has declared! 37The LORD has
always helped you, our king. May he also
help Solomon and make King Solomon's
throne an even greater throne than yours."

38So Zadok the priest, Nathan the prophet,
and Benaiah son of Jehoiada left with the
Kerethites and Pelethites.[n] They put
Solomon on King David's mule and took
him to the spring called Gihon. 39Zadok the
priest took the container of olive oil from
the Holy Tent and poured the oil on
Solomon's head to show he was the king.
Then they blew the trumpet, and all the
people shouted, "Long live King Solomon!"
40All the people followed Solomon into the
city. Playing flutes and shouting for joy, they
made so much noise the ground shook.

41At this time Adonijah and all the guests
with him were finishing their meal. When
he heard the sound from the trumpet, Joab
asked, "What does all that noise from the
city mean?"

42While Joab was speaking, Jonathan son
of Abiathar the priest arrived. Adonijah said,
"Come in! You are an important man, so you
must be bringing good news."

43But Jonathan answered, "No! Our master
King David has made Solomon the new
king. 44King David sent Zadok the priest,
Nathan the prophet, Benaiah son of
Jehoiada, and all the king's bodyguards with
him, and they have put Solomon on the
king's own mule. 45Then Zadok the priest
and Nathan the prophet poured olive oil on
Solomon at Gihon to make him king. After
that they went into the city, shouting with
joy. Now the whole city is excited, and that is
the noise you hear. 46Solomon has now
become the king. 47All the king's officers
have come to tell King David that he has
done a good thing. They are saying, 'May
your God make Solomon even more famous
than you and an even greater king than
you.' " Jonathan continued, "And King David
bowed down on his bed to worship God,
48saying, 'Bless the LORD, the God of Israel.
Today he has made one of my sons the king
and allowed me to see it.' "

49Then all of Adonijah's guests were
afraid, and they left quickly and scattered.
50Adonijah was also afraid of Solomon, so he
went and took hold of the corners of the
altar.[n] 51Then someone told Solomon,
"Adonijah is afraid of you, so he is at the
altar, holding on to its corners. He says, 'Tell
King Solomon to promise me today that he
will not kill me.' "

52So Solomon answered, "Adonijah must
show that he is a man of honor. If he does
that, I promise he will not lose even a single
hair from his head. But if he does anything
wrong, he will die." 53Then King Solomon
sent some men to get Adonijah. When he
was brought from the altar, he came before
King Solomon and bowed down. Solomon
told him, "Go home."

The Death of David

2 Since it was almost time for David to die,
he gave his son Solomon his last
commands. 2David said, "My time to die is
near. Be a good and strong leader. 3Obey the
LORD your God. Follow him by obeying his
demands, his commands, his laws, and his
rules that are written in the teachings of
Moses. If you do these things, you will be
successful in all you do and wherever you go.
4And if you obey the LORD, he will keep the
promise he made to me. He said: 'If your
descendants live as I tell them and have
complete faith in me, a man from your family
will always be king over the people of Israel.'

5"Also, you remember what Joab son of
Zeruiah did to me. He killed the two
commanders of Israel's armies: Abner son of
Ner and Amasa son of Jether. He did this as if
he and they were at war, although it was a
time of peace. He put their blood on the belt
around his waist and on his sandals on his
feet. 6Punish him in the way you think is
wisest, but do not let him die peacefully of
old age.

1:38 Kerethites and Pelethites These were probably special units of the army that were responsible for the king's safety, a kind of palace guard.
1:50 corners of the altar If a person were innocent of a crime, he could run into the Holy Place where the altar was. If he held on to the corners of the altar, which looked like horns, he would be safe.

7"Be kind to the children of Barzillai of
Gilead, and allow them to eat at your table.
They welcomed me when I ran away from
your brother Absalom.
8"And remember, Shimei son of Gera, the
Benjaminite, is here with you. He cursed me
the day I went to Mahanaim. But when he
came down to meet me at the Jordan River, I
promised him before the Lord, 'Shimei, I will
not kill you.' 9But you should not leave him
unpunished. You are a wise man, and you
will know what to do to him, but you must
be sure he is killed."
10Then David died and was buried with
his ancestors in Jerusalem. 11He had ruled
over Israel forty years—seven years in
Hebron and thirty-three years in Jerusalem.

Solomon Takes Control as King

12Solomon became king after David, his
father, and he was in firm control of his
kingdom.
13At this time Adonijah son of Haggith
went to Bathsheba, Solomon's mother. "Do
you come in peace?" Bathsheba asked.

"Yes. This is a peaceful visit," Adonijah
answered. 14"I have something to say to you."

"You may speak," she said.
15"You remember that at one time the
kingdom was mine," Adonijah said. "All the
people of Israel recognized me as their king,
but things have changed. Now my brother is
the king, because the LORD chose him. 16Now
I have one thing to ask you; please do not
refuse me."

Bathsheba answered, "What do you
want?"
17"I know King Solomon will do anything
you ask him," Adonijah continued. "Please
ask him to give me Abishag the
Shunammite to be my wife."
18"Very well," she answered. "I will speak
to the king for you."
19So Bathsheba went to King Solomon to
speak to him for Adonijah. When Solomon
saw her, he stood up to meet her, then
bowed down, and sat on the throne. He told
some servants to bring another throne for
his mother. Then she sat down at his right
side.
20Bathsheba said, "I have one small thing
to ask you. Please do not refuse me."

"Ask, mother," the king answered. "I will
not refuse you."
21So she said, "Allow Abishag the
Shunammite to marry your brother
Adonijah."
22King Solomon answered his mother,
"Why do you ask me to give him Abishag?
Why don't you also ask for him to become
the king since he is my older brother?
Abiathar the priest and Joab son of Zeruiah
would support him!"
23Then King Solomon swore by the name
of the LORD, saying, "May God punish me
terribly if this doesn't cost Adonijah his life!
24By the LORD who has given me the throne
that belonged to my father David and who
has kept his promise and given the kingdom
to me and my people, Adonijah will die
today!" 25Then King Solomon gave orders to
Benaiah son of Jehoiada, and he went and
killed Adonijah.
26King Solomon said to Abiathar the
priest, "I should kill you too, but I will allow
you to go back to your fields in Anathoth. I
will not kill you at this time, because you
helped carry the Ark of the Lord GOD while
marching with my father David. And I know
you shared in all the hard times with him."
27Then Solomon removed Abiathar from
being the LORD's priest. This happened as the
LORD had said it would, when he was
speaking in Shiloh about the priest Eli and
his descendants.
28When Joab heard about what had
happened, he was afraid. He had supported
Adonijah but not Absalom. So Joab ran to
the Tent of the LORD and took hold of the
corners of the altar.[n] 29Someone told King
Solomon that Joab had run to the Tent of the
LORD and was beside the altar. Then
Solomon ordered Benaiah to go and kill him.
30Benaiah went into the Tent of the LORD
and said to Joab, "The king says, 'Come out!' "

But Joab answered, "No, I will die here."

So Benaiah went back to the king and told
him what Joab had said. 31Then the king
ordered Benaiah, "Do as he says! Kill him
there and bury him. Then my family and I
will be free of the guilt of Joab, who has
killed innocent people. 32Without my father

2:28 corners of the altar If a person were innocent of a crime, he could run into the Holy Place where the altar was. If he held on to the corners of the altar, which looked like horns, he would be safe.

knowing it, he killed two men who were
much better than he was—Abner son of Ner,
the commander of Israel's army, and Amasa
son of Jether, the commander of Judah's
army. So the LORD will pay him back for
those deaths. 33Joab and his family will be
forever guilty for their deaths, but there will
be peace from the LORD for David, his
descendants, his family, and his throne
forever."

34So Benaiah son of Jehoiada killed Joab,
and he was buried near his home in the
desert. 35The king then made Benaiah son of
Jehoiada commander of the army in Joab's
place. He also made Zadok the new high
priest in Abiathar's place.

36Next the king sent for Shimei. Solomon
said to him, "Build a house for yourself in
Jerusalem and live there. Don't leave the city.
37The very day you leave and cross the
Kidron Valley, someone will kill you, and it
will be your own fault."

38So Shimei answered the king, "I agree
with what you say. I will do what you say,
my master and king." So Shimei lived in
Jerusalem for a long time.

39But three years later two of Shimei's
slaves ran away to Achish king of Gath, who
was the son of Maacah. Shimei heard that
his slaves were in Gath, 40so he put his
saddle on his donkey and went to Achish at
Gath to find them. Then he brought them
back from Gath.

41Someone told Solomon that Shimei had
gone from Jerusalem to Gath and had
returned. 42So Solomon sent for Shimei and
said, "I made you promise in the name of the
LORD not to leave Jerusalem. I warned you if
you went out anywhere you would die, and
you agreed to what I said. 43Why did you
break your promise to the LORD and disobey
my command?" 44The king also said, "You
know the many wrong things you did to my
father David, so now the LORD will punish
you for those wrongs. 45But the LORD will
bless me and make the rule of David safe
before the LORD forever."

46Then the king ordered Benaiah to kill
Shimei, and he did. Now Solomon was in
full control of his kingdom.

Solomon Asks for Wisdom

3 Solomon made an agreement with the
king of Egypt by marrying his daughter
and bringing her to Jerusalem. At this time
Solomon was still building his palace and the
Temple of the LORD, as well as a wall around
Jerusalem. 2The Temple for the worship of
the LORD had not yet been finished, so people
were still sacrificing at altars in many places
of worship. 3Solomon showed he loved the
LORD by following the commands his father
David had given him, except many other
places of worship were still used to offer sacrifices and to burn incense.

4King Solomon went to Gibeon to offer a
sacrifice, because it was the most important
place of worship. He offered a thousand
burnt offerings on that altar. 5While he was
at Gibeon, the LORD appeared to him in a
dream during the night. God said, "Ask for
whatever you want me to give you."

6Solomon answered, "You were very kind
to your servant, my father David. He obeyed
you, and he was honest and lived right. You
showed great kindness to him when you
allowed his son to be king after him. 7LORD
my God, now you have made me, your
servant, king in my father's place. But I am
like a little child; I don't know how to do
what must be done. 8I, your servant, am here
among your chosen people, and there are too
many of them to count. 9I ask that you give
me a heart that understands, so I can rule the
people in the right way and will know the
difference between right and wrong.
Otherwise, it is impossible to rule this great
people of yours."

10The Lord was pleased that Solomon had
asked this. 11So God said to him, "You did not
ask for a long life, or riches for yourself, or
the death of your enemies. Since you asked
for wisdom to make the right decisions, 12I
will do what you asked. I will give you
wisdom and understanding that is greater
than anyone has had in the past or will have
in the future. 13I will also give you what you
did not ask for: riches and honor. During
your life no other king will be as great as
you. 14If you follow me and obey my laws
and commands, as your father David did, I
will also give you a long life."

15After Solomon woke up from the dream,
he went to Jerusalem. He stood before the
Ark of the Agreement with the LORD, where
he made burnt offerings and fellowship
offerings. After that, he gave a feast for all his
leaders and officers.

devotion 89

1 KINGS 3:9–14

WHO SAYS?!

The other day a friend told me about a woman who approached her and asked, "Do you really think women ever change?" I've thought about that question every day since, and it makes me mad, furious even, when we women are perceived as or settle for anything less than what God intended us to be. We can change. I have changed. I have seen women grow into beautiful, mature believers that kick it for Jesus, loving their husbands with abandon, growing their children into dedicated followers of Christ, and reaching out to everyone around them with God's care and compassion.

If you want to see your life changed, train your mind and your body with Scripture, meditate on it, and ask God everyday for wisdom. Seek him just as Solomon did. Photocopy Solomon's request for wisdom. Put it in your Bible, in your car, in your magazine, on your fridge, on your desktop. Everywhere you go, take it along and respect it as your trainer. If you do this for the next thirty days (they say twenty-one days makes a habit), and you are obedient to its instruction, you will have transformed your mind to seek God alone for his wisdom. Then an unbelieving world will see a changed woman who looks a lot like the one described in Proverbs 31: "She speaks wise words and teaches others to be kind" (verse 26). Then we can all go look for this cynical chick together!

Solomon Makes a Wise Decision

16One day two women who were
prostitutes came to Solomon. As they stood
before him, 17one of the women said, "My
master, this woman and I live in the same
house. I gave birth to a baby while she was
there with me. 18Three days later this
woman also gave birth to a baby. No one else
was in the house with us; it was just the two
of us. 19One night this woman rolled over on
her baby, and he died. 20So she took my son
from my bed during the night while I was
asleep, and she carried him to her bed. Then
she put the dead baby in my bed. 21The next
morning when I got up to feed my baby, I
saw that he was dead! When I looked at him
more closely, I realized he was not my son."
22"No!" the other woman cried. "The living
baby is my son, and the dead baby is yours!"
But the first woman said, "No! The dead
baby is yours, and the living one is mine!" So
the two women argued before the king.
23Then King Solomon said, "One of you
says, 'My son is alive and your son is dead.'
Then the other one says, 'No! Your son is
dead and my son is alive.' "
24The king sent his servants to get a
sword. When they brought it to him, 25he
said, "Cut the living baby into two pieces,
and give each woman half."
26The real mother of the living child was
full of love for her son. So she said to the
king, "Please, my master, don't kill him! Give
the baby to her!"
But the other woman said, "Neither of us
will have him. Cut him into two pieces!"
27Then King Solomon said, "Don't kill
him. Give the baby to the first woman,
because she is the real mother."
28When the people of Israel heard about
King Solomon's decision, they respected him
very much. They saw he had wisdom from
God to make the right decisions.

Solomon's Officers

4 King Solomon ruled over all Israel.
2These are the names of his leading
officers:

Azariah son of Zadok was the priest;

3Elihoreph and Ahijah, sons of Shisha, recorded what happened in the courts;

Jehoshaphat son of Ahilud recorded the history of the people;

4Benaiah son of Jehoiada was commander of the army;

Zadok and Abiathar were priests;

5Azariah son of Nathan was in charge of the district governors;

Zabud son of Nathan was a priest and adviser to the king;

6Ahishar was responsible for everything in the palace;

Adoniram son of Abda was in charge of the labor force.

7Solomon placed twelve governors over the districts of Israel, who gathered food from their districts for the king and his family. Each governor was responsible for bringing food to the king one month of each year. 8These are the names of the twelve governors:

Ben-Hur was governor of the mountain country of Ephraim.

9Ben-Deker was governor of Makaz, Shaalbim, Beth Shemesh, and Elon Bethhanan.

10Ben-Hesed was governor of Arubboth, Socoh, and all the land of Hepher.

11Ben-Abinadab was governor of Naphoth Dor. (He was married to Taphath, Solomon's daughter.)

12Baana son of Ahilud was governor of Taanach, Megiddo, and all of Beth Shan next to Zarethan. This was below Jezreel from Beth Shan to Abel Meholah across from Jokmeam.

13Ben-Geber was governor of Ramoth in Gilead. (He was governor of all the towns of Jair in Gilead. Jair was the son of Manasseh. Ben-Geber was also over the district of Argob in Bashan, which had sixty large, walled cities with bronze bars on their gates.)

14Ahinadab son of Iddo was governor of Mahanaim.

15Ahimaaz was governor of Naphtali. (He was married to Basemath, Solomon's daughter.)

16Baana son of Hushai was governor of Asher and Aloth.

17Jehoshaphat son of Paruah was governor of Issachar.

18Shimei son of Ela was governor of Benjamin.

19Geber son of Uri was governor of Gilead. Gilead had been the country of Sihon king of the Amorites and Og king of Bashan. But Geber was the only governor over this district.

Solomon's Kingdom

20There were as many people in Judah and Israel as grains of sand on the seashore. The people ate, drank, and were happy.
21Solomon ruled over all the kingdoms from the Euphrates River to the land of the Philistines, as far as the border of Egypt. These countries brought Solomon the payments he demanded, and they were under his control all his life.

22Solomon needed much food each day to feed himself and all the people who ate at his table: one hundred ninety-five bushels of fine flour, three hundred ninety bushels of
grain, 23ten cows that were fed on good grain, twenty cows that were raised in the fields, one hundred sheep, three kinds of deer, and fattened birds.

24Solomon controlled all the countries west of the Euphrates River—the land from Tiphsah to Gaza. And he had peace on all
sides of his kingdom. 25During Solomon's life Judah and Israel, from Dan to Beersheba,[n] also lived in peace; all of his people were able to sit under their own fig trees and grapevines.

26Solomon had four thousand stalls for his chariot horses and twelve thousand horses.
27Each month one of the district governors gave King Solomon all the food he needed—enough for every person who ate at the king's table. The governors made sure he had
everything he needed. 28They also brought enough barley and straw for Solomon's chariot and work horses; each person brought this grain to the right place.

Solomon's Wisdom

29God gave Solomon great wisdom so he could understand many things. His wisdom was as hard to measure as the grains of sand
on the seashore. 30His wisdom was greater than any wisdom of the East, or any wisdom
in Egypt. 31He was wiser than anyone on

4:25 Dan to Beersheba Dan was the city farthest north in Israel, and Beersheba was the city farthest south. So this means all the people of Israel.

earth. He was even wiser than Ethan the Ezrahite, as well as Heman, Calcol, and Darda—the three sons of Mahol. King Solomon became famous in all the surrounding countries. 32 During his life he spoke three thousand wise sayings and also wrote one thousand five songs. 33 He taught about many kinds of plants—everything from the great cedar trees of Lebanon to the weeds that grow out of the walls. He also taught about animals, birds, crawling things, and fish. 34 People from all nations came to listen to King Solomon's wisdom. The kings of all nations sent them to him, because they had heard of Solomon's wisdom.

Preparing to Build the Temple

5 Hiram, the king of Tyre, had always been David's friend. When Hiram heard that Solomon had been made king in David's place, he sent his messengers to Solomon. 2 Solomon sent this message back to King Hiram: 3 "You remember my father David had to fight many wars with the countries around him, so he was never able to build a temple for worshiping the LORD his God. David was waiting until the LORD allowed him to defeat all his enemies. 4 But now the LORD my God has given me peace on all sides of my country. I have no enemies now, and no danger threatens my people.

5 "The LORD promised my father David, 'I will make your son king after you, and he will build a temple for worshiping me.' Now, I plan to build that temple for worshiping the LORD my God. 6 So send your men to cut down cedar trees for me from Lebanon. My servants will work with yours, and I will pay them whatever wages you decide. We don't have anyone who can cut down trees as well as the people of Sidon."

7 When Hiram heard what Solomon asked, he was very happy. He said, "Praise the LORD today! He has given David a wise son to rule over this great nation!" 8 Then Hiram sent back this message to Solomon: "I received the message you sent, and I will give you all the cedar and pine trees you want. 9 My servants will bring them down from Lebanon to the sea. There I will tie them together and float them along the shore to the place you choose. Then I will separate the logs there, and you can take them away. In return it is my wish that you give food to all those who live with me." 10 So Hiram gave Solomon as much cedar and pine as he wanted. 11 And Solomon gave Hiram about one hundred twenty-five thousand bushels of wheat each year to feed the people who lived with him. Solomon also gave him about one hundred fifteen thousand gallons of pure olive oil every year.

12 The LORD gave Solomon wisdom as he had promised. And there was peace between Hiram and Solomon; these two kings made a treaty between themselves.

13 King Solomon forced thirty thousand men of Israel to help in this work. 14 He sent a group of ten thousand men each month to Lebanon. Each group worked in Lebanon one month, then went home for two months. A man named Adoniram was in charge. 15 Solomon forced eighty thousand men to work in the hill country, cutting stone, and he had seventy thousand men to carry the stones. 16 There were also thirty-three hundred men who directed the workers. 17 King Solomon commanded them to cut large blocks of fine stone to be used for the foundation of the Temple. 18 Solomon's and Hiram's builders and the men from Byblos carved the stones and prepared the stones and the logs for building the Temple.

Solomon Builds the Temple

6 Solomon began to build the Temple four hundred eighty years after the people of Israel had left Egypt. This was during the fourth year of King Solomon's rule over Israel. It was the second month, the month of Ziv.

2 The Temple was ninety feet long, thirty feet wide, and forty-five feet high. 3 The porch in front of the main room of the Temple was fifteen feet deep and thirty feet wide. This room ran along the front of the Temple itself. Its width was equal to that of the Temple. 4 The Temple also had windows that opened and closed. 5 Solomon also built some side rooms against the walls of the main room and the inner room of the Temple. He built rooms all around. 6 The rooms on the bottom floor were seven and one-half feet wide. Those on the middle floor were nine feet wide, and the rooms above them were ten and one-half feet wide. The Temple wall that formed the side of each

room was thinner than the wall in the room
below. These rooms were pushed against the
Temple wall, but they did not have their
main beams built into this wall.
7The stones were prepared at the same
place where they were cut from the ground.
Since these stones were the only ones used
to build the Temple, there was no noise of
hammers, axes, or any other iron tools at the
Temple.
8The entrance to the lower rooms beside
the Temple was on the south side. From
there, stairs went up to the second-floor
rooms. And from there, stairs went on to the
third-floor rooms. 9Solomon put a roof made
from beams and cedar boards on the Temple.
So he finished building the Temple 10as well
as the bottom floor that was beside the
Temple. This bottom floor was seven and
one-half feet high and was attached to the
Temple by cedar beams.
11The LORD said to Solomon: 12"If you obey
all my laws and commands, I will do for you
what I promised your father David. 13I will
live among the Israelites in this Temple, and
I will never leave my people Israel."
14So Solomon finished building the
Temple. 15The inside walls were covered from
floor to ceiling with cedar boards. The floor
was made from pine boards. 16A room thirty
feet long was built in the back part of the
Temple. This room, called the Most Holy
Place, was separated from the rest of the
Temple by cedar boards which reached from
floor to ceiling. 17The main room, the one in
front of the Most Holy Place, was sixty feet
long. 18Everything inside the Temple was
covered with cedar, which was carved with
pictures of flowers and plants. A person could
not see the stones of the wall, only the cedar.
19Solomon prepared the inner room at the
back of the Temple to keep the Ark of the
Agreement with the LORD. 20This inner room
was thirty feet long, thirty feet wide, and
thirty feet high. He covered this room with
pure gold, and he also covered the altar of
cedar. 21He covered the inside of the Temple
with pure gold, placing gold chains across
the front of the inner room, which was also
covered with gold. 22So all the inside of the
Temple, as well as the altar of the Most Holy
Place, was covered with gold.
23Solomon made two creatures from olive
wood and placed them in the Most Holy
Place. Each creature was fifteen feet tall 24and
had two wings. Each wing was seven and
one-half feet long, so it was fifteen feet from
the end of one wing to the end of the other.
25The creatures were the same size and shape;
26each was fifteen feet tall. 27These creatures
were put beside each other in the Most Holy
Place with their wings spread out. One
creature's wing touched one wall, and the
other creature's wing touched the other wall
with their wings touching each other in the
middle of the room. 28These two creatures
were covered with gold.
29All the walls around the Temple were
carved with pictures of creatures with wings,
as well as palm trees and flowers. This was
true for both the main room and the inner
room. 30The floors of both rooms were
covered with gold.
31Doors made from olive wood were placed
at the entrance to the Most Holy Place. These
doors had five-sided frames. 32Creatures with
wings, as well as palm trees and flowers, were
also carved on the two olive wood doors that
were covered with gold. The creatures and
the palm trees on the doors were covered
with gold as well. 33At the entrance to the
main room there was a square door frame
made of olive wood. 34Two doors were made
from pine. Each door had two parts so the
doors folded. 35The doors were covered with
pictures of creatures with wings, as well as
palm trees and flowers. All of the carvings
were covered with gold, which was evenly
spread over them.
36The inner courtyard was enclosed by
walls, which were made of three rows of cut
stones and one row of cedar boards.
37Work began on the Temple in Ziv, the
second month, during the fourth year
Solomon was king over Israel. 38The Temple
was finished during the eleventh year he
was king, in the eighth month, the month of
Bul. It was built exactly as it was planned.
Solomon had spent seven years building it.

Solomon's Palace

7 King Solomon also built a palace for
himself; it took him thirteen years to
finish it. 2Built of cedars from the Forest of
Lebanon, it was one hundred fifty feet long,
seventy-five feet wide, and forty-five feet
high. It had four rows of cedar columns
which supported the cedar beams. 3There

were forty-five beams on the roof, with
fifteen beams in each row, and the ceiling
was covered with cedar above the beams.
4Windows were placed in three rows facing
each other. 5All the doors were square, and
the three doors at each end faced each other.

6Solomon also built the porch that had
pillars. This porch was seventy-five feet long
and forty-five feet wide. Along the front of
the porch was a roof supported by pillars.

7Solomon also built a throne room where
he judged people, called the Hall of Justice.
This room was covered with cedar from the
floor to the ceiling. 8The palace where
Solomon lived was built like the Hall of
Justice, and it was behind this hall. Solomon
also built the same kind of palace for his
wife, who was the daughter of the king of
Egypt.

9All these buildings were made with
blocks of fine stone. First they were carefully
cut. Then they were trimmed with a saw in
the front and back. These fine stones went
from the foundations of the buildings to the
top of the walls. Even the courtyard was
made with blocks of stone. 10The
foundations were made with large blocks of
fine stone, some as long as fifteen feet.
Others were twelve feet long. 11On top of
these foundation stones were other blocks of
fine stone and cedar beams. 12The palace
courtyard, the courtyard inside the Temple,
and the porch of the Temple were
surrounded by walls. All of these walls had
three rows of stone blocks and one row of
cedar beams.

The Temple Is Completed Inside

13King Solomon sent to Tyre and had
Huram brought to him. 14Huram's mother
was a widow from the tribe of Naphtali. His
father was from Tyre and had been skilled in
making things from bronze. Huram was also
very skilled and experienced in bronze work.
So he came to King Solomon and did all the
bronze work.

15He made two bronze pillars, each one
twenty-seven feet tall and eighteen feet
around. 16He also made two bronze capitals
that were seven and one-half feet tall, and he
put them on top of the pillars. 17Then he
made a net of seven chains for each capital,
which covered the capitals on top of the two
pillars. 18He made two rows of bronze
pomegranates to go on the nets. These
covered the capitals at the top of the pillars.
19The capitals on top of the pillars in the
porch were shaped like lilies, and they were
six feet tall. 20The capitals were on top of
both pillars, above the bowl-shaped section
and next to the nets. At that place there were
two hundred pomegranates in rows all
around the capitals. 21Huram put these two
bronze pillars at the porch of the Temple. He
named the south pillar He Establishes and
the north pillar In Him Is Strength. 22The
capitals on top of the pillars were shaped
like lilies. So the work on the pillars was
finished.

23Then Huram made from bronze a large
round bowl, which was called the Sea. It was
forty-five feet around, fifteen feet across, and
seven and one-half feet deep. 24Around the
outer edge of the bowl was a rim. Under this
rim were two rows of bronze plants which
surrounded the bowl. There were ten plants
every eighteen inches, and these plants were
made in one piece with the bowl. 25The bowl
rested on the backs of twelve bronze bulls
that faced outward from the center of the
bowl. Three bulls faced north, three faced
west, three faced south, and three faced east.
26The sides of the bowl were four inches
thick, and it held about eleven thousand
gallons. The rim of the bowl was like the rim
of a cup or like a lily blossom.

27Then Huram made ten bronze stands,
each one six feet long, six feet wide, and four
and one-half feet high. 28The stands were
made from square sides, which were put on
frames. 29On the sides were bronze lions,
bulls, and creatures with wings. On the
frames above and below the lions and bulls
were designs of flowers hammered into the
bronze. 30Each stand had four bronze wheels
with bronze axles. At the corners there were
bronze supports for a large bowl, and the
supports had designs of flowers. 31There was
a frame on top of the bowls, eighteen inches
high above the bowls. The opening of the
bowl was round, twenty-seven inches deep.
Designs were carved into the bronze on the
frame, which was square, not round. 32The
four wheels, placed under the frame, were
twenty-seven inches high. The axles
between the wheels were made as one piece
with the stand. 33The wheels were like a
chariot's wheels. Everything on the

wheels—the axles, rims, spokes, and hubs—
were made of bronze.
34The four supports were on the four
corners of each stand. They were made as
one piece with the stand. 35A strip of bronze
around the top of each stand was nine
inches deep. It was also made as one piece
with the stand. 36The sides of the stand and
the frames were covered with carvings of
creatures with wings, as well as lions, palm
trees, and flowers. 37This is the way Huram
made the ten stands. The bronze for each
stand was melted and poured into a mold, so
all the stands were the same size and shape.
38Huram also made ten bronze bowls, one
bowl for each of the ten stands. Each bowl
was six feet across and could hold about two
hundred thirty gallons. 39Huram put five
stands on the south side of the Temple and
five on the north side. He put the large bowl
in the southeast corner of the Temple.
40Huram also made bowls, shovels, and
small bowls.

So Huram finished all his work for King
Solomon on the Temple of the LORD:

41two pillars;
two large bowls for the capitals on top of the pillars;
two nets to cover the two large bowls for the capitals on top of the pillars;
42four hundred pomegranates for the two nets (there were two rows of pomegranates for each net covering the bowls for the capitals on top of the pillars);
43ten stands with a bowl on each stand;
44the large bowl with twelve bulls under it;
45the pots, shovels, small bowls, and all the utensils for the Temple of the LORD.

Huram made everything King Solomon
wanted from polished bronze. 46The king
had these things poured into clay molds that
were made in the plain of the Jordan River
between Succoth and Zarethan. 47Solomon
never weighed the bronze used to make
these things, because there was too much to
weigh. So the total weight of all the bronze
was never known.
48Solomon also made all the items for the
Temple of the LORD:

the golden altar;
the golden table which held the bread that shows God's people are in his presence;
49the lampstands of pure gold (five on the right side and five on the left side in front of the Most Holy Place);
the flowers, lamps, and tongs of gold;
50the pure gold bowls, wick trimmers, small bowls, pans, and dishes used to carry coals;
the gold hinges for the doors of the Most Holy Place and the main room of the Temple.

51Finally the work King Solomon did for
the Temple of the LORD was finished.
Solomon brought in everything his father
David had set apart for the Temple—silver,
gold, and other articles. He put everything in
the treasuries of the Temple of the LORD.

The Ark Is Brought into the Temple

8 King Solomon called for the elders of
Israel, the heads of the tribes, and the
leaders of the families to come to him in
Jerusalem. He wanted them to bring the Ark
of the Agreement with the LORD from the
older part of the city. 2So all the Israelites
came together with King Solomon during
the festival in the month of Ethanim, the
seventh month.
3When all the elders of Israel arrived, the
priests lifted up the Ark. 4They carried the
Ark of the LORD, the Meeting Tent, and the
holy utensils; the priests and the Levites
brought them up. 5King Solomon and all the
Israelites gathered before the Ark and
sacrificed so many sheep and cattle no one
could count them all. 6Then the priests put
the Ark of the Agreement with the LORD in
its place inside the Most Holy Place in the
Temple, under the wings of the golden
creatures. 7The wings of these creatures were
spread out over the place for the Ark,
covering it and its carrying poles. 8The
carrying poles were so long that anyone
standing in the Holy Place in front of the
Most Holy Place could see the ends of the
poles, but no one could see them from
outside the Holy Place. The poles are still
there today. 9The only things inside the Ark
were two stone tablets[n] that Moses had put
in the Ark at Mount Sinai. That was where

8:9 stone tablets They were the two tablets on which God wrote the Ten Commandments.

the LORD made his agreement with the
Israelites after they came out of Egypt.
[10]When the priests left the Holy Place, a
cloud filled the Temple of the LORD. [11]The
priests could not continue their work,
because the Temple was filled with the glory
of the LORD.

Solomon Speaks to the People

[12]Then Solomon said, "The LORD said he
would live in a dark cloud. [13]LORD, I have
truly built a wonderful Temple for you—a
place for you to live forever."
[14]While all the Israelites were standing
there, King Solomon turned to them and
blessed them.
[15]Then he said, "Praise the LORD, the God
of Israel. He has done what he promised to
my father David. The LORD said, [16]'Since the
time I brought my people Israel out of Egypt,
I have not chosen a city in any tribe of Israel
where a temple will be built for me. But I
have chosen David to lead my people Israel.'
[17]"My father David wanted to build a
temple for the LORD, the God of Israel. [18]But
the LORD said to my father David, 'It was
good that you wanted to build a temple for
me. [19]But you are not the one to build it.
Your son, who comes from your own body, is
the one who will build my temple.'
[20]"Now the LORD has kept his promise. I
am the king now in place of David my
father. Now I rule Israel as the LORD
promised, and I have built the Temple for
the LORD, the God of Israel. [21]I have made a
place there for the Ark, in which is the
Agreement the LORD made with our
ancestors when he brought them out of
Egypt."

Solomon's Prayer

[22]Then Solomon stood facing the LORD's
altar, and all the Israelites were standing
behind him. He spread out his hands toward
the sky [23]and said:
"LORD, God of Israel, there is no god like
you in heaven above or on earth below. You
keep your agreement of love with your
servants who truly follow you. [24]You have
kept the promise you made to your servant
David, my father. You spoke it with your
own mouth and finished it with your hands
today. [25]Now LORD, God of Israel, keep the
promise you made to your servant David, my
father. You said, 'If your sons are careful to
obey me as you have obeyed me, there will
always be someone from your family ruling
Israel.' [26]Now, God of Israel, please continue
to keep that promise you made to your
servant David, my father.
[27]"But, God, can you really live here on the
earth? The sky and the highest place in
heaven cannot contain you. Surely this
house which I have built cannot contain
you. [28]But please listen to my prayer and my
request, because I am your servant. LORD my
God, hear this prayer your servant prays to
you today. [29]Night and day please watch
over this Temple where you have said, 'I will
be worshiped there.' Hear the prayer I pray
facing this Temple. [30]Hear my prayers and
the prayers of your people Israel when we
pray facing this place. Hear from your home
in heaven, and when you hear, forgive us.
[31]"If someone wrongs another person, he
will be brought to the altar in this Temple. If
he swears an oath that he is not guilty,
[32]then hear in heaven. Judge the case, punish
the guilty, but declare that the innocent
person is not guilty.
[33]"When your people, the Israelites, sin
against you, their enemies will defeat them.
But if they come back to you and praise you
and pray to you in this Temple, [34]then hear
them in heaven. Forgive the sins of your
people Israel, and bring them back to the
land you gave to their ancestors.
[35]"When they sin against you, you will
stop the rain from falling on their land. Then
they will pray, facing this place and praising
you; they will stop sinning when you make
them suffer. [36]When this happens, please
hear their prayer in heaven, and forgive the
sins of your servants, the Israelites. Teach
them to do what is right. Then please send
rain to this land you have given particularly
to them.
[37]"At times the land will become so dry
that no food will grow, or a great sickness
will spread among the people. Sometimes all
the crops will be destroyed by locusts or
grasshoppers. Your people will be attacked
in their cities by their enemy or will become
sick. [38]When any of these things happen, the
people will become truly sorry. If your
people spread their hands in prayer toward
this Temple, [39]then hear their prayers from
your home in heaven. Forgive and treat each

person as he should be treated because you
know what is in a person's heart. Only you
know what is in everyone's heart. 40Then
your people will respect you as long as they
live in this land you gave to our ancestors.

41-42"People who are not Israelites,
foreigners from other lands, will hear about
your greatness and power. They will come
from far away to pray at this Temple. 43Then
hear from your home in heaven, and do
whatever they ask you. Then people
everywhere will know you and respect you,
just as your people in Israel do. Then
everyone will know I built this Temple as a
place to worship you.

44"When your people go out to fight their
enemies along some road on which you send
them, your people will pray to you, facing
the city which you have chosen and the
Temple I have built for you. 45Then hear in
heaven their prayers, and do what is right.

46"Everyone sins, so your people will also
sin against you. You will become angry with
them and hand them over to their enemies.
Their enemies will capture them and take
them away to their countries far or near.
47Your people will be sorry for their sins
when they are held as prisoners in another
country. They will be sorry and pray to you
in the land where they are held as prisoners,
saying, 'We have sinned. We have done
wrong and acted wickedly.' 48They will truly
turn back to you in the land of their
enemies. They will pray to you, facing this
land you gave their ancestors, this city you
have chosen, and the Temple I have built for
you. 49Then hear their prayers from your
home in heaven, and do what is right.
50Forgive your people of all their sins and for
turning against you. Make those who have
captured them show them mercy.
51Remember, they are your special people.
You brought them out of Egypt, as if you
were pulling them out of a blazing furnace.

52"Give your attention to my prayers and
the prayers of your people Israel. Listen to
them anytime they ask you for help. 53You
chose them from all the nations on earth to
be your very own people. This is what you
promised through Moses your servant when
you brought our ancestors out of Egypt, Lord
GOD."

54Solomon prayed this prayer to the LORD,
kneeling in front of the altar with his arms
raised toward heaven. When he finished
praying, he got up. 55Then, in a loud voice,
he stood and blessed all the people of Israel,
saying: 56"Praise the LORD! He promised he
would give rest to his people Israel, and he
has given us rest. The LORD has kept all the
good promises he gave through his servant
Moses. 57May the LORD our God be with us as
he was with our ancestors. May he never
leave us, 58and may he turn us to himself so
we will follow him. Let us obey all the laws
and commands he gave our ancestors. 59May
the LORD our God remember this prayer day
and night and do what is right for his
servant and his people Israel day by day.
60Then all the people of the world will know
the LORD is the only true God. 61You must
fully obey the LORD our God and follow all
his laws and commands. Continue to obey in
the future as you do now."

Sacrifices Are Offered

62Then King Solomon and all Israel with
him offered sacrifices to the LORD. 63Solomon
killed twenty-two thousand cattle and one
hundred twenty thousand sheep as
fellowship offerings. So the king and all the
people gave the Temple to the LORD.

64On that day King Solomon made holy
the middle part of the courtyard which is
in front of the Temple of the LORD. There
he offered whole burnt offerings, grain
offerings, and the fat of the fellowship
offerings. He offered them in the courtyard,
because the bronze altar before the LORD was
too small to hold all the burnt offerings, the
grain offerings, and the fat of the fellowship
offerings.

65Solomon and all the Israelites celebrated
the other festival that came at that time.
People came from as far away as Lebo
Hamath and the brook of Egypt. A great
many people celebrated before the LORD for
seven days, then seven more days, for a total
of fourteen days. 66On the following day
Solomon sent the people home. They blessed
the king as they went, happy because of all
the good things the LORD had done for his
servant David and his people Israel.

The Lord Appears to Solomon Again

9 Solomon finished building the Temple
of the LORD and his royal palace and
everything he wanted to build. 2Then the

devotion 90

1 KINGS 9:3-5

HOW LONG DID YOU TAKE A PACIFIER?

God described David as "sincere." What does it mean to be sincere? My dictionary says "without hypocrisy or pretense." Yet I often hear unbelievers talk about Christians who are hypocrites, and unfortunately, I also see a lot of pretentious believers. Why can't we be real with each other?

My daughter used a pacifier until she was four years old. We hid it well until one day my husband got up in front of our church to make an announcement and took her with him. To my horror, I saw the pacifier in her hand and just prayed she would not put it in her mouth. You guessed it—she popped it right in her mouth for all to see. I got more criticism for that pacifier than you can imagine. I wanted to preach a sermon about not judging others.

We need to learn to be obedient to the Lord, but we also need to learn to be fair and sincere with one another. Believers who have an image of how a Christian should look often like to make up extra rules to add to God's commands. And they want everyone to fit their image! But God made us all differently. (Some of us may even suck a pacifier until we are four years old!) Look up Matthew 22:34-40. The most important commandments are to love the Lord and love your neighbor. The great part about these commands is that sincere love doesn't leave any room for pretenses or critical spirits.

LORD appeared to him again just as he had
done before, in Gibeon. 3The LORD said to
him: "I have heard your prayer and what you
have asked me to do. You built this Temple,
and I have made it a holy place. I will be
worshiped there forever and will watch over
it and protect it always.

4"But you must serve me as your father
David did; he was fair and sincere. You must
obey all I have commanded and keep my
laws and rules. 5If you do, I will make your
kingdom strong. This is the promise I made
to your father David—that someone from
his family would always rule Israel.

6"But you and your children must follow
me and obey the laws and commands I have
given you. You must not serve or worship
other gods. 7If you do, I will force Israel to
leave the land I have given them, and I will
leave this Temple that I have made holy. All
the nations will make fun of Israel and speak
evil about them. 8If the Temple is destroyed,
everyone who passes by will be shocked.
They will make fun of you and ask, 'Why did
the LORD do this terrible thing to this land
and this Temple?' 9People will answer, 'This
happened because they left the LORD their
God. This was the God who brought their
ancestors out of Egypt, but they decided to
follow other gods. They worshiped and
served those gods, so the LORD brought all
this disaster on them.'"

Solomon's Other Achievements

10By the end of twenty years, King
Solomon had built two buildings—the
Temple of the LORD and the royal palace. 11At
that time King Solomon gave twenty towns
in Galilee to Hiram king of Tyre, because
Hiram had helped with the buildings. Hiram
had given Solomon all the cedar, pine, and
gold he wanted. 12So Hiram traveled from
Tyre to see the towns Solomon had given
him, but when he saw them, he was not
pleased. 13He asked, "What good are these
towns you have given me, my brother?" So

he named them the Land of Cabul,[n] and they
are still called that today. 14Hiram had sent
Solomon about nine thousand pounds of
gold.

15This is the account of the forced labor
Solomon used to build the Temple and the
palace. He had them fill in the land and
build the wall around Jerusalem. He also had
them rebuild the cities of Hazor, Megiddo,
and Gezer. 16(In the past the king of Egypt
had attacked and captured Gezer. After
burning it, he killed the Canaanites who
lived there. Then he gave it as a wedding
present to his daughter, who married
Solomon. 17So Solomon rebuilt it.) He also
built the cities of Lower Beth Horon 18and
Baalath, as well as Tadmor, which is in the
desert. 19King Solomon also built cities for
storing grain and supplies and cities for his
chariots and horses. He built whatever he
wanted in Jerusalem, Lebanon, and
everywhere he ruled.

20There were other people in the land
who were not Israelites—Amorites, Hittites,
Perizzites, Hivites, and Jebusites. 21They were
descendants of people that the Israelites had
not destroyed. Solomon forced them to work
for him as slaves, as is still true today. 22But
Solomon did not make slaves of the
Israelites. They were his soldiers,
government leaders, officers, captains,
chariot commanders, and drivers.

23These were his most important officers
over the work. There were five hundred fifty
supervisors over the people who did the
work on Solomon's projects.

24The daughter of the king of Egypt
moved from the old part of Jerusalem to the
palace that Solomon had built for her. Then
Solomon filled in the surrounding land.

25Three times each year Solomon offered
whole burnt offerings and fellowship
offerings on the altar he had built for the
LORD. He also burned incense before the
LORD. So he finished the work on the
Temple.

26King Solomon also built ships at Ezion
Geber, a town near Elath on the shore of the
Red Sea, in the land of Edom. 27Hiram had
skilled sailors, so he sent them to serve in
these ships with Solomon's men. 28The ships
sailed to Ophir and brought back about
thirty-two thousand pounds of gold to King
Solomon.

The Queen of Sheba Visits Solomon

10 When the queen of Sheba heard about
Solomon, she came to test him with
hard questions. 2She traveled to Jerusalem
with a large group of servants and camels
carrying spices, jewels, and much gold.
When she came to Solomon, she talked with
him about all she had in mind, 3and Solomon
answered all her questions. Nothing was too
hard for him to explain to her. 4The queen of
Sheba learned that Solomon was very wise.
She saw the palace he had built, 5the food on
his table, his many officers, the palace
servants, and their good clothes. She saw the
servants who served him at feasts and the
whole burnt offerings he made in the Temple
of the LORD. All these things amazed her.

6So she said to King Solomon, "What I
heard in my own country about your
achievements and wisdom is true. 7I could
not believe it then, but now I have come and
seen it with my own eyes. I was not told
even half of it! Your wisdom and wealth are
much greater than I had heard. 8Your men
and officers are very lucky, because in
always serving you, they are able to hear
your wisdom. 9Praise the LORD your God,
who was pleased to make you king of Israel.
The LORD has constant love for Israel, so he
made you king to keep justice and to rule
fairly."

10Then she gave the king about nine
thousand pounds of gold and many spices
and jewels. No one since that time has
brought more spices than the queen of
Sheba gave to King Solomon.

11(Hiram's ships brought gold from Ophir,
as well as much juniper wood and jewels.
12Solomon used the juniper wood to build
supports for the Temple of the LORD and the
palace, and to make harps and lyres for the
musicians. Such fine juniper wood has not
been brought in or been seen since that
time.)

13King Solomon gave the queen of Sheba
everything she wanted and asked for, in
addition to what he had already given her of
his wealth. Then she and her servants
returned to her own country.

9:13 Cabul This name sounds like the Hebrew word for "worthless."

Solomon's Wealth

14 Every year King Solomon received about fifty thousand pounds of gold. 15 Besides that, he also received gold from the traders and merchants, as well as from the kings of Arabia and governors of the land.

16 King Solomon made two hundred large shields of hammered gold, each of which contained about seven and one-half pounds of gold. 17 He also made three hundred smaller shields of hammered gold, each of which contained about four pounds of gold. The king put them in the Palace of the Forest of Lebanon.

18 The king built a large throne of ivory and covered it with fine gold. 19 The throne had six steps on it, and its back was round at the top. There were armrests on both sides of the chair, and each armrest had a lion beside it. 20 Twelve lions stood on the six steps, one lion at each end of each step. Nothing like this had ever been made for any other kingdom. 21 All of Solomon's drinking cups, as well as the dishes in the Palace of the Forest of Lebanon, were made of pure gold. Nothing was made from silver, because silver was not valuable in Solomon's time.

22 King Solomon also had many trading ships at sea, along with Hiram's ships. Every three years the ships returned, bringing back gold, silver, ivory, apes, and baboons.

23 So Solomon had more riches and wisdom than all the other kings on earth. 24 People everywhere wanted to see King Solomon and listen to the wisdom God had given him. 25 Every year those who came brought gifts of silver and gold, clothes, weapons, spices, horses, and mules.

26 Solomon had fourteen hundred chariots and twelve thousand horses. He kept some in special cities for the chariots, and others he kept with him in Jerusalem. 27 In Jerusalem Solomon made silver as common as stones and cedar trees as common as the fig trees on the western hills. 28 He imported horses from Egypt and Kue. His traders bought them in Kue. 29 A chariot from Egypt cost about fifteen pounds of silver, and a horse cost nearly four pounds of silver. Solomon's traders also sold horses and chariots to all the kings of the Hittites and the Arameans.

Solomon's Many Wives

11 King Solomon loved many women who were not from Israel. He loved the daughter of the king of Egypt, as well as women of the Moabites, Ammonites, Edomites, Sidonians, and Hittites. 2 The LORD had told the Israelites, "You must not marry people of other nations. If you do, they will cause you to follow their gods." But Solomon fell in love with these women. 3 He had seven hundred wives who were from royal families and three hundred slave women who gave birth to his children. His wives caused him to turn away from God. 4 As Solomon grew old, his wives caused him to follow other gods. He did not follow the LORD completely as his father David had done. 5 Solomon worshiped Ashtoreth, the goddess of the people of Sidon, and Molech, the hated god of the Ammonites. 6 So Solomon did what the LORD said was wrong and did not follow the LORD completely as his father David had done.

7 On a hill east of Jerusalem, Solomon built two places for worship. One was a place to worship Chemosh, the hated god of the Moabites, and the other was a place to worship Molech, the hated god of the Ammonites. 8 Solomon did the same thing for all his foreign wives so they could burn incense and offer sacrifices to their gods.

9 The LORD had appeared to Solomon twice, but the king turned away from following the LORD, the God of Israel. The LORD was angry with Solomon, 10 because he had commanded Solomon not to follow other gods. But Solomon did not obey the LORD's command. 11 So the LORD said to Solomon, "Because you have chosen to break your agreement with me and have not obeyed my commands, I will tear your kingdom away from you and give it to one of your officers. 12 But I will not take it away while you are alive because of my love for your father David. I will tear it away from your son when he becomes king. 13 I will not tear away all the kingdom from him, but I will leave him one tribe to rule. I will do this because of David, my servant, and because of Jerusalem, the city I have chosen."

Solomon's Enemies

14 The LORD caused Hadad the Edomite, a member of the family of the king of Edom,

to become Solomon's enemy. 15Earlier, David
had defeated Edom. When Joab, the
commander of David's army, went into
Edom to bury the dead, he killed all the
males. 16Joab and all the Israelites stayed in
Edom for six months and killed every male
in Edom. 17At that time Hadad was only a
young boy, so he ran away to Egypt with
some of his father's officers. 18They left
Midian and went to Paran, where they were
joined by other men. Then they all went to
Egypt to see the king, who gave Hadad a
house, some food, and some land.

19The king liked Hadad so much he gave
Hadad a wife—the sister of Tahpenes, the
king's wife. 20They had a son named
Genubath. Queen Tahpenes brought him up
in the royal palace with the king's own
children.

21While he was in Egypt, Hadad heard
that David had died and that Joab, the
commander of the army, was dead also. So
Hadad said to the king, "Let me go; I will
return to my own country."

22"Why do you want to go back to your
own country?" the king asked. "What
haven't I given you here?"

"Nothing," Hadad answered, "but please,
let me go."

23God also caused another man to be
Solomon's enemy—Rezon son of Eliada.
Rezon had run away from his master,
Hadadezer king of Zobah. 24After David
defeated the army of Zobah, Rezon gathered
some men and became the leader of a small
army. They went to Damascus and settled
there, and Rezon became king of Damascus.
25Rezon ruled Aram, and he hated Israel. So
he was an enemy of Israel all the time
Solomon was alive. Both Rezon and Hadad
made trouble for Israel.

26Jeroboam son of Nebat was one of
Solomon's officers. He was an Ephraimite
from the town of Zeredah, and he was the
son of a widow named Zeruah. Jeroboam
turned against the king.

27This is the story of how Jeroboam
turned against the king. Solomon was filling
in the land and repairing the wall of
Jerusalem, the city of David, his father.
28Jeroboam was a capable man, and Solomon
saw that this young man was a good worker.
So Solomon put him over all the workers
from the tribes of Ephraim and Manasseh.

29One day as Jeroboam was leaving
Jerusalem, Ahijah, the prophet from Shiloh,
who was wearing a new coat, met him on
the road. The two men were alone out in the
country. 30Ahijah took his new coat and tore
it into twelve pieces. 31Then he said to
Jeroboam, "Take ten pieces of this coat for
yourself. The LORD, the God of Israel, says: 'I
will tear the kingdom away from Solomon
and give you ten tribes. 32But I will allow
him to control one tribe. I will do this for the
sake of my servant David and for Jerusalem,
the city I have chosen from all the tribes of
Israel. 33I will do this because Solomon has
stopped following me and has worshiped
the Sidonian god Ashtoreth, the Moabite god
Chemosh, and the Ammonite god Molech.
Solomon has not obeyed me by doing what I
said is right and obeying my laws and
commands, as his father David did.

34" 'But I will not take all the kingdom
away from Solomon. I will let him rule all
his life because of my servant David, whom
I chose, who obeyed all my commands and
laws. 35But I will take the kingdom away
from his son, and I will allow you to rule
over the ten tribes. 36I will allow Solomon's
son to continue to rule over one tribe so
that there will always be a descendant of
David, my servant, in Jerusalem, the city
where I chose to be worshiped. 37But I will
make you rule over everything you want.
You will rule over all of Israel, 38and I will
always be with you if you do what I say is
right. You must obey all my commands. If
you obey my laws and commands as David
did, I will be with you. I will make your
family a lasting family of kings, as I did for
David, and give Israel to you. 39I will punish
David's children because of this, but I will
not punish them forever.' "

Solomon's Death

40Solomon tried to kill Jeroboam, but he
ran away to Egypt, to Shishak king of Egypt,
where he stayed until Solomon died.

41Everything else King Solomon did, and
the wisdom he showed, is written in the
book of the history of Solomon. 42Solomon
ruled in Jerusalem over all Israel for forty
years. 43Then he died and was buried in
Jerusalem, the city of David, his father.
And his son Rehoboam became king in his
place.

Israel Turns Against Rehoboam

12 Rehoboam went to Shechem, where
all the Israelites had gone to make
him king. 2Jeroboam son of Nebat was still
in Egypt, where he had gone to escape from
Solomon. When Jeroboam heard about
Rehoboam being made king, he was living in
Egypt. 3After the people sent for him, he and
the people went to Rehoboam and said to
him, 4"Your father forced us to work very
hard. Now, make it easier for us, and don't
make us work as hard as he did. Then we
will serve you."
5Rehoboam answered, "Go away for three
days, and then come back to me." So the
people left.
6King Rehoboam asked the elders who
had advised Solomon during his lifetime,
"How do you think I should answer these
people?"
7They said, "You should be like a servant to
them today. If you serve them and give them
a kind answer, they will serve you always."
8But Rehoboam rejected this advice.
Instead, he asked the young men who had
grown up with him and who served as his
advisers. 9Rehoboam asked them, "What is
your advice? How should we answer these
people who said, 'Don't make us work as
hard as your father did'?"
10The young men who had grown up with
him answered, "Those people said to you,
'Your father forced us to work very hard.
Now make our work easier.' You should tell
them, 'My little finger is bigger than my
father's legs. 11He forced you to work hard,
but I will make you work even harder. My
father beat you with whips, but I will beat
you with whips that have sharp points.' "
12Rehoboam had told the people, "Come
back to me in three days." So after three days
Jeroboam and all the people returned to
Rehoboam. 13King Rehoboam spoke cruel
words to them, because he had rejected the
advice the elders had given him. 14He
followed the advice of the young men and
said to the people, "My father forced you to
work hard, but I will make you work even
harder. My father beat you with whips, but I
will beat you with whips that have sharp
points." 15So the king did not listen to the
people. The LORD caused this to happen to
keep the promise he had made to Jeroboam
son of Nebat through Ahijah, a prophet from
Shiloh.
16When all the Israelites saw that the new
king refused to listen to them, they said to
the king,

"We have no share in David!
We have no part in the son of Jesse!
People of Israel, let's go to our own homes!
Let David's son rule his own people!"

So the Israelites went home. 17But Rehoboam
still ruled over the Israelites who lived in the
towns of Judah.
18Adoniram was in charge of the forced
labor. When Rehoboam sent him to the
people of Israel, they threw stones at him
until he died. But King Rehoboam ran to his
chariot and escaped to Jerusalem. 19Since
then, Israel has been against the family of
David.
20When all the Israelites heard that
Jeroboam had returned, they called him to a
meeting and made him king over all Israel.
Only the tribe of Judah continued to follow
the family of David.
21When Rehoboam arrived in Jerusalem,
he gathered one hundred eighty thousand of
the best soldiers from the tribes of Judah and
Benjamin. As son of Solomon, Rehoboam
wanted to fight the people of Israel to take
back his kingdom.
22But God spoke his word to Shemaiah, a
man of God, saying, 23"Speak to Solomon's
son Rehoboam, the king of Judah, and to all
the people of Judah and Benjamin and the
rest of the people. Say to them, 24'The LORD
says you must not go to war against your
brothers, the Israelites. Every one of you
should go home, because I made all these
things happen.' " So they obeyed the LORD's
command and went home as the LORD had
commanded.
25Then Jeroboam made Shechem in the
mountains of Ephraim a very strong city,
and he lived there. He also went to the city
of Peniel and made it stronger.

Jeroboam Builds Golden Calves

26Jeroboam said to himself, "The kingdom
will probably go back to David's family. 27If
the people continue going to the Temple of
the LORD in Jerusalem to offer sacrifices, they
will want to be ruled again by Rehoboam.
Then they will kill me and follow Rehoboam
king of Judah."

[28]King Jeroboam asked for advice. Then he
made two golden calves. "It is too long a
journey for you to go to Jerusalem to
worship," he said to the people. "Israel, here
are your gods who brought you out of
Egypt." [29]Jeroboam put one golden calf in
the city of Bethel and the other in the city of
Dan. [30]This became a very great sin, because
the people traveled as far as Dan to worship
the calf there.

[31]Jeroboam built temples on the places of
worship. He also chose priests from all the
people, not just from the tribe of Levi. [32]And
he started a new festival on the fifteenth day
of the eighth month, just like the festival in
Judah. During that time the king offered
sacrifices on the altar, along with sacrifices
to the calves in Bethel he had made. He also
chose priests in Bethel to serve at the places
of worship he had made. [33]So Jeroboam
chose his own time for a festival for the
Israelites—the fifteenth day of the eighth
month. During that time he offered
sacrifices on the altar he had built in Bethel.
He set up a festival for the Israelites and
offered sacrifices on the altar.

The Man of God Speaks Against Bethel

13 The LORD commanded a man of God
from Judah to go to Bethel. When he
arrived, Jeroboam was standing by the altar
to offer a sacrifice. [2]The LORD had
commanded the man of God to speak
against the altar. The man said, "Altar, altar,
the LORD says to you: 'David's family will
have a son named Josiah. The priests for the
places of worship now make their sacrifices
on you, but Josiah will sacrifice those priests
on you. Human bones will be burned on
you.' " [3]That same day the man of God gave
proof that these things would happen. "This
is the LORD's sign that this will happen," he
said. "This altar will break apart, and the
ashes on it will fall to the ground."

[4]When King Jeroboam heard what the
man of God said about the altar in Bethel,
the king raised his hand from the altar and
pointed at the man. "Take him!" he said. But
when the king said this, his arm was
paralyzed, and he could not move it. [5]The
altar also broke into pieces, and its ashes fell
to the ground. This was the sign the LORD
had told the man of God to give.

[6]Then the king said to the man of God,
"Please pray to the LORD your God for me,
and ask him to heal my arm."

So the man of God prayed to the LORD, and
the king's arm was healed, becoming as it
was before.

[7]Then the king said to the man of God,
"Please come home and eat with me, and I
will give you a gift."

[8]But the man of God answered the king,
"Even if you gave me half of your kingdom, I
would not go with you. I will not eat or
drink anything in this place. [9]The LORD
commanded me not to eat or drink anything
nor to return on the same road by which I
came." [10]So he took a different road and did
not return on the same road by which he
had come to Bethel.

[11]Now an old prophet was living in
Bethel. His sons came and told him what the
man of God had done there that day. They
also told their father what he had said to
King Jeroboam. [12]The father asked, "Which
road did he use when he left?" So his sons
showed him the road the man of God from
Judah had taken. [13]Then the prophet told his
sons to put a saddle on his donkey. So they
saddled the donkey, and he left.

[14]He went after the man of God and found
him sitting under an oak tree. The prophet
asked, "Are you the man of God who came
from Judah?"

The man answered, "Yes, I am."

[15]The prophet said, "Please come home
and eat with me."

[16]"I can't go home with you," the man of
God answered. "I can't eat or drink with you
in this place. [17]The LORD said to me, 'Don't
eat or drink anything there or return on the
same road by which you came.' "

[18]Then the old prophet said, "But I also am
a prophet like you." Then he told a lie. He
said, "An angel from the LORD came to me
and told me to bring you to my home. He
said you should eat and drink with me." [19]So
the man of God went to the old prophet's
house, and he ate and drank with him there.

[20]While they were sitting at the table, the
LORD spoke his word to the old prophet.
[21]The old prophet cried out to the man of
God from Judah, "The LORD said you did not
obey him! He said you did not do what the
LORD your God commanded you. [22]The LORD
commanded you not to eat or drink
anything in this place, but you came back

and ate and drank. So your body will not be
buried in your family grave."
23 After the man of God finished eating
and drinking, the prophet put a saddle on
his donkey for him, and the man left. 24 As he
was traveling home, a lion attacked and
killed him. His body lay on the road, with
the donkey and the lion standing nearby.
25 Some men who were traveling on that
road saw the body and the lion standing
nearby. So they went to the city where the
old prophet lived and told what they had
seen.
26 The old prophet who had brought back
the man of God heard what had happened.
"It is the man of God who did not obey the
LORD's command," he said. "So the LORD sent
a lion to kill him, just as he said he would."
27 Then the prophet said to his sons, "Put a
saddle on my donkey," which they did. 28 The
old prophet went out and found the body
lying on the road, with the donkey and the
lion still standing nearby. The lion had not
eaten the body or hurt the donkey. 29 The
prophet put the body on his donkey and
carried it back to the city to have a time of
sadness for him and to bury him. 30 The
prophet buried the body in his own family
grave, and they were sad for the man of God
and said, "Oh, my brother."
31 After the prophet buried the body, he
said to his sons, "When I die, bury me in this
same grave. Put my bones next to his.
32 Through him the LORD spoke against the
altar at Bethel and against the places of
worship in the towns of Samaria. What the
LORD spoke through him will certainly come
true."
33 After this incident King Jeroboam did
not stop doing evil. He continued to choose
priests for the places of worship from among
all the people. Anyone who wanted to be a
priest for the places of worship was allowed
to be one. 34 In this way the family of
Jeroboam sinned, and this sin caused its ruin
and destruction from the earth.

Jeroboam's Son Dies

14 At that time Jeroboam's son Abijah
became very sick. 2 So Jeroboam said
to his wife, "Go to Shiloh to see the prophet
Ahijah. He is the one who said I would
become king of Israel. But dress yourself so
people won't know you are my wife. 3 Take
the prophet ten loaves of bread, some cakes,
and a jar of honey. Then ask him what will
happen to our son, and he will tell you." 4 So
the king's wife did as he said and went to
Ahijah's home in Shiloh.
Now Ahijah was very old and blind. 5 The
LORD said to him, "Jeroboam's son is sick, and
Jeroboam's wife is coming to ask you about
him. When she arrives, she will pretend to
be someone else." Then the LORD told Ahijah
what to say.
6 When Ahijah heard her walking to the
door, he said, "Come in, wife of Jeroboam.
Why are you pretending to be someone else?
I have bad news for you. 7 Go back and tell
Jeroboam that this is what the LORD, the God
of Israel, says: 'Jeroboam, I chose you from
among all the people and made you the
leader of my people Israel. 8 I tore the
kingdom away from David's family, and I
gave it to you. But you are not like my
servant David, who always obeyed my
commands and followed me with all his
heart. He did only what I said was right. 9 But
you have done more evil than anyone who
ruled before you. You have quit following
me and have made other gods and idols of
metal. This has made me very angry, 10 so I
will soon bring disaster to your family. I will
kill all the men in your family, both slaves
and free men. I will destroy your family as
completely as fire burns up manure.
11 Anyone from your family who dies in the
city will be eaten by dogs, and those who die
in the fields will be eaten by the birds. The
LORD has spoken.' "
12 Then Ahijah said to Jeroboam's wife, "Go
home now. As soon as you enter your city,
your son will die, 13 and all Israel will be sad
for him and bury him. He is the only one of
Jeroboam's family who will be buried,
because he is the only one in the king's
family who pleased the LORD, the God of
Israel.
14 "The LORD will put a new king over
Israel, who will destroy Jeroboam's family,
and this will happen soon. 15 Then the LORD
will punish Israel, which will be like reeds
swaying in the water. The LORD will pull up
Israel from this good land, the land he gave
their ancestors. He will scatter Israel beyond
the Euphrates River, because he is angry
with the people. They made the LORD angry
when they set up idols to worship Asherah.

16Jeroboam sinned, and then he made the
people of Israel sin. So the LORD will let the
people of Israel be defeated."
17Then Jeroboam's wife left and returned
to Tirzah. As soon as she entered her home,
the boy died. 18After they buried him, all
Israel had a time of sadness for him, just as
the LORD had said through his servant, the
prophet Ahijah.
19Everything else Jeroboam did is written
in the book of the history of the kings of
Israel. He fought wars and continued to rule
the people, 20serving as king for twenty-two
years. Then he died, and his son Nadab
became king in his place.

The Death of Rehoboam

21Solomon's son Rehoboam was forty-one
years old when he became king of Judah. His
mother was Naamah from Ammon.
Rehoboam ruled in Jerusalem for seventeen
years. (The LORD had chosen that city from
all the land of Israel as the place where he
would be worshiped.)
22The people of Judah did what the LORD
said was wrong. Their sins made the LORD
very angry, even more angry than he had
been at their ancestors. 23The people built
stone pillars and places to worship gods and
Asherah idols on every high hill and under
every green tree. 24There were even male
prostitutes in the land. They acted like the
people who had lived in the land before the
Israelites. They had done many evil things,
and God had taken the land away from
them.
25During the fifth year Rehoboam was
king, Shishak king of Egypt attacked
Jerusalem. 26He took the treasures from the
Temple of the LORD and the king's palace. He
took everything, even the gold shields
Solomon had made. 27So King Rehoboam
made bronze shields to put in their place
and gave them to the commanders of the
guards for the palace gates. 28Whenever the
king went to the Temple of the LORD, the
guards carried the shields. Later, they would
put them back in the guardroom.
29Everything else King Rehoboam did is
written in the book of the history of the
kings of Judah. 30There was war between
Rehoboam and Jeroboam the whole time.
31Rehoboam, son of Naamah from Ammon,
died and was buried with his ancestors in
Jerusalem, and his son Abijam[n] became king
in his place.

Abijam King of Judah

15 Abijam became king of Judah during
the eighteenth year Jeroboam son of
Nebat was king of Israel. 2Abijam ruled in
Jerusalem for three years. His mother was
Maacah daughter of Abishalom. 3He did all
the same sins his father before him had
done. Abijam was not faithful to the LORD
his God as David, his great-grandfather, had
been. 4Because the LORD loved David, the
LORD gave him a kingdom in Jerusalem and
allowed him to have a son to be king after
him. The LORD also kept Jerusalem safe.
5David always did what the LORD said was
right and obeyed his commands all his life,
except the one time when David sinned
against Uriah the Hittite.
6There was war between Abijam and
Jeroboam during Abijam's lifetime.
7Everything else Abijam did is written in the
book of the history of the kings of Judah.
During the time Abijam ruled, there was war
between Abijam and Jeroboam. 8Abijam died
and was buried in Jerusalem, and his son Asa
became king in his place.

Asa King of Judah

9During the twentieth year Jeroboam was
king of Israel, Asa became king of Judah.
10His grandmother's name was Maacah, the
daughter of Abishalom. Asa ruled in
Jerusalem for forty-one years.
11Asa did what the LORD said was right, as
his ancestor David had done. 12He forced the
male prostitutes at the worship places to
leave the country. He also took away the
idols that his ancestors had made. 13His
grandmother Maacah had made a terrible
Asherah idol, so Asa removed her from
being queen mother. He cut down that idol
and burned it in the Kidron Valley. 14The
places of worship to gods were not removed.
Even so, Asa was faithful to the LORD all his
life. 15Asa brought into the Temple of the
LORD the gifts he and his father had given:
gold, silver, and utensils.
16There was war between Asa and Baasha

14:31 Abijam A negative name for Abijah. See 2 Chronicles 13.

God's will

Most of us view God's will as a great mystery. We want to know what God wants for our lives, but we feel as though we are running up the down escalator and can never quite make it to the top. We constantly ask ourselves, "Am I in God's will?" We think the answer is somehow found in our behavior. We think if we are good enough, then maybe we are in his will.

The first step to seeking God's will is simply to seek God. Read Matthew 6:33. This verse tells us that what we should want the most is to do what God wants. He'll take care of the rest. God is preparing you from within to be all that he has called you to be. You need to know God in order to serve him. Spend time in his Word and learn under a pastor that teaches the Word of God. The more you understand the heart of God, the better equipped you will be to serve him.

The second step is believing the promises of God. Once you begin to know the ways of God, you have to apply them to your life every day. So many Christians get caught up in the routines of life and forget to practice what they know to be true. Step out in faith and minister to those in need or encourage a neighbor to come to church. These are such simple ways of serving God that are often overlooked.

Finally, learn to hear God's voice as you go about your day. The Spirit of God lives within us, and he will speak to our thoughts with ideas and encouragement when we give him the opportunity. God's will for your life is a daily occurrence. Wake up each day and ask God to show you what he has for you to do that day.

THINK ABOUT IT: Are you in the will of God?
Are you equipped to serve the Lord?
Have you connected with God lately?

DIG DEEPER: Psalm 37:5 (trust), Psalm 40:8 (obedience), and Luke 9:23 (sacrifice)

being with God

I have often wondered what it would be like to be 100 percent steady in spending time loving the Lord. It seems that in this freeway-fast lifestyle of microwaves and airplanes, there's not much that points to simply being with him. Because of that, I grab a plane ride in prayer or a commute of listening to beautiful music that reminds me of God's beauty.

Each day is a choice, an investment. There have been days I've given God much of my heart; other days, it's been pennies' worth. This sheepish soul of mine is learning that it is not in the doing with (or for) Christ so much as it is in the being with Christ that matters most to him. If you are like me, you never pray harder or listen more for God's voice than when you are broken. Tough situations often bring us to our knees. But what about when life is ironed out a bit?

God offers steady love in a chaotic world. Cars crash, people fall in love, children grow up, gas prices increase—so much of life changes about us, but not the Father. And while a daily quiet time with Christ is important, God wants so much more than a simple "check-marks-the-spot" quiet time. Whether it's quick prayers throughout the day, a verse read before going to bed, or a great coffee conversation with a friend about what Heaven is teaching you in this life, you have spent time conversing with Jesus.

In the midst of all the chaos, know that looking up is the best choice when you need a moment of quiet. God speaks in the mundane tasks of life as well as in the vibrant mountaintop experiences. Jesus wants to be with you today.

THINK ABOUT IT: What are the pressures that keep you from time with Jesus? Think about times you've been "doing" more than "being" with Christ. What steps can you take to enlarge the "being" side of that relationship?

DIG DEEPER: Isaiah 40:29–31 (God's strength for us), 1 Timothy 6:11–16 (proactive living), and Esther 4:12–14 (purpose)

redemption

When a woman talks about the life she used to live and what God is doing for her now, she is essentially saying, "I came to God with a worthless coupon and he redeemed it. He exchanged my sack of ashes for a crown of beauty. He replaced my despair with an unshakable hope."

Do you know any women who wear crowns of beauty? They are not haughty. They are thankful, lovely, and peaceful. Being pursued and embraced by God while you still smell like a fireplace is very humbling. These women walk with their heads held high, yet hearts bowed low in reverence. They speak with the wisdom of one who has known the mercy of God instead of the rambling words that come from those who have only read about him. They ache for the lost and rejoice with the found. They cry with the sinners and celebrate with the forgiven. They walk in confidence, not perfection. They have stood in the dark until God came to the rescue. They know God is present and able. They know the depths of his great love.

Receiving a crown of beauty makes these women vessels of God's grace and mercy. Women who have been forgiven much are not so quick to judge. Women who have been relieved of their debts want to release others from their bondage. These women never forget where the crown came from. It was undeserved. It replaced the ashes of brokenness and pain.

The same offer is extended to you and to me. Amazing, I know. Got some ashes you'd like to trade? The God of heaven is just waiting to see what you'll look like underneath a crown of beauty.

THINK ABOUT IT: Do you have a sack full of ashes or pain? How long have you been accumulating ashes, and how does the weight of them make you feel?
Do you know a woman who wears a crown of beauty? Describe her.
How do you redeem a coupon? How does God redeem ashes?

DIG DEEPER: Psalm 45:10–11 (your beauty), Isaiah 61:1–3 (spiritual trading), and Micah 7:18 (God's mercy)

authenticity

A friend of mine recently told me a story about her youngest son. His older brothers were in school, so her son entertained himself by making up stories and reciting them out loud while his mom, my friend, drove around in their minivan. Recently, she noticed he was making strange squeaking sounds in the middle of a story. She looked in the rearview mirror and asked, "What's wrong, honey?"

He looked up innocently and said, "I'm just fast-forwarding through the bad parts, Momma." There's a familiar story in the Gospels about an attorney who wouldn't admit he was a sinner. He tried to fast-forward through the bad parts of his life, too:

"Then an expert on the law stood up to test Jesus, saying, 'Teacher, what must I do to get life forever?'

Jesus said, 'What is written in the law? What do you read there?'

The man answered, 'Love the Lord your God with all your heart, all your soul, all your strength and all your mind.' Also, 'Love your neighbor as you love yourself.'

Jesus said to him, 'Your answer is right. Do this and you will live.'

But the man, wanting to show the importance of his question, said to Jesus, 'And who is my neighbor?'" (Luke 10:25–29).

If this guy had been honest, he would've said, "I know what the law says, Jesus, but I can't possibly live it out. I've tried, really I have, but I just can't do it! I'm a selfish nerd, and I have a tendency to cuss in traffic. Plus, I don't even like some of my neighbors, much less love them!" But instead of confessing his imperfections, this lawyer sidestepped the truth with a silly question. Mercifully, Jesus didn't punish the man's haughtiness. Instead, he tutored him on humility with a wonderful story about a kind Samaritan (Luke 10:30–37).

THINK ABOUT IT: In what circumstances are you most likely to downplay your sin and pretend you have it all together?
How can attempting to look "super spiritual" actually be harmful to your heart?

DIG DEEPER: Matthew 5:5 (humility) and 1 John 1:8–10 (forgiveness)

The Widow of Zarephath

1 KINGS 17

She blinks back tears as she gathers small pieces of wood. Her arms are thin, and the bones in her hands protrude. Her husband died before the drought, but even he could not have yielded a crop from the dry ground. Her son sleeps inside their tiny home, and she knows it won't be long before they both die.

"Would you bring me a little water in a cup so I may have a drink?" She nods to the stranger and turns to fetch the water. "Please bring me a piece of bread, too." She turns to look at him. Surely he knows there is no food! She explains that the little flour she has left was intended to feed herself and her son before they die. He takes a step toward her and speaks.

"The Lord, the God of Israel, says, 'That jar of flour will never be empty, and the jug will always have oil in it, until the day the Lord sends rain to the land.' "

She walks home and ponders the words of the man as she makes a loaf of bread. She looks into the flour pot—there seems to be enough for another loaf! She rushes the bread to the man and quickly makes another loaf for her and her son. She peeks into the pot and it isn't empty. Can it be? It will never be empty again!

God will always be our provider, sometimes giving us what we need in unexpected ways.

Elijah Brings a Boy Back to Life

17Some time later the son of the woman
who owned the house became sick. He grew
worse and worse and finally stopped
breathing. 18The woman said to Elijah, "Man
of God, what have you done to me? Did you
come here to remind me of my sin and to
kill my son?"
19Elijah said to her, "Give me your son."
Elijah took the boy from her, carried him
upstairs, and laid him on the bed in the
room where he was staying. 20Then he
prayed to the LORD: "LORD my God, this
widow is letting me stay in her house. Why
have you done this terrible thing to her and
caused her son to die?" 21Then Elijah lay on
top of the boy three times. He prayed to the
LORD, "LORD my God, let this boy live again!"
22The LORD answered Elijah's prayer; the
boy began breathing again and was alive.
23Elijah carried the boy downstairs and gave
him to his mother and said, "See! Your son is
alive!"
24"Now I know you really are a man from
God," the woman said to Elijah. "I know that
the LORD truly speaks through you!"

Elijah Kills the Prophets of Baal

18 During the third year without rain,
the LORD spoke his word to Elijah: "Go
and meet King Ahab, and I will soon send
rain." 2So Elijah went to meet Ahab.
By this time there was no food in Samaria.
3King Ahab sent for Obadiah, who was in
charge of the king's palace. (Obadiah was a
true follower of the LORD. 4When Jezebel was
killing all the LORD's prophets, Obadiah hid a
hundred of them in two caves, fifty in one
cave and fifty in another. He also brought
them food and water.) 5Ahab said to
Obadiah, "Let's check every spring and
valley in the land. Maybe we can find
enough grass to keep our horses and mules
alive and not have to kill our animals." 6So
each one chose a part of the country to
search; Ahab went in one direction and
Obadiah in another.
7While Obadiah was on his way, Elijah
met him. Obadiah recognized Elijah, so he
bowed down to the ground and said, "Elijah?
Is it really you, master?"
8"Yes," Elijah answered. "Go tell your
master that I am here."

son of Ginath to be king, while the other
half wanted Omri. 22Omri's followers were
stronger than the followers of Tibni son of
Ginath, so Tibni died, and Omri became
king.
23Omri became king of Israel during the
thirty-first year Asa was king of Judah. Omri
ruled Israel for twelve years, six of those
years in the city of Tirzah. 24He bought the
hill of Samaria from Shemer for about one
hundred fifty pounds of silver. Omri built a
city on that hill and called it Samaria after
the name of its earlier owner, Shemer.
25But Omri did what the LORD said was
wrong; he did more evil than all the kings
who came before him. 26Jeroboam son of
Nebat had led the people of Israel to sin, and
Omri sinned in the same way as Jeroboam.
The Israelites made the LORD, the God of
Israel, very angry because they worshiped
worthless idols.
27Everything else Omri did and all his
successes are written in the book of the
history of the kings of Israel. 28So Omri died
and was buried in Samaria, and his son Ahab
became king in his place.

Ahab King of Israel

29Ahab son of Omri became king of Israel
during Asa's thirty-eighth year as king of
Judah, and Ahab ruled Israel in the city of
Samaria for twenty-two years. 30More than
any king before him, Ahab son of Omri did
many things the LORD said were wrong. 31He
sinned in the same ways as Jeroboam son of
Nebat, but he did even worse things. He
married Jezebel daughter of Ethbaal, the
king of Sidon. Then Ahab began to serve
Baal and worship him. 32He built a temple in
Samaria for worshiping Baal and put an altar
there for Baal. 33Ahab also made an idol for
worshiping Asherah. He did more things to
make the LORD, the God of Israel, angry than
all the other kings before him.
34During the time of Ahab, Hiel from
Bethel rebuilt the city of Jericho. It cost Hiel
the life of Abiram, his oldest son, to begin
work on the city, and it cost the life of
Segub, his youngest son, to build the city
gates. This happened just as the LORD,
speaking through Joshua son of Nun, said it
would happen.[n]

Elijah Stops the Rain

17 Now Elijah the Tishbite was a
prophet from the settlers in Gilead. "I
serve the LORD, the God of Israel," Elijah said
to Ahab. "As surely as the LORD lives, no rain
or dew will fall during the next few years
unless I command it."
2Then the LORD spoke his word to Elijah:
3"Leave this place and go east and hide near
Kerith Ravine east of the Jordan River. 4You
may drink from the stream, and I have
commanded ravens to bring you food there."
5So Elijah did what the LORD said; he went to
Kerith Ravine, east of the Jordan, and lived
there. 6The birds brought Elijah bread and
meat every morning and evening, and he
drank water from the stream.
7After a while the stream dried up because
there was no rain. 8Then the LORD spoke his
word to Elijah, 9"Go to Zarephath in Sidon
and live there. I have commanded a widow
there to take care of you."
10So Elijah went to Zarephath. When he
reached the town gate, he saw a widow
gathering wood for a fire. Elijah asked her,
"Would you bring me a little water in a cup
so I may have a drink?" 11As she was going to
get his water, Elijah said, "Please bring me a
piece of bread, too."
12The woman answered, "As surely as the
LORD your God lives, I have no bread. I have
only a handful of flour in a jar and only a
little olive oil in a jug. I came here to gather
some wood so I could go home and cook our
last meal. My son and I will eat it and then
die from hunger."
13"Don't worry," Elijah said to her. "Go
home and cook your food as you have said.
But first make a small loaf of bread from the
flour you have, and bring it to me. Then
cook something for yourself and your son.
14The LORD, the God of Israel, says, 'That jar
of flour will never be empty, and the jug will
always have oil in it, until the day the LORD
sends rain to the land.' "
15So the woman went home and did what
Elijah told her to do. And the woman and
her son and Elijah had enough food every
day. 16The jar of flour and the jug of oil were
never empty, just as the LORD, through
Elijah, had promised.

16:34 the LORD . . . happen When Joshua destroyed Jericho, he said whoever rebuilt the city would lose his oldest and youngest sons. See Joshua 6:26.

9Then Obadiah said, "What wrong have I
done for you to hand me over to Ahab like
this? He will put me to death. 10As surely as
the LORD your God lives, the king has sent
people to every country to search for you. If
the ruler said you were not there, Ahab
forced the ruler to swear you could not be
found in his country. 11Now you want me to
go to my master and tell him, 'Elijah is here'?
12The Spirit of the LORD may carry you to
some other place after I leave. If I go tell
King Ahab you are here, and he comes and
doesn't find you, he will kill me! I have
followed the LORD since I was a boy.
13Haven't you been told what I did? When
Jezebel was killing the LORD's prophets, I hid
a hundred of them, fifty in one cave and fifty
in another. I brought them food and water.
14Now you want me to go and tell my master
you are here? He will kill me!"

15Elijah answered, "As surely as the LORD
All-Powerful lives, whom I serve, I will be
seen by Ahab today."

16So Obadiah went to Ahab and told him
where Elijah was. Then Ahab went to meet
Elijah.

17When he saw Elijah, he asked, "Is it
you—the biggest troublemaker in Israel?"

18Elijah answered, "I have not made
trouble in Israel. You and your father's
family have made all this trouble by not
obeying the LORD's commands. You have
gone after the Baals. 19Now tell all Israel to
meet me at Mount Carmel. Also bring the
four hundred fifty prophets of Baal and the
four hundred prophets of Asherah, who eat
at Jezebel's table."

20So Ahab called all the Israelites and
those prophets to Mount Carmel. 21Elijah
approached the people and said, "How long
will you not decide between two choices? If
the LORD is the true God, follow him, but if
Baal is the true God, follow him!" But the
people said nothing.

22Elijah said, "I am the only prophet of the
LORD here, but there are four hundred fifty
prophets of Baal. 23Bring two bulls. Let the
prophets of Baal choose one bull and kill it
and cut it into pieces. Then let them put the
meat on the wood, but they are not to set fire
to it. I will prepare the other bull, putting
the meat on the wood but not setting fire to
it. 24You prophets of Baal, pray to your god,
and I will pray to the LORD. The god who
answers by setting fire to his wood is the
true God."

All the people agreed that this was a good
idea.

25Then Elijah said to the prophets of Baal,
"There are many of you, so you go first.
Choose a bull and prepare it. Pray to your
god, but don't start the fire."

26So they took the bull that was given to
them and prepared it. They prayed to Baal
from morning until noon, shouting "Baal,
answer us!" But there was no sound, and no
one answered. They danced around the altar
they had built.

27At noon Elijah began to make fun of
them. "Pray louder!" he said. "If Baal really is
a god, maybe he is thinking, or busy, or
traveling! Maybe he is sleeping so you will
have to wake him!" 28The prophets prayed
louder, cutting themselves with swords and
spears until their blood flowed, which was
the way they worshiped. 29The afternoon
passed, and the prophets continued to act
like this until it was time for the evening
sacrifice. But no voice was heard; Baal did
not answer, and no one paid attention.

30Then Elijah said to all the people, "Now
come to me." So they gathered around him,
and Elijah rebuilt the altar of the LORD,
which had been torn down. 31He took twelve
stones, one stone for each of the twelve
tribes, the number of Jacob's sons. (The LORD
changed Jacob's name to Israel.) 32Elijah used
these stones to rebuild the altar in honor of
the LORD. Then he dug a ditch around the
altar that was big enough to hold about
thirteen quarts of seed. 33Elijah put the wood
on the altar, cut the bull into pieces, and laid
the pieces on the wood. 34Then he said, "Fill
four jars with water, and pour it on the meat
and on the wood." Then Elijah said, "Do it
again," and they did it again. Then he said,
"Do it a third time," and they did it the third
time. 35So the water ran off the altar and
filled the ditch.

36At the time for the evening sacrifice, the
prophet Elijah went near the altar. "LORD, you
are the God of Abraham, Isaac, and Israel," he
prayed. "Prove that you are the God of Israel
and that I am your servant. Show these
people that you commanded me to do all
these things. 37LORD, answer my prayer so
these people will know that you, LORD, are
God and that you will change their minds."

38Then fire from the LORD came down and
burned the sacrifice, the wood, the stones,
and the ground around the altar. It also dried
up the water in the ditch. 39When all the
people saw this, they fell down to the
ground, crying, "The LORD is God! The LORD
is God!"
40Then Elijah said, "Capture the prophets
of Baal! Don't let any of them run away!" The
people captured all the prophets. Then
Elijah led them down to the Kishon Valley,
where he killed them.

The Rain Comes Again

41Then Elijah said to Ahab, "Now, go, eat,
and drink, because a heavy rain is coming."
42So King Ahab went to eat and drink. At the
same time Elijah climbed to the top of
Mount Carmel, where he bent down to the
ground with his head between his knees.
43Then Elijah said to his servant, "Go and
look toward the sea."

The servant went and looked. "I see nothing," he said.

Elijah told him to go and look again. This
happened seven times. 44The seventh time,
the servant said, "I see a small cloud, the size
of a human fist, coming from the sea."

Elijah told the servant, "Go to Ahab and tell him to get his chariot ready and go home now. Otherwise, the rain will stop him."

45After a short time the sky was covered
with dark clouds. The wind began to blow,
and soon a heavy rain began to fall. Ahab got
in his chariot and started back to Jezreel.
46The LORD gave his power to Elijah, who
tightened his clothes around him and ran
ahead of King Ahab all the way to Jezreel.

Elijah Runs Away

19 King Ahab told Jezebel every thing
Elijah had done and how Elijah had
killed all the prophets with a sword. 2So
Jezebel sent a messenger to Elijah, saying,
"May the gods punish me terribly if by this
time tomorrow I don't kill you just as you
killed those prophets."
3When Elijah heard this, he was afraid
and ran for his life, taking his servant with
him. When they came to Beersheba in
Judah, Elijah left his servant there. 4Then
Elijah walked for a whole day into the
desert. He sat down under a bush and asked
to die. "I have had enough, LORD," he prayed.
"Let me die. I am no better than my
ancestors." 5Then he lay down under the tree
and slept.

Suddenly an angel came to him and
touched him. "Get up and eat," the angel
said. 6Elijah saw near his head a loaf baked
over coals and a jar of water, so he ate and
drank. Then he went back to sleep.
7Later the LORD's angel came to him a
second time. The angel touched him and
said, "Get up and eat. If you don't, the
journey will be too hard for you." 8So Elijah
got up and ate and drank. The food made
him strong enough to walk for forty days
and nights to Mount Sinai, the mountain of
God. 9There Elijah went into a cave and
stayed all night.

Then the LORD spoke his word to him: "Elijah! Why are you here?"

10He answered, "LORD God All-Powerful, I
have always served you as well as I could.
But the people of Israel have broken their
agreement with you, destroyed your altars,
and killed your prophets with swords. I am
the only prophet left, and now they are
trying to kill me, too."
11The LORD said to Elijah, "Go, stand in
front of me on the mountain, and I will pass
by you." Then a very strong wind blew until
it caused the mountains to fall apart and
large rocks to break in front of the LORD. But
the LORD was not in the wind. After the
wind, there was an earthquake, but the LORD
was not in the earthquake. 12After the
earthquake, there was a fire, but the LORD
was not in the fire. After the fire, there was a
quiet, gentle sound. 13When Elijah heard it,
he covered his face with his coat and went
out and stood at the entrance to the cave.

Then a voice said to him, "Elijah! Why are you here?"

14He answered, "LORD God All-Powerful, I
have always served you as well as I could.
But the people of Israel have broken their
agreement with you, destroyed your altars,
and killed your prophets with swords. I am
the only prophet left, and now they are
trying to kill me, too."
15The LORD said to him, "Go back on the
road that leads to the desert around
Damascus. Enter that city, and pour olive oil
on Hazael to make him king over Aram.
16Then pour oil on Jehu son of Nimshi to
make him king over Israel. Next, pour oil on

devotion 92

1 KINGS 19:11–12

THE WHISPERS OF GOD

Sometimes God comes as a whisper. I think I would recognize him more easily if he would come as an earthquake to get my attention or a pillar of fire to show me where to go. But mostly, God comes to me softly.

My life is like yours—ridiculous. Almost all I can hear clearly is one of the kids shouting, "Mommmm!" Sometimes they even yell in unison. I love them and I love my loud life, but I really want to hear the quiet, gentle sound of God. What I am learning is that I have to build time into my day to hear his whispers.

This is not some super-spiritual technique, nor is it guaranteed to work for you. But I cancel out a lot of distractions when I go into my closet or just into my bedroom, close the door, and lie on my face. There is something about the physical act of lying down in front of God that gives my soul perspective. In that moment I remember who I am and how big God is. Many times, I lie down and begin babbling. There's so much that I need to say to God. But more often, I remember to just be quiet. I expect and wait for a quiet, gentle sound that will give me stand-up instructions.

The next time you can, lie on your face and let yourself become reacquainted with quiet. I expect you'll begin to meet with God and learn to recognize his whispers.

Elisha son of Shaphat from Abel Meholah to
make him a prophet in your place. 17Jehu
will kill anyone who escapes from Hazael's
sword, and Elisha will kill anyone who
escapes from Jehu's sword. 18I have seven
thousand people left in Israel who have
never bowed down before Baal and whose
mouths have never kissed his idol."

Elisha Becomes a Prophet

19So Elijah left that place and found Elisha
son of Shaphat plowing a field with a team
of oxen. He owned twelve teams of oxen and
was plowing with the twelfth team. Elijah
came up to Elisha, took off his coat, and put
it on Elisha. 20Then Elisha left his oxen and
ran to follow Elijah. "Let me kiss my father
and my mother good-bye," Elisha said. "Then
I will go with you."

Elijah answered, "Go back. It does not
matter to me."

21So Elisha went back and took his pair of
oxen and killed them. He used their wooden
yoke for a fire. Then he cooked the meat and
gave it to the people. After they ate it, Elisha
left and followed Elijah and became his
helper.

Ben-Hadad and Ahab Go to War

20 Ben-Hadad king of Aram gathered
together all his army. There were
thirty-two kings with their horses and
chariots who went with him and surrounded
Samaria and attacked it. 2The king sent
messengers into the city to Ahab king of
Israel.

This was his message: "Ben-Hadad says,
3'Your silver and gold belong to me, as well
as the best of your wives and children.' "

4Ahab king of Israel answered, "My master
and king, I agree to what you say. I and
everything I have belong to you."

5Then the messengers came to Ahab
again. They said, "Ben-Hadad says, 'I told
you before that you must give me your
silver and gold, your wives and your
children. 6About this time tomorrow I will
send my men, who will search everywhere

in your palace and in the homes of your officers. Whatever they want they will take and carry off.' "

[7]Then Ahab called a meeting of all the elders of his country. He said, "Ben-Hadad is looking for trouble. First he said I had to give him my wives, my children, my silver, and my gold, and I have not refused him."

[8]The elders and all the people said, "Don't listen to him or agree to this."

[9]So Ahab said to Ben-Hadad's messengers, "Tell my master the king: 'I will do what you said at first, but I cannot allow this second command.' " And King Ben-Hadad's men carried the message back to him.

[10]Then Ben-Hadad sent another message to Ahab: "May the gods punish me terribly if I don't completely destroy Samaria. There won't be enough left for each of my men to get a handful of dust!"

[11]Ahab answered, "Tell Ben-Hadad, 'The man who puts on his armor should not brag. It's the man who lives to take it off who has the right to brag.' "

[12]Ben-Hadad was drinking in his tent with the other rulers when the message came from Ahab. Ben-Hadad commanded his men to prepare to attack the city, and they moved into place for battle.

[13]At the same time a prophet came to Ahab king of Israel. The prophet said, "Ahab, the LORD says to you, 'Do you see that big army? I will hand it over to you today so you will know I am the LORD.' "

[14]Ahab asked, "Who will you use to defeat them?"

The prophet answered, "The LORD says, 'The young officers of the district governors will defeat them.' "

Then the king asked, "Who will command the main army?"

The prophet answered, "You will."

[15]So Ahab gathered the young officers of the district governors, two hundred thirty-two of them. Then he called together the army of Israel, about seven thousand people in all.

[16]They marched out at noon, while Ben-Hadad and the thirty-two rulers helping him were getting drunk in their tents. [17]The young officers of the district governors attacked first. Ben-Hadad sent out scouts who told him that soldiers were coming from Samaria. [18]Ben-Hadad said, "They may be coming to fight, or they may be coming to ask for peace. In either case capture them alive."

[19]The young officers of the district governors led the attack, followed by the army of Israel. [20]Each officer of Israel killed the man who came against him. The men from Aram ran away as Israel chased them, but Ben-Hadad king of Aram escaped on a horse with some of his horsemen. [21]Ahab king of Israel led the army and destroyed the Arameans' horses and chariots. King Ahab thoroughly defeated the Aramean army.

[22]Then the prophet went to Ahab king of Israel and said, "The king of Aram will attack you again next spring. So go home now and strengthen your army and see what you need to do."

[23]Meanwhile the officers of Ben-Hadad king of Aram said to him, "The gods of Israel are mountain gods. Since we fought in a mountain area, Israel won. Let's fight them on the flat land, and then we will win. [24]This is what you should do. Don't allow the thirty-two rulers to command the armies, but put other commanders in their places. [25]Gather an army like the one that was destroyed and as many horses and chariots as before. We will fight the Israelites on flat land, and then we will win." Ben-Hadad agreed with their advice and did what they said.

[26]The next spring Ben-Hadad gathered the army of Aram and went up to Aphek to fight against Israel.

[27]The Israelites also had prepared for war. They marched out to meet the Arameans and camped opposite them. The Israelites looked like two small flocks of goats, but the Arameans covered the area.

[28]A man of God came to the king of Israel with this message: "The LORD says, 'The people of Aram say that I, the LORD, am a god of the mountains, not a god of the valleys. So I will allow you to defeat this huge army, and then you will know I am the LORD.' "

[29]The armies were camped across from each other for seven days. On the seventh day the battle began. The Israelites killed one hundred thousand Aramean soldiers in one day. [30]The rest of them ran away to the city of Aphek, where a city wall fell on twenty-seven thousand of them. Ben-Hadad also ran away to the city and hid in a room.

[31]His officers said to him, "We have heard

that the kings of Israel are trustworthy. Let's
dress in rough cloth to show our sadness,
and wear ropes on our heads. Then we will
go to the king of Israel, and perhaps he will
let you live."
[32]So they dressed in rough cloth and wore
ropes on their heads and went to the king of
Israel. They said, "Your servant Ben-Hadad
says, 'Please let me live.' "
Ahab answered, "Is he still alive? He is my
brother."
[33]Ben-Hadad's men had wanted a sign
from Ahab. So when Ahab called Ben-Hadad
his brother, they quickly said, "Yes!
Ben-Hadad is your brother."
Ahab said, "Bring him to me." When
Ben-Hadad came, Ahab asked him to join
him in the chariot.
[34]Ben-Hadad said to him, "Ahab, I will give
you back the cities my father took from your
father. And you may put shops in Damascus,
as my father did in Samaria."
Ahab said, "If you agree to this, I will
allow you to go free." So the two kings
made a peace agreement. Then Ahab let
Ben-Hadad go free.

A Prophet Speaks Against Ahab

[35]One prophet from one of the groups of
prophets told another, "Hit me!" He said this
because the LORD had commanded it, but the
other man refused. [36]The prophet said, "You
did not obey the LORD's command, so a lion
will kill you as soon as you leave me." When
the man left, a lion found him and killed
him.
[37]The prophet went to another man and
said, "Hit me, please!" So the man hit him
and hurt him. [38]The prophet wrapped his
face in a cloth so no one could tell who he
was. Then he went and waited by the road
for the king. [39]As Ahab king of Israel passed
by, the prophet called out to him. "I went to
fight in the battle," the prophet said. "One of
our men brought an enemy soldier to me.
Our man said, 'Guard this man. If he runs
away, you will have to give your life in his
place. Or, you will have to pay a fine of
seventy-five pounds of silver.' [40]But I was
busy doing other things, so the man ran
away."
The king of Israel answered, "You have
already said what the punishment is. You
must do what the man said."
[41]Then the prophet quickly took the cloth
from his face. When the king of Israel saw
him, he knew he was one of the prophets.
[42]The prophet said to the king, "This is what
the LORD says: 'You freed the man I said
should die, so your life will be taken instead
of his. The lives of your people will also be
taken instead of the lives of his people.' "
[43]Then King Ahab went back to his palace
in Samaria, angry and upset.

Ahab Takes Naboth's Vineyard

21 After these things had happened, this
is what followed. A man named
Naboth owned a vineyard in Jezreel, near the
palace of Ahab king of Israel. [2]One day Ahab
said to Naboth, "Give me your vineyard. It is
near my palace, and I want to make it into a
vegetable garden. I will give you a better
vineyard in its place, or, if you prefer, I will
pay you what it is worth."
[3]Naboth answered, "May the LORD keep
me from ever giving my land to you. It
belongs to my family."
[4]Ahab went home angry and upset,
because he did not like what Naboth from
Jezreel had said. (Naboth had said, "I will not
give you my family's land.") Ahab lay down
on his bed, turned his face to the wall, and
refused to eat.
[5]His wife, Jezebel, came in and asked him,
"Why are you so upset that you refuse to
eat?"
[6]Ahab answered, "I talked to Naboth, the
man from Jezreel. I said, 'Sell me your
vineyard, or, if you prefer, I will give you
another vineyard for it.' But Naboth refused."
[7]Jezebel answered, "Is this how you rule as
king over Israel? Get up, eat something, and
cheer up. I will get Naboth's vineyard for
you."
[8]So Jezebel wrote some letters, signed
Ahab's name to them, and used his own seal
to seal them. Then she sent them to the
elders and important men who lived in
Naboth's town. [9]The letter she wrote said:
"Declare a day during which the people are
to fast. Call the people together, and give
Naboth a place of honor among them. [10]Seat
two troublemakers across from him, and
have them say they heard Naboth speak
against God and the king. Then take Naboth
out of the city and kill him with stones."
[11]The elders and important men of Jezreel

obeyed Jezebel's command, just as she wrote
in the letters. 12They declared a special day
on which the people were to fast. And they
put Naboth in a place of honor before the
people. 13Two troublemakers sat across from
Naboth and said in front of everybody that
they had heard him speak against God and
the king. So the people carried Naboth out
of the city and killed him with stones.
14Then the leaders sent a message to Jezebel,
saying, "Naboth has been killed."
15When Jezebel heard that Naboth had
been killed, she told Ahab, "Naboth of Jezreel
is dead. Now you may go and take for
yourself the vineyard he would not sell to
you." 16When Ahab heard that Naboth of
Jezreel was dead, he got up and went to the
vineyard to take it for his own.
17At this time the LORD spoke his word to
the prophet Elijah the Tishbite. The LORD
said, 18"Go to Ahab king of Israel in Samaria.
He is at Naboth's vineyard, where he has
gone to take it as his own. 19Tell Ahab that I,
the LORD, say to him, 'You have murdered
Naboth and taken his land. So I tell you this:
In the same place the dogs licked up
Naboth's blood, they will also lick up your
blood!' "
20When Ahab saw Elijah, he said, "So you
have found me, my enemy!"
Elijah answered, "Yes, I have found you.
You have always chosen to do what the LORD
says is wrong. 21So the LORD says to you, 'I
will soon destroy you. I will kill you and
every male in your family, both slave and
free. 22Your family will be like the family of
King Jeroboam son of Nebat and like the
family of King Baasha son of Ahijah. I will
destroy you, because you have made me
angry and have led the people of Israel to
sin.'
23"And the LORD also says, 'Dogs will eat
the body of Jezebel in the city of Jezreel.'
24"Anyone in your family who dies in the
city will be eaten by dogs, and anyone who
dies in the fields will be eaten by birds."
25There was no one like Ahab who had
chosen so often to do what the LORD said was
wrong, because his wife Jezebel influenced
him to do evil. 26Ahab sinned terribly by
worshiping idols, just as the Amorite people
did. And the LORD had taken away their land
and given it to the people of Israel.
27After Elijah finished speaking, Ahab tore
his clothes. He put on rough cloth, fasted,
and even slept in the rough cloth to show
how sad and upset he was.
28The LORD spoke his word to Elijah the
Tishbite: 29"I see that Ahab is now sorry for
what he has done. So I will not cause the
trouble to come to him during his life, but I
will wait until his son is king. Then I will
bring this trouble to Ahab's family."

The Death of Ahab

22 For three years there was peace
between Israel and Aram. 2During the
third year Jehoshaphat king of Judah went to
visit Ahab king of Israel.
3At that time Ahab asked his officers, "Do
you remember that the king of Aram took
Ramoth in Gilead from us? Why have we
done nothing to get it back?" 4So Ahab asked
King Jehoshaphat, "Will you go with me to
fight at Ramoth in Gilead?"
"I will go with you," Jehoshaphat
answered. "My soldiers are yours, and my
horses are yours." 5Jehoshaphat also said to
Ahab, "But first we should ask if this is the
LORD's will."
6Ahab called about four hundred prophets
together and asked them, "Should I go to war
against Ramoth in Gilead or not?"
They answered, "Go, because the Lord will
hand them over to you."
7But Jehoshaphat asked, "Isn't there a
prophet of the LORD here? Let's ask him what
we should do."
8Then King Ahab said to Jehoshaphat,
"There is one other prophet. We could ask
the LORD through him, but I hate him. He
never prophesies anything good about me,
but something bad. He is Micaiah son of
Imlah."
Jehoshaphat said, "King Ahab, you
shouldn't say that!"
9So Ahab king of Israel told one of his
officers to bring Micaiah to him at once.
10Ahab king of Israel and Jehoshaphat
king of Judah had on their royal robes and
were sitting on their thrones at the threshing
floor, near the entrance to the gate of
Samaria. All the prophets were standing
before them, speaking their messages.
11Zedekiah son of Kenaanah had made some
iron horns. He said to Ahab, "This is what the
LORD says, 'You will use these horns to fight
the Arameans until they are destroyed.' "

[12]All the other prophets said the same
thing. "Attack Ramoth in Gilead and win,
because the LORD will hand the Arameans
over to you."

[13]The messenger who had gone to get
Micaiah said to him, "All the other prophets
are saying King Ahab will succeed. You
should agree with them and give the king a
good answer."

[14]But Micaiah answered, "As surely as the
LORD lives, I can tell him only what the LORD
tells me."

[15]When Micaiah came to Ahab, the king
asked him, "Micaiah, should we attack
Ramoth in Gilead or not?"

Micaiah answered, "Attack and win! The
LORD will hand them over to you."

[16]But Ahab said to Micaiah, "How many
times do I have to tell you to speak only the
truth to me in the name of the LORD?"

[17]So Micaiah answered, "I saw the army
of Israel scattered over the hills like sheep
without a shepherd. The LORD said, 'They
have no leaders. They should go home and
not fight.' "

[18]Then Ahab king of Israel said to
Jehoshaphat, "I told you! He never
prophesies anything good about me, but
only bad."

[19]But Micaiah said, "Hear the message
from the LORD: I saw the LORD sitting on his
throne with his heavenly army standing
near him on his right and on his left. [20]The
LORD said, 'Who will trick Ahab into
attacking Ramoth in Gilead where he will
be killed?'

"Some said one thing; some said another.
[21]Then one spirit came and stood before the
LORD and said, 'I will trick him.'

[22]"The LORD asked, 'How will you do it?'

"The spirit answered, 'I will go to Ahab's
prophets and make them tell lies.'

"So the LORD said, 'You will succeed in
tricking him. Go and do it.' "

[23]Micaiah said, "Ahab, the LORD has made
your prophets lie to you, and the LORD has
decided that disaster should come to you."

[24]Then Zedekiah son of Kenaanah went
up to Micaiah and slapped him in the face.
Zedekiah said, "Has the LORD's spirit left me
to speak through you?"

[25]Micaiah answered, "You will find out on
the day you go to hide in an inside room."

[26]Then Ahab king of Israel ordered, "Take
Micaiah and send him to Amon, the
governor of the city, and to Joash, the king's
son. [27]Tell them I said to put this man in
prison and give him only bread and water
until I return safely from the battle."

[28]Micaiah said, "Ahab, if you come back
safely from battle, the LORD has not spoken
through me. Remember my words, all you
people!"

[29]So Ahab king of Israel and Jehoshaphat
king of Judah went to Ramoth in Gilead.
[30]King Ahab said to Jehoshaphat, "I will go
into battle, but I will wear other clothes so
no one will recognize me. But you wear
your royal clothes." So Ahab wore other
clothes and went into battle.

[31]The king of Aram had ordered his
thirty-two chariot commanders, "Don't fight
with anyone—important or unimportant—
except the king of Israel." [32]When these
commanders saw Jehoshaphat, they thought
he was certainly the king of Israel, so they
turned to attack him. But Jehoshaphat began
shouting. [33]When they saw he was not King
Ahab, they stopped chasing him.

[34]By chance, a soldier shot an arrow, but
he hit Ahab king of Israel between the
pieces of his armor. King Ahab said to his
chariot driver, "Turn around and get me out
of the battle, because I am hurt!" [35]The
battle continued all day. King Ahab was
held up in his chariot and faced the
Arameans. His blood flowed down to the
bottom of the chariot. That evening he died.
[36]Near sunset a cry went out through the
army of Israel: "Each man go back to his
own city and land."

[37]In that way King Ahab died. His body
was carried to Samaria and buried there.
[38]The men cleaned Ahab's chariot at a pool
in Samaria where prostitutes bathed, and
the dogs licked his blood from the chariot.
These things happened as the LORD had said
they would.

[39]Everything else Ahab did is written in
the book of the history of the kings of Israel.
It tells about the palace Ahab built and
decorated with ivory and the cities he built.
[40]So Ahab died, and his son Ahaziah
became king in his place.

Jehoshaphat King of Judah

[41]Jehoshaphat son of Asa became king
of Judah during Ahab's fourth year as king of

Israel. 42Jehoshaphat was thirty-five years
old when he became king, and he ruled in
Jerusalem for twenty-five years. His mother's
name was Azubah daughter of Shilhi.
43Jehoshaphat was good, like his father Asa,
and he did what the LORD said was right. But
Jehoshaphat did not destroy the places
where gods were worshiped, so the people
continued offering sacrifices and burning
incense there. 44Jehoshaphat was at peace
with the king of Israel. 45Jehoshaphat fought
many wars, and these wars and his successes
are written in the book of the history of the
kings of Judah. 46There were male
prostitutes still in the places of worship
from the days of his father, Asa. So
Jehoshaphat forced them to leave.

47During this time the land of Edom had
no king; it was ruled by a governor.

48King Jehoshaphat built trading ships to
sail to Ophir for gold. But the ships were
wrecked at Ezion Geber, so they never set
sail. 49Ahaziah son of Ahab went to help
Jehoshaphat, offering to give Jehoshaphat
some men to sail with his men, but
Jehoshaphat refused.

50Jehoshaphat died and was buried with
his ancestors in Jerusalem, the city of David,
his ancestor. Then his son Jehoram became
king in his place.

Ahaziah King of Israel

51Ahaziah son of Ahab became king of
Israel in Samaria during Jehoshaphat's
seventeenth year as king over Judah.
Ahaziah ruled Israel for two years, 52and he
did what the LORD said was wrong. He did
the same evil his father Ahab, his mother
Jezebel, and Jeroboam son of Nebat had
done. All these rulers led the people of Israel
into more sin. 53Ahaziah worshiped and
served the god Baal, and this made the LORD,
the God of Israel, very angry. In these ways
Ahaziah did what his father had done.

2 Kings

Person Holding the Pen God Wrote With: Author is unknown (see explanation under 1 Kin.).

When the Text Was Written: Between 561 and 538 B.C.

Spiritual Posture of the Original Recipients: Just like the atmosphere of 1 Kings, God's people are still exhibiting signs of spiritual ADD, wavering in their commitment to him and his laws. This unfaithful behavior is compounded by the fact that many of their kings are evil idolaters.

Storyline Synopsis: Second Kings is a seamless continuation of 1 Kings. At this point in Israel's history, the original kingdom has splintered into two distinct regions: Judah, the southern kingdom that retained the holy city of Jerusalem; and Israel, the northern kingdom that retained the unique name of what had been a "theocracy" (a people and place that God claimed as his own). Second Kings chronicles over five centuries of mostly bad rulers and waning godliness in both Judah and Israel. It also covers the eventual defeat Israel suffered at the hands of Assyria (2 Kin. 17:22–23) and Babylon's capture of Judah, resulting in what's commonly called the Jewish "exile" (chapter 25). Perhaps an apt title for these twenty-five chapters would be: *God's Children's Persistent Rebellion Has Very Painful Consequences.*

A Moment Worth Discussing: The ministry of the prophet Elisha, who followed in the mostly faithful footsteps of his mentor, Elijah the Tishbite, provides many of the bright spots in this book. Comparing and contrasting the careers of these two representatives of God would make for a fascinating discussion. One of the most interesting déjà vu miracles that God accomplishes through these two prophets involves a woman, her only expired son, and some life-giving, full-body contact (1 Kin. 17:17–24 and 2 Kin. 4:8–37). This serves as yet another example that the Bible is definitely not boring!

Interesting (But Likely to Be Overlooked) Character: *Jehosheba*, a very brave young girl who just happens to be the daughter of a king. (See the connection?) Her selfless actions save a little boy's life, protecting him from his wicked grandmother, a total witch of a woman who was bent on his murder (2 Kin. 11:1–3).

Elijah and King Ahaziah

1 After Ahab died, Moab broke away from Israel's rule. 2 Ahaziah fell down through the wooden bars in his upstairs room in Samaria and was badly hurt. He sent messengers and told them, "Go, ask Baal-Zebub, god of Ekron, if I will recover from my injuries."

3 But the LORD's angel said to Elijah the Tishbite, "Go up and meet the messengers sent by the king of Samaria. Ask them, 'Why are you going to ask questions of Baal-Zebub, god of Ekron? Is it because you think there is no God in Israel?' 4 This is what the LORD says: 'You will never get up from the bed you are lying on; you will die.' " Then Elijah left.

5 When the messengers returned to Ahaziah, he asked them, "Why have you returned?"

6 They said, "A man came to meet us. He said, 'Go back to the king who sent you and tell him what the LORD says: "Why do you send messengers to ask questions of Baal-Zebub, god of Ekron? Is it because you think there is no God in Israel? You will never get up from the bed you are lying on; you will die." ' "

7 Ahaziah asked them, "What did the man look like who met you and told you this?"

8 They answered, "He was a hairy man and wore a leather belt around his waist."

Ahaziah said, "It was Elijah the Tishbite."

9 Then he sent a captain with his fifty men to Elijah. The captain went to Elijah, who was sitting on top of the hill, and said to him, "Man of God, the king says, 'Come down!' "

10 Elijah answered the captain, "If I am a man of God, let fire come down from heaven and burn up you and your fifty men." Then fire came down from heaven and burned up the captain and his fifty men.

11 Ahaziah sent another captain and fifty men to Elijah. The captain said to him, "Man of God, this is what the king says: 'Come down quickly!' "

12 Elijah answered, "If I am a man of God, let fire come down from heaven and burn up you and your fifty men!" Then fire came down from heaven and burned up the captain and his fifty men.

13 Ahaziah then sent a third captain with his fifty men. The third captain came and fell down on his knees before Elijah and begged, "Man of God, please respect my life and the lives of your fifty servants. 14 See, fire came down from heaven and burned up the first two captains of fifty with all their men. But now, respect my life."

15 The LORD's angel said to Elijah, "Go down with him and don't be afraid of him." So Elijah got up and went down with him to see the king.

16 Elijah told Ahaziah, "This is what the LORD says: 'You have sent messengers to ask questions of Baal-Zebub, god of Ekron. Is it because you think there is no God in Israel to ask? Because of this, you will never get up from your bed; you will die.' " 17 So Ahaziah died, just as the LORD, through Elijah, had said he would.

Joram became king in Ahaziah's place during the second year Jehoram son of Jehoshaphat was king of Judah. Joram ruled because Ahaziah had no son to take his place. 18 The other things Ahaziah did are written in the book of the history of the kings of Israel.

Elijah Is Taken to Heaven

2 It was almost time for the LORD to take Elijah by a whirlwind up into heaven. While Elijah and Elisha were leaving Gilgal, 2 Elijah said to Elisha, "Please stay here. The LORD has told me to go to Bethel."

But Elisha said, "As the LORD lives, and as you live, I won't leave you." So they went down to Bethel. 3 The groups of prophets at Bethel came out to Elisha and said to him, "Do you know the LORD will take your master away from you today?"

Elisha said, "Yes, I know, but don't talk about it."

4 Elijah said to him, "Stay here, Elisha, because the LORD has sent me to Jericho."

But Elisha said, "As the LORD lives, and as you live, I won't leave you."

So they went to Jericho. 5 The groups of prophets at Jericho came to Elisha and said, "Do you know that the LORD will take your master away from you today?"

Elisha answered, "Yes, I know, but don't talk about it."

6 Elijah said to Elisha, "Stay here. The LORD has sent me to the Jordan River."

Elisha answered, "As the LORD lives, and as you live, I won't leave you."

So the two of them went on. 7Fifty men of the groups of prophets came and stood far from where Elijah and Elisha were by the Jordan. 8Elijah took off his coat, rolled it up, and hit the water. The water divided to the right and to the left, and Elijah and Elisha crossed over on dry ground.

9After they had crossed over, Elijah said to Elisha, "What can I do for you before I am taken from you?"

Elisha said, "Leave me a double share of your spirit."[n]

10Elijah said, "You have asked a hard thing. But if you see me when I am taken from you, it will be yours. If you don't, it won't happen."

11As they were walking and talking, a chariot and horses of fire appeared and separated Elijah from Elisha. Then Elijah went up to heaven in a whirlwind. 12Elisha saw it and shouted, "My father! My father! The chariots of Israel and their horsemen!" And Elisha did not see him anymore. Then Elisha grabbed his own clothes and tore them to show how sad he was.

13He picked up Elijah's coat that had fallen from him. Then he returned and stood on the bank of the Jordan. 14Elisha hit the water with Elijah's coat and said, "Where is the LORD, the God of Elijah?" When he hit the water, it divided to the right and to the left, and Elisha crossed over.

15The groups of prophets at Jericho were watching and said, "Elisha now has the spirit Elijah had." And they came to meet him, bowing down to the ground before him. 16They said to him, "There are fifty strong men with us. Please let them go and look for your master. Maybe the Spirit of the LORD has taken Elijah up and set him down on some mountain or in some valley."

But Elisha answered, "No, don't send them."

17When the groups of prophets had begged Elisha until he couldn't refuse them anymore, he said, "Send them." So they sent fifty men who looked for three days, but they could not find him. 18Then they came back to Elisha at Jericho where he was staying. He said to them, "I told you not to go, didn't I?"

Elisha Makes the Water Pure

19The people of the city said to Elisha, "Look, master, this city is a nice place to live as you can see. But the water is so bad the land cannot grow crops."

20Elisha said, "Bring me a new bowl and put salt in it." So they brought it to him.

21Then he went out to the spring and threw the salt in it. He said, "This is what the LORD says: 'I have healed this water. From now on it won't cause death, and it won't keep the land from growing crops.' " 22So the water has been healed to this day just as Elisha had said.

Boys Make Fun of Elisha

23From there Elisha went up to Bethel. On the way some boys came out of the city and made fun of him. They said to him, "Go up too, you baldhead! Go up too, you baldhead!" 24Elisha turned around, looked at them, and put a curse on them in the name of the LORD. Then two mother bears came out of the woods and tore forty-two of the boys to pieces. 25Elisha went to Mount Carmel and from there he returned to Samaria.

War Between Israel and Moab

3 Joram son of Ahab became king over Israel at Samaria in Jehoshaphat's eighteenth year as king of Judah. And Joram ruled twelve years. 2He did what the LORD said was wrong, but he was not like his father and mother; he removed the stone pillars his father had made for Baal. 3But he continued to sin like Jeroboam son of Nebat who had led Israel to sin. Joram did not stop doing these same sins.

4Mesha king of Moab raised sheep. He paid the king of Israel one hundred thousand lambs and the wool of one hundred thousand sheep. 5But when Ahab died, the king of Moab turned against the king of Israel. 6So King Joram went out from Samaria and gathered Israel's army. 7He also sent messengers to Jehoshaphat king of Judah. "The king of Moab has turned against me," he said. "Will you go with me to fight Moab?"

Jehoshaphat replied, "I will go with you. My soldiers and my horses are yours."

2:9 Leave . . . spirit By law, the first son in a family would inherit a double share of his father's possessions. Elisha is asking to inherit a share of his master's power as his follower. He is not asking for twice as much power as Elijah had.

[8]Jehoshaphat asked, "Which way should
we attack?"
Joram answered, "Through the Desert of
Edom."
[9]So the king of Israel went with the king
of Judah and the king of Edom. After they
had marched seven days, there was no more
water for the army or for their animals that
were with them. [10]The king of Israel said,
"This is terrible! The LORD has called us three
kings together to hand us over to the
Moabites!"
[11]But Jehoshaphat asked, "Is there a
prophet of the LORD here? We can ask the
LORD through him."
An officer of the king of Israel answered,
"Elisha son of Shaphat is here. He was
Elijah's servant."
[12]Jehoshaphat said, "He speaks the LORD's
truth." So the king of Israel and Jehoshaphat
and the king of Edom went down to see
Elisha.
[13]Elisha said to the king of Israel, "I have
nothing to do with you. Go to the prophets
of your father and to the prophets of your
mother!"
The king of Israel said to Elisha, "No, the
LORD has called us three kings together to
hand us over to the Moabites."
[14]Elisha said, "As surely as the LORD
All-Powerful lives, whom I serve, I tell you
the truth. I wouldn't even look at you or
notice you if Jehoshaphat king of Judah were
not here. I respect him. [15]Now bring me
someone who plays the harp."
While the harp was being played, the
LORD gave Elisha power. [16]Then Elisha said,
"The LORD says to dig holes in the valley.
[17]The LORD says you won't see wind or rain,
but the valley will be filled with water. Then
you, your cattle, and your other animals can
drink. [18]This is easy for the LORD to do; he
will also hand Moab over to you. [19]You will
destroy every strong, walled city and every
important town. You will cut down every
good tree and stop up all springs. You will
ruin every good field with rocks."
[20]The next morning, about the time the
sacrifice was offered, water came from the
direction of Edom and filled the valley.
[21]All the Moabites heard that the kings
had come up to fight against them. So they
gathered everyone old enough to put on
armor and waited at the border. [22]But
when the Moabites got up early in the
morning, the sun was shining on the water.
They saw the water across from them, and it
looked as red as blood. [23]Then they said,
"This is blood! The kings must have fought
and killed each other! Come, Moabites, let's
take the valuables from the dead bodies!"
[24]When the Moabites came to the camp of
Israel, the Israelites came out and fought
them until they ran away. Then the Israelites
went on into the land, killing the Moabites.
[25]They tore down the cities and threw rocks
all over every good field. They stopped up all
the springs and cut down all the good trees.
Kir Hareseth was the only city with its stones
still in place, but the men with slingshots
surrounded it and conquered it, too.
[26]When the king of Moab saw that the
battle was too much for him, he took seven
hundred men with swords to try to break
through to the king of Edom. But they could
not break through. [27]Then the king of Moab
took his oldest son, who would have been
king after him, and offered him as a burnt
offering on the wall. So there was great
anger against the Israelites, who left and
went back to their own land.

A Widow Asks Elisha for Help

4 The wife of a man from the groups of
prophets said to Elisha, "Your servant, my
husband, is dead. You know he honored the
LORD. But now the man he owes money to is
coming to take my two boys as his slaves!"
[2]Elisha answered, "How can I help you?
Tell me, what do you have in your house?"
The woman said, "I don't have anything
there except a pot of oil."
[3]Then Elisha said, "Go and get empty jars
from all your neighbors. Don't ask for just a
few. [4]Then go into your house and shut the
door behind you and your sons. Pour oil into
all the jars, and set the full ones aside."
[5]So she left Elisha and shut the door
behind her and her sons. As they brought
the jars to her, she poured out the oil. [6]When
the jars were all full, she said to her son,
"Bring me another jar."
But he said, "There are no more jars." Then
the oil stopped flowing.
[7]She went and told Elisha. And the
prophet said to her, "Go, sell the oil and pay
what you owe. You and your sons can live on
what is left."

devotion 93

2 KINGS 3:18

IS SEX LIKE DIGGING DITCHES?

The women I counsel consistently share with me that they have sex with their spouses less than two or three times a month. When I ask why, I get a list of reasons: the kids, our schedules, too tired, insecurities, no desire, and poor communication. The problem is, Christian men are attacked by Satan just like all men are. Satan pushes on this door constantly. If you've left the door cracked by withholding sex or by not making it a priority, Satan doesn't even need to use pretty women and pornography. He can use the lack of intimacy in your own home.

Even if sex sometimes (or usually) feels like one more to-do before bedtime, I want to encourage you to clear your list of excuses. If your schedule is crazy, plan it! Put the kids in bed early—*their* beds! And wear whatever makes you feel the sexiest. For me, it's my husband's white button-down shirt that is three times too big. It makes me feel three sizes smaller! If the desire's not there, ask God to provide it.

In Elisha's day, God told the people to dig ditches and they would receive water. Just like God met Israel's need, sexual intimacy meets a very real marital need. Making intimacy a priority is like water for your relationship—it brings new vitality and refreshment to the driest days. Start putting these ideas into practice—you'll find that you and your husband will be operating in some new, very beautiful ways.

The Shunammite Woman

8One day Elisha went to Shunem, where
an important woman lived. She begged
Elisha to stay and eat. So every time Elisha
passed by, he stopped there to eat. 9The
woman said to her husband, "I know that
this is a holy man of God who passes by our
house all the time. 10Let's make a small room
on the roof[n] and put a bed in the room for
him. We can put a table, a chair, and a
lampstand there. Then when he comes by,
he can stay there."

11One day Elisha came to the woman's
house. After he went to his room and rested,
12he said to his servant Gehazi, "Call the
Shunammite woman."

When the servant had called her, she
stood in front of him. 13Elisha had told his
servant, "Now say to her, 'You have gone to
all this trouble for us. What can I do for you?
Do you want me to speak to the king or the
commander of the army for you?' "

She answered, "I live among my own
people."

14Elisha said to Gehazi, "But what can we
do for her?"

He answered, "She has no son, and her
husband is old."

15Then Elisha said to Gehazi, "Call her."
When he called her, she stood in the
doorway. 16Then Elisha said, "About this
time next year, you will hold a son in your
arms."

The woman said, "No, master, man of God,
don't lie to me, your servant!"

17But the woman became pregnant and
gave birth to a son at that time the next year,
just as Elisha had told her.

18The boy grew up and one day went out
to his father, who was with the grain

4:10 roof In Bible times houses were built with flat roofs. The roof was used for drying things such as flax and fruit. And it was used as an extra room, as a place for worship, and as a cool place to sleep in the summer.

harvesters. 19The boy said to his father, "My
head! My head!"
The father said to his servant, "Take him
to his mother!" 20The servant took him to his
mother, and he lay on his mother's lap until
noon. Then he died. 21So she took him up
and laid him on Elisha's bed. Then she shut
the door and left.
22She called to her husband, "Send me one
of the servants and one of the donkeys. Then
I can go quickly to the man of God and
return."
23The husband said, "Why do you want to
go to him today? It isn't the New Moon or
the Sabbath day."
She said, "It will be all right."
24Then she saddled the donkey and said to
her servant, "Lead on. Don't slow down for
me unless I tell you." 25So she went to Elisha,
the man of God, at Mount Carmel.
When he saw her coming from far away,
he said to his servant Gehazi, "Look, there's
the Shunammite woman! 26Run to meet her
and ask, 'Are you all right? Is your husband
all right? Is the boy all right?' "
She answered, "Everything is all right."
27Then she came to Elisha at the hill and
grabbed his feet. Gehazi came near to pull
her away, but Elisha said to him, "Leave her
alone. She's very upset, and the LORD has not
told me about it. He has hidden it from me."
28She said, "Master, did I ask you for a son?
Didn't I tell you not to lie to me?"
29Then Elisha said to Gehazi, "Get ready.
Take my walking stick in your hand and go
quickly. If you meet anyone, don't say hello.
If anyone greets you, don't respond. Lay my
walking stick on the boy's face."
30The boy's mother said, "As surely as the
LORD lives and as you live, I won't leave you!"
So Elisha got up and followed her.
31Gehazi went on ahead and laid the
walking stick on the boy's face, but the boy
did not talk or move. Then Gehazi went
back to meet Elisha. "The boy has not
awakened," he said.
32When Elisha came into the house, the
boy was lying dead on his bed. 33Elisha
entered the room and shut the door, so only
he and the boy were in the room. Then he
prayed to the LORD. 34He went to the bed and
lay on the boy, putting his mouth on the
boy's mouth, his eyes on the boy's eyes, and
his hands on the boy's hands. He stretched
himself out on top of the boy. Soon the boy's
skin became warm. 35Elisha turned away and
walked around the room. Then he went back
and put himself on the boy again. The boy
sneezed seven times and opened his eyes.
36Elisha called Gehazi and said, "Call the
Shunammite!" So he did. When she came,
Elisha said, "Pick up your son." 37She came
in and fell at Elisha's feet, bowing facedown
to the floor. Then she picked up her son and
went out.

Elisha and the Stew

38When Elisha returned to Gilgal, there
was a shortage of food in the land. While the
groups of prophets were sitting in front of
him, he said to his servant, "Put the large pot
on the fire, and boil some stew for these
men."
39One of them went out into the field to
gather plants. Finding a wild vine, he picked
fruit from the vine and filled his robe with it.
Then he came and cut up the fruit into the
pot. But they didn't know what kind of fruit
it was. 40They poured out the stew for the
others to eat. When they began to eat it, they
shouted, "Man of God, there's death in the
pot!" And they could not eat it.
41Elisha told them to bring some flour. He
threw it into the pot and said, "Pour it out for
the people to eat." Then there was nothing
harmful in the pot.

Elisha Feeds the People

42A man from Baal Shalishah came to
Elisha, bringing him twenty loaves of barley
bread from the first harvest. He also brought
fresh grain in his sack. Elisha said, "Give it to
the people to eat."
43Elisha's servant asked, "How can I feed a
hundred people with so little?"
"Give the bread to the people to eat,"
Elisha said. "This is what the LORD says:
'They will eat and will have food left over.' "
44After he gave it to them, the people ate and
had food left over, as the LORD had said.

Naaman Is Healed

5 Naaman was commander of the army of
the king of Aram. He was honored by his
master, and he had much respect because
the LORD used him to give victory to Aram.
He was a mighty and brave man, but he had
a skin disease.

2 The Arameans had gone out to raid the
Israelites and had taken a little girl as a
captive. This little girl served Naaman's wife.
3 She said to her mistress, "I wish my master
would meet the prophet who lives in
Samaria. He would cure him of his disease."

4 Naaman went to the king and told him
what the girl from Israel had said. 5 The king
of Aram said, "Go ahead, and I will send a
letter to the king of Israel." So Naaman left
and took with him about seven hundred
fifty pounds of silver, as well as one hundred
fifty pounds of gold and ten changes of
clothes. 6 He brought the letter to the king of
Israel, which read, "I am sending my servant
Naaman to you so you can heal him of his
skin disease."

7 When the king of Israel read the letter,
he tore his clothes to show how upset he
was. He said, "I'm not God! I can't kill and
make alive again! Why does this man send
someone with a skin disease for me to heal?
You can see that the king of Aram is trying
to start trouble with me."

8 When Elisha, the man of God, heard that
the king of Israel had torn his clothes, he
sent the king this message: "Why have you
torn your clothes? Let Naaman come to me.
Then he will know there is a prophet in
Israel." 9 So Naaman went with his horses
and chariots to Elisha's house and stood
outside the door.

10 Elisha sent Naaman a messenger who
said, "Go and wash in the Jordan River seven
times. Then your skin will be healed, and
you will be clean."

11 Naaman became angry and left. He said,
"I thought Elisha would surely come out and
stand before me and call on the name of the
LORD his God. I thought he would wave his
hand over the place and heal the disease.
12 The Abana and the Pharpar, the rivers of
Damascus, are better than all the waters of
Israel. Why can't I wash in them and become
clean?" So Naaman went away very angry.

13 Naaman's servants came near and said to
him, "My father, if the prophet had told you
to do some great thing, wouldn't you have
done it? Doesn't it make more sense just to
do it? After all, he only told you, 'Wash, and
you will be clean.' " 14 So Naaman went down
and dipped in the Jordan seven times, just as
Elisha had said. Then his skin became new
again, like the skin of a child. And he was
clean.

15 Naaman and all his group returned to
Elisha. He stood before Elisha and said,
"Look, I now know there is no God in all the
earth except in Israel. Now please accept a
gift from me."

16 But Elisha said, "As surely as the LORD
lives whom I serve, I won't accept anything."
Naaman urged him to take the gift, but he
refused.

17 Then Naaman said, "If you won't take
the gift, then please give me some soil—as
much as two of my mules can carry. From
now on I'll not offer any burnt offering or
sacrifice to any other gods but the LORD.
18 But let the LORD pardon me for this: When
my master goes into the temple of Rimmon[n]
to worship, he leans on my arm. Then I must
bow in that temple. May the LORD pardon
me when I do that."

19 Elisha said to him, "Go in peace."

Naaman left Elisha and went a short way.
20 Gehazi, the servant of Elisha the man of
God, thought, "My master has not accepted
what Naaman the Aramean brought. As
surely as the LORD lives, I'll run after him and
get something from him." 21 So Gehazi went
after Naaman.

When Naaman saw someone running
after him, he got off the chariot to meet
Gehazi. He asked, "Is everything all right?"

22 Gehazi said, "Everything is all right. My
master has sent me. He said, 'Two young
men from the groups of prophets in the
mountains of Ephraim just came to me.
Please give them seventy-five pounds of
silver and two changes of clothes.' "

23 Naaman said, "Please take one hundred
fifty pounds," and he urged Gehazi to take it.
He tied one hundred fifty pounds of silver in
two bags with two changes of clothes. Then
he gave them to two of his servants to carry
for Gehazi. 24 When they came to the hill,
Gehazi took these things from Naaman's
servants and put them in the house. Then he
let Naaman's servants go, and they left.

25 When he came in and stood before his
master, Elisha said to him, "Where have you
been, Gehazi?"

"I didn't go anywhere," he answered.

5:18 temple of Rimmon The place where the Aramean people worshiped the god Rimmon.

26But Elisha said to him, "My spirit was
with you. I knew when the man turned from
his chariot to meet you. This isn't a time to
take money, clothes, olives, grapes, sheep,
oxen, male servants, or female servants. 27So
Naaman's skin disease will come on you and
your children forever." When Gehazi left
Elisha, he had the disease and was as white
as snow.

An Axhead Floats

6 The groups of prophets said to Elisha,
"The place where we meet with you is
too small for us. 2Let's go to the Jordan River.
There everyone can get a log, and let's build
a place there to live."
Elisha said, "Go."
3One of them said, "Please go with us."
Elisha answered, "I will go," 4so he went
with them. When they arrived at the Jordan,
they cut down some trees. 5As one man was
cutting down a tree, the head of his ax fell
into the water. He yelled, "Oh, my master! I
borrowed that ax!"
6Elisha asked, "Where did it fall?" The
man showed him the place. Then Elisha cut
down a stick and threw it into the water, and
it made the iron head float. 7Elisha said,
"Pick up the axhead." Then the man reached
out and took it.

Elisha and the Blinded Arameans

8The king of Aram was at war with Israel.
He had a council meeting with his officers
and said, "I will set up my camp in this
place."
9Elisha, the man of God, sent a message to
the king of Israel, saying, "Be careful! Don't
pass that place, because the Arameans are
going down there!"
10The king of Israel checked the place
about which Elisha had warned him. Elisha
warned him several times, so the king
protected himself there.
11The king of Aram was angry about this.
He called his officers together and
demanded, "Tell me who of us is working for
the king of Israel."
12One of the officers said, "None, my
master and king. It's Elisha, the prophet
from Israel. He can tell you what you speak
in your bedroom."
13The king said, "Go and find him so I can
send men and catch him."
The servants came back and reported, "He
is in Dothan."
14Then the king sent horses, chariots, and
many troops to Dothan. They arrived at
night and surrounded the city.
15Elisha's servant got up early, and when
he went out, he saw an army with horses
and chariots all around the city. The servant
said to Elisha, "Oh, my master, what can we
do?"
16Elisha said, "Don't be afraid. The army
that fights for us is larger than the one
against us."
17Then Elisha prayed, "LORD, open my
servant's eyes, and let him see."
The LORD opened the eyes of the young
man, and he saw that the mountain was full
of horses and chariots of fire all around
Elisha.
18As the enemy came down toward Elisha,
he prayed to the LORD, "Make these people
blind." So he made the Aramean army blind,
as Elisha had asked.
19Elisha said to them, "This is not the
right road or the right city. Follow me and I'll
take you to the man you are looking for."
Then Elisha led them to Samaria.
20After they entered Samaria, Elisha said,
"LORD, open these men's eyes so they can
see." So the LORD opened their eyes, and the
Aramean army saw that they were inside the
city of Samaria!
21When the king of Israel saw the
Aramean army, he said to Elisha, "My father,
should I kill them? Should I kill them?"
22Elisha answered, "Don't kill them. You
wouldn't kill people whom you captured
with your sword and bow. Give them food
and water, and let them eat and drink and
then go home to their master." 23So he
prepared a great feast for the Aramean army.
After they ate and drank, the king sent them
away, and they went home to their master.
The soldiers of Aram did not come anymore
into the land of Israel.

A Shortage of Food

24Later, Ben-Hadad king of Aram gathered
his whole army and surrounded and
attacked Samaria. 25There was a shortage of
food in Samaria. It was so bad that a
donkey's head sold for about two pounds of
silver, and half of a pint of dove's dung sold
for about two ounces of silver.

devotion 94

2 KINGS 6:16–17

DO YOU SEE THEM?

We left the dentist's office and headed toward the mall. My three-year-old was in her car seat as I drove. It happened so quickly that I didn't have time to react. Another car hit us broadside, and our minivan flipped over. Immediately, someone was at the side of our van calling my daughter's name. "You're okay! We're going to get you out." He opened the back door and crawled through to my daughter, talking to her as he came. He reached over me and turned off the car engine. I undid my seatbelt, got my baby, and we climbed out of the van.

I sat on the side of the road with the paramedic while he checked us out. He told me that he had never seen an accident where the car flipped over and the people inside didn't even have a scratch. We were not even *bruised*. I told the paramedic that someone had helped us when the accident first happened. I assumed the man was someone from our church because he knew my child's name. The paramedic told me that no one was around when he arrived. At that moment, I knew God sent us an angel that day.

When Elisha prayed that God would open the young man's eyes, the man could suddenly see angels all around even though he hadn't known they were there. That's what God did for me. You never know—he may send an angel to you, too, when you least expect it.

26As the king of Israel was passing by on
the wall, a woman yelled out to him, "Help
me, my master and king!"
27The king said, "If the LORD doesn't help
you, how can I? Can I get help from the
threshing floor or from the winepress?"
28Then the king said to her, "What is your
trouble?"
She answered, "This woman said to me,
'Give up your son so we can eat him today.
Then we will eat my son tomorrow.' 29So we
boiled my son and ate him. Then the next
day I said to her, 'Give up your son so we can
eat him.' But she had hidden him."
30When the king heard the woman's
words, he tore his clothes in grief. As he
walked along the wall, the people looked
and saw he had on rough cloth under his
clothes to show his sadness. 31He said, "May
God punish me terribly if the head of Elisha
son of Shaphat isn't cut off from his body
today!"
32The king sent a messenger to Elisha,
who was sitting in his house with the elders.
But before the messenger arrived, Elisha said
to them, "See, this murderer is sending men
to cut off my head. When the messenger
arrives, shut the door and hold it; don't let
him in. The sound of his master's feet is
behind him."
33Elisha was still talking with the leaders
when the messenger arrived. The king said,
"This trouble has come from the LORD. Why
should I wait for the LORD any longer?"
7 Elisha said, "Listen to the LORD's word.
This is what the LORD says: 'About this
time tomorrow seven quarts of fine flour
will be sold for two-fifths of an ounce of
silver, and thirteen quarts of barley will
be sold for two-fifths of an ounce of
silver. This will happen at the gate of
Samaria.' "
2Then the officer who was close to the
king answered Elisha, "Even if the LORD
opened windows in the sky, that couldn't
happen."
Elisha said, "You will see it with your eyes,
but you will not eat any of it."

3There were four men with a skin disease at the entrance to the city gate. They said to each other, "Why do we sit here until we die? 4There is no food in the city. So if we go into the city, we will die there. If we stay here, we will die. So let's go to the Aramean camp. If they let us live, we will live. If they kill us, we die."

5So they got up at twilight and went to the Aramean camp, but when they arrived, no one was there. 6The Lord had caused the Aramean army to hear the sound of chariots, horses, and a large army. They had said to each other, "The king of Israel has hired the Hittite and Egyptian kings to attack us!" 7So they got up and ran away in the twilight, leaving their tents, horses, and donkeys. They left the camp standing and ran for their lives.

8When the men with the skin disease came to the edge of the camp, they went into one of the tents and ate and drank. They carried silver, gold, and clothes out of the camp and hid them. Then they came back and entered another tent. They carried things from this tent and hid them, also. 9Then they said to each other, "We're doing wrong. Today we have good news, but we are silent. If we wait until the sun comes up, we'll be discovered. Let's go right now and tell the people in the king's palace."

10So they went and called to the gatekeepers of the city. They said, "We went to the Aramean camp, but no one is there; we didn't hear anyone. The horses and donkeys were still tied up, and the tents were still standing." 11Then the gatekeepers shouted out and told the people in the palace.

12The king got up in the night and said to his officers, "I'll tell you what the Arameans are doing to us. They know we are starving. They have gone out of the camp to hide in the field. They're saying, 'When the Israelites come out of the city, we'll capture them alive. Then we'll enter the city.' "

13One of his officers answered, "Let some men take five of the horses that are still left in the city. These men are like all the Israelites who are left; they are also about to die. Let's send them to see what has happened."

14So the men took two chariots with horses. The king sent them after the Aramean army, saying, "Go and see what has happened." 15The men followed the Aramean army as far as the Jordan River. The road was full of clothes and equipment that the Arameans had thrown away as they had hurriedly left. So the messengers returned and told the king. 16Then the people went out and took valuables from the Aramean camp. So seven quarts of fine flour were sold for two-fifths of an ounce of silver, and thirteen quarts of barley were sold for two-fifths of an ounce of silver, just as the LORD had said.

17The king chose the officer who was close to him to guard the gate, but the people trampled the officer to death. This happened just as Elisha had told the king when the king came to his house. 18He had said, "Thirteen quarts of barley and seven quarts of fine flour will each sell for two-fifths of an ounce of silver about this time tomorrow at the gate of Samaria."

19But the officer had answered, "Even if the LORD opened windows in the sky, that couldn't happen." And Elisha had told him, "You will see it with your eyes, but you won't eat any of it." 20It happened to the officer just that way. The people trampled him in the gateway, and he died.

The Shunammite Regains Her Land

8 Elisha spoke to the woman whose son he had brought back to life. He said, "Get up and go with your family. Stay any place you can, because the LORD has called for a time without food that will last seven years." 2So the woman got up and did as the man of God had said. She left with her family, and they stayed in the land of the Philistines for seven years. 3After seven years she returned from the land of the Philistines and went to beg the king for her house and land. 4The king was talking with Gehazi, the servant of the man of God. The king had said, "Please tell me all the great things Elisha has done." 5Gehazi was telling the king how Elisha had brought a dead boy back to life. Just then the woman whose son Elisha had brought back to life came and begged the king for her house and land.

Gehazi said, "My master and king, this is the woman, and this is the son Elisha brought back to life."

6The king asked the woman, and she told

him about it. Then the king chose an officer to help her. "Give the woman everything that is hers," the king said. "Give her all the money made from her land from the day she left until now."

Ben-Hadad Is Killed

7 Then Elisha went to Damascus, where Ben-Hadad king of Aram was sick. Someone told him, "The man of God has arrived."

8 The king said to Hazael, "Take a gift in your hand and go meet him. Ask the LORD through him if I will recover from my sickness."

9 So Hazael went to meet Elisha, taking with him a gift of forty camels loaded with every good thing in Damascus. He came and stood before Elisha and said, "Your son Ben-Hadad king of Aram sent me to you. He asks if he will recover from his sickness."

10 Elisha said to Hazael, "Go and tell Ben-Hadad, 'You will surely recover,' but the LORD has told me he will really die." 11 Hazael stared at Elisha until he felt ashamed. Then Elisha cried.

12 Hazael asked, "Why are you crying, master?"

Elisha answered, "Because I know what evil you will do to the Israelites. You will burn their strong, walled cities with fire and kill their young men with swords. You will throw their babies to the ground and split open their pregnant women."

13 Hazael said, "Am I a dog? How could I do such things?"

Elisha answered, "The LORD has shown me that you will be king over Aram."

14 Then Hazael left Elisha and came to his master. Ben-Hadad said to him, "What did Elisha say to you?"

Hazael answered, "He told me that you will surely recover." 15 But the next day Hazael took a blanket and dipped it in water. Then he put it over Ben-Hadad's face, and he died. So Hazael became king in Ben-Hadad's place.

Jehoram King of Judah

16 While Jehoshaphat was king in Judah, Jehoram son of Jehoshaphat became king of Judah. This was during the fifth year Joram son of Ahab was king of Israel. 17 Jehoram was thirty-two years old when he began to rule, and he ruled eight years in Jerusalem. 18 He followed the ways of the kings of Israel, just as the family of Ahab had done, because he married Ahab's daughter. Jehoram did what the LORD said was wrong. 19 But the LORD would not destroy Judah because of his servant David. The LORD had promised that one of David's descendants would always rule.

20 In Jehoram's time Edom broke away from Judah's rule and chose their own king. 21 So Jehoram and all his chariots went to Zair. The Edomites surrounded him and his chariot commanders. Jehoram got up and attacked the Edomites at night, but his army ran away to their tents. 22 From then until now the country of Edom has fought against the rule of Judah. At the same time Libnah also broke away from Judah's rule.

23 The other acts of Jehoram and all the things he did are written in the book of the history of the kings of Judah. 24 Jehoram died and was buried with his ancestors in Jerusalem, and Jehoram's son Ahaziah ruled in his place.

25 Ahaziah son of Jehoram became king of Judah during the twelfth year Joram son of Ahab was king of Israel. 26 Ahaziah was twenty-two years old when he became king, and he ruled one year in Jerusalem. His mother's name was Athaliah, a granddaughter of Omri king of Israel. 27 Ahaziah followed the ways of Ahab's family. He did what the LORD said was wrong, as Ahab's family had done, because he was a son-in-law to Ahab.

28 Ahaziah went with Joram son of Ahab to Ramoth in Gilead, where they fought against Hazael king of Aram. The Arameans wounded Joram. 29 So King Joram returned to Jezreel to heal from the wound he had received from the Arameans at Ramoth when he fought Hazael king of Aram. Ahaziah son of Jehoram king of Judah went down to visit Joram son of Ahab at Jezreel, because he had been wounded.

Jehu Is Chosen King

9 At the same time, Elisha the prophet called a man from the groups of prophets. Elisha said, "Get ready, and take this small bottle of olive oil in your hand. Go to Ramoth in Gilead. 2 When you arrive, find Jehu son of Jehoshaphat, the son of Nimshi. Go in and make Jehu get up from among his brothers,

Jezebel

2 KINGS 9

Jezebel sits in front of the mirror, applying a stroke of blue shadow above her eye. She examines her work and duplicates the shade on the other eye before adding dark colors on the brow bone. She smoothes her hair, setting it in place, and brushes her lips with red. She has heard that Jehu, the new King of Israel, is in Jezreel. She stands by the window and waits.

As Queen of Israel, she is a powerful woman, able to kill hundreds of God's prophets with one command. To her, God is weak—and belief in him is a sign of weakness. Each time one of his prophets is killed, she replaces him with a prophet of Baal. But she could never get to Elijah, the prophet she most wanted killed, who warned Israel not to fall away from God. He had killed 450 of her prophets in the name of God. "Dogs will eat the body of Jezebel in the city of Jezreel," Elijah had told Ahab. Ahab should have commanded Elijah destroyed at that moment but he didn't. Ahab was weak.

She watches as Jehu walks through the city gate. "Have you come in peace, you Zimri?" (Zimri was a well-known traitor.) Jehu lifts his head to see her, and the servants at Jezebel's side look down at him. "Throw her down," Jehu says. And without hesitation, the servants toss her out the window.

Jezebel chose to harden her heart toward God. What choice have you made?

and take him to an inner room. 3Then take
the bottle and pour the oil on Jehu's head and
say, 'This is what the LORD says: I have
appointed you king over Israel.' Then open
the door and run away. Don't wait!"

4So the young man, the prophet, went to
Ramoth in Gilead. 5When he arrived, he saw
the officers of the army sitting together. He
said, "Commander, I have a message for you."

Jehu asked, "For which one of us?"

The young man said, "For you,
commander."

6Jehu got up and went into the house.
Then the young prophet poured the olive oil
on Jehu's head and said to him, "This is what
the LORD, the God of Israel says: 'I have
appointed you king over the LORD's people
Israel. 7You must destroy the family of Ahab
your master. I will punish Jezebel for the
deaths of my servants the prophets and for
all the LORD's servants who were murdered.
8All of Ahab's family must die. I will not let
any male child in Ahab's family live in
Israel, whether slave or free. 9I will make
Ahab's family like the family of Jeroboam
son of Nebat and like the family of Baasha
son of Ahijah. 10The dogs will eat Jezebel at
Jezreel, and no one will bury her.' "

Then the young prophet opened the door
and ran away.

11When Jehu went back to his master's
officers, one of them said to Jehu, "Is
everything all right? Why did this crazy man
come to you?"

Jehu answered, "You know the man and
how he talks."

12They answered, "That's not true. Tell us."

Jehu said, "He said to me, 'This is what the
LORD says: I have appointed you to be king
over Israel.' "

13Then the officers hurried, and each man
took off his own coat and put it on the stairs
for Jehu. They blew the trumpet and
shouted, "Jehu is king!"

Joram and Ahaziah Are Killed

14So Jehu son of Jehoshaphat, the son of
Nimshi, made plans against Joram. Now
Joram and all Israel had been defending
Ramoth in Gilead from Hazael king of Aram.
15But King Joram had to return to Jezreel to
heal from the injuries the Arameans had
given him when he fought against Hazael
king of Aram.

Jehu said, "If you agree with this, don't let
anyone leave the city. They might tell the
news in Jezreel." 16 Then he got into his
chariot and set out for Jezreel, where Joram
was resting. Ahaziah king of Judah had gone
down to see him.
17 The lookout was standing on the
watchtower in Jezreel when he saw Jehu's
troops coming. He said, "I see some soldiers!"
Joram said, "Take a horseman and send
him to meet them. Tell him to ask, 'Is all in
order?' "
18 The horseman rode out to meet Jehu,
and he said, "This is what the king says: 'Is
all in order?' "
Jehu said, "Why bother yourself with
order? Come along behind me."
The lookout reported, "The messenger
reached them, but he is not coming back."
19 Then Joram sent out a second horseman.
This rider came to Jehu's group and said,
"This is what the king says: 'Is all in order?' "
Jehu answered, "Why bother yourself
with order? Come along behind me."
20 The lookout reported, "The second man
reached them, but he is not coming back.
The man in the chariot is driving like Jehu
son of Nimshi. He drives as if he were crazy!"
21 Joram said, "Get my chariot ready." Then
the servant got Joram's chariot ready. Joram
king of Israel and Ahaziah king of Judah
went out, each in his own chariot, to meet
Jehu at the property of Naboth the Jezreelite.
22 When Joram saw Jehu, he said, "Is all in
order, Jehu?"
Jehu answered, "There will never be any
order as long as your mother Jezebel
worships idols and uses witchcraft."
23 Joram turned the horses to run away
and yelled to Ahaziah, "It's a trick, Ahaziah!"
24 Then Jehu drew his bow and shot Joram
between his shoulders. The arrow went
through Joram's heart, and he fell down in
his chariot.
25 Jehu ordered Bidkar, his chariot officer,
"Pick up Joram's body, and throw it into the
field of Naboth the Jezreelite. Remember
when you and I rode together with Joram's
father Ahab. The LORD made this prophecy
against him: 26 'Yesterday I saw the blood of
Naboth and his sons, says the LORD, so I will
punish Ahab in his field, says the LORD.' Take
Joram's body and throw it into the field, as
the LORD has said."
27 When Ahaziah king of Judah saw this,
he ran away toward Beth Haggan. Jehu
chased him, saying, "Shoot Ahaziah, too!"
Ahaziah was wounded in his chariot on the
way up to Gur near Ibleam. He got as far as
Megiddo but died there. 28 Ahaziah's servants
carried his body in a chariot to Jerusalem
and buried him with his ancestors in his
tomb in Jerusalem. 29 (Ahaziah had become
king over Judah in the eleventh year Joram
son of Ahab was king.)

Death of Jezebel

30 When Jehu came to Jezreel, Jezebel
heard about it. She put on her eye makeup
and fixed her hair. Then she looked out the
window. 31 When Jehu entered the city gate,
Jezebel said, "Have you come in peace, you
Zimri,[n] you who killed your master?"
32 Jehu looked up at the window and said,
"Who is on my side? Who?" Two or three
servants looked out the window at Jehu.
33 He said to them, "Throw her down." So
they threw Jezebel down, and the horses ran
over her. Some of her blood splashed on the
wall and on the horses.
34 Jehu went into the house and ate and
drank. Then he said, "Now see about this
cursed woman. Bury her, because she is a
king's daughter."
35 The men went to bury Jezebel, but they
could not find her. They found only her
skull, feet, and the palms of her hands.
36 When they came back and told Jehu, he
said, "The LORD said this through his servant
Elijah the Tishbite: 'The dogs will eat Jezebel
at Jezreel. 37 Her body will be like manure on
the field in the land at Jezreel. No one will be
able to say that this is Jezebel.' "

Families of Ahab and Ahaziah Killed

10 Ahab had seventy sons in Samaria.
Jehu wrote letters and sent them to
Samaria to the officers and elders of Jezreel
and to the guardians of the sons of Ahab.
Jehu said, 2 "You have your master's sons
with you, and you have chariots, horses, a
city with strong walls, and weapons. When
you get this letter, 3 choose the best and most
worthy person among your master's sons,

9:31 Zimri He was the man who killed Elah and the family of Baasha. Read 1 Kings 16:8–12.

and make him king. Then fight for your
master's family."
4But the officers and leaders of Jezreel
were frightened. They said, "Two kings could
not stand up to Jehu, so how can we?"
5The palace manager, the city governor,
the leaders, and the guardians sent a
message to Jehu. "We are your servants,"
they said. "We will do everything you tell us
to do. We won't make any man king, so do
whatever you think is best."
6Then Jehu wrote a second letter, saying,
"If you are on my side and will obey me, cut
off the heads of your master's sons and come
to me at Jezreel tomorrow about this time."
Now the seventy sons of the king's family
were with the leading men of the city who
were their guardians. 7When the leaders
received the letter, they took the king's sons
and killed all seventy of them. They put
their heads in baskets and sent them to Jehu
at Jezreel. 8The messenger came to Jehu and
told him, "They have brought the heads of
the king's sons."
Then Jehu said, "Lay the heads in two
piles at the city gate until morning."
9In the morning, Jehu went out and stood
before the people and said to them, "You are
innocent. Look, I made plans against my
master and killed him. But who killed all
these? 10You should know that everything
the LORD said about Ahab's family will come
true. The LORD has spoken through his
servant Elijah, and the LORD has done what
he said." 11So Jehu killed everyone of Ahab's
family in Jezreel who was still alive. He also
killed all Ahab's leading men, close friends,
and priests. No one who had helped Ahab
was left alive.
12Then Jehu left and went to Samaria by
way of the road to Beth Eked of the
Shepherds. 13There Jehu met some relatives
of Ahaziah king of Judah. Jehu asked, "Who
are you?"
They answered, "We are relatives of
Ahaziah. We have come down to get revenge
for the families of the king and the king's
mother."
14Then Jehu said, "Take them alive!" So
they captured Ahaziah's relatives alive and
killed them at the well near Beth Eked—
forty-two of them. Jehu did not leave anyone
alive.
15After Jehu left there, he met Jehonadab
son of Recab, who was also on his way to
meet Jehu. Jehu greeted him and said, "Are
you as good a friend to me as I am to you?"
Jehonadab answered, "Yes, I am."
Jehu said, "If you are, then give me your
hand." So Jehonadab gave him his hand, and
Jehu pulled him into the chariot. 16"Come
with me," Jehu said. "You can see how strong
my feelings are for the LORD." So Jehu had
Jehonadab ride in his chariot.
17When Jehu came to Samaria, he killed
all of Ahab's family in Samaria. He destroyed
all those who were left, just as the LORD had
told Elijah it would happen.

Baal Worshipers Killed

18Then Jehu gathered all the people
together and said to them, "Ahab served Baal
a little, but Jehu will serve Baal much. 19Now
call for me all Baal's prophets and priests and
all the people who worship Baal. Don't let
anyone miss this meeting, because I have a
great sacrifice for Baal. Anyone who is not
there will not live." But Jehu was tricking
them so he could destroy the worshipers of
Baal. 20He said, "Prepare a holy meeting for
Baal." So they announced the meeting.
21Then Jehu sent word through all Israel,
and all the worshipers of Baal came; not one
stayed home. They came into the temple of
Baal, and the temple was filled from one side
to the other.
22Jehu said to the man who kept the robes,
"Bring out robes for all the worshipers of
Baal." After he brought out robes for them,
23Jehu and Jehonadab son of Recab went into
the temple of Baal. Jehu said to the
worshipers of Baal, "Look around, and make
sure there are no servants of the LORD with
you. Be sure there are only worshipers of
Baal." 24Then the worshipers of Baal went in
to offer sacrifices and burnt offerings.
Jehu had eighty men waiting outside. He
had told them, "Don't let anyone escape. If
you do, you must pay with your own life."
25As soon as Jehu finished offering the
burnt offering, he ordered the guards and the
captains, "Go in and kill the worshipers of
Baal. Don't let anyone come out." So the
guards and captains killed the worshipers of
Baal with the sword and threw their bodies
out. Then they went to the inner rooms of
the temple 26and brought out the pillars of
the temple of Baal and burned them. 27They

tore down the stone pillar of Baal, as well as the temple of Baal. And they made it into a sewage pit, as it is today.

28So Jehu destroyed Baal worship in Israel, 29but he did not stop doing the sins Jeroboam son of Nebat had done. Jeroboam had led Israel to sin by worshiping the golden calves in Bethel and Dan.

30The LORD said to Jehu, "You have done well in obeying what I said was right. You have done to the family of Ahab as I wanted. Because of this, your descendants as far as your great-great-grandchildren will be kings of Israel." 31But Jehu was not careful to follow the teachings of the LORD, the God of Israel, with all his heart. He did not stop doing the same sins Jeroboam had done, by which he had led Israel to sin.

32At that time the LORD began to make Israel smaller. Hazael defeated the Israelites in all the land of Israel, 33taking all the land of the Jordan known as the land of Gilead. (It was the region of Gad, Reuben, and Manasseh.) He took land from Aroer by the Arnon Ravine through Gilead to Bashan.

34The other things Jehu did—everything he did and all his victories—are recorded in the book of the history of the kings of Israel. 35Jehu died and was buried in Samaria, and his son Jehoahaz became king in his place. 36Jehu was king over Israel in Samaria for twenty-eight years.

Athaliah and Joash

11 When Ahaziah's mother, Athaliah, saw that her son was dead, she killed all the royal family. 2But Jehosheba, King Jehoram's daughter and Ahaziah's sister, took Joash, Ahaziah's son. She stole him from among the other sons of the king who were about to be murdered. She put Joash and his nurse in a bedroom to hide him from Athaliah, so he was not killed. 3He hid with her in the Temple of the LORD for six years. During that time Athaliah ruled the land.

4In the seventh year Jehoiada sent for the commanders of groups of a hundred men, as well as the Carites.[n] He brought them together in the Temple of the LORD and made an agreement with them. There, in the Temple of the LORD, he made them promise loyalty, and then he showed them the king's son. 5He commanded them, "This is what you must do. A third of you who go on duty on the Sabbath will guard the king's palace. 6A third of you will be at the Sur Gate, and another third will be at the gate behind the guard. This way you will guard the Temple. 7The two groups who go off duty on the Sabbath must protect the Temple of the LORD for the king. 8All of you must stand around the king, with weapons in hand. Kill anyone who comes near. Stay close to the king when he goes out and when he comes in."

9The commanders over a hundred men obeyed everything Jehoiada the priest had commanded. Each one took his men who came on duty on the Sabbath and those who went off duty on the Sabbath, and they came to Jehoiada the priest. 10He gave the commanders the spears and shields that had belonged to King David and that were kept in the Temple of the LORD.

Joash Becomes King

11Then each guard took his place with his weapons in his hand. There were guards from the south side of the Temple to the north side. They stood by the altar and the Temple and around the king. 12Jehoiada brought out the king's son and put the crown on him and gave him a copy of the agreement. They appointed him king and poured olive oil on him. Then they clapped their hands and said, "Long live the king!"

13When Athaliah heard the noise of the guards and the people, she went to them at the Temple of the LORD. 14She looked, and there was the king, standing by the pillar, as the custom was. The officers and trumpeters were standing beside him, and all the people of the land were very happy and were blowing trumpets. Then Athaliah tore her clothes and screamed, "Traitors! Traitors!"

15Jehoiada the priest gave orders to the commanders of a hundred men, who led the army. He said, "Surround her with soldiers and kill with a sword anyone who follows her." He commanded this because he had said, "Don't put Athaliah to death in the Temple of the LORD." 16So they caught her

11:4 Carites This was probably a special unit of the army that was responsible for the king's safety, a kind of palace guard similar to the Kerethites and the Pelethites.

Jehosheba

2 KINGS 11

Word reaches Jehosheba that her brother, King Ahaziah of Judah, has been killed. Her heart races because the king's mother—her own stepmother, Athaliah—has ordered all of the king's heirs to be killed. Her own grandchildren! Jehosheba thinks.

Evil comes naturally to Athaliah. Her mother, Jezebel, had killed hundreds of God's prophets. Jehosheba had married the high priest, Jehoiada, and together they lived for God and followed his commands. She finds her nephew Joash and rushes him into a bedroom with his nurse. "Don't make a sound," she says whispering. "Don't open this door until I come for you."

For some reason, Jehosheba has always felt that the Lord's hand was on Joash. She knows she has to be the one to save him from this evil. The murders of her other nephews are swift. In the aftermath, Jehosheba runs back to the bedroom and clutches Joash to her chest, covering him with a blanket. "Follow me," she says, instructing the nurse. Her heart pounds within her as she runs through the palace.

Once outside the grounds she flees to the Temple of God, the one place she knows Athaliah will not think to look for Joash. She closes the door of the Temple and tries to catch her breath, not realizing that she has preserved the royal line of the Messiah himself.

Jehosheba was part of the royal family but wouldn't worship their idols. Instead, she set her mind to live for God. Who are you living for?

when she came to the horses' entrance
near the palace. There she was put to
death.
17Then Jehoiada made an agreement
between the LORD and the king and the
people that they would be the LORD's special
people. He also made an agreement between
the king and the people. 18All the people of
the land went to the temple of Baal and tore
it down, smashing the altars and idols. They
also killed Mattan, the priest of Baal, in front
of the altars.
Then Jehoiada the priest placed guards at
the Temple of the LORD. 19He took with him
the commanders of a hundred men and the
Carites, the royal bodyguards, as well as the
guards and all the people of the land.
Together they took the king out of the
Temple of the LORD and went into the palace
through the gate of the guards. Then the
king sat on the royal throne. 20So all the
people of the land were very happy, and
Jerusalem had peace, because Athaliah had
been put to death with the sword at the
palace.
21Joash was seven years old when he
became king.

12 Joash became king of Judah in Jehu's
seventh year as king of Israel, and he
ruled for forty years in Jerusalem. His
mother's name was Zibiah, and she was from
Beersheba. 2Joash did what the LORD said was
right as long as Jehoiada the priest taught
him. 3But the places where gods were
worshiped were not removed; the people
still made sacrifices and burned incense
there.

Joash Repairs the Temple

4Joash said to the priests, "Take all the
money brought as offerings to the Temple
of the LORD. This includes the money each
person owes in taxes and the money each
person promises or brings freely to the
LORD. 5Each priest will take the money
from the people he serves. Then the priests
must repair any damage they find in the
Temple."
6But by the twenty-third year Joash was
king, the priests still had not repaired the
Temple. 7So King Joash called for Jehoiada
the priest and the other priests and said to
them, "Why aren't you repairing the damage
of the Temple? Don't take any more money

from the people you serve, but hand over the
money for the repair of the Temple." 8The
priests agreed not to take any more money
from the people and not to repair the
Temple themselves.
9Jehoiada the priest took a box and made a
hole in the top of it. Then he put it by the
altar, on the right side as the people came
into the Temple of the LORD. The priests
guarding the doorway put all the money
brought to the Temple of the LORD into the
box.
10Each time the priests saw that the box
was full of money, the king's royal secretary
and the high priest came. They counted the
money that had been brought to the Temple
of the LORD, and they put it into bags. 11Next
they weighed the money and gave it to the
people in charge of the work on the Temple.
With it they paid the carpenters and the
builders who worked on the Temple of the
LORD, 12as well as the bricklayers and
stonecutters. They also used the money to
buy timber and cut stone to repair the
damage of the Temple of the LORD. It paid for
everything.
13The money brought into the Temple of
the LORD was not used to make silver cups,
wick trimmers, bowls, trumpets, or gold or
silver vessels. 14They paid the money to the
workers, who used it to repair the Temple of
the LORD. 15They did not demand to know
how the money was spent, because the
workers were honest. 16The money from the
penalty offerings and sin offerings was not
brought into the Temple of the LORD,
because it belonged to the priests.

Joash Saves Jerusalem

17About this time Hazael king of Aram
attacked Gath and captured it. Then he went
to attack Jerusalem. 18Joash king of Judah
took all the holy things given by his
ancestors, the kings of Judah—Jehoshaphat,
Jehoram, and Ahaziah. He also took his own
holy things as well as the gold that was
found in the treasuries of the Temple of the
LORD and the gold from the palace. Joash
sent all this treasure to Hazael king of Aram,
who turned away from Jerusalem.
19Everything else Joash did is written in
the book of the history of the kings of Judah.
20His officers made plans against him and
killed him at Beth Millo on the road down to

devotion 95

2 KINGS 12:15

GOT ANY ROCKS IN YOUR PURSE?

One day my daughter and I were shopping. She was playing with these little pink rocks on a display while I looked at art supplies. As we were walking to the car, I noticed something pink tucked into her little fist. I picked her up and explained to her that she couldn't take things from a store without paying for them. We went back inside the store so she could put the rock back. That evening at dinner I asked her to tell her father about the rock in the store that day. She looked at him and said, "Well, actually the rock is in Mommy's purse." She had dropped it in there when I picked her up to talk to her.

How often do we do this in our lives? We look like we're being honest, but really we have our little rocks hidden where we think others won't find them. Whether it's cheating on your taxes or cheating on your husband, honesty is rare in today's culture. Honesty sets us apart from the world. Have you ever shocked a clerk by returning change that was counted incorrectly? The world says little white lies don't really hurt anyone, but the world is wrong. Being honest is one of the greatest attributes you can have as a Christian. Check your pockets, your purse—your heart—and make sure there aren't any little rocks hidden inside. Make honesty a part of who you are in every area of your life.

Silla. 21The officers who killed him were
Jozabad son of Shimeath and Jehozabad son
of Shomer. Joash was buried with his
ancestors in Jerusalem, and Amaziah, his
son, became king in his place.

Jehoahaz King of Israel

13 Jehoahaz son of Jehu became king
over Israel in Samaria during the
twenty-third year Joash son of Ahaziah was
king of Judah. Jehoahaz ruled seventeen years,
2and he did what the LORD said was wrong.
Jehoahaz did the same sins Jeroboam son of
Nebat had done. Jeroboam had led Israel to
sin, and Jehoahaz did not stop doing these
same sins. 3So the LORD was angry with Israel
and handed them over to Hazael king of
Aram and his son Ben-Hadad for a long time.
4Then Jehoahaz begged the LORD, and the
LORD listened to him. The LORD had seen the
troubles of Israel; he saw how terribly the
king of Aram was treating them. 5He gave
Israel a man to save them, and they escaped
from the Arameans. The Israelites then lived
in their own homes as they had before, 6but
they still did not stop doing the same sins
that the family of Jeroboam had done. He
had led Israel to sin, and they continued
doing those sins. The Asherah idol also was
left standing in Samaria.
7Nothing was left of Jehoahaz's army
except fifty horsemen, ten chariots, and ten
thousand foot soldiers. The king of Aram had
destroyed them and made them like chaff.
8Everything else Jehoahaz did and all his
victories are written in the book of the
history of the kings of Israel. 9Jehoahaz died
and was buried in Samaria, and his son
Jehoash became king in his place.

Jehoash King of Israel

10Jehoash son of Jehoahaz became
king of Israel in Samaria during Joash's
thirty-seventh year as king of Judah. Jehoash
ruled sixteen years, 11and he did what the
LORD said was wrong. He did not stop doing
the same sins Jeroboam son of Nebat had
done. Jeroboam had led Israel to sin, and
Jehoash continued to do the same thing.
12Everything else he did and all his victories,
including his war against Amaziah king of
Judah, are written in the book of the history
of the kings of Israel. 13Jehoash died, and
Jeroboam took his place on the throne.
Jehoash was buried in Samaria with the
kings of Israel.

The Death of Elisha

14At this time Elisha became sick. Before
he died, Jehoash king of Israel went to Elisha
and cried for him. Jehoash said, "My father,
my father! The chariots of Israel and their
horsemen!"
15Elisha said to Jehoash, "Take a bow and
arrows." So he took a bow and arrows.
16Then Elisha said to him, "Put your hand on
the bow." So Jehoash put his hand on the
bow. Then Elisha put his hands on the king's
hands. 17Elisha said, "Open the east window."
So Jehoash opened the window. Then Elisha
said, "Shoot," and Jehoash shot. Elisha said,
"The LORD's arrow of victory over Aram! You
will defeat the Arameans at Aphek until you
destroy them."
18Elisha said, "Take the arrows." So
Jehoash took them. Then Elisha said to him,
"Strike the ground." So Jehoash struck the
ground three times and stopped. 19The man
of God was angry with him. "You should
have struck five or six times!" Elisha said.
"Then you would have struck Aram until
you had completely destroyed it. But now
you will defeat it only three times."
20Then Elisha died and was buried.
At that time groups of Moabites would
rob the land in the springtime. 21Once as
some Israelites were burying a man,
suddenly they saw a group of Moabites
coming. The Israelites threw the dead man
into Elisha's grave. When the man touched
Elisha's bones, the man came back to life and
stood on his feet.

War with Aram

22During all the days Jehoahaz was king,
Hazael king of Aram troubled Israel. 23But
the LORD was kind to the Israelites; he had
mercy on them and helped them because of
his agreement with Abraham, Isaac, and
Jacob. To this day he has never wanted to
destroy them or reject them.
24When Hazael king of Aram died, his son
Ben-Hadad became king in his place.
25During a war Hazael had taken some cities
from Jehoahaz, Jehoash's father. Now
Jehoash took back those cities from Hazael's
son Ben-Hadad. He defeated Ben-Hadad three
times and took back the cities of Israel.

Amaziah King of Judah

14 Amaziah son of Joash became king of
Judah during the second year Jehoash
son of Jehoahaz was king of Israel. [2]Amaziah
was twenty-five years old when he became
king, and he ruled twenty-nine years in
Jerusalem. His mother was named
Jehoaddin, and she was from Jerusalem.
[3]Amaziah did what the LORD said was right.
He did everything his father Joash had done,
but he did not do as his ancestor David had
done. [4]The places where gods were
worshiped were not removed, so the people
still sacrificed and burned incense there.
[5]As soon as Amaziah took control of the
kingdom, he executed the officers who had
murdered his father the king. [6]But he did not
put to death the children of the murderers
because of the rule written in the Book of
the Teachings of Moses. The LORD had
commanded: "Parents must not be put to
death when their children do wrong, and
children must not be put to death when
their parents do wrong. Each must die for
his own sins."[n]
[7]In battle Amaziah killed ten thousand
Edomites in the Valley of Salt. He also took
the city of Sela. He called it Joktheel, as it is
still called today.
[8]Amaziah sent messengers to Jehoash son
of Jehoahaz, the son of Jehu, king of Israel.
They said, "Come, let's meet face to face."
[9]Then Jehoash king of Israel answered
Amaziah king of Judah, "A thornbush in
Lebanon sent a message to a cedar tree in
Lebanon. It said, 'Let your daughter marry
my son.' But then a wild animal from
Lebanon came by, walking on and crushing
the thornbush. [10]You have defeated Edom,
but you have become proud. Stay at home
and brag. Don't ask for trouble, or you and
Judah will be defeated."
[11]But Amaziah would not listen, so
Jehoash king of Israel went to attack. He and
Amaziah king of Judah faced each other in
battle at Beth Shemesh in Judah. [12]Israel
defeated Judah, and every man of Judah ran
away to his home. [13]At Beth Shemesh
Jehoash king of Israel captured Amaziah
king of Judah. (Amaziah was the son of
Joash, who was the son of Ahaziah.) Jehoash
went up to Jerusalem and broke down the
wall of Jerusalem from the Gate of Ephraim
to the Corner Gate, which was about six
hundred feet. [14]He took all the gold and
silver and all the utensils in the Temple of
the LORD, and he took the treasures of the
palace and some hostages. Then he returned
to Samaria.
[15]The other acts of Jehoash and his
victories, including his war against Amaziah
king of Judah, are written in the book of the
history of the kings of Israel. [16]Jehoash died
and was buried in Samaria with the kings of
Israel, and his son Jeroboam became king in
his place.
[17]Amaziah son of Joash, the king of Judah,
lived fifteen years after the death of Jehoash
son of Jehoahaz, the king of Israel. [18]The
other things Amaziah did are written in the
book of the history of the kings of Judah.
[19]The people in Jerusalem made plans
against him. So he ran away to the town of
Lachish, but they sent men after him to
Lachish and killed him. [20]They brought his
body back on horses, and he was buried with
his ancestors in Jerusalem, in the city of
David.
[21]Then all the people of Judah made
Uzziah[n] king in place of his father Amaziah.
Uzziah was sixteen years old. [22]He rebuilt
the town of Elath and made it part of Judah
again after Amaziah died.

Jeroboam King of Israel

[23]Jeroboam son of Jehoash became king
of Israel in Samaria during the fifteenth
year Amaziah was king of Judah. (Amaziah
was the son of Joash.) Jeroboam ruled
forty-one years, [24]and he did what the LORD
said was wrong. Jeroboam son of Nebat had
led Israel to sin, and Jeroboam son of
Jehoash did not stop doing the same sins.
[25]Jeroboam won back Israel's border from
Lebo Hamath to the Dead Sea. This
happened as the LORD, the God of Israel, had
said through his servant Jonah son of
Amittai, the prophet from Gath Hepher.
[26]The LORD had seen how the Israelites, both
slave and free, were suffering terribly. No
one was left who could help Israel. [27]The
LORD had not said he would completely
destroy Israel from the world, so he saved

14:6 "Parents . . . sins." See Deuteronomy 24:16. **14:21 Uzziah** Also called Azariah.

the Israelites through Jeroboam son of
Jehoash.
28 Everything else Jeroboam did is written
down—all his victories and how he won
back from Judah the towns of Damascus and
Hamath for Israel. All this is written in the
book of the history of the kings of Israel.
29 Jeroboam died and was buried with his
ancestors, the kings of Israel. Jeroboam's son
Zechariah became king in his place.

Uzziah King of Judah

15 Uzziah son of Amaziah became
king of Judah during Jeroboam's
twenty-seventh year as king of Israel. 2 Uzziah
was sixteen years old when he became king,
and he ruled fifty-two years in Jerusalem. His
mother was named Jecoliah, and she was
from Jerusalem. 3 He did what the LORD said
was right, just as his father Amaziah had
done. 4 But the places where gods were
worshiped were not removed, so the people
still made sacrifices and burned incense there.
5 The LORD struck Uzziah with a skin
disease, which he had until the day he died.
So he had to live in a separate house. Jotham,
the king's son, was in charge of the palace,
and he governed the people of the land.
6 All the other things Uzziah did are
written in the book of the history of the
kings of Judah. 7 Uzziah died and was buried
near his ancestors in Jerusalem, and his son
Jotham became king in his place.

Zechariah King of Israel

8 Zechariah son of Jeroboam was king over
Israel in Samaria. He ruled for six months
during Uzziah's[n] thirty-eighth year as king of
Judah. 9 Zechariah did what the LORD said
was wrong, just as his ancestors had done.
Jeroboam son of Nebat had led the people of
Israel to sin, and Zechariah did not stop
doing the same sins.
10 Shallum son of Jabesh made plans
against Zechariah and killed him in front of
the people. Then Shallum became king in
his place. 11 The other acts of Zechariah are
written in the book of the history of the
kings of Israel. 12 The LORD had told Jehu:
"Your sons down to your great-great-
grandchildren will be kings of Israel," and
the LORD's word came true.

Shallum King of Israel

13 Shallum son of Jabesh became king
during Uzziah's thirty-ninth year as king of
Judah. Shallum ruled for a month in
Samaria. 14 Then Menahem son of Gadi came
up from Tirzah to Samaria and attacked
Shallum son of Jabesh in Samaria. He killed
him and became king in Shallum's place.
15 The other acts of Shallum and his secret
plans are written in the book of the history
of the kings of Israel.

Menahem King of Israel

16 Menahem started out from Tirzah and
attacked Tiphsah, destroying the city and
the area nearby. This was because the people
had refused to open the city gate for him. He
defeated them and ripped open all their
pregnant women.
17 Menahem son of Gadi became king over
Israel during Uzziah's thirty-ninth year as
king of Judah. Menahem ruled ten years in
Samaria, 18 and he did what the LORD said was
wrong. Jeroboam son of Nebat had led Israel
to sin, and all the time Menahem was king,
he did not stop doing the same sins.
19 Pul king of Assyria came to attack the
land. Menahem gave him about seventy-four
thousand pounds of silver so Pul would
support him and make his hold on the
kingdom stronger. 20 Menahem taxed Israel
to pay about one and one-fourth pounds of
silver to each soldier of the king of Assyria.
So the king left and did not stay in the land.
21 Everything else Menahem did is written
in the book of the history of the kings of
Israel. 22 Then Menahem died, and his son
Pekahiah became king in his place.

Pekahiah King of Israel

23 Pekahiah son of Menahem became king
over Israel in Samaria during Uzziah's[n]
fiftieth year as king of Judah. Pekahiah ruled
two years, 24 and he did what the LORD said
was wrong. Jeroboam son of Nebat had led
Israel to sin, and Pekahiah did not stop doing
the same sins.
25 Pekah son of Remaliah was one of
Pekahiah's captains, and he made plans
against Pekahiah. He took fifty men of
Gilead with him and killed Pekahiah, as
well as Argob and Arieh, in the palace at

15:8, 23 Uzziah Also called Azariah.

Samaria. Then Pekah became king in
Pekahiah's place.
26 Everything else Pekahiah did is written
in the book of the history of the kings of
Israel.

Pekah King of Israel

27 Pekah son of Remaliah became king
over Israel in Samaria during Uzziah's[n]
fifty-second year as king of Judah. Pekah
ruled twenty years, 28 and he did what the
LORD said was wrong. Jeroboam son of Nebat
had led Israel to sin, and Pekah did not
stop doing the same sins.
29 Tiglath-Pileser[n] was king of Assyria. He
attacked while Pekah was king of Israel,
capturing the cities of Ijon, Abel Beth
Maacah, Janoah, Kedesh, and Hazor. He also
captured Gilead and Galilee and all the land
of Naphtali and carried the people away to
Assyria. 30 Then Hoshea son of Elah made
plans against Pekah son of Remaliah and
attacked and killed him. Then Hoshea
became king in Pekah's place during the
twentieth year Jotham son of Uzziah was
king.
31 Everything else Pekah did is written in
the book of the history of the kings of Israel.

Jotham King of Judah

32 Jotham son of Uzziah became king of
Judah during the second year Pekah son of
Remaliah was king of Israel. 33 Jotham was
twenty-five years old when he became king,
and he ruled sixteen years in Jerusalem. His
mother's name was Jerusha daughter of
Zadok. 34 Jotham did what the LORD said was
right, just as his father Uzziah had done.
35 But the places where gods were worshiped
were not removed, and the people still made
sacrifices and burned incense there. Jotham
rebuilt the Upper Gate of the Temple of the
LORD.
36 The other things Jotham did while he
was king are written in the book of the
history of the kings of Judah. 37 At that time
the LORD began to send Rezin king of Aram
and Pekah son of Remaliah against Judah.
38 Jotham died and was buried with his
ancestors in Jerusalem, the city of David, his
ancestor. Then Jotham's son Ahaz became
king in his place.

Ahaz King of Judah

16 Ahaz was the son of Jotham king of
Judah. Ahaz became king of Judah in
the seventeenth year Pekah son of Remaliah
was king of Israel. 2 Ahaz was twenty years
old when he became king, and he ruled
sixteen years in Jerusalem. Unlike his
ancestor David, he did not do what the LORD
his God said was right. 3 Ahaz did the same
things the kings of Israel had done. He even
made his son pass through fire. He did the
same hateful sins as the nations had done
whom the LORD had forced out of the land
ahead of the Israelites. 4 Ahaz offered
sacrifices and burned incense at the places
where gods were worshiped, on the hills,
and under every green tree.
5 Rezin king of Aram and Pekah son of
Remaliah, the king of Israel, came up to
attack Jerusalem. They surrounded Ahaz but
could not defeat him. 6 At that time Rezin
king of Aram took back the city of Elath for
Aram, and he forced out all the people of
Judah. Then Edomites moved into Elath, and
they still live there today.
7 Ahaz sent messengers to Tiglath-Pileser
king of Assyria, saying, "I am your servant
and your friend. Come and save me from the
king of Aram and the king of Israel, who are
attacking me." 8 Ahaz took the silver and
gold that was in the Temple of the LORD and
in the treasuries of the palace, and he sent
these as a gift to the king of Assyria. 9 So the
king of Assyria listened to Ahaz. He attacked
Damascus and captured it and sent all its
people away to Kir. And he killed Rezin.
10 Then King Ahaz went to Damascus to
meet Tiglath-Pileser king of Assyria. Ahaz
saw an altar at Damascus, and he sent plans
and a pattern of this altar to Uriah the priest.
11 So Uriah the priest built an altar, just like
the plans King Ahaz had sent him from
Damascus. Uriah finished the altar before
King Ahaz came back from Damascus.
12 When the king arrived from Damascus, he
saw the altar and went near and offered
sacrifices on it. 13 He burned his burnt
offerings and grain offerings and poured out
his drink offering. He also sprinkled the
blood of his fellowship offerings on the altar.
14 Ahaz moved the bronze altar that was

15:27 Uzziah Also called Azariah. **15:29 Tiglath-Pileser** Also called Pul.

before the LORD at the front of the Temple. It
was between Ahaz's altar and the Temple of
the LORD, but he put it on the north side of
his altar. 15King Ahaz commanded Uriah the
priest, "On the large altar burn the morning
burnt offering, the evening grain offering,
the king's burnt offering and grain offering,
and the whole burnt offering, the grain
offering, and the drink offering for all the
people of the land. Sprinkle on the altar all
the blood of the burnt offering and of the
sacrifice. But I will use the bronze altar to
ask questions of God." 16So Uriah the priest
did everything as King Ahaz commanded
him.

17Then King Ahaz took off the side panels
from the bases and removed the washing
bowls from the top of the bases. He also took
the large bowl, which was called the Sea, off
the bronze bulls that held it up, and he put it
on a stone base. 18Ahaz took away the
platform for the royal throne, which had
been built at the Temple of the LORD. He also
took away the outside entrance for the king.
He did these things because of the king of
Assyria.

19The other things Ahaz did as king are
written in the book of the history of the
kings of Judah. 20Ahaz died and was buried
with his ancestors in Jerusalem, and Ahaz's
son Hezekiah became king in his place.

Hoshea, Last King of Israel

17 Hoshea son of Elah became king over
Israel during Ahaz's twelfth year as
king of Judah. Hoshea ruled in Samaria nine
years. 2He did what the LORD said was wrong,
but he was not as bad as the kings of Israel
who had ruled before him.

3Shalmaneser king of Assyria came to
attack Hoshea. Hoshea had been
Shalmaneser's servant and had made the
payments to Shalmaneser that he had
demanded. 4But the king of Assyria found
out that Hoshea had made plans against him
by sending messengers to So, the king of
Egypt. Hoshea had also stopped giving
Shalmaneser the payments, which he had
paid every year in the past. For that, the king
put Hoshea in prison. 5Then the king of
Assyria came and attacked all the land of
Israel. He surrounded Samaria and attacked
it for three years. 6He defeated Samaria in
the ninth year Hoshea was king, and he took
the Israelites away to Assyria. He settled
them in Halah, in Gozan on the Habor River,
and in the cities of the Medes.

Israelites Punished for Sin

7All these things happened because the
Israelites had sinned against the LORD their
God. He had brought them out of Egypt and
had rescued them from the power of the
king of Egypt, but the Israelites had honored
other gods. 8They lived like the nations the
LORD had forced out of the land ahead of
them. They lived as their evil kings had
shown them, 9secretly sinning against the
LORD their God. They built places to worship
gods in all their cities, from the watchtower
to the strong, walled city. 10They put up
stone pillars to gods and Asherah idols on
every high hill and under every green tree.
11The Israelites burned incense everywhere
gods were worshiped, just as the nations
who lived there before them had done,
whom the LORD had forced out of the land.
The Israelites did wicked things that made
the LORD angry. 12They served idols when the
LORD had said, "You must not do this." 13The
LORD used every prophet and seer to warn
Israel and Judah. He said, "Stop your evil
ways and obey my commands and laws.
Follow all the teachings that I commanded
your ancestors, the teachings that I gave you
through my servants the prophets."

14But the people would not listen. They
were stubborn, just as their ancestors had
been who did not believe in the LORD their
God. 15They rejected the LORD's laws and the
agreement he had made with their ancestors.
And they refused to listen to his warnings.
They worshiped useless idols and became
useless themselves. They did what the
nations around them did, which the LORD
had warned them not to do.

16The people rejected all the commands of
the LORD their God. They molded statues of
two calves, and they made an Asherah idol.
They worshiped all the stars of the sky and
served Baal. 17They made their sons and
daughters pass through fire and tried to find
out the future by magic and witchcraft. They
always chose to do what the LORD said was
wrong, which made him angry. 18Because he
was very angry with the people of Israel, he
removed them from his presence. Only the
tribe of Judah was left.

Judah Is Also Guilty

19 But even Judah did not obey the commands of the LORD their God. They did what the Israelites had done, 20 so the LORD rejected all the people of Israel. He punished them and let others destroy them; he threw them out of his presence. 21 When the LORD separated them from the family of David, the Israelites made Jeroboam son of Nebat their king. Jeroboam led the Israelites away from the LORD and led them to sin greatly. 22 So they continued to do all the sins Jeroboam did. They did not stop doing these sins 23 until the LORD removed the Israelites from his presence, just as he had said through all his servants the prophets. So the Israelites were taken out of their land to Assyria, and they have been there to this day.

The Beginning of the Samaritan People

24 The king of Assyria brought people from Babylon, Cuthah, Avva, Hamath, and Sepharvaim and put them in the cities of Samaria to replace the Israelites. These people took over Samaria and lived in the cities. 25 At first they did not worship the LORD, so he sent lions among them which killed some of them. 26 The king of Assyria was told, "You sent foreigners into the cities of Samaria who do not know the law of the god of the land. This is why he has sent lions among them. The lions are killing them because they don't know what the god wants."

27 Then the king of Assyria commanded, "Send back one of the priests you took away. Let him live there and teach the people what the god wants." 28 So one of the priests who had been carried away from Samaria returned to live in Bethel. And he taught the people how to honor the LORD.

29 But each nation made gods of its own and put them in the cities where they lived and in the temples where gods were worshiped. These temples had been built by the Samaritans. 30 The people from Babylon made Succoth Benoth their god. The people from Cuthah worshiped Nergal. The people of Hamath worshiped Ashima. 31 The Avvites worshiped Nibhaz and Tartak. The Sepharvites burned their children in the fire, sacrificing them to Adrammelech and Anammelech, the gods of Sepharvaim. 32 They also honored the LORD, but they chose priests for the places where gods were worshiped. The priests were chosen from among themselves, and they made sacrifices for the people. 33 The people honored the LORD but also served their own gods, just as the nations did from which they had been brought. 34 Even today they do as they did in the past. They do not worship the LORD nor obey his rules and commands. They do not obey the teachings or the commands of the LORD, which he gave to the children of Jacob, whom he had named Israel. 35 The LORD had made an agreement with them and had commanded them, "Do not honor other gods. Do not bow down to them or worship them or offer sacrifices to them. 36 Worship the LORD who brought you up out of the land of Egypt with great power and strength. Bow down to him and offer sacrifices to him. 37 Always obey the rules, orders, teachings, and commands he wrote for you. Do not honor other gods. 38 Do not forget the agreement I made with you, and do not honor other gods. 39 Instead worship the LORD your God, who will save you from all your enemies."

40 But the Israelites did not listen. They kept on doing the same things they had done before. 41 So these nations honored the LORD but also worshiped their idols, and their children and grandchildren still do as their ancestors did.

Hezekiah King of Judah

18 Hezekiah son of Ahaz king of Judah became king during the third year Hoshea son of Elah was king of Israel. 2 Hezekiah was twenty-five years old when he became king, and he ruled twenty-nine years in Jerusalem. His mother's name was Abijah daughter of Zechariah. 3 Hezekiah did what the LORD said was right, just as his ancestor David had done. 4 He removed the places where gods were worshiped. He smashed the stone pillars and cut down the Asherah idols. Also the Israelites had been burning incense to Nehushtan, the bronze snake Moses had made. But Hezekiah broke it into pieces.

5 Hezekiah trusted in the LORD, the God of Israel. There was no one like him among all the kings of Judah, either before him or after him. 6 Hezekiah was loyal to the LORD and did not stop following him; he obeyed the commands the LORD had given Moses. 7 And

the LORD was with Hezekiah, so he had
success in everything he did. He turned
against the king of Assyria and stopped
serving him. [8]Hezekiah defeated the
Philistines all the way to Gaza and its
borders, including the watchtowers and the
strong, walled cities.

The Assyrians Capture Samaria

[9]Shalmaneser king of Assyria surrounded
Samaria and attacked it in the fourth year
Hezekiah was king. This was the seventh
year Hoshea son of Elah was king of Israel.
[10]After three years the Assyrians captured
Samaria. This was in the sixth year Hezekiah
was king, which was Hoshea's ninth year as
king of Israel. [11]The king of Assyria took the
Israelites away to Assyria and settled them
in Halah, in Gozan on the Habor River, and
in the cities of the Medes. [12]This happened
because they did not obey the LORD their
God. They broke his agreement and did not
obey all that Moses, the LORD's servant, had
commanded. They would not listen to the
commands or do them.

Assyria Attacks Judah

[13]During Hezekiah's fourteenth year as
king, Sennacherib king of Assyria attacked
all the strong, walled cities of Judah and
captured them. [14]Then Hezekiah king of
Judah sent a message to the king of Assyria
at Lachish. He said, "I have done wrong.
Leave me alone, and I will pay anything you
ask." So the king of Assyria made Hezekiah
pay about twenty-two thousand pounds of
silver and two thousand pounds of gold.
[15]Hezekiah gave him all the silver that was
in the Temple of the LORD and in the palace
treasuries. [16]Hezekiah stripped all the gold
that covered the doors and doorposts of the
Temple of the LORD. Hezekiah had put gold
on these doors himself, but he gave it all to
the king of Assyria.

[17]The king of Assyria sent out his
supreme commander, his chief officer, and
his field commander. They went with a large
army from Lachish to King Hezekiah in
Jerusalem. When they came near the
waterway from the upper pool on the road
where people do their laundry, they stopped.
[18]They called for the king, so the king sent
Eliakim, Shebna, and Joah out to meet them.
Eliakim son of Hilkiah was the palace
manager, Shebna was the royal secretary,
and Joah son of Asaph was the recorder.

[19]The field commander said to them, "Tell
Hezekiah this:

" 'The great king, the king of Assyria, says:
What can you trust in now? [20]You say you
have battle plans and power for war, but
your words mean nothing. Whom are you
trusting for help so that you turn against
me? [21]Look, you are depending on Egypt to
help you, but Egypt is like a splintered
walking stick. If you lean on it for help, it
will stab your hand and hurt you. The king
of Egypt will hurt all those who depend on
him. [22]You might say, "We are depending on
the LORD our God," but Hezekiah destroyed
the LORD's altars and the places of worship.
Hezekiah told Judah and Jerusalem, "You
must worship only at this one altar in
Jerusalem."

[23]" 'Now make an agreement with my
master, the king of Assyria: I will give you
two thousand horses if you can find enough
men to ride them. [24]You cannot defeat one of
my master's least important officers, so why
do you depend on Egypt to give you chariots
and horsemen? [25]I have not come to attack
and destroy this place without an order from
the LORD. The LORD himself told me to come
to this country and destroy it.' "

[26]Then Eliakim son of Hilkiah, Shebna,
and Joah said to the field commander,
"Please speak to us in the Aramaic language.
We understand it. Don't speak to us in
Hebrew, because the people on the city wall
can hear you."

[27]"No," the commander said, "my master
did not send me to tell these things only to
you and your king. He sent me to speak also
to those people sitting on the wall who will
have to eat their own dung and drink their
own urine like you."

[28]Then the commander stood and shouted
loudly in the Hebrew language, "Listen to
what the great king, the king of Assyria,
says! [29]The king says you should not let
Hezekiah fool you, because he can't save you
from my power. [30]Don't let Hezekiah talk
you into trusting the LORD by saying, 'The
LORD will surely save us. This city won't be
handed over to the king of Assyria.'

[31]"Don't listen to Hezekiah. The king of
Assyria says, 'Make peace with me, and come
out of the city to me. Then everyone will be

free to eat the fruit from his own grapevine
and fig tree and to drink water from his own
well. 32After that I will come and take you to
a land like your own—a land with grain and
new wine, bread and vineyards, olives, and
honey. Choose to live and not to die!'
"Don't listen to Hezekiah. He is fooling
you when he says, 'The LORD will save us.'
33Has a god of any other nation saved his
people from the power of the king of
Assyria? 34Where are the gods of Hamath
and Arpad? Where are the gods of
Sepharvaim, Hena, and Ivvah? They did not
save Samaria from my power. 35Not one of
all the gods of these countries has saved his
people from me. Neither can the LORD save
Jerusalem from my power."
36The people were silent. They didn't
answer the commander at all, because King
Hezekiah had ordered, "Don't answer him."
37Then Eliakim, Shebna, and Joah tore
their clothes to show how upset they were.
(Eliakim son of Hilkiah was the palace
manager, Shebna was the royal secretary,
and Joah son of Asaph was the recorder.) The
three men went to Hezekiah and told him
what the field commander had said.

Jerusalem Will Be Saved

19 When King Hezekiah heard the
message, he tore his clothes and put
on rough cloth to show how sad he was.
Then he went into the Temple of the LORD.
2Hezekiah sent Eliakim, the palace manager,
and Shebna, the royal secretary, and the
older priests to Isaiah. They were all wearing
rough cloth when they came to Isaiah the
prophet, the son of Amoz. 3They told Isaiah,
"This is what Hezekiah says: Today is a day
of sorrow and punishment and disgrace, as
when a child should be born, but the mother
is not strong enough to give birth to it. 4The
king of Assyria sent his field commander to
make fun of the living God. Maybe the LORD
your God will hear what the commander
said and will punish him for it. So pray for
the few of us who are left alive."
5When Hezekiah's officers came to Isaiah,
6he said to them, "Tell your master this: The
LORD says, 'Don't be afraid of what you have
heard. Don't be frightened by the words the
servants of the king of Assyria have spoken
against me. 7Listen! I am going to put a spirit
in the king of Assyria. He will hear a report
that will make him return to his own
country, and I will cause him to die by the
sword there.' "
8The field commander heard that the king
of Assyria had left Lachish. When he went
back, he found the king fighting against the
city of Libnah.
9The king received a report that Tirhakah,
the Cushite king of Egypt, was coming to
attack him. When the king of Assyria heard
this, he sent messengers to Hezekiah, saying,
10"Tell Hezekiah king of Judah: Don't be
fooled by the god you trust. Don't believe
him when he says Jerusalem will not be
handed over to the king of Assyria. 11You
have heard what the kings of Assyria have
done. They have completely defeated every
country, so do not think you will be saved.
12Did the gods of those people save them? My
ancestors destroyed them, defeating the cities
of Gozan, Haran, and Rezeph, and the people
of Eden living in Tel Assar. 13Where are the
kings of Hamath and Arpad? Where are the
kings of Sepharvaim, Hena, and Ivvah?"

Hezekiah Prays to the Lord

14When Hezekiah received the letter from
the messengers and read it, he went up to
the Temple of the LORD. He spread the letter
out before the LORD 15and prayed to the LORD:
"LORD, God of Israel, whose throne is
between the gold creatures with wings, only
you are God of all the kingdoms of the earth.
You made the heavens and the earth. 16Hear,
LORD, and listen. Open your eyes, LORD, and
see. Listen to the words Sennacherib has said
to insult the living God. 17It is true, LORD,
that the kings of Assyria have destroyed
these countries and their lands. 18They have
thrown the gods of these nations into the
fire, but they were only wood and rock
statues that people made. So the kings have
destroyed them. 19Now, LORD our God, save
us from the king's power so that all the
kingdoms of the earth will know that you,
LORD, are the only God."

God Answers Hezekiah

20Then Isaiah son of Amoz sent a message
to Hezekiah that said, "This is what the LORD,
the God of Israel, says: I have heard your
prayer to me about Sennacherib king of
Assyria. 21This is what the LORD has said
against Sennacherib:

devotion 96

2 KINGS 19:14–19

MAKE YOUR GLORY KNOWN!

Lord, make your glory known! Some days we might have to pray that all day long. Lord, come into my kitchen, see my desperate heart, and show me your glory. Step into my loneliness and light up the room with your presence. Come with power. Come deliver me from my enemies. Come into my weakness with your strength. Lord God, you have to add your spirit to my feeble life or I will surely succumb. I need supernatural help.

Hezekiah gave an account of his serious circumstances, and then he begged God to show himself, to prove himself as the King of heaven and earth, the only God. Do you need God to reveal himself today? Do you need to see his power and hear him speak? Then pray like Hezekiah and plead your case before God. Report to the Lord all the assaults on your life. Tell him of your overwhelming commitments. Let him know that there isn't enough of you to go around. Be honest about every ache and disappointment and insecurity. Beg for his presence and his glory and his very real assistance in your need.

Commit again that you will walk through this day with integrity. You will not take the easy way out, nor will you forsake all the Lord has already shown you and done for you. But if you need his glory, if you need his voice, then shout out, "God, I need you more than anything! Come and make your glory known!"

'The people of Jerusalem
    hate you and make fun of you.
The people of Jerusalem
    laugh at you as you run away.
22 You have insulted me and spoken
        against me;
    you have raised your voice
        against me.
You have a proud look on your face,
    which is against me, the Holy One of
        Israel.
23 You have sent your messengers to insult
        the Lord.
    You have said, "With my many chariots
I have gone to the tops of the mountains,
    to the highest mountains of Lebanon.
I have cut down its tallest cedars
    and its best pine trees.
I have gone to its farthest places
    and to its best forests.
24 I have dug wells in foreign countries
    and drunk water there.
By the soles of my feet,
    I have dried up all the rivers of Egypt."

25 " 'King of Assyria, surely you have heard.
    Long ago I, the LORD, planned these
        things.
Long ago I designed them,
    and now I have made them happen.
I allowed you to turn those strong, walled
        cities
    into piles of rocks.
26 The people in those cities were weak;
    they were frightened and put to
        shame.
They were like grass in the field,
    like tender, young grass,
like grass on the housetop
    that is burned by the wind before it can
        grow.

27 " 'I know when you rest,
    when you come and go,
    and how you rage against me.
28 Because you rage against me,
    and because I have heard your proud
        words,
I will put my hook in your nose
    and my bit in your mouth.

Then I will force you to leave my country
the same way you came.'
29"Then the LORD said, 'Hezekiah, I will
give you this sign:
This year you will eat the grain that grows
wild,
and the second year you will eat what
grows wild from that.
But in the third year, plant grain and
harvest it.
Plant vineyards and eat their fruit.
30Some of the people in the family of Judah
will escape.
Like plants that take root,
they will grow strong and have many
children.
31A few people will come out of Jerusalem
alive;
a few from Mount Zion will live.
The strong love of the LORD All-Powerful
will make this happen.'
32"So this is what the LORD says about the
king of Assyria:
'He will not enter this city
or even shoot an arrow here.
He will not fight against it with shields
or build a ramp to attack the city walls.
33He will return to his country the same
way he came,
and he will not enter this city,'
says the LORD.
34'I will defend and save this city
for my sake and for the sake of David,
my servant.'"
35That night the angel of the LORD went
out and killed one hundred eighty-five
thousand men in the Assyrian camp.
When the people got up early the next
morning, they saw all the dead bodies. 36So
Sennacherib king of Assyria left and went
back to Nineveh and stayed there.
37One day as Sennacherib was worshiping
in the temple of his god Nisroch, his sons
Adrammelech and Sharezer killed him with
a sword. Then they escaped to the land of
Ararat. So Sennacherib's son Esarhaddon
became king of Assyria.

Hezekiah's Illness

20 At that time Hezekiah became so sick
he almost died. The prophet Isaiah son
of Amoz went to see him and told him, "This
is what the LORD says: Make arrangements
because you are not going to live, but die."
2Hezekiah turned toward the wall and
prayed to the LORD, 3"LORD, please remember
that I have always obeyed you. I have given
myself completely to you and have done
what you said was right." Then Hezekiah
cried loudly.
4Before Isaiah had left the middle
courtyard, the LORD spoke his word to Isaiah:
5"Go back and tell Hezekiah, the leader of my
people: 'This is what the LORD, the God of
your ancestor David, says: I have heard your
prayer and seen your tears, so I will heal you.
Three days from now you will go up to the
Temple of the LORD. 6I will add fifteen years
to your life. I will save you and this city from
the king of Assyria; I will protect the city for
my sake and for the sake of my servant
David.'"
7Then Isaiah said, "Make a paste from
figs." So they made it and put it on
Hezekiah's boil, and he got well.
8Hezekiah had asked Isaiah, "What will be
the sign that the LORD will heal me and that I
will go up to the Temple of the LORD on the
third day?"
9Isaiah said, "The LORD will do what he
says. This is the sign from the LORD to show
you: Do you want the shadow to go forward
ten steps or back ten steps?"
10Hezekiah answered, "It's easy for the
shadow to go forward ten steps. Instead, let it
go back ten steps."
11Then Isaiah the prophet called to the
LORD, and the LORD brought the shadow ten
steps back up the stairway of Ahaz that it
had gone down.

Messengers from Babylon

12At that time Merodach-Baladan son of
Baladan was king of Babylon. He sent letters
and a gift to Hezekiah, because he had heard
that Hezekiah was sick. 13Hezekiah listened
to the messengers, so he showed them what
was in his storehouses: the silver, gold,
spices, expensive perfumes, his swords and
shields, and all his wealth. He showed them
everything in his palace and his kingdom.
14Then Isaiah the prophet went to King
Hezekiah and asked him, "What did these
men say? Where did they come from?"
Hezekiah said, "They came from a faraway
country—from Babylon."
15So Isaiah asked him, "What did they see
in your palace?"

Hezekiah said, "They saw everything in
my palace. I showed them all my wealth."
16Then Isaiah said to Hezekiah, "Listen to
the words of the LORD: 17'In the future
everything in your palace and everything
your ancestors have stored up until this day
will be taken away to Babylon. Nothing will
be left,' says the LORD. 18'Some of your own
children, those who will be born to you, will
be taken away. And they will become
servants in the palace of the king of
Babylon.' "
19Hezekiah told Isaiah, "These words from
the LORD are good." He said this because he
thought, "There will be peace and security in
my lifetime."
20Everything else Hezekiah did—all his
victories, his work on the pool, his work on
the tunnel to bring water into the city—is
written in the book of the history of the
kings of Judah. 21Then Hezekiah died, and
his son Manasseh became king in his place.

Manasseh King of Judah

21 Manasseh was twelve years old when
he became king, and he was king
fifty-five years in Jerusalem. His mother's
name was Hephzibah. 2He did what the LORD
said was wrong. He did the hateful things the
other nations had done—the nations that the
LORD had forced out of the land ahead of the
Israelites. 3Manasseh's father, Hezekiah, had
destroyed the places where gods were
worshiped, but Manasseh rebuilt them. He
built altars for Baal, and he made an Asherah
idol as Ahab king of Israel had done.
Manasseh also worshiped all the stars of the
sky and served them. 4The LORD had said
about the Temple, "I will be worshiped in
Jerusalem," but Manasseh built altars in the
Temple of the LORD. 5He built altars to
worship the stars in the two courtyards of the
Temple of the LORD. 6He made his own son
pass through fire. He practiced magic and told
the future by explaining signs and dreams,
and he got advice from mediums and
fortune-tellers. He did many things the LORD
said were wrong, which made the LORD angry.
7Manasseh carved an Asherah idol and
put it in the Temple. The LORD had said to
David and his son Solomon about the
Temple, "I will be worshiped forever in this
Temple and in Jerusalem, which I have
chosen from all the tribes of Israel. 8I will
never again make the Israelites wander out
of the land I gave their ancestors. But they
must obey everything I have commanded
them and all the teachings my servant
Moses gave them." 9But the people did not
listen. Manasseh led them to do more evil
than the nations the LORD had destroyed
ahead of the Israelites.
10The LORD said through his servants the
prophets, 11"Manasseh king of Judah has
done these hateful things. He has done more
evil than the Amorites before him. He also
has led Judah to sin with his idols. 12So this
is what the LORD, the God of Israel, says: 'I
will bring so much trouble on Jerusalem and
Judah that anyone who hears about it will be
shocked. 13I will stretch the measuring line
of Samaria over Jerusalem, and the plumb
line used against Ahab's family will be used
on Jerusalem. I will wipe out Jerusalem as a
person wipes a dish and turns it upside
down. 14I will throw away the rest of my
people who are left. I will give them to their
enemies, and they will be robbed by all their
enemies, 15because my people did what I
said was wrong. They have made me angry
from the day their ancestors left Egypt until
now.' "
16Manasseh also killed many innocent
people, filling Jerusalem from one end to the
other with their blood. This was besides the
sin he led Judah to do; he led Judah to do
what the LORD said was wrong.
17The other things Manasseh did as king,
even the sin he did, are written in the book
of the history of the kings of Judah.
18Manasseh died and was buried in the
garden of his own palace, the garden of Uzza.
Then Manasseh's son Amon became king in
his place.

Amon King of Judah

19Amon was twenty-two years old when
he became king, and he was king for two
years in Jerusalem. His mother's name was
Meshullemeth daughter of Haruz, who was
from Jotbah. 20Amon did what the LORD said
was wrong, as his father Manasseh had done.
21He lived in the same way his father had
lived: he worshiped the idols his father had
worshiped, and he bowed down before them.
22Amon rejected the LORD, the God of his
ancestors, and did not follow the ways of the
LORD.

23Amon's officers made plans against him
and killed him in his palace. 24Then the
people of the land killed all those who had
made plans to kill King Amon, and they
made his son Josiah king in his place.
25Everything else Amon did is written in
the book of the history of the kings of Judah.
26He was buried in his grave in the garden of
Uzza, and his son Josiah became king in his
place.

Josiah King of Judah

22 Josiah was eight years old when he
became king, and he ruled thirty-one
years in Jerusalem. His mother's name was
Jedidah daughter of Adaiah, who was from
Bozkath. 2Josiah did what the LORD said was
right. He lived as his ancestor David had
lived, and he did not stop doing what was
right.
3In Josiah's eighteenth year as king, he
sent Shaphan to the Temple of the LORD.
Shaphan son of Azaliah, the son of
Meshullam, was the royal secretary. Josiah
said, 4"Go up to Hilkiah the high priest, and
have him empty out the money the
gatekeepers have gathered from the people.
This is the money they have brought into
the Temple of the LORD. 5Have him give the
money to the supervisors of the work on the
Temple of the LORD. They must pay the
workers who repair the Temple of the
LORD— 6the carpenters, builders, and
bricklayers. Also use the money to buy
timber and cut stone to repair the Temple.
7They do not need to report how they use
the money given to them, because they are
working honestly."

The Book of the Teachings Is Found

8Hilkiah the high priest said to Shaphan
the royal secretary, "I've found the Book of
the Teachings in the Temple of the LORD." He
gave it to Shaphan, who read it.
9Then Shaphan the royal secretary went
to the king and reported to Josiah, "Your
officers have paid out the money that was in
the Temple of the LORD. They have given it to
the workers and supervisors at the Temple."
10Then Shaphan the royal secretary told the
king, "Hilkiah the priest has given me a
book." And Shaphan read from the book to
the king.
11When the king heard the words of the
Book of the Teachings, he tore his clothes to
show how upset he was. 12He gave orders to
Hilkiah the priest, Ahikam son of Shaphan,
Acbor son of Micaiah, Shaphan the royal
secretary, and Asaiah the king's servant.
These were the orders: 13"Go and ask the
LORD about the words in the book that was
found. Ask for me, for all the people, and for
all Judah. The LORD's anger is burning
against us, because our ancestors did not
obey the words of this book; they did not do
all the things written for us to do."
14So Hilkiah the priest, Ahikam, Acbor,
Shaphan, and Asaiah went to talk to Huldah
the prophetess. She was the wife of Shallum
son of Tikvah, the son of Harhas, who took
care of the king's clothes. Huldah lived in
Jerusalem, in the new area of the city.
15She said to them, "This is what the LORD,
the God of Israel, says: Tell the man who sent
you to me, 16'This is what the LORD says: I
will bring trouble to this place and to the
people living here, as it is written in the
book which the king of Judah has read.
17The people of Judah have left me and have
burned incense to other gods. They have
made me angry by all that they have done.
My anger burns against this place like a fire,
and it will not be put out.' 18Tell the king of
Judah, who sent you to ask the LORD, 'This is
what the LORD, the God of Israel, says about
the words you heard: 19When you heard my
words against this place and its people, you
became sorry for what you had done and
humbled yourself before me. I said they
would be cursed and would be destroyed.
You tore your clothes to show how upset
you were, and you cried in my presence. This
is why I have heard you, says the LORD. 20So I
will let you die, and you will be buried in
peace. You won't see all the trouble I will
bring to this place.' "
So they took her message back to the king.

The People Hear the Agreement

23 Then the king gathered all the elders
of Judah and Jerusalem together. 2He
went up to the Temple of the LORD, and all
the people from Judah and Jerusalem went
with him. The priests, prophets, and all the
people—from the least important to the
most important—went with him. He read to
them all the words of the Book of the
Agreement that was found in the Temple of
the LORD. 3The king stood by the pillar and

devotion 97

2 KINGS 22:19

DO YOU LIKE MY PEARLS?

I love my pearls. They were a gift from my husband on my thirtieth birthday, and when I wear those pearls, there is something about them that makes me feel beautiful and sophisticated. As the little oyster struggled to rid the irritation inside his shell, he found that with each pass of the concentric layer of nacre, there was relief. Little did he know that out of his suffering would come my beautiful treasure.

Jesus took each word of God and wrapped it around everyday people who were suffering. Then he took his body and allowed it to be put to death on a cross so that when the suffering was over, we too would have a jewel of great price—the way to eternal life. It's no mistake that the twelve gates in heaven are pearls, each representing the pain and suffering of one of Jesus' twelve followers (Rev. 21:21).

Although he was God in the flesh, Jesus wore his humility like a jewel. He never used his power out of anger or used the Word as a weapon. He changed lives by ministering truth. Humility doesn't mean you are stupid, a pushover, or even weak. Humility means that you conduct yourself in a manner that seeks others' best interests first. Instead of straining to be right, settle for serving. God can take life's little irritations and create beauty out of them—the inner beauty of humility and self-sacrifice that shines just as brightly as my favorite pearls.

made an agreement in the presence of the LORD to follow the LORD and obey his commands, rules, and laws with his whole being, and to obey the words of the agreement written in this book. Then all the people promised to obey the agreement.

Josiah Destroys the Places for Idol Worship

4The king commanded Hilkiah the high
priest and the priests of the next rank and
the gatekeepers to bring out of the Temple of
the LORD everything made for Baal, Asherah,
and all the stars of the sky. Then Josiah
burned them outside Jerusalem in the open
country of the Kidron Valley and carried
their ashes to Bethel. 5The kings of Judah
had chosen priests for these gods. These
priests burned incense in the places where
gods were worshiped in the cities of Judah
and the towns around Jerusalem. They
burned incense to Baal, the sun, the moon,
the planets, and all the stars of the sky. But
Josiah took those priests away. 6He removed
the Asherah idol from the Temple of the
LORD and took it outside Jerusalem to the
Kidron Valley, where he burned it and beat it
into dust. Then he threw the dust on the
graves of the common people. 7He also tore
down the houses of the male prostitutes
who were in the Temple of the LORD, where
the women did weaving for Asherah.

8King Josiah brought all the false priests
from the cities of Judah. He ruined the places
where gods were worshiped, where the
priests had burned incense, from Geba to
Beersheba. He destroyed the places of
worship at the entrance to the Gate of
Joshua, the ruler of the city, on the left side
of the city gate. 9The priests at the places
where gods were worshiped were not
allowed to serve at the LORD's altar in
Jerusalem. But they could eat bread made
without yeast with their brothers.

10Josiah ruined Topheth, in the Valley of

Ben Hinnom, so no one could sacrifice his
son or daughter to Molech. [11]Judah's kings
had placed horses at the front door of the
Temple of the LORD in the courtyard near the
room of Nathan-Melech, an officer. These
horses were for the worship of the sun. So
Josiah removed them and burned the
chariots that were for sun worship also.
[12]The kings of Judah had built altars on
the roof[n] of the upstairs room of Ahaz.
Josiah broke down these altars and the altars
Manasseh had made in the two courtyards of
the Temple of the LORD. Josiah smashed
them to pieces and threw their dust into the
Kidron Valley. [13]King Josiah ruined the
places where gods were worshiped east of
Jerusalem, south of the Mount of Olives.[n]
Solomon king of Israel had built these
places. One was for Ashtoreth, the hated
goddess of the Sidonians. One was for
Chemosh, the hated god of Moab. And one
was for Molech, the hated god of the
Ammonites. [14]Josiah smashed to pieces the
stone pillars they worshiped, and he cut
down the Asherah idols. Then he covered
the places with human bones.
[15]Josiah also broke down the altar at
Bethel—the place of worship made by
Jeroboam son of Nebat, who had led Israel to
sin. Josiah burned that place, broke the
stones of the altar into pieces, then beat
them into dust. He also burned the Asherah
idol. [16]When he turned around, he saw the
graves on the mountain. He had the bones
taken from the graves, and he burned them
on the altar to ruin it. This happened as the
LORD had said it would through the man of
God.
[17]Josiah asked, "What is that monument I
see?"

The people of the city answered, "It's the
grave of the man of God who came from
Judah. This prophet announced the things
you have done against the altar of Bethel."
[18]Josiah said, "Leave the grave alone. No
one may move this man's bones." So they left
his bones and the bones of the prophet who
had come from Samaria.
[19]The kings of Israel had built temples for
worshiping gods in the cities of Samaria,
which had caused the LORD to be angry.
Josiah removed all those temples and did the
same things as he had done at Bethel. [20]He
killed all the priests of those places of
worship; he killed them on the altars and
burned human bones on the altars. Then he
went back to Jerusalem.

Josiah Celebrates the Passover

[21]The king commanded all the people,
"Celebrate the Passover to the LORD your God
as it is written in this Book of the
Agreement." [22]The Passover had not been
celebrated like this since the judges led
Israel. Nor had one like it happened while
there were kings of Israel and kings of Judah.
[23]This Passover was celebrated to the LORD in
Jerusalem in the eighteenth year of King
Josiah's rule.
[24]Josiah destroyed the mediums, fortune-
tellers, house gods, and idols. He also
destroyed all the hated gods seen in the land
of Judah and Jerusalem. This was to obey the
words of the teachings written in the book
Hilkiah the priest had found in the Temple
of the LORD.
[25]There was no king like Josiah before or
after him. He obeyed the LORD with all his
heart, soul, and strength, following all the
Teachings of Moses.
[26]Even so, the LORD did not stop his strong
and terrible anger. His anger burned against
Judah because of all Manasseh had done to
make him angry. [27]The LORD said, "I will
send Judah out of my sight, as I have sent
Israel away. I will reject Jerusalem, which I
chose. And I will take away the Temple
about which I said, 'I will be worshiped
there.' "
[28]Everything else Josiah did is written in
the book of the history of the kings of Judah.
[29]While Josiah was king, Neco king of
Egypt went to help the king of Assyria at the
Euphrates River. King Josiah marched out to
fight against Neco, but at Megiddo, Neco
faced him and killed him. [30]Josiah's servants
carried his body in a chariot from Megiddo
to Jerusalem and buried him in his own
grave. Then the people of Judah chose
Josiah's son Jehoahaz and poured olive oil
on him to make him king in his father's
place.

23:12 roof In Bible times houses were built with flat roofs. The roof was used for drying things such as flax and fruit. And it was used as an extra room, as a place for worship, and as a cool place to sleep in the summer. **23:13 Mount of Olives** Literally, "The Mountain of Ruin."

Jehoahaz King of Judah

31 Jehoahaz was twenty-three years old when he became king, and he was king in Jerusalem for three months. His mother's name was Hamutal, who was the daughter of Jeremiah from Libnah. 32 Jehoahaz did what the LORD said was wrong, just as his ancestors had done.

33 King Neco took Jehoahaz prisoner at Riblah in the land of Hamath so that Jehoahaz could not rule in Jerusalem. Neco made the people of Judah pay about seventy-five hundred pounds of silver and about seventy-five pounds of gold.

34 King Neco made Josiah's son Eliakim the king in place of Josiah his father. Then Neco changed Eliakim's name to Jehoiakim. But Neco took Jehoahaz to Egypt, where he died. 35 Jehoiakim gave King Neco the silver and gold he demanded. Jehoiakim taxed the land and took silver and gold from the people of the land to give to King Neco. Each person had to pay his share.

Jehoiakim King of Judah

36 Jehoiakim was twenty-five years old when he became king, and he was king in Jerusalem for eleven years. His mother's name was Zebidah daughter of Pedaiah, who was from Rumah. 37 Jehoiakim did what the LORD said was wrong, just as his ancestors had done.

24 While Jehoiakim was king, Nebuchadnezzar king of Babylon attacked the land of Judah. So Jehoiakim became Nebuchadnezzar's servant for three years. Then he turned against Nebuchadnezzar and broke away from his rule. 2 The LORD sent raiding parties from Babylon, Aram, Moab, and Ammon against Jehoiakim to destroy Judah. This happened as the LORD had said it would through his servants the prophets.

3 The LORD commanded this to happen to the people of Judah, to remove them from his presence, because of all the sins of Manasseh. 4 He had killed many innocent people and had filled Jerusalem with their blood. And the LORD would not forgive these sins.

5 The other things that happened while Jehoiakim was king and all he did are written in the book of the history of the kings of Judah. 6 Jehoiakim died, and his son Jehoiachin became king in his place.

7 The king of Egypt did not leave his land again, because the king of Babylon had captured all that belonged to the king of Egypt, from the brook of Egypt to the Euphrates River.

Jehoiachin King of Judah

8 Jehoiachin was eighteen years old when he became king, and he was king three months in Jerusalem. His mother's name was Nehushta daughter of Elnathan from Jerusalem. 9 Jehoiachin did what the LORD said was wrong, just as his father had done.

10 At that time the officers of Nebuchadnezzar king of Babylon came up to Jerusalem. When they reached the city, they attacked it. 11 Nebuchadnezzar himself came to the city while his officers were attacking it. 12 Jehoiachin king of Judah surrendered to the king of Babylon, along with Jehoiachin's mother, servants, nobles, and officers. So Nebuchadnezzar made Jehoiachin a prisoner in the eighth year he was king of Babylon. 13 Nebuchadnezzar took all the treasures from the Temple of the LORD and from the palace. He cut up all the gold objects Solomon king of Israel had made for the Temple of the LORD. This happened as the LORD had said it would. 14 Nebuchadnezzar took away all the people of Jerusalem, including all the leaders, all the wealthy people, and all the craftsmen and metal workers. There were ten thousand prisoners in all. Only the poorest people in the land were left. 15 Nebuchadnezzar carried away Jehoiachin to Babylon, as well as the king's mother and his wives, the officers, and the leading men of the land. They were taken captive from Jerusalem to Babylon. 16 The king of Babylon also took all seven thousand soldiers, who were strong and able to fight in war, and about a thousand craftsmen and metal workers. Nebuchadnezzar took them as prisoners to Babylon. 17 Then he made Mattaniah, Jehoiachin's uncle, king in Jehoiachin's place. He also changed Mattaniah's name to Zedekiah.

Zedekiah King of Judah

18 Zedekiah was twenty-one years old when he became king, and he was king in Jerusalem for eleven years. His mother's

name was Hamutal daughter of Jeremiah[n] from Libnah. 19 Zedekiah did what the LORD said was wrong, just as Jehoiakim had done. 20 All this happened in Jerusalem and Judah because the LORD was angry with them. Finally, he threw them out of his presence.

The Fall of Jerusalem

Zedekiah turned against the king of Babylon.

25 Nebuchadnezzar king of Babylon marched against Jerusalem with his whole army during Zedekiah's ninth year as king, on the tenth day of the tenth month. He made a camp around the city and piled dirt against the city walls to attack it. 2 The city was under attack until Zedekiah's eleventh year as king. 3 By the ninth day of the fourth month, the hunger was terrible in the city. There was no food for the people to eat. 4 Then the city was broken into, and the whole army ran away at night through the gate between the two walls by the king's garden. While the Babylonians were still surrounding the city, Zedekiah and his men ran away toward the Jordan Valley. 5 But the Babylonian army chased King Zedekiah and caught up with him in the plains of Jericho. All of his army was scattered from him, 6 so they captured Zedekiah and took him to the king of Babylon at Riblah. There he passed sentence on Zedekiah. 7 They killed Zedekiah's sons as he watched. Then they put out his eyes and put bronze chains on him and took him to Babylon.

8 Nebuzaradan was the commander of the king's special guards. This officer of the king of Babylon came to Jerusalem on the seventh day of the fifth month, in Nebuchadnezzar's nineteenth year as king of Babylon. 9 Nebuzaradan set fire to the Temple of the LORD and the palace and all the houses of Jerusalem. Every important building was burned.

10 The whole Babylonian army, led by the commander of the king's special guards, broke down the walls around Jerusalem. 11 Nebuzaradan, the commander of the guards, captured the people left in Jerusalem, those who had surrendered to the king of Babylon, and the rest of the people. 12 But the commander left behind some of the poorest people of the land to take care of the vineyards and fields.

13 The Babylonians broke up the bronze pillars, the bronze stands, and the large bronze bowl, which was called the Sea, in the Temple of the LORD. Then they carried the bronze to Babylon. 14 They also took the pots, shovels, wick trimmers, dishes, and all the bronze objects used to serve in the Temple. 15 The commander of the king's special guards took away the pans for carrying hot coals, the bowls, and everything made of pure gold or silver. 16 There were two pillars and the large bronze bowl and the movable stands which Solomon had made for the Temple of the LORD. There was so much bronze that it could not be weighed. 17 Each pillar was about twenty-seven feet high. The bronze capital on top of the pillar was about four and one-half feet high. It was decorated with a net design and bronze pomegranates all around it. The other pillar also had a net design and was like the first pillar.

Judah Is Taken Prisoner

18 The commander of the guards took some prisoners—Seraiah the chief priest, Zephaniah the priest next in rank, and the three doorkeepers. 19 Of the people who were still in the city, he took the officer in charge of the fighting men, as well as five people who advised the king. He took the royal secretary who selected people for the army and sixty other men who were in the city. 20 Nebuzaradan, the commander, took all these people and brought them to the king of Babylon at Riblah. 21 There at Riblah, in the land of Hamath, the king had them killed. So the people of Judah were led away from their country as captives.

Gedaliah Becomes Governor

22 Nebuchadnezzar king of Babylon left some people in the land of Judah. He appointed Gedaliah son of Ahikam, the son of Shaphan, as governor.

23 The army captains and their men heard that the king of Babylon had made Gedaliah

24:18 Jeremiah This is not the prophet Jeremiah, but a different man with the same name.

governor, so they came to Gedaliah at
Mizpah. They were Ishmael son of
Nethaniah, Johanan son of Kareah, Seraiah
son of Tanhumeth the Netophathite,
Jaazaniah son of the Maacathite, and their
men. 24Then Gedaliah promised these army
captains and their men, "Don't be afraid of
the Babylonian officers. Live in the land and
serve the king of Babylon, and everything
will go well for you."

25In the seventh month Ishmael son of
Nethaniah, son of Elishama from the king's
family, came with ten men and killed
Gedaliah. They also killed the men of Judah
and Babylon who were with Gedaliah at
Mizpah. 26Then all the people, from the least
important to the most important, along with
the army leaders, ran away to Egypt, because
they were afraid of the Babylonians.

Jehoiachin Is Set Free

27Jehoiachin king of Judah was held in
Babylon for thirty-seven years. In the
thirty-seventh year Evil-Merodach became
king of Babylon, and he let Jehoiachin out of
prison on the twenty-seventh day of the
twelfth month. 28Evil-Merodach spoke
kindly to Jehoiachin and gave him a seat of
honor above the seats of the other kings who
were with him in Babylon. 29So Jehoiachin
put away his prison clothes. For the rest of
his life, he ate at the king's table. 30Every day,
for as long as Jehoiachin lived, the king gave
him an allowance.

1 Chronicles

The Latin Vulgate (the first common translation from the original Hebrew and Aramaic texts) used this longer title: "The Chronicles of the Entire Sacred History."

Person Holding the Pen God Wrote With: The author doesn't identify himself, but most assume it was *Ezra,* whose qualifications are spelled out in the Old Testament book bearing his name (Ezra 7:1–6).

When the Text Was Written: Most likely between 450 and 430 B.C.

Spiritual Posture of the Original Recipients: The Jews from the southern kingdom (Judah) had returned from captivity in Babylon to find a very different Jerusalem. The magnificent first Temple was demolished, their security system was breached, and there was a Persian king in power instead of a Jewish monarch. While they rebuilt the Temple and overhauled the wall around the city, the new church paled in comparison to "Solomon's Temple"—and the Jews were now viewed as second-class citizens. The Israelites were most likely feeling insecure about their status as God's chosen people.

Storyline Synopsis: The Chronicles are sort of like the very first Bible commentaries, with their subject matter being 1 and 2 Samuel and 1 and 2 Kings. This book covers the genealogies of the patriarchs (chapters 1—9), the twelve tribes of Israel (chapters 2—8), the return to Jerusalem (chapter 9), the highlights of King David's reign (chapters 10—29), and the introduction of King Solomon (1 Chr. 29:21–30). It's as if the author has compiled a "best of" journal to remind the Israelites that God's promises for them were still in effect in spite of their difficult circumstances.

A Moment Worth Discussing: Saul is vilified in light of his *spiritual* adultery (1 Chr. 10:13–14), yet this text doesn't even mention David's *physical* adultery with Bathsheba! The chronicler is so committed to proving God's faithfulness throughout Israel's eyebrow-raising history that he pointedly excludes David's big blunder. Instead of bringing up the mistakes of the past, he focuses on the overarching theme of Jehovah's mercy.

Interesting (But Likely to Be Overlooked) Characters: David's small team of *"mighty men"* mentioned in 1 Chronicles 11:10–47 was an impressive group of soldiers. (Also see 2 Sam. 23:24–39.) Included in this select fraternity were brave brawlers who defeated scores of enemy troops—and one who killed a ferocious lion with his bare hands!

From Adam to Abraham

1 Adam was the father of Seth. Seth was the father of Enosh. Enosh was the father of Kenan. 2Kenan was the father of Mahalalel. Mahalalel was the father of Jared. Jared was the father of Enoch. 3Enoch was the father of Methuselah. Methuselah was the father of Lamech, and Lamech was the father of Noah.

4The sons of Noah were Shem, Ham, and Japheth.

5Japheth's sons were Gomer, Magog, Madai, Javan, Tubal, Meshech, and Tiras.

6Gomer's sons were Ashkenaz, Riphath, and Togarmah.

7Javan's sons were Elishah, Tarshish, Kittim,[n] and Rodanim.

8Ham's sons were Cush, Mizraim,[n] Put, and Canaan.

9Cush's sons were Seba, Havilah, Sabta, Raamah, and Sabteca.

Raamah's sons were Sheba and Dedan.

10Cush was the father of Nimrod, who grew up to become a mighty warrior on the earth.

11Mizraim was the father of the Ludites, Anamites, Lehabites, and Naphtuhites, 12Pathrusites, Casluhites, and Caphtorites. (The Philistines came from the Casluhites.)

13Canaan's first child was Sidon. He was also the father of the Hittites, 14Jebusites, Amorites, Girgashites, 15Hivites, Arkites, Sinites, 16Arvadites, Zemarites, and Hamathites.

17Shem's sons were Elam, Asshur, Arphaxad, Lud, and Aram.

Aram's sons were Uz, Hul, Gether, and Meshech.

18Arphaxad was the father of Shelah, who was the father of Eber.

19Eber had two sons. One son was named Peleg,[n] because the people on the earth were divided into different languages during his life. Peleg's brother was named Joktan.

20Joktan was the father of Almodad, Sheleph, Hazarmaveth, Jerah, 21Hadoram, Uzal, Diklah, 22Obal, Abimael, Sheba, 23Ophir, Havilah, and Jobab. All these were Joktan's sons. 24The family line included Shem, Arphaxad, Shelah, 25Eber, Peleg, Reu, 26Serug, Nahor, Terah, 27and Abram, who was called Abraham.

Abraham's Family

28Abraham's sons were Isaac and Ishmael.

29These were the sons of Isaac and Ishmael. Ishmael's first son was Nebaioth. His other sons were Kedar, Adbeel, Mibsam, 30Mishma, Dumah, Massa, Hadad, Tema, 31Jetur, Naphish, and Kedemah. These were Ishmael's sons. 32Keturah, Abraham's slave woman, gave birth to Zimran, Jokshan, Medan, Midian, Ishbak, and Shuah.

Jokshan's sons were Sheba and Dedan.

33Midian's sons were Ephah, Epher, Hanoch, Abida, and Eldaah. All these were descendants of Keturah.

34Abraham was the father of Isaac, and Isaac's sons were Esau and Israel.

35Esau's sons were Eliphaz, Reuel, Jeush, Jalam, and Korah.

36Eliphaz's sons were Teman, Omar, Zepho, Gatam, Kenaz, Timna, and Amalek.

37Reuel's sons were Nahath, Zerah, Shammah, and Mizzah.

The Edomites from Seir

38Seir's sons were Lotan, Shobal, Zibeon, Anah, Dishon, Ezer, and Dishan.

39Lotan's sons were Hori and Homam, and his sister was Timna.

40Shobal's sons were Alvan, Manahath, Ebal, Shepho, and Onam.

Zibeon's sons were Aiah and Anah.

41Anah's son was Dishon.

Dishon's sons were Hemdan, Eshban, Ithran, and Keran.

42Ezer's sons were Bilhan, Zaavan, and Akan.

Dishan's sons were Uz and Aran.

The Kings of Edom

43These kings ruled in Edom before there were kings in Israel. Bela son of Beor was king of Edom, and his city was named Dinhabah.

44When Bela died, Jobab son of Zerah became king. He was from Bozrah.

45When Jobab died, Husham became king. He was from the land of the Temanites.

46When Husham died, Hadad son of Bedad became king, and his city was named Avith. Hadad defeated Midian in the country of Moab.

1:7 Kittim His descendants were the people of Cyprus. **1:8 Mizraim** This is another name for Egypt. **1:19 Peleg** This name sounds like the Hebrew word for "divided."

47 When Hadad died, Samlah became king.
He was from Masrekah.
48 When Samlah died, Shaul became king.
He was from Rehoboth by the river.
49 When Shaul died, Baal-Hanan son of
Acbor became king.
50 When Baal-Hanan died, Hadad became
king, and his city was named Pau. Hadad's
wife was named Mehetabel, and she was the
daughter of Matred, who was the daughter
of Me-Zahab. 51 Then Hadad died.
The leaders of the family groups of Edom
were Timna, Alvah, Jetheth, 52 Oholibamah,
Elah, Pinon, 53 Kenaz, Teman, Mibzar,
54 Magdiel, and Iram. These were the leaders
of Edom.

Israel's Family

2 The sons of Israel[n] were Reuben, Simeon,
Levi, Judah, Issachar, Zebulun, 2 Dan,
Joseph, Benjamin, Naphtali, Gad, and Asher.

Judah's Family

3 Judah's sons were Er, Onan, and Shelah. A
Canaanite woman, the daughter of Shua,
was their mother. Judah's first son, Er, did
what the LORD said was wicked, so the LORD
put him to death. 4 Judah's daughter-in-law
Tamar gave birth to Perez and Zerah. Judah
was the father, so Judah had five sons.
5 Perez's sons were Hezron and Hamul.
6 Zerah had five sons: Zimri, Ethan,
Heman, Calcol, and Darda.
7 Carmi's son was Achan, who caused
trouble for Israel because he took things that
had been given to the LORD to be destroyed.
8 Ethan's son was Azariah.
9 Hezron's sons were Jerahmeel, Ram, and
Caleb.
10 Ram was Amminadab's father, and
Amminadab was Nahshon's father. Nahshon
was the leader of the people of Judah.
11 Nahshon was the father of Salmon, who
was the father of Boaz. 12 Boaz was the father
of Obed, and Obed was the father of Jesse.
13 Jesse's first son was Eliab. His second son
was Abinadab, his third was Shimea, 14 his
fourth was Nethanel, his fifth was Raddai,
15 his sixth was Ozem, and his seventh son
was David. 16 Their sisters were Zeruiah and
Abigail. Zeruiah's three sons were Abishai,
Joab, and Asahel. 17 Abigail was the mother of
Amasa, and his father was Jether, an
Ishmaelite.

Caleb's Family

18 Caleb son of Hezron had children by his
wife Azubah and by Jerioth. Caleb and
Azubah's sons were Jesher, Shobab, and
Ardon. 19 When Azubah died, Caleb married
Ephrath. They had a son named Hur, 20 who
was the father of Uri, who was the father of
Bezalel.
21 Later, when Hezron was sixty years old,
he married the daughter of Makir, Gilead's
father. Hezron had sexual relations with
Makir's daughter, and she had a son named
Segub. 22 Segub was the father of Jair. Jair
controlled twenty-three cities in the country
of Gilead. 23 (But Geshur and Aram captured
the Towns of Jair, as well as Kenath and the
small towns around it—sixty towns in all.)
All these were descendants of Makir, the
father of Gilead.
24 After Hezron died in Caleb Ephrathah,
his wife Abijah had his son, named Ashhur.
Ashhur became the father of Tekoa.

Jerahmeel's Family

25 Hezron's first son was Jerahmeel.
Jerahmeel's sons were Ram, Bunah, Oren,
Ozem, and Ahijah. Ram was Jerahmeel's
first son. 26 Jerahmeel had another wife,
named Atarah. She was the mother of
Onam.
27 Jerahmeel's first son, Ram, had sons.
They were Maaz, Jamin, and Eker.
28 Onam's sons were Shammai and Jada.
Shammai's sons were Nadab and Abishur.
29 Abishur's wife was named Abihail, and
their sons were Ahban and Molid.
30 Nadab's sons were Seled and Appaim.
Seled died without having children.
31 Appaim's son was Ishi, who became the
father of Sheshan.
Sheshan was the father of Ahlai.
32 Jada was Shammai's brother, and Jada's
sons were Jether and Jonathan. Jether died
without having children.
33 Jonathan's sons were Peleth and Zaza.
These were Jerahmeel's descendants.
34 Sheshan did not have any sons, only
daughters. He had a servant from Egypt
named Jarha. 35 Sheshan let his daughter

2:1 Israel Another name for Jacob.

marry his servant Jarha, and she had a son
named Attai.
36Attai was the father of Nathan. Nathan
was the father of Zabad. 37Zabad was the
father of Ephlal. Ephlal was the father of
Obed. 38Obed was the father of Jehu. Jehu
was the father of Azariah. 39Azariah was the
father of Helez. Helez was the father of
Eleasah. 40Eleasah was the father of Sismai.
Sismai was the father of Shallum. 41Shallum
was the father of Jekamiah, and Jekamiah
was the father of Elishama.

Caleb's Family

42Caleb was Jerahmeel's brother. Caleb's
first son was Mesha. Mesha was the father of
Ziph, and his son Mareshah was the father of
Hebron.
43Hebron's sons were Korah, Tappuah,
Rekem, and Shema. 44Shema was the father
of Raham, who was the father of Jorkeam.
Rekem was the father of Shammai.
45Shammai was the father of Maon, and
Maon was the father of Beth Zur.
46Caleb's slave woman was named Ephah,
and she was the mother of Haran, Moza, and
Gazez. Haran was the father of Gazez.
47Jahdai's sons were Regem, Jotham,
Geshan, Pelet, Ephah, and Shaaph.
48Caleb had another slave woman named
Maacah. She was the mother of Sheber,
Tirhanah, 49Shaaph, and Sheva. Shaaph was
the father of Madmannah. Sheva was the
father of Macbenah and Gibea. Caleb's
daughter was Acsah.
50-51These were Caleb's descendants:
Caleb's son Hur was the first son of his
mother Ephrathah. Hur's sons were Shobal,
Salma, and Hareph. Shobal was the father of
Kiriath Jearim. Salma was the father of
Bethlehem. And Hareph was the father of
Beth Gader.
52Shobal was the father of Kiriath Jearim.
Shobal's descendants were Haroeh, half the
Manahathites, 53and the family groups of
Kiriath Jearim: the Ithrites, Puthites,
Shumathites, and Mishraites. The Zorathites
and the Eshtaolites came from the Mishraite
people.
54Salma's descendants were Bethlehem,
the Netophathites, Atroth Beth Joab, half the
Manahathites, and the Zorites. 55His
descendants included the families who lived
at Jabez, who wrote and copied important
papers. They were called the Tirathites,
Shimeathites, and Sucathites and were from
the Kenite family group who came from
Hammath. He was the father of the people
living in Recab.

David's Family

3 These are David's sons who were born in
Hebron. The first was Amnon, whose
mother was Ahinoam from Jezreel. The
second son was Daniel, whose mother was
Abigail from Carmel. 2The third son was
Absalom, whose mother was Maacah
daughter of Talmai, the king of Geshur. The
fourth son was Adonijah, whose mother was
Haggith. 3The fifth son was Shephatiah,
whose mother was Abital. The sixth son was
Ithream, whose mother was Eglah. 4These
six sons of David were born to him in
Hebron, where David ruled for seven and
one-half years.
David ruled in Jerusalem thirty-three
years. 5These were his children who were
born in Jerusalem: Shammua, Shobab,
Nathan, and Solomon—the four children of
David and Bathsheba, Ammiel's daughter.
6-8David's other nine children were Ibhar,
Elishua, Eliphelet, Nogah, Nepheg, Japhia,
Elishama, Eliada, and Eliphelet. 9These were
all of David's sons, except for those born to
his slave women. David also had a daughter
named Tamar.

The Kings of Judah

10Solomon's son was Rehoboam.
Rehoboam's son was Abijah. Abijah's son
was Asa. Asa's son was Jehoshaphat.
11Jehoshaphat's son was Jehoram. Jehoram's
son was Ahaziah. Ahaziah's son was Joash.
12Joash's son was Amaziah. Amaziah's son
was Azariah. Azariah's son was Jotham.
13Jotham's son was Ahaz. Ahaz's son was
Hezekiah. Hezekiah's son was Manasseh.
14Manasseh's son was Amon, and Amon's
son was Josiah.
15These were Josiah's sons: His first son
was Johanan, his second was Jehoiakim, his
third was Zedekiah, and his fourth was
Shallum.
16Jehoiakim was followed by Jehoiachin,
and he was followed by Zedekiah.

David's Descendants After the Babylonian Captivity

17Jehoiachin was taken as a prisoner. His
sons were Shealtiel, 18Malkiram, Pedaiah,

Shenazzar, Jekamiah, Hoshama, and
Nedabiah.
19 Pedaiah's sons were Zerubbabel and
Shimei.
Zerubbabel's sons were Meshullam and
Hananiah, and their sister was Shelomith.
20 Zerubbabel also had five other sons:
Hashubah, Ohel, Berekiah, Hasadiah, and
Jushab-Hesed.
21 Hananiah's descendants were Pelatiah
and Jeshaiah, and the sons of Rephaiah,
Arnan, Obadiah, and Shecaniah.
22 Shecaniah's son was Shemaiah.
Shemaiah's sons were Hattush, Igal, Bariah,
Neariah, and Shaphat. There were six in all.
23 Neariah had three sons: Elioenai,
Hizkiah, and Azrikam.
24 Elioenai had seven sons: Hodaviah,
Eliashib, Pelaiah, Akkub, Johanan, Delaiah,
and Anani.

Other Family Groups of Judah

4 Judah's descendants were Perez, Hezron,
Carmi, Hur, and Shobal.
2 Reaiah was Shobal's son. Reaiah was the
father of Jahath, and Jahath was the father of
Ahumai and Lahad. They were the family
groups of the Zorathite people.
3-4 Hur was the oldest son of Caleb and his
wife Ephrathah. Hur was the leader of
Bethlehem. His three sons were Etam,
Penuel, and Ezer. Etam's sons were Jezreel,
Ishma, and Idbash. They had a sister named
Hazzelelponi. Penuel was the father of
Gedor, and Ezer was the father of Hushah.
5 Tekoa's father was Ashhur. Ashhur had
two wives named Helah and Naarah.
6 The sons of Ashhur and Naarah were
Ahuzzam, Hepher, Temeni, and Haahashtari.
These were the descendants of Naarah.
7 Helah's sons were Zereth, Zohar, Ethnan,
8 and Koz. Koz was the father of Anub,
Hazzobebah, and the Aharhel family group.
Aharhel was the son of Harum.
9 There was a man named Jabez, who
was respected more than his brothers. His
mother named him Jabez[n] because she said,
"I was in much pain when I gave birth to
him." 10 Jabez prayed to the God of Israel,
"Please do good things for me and give
me more land. Stay with me, and don't
let anyone hurt me. Then I won't have
any pain." And God did what Jabez had
asked.
11 Kelub, Shuhah's brother, was the father
of Mehir. Mehir was the father of Eshton.
12 Eshton was the father of Beth Rapha,
Paseah, and Tehinnah. Tehinnah was the
father of the people from the town of
Nahash. These people were from Recah.
13 The sons of Kenaz were Othniel and
Seraiah.
Othniel's sons were Hathath and
Meonothai. 14 Meonothai was the father of
Ophrah.
Seraiah was the father of Joab. Joab was
the ancestor of the people from Craftsmen's
Valley, named that because the people living
there were craftsmen.
15 Caleb was Jephunneh's son. Caleb's sons
were Iru, Elah, and Naam. Elah's son was
Kenaz.
16 Jehallelel's sons were Ziph, Ziphah,
Tiria, and Asarel.
17-18 Ezrah's sons were Jether, Mered,
Epher, and Jalon. Mered married Bithiah,
the daughter of the king of Egypt. The
children of Mered and Bithiah were
Miriam, Shammai, and Ishbah. Ishbah was
the father of Eshtemoa. Mered also had a
wife from Judah, who gave birth to Jered,
Heber, and Jekuthiel. Jered became the
father of Gedor. Heber became the father of
Soco. And Jekuthiel became the father of
Zanoah.
19 Hodiah's wife was Naham's sister. The
sons of Hodiah's wife were Eshtemoa and the
father of Keilah. Keilah was from the
Garmite people, and Eshtemoa was from the
Maacathite people.
20 Shimon's sons were Amnon, Rinnah,
Ben-Hanan, and Tilon.
Ishi's sons were Zoheth and Ben-Zoheth.
21-22 Shelah was Judah's son. Shelah's sons
were Er, Laadah, Jokim, the men from
Cozeba, Joash, and Saraph. Er was the father
of Lecah. Laadah was the father of Mareshah
and the family groups of linen workers at
Beth Ashbea. Joash and Saraph ruled in
Moab and Jashubi Lehem. The writings
about this family are very old. 23 These sons
of Shelah were potters. They lived in
Netaim and Gederah and worked for the
king.

4:9 Jabez This name in Hebrew sounds like the word for "pain."

Simeon's Children

24 Simeon's sons were Nemuel, Jamin, Jarib, Zerah, and Shaul. 25 Shaul's son was Shallum. Shallum's son was Mibsam. Mibsam's son was Mishma.

26 Mishma's son was Hammuel. Hammuel's son was Zaccur. Zaccur's son was Shimei. 27 Shimei had sixteen sons and six daughters, but his brothers did not have many children, so there were not as many people in their family group as there were in Judah.

28 Shimei's children lived in Beersheba, Moladah, Hazar Shual, 29 Bilhah, Ezem, Tolad, 30 Bethuel, Hormah, Ziklag, 31 Beth Marcaboth, Hazar Susim, Beth Biri, and Shaaraim. They lived in these cities until David became king. 32 The five villages near these cities were Etam, Ain, Rimmon, Token, and Ashan. 33 There were also other villages as far away as Baalath. This is where they lived. And they wrote the history of their family.

34-38 The men in this list were leaders of their family groups: Meshobab, Jamlech, Joshah son of Amaziah, Joel, Jehu son of Joshibiah (Joshibiah was the son of Seraiah, who was the son of Asiel), Elioenai, Jaakobah, Jeshohaiah, Asaiah, Adiel, Jesimiel, Benaiah, and Ziza. (Ziza was the son of Shiphi, who was the son of Allon. Allon was the son of Jedaiah, who was the son of Shimri. And Shimri was the son of Shemaiah.)

These families grew very large. 39 They went outside the city of Gedor to the east side of the valley to look for pasture for their flocks. 40 They found good pastures with plenty of grass, and the land was open country and peaceful and quiet. Ham's descendants had lived there in the past.

41 These men who were listed came to Gedor while Hezekiah was king of Judah. They fought against the Hamites, destroying their tents, and also against the Meunites who lived there, and completely destroyed them. So there are no Meunites there even today. Then these men began to live there, because there was pasture for their flocks. 42 Ishi's sons, Pelatiah, Neariah, Rephaiah, and Uzziel, led five hundred of the Simeonites and attacked the people living in the mountains of Edom. 43 They killed the few Amalekites who were still alive. From that time until now these Simeonites have lived in Edom.

Reuben's Children

5 Reuben was Israel's first son. Reuben should have received the special privileges of the oldest son, but he had sexual relations with his father's slave woman. So those special privileges were given to Joseph's sons. (Joseph was a son of Israel.) In the family history Reuben's name is not listed as the first son. 2 Judah became stronger than his brothers, and a leader came from his family. But Joseph's family received the privileges that belonged to the oldest son. 3 Reuben was Israel's first son. Reuben's sons were Hanoch, Pallu, Hezron, and Carmi.

4 These were the children of Joel: Shemaiah was Joel's son. Gog was Shemaiah's son. Shimei was Gog's son. 5 Micah was Shimei's son. Reaiah was Micah's son. Baal was Reaiah's son. 6 Beerah was Baal's son. Beerah was a leader of the tribe of Reuben. Tiglath-Pileser king of Assyria captured him and took him away.

7 Joel's brothers and all his family groups are listed just as they are written in their family histories: Jeiel was the first, then Zechariah, 8 and Bela. (Bela was the son of Azaz. Azaz was the son of Shema, and Shema was the son of Joel.) They lived in the area of Aroer all the way to Nebo and Baal Meon. 9 Bela's people lived to the east—as far as the edge of the desert, which is beside the Euphrates River—because they had too many cattle for the land of Gilead.

10 When Saul was king, Bela's people fought a war against the Hagrite people and defeated them. Then Bela's people lived in the tents that had belonged to the Hagrites in all the area east of Gilead.

Gad's Children

11 The people from the tribe of Gad lived near the Reubenites. The Gadites lived in the area of Bashan all the way to Salecah. 12 Joel was the main leader, Shapham was second, and then Janai and Shaphat were leaders in Bashan.

13 The seven relatives in their families were Michael, Meshullam, Sheba, Jorai, Jacan, Zia, and Eber. 14 They were the descendants of Abihail. Abihail was Huri's son. Huri was Jaroah's son. Jaroah was

Gilead's son. Gilead was Michael's son.
Michael was Jeshishai's son. Jeshishai was
Jahdo's son, and Jahdo was the son of Buz.
15Ahi was Abdiel's son, and Abdiel was
Guni's son. Ahi was the leader of their
family.
16The Gadites lived in Gilead, Bashan and
the small towns around it, and on all the
pasturelands in the Plain of Sharon all the
way to the borders.
17All these names were written in the
family history of Gad during the time
Jotham was king of Judah and Jeroboam was
king of Israel.

Soldiers Skilled in War

18There were forty-four thousand seven
hundred sixty soldiers from the tribes of
Reuben and Gad and East Manasseh who
carried shields and swords and bows. They
were skilled in war. 19They started a war
against the Hagrites and the people of Jetur,
Naphish, and Nodab. 20The men from the
tribes of Manasseh, Reuben, and Gad prayed
to God during the war, asking him to help
them. So he helped them because they
trusted him. He handed over to them the
Hagrites and all those who were with them.
21They took the animals that belonged to the
Hagrites: fifty thousand camels, two
hundred fifty thousand sheep, and two
thousand donkeys. They also captured one
hundred thousand people. 22Many Hagrites
were killed because God helped the people
of Reuben, Gad, and Manasseh. Then they
lived there until Babylon captured them and
took them away.

East Manasseh

23There were many people in East
Manasseh, and they lived in the area of
Bashan all the way to Baal Hermon, Senir,
and Mount Hermon.
24These were the family leaders: Epher,
Ishi, Eliel, Azriel, Jeremiah, Hodaviah, and
Jahdiel. They were all strong, brave, and
famous men, and leaders in their families.
25But they sinned against the God that their
ancestors had worshiped. They began
worshiping the gods of the people in that
land, and those were the people God was
destroying. 26So the God of Israel made Pul

devotion 98

1 CHRONICLES 5:20

WHAT IF IT'S NOT OKAY?

When my sister had cancer, I felt constantly confused. I wanted to trust God with my sister's life, but I knew everyone around me thought she was going to die. My husband's parents happened to be in town, and we went to lunch with them. I was convinced they would be able to make sense of it all for me. As we sat at lunch, I told them that I was really trying to have faith that my sister would be healed. My mother-in-law looked at me and said, "It is a lot easier to have faith in the hopes of healing than it is to have faith in the face of death." That was not what I wanted to hear, but I knew she was right. Faith is about trusting the Lord, not only regardless of the circumstances but also regardless of the outcome.

Look up Hebrews 11. This chapter is often called the "Hall of Faith." Each of these men and women trusted God in the midst of difficult circumstances and impossible odds, even though many of them died before they saw God's faithfulness. But as we read their stories thousands of years later, we know that God was faithful in each of their lives. God can be trusted. That's what faith is all about. God wants to help you if you will only trust him. You may not know the outcome of your circumstance, but you know the One who holds it all in his hands. Trust him.

king of Assyria want to go to war. (Pul was
also called Tiglath-Pileser.) He captured the
people of Reuben, Gad, and East Manasseh,
and he took them away to Halah, Habor,
Hara, and near the Gozan River. They have
lived there from that time until this day.

Levi's Children

6 Levi's sons were Gershon, Kohath, and
Merari.
2Kohath's sons were Amram, Izhar,
Hebron, and Uzziel.
3Amram's children were Aaron, Moses,
and Miriam.
Aaron's sons were Nadab, Abihu, Eleazar,
and Ithamar. 4Eleazar was the father of
Phinehas. Phinehas was the father of
Abishua. 5Abishua was the father of Bukki.
Bukki was the father of Uzzi. 6Uzzi was the
father of Zerahiah. Zerahiah was the father
of Meraioth. 7Meraioth was the father of
Amariah. Amariah was the father of Ahitub.
8Ahitub was the father of Zadok. Zadok was
the father of Ahimaaz. 9Ahimaaz was the
father of Azariah. Azariah was the father of
Johanan. 10Johanan was the father of
Azariah. (Azariah was a priest in the Temple
Solomon built in Jerusalem.) 11Azariah was
the father of Amariah. Amariah was the
father of Ahitub. 12Ahitub was the father of
Zadok. Zadok was the father of Shallum.
13Shallum was the father of Hilkiah. Hilkiah
was the father of Azariah. 14Azariah was the
father of Seraiah, and Seraiah was the father
of Jehozadak.
15Jehozadak was forced to leave his home
when the LORD sent Judah and Jerusalem
into captivity under the control of
Nebuchadnezzar.
16Levi's sons were Gershon, Kohath, and
Merari.
17The names of Gershon's sons were Libni
and Shimei.
18Kohath's sons were Amram, Izhar,
Hebron, and Uzziel.
19Merari's sons were Mahli and Mushi.
This is a list of the family groups of Levi,
listed by the name of the father of each
group.
20Gershon's son was Libni. Libni's son was
Jehath. Jehath's son was Zimmah.
21Zimmah's son was Joah. Joah's son was
Iddo. Iddo's son was Zerah. And Zerah's son
was Jeatherai.
22Kohath's son was Amminadab.
Amminadab's son was Korah. Korah's son
was Assir. 23Assir's son was Elkanah.
Elkanah's son was Ebiasaph. Ebiasaph's son
was Assir. 24Assir's son was Tahath. Tahath's
son was Uriel. Uriel's son was Uzziah, and
Uzziah's son was Shaul.
25Elkanah's sons were Amasai and
Ahimoth. 26Ahimoth's son was Elkanah.
Elkanah's son was Zophai. Zophai's son was
Nahath. 27Nahath's son was Eliab. Eliab's son
was Jeroham. Jeroham's son was Elkanah,
and Elkanah's son was Samuel.
28Samuel's sons were Joel, the first son,
and Abijah, the second son.
29Merari's son was Mahli. Mahli's son was
Libni. Libni's son was Shimei. Shimei's son
was Uzzah. 30Uzzah's son was Shimea.
Shimea's son was Haggiah, and Haggiah's
son was Asaiah.

The Temple Musicians

31David chose some people to be in charge
of the music in the house of the LORD. They
began their work after the Ark of the
Agreement was put there. 32They served by
making music at the Holy Tent (also called
the Meeting Tent), and they served until
Solomon built the Temple of the LORD in
Jerusalem. They followed the rules for their
work.
33These are the musicians and their sons:
From Kohath's family there was Heman
the singer. Heman was Joel's son. Joel was
Samuel's son. 34Samuel was Elkanah's son.
Elkanah was Jeroham's son. Jeroham was
Eliel's son. Eliel was Toah's son. 35Toah was
Zuph's son. Zuph was Elkanah's son.
Elkanah was Mahath's son. Mahath was
Amasai's son. 36Amasai was Elkanah's son.
Elkanah was Joel's son. Joel was Azariah's
son. Azariah was Zephaniah's son.
37Zephaniah was Tahath's son. Tahath was
Assir's son. Assir was Ebiasaph's son.
Ebiasaph was Korah's son. 38Korah was
Izhar's son. Izhar was Kohath's son. Kohath
was Levi's son. Levi was Israel's son.
39There was Heman's helper Asaph, whose
group stood by Heman's right side. Asaph
was Berekiah's son. Berekiah was Shimea's
son. 40Shimea was Michael's son. Michael
was Baaseiah's son. Baaseiah was Malkijah's
son. 41Malkijah was Ethni's son. Ethni was
Zerah's son. Zerah was Adaiah's son.

42 Adaiah was Ethan's son. Ethan was
Zimmah's son. Zimmah was Shimei's son.
43 Shimei was Jahath's son. Jahath was
Gershon's son, and Gershon was Levi's son.
44 Merari's family were the helpers of
Heman and Asaph, and they stood by
Heman's left side. In this group was Ethan
son of Kishi. Kishi was Abdi's son. Abdi was
Malluch's son. 45 Malluch was Hashabiah's
son. Hashabiah was Amaziah's son. Amaziah
was Hilkiah's son. 46 Hilkiah was Amzi's son.
Amzi was Bani's son. Bani was Shemer's son.
47 Shemer was Mahli's son. Mahli was
Mushi's son. Mushi was Merari's son, and
Merari was Levi's son.
48 The other Levites served by doing their
own special work in the Holy Tent, the
house of God. 49 Aaron and his descendants
offered the sacrifices on the altar of burnt
offering and burned the incense on the altar
of incense. They offered the sacrifices that
removed the Israelites' sins so they could
belong to God. They did all the work in the
Most Holy Place and followed all the laws
that Moses, God's servant, had commanded.
50 These were Aaron's sons: Eleazar was
Aaron's son. Phinehas was Eleazar's son.
Abishua was Phinehas' son. 51 Bukki was
Abishua's son. Uzzi was Bukki's son.
Zerahiah was Uzzi's son. 52 Meraioth was
Zerahiah's son. Amariah was Meraioth's
son. Ahitub was Amariah's son. 53 Zadok
was Ahitub's son, and Ahimaaz was Zadok's
son.

Land for the Levites

54 These are the places where Aaron's
descendants lived. His descendants from the
Kohath family group received the first share
of the land.
55 They were given the city of Hebron in
Judah and the pastures around it, 56 but the
fields farther from the city and the villages
near Hebron were given to Caleb son of
Jephunneh. 57 So the descendants of Aaron
were given Hebron, one of the cities of
safety. They also received the towns and
pastures of Libnah, Jattir, Eshtemoa, 58 Hilen,
Debir, 59 Ashan, Juttah, and Beth Shemesh.
60 They also received these towns and
pastures from the tribe of Benjamin: Gibeon,
Geba, Alemeth, and Anathoth.

The Kohath family groups received a total
of thirteen towns.
61 The rest of the Kohath family group was
given ten towns from the family groups of
West Manasseh. The towns were chosen by
throwing lots.
62 The Gershon family group received
thirteen towns from the tribes of Issachar,
Asher, Naphtali, and the part of Manasseh
living in Bashan.
63 The Merari family group received
twelve towns from the tribes of Reuben, Gad,
and Zebulun. Those towns were chosen by
throwing lots.
64 So the Israelites gave these towns and
their pastures to the Levites. 65 The towns
from the tribes of Judah, Simeon, and
Benjamin, which were named, were chosen
by throwing lots.
66 Some of the Kohath family groups
received towns and pastures from the tribe
of Ephraim. 67 They received Shechem, one of
the cities of safety,[n] with its pastures in the
mountains of Ephraim. They also received
the towns and pastures of Gezer, 68 Jokmeam,
Beth Horon, 69 Aijalon, and Gath Rimmon.
70 The rest of the people in the Kohath
family group received the towns of Aner and
Bileam and their pastures from West
Manasseh.
71 From East Manasseh, the Gershon
family received the towns and pastures of
Golan in Bashan and Ashtaroth.
72-73 From the tribe of Issachar, the
Gershon family received the towns and
pastures of Kedesh, Daberath, Ramoth, and
Anem.
74-75 From the tribe of Asher, the Gershon
family received the towns and pastures of
Mashal, Abdon, Hukok, and Rehob.
76 From the tribe of Naphtali, the Gershon
family received the towns and pastures of
Kedesh in Galilee, Hammon, and Kiriathaim.
77 The rest of the Levites, the people from
the Merari family, received from the tribe of
Zebulun the towns and pastures of Jokneam,
Kartah, Rimmono, and Tabor.
78-79 From the tribe of Reuben, the Merari
family received the towns and pastures of
Bezer in the desert, Jahzah, Kedemoth, and
Mephaath. (The tribe of Reuben lived east of
the Jordan River, across from Jericho.)

6:67 cities of safety A person who had accidentally killed someone could go to one of the six cities of safety to receive protection and a fair trial.

80-81From the tribe of Gad, the Merari family
received the towns and pastures of Ramoth in
Gilead, Mahanaim, Heshbon, and Jazer.

Issachar's Children

7 Issachar had four sons: Tola, Puah,
Jashub, and Shimron.
2Tola's sons were Uzzi, Rephaiah, Jeriel,
Jahmai, Ibsam, and Samuel, and they were
leaders of their families. In the family history
of Tola's descendants, twenty-two thousand
six hundred men were listed as fighting men
during the time David was king.
3Uzzi's son was Izrahiah.
Izrahiah's sons were Michael, Obadiah,
Joel, and Isshiah. All five of them were
leaders. 4Their family history shows they
had thirty-six thousand men ready to serve
in the army, because they had many wives
and children.
5The records of the family groups of
Issachar show there were eighty-seven
thousand fighting men.

Benjamin's Children

6Benjamin had three sons: Bela, Beker, and
Jediael.
7Bela had five sons: Ezbon, Uzzi, Uzziel,
Jerimoth, and Iri, and they were leaders of
their families. Their family history shows
they had twenty-two thousand thirty-four
fighting men.
8Beker's sons were Zemirah, Joash, Eliezer,
Elioenai, Omri, Jeremoth, Abijah, Anathoth,
and Alemeth. They all were Beker's sons.
9Their family history listed the family
leaders and twenty thousand two hundred
fighting men.
10Jediael's son was Bilhan.
Bilhan's sons were Jeush, Benjamin, Ehud,
Kenaanah, Zethan, Tarshish, and Ahishahar.
11All these sons of Jediael were leaders of
their families. They had seventeen thousand
two hundred fighting men ready to serve in
the army.
12The Shuppites and Huppites were
descendants of Ir, and the Hushites were
descendants of Aher.

Naphtali's Children

13Naphtali's sons were Jahziel, Guni, Jezer,
and Shillem. They were Bilhah's grandsons.

Manasseh's Children

14These are Manasseh's descendants.
Manasseh had an Aramean slave woman,
who was the mother of Asriel and Makir.
Makir was Gilead's father. 15Makir took a
wife from the Huppites and Shuppites. His
sister was named Maacah. His second son
was named Zelophehad, and he had only
daughters. 16Makir's wife Maacah had a son
whom she named Peresh. Peresh's brother
was named Sheresh. Sheresh's sons were
Ulam and Rakem.
17Ulam's son was Bedan.
These were the sons of Gilead, who was
the son of Makir. Makir was Manasseh's son.
18Makir's sister Hammoleketh gave birth to
Ishhod, Abiezer, and Mahlah.
19The sons of Shemida were Ahian,
Shechem, Likhi, and Aniam.

Ephraim's Children

20These are the names of Ephraim's
descendants. Ephraim's son was Shuthelah.
Shuthelah's son was Bered. Bered's son was
Tahath. Tahath's son was Eleadah. Eleadah's
son was Tahath. 21Tahath's son was Zabad.
Zabad's son was Shuthelah.
Ezer and Elead went to Gath to steal cows
and sheep and were killed by some men who
grew up in that city. 22Their father Ephraim
cried for them many days, and his family
came to comfort him. 23Then he had sexual
relations with his wife again. She became
pregnant and gave birth to a son whom
Ephraim named Beriah[n] because of the
trouble that had happened to his family.
24Ephraim's daughter was Sheerah. She built
Lower Beth Horon, Upper Beth Horon, and
Uzzen Sheerah.
25Rephah was Ephraim's son. Resheph was
Rephah's son. Telah was Resheph's son.
Tahan was Telah's son. 26Ladan was Tahan's
son. Ammihud was Ladan's son. Elishama
was Ammihud's son. 27Nun was Elishama's
son, and Joshua was the son of Nun.
28Ephraim's descendants lived in these
lands and towns: Bethel and the villages near
it, Naaran on the east, Gezer and the villages
near it on the west, and Shechem and the
villages near it. These villages went all the
way to Ayyah and its villages. 29Along the
borders of Manasseh's land were the towns

7:23 Beriah This name sounds like the Hebrew word for "trouble."

Issachar, made plans to kill Nadab. Nadab
and all Israel were attacking the Philistine
town of Gibbethon, so Baasha killed Nadab
there. [28]This happened during Asa's third
year as king of Judah, and Baasha became the
next king of Israel.

Baasha King of Israel

[29]As soon as Baasha became king, he
killed all of Jeroboam's family, leaving no
one in Jeroboam's family alive. He destroyed
them all as the LORD had said would happen
through his servant Ahijah from Shiloh.
[30]King Jeroboam had sinned very much
and had led the people of Israel to sin, so
he made the LORD, the God of Israel, very
angry.

[31]Everything else Nadab did is written in
the book of the history of the kings of Israel.
[32]There was war between Asa king of Judah
and Baasha king of Israel all the time they
ruled.

[33]Baasha son of Ahijah became king of
Israel during Asa's third year as king of
Judah. Baasha ruled in Tirzah for twenty-
four years, [34]and he did what the LORD said
was wrong. Jeroboam had led the people of
Israel to sin, and Baasha sinned in the same
way as Jeroboam.

16 Jehu son of Hanani spoke the word of
the LORD against King Baasha. [2]The
LORD said, "You were nothing, but I took
you and made you a leader over my people
Israel. But you have followed the ways of
Jeroboam and have led my people Israel
to sin. Their sins have made me angry,
[3]so, Baasha, I will soon destroy you and
your family. I will do to you what I did to the
family of Jeroboam son of Nebat. [4]Anyone
from your family who dies in the city will
be eaten by dogs, and anyone from your
family who dies in the fields will be eaten
by birds."

[5]Everything else Baasha did and all his
victories are written down in the book of the
history of the kings of Israel. [6]So Baasha died
and was buried in Tirzah, and his son Elah
became king in his place.

[7]The LORD spoke his word against Baasha
and his family through the prophet Jehu son
of Hanani. Baasha had done many things the
LORD said were wrong, which made the LORD
very angry. He did the same evil deeds that
Jeroboam's family had done before him. The
LORD also spoke against Baasha because he
killed all of Jeroboam's family.

Elah King of Israel

[8]Elah son of Baasha became king of Israel
during Asa's twenty-sixth year as king of
Judah, and Elah ruled in Tirzah for two years.

[9]Zimri, one of Elah's officers, commanded
half of Elah's chariots. Zimri made plans
against Elah while the king was in Tirzah,
getting drunk at Arza's home. (Arza was in
charge of the palace at Tirzah.) [10]Zimri went
into Arza's house and killed Elah during Asa's
twenty-seventh year as king of Judah. Then
Zimri became king of Israel in Elah's place.

Zimri King of Israel

[11]As soon as Zimri became king, he killed
all of Baasha's family, not allowing any of
Baasha's family or friends to live. [12]So Zimri
destroyed all of Baasha's family just as the
LORD had said it would happen through the
prophet Jehu. [13]Baasha and his son Elah
sinned and led the people of Israel to sin, and
they made the LORD, the God of Israel, angry
because of their worthless idols.

[14]Everything else Elah did is written in
the book of the history of the kings of Israel.

[15]So during Asa's twenty-seventh year as
king of Judah, Zimri became king of Israel
and ruled in Tirzah seven days.

The army of Israel was camped near
Gibbethon, a Philistine town. [16]The men in
the camp heard that Zimri had made secret
plans against King Elah and had killed him.
So that day in the camp they made Omri, the
commander of the army, king over Israel.
[17]So Omri and all the Israelite army left
Gibbethon and attacked Tirzah. [18]When
Zimri saw that the city had been captured,
he went into the palace and set it on fire,
burning the palace and himself with it. [19]So
Zimri died because he had sinned by doing
what the LORD said was wrong. Jeroboam
had led the people of Israel to sin, and Zimri
sinned in the same way as Jeroboam.

[20]Everything else Zimri did and the story
of how he turned against King Elah are
written down in the book of the history of
the kings of Israel.

Omri King of Israel

[21]The people of Israel were divided into
two groups. Half of the people wanted Tibni

devotion 91

1 KINGS 15:14–15

"IN CONSTRUCTION"

I never liked the term "under construction." It gives some sort of immediate visual that we are trapped under something. I like to say "*in* construction"—I am here, I am happy to be here, and I want to be built up.

King Asa was a work in progress. He was in the process of being built up. He did not always do the right things, but his willing heart kept him on the right track for godly success. When contractors construct a new home, they do not just lay the foundation and then say to the owners, "Hi, here is your house." No, the house is not complete. The first part is done, but now they have to put up the walls, trim out the interior, and put the roof on—then the house is complete. That is the process of construction.

As believers, we get discouraged if we do not become spiritual mansions overnight. If you are a believer and there are some things still not completed, don't be discouraged. You're on your way. Lay the foundations that need to be in place before your walls and roof can be added. If it's your relationships, your finances, or your workplace, know that your spiritual growth is progressing even in the midst of the imperfections. I love being in construction. God is constantly doing something new, and there is always an opportunity to allow the Holy Spirit to create a spiritual masterpiece in my life.

king of Israel all the time they were kings.
17Baasha attacked Judah, and he made the
town of Ramah strong so he could keep
people from leaving or entering Judah, Asa's
country.
18Asa took the rest of the silver and gold
from the treasuries of the Temple of the LORD
and his own palace and gave it to his officers.
Then he sent them to Ben-Hadad son of
Tabrimmon, who was the son of Hezion.
Ben-Hadad was the king of Aram and ruled
in the city of Damascus. Asa said, 19"Let there
be a treaty between you and me as there was
between my father and your father. I am
sending you a gift of silver and gold. Break
your treaty with Baasha king of Israel so he
will leave my land."
20Ben-Hadad agreed with King Asa, so he
sent the commanders of his armies to attack
the towns of Israel. They defeated the towns
of Ijon, Dan, and Abel Beth Maacah, as well
as all Galilee and the area of Naphtali.
21When Baasha heard about these attacks, he
stopped building up Ramah and returned to
Tirzah. 22Then King Asa gave an order to all
the people of Judah; everyone had to help.
They carried away all the stones and wood
Baasha had been using in Ramah, and they
used them to build up Geba and Mizpah in
the land of Benjamin.
23Everything else Asa did—his victories
and the cities he built—is written in the
book of the history of the kings of Judah.
When he became old, he got a disease in his
feet. 24After Asa died, he was buried with his
ancestors in Jerusalem, the city of David,
his ancestor. Then Jehoshaphat, Asa's son,
became king in his place.

Nadab King of Israel

25Nadab son of Jeroboam became king of
Israel during the second year Asa was king of
Judah. Nadab was king of Israel for two
years, 26and he did what the LORD said was
wrong. Jeroboam had led the people of Israel
to sin, and Nadab sinned in the same way as
his father Jeroboam.
27Baasha son of Ahijah, from the tribe of

9 The names of all the people of Israel
were listed in their family histories, and
those family histories were put in the book
of the kings of Israel.

The People in Jerusalem

The people of Judah were captured and
forced to go to Babylon, because they were
not faithful to God. 2The first people to come
back and live in their own lands and towns
were some Israelites, priests, Levites, and
Temple servants.
3People from the tribes of Judah,
Benjamin, Ephraim, and Manasseh lived in
Jerusalem. This is a list of those people.
4There was Uthai son of Ammihud.
(Ammihud was Omri's son. Omri was Imri's
son. Imri was Bani's son. Bani was a
descendant of Perez, and Perez was Judah's
son.)
5Of the Shilonite people there were
Asaiah and his sons. Asaiah was the oldest
son in his family.
6Of the Zerahite people there were Jeuel
and other relatives of Zerah. There were six
hundred ninety of them in all.
7From the tribe of Benjamin there was
Sallu son of Meshullam. (Meshullam was
Hodaviah's son, and Hodaviah was
Hassenuah's son.) 8There was also Ibneiah
son of Jeroham and Elah son of Uzzi. (Uzzi
was Micri's son.) And there was Meshullam
son of Shephatiah. (Shephatiah was Reuel's
son, and Reuel was Ibnijah's son.) 9The
family history of Benjamin lists nine
hundred fifty-six people living in Jerusalem,
and all these were leaders of their families.
10Of the priests there were Jedaiah,
Jehoiarib, Jakin, and 11Azariah son of
Hilkiah. (Hilkiah was Meshullam's son.
Meshullam was Zadok's son. Zadok was
Meraioth's son. Meraioth was Ahitub's son.
Ahitub was the officer responsible for the
Temple of God.) 12Also there was Adaiah son
of Jeroham. (Jeroham was Pashhur's son, and
Pashhur was Malkijah's son.) And there was
Maasai son of Adiel. (Adiel was Jahzerah's
son. Jahzerah was Meshullam's son.
Meshullam was Meshillemith's son, and

devotion 99

1 CHRONICLES 9:1

THE OTHER WOMAN, THE OTHER GOD

How are we unfaithful to God? Think of a marriage; a spouse is unfaithful when he or she physically joins to another. Now apply this to God. We are unfaithful to God when we give ourselves spiritually to something else. The Israelites were continually surrounded by people who worshiped multiple gods. The other religions of the day made sacrifices to a variety of gods. The peer pressure seemed to be more than the Israelites could take. They were continually falling back into idol worship.

The Bible says that the devil is a roaring lion, seeking whom he may devour. He knows that in our culture, idol worship is not tempting to a Christian. So how does he tempt us to be unfaithful to God? I believe Satan uses materialism to draw people away from God. When we shop, are we buying to fulfill a need or to impress the world around us? I have two teenage daughters, and I can tell you that purses in our home can be idols. My girls see their friends with two-hundred-dollar purses, and they want one too. The peer pressure to conform to the world is constantly upon us.

So how do you remain faithful to God so that you are not captured by the world? Stay on your knees. Ask God for direction and guidance when you're shopping, when you're watching television, and when you're making decisions. The world is screaming for your attention. Don't listen. God has a better way.

of Beth Shan, Taanach, Megiddo, and Dor,
and the villages near them. The descendants
of Joseph son of Israel lived in these towns.

Asher's Children

30 Asher's sons were Imnah, Ishvah, Ishvi,
and Beriah. Their sister was Serah.
31 Beriah's sons were Heber and Malkiel.
Malkiel was Birzaith's father.
32 Heber was the father of Japhlet, Shomer,
Hotham, and their sister Shua.
33 Japhlet's sons were Pasach, Bimhal, and
Ashvath. They were Japhlet's children.
34 Japhlet's brother was Shomer. Shomer's
sons were Rohgah, Hubbah, and Aram.
35 Shomer's brother was Hotham.
Hotham's sons were Zophah, Imna, Shelesh,
and Amal.
36 Zophah's sons were Suah, Harnepher,
Shual, Beri, Imrah, 37 Bezer, Hod, Shamma,
Shilshah, Ithran, and Beera.
38 Jether's sons were Jephunneh, Pispah,
and Ara.
39 Ulla's sons were Arah, Hanniel, and
Rizia.
40 All these men were descendants of
Asher and leaders of their families. They
were powerful warriors and outstanding
leaders. Their family history lists that they
had twenty-six thousand soldiers ready to
serve in the army.

The Family History of King Saul

8 Benjamin was the father of Bela, his first
son. Ashbel was his second son, Aharah
was his third, 2 Nohah was his fourth, and
Rapha was his fifth son.
3 Bela's sons were Addar, Gera, Abihud,
4 Abishua, Naaman, Ahoah, 5 Gera,
Shephuphan, and Huram.
6 These were the descendants of Ehud and
leaders of their families in Geba. They were
forced to move to Manahath. 7 Ehud's
descendants were Naaman, Ahijah, and Gera.
Gera forced them to leave. He was the father
of Uzza and Ahihud.
8-11 Shaharaim and his wife Hushim had
sons named Abitub and Elpaal. In Moab,
Shaharaim divorced his wives Hushim and
Baara. Shaharaim and his wife Hodesh had
these sons: Jobab, Zibia, Mesha, Malcam,
Jeuz, Sakia, and Mirmah. They were leaders
of their families.
12-13 Elpaal's sons were Eber, Misham,
Shemed, Beriah, and Shema. Shemed built
the towns of Ono and Lod and the villages
around them. Beriah and Shema were leaders
of the families living in Aijalon, and they
forced out the people who lived in Gath.
14 Beriah's sons were Ahio, Shashak,
Jeremoth, 15 Zebadiah, Arad, Eder, 16 Michael,
Ishpah, and Joha.
17 Elpaal's sons were Zebadiah,
Meshullam, Hizki, Heber, 18 Ishmerai, Izliah,
and Jobab.
19 Shimei's sons were Jakim, Zicri, Zabdi,
20 Elienai, Zillethai, Eliel, 21 Adaiah, Beraiah,
and Shimrath.
22 Shashak's sons were Ishpan, Eber, Eliel,
23 Abdon, Zicri, Hanan, 24 Hananiah, Elam,
Anthothijah, 25 Iphdeiah, and Penuel.
26 Jeroham's sons were Shamsherai,
Shehariah, Athaliah, 27 Jaareshiah, Elijah, and
Zicri.
28 The family histories show that all these
men were leaders of their families and lived
in Jerusalem.
29 Jeiel lived in the town of Gibeon, where
he was the leader. His wife was named
Maacah. 30 Jeiel's first son was Abdon. His
other sons were Zur, Kish, Baal, Ner, Nadab,
31 Gedor, Ahio, Zeker, 32 and Mikloth. Mikloth
was the father of Shimeah. These sons also
lived near their relatives in Jerusalem.
33 Ner was the father of Kish. Kish was the
father of Saul, and Saul was the father of
Jonathan, Malki-Shua, Abinadab, and
Esh-Baal.
34 Jonathan's son was Merib-Baal, who was
the father of Micah.
35 Micah's sons were Pithon, Melech, Tarea,
and Ahaz. 36 Ahaz was the father of
Jehoaddah. Jehoaddah was the father of
Alemeth, Azmaveth, and Zimri. Zimri was
the father of Moza. 37 Moza was the father of
Binea. Raphah was Binea's son. Eleasah was
Raphah's son, and Azel was Eleasah's son.
38 Azel had six sons: Azrikam, Bokeru,
Ishmael, Sheariah, Obadiah, and Hanan. All
these were Azel's sons.
39 Azel's brother was Eshek. Eshek's first
son was Ulam, his second was Jeush, and
Eliphelet was his third. 40 Ulam's sons were
mighty warriors and good archers. They had
many sons and grandsons—one hundred
fifty of them in all.
All these men were Benjamin's
descendants.

Meshillemith was Immer's son.) 13There
were one thousand seven hundred sixty
priests. They were leaders of their families,
and they were responsible for serving in the
Temple of God.

14Of the Levites there was Shemaiah son
of Hasshub. (Hasshub was Azrikam's son,
and Azrikam was Hashabiah's son.
Hashabiah was from the family of Merari.)
15There were also Bakbakkar, Heresh, Galal,
and Mattaniah son of Mica. (Mica was Zicri's
son, and Zicri was Asaph's son.) 16There was
also Obadiah son of Shemaiah. (Shemaiah
was Galal's son, and Galal was Jeduthun's
son.) And there was Berekiah son of Asa.
(Asa was the son of Elkanah, who lived in
the villages of the Netophathites.)

17Of the gatekeepers there were Shallum,
Akkub, Talmon, Ahiman, and their relatives.
Shallum was their leader. 18These
gatekeepers from the tribe of Levi still stand
next to the King's Gate on the east side of the
city. 19Shallum was Kore's son. Kore was
Ebiasaph's son, and Ebiasaph was Korah's
son. Shallum and his relatives from the
family of Korah were gatekeepers and were
responsible for guarding the gates of the
Temple. Their ancestors had also been
responsible for guarding the entrance to the
Temple of the LORD. 20In the past Phinehas,
Eleazar's son, was in charge of the
gatekeepers, and the LORD was with
Phinehas. 21Zechariah son of Meshelemiah
was the gatekeeper at the entrance to the
Temple.

22In all, two hundred twelve men were
chosen to guard the gates, and their names
were written in their family histories in
their villages. David and Samuel the seer
chose these men because they were
dependable. 23The gatekeepers and their
descendants had to guard the gates of the
Temple of the LORD. (The Temple took the
place of the Holy Tent.) 24There were
gatekeepers on all four sides of the Temple:
east, west, north, and south. 25The
gatekeepers' relatives who lived in the
villages had to come and help them at times.
Each time they came they helped the
gatekeepers for seven days. 26Because they
were dependable, four gatekeepers were
made the leaders of all the gatekeepers. They
were Levites, and they were responsible for
the rooms and treasures in the Temple of
God. 27They stayed up all night guarding the
Temple of God, and they opened it every
morning.

28Some of the gatekeepers were
responsible for the utensils used in the
Temple services. They counted these
utensils when people took them out and
when they brought them back. 29Other
gatekeepers were chosen to take care of the
furniture and utensils in the Holy Place.
They also took care of the flour, wine, oil,
incense, and spices, 30but some of the priests
took care of mixing the spices. 31There was
a Levite named Mattithiah who was
dependable and had the job of baking the
bread used for the offerings. He was the first
son of Shallum, who was from the family of
Korah. 32Some of the gatekeepers from the
Kohath family had the job of preparing the
special bread that was put on the table
every Sabbath day.

33Some of the Levites were musicians in
the Temple. The leaders of these families
stayed in the rooms of the Temple. Since
they were on duty day and night, they did
not do other work in the Temple.

34These are the leaders of the Levite
families. Their names were listed in their
family histories, and they lived in Jerusalem.

The Family History of King Saul

35Jeiel lived in the town of Gibeon, where
he was the leader. His wife was named
Maacah. 36Jeiel's first son was Abdon. His
other sons were Zur, Kish, Baal, Ner, Nadab,
37Gedor, Ahio, Zechariah, and Mikloth.
38Mikloth was Shimeam's father. Jeiel's
family lived near their relatives in
Jerusalem.

39Ner was Kish's father. Kish was Saul's
father. Saul was the father of Jonathan,
Malki-Shua, Abinadab, and Esh-Baal.

40Jonathan's son was Merib-Baal, who was
the father of Micah.

41Micah's sons were Pithon, Melech,
Tahrea, and Ahaz. 42Ahaz was Jadah's father.
Jadah was the father of Alemeth, Azmaveth,
and Zimri. Zimri was Moza's father. 43Moza
was Binea's father. Rephaiah was Binea's son.
Eleasah was Rephaiah's son, and Azel was
Eleasah's son.

44Azel had six sons: Azrikam, Bokeru,
Ishmael, Sheariah, Obadiah, and Hanan.
They were Azel's sons.

The Death of King Saul

10 The Philistines fought against Israel, and the Israelites ran away from them. Many Israelites were killed on Mount Gilboa. 2The Philistines fought hard against Saul and his sons, killing his sons Jonathan, Abinadab, and Malki-Shua. 3The fighting was heavy around Saul, and the archers shot him with their arrows and wounded him.

4Then Saul said to the officer who carried his armor, "Pull out your sword and stab me. If you don't, these Philistines who are not circumcised will come and hurt me." But Saul's officer refused, because he was afraid. So Saul took his own sword and threw himself on it. 5When the officer saw that Saul was dead, he threw himself on his own sword and died. 6So Saul and three of his sons died; all his family died together.

7When the Israelites living in the valley saw that their army had run away and that Saul and his sons were dead, they left their towns and ran away. Then the Philistines came and settled in them.

8The next day when the Philistines came to strip the dead soldiers, they found Saul and his sons dead on Mount Gilboa. 9The Philistines stripped Saul's body and took his head and his armor. Then they sent messengers through all their country to tell the news to their idols and to their people. 10The Philistines put Saul's armor in the temple of their idols and hung his head in the temple of Dagon.

11All the people in Jabesh Gilead heard what the Philistines had done to Saul. 12So the brave men of Jabesh went and got the bodies of Saul and his sons and brought them to Jabesh. They buried their bones under the large tree in Jabesh. Then the people of Jabesh fasted for seven days.

13Saul died because he was not faithful to the LORD and did not obey the LORD. He even went to a medium and asked her for advice 14instead of asking the LORD. This is why the LORD put Saul to death and gave the kingdom to Jesse's son David.

David Becomes King

11 Then the people of Israel came to David at the town of Hebron and said, "Look, we are your own family. 2Even when Saul was king, you were the one who led Israel in battle. The LORD your God said to you, 'You will be the shepherd for my people Israel. You will be their leader.' "

3So all the elders of Israel came to King David at Hebron. He made an agreement with them in Hebron in the presence of the LORD. Then they poured oil on David to make him king over Israel. The LORD had promised through Samuel that this would happen.

David Captures Jerusalem

4David and all the Israelites went to the city of Jerusalem. At that time Jerusalem was called Jebus, and the people living there were named Jebusites. 5They said to David, "You can't get inside our city." But David did take the city of Jerusalem with its strong walls, and it became the City of David.

6David had said, "The person who leads the attack against the Jebusites will become the commander over all my army." Joab son of Zeruiah led the attack, so he became the commander of the army.

7Then David made his home in the strong, walled city, which is why it was named the City of David. 8David rebuilt the city, beginning where the land was filled in and going to the wall that was around the city. Joab repaired the other parts of the city. 9David became stronger and stronger, and the LORD All-Powerful was with him.

David's Mighty Warriors

10This is a list of the leaders over David's warriors who helped make David's kingdom strong. All the people of Israel also supported David's kingdom. These heroes and all the people of Israel made David king, just as the LORD had promised.

11This is a list of David's warriors:

Jashobeam was from the Hacmonite people. He was the head of the Three,[n] David's most powerful soldiers. He used his spear to fight three hundred men at one time, and he killed them all.

12Next was Eleazar, one of the Three. Eleazar was Dodai's son from the Ahohite people. 13Eleazar was with David at Pas Dammim when the Philistines came there to

11:11 Three Or maybe "Thirty." These were David's most powerful soldiers. See 2 Samuel 23:8.

fight. There was a field of barley at that
place. The Israelites ran away from the
Philistines, 14but they stopped in the middle
of that field and fought for it and killed the
Philistines. The LORD gave them a great
victory.
15Once, three of the Thirty, David's chief
soldiers, came down to him at the rock by
the cave near Adullam. At the same time the
Philistine army had camped in the Valley of
Rephaim.
16At that time David was in a stronghold,
and some of the Philistines were in
Bethlehem. 17David had a strong desire for
some water. He said, "Oh, I wish someone
would get me water from the well near the
city gate of Bethlehem!" 18So the Three broke
through the Philistine army and took water
from the well near the city gate in
Bethlehem. Then they brought it to David,
but he refused to drink it. He poured it out
before the LORD, 19saying, "May God keep me
from drinking this water! It would be like
drinking the blood of the men who risked
their lives to bring it to me!" So David
refused to drink it.

These were the brave things that the three warriors did.

20Abishai brother of Joab was the captain
of the Three. Abishai fought three hundred
soldiers with his spear and killed them. He
became as famous as the Three 21and was
more honored than the Three. He became
their commander even though he was not
one of them.
22Benaiah son of Jehoiada was a brave
fighter from Kabzeel who did mighty things.
He killed two of the best warriors from
Moab. He also went down into a pit and
killed a lion on a snowy day. 23Benaiah killed
an Egyptian who was about seven and
one-half feet tall and had a spear as large as a
weaver's rod. Benaiah had a club, but he
grabbed the spear from the Egyptian's hand
and killed him with his own spear. 24These
were the things Benaiah son of Jehoiada did.
He was as famous as the Three. 25He received
more honor than the Thirty, but he did not
become a member of the Three. David made
him leader of his bodyguards.

The Thirty Chief Soldiers

26These were also mighty warriors:
Asahel brother of Joab;
Elhanan son of Dodo from Bethlehem;
27Shammoth the Harorite;
Helez the Pelonite;
28Ira son of Ikkesh from Tekoa;
Abiezer the Anathothite;
29Sibbecai the Hushathite;
Ilai the Ahohite;
30Maharai the Netophathite;
Heled son of Baanah the Netophathite;
31Ithai son of Ribai from Gibeah in Benjamin;
Benaiah the Pirathonite;
32Hurai from the ravines of Gaash;
Abiel the Arbathite;
33Azmaveth the Baharumite;
Eliahba the Shaalbonite;
34the sons of Hashem the Gizonite;
Jonathan son of Shagee the Hararite;
35Ahiam son of Sacar the Hararite;
Eliphal son of Ur;
36Hepher the Mekerathite;
Ahijah the Pelonite;
37Hezro the Carmelite;
Naarai son of Ezbai;
38Joel brother of Nathan;
Mibhar son of Hagri;
39Zelek the Ammonite;
Naharai the Berothite, the officer who carried the armor for Joab son of Zeruiah;
40Ira the Ithrite;
Gareb the Ithrite;
41Uriah the Hittite;
Zabad son of Ahlai;
42Adina son of Shiza the Reubenite, who was the leader of the Reubenites, and his thirty soldiers;
43Hanan son of Maacah;
Joshaphat the Mithnite;
44Uzzia the Ashterathite;
Shama and Jeiel sons of Hotham the Aroerite;
45Jediael son of Shimri;
Joha, Jediael's brother, the Tizite;
46Eliel the Mahavite;
Jeribai and Joshaviah, Elnaam's sons;
Ithmah the Moabite;
47Eliel, Obed, and Jaasiel the Mezobaites.

Warriors Join David

12 These were the men who came to
David at Ziklag when David was
hiding from Saul son of Kish. They were

among the warriors who helped David in
battle. [2]They came with bows for weapons
and could use either their right or left hands
to shoot arrows or to sling rocks. They were
Saul's relatives from the tribe of Benjamin.
[3]Ahiezer was their leader, and there was
Joash. (Ahiezer and Joash were sons of
Shemaah, who was from the town of
Gibeah.) There were also Jeziel and Pelet,
the sons of Azmaveth. There were Beracah
and Jehu from the town of Anathoth. [4]And
there was Ishmaiah from the town of
Gibeon; he was one of the Thirty. In fact, he
was the leader of the Thirty. There were
Jeremiah, Jahaziel, Johanan, and Jozabad
from Gederah. [5]There were Eluzai,
Jerimoth, Bealiah, and Shemariah. There
was Shephatiah from Haruph. [6]There were
Elkanah, Isshiah, Azarel, Joezer, and
Jashobeam from the family group of
Korah. [7]And there were Joelah and
Zebadiah, the sons of Jeroham, from the
town of Gedor.

[8]Part of the people of Gad joined David at
his stronghold in the desert. They were
brave warriors trained for war and skilled
with shields and spears. They were as
fierce as lions and as fast as gazelles over the
hills.

[9]Ezer was the leader of Gad's army, and
Obadiah was second in command. Eliab was
third, [10]Mishmannah was fourth, Jeremiah
was fifth, [11]Attai was sixth, Eliel was
seventh, [12]Johanan was eighth, Elzabad was
ninth, [13]Jeremiah was tenth, and Macbannai
was eleventh in command.

[14]They were the commanders of the army
from Gad. The least of these leaders was in
charge of a hundred soldiers, and the
greatest was in charge of a thousand. [15]They
crossed the Jordan River and chased away
the people living in the valleys, to the east
and to the west. This happened in the first
month of the year when the Jordan floods
the valley.

[16]Other people from the tribes of
Benjamin and Judah also came to David at
his stronghold. [17]David went out to meet
them and said to them, "If you have come
peacefully to help me, I welcome you. Join
me. But if you have come to turn me over to
my enemies, even though I have done
nothing wrong, the God of our ancestors will
see this and punish you."

[18]Then the Spirit entered Amasai, the
leader of the Thirty, and he said:

"We belong to you, David.
We are with you, son of Jesse.
Success, success to you.
Success to those who help you,
because your God helps you."

So David welcomed these men and made
them leaders of his army.

[19]Some of the men from Manasseh also
joined David when he went with the
Philistines to fight Saul. But David and his
men did not really help the Philistines. After
talking about it, the Philistine leaders
decided to send David away. They said, "If
David goes back to his master Saul, we will
be killed." [20]These are the men from
Manasseh who joined David when he went
to Ziklag: Adnah, Jozabad, Jediael, Michael,
Jozabad, Elihu, and Zillethai. Each of them
was a leader of a thousand men from
Manasseh. [21]All these men of Manasseh were
brave soldiers, and they helped David fight
against groups of men who went around the
country robbing people. These soldiers
became commanders in David's army.
[22]Every day more men joined David, and
his army became large, like the army of
God.

Others Join David at Hebron

[23]These are the numbers of the soldiers
ready for battle who joined David at Hebron.
They came to help turn the kingdom of Saul
over to David, just as the LORD had said.

[24]There were sixty-eight hundred men
with their weapons from Judah. They carried
shields and spears.

[25]There were seventy-one hundred men
from Simeon. They were warriors ready for
war.

[26]There were forty-six hundred men from
Levi. [27]Jehoiada, a leader from Aaron's
family, was in that group. There were
thirty-seven hundred with him. [28]Zadok
was also in that group. He was a strong
young warrior, and with him came
twenty-two leaders from his family.

[29]There were three thousand men from
Benjamin, who were Saul's relatives. Most of
them had remained loyal to Saul's family
until then.

[30]There were twenty thousand eight
hundred men from Ephraim. They were

brave warriors and were famous men in
their own family groups.
31There were eighteen thousand men
from West Manasseh. Each one was
especially chosen to make David king.
32There were two hundred leaders from
Issachar. They knew what Israel should do,
and they knew the right time to do it. Their
relatives were with them and under their
command.
33There were fifty thousand men from
Zebulun. They were trained soldiers and
knew how to use every kind of weapon of
war. They followed David completely.
34There were one thousand officers from
Naphtali. They had thirty-seven thousand
soldiers with them who carried shields and
spears.
35There were twenty-eight thousand six
hundred men from Dan, who were ready for
war.
36There were forty thousand trained
soldiers from Asher, who were ready for war.
37There were one hundred twenty
thousand soldiers from the east side of the
Jordan River from the people of Reuben, Gad,
and East Manasseh. They had every kind of
weapon.
38All these fighting men were ready to go
to war. They came to Hebron fully agreed to
make David king of all Israel. All the other
Israelites also agreed to make David king.
39They spent three days there with David,
eating and drinking, because their relatives
had prepared food for them. 40Also, their
neighbors came from as far away as Issachar,
Zebulun, and Naphtali, bringing food on
donkeys, camels, mules, and oxen. They
brought much flour, fig cakes, raisins, wine,
oil, cows, and sheep, because the people of
Israel were very happy.

Bringing Back the Ark

13 David talked with all the officers of
his army, the commanders of a
hundred men and the commanders of a
thousand men. 2Then David called the
people of Israel together and said, "If you
think it is a good idea, and if it is what the
LORD our God wants, let's send a message.
Let's tell our fellow Israelites in all the areas
of Israel and the priests and Levites living
with them in their towns and pastures to
come and join us. 3Let's bring the Ark of our
God back to us. We did not use it to ask God
for help while Saul was king." 4All the
people agreed with David, because they all
thought it was the right thing to do.
5So David gathered all the Israelites, from
the Shihor River in Egypt to Lebo Hamath,
to bring the Ark of God back from the town
of Kiriath Jearim. 6David and all the
Israelites with him went to Baalah of Judah,
which is Kiriath Jearim, to get the Ark of
God the LORD. God's throne is between the
golden, winged creatures on the Ark, and the
Ark is called by his name.
7The people carried the Ark of God from
Abinadab's house on a new cart, and Uzzah
and Ahio guided it. 8David and all the
Israelites were celebrating in the presence of
God. With all their strength they were
singing and playing lyres, harps,
tambourines, cymbals, and trumpets.
9When David's men came to the threshing
floor of Kidon, the oxen stumbled, and Uzzah
reached out his hand to steady the Ark. 10The
LORD was angry with Uzzah and killed him,
because he had touched the Ark. So Uzzah
died there in the presence of God.
11David was angry because the LORD had
punished Uzzah in his anger. Now that place
is called The Punishment of Uzzah.
12David was afraid of God that day and
asked, "How can I bring the Ark of God
home to me?" 13So David did not take the
Ark with him to Jerusalem. Instead, he took
it to the house of Obed-Edom who was from
Gath. 14The Ark of God stayed with Obed-
Edom's family in his house for three months,
and the LORD blessed Obed-Edom's family
and everything he owned.

David's Kingdom Grows

14 Hiram king of the city of Tyre sent
messengers to David. He also sent
cedar logs, bricklayers, and carpenters to
build a palace for David. 2Then David knew
that the LORD really had made him king of
Israel and that he had made his kingdom
great. The LORD did this because he loved his
people Israel.
3David married more women in Jerusalem
and had more sons and daughters. 4These
are the names of David's children born in
Jerusalem: Shammua, Shobab, Nathan,
Solomon, 5Ibhar, Elishua, Elpelet, 6Nogah,
Nepheg, Japhia, 7Elishama, Beeliada, and
Eliphelet.

devotion 100

1 CHRONICLES 13:11–12

A GOOD IDEA GONE BAD

David had an idea. He wanted to return the Ark of God from Kiriath to Jerusalem. He talked with three different groups of people to get a consensus for the move. He basically said, "If you think this is a good idea, let's retrieve it and celebrate its return." They all agreed with their king, and off they went to retrieve the Ark. Everything appeared to be going as David planned. There was celebration and joy—but then, on the way home, tragedy struck. Uzzah reached out to steady the Ark, touched it, and died.

We can always round people up to agree with our ideas, but ultimately those conversations should start with God first. David made his first mistake by talking with others and not the Lord. Poor Uzzah. It appears he met a fate that should not have been his except that God's instructions were clear about how the Ark was to be moved: with poles through its rings and carried on the shoulders of the Levites. Instead, it was placed on a cart, pulled by an ox, and guided by a man who was not a Levite.

David's anger rose against the Lord because Uzzah died, but David knew he had moved the Ark in his own strength. God wants us to be obedient first. Our enthusiasm for service does not replace his instructions. If it sounds like a great idea, make sure you can line it up with the Word before you act.

David Defeats the Philistines

[8]When the Philistines heard that David
had been made king of all Israel, they went
to look for him. But David heard about it and
went out to fight them. [9]The Philistines had
attacked and robbed the people in the Valley
of Rephaim. [10]David asked God, "Should I go
and attack the Philistines? Will you hand
them over to me?"

The LORD answered him, "Go, I will hand
them over to you."

[11]So David and his men went up to the
town of Baal Perazim and defeated the
Philistines. David said, "Like a flood of water,
God has broken through my enemies by
using me." So that place was named Baal
Perazim.[n] [12]The Philistines had left their
idols there, so David ordered his men to
burn them.

[13]Soon the Philistines attacked the people
in the valley again. [14]David prayed to God
again, and God answered him, saying, "Don't
attack the Philistines from the front. Instead,
go around them and attack them in front of
the balsam trees. [15]When you hear the
sound of marching in the tops of the balsam
trees, then attack. I, God, will have gone out
before you to defeat the Philistine army."
[16]David did as God commanded, and he and
his men defeated the Philistine army all the
way from Gibeon to Gezer.

[17]So David became famous in all the
countries, and the LORD made all nations
afraid of him.

The Ark Is Brought to Jerusalem

15 David built houses for himself in
Jerusalem. Then he prepared a place
for the Ark of God, and he set up a tent for it.
[2]David said, "Only the Levites may carry the
Ark of God. The LORD chose them to carry the
Ark of the LORD and to serve him forever."
[3]David called all the people of Israel to
come to Jerusalem. He wanted to bring the

14:11 Baal Perazim This name means "the Lord breaks through."

Ark of the LORD to the place he had made for it. 4David called together the descendants of Aaron and the Levites. 5There were one hundred twenty people from Kohath's family group, with Uriel as their leader. 6There were two hundred twenty people from Merari's family group, with Asaiah as their leader. 7There were one hundred thirty people from Gershon's family group, with Joel as their leader. 8There were two hundred people from Elizaphan's family group, with Shemaiah as their leader. 9There were eighty people from Hebron's family group, with Eliel as their leader. 10And there were one hundred twelve people from Uzziel's family group, with Amminadab as their leader.

11Then David asked the priests Zadok and Abiathar and these Levites to come to him: Uriel, Asaiah, Joel, Shemaiah, Eliel, and Amminadab. 12David said to them, "You are the leaders of the families of Levi. You and the other Levites must give yourselves for service to the LORD. Bring up the Ark of the LORD, the God of Israel, to the place I have made for it. 13The last time we did not ask the LORD how to carry it. You Levites didn't carry it, so the LORD our God punished us."

14Then the priests and Levites prepared themselves for service to the LORD so they could carry the Ark of the LORD, the God of Israel. 15The Levites used special poles to carry the Ark of God on their shoulders, as Moses had commanded, just as the LORD had said they should.

16David told the leaders of the Levites to appoint their brothers as singers to play their lyres, harps, and cymbals and to sing happy songs.

17So the Levites appointed Heman and his relatives Asaph and Ethan. Heman was Joel's son. Asaph was Berekiah's son. And Ethan, from the Merari family group, was Kushaiah's son. 18There was also a second group of Levites: Zechariah, Jaaziel, Shemiramoth, Jehiel, Unni, Eliab, Benaiah, Maaseiah, Mattithiah, Eliphelehu, Mikneiah, Obed-Edom, and Jeiel. They were the Levite guards.

19The singers Heman, Asaph, and Ethan played bronze cymbals. 20Zechariah, Jaaziel, Shemiramoth, Jehiel, Unni, Eliab, Maaseiah, and Benaiah played the lyres. 21Mattithiah, Eliphelehu, Mikneiah, Obed-Edom, Jeiel, and Azaziah played the harps. 22The Levite leader Kenaniah was in charge of the singing, because he was very good at it.

23Berekiah and Elkanah were two of the guards for the Ark of the Agreement. 24The priests Shebaniah, Joshaphat, Nethanel, Amasai, Zechariah, Benaiah, and Eliezer had the job of blowing trumpets in front of the Ark of God. Obed-Edom and Jehiah were also guards for the Ark.

25David, the leaders of Israel, and the commanders of a thousand soldiers went to get the Ark of the Agreement with the LORD. They all went to bring the Ark from Obed-Edom's house with great joy. 26Because God helped the Levites who carried the Ark of the Agreement with the LORD, they sacrificed seven bulls and seven male sheep. 27All the Levites who carried the Ark, and Kenaniah, the man in charge of the singing, and all the singers wore robes of fine linen. David also wore a robe of fine linen and a holy vest of fine linen. 28So all the people of Israel brought up the Ark of the Agreement with the LORD. They shouted, blew horns and trumpets, and played cymbals, lyres, and harps.

29As the Ark of the Agreement with the LORD entered Jerusalem, Saul's daughter Michal watched from a window. When she saw King David dancing and celebrating, she hated him.

16 They brought the Ark of God and put it inside the tent that David had set up for it. Then they offered burnt offerings and fellowship offerings to God. 2When David had finished giving the burnt offerings and fellowship offerings, he blessed the people in the name of the LORD. 3He gave a loaf of bread, some dates, and raisins to every Israelite man and woman.

4Then David appointed some of the Levites to serve before the Ark of the LORD. They had the job of leading the worship and giving thanks and praising the LORD, the God of Israel. 5Asaph, who played the cymbals, was the leader. Zechariah was second to him. The other Levites were Jaaziel, Shemiramoth, Jehiel, Mattithiah, Eliab, Benaiah, Obed-Edom, and Jeiel. They played the lyres and harps. 6Benaiah and Jahaziel were priests who blew the trumpets regularly before the Ark of the Agreement with God. 7That day David first gave Asaph

and his relatives the job of singing praises to
the LORD.

David's Song of Thanks

[8]Give thanks to the LORD and pray to him.
Tell the nations what he has done.
[9]Sing to him; sing praises to him.
Tell about all his miracles.
[10]Be glad that you are his;
let those who seek the LORD be happy.
[11]Depend on the LORD and his strength;
always go to him for help.
[12]Remember the miracles he has done,
his wonders, and his decisions.
[13]You are the descendants of his servant, Israel;
you are the children of Jacob, his chosen people.

[14]He is the LORD our God.
His laws are for all the world.
[15]He will keep his agreement forever;
he will keep his promises always.
[16]He will keep the agreement he made with Abraham
and the promise he made to Isaac.
[17]He made it a law for the people of Jacob;
he made it an agreement with Israel to last forever.
[18]He said, "I will give the land of Canaan to you,
to belong to you."

[19]Then God's people were few in number,
and they were strangers in the land.
[20]They went from one nation to another,
from one kingdom to another.
[21]But he did not let anyone hurt them;
he warned kings not to harm them.
[22]He said, "Don't touch my chosen people,
and don't harm my prophets."

[23]Sing to the LORD, all the earth.
Every day tell how he saves us.
[24]Tell the nations about his glory;
tell all peoples the miracles he does.
[25]The LORD is great; he should be praised.
He should be respected more than all the gods.
[26]All the gods of the nations are only idols,
but the LORD made the skies.
[27]He has glory and majesty;
he has power and joy in his Temple.

[28]Praise the LORD, all nations on earth.
Praise the LORD's glory and power;
[29]praise the glory of the LORD's name.
Bring an offering and come to him.
Worship the LORD because he is holy.
[30]Tremble before him, everyone on earth.
The earth is set, and it cannot be moved.
[31]Let the skies rejoice and the earth be glad.
Let people everywhere say, "The LORD is king!"
[32]Let the sea and everything in it shout;
let the fields and everything in them rejoice.
[33]Then the trees of the forest will sing
for joy before the LORD.
They will sing because he is coming to judge the world.

[34]Thank the LORD because he is good.
His love continues forever.
[35]Say to him, "Save us, God our Savior,
and bring us back and save us from other nations.
Then we will thank you
and will gladly praise you."
[36]Praise the LORD, the God of Israel.
He always was and always will be.

All the people said "Amen" and praised the LORD.

[37]Then David left Asaph and the other
Levites there in front of the Ark of the
Agreement with the LORD. They were to
serve there every day. [38]David also left
Obed-Edom and sixty-eight other Levites to
serve with them. Hosah and Obed-Edom
son of Jeduthun were guards.

[39]David left Zadok the priest and the
other priests who served with him in front
of the Tent of the LORD at the place of
worship in Gibeon. [40]Every morning and
evening they offered burnt offerings on the
altar of burnt offerings, following the rules
written in the Teachings of the LORD, which
he had given Israel. [41]With them were
Heman and Jeduthun and other Levites.
They were chosen by name to sing praises
to the LORD because his love continues
forever. [42]Heman and Jeduthun also had the
job of playing the trumpets and cymbals
and other musical instruments when songs
were sung to God. Jeduthun's sons guarded
the gates.

[43]Then all the people left. Each person
went home, and David also went home to
bless the people in his home.

God's Promise to David

17 When David moved into his palace,
he said to Nathan the prophet, "Look,
I am living in a palace made of cedar, but the
Ark of the Agreement with the LORD sits in a
tent."
2Nathan said to David, "Do what you want
to do, because God is with you."
3But that night God spoke his word to
Nathan, saying, 4"Go and tell David my
servant, 'This is what the LORD says: You are
not the person to build a house for me to live
in. 5From the time I brought Israel out of
Egypt until now I have not lived in a house. I
have moved from one tent site to another
and from one place to another. 6As I have
moved with the Israelites to different places,
I have never said to the leaders, whom I
commanded to take care of my people,
"Why haven't you built me a house of
cedar?" '
7"Now, tell my servant David: 'This is what
the LORD All-Powerful says: I took you from
the pasture and from tending the sheep and
made you king of my people Israel. 8I have
been with you everywhere you have gone. I
have defeated your enemies for you. I will
make you as famous as any of the great
people on the earth. 9I will choose a place for
my people Israel, and I will plant them so
they can live in their own homes. They will
not be bothered anymore. Wicked people
will no longer hurt them as they have in the
past 10when I chose judges for my people
Israel. I will defeat all your enemies.
" 'I tell you that the LORD will make your
descendants kings of Israel after you.
11When you die and join your ancestors, I
will make one of your sons the new king,
and I will set up his kingdom. 12He will
build a house for me, and I will let his
kingdom rule always. 13I will be his father,
and he will be my son. I took away my love
from Saul, who ruled before you, but I will
never stop loving your son. 14I will put him
in charge of my house and kingdom forever.
His family will rule forever.' "
15Nathan told David everything God had
said in this vision.

David Prays to God

16Then King David went in and sat in
front of the LORD. David said, "LORD God,
who am I? What is my family? Why did you
bring me to this point? 17But that was not
enough for you, God. You have also made
promises about my future family. LORD God,
you have treated me like a very important
person.
18"What more can I say to you for
honoring me, your servant? You know me so
well. 19LORD, you have done this wonderful
thing for my sake and because you wanted
to. You have made known all these great
things.
20"There is no one like you, LORD. There is
no God except you. We have heard all this
ourselves! 21There is no nation like your
people Israel. They are the only people on
earth that God chose to be his own. You
made your name well known by the great
and wonderful things you did for them. You
went ahead of them and forced other nations
out of the land. You freed your people from
slavery in Egypt. 22You made the people of
Israel your very own people forever, and,
LORD, you are their God.
23"LORD, keep the promise forever that you
made about my family and me, your servant.
Do what you have said. 24Then you will be
honored always, and people will say, 'The
LORD All-Powerful, the God over Israel, is
Israel's God!' And the family of your servant
David will continue before you.
25"My God, you have told me that you
would make my family great. So I, your
servant, am brave enough to pray to you.
26LORD, you are God, and you have promised
these good things to me, your servant. 27You
have chosen to bless my family. Let it
continue before you always. LORD, you have
blessed my family, so it will always be
blessed."

David Defeats Nations

18 Later, David defeated the Philistines,
conquered them, and took the city of
Gath and the small towns around it.
2He also defeated the people of Moab. So
the people of Moab became servants of
David and gave him the payment he
demanded.
3David also defeated Hadadezer king of
Zobah all the way to the town of Hamath as
he tried to spread his kingdom to the
Euphrates River. 4David captured one
thousand of his chariots, seven thousand

devotion 101

1 CHRONICLES 17:26–27

YOU CAN TAKE IT TO THE BANK

When you make a deposit at the bank on Monday, you surely expect it to be there on Tuesday if you need to withdraw it, right? It is the legal principal at our banking institutions that what you deposit into your account will be there when you need to withdraw it.

God's Word and his promises are a similar spiritual principal: when we deposit them into our hearts, we have something to withdraw. When we need encouragement or compassion or even conviction, we are able to draw it out for our use. The whole second half of 1 Chronicles 17 shows David modeling a prayer life that is prepared to make godly deposits. He starts by humbling himself before the Lord, acknowledging his weaknesses and sins, and then moves right into praises. Lastly, he expresses his requests for himself and his household.

We should desire to have a spiritual richness that we draw from all the days of our lives. If you are feeling like your bank is empty, start with a list of God's promises and give yourself fully to understanding what they mean to you personally. He wants to take you and your family to places that you have never even imagined. God wants nothing more than for you to know that he is beyond crazy about you and that he has instruction, guidance, and blessings just waiting for you. There is nothing preventing you from going to the bank. So take his Word and deposit it into your heart!

men who rode in chariots, and twenty
thousand foot soldiers. He crippled all but a
hundred of the chariot horses.
5Arameans from Damascus came to help
Hadadezer king of Zobah, but David killed
twenty-two thousand of them. 6Then David
put groups of soldiers in Damascus in Aram.
The Arameans became David's servants and
gave him the payments he demanded. So the
LORD gave David victory everywhere he
went.
7David took the shields of gold that had
belonged to Hadadezer's officers and
brought them to Jerusalem. 8David also took
many things made of bronze from Tebah and
Cun, which had been cities under
Hadadezer's control. Later, Solomon used
this bronze to make things for the Temple:
the large bronze bowl, which was called the
Sea, the pillars, and other bronze utensils.
9Toi king of Hamath heard that David had
defeated all the army of Hadadezer king of
Zobah. 10So Toi sent his son Hadoram to
greet and congratulate King David for
defeating Hadadezer. (Hadadezer had been at
war with Toi.) Hadoram brought items made
of gold, silver, and bronze. 11King David gave
them to the LORD, along with the silver and
gold he had taken from these nations: Edom,
Moab, the Ammonites, the Philistines, and
Amalek.
12Abishai son of Zeruiah killed eighteen
thousand Edomites in the Valley of Salt.
13David put groups of soldiers in Edom, and
all the Edomites became his servants. The
LORD gave David victory everywhere he
went.

David's Important Officers

14David was king over all of Israel, and he
did what was fair and right for all his people.
15Joab son of Zeruiah was commander over
the army. Jehoshaphat son of Ahilud was the
recorder. 16Zadok son of Ahitub and

Abiathar son of Ahimelech were priests. Shavsha was the royal secretary. 17Benaiah son of Jehoiada was over the Kerethites and Pelethites.[n] And David's sons were important officers who served at his side.

War with the Ammonites and Arameans

19 When Nahash king of the Ammonites died, his son became king after him. 2David said, "Nahash was loyal to me, so I will be loyal to his son Hanun." So David sent messengers to comfort Hanun about his father's death.

David's officers went to the land of the Ammonites to comfort Hanun. 3But the Ammonite leaders said to Hanun, "Do you think David wants to honor your father by sending men to comfort you? No! David sent them to study the land and capture it and spy it out." 4So Hanun arrested David's officers. To shame them he shaved their beards and cut off their clothes at the hips. Then he sent them away.

5When the people told David what had happened to his officers, he sent messengers to meet them, because they were very ashamed. King David said, "Stay in Jericho until your beards have grown back. Then come home."

6The Ammonites knew that they had insulted David. So Hanun and the Ammonites sent about seventy-four thousand pounds of silver to hire chariots and chariot drivers from Northwest Mesopotamia, Aram Maacah, and Zobah. 7The Ammonites hired thirty-two thousand chariots and the king of Maacah and his army. So they came and set up camp near the town of Medeba. The Ammonites themselves came out of their towns and got ready for battle.

8When David heard about this, he sent Joab with the whole army. 9The Ammonites came out and prepared for battle at the city gate. The kings who had come to help were out in the field by themselves.

10Joab saw that there were enemies both in front of him and behind him. So he chose some of the best soldiers of Israel and sent them out to fight the Arameans. 11Joab put the rest of the army under the command of Abishai, his brother. Then they went out to fight the Ammonites. 12Joab said to Abishai, "If the Arameans are too strong for me, you must help me. Or, if the Ammonites are too strong for you, I will help you. 13Be strong. We must fight bravely for our people and the cities of our God. The LORD will do what he thinks is right."

14Then Joab and the army with him went to attack the Arameans, and the Arameans ran away. 15When the Ammonites saw that the Arameans were running away, they also ran away from Joab's brother Abishai and went back to their city. So Joab went back to Jerusalem.

16When the Arameans saw that Israel had defeated them, they sent messengers to bring other Arameans from east of the Euphrates River. Their leader was Shophach, the commander of Hadadezer's army.

17When David heard about this, he gathered all the Israelites, and they crossed over the Jordan River. He prepared them for battle, facing the Arameans. The Arameans fought with him, 18but they ran away from the Israelites. David killed seven thousand Aramean chariot drivers and forty thousand Aramean foot soldiers. He also killed Shophach, the commander of the Aramean army.

19When those who served Hadadezer saw that the Israelites had defeated them, they made peace with David and served him. So the Arameans refused to help the Ammonites again.

Joab Destroys the Ammonites

20 In the spring, the time of year when kings normally went out to battle, Joab led out the army of Israel. But David stayed in Jerusalem. The army of Israel destroyed the land of Ammon and went to the city of Rabbah and attacked it. 2David took the crown off the head of their king,[n] and had it placed on his own head. That gold crown weighed about seventy-five pounds, and it had valuable gems in it. And David took many valuable things from the city. 3He also brought out the people of the city and forced them to work with saws, iron picks, and axes. David did this to all the Ammonite

18:17 Kerethites and Pelethites These were probably special units of the army that were responsible for the king's safety, a kind of palace guard. **20:2 their king** Or, "Milcom," the god of the Ammonite people.

cities. Then David and all his army returned
to Jerusalem.

Philistine Giants Are Killed

4 Later, at Gezer, war broke out with the
Philistines. Sibbecai the Hushathite killed
Sippai, who was one of the descendants of
the Rephaites. So those Philistines were
defeated.

5 Later, there was another battle with the
Philistines. Elhanan son of Jair killed Lahmi,
the brother of Goliath, who was from the
town of Gath. His spear was as large as a
weaver's rod.

6 At Gath another battle took place. A huge
man was there; he had six fingers on each
hand and six toes on each foot—twenty-four
fingers and toes in all. This man also was one
of the sons of Rapha. 7 When he spoke
against Israel, Jonathan son of Shimea,
David's brother, killed him.

8 These descendants of Rapha from Gath
were killed by David and his men.

David Counts the Israelites

21 Satan was against Israel, and he
caused David to count the people of
Israel. 2 So David said to Joab and the
commanders of the troops, "Go and count all
the Israelites from Beersheba to Dan.[n] Then
tell me so I will know how many there are."

3 But Joab said, "May the LORD give the
nation a hundred times more people. My
master the king, all the Israelites are your
servants. Why do you want to do this, my
master? You will make Israel guilty of sin."

4 But the king commanded Joab, so Joab
left and went through all Israel. Then he
returned to Jerusalem. 5 Joab gave the list of
the people to David. There were one million
one hundred thousand men in all of Israel
who could use the sword, and there were
four hundred seventy thousand men in
Judah who could use the sword. 6 But Joab
did not count the tribes of Levi and
Benjamin, because he didn't like King
David's order. 7 David had done something
God had said was wrong, so God punished
Israel.

8 Then David said to God, "I have sinned
greatly by what I have done! Now, I beg you
to forgive me, your servant, because I have
been very foolish."

9 The LORD said to Gad, who was David's
seer, 10 "Go and tell David, 'This is what the
LORD says: I offer you three choices. Choose
one of them and I will do it.' "

11 So Gad went to David and said to him,
"This is what the LORD says: 'Choose for
yourself 12 three years of hunger. Or choose
three months of running from your enemies
as they chase you with their swords. Or
choose three days of punishment from the
LORD, in which a terrible disease will spread
through the country. The angel of the LORD
will go through Israel destroying the people.'
Now, David, decide which of these things I
should tell the LORD who sent me."

13 David said to Gad, "I am in great trouble.
Let the LORD punish me, because the LORD is
very merciful. Don't let my punishment
come from human beings."

14 So the LORD sent a terrible disease on
Israel, and seventy thousand people died.
15 God sent an angel to destroy Jerusalem, but
when the angel started to destroy it, the LORD
saw it and felt very sorry about the terrible
things that had happened. So he said to the
angel who was destroying, "That is enough!
Put down your arm!" The angel of the LORD
was then standing at the threshing floor of
Araunah the Jebusite.

16 David looked up and saw the angel of
the LORD in the sky, holding his sword drawn
and pointed at Jerusalem. Then David and
the elders bowed facedown on the ground.
They were wearing rough cloth to show
their grief. 17 David said to God, "I am the one
who sinned and did wrong. I gave the order
for the people to be counted. These people
only followed me like sheep. They did
nothing wrong. LORD my God, please punish
me and my family, but stop the terrible
disease that is killing your people."

18 Then the angel of the LORD told Gad to
tell David that he should build an altar to
the LORD on the threshing floor of Araunah
the Jebusite. 19 So David did what Gad told
him to do, in the name of the LORD.

20 Araunah was separating the wheat from
the straw. When he turned around, he saw
the angel. Araunah's four sons who were
with him hid. 21 David came to Araunah,

21:2 Beersheba to Dan Beersheba was the city farthest south in Israel. Dan was the city farthest north. So this means all the people of Israel.

devotion 102

1 CHRONICLES 21:17–28

DON'T BUY IT ON THE SALE RACK

David was the kind of man God wanted as the King of Israel (Acts 13:22). He had the utmost respect for his God, and he would never give God something cheap. David knew that sacrifice was precious to the Lord, and he wanted to give him an offering that had cost something. David was not willing to take the easy way out.

Why does God put such a high value on sacrifice? God knows the heart of man and how selfish man can be. God asked the Israelites for sacrifices because he was preparing them for a Messiah who would come and be the ultimate sacrifice for their sins. God would be the One to make the greatest sacrifice by giving humanity his only son.

How often in our own lives do we cheat God, thinking we deserve more and should sacrifice less? We neglect to seek after God's heart and continue to rely on the whims of our own hearts. The Bible says, "You may believe you are doing right, but the Lord judges your reasons" (Prov. 21:2). Think of your own life. Have you sacrificed for the Lord recently? What is it you could do for God today that would involve a sacrifice? Remember that you can never out-give God. His blessings abound in our lives when our heart is willing to sacrifice. David bought the land for God that day, not knowing it would be the place where God would one day build his Temple.

and when Araunah saw him, he left the threshing floor and bowed facedown on the ground before David.

22David said to him, "Sell me your
threshing floor so I can build an altar to the LORD here. Then the terrible disease will stop. Sell it to me for the full price."

23Araunah said to David, "Take this
threshing floor. My master the king, do anything you want. Look, I will also give you oxen for the whole burnt offerings, the threshing boards for the wood, and wheat for the grain offering. I give everything to you."

24But King David answered Araunah, "No,
I will pay the full price for the land. I won't take anything that is yours and give it to the LORD. I won't offer a burnt offering that costs me nothing."

25So David paid Araunah about fifteen
pounds of gold for the place. 26David built an
altar to the LORD there and offered whole burnt offerings and fellowship offerings. David prayed to the LORD, and he answered him by sending down fire from heaven on
the altar of burnt offering. 27Then the LORD
commanded the angel to put his sword back into its holder.

28When David saw that the LORD had
answered him on the threshing floor of
Araunah, he offered sacrifices there. 29The
Holy Tent that Moses made while the Israelites were in the desert and the altar of burnt offerings were in Gibeon at the place
of worship. 30But David could not go to the
Holy Tent to speak with God, because he was afraid of the angel of the LORD and his sword.

22 David said, "The Temple of the LORD God and the altar for Israel's burnt offerings will be built here."

David Makes Plans for the Temple

2So David ordered all foreigners living in
Israel to gather together. From that group David chose stonecutters to cut stones to be used in building the Temple of God. 3David
supplied a large amount of iron to be used

for making nails and hinges for the gate
doors. He also supplied more bronze than
could be weighed, [4]and he supplied more
cedar logs than could be counted. Much of
the cedar had been brought to David by the
people from Sidon and Tyre.
[5]David said, "We should build a great
Temple for the LORD, which will be famous
everywhere for its greatness and beauty.
But my son Solomon is young. He hasn't
yet learned what he needs to know, so I
will prepare for the building of it." So David
got many of the materials ready before
he died.
[6]Then David called for his son Solomon
and told him to build the Temple for the
LORD, the God of Israel. [7]David said to him,
"My son, I wanted to build a temple for
worshiping the LORD my God. [8]But the LORD
spoke his word to me, 'David, you have
killed many people. You have fought many
wars. You cannot build a temple for worship
to me, because you have killed many people.
[9]But, you will have a son, a man of peace and
rest. I will give him rest from all his enemies
around him. His name will be Solomon,[n] and
I will give Israel peace and quiet while he is
king. [10]Solomon will build a temple for
worship to me. He will be my son, and I will
be his father. I will make his kingdom
strong; someone from his family will rule
Israel forever.' "
[11]David said, "Now, my son, may the LORD
be with you. May you build a temple for the
LORD your God, as he said you would. [12]He
will make you the king of Israel. May the
LORD give you wisdom and understanding so
you will be able to obey the teachings of the
LORD your God. [13]Be careful to obey the rules
and laws the LORD gave Moses for Israel. If
you obey them, you will have success. Be
strong and brave. Don't be afraid or
discouraged.
[14]"Solomon, I have worked hard getting
many of the materials for building the
Temple of the LORD. I have supplied about
seven and one-half million pounds of gold,
about seventy-five million pounds of silver,
so much bronze and iron it cannot be
weighed, and wood and stone. You may add
to them. [15]You have many workmen—
stonecutters, bricklayers, carpenters, and
people skilled in every kind of work. [16]They
are skilled in working with gold, silver,
bronze, and iron. You have more craftsmen
than can be counted. Now begin the work,
and may the LORD be with you."
[17]Then David ordered all the leaders of
Israel to help his son Solomon. [18]David said
to them, "The LORD your God is with you.
He has given you rest from our enemies. He
has handed over to me the people living
around us. The LORD and his people are in
control of this land. [19]Now give yourselves
completely to obeying the LORD your God.
Build the holy place of the LORD God; build
the Temple for worship to the LORD. Then
bring the Ark of the Agreement with the
LORD and the holy items that belong to God
into the Temple."

The Levites

23 After David had lived long and was
old, he made his son Solomon the
new king of Israel. [2]David gathered all the
leaders of Israel, along with the priests and
Levites. [3]He counted the Levites who were
thirty years old and older. In all, there were
thirty-eight thousand Levites. [4]David said,
"Of these, twenty-four thousand Levites will
direct the work of the Temple of the LORD,
six thousand Levites will be officers and
judges, [5]four thousand Levites will be
gatekeepers, and four thousand Levites will
praise the LORD with musical instruments I
made for giving praise."
[6]David separated the Levites into three
groups that were led by Levi's three sons:
Gershon, Kohath, and Merari.

The People of Gershon

[7]From the people of Gershon, there were
Ladan and Shimei.
[8]Ladan had three sons. His first son was
Jehiel, and his other sons were Zetham and
Joel.
[9]Shimei's sons were Shelomoth, Haziel,
and Haran. These three sons were leaders of
Ladan's families. [10]Shimei had four sons:
Jahath, Ziza, Jeush, and Beriah. [11]Jahath was
the first son, and Ziza was the second son.
But Jeush and Beriah did not have many
children, so they were counted as if they
were one family.

22:9 Solomon This name sounds like the Hebrew word for "peace."

The People of Kohath

12Kohath had four sons: Amram, Izhar,
Hebron, and Uzziel.
13Amram's sons were Aaron and Moses.
Aaron and his descendants were chosen to
be special forever. They were chosen to
prepare the holy things for the LORD's
service, to offer sacrifices before the LORD,
and to serve him as priests. They were to
give blessings in his name forever.
14Moses was the man of God, and his sons
were counted as part of the tribe of Levi.
15Moses' sons were Gershom and Eliezer.
16Gershom's first son was Shubael. 17Eliezer's
first son was Rehabiah. Eliezer had no other
sons, but Rehabiah had many sons.
18Izhar's first son was Shelomith.
19Hebron's first son was Jeriah, his second
was Amariah, his third was Jahaziel, and his
fourth was Jekameam.
20Uzziel's first son was Micah and his
second was Isshiah.

The People of Merari

21Merari's sons were Mahli and Mushi.
Mahli's sons were Eleazar and Kish.
22Eleazar died without sons; he had only
daughters. Eleazar's daughters married their
cousins, the sons of Kish. 23Mushi's three
sons were Mahli, Eder, and Jerimoth.

The Levites' Work

24These were Levi's descendants listed by
their families. They were the leaders of
families. Each person who was twenty years
old or older was listed. They served in the
LORD's Temple.
25David had said, "The LORD, the God of
Israel, has given rest to his people. He has
come to live in Jerusalem forever. 26So the
Levites don't need to carry the Holy Tent or
any of the things used in its services
anymore." 27David's last instructions were to
count the Levites who were twenty years old
and older.
28The Levites had the job of helping
Aaron's descendants in the service of the
Temple of the LORD. They cared for the
Temple courtyard and side rooms, and they
made all the holy things pure. Their job was
to serve in the Temple of God. 29They were
responsible for putting the holy bread on the
table, for the flour in the grain offerings, for
the bread made without yeast, for the baking
and mixing, and for the measuring. 30The
Levites also stood every morning and gave
thanks and praise to the LORD. They also did
this every evening. 31The Levites offered all
the burnt offerings to the LORD on the special
days of rest, at the New Moon festivals, and
at all appointed feasts. They served before
the LORD every day. They were to follow the
rules for how many Levites should serve
each time. 32So the Levites took care of the
Meeting Tent and the Holy Place. And they
helped their relatives, Aaron's descendants,
with the services at the Temple of the LORD.

The Groups of the Priests

24 These were the groups of Aaron's
sons: Aaron's sons were Nadab, Abihu,
Eleazar, and Ithamar. 2But Nadab and Abihu
died before their father did, and they had no
sons. So Eleazar and Ithamar served as the
priests. 3David, with the help of Zadok, a
descendant of Eleazar, and Ahimelech, a
descendant of Ithamar, separated their
family groups into two different groups.
Each group had certain duties. 4There were
more leaders from Eleazar's family than
from Ithamar's—sixteen leaders from
Eleazar's family and eight leaders from
Ithamar's family. 5Men were chosen from
Eleazar's and Ithamar's families by throwing
lots. Some men from each family were
chosen to be in charge of the Holy Place, and
some were chosen to serve as priests.
6Shemaiah son of Nethanel, from the tribe
of Levi, was the secretary. He recorded the
names of those descendants in front of King
David, the officers, Zadok the priest,
Ahimelech son of Abiathar, and the leaders
of the families of the priests and Levites. The
work was divided by lots among the families
of Eleazar and Ithamar. The following men
with their groups were chosen.
7The first one chosen was Jehoiarib. The
second was Jedaiah. 8The third was Harim.
The fourth was Seorim. 9The fifth was
Malkijah. The sixth was Mijamin. 10The
seventh was Hakkoz. The eighth was Abijah.
11The ninth was Jeshua. The tenth was
Shecaniah. 12The eleventh was Eliashib. The
twelfth was Jakim. 13The thirteenth was
Huppah. The fourteenth was Jeshebeab.
14The fifteenth was Bilgah. The sixteenth
was Immer. 15The seventeenth was Hezir.
The eighteenth was Happizzez. 16The

nineteenth was Pethahiah. The twentieth
was Jehezkel. 17The twenty-first was Jakin.
The twenty-second was Gamul. 18The
twenty-third was Delaiah. The twenty-fourth
was Maaziah.
19These were the groups chosen to serve
in the Temple of the LORD. They obeyed the
rules given them by Aaron, just as the LORD,
the God of Israel, had commanded him.

The Other Levites

20These are the names of the rest of Levi's
descendants:
Shubael was a descendant of Amram, and
Jehdeiah was a descendant of Shubael.
21Isshiah was the first son of Rehabiah.
22From the Izhar family group, there was
Shelomoth, and Jahath was a descendant of
Shelomoth.
23Hebron's first son was Jeriah, Amariah
was his second, Jahaziel was his third, and
Jekameam was his fourth.
24Uzziel's son was Micah. Micah's son was
Shamir. 25Micah's brother was Isshiah, and
Isshiah's son was Zechariah.
26Merari's descendants were Mahli and
Mushi. Merari's son was Jaaziah. 27Jaaziah
son of Merari had sons named Shoham,
Zaccur, and Ibri. 28Mahli's son was Eleazar,
but Eleazar did not have any sons.
29Kish's son was Jerahmeel.
30Mushi's sons were Mahli, Eder, and
Jerimoth.
These are the Levites, listed by their
families. 31They were chosen for special jobs
by throwing lots in front of King David,
Zadok, Ahimelech, the leaders of the
families of the priests, and the Levites. They
did this just as their relatives, the priests,
Aaron's descendants, had done. The families
of the oldest brother and the youngest
brother were treated the same.

The Music Groups

25 David and the commanders of the
army chose some of the sons of
Asaph, Heman, and Jeduthun to preach and
play harps, lyres, and cymbals. Here is a list
of the men who served in this way:
2Asaph's sons who served were Zaccur,
Joseph, Nethaniah, and Asarelah. King David
chose Asaph to preach, and Asaph directed
his sons.
3Jeduthun's sons who served were
Gedaliah, Zeri, Jeshaiah, Shimei, Hashabiah,
and Mattithiah. There were six of them, and
Jeduthun directed them. He preached and
used a harp to give thanks and praise to the
LORD.
4Heman's sons who served were Bukkiah,
Mattaniah, Uzziel, Shubael, Jerimoth,
Hananiah, Hanani, Eliathah, Giddalti,
Romamti-Ezer, Joshbekashah, Mallothi,
Hothir, and Mahazioth. 5All these were sons
of Heman, David's seer. God promised to
make Heman strong, so Heman had many
sons. God gave him fourteen sons and three
daughters. 6Heman directed all his sons in
making music for the Temple of the LORD
with cymbals, lyres, and harps; that was
their way of serving in the Temple of God.
King David was in charge of Asaph,
Jeduthun, and Heman. 7These men and
their relatives were trained and skilled in
making music for the LORD. There were two
hundred eighty-eight of them. 8Everyone
threw lots to choose the time his family was
to serve at the Temple. The young and the
old, the teacher and the student, had to
throw lots.
9First, the lot fell to Joseph, from the
family of Asaph.
Second, twelve men were chosen from
Gedaliah, his sons and relatives.
10Third, twelve men were chosen from
Zaccur, his sons and relatives.
11Fourth, twelve men were chosen from
Izri, his sons and relatives.
12Fifth, twelve men were chosen from
Nethaniah, his sons and relatives.
13Sixth, twelve men were chosen from
Bukkiah, his sons and relatives.
14Seventh, twelve men were chosen from
Jesarelah, his sons and relatives.
15Eighth, twelve men were chosen from
Jeshaiah, his sons and relatives.
16Ninth, twelve men were chosen from
Mattaniah, his sons and relatives.
17Tenth, twelve men were chosen from
Shimei, his sons and relatives.
18Eleventh, twelve men were chosen from
Azarel, his sons and relatives.
19Twelfth, twelve men were chosen from
Hashabiah, his sons and relatives.
20Thirteenth, twelve men were chosen
from Shubael, his sons and relatives.
21Fourteenth, twelve men were chosen
from Mattithiah, his sons and relatives.

[22]Fifteenth, twelve men were chosen from
Jerimoth, his sons and relatives.
[23]Sixteenth, twelve men were chosen
from Hananiah, his sons and relatives.
[24]Seventeenth, twelve men were chosen
from Joshbekashah, his sons and relatives.
[25]Eighteenth, twelve men were chosen
from Hanani, his sons and relatives.
[26]Nineteenth, twelve men were chosen
from Mallothi, his sons and relatives.
[27]Twentieth, twelve men were chosen
from Eliathah, his sons and relatives.
[28]Twenty-first, twelve men were chosen
from Hothir, his sons and relatives.
[29]Twenty-second, twelve men were
chosen from Giddalti, his sons and relatives.
[30]Twenty-third, twelve men were chosen
from Mahazioth, his sons and relatives.
[31]Twenty-fourth, twelve men were chosen
from Romamti-Ezer, his sons and relatives.

The Gatekeepers

26 These are the groups of the
gatekeepers. From the family of
Korah, there was Meshelemiah son of Kore,
who was from Asaph's family. [2]Meshelemiah
had sons. Zechariah was his first son, Jediael
was second, Zebadiah was third, Jathniel was
fourth, [3]Elam was fifth, Jehohanan was
sixth, and Eliehoenai was seventh.
[4]Obed-Edom had sons. Shemaiah was his
first son, Jehozabad was second, Joah was
third, Sacar was fourth, Nethanel was fifth,
[5]Ammiel was sixth, Issachar was seventh,
and Peullethai was eighth. God blessed
Obed-Edom with children.
[6]Obed-Edom's son Shemaiah also had
sons. They were leaders in their father's
family because they were capable men.
[7]Shemaiah's sons were Othni, Rephael, Obed,
Elzabad, Elihu, and Semakiah. Elihu, and
Semakiah were skilled workers. [8]All these
were Obed-Edom's descendants. They and
their sons and relatives were capable men
and strong workers. Obed-Edom had
sixty-two descendants in all.
[9]Meshelemiah had sons and relatives who
were skilled workers. In all, there were
eighteen.
[10]From the Merari family, Hosah had sons.
Shimri was chosen to be in charge. Although
he was not the oldest son, his father chose
him to be in charge. [11]Hilkiah was his
second son, Tabaliah was third, and
Zechariah was fourth. In all, Hosah had
thirteen sons and relatives.
[12]These were the leaders of the groups of
gatekeepers, and they served in the Temple
of the LORD. Their relatives also worked in
the Temple. [13]By throwing lots, each family
chose a gate to guard. Young and old threw
lots.
[14]Meshelemiah was chosen by lot to
guard the East Gate. Then lots were thrown
for Meshelemiah's son Zechariah. He was a
wise counselor and was chosen for the North
Gate. [15]Obed-Edom was chosen for the South
Gate, and Obed-Edom's sons were chosen to
guard the storehouse. [16]Shuppim and Hosah
were chosen for the West Gate and the
Shalleketh Gate on the upper road.

Guards stood side by side with guards.
[17]Six Levites stood guard every day at the
East Gate; four Levites stood guard every day
at the North Gate; four Levites stood guard
every day at the South Gate; and two Levites
at a time guarded the storehouse. [18]There
were two guards at the western court and
four guards on the road to the court.
[19]These were the groups of the
gatekeepers from the families of Korah and
Merari.

Other Leaders

[20]Other Levites were responsible for
guarding the treasuries of the Temple of God
and for the places where the holy items were
kept.
[21]Ladan was Gershon's son and the
ancestor of several family groups. Jehiel was
a leader of one of the family groups. [22]His
sons were Zetham and Joel his brother, and
they were responsible for the treasuries of
the Temple of the LORD.
[23]Other leaders were chosen from the
family groups of Amram, Izhar, Hebron, and
Uzziel. [24]Shubael, the descendant of
Gershom, who was Moses' son, was the
leader responsible for the treasuries. [25]These
were Shubael's relatives from Eliezer:
Eliezer's son Rehabiah, Rehabiah's son
Jeshaiah, Jeshaiah's son Joram, Joram's son
Zicri, and Zicri's son Shelomith. [26]Shelomith
and his relatives were responsible for
everything that had been collected for the
Temple by King David, by the heads of
families, by the commanders of a thousand
men and of a hundred men, and by other

army commanders. 27They also gave some of the things they had taken in wars to be used in repairing the Temple of the LORD. 28Shelomith and his relatives took care of all the holy items. Some had been given by Samuel the seer, Saul son of Kish, Abner son of Ner, and Joab son of Zeruiah.

29Kenaniah was from the Izhar family. He and his sons worked outside the Temple as officers and judges in different places in Israel.

30Hashabiah was from the Hebron family. He and his relatives were responsible for the LORD's work and the king's business in Israel west of the Jordan River. There were seventeen hundred skilled men in Hashabiah's group. 31The history of the Hebron family shows that Jeriah was their leader. In David's fortieth year as king, the records were searched, and some capable men of the Hebron family were found living at Jazer in Gilead. 32Jeriah had twenty-seven hundred relatives who were skilled men and leaders of families. King David gave them the responsibility of directing the tribes of Reuben, Gad, and East Manasseh in God's work and the king's business.

Army Divisions

27 This is the list of the Israelites who served the king in the army. Each division was on duty one month each year. There were leaders of families, commanders of a hundred men, commanders of a thousand men, and other officers. Each division had twenty-four thousand men.

2Jashobeam son of Zabdiel was in charge of the first division for the first month. There were twenty-four thousand men in his division. 3Jashobeam, one of the descendants of Perez, was leader of all the army officers for the first month.

4Dodai, from the Ahohites, was in charge of the division for the second month. Mikloth was a leader in the division. There were twenty-four thousand men in Dodai's division.

5The third commander, for the third month, was Benaiah son of Jehoiada the priest. There were twenty-four thousand men in his division. 6He was the Benaiah who was one of the Thirty[n] soldiers. Benaiah was a brave warrior who led those men. Benaiah's son Ammizabad was in charge of Benaiah's division.

7The fourth commander, for the fourth month, was Asahel, the brother of Joab. Later, Asahel's son Zebadiah took his place as commander. There were twenty-four thousand men in his division.

8The fifth commander, for the fifth month, was Shamhuth, from Izrah's family. There were twenty-four thousand men in his division.

9The sixth commander, for the sixth month, was Ira son of Ikkesh from the town of Tekoa. There were twenty-four thousand men in his division.

10The seventh commander, for the seventh month, was Helez. He was from the Pelonites and a descendant of Ephraim. There were twenty-four thousand men in his division.

11The eighth commander, for the eighth month, was Sibbecai. He was from Hushah and was from Zerah's family. There were twenty-four thousand men in his division.

12The ninth commander, for the ninth month, was Abiezer. He was from Anathoth in Benjamin. There were twenty-four thousand men in his division.

13The tenth commander, for the tenth month, was Maharai. He was from Netophah and was from Zerah's family. There were twenty-four thousand men in his division.

14The eleventh commander, for the eleventh month, was Benaiah. He was from Pirathon in Ephraim. There were twenty-four thousand men in his division.

15The twelfth commander, for the twelfth month, was Heldai. He was from Netophah and was from Othniel's family. There were twenty-four thousand men in his division.

Leaders of the Tribes

16These were the leaders of the tribes of Israel. Eliezer son of Zicri was over the tribe of Reuben. Shephatiah son of Maacah was over the tribe of Simeon. 17Hashabiah son of Kemuel was over the tribe of Levi. Zadok was over the people of Aaron. 18Elihu, one of David's brothers, was over the tribe of Judah. Omri son of Michael was over the tribe of Issachar. 19Ishmaiah son of Obadiah was

27:6 Thirty These were David's most powerful soldiers. See 2 Samuel 23:24.

over the tribe of Zebulun. Jerimoth son of
Azriel was over the tribe of Naphtali.
20Hoshea son of Azaziah was over the tribe
of Ephraim. Joel son of Pedaiah was over
West Manasseh. 21Iddo son of Zechariah was
over East Manasseh. Jaasiel son of Abner was
over the tribe of Benjamin. 22Azarel son of
Jeroham was over the tribe of Dan.

These were the leaders of the tribes of
Israel.

23The LORD had promised to make the
Israelites as many as the stars in the sky. So
David only counted the men who were
twenty years old and older. 24Joab son of
Zeruiah began to count the people, but he
did not finish. God became angry with Israel
for counting the people, so the number of
the people was not put in the history book
about King David's rule.

The King's Directors

25Azmaveth son of Adiel was in charge of
the royal storehouses.

Jonathan son of Uzziah was in charge of
the storehouses in the country, towns,
villages, and towers.

26Ezri son of Kelub was in charge of the
field workers who farmed the land.

27Shimei, from the town of Ramah, was in
charge of the vineyards.

Zabdi, from Shapham, was in charge of
storing the wine that came from the
vineyards.

28Baal-Hanan, from Geder, was in charge
of the olive trees and sycamore trees in the
western hills.

Joash was in charge of storing the olive
oil.

29Shitrai, from Sharon, was in charge of
the herds that fed in the Plain of Sharon.

Shaphat son of Adlai was in charge of the
herds in the valleys.

30Obil, an Ishmaelite, was in charge of the
camels.

Jehdeiah, from Meronoth, was in charge of
the donkeys.

31Jaziz, from the Hagrites, was in charge of
the flocks.

All these men were the officers who took
care of King David's property.

32Jonathan was David's uncle, and he
advised David. Jonathan was a wise man and
a teacher of the law. Jehiel son of Hacmoni
took care of the king's sons. 33Ahithophel
advised the king. Hushai, from the Arkite
people, was the king's friend. 34Jehoiada and
Abiathar later took Ahithophel's place in
advising the king. Jehoiada was Benaiah's
son. Joab was the commander of the king's
army.

David's Plans for the Temple

28 David commanded all the leaders of
Israel to come to Jerusalem. There
were the leaders of the tribes, commanders
of the divisions serving the king, commanders
of a thousand men and of a hundred men,
leaders who took care of the property and
animals that belonged to the king and his
sons, men over the palace, the powerful
men, and all the brave warriors.

2King David stood up and said, "Listen to
me, my relatives and my people. I wanted to
build a place to keep the Ark of the
Agreement with the LORD. I wanted it to be
God's footstool. So I made plans to build a
temple. 3But God said to me, 'You must not
build a temple for worshiping me, because
you are a soldier and have killed many
people.'

4"But the LORD, the God of Israel, chose me
from my whole family to be king of Israel
forever. He chose the tribe of Judah to lead,
and from the people of Judah, he chose my
father's family. From that family God was
pleased to make me king of Israel. 5The LORD
has given me many sons, and from those
sons he has chosen Solomon to be the new
king of Israel. Israel is the LORD's kingdom.
6The LORD said to me, 'Your son Solomon
will build my Temple and its courtyards. I
have chosen Solomon to be my son, and I
will be his father. 7He is obeying my laws
and commands now. If he continues to obey
them, I will make his kingdom strong
forever.' "

8David said, "Now, in front of all Israel, the
assembly of the LORD, and in the hearing of
God, I tell you these things: Be careful to
obey all the commands of the LORD your
God. Then you will keep this good land and
pass it on to your descendants forever.

9"And you, my son Solomon, accept the
God of your father. Serve him completely
and willingly, because the LORD knows what
is in everyone's mind. He understands
everything you think. If you go to him for
help, you will get an answer. But if you turn

devotion 103

1 CHRONICLES 28:9

COME OUT, COME OUT WHEREVER YOU ARE!

Have you ever tried to hide something from God? Maybe you have wanted to hide your real motives, your secret sin, or even the consequences you are already suffering. We often try to hide our very hearts from God, hoping that he won't see our spiritual poverty or discover our pitiful thoughts.

But if you remember that God is already privy to everything that concerns you, would that truth coax you out? If you heard that the God who knows you truly and loves you still wants to wrap you in his embrace, would you fall into his great big arms of love? I am so grateful that God can see through my mustered smile or my best efforts or the big mess I have made right down into my aching heart. He knows his daughter intimately. He smiles over your beautiful design because you are his amazing idea. So why do we forget David's instructions to Solomon?

God understands everything you think, why you think that way, and even what confuses you. He *gets* you. He knows you inside and out and still promises that every time you come out of hiding and move toward him for help, he will answer. We waste too much time in hiding. What if every day was an honest day with God? What if you could trust his good heart and seek him quickly for answers? What if you served him willingly and came to him honestly because he knows and loves you so completely?

away from him, he will leave you forever.
[10]Solomon, you must understand this. The
LORD has chosen you to build the Temple as
his holy place. Be strong and finish the job."
[11]Then David gave his son Solomon the
plans for building the Temple and the
courtyard around the Temple. They included
its buildings, its storerooms, its upper rooms,
its inside rooms, and the place where the
people's sins were removed. [12]David gave
him plans for everything he had in mind:
the courtyards around the LORD's Temple
and all the rooms around it, the Temple
treasuries, and the treasuries of the holy
items used in the Temple. [13]David gave
Solomon directions for the groups of the
priests and Levites. David told him about all
the work of serving in the Temple of the
LORD and about the items to be used in the
Temple service [14]that were made of gold or
silver. David told Solomon how much gold
or silver should be used to make each thing.
[15]David told him how much gold to use for
each gold lampstand and its lamps and how
much silver to use for each silver lampstand
and its lamps. The different lampstands were
to be used where needed. [16]David told how
much gold should be used for each table that
held the holy bread and how much silver
should be used for the silver tables. [17]He told
how much pure gold should be used to
make the forks, bowls, and pitchers and how
much gold should be used to make each gold
dish. He told how much silver should be
used to make each silver dish [18]and how
much pure gold should be used for the altar
of incense. He also gave Solomon the plans
for the chariot of the golden creatures that
spread their wings over the Ark of the
Agreement with the LORD.
[19]David said, "All these plans were written
with the LORD guiding me. He helped me
understand everything in the plans."
[20]David also said to his son Solomon, "Be

strong and brave, and do the work. Don't be
afraid or discouraged, because the LORD God,
my God, is with you. He will not fail you or
leave you until all the work for the Temple
of the LORD is finished. 21The groups of the
priests and Levites are ready for all the work
on the Temple of God. Every skilled worker
is ready to help you with all the work. The
leaders and all the people will obey every
command you give."

Gifts for Building the Temple

29 King David said to all the Israelites
who were gathered, "God chose my
son Solomon, who is young and hasn't yet
learned what he needs to know, but the work
is important. This palace is not for people; it
is for the LORD God. 2I have done my best to
prepare for building the Temple of God. I
have given gold for the things made of gold
and silver for the things made of silver. I have
given bronze for the things made of bronze
and iron for the things made of iron. I have
given wood for the things made of wood and
onyx for the settings. I have given turquoise
gems of many different colors, valuable
stones, and white marble. I have given much
of all these things. 3I have already given this
for the Temple, but now I am also giving my
own treasures of gold and silver, because I
really want the Temple of my God to be built.
4I have given about two hundred twenty
thousand pounds of pure gold from Ophir
and about five hundred twenty thousand
pounds of pure silver. They will be used to
cover the walls of the buildings 5and for all
the gold and silver work. Skilled men may
use the gold and silver to make things for the
Temple. Now, who is ready to give himself to
the service of the LORD today?"

6The family leaders and the leaders of the
tribes of Israel, the commanders of a
thousand men and of a hundred men, and
the leaders responsible for the king's work
gave their valuable things. 7They donated
about three hundred eighty thousand
pounds of gold, about seven hundred fifty
thousand pounds of silver, about one million
three hundred fifty thousand pounds of
bronze, and about seven million five
hundred thousand pounds of iron to the
Temple of God. 8People who had valuable
gems gave them to the treasury of the
Temple of the LORD, and Jehiel, from the
Gershon family, took care of the valuable
gems. 9The leaders gave willingly and
completely to the LORD. The people rejoiced
to see their leaders give so gladly, and King
David was also very happy.

David's Prayer

10David praised the LORD in front of all the
people who were gathered. He said:

"We praise you, LORD,
God of our father Israel.
We praise you forever and ever.
11LORD, you are great and powerful.
You have glory, victory, and honor.
Everything in heaven and on earth
belongs to you.
The kingdom belongs to you, LORD;
you are the ruler over everything.
12Riches and honor come from you.
You rule everything.
You have the power and strength
to make anyone great and strong.
13Now, our God, we thank you
and praise your glorious name.

14"These things did not really come from
me and my people.
Everything comes from you;
we have given you back what you
gave us.
15We are like foreigners and strangers,
as our ancestors were.
Our time on earth is like a shadow.
There is no hope.
16LORD our God, we have gathered all this
to build your Temple for worship to you.
But everything has come from you;
everything belongs to you.
17I know, my God, that you test people's
hearts.
You are happy when people do what is
right.
I was happy to give all these things,
and I gave with an honest heart.
Your people gathered here are happy to
give to you,
and I rejoice to see their giving.
18LORD, you are the God of our ancestors,
the God of Abraham, Isaac, and Jacob.
Make your people want to serve you
always,
and make them want to obey you.
19Give my son Solomon a desire to serve
you.

Help him always obey your commands,
laws, and rules.
Help him build the Temple
for which I have prepared."
20Then David said to all the people who
were gathered, "Praise the LORD your God."
So they all praised the LORD, the God of their
ancestors, and they bowed to the ground to
give honor to the LORD and the king.

Solomon Becomes King

21The next day the people sacrificed to the
LORD. They offered burnt offerings to him of
a thousand bulls, a thousand male sheep,
and a thousand male lambs. They also
brought drink offerings. Many sacrifices
were made for all the people of Israel. 22That
day the people ate and drank with much joy,
and the LORD was with them.

And they made David's son Solomon king
for the second time. They poured olive oil on
Solomon to appoint him king in the presence
of the LORD. And they poured oil on Zadok to
appoint him as priest. 23Then Solomon sat on
the LORD's throne as king and took his father
David's place. Solomon was very successful,
and all the people of Israel obeyed him. 24All
the leaders and soldiers and King David's sons
accepted Solomon as king and promised to
obey him. 25The LORD made Solomon great
before all the Israelites and gave Solomon
much honor. No king of Israel before
Solomon had such honor.

David's Death

26David son of Jesse was king over all
Israel. 27He had ruled over Israel forty
years—seven years in Hebron and
thirty-three years in Jerusalem. 28David died
when he was old. He had lived a good, long
life and had received many riches and honors.
His son Solomon became king after him.
29Everything David did as king, from
beginning to end, is recorded in the records
of Samuel the seer, the records of Nathan the
prophet, and the records of Gad the seer.
30Those writings tell what David did as king
of Israel. They tell about his power and what
happened to him and to Israel and to all the
kingdoms around them.

2 Chronicles

Originally one unit, 1 and 2 Chronicles weren't divided into separate volumes until the Greek version of the Old Testament (the Septuagint) was translated around 200 B.C.

Person Holding the Pen God Wrote With: Jewish tradition points to *Ezra* (see explanation under 1 Chr.).

When the Text Was Written: Most likely between 450 and 430 B.C.

Spiritual Posture of the Original Recipients: Just as in 1 Chronicles, the Jews from Judah had returned from captivity in Babylon to Jerusalem, a city that had experienced great change. While they'd done their best to recapture its former glory with ambitious building and restoration projects, the city wasn't nearly as beautiful nor were they as powerful a people group as they'd been before the exile. Their confidence as God's chosen people was shaken.

Storyline Synopsis: While 1 Chronicles is mostly an overview of 1 and 2 Samuel, with David taking up most of the ink, Solomon is the main character in 2 Chronicles. In this volume, the chronicler covers the territory of 1 and 2 Kings, beginning with the establishment of Solomon's rule and quickly proceeding to the construction and dedication of the first Temple in Jerusalem. The book concludes with a recap of the remaining monarchs who succeeded Solomon and presided over a divided Jewish kingdom. The author maintains his pattern of not bringing up ugly past errors by omitting the spiritual decline of Solomon's latter days.

A Moment Worth Discussing: Chapters 4 and 5 narrate the unprecedented Temple building project. It took over seven years to complete, and when finished, it rivaled any structure celebrated on *Lifestyles of the Rich and Famous*! This impressive building served as God's tangible dwelling place on earth, symbolized his mercy and grace, and gave the Israelites a place to gather for formal worship. It's pretty amazing to ponder that God's "Temple" now resides in the hearts of those who know and love him (1 Cor. 3:16 and 2 Cor. 6:16).

Interesting (But Likely to Be Overlooked) Character: The *Queen of Sheba* paid Solomon a visit with the haughty intention of proving that he simply couldn't be as extraordinary as his reputation. But she was so impressed and amazed by his wisdom and the opulence of his palace that she exclaimed praises to God (2 Chr. 9:1–8).

Solomon Asks for Wisdom

1 Solomon, David's son, became a powerful
king, because the LORD his God was with
him and made him very great.
[2]Solomon spoke to all the people of
Israel—the commanders of a hundred men
and of a thousand men, the judges, every
leader in all Israel, and the leaders of the
families. [3]Then Solomon and all the people
with him went to the place of worship at the
town of Gibeon. God's Meeting Tent, which
Moses the LORD's servant had made in the
desert, was there. [4]David had brought the
Ark of God from Kiriath Jearim to Jerusalem,
where he had made a place for it and had set
up a tent for it. [5]The bronze altar that Bezalel
son of Uri, who was the son of Hur, had
made was in Gibeon in front of the Holy
Tent. So Solomon and the people worshiped
there. [6]Solomon went up to the bronze altar
in the presence of the LORD at the Meeting
Tent and offered a thousand burnt offerings
on it.
[7]That night God appeared to Solomon and
said to him, "Ask for whatever you want me
to give you."
[8]Solomon answered, "You have been very
kind to my father David, and you have made
me king in his place. [9]Now, LORD God, may
your promise to my father David come true.
You have made me king of a people who are
as many as the dust of the earth. [10]Now give
me wisdom and knowledge so I can lead
these people in the right way, because no
one can rule them without your help."
[11]God said to Solomon, "You have not
asked for wealth or riches or honor, or for
the death of your enemies, or for a long life.
But since you have asked for wisdom and
knowledge to lead my people, over whom I
have made you king, [12]I will give you
wisdom and knowledge. I will also give you
more wealth, riches, and honor than any
king who has lived before you or any who
will live after you."
[13]Then Solomon left the place of worship,
the Meeting Tent, at Gibeon and went back
to Jerusalem. There King Solomon ruled
over Israel.

Solomon's Wealth

[14]Solomon had fourteen hundred chariots
and twelve thousand horses. He kept some
in special cities for the chariots, and others

devotion 104

2 CHRONICLES 1:7–12

IF I HAD $28 MILLION . . .

In my line of work, I have watched many people get rich only to lose every single penny of it in the end. I had a client that earned $28 million in just one year. I remember telling him one afternoon that what I was about to say to him would either be a blessing or haunt him all the days of his life. I told him that if he did not get control and be wise with his money, there was going to come a day when he would wish that he had what was spent on his credit card for just one month, and he would realize that one monthly payment could have provided two years of income. I wish I could say he listened to me, but the last time I heard news about him, he had lost everything that he acquired.

Without wisdom and knowledge, people do not know what to do with their blessings; and wisdom is not just isolated to financial matters. It includes cultivating and nurturing relationships and how to conduct ourselves in a godly manner. I have seen more Christians get into trouble with their finances than you can imagine. They rationalize that if they just had more money, their problems would be solved. But the truth of it is that they would still struggle because they are not putting God's wisdom in its rightful place. Ask God for wisdom first, and he will provide the blessings.

he kept with him in Jerusalem. [15]In
Jerusalem Solomon made silver and gold as
plentiful as stones and cedar trees as
plentiful as the fig trees on the western hills.
[16]He imported horses from Egypt and Kue;
his traders bought them in Kue. [17]They
imported chariots from Egypt for about
fifteen pounds of silver apiece, and horses
cost nearly four pounds of silver apiece.
Then they sold the horses and chariots to all
the kings of the Hittites and the Arameans.

Solomon Prepares for the Temple

2 Solomon decided to build a temple as a
place to worship the LORD and also a
palace for himself. [2]He chose seventy
thousand men to carry loads, eighty thousand
men to cut stone in the hill country, and
thirty-six hundred men to direct the workers.

[3]Solomon sent this message to Hiram
king of the city of Tyre: "Help me as you
helped my father David by sending him
cedar logs so he could build himself a palace
to live in. [4]I will build a temple for
worshiping the LORD my God, and I will give
this temple to him. There we will burn
sweet-smelling spices in his presence. We
will continually set out the holy bread in
God's presence. And we will burn sacrifices
every morning and evening, on Sabbath days
and New Moons, and on the other feast days
commanded by the LORD our God. This is a
rule for Israel to obey forever.

[5]"The temple I build will be great, because
our God is greater than all gods. [6]But no one
can really build a house for our God. Not
even the highest of heavens can hold him.
How then can I build a temple for him
except as a place to burn sacrifices to him?

[7]"Now send me a man skilled in working
with gold, silver, bronze, and iron, and with
purple, red, and blue thread. He must also
know how to make engravings. He will
work with my skilled craftsmen in Judah
and Jerusalem, whom my father David
chose.

[8]"Also send me cedar, pine, and juniper
logs from Lebanon. I know your servants are
experienced at cutting down the trees in
Lebanon, and my servants will help them.
[9]Send me a lot of wood, because the temple I
am going to build will be large and
wonderful. [10]I will give your servants who
cut the wood one hundred twenty-five
thousand bushels of wheat, one hundred
twenty-five thousand bushels of barley, one
hundred fifteen thousand gallons of wine,
and one hundred fifteen thousand gallons of
oil."

[11]Then Hiram king of Tyre answered
Solomon with this letter: "Solomon, because
the LORD loves his people, he chose you to be
their king." [12]Hiram also said: "Praise the
LORD, the God of Israel, who made heaven
and earth! He has given King David a wise
son, one with wisdom and understanding,
who will build a temple for the LORD and a
palace for himself.

[13]"I will send you a skilled and wise man
named Huram-Abi. [14]His mother was from
the people of Dan, and his father was from
Tyre. Huram-Abi is skilled in working with
gold, silver, bronze, iron, stone, and wood,
and with purple, blue, and red thread, and
expensive linen. He is skilled in making
engravings and can make any design you
show him. He will help your craftsmen and
the craftsmen of your father David.

[15]"Now send my servants the wheat,
barley, oil, and wine you promised. [16]We will
cut as much wood from Lebanon as you
need and will bring it on rafts by sea to
Joppa. Then you may carry it to Jerusalem."

[17]Solomon counted all the foreigners
living in Israel. (This was after the time his
father David had counted the people.) There
were one hundred fifty-three thousand six
hundred foreigners in the country.
[18]Solomon chose seventy thousand of them
to carry loads, eighty thousand of them to
cut stone in the mountains, and thirty-six
hundred of them to direct the workers and
to keep the people working.

Solomon Builds the Temple

3 Then Solomon began to build the
Temple of the LORD in Jerusalem on
Mount Moriah. This was where the LORD had
appeared to David, Solomon's father.
Solomon built the Temple on the place
David had prepared on the threshing floor of
Araunah the Jebusite. [2]Solomon began
building in the second month of the fourth
year he ruled Israel.

[3]Solomon used these measurements for
building the Temple of God. It was ninety
feet long and thirty feet wide, using the old
measurement. [4]The porch in front of the

main room of the Temple was thirty feet
long and thirty feet high.
He covered the inside of the porch with
pure gold. 5He put panels of pine on the walls
of the main room and covered them with
pure gold. Then he put designs of palm trees
and chains in the gold. 6He decorated the
Temple with gems and gold from Parvaim.[n]
7He put gold on the Temple's ceiling beams,
doorposts, walls, and doors, and he carved
creatures with wings on the walls.
8Then he made the Most Holy Place. It
was thirty feet long and thirty feet wide, as
wide as the Temple. He covered its walls
with about forty-six thousand pounds of
pure gold. 9The gold nails weighed over a
pound. He also covered the upper rooms
with gold.
10He made two creatures with wings for
the Most Holy Place and covered them with
gold. 11The wings of the gold creatures were
thirty feet across. One wing of one creature
was seven and one-half feet long and
touched the Temple wall. The creature's
other wing was also seven and one-half feet
long, and it touched a wing of the second
creature. 12One wing of the second creature
touched the other side of the room and was
also seven and one-half feet long. The second
creature's other wing touched the first
creature's wing, and it was also seven and
one-half feet long. 13Together, the creatures'
wings were thirty feet across. The creatures
stood on their feet, facing the main room.
14He made the curtain of blue, purple, and
red thread, and expensive linen, and he put
designs of creatures with wings in it.
15He made two pillars to stand in front of
the Temple. They were about fifty-two feet
tall, and the capital of each pillar was over
seven feet tall. 16He made a net of chains and
put them on the tops of the pillars. He made
a hundred pomegranates and put them on
the chains. 17Then he put the pillars up in
front of the Temple. One pillar stood on the
south side, the other on the north. He named
the south pillar He Establishes and the north
pillar In Him Is Strength.

Things for the Temple

4 He made a bronze altar thirty feet long,
thirty feet wide, and fifteen feet tall.
2Then he made from bronze a large round
bowl, which was called the Sea. It was
forty-five feet around, fifteen feet across, and
seven and one-half feet deep. 3There were
carvings of bulls under the rim of the
bowl—ten bulls every eighteen inches. They
were in two rows and were made in one
piece with the bowl.
4The bowl rested on the backs of twelve
bronze bulls that faced outward from the
center of the bowl. Three bulls faced north,
three faced west, three faced south, and three
faced east. 5The sides of the bowl were four
inches thick, and it held about seventeen
thousand five hundred gallons. The rim of
the bowl was like the rim of a cup or like a
lily blossom.
6He made ten smaller bowls and put five
on the south side and five on the north. They
were for washing the animals for the burnt
offerings, but the large bowl was for the
priests to wash in.
7He made ten lampstands of gold,
following the plans. He put them in the
Temple, five on the south side and five on
the north.
8He made ten tables and put them in the
Temple, five on the south side and five on
the north. And he used gold to make a
hundred other bowls.
9He also made the priests' courtyard and
the large courtyard. He made the doors that
opened to the courtyard and covered them
with bronze. 10Then he put the large bowl in
the southeast corner of the Temple.
11Huram also made bowls, shovels, and
small bowls. So he finished his work for
King Solomon on the Temple of God:
12two pillars;
two large bowls for the capitals on top of
the pillars;
two nets to cover the two large bowls for
the capitals on top of the pillars;
13four hundred pomegranates for the
two nets (there were two rows of
pomegranates for each net
covering the bowls for the capitals
on top of the pillars);
14the stands with a bowl on each
stand;
15the large bowl with twelve bulls
under it;

3:6 Parvaim There was much gold there. It may have been in the country of Ophir.

16the pots, shovels, forks, and all the
things to go with them.
All the things that Huram-Abi made for
King Solomon for the Temple of the LORD
were made of polished bronze. 17The king
had these things poured into clay molds that
were made in the plain of the Jordan River
between Succoth and Zarethan. 18Solomon
had so many things made that the total
weight of all the bronze was never known.
19Solomon also made all the things for
God's Temple: the golden altar; tables which
held the bread that shows God's people are
in his presence; 20the lampstands and their
lamps of pure gold, to burn in front of the
Most Holy Place as planned; 21the flowers,
lamps, and tongs of pure gold; 22the pure
gold wick trimmers, small bowls, pans, and
dishes used to carry coals, the gold doors for
the Temple, and the inside doors of the Most
Holy Place and of the main room.
5 Finally all the work Solomon did for
the Temple of the LORD was finished. He
brought in everything his father David
had set apart for the Temple—all the silver
and gold and other articles. And he put
everything in the treasuries of God's
Temple.

The Ark Is Brought into the Temple

2Solomon called for the elders of Israel,
the heads of the tribes, and the leaders of the
families to come to him in Jerusalem. He
wanted them to bring the Ark of the
Agreement with the LORD from the older
part of the city. 3So all the Israelites came
together with the king during the festival in
the seventh month.
4When all the elders of Israel arrived, the
Levites lifted up the Ark. 5They carried the
Ark of the Agreement, the Meeting Tent, and
the holy utensils in it; the priests and the
Levites brought them up. 6King Solomon
and all the Israelites gathered before the
Ark of the Agreement and sacrificed so
many sheep and bulls no one could count
them.
7Then the priests put the Ark of the
Agreement with the LORD in its place inside
the Most Holy Place in the Temple, under
the wings of the golden creatures. 8The
wings of these creatures were spread out
over the place for the Ark, covering it and its
carrying poles. 9The carrying poles were so
long that anyone standing in the Holy Place
in front of the Most Holy Place could see the
ends of the poles. But no one could see them
from outside the Holy Place. The poles are
still there today. 10The only things inside the
Ark were two stone tablets[n] that Moses had
put in the Ark at Mount Sinai. That was
where the LORD made his agreement with
the Israelites after they came out of Egypt.
11Then all the priests left the Holy Place.
(All the priests from each group had made
themselves ready to serve the LORD.) 12All the
Levite musicians—Asaph, Heman, Jeduthun,
and all their sons and relatives—stood on
the east side of the altar. They were dressed
in white linen and played cymbals, harps,
and lyres. With them were one hundred
twenty priests who blew trumpets. 13Those
who blew the trumpets and those who sang
together sounded like one person as they
praised and thanked the LORD. They sang as
others played their trumpets, cymbals, and
other instruments. They praised the LORD
with this song:

"He is good;
his love continues forever."

Then the Temple of the LORD was filled
with a cloud. 14The priests could not
continue their work because of the cloud,
because the LORD's glory filled the Temple of
God.

Solomon Speaks to the People

6 Then Solomon said, "The LORD said he
would live in the dark cloud. 2LORD, I
have built a wonderful Temple for you—a
place for you to live forever."
3While all the Israelites were standing
there, King Solomon turned to them and
blessed them. 4Then he said, "Praise the
LORD, the God of Israel. He has done what
he promised to my father David. The LORD
said, 5'Since the time I brought my people
out of Egypt, I have not chosen a city in any
tribe of Israel where a temple will be built
for me. I did not choose a man to lead my
people Israel. 6But now I have chosen
Jerusalem as the place I am to be
worshiped, and I have chosen David to lead
my people Israel.'

5:10 stone tablets They were the two stone tablets on which God wrote the Ten Commandments.

[7]"My father David wanted to build a
temple for the LORD, the God of Israel. [8]But
the LORD said to my father David, 'It was
good that you wanted to build a temple for
me. [9]But you are not the one to build it. Your
son, who comes from your own body, is the
one who will build my temple.'
[10]"Now the LORD has kept his promise. I
am the king now in place of David my
father. Now I rule Israel as the LORD
promised, and I have built the Temple for
the LORD, the God of Israel. [11]There I have
put the Ark, in which is the Agreement the
LORD made with the Israelites."

Solomon's Prayer

[12]Then Solomon stood facing the LORD's
altar, and all the Israelites were standing
behind him. He spread out his hands. [13]He
had made a bronze platform seven and
one-half feet long, seven and one-half feet
wide, and seven and one-half feet high, and
he had placed it in the middle of the outer
courtyard. Solomon stood on the platform.
Then he kneeled in front of all the people of
Israel gathered there, and he spread out his
hands toward the sky. [14]He said, "LORD, God
of Israel, there is no god like you in heaven
or on earth. You keep your agreement of love
with your servants who truly follow you.
[15]You have kept the promise you made to
your servant David, my father. You spoke it
with your own mouth and finished it with
your hands today.
[16]"Now, LORD, God of Israel, keep the
promise you made to your servant David, my
father. You said, 'If your sons are careful to
obey my teachings as you have obeyed, there
will always be someone from your family
ruling Israel.' [17]Now, LORD, God of Israel,
please continue to keep that promise you
made to your servant.
[18]"But, God, can you really live here on the
earth with people? The sky and the highest
place in heaven cannot contain you. Surely
this house which I have built cannot contain
you. [19]But please listen to my prayer and my
request, because I am your servant. LORD my
God, hear this prayer your servant prays to
you. [20]Day and night please watch over this
Temple where you have said you would be
worshiped. Hear the prayer I pray facing this
Temple. [21]Hear my prayers and the prayers
of your people Israel when we pray facing
this place. Hear from your home in heaven,
and when you hear, forgive us.
[22]"If someone wrongs another person, he
will be brought to the altar in this Temple. If
he swears an oath that he is not guilty,
[23]then hear in heaven. Judge the case, punish
the guilty, but declare that the innocent
person is not guilty.
[24]"When your people, the Israelites, sin
against you, their enemies will defeat them.
But if they come back to you and praise you
and pray to you in this Temple, [25]then listen
from heaven. Forgive the sin of your people
Israel, and bring them back to the land you
gave to them and their ancestors.
[26]"When they sin against you, you will
stop the rain from falling on their land. Then
they will pray, facing this place and praising
you; they will stop sinning when you make
them suffer. [27]When this happens, hear their
prayer in heaven, and forgive the sins of your
servants, the Israelites. Teach them to do
what is right. Then please send rain to this
land you have given particularly to them.
[28]"At times the land will get so dry that no
food will grow, or a great sickness will
spread among the people. Sometimes the
crops will be destroyed by locusts or
grasshoppers. Your people will be attacked
in their cities by their enemies, or will
become sick. [29]When any of these things
happens, the people will become truly sorry.
If your people spread their hands in prayer
toward this Temple, [30]then hear their
prayers from your home in heaven. Forgive
and treat each person as he should be treated
because you know what is in a person's
heart. Only you know what is in people's
hearts. [31]Then the people will respect and
obey you as long as they live in this land you
gave our ancestors.
[32]"People who are not Israelites, foreigners
from other lands, will hear about your
greatness and power. They will come from
far away to pray at this Temple. [33]Then hear
from your home in heaven, and do whatever
they ask you. Then people everywhere will
know you and respect you, just as your
people Israel do. Then everyone will know
that I built this Temple as a place to worship
you.
[34]"When your people go out to fight their
enemies along some road on which you send
them, your people will pray to you, facing

devotion 105

2 CHRONICLES 6:18–21

THE PRAYERS OF THE WORLD

Does God really hear our prayers? I love the scene from the movie *Bruce Almighty* when Bruce is trying to answer all the prayers of all the people at the same time. It makes you appreciate God a bit more. But God is not a man, and he is able to hear the prayers of all people at all times. This is why he is God. The other question you have to ask yourself is whether or not your prayers make any difference in your life and in the lives of others. The answer is an important one. You see, if your prayers can really make a difference, then the importance of prayer in the life of a Christian is monumental.

Look up James 5:16. This scripture tells us that when a believing person prays, great things happen. Those prayers are powerful and effective. Prayer makes all the difference. How committed are you to prayer? Is it something you do occasionally or something you do continually? I remember as a teenager thinking that being a prayer warrior must be a boring calling on your life. It would be much more exciting to be a missionary or an evangelist. As I grew in the Lord, I began to realize that the Christians with the most exciting lives were those who made prayer a priority. How can we serve God if we never talk to him about where and how to serve? Make prayer a priority today. It will change your life.

this city which you have chosen and the
Temple I have built for you. 35Then hear in
heaven their prayers, and do what is right.
36"Everyone sins, so your people will also
sin against you. You will become angry with
them and will hand them over to their
enemies. Their enemies will capture them
and take them away to a country far or near.
37Your people will be sorry for their sins
when they are held as prisoners in another
country. They will be sorry and pray to you
in the land where they are held as prisoners,
saying, 'We have sinned. We have done
wrong and acted wickedly.' 38They will truly
turn back to you in the land where they are
captives. They will pray, facing this land you
gave their ancestors, this city you have
chosen, and the Temple I have built for you.
39Then hear their prayers from your home in
heaven and do what is right. Forgive your
people who have sinned against you.
40"Now, my God, look at us. Listen to the
prayers we pray in this place.
41Now, rise, LORD God, and come to your
resting place.
Come with the Ark of the Agreement
that shows your strength.
Let your priests receive your salvation,
LORD God,
and may your holy people be happy
because of your goodness.
42LORD God, do not reject your appointed
one.
Remember your love for your servant
David."

The Temple Is Given to the Lord

7 When Solomon finished praying, fire
came down from the sky and burned up
the burnt offering and the sacrifices. The
LORD's glory filled the Temple. 2The priests
could not enter the Temple of the LORD,
because the LORD's glory filled it. 3When all
the people of Israel saw the fire come down
from heaven and the LORD's glory on the
Temple, they bowed down on the pavement
with their faces to the ground. They
worshiped and thanked the LORD, saying,
"He is good;
his love continues forever."

[4]Then King Solomon and all the people
offered sacrifices to the LORD. [5]King Solomon
offered a sacrifice of twenty-two thousand
cattle and one hundred twenty thousand
sheep. So the king and all the people gave
the Temple to God. [6]The priests stood ready
to do their work. The Levites also stood with
the instruments of the LORD's music that
King David had made for praising the LORD.
The priests and Levites were saying, "His
love continues forever." The priests, who
stood across from the Levites, blew their
trumpets, and all the Israelites were
standing.

[7]Solomon made holy the middle part of
the courtyard, which is in front of the
Temple of the LORD. There he offered whole
burnt offerings and the fat of the fellowship
offerings. He offered them in the courtyard,
because the bronze altar he had made could
not hold the burnt offerings, grain offerings,
and fat.

[8]Solomon and all the Israelites celebrated
the festival for seven days. There were many
people, and they came from as far away as
Lebo Hamath and the brook of Egypt. [9]For
seven days they celebrated giving the altar
for the worship of God. Then they celebrated
the festival for seven days. On the eighth day
they had a meeting. [10]On the twenty-third
day of the seventh month Solomon sent the
people home, full of joy. They were happy
because the LORD had been so good to David,
Solomon, and his people Israel.

The Lord Appears to Solomon

[11]Solomon finished the Temple of the
LORD and his royal palace. He had success in
doing everything he planned in the Temple
of the LORD and his own palace. [12]Then the
LORD appeared to Solomon at night and said
to him, "I have heard your prayer and have
chosen this place for myself to be a Temple
for sacrifices.

[13]"I may stop the sky from sending rain. I
may command the locusts to destroy the
land. I may send sicknesses to my people.
[14]Then if my people, who are called by my
name, will humble themselves, if they will
pray and seek me and stop their evil ways, I
will hear them from heaven. I will forgive
their sin, and I will heal their land. [15]Now I
will see them, and I will listen to the prayers
prayed in this place. [16]I have chosen this
Temple and made it holy. So I will be
worshiped there forever. Yes, I will always
watch over it and love it.

[17]"But you must serve me as your father
David did. You must obey all I have
commanded and keep my laws and rules. [18]If
you do, I will make your kingdom strong.
This is the agreement I made with your
father David, saying, 'Someone from your
family will always rule in Israel.'

[19]"But you must follow me and obey the
laws and commands I have given you. You
must not serve or worship other gods. [20]If
you do, I will take the Israelites out of my
land, the land I have given them, and I will
leave this Temple that I have made holy. All
the nations will make fun of it and speak
evil about it. [21]This Temple is honored now,
but then, everyone who passes by will be
shocked. They will ask, 'Why did the LORD
do this terrible thing to this land and this
Temple?' [22]People will answer, 'This
happened because they left the LORD, the
God of their ancestors, the God who brought
them out of Egypt. They decided to follow
other gods and worshiped and served them,
so he brought all this disaster on them.' "

Solomon's Other Achievements

8 By the end of twenty years, Solomon had
built the Temple of the LORD and the
royal palace. [2]Solomon rebuilt the towns
that Hiram had given him, and Solomon
sent Israelites to live in them. [3]Then he went
to Hamath Zobah and captured it. [4]Solomon
also built the town of Tadmor in the desert,
and he built all the towns in Hamath as
towns for storing grain and supplies. [5]He
rebuilt the towns of Upper Beth Horon and
Lower Beth Horon, protecting them with
strong walls, gates, and bars in the gates. [6]He
also rebuilt the town of Baalath. And he
built all the other towns for storage and all
the cities for his chariots and horses. He
built all he wanted in Jerusalem, Lebanon,
and everywhere he ruled.

[7]There were other people in the land who
were not Israelites—the Hittites, Amorites,
Perizzites, Hivites, and Jebusites. [8]They were
descendants of the people that the Israelites
had not destroyed. Solomon forced them to
be slave workers, as is still true today. [9]But
Solomon did not make slaves of the
Israelites. They were his soldiers, chief

captains, commanders of his chariots, and
his chariot drivers. 10These were his most
important officers. There were two hundred
fifty of them to direct the people.
11Solomon brought the daughter of the
king of Egypt from the older part of
Jerusalem to the palace he had built for her.
Solomon said, "My wife must not live in
King David's palace, because the places
where the Ark of the Agreement has been
are holy."
12Then Solomon offered burnt offerings to
the LORD on the altar he had built for the
LORD in front of the Temple porch. 13He
offered sacrifices every day as Moses had
commanded. They were offered on the
Sabbath days, New Moons, and the three
yearly feasts—the Feast of Unleavened
Bread, the Feast of Weeks, and the Feast of
Shelters. 14Solomon followed his father
David's instructions and chose the groups of
priests for their service and the Levites to
lead the praise and to help the priests do
their daily work. And he chose the
gatekeepers by their groups to serve at each
gate, as David, the man of God, had
commanded. 15They obeyed all of Solomon's
commands to the priests and Levites, as well
as his commands about the treasuries.
16All Solomon's work was done as he had
said from the day the foundation of the
Temple of the LORD was begun, until it was
finished. So the Temple was finished.
17Then Solomon went to the towns of
Ezion Geber and Elath near the Red Sea in
the land of Edom. 18Hiram sent ships to
Solomon that were commanded by his own
men, who were skilled sailors. Hiram's men
went with Solomon's men to Ophir and
brought back about thirty-four thousand
pounds of gold to King Solomon.

The Queen of Sheba Visits

9 When the queen of Sheba heard about
Solomon's fame, she came to Jerusalem
to test him with hard questions. She had a
large group of servants with her and camels
carrying spices, jewels, and much gold.
When she came to Solomon, she talked with
him about all she had in mind, 2and
Solomon answered all her questions.
Nothing was too hard for him to explain to
her. 3The queen of Sheba saw that Solomon
was very wise. She saw the palace he had
built, 4the food on his table, his many
officers, the palace servants and their good
clothes, the servants who served Solomon
his wine and their good clothes. She saw the
whole burnt offerings he made in the
Temple of the LORD. All these things amazed
her.
5So she said to King Solomon, "What I
heard in my own country about your
achievements and wisdom is true. 6I did not
believe it then, but now I have come and
seen it with my own eyes. I was not told
even half of your great wisdom! You are
much greater than I had heard. 7Your people
and officials are very lucky, because in
always serving you, they are able to hear
your wisdom. 8Praise the LORD your God
who was pleased to make you king. He has
put you on his throne to rule for the LORD
your God, because your God loves the people
of Israel and supports them forever. He has
made you king over them to keep justice and
to rule fairly."
9Then she gave the king about nine
thousand pounds of gold and many spices
and jewels. No one had ever given such
spices as the queen of Sheba gave to King
Solomon.
10Hiram's men and Solomon's men
brought gold from Ophir, juniper wood, and
jewels. 11King Solomon used the juniper
wood to build steps for the Temple of the
LORD and the palace and to make lyres and
harps for the musicians. No one in Judah had
ever seen such beautiful things as these.
12King Solomon gave the queen of Sheba
everything she wanted and asked for, even
more than she had brought to him. Then she
and her servants returned to her own
country.

Solomon's Wealth

13Every year King Solomon received about
fifty thousand pounds of gold. 14Besides that,
he also received gold from traders and
merchants. All the kings of Arabia and the
governors of the land also brought gold and
silver.
15King Solomon made two hundred large
shields of hammered gold, each of which
contained about seven and one-half pounds
of hammered gold. 16He also made three
hundred smaller shields of hammered gold,
each of which contained about four pounds

of gold. The king put them in the Palace of
the Forest of Lebanon.
17The king built a large throne of ivory
and covered it with pure gold. 18The throne
had six steps on it and a gold footstool. There
were armrests on both sides of the chair, and
each armrest had a lion beside it. 19Twelve
lions stood on the six steps, one lion at each
end of each step. Nothing like this had ever
been made for any other kingdom. 20All of
Solomon's drinking cups, as well as the
dishes in the Palace of the Forest of Lebanon,
were made of pure gold. In Solomon's time
people did not think silver was valuable.
21King Solomon had many ships that he
sent out to trade, with Hiram's men as the
crews. Every three years the ships returned,
bringing back gold, silver, ivory, apes, and
baboons.
22King Solomon had more riches and
wisdom than all the other kings on earth.
23All the kings of the earth wanted to see
Solomon and listen to the wisdom God had
given him. 24Year after year everyone who
came brought gifts of silver and gold,
clothes, weapons, spices, horses, and mules.
25Solomon had four thousand stalls for
horses and chariots, and he had twelve
thousand horses. He kept some in special
cities for the chariots, and others he kept
with him in Jerusalem. 26Solomon ruled
over all the kingdoms from the Euphrates
River to the land of the Philistines, as far as
the border of Egypt. 27In Jerusalem the king
made silver as common as stones and cedar
trees as plentiful as the fig trees on the
western hills. 28Solomon imported horses
from Egypt and all other countries.

Solomon's Death

29Everything else Solomon did, from the
beginning to the end, is written in the records
of Nathan the prophet, and in the prophecy
of Ahijah the Shilonite, and in the visions of
Iddo the seer, who wrote about Jeroboam,
Nebat's son. 30Solomon ruled in Jerusalem
over all Israel for forty years. 31Then Solomon
died and was buried in Jerusalem, the city of
David, his father. And Solomon's son
Rehoboam became king in his place.

Israel Turns Against Rehoboam

10 Rehoboam went to Shechem, where
all the Israelites had gone to make
him king. 2Jeroboam son of Nebat was in
Egypt, where he had gone to escape from
King Solomon. When Jeroboam heard about
Rehoboam being made king, he returned
from Egypt. 3After the people sent for him,
he and the people went to Rehoboam and
said to him, 4"Your father forced us to work
very hard. Now, make it easier for us, and
don't make us work as he did. Then we will
serve you."
5Rehoboam answered, "Come back to me
in three days." So the people left.
6King Rehoboam asked the elders who
had advised Solomon during his lifetime,
"How do you think I should answer these
people?"
7They answered, "Be kind to these people.
If you please them and give them a kind
answer, they will serve you always."
8But Rehoboam rejected this advice.
Instead, he asked the young men who had
grown up with him and who served as his
advisers. 9Rehoboam asked them, "What is
your advice? How should we answer these
people who said, 'Don't make us work as
hard as your father did'?"
10The young men who had grown up with
him answered, "The people said to you, 'Your
father forced us to work very hard. Now
make our work easier.' You should tell them,
'My little finger is bigger than my father's
legs. 11He forced you to work hard, but I will
make you work even harder. My father beat
you with whips, but I will beat you with
whips that have sharp points.' "
12Rehoboam had told the people, "Come
back to me in three days." So after three days
Jeroboam and all the people returned to
Rehoboam. 13King Rehoboam spoke cruel
words to them, because he had rejected the
advice of the elders. 14He followed the advice
of the young men and said, "My father forced
you to work hard, but I will make you work
even harder. My father beat you with whips,
but I will beat you with whips that have
sharp points." 15So the king did not listen to
the people. God caused this to happen so
that the LORD could keep the promise he had
made to Jeroboam son of Nebat through
Ahijah, a prophet from Shiloh.
16When all the Israelites saw that the king
refused to listen to them, they said to the
king,
"We have no share in David!
We have no part in the son of Jesse!

People of Israel, let's go to our own
homes!
Let David's son rule his own people."
So all the Israelites went home. 17But
Rehoboam still ruled over the Israelites who
lived in the towns of Judah.

18Adoniram was in charge of the forced
labor. When Rehoboam sent him to the
people, they threw stones at him until he
died. But King Rehoboam ran to his chariot
and escaped to Jerusalem. 19Since then, Israel
has been against the family of David.

11 When Rehoboam arrived in
Jerusalem, he gathered one hundred
eighty thousand of the best soldiers from
Judah and Benjamin. He wanted to fight
Israel to take back his kingdom. 2But the
LORD spoke his word to Shemaiah, a man of
God, saying, 3"Speak to Solomon's son
Rehoboam, the king of Judah, and to all the
Israelites living in Judah and Benjamin. Say
to them, 4'The LORD says you must not go to
war against your brothers. Every one of you
should go home, because I made all these
things happen.'" So they obeyed the LORD's
command and turned back and did not
attack Jeroboam.

Rehoboam Makes Judah Strong

5Rehoboam lived in Jerusalem and built
strong cities in Judah to defend it. 6He built
up the cities of Bethlehem, Etam, Tekoa,
7Beth Zur, Soco, Adullam, 8Gath, Mareshah,
Ziph, 9Adoraim, Lachish, Azekah, 10Zorah,
Aijalon, and Hebron. These were strong,
walled cities in Judah and Benjamin. 11When
Rehoboam made those cities strong, he put
commanders and supplies of food, oil, and
wine in them. 12Also, Rehoboam put shields
and spears in all the cities and made them
very strong. Rehoboam kept the people of
Judah and Benjamin under his control.

13The priests and the Levites from all over
Israel joined Rehoboam. 14The Levites even
left their pasturelands and property and
came to Judah and Jerusalem, because
Jeroboam and his sons refused to let them
serve as priests to the LORD. 15Jeroboam
chose his own priests for the places of
worship and for the goat and calf idols he
had made. 16There were people from all the
tribes of Israel who wanted to obey the LORD,
the God of Israel. So they went to Jerusalem
with the Levites to sacrifice to the LORD, the
God of their ancestors. 17These people made
the kingdom of Judah strong, and they
supported Solomon's son Rehoboam for
three years. During this time they lived the
way David and Solomon had lived.

Rehoboam's Family

18Rehoboam married Mahalath, the
daughter of Jerimoth and Abihail. Jerimoth
was David's son, and Abihail was the
daughter of Eliab, Jesse's son. 19Mahalath
gave Rehoboam these sons: Jeush,
Shemariah, and Zaham. 20Then Rehoboam
married Absalom's daughter Maacah, and
she gave Rehoboam these children: Abijah,
Attai, Ziza, and Shelomith. 21Rehoboam
loved Maacah more than his other wives and
slave women. Rehoboam had eighteen wives
and sixty slave women and was the father of
twenty-eight sons and sixty daughters.

22Rehoboam chose Abijah son of Maacah
to be the leader of his own brothers, because
he planned to make Abijah king.
23Rehoboam acted wisely. He spread his sons
through all the areas of Judah and Benjamin,
sending them to every strong, walled city. He
gave plenty of supplies to his sons, and he
also found wives for them.

Shishak Attacks Jerusalem

12 After Rehoboam's kingdom was set up
and he became strong, he and the
people of Judah stopped obeying the
teachings of the LORD. 2During the fifth year
Rehoboam was king, Shishak king of Egypt
attacked Jerusalem, because Rehoboam and
the people were unfaithful to the LORD.
3Shishak had twelve hundred chariots and
sixty thousand horsemen. He brought troops
of Libyans, Sukkites, and Cushites from Egypt
with him, so many they couldn't be counted.
4Shishak captured the strong, walled cities of
Judah and came as far as Jerusalem.

5Then Shemaiah the prophet came to
Rehoboam and the leaders of Judah who had
gathered in Jerusalem because they were
afraid of Shishak. Shemaiah said to them,
"This is what the LORD says: 'You have left
me, so now I will leave you to face Shishak
alone.'"

6Then the leaders of Judah and King
Rehoboam were sorry for what they had
done. They said, "The LORD does what is
right."

devotion 106

2 CHRONICLES 12:6

SORRY? OR SORRY YOU GOT CAUGHT?

King Rehoboam turned his back on God. He thought he could rule in his own strength. Because of that, God allowed another nation to rise up against Israel to destroy them. It seems that Rehoboam was truly sorry for what he had done because he was willing to accept the Lord's consequences for his actions. He said, "The Lord does what is right." He was about to be destroyed by another nation, and yet he was telling God that he was right. How often do we repent and then ask God to take away our consequences in the same breath? God sees the motives of our heart. He knows when we are truly sorry and when we are looking for a way out. Read the end of this story and see whether or not God allowed the other nation to be victorious over Israel.

I often say to my kids, "Are you sorry for what you have done or sorry that you got caught?" There is a big difference. This is something we can all ask ourselves when we get caught in sin. Hebrews 12:1 talks about removing sin and anything else that would prevent us from running the race marked out for us. Sin keeps you from God's best for your life. Look at your life and ask God to show you if there is sin that has crept in. Tell God you are sorry and get back on track to finish the race he has set before you.

7When the LORD saw they were sorry for
what they had done, the LORD spoke his
word to Shemaiah, saying, "The king and the
leaders are sorry. So I will not destroy them
but will save them soon. I will not use
Shishak to punish Jerusalem in my anger.
8But the people of Jerusalem will become
Shishak's servants so they may learn that
serving me is different than serving the
kings of other nations."
9Shishak king of Egypt attacked Jerusalem
and took the treasures from the Temple of
the LORD and the king's palace. He took
everything, even the gold shields Solomon
had made. 10So King Rehoboam made
bronze shields to take their place and gave
them to the commanders of the guards for
the palace gates. 11Whenever the king went
to the Temple of the LORD, the guards went
with him, carrying the shields. Later, they
would put them back in the guardroom.
12When Rehoboam was sorry for what he
had done, the LORD held his anger back and
did not fully destroy Rehoboam. There was
some good in Judah.
13King Rehoboam made himself a strong
king in Jerusalem. He was forty-one years old
when he became king, and he was king in
Jerusalem for seventeen years. Jerusalem is
the city that the LORD chose from all the
tribes of Israel in which he was to be
worshiped. Rehoboam's mother was Naamah
from the country of Ammon. 14Rehoboam
did evil because he did not want to obey the
LORD.
15The things Rehoboam did as king, from
the beginning to the end, are written in the
records of Shemaiah the prophet and Iddo
the seer, in the family histories. There were
wars between Rehoboam and Jeroboam all
the time they ruled. 16Rehoboam died and
was buried in Jerusalem, and his son Abijah
became king in his place.

Abijah King of Judah

13 Abijah became the king of Judah
during the eighteenth year Jeroboam
was king of Israel. 2Abijah ruled in Jerusalem
for three years. His mother was Maacah
daughter of Uriel from the town of Gibeah.

And there was war between Abijah and
Jeroboam. 3Abijah led an army of four
hundred thousand capable soldiers into
battle, and Jeroboam prepared to fight him
with eight hundred thousand capable
soldiers.
4Abijah stood on Mount Zemaraim in the
mountains of Ephraim and said, "Jeroboam
and all Israel, listen to me! 5You should
know that the LORD, the God of Israel, gave
David and his sons the right to rule Israel
forever by an agreement of salt. 6But
Jeroboam son of Nebat, one of the officers of
Solomon, David's son, turned against his
master. 7Then worthless, evil men joined
Jeroboam against Rehoboam, Solomon's son.
He was young and didn't know what to do,
so he could not stop them.
8"Now you people are making plans
against the LORD's kingdom, which belongs
to David's sons. There are many of you, and
you have the gold calves Jeroboam made for
you as gods. 9You have thrown out the
Levites and the LORD's priests, Aaron's sons.
You have chosen your own priests as
people in other countries do. Anyone who
comes with a young bull and seven male
sheep can become a priest of idols that are
not gods.
10"But as for us, the LORD is our God; we
have not left him. The priests who serve the
LORD are Aaron's sons, and the Levites help
them. 11They offer burnt offerings and
sweet-smelling incense to the LORD every
morning and evening. They put the bread on
the special table in the Temple. And they
light the lamps on the gold lampstand every
evening. We obey the command of the LORD
our God, but you have left him. 12God
himself is with us as our ruler. His priests
blow the trumpet to call us to war against
you. Men of Israel, don't fight against the
LORD, the God of your ancestors, because you
won't succeed."
13But Jeroboam had sent some troops to
sneak behind Judah's army. So while
Jeroboam was in front of Judah's army,
Jeroboam's soldiers were behind them.
14When the soldiers of Judah turned around,
they saw Jeroboam's army attacking both in
front and back. So they cried out to the LORD,
and the priests blew the trumpets. 15Then
the men of Judah gave a battle cry. When
they shouted, God caused Jeroboam and the
army of Israel to run away from Abijah and
the army of Judah. 16When the army of
Israel ran away from the men of Judah, God
handed them over to Judah. 17Abijah's army
struck Israel so that five hundred thousand
of Israel's best men were killed. 18So at that
time the people of Israel were defeated. And
the people of Judah won, because they
depended on the LORD, the God of their
ancestors.
19Abijah's army chased Jeroboam's army
and captured from him the towns of Bethel,
Jeshanah, and Ephron, and the small villages
near them. 20Jeroboam never became strong
again while Abijah was alive. The LORD
struck Jeroboam, and he died.
21But Abijah became strong. He married
fourteen women and was the father of
twenty-two sons and sixteen daughters.
22Everything else Abijah did—what he said
and what he did—is recorded in the writings
of the prophet Iddo.

14 Abijah died and was buried in
Jerusalem. His son Asa became king
in his place, and there was peace in the
country for ten years during Asa's time.

Asa King of Judah

2Asa did what the LORD his God said was
good and right. 3He removed the foreign
altars and the places where gods were
worshiped. He smashed the stone pillars that
honored other gods, and he tore down the
Asherah idols. 4Asa commanded the people
of Judah to follow the LORD, the God of their
ancestors, and to obey his teachings and
commandments. 5He also removed the
places where gods were worshiped and the
incense altars from every town in Judah. So
the kingdom had peace while Asa was king.
6Asa built strong, walled cities in Judah
during the time of peace. He had no war in
these years, because the LORD gave him
peace.
7Asa said to the people of Judah, "Let's
build up these towns and put walls
around them. Let's make towers, gates, and
bars in the gates. This country is ours,
because we have obeyed the LORD our God.
We have followed him, and he has given us
peace all around." So they built and had
success.
8Asa had an army of three hundred
thousand men from Judah and two hundred

eighty thousand men from Benjamin. The
men from Judah carried large shields and
spears. The men from Benjamin carried
small shields and bows and arrows. All of
them were brave fighting men.
9 Then Zerah from Cush came out to fight
them with an enormous army and three
hundred chariots. They came as far as the
town of Mareshah. 10 So Asa went out to
fight Zerah and prepared for battle in the
Valley of Zephathah at Mareshah.
11 Asa called out to the LORD his God,
saying, "LORD, only you can help weak
people against the strong. Help us, LORD our
God, because we depend on you. We fight
against this enormous army in your name.
LORD, you are our God. Don't let anyone win
against you."
12 So the LORD defeated the Cushites when
Asa's army from Judah attacked them, and
the Cushites ran away. 13 Asa's army chased
them as far as the town of Gerar. So many
Cushites were killed that the army could not
fight again; they were crushed by the LORD
and his army. Asa and his army carried many
valuable things away from the enemy.
14 They destroyed all the towns near Gerar,
because the people living in these towns
were afraid of the LORD. Since these towns
had many valuable things, Asa's army took
them away. 15 Asa's army also attacked the
camps where the shepherds lived and took
many sheep and camels. Then they returned
to Jerusalem.

Asa's Changes

15 The Spirit of God entered Azariah son
of Oded. 2 Azariah went to meet Asa
and said, "Listen to me, Asa and all you
people of Judah and Benjamin. The LORD is
with you when you are with him. If you
obey him, you will find him, but if you
leave him, he will leave you. 3 For a long
time Israel was without the true God and
without a priest to teach them and without
the teachings. 4 But when they were in
trouble, they turned to the LORD, the God of
Israel. They looked for him and found him.
5 In those days no one could travel safely.
There was much trouble in all the nations.
6 One nation would destroy another nation,
and one city would destroy another city,
because God troubled them with all kinds
of distress. 7 But you should be strong. Don't
give up, because you will get a reward for
your good work."
8 Asa felt brave when he heard these words
and the message from Azariah son of Oded
the prophet. So he removed the hateful idols
from all of Judah and Benjamin and from the
towns he had captured in the hills of
Ephraim. He repaired the LORD's altar that
was in front of the porch of the Temple of
the LORD.
9 Then Asa gathered all the people from
Judah and Benjamin and from the tribes of
Ephraim, Manasseh, and Simeon who were
living in Judah. Many people came to Asa
even from Israel, because they saw that the
LORD, Asa's God, was with him.
10 Asa and these people gathered in
Jerusalem in the third month of the fifteenth
year of Asa's rule. 11 At that time they
sacrificed to the LORD seven hundred bulls
and seven thousand sheep and goats from
the valuable things Asa's army had taken
from their enemies. 12 Then they made an
agreement to obey the LORD, the God of their
ancestors, with their whole being. 13 Anyone
who refused to obey the LORD, the God of
Israel, was to be killed. It did not matter if
that person was important or unimportant, a
man or woman. 14 Then Asa and the people
made a promise before the LORD, shouting
with a loud voice and blowing trumpets and
sheep's horns. 15 All the people of Judah were
happy about the promise, because they had
promised with all their heart. They looked
for God and found him. So the LORD gave
them peace in all the country.
16 King Asa also removed Maacah, his
grandmother, from being queen mother,
because she had made a terrible Asherah
idol. Asa cut down that idol, smashed it into
pieces, and burned it in the Kidron Valley.
17 But the places of worship to gods were not
removed from Judah. Even so, Asa was
faithful all his life.
18 Asa brought into the Temple of God the
gifts he and his father had given: silver, gold,
and utensils.
19 There was no more war until the
thirty-fifth year of Asa's rule.

Asa's Last Years

16 In the thirty-sixth year of Asa's rule,
Baasha king of Israel attacked Judah.
He made the town of Ramah strong so he

could keep people from leaving or entering
Judah, Asa's country.
2Asa took silver and gold from the
treasuries of the Temple of the LORD and out
of his own palace. Then he sent it with
messengers to Ben-Hadad king of Aram, who
lived in Damascus. Asa said, 3"Let there be a
treaty between you and me as there was
between my father and your father. I am
sending you silver and gold. Break your
treaty with Baasha king of Israel so he will
leave my land."
4Ben-Hadad agreed with King Asa and
sent the commanders of his armies to attack
the towns of Israel. They defeated the towns
of Ijon, Dan, and Abel Beth Maacah, and all
the towns in Naphtali where treasures were
stored. 5When Baasha heard about this, he
stopped building up Ramah and left his
work. 6Then King Asa brought all the people
of Judah to Ramah, and they carried away
the rocks and wood that Baasha had used.
And they used them to build up Geba and
Mizpah.
7At that time Hanani the seer came to Asa
king of Judah and said to him, "You
depended on the king of Aram to help you
and not on the LORD your God. So the king of
Aram's army escaped from you. 8The
Cushites and Libyans had a large and
powerful army and many chariots and
horsemen. But you depended on the LORD to
help you, so he handed them over to you.
9The LORD searches all the earth for people
who have given themselves completely to
him. He wants to make them strong. Asa,
you did a foolish thing, so from now on you
will have wars."
10Asa was angry with Hanani the seer
because of what he had said; he was so angry
that he put Hanani in prison. And Asa was
cruel to some of the people at the same time.
11Everything Asa did as king, from the
beginning to the end, is written in the book
of the kings of Judah and Israel. 12In the
thirty-ninth year of his rule, Asa got a
disease in his feet. Though his disease was
very bad, he did not ask for help from the
LORD, but only from the doctors. 13Then Asa
died in the forty-first year of his rule. 14The
people buried Asa in the tomb he had made
for himself in Jerusalem. They laid him on a

devotion 107

2 CHRONICLES 16:9

SOUVENIRS FROM LIBERIA

She was a beautiful young woman with long blonde hair and big blue eyes when I met her. She had grown up in Boca Raton, Florida, in a wonderful Christian family. She had attended private schools in nice clothes. She had married a wonderful Christian man, and they were expecting their first baby. She was also on her way to the mission field in Liberia, a far cry from Boca. The country was in the middle of a civil war, and the poverty was extensive. Their house had no electricity and no security, yet they knew God had called them to go.

Giving yourself completely to God is an amazing way to live your life. Andrea could fill a book with the stories from her time on the mission field in Liberia. She could tell you stories of how God protected them, stories of how God provided for them, and stories of how God saved the many lives that they touched. People often ask her how she did it. How do you go from the comforts of southern Florida to a place like Liberia? God made her strong. It is a promise that he makes to each of us. No matter what road God has called you to walk down, if you will give yourself completely to him, he will make you strong. Andrea now has eight children. Three of them are her adopted sons from Africa. Perhaps they are three of the reasons she went in the first place.

bed filled with spices and different kinds of mixed perfumes, and they made a large fire to honor him.

Jehoshaphat King of Judah

17 Jehoshaphat, Asa's son, became king of Judah in his place. Jehoshaphat made Judah strong so they could fight against Israel. 2He put troops in all the strong, walled cities of Judah, in the land of Judah, and in the towns of Ephraim that his father Asa had captured.

3The LORD was with Jehoshaphat, because he lived as his ancestor David had lived when he first became king. Jehoshaphat did not ask for help from the Baal idols, 4but from the God of his father. He obeyed God's commands and did not live as the people of Israel lived. 5The LORD made Jehoshaphat a strong king over Judah. All the people of Judah brought gifts to Jehoshaphat, so he had much wealth and honor. 6He wanted very much to obey the LORD. He also removed the places for worshiping gods and the Asherah idols from Judah.

7During the third year of his rule, Jehoshaphat sent his officers to teach in the towns of Judah. These officers were Ben-Hail, Obadiah, Zechariah, Nethanel, and Micaiah. 8Jehoshaphat sent with them these Levites: Shemaiah, Nethaniah, Zebadiah, Asahel, Shemiramoth, Jehonathan, Adonijah, Tobijah, and Tob-Adonijah. He also sent the priests Elishama and Jehoram. 9These leaders, Levites, and priests taught the people in Judah. They took the Book of the Teachings of the LORD and went through all the towns of Judah and taught the people.

10The nations near Judah were afraid of the LORD, so they did not start a war against Jehoshaphat. 11Some of the Philistines brought gifts and silver to Jehoshaphat as he demanded. Some Arabs brought him flocks: seventy-seven hundred sheep and seventy-seven hundred goats.

12Jehoshaphat grew more and more powerful. He built strong, walled cities and towns for storing supplies in Judah. 13He kept many supplies in the towns of Judah, and he kept trained soldiers in Jerusalem. 14These soldiers were listed by families. From the families of Judah, these were the commanders of groups of a thousand men: Adnah was the commander of three hundred thousand soldiers; 15Jehohanan was the commander of two hundred eighty thousand soldiers; 16Amasiah was the commander of two hundred thousand soldiers. Amasiah son of Zicri had volunteered to serve the LORD.

17These were the commanders from the families of Benjamin: Eliada, a brave soldier, had two hundred thousand soldiers who used bows and shields. 18And Jehozabad had one hundred eighty thousand men armed for war.

19All these soldiers served King Jehoshaphat. The king also put other men in the strong, walled cities through all of Judah.

Micaiah Warns King Ahab

18 Jehoshaphat had much wealth and honor, and he made an agreement with King Ahab through marriage.[n] 2A few years later Jehoshaphat went to visit Ahab in Samaria. Ahab sacrificed many sheep and cattle as a great feast to honor Jehoshaphat and the people with him. He encouraged Jehoshaphat to attack Ramoth in Gilead. 3Ahab king of Israel asked Jehoshaphat king of Judah, "Will you go with me to attack Ramoth in Gilead?"

Jehoshaphat answered, "I will go with you, and my soldiers are yours. We will join you in the battle." 4Jehoshaphat also said to Ahab, "But first we should ask if this is the LORD's will."

5So King Ahab called four hundred prophets together and asked them, "Should we go to war against Ramoth in Gilead or not?"

They answered, "Go, because God will hand them over to you."

6But Jehoshaphat asked, "Isn't there a prophet of the LORD here? Let's ask him what we should do."

7Then King Ahab said to Jehoshaphat, "There is one other prophet. We could ask the LORD through him, but I hate him. He never prophesies anything good about me, but always something bad. He is Micaiah son of Imlah."

Jehoshaphat said, "King Ahab, you shouldn't say that!"

18:1 agreement . . . through marriage Jehoshaphat's son Jehoram married Athaliah, Ahab's daughter. See 2 Chronicles 21:6.

8 So Ahab king of Israel told one of his officers to bring Micaiah to him at once.

9 Ahab king of Israel and Jehoshaphat king of Judah had on their royal robes and were sitting on their thrones at the threshing floor, near the entrance to the gate of Samaria. All the prophets were standing before them speaking their messages. 10 Zedekiah son of Kenaanah had made some iron horns. He said to Ahab, "This is what the LORD says: 'You will use these horns to fight the Arameans until they are destroyed.' "

11 All the other prophets said the same thing, "Attack Ramoth in Gilead and win, because the LORD will hand the Arameans over to you."

12 The messenger who had gone to get Micaiah said to him, "All the other prophets are saying King Ahab will win. You should agree with them and give the king a good answer."

13 But Micaiah answered, "As surely as the LORD lives, I can tell him only what my God says."

14 When Micaiah came to Ahab, the king asked him, "Micaiah, should we attack Ramoth in Gilead or not?"

Micaiah answered, "Attack and win! They will be handed over to you."

15 But Ahab said to Micaiah, "How many times do I have to tell you to speak only the truth to me in the name of the LORD?"

16 So Micaiah answered, "I saw the army of Israel scattered over the hills like sheep without a shepherd. The LORD said, 'They have no leaders. They should go home and not fight.' "

17 Then Ahab king of Israel said to Jehoshaphat, "I told you! He never prophesies anything good about me, but only bad."

18 But Micaiah said, "Hear the message from the LORD: I saw the LORD sitting on his throne with his heavenly army standing on his right and on his left. 19 The LORD said, 'Who will trick King Ahab of Israel into attacking Ramoth in Gilead where he will be killed?'

"Some said one thing; some said another. 20 Then one spirit came and stood before the LORD and said, 'I will trick him.'

"The LORD asked, 'How will you do it?'

21 "The spirit answered, 'I will go to Ahab's prophets and make them tell lies.'

"So the LORD said, 'You will succeed in tricking him. Go and do it.' "

22 Micaiah said, "Ahab, the LORD has made your prophets lie to you, and the LORD has decided that disaster should come to you."

23 Then Zedekiah son of Kenaanah went up to Micaiah and slapped him in the face. Zedekiah said, "Has the LORD's Spirit left me to speak through you?"

24 Micaiah answered, "You will find out on the day you go to hide in an inside room."

25 Then Ahab king of Israel ordered, "Take Micaiah and send him to Amon, the governor of the city, and to Joash, the king's son. 26 Tell them I said to put this man in prison and give him only bread and water until I return safely from the battle."

27 Micaiah said, "Ahab, if you come back safely from the battle, the LORD has not spoken through me. Remember my words, all you people!"

Ahab Is Killed

28 So Ahab king of Israel and Jehoshaphat king of Judah went to Ramoth in Gilead. 29 King Ahab said to Jehoshaphat, "I will go into battle, but I will wear other clothes so no one will recognize me. But you wear your royal clothes." So Ahab wore other clothes, and they went into battle.

30 The king of Aram ordered his chariot commanders, "Don't fight with anyone—important or unimportant—except the king of Israel." 31 When these commanders saw Jehoshaphat, they thought he was the king of Israel, so they turned to attack him. But Jehoshaphat began shouting, and the LORD helped him. God made the chariot commanders turn away from Jehoshaphat. 32 When they saw he was not King Ahab, they stopped chasing him.

33 By chance, a soldier shot an arrow which hit Ahab king of Israel between the pieces of his armor. King Ahab said to his chariot driver, "Turn around and get me out of the battle, because I am hurt!" 34 The battle continued all day. King Ahab held himself up in his chariot and faced the Arameans until evening. Then he died at sunset.

19 Jehoshaphat king of Judah came back safely to his palace in Jerusalem. 2 Jehu son of Hanani, a seer, went out to meet him and said to the king, "Why did you help evil people? Why do you love those who hate the LORD? That is the reason the LORD is angry with you. 3But there is some good in you. You took the Asherah idols out of this country, and you have tried to obey God."

Jehoshaphat Chooses Judges

4Jehoshaphat lived in Jerusalem. He went out again to be with the people, from Beersheba to the mountains of Ephraim, and he turned them back to the LORD, the God of their ancestors. 5Jehoshaphat appointed judges in all the land, in each of the strong, walled cities of Judah. 6Jehoshaphat said to them, "Watch what you do, because you are not judging for people but for the LORD. He will be with you when you make a decision. 7Now let each of you fear the LORD. Watch what you do, because the LORD our God wants people to be fair. He wants all people to be treated the same, and he doesn't want decisions influenced by money."

8And in Jerusalem Jehoshaphat appointed some of the Levites, priests, and leaders of Israelite families to be judges. They were to decide cases about the law of the LORD and settle problems between the people who lived in Jerusalem. 9Jehoshaphat commanded them, "You must always serve the LORD completely, and you must fear him. 10Your people living in the cities will bring you cases about killing, about the teachings, commands, rules, or some other law. In all these cases you must warn the people not to sin against the LORD. If you don't, he will be angry with you and your people. But if you warn them, you won't be guilty.

11"Amariah, the leading priest, will be over you in all cases about the LORD. Zebadiah son of Ishmael, a leader in the tribe of Judah, will be over you in all cases about the king. Also, the Levites will serve as officers for you. Have courage. May the LORD be with those who do what is right."

Jehoshaphat Faces War

20 Later the Moabites, Ammonites, and some Meunites came to start a war with Jehoshaphat. 2Messengers came and told Jehoshaphat, "A large army is coming against you from Edom, from the other side of the Dead Sea. They are already in Hazazon Tamar!" (Hazazon Tamar is also called En Gedi.) 3Jehoshaphat was afraid, so he decided to ask the LORD what to do. He announced that everyone in Judah should fast during this special time of prayer to God. 4The people of Judah came together to ask the LORD for help; they came from every town in Judah.

5The people of Judah and Jerusalem met in front of the new courtyard in the Temple of the LORD. Then Jehoshaphat stood up, 6and he said, "LORD, God of our ancestors, you are the God in heaven. You rule over all the kingdoms of the nations. You have power and strength, so no one can stand against you. 7Our God, you forced out the people who lived in this land as your people Israel moved in. And you gave this land forever to the descendants of your friend Abraham. 8They lived in this land and built a Temple for you. They said, 9'If trouble comes upon us, or war, punishment, sickness, or hunger, we will stand before you and before this Temple where you have chosen to be worshiped. We will cry out to you when we are in trouble. Then you will hear and save us.'

10"But now here are men from Ammon, Moab, and Edom. You wouldn't let the Israelites enter their lands when the Israelites came from Egypt. So the Israelites turned away and did not destroy them. 11But see how they repay us for not destroying them! They have come to force us out of your land, which you gave us as our own. 12Our God, punish those people. We have no power against this large army that is attacking us. We don't know what to do, so we look to you for help."

13All the men of Judah stood before the LORD with their babies, wives, and children. 14Then the Spirit of the LORD entered Jahaziel. (Jahaziel was Zechariah's son. Zechariah was Benaiah's son. Benaiah was Jeiel's son, and Jeiel was Mattaniah's son.) Jahaziel, a Levite and a descendant of Asaph, stood up in the meeting. 15He said, "Listen to me, King Jehoshaphat and all you people living in Judah and Jerusalem. The LORD says this to you: 'Don't be afraid or discouraged because of this large army. The battle is not your battle, it is God's. 16Tomorrow go down there and fight those people. They will come up through the Pass of Ziz. You will find them at the end of the ravine that leads to

devotion 108

2 CHRONICLES 20:15–21

ORGANIZED FOR JESUS

Jehoshaphat had it going on. He was thirty-five years old when his reign began. He possessed riches and honor, eradicated the houses of male prostitutes, and started wars. He also ended wars, made peace, brought tribute to Judah, appointed judges, handled decisions and disputes, and even took rebuke. Jehoshaphat was so widely known in the land that the surrounding nations took note of his strength. They recognized that the presence of the Lord was strong in his life and that they should honor him instead of attacking him. Jehoshaphat had a strong character and a deliberate countenance that persevered in the strength of the Lord. He must have been exhausted at the end of the day . . . I hope he had a great wife!

We all have responsibilities that need to be accomplished each day, but we will not be able to establish order until we get organized. You can't enjoy your kitchen if you have to battle the Tupperware every time you open the cabinets. You can't enjoy your children's activities if you keep missing them because they are not written down. You can't have friends if you are not one, and you can't be refreshed by Jesus if you never take time to meet with him. Jehoshaphat had faith that he would succeed because he knew he was meeting God for direction, and he executed the plans that God showed him. Be a woman that executes the plan, and get organized for Jesus.

the Desert of Jeruel. [17]You won't need to fight
in this battle. Just stand strong in your
places, and you will see the LORD save you.
Judah and Jerusalem, don't be afraid or
discouraged, because the LORD is with you.
So go out against those people tomorrow.' "
[18]Jehoshaphat bowed facedown on the
ground. All the people of Judah and
Jerusalem bowed down before the LORD and
worshiped him. [19]Then some Levites from
the Kohathite and Korahite people stood up
and praised the LORD, the God of Israel, with
very loud voices.
[20]Jehoshaphat's army went out into the
Desert of Tekoa early in the morning. As
they were starting out, Jehoshaphat stood
and said, "Listen to me, people of Judah
and Jerusalem. Have faith in the LORD your
God, and you will stand strong. Have faith
in his prophets, and you will succeed."
[21]Jehoshaphat listened to the people's
advice. Then he chose men to be singers to
the LORD, to praise him because he is holy
and wonderful. As they marched in front of
the army, they said,

"Thank the LORD,
because his love continues forever."

[22]As they began to sing and praise God,
the LORD set ambushes for the people of
Ammon, Moab, and Edom who had come to
attack Judah. And they were defeated. [23]The
Ammonites and Moabites attacked the
Edomites, destroying them completely. After
they had killed the Edomites, they killed
each other.
[24]When the men from Judah came to a
place where they could see the desert, they
looked at the enemy's large army. But they
only saw dead bodies lying on the ground;
no one had escaped. [25]When Jehoshaphat
and his army came to take their valuables,
they found many supplies, much clothing,
and other valuable things. There was more
than they could carry away; there was so
much it took three days to gather it all. [26]On
the fourth day Jehoshaphat and his army

met in the Valley of Beracah and praised the LORD. That is why that place has been called the Valley of Beracah[n] to this day.

27Then Jehoshaphat led all the men from Judah and Jerusalem back to Jerusalem. The LORD had made them happy because their enemies were defeated. 28They entered Jerusalem with harps, lyres, and trumpets and went to the Temple of the LORD.

29When all the kingdoms of the lands around them heard how the LORD had fought Israel's enemies, they feared God. 30So Jehoshaphat's kingdom was not at war. His God gave him peace from all the countries around him.

Jehoshaphat's Rule Ends

31Jehoshaphat ruled over the country of Judah. He was thirty-five years old when he became king, and he ruled in Jerusalem for twenty-five years. His mother's name was Azubah daughter of Shilhi. 32Jehoshaphat was good like his father Asa, and he did what the LORD said was right. 33But the places where gods were worshiped were not removed, and the people did not really want to follow the God of their ancestors.

34The other things Jehoshaphat did as king, from the beginning to the end, are written in the records of Jehu son of Hanani, which are in the book of the kings of Israel.

35Later, Jehoshaphat king of Judah made a treaty with Ahaziah king of Israel, which was a wrong thing to do. 36Jehoshaphat agreed with Ahaziah to build trading ships, which they built in the town of Ezion Geber. 37Then Eliezer son of Dodavahu from the town of Mareshah spoke against Jehoshaphat. He said, "Jehoshaphat, because you joined with Ahaziah, the LORD will destroy what you have made." The ships were wrecked so they could not sail out to trade.

21 Jehoshaphat died and was buried with his ancestors in Jerusalem, the city of David. Then his son Jehoram became king in his place. 2Jehoram's brothers were Azariah, Jehiel, Zechariah, Azariahu, Michael, and Shephatiah. They were the sons of Jehoshaphat king of Judah. 3Jehoshaphat gave his sons many gifts of silver, gold, and valuable things, and he gave them strong, walled cities in Judah. But Jehoshaphat gave the kingdom to Jehoram, because he was the first son.

Jehoram King of Judah

4When Jehoram took control of his father's kingdom, he killed all his brothers with a sword and also killed some of the leaders of Judah. 5He was thirty-two years old when he began to rule, and he ruled eight years in Jerusalem. 6He followed in the ways of the kings of Israel, just as the family of Ahab had done, because he married Ahab's daughter. Jehoram did what the LORD said was wrong. 7But the LORD would not destroy David's family because of the agreement he had made with David. He had promised that one of David's descendants would always rule.

8In Jehoram's time, Edom broke away from Judah's rule and chose their own king. 9So Jehoram went to Edom with all his commanders and chariots. The Edomites surrounded him and his chariot commanders, but Jehoram got up and attacked the Edomites at night. 10From then until now the country of Edom has fought against the rule of Judah. At the same time the people of Libnah also broke away from Jehoram because Jehoram left the LORD, the God of his ancestors.

11Jehoram also built places to worship gods on the hills in Judah. He led the people of Jerusalem to sin, and he led the people of Judah away from the LORD. 12Then Jehoram received this letter from Elijah the prophet:

> This is what the LORD, the God of your ancestor David, says, "Jehoram, you have not lived as your father Jehoshaphat lived and as Asa king of Judah lived. 13But you have lived as the kings of Israel lived, leading the people of Judah and Jerusalem to sin against God, as Ahab and his family did. You have killed your brothers, and they were better than you. 14So now the LORD is about to punish your people, your children, wives,

20:26 Beracah This name means "blessing" or "praise."

and everything you own. [15]You
will have a terrible disease in your
intestines that will become worse
every day. Finally it will cause
your intestines to come out."

[16]The LORD caused the Philistines and the
Arabs who lived near the Cushites to be
angry with Jehoram. [17]So the Philistines and
Arabs attacked Judah and carried away all
the wealth of Jehoram's palace, as well as his
sons and wives. Only Jehoram's youngest
son, Ahaziah, was left.

[18]After these things happened, the LORD
gave Jehoram a disease in his intestines that
could not be cured. [19]After he was sick for
two years, Jehoram's intestines came out
because of the disease, and he died in terrible
pain. The people did not make a fire to
honor Jehoram as they had done for his
ancestors.

[20]Jehoram was thirty-two years old when
he became king, and he ruled eight years in
Jerusalem. No one was sad when he died. He
was buried in Jerusalem, but not in the
graves for the kings.

Ahaziah King of Judah

22 The people of Jerusalem chose
Ahaziah, Jehoram's youngest son, to be
king in his place. The robbers who had come
with the Arabs to attack Jehoram's camp had
killed all of Jehoram's older sons. So Ahaziah
began to rule Judah. [2]Ahaziah was twenty-two
years old when he became king, and he ruled
one year in Jerusalem. His mother's name
was Athaliah, a granddaughter of Omri.
[3]Ahaziah followed the ways of Ahab's family,
because his mother encouraged him to do
wrong. [4]Ahaziah did what the LORD said was
wrong, as Ahab's family had done. They gave
advice to Ahaziah after his father died, and
their bad advice led to his death. [5]Following
their advice, Ahaziah went with Joram son of
Ahab to Ramoth in Gilead, where they fought
against Hazael king of Aram. The Arameans
wounded Joram. [6]So Joram returned to
Jezreel to heal from the wounds he received
at Ramoth when he fought Hazael king of
Aram.

Ahaziah son of Jehoram and king of Judah
went down to visit Joram son of Ahab at
Jezreel because he had been wounded.

[7]God caused Ahaziah's death when he
went to visit Joram. Ahaziah arrived and
went out with Joram to meet Jehu son of
Nimshi, whom the LORD had appointed to
destroy Ahab's family. [8]While Jehu was
punishing Ahab's family, he found the
leaders of Judah and the sons of Ahaziah's
relatives who served Ahaziah, and Jehu
killed them all. [9]Then Jehu looked for
Ahaziah. Jehu's men caught him hiding in
Samaria, so they brought him to Jehu. Then
they killed and buried him. They said,
"Ahaziah is a descendant of Jehoshaphat, and
Jehoshaphat obeyed the LORD with all his
heart." No one in Ahaziah's family had the
power to take control of the kingdom of
Judah.

Athaliah and Joash

[10]When Ahaziah's mother, Athaliah, saw
that her son was dead, she killed all the royal
family in Judah. [11]But Jehosheba, King
Jehoram's daughter, took Joash, Ahaziah's
son. She stole him from among the other
sons of the king who were going to be
murdered and put him and his nurse in a
bedroom. So Jehosheba, who was King
Jehoram's daughter and Ahaziah's sister
and the wife of Jehoiada the priest, hid
Joash so Athaliah could not kill him. [12]He
hid with them in the Temple of God for six
years. During that time Athaliah ruled the
land.

23 In the seventh year Jehoiada decided
to do something. He made an
agreement with the commanders of the
groups of a hundred men: Azariah son of
Jeroham, Ishmael son of Jehohanan, Azariah
son of Obed, Maaseiah son of Adaiah, and
Elishaphat son of Zicri. [2]They went around
in Judah and gathered the Levites from all
the towns, and they gathered the leaders of
the families of Judah. Then they went to
Jerusalem. [3]All the people together made
an agreement with the king in the Temple
of God.

Jehoiada said to them, "The king's son will
rule, as the LORD promised about David's
descendants. [4]Now this is what you must do:
You priests and Levites go on duty on the
Sabbath. A third of you will guard the doors.
[5]A third of you will be at the king's palace,
and a third of you will be at the Foundation
Gate. All the other people will stay in the
courtyards of the Temple of the LORD. [6]Don't

let anyone come into the Temple of the LORD
except the priests and Levites who serve.
They may come because they have been
made ready to serve the LORD, but all the
others must do the job the LORD has given
them. 7The Levites must stay near the king,
each man with his weapon in his hand. If
anyone tries to enter the Temple, kill him.
Stay close to the king when he goes in and
when he goes out."

Joash Becomes King

8The Levites and all the people of Judah
obeyed everything Jehoiada the priest
had commanded. He did not excuse anyone
from the groups of the priests. So each
commander took his men who came on duty
on the Sabbath with those who went off
duty on the Sabbath. 9Jehoiada gave the
commanders of a hundred men the spears
and the large and small shields that had
belonged to King David and that were kept
in the Temple of God. 10Then Jehoiada told
the soldiers where to stand with weapon in
hand. There were guards from the south side
of the Temple to the north side. They stood
by the altar and the Temple and around the
king.

11Jehoiada and his sons brought out the
king's son and put the crown on him and
gave him a copy of the agreement. Then they
appointed him king and poured olive oil on
him and shouted, "Long live the king!"

12When Athaliah heard the noise of the
people running and praising the king, she
went to them at the Temple of the LORD.
13She looked, and there was the king
standing by his pillar at the entrance. The
officers and the trumpeters were standing
beside him, and all the people of the land
were happy and blowing trumpets. The
singers were playing musical instruments
and leading praises. Then Athaliah tore her
clothes and screamed, "Traitors! Traitors!"

14Jehoiada the priest sent out the
commanders of a hundred men, who led the
army. He said, "Surround her with soldiers
and take her out of the Temple area. Kill
with a sword anyone who follows her." He
had said, "Don't put Athaliah to death in the
Temple of the LORD." 15So they caught her
when she came to the entrance of the Horse
Gate near the palace. There they put her to
death.

16Then Jehoiada made an agreement with
the people and the king that they would be
the LORD's special people. 17All the people
went to the temple of Baal and tore it down,
smashing the altars and idols. They killed
Mattan, the priest of Baal, in front of the
altars.

18Then Jehoiada chose the priests, who
were Levites, to be responsible for the
Temple of the LORD. David had given them
duties in the Temple of the LORD. They were
to offer the burnt offerings to the LORD as the
Teachings of Moses commanded, and they
were to offer them with much joy and
singing as David had commanded.
19Jehoiada put guards at the gates of the
Temple of the LORD so that anyone who was
unclean in any way could not enter.

20Jehoiada took with him the
commanders of a hundred men, the
important men, the rulers of the people, and
all the people of the land to take the king
out of the Temple of the LORD. They went
through the Upper Gate into the palace, and
then they seated the king on the throne. 21So
all the people of the land were very happy,
and Jerusalem had peace, because Athaliah
had been put to death with the sword.

Joash Repairs the Temple

24 Joash was seven years old when he
became king, and he ruled forty years
in Jerusalem. His mother's name was Zibiah,
and she was from Beersheba. 2Joash did what
the LORD said was right as long as Jehoiada
the priest was alive. 3Jehoiada chose two
wives for Joash, and Joash had sons and
daughters.

4Later, Joash decided to repair the Temple
of the LORD. 5He called the priests and the
Levites together and said to them, "Go to the
towns of Judah and gather the money all the
Israelites have to pay every year. Use it to
repair the Temple of your God. Do this now."
But the Levites did not hurry.

6So King Joash called for Jehoiada the
leading priest and said to him, "Why haven't
you made the Levites bring in from Judah
and Jerusalem the tax money that Moses, the
LORD's servant, and the people of Israel used
for the Holy Tent?"

7In the past the sons of wicked Athaliah
had broken into the Temple of God and used
its holy things for worshiping the Baal idols.

8King Joash commanded that a box for contributions be made. They put it outside, at the gate of the Temple of the LORD. 9Then the Levites made an announcement in Judah and Jerusalem, telling people to bring to the LORD the tax money Moses, the servant of God, had made the Israelites give while they were in the desert. 10All the officers and people were happy to bring their money, and they put it in the box until the box was full. 11When the Levites would take the box to the king's officers, they would see that it was full of money. Then the king's royal secretary and the leading priest's officer would come and take out the money and return the box to its place. They did this often and gathered much money. 12King Joash and Jehoiada gave the money to the people who worked on the Temple of the LORD. And they hired stoneworkers and carpenters to repair the Temple of the LORD. They also hired people to work with iron and bronze to repair the Temple.

13The people worked hard, and the work to repair the Temple went well. They rebuilt the Temple of God to be as it was before, but even stronger. 14When the workers finished, they brought the money that was left to King Joash and Jehoiada. They used that money to make utensils for the Temple of the LORD, utensils for the service in the Temple and for the burnt offerings, and bowls and other utensils from gold and silver. Burnt offerings were given every day in the Temple of the LORD while Jehoiada was alive.

15Jehoiada grew old and lived many years. Then he died when he was one hundred thirty years old. 16Jehoiada was buried in Jerusalem with the kings, because he had done much good in Judah for God and his Temple.

Joash Does Evil

17After Jehoiada died, the officers of Judah came and bowed down to King Joash, and he listened to them. 18The king and these leaders stopped worshiping in the Temple of the LORD, the God of their ancestors. Instead, they began to worship the Asherah idols and other idols. Because they did wrong, God was angry with the people of Judah and Jerusalem. 19Even though the LORD sent prophets to the people to turn them back to him and even though the prophets warned them, they refused to listen.

20Then the Spirit of God entered Zechariah son of Jehoiada the priest. Zechariah stood before the people and said, "This is what God says: 'Why do you disobey the LORD's commands? You will not be successful. Because you have left the LORD, he has also left you.' "

21But the king and his officers made plans against Zechariah. At the king's command they threw stones at him in the courtyard of the Temple of the LORD until he died. 22King Joash did not remember Jehoiada's kindness to him, so Joash killed Zechariah, Jehoiada's son. Before Zechariah died, he said, "May the LORD see what you are doing and punish you."

23At the end of the year, the Aramean army came against Joash. They attacked Judah and Jerusalem, killed all the leaders of the people, and sent all the valuable things to their king in Damascus. 24The Aramean army came with only a small group of men, but the LORD handed over to them a very large army from Judah, because the people of Judah had left the LORD, the God of their ancestors. So Joash was punished. 25When the Arameans left, Joash was badly wounded. His own officers made plans against him because he had killed Zechariah son of Jehoiada the priest. So they killed Joash in his own bed. He died and was buried in Jerusalem but not in the graves of the kings.

26The officers who made plans against Joash were Jozabad and Jehozabad. Jozabad was the son of Shimeath, a woman from Ammon. And Jehozabad was the son of Shimrith, a woman from Moab. 27The story of Joash's sons, the great prophecies against him, and how he repaired the Temple of God are written in the book of the kings. Joash's son Amaziah became king in his place.

Amaziah King of Judah

25 Amaziah was twenty-five years old when he became king, and he ruled for twenty-nine years in Jerusalem. His mother's name was Jehoaddin, and she was from Jerusalem. 2Amaziah did what the LORD said was right, but he did not really want to obey him. 3As soon as Amaziah took strong control of the kingdom, he

executed the officers who had murdered his
father the king. [4]But Amaziah did not put to
death their children. He obeyed what was
written in the Book of Moses, where the
LORD commanded, "Parents must not be put
to death when their children do wrong, and
children must not be put to death when
their parents do wrong. Each must die for
his own sins."[n]

[5]Amaziah gathered the people of Judah
together. He grouped all the people of Judah
and Benjamin by families, and he put
commanders over groups of a thousand and
over groups of a hundred. He counted the
men who were twenty years old and older.
In all there were three hundred thousand
soldiers ready to fight and skilled with
spears and shields. [6]Amaziah also hired one
hundred thousand soldiers from Israel for
about seventy-five hundred pounds of silver.
[7]But a man of God came to Amaziah and
said, "My king, don't let the army of Israel go
with you. The LORD is not with Israel or the
people from the tribe of Ephraim. [8]You can
make yourself strong for war, but God will
defeat you. He has the power to help you or
to defeat you."

[9]Amaziah said to the man of God, "But
what about the seventy-five hundred pounds
of silver I paid to the Israelite army?"

The man of God answered, "The LORD can
give you much more than that."

[10]So Amaziah sent the Israelite army back
home to Ephraim. They were very angry
with the people of Judah and went home
angry.

[11]Then Amaziah became very brave and
led his army to the Valley of Salt in the
country of Edom. There Amaziah's army
killed ten thousand Edomites. [12]The army of
Judah also captured ten thousand and took
them to the top of a cliff and threw them off
so that they split open.

[13]At the same time the Israelite troops
that Amaziah had not let fight in the war
were robbing towns in Judah. From Samaria
to Beth Horon they killed three thousand
people and took many valuable things.

[14]When Amaziah came home after
defeating the Edomites, he brought back the
idols they worshiped and started to worship
them himself. He bowed down to them and
offered sacrifices to them. [15]The LORD was
very angry with Amaziah, so he sent a
prophet to him who said, "Why have you
asked their gods for help? They could not
even save their own people from you!"

[16]As the prophet spoke, Amaziah said to
him, "We never gave you the job of advising
the king. Stop, or you will be killed."

The prophet stopped speaking except to
say, "I know that God has decided to destroy
you because you have done this. You did not
listen to my advice."

[17]Amaziah king of Judah talked with
those who advised him. Then he sent a
message to Jehoash son of Jehoahaz, who
was the son of Jehu king of Israel. Amaziah
said to Jehoash, "Come, let's meet face to
face."

[18]Then Jehoash king of Israel answered
Amaziah king of Judah, "A thornbush in
Lebanon sent a message to a cedar tree in
Lebanon. It said, 'Let your daughter marry
my son.' But then a wild animal from
Lebanon came by, walking on and crushing
the thornbush. [19]You say to yourself that you
have defeated Edom, but you have become
proud, and you brag. But you stay at home!
Don't ask for trouble, or you and Judah will
be defeated."

[20]But Amaziah would not listen. God
caused this to happen so that Jehoash
would defeat Judah, because Judah asked for
help from the gods of Edom. [21]So Jehoash
king of Israel went to attack. He and
Amaziah king of Judah faced each other in
battle at Beth Shemesh in Judah. [22]Israel
defeated Judah, and every man of Judah ran
away to his home. [23]At Beth Shemesh
Jehoash king of Israel captured Amaziah
king of Judah. (Amaziah was the son of
Joash, who was the son of Ahaziah.) Then
Jehoash brought him to Jerusalem. Jehoash
broke down the wall of Jerusalem, from the
Gate of Ephraim to the Corner Gate, about
six hundred feet. [24]He took all the gold and
silver and all the utensils from the Temple
of God that Obed-Edom had taken care of.
He also took the treasures from the palace
and some hostages. Then he returned to
Samaria.

[25]Amaziah son of Joash, the king of Judah,
lived fifteen years after the death of Jehoash

25:4 "Parents . . . sins." See Deuteronomy 24:16.

son of Jehoahaz, the king of Israel. [26]The
other things Amaziah did as king, from the
beginning to the end, are written in the book
of the kings of Judah and Israel. [27]When
Amaziah stopped obeying the LORD, the
people in Jerusalem made plans against him.
So he ran away to the town of Lachish, but
they sent men after him to Lachish and
killed him. [28]They brought his body back on
horses, and he was buried with his ancestors
in Jerusalem, the city of David.

Uzziah King of Judah

26 Then all the people of Judah made
Uzziah[n] king in place of his father
Amaziah. Uzziah was sixteen years old. [2]He
rebuilt the town of Elath and made it part of
Judah again after Amaziah died.

[3]Uzziah was sixteen years old when he
became king, and he ruled fifty-two years in
Jerusalem. His mother's name was Jecoliah,
and she was from Jerusalem. [4]He did what
the LORD said was right, just as his father
Amaziah had done. [5]Uzziah obeyed God
while Zechariah was alive, because he
taught Uzziah how to respect and obey God.
And as long as Uzziah obeyed the LORD, God
gave him success.

[6]Uzziah fought a war against the
Philistines. He tore down the walls around
their towns of Gath, Jabneh, and Ashdod and
built new towns near Ashdod and in other
places among the Philistines. [7]God helped
Uzziah fight the Philistines, the Arabs living
in Gur Baal, and the Meunites. [8]Also, the
Ammonites made the payments Uzziah
demanded. He was very powerful, so his
name became famous all the way to the
border of Egypt.

[9]Uzziah built towers in Jerusalem at the
Corner Gate, the Valley Gate, and where the
wall turned, and he made them strong. [10]He
also built towers in the desert and dug many
wells, because he had many cattle on the
western hills and in the plains. He had
people who worked his fields and vineyards
in the hills and in the fertile lands, because
he loved the land.

[11]Uzziah had an army of trained soldiers.
They were counted and put in groups by
Jeiel the royal secretary and Maaseiah the
officer. Hananiah, one of the king's
commanders, was their leader. [12]There were
twenty-six hundred leaders over the soldiers.
[13]They were in charge of an army of three
hundred seven thousand five hundred men
who fought with great power to help the
king against the enemy. [14]Uzziah gave his
army shields, spears, helmets, armor, bows,
and stones for their slings. [15]In Jerusalem
Uzziah made cleverly designed devices.
These devices on the towers and corners of
the city walls were used to shoot arrows and
large rocks. So Uzziah became famous in
faraway places, because he had much help
until he became powerful.

[16]But when Uzziah became powerful, his
pride led to his ruin. He was unfaithful to
the LORD his God; he went into the Temple of
the LORD to burn incense on the altar for
incense. [17]Azariah and eighty other brave
priests who served the LORD followed Uzziah
into the Temple. [18]They told him he was
wrong and said to him, "You don't have the
right to burn incense to the LORD. Only the
priests, Aaron's descendants, should burn the
incense, because they have been made holy.
Leave this holy place. You have been
unfaithful, and the LORD God will not honor
you for this."

[19]Uzziah was standing beside the altar for
incense in the Temple of the LORD, and in his
hand was a pan for burning incense. He was
very angry with the priests. As he was
standing in front of the priests, a skin disease
broke out on his forehead. [20]Azariah, the
leading priest, and all the other priests
looked at him and saw the skin disease on
his forehead. So they hurried him out of the
Temple. Uzziah also rushed out, because the
LORD was punishing him. [21]So King Uzziah
had the skin disease until the day he died. He
had to live in a separate house and could not
enter the Temple of the LORD. His son Jotham
was in charge of the palace, and he governed
the people of the land.

[22]The other things Uzziah did as king,
from beginning to end, were written down
by the prophet Isaiah son of Amoz. [23]Uzziah
died and was buried near his ancestors in a
graveyard that belonged to the kings. This
was because people said, "He had a skin
disease." And his son Jotham became king in
his place.

26:1 Uzziah Also called Azariah.

devotion 109

2 CHRONICLES 26:16

FROM POWER TO PRIDE AND BACK AGAIN

Do you see the progression of sin in Uzziah's life? His power led to his pride, which led to his unfaithfulness. This has been the human pattern since the beginning of time. Look at Eve. She had the power to eat anything in the garden. Satan tempted her by telling her that God was trying to keep her from something good that she deserved. Eve's pride led to her unfaithfulness.

There is one tool we can use to combat the power that leads to pride. We can be humble. My husband often says, "The most amazing thing about the life of Christ is not the miracles he did—it is the ones he *didn't* do." Jesus had the power to do anything. He could have healed *all* the sick and destroyed *all* the evil men of that day. But he didn't. Satan tempted him to use that power three times in the desert. Each time Jesus refused. Jesus, who was all-powerful, lived a life of humility. He never defended his actions or demanded attention. He was here to fulfill the will of his Father. He was humble to the point of death. When you look at your own life, do you see pride or humility? Are you seeking your own agenda or the will of the Father? God wants us to be humble, just as Christ was humble. He asks us to lay down our lives and our agenda, just as Christ willingly laid down his life for our salvation.

Jotham King of Judah

27 Jotham was twenty-five years old
when he became king, and he ruled
sixteen years in Jerusalem. His mother's
name was Jerusha daughter of Zadok.
2 Jotham did what the LORD said was right,
just as his father Uzziah had done. But
Jotham did not enter the Temple of the LORD
to burn incense as his father had. But the
people continued doing wrong. 3 Jotham
rebuilt the Upper Gate of the Temple of the
LORD, and he added greatly to the wall at
Ophel. 4 He also built towns in the hill
country of Judah, as well as walled cities and
towers in the forests.
5 Jotham also fought the king of the
Ammonites and defeated them. So each year
for three years they gave Jotham about
seventy-five hundred pounds of silver, about
sixty-two thousand bushels of wheat, and
about sixty-two thousand bushels of barley.
6 Jotham became powerful, because he
always obeyed the LORD his God.
7 The other things Jotham did while he
was king and all his wars are written in the
book of the kings of Israel and Judah.
8 Jotham was twenty-five years old when he
became king, and he ruled sixteen years in
Jerusalem. 9 Jotham died and was buried in
Jerusalem, the city of David. Then Jotham's
son Ahaz became king in his place.

Ahaz King of Judah

28 Ahaz was twenty years old when he
became king, and he ruled sixteen
years in Jerusalem. Unlike his ancestor David,
he did not do what the LORD said was right.
2 Ahaz did the same things the kings of Israel
had done. He made metal idols to worship
Baal. 3 He burned incense in the Valley of Ben
Hinnom and made his children pass through
the fire. He did the same hateful sins as the
nations had done whom the LORD had forced
out of the land ahead of the Israelites. 4 Ahaz
offered sacrifices and burned incense at the
places where gods were worshiped, and on
the hills, and under every green tree.
5 So the LORD his God handed over Ahaz to

the king of Aram. The Arameans defeated
Ahaz and took many people of Judah as
prisoners to Damascus.
He also handed over Ahaz to Pekah king
of Israel, and Pekah's army killed many
soldiers of Ahaz. [6]The army of Pekah son of
Remaliah killed one hundred twenty
thousand brave soldiers from Judah in one
day. Pekah defeated them because they had
left the LORD, the God of their ancestors.
[7]Zicri, a warrior from Ephraim, killed King
Ahaz's son Maaseiah. He also killed
Azrikam, the officer in charge of the palace,
and Elkanah, who was second in command
to the king. [8]The Israelite army captured two
hundred thousand of their own relatives.
They took women, sons and daughters, and
many valuable things from Judah and
carried them back to Samaria. [9]But a prophet
of the LORD named Oded was there. He met
the Israelite army when it returned to
Samaria and said to them, "The LORD, the
God of your ancestors, handed Judah over to
you, because he was angry with those
people. But God has seen the cruel way you
killed them. [10]Now you plan to make the
people of Judah and Jerusalem your slaves,
but you also have sinned against the LORD
your God. [11]Now listen to me. Send back
your brothers and sisters whom you
captured, because the LORD is very angry
with you."
[12]Then some of the leaders in Ephraim—
Azariah son of Jehohanan, Berekiah son of
Meshillemoth, Jehizkiah son of Shallum, and
Amasa son of Hadlai—met the Israelite
soldiers coming home from war. [13]They
warned the soldiers, "Don't bring the
prisoners from Judah here. If you do, we will
be guilty of sin against the LORD, and that
will make our sin and guilt even worse. Our
guilt is already so great that he is angry with
Israel."
[14]So the soldiers left the prisoners and
valuable things in front of the officers and
people there. [15]The leaders who were named
took the prisoners and gave those who were
naked the clothes that the Israelite army had
taken. They gave the prisoners clothes,
sandals, food, drink, and medicine. They put
the weak prisoners on donkeys and took
them back to their families in Jericho, the
city of palm trees. Then they returned home
to Samaria.

[16-17]At that time the Edomites came again
and attacked Judah and carried away
prisoners. So King Ahaz sent to the king of
Assyria for help. [18]The Philistines also
robbed the towns in the western hills and in
southern Judah. They captured the towns of
Beth Shemesh, Aijalon, Gederoth, Soco,
Timnah, and Gimzo, and the villages around
them. Then the Philistines lived in those
towns. [19]The LORD brought trouble on Judah
because Ahaz their king led the people of
Judah to sin, and he was unfaithful to the
LORD. [20]Tiglath-Pileser king of Assyria came
to Ahaz, but he gave Ahaz trouble instead of
help. [21]Ahaz took some valuable things from
the Temple of the LORD, from the palace, and
from the princes, and he gave them to the
king of Assyria, but it did not help.
[22]During Ahaz's troubles he was even
more unfaithful to the LORD. [23]He offered
sacrifices to the gods of the people of
Damascus, who had defeated him. He
thought, "The gods of the kings of Aram
helped them. If I offer sacrifices to them,
they will help me also." But this brought
ruin to Ahaz and all Israel.
[24]Ahaz gathered the things from the
Temple of God and broke them into pieces.
Then he closed the doors of the Temple of
the LORD. He made altars and put them on
every street corner in Jerusalem. [25]In every
town in Judah, Ahaz made places for
burning sacrifices to worship other gods. So
he made the LORD, the God of his ancestors,
very angry.
[26]The other things Ahaz did as king, from
beginning to end, are written in the book of
the kings of Judah and Israel. [27]Ahaz died
and was buried in the city of Jerusalem, but
not in the graves of the kings of Israel.
Ahaz's son Hezekiah became king in his
place.

Hezekiah Purifies the Temple

29 Hezekiah was twenty-five years old
when he became king, and he ruled
twenty-nine years in Jerusalem. His mother's
name was Abijah daughter of Zechariah.
[2]Hezekiah did what the LORD said was right,
just as his ancestor David had done.
[3]Hezekiah opened the doors of the Temple
of the LORD and repaired them in the first
month of the first year he was king.
[4]Hezekiah brought in the priests and Levites

devotion 110

2 CHRONICLES 29:1–2

OF ALL THE DYSFUNCTIONAL FAMILIES IN THE WORLD

How many times have you said to yourself or heard from another, "You do not understand. I come from a dysfunctional family." Well I say, welcome to the club! Who *hasn't* come from a dysfunctional family? If you've read Genesis, you know the story about Adam and Eve. What about Abraham? He carried his almost-grown son to the altar to sacrifice him. And let's not forget about Jesus himself who had Rahab, a harlot, in his lineage. And in ancient Israel, there was Hezekiah, whose father liked to sacrifice his sons to false gods. But look at how things turned out for Hezekiah. By the time he was twenty-five, he was the King of Israel because he did what was right in the sight of the Lord.

Coming from a dysfunctional family is not a death sentence for your life. God is not a respecter of persons, which means that everyone is level at the cross. And his atonement for sin is available to all, regardless of what your family tree resembles. If you want to be healed, take the bitterness and disappointment from your mind and lay it down. Celebrate the fact that God has lifted you up out of the muck and mire, and if you want to be really radical, reach into the depths of your soul and grant forgiveness to all those who need it from you. Who knows? Maybe you will be the First Lady someday, but if not, you are still a princess to the Lord.

and gathered them in the courtyard on the
east side of the Temple. 5Hezekiah said,
"Listen to me, Levites. Make yourselves
ready for the LORD's service, and make holy
the Temple of the LORD, the God of your
ancestors. Remove from the Temple
everything that makes it impure. 6Our
ancestors were unfaithful to God and did
what the LORD said was wrong. They left the
LORD and stopped worshiping at the Temple
where he lives. They rejected him. 7They
shut the doors of the porch of the Temple,
and they let the fire go out in the lamps.
They stopped burning incense and offering
burnt offerings in the holy place to the God
of Israel. 8So the LORD became very angry
with the people of Judah and Jerusalem, and
he punished them. Other people are
frightened and shocked by what he did to
them. So they insult the people of Judah. You
know these things are true. 9That is why our
ancestors were killed in battle and our sons,
daughters, and wives were taken captive.
10Now I, Hezekiah, have decided to make an
agreement with the LORD, the God of Israel,
so he will not be angry with us anymore.
11My sons, don't waste any more time. The
LORD chose you to stand before him, to serve
him, to be his servants, and to burn incense
to him."

12These are the Levites who started to
work. From the Kohathite family there were
Mahath son of Amasai and Joel son of
Azariah. From the Merarite family there
were Kish son of Abdi and Azariah son of
Jehallelel. From the Gershonite family there
were Joah son of Zimmah and Eden son of
Joah. 13From Elizaphan's family there were
Shimri and Jeiel. From Asaph's family there
were Zechariah and Mattaniah. 14From
Heman's family there were Jehiel and
Shimei. From Jeduthun's family there were
Shemaiah and Uzziel.

15These Levites gathered their brothers
together and made themselves holy for
service in the Temple. Then they went into
the Temple of the LORD to purify it. They
obeyed the king's command that had come

from the LORD. 16When the priests went into
the Temple of the LORD to purify it, they took
out all the unclean things they found in the
Temple of the LORD and put them in the
Temple courtyard. Then the Levites took
these things out to the Kidron Valley.
17Beginning on the first day of the first
month, they made the Temple holy for the
LORD's service. On the eighth day of the
month, they came to the porch of the
Temple, and for eight more days they made
the Temple of the LORD holy. So they finished
on the sixteenth day of the first month.

18Then they went to King Hezekiah and
said, "We have purified the entire Temple of
the LORD, the altar for burnt offerings and its
utensils, and the table for the holy bread and
all its utensils. 19When Ahaz was king, he
was unfaithful to God and removed some
things from the Temple. But we have put
them back and made them holy for the LORD.
They are now in front of the LORD's altar."

20Early the next morning King Hezekiah
gathered the leaders of the city and went up
to the Temple of the LORD. 21They brought
seven bulls, seven male sheep, seven lambs,
and seven male goats. These animals were
an offering to remove the sin of the people
and the kingdom of Judah and to make the
Temple ready for service to God. King
Hezekiah commanded the priests, the
descendants of Aaron, to offer these animals
on the LORD's altar. 22So the priests killed the
bulls and sprinkled their blood on the altar.
They killed the sheep and sprinkled their
blood on the altar. Then they killed the
lambs and sprinkled their blood on the altar.
23Then the priests brought the male goats
for the sin offering before the king and the
people there. After the king and the people
put their hands on the goats, 24the priests
killed them. With the goats' blood they
made an offering on the altar to remove the
sins of the Israelites so they would belong to
God. The king had said that the burnt
offering and sin offering should be made for
all Israel.

25King Hezekiah put the Levites in the
Temple of the LORD with cymbals, harps, and
lyres, as David, Gad, and Nathan had
commanded. (Gad was the king's seer, and
Nathan was a prophet.) This command came
from the LORD through his prophets. 26So the
Levites stood ready with David's
instruments of music, and the priests stood
ready with their trumpets.

27Then Hezekiah gave the order to
sacrifice the burnt offering on the altar.
When the burnt offering began, the singing
to the LORD also began. The trumpets were
blown, and the musical instruments of
David king of Israel were played. 28All the
people worshiped, the singers sang, and the
trumpeters blew their trumpets until the
burnt offering was finished.

29When the sacrifices were completed,
King Hezekiah and everyone with him
bowed down and worshiped. 30King
Hezekiah and his officers ordered the Levites
to praise the LORD, using the words David
and Asaph the seer had used. So they praised
God with joy and bowed down and
worshiped.

31Then Hezekiah said, "Now that you
people of Judah have given yourselves to the
LORD, come near to the Temple of the LORD.
Bring sacrifices and offerings, to show
thanks to him." So the people brought
sacrifices and thank offerings, and anyone
who was willing also brought burnt
offerings. 32For burnt offerings they brought
a total of seventy bulls, one hundred male
sheep, and two hundred lambs; all these
animals were sacrificed as burnt offerings to
the LORD. 33The holy offerings totaled six
hundred bulls and three thousand sheep and
goats. 34There were not enough priests to
skin all the animals for the burnt offerings.
So their relatives the Levites helped them
until the work was finished and other priests
could be made holy. The Levites had been
more careful to make themselves holy for
the LORD's service than the priests. 35There
were many burnt offerings along with the
fat of fellowship offerings and drink
offerings. So the service in the Temple of the
LORD began again. 36And Hezekiah and the
people were very happy that God had made
it happen so quickly for his people.

The Passover Celebration

30 King Hezekiah sent messages to all
the people of Israel and Judah, and he
wrote letters to the people of Ephraim and
Manasseh. Hezekiah invited all these people
to come to the Temple of the LORD in
Jerusalem to celebrate the Passover for the
LORD, the God of Israel. 2King Hezekiah, his

officers, and all the people in Jerusalem
agreed to celebrate the Passover in the
second month. 3They could not celebrate it
at the normal time, because not enough
priests had made themselves ready to serve
the LORD, and the people had not yet
gathered in Jerusalem. 4This plan satisfied
King Hezekiah and all the people. 5So they
made an announcement everywhere in
Israel, from Beersheba to Dan,[n] telling the
people to come to Jerusalem to celebrate the
Passover for the LORD, the God of Israel. For a
long time most of the people had not celebrated the Passover as the law commanded.
6At the king's command, the messengers
took letters from him and his officers all
through Israel and Judah. This is what the
letters said:

> People of Israel, return to the
> LORD, the God of Abraham, Isaac,
> and Israel. Then God will return to
> you who are still alive, who have
> escaped from the kings of Assyria.
> 7Don't be like your ancestors
> or your relatives. They turned
> against the LORD, the God of their
> ancestors, so he caused other
> people to be disgusted with them.
> You know this is true. 8Don't be
> stubborn as your ancestors were,
> but obey the LORD willingly. Come
> to the Temple, which he has made
> holy forever. Serve the LORD your
> God so he will not be angry with
> you. 9Come back to the LORD. Then
> the people who captured your
> relatives and children will be kind
> to them and will let them return
> to this land. The LORD your God is
> kind and merciful. He will not
> turn away from you if you return
> to him.

10The messengers went to every town in
Ephraim and Manasseh, and all the way to
Zebulun, but the people laughed at them
and made fun of them. 11But some men from
Asher, Manasseh, and Zebulun were sorry
for what they had done and went to
Jerusalem. 12And God united all the people
of Judah in obeying King Hezekiah and his
officers, because their command had come
from the LORD.

13In the second month a large crowd came
together in Jerusalem to celebrate the Feast
of Unleavened Bread. 14The people removed
the altars and incense altars to gods in
Jerusalem and threw them into the Kidron
Valley.

15They killed the Passover lamb on the
fourteenth day of the second month. The
priests and the Levites were ashamed, so
they made themselves holy and brought
burnt offerings into the Temple of the LORD.
16They took their regular places in the
Temple as the Teachings of Moses, the man
of God, commanded. The Levites gave the
blood of the sacrifices to the priests, who
sprinkled it on the altar. 17Since many
people in the crowd had not made
themselves holy, the Levites killed the
Passover lambs for everyone who was not
clean. The Levites made each lamb holy for
the LORD. 18-19Although many people from
Ephraim, Manasseh, Issachar, and Zebulun
had not purified themselves for the feast,
they ate the Passover even though it was
against the law. So Hezekiah prayed for
them, saying, "LORD, you are good. You are
the LORD, the God of our ancestors. Please
forgive all those who try to obey you even if
they did not make themselves clean as the
rules of the Temple command." 20The LORD
listened to Hezekiah's prayer, and he healed
the people. 21The Israelites in Jerusalem
celebrated the Feast of Unleavened Bread for
seven days with great joy to the LORD. The
Levites and priests praised the LORD every
day with loud music. 22Hezekiah encouraged
all the Levites who showed they understood
well how to do their service for the LORD.
The people ate the feast for seven days,
offered fellowship offerings, and praised the
LORD, the God of their ancestors.

23Then all the people agreed to stay seven
more days, so they celebrated with joy for
seven more days. 24Hezekiah king of Judah
gave one thousand bulls and seven thousand
sheep to the people. The officers gave one
thousand bulls and ten thousand sheep to
the people. Many priests made themselves
holy. 25All the people of Judah, the priests,
the Levites, those who came from Israel, the

30:5 Beersheba to Dan Dan was the city farthest north in Israel, and Beersheba was the city farthest south. So this means all the people of Israel.

foreigners from Israel, and the foreigners
living in Judah were very happy. 26There was
much joy in Jerusalem, because there had
not been a celebration like this since the
time of Solomon son of David and king of
Israel. 27The priests and Levites stood up and
blessed the people, and God heard them
because their prayer reached heaven, his
holy home.

The Collection for the Priests

31 When the Passover celebration was
finished, all the Israelites in Jerusalem
went out to the towns of Judah. There they
smashed the stone pillars used to worship
gods. They cut down the Asherah idols and
destroyed the altars and places for
worshiping gods in all of Judah, Benjamin,
Ephraim, and Manasseh. After they had
destroyed all of them, the Israelites returned
to their own towns and homes.
2King Hezekiah appointed groups of
priests and Levites for their special duties.
They were to offer burnt offerings and
fellowship offerings, to worship, and to give
thanks and praise at the gates of the LORD's
house. 3Hezekiah gave some of his own
animals for the burnt offerings, which were
given every morning and evening, on
Sabbath days, during New Moons, and at
other feasts commanded in the LORD's
Teachings.
4Hezekiah commanded the people living
in Jerusalem to give the priests and Levites
the portion that belonged to them. Then the
priests and Levites could give all their time
to the LORD's Teachings. 5As soon as the
king's command went out to the Israelites,
they gave freely of the first portion of their
grain, new wine, oil, honey, and everything
they grew in their fields. They brought a
large amount, one-tenth of everything. 6The
people of Israel and Judah who lived in
Judah also brought one-tenth of their cattle
and sheep and one-tenth of the holy things
that were given to the LORD their God, and
they put all of them in piles. 7The people
began the piles in the third month and
finished in the seventh month. 8When
Hezekiah and his officers came and saw the
piles, they praised the LORD and his people,
the people of Israel. 9Hezekiah asked the
priests and Levites about the piles. 10Azariah,
the leading priest from Zadok's family,
answered Hezekiah, "Since the people began
to bring their offerings to the Temple of the
LORD, we have had plenty to eat and plenty
left over, because the LORD has blessed his
people. So we have all this left over."
11Then Hezekiah commanded the priests
to prepare the storerooms in the Temple of
the LORD. So this was done. 12Then the
priests brought in the offerings and the
things given to the LORD and one-tenth of
everything the people had given. Conaniah
the Levite was in charge of these things, and
his brother Shimei was second to him.
13Conaniah and his brother Shimei were
over these supervisors: Jehiel, Azaziah,
Nahath, Asahel, Jerimoth, Jozabad, Eliel,
Ismakiah, Mahath, and Benaiah. King
Hezekiah and Azariah the officer in charge
of the Temple of God had chosen them.
14Kore son of Imnah the Levite was in
charge of the special gifts the people wanted
to give to God. He was responsible for giving
out the contributions made to the LORD and
the holy gifts. Kore was the guard at the East
Gate. 15Eden, Miniamin, Jeshua, Shemaiah,
Amariah, and Shecaniah helped Kore in the
towns where the priests lived. They gave
from what was collected to the other groups
of priests, both young and old.
16From what was collected, these men also
gave to the males three years old and older
who had their names in the Levite family
histories. They were to enter the Temple of
the LORD for their daily service, each group
having its own responsibilities. 17The priests
were given their part of the collection, by
families, as listed in the family histories. The
Levites twenty years old and older were
given their part of the collection, based on
their responsibilities and their groups. 18The
Levites' babies, wives, sons, and daughters
also got part of the collection. This was done
for all the Levites who were listed in the
family histories, because they always kept
themselves ready to serve the LORD.
19Some of Aaron's descendants, the
priests, lived on the farmlands near the
towns or in the towns. Men were chosen by
name to give part of the collection to these
priests. All the males and those named in the
family histories of the Levites received part
of the collection.
20This is what King Hezekiah did in
Judah. He did what was good and right

and obedient before the LORD his God.
21 Hezekiah tried to obey God in his service
of the Temple of God, and he tried to obey
God's teachings and commands. He gave
himself fully to his work for God. So he had
success.

Assyria Attacks Judah

32 After Hezekiah did all these things to
serve the LORD, Sennacherib king of
Assyria came and attacked Judah. He and his
army surrounded and attacked the strong,
walled cities, hoping to take them for himself.
2 Hezekiah knew that Sennacherib had come
to Jerusalem to attack it. 3 So Hezekiah and his
officers and army commanders decided to cut
off the water from the springs outside the
city. So the officers and commanders helped
Hezekiah. 4 Many people came and cut off all
the springs and the stream that flowed
through the land. They said, "The king of
Assyria will not find much water when he
comes here." 5 Then Hezekiah made Jerusalem
stronger. He rebuilt all the broken parts of the
wall and put towers on it. He also built
another wall outside the first one and
strengthened the area that was filled in on
the east side of the old part of Jerusalem. He
also made many weapons and shields.

6 Hezekiah put army commanders over
the people and met with them at the open
place near the city gate. Hezekiah
encouraged them, saying, 7 "Be strong and
brave. Don't be afraid or worried because of
the king of Assyria or his large army. There is
a greater power with us than with him. 8 He
only has men, but we have the LORD our God
to help us and to fight our battles." The
people were encouraged by the words of
Hezekiah king of Judah.

9 After this King Sennacherib of Assyria
and all his army surrounded and attacked
Lachish. Then he sent his officers to
Jerusalem with this message for King
Hezekiah of Judah and all the people of
Judah in Jerusalem:

> 10 Sennacherib king of Assyria
> says this: "You have nothing to
> trust in to help you. It is no use for
> you to stay in Jerusalem under
> attack. 11 Hezekiah says to you,
> 'The LORD our God will save us
> from the king of Assyria,' but he is
> fooling you. If you stay in
> Jerusalem, you will die from
> hunger and thirst. 12 Hezekiah
> himself removed your LORD's
> places of worship and altars. He
> told you people of Judah and
> Jerusalem that you must worship
> and burn incense on only one
> altar.
>
> 13 "You know what my ancestors
> and I have done to all the people
> in other nations. The gods of those
> nations could not save their
> people from my power. 14 My
> ancestors destroyed those nations;
> none of their gods could save
> them from me. So your god cannot
> save you from my power. 15 Do not
> let Hezekiah fool you or trick you,
> and do not believe him. No god of
> any nation or kingdom has been
> able to save his people from me or
> my ancestors. Your god is even less
> able to save you from me."

16 Sennacherib's officers said worse things
against the LORD God and his servant
Hezekiah. 17 King Sennacherib also wrote
letters insulting the LORD, the God of Israel.
They spoke against him, saying, "The gods of
the other nations could not save their people
from me. In the same way Hezekiah's god
won't be able to save his people from me."
18 Then the king's officers shouted in
Hebrew, calling out to the people of
Jerusalem who were on the city wall. The
officers wanted to scare the people away so
they could capture Jerusalem. 19 They spoke
about the God of Jerusalem as though he
were like the gods the people of the world
worshiped, which are made by human
hands.

20 King Hezekiah and the prophet Isaiah
son of Amoz prayed to heaven about this.
21 Then the LORD sent an angel who killed all
the soldiers, leaders, and officers in the camp
of the king of Assyria. So the king went back
to his own country in disgrace. When he
went into the temple of his god, some of his
own sons killed him with a sword.

22 So the LORD saved Hezekiah and the
people in Jerusalem from Sennacherib king
of Assyria and from all other people. He took
care of them on every side. 23 Many people

brought gifts for the LORD to Jerusalem, and they also brought valuable gifts to King Hezekiah of Judah. From then on all the nations respected Hezekiah.

Hezekiah Dies

24At that time Hezekiah became so sick he almost died. When he prayed to the LORD, the LORD spoke to him and gave him a sign.[n] 25But Hezekiah did not thank God for his kindness, because he was so proud. So the LORD was angry with him and the people of Judah and Jerusalem. 26But later Hezekiah and the people of Jerusalem were sorry and stopped being proud, so the LORD did not punish them while Hezekiah was alive.

27Hezekiah had many riches and much honor. He made treasuries for his silver, gold, gems, spices, shields, and other valuable things. 28He built storage buildings for grain, new wine, and oil and stalls for all the cattle and pens for the sheep. 29He also built many towns. He had many flocks and herds, because God had given Hezekiah much wealth.

30It was Hezekiah who cut off the upper pool of the Gihon spring and made those waters flow straight down to the west side of the older part of Jerusalem. And Hezekiah was successful in everything he did. 31But one time the leaders of Babylon sent messengers to Hezekiah, asking him about a strange sign that had happened in the land. When they came, God left Hezekiah alone to test him so he could know everything that was in Hezekiah's heart.[n]

32Hezekiah's love for God and the other things he did as king are written in the vision of the prophet Isaiah son of Amoz. This is in the book of the kings of Judah and Israel. 33Hezekiah died and was buried on a hill, where the graves of David's ancestors are. All the people of Judah and Jerusalem honored Hezekiah when he died, and his son Manasseh became king in his place.

Manasseh King of Judah

33 Manasseh was twelve years old when he became king, and he was king for fifty-five years in Jerusalem. 2He did what the LORD said was wrong. He did the hateful things the nations had done—the nations that the LORD had forced out of the land ahead of the Israelites. 3Manasseh's father, Hezekiah, had torn down the places where gods were worshiped, but Manasseh rebuilt them. He also built altars for the Baal gods, and he made Asherah idols and worshiped all the stars of the sky and served them. 4The LORD had said about the Temple, "I will be worshiped in Jerusalem forever," but Manasseh built altars in the Temple of the LORD. 5He built altars to worship the stars in the two courtyards of the Temple of the LORD. 6He made his children pass through fire in the Valley of Ben Hinnom. He practiced magic and witchcraft and told the future by explaining signs and dreams. He got advice from mediums and fortune-tellers. He did many things the LORD said were wrong, which made the LORD angry.

7Manasseh carved an idol and put it in the Temple of God. God had said to David and his son Solomon about the Temple, "I will be worshiped forever in this Temple and in Jerusalem, which I have chosen from all the tribes of Israel. 8I will never again make the Israelites leave the land I gave to their ancestors. But they must obey everything I have commanded them in all the teachings, rules, and commands I gave them through Moses." 9But Manasseh led the people of Judah and Jerusalem to do wrong. They did more evil than the nations the LORD had destroyed ahead of the Israelites.

10The LORD spoke to Manasseh and his people, but they did not listen. 11So the LORD brought the king of Assyria's army commanders to attack Judah. They captured Manasseh, put hooks in him, placed bronze chains on his hands, and took him to Babylon. 12As Manasseh suffered, he begged the LORD his God for help and humbled himself before the God of his ancestors. 13When Manasseh prayed, the LORD heard him and had pity on him. So the LORD let him return to Jerusalem and to his kingdom. Then Manasseh knew that the LORD is the true God.

14After that happened, Manasseh rebuilt the outer wall of Jerusalem and made it higher. It was in the valley on the west side

32:24 sign See Isaiah 38:1–8. It tells the story about the sign and how the Lord gave Hezekiah fifteen more years to live.

32:31 God . . . heart See 2 Kings 20:12–19.

devotion 111

2 CHRONICLES 33:12–13

MERCY POURS ON THE UNDESERVING

Manasseh had disobeyed God, and not just a little, mind you. Manasseh led the people of Judah into doing more evil than any other king before him. Manasseh's punishment from God was swift and deliberate and serious. His captors were ruthless. They bound him, put hooks through his body like he was a wild animal, and imprisoned him in Babylon. As Manasseh suffered, he became broken and sorry for his evil. (Consequences have a way of getting our attention, don't they?) Eventually Manasseh's heart was humbled before God. What is so amazing is that when this rebellious, wicked man prayed to God with pure remorse, God heard him. The same God who had punished Manasseh's evil was drawn by compassion to have pity on him.

This story gives me so much hope. Sometimes my suffering is the result of my poor choices or my laziness or my lack of knowledge. Sometimes I could have tried harder or sought God more earnestly. Many of my heartaches probably could have been avoided with greater wisdom or patience on my part. But our God is a merciful God. He hears the contrite prayers of the broken.

Maybe you are suffering in the shame of your choices. If so, then hear this wild, wonderful truth: God listens when we have come to the end of ourselves. Our God moves and abides in a lavish love that never runs out. He delights in showing mercy without end.

of the Gihon spring and went to the
entrance of the Fish Gate and around the hill
of Ophel. Then he put commanders in all the
strong, walled cities in Judah.
15Manasseh removed the idols of other
nations, including the idol in the Temple of
the LORD. He removed all the altars he had
built on the Temple hill and in Jerusalem
and threw them out of the city. 16Then he set
up the LORD's altar and sacrificed on it
fellowship offerings and offerings to show
thanks to God. Manasseh commanded all the
people of Judah to serve the LORD, the God of
Israel. 17The people continued to offer
sacrifices at the places of worship, but their
sacrifices were only to the LORD their God.
18The other things Manasseh did as king, his
prayer to his God, and what the seers said to
him in the name of the LORD, the God of
Israel—all are recorded in the book of the
history of the kings of Israel. 19Manasseh's
prayer and God's pity for him, his sins, his
unfaithfulness, the places he built for
worshiping gods and the Asherah idols
before he humbled himself—all are written
in the book of the seers. 20Manasseh died and
was buried in his palace. Then Manasseh's
son Amon became king in his place.

Amon King of Judah

21Amon was twenty-two years old when
he became king, and he was king for two
years in Jerusalem. 22He did what the LORD
said was wrong, as his father Manasseh had
done. Amon worshiped and offered sacrifices
to all the carved idols Manasseh had made.
23Amon did not humble himself before the
LORD as his father Manasseh had done.
Instead, Amon sinned even more.
24King Amon's officers made plans against
him and killed him in his palace. 25Then the
people of the land killed all those who had
made plans to kill King Amon, and they
made his son Josiah king in his place.

Josiah King of Judah

34 Josiah was eight years old when he
became king, and he ruled thirty-one
years in Jerusalem. 2He did what the LORD
said was right. He lived as his ancestor David
had lived, and he did not stop doing what
was right.
3In his eighth year as king while he was
still young, Josiah began to obey the God of
his ancestor David. In his twelfth year as
king, Josiah began to remove from Judah and
Jerusalem the gods, the places for
worshiping gods, the Asherah idols, and the
wooden and metal idols. 4The people tore
down the altars for the Baal gods as Josiah
directed. Then Josiah cut down the incense
altars that were above them. He broke up the
Asherah idols and the wooden and metal
idols and beat them into powder. Then he
sprinkled the powder on the graves of the
people who had offered sacrifices to these
gods. 5He burned the bones of their priests
on their own altars. So Josiah removed idol
worship from Judah and Jerusalem, 6and
from the towns in the areas of Manasseh,
Ephraim, and Simeon all the way to
Naphtali, and in the ruins near these towns.
7Josiah broke down the altars and Asherah
idols and beat the idols into powder. He cut
down all the incense altars in all of Israel.
Then he went back to Jerusalem.
8In Josiah's eighteenth year as king, he
made Judah and the Temple pure again. He
sent Shaphan son of Azaliah, Maaseiah the
city leader, and Joah son of Joahaz the
recorder to repair the Temple of the LORD,
the God of Josiah. 9These men went to
Hilkiah the high priest and gave him the
money the Levite gatekeepers had gathered
from the people of Manasseh, Ephraim, and
all the Israelites who were left alive, and also
from all the people of Judah, Benjamin, and
Jerusalem. This is the money they had
brought into the Temple of God. 10Then the
Levites gave it to the supervisors of the work
on the Temple of the LORD, and they paid the
workers who rebuilt and repaired the
Temple. 11They gave money to carpenters
and builders to buy cut stone and wood. The
wood was used to rebuild the buildings and
to make beams for them, because the kings
of Judah had let the buildings fall into ruin.
12The men did their work well. Their
supervisors were Jahath and Obadiah, who
were Levites from the family of Merari, and
Zechariah and Meshullam, who were from
the family of Kohath. These Levites were all
skilled musicians. 13They were also in charge
of the workers who carried loads and all the
other workers. Some Levites worked as
secretaries, officers, and gatekeepers.

The Book of the Teachings Is Found

14The Levites brought out the money that
was in the Temple of the LORD. As they were
doing this, Hilkiah the priest found the Book
of the LORD's Teachings that had been given
through Moses. 15Hilkiah said to Shaphan
the royal secretary, "I've found the Book of
the Teachings in the Temple of the LORD!"
Then he gave it to Shaphan.
16Shaphan took the book to the king and
reported to Josiah, "Your officers are doing
everything you told them to do. 17They have
paid out the money that was in the Temple
of the LORD and have given it to the
supervisors and the workers." 18Then
Shaphan the royal secretary told the king,
"Hilkiah the priest has given me a book."
And Shaphan read from the book to the
king.
19When the king heard the words of the
Teachings, he tore his clothes to show how
upset he was. 20He gave orders to Hilkiah,
Ahikam son of Shaphan, Acbor son of
Micaiah, Shaphan the royal secretary, and
Asaiah, the king's servant. These were the
orders: 21"Go and ask the LORD about the
words in the book that was found. Ask for
me and for the people who are left alive in
Israel and Judah. The LORD is very angry with
us, because our ancestors did not obey the
LORD's word; they did not do everything this
book says to do."
22So Hilkiah and those the king sent with
him went to talk to Huldah the prophetess.
She was the wife of Shallum son of Tikvah,
the son of Harhas, who took care of the
king's clothes. Huldah lived in Jerusalem, in
the new area of the city.
23She said to them, "This is what the LORD,
the God of Israel, says: Tell the man who sent
you to me, 24'This is what the LORD says: I
will bring trouble to this place and to the
people living here. I will bring all the curses
that are written in the book that was read to
the king of Judah. 25The people of Judah

have left me and have burned incense to
other gods. They have made me angry by all
the evil things they have made. So I will
punish them in my anger, which will not be
put out.' 26 Tell the king of Judah, who sent
you to ask the LORD, 'This is what the LORD,
the God of Israel, says about the words you
heard: 27 When you heard my words against
this place and its people, you became sorry
for what you had done and you humbled
yourself before me. You tore your clothes to
show how upset you were, and you cried in
my presence. This is why I have heard you,
says the LORD. 28 So I will let you die and be
buried in peace. You won't see all the trouble
I will bring to this place and the people
living here.' "

So they took her message back to the king.
29 Then the king gathered all the elders of
Judah and Jerusalem together. 30 He went up
to the Temple of the LORD, and all the people
from Judah and from Jerusalem went with
him. The priests, the Levites, and all the
people—from the most important to the
least important—went with him. He read to
them all the words in the Book of the
Agreement that was found in the Temple of
the LORD. 31 The king stood by his pillar and
made an agreement in the presence of the
LORD to follow the LORD and obey his
commands, rules, and laws with his whole
being and to obey the words of the
agreement written in this book. 32 Then
Josiah made all the people in Jerusalem and
Benjamin promise to accept the agreement.
So the people of Jerusalem obeyed the
agreement of God, the God of their
ancestors.

33 And Josiah threw out the hateful idols
from all the land that belonged to the
Israelites. He led everyone in Israel to serve
the LORD their God. While Josiah lived, the
people obeyed the LORD, the God of their
ancestors.

Josiah Celebrates the Passover

35 King Josiah celebrated the Passover to
the LORD in Jerusalem. The Passover
lamb was killed on the fourteenth day of the
first month. 2 Josiah chose the priests to do
their duties, and he encouraged them as they
served in the Temple of the LORD. 3 The
Levites taught the Israelites and were made
holy for service to the LORD. Josiah said to
them, "Put the Holy Ark in the Temple that
David's son Solomon, the king of Israel,
built. Do not carry it from place to place on
your shoulders anymore. Now serve the
LORD your God and his people Israel.
4 Prepare yourselves by your family groups
for service, and do the jobs that King David
and his son Solomon gave you to do.

5 "Stand in the holy place with a group of
the Levites for each family group of the
people. 6 Kill the Passover lambs, and make
yourselves holy to the LORD. Prepare the
lambs for your relatives, the people of Israel,
as the LORD through Moses commanded us
to do."

7 Josiah gave the Israelites thirty thousand
sheep and goats to kill for the Passover
sacrifices, and he gave them three thousand
cattle. They were all his own animals.

8 Josiah's officers also gave willingly to the
people, the priests, and the Levites. Hilkiah,
Zechariah, and Jehiel, the officers in charge
of the Temple, gave the priests twenty-six
hundred lambs and goats and three hundred
cattle for Passover sacrifices. 9 Conaniah, his
brothers Shemaiah and Nethanel, and
Hashabiah, Jeiel, and Jozabad gave the
Levites five thousand sheep and goats and
five hundred cattle for Passover sacrifices.
These men were leaders of the Levites.

10 When everything was ready for the
Passover service, the priests and Levites went
to their places, as the king had commanded.
11 The Passover lambs were killed. Then the
Levites skinned the animals and gave the
blood to the priests, who sprinkled it on the
altar. 12 Then they gave the animals for the
burnt offerings to the different family
groups so the burnt offerings could be
offered to the LORD as was written in the
book of Moses. They also did this with the
cattle. 13 The Levites roasted the Passover
sacrifices over the fire as they were
commanded, and they boiled the holy
offerings in pots, kettles, and pans. Then
they quickly gave the meat to the people.
14 After this was finished, the Levites
prepared meat for themselves and for the
priests, the descendants of Aaron. The priests
worked until night, offering the burnt
offerings and burning the fat of the
sacrifices.

15 The Levite singers from Asaph's family
stood in the places chosen for them by King

David, Asaph, Heman, and Jeduthun, the
king's seer. The gatekeepers at each gate did
not have to leave their places, because their
fellow Levites had prepared everything for
them for the Passover.
16So everything was done that day for the
worship of the LORD, as King Josiah
commanded. The Passover was celebrated,
and the burnt offerings were offered on the
LORD's altar. 17The Israelites who were there
celebrated the Passover and the Feast of
Unleavened Bread for seven days. 18The
Passover had not been celebrated like this in
Israel since the prophet Samuel was alive.
None of the kings of Israel had ever
celebrated a Passover like it was celebrated
by King Josiah, the priests, the Levites, the
people of Judah and Israel who were there,
and the people of Jerusalem. 19This Passover
was celebrated in the eighteenth year Josiah
was king.

The Death of Josiah

20After Josiah did all this for the Temple,
Neco king of Egypt led an army to attack
Carchemish, a town on the Euphrates River.
And Josiah marched out to fight against
Neco. 21But Neco sent messengers to Josiah,
saying, "King Josiah, there should not be war
between us. I did not come to fight you, but
my enemies. God told me to hurry, and he is
on my side. So don't fight God, or he will
destroy you."
22But Josiah did not go away. He wore
different clothes so no one would know who
he was. Refusing to listen to what Neco said
at God's command, Josiah went to fight on
the plain of Megiddo. 23In the battle King
Josiah was shot by archers. He told his
servants, "Take me away because I am badly
wounded." 24So they took him out of his
chariot and put him in another chariot and
carried him to Jerusalem. There he died and
was buried in the graves where his ancestors
were buried. All the people of Judah and
Jerusalem were very sad because he was
dead.
25Jeremiah wrote some sad songs about
Josiah. Even to this day all the men and
women singers remember and honor Josiah
with these songs. It became a custom in
Israel to sing these songs that are written in
the collection of sad songs.
26-27The other things Josiah did as king,
from beginning to end, are written in the
book of the kings of Israel and Judah. It tells
how he loved what was written in the LORD's
teachings.

Jehoahaz King of Judah

36 The people of Judah chose Josiah's son
Jehoahaz and made him king in
Jerusalem in his father's place.
2Jehoahaz was twenty-three years old
when he became king, and he was king in
Jerusalem for three months. 3Then King
Neco of Egypt removed Jehoahaz from being
king in Jerusalem. Neco made the people of
Judah pay about seventy-five hundred
pounds of silver and about seventy-five
pounds of gold. 4The king of Egypt made
Jehoahaz's brother Eliakim the king of Judah
and Jerusalem and changed his name to
Jehoiakim. But Neco took his brother
Jehoahaz to Egypt.

Jehoiakim King of Judah

5Jehoiakim was twenty-five years old
when he became king, and he was king in
Jerusalem for eleven years. He did what the
LORD his God said was wrong. 6King
Nebuchadnezzar of Babylon attacked Judah,
captured Jehoiakim, put bronze chains on
him, and took him to Babylon.
7Nebuchadnezzar removed some of the
things from the Temple of the LORD, took
them to Babylon, and put them in his own
palace.
8The other things Jehoiakim did as king,
the hateful things he did, and everything he
was guilty of doing, are written in the book
of the kings of Israel and Judah. And
Jehoiakim's son Jehoiachin became king in
his place.

Jehoiachin King of Judah

9Jehoiachin was eighteen years old
when he became king of Judah, and he
was king in Jerusalem for three months
and ten days. He did what the LORD said was
wrong. 10In the spring King Nebuchadnezzar
sent for Jehoiachin and brought him and
some valuable treasures from the Temple of
the LORD to Babylon. Then Nebuchadnezzar
made Jehoiachin's uncle Zedekiah the king
of Judah and Jerusalem.

Zedekiah King of Judah

[11]Zedekiah was twenty-one years old
when he became king of Judah, and he was
king in Jerusalem for eleven years.
[12]Zedekiah did what the LORD his God said
was wrong. The prophet Jeremiah spoke
messages from the LORD, but Zedekiah did
not obey. [13]Zedekiah turned against King
Nebuchadnezzar, who had forced him to
swear in God's name to be loyal to him. But
Zedekiah became stubborn and refused to
obey the LORD, the God of Israel. [14]Also, all
the leaders of the priests and the people of
Judah became more wicked, following the
evil example of the other nations. The LORD
had made the Temple in Jerusalem holy, but
the leaders made it unholy.

The Fall of Jerusalem

[15]The LORD, the God of their ancestors,
sent prophets again and again to warn his
people, because he had pity on them and on
his Temple. [16]But they made fun of God's
prophets and hated God's messages. They
refused to listen to the prophets until,
finally, the LORD became so angry with his
people that he could not be stopped. [17]So
God brought the king of Babylon to attack
them. The king killed the young men even
when they were in the Temple. He had no
mercy on the young men or women, the old
men or those who were sick. God handed all
of them over to Nebuchadnezzar.
[18]Nebuchadnezzar carried away to Babylon
all the things from the Temple of God, both
large and small, and all the treasures from
the Temple of the LORD and from the king
and his officers. [19]Nebuchadnezzar and his
army set fire to God's Temple and broke
down Jerusalem's wall and burned all the
palaces. They took or destroyed every
valuable thing in Jerusalem.

[20]Nebuchadnezzar took captive to
Babylon the people who were left alive, and
he forced them to be slaves for him and his
descendants. They remained there as slaves
until the Persian kingdom defeated Babylon.
[21]And so what the LORD had told Israel
through the prophet Jeremiah happened:
The country was an empty wasteland for
seventy years to make up for the years of
Sabbath rest[n] that the people had not kept.

[22]In the first year Cyrus was king of Persia,
the LORD had Cyrus send an announcement
to his whole kingdom. This happened so the
LORD's message spoken by Jeremiah would
come true. He wrote:

[23]This is what Cyrus king of Persia says:

> The LORD, the God of heaven,
> has given me all the kingdoms of
> the earth, and he has appointed
> me to build a Temple for him at
> Jerusalem in Judah. Now may the
> LORD your God be with all of you
> who are his people. You are free to
> go to Jerusalem.

36:21 Sabbath rest The law said that every seventh year the land was not to be farmed. See Leviticus 25:1–7.

Ezra

A name that means "Jehovah helps"

Person Holding the Pen God Wrote With: *Ezra*, an important Jewish priest and scribe who descended from the bloodline of Moses' brother Aaron (Ezra 7:1–5), is the most likely author.

When the Text Was Written: Since Ezra led the second sprint out of Babylon around 458 B.C., this book was probably written in the following decades, between 457 and 437 B.C.

Spiritual Posture of the Original Recipients: The people of God are initially gleeful because they have just heard the King of Persia and world leader, Cyrus, announce the end of their Babylonian captivity (Ezra 1:1–4). Then reality sets in over the next century as they stream back home and get to work refurbishing the land of milk and honey.

Storyline Synopsis: The newly freed Israelites hurriedly grab their backpacks and start trekking back to Jerusalem under the leadership of Zerubbabel in 538 B.C. (chapter 2). As soon as their tired feet hit the sands of Jerusalem, God's ragtag team of survivors begin rebuilding the Temple (chapters 3—6). After they restore Jehovah's royal residence to the best of their ability (the second Temple paled next to the original constructed by Solomon), they celebrate Passover (Ezra 6:19–22). Eighty years later, in 458 B.C., a new Persian king, Artaxerxes, appoints Ezra to organize and lead the remaining Jewish exiles languishing in Babylon back home. Basically, this book is Ezra's narration of God's fulfillment of his promise to restore a faithful remnant of believers to the holy city of Jerusalem.

A Moment Worth Discussing: Ezra 3:10–13 records the juxtaposed reaction from God's people—both joyful shouting and loud weeping—when the foundation for the new Temple was laid. The reason some old men were crying is because they'd seen the first Temple in all its glory, and they were grieving the fact that God's "new house" was so dinky by comparison and didn't have the same feeling of God's tangible presence (see also Hag. 2:1–4 and Zech. 4:9–10). Their lament regarding the noticeable difference between the first and second Temples is a good catalyst to discuss the inevitable consequences of rebellion. Just because we repent after disobeying God doesn't mean everything will be hunky-dory again; bad spiritual behavior leaves scars.

Interesting (But Likely to Be Overlooked) Character: *Zerubbabel's* leadership points to the sovereign mercy of God because "Z" was technically sullied by a curse on his ancestors (Jer. 22:24–30). Nonetheless, God appointed him to lead the first freedom tour.

Cyrus Helps the Captives Return

1 In the first year Cyrus was king of Persia,
the LORD caused Cyrus to send an
announcement to his whole kingdom and to
put it in writing. This happened so the
LORD's message spoken by Jeremiah would
come true. He wrote:

> 2 This is what Cyrus king of Persia says:
> The LORD, the God of heaven,
> has given all the kingdoms of the
> earth to me, and he has appointed
> me to build a Temple for him at
> Jerusalem in Judah. 3 May God be
> with all of you who are his people.
> You are free to go to Jerusalem in
> Judah and build the Temple of the
> LORD, the God of Israel, who is in
> Jerusalem. 4 Those who stay
> behind, wherever they live, should
> support those who want to go.
> Give them silver and gold,
> supplies and cattle, and special
> gifts for the Temple of God in
> Jerusalem.

5 Then the family leaders of Judah and
Benjamin and the priests and Levites got
ready to go to Jerusalem—everyone God had
caused to want to go to Jerusalem to build
the Temple of the LORD. 6 All their neighbors
helped them, giving them things made of
silver and gold, along with supplies, cattle,
valuable gifts, and special gifts for the
Temple. 7 Also, King Cyrus brought out the
bowls and pans that belonged in the Temple
of the LORD, which Nebuchadnezzar had
taken from Jerusalem and put in the temple
of his own god. 8 Cyrus king of Persia had
Mithredath the treasurer bring them and
count them out for Sheshbazzar, the prince
of Judah.

9 He listed thirty gold dishes, one thousand
silver dishes, twenty-nine pans, 10 thirty gold
bowls, four hundred ten matching silver
bowls, and one thousand other pieces.

11 There was a total of fifty-four hundred
pieces of gold and silver. Sheshbazzar
brought all these things along when the
captives went from Babylon to Jerusalem.

The Captives Who Returned

2 These are the people of the area who
returned from captivity, whom
Nebuchadnezzar king of Babylon had taken
away to Babylon. They returned to Jerusalem
and Judah, each going back to his own town.
2 These people returned with Zerubbabel,
Jeshua, Nehemiah, Seraiah, Reelaiah,
Mordecai, Bilshan, Mispar, Bigvai, Rehum,
and Baanah.

These are the people from Israel: 3 the
descendants of Parosh—2,172; 4 the
descendants of Shephatiah—372; 5 the
descendants of Arah—775; 6 the descendants
of Pahath-Moab (through the family of
Jeshua and Joab)—2,812; 7 the descendants of
Elam—1,254; 8 the descendants of Zattu—
945; 9 the descendants of Zaccai—760; 10 the
descendants of Bani—642; 11 the descendants
of Bebai—623; 12 the descendants of Azgad—
1,222; 13 the descendants of Adonikam—666;
14 the descendants of Bigvai—2,056; 15 the
descendants of Adin—454; 16 the descendants
of Ater (through the family of Hezekiah)—
98; 17 the descendants of Bezai—323; 18 the
descendants of Jorah—112; 19 the descendants
of Hashum—223; 20 the descendants of
Gibbar—95.

21 These are the people from the towns: of
Bethlehem—123; 22 of Netophah—56; 23 of
Anathoth—128; 24 of Azmaveth—42; 25 of
Kiriath Jearim, Kephirah, and Beeroth—743;
26 of Ramah and Geba—621; 27 of Micmash—
122; 28 of Bethel and Ai—223; 29 of Nebo—52;
30 of Magbish—156; 31 of the other town of
Elam—1,254; 32 of Harim—320; 33 of Lod,
Hadid and Ono—725; 34 of Jericho—345; 35 of
Senaah—3,630.

36 These are the priests: the descendants of
Jedaiah (through the family of Jeshua)—973;
37 the descendants of Immer—1,052; 38 the
descendants of Pashhur—1,247; 39 the
descendants of Harim—1,017.

40 These are the Levites: the descendants of
Jeshua and Kadmiel (through the family of
Hodaviah)—74.

41 These are the singers: the descendants of
Asaph—128.

42 These are the gatekeepers of the Temple:
the descendants of Shallum, Ater, Talmon,
Akkub, Hatita, and Shobai—139.

43 These are the Temple servants: the
descendants of Ziha, Hasupha, Tabbaoth,
44 Keros, Siaha, Padon, 45 Lebanah, Hagabah,
Akkub, 46 Hagab, Shalmai, Hanan, 47 Giddel,
Gahar, Reaiah, 48 Rezin, Nekoda, Gazzam,
49 Uzza, Paseah, Besai, 50 Asnah, Meunim,

Nephussim, 51Bakbuk, Hakupha, Harhur,
52Bazluth, Mehida, Harsha, 53Barkos, Sisera,
Temah, 54Neziah, and Hatipha.

55These are the descendants of the
servants of Solomon: the descendants of
Sotai, Hassophereth, Peruda, 56Jaala, Darkon,
Giddel, 57Shephatiah, Hattil, Pokereth-
Hazzebaim, and Ami.

58The Temple servants and the
descendants of the servants of Solomon
numbered 392.

59Some people came to Jerusalem from
the towns of Tel Melah, Tel Harsha, Kerub,
Addon, and Immer, but they could not prove
that their ancestors came from Israel. 60They
were the descendants of Delaiah, Tobiah, and
Nekoda—652.

61Also these priests: the descendants of
Hobaiah, Hakkoz, and Barzillai, who had
married a daughter of Barzillai from Gilead
and was called by her family name.

62These people searched for their family
records but could not find them. So they
could not be priests, because they were
thought to be unclean. 63The governor
ordered them not to eat any of the food
offered to God until a priest had settled this
matter by using the Urim and Thummim.

64The total number of those who returned
was 42,360. 65This is not counting their 7,337
male and female servants and the 200 male
and female singers they had with them.
66They had 736 horses, 245 mules, 67435
camels, and 6,720 donkeys.

68When they arrived at the Temple of the
LORD in Jerusalem, some of the leaders of
families gave offerings to rebuild the Temple
of God on the same site as before. 69They
gave as much as they could to the treasury to
rebuild the Temple—about 1,100 pounds of
gold, about 6,000 pounds of silver, and 100
pieces of clothing for the priests.

70All the Israelites settled in their
hometowns. The priests, Levites, singers,
gatekeepers, and Temple servants, along
with some of the other people, settled in
their own towns as well.

Rebuilding the Altar

3 In the seventh month, after the Israelites
were settled in their hometowns, they
met together in Jerusalem. 2Then Jeshua son
of Jozadak and his fellow priests joined
Zerubbabel son of Shealtiel and began to
build the altar of the God of Israel where
they could offer burnt offerings, just as it is
written in the Teachings of Moses, the man
of God. 3Even though they were afraid of the
people living around them, they built the
altar where it had been before. And they
offered burnt offerings on it to the LORD
morning and evening. 4Then, to obey what
was written, they celebrated the Feast of
Shelters. They offered the right number of
sacrifices for each day of the festival. 5After
the Feast of Shelters, they had regular
sacrifices every day, as well as sacrifices for
the New Moon and all the festivals
commanded by the LORD. Also there were
special offerings brought as gifts to the LORD.
6On the first day of the seventh month they
began to bring burnt offerings to the LORD,
but the foundation of the LORD's Temple had
not yet been laid.

Rebuilding the Temple

7Then they gave money to the bricklayers
and carpenters. They also gave food, wine,
and oil to the cities of Sidon and Tyre so they
would float cedar logs from Lebanon to the
seacoast town of Joppa. Cyrus king of Persia
had given permission for this.

8In the second month of the second year
after their arrival at the Temple of God in
Jerusalem, Zerubbabel son of Shealtiel,
Jeshua son of Jozadak, their fellow priests
and Levites, and all who had returned from
captivity to Jerusalem began to work. They
chose Levites twenty years old and older to
be in charge of the building of the Temple of
the LORD. 9These men were in charge of the
work of building the Temple of God: Jeshua
and his sons and brothers; Kadmiel and his
sons who were the descendants of Hodaviah;
and the sons of Henadad and their sons and
brothers. They were all Levites.

10The builders finished laying the
foundation of the Temple of the LORD. Then
the priests, dressed in their robes, stood with
their trumpets, and the Levites, the sons of
Asaph, stood with their cymbals. They all
took their places and praised the LORD just as
David king of Israel had said to do. 11With
praise and thanksgiving, they sang to the
LORD:

"He is good;
his love for Israel continues forever."

And then all the people shouted loudly,

devotion 112

EZRA 3:11-12

WHEN IT ALL COMES TOGETHER

In 1998 my husband and I vacationed in North Carolina with our best friends. Each morning Cindy and I would drink coffee on the deck and do our devotions. One morning Cindy said she had a vision that the four of us were in some sort of ministry together, and she had even drawn a picture of the building where she saw us. Several years later, Rob and I left Florida to answer his call as a pastor in Brentwood, Tennessee. By the summer of 2002, our home Bible study was ready for a building, so we put in an offer and waited. That same week I returned to Florida to visit with Cindy. I asked her if she had her journal from 1998, and I started to cry when I saw her drawing. The building she had drawn was exactly like the one we had just put the offer on. I knew at that moment that the building would be ours and that Cindy and RJ would soon be joining us in ministry. They moved to Tennessee in 2003.

It's hard to describe the joy that comes from God. Ezra was overcome with joy when he saw the foundation of the Temple being laid—not because it was a building, but because God's will was being done. I was not excited about the building; I was excited because I knew we were exactly where God wanted us. Take joy, for where you are today is not where you were yesterday!

"Praise the LORD! The foundation of his
Temple has been laid." 12But many of the
older priests, Levites, and family leaders who
had seen the first Temple cried when they
saw the foundation of this Temple. Most of
the other people were shouting with joy.
13The people made so much noise it could be
heard far away, and no one could tell the
difference between the joyful shouting and
the sad crying.

Enemies of the Rebuilding

4 When the enemies of the people of
Judah and Benjamin heard that the
returned captives were building a Temple for
the LORD, the God of Israel, 2they came to
Zerubbabel and the leaders of the families.
The enemies said, "Let us help you build,
because we are like you and want to worship
your God. We have been offering sacrifices
to him since the time of Esarhaddon king of
Assyria, who brought us here."
3But Zerubbabel, Jeshua, and the leaders of
Israel answered, "You will not help us build a
Temple to our God. We will build it
ourselves for the LORD, the God of Israel, as
King Cyrus, the king of Persia, commanded
us to do."
4Then the people around them tried to
discourage the people of Judah by making
them afraid to build. 5Their enemies hired
others to delay the building plans during the
time Cyrus was king of Persia. And it
continued to the time Darius was king of
Persia.

More Problems for the Builders

6When Xerxes first became king, those
enemies wrote a letter against the people of
Judah and Jerusalem.
7When Artaxerxes became king of Persia,
Bishlam, Mithredath, Tabeel, and those with
them wrote a letter to Artaxerxes. It was
written in the Aramaic language and
translated.
8Rehum the governor and Shimshai the
governor's secretary wrote a letter against
Jerusalem to Artaxerxes the king. It said:

[9]This letter is from Rehum the governor, Shimshai the secretary, and their fellow workers—the judges and important officers over the men who came from Tripolis, Persia, Erech, and Babylon, the Elamite people of Susa, [10]and those whom the great and honorable Ashurbanipal forced out of their countries and settled in the city of Samaria and in other places of the Trans-Euphrates.

[11](This is a copy of the letter they sent to Artaxerxes.)

To King Artaxerxes.
From your servants who live in Trans-Euphrates.

[12]King Artaxerxes, you should know that the Jewish people who came to us from you have gone to Jerusalem to rebuild that evil city that refuses to obey. They are fixing the walls and repairing the foundations of the buildings.

[13]Now, King Artaxerxes, you should know that if Jerusalem is built and its walls are fixed, Jerusalem will not pay taxes of any kind. Then the amount of money your government collects will be less. [14]Since we must be loyal to the government, we don't want to see the king dishonored. So we are writing to let the king know. [15]We suggest you search the records of the kings who ruled before you. You will find out that the city of Jerusalem refuses to obey and makes trouble for kings and areas controlled by Persia. Since long ago it has been a place where disobedience has started. That is why it was destroyed. [16]We want you to know, King Artaxerxes, that if this city is rebuilt and its walls fixed, you will be left with nothing in Trans-Euphrates.

[17]King Artaxerxes sent this answer:

To Rehum the governor and Shimshai the secretary, to all their fellow workers living in Samaria, and to those in other places in Trans-Euphrates.

Greetings.

[18]The letter you sent to us has been translated and read to me. [19]I ordered the records to be searched, and it was done. We found that Jerusalem has a history of disobedience to kings and has been a place of problems and trouble. [20]Jerusalem has had powerful kings who have ruled over the whole area of Trans-Euphrates, and taxes of all kinds have been paid to them. [21]Now, give an order for those men to stop work. The city of Jerusalem will not be rebuilt until I say so. [22]Make sure you do this, because if they continue, it will hurt the government.

[23]A copy of the letter that King Artaxerxes sent was read to Rehum and Shimshai the secretary and the others. Then they quickly went to the Jewish people in Jerusalem and forced them to stop building.

[24]So the work on the Temple of God in Jerusalem stopped until the second year Darius was king of Persia.

Tattenai's Letter to Darius

5 The prophets Haggai and Zechariah, a descendant of Iddo, prophesied to the Jewish people in Judah and Jerusalem in the name of the God of Israel, who was over them. [2]Then Zerubbabel son of Shealtiel and Jeshua son of Jozadak started working again to rebuild the Temple of God in Jerusalem. And the prophets of God were there, helping them.

[3]At that time Tattenai, the governor of Trans-Euphrates, and Shethar-Bozenai, and their fellow workers went to the Jewish people and asked, "Who gave you permission to rebuild this Temple and fix these walls?" [4]They also asked, "What are the names of the men working on this building?" [5]But their God was watching over the elders of the Jewish people. The builders were not stopped until a report could go to King Darius and his written answer could be received.

[6]This is a copy of the letter that was sent
to King Darius by Tattenai, the governor of
Trans-Euphrates, Shethar-Bozenai, and the
other important officers of Trans-Euphrates.
[7]This is what was said in the report they sent
to him:

To King Darius.

Greetings. May you have peace.

[8]King Darius, you should know
that we went to the district of
Judah where the Temple of the
great God is. The people are
building that Temple with large
stones, and they are putting
timbers in the walls. They are
working very hard and are
building very fast.

[9]We asked their elders, "Who
gave you permission to rebuild
this Temple and these walls?"
[10]We also asked for their names,
and we wrote down the names of
their leaders so you would know
who they are.

[11]This is the answer they gave
to us: "We are the servants of the
God of heaven and earth. We are
rebuilding the Temple that a
great king of Israel built and
finished many years ago. [12]But our
ancestors made the God of heaven
angry, so he handed them over to
Nebuchadnezzar king of Babylon,
who destroyed this Temple and
took the people to Babylon as
captives.

[13]"Later, in the first year Cyrus
was king of Babylon, he gave a
special order for this Temple to be
rebuilt. [14]Cyrus brought out from
the temple in Babylon the gold
and silver bowls and pans that
came from the Temple of God.
Nebuchadnezzar had taken them
from the Temple in Jerusalem and
had put them in the temple in
Babylon.

"Then King Cyrus gave them to
Sheshbazzar, his appointed
governor. [15]Cyrus said to him,
'Take these gold and silver bowls
and pans, and put them back in
the Temple in Jerusalem and
rebuild the Temple of God where
it was.' [16]So Sheshbazzar came and
laid the foundations of the Temple
of God in Jerusalem. From that day
until now the work has been
going on, but it is not yet finished."

[17]Now, if the king wishes, let a
search be made in the royal
records of Babylon. See if King
Cyrus gave an order to rebuild this
Temple in Jerusalem. Then let the
king write us and tell us what he
has decided.

The Order of Darius

6 So King Darius gave an order to search
the records kept in the treasury in
Babylon. [2]A scroll was found in Ecbatana,
the capital city of Media. This is what was
written on it:

Note:

[3]King Cyrus gave an order about
the Temple of God in Jerusalem in
the first year he was king. This
was the order:

"Let the Temple be rebuilt as a
place to present sacrifices. Let its
foundations be laid; it should be
ninety feet high and ninety feet
wide. [4]It must have three layers of
large stones and then one layer of
timbers. The costs should be paid
from the king's treasury. [5]The gold
and silver utensils from the
Temple of God should be put back
in their places. Nebuchadnezzar
took them from the Temple in
Jerusalem and brought them to
Babylon, but they are to be put
back in the Temple of God in
Jerusalem."

[6]Now then, Tattenai, governor
of Trans-Euphrates, Shethar-
Bozenai, and all the officers of that
area, stay away from there. [7]Do
not bother the work on that
Temple of God. Let the governor of
the Jewish people and the Jewish
elders rebuild this Temple where it
was before.

[8]Also, I order you to do this for
those elders of the Jewish people
who are building this Temple: The
cost of the building is to be fully

paid from the royal treasury,
from taxes collected from
Trans-Euphrates. Do this so the
work will not stop. 9Give those
people anything they need—
young bulls, male sheep, or lambs
for burnt offerings to the God of
heaven, or wheat, salt, wine, or
olive oil. Give the priests in
Jerusalem anything they ask for
every day without fail. 10Then
they may offer sacrifices pleasing
to the God of heaven, and they
may pray for the life of the king
and his sons.
11Also, I give this order: If
anyone changes this order, a wood
beam is to be pulled from his
house and driven through his
body. Because of his crime, make
his house a pile of ruins. 12God has
chosen Jerusalem as the place he is
to be worshiped. May he punish
any king or person who tries to
change this order and destroy this
Temple.
I, Darius, have given this order.
Let it be obeyed quickly and
carefully.

Completion of the Temple

13So, Tattenai, the governor of Trans-
Euphrates, Shethar-Bozenai, and their fellow
workers carried out King Darius' order
quickly and carefully. 14The Jewish elders
continued to build and were successful
because of the preaching of Haggai the
prophet and Zechariah, a descendant of Iddo.
They finished building the Temple as the
God of Israel had commanded and as kings
Cyrus, Darius, and Artaxerxes of Persia had
ordered. 15The Temple was finished on the
third day of the month of Adar in the sixth
year Darius was king.
16Then the people of Israel celebrated and
gave the Temple to God to honor him.
Everybody was happy: the priests, the
Levites, and the rest of the Jewish people
who had returned from captivity. 17They
gave the Temple to God by offering a
hundred bulls, two hundred male sheep, and
four hundred lambs as sacrifices. And as an
offering to forgive the sins of all Israel, they
offered twelve male goats, one goat for each
tribe in Israel. 18Then they put the priests
and the Levites into their separate groups.
Each group had a certain time to serve God
in the Temple at Jerusalem as it is written in
the Book of Moses.

The Passover Is Celebrated

19The Jewish people who returned from
captivity celebrated the Passover on the
fourteenth day of the first month. 20The
priests and Levites had made themselves
clean. Then the Levites killed the Passover
lambs for all the people who had returned
from captivity, for their relatives the priests,
and for themselves. 21So all the people of
Israel who returned from captivity ate the
Passover lamb. So did the people who had
given up the unclean ways of their
non-Jewish neighbors in order to worship
the LORD, the God of Israel. 22For seven days
they celebrated the Feast of Unleavened
Bread in a very joyful way. The LORD had
made them happy by changing the mind of
the king of Assyria so that he helped them in
the work on the Temple of the God of Israel.

Ezra Comes to Jerusalem

7 After these things[n] during the rule of
Artaxerxes king of Persia, Ezra came up
from Babylon. Ezra was the son of Seraiah,
the son of Azariah, the son of Hilkiah, 2the
son of Shallum, the son of Zadok, the son of
Ahitub, 3the son of Amariah, the son of
Azariah, the son of Meraioth, 4the son of
Zerahiah, the son of Uzzi, the son of Bukki,
5the son of Abishua, the son of Phinehas, the
son of Eleazar, the son of Aaron the high
priest. 6This Ezra came to Jerusalem from
Babylon. He was a teacher and knew well the
Teachings of Moses that had been given by
the LORD, the God of Israel. Ezra received
everything he asked for from the king,
because the LORD his God was helping him.
7In the seventh year of King Artaxerxes
more Israelites came to Jerusalem. Among
them were priests, Levites, singers, gatekeepers, and Temple servants.
8Ezra arrived in Jerusalem in the fifth
month of Artaxerxes' seventh year as king.
9Ezra had left Babylon on the first day of the

7:1 After these things There is a time period of about sixty years between chapters six and seven.

first month, and he arrived in Jerusalem on the first day of the fifth month, because God was helping him. 10 Ezra had worked hard to know and obey the Teachings of the LORD and to teach his rules and commands to the Israelites.

Artaxerxes' Letter to Ezra

11 King Artaxerxes had given a letter to Ezra, a priest and teacher who taught about the commands and laws the LORD gave Israel. This is a copy of the letter:

> 12 From Artaxerxes, king of kings, to Ezra the priest, a teacher of the Law of the God of heaven.
>
> Greetings.
>
> 13 Now I give this order: Any Israelite in my kingdom who wishes may go with you to Jerusalem, including priests and Levites. 14 Ezra, you are sent by the king and the seven people who advise him to ask how Judah and Jerusalem are obeying the Law of your God, which you are carrying with you. 15 Also take with you the silver and gold that the king and those who advise him have given freely to the God of Israel, whose Temple is in Jerusalem. 16 Also take the silver and gold you receive from the area of Babylon. Take the offerings the Israelites and their priests have given as gifts for the Temple of your God in Jerusalem. 17 With this money buy bulls, male sheep, and lambs, and the grain offerings and drink offerings that go with those sacrifices. Then sacrifice them on the altar in the Temple of your God in Jerusalem.
>
> 18 You and your fellow Jews may spend the silver and gold left over as you want and as God wishes. 19 Take to the God of Jerusalem all the utensils for worship in the Temple of your God, 20 which we have given you. Use the royal treasury to pay for anything else you need for the Temple of your God.
>
> 21 Now I, King Artaxerxes, give this order to all the men in charge of the treasury of Trans-Euphrates: Give Ezra, a priest and a teacher of the Law of the God of heaven, whatever he asks for. 22 Give him up to seventy-five hundred pounds of silver, six hundred bushels of wheat, six hundred gallons of wine, and six hundred gallons of olive oil. And give him as much salt as he wants. 23 Carefully give him whatever the God of heaven wants for the Temple of the God of heaven. We do not want God to be angry with the king and his sons.
>
> 24 Remember, you must not make these people pay taxes of any kind: priests, Levites, singers, gatekeepers, Temple servants, and other workers in this Temple of God.
>
> 25 And you, Ezra, use the wisdom you have from your God to choose judges and lawmakers to rule the Jewish people of Trans-Euphrates. They know the laws of your God, and you may teach anyone who does not know them. 26 Whoever does not obey the law of your God or of the king must be punished. He will be killed, or sent away, or have his property taken away, or be put in jail.

27 Praise the LORD, the God of our ancestors. He caused the king to want to honor the Temple of the LORD in Jerusalem. 28 The LORD has shown me, Ezra, his love in the presence of the king, those who advise the king, and the royal officers. Because the LORD my God was helping me, I had courage, and I gathered the leaders of Israel to return with me.

Leaders Who Returned with Ezra

8 These are the leaders of the family groups and those who were listed with them who came back with me from Babylon during the rule of King Artaxerxes.

2 From the descendants of Phinehas: Gershom.

From the descendants of Ithamar: Daniel.

From the descendants of David: Hattush 3 of the descendants of Shecaniah.

From the descendants of Parosh:
Zechariah, with one hundred fifty men.
4 From the descendants of Pahath-Moab:
Eliehoenai son of Zerahiah, with two
hundred men.
5 From the descendants of Zattu:
Shecaniah son of Jahaziel, with three
hundred men.
6 From the descendants of Adin: Ebed son
of Jonathan, with fifty men.
7 From the descendants of Elam: Jeshaiah
son of Athaliah, with seventy men.
8 From the descendants of Shephatiah:
Zebadiah son of Michael, with eighty men.
9 From the descendants of Joab: Obadiah
son of Jehiel, with two hundred eighteen
men.
10 From the descendants of Bani:
Shelomith son of Josiphiah, with one
hundred sixty men.
11 From the descendants of Bebai:
Zechariah son of Bebai, with twenty-eight
men.
12 From the descendants of Azgad: Johanan
son of Hakkatan, with one hundred ten men.
13 From the descendants of Adonikam,
these were the last ones: Eliphelet, Jeuel, and
Shemaiah, with sixty men.
14 From the descendants of Bigvai: Uthai
and Zaccur, with seventy men.

The Return to Jerusalem

15 I called all those people together at the
canal that flows toward Ahava, where we
camped for three days. I checked all the
people and the priests, but I did not find any
Levites. 16 So I called these leaders: Eliezer,
Ariel, Shemaiah, Elnathan, Jarib, Elnathan,
Nathan, Zechariah, and Meshullam. And I
called Joiarib and Elnathan, who were
teachers. 17 I sent these men to Iddo, the
leader at Casiphia, and told them what to say
to Iddo and his relatives, who are the Temple
servants in Casiphia. I sent them to bring
servants to us for the Temple of our God.
18 Our God was helping us, so Iddo's relatives
gave us Sherebiah, a wise man from the
descendants of Mahli son of Levi, who was
the son of Israel. And they brought
Sherebiah's sons and brothers, for a total of
eighteen men. 19 And they brought to us
Hashabiah and Jeshaiah from the
descendants of Merari, and his brothers and
nephews. In all there were twenty men.
20 They also brought two hundred twenty of
the Temple servants, a group David and the
officers had set up to help the Levites. All of
those men were listed by name.
21 There by the Ahava Canal, I announced
we would all fast and deny ourselves before
our God. We would ask God for a safe trip for
ourselves, our children, and all our
possessions. 22 I was ashamed to ask the king
for soldiers and horsemen to protect us from
enemies on the road. We had said to the
king, "Our God helps everyone who obeys
him, but he is very angry with all who reject
him." 23 So we fasted and prayed to our God
about our trip, and he answered our prayers.
24 Then I chose twelve of the priests who
were leaders, Sherebiah, Hashabiah, and ten
of their relatives. 25 I weighed the offering of
silver and gold and the utensils given for the
Temple of our God, and I gave them to the
twelve priests I had chosen. The king, the
people who advised him, his officers, and all
the Israelites there with us had given these
things for the Temple. 26 I weighed out and
gave them about fifty thousand pounds of
silver, about seventy-five hundred pounds of
silver objects, and about seventy-five
hundred pounds of gold. 27 I gave them
twenty gold bowls that weighed about
nineteen pounds and two fine pieces of
polished bronze that were as valuable as
gold.
28 Then I said to the priests, "You and these
utensils belong to the LORD for his service.
The silver and gold are gifts to the LORD, the
God of your ancestors. 29 Guard these things
carefully. In Jerusalem, weigh them in front
of the leading priests, Levites, and the leaders
of the family groups of Israel in the rooms of
the Temple of the LORD." 30 So the priests and
Levites accepted the silver, the gold, and the
utensils that had been weighed to take them
to the Temple of our God in Jerusalem.
31 On the twelfth day of the first month we
left the Ahava Canal and started toward
Jerusalem. Our God helped us and protected
us from enemies and robbers along the way.
32 Finally we arrived in Jerusalem where we
rested three days.
33 On the fourth day we weighed out the
silver, the gold, and the utensils in the
Temple of our God. We handed them to the
priest Meremoth son of Uriah. Eleazar son of
Phinehas was with him, as were the Levites

devotion 113

EZRA 8:21–23

A MEAL . . . OR AN ANSWER?

Mark 9:14-29 tells the story of Jesus' followers being unable to cast out a demon. Jesus had sent out his followers throughout Israel to do miracles in his name. They had been healing and casting out demons until they came upon this one boy for whom they seemed unable to do anything. Then Jesus showed up and cast out the demon. The followers were confused. They asked Jesus why they were unable to do what he had done. Jesus answered them in verse 29 saying, "That kind of spirit can only be forced out by prayer." Some versions of the Bible say *prayer and fasting*.

You see the same thing in Ezra's story. The people of Israel were traveling back to Jerusalem after being captives in Babylon. They were scared and seeking God for their journey. Ezra told the people, just as Jesus later told his followers, that they needed to pray and fast. And God answered their prayers.

When you are faced with moments in your life that you feel are beyond your ability to cope with, there is only one thing to do. You need to pray and fast. If you have never fasted before, try just giving up one meal. Rather than having lunch, for example, spend that time in prayer for your particular situation. Prayer and fasting is not a magic solution for getting the answers you want, but it is a powerful way to pray. Know that the Lord will hear your prayers!

Jozabad son of Jeshua and Noadiah son of
Binnui. 34We checked everything by number
and by weight, and the total weight was
written down.

35Then the captives who returned made
burnt offerings to the God of Israel. They
sacrificed twelve bulls for all Israel, ninety-
six male sheep, and seventy-seven lambs. For
a sin offering there were twelve male goats.
All this was a burnt offering to the LORD.
36They took King Artaxerxes' orders to the
royal officers and to the governors of Trans-
Euphrates. Then these men gave help to the
people and the Temple of God.

Ezra's Prayer

9 After these things had been done, the
leaders came to me and said, "Ezra, the
Israelites, including the priests and Levites,
have not kept themselves separate from the
people around us. Those neighbors do evil
things, as the Canaanites, Hittites, Perizzites,
Jebusites, Ammonites, Moabites, Egyptians,
and Amorites did. 2The Israelite men and
their sons have married these women. They
have mixed the people who belong to God
with the people around them. The leaders
and officers of Israel have led the rest of the
Israelites to do this unfaithful thing."

3When I heard this, I angrily tore my robe
and coat, pulled hair from my head and
beard, and sat down in shock. 4Everyone
who trembled in fear at the word of the God
of Israel gathered around me because of the
unfaithfulness of the captives who had
returned. I sat there in shock until the
evening sacrifice.

5At the evening sacrifice I got up from
where I had shown my shame. My robe and
coat were torn, and I fell on my knees with
my hands spread out to the LORD my God. 6I
prayed,

"My God, I am too ashamed and
embarrassed to lift up my face to you, my
God, because our sins are so many. They are
higher than our heads. Our guilt even

reaches up to the sky. [7]From the days of our
ancestors until now, our guilt has been great.
Because of our sins, we, our kings, and our
priests have been punished by the sword and
captivity. Foreign kings have taken away our
things and shamed us, even as it is today.

[8]"But now, for a short time, the LORD our
God has been kind to us. He has let some of
us come back from captivity and has let us
live in safety in his holy place. And so our
God gives us hope and a little relief from our
slavery. [9]Even though we are slaves, our God
has not left us. He caused the kings of Persia
to be kind to us and has given us new life.
We can rebuild the Temple and repair its
ruins. And he has given us a wall to protect
us in Judah and Jerusalem.

[10]"But now, our God, what can we say
after you have done all this? We have
disobeyed your commands [11]that you gave
through your servants the prophets. You
said, 'The land you are entering to own is
ruined; the people living there have spoiled
it by the evil they do. Their evil filled the
land with uncleanness from one end to the
other. [12]So do not let your daughters marry
their sons, and do not let their daughters
marry your sons. Do not wish for their peace
or success. Then you will be strong and eat
the good things of the land. Then you can
leave this land to your descendants forever.'

[13]"What has happened to us is our own
fault. We have done evil things, and our guilt
is great. But you, our God, have punished us
less than we deserve; you have left a few of
us alive. [14]We should not again break your
commands by allowing marriages with these
wicked people. If we did, you would get
angry enough to destroy us, and none of us
would be left alive. [15]LORD, God of Israel, by
your goodness a few of us are left alive today.
We admit that we are guilty and none of us
should be allowed to stand before you."

The People Confess Sin

10 As Ezra was praying and confessing
and crying and throwing himself
down in front of the Temple, a large group of
Israelite men, women, and children gathered
around him who were also crying loudly.
[2]Then Shecaniah son of Jehiel the Elamite
said to Ezra, "We have been unfaithful to our
God by marrying women from the peoples
around us. But even so, there is still hope for
Israel. [3]Now let us make an agreement
before our God. We will send away all these
women and their children as you and those
who respect the commands of our God
advise. Let it be done to obey God's
Teachings. [4]Get up, Ezra. You are in charge,
and we will support you. Have courage and
do it."

[5]So Ezra got up and made the priests,
Levites, and all the people of Israel promise
to do what was suggested; and they
promised. [6]Then Ezra left the Temple and
went to the room of Jehohanan son of
Eliashib. While Ezra was there, he did not
eat or drink, because he was still sad about
the unfaithfulness of the captives who had
returned.

[7]They sent an order in Judah and
Jerusalem for all the captives who had
returned to meet together in Jerusalem.
[8]Whoever did not come to Jerusalem within
three days would lose his property and
would no longer be a member of the
community of the returned captives. That
was the decision of the officers and elders.

[9]So within three days all the men of Judah
and Benjamin gathered in Jerusalem. It was
the twentieth day of the ninth month. All
the men were sitting in the open place in
front of the Temple and were upset because
of the meeting and because it was raining.
[10]Ezra the priest stood up and said to them,
"You have been unfaithful and have married
non-Jewish women. You have made Israel
more guilty. [11]Now, confess it to the LORD,
the God of your ancestors. Do his will and
separate yourselves from the people living
around you and from your non-Jewish
wives."

[12]Then the whole group answered Ezra
with a loud voice, "Ezra, you're right! We
must do what you say. [13]But there are many
people here, and it's the rainy season. We
can't stand outside, and this problem can't be
solved in a day or two, because we have
sinned badly. [14]Let our officers make a
decision for the whole group. Then let
everyone in our towns who has married a
non-Jewish woman meet with the elders and
judges of each town at a planned time, until
the hot anger of our God turns away from
us." [15]Only Jonathan son of Asahel, Jahzeiah
son of Tikvah, Meshullam, and Shabbethai
the Levite were against the plan.

16So the returned captives did what was
suggested. Ezra the priest chose men who
were leaders of the family groups and
named one from each family division. On
the first day of the tenth month they sat
down to study each case. 17By the first day of
the first month, they had finished with all
the men who had married non-Jewish
women.

Those Guilty of Marrying Non-Jewish Women

18These are the descendants of the priests
who had married foreign women:

From the descendants of Jeshua son of
Jozadak and Jeshua's brothers: Maaseiah,
Eliezer, Jarib, and Gedaliah. 19(They all
promised to divorce their wives, and each
one brought a male sheep from the flock as a
penalty offering.)

20From the descendants of Immer: Hanani
and Zebadiah.

21From the descendants of Harim:
Maaseiah, Elijah, Shemaiah, Jehiel, and
Uzziah.

22From the descendants of Pashhur:
Elioenai, Maaseiah, Ishmael, Nethanel,
Jozabad, and Elasah.

23Among the Levites: Jozabad, Shimei,
Kelaiah (also called Kelita), Pethahiah, Judah,
and Eliezer.

24Among the singers: Eliashib.

Among the gatekeepers: Shallum, Telem,
and Uri.

25And among the other Israelites, these
married non-Jewish women:

From the descendants of Parosh: Ramiah,
Izziah, Malkijah, Mijamin, Eleazar, Malkijah,
and Benaiah.

26From the descendants of Elam:
Mattaniah, Zechariah, Jehiel, Abdi, Jeremoth,
and Elijah.

27From the descendants of Zattu: Elioenai,
Eliashib, Mattaniah, Jeremoth, Zabad, and
Aziza.

28From the descendants of Bebai:
Jehohanan, Hananiah, Zabbai, and Athlai.

29From the descendants of Bani:
Meshullam, Malluch, Adaiah, Jashub, Sheal,
and Jeremoth.

30From the descendants of Pahath-Moab:
Adna, Kelal, Benaiah, Maaseiah, Mattaniah,
Bezalel, Binnui, and Manasseh.

31From the descendants of Harim: Eliezer,
Ishijah, Malkijah, Shemaiah, Shimeon,
32Benjamin, Malluch, and Shemariah.

33From the descendants of Hashum:
Mattenai, Mattattah, Zabad, Eliphelet,
Jeremai, Manasseh, and Shimei.

34From the descendants of Bani: Maadai,
Amram, Uel, 35Benaiah, Bedeiah, Keluhi,
36Vaniah, Meremoth, Eliashib, 37Mattaniah,
Mattenai, and Jaasu.

38From the descendants of Binnui: Shimei,
39Shelemiah, Nathan, Adaiah, 40Macnadebai,
Shashai, Sharai, 41Azarel, Shelemiah,
Shemariah, 42Shallum, Amariah, and Joseph.

43From the descendants of Nebo: Jeiel,
Mattithiah, Zabad, Zebina, Jaddai, Joel, and
Benaiah.

44All these men had married non-Jewish
women, and some of them had children by
these wives.

Nehemiah

A name that means "Jehovah comforts"

Person Holding the Pen God Wrote With: *Ezra* wrote this book, but he gathered most of the information from Nehemiah's personal journal.

When the Text Was Written: This book was penned during Nehemiah's second term as governor of Jerusalem (from around 424 to 400 B.C.).

Spiritual Posture of the Original Recipients: The second wave of Jewish exiles have just returned from captivity in Babylon, led by Ezra. They're extremely glad to be home, but with their confinement still fresh on their minds, they're now focused on protecting themselves and the city they reside in.

Storyline Synopsis: Nehemiah resigns from his job as a royal assistant in Persia to return to Jerusalem and serve as governor. When he takes an official tour of the city walls, he finds them in such a sorry state that he spearheads a "Rebuild the Barrier" campaign. After dealing with some dicey opposition from a gang of bullies, Nehemiah succeeds in completing this capital campaign project in record time. Once the wall is rebuilt, confession and repentance roll through town, and God-centered worship is reestablished. This book reads like part two of *God's Promise of Restoring a Faithful Remnant in Jerusalem*!

A Moment Worth Discussing: Chapter 9 records an incredible spiritual revival. For three hours, the inhabitants of Jerusalem confess the sins of their forefathers, after which they confess their own ungodly behavior for another three hours. Then they spend the same amount of time celebrating their heavenly Father's forgiveness and faithfulness throughout Israel's turbulent history. At the very end of this emotional day of repentance and worship, God's people make a formalized national agreement, signed and sealed by their leaders, to obey him in the future (Neh. 9:38). Ponder why the best intentions made during revivals typically melt away in the heat of real life.

Interesting (But Likely to Be Overlooked) Character: *Artaxerxes* was a non-Jewish (Persian) king whose trust in the Jewish Nehemiah was evident. The king hired Nehemiah to be his cupbearer (Neh. 2:1)—the guy who sipped the king's wine from his goblet to make sure it wasn't poisoned. Only Art had the political power to grant Nehemiah's wish to rebuild Jerusalem's rock walls (2:2–9).

Nehemiah's Prayer

1 These are the words of Nehemiah son of Hacaliah.

In the month of Kislev in the twentieth year,[n] I, Nehemiah, was in the capital city of Susa. 2One of my brothers named Hanani came with some other men from Judah. I asked them about Jerusalem and the Jewish people who lived through the captivity.

3They answered me, "Those who are left from the captivity are back in Judah, but they are in much trouble and are full of shame. The wall around Jerusalem is broken down, and its gates have been burned."

4When I heard these things, I sat down and cried for several days. I was sad and fasted. I prayed to the God of heaven, 5"LORD, God of heaven, you are the great God who is to be respected. You are loyal, and you keep your agreement with those who love you and obey your commands. 6Look and listen carefully. Hear the prayer that I, your servant, am praying to you day and night for your servants, the Israelites. I confess the sins we Israelites have done against you. My father's family and I have sinned against you. 7We have been wicked toward you and have not obeyed the commands, rules, and laws you gave your servant Moses.

8"Remember what you taught your servant Moses, saying, 'If you are unfaithful, I will scatter you among the nations. 9But if you return to me and obey my commands, I will gather your people from the far ends of the earth. And I will bring them from captivity to where I have chosen to be worshiped.'

10"They are your servants and your people, whom you have saved with your great strength and power. 11Lord, listen carefully to the prayer of your servant and the prayers of your servants who love to honor you. Give me, your servant, success today; allow this king to show kindness to me."

I was the one who served wine to the king.

Nehemiah Is Sent to Jerusalem

2 It was the month of Nisan in the twentieth year Artaxerxes was king. He wanted some wine, so I took some and gave it to the king. I had not been sad in his presence before. 2So the king said, "Why does your face look sad even though you are not sick? Your heart must be sad."

Then I was very afraid. 3I said to the king, "May the king live forever! My face is sad because the city where my ancestors are buried lies in ruins, and its gates have been destroyed by fire."

4Then the king said to me, "What do you want?"

First I prayed to the God of heaven. 5Then I answered the king, "If you are willing and if I have pleased you, send me to the city in Judah where my ancestors are buried so I can rebuild it."

6The queen was sitting next to the king. He asked me, "How long will your trip take, and when will you get back?" It pleased the king to send me, so I set a time.

7I also said to him, "If you are willing, give me letters for the governors of Trans-Euphrates. Tell them to let me pass safely through their lands on my way to Judah. 8And may I have a letter for Asaph, the keeper of the king's forest, telling him to give me timber? I will need it to make boards for the gates of the palace, which is by the Temple, and for the city wall, and for the house in which I will live." So the king gave me the letters, because God was showing kindness to me. 9Then I went to the governors of Trans-Euphrates and gave them the king's letters. The king had also sent army officers and soldiers on horses with me.

10When Sanballat the Horonite and Tobiah the Ammonite officer heard about this, they were upset that someone had come to help the Israelites.

Nehemiah Inspects Jerusalem

11I went to Jerusalem and stayed there three days. 12Then at night I started out with a few men. I had not told anyone what God had caused me to do for Jerusalem. There were no animals with me except the one I was riding.

13I went out at night through the Valley Gate. I rode toward the Dragon Well and the Trash Gate, inspecting the walls of Jerusalem that had been broken down and the gates

1:1 twentieth year This is probably referring to the twentieth year King Artaxerxes I ruled Persia.

devotion 114

NEHEMIAH 2:1-9

DON'T FEED THE FEARS

Being afraid comes with the territory of humanity. It sneaks up on us at the weirdest times, though it can also seem ever-present and overwhelming. I love Nehemiah's honesty about his fear of the king. I have also been very afraid. Some days I'm afraid that I'm not a good mom. Other days I'm afraid of the world's depravity. Many times I've been afraid of failure or afraid that I will never know a lasting romantic love.

Every time we feel ourselves becoming afraid, we have two options. Our first option is to feed the fear. We can remember our flaws and inadequacies. We can incline our ear toward the accuser's lies. We can believe those lies and make choices as if everything the accuser has said about us is true.

Or when we feel afraid, before we give up or give in to our weakness, our second option is to pray to the God of heaven as Nehemiah did. We can lay our fear on God's altar. We can entrust our fear to the only One who overcomes.

I am sure that when Nehemiah spoke to the king, there was a part of him that was still afraid—even after praying. But I am also sure that the power of God in him was the reason he was not paralyzed by his fear. By the power of the Holy Spirit in us, you and I have been given the way to walk in strength, even through our fears.

that had been destroyed by fire. 14Then I
rode on toward the Fountain Gate and the
King's Pool, but there was not enough room
for the animal I was riding to pass through.
15So I went up the valley at night, inspecting
the wall. Finally, I turned and went back in
through the Valley Gate. 16The guards did
not know where I had gone or what I was
doing. I had not yet said anything to the
Jewish people, the priests, the important
men, the officers, or any of the others who
would do the work.

17Then I said to them, "You can see the
trouble we have here. Jerusalem is a pile of
ruins, and its gates have been burned. Come,
let's rebuild the wall of Jerusalem so we
won't be full of shame any longer." 18I also
told them how God had been kind to me and
what the king had said to me.

Then they answered, "Let's start
rebuilding." So they began to work hard.

19But when Sanballat the Horonite,
Tobiah the Ammonite officer, and Geshem
the Arab heard about it, they made fun of us
and laughed at us. They said, "What are you
doing? Are you turning against the king?"

20But I answered them, "The God of
heaven will give us success. We, his servants,
will start rebuilding, but you have no share,
claim, or memorial in Jerusalem."

Builders of the Wall

3 Eliashib the high priest and his fellow
priests went to work and rebuilt the
Sheep Gate. They gave it to the Lord's service
and set its doors in place. They worked as far
as the Tower of the Hundred and gave it to
the Lord's service. Then they went on to the
Tower of Hananel. 2Next to them, the people
of Jericho built part of the wall, and Zaccur
son of Imri built next to them.

3The sons of Hassenaah rebuilt the Fish
Gate, laying its boards and setting its doors,
bolts, and bars in place. 4Meremoth son of
Uriah, the son of Hakkoz, made repairs next
to them. Meshullam son of Berekiah, the son
of Meshezabel, made repairs next to
Meremoth. And Zadok son of Baana made

repairs next to Meshullam. [5]The people from
Tekoa made repairs next to them, but the
leading men of Tekoa would not work under
their supervisors.

[6]Joiada son of Paseah and Meshullam son
of Besodeiah repaired the Old Gate. They laid
its boards and set its doors, bolts, and bars in
place. [7]Next to them, Melatiah from Gibeon,
other men from Gibeon and Mizpah, and
Jadon from Meronoth made repairs. These
places were ruled by the governor of
Trans-Euphrates. [8]Next to them, Uzziel son
of Harhaiah, a goldsmith, made repairs. And
next to him, Hananiah, a perfume maker,
made repairs. These men rebuilt Jerusalem
as far as the Broad Wall. [9]The next part of
the wall was repaired by Rephaiah son of
Hur, the ruler of half of the district of
Jerusalem. [10]Next to him, Jedaiah son of
Harumaph made repairs opposite his own
house. And next to him, Hattush son of
Hashabneiah made repairs. [11]Malkijah son of
Harim and Hasshub son of Pahath-Moab
repaired another part of the wall and the
Tower of the Ovens. [12]Next to them Shallum
son of Hallohesh, the ruler of half of the
district of Jerusalem, and his daughters made
repairs.

[13]Hanun and the people of Zanoah
repaired the Valley Gate, rebuilding it and
setting its doors, bolts, and bars in place.
They also repaired the five hundred yards of
the wall to the Trash Gate.

[14]Malkijah son of Recab, the ruler of the
district of Beth Hakkerem, repaired the
Trash Gate. He rebuilt that gate and set its
doors, bolts, and bars in place.

[15]Shallun son of Col-Hozeh, the ruler of
the district of Mizpah, repaired the Fountain
Gate. He rebuilt it, put a roof over it, and set
its doors, bolts, and bars in place. He also
repaired the wall of the Pool of Siloam next
to the King's Garden all the way to the steps
that went down from the older part of the
city. [16]Next to Shallun was Nehemiah[n] son of
Azbuk, the ruler of half of the district of Beth
Zur. He made repairs opposite the tombs of
David and as far as the man-made pool and
the House of the Heroes.

[17]Next to him, the Levites made repairs,
working under Rehum son of Bani. Next to
him, Hashabiah, the ruler of half of the
district of Keilah, for his district. [18]Next to
him, Binnui son of Henadad and his relatives
made repairs. Binnui was the ruler of the
other half of the district of Keilah. [19]Next to
them, Ezer son of Jeshua, the ruler of
Mizpah, repaired another part of the wall.
He worked across from the way up to the
armory, as far as the bend. [20]Next to him,
Baruch son of Zabbai worked hard on the
wall that went from the bend to the entrance
to the house of Eliashib, the high priest.
[21]Next to him, Meremoth son of Uriah, the
son of Hakkoz, repaired the wall that went
from the entrance to Eliashib's house to the
far end of it.

[22]Next to him worked the priests from the
surrounding area. [23]Next to them, Benjamin
and Hasshub made repairs in front of their
own house. Next to them, Azariah son of
Maaseiah, the son of Ananiah, made repairs
beside his own house. [24]Next to him, Binnui
son of Henadad repaired the wall that went
from Azariah's house to the bend and on to
the corner. [25]Palal son of Uzai worked across
from the bend and by the tower on the
upper palace, which is near the courtyard of
the king's guard. Next to Palal, Pedaiah son
of Parosh made repairs. [26]The Temple
servants who lived on the hill of Ophel made
repairs as far as a point opposite the Water
Gate. They worked toward the east and the
tower that extends from the palace. [27]Next to
them, the people of Tekoa repaired the wall
from the great tower that extends from the
palace to the wall of Ophel.

[28]The priests made repairs above the
Horse Gate, each working in front of his own
house. [29]Next to them, Zadok son of Immer
made repairs across from his own house.
Next to him, Shemaiah son of Shecaniah, the
guard of the East Gate, made repairs. [30]Next
to him, Hananiah son of Shelemiah, and
Hanun, the sixth son of Zalaph, made repairs
on another part of the wall. Next to them,
Meshullam son of Berekiah made repairs
across from where he lived. [31]Next to him,
Malkijah, one of the goldsmiths, made
repairs. He worked as far as the house of the
Temple servants and the traders, which is
across from the Inspection Gate, and as far as
the room above the corner of the wall. [32]The
goldsmiths and the traders made repairs

3:16 Nehemiah This is a different Nehemiah than the one who wrote this book.

between the room above the corner of the
wall and the Sheep Gate.

Those Against the Rebuilding

4 When Sanballat heard we were
rebuilding the wall, he was very angry,
even furious. He made fun of the Jewish
people. 2He said to his friends and those
with power in Samaria, "What are these
weak Jews doing? Will they rebuild the
wall? Will they offer sacrifices? Can they
finish it in one day? Can they bring stones
back to life from piles of trash and ashes?"
3Tobiah the Ammonite, who was next to
Sanballat, said, "If a fox climbed up on the
stone wall they are building, it would break
it down."
4I prayed, "Hear us, our God. We are hated.
Turn the insults of Sanballat and Tobiah
back on their own heads. Let them be
captured and stolen like valuables. 5Do not
hide their guilt or take away their sins so
that you can't see them, because they have
insulted the builders."
6So we rebuilt the wall to half its height,
because the people were willing to work.
7But Sanballat, Tobiah, the Arabs, the
Ammonites, and the people from Ashdod
were very angry when they heard that the
repairs to Jerusalem's walls were continuing
and that the holes in the wall were being
closed. 8So they all made plans to come to
Jerusalem and fight and stir up trouble. 9But
we prayed to our God and appointed guards
to watch for them day and night.
10The people of Judah said, "The workers
are getting tired. There is so much trash we
cannot rebuild the wall."
11And our enemies said, "The Jews won't
know or see anything until we come among
them and kill them and stop the work."
12Then the Jewish people who lived near
our enemies came and told us ten times,
"Everywhere you turn, the enemy will attack
us." 13So I put people behind the lowest
places along the wall—the open places—
and I put families together with their
swords, spears, and bows. 14Then I looked
around and stood up and said to the
important men, the leaders, and the rest of
the people: "Don't be afraid of them.
Remember the Lord, who is great and
powerful. Fight for your brothers, your sons
and daughters, your wives, and your homes."
15Then our enemies heard that we knew
about their plans and that God had ruined
their plans. So we all went back to the wall,
each to his own work.
16From that day on, half my people
worked on the wall. The other half was
ready with spears, shields, bows, and armor.
The officers stood in back of the people of
Judah 17who were building the wall. Those
who carried materials did their work with
one hand and carried a weapon with the
other. 18Each builder wore his sword at his
side as he worked. The man who blew the
trumpet to warn the people stayed next to
me.
19Then I said to the important people, the
leaders, and everyone else, "This is a very big
job. We are spreading out along the wall so
that we are far apart. 20Wherever you hear
the sound of the trumpet, assemble there.
Our God will fight for us."
21So we continued to work with half the
men holding spears from sunrise till the
stars came out. 22At that time I also said to
the people, "Let every man and his helper
stay inside Jerusalem at night. They can be
our guards at night and workmen during the
day." 23Neither I, my brothers, my workers,
nor the guards with me ever took off our
clothes. Each person carried his weapon
even when he went for water.

Nehemiah Helps Poor People

5 The men and their wives complained
loudly against their fellow Jews. 2Some
of them were saying, "We have many sons
and daughters in our families. To eat and
stay alive, we need grain."
3Others were saying, "We are borrowing
money against our fields, vineyards, and
homes to get grain because there is not
much food."
4And still others were saying, "We are
borrowing money to pay the king's tax on
our fields and vineyards. 5We are just like
our fellow Jews, and our sons are like their
sons. But we have to sell our sons and
daughters as slaves. Some of our daughters
have already been sold. But there is nothing
we can do, because our fields and vineyards
already belong to other people."
6When I heard their complaints about
these things, I was very angry. 7After I
thought about it, I accused the important

people and the leaders, "You are charging
your own brothers too much interest." So I
called a large meeting to deal with them. 8I
said to them, "As much as possible, we have
bought freedom for our fellow Jews who had
been sold to foreigners. Now you are selling
your fellow Jews to us!" The leaders were
quiet and had nothing to say.
9Then I said, "What you are doing is not
right. Don't you fear God? Don't let our
foreign enemies shame us. 10I, my brothers,
and my men are also lending money and
grain to the people. But stop charging them
so much for this. 11Give back their fields,
vineyards, olive trees, and houses right now.
Also give back the extra amount you
charged—the hundredth part of the money,
grain, new wine, and oil."
12They said, "We will give it back and not
demand anything more from them. We will
do as you say."
Then I called for the priests, and I made
the important people and leaders take an
oath to do what they had said. 13Also I shook
out the folds of my robe and said, "In this
way may God shake out everyone who does
not keep his promise. May God shake him
out of his house and out of the things that
are his. Let that person be shaken out and
emptied!"
Then the whole group said, "Amen," and
they praised the LORD. So the people did
what they had promised.
14I was appointed governor in the land of
Judah in the twentieth year of King
Artaxerxes' rule. I was governor of Judah for
twelve years, until his thirty-second year.
During that time neither my brothers nor I
ate the food that was allowed for a governor.
15But the governors before me had placed a
heavy load on the people. They took about
one pound of silver from each person, along
with food and wine. The governors' helpers
before me also controlled the people, but I
did not do that, because I feared God. 16I
worked on the wall, as did all my men who
were gathered there. We did not buy any
fields.

devotion 115

NEHEMIAH 5:1–13

SELLING YOUR BROTHER OUT . . . LITERALLY

The people of Judah had already rebuilt the Temple in Jerusalem. Nehemiah came to guide them in rebuilding the city walls and reordering their lives. His mission was to restore the protection they needed to keep their enemies out. But in the middle of the project, an attack by the dreaded enemy became a secondary threat. One of Nehemiah's biggest challenges was happening inside the hearts of the people.

His people had turned on one another. They were charging ridiculous rates of interest on grain. Families were having to sell their children into slavery just to pay the exorbitant rates charged by fellow Jews. This poverty and mistreatment had left the people bitter and hopeless. Nehemiah made them promise before God to deal fairly and compassionately with one another.

The people of God should be compassionate every chance we get. Life is just too hard. Almost everyone has more to carry than is reasonable. Emotional neglect is rampant, not to mention the strain of just paying the bills and getting to the end of the month. What if believers always responded fairly? What if people felt the compassion of God in our presence? What if our words brought encouragement to them instead of more guilt and pain? What if we stood under burdens with one another instead of adding more weight?

What if, indeed. Not only would God be glorified but hearts would be healed and lives restored. And people would truly come to know the beauty of compassion.

17 Also, I fed one hundred fifty Jewish
people and officers at my table, as well as
those who came from the nations around us.
18 This is what was prepared every day: one
ox, six good sheep, and birds. And every ten
days there were all kinds of wine. But I never
demanded the food that was due a governor,
because the people were already working
very hard.
19 Remember to be kind to me, my God, for
all the good I have done for these people.

More Problems for Nehemiah

6 Then Sanballat, Tobiah, Geshem the
Arab, and our other enemies heard that
I had rebuilt the wall and that there was not
one gap in it. But I had not yet set the doors
in the gates. 2 So Sanballat and Geshem sent
me this message: "Come, Nehemiah, let's
meet together in Kephirim on the plain
But they were planning to harm me. 3 So
I sent messengers to them with this answer:
"I am doing a great work, and I can't come
down. I don't want the work to stop while
I leave to meet you." 4 Sanballat and
Geshem sent the same message to me four
times, and each time I sent back the same
answer.
5 The fifth time Sanballat sent his helper
to me with the message, and in his hand
was an unsealed letter. 6 This is what was
written:

> A report is going around to all
> the nations, and Geshem says it is
> true, that you and the Jewish
> people are planning to turn
> against the king and that you are
> rebuilding the wall. They say you
> are going to be their king 7 and
> that you have appointed prophets
> to announce in Jerusalem: "There
> is a king of Judah!" The king will
> hear about this. So come, let's
> discuss this together.

8 So I sent him back this answer: "Nothing
you are saying is really happening. You are
just making it up in your own mind."
9 Our enemies were trying to scare us,
thinking, "They will get too weak to work.
Then the wall will not be finished."
But I prayed, "God, make me strong."
10 One day I went to the house of
Shemaiah son of Delaiah, the son of
Mehetabel. Shemaiah had to stay at home.
He said, "Nehemiah, let's meet in the Temple
of God. Let's go inside the Temple and close
the doors, because men are coming at night
to kill you."
11 But I said, "Should a man like me run
away? Should I run for my life into the
Temple? I will not go." 12 I knew that God
had not sent him but that Tobiah and
Sanballat had paid him to prophesy against
me. 13 They paid him to frighten me so I
would do this and sin. Then they could give
me a bad name to shame me.
14 I prayed, "My God, remember Tobiah
and Sanballat and what they have done. Also
remember the prophetess Noadiah and the
other prophets who have been trying to
frighten me."

The Wall Is Finished

15 The wall of Jerusalem was completed on
the twenty-fifth day of the month of Elul. It
took fifty-two days to rebuild. 16 When all
our enemies heard about it and all the
nations around us saw it, they were shamed.
They then understood that the work had
been done with the help of our God.
17 Also in those days the important people
of Judah sent many letters to Tobiah, and he
answered them. 18 Many Jewish people had
promised to be faithful to Tobiah, because he
was the son-in-law of Shecaniah son of Arah.
And Tobiah's son Jehohanan had married the
daughter of Meshullam son of Berekiah.
19 These important people kept telling me
about the good things Tobiah was doing, and
then they would tell Tobiah what I said
about him. So Tobiah sent letters to
frighten me.
7 After the wall had been rebuilt and I had
set the doors in place, the gatekeepers,
singers, and Levites were chosen. 2 I put my
brother Hanani, along with Hananiah, the
commander of the palace, in charge of
Jerusalem. Hananiah was honest and feared
God more than most people. 3 I said to them,
"The gates of Jerusalem should not be
opened until the sun is hot. While the
gatekeepers are still on duty, have them
shut and bolt the doors. Appoint people
who live in Jerusalem as guards, and put
some at guard posts and some near their
own houses."

The Captives Who Returned

4 The city was large and roomy, but there
were few people in it, and the houses had
not yet been rebuilt. 5 Then my God caused
me to gather the important people, the
leaders, and the common people so I could
register them by families. I found the family
history of those who had returned first. This
is what I found written there:

6 These are the people of the area who
returned from captivity, whom
Nebuchadnezzar king of Babylon had taken
away. They returned to Jerusalem and Judah,
each going back to his own town. 7 These
people returned with Zerubbabel, Jeshua,
Nehemiah, Azariah, Raamiah, Nahamani,
Mordecai, Bilshan, Mispereth, Bigvai,
Nehum, and Baanah.

These are the people from Israel: 8 the
descendants of Parosh—2,172; 9 the
descendants of Shephatiah—372; 10 the
descendants of Arah—652; 11 the
descendants of Pahath-Moab (through the
family of Jeshua and Joab)—2,818; 12 the
descendants of Elam—1,254; 13 the
descendants of Zattu—845; 14 the
descendants of Zaccai—760; 15 the
descendants of Binnui—648; 16 the
descendants of Bebai—628; 17 the
descendants of Azgad—2,322; 18 the
descendants of Adonikam—667; 19 the
descendants of Bigvai—2,067; 20 the
descendants of Adin—655; 21 the descendants
of Ater (through Hezekiah)—98; 22 the
descendants of Hashum—328; 23 the
descendants of Bezai—324; 24 the
descendants of Hariph—112; 25 the
descendants of Gibeon—95.

26 These are the people from the towns of
Bethlehem and Netophah—188; 27 of
Anathoth—128; 28 of Beth Azmaveth—42;
29 of Kiriath Jearim, Kephirah, and Beeroth—
743; 30 of Ramah and Geba—621; 31 of
Micmash—122; 32 of Bethel and Ai—123; 33 of
the other Nebo—52; 34 of the other Elam—
1,254; 35 of Harim—320; 36 of Jericho—345;
37 of Lod, Hadid, and Ono—721; 38 of
Senaah—3,930.

39 These are the priests: the descendants of
Jedaiah (through the family of Jeshua)—973;
40 the descendants of Immer—1,052; 41 the
descendants of Pashhur—1,247; 42 the
descendants of Harim—1,017.

43 These are the Levites: the descendants of
Jeshua (through Kadmiel through the family
of Hodaviah)—74.

44 These are the singers: the descendants of
Asaph—148.

45 These are the gatekeepers: the
descendants of Shallum, Ater, Talmon,
Akkub, Hatita, and Shobai—138.

46 These are the Temple servants: the
descendants of Ziha, Hasupha, Tabbaoth,
47 Keros, Sia, Padon, 48 Lebana, Hagaba,
Shalmai, 49 Hanan, Giddel, Gahar, 50 Reaiah,
Rezin, Nekoda, 51 Gazzam, Uzza, Paseah,
52 Besai, Meunim, Nephussim, 53 Bakbuk,
Hakupha, Harhur, 54 Bazluth, Mehida,
Harsha, 55 Barkos, Sisera, Temah, 56 Neziah,
and Hatipha.

57 These are the descendants of the
servants of Solomon: the descendants of
Sotai, Sophereth, Perida, 58 Jaala, Darkon,
Giddel, 59 Shephatiah, Hattil, Pokereth-
Hazzebaim, and Amon.

60 The Temple servants and the
descendants of the servants of Solomon
totaled 392 people.

61 Some people came to Jerusalem from
the towns of Tel Melah, Tel Harsha, Kerub,
Addon, and Immer, but they could not prove
that their ancestors came from Israel. Here
are their names and their number: 62 the
descendants of Delaiah, Tobiah, and
Nekoda—642.

63 And these priests could not prove that
their ancestors came from Israel: the
descendants of Hobaiah, Hakkoz, and
Barzillai. (He had married a daughter of
Barzillai from Gilead and was called by her
family name.)

64 These people searched for their family
records, but they could not find them. So
they could not be priests, because they were
thought to be unclean. 65 The governor
ordered them not to eat any of the holy food
until a priest settled this matter by using the
Urim and Thummim.

66 The total number of those who returned
was 42,360. 67 This is not counting their 7,337
male and female servants and the 245 male
and female singers with them. 68 They had
736 horses, 245 mules, 69 435 camels, and
6,720 donkeys.

70 Some of the family leaders gave to the
work. The governor gave to the treasury
about 19 pounds of gold, 50 bowls, and 530

pieces of clothing for the priests. [71]Some of
the family leaders gave about 375 pounds of
gold and about 2,660 pounds of silver to the
treasury for the work. [72]The total of what the
other people gave was about 375 pounds of
gold, about 2,250 pounds of silver, and 67
pieces of clothing for the priests. [73]So these
people all settled in their own towns: the
priests, the Levites, the gatekeepers, the
singers, the Temple servants, and all the
other people of Israel.

Ezra Reads the Teachings

By the seventh month the Israelites were
settled in their own towns.

8 All the people of Israel gathered together
in the square by the Water Gate. They
asked Ezra the teacher to bring out the Book
of the Teachings of Moses, which the LORD
had given to Israel.
[2]So on the first day of the seventh month,
Ezra the priest brought out the Teachings for
the crowd. Men, women, and all who could
listen and understand had gathered. [3]At the
square by the Water Gate Ezra read the
Teachings out loud from early morning until
noon to the men, women, and everyone who
could listen and understand. All the people
listened carefully to the Book of the
Teachings.
[4]Ezra the teacher stood on a high wooden
platform that had been built just for this
time. On his right were Mattithiah, Shema,
Anaiah, Uriah, Hilkiah, and Maaseiah. And
on his left were Pedaiah, Mishael, Malkijah,
Hashum, Hashbaddanah, Zechariah, and
Meshullam.
[5]Ezra opened the book in full view of
everyone, because he was above them. As he
opened it, all the people stood up. [6]Ezra
praised the LORD, the great God, and all the
people held up their hands and said, "Amen!
Amen!" Then they bowed down and
worshiped the LORD with their faces to the
ground.
[7]These Levites explained the Teachings to
the people as they stood there: Jeshua, Bani,
Sherebiah, Jamin, Akkub, Shabbethai,
Hodiah, Maaseiah, Kelita, Azariah, Jozabad,
Hanan, and Pelaiah. [8]They read from the
Book of the Teachings of God and explained
what it meant so the people understood
what was being read.
[9]Then Nehemiah the governor, Ezra the
priest and teacher, and the Levites who were
teaching said to all the people, "This is a
holy day to the LORD your God. Don't be
sad or cry." All the people had been crying
as they listened to the words of the
Teachings.
[10]Nehemiah said, "Go and enjoy good food
and sweet drinks. Send some to people who
have none, because today is a holy day to the
Lord. Don't be sad, because the joy of the
LORD will make you strong."
[11]The Levites helped calm the people,
saying, "Be quiet, because this is a holy day.
Don't be sad."
[12]Then all the people went away to eat
and drink, to send some of their food to
others, and to celebrate with great joy. They
finally understood what they had been
taught.
[13]On the second day of the month, the
leaders of all the families, the priests, and the
Levites met with Ezra the teacher. They
gathered to study the words of the
Teachings. [14]This is what they found written
in the Teachings: The LORD commanded
through Moses that the people of Israel were
to live in shelters during the feast of the
seventh month. [15]The people were supposed
to preach this message and spread it through
all their towns and in Jerusalem: "Go out
into the mountains, and bring back branches
from olive and wild olive trees, myrtle trees,
palms, and shade trees. Make shelters with
them, as it is written."
[16]So the people went out and got tree
branches. They built shelters on their roofs,[n]
in their courtyards, in the courtyards of the
Temple, in the square by the Water Gate, and
in the square next to the Gate of Ephraim.
[17]The whole group that had come back from
captivity built shelters and lived in them.
The Israelites had not done this since the
time of Joshua son of Nun. And they were
very happy.
[18]Ezra read to them every day from the
Book of the Teachings, from the first day
to the last. The people of Israel celebrated
the feast for seven days, and then on the

8:16 roofs In Bible times houses were built with flat roofs. The roof was used for drying things such as flax and fruit. And it was used as an extra room, as a place for worship, and as a cool place to sleep in the summer.

devotion 116

NEHEMIAH 8:10

KNOW WHEN TO LOOK UP

Nehemiah's heart desire was for the people to stop weeping about their inferior, sinful souls and be encouraged in the joy of the Lord. He wanted them to eat, drink, and honor a holy day of celebration. As a pastor's wife, I can relate. Today it seems like churches are having condemnation parties with a pastor in the pulpit making people feeling worse than they already do. Don't get me wrong, there is a place for the conviction of the Holy Spirit, but to beat people up is deadening. As my husband leaves his seat next to me each week, he always leans over to give me a kiss, and I whisper to him, "Give them hope."

I want people to leave our fellowship encouraged as well as spiritually grown up and ready to serve. Do you run in, make sure your kids are settled, grab a cup of coffee, and then take a seat? What about greeting someone new? What about listening to the Holy Spirit say, "Go pray with that hurting woman"? God is speaking to you, giving you an opportunity to bless someone. Share what you have. How many clothes do you have in your closet that you do not wear? How many bikes are hanging in your garage that you don't ride? How many new mothers do you know that would enjoy a lunch date out of the house? Celebrate, woman! You have a God that has equipped you to receive joy and be contagious. Now that's church!

eighth day the people gathered as the law said.

Israel Confesses Sins

9 On the twenty-fourth day of that same
month, the people of Israel gathered.
They fasted, and they wore rough cloth and
put dust on their heads to show their
sadness. 2Those people whose ancestors
were from Israel had separated themselves
from all foreigners. They stood and
confessed their sins and their ancestors'
sins. 3For a fourth of the day they stood
where they were and read from the Book of
the Teachings of the LORD their God. For
another fourth of the day they confessed
their sins and worshiped the LORD their
God. 4These Levites were standing on the
stairs: Jeshua, Bani, Kadmiel, Shebaniah,
Bunni, Sherebiah, Bani, and Kenani. They
called out to the LORD their God with loud
voices. 5Then these Levites spoke: Jeshua,
Kadmiel, Bani, Hashabneiah, Sherebiah,
Hodiah, Shebaniah, and Pethahiah. They
said, "Stand up and praise the LORD your
God, who lives forever and ever."

The People's Prayer

"Blessed be your wonderful name.
It is more wonderful than all blessing
and praise.
6You are the only LORD.
You made the heavens, even the highest
heavens,
with all the stars.
You made the earth and everything on it,
the seas and everything in them;
you give life to everything.
The heavenly army worships you.

7"You are the LORD,
the God who chose Abram
and brought him out of Ur in Babylonia
and named him Abraham.
8You found him faithful to you,
so you made an agreement with him
to give his descendants the land of the
Canaanites,

Hittites, Amorites,
Perizzites, Jebusites, and Girgashites.
You have kept your promise,
because you do what is right.

9"You saw our ancestors suffering in Egypt
and heard them cry out at the Red Sea.
10You did signs and miracles against the king of Egypt,
and against all his officers and all his people,
because you knew how proud they were.
You became as famous as you are today.
11You divided the sea in front of our ancestors;
they walked through on dry ground.
But you threw the people chasing them into the deep water,
like a stone thrown into mighty waters.
12You led our ancestors with a pillar of cloud by day
and with a pillar of fire at night.
It lit the way
they were supposed to go.
13You came down to Mount Sinai
and spoke from heaven to our ancestors.
You gave them fair rules and true teachings,
good orders and commands.
14You told them about your holy Sabbath
and gave them commands, orders, and teachings
through your servant Moses.
15When they were hungry, you gave them bread from heaven.
When they were thirsty, you brought them water from the rock.
You told them to enter and take over
the land you had promised to give them.

16"But our ancestors were proud and stubborn
and did not obey your commands.
17They refused to listen;
they forgot the miracles you did for them.
So they became stubborn and turned against you,
choosing a leader to take them back to slavery.
But you are a forgiving God.
You are kind and full of mercy.
You do not become angry quickly, and you have great love.
So you did not leave them.
18Our ancestors even made an idol of a calf for themselves.
They said, 'This is your god, Israel,
who brought you up out of Egypt.'
They spoke against you.

19"You have great mercy,
so you did not leave them in the desert.
The pillar of cloud guided them by day,
and the pillar of fire led them at night,
lighting the way they were to go.
20You gave your good Spirit to teach them.
You gave them manna to eat
and water when they were thirsty.
21You took care of them for forty years in the desert;
they needed nothing.
Their clothes did not wear out,
and their feet did not swell.

22"You gave them kingdoms and nations;
you gave them more land.
They took over the country of Sihon king of Heshbon
and the country of Og king of Bashan.
23You made their children as many as the stars in the sky,
and you brought them into the land
that you told their ancestors to enter and take over.
24So their children went into the land and took over.
The Canaanites lived there, but you defeated them for our ancestors.
You handed over to them the Canaanites,
their kings, and the people of the land.
Our ancestors could do what they wanted with them.
25They captured strong, walled cities and fertile land.
They took over houses full of good things,
wells that were already dug,
vineyards, olive trees, and many fruit trees.
They ate until they were full and grew fat;
they enjoyed your great goodness.

26"But they were disobedient and turned against you
and ignored your teachings.

Your prophets warned them to come back
to you,
but they killed those prophets
and spoke against you.
27 So you handed them over to their enemies,
and their enemies treated them badly.
But in this time of trouble our ancestors
cried out to you,
and you heard from heaven.
You had great mercy
and gave them saviors who saved them
from the power of their enemies.
28 But as soon as they had rest,
they again did what was evil.
So you left them to their enemies
who ruled over them.
When they cried out to you again,
you heard from heaven.
Because of your mercy, you saved them
again and again.
29 You warned them to return to your
teachings,
but they were proud and did not obey
your commands.
If someone obeys your laws, he will live,
but they sinned against your laws.
They were stubborn, unwilling, and
disobedient.
30 You were patient with them for many
years
and warned them by your Spirit
through the prophets,
but they did not pay attention.
So you handed them over to other
countries.
31 But because your mercy is great, you did
not kill them all or leave them.
You are a kind and merciful God.

32 "And so, our God, you are the great and
mighty and wonderful God.
You keep your agreement of love.
Do not let all our trouble seem
unimportant to you.
This trouble has come to us, to our kings
and our leaders,
to our priests and prophets,
to our ancestors and all your people
from the days of the kings of Assyria until
today.
33 You have been fair in everything that has
happened to us;
you have been loyal, but we have been
wicked.
34 Our kings, leaders, priests, and ancestors
did not obey your teachings;
they did not pay attention to the
commands and warnings you gave
them.
35 Even when our ancestors were living in
their kingdom,
enjoying all the good things you had
given them,
enjoying the land that was fertile and
full of room,
they did not stop their evil ways.

36 "Look, we are slaves today
in the land you gave our ancestors.
They were to enjoy its fruit and its good
things,
but look, we are slaves here.
37 The land's great harvest belongs to the
kings you have put over us
because of our sins.
Those kings rule over us and our cattle as
they please,
so we are in much trouble.

The People's Agreement

38 "Because of all this, we are making an
agreement in writing, and our leaders,
Levites, and priests are putting their seals
on it."

10 These are the men who sealed the
agreement:

Nehemiah the governor, son of
Hacaliah.

Zedekiah, 2 Seraiah, Azariah, Jeremiah,
3 Pashhur, Amariah, Malkijah, 4 Hattush,
Shebaniah, Malluch, 5 Harim, Meremoth,
Obadiah, 6 Daniel, Ginnethon, Baruch,
7 Meshullam, Abijah, Mijamin, 8 Maaziah,
Bilgai, and Shemaiah. These are the
priests.

9 These are the Levites who sealed it:
Jeshua son of Azaniah, Binnui of the sons of
Henadad, Kadmiel, 10 and their fellow
Levites: Shebaniah, Hodiah, Kelita, Pelaiah,
Hanan, 11 Mica, Rehob, Hashabiah, 12 Zaccur,
Sherebiah, Shebaniah, 13 Hodiah, Bani, and
Beninu.

14 These are the leaders of the people who
sealed the agreement: Parosh, Pahath-Moab,
Elam, Zattu, Bani, 15 Bunni, Azgad, Bebai,
16 Adonijah, Bigvai, Adin, 17 Ater, Hezekiah,
Azzur, 18 Hodiah, Hashum, Bezai, 19 Hariph,
Anathoth, Nebai, 20 Magpiash, Meshullam,

Hezir, 21 Meshezabel, Zadok, Jaddua,
22 Pelatiah, Hanan, Anaiah, 23 Hoshea,
Hananiah, Hasshub, 24 Hallohesh, Pilha,
Shobek, 25 Rehum, Hashabnah, Maaseiah,
26 Ahiah, Hanan, Anan, 27 Malluch, Harim,
and Baanah.

28 The rest of the people took an oath.
They were the priests, Levites, gatekeepers,
singers, Temple servants, all those who
separated themselves from foreigners to
keep the Teachings of God, and also their
wives and their sons and daughters who
could understand. 29 They joined their fellow
Israelites and their leading men in taking an
oath, which was tied to a curse in case they
broke the oath. They promised to follow the
Teachings of God, which they had been
given through Moses the servant of God, and
to obey all the commands, rules, and laws of
the LORD our God.

> We promise not to let our
> daughters marry foreigners nor to
> let our sons marry their daughters.
> 31 Foreigners may bring goods or
> grain to sell on the Sabbath, but
> we will not buy on the Sabbath or
> any holy day. Every seventh year
> we will not plant, and that year we
> will forget all that people owe us.
>
> 32 We will be responsible for the
> commands to pay for the service
> of the Temple of our God. We will
> give an eighth of an ounce of
> silver each year. 33 It is for the
> bread that is set out on the table;
> the regular grain offerings and
> burnt offerings; the offerings on
> the Sabbaths, New Moon festivals,
> and special feasts; the holy
> offerings; the offerings to remove
> the sins of the Israelites so they
> will belong to God; and for the
> work of the Temple of our God.
>
> 34 We, the priests, the Levites,
> and the people, have thrown lots
> to decide at what time of year each
> family must bring wood to the
> Temple. The wood is for burning
> on the altar of the LORD our God,
> and we will do this as it is written
> in the Teachings.
>
> 35 We also will bring the
> firstfruits from our crops and the
> firstfruits of every tree to the
> Temple each year.
>
> 36 We will bring to the Temple
> our firstborn sons and cattle and
> the firstborn of our herds and
> flocks, as it is written in the
> Teachings. We will bring them to
> the priests who are serving in the
> Temple.
>
> 37 We will bring to the priests at
> the storerooms of the Temple the
> first of our ground meal, our
> offerings, the fruit from all our
> trees, and our new wine and oil.
> And we will bring a tenth of our
> crops to the Levites, who will
> collect these things in all the
> towns where we work. 38 A priest
> of Aaron's family must be with the
> Levites when they receive the
> tenth of the people's crops. The
> Levites must bring a tenth of all
> they receive to the Temple of our
> God to put in the storerooms of
> the treasury. 39 The people of Israel
> and the Levites are to bring to the
> storerooms the gifts of grain, new
> wine, and oil. That is where the
> utensils for the Temple are kept
> and where the priests who are
> serving, the gatekeepers, and
> singers stay.
>
> We will not ignore the Temple
> of our God.

New People Move into Jerusalem

11 The leaders of Israel lived in
Jerusalem. But the rest of the people
threw lots to choose one person out of every
ten to come and live in Jerusalem, the holy
city. The other nine could stay in their own
cities. 2 The people blessed those who
volunteered to live in Jerusalem.

3 These are the area leaders who lived in
Jerusalem. (Some people lived on their own
land in the cities of Judah. These included
Israelites, priests, Levites, Temple servants,
and descendants of Solomon's servants.
4 Others from the families of Judah and
Benjamin lived in Jerusalem.)

These are the descendants of Judah who
moved into Jerusalem. There was Athaiah
son of Uzziah. (Uzziah was the son of

Zechariah, the son of Amariah. Amariah was
the son of Shephatiah, the son of Mahalalel.
Mahalalel was a descendant of Perez.) [5]There
was also Maaseiah son of Baruch. (Baruch
was the son of Col-Hozeh, the son of
Hazaiah. Hazaiah was the son of Adaiah, the
son of Joiarib. Joiarib was the son of
Zechariah, a descendant of Shelah.) [6]All the
descendants of Perez who lived in Jerusalem
totaled 468 men. They were soldiers.
[7]These are descendants of Benjamin who
moved into Jerusalem. There was Sallu son
of Meshullam. (Meshullam was the son of
Joed, the son of Pedaiah. Pedaiah was the son
of Kolaiah, the son of Maaseiah. Maaseiah
was the son of Ithiel, the son of Jeshaiah.)
[8]Following him were Gabbai and Sallai, for a
total of 928 men. [9]Joel son of Zicri was
appointed over them, and Judah son of
Hassenuah was second in charge of the new
area of the city.
[10]These are the priests who moved into
Jerusalem. There was Jedaiah son of Joiarib,
Jakin, [11]and Seraiah son of Hilkiah, the
supervisor in the Temple. (Hilkiah was the
son of Meshullam, the son of Zadok. Zadok
was the son of Meraioth, the son of Ahitub.)
[12]And there were others with them who did
the work for the Temple. All together there
were 822 men. Also there was Adaiah son of
Jeroham. (Jeroham was the son of Pelaliah,
the son of Amzi. Amzi was the son of
Zechariah, the son of Pashhur. Pashhur was
the son of Malkijah.) [13]And there were
family heads with him. All together there
were 242 men. Also there was Amashsai son
of Azarel. (Azarel was the son of Ahzai, the
son of Meshillemoth. Meshillemoth was the
son of Immer.) [14]And there were brave men
with Amashsai. All together there were 128
men. Zabdiel son of Haggedolim was
appointed over them.
[15]These are the Levites who moved into
Jerusalem. There was Shemaiah son of
Hasshub. (Hasshub was the son of Azrikam,
the son of Hashabiah. Hashabiah was the
son of Bunni.) [16]And there were Shabbethai
and Jozabad, two of the leaders of the Levites
who were in charge of the work outside the
Temple. [17]There was Mattaniah son of Mica.
(Mica was the son of Zabdi, the son of
Asaph.) Mattaniah was the director who led
the people in thanksgiving and prayer. There
was Bakbukiah, who was second in charge
over his fellow Levites. And there was Abda
son of Shammua. (Shammua was the son of
Galal, the son of Jeduthun.) [18]All together
284 Levites lived in the holy city of
Jerusalem.
[19]The gatekeepers who moved into
Jerusalem were Akkub, Talmon, and others
with them. There was a total of 172 men
who guarded the city gates.
[20]The other Israelites, priests, and Levites
lived on their own land in all the cities of
Judah.
[21]The Temple servants lived on the hill of
Ophel, and Ziha and Gishpa were in charge
of them.
[22]Uzzi son of Bani was appointed over the
Levites in Jerusalem. (Bani was the son of
Hashabiah, the son of Mattaniah. Mattaniah
was the son of Mica.) Uzzi was one of
Asaph's descendants, who were the singers
responsible for the servi[illegible]
[23]The singers were under the king's orders,
which regulated them day by day.
[24]Pethahiah son of Meshezabel was the
king's spokesman. (Meshezabel was a
descendant of Zerah, the son of Judah.)
[25]Some of the people of Judah lived in
villages with their surrounding fields. They
lived in Kiriath Arba and its surroundings, in
Dibon and its surroundings, in Jekabzeel and
its surroundings, [26]in Jeshua, Moladah, Beth
Pelet, [27]Hazar Shual, Beersheba and its
surroundings, [28]in Ziklag and Meconah and
its surroundings, [29]in En Rimmon, Zorah,
Jarmuth, [30]Zanoah, Adullam and their
villages, in Lachish and the fields around it,
and in Azekah and its surroundings. So they
settled from Beersheba all the way to the
Valley of Hinnom.
[31]The descendants of the Benjaminites
from Geba lived in Micmash, Aija, Bethel
and its surroundings, [32]in Anathoth, Nob,
Ananiah, [33]Hazor, Ramah, Gittaim, [34]Hadid,
Zeboim, Neballat, [35]Lod, Ono, and in the
Valley of the Craftsmen.
[36]Some groups of the Levites from Judah
settled in the land of Benjamin.

Priests and Levites

12 These are the priests and Levites who
returned with Zerubbabel son of
Shealtiel and with Jeshua. There were
Seraiah, Jeremiah, Ezra, [2]Amariah, Malluch,
Hattush, [3]Shecaniah, Rehum, Meremoth,

4Iddo, Ginnethon, Abijah, 5Mijamin,
Moadiah, Bilgah, 6Shemaiah, Joiarib, Jedaiah,
7Sallu, Amok, Hilkiah, and Jedaiah. They
were the leaders of the priests and their
relatives in the days of Jeshua.
8The Levites were Jeshua, Binnui,
Kadmiel, Sherebiah, Judah, and Mattaniah.
Mattaniah and his relatives were in charge
of the songs of thanksgiving. 9Bakbukiah
and Unni, their relatives, stood across from
them in the services.
10Jeshua was the father of Joiakim.
Joiakim was the father of Eliashib. Eliashib
was the father of Joiada. 11Joiada was the
father of Jonathan, and Jonathan was the
father of Jaddua.
12In the days of Joiakim, these priests were
the leaders of the families of priests:
Meraiah, from Seraiah's family; Hananiah,
from Jeremiah's family; 13Meshullam, from
Amariah's
family; 14Jonathan, from Malluch's family;
Joseph, from Shecaniah's family; 15Adna,
from Harim's family; Helkai, from
Meremoth's family; 16Zechariah, from Iddo's
family; Meshullam, from Ginnethon's
family; 17Zicri, from Abijah's family; Piltai,
from Miniamin's and Moadiah's families;
18Shammua, from Bilgah's family;
Jehonathan, from Shemaiah's family;
19Mattenai, from Joiarib's family; Uzzi, from
Jedaiah's family; 20Kallai, from Sallu's family;
Eber, from Amok's family; 21Hashabiah,
from Hilkiah's family; and Nethanel, from
Jedaiah's family.
22The leaders of the families of the Levites
and the priests were written down in the
days of Eliashib, Joiada, Johanan, and Jaddua,
while Darius the Persian was king. 23The
family leaders among the Levites were
written down in the history book, but only
up to the time of Johanan son of Eliashib.
24The leaders of the Levites were Hashabiah,
Sherebiah, Jeshua son of Kadmiel, and their
relatives. Their relatives stood across from
them and gave praise and thanksgiving to
God. One group answered the other group,
as David, the man of God, had commanded.
25These were the gatekeepers who
guarded the storerooms next to the gates:
Mattaniah, Bakbukiah, Obadiah, Meshullam,
Talmon, and Akkub. 26They served in the
days of Joiakim son of Jeshua, the son of
Jozadak. They also served in the days of
Nehemiah the governor and Ezra the priest
and teacher.

The Wall of Jerusalem

27When the wall of Jerusalem was offered
as a gift to God, they asked the Levites to
come from wherever they lived to Jerusalem
to celebrate with joy the gift of the wall.
They were to celebrate with songs of
thanksgiving and with the music of
cymbals, harps, and lyres. 28They also
brought together singers from all around
Jerusalem, from the Netophathite villages,
29from Beth Gilgal, and from the areas of
Geba and Azmaveth. The singers had built
villages for themselves around Jerusalem.
30The priests and Levites made themselves
pure, and they also made the people, the
gates, and the wall of Jerusalem pure.
31I had the leaders of Judah go up on top
of the wall, and I appointed two large
choruses to give thanks. One chorus went to
the right on top of the wall, toward the
Trash Gate. 32Behind them went Hoshaiah
and half the leaders of Judah. 33Azariah, Ezra,
Meshullam, 34Judah, Benjamin, Shemaiah,
and Jeremiah also went. 35Some priests with
trumpets also went, along with Zechariah
son of Jonathan. (Jonathan was the son of
Shemaiah, the son of Mattaniah. Mattaniah
was the son of Micaiah, the son of Zaccur.
Zaccur was the son of Asaph.) 36Zechariah's
relatives also went. They were Shemaiah,
Azarel, Milalai, Gilalai, Maai, Nethanel,
Judah, and Hanani. These men played the
musical instruments of David, the man of
God, and Ezra the teacher walked in front of
them. 37They went from the Fountain Gate
straight up the steps to the highest part of
the wall by the older part of the city. They
went on above the house of David to the
Water Gate on the east.
38The second chorus went to the left,
while I followed them on top of the wall
with half the people. We went from the
Tower of the Ovens to the Broad Wall, 39over
the Gate of Ephraim to the Old Gate and the
Fish Gate, to the Tower of Hananel and the
Tower of the Hundred. We went as far as the
Sheep Gate and stopped at the Gate of the
Guard.
40The two choruses took their places at
the Temple. Half of the leaders and I did also.
41These priests were there with their

trumpets: Eliakim, Maaseiah, Miniamin,
Micaiah, Elioenai, Zechariah, and Hananiah.
42These people were also there: Maaseiah,
Shemaiah, Eleazar, Uzzi, Jehohanan,
Malkijah, Elam, and Ezer. The choruses sang,
led by Jezrahiah. 43The people offered many
sacrifices that day and were happy because
God had given them great joy. The women
and children were happy. The sound of
happiness in Jerusalem could be heard far
away.
44At that time the leaders appointed men
to be in charge of the storerooms. These
rooms were for the gifts, the firstfruits, and
the ten percent that the people brought. The
Teachings said they should bring a share for
the priests and Levites from the fields
around the towns. The people of Judah were
happy to do this for the priests and Levites
who served. 45They performed the service of
their God in making things pure. The singers
and gatekeepers also did their jobs, as David
had commanded his son Solomon. 46Earlier,
in the time of David and Asaph, there was a
leader of the singers and of the songs of
praise and thanksgiving to God. 47So it was
in the days of Zerubbabel and Nehemiah. All
the people of Israel gave something to the
singers and gatekeepers, and they also set
aside part for the Levites. Then the Levites
set aside part for the descendants of Aaron.

Foreign People Are Sent Away

13 On that day they read the Book of
Moses to the people, and they found
that it said no Ammonite or Moabite should
ever be allowed in the meeting to worship.
2The Ammonites and Moabites had not
welcomed the Israelites with food and water.
Instead, they had hired Balaam to put a curse
on Israel. (But our God turned the curse into
a blessing.) 3When the people heard this
teaching, they separated all foreigners from
Israel.

Nehemiah Returns to Jerusalem

4Before that happened, Eliashib the priest,
who was in charge of the Temple
storerooms, was friendly with Tobiah.
5Eliashib let Tobiah use one of the large
storerooms. Earlier it had been used for grain
offerings, incense, the utensils, and the tenth
offerings of grain, new wine, and olive oil
that belonged to the Levites, singers, and
gatekeepers. It had also been used for gifts
for the priests.
6I was not in Jerusalem when this
happened. I had gone back to Artaxerxes
king of Babylon in the thirty-second year he
was king. Finally I asked the king to let me
leave. 7When I returned to Jerusalem, I
found out the evil Eliashib had done by
letting Tobiah have a room in the Temple
courtyard. 8I was very upset at this, so I
threw all of Tobiah's goods out of the room.
9I ordered the rooms to be purified, and I
brought back the utensils for God's Temple,
the grain offerings, and the incense.
10Then I found out the people were not
giving the Levites their shares. So the Levites
and singers who served had gone back to
their own farms. 11I argued with the officers,
saying, "Why haven't you taken care of the
Temple?" Then I gathered the Levites and
singers and put them back at their
12All the people of Judah then brought to
the storerooms a tenth of their crops, new
wine, and olive oil. 13I put these men in
charge of the storerooms: Shelemiah the
priest, Zadok the teacher, and Pedaiah a
Levite. I made Hanan son of Zaccur, the son
of Mattaniah, their helper. Everyone knew
they were honest. They gave out the
portions that went to their relatives.
14Remember me, my God, for this. Do not
ignore my love for the Temple and its
service.
15In those days I saw people in Judah
working in the winepresses on the Sabbath
day. They were bringing in grain and loading
it on donkeys. And they were bringing loads
of wine, grapes, and figs into Jerusalem on
the Sabbath day. So I warned them about
selling food on that day. 16People from the
city of Tyre who were living in Jerusalem
brought in fish and other things and sold
them there on the Sabbath day to the people
of Judah. 17I argued with the important men
of Judah and said to them, "What is this evil
thing you are doing? You are ruining the
Sabbath day. 18This is just what your
ancestors did. So our God did terrible things
to us and this city. Now you are making him
even more angry at Israel by ruining the
Sabbath day."
19So I ordered that the doors be shut at
sunset before the Sabbath and not be
opened until the Sabbath was over. I put my

servants at the gates so no load could come
in on the Sabbath. [20]Once or twice traders
and sellers of all kinds of goods spent the
night outside Jerusalem. [21]So I warned
them, "Why are you spending the night by
the wall? If you do it again, I will force you
away." After that, they did not come back
on the Sabbath. [22]Then I ordered the
Levites to purify themselves and to guard
the city gates to make sure the Sabbath
remained holy.

Remember me, my God, for this. Have
mercy on me because of your great love.

[23]In those days I saw men of Judah who
had married women from Ashdod, Ammon,
and Moab. [24]Half their children were
speaking the language of Ashdod or some
other place, and they couldn't speak the
language of Judah. [25]I argued with those
people, put curses on them, hit some of
them, and pulled out their hair. I forced
them to make a promise to God, saying, "Do
not let your daughters marry the sons of
foreigners, and do not take the daughters of
foreigners as wives for your sons or
yourselves. [26]Foreign women made King
Solomon of Israel sin. There was never a
king like him in any of the nations. God
loved Solomon and made him king over all
Israel, but foreign women made him sin.
[27]And now you are not obedient when you
do this evil thing. You are unfaithful to our
God when you marry foreign wives."

[28]Joiada was the son of Eliashib the high
priest. One of Joiada's sons married a
daughter of Sanballat the Horonite, so I sent
him away from me.

[29]Remember them, my God, because they
made the priesthood unclean and the
agreement of the priests and Levites
unclean.

[30]So I purified them of everything that
was foreign. I appointed duties for the
priests and Levites, giving each man his own
job. [31]I also made sure wood was brought for
the altar at regular times and that the
firstfruits were brought.

Remember me, my God; be kind to me.

Esther

The second of only two books in the Bible named after a woman (the other is Ruth), this book is the last of the Old Testament historical books.

Person Holding the Pen God Wrote With: Officially the author is anonymous, although some theologians believe the author to be Esther's cousin *Mordecai.* Other possible authors include *Ezra* and *Nehemiah.*

When the Text Was Written: Because of the Persian themes throughout, Esther was probably written prior to Greece's victory over Persia in 331 B.C. In light of the way it is "casually assumed" that King Xerxes' monarchy is over at the end of the story (Esth. 10:2), it's unlikely that it was recorded after his assassination around 465 B.C.

Spiritual Posture of the Original Recipients: Esther records a slice of history when Persia ruled the ancient world, including the country of Israel. This text coincides with the time frame of Ezra when God's people were enjoying their liberation from Babylon and praising Jehovah's faithfulness. But they were also struggling with the hardship of resettling their homeland and facing oppression from other people groups.

Storyline Synopsis: This particular event takes place during a ten-year segment of Persian king Xerxes' reign. The gist of the story is that Xerxes has dethroned his queen in a fit of chauvinistic rage and needs a replacement—so he stages a massive beauty pageant to find a new mate. An exceptionally lovely young Jewish woman named Esther wins his favor and gets the tiara. More importantly, God uses Esther's courage—spurred on by her godly cousin Mordecai—to sabotage a wicked plot to annihilate the Jewish people.

A Moment Worth Discussing: Esther's predecessor, the woman formerly known as Queen Vashti, is an interesting character to chat about. Her refusal of King Xerxes' request to "come join the party" (Esth. 1:10–12) is sometimes defined as an act of rebellion, but her mettle actually deserves admiration. She essentially risked life and limb—not to mention a cushy job and an amazing house—when she told her inebriated husband that she wasn't about to parade around in front of his leering buddies. While her stand cost her the crown, her dignity was still intact!

Interesting (But Likely to Be Overlooked) Character: A guy named *Hegai,* who had the responsibility of caring for and coordinating all the gorgeous girls vying for Queen Vashti's vacated position (Esth. 2:8–9). One can only imagine how difficult it was to manage all those debutantes!

Queen Vashti Disobeys the King

1 This is what happened during the time of
King Xerxes, the king who ruled the one
hundred twenty-seven states from India
to Cush. 2In those days King Xerxes ruled
from his capital city of Susa. 3In the third
year of his rule, he gave a banquet for all his
important men and royal officers. The army
leaders from the countries of Persia and
Media and the important men from all
Xerxes' empire were there.
4The banquet lasted one hundred eighty
days. All during that time King Xerxes was
showing off the great wealth of his kingdom
and his own great riches and glory. 5When
the one hundred eighty days were over, the
king gave another banquet. It was held in
the courtyard of the palace garden for seven
days, and it was for everybody in the palace
at Susa, from the greatest to the least. 6The
courtyard had fine white curtains and
purple drapes that were tied to silver rings
on marble pillars by white and purple cords.
And there were gold and silver couches on a
floor set with tiles of white marble, shells,
and gems. 7Wine was served in gold cups of
various kinds. And there was plenty of the
king's wine, because he was very generous.
8The king commanded that the guests be
permitted to drink as much as they wished.
He told the wine servers to serve each man
what he wanted.
9Queen Vashti also gave a banquet for the
women in the royal palace of King Xerxes.
10On the seventh day of the banquet, King
Xerxes was very happy, because he had been
drinking much wine. He gave a command to
the seven eunuchs who served him—
Mehuman, Biztha, Harbona, Bigtha, Abagtha,
Zethar, and Carcas. 11He commanded them
to bring him Queen Vashti, wearing her
royal crown. She was to come to show her
beauty to the people and important men,
because she was very beautiful. 12The
eunuchs told Queen Vashti about the king's
command, but she refused to come. Then the
king became very angry; his anger was like a
burning fire.
13It was a custom for the king to ask
advice from experts about law and order. So
King Xerxes spoke with the wise men who
would know the right thing to do. 14The
wise men the king usually talked to were
Carshena, Shethar, Admatha, Tarshish,
Meres, Marsena, and Memucan, seven of the
important men of Persia and Media. These
seven had special privileges to see the king
and had the highest rank in the kingdom.
15The king asked them, "What does the law
say must be done to Queen Vashti? She has
not obeyed the command of King Xerxes,
which the eunuchs took to her."
16Then Memucan said to the king and the
other important men, "Queen Vashti has not
done wrong to the king alone. She has also
done wrong to all the important men and all
the people in all the empire of King Xerxes.
17All the wives of the important men of
Persia and Media will hear about the queen's
actions. Then they will no longer honor
their husbands. They will say, 'King Xerxes
commanded Queen Vashti to be brought to
him, but she refused to come.' 18Today the
wives of the important men of Persia and
Media have heard about the queen's actions.
So they will speak in the same way to their
husbands, and there will be no end to
disrespect and anger.
19"So, our king, if it pleases you, give a
royal order, and let it be written in the laws
of Persia and Media, which cannot be
changed. The law should say Vashti is never
again to enter the presence of King Xerxes.
Also let the king give her place as queen to
someone who is better than she is. 20And let
the king's order be announced everywhere
in his enormous kingdom. Then all the
women will respect their husbands, from the
greatest to the least."
21The king and his important men were
happy with this advice, so King Xerxes did as
Memucan suggested. 22He sent letters to all
the states of the kingdom in the writing of
each state and in the language of each group
of people. These letters announced that each
man was to be the ruler of his own family.

Esther Is Made Queen

2 Later, when King Xerxes was not so
angry, he remembered Vashti and what
she had done and his order about her. 2Then
the king's personal servants suggested, "Let a
search be made for beautiful young girls for
the king. 3Let the king choose supervisors in
every state of his kingdom to bring every
beautiful young girl to the palace at Susa.
They should be taken to the women's

Esther

Queen Esther listens as her servant delivers word from her cousin Mordecai. It is fantastical, but she knows in her heart that it's true: Haman, one of the king's high-ranking officers, has convinced the king to order all the Jews killed. She and Mordecai are both Jewish.

But what Mordecai has asked is too much for her. She cannot go before the king! Anyone who approaches the king's throne without being summoned is subject to death. Mordecai receives Esther's message declining the dangerous task, but he sends another message for the woman he adopted as his own child.

Esther listens as the servant repeats the words of Mordecai: "And who knows, you may have been chosen queen for just such a time as this." Esther's heart is pierced. This seems like an impossible request, but her entire life was a tale of the impossible—a Jewish orphan was now queen of a great empire.

She sends word to Mordecai to have the Jewish people fast for three days. She clutches the hands of her servant girls. "Fast and pray with me," she says. Esther is willing to lay her life on the line and knows that it will only be through prayer that the king's heart will be softened to see her. Even then, she may die—but it is a risk she must take.

God lifts up ordinary people to accomplish his purposes but doesn't ask us to be extraordinary. He just asks us to be willing.

quarters and put under the care of Hegai, the
king's eunuch in charge of the women. And
let beauty treatments be given to them.
4 Then let the girl who most pleases the king
become queen in place of Vashti." The king
liked this idea, so he did as they said.
5 Now there was a Jewish man in the
palace of Susa whose name was Mordecai
son of Jair. Jair was the son of Shimei, the
son of Kish. Mordecai was from the tribe of
Benjamin, 6 which had been taken captive
from Jerusalem by Nebuchadnezzar king of
Babylon. They were part of the group taken
into captivity with Jehoiachin king of
Judah. 7 Mordecai had a cousin named
Hadassah, who had no father or mother, so
Mordecai took care of her. Hadassah was
also called Esther, and she had a very pretty
figure and face. Mordecai had adopted her
as his own daughter when her father and
mother died.
8 When the king's command and order
had been heard, many girls had been
brought to the palace in Susa and put under
the care of Hegai. Esther was also taken to
the king's palace and put under the care of
Hegai, who was in charge of the women.
9 Esther pleased Hegai, and he liked her. So
Hegai quickly began giving Esther her
beauty treatments and special food. He gave
her seven servant girls chosen from the
king's palace. Then he moved her and her
seven servant girls to the best part of the
women's quarters.
10 Esther did not tell anyone about her
family or who her people were, because
Mordecai had told her not to. 11 Every day
Mordecai walked back and forth near the
courtyard where the king's women lived to
find out how Esther was and what was
happening to her.
12 Before a girl could take her turn with
King Xerxes, she had to complete twelve
months of beauty treatments that were
ordered for the women. For six months she
was treated with oil and myrrh and for six
months with perfumes and cosmetics.
13 Then she was ready to go to the king.
Anything she asked for was given to her to
take with her from the women's quarters to
the king's palace. 14 In the evening she would
go to the king's palace, and in the morning
she would return to another part of the
women's quarters. There she would be

placed under the care of Shaashgaz, the
king's eunuch in charge of the slave women.
The girl would not go back to the king again
unless he was pleased with her and asked for
her by name.
15The time came for Esther daughter of
Abihail, Mordecai's uncle, who had been
adopted by Mordecai, to go to the king. She
asked for only what Hegai suggested she
should take. (Hegai was the king's eunuch
who was in charge of the women.) Everyone
who saw Esther liked her. 16So Esther was
taken to King Xerxes in the royal palace in
the tenth month, the month of Tebeth,
during Xerxes' seventh year as king.
17And the king was pleased with Esther
more than with any of the other virgins. He
liked her more than any of the others, so he
put a royal crown on her head and made her
queen in place of Vashti. 18Then the king
gave a great banquet for Esther and invited
all his important men and royal officers. He
announced a holiday for all the empire and
had the government give away gifts.

Mordecai Discovers an Evil Plan

19Now Mordecai was sitting at the king's
gate when the girls were gathered the
second time. 20Esther still had not told
anyone about her family or who her people
were, just as Mordecai had commanded her.
She obeyed Mordecai just as she had done
when she was under his care.
21Now Bigthana and Teresh were two of
the king's eunuchs who guarded the
doorway. While Mordecai was sitting at the
king's gate, they became angry and began to
make plans to kill King Xerxes. 22But
Mordecai found out about their plans and
told Queen Esther. Then Esther told the king
how Mordecai had discovered the evil plan.
23When the report was investigated, it was
found to be true, and the two officers who
had planned to kill the king were hanged.
All this was written down in the daily court
record in the king's presence.

Haman Plans to Destroy the Jewish People

3 After these things happened, King Xerxes
honored Haman son of Hammedatha the
Agagite. He gave him a new rank that was
higher than all the important men. 2All the
royal officers at the king's gate would bow
down and kneel before Haman, as the king
had ordered. But Mordecai would not bow
down or show him honor.
3Then the royal officers at the king's gate
asked Mordecai, "Why don't you obey the
king's command?" 4And they said this to
him every day. When he did not listen to
them, they told Haman about it. They
wanted to see if Haman would accept
Mordecai's behavior because Mordecai had
told them he was Jewish.
5When Haman saw that Mordecai would
not bow down to him or honor him, he
became very angry. 6He thought of himself
as too important to try to kill only Mordecai.
He had been told who the people of
Mordecai were, so he looked for a way to
destroy all of Mordecai's people, the Jews, in
all of Xerxes' kingdom.
7It was in the first month of the twelfth
year of King Xerxes' rule—the month of
Nisan. Pur (that is, the lot) was thrown
before Haman to choose a day and a month.
So the twelfth month, the month of Adar,
was chosen.
8Then Haman said to King Xerxes, "There
is a certain group of people scattered among
the other people in all the states of your
kingdom. Their customs are different from
those of all the other people, and they do
not obey the king's laws. It is not right for
you to allow them to continue living in
your kingdom. 9If it pleases the king, let an
order be given to destroy those people. Then
I will pay seven hundred fifty thousand
pounds of silver to those who do the king's
business, and they will put it into the royal
treasury."
10So the king took his signet ring off and
gave it to Haman son of Hammedatha, the
Agagite, the enemy of the Jewish people.
11Then the king said to Haman, "The money
and the people are yours. Do with them as
you please."
12On the thirteenth day of the first month,
the royal secretaries were called, and they
wrote out all of Haman's orders. They wrote
to the king's governors and to the captains of
the soldiers in each state and to the
important men of each group of people. The
orders were written in the writing of each
state and in the language of each people.
They were written in the name of King
Xerxes and sealed with his signet ring.
13Letters were sent by messengers to all the

king's empire ordering them to destroy, kill,
and completely wipe out all the Jewish
people. That meant young and old, women
and little children, too. It was to happen on a
single day—the thirteenth day of the twelfth
month, which was Adar. And they could
take everything the Jewish people owned.
[14]A copy of the order was given out as a law
in every state so all the people would be
ready for that day.
[15]The messengers set out, hurried by the
king's command, as soon as the order was
given in the palace at Susa. The king and
Haman sat down to drink, but the city of
Susa was in confusion.

Mordecai Asks Esther to Help

4 When Mordecai heard about all that had
been done, he tore his clothes, put on
rough cloth and ashes, and went out into the
city crying loudly and painfully. [2]But
Mordecai went only as far as the king's gate,
because no one was allowed to enter that
gate dressed in rough cloth. [3]As the king's
order reached every area, there was great
sadness and loud crying among the Jewish
people. They fasted and cried out loud, and
many of them lay down on rough cloth and
ashes to show how sad they were.
[4]When Esther's servant girls and eunuchs
came to her and told her about Mordecai,
she was very upset and afraid. She sent
clothes for Mordecai to put on instead of the
rough cloth, but he would not wear them.
[5]Then Esther called for Hathach, one of the
king's eunuchs chosen by the king to serve
her. Esther ordered him to find out what was
bothering Mordecai and why.
[6]So Hathach went to Mordecai, who was
in the city square in front of the king's gate.
[7]Mordecai told Hathach everything that had
happened to him, and he told Hathach about
the amount of money Haman had promised
to pay into the king's treasury for the killing
of the Jewish people. [8]Mordecai also gave
him a copy of the order to kill the Jewish
people, which had been given in Susa. He
wanted Hathach to show it to Esther and to
tell her about it. And Mordecai told him to
order Esther to go into the king's presence to
beg for mercy and to plead with him for her
people.

devotion 117

ESTHER 4:14

THE RIGHT WOMAN FOR THE JOB

The story of Esther is an amazing one. I remember being in the sixth grade at a Christian school and hearing this story for the first time. Our teacher would only read one chapter a day, and I couldn't wait to hear the rest of the story. I also remember thinking how exciting it would be to be used by God in such an incredible way. Esther was a young Jewish girl who became a queen in a foreign land. Who would have guessed that God would use her to save the Jewish people from being massacred? She was chosen to be queen for "just such a time as this."

You have been chosen for such a time as this. God has a plan and a purpose for your life. You never know when that time will be or what God will use you for, but you can know that he will use you. You just have to let him. How often do we keep quiet or not step out when God wants to use us? God will find someone else to do the job he intends to be done, but we will miss out on the excitement of being used by God in that particular situation. God uses us to bless us, and I've often heard people say how honored and encouraged they feel when they are used by God. Be bold when God brings a task for you to do for him. You never know what blessings God will bring!

9 Hathach went back and reported to
Esther everything Mordecai had said. 10 Then
Esther told Hathach to tell Mordecai, 11 "All
the royal officers and people of the royal
states know that no man or woman may go
to the king in the inner courtyard without
being called. There is only one law about
this: Anyone who enters must be put to
death unless the king holds out his gold
scepter. Then that person may live. And I
have not been called to go to the king for
thirty days."
12 Esther's message was given to Mordecai.
13 Then Mordecai sent back word to Esther:
"Just because you live in the king's palace,
don't think that out of all the Jewish people
you alone will escape. 14 If you keep quiet at
this time, someone else will help and save
the Jewish people, but you and your father's
family will all die. And who knows, you may
have been chosen queen for just such a time
as this."
15 Then Esther sent this answer to
Mordecai: 16 "Go and get all the Jewish people
in Susa together. For my sake, fast; do not eat
or drink for three days, night and day. I and
my servant girls will also fast. Then I will go
to the king, even though it is against the law,
and if I die, I die."
17 So Mordecai went away and did
everything Esther had told him to do.

Esther Speaks to the King

5 On the third day Esther put on her royal
robes and stood in the inner courtyard of
the king's palace, facing the king's hall. The
king was sitting on his royal throne in the
hall, facing the doorway. 2 When the king
saw Queen Esther standing in the courtyard,
he was pleased. He held out to her the gold
scepter that was in his hand, so Esther went
forward and touched the end of it.
3 The king asked, "What is it, Queen
Esther? What do you want to ask me? I will
give you as much as half of my kingdom."
4 Esther answered, "My king, if it pleases
you, come today with Haman to a banquet
that I have prepared for you."
5 Then the king said, "Bring Haman
quickly so we may do what Esther asks."
So the king and Haman went to the
banquet Esther had prepared for them. 6 As
they were drinking wine, the king said to
Esther, "Now, what are you asking for? I will
give it to you. What is it you want? I will
give you as much as half of my kingdom."
7 Esther answered, "This is what I want
and what I ask for. 8 My king, if you are
pleased with me and if it pleases you, give
me what I ask for and do what I want. Come
with Haman tomorrow to the banquet I will
prepare for you. Then I will answer your
question about what I want."

Haman's Plans Against Mordecai

9 Haman left the king's palace that day
happy and content. But when he saw
Mordecai at the king's gate and saw that
Mordecai did not stand up or tremble with
fear before him, Haman became very angry
with Mordecai. 10 But he controlled his anger
and went home.
Then Haman called together his friends
and his wife, Zeresh. 11 He told them how
wealthy he was and how many sons he had.
He also told them all the ways the king had
honored him and how the king had placed
him higher than his important men and his
royal officers. 12 He also said, "I'm the only
person Queen Esther invited to come with
the king to the banquet she gave. And
tomorrow also the queen has asked me to be
her guest with the king. 13 But all this does
not really make me happy when I see that
Jew Mordecai sitting at the king's gate."
14 Then Haman's wife, Zeresh, and all his
friends said, "Have a seventy-five foot
platform built, and in the morning ask the
king to have Mordecai hanged on it. Then go
to the banquet with the king and be happy."
Haman liked this suggestion, so he ordered
the platform to be built.

Mordecai Is Honored

6 That same night the king could not
sleep. So he gave an order for the daily
court record to be brought in and read to
him. 2 It was found recorded that Mordecai
had warned the king about Bigthana and
Teresh, two of the king's officers who
guarded the doorway and who had planned
to kill the king.
3 The king asked, "What honor and reward
have been given to Mordecai for this?"
The king's personal servants answered,
"Nothing has been done for Mordecai."

devotion 118

ESTHER 6:1–2

WHAT IF . . .

What if you lived like God is going before you to prepare the way? What if you trusted God to speak to your spirit about all that concerns you and knew that he will outline your steps, protect you from harm, fight your enemies, and open wide the doors that have been shut? Esther did. She knew that God wants to do all that and more for his beloved. Inside the strong arms of his embrace is every protection you will need. With his guidance, you will learn to hear his voice of warning and confidently follow his promptings.

Many of us don't know what the Holy Spirit's voice sounds like, so we must learn. We must go alongside people who walk with the Lord. We must begin to hang out where we are sure that God is. We must become familiar with what it feels like and looks like when God is near. We all need to live in a home where the Spirit abides so that we will know where the Spirit is not. It shouldn't feel right outside his presence, just like it shouldn't "sit well" with our spirits when evil is present.

God is making a way, but we must become students of his character and lovers of his presence. I fully believe this statement I once heard: "God does not reveal himself to the casual observer, but only to the passionate pursuer." May we become passionate in the pursuit of his presence and his voice.

4The king said, "Who is in the courtyard?"
Now Haman had just entered the outer court
of the king's palace. He had come to ask the
king about hanging Mordecai on the
platform he had prepared.
5The king's personal servants said,
"Haman is standing in the courtyard."
The king said, "Bring him in."
6So Haman came in. And the king asked
him, "What should be done for a man whom
the king wants very much to honor?"
And Haman thought to himself, "Whom
would the king want to honor more than
me?" 7So he answered the king, "This is what
you could do for the man you want very
much to honor. 8Have the servants bring a
royal robe that the king himself has worn.
And also bring a horse with a royal crown on
its head, a horse that the king himself has
ridden. 9Let the robe and the horse be given
to one of the king's most important men. Let
the servants put the robe on the man the
king wants to honor, and let them lead him
on the horse through the city streets. As they
are leading him, let them announce: 'This is
what is done for the man whom the king
wants to honor!' "
10The king commanded Haman, "Go
quickly. Take the robe and the horse just as
you have said, and do all this for Mordecai
the Jew who sits at the king's gate. Do not
leave out anything you have suggested."
11So Haman took the robe and the horse,
and he put the robe on Mordecai. Then he
led him on horseback through the city
streets, announcing before Mordecai: "This is
what is done for the man whom the king
wants to honor!"
12Then Mordecai returned to the king's
gate, but Haman hurried home with his
head covered, because he was embarrassed
and ashamed. 13He told his wife, Zeresh, and
all his friends everything that had happened
to him.
Haman's wife and the men who gave him
advice said, "You are starting to lose power to
Mordecai. Since he is a Jew, you cannot win
against him. You will surely be ruined."

14While they were still talking, the king's
eunuchs came to Haman's house and made
him hurry to the banquet Esther had
prepared.

Haman Is Hanged

7 So the king and Haman went in to eat
with Queen Esther. 2As they were
drinking wine on the second day, the king
asked Esther again, "What are you asking
for? I will give it to you. What is it you
want? I will give you as much as half of my
kingdom."

3Then Queen Esther answered, "My king,
if you are pleased with me, and if it pleases
you, let me live. This is what I ask. And let
my people live, too. This is what I want. 4My
people and I have been sold to be destroyed,
to be killed and completely wiped out. If we
had been sold as male and female slaves, I
would have kept quiet, because that would
not be enough of a problem to bother the
king."

5Then King Xerxes asked Queen Esther,
"Who is he, and where is he? Who has done
such a thing?"

6Esther said, "Our enemy and foe is this
wicked Haman!"

Then Haman was filled with terror before
the king and queen. 7The king was very
angry, so he got up, left his wine, and went
out into the palace garden. But Haman
stayed inside to beg Queen Esther to save his
life. He could see that the king had already
decided to kill him.

8When the king returned from the palace
garden to the banquet hall, he saw Haman
falling on the couch where Esther was lying.
The king said, "Will he even attack the
queen while I am in the house?"

As soon as the king said that, servants
came in and covered Haman's face.
9Harbona, one of the eunuchs there serving
the king, said, "Look, a seventy-five foot
platform stands near Haman's house. This is
the one Haman had prepared for Mordecai,
who gave the warning that saved the king."

The king said, "Hang Haman on it!" 10So
they hanged Haman on the platform he had
prepared for Mordecai. Then the king was
not so angry anymore.

The King Helps the Jewish People

8 That same day King Xerxes gave Queen
Esther everything Haman, the enemy of
the Jewish people, had left when he died.
And Mordecai came in to see the king,
because Esther had told the king how he was
related to her. 2Then the king took off his
signet ring that he had taken back from
Haman, and he gave it to Mordecai. Esther
put Mordecai in charge of everything
Haman left when he died.

3Once again Esther spoke to the king. She
fell at the king's feet and cried and begged
him to stop the evil plan that Haman the
Agagite had planned against the Jews. 4The
king held out the gold scepter to Esther. So
Esther got up and stood in front of him.

5She said, "My king, if you are pleased
with me, and if it pleases you to do this, if
you think it is the right thing to do, and if
you are happy with me, let an order be
written to cancel the letters Haman wrote.
Haman the Agagite sent messages to destroy
all the Jewish people in all of your kingdom.
6I could not stand to see that terrible thing
happen to my people. I could not stand to
see my family killed."

7King Xerxes answered Queen Esther and
Mordecai the Jew, "Because Haman was
against the Jewish people, I have given his
things to Esther, and my soldiers have
hanged him. 8Now, in the king's name, write
another order to the Jewish people as it
seems best to you. Then seal the order with
the king's signet ring, because no letter
written in the king's name and sealed with
his signet ring can be canceled."

9At that time the king's secretaries were
called. This was the twenty-third day of the
third month, which is Sivan. The secretaries
wrote out all of Mordecai's orders to the
Jews, to the governors, to the captains of the
soldiers in each state, and to the important
men of the one hundred twenty-seven states
that reached from India to Cush. They wrote
in the writing of each state and in the
language of each people. They also wrote to
the Jewish people in their own writing and
language. 10Mordecai wrote orders in the
name of King Xerxes and sealed the letters
with the king's signet ring. Then he sent the
king's orders by messengers on fast horses,
horses that were raised just for the king.

11These were the king's orders: The Jewish
people in every city have the right to gather
together to protect themselves. They may
destroy, kill, and completely wipe out the

army of any state or people who attack
them. And they are to do the same to the
women and children of that army. They may
also take by force the property of their
enemies. 12The one day set for the Jewish
people to do this in all the empire of King
Xerxes was the thirteenth day of the twelfth
month, the month of Adar. 13A copy of the
king's order was to be sent out as a law in
every state. It was to be made known to the
people of every nation living in the kingdom
so the Jewish people would be ready on that
set day to strike back at their enemies.

14The messengers hurried out, riding on
the royal horses, because the king
commanded those messengers to hurry. And
the order was also given in the palace at Susa.

15Mordecai left the king's presence
wearing royal clothes of blue and white and
a large gold crown. He also had a purple robe
made of the best linen. And the people of
Susa shouted for joy. 16It was a time of
happiness, joy, gladness, and honor for the
Jewish people. 17As the king's order went to
every state and city, there was joy and
gladness among the Jewish people. In every
state and city to which the king's order went,
they were having feasts and celebrating. And
many people through all the empire became
Jews, because they were afraid of the Jewish
people.

Victory for the Jewish People

9 The order the king had commanded was
to be done on the thirteenth day of the
twelfth month, the month of Adar. That was
the day the enemies of the Jewish people had
hoped to defeat them, but that was changed.
So the Jewish people themselves defeated
those who hated them. 2The Jews met in
their cities in all the empire of King Xerxes
in order to attack those who wanted to harm
them. No one was strong enough to fight
against them, because all the other people
living in the empire were afraid of them.
3All the important men of the states, the
governors, captains of the soldiers, and the
king's officers helped the Jewish people,
because they were afraid of Mordecai.
4Mordecai was very important in the king's
palace. He was famous in all the empire,
because he was becoming a leader of more
and more people.

5And, with their swords, the Jewish
people defeated all their enemies, killing and
destroying them. And they did what they
wanted with those people who hated them.
6In the palace at Susa, they killed and
destroyed five hundred men. 7They also
killed: Parshandatha, Dalphon, Aspatha,
8Poratha, Adalia, Aridatha, 9Parmashta,
Arisai, Aridai, and Vaizatha, 10the ten sons of
Haman, son of Hammedatha, the enemy of
the Jewish people. But the Jewish people did
not take their belongings.

11On that day the number killed in the
palace at Susa was reported to the king.
12The king said to Queen Esther, "The Jewish
people have killed and destroyed five
hundred people in the palace at Susa, and
they have also killed Haman's ten sons.
What have they done in the rest of the king's
empire! Now what else are you asking? I will
do it! What else do you want? It will be
done!"

13Esther answered, "If it pleases the king,
give the Jewish people who are in Susa
permission to do again tomorrow what the
king ordered for today. And let the bodies of
Haman's ten sons be hanged on the platform."

14So the king ordered that it be done. A
law was given in Susa, and the bodies of the
ten sons of Haman were hanged. 15The
Jewish people in Susa came together on the
fourteenth day of the month of Adar. They
killed three hundred people in Susa, but
they did not take their belongings.

16At that same time, all the Jewish people
in the king's empire also met to protect
themselves and get rid of their enemies.
They killed seventy-five thousand of those
who hated them, but they did not take their
belongings. 17This happened on the
thirteenth day of the month of Adar. On the
fourteenth day they rested and made it a day
of joyful feasting.

The Feast of Purim

18But the Jewish people in Susa met on the
thirteenth and fourteenth days of the month
of Adar. Then they rested on the fifteenth
day and made it a day of joyful feasting.

19This is why the Jewish people who live
in the country and small villages celebrate
on the fourteenth day of the month of Adar.
It is a day of joyful feasting and a day for
exchanging gifts.

20Mordecai wrote down everything that

had happened. Then he sent letters to all the Jewish people in all the empire of King Xerxes, far and near. 21 He told them to celebrate every year on the fourteenth and fifteenth days of the month of Adar, 22 because that was when the Jewish people got rid of their enemies. They were also to celebrate it as the month their sadness was turned to joy and their crying for the dead was turned into celebration. He told them to celebrate those days as days of joyful feasting and as a time for giving food to each other and presents to the poor.

23 So the Jewish people agreed to do what Mordecai had written to them, and they agreed to hold the celebration every year. 24 Haman son of Hammedatha, the Agagite, was the enemy of all the Jewish people. He had made an evil plan against the Jewish people to destroy them, and he had thrown the Pur (that is, the lot) to choose a day to ruin and destroy them. 25 But when the king learned of the evil plan, he sent out written orders that the evil plans Haman had made against the Jewish people would be used against him. And those orders said that Haman and his sons should be hanged on the platform. 26 So these days were called Purim, which comes from the word "Pur" (the lot). Because of everything written in this letter and what they had seen and what happened to them, 27 the Jewish people set up this custom. They and their descendants and all those who join them are always to celebrate these two days every year. They should do it in the right way and at the time Mordecai had ordered them in the letter. 28 These two days should be remembered and celebrated from now on in every family, in every state, and in every city. These days of Purim should always be celebrated by the Jewish people, and their descendants should always remember to celebrate them, too.

29 So Queen Esther daughter of Abihail, along with Mordecai the Jew, wrote this second letter about Purim. Using the power they had, they wrote to prove the first letter was true. 30 And Mordecai sent letters to all the Jewish people in the one hundred twenty-seven states of the kingdom of Xerxes, writing them a message of peace and truth. 31 He wrote to set up these days of Purim at the chosen times. Mordecai the Jew and Queen Esther had sent out the order for the Jewish people, just as they had set up things for themselves and their descendants: On these two days the people should fast and cry loudly. 32 Esther's letter set up the rules for Purim, and they were written down in the records.

The Greatness of Mordecai

10 King Xerxes demanded taxes everywhere, even from the cities on the seacoast. 2 And all the great things Xerxes did by his power and strength are written in the record books of the kings of Media and Persia. Also written in those record books are all the things done by Mordecai, whom the king made great. 3 Mordecai the Jew was second in importance to King Xerxes, and he was the most important man among the Jewish people. His fellow Jews respected him very much, because he worked for the good of his people and spoke up for the safety of all the Jewish people.

Job

The primary character in this story, Job's name in Hebrew means "afflicted one."

Person Holding the Pen God Wrote With: Like many of the Old Testament books, we can't be sure who wrote this.

When the Text Was Written: Sometime between the lifetimes of Moses and Ezra—from around 1400 to 450 B.C.

Spiritual Posture of the Original Recipients: While it is likely that Job was a historical character (Job 1:1) who lived in the ancient Near East, we don't know who the original audience for his saga was. We can be sure, however, that those who first heard it were familiar with hardship, which is a running theme in this drama.

Storyline Synopsis: The premise of this book deals with two basic questions: *Why does God allow suffering in a world under his control?* and *How should God's people respond when they suffer pain, disappointment, and loss?* Job wrestles with the first question to the point of demanding to have a little talk with God (Job 31:35–37). But Job finally learns how to graciously submit to God's merciful sovereignty—even in the midst of awful circumstances—after God puts him in his place with statements like, "Where were you when I made the earth's foundation?" (38:4–11). It's important to note that God didn't accuse Job of sin when Job revealed his frustration. Instead, God honored Job's honesty with compassion and blessings for his faith under pressure.

A Moment Worth Discussing: Chapters 32—37 cover what academics call "the Elihu Interruption." This is the moment when a godly guy named Elihu talks about the limitations of man's understanding as he contradicts the bad theology of Job's friends, Eliphaz, Bildad, and Zophar. These three had basically told Job that he must have committed some whopper sins to incur the kind of problems he was facing. But Elihu explains that a relationship with God doesn't exempt us from pain, nor does human suffering mean that God doesn't care about his people. This section provides great fodder for the age-old question, *If God is so loving, why do bad things happen to good people?*

Interesting (But Likely to Be Overlooked) Characters: Job's second set of daughters had wonderful prophetic names: *Jemimah* means "day light" and *Keziah* means "sweet smelling." They were gorgeous women and were given the same inheritance as their brothers (Job 42:13–15), which was highly unusual in this ancient culture.

Job, the Good Man

1 A man named Job lived in the land of Uz. He was an honest and innocent man; he honored God and stayed away from evil. 2Job had seven sons and three daughters. 3He owned seven thousand sheep, three thousand camels, five hundred teams of oxen, and five hundred female donkeys. He also had a large number of servants. He was the greatest man among all the people of the East.

4Job's sons took turns holding feasts in their homes and invited their sisters to eat and drink with them. 5After a feast was over, Job would send and have them made clean. Early in the morning Job would offer a burnt offering for each of them, because he thought, "My children may have sinned and cursed God in their hearts." Job did this every time.

Satan Appears Before the Lord

6One day the angels came to show themselves before the LORD, and Satan[n] was with them. 7The LORD said to Satan, "Where have you come from?"

Satan answered the LORD, "I have been wandering around the earth, going back and forth in it."

8Then the LORD said to Satan, "Have you noticed my servant Job? No one else on earth is like him. He is an honest and innocent man, honoring God and staying away from evil."

9But Satan answered the LORD, "Job honors God for a good reason. 10You have put a wall around him, his family, and everything he owns. You have blessed the things he has done. His flocks and herds are so large they almost cover the land. 11But reach out your hand and destroy everything he has, and he will curse you to your face."

12The LORD said to Satan, "All right, then. Everything Job has is in your power, but you must not touch Job himself." Then Satan left the LORD's presence.

13One day Job's sons and daughters were eating and drinking wine together at the oldest brother's house. 14A messenger came to Job and said, "The oxen were plowing and the donkeys were eating grass nearby, 15when the Sabeans attacked and carried them away. They killed the servants with swords, and I am the only one who escaped to tell you!"

16The messenger was still speaking when another messenger arrived and said, "Lightning from God fell from the sky. It burned up the sheep and the servants, and I am the only one who escaped to tell you!"

17The second messenger was still speaking when another messenger arrived and said, "The Babylonians sent three groups of attackers that swept down and stole your camels and killed the servants. I am the only one who escaped to tell you!"

18The third messenger was still speaking when another messenger arrived and said, "Your sons and daughters were eating and drinking wine together at the oldest brother's house. 19Suddenly a great wind came from the desert, hitting all four corners of the house at once. The house fell in on the young people, and they are all dead. I am the only one who escaped to tell you!"

20When Job heard this, he got up and tore his robe and shaved his head to show how sad he was. Then he bowed down to the ground to worship God. 21He said:

"I was naked when I was born,
    and I will be naked when I die.
The LORD gave these things to me,
    and he has taken them away.
    Praise the name of the LORD."

22In all this Job did not sin or blame God.

Satan Appears Before the Lord Again

2 On another day the angels came to show themselves before the LORD, and Satan was with them again. 2The LORD said to Satan, "Where have you come from?"

Satan answered the LORD, "I have been wandering around the earth, going back and forth in it."

3Then the LORD said to Satan, "Have you noticed my servant Job? No one else on earth is like him. He is an honest and innocent man, honoring God and staying away from evil. You caused me to ruin him for no good reason, but he continues to be without blame."

4"One skin for another!" Satan answered. "A man will give all he has to save his own

1:6 Satan Or "the accuser."

devotion 119

JOB 1:20–22

WHEN TRAGEDY COMES—AND IT WILL

Are you prepared to bless God in the day of your calamity? Will you be able to worship God as your Father, no matter how intense your grief or how deep the pain he allows?

Mark it down—virtually every one of us will experience a severe tragedy. And tragedy always seems meaningless, undeserved, and cruel. Most of our pain does not come as clear punishment for sin. Most of it seems to come from nowhere, confusing us with its randomness and injustice.

That's why Job's suffering is so relevant to us. His afflictions seemed to come out of nowhere, and they had no connection to his character. Job's story was recorded so that we will have help in living through the certain heartbreaks still to come. Job did more than keep a stiff upper lip. He showed us how to bow reverently in trust before the goodness of God Almighty. Job worshiped God even in his catastrophic loss, and therein lies the victory. The triumphant power of God was revealed in Job's character.

How will you respond to devastating news when it arrives? Will the truth of your character reveal God's glory, or will your emptiness be laid bare for all to see? Job could praise the Lord because he trusted God's supreme authority. He also trusted the good heart of God. Will you build a monument to God's authority in your heart so that when the day of testing comes, you will stand sure on the power of his love?

life. 5But reach out your hand and destroy
his flesh and bones, and he will curse you to
your face."

6The LORD said to Satan, "All right, then.
Job is in your power, but you may not take
his life."

7So Satan left the LORD's presence. He put
painful sores on Job's body, from the top of
his head to the soles of his feet. 8Job took a
piece of broken pottery to scrape himself,
and he sat in ashes in misery.

9Job's wife said to him, "Why are you
trying to stay innocent? Curse God and die!"

10Job answered, "You are talking like a
foolish woman. Should we take only good
things from God and not trouble?" In spite of
all this Job did not sin in what he said.

Job's Three Friends Come to Help

11Now Job had three friends: Eliphaz the
Temanite, Bildad the Shuhite, and Zophar
the Naamathite. When these friends heard
about Job's troubles, they agreed to meet and
visit him. They wanted to show their
concern and to comfort him. 12They saw Job
from far away, but he looked so different
they almost didn't recognize him. They
began to cry loudly and tore their robes and
put dirt on their heads to show how sad they
were. 13Then they sat on the ground with Job
seven days and seven nights. No one said a
word to him because they saw how much he
was suffering.

Job Curses His Birth

3 After seven days Job cried out and cursed
the day he had been born, 2saying:

3"Let the day I was born be destroyed,
and the night it was said, 'A boy is born!'
4Let that day turn to darkness.
Don't let God care about it.
Don't let light shine on it.
5Let darkness and gloom have that day.
Let a cloud hide it.
Let thick darkness cover its light.
6Let thick darkness capture that night.

Don't count it among the days of the
year
or put it in any of the months.
7 Let that night be empty,
with no shout of joy to be heard.
8 Let those who curse days curse that day.
Let them prepare to wake up the sea
monster Leviathan.
9 Let that day's morning stars never appear;
let it wait for daylight that never
comes.
Don't let it see the first light of dawn,
10 because it allowed me to be born
and did not hide trouble from my eyes.

11 "Why didn't I die as soon as I was born?
Why didn't I die when I came out of the
womb?
12 Why did my mother's knees receive me,
and my mother's breasts feed me?
13 If they had not been there,
I would be lying dead in peace;
I would be asleep and at rest
14 with kings and wise men of the earth
who built places for themselves that are
now ruined.
15 I would be asleep with rulers
who filled their houses with gold and
silver.
16 Why was I not buried like a child born
dead,
like a baby who never saw the light of
day?
17 In the grave the wicked stop making
trouble,
and the weary workers are at rest.
18 In the grave there is rest for the captives
who no longer hear the shout of the
slave driver.
19 People great and small are in the grave,
and the slave is freed from his master.

20 "Why is light given to those in misery?
Why is life given to those who are so
unhappy?
21 They want to die, but death does not
come.
They search for death more than for
hidden treasure.
22 They are very happy
when they get to the grave.
23 They cannot see where they are going.
God has hidden the road ahead.
24 I make sad sounds as I eat;
my groans pour out like water.
25 Everything I feared and dreaded
has happened to me.
26 I have no peace or quietness.
I have no rest, only trouble."

Eliphaz Speaks

4 Then Eliphaz the Temanite answered:
2 "If someone tried to speak with you,
would you be upset?
I cannot keep from speaking.
3 Think about the many people you have
taught
and the weak hands you have made
strong.
4 Your words have comforted those who
fell,
and you have strengthened those who
could not stand.
5 But now trouble comes to you, and you
are discouraged;
trouble hits you, and you are terrified.
6 You should have confidence because you
respect God;
you should have hope because you are
innocent.

7 "Remember that the innocent will not die;
honest people will never be destroyed.
8 I have noticed that people who plow evil
and plant trouble, harvest it.
9 God's breath destroys them,
and a blast of his anger kills them.
10 Lions may roar and growl,
but when the teeth of a strong lion are
broken,
11 that lion dies of hunger.
The cubs of the mother lion are
scattered.

12 "A word was brought to me in secret,
and my ears heard a whisper of it.
13 It was during a nightmare
when people are in deep sleep.
14 I was trembling with fear;
all my bones were shaking.
15 A spirit glided past my face,
and the hair on my body stood
on end.
16 The spirit stopped,
but I could not see what it was.
A shape stood before my eyes,
and I heard a quiet voice.
17 It said, 'Can a human be more right than
God?
Can a person be pure before his maker?

Job's Wife

JOB

She watches as her husband scrapes the painful boils on his body. He screams in pain as the boils burst open on his leg and ooze over his marred calf. Everything they had is now gone. Their ten children and all their flocks are dead. Her heart aches as she watches Job sit in the midst of ashes. *How could this happen to him?* she thinks. *He is an honest and innocent man.* All his life, Job had honored God and stayed away from evil.

She kneels down before him and from the depths of her soul says, "Why are you trying to stay innocent? Curse God and die!" She doesn't say it with evil on her lips, but with anguish. She cannot stand to sit back and watch her husband suffer any longer. She is the one who always hears his moans of agony. She is the one who watches his body twist in pain. She is the one who hears his cries at night for their children. Death seems a better answer than his continued suffering.

Job looks upon her, and tension eases from his face. His words are soft, not hard. "You are talking like a foolish woman. Should we take only good things from God and not trouble?" She nods and smiles. Job is still honoring God.

It honors God when we wait. Job's wife would have missed the blessing of their restored life together if Job had listened to her and not waited on God.

18God does not trust his angels;
he blames them for mistakes.
19So he puts even more blame on people
who live in clay houses,[n]
whose foundations are made of dust,
who can be crushed like a moth.
20Between dawn and sunset many people
are broken to pieces;
without being noticed, they die and are
gone forever.
21The ropes of their tents are pulled up,
and they die without wisdom.'

5 "Call if you want to, Job, but no one will
answer you.
You can't turn to any of the holy ones.
2Anger kills the fool,
and jealousy slays the stupid.
3I have seen a fool succeed,
but I cursed his home immediately.
4His children are far from safety
and are crushed in court with no
defense.
5The hungry eat his harvest,
even taking what grew among the
thorns,
and thirsty people want his wealth.
6Hard times do not come up from the
ground,
and trouble does not grow from the
earth.
7People produce trouble
as surely as sparks fly upward.

8"But if I were you, I would call on God
and bring my problem before him.
9God does wonders that cannot be
understood;
he does so many miracles they cannot
be counted.
10He gives rain to the earth
and sends water on the fields.
11He makes the humble person important
and lifts the sad to places of safety.
12He ruins the plans of those who trick
others
so they have no success.
13He catches the wise in their own clever
traps
and sweeps away the plans of those
who try to trick others.

4:19 clay houses This is probably talking about people's bodies.

devotion 120

JOB 5:2

ROOTS AND FRUIT

Does it take much to make you angry? Anger is not an emotion that is banned from our lives—even Jesus was angry with those who were buying and selling in the Temple. He was not sheepish about it either. He was *mad*. So mad that he physically turned over their tables and drove them out (Matt. 21:12-13). We have all known that kind of anger. It's the anger that turns us into giant mama bears the minute someone messes with our children, treats the innocent unjustly, or decides to mess with our men. Oh yeah, baby, mama is in the house, and you might as well substitute "wrath" for "anger."

However, the anger I am asking about is different from righteous anger. This other anger lives so close to the edge of your being that even when it is unprovoked, it still comes raging to the surface, destroying everything in its path. That anger that lives below the surface often has deep roots. Begin today by walking through your heart and life to figure out what you are holding on to, or not letting go of, that is causing this inferno of anger to be stoked. Spend some quiet time now and ask the Lord by the power of the Holy Spirit to show you the root of this unwanted anger. And may I make a suggestion? Retrieve a spiritual shovel, remove the roots, and replace them with the fruit of the Spirit (Gal. 5:22-23). Enjoy the harvest!

14 Darkness covers them up in the daytime;
even at noon they feel around in the dark.
15 God saves the needy from their lies
and from the harm done by powerful people.
16 So the poor have hope,
while those who are unfair are silenced.

17 "The one whom God corrects is happy,
so do not hate being corrected by the Almighty.
18 God hurts, but he also bandages up;
he injures, but his hands also heal.
19 He will save you from six troubles;
even seven troubles will not harm you.
20 God will buy you back from death in times of hunger,
and in battle he will save you from the sword.
21 You will be protected from the tongue that strikes like a whip,
and you will not be afraid when destruction comes.
22 You will laugh at destruction and hunger,
and you will not fear the wild animals,
23 because you will have an agreement with the stones in the field,
and the wild animals will be at peace with you.
24 You will know that your tent is safe,
because you will check the things you own and find nothing missing.
25 You will know that you will have many children,
and your descendants will be like the grass on the earth.
26 You will come to the grave with all your strength,
like bundles of grain gathered at the right time.

27 "We have checked this, and it is true,
so hear it and decide what it means to you."

Job Answers Eliphaz

6 Then Job answered:
2 "I wish my suffering could be weighed
and my misery put on scales.

3 My sadness would be heavier than the
sand of the seas.
No wonder my words seem careless.
4 The arrows of the Almighty are in me;
my spirit drinks in their poison;
God's terrors are gathered against me.
5 A wild donkey does not bray when it has
grass to eat,
and an ox is quiet when it has feed.
6 Tasteless food is not eaten without salt,
and there is no flavor in the white of an
egg.
7 I refuse to touch it;
such food makes me sick.

8 "How I wish that I might have what I ask
for
and that God would give me what I
hope for.
9 How I wish God would crush me
and reach out his hand to destroy me.
10 Then I would have this comfort
and be glad even in this unending pain,
because I would know I did not reject
the words of the Holy One.

11 "I do not have the strength to wait.
There is nothing to hope for,
so why should I be patient?
12 I do not have the strength of stone;
my flesh is not bronze.
13 I have no power to help myself,
because success has been taken away
from me.

14 "They say, 'A person's friends should be
kind to him when he is in trouble,
even if he stops fearing the Almighty.'
15 But my brothers cannot be counted on.
They are like streams that do not
always flow,
streams that sometimes run over.
16 They are made dark by melting ice
and rise with melting snow.
17 But they stop flowing in the dry season;
they disappear when it is hot.
18 Travelers turn away from their paths
and go into the desert and die.
19 The groups of travelers from Tema look
for water,
and the traders of Sheba look hopefully.
20 They are upset because they had been
sure;
when they arrive, they are
disappointed.
21 You also have been no help.
You see something terrible, and you are
afraid.
22 I have never said, 'Give me a gift.
Use your wealth to pay my debt.
23 Save me from the enemy's power.
Buy me back from the clutches of cruel
people.'

24 "Teach me, and I will be quiet.
Show me where I have been wrong.
25 Honest words are painful,
but your arguments prove nothing.
26 Do you mean to correct what I say?
Will you treat the words of a troubled
man as if they were only wind?
27 You would even gamble for orphans
and would trade away your friend.

28 "But now please look at me.
I would not lie to your face.
29 Change your mind; do not be unfair;
think again, because my innocence is
being questioned.
30 What I am saying is not wicked;
I can tell the difference between right
and wrong.

7 "People have a hard task on earth,
and their days are like those of a
laborer.
2 They are like a slave wishing for the
evening shadows,
like a laborer waiting to be paid.
3 But I am given months that are empty,
and nights of misery have been given
to me.
4 When I lie down, I think, 'How long until
I get up?'
The night is long, and I toss until dawn.
5 My body is covered with worms and
scabs,
and my skin is broken and full of sores.

6 "My days go by faster than a weaver's tool,
and they come to an end without hope.
7 Remember, God, that my life is only a
breath.
My eyes will never see happy times
again.
8 Those who see me now will see me no
more;
you will look for me, but I will be gone.
9 As a cloud disappears and is gone,
people go to the grave and never return.

[10]They will never come back to their
houses again,
and their places will not know them
anymore.

[11]"So I will not stay quiet;
I will speak out in the suffering of my
spirit.
I will complain because I am so
unhappy.
[12]I am not the sea or the sea monster.
So why have you set a guard over me?
[13]Sometimes I think my bed will comfort
me
or that my couch will stop my
complaint.
[14]Then you frighten me with dreams
and terrify me with visions.
[15]My throat prefers to be choked;
my bones welcome death.
[16]I hate my life; I don't want to live forever.
Leave me alone, because my days have
no meaning.

[17]"Why do you make people so important
and give them so much attention?
[18]You examine them every morning
and test them every moment.
[19]Will you never look away from me
or leave me alone even long enough to
swallow?
[20]If I have sinned, what have I done to you,
you watcher of humans?
Why have you made me your target?
Have I become a heavy load for you?
[21]Why don't you pardon my wrongs
and forgive my sins?
I will soon lie down in the dust of death.
Then you will search for me, but I will
be no more."

Bildad Speaks to Job

8 Then Bildad the Shuhite answered:
[2]"How long will you say such things?
Your words are no more than wind.
[3]God does not twist justice;
the Almighty does not make wrong
what is right.
[4]Your children sinned against God,
and he punished them for their sins.
[5]But you should ask God for help
and pray to the Almighty for mercy.
[6]If you are good and honest,
he will stand up for you
and bring you back where you belong.
[7]Where you began will seem unimportant,
because your future will be so
successful.

[8]"Ask old people;
find out what their ancestors learned,
[9]because we were only born yesterday and
know nothing.
Our days on earth are only a shadow.
[10]Those people will teach you and tell you
and speak about what they know.
[11]Papyrus plants cannot grow where there
is no swamp,
and reeds cannot grow tall without
water.
[12]While they are still growing and not yet
cut,
they will dry up quicker than grass.
[13]That is what will happen to those who
forget God;
the hope of the wicked will be gone.
[14]What they hope in is easily broken;
what they trust is like a spider's web.
[15]They lean on the spider's web, but it
breaks.
They grab it, but it does not hold up.
[16]They are like well-watered plants in the
sunshine
that spread their roots all through the
garden.
[17]They wrap their roots around a pile of
rocks
and look for a place among the stones.
[18]But if a plant is torn from its place,
then that place rejects it and says, 'I
never saw you.'
[19]Now joy has gone away;
other plants grow up from the same
dirt.

[20]"Surely God does not reject the innocent
or give strength to those who do evil.
[21]God will yet fill your mouth with
laughter
and your lips with shouts of joy.
[22]Your enemies will be covered with shame,
and the tents of the wicked will be
gone."

Job Answers Bildad

9 Then Job answered:
[2]"Yes, I know that this is true,
but how can anyone be right in the
presence of God?
[3]Someone might want to argue with God,

but no one could answer God,
not one time out of a thousand.
4 God's wisdom is deep, and his power is great;
no one can fight him without getting hurt.
5 God moves mountains without anyone knowing it
and turns them over when he is angry.
6 He shakes the earth out of its place
and makes its foundations tremble.
7 He commands the sun not to shine
and shuts off the light of the stars.
8 He alone stretches out the skies
and walks on the waves of the sea.
9 It is God who made the Bear, Orion, and the Pleiades[n]
and the groups of stars in the southern sky.
10 He does wonders that cannot be understood;
he does so many miracles they cannot be counted.
11 When he passes me, I cannot see him;
when he goes by me, I do not recognize him.
12 If he snatches something away, no one can stop him
or say to him, 'What are you doing?'
13 God will not hold back his anger.
Even the helpers of the monster Rahab lie at his feet in fear.
14 So how can I argue with God,
or even find words to argue with him?
15 Even if I were right, I could not answer him;
I could only beg God, my Judge, for mercy.
16 If I called to him and he answered,
I still don't believe he would listen to me.
17 He would crush me with a storm
and multiply my wounds for no reason.
18 He would not let me catch my breath
but would overwhelm me with misery.
19 When it comes to strength, God is stronger than I;
when it comes to justice, no one can accuse him.
20 Even if I were right, my own mouth would say I was wrong;
if I were innocent, my mouth would say I was guilty.

21 "I am innocent,
but I don't care about myself.
I hate my own life.
22 It is all the same. That is why I say,
'God destroys both the innocent and the guilty.'
23 If the whip brings sudden death,
God will laugh at the suffering of the innocent.
24 When the land falls into the hands of evil people,
he covers the judges' faces so they can't see it.
If it is not God who does this, then who is it?

25 "My days go by faster than a runner;
they fly away without my seeing any joy.
26 They glide past like paper boats.
They attack like eagles swooping down to feed.
27 Even though I say, 'I will forget my complaint;
I will change the look on my face and smile,'
28 I still dread all my suffering.
I know you will hold me guilty.
29 I have already been found guilty,
so why should I struggle for no reason?
30 I might wash myself with soap
and scrub my hands with strong soap,
31 but you would push me into a dirty pit,
and even my clothes would hate me.

32 "God is not human like me, so I cannot answer him.
We cannot meet each other in court.
33 I wish there were someone to make peace between us,
someone to decide our case.
34 Maybe he could remove God's punishment
so his terror would no longer frighten me.
35 Then I could speak without being afraid,
but I am not able to do that.

10 "I hate my life,
so I will complain without holding back;
I will speak because I am so unhappy.
2 I will say to God: Do not hold me guilty,
but tell me what you have against me.

9:9 Bear . . . Pleiades Names of well-known groups of stars.

devotion 121

JOB 9:10

MIRACLES AND WONDERS

One of my favorite places in the world is the Florida Keys. The sunsets are amazing as the sun slips over the edge of the ocean. The water is crystal clear, and the ocean breezes just kiss your face. I love to snorkel on the reefs with my children. They get so excited to see the brightly colored fish and the stingrays that swim beneath us. Even the nurse sharks bring a cry of delight to their lips as we become a part of God's underwater wonderland. After just one hour snorkeling down there, you'd have to agree with Job that God's wonders are beyond understanding.

God's miracles seem to be a little more hidden than his wonders, though. I think they happen in each of our lives every day, and we just don't know it. I believe he heals me from disease, he protects my children, he guards my marriage, and he even parts the interstate traffic some days. There are also miracles that God wants us to ask for in faith. He teaches us so much through those experiences when we have to believe even though we do not see the answers right away. I also believe that some day he will allow his miracles to be more visible. This will be a time when he is preparing his people for his return. Many Christians don't believe miracles exist today. But I say we have to believe—or we may miss the greatest miracle of all.

3 Does it make you happy to trouble me?
Don't you care about me, the work of your hands?
Are you happy with the plans of evil people?
4 Do you have human eyes
that see as we see?
5 Are your days like the days of humans,
and your years like our years?
6 You look for the evil I have done
and search for my sin.
7 You know I am not guilty,
but no one can save me from your power.

8 "Your hands shaped and made me.
Do you now turn around and destroy me?
9 Remember that you molded me like a piece of clay.
Will you now turn me back into dust?
10 You formed me inside my mother
like cheese formed from milk.
11 You dressed me with skin and flesh;
you sewed me together with bones and muscles.
12 You gave me life and showed me kindness,
and in your care you watched over my life.

13 "But in your heart you hid other plans.
I know this was in your mind.
14 If I sinned, you would watch me
and would not let my sin go unpunished.
15 How terrible it will be for me if I am guilty!
Even if I am right, I cannot lift my head.
I am full of shame
and experience only pain.
16 If I hold up my head, you hunt me like a lion
and again show your terrible power against me.
17 You bring new witnesses against me
and increase your anger against me.
Your armies come against me.

18"So why did you allow me to be born?
I wish I had died before anyone saw me.
19I wish I had never lived,
but had been carried straight from birth
to the grave.
20The few days of my life are almost over.
Leave me alone so I can have a moment
of joy.
21Soon I will leave; I will not return
from the land of darkness and gloom,
22the land of darkest night,
from the land of gloom and confusion,
where even the light is darkness."

Zophar Speaks to Job

11 Then Zophar the Naamathite
answered:
2"Should these words go unanswered?
Is this talker in the right?
3Your lies do not make people quiet;
people should correct you when you
make fun of God.
4You say, 'My teachings are right,
and I am clean in God's sight.'
5I wish God would speak
and open his lips against you
6and tell you the secrets of wisdom,
because wisdom has two sides.
Know this: God has even forgotten some
of your sin.

7"Can you understand the secrets of God?
Can you search the limits of the
Almighty?
8His limits are higher than the heavens;
you cannot reach them!
They are deeper than the grave; you
cannot understand them!
9His limits are longer than the earth
and wider than the sea.

10"If God comes along and puts you in
prison
or calls you into court, no one can stop
him.
11God knows who is evil,
and when he sees evil, he takes note
of it.
12A fool cannot become wise
any more than a wild donkey can be
born tame.

13"You must give your whole heart to him
and hold out your hands to him for
help.
14Put away the sin that is in your hand;
let no evil remain in your tent.
15Then you can lift up your face without
shame,
and you can stand strong without fear.
16You will forget your trouble
and remember it only as water gone by.
17Your life will be as bright as the noonday
sun,
and darkness will seem like morning.
18You will feel safe because there is hope;
you will look around and rest in safety.
19You will lie down, and no one will scare
you.
Many people will want favors from
you.
20But the wicked will not be able to see,
so they will not escape.
Their only hope will be to die."

Job Answers Zophar

12 Then Job answered:
2"You really think you are the only
wise people
and that when you die, wisdom will die
with you!
3But my mind is as good as yours;
you are not better than I am.
Everyone knows all these things.
4My friends all laugh at me
when I call on God and expect him to
answer me;
they laugh at me even though I am
right and innocent!
5Those who are comfortable don't care that
others have trouble;
they think it right that those people
should have troubles.
6The tents of robbers are not bothered,
and those who make God angry are
safe.
They have their god in their pocket.

7"But ask the animals, and they will teach
you,
or ask the birds of the air, and they will
tell you.
8Speak to the earth, and it will teach you,
or let the fish of the sea tell you.
9Every one of these knows
that the hand of the LORD has done this.
10The life of every creature
and the breath of all people are in God's
hand.

11The ear tests words
as the tongue tastes food.
12Older people are wise,
and long life brings understanding.

13"But only God has wisdom and power,
good advice and understanding.
14What he tears down cannot be rebuilt;
anyone he puts in prison cannot be let out.
15If God holds back the waters, there is no rain;
if he lets the waters go, they flood the land.
16He is strong and victorious;
both the one who fools others and the one who is fooled belong to him.
17God leads the wise away as captives
and turns judges into fools.
18He takes off chains that kings put on
and puts a garment on their bodies.
19He leads priests away naked
and destroys the powerful.
20He makes trusted people be silent
and takes away the wisdom of elders.
21He brings disgrace on important people
and takes away the weapons of the strong.
22He uncovers the deep things of darkness
and brings dark shadows into the light.
23He makes nations great and then destroys them;
he makes nations large and then scatters them.
24He takes understanding away from the leaders of the earth
and makes them wander through a pathless desert.
25They feel around in darkness with no light;
he makes them stumble like drunks.

13 "Now my eyes have seen all this;
my ears have heard and understood it.
2What you know, I also know.
You are not better than I am.
3But I want to speak to the Almighty
and to argue my case with God.
4But you smear me with lies.
You are worthless doctors, all of you!
5I wish you would just stop talking;
then you would really be wise!
6Listen to my argument,
and hear the pleading of my lips.
7You should not speak evil in the name of God;
you cannot speak God's truth by telling lies.
8You should not unfairly choose his side against mine;
you should not argue the case for God.
9You will not do well if he examines you;
you cannot fool God as you might fool humans.
10God would surely scold you
if you unfairly took one person's side.
11His bright glory would scare you,
and you would be very much afraid of him.
12Your wise sayings are worth no more than ashes,
and your arguments are as weak as clay.

13"Be quiet and let me speak.
Let things happen to me as they will.
14Why should I put myself in danger
and take my life in my own hands?
15Even if God kills me, I have hope in him;
I will still defend my ways to his face.
16This is my salvation.
The wicked cannot come before him.
17Listen carefully to my words;
let your ears hear what I say.
18See, I have prepared my case,
and I know I will be proved right.
19No one can accuse me of doing wrong.
If someone can, I will be quiet and die.

20"God, please just give me these two things,
and then I will not hide from you:
21Take your punishment away from me,
and stop frightening me with your terrors.
22Then call me, and I will answer,
or let me speak, and you answer.
23How many evil things and sins have I done?
Show me my wrong and my sin.
24Don't hide your face from me;
don't think of me as your enemy.
25Don't punish a leaf that is blown by the wind;
don't chase after straw.
26You write down cruel things against me
and make me suffer for my boyhood sins.

devotion 122

JOB 13:15

WHAT'S WAITING FOR ME THERE

My sister is my best friend. She has long red hair and beautiful blue eyes, and her name is Julie. She is an incredible person. You always laugh when you are with her. Julie sees the best in life regardless of the circumstances.

She was diagnosed with cancer when she was only twenty-seven years old. We thought the worst part would be for Julie to lose her beautiful hair. We were wrong. After chemotherapy and radiation, we realized her cancer was aggressive. A miracle from the Lord was our only hope. We began having weekly prayer meetings for Julie as a family. One night Julie looked at us after we prayed, and she said, "I'll love the Lord if I live, and I'll love the Lord if I die." And at that moment, we all realized that she had summed up what being a Christian is all about.

Job says something similar: "Even if God kills me, I have hope in him." The length of our life is in God's hands. Since my sister died, I look at birthdays a bit differently. I appreciate the gift of each year and never take it for granted. I also look forward to heaven a bit more. I know that my best friend is waiting for me. I have so much to tell her—so many memories to relive. But mostly I just want to look into those beautiful blue eyes, stroke that beautiful red hair, and tell her how much I have missed her.

27 You put my feet in chains
and keep close watch wherever I go.
You even mark the soles of my feet.
28 "Everyone wears out like something rotten,
like clothing eaten by moths.

14 "All of us born to women
live only a few days and have lots of trouble.
2 We grow up like flowers and then dry up and die.
We are like a passing shadow that does not last.
3 Lord, do you need to watch me like this?
Must you bring me before you to be judged?
4 No one can bring something clean from something dirty.
5 Our time is limited.
You have given us only so many months to live
and have set limits we cannot go beyond.
6 So look away from us and leave us alone
until we put in our time like a laborer.
7 "If a tree is cut down,
there is hope that it will grow again
and will send out new branches.
8 Even if its roots grow old in the ground,
and its stump dies in the dirt,
9 at the smell of water it will bud
and put out new shoots like a plant.
10 But we die, and our bodies are laid in the ground;
we take our last breath and are gone.
11 Water disappears from a lake,
and a river loses its water and dries up.
12 In the same way, we lie down and do not rise again;
we will not get up or be awakened
until the heavens disappear.
13 "I wish you would hide me in the grave;
hide me until your anger is gone.

I wish you would set a time
and then remember me!
14 Will the dead live again?
All my days are a struggle;
I will wait until my change comes.
15 You will call, and I will answer you;
you will desire the creature your hands have made.
16 Then you will count my steps,
but you will not keep track of my sin.
17 My wrongs will be closed up in a bag,
and you will cover up my sin.

18 "A mountain washes away and crumbles;
and a rock can be moved from its place.
19 Water washes over stones and wears them down,
and rushing waters wash away the dirt.
In the same way, you destroy hope.
20 You defeat people forever, and they are gone;
you change their appearance and send them away.
21 Their children are honored, but they do not know it;
their children are disgraced, but they do not see it.
22 They only feel the pain of their body
and feel sorry for themselves."

Eliphaz Answers Job

15 Then Eliphaz the Temanite answered:
2 "A wise person would not answer with empty words
or fill his stomach with the hot east wind.
3 He would not argue with useless words
or make speeches that have no value.
4 But you even destroy respect for God
and limit the worship of him.
5 Your sin teaches your mouth what to say;
you use words to trick others.
6 It is your own mouth, not mine, that shows you are wicked;
your own lips testify against you.

7 "You are not the first man ever born;
you are not older than the hills.
8 You did not listen in on God's secret council.
But you limit wisdom to yourself.
9 You don't know any more than we know.
You don't understand any more than we understand.
10 Old people with gray hair are on our side;
they are even older than your father.
11 Is the comfort God gives you not enough for you,
even when words are spoken gently to you?
12 Has your heart carried you away from God?
Why do your eyes flash with anger?
13 Why do you speak out your anger against God?
Why do these words pour out of your mouth?
14 "How can anyone be pure?
How can someone born to a woman be good?
15 God places no trust in his holy ones,
and even the heavens are not pure in his eyes.
16 How much less pure is one who is terrible and rotten
and drinks up evil as if it were water!

17 "Listen to me, and I will tell you about it;
I will tell you what I have seen.
18 These are things wise men have told;
their ancestors told them, and they have hidden nothing.
19 (The land was given to their fathers only,
and no foreigner lived among them.)
20 The wicked suffer pain all their lives;
the cruel suffer during all the years saved up for them.
21 Terrible sounds fill their ears,
and when things seem to be going well, robbers attack them.
22 Evil people give up trying to escape from the darkness;
it has been decided that they will die by the sword.
23 They wander around and will become food for vultures.
They know darkness will soon come.
24 Worry and suffering terrify them;
they overwhelm them, like a king ready to attack,
25 because they shake their fists at God
and try to get their own way against the Almighty.
26 They stubbornly charge at God
with thick, strong shields.

27 "Although the faces of the wicked are thick with fat,
and their bellies are fat with flesh,

devotion 123

JOB 15:5–10

WITH FRIENDS LIKE THAT . . .

You've probably heard all the jokes about Job's friends. In case you haven't, his friends were lousy. Each one seemed called to the ministry of discouragement. All of them were without spiritual eyes to see God's hand or truly discern the truth of Job's heart. Put the bunch of them together, and they still couldn't understand what God was doing. They lacked wisdom, maturity, and were excruciatingly without compassion.

How about your friends? Are you surrounded by a bunch of friends who give you bad advice and pour spiritual salt into your gaping wounds? What kind of people have permission to speak into your heart and give direction for your decisions? When choosing wise counsel, be sure to look for the following:

- *A biblical mindset.* Do they know the truths of Scripture, and can they apply them?
- *A prayerful heart.* None of us are truly wise. Look for a person who will join you in seeking God's best in prayer.
- *A life of character and spiritual fruit.* Does their life bear any likeness to the life of Jesus? Does their character resemble his?
- *Humility.* A wise counselor is gentle, compassionate, completely dependent on God for insight, and unmarked by pride or arrogance.

Maybe it's time to take a friend inventory. Decide today to only receive advice from the men and women who are qualified by the Holy Spirit to encourage you and direct your path. God will honor your faithfulness in choosing your inner circle wisely.

28 they will live in towns that are ruined,
in houses where no one lives,
which are crumbling into ruins.
29 The wicked will no longer get rich,
and the riches they have will not last;
the things they own will no longer
spread over the land.
30 They will not escape the darkness.
A flame will dry up their branches;
God's breath will carry the wicked
away.
31 The wicked should not fool themselves by
trusting what is useless.
If they do, they will get nothing in
return.
32 Their branches will dry up before they
finish growing
and will never turn green.
33 They will be like a vine whose grapes are
pulled off before they are ripe,
like an olive tree that loses its blossoms.
34 People without God can produce
nothing.
Fire will destroy the tents of those who
take money to do evil,
35 who plan trouble and give birth to evil,
whose hearts plan ways to trick others."

Job Answers Eliphaz

16 Then Job answered:
2 "I have heard many things like these.
You are all painful comforters!
3 Will your long-winded speeches never
end?
What makes you keep on arguing?
4 I also could speak as you do
if you were in my place.
I could make great speeches against you
and shake my head at you.
5 But, instead, I would encourage you,
and my words would bring you relief.

6"Even if I speak, my pain is not less,
and if I don't speak, it still does not go away.
7God, you have surely taken away my strength
and destroyed my whole family.
8You have made me thin and weak,
and this shows I have done wrong.
9God attacks me and tears me with anger;
he grinds his teeth at me;
my enemy stares at me with his angry eyes.
10People open their mouths to make fun of me
and hit my cheeks to insult me.
They join together against me.
11God has turned me over to evil people
and has handed me over to the wicked.
12Everything was fine with me,
but God broke me into pieces;
he held me by the neck and crushed me.
He has made me his target;
13 his archers surround me.
He stabs my kidneys without mercy;
he spills my blood on the ground.
14Again and again God attacks me;
he runs at me like a soldier.

15"I have sewed rough cloth over my skin to show my sadness
and have buried my face in the dust.
16My face is red from crying;
I have dark circles around my eyes.
17Yet my hands have never done anything cruel,
and my prayer is pure.

18"Earth, please do not cover up my blood.
Don't let my cry ever stop being heard!
19Even now I have one who speaks for me in heaven;
the one who is on my side is high above.
20The one who speaks for me is my friend.
My eyes pour out tears to God.
21He begs God on behalf of a human
as a person begs for his friend.

22"Only a few years will pass
before I go on the journey of no return.
17 My spirit is broken;
the days of my life are almost gone.
The grave is waiting for me.
2Those who laugh at me surround me;
I watch them insult me.

3"God, make me a promise.
No one will make a pledge for me.
4You have closed their minds to understanding.
Do not let them win over me.
5People might speak against their friends for money,
but if they do, the eyes of their children go blind.

6"God has made my name a curse word;
people spit in my face.
7My sight has grown weak because of my sadness,
and my body is as thin as a shadow.
8Honest people are upset about this;
innocent people are upset with those who do wrong.
9But those who do right will continue to do right,
and those whose hands are not dirty with sin will grow stronger.

10"But, all of you, come and try again!
I do not find a wise person among you.
11My days are gone, and my plans have been destroyed,
along with the desires of my heart.
12These men think night is day;
when it is dark, they say, 'Light is near.'
13If the only home I hope for is the grave,
if I spread out my bed in darkness,
14if I say to the grave, 'You are my father,'
and to the worm, 'You are my mother'
or 'You are my sister,'
15where, then, is my hope?
Who can see any hope for me?
16Will hope go down to the gates of death?
Will we go down together into the dust?"

Bildad Answers Job

18 Then Bildad the Shuhite answered:
2"When will you stop these speeches?
Be sensible, and then we can talk.
3You think of us as cattle,
as if we are stupid.
4You tear yourself to pieces in your anger.
Should the earth be vacant just for you?
Should the rocks move from their places?

5"The lamp of the wicked will be put out,
and the flame in their lamps will stop burning.
6The light in their tents will grow dark,
and the lamps by their sides will go out.
7Their strong steps will grow weak;
they will fall into their own evil traps.
8Their feet will be caught in a net
when they walk into its web.
9A trap will catch them by the heel
and hold them tight.
10A trap for them is hidden on the ground,
right in their path.
11Terrible things startle them from every side
and chase them at every step.
12Hunger takes away their strength,
and disaster is at their side.
13Disease eats away parts of their skin;
death gnaws at their arms and legs.
14They are torn from the safety of their tents
and dragged off to Death, the King of Terrors.
15Their tents are set on fire,
and sulfur is scattered over their homes.
16Their roots dry up below ground,
and their branches die above ground.
17People on earth will not remember them;
their names will be forgotten in the land.
18They will be driven from light into darkness
and chased out of the world.
19They have no children or descendants among their people,
and no one will be left alive where they once lived.
20People of the west will be shocked at what has happened to them,
and people of the east will be very frightened.
21Surely this is what will happen to the wicked;
such is the place of one who does not know God."

Job Answers Bildad

19 Then Job answered:
2"How long will you hurt me
and crush me with your words?
3You have insulted me ten times now
and attacked me without shame.
4Even if I have sinned,
it is my worry alone.
5If you want to make yourselves look better than I,
you can blame me for my suffering.
6Then know that God has wronged me
and pulled his net around me.

7"I shout, 'I have been wronged!'
But I get no answer.
I scream for help
but I get no justice.
8God has blocked my way so I cannot pass;
he has covered my paths with darkness.
9He has taken away my honor
and removed the crown from my head.
10He beats me down on every side until I am gone;
he destroys my hope like a fallen tree.
11His anger burns against me,
and he treats me like an enemy.
12His armies gather;
they prepare to attack me.
They camp around my tent.

13"God has made my brothers my enemies,
and my friends have become strangers.
14My relatives have gone away,
and my friends have forgotten me.
15My guests and my female servants treat me like a stranger;
they look at me as if I were a foreigner.
16I call for my servant, but he does not answer,
even when I beg him with my own mouth.
17My wife can't stand my breath,
and my own family dislikes me.
18Even the little boys hate me
and talk about me when I leave.
19All my close friends hate me;
even those I love have turned against me.
20I am nothing but skin and bones;
I have escaped by the skin of my teeth.
21Pity me, my friends, pity me,
because the hand of God has hit me.
22Why do you chase me as God does?
Haven't you hurt me enough?

23"How I wish my words were written down,
written on a scroll.
24I wish they were carved with an iron pen into lead,
or carved into stone forever.

25I know that my Defender lives,
and in the end he will stand upon the earth.
26Even after my skin has been destroyed,
in my flesh I will see God.
27I will see him myself;
I will see him with my very own eyes.
How my heart wants that to happen!

28"If you say, 'We will continue to trouble Job,
because the problem lies with him,'
29you should be afraid of the sword yourselves.
God's anger will bring punishment by the sword.
Then you will know there is judgment."

Zophar Answers

20 Then Zophar the Naamathite answered:
2"My troubled thoughts cause me to answer,
because I am very upset.
3You correct me and I am insulted,
but I understand how to answer you.

4"You know how it has been for a long time,
ever since people were first put on the earth.
5The happiness of evil people is brief,
and the joy of the wicked lasts only a moment.
6Their pride may be as high as the heavens,
and their heads may touch the clouds,
7but they will be gone forever, like their own dung.
People who knew them will say,
'Where are they?'
8They will fly away like a dream
and not be found again;
they will be chased away like a vision in the night.
9Those who saw them will not see them again;
the places where they lived will see them no more.
10Their children will have to pay back the poor,
and they will have to give up their wealth.
11They had the strength of their youth in their bones,
but it will lie with them in the dust of death.

devotion 124

JOB 19:25–26

BUMPER STICKERS AND BAD MANNERS

Jesus is your defender, but there will still be times when you experience resistance and even mockery because of your faith. One particularly hot Florida afternoon comes to mind. I was driving down the road, and I noticed a car in my rear view mirror moving very fast and gaining on me quickly. The car rushed past and just as quickly returned to my lane, then slowed down. I was very perplexed—and then I noticed it—his Darwin fish sticker with legs was eating the Christian fish. He was making a mockery of my Lord, and it was no mistake that he chose me since my fish was proudly displayed on my bumper.

Good thing for me, I was driving a fast car with a V8 engine, so overtaking him was easy. As I was displaying my "mature" Christian road rage, the Holy Spirit spoke to my heart and said, "Do not worry. 'Every knee will bow to the name of Jesus'" (Phil. 2:10-11).

Yes, my sweet Christian, hide this verse in your heart for all the times you will be challenged because of your love for Christ. He is your defender, and we do not need to win drag races or conduct Bible-thumping wars to convince people that his Word is true. We just need to be an example of Christ and rest knowing that every single soul will one day see Jesus and confess that he is Lord. Amen!

12"Evil may taste sweet in their mouths,
and they may hide it under their tongues.
13They cannot stand to let go of it;
they keep it in their mouths.
14But their food will turn sour in their stomachs,
like the poison of a snake inside them.
15They have swallowed riches, but they will spit them out;
God will make them vomit their riches up.
16They will suck the poison of snakes,
and the snake's fangs will kill them.
17They will not admire the sparkling streams
or the rivers flowing with honey and cream.
18They must give back what they worked for without eating it;
they will not enjoy the money they made from their trading,
19because they troubled the poor and left them with nothing.
They have taken houses they did not build.

20"Evil people never lack an appetite,
and nothing escapes their selfishness.
21But nothing will be left for them to eat;
their riches will not continue.
22When they still have plenty, trouble will catch up to them,
and great misery will come down on them.
23When the wicked fill their stomachs,
God will send his burning anger against them,
and blows of punishment will fall on them like rain.
24The wicked may run away from an iron weapon,
but a bronze arrow will stab them.
25They will pull the arrows out of their backs
and pull the points out of their livers.
Terrors will come over them;
26 total darkness waits for their treasure.
A fire not fanned by people will destroy them
and burn up what is left of their tents.
27The heavens will show their guilt,
and the earth will rise up against them.
28A flood will carry their houses away,
swept away on the day of God's anger.
29This is what God plans for evil people;
this is what he has decided they will receive."

Job Answers Zophar

21 Then Job answered:
2"Listen carefully to my words,
and let this be the way you comfort me.
3Be patient while I speak.
After I have finished, you may continue to make fun of me.

4"My complaint is not just against people;
I have reason to be impatient.
5Look at me and be shocked;
put your hand over your mouth in shock.
6When I think about this, I am terribly afraid
and my body shakes.
7Why do evil people live a long time?
They grow old and become more powerful.
8They see their children around them;
they watch them grow up.
9Their homes are safe and without fear;
God does not punish them.
10Their bulls never fail to mate;
their cows have healthy calves.
11They send out their children like a flock;
their little ones dance about.
12They sing to the music of tambourines and harps,
and the sound of the flute makes them happy.
13Evil people enjoy successful lives
and then go peacefully to the grave.
14They say to God, 'Leave us alone!
We don't want to know your ways.
15Who is the Almighty that we should serve him?
What would we gain by praying to him?'
16The success of the wicked is not their own doing.
Their way of thinking is different from mine.
17Yet how often are the lamps of evil people turned off?
How often does trouble come to them?
How often do they suffer God's angry punishment?

18 How often are they like straw in the wind
or like chaff that is blown away by a
storm?
19 It is said, 'God saves up a person's
punishment for his children.'
But God should punish the wicked
themselves so they will know it.
20 Their eyes should see their own
destruction,
and they should suffer the anger of the
Almighty.
21 They do not care about the families they
leave behind
when their lives have come to an end.

22 "No one can teach knowledge to God;
he is the one who judges even the most
important people.
23 One person dies while he still has all his
strength,
feeling completely safe and comfortable.
24 His body was well fed,
and his bones were strong and healthy.
25 But another person dies with an unhappy
heart,
never enjoying any happiness.
26 They are buried next to each other,
and worms cover them both.

27 "I know very well your thoughts
and your plans to wrong me.
28 You ask about me, 'Where is this great
man's house?
Where are the tents where the wicked
live?'
29 Have you never asked those who travel?
Have you never listened to their
stories?
30 On the day of God's anger and
punishment,
it is the wicked who are spared.
31 Who will accuse them to their faces?
Who will pay them back for the evil
they have done?
32 They are carried to their graves,
and someone keeps watch over their
tombs.
33 The dirt in the valley seems sweet to
them.
Everybody follows after them,
and many people go before them.

34 "So how can you comfort me with this
nonsense?
Your answers are only lies!"

Eliphaz Answers

22 Then Eliphaz the Temanite answered:
2 "Can anyone be of real use to God?
Can even a wise person do him good?
3 Does it help the Almighty for you to be
good?
Does he gain anything if you are
innocent?
4 Does God punish you for respecting him?
Does he bring you into court for this?
5 No! It is because your evil is without
limits
and your sins have no end.
6 You took your brothers' things for a debt
they didn't owe;
you took clothes from people and left
them naked.
7 You did not give water to tired people,
and you kept food from the hungry.
8 You were a powerful man who owned
land;
you were honored and lived in the land.
9 But you sent widows away empty-handed,
and you mistreated orphans.
10 That is why traps are all around you
and sudden danger frightens you.
11 That is why it is so dark you cannot see
and a flood of water covers you.

12 "God is in the highest part of heaven.
See how high the highest stars are!
13 But you ask, 'What does God know?
Can he judge us through the dark
clouds?
14 Thick clouds cover him so he cannot see
us
as he walks around high up in the
sky.'
15 Are you going to stay on the old path
where evil people walk?
16 They were carried away before their time
was up,
and their foundations were washed
away by a flood.
17 They said to God, 'Leave us alone!
The Almighty can do nothing to us.'
18 But it was God who filled their houses
with good things.
Their way of thinking is different from
mine.

19 "Good people can watch and be glad;
the innocent can laugh at them and
say,

20'Surely our enemies are destroyed,
and fire burns up their wealth.'

21"Obey God and be at peace with him;
this is the way to happiness.
22Accept teaching from his mouth,
and keep his words in your heart.
23If you return to the Almighty, you will be
blessed again.
So remove evil from your house.
24Throw your gold nuggets into the dust
and your fine gold among the rocks in
the ravines.
25Then the Almighty will be your gold
and the best silver for you.
26You will find pleasure in the Almighty,
and you will look up to him.
27You will pray to him, and he will hear you,
and you will keep your promises to
him.
28Anything you decide will be done,
and light will shine on your ways.
29When people are made humble and you
say, 'Have courage,'
then the humble will be saved.
30Even a guilty person will escape
and be saved because your hands are
clean."

Job Answers

23 Then Job answered:
2"My complaint is still bitter today.
I groan because God's heavy hand is
on me.
3I wish I knew where to find God
so I could go to where he lives.
4I would present my case before him
and fill my mouth with arguments.
5I would learn how he would answer me
and would think about what he would
say.
6Would he not argue strongly against me?
No, he would really listen to me.
7Then an honest person could present his
case to God,
and I would be saved forever by my
judge.

8"If I go to the east, God is not there;
if I go to the west, I do not see him.
9When he is at work in the north, I catch
no sight of him;
when he turns to the south, I cannot
see him.
10But God knows the way that I take,
and when he has tested me, I will come
out like gold.

devotion 125

JOB 23:10–12

THE SCHOOL OF LOSS

When my sister died, I knew that God was testing me. I went through a season where I didn't want to talk to God or even read my Bible. I never turned my back on God or even blamed God for allowing her to die. But in the days and months after my loss, I honestly felt as though I couldn't trust him anymore. I felt that he had let me down. I remember one night waking up with that sickening feeling of loss and making my way to the stairs to cry. I asked the Lord to forgive me for avoiding him. Then I heard his quiet whisper in my heart, "I'll be here when you're ready to talk again. I love you." It was exactly what I needed to hear.

When testing comes your way, remember to give yourself a little time to sort through it. I slowly made my way back to the Lord, but I needed time to heal from my loss and remember how to confidently trust God again. We often pretend everything is okay when in reality, our heart is breaking. We need to be honest with ourselves and trust God to make sense of our pain. Seasons of testing can be difficult, but when it's over, you will see the gold. Your steps will follow a little closer to his steps. You will listen a little more carefully to his words. You will treasure his ways a little bit more.

[11]My feet have closely followed his steps;
I have stayed in his way;
I did not turn aside.
[12]I have never left the commands he has spoken;
I have treasured his words more than my own.

[13]"But he is the only God.
Who can come against him?
He does anything he wants.
[14]He will do to me what he said he would do,
and he has many plans like this.
[15]That is why I am frightened of him;
when I think of this, I am afraid of him.
[16]God has made me afraid;
the Almighty terrifies me.
[17]But I am not hidden by the darkness,
by the thick darkness that covers my face.

24 "I wish the Almighty would set a time for judging.
Those who know God do not see such a day.
[2]Wicked people take other people's land;
they steal flocks and take them to new pastures.
[3]They chase away the orphan's donkey
and take the widow's ox when she has no money.
[4]They push needy people off the path;
all the poor of the land hide from them.
[5]The poor become like wild donkeys in the desert
who go about their job of finding food.
The desert gives them food for their children.
[6]They gather hay and straw in the fields
and pick up leftover grapes from the vineyard of the wicked.
[7]They spend the night naked, because they have no clothes,
nothing to cover themselves in the cold.
[8]They are soaked from mountain rains
and stay near the large rocks because they have no shelter.
[9]The fatherless child is grabbed from its mother's breast;
they take a poor mother's baby to pay for what she owes.
[10]So the poor go around naked without any clothes;
they carry bundles of grain but still go hungry;
[11]they crush olives to get oil
and grapes to get wine, but they still go thirsty.
[12]Dying people groan in the city,
and the injured cry out for help,
but God accuses no one of doing wrong.

[13]"Those who fight against the light
do not know God's ways
or stay in his paths.
[14]When the day is over, the murderers get up
to kill the poor and needy.
At night they go about like thieves.
[15]Those who are guilty of adultery watch for the night,
thinking, 'No one will see us,'
and they keep their faces covered.
[16]In the dark, evil people break into houses.
In the daytime they shut themselves up in their own houses,
because they want nothing to do with the light.
[17]Darkness is like morning to all these evil people
who make friends with the terrors of darkness.

[18]"They are like foam floating on the water.
Their part of the land is cursed;
no one uses the road that goes by their vineyards.
[19]As heat and dryness quickly melt the snow,
so the grave quickly takes away the sinners.
[20]Their mothers forget them,
and worms will eat their bodies.
They will not be remembered,
so wickedness is broken in pieces like a stick.
[21]These evil people abuse women who cannot have children
and show no kindness to widows.
[22]But God drags away the strong by his power.
Even though they seem strong, they do not know how long they will live.
[23]God may let these evil people feel safe,
but he is watching their ways.
[24]For a little while they are important, and then they die;

they are laid low and buried like
everyone else;
they are cut off like the heads of grain.
25 If this is not true, who can prove I am
wrong?
Who can show that my words are
worth nothing?"

Bildad Answers

25 Then Bildad the Shuhite answered:
2 "God rules and he must be honored;
he set up order in his high heaven.
3 No one can count God's armies.
His light shines on all people.
4 So no one can be good in the presence of
God,
and no one born to a woman can be
pure.
5 Even the moon is not bright
and the stars are not pure in his eyes.
6 People are much less! They are like
insects.
They are only worms!"

Job Answers Bildad

26 Then Job answered:
2 "You are no help to the helpless!
You have not aided the weak!
3 Your advice lacks wisdom!
You have shown little understanding!
4 Who has helped you say these words?
And where did you get these ideas?
5 "The spirits of the dead tremble,
those who are beneath and in the
waters.
6 Death is naked before God;
destruction is uncovered before him.
7 God stretches the northern sky out over
empty space
and hangs the earth on nothing.
8 He wraps up the waters in his thick
clouds,
but the clouds do not break under their
weight.
9 He covers the face of the moon,
spreading his clouds over it.
10 He draws the horizon like a circle on the
water
at the place where light and darkness
meet.
11 Heaven's foundations shake
when he thunders at them.
12 With his power he quiets the sea;
by his wisdom he destroys Rahab, the
sea monster.
13 He breathes, and the sky clears.
His hand stabs the fleeing snake.
14 And these are only a small part of God's
works.
We only hear a small whisper of him.
Who could understand God's
thundering power?"

27 And Job continued speaking:
2 "As surely as God lives, who has
taken away my rights,
the Almighty, who has made me
unhappy,
3 as long as I am alive
and God's breath of life is in my nose,
4 my lips will not speak evil,
and my tongue will not tell a lie.
5 I will never agree you are right;
until I die, I will never stop saying I am
innocent.
6 I will insist that I am right; I will not back
down.
My conscience will never bother me.
7 "Let my enemies be like evil people,
my foes like those who are wrong.
8 What hope do the wicked have when
they die,
when God takes their life away?
9 God will not listen to their cries
when trouble comes to them.
10 They will not find joy in the Almighty,
even though they call out to God all the
time.
11 "I will teach you about the power of God
and will not hide the ways of the
Almighty.
12 You have all seen this yourselves.
So why are we having all this talk that
means nothing?
13 "Here is what God has planned for evil
people,
and what the Almighty will give to
cruel people:
14 They may have many children, but the
sword will kill them.
Their children who are left will never
have enough to eat.
15 Then they will die of disease and be
buried,
and the widows will not even cry for
them.

16The wicked may heap up silver like piles
of dirt
and have so many clothes they are like
piles of clay.
17But good people will wear what evil
people have gathered,
and the innocent will divide up their
silver.
18The houses the wicked build are like a
spider's web,
like a hut that a guard builds.
19The wicked are rich when they go to bed,
but they are rich for the last time;
when they open their eyes, everything
is gone.
20Fears come over them like a flood,
and a storm snatches them away in the
night.
21The east wind will carry them away, and
then they are gone,
because it sweeps them out of their
place.
22The wind will hit them without mercy
as they try to run away from its power.
23It will be as if the wind is clapping its
hands;
it will whistle at them as they run from
their place.

28 "There are mines where people dig
silver
and places where gold is made pure.
2Iron is taken from the ground,
and copper is melted out of rocks.
3Miners bring lights
and search deep into the mines
for ore in thick darkness.
4Miners dig a tunnel far from where
people live,
where no one has ever walked;
they work far from people, swinging
and swaying from ropes.
5Food grows on top of the earth,
but below ground things are changed as
if by fire.
6Sapphires are found in rocks,
and gold dust is also found there.
7No hawk knows that path;
the falcon has not seen it.
8Proud animals have not walked there,
and no lions cross over it.
9Miners hit the rocks of flint
and dig away at the bottom of the
mountains.
10They cut tunnels through the rock
and see all the treasures there.
11They search for places where rivers begin
and bring things hidden out into the
light.

12"But where can wisdom be found,
and where does understanding live?
13People do not understand the value of
wisdom;
it cannot be found among those who
are alive.
14The deep ocean says, 'It's not in me;'
the sea says, 'It's not in me.'
15Wisdom cannot be bought with gold,
and its cost cannot be weighed in silver.
16Wisdom cannot be bought with fine gold
or with valuable onyx or sapphire
gems.
17Gold and crystal are not as valuable as
wisdom,
and you cannot buy it with jewels of
gold.
18Coral and jasper are not worth talking
about,
and the price of wisdom is much
greater than rubies.
19The topaz from Cush cannot compare to
wisdom;
it cannot be bought with the purest
gold.

20"So where does wisdom come from,
and where does understanding live?
21It is hidden from the eyes of every living
thing,
even from the birds of the air.
22The places of destruction and death say,
'We have heard reports about it.'
23Only God understands the way to wisdom,
and he alone knows where it lives,
24because he looks to the farthest parts of
the earth
and sees everything under the sky.
25When God gave power to the wind
and measured the water,
26when he made rules for the rain
and set a path for a thunderstorm to
follow,
27then he looked at wisdom and decided its
worth;
he set wisdom up and tested it.
28Then he said to humans,
'The fear of the Lord is wisdom;
to stay away from evil is
understanding.' "

devotion 126

JOB 28:28

WHEN YOU ARE IN PAIN

Job has always been one of my favorite characters in the Bible. This man, who was tested beyond human limits, lost everything on earth he called precious: his children, his home, his assets . . . all gone in the blink of an eye. What might be your response to such life-shattering tests? Would you hide? Would you shake your angry fist at heaven? Would you turn from the One you believed in because tragedy came and cut like a knife?

Pain has a way of either teaching or tearing a heart. Wisdom or bitterness can be found through such suffering, but the choice is largely ours. Wisdom brings us one step closer to letting go of the question, "Why me?" and asking God instead, "What do you wish to teach me?" Wisdom can be found through the jaw-dropping recognition of God's awesome power. He is intimately involved in our lives. He knows our pain. Though knowing God and seeking wisdom are not fireproof blockades against pain or tragedy, we can know like Job that such trials are not off God's radar screen. This knowledge helps equip us for the journey onward.

While evil calls us to forsake God when pain strikes, wisdom calls us to cling to the One who knows the outcome of such challenges. As this saying illustrates, those same challenges often cause us to seek God in the midst of our deepest pain: "Those who've walked most intimately with the Lord are often those with the most battle scars."

Job Continues

29 Job continued to speak:
2"How I wish for the months that
have passed
and the days when God watched
over me.
3God's lamp shined on my head,
and I walked through darkness by his
light.
4I wish for the days when I was strong,
when God's close friendship blessed my
house.
5The Almighty was still with me,
and my children were all around me.
6It was as if my path were covered with
cream
and the rocks poured out olive oil
for me.
7I would go to the city gate
and sit in the public square.
8When the young men saw me, they
would step aside,
and the old men would stand up in
respect.
9The leading men stopped speaking
and covered their mouths with their
hands.
10The voices of the important men were
quiet,
as if their tongues stuck to the roof of
their mouths.
11Anyone who heard me spoke well of me,
and those who saw me praised me,
12because I saved the poor who called out
and the orphan who had no one to
help.
13The dying person blessed me,
and I made the widow's heart sing.
14I put on right living as if it were clothing;
I wore fairness like a robe and a turban.
15I was eyes for the blind
and feet for the lame.
16I was like a father to needy people,
and I took the side of strangers who
were in trouble.

[17]I broke the fangs of evil people
and snatched the captives from their teeth.
[18]"I thought, 'I will live for as many days as there are grains of sand,
and I will die in my own house.
[19]My roots will reach down to the water.
The dew will lie on the branches all night.
[20]New honors will come to me continually,
and I will always have great strength.'
[21]"People listened to me carefully
and waited quietly for my advice.
[22]After I finished speaking, they spoke no more.
My words fell very gently on their ears.
[23]They waited for me as they would for rain
and drank in my words like spring rain.
[24]I smiled at them when they doubted,
and my approval was important to them.
[25]I chose the way for them and was their leader.
I lived like a king among his army,
like a person who comforts sad people.

30 "But now those who are younger than I make fun of me.
I would not have even let their fathers
sit with my sheep dogs.
[2]What use did I have for their strength
since they had lost their strength to work?
[3]They were thin from hunger
and wandered the dry and ruined land at night.
[4]They gathered desert plants among the brush
and ate the root of the broom tree.
[5]They were forced to live away from people;
people shouted at them as if they were thieves.
[6]They lived in dried-up streambeds,
in caves, and among the rocks.
[7]They howled like animals among the bushes
and huddled together in the brush.
[8]They are worthless people without names
and were forced to leave the land.
[9]"Now they make fun of me with songs;
my name is a joke among them.
[10]They hate me and stay far away from me,
but they do not mind spitting in my face.
[11]God has taken away my strength and made me suffer,
so they attack me with all their anger.
[12]On my right side they rise up like a mob.
They lay traps for my feet
and prepare to attack me.
[13]They break up my road
and work to destroy me,
and no one helps me.
[14]They come at me as if through a hole in the wall,
and they roll in among the ruins.
[15]Great fears overwhelm me.
They blow my honor away as if by a great wind,
and my safety disappears like a cloud.

[16]"Now my life is almost over;
my days are full of suffering.
[17]At night my bones ache;
gnawing pains never stop.
[18]In his great power God grabs hold of my clothing
and chokes me with the collar of my coat.
[19]He throws me into the mud,
and I become like dirt and ashes.

[20]"I cry out to you, God, but you do not answer;
I stand up, but you just look at me.
[21]You have turned on me without mercy;
with your powerful hand you attacked me.
[22]You snatched me up and threw me into the wind
and tossed me about in the storm.
[23]I know you will bring me down to death,
to the place where all living people must go.

[24]"Surely no one would hurt those who are ruined
when they cry for help in their time of trouble.
[25]I cried for those who were in trouble;
I have been very sad for poor people.
[26]But when I hoped for good, only evil came to me;
when I looked for light, darkness came.
[27]I never stop being upset;
days of suffering are ahead of me.

28 I have turned black, but not by the sun.
I stand up in public and cry for help.
29 I have become a brother to wild dogs
and a friend to ostriches.
30 My skin has become black and peels off,
as my body burns with fever.
31 My harp is tuned to sing a sad song,
and my flute is tuned to moaning.

31 "But I made an agreement with my
eyes
not to look with desire at a girl.
2 What has God above promised for
people?
What has the Almighty planned from
on high?
3 It is ruin for evil people
and disaster for those who do wrong.
4 God sees my ways
and counts every step I take.

5 "If I have been dishonest
or lied to others,
6 then let God weigh me on honest scales.
Then he will know I have done nothing
wrong.
7 If I have turned away from doing what is
right,
or my heart has been led by my eyes to
do wrong,
or my hands have been made unclean,
8 then let other people eat what I have
planted,
and let my crops be plowed up.

9 "If I have desired another woman
or have waited at my neighbor's door
for his wife,
10 then let my wife grind another man's
grain,
and let other men have sexual relations
with her.
11 That would be shameful,
a sin to be punished.
12 It is like a fire that burns and destroys;
all I have done would be plowed up.

13 "If I have been unfair to my male and
female slaves
when they had a complaint against me,
14 how could I tell God what I did?
What will I answer when he asks me to
explain what I've done?
15 God made me in my mother's womb, and
he also made them;
the same God formed both of us in our
mothers' wombs.

16 "I have never refused the appeals of the
poor
or let widows give up hope while
looking for help.
17 I have not kept my food to myself
but have given it to the orphans.
18 Since I was young, I have been like a
father to the orphans.
From my birth I guided the widows.
19 I have not let anyone die for lack of clothes
or let a needy person go without a coat.
20 That person's heart blessed me,
because I warmed him with the wool of
my sheep.
21 I have never hurt an orphan
even when I knew I could win in court.
22 If I have, then let my arm fall off my
shoulder
and be broken at the joint.
23 I fear destruction from God,
and I fear his majesty, so I could not do
such things.

24 "I have not put my trust in gold
or said to pure gold, 'You are my
security.'
25 I have not celebrated my great wealth
or the riches my hands had gained.
26 I have not thought about worshiping the
sun in its brightness
nor admired the moon moving in glory
27 so that my heart was pulled away from
God.
My hand has never offered the sun and
moon a kiss of worship.
28 If I had, these also would have been sins
to be punished,
because I would have been unfaithful
to God.

29 "I have not been happy when my enemies
fell
or laughed when they had trouble.
30 I have not let my mouth sin
by cursing my enemies' life.
31 The servants of my house have always
said,
'All have eaten what they want of Job's
food.'
32 No stranger ever had to spend the night in
the street,
because I always let travelers stay in my
home.

devotion 127

JOB 31:24–28

WHAT'S A CLEAN CONSCIENCE WORTH TO YOU?

Job essentially said to his friends, "I'm clean. I don't have anything to hide. I haven't done what you're accusing me of. I know in my heart that I am not the man you say that I am. Before God, I am clean."

Wow. What incredible power comes from keeping a clean life. If your conscience is not clear, you spend a lot of mental and emotional energy trying to cover things up. A murky conscience requires a great deal of wrangling and rationalizing. This burdened conscience is a heavy chain that will keep you shackled to a wall of guilt.

But we belong to God, and he has made a way for us to live in the light. We can be like Job and live with a clear conscience because of the freedom Christ gives. We can pursue a clean life even if no one else around us wants to go there, and even if others continue to remind us of our mistakes.

Here's the best part: when you get clean before God every day, no one can condemn you. They may accuse you, but if you're clean, it won't stick. They may gossip, but when you're clean, it won't last. And even better, God has promised that when you ask, he will make you clean. Bow in his presence this day. Ask him to make you clean. Decide to make choices that purify your life. And then walk in the strength that comes from a clear conscience.

33 I have not hidden my sin as others do,
secretly keeping my guilt to myself.
34 I was not so afraid of the crowd
that I kept quiet and stayed inside
because I feared being hated by other families.

35 ("How I wish a court would hear my case!
Here I sign my name to show I have told the truth.
Now let the Almighty answer me;
let the one who accuses me write it down.
36 I would wear the writing on my shoulder;
I would put it on like a crown.
37 I would explain to God every step I took,
and I would come near to him like a prince.)
38 "If my land cries out against me
and its plowed rows are not wet with tears,
39 if I have taken the land's harvest without paying
or have broken the spirit of those who worked the land,
40 then let thorns come up instead of wheat,
and let weeds come up instead of barley."
The words of Job are finished.

Elihu Speaks

32 These three men stopped trying to
answer Job, because he was so sure he
was right. 2 But Elihu son of Barakel the
Buzite, from the family of Ram, became very
angry with Job, because Job claimed he was
right instead of God. 3 Elihu was also angry
with Job's three friends who had no answer
to show that Job was wrong, yet continued
to blame him. 4 Elihu had waited before
speaking to Job, because the three friends
were older than he was. 5 But when Elihu
saw that the three men had nothing more to
say, he became very angry.
6 So Elihu son of Barakel the Buzite said
this:

"I am young,
and you are old.
That is why I was afraid
to tell you what I know.
7I thought, 'Older people should speak,
and those who have lived many years
should teach wisdom.'
8But it is the spirit in a person,
the breath of the Almighty, that gives
understanding.
9It is not just older people who are wise;
they are not the only ones who
understand what is right.
10So I say, listen to me.
I too will tell you what I know.
11I waited while you three spoke,
and listened to your explanations.
While you looked for words to use,
12 I paid close attention to you.
But not one of you has proved Job
wrong;
none of you has answered his
arguments.
13Don't say, 'We have found wisdom;
only God will show Job to be wrong,
not people.'
14Job has not spoken his words against me,
so I will not use your arguments to
answer Job.

15"These three friends are defeated and have
no more to say;
words have failed them.
16Now they are standing there with no
answers for Job.
Now that they are quiet, must I wait to
speak?
17No, I too will speak
and tell what I know.
18I am full of words,
and the spirit in me causes me to speak.
19I am like wine that has been bottled up;
I am ready to burst like a new leather
wine bag.
20I must speak so I will feel relief;
I must open my mouth and answer.
21I will be fair to everyone
and not flatter anyone.
22I don't know how to flatter,
and if I did, my Maker would quickly
take me away.

33 "Now, Job, listen to my words.
Pay attention to everything I say.
2I open my mouth
and am ready to speak.
3My words come from an honest heart,
and I am sincere in saying what I know.
4The Spirit of God created me,
and the breath of the Almighty gave me
life.
5Answer me if you can;
get yourself ready and stand before me.
6I am just like you before God;
I too am made out of clay.
7Don't be afraid of me;
I will not be hard on you.

8"But I heard what you have said;
I heard every word.
9You said, 'I am pure and without sin;
I am innocent and free from guilt.
10But God has found fault with me;
he considers me his enemy.
11He locks my feet in chains
and closely watches everywhere I go.'

12"But I tell you, you are not right in saying
this,
because God is greater than we are.
13Why do you accuse God
of not answering anyone?
14God does speak—sometimes one way and
sometimes another—
even though people may not
understand it.
15He speaks in a dream or a vision of the
night
when people are in a deep sleep,
lying on their beds.
16He speaks in their ears
and frightens them with warnings
17to turn them away from doing wrong
and to keep them from being proud.
18God does this to save people from death,
to keep them from dying.
19People may be corrected while in bed in
great pain;
they may have continual pain in their
very bones.
20They may be in such pain that they even
hate food,
even the very best meal.
21Their body becomes so thin there is
almost nothing left of it,
and their bones that were hidden now
stick out.
22They are near death,
and their life is almost over.

23"But there may be an angel to speak for
him,
one out of a thousand, who will tell
him what to do.
24The angel will beg for mercy and say:
'Save him from death.
I have found a way to pay for his life.'
25Then his body is made new like a child's.
It will return to the way it was when he
was young.
26That person will pray to God, and God
will listen to him.
He will see God's face and will shout
with happiness.
And God will set things right for him
again.
27Then he will say to others,
'I sinned and twisted what was right,
but I did not receive the punishment I
should have received.
28God bought my life back from death,
and I will continue to enjoy life.'

29"God does all these things to a person
two or even three times
30so he won't die as punishment for his sins
and so he may still enjoy life.

31"Job, pay attention and listen to me;
be quiet, and I will speak.
32If you have anything to say, answer me;
speak up, because I want to prove you
right.
33But if you have nothing to say, then listen
to me;
be quiet, and I will teach you wisdom."

34 Then Elihu said:
2"Hear my words, you wise men;
listen to me, you who know a lot.
3The ear tests words
as the tongue tastes food.
4Let's decide for ourselves what is right,
and let's learn together what is good.

5"Job says, 'I am not guilty,
and God has refused me a fair trial.
6Instead of getting a fair trial,
I am called a liar.
I have been seriously hurt,
even though I have not sinned.'
7There is no other man like Job;
he takes insults as if he were drinking
water.
8He keeps company with those who do
evil
and spends time with wicked men,
9because he says, 'It is no use
to try to please God.'

10"So listen to me, you who can understand.
God can never do wrong!
It is impossible for the Almighty to do
evil.
11God pays people back for what they have
done
and gives them what their actions
deserve.
12Truly God will never do wrong;
the Almighty will never twist what is
right.
13No one chose God to rule over the earth
or put him in charge of the whole
world.
14If God should decide
to take away life and breath,
15then everyone would die together
and turn back into dust.

16"If you can understand, hear this;
listen to what I have to say.
17Can anyone govern who hates what is
right?
How can you blame God who is both
fair and powerful?
18God is the one who says to kings, 'You are
worthless,'
or to important people, 'You are evil.'
19He is not nicer to princes than other
people,
nor kinder to rich people than poor
people,
because he made them all with his own
hands.
20They can die in a moment, in the middle
of the night.
They are struck down, and then they
pass away;
powerful people die without help.

21"God watches where people go;
he sees every step they take.
22There is no dark place or deep shadow
where those who do evil can hide from
him.
23He does not set a time
for people to come before him for
judging.
24Without asking questions, God breaks
powerful people into pieces
and puts others in their place.

devotion 128

JOB 34:10

GOD, ARE YOU TRYING TO TAKE ME OUT?

If you are feeling like God is trying to kill you, remember that it is impossible for him to do evil! I am not kidding. What did you think when you read the title? Believing that God cares about all the details of your life is the first step to dispelling your thoughts of the Creator wanting to take you out. He cares about every single little detail of your being and your emotions. He cares when you are brokenhearted and tired, afraid and alone. Where are you today? Maybe illness has overtaken someone in your family, maybe one of your children is making poor decisions, maybe you are brokenhearted because your husband's heart is cold . . . I don't know where you are today, but there is hope in Christ. And he knows right where you are.

Draw yourself into the Word and read about Job's conversations with God and Job's victory. Purpose to not let your heart be discouraged, but rather be filled with hope and praise. Nurture your heart and mind with the truth of the Word so you will have spiritual strength to trust him even when you cannot see the outcome of your circumstances. Dear child, you will see the power of his Word at work in your life. Job did not come to understand the fullness of God until he walked through his season of affliction. "Although he brings sorrow, he also has mercy and great love" (Lam. 3:32).

25Because God knows what people do,
he defeats them in the night, and they are crushed.
26He punishes them for the evil they do
so that everyone else can watch,
27because they stopped following God
and did not care about any of his ways.
28The cry of the poor comes to God;
he hears the cry of the needy.
29But if God keeps quiet, who can blame him?
If he hides his face, who can see him?
God still rules over both nations and persons alike.
30 He keeps the wicked from ruling
and from trapping others.

31"But suppose someone says to God,
'I am guilty, but I will not sin anymore.
32Teach me what I cannot see.
If I have done wrong, I will not do it again.'
33So, Job, should God reward you as you want
when you refuse to change?
You must decide, not I,
so tell me what you know.

34"Those who understand speak,
and the wise who hear me say,
35'Job speaks without knowing what is true;
his words show he does not understand.'
36I wish Job would be tested completely,
because he answered like an evil man!
37Job now adds to his sin by turning against God.
He claps his hands in protest,
speaking more and more against God."

35 Then Elihu said:
2"Do you think this is fair?
You say, 'God will show that I am right,'
3but you also ask, 'What's the use?
I don't gain anything by not sinning.'

4"I will answer you
and your friends who are with you.
5Look up at the sky
and see the clouds so high above you.

[6]If you sin, it does nothing to God;
even if your sins are many, they do nothing to him.
[7]If you are good, you give nothing to God;
he receives nothing from your hand.
[8]Your evil ways only hurt others like yourself,
and the good you do only helps other human beings.

[9]"People cry out when they are in trouble;
they beg for relief from powerful people.
[10]But no one asks, 'Where is God, my Maker,
who gives us songs in the night,
[11]who makes us smarter than the animals of the earth
and wiser than the birds of the air?'
[12]God does not answer evil people when they cry out,
because the wicked are proud.
[13]God does not listen to their useless begging;
the Almighty pays no attention to them.
[14]He will listen to you even less
when you say that you do not see him,
that your case is before him,
that you must wait for him,
[15] that his anger never punishes,
and that he doesn't notice evil.
[16]So Job is only speaking nonsense,
saying many words without knowing what is true."

Elihu's Speech Continues

36 Elihu continued:
[2]"Listen to me a little longer, and I will show you
that there is more to be said for God.
[3]What I know comes from far away.
I will show that my Maker is right.
[4]You can be sure that my words are not false;
one who really knows is with you.

[5]"God is powerful, but he does not hate people;
he is powerful and sure of what he wants to do.
[6]He will not keep evil people alive,
but he gives the poor their rights.
[7]He always watches over those who do right;
he sets them on thrones with kings
and they are honored forever.
[8]If people are bound in chains,
or if trouble, like ropes, ties them up,
[9]God tells them what they have done,
that they have sinned in their pride.
[10]God makes them listen to his warning
and commands them to change from doing evil.
[11]If they obey and serve him,
the rest of their lives will be successful,
and the rest of their years will be happy.
[12]But if they do not listen,
they will die by the sword,
and they will die without knowing why.

[13]"Those who have wicked hearts hold on to anger.
Even when God punishes them, they do not cry for help.
[14]They die while they are still young,
and their lives end in disgrace.
[15]But God saves those who suffer through their suffering;
he gets them to listen through their pain.

[16]"God is gently calling you from the jaws of trouble
to an open place of freedom
where he has set your table full of the best food.
[17]But now you are being punished like the wicked;
you are getting justice.
[18]Be careful! Don't be led away from God by riches;
don't let much money turn you away.
[19]Neither your wealth nor all your great strength
will keep you out of trouble.
[20]Don't wish for the night
when people are taken from their homes.
[21]Be careful not to turn to evil,
which you seem to want more than suffering.

[22]"God is great and powerful;
no other teacher is like him.
[23]No one has planned his ways for him;
no one can say to God, 'You have done wrong.'
[24]Remember to praise his work,
about which people have sung.

25Everybody has seen it;
people look at it from far off.
26God is so great, greater than we can understand!
No one knows how old he is.

27"He evaporates the drops of water from the earth
and turns them into rain.
28The rain then pours down from the clouds,
and showers fall on people.
29No one understands how God spreads out the clouds
or how he sends thunder from where he lives.
30Watch how God scatters his lightning around him,
lighting up the deepest parts of the sea.
31This is the way God governs the nations;
this is how he gives us enough food.
32God fills his hands with lightning
and commands it to strike its target.
33His thunder announces the coming storm,
and even the cattle know it is near.

37 "At the sound of his thunder, my heart pounds
as if it will jump out of my chest.
2Listen! Listen to the thunder of God's voice
and to the rumbling that comes from his mouth.
3He turns his lightning loose under the whole sky
and sends it to the farthest parts of the earth.
4After that you can hear the roar
when he thunders with a great sound.
He does not hold back the flashing
when his voice is heard.
5God's voice thunders in wonderful ways;
he does great things we cannot understand.
6He says to the snow, 'Fall on the earth,'
and to the shower, 'Be a heavy rain.'
7With it, he stops everyone from working
so everyone knows it is the work of God.
8The animals take cover from the rain
and stay in their dens.
9The storm comes from where it was stored;
the cold comes with the strong winds.
10The breath of God makes ice,
and the wide waters become frozen.
11He fills the clouds with water
and scatters his lightning through them.
12At his command they swirl around
over the whole earth,
doing whatever he commands.
13He uses the clouds to punish people
or to water his earth and show his love.

14"Job, listen to this:
Stop and notice God's miracles.
15Do you know how God controls the clouds
and makes his lightning flash?
16Do you know how the clouds hang in the sky?
Do you know the miracles of God, who knows everything?
17You suffer in your clothes
when the land is silenced by the hot, south wind.
18You cannot stretch out the sky like God
and make it look as hard as polished bronze.
19Tell us what we should say to him;
we cannot get our arguments ready
because we do not have enough understanding.
20Should God be told that I want to speak?
Would a person ask to be swallowed up?
21No one can look at the sun
when it is bright in the sky
after the wind has blown all the clouds away.
22God comes out of the north in golden light,
in overwhelming greatness.
23The Almighty is too high for us to reach.
He has great strength;
he is always right and never punishes unfairly.
24That is why people honor him;
he does not respect those who say they are wise."

The Lord Questions Job

38 Then the LORD answered Job from the storm. He said:
2"Who is this that makes my purpose unclear

by saying things that are not true?
3 Be strong like a man!
I will ask you questions,
and you must answer me.
4 Where were you when I made the earth's
foundation?
Tell me, if you understand.
5 Who marked off how big it should be?
Surely you know!
Who stretched a ruler across it?
6 What were the earth's foundations set on,
or who put its cornerstone in place
7 while the morning stars sang together
and all the angels shouted with joy?

8 "Who shut the doors to keep the sea in
when it broke through and was born,
9 when I made the clouds like a coat for the
sea
and wrapped it in dark clouds,
10 when I put limits on the sea
and put its doors and bars in place,
11 when I said to the sea, 'You may come this
far, but no farther;
this is where your proud waves must
stop'?

12 "Have you ever ordered the morning to
begin,
or shown the dawn where its place was
13 in order to take hold of the earth by its
edges
and shake evil people out of it?
14 At dawn the earth changes like clay being
pressed by a seal;
the hills and valleys stand out like folds
in a coat.
15 Light is not given to evil people;
their arm is raised to do harm, but it is
broken.

16 "Have you ever gone to where the sea
begins
or walked in the valleys under the sea?
17 Have the gates of death been opened to
you?
Have you seen the gates of the deep
darkness?
18 Do you understand how wide the earth is?
Tell me, if you know all these things.

19 "What is the path to light's home,
and where does darkness live?

devotion 129

JOB 38:4–5

MYSTERIES OF GOD

My husband and I were in charge of a youth group for high school kids for ten years. Teenagers are such fun. They live life to the fullest and always find something to laugh about. They are a bit like sponges—taking in everything you say and often giving it right back to you when you least expect it. When we were in youth ministry, our own children were toddlers. We often wondered what it would be like to parent teenagers as compared to being their youth pastor. Now our children are teenagers ages seventeen, fifteen, and fourteen years old. Now we know!

When I read these verses, I can hear my husband giving one of our teenagers a much-needed lecture. Teens think they have all the answers and wonder how you have survived all these years. Everything you say tends to go in one ear and out the other. How often do we have the same attitude with God? We want God to do things our way. We are convinced that we know how our life should be played out.

Take time today and consider how God might have made the earth's foundation or carved out the ocean depths. How did God figure out how big the earth should be? We cannot even fathom the mysteries of God. Think about it: what we cannot even begin to understand, God simply spoke into existence. If he can do that, he certainly has the wisdom to guide our lives. Trust him!

20Can you take them to their places?
Do you know the way to their homes?
21Surely you know, if you were already born
when all this happened!
Have you lived that many years?

22"Have you ever gone into the storehouse
of the snow
or seen the storehouses for hail,
23which I save for times of trouble,
for days of war and battle?
24Where is the place from which light
comes?
Where is the place from which the east
winds blow over the earth?
25Who cuts a waterway for the heavy rains
and sets a path for the thunderstorm?
26Who waters the land where no one lives,
the desert that has no one in it?
27Who sends rain to satisfy the empty land
so the grass begins to grow?
28Does the rain have a father?
Who is father to the drops of dew?
29Who is the mother of the ice?
Who gives birth to the frost from the
sky
30when the water becomes hard as stone,
and even the surface of the ocean is
frozen?

31"Can you tie up the stars of the Pleiades
or loosen the ropes of the stars in
Orion?
32Can you bring out the stars on time
or lead out the stars of the Bear with its
cubs?
33Do you know the laws of the sky
and understand their rule over the
earth?

34"Can you shout an order to the clouds
and cover yourself with a flood of water?
35Can you send lightning bolts on their
way?
Do they come to you and say, 'Here we
are'?
36Who put wisdom inside the mind
or understanding in the heart?
37Who has the wisdom to count the clouds?
Who can pour water from the jars of
the sky
38when the dust becomes hard
and the clumps of dirt stick together?

39"Do you hunt food for the female lion
to satisfy the hunger of the young lions
40while they lie in their dens
or hide in the bushes waiting to attack?
41Who gives food to the birds
when their young cry out to God
and wander about without food?

39 "Do you know when the mountain
goats give birth?
Do you watch when the deer gives
birth to her fawn?
2Do you count the months until they give
birth
and know the right time for them to
give birth?
3They lie down, their young are born,
and then the pain of giving birth is
over.
4Their young ones grow big and strong in
the wild country.
Then they leave their homes and do not
return.

5"Who let the wild donkey go free?
Who untied its ropes?
6I am the one who gave the donkey the
desert as its home;
I gave it the desert lands as a place to
live.
7The wild donkey laughs at the confusion
in the city,
and it does not hear the drivers shout.
8It roams the hills looking for pasture,
looking for anything green to eat.

9"Will the wild ox agree to serve you
and stay by your feeding box at night?
10Can you hold it to the plowed row with a
harness
so it will plow the valleys for you?
11Will you depend on the wild ox for its
great strength
and leave your heavy work for it to do?
12Can you trust the ox to bring in your
grain
and gather it to your threshing floor?

13"The wings of the ostrich flap happily,
but they are not like the feathers of the
stork.
14The ostrich lays its eggs on the ground
and lets them warm in the sand.
15It does not stop to think that a foot might
step on them and crush them;
it does not care that some animal might
walk on them.

30Its young eat blood,
and where there is something dead, the
eagle is there."

40

The LORD said to Job:
2"Will the person who argues with
the Almighty correct him?
Let the person who accuses God answer
him."

3Then Job answered the LORD:
4"I am not worthy; I cannot answer you
anything,
so I will put my hand over my mouth.
5I spoke one time, but I will not answer
again;
I even spoke two times, but I will say
nothing more."

6Then the LORD spoke to Job from the
storm:
7"Be strong, like a man!
I will ask you questions,
and you must answer me.
8Would you say that I am unfair?
Would you blame me to make yourself
look right?
9Are you as strong as God?
Can your voice thunder like his?
10If so, then decorate yourself with glory
and beauty;
dress in honor and greatness as if they
were clothing.
11Let your great anger punish;
look at the proud and bring them
down.
12Look at the proud and make them
humble.
Crush the wicked wherever they are.
13Bury them all in the dirt together;
cover their faces in the grave.
14If you can do that, then I myself will
praise you,
because you are strong enough to save
yourself.

15"Look at Behemoth,[n]
which I made just as I made you.
It eats grass like an ox.
16Look at the strength it has in its body;
the muscles of its stomach are
powerful.
17Its tail is like a cedar tree;
the muscles of its thighs are woven
together.
18Its bones are like tubes of bronze;
its legs are like bars of iron.
19It is one of the first of God's works,
but its Maker can destroy it.
20The hills, where the wild animals play,
provide food for it.
21It lies under the lotus plants,
hidden by the tall grass in the swamp.
22The lotus plants hide it in their shadow;
the poplar trees by the streams
surround it.
23If the river floods, it will not be afraid;
it is safe even if the Jordan River rushes
to its mouth.
24Can anyone blind its eyes and capture it?
Can anyone put hooks in its nose?

41

"Can you catch Leviathan[n] on a
fishhook
or tie its tongue down with a rope?
2Can you put a cord through its nose
or a hook in its jaw?
3Will it keep begging you for mercy
and speak to you with gentle words?
4Will it make an agreement with you
and let you take it as your slave for life?
5Can you make a pet of Leviathan as you
would a bird
or put it on a leash for your girls?
6Will traders try to bargain with you for it?
Will they divide it up among the
merchants?
7Can you stick darts all over its skin
or fill its head with fishing spears?
8If you put one hand on it,
you will never forget the battle,
and you will never do it again!
9There is no hope of defeating it;
just seeing it overwhelms people.
10No one is brave enough to make it angry,
so who would be able to stand up
against me?
11No one has ever given me anything that I
must pay back,
because everything under the sky
belongs to me.

12"I will speak about Leviathan's arms and
legs,
its great strength and well-formed body.

40:15 Behemoth A large land animal, exact identity unknown. **41:1 Leviathan** A sea creature, exact identity unknown.

16The ostrich is cruel to its young, as if they
were not even its own.
It does not care that its work is for
nothing,
17because God did not give the ostrich
wisdom;
God did not give it a share of good
sense.
18But when the ostrich gets up to run, it is
so fast
that it laughs at the horse and its
rider.

19"Job, are you the one who gives the horse
its strength
or puts a flowing mane on its neck?
20Do you make the horse jump like a
locust?
It scares people with its proud snorting.
21It paws wildly, enjoying its strength,
and charges into battle.
22It laughs at fear and is afraid of nothing;
it does not run away from the sword.
23The bag of arrows rattles against the
horse's side,
along with the flashing spears and
swords.
24With great excitement, the horse races
over the ground;
and it cannot stand still when it hears
the trumpet.
25When the trumpet blows, the horse
snorts, 'Aha!'
It smells the battle from far away;
it hears the shouts of commanders and
the battle cry.

26"Is it through your wisdom that the hawk
flies
and spreads its wings toward the
south?
27Are you the one that commands the eagle
to fly
and build its nest so high?
28It lives on a high cliff and stays there at
night;
the rocky peak is its protected place.
29From there it looks for its food;
its eyes can see it from far away.

devotion 130

JOB 40:1–5

GOD DOESN'T SIGN ON THE DOTTED LINE

Some of the answers to life's questions are reserved only for the Maker of the heavens. We may think we know why God is bringing a certain difficult circumstance into our life, but our expectations often fall short of the glory God intends that pain to foster in us. We hand him bronze, but he has fired up the furnace to make twenty-four karat gold. We cannot see the full reality of the intense purifying process he uses to bring out the gold in our lives.

There have been many times I wanted God to sign on the dotted line of my personal contract for life. One of the things I wanted him to promise me was that I would feel no pain. Never leave disappointed. I wanted him to fill me in every time he was making a move in the cosmos. But I have learned it is not my job to be the general manager of the universe. There are mysteries to this life that will never be explained here. There are mysterious ways God uses tragedies that would baffle the mind. It is not for us to require an answer of the One who made us in the first place.

It doesn't mean that God doesn't care about how such suffering affects our lives. It doesn't mean that God is a power-hungry, Zeus-like character ready to throw down lightning at the first question. On the contrary, wrestling with God brings us closer to him and farther from ourselves.

13No one can tear off its outer hide
or poke through its double armor.
14No one can force open its great jaws;
they are filled with frightening teeth.
15It has rows of shields on its back
that are tightly sealed together.
16Each shield is so close to the next one
that no air can go between them.
17They are joined strongly to one another;
they hold on to each other and cannot be separated.
18When it snorts, flashes of light are thrown out,
and its eyes look like the light at dawn.
19Flames blaze from its mouth;
sparks of fire shoot out.
20Smoke pours out of its nose,
as if coming from a large pot over a hot fire.
21Its breath sets coals on fire,
and flames come out of its mouth.
22There is great strength in its neck.
People are afraid and run away.
23The folds of its skin are tightly joined;
they are set and cannot be moved.
24Its chest is as hard as a rock,
even as hard as a grinding stone.
25The powerful fear its terrible looks
and draw back in fear as it moves.
26The sword that hits it does not hurt it,
nor the arrows, darts, and spears.
27It treats iron as if it were straw
and bronze metal as if it were rotten wood.
28It does not run away from arrows;
stones from slings are like chaff to it.
29Clubs feel like pieces of straw to it,
and it laughs when they shake a spear at it.
30The underside of its body is like broken pieces of pottery.
It leaves a trail in the mud like a threshing board.
31It makes the deep sea bubble like a boiling pot;
it stirs up the sea like a pot of oil.
32When it swims, it leaves a shining path in the water

devotion 131

JOB 42:1–2

IT'S ALL A MATTER OF FOCUS

In the end, as a broken and changed man, Job confessed God's sovereignty. Job was changed because he had begun to really see God as he is. Before we begin to see God, we are inclined to believe that we have something to do with the goodness or the blessings we have enjoyed. Maybe we think that good things have come to us because we're educated or we have persevered or we have chosen wisely. When you and I really begin to see God as he is—holy, almighty, supreme, and yet loving—then we are also confronted with who we are not. And that perspective changes everything.

Every good thing has come to us from the sovereign hand of God. We are given our next breath because of his divine permission. Time moves at his bidding. Life stops as he has decided. His plans will not be ruined. He is God and we are not. He is the Creator and we are the created.

When you begin to see God, you will sense a change in your spirit. You will feel yourself begin to bow your life before his greatness. You will seek him as your divine authority and counsel. Pride will be replaced by humility. Self-importance will be changed by service. You will grieve the presence of sin in your life. May we all, like Job, have eyes to see God as he is. Sovereign. Invincible. Worthy of a life of praise and devotion.

that makes the sea look as if it had
white hair.
33 Nothing else on earth is equal to it;
it is a creature without fear.
34 It looks down on all those who are too
proud;
it is king over all proud creatures."

Job Answers the Lord

42 Then Job answered the LORD:
2 "I know that you can do all things
and that no plan of yours can be
ruined.
3 You asked, 'Who is this that made my
purpose unclear by saying things
that are not true?'
Surely I spoke of things I did not
understand;
I talked of things too wonderful for me
to know.
4 You said, 'Listen now, and I will speak.
I will ask you questions,
and you must answer me.'
5 My ears had heard of you before,
but now my eyes have seen you.
6 So now I hate myself;
I will change my heart and life.
I will sit in the dust and ashes."

End of the Story

7 After the LORD had said these things to
Job, he said to Eliphaz the Temanite, "I am
angry with you and your two friends,
because you have not said what is right
about me, as my servant Job did. 8 Now take
seven bulls and seven male sheep, and go to
my servant Job, and offer a burnt offering for
yourselves. My servant Job will pray for you,
and I will listen to his prayer. Then I will not
punish you for being foolish. You have not
said what is right about me, as my servant
Job did." 9 So Eliphaz the Temanite, Bildad
the Shuhite, and Zophar the Naamathite did
as the LORD said, and the LORD listened to
Job's prayer.

10 After Job had prayed for his friends, the
LORD gave him success again. The LORD gave
Job twice as much as he had owned before.
11 Job's brothers and sisters came to his
house, along with everyone who had known
him before, and they all ate with him there.
They comforted him and made him feel
better about the trouble the LORD had
brought on him, and each one gave Job a
piece of silver and a gold ring.

12 The LORD blessed the last part of Job's
life even more than the first part. Job had
fourteen thousand sheep, six thousand
camels, a thousand teams of oxen, and a
thousand female donkeys. 13 Job also had
seven sons and three daughters. 14 He named
the first daughter Jemimah, the second
daughter Keziah, and the third daughter
Keren-Happuch. 15 There were no other
women in all the land as beautiful as Job's
daughters. And their father Job gave them
land to own along with their brothers.

16 After this, Job lived one hundred forty
years. He lived to see his children,
grandchildren, great-grandchildren, and
great-great-grandchildren. 17 Then Job died;
he was old and had lived many years.

Psalms

From a Hebrew word meaning "praises," this collection of biblical songs, sometimes formally referred to as "the Psalter," is the Old Testament book most frequently quoted in the New Testament.

Person Holding the Pen God Wrote With: *King David* is commonly assumed to be the author of Psalms, but he actually only wrote about half of them. Other authors include *Asaph, Solomon, Moses, Heman, Ethan,* and the *sons of Korah.* Nearly a third of the psalms are anonymous.

When the Text Was Written: These 150 individual psalms were written over the time span of almost nine hundred years, from Moses' era (1400 B.C.) until after the Jewish people returned from captivity in Babylon (around 500 B.C.).

Spiritual Posture of the Original Recipients: Since this book was written over a broad time frame, the recipients exhibited every imaginable spiritual posture. Sometimes they were faithful to God, and sometimes they were angry with him. At times they were jubilant; at others they were repentant. Sometimes they simply felt sorry for themselves and didn't trust God.

Storyline Synopsis: While the central purpose of Psalms is to give praise to God, it also serves as a sort of diary of man's relationship with God. John Calvin, an ancient church "father," called Psalms an "anatomy of all parts of the soul"—and it certainly reflects the pendulum of emotion in human spirituality. Psalms journals the complexity of human nature—the good, the bad, and the ugly—and has heartened believers throughout history because of its authentic reflection of real life in all its messy glory. Consequently, the psalms cover a wide range of subjects and are formally classified into several types, including *wisdom* psalms, *penitential* psalms, *royal* or *Messianic* psalms, *thanksgiving* psalms, *imprecatory* psalms, psalms of *ascent* or *pilgrimage,* and psalms of *lament.* The book as a whole is traditionally organized into an introduction (chapters 1—2); five "books" (chapters 3—41, 42—72, 73—89, 90—106, and 107—145) that are each followed by a doxology; and a conclusion (chapters 146—150).

A Moment Worth Discussing: David recognizes that his sexual dalliance with Bathsheba has damaged the intimacy he once shared with God, and he pours out his poetical grief (Ps. 51). This is one of the most beautiful portraits of repentance in Scripture, and it serves as a model for the posture Christians should assume before our holy God.

Interesting (But Likely to Be Overlooked) Character: *Ethan the Ezrahite,* who penned one psalm (Ps. 89), wasn't as book smart as David's son Solomon (1 Kin. 4:31) but might have been a more talented musician (1 Chr. 6:42, 15:17–19).

Book 1

Two Ways to Live

1 Happy are those who don't listen to the
wicked,
who don't go where sinners go,
who don't do what evil people do.
2 They love the LORD's teachings,
and they think about those teachings
day and night.
3 They are strong, like a tree planted by a
river.
The tree produces fruit in season,
and its leaves don't die.
Everything they do will succeed.

4 But wicked people are not like that.
They are like chaff that the wind blows
away.
5 So the wicked will not escape God's
punishment.
Sinners will not worship with God's
people.
6 This is because the LORD takes care of his
people,
but the wicked will be destroyed.

The Lord's Chosen King

2 Why are the nations so angry?
Why are the people making useless
plans?
2 The kings of the earth prepare to fight,
and their leaders make plans together
against the LORD
and his appointed one.
3 They say, "Let's break the chains that hold
us back
and throw off the ropes that tie us
down."

4 But the one who sits in heaven laughs;
the Lord makes fun of them.
5 Then the LORD warns them
and frightens them with his anger.
6 He says, "I have appointed my own king
to rule in Jerusalem on my holy
mountain, Zion."

7 Now I will tell you what the LORD has
declared:
He said to me, "You are my son.
Today I have become your father.
8 If you ask me, I will give you the nations;
all the people on earth will be yours.
9 You will rule over them with an iron rod.
You will break them into pieces like
pottery."
10 So, kings, be wise;
rulers, learn this lesson.
11 Obey the LORD with great fear.
Be happy, but tremble.
12 Show that you are loyal to his son,
or you will be destroyed by his anger,
because he can quickly become angry.
But happy are those who trust him for
protection.

A Morning Prayer

David sang this when he ran away from his son Absalom.

3 LORD, I have many enemies!
Many people have turned against me.
2 Many are saying about me,
"God won't rescue him." *Selah*
3 But, LORD, you are my shield,
my wonderful God who gives me
courage.
4 I will pray to the LORD,
and he will answer me from his holy
mountain. *Selah*

5 I can lie down and go to sleep,
and I will wake up again,
because the LORD gives me strength.
6 Thousands of troops may surround me,
but I am not afraid.

7 LORD, rise up!
My God, come save me!
You have struck my enemies on the cheek;
you have broken the teeth of the
wicked.
8 The LORD can save his people.
LORD, bless your people. *Selah*

An Evening Prayer

For the director of music. With stringed instruments. A psalm of David.

4 Answer me when I pray to you,
my God who does what is right.
Make things easier for me when I am in
trouble.
Have mercy on me and hear my prayer.

2 People, how long will you turn my honor
into shame?
How long will you love what is false
and look for new lies? *Selah*
3 You know that the LORD has chosen for
himself those who are loyal to him.
The LORD listens when I pray to him.

4When you are angry, do not sin.
Think about these things quietly
as you go to bed. *Selah*
5Do what is right as a sacrifice to the LORD
and trust the LORD.

6Many people ask,
"Who will give us anything good?"
LORD, be kind to us.
7But you have made me very happy,
happier than they are,
even with all their grain and new wine.
8I go to bed and sleep in peace,
because, LORD, only you keep me safe.

A Morning Prayer for Protection

For the director of music. For flutes. A psalm of David.

5 LORD, listen to my words.
Understand my sadness.
2Listen to my cry for help, my King and my God,
because I pray to you.
3LORD, every morning you hear my voice.
Every morning, I tell you what I need,
and I wait for your answer.

4You are not a God who is pleased with the wicked;
you do not live with those who do evil.
5Those people who make fun of you
cannot stand before you.
You hate all those who do evil.
6You destroy liars;
the LORD hates those who kill and trick others.

7Because of your great love,
I can come into your Temple.
Because I fear and respect you,
I can worship in your holy Temple.
8LORD, since I have many enemies,
show me the right thing to do.
Show me clearly how you want me to live.

9My enemies' mouths do not tell the truth;
in their hearts they want to destroy others.
Their throats are like open graves;
they use their tongues for telling lies.
10God, declare them guilty!
Let them fall into their own traps.
Send them away because their sins are many;
they have turned against you.

devotion 132

PSALM 4:3–5

ARE YOU IN "THE BAD PLACE"?

There are times when I make the Wicked Witch of the West look like Glenda the Good Witch's twin sister. When I get in what I call the "bad place," I quickly need to get alone with the Lord, get heart-to-heart with him, and be totally honest. When anger starts to show itself in my life, I know that my frustration level has topped out. Believe me, it is ugly—Wicked Witch of the West ugly! Frustration is the spark that starts the fire of anger. With life's everyday needs, demands, and even failures, it can cause you to step out into the "bad place" where you sin in your anger, hurt others' feelings, or even worse, be a spirit killer. It is humbling to have to clean up all the emotional damage caused by your own anger.

Galatians 5:22-23 says that the Spirit produces the fruit of self-control. Yes, it is a fruit, which means it doesn't just appear like magic (unless of course you are a Chia Pet). It is a seed that is planted in your heart through the Word and a discipline that is nurtured through your circumstances. This is the secret for growing your seedlings into fruit: be still and call out to God. He can't hear you if you're not talking to him. Want more tips on growing your seedlings into mature fruit? Trust God, be honest, and be heart-to-heart with your Lord. Today is the day your seed of self-control is being watered.

[11]But let everyone who trusts you be happy;
let them sing glad songs forever.
Protect those who love you
and who are happy because of you.
[12]LORD, you bless those who do what is right;
you protect them like a soldier's shield.

A Prayer for Mercy in Troubled Times

For the director of music. With stringed instruments. Upon the sheminith. A psalm of David.

6 LORD, don't correct me when you are angry;
don't punish me when you are very angry.
[2]LORD, have mercy on me because I am weak.
Heal me, LORD, because my bones ache.
[3]I am very upset.
LORD, how long will it be?

[4]LORD, return and save me;
save me because of your kindness.
[5]Dead people don't remember you;
those in the grave don't praise you.

[6]I am tired of crying to you.
Every night my bed is wet with tears;
my bed is soaked from my crying.
[7]My eyes are weak from so much crying;
they are weak from crying about my enemies.

[8]Get away from me, all you who do evil,
because the LORD has heard my crying.
[9]The LORD has heard my cry for help;
the LORD will answer my prayer.
[10]All my enemies will be ashamed and troubled.
They will turn and suddenly leave in shame.

A Prayer for Fairness

A shiggaion of David which he sang to the LORD about Cush, from the tribe of Benjamin.

7 LORD my God, I trust in you for protection.
Save me and rescue me
from those who are chasing me.
[2]Otherwise, like a lion they will tear me apart.
They will rip me to pieces, and no one can save me.

[3]LORD my God, what have I done?
Have my hands done something wrong?
[4]Have I done wrong to my friend
or stolen without reason from my enemy?
[5]If I have, let my enemy chase me and capture me.
Let him trample me into the dust
and bury me in the ground. *Selah*

[6]LORD, rise up in your anger;
stand up against my enemies' anger.
Get up and demand fairness.
[7]Gather the nations around you
and rule them from above.
[8]LORD, judge the people.
LORD, defend me because I am right,
because I have done no wrong, God Most High.
[9]God, you do what is right.
You know our thoughts and feelings.
Stop those wicked actions done by evil people,
and help those who do what is right.
[10]God protects me like a shield;
he saves those whose hearts are right.
[11]God judges by what is right,
and God is always ready to punish the wicked.
[12]If they do not change their lives,
God will sharpen his sword;
he will string his bow and take aim.
[13]He has prepared his deadly weapons;
he has made his flaming arrows.

[14]There are people who think up evil
and plan trouble and tell lies.
[15]They dig a hole to trap others,
but they will fall into it themselves.
[16]They will get themselves into trouble;
the violence they cause will hurt only themselves.

[17]I praise the LORD because he does what is right.
I sing praises to the LORD Most High.

The Lord's Greatness

For the director of music. On the gittith. A psalm of David.

8 LORD our Lord,
your name is the most wonderful name in all the earth!
It brings you praise in heaven above.
[2]You have taught children and babies
to sing praises to you
because of your enemies.

And so you silence your enemies
and destroy those who try to get even.

3 I look at your heavens,
which you made with your fingers.
I see the moon and stars,
which you created.
4 But why are people even important to you?
Why do you take care of human beings?
5 You made them a little lower than the angels
and crowned them with glory and honor.
6 You put them in charge of everything you made.
You put all things under their control:
7 all the sheep, the cattle,
and the wild animals,
8 the birds in the sky,
the fish in the sea,
and everything that lives under water.

9 LORD our Lord,
your name is the most wonderful name in all the earth!

Thanksgiving for Victory

For the director of music. To the tune of "The Death of the Son." A psalm of David.

9 I will praise you, LORD, with all my heart.
I will tell all the miracles you have done.
2 I will be happy because of you;
God Most High, I will sing praises to your name.
3 My enemies turn back;
they are overwhelmed and die because of you.
4 You have heard my complaint;
you sat on your throne and judged by what was right.
5 You spoke strongly against the foreign nations and destroyed the wicked;
you wiped out their names forever and ever.
6 The enemy is gone forever.
You destroyed their cities;
no one even remembers them.

7 But the LORD rules forever.
He sits on his throne to judge,
8 and he will judge the world in fairness;
he will decide what is fair for the nations.

devotion 133

PSALM 8:4–6

PEGGING AWAY

God amazes me. Why did he put us in charge of all that he made? He knew that we would mess it all up, yet he did it anyway. I look at my little portion of creation and wonder if I'm caring for it the way I should. I often tell my husband that doing housework is such a thankless job. We make the beds, wash the clothes, and do the dishes—all of which is undone before the day is through. Our children, our pets, and our homes are all part of God's creation, which he has placed in our care. These verses cause me to look at my housework a little differently. Am I caring for my home in a way that honors God, or do I live in chaos most of the time? Does my yard bring glory to God, or is it the eyesore of the neighborhood?

The Bible talks about us ruling with God someday in heaven. I think this life is all part of our training. One of my family members has a plaque over her kitchen sink that she had re-created for all her grandchildren that says, "Praise and Pray and Peg Away." I love the simplicity of that. It reminds me to keep on doing the things that need to be done, but do it in an attitude of praise and prayer. I need to be diligent with the little that God has put under my control so that one day I will be worthy of the honor of ruling beside him.

9The LORD defends those who suffer;
he defends them in times of trouble.
10Those who know the LORD trust him,
because he will not leave those who come to him.

11Sing praises to the LORD who is king on Mount Zion.
Tell the nations what he has done.
12He remembers who the murderers are;
he will not forget the cries of those who suffer.
13LORD, have mercy on me.
See how my enemies hurt me.
Do not let me go through the gates of death.
14Then, at the gates of Jerusalem, I will praise you;
I will rejoice because you saved me.

15The nations have fallen into the pit they dug.
Their feet are caught in the nets they laid.
16The LORD has made himself known by his fair decisions;
the wicked get trapped by what they do. *Higgaion. Selah*

17Wicked people will go to the grave,
and so will all those who forget God.
18But those who have troubles will not be forgotten.
The hopes of the poor will never die.

19LORD, rise up and judge the nations.
Don't let people think they are strong.
20Teach them to fear you, LORD.
The nations must learn that they are only human. *Selah*

A Complaint About Evil People

10 LORD, why are you so far away?
Why do you hide when there is trouble?
2Proudly the wicked chase down those who suffer.
Let them be caught in their own traps.
3They brag about the things they want.
They bless the greedy but hate the LORD.
4The wicked people are too proud.
They do not look for God;
there is no room for God in their thoughts.
5They always succeed.
They are far from keeping your laws;
they make fun of their enemies.
6They say to themselves, "Nothing bad will ever happen to me;
I will never be ruined."
7Their mouths are full of curses, lies, and threats;
they use their tongues for sin and evil.
8They hide near the villages.
They look for innocent people to kill;
they watch in secret for the helpless.
9They wait in hiding like a lion.
They wait to catch poor people;
they catch the poor in nets.
10The poor are thrown down and crushed;
they are defeated because the others are stronger.
11The wicked think, "God has forgotten us.
He doesn't see what is happening."

12LORD, rise up and punish the wicked.
Don't forget those who need help.
13Why do wicked people hate God?
They say to themselves, "God won't punish us."
14LORD, surely you see these cruel and evil things;
look at them and do something.
People in trouble look to you for help.
You are the one who helps the orphans.
15Break the power of wicked people.
Punish them for the evil they have done.

16The LORD is King forever and ever.
Destroy from your land those nations that do not worship you.
17LORD, you have heard what the poor people want.
Do what they ask, and listen to them.
18Protect the orphans and put an end to suffering
so they will no longer be afraid of evil people.

Trust in the Lord

For the director of music. Of David.

11 I trust in the LORD for protection.
So why do you say to me,
"Fly like a bird to your mountain.
2Like hunters, the wicked string their bows;
they set their arrows on the bowstrings.
They shoot from dark places
at those who are honest.

3When the foundations for good collapse,
what can good people do?"

4The LORD is in his holy temple;
the LORD sits on his throne in heaven.
He sees what people do;
he keeps his eye on them.
5The LORD tests those who do right,
but he hates the wicked and those who love to hurt others.
6He will send hot coals and burning sulfur on the wicked.
A whirlwind is what they will get.
7The LORD does what is right, and he loves justice,
so honest people will see his face.

A Prayer Against Liars

For the director of music. Upon the sheminith. A psalm of David.

12 Save me, LORD, because the good people are all gone;
no true believers are left on earth.
2Everyone lies to his neighbors;
they say one thing and mean another.

3The LORD will stop those flattering lips
and cut off those bragging tongues.
4They say, "Our tongues will help us win.
We can say what we wish; no one is our master."

5But the LORD says,
"I will now rise up,
because the poor are being hurt.
Because of the moans of the helpless,
I will give them the help they want."
6The LORD's words are pure,
like silver purified by fire,
like silver purified seven times over.

7LORD, you will keep us safe;
you will always protect us from such people.
8But the wicked are all around us;
everyone loves what is wrong.

A Prayer for God to Be Near

For the director of music. A psalm of David.

13 How long will you forget me, LORD? Forever?
How long will you hide from me?
2How long must I worry
and feel sad in my heart all day?
How long will my enemy win over me?

devotion 134

PSALM 11:7

WHAT DO TAXES HAVE TO DO WITH GOD'S PRESENCE?

When David said that people will see the face of God, he meant that honest people will be admitted into the Lord's presence and will enjoy his blessings. Sometimes God is asking us to be honest with him in private, to tell the truth of our motives, to confess our sin, or to own up to our weaknesses. But God also promises his presence to those who *live* honestly. God is concerned with the ordinary details of our lives—pumping gas, interacting with teachers and coaches, punching a time card, or paying taxes. He is offering the glory of his presence and the blessings of his pleasure to those who take care to tell the truth and conduct business and family matters with integrity.

It's so easy to rationalize the little things. Skim here, round off there, tell a "little" white lie. But God is waiting for moral and trustworthy people to honor him, even in the mundane routines of life. He waits for honest people to show themselves, and then he blesses them with the bounty of his presence.

Here's the deal. If you really believe that God is God, that he has your best interests at heart, that his plans for your life are beyond anything you could hope for, then there is no need to fudge on taxes or lie for your own benefit. When you trust God for your happiness and live honestly, even in the ordinary, he promises you will see his face and receive his blessing.

3LORD, look at me.
Answer me, my God;
tell me, or I will die.
4Otherwise my enemy will say, "I have won!"
Those against me will rejoice that I've been defeated.
5I trust in your love.
My heart is happy because you saved me.
6I sing to the LORD
because he has taken care of me.

The Unbelieving Fool

For the director of music. Of David.

14 Fools say to themselves,
"There is no God."
Fools are evil and do terrible things;
there is no one who does anything good.
2The LORD looked down from heaven on all people
to see if anyone understood,
if anyone was looking to God for help.
3But all have turned away.
Together, everyone has become evil.
There is no one who does anything good,
not even one.

4Don't the wicked understand?
They destroy my people as if they were eating bread.
They do not ask the LORD for help.
5But the wicked are filled with terror,
because God is with those who do what is right.
6The wicked upset the plans of the poor,
but the LORD will protect them.

7I pray that victory will come to Israel from Mount Zion!
May the LORD bring them back.
Then the people of Jacob will rejoice,
and the people of Israel will be glad.

What the Lord Demands

A psalm of David.

15 LORD, who may enter your Holy Tent?
Who may live on your holy mountain?

2Only those who are innocent
and who do what is right.
Such people speak the truth from their hearts
3 and do not tell lies about others.
They do no wrong to their neighbors
and do not gossip.
4They do not respect hateful people
but honor those who honor the LORD.
They keep their promises to their neighbors,
even when it hurts.
5They do not charge interest on money they lend
and do not take money to hurt innocent people.

Whoever does all these things will never be destroyed.

The Lord Takes Care of His People

A miktam of David.

16 Protect me, God,
because I trust in you.
2I said to the LORD, "You are my Lord.
Every good thing I have comes from you."
3As for the godly people in the world,
they are the wonderful ones I enjoy.
4But those who turn to idols
will have much pain.
I will not offer blood to those idols
or even speak their names.

5No, the LORD is all I need.
He takes care of me.
6My share in life has been pleasant;
my part has been beautiful.

7I praise the LORD because he advises me.
Even at night, I feel his leading.
8I keep the LORD before me always.
Because he is close by my side,
I will not be hurt.
9So I rejoice and am glad.
Even my body has hope,
10because you will not leave me in the grave.
You will not let your holy one rot.
11You will teach me how to live a holy life.
Being with you will fill me with joy;
at your right hand I will find pleasure forever.

A Prayer for Protection

A prayer of David.

17 LORD, hear me begging for fairness;
listen to my cry for help.

devotion 135

PSALM 16:2–11

A SPIRITUAL SKIP IN YOUR STEP

Have you ever been so full of happiness that you said hello to everyone you passed and your eyes saw beauty in each glance? God's glory was blazing all around you. Your heartache was forgotten. You were bursting with joy, and you just couldn't keep it in. That's David's heart in Psalm 16.

God has promised all through Scripture that fellowship with him will make us full of joy. Spiritual and emotional fullness frees us to see his glory, enjoy his good gifts, and praise him for the whole, wide world to see. And when we have become full from our fellowship with God, we begin to overflow, sloshing out the goodness of God onto others—spilling his glory.

But this kind of fullness, this spiritual skip in your step, begins in private—you and God enjoying lots of alone time. It's you pursuing him in the unseen. Living through trials with integrity. Praying. Reading his words to you. Choosing holiness and right living. Changing when the Holy Spirit prompts. Giving in secret. Loving. Forgiving. Running from the old person you used to be.

That kind of fellowship, day after day, consistent and sustained, brings the fellowship that makes us full. When we are full, we won't make empty choices and suffer miserable consequences. When we are full, God's Spirit is guiding us. Working through us. Walking us through the life he dreamed of before we were even born. Be alone with God today and watch how he fills you up with his joy.

Pay attention to my prayer,
because I speak the truth.
2 You will judge that I am right;
your eyes can see what is true.
3 You have examined my heart;
you have tested me all night.
You questioned me without finding
anything wrong;
I have not sinned with my mouth.
4 I have obeyed your commands,
so I have not done what evil people do.
5 I have done what you told me;
I have not failed.

6 I call to you, God,
and you answer me.
Listen to me now,
and hear what I say.
7 Your love is wonderful.
By your power you save those who
trust you
from their enemies.
8 Protect me as you would protect your
own eye.
Hide me under the shadow of your
wings.
9 Keep me from the wicked who attack me,
from my enemies who surround me.
10 They are selfish
and brag about themselves.
11 They have chased me until they have
surrounded me.
They plan to throw me to the ground.
12 They are like lions ready to kill;
like lions, they sit in hiding.

13 LORD, rise up, face the enemy, and throw
them down.
Save me from the wicked with your
sword.
14 LORD, save me by your power
from those whose reward is in this life.
They have plenty of food.
They have many sons

and leave much money to their
children.
15 Because I have lived right, I will see your
face.
When I wake up, I will see your
likeness and be satisfied.

A Song of Victory

For the director of music. By the LORD's servant, David. David sang this song to the LORD when the Lord had saved him from Saul and all his other enemies.

18 I love you, LORD. You are my strength.
2 The LORD is my rock, my protection,
my Savior.
My God is my rock.
I can run to him for safety.
He is my shield and my saving strength,
my defender.
3 I will call to the LORD, who is worthy of
praise,
and I will be saved from my enemies.

4 The ropes of death came around me;
the deadly rivers overwhelmed me.
5 The ropes of death wrapped around me.
The traps of death were before me.
6 In my trouble I called to the LORD.
I cried out to my God for help.
From his temple he heard my voice;
my call for help reached his ears.

7 The earth trembled and shook.
The foundations of the mountains
began to shake.
They trembled because the LORD was
angry.
8 Smoke came out of his nose,
and burning fire came out of his mouth.
Burning coals went before him.
9 He tore open the sky and came down
with dark clouds under his feet.
10 He rode a creature with wings and flew.
He raced on the wings of the wind.
11 He made darkness his covering, his
shelter around him,
surrounded by fog and clouds.
12 Out of the brightness of his presence came
clouds
with hail and lightning.
13 The LORD thundered from heaven;
the Most High raised his voice,
and there was hail and lightning.
14 He shot his arrows and scattered his
enemies.
His many bolts of lightning confused
them with fear.
15 LORD, you spoke strongly.
The wind blew from your nose.
Then the valleys of the sea appeared,
and the foundations of the earth were
seen.

16 The LORD reached down from above and
took me;
he pulled me from the deep water.
17 He saved me from my powerful enemies,
from those who hated me, because they
were too strong for me.
18 They attacked me at my time of trouble,
but the LORD supported me.
19 He took me to a safe place.
Because he delights in me, he saved me.

20 The LORD spared me because I did what
was right.
Because I have not done evil, he has
rewarded me.
21 I have followed the ways of the LORD;
I have not done evil by turning away
from my God.
22 I remember all his laws
and have not broken his rules.
23 I am innocent before him;
I have kept myself from doing evil.
24 The LORD rewarded me because I did what
was right,
because I did what the LORD said was
right.

25 LORD, you are loyal to those who are loyal,
and you are good to those who are
good.
26 You are pure to those who are pure,
but you are against those who are bad.
27 You save the humble,
but you bring down those who are
proud.
28 LORD, you give light to my lamp.
My God brightens the darkness
around me.
29 With your help I can attack an army.
With God's help I can jump over a wall.

30 The ways of God are without fault.
The LORD's words are pure.
He is a shield to those who trust him.
31 Who is God? Only the LORD.
Who is the Rock? Only our God.
32 God is my protection.
He makes my way free from fault.

devotion 136

PSALM 18:28–30

JUMP THAT WALL!

If you feel like running to the nearest church or ministry to seek new employment, I implore you to stop, drop, and pray. Of course, if the Lord is opening that door for you and it is a desire of your heart, then go for it. However, if you are one of those Christians who believes that you are not useful in advancing the kingdom if you have a secular job, then I am talking to you. You are a vessel, a lamp if you will, that is being used by the Holy Spirit to light the way in a dark place. How would people ever see or hear about the goodness of God if you were not there working side by side with them everyday?

So get ready and jump that wall! Ask God for his help and a double portion of discernment for what is going on in others' lives around you so you may impact their lives for his glory. If you want a ministry that rocks, share your hope with those who desire to revive their dried-up, dead lives with living water. When the Holy Spirit starts to march little lost souls into your office for advice, be prepared to boldly and confidently counsel and encourage them with the Word. I want to remind you, Christian, that the Lord told Joshua that everywhere he placed his feet, God would give him that land. Place your feet firmly in your workplace and rock it out for Jesus.

33 He makes me like a deer that does not
stumble;
he helps me stand on the steep
mountains.
34 He trains my hands for battle
so my arms can bend a bronze bow.
35 You protect me with your saving shield.
You support me with your right hand.
You have stooped to make me great.
36 You give me a better way to live,
so I live as you want me to.
37 I chased my enemies and caught them.
I did not quit until they were destroyed.
38 I crushed them so they couldn't rise up
again.
They fell beneath my feet.
39 You gave me strength in battle.
You made my enemies bow before me.
40 You made my enemies turn back,
and I destroyed those who hated me.
41 They called for help,
but no one came to save them.
They called to the LORD,
but he did not answer them.
42 I beat my enemies into pieces, like dust in
the wind.
I poured them out like mud in the
streets.

43 You saved me when the people attacked me.
You made me the leader of nations.
People I never knew serve me.
44 As soon as they hear me, they obey me.
Foreigners obey me.
45 They all become afraid
and tremble in their hiding places.

46 The LORD lives!
May my Rock be praised.
Praise the God who saves me!
47 God gives me victory over my enemies
and brings people under my rule.
48 He saves me from my enemies.

You set me over those who hate me.
You saved me from violent people.
49 So I will praise you, LORD, among the
nations.
I will sing praises to your name.

50 The LORD gives great victories to his
king.
He is loyal to his appointed king,
to David and his descendants forever.

God's Works and Word

For the director of music. A psalm of David.

19 The heavens declare the glory of God,
and the skies announce what his
hands have made.
2 Day after day they tell the story;
night after night they tell it again.
3 They have no speech or words;
they have no voice to be heard.
4 But their message goes out through all the
world;
their words go everywhere on earth.
The sky is like a home for the sun.
5 The sun comes out like a bridegroom
from his bedroom.
It rejoices like an athlete eager to run a
race.
6 The sun rises at one end of the sky
and follows its path to the other end.
Nothing hides from its heat.

7 The teachings of the LORD are perfect;
they give new strength.
The rules of the LORD can be trusted;
they make plain people wise.
8 The orders of the LORD are right;
they make people happy.
The commands of the LORD are pure;
they light up the way.
9 Respect for the LORD is good;
it will last forever.
The judgments of the LORD are true;
they are completely right.
10 They are worth more than gold,
even the purest gold.
They are sweeter than honey,
even the finest honey.
11 By them your servant is warned.
Keeping them brings great reward.

12 People cannot see their own mistakes.
Forgive me for my secret sins.
13 Keep me from the sins of pride;
don't let them rule me.
Then I can be pure
and innocent of the greatest of sins.

14 I hope my words and thoughts please you.
LORD, you are my Rock, the one who
saves me.

A Prayer for the King

For the director of music. A psalm of David.

20 May the LORD answer you in times of
trouble.
May the God of Jacob protect you.
2 May he send you help from his Temple
and support you from Mount Zion.
3 May he remember all your offerings
and accept all your sacrifices. *Selah*
4 May he give you what you want
and make all your plans succeed,
5 and we will shout for joy when you
succeed,
and we will raise a flag in the name of
our God.
May the LORD give you all that you ask
for.

6 Now I know the LORD helps his appointed
king.
He answers him from his holy heaven
and saves him with his strong right
hand.
7 Some trust in chariots, others in horses,
but we trust the LORD our God.
8 They are overwhelmed and defeated,
but we march forward and win.
9 LORD, save the king!
Answer us when we call for help.

Thanksgiving for the King

For the director of music. A psalm of David.

21 LORD, the king rejoices because of your
strength;
he is so happy when you save him!
2 You gave the king what he wanted
and did not refuse what he asked
for. *Selah*
3 You put good things before him
and placed a gold crown on his head.
4 He asked you for life,
and you gave it to him,
so his years go on and on.
5 He has great glory because you gave him
victories;
you gave him honor and praise.
6 You always gave him blessings;
you made him glad because you were
with him.
7 The king truly trusts the LORD.
Because God Most High always loves
him,
he will not be overwhelmed.
8 Your hand is against all your enemies;

devotion 137

PSALM 20:7–8

CHARIOTS AND HURRICANES

I have lived in southern Florida all my life. My grandparents came here in 1945, so my family has lived through many a hurricane. I have never worried about hurricanes because my family never seemed too bothered by them. Then last year we had three major storms in six weeks. Family and friends just north of us lived through loss and chaos for months afterward. I think quite differently about hurricanes now. This summer, we did some renovations to our home, and I thought about the possibility of how, in just a moment, a hurricane could destroy everything we were doing. Are we pouring ourselves into things that will eventually be destroyed?

Where have you placed your trust? Just as the Scriptures talk about placing trust in horses and chariots, we place our trust in people and things. We often accumulate so much stuff in our lives that we spend most of our time taking care of those things. We also build relationships that are unhealthy because we are searching for our value in the relationship rather than God. The fact is, things will deteriorate and people will eventually disappoint us. We need to place our trust in our eternal Lord because he never disappoints. Look up the parable of the house built on the rock in Matthew 7:24-27. Where you place your trust is where you are building your house. Are you building on the Rock or on things that could be destroyed in a moment?

those who hate you will feel your
power.
9When you appear,
you will burn them as in a furnace.
In your anger you will swallow them up,
and fire will burn them up.
10You will destroy their families from the
earth;
their children will not live.
11They made evil plans against you,
but their traps won't work.
12You will make them turn their backs
when you aim your arrows at them.
13Be supreme, LORD, in your power.
We sing and praise your greatness.

The Prayer of a Suffering Man

For the director of music. To the tune of "The Doe of Dawn." A psalm of David.

22 My God, my God, why have you
abandoned me?
You seem far from saving me,
far away from my groans.
2My God, I call to you during the day,
but you do not answer.
I call at night;
I am not silent.
3You sit as the Holy One.
The praises of Israel are your
throne.
4Our ancestors trusted you;
they trusted, and you saved them.
5They called to you for help
and were rescued.
They trusted you
and were not disappointed.
6But I am like a worm instead of a man.
People make fun of me and hate me.
7Those who look at me laugh.
They stick out their tongues and shake
their heads.
8They say, "Turn to the LORD for help.
Maybe he will save you.
If he likes you,
maybe he will rescue you."

9 You had my mother give birth to me.
You made me trust you
while I was just a baby.
10 I have leaned on you since the day I was born;
you have been my God since my mother gave me birth.
11 So don't be far away from me.
Now trouble is near,
and there is no one to help.
12 People have surrounded me like angry bulls.
Like the strong bulls of Bashan, they are on every side.
13 Like hungry, roaring lions
they open their mouths at me.
14 My strength is gone,
like water poured out onto the ground,
and my bones are out of joint.
My heart is like wax;
it has melted inside me.
15 My strength has dried up like a clay pot,
and my tongue sticks to the top of my mouth.
You laid me in the dust of death.
16 Evil people have surrounded me;
like dogs they have trapped me.
They have bitten my arms and legs.
17 I can count all my bones;
people look and stare at me.
18 They divided my clothes among them,
and they threw lots for my clothing.

19 But, LORD, don't be far away.
You are my strength; hurry to help me.
20 Save me from the sword;
save my life from the dogs.
21 Rescue me from the lion's mouth;
save me from the horns of the bulls.

22 Then I will tell my brothers and sisters about you;
I will praise you in the public meeting.
23 Praise the LORD, all you who respect him.
All you descendants of Jacob, honor him;
fear him, all you Israelites.
24 He does not ignore those in trouble.
He doesn't hide from them
but listens when they call out to him.
25 LORD, I praise you in the great meeting of your people;
these worshipers will see me do what I promised.
26 Poor people will eat until they are full;
those who look to the LORD will praise him.
May your hearts live forever!
27 People everywhere will remember
and will turn to the LORD.
All the families of the nations
will worship him
28 because the LORD is King,
and he rules the nations.

29 All the powerful people on earth will eat and worship.
Everyone will bow down to him,
all who will one day die.
30 The people in the future will serve him;
they will always be told about the Lord.
31 They will tell that he does what is right.
People who are not yet born
will hear what God has done.

The Lord the Shepherd

A psalm of David.

23 The LORD is my shepherd;
I have everything I need.
2 He lets me rest in green pastures.
He leads me to calm water.
3 He gives me new strength.
He leads me on paths that are right
for the good of his name.
4 Even if I walk through a very dark valley,
I will not be afraid,
because you are with me.
Your rod and your shepherd's staff
comfort me.

5 You prepare a meal for me
in front of my enemies.
You pour oil of blessing on my head;[n]
you fill my cup to overflowing.
6 Surely your goodness and love will be with me
all my life,
and I will live in the house of the LORD forever.

A Welcome for God into the Temple

A psalm of David.

24 The earth belongs to the LORD, and everything in it—
the world and all its people.

23:5 pour oil . . . head This can mean that God gave him great wealth and blessed him.

2He built it on the waters
and set it on the rivers.

3Who may go up on the mountain of the LORD?
Who may stand in his holy Temple?
4Only those with clean hands and pure hearts,
who have not worshiped idols,
who have not made promises in the name of a false god.
5They will receive a blessing from the LORD;
the God who saves them will declare them right.
6They try to follow God;
they look to the God of Jacob for help. *Selah*

7Open up, you gates.
Open wide, you aged doors
and the glorious King will come in.
8Who is this glorious King?
The LORD, strong and mighty.
The LORD, the powerful warrior.
9Open up, you gates.
Open wide, you aged doors
and the glorious King will come in.
10Who is this glorious King?
The LORD All-Powerful—
he is the glorious King. *Selah*

A Prayer for God to Guide

Of David.

25 LORD, I give myself to you;
2 my God, I trust you.
Do not let me be disgraced;
do not let my enemies laugh at me.
3No one who trusts you will be disgraced,
but those who sin without excuse will be disgraced.

4LORD, tell me your ways.
Show me how to live.
5Guide me in your truth,
and teach me, my God, my Savior.
I trust you all day long.
6LORD, remember your mercy and love
that you have shown since long ago.
7Do not remember the sins
and wrong things I did when I was young.

devotion 138

PSALM 25:1-5

NO PICKING AND CHOOSING

What if Jesus walked into your kitchen this morning and said, "Hi, I'm Jesus. I am the Son of God. I came into the world to save sinners, give them everlasting life, and provide true joy. My death and resurrection has atoned for sin. And by my wisdom, I can show you how to make the best choices that will bring you the greatest life and joy. Will you trust me?"

And what if you said, "I want to be forgiven, so thanks for the forgiveness. But I'm not sure you know how to make choices that will bring me true joy, so I'm just going to go my own way on that one."

The same God who has saved you wants to direct your life. He wants to show you the best choices you can make and guide you in every step you have before you. It's amazing how many of us want a part of God but not all of him. And then we wonder why we are lacking or empty or lost. If you've trusted him to save you for eternity, will you trust him with the decisions you face this day? Will you wait for his wisdom? Will you consult him in everything that concerns you?

Say with David, "Lord, I give myself to you; my God, I trust you" (verse 1). Humble yourself before the Lord. Be reverent, for he is almighty. And trust his mercy and counsel with all your heart.

But remember to love me always
because you are good, LORD.
[8]The LORD is good and right;
he points sinners to the right way.
[9]He shows those who are humble how to do right,
and he teaches them his ways.
[10]All the LORD's ways are loving and true
for those who follow the demands of his agreement.
[11]For the sake of your name, LORD,
forgive my many sins.
[12]Are there those who respect the LORD?
He will point them to the best way.
[13]They will enjoy a good life,
and their children will inherit the land.
[14]The LORD tells his secrets to those who respect him;
he tells them about his agreement.
[15]My eyes are always looking to the LORD for help.
He will keep me from any traps.
[16]Turn to me and have mercy on me,
because I am lonely and hurting.
[17]My troubles have grown larger;
free me from my problems.
[18]Look at my suffering and troubles,
and take away all my sins.
[19]Look at how many enemies I have!
See how much they hate me!
[20]Protect me and save me.
I trust you, so do not let me be disgraced.
[21]My hope is in you,
so may goodness and honesty guard me.
[22]God, save Israel from all their troubles!

The Prayer of an Innocent Believer

Of David.

26 LORD, defend me because I have lived an innocent life.
I have trusted the LORD and never doubted.
[2]LORD, try me and test me;
look closely into my heart and mind.
[3]I see your love,
and I live by your truth.
[4]I do not spend time with liars,
nor do I make friends with those who hide their sin.
[5]I hate the company of evil people,
and I won't sit with the wicked.
[6]I wash my hands to show I am innocent,
and I come to your altar, LORD.
[7]I raise my voice in praise
and tell of all the miracles you have done.
[8]LORD, I love the Temple where you live,
where your glory is.
[9]Do not kill me with those sinners
or take my life with those murderers.
[10]Evil is in their hands,
and they do wrong for money.
[11]But I have lived an innocent life,
so save me and have mercy on me.
[12]I stand in a safe place.
LORD, I praise you in the great meeting.

A Song of Trust in God

Of David.

27 The LORD is my light and the one who saves me.
So why should I fear anyone?
The LORD protects my life.
So why should I be afraid?
[2]Evil people may try to destroy my body.
My enemies and those who hate me attack me,
but they are overwhelmed and defeated.
[3]If an army surrounds me,
I will not be afraid.
If war breaks out,
I will trust the LORD.

[4]I ask only one thing from the LORD.
This is what I want:
Let me live in the LORD's house
all my life.
Let me see the LORD's beauty
and look with my own eyes at his Temple.
[5]During danger he will keep me safe in his shelter.
He will hide me in his Holy Tent,
or he will keep me safe on a high mountain.
[6]My head is higher than my enemies around me.
I will offer joyful sacrifices in his Holy Tent.
I will sing and praise the LORD.

[7]LORD, hear me when I call;
have mercy and answer me.
[8]My heart said of you, "Go, worship him."
So I come to worship you, LORD.
[9]Do not turn away from me.
Do not turn your servant away in anger;
you have helped me.

devotion 139

PSALM 27

BULLIES ON OUR PLAYGROUND

Most women I know are beset with fear. We are all constantly battling spiritual enemies that loom in the shadows and bully us with unrelenting intimidation. Fear kicks us under the table, elbows us in the ribs, and pinches us when no one is looking. Fear tells us that we deserve punishment and then keeps us in a headlock until we scream, "Uncle! Okay, okay, I believe it."

The bullies yell, "You can't!" to make us stop trying.

The enemies cry, "You could get hurt!" to send our dreams packing.

Fear asks, "What if they knew all your sin?" to steal our forgiveness.

These adversaries snicker, "You don't deserve anything," and we fall for it again and again. This kind of fear will play with your head, rip out your heart, and empty your soul.

Are you battling with the bully of fear? Have the enemies of your dreams ambushed you again? Then look at where David turned when his enemies attacked. He decided to trust God more than the fierceness of his assailants. He believed that God was his protector and rested in that truth.

You and I will face enemies until we stand in the presence of God. There will be new battles and old ones that flare up again. But each time, we must decide in our hearts and reflect with our lives: I truly believe. I am living to see his goodness. I will be strong and brave and wait for God's deliverance.

Do not push me away or leave me alone,
God, my Savior.
10 If my father and mother leave me,
the LORD will take me in.
11 LORD, teach me your ways,
and guide me to do what is right
because I have enemies.
12 Do not hand me over to my enemies,
because they tell lies about me
and say they will hurt me.

13 I truly believe
I will live to see the LORD's goodness.
14 Wait for the LORD's help.
Be strong and brave,
and wait for the LORD's help.

A Prayer in Troubled Times

Of David.

28 LORD, my Rock, I call out to you for help.
Do not be deaf to me.
If you are silent,
I will be like those in the grave.
2 Hear the sound of my prayer,
when I cry out to you for help.
I raise my hands
toward your Most Holy Place.
3 Don't drag me away with the wicked,
with those who do evil.
They say "Peace" to their neighbors,
but evil is in their hearts.
4 Pay them back for what they have done,
for their evil deeds.
Pay them back for what they have done;
give them their reward.
5 They don't understand what the LORD has done
or what he has made.
So he will knock them down
and not lift them up.

6 Praise the LORD,
because he heard my prayer for help.
7 The LORD is my strength and shield.
I trust him, and he helps me.

I am very happy,
and I praise him with my song.
8The LORD is powerful;
he gives victory to his chosen one.
9Save your people
and bless those who are your own.
Be their shepherd and carry them
forever.

God in the Thunderstorm

A psalm of David.

29 Praise the LORD, you angels;
praise the LORD's glory and power.
2Praise the LORD for the glory of his name;
worship the LORD because he is holy.

3The LORD's voice is heard over the sea.
The glorious God thunders;
the LORD thunders over the ocean.
4The LORD's voice is powerful;
the LORD's voice is majestic.
5The LORD's voice breaks the trees;
the LORD breaks the cedars of
Lebanon.
6He makes the land of Lebanon dance like
a calf
and Mount Hermon jump like a baby
bull.
7The LORD's voice makes the lightning
flash.
8The LORD's voice shakes the desert;
the LORD shakes the Desert of Kadesh.
9The LORD's voice shakes the oaks
and strips the leaves off the trees.
In his Temple everyone says, "Glory to
God!"

10The LORD controls the flood.
The LORD will be King forever.
11The LORD gives strength to his people;
the LORD blesses his people with peace.

Thanksgiving for Escaping Death

A psalm of David. A song for giving the Temple to the LORD.

30 I will praise you, LORD,
because you rescued me.
You did not let my enemies laugh
at me.

devotion 140

PSALM 29:10–11

STORM WARNING!

Coming from southern Florida, I know about scary storms! They are dangerous, loud, and they bring uncertainty and fear. The only thing comforting about Florida's storms is that they are fairly predictable. When a major storm like a hurricane approaches, you know for days that it is coming and where it will make landfall. You take comfort in knowing you can prevent yourself from being in its path and avoid destruction since you know where the storm is headed.

Is there a storm heading your way? You can be fairly certain that if you are currently in a wrong relationship, continuing in a certain sin, or struggling with a lack of self-control that the storm warning is upon you. What is causing a separation between you and your King?

Storm warnings are a good thing because they allow you to get out before the storm comes. Sweet Christian, get out of the way! Unless you are crazy, I do not know anyone who purposely welcomes suffering. Lay down everything that is keeping you in the path of harm's way. The Lord will provide you with strength to tackle each issue and clear it from your life. When you are tired or afraid, remember you can be encouraged by **F**inding **A**nswers in **I**ntimate **T**imes with **H**im—FAITH. When you start to freak out about all that is going on around you, draw tight into the Lord and remind yourself that he alone is your protection. He will bless you with peace.

2 LORD, my God, I prayed to you,
and you healed me.
3 You lifted me out of the grave;
you spared me from going down to the place of the dead.

4 Sing praises to the LORD, you who belong to him;
praise his holy name.
5 His anger lasts only a moment,
but his kindness lasts for a lifetime.
Crying may last for a night,
but joy comes in the morning.

6 When I felt safe, I said,
"I will never fear."
7 LORD, in your kindness you made my mountain safe.
But when you turned away, I was frightened.

8 I called to you, LORD,
and asked you to have mercy on me.
9 I said, "What good will it do if I die
or if I go down to the grave?
Dust cannot praise you;
it cannot speak about your truth.
10 LORD, hear me and have mercy on me.
LORD, help me."

11 You changed my sorrow into dancing.
You took away my clothes of sadness,
and clothed me in happiness.
12 I will sing to you and not be silent.
LORD, my God, I will praise you forever.

A Prayer of Faith in Troubled Times

For the director of music. A psalm of David.

31 LORD, I trust in you;
let me never be disgraced.
Save me because you do what is right.
2 Listen to me
and save me quickly.
Be my rock of protection,
a strong city to save me.
3 You are my rock and my protection.
For the good of your name, lead me and guide me.
4 Set me free from the trap they set for me,
because you are my protection.
5 I give you my life.
Save me, LORD, God of truth.

6 I hate those who worship false gods.
I trust only in the LORD.
7 I will be glad and rejoice in your love,
because you saw my suffering;
you knew my troubles.
8 You have not handed me over to my enemies
but have set me in a safe place.

9 LORD, have mercy, because I am in misery.
My eyes are weak from so much crying,
and my whole being is tired from grief.
10 My life is ending in sadness,
and my years are spent in crying.
My troubles are using up my strength,
and my bones are getting weaker.
11 Because of all my troubles, my enemies hate me,
and even my neighbors look down on me.
When my friends see me,
they are afraid and run.
12 I am like a piece of a broken pot.
I am forgotten as if I were dead.
13 I have heard many insults.
Terror is all around me.
They make plans against me
and want to kill me.
14 LORD, I trust you.
I have said, "You are my God."
15 My life is in your hands.
Save me from my enemies
and from those who are chasing me.
16 Show your kindness to me, your servant.
Save me because of your love.
17 LORD, I called to you,
so do not let me be disgraced.
Let the wicked be disgraced
and lie silent in the grave.
18 With pride and hatred
they speak against those who do right.
So silence their lying lips.

19 How great is your goodness
that you have stored up for those who fear you,
that you have given to those who trust you.
You do this for all to see.
20 You protect them by your presence
from what people plan against them.
You shelter them from evil words.
21 Praise the LORD.
His love to me was wonderful
when my city was attacked.
22 In my distress, I said,
"God cannot see me!"

But you heard my prayer
when I cried out to you for help.
23 Love the LORD, all you who belong to him.
The LORD protects those who truly believe,
but he punishes the proud as much as they have sinned.
24 All you who put your hope in the LORD
be strong and brave.

It Is Better to Confess Sin

A maskil of David.

32 Happy is the person
whose sins are forgiven,
whose wrongs are pardoned.
2 Happy is the person
whom the LORD does not consider guilty
and in whom there is nothing false.
3 When I kept things to myself,
I felt weak deep inside me.
I moaned all day long.
4 Day and night you punished me.
My strength was gone as in the summer heat. *Selah*
5 Then I confessed my sins to you
and didn't hide my guilt.
I said, "I will confess my sins to the LORD,"
and you forgave my guilt. *Selah*
6 For this reason, all who obey you
should pray to you while they still can.
When troubles rise like a flood,
they will not reach them.
7 You are my hiding place.
You protect me from my troubles
and fill me with songs of salvation. *Selah*
8 The LORD says, "I will make you wise and show you where to go.
I will guide you and watch over you.
9 So don't be like a horse or donkey,
that doesn't understand.
They must be led with bits and reins,
or they will not come near you."
10 Wicked people have many troubles,
but the LORD's love surrounds those who trust him.
11 Good people, rejoice and be happy in the LORD.
Sing all you whose hearts are right.

Praise God Who Creates and Saves

33 Sing to the LORD, you who do what is right;
honest people should praise him.

devotion 141

PSALM 32:7–9

HIKING THE GRAND CANYON

Several years ago, we took our four children to the Grand Canyon. My husband, who is an avid hiker, planned an excursion for us to hike eight miles through the canyon and stay on an Indian reservation called Havasupi. The only problems were that we were hiking in August, we started our hike at noon, and it was one hundred degrees out there. As we started out, I asked my son where the water I had packed for him was. "Don't worry," he said, "I had a Gatorade in the car." We were in trouble. About a mile into the hike, my children and I thought we were going to die before the trip was over. I have never been more focused on the Lord than I was during the next four hours of hiking.

So often in our lives, we think we are wise. We assume that we know which way to go and continue on our path until trouble comes our way. The Lord wants us to look to him for direction so we will be protected from troubles *before* they come our way. We had planned our trip to the Grand Canyon months in advance and thought we were prepared for the journey. We were wrong. How often we do the same thing in our everyday lives. Allow God to guide you and protect you from troubles by seeking direction from him. He will show you where to go and the best path to take to get there.

2Praise the LORD on the harp;
make music for him on a ten-stringed lyre.
3Sing a new song to him;
play well and joyfully.

4God's word is true,
and everything he does is right.
5He loves what is right and fair;
the LORD's love fills the earth.

6The sky was made at the LORD's command.
By the breath from his mouth, he made all the stars.
7He gathered the water of the sea into a heap.
He made the great ocean stay in its place.
8All the earth should worship the LORD;
the whole world should fear him.
9He spoke, and it happened.
He commanded, and it appeared.
10The LORD upsets the plans of nations;
he ruins all their plans.
11But the LORD's plans will stand forever;
his ideas will last from now on.
12Happy is the nation whose God is the LORD,
the people he chose for his very own.
13The LORD looks down from heaven
and sees every person.
14From his throne he watches
all who live on earth.
15He made their hearts
and understands everything they do.
16No king is saved by his great army.
No warrior escapes by his great strength.
17Horses can't bring victory;
they can't save by their strength.
18But the LORD looks after those who fear him,
those who put their hope in his love.
19He saves them from death
and spares their lives in times of hunger.
20So our hope is in the LORD.
He is our help, our shield to protect us.
21We rejoice in him,
because we trust his holy name.
22LORD, show your love to us
as we put our hope in you.

Praise God Who Judges and Saves

David's song from the time he acted crazy so Abimelech would send him away, and David did leave.

34 I will praise the LORD at all times;
his praise is always on my lips.
2My whole being praises the LORD.
The poor will hear and be glad.
3Glorify the LORD with me,
and let us praise his name together.

4I asked the LORD for help, and he answered me.
He saved me from all that I feared.
5Those who go to him for help are happy,
and they are never disgraced.
6This poor man called, and the LORD heard him
and saved him from all his troubles.
7The angel of the LORD camps around those who fear God,
and he saves them.

8Examine and see how good the LORD is.
Happy is the person who trusts him.
9You who belong to the LORD, fear him!
Those who fear him will have everything they need.
10Even lions may get weak and hungry,
but those who look to the LORD will have every good thing.
11Children, come and listen to me.
I will teach you to worship the LORD.
12You must do these things
to enjoy life and have many happy days.
13You must not say evil things,
and you must not tell lies.
14Stop doing evil and do good.
Look for peace and work for it.

15The LORD sees the good people
and listens to their prayers.
16But the LORD is against those who do evil;
he makes the world forget them.
17The LORD hears good people when they cry out to him,
and he saves them from all their troubles.
18The LORD is close to the brokenhearted,
and he saves those whose spirits have been crushed.

19People who do what is right may have many problems,
but the LORD will solve them all.

20He will protect their very bones;
not one of them will be broken.
21Evil will kill the wicked;
those who hate good people will be judged guilty.
22But the LORD saves his servants' lives;
no one who trusts him will be judged guilty.

A Prayer for Help

Of David.

35 LORD, battle with those who battle with me.
Fight against those who fight against me.
2Pick up the shield and armor.
Rise up and help me.
3Lift up your spears, both large and small,
against those who chase me.
Tell me, "I will save you."

4Make those who want to kill me
be ashamed and disgraced.
Make those who plan to harm me
turn back and run away.
5Make them like chaff blown by the wind
as the angel of the LORD forces them away.
6Let their road be dark and slippery
as the angel of the LORD chases them.
7For no reason they spread out their net to trap me;
for no reason they dug a pit for me.
8So let ruin strike them suddenly.
Let them be caught in their own nets;
let them fall into the pit and die.
9Then I will rejoice in the LORD;
I will be happy when he saves me.
10Even my bones will say,
"LORD, who is like you?
You save the weak from the strong,
the weak and poor from robbers."

11Men without mercy stand up to testify.
They ask me things I do not know.
12They repay me with evil for the good I have done,
and they make me very sad.
13Yet when they were sick, I put on clothes of sadness
and showed my sorrow by fasting.
But my prayers were not answered.
14 I acted as if they were my friends or brothers.
I bowed in sadness as if I were crying for my mother.

15But when I was in trouble, they gathered and laughed;
they gathered to attack before I knew it.
They insulted me without stopping.
16They made fun of me and were cruel to me
and ground their teeth at me in anger.
17Lord, how long will you watch this happen?
Save my life from their attacks;
save me from these people who are like lions.
18I will praise you in the great meeting.
I will praise you among crowds of people.
19Do not let my enemies laugh at me;
they hate me for no reason.
Do not let them make fun of me;
they have no cause to hate me.
20Their words are not friendly
but are lies about peace-loving people.
21They speak against me
and say, "Aha! We saw what you did!"

22LORD, you have been watching. Do not keep quiet.
Lord, do not leave me alone.
23Wake up! Come and defend me!
My God and Lord, fight for me!
24LORD my God, defend me with your justice.
Don't let them laugh at me.
25Don't let them think, "Aha! We got what we wanted!"
Don't let them say, "We destroyed him."
26Let them be ashamed and embarrassed,
because they were happy when I hurt.
Cover them with shame and disgrace,
because they thought they were better than I was.
27May my friends sing and shout for joy.
May they always say, "Praise the greatness of the LORD,
who loves to see his servants do well."
28I will tell of your goodness
and will praise you every day.

Wicked People and a Good God

For the director of music. Of David, the servant of the LORD.

36 Sin speaks to the wicked in their hearts.
They have no fear of God.
2They think too much of themselves
so they don't see their sin and hate it.
3Their words are wicked lies;
they are no longer wise or good.

4At night they make evil plans;
what they do leads to nothing good.
They don't refuse things that are evil.

5LORD, your love reaches to the heavens,
your loyalty to the skies.
6Your goodness is as high as the mountains.
Your justice is as deep as the great ocean.
LORD, you protect both people and animals.
7God, your love is so precious!
You protect people in the shadow of your wings.
8They eat the rich food in your house,
and you let them drink from your river of pleasure.
9You are the giver of life.
Your light lets us enjoy life.

10Continue to love those who know you
and to do good to those who are good.
11Don't let proud people attack me
and the wicked force me away.
12Those who do evil have been defeated.
They are overwhelmed;
they cannot do evil any longer.

God Will Reward Fairly

Of David.

37 Don't be upset because of evil people.
Don't be jealous of those who do wrong,
2because like the grass, they will soon dry up.
Like green plants, they will soon die away.

3Trust the LORD and do good.
Live in the land and feed on truth.
4Enjoy serving the LORD,
and he will give you what you want.
5Depend on the LORD;
trust him, and he will take care of you.
6Then your goodness will shine like the sun,
and your fairness like the noonday sun.

7Wait and trust the LORD.
Don't be upset when others get rich
or when someone else's plans succeed.
8Don't get angry.
Don't be upset; it only leads to trouble.

devotion 142

PSALM 37:16-24

GRAB HIS HAND

I recall a time as a child when I was walking in the park with my dad. The path was rocky, and I kept stumbling along the way. When the path got too difficult for my little legs to walk on, I ended up falling down. As I fought tears, I looked up to see my dad extending his hand out to me. Taking it, I suddenly felt lifted up and was able to walk over the rockiest parts. Isn't that exactly what our heavenly Father does for us? Just when we think we can't go on anymore, he reaches out to help us up, and while holding our hand, he keeps us from falling. Unfortunately, it seems like we frequently don't accept God's outstretched hand.

Sometimes as we travel through life, we seem bent on stumbling along all by ourselves without ever depending on God's help. Many times, we even try to forge our own paths instead of walking the path that God has already lovingly laid out for us. How many times do we find ourselves lost along a path that we never fully intended to go on? We've made one too many wrong decisions and chosen a road that ultimately leads to a dead end. But even then, we can reach out to God, grab his hand, and let him lift us up. God is always pleased when we hold his hand, and it's at that point in our walk that he can keep us from falling.

9Evil people will be sent away,
but those who trust the LORD will inherit the land.
10In a little while the wicked will be no more.
You may look for them, but they will be gone.
11People who are not proud will inherit the land
and will enjoy complete peace.

12The wicked make evil plans against good people.
They grind their teeth at them in anger.
13But the Lord laughs at the wicked,
because he sees that their day is coming.
14The wicked draw their swords
and bend their bows
to kill the poor and helpless,
to kill those who are honest.
15But their swords will stab their own hearts,
and their bows will break.

16It is better to have little and be right
than to have much and be wrong.
17The power of the wicked will be broken,
but the LORD supports those who do right.
18The LORD watches over the lives of the innocent,
and their reward will last forever.
19They will not be ashamed when trouble comes.
They will be full in times of hunger.
20But the wicked will die.
The LORD's enemies will be like the flowers of the fields;
they will disappear like smoke.
21The wicked borrow and don't pay back,
but those who do right give freely to others.
22Those whom the LORD blesses will inherit the land,
but those he curses will be sent away.

23When people's steps follow the LORD,
God is pleased with their ways.
24If they stumble, they will not fall,
because the LORD holds their hand.

25I was young, and now I am old,
but I have never seen good people left helpless
or their children begging for food.
26Good people always lend freely to others,
and their children are a blessing.

27Stop doing evil and do good,
so you will live forever.
28The LORD loves justice
and will not leave those who worship him.
He will always protect them,
but the children of the wicked will die.
29Good people will inherit the land
and will live in it forever.

30Good people speak with wisdom,
and they say what is fair.
31The teachings of their God are in their heart,
so they do not fail to keep them.
32The wicked watch for good people
so that they may kill them.
33But the LORD will not take away his protection
or let good people be judged guilty.

34Wait for the LORD's help
and follow him.
He will honor you and give you the land,
and you will see the wicked sent away.

35I saw a wicked and cruel man
who looked strong like a healthy tree in good soil.
36But he died and was gone;
I looked for him, but he couldn't be found.
37Think of the innocent person,
and watch the honest one.
The man who has peace
will have children to live after him.
38But sinners will be destroyed;
in the end the wicked will die.

39The LORD saves good people;
he is their strength in times of trouble.
40The LORD helps them and saves them;
he saves them from the wicked,
because they trust in him for protection.

A Prayer in Time of Sickness

A psalm of David to remember.

38 LORD, don't correct me when you are angry.

Don't punish me when you are
furious.
2Your arrows have wounded me,
and your hand has come down
on me.
3My body is sick from your punishment.
Even my bones are not healthy because
of my sin.
4My guilt has overwhelmed me;
like a load it weighs me down.

5My sores stink and become infected
because I was foolish.
6I am bent over and bowed down;
I am sad all day long.
7I am burning with fever,
and my whole body is sore.
8I am weak and faint.
I moan from the pain I feel.

9Lord, you know everything I want;
my cries are not hidden from you.
10My heart pounds, and my strength is
gone.
I am losing my sight.
11Because of my wounds, my friends and
neighbors avoid me,
and my relatives stay far away.
12Some people set traps to kill me.
Those who want to hurt me plan
trouble;
all day long they think up lies.

13I am like the deaf; I cannot hear.
Like the mute, I cannot speak.
14I am like those who do not hear,
who have no answer to give.
15I trust you, LORD.
You will answer, my Lord and God.
16I said, "Don't let them laugh at me
or brag when I am defeated."
17I am about to die,
and I cannot forget my pain.
18I confess my guilt;
I am troubled by my sin.
19My enemies are strong and healthy,
and many hate me for no reason.
20They repay me with evil for the good I
did.
They lie about me because I try to do
good.

21LORD, don't leave me;
my God, don't go away.

devotion 143

PSALM 40:1–3

WHEN LIFE IS THE PITS

David had fallen into a pit. Maybe it was a time of spiritual dryness or a physical trial or an overwhelming circumstance. Whatever it was, the situation had taken a godly man down, and he called on God. To love God does not exclude us from the very difficult and disappointing trials that come to all of us. David had fallen, and each one of us knows firsthand what that feels like.

But our goal as believers is to learn from David's path toward restoration. From his love for God, he has shown us where to go and how to get to God when we find ourselves in despair. Let's look at the six stages of his experience, and then follow him closely.

First, David was in a muddy pit. Second, he cried out to God for help. Third, he waited for the Lord. Fourth, God lifted him out to safety. Fifth, God gave David a new song. And sixth, others trusted God when they saw the pattern of David's life.

We can cry out to God in our distress, and then wait humbly and hopefully for the Lord. When God comes in his own time and in his own way to make us secure, it's time to begin a new song of praise for his provision. Others will see how our lives worship God, and they will learn to cry out from their pit and call on his awesome name. What an amazing lesson from an amazing life.

22 Quickly come and help me,
my Lord and Savior.

Life Is Short

For the director of music. For Jeduthun. A psalm of David.

39 I said, "I will be careful how I act
and will not sin by what I say.
I will be careful what I say
around wicked people."
2 So I kept very quiet.
I didn't even say anything good,
but I became even more upset.
3 I became very angry inside,
and as I thought about it, my anger
burned.
So I spoke:
4 "LORD, tell me when the end will come
and how long I will live.
Let me know how long I have.
5 You have given me only a short life;
my lifetime is like nothing to you.
Everyone's life is only a breath. *Selah*
6 People are like shadows moving about.
All their work is for nothing;
they collect things but don't know who
will get them.

7 "So, Lord, what hope do I have?
You are my hope.
8 Save me from all my sins.
Don't let wicked fools make fun of me.
9 I am quiet; I do not open my mouth,
because you are the one who has done
this.
10 Quit punishing me;
your beating is about to kill me.
11 You correct and punish people for their
sins;
like a moth, you destroy what they
love.
Everyone's life is only a breath. *Selah*

12 "LORD, hear my prayer,
and listen to my cry.
Do not ignore my tears.
I am like a visitor with you.
Like my ancestors, I'm only here a short
time.
13 Leave me alone so I can be happy
before I leave and am no more."

Praise and Prayer for Help

For the director of music. A psalm of David.

40 I waited patiently for the LORD.
He turned to me and heard my cry.
2 He lifted me out of the pit of destruction,
out of the sticky mud.
He stood me on a rock
and made my feet steady.
3 He put a new song in my mouth,
a song of praise to our God.
Many people will see this and worship
him.
Then they will trust the LORD.

4 Happy is the person
who trusts the LORD,
who doesn't turn to those who are proud
or to those who worship false gods.
5 LORD my God, you have done many
miracles.
Your plans for us are many.
If I tried to tell them all,
there would be too many to count.

6 You do not want sacrifices and offerings.
But you have made a hole in my ear
to show that my body and life are yours.
You do not ask for burnt offerings
and sacrifices to take away sins.
7 Then I said, "Look, I have come.
It is written about me in the book.
8 My God, I want to do what you want.
Your teachings are in my heart."

9 I will tell about your goodness in the
great meeting of your people.
LORD, you know my lips are not silent.
10 I do not hide your goodness in my heart;
I speak about your loyalty and salvation.
I do not hide your love and truth
from the people in the great meeting.

11 LORD, do not hold back your mercy
from me;
let your love and truth always
protect me.
12 Troubles have surrounded me;
there are too many to count.
My sins have caught me
so that I cannot see a way to escape.
I have more sins than hairs on my head,
and I have lost my courage.
13 Please, LORD, save me.
Hurry, LORD, to help me.
14 People are trying to kill me.
Shame them and disgrace them.
People want to hurt me.
Let them run away in disgrace.
15 People are making fun of me.
Let them be shamed into silence.

16 But let those who follow you
be happy and glad.
They love you for saving them.
May they always say, "Praise the
LORD!"

17 Lord, because I am poor and helpless,
please remember me.
You are my helper and savior.
My God, do not wait.

A Prayer in Time of Sickness

For the director of music. A psalm of David.

41 Happy are those who think about the
poor.
When trouble comes, the LORD will
save them.
2 The LORD will protect them and spare
their life
and will bless them in the land.
He will not let their enemies take
them.
3 The LORD will give them strength when
they are sick,
and he will make them well again.

4 I said, "LORD, have mercy on me.
Heal me, because I have sinned against
you."
5 My enemies are saying evil things about
me.
They say, "When will he die and be
forgotten?"
6 Some people come to see me,
but they lie.
They just come to get bad news.
Then they go and gossip.
7 All my enemies whisper about me
and think the worst about me.
8 They say, "He has a terrible disease.
He will never get out of bed again."
9 My best and truest friend, who ate at my
table,
has even turned against me.

10 LORD, have mercy on me.
Give me strength so I can pay them
back.
11 Because my enemies do not defeat me,
I know you are pleased with me.
12 Because I am innocent, you support me
and will let me be with you forever.

devotion 144

PSALM 42:1–2

MEETING THE LORD

When David wrote Psalm 42, he painted a picture for us of what an intense thirst for God looks like: a sweet deer after a long day's journey looking for a crystal brook to quench his thirst. I cannot imagine going an entire day without water; in fact, if I deprive my body of that provision, dehydration and a headache soon follow. How much more does your spirit need watering when precious communion time is missing with the Lord? There is nothing I desire more than to get alone with the Lord, to see what he has to say to me, to pray with him, and to get into his Word. Those are the true desires of my heart and the intentions of my spirit.

But somewhere between desire and intention, life happens. Before my feet hit the floor, schedules, commitments, and everything in between take over. The only way to overcome life and get to the stream is to make a commitment to meet the Lord anyway and anywhere we can. If life interrupts before your feet hit the floor, then you need to meet him before you set one little toe down. If your lunch hour is the only time you can get to the brook, then go alone. If late in the evening immersed in your tub is the only piece of quiet you have, ask the Lord to share it with you. God wants to satisfy your thirst, and I promise he will meet you anywhere.

13 Praise the LORD, the God of Israel.
He has always been,
and he will always be.
Amen and amen.

Book 2

Wishing to Be Near God

For the director of music. A maskil of the sons of Korah.

42 As a deer thirsts for streams of water,
so I thirst for you, God.
2 I thirst for the living God.
When can I go to meet with him?
3 Day and night, my tears have been my food.
People are always saying,
"Where is your God?"
4 When I remember these things,
I speak with a broken heart.
I used to walk with the crowd
and lead them to God's Temple
with songs of praise.

5 Why am I so sad?
Why am I so upset?
I should put my hope in God
and keep praising him,
my Savior and 6 my God.

I am very sad.
So I remember you where the Jordan
River begins,
near the peaks of Hermon and Mount
Mizar.
7 Troubles have come again and again,
sounding like waterfalls.
Your waves are crashing all around me.
8 The LORD shows his true love every day.
At night I have a song,
and I pray to my living God.
9 I say to God, my Rock,
"Why have you forgotten me?
Why am I sad
and troubled by my enemies?"
10 My enemies' insults make me feel
as if my bones were broken.
They are always saying,
"Where is your God?"

11 Why am I so sad?
Why am I so upset?
I should put my hope in God
and keep praising him,
my Savior and my God.

A Prayer for Protection

43 God, defend me.
Argue my case against those who
don't follow you.
Save me from liars and those who do
evil.
2 God, you are my strength.
Why have you rejected me?
Why am I sad
and troubled by my enemies?
3 Send me your light and truth
to guide me.
Let them lead me to your holy
mountain,
to where you live.
4 Then I will go to the altar of God,
to God who is my joy and happiness.
I will praise you with a harp,
God, my God.

5 Why am I so sad?
Why am I so upset?
I should put my hope in God
and keep praising him,
my Savior and my God.

A Prayer for Help

For the director of music. A maskil of the sons of Korah.

44 God, we have heard about you.
Our ancestors told us
what you did in their days,
in days long ago.
2 With your power you forced the nations
out of the land
and placed our ancestors here.
You destroyed those other nations,
but you made our ancestors grow
strong.
3 It wasn't their swords that took the land.
It wasn't their power that gave them
victory.
But it was your great power and strength.
You were with them because you loved
them.

4 My God, you are my King.
Your commands led Jacob's people to
victory.
5 With your help we pushed back our
enemies.
In your name we trampled those who
came against us.
6 I don't trust my bow to help me,
and my sword can't save me.

7You saved us from our foes,
and you made our enemies ashamed.
8We will praise God every day;
we will praise your name forever. *Selah*

9But you have rejected us and shamed us.
You don't march with our armies
anymore.
10You let our enemies push us back,
and those who hate us have taken our
wealth.
11You gave us away like sheep to be eaten
and have scattered us among the
nations.
12You sold your people for nothing
and made no profit on the sale.

13You made us a joke to our neighbors;
those around us laugh and make fun
of us.
14You made us a joke to the other nations;
people shake their heads.
15I am always in disgrace,
and I am covered with shame.
16My enemy is getting even
with insults and curses.

17All these things have happened to us,
but we have not forgotten you
or failed to keep our agreement with
you.
18Our hearts haven't turned away from you,
and we haven't stopped following you.
19But you crushed us in this place where
wild dogs live,
and you covered us with deep darkness.

20If we had forgotten our God
or lifted our hands in prayer to foreign
gods,
21God would have known,
because he knows what is in our hearts.
22But for you we are in danger of death all
the time.
People think we are worth no more
than sheep to be killed.

23Wake up, Lord! Why are you sleeping?
Get up! Don't reject us forever.
24Why do you hide from us?
Have you forgotten our pain and
troubles?

25We have been pushed down into the
dirt;
we are flat on the ground.
26Get up and help us.
Because of your love, save us.

devotion 145

PSALM 44:3

THE BABY THAT LEARNED TO SMILE

They called her the baby that never smiled. She came to us at eight months old with allergies and a rash all over her body. We began the process of assessing her needs, taking her to the doctor, and loving her. A month later, she was a different baby. Physically, her skin had returned to a beautiful color, and her allergies had subsided. But the biggest change was in her personality. She became the baby who never stops smiling. She loves to sing, dance, and clap. She crawls after me looking for my attention and a way to make me laugh. She captures the heart of anyone who walks into the room.

The power of love is an amazing thing. God loved the Israelites so much that he used his power and strength to defeat godless nations for a people he called his own. God wants to do the same in your life. We just have to accept his love. Babies easily accept love if it is given consistently. I am often amazed at how easily our foster babies take to us. I expect them to cry the first few days that we have them, but they just watch us and wait to see what we have to offer. When they experience our love, they quickly love us right back. Jesus said we should come to him as little children. Come willing to accept his love and trust him with your life. He will turn you into a child who always smiles.

A Song for the King's Wedding

For the director of music. To the tune of "Lilies." A maskil. A love song of the sons of Korah.

45 Beautiful words fill my mind.
I am speaking of royal things.
My tongue is like the pen of a skilled writer.

2 You are more handsome than anyone,
and you are an excellent speaker,
so God has blessed you forever.
3 Put on your sword, powerful warrior.
Show your glory and majesty.
4 In your majesty win the victory
for what is true and right.
Your power will do amazing things.
5 Your sharp arrows will enter
the hearts of the king's enemies.
Nations will be defeated before you.
6 God, your throne will last forever and ever.
You will rule your kingdom with fairness.
7 You love right and hate evil,
so God has chosen you from among your friends;
he has set you apart with much joy.
8 Your clothes smell like myrrh, aloes, and cassia.
From palaces of ivory
music comes to make you happy.
9 Kings' daughters are among your honored women.
Your bride stands at your right side
wearing gold from Ophir.

10 Listen to me, daughter; look and pay attention.
Forget your people and your father's family.
11 The king loves your beauty.
Because he is your master, you should obey him.
12 People from the city of Tyre have brought a gift.
Wealthy people will want to meet you.
13 The princess is very beautiful.
Her gown is woven with gold.
14 In her beautiful clothes she is brought to the king.

devotion 146

PSALM 46:1-10

REASONS UNREVEALED

My mind is still flooded with television images from those first days after the 2004 tsunami. I know they'll grip my heart forever. Perhaps most heartbreaking were the accounts of hundreds of children who perished in the deluge. I hope they weren't afraid and were carried straight home to God!

As I watched the footage of the disaster, I cried out to God for the people of Indonesia. I didn't understand why so many souls, so many of them children, were taken in one fell swoop; but I did know that we'd seen the power of nature unleashed in a way that had never occurred in our lifetime. I felt insignificant in comparison, and one question was foremost in my mind: "Why Lord?"

As difficult as it is to accept, I've come to realize it's not my job to understand why God allows nature to unleash its power when human beings are in its path. I choose to believe that he is a God of justice—even when his reasons haven't been revealed. Maybe when natural disasters strike we can see them as a reminder that our God is both gentle enough to orchestrate the birth of a child and mighty enough to shake the mountains.

While we might feel insignificant compared to the mountains or the earth's beauty and power, it's pretty astounding to know that the Creator of those things is the same amazing God who created and loves us. And he invites us to be still in his presence.

moods

"On the broom" is a term I use when referring to my mood. I have days when, for no apparent reason at all, I feel like calling that broom out of the corner and jumping on for a frenzied ride, terrorizing anyone or anything that gets in my path, including my co-workers, my husband, my friends, or even unsuspecting strangers. What causes me to get so harried that I lose control? It's called being empty—poured out with nothing left in the well, not a single drop.

As women, we can just keep going and going on nothing but fumes. Then at the worst time possible, one of those fumes can fuel a spark that rages into a fire. I hate when empty explodes like that. If my car runs out of gas, whose fault is it? The gas station hasn't moved; I just drove on by and didn't stop for a refill.

When we are empty and OTB, we wind up hurting the people we love the most, the ones that we most want to protect. Then comes the conviction and humility of making things right. You'll also have to deal with the guilt that comes from knowing that your rapid-fire flame burned someone else and left a singe on your own spirit as well. And you're not off the hook when you offend a stranger. The Holy Spirit will just make sure, for instance, that they wind up in the prayer line at church while you are a prayer counselor!

Here's the point: stop and get filled up! Don't keep passing by the Word on your nightstand. Dust it off and fill your heart and soul with the spiritual fuel you so desperately need. I would much rather enjoy a peaceful drive through the countryside than an OTB ride on the wild side!

THINK ABOUT IT: How often do you fill your well?
What are your greatest struggles when the negative attitudes of your heart manifest in your actions?

DIG DEEPER: Proverbs 22:11 (reputation), Jeremiah 6:16 (choices), 2 Corinthians 9:8 (God's ample supply), and 1 Peter 3:8–11 (kindness)

marriage

Marriage is one of the greatest gifts the Lord has given us. He saw Adam in the Garden of Eden and said that it was not good for man to be alone. Thus, he created Eve. So how is it that thousands of years later we have marriages that continue to end in divorce with two broken people (not to mention children) left in the wake? My husband and I have counseled many couples over the years whose marriages are falling apart. So often, the root of the problem stems from two people trying to live two lives rather than becoming one. We see husbands who feel abandoned by their wives and wives who feel ignored by their husbands. Couples today are seeking relationships outside their marriages because they are lonely, and this is exactly what God said is not good.

Stephan and I have struggled with living two lives in our own marriage, so I can speak from experience. We now have identified a pattern that we fall into that we call "The Spiral." Stephan gets busy with work, I get busy with the kids, and we quickly become two ships that pass in the night.

In Ephesians 5:22–25, the Bible tells wives to yield to their husbands as to the Lord and husbands to love their wives as Christ loved the church. One way we yield to our husbands is by getting involved in their lives. We have to make a conscious effort to be a part of their world. I am always amazed how quickly my husband responds when I begin to reach out to him. Living life together rather than separately is so much more fun than being alone. Reach out to your husband today, and see how God will make your marriage stronger.

THINK ABOUT IT: Are you and your husband living two lives or one?
Do you see your marriage as a gift?
Have you had fun with your husband lately?

DIG DEEPER: 1 Corinthians 7:3–4 (marriage), Philippians 2:3–5 (humility), and 1 Peter 5:7 (anxiety)

patience

I will never forget the phone call I received from my mother eight months ago: "Your sister is in the hospital. She's had a brain aneurysm." The words were a stab to my soul. My sister was in intensive care with blood on the brain. Life or death situations always seemed like something other families had to deal with . . . until that day. Hearing "she may not make it through the night" shattered every other priority I had in my life.

As Sara moved from bad to worse, brain surgery became vital for her recovery. I watched her blonde locks shaved down to a five o'clock shadow, and I could only pray that the doctors would carefully maneuver through her cranium to remove the mass within her skull. By heaven's mercy, it was a success.

Something I didn't count on was the dramatic effect the surgery would have on my sister. While our family was so grateful to have her around at all, we missed the brilliant, carbonated Sara we'd all grown to know and love. I became frustrated with her extremely slow recovery time. Finally, I realized I was growing impatient with my sister because of my personal expectations. In truth, she was healing rapidly (though minutely) each day! It was my impatience that clouded my ability to see the daily miracles God was performing in my sister's life.

Sara's slow recovery has silently helped me realize something: God's love for each one of us is patient, without rigid expectations, and without a "daily planner" kind of pacing. God sovereignly loves us without reservation and regardless of how we daily respond. We are all, like Sara, broken but healing, growing little by little in the gracious love of the Father.

THINK ABOUT IT: Do you accept that kind of patient, Christ-like love personally? Do you extend it to others?
Who are the people you need God to help you love more selflessly today?

DIG DEEPER: Psalm 31:14–16 (rescue), Psalm 56:3–4 (protection), Zechariah 4:6–7 (deliverance), and 1 Corinthians 15:10 (grace)

single moms

Lord God, you know that I love these kids like crazy, but parenting was never meant to be like this. Children shouldn't have to feel torn about whom to sit with at the baseball game. The schedules make us crazy. My kids never want to pack an overnight bag again as long as they live. I am so sad for the brokenness they have already known. And my heart keeps breaking over and over. Some days it's all I can do to get the children to school, go to my job, and then fall into bed as soon as it's over.

And the internal loneliness is almost unbearable. I ache on the inside, truly a physical ache, to be held and loved. Help me to be strong when I'd rather be cared for. Carry me from one day to the next with integrity. I want to walk this out with strength. Please replenish my soul. Please come with a love that fills me up and makes me whole. I feel incomplete and barely connected—a single mom in a family world. I just don't fit sometimes.

Lord, more than anything, I want to glorify you. I want to love my children with the Holy Spirit's tenderness. Please add patience to my exhaustion. Give me eyes to see your power. Don't let me miss your guidance.

Father, I know that my children belong to you. They always have. In the name of Jesus, will you come and cover them with your goodness? Will you protect them with your greatness? Will you fill in every missing piece? Let them become adults with great character and kind hearts. Let us persevere together in this house as a complete family for your glory and to make you known. Amen.

THINK ABOUT IT: What's your most difficult struggle as a single mom?
How do you see God's authority in using that struggle to shape your character?
What's the next step you can take toward keeping a spiritually healthy home while you're a single mom?

DIG DEEPER: Psalm 63:1–8 (seeking God), Matthew 6:33 (spiritual priorities), and Ephesians 3:14–21 (spiritual strength)

Her bridesmaids follow behind her,
and they are also brought to him.
15They come with happiness and joy;
they enter the king's palace.

16You will have sons to replace your fathers.
You will make them rulers through all the land.
17I will make your name famous from now on,
so people will praise you forever and ever.

God Protects His People

For the director of music. By alamoth. A psalm of the sons of Korah.

46 God is our protection and our strength.
He always helps in times of trouble.
2So we will not be afraid even if the earth shakes,
or the mountains fall into the sea,
3even if the oceans roar and foam,
or the mountains shake at the raging sea. *Selah*

4There is a river that brings joy to the city of God,
the holy place where God Most High lives.
5God is in that city, and so it will not be shaken.
God will help her at dawn.
6Nations tremble and kingdoms shake.
God shouts and the earth crumbles.

7The LORD All-Powerful is with us;
the God of Jacob is our defender. *Selah*

8Come and see what the LORD has done,
the amazing things he has done on the earth.
9He stops wars everywhere on the earth.
He breaks all bows and spears
and burns up the chariots with fire.
10God says, "Be still and know that I am God.
I will be praised in all the nations;
I will be praised throughout the earth."

11The LORD All-Powerful is with us;
the God of Jacob is our defender. *Selah*

God, the King of the World

For the director of music. A psalm of the sons of Korah.

47 Clap your hands, all you people.
Shout to God with joy.
2The LORD Most High is wonderful.
He is the great King over all the earth!
3He defeated nations for us
and put them under our control.
4He chose the land we would inherit.
We are the children of Jacob, whom he loved. *Selah*

5God has risen with a shout of joy;
the LORD has risen as the trumpets sounded.
6Sing praises to God. Sing praises.
Sing praises to our King. Sing praises.
7God is King of all the earth,
so sing a song of praise to him.
8God is King over the nations.
God sits on his holy throne.
9The leaders of the nations meet
with the people of the God of Abraham,
because the leaders of the earth belong to God.
He is supreme.

Jerusalem, the City of God

A psalm of the sons of Korah.

48 The LORD is great; he should be praised
in the city of our God, on his holy mountain.
2It is high and beautiful
and brings joy to the whole world.
Mount Zion is like the high mountains of the north;
it is the city of the Great King.
3God is within its palaces;
he is known as its defender.
4Kings joined together
and came to attack the city.
5But when they saw it, they were amazed.
They ran away in fear.
6Fear took hold of them;
they hurt like a woman having a baby.
7You destroyed the large trading ships
with an east wind.

8First we heard
and now we have seen
that God will always keep his city safe.
It is the city of the LORD All-Powerful,
the city of our God. *Selah*

9God, we come into your Temple
to think about your love.

[10]God, your name is known everywhere;
all over the earth people praise you.
Your right hand is full of goodness.
[11]Mount Zion is happy
and all the towns of Judah rejoice,
because your decisions are fair.

[12]Walk around Jerusalem
and count its towers.
[13]Notice how strong they are.
Look at the palaces.
Then you can tell your children about them.
[14]This God is our God forever and ever.
He will guide us from now on.

Trusting Money Is Foolish

For the director of music. A psalm of the sons of Korah.

49 Listen to this, all you nations;
listen, all you who live on earth.
[2]Listen, both great and small,
rich and poor together.
[3]What I say is wise,
and my heart speaks with understanding.
[4]I will pay attention to a wise saying;
I will explain my riddle on the harp.

[5]Why should I be afraid of bad days?
Why should I fear when evil people surround me?
[6]They trust in their money
and brag about their riches.
[7]No one can buy back the life of another.
No one can pay God for his own life,
[8]because the price of a life is high.
No payment is ever enough.
[9]Do people live forever?
Don't they all face death?
[10]See, even wise people die.
Fools and stupid people also die
and leave their wealth to others.
[11]Their graves will always be their homes.
They will live there from now on,
even though they named places after themselves.

devotion 147

PSALM 49:16–20

WITH ETERNITY IN VIEW

When all we can see is the accumulation of wealth, the amount or lack in the checkbook, the size of the house or the model of the car, then the writer of Psalm 49 says we have missed what matters more than anything.

Learning what matters means that we keep eternity in view. It means we value what God values. With eternity in view, we can hear God whisper truths that keep our eyes focused on the kingdom inheritance. We will begin to feel in our spirit what really matters to him and discern what has no value for God's work. Keeping eternity in view also takes the pressure off.

An executive position is cool, but what matters more is being able to hear the voice of the Father. Kids with straight As are something to celebrate, but their accomplishments are meaningless without tender hearts for God. A big house is a gift to be enjoyed, but it adds nothing to a shallow, empty life.

When you are wrapped up in the arms of God trying to live a godly life, he will keep realigning your heart. Earthly riches won't mean as much as they told you they should in college. The intense pressure to succeed will take a back seat to becoming a beautiful woman of righteous confidence. With eternity in view, you can take a deep breath, rest on your trust in God, and watch your everyday living become an extraordinary testimony to the faithfulness of God.

12Even rich people do not live forever;
like the animals, people die.

13This is what will happen to those who
trust in themselves
and to their followers who believe
them. *Selah*
14Like sheep, they must die,
and death will be their shepherd.
Honest people will rule over them in the
morning,
and their bodies will rot in a grave far
from home.
15But God will save my life
and will take me from the grave. *Selah*

16Don't be afraid of rich people
because their houses are more
beautiful.
17They don't take anything to the grave;
their wealth won't go down with them.
18Even though they were praised when they
were alive—
and people may praise you when you
succeed—
19they will go to where their ancestors are.
They will never see light again.
20Rich people with no understanding
are just like animals that die.

God Wants True Worship

A psalm of Asaph.

50 The God of gods, the LORD, speaks.
He calls the earth from the rising to
the setting sun.
2God shines from Jerusalem,
whose beauty is perfect.
3Our God comes, and he will not be silent.
A fire burns in front of him,
and a powerful storm surrounds him.
4He calls to the sky above and to the earth
that he might judge his people.
5He says, "Gather around, you who
worship me,
who have made an agreement with me,
using a sacrifice."
6God is the judge,
and even the skies say he is right. *Selah*
7God says, "My people, listen to me;
Israel, I will testify against you.
I am God, your God.
8I do not scold you for your sacrifices.
You always bring me your burnt
offerings.
9But I do not need bulls from your stalls
or goats from your pens,
10because every animal of the forest is
already mine.
The cattle on a thousand hills are
mine.
11I know every bird on the mountains,
and every living thing in the fields is
mine.
12If I were hungry, I would not tell you,
because the earth and everything in it
are mine.
13I don't eat the meat of bulls
or drink the blood of goats.
14Give an offering to show thanks to God.
Give God Most High what you have
promised.
15Call to me in times of trouble.
I will save you, and you will honor me."

16But God says to the wicked,
"Why do you talk about my laws?
Why do you mention my agreement?
17You hate my teachings
and turn your back on what I say.
18When you see a thief, you join him.
You take part in adultery.
19You don't stop your mouth from speaking
evil,
and your tongue makes up lies.
20You speak against your brother
and lie about your mother's son.
21I have kept quiet while you did these
things,
so you thought I was just like you.
But I will scold you
and accuse you to your face.

22"Think about this, you who forget God.
Otherwise, I will tear you apart,
and no one will save you.
23Those people honor me
who bring me offerings to show
thanks.
And I, God, will save those who do that."

A Prayer for Forgiveness

For the director of music. A psalm of David when the prophet Nathan came to David after David's sin with Bathsheba.

51 God, be merciful to me
because you are loving.
Because you are always ready to be
merciful,
wipe out all my wrongs.

2 Wash away all my guilt
and make me clean again.

3 I know about my wrongs,
and I can't forget my sin.
4 You are the only one I have sinned against;
I have done what you say is wrong.
You are right when you speak
and fair when you judge.
5 I was brought into this world in sin.
In sin my mother gave birth to me.

6 You want me to be completely truthful,
so teach me wisdom.
7 Take away my sin, and I will be clean.
Wash me, and I will be whiter than snow.
8 Make me hear sounds of joy and gladness;
let the bones you crushed be happy again.
9 Turn your face from my sins
and wipe out all my guilt.

10 Create in me a pure heart, God,
and make my spirit right again.
11 Do not send me away from you
or take your Holy Spirit away from me.
12 Give me back the joy of your salvation.
Keep me strong by giving me a willing spirit.
13 Then I will teach your ways to those who do wrong,
and sinners will turn back to you.
14 God, save me from the guilt of murder,
God of my salvation,
and I will sing about your goodness.
15 Lord, let me speak
so I may praise you.
16 You are not pleased by sacrifices, or I would give them.
You don't want burnt offerings.
17 The sacrifice God wants is a broken spirit.
God, you will not reject a heart that is broken and sorry for sin.

18 Do whatever good you wish for Jerusalem.
Rebuild the walls of Jerusalem.
19 Then you will be pleased with right sacrifices and whole burnt offerings,
and bulls will be offered on your altar.

God Will Punish the Proud

For the director of music. A maskil of David. When Doeg the Edomite came to Saul and said to him, "David is in Ahimelech's house."

52 Mighty warrior, why do you brag
about the evil you do?
God's love will continue forever.

devotion 148

PSALM 51:5–17

PARTY FAVOR OR TEMPLE? YOU DECIDE.

I wish I could tell you that I have been walking with the Lord all my life, but the truth is, I walked in the flesh in my early years. I was a good person but found myself buying into what the world considered acceptable behavior. You name it, I did it. I worked hard and played even harder. Cocaine was a weekend accessory that went nicely with my bottle of wine, and I treated my body more like a party favor than a temple. This was my life, and the years of this kind of partying left me with many soul ties and deadening guilt I thought I would never be able to shake.

When I was saved, I hid in the church for about a year. I did not want anyone to know me or what my life was like. How could this holy God use me? Then one day, as Pastor Bob went through his testimony, I was shocked to learn that his story was not much different than mine. Through the pain and the brokenness of his spirit, God called him to a new life. My new life is a husband that loves the Lord and rocks my world, a clean heart that is after God's, and a ministry of offering redemption out of personal experience. If your spirit is broken and empty today, let your heart receive Christ. He alone can make you truly new and remove the guilt of your sins.

2You think up evil plans.
Your tongue is like a sharp razor,
making up lies.
3You love wrong more than right
and lies more than truth. *Selah*
4You love words that bite
and tongues that lie.
5But God will ruin you forever.
He will grab you and throw you out of
your tent;
he will tear you away from the land of
the living. *Selah*
6Those who do right will see this and fear
God.
They will laugh at you and say,
7"Look what happened to the man
who did not depend on God
but depended on his money.
He grew strong by his evil plans."
8But I am like an olive tree
growing in God's Temple.
I trust God's love
forever and ever.
9God, I will thank you forever for what you
have done.
With those who worship you, I will
trust you because you are good.

The Unbelieving Fool

For the director of music. By mahalath. A maskil of David.

53 Fools say to themselves,
"There is no God."
Fools are evil and do terrible things;
none of them does anything good.

2God looked down from heaven on all
people
to see if anyone was wise,
if anyone was looking to God for help.
3But all have turned away.
Together, everyone has become evil;
none of them does anything good.
Not a single person.

4Don't the wicked understand?
They destroy my people as if they were
eating bread.
They do not ask God for help.
5The wicked are filled with terror
where there had been nothing to fear.
God will scatter the bones of your
enemies.

devotion 149

PSALM 52:8–9

GOD'S GOODNESS

Have you ever met people you have reservations about? Perhaps your internal radar sensed that you might not be able to trust them. I once had a person in my life who was a Christian, but I always wondered about his motivations in any given situation. It seemed he was most concerned with his well-being rather than the well-being of others. I questioned every decision he made that concerned me. People like that are self-reliant rather than God-reliant. They think they have to look out for themselves because no one else will. They believe they can fix their lives by working harder or manipulating those around them.

God is good. You never have to question God's motives. He is always looking out for your best interests. You can trust him. When you talk to those who have been Christians for a long time, they will always tell you of God's faithfulness in their lives. As a pastor's wife, I hear a lot of stories about how God has worked through many types of situations. Our church once put a collection of these stories into a book. You cannot read that book without realizing that there is a God and that he is in the business of restoring lives. There is story after story of impossible situations, and each time God showed up beyond what was expected. God can fix the things in your life that need fixing. He is writing your story today, and remember—God only writes bestsellers.

You will defeat them,
because God has rejected them.

6 I pray that victory will come to Israel
from Mount Zion!
May God bring them back.
Then the people of Jacob will rejoice,
and the people of Israel will be glad.

A Prayer for Help

For the director of music. With stringed instruments. A maskil of David when the Ziphites went to Saul and said, "We think David is hiding among our people."

54 God, save me because of who you are.
By your strength show that I am
innocent.
2 Hear my prayer, God;
listen to what I say.
3 Strangers turn against me,
and cruel people want to kill me.
They do not care about God. *Selah*

4 See, God will help me;
the Lord will support me.
5 Let my enemies be punished with their
own evil.
Destroy them because you are loyal
to me.

6 I will offer a sacrifice as a special gift to you.
I will thank you, LORD, because you are
good.
7 You have saved me from all my troubles,
and I have seen my enemies defeated.

A Prayer About a False Friend

For the director of music. With stringed instruments. A maskil of David.

55 God, listen to my prayer
and do not ignore my cry for help.
2 Pay attention to me and answer me.
I am troubled and upset
3 by what the enemy says
and how the wicked look at me.
They bring troubles down on me,
and in anger they attack me.

4 I am frightened inside;
the terror of death has attacked me.
5 I am scared and shaking,
and terror grips me.
6 I said, "I wish I had wings like a dove.
Then I would fly away and rest.
7 I would wander far away
and stay in the desert. *Selah*
8 I would hurry to my place of escape,
far away from the wind and storm."

9 Lord, destroy and confuse their words,
because I see violence and fighting in
the city.
10 Day and night they are all around its walls,
and evil and trouble are everywhere
inside.
11 Destruction is everywhere in the city;
trouble and lying never leave its streets.

12 It was not an enemy insulting me.
I could stand that.
It was not someone who hated me.
I could hide from him.
13 But it is you, a person like me,
my companion and good friend.
14 We had a good friendship
and walked together to God's Temple.

15 Let death take away my enemies.
Let them die while they are still young
because evil lives with them.
16 But I will call to God for help,
and the LORD will save me.
17 Morning, noon, and night I am troubled
and upset,
but he will listen to me.
18 Many are against me,
but he keeps me safe in battle.
19 God who lives forever
will hear me and punish them. *Selah*
But they will not change;
they do not fear God.

20 The one who was my friend attacks his
friends
and breaks his promises.
21 His words are slippery like butter,
but war is in his heart.
His words are smoother than oil,
but they cut like knives.
22 Give your worries to the LORD,
and he will take care of you.
He will never let good people down.
23 But, God, you will bring down
the wicked to the grave.
Murderers and liars will live
only half a lifetime.
But I will trust in you.

Trusting God for Help

For the director of music. To the tune of "The Dove in the Distant Oak." A miktam of David when the Philistines captured him in Gath.

56 God, be merciful to me because
people are chasing me;
the battle has pressed me all day long.

2My enemies have chased me all day;
there are many proud people
fighting me.
3When I am afraid,
I will trust you.
4I praise God for his word.
I trust God, so I am not afraid.
What can human beings do to me?

5All day long they twist my words;
all their evil plans are against me.
6They wait. They hide.
They watch my steps,
hoping to kill me.
7God, do not let them escape;
punish the foreign nations in your anger.
8You have recorded my troubles.
You have kept a list of my tears.
Aren't they in your records?

9On the day I call for help, my enemies will
be defeated.
I know that God is on my side.
10I praise God for his word to me;
I praise the LORD for his word.
11I trust in God. I will not be afraid.
What can people do to me?

12God, I must keep my promises to you.
I will give you my offerings to thank
you,
13because you have saved me from death.
You have kept me from being defeated.
So I will walk with God
in light among the living.

A Prayer in Troubled Times

For the director of music. To the tune of "Do Not Destroy." A miktam of David when he escaped from Saul in the cave.

57 Be merciful to me, God; be merciful
to me
because I come to you for protection.
Let me hide under the shadow of your
wings
until the trouble has passed.

2I cry out to God Most High,
to the God who does everything for me.
3He sends help from heaven and saves me.
He punishes those who chase me. *Selah*
God sends me his love and truth.

4Enemies, like lions, are all around me;
I must lie down among them.
Their teeth are like spears and arrows,
their tongues as sharp as swords.

devotion 150

PSALM 56:1–4

PLEASING THE PROFESSOR

The professor was unbelievably hard on her, and his expectations seemed entirely unrealistic. Like the psalmist, she felt chased. Every time she raised her hand to comment on a subject, her enemy belittled her answer, leaving her feeling dim-witted and foolish. She knew the subject inside and out and studied the text thoroughly before each class. This instructor had something against her from the day she walked into his class, and it seemed that nothing she did would please him. She felt that taking the course was futile and seriously considered dropping it. One night she cried out to God in prayer asking him to help her understand what her professor was looking for and what she needed to do to win his favor. However, the answer she received was not what she expected. God did not want her to focus on making her instructor happy—God wanted her to trust *him* to lead her through the course.

Have you experienced a situation like this? A supervisor who was impossible to please? An in-law who seemed determined to cause turbulence in your marriage? It's a difficult road to walk, but we have to remember to seek God's approval, not simply man's praise. As the psalmist said, "I trust God, so I am not afraid. What can human beings do to me?" (verse 4). No matter where it is that you feel chased, marginalized, or attacked, know that you don't have to be afraid. Trust God for victory in the battles you're facing today.

5God is supreme over the skies;
his majesty covers the earth.

6They set a trap for me.
I am very worried.
They dug a pit in my path,
but they fell into it themselves. *Selah*

7My heart is steady, God; my heart is steady.
I will sing and praise you.
8Wake up, my soul.
Wake up, harp and lyre!
I will wake up the dawn.
9Lord, I will praise you among the nations;
I will sing songs of praise about you to
all the nations.
10Your great love reaches to the skies,
your truth to the clouds.
11God, you are supreme above the skies.
Let your glory be over all the earth.

Unfair Judges

For the director of music. To the tune of "Do Not Destroy." A miktam of David.

58 Do you rulers really say what is right?
Do you judge people fairly?
2No, in your heart you plan evil;
you think up violent crimes in the land.
3From birth, evil people turn away from
God;
they wander off and tell lies as soon as
they are born.
4They are like poisonous snakes,
like deaf cobras that stop up their ears
5so they cannot hear the music of the
snake charmer
no matter how well he plays.

6God, break the teeth in their mouths!
Tear out the fangs of those lions, LORD!
7Let them disappear like water that flows
away.
Let them be cut short like a broken
arrow.
8Let them be like snails that melt as they
move.
Let them be like a child born dead who
never saw the sun.
9His anger will blow them away alive
faster than burning thorns can heat a
pot.
10Good people will be glad when they see
him get even.
They will wash their feet in the blood
of the wicked.
11Then people will say,
"There really are rewards for doing
what is right.
There really is a God who judges the
world."

A Prayer for Protection

For the director of music. To the tune of "Do Not Destroy." A miktam of David when Saul sent men to watch David's house to kill him.

59 God, save me from my enemies.
Protect me from those who come
against me.
2Save me from those who do evil
and from murderers.

3Look, they are waiting to ambush me.
Cruel people attack me,
but I have not sinned or done wrong,
LORD.
4I have done nothing wrong, but they are
ready to attack me.
Wake up to help me, and look.
5You are the LORD God All-Powerful, the
God of Israel.
Arise and punish those people.
Do not give those traitors any
mercy. *Selah*

6They come back at night.
Like dogs they growl and roam around
the city.
7Notice what comes from their mouths.
Insults come from their lips,
because they say, "Who's listening?"
8But, LORD, you laugh at them;
you make fun of all of them.

9God, my strength, I am looking to you,
because God is my defender.
10My God loves me, and he goes in front
of me.
He will help me defeat my enemies.
11Lord, our protector, do not kill them, or
my people will forget.
With your power scatter them and
defeat them.
12They sin by what they say;
they sin with their words.
They curse and tell lies,
so let their pride trap them.
13Destroy them in your anger;
destroy them completely!
Then they will know
that God rules over Israel
and to the ends of the earth. *Selah*

14They come back at night.
Like dogs they growl
and roam around the city.
15They wander about looking for food,
and they howl if they do not find
enough.
16But I will sing about your strength.
In the morning I will sing about your
love.
You are my defender,
my place of safety in times of trouble.
17God, my strength, I will sing praises to
you.
God, my defender, you are the God who
loves me.

A Prayer After a Defeat

For the director of music. To the tune of "Lily of the Agreement." A miktam of David. For teaching. When David fought the Arameans of Northwest Mesopotamia and Zobah, and when Joab returned and defeated twelve thousand Edomites at the Valley of Salt.

60 God, you have rejected us and
scattered us.
You have been angry, but please come
back to us.
2You made the earth shake and crack.
Heal its breaks because it is shaking.
3You have given your people trouble.
You made us unable to walk straight,
like people drunk with wine.
4You have raised a banner to gather those
who fear you.
Now they can stand up against the
enemy. *Selah*

5Answer us and save us by your power
so the people you love will be rescued.

6God has said from his Temple,
"When I win, I will divide Shechem
and measure off the Valley of Succoth.
7Gilead and Manasseh are mine.
Ephraim is like my helmet.
Judah holds my royal scepter.
8Moab is like my washbowl.
I throw my sandals at Edom.
I shout at Philistia."

9Who will bring me to the strong, walled
city?
Who will lead me to Edom?

devotion 151

PSALM 59:16–17

ONLY ONE HERO

I believe in the heart of the feminine soul is a woman who longs to be protected, cared for, and rescued. There is a woman who cries out, "God, will you be my defender?" It's just that you have to probe a woman to get to this longing. We've stuffed it all down, trying to believe we can do everything all by ourselves.

Actually, we've been applauded for enduring great difficulty alone. We call women who don't need help "superwomen" and set them apart as inspirational. They write books and appear on talk shows to train us how to emotionally, mentally, and physically do it all—alone.

But over and over in Scripture, we hear godly men and women cry out, "Oh Lord, help me." And then we watch the God of the universe rescue those who belong to him. He saves any who would call him Lord. Our God is a rescuing God. He is strong and safe, and he has promised to defend his beloved.

The seasons of a woman's life are incredibly varied, but each of us faces those times that seem to lay us across the tracks of an oncoming train—lonely, desperate, and even hopeless. What God promises is that he always, always comes through. He always shows up. He always saves. He always defends. His timing is not ours. His methods are usually unconventional. But what we can know, what we can settle in our soul, is that he is faithful to come when we call.

10God, surely you have rejected us;
you do not go out with our armies.
11Help us fight the enemy.
Human help is useless,
12but we can win with God's help.
He will defeat our enemies.

A Prayer for Protection

For the director of music. With stringed instruments. Of David.

61 God, hear my cry;
listen to my prayer.
2I call to you from the ends of the earth
when I am afraid.
Carry me away to a high mountain.
3You have been my protection,
like a strong tower against my enemies.

4Let me live in your Holy Tent forever.
Let me find safety in the shelter of your
wings. *Selah*

5God, you have heard my promises.
You have given me what belongs to
those who fear you.

6Give the king a long life;
let him live many years.
7Let him rule in the presence of God
forever.
Protect him with your love and truth.
8Then I will praise your name forever,
and every day I will keep my promises.

Trust Only in God

For the director of music. For Jeduthun. A psalm of David.

62 I find rest in God;
only he can save me.
2He is my rock and my salvation.
He is my defender;
I will not be defeated.

3How long will you attack someone?
Will all of you kill that person?
Who is like a leaning wall, like a fence
ready to fall?
4They are planning to make that person
fall.
They enjoy telling lies.
With their mouths they bless,
but in their hearts they curse. *Selah*

5I find rest in God;
only he gives me hope.

devotion 152

PSALM 62:5–8

WHAT DISAPPOINTMENTS REVEAL

Anger is an emotion that destroys many things, including trust. Trust cannot be present when the heart is furious. I remember a time when my heart was a dark and angry place. I wondered where the woman went who loved her Lord, who loved people, and whose joy was considered contagious. I felt like a complete failure, and one night I poured myself out in the dark before the Lord. "Why am I so angry? Where did I go? I feel like I am losing me, Father. Please speak to my heart."

Out of the light, the Holy Spirit answered, "You are angry because you do not trust me. You had your own expectations, and those unmet expectations turned into disappointments, and disappointments into frustrations, and frustrations into anger."

I thought hard about what the Spirit had said, and I reflected on all the things I could identify as a source of frustration or anger. And you know what? He was right. I could track every single thing back to an unmet expectation—how I thought things should have gone, how a relationship was supposed to be, what my business should look like, you get the picture. All the while, I was telling myself I wanted God's will, but in reality, I wanted God's will to fulfill my own hopes and expectations. Is the Lord asking you to loosen your fearful grip on an unmet expectation? Allow God to fill you with the hopes, dreams, and expectations he has for your life.

6He is my rock and my salvation.
He is my defender;
I will not be defeated.
7My honor and salvation come from God.
He is my mighty rock and my
protection.

8People, trust God all the time.
Tell him all your problems,
because God is our protection. *Selah*

9The least of people are only a breath,
and even the greatest are just a lie.
On the scales, they weigh nothing;
together they are only a breath.
10Do not trust in force.
Stealing is of no use.
Even if you gain more riches,
don't put your trust in them.

11God has said this,
and I have heard it over and over:
God is strong.
12The Lord is loving.
You reward people for what they have
done.

Wishing to Be Near God

A psalm of David when he was in the desert of Judah.

63 God, you are my God.
I search for you.
I thirst for you
like someone in a dry, empty land
where there is no water.
2I have seen you in the Temple
and have seen your strength and glory.
3Because your love is better than life,
I will praise you.
4I will praise you as long as I live.
I will lift up my hands in prayer to your
name.
5I will be content as if I had eaten the best
foods.
My lips will sing, and my mouth will
praise you.

6I remember you while I'm lying in bed;
I think about you through the night.
7You are my help.
Because of your protection, I sing.
8I stay close to you;
you support me with your right hand.

9Some people are trying to kill me,
but they will go down to the grave.
10They will be killed with swords
and eaten by wild dogs.

11But the king will rejoice in his God.
All who make promises in his name
will praise him,
but the mouths of liars will be shut.

A Prayer Against Enemies

For the director of music. A psalm of David.

64 God, listen to my complaint.
I am afraid of my enemies;
protect my life from them.
2Hide me from those who plan wicked
things,
from that gang who does evil.
3They sharpen their tongues like swords
and shoot bitter words like arrows.
4From their hiding places they shoot at
innocent people;
they shoot suddenly and are not afraid.
5They encourage each other to do wrong.
They talk about setting traps,
thinking no one will see them.
6They plan wicked things and say,
"We have a perfect plan."
The mind of human beings is hard to
understand.

7But God will shoot them with arrows;
they will suddenly be struck down.
8Their own words will be used against
them.
All who see them will shake their
heads.
9Then everyone will fear God.
They will tell what God has done,
and they will learn from what he has
done.
10Good people will be happy in the LORD
and will find protection in him.
Let everyone who is honest praise the
LORD.

A Hymn of Thanksgiving

For the director of music. A psalm of David. A song.

65 God, you will be praised in Jerusalem.
We will keep our promises to you.
2You hear our prayers.
All people will come to you.
3Our guilt overwhelms us,
but you forgive our sins.
4Happy are the people you choose
and invite to stay in your court.
We are filled with good things in your
house,
your holy Temple.

5You answer us in amazing ways,
God our Savior.
People everywhere on the earth
and beyond the sea trust you.
6You made the mountains by your strength;
you are dressed in power.
7You stopped the roaring seas,
the roaring waves,
and the uproar of the nations.
8Even those people at the ends of the earth fear your miracles.
You are praised from where the sun rises to where it sets.

9You take care of the land and water it;
you make it very fertile.
The rivers of God are full of water.
Grain grows because you make it grow.
10You send rain to the plowed fields;
you fill the rows with water.
You soften the ground with rain,
and then you bless it with crops.
11You give the year a good harvest,
and you load the wagons with many crops.
12The desert is covered with grass
and the hills with happiness.
13The pastures are full of flocks,
and the valleys are covered with grain.
Everything shouts and sings for joy.

Praise God for What He Has Done

For the director of music. A song. A psalm.

66 Everything on earth, shout with joy to God!
2Sing about his glory!
Make his praise glorious!
3Say to God, "Your works are amazing!
Because your power is great,
your enemies fall before you.
4All the earth worships you
and sings praises to you.
They sing praises to your name." *Selah*

5Come and see what God has done,
the amazing things he has done for people.
6He turned the sea into dry land.
The people crossed the river on foot.
So let us rejoice because of what he did.
7He rules forever with his power.
He keeps his eye on the nations,
so people should not turn against him. *Selah*

8You people, praise our God;
loudly sing his praise.
9He protects our lives
and does not let us be defeated.
10God, you have tested us;
you have purified us like silver.
11You let us be trapped
and put a heavy load on us.
12You let our enemies walk on our heads.
We went through fire and flood,
but you brought us to a place with good things.

13I will come to your Temple with burnt offerings.
I will give you what I promised,
14 things I promised when I was in trouble.
15I will bring you offerings of fat animals,
and I will offer sheep, bulls, and goats. *Selah*

16All of you who fear God, come and listen,
and I will tell you what he has done for me.
17I cried out to him with my mouth
and praised him with my tongue.
18If I had known of any sin in my heart,
the Lord would not have listened to me.
19But God has listened;
he has heard my prayer.
20Praise God,
who did not ignore my prayer
or hold back his love from me.

Everyone Should Praise God

For the director of music. With stringed instruments. A psalm. A song.

67 God, have mercy on us and bless us
and show us your kindness *Selah*
2so the world will learn your ways,
and all nations will learn that you can save.

3God, the people should praise you;
all people should praise you.
4The nations should be glad and sing
because you judge people fairly.
You guide all the nations on earth. *Selah*
5God, the people should praise you;
all people should praise you.

6The land has given its crops.
God, our God, blesses us.
7God blesses us
so people all over the earth will fear him.

devotion 153

PSALM 66:17–19

SINS OF THE HEART

Sins of the heart are not an easy thing to think about. They are the best-kept secrets because we often keep them from ourselves. I grew up in a wonderful Christian family. But it was a family of strong personalities. Being right was an important thing, and being wrong was hard to admit. As I began my own family, I brought some of my family secrets along. I remember having an argument with my husband one day, and he said to me, "You can't ever be wrong." Then he headed out the door with our kids to an event we were supposed to attend together. I had refused to go. My four-year-old son came into my bedroom and begged me to come with them. I realized in that instant how wrong I was to allow this argument to get to the point that I had my precious little boy in tears all because I wanted to be right.

Sins of the heart are attitudes of pride, selfishness, and unforgiveness. We allow them to ruin relationships and cloud our judgment. The Bible also says that sin in our hearts keeps the Lord from listening to us. Our prayers are hindered because our motivations are selfish and prideful. We have to continually come to the Lord and ask him to reveal our sins so that we can ask for his forgiveness. It will open up the gates of heaven, and God will again hear our prayers.

Praise God Who Saved the Nation

For the director of music. A psalm of David. A song.

68 Let God rise up and scatter his
enemies;
let those who hate him run away from
him.
2Blow them away as smoke
is driven away by the wind.
As wax melts before a fire,
let the wicked be destroyed before God.
3But those who do right should be glad
and should rejoice before God;
they should be happy and glad.

4Sing to God; sing praises to his name.
Prepare the way for him
who rides through the desert,
whose name is the LORD.
Rejoice before him.
5God is in his holy Temple.
He is a father to orphans,
and he defends the widows.
6God gives the lonely a home.
He leads prisoners out with joy,
but those who turn against God will
live in a dry land.

7God, you led your people out
when you marched through the
desert. *Selah*

8The ground shook
and the sky poured down rain
before God, the God of Mount Sinai,
before God, the God of Israel.
9God, you sent much rain;
you refreshed your tired land.
10Your people settled there.
God, in your goodness
you took care of the poor.

11The Lord gave the command,
and a great army told the news:
12"Kings and their armies run away.
In camp they divide the wealth taken
in war.
13Those who stayed by the campfires
will share the riches taken in battle."
14The Almighty scattered kings
like snow on Mount Zalmon.

15The mountains of Bashan are high;
the mountains of Bashan have many peaks.
16Why do you mountains with many peaks look with envy
on the mountain that God chose for his home?
The LORD will live there forever.
17God comes with millions of chariots;
the Lord comes from Mount Sinai to his holy place.
18When you went up to the heights,
you led a parade of captives.
You received gifts from the people,
even from those who turned against you.
And the LORD God will live there.

19Praise the Lord, God our Savior,
who helps us every day. *Selah*
20Our God is a God who saves us;
the LORD God saves us from death.

21God will crush his enemies' heads,
the hairy skulls of those who continue to sin.
22The Lord said, "I will bring the enemy back from Bashan;
I will bring them back from the depths of the sea.
23Then you can stick your feet in their blood,
and your dogs can lick their share."

24God, people have seen your victory march;
God my King marched into the holy place.
25The singers are in front and the instruments are behind.
In the middle are the girls with the tambourines.
26Praise God in the meeting place;
praise the LORD in the gathering of Israel.
27There is the smallest tribe, Benjamin, leading them.
And there are the leaders of Judah with their group.
There also are the leaders of Zebulun and of Naphtali.

28God, order up your power;
show the mighty power you have used for us before.
29Kings will bring their wealth to you,
to your Temple in Jerusalem.
30Punish Egypt, the beast in the tall grass along the river.
Punish the leaders of nations, those bulls among the cows.
Defeated, they will bring you their silver.
Scatter those nations that love war.
31Messengers will come from Egypt;
the people of Cush will pray to God.

32Kingdoms of the earth, sing to God;
sing praises to the Lord. *Selah*
33Sing to the one who rides through the skies, which are from long ago.
He speaks with a thundering voice.
34Announce that God is powerful.
He rules over Israel,
and his power is in the skies.
35God, you are wonderful in your Temple.
The God of Israel gives his people strength and power.

Praise God!

A Cry for Help

For the director of music. To the tune of "Lilies." A psalm of David.

69 God, save me,
because the water has risen to my neck.
2I'm sinking down into the mud,
and there is nothing to stand on.
I am in deep water,
and the flood covers me.
3I am tired from calling for help;
my throat is sore.
My eyes are tired from waiting
for God to help me.
4There are more people who hate me for no reason than hairs on my head;
powerful enemies want to destroy me for no reason.
They make me pay back
what I did not steal.

5God, you know what I have done wrong;
I cannot hide my guilt from you.
6Lord GOD All-Powerful,
do not let those who hope in you be ashamed because of me.
God of Israel,
do not let your worshipers be disgraced because of me.
7For you, I carry this shame,
and my face is covered with disgrace.
8I am like a stranger to my closest relatives
and a foreigner to my mother's children.

9My strong love for your Temple
completely controls me.
When people insult you, it hurts me.
10When I cry and fast,
they make fun of me.
11When I wear clothes of sadness,
they joke about me.
12They make fun of me in public places,
and the drunkards make up songs
about me.

13But I pray to you, LORD, for favor.
God, because of your great love, answer
me.
You are truly able to save.
14Pull me from the mud,
and do not let me sink.
Save me from those who hate me
and from the deep water.
15Do not let the flood drown me
or the deep water swallow me
or the grave close its mouth over me.
16LORD, answer me because your love is so
good.
Because of your great kindness, turn
to me.
17Do not hide from me, your servant.
I am in trouble. Hurry to help me!
18Come near and save me;
rescue me from my enemies.

19You see my shame and disgrace.
You know all my enemies and what
they have said.
20Insults have broken my heart
and left me weak.
I looked for sympathy, but there was
none;
I found no one to comfort me.
21They put poison in my food
and gave me vinegar to drink.
22Let their own feasts cause their ruin;
let their feasts trap them and pay them
back.
23Let their eyes be closed so they cannot see
and their backs be forever weak from
troubles.
24Pour your anger out on them;
let your anger catch up with them.
25May their place be empty;
leave no one to live in their tents.
26They chase after those you have hurt,
and they talk about the pain of those
you have wounded.
27Charge them with crime after crime,
and do not let them have anything
good.
28Wipe their names from the book of life,
and do not list them with those who do
what is right.
29I am sad and hurting.
God, save me and protect me.

30I will praise God in a song
and will honor him by giving thanks.
31That will please the LORD more than
offering him cattle,
more than sacrificing a bull with horns
and hoofs.
32Poor people will see this and be glad.
Be encouraged, you who worship God.
33The LORD listens to those in need
and does not look down on captives.

34Heaven and earth should praise him,
the seas and everything in them.
35God will save Jerusalem
and rebuild the cities of Judah.
Then people will live there and own the
land.
36 The descendants of his servants will
inherit that land,
and those who love him will live there.

A Cry for God to Help Quickly

For the director of music. A psalm of David. To help people remember.

70 God, come quickly and save me.
LORD, hurry to help me.
2Let those who are trying to kill me
be ashamed and disgraced.
Let those who want to hurt me
run away in disgrace.
3Let those who make fun of me
stop because of their shame.
4But let all those who worship you
rejoice and be glad.
Let those who love your salvation
always say, "Praise the greatness of
God."
5I am poor and helpless;
God, hurry to me.
You help me and save me.
LORD, do not wait.

An Old Person's Prayer

71 In you, LORD, is my protection.
Never let me be ashamed.

[2]Because you do what is right, save and
rescue me;
listen to me and save me.
[3]Be my place of safety
where I can always come.
Give the command to save me,
because you are my rock and my
strong, walled city.
[4]My God, save me from the power of the
wicked
and from the hold of evil and cruel
people.
[5]LORD, you are my hope.
LORD, I have trusted you since I was
young.
[6]I have depended on you since I was born;
you helped me even on the day of my
birth.
I will always praise you.

[7]I am an example to many people,
because you are my strong protection.
[8]I am always praising you;
all day long I honor you.
[9]Do not reject me when I am old;
do not leave me when my strength is
gone.
[10]My enemies make plans against me,
and they meet together to kill me.
[11]They say, "God has left him.
Go after him and take him,
because no one will save him."

[12]God, don't be far off.
My God, hurry to help me.
[13]Let those who accuse me
be ashamed and destroyed.
Let those who are trying to hurt me
be covered with shame and disgrace.
[14]But I will always have hope
and will praise you more and more.
[15]I will tell how you do what is right.
I will tell about your salvation all day
long,
even though it is more than I can
tell.
[16]I will come and tell about your powerful
works, Lord GOD.

devotion 154

PSALM 71:14

YOUNG BRIDE, YOUNG WIDOW

She was a bride in April and a widow in July. She was twenty-four years old at the time of her husband's death and had only just begun to develop pictures from their honeymoon. She'd planned to create a scrapbook of their trip and had taken many wonderful pictures in Hawaii, most of them of her adventurous husband. The last picture she took of her husband was in a small plane just before takeoff. The smile on his face was evidence that he'd never been happier than at that moment with his beautiful wife snapping pictures. She was obviously so impressed and proud of him as he was about to embark on another great adventure!

It was the last adventure he took before he woke up in paradise.

The funeral was heartrending, but people commented on how composed his beautiful widow seemed to be. While she'd had a few days to cry, and there would no doubt be more tears later when she laid her head on her pillow to face another restless night, her composure at the funeral was remarkable. Some people said, "My goodness! What a rock she is!"

Well, she wasn't a rock at all, but she clung to something people don't always remember during a funeral. Her husband knew Christ as his Savior, so in her grief she chose to praise God. She would miss her husband tremendously, but she had a great deal of hope because she knew she would see him again in paradise.

I will remind people that only you do
what is right.

17God, you have taught me since I was
young.
To this day I tell about the miracles
you do.
18Even though I am old and gray,
do not leave me, God.
I will tell the children about your power;
I will tell those who live after me about
your might.

19God, your justice reaches to the skies.
You have done great things;
God, there is no one like you.
20You have given me many troubles and bad
times,
but you will give me life again.
When I am almost dead,
you will keep me alive.
21You will make me greater than ever,
and you will comfort me again.

22I will praise you with the harp.
I trust you, my God.
I will sing to you with the lyre,
Holy One of Israel.
23I will shout for joy when I sing praises to
you.
You have saved me.
24I will tell about your justice all day long.
And those who want to hurt me
will be ashamed and disgraced.

A Prayer for the King

Of Solomon.

72 God, give the king your good
judgment
and the king's son your goodness.
2Help him judge your people fairly
and decide what is right for the poor.
3Let there be peace on the mountains
and goodness on the hills for the people.
4Help him be fair to the poor
and save the needy
and punish those who hurt them.

5May they respect you as long as the sun
shines
and as long as the moon glows.
6Let him be like rain on the grass,
like showers that water the earth.
7Let goodness be plentiful while he lives.
Let peace continue as long as there is a
moon.

8Let his kingdom go from sea to sea,
and from the Euphrates River to the
ends of the earth.
9Let the people of the desert bow down to
him,
and make his enemies lick the dust.
10Let the kings of Tarshish and the faraway
lands
bring him gifts.
Let the kings of Sheba and Seba
bring their presents to him.
11Let all kings bow down to him
and all nations serve him.

12He will help the poor when they cry out
and will save the needy when no one
else will help.
13He will be kind to the weak and poor,
and he will save their lives.
14He will save them from cruel people who
try to hurt them,
because their lives are precious to him.

15Long live the king!
Let him receive gold from Sheba.
Let people always pray for him
and bless him all day long.
16Let the fields grow plenty of grain
and the hills be covered with crops.
Let the land be as fertile as Lebanon,
and let the cities grow like the grass in
a field.
17Let the king be famous forever;
let him be remembered as long as the
sun shines.
Let the nations be blessed because of him,
and may they all bless him.

18Praise the LORD God, the God of Israel,
who alone does such miracles.
19Praise his glorious name forever.
Let his glory fill the whole world.
Amen and amen.

20This ends the prayers of David son of
Jesse.

Book 3

Should the Wicked Be Rich?

A psalm of Asaph.

73 God is truly good to Israel,
to those who have pure hearts.
2But I had almost stopped believing;
I had almost lost my faith

3because I was jealous of proud people.
I saw wicked people doing well.

4They are not suffering;
they are healthy and strong.
5They don't have troubles like the rest
of us;
they don't have problems like other
people.
6They wear pride like a necklace
and put on violence as their clothing.
7They are looking for profits
and do not control their selfish
desires.
8They make fun of others and speak evil;
proudly they speak of hurting others.
9They brag to the sky.
They say that they own the earth.
10So their people turn to them
and give them whatever they want.
11They say, "How can God know?
What does God Most High know?"
12These people are wicked,
always at ease, and getting richer.
13So why have I kept my heart pure?
Why have I kept my hands from doing
wrong?
14I have suffered all day long;
I have been punished every morning.

15God, if I had decided to talk like this,
I would have let your people down.
16I tried to understand all this,
but it was too hard for me to see
17until I went to the Temple of God.
Then I understood what will happen to
them.
18You have put them in danger;
you cause them to be destroyed.
19They are destroyed in a moment;
they are swept away by terrors.
20It will be like waking from a dream.
Lord, when you rise up, they will
disappear.

21When my heart was sad
and I was angry,
22I was senseless and stupid.
I acted like an animal toward you.
23But I am always with you;
you have held my hand.
24You guide me with your advice,
and later you will receive me in
honor.

devotion 155

PSALM 73:23–28

WHEN EVERYTHING IS GONE

We've seen the pictures of tsunamis. We've witnessed the devastation of hurricanes. We've watched as families lose everything they had and sometimes everyone they loved. I cannot imagine what it would be like to lose my worldly accumulation and literally have nothing left on this earth. And when I try to think of that kind of loss, I ask myself, "Is everything I desire truly in heaven?" Would the strength of God be enough? Is my faith tethered to the unchanging faithfulness of God? If my whole world blows away tomorrow, will I still bow down and worship my King? Will I cry out to Jesus?

Maybe a physical hurricane has torn your life away, or maybe a spiritual hurricane has left you standing alone in one of the most difficult seasons of your life. Has the earth been rumbling underneath your feet? Are you afraid of your circumstances or your accusers or the rumors? Do you fear that the gale-force winds of life will surely blow you away? Then hear these words of assurance and refuge: our great God has not left you. He will never leave you. He holds your hand, even in this moment. Our only and best hope still is and forever will be the Lord God Almighty. Our Invincible Warrior. Fearless Protector. Merciful Father. When we have nothing left on this earth, we can still trust that our hope remains secure. We are held and delivered by the God who promises to be our strength.

25 I have no one in heaven but you;
I want nothing on earth besides you.
26 My body and my mind may become weak,
but God is my strength.
He is mine forever.

27 Those who are far from God will die;
you destroy those who are unfaithful.
28 But I am close to God, and that is good.
The Lord GOD is my protection.
I will tell all that you have done.

A Nation in Trouble Prays

A maskil of Asaph.

74 God, why have you rejected us for so long?
Why are you angry with us, the sheep of your pasture?
2 Remember the people you bought long ago.
You saved us, and we are your very own.
After all, you live on Mount Zion.
3 Make your way through these old ruins;
the enemy wrecked everything in the Temple.

4 Those who were against you shouted in your meeting place
and raised their flags there.
5 They came with axes raised
as if to cut down a forest of trees.
6 They smashed the carved panels
with their axes and hatchets.
7 They burned your Temple to the ground;
they have made the place where you live unclean.
8 They thought, "We will completely crush them!"
They burned every place where God was worshiped in the land.
9 We do not see any signs.
There are no more prophets,
and no one knows how long this will last.
10 God, how much longer will the enemy make fun of you?
Will they insult you forever?
11 Why do you hold back your power?
Bring your power out in the open and destroy them!

12 God, you have been our king for a long time.
You bring salvation to the earth.
13 You split open the sea by your power
and broke the heads of the sea monster.
14 You smashed the heads of the monster Leviathan
and gave it to the desert creatures as food.
15 You opened up the springs and streams
and made the flowing rivers run dry.
16 Both the day and the night are yours;
you made the sun and the moon.
17 You set all the limits on the earth;
you created summer and winter.

18 LORD, remember how the enemy insulted you.
Remember how those foolish people made fun of you.
19 Do not give us, your doves, to those wild animals.
Never forget your poor people.
20 Remember the agreement you made with us,
because violence fills every dark corner of this land.
21 Do not let your suffering people be disgraced.
Let the poor and helpless praise you.

22 God, arise and defend yourself.
Remember the insults that come from those foolish people all day long.
23 Don't forget what your enemies said;
don't forget their roar as they rise against you always.

God the Judge

For the director of music. To the tune of "Do Not Destroy." A psalm of Asaph. A song.

75 God, we thank you;
we thank you because you are near.
We tell about the miracles you do.

2 You say, "I set the time for trial,
and I will judge fairly.
3 The earth with all its people may shake,
but I am the one who holds it steady. *Selah*
4 I say to those who are proud, 'Don't brag,'
and to the wicked, 'Don't show your power.
5 Don't try to use your power against heaven.
Don't be stubborn.' "

6 No one from the east or the west
or the desert can judge you.
7 God is the judge;
he judges one person as guilty and another as innocent.

devotion 156

PSALM 75:7

MISUNDERSTOOD AND WRONGLY ACCUSED

Is this one of those days when all you want to do is scream out for justice? Have you been wrongly accused, misunderstood, or offended? When these types of events unfold in life, they seem monumental, and I find myself with a sick heart, going over all of the details to make sure I have not allowed one single word or action to slip from my memory. I ask over and over, what if I had done one more thing, said one more thing, or not said one more thing—could I have changed the outcome?

We encourage one another to seek the Scriptures for comfort and counsel; however, when we are personally in the middle of a storm of accusations, all we want to do is hide in the smallest, most confined space we can find. Our minds run rampant—*I will never talk to another person as long as I live! Who needs friends? They're just a lot of work. I'll quit this job, and no one will even notice if I am gone*—and a sick heart follows close behind.

The Word is your comfort, and so is God's heart toward you. The Lord loves you, and not one thing goes unnoticed. He sees every wrong deed orchestrated, hears every coarse word spoken, witnesses every plot contrived, and knows each tear you've shed. Rest with a joyful heart knowing that the Lord requires no assistance on your part except to trust him and be confident in his justice.

8 The LORD holds a cup of anger in his hand;
it is full of wine mixed with spices.
He pours it out even to the last drop,
and the wicked drink it all.

9 I will tell about this forever;
I will sing praise to the God of Jacob.
10 He will take all power away from the wicked,
but the power of good people will grow.

The God Who Always Wins

For the director of music. With stringed instruments. A psalm of Asaph. A song.

76 People in Judah know God;
his fame is great in Israel.
2 His Tent is in Jerusalem;
his home is on Mount Zion.
3 There God broke the flaming arrows,
the shields, the swords, and the weapons of war. *Selah*

4 God, how wonderful you are!
You are more splendid than the hills full of animals.
5 The brave soldiers were stripped
as they lay asleep in death.
Not one warrior
had the strength to stop it.
6 God of Jacob, when you spoke strongly,
horses and riders fell dead.
7 You are feared;
no one can stand against you when you are angry.
8 From heaven you gave the decision,
and the earth was afraid and silent.
9 God, you stood up to judge
and to save the needy people of the earth. *Selah*
10 People praise you for your anger against evil.
Those who live through your anger are stopped from doing more evil.

11 Make and keep your promises to the LORD your God.
From all around, gifts should come to the God we worship.
12 God breaks the spirits of great leaders;
the kings on earth fear him.

Remembering God's Help

For the director of music. For Jeduthun. A psalm of Asaph.

77 I cry out to God;
I call to God, and he will hear me.
2 I look for the Lord on the day of
trouble.
All night long I reach out my hands,
but I cannot be comforted.
3 When I remember God, I become upset;
when I think, I become afraid. *Selah*
4 You keep my eyes from closing.
I am too upset to say anything.
5 I keep thinking about the old days,
the years of long ago.
6 At night I remember my songs.
I think and I ask myself:
7 "Will the Lord reject us forever?
Will he never be kind to us again?
8 Is his love gone forever?
Has he stopped speaking for all time?
9 Has God forgotten mercy?
Is he too angry to pity us?" *Selah*
10 Then I say, "This is what makes me sad:
For years the power of God Most High
was with us."

11 I remember what the LORD did;
I remember the miracles you did long
ago.
12 I think about all the things you did
and consider your deeds.

13 God, your ways are holy.
No god is as great as our God.
14 You are the God who does miracles;
you have shown people your power.
15 By your power you have saved your
people,
the descendants of Jacob and
Joseph. *Selah*

16 God, the waters saw you;
they saw you and became afraid;
the deep waters shook with fear.
17 The clouds poured down their rain.
The sky thundered.
Your lightning flashed back and forth
like arrows.
18 Your thunder sounded in the whirlwind.
Lightning lit up the world.
The earth trembled and shook.
19 You made a way through the sea
and paths through the deep waters,
but your footprints were not seen.
20 You led your people like a flock
by using Moses and Aaron.

God Saved Israel from Egypt

A maskil of Asaph.

78 My people, listen to my teaching;
listen to what I say.
2 I will speak using stories;
I will tell secret things from long ago.
3 We have heard them and known them
by what our ancestors have told us.
4 We will not keep them from our children;
we will tell those who come later
about the praises of the LORD.
We will tell about his power
and the miracles he has done.

5 The LORD made an agreement with Jacob
and gave the teachings to Israel,
which he commanded our ancestors
to teach to their children.
6 Then their children would know them,
even their children not yet born.
And they would tell their children.
7 So they would all trust God
and would not forget what he had done
but would obey his commands.
8 They would not be like their ancestors
who were stubborn and disobedient.
Their hearts were not loyal to God,
and they were not true to him.

9 The men of Ephraim had bows for
weapons,
but they ran away on the day of battle.
10 They didn't keep their agreement with
God
and refused to live by his teachings.
11 They forgot what he had done
and the miracles he had shown them.
12 He did miracles while their ancestors
watched,
in the fields of Zoan in Egypt.
13 He divided the Red Sea and led them
through.
He made the water stand up like a wall.
14 He led them with a cloud by day
and by the light of a fire by night.
15 He split the rocks in the desert
and gave them more than enough
water, as if from the deep ocean.
16 He brought streams out of the rock
and caused water to flow down like
rivers.

17But the people continued to sin against him;
in the desert they turned against God Most High.
18They decided to test God
by asking for the food they wanted.
19Then they spoke against God,
saying, "Can God prepare food in the desert?
20When he hit the rock, water poured out
and rivers flowed down.
But can he give us bread also?
Will he provide his people with meat?"
21When the LORD heard them, he was very angry.
His anger was like fire to the people of Jacob;
his anger grew against the people of Israel.
22They had not believed God
and had not trusted him to save them.
23But he gave a command to the clouds above
and opened the doors of heaven.
24He rained manna down on them to eat;
he gave them grain from heaven.
25So they ate the bread of angels.
He sent them all the food they could eat.
26He sent the east wind from heaven
and led the south wind by his power.
27He rained meat on them like dust.
The birds were as many as the sand of the sea.
28He made the birds fall inside the camp,
all around the tents.
29So the people ate and became very full.
God had given them what they wanted.
30While they were still eating,
and while the food was still in their mouths,
31God became angry with them.
He killed some of the healthiest of them;
he struck down the best young men of Israel.
32But they kept on sinning;
they did not believe even with the miracles.
33So he ended their days without meaning
and their years in terror.
34Anytime he killed them, they would look to him for help;
they would come back to God and follow him.
35They would remember that God was their Rock,
that God Most High had saved them.
36But their words were false,
and their tongues lied to him.
37Their hearts were not really loyal to God;
they did not keep his agreement.
38Still God was merciful.
He forgave their sins
and did not destroy them.
Many times he held back his anger
and did not stir up all his anger.
39He remembered that they were only human,
like a wind that blows and does not come back.
40They turned against God so often in the desert
and grieved him there.
41Again and again they tested God
and brought pain to the Holy One of Israel.
42They did not remember his power
or the time he saved them from the enemy.
43They forgot the signs he did in Egypt
and his wonders in the fields of Zoan.
44He turned their rivers to blood
so no one could drink the water.
45He sent flies that bit the people.
He sent frogs that destroyed them.
46He gave their crops to grasshoppers
and what they worked for to locusts.
47He destroyed their vines with hail
and their sycamore trees with sleet.
48He killed their animals with hail
and their cattle with lightning.
49He showed them his hot anger.
He sent his strong anger against them,
his destroying angels.
50He found a way to show his anger.
He did not keep them from dying
but let them die by a terrible disease.
51God killed all the firstborn sons in Egypt,
the oldest son of each family of Ham.[n]
52But God led his people out like sheep

78:51 Ham The people in Egypt were descendants of Ham, one of Noah's sons. See Genesis 10:6.

and he guided them like a flock
through the desert.
53He led them to safety so they had nothing
to fear,
but their enemies drowned in the sea.
54So God brought them to his holy land,
to the mountain country he took with
his own power.
55He forced out the other nations,
and he had his people inherit the land.
He let the tribes of Israel settle there in
tents.

56But they tested God
and turned against God Most High;
they did not keep his rules.
57They turned away and were disloyal just
like their ancestors.
They were like a crooked bow that does
not shoot straight.
58They made God angry by building places
to worship gods;
they made him jealous with their idols.
59When God heard them, he became very
angry
and rejected the people of Israel
completely.
60He left his dwelling at Shiloh,
the Tent where he lived among the
people.
61He let the Ark, his power, be captured;
he let the Ark, his glory, be taken by
enemies.
62He let his people be killed;
he was very angry with his children.
63The young men died by fire,
and the young women had no one to
marry.
64Their priests fell by the sword,
but their widows were not allowed to
cry.

65Then the Lord got up as if he had been
asleep;
he awoke like a man who had been
drunk with wine.
66He struck down his enemies
and disgraced them forever.
67But God rejected the family of Joseph;
he did not choose the tribe of Ephraim.
68Instead, he chose the tribe of Judah
and Mount Zion, which he loves.
69And he built his Temple high like the
mountains.
Like the earth, he built it to last forever.
70He chose David to be his servant
and took him from the sheep pens.
71He brought him from tending the sheep
so he could lead the flock, the people of
Jacob,
his own people, the people of Israel.
72And David led them with an innocent
heart
and guided them with skillful hands.

The Nation Cries for Jerusalem

A psalm of Asaph.

79 God, nations have come against your
chosen people.
They have ruined your holy Temple.
They have turned Jerusalem into ruins.
2They have given the bodies of your
servants as food to the wild birds.
They have given the bodies of those who
worship you to the wild animals.
3They have spilled blood like water all
around Jerusalem.
No one was left to bury the dead.
4We are a joke to the other nations;
they laugh and make fun of us.

5LORD, how long will this last?
Will you be angry forever?
How long will your jealousy burn like a
fire?
6Be angry with the nations that do not
know you
and with the kingdoms that do not
honor you.
7They have gobbled up the people of
Jacob
and destroyed their land.
8Don't punish us for our past sins.
Show your mercy to us soon,
because we are helpless!
9God our Savior, help us
so people will praise you.
Save us and forgive our sins
so people will honor you.
10Why should the nations say,
"Where is their God?"
Tell the other nations in our presence
that you punish those who kill your
servants.
11Hear the moans of the prisoners.
Use your great power
to save those sentenced to die.
12Repay those around us seven times over
for their insults to you, Lord.

13 We are your people, the sheep of your flock.
We will thank you always;
forever and ever we will praise you.

A Prayer to Bring Israel Back

For the director of music. To the tune of "Lilies of the Agreement." A psalm of Asaph.

80 Shepherd of Israel, listen to us.
You lead the people of Joseph like a flock.
You sit on your throne between the gold creatures with wings.
Show your greatness 2 to the people of Ephraim, Benjamin, and Manasseh.
Use your strength,
and come to save us.

3 God, take us back.
Show us your kindness so we can be saved.

4 LORD God All-Powerful,
how long will you be angry
at the prayers of your people?
5 You have fed your people with tears;
you have made them drink many tears.
6 You made those around us fight over us,
and our enemies make fun of us.

7 God All-Powerful, take us back.
Show us your kindness so we can be saved.

8 You brought us out of Egypt as if we were a vine.
You forced out other nations and planted us in the land.
9 You cleared the ground for us.
Like a vine, we took root and filled the land.
10 We covered the mountains with our shade.
We had limbs like the mighty cedar tree.
11 Our branches reached the Mediterranean Sea,
and our shoots went to the Euphrates River.

12 So why did you pull down our walls?
Now everyone who passes by steals from us.
13 Like wild pigs they walk over us;
like wild animals they feed on us.
14 God All-Powerful, come back.
Look down from heaven and see.
Take care of us, your vine.
15 You planted this shoot with your own hands
and strengthened this child.
16 Now it is cut down and burned with fire;
you destroyed us by your angry looks.
17 With your hand,
strengthen the one you have chosen for yourself.
18 Then we will not turn away from you.
Give us life again, and we will call to you for help.
19 LORD God All-Powerful, take us back.
Show us your kindness so we can be saved.

A Song for a Holiday

For the director of music. By the gittith. A psalm of Asaph.

81 Sing for joy to God, our strength;
shout out loud to the God of Jacob.
2 Begin the music. Play the tambourines.
Play pleasant music on the harps and lyres.
3 Blow the trumpet at the time of the New Moon,
when the moon is full, when our feast begins.
4 This is the law for Israel;
it is the command of the God of Jacob.
5 He gave this rule to the people of Joseph
when they went out of the land of Egypt.

I heard a language I did not know, saying:
6 "I took the load off their shoulders;
I let them put down their baskets.
7 When you were in trouble, you called,
and I saved you.
I answered you with thunder.
I tested you at the waters of Meribah. *Selah*
8 My people, listen. I am warning you.
Israel, please listen to me!
9 You must not have foreign gods;
you must not worship any false god.
10 I, the LORD, am your God,
who brought you out of Egypt.
Open your mouth and I will feed you.

11 "But my people did not listen to me;
Israel did not want me.

devotion 157

PSALM 81:8-16

EXTERMINATE THE CHRISTMAS TREE?

Christmas Eve is always a busy time for our family—preparing food, wrapping last-minute gifts, and planning for the Christmas Eve service. As I made my way to the coffee pot a few years ago on Christmas Eve morning, I noticed a small bug on one of the packages. I looked closer and realized the bugs were all over the tree, the packages, and were crawling up my walls. We spent the next two hours disposing of the tree and debugging the house. It was quite a disappointment. That night as we sat in our living room, we talked about the day's events. My daughter had an amazing observation. "Our tree was so beautiful with all the lights and ornaments," she said, "but the bugs were like sin in our lives. We might look beautiful on the outside, but if we have sin in our lives, it will eventually ruin us just like the bugs ruined our tree."

This is exactly what God was warning the Israelites about. He begged them to listen to him. He wanted them to understand that having foreign gods in their lives would destroy them. Sin always seems harmless in the beginning. Similarly, our tree seemed beautiful when the bugs were still in their eggs. But as soon as the eggs hatched, the tree was quickly destroyed. Hear God's warning. Don't allow sin to hide in your life. Get rid of it, just as the Israelites had to rid themselves of foreign gods. Exterminate if necessary!

12 So I let them go their stubborn way
and follow their own advice.
13 I wish my people would listen to me;
I wish Israel would live my way.
14 Then I would quickly defeat their
enemies
and turn my hand against their foes.
15 Those who hate the LORD would bow
before him.
Their punishment would continue
forever.
16 But I would give you the finest wheat
and fill you with honey from the
rocks."

A Cry for Justice

A psalm of Asaph.

82 God is in charge of the great meeting;
he judges among the "gods."
2 He says, "How long will you defend evil
people?
How long will you show greater
kindness to the wicked? *Selah*
3 Defend the weak and the orphans;
defend the rights of the poor and
suffering.
4 Save the weak and helpless;
free them from the power of the
wicked.

5 "You know nothing. You don't
understand.
You walk in the dark,
while the world is falling apart.
6 I said, 'You are "gods."
You are all sons of God Most High.'
7 But you will die like any other person;
you will fall like all the leaders."

8 God, come and judge the earth,
because you own all the nations.

A Prayer Against the Enemies

A song. A psalm of Asaph.

83 God, do not keep quiet;
God, do not be silent or still.
2 Your enemies are making noises;
those who hate you are getting ready to
attack.

3They are making secret plans against your
people;
they plot against those you love.
4They say, "Come, let's destroy them as a
nation.
Then no one will ever remember the
name 'Israel.' "
5They are united in their plan.
These have made an agreement against
you:
6the families of Edom and the Ishmaelites,
Moab and the Hagrites,
7the people of Byblos, Ammon, Amalek,
Philistia, and Tyre.
8Even Assyria has joined them
to help Ammon and Moab, the
descendants of Lot. *Selah*

9God, do to them what you did to Midian,
what you did to Sisera and Jabin at the
Kishon River.
10They died at Endor,
and their bodies rotted on the ground.
11Do to their important leaders what you
did to Oreb and Zeeb.
Do to their princes what you did to
Zebah and Zalmunna.
12They said, "Let's take for ourselves
the pasturelands that belong to God."
13My God, make them like tumbleweed,
like chaff blown away by the wind.
14Be like a fire that burns a forest
or like flames that blaze through the
hills.
15Chase them with your storm,
and frighten them with your wind.
16Cover them with shame.
Then people will look for you, LORD.
17Make them afraid and ashamed forever.
Disgrace them and destroy them.
18Then they will know that you are the
LORD,
that only you are God Most High over
all the earth.

Wishing to Be in the Temple

For the director of music. On the gittith. A psalm of the sons of Korah.

84 LORD All-Powerful,
how lovely is your Temple!
2I want more than anything
to be in the courtyards of the LORD's
Temple.
My whole being wants
to be with the living God.
3The sparrows have found a home,
and the swallows have nests.
They raise their young near your altars,
LORD All-Powerful, my King and my
God.
4Happy are the people who live at your
Temple;
they are always praising you. *Selah*
5Happy are those whose strength comes
from you,
who want to travel to Jerusalem.
6As they pass through the Valley of Baca,
they make it like a spring.
The autumn rains fill it with pools of
water.
7The people get stronger as they go,
and everyone meets with God in
Jerusalem.
8LORD God All-Powerful, hear my prayer;
God of Jacob, listen to me. *Selah*
9God, look at our shield;
be kind to your appointed king.
10One day in the courtyards of your Temple
is better
than a thousand days anywhere else.
I would rather be a doorkeeper in the
Temple of my God
than live in the homes of the wicked.
11The LORD God is like a sun and shield;
the LORD gives us kindness and honor.
He does not hold back anything good
from those whose lives are innocent.
12LORD All-Powerful,
happy are the people who trust you!

A Prayer for the Nation

For the director of music. A psalm of the sons of Korah.

85 LORD, you have been kind to your land;
you brought back the people of
Jacob.
2You forgave the guilt of the people
and covered all their sins. *Selah*
3You stopped all your anger;
you turned back from your strong anger.

4God our Savior, bring us back again.
Stop being angry with us.
5Will you be angry with us forever?
Will you stay angry from now on?
6Won't you give us life again?
Your people would rejoice in you.
7LORD, show us your love,
and save us.

[8]I will listen to God the LORD.
He has ordered peace for those who worship him.
Don't let them go back to foolishness.
[9]God will soon save those who respect him,
and his glory will be seen in our land.
[10]Love and truth belong to God's people;
goodness and peace will be theirs.
[11]On earth people will be loyal to God,
and God's goodness will shine down from heaven.
[12]The LORD will give his goodness,
and the land will give its crops.
[13]Goodness will go before God
and prepare the way for him.

A Cry for Help

A prayer of David.

86 LORD, listen to me and answer me.
I am poor and helpless.
[2]Protect me, because I worship you.
My God, save me, your servant who trusts in you.
[3]Lord, have mercy on me,
because I have called to you all day.
[4]Give happiness to me, your servant,
because I give my life to you, Lord.
[5]Lord, you are kind and forgiving
and have great love for those who call to you.
[6]LORD, hear my prayer,
and listen when I ask for mercy.
[7]I call to you in times of trouble,
because you will answer me.

[8]Lord, there is no god like you
and no works like yours.
[9]Lord, all the nations you have made
will come and worship you.
They will honor you.
[10]You are great and you do miracles.
Only you are God.
[11]LORD, teach me what you want me to do,
and I will live by your truth.
Teach me to respect you completely.
[12]Lord, my God, I will praise you with all my heart,
and I will honor your name forever.

devotion 158

PSALM 86:11–13

LIVING AN UNMANAGEABLE LIFE?

How often do we actually lay aside our desires and ask God what he wants us to do in a situation? Many of us don't seek God's counsel often enough, but decision making would be easier if we did. Why do we embark upon decisions on our own? Is it because we're stubborn, impatient, forgetful, or just too proud? Whatever the reason, it pulls us off our course, and we are fooled into thinking we can live life on our own. That is, until we find ourselves in deep trouble.

In Psalm 86, David prays to his Lord about a life-threatening situation, so fear is probably the motivation behind his plea. But God wants to be there for us in every situation—before it turns bad. We make better decisions in our lives when we seek God's guidance and direction in everything, whether it's how to deal with a difficult boss, a tumultuous marriage, or a stressful situation with our kids. Whatever it is, let's give it to God and let him lead us to the answer. He will guide his children in the right direction.

I encourage you to use David's prayer if you're struggling in your life. Don't forget to show your honor to God in everything you do. God loves his children. He'll be there to save you when your life seems unmanageable, so be sure to take a moment to praise and thank him for walking with you today.

13 You have great love for me.
You have saved me from death.

14 God, proud people are attacking me;
a gang of cruel people is trying to kill me.
They do not respect you.
15 But, Lord, you are a God who shows mercy and is kind.
You don't become angry quickly.
You have great love and faithfulness.
16 Turn to me and have mercy.
Give me, your servant, strength.
Save me, the son of your female servant.
17 Show me a sign of your goodness.
When my enemies look, they will be ashamed.
You, LORD, have helped me and comforted me.

God Loves Jerusalem

A song. A psalm of the sons of Korah.

87 The LORD built Jerusalem on the holy mountain.
2 He loves its gates more than any other place in Israel.
3 City of God,
wonderful things are said about you. *Selah*
4 God says, "I will put Egypt and Babylonia
on the list of nations that know me.
People from Philistia, Tyre, and Cush
will be born there."

5 They will say about Jerusalem,
"This one and that one were born there.
God Most High will strengthen her."
6 The LORD will keep a list of the nations.
He will note, "This person was born there." *Selah*

7 They will dance and sing,
"All good things come from Jerusalem."

A Sad Complaint

A song. A psalm of the sons of Korah. For the director of music. By the mahalath leannoth. A maskil of Heman the Ezrahite.

88 LORD, you are the God who saves me.
I cry out to you day and night.
2 Receive my prayer,
and listen to my cry.

3 My life is full of troubles,
and I am nearly dead.
4 They think I am on the way to my grave.
I am like a man with no strength.
5 I have been left as dead,
like a body lying in a grave
whom you don't remember anymore,
cut off from your care.
6 You have brought me close to death;
I am almost in the dark place of the dead.
7 You have been very angry with me;
all your waves crush me. *Selah*
8 You have taken my friends away from me
and have made them hate me.
I am trapped and cannot escape.
9 My eyes are weak from crying.
LORD, I have prayed to you every day;
I have lifted my hands in prayer to you.

10 Do you show your miracles for the dead?
Do their spirits rise up and praise you? *Selah*
11 Will your love be told in the grave?
Will your loyalty be told in the place of death?
12 Will your miracles be known in the dark grave?
Will your goodness be known in the land of forgetfulness?

13 But, LORD, I have called out to you for help;
every morning I pray to you.
14 LORD, why do you reject me?
Why do you hide from me?
15 I have been weak and dying since I was young.
I suffer from your terrors, and I am helpless.
16 You have been angry with me,
and your terrors have destroyed me.
17 They surround me daily like a flood;
they are all around me.
18 You have taken away my loved ones and friends.
Darkness is my only friend.

A Song About God's Loyalty

A maskil of Ethan the Ezrahite.

89 I will always sing about the LORD's love;
I will tell of his loyalty from now on.
2 I will say, "Your love continues forever;
your loyalty goes on and on like the sky."
3 You said, "I made an agreement with the man of my choice;

I made a promise to my servant David.
4I told him, 'I will make your family
continue forever.
Your kingdom will go on and on.' " *Selah*

5LORD, the heavens praise you for your
miracles
and for your loyalty in the meeting of
your holy ones.
6Who in heaven is equal to the LORD?
None of the angels is like the LORD.
7When the holy ones meet, it is God they
fear.
He is more frightening than all who
surround him.
8LORD God All-Powerful, who is like you?
LORD, you are powerful and completely
trustworthy.
9You rule the mighty sea
and calm the stormy waves.
10You crushed the sea monster Rahab;
by your power you scattered your
enemies.
11The skies and the earth belong to you.
You made the world and everything
in it.
12You created the north and the south.
Mount Tabor and Mount Hermon sing
for joy at your name.
13Your arm has great power.
Your hand is strong; your right hand is
lifted up.
14Your kingdom is built on what is right
and fair.
Love and truth are in all you do.
15Happy are the people who know how to
praise you.
LORD, let them live in the light of your
presence.
16In your name they rejoice
and continually praise your goodness.
17You are their glorious strength,
and in your kindness you honor our
king.
18Our king, our shield, belongs to the LORD,
to the Holy One of Israel.

19Once, in a vision, you spoke
to those who worship you.
You said, "I have given strength to a
warrior;
I have raised up a young man from my
people.
20I have found my servant David;
I appointed him by pouring holy oil on
him.
21I will steady him with my hand
and strengthen him with my arm.
22No enemy will make him give forced
payments,
and wicked people will not defeat him.
23I will crush his enemies in front of him;
I will defeat those who hate him.
24My loyalty and love will be with him.
Through me he will be strong.
25I will give him power over the sea
and control over the rivers.
26He will say to me, 'You are my father,
my God, the Rock, my Savior.'
27I will make him my firstborn son,
the greatest king on earth.
28My love will watch over him forever,
and my agreement with him will never
end.
29I will make his family continue,
and his kingdom will last as long as the
skies.

30"If his descendants reject my teachings
and do not follow my laws,
31if they ignore my demands
and disobey my commands,
32then I will punish their sins with a rod
and their wrongs with a whip.
33But I will not hold back my love from
David,
nor will I stop being loyal.
34I will not break my agreement
nor change what I have said.
35I have promised by my holiness,
I will not lie to David.
36His family will go on forever.
His kingdom will last before me like
the sun.
37It will continue forever, like the moon,
like a dependable witness in the
sky." *Selah*

38But now you have refused and rejected
your appointed king.
You have been angry with him.
39You have abandoned the agreement with
your servant
and thrown his crown to the ground.
40You have torn down all his city walls;
you have turned his strong cities into
ruins.
41Everyone who passes by steals from him.
His neighbors insult him.

42You have given strength to his enemies
and have made them all happy.
43You have made his sword useless;
you did not help him stand in battle.
44You have kept him from winning
and have thrown his throne to the ground.
45You have cut his life short
and covered him with shame. *Selah*

46LORD, how long will this go on?
Will you ignore us forever?
How long will your anger burn like a fire?
47Remember how short my life is.
Why did you create us? For nothing?
48What person alive will not die?
Who can escape the grave? *Selah*

49Lord, where is your love from times past,
which in your loyalty you promised to David?
50Lord, remember how they insulted your servant;
remember how I have suffered the insults of the nations.
51LORD, remember how your enemies insulted you
and how they insulted your appointed king wherever he went.

52Praise the LORD forever!
Amen and amen.

Book 4

God Is Eternal, and We Are Not

A prayer of Moses, the man of God.

90 Lord, you have been our home
since the beginning.
2Before the mountains were born
and before you created the earth and the world,
you are God.
You have always been, and you will always be.

3You turn people back into dust.
You say, "Go back into dust, human beings."
4To you, a thousand years

devotion 159

PSALM 90:2

GURU OF THE MOMENT

In every generation, there are those who question the authority of God, people who try to find other words to live by instead of God's words. They live their lives blown around by the latest trend or rumored guru technique. They go from book to book and seminar to seminar, searching for anything that will enlighten their lives, anything except the unchanging, eternal person of God.

But what we know is that from generation to generation, God endures. His words remain powerful and life giving. And his relationship with us is built on the foundation of Jesus Christ, who is the same yesterday, today, and forever.

Here is the great news. You can build your life on something that lasts! You do not have to build on shifting sand or put your hope inside a bubble that will shimmer for a moment and pop. You do not have to treat your heartache with a temporary remedy. God is available to you, the God who has always been and always will be.

God has outlived all the fads and broken all the criticism, and he continues to offer you the place of greatest healing and utmost fulfillment. You and I can live every single day looking back with thankfulness on all that God has done for us and looking forward to all God promises to do for us because of Christ. He is the God of every generation. Won't you come and find your rest in the One who existed before Creation?

is like the passing of a day,
or like a few hours in the night.
5 While people sleep, you take their lives.
They are like grass that grows up in the morning.
6 In the morning they are fresh and new,
but by evening they dry up and die.

7 We are destroyed by your anger;
we are terrified by your hot anger.
8 You have put the evil we have done right in front of you;
you clearly see our secret sins.
9 All our days pass while you are angry.
Our years end with a moan.
10 Our lifetime is seventy years
or, if we are strong, eighty years.
But the years are full of hard work and pain.
They pass quickly, and then we are gone.

11 Who knows the full power of your anger?
Your anger is as great as our fear of you should be.
12 Teach us how short our lives really are
so that we may be wise.

13 LORD, how long before you return
and show kindness to your servants?
14 Fill us with your love every morning.
Then we will sing and rejoice all our lives.
15 We have seen years of trouble.
Now give us as much joy as you gave us sorrow.
16 Show your servants the wonderful things you do;
show your greatness to their children.
17 Lord our God, treat us well.
Give us success in what we do;
yes, give us success in what we do.

Safe in the Lord

91 Those who go to God Most High for safety
will be protected by the Almighty.
2 I will say to the LORD, "You are my place of safety and protection.
You are my God and I trust you."
3 God will save you from hidden traps
and from deadly diseases.
4 He will cover you with his feathers,
and under his wings you can hide.
His truth will be your shield and protection.
5 You will not fear any danger by night
or an arrow during the day.
6 You will not be afraid of diseases that come in the dark
or sickness that strikes at noon.
7 At your side one thousand people may die,
or even ten thousand right beside you,
but you will not be hurt.
8 You will only watch
and see the wicked punished.

9 The LORD is your protection;
you have made God Most High your place of safety.
10 Nothing bad will happen to you;
no disaster will come to your home.
11 He has put his angels in charge of you
to watch over you wherever you go.
12 They will catch you in their hands
so that you will not hit your foot on a rock.
13 You will walk on lions and cobras;
you will step on strong lions and snakes.

14 The LORD says, "Whoever loves me, I will save.
I will protect those who know me.
15 They will call to me, and I will answer them.
I will be with them in trouble;
I will rescue them and honor them.
16 I will give them a long, full life,
and they will see how I can save."

Thanksgiving for God's Goodness

A psalm. A song for the Sabbath day.

92 It is good to praise you, LORD,
to sing praises to God Most High.
2 It is good to tell of your love in the morning
and of your loyalty at night.
3 It is good to praise you with the ten-stringed lyre
and with the soft-sounding harp.

4 LORD, you have made me happy by what you have done;
I will sing for joy about what your hands have done.
5 LORD, you have done such great things!
How deep are your thoughts!
6 Stupid people don't know these things,
and fools don't understand.

7Wicked people grow like the grass.
Evil people seem to do well,
but they will be destroyed forever.
8But, LORD, you will be honored forever.

9LORD, surely your enemies,
surely your enemies will be destroyed,
and all who do evil will be scattered.
10But you have made me as strong as an ox.
You have poured fine oils on me.
11When I looked, I saw my enemies;
I heard the cries of those who are against me.

12But good people will grow like palm trees;
they will be tall like the cedars of Lebanon.
13Like trees planted in the Temple of the LORD,
they will grow strong in the courtyards of our God.
14When they are old, they will still produce fruit;
they will be healthy and fresh.
15They will say that the LORD is good.
He is my Rock, and there is no wrong in him.

The Majesty of the Lord

93 The LORD is king. He is clothed in majesty.
The LORD is clothed in majesty
and armed with strength.
The world is set,
and it cannot be moved.
2LORD, your kingdom was set up long ago;
you are everlasting.

3LORD, the seas raise,
the seas raise their voice.
The seas raise up their pounding waves.
4The sound of the water is loud;
the ocean waves are powerful,
but the LORD above is much greater.

5LORD, your laws will stand forever.
Your Temple will be holy forevermore.

devotion 160

PSALM 94:12

PAID TUITION AND A FULL-TIME TUTOR

If the words "correct" and "law" are in the same sentence, do you experience anxiety or joy in your heart? It is not part of God's plan for you to live a hopeless, defeated, or ashamed life. His Word was not meant as a benchmark to measure your personal failures. These beautiful Scriptures are alive and intended to strengthen you, encourage your faith, and fill your heart and mind with wisdom. There is evidence all throughout Scripture of God transforming ordinary men and women into the extraordinary.

All along my walk, I have witnessed how the truth of godly teaching works in our lives and is manifested in our relationships. Do you realize that every time you take in the Word, the Lord is lovingly instructing you? When you read the Scriptures, when you quiet your heart with devotions, when you gather together on Sundays, and when faithful friends speak into your life, you are being educated and transformed. As a believer, your tuition is paid, you have a great teacher, a full-time tutor, and a God that is the lover of your soul. You are a student attending the school of the Holy Spirit.

The Holy Spirit reveals the truth about God and his activity in your life, and in turn, that truth causes you to bring about change that will line up with God's Word. You are an extraordinary woman. Celebrate your higher education and hurry up—your next class is waiting for you.

God Will Pay Back His Enemies

94 The LORD is a God who punishes.
God, show your greatness and punish!
2Rise up, Judge of the earth,
and give the proud what they deserve.
3How long will the wicked be happy?
How long, LORD?
4They are full of proud words;
those who do evil brag about what they have done.
5LORD, they crush your people
and make your children suffer.
6They kill widows and foreigners
and murder orphans.
7They say, "The LORD doesn't see;
the God of Jacob doesn't notice."

8You stupid ones among the people, pay attention.
You fools, when will you understand?
9Can't the creator of ears hear?
Can't the maker of eyes see?
10Won't the one who corrects nations punish you?
Doesn't the teacher of people know everything?
11The LORD knows what people think.
He knows their thoughts are just a puff of wind.

12LORD, those you correct are happy;
you teach them from your law.
13You give them rest from times of trouble
until a pit is dug for the wicked.
14The LORD won't leave his people
nor give up his children.
15Judgment will again be fair,
and all who are honest will follow it.

16Who will help me fight against the wicked?
Who will stand with me against those who do evil?
17If the LORD had not helped me,
I would have died in a minute.
18I said, "I am about to fall,"
but, LORD, your love kept me safe.
19I was very worried,
but you comforted me and made me happy.
20Crooked leaders cannot be your friends.
They use the law to cause suffering.
21They join forces against people who do right
and sentence to death the innocent.
22But the LORD is my defender;
my God is the rock of my protection.
23God will pay them back for their sins
and will destroy them for their evil.
The LORD our God will destroy them.

A Call to Praise and Obedience

95 Come, let's sing for joy to the LORD.
Let's shout praises to the Rock who saves us.
2Let's come to him with thanksgiving.
Let's sing songs to him,
3because the LORD is the great God,
the great King over all gods.
4The deepest places on earth are his,
and the highest mountains belong to him.
5The sea is his because he made it,
and he created the land with his own hands.

6Come, let's worship him and bow down.
Let's kneel before the LORD who made us,
7because he is our God
and we are the people he takes care of,
the sheep that he tends.

Today listen to what he says:
8 "Do not be stubborn, as your ancestors were at Meribah,
as they were that day at Massah in the desert.
9There your ancestors tested me
and tried me even though they saw what I did.
10I was angry with those people for forty years.
I said, 'They are not loyal to me
and have not understood my ways.'
11I was angry and made a promise,
'They will never enter my rest.' "

Praise for the Lord's Glory

96 Sing to the LORD a new song;
sing to the LORD, all the earth.
2Sing to the LORD and praise his name;
every day tell how he saves us.

3 Tell the nations of his glory;
tell all peoples the miracles he does,
4 because the LORD is great; he should be praised at all times.
He should be honored more than all the gods,
5 because all the gods of the nations are only idols,
but the LORD made the heavens.
6 The LORD has glory and majesty;
he has power and beauty in his Temple.

7 Praise the LORD, all nations on earth;
praise the LORD's glory and power.
8 Praise the glory of the LORD's name.
Bring an offering and come into his Temple courtyards.
9 Worship the LORD because he is holy.
Tremble before him, everyone on earth.
10 Tell the nations, "The LORD is king."
The earth is set, and it cannot be moved.
He will judge the people fairly.
11 Let the skies rejoice and the earth be glad;
let the sea and everything in it shout.
12 Let the fields and everything in them rejoice.
Then all the trees of the forest will sing for joy
13 before the LORD, because he is coming.
He is coming to judge the world;
he will judge the world with fairness
and the peoples with truth.

A Hymn About the Lord's Power

97 The LORD is king. Let the earth rejoice;
faraway lands should be glad.
2 Thick, dark clouds surround him.
His kingdom is built on what is right and fair.
3 A fire goes before him
and burns up his enemies all around.
4 His lightning lights up the world;
when the people see it, they tremble.
5 The mountains melt like wax before the LORD,
before the Lord of all the earth.
6 The heavens tell about his goodness,
and all the people see his glory.

7 Those who worship idols should be ashamed;
they brag about their gods.
All the gods should worship the LORD.
8 When Jerusalem hears this, she is glad,

devotion 161

PSALM 96:6–13

LIFE ISN'T FAIR, BUT IS KINDERGARTEN?

I had three children in three years. They were each other's best friends when they were little, but they also were in constant competition to be first. It was always who got to go first, who got to sit in the front seat, who got to push the elevator button, and on and on. They would always say to me, "That's not fair." So my usual response was, "Life isn't fair." When the youngest of the three went to kindergarten, her teacher explained the different jobs that each student would do in the classroom on a rotating basis. She finished her explanation with, "It will always be fair." My daughter raised her hand and said, "But my mother said that life isn't fair." The teacher, taken aback, answered, "Well, honey, life isn't fair, but kindergarten is."

I'll take it one step further. Life isn't fair, but God is. The Bible tells us that he will judge the people fairly. One of the greatest rewards we will have in heaven will be to live in a world that is fair. I believe that is why the skies will rejoice, the seas will shout, and the trees will sing for joy. He is coming to judge the world, and when he does, he will set up his kingdom here on earth. It will be a glorious kingdom to live in and everything will be fair. Our God-given desire for fairness and justice will one day be satisfied by Jesus himself!

and the towns of Judah rejoice.
They are happy because of your
judgments, LORD.
9 You are the LORD Most High over all the
earth;
you are supreme over all gods.

10 People who love the LORD hate evil.
The LORD watches over those who
follow him
and frees them from the power of the
wicked.
11 Light shines on those who do right;
joy belongs to those who are honest.
12 Rejoice in the LORD, you who do right.
Praise his holy name.

The Lord of Power and Justice

A psalm.

98 Sing to the LORD a new song,
because he has done miracles.
By his right hand and holy arm
he has won the victory.
2 The LORD has made known his power to
save;
he has shown the other nations his
victory for his people.
3 He has remembered his love
and his loyalty to the people of Israel.
All the ends of the earth have seen
God's power to save.

4 Shout with joy to the LORD, all the earth;
burst into songs and make music.
5 Make music to the LORD with harps,
with harps and the sound of singing.
6 Blow the trumpets and the sheep's horns;
shout for joy to the LORD the King.

7 Let the sea and everything in it shout;
let the world and everyone in it sing.
8 Let the rivers clap their hands;
let the mountains sing together for joy.
9 Let them sing before the LORD,
because he is coming to judge the
world.
He will judge the world fairly;
he will judge the peoples with fairness.

The Lord, the Fair and Holy King

99 The LORD is king.
Let the peoples shake with fear.
He sits between the gold creatures with
wings.
Let the earth shake.
2 The LORD in Jerusalem is great;
he is supreme over all the peoples.
3 Let them praise your name;
it is great, holy and to be feared.

4 The King is powerful and loves justice.
LORD, you made things fair;
you have done what is fair and right
for the people of Jacob.
5 Praise the LORD our God,
and worship at the Temple, his footstool.
He is holy.

6 Moses and Aaron were among his priests,
and Samuel was among his worshipers.
They called to the LORD,
and he answered them.
7 He spoke to them from the pillar of cloud.
They kept the rules and laws he gave
them.

8 LORD our God, you answered them.
You showed them that you are a
forgiving God,
but you punished them for their
wrongs.
9 Praise the LORD our God,
and worship at his holy mountain,
because the LORD our God is holy.

A Call to Praise the Lord

A psalm of thanks.

100 Shout to the LORD, all the earth.
2 Serve the Lord with joy;
come before him with singing.
3 Know that the LORD is God.
He made us, and we belong to him;
we are his people, the sheep he tends.

4 Come into his city with songs of
thanksgiving
and into his courtyards with songs of
praise.
Thank him and praise his name.
5 The LORD is good. His love is forever,
and his loyalty goes on and on.

A Promise to Rule Well

A psalm of David.

101 I will sing of your love and
fairness;
LORD, I will sing praises to you.
2 I will be careful to live an innocent life.
When will you come to me?

I will live an innocent life in my house.
3 I will not look at anything wicked.

devotion 162

PSALM 101:2–4

MARY'S PROMISE

On the day that my friend Mary received Christ, she made promises to the Lord—and to anyone who would listen—about the improved life she planned to live: no more partying, no more going out with men who didn't respect her, and no more gossiping. As someone who is blessed to have been a Christian for many years, I listened patiently to her proclamation.

On one hand, I felt inspired to do a better job myself, since I certainly wasn't in the clear. I was impatient with my husband, I'd participated in a conversation earlier in the week that I should have walked away from, and I'd even shaken my fist at another driver. Some Christian example I was! On the other hand, I silently prayed that Mary would have patience with herself when she realized that she still could, and would, fall.

Each time we choose Christ, Satan knows he has lost, and he'll be relentless in his efforts to pull us off our course. But we need to continue to choose Christ anyway. I've no doubt the psalmist's words in this passage were a sincere promise to try, and I echo his words when he asked God, "When will you come to me?" It's difficult, actually impossible, to live a blameless life, and sometimes we might wonder where God is when we need him most. However, he's always there to guide us, and we make him happy when he knows we are doing our best.

I hate those who turn against you;
they will not be found near me.
4 Let those who want to do wrong stay away from me;
I will have nothing to do with evil.
5 If anyone secretly says things against his neighbor,
I will stop him.
I will not allow people
to be proud and look down on others.

6 I will look for trustworthy people
so I can live with them in the land.
Only those who live innocent lives
will be my servants.
7 No one who is dishonest will live in my house;
no liars will stay around me.
8 Every morning I will destroy the wicked in the land.
I will rid the LORD's city of people who do evil.

A Cry for Help

A prayer of a person who is suffering when he is discouraged and tells the LORD his complaints.

102 LORD, listen to my prayer;
let my cry for help come to you.
2 Do not hide from me
in my time of trouble.
Pay attention to me.
When I cry for help, answer me quickly.

3 My life is passing away like smoke,
and my bones are burned up with fire.
4 My heart is like grass
that has been cut and dried.
I forget to eat.
5 Because of my grief,
my skin hangs on my bones.
6 I am like a desert owl,
like an owl living among the ruins.
7 I lie awake.
I am like a lonely bird on a housetop.

8All day long enemies insult me;
those who make fun of me use my name as a curse.
9I eat ashes for food,
and my tears fall into my drinks.
10Because of your great anger,
you have picked me up and thrown me away.
11My days are like a passing shadow;
I am like dried grass.

12But, LORD, you rule forever,
and your fame goes on and on.
13You will come and have mercy on Jerusalem,
because the time has now come to be kind to her;
the right time has come.
14Your servants love even her stones;
they even care about her dust.
15Nations will fear the name of the LORD,
and all the kings on earth will honor you.
16The LORD will rebuild Jerusalem;
there his glory will be seen.
17He will answer the prayers of the needy;
he will not reject their prayers.

18Write these things for the future
so that people who are not yet born will praise the LORD.
19The LORD looked down from his holy place above;
from heaven he looked down at the earth.
20He heard the moans of the prisoners,
and he freed those sentenced to die.
21The name of the LORD will be heard in Jerusalem;
his praise will be heard there.
22People will come together,
and kingdoms will serve the LORD.

23God has made me tired of living;
he has cut short my life.
24So I said, "My God, do not take me in the middle of my life.
Your years go on and on.
25In the beginning you made the earth,
and your hands made the skies.
26They will be destroyed, but you will remain.
They will all wear out like clothes.
And, like clothes, you will change them
and throw them away.
27But you never change,
and your life will never end.
28Our children will live in your presence,
and their children will remain with you."

Praise to the Lord of Love

Of David.

103 All that I am, praise the LORD;
everything in me, praise his holy name.
2My whole being, praise the LORD
and do not forget all his kindnesses.
3He forgives all my sins
and heals all my diseases.
4He saves my life from the grave
and loads me with love and mercy.
5He satisfies me with good things
and makes me young again, like the eagle.

6The LORD does what is right and fair
for all who are wronged by others.
7He showed his ways to Moses
and his deeds to the people of Israel.
8The LORD shows mercy and is kind.
He does not become angry quickly, and he has great love.
9He will not always accuse us,
and he will not be angry forever.
10He has not punished us as our sins should be punished;
he has not repaid us for the evil we have done.
11As high as the sky is above the earth,
so great is his love for those who respect him.
12He has taken our sins away from us
as far as the east is from west.
13The LORD has mercy on those who respect him,
as a father has mercy on his children.
14He knows how we were made;
he remembers that we are dust.

15Human life is like grass;
we grow like a flower in the field.
16After the wind blows, the flower is gone,
and there is no sign of where it was.
17But the LORD's love for those who respect him
continues forever and ever,
and his goodness continues to their grandchildren
18and to those who keep his agreement
and who remember to obey his orders.

devotion 163

PSALM 103:1–4

REMEMBERING NOT TO FORGET

Have you ever had an experience in which you felt the goodness and faithfulness of God so intensely that you leaped into the air, hugged your children, and even cried out, "Thank you, God. Thank you for your blessings"? You may have even said something like, "God, I will never doubt you again. I have seen with my own eyes your mercy and kindness!"

And then, maybe some months later, there you were—discouraged, doubting, and without confidence. Why does this happen to us? It happens because we operate inside the weakness of our humanity. And the human heart is prone to forget. We even forget our actual experiences, not to mention the truths we've learned from Scripture. The psalmist said that we have to remember not to forget. We are supposed to keep in mind the goodness of God and glorify him with our whole beings. But how? How can we live this kind of praise?

What if a life of praise means that in every area of our lives, we live gratefully? What if we were grateful for every gift and circumstance, the trials as well as the mountaintops? What if we were thankful for people who come into our lives, the short time we have with them, and the things they teach us about having character? I believe if we commit to living gratefully with every breath, then God will be praised with our whole being. And we will remember what we have been inclined to forget.

19 The LORD has set his throne in heaven,
and his kingdom rules over everything.
20 You who are his angels, praise the LORD.
You are the mighty warriors who do what he says
and who obey his voice.
21 You, his armies, praise the LORD;
you are his servants who do what he wants.
22 Everything the LORD has made
should praise him in all the places he rules.
My whole being, praise the LORD.

Praise to God Who Made the World

104 My whole being, praise the LORD.
LORD my God, you are very great.
You are clothed with glory and majesty;
2 you wear light like a robe.
You stretch out the skies like a tent.
3 You build your room above the clouds.
You make the clouds your chariot,
and you ride on the wings of the wind.
4 You make the winds your messengers,
and flames of fire are your servants.

5 You built the earth on its foundations
so it can never be moved.
6 You covered the earth with oceans;
the water was above the mountains.
7 But at your command, the water rushed away.
When you thundered your orders, it hurried away.
8 The mountains rose; the valleys sank.
The water went to the places you made for it.
9 You set borders for the seas that they cannot cross,
so water will never cover the earth again.

10 You make springs pour into the ravines;
they flow between the mountains.
11 They water all the wild animals;
the wild donkeys come there to drink.
12 Wild birds make nests by the water;
they sing among the tree branches.

13 You water the mountains from above.
The earth is full of the things you made.
14 You make the grass for cattle
and vegetables for the people.
You make food grow from the earth.
15 You give us wine that makes happy hearts
and olive oil that makes our faces shine.
You give us bread that gives us strength.
16 The LORD's trees have plenty of water;
they are the cedars of Lebanon, which he planted.
17 The birds make their nests there;
the stork's home is in the fir trees.
18 The high mountains belong to the wild goats.
The rocks are hiding places for the badgers.

19 You made the moon to mark the seasons,
and the sun always knows when to set.
20 You make it dark, and it becomes night.
Then all the wild animals creep around.
21 The lions roar as they attack.
They look to God for food.
22 When the sun rises, they leave
and go back to their dens to lie down.
23 Then people go to work
and work until evening.

24 LORD, you have made many things;
with your wisdom you made them all.
The earth is full of your riches.
25 Look at the sea, so big and wide,
with creatures large and small that cannot be counted.
26 Ships travel over the ocean,
and there is the sea monster Leviathan,
which you made to play there.

27 All these things depend on you
to give them their food at the right time.
28 When you give it to them,
they gather it up.
When you open your hand,
they are filled with good food.
29 When you turn away from them,
they become frightened.
When you take away their breath,
they die and turn to dust.
30 When you breathe on them,
they are created,
and you make the land new again.

31 May the glory of the LORD be forever.
May the LORD enjoy what he has made.
32 He just looks at the earth, and it shakes.
He touches the mountains, and they smoke.

33 I will sing to the LORD all my life;
I will sing praises to my God as long as I live.
34 May my thoughts please him;
I am happy in the LORD.
35 Let sinners be destroyed from the earth,
and let the wicked live no longer.
My whole being, praise the LORD.
Praise the LORD.

God's Love for Israel

105 Give thanks to the LORD and pray to him.
Tell the nations what he has done.
2 Sing to him; sing praises to him.
Tell about all his miracles.
3 Be glad that you are his;
let those who seek the LORD be happy.
4 Depend on the LORD and his strength;
always go to him for help.
5 Remember the miracles he has done;
remember his wonders and his decisions.
6 You are descendants of his servant Abraham,
the children of Jacob, his chosen people.
7 He is the LORD our God.
His laws are for all the world.

8 He will keep his agreement forever;
he will keep his promises always.
9 He will keep the agreement he made with Abraham
and the promise he made to Isaac.
10 He made it a law for the people of Jacob;
he made it an agreement with Israel to last forever.
11 The LORD said, "I will give you the land of Canaan,
and it will belong to you."

12 Then God's people were few in number.
They were strangers in the land.
13 They went from one nation to another,
from one kingdom to another.
14 But the LORD did not let anyone hurt them;
he warned kings not to harm them.
15 He said, "Don't touch my chosen people,
and don't harm my prophets."

16God ordered a time of hunger in the land,
and he destroyed all the food.
17Then he sent a man ahead of them—
Joseph, who was sold as a slave.
18They put chains around his feet
and an iron ring around his neck.
19Then the time he had spoken of came,
and the LORD's words proved that
Joseph was right.
20The king of Egypt sent for Joseph and
freed him;
the ruler of the people set him free.
21He made him the master of his house;
Joseph was in charge of his riches.
22He could order the princes as he wished.
He taught the older men to be wise.
23Then his father Israel came to Egypt;
Jacob[n] lived in Egypt.[n]
24The LORD made his people grow in
number,
and he made them stronger than their
enemies.
25He caused the Egyptians to hate his
people
and to make plans against his servants.
26Then he sent his servant Moses,
and Aaron, whom he had chosen.
27They did many signs among the
Egyptians
and worked wonders in Egypt.
28The LORD sent darkness and made the
land dark,
but the Egyptians turned against what
he said.
29So he changed their water into blood
and made their fish die.
30Then their country was filled with frogs,
even in the bedrooms of their rulers.
31The LORD spoke and flies came,
and gnats were everywhere in the
country.
32He made hail fall like rain
and sent lightning through their land.
33He struck down their grapevines and fig
trees,
and he destroyed every tree in the
country.
34He spoke and grasshoppers came;
the locusts were too many to count.
35They ate all the plants in the land
and everything the earth produced.
36The LORD also killed all the firstborn sons
in the land,
the oldest son of each family.

37Then he brought his people out,
and they carried with them silver and
gold.
Not one of his people stumbled.
38The Egyptians were glad when they left,
because the Egyptians were afraid of
them.
39The LORD covered them with a cloud
and lit up the night with fire.
40When they asked, he brought them quail
and filled them with bread from heaven.
41God split the rock, and water flowed out;
it ran like a river through the desert.
42He remembered his holy promise
to his servant Abraham.

43So God brought his people out with joy,
his chosen ones with singing.
44He gave them lands of other nations,
so they received what others had
worked for.
45This was so they would keep his orders
and obey his teachings.

Praise the LORD!

Israel's Failure to Trust God

106 Praise the LORD!

Thank the LORD because he is
good.
His love continues forever.
2No one can tell all the mighty things the
LORD has done;
no one can speak all his praise.
3Happy are those who do right,
who do what is fair at all times.

4LORD, remember me when you are kind to
your people;
help me when you save them.
5Let me see the good things you do for
your chosen people.
Let me be happy along with your
happy nation;
let me join your own people in praising
you.

6We have sinned just as our ancestors did.
We have done wrong; we have done
evil.

105:23 Jacob Also called Israel. **105:23 Egypt** Literally, "the land of Ham." Also in verse 27. The people in Egypt were descendants of Ham, one of Noah's sons. See Genesis 10:6.

40 So the LORD became angry with his people
and hated his own children.
41 He handed them over to other nations
and let their enemies rule over them.
42 Their enemies were cruel to them
and kept them under their power.
43 The LORD saved his people many times,
but they continued to turn against him.
So they became even more wicked.

44 But God saw their misery
when he heard their cry.
45 He remembered his agreement with
them,
and he felt sorry for them because of
his great love.
46 He caused them to be pitied
by those who held them captive.

47 LORD our God, save us
and bring us back from other nations.
Then we will thank you
and will gladly praise you.

48 Praise the LORD, the God of Israel.
He always was and always will be.
Let all the people say, "Amen!"

Praise the LORD!

Book 5

God Saves from Many Dangers

107 Thank the LORD because he is good.
His love continues forever.
2 That is what those whom the LORD has
saved should say.
He has saved them from the enemy
3 and has gathered them from other
lands,
from east and west, north and south.

4 Some people had wandered in the desert
lands.
They found no city in which to live.
5 They were hungry and thirsty,
and they were discouraged.
6 In their misery they cried out to the LORD,
and he saved them from their troubles.
7 He led them on a straight road
to a city where they could live.
8 Let them give thanks to the LORD for his
love
and for the miracles he does for people.
9 He satisfies the thirsty
and fills up the hungry.
10 Some sat in gloom and darkness;
they were prisoners suffering in chains.
11 They had turned against the words of God
and had refused the advice of God Most
High.
12 So he broke their pride by hard work.
They stumbled, and no one helped.
13 In their misery they cried out to the LORD,
and he saved them from their
troubles.
14 He brought them out of their gloom and
darkness
and broke their chains.
15 Let them give thanks to the LORD for his
love
and for the miracles he does for people.
16 He breaks down bronze gates
and cuts apart iron bars.

17 Some fools turned against God
and suffered for the evil they did.
18 They refused to eat anything,
so they almost died.
19 In their misery they cried out to the LORD,
and he saved them from their troubles.
20 God gave the command and healed them,
so they were saved from dying.
21 Let them give thanks to the LORD for his
love
and for the miracles he does for people.
22 Let them offer sacrifices to thank him.
With joy they should tell what he has
done.

23 Others went out to sea in ships
and did business on the great oceans.
24 They saw what the LORD could do,
the miracles he did in the deep oceans.
25 He spoke, and a storm came up,
which blew up high waves.
26 The ships were tossed as high as the sky
and fell low to the depths.
The storm was so bad that they lost
their courage.
27 They stumbled and fell like people who
were drunk.
They did not know what to do.
28 In their misery they cried out to the LORD,
and he saved them from their
troubles.
29 He stilled the storm
and calmed the waves.
30 They were happy that it was quiet,
and God guided them to the port they
wanted.

7Our ancestors in Egypt
did not learn from your miracles.
They did not remember all your kindnesses,
so they turned against you at the Red Sea.
8But the LORD saved them for his own sake,
to show his great power.
9He commanded the Red Sea, and it dried up.
He led them through the deep sea as if it were a desert.
10He saved them from those who hated them.
He saved them from their enemies,
11and the water covered their foes.
Not one of them escaped.
12Then the people believed what the LORD said,
and they sang praises to him.

13But they quickly forgot what he had done;
they did not wait for his advice.
14They became greedy for food in the desert,
and they tested God there.
15So he gave them what they wanted,
but he also sent a terrible disease among them.

16The people in the camp were jealous of Moses
and of Aaron, the holy priest of the LORD.
17Then the ground opened up and swallowed Dathan
and closed over Abiram's group.
18A fire burned among their followers,
and flames burned up the wicked.

19The people made a gold calf at Mount Sinai
and worshiped a metal statue.
20They exchanged their glorious God
for a statue of a bull that eats grass.
21They forgot the God who saved them,
who had done great things in Egypt,
22who had done miracles in Egypt[n]
and amazing things by the Red Sea.
23So God said he would destroy them.
But Moses, his chosen one, stood before him
and stopped God's anger from destroying them.

24Then they refused to go into the beautiful land of Canaan;
they did not believe what God promised.
25They grumbled in their tents
and did not obey the LORD.
26So he swore to them
that they would die in the desert.
27He said their children would be killed by other nations
and that they would be scattered among other countries.

28They joined in worshiping Baal at Peor
and ate meat that had been sacrificed to lifeless statues.
29They made the LORD angry by what they did,
so many people became sick with a terrible disease.
30But Phinehas prayed to the LORD,
and the disease stopped.
31Phinehas did what was right,
and it will be remembered from now on.

32The people also made the LORD angry at Meribah,
and Moses was in trouble because of them.
33The people turned against the Spirit of God,
so Moses spoke without stopping to think.

34The people did not destroy the other nations
as the LORD had told them to do.
35Instead, they mixed with the other nations
and learned their customs.
36They worshiped other nations' idols
and were trapped by them.
37They even killed their sons and daughters
as sacrifices to demons.
38They killed innocent people,
their own sons and daughters,
as sacrifices to the idols of Canaan.
So the land was made unholy by their blood.
39The people became unholy by their sins;
they were unfaithful to God in what they did.

106:22 Egypt Literally, "the land of Ham." The people in Egypt were descendants of Ham, one of Noah's sons. See Genesis 10:6.

31Let them give thanks to the LORD for his
love
and for the miracles he does for people.
32Let them praise his greatness in the
meeting of the people;
let them praise him in the meeting of
the elders.

33He changed rivers into a desert
and springs of water into dry ground.
34He made fertile land salty,
because the people there did evil.
35He changed the desert into pools of water
and dry ground into springs of water.
36He had the hungry settle there
so they could build a city in which to
live.
37They planted seeds in the fields and
vineyards,
and they had a good harvest.
38God blessed them, and they grew in
number.
Their cattle did not become fewer.

39Because of disaster, troubles, and sadness,
their families grew smaller and weaker.
40He showed he was displeased with their
leaders
and made them wander in a pathless
desert.
41But he lifted the poor out of their
suffering
and made their families grow like
flocks of sheep.
42Good people see this and are happy,
but the wicked say nothing.

43Whoever is wise will remember these
things
and will think about the love of the
LORD.

A Prayer for Victory

A song. A psalm of David.

108 God, my heart is steady.
I will sing and praise you with
all my being.
2Wake up, harp and lyre!
I will wake up the dawn.
3LORD, I will praise you among the nations;
I will sing songs of praise about you to
all the nations.
4Your great love reaches to the skies,
your truth to the heavens.
5God, you are supreme above the skies.
Let your glory be over all the earth.

devotion 164

PSALM 107:43

THINK ABOUT HIS LOVE

Psalm 107 recounts all the times the Lord heard the cries of the children of Israel and delivered them from their oppression. He broke the chains of slavery that bound them in Egypt, delivered food and water in the desert, and defeated all of their enemies along the way to the land he had promised their ancestors. Despite his provisions, the Israelites' sin was that they forgot God's goodness. Their doubting hearts didn't trust God. It is so easy to fall into focusing on everything that is wrong in our lives and become whining, complaining children. God wants us to have hearts that trust him in all circumstances, but somehow when our world is rocked just a bit, we forget that he is there ready to help.

God wants us to be wise women. Wise women do not freak out or complain about every little thing. A wise woman has a steadfast heart that reflects on the very present and evident hand of God in her life even when she cannot determine the outcome of her circumstances. If your heart is heavy and you're struggling with issues today, first pour out praise to the Lord, and then quietly remind yourself of the miracles you have witnessed in your life and the lives of others. God calls you to be a wise woman. He has given you a family to love, he has given you the ability to read his Word, and he has given you evidence of his love toward you.

6Answer us and save us by your power
so the people you love will be rescued.
7God has said from his Temple,
"When I win, I will divide Shechem
and measure off the Valley of Succoth.
8Gilead and Manasseh are mine.
Ephraim is like my helmet.
Judah holds my royal scepter.
9Moab is like my washbowl.
I throw my sandals at Edom.
I shout at Philistia."

10Who will bring me to the strong, walled city?
Who will lead me to Edom?
11God, surely you have rejected us;
you do not go out with our armies.
12Help us fight the enemy.
Human help is useless,
13but we can win with God's help.
He will defeat our enemies.

A Prayer Against an Enemy

For the director of music. A psalm of David.

109 God, I praise you.
Do not be silent.
2Wicked people and liars have spoken against me;
they have told lies about me.
3They have said hateful things about me
and attack me for no reason.
4They attacked me, even though I loved them
and prayed for them.
5I was good to them, but they repay me with evil.
I loved them, but they hate me in return.

6They say about me, "Have an evil person work against him,
and let an accuser stand against him.
7When he is judged, let him be found guilty,
and let even his prayers show his guilt.
8Let his life be cut short,
and let another man replace him as leader.
9Let his children become orphans
and his wife a widow.
10Make his children wander around,
begging for food.
Let them be forced out of the ruins in which they live.
11Let the people to whom he owes money
take everything he owns,
and let strangers steal everything he has worked for.
12Let no one show him love
or have mercy on his orphaned children.
13Let all his descendants die
and be forgotten by those who live after him.
14LORD, remember how wicked his ancestors were,
and don't let the sins of his mother be wiped out.
15LORD, always remember their sins.
Then make people forget about them completely.

16"He did not remember to be loving.
He hurt the poor, the needy, and those who were sad
until they were nearly dead.
17He loved to put curses on others,
so let those same curses fall on him.
He did not like to bless others,
so do not let good things happen to him.
18He cursed others as often as he wore clothes.
Cursing others filled his body and his life,
like drinking water and using olive oil.
19So let curses cover him like clothes
and wrap around him like a belt."
20May the LORD do these things to those who accuse me,
to those who speak evil against me.

21But you, Lord GOD,
be kind to me so others will know you are good.
Because your love is good, save me.
22I am poor and helpless
and very sad.
23I am dying like an evening shadow;
I am shaken off like a locust.
24My knees are weak from fasting,
and I have grown thin.
25My enemies insult me;
they look at me and shake their heads.
26LORD my God, help me;
because you are loving, save me.
27Then they will know that your power has done this;
they will know that you have done it, LORD.

28They may curse me, but you bless me.
They may attack me, but they will be disgraced.
Then I, your servant, will be glad.
29Let those who accuse me be disgraced
and covered with shame like a coat.

30I will thank the LORD very much;
I will praise him in front of many people.
31He defends the helpless
and saves them from those who accuse them.

The Lord Appoints a King

A psalm of David.

110 The LORD said to my Lord,
"Sit by me at my right side
until I put your enemies under your control."
2The LORD will enlarge your kingdom
beyond Jerusalem,
and you will rule over your enemies.
3Your people will join you on your day of battle.
You have been dressed in holiness from birth;
you have the freshness of a child.

4The LORD has made a promise
and will not change his mind.
He said, "You are a priest forever,
a priest like Melchizedek."

5The Lord is beside you to help you.
When he becomes angry, he will crush kings.
6He will judge those nations, filling them with dead bodies;
he will defeat rulers all over the world.
7The king will drink from the brook on the way.
Then he will be strengthened.

Praise the Lord's Goodness

111 Praise the LORD!

I will thank the LORD with all my heart
in the meeting of his good people.
2The LORD does great things;
those who enjoy them seek them.
3What he does is glorious and splendid,
and his goodness continues forever.
4His miracles are unforgettable.
The LORD is kind and merciful.
5He gives food to those who fear him.
He remembers his agreement forever.
6He has shown his people his power
when he gave them the lands of other nations.

7Everything he does is good and fair;
all his orders can be trusted.
8They will continue forever.
They were made true and right.
9He sets his people free.
He made his agreement everlasting.
He is holy and wonderful.

10Wisdom begins with respect for the LORD;
those who obey his orders have good understanding.
He should be praised forever.

Honest People Are Blessed

112 Praise the LORD!

Happy are those who respect the LORD,
who want what he commands.
2Their descendants will be powerful in the land;
the children of honest people will be blessed.

3Their houses will be full of wealth and riches,
and their goodness will continue forever.
4A light shines in the dark for honest people,
for those who are merciful and kind and good.
5It is good to be merciful and generous.
Those who are fair in their business
6will never be defeated.
Good people will always be remembered.
7They won't be afraid of bad news;
their hearts are steady because they trust the LORD.
8They are confident and will not be afraid;
they will look down on their enemies.
9They give freely to the poor.
The things they do are right and will continue forever.
They will be given great honor.
10The wicked will see this and become angry;
they will grind their teeth in anger and then disappear.

devotion 165

PSALM 111:10

WISDOM BEGINS WITH RESPECT

I was twenty-one years old when I fell in love with my husband, who is the oldest grandson of the Reverend Billy Graham, and I never dreamed of being a part of such a wonderful family. We had been dating for several months when he invited me to attend one of his grandfather's crusades in Washington DC. I was so nervous to meet his grandfather for the first time. As we arrived at the hotel the first day, Stephan's younger siblings were standing in the lobby. "Hurry," they excitedly told us. "Go change. We are going with Daddy Bill to Vice President Bush's house for dinner." I was overwhelmed. Meeting Billy Graham was intimidating enough without having to meet Vice President George Bush at the same time.

I think of that day as such an honor. I have great respect for both men. I know that if either man asked me to do something, I would do it without a moment's hesitation. I often wonder if I truly hold the same kind of respect for the King of Kings. Do I obey him without a moment's hesitation? If I really understood who he is and watched him rule earth with my eyes, I believe my respect would be much greater. The Bible says that wisdom begins with respect. Do you respect the Lord, or are you complacent about your relationship with him? Take time today to praise the King of Kings for who he is. It will make you a little wiser.

The wishes of the wicked will come to
nothing.

Praise for the Lord's Kindness

113 Praise the LORD!
Praise him, you servants of the
LORD;
praise the name of the LORD.
2The LORD's name should be praised
now and forever.
3The LORD's name should be praised
from where the sun rises to where it sets.
4The LORD is supreme over all the nations;
his glory reaches to the skies.

5No one is like the LORD our God,
who rules from heaven,
6who bends down to look
at the skies and the earth.
7The LORD lifts the poor from the dirt
and takes the helpless from the ashes.
8He seats them with princes,
the princes of his people.
9He gives children to the woman who has
none
and makes her a happy mother.
Praise the LORD!

God Brought Israel from Egypt

114 When the Israelites went out of
Egypt,
the people of Jacob left that foreign
country.
2Then Judah became God's holy place;
Israel became the land he ruled.

3The Red Sea looked and ran away;
the Jordan River turned back.
4The mountains danced like sheep
and the hills like little lambs.
5Sea, why did you run away?
Jordan, why did you turn back?
6Mountains, why did you dance like
sheep?
Hills, why did you dance like little
lambs?

7Earth, shake with fear before the Lord,
before the God of Jacob.
8He turned a rock into a pool of water,
a hard rock into a spring of water.

The One True God

115 It does not belong to us, LORD.
The glory belongs to you
because of your love and loyalty.

2Why do the nations ask,
"Where is their God?"
3Our God is in heaven.
He does what he pleases.
4Their idols are made of silver and gold,
the work of human hands.
5They have mouths, but they cannot
speak.
They have eyes, but they cannot see.
6They have ears, but they cannot hear.
They have noses, but they cannot
smell.
7They have hands, but they cannot feel.
They have feet, but they cannot walk.
No sounds come from their throats.
8People who make idols will be like them,
and so will those who trust them.
9Family of Israel, trust the LORD;
he is your helper and your protection.
10Family of Aaron, trust the LORD;
he is your helper and your protection.
11You who respect the LORD should trust
him;
he is your helper and your protection.

12The LORD remembers us and will bless us.
He will bless the family of Israel;
he will bless the family of Aaron.
13The LORD will bless those who respect
him,
from the smallest to the greatest.

14May the LORD give you success,
and may he give you and your children
success.
15May you be blessed by the LORD,
who made heaven and earth.

16Heaven belongs to the LORD,
but he gave the earth to people.
17Dead people do not praise the LORD;
those in the grave are silent.
18But we will praise the LORD
now and forever.

Praise the LORD!

Thanksgiving for Escaping Death

116 I love the LORD,
because he listens to my prayers
for help.
2He paid attention to me,
so I will call to him for help as long as I
live.
3The ropes of death bound me,
and the fear of the grave took hold
of me.
I was troubled and sad.
4Then I called out the name of the LORD.
I said, "Please, LORD, save me!"

5The LORD is kind and does what is
right;
our God is merciful.
6The LORD watches over the foolish;
when I was helpless, he saved me.
7I said to myself, "Relax,
because the LORD takes care of you."
8LORD, you saved me from death.
You stopped my eyes from crying;
you kept me from being defeated.
9So I will walk with the LORD
in the land of the living.
10I believed, so I said,
"I am completely ruined."
11In my distress I said,
"All people are liars."

12What can I give the LORD
for all the good things he has given
to me?
13I will lift up the cup of salvation,
and I will pray to the LORD.
14I will give the LORD what I promised
in front of all his people.

15The death of one that belongs to the
LORD
is precious in his sight.
16LORD, I am your servant;
I am your servant and the son of your
female servant.
You have freed me from my chains.
17I will give you an offering to show thanks
to you,
and I will pray to the LORD.
18I will give the LORD what I promised
in front of all his people,
19in the Temple courtyards
in Jerusalem.

Praise the LORD!

devotion 166

PSALM 116:5–7

SISTERS AND MOMS

Psalm 116 reminds me of my friendships with all kinds of moms and how the Lord preserves them through their often exhausting days. I continue to be amazed as they juggle their children with careers, marriages, volunteer work, and an array of other responsibilities.

One single mom illustrated her responsibility perfectly when she said, "Sometimes I don't know if I can go on another day, and at bedtime I barely cry out to God before I fall asleep exhausted. But the next morning I know that I can go on, and I know what my assignment is. God usually wakes me up with a crying child or a small hand tugging at my pillow."

This mother knew two important things. The first was that she needed rest, and the other was that her assignment was to be a mom. If you are a mom, God knows your struggles, and you make him proud when you take care of your children no matter the circumstance.

When you fall asleep at night, don't worry. Know that you're doing the right thing, and let your thoughts drift to your Lord for rejuvenation of your body and soul. And for those of us who are not yet moms, we know that God calls us according to his purpose. For now, we can still reach out and touch the lives of children by supporting their moms. Let us pray for our sisters in Christ who are moms that they will find strength and energy each morning.

A Hymn of Praise

117 All you nations, praise the LORD.
All you people, praise him
2 because the LORD loves us very much,
and his truth is everlasting.

Praise the LORD!

Thanksgiving for Victory

118 Thank the LORD because he is good.
His love continues forever.
2 Let the people of Israel say,
"His love continues forever."
3 Let the family of Aaron say,
"His love continues forever."
4 Let those who respect the LORD say,
"His love continues forever."

5 I was in trouble, so I called to the LORD.
The LORD answered me and set me free.
6 I will not be afraid, because the LORD is with me.
People can't do anything to me.
7 The LORD is with me to help me,
so I will see my enemies defeated.
8 It is better to trust the LORD
than to trust people.
9 It is better to trust the LORD
than to trust princes.
10 All the nations surrounded me,
but I defeated them in the name of the LORD.
11 They surrounded me on every side,
but with the LORD's power I defeated them.
12 They surrounded me like a swarm of bees,
but they died as quickly as thorns burn.
By the LORD's power, I defeated them.

13 They chased me until I was almost
defeated,
but the LORD helped me.
14 The LORD gives me strength and a song.
He has saved me.

15 Shouts of joy and victory
come from the tents of those who do
right:
"The LORD has done powerful things."
16 The power of the LORD has won the
victory;
with his power the LORD has done
mighty things.

17 I will not die, but live,
and I will tell what the LORD has done.
18 The LORD has taught me a hard lesson,
but he did not let me die.

19 Open for me the Temple gates.
Then I will come in and thank the LORD.
20 This is the LORD's gate;
only those who are good may enter
through it.
21 LORD, I thank you for answering me.
You have saved me.

22 The stone that the builders rejected
became the cornerstone.
23 The LORD did this,
and it is wonderful to us.
24 This is the day that the LORD has made.
Let us rejoice and be glad today!
25 Please, LORD, save us;
please, LORD, give us success.
26 God bless the one who comes in the name
of the LORD.
We bless all of you from the Temple of
the LORD.
27 The LORD is God,
and he has shown kindness to us.
With branches in your hands, join the
feast.
Come to the corners of the altar.

28 You are my God, and I will thank you;
you are my God, and I will praise your
greatness.

29 Thank the LORD because he is good.
His love continues forever.

The Word of God

119 Happy are those who live pure
lives,
who follow the LORD's teachings.
2 Happy are those who keep his rules,
who try to obey him with their whole
heart.
3 They don't do what is wrong;
they follow his ways.
4 LORD, you gave your orders
to be obeyed completely.
5 I wish I were more loyal
in obeying your demands.
6 Then I would not be ashamed
when I study your commands.
7 When I learned that your laws are fair,
I praised you with an honest heart.
8 I will obey your demands,
so please don't ever leave me.

9 How can a young person live a pure life?
By obeying your word.
10 With all my heart I try to obey you.
Don't let me break your commands.
11 I have taken your words to heart
so I would not sin against you.
12 LORD, you should be praised.
Teach me your demands.
13 My lips will tell about
all the laws you have spoken.
14 I enjoy living by your rules
as people enjoy great riches.
15 I think about your orders
and study your ways.
16 I enjoy obeying your demands,
and I will not forget your word.

17 Do good to me, your servant, so I can
live,
so I can obey your word.
18 Open my eyes to see
the miracles in your teachings.
19 I am a stranger on earth.
Do not hide your commands from me.
20 I wear myself out with desire
for your laws all the time.
21 You scold proud people;
those who ignore your commands are
cursed.
22 Don't let me be insulted and hated
because I keep your rules.
23 Even if princes speak against me,
I, your servant, will think about your
demands.
24 Your rules give me pleasure;
they give me good advice.
25 I am about to die.
Give me life, as you have promised.

devotion 167

PSALM 119:19, 89–93

WHOSE WORDS COME TO YOUR MIND?

Would you consider your faith strong or weak? It seems like most of the strong Christian women I meet are women who have the words of God stored in their hearts. They have taken the time to memorize Scripture, and God's truths have become an integral part of their thoughts and their character.

God made us so that our faith would feed on Scripture in order for our minds and hearts to be sustained. When we don't know what the Word of God says, our faith may wane or crumble underneath difficult decisions or circumstances. With God's Word inside of us, we are able to trust him. Rest in his supreme authority. Recall his goodness and his promises.

So many times we think that we cannot memorize Scripture. You can if you try—I promise. My favorite memory routine is to write Scriptures that have been especially meaningful to me on spiral-bound note cards. Other times, in my own study, I will be stirred to memorize a passage I have read. With these little spiral-bound cards, I can flip through my verses for a quick review when I'm in the car or having time with God. Most of the time, these are the verses that come to mind when I am counseling with a friend or just speaking to someone about my life with God.

Do you want to have a strong faith? Then love the teachings of God and take the time to keep them in your heart.

26 I told you about my life, and you
answered me.
Teach me your demands.
27 Help me understand your orders.
Then I will think about your miracles.
28 I am sad and tired.
Make me strong again as you have
promised.
29 Don't let me be dishonest;
have mercy on me by helping me obey
your teachings.
30 I have chosen the way of truth;
I have obeyed your laws.
31 I hold on to your rules.
LORD, do not let me be disgraced.
32 I will quickly obey your commands,
because you have made me happy.

33 LORD, teach me your demands,
and I will keep them until the end.
34 Help me understand, so I can keep your
teachings,
obeying them with all my heart.
35 Lead me in the path of your commands,
because that makes me happy.
36 Make me want to keep your rules
instead of wishing for riches.
37 Keep me from looking at worthless
things.
Let me live by your word.
38 Keep your promise to me, your servant,
so you will be respected.
39 Take away the shame I fear,
because your laws are good.
40 How I want to follow your orders.
Give me life because of your goodness.

41 LORD, show me your love,
and save me as you have promised.
42 I have an answer for people who
insult me,
because I trust what you say.
43 Never keep me from speaking your truth,
because I depend on your fair laws.
44 I will obey your teachings
forever and ever.

45So I will live in freedom,
because I want to follow your orders.
46I will discuss your rules with kings
and will not be ashamed.
47I enjoy obeying your commands,
which I love.
48I praise your commands, which I love,
and I think about your demands.

49Remember your promise to me, your servant;
it gives me hope.
50When I suffer, this comforts me:
Your promise gives me life.
51Proud people always make fun of me,
but I do not reject your teachings.
52I remember your laws from long ago,
and they comfort me, LORD.
53I become angry with wicked people
who do not keep your teachings.
54I sing about your demands
wherever I live.
55LORD, I remember you at night,
and I will obey your teachings.
56This is what I do:
I follow your orders.

57LORD, you are my share in life;
I have promised to obey your words.
58I prayed to you with all my heart.
Have mercy on me as you have promised.
59I thought about my life,
and I decided to follow your rules.
60I hurried and did not wait
to obey your commands.
61Wicked people have tied me up,
but I have not forgotten your teachings.
62In the middle of the night, I get up to thank you
because your laws are right.
63I am a friend to everyone who fears you,
to anyone who obeys your orders.
64LORD, your love fills the earth.
Teach me your demands.

65You have done good things for your servant,
as you have promised, LORD.
66Teach me wisdom and knowledge
because I trust your commands.
67Before I suffered, I did wrong,
but now I obey your word.
68You are good, and you do what is good.
Teach me your demands.
69Proud people have made up lies about me,
but I will follow your orders with all my heart.
70Those people have no feelings,
but I love your teachings.
71It was good for me to suffer
so I would learn your demands.
72Your teachings are worth more to me
than thousands of pieces of gold and silver.

73You made me and formed me with your hands.
Give me understanding so I can learn your commands.
74Let those who respect you rejoice when they see me,
because I put my hope in your word.
75LORD, I know that your laws are right
and that it was right for you to punish me.
76Comfort me with your love,
as you promised me, your servant.
77Have mercy on me so that I may live.
I love your teachings.
78Make proud people ashamed because they lied about me.
But I will think about your orders.
79Let those who respect you return to me,
those who know your rules.
80Let me obey your demands perfectly
so I will not be ashamed.

81I am weak from waiting for you to save me,
but I hope in your word.
82My eyes are tired from looking for your promise.
When will you comfort me?
83Even though I am like a wine bag going up in smoke,
I do not forget your demands.
84How long will I live?
When will you judge those who are hurting me?
85Proud people have dug pits to trap me.
They have nothing to do with your teachings.
86All of your commands can be trusted.
Liars are hurting me. Help me!
87They have almost put me in the grave,
but I have not rejected your orders.
88Give me life by your love
so I can obey your rules.

89LORD, your word is everlasting;
it continues forever in heaven.

90Your loyalty will go on and on;
you made the earth, and it still stands.
91All things continue to this day because of
your laws,
because all things serve you.
92If I had not loved your teachings,
I would have died from my sufferings.
93I will never forget your orders,
because you have given me life by them.
94I am yours. Save me.
I want to obey your orders.
95Wicked people are waiting to destroy me,
but I will think about your rules.
96Everything I see has its limits,
but your commands have none.

97How I love your teachings!
I think about them all day long.
98Your commands make me wiser than my
enemies,
because they are mine forever.
99I am wiser than all my teachers,
because I think about your rules.
100I have more understanding than the
elders,
because I follow your orders.
101I have avoided every evil way
so I could obey your word.
102I haven't walked away from your laws,
because you yourself are my teacher.
103Your promises are sweet to me,
sweeter than honey in my mouth!
104Your orders give me understanding,
so I hate lying ways.

105Your word is like a lamp for my feet
and a light for my path.
106I will do what I have promised
and obey your fair laws.
107I have suffered for a long time.
LORD, give me life by your word.
108LORD, accept my willing praise
and teach me your laws.
109My life is always in danger,
but I haven't forgotten your teachings.
110Wicked people have set a trap for me,
but I haven't strayed from your orders.
111I will follow your rules forever,
because they make me happy.
112I will try to do what you demand
forever, until the end.
113I hate disloyal people,
but I love your teachings.
114You are my hiding place and my shield;
I hope in your word.
115Get away from me, you who do evil,
so I can keep my God's commands.
116Support me as you promised so I can live.
Don't let me be embarrassed because of
my hopes.
117Help me, and I will be saved.
I will always respect your demands.
118You reject those who ignore your demands,
because their lies mislead them.
119You throw away the wicked of the world
like trash.
So I will love your rules.
120I shake in fear of you;
I respect your laws.

121I have done what is fair and right.
Don't leave me to those who wrong me.
122Promise that you will help me, your
servant.
Don't let proud people wrong me.
123My eyes are tired from looking for your
salvation
and for your good promise.
124Show your love to me, your servant,
and teach me your demands.
125I am your servant. Give me wisdom
so I can understand your rules.
126LORD, it is time for you to do something,
because people have disobeyed your
teachings.
127I love your commands
more than the purest gold.
128I respect all your orders,
so I hate lying ways.

129Your rules are wonderful.
That is why I keep them.
130Learning your words gives wisdom
and understanding for the foolish.
131I am nearly out of breath.
I really want to learn your commands.
132Look at me and have mercy on me
as you do for those who love you.
133Guide my steps as you promised;
don't let any sin control me.
134Save me from harmful people
so I can obey your orders.
135Show your kindness to me, your servant.
Teach me your demands.
136Tears stream from my eyes,
because people do not obey your
teachings.

137LORD, you do what is right,
and your laws are fair.

138The rules you commanded are right
and completely trustworthy.
139I am so upset I am worn out,
because my enemies have forgotten
your words.
140Your promises are proven,
so I, your servant, love them.
141I am unimportant and hated,
but I have not forgotten your orders.
142Your goodness continues forever,
and your teachings are true.
143I have had troubles and misery,
but I love your commands.
144Your rules are always good.
Help me understand so I can live.

145LORD, I call to you with all my heart.
Answer me, and I will keep your
demands.
146I call to you.
Save me so I can obey your rules.
147I wake up early in the morning and cry
out.
I hope in your word.
148I stay awake all night
so I can think about your promises.
149Listen to me because of your love;
LORD, give me life by your laws.
150Those who love evil are near,
but they are far from your teachings.
151But, LORD, you are also near,
and all your commands are true.
152Long ago I learned from your rules
that you made them to continue
forever.

153See my suffering and rescue me,
because I have not forgotten your
teachings.
154Argue my case and save me.
Let me live by your promises.
155Wicked people are far from being saved,
because they do not want your
demands.
156LORD, you are very kind;
give me life by your laws.
157Many enemies are after me,
but I have not rejected your rules.
158I see those traitors, and I hate them,
because they do not obey what you say.
159See how I love your orders.
LORD, give me life by your love.
160Your words are true from the start,
and all your laws will be fair forever.

devotion 168

PSALM 123:1–2

JUST STAND

Depending on the Lord is an act of worship. It is a sweet trust that can only be understood like a child who never doubts the intent of his parent's heart. Depending on God means that no matter what has transpired in our world, we know God is in control of the circumstances. We need to be reminded all the time of God's faithfulness and that we can literally depend on him. Seeing his hand move in our own lives and the lives of other people is much more than just talk. Our God is a God of action! This is the hope that each of us shares when we start to cave in under the heaviness this world can dish out.

When you have sought the Lord with all your heart, and you do not hear a prompting from the Holy Spirit to move one way or another, you need to dig in your heels and your heart and just stand. When you are tempted to take matters into your own hands—stop! I know it's hard, and it requires our spirits to be disciplined and self-controlled. If you are one of those sisters that can make things happen just because you are capable, don't! Look up to heaven and hold captive every thought that assaults your mind. Allow the mercy of the Lord to direct you. In Ephesians 6:13, the Word instructs us to stand. When you have done everything you know to do, stand! What a beautiful act of worship!

161 Leaders attack me for no reason,
but I fear your law in my heart.
162 I am as happy over your promises
as if I had found a great treasure.
163 I hate and despise lies,
but I love your teachings.
164 Seven times a day I praise you
for your fair laws.
165 Those who love your teachings will find
true peace,
and nothing will defeat them.
166 I am waiting for you to save me, LORD.
I will obey your commands.
167 I obey your rules,
and I love them very much.
168 I obey your orders and rules,
because you know everything I do.

169 Hear my cry to you, LORD.
Let your word help me understand.
170 Listen to my prayer;
save me as you promised.
171 Let me speak your praise,
because you have taught me your
demands.
172 Let me sing about your promises,
because all your commands are fair.
173 Give me your helping hand,
because I have chosen your commands.
174 I want you to save me, LORD.
I love your teachings.
175 Let me live so I can praise you,
and let your laws help me.
176 I have wandered like a lost sheep.
Look for your servant, because I have
not forgotten your commands.

A Prayer of Someone Far from Home

A psalm for going up to worship.

120 When I was in trouble, I called to
the LORD,
and he answered me.
2 LORD, save me from liars
and from those who plan evil.

3 You who plan evil, what will God do to
you?
How will he punish you?
4 He will punish you with the sharp arrows
of a warrior
and with burning coals of wood.

5 How terrible it is for me to live in the land
of Meshech,
to live among the people of Kedar.
6 I have lived too long
with people who hate peace.
7 When I talk peace,
they want war.

The Lord Guards His People

A song for going up to worship.

121 I look up to the hills,
but where does my help come
from?
2 My help comes from the LORD,
who made heaven and earth.

3 He will not let you be defeated.
He who guards you never sleeps.
4 He who guards Israel
never rests or sleeps.
5 The LORD guards you.
The LORD is the shade that protects you
from the sun.
6 The sun cannot hurt you during the day,
and the moon cannot hurt you at night.
7 The LORD will protect you from all
dangers;
he will guard your life.
8 The LORD will guard you as you come
and go,
both now and forever.

Happy People in Jerusalem

A song for going up to worship. Of David.

122 I was happy when they said to me,
"Let's go to the Temple of the
LORD."
2 Jerusalem, we are standing
at your gates.

3 Jerusalem is built as a city
with the buildings close together.
4 The tribes go up there,
the tribes who belong to the LORD.
It is the rule in Israel
to praise the LORD at Jerusalem.
5 There the descendants of David
set their thrones to judge the people.

6 Pray for peace in Jerusalem:
"May those who love her be safe.
7 May there be peace within her walls
and safety within her strong towers."
8 To help my relatives and friends,
I say, "Let Jerusalem have peace."
9 For the sake of the Temple of the LORD our
God,
I wish good for her.

A Prayer for Mercy

A song for going up to worship.

123 LORD, I look upward to you,
you who live in heaven.
2 Slaves depend on their masters,
and a female servant depends on her mistress.
In the same way, we depend on the LORD our God;
we wait for him to show us mercy.

3 Have mercy on us, LORD. Have mercy on us,
because we have been insulted.
4 We have suffered many insults from lazy people
and much cruelty from the proud.

The Lord Saves His People

A song for going up to worship. Of David.

124 What if the LORD had not been on our side?
(Let Israel repeat this.)
2 What if the LORD had not been on our side
when we were attacked?
3 When they were angry with us,
they would have swallowed us alive.
4 They would have been like a flood drowning us;
they would have poured over us like a river.
5 They would have swept us away like a mighty stream.

6 Praise the LORD,
who did not let them chew us up.
7 We escaped like a bird
from the hunter's trap.
The trap broke,
and we escaped.
8 Our help comes from the LORD,
who made heaven and earth.

God Protects Those Who Trust Him

A song for going up to worship.

125 Those who trust the LORD are like Mount Zion,
which sits unmoved forever.
2 As the mountains surround Jerusalem,
the LORD surrounds his people
now and forever.

devotion 169

PSALM 125:1-2

STAND LIKE A MOUNTAIN

I love the mountains. They have such an awe-inspiring, majestic presence about them. We traveled through Switzerland one summer with our children and hiked up and down mountains. Sometimes we barely made it up the mountain because the climb was so steep, and other times we would race to the top. But the view from any mountaintop was always breathtaking. When you stand at the top of a mountain, you also realize why towns used to be built in valleys surrounded by mountains. As the saying goes, "On a clear day you can see forever," and that is a military advantage for protecting those below.

God is like a mountain surrounding his people. He is strong and unmovable. He is our protector. The Bible also compares a believer who trusts in the Lord to a mountain. Trusting God makes us sturdy and unshakeable. James 1:6-8 describes what doubting God (the opposite of trusting) looks like: "Anyone who doubts is like a wave in the sea, blown up and down by the wind. Such doubters . . . cannot decide about anything they do." Because people who doubt are always moving, they're weak and unstable. Unfortunately, doubting comes much more easily to us than trust does; it's part of being human. But we need to battle with our doubts and learn to trust God. He is surrounding us with his protection and love now and forever. When we're faced with the choice, let's choose to be a mountain of trust instead of a wave of doubt.

3The wicked will not rule
over those who do right.
If they did, the people who do right
might use their power to do evil.
4LORD, be good to those who are good,
whose hearts are honest.
5But, LORD, when you remove those who do evil,
also remove those who stop following you.

Let there be peace in Israel.

Lord, Bring Your People Back

A song for going up to worship.

126 When the LORD brought the prisoners back to Jerusalem,
it seemed as if we were dreaming.
2Then we were filled with laughter,
and we sang happy songs.
Then the other nations said,
"The LORD has done great things for them."
3The LORD has done great things for us,
and we are very glad.

4LORD, return our prisoners again,
as you bring streams to the desert.
5Those who cry as they plant crops
will sing at harvest time.
6Those who cry
as they carry out the seeds
will return singing
and carrying bundles of grain.

All Good Things Come from God

A song for going up to worship. Of Solomon.

127 If the LORD doesn't build the house,
the builders are working for nothing.
If the LORD doesn't guard the city,
the guards are watching for nothing.
2It is no use for you to get up early
and stay up late,
working for a living.
The LORD gives sleep to those he loves.
3Children are a gift from the LORD;
babies are a reward.
4Children who are born to a young man
are like arrows in the hand of a warrior.
5Happy is the man
who has his bag full of arrows.
They will not be defeated
when they fight their enemies at the city gate.

The Happy Home

A song for going up to worship.

128 Happy are those who respect the LORD and obey him.
2You will enjoy what you work for,
and you will be blessed with good things.
3Your wife will give you many children,
like a vine that produces much fruit.
Your children will bring you much good,
like olive branches that produce many olives.
4This is how the man who respects the LORD
will be blessed.
5May the LORD bless you from Mount Zion;
may you enjoy the good things of Jerusalem all your life.
6May you see your grandchildren.

Let there be peace in Israel.

A Prayer Against the Enemies

A song for going up to worship.

129 They have treated me badly all my life.
(Let Israel repeat this.)
2They have treated me badly all my life,
but they have not defeated me.
3Like farmers plowing, they plowed over my back,
making long wounds.
4But the LORD does what is right;
he has set me free from those wicked people.

5Let those who hate Jerusalem
be turned back in shame.
6Let them be like the grass on the roof
that dries up before it has grown.
7There is not enough of it to fill a hand
or to make into a bundle to fill one's arms.
8Let those who pass by them not say,
"May the LORD bless you.
We bless you by the power of the LORD."

A Prayer for Mercy

A song for going up to worship.

130 LORD, I am in great trouble,
so I call out to you.
2 Lord, hear my voice;
listen to my prayer for help.
3 LORD, if you punished people for all their sins,
no one would be left, Lord.
4 But you forgive us,
so you are respected.

5 I wait for the LORD to help me,
and I trust his word.
6 I wait for the Lord to help me
more than night watchmen wait for the dawn,
more than night watchmen wait for the dawn.

7 People of Israel, put your hope in the LORD
because he is loving
and able to save.
8 He will save Israel
from all their sins.

Childlike Trust in the Lord

A song for going up to worship. Of David.

131 LORD, my heart is not proud;
I don't look down on others.
I don't do great things,
and I can't do miracles.
2 But I am calm and quiet,
like a baby with its mother.
I am at peace, like a baby with its mother.

3 People of Israel, put your hope in the LORD
now and forever.

In Praise of the Temple

A song for going up to worship.

132 LORD, remember David
and all his suffering.
2 He made an oath to the LORD,
a promise to the Mighty God of Jacob.
3 He said, "I will not go home to my house,
or lie down on my bed,
4 or close my eyes,
or let myself sleep
5 until I find a place for the LORD.

devotion 170

PSALM 131:1

THE MYTH OF DOING EVERYTHING RIGHT

Proud people often spend so much time being concerned about doing everything right that they can't relax and enjoy what it is they're actually doing. While we all might know a good example of a person in our life who struggles with pride, it might also do us some good to look inwardly at ourselves. Sometimes we can be blind to our own prideful feelings and not even notice when we have unreachable expectations for our husbands, children, or friends. We set our loved ones up to fail and ourselves up for disappointment when a person or situation doesn't live up to the unrealistic standards we've set.

The psalmist who wrote Psalm 131 admitted that he couldn't do great things or miracles. His words remind us that there isn't a reason to be proud or look down on others. It's true God has given us many talents, and to some he has even given skills that are considerably exceptional in comparison to the rest of us. However, anything we do can never be as great as when God gives us a rainbow, makes the wind blow, or causes raindrops to fall from the sky. And we certainly can't turn water into wine, part the waters of the sea, or count the number of stars in the heavens. So when we begin putting too much pressure on ourselves and others to conform to a certain standard, we might consider giving them (and ourselves) a break and giving God the glory.

I want to provide a home for the
Mighty God of Jacob."

6We heard about the Ark in Bethlehem.
We found it at Kiriath Jearim.
7Let's go to the LORD's house.
Let's worship at his footstool.
8Rise, LORD, and come to your resting place;
come with the Ark that shows your strength.
9May your priests do what is right.
May your people sing for joy.

10For the sake of your servant David,
do not reject your appointed king.
11The LORD made a promise to David,
a sure promise that he will not take back.
He promised, "I will make one of your descendants
rule as king after you.
12If your sons keep my agreement
and the rules that I teach them,
then their sons after them will rule
on your throne forever and ever."

13The LORD has chosen Jerusalem;
he wants it for his home.
14He says, "This is my resting place forever.
Here is where I want to stay.
15I will bless her with plenty;
I will fill her poor with food.
16I will cover her priests with salvation,
and those who worship me will really sing for joy.

17"I will make a king come from the family of David.
I will provide my appointed one
descendants to rule after him.
18I will cover his enemies with shame,
but his crown will shine."

The Love of God's People

A song for going up to worship. Of David.

133 It is good and pleasant
when God's people live together in peace!
2It is like perfumed oil poured on the priest's head
and running down his beard.
It ran down Aaron's beard
and on to the collar of his robes.
3It is like the dew of Mount Hermon
falling on the hills of Jerusalem.
There the LORD gives his blessing
of life forever.

Temple Guards, Praise the Lord

A song for going up to worship.

134 Praise the LORD, all you servants of the LORD,
you who serve at night in the Temple of the LORD.
2Raise your hands in the Temple
and praise the LORD.

3May the LORD bless you from Mount Zion,
he who made heaven and earth.

The Lord Saves, Idols Do Not

135 Praise the LORD!

Praise the name of the LORD;
praise him, you servants of the LORD,
2you who stand in the LORD's Temple
and in the Temple courtyards.
3Praise the LORD, because he is good;
sing praises to him, because it is pleasant.

4The LORD has chosen the people of Jacob for himself;
he has chosen the people of Israel for his very own.
5I know that the LORD is great.
Our Lord is greater than all the gods.
6The LORD does what he pleases,
in heaven and on earth,
in the seas and the deep oceans.
7He brings the clouds from the ends of the earth.
He sends the lightning with the rain.
He brings out the wind from his storehouses.

8He destroyed the firstborn sons in Egypt
the firstborn of both people and animals.
9He did many signs and miracles in Egypt
against the king and his servants.
10He defeated many nations
and killed powerful kings:
11Sihon king of the Amorites,
Og king of Bashan,
and all the kings of Canaan.
12Then he gave their land as a gift,
a gift to his people, the Israelites.

13LORD, your name is everlasting;
LORD, you will be remembered forever.

14The LORD defends his people
and has mercy on his servants.

15The idols of other nations are made of
silver and gold,
the work of human hands.
16They have mouths, but they cannot speak.
They have eyes, but they cannot see.
17They have ears, but they cannot hear.
They have no breath in their mouths.
18People who make idols will be like them,
and so will those who trust them.

19Family of Israel, praise the LORD.
Family of Aaron, praise the LORD.
20Family of Levi, praise the LORD.
You who respect the LORD should praise
him.
21You people of Jerusalem, praise the LORD
on Mount Zion.
Praise the LORD!

God's Love Continues Forever

136 Give thanks to the LORD because he
is good.
His love continues forever.
2Give thanks to the God of gods.
His love continues forever.
3Give thanks to the Lord of lords.
His love continues forever.

4Only he can do great miracles.
His love continues forever.
5With his wisdom he made the skies.
His love continues forever.
6He spread out the earth on the seas.
His love continues forever.
7He made the sun and the moon.
His love continues forever.
8He made the sun to rule the day.
His love continues forever.
9He made the moon and stars to rule the
night.
His love continues forever.

10He killed the firstborn sons of the
Egyptians.
His love continues forever.
11He brought the people of Israel out of
Egypt.
His love continues forever.
12He did it with his great power and
strength.

devotion 171

PSALM 136:26

WHO WANTS JUST A TASTE?

We cultivate many different relationships in life. Many times, we make lasting commitments to marriage or lifelong friendships. Then things happen, or nothing happens, and what once mattered more than anything fades and eventually goes away. Many of us could tell a hundred versions of this story. There is rarely a woman who has not tasted a broken relationship.

Because we have experienced the ebb and flow of human love, we might believe that God is also capable of breaking our heart. We may worry his love will fade or leave us high and dry. Some of us even think we have already used up all the love rations God allotted for us. We may think, *He must surely be out of love by now.*

But that is not God's love. God's love for you is a divine love that never fails. His love is the kind that runs toward you, even when you believe you are unlovely. His love will come to find you when you are hiding. His love will never let you go. It is without end. His love will never, ever fail—it's just impossible!

Maybe you have tasted the love of God and thought that a taste was all you deserved. But one of the reasons we praise God, the reason we get down on our knees and worship him, is because God's love is more than a taste. His love will continue forever in heaven, where the Lord waits to give you a feast.

His love continues forever.
[13]He parted the water of the Red Sea.
His love continues forever.
[14]He brought the Israelites through the middle of it.
His love continues forever.
[15]But the king of Egypt and his army drowned in the Red Sea.
His love continues forever.

[16]He led his people through the desert.
His love continues forever.
[17]He defeated great kings.
His love continues forever.
[18]He killed powerful kings.
His love continues forever.
[19]He defeated Sihon king of the Amorites.
His love continues forever.
[20]He defeated Og king of Bashan.
His love continues forever.
[21]He gave their land as a gift.
His love continues forever.
[22]It was a gift to his servants, the Israelites.
His love continues forever.

[23]He remembered us when we were in trouble.
His love continues forever.
[24]He freed us from our enemies.
His love continues forever.
[25]He gives food to every living creature.
His love continues forever.

[26]Give thanks to the God of heaven.
His love continues forever.

Israelites in Captivity

137 By the rivers in Babylon we sat and cried
when we remembered Jerusalem.
[2]On the poplar trees nearby
we hung our harps.
[3]Those who captured us asked us to sing;
our enemies wanted happy songs.
They said, "Sing us a song about Jerusalem!"

[4]But we cannot sing songs about the LORD
while we are in this foreign country!
[5]Jerusalem, if I forget you,
let my right hand lose its skill.
[6]Let my tongue stick to the roof of my mouth
if I do not remember you,
if I do not think about Jerusalem
as my greatest joy.

[7]LORD, remember what the Edomites did
on the day Jerusalem fell.
They said, "Tear it down!
Tear it down to its foundations!"
[8]People of Babylon, you will be destroyed.
The people who pay you back for what you did to us will be happy.
[9]They will grab your babies
and throw them against the rocks.

A Hymn of Thanksgiving

A psalm of David.

138 LORD, I will thank you with all my heart;
I will sing to you before the gods.
[2]I will bow down facing your holy Temple,
and I will thank you for your love and loyalty.
You have made your name and your word
greater than anything.
[3]On the day I called to you, you answered me.
You made me strong and brave.

[4]LORD, let all the kings of the earth praise you
when they hear the words you speak.
[5]They will sing about what the LORD has done,
because the LORD's glory is great.
[6]Though the LORD is supreme,
he takes care of those who are humble,
but he stays away from the proud.
[7]LORD, even when I have trouble all around me,
you will keep me alive.
When my enemies are angry,
you will reach down and save me by your power.
[8]LORD, you do everything for me.
LORD, your love continues forever.
Do not leave us, whom you made.

God Knows Everything

For the director of music. A psalm of David.

139 LORD, you have examined me
and know all about me.
[2]You know when I sit down and when I get up.

You know my thoughts before I think
them.
3 You know where I go and where I lie
down.
You know everything I do.
4 LORD, even before I say a word,
you already know it.
5 You are all around me—in front and in
back—
and have put your hand on me.
6 Your knowledge is amazing to me;
it is more than I can understand.

7 Where can I go to get away from your
Spirit?
Where can I run from you?
8 If I go up to the heavens, you are there.
If I lie down in the grave, you are there.
9 If I rise with the sun in the east
and settle in the west beyond the sea,
10 even there you would guide me.
With your right hand you would
hold me.

11 I could say, "The darkness will hide me.
Let the light around me turn into
night."
12 But even the darkness is not dark to you.
The night is as light as the day;
darkness and light are the same to you.

13 You made my whole being;
you formed me in my mother's body.
14 I praise you because you made me in an
amazing and wonderful way.
What you have done is wonderful.
I know this very well.
15 You saw my bones being formed
as I took shape in my mother's body.
When I was put together there,
16 you saw my body as it was formed.
All the days planned for me
were written in your book
before I was one day old.

17 God, your thoughts are precious to me.
They are so many!
18 If I could count them,
they would be more than all the grains
of sand.
When I wake up,
I am still with you.

19 God, I wish you would kill the wicked!
Get away from me, you murderers!

devotion 172

PSALM 139:1-10

TRUST HIM WITH ALL OF YOU

All of us are going to deal with trust issues at some point in our lives. It is the law of human nature to feel like we need to be guarded and suspect when it comes to exposing ourselves to others. I know I have long struggled with who I allow to know me, and I mean all of me. Sometimes letting people in can be a beautiful experience that creates lifelong friendships and solid confidants. Then there are those who ravage us after we let them in. They are wolves in sheep's clothing with selfish and harmful intentions. Those are the people that make me want to be a hermit and live in a spiritual space that is so tight even the Holy Spirit gets squeezed out.

The desire to live as a recluse usually comes out of fear of having to open ourselves up to trust people yet again. David knew that he could always be sure of the love that God had for him. Even when he could not trust servants, lovers, or even his own son, he could count on the Lord. The truth is that nothing in your life or your spirit happens without God's knowledge. He is your protector and your provision. Human relationships are meant to be blessings (even though some can be curses), but your relationship with the Lord is constant, and his love toward you is never-ending. He is holding your hand, so go ahead and trust him with all of you.

20They say evil things about you.
Your enemies use your name
thoughtlessly.
21LORD, I hate those who hate you;
I hate those who rise up against you.
22I feel only hate for them;
they are my enemies.

23God, examine me and know my heart;
test me and know my anxious
thoughts.
24See if there is any bad thing in me.
Lead me on the road to everlasting life.

A Prayer for Protection

For the director of music. A psalm of David.

140 LORD, rescue me from evil people;
protect me from cruel people
2who make evil plans,
who always start fights.
3They make their tongues sharp as a
snake's;
their words are like snake poison. *Selah*

4LORD, guard me from the power of wicked
people;
protect me from cruel people
who plan to trip me up.
5The proud hid a trap for me.
They spread out a net beside the road;
they set traps for me. *Selah*

6I said to the LORD, "You are my God."
LORD, listen to my prayer for help.
7LORD God, my mighty savior,
you protect me in battle.
8LORD, do not give the wicked what they
want.
Don't let their plans succeed,
or they will become proud. *Selah*

9Those around me have planned trouble.
Now let it come to them.
10Let burning coals fall on them.
Throw them into the fire
or into pits from which they cannot
escape.
11Don't let liars settle in the land.
Let evil quickly hunt down cruel
people.
12I know the LORD will get justice for the
poor
and will defend the needy in court.
13Good people will praise his name;
honest people will live in his presence.

A Prayer Not to Sin

A psalm of David.

141 LORD, I call to you. Come quickly.
Listen to me when I call to you.
2Let my prayer be like incense placed
before you,
and my praise like the evening
sacrifice.

3LORD, help me control my tongue;
help me be careful about what I say.
4Take away my desire to do evil
or to join others in doing wrong.
Don't let me eat tasty food
with those who do evil.

5If a good person punished me, that would
be kind.
If he corrected me, that would be like
perfumed oil on my head.
I shouldn't refuse it.
But I pray against those who do evil.
6 Let their leaders be thrown down the
cliffs.
Then people will know that I have
spoken correctly:
7"The ground is plowed and broken up.
In the same way, our bones have been
scattered at the grave."

8GOD, I look to you for help.
I trust in you, LORD. Don't let me
die.
9Protect me from the traps they set
for me
and from the net that evil people have
spread.
10Let the wicked fall into their own nets,
but let me pass by safely.

A Prayer for Safety

A maskil of David when he was in the cave. A prayer.

142 I cry out to the LORD;
I pray to the LORD for mercy.
2I pour out my problems to him;
I tell him my troubles.
3When I am afraid,
you, LORD, know the way out.
In the path where I walk,
a trap is hidden for me.
4Look around me and see.
No one cares about me.
I have no place of safety;
no one cares if I live.

5 LORD, I cry out to you.
I say, "You are my protection.
You are all I want in this life."
6 Listen to my cry,
because I am helpless.
Save me from those who are chasing me,
because they are too strong for me.
7 Free me from my prison,
and then I will praise your name.
Then good people will surround me,
because you have taken care of me.

A Prayer Not to Be Killed

A psalm of David.

143 LORD, hear my prayer;
listen to my cry for mercy.
Answer me
because you are loyal and good.
2 Don't judge me, your servant,
because no one alive is right before you.
3 My enemies are chasing me;
they crushed me to the ground.
They made me live in darkness
like those long dead.
4 I am afraid;
my courage is gone.

5 I remember what happened long ago;
I consider everything you have done.
I think about all you have made.
6 I lift my hands to you in prayer.
As a dry land needs rain, I thirst for you. *Selah*

7 LORD, answer me quickly,
because I am getting weak.
Don't turn away from me,
or I will be like those who are dead.
8 Tell me in the morning about your love,
because I trust you.
Show me what I should do,
because my prayers go up to you.
9 LORD, save me from my enemies;
I hide in you.
10 Teach me to do what you want,
because you are my God.
Let your good Spirit
lead me on level ground.

11 LORD, let me live
so people will praise you.
In your goodness
save me from my troubles.
12 In your love defeat my enemies.
Destroy all those who trouble me,
because I am your servant.

A Prayer for Victory

Of David.

144 Praise the LORD, my Rock,
who trains me for war,
who trains me for battle.
2 He protects me like a strong, walled city,
and he loves me.
He is my defender and my Savior,
my shield and my protection.
He helps me keep my people under control.
3 LORD, why are people important to you?
Why do you even think about human beings?
4 People are like a breath;
their lives are like passing shadows.

5 LORD, tear open the sky and come down.
Touch the mountains so they will smoke.
6 Send the lightning and scatter my enemies.
Shoot your arrows and force them away.
7 Reach down from above.
Save me and rescue me out of this sea of enemies,
from these foreigners.
8 They are liars;
they are dishonest.

9 God, I will sing a new song to you;
I will play to you on the ten-stringed harp.
10 You give victory to kings.
You save your servant David from cruel swords.
11 Save me, rescue me from these foreigners.
They are liars; they are dishonest.

12 Let our sons in their youth
grow like plants.
Let our daughters be
like the decorated stones in the Temple.
13 Let our barns be filled
with crops of all kinds.
Let our sheep in the fields have
thousands and tens of thousands of lambs.
14 Let our cattle be strong.
Let no one break in.

devotion 173

PSALM 144:3–4

ETERNAL PERSPECTIVE

Our lives on earth are like a breath compared to eternity. Think about taking one breath. You probably take thousands of them each day. Sometimes we forget about the brevity of life. We spend our lives accumulating stuff and seeking fame and fortune rather than seeking things that have eternal value. When Jesus walked on the earth, he continually spoke about the kingdom of God. He wanted us to understand that everything on this earth is temporary. He wanted us to learn to have an eternal perspective.

So how do we have an eternal perspective? Read Matthew 6:19-21. Jesus tells us that our hearts will be where our treasure is. Am I storing up treasure in heaven or on earth? When I evaluate my life, I often look to see where it is that I spend most of my time. This is a true test of what it is that I treasure. It is also an eye-opener to where my heart really is.

One of my children once asked me how we are to store treasure in heaven. I believe one of the ways to do it is right in Psalm 144. People are important to God. By investing in people, we are storing up treasure in heaven. Jesus said in Matthew 25:40, "I tell you the truth, anything you did for even the least of my people here, you also did for me." So spend some time today investing in people. You will be collecting treasure that will last forever.

Let there be no war,
no screams in our streets.

15 Happy are those who are like this;
happy are the people whose God is the LORD.

Praise to God the King

A psalm of praise. Of David.

145 I praise your greatness, my God the King;
I will praise you forever and ever.
2 I will praise you every day;
I will praise you forever and ever.
3 The LORD is great and worthy of our praise;
no one can understand how great he is.
4 Parents will tell their children what you have done.
They will retell your mighty acts,
5 wonderful majesty, and glory.
And I will think about your miracles.
6 They will tell about the amazing things you do,
and I will tell how great you are.
7 They will remember your great goodness
and will sing about your fairness.

8 The LORD is kind and shows mercy.
He does not become angry quickly but is full of love.
9 The LORD is good to everyone;
he is merciful to all he has made.
10 LORD, everything you have made will praise you;
those who belong to you will bless you.
11 They will tell about the glory of your kingdom
and will speak about your power.
12 Then everyone will know the mighty things you do
and the glory and majesty of your kingdom.
13 Your kingdom will go on and on,
and you will rule forever.

The LORD will keep all his promises;
he is loyal to all he has made.

14The LORD helps those who have been
defeated
and takes care of those who are in
trouble.
15All living things look to you for food,
and you give it to them at the right
time.
16You open your hand,
and you satisfy all living things.

17Everything the LORD does is right.
He is loyal to all he has made.
18The LORD is close to everyone who prays
to him,
to all who truly pray to him.
19He gives those who respect him what
they want.
He listens when they cry, and he saves
them.
20The LORD protects everyone who loves
him,
but he will destroy the wicked.

21I will praise the LORD.
Let everyone praise his holy name
forever.

Praise God Who Helps the Weak

146 Praise the LORD!
My whole being, praise the LORD.
2I will praise the LORD all my life;
I will sing praises to my God as long as I
live.
3Do not put your trust in princes
or other people, who cannot save you.
4When people die, they are buried.
Then all of their plans come to an end.
5Happy are those who are helped by the
God of Jacob.
Their hope is in the LORD their God.
6He made heaven and earth,
the sea and everything in it.
He remains loyal forever.
7He does what is fair for those who have
been wronged.
He gives food to the hungry.
The LORD sets the prisoners free.
8 The LORD gives sight to the blind.
The LORD lifts up people who are in
trouble.
The LORD loves those who do right.
9The LORD protects the foreigners.
He defends the orphans and widows,
but he blocks the way of the wicked.

10The LORD will be King forever.
Jerusalem, your God is everlasting.

Praise the LORD!

Praise God Who Helps His People

147 Praise the LORD!
It is good to sing praises to our God;
it is good and pleasant to praise him.
2The LORD rebuilds Jerusalem;
he brings back the captured
Israelites.
3He heals the brokenhearted
and bandages their wounds.
4He counts the stars
and names each one.
5Our Lord is great and very powerful.
There is no limit to what he knows.
6The LORD defends the humble,
but he throws the wicked to the
ground.

7Sing praises to the LORD;
praise our God with harps.
8He fills the sky with clouds
and sends rain to the earth
and makes grass grow on the hills.
9He gives food to cattle
and to the little birds that call.

10He is not impressed with the strength of a
horse
or with human might.
11The LORD is pleased with those who
respect him,
with those who trust his love.

12Jerusalem, praise the LORD;
Jerusalem, praise your God.
13He makes your city gates strong
and blesses your children inside.
14He brings peace to your country
and fills you with the finest grain.

15He gives a command to the earth,
and it quickly obeys him.
16He spreads the snow like wool
and scatters the frost like ashes.
17He throws down hail like rocks.
No one can stand the cold he sends.
18Then he gives a command, and it melts.
He sends the breezes, and the waters
flow.

19He gave his word to Jacob,
his laws and demands to Israel.

devotion 174

PSALM 147:10–11

BUST THAT BRONC!

Have you ever witnessed a wild bronc riding competition at a rodeo or on television? As soon as horse and rider explode out of the chute into the arena, their strength is apparent. The horses usually win, but the cowboys often stay on for several seconds before being bucked off or rescued. Just seeing a cowboy's body whipping dangerously back and forth on a horse is enough to make me really glad that my physical strength is not what God is looking for.

What pleases God is respect and trust, but I have to admit that it isn't always easy. There are times that I'm so filled with doubt and disobedience to the Lord that the prospect of riding a bucking horse actually seems easier. To respect our Lord and trust his love should not be difficult, but because we are human, we all too often lose sight of his devotion to us and guidance in our lives.

One thing about a wild bronc ride is that neither the cowboy nor the horse trusts each other, but our relationship with our Father can be different. Take off your cowboy hat and trust God! Even when life seems like a struggle, I encourage you to keep your eyes fixed on him because he will not fail you. Take comfort in knowing that surrendering to him is more pleasing than being strong. It is his strength that we ought to seek and his power that will see us through.

20 He didn't do this for any other nation.
They don't know his laws.

Praise the LORD!

The World Should Praise the Lord

148 Praise the LORD!

Praise the LORD from the skies.
Praise him high above the earth.
2 Praise him, all you angels.
Praise him, all you armies of heaven.
3 Praise him, sun and moon.
Praise him, all you shining stars.
4 Praise him, highest heavens
and you waters above the sky.
5 Let them praise the LORD,
because they were created by his command.
6 He put them in place forever and ever;
he made a law that will never change.

7 Praise the LORD from the earth,
you large sea animals and all the oceans,
8 lightning and hail, snow and mist,
and stormy winds that obey him,
9 mountains and all hills,
fruit trees and all cedars,
10 wild animals and all cattle,
crawling animals and birds,
11 kings of the earth and all nations,
princes and all rulers of the earth,
12 young men and women,
old people and children.

13 Praise the LORD,
because he alone is great.
He is more wonderful than heaven and earth.
14 God has given his people a king.
He should be praised by all who belong to him;
he should be praised by the Israelites, the people closest to his heart.

Praise the LORD!

Praise the God of Israel

149 Praise the LORD!

Sing a new song to the LORD;
sing his praise in the meeting of his people.

2 Let the Israelites be happy because of God, their Maker.
Let the people of Jerusalem rejoice because of their King.
3 They should praise him with dancing.
They should sing praises to him with tambourines and harps.
4 The LORD is pleased with his people;
he saves the humble.
5 Let those who worship him rejoice in his glory.
Let them sing for joy even in bed!

6 Let them shout his praise
with their two-edged swords in their hands.
7 They will punish the nations
and defeat the people.
8 They will put those kings in chains
and those important men in iron bands.
9 They will punish them as God has written.
God is honored by all who worship him.

Praise the LORD!

Praise the Lord with Music

150 Praise the LORD!

Praise God in his Temple;
praise him in his mighty heaven.
2 Praise him for his strength;
praise him for his greatness.
3 Praise him with trumpet blasts;
praise him with harps and lyres.
4 Praise him with tambourines and dancing;
praise him with stringed instruments and flutes.
5 Praise him with loud cymbals;
praise him with crashing cymbals.
6 Let everything that breathes praise the LORD.

Praise the LORD!

Proverbs

Titled "The Proverbs of Solomon" in the Hebrew Bible, Proverbs is referred to as a wisdom book (along with Job, Psalms, Ecclesiastes, and the Song of Songs).

Person Holding the Pen God Wrote With: *Solomon*, who asked God for a "heart that understands" early in his tenure as Israel's king (1 Kin. 3:9), compiled most of these wise sayings. Other unnamed authors, along with a guy named *Agur* (chapter 30) and a king named *Lemuel* (chapter 31)—both of which could have been pen names for Solomon—did some of the writing as well.

When the Text Was Written: Solomon ruled Israel from 971 to 931 B.C., and certainly much of this text was composed and collected during that time period. However, the entire Book of Proverbs wasn't amassed until King Hezekiah's reign from 715 to 686 B.C.

Spiritual Posture of the Original Recipients: Much like the extended time period in which Psalms was written, the Israelites reflected a myriad of spiritual positions throughout this season. Solomon himself deviated from his father's faithful footsteps toward the idol worship practiced by his pagan wives and slave women (1 Kin. 11:1–13).

Storyline Synopsis: It has been suggested that Proverbs is like a biblical multi-vitamin—you should read one every day! This book is soul enriching because it overflows with practical advice for people of faith. Proverbs deals with everyday issues such as our relationship with God, self-image, and how to successfully interact with others. The two "voices" running through the text are wisdom and foolishness. Wisdom comes from knowing God (Prov. 1:7); foolishness occurs when people feed their own selfish desires (1:28–33).

A Moment Worth Discussing: Proverbs 11:22, "A beautiful woman without good sense is like a gold ring in a pig's snout," will probably encourage wise, plain-looking girls in book clubs everywhere to clear their throats and grin! A similar adage that praises a woman's inward character versus her outward appearance is found in the last female-friendly chapter of this book (Prov. 31:30). Both proverbs prompt the question, "How would God describe an attractive woman?"

Interesting (But Likely to Be Overlooked) Characters: *Ithiel* and *Ucal*, the two recipients of Agur's dedication in chapter 30. Some suggest they were his favorite students, much like Theophilus was with Luke (Luke 1:1–4).

The Importance of Proverbs

1 These are the wise words of Solomon son of David, king of Israel.

2 They teach wisdom and self-control;
they will help you understand wise words.
3 They will teach you how to be wise and self-controlled
and will teach you to do what is honest and fair and right.
4 They make the uneducated wise
and give knowledge and sense to the young.
5 Wise people can also listen and learn;
even they can find good advice in these words.
6 Then anyone can understand wise words and stories,
the words of the wise and their riddles.
7 Knowledge begins with respect for the LORD,
but fools hate wisdom and discipline.

Warnings Against Evil

8 My child, listen to your father's teaching
and do not forget your mother's advice.
9 Their teaching will be like flowers in your hair
or a necklace around your neck.

10 My child, if sinners try to lead you into sin,
do not follow them.
11 They will say, "Come with us.
Let's ambush and kill someone;
let's attack some innocent people just for fun.
12 Let's swallow them alive, as death does;
let's swallow them whole, as the grave does.
13 We will take all kinds of valuable things
and fill our houses with stolen goods.
14 Come join us,
and we will share with you stolen goods."
15 My child, do not go along with them;
do not do what they do.
16 They are eager to do evil
and are quick to kill.
17 It is useless to spread out a net
right where the birds can see it.
18 But sinners will fall into their own traps;
they will only catch themselves!
19 All greedy people end up this way;
greed kills selfish people.

Wisdom Speaks

20 Wisdom is like a woman shouting in the street;
she raises her voice in the city squares.
21 She cries out in the noisy street
and shouts at the city gates:
22 "You fools, how long will you be foolish?
How long will you make fun of wisdom
and hate knowledge?
23 If only you had listened when I corrected you,
I would have told you what's in my heart;
I would have told you what I am thinking.
24 I called, but you refused to listen;
I held out my hand, but you paid no attention.
25 You did not follow my advice
and did not listen when I corrected you.
26 So I will laugh when you are in trouble.
I will make fun when disaster strikes you,
27 when disaster comes over you like a storm,
when trouble strikes you like a whirlwind,
when pain and trouble overwhelm you.

28 "Then you will call to me,
but I will not answer.
You will look for me,
but you will not find me.
29 It is because you rejected knowledge
and did not choose to respect the LORD.
30 You did not accept my advice,
and you rejected my correction.
31 So you will get what you deserve;
you will get what you planned for others.
32 Fools will die because they refuse to listen;
they will be destroyed because they do not care.
33 But those who listen to me will live in safety
and be at peace, without fear of injury."

Rewards of Wisdom

2 My child, listen to what I say
and remember what I command you.

2 Listen carefully to wisdom;
set your mind on understanding.
3 Cry out for wisdom,
and beg for understanding.
4 Search for it like silver,
and hunt for it like hidden treasure.
5 Then you will understand respect for the LORD,
and you will find that you know God.
6 Only the LORD gives wisdom;
he gives knowledge and understanding.
7 He stores up wisdom for those who are honest.
Like a shield he protects the innocent.
8 He makes sure that justice is done,
and he protects those who are loyal to him.

9 Then you will understand what is honest and fair
and what is the good and right thing to do.
10 Wisdom will come into your mind,
and knowledge will be pleasing to you.
11 Good sense will protect you;
understanding will guard you.
12 It will keep you from the wicked,
from those whose words are bad,
13 who don't do what is right
but what is evil.
14 They enjoy doing wrong
and are happy to do what is crooked and evil.
15 What they do is wrong,
and their ways are dishonest.
16 It will save you from the unfaithful wife
who tries to lead you into adultery with pleasing words.
17 She leaves the husband she married when she was young.
She ignores the promise she made before God.
18 Her house is on the way to death;
those who took that path are now all dead.
19 No one who goes to her comes back
or walks the path of life again.
20 But wisdom will help you be good
and do what is right.
21 Those who are honest will live in the land,
and those who are innocent will remain in it.
22 But the wicked will be removed from the land,
and the unfaithful will be thrown out of it.

Advice to Children

3 My child, do not forget my teaching,
but keep my commands in mind.
2 Then you will live a long time,
and your life will be successful.

3 Don't ever forget kindness and truth.
Wear them like a necklace.
Write them on your heart as if on a tablet.
4 Then you will be respected
and will please both God and people.
5 Trust the LORD with all your heart,
and don't depend on your own understanding.
6 Remember the LORD in all you do,
and he will give you success.

7 Don't depend on your own wisdom.
Respect the LORD and refuse to do wrong.
8 Then your body will be healthy,
and your bones will be strong.
9 Honor the LORD with your wealth
and the firstfruits from all your crops.
10 Then your barns will be full,
and your wine barrels will overflow with new wine.
11 My child, do not reject the LORD's discipline,
and don't get angry when he corrects you.
12 The LORD corrects those he loves,
just as parents correct the child they delight in.

13 Happy is the person who finds wisdom,
the one who gets understanding.
14 Wisdom is worth more than silver;
it brings more profit than gold.
15 Wisdom is more precious than rubies;
nothing you could want is equal to it.
16 With her right hand wisdom offers you a long life,
and with her left hand she gives you riches and honor.
17 Wisdom will make your life pleasant
and will bring you peace.

devotion 175

PROVERBS 3:5–7

A SWEETER DEAL THAN YOU KNOW

When you give your heart to Christ, you are essentially saying, "Here I am laying down everything that I have tried to accomplish in my own strength, my own mind, and my own flesh." When you read that statement, is your immediate interpretation, "Oh, I have to give up the things that are fun, lay down the dreams that I have, blend in, or no longer stand out as an accomplished success"? If those are your thoughts, you are in for a real treat!

Christ wants to rock your world; he does not want you to live in the doldrums of a Christian life. He wants you to be more vibrant, peaceful, and more successful than ever before. He is asking your heart and your mind to trust him and to leave behind your days of depending on your own understanding. So much of our Christian walk is learning to depend on him and believing that what he has for us is so much better than what we could create ourselves. If you are tempted today to return to any part of your old life or your old self, run as fast as you can to the Lord and refuse to interfere with the awesome process of change that is happening in your life right now. Pour your heart out to him today, tell him everything that is making you fearful, tell him everything that you want to be, and let your Lord ignite a fire of strength in your soul.

18 As a tree produces fruit, wisdom gives life
to those who use it,
and everyone who uses it will be happy.

19 The LORD made the earth, using his
wisdom.
He set the sky in place, using his
understanding.
20 With his knowledge, he made springs
flow into rivers
and the clouds drop rain on the earth.

21 My child, hold on to wisdom and good
sense.
Don't let them out of your sight.
22 They will give you life
and beauty like a necklace around your
neck.
23 Then you will go your way in safety,
and you will not get hurt.
24 When you lie down, you won't be afraid;
when you lie down, you will sleep in
peace.
25 You won't be afraid of sudden trouble;
you won't fear the ruin that comes to
the wicked,
26 because the LORD will keep you safe.
He will keep you from being trapped.

27 Whenever you are able,
do good to people who need help.
28 If you have what your neighbor asks for,
don't say, "Come back later.
I will give it to you tomorrow."
29 Don't make plans to hurt your neighbor
who lives nearby and trusts you.
30 Don't accuse a person for no good reason;
don't accuse someone who has not
harmed you.
31 Don't be jealous of those who use
violence,
and don't choose to be like them.
32 The LORD hates those who do wrong,
but he is a friend to those who are
honest.
33 The LORD will curse the evil person's
house,
but he will bless the home of those who
do right.
34 The LORD laughs at those who laugh at
him,

but he gives grace to those who are not
proud.
35 Wise people will receive honor,
but fools will be disgraced.

Wisdom Is Important

4 My children, listen to your father's
teaching;
pay attention so you will understand.
2 What I am telling you is good,
so do not forget what I teach you.
3 When I was a young boy in my father's
house
and like an only child to my mother,
4 my father taught me and said,
"Hold on to my words with all your
heart.
Keep my commands and you will live.
5 Get wisdom and understanding.
Don't forget or ignore my words.
6 Hold on to wisdom, and it will take care
of you.
Love it, and it will keep you safe.
7 Wisdom is the most important thing; so
get wisdom.
If it costs everything you have, get
understanding.
8 Treasure wisdom, and it will make you
great;
hold on to it, and it will bring you
honor.
9 It will be like flowers in your hair
and like a beautiful crown on your
head."

10 My child, listen and accept what I say.
Then you will have a long life.
11 I am guiding you in the way of wisdom,
and I am leading you on the right
path.
12 Nothing will hold you back;
you will not be overwhelmed.
13 Always remember what you have been
taught,
and don't let go of it.
Keep all that you have learned;
it is the most important thing in life.
14 Don't follow the ways of the wicked;
don't do what evil people do.
15 Avoid their ways, and don't follow them.
Stay away from them and keep on
going,
16 because they cannot sleep until they do
evil.
They cannot rest until they harm
someone.
17 They feast on wickedness and cruelty
as if they were eating bread and
drinking wine.

18 The way of the good person is like the
light of dawn,
growing brighter and brighter until full
daylight.
19 But the wicked walk around in the dark;
they can't even see what makes them
stumble.

20 My child, pay attention to my words;
listen closely to what I say.
21 Don't ever forget my words;
keep them always in mind.
22 They are the key to life for those who find
them;
they bring health to the whole body.
23 Be careful what you think,
because your thoughts run your life.
24 Don't use your mouth to tell lies;
don't ever say things that are not true.
25 Keep your eyes focused on what is right,
and look straight ahead to what is good.
26 Be careful what you do,
and always do what is right.
27 Don't turn off the road of goodness;
keep away from evil paths.

Warning About Adultery

5 My son, pay attention to my wisdom;
listen to my words of understanding.
2 Be careful to use good sense,
and watch what you say.
3 The words of another man's wife may
seem sweet as honey;
they may be as smooth as olive oil.
4 But in the end she will bring you sorrow,
causing you pain like a two-edged
sword.
5 She is on the way to death;
her steps are headed straight to the
grave.
6 She gives little thought to life.
She doesn't even know that her ways
are wrong.

7 Now, my sons, listen to me,
and don't ignore what I say.
8 Stay away from such a woman.
Don't even go near the door of her
house,

9or you will give your riches to others,
and the best years of your life will be given to someone cruel.
10Strangers will enjoy your wealth,
and what you worked so hard for will go to someone else.
11You will groan at the end of your life
when your health is gone.
12Then you will say, "I hated being told what to do!
I would not listen to correction!
13I would not listen to my teachers
or pay attention to my instructors.
14I came close to being completely ruined
in front of a whole group of people."

15Be faithful to your own wife,
just as you drink water from your own well.
16Don't pour your water in the streets;
don't give your love to just any woman.
17These things are yours alone
and shouldn't be shared with strangers.
18Be happy with the wife you married when you were young.
She gives you joy, as your fountain gives you water.
19She is as lovely and graceful as a deer.
Let her love always make you happy;
let her love always hold you captive.
20My son, don't be held captive by a woman who takes part in adultery.
Don't fondle a woman who is not your wife.

21The LORD sees everything you do,
and he watches where you go.
22An evil man will be caught in his wicked ways;
the ropes of his sins will tie him up.
23He will die because he does not control himself,
and he will be held captive by his foolishness.

Dangers of Being Foolish

6 My child, be careful about giving a guarantee for somebody else's loan,
about promising to pay what someone else owes.
2You might get trapped by what you say;
you might be caught by your own words.
3My child, if you have done this and are under your neighbor's control,
here is how to get free.
Don't be proud. Go to your neighbor
and beg to be free from your promise.
4Don't go to sleep
or even rest your eyes,
5but free yourself like a deer running from a hunter,
like a bird flying away from a trapper.

6Go watch the ants, you lazy person.
Watch what they do and be wise.
7Ants have no commander,
no leader or ruler,
8but they store up food in the summer
and gather their supplies at harvest.
9How long will you lie there, you lazy person?
When will you get up from sleeping?
10You sleep a little; you take a nap.
You fold your hands and lie down to rest.
11So you will be as poor as if you had been robbed;
you will have as little as if you had been held up.

12Some people are wicked and no good.
They go around telling lies,
13winking with their eyes, tapping with their feet,
and making signs with their fingers.
14They make evil plans in their hearts
and are always starting arguments.
15So trouble will strike them in an instant;
suddenly they will be so hurt no one can help them.

16There are six things the LORD hates.
There are seven things he cannot stand:
17 a proud look,
a lying tongue,
hands that kill innocent people,
18 a mind that thinks up evil plans,
feet that are quick to do evil,
19 a witness who lies,
and someone who starts arguments among families.

Warning About Adultery

20My son, keep your father's commands,
and don't forget your mother's teaching.
21Keep their words in mind forever
as though you had them tied around your neck.

devotion 176

PROVERBS 6:20–23

HOW YOUNG IS TOO YOUNG?

My son was only a year old when we began reading to him from the Bible every night before he went to bed. It was my husband's idea. I thought he was too young to understand. I found this little children's Bible, and we started with the story of Creation. The first time we read it, I simply pointed out the animals in the pictures and let him turn the pages. We must have read the same little Bible to him a hundred times over the next two years of his life. The Bible had little teeth marks, dirty fingerprints, and scribbles, but by the time he was three, he could tell you every story just by looking at the pictures.

Now my children have their own devotional lives. Whenever they are being really difficult, the first thing I ask them is if they've had their devotions that day. The kids will tease me and say that I find God in everything. They think this is an insult because I over-spiritualize everything (by their standards). I think this is a compliment! We were vacationing with my parents recently, and my mother began telling the kids a story about how God helped us find a lobster in the Florida Keys years ago. The kids were laughing at her story, and then my son turned to me and said, "Now we know where you get it."

"Yep," I thought to myself, "and someday you'll do the same for your children."

22 They will guide you when you walk.
They will guard you when you sleep.
They will speak to you when you are awake.
23 These commands are like a lamp;
this teaching is like a light.
And the correction that comes from them
will help you have life.
24 They will keep you from sinful women
and from the pleasing words of another man's unfaithful wife.
25 Don't desire her because she is beautiful.
Don't let her capture you by the way she looks at you.
26 A prostitute will treat you like a loaf of bread,
and a woman who takes part in adultery may cost you your life.
27 You cannot carry hot coals against your chest
without burning your clothes,
28 and you cannot walk on hot coals
without burning your feet.
29 The same is true if you have sexual relations with another man's wife.
Anyone who does so will be punished.
30 People don't hate a thief
when he steals because he is hungry.
31 But if he is caught, he must pay back seven times what he stole,
and it may cost him everything he owns.
32 A man who takes part in adultery has no sense;
he will destroy himself.
33 He will be beaten up and disgraced,
and his shame will never go away.
34 Jealousy makes a husband very angry,
and he will have no pity when he gets revenge.
35 He will accept no payment for the wrong;
he will take no amount of money.

The Woman of Adultery

7 My son, remember what I say, and treasure my commands.
2 Obey my commands, and you will live.
Guard my teachings as you would your own eyes.
3 Remind yourself of them;
write them on your heart as if on a tablet.

4Treat wisdom as a sister,
and make understanding your closest friend.
5Wisdom and understanding will keep you away from adultery,
away from the unfaithful wife and her pleasing words.

6Once while I was at the window of my house
I looked out through the shutters
7and saw some foolish, young men.
I noticed one of them had no wisdom.
8He was walking down the street near the corner
on the road leading to her house.
9It was the twilight of the evening;
the darkness of the night was just beginning.
10Then the woman approached him,
dressed like a prostitute
and planning to trick him.
11She was loud and stubborn
and never stayed at home.
12She was always out in the streets or in the city squares,
waiting around on the corners of the streets.
13She grabbed him and kissed him.
Without shame she said to him,
14"I made my fellowship offering and took some of the meat home.
Today I have kept my special promises.
15So I have come out to meet you;
I have been looking for you and have found you.
16I have covered my bed
with colored sheets from Egypt.
17I have made my bed smell sweet
with myrrh, aloes, and cinnamon.
18Come, let's make love until morning.
Let's enjoy each other's love.
19My husband is not home;
he has gone on a long trip.
20He took a lot of money with him
and won't be home for weeks."
21By her clever words she made him give in;
by her pleasing words she led him into doing wrong.
22All at once he followed her,
like an ox led to the butcher,
like a deer caught in a trap
23 and shot through the liver with an arrow.
Like a bird caught in a trap,
he didn't know what he did would kill him.

24Now, my sons, listen to me;
pay attention to what I say.
25Don't let yourself be tricked by such a woman;
don't go where she leads you.
26She has ruined many good men,
and many have died because of her.
27Her house is on the road to death,
the road that leads down to the grave.

Listen to Wisdom

8 Wisdom calls to you like someone shouting;
understanding raises her voice.
2On the hilltops along the road
and at the crossroads, she stands calling.
3Beside the city gates,
at the entrances into the city, she calls out:
4"Listen, everyone, I'm calling out to you;
I am shouting to all people.
5You who are uneducated, seek wisdom.
You who are foolish, get understanding.
6Listen, because I have important things to say,
and what I tell you is right.
7What I say is true,
I refuse to speak evil.
8Everything I say is honest;
nothing I say is crooked or false.
9People with good sense know what I say is true;
and those with knowledge know my words are right.
10Choose my teachings instead of silver,
and knowledge rather than the finest gold.
11Wisdom is more precious than rubies.
Nothing you could want is equal to it.

12"I am wisdom, and I have good judgment.
I also have knowledge and good sense.
13If you respect the LORD, you will also hate evil.
I hate pride and bragging,
evil ways and lies.
14I have good sense and advice,
and I have understanding and power.
15I help kings to govern
and rulers to make fair laws.

16Princes use me to lead,
and so do all important people who judge fairly.
17I love those who love me,
and those who seek me find me.
18Riches and honor are mine to give.
So are wealth and lasting success.
19What I give is better than the finest gold,
better than the purest silver.
20I do what is right
and follow the path of justice.
21I give wealth to those who love me,
filling their houses with treasures.

22"I, wisdom, was with the LORD when he began his work,
long before he made anything else.
23I was created in the very beginning,
even before the world began.
24I was born before there were oceans,
or springs overflowing with water,
25before the hills were there,
before the mountains were put in place.
26God had not made the earth or fields,
not even the first dust of the earth.
27I was there when God put the skies in place,
when he stretched the horizon over the oceans,
28when he made the clouds above
and put the deep underground springs in place.
29I was there when he ordered the sea
not to go beyond the borders he had set.
I was there when he laid the earth's foundation.
30 I was like a child by his side.
I was delighted every day,
enjoying his presence all the time,
31enjoying the whole world,
and delighted with all its people.

32"Now, my children, listen to me,
because those who follow my ways are happy.
33Listen to my teaching, and you will be wise;
do not ignore it.
34Happy are those who listen to me,
watching at my door every day,
waiting at my open doorway.
35Those who find me find life,
and the LORD will be pleased with them.
36Those who do not find me hurt themselves.
Those who hate me love death."

Being Wise or Foolish

9 Wisdom has built her house;
she has made its seven columns.
2She has prepared her food and wine;
she has set her table.
3She has sent out her servant girls,
and she calls out from the highest place in the city.
4She says to those who are uneducated,
"Come in here, you foolish people!
5Come and eat my food
and drink the wine I have prepared.
6Stop your foolish ways, and you will live;
take the road of understanding.

7"If you correct someone who makes fun of wisdom, you will be insulted.
If you correct an evil person, you will get hurt.
8Do not correct those who make fun of wisdom, or they will hate you.
But correct the wise, and they will love you.
9Teach the wise, and they will become even wiser;
teach good people, and they will learn even more.

10"Wisdom begins with respect for the LORD,
and understanding begins with knowing the Holy One.
11If you live wisely, you will live a long time;
wisdom will add years to your life.
12The wise person is rewarded by wisdom,
but whoever makes fun of wisdom will suffer for it."

13Foolishness is like a loud woman;
she does not have wisdom or knowledge.
14She sits at the door of her house
at the highest place in the city.
15She calls out to those who are passing by,
who are going along, minding their own business.
16She says to those who are uneducated,
"Come in here, you foolish people!
17Stolen water is sweeter,
and food eaten in secret tastes better."
18But these people don't know that everyone who goes there dies,
that her guests end up deep in the grave.

The Wise Words of Solomon

10 These are the wise words of Solomon:
Wise children make their father happy,
but foolish children make their mother sad.

2 Riches gotten by doing wrong have no value,
but right living will save you from death.

3 The LORD does not let good people go hungry,
but he keeps evil people from getting what they want.

4 A lazy person will end up poor,
but a hard worker will become rich.

5 Those who gather crops on time are wise,
but those who sleep through the harvest are a disgrace.

6 Good people will have rich blessings,
but the wicked will be overwhelmed by violence.

7 Good people will be remembered as a blessing,
but evil people will soon be forgotten.

8 The wise do what they are told,
but a talkative fool will be ruined.

9 The honest person will live in safety,
but the dishonest will be caught.

10 A wink may get you into trouble,
and foolish talk will lead to your ruin.

11 The words of a good person give life, like a fountain of water,
but the words of the wicked contain nothing but violence.

12 Hatred stirs up trouble,
but love forgives all wrongs.

13 Wise people speak with understanding,
but people without wisdom should be punished.

14 The wise don't tell everything they know,
but the foolish talk too much and are ruined.

devotion 177

PROVERBS 10:12

"I DON'T HATE ANYONE"

It's surprising when we see fellow women causing so much pain in each other as a result of envy or jealousy. Proverbs 10:12 explains it all when it says, "Hatred stirs up trouble."

"Oh," you might be thinking, "I don't *hate* anyone." That is probably true; but when we deal with our sisters in Christ or anyone else in a way that is mean-spirited, we are stirring up trouble that is, by its very nature, hateful. Perhaps you've been the target of hateful actions or words sometime during your life, or maybe you are even guilty of letting an occasional rumor slip from your tongue without thinking first. The trouble hatred causes us ranges from hurt feelings to devastation.

We've all seen or heard of marriages destroyed, careers ended, or reputations tarnished because of a person or a group of people who seem to thrive on the unhappiness of others. We see it on the news when politicians are "exposed." We read it in the magazines when entertainment reporters describe the broken relationships of celebrities, and it happens in our own homes, workplaces, and churches. Fortunately, the second part of this verse reminds us that there is a way to recover from the wrongs that occur from hateful situations. We can ask our friends and families to forgive us and choose to be more loving and careful in our interactions with others. And if we've been victims of a wrong, we can forgive those who have hurt us.

15Having lots of money protects the rich,
but having no money destroys the poor.

16Good people are rewarded with life,
but evil people are paid with punishment.

17Whoever accepts correction is on the way to life,
but whoever ignores correction will lead others away from life.

18Whoever hides hate is a liar.
Whoever tells lies is a fool.

19If you talk a lot, you are sure to sin;
if you are wise, you will keep quiet.

20The words of a good person are like pure silver,
but an evil person's thoughts are worth very little.

21Good people's words will help many others,
but fools will die because they don't have wisdom.

22The LORD's blessing brings wealth,
and no sorrow comes with it.

23A foolish person enjoys doing wrong,
but a person with understanding enjoys doing what is wise.

24Evil people will get what they fear most,
but good people will get what they want most.

25A storm will blow the evil person away,
but a good person will always be safe.

26A lazy person affects the one he works for
like vinegar on the teeth or smoke in the eyes.

27Whoever respects the LORD will have a long life,
but the life of an evil person will be cut short.

28A good person can look forward to happiness,
but an evil person can expect nothing.

29The LORD will protect good people
but will ruin those who do evil.

30Good people will always be safe,
but evil people will not remain in the land.

31A good person says wise things,
but a liar's tongue will be stopped.

32Good people know the right thing to say,
but evil people only tell lies.

11 The LORD hates dishonest scales,
but he is pleased with honest weights.

2Pride leads only to shame;
it is wise to be humble.

3Good people will be guided by honesty;
dishonesty will destroy those who are not trustworthy.

4Riches will not help when it's time to die,
but right living will save you from death.

5The goodness of the innocent makes life easier,
but the wicked will be destroyed by their wickedness.

6Doing right brings freedom to honest people,
but those who are not trustworthy will be caught by their own desires.

7When the wicked die, hope dies with them;
their hope in riches will come to nothing.

8The good person is saved from trouble;
it comes to the wicked instead.

9With words an evil person can destroy a neighbor,
but a good person will escape by being resourceful.

10When good people succeed, the city is happy.
When evil people die, there are shouts of joy.

11Good people bless and build up their city,
but the wicked can destroy it with their words.

12People without good sense find fault with their neighbors,
but those with understanding keep quiet.

13Gossips can't keep secrets,
but a trustworthy person can.

14Without leadership a nation falls,
but lots of good advice will save it.

15Whoever guarantees to pay somebody else's loan will suffer.
It is safer to avoid such promises.

16A kind woman gets respect,
but cruel men get only wealth.

17Kind people do themselves a favor,
but cruel people bring trouble on themselves.

18An evil person really earns nothing,
but a good person will surely be rewarded.

19Those who are truly good will live,
but those who chase after evil will die.

20The LORD hates those with evil hearts
but is pleased with those who are innocent.

21Evil people will certainly be punished,
but those who do right will be set free.

22A beautiful woman without good sense
is like a gold ring in a pig's snout.

23Those who do right only wish for good,
but the wicked can expect to be defeated by God's anger.

24Some people give much but get back even more.
Others don't give what they should and end up poor.

25Whoever gives to others will get richer;
those who help others will themselves be helped.

26People curse those who keep all the grain,
but they bless the one who is willing to sell it.

27Whoever looks for good will find kindness,
but whoever looks for evil will find trouble.

28Those who trust in riches will be ruined,
but a good person will be healthy like a green leaf.

29Whoever brings trouble to his family
will be left with nothing but the wind.
A fool will be a servant to the wise.

30A good person gives life to others;
the wise person teaches others how to live.

31Good people will be rewarded on earth,
and the wicked and the sinners will be punished.

12

Anyone who loves learning accepts correction,
but a person who hates being corrected is stupid.

2The LORD is pleased with a good person,
but he will punish anyone who plans evil.

3Doing evil brings no safety at all,
but a good person has safety and security.

4A good wife is like a crown for her husband,
but a disgraceful wife is like a disease in his bones.

5The plans that good people make are fair,
but the advice of the wicked will trick you.

6The wicked talk about killing people,
but the words of good people will save them.

7Wicked people die and they are no more,
but a good person's family continues.

8The wisdom of the wise wins praise,
but there is no respect for the stupid.

9A person who is not important but has a servant is better off
than someone who acts important but has no food.

10Good people take care of their animals,
but even the kindest acts of the wicked are cruel.

11Those who work their land will have plenty of food,
but the one who chases empty dreams is not wise.

12The wicked want what other evil people have stolen,
but good people want to give what they have to others.

13Evil people are trapped by their evil talk,
but good people stay out of trouble.

14 People will be rewarded for what they say,
and they will also be rewarded for what they do.

15 Fools think they are doing right,
but the wise listen to advice.

16 Fools quickly show that they are upset,
but the wise ignore insults.

17 An honest witness tells the truth,
but a dishonest witness tells lies.

18 Careless words stab like a sword,
but wise words bring healing.

19 Truth will continue forever,
but lies are only for a moment.

20 Those who plan evil are full of lies,
but those who plan peace are happy.

21 No harm comes to a good person,
but an evil person's life is full of trouble.

22 The LORD hates those who tell lies
but is pleased with those who keep their promises.

23 Wise people keep what they know to themselves,
but fools can't keep from showing how foolish they are.

24 Hard workers will become leaders,
but those who are lazy will be slaves.

25 Worry is a heavy load,
but a kind word cheers you up.

26 Good people take advice from their friends,
but an evil person is easily led to do wrong.

27 The lazy catch no food to cook,
but a hard worker will have great wealth.

28 Doing what is right is the way to life,
but there is another way that leads to death.

13 Wise children take their parents' advice,
but whoever makes fun of wisdom won't listen to correction.

2 People will be rewarded for what they say,
but those who can't be trusted want only violence.

devotion 178

PROVERBS 12:16

MADE A FOOL OF YOURSELF LATELY?

"Upset" is a word that describes my mood when I have to wait in the checkout line too long or my hairdresser puts the wrong color on my roots. Being upset, in and of itself, is not a sin. It is, however, a sin when that emotion gets you into action and you resemble a crazy woman, or as the Lord puts it—a fool. I find the fool in me comes out when the circumstances of my day have topped me off. I mean, even our gas tanks warn us, "Do not top off your tank—could cause an explosion." Maybe I need a label! Maybe my husband and employees would think twice about making me their dumping ground if I wore one that said, "Warning! Dump at your own risk. Very close to being topped off."

Proverbs says if we are to be wise, we are to ignore insults. What insults you to the point of outburst? Is it your friends? Is it your children being disobedient? Is your husband working your last nerve? If you answered yes to just one of the above, you are in danger of exploding and making a fool of yourself. I am going to suggest that you simply need to take a break. It does not need to be a beach vacation. It just needs to be a break from the usual. Get alone with the Lord and get your perspective back so you can center your heart and mind. I mean it. Go do it!

3 Those who are careful about what they
say protect their lives,
but whoever speaks without thinking
will be ruined.

4 The lazy will not get what they want,
but those who work hard will.

5 Good people hate what is false,
but the wicked do shameful and
disgraceful things.

6 Doing what is right protects the honest
person,
but doing evil ruins the sinner.

7 Some people pretend to be rich but really
have nothing.
Others pretend to be poor but really are
wealthy.

8 The rich may have to pay a ransom for
their lives,
but the poor will face no such danger.

9 Good people can look forward to a bright
future,
but the future of the wicked is like a
flame going out.

10 Pride only leads to arguments,
but those who take advice are wise.

11 Money that comes easily disappears
quickly,
but money that is gathered little by
little will grow.

12 It is sad not to get what you hoped for.
But wishes that come true are like
eating fruit from the tree of life.

13 Those who reject what they are taught
will pay for it,
but those who obey what they are told
will be rewarded.

14 The teaching of a wise person gives life.
It is like a fountain that can save people
from death.

15 People with good understanding will be
well liked,
but the lives of those who are not
trustworthy are hard.

16 Every wise person acts with good sense,
but fools show how foolish they are.

17 A wicked messenger brings nothing but
trouble,
but a trustworthy one makes
everything right.

18 A person who refuses correction will end
up poor and disgraced,
but the one who accepts correction will
be honored.

19 It is so good when wishes come true,
but fools hate to stop doing evil.

20 Spend time with the wise and you will
become wise,
but the friends of fools will suffer.

21 Trouble always comes to sinners,
but good people enjoy success.

22 Good people leave their wealth to their
grandchildren,
but a sinner's wealth is stored up for
good people.

23 A poor person's field might produce
plenty of food,
but others often steal it away.

24 If you do not punish your children, you
don't love them,
but if you love your children, you will
correct them.

25 Good people have enough to eat,
but the wicked will go hungry.

14 A wise woman strengthens her
family,
but a foolish woman destroys hers by
what she does.

2 People who live good lives respect the
LORD,
but those who live evil lives don't.

3 Fools will be punished for their proud
words,
but the words of the wise will protect
them.

4 When there are no oxen, no food is in the
barn.
But with a strong ox, much grain can be
grown.

5 A truthful witness does not lie,
but a false witness tells nothing but
lies.

6 Those who make fun of wisdom look for
it and do not find it,

but knowledge comes easily to those
with understanding.

7Stay away from fools,
because they can't teach you anything.

8A wise person will understand what to do,
but a foolish person is dishonest.

9Fools don't care if they sin,
but honest people work at being right.

10No one else can know your sadness,
and strangers cannot share your joy.

11The wicked person's house will be
destroyed,
but a good person's tent will still be
standing.

12Some people think they are doing right,
but in the end it leads to death.

13Someone who is laughing may be sad
inside,
and joy may end in sadness.

14Evil people will be paid back for their evil
ways,
and good people will be rewarded for
their good ones.

15Fools will believe anything,
but the wise think about what they do.

16Wise people are careful and stay out of
trouble,
but fools are careless and quick to act.

17Someone with a quick temper does
foolish things,
but someone with understanding
remains calm.

18Fools are rewarded with nothing but
more foolishness,
but the wise are rewarded with
knowledge.

19Evil people will bow down to those who
are good;
the wicked will bow down at the door
of those who do right.

20The poor are rejected, even by their
neighbors,
but the rich have many friends.

21It is a sin to hate your neighbor,
but being kind to the needy brings
happiness.

22Those who make evil plans will be ruined,
but those who plan to do good will be
loved and trusted.

23Those who work hard make a profit,
but those who only talk will be poor.

24Wise people are rewarded with wealth,
but fools only get more foolishness.

25A truthful witness saves lives,
but a false witness is a traitor.

26Those who respect the LORD will have
security,
and their children will be protected.

27Respect for the LORD gives life.
It is like a fountain that can save people
from death.

28A king is honored when he has many
people to rule,
but a prince is ruined if he has none.

29Patient people have great understanding,
but people with quick tempers show
their foolishness.

30Peace of mind means a healthy body,
but jealousy will rot your bones.

31Whoever mistreats the poor insults their
Maker,
but whoever is kind to the needy
honors God.

32The wicked are ruined by their own evil,
but those who do right are protected
even in death.

33Wisdom lives in those with
understanding,
and even fools recognize it.

34Doing what is right makes a nation great,
but sin will bring disgrace to any
people.

35A king is pleased with a wise servant,
but he will become angry with one
who causes him shame.

15

A gentle answer will calm a person's
anger,
but an unkind answer will cause more
anger.

2Wise people use knowledge when they
speak,
but fools pour out foolishness.

devotion 179

PROVERBS 15:1

THE POWER OF GENTLENESS

One day when my children were in elementary school, they were playing a game across the street with the neighbors. As they played, they crossed the street as a car was coming down the road. Moments later, a little boy who was in preschool followed after them and was almost hit by the car. The child's mother was so upset with my children for not watching out for him that she yelled at them and sent them home. My kids came into the house extremely mad at our neighbor because the little boy hadn't even been playing with them.

As a mother, your first instinct is to defend your children. I understood why my neighbor was upset, but I also understood that my children were unaware of the situation. I had a choice to make. I could go outside and defend my children, or I could find a gentle way to respond. I told the kids that we needed to go and tell our neighbor that we were sorry about the little boy almost getting hurt. And we did. So what could have started a neighborhood feud was turned into a round of apologies and neighbors who remained friends.

We can't avoid feeling anger when situations happen that are unsettling. The Bible doesn't tell us it is wrong to be angry, it just tells us that we need to be careful in how we express that anger. A gentle answer seems to be a good first step.

3 The LORD's eyes see everything;
he watches both evil and good people.

4 As a tree gives fruit, healing words give life,
but dishonest words crush the spirit.

5 Fools reject their parents' correction,
but anyone who accepts correction is wise.

6 Much wealth is in the houses of good people,
but evil people get nothing but trouble.

7 Wise people use their words to spread knowledge,
but there is no knowledge in the thoughts of fools.

8 The LORD hates the sacrifice that the wicked offer,
but he likes the prayers of honest people.

9 The LORD hates what evil people do,
but he loves those who do what is right.

10 The person who quits doing what is right will be punished,
and the one who hates to be corrected will die.

11 The LORD knows what is happening in the world of the dead,
so he surely knows the thoughts of the living.

12 Those who make fun of wisdom don't like to be corrected;
they will not ask the wise for advice.

13 Happiness makes a person smile,
but sadness can break a person's spirit.

14 People with understanding want more knowledge,
but fools just want more foolishness.

15 Every day is hard for those who suffer,
but a happy heart is like a continual feast.

16 It is better to be poor and respect the LORD
than to be wealthy and have much
trouble.

17 It is better to eat vegetables with those
who love you
than to eat meat with those who hate
you.

18 People with quick tempers cause trouble,
but those who control their tempers
stop a quarrel.

19 A lazy person's life is like a patch of
thorns,
but an honest person's life is like a
smooth highway.

20 Wise children make their father happy,
but foolish children disrespect their
mother.

21 A person without wisdom enjoys being
foolish,
but someone with understanding does
what is right.

22 Plans fail without good advice,
but they succeed with the advice of
many others.

23 People enjoy giving good advice.
Saying the right word at the right time
is so pleasing.

24 Wise people's lives get better and better.
They avoid whatever would cause their
death.

25 The LORD will tear down the proud
person's house,
but he will protect the widow's
property.

26 The LORD hates evil thoughts
but is pleased with kind words.

27 Greedy people bring trouble to their
families,
but the person who can't be paid to do
wrong will live.

28 Good people think before they answer,
but the wicked simply pour out evil.

29 The LORD does not listen to the wicked,
but he hears the prayers of those who
do right.

30 Good news makes you feel better.
Your happiness will show in your eyes.

31 If you listen to correction to improve your
life,
you will live among the wise.

32 Those who refuse correction hate
themselves,
but those who accept correction gain
understanding.

33 Respect for the LORD will teach you
wisdom.
If you want to be honored, you must be
humble.

16 People may make plans in their minds,
but only the LORD can make them
come true.

2 You may believe you are doing right,
but the LORD will judge your reasons.

3 Depend on the LORD in whatever you do,
and your plans will succeed.

4 The LORD makes everything go as he
pleases.
He has even prepared a day of disaster
for evil people.

5 The LORD hates those who are proud.
They will surely be punished.

6 Love and truth bring forgiveness of sin.
By respecting the LORD you will avoid
evil.

7 When people live so that they please the
LORD,
even their enemies will make peace
with them.

8 It is better to be poor and right
than to be wealthy and dishonest.

9 People may make plans in their minds,
but the LORD decides what they will do.

10 The words of a king are like a message
from God,
so his decisions should be fair.

11 The LORD wants honest balances and scales;
all the weights are his work.

12 Kings hate those who do wrong,
because governments only continue if
they are fair.

13 Kings like honest people;
they value someone who speaks the
truth.

14 An angry king can put someone to
death,
so a wise person will try to make him
happy.

15 A smiling king can give people life;
his kindness is like a spring shower.

16 It is better to get wisdom than gold,
and to choose understanding rather
than silver!

17 Good people stay away from evil.
By watching what they do, they protect
their lives.

18 Pride leads to destruction;
a proud attitude brings ruin.

19 It is better to be humble and be with those
who suffer
than to share stolen property with the
proud.

20 Whoever listens to what is taught will
succeed,
and whoever trusts the LORD will be
happy.

21 The wise are known for their
understanding.
Their pleasant words make them better
teachers.

22 Understanding is like a fountain which
gives life to those who use it,
but foolishness brings punishment to
fools.

23 Wise people's minds tell them what to
say,
and that helps them be better teachers.

24 Pleasant words are like a honeycomb,
making people happy and healthy.

25 Some people think they are doing right,
but in the end it leads to death.

26 The workers' hunger helps them,
because their desire to eat makes them
work.

27 Useless people make evil plans,
and their words are like a burning fire.

28 A useless person causes trouble,
and a gossip ruins friendships.

29 Cruel people trick their neighbors
and lead them to do wrong.

30 Someone who winks is planning evil,
and the one who grins is planning
something wrong.

31 Gray hair is like a crown of honor;
it is earned by living a good life.

32 Patience is better than strength.
Controlling your temper is better than
capturing a city.

33 People throw lots to make a decision,
but the answer comes from the LORD.

17 It is better to eat a dry crust of bread in
peace
than to have a feast where there is
quarreling.

2 A wise servant will rule over the master's
disgraceful child
and will even inherit a share of what
the master leaves his children.

3 A hot furnace tests silver and gold,
but the LORD tests hearts.

4 Evil people listen to evil words.
Liars pay attention to cruel words.

5 Whoever mistreats the poor insults their
Maker;
whoever enjoys someone's trouble will be
punished.

6 Old people are proud of their
grandchildren,
and children are proud of their
parents.

7 Fools should not be proud,
and rulers should not be liars.

8 Some people think they can pay others to
do anything they ask.
They think it will work every time.

9 Whoever forgives someone's sin makes a
friend,
but gossiping about the sin breaks up
friendships.

10 A wise person will learn more from a
warning
than a fool will learn from a hundred
lashings.

11 Disobedient people look only for trouble,
so a cruel messenger will be sent
against them.

12 It is better to meet a bear robbed of her cubs
than to meet a fool doing foolish things.

13 Whoever gives evil in return for good
will always have trouble at home.

14 Starting a quarrel is like a leak in a dam,
so stop it before a fight breaks out.

15 The LORD hates both of these things:
freeing the guilty and punishing the innocent.

16 It won't do a fool any good to try to buy wisdom,
because he doesn't have the ability to be wise.

17 A friend loves you all the time,
and a brother helps in time of trouble.

18 It is not wise to promise
to pay what your neighbor owes.

19 Whoever loves to argue loves to sin.
Whoever brags a lot is asking for trouble.

20 A person with an evil heart will find no success,
and the person whose words are evil will get into trouble.

21 It is sad to have a foolish child;
there is no joy in being the parent of a fool.

22 A happy heart is like good medicine,
but a broken spirit drains your strength.

23 When the wicked accept money to do wrong
there can be no justice.

24 The person with understanding is always looking for wisdom,
but the mind of a fool wanders everywhere.

25 Foolish children make their father sad
and cause their mother great sorrow.

26 It is not good to punish the innocent
or to beat leaders for being honest.

27 The wise say very little,
and those with understanding stay calm.

28 Even fools seem to be wise if they keep quiet;
if they don't speak, they appear to understand.

18

Unfriendly people are selfish
and hate all good sense.

2 Fools do not want to understand anything.
They only want to tell others what they think.

3 Do something evil, and people won't like you.
Do something shameful, and they will make fun of you.

4 Spoken words can be like deep water,
but wisdom is like a flowing stream.

5 It is not good to honor the wicked
or to be unfair to the innocent.

6 The words of fools start quarrels.
They make people want to beat them.

7 The words of fools will ruin them;
their own words will trap them.

8 The words of a gossip are like tasty bits of food.
People like to gobble them up.

9 A person who doesn't work hard
is just like someone who destroys things.

10 The LORD is like a strong tower;
those who do right can run to him for safety.

11 Rich people trust their wealth to protect them.
They think it is like the high walls of a city.

12 Proud people will be ruined,
but the humble will be honored.

13 Anyone who answers without listening
is foolish and confused.

14 The will to live can get you through sickness,
but no one can live with a broken spirit.

15 The mind of a person with understanding gets knowledge;
the wise person listens to learn more.

devotion 180

PROVERBS 18:2

DON'T LISTEN TO A FOOL

Why would a fool not want to understand anything? The answer? He thinks he knows it all. The scary thing is that fools can be very religious people. Look up Luke 12:1-3. Jesus said the religious men of his day were hypocrites because they told everyone else how to live their lives, but in secret they lived any way they wanted to. Jesus also told his followers to beware of the Pharisees' yeast, which might sound strange, but he was saying that in the same way yeast has a dramatic effect on bread dough, following the words and actions of the Pharisees would have a dramatically *negative* effect on anyone who listened to these religious hypocrites.

We need to be discerning Christians. Don't listen to everything you hear as if it is coming from God. Christians are human and they can make mistakes. Sometimes well-meaning Christians speak out of ignorance or pride. When someone's words wrongly discourage us, they can keep us from doing what God has called us to do. In the same manner, when someone pressures us to be something we were never meant to be, it can cause us to want to give up on God. Jesus came to earth so that we could have a relationship with God without having to go through someone else. He wants you to hear his words with your own ears. Spend time listening to him everyday by spending time in his Word. The Bible will help any fool understand.

16 Taking gifts to important people
will help get you in to see them.

17 The person who tells one side of a story
seems right,
until someone else comes and asks
questions.

18 Throwing lots can settle arguments
and keep the two sides from fighting.

19 A brother who has been insulted is harder
to win back than a walled city,
and arguments separate people like the
barred gates of a palace.

20 People will be rewarded for what they say;
they will be rewarded by how they
speak.

21 What you say can mean life or death.
Those who speak with care will be
rewarded.

22 When a man finds a wife, he finds
something good.
It shows that the LORD is pleased with
him.

23 The poor beg for mercy,
but the rich give rude answers.

24 Some friends may ruin you,
but a real friend will be more loyal than
a brother.

19 It is better to be poor and honest
than to be foolish and tell lies.

2 Enthusiasm without knowledge is not
good.
If you act too quickly, you might make
a mistake.

3 People's own foolishness ruins their
lives,
but in their minds they blame the LORD.

4 Wealthy people are always finding more
friends,
but the poor lose all theirs.

5A witness who lies will not go free;
liars will never escape.

6Many people want to please a leader,
and everyone is friends with those who give gifts.

7Poor people's relatives avoid them;
even their friends stay far away.
They run after them, begging,
but they are gone.

8Those who get wisdom do themselves a favor,
and those who love learning will succeed.

9A witness who lies will not go free,
liars will die.

10A fool should not live in luxury.
A slave should not rule over princes.

11The wise are patient;
they will be honored if they ignore insults.

12An angry king is like a roaring lion,
but his kindness is like the dew on the grass.

13A foolish child brings disaster to a father,
and a quarreling wife is like dripping water.

14Houses and wealth are inherited from parents,
but a wise wife is a gift from the LORD.

15Lazy people sleep a lot,
and idle people will go hungry.

16Those who obey the commands protect themselves,
but those who are careless will die.

17Being kind to the poor is like lending to the LORD;
he will reward you for what you have done.

18Correct your children while there is still hope;
do not let them destroy themselves.

19People with quick tempers will have to pay for it.
If you help them out once, you will have to do it again.

20Listen to advice and accept correction,
and in the end you will be wise.

21People can make all kinds of plans,
but only the LORD's plan will happen.

22People want others to be loyal,
so it is better to be poor than to be a liar.

23Those who respect the LORD will live
and be satisfied, unbothered by trouble.

24Though the lazy person puts his hand in the dish,
he won't lift the food to his mouth.

25Whip those who make fun of wisdom,
and perhaps foolish people will gain some wisdom.
Correct those with understanding, and they will gain knowledge.

26A child who robs his father and sends away his mother
brings shame and disgrace on himself.

27Don't stop listening to correction, my child,
or you will forget what you have already learned.

28An evil witness makes fun of fairness,
and wicked people love what is evil.

29People who make fun of wisdom will be punished,
and the backs of foolish people will be beaten.

20 Wine and beer make people loud and uncontrolled;
it is not wise to get drunk on them.

2An angry king is like a roaring lion.
Making him angry may cost you your life.

3Foolish people are always fighting,
but avoiding quarrels will bring you honor.

4Lazy farmers don't plow when they should;
they expect a harvest, but there is none.

5People's thoughts can be like a deep well,
but someone with understanding can find the wisdom there.

6Many people claim to be loyal,
but it is hard to find a trustworthy person.

7The good people who live honest lives
will be a blessing to their children.

8When a king sits on his throne to judge,
he knows evil when he sees it.

9No one can say, "I am innocent;
I have never done anything wrong."

10The LORD hates both these things:
dishonest weights and dishonest measures.

11Even children are known by their behavior;
their actions show if they are innocent and good.

12The LORD has made both these things:
ears to hear and eyes to see.

13If you love to sleep, you will be poor.
If you stay awake, you will have plenty of food.

14Buyers say, "This is bad. It's no good."
Then they go away and brag about what they bought.

15There is gold and plenty of rubies,
but only a few people speak with knowledge.

16Take the coat of someone who promises to pay a stranger's debts,
and keep it until he pays what the stranger owes.

17Stolen food may taste sweet at first,
but later it will feel like a mouth full of gravel.

18Get advice if you want your plans to work.
If you go to war, get the advice of others.

19Gossips can't keep secrets,
so avoid people who talk too much.

20Those who curse their father or mother
will be like a light going out in darkness.

21Wealth inherited quickly in the beginning
will do you no good in the end.

22Don't say, "I'll pay you back for the wrong you did."
Wait for the LORD, and he will make things right.

23The LORD hates dishonest weights,
and dishonest scales do not please him.

24The LORD decides what a person will do;
no one understands what his life is all about.

25It's dangerous to promise something to God too quickly.
After you've thought about it, it may be too late.

26A wise king sorts out the evil people,
and he punishes them as they deserve.

27The LORD looks deep inside people
and searches through their thoughts.

28Loyalty and truth keep a king in power;
he continues to rule if he is loyal.

29The young glory in their strength,
and the old are honored for their gray hair.

30Hard punishment will get rid of evil,
and whippings can change an evil heart.

21

The LORD can control a king's mind as he controls a river;
he can direct it as he pleases.

2You may believe you are doing right,
but the LORD judges your reasons.

3Doing what is right and fair
is more important to the LORD than sacrifices.

4Proud looks, proud thoughts,
and evil actions are sin.

5The plans of hard-working people earn a profit,
but those who act too quickly become poor.

6Wealth that comes from telling lies
vanishes like a mist and leads to death.

7The violence of the wicked will destroy them,
because they refuse to do what is right.

8Guilty people live dishonest lives,
but honest people do right.

9 It is better to live in a corner on the roof[n]
than inside the house with a quarreling wife.
10 Evil people only want to harm others.
Their neighbors get no mercy from them.
11 If you punish those who make fun of wisdom, a foolish person may gain some wisdom.
But if you teach the wise, they will get knowledge.
12 God, who is always right, watches the house of the wicked
and brings ruin on every evil person.
13 Whoever ignores the poor when they cry for help
will also cry for help and not be answered.
14 A secret gift will calm an angry person;
a present given in secrecy will quiet great anger.
15 When justice is done, good people are happy,
but evil people are ruined.
16 Whoever does not use good sense
will end up among the dead.
17 Whoever loves pleasure will become poor;
whoever loves wine and perfume will never be rich.
18 Wicked people will suffer instead of good people,
and those who cannot be trusted will suffer instead of those who do right.
19 It is better to live alone in the desert
than with a quarreling and complaining wife.
20 Wise people's houses are full of the best foods and olive oil,
but fools waste everything they have.
21 Whoever tries to live right and be loyal
finds life, success, and honor.
22 A wise person can defeat a city full of warriors
and tear down the defenses they trust in.
23 Those who are careful about what they say
keep themselves out of trouble.
24 People who act with stubborn pride
are called "proud," "bragger," and "mocker."
25 Lazy people's desire for sleep will kill them,
because they refuse to work.
26 All day long they wish for more,
but good people give without holding back.
27 The LORD hates sacrifices brought by evil people,
particularly when they offer them for the wrong reasons.
28 A lying witness will be forgotten,
but a truthful witness will speak on.
29 Wicked people are stubborn,
but good people think carefully about what they do.
30 There is no wisdom, understanding, or advice
that can succeed against the LORD.
31 You can get the horses ready for battle,
but it is the LORD who gives the victory.

22 Being respected is more important than having great riches.
To be well thought of is better than silver or gold.
2 The rich and the poor are alike
in that the LORD made them all.
3 The wise see danger ahead and avoid it,
but fools keep going and get into trouble.
4 Respecting the LORD and not being proud
will bring you wealth, honor, and life.
5 Evil people's lives are like paths covered with thorns and traps.
People who guard themselves don't have such problems.

21:9 roof In Bible times houses were built with flat roofs. The roof was used for drying things such as flax and fruit. And it was used as an extra room, as a place for worship, and as a cool place to sleep in the summer.

6 Train children to live the right way,
and when they are old, they will not stray from it.

7 The rich rule over the poor,
and borrowers are servants to lenders.

8 Those who plan evil will receive trouble.
Their cruel anger will come to an end.

9 Generous people will be blessed,
because they share their food with the poor.

10 Get rid of the one who makes fun of wisdom.
Then fighting, quarrels, and insults will stop.

11 Whoever loves pure thoughts and kind words
will have even the king as a friend.

12 The LORD guards knowledge,
but he destroys false words.

13 The lazy person says, "There's a lion outside!
I might get killed out in the street!"

14 The words of an unfaithful wife are like a deep trap.
Those who make the LORD angry will get caught by them.

15 Every child is full of foolishness,
but punishment can get rid of it.

16 Whoever gets rich by mistreating the poor,
and gives presents to the wealthy, will become poor.

Other Wise Sayings

17 Listen carefully to what wise people say;
pay attention to what I am teaching you.

18 It will be good to keep these things in mind
so that you are ready to repeat them.

devotion 181

PROVERBS 22:6

HOPE FOR PARENTS

What if you've done everything you know to do to train your children, but they've chosen a different path? You read the books. You prayed for them and taught them how to pray for themselves. You modeled right living, poured good things into their spirits, disciplined with appropriate authority, and loved them like crazy. What if you've done your best, and still they live rebelliously? Do you somehow believe it's your fault? Do you wonder if there was something you could have done differently because this proverb isn't working for you? If so, you may read Proverbs 22:6 and feel the brokenhearted weight of guilt.

But take heart. Remember, a proverb is a general truth. Here is the essence of this verse: parents are responsible for training. God takes our parenting tasks seriously and expects us to do likewise. And generally, when the right living has been modeled and the right training has happened, children return to their training, even when they are old. But Scripture also teaches personal responsibility. A child becomes an adult who is responsible for the truths they've been taught. The father of the prodigal wasn't blamed for his son's recklessness. Joseph's parents weren't held accountable for his brothers being scoundrels.

Let us train our children with all our hearts, and then let's entrust them to the Lord, begging him to make them responsible. A godly mother may be brokenhearted for her rebellious child, but she doesn't have to carry a guilt that comes from misunderstanding this verse.

19I am teaching them to you now
so that you will put your trust in the
LORD.
20I have written thirty sayings for you,
which give knowledge and good advice.
21I am teaching you true and reliable words
so that you can give true answers to
anyone who asks.

22Do not abuse poor people because they
are poor,
and do not take away the rights of the
needy in court.
23The LORD will defend them in court
and will take the life of those who take
away their rights.

24Don't make friends with quick-tempered
people
or spend time with those who have bad
tempers.
25If you do, you will be like them.
Then you will be in real danger.

26Don't promise to pay what someone else
owes,
and don't guarantee anyone's loan.
27If you cannot pay the loan,
your own bed may be taken right out
from under you.

28Don't move an old stone that marks a
border,
because those stones were set up by
your ancestors.
29Do you see people skilled in their work?
They will work for kings, not for
ordinary people.

23 If you sit down to eat with a ruler,
notice the food that is in front of
you.
2Control yourself
if you have a big appetite.
3Don't be greedy for his fine foods,
because that food might be a trick.
4Don't wear yourself out trying to get rich;
be wise enough to control yourself.
5Wealth can vanish in the wink of an eye.
It can seem to grow wings
and fly away like an eagle.

6Don't eat the food of selfish people;
don't be greedy for their fine foods.
7Selfish people are always worrying
about how much the food costs.
They tell you, "Eat and drink,"
but they don't really mean it.
8You will throw up the little you have eaten,
and you will have wasted your kind
words.

9Don't speak to fools;
they will only ignore your wise words.

10Don't move an old stone that marks a
border,
and don't take fields that belong to
orphans.
11God, their defender, is strong;
he will take their side against you.

12Remember what you are taught,
and listen carefully to words of
knowledge.

13Don't fail to punish children.
If you spank them, they won't die.
14If you spank them,
you will save them from death.

15My child, if you are wise,
then I will be happy.
16I will be so pleased
if you speak what is right.

17Don't envy sinners,
but always respect the LORD.
18Then you will have hope for the future,
and your wishes will come true.

19Listen, my child, and be wise.
Keep your mind on what is right.
20Don't drink too much wine
or eat too much food.
21Those who drink and eat too much
become poor.
They sleep too much and end up
wearing rags.

22Listen to your father, who gave you life,
and do not forget your mother when
she is old.
23Learn the truth and never reject it.
Get wisdom, self-control, and
understanding.
24The father of a good child is very happy;
parents who have wise children are
glad because of them.
25Make your father and mother happy;
give your mother a reason to be glad.

26My son, pay attention to me,
and watch closely what I do.

27A prostitute is as dangerous as a deep pit,
and an unfaithful wife is like a narrow well.
28They ambush you like robbers
and cause many men to be unfaithful to their wives.

29Who has trouble? Who has pain?
Who fights? Who complains?
Who has unnecessary bruises?
Who has bloodshot eyes?
30It is people who drink too much wine,
who try out all different kinds of strong drinks.
31Don't stare at the wine when it is red,
when it sparkles in the cup,
when it goes down smoothly.
32Later it bites like a snake
with poison in its fangs.
33Your eyes will see strange sights,
and your mind will be confused.
34You will feel dizzy as if you're in a storm on the ocean,
as if you're on top of a ship's sails.
35You will think, "They hit me, but I'm not hurt.
They beat me up, but I don't remember it.
I wish I could wake up.
Then I would get another drink."

24 Don't envy evil people
or try to be friends with them.
2Their minds are always planning violence,
and they always talk about making trouble.

3It takes wisdom to have a good family,
and it takes understanding to make it strong.
4It takes knowledge to fill a home
with rare and beautiful treasures.

5Wise people have great power,
and those with knowledge have great strength.
6So you need advice when you go to war.
If you have lots of good advice, you will win.

7Foolish people cannot understand wisdom.
They have nothing to say in a discussion.

devotion 182

PROVERBS 24:3–4

TAKE FIVE STEPS TOWARD WISDOM

The Book of Proverbs is an amazing book of life instruction. Solomon, who recorded many of the proverbs, said that those who choose disobedience suffer consequences and those who obey wisdom receive blessings. He esteemed the importance of wisdom and reminded us to do whatever it takes to become wise in the counsel of God. But how? How in the world do I just go out and find wisdom? And while we're at it, where do I start?

First, desire wisdom. What is valuable to God must become valuable to you. Push away from foolishness and turn toward godly understanding. Second, study wisdom, both in the written Word and in the lives of women and men around you. When you come across wisdom, stop, take it in, and learn from the words or the person. Third, pray. God says if any of us need wisdom, we should ask him for it (James 1:5). The wisdom that gives help will come to you as a supernatural gift from God. Fourth, remember eternity. Remind yourself that this life is just a vapor compared to the eternity God has prepared for us. When you are tempted to act or think like the world, remember what matters for eternity. And fifth, run to Jesus. To know Jesus is to know wisdom. To see his character is to see how wisdom responds. To imitate his heart is to live in Christ's wisdom.

My sister, pursue wisdom and watch your life be filled with rare and beautiful treasures.

[8]Whoever makes evil plans
will be known as a troublemaker.
[9]Making foolish plans is sinful,
and making fun of wisdom is hateful.

[10]If you give up when trouble comes,
it shows that you are weak.

[11]Save those who are being led to their death;
rescue those who are about to be killed.
[12]If you say, "We don't know anything about this,"
God, who knows what's in your mind, will notice.
He is watching you, and he will know.
He will reward each person for what he has done.

[13]My child, eat honey because it is good.
Honey from the honeycomb tastes sweet.
[14]In the same way, wisdom is pleasing to you.
If you find it, you have hope for the future,
and your wishes will come true.

[15]Don't be wicked and attack a good family's house;
don't rob the place where they live.
[16]Even though good people may be bothered by trouble seven times,
they are never defeated,
but the wicked are overwhelmed by trouble.

[17]Don't be happy when your enemy is defeated;
don't be glad when he is overwhelmed.
[18]The LORD will notice and be displeased.
He may not be angry with them anymore.

[19]Don't envy evil people,
and don't be jealous of the wicked.
[20]An evil person has nothing to hope for;
the wicked will die like a flame that is put out.
[21]My child, respect the LORD and the king.
Don't join those people who refuse to obey them.
[22]The LORD and the king will quickly destroy such people.
Those two can cause great disaster!

More Words of Wisdom

[23]These are also sayings of the wise:
It is not good to take sides when you are the judge.
[24]Don't tell the wicked that they are innocent;
people will curse you, and nations will hate you.
[25]But things will go well if you punish the guilty,
and you will receive rich blessings.

[26]An honest answer is as pleasing
as a kiss on the lips.

[27]First, finish your outside work
and prepare your fields.
After that, you can build your house.

[28]Don't testify against your neighbor for no good reason.
Don't say things that are false.
[29]Don't say, "I'll get even;
I'll do to him what he did to me."

[30]I passed by a lazy person's field
and by the vineyard of someone with no sense.
[31]Thorns had grown up everywhere.
The ground was covered with weeds,
and the stone walls had fallen down.
[32]I thought about what I had seen;
I learned this lesson from what I saw.
[33]You sleep a little; you take a nap.
You fold your hands and lie down to rest.
[34]Soon you will be as poor as if you had been robbed;
you will have as little as if you had been held up.

More Wise Sayings of Solomon

25 These are more wise sayings of Solomon, copied by the men of Hezekiah king of Judah.

[2]God is honored for what he keeps secret.
Kings are honored for what they can discover.

[3]No one can measure the height of the skies or the depth of the earth.
So also no one can understand the mind of a king.

5Answer fools when they speak foolishly,
or they will think they are really wise.

6Sending a message by a foolish person
is like cutting off your feet or drinking poison.

7A wise saying spoken by a fool
is as useless as the legs of a crippled person.

8Giving honor to a foolish person
is like tying a stone in a slingshot.

9A wise saying spoken by a fool
is like a thorn stuck in the hand of a drunk.

10Hiring a foolish person or anyone just passing by
is like an archer shooting at just anything.

11A fool who repeats his foolishness
is like a dog that goes back to what it has thrown up.

12There is more hope for a foolish person
than for those who think they are wise.

13The lazy person says, "There's a lion in the road!
There's a lion in the streets!"

14Like a door turning back and forth on its hinges,
the lazy person turns over and over in bed.

15Lazy people may put their hands in the dish,
but they are too tired to lift the food to their mouths.

16The lazy person thinks he is wiser
than seven people who give sensible answers.

17Interfering in someone else's quarrel as you pass by
is like grabbing a dog by the ears.

18Like a madman shooting
deadly, burning arrows
19is the one who tricks a neighbor
and then says, "I was just joking."

20Without wood, a fire will go out,
and without gossip, quarreling will stop.

21Just as charcoal and wood keep a fire going,
a quarrelsome person keeps an argument going.

22The words of a gossip are like tasty bits of food;
people like to gobble them up.

23Kind words from a wicked mind
are like a shiny coating on a clay pot.

24Those who hate you may try to fool you with their words,
but in their minds they are planning evil.

25People's words may be kind, but don't believe them,
because their minds are full of evil thoughts.

26Lies can hide hate,
but the evil will be plain to everyone.

27Whoever digs a pit for others will fall into it.
Whoever tries to roll a boulder down on others will be crushed by it.

28Liars hate the people they hurt,
and false praise can ruin others.

27 Don't brag about tomorrow;
you don't know what may happen then.

2Don't praise yourself. Let someone else do it.
Let the praise come from a stranger and not from your own mouth.

3Stone is heavy, and sand is weighty,
but a complaining fool is worse than either.

4Anger is cruel and destroys like a flood,
but no one can put up with jealousy!

5It is better to correct someone openly
than to have love and not show it.

6The slap of a friend can be trusted to help you,
but the kisses of an enemy are nothing but lies.

7When you are full, not even honey tastes good,
but when you are hungry, even something bitter tastes sweet.

4 Remove the scum from the silver,
so the silver can be used by the silversmith.
5 Remove wicked people from the king's presence;
then his government will be honest and last a long time.

6 Don't brag to the king
and act as if you are great.
7 It is better for him to give you a higher position
than to bring you down in front of the prince.

Because of something you have seen,
8 do not quickly take someone to court.
What will you do later
when your neighbor proves you wrong?

9 If you have an argument with your neighbor,
don't tell other people what was said.
10 Whoever hears it might shame you,
and you might not ever be respected again.
11 The right word spoken at the right time
is as beautiful as gold apples in a silver bowl.

12 A wise warning to someone who will listen
is as valuable as gold earrings or fine gold jewelry.
13 Trustworthy messengers refresh those who send them,
like the coolness of snow in the summertime.

14 People who brag about gifts they never give
are like clouds and wind that give no rain.

15 With patience you can convince a ruler,
and a gentle word can get through to the hard-headed.

16 If you find honey, don't eat too much,
or it will make you throw up.
17 Don't go to your neighbor's house too often;
too much of you will make him hate you.

18 When you lie about your neighbors,
it hurts them as much as a club, a sword, or a sharp arrow.

19 Trusting unfaithful people when you are in trouble
is like eating with a broken tooth or walking with a crippled foot.

20 Singing songs to someone who is sad
is like taking away his coat on a cold day
or pouring vinegar on soda.

21 If your enemy is hungry, feed him.
If he is thirsty, give him a drink.
22 Doing this will be like pouring burning coals on his head,
and the LORD will reward you.

23 As the north wind brings rain,
telling gossip brings angry looks.

24 It is better to live in a corner on the roof[n]
than inside the house with a quarreling wife.

25 Good news from a faraway place
is like a cool drink when you are tired.

26 A good person who gives in to evil
is like a muddy spring or a dirty well.

27 It is not good to eat too much honey,
nor does it bring you honor to brag about yourself.

28 Those who do not control themselves
are like a city whose walls are broken down.

26 It shouldn't snow in summer or rain at harvest.
Neither should a foolish person ever be honored.

2 Curses will not harm someone who is innocent;
they are like sparrows or swallows that fly around and never land.

3 Whips are for horses, and harnesses are for donkeys,
so paddles are good for fools.

4 Don't answer fools when they speak foolishly,
or you will be just like them.

25:24 roof In Bible times houses were built with flat roofs. The roof was used for drying things such as flax and fruit. And it was used as an extra room, as a place for worship, and as a cool place to sleep in the summer.

[8]A person who leaves his home
is like a bird that leaves its nest.

[9]The sweet smell of perfume and oils is
pleasant,
and so is good advice from a friend.

[10]Don't forget your friend or your parent's
friend.
Don't always go to your family for help
when trouble comes.
A neighbor close by is better than a
family far away.

[11]Be wise, my child, and make me happy.
Then I can respond to any insult.

[12]The wise see danger ahead and avoid it,
but fools keep going and get into
trouble.

[13]Take the coat of someone who promises
to pay a stranger's loan,
and keep it until he pays what the
stranger owes.

[14]If you loudly greet your neighbor early in
the morning,
he will think of it as a curse.

[15]A quarreling wife is as bothersome
as a continual dripping on a rainy day.
[16]Stopping her is like stopping the wind
or trying to grab oil in your hand.

[17]As iron sharpens iron,
so people can improve each other.
[18]Whoever tends a fig tree gets to eat its
fruit,
and whoever takes care of his master
will receive honor.

[19]As water reflects your face,
so your mind shows what kind of
person you are.

[20]People will never stop dying and being
destroyed,
and they will never stop wanting more
than they have.
[21]A hot furnace tests silver and gold,
and people are tested by the praise they
receive.

[22]Even if you ground up a foolish person
like grain in a bowl,
you couldn't remove the foolishness.

devotion 183

PROVERBS 27:17

WHERE ARE YOU IN THE PACK?

Sometimes you just have to stop where you are, look around your life, and take inventory of the people who have permission to be there. You didn't get to choose some of the folks in your life, but you do get to choose who will speak into your heart, who will give you counsel, and who will help you run faster toward God.

They say that you pace yourself according to the people you run beside. If you are back in the pack of slow runners, then guess what—you are pacing slow. But if you set your stride alongside someone who is pursuing the Lord with passion, then you both pick up the pace. Their iron is sharpening your iron. Today might be a good day to examine your friendships. Are you being held back in the pack of "slow runners" when your soul longs to pull away from the pack and quicken the pace?

To become a godly woman, you will have to guard your heart from women who do not pursue the counsel of God. You will need to step back from those who aren't really hungry for God and detach from the women who discourage or lead you astray. It might mean that you stop seeking someone's input and consciously turn to someone else for strength and wisdom.

A godly friend will make you a better woman. I'm not sure that great spiritual depth will be attained without the sharpening she will bring into your life.

23 Be sure you know how your sheep are
doing,
and pay attention to the condition of
your cattle.
24 Riches will not go on forever,
nor do governments go on forever.
25 Bring in the hay, and let the new grass
appear.
Gather the grass from the hills.
26 Make clothes from the lambs' wool,
and sell some goats to buy a field.
27 There will be plenty of goat's milk
to feed you and your family
and to make your servant girls healthy.

28 Evil people run even though no one is
chasing them,
but good people are as brave as a lion.

2 When a country is lawless, it has one
ruler after another;
but when it is led by a leader with
understanding and knowledge, it
continues strong.

3 Rulers who mistreat the poor
are like a hard rain that destroys the
crops.

4 Those who disobey what they have been
taught praise the wicked,
but those who obey what they have
been taught are against them.

5 Evil people do not understand justice,
but those who follow the LORD
understand it completely.

6 It is better to be poor and innocent
than to be rich and wicked.

7 Children who obey what they have been
taught are wise,
but friends of troublemakers disgrace
their parents.

8 Some people get rich by overcharging
others,
but their wealth will be given to those
who are kind to the poor.

9 If you refuse to obey what you have been
taught,
your prayers will not be heard.

10 Those who lead good people to do
wrong
will be ruined by their own evil,
but the innocent will be rewarded with
good things.

11 Rich people may think they are wise,
but the poor with understanding will
prove them wrong.

12 When good people triumph, there is great
happiness,
but when the wicked get control,
everybody hides.

13 If you hide your sins, you will not
succeed.
If you confess and reject them, you will
receive mercy.

14 Those who are always respectful will be
happy,
but those who are stubborn will get
into trouble.

15 A wicked ruler is as dangerous to poor
people
as a roaring lion or a charging bear.

16 A ruler without wisdom will be cruel,
but the one who refuses to take
dishonest money will rule a long
time.

17 Don't help those who are guilty of
murder;
let them run until they die.

18 Innocent people will be kept safe,
but those who are dishonest will
suddenly be ruined.

19 Those who work their land will have
plenty of food,
but the ones who chase empty dreams
instead will end up poor.

20 A truthful person will have many
blessings,
but those eager to get rich will be
punished.

21 It is not good for a judge to take sides,
but some will sin for only a piece of
bread.

22 Selfish people are in a hurry to get rich
and do not realize they soon will be
poor.

23 Those who correct others will later be
liked
more than those who give false praise.

24 Whoever robs father or mother
and says, "It's not wrong,"
is just like someone who destroys things.

25 A greedy person causes trouble,
but the one who trusts the LORD will
succeed.

26 Those who trust in themselves are
foolish,
but those who live wisely will be kept
safe.

27 Whoever gives to the poor will have
everything he needs,
but the one who ignores the poor will
receive many curses.

28 When the wicked get control, everybody
hides,
but when they die, good people do well.

29 Whoever is stubborn after being
corrected many times
will suddenly be hurt beyond cure.

2 When good people do well, everyone is
happy,
but when evil people rule, everyone
groans.

3 Those who love wisdom make their
parents happy,
but friends of prostitutes waste their
money.

4 If a king is fair, he makes his country
strong,
but if he takes gifts dishonestly, he tears
his country down.

5 Those who give false praise to their
neighbors
are setting a trap for them.

6 Evil people are trapped by their own sin,
but good people can sing and be happy.

7 Good people care about justice for the
poor,
but the wicked are not concerned.

8 People who make fun of wisdom cause
trouble in a city,
but wise people calm anger down.

9 When a wise person takes a foolish
person to court,
the fool only shouts or laughs, and
there is no peace.

10 Murderers hate an honest person
and try to kill those who do right.

11 Foolish people lose their tempers,
but wise people control theirs.

12 If a ruler pays attention to lies,
all his officers will become wicked.

13 The poor person and the cruel person are
alike
in that the LORD gave eyes to both of
them.

14 If a king judges poor people fairly,
his government will continue forever.

15 Correction and punishment make
children wise,
but those left alone will disgrace their
mother.

16 When there are many wicked people,
there is much sin,
but those who do right will see them
destroyed.

17 Correct your children, and you will be
proud;
they will give you satisfaction.

18 Where there is no word from God, people
are uncontrolled,
but those who obey what they have
been taught are happy.

19 Words alone cannot correct a servant,
because even if they understand, they
won't respond.

20 Do you see people who speak too quickly?
There is more hope for a foolish person
than for them.

21 If you spoil your servants when they are
young,
they will bring you grief later on.

22 An angry person causes trouble;
a person with a quick temper sins a lot.

23 Pride will ruin people,
but those who are humble will be
honored.

24 Partners of thieves are their own worst
enemies.
If they have to testify in court, they are
afraid to say anything.

25 Being afraid of people can get you into
trouble,

The Proverbs 31 Woman

Hers is a large household with much to do, so she rises early to prepare breakfast. She is not sluggish in her work but labors with energy and strength, knowing that laziness will not feed her children. After her sons and daughters are in bed, she sits at the loom and weaves into the night. It is a time-consuming task—it seems the spindle and distaff never leave her hands. But she likes the work and knows she can sell her fabrics at market for a good price. It's not that they're cramped for money; her husband is one of the leaders of the land. But she doesn't rest on her laurels.

Her children respect her. She speaks with wisdom and teaches them how to be kind, always treating them as she teaches them to treat others. Raising the children is a daunting task, but she looks to the future with joy. She knows there will be the blessing of sweet kisses from grandchildren. She looks forward to growing old with her husband.

She doesn't let her busyness take her eyes off the poor. She helps the needy as she can. She can't do everything, but she is wise and knows that time is too precious to waste. Her husband's praise falls sweetly on her ears: "There are many fine women, but you are better than all of them." And with that, she slips into bed and falls asleep.

Do you use your time wisely?

but if you trust the LORD, you will be
safe.
26Many people want to speak to a ruler,
but justice comes only from the LORD.
27Good people hate those who are
dishonest,
and the wicked hate those who are
honest.

Wise Words from Agur

30 These are the words of Agur son of
Jakeh.
This is his message to Ithiel and Ucal:
2"I am the most stupid person there is,
and I have no understanding.
3I have not learned to be wise,
and I don't know much about God, the
Holy One.
4Who has gone up to heaven and come
back down?
Who can hold the wind in his hand?
Who can gather up the waters in his coat?
Who has set in place the ends of the
earth?
What is his name or his son's name?
Tell me, if you know!

5"Every word of God is true.
He guards those who come to him for
safety.
6Do not add to his words,
or he will correct you and prove you are
a liar.

7"I ask two things from you, LORD.
Don't refuse me before I die.
8Keep me from lying and being dishonest.
And don't make me either rich or poor;
just give me enough food for each day.
9If I have too much, I might reject you
and say, 'I don't know the LORD.'
If I am poor, I might steal
and disgrace the name of my God.

10"Do not say bad things about servants to
their masters,
or they will curse you, and you will
suffer for it.

11"Some people curse their fathers
and do not bless their mothers.
12Some people think they are pure,
but they are not really free from evil.
13Some people have such a proud look!
They look down on others.

14Some people have teeth like swords;
their jaws seem full of knives.
They want to remove the poor from the earth
and the needy from the land.

15"Greed has two daughters
named 'Give' and 'Give.'
There are three things that are never satisfied,
really four that never say, 'I've had enough!':
16the cemetery, the childless mother,
the land that never gets enough rain,
and fire that never says, 'I've had enough!'

17"If you make fun of your father
and refuse to obey your mother,
the birds of the valley will peck out your eyes,
and the vultures will eat them.

18"There are three things that are too hard for me,
really four I don't understand:
19the way an eagle flies in the sky,
the way a snake slides over a rock,
the way a ship sails on the sea,
and the way a man and a woman fall in love.

20"This is the way of a woman who takes part in adultery:
She acts as if she had eaten and washed her face;
she says, 'I haven't done anything wrong.'

21"There are three things that make the earth tremble,
really four it cannot stand:
22a servant who becomes a king,
a foolish person who has plenty to eat,
23a hated woman who gets married,
and a maid who replaces her mistress.

24"There are four things on earth that are small,
but they are very wise:
25Ants are not very strong,
but they store up food in the summer.
26Rock badgers are not very powerful,
but they can live among the rocks.
27Locusts have no king,
but they all go forward in formation.
28Lizards can be caught in the hand,
but they are found even in kings' palaces.

29"There are three things that strut proudly,
really four that walk as if they were important:
30a lion, the proudest animal,
which is strong and runs from nothing,
31a rooster, a male goat,
and a king when his army is around him.

32"If you have been foolish and proud,
or if you have planned evil, shut your mouth.
33Just as stirring milk makes butter,
and twisting noses makes them bleed,
so stirring up anger causes trouble."

Wise Words of King Lemuel

31 These are the words of King Lemuel,
the message his mother taught him:
2"My son, I gave birth to you.
You are the son I prayed for.
3Don't waste your strength on women
or your time on those who ruin kings.

4"Kings should not drink wine, Lemuel,
and rulers should not desire beer.
5If they drink, they might forget the law
and keep the needy from getting their rights.
6Give beer to people who are dying
and wine to those who are sad.
7Let them drink and forget their need
and remember their misery no more.

8"Speak up for those who cannot speak for themselves;
defend the rights of all those who have nothing.
9Speak up and judge fairly,
and defend the rights of the poor and needy."

The Good Wife

10It is hard to find a good wife,
because she is worth more than rubies.
11Her husband trusts her completely.
With her, he has everything he needs.
12She does him good and not harm
for as long as she lives.
13She looks for wool and flax
and likes to work with her hands.
14She is like a trader's ship,

devotion 184

PROVERBS 31:30

PLEASING GOD

Proverbs 31 will strike fear into any woman's heart. When one of my daughters was twelve years old, I took her to a Women of Faith Conference. There was a comedian who did a skit about the different hats we wear as women. The hats were too numerous for her to handle with grace, and the skit was hilarious because every wife and mother feels that way at times. On our way home that night, my daughter asked me if the skit really portrayed what it is like to be a wife and mother. "Yes," I said with a smile, "at times it can feel overwhelming."

"Oh, mom," she said with fear in her voice, "I'll never be able to do it all." She didn't think the skit was funny at all.

The one comforting thought about the Proverbs 31 woman is that she wasn't a real woman. She was an *example* of a woman. The most important thing said about her in this proverb is that she respected the Lord. Everything that she did was done to the glory of God. I have to remind myself of this every day. I can get so caught up in pleasing my husband, pleasing my children, pleasing my family, and pleasing my friends that I forget to make sure that everything I do is pleasing to God. Tell God how much you respect him and try pleasing him today. Somehow, all the rest falls into place when you do.

bringing food from far away.
15 She gets up while it is still dark
and prepares food for her family
and feeds her servant girls.
16 She inspects a field and buys it.
With money she earned, she plants a vineyard.
17 She does her work with energy,
and her arms are strong.
18 She knows that what she makes is good.
Her lamp burns late into the night.
19 She makes thread with her hands
and weaves her own cloth.
20 She welcomes the poor
and helps the needy.
21 She does not worry about her family when it snows,
because they all have fine clothes to keep them warm.
22 She makes coverings for herself;
her clothes are made of linen and other expensive material.
23 Her husband is known at the city meetings,
where he makes decisions as one of the leaders of the land.
24 She makes linen clothes and sells them
and provides belts to the merchants.
25 She is strong and is respected by the people.
She looks forward to the future with joy.
26 She speaks wise words
and teaches others to be kind.
27 She watches over her family
and never wastes her time.
28 Her children speak well of her.
Her husband also praises her,
29 saying, "There are many fine women,
but you are better than all of them."
30 Charm can fool you, and beauty can trick you,
but a woman who respects the LORD should be praised.
31 Give her the reward she has earned;
she should be praised in public for what she has done.

Ecclesiastes

From a Greek word meaning "the preacher"
This book is also one of the "Megilloth" or "five scrolls" that were read out loud during significant Jewish festivals. It was also read on the day of Pentecost.

Person Holding the Pen God Wrote With: The author was likely *Solomon*, especially in light of the author's description of himself as "a son of David, king in Jerusalem" (Eccl. 1:1). However, some scholars think the author was simply writing in Solomon's "voice" in an attempt to be more widely accepted.

When the Text Was Written: Probably late in Solomon's life, but certainly prior to his death in 931 B.C.

Spiritual Posture of the Original Recipients: Ecclesiastes seems to be addressed to all of Israel during Solomon's monarchy. The language used conjures up the image of a teacher lecturing to a classroom of wide-eyed students. Better yet, picture a wise old sage holding court with a motley crew of disaffected college students in Starbucks.

Storyline Synopsis: Ecclesiastes is unique in biblical literature because of its "coffee house" philosophizing, heavenward glances, and musings about transcendence. (However, this writing style was rather common in the ancient Near East when Ecclesiastes was written.) The author ponders truths about God and life in general, asking big questions that don't always have black and white answers. The overall themes throughout the book are the vanity of human understanding and human undertakings. The bottom line from this Old Testament thinker is that God is in complete control of the universe, but the human mind is too dinky to really fathom the vastness of his plans and purposes.

A Moment Worth Discussing: The middle of this distinctive sermon (Eccl. 4:7–12) includes a message about the necessity of community. The preacher calls to attention the loneliness of driven people who sacrifice relationship for riches. This passage points to the futility of a "Lone Ranger" mentality and underscores the biblical macro-theme that people matter to God—and they should matter to us.

Interesting (But Likely to Be Overlooked) Character: The *seductress* who is so eloquently vilified in Ecclesiastes 7:26. Some people think she's the same trashy girl Solomon repeatedly warned young men about in Proverbs (2:16–19; 5:1–14; 6:24–29; 7:1–27).

1 These are the words of the Teacher, a son of David, king in Jerusalem.

2 The Teacher says,
"Useless! Useless!
Completely useless!
Everything is useless."

3 What do people really gain
from all the hard work they do here on earth?

Things Never Change

4 People live, and people die,
but the earth continues forever.
5 The sun rises, the sun sets,
and then it hurries back to where it rises again.
6 The wind blows to the south;
it blows to the north.
It blows from one direction and then another.
Then it turns around and repeats the same pattern, going nowhere.
7 All the rivers flow to the sea,
but the sea never becomes full.
8 Everything is boring,
so boring that you don't even want to talk about it.
Words come again and again to our ears,
but we never hear enough,
nor can we ever really see all we want to see.
9 All things continue the way they have been since the beginning.
What has happened will happen again;
there is nothing new here on earth.
10 Someone might say,
"Look, this is new,"
but really it has always been here.
It was here before we were.
11 People don't remember what happened long ago,
and in the future people will not remember what happens now.
Even later, other people will not remember what was done before them.

Does Wisdom Bring Happiness?

12 I, the Teacher, was king over Israel in
Jerusalem. 13 I decided to use my wisdom to
learn about everything that happens on
earth. I learned that God has given us
terrible things to face. 14 I looked at
everything done on earth and saw that it is
all useless, like chasing the wind.

15 If something is crooked,
you can't make it straight.
If something is missing,
you can't say it is there.

16 I said to myself, "I have become very wise
and am now wiser than anyone who ruled
Jerusalem before me. I know what wisdom
and knowledge really are." 17 So I decided to
find out about wisdom and knowledge and
also about foolish thinking, but this turned
out to be like chasing the wind.

18 With much wisdom comes much disappointment;
the person who gains more knowledge also gains more sorrow.

Does "Having Fun" Bring Happiness?

2 I said to myself, "I will try having fun. I
will enjoy myself." But I found that this
is also useless. 2 It is foolish to laugh all the
time, and having fun doesn't accomplish
anything. 3 I decided to cheer myself up with
wine while my mind was still thinking
wisely. I wanted to find a way to enjoy
myself and see what was good for people to
do during their few days of life.

Does Hard Work Bring Happiness?

4 Then I did great things: I built houses
and planted vineyards for myself. 5 I made
gardens and parks, and I planted all kinds of
fruit trees in them. 6 I made pools of water
for myself and used them to water my
growing trees. 7 I bought male and female
slaves, and slaves were also born in my
house. I had large herds and flocks, more
than anyone in Jerusalem had ever had
before. 8 I also gathered silver and gold for
myself, treasures from kings and other areas.
I had male and female singers and all the
women a man could ever want. 9 I became
very famous, even greater than anyone who
had lived in Jerusalem before me. My
wisdom helped me in all this.

10 Anything I saw and wanted, I got for myself;
I did not miss any pleasure I desired.
I was pleased with everything I did,
and this pleasure was the reward for all my hard work.
11 But then I looked at what I had done,
and I thought about all the hard work.

Suddenly I realized it was useless, like
chasing the wind.
There is nothing to gain from anything
we do here on earth.

Maybe Wisdom Is the Answer

12 Then I began to think again about being
wise,
and also about being foolish and doing
crazy things.
But after all, what more can anyone do?
He can't do more than what the other
king has already done.
13 I saw that being wise is certainly better
than being foolish,
just as light is better than darkness.
14 Wise people see where they are going,
but fools walk around in the dark.
Yet I saw that
both wise and foolish people end the
same way.
15 I thought to myself,
"What happens to a fool will happen to
me, too,
so what is the reward for being wise?"
I said to myself,
"Being wise is also useless."
16 The wise person and the fool
will both die,
and no one will remember either one for
long.
In the future, both will be forgotten.

Is There Real Happiness in Life?

17 So I hated life. It made me sad to think
that everything here on earth is useless, like
chasing the wind. 18 I hated all the things I
had worked for here on earth, because I
must leave them to someone who will live
after me. 19 Someone else will control
everything for which I worked so hard here
on earth, and I don't know if he will be wise
or foolish. This is also useless. 20 So I became
sad about all the hard work I had done here
on earth. 21 People can work hard using all
their wisdom, knowledge, and skill, but
they will die, and other people will get the
things for which they worked. They did not
do the work, but they will get everything.
This is also unfair and useless. 22 What do
people get for all their work and struggling
here on earth? 23 All of their lives their
work is full of pain and sorrow, and even at
night their minds don't rest. This is also
useless.

24 The best that people can do is eat,
drink, and enjoy their work. I saw that even
this comes from God, 25 because no one can
eat or enjoy life without him. 26 If people
please God, God will give them wisdom,
knowledge, and joy. But sinners will get only
the work of gathering and storing wealth
that they will have to give to the ones who
please God. So all their work is useless, like
chasing the wind.

There Is a Time for Everything

3 There is a time for everything,
and everything on earth has its special
season.
2 There is a time to be born
and a time to die.
There is a time to plant
and a time to pull up plants.
3 There is a time to kill
and a time to heal.
There is a time to destroy
and a time to build.
4 There is a time to cry
and a time to laugh.
There is a time to be sad
and a time to dance.
5 There is a time to throw away stones
and a time to gather them.
There is a time to hug
and a time not to hug.
6 There is a time to look for something
and a time to stop looking for it.
There is a time to keep things
and a time to throw things away.
7 There is a time to tear apart
and a time to sew together.
There is a time to be silent
and a time to speak.
8 There is a time to love
and a time to hate.
There is a time for war
and a time for peace.

God Controls His World

9 Do people really gain anything from
their work? 10 I saw the hard work God
has given people to do. 11 God has given
them a desire to know the future. He does
everything just right and on time, but people
can never completely understand what he is
doing. 12 So I realize that the best thing for

devotion 185

ECCLESIASTES 3:11

GOD ALWAYS COMES THROUGH

We often tell our teenagers that they will probably have to make the most important decisions in their lives with the least amount of information. In the next several years, they will be choosing their careers and their spouses and beginning their families. As parents, we do the best we can with raising our kids, and then we have to release them to the Lord. I have talked to so many parents of young adults who are heartbroken over some of the decisions their children have made. They feel guilty and somehow responsible for their children, and they are at a loss as to how to reach them.

Ecclesiastes 3:11 is such a comfort to those who are struggling with loved ones who have chosen to follow the world. "He does everything just right and on time." This is a promise. We can't understand all of God's ways, and we hate to see our loved ones suffer, but God has not abandoned you or them. He created us with a desire to know the future; however, he does not tell us the future so that we will depend on him. For those of you who wait for a prodigal child or even a spouse to come home, know the Lord is working in their lives. The Lord loves them even more than you do, and he knows how to reach them. As my father always says, "God always comes through. Sometimes it is 11:59 when he does, but he always comes through."

them is to be happy and enjoy themselves as
long as they live. [13]God wants all people to
eat and drink and be happy in their work,
which are gifts from God. [14]I know that
everything God does will continue forever.
People cannot add anything to what God has
done, and they cannot take anything away
from it. God does it this way to make people
respect him.

[15]What happens now has happened in the past,
and what will happen in the future has happened before.
God makes the same things happen again and again.

Unfairness on Earth

[16]I also saw this here on earth:
Where there should have been justice, there was evil;
where there should have been right, there was wrong.
[17]I said to myself,
God has planned a time for every thing and every action,
so he will judge both good people and bad.

[18]I decided that God leaves it the way it is
to test people and to show them they are just
like animals. [19]The same thing happens to
animals and to people; they both have the
same breath, so they both die. People are no
better off than the animals, because
everything is useless. [20]Both end up the
same way; both came from dust and both
will go back to dust. [21]Who can be sure that
the human spirit goes up to God and that
the spirit of an animal goes down into the
ground? [22]So I saw that the best thing people
can do is to enjoy their work, because that is
all they have. No one can help another
person see what will happen in the future.

Is It Better to Be Dead?

4 Again I saw all the people who were mistreated here on earth.

I saw their tears
and that they had no one to comfort them.
Cruel people had all the power,
and there was no one to comfort those they hurt.
2I decided that the dead
are better off than the living.
3But those who have never been born
are better off still;
they have not seen the evil
that is done here on earth.

Why Work So Hard?

4I realized the reason people work hard
and try to succeed: They are jealous of each
other. This, too, is useless, like chasing the
wind.

5Some say it is foolish to fold your hands
and do nothing,
because you will starve to death.
6Maybe so, but I say it is better to be content
with what little you have.
Otherwise, you will always be struggling
for more,
and that is like chasing the wind.

7Again I saw something here on earth that
was useless:
8I saw a man who had no family,
no son or brother.
He always worked hard
but was never satisfied with what he had.
He never asked himself, "For whom am I
working so hard?
Why don't I let myself enjoy life?"
This also is very sad and useless.

Friends and Family Give Strength

9Two people are better than one,
because they get more done by working together.
10If one falls down,
the other can help him up.
But it is bad for the person who is alone
and falls,
because no one is there to help.
11If two lie down together, they will be warm,
but a person alone will not be warm.
12An enemy might defeat one person,
but two people together can defend themselves;
a rope that is woven of three strings is
hard to break.

Fame and Power Are Useless

13A poor but wise boy is better than a
foolish but old king who doesn't listen to
advice. 14A boy became king. He had been
born poor in the kingdom and had even
gone to prison before becoming king. 15I
watched all the people who live on earth
follow him and make him their king.
16Many followed him at first, but later, they
did not like him, either. So fame and power
are useless, like chasing the wind.

Be Careful About Making Promises

5 Be careful when you go to worship at the
Temple. It is better to listen than to offer
foolish sacrifices without even knowing you
are doing wrong.

2Think before you speak,
and be careful about what you say to God.
God is in heaven,
and you are on the earth,
so say only a few words to God.
3The saying is true: Bad dreams come from
too much worrying,
and too many words come from foolish people.

4If you make a promise to God, don't be
slow to keep it. God is not happy with fools,
so give God what you promised. 5It is better
not to promise anything than to promise
something and not do it. 6Don't let your
words cause you to sin, and don't say to the
priest at the Temple, "I didn't mean what I
promised." If you do, God will become
angry with your words and will destroy
everything you have worked for. 7Many
useless promises are like so many dreams;
they mean nothing. You should respect
God.

Officers Cheat Each Other

8In some places you will see poor people
mistreated. Don't be surprised when they are
not treated fairly or given their rights. One
officer is cheated by a higher officer who in
turn is cheated by even higher officers. 9The
wealth of the country is divided up among
them all. Even the king makes sure he gets
his share of the profits.

Wealth Cannot Buy Happiness

10 Whoever loves money
will never have enough money;
Whoever loves wealth
will not be satisfied with it.
This is also useless.
11 The more wealth people have,
the more friends they have to help
spend it.
So what do people really gain?
They gain nothing except to look at
their riches.
12 Those who work hard sleep in peace;
it is not important if they eat little or
much.
But rich people worry about their
wealth
and cannot sleep.

13 I have seen real misery here on earth:
Money saved is a curse to its owners.
14 They lose it all in a bad deal
and have nothing to give to their children.
15 People come into this world with nothing,
and when they die they leave with
nothing.
In spite of all their hard work,
they leave just as they came.
16 This, too, is real misery:
They leave just as they came.
So what do they gain from chasing the
wind?
17 All they get are days full of sadness and
sorrow,
and they end up sick, defeated, and
angry.

Enjoy Your Life's Work

18 I have seen what is best for people here
on earth. They should eat and drink and
enjoy their work, because the life God has
given them on earth is short. 19 God gives
some people the ability to enjoy the wealth
and property he gives them, as well as the
ability to accept their state in life and enjoy
their work. 20 They do not worry about how
short life is, because God keeps them busy
with what they love to do.

6 I have seen something else wrong here
on earth that causes serious problems for
people. 2 God gives great wealth, riches, and
honor to some people; they have everything
they want. But God does not let them enjoy
such things; a stranger enjoys them instead.
This is useless and very wrong. 3 A man
might have a hundred children and live a

devotion 186

ECCLESIASTES 5:18

ENJOY THE JOURNEY

I love my life! God has blessed me with a sexy, godly husband that loves the Lord, a challenging but exciting job, and the ability to love people hardcore! In our Christian walk, my husband and I have taken the Lord's instructions for godly living literally. We love each other madly. We have been married for seventeen years and still laugh and really enjoy the life and ministry God has given to us. There are a lot of times when I am fully aware that there are those who wonder how we got to where we are together.

Rob and I traveled this life together by holding onto what the Lord spoke to us through his Word. When our finances were dire, he told us to test him with tithing and watch his blessing. We did and he blessed us. When we had fights, he told us not to sin in our anger, so we didn't and survived. When communication started to get a little sparse, he told us above all things to pray for one another, so we did and fell deeper in love. Each milestone in our walk required instruction from the Word and obedience from us both, and because of that heart, we have seen the best in each other. Do not miss out on the blessings that the Lord has for you right now! Walk with Jesus through this life and savor the taste of heaven he brings to each day on earth. Enjoy the journey!

long time, but what good is it if he can't
enjoy the good God gives him or have a
proper burial? I say a baby born dead is
better off than he is. 4A baby born dead is
useless. It returns to darkness without even a
name. 5That baby never saw the sun and
never knew anything, but it finds more rest
than that man. 6Even if he lives two
thousand years, he doesn't enjoy the good
God gives him. Everyone is going to the
same place.

7People work just to feed themselves,
but they never seem to get enough to
eat.
8In this way a wise person
is no better off than a fool.
Then, too, it does a poor person little
good
to know how to get along in life.
9It is better to see what you have
than to want more.
Wanting more is useless—
like chasing the wind.

Who Can Understand God's Plan?

10Whatever happens was planned long ago.
Everyone knows what people are like.
No one can argue with God,
who is stronger than anyone.
11The more you say,
the more useless it is.
What good does it do?

12People have only a few useless days of
life on the earth; their short life passes like a
shadow. Who knows what is best for them
while they live? Who can tell them what the
future will bring?

Some Benefits of Serious Thinking

7 It is better to have respect than good
perfume.
The day of death is better than the day of
birth.
2It is better to go to a funeral
than to a party.
We all must die,
and everyone living should think about
this.
3Sorrow is better than laughter,
and sadness has a good influence on
you.
4A wise person thinks about death,
but a fool thinks only about having a
good time.
5It is better to be criticized by a wise
person
than to be praised by a fool.
6The laughter of fools
is like the crackling of thorns in a
cooking fire.
Both are useless.

7Even wise people are fools
if they let money change their
thinking.

8It is better to finish something
than to start it.
It is better to be patient
than to be proud.
9Don't become angry quickly,
because getting angry is foolish.

10Don't ask, "Why was life better in the
'good old days'?"
It is not wise to ask such questions.

11Wisdom is better when it comes with
money.
They both help those who are alive.
12Wisdom is like money:
they both help.
But wisdom is better,
because it can save whoever has it.

13Look at what God has done:
No one can straighten what he has
bent.
14When life is good, enjoy it.
But when life is hard, remember:
God gives good times and hard times,
and no one knows what tomorrow will
bring.

It Is Impossible to Be Truly Good

15In my useless life I have seen both of
these:
I have seen good people die in spite of
their goodness
and evil people live a long time in spite
of their evil.
16Don't be too right,
and don't be too wise.
Why destroy yourself?
17Don't be too wicked,
and don't be foolish.
Why die before your time?
18It is good to grab the one and not let go of
the other;
those who honor God will hold them
both.

19 Wisdom makes a person stronger
than ten leaders in a city.

20 Surely there is not a good person on earth
who always does good and never sins.

21 Don't listen to everything people say,
or you might hear your servant insulting you.
22 You know that many times
you have insulted others.

23 I used wisdom to test all these things.
I wanted to be wise,
but it was too hard for me.
24 I cannot understand why things are as they are.
It is too hard for anyone to understand.
25 I studied and tried very hard to find wisdom,
to find some meaning for everything.
I learned that it is foolish to be evil,
and it is crazy to act like a fool.

26 I found that some women are worse than death
and are as dangerous as traps.
Their love is like a net,
and their arms hold men like chains.
A man who pleases God will be saved from them,
but a sinner will be caught by them.
27 The Teacher says, "This is what I learned:
I added all these things together
to find some meaning for everything.
28 While I was searching,
I did not find one man among the thousands I found.
Nor did I find a woman among all these.
29 One thing I have learned:
God made people good,
but they have found all kinds of ways to be bad."

Obey the King

8 No one is like the wise person
who can understand what things mean.
Wisdom brings happiness;
it makes sad faces happy.

2 Obey the king's command, because you
made a promise to God. 3 Don't be too quick
to leave the king. Don't support something
that is wrong, because the king does
whatever he pleases. 4 What the king says is
law; no one tells him what to do.

5 Whoever obeys the king's command will be safe.
A wise person does the right thing at the right time.
6 There is a right time and a right way for everything,
yet people often have many troubles.
7 They do not know what the future holds,
and no one can tell them what will happen.
8 No one can control the wind
or stop his own death.
No soldier is released in times of war,
and evil does not set free those who do evil.

Justice, Rewards, and Punishment

9 I saw all of this as I considered all that is
done here on earth. Sometimes people harm
those they control. 10 I saw the funerals of
evil people who used to go in and out of the
holy place. They were honored in the same
towns where they had done evil. This is
useless, too.

11 When evil people are not punished
right away, it makes others want to do evil,
too. 12 Though a sinner might do a hundred
evil things and might live a long time, I
know it will be better for those who honor
God. 13 I also know it will not go well for evil
people, because they do not honor God. Like
a shadow, they will not last. 14 Sometimes
something useless happens on earth. Bad
things happen to good people, and good
things happen to bad people. I say that this
is also useless. 15 So I decided it was more
important to enjoy life. The best that people
can do here on earth is to eat, drink, and
enjoy life, because these joys will help them
do the hard work God gives them here on
earth.

We Cannot Understand All God Does

16 I tried to understand all that happens on
earth. I saw how busy people are, working
day and night and hardly ever sleeping. 17 I
also saw all that God has done. Nobody can
understand what God does here on earth. No
matter how hard people try to understand it,
they cannot. Even if wise people say they
understand, they cannot; no one can really
understand it.

Is Death Fair?

9 I thought about all this and tried to understand it. I saw that God controls good people and wise people and what they do, but no one knows if they will experience love or hate.

2Good and bad people end up the same—
those who are right and those who are wrong,
those who are good and those who are evil,
those who are clean and those who are unclean,
those who sacrifice and those who do not.
The same things happen to a good person
as happen to a sinner,
to a person who makes promises to God
and to one who does not.

3This is something wrong that happens
here on earth: What happens to one
happens to all. So people's minds are full of
evil and foolish thoughts while they live.
After that, they join the dead. 4But anyone
still alive has hope; even a live dog is better
off than a dead lion!

5The living know they will die,
but the dead know nothing.
Dead people have no more reward,
and people forget them.
6After people are dead,
they can no longer love or hate or envy.
They will never again share
in what happens here on earth.

Enjoy Life While You Can

7So go eat your food and enjoy it;
drink your wine and be happy,
because that is what God wants you to do.
8Put on nice clothes
and make yourself look good.

9Enjoy life with the wife you love. Enjoy
all the useless days of this useless life God
has given you here on earth, because it is all
you have. So enjoy the work you do here on
earth. 10Whatever work you do, do your best,
because you are going to the grave, where

devotion 187

ECCLESIASTES 9:3

BIRTH, DEATH, AND PAYING TAXES

Solomon said that ultimately, every living person will meet the same end. What happens to one of us will happen to us all. On this earth, a person may choose a life full of evil or choose to walk in wisdom, but both are assured to face the same certain end. Death is our definite eventuality.

While you can't choose how or when you will exit this life, you *can* choose your eternity. Either you will believe that God is who he says he is or you will deny his existence. Scripture says that one day every knee will bow before the King of heaven. Some will bow and receive the judgment of their disbelief. But those who know God will bow before the inheritance of their eternal reward.

Have you made a decision about eternity? Death is such a scary proposition that many people put off deciding because of fear. But if death is certain, doesn't it make more sense to decide your eternity sooner than live all the days of your life afraid of the unknown?

The Bible says that any who call on Jesus' name will be saved (Acts 2:21). Everyone who asks for forgiveness will receive it. All who believe that Jesus is the Son of God will be rescued from judgment, and their lives will be secure for eternity. Death is a sure thing. But what's even more sure is God's promise to save. Call out to Jesus, and let him take all your fears about death away.

there is no working, no planning, no
knowledge, and no wisdom.

Time and Chance

[11]I also saw something else here on earth:
The fastest runner does not always win
the race,
the strongest soldier does not always
win the battle,
the wisest does not always have food,
the smartest does not always become
wealthy,
and the talented one does not always
receive praise.
Time and chance happen to everyone.
[12]No one knows what will happen next.
Like a fish caught in a net,
or a bird caught in a trap,
people are trapped by evil
when it suddenly falls on them.

Wisdom Does Not Always Win

[13]I also saw something wise here on earth
that impressed me. [14]There was a small town
with only a few people in it. A great king
fought against it and put his armies all
around it. [15]Now there was a poor but wise
man in the town who used his wisdom to
save his town. But later on, everyone forgot
about him. [16]I still think wisdom is better
than strength. But those people forgot about
the poor man's wisdom and stopped
listening to what he said.
[17]The quiet words of a wise person are
better
than the shouts of a foolish ruler.
[18]Wisdom is better than weapons of war,
but one sinner can destroy much good.

10 Dead flies can make even perfume
stink.
In the same way, a little foolishness can
spoil wisdom.
[2]The heart of the wise leads to right,
but the heart of a fool leads to wrong.
[3]Even in the way fools walk along the
road,
they show they are not wise;
they show everyone how stupid they are.
[4]Don't leave your job
just because your boss is angry with you.
Remaining calm solves great problems.

[5]There is something else wrong that
happens here on earth.
It is the kind of mistake rulers make:
[6]Fools are given important positions
while gifted people are given lower
ones;
[7]I have seen servants ride horses
while princes walk like servants on
foot.
[8]Anyone who digs a pit might fall into it;
anyone who knocks down a wall might
be bitten by a snake;
[9]anyone who moves boulders might be
hurt by them;
and anyone who cuts logs might be
harmed by them.
[10]A dull ax means
harder work.
Being wise will make it easier.
[11]If a snake bites the tamer before it is
tamed,
what good is the tamer?

[12]The words of the wise bring them
praise,
but the words of a fool will destroy
them.
[13]A fool begins by saying foolish things
and ends by saying crazy and wicked
things.
[14]A fool talks too much.
No one knows the future,
and no one can tell what will happen
after death.
[15]Work wears fools out;
they don't even know how to get
home.

The Value of Work

[16]How terrible it is for a country whose
king is a child
and whose leaders eat all morning.
[17]How lucky a country is whose king comes
from a good family,
whose leaders eat only at mealtime
and for strength, not to get drunk.

[18]If someone is lazy, the roof will begin to
fall.
If he doesn't fix it, the house will leak.

[19]A party makes you feel good,
wine makes you feel happy,
and money buys anything.

[20]Don't make fun of the king,
and don't make fun of rich people, even
in your bedroom.

A little bird might carry your words;
a bird might fly and tell what you said.

Boldly Face the Future

11 Invest what you have,
because after a while you will get a return.
2 Invest what you have in several different businesses,
because you don't know what disasters might happen.

3 If clouds are full of rain,
they will shower on the earth.
A tree can fall to the north or south,
but it will stay where it falls.
4 Those who wait for perfect weather
will never plant seeds;
those who look at every cloud
will never harvest crops.
5 You don't know where the wind will blow,
and you don't know how a baby grows inside the mother.
In the same way, you don't know what God is doing,
or how he created everything.
6 Plant early in the morning,
and work until evening,
because you don't know if this or that will succeed.
They might both do well.

Serve God While You Are Young

7 Sunshine is sweet;
it is good to see the light of day.
8 People ought to enjoy every day of their lives,
no matter how long they live.
But they should also remember this:
You will be dead a long time.
Everything that happens then is useless.
9 Young people, enjoy yourselves while you are young;
be happy while you are young.
Do whatever your heart desires,
whatever you want to do.
But remember that God will judge you
for everything you do.
10 Don't worry,
and forget the troubles of your body,
because youth and childhood are useless.

The Problems of Old Age

12 Remember your Creator
while you are young,
before the days of trouble come
and the years when you say,
"I find no pleasure in them."
2 When you get old,
the light from the sun, moon, and stars will grow dark;
the rain clouds will never seem to go away.
3 At that time your arms will shake
and your legs will become weak.
Your teeth will fall out so you cannot chew,
and your eyes will not see clearly.
4 Your ears will be deaf to the noise in the streets,
and you will barely hear the millstone grinding grain.
You'll wake up when a bird starts singing,
but you will barely hear singing.
5 You will fear high places
and will be afraid to go for a walk.
Your hair will become white like the flowers on an almond tree.
You will limp along like a grasshopper when you walk.
Your appetite will be gone.
Then you will go to your everlasting home,
and people will go to your funeral.

6 Soon your life will snap like a silver chain
or break like a golden bowl.
You will be like a broken pitcher at a spring,
or a broken wheel at a well.
7 You will turn back into the dust of the earth again,
but your spirit will return to God who gave it.

8 Everything is useless!
The Teacher says that everything is useless.

Conclusion: Honor God

9 The Teacher was very wise and taught
the people what he knew. He very carefully
thought about, studied, and set in order
many wise teachings.
10 The Teacher looked
for just the right words to write what is
dependable and true.
11 Words from wise people are like sharp

devotion 188

ECCLESIASTES 12:13

MORE THAN FRIENDS

The interesting thing about my relationship with one of my dear friends is that we work together. In fact, I am her boss. And although we are dear friends, I expect submission and even obedience when it comes to the affairs at the office. In our personal friendship, she has complete freedom to get heart-to-heart and even nose-to-nose with me. We are constantly holding one another spiritually accountable. She has no problem telling me like it is. I am confident that there have been seasons at work when she would've liked to use that freedom, but she honored me out of respect for authority.

God loved Moses so much that Scripture says that the two of them talked together face-to-face just as any man would with his best friend. God performed many miracles through Moses and blessed him in rich, personal ways. And although God's affinity toward Moses was like that of a best friend, the Lord still required Moses to respect him and obey his commands. God still wanted honor from Moses: "Take off your sandals, because you are standing on holy ground" (Ex. 3:5). If your body is the temple of the Holy Spirit (check out 1 Cor. 6:19-20), then you are standing on holy ground everywhere you walk. Do not ever forget that you are on a journey with a holy God that desires both honor and obedience from the children he loves.

sticks used to guide animals. They are like nails that have been driven in firmly. Altogether they are wise teachings that
come from one Shepherd. 12 So be careful,
my son, about other teachings. People are always writing books, and too much study will make you tired.

13 Now, everything has been heard,
so I give my final advice:
Honor God and obey his commands,
because this is all people must do.
14 God will judge everything,
even what is done in secret,
the good and the evil.

Song of Songs

A Hebrew idiom expressing the superlative—as in the song of all songs (just as Jesus is the King of all kings) The book is commonly referred to as the "Song of Solomon" because Solomon is the central male character in the story.

Person Holding the Pen God Wrote With: The assumption is that *King Solomon* wrote this poetic book. However, there are several linguistic issues casting doubt on sole Solomonic authorship, begging the question that perhaps *Solomon's royal poets* wrote it in honor of their king. None of these issues are compelling enough to completely eliminate Solomon as a possible author.

When the Text Was Written: This book was most likely written during the tenth century B.C. Rabbinic tradition holds that Solomon wrote the Song of Songs early in life—prior to amassing his harem of seven hundred wives and three hundred slave women (1 Kin. 11:3–4).

Spiritual Posture of the Original Recipients: The two central characters in this book are Solomon and his beloved, the woman of Shulam. There's a small supporting cast, which includes the woman's brothers, her girlfriends (the Women of Jerusalem), some grouchy night watchmen, and a sprinkling of wedding guests. Solomon was a committed follower of Jehovah as a young man and monarch (1 Kin. 3), but he strayed from God in his later years (11:4). Based on her dialogue and character, it is likely that Solomon's beloved worshiped Jehovah as well.

Storyline Synopsis: Song of Songs is a colorful poem that stands out in biblical literature like white shoes after Labor Day! The lyrics in this book are shockingly explicit and may appear more like a Danielle Steele novel than the inspired Word of God at first glance. Themes of sexuality and marital fidelity are woven throughout the book, but Bible scholars debate how to interpret its erotic motif. The inclusive Christocentric (Christ-centered) approach allows for the literal, historical romance between Solomon and the woman of Shulam, but it also considers how the recurrent themes of faithfulness and intimacy illustrate a believer's relationship with God.

A Moment Worth Discussing: In Song of Songs 4:9, Solomon looks at his blushing bride—just prior to consummating their marriage in a pyrotechnic display of passion—and tells her that she's captivated his heart with one glance. It's even better than when Renee Zellweger tells Tom Cruise, "You had me at hello," in *Jerry Maguire*.

Interesting (But Likely to Be Overlooked) Characters: The *Women of Jerusalem* operate under the radar most of the time, but they surface at the most opportune moments!

The Shulammite Woman

SONG OF SONGS

She has always dreamed of the man she would marry and her wedding day. But even in her wildest dreams, she never imagined him—or the love that would fill her heart. "Kiss me with the kisses of your mouth, because your love is better than wine," she says.

He gazes at her, and she feels her breath catch. "You are the most beautiful of women. Oh, you are beautiful. Your love is so sweet." Her heart swells—she is certain it will burst! Her voice is soft. "You are so handsome, my lover."

She recalls their courtship, the early days of exchanged glances and warm smiles. Once she even dreamed that she couldn't find her lover. She went around the city searching the streets and squares. When she found him, she held him tightly and would not let him go. Then he proposed, "Get up, my darling; let's go away, my beautiful one."

Now she stands at the threshold of marriage to the man she loves—she can barely contain her excitement! Each declaration of love she makes for her groom elicits an equally passionate response from him. She feels treasured, worthy, and beloved. "Even much water cannot put out the flame of love; floods cannot drown love," he says. She smiles, letting the waters of his love fill her heart.

God promises to love us with the depth of love found between this bride and groom, and his love is more passionate than we can imagine.

1 Solomon's Song of Songs.

The Woman Speaks to the Man She Loves

[2]Kiss me with the kisses of your mouth,
because your love is better than wine.
[3]The smell of your perfume is pleasant,
and your name is pleasant like
expensive perfume.
That's why the young women love
you.
[4]Take me with you; let's run together.
The king takes me into his rooms.

Friends Speak to the Man

We will rejoice and be happy with you;
we praise your love more than wine.
With good reason, the young women
love you.

The Woman Speaks

[5]I'm dark but lovely,
women of Jerusalem,
dark like the tents of Kedar,
like the curtains of Solomon.
[6]Don't look at how dark I am,
at how dark the sun has made me.
My brothers were angry with me
and made me tend the vineyards,
so I haven't tended my own vineyard!
[7]Tell me, you whom I love,
where do you feed your sheep?
Where do you let them rest at noon?
Why should I look for you near your
friend's sheep,
like a woman who wears a veil?[n]

The Man Speaks to the Woman

[8]You are the most beautiful of women.
Surely you know to follow the sheep
and feed your young goats
near the shepherds' tents.
[9]My darling, you are like a mare
among the king's stallions.
[10]Your cheeks are beautiful with
ornaments,
and your neck with jewels.
[11]We will make for you gold earrings
with silver hooks.

The Woman Speaks

[12]The smell of my perfume spreads out
to the king on his couch.

1:7 veil This was the way a prostitute usually dressed.

13My lover is like a bag of myrrh
that lies all night between my
breasts.
14My lover is like a bunch of flowers
from the vineyards at En Gedi.

The Man Speaks

15My darling, you are beautiful!
Oh, you are beautiful,
and your eyes are like doves.

The Woman Answers the Man

16You are so handsome, my lover,
and so pleasant!
Our bed is the grass.
17Cedar trees form our roof;
our ceiling is made of juniper wood.

The Woman Speaks Again

2 I am a rose in the Plain of Sharon,
a lily in the valleys.

The Man Speaks Again

2Among the young women, my darling
is like a lily among thorns!

The Woman Answers

3Among the young men, my lover
is like an apple tree in the woods!
I enjoy sitting in his shadow;
his fruit is sweet to my taste.
4He brought me to the banquet room,
and his banner over me is love.
5Strengthen me with raisins,
and refresh me with apples,
because I am weak with love.
6My lover's left hand is under my head,
and his right arm holds me tight.

The Woman Speaks to the Friends

7Women of Jerusalem, promise me
by the gazelles and the deer
not to awaken
or excite my feelings of love
until it is ready.

The Woman Speaks Again

8I hear my lover's voice.
Here he comes jumping across the
mountains,
skipping over the hills.
9My lover is like a gazelle or a young deer.
Look, he stands behind our wall
peeking through the windows,
looking through the blinds.
10My lover spoke and said to me,
"Get up, my darling;
let's go away, my beautiful one.

devotion 189

SONG OF SONGS 2:4

DO YOU SEE YOUR BANNER?

Solomon did two things for the woman he loved. He brought her into the banquet hall to give her a wonderful feast of delicious foods. He also put his banner of love over her for protection. He provided for her physically and emotionally. This is a beautiful picture of how God loves us. We are precious in his sight. He wants to treat us like a queen, and we need to realize how much God loves us so we can begin to love him in the same way.

On my way to teach a Bible study one morning, I stopped for a cup of coffee. I looked in my purse for some change and realized that I had forty dollars that I had forgotten about. As I reached for it, I sensed that the Lord wanted me to give it to someone that I would meet that day. After Bible study, a woman approached me for prayer. Her husband had lost his job, and they were really struggling. I told her about the forty dollars and gave her the money. Another woman overheard the conversation and told us she had brought a bag of little girl clothes for a friend who hadn't shown up that morning. The clothes were just the right size for the woman's daughter. Isn't it amazing when God shows up in unexpected ways? He will provide for us physically and emotionally because his banner over us is love.

[11]Look, the winter is past;
the rains are over and gone.
[12]Blossoms appear through all the land.
The time has come to sing;
the cooing of doves is heard in our land.
[13]There are young figs on the fig trees,
and the blossoms on the vines smell sweet.
Get up, my darling;
let's go away, my beautiful one."

The Man Speaks

[14]My beloved is like a dove hiding in the cracks of the rock,
in the secret places of the cliff.
Show me your face,
and let me hear your voice.
Your voice is sweet,
and your face is lovely.
[15]Catch the foxes for us—
the little foxes that ruin the vineyards
while they are in blossom.

The Woman Speaks

[16]My lover is mine, and I am his.
He feeds among the lilies
[17]until the day dawns
and the shadows disappear.
Turn, my lover.
Be like a gazelle or a young deer
on the mountain valleys.

The Woman Dreams

3 At night on my bed,
I looked for the one I love;
I looked for him, but I could not find him.
[2]I got up and went around the city,
in the streets and squares,
looking for the one I love.
I looked for him, but I could not find him.
[3]The watchmen found me as they patrolled the city,
so I asked, "Have you seen the one I love?"
[4]As soon as I had left them,
I found the one I love.
I held him and would not let him go
until I brought him to my mother's house,
to the room where I was born.

The Woman Speaks to the Friends

[5]Women of Jerusalem, promise me
by the gazelles and the deer
not to awaken
or excite my feelings of love
until it is ready.
[6]Who is this coming out of the desert
like a cloud of smoke?
Who is this that smells like myrrh, incense,
and other spices?
[7]Look, it's Solomon's couch[n]
with sixty soldiers around it,
the finest soldiers of Israel.
[8]These soldiers all carry swords
and have been trained in war.
Every man wears a sword at his side
and is ready for the dangers of the night.
[9]King Solomon had a couch made for himself
of wood from Lebanon.
[10]He made its posts of silver
and its braces of gold.
The seat was covered with purple cloth
that the women of Jerusalem wove with love.
[11]Women of Jerusalem, go out and see King Solomon.
He is wearing the crown his mother put on his head
on his wedding day,
when his heart was happy!

The Man Speaks to the Woman

4 How beautiful you are, my darling!
Oh, you are beautiful!
Your eyes behind your veil are like doves.
Your hair is like a flock of goats
streaming down Mount Gilead.
[2]Your teeth are white like newly sheared sheep
just coming from their bath.
Each one has a twin,
and none of them is missing.
[3]Your lips are like red silk thread,
and your mouth is lovely.
Your cheeks behind your veil
are like slices of a pomegranate.
[4]Your neck is like David's tower,
built with rows of stones.
A thousand shields hang on its walls;
each shield belongs to a strong soldier.

3:7 couch Something like a bed carried by slaves on which the king lay or sat while traveling.

5Your breasts are like two fawns,
like twins of a gazelle,
feeding among the lilies.
6Until the day dawns
and the shadows disappear,
I will go to that mountain of myrrh
and to that hill of incense.
7My darling, everything about you is beautiful,
and there is nothing at all wrong with you.
8Come with me from Lebanon, my bride.
Come with me from Lebanon,
from the top of Mount Amana,
from the tops of Mount Senir and Mount Hermon.
Come from the lions' dens
and from the leopards' hills.
9My sister, my bride,
you have thrilled my heart;
you have thrilled my heart
with a glance of your eyes,
with one sparkle from your necklace.
10Your love is so sweet, my sister, my bride.
Your love is better than wine,
and your perfume smells better than any spice.
11My bride, your lips drip honey;
honey and milk are under your tongue.
Your clothes smell like the cedars of Lebanon.
12My sister, my bride, you are like a garden locked up,
like a walled-in spring, a closed-up fountain.
13Your limbs are like an orchard
of pomegranates with all the best fruit,
filled with flowers and nard,
14nard and saffron, calamus, and cinnamon,
with trees of incense, myrrh, and aloes—
all the best spices.
15You are like a garden fountain—
a well of fresh water
flowing down from the mountains of Lebanon.

The Woman Speaks

16Awake, north wind.
Come, south wind.
Blow on my garden,
and let its sweet smells flow out.
Let my lover enter the garden
and eat its best fruits.

The Man Speaks

5 I have entered my garden, my sister, my bride.
I have gathered my myrrh with my spice.
I have eaten my honeycomb and my honey.
I have drunk my wine and my milk.

The Friends Speak

Eat, friends, and drink;
yes, drink deeply, lovers.

The Woman Dreams

2I sleep, but my heart is awake.
I hear my lover knocking.
"Open to me, my sister, my darling,
my dove, my perfect one.
My head is wet with dew,
and my hair with the dampness of the night."
3I have taken off my garment
and don't want to put it on again.
I have washed my feet
and don't want to get them dirty again.
4My lover put his hand through the opening,
and I felt excited inside.
5I got up to open the door for my lover.
Myrrh was dripping from my hands
and flowing from my fingers,
onto the handles of the lock.
6I opened the door for my lover,
but my lover had left and was gone.
When he spoke, he took my breath away.
I looked for him, but I could not find him;
I called for him, but he did not answer.
7The watchmen found me
as they patrolled the city.
They hit me and hurt me;
the guards on the wall took away my veil.
8Promise me, women of Jerusalem,
if you find my lover,
tell him I am weak with love.

The Friends Answer the Woman

9How is your lover better than other lovers,
most beautiful of women?
How is your lover better than other lovers?
Why do you want us to promise this?

The Woman Answers the Friends

[10]My lover is healthy and tan,
the best of ten thousand men.
[11]His head is like the finest gold;
his hair is wavy and black like a raven.
[12]His eyes are like doves
by springs of water.
They seem to be bathed in cream
and are set like jewels.
[13]His cheeks are like beds of spices;
they smell like mounds of perfume.
His lips are like lilies
flowing with myrrh.
[14]His hands are like gold hinges,
filled with jewels.
His body is like shiny ivory
covered with sapphires.
[15]His legs are like large marble posts,
standing on bases of fine gold.
He is like a cedar of Lebanon,
like the finest of the trees.
[16]His mouth is sweet to kiss,
and I desire him very much.
Yes, daughters of Jerusalem,
this is my lover
and my friend.

The Friends Speak to the Woman

6 Where has your lover gone,
most beautiful of women?
Which way did your lover turn?
We will look for him with you.

The Woman Answers the Friends

[2]My lover has gone down to his garden,
to the beds of spices,
to feed in the gardens
and to gather lilies.
[3]I belong to my lover,
and my lover belongs to me.
He feeds among the lilies.

The Man Speaks to the Woman

[4]My darling, you are as beautiful as
the city of Tirzah,
as lovely as the city of Jerusalem,
like an army flying flags.
[5]Turn your eyes from me,
because they excite me too much.
Your hair is like a flock of goats
streaming down Mount Gilead.
[6]Your teeth are white like sheep
just coming from their bath;

devotion 190

SONG OF SONGS 6:3

THE GIFT OF BELONGING

My husband and I have been married for almost twenty years. We have so enjoyed our life together, and yet we will tell anyone who asks that marriage is hard work. So many people come into marriage thinking that their spouse will fulfill all their dreams and desires. The reality is that you have two very different people with very different dreams just trying to survive. However, you as a couple belong to one another. This means that you will have to give in a lot of the time but never give up on one another. There is a security in belonging that we should never take for granted. We believe it is the belonging and the security that make our sex life complete.

Marriage is also a beautiful example of our relationship with God. We belong to God, and God belongs to us. Belonging is so important when you consider that the opposite of belonging is *being left out*. As a foster parent, I deal with the issue of belonging on a daily basis. I want to tell my little ones that they belong to me, but they don't. What I do tell them is that they belong to God, and he will never leave them or forsake them. I have to believe this with everything in me or I would not be able to continue foster parenting. We belong to God, and belonging is the greatest gift of all.

each one has a twin,
and none of them is missing.
7 Your cheeks behind your veil
are like slices of a pomegranate.
8 There may be sixty queens and eighty
slave women
and so many girls you cannot count
them,
9 but there is only one like my dove, my
perfect one.
She is her mother's only daughter,
the brightest of the one who gave her
birth.
The young women saw her and called her
happy;
the queens and the slave women also
praised her.

The Young Women Praise the Woman

10 Who is that young woman
that shines out like the dawn?
She is as pretty as the moon,
as bright as the sun,
as wonderful as an army flying flags.

The Man Speaks

11 I went down into the orchard of nut trees
to see the blossoms of the valley,
to look for buds on the vines,
to see if the pomegranate trees had
bloomed.
12 Before I realized it, my desire for you
made me feel
like a prince in a chariot.

The Friends Call to the Woman

13 Come back, come back, woman of
Shulam.
Come back, come back,
so we may look at you!

The Woman Answers the Friends

Why do you want to look at the woman
of Shulam
as you would at the dance of two
armies?

The Man Speaks to the Woman

7 Your feet are beautiful in sandals,
you daughter of a prince.
Your round thighs are like jewels
shaped by an artist.
2 Your navel is like a round drinking cup
always filled with wine.
Your stomach is like a pile of wheat
surrounded with lilies.
3 Your breasts are like two fawns,
like twins of a gazelle.
4 Your neck is like an ivory tower.
Your eyes are like the pools in Heshbon
near the gate of Bath Rabbim.
Your nose is like the mountain of Lebanon
that looks down on Damascus.
5 Your head is like Mount Carmel,
and your hair is like purple cloth;
the king is captured in its folds.
6 You are beautiful and pleasant;
my love, you are full of delights.
7 You are tall like a palm tree,
and your breasts are like its bunches of
fruit.
8 I said, "I will climb up the palm tree
and take hold of its fruit."
Let your breasts be like bunches of grapes,
the smell of your breath like apples,
9 and your mouth like the best
wine.

The Woman Speaks to the Man

Let this wine go down sweetly for my
lover;
may it flow gently past the lips and
teeth.
10 I belong to my lover,
and he desires only me.
11 Come, my lover,
let's go out into the country
and spend the night in the fields.
12 Let's go early to the vineyards
and see if the buds are on the vines.
Let's see if the blossoms have already
opened
and if the pomegranates have bloomed.
There I will give you my love.
13 The mandrake flowers give their sweet
smell,
and all the best fruits are at our gates.
I have saved them for you, my lover,
the old delights and the new.

8 I wish you were like my brother
who fed at my mother's breasts.
If I found you outside,
I would kiss you,
and no one would look down on me.
2 I would lead you and bring you
to my mother's house;
she is the one who taught me.

I would give you a drink of spiced wine
from my pomegranates.

The Woman Speaks to the Friends

3 My lover's left hand is under my head,
and his right arm holds me tight.
4 Women of Jerusalem,
promise not to awaken
or excite my feelings of love
until it is ready.

The Friends Speak

5 Who is this coming out of the desert,
leaning on her lover?

The Man Speaks to the Woman

I woke you under the apple tree
where you were born;
there your mother gave birth to you.
6 Put me like a seal on your heart,
like a seal on your arm.
Love is as strong as death;
jealousy is as strong as the grave.
Love bursts into flames
and burns like a hot fire.
7 Even much water cannot put out the
flame of love;
floods cannot drown love.
If a man offered everything in his house
for love,
people would totally reject it.

The Woman's Brothers Speak

8 We have a little sister,
and her breasts are not yet grown.
What should we do for our sister
on the day she becomes engaged?
9 If she is a wall,
we will put silver towers on her.
If she is a door,
we will protect her with cedar boards.

The Woman Speaks

10 I am a wall,
and my breasts are like towers.
So I was to him,
as one who brings happiness.
11 Solomon had a vineyard at Baal Hamon.
He rented the vineyards for others to
tend,
and everyone who rented had to pay
twenty-five pounds of silver for the
fruit.
12 But my own vineyard is mine to give.
Solomon, the twenty-five pounds of
silver are for you,
and five pounds are for those who tend
the fruit.

The Man Speaks to the Woman

13 You who live in the gardens,
my friends are listening for your
voice;
let me hear it.

The Woman Speaks to the Man

14 Hurry, my lover,
be like a gazelle
or a young deer
on the mountains where spices grow.

Isaiah

A Hebrew word that means "the Lord is salvation"

Person Holding the Pen God Wrote With: The Jewish prophet, *Isaiah*, who is quoted in the New Testament more often than any other Old Testament prophet, authored this book that bears his name. He was married with two children and probably came from an influential family, as he was able to easily arrange an audience with the king and a high priest (Is. 7:3, 8:2). Tradition holds that Isaiah was martyred by being cut in half during the reign of wicked King Manasseh (Heb. 11:37).

When the Text Was Written: Sometime during the later seventh century since Isaiah recorded Sennacherib's death (Is. 37:38), which occurred in 681 B.C.

Spiritual Posture of the Original Recipients: Isaiah's ministry took place around the holy city of Jerusalem during the period of the "divided kingdom" (739–686 B.C.). His prophesying spanned the reigns of four separate kings of Judah: Uzziah, Jotham, Ahaz, and Hezekiah (Is. 1:1). With a few notable exceptions (particularly during Jotham and Hezekiah's leadership), the people of Judah grew increasingly distant from Jehovah. They were especially enamored with the wealth and power of nearby pagan nations.

Storyline Synopsis: Because Isaiah's prophecy is so lengthy and detailed, it is difficult to condense. This is further complicated by the fact that Isaiah's words bounce back and forth between God's temporal kingdom of Israel and the future realm of eternal glory. For instance, Isaiah forecasts that the Israelites will be literally punished for their rebellion by the Babylonian captivity, and then he rhapsodizes about the type of gemstones that will decorate heaven. In short, God anointed Isaiah's lips with a hot coal straight from his personal fireplace (Is. 6:6–10), which purified Isaiah's heart and enabled him to be one of the most prolific divine mouthpieces in history.

A Moment Worth Discussing: Chapter 53 is undoubtedly Isaiah's literary masterpiece. He depicts the coming Messiah as a spotless lamb being led to its slaughter. This colorful, detailed description points unmistakably to the cross of Calvary, where Jesus willingly stretched out his arms and died for the sins of all humanity. It is especially interesting to contrast this sobering Old Testament commentary with the actual eyewitness accounts of the crucifixion in each of the Gospels (see Matt. 27:1–55; Mark 15:1–41; Luke 23:1–49; John 19:1–37).

Interesting (But Likely to Be Overlooked) Characters: The "*backsliders*" Isaiah prophesies about certainly don't deserve God's healing and restoration (Is. 57:14–19), but they are still highlighted as recipients of his amazing grace. This passage should galvanize feeble hearts everywhere!

1 This is the vision Isaiah son of Amoz saw about what would happen to Judah and Jerusalem. Isaiah saw these things while Uzziah, Jotham, Ahaz, and Hezekiah were kings of Judah.

God's Case Against His Children

2 Heaven and earth, listen,
because the LORD is speaking:
"I raised my children and helped them grow up,
but they have turned against me.
3 An ox knows its master,
and a donkey knows where its owner feeds it,
but the people of Israel do not know me;
my people do not understand."

4 How terrible! Israel is a nation of sin,
a people loaded down with guilt,
a group of children doing evil,
children who are full of evil.
They have left the LORD;
they hate God, the Holy One of Israel,
and have turned away from him as if he were a stranger.

5 Why should you continue to be punished?
Why do you continue to turn against him?
Your whole head is hurt,
and your whole heart is sick.
6 There is no healthy spot
from the bottom of your foot to the top of your head;
you are covered with wounds, hurts, and open sores
that are not cleaned and covered,
and no medicine takes away the pain.

7 Your land is ruined;
your cities have been burned with fire.
While you watch,
your enemies are stealing everything from your land;
it is ruined like a country destroyed by enemies.
8 Jerusalem is left alone
like an empty shelter in a vineyard,
like a hut left in a field of melons,
like a city surrounded by enemies.
9 The LORD All-Powerful
allowed a few of our people to live.
Otherwise we would have been completely destroyed
like the cities of Sodom and Gomorrah.

10 Jerusalem, your rulers are like those of Sodom,
and your people are like those of Gomorrah.
Hear the word of the LORD;
listen to the teaching of our God!
11 The LORD says,
"I do not want all these sacrifices.
I have had enough of your burnt sacrifices
of male sheep and fat from fine animals.
I am not pleased
by the blood of bulls, lambs, and goats.
12 You come to meet with me,
but who asked you to do
all this running in and out of my Temple's rooms?
13 Don't continue bringing me worthless sacrifices!
I hate the incense you burn.
I can't stand your New Moons, Sabbaths, and other feast days;
I can't stand the evil you do in your holy meetings.
14 I hate your New Moon feasts
and your other yearly feasts.
They have become a heavy weight on me,
and I am tired of carrying it.
15 When you raise your arms to me in prayer,
I will refuse to look at you.
Even if you say many prayers,
I will not listen to you,
because your hands are full of blood.
16 Wash yourselves and make yourselves clean.
Stop doing the evil things I see you do.
Stop doing wrong.
17 Learn to do good.
Seek justice.
Punish those who hurt others.
Help the orphans.
Stand up for the rights of widows."

18 The LORD says,
"Come, let us talk about these things.
Though your sins are like scarlet,
they can be as white as snow.
Though your sins are deep red,
they can be white like wool.
19 If you become willing and obey me,
you will eat good crops from the land.

devotion 191

ISAIAH 1:18

WASHED-WHITE-AS-SNOW WOMAN

Because of God's love and because of Jesus' death on the cross, you and I can be made clean. Forgiven. The ugliness taken away. The scarlet stains of our mistakes washed white as snow. It's a promise God makes to us all through his Word.

But Satan doesn't want you to believe it. He knows that if you really begin to live in this kind of truth, your life will become powerful. The enemy knows that God will use the transformed, washed-white-as-snow woman to glorify himself. He realizes that when you live in the strength and humility of being made clean, then you will begin to change and affect every circumstance you step into with God-ordained wisdom and power.

So the accuser whispers in your ear, "Don't believe it. That might be true for someone else, but it could never be true for you." He keeps bringing up your old sin. He tells you that you still deserve punishment. He bullies you with his taunting. Satan wants to neutralize the power of God's forgiveness.

But God's love is like an authoritative shout that comes to quiet the whispers. When the Maker of heaven and earth says that you are forgiven, then you are irreversibly and eternally pardoned. Will you let the truth of God's love be the exclamation that silences the whispers of the accuser?

Believe in the truth of God's word. Put your full weight down on it. Trust in God's promises, and live like a woman who has been forgiven!

20 But if you refuse to obey and if you turn
against me,
you will be destroyed by your enemies'
swords."
The LORD himself said these things.

Jerusalem Is Not Loyal to God

21 The city of Jerusalem once followed the
LORD,
but she is no longer loyal to him.
She used to be filled with fairness;
people there lived the way God wanted.
But now, murderers live there.
22 Jerusalem, you have become like the
scum left when silver is purified;
you are like wine mixed with water.
23 Your rulers are rebels
and friends of thieves.
They all accept money for doing wrong,
and they are paid to cheat people.
They don't seek justice for the orphans
or listen to the widows' needs.

24 So the Lord GOD All-Powerful,
the Mighty One of Israel, says:
"You, my enemies, will not cause me any
more trouble.
I will pay you back for what you
did.
25 I will turn against you
and clean away all your wrongs as if
with soap;
I will take all the worthless things out
of you.
26 I will bring back judges as you had long
ago;
your counselors will be like those you
had in the beginning.
Then you will be called the City That Is
Right with God,
the Loyal City."
27 By doing what is fair,
Jerusalem will be free again.
By doing what is right,

her people who come back to the LORD
will have freedom.
28But sinners and those who turn against
him will be destroyed;
those who have left the LORD will die.

29"You will be ashamed,
because you have worshiped gods
under the oak trees.
You will be disgraced,
because you have worshiped idols in
your gardens.
30You will be like an oak whose leaves are
dying
or like a garden without water.
31Powerful people will be like small, dry
pieces of wood,
and their works will be like sparks.
They will burn together,
and no one will be able to put out that
fire."

The Message About Jerusalem

2 Isaiah son of Amoz saw this message
about Judah and Jerusalem:
2 In the last days
the mountain on which the LORD's
Temple stands
will become the most important of all
mountains.
It will be raised above the hills,
and people from all nations will come
streaming to it.
3Many nations will come and say,
"Come, let us go up to the mountain of
the LORD,
to the Temple of the God of Jacob.
Then God will teach us his ways,
and we will obey his teachings."
His teachings will go out from Jerusalem;
the message of the LORD will go out
from Jerusalem.
4He will settle arguments among the
nations
and will make decisions for many
nations.
Then they will make their swords into
plows
and their spears into hooks for
trimming trees.
Nations will no longer fight other nations,
nor will they train for war anymore.

5Come, family of Jacob,
and let us follow the way of the LORD.

A Terrible Day Is Coming

6LORD, you have left your people,
the family of Jacob,
because they have become filled with
wrong ideas from people in the
East.
They try to tell the future like the
Philistines,
and they have completely accepted
those foreign ideas.
7Their land has been filled with silver and
gold;
there are a great many treasures there.
Their land has been filled with horses;
there are many chariots there.
8Their land is full of idols.
The people worship these idols they
made with their own hands
and shaped with their own fingers.
9People will not be proud any longer
but will bow low with shame.
God, do not forgive them.

10Go into the caves of the cliffs;
dig holes and hide in the ground
from the anger of the LORD
and from his great power!
11Proud people will be made humble,
and they will bow low with shame.
At that time only the LORD will still be
praised.

12The LORD All-Powerful has a certain day
planned
when he will punish the proud and
those who brag,
and they will no longer be important.
13He will bring down the tall cedar trees
from Lebanon
and the great oak trees of Bashan,
14all the tall mountains
and the high hills,
15every tall tower
and every high, strong wall,
16all the trading ships
and the beautiful ships.
17At that time proud people will be made
humble,
and they will bow low with shame.
At that time only the LORD will be praised,
18 but all the idols will be gone.
19People will run to caves in the rocky cliffs
and will dig holes and hide in the
ground

from the anger of the LORD
and his great power,
when he stands to shake the earth.
20At that time people will throw away
their gold and silver idols,
which they made for themselves to
worship;
they will throw them away to the bats
and moles.
21Then the people will hide in caves
and cracks in the rocks
from the anger of the LORD
and his great power,
when he stands to shake the earth.

22You should stop trusting in people to save
you,
because people are only human;
they aren't able to help you.

God Will Punish Judah and Jerusalem

3 Understand this:
The Lord GOD All-Powerful
will take away everything Judah and
Jerusalem need—
all the food and water,
2the heroes and great soldiers,
the judges and prophets,
people who do magic and elders,
3the military leaders and government
leaders,
the counselors, the skilled craftsmen,
and those who try to tell the
future.
4The LORD says, "I will cause young boys to
be your leaders,
and foolish children will rule over you.
5People will be against each other;
everyone will be against his
neighbor.
Young people will not respect older
people,
and common people will not respect
important people."
6At that time a man will grab one of his
brothers
from his own family and say,
"You have a coat, so you will be our leader.
These ruins will be under your control."
7But that brother will stand up and say,
"I cannot help you,
because I do not have food or clothes in
my house.
You will not make me your leader."

8This will happen because Jerusalem has
stumbled,
and Judah has fallen.
The things they say and do are against the
LORD;
they turn against him.
9The look on their faces shows they are
guilty;
like the people of Sodom, they are
proud of their sin.
They don't care who sees it.
How terrible it will be for them,
because they have brought much
trouble on themselves.

10Tell those who do what is right that
things will go well for them,
because they will receive a reward for
what they do.
11But how terrible it will be for the wicked!
They will be punished for all the wrong
they have done.
12Children treat my people cruelly,
and women rule over them.
My people, your guides lead you in the
wrong way
and turn you away from what is right.

13The LORD takes his place in court
and stands to judge the people.
14The LORD presents his case
against the elders and other leaders of
his people:
"You have burned the vineyard.
Your houses are full of what you took
from the poor.
15What gives you the right to crush my
people
and grind the faces of the poor into the
dirt?"
The Lord GOD All-Powerful says this.

A Warning to Women of Jerusalem

16The LORD says,
"The women of Jerusalem are proud.
They walk around with their heads held
high,
and they flirt with their eyes.
They take quick, short steps,
making noise with their ankle
bracelets."
17So the Lord will put sores on the heads of
those women in Jerusalem,
and he will make them lose their hair.
18At that time the Lord will take away

everything that makes them proud: their
beautiful ankle bracelets, their headbands,
their necklaces shaped like the moon, 19their
earrings, bracelets, and veils, 20their scarves,
ankle chains, the cloth belts worn around
their waists, their bottles of perfume, and
charms, 21their signet rings, nose rings,
22their fine robes, capes, shawls, and purses,
23their mirrors, linen dresses, turbans, and
long shawls.

24Instead of wearing sweet-smelling
perfume, they will stink.
Instead of fine cloth belts, they will
wear the ropes of captives.
Instead of having their hair fixed in fancy
ways, they will be bald.
Instead of fine clothes, they will wear
clothes of sadness.
Instead of being beautiful, they will
wear the brand of a captive.
25At that time your men will be killed with
swords,
and your heroes will die in war.
26There will be crying and sadness near the
city gates.
Jerusalem will be like a woman who
has lost everything and sits on the
ground.

4 At that time seven women will grab one
man
and say, "We will eat our own bread
and make our own clothes,
but please marry us!
Please, take away our shame."

The Branch of the Lord

2At that time the LORD's branch will be
very beautiful and great. The people still
living in Israel will be proud of what the
land grows. 3Those who are still living in
Jerusalem will be called holy; their names
are recorded among the living in Jerusalem.
4The Lord will wash away the filth from the
women of Jerusalem. He will wash the
bloodstains out of Jerusalem and clean the
city with the spirit of fairness and the spirit
of fire. 5Then the LORD will cover Mount
Zion and the people who meet there with a
cloud of smoke during the day and with a
bright, flaming fire at night. There will be a
covering over every person. 6This covering
will protect the people from the heat of the
sun and will provide a safe place to hide
from the storm and rain.

Israel, the Lord's Vineyard

5 Now I will sing for my friend a song
about his vineyard.
My friend had a vineyard
on a hill with very rich soil.
2He dug and cleared the field of stones
and planted the best grapevines there.
He built a tower in the middle of it
and cut out a winepress as well.
He hoped good grapes would grow
there,
but only bad ones grew.
3My friend says, "You people living in
Jerusalem,
and you people of Judah,
judge between me and my vineyard.
4What more could I have done for my
vineyard
than I have already done?
Although I expected good grapes to grow,
why were there only bad ones?
5Now I will tell you
what I will do to my vineyard:
I will remove the hedge,
and it will be burned.
I will break down the stone wall,
and it will be walked on.
6I will ruin my field.
It will not be trimmed or hoed,
and weeds and thorns will grow there.
I will command the clouds
not to rain on it."

7The vineyard belonging to the LORD
All-Powerful
is the nation of Israel;
the garden that he loves
is the people of Judah.
He looked for justice, but there was only
killing.
He hoped for right living, but there
were only cries of pain.

8How terrible it will be for you who add
more houses to your houses
and more fields to your fields
until there is no room left for other
people.
Then you are left alone in the land.
9The LORD All-Powerful said this to me:
"The fine houses will be destroyed;

the large and beautiful houses will be
left empty.
10At that time a ten-acre vineyard will make
only six gallons of wine,
and ten bushels of seed will grow only
half a bushel of grain."

11How terrible it will be for people who rise
early in the morning
to look for strong drink,
who stay awake late at night,
becoming drunk with wine.
12At their parties they have lyres, harps,
tambourines, flutes, and wine.
They don't see what the LORD has done
or notice the work of his hands.
13So my people will be captured and taken
away,
because they don't really know me.
All the great people will die of hunger,
and the common people will die of
thirst.
14So the place of the dead wants more and
more people,
and it opens wide its mouth.
Jerusalem's important people and
common people will go down
into it,
with their happy and noisy ones.
15So the common people and the great
people will be brought down;
those who are proud will be humbled.
16The LORD All-Powerful will receive glory
by judging fairly;
the holy God will show himself holy by
doing what is right.
17Then the sheep will go anywhere they
want,
and lambs will feed on the land that
rich people once owned.

18How terrible it will be for those people!
They pull their guilt and sins behind
them
as people pull wagons with ropes.
19They say, "Let God hurry;
let him do his work soon
so we may see it.
Let the plan of the Holy One of Israel
happen soon
so that we will know what it is."

20How terrible it will be for people who call
good things bad
and bad things good,
who think darkness is light
and light is darkness,
who think sour is sweet
and sweet is sour.

21How terrible it will be for people who
think they are wise
and believe they are clever.

22How terrible it will be for people who are
famous for drinking wine
and are champions at mixing drinks.
23They take money to set the guilty free
and don't allow good people to be
judged fairly.
24They will be destroyed
just as fire burns straw or dry grass.
They will be destroyed
like a plant whose roots rot
and whose flower dies and blows away
like dust.
They have refused to obey the teachings
of the LORD All-Powerful
and have hated the message from the
Holy God of Israel.
25So the LORD has become very angry with
his people,
and he has raised his hand to punish
them.
Even the mountains are frightened.
Dead bodies lie in the streets like
garbage.

But the LORD is still angry;
his hand is still raised to strike down
the people.

26He raises a banner for the nations far
away.
He whistles to call those people from
the ends of the earth.
Look! The enemy comes quickly!
27Not one of them becomes tired or falls
down.
Not one of them gets sleepy and falls
asleep.
Their weapons are close at hand,
and their sandal straps are not broken.
28Their arrows are sharp,
and all of their bows are ready to shoot.
The horses' hoofs are hard as rocks,
and their chariot wheels move like a
whirlwind.
29Their shout is like the roar of a lion;
it is loud like a young lion.
They growl as they grab their captives.

There is no one to stop them from
taking their captives away.
30 On that day they will roar
like the waves of the sea.
And when people look at the land,
they will see only darkness and pain;
all light will become dark in this thick
cloud.

Isaiah Becomes a Prophet

6 In the year that King Uzziah died, I saw
the Lord sitting on a very high throne.
His long robe filled the Temple. 2 Heavenly
creatures of fire stood above him. Each
creature had six wings: It used two wings to
cover its face, two wings to cover its feet, and
two wings for flying. 3 Each creature was
calling to the others:
"Holy, holy, holy is the LORD All-Powerful.
His glory fills the whole earth."
4 Their calling caused the frame around the
door to shake, as the Temple filled with
smoke.
5 I said, "Oh, no! I will be destroyed. I am
not pure, and I live among people who are
not pure, but I have seen the King, the LORD
All-Powerful."
6 One of the heavenly creatures used a pair
of tongs to take a hot coal from the altar.
Then he flew to me with the hot coal in his
hand. 7 The creature touched my mouth with
the hot coal and said, "Look, your guilt is
taken away, because this hot coal has
touched your lips. Your sin is taken away."
8 Then I heard the Lord's voice, saying,
"Whom can I send? Who will go for us?"
So I said, "Here I am. Send me!"
9 Then the Lord said, "Go and tell this to
the people:
'You will listen and listen, but you will
not understand.
You will look and look, but you will not
learn.'
10 Make the minds of these people dumb.
Shut their ears. Cover their eyes.
Otherwise, they might really understand
what they see with their eyes
and hear with their ears.
They might really understand in their
minds
and come back to me and be healed."
11 Then I asked, "Lord, how long should I
do this?"
He answered,

devotion 192

ISAIAH 6:1–5

UNLOCKED CHAINS

You and I, in our bodily state, will always deal with dying to a sinful nature. It is a spiritual law that sin will exist here on earth. Living here requires us to continually crucify the desires of the flesh to fulfill the power of the Spirit. Part of living in his power means totally believing that there is forgiveness for sin. There is not one sin that Christ's blood did not cover, not one! It is sad to meet believers who are bound up by their sin, and I am not talking about continuing in sin—I am talking about living like there is no forgiveness and being paralyzed by life. It's like sitting in an open jail cell with unlocked chains but not going free. It's time to walk away!

We must never put sin above the throne of God. If you are stuck believing that forgiveness is not available to you, then you are telling the Lord that your sin is beyond the reach of Christ's sacrifice. True conviction is when the Holy Spirit reminds us that there is sin present and then moves in our soul to seek forgiveness. That conviction is prompting you to go to the throne and receive the grace that God has made available to you. Do not take the power of grace and the position of the throne and put your sin above it. You are made whole by Christ and his blood. You are good enough, and there is NOTHING that can separate you from the love of your God.

"Until the cities are destroyed
and the people are gone,
until there are no people left in the houses,
until the land is destroyed and left empty.
12The LORD will send the people far away,
and the land will be left empty.
13One-tenth of the people will be left in the land,
but it will be destroyed again.
These people will be like an oak tree
whose stump is left when the tree is chopped down.
The people who remain will be like a stump that will sprout again."

Trouble with Aram

7 Now Ahaz was the son of Jotham, who was the son of Uzziah. When Ahaz was king of Judah, Rezin king of Aram and Pekah son of Remaliah, the king of Israel, went up to Jerusalem to fight against it. But they were not able to defeat the city.

2Ahaz king of Judah received a message saying, "The armies of Aram and Israel[n] have joined together."

When Ahaz heard this, he and the people were frightened. They shook with fear like trees of the forest blown by the wind.

3Then the LORD told Isaiah, "You and your son Shear-Jashub[n] should go and meet Ahaz at the place where the water flows into the upper pool, on the road where people do their laundry. 4Tell Ahaz, 'Be careful. Be calm and don't worry. Don't let those two men, Rezin and Pekah son of Remaliah, scare you. Don't be afraid of their anger or Aram's anger, because they are like two barely burning sticks that are ready to go out. 5They have made plans against you, saying, 6"Let's fight against Judah and tear it apart. We will divide the land for ourselves and make the son of Tabeel the new king of Judah." 7But I, the Lord GOD, say,

" 'Their plan will not succeed;
it will not happen,
8because Aram is led by the city of Damascus,
and Damascus is led by its weak king, Rezin.
Within sixty-five years Israel will no longer be a nation.
9Israel is led by the city of Samaria,
and Samaria is led by its weak king, the son of Remaliah.
If your faith is not strong,
you will not have strength enough to last.' "

Immanuel—God Is with Us

10Then the LORD spoke to Ahaz again, saying, 11"Ask for a sign from the LORD your God to prove to yourself that these things are true. It may be a sign from as deep as the place of the dead or as high as the heavens."

12But Ahaz said, "I will not ask for a sign or test the LORD."

13Then Isaiah said, "Ahaz, descendant of David, listen carefully! Isn't it bad enough that you wear out the patience of people? Do you also have to wear out the patience of my God? 14The Lord himself will give you a sign: The virgin[n] will be pregnant. She will have a son, and she will name him Immanuel.[n] 15He will be eating milk curds and honey when he learns to reject what is evil and to choose what is good. 16You are afraid of the kings of Israel and Aram now. But before the child learns to choose good and reject evil, the lands of Israel and Aram will be empty. 17The LORD will bring troubled times to you, your people, and to the people of your father's family. They will be worse than anything that has happened since Israel separated from Judah. The LORD will bring the king of Assyria to fight against you.

18"At that time the LORD will whistle for the Egyptians, and they will come like flies from Egypt's faraway streams. He will call for the Assyrians, and they will come like bees. 19These enemies will camp in the deep ravines and in the cliffs, by the thornbushes and watering holes. 20The Lord will hire Assyria and use it like a razor to punish Judah. It will be as if the Lord is shaving the hair from Judah's head and legs and removing Judah's beard.

21"At that time a person will be able to keep only one young cow and two sheep alive. 22There will be only enough milk for that person to eat milk curds. All who

7:2 Israel Literally, "Ephraim." Isaiah often uses "Ephraim" to mean all of Israel. **7:3 Shear-Jashub** This name means "a part of the people will come back." **7:14 virgin** The Hebrew word means "a young woman." Often this meant a girl who was not married and had not yet had sexual relations with anyone. **7:14 Immanuel** This name means "God is with us."

remain in the land will go back to eating just
milk curds and honey. 23 In this land there
are now vineyards that have a thousand
grapevines, which are worth about twenty-
five pounds of silver. But these fields will
become full of weeds and thorns. 24 The land
will become wild and useful only as a
hunting ground. 25 People once worked and
grew food on these hills, but at that time
people will not go there, because the land
will be filled with weeds and thorns. Only
sheep and cattle will go to those places."

Assyria Will Come Soon

8 The LORD told me, "Take a large scroll
and write on it with an ordinary pen:
'Maher-Shalal-Hash-Baz.' 2 I will gather some
men to be reliable witnesses: Uriah the priest
and Zechariah son of Jeberekiah."

3 Then I went to the prophetess, and she
became pregnant and had a son. The LORD
told me, "Name the boy Maher-Shalal-Hash-
Baz,[n] 4 because the king of Assyria will take
away all the wealth and possessions of
Damascus and Samaria before the boy learns
to say 'my father' or 'my mother.' "

5 Again the LORD spoke to me, saying,

6 "These people refuse to accept
the slow-moving waters of the pool of Shiloah
and are terrified of Rezin
and Pekah son of Remaliah.
7 So I, the Lord, will bring
the king of Assyria and all his power against them,
like a powerful flood of water from the Euphrates River.
The Assyrians will be like water rising over the banks of the river,
flowing over the land.
8 That water will flow into Judah and pass through it,
rising to Judah's throat.
Immanuel, this army will spread its wings like a bird
until it covers your whole country."

9 Be broken, all you nations,
and be smashed to pieces.
Listen, all you faraway countries.
Prepare for battle and be smashed to pieces!
Prepare for battle and be smashed to pieces!
10 Make your plans for the fight,
but they will be defeated.
Give orders to your armies,
but they will be useless,
because God is with us.

Warnings to Isaiah

11 The LORD spoke to me with his great
power and warned me not to follow the lead
of the rest of the people. He said,

12 "People are saying that others make plans against them,
but you should not believe them.
Don't be afraid of what they fear;
do not dread those things.
13 But remember that the LORD All-Powerful is holy.
He is the one you should fear;
he is the one you should dread.
14 Then he will be a place of safety for you.
But for the two families of Israel,
he will be like a stone that causes people to stumble,
like a rock that makes them fall.
He will be like a trap for the people of Jerusalem,
and he will catch them in his trap.
15 Many people will fall over this rock.
They will fall and be broken;
they will be trapped and caught."
16 Make an agreement.
Seal up the teaching while my followers are watching.
17 I will wait for the LORD to help us,
the LORD who is ashamed of the family of Israel.
I will wait for him.

18 I am here, and with me are the children
the LORD has given me. We are signs and
proofs for the people of Israel from the
LORD All-Powerful, who lives on Mount
Zion.

19 Some people say, "Ask the mediums and
fortune-tellers, who whisper and mutter,
what to do." But I tell you that people
should ask their God for help. Why should
people who are still alive ask something
from the dead? 20 You should follow the
teachings and the agreement with the LORD.

8:3 Maher-Shalal-Hash-Baz This name means "there will soon be looting and stealing."

The mediums and fortune-tellers do not
speak the word of the LORD, so their words
are worth nothing.
21 People will wander through the land
troubled and hungry. When they become
hungry, they will become angry and will
look up and curse their king and their God.
22 They will look around them at their land
and see only trouble, darkness, and awful
gloom. And they will be forced into the
darkness.

A New Day Is Coming

9 But suddenly there will be no more
gloom for the land that suffered. In the
past God made the lands of Zebulun and
Naphtali hang their heads in shame, but in
the future those lands will be made great.
They will stretch from the road along the
Mediterranean Sea to the land beyond the
Jordan River and north to Galilee, the land of
people who are not Israelites.

2 Before those people lived in darkness,
but now they have seen a great light.
They lived in a dark land,
but a light has shined on them.
3 God, you have caused the nation to grow
and made the people happy.
And they have shown their happiness to
you,
like the joy during harvest time,
like the joy of people
taking what they have won in war.
4 Like the time you defeated Midian,
you have taken away their heavy load
and the heavy pole from their backs
and the rod the enemy used to punish
them.
5 Every boot that marched in battle
and every uniform stained with blood
has been thrown into the fire.
6 A child has been born to us;
God has given a son to us.
He will be responsible for leading the
people.
His name will be Wonderful Counselor,
Powerful God,
Father Who Lives Forever, Prince of
Peace.
7 Power and peace will be in his kingdom
and will continue to grow forever.
He will rule as king on David's throne
and over David's kingdom.
He will make it strong
by ruling with justice and goodness
from now on and forever.

devotion 193

ISAIAH 9:6

"NOSE THAT CASTS SHADOW"

Have you ever seen the movie *Dances with Wolves*? I love how the Native Americans give their children names that describe their personalities or physical characteristics. After we saw this movie, my husband and I tried giving our family members names like that. My husband was "Nose that Casts Shadow," and I was "Always with Child." We named our son "Little Nervous One" and named our daughter "Head on Fire." I don't even have to explain to you the meanings because they are so descriptive.

This is the same thing Isaiah did in Scripture. The names he used for God are so precious because they describe for us our Savior in such vivid detail. Jesus is our Wonderful Counselor. He understands each of us so personally that he will lead and guide us through life. He is also our Powerful God and is able to do more than we could ever think or imagine. God is eternal, our Father Who Lives Forever, and he offers us the opportunity to live forever with him in heaven. Jesus is also the Prince of Peace. Living in a world where war is on the news every night, we all desire peace more than ever before. Jesus came to earth to die for our sins so that one day he could return and bring peace to earth forever. He came the first time as a child, but he will return ready to rule his people as the King of Kings.

The LORD All-Powerful will do this
because of his strong love for his
people.

God Will Punish Israel

8The Lord sent a message against the
people of Jacob;
it says that God will judge Israel.
9Then everyone in Israel, even the leaders
in Samaria,
will know that God has sent it.
Those people are proud and brag by
saying,
10"These bricks have fallen,
but we will build again with cut stones.
These small trees have been chopped
down,
but we will put great cedars there."
11But the LORD has brought the enemies of
Rezin against them;
he has stirred up their enemies against
them.
12The Arameans came from the east
and the Philistines from the west,
and they ate up Israel with their armies.
But the LORD was still angry;
his hand was still raised to punish the
people.

13But the people did not return to the one
who had struck them;
they did not follow the LORD
All-Powerful.
14So the LORD cut off Israel's head and tail,
taking away both the branch and stalk
in one day.
15The elders and important men were the
head,
and the prophets who speak lies were
the tail.
16Those who led the people led them in the
wrong direction,
and those who followed them were
destroyed.
17So the Lord is not happy with the young
people,
nor will he show mercy to the orphans
and widows.
All the people are separated from God and
are very evil;
they all speak lies.

But the LORD is still angry;
his hand is still raised to strike down
the people.

18Evil is like a small fire.
First, it burns weeds and thorns.
Next, it burns the larger bushes in the
forest,
and they all go up in a column of
smoke.
19The LORD All-Powerful is angry,
so the land will be burned.
The people are like fuel for the fire;
no one will try to save his brother or
sister.
20People will grab something on the right,
but they will still be hungry.
They will eat something on the left,
but they will not be filled.
Then they will each turn and eat their
own children.
21The people of Manasseh will fight against
the people of Ephraim,
and Ephraim will fight against
Manasseh.
Then both of them will turn against
Judah.
But the LORD is still angry;
his hand is still raised to strike down
the people.

10 How terrible it will be for those who
make unfair laws,
and those who write laws that make
life hard for people.
2They are not fair to the poor,
and they rob my people of their rights.
They allow people to steal from widows
and to take from orphans what really
belongs to them.
3How will you explain the things you have
done?
What will you do when your
destruction comes from far away?
Where will you run for help?
Where will you hide your riches then?
4You will have to bow down among the
captives
or fall down among the dead bodies.
But the LORD is still angry;
his hand is still raised to strike down
the people.

God Will Punish Assyria

5God says, "How terrible it will be for the
king of Assyria.
I use him like a rod to show my anger;
in anger I use Assyria like a club.

6I send it to fight against a nation that is
separated from God.
I am angry with those people,
so I command Assyria to fight against
them,
to take their wealth from them,
to trample them down like dirt in the
streets.
7But Assyria's king doesn't understand that
I am using him;
he doesn't know he is a tool for me.
He only wants to destroy other people
and to defeat many nations.
8The king of Assyria says to himself,
'All of my commanders are like kings.
9The city Calno is like the city
Carchemish.
The city Hamath is like the city Arpad.
The city Samaria is like the city
Damascus.
10I defeated those kingdoms that worship
idols,
and those idols were more than the
idols of Jerusalem and Samaria.
11As I defeated Samaria and her idols,
I will also defeat Jerusalem and her
idols.' "
12When the Lord finishes doing what he
planned to Mount Zion and Jerusalem, he
will punish Assyria. The king of Assyria is
very proud, and his pride has made him do
these evil things, so God will punish him.
13The king of Assyria says this:
"By my own power I have done these
things;
by my wisdom I have defeated many
nations.
I have taken their wealth,
and, like a mighty one, I have taken
their people.
14I have taken the riches of all these people,
like a person reaching into a bird's nest.
I have taken these nations,
like a person taking eggs.
Not one raised a hand
or opened its mouth to stop me."

15An ax is not better than the person who
swings it.
A saw is not better than the one who
uses it.
A stick cannot control the person who
picks it up.
A club cannot pick up the person!
16So the Lord GOD All-Powerful
will send a terrible disease upon
Assyria's soldiers.
The strength of Assyria will be burned up
like a fire burning until everything is
gone.
17God, the Light of Israel, will be like a fire;
the Holy One will be like a flame.
He will be like a fire
that suddenly burns the weeds and
thorns.
18The fire burns away the great trees and
rich farmlands,
destroying everything.
It will be like a sick person who wastes
away.
19The trees left standing will be so few
that even a child could count them.

20At that time some people will be left alive
in Israel
from the family of Jacob.
They will not continue to depend
on the person who defeated them.
They will learn truly to depend on the
LORD,
the Holy One of Israel.
21Those who are left alive in Jacob's family
will again follow the powerful God.
22Israel, your people are many,
like the grains of sand by the sea.
But only a few of them will be left alive
to return to the LORD.
God has announced that he will destroy
the land
completely and fairly.
23The Lord GOD All-Powerful will certainly
destroy this land,
as he has announced.
24This is what the Lord GOD All-Powerful
says:
"My people living in Jerusalem,
don't be afraid of the Assyrians,
who beat you with a rod
and raise a stick against you, as Egypt
did.
25After a short time my anger against you
will stop,
and then I will turn my anger to
destroying them."

26Then the LORD All-Powerful will beat the
Assyrians with a whip
as he defeated Midian at the rock of
Oreb.

He will raise his stick over the waters
as he did in Egypt.
27Then the troubles that Assyria puts on you
will be removed,
and the load they make you carry
will be taken away.

Assyria Invades Israel

28The army of Assyria will enter near Aiath.
Its soldiers will walk through Migron.
They will store their food in Micmash.
29The army will go over the pass.
The soldiers will sleep at Geba.
The people of Ramah will be afraid,
and the people at Gibeah of Saul will run away.
30Cry out, Bath Gallim!
Laishah, listen!
Poor Anathoth!
31The people of Madmenah are running away;
the people of Gebim are hiding.
32This day the army will stop at Nob.
They will shake their fist at Mount Zion,
at the hill of Jerusalem.

33Watch! The Lord GOD All-Powerful
with his great power will chop them down like a great tree.
Those who are great will be cut down;
those who are important will fall to the ground.
34He will cut them down
as a forest is cut down with an ax.
And the great trees of Lebanon
will fall by the power of the Mighty One.

The King of Peace Is Coming

11 A new branch will grow
from a stump of a tree;
so a new king will come
from the family of Jesse.[n]
2The Spirit of the LORD will rest upon that king.
The Spirit will give him wisdom and understanding, guidance and power.
The Spirit will teach him to know and respect the LORD.
3This king will be glad to obey the LORD.
He will not judge by the way things look
or decide by what he hears.
4But he will judge the poor honestly;
he will be fair in his decisions for the poor people of the land.
At his command evil people will be punished,
and by his words the wicked will be put to death.
5Goodness and fairness will give him strength,
like a belt around his waist.

6Then wolves will live in peace with lambs,
and leopards will lie down to rest with goats.
Calves, lions, and young bulls will eat together,
and a little child will lead them.
7Cows and bears will eat together in peace.
Their young will lie down to rest together.
Lions will eat hay as oxen do.
8A baby will be able to play near a cobra's hole,
and a child will be able to put his hand into the nest of a poisonous snake.
9They will not hurt or destroy each other
on all my holy mountain,
because the earth will be full of the knowledge of the LORD,
as the sea is full of water.

10At that time the new king from the
family of Jesse will stand as a banner for all
peoples. The nations will come together
around him, and the place where he lives
will be filled with glory. 11At that time the
Lord will again reach out and take his people
who are left alive in Assyria, North Egypt,
South Egypt, Cush, Elam, Babylonia,
Hamath, and all the islands of the sea.
12God will raise a banner as a sign for all nations,
and he will gather the people of Israel who were forced from their country.
He will gather the scattered people of Judah
from all parts of the earth.
13At that time Israel will not be jealous anymore,

11:1 Jesse King David's father.

and Judah will have no more enemies.
Israel will not be jealous of Judah,
and Judah will not hate Israel.
14But Israel and Judah will attack the
Philistines on the west.
Together they will take the riches from
the people of the east.
They will conquer Edom and Moab,
and the people of Ammon will be
under their control.
15The LORD will dry up
the Red Sea of Egypt.
He will wave his arm over the Euphrates
River
and dry it up with a scorching wind.
He will divide it into seven small rivers
so that people can walk across them
with their sandals on.
16So God's people who are left alive
will have a way to leave Assyria,
just like the time the Israelites
came out of Egypt.

A Song of Praise to God

12 At that time you will say:
"I praise you, LORD!
You were angry with me,
but you are not angry with me now!
You have comforted me.
2God is the one who saves me;
I will trust him and not be afraid.
The LORD, the LORD gives me strength and
makes me sing.
He has saved me."
3You will receive your salvation with joy
as you would draw water from a well.
4At that time you will say,
"Praise the LORD and worship him.
Tell everyone what he has done
and how great he is.
5Sing praise to the LORD, because he has
done great things.
Let all the world know what he has
done.
6Shout and sing for joy, you people of
Jerusalem,
because the Holy One of Israel does
great things before your eyes."

God's Message to Babylon

13 God showed Isaiah son of Amoz this
message about Babylon:

devotion 194

ISAIAH 12:1-6

ANCIENT WATER COOLER TALK

Isaiah foretold the exact scene in John 4 between Jesus and the Samaritan woman in these verses from Isaiah 12. The Samaritan woman came to draw from the well at a different time than all the other women. She was a woman of reputation (not a good one), and she wanted to avoid explaining why she was living with yet another man. As she came to the well, she met Jesus. During their time together, she changed her mind three times about who he was; first he was a Jew (John 4:9), then he was a prophet (4:19), and finally she realized he was the Messiah (4:25-26). Excited and bold about being made whole, she ran into the city to speak with the same people she had so desperately tried to avoid, "Come and see a man who told me everything I ever did. Do you think he might be the Christ?" (4:29).

The townspeople rushed to meet Jesus because of her testimony, and although they came first because of her words, many became believers because they heard Jesus for themselves (John 4:42). People should be drawn to your life because of Jesus. You are at the well when you meet him everyday. As you go about your business, you are the vessel that he can use to draw people to himself. Now go tell everyone the amazing things that the Lord has done for you. Encourage them with your testimony. Go let it be your testimony for a reason.

2Raise a flag on the bare mountain.
Call out to the men.
Raise your hand to signal them
to enter through the gates for
important people.
3I myself have commanded those people
whom I have separated as mine.
I have called those warriors to carry out
my anger.
They rejoice and are glad to do my will.

4Listen to the loud noise in the mountains,
the sound of many people.
Listen to the noise among the kingdoms,
the sound of nations gathering together.
The LORD All-Powerful is calling
his army together for battle.
5This army is coming from a faraway land,
from the edge of the horizon.
In anger the LORD is using this army like a
weapon
to destroy the whole country.

6Cry, because the LORD's day of judging is
near;
the Almighty is sending destruction.
7People will be weak with fear,
and their courage will melt away.
8Everyone will be afraid.
Pain and hurt will grab them;
they will hurt like a woman giving
birth to a baby.
They will look at each other in fear,
with their faces red like fire.

God's Judgment Against Babylon

9Look, the LORD's day of judging is
coming—
a terrible day, a day of God's anger.
He will destroy the land
and the sinners who live in it.
10The stars will not show their light;
the skies will be dark.
The sun will grow dark as it rises,
and the moon will not give its light.
11The LORD says, "I will punish the world
for its evil
and wicked people for their sins.
I will cause proud people to lose their
pride,
and I will destroy the pride of those
who are cruel to others.
12People will be harder to find than pure
gold;
there will be fewer people than there is
fine gold in Ophir.
13I will make the sky shake,
and the earth will be moved from its
place
by the anger of the LORD All-Powerful
at the time of his burning anger.

14"Then the people from Babylon will run
away like hunted deer
or like sheep who have no shepherd.
Everyone will turn back to his own
people;
each will run back to his own land.
15Everyone who is captured will be killed;
everyone who is caught will be killed
with a sword.
16Their little children will be beaten to
death in front of them.
Their houses will be robbed
and their wives raped.

17"Look, I will cause the armies of Media to
attack Babylon.
They do not care about silver
or delight in gold.
18Their soldiers will shoot the young men
with arrows;
they will show no mercy on children,
nor will they feel sorry for little ones.
19Babylon is the most beautiful of all
kingdoms,
and the Babylonians are very proud
of it.
But God will destroy it
like Sodom and Gomorrah.
20No one will ever live there
or settle there again.
No Arab will put a tent there;
no shepherd will bring sheep there.
21Only desert animals will live there,
and their houses will be full of wild
dogs.
Owls will live there,
and wild goats will leap about in the
houses.
22Wolves will howl within the strong walls,
and wild dogs will bark in the beautiful
buildings.
The end of Babylon is near;
its time is almost over."

Israel Will Return Home

14 The LORD will show mercy to the
people of Jacob, and he will again

choose the people of Israel. He will settle them in their own land. Then non-Israelite people will join the Israelites and will become a part of the family of Jacob.
2Nations will take the Israelites back to their land. Then those men and women from the other nations will become slaves to Israel in the LORD's land. In the past the Israelites were their slaves, but now the Israelites will defeat those nations and rule over them.

The King of Babylon Will Fall

3The LORD will take away the Israelites' hard work and will comfort them. They will
no longer have to work hard as slaves. 4On
that day Israel will sing this song about the king of Babylon:

The cruel king who ruled us is finished;
his angry rule is finished!
5The LORD has broken the scepter of evil rulers
and taken away their power.
6The king of Babylon struck people in anger
again and again.
He ruled nations in anger
and continued to hurt them.
7But now, the whole world rests and is quiet.
Now the people begin to sing.
8Even the pine trees are happy,
and the cedar trees of Lebanon rejoice.
They say, "The king has fallen,
so no one will ever cut us down again."

9The place of the dead is excited
to meet you when you come.
It wakes the spirits of the dead,
the leaders of the world.
It makes kings of all nations
stand up from their thrones to greet you.
10All these leaders will make fun of you
and will say,
"Now you are weak, as we are.
Now you are just like us."
11Your pride has been sent down to the place of the dead.
The music from your harps goes with it.
Flies are spread out like your bed beneath you,
and worms cover your body like a blanket.

12King of Babylon, morning star, you have fallen from heaven,
even though you were as bright as the rising sun!
In the past all the nations on earth bowed down before you,
but now you have been cut down.
13You told yourself,
"I will go up to heaven.
I will put my throne
above God's stars.
I will sit on the mountain of the gods,
on the slopes of the sacred mountain.
14I will go up above the tops of the clouds.
I will be like God Most High."
15But you were brought down to the grave,
to the deep places where the dead are.

16Those who see you stare at you.
They think about what has happened to you
and say, "Is this the same man who caused great fear on earth,
who shook the kingdoms,
17who turned the world into a desert,
who destroyed its cities,
who captured people in war
and would not let them go home?"

18Every king of the earth has been buried with honor,
each in his own grave.
19But you are thrown out of your grave,
like an unwanted branch.
You are covered by bodies
that died in battle,
by bodies to be buried in a rocky pit.
You are like a dead body other soldiers walk on.
20 You will not be buried with those bodies,
because you ruined your own country
and killed your own people.
The children of evil people
will never be mentioned again.

21Prepare to kill his children,
because their father is guilty.
They will never again take control of the earth;
they will never again fill the world with their cities.

22The LORD All-Powerful says this:
"I will fight against those people;
I will destroy Babylon and its people,

its children and their descendants," says
the LORD.
23"I will make Babylon fit only for owls
and for swamps.
I will sweep Babylon as with a broom of
destruction,"
says the LORD All-Powerful.

God Will Punish Assyria

24The LORD All-Powerful has made this
promise:
"These things will happen exactly as I
planned them;
they will happen exactly as I set them
up.
25I will destroy the king of Assyria in my
country;
I will trample him on my mountains.
He placed a heavy load on my people,
but that weight will be removed.

26"This is what I plan to do for all the earth.
And this is the hand that I have raised
over all nations."

27When the LORD All-Powerful makes a plan,
no one can stop it.
When the LORD raises his hand to punish
people,
no one can stop it.

God's Message to Philistia

28This message was given in the year that
King Ahaz died:
29Country of Philistia, don't be happy
that the king who struck you is now
dead.
He is like a snake that will give birth to
another dangerous snake.
The new king will be like a quick,
dangerous snake to bite you.
30Even the poorest of my people will be
able to eat safely,
and people in need will be able to lie
down in safety.
But I will kill your family with hunger,
and all your people who are left will die.

31People near the city gates, cry out!
Philistines, be frightened,
because a cloud of dust comes from the
north.
It is an army, full of men ready to fight.
32What shall we tell the messengers from
Philistia?
Say that the LORD has made Jerusalem
strong
and that his poor people will go there
for safety.

God's Message to Moab

15 This is a message about Moab:
In one night armies took the wealth
from Ar in Moab,
and it was destroyed.
In one night armies took the wealth from
Kir in Moab,
and it was destroyed.
2The people of Dibon go to the places of
worship to cry.
The people of Moab cry for the cities of
Nebo and Medeba.
Every head and beard has been shaved to
show how sad Moab is.
3In the streets they wear rough cloth to
show their sadness.
On the roofs[n] and in the public squares,
they are crying loudly.
4People in the cities Heshbon and Elealeh
cry out loud.
You can hear their voices far away in
the city Jahaz.
Even the soldiers are frightened;
they are shaking with fear.

5My heart cries with sorrow for Moab.
Its people run away to Zoar for safety;
they run to Eglath Shelishiyah.
People are going up the mountain road to
Luhith,
crying as they go.
People are going on the road to Horonaim,
crying over their destruction.
6But the water of Nimrim has dried up.
The grass has dried up,
and all the plants are dead;
nothing green is left.
7So the people gather up what they have
saved
and carry it across the Ravine of the
Poplars.
8Crying is heard everywhere in Moab.
Their crying is heard as far away as the
city Eglaim;
it is heard as far away as Beer Elim.

15:3 roofs In Bible times houses were built with flat roofs. The roof was used for drying things such as flax and fruit. And it was used as an extra room, as a place for worship, and as a cool place to sleep in the summer.

9The water of the city Dibon is full of
blood,
and I, the LORD, will bring even more
troubles to Dibon.
A few people living in Moab have escaped
the enemy,
but I will send lions to kill them.

16 Send the king of the land
the payment he demands.
Send a lamb from Sela through the desert
to the mountain of Jerusalem.
2The women of Moab
try to cross the river Arnon
like little birds
that have fallen from their nest.
3They say: "Help us.
Tell us what to do.
Protect us from our enemies
as shade protects us from the noon sun.
Hide us, because we are running for
safety!
Don't give us to our enemies.
4Let those of us who were forced out of
Moab live in your land.
Hide us from our enemies."

The robbing of Moab will stop.
The enemy will be defeated;
those who hurt others will disappear
from the land.
5Then a new loyal king will come;
this faithful king will be from the
family of David.
He will judge fairly
and do what is right.
6We have heard that the people of Moab
are proud
and very conceited.
They are very proud and angry,
but their bragging means nothing.
7So the people of Moab will cry;
they will all be sad.
They will moan and groan
for the raisin cakes they had in Kir
Hareseth.
8But the fields of Heshbon and the vines of
Sibmah cannot grow grapes;
foreign rulers have destroyed the
grapevines.
The grapevines once spread as far as the
city of Jazer and into the desert;
they had spread as far as the sea.
9I cry with the people of Jazer
for the grapevines of Sibmah.
I will cry with the people of Heshbon and
Elealeh.
There will be no shouts of joy,
because there will be no harvest or ripe
fruit.
10There will be no joy and happiness in the
orchards
and no songs or shouts of joy in the
vineyards.
No one makes wine in the winepresses,
because I have put an end to shouts of
joy.
11My heart cries for Moab like a harp
playing a funeral song;
I am very sad for Kir Hareseth.
12The people of Moab will go to their places
of worship
and will try to pray.
But when they go to their temple to pray,
they will not be able.

13Earlier the LORD said these things about
Moab. 14Now the LORD says, "In three years
all those people and what they take pride in
will be hated. (This is three years as a hired
helper would count time.) There will be a
few people left, but they will be weak."

God's Message to Aram

17 This is a message about Damascus:
"The city of Damascus will be
destroyed;
only ruins will remain.
2People will leave the cities of Aroer.
Flocks will wander freely in those
empty towns,
and there will be no one to bother them.
3The strong, walled cities of Israel will be
destroyed.
The government in Damascus will end.
Those left alive of Aram will be
like the glory of Israel," says the LORD
All-Powerful.

4"At that time Israel's wealth will all be
gone.
Israel will be like someone who has lost
much weight from sickness.
5That time will be like the grain harvest in
the Valley of Rephaim.
The workers cut the wheat.
Then they cut the heads of grain from
the plants
and collect the grain.

[6]That time will also be like the olive harvest,
when a few olives are left.
Two or three olives are left in the top branches.
Four or five olives are left on full branches," says the LORD, the God of Israel.

[7]At that time people will look to God, their Maker;
their eyes will see the Holy One of Israel.
[8]They will not trust the altars they have made,
nor will they trust what their hands have made,
not even the Asherah idols and altars.
[9]In that day all their strong cities will be
empty. They will be like the cities the
Hivites and the Amorites left when the
Israelites came to take the land. Everything
will be ruined.
[10]You have forgotten the God who saves you;
you have not remembered that God is your place of safety.
You plant the finest grapevines
and grapevines from faraway places.
[11]You plant your grapevines one day and try to make them grow,
and the next day you make them blossom.
But at harvest time everything will be dead;
a sickness will kill all the plants.

[12]Listen to the many people!
Their crying is like the noise from the sea.
Listen to the nations!
Their crying is like the crashing of great waves.
[13]The people roar like the waves,
but when God speaks harshly to them,
they will run away.
They will be like chaff on the hills being blown by the wind,
or like tumbleweeds blown away by a storm.
[14]At night the people will be very frightened.
Before morning, no one will be left.
So our enemies will come to our land,
but they will become nothing.

God's Message to Cush

18 How terrible it will be for the land beyond the rivers of Cush.
It is filled with the sound of wings.
[2]That land sends messengers across the sea;
they go on the water in boats made of reeds.

Go, quick messengers,
to a people who are tall and smooth-skinned,
who are feared everywhere.
They are a powerful nation that defeats other nations.
Their land is divided by rivers.

[3]All you people of the world, look!
Everyone who lives in the world, look!
You will see a banner raised on a mountain.
You will hear a trumpet sound.
[4]The LORD said to me,
"I will quietly watch from where I live,
like heat in the sunshine,
like the dew in the heat of harvest time."
[5]The time will come, after the flowers have bloomed and before the harvest,
when new grapes will be budding and growing.
The enemy will cut the plants with knives;
he will cut down the vines and take them away.
[6]They will be left for the birds of the mountains
and for the wild animals.
Birds will feed on them all summer,
and wild animals will eat them that winter."

[7]At that time a gift will be brought to the LORD All-Powerful
from the people who are tall and smooth-skinned,
who are feared everywhere.
They are a powerful nation that defeats other nations.
Their land is divided by rivers.
These gifts will be brought to the place of the LORD All-Powerful,
to Mount Zion.

God's Message to Egypt

19 This is a message about Egypt:
Look, the LORD is coming on a fast
cloud
to enter Egypt.
The idols of Egypt will tremble before him,
and Egypt's courage will melt away.

2 The LORD says, "I will cause the Egyptians
to fight against themselves.
People will fight with their relatives;
neighbors will fight neighbors;
cities will fight cities;
kingdoms will fight kingdoms.
3 The Egyptians will be afraid,
and I will ruin their plans.
They will ask advice from their idols and
spirits of the dead,
from their mediums and
fortune-tellers."
4 The Lord GOD All-Powerful says,
"I will hand Egypt over to a hard
master,
and a powerful king will rule over
them."

5 The sea will become dry,
and the water will disappear from the
Nile River.
6 The canals will stink;
the streams of Egypt will decrease and
dry up.
All the water plants will rot;
7 all the plants along the banks of the
Nile will die.
Even the planted fields by the Nile
will dry up, blow away, and disappear.
8 The fishermen, all those who catch fish
from the Nile,
will groan and cry;
those who fish in the Nile will be sad.
9 All the people who make cloth from flax
will be sad,
and those who weave linen will lose
hope.
10 Those who weave cloth will be broken.
All those who work for money will be
sad.

11 The officers of the city of Zoan are fools;
the wise men who advise the king of
Egypt give wrong advice.
How can you say to him, 'I am wise'?
How can you say, 'I am from the old
family of the kings'?
12 Egypt, where are your wise men?
Let them show you
what the LORD All-Powerful has planned
for Egypt.
13 The officers of Zoan have been fooled;
the leaders of Memphis have believed
false things.
So the leaders of Egypt
lead that nation the wrong way.
14 The LORD has made the leaders confused.
They have led Egypt to wander in the
wrong ways,
like drunk people stumbling in their
own vomit.
15 There is nothing Egypt can do;
no one there can help.

16 In that day the Egyptians will be like
women. They will be afraid of the LORD
All-Powerful, because he will raise his hand
to strike them down. 17 The land of Judah
will bring fear to Egypt. Anyone there who
hears the name Judah will be afraid, because
the LORD All-Powerful has planned terrible
things for them. 18 At that time five cities in
Egypt will speak Hebrew, the language of
Canaan, and they will promise to be loyal to
the LORD All-Powerful. One of these cities
will be named the City of Destruction. 19 At
that time there will be an altar for the LORD
in the middle of Egypt and a monument to
the LORD at the border of Egypt. 20 This will
be a sign and a witness to the LORD
All-Powerful in the land of Egypt. When the
people cry to the LORD for help, he will send
someone to save and defend them. He will
rescue them from those who hurt them.

21 So the LORD will show himself to the
Egyptians, and then they will know he is the
LORD. They will worship God and offer many
sacrifices. They will make promises to the
LORD and will keep them. 22 The LORD will
punish the Egyptians, but then he will heal
them. They will come back to the LORD, and
he will listen to their prayers and heal them.

23 At that time there will be a highway
from Egypt to Assyria, and the Assyrians will
go to Egypt, and the Egyptians will go to
Assyria. The Egyptians and Assyrians will
worship God together. 24 At that time Israel,
Assyria, and Egypt will join together, which
will be a blessing for the earth. 25 The LORD
All-Powerful will bless them, saying, "Egypt,
you are my people. Assyria, I made you.
Israel, I own you. You are all blessed!"

devotion 195

ISAIAH 19:20

ENEMY ACROSS STATE LINES

Is there someone plotting, manipulating, and gossiping about you right now? Do not be afraid, for the Lord is with you. I had an unusual experience with a very troubled woman who made up lies about others that were hurtful and devastating. Her deception was deep and well organized, and her beauty was captivating. I have never encountered anyone in my walk that was as dangerous as she was, and the funny thing is, we were good friends for a long time before I figured that out. If she suspected someone was beginning to expose her or challenge her stories, she would begin a full-on assault campaign against them, even in church.

It wasn't long before I became a target, and she decided to use my husband as the center of her battle plan. I was madder than a rattlesnake being tormented with a stick, and believe me, I had her within striking distance more than once. I knew that God would not want me to defend myself or retaliate. Like Isaiah, I prayed for God to do the defending. This was my message from God, "Don't say, 'I'll pay you back for the wrong you did.' Wait for the Lord, and he will make things right" (Prov. 20:22). Within weeks, her husband received a job offer in another state and they moved! God doesn't always move our problems across state lines, but he does deal with them as he sees fit. I have learned to let God deal with the evil people.

Assyria Will Defeat Egypt and Cush

20 Sargon king of Assyria sent a military
commander to Ashdod to attack
that city. So the commander attacked and
captured it. 2Then the LORD spoke through
Isaiah son of Amoz, saying, "Take the rough
cloth off your body, and take your sandals
off your feet." So Isaiah obeyed and walked
around naked and barefoot.

3Then the LORD said, "Isaiah my servant
has walked around naked and barefoot for
three years as a sign against Egypt and Cush.
4The king of Assyria will carry away
prisoners from Egypt and Cush. Old people
and young people will be led away naked
and barefoot, with their buttocks bare. So
the Egyptians will be shamed. 5People who
looked to Cush for help will be afraid, and
those who were amazed by Egypt's glory will
be shamed. 6People who live near the sea
will say, 'Look at those countries. We trusted
them to help us. We ran to them so they
would save us from the king of Assyria. So
how will we be able to escape?' "

God's Message to Babylon

21 This is a message about the Desert by
the Sea:[n]

Disaster is coming from the desert
like wind blowing in the south.
It is coming from a terrible country.
2I have seen a terrible vision.
I see traitors turning against you
and people taking your wealth.

Elam, attack the people!
Media, surround the city and attack it!
I will bring an end to the pain the city
causes.

3I saw those terrible things, and now I am
in pain;
my pains are like the pains of giving
birth.

21:1 Desert by the Sea Probably Babylon.

What I hear makes me very afraid;
what I see causes me to shake with fear.
4 I am worried,
and I am shaking with fear.
My pleasant evening
has become a night of fear.

5 They set the table;
they spread the rugs;
they eat and drink.
Leaders, stand up.
Prepare the shields for battle!

6 The Lord said to me,
"Go, place a lookout for the city
and have him report what he sees.
7 If he sees chariots and teams of horses,
donkeys, or camels,
he should pay very close attention."

8 Then the lookout called out,
"My master, each day I stand in the
watchtower watching;
every night I have been on guard.
9 Look, I see a man coming in a chariot
with a team of horses."
The man gives back the answer,
"Babylon has fallen. It has fallen!
All the statues of her gods
lie broken on the ground."
10 My people are crushed like grain on the
threshing floor.
My people, I tell you what I have heard
from the LORD All-Powerful,
from the God of Israel.

God's Message to Edom

11 This is a message about Dumah:[n]
Someone calls to me from Edom,
"Watchman, how much of the night is
left?
Watchman, how much longer will it be
night?"
12 The watchman answers,
"Morning is coming, but then night
will come again.
If you have something to ask,
then come back and ask."

God's Message to Arabia

13 This is a message about Arabia:
A group of traders from Dedan
spent the night near some trees in
Arabia.
14 They gave water to thirsty travelers;
the people of Tema gave food
to those who were escaping.
15 They were running from swords,
from swords ready to kill,
from bows ready to shoot,
from a hard battle.

16 This is what the Lord said to me: "In one
year all the glory of the country of Kedar will
be gone. (This is a year as a hired helper
counts time.) 17 At that time only a few of the
archers, the soldiers of Kedar, will be left
alive." The LORD, the God of Israel, has
spoken.

God's Message to Jerusalem

22 This is a message about the Valley of Vision:[n]

What is wrong with you people?
Why are you on your roofs?[n]
2 This city was a very busy city,
full of noise and wild parties.
Now your people have been killed,
but not with swords,
nor did they die in battle.
3 All your leaders ran away together,
but they have been captured without
using a bow.
All you who were captured
tried to run away before the enemy
came.
4 So I say, "Don't look at me.
Let me cry loudly.
Don't hurry to comfort me
about the destruction of Jerusalem."
5 The Lord GOD All-Powerful has chosen a
special day
of riots and confusion.
People will trample each other in the
Valley of Vision.
The city walls will be knocked down,
and the people will cry out to the
mountain.
6 The soldiers from Elam will gather their
arrows
and their chariots and men on horses.
Kir will prepare their shields.
7 Your nicest valleys will be filled with
chariots.

21:11 Dumah Another name for Edom. **22:1 Valley of Vision** This probably means a valley near Jerusalem.
22:1 roofs In Bible times houses were built with flat roofs. The roof was used for drying things such as flax and fruit. And it was used as an extra room, as a place for worship, and as a cool place to sleep in the summer.

Horsemen will be ordered to guard the
gates of the city.
8 The walls protecting Judah will fall.

At that time the people of Jerusalem
depended on
the weapons kept at the Palace of the
Forest.
9 You saw that the walls of Jerusalem
had many cracks that needed repairing.
You stored up water in the lower pool.
10 You counted the houses of Jerusalem,
and you tore down houses to repair the
walls with their stones.
11 You made a pool between the two walls
to save water from the old pool,
but you did not trust the God who made
these things;
you did not respect the One who
planned them long ago.

12 The Lord God All-Powerful told the
people
to cry and be sad,
to shave their heads and wear rough
cloth.
13 But look, the people are happy
and are having wild parties.
They kill the cattle and the sheep;
they eat the food and drink the wine.
They say, "Let us eat and drink,
because tomorrow we will die."
14 The Lord All-Powerful said to me: "You
people will die before this guilt is forgiven."
The Lord God All-Powerful said this.

God's Message to Shebna

15 This is what the Lord God All-Powerful
says:
"Go to this servant Shebna,
the manager of the palace.
16 Say to him, 'What are you doing here?
Who said you could cut out a tomb for
yourself here?
Why are you preparing your tomb in a
high place?
Why are you carving out a tomb from
the rock?
17 Look, mighty one! The Lord will throw
you away.
He will take firm hold of you

devotion 196

ISAIAH 22:8–11

WHOSE RESOURCES ARE YOU DEPENDING ON?

The exact opposite of believing God and depending on God is trusting in your own strength and resources. When we begin to think that we have the answers or the resources or the wisdom apart from God, then we have begun to live in pride. There is a very close relationship between pride and unbelief. Pride means that you have turned away from God to take satisfaction in your own plans or your own promotion. This arrogant spirit is a sad reflection of an unbelieving heart.

Very simply, the battle against pride is a battle against unbelief. We must believe God more than anything and trust his plans before we trust ourselves. Real faith results in humility of spirit. Pride fades in the light of great faith.

To counter the inevitable, Scripture gives us some wise counsel. First, boast only in the Lord. Make a big deal out of God in every experience and every circumstance. Speak his name out loud. Tell others what God has done and make sure they see him instead of you and your gifts. Second, draw near to God and watch him give you humility (James 4:6-8). And third, give your worries to the Lord. He will carry them and give you humility because of his strength (1 Pet. 5:5-7).

Believing in God more than you believe in yourself will counter every act of pride and restore to your countenance a beautiful humility that gives glory to his name.

22They will be gathered together
like prisoners thrown into a dungeon;
they will be shut up in prison.
After much time they will be punished.
23The moon will be embarrassed,
and the sun will be ashamed,
because the LORD All-Powerful will rule as king
on Mount Zion in Jerusalem.
Jerusalem's leaders will see his greatness.

A Song of Praise to God

25 LORD, you are my God.
I honor you and praise you,
because you have done amazing things.
You have always done what you said you would do;
you have done what you planned long ago.
2You have made the city a pile of rocks
and have destroyed her walls.
The city our enemies built with strong walls is gone;
it will never be built again.
3People from powerful nations will honor you;
cruel people from strong cities will fear you.
4You protect the poor;
you protect the helpless when they are in danger.
You are like a shelter from storms,
like shade that protects them from the heat.
The cruel people attack
like a rainstorm beating against the wall,
5 like the heat in the desert.
But you, God, stop their violent attack.
As a cloud cools a hot day,
you silence the songs of those who have no mercy.

God's Banquet for His Servants

6The LORD All-Powerful will prepare a feast
on this mountain for all people.
It will be a feast with all the best food and wine,
the finest meat and wine.
7On this mountain God will destroy
the veil that covers all nations,
the veil that stretches over all peoples;
8 he will destroy death forever.
The Lord GOD will wipe away every tear from every face.
He will take away the shame of his people from the earth.
The LORD has spoken.

9At that time people will say,
"Our God is doing this!
We have waited for him, and he has come to save us.
This is the LORD. We waited for him,
so we will rejoice and be happy when he saves us."
10The LORD will protect Jerusalem,
but he will crush our enemy Moab
like straw that is trampled down in the manure.
11They will spread their arms in it
like a person who is swimming.
But God will bring down their pride,
and all the clever things they have made will mean nothing.
12Moab's high walls protect them,
but God will destroy these walls.
He will throw them down to the ground,
even to the dust.

A Song of Praise to God

26 At that time people will sing this song in Judah:
We have a strong city.
God protects us with its strong walls and defenses.
2Open the gates,
and the good people will enter,
those who follow God.
3You, LORD, give true peace
to those who depend on you,
because they trust you.
4So, trust the LORD always,
because he is our Rock forever.
5He will destroy the proud city,
and he will punish the people living there.
He will bring that high city down to the ground
and throw it down into the dust.
6Then those who were hurt by the city will walk on its ruins;
those who were made poor by the city will trample it under their feet.

7The path of life is level for those who are right with God;
LORD, you make the way of life smooth for those people.

devotion 197

ISAIAH 26:3–4

IN CASE OF NUCLEAR ATTACK . . .

One of my favorite Scripture passages is Philippians 4:6-7. Take a minute to look it up. Maybe one of the reasons I like it so much is because I come from a family of worriers. We like to think about every worst-case scenario and figure out how we will solve the problem. This drives my husband crazy, but he puts up with us. We even have a plan for a nuclear attack. I'm not kidding. So when I read Paul's words in Philippians, they put my mind at ease: "Do not worry about anything, but pray and ask God for everything you need" (Phil. 4:6). God is in control. As Isaiah said, he is "our Rock forever" (Is. 26:4). He is our strength when we feel like we can't go on.

When we depend on God by taking our needs to him, he will give us his peace that is beyond our understanding and will guard our hearts and minds. He will calm us even when we have every reason to be anxious. Jesus displayed this picture of peace when he literally slept in the back of a boat while a storm raged all around. No matter what storm you're facing, God will give you his peace if only you will depend on him. Allow God to be your rock in whatever situation you face today. Ask him for that peace that is beyond understanding, and watch how your mind will cease to worry. You will learn to truly trust him.

8But, LORD, we are waiting
for your way of justice.
Our souls want to remember
you and your name.
9My soul wants to be with you at night,
and my spirit wants to be with you at the dawn of every day.
When your way of justice comes to the land,
people of the world will learn the right way of living.
10Evil people will not learn to do good
even if you show them kindness.
They will continue doing evil, even if they live in a good world;
they never see the LORD's greatness.
11LORD, you are ready to punish those people,
but they do not see that.
Show them your strong love for your people.
Then those who are evil will be ashamed.
Burn them in the fire
you have prepared for your enemies.

12LORD, all our success is because of what you have done,
so give us peace.
13LORD, our God, other masters besides you have ruled us,
but we honor only you.
14Those masters are now dead;
their ghosts will not rise from death.
You punished and destroyed them
and erased any memory of them.
15LORD, you multiplied the number of your people;
you multiplied them and brought honor to yourself.
You made the borders of the land wide.
16LORD, people remember you when they are in trouble;
they say quiet prayers to you when you punish them.
17LORD, when we are with you,
we are like a woman giving birth to a baby;
she cries and has pain from the birth.
18In the same way, we had pain.
We gave birth, but only to wind.

We don't bring salvation to the land
or make new people for the world.
19 Your people have died, but they will live again;
their bodies will rise from death.
You who lie in the ground,
wake up and be happy!
The dew covering you is like the dew of a new day;
the ground will give birth to the dead.

Judgment: Reward or Punishment

20 My people, go into your rooms
and shut your doors behind you.
Hide in your rooms for a short time
until God's anger is finished.
21 The LORD will leave his place
to punish the people of the world for their sins.
The earth will show the blood of the people who have been killed;
it will not cover the dead any longer.

27 At that time the LORD will punish
Leviathan, the gliding snake.
He will punish Leviathan, the coiled snake,
with his great and hard and powerful sword.
He will kill the monster in the sea.

2 At that time
people will sing about the pleasant vineyard.
3 "I, the LORD, will care for that vineyard;
I will water it at the right time.
No one will hurt it,
because I will guard it day and night.
4 I am not angry.
If anyone builds a wall of thornbushes in war,
I will march to it and burn it.
5 But if anyone comes to me for safety
and wants to make peace with me,
he should come and make peace with me."
6 In the days to come, the people of Jacob
will be like a plant with good roots;
Israel will grow like a plant beginning to bloom.
Then the world will be filled with their children.

The Lord Will Send Israel Away

7 The LORD has not hurt his people as he hurt their enemies;
his people have not been killed like those who tried to kill them.
8 He will settle his argument with Israel by sending it far away.
Like a hot desert wind, he will drive it away.
9 This is how Israel's guilt will be forgiven;
this is how its sins will be taken away:
Israel will crush the rocks of the altar to dust,
and no statues or altars will be left standing for the Asherah idols.
10 At that time the strong, walled city will be empty
like a desert.
Calves will eat grass there.
They will lie down there
and eat leaves from the branches.
11 The limbs will become dry and break off,
so women will use them for firewood.
The people refuse to understand,
so God will not comfort them;
their Maker will not be kind to them.

12 At that time the LORD will begin
gathering his people one by one from the
Euphrates River to the brook of Egypt. He
will separate them from others as grain is
separated from chaff. 13 Many of my people
are now lost in Assyria. Some have run away
to Egypt. But at that time a great trumpet
will be blown, and all those people will
come and worship the LORD on that holy
mountain in Jerusalem.

Warnings to Israel

28 How terrible it will be for Samaria,
the pride of Israel's drunken people!
That beautiful crown of flowers is just a dying plant
set on a hill above a rich valley where drunkards live.
2 Look, the Lord has someone who is strong and powerful.
Like a storm of hail and strong wind,
like a sudden flood of water pouring over the country,
he will throw Samaria down to the ground.

3That city, the pride of Israel's drunken people,
will be trampled underfoot.
4That beautiful crown of flowers is just a dying plant
set on a hill above a rich valley.
That city will be like the first fig of summer.
Anyone who sees it
quickly picks it and eats it.

5At that time the LORD All-Powerful
will be like a beautiful crown,
like a wonderful crown of flowers
for his people who are left alive.
6Then he will give wisdom to the judges
who must decide cases
and strength to those who battle at the city gate.
7But now those leaders are drunk with wine;
they stumble from drinking too much beer.
The priests and prophets are drunk with beer
and are filled with wine.
They stumble from too much beer.
The prophets are drunk when they see their visions;
the judges stumble when they make their decisions.
8Every table is covered with vomit,
so there is not a clean place anywhere.

9The LORD is trying to teach the people a lesson;
he is trying to make them understand his teachings.
But the people are like babies too old for breast milk,
like those who no longer nurse at their mother's breast.
10So they make fun of the LORD's prophet and say:
"A command here, a command there.
A rule here, a rule there.
A little lesson here, a little lesson there."
11So the LORD will use strange words and foreign languages
to speak to these people.
12God said to them,
"Here is a place of rest;
let the tired people come and rest.
This is the place of peace."
But the people would not listen.
13So the words of the LORD will be,
"A command here, a command there.
A rule here, a rule there.
A little lesson here, a little lesson there."
They will fall back and be defeated;
they will be trapped and captured.

14So listen to the LORD's message, you who brag,
you leaders in Jerusalem.
15You say, "We have made an agreement with death;
we have a contract with death.
When terrible punishment passes by,
it won't hurt us.
Our lies will keep us safe,
and our tricks will hide us."
16Because of these things, this is what the
Lord GOD says:
"I will put a stone in the ground in Jerusalem,
a tested stone.
Everything will be built on this important and precious rock.
Anyone who trusts in it will never be disappointed.
17I will use justice as a measuring line
and goodness as the standard.
The lies you hide behind will be destroyed as if by hail.
They will be washed away as if in a flood.
18Your agreement with death will be erased;
your contract with death will not help you.
When terrible punishment comes,
you will be crushed by it.
19Whenever punishment comes, it will take you away.
It will come morning after morning;
it will defeat you by day and by night.
Those who understand this punishment will be terrified."
20You will be like the person who tried to sleep
on a bed that was too short
and with a blanket that was too narrow
to wrap around himself.
21The LORD will fight as he did at Mount Perazim.
He will be angry as he was in the Valley of Gibeon.
He will do his work, his strange work.
He will finish his job, his strange job.

[22]Now, you must not make fun of these things,
or the ropes around you will become tighter.
The Lord God All-Powerful has told me
how the whole earth will be destroyed.

The Lord Punishes Fairly

[23]Listen closely to what I tell you;
listen carefully to what I say.
[24]A farmer does not plow his field all the time;
he does not go on working the soil.
[25]He makes the ground flat and smooth.
Then he plants the dill and scatters the cumin.
He plants the wheat in rows,
the barley in its special place,
and other wheat as a border around the field.
[26]His God teaches him
and shows him the right way.
[27]A farmer doesn't use heavy boards to crush dill;
he doesn't use a wagon wheel to crush cumin.
He uses a small stick to break open the dill,
and with a stick he opens the cumin.
[28]The grain is ground to make bread.
People do not ruin it by crushing it forever.
The farmer separates the wheat from the chaff with his cart,
but he does not let his horses grind it.
[29]This lesson also comes from the Lord All-Powerful,
who gives wonderful advice, who is very wise.

Warnings to Jerusalem

29 How terrible it will be for you, Jerusalem,
the city where David camped.
Your festivals have continued
year after year.
[2]I will attack Jerusalem,
and that city will be filled with sadness and crying.
It will be like an altar to me.
[3]I will put armies all around you, Jerusalem;
I will surround you with towers
and with devices to attack you.
[4]You will be pulled down and will speak from the ground;
I will hear your voice rising from the ground.
It will sound like the voice of a ghost;
your words will come like a whisper from the dirt.

[5]Your many enemies will become like fine dust;
the many cruel people will be like chaff that is blown away.
Everything will happen very quickly.
[6] The Lord All-Powerful will come
with thunder, earthquakes, and great noises,
with storms, strong winds, and a fire that destroys.
[7]Then all the nations that fight against Jerusalem
will be like a dream;
all the nations that attack her
will be like a vision in the night.
[8]They will be like a hungry man who dreams he is eating,
but when he awakens, he is still hungry.
They will be like a thirsty man who dreams he is drinking,
but when he awakens, he is still weak and thirsty.
It will be the same way with all the nations
who fight against Mount Zion.

[9]Be surprised and amazed.
Blind yourselves so that you cannot see.
Become drunk, but not from wine.
Trip and fall, but not from beer.
[10]The Lord has made you go into a deep sleep.
He has closed your eyes. (The prophets are your eyes.)
He has covered your heads. (The seers are your heads.)

[11]This vision is like the words of a book
that is closed and sealed. You may give the
book to someone who can read and tell that
person to read it. But he will say, "I can't read
the book, because it is sealed." [12]Or you may
give the book to someone who cannot read
and tell him to read it. But he will say, "I
don't know how to read."

[13]The Lord says:
"These people worship me with their mouths,
and honor me with their lips,
but their hearts are far from me.

Their worship is based on
nothing but human rules.
14So I will continue to amaze these
people
by doing more and more miracles.
Their wise men will lose their wisdom;
their wise men will not be able to
understand."

Warnings About Other Nations

15How terrible it will be for those who try
to hide things from the LORD
and who do their work in darkness.
They think no one will see them or
know what they do.
16You are confused.
You think the clay is equal to the potter.
You think that an object can tell the one
who made it,
"You didn't make me."
This is like a pot telling its maker,
"You don't know anything."

A Better Time Is Coming

17In a very short time, Lebanon will become
rich farmland,
and the rich farmland will seem like a
forest.
18At that time the deaf will hear the words
in a book.
Instead of having darkness and gloom,
the blind will see.
19The LORD will make the poor people
happy;
they will rejoice in the Holy One of
Israel.
20Then the people without mercy will come
to an end;
those who do not respect God will
disappear.
Those who enjoy doing evil will be
gone:
21those who lie about others in court,
those who trap people in court,
those who lie and take justice from
innocent people in court.
22This is what the LORD who set Abraham
free says to the family of Jacob:
"Now the people of Jacob will not be
ashamed
or disgraced any longer.
23When they see all their children,
the children I made with my hands,
they will say my name is holy.
They will agree that the Holy One of
Jacob is holy,
and they will respect the God of Israel.
24People who do wrong will now
understand.
Those who complain will accept being
taught."

Warnings to the Stubborn Nation

30 The LORD said,
"How terrible it will be for these
stubborn children.
They make plans, but they don't ask me to
help them.
They make agreements with other
nations, without asking my Spirit.
They are adding more and more sins to
themselves.
2They go down to Egypt for help
without asking me about it first.
They hope they will be saved by the king
of Egypt;
they want Egypt to protect them.
3But hiding in Egypt will bring you only
shame;
Egypt's protection will only disappoint
you.
4Your officers have gone to Zoan,
and your messengers have gone to
Hanes,
5but they will be put to shame,
because Egypt is useless to them.
It will give no help and will be of no use;
it will cause them only shame and
embarrassment."

God's Message to Judah

6This is a message about the animals in
southern Judah:
Southern Judah is a dangerous place
full of lions and lionesses,
poisonous snakes and darting snakes.
The messengers travel through there with
their wealth on the backs of
donkeys
and their treasure on the backs of
camels.
They carry them to a nation that cannot
help them,
7 to Egypt whose help is useless.
So I call that country Rahab the
Do-Nothing.
8Now write this on a sign for the people,
write this on a scroll,

so that for the days to come
this will be a witness forever.
9These people are like children who lie
and refuse to obey;
they refuse to listen to the LORD's
teachings.
10They tell the seers,
"Don't see any more visions!"
They say to the prophets,
"Don't tell us the truth!
Say things that will make us feel good;
see only good things for us.
11Stop blocking our path.
Get out of our way.
Stop telling us
about God, the Holy One of Israel."
12So this is what the Holy One of Israel
says:
"You people have refused to accept this
message
and have depended on cruelty and lies
to help you.
13You are guilty of these things.
So you will be like a high wall with
cracks in it
that falls suddenly and breaks into
small pieces.
14You will be like a clay jar that breaks,
smashed into many pieces.
Those pieces will be too small
to take coals from the fire
or to get water from a well."
15This is what the Lord GOD, the Holy One
of Israel, says:
"If you come back to me and trust me, you
will be saved.
If you will be calm and trust me, you
will be strong."
But you don't want to do that.
16You say, "No, we need horses to run
away on."
So you will run away on horses.
You say, "We will ride away on fast horses."
So those who chase you will be fast.
17One enemy will make threats,
and a thousand of your men will run
away.
Five enemies will make threats,
and all of you will run from them.
You will be left alone like a flagpole on a
hilltop,
like a banner on a hill.
18The LORD wants to show his mercy to you.
He wants to rise and comfort you.

devotion 198

ISAIAH 30:15-21

FOR CRYING OUT LOUD, JUST STOP AND ASK DIRECTIONS!

You would think that if Judah could listen and hear God's voice telling them which direction was the right way to go, they would not have been so stubborn. Come to think of it, that sounds like a lot of people I know, including myself at times.

Have you ever been the unfortunate passenger in the car with someone who wouldn't stop and ask directions? Perhaps the driver was your husband—or maybe it was you! I remember a time that a friend and I were traveling in an unfamiliar place, and we wandered around aimlessly until we were more lost than when we started. Eventually, we gave up and stopped to ask directions at a gas station. The person behind the cash register rattled off directions that were so simple they were embarrassing. We'd passed that gas station at least four times as we drove in circles. If only we'd stopped sooner, we could have received the exact directions and saved ourselves a load of time.

That's how we are sometimes with God. We get lost and perhaps we hear his voice, but we keep going, thinking we'll eventually figure it out. It's amazing how much time we waste when we could just follow his directions. We run ahead of him or drag our heels when he's trying to lead us. What we need to do is listen. If we listen, we'll hear his voice in our hearts, and he will lead us in the right direction.

The LORD is a fair God,
and everyone who waits for his help
will be happy.

The Lord Will Help His People

[19]You people who live on Mount Zion in
Jerusalem will not cry anymore. The LORD
will hear your crying, and he will comfort
you. When he hears you, he will help you.
[20]The Lord has given you sorrow and hurt
like the bread and water you ate every day.
He is your teacher; he will not continue to
hide from you, but you will see your teacher
with your own eyes. [21]If you go the wrong
way—to the right or to the left—you will
hear a voice behind you saying, "This is the
right way. You should go this way." [22]You
have statues covered with silver and gold,
but you will ruin them for further use. You
will throw them away like filthy rags and
say, "Go away!"

[23]At that time the LORD will send rain for
the seeds you plant in the ground, and the
ground will grow food for you. The harvest
will be rich and great, and you will have
plenty of food in the fields for your animals.
[24]Your oxen and donkeys that work the soil
will have all the food they need. You will
have to use shovels and pitchforks to spread
all their food. [25]Every mountain and hill will
have streams filled with water. These things
will happen after many people are killed
and the towers are pulled down. [26]At that
time the light from the moon will be bright
like the sun, and the light from the sun will
be seven times brighter than now, like the
light of seven days. These things will happen
when the LORD bandages his broken people
and heals the hurts he gave them.

[27]Look! The LORD comes from far away.
His anger is like a fire with thick clouds
of smoke.
His mouth is filled with anger,
and his tongue is like a burning fire.
[28]His breath is like a rushing river,
which rises to the throat.
He will judge the nations as if he is sifting
them through the strainer of
destruction.
He will place in their mouths a bit that
will lead them the wrong way.
[29]You will sing happy songs
as on the nights you begin a festival.
You will be happy like people listening to
flutes
as they come to the mountain of the
LORD,
to the Rock of Israel.
[30]The LORD will cause all people to hear his
great voice
and to see his powerful arm come
down with anger,
like a great fire that burns everything,
like a great storm with much rain and
hail.
[31]Assyria will be afraid when it hears the
voice of the LORD,
because he will strike Assyria with a
rod.
[32]When the LORD punishes Assyria with a
rod,
he will beat them to the music of
tambourines and harps;
he will fight against them with his
mighty weapons.
[33]Topheth[n] has been made ready for a long
time;
it is ready for the king.
It was made deep and wide
with much wood and fire.
And the LORD's breath will come
like a stream of burning sulfur and set
it on fire.

Warnings About Relying on Egypt

31 How terrible it will be for those people
who go down to Egypt for help.
They think horses will save them.
They think their many chariots
and strong horsemen will save them.
But they don't trust God, the Holy One of
Israel,
or ask the LORD for help.
[2]But he is wise and can bring them
disaster.
He does not change his warnings.
He will rise up and fight against the evil
people
and against those who try to help evil
people.
[3]The Egyptians are only people and are not
God.
Their horses are only animals and are
not spirit.

30:33 Topheth Gehenna; the Valley of Hinnom. Here people burned the bodies of criminals and animals, along with garbage.

The LORD will stretch out his arm,
and the one who helps will stumble,
and the people who wanted help will fall.
All of them will be destroyed together.
4The LORD says this to me:
"When a lion or a lion's cub kills an animal to eat,
it stands over the dead animal and roars.
A band of shepherds
may be assembled against it,
but the lion will not be afraid of their yelling
or upset by their noise.
So the LORD All-Powerful will come down
to fight on Mount Zion and on its hill.
5The LORD All-Powerful will defend Jerusalem
like birds flying over their nests.
He will defend and save it;
he will 'pass over' and save Jerusalem."
6You children of Israel, come back to the
God you fought against. 7The time is coming
when each of you will stop worshiping idols
of gold and silver, which you sinned by
making.
8"Assyria will be defeated by a sword, but not the sword of a person;
Assyria will be destroyed, but not by a person's sword.
Assyria will run away from the sword of God,
but its young men will be caught and made slaves.
9They will panic, and their protection will be destroyed.
Their commanders will be terrified
when they see God's battle flag,"
says the LORD,
whose fire is in Jerusalem
and whose furnace is in Jerusalem.

A Good Kingdom Is Coming

32 A king will rule in a way that brings justice,
and leaders will make fair decisions.
2Then each ruler will be like a shelter from the wind,
like a safe place in a storm,
like streams of water in a dry land,
like a cool shadow from a large rock in a hot land.
3People will look to the king for help,
and they will truly listen to what he says.
4People who are now worried will be able to understand.
Those who cannot speak clearly now
will then be able to speak clearly and quickly.
5Fools will not be called great,
and people will not respect the wicked.
6A fool says foolish things,
and in his mind he plans evil.
A fool does things that are wicked,
and he says wrong things about the LORD.
A fool does not feed the hungry
or let thirsty people drink water.
7The wicked person uses evil like a tool.
He plans ways to take everything from the poor.
He destroys the poor with lies,
even when the poor person is in the right.
8But a good leader plans to do good,
and those good things make him a good leader.

Hard Times Are Coming

9You women who are calm now,
stand up and listen to me.
You women who feel safe now,
hear what I say.
10You women feel safe now,
but after one year you will be afraid.
There will be no grape harvest
and no summer fruit to gather.
11Women, you are calm now, but you should shake with fear.
Women, you feel safe now, but you should tremble.
Take off your nice clothes
and put rough cloth around your waist to show your sadness.
12Beat your breasts in grief, because the fields that were pleasant are now empty.
Cry, because the vines that once had fruit now have no more grapes.
13Cry for the land of my people,
in which only thorns and weeds now grow.
Cry for the city that once was happy
and for all the houses that once were filled with joy.

14The palace will be empty;
people will leave the noisy city.
Strong cities and towers will be empty.
Wild donkeys will love to live there,
and sheep will go there to eat.

Things Will Get Better

15This will continue until God pours his
Spirit from above upon us.
Then the desert will be like a fertile
field
and the fertile field like a forest.
16Justice will be found even in the desert,
and fairness will be found in the fertile
fields.
17That fairness will bring peace,
and it will bring calm and safety forever.
18My people will live in peaceful places
and in safe homes
and in calm places of rest.
19Hail will destroy the forest,
and the city will be completely
destroyed.
20But you will be happy as you plant seeds
near every stream
and as you let your cattle and donkeys
wander freely.

Warnings to Assyria and Promises to God's People

33 How terrible it will be for you who
destroy others
but have not been destroyed yet.
How terrible it will be for you, traitor,
whom no one has turned against yet.
When you stop destroying,
others will destroy you.
When you stop turning against others,
they will turn against you.

2LORD, be kind to us.
We have waited for your help.
Give us strength every morning.
Save us when we are in trouble.
3Your powerful voice makes people run
away in fear;
your greatness causes the nations to
run away.
4Like locusts, your enemies will take away
the things you stole in war.
Like locusts rushing about, they will
take your wealth.
5The LORD is very great, and he lives in a
high place.
He fills Jerusalem with fairness and
justice.
6He will be your safety.
He is full of salvation, wisdom, and
knowledge.
Respect for the LORD is the greatest
treasure.

7See, brave people are crying out in the
streets;
those who tried to bring peace are
weeping loudly.
8There is no one on the roads,
no one walking in the paths.
People have broken the agreements they
made.
They refuse to believe the proof from
witnesses.
No one respects other people.
9The land is sick and dying;
Lebanon is ashamed and dying.
The Plain of Sharon is dry like the desert,
and the trees of Bashan and Carmel are
dying.
10The LORD says, "Now, I will stand up
and show my greatness.
Now, I will become important to the
people.
11You people do useless things
that are like hay and straw.
A destructive wind will burn you like
fire.
12People will be burned until their bones
become like lime;
they will burn quickly like dry
thornbushes."

13You people in faraway lands, hear what I
have done.
You people who are near me, learn
about my power.
14The sinners in Jerusalem are afraid;
those who are separated from God
shake with fear.
They say, "Can any of us live through this
fire that destroys?
Who can live near this fire that burns
on and on?"
15A person who does what is right
and speaks what is right,
who refuses to take money unfairly,
who refuses to take money to hurt
others,
who does not listen to plans of murder,
who refuses to think about evil—

16this is the kind of person who will be safe.
He will be protected as he would be in a high, walled city.
He will always have bread,
and he will not run out of water.
17Your eyes will see the king in his beauty.
You will see the land that stretches far away.
18You will think about the terror of the past:
"Where is that officer?
Where is the one who collected the taxes?
Where is the officer in charge of our defense towers?"
19No longer will you see those proud people from other countries,
whose strange language you couldn't understand.

God Will Protect Jerusalem

20Look at Jerusalem, the city of our festivals.
Look at Jerusalem, that beautiful place of rest.
It is like a tent that will never be moved;
the pegs that hold her in place will never be pulled up,
and her ropes will never be broken.
21There the LORD will be our Mighty One.
That land is a place with streams and wide rivers,
but there will be no enemy boats on those rivers;
no powerful ship will sail on them.
22This is because the LORD is our judge.
The LORD makes our laws.
The LORD is our king.
He will save us.
23You sailors from other lands, hear:
The ropes on your boats hang loose.
The mast is not held firm.
The sails are not spread open.
Then your great wealth will be divided.
There will be so much wealth that even the crippled people will carry off a share.
24No one living in Jerusalem will say, "I am sick."
The people who live there will have their sins forgiven.

God Will Punish His Enemies

34 All you nations, come near and listen.
Pay attention, you peoples!
The earth and all the people in it should listen,
the world and everything in it.
2The LORD is angry with all the nations;
he is angry with their armies.
He will destroy them and kill them all.
3Their bodies will be thrown outside.
The stink will rise from the bodies,
and the blood will flow down the mountains.
4The sun, moon, and stars will dissolve,
and the sky will be rolled up like a scroll.
The stars will fall
like dead leaves from a vine
or dried-up figs from a fig tree.
5The LORD's sword in the sky is covered with blood.
It will cut through Edom
and destroy those people as an offering to the LORD.
6The LORD's sword will be covered with blood;
it will be covered with fat,
with the blood from lambs and goats,
with the fat from the kidneys of sheep.
This is because the LORD decided there will be a sacrifice in Bozrah
and much killing in Edom.
7The oxen will be killed,
and the cattle and the strong bulls.
The land will be filled with their blood,
and the dirt will be covered with their fat.

8The LORD has chosen a time for punishment.
He has chosen a year when people must pay for the wrongs they did to Jerusalem.
9Edom's rivers will be like hot tar.
Its dirt will be like burning sulfur.
Its land will be like burning tar.
10The fires will burn night and day;
the smoke will rise from Edom forever.
Year after year that land will be empty;
no one will ever travel through that land again.
11Birds and small animals will own that land,
and owls and ravens will live there.
God will make it an empty wasteland;
it will have nothing left in it.

[12]The important people will have no one
left to rule them;
the leaders will all be gone.
[13]Thorns will take over the strong towers,
and wild bushes will grow in the
walled cities.
It will be a home for wild dogs
and a place for owls to live.
[14]Desert animals will live with the hyenas,
and wild goats will call to their friends.
Night animals will live there
and find a place of rest.
[15]Owls will nest there and lay eggs.
When they hatch open, the owls will
gather their young under their
wings.
Hawks will gather
with their own kind.

[16]Look at the LORD's scroll and read what
is written there:
None of these will be missing;
none will be without its mate.
God has given the command,
so his Spirit will gather them
together.
[17]God has divided the land among them,
and he has given them each their
portion.
So they will own that land forever
and will live there year after year.

God Will Comfort His People

35 The desert and dry land will become
happy;
the desert will be glad and will produce
flowers.
Like a flower, [2]it will have many blooms.
It will show its happiness, as if it were
shouting with joy.
It will be beautiful like the forest of
Lebanon,
as beautiful as the hill of Carmel and
the Plain of Sharon.
Everyone will see the glory of the LORD
and the splendor of our God.
[3]Make the weak hands strong
and the weak knees steady.
[4]Say to people who are frightened,
"Be strong. Don't be afraid.
Look, your God will come,
and he will punish your enemies.
He will make them pay for the wrongs
they did,
but he will save you."
[5]Then the blind people will see again,
and the deaf will hear.
[6]Crippled people will jump like deer,
and those who can't talk now will
shout with joy.
Water will flow in the desert,
and streams will flow in the dry land.
[7]The burning desert will have pools of
water,
and the dry ground will have springs.
Where wild dogs once lived,
grass and water plants will grow.
[8]A road will be there;
this highway will be called "The Road
to Being Holy."
Evil people will not be allowed to walk on
that road;
only good people will walk on it.
No fools will go on it.
[9]No lions will be there,
nor will dangerous animals be on that
road.
They will not be found there.
That road will be for the people God
saves;
[10] the people the LORD has freed will
return there.
They will enter Jerusalem with joy,
and their happiness will last forever.
Their gladness and joy will fill them
completely,
and sorrow and sadness will go far
away.

The Assyrians Invade Judah

36 During Hezekiah's fourteenth year as
king, Sennacherib king of Assyria
attacked all the strong, walled cities of Judah
and captured them. [2]The king of Assyria sent
out his field commander with a large army
from Lachish to King Hezekiah in Jerusalem.
When the commander came near the
waterway from the upper pool on the road
where people do their laundry, he stopped.
[3]Eliakim, Shebna, and Joah went out to meet
him. Eliakim son of Hilkiah was the palace
manager, Shebna was the royal secretary, and
Joah son of Asaph was the recorder.
[4]The field commander said to them, "Tell
Hezekiah this:
" 'The great king, the king of Assyria, says:
What can you trust in now? [5]You say you
have battle plans and power for war, but
your words mean nothing. Whom are you

devotion 199

ISAIAH 35:8-10

A WORLD WITHOUT HEARTBREAK

Did you hear Isaiah's prophecy filled with guarantees that God has made to all who call him Lord? God's reign will be beyond anything we can comprehend on this earth. He has an eternal future waiting that is fit for the beloved of a king. Still to come for us is a place where evil will not be allowed to enter. Can you imagine? No sin inside your heart—or your neighbor's. Pure motives. Compassionate understanding. Freedom to love and enjoy and celebrate. Goodness will reign and evil will be banned.

There will be no danger in the future that awaits us. We won't live in fear for our children or their safety. No bullies or scoundrels or criminals allowed. No fear of the threat of darkness or the corruption that hides in the shadows. No more terrorists or rumors of war. Joy and happiness will last forever. During our days on earth, the joy we taste is only a portion of what we will live in for eternity. Our momentary delights will become permanent and everlasting. Joy and gladness will completely fill every emptiness. Sorrow and sadness will be banished. Our hearts will never have to grieve again.

What if you lived this day in the light of these promises? You can live like you have hope—because you do. Live strong and assured. The King of heaven has promised to reign on this earth in majesty. If you belong to God, then your future is sure and beyond your imagination.

trusting for help so that you turn against
me? 6Look, you are depending on Egypt to
help you, but Egypt is like a splintered
walking stick. If you lean on it for help, it
will stab your hand and hurt you. The king
of Egypt will hurt all those who depend on
him. 7You might say, "We are depending on
the LORD our God," but Hezekiah destroyed
the LORD's altars and the places of worship.
Hezekiah told Judah and Jerusalem, "You
must worship only at this one altar."

8" 'Now make an agreement with my
master, the king of Assyria: I will give you
two thousand horses if you can find enough
men to ride them. 9You cannot defeat one of
my master's least important officers, so why
do you depend on Egypt to give you chariots
and horsemen? 10I have not come to attack
and destroy this country without an order
from the LORD. The LORD himself told me to
come to this country and destroy it.' "

11Then Eliakim, Shebna, and Joah said to
the field commander, "Please speak to us in
the Aramaic language. We understand it.
Don't speak to us in Hebrew, because the
people on the city wall can hear you."

12But the commander said, "My master did
not send me to tell these things only to you
and your king. He sent me to speak also to
those people sitting on the wall who will
have to eat their own dung and drink their
own urine like you."

13Then the commander stood and shouted
loudly in the Hebrew language, "Listen to
what the great king, the king of Assyria says,
14The king says you should not let Hezekiah
fool you, because he can't save you. 15Don't
let Hezekiah talk you into trusting the LORD
by saying, 'The LORD will surely save us. This
city won't be handed over to the king of
Assyria.'

16"Don't listen to Hezekiah. The king of
Assyria says, 'Make peace with me, and come
out of the city to me. Then everyone will be
free to eat the fruit from his own grapevine
and fig tree and to drink water from his own

well. 17After that I will come and take you to
a land like your own—a land with grain and
new wine, bread and vineyards.'
18"Don't let Hezekiah fool you, saying,
'The LORD will save us.' Has a god of any
other nation saved his people from the
power of the king of Assyria? 19Where are
the gods of Hamath and Arpad? Where are
the gods of Sepharvaim? They did not save
Samaria from my power. 20Not one of all the
gods of these countries has saved his people
from me. Neither can the LORD save
Jerusalem from my power."
21The people were silent. They didn't
answer the commander at all, because King
Hezekiah had ordered, "Don't answer him."
22Then Eliakim, Shebna, and Joah tore
their clothes to show how upset they were.
(Eliakim son of Hilkiah was the palace
manager, Shebna was the royal secretary,
and Joah son of Asaph was the recorder.) The
three men went to Hezekiah and told him
what the field commander had said.

Hezekiah Asks God to Help

37 When King Hezekiah heard the
message, he tore his clothes and put
on rough cloth to show how sad he was.
Then he went into the Temple of the LORD.
2Hezekiah sent Eliakim, the palace manager,
and Shebna, the royal secretary, and the
older priests to Isaiah. They were all wearing
rough cloth when they came to Isaiah the
prophet, the son of Amoz. 3They told Isaiah,
"This is what Hezekiah says: Today is a day
of sorrow and punishment and disgrace, as
when a child should be born, but the mother
is not strong enough to give birth to it. 4The
king of Assyria sent his field commander to
make fun of the living God. Maybe the LORD
your God will hear what the commander
said and will punish him for it. So pray for
the few of us who are left alive."
5When Hezekiah's officers came to Isaiah,
6he said to them, "Tell your master this: The
LORD says, 'Don't be afraid of what you have
heard. Don't be frightened by the words the
servants of the king of Assyria have spoken
against me. 7Listen! I am going to put a spirit
in the king of Assyria. He will hear a report
that will make him return to his own
country, and I will cause him to die by the
sword there.' "
8The field commander heard that the king
of Assyria had left Lachish. When he went
back, he found the king fighting against the
city of Libnah.
9The king received a report that Tirhakah,
the Cushite king of Egypt, was coming to
attack him. When the king of Assyria heard
this, he sent messengers to Hezekiah, saying,
10"Tell Hezekiah king of Judah: Don't be
fooled by the god you trust. Don't believe
him when he says Jerusalem will not be
handed over to the king of Assyria. 11You
have heard what the kings of Assyria have
done. They have completely defeated every
country, so do not think you will be saved.
12Did the gods of those people save them?
My ancestors destroyed them, defeating the
cities of Gozan, Haran, and Rezeph, and the
people of Eden living in Tel Assar. 13Where
are the kings of Hamath and Arpad? Where
are the kings of Sepharvaim, Hena, and
Ivvah?"

Hezekiah Prays to the Lord

14When Hezekiah received the letter from
the messengers and read it, he went up to
the Temple of the LORD. He spread the letter
out before the LORD 15and prayed to the LORD:
16"LORD All-Powerful, you are the God of
Israel, whose throne is between the gold
creatures with wings, only you are God of all
the kingdoms of the earth. You made the
heavens and the earth. 17Hear, LORD, and
listen. Open your eyes, LORD, and see. Listen
to all the words Sennacherib has said to
insult the living God.
18"It is true, LORD, that the kings of Assyria
have destroyed all these countries and their
lands. 19They have thrown the gods of these
nations into the fire, but they were only
wood and rock statues that people made. So
the kings have destroyed them. 20Now, LORD
our God, save us from the king's power so
that all the kingdoms of the earth will know
that you, LORD, are the only God."

The Lord Answers Hezekiah

21Then Isaiah son of Amoz sent a message
to Hezekiah that said, "This is what the LORD,
the God of Israel, says: 'You prayed to me
about Sennacherib king of Assyria. 22So this
is what the LORD has said against
Sennacherib:

The people of Jerusalem
  hate you and make fun of you;

the people of Jerusalem
laugh at you as you run away.
23You have insulted me and spoken against me;
you have raised your voice against me.
You have a proud look on your face,
which is against me, the Holy One of Israel!
24You have sent your messengers to insult the Lord.
You have said, "With my many chariots
I have gone to the tops of the mountains,
to the highest mountains of Lebanon.
I have cut down its tallest cedars
and its best pine trees.
I have gone to its greatest heights
and its best forests.
25I have dug wells in foreign countries
and drunk water there.
By the soles of my feet,
I have dried up all the rivers of Egypt."

26" 'King of Assyria, surely you have heard.
Long ago I, the LORD, planned these things.
Long ago I designed them,
and now I have made them happen.
I allowed you to turn those strong, walled cities
into piles of rocks.
27The people in those cities were weak;
they were frightened and put to shame.
They were like grass in the field,
like tender, young grass,
like grass on the housetop
that is burned by the wind before it can grow.

28" 'I know when you rest,
when you come and go,
and how you rage against me.
29Because you rage against me,
and because I have heard your proud words,
I will put my hook in your nose
and my bit in your mouth.
Then I will force you to leave my country
the same way you came.'
30"Then the LORD said, 'Hezekiah, I will
give you this sign:
This year you will eat the grain that grows wild,
and the second year you will eat what grows wild from that.
But in the third year, plant grain and harvest it.
Plant vineyards and eat their fruit.
31Some of the people in the family of Judah will escape.
Like plants that take root,
they will grow strong and have many children.
32A few people will come out of Jerusalem alive;
a few from Mount Zion will live.
The strong love of the LORD All-Powerful
will make this happen.'
33"So this is what the LORD says about the
king of Assyria:
'He will not enter this city
or even shoot an arrow here.
He will not fight against it with shields
or build a ramp to attack the city walls.
34He will return to his country the same way he came,
and he will not enter this city,'
says the LORD.
35'I will defend and save this city
for my sake and for David, my servant.' "
36Then the angel of the LORD went out and
killed one hundred eighty-five thousand
men in the Assyrian camp. When the people
got up early the next morning, they saw all
the dead bodies. 37So Sennacherib king of
Assyria left and went back to Nineveh and
stayed there.
38One day as Sennacherib was worshiping
in the temple of his god Nisroch, his sons
Adrammelech and Sharezer killed him with
a sword. Then they escaped to the land of
Ararat. So Sennacherib's son Esarhaddon became king of Assyria.

Hezekiah's Illness

38 At that time Hezekiah became very
sick; he was almost dead. The prophet
Isaiah son of Amoz went to see him and told
him, "This is what the LORD says: Make
arrangements, because you are not going to
live, but die."
2Hezekiah turned toward the wall and
prayed to the LORD, 3"LORD, please remember
that I have always obeyed you. I have given
myself completely to you and have done
what you said was right." Then Hezekiah
cried loudly.
4Then the LORD spoke his word to Isaiah:
5"Go to Hezekiah and tell him: 'This is what
the LORD, the God of your ancestor David,
says: I have heard your prayer and seen your

tears. So I will add fifteen years to your life.
6I will save you and this city from the king
of Assyria; I will defend this city.
7" 'The LORD will do what he says. This is
the sign from the LORD to show you: 8The
sun has made a shadow go down the
stairway of Ahaz, but I will make it go back
ten steps.' " So the shadow made by the sun
went back up the ten steps it had gone down.
9After Hezekiah king of Judah got well, he
wrote this song:

10I said, "I am in the middle of my life.
Do I have to go through the gates of death?
Will I have the rest of my life taken away from me?"
11I said, "I will not see the LORD
in the land of the living again.
I will not again see the people
who live on the earth.
12Like a shepherd's tent,
my home has been pulled down and taken from me.
I am finished
like the cloth a weaver rolls up and cuts from the loom.[n]
In one day you brought me to this end.
13All night I cried loudly.
Like a lion, he crushed all my bones.
In one day you brought me to this end.
14I cried like a bird
and moaned like a dove.
My eyes became tired as I looked to the heavens.
Lord, I have troubles. Please help me."

15What can I say?
The Lord told me what would happen
and then made it happen.
I have had these troubles in my soul,
so now I will be humble all my life.
16Lord, because of you, people live.
Because of you, my spirit also lives;
you made me well and let me live.
17It was for my own good
that I had such troubles.
Because you love me very much,
you did not let me die
but threw my sins
far away.
18People in the place of the dead cannot praise you;
those who have died cannot sing praises to you;
those who die don't trust you
to help them.
19The people who are alive are the ones who praise you.
They praise you as I praise you today.
A father should tell his children
that you provide help.
20The LORD saved me,
so we will play songs on stringed instruments
in the Temple of the LORD
all the days of our lives.

21Then Isaiah said, "Make a paste from figs
and put it on Hezekiah's boil. Then he will
get well." 22Hezekiah then asked Isaiah,
"What will be the sign? What will show that
I will go up to the Temple of the LORD?"

Messengers from Babylon

39 At that time Merodach-Baladan son of
Baladan was king of Babylon. He sent
letters and a gift to Hezekiah, because he had
heard that Hezekiah had been sick and was
now well. 2Hezekiah was pleased and
showed the messengers what was in his
storehouses: the silver, gold, spices,
expensive perfumes, his swords and shields,
and all his wealth. He showed them
everything in his palace and in his kingdom.
3Then Isaiah the prophet went to King
Hezekiah and asked him, "What did these
men say? Where did they come from?"
Hezekiah said, "They came from a faraway
country—from Babylon."
4So Isaiah asked him, "What did they see
in your palace?"
Hezekiah said, "They saw everything in
my palace. I showed them all my wealth."
5Then Isaiah said to Hezekiah: "Listen to
the words of the LORD All-Powerful: 6'In the
future everything in your palace and
everything your ancestors have stored up
until this day will be taken away to Babylon.
Nothing will be left,' says the LORD. 7Some of
your own children, those who will be born
to you, will be taken away, and they will
become servants in the palace of the king of
Babylon."
8Hezekiah told Isaiah, "These words from
the LORD are good." He said this because he

38:12 loom A machine for making cloth from thread.

thought, "There will be peace and security in my lifetime."

Israel's Punishment Will End

40 Your God says,
"Comfort, comfort my people.
2Speak kindly to the people of Jerusalem
and tell them
that their time of service is finished,
that they have paid for their sins,
that the LORD has punished Jerusalem
twice for every sin they did."
3This is the voice of one who calls out:
"Prepare in the desert
the way for the LORD.
Make a straight road in the dry lands
for our God.
4Every valley should be raised up,
and every mountain and hill should be
made flat.
The rough ground should be made level,
and the rugged ground should be made
smooth.
5Then the glory of the LORD will be shown,
and all people together will see it.
The LORD himself said these things."
6A voice says, "Cry out!"
Then I said, "What shall I cry out?"
"Say all people are like the grass,
and all their glory is like the flowers of
the field.
7The grass dies and the flowers fall
when the breath of the LORD blows on
them.
Surely the people are like grass.
8The grass dies and the flowers fall,
but the word of our God will live
forever."
9Jerusalem, you have good news to tell.
Go up on a high mountain.
Jerusalem, you have good news to tell.
Shout out loud the good news.
Shout it out and don't be afraid.
Say to the towns of Judah,
"Here is your God."
10Look, the Lord GOD is coming with power
to rule all the people.
Look, he will bring reward for his
people;
he will have their payment with him.
11He takes care of his people like a
shepherd.

devotion 200

ISAIAH 40:6–8

IN THE END

Isaiah was clear. He wanted to make sure that we know that like the grass, our flesh will wither, and like the flower, we all will die (or at least our bodies will). What will be left is the infallible Word of the Lord. Everything that has been breathed into Scripture by the Holy Spirit will not only come to pass but will be the only thing still standing as we know it. God is the Alpha and the Omega, the author and the finisher of our faith, and every single day that passes, he is working toward establishing the fulfillment of the biblical prophecy that is yet to come.

It is hard to really get our arms around what the end times will be like, and I am sure every generation before us has thought that they would see it come. Even Jesus' followers kept gazing up into the clouds, expecting the return of Jesus. We are witnessing the perpetual forward movement of the Word, so we too should be expecting his return. However, I want to make sure that I personally participate in preventing as many souls as possible from going anywhere other than heaven. Do not get locked up in who, what, and when it will happen; just be ready for it to happen at any time. There are so many people who are not ready, and they need to know Jesus. In the end, that is all that is going to matter.

He gathers them like lambs in his arms
and carries them close to him.
He gently leads the mothers of the lambs.

God Is Supreme

12 Who has measured the oceans in the palm of his hand?
Who has used his hand to measure the sky?
Who has used a bowl to measure all the dust of the earth
and scales to weigh the mountains and hills?
13 Who has known the mind of the LORD
or been able to give him advice?
14 Whom did he ask for help?
Who taught him the right way?
Who taught him knowledge
and showed him the way to understanding?

15 The nations are like one small drop in a bucket;
they are no more than the dust on his measuring scales.
To him the islands are no more than fine dust on his scales.
16 All the trees in Lebanon are not enough for the altar fires,
and all the animals in Lebanon are not enough for burnt offerings.
17 Compared to the LORD all the nations are worth nothing;
to him they are less than nothing.

18 Can you compare God to anything?
Can you compare him to an image of anything?
19 An idol is formed by a craftsman,
and a goldsmith covers it with gold
and makes silver chains for it.
20 A poor person cannot buy those expensive statues,
so he finds a tree that will not rot.
Then he finds a skilled craftsman
to make it into an idol that will not fall over.

21 Surely you know. Surely you have heard.
Surely from the beginning someone told you.
Surely you understand how the earth was created.
22 God sits on his throne above the circle of the earth,
and compared to him, people are like grasshoppers.
He stretches out the skies like a piece of cloth
and spreads them out like a tent to sit under.
23 He makes rulers unimportant
and the judges of this world worth nothing.
24 They are like plants that are placed in the ground,
like seeds that are planted.
As soon as they begin to grow strong,
he blows on them and they die,
and the wind blows them away like chaff.

25 God, the Holy One, says, "Can you compare me to anyone?
Is anyone equal to me?"
26 Look up to the skies.
Who created all these stars?
He leads out the army of heaven one by one
and calls all the stars by name.
Because he is strong and powerful,
not one of them is missing.

27 People of Jacob, why do you complain?
People of Israel, why do you say,
"The LORD does not see what happens to me;
he does not care if I am treated fairly"?
28 Surely you know.
Surely you have heard.
The LORD is the God who lives forever,
who created all the world.
He does not become tired or need to rest.
No one can understand how great his wisdom is.
29 He gives strength to those who are tired
and more power to those who are weak.
30 Even children become tired and need to rest,
and young people trip and fall.
31 But the people who trust the LORD will become strong again.
They will rise up as an eagle in the sky;
they will run and not need rest;
they will walk and not become tired.

The Lord Will Help Israel

41 The LORD says, "Faraway countries, listen to me.
Let the nations become strong.

Come to me and speak;
we will meet together to decide who is right.

2 "Who caused the one to come from the east?
Who gives him victories everywhere he goes?
The one who brought him gives nations over to him
and defeats kings.
He uses his sword, and kings become like dust.
He uses his bow, and they are blown away like chaff.
3 He chases them and is never hurt,
going places he has never been before.
4 Who caused this to happen?
Who has controlled history since the beginning?
I, the LORD, am the one. I was here at the beginning,
and I will be here when all things are finished."

5 All you faraway places, look and be afraid;
all you places far away on the earth, shake with fear.
Come close and listen to me.
6 The workers help each other
and say to each other, "Be strong!"
7 The craftsman encourages the goldsmith,
and the workman who smooths the metal with a hammer encourages the one who shapes the metal.
He says, "This metal work is good."
He nails the statue to a base so it can't fall over.

Only the Lord Can Save Us

8 The LORD says, "People of Israel, you are my servants.
People of Jacob, I chose you.
You are from the family of my friend Abraham.
9 I took you from places far away on the earth
and called you from a faraway country.
I said, 'You are my servants.'
I have chosen you and have not turned against you.
10 So don't worry, because I am with you.
Don't be afraid, because I am your God.
I will make you strong and will help you;
I will support you with my right hand that saves you.

11 "All those people who are angry with you
will be ashamed and disgraced.
Those who are against you
will disappear and be lost.
12 You will look for your enemies,
but you will not find them.
Those who fought against you
will vanish completely.
13 I am the LORD your God,
who holds your right hand,
and I tell you, 'Don't be afraid.
I will help you.'
14 You few people of Israel who are left,
do not be afraid even though you are weak as a worm.
I myself will help you," says the LORD.
"The one who saves you is the Holy One of Israel.
15 Look, I have made you like a new threshing board
with many sharp teeth.
So you will walk on mountains and crush them;
you will make the hills like chaff.
16 You will throw them into the air, and the wind will carry them away;
a windstorm will scatter them.
Then you will be happy in the LORD;
you will be proud of the Holy One of Israel.

17 "The poor and needy people look for water,
but they can't find any.
Their tongues are dry with thirst.
But I, the LORD, will answer their prayers;
I, the God of Israel, will not leave them to die.
18 I will make rivers flow on the dry hills
and springs flow through the valleys.
I will change the desert into a lake of water
and the dry land into fountains of water.
19 I will make trees grow in the desert—
cedars, acacia, myrtle, and olive trees.
I will put pine, fir, and cypress trees
growing together in the desert.
20 People will see these things and understand;
they will think carefully about these things and learn
that the LORD's power did this,
that the Holy One of Israel made these things."

The Lord Challenges False Gods

21 The LORD says, "Present your case."
The King of Jacob says, "Tell me your arguments.
22 Bring in your idols to tell us
what is going to happen.
Have them tell us what happened in the beginning.
Then we will think about these things,
and we will know how they will turn out.
Or tell us what will happen in the future.
23 Tell us what is coming next
so we will believe that you are gods.
Do something, whether it is good or bad,
and make us afraid.
24 You gods are less than nothing;
you can't do anything.
Those who worship you should be hated.

25 "I have brought someone to come out of the north[n]
I have called by name a man from the east, and he knows me.
He walks on kings as if they were mud,
just as a potter walks on the clay.
26 Who told us about this before it happened?
Who told us ahead of time so we could say, 'He was right'?
None of you told us anything;
none of you told us before it happened;
no one heard you tell about it.
27 I, the LORD, was the first one to tell
Jerusalem that the people were coming home.
I sent a messenger to Jerusalem with the good news.
28 I look at the idols, but there is not one that can answer.
None of them can give advice;
none of them can answer my questions.
29 Look, all these idols are false.
They cannot do anything;
they are worth nothing.

The Lord's Special Servant

42 "Here is my servant, the one I support.
He is the one I chose, and I am pleased with him.
I have put my Spirit upon him,
and he will bring justice to all nations.
2 He will not cry out or yell
or speak loudly in the streets.
3 He will not break a crushed blade of grass
or put out even a weak flame.
He will truly bring justice;
4 he will not lose hope or give up
until he brings justice to the world.
And people far away will trust his teachings."

5 God, the LORD, said these things.
He created the skies and stretched them out.
He spread out the earth and everything on it.
He gives life to all people on earth,
to everyone who walks on the earth.
6 The LORD says, "I, the LORD, called you to do right,
and I will hold your hand
and protect you.
You will be the sign of my agreement with the people,
a light to shine for all people.
7 You will help the blind to see.
You will free those who are in prison,
and you will lead those who live in darkness out of their prison.

8 "I am the LORD. That is my name.
I will not give my glory to another;
I will not let idols take the praise that should be mine.
9 The things I said would happen have happened,
and now I tell you about new things.
Before those things happen,
I tell you about them."

A Song of Praise to the Lord

10 Sing a new song to the LORD;
sing his praise everywhere on the earth.
Praise him, you people who sail on the seas and you animals who live in them.
Praise him, you people living in faraway places.
11 The deserts and their cities should praise him.
The settlements of Kedar should praise him.
The people living in Sela should sing for joy;

41:25 someone . . . north This probably means Cyrus, a king of Persia.

they should shout from the
mountaintops.
12 They should give glory to the LORD.
People in faraway lands should praise
him.
13 The LORD will march out like a strong
soldier;
he will be excited like a man ready to
fight a war.
He will shout out the battle cry
and defeat his enemies.

14 The LORD says, "For a long time I have said
nothing;
I have been quiet and held myself
back.
But now I will cry out
and strain like a woman giving birth to
a child.
15 I will destroy the hills and mountains
and dry up all their plants.
I will make the rivers become dry land
and dry up the pools of water.
16 Then I will lead the blind along a way
they never knew;
I will guide them along paths they have
not known.
I will make the darkness become light for
them,
and the rough ground smooth.
These are the things I will do;
I will not leave my people.
17 But those who trust in idols,
who say to their statues,
'You are our gods'
will be rejected in disgrace.

Israel Refused to Listen to the Lord

18 "You who are deaf, hear me.
You who are blind, look and see.
19 No one is more blind than my servant
Israel
or more deaf than the messenger I send.
No one is more blind than the person I
own
or more blind than the servant of the
LORD.
20 Israel, you have seen much, but you have
not obeyed.
You hear, but you refuse to listen."
21 The LORD made his teachings wonderful,
because he is good.
22 These people have been defeated and
robbed.
They are trapped in pits
or locked up in prison.
Like robbers, enemies have taken them
away,
and there is no one to save them.
Enemies carried them off,
and no one said, "Bring them back."
23 Will any of you listen to this?
Will you listen carefully in the future?
24 Who let the people of Jacob be carried off?
Who let robbers take Israel away?
The LORD allowed this to happen,
because we sinned against him.
We did not live the way he wanted us to
live
and did not obey his teaching.
25 So he became very angry with us
and brought terrible wars against us.
It was as if the people of Israel had fire all
around them,
but they didn't know what was
happening.
It was as if they were burning,
but they didn't pay any attention.

God Is Always with His People

43 Now this is what the Lord says.
He created you, people of Jacob;
he formed you, people of Israel.
He says, "Don't be afraid, because I have
saved you.
I have called you by name, and you are
mine.
2 When you pass through the waters, I will
be with you.
When you cross rivers, you will not
drown.
When you walk through fire, you will not
be burned,
nor will the flames hurt you.
3 This is because I, the LORD, am your God,
the Holy One of Israel, your Savior.
I gave Egypt to pay for you,
and I gave Cush and Seba to make you
mine.
4 Because you are precious to me,
because I give you honor and love you,
I will give other people in your place;
I will give other nations to save your
life.
5 Don't be afraid, because I am with you.
I will bring your children from the east
and gather you from the west.

devotion 201

ISAIAH 43:4-7

NADIA'S PERFECT FAMILY

We traveled to Russia on a mission trip several years ago. We went to an orphanage one day to spend time with the children. When my husband and I walked into the nursery to play with the toddlers, a little girl named Nadia simply attached herself to me and wouldn't let go. She had blonde hair and blue eyes and a beautiful round face, but she was blind. By the end of the day, Stephan and I fell in love with her and had a hard time leaving. As we talked that night, we began to think about adopting her. We had three children at home, so we had to ask ourselves if we could handle another child, much less one with special needs.

That night we read Isaiah 43:4-7 and began praying earnestly for little Nadia. We knew that the Lord wanted to bring her out of the orphanage, so we just needed to pray about whether it was our home she was to come to. We also prayed for the Lord to provide the money if he wanted us to adopt her. Eventually, another couple that had no other children came forward. Even better? The wife was a nurse! God had provided the perfect family for Nadia. We then realized our job had simply been prayer.

Pray for the little orphans of the world today. The Lord wants each of them to have a home, and our prayers make a difference.

6 I will tell the north: Give my people to me.
I will tell the south: Don't keep my people in prison.
Bring my sons from far away
and my daughters from faraway places.
7 Bring to me all the people who are mine,
whom I made for my glory,
whom I formed and made."

Judah Is God's Witness

8 Bring out the people who have eyes but don't see
and those who have ears but don't hear.
9 All the nations gather together,
and all the people come together.
Which of their gods said this would happen?
Which of their gods can tell what happened in the beginning?
Let them bring their witnesses to prove they were right.
Then others will say, "It is true."
10 The LORD says, "You are my witnesses
and the servant I chose.
I chose you so you would know and believe me,
so you would understand that I am the true God.
There was no God before me,
and there will be no God after me.
11 I myself am the LORD;
I am the only Savior.
12 I myself have spoken to you, saved you,
and told you these things.
It was not some foreign god among you.
You are my witnesses, and I am God,"
says the LORD.
13 "I have always been God.
No one can save people from my power;
when I do something, no one can change it."

14 This is what the LORD, who saves you,
the Holy One of Israel, says:
"I will send armies to Babylon for you,
and I will knock down all its locked gates.

The Babylonians will shout their cries of
sorrow.
15I am the LORD, your Holy One,
the Creator of Israel, your King."

God Will Save His People Again

16This is what the LORD says.
He is the one who made a road through
the sea
and a path through rough waters.
17He is the one who defeated the chariots
and horses
and the mighty armies.
They fell together and will never rise
again.
They were destroyed as a flame is put
out.
18The LORD says, "Forget what happened
before,
and do not think about the past.
19Look at the new thing I am going to do.
It is already happening. Don't you
see it?
I will make a road in the desert
and rivers in the dry land.
20Even the wild animals will be thankful
to me—
the wild dogs and owls.
They will honor me when I put water in
the desert
and rivers in the dry land
to give water to my people, the ones I
chose.
21The people I made
will sing songs to praise me.

22"People of Jacob, you have not called
to me;
people of Israel, you have become tired
of me.
23You have not brought me your sacrifices
of sheep
nor honored me with your sacrifices.
I did not weigh you down with sacrifices
to offer
or make you tired with incense to
burn.
24So you did not buy incense for me;
you did not freely bring me fat from
your sacrifices.
Instead you have weighed me down with
your many sins;
you have made me tired of your many
wrongs.
25"I, I am the One who erases all your sins,
for my sake;
I will not remember your sins.
26But you should remind me.
Let's meet and decide what is right.
Tell what you have done and show you
are right.
27Your first father sinned,
and your leaders have turned
against me.
28So I will make your holy rulers unholy.
I will bring destruction on the people of
Jacob,
and I will let Israel be insulted."

The Lord Is the Only God

44 The LORD says, "People of Jacob, you
are my servants. Listen to me!
People of Israel, I chose you."
2This is what the LORD says, who made
you,
who formed you in your mother's body,
who will help you:
"People of Jacob, my servants, don't be
afraid.
Israel, I chose you.
3I will pour out water for the thirsty land
and make streams flow on dry land.
I will pour out my Spirit into your
children
and my blessing on your descendants.
4Your children will grow like a tree in the
grass,
like poplar trees growing beside
streams of water.
5One person will say, 'I belong to the LORD,'
and another will use the name Jacob.
Another will sign his name 'I am the
LORD's,'
and another will use the name Israel."

6The LORD, the king of Israel,
is the LORD All-Powerful, who saves
Israel.
This is what he says: "I am the beginning
and the end.
I am the only God.
7Who is a god like me?
That god should come and prove it.
Let him tell and explain all that has
happened since I set up my
ancient people.
He should also tell what will happen in
the future.

8Don't be afraid! Don't worry!
I have always told you what will happen.
You are my witnesses.
There is no other God but me.
I know of no other Rock; I am the only One."

Idols Are Useless

9Some people make idols, but they are worth nothing.
People treasure them, but they are useless.
Those people are witnesses for the statues,
but those people cannot see.
They know nothing, so they will be ashamed.
10Who made these gods?
Who made these useless idols?
11The workmen who made them will be ashamed,
because they are only human.
If they all would come together,
they would all be ashamed and afraid.

12One workman uses tools to heat iron,
and he works over hot coals.
With his hammer he beats the metal and makes a statue,
using his powerful arms.
But when he becomes hungry, he loses his power.
If he does not drink water, he becomes tired.
13Another workman uses a line and a compass
to draw on the wood.
Then he uses his chisels to cut a statue
and his calipers to measure the statue.
In this way, the workman makes the wood look exactly like a person,
and this statue of a person sits in the house.
14He cuts down cedars
or cypress or oak trees.
Those trees grew by their own power in the forest.
Or he plants a pine tree, and the rain makes it grow.
15Then he burns the tree.
He uses some of the wood for a fire to keep himself warm.
He also starts a fire to bake his bread.
But he uses part of the wood to make a god, and then he worships it!
He makes the idol and bows down to it!
16The man burns half of the wood in the fire.
He uses the fire to cook his meat,
and he eats the meat until he is full.
He also burns the wood to keep himself warm. He says,
"Good! Now I am warm. I can see because of the fire's light."
17But he makes a statue from the wood that is left and calls it his god.
He bows down to it and worships it.
He prays to it and says,
"You are my god. Save me!"
18Those people don't know what they are doing. They don't understand!
It is as if their eyes are covered so they can't see.
Their minds don't understand.
19They have not thought about these things;
they don't understand.
They have never thought to themselves,
"I burned half of the wood in the fire
and used the hot coals to bake my bread.
I cooked and ate my meat.
And I used the wood that was left to make this hateful thing.
I am worshiping a block of wood!"
20He doesn't know what he is doing;
his confused mind leads him the wrong way.
He cannot save himself
or say, "This statue I am holding is a false god."

The Lord Is the True God

21"People of Jacob, remember these things!
People of Israel, remember you are my servants.
I made you, and you are my servants.
So Israel, I will not forget you.
22I have swept away your sins like a big cloud;
I have removed your sins like a cloud that disappears into the air.
Come back to me because I saved you."

23Skies, sing for joy because the LORD did great things!
Earth, shout for joy, even in your deepest parts!

Sing, you mountains, with thanks to God.
Sing, too, you trees in the forest!
The LORD saved the people of Jacob!
He showed his glory when he saved Israel.
24This is what the LORD says, who saved you,
who formed you in your mother's body:
"I, the LORD, made everything,
stretching out the skies by myself
and spreading out the earth all alone.
25I show that the signs of the lying prophets are false;
I make fools of those who do magic.
I confuse even the wise;
they think they know much, but I make them look foolish.
26I make the messages of my servants come true;
I make the advice of my messengers come true.
I say to Jerusalem,
'People will live in you again!'
I say to the towns of Judah,
'You will be built again!'
I say to Jerusalem's ruins,
'I will repair you.'
27I tell the deep waters, 'Become dry!
I will make your streams become dry!'
28I say of Cyrus,[n] 'He is my shepherd
and will do all that I want him to do.
He will say to Jerusalem, "You will be built again!"
He will tell the Temple, "Your foundations will be rebuilt." ' "

God Chooses Cyrus to Free Israel

45 This is what the LORD says to Cyrus, his appointed king:
"I hold your right hand
and will help you defeat nations
and take away other kings' power.
I will open doors for you
so city gates will not stop you.
2I will go before you
and make the mountains flat.
I will break down the bronze gates of the cities
and cut through their iron bars.
3I will give you the wealth that is stored away
and the hidden riches
so you will know I am the LORD,
the God of Israel, who calls you by name.
4I do these things for my servants, the people of Jacob,
and for my chosen people, the Israelites.
Cyrus, I call you by name,
and I give you a title of honor even though you don't know me.
5I am the LORD. There is no other God;
I am the only God.
I will make you strong,
even though you don't know me,
6so that everyone will know
there is no other God.
From the east to the west they will know
I alone am the LORD.
7I made the light and the darkness.
I bring peace, and I cause troubles.
I, the LORD, do all these things.

8"Sky above, make victory fall like rain;
clouds, pour down victory.
Let the earth receive it,
and let salvation grow,
and let victory grow with it.
I, the LORD, have created it.

9"How terrible it will be for those who argue with the God who made them.
They are like a piece of broken pottery among many pieces.
The clay does not ask the potter,
'What are you doing?'
The thing that is made doesn't say to its maker,
'You have no hands.'
10How terrible it will be for the child who says to his father,
'Why are you giving me life?'
How terrible it will be for the child who says to his mother,
'Why are you giving birth to me?' "

11This is what the LORD,
the Holy One of Israel, and its Maker, says:
"You ask me about what will happen.
You question me about my children.
You give me orders about what I have made.

44:28 Cyrus A king of Persia who ruled from about 550–530 B.C.

12 I made the earth
and all the people living on it.
With my own hands I stretched out the skies,
and I commanded all the armies in the sky.
13 I will bring Cyrus to do good things,
and I will make his work easy.
He will rebuild my city
and set my people free
without any payment or reward.
The LORD All-Powerful says this."

14 The LORD says,
"The goods made in Egypt and Cush
and the tall people of Seba
will come to you
and will become yours.
The Sabeans will walk behind you,
coming along in chains.
They will bow down before you
and pray to you, saying,
'God is with you,
and there is no other God.' "

15 God and Savior of Israel,
you are a God that people cannot see.
16 All the people who make idols will be put to great shame;
they will go off together in disgrace.
17 But Israel will be saved by the LORD,
and that salvation will continue forever.
Never again will Israel be put to shame.

18 The LORD created the heavens.
He is the God who formed the earth and made it.
He did not want it to be empty,
but he wanted life on the earth.
This is what the LORD says:
"I am the LORD. There is no other God.
19 I did not speak in secret
or hide my words in some dark place.
I did not tell the family of Jacob
to look for me in empty places.
I am the LORD, and I speak the truth;
I say what is right.

20 "You people who have escaped from other nations,
gather together and come before me;
come near together.
People who carry idols of wood don't know what they are doing.
They pray to a god who cannot save them.
21 Tell these people to come to me.
Let them talk about these things together.
Who told you long ago that this would happen?
Who told about it long ago?
I, the LORD, said these things.
There is no other God besides me.
I am the only good God. I am the Savior.
There is no other God.

22 "All people everywhere,
follow me and be saved.
I am God. There is no other God.
23 I will make a promise by my own power,
and my promise is true;
what I say will not be changed.
I promise that everyone will bow before me
and will promise to follow me.
24 People will say about me, 'Goodness and power
come only from the LORD.' "
Everyone who has been angry with him
will come to him and be ashamed.
25 But with the LORD's help, the people of Israel
will be found to be good,
and they will praise him.

False Gods Are Useless

46 Bel and Nebo bow down.
Their idols are carried by animals.
The statues are only heavy loads that must be carried;
they only make people tired.
2 These gods will all bow down.
They cannot save themselves
but will all be carried away like prisoners.

3 "Family of Jacob, listen to me!
All you people from Israel who are still alive, listen!
I have carried you since you were born;
I have taken care of you from your birth.
4 Even when you are old, I will be the same.
Even when your hair has turned gray, I will take care of you.
I made you and will take care of you.
I will carry you and save you.

5 "Can you compare me to anyone?
No one is equal to me or like me.

devotion 202

ISAIAH 46:3–4

"I LOVE GETTING OLDER"

Billy and Ruth Graham are getting older and looking forward to heaven more every day. God has done so much with their lives. Daddy Bill, as he is called by family, has been used by God to bring thousands and thousands to Christ, and Ruth, or Tai Tai to her grandchildren, has written books and encouraged thousands in the Lord. But now, their hair has turned gray, and they are battling different ailments. Tai Tai is unable to read. Being unable to read her Bible has been the hardest part for her. "I cut my teeth on the Bible," she says. "I miss it more than anything else." Daddy Bill says that no one prepares you for getting older—it takes you by surprise.

Despite the surprises, Ruth says something about aging that is hard to understand. She says, "I love getting older." Baffling. How can you enjoy the limitations, the illness, and even the pain that the two of them have suffered through in their old age? But Isaiah 46:3-4 explains it. God says, "Even when you are old, I will be the same. Even when your hair has turned gray, I will take care of you" (verse 4). Maybe now the Lord is caring for the two of them because they can't care for themselves like they used to. They have both lived such full and rich lives, but now it is their turn to enjoy the simplicities of the Lord. Now it is their turn to rest until the Lord carries them to heaven.

6 Some people are rich with gold
and weigh their silver on the scales.
They hire a goldsmith, and he makes it into a god.
Then they bow down and worship it.
7 They put it on their shoulders and carry it.
They set it in its place, and there it stands;
it cannot move from its place.
People may yell at it, but it cannot answer.
It cannot save them from their troubles.

8 "Remember this, and do not forget it!
Think about these things, you who turn against God.
9 Remember what happened long ago.
Remember that I am God, and there is no other God.
I am God, and there is no one like me.
10 From the beginning I told you what would happen in the end.
A long time ago I told you things that have not yet happened.
When I plan something, it happens.
What I want to do, I will do.
11 I am calling a man from the east to carry out my plan;
he will come like a hawk from a country far away.
I will make what I have said come true;
I will do what I have planned.
12 Listen to me, you stubborn people,
who are far from what is right.
13 I will soon do the things that are right.
I will bring salvation soon.
I will save Jerusalem
and bring glory to Israel."

God Will Destroy Babylon

47 The LORD says, "City of Babylon, go down and sit in the dirt.
People of Babylon, sit on the ground.
You are no longer the ruler.
You will no longer be called
tender or beautiful.
2 You must use large stones to grind grain into flour.

Remove your veil and your nice skirts.
Uncover your legs and cross the rivers.
3 People will see your nakedness;
they will see your shame.
I will punish you;
I will punish every one of you."

4 Our Savior is named the LORD
All-Powerful;
he is the Holy One of Israel.

5 "Babylon, sit in darkness and say nothing.
You will no longer be called the queen
of kingdoms.
6 I was angry with my people,
so I rejected those who belonged to me.
I gave them to you,
but you showed them no mercy.
You even made the old people
work very hard.
7 You said, 'I will live forever
as the queen.'
But you did not think about these things
or consider what would happen.
8 "Now, listen, you lover of pleasure.
You think you are safe.
You tell yourself,
'I am the only important person.
I will never be a widow
or lose my children.'
9 Two things will happen to you suddenly,
in a single day.
You will lose your children and your
husband.
These things will truly happen to you,
in spite of all your magic,
in spite of your powerful tricks.
10 You do evil things, but you feel safe
and say, 'No one sees what I do.'
Your wisdom and knowledge
have fooled you.
You say to yourself,
'I am God, and no one is equal to me.'
11 But troubles will come to you,
and you will not know how to stop
them.
Disaster will fall on you,
and you will not be able to keep it away.
You will be destroyed quickly;
you will not even see it coming.

12 "Keep on using your tricks
and doing all your magic
that you have used since you were
young.
Maybe they will help you;
maybe you will be able to scare
someone.
13 You are tired of the advice you have
received.
So let those who study the sky—
those who tell the future by looking at
the stars and the new moons—
let them save you from what is about to
happen to you.
14 But they are like straw;
fire will quickly burn them up.
They cannot save themselves
from the power of the fire.
They are not like coals that give warmth
nor like a fire that you may sit beside.
15 You have worked with these people,
and they have been with you since you
were young,
but they will not be able to help you.
Everyone will go his own way,
and there will be no one left to save
you."

God Controls the Future

48 The LORD says, "Family of Jacob, listen
to me.
You are called Israel,
and you come from the family of Judah.
You swear by the LORD's name
and praise the God of Israel,
but you are not honest or sincere.
2 You call yourselves people of the holy
city,
and you depend on the God of Israel,
who is named the LORD All-Powerful.
3 Long ago I told you what would happen.
I said these things and made them
known;
suddenly I acted, and these things
happened.
4 I knew you were stubborn;
your neck was like an iron muscle,
and your head was like bronze.
5 So a long time ago I told you about these
things;
I told you about them before they
happened
so you couldn't say, 'My idols did this,
and my wooden and metal statues
made these things happen.'
6 "You heard and saw everything that
happened,

so you should tell this news to others.
Now I will tell you about new things,
hidden things that you don't know yet.
7These things are happening now, not long ago;
you have not heard about them before today.
So you cannot say, 'We already knew about that.'
8But you have not heard me; you have not understood.
Even long ago you did not listen to me.
I knew you would surely turn against me;
you have fought against me since you were born.
9But for my own sake I will be patient.
People will praise me for not becoming angry
and destroying you.
10I have made you pure, but not by fire, as silver is made pure.
I have purified you by giving you troubles.
11I do this for myself, for my own sake.
I will not let people speak evil against me,
and I will not let some god take my glory.

Israel Will Be Free

12"People of Jacob, listen to me.
People of Israel, I have called you to be my people.
I am God;
I am the beginning and the end.
13I made the earth with my own hands.
With my right hand I spread out the skies.
When I call them,
they come together before me."

14All of you, come together and listen.
None of the gods said these things would happen.
The LORD has chosen someone
to attack the Babylonians;
he will carry out his wishes against Babylon.

15"I have spoken; I have called him.[n]
I have brought him, and I will make him successful.
16Come to me and listen to this.
From the beginning I have spoken openly.
From the time it began, I was there."

Now, the Lord GOD
has sent me with his Spirit.
17This is what the LORD, who saves you,
the Holy One of Israel, says:
"I am the LORD your God,
who teaches you to do what is good,
who leads you in the way you should go.
18If you had obeyed me,
you would have had peace like a full-flowing river.
Good things would have flowed to you like the waves of the sea.
19You would have had many children,
as many as the grains of sand.
They would never have died out
nor been destroyed."

20My people, leave Babylon!
Run from the Babylonians!
Tell this news with shouts of joy to the people;
spread it everywhere on earth.
Say, "The LORD has saved his servants, the people of Jacob."
21They did not become thirsty when he led them through the deserts.
He made water flow from a rock for them.
He split the rock,
and water flowed out.

22"There is no peace for evil people," says the LORD.

God Calls His Special Servant

49 All of you people in faraway places,
listen to me.
Listen, all you nations far away.
Before I was born, the LORD called me to serve him.
The LORD named me while I was still in my mother's womb.
2He made my tongue like a sharp sword.
He hid me in the shadow of his hand.
He made me like a sharp arrow.
He hid me in the holder for his arrows.

48:15 him This probably refers to Cyrus king of Persia.

3He told me, "Israel, you are my servant.
I will show my glory through you."
4But I said, "I have worked hard for nothing;
I have used all my power, but I did nothing useful.
But the LORD will decide what my work is worth;
God will decide my reward."
5The LORD made me in the body of my mother
to be his servant,
to lead the people of Jacob back to him
so that Israel might be gathered to him.
The LORD will honor me,
and I will get my strength from my God.
6Now he told me,
"You are an important servant to me
to bring back the tribes of Jacob,
to bring back the people of Israel who are left alive.
But, more importantly, I will make you a light for all nations
to show people all over the world the way to be saved."

7The LORD who saves you
is the Holy One of Israel.
He speaks to the one who is hated by the people,
to the servant of rulers.
This is what he says: "Kings will see you
and stand to honor you;
great leaders will bow down before you,
because the LORD can be trusted.
He is the Holy One of Israel, who has chosen you."

The Day of Salvation

8This is what the LORD says:
"At the right time I will hear your prayers.
On the day of salvation I will help you.
I will protect you,
and you will be the sign of my agreement with the people.
You will bring back the people to the land
and give the land that is now ruined back to its owners.
9You will tell the prisoners, 'Come out of your prison.'
You will tell those in darkness, 'Come into the light.'
The people will eat beside the roads,
and they will find food even on bare hills.
10They will not be hungry or thirsty.
Neither the hot sun nor the desert wind will hurt them.
The God who comforts them will lead them
and guide them by springs of water.
11I will make my mountains into roads,
and the roads will be raised up.
12Look, people are coming to me from far away,
from the north and from the west,
from Aswan in southern Egypt."

13Heavens and earth, be happy.
Mountains, shout with joy,
because the LORD comforts his people
and will have pity on those who suffer.

Jerusalem and Her Children

14But Jerusalem said, "The LORD has left me;
the Lord has forgotten me."

15The LORD answers, "Can a woman forget the baby she nurses?
Can she feel no kindness for the child to which she gave birth?
Even if she could forget her children,
I will not forget you.
16See, I have written your name on my hand.
Jerusalem, I always think about your walls.
17Your children will soon return to you,
and the people who defeated you and destroyed you will leave.
18Look up and look around you.
All your children are gathering to return to you."
The LORD says, "As surely as I live,
your children will be like jewels
that a bride wears proudly.

19"You were destroyed and defeated,
and your land was made useless.
But now you will have more people than the land can hold,
and those people who destroyed you will be far away.
20Children were born to you while you were sad,
but they will say to you,
'This place is too small for us.
Give us a bigger place to live.'

21 Then you will say to yourself,
'Who gave me all these children?
I was sad and lonely,
defeated and separated from my people.
So who reared these children?
I was left all alone.
Where did all these children come from?' "

22 This is what the Lord GOD says:
"See, I will lift my hand to signal the nations;
I will raise my banner for all the people to see.
Then they will bring your sons back to you in their arms,
and they will carry your daughters on their shoulders.
23 Kings will teach your children,
and daughters of kings will take care of them.
They will bow down before you
and kiss the dirt at your feet.
Then you will know I am the LORD.
Anyone who trusts in me will not be disappointed."

24 Can the wealth a soldier wins in war be taken away from him?
Can a prisoner be freed from a powerful soldier?
25 This is what the LORD says:
"The prisoners will be taken from the strong soldiers.
What the soldiers have taken will be saved.
I will fight your enemies,
and I will save your children.
26 I will force those who trouble you to eat their own flesh.
Their own blood will be the wine that makes them drunk.
Then everyone will know
I, the LORD, am the One who saves you;
I am the Powerful One of Jacob who saves you."

Israel Was Punished for Its Sin

50 This is what the LORD says:
"People of Israel, you say I divorced your mother.
Then where is the paper that proves it?

devotion 203

ISAIAH 50:10–11

BARBIE AND KEN'S FOREST FIRE

When I was eight and my brother was four, we took Barbie and Ken, along with their camper, and went on a camping trip in the woods in our backyard. Ken was not too swift, so I had to help him build the campfire. Within minutes the campfire had grown to a roaring blaze in the woods. Scared, my brother and I ran into the house and retreated to our rooms. It was not long before someone saw the flames and called the fire department. Boy, we knew we were going to get it. The fire marshal was a pretty astute guy and grateful that Mattel did such a good job with Barbie and Ken that there was enough evidence to point to the parties responsible for starting the blaze. Lying "down in a place of pain" is an understatement (verse 11), and both of us learned the lesson of a lifetime—play with fire and you will get burned (or at least red heinies).

Isaiah's message and encouragement is to not walk in your own ways. As children, my brother and I made our own way without permission or guidance, and we experienced a devastating outcome that affected more than just our family. Do not try to light your path with the fire of self-will. Let your heart trust and depend on a heavenly Father that will make sure that when you lie down, it will be in peace, not pain. If you are playing with fire today, put it out!

Or do you think I sold you
to pay a debt?
Because of the evil things you did, I sold
you.
Because of the times she turned against
me, your mother was sent away.
2I came home and found no one there;
I called, but no one answered.
Do you think I am not able to save you?
Do I not have the power to save you?
Look, I need only to shout and the sea
becomes dry.
I change rivers into a desert,
and their fish rot because there is no water;
they die of thirst.
3I can make the skies dark;
I can make them black like clothes of
sadness."

God's Servant Obeys

4The Lord GOD gave me the ability to teach
so that I know what to say to make the
weak strong.
Every morning he wakes me.
He teaches me to listen like a student.
5The Lord GOD helps me learn,
and I have not turned against him
nor stopped following him.
6I offered my back to those who beat me.
I offered my cheeks to those who
pulled my beard.
I won't hide my face from them
when they make fun of me and spit
at me.
7The Lord GOD helps me,
so I will not be ashamed.
I will be determined,
and I know I will not be disgraced.
8He shows that I am innocent, and he is
close to me.
So who can accuse me?
If there is someone, let us go to court
together.
If someone wants to prove I have done
wrong,
he should come and tell me.
9Look! It is the Lord GOD who helps me.
So who can prove me guilty?
Look! All those who try will become
useless like old clothes;
moths will eat them.
10Who among you fears the LORD
and obeys his servant?
That person may walk in the dark
and have no light.
Then let him trust in the LORD
and yet depend on his God.
11But instead, some of you want to light
your own fires
and make your own light.
So, go, walk in the light of your fires,
and trust your own light to guide you.
But this is what you will receive
from me:
You will lie down in a place of pain.

Jerusalem Will Be Saved

51 The LORD says, "Listen to me,
those of you who try to live right
and follow the LORD.
Look at the rock from which you were
cut;
look at the stone quarry from which
you were dug.
2Look at Abraham, your ancestor,
and Sarah, who gave birth to your
ancestors.
Abraham had no children when I called
him,
but I blessed him and gave him many
descendants.
3So the LORD will comfort Jerusalem;
he will show mercy to those who live
in her ruins.
He will change her deserts into a garden
like Eden;
he will make her empty lands like the
garden of the LORD.
People there will be very happy;
they will give thanks and sing songs.
4"My people, listen to me;
my nation, pay attention to me.
I will give the people my teachings,
and my decisions will be like a light to
all people.
5I will soon show that I do what is right.
I will soon save you.
I will use my power and judge all
nations.
All the faraway places are waiting
for me;
they wait for my power to help them.
6Look up to the heavens.
Look around you at the earth below.
The skies will disappear like clouds of
smoke.

The earth will become useless like old clothes,
and its people will die like flies.
But my salvation will continue forever,
and my goodness will never end.

7 "You people who know what is right should listen to me;
you people who follow my teachings should hear what I say.
Don't be afraid of the evil things people say,
and don't be upset by their insults.
8 Moths will eat those people as if they were clothes,
and worms will eat them as if they were wool.
But my goodness will continue forever,
and my salvation will continue from now on."

9 Wake up, wake up, and use your strength, powerful LORD.
Wake up as you did in the old times,
as you did a long time ago.
With your own power, you cut Rahab into pieces
and killed that sea monster.
10 You dried up the sea
and the waters of the deep ocean.
You made the deepest parts of the sea into a road
for your people to cross over and be saved.
11 The people the LORD has freed will return
and enter Jerusalem with joy.
Their happiness will last forever.
They will have joy and gladness,
and all sadness and sorrow will be gone far away.

12 The LORD says, "I am the one who comforts you.
So why should you be afraid of people, who die?
Why should you fear people who die like the grass?
13 Have you forgotten the LORD who made you,
who stretched out the skies
and made the earth?
Why are you always afraid
of those angry people who trouble you
and who want to destroy?
But where are those angry people now?
14 People in prison will soon be set free;

devotion 204

ISAIAH 51:6

LOOK UP

Look up, my dear woman, and see the salvation of the Lord. What an encouragement to know that when all of this life and its unknowns are finished, we know exactly what we will be looking at—the heavens of God. You may not know how many years you will live, how many children or grandchildren you will have, or where you will call home when retirement comes. But you do know that when the Lord calls a believer home, that believer will be in his presence with all those who have gone before. He will meet you there in the new heaven with giant gates of pearls and streets that are paved with gold. This is the joy set before us that he has given us a promise of eternal life.

During this season, fix your heart and mind to live looking up. It is so easy with the weight of the world on our shoulders to be in a state of defeat and go looking to other resources to lighten our load. But be of good cheer—Jesus has overcome the world. Look up! Look up to find comfort for your grieving heart. Look up to rid your life of sin. Look up to celebrate the joys of birth. Look up when you need strength, and look up even when you don't feel like it. Up is the only place where you will find a forever King that loves you with everything he has. A King whose goodness will never end!

they will not die in prison,
and they will have enough food.
15I am the LORD your God,
who stirs the sea and makes the waves roar.
My name is the LORD All-Powerful.
16I will give you the words I want you to say.
I will cover you with my hands and protect you.
I made the heavens and the earth,
and I say to Jerusalem, 'You are my people.' "

God Punished Israel

17Awake! Awake!
Get up, Jerusalem.
The LORD was very angry with you;
your punishment was like wine in a cup.
The LORD made you drink that wine;
you drank the whole cup until you stumbled.
18Jerusalem had many people,
but there was not one to lead her.
Of all the people who grew up there,
no one was there to guide her.
19Troubles came to you two by two,
but no one will feel sorry for you.
There was ruin and disaster, great hunger and fighting.
No one can comfort you.
20Your people have become weak.
They fall down and lie on every street corner,
like animals caught in a net.
They have felt the full anger of the LORD
and have heard God's angry shout.
21So listen to me, poor Jerusalem,
you who are drunk but not from wine.
22Your God will defend his people.
This is what the LORD your God says:
"The punishment I gave you is like a cup of wine.
You drank it and could not walk straight.
But I am taking that cup of my anger away from you,
and you will never be punished by my anger again.
23I will now give that cup of punishment to those who gave you pain,
who told you,
'Bow down so we can walk over you.'
They made your back like dirt for them to walk on;
you were like a street for them to travel on."

Jerusalem Will Be Saved

52 Wake up, wake up, Jerusalem!
Become strong!
Be beautiful again,
holy city of Jerusalem.
The people who do not worship God and who are not pure
will not enter you again.
2Jerusalem, you once were a prisoner.
Now shake off the dust and stand up.
Jerusalem, you once were a prisoner.
Now free yourself from the chains around your neck.
3This is what the LORD says:
"You were not sold for a price,
so you will be saved without cost."
4This is what the Lord GOD says:
"First my people went down to Egypt to live.
Later Assyria made them slaves.
5"Now see what has happened," says the LORD.
"Another nation has taken away my people for nothing.
This nation who rules them makes fun of me," says the LORD.
"All day long they speak against me.
6This has happened so my people will know who I am,
and so, on that future day, they will know
that I am the one speaking to them.
It will really be me."
7How beautiful is the person
who comes over the mountains to bring good news,
who announces peace
and brings good news,
who announces salvation
and says to Jerusalem,
"Your God is King."
8Listen! Your guards are shouting.
They are all shouting for joy!
They all will see with their own eyes
when the LORD returns to Jerusalem.
9Jerusalem, your buildings are destroyed now,
but shout and rejoice together,

because the LORD has comforted his people.
He has saved Jerusalem.
10 The LORD will show his holy power
to all the nations.
Then everyone on earth
will see the salvation of our God.

11 You people, leave, leave; get out of
Babylon!
Touch nothing that is unclean.
You men who carry the LORD's things used
in worship,
leave there and make yourselves pure.
12 You will not be forced to leave Babylon
quickly;
you will not be forced to run away,
because the LORD will go before you,
and the God of Israel will guard you
from behind.

The Lord's Suffering Servant

13 The LORD says, "See, my servant will act
wisely.
People will greatly honor and respect
him.
14 Many people were shocked when they
saw him.
His appearance was so damaged he did
not look like a man;
his form was so changed they could
barely tell he was human.
15 But now he will surprise many nations.
Kings will be amazed and shut their
mouths.
They will see things they had not been
told about him,
and they will understand things they
had not heard."

53 Who would have believed what we
heard?
Who saw the LORD's power in this?
2 He grew up like a small plant before the
LORD,
like a root growing in a dry land.
He had no special beauty or form to make
us notice him;
there was nothing in his appearance to
make us desire him.
3 He was hated and rejected by people.
He had much pain and suffering.
People would not even look at him.
He was hated, and we didn't even notice
him.
4 But he took our suffering on him
and felt our pain for us.
We saw his suffering
and thought God was punishing him.
5 But he was wounded for the wrong we
did;
he was crushed for the evil we did.
The punishment, which made us well,
was given to him,
and we are healed because of his
wounds.
6 We all have wandered away like sheep;
each of us has gone his own way.
But the LORD has put on him the
punishment
for all the evil we have done.

7 He was beaten down and punished,
but he didn't say a word.
He was like a lamb being led to be killed.
He was quiet, as a sheep is quiet while
its wool is being cut;
he never opened his mouth.
8 Men took him away roughly and unfairly.
He died without children to continue
his family.
He was put to death;
he was punished for the sins of my
people.
9 He was buried with wicked men,
and he died with the rich.
He had done nothing wrong,
and he had never lied.

10 But it was the LORD who decided
to crush him and make him suffer.
The LORD made his life a penalty
offering,
but he will still see his descendants and
live a long life.
He will complete the things the LORD
wants him to do.
11 "After his soul suffers many things,
he will see life and be satisfied.
My good servant will make many people
right with God;
he will carry away their sins.
12 For this reason I will make him a great
man among people,
and he will share in all things with
those who are strong.
He willingly gave his life
and was treated like a criminal.
But he carried away the sins of many
people

and asked forgiveness for those who
sinned."

People Will Return to Jerusalem

54 The LORD says, "Sing, Jerusalem.
You are like a woman who never
gave birth to children.
Start singing and shout for joy.
You never felt the pain of giving birth,
but you will have more children
than the woman who has a husband.
2 Make your tent bigger;
stretch it out and make it wider.
Do not hold back.
Make the ropes longer
and its stakes stronger,
3 because you will spread out to the right
and to the left.
Your children will take over other
nations,
and they will again live in cities that
once were destroyed.
4 "Don't be afraid, because you will not be
ashamed.
Don't be embarrassed, because you will
not be disgraced.
You will forget the shame you felt
earlier;
you will not remember the shame you
felt when you lost your husband.
5 The God who made you is like your
husband.
His name is the LORD All-Powerful.
The Holy One of Israel is the one who
saves you.
He is called the God of all the earth.
6 You were like a woman whose husband
left her,
and you were very sad.
You were like a wife who married young
and then her husband left her.
But the LORD called you to be his,"
says your God.
7 God says, "I left you for a short time,
but with great kindness I will bring you
back again.
8 I became very angry
and hid from you for a time,
but I will show you mercy with kindness
forever,"
says the LORD who saves you.
9 The LORD says, "This day is like the time
of Noah to me.
I promised then that I would never
flood the world again.
In the same way, I promise I will not be
angry with you
or punish you again.
10 The mountains may disappear,
and the hills may come to an end,
but my love will never disappear;
my promise of peace will not come to
an end,"
says the LORD who shows mercy to you.

11 "You poor city. Storms have hurt you,
and you have not been comforted.
But I will rebuild you with turquoise
stones,
and I will build your foundations with
sapphires.
12 I will use rubies to build your walls
and shining jewels for the gates
and precious jewels for all your outer
walls.
13 All your children will be taught by the
LORD,
and they will have much peace.
14 I will build you using fairness.
You will be safe from those who would
hurt you,
so you will have nothing to fear.
Nothing will come to make you afraid.
15 I will not send anyone to attack you,
and you will defeat those who do attack
you.
16 "See, I made the blacksmith.
He fans the fire to make it hotter,
and he makes the kind of tool he wants.
In the same way I have made the
destroyer to destroy.
17 So no weapon that is used against you
will defeat you.
You will show that those who speak
against you are wrong.
These are the good things my servants
receive.
Their victory comes from me," says the
LORD.

God Gives What Is Good

55 The LORD says, "All you who are thirsty,
come and drink.
Those of you who do not have money,
come, buy and eat!
Come buy wine and milk
without money and without cost.

2 Why spend your money on something
that is not real food?
Why work for something that doesn't
really satisfy you?
Listen closely to me, and you will eat
what is good;
your soul will enjoy the rich food that
satisfies.
3 Come to me and listen;
listen to me so you may live.
I will make an agreement with you that
will last forever.
I will give you the blessings I promised
to David.
4 I made David a witness of my power for
all nations,
a ruler and commander of many
nations.
5 You will call for nations that you don't yet
know.
And these nations that do not know
you will run to you
because of the LORD your God,
because of the Holy One of Israel who
honors you."

6 So you should look for the LORD before it
is too late;
you should call to him while he is near.
7 The wicked should stop doing wrong,
and they should stop their evil
thoughts.
They should return to the LORD so he may
have mercy on them.
They should come to our God, because
he will freely forgive them.

8 The LORD says, "My thoughts are not like
your thoughts.
Your ways are not like my ways.
9 Just as the heavens are higher than the
earth,
so are my ways higher than your ways
and my thoughts higher than your
thoughts.
10 Rain and snow fall from the sky
and don't return without watering the
ground.
They cause the plants to sprout and grow,
making seeds for the farmer
and bread for the people.
11 The same thing is true of the words I
speak.
They will not return to me empty.
They make the things happen that I want
to happen,

devotion 205

ISAIAH 55:8–9

WHAT DOES IT TAKE TO CHANGE?

My thoughts and ways are different than the Lord's, yet I want to become more and more like him. So how do I go about doing this? Romans 12:2 says that we need to be "changed within by a new way of thinking." God's thoughts and ways are right here in your hands in the Word of God. If we want to know God's thoughts, we just need to spend time in the Bible. Hebrews 4:12 says that God's Word is alive and "sharper than a double-edged sword." Its words reach our core and cut away at any thoughts and feelings that don't align with Scripture. It changes us through the power of the Holy Spirit.

We are not capable of changing ourselves. God has given us salvation through faith by grace. Grace is receiving something we don't reserve. Paul asks in Galatians 3:3, "You began your life in Christ by the Spirit. Now are you trying to make it complete by your own power?" We can try to follow Christ in our own strength, but we will fail. His ways are not our ways. We have to depend on the Holy Spirit to do the work in us to make us more and more like Christ. Our thoughts and ways are not God's, but when we have the Spirit of God living in us and the Word of God flowing through us, we will be changed and become more and more like Jesus every day.

and they succeed in doing what I send
them to do.

12"So you will go out with joy
and be led out in peace.
The mountains and hills will burst into
song before you,
and all the trees in the fields will clap
their hands.
13Large cypress trees will grow where
thornbushes were.
Myrtle trees will grow where weeds
were.
These things will be a reminder of the
LORD's promise,
and this reminder will never be
destroyed."

All Nations Will Obey the Lord

56 This is what the LORD says:
"Give justice to all people,
and do what is right,
because my salvation will come to you
soon.
Soon everyone will know that I do
what is right.
2The person who obeys the law about the
Sabbath
will be blessed,
and the person who does no evil
will be blessed."

3Foreigners who have joined the LORD
should not say,
"The LORD will not accept me with his
people."
The eunuch should not say,
"Because I cannot have children, the
LORD will not accept me."
4This is what the LORD says:
"The eunuchs should obey the law about
the Sabbath
and do what I want
and keep my agreement.
5If they do, I will make their names
remembered
within my Temple and its walls.
It will be better for them than children.
I will give them a name that will last
forever,
that will never be forgotten.
6Foreigners will join the LORD
to worship him and love him,
to serve him,
to obey the law about the Sabbath,
and to keep my agreement.
7I will bring these people to my holy
mountain
and give them joy in my house of
prayer.
The offerings and sacrifices
they place on my altar will please me,
because my Temple will be called
a house for prayer for people from all
nations."
8The Lord GOD says—
he who gathers the Israelites that were
forced to leave their country:
"I will bring together other people
to join those who are already gathered."

Israel's Leaders Are Evil

9All you animals of the field,
all you animals of the forest, come to
eat.
10The leaders who are to guard the people
are blind;
they don't know what they are doing.
All of them are like quiet dogs
that don't know how to bark.
They lie down and dream
and love to sleep.
11They are like hungry dogs
that are never satisfied.
They are like shepherds
who don't know what they are doing.
They all have gone their own way;
all they want to do is satisfy
themselves.
12They say, "Come, let's drink some wine;
let's drink all the beer we want.
And tomorrow we will do this again,
or, maybe we will have an even better
time."

Israel Does Not Follow God

57 Those who are right with God may die,
but no one pays attention.
Good people are taken away,
but no one understands.
Those who do right are being taken away
from evil
2 and are given peace.
Those who live as God wants
find rest in death.

3"Come here, you magicians!
Come here, you children of prostitutes
and those who take part in
adultery!

4 Of whom are you making fun?
Whom are you insulting?
At whom do you stick out your tongue?
You turn against God,
and you are liars.
5 You have sexual relations under every green tree
to worship your gods.
You kill children in the ravines
and sacrifice them in the rocky places.
6 You take the smooth rocks from the ravines
as your portion.
You pour drink offerings on them to worship them,
and you give grain offerings to them.
Do you think this makes me want to show you mercy?
7 You make your bed on every hill and mountain,
and there you offer sacrifices.
8 You have hidden your idols
behind your doors and doorposts.
You have left me, and you have uncovered yourself.
You have pulled back the covers and climbed into bed.
You have made an agreement with those whose beds you love,
and you have looked at their nakedness.
9 You use your oils and perfumes
to look nice for Molech.
You have sent your messengers to faraway lands;
you even tried to send them to the place of the dead.
10 You were tired from doing these things,
but you never gave up.
You found new strength,
so you did not quit.

11 "Whom were you so afraid of
that you lied to me?
You have not remembered me
or even thought about me.
I have been quiet for a long time.
Is that why you are not afraid of me?
12 I will tell about your 'goodness' and what you do,
and those things will do you no good.
13 When you cry out for help,
let the gods you have gathered help you.
The wind will blow them all away;
just a puff of wind will take them away.
But the person who depends on me will receive the land
and own my holy mountain."

The Lord Will Save His People

14 Someone will say, "Build a road! Build a road! Prepare the way!
Make the way clear for my people."
15 And this is the reason: God lives forever and is holy.
He is high and lifted up.
He says, "I live in a high and holy place,
but I also live with people who are sad and humble.
I give new life to those who are humble
and to those whose hearts are broken.
16 I will not accuse forever,
nor will I always be angry,
because then human life would grow weak.
Human beings, whom I created, would die.
17 I was angry because they were dishonest in order to make money.
I punished them and turned away from them in anger,
but they continued to do evil.
18 I have seen what they have done, but I will heal them.
I will guide them and comfort them
and those who felt sad for them.
They will all praise me.
19 I will give peace, real peace, to those far and near,
and I will heal them," says the LORD.
20 But evil people are like the angry sea,
which cannot rest,
whose waves toss up waste and mud.
21 "There is no peace for evil people," says my God.

How to Honor God

58 The LORD says, "Shout out loud. Don't hold back.
Shout out loud like a trumpet.
Tell my people what they have done against their God;
tell the family of Jacob about their sins.
2 They still come every day looking for me
and want to learn my ways.
They act just like a nation that does what is right,
that obeys the commands of its God.

They ask me to judge them fairly.
They want God to be near them.
3 They say, 'To honor you we had special days when we fasted,
but you didn't see.
We humbled ourselves to honor you,
but you didn't notice.' "

But the LORD says, "You do what pleases yourselves on these special days,
and you are unfair to your workers.
4 On these special days when you fast, you argue and fight
and hit each other with your fists.
You cannot do these things as you do now
and believe your prayers are heard in heaven.
5 This kind of special day is not what I want.
This is not the way I want people to be sorry for what they have done.
I don't want people just to bow their heads like a plant
and wear rough cloth and lie in ashes to show their sadness.
This is what you do on your special days when you fast,
but do you think this is what the LORD wants?

6 "I will tell you the kind of fast I want:
Free the people you have put in prison unfairly
and undo their chains.
Free those to whom you are unfair
and stop their hard labor.
7 Share your food with the hungry
and bring poor, homeless people into your own homes.
When you see someone who has no clothes, give him yours,
and don't refuse to help your own relatives.
8 Then your light will shine like the dawn,
and your wounds will quickly heal.
Your God will walk before you,
and the glory of the LORD will protect you from behind.
9 Then you will call out, and the LORD will answer.
You will cry out, and he will say, 'Here I am.'

"If you stop making trouble for others,
if you stop using cruel words and pointing your finger at others,
10 if you feed those who are hungry
and take care of the needs of those who are troubled,
then your light will shine in the darkness,
and you will be bright like sunshine at noon.
11 The LORD will always lead you.
He will satisfy your needs in dry lands
and give strength to your bones.
You will be like a garden that has much water,
like a spring that never runs dry.
12 Your people will rebuild the old cities that are now in ruins;
you will rebuild their foundations.
You will be known for repairing the broken places
and for rebuilding the roads and houses.

13 "You must obey God's law about the Sabbath
and not do what pleases yourselves on that holy day.
You should call the Sabbath a joyful day
and honor it as the LORD's holy day.
You should honor it by not doing whatever you please
nor saying whatever you please on that day.
14 Then you will find joy in the LORD,
and I will carry you to the high places above the earth.
I will let you eat the crops of the land your ancestor Jacob had."
The LORD has said these things.

The Evil That People Do

59 Surely the LORD's power is enough to save you.
He can hear you when you ask him for help.
2 It is your evil that has separated you from your God.
Your sins cause him to turn away from you,
so he does not hear you.
3 With your hands you have killed others,
and with your fingers you have done wrong.
With your lips you have lied,
and with your tongue you say evil things.
4 People take each other to court unfairly,

and no one tells the truth in arguing his case.
They accuse each other falsely and tell lies.
They cause trouble and create more evil.
5 They hatch evil like eggs from poisonous snakes.
If you eat one of those eggs, you will die,
and if you break one open, a poisonous snake comes out.
People tell lies as they would spin a spider's web.
6 The webs they make cannot be used for clothes;
you can't cover yourself with those webs.
The things they do are evil,
and they use their hands to hurt others.
7 They eagerly run to do evil,
and they are always ready to kill innocent people.
They think evil thoughts.
Everywhere they go they cause ruin and destruction.
8 They don't know how to live in peace,
and there is no fairness in their lives.
They are dishonest.
Anyone who lives as they live will never have peace.

Israel's Sin Brings Trouble

9 Fairness has gone far away;
goodness is nowhere to be found.
We wait for the light, but there is only darkness now.
We hope for a bright light, but all we have is darkness.
10 We are like the blind feeling our way along a wall.
We feel our way as if we had no eyes.
In the brightness of day we trip as if it were night.
We are like dead men among the strong.
11 All of us growl like the bears.
We call out sadly like the doves.
We look for justice, but there isn't any.
We want to be saved, but salvation is far away.

12 We have done many wrong things against our God;
our sins show we are wrong.
We know we have turned against God;
we know the evil things we have done:
13 sinning and rejecting the LORD,
turning away from our God,
planning to hurt others and to disobey God,
planning and speaking lies.
14 So we have driven away justice,
and we have kept away from what is right.
Truth is not spoken in the streets;
what is honest is not allowed to enter the city.
15 Truth cannot be found anywhere,
and people who refuse to do evil are attacked.

The LORD looked and could not find any justice,
and he was displeased.
16 He could not find anyone to help the people,
and he was surprised that there was no one to help.
So he used his own power to save the people;
his own goodness gave him strength.
17 He covered himself with goodness like armor.
He put the helmet of salvation on his head.
He put on his clothes for punishing
and wrapped himself in the coat of his strong love.
18 The LORD will pay back his enemies for what they have done.
He will show his anger to those who were against him;
he will punish the people in faraway places as they deserve.
19 Then people from the west will fear the LORD,
and people from the east will fear his glory.
The LORD will come quickly like a fast-flowing river,
driven by the breath of the LORD.

20 "Then a Savior will come to Jerusalem
and to the people of Jacob who have turned from sin,"
says the LORD.
21 The LORD says, "This is my agreement
with these people: My Spirit and my words
that I give you will never leave you or your

children or your grandchildren, now and
forever."

Jerusalem Will Be Great

60 "Jerusalem, get up and shine, because
your light has come,
and the glory of the LORD shines on you.
2 Darkness now covers the earth;
deep darkness covers her people.
But the LORD shines on you,
and people see his glory around you.
3 Nations will come to your light;
kings will come to the brightness of
your sunrise.

4 "Look around you.
People are gathering and coming to
you.
Your sons are coming from far away,
and your daughters are coming with
them.
5 When you see them, you will shine with
happiness;
you will be excited and full of joy,
because the wealth of the nations across
the seas will be given to you;
the riches of the nations will come to
you.
6 Herds of camels will cover your land,
young camels from Midian and
Ephah.
People will come from Sheba
bringing gold and incense,
and they will sing praises to the LORD.
7 All the sheep from Kedar will be given to
you;
the sheep from Nebaioth will be
brought to you.
They will be pleasing sacrifices on my
altar,
and I will make my beautiful Temple
more beautiful.

8 "The people are returning to you like
clouds,
like doves flying to their nests.
9 People in faraway lands are waiting
for me.
The great trading ships will come first,
bringing your children from faraway
lands,
and with them silver and gold.
This will honor the LORD your God,
the Holy One of Israel,
who does wonderful things for you.

10 "Jerusalem, foreigners will rebuild your
walls,
and their kings will serve you.
When I was angry, I hurt you,
but now I want to be kind to you and
comfort you.
11 Your gates will always be open;
they will not be closed day or night
so the nations can bring their wealth to
you,
and their kings will be led to you.
12 The nation or kingdom that doesn't serve
you will be destroyed;
it will be completely ruined.

13 "The great trees of Lebanon will be given
to you:
its pine, fir, and cypress trees together.
You will use them to make my Temple
beautiful,
and I will give much honor to this
place where I rest my feet.
14 The people who have hurt you will bow
down to you;
those who hated you will bow down at
your feet.
They will call you The City of the LORD,
Jerusalem, city of the Holy One of
Israel.

15 "You have been hated and left empty
with no one passing through.
But I will make you great from now on;
you will be a place of happiness forever
and ever.
16 You will be given what you need from the
nations,
like a child drinking milk from its
mother.
Then you will know that it is I, the LORD,
who saves you.
You will know that the Powerful One of
Jacob protects you.
17 I will bring you gold in place of bronze,
silver in place of iron,
bronze in place of wood,
iron in place of rocks.
I will change your punishment into
peace,
and you will be ruled by what is right.
18 There will be no more violence in your
country;
it will not be ruined or destroyed.
You will name your walls Salvation
and your gates Praise.

19The sun will no longer be your light
during the day
nor will the brightness from the moon
be your light,
because the LORD will be your light
forever,
and your God will be your glory.
20Your sun will never set again,
and your moon will never be dark,
because the LORD will be your light
forever,
and your time of sadness will end.
21All of your people will do what is right.
They will receive the earth forever.
They are the plant I have planted,
the work of my own hands
to show my greatness.
22The smallest family will grow to a
thousand.
The least important of you will become
a powerful nation.
I am the LORD,
and when it is time, I will make these
things happen quickly."

The Lord's Message of Freedom

61 The Lord GOD has put his Spirit in me,
because the LORD has appointed me
to tell the good news to the
poor.
He has sent me to comfort those whose
hearts are broken,
to tell the captives they are free,
and to tell the prisoners they are
released.
2He has sent me to announce the time when
the LORD will show his kindness
and the time when our God will punish
evil people.
He has sent me to comfort all those who
are sad
3 and to help the sorrowing people of
Jerusalem.
I will give them a crown to replace their
ashes,
and the oil of gladness to replace their
sorrow,
and clothes of praise to replace their
spirit of sadness.

devotion 206

ISAIAH 61:1-3

NO IMPOSTER HERE

In chapter 61 we read about Isaiah's prophecy of the Messiah and about the things he would do for the world when he came. He would bring deliverance to the Israelites—and to us, too. Isn't it amazing how the coming of Jesus was foretold long before he arrived on earth as a baby?

Luke 4:18-21 tells us that years later, Jesus read the words of Isaiah to a crowd. He said, "'The Lord has put his Spirit in me, because he appointed me to tell the Good News to the poor. He has sent me to tell the captives they are free and to tell the blind that they can see again'" (verse 18). He ends by telling the crowd, "'While you heard these words just now, they were coming true!'" (verse 20).

By reading the prophecy to the crowd, Jesus boldly proclaimed himself to be the one Isaiah talked about. Nevertheless, some still rejected Jesus. However, the skeptics were wrong because we see in Luke 7:21 that Jesus "healed many people of their sicknesses, diseases, and evils spirits, and he gave sight to many blind people." Truly, Jesus came to set the captives free!

Digging into prophecy can seem daunting, but the burden of proof is on us as Christians. If we make ourselves aware of prophecy in the Bible, we have a tool to show others and one that will strengthen our own faith. We can find great comfort in knowing that yes, Jesus did what was prophesied. He is who the prophets said he would be!

Then they will be called Trees of Goodness,
trees planted by the LORD to show his greatness.
4 They will rebuild the old ruins
and restore the places destroyed long ago.
They will repair the ruined cities
that were destroyed for so long.
5 My people, foreigners will come to tend your sheep.
People from other countries will tend your fields and vineyards.
6 You will be called priests of the LORD;
you will be named the servants of our God.
You will have riches from all the nations on earth,
and you will take pride in them.
7 Instead of being ashamed, my people will receive twice as much wealth.
Instead of being disgraced, they will be happy because of what they receive.
They will receive a double share of the land,
so their happiness will continue forever.
8 "I, the LORD, love justice.
I hate stealing and everything that is wrong.
I will be fair and give my people what they should have,
and I will make an agreement with them that will continue forever.
9 Everyone in all nations will know the children of my people,
and their children will be known among the nations.
Anyone who sees them will know
that they are people the LORD has blessed."
10 The LORD makes me very happy;
all that I am rejoices in my God.
He has covered me with clothes of salvation
and wrapped me with a coat of goodness,
like a bridegroom dressed for his wedding,
like a bride dressed in jewels.
11 The earth causes plants to grow,
and a garden causes the seeds planted in it to grow.
In the same way the Lord GOD will make goodness and praise
come from all the nations.

New Jerusalem

62 Because I love Jerusalem, I will continue to speak for her;
for Jerusalem's sake I will not stop speaking
until her goodness shines like a bright light,
until her salvation burns bright like a flame.
2 Jerusalem, the nations will see your goodness,
and all kings will see your glory.
Then you will have a new name,
which the LORD himself will give you.
3 You will be like a beautiful crown in the LORD's hand,
like a king's crown in your God's hand.
4 You will never again be called the People that God Left,
nor your land the Land that God Destroyed.
You will be called the People God Loves,
and your land will be called the Bride of God,
because the LORD loves you.
And your land will belong to him as a bride belongs to her husband.
5 As a young man marries a woman,
so your children will marry your land.
As a man rejoices over his new wife,
so your God will rejoice over you.

6 Jerusalem, I have put guards on the walls to watch.
They must not be silent day or night.
You people who remind the LORD of your needs in prayer
should never be quiet.
7 You should not stop praying to him until he builds up Jerusalem
and makes it a city all people will praise.
8 The LORD has made a promise,
and by his power he will keep his promise.
He said, "I will never again give your grain as food to your enemies.
I will not let your enemies drink the new wine
that you have worked to make.
9 Those who gather food will eat it,
and they will praise the LORD.
Those who gather the grapes will drink the wine
in the courts of my Temple."

devotion 207

ISAIAH 61:10

HERE COMES THE BRIDE

I don't think it's any coincidence that all throughout the Bible, God uses bridal imagery to refer to his own. We are his bride, and he is our Bridegroom. When we are finally standing in his presence, there will be a celebration in heaven that he calls the wedding meal of the Lamb (Rev. 19:7-9). How completely he knows the feminine soul. How well he knows that we long to be the bride. How wonderful he is to make it so.

I'm not sure that men grasp the depth of this imagery the way women do. We women get this. God has set in our hearts a longing for beauty and romance. To be called the bride is to imagine we have become everything we were meant to be.

What if we decided that when God calls us his bride, it is unequivocally, unquestionably, and irrevocably so? Can you imagine how your life would change if you really believed this? Embracing your position as the bride of Christ means being held in his strong arms of love and passion every single day.

Do you remember the last bride you saw? I bet she was beautiful. It was her day. She was confident—maybe more confident than any other day of her life. Finally, the one she longed for had come. As the bride of Christ, the same life is available to you day after day. You can be beautiful, confident, and live inside the truth of eternal hope.

10 Go through, go through the gates!
Make the way ready for the people.
Build up, build up the road!
Move all the stones off the road.
Raise the banner as a sign for the people.
11 The LORD is speaking
to all the faraway lands:
"Tell the people of Jerusalem,
'Look, your Savior is coming.
He is bringing your reward to you;
he is bringing his payment with him.' "
12 His people will be called the Holy People,
the Saved People of the LORD,
and Jerusalem will be called the City God Wants,
the City God Has Not Rejected.

The Lord Judges His People

63 Who is this coming from Edom,
from the city of Bozrah, dressed in red?
Who is this dressed in fine clothes
and marching forward with his great power?
He says, "I, the LORD, speak what is right.
I have the power to save you."
2 Someone asks, "Why are your clothes bright red
as if you had walked on the grapes to make wine?"
3 The LORD answers, "I have walked in the winepress alone,
and no one among the nations helped me.
I was angry and walked on the nations
and crushed them because of my anger.
Blood splashed on my clothes,
and I stained all my clothing.
4 I chose a time to punish people,
and the time has come for me to save.
5 I looked around, but I saw no one to help me.
I was surprised that no one supported me.
So I used my own power to save my people;
my own anger supported me.

6While I was angry, I walked on the
nations.
In my anger I punished them
and poured their blood on the
ground."

The Lord's Kindness to His People

7I will tell about the LORD's kindness
and praise him for everything he has
done.
I will praise the LORD for the many good
things he has given us
and for his goodness to the people of
Israel.
He has shown great mercy to us
and has been very kind to us.
8He said, "These are my people;
my children will not lie to me."
So he saved them.
9When they suffered, he suffered also.
He sent his own angel to save them.
Because of his love and kindness, he saved
them.
Since long ago he has picked them up
and carried them.
10But they turned against him
and made his Holy Spirit very sad.
So he became their enemy,
and he fought against them.

11But then his people remembered what
happened long ago,
in the days of Moses and the Israelites
with him.
Where is the LORD who brought the
people through the sea,
with the leaders of his people?
Where is the one
who put his Holy Spirit among them,
12who led Moses by the right hand
with his wonderful power,
who divided the water before them
to make his name famous forever,
13who led the people through the deep
waters?
Like a horse walking through a desert,
the people did not stumble.
14Like cattle that go down to the valley,
the Spirit of the LORD gave the people a
place to rest.
LORD, that is the way you led your
people,
and by this you won for yourself
wonderful fame.

A Prayer for Help

15LORD, look down from the heavens and
see;
look at us from your wonderful and
holy home in heaven.
Where is your strong love and power?
Why are you keeping your love and
mercy from us?
16You are our father.
Abraham doesn't know we are his
children,
and Israel doesn't recognize us.
LORD, you are our father.
You are called "the one who has always
saved us."
17LORD, why are you making us wander
from your ways?
Why do you make us stubborn so that
we don't honor you?
For our sake come back to us,
your servants, who belong to you.
18Your people had your Temple for a
while,
but now our enemies have walked on
your holy place and crushed it.
19We have become like people you never
ruled over,
like those who have never worn your
name.

64 Tear open the skies and come down to
earth
so that the mountains will tremble
before you.
2Like a fire that burns twigs,
like a fire that makes water boil,
let your enemies know who you are.
Then all nations will shake with fear
when they see you.
3You have done amazing things we did not
expect.
You came down, and the mountains
trembled before you.
4From long ago no one has ever heard of a
God like you.
No one has ever seen a God besides you,
who helps the people who trust you.
5You help those who enjoy doing good,
who remember how you want them to
live.
But you were angry because we sinned.
For a long time we disobeyed,
so how can we be saved?
6All of us are dirty with sin.

All the right things we have done are
like filthy pieces of cloth.
All of us are like dead leaves,
and our sins, like the wind, have carried
us away.
7No one worships you
or even asks you to help us.
That is because you have turned away
from us
and have let our sins destroy us.

8But LORD, you are our father.
We are like clay, and you are the potter;
your hands made us all.
9LORD, don't continue to be angry with us;
don't remember our sins forever.
Please, look at us,
because we are your people.
10Your holy cities are empty like the desert.
Jerusalem is like a desert;
it is destroyed.
11Our ancestors worshiped you
in our holy and wonderful Temple,
but now it has been burned with fire,
and all our precious things have been
destroyed.
12When you see these things, will you hold
yourself back from helping us,
LORD?
Will you be silent and punish us
beyond what we can stand?

All People Will Learn About God

65 The LORD says, "I made myself known
to people who were not looking
for me.
I was found by those who were not
asking me for help.
I said, 'Here I am. Here I am,'
to a nation that was not praying to me.
2All day long I stood ready to accept
people who turned against me,
but the way they continue to live is not
good;
they do anything they want to do.
3Right in front of me
they continue to do things that make
me angry.
They offer sacrifices to their gods in
their gardens,
and they burn incense on altars of brick.
4They sit among the graves
and spend their nights waiting to get
messages from the dead.
They eat the meat of pigs,
and their pots are full of soup made
from meat that is wrong to eat.
5But they tell others, 'Stay away, and don't
come near me.
I am too holy for you.'
These people are like smoke in my nose.
Like a fire that burns all the time, they
continue to make me angry.

6"Look, it is written here before me.
I will not be quiet; instead, I will repay
you in full.
I will punish you for what you have
done.
7I will punish you for your sins and your
ancestors' sins,"
says the LORD.
"They burned incense to gods on the
mountains
and shamed me on those hills.
So I will punish them as they should be
punished
for what they did."

8This is what the LORD says:
"When there is juice left in the grapes,
people do not destroy them,
because they know there is good left in
them.
So I will do the same thing to my
servants—
I will not completely destroy them.
9I will leave some of the children of
Jacob,
and some of the people of Judah will
receive my mountain.
I will choose the people who will live
there;
my servants will live there.
10Then the Plain of Sharon will be a field
for flocks,
and the Valley of Achor will be a place
for herds to rest.
They will be for the people who want
to follow me.
11"But as for you who left the LORD,
who forgot about my holy mountain,
who worship the god Luck,
who hold religious feasts for the god
Fate,
12I decide your fate, and I will punish you
with my sword.
You will all be killed,

because I called you, but you refused to answer.
I spoke to you, but you wouldn't listen.
You did the things I said were evil
and chose to do things that displease me."
13 So this is what the Lord GOD says:
"My servants will eat,
but you evil people will be hungry.
My servants will drink,
but you evil people will be thirsty.
My servants will be happy,
but you evil people will be shamed.
14 My servants will shout for joy
because of the goodness of their hearts,
but you evil people will cry,
because you will be sad.
You will cry loudly, because your spirits will be broken.
15 Your names will be like curses to my servants,
and the Lord GOD will put you to death.
But he will call his servants by another name.
16 People in the land who ask for blessings
will ask for them from the faithful God.
And people in the land who make a promise
will promise in the name of the faithful God,
because the troubles of the past will be forgotten.
I will make those troubles go away.

A New Time Is Coming

17 "Look, I will make new heavens and a new earth,
and people will not remember the past
or think about those things.
18 My people will be happy forever
because of the things I will make.
I will make a Jerusalem that is full of joy,
and I will make her people a delight.
19 Then I will rejoice over Jerusalem
and be delighted with my people.
There will never again be heard in that city
the sounds of crying and sadness.
20 There will never be a baby from that city
who lives only a few days.
And there will never be an older person
who doesn't have a long life.
A person who lives a hundred years will be called young,
and a person who dies before he is a hundred will be thought of as a sinner.
21 In that city those who build houses will live there.
Those who plant vineyards will get to eat their grapes.
22 No more will one person build a house and someone else live there.
One person will not plant a garden and someone else eat its fruit.
My people will live a long time,
as trees live long.
My chosen people will live there
and enjoy the things they make.
23 They will never again work for nothing.
They will never again give birth to children who die young.
All my people will be blessed by the LORD;
they and their children will be blessed.
24 I will provide for their needs before they ask,
and I will help them while they are still asking for help.
25 Wolves and lambs will eat together in peace.
Lions will eat hay like oxen,
and a snake on the ground will not hurt anyone.
They will not hurt or destroy each other
on all my holy mountain,"
says the LORD.

The Lord Will Judge All Nations

66 This is what the LORD says:
"Heaven is my throne,
and the earth is my footstool.
So do you think you can build a house for me?
Do I need a place to rest?
2 My hand made all things.
All things are here because I made them,"
says the LORD.

"These are the people I am pleased with:
those who are not proud or stubborn
and who fear my word.
3 But those people who kill bulls as a sacrifice to me
are like those who kill people.
Those who kill sheep as a sacrifice
are like those who break the necks of dogs.

Those who give me grain offerings
are like those who offer me the blood of pigs.[n]
Those who burn incense
are like those who worship idols.
These people choose their own ways, not mine,
and they love the terrible things they do.
4So I will choose their punishments,
and I will punish them with what they fear most.
This is because I called to them, but they did not listen.
I spoke to them, but they did not hear me.
They did things I said were evil;
they chose to do things I did not like."

5You people who obey the words of the LORD,
listen to what he says:
"Your brothers hated you
and turned against you because you followed me.
Your brothers said, 'Let the LORD be honored
so we may see you rejoice,'
but they will be punished.
6Listen to the loud noise coming from the city;
hear the noise from the Temple.
It is the LORD punishing his enemies,
giving them the punishment they should have.

7"A woman does not give birth before she feels the pain;
she does not give birth to a son before the pain starts.
8No one has ever heard of that happening;
no one has ever seen that happen.
In the same way no one ever saw a country begin in one day;
no one has ever heard of a new nation beginning in one moment.
But Jerusalem will give birth to her children
just as soon as she feels the birth pains.
9In the same way I will not cause pain
without allowing something new to be born," says the LORD.
"If I cause you the pain,
I will not stop you from giving birth to your new nation," says your God.
10"Jerusalem, rejoice.
All you people who love Jerusalem, be happy.
Those of you who felt sad for Jerusalem
should now feel happy with her.
11You will take comfort from her and be satisfied,
as a child is nursed by its mother.
You will receive her good things
and enjoy her wealth."
12This is what the LORD says:
"I will give her peace that will flow to her like a river.
The wealth of the nations will come to her like a river overflowing its banks.
Like babies you will be nursed and held in my arms
and bounced on my knees.
13I will comfort you
as a mother comforts her child.
You will be comforted in Jerusalem."

14When you see these things, you will be happy,
and you will grow like the grass.
The LORD's servants will see his power,
but his enemies will see his anger.
15Look, the LORD is coming with fire
and his armies with clouds of dust.
He will punish those people with his anger;
he will punish them with flames of fire.
16The LORD will judge the people with fire,
and he will destroy many people with his sword;
he will kill many people.

17"These people make themselves holy
and pure to go to worship their gods in their
gardens. Following each other into their
special gardens, they eat the meat of pigs and
rats and other hateful things. But they will
all be destroyed together," says the LORD.
18"I know they have evil thoughts and do
evil things, so I am coming to punish them. I
will gather all nations and all people, and
they will come together and see my glory.
19"I will put a mark on some of the people,
and I will send some of these saved people to

66:3 dogs . . . pigs God did not want his people to offer dogs and pigs as sacrifices because they were unclean animals.

the nations: to Tarshish, Libya, Lud (the land
of archers), Tubal, Greece, and all the
faraway lands. These people have never
heard about what I have done nor seen my
glory. So the saved people will tell the
nations about my glory. [20]And they will
bring all your fellow Israelites from all
nations to my holy mountain in Jerusalem.
Your fellow Israelites will come on horses,
donkeys, and camels and in chariots and
wagons. They will be like the grain offerings
that the people bring in clean containers to
the Temple," says the LORD. [21]"And I will
choose even some of these people to be
priests and Levites," says the LORD.
[22]"I will make new heavens and the new
earth, which will last forever," says the LORD.
"In the same way, your names and your
children will always be with me. [23]All
people will come to worship me every
Sabbath and every New Moon," says the
LORD. [24]"They will go out and see the dead
bodies of the people who sinned against me.
The worms that eat them will never die, and
the fires that burn them will never stop, and
everyone will hate to see those bodies."

Jeremiah

A Hebrew word that literally means "Jehovah throws"
(The implied meaning is that God is appointing or sending out his prophet.)

Person Holding the Pen God Wrote With: *Jeremiah,* who is often referred to as the "weeping prophet" in light of the way he grieved over Judah's spiritual rebellion

When the Text Was Written: Sometime between 627 B.C. (Jer. 1:2) and 561 B.C. (52:31–34)

Spiritual Posture of the Original Recipients: Israel was basically thumbing her nose at Jehovah, engaging in flagrant idolatry and pagan worship rituals.

Storyline Synopsis: The theme of this season in Israel's history could be summed up with the title of an old country song: *Looking for Love in All the Wrong Places.* God calls a prophet, this single guy named Jeremiah, to pick up a bullhorn and announce a warning about the imminent wrath their behavior has earned the Israelites (chapter 1). The opening of his pronouncement deals with the pitiful spiritual condition of God's people (chapters 2—10). Next Jeremiah details his own emotional struggles regarding his ministry, which wasn't yielding the positive results he had hoped for (chapters 11—20). Third comes a stinging indictment about Judah's leaders and the dumb decisions they were making (chapters 21—39). Jeremiah's parting words describe the inevitable fall of Jerusalem to Babylon and God's future judgment on other pagan nations (chapters 40—52).

A Moment Worth Discussing: While this Old Testament prophecy can be pretty depressing—at one point in the story, God instructs Jeremiah to literally wear a yoke around his neck to symbolize Judah's future captivity in Babylon (chapters 27—28)—there's a big bright spot in the middle! Chapters 30—33 are sometimes called "The Book of Comfort" because they include Jehovah's promise to restore his people. The Israelites were definitely going to have to "face the music" and endure the righteous punishment that their sin deserved, but they were also given the assurance of great joy to come. Jeremiah's prophecy points to Jesus, the Savior of the world!

Interesting (But Likely to Be Overlooked) Character: *Seraiah* was the man Jeremiah appointed to read this scroll of destruction to the King of Babylon before tossing the whole thing into the Euphrates River to symbolize Babylon's eventual fall (Jer. 51:59–64). Seraiah's mission brings to mind the phrase, "Don't shoot the messenger!"

1 These are the words of Jeremiah son of
Hilkiah. He belonged to the family of
priests who lived in the town of Anathoth in
the land of Benjamin. 2 The LORD spoke his
word to Jeremiah during the thirteenth year
that Josiah son of Amon was king of Judah.
3 The LORD also spoke to Jeremiah while
Jehoiakim son of Josiah was king of Judah
and during the eleven years that Zedekiah
son of Josiah was king of Judah. In the fifth
month of his last year, the people of
Jerusalem were taken away as captives.

The Lord Calls Jeremiah

4 The LORD spoke his word to me, saying:
5 "Before I made you in your mother's
womb, I chose you.
Before you were born, I set you apart
for a special work.
I appointed you as a prophet to the
nations."
6 Then I said, "But Lord GOD, I don't know
how to speak. I am only a boy."
7 But the LORD said to me, "Don't say, 'I am
only a boy.' You must go everywhere I send
you, and you must say everything I tell you
to say. 8 Don't be afraid of anyone, because I
am with you to protect you," says the LORD.
9 Then the LORD reached out his hand and
touched my mouth. He said to me, "See, I am
putting my words in your mouth. 10 Today I
have put you in charge of nations and
kingdoms. You will pull up and tear down,
destroy and overthrow, build up and plant."

Jeremiah Sees Two Visions

11 The LORD spoke his word to me, saying:
"Jeremiah, what do you see?"
I answered, "I see a stick of almond wood."
12 The LORD said to me, "You have seen
correctly, because I am watching to make
sure my words come true."
13 The LORD spoke his word to me again:
"What do you see?"
I answered, "I see a pot of boiling water,
tipping over from the north."
14 The LORD said to me, "Disaster will come
from the north and strike all the people who
live in this country. 15 In a short time I will
call all of the people in the northern
kingdoms," said the LORD.
"Those kings will come and set up their
thrones
near the entrance of the gates of
Jerusalem.
They will attack all the city walls around
Jerusalem
and all the cities in Judah.

devotion 208

JEREMIAH 1:7–9

GET GOING!

When the voice of the Holy Spirit calls out to your heart, is your first response, "No way. Not me, Lord. I am not qualified!" If so, I can assure you that you are destined to get a lesson about the confession of your mouth. We all have deep desires in our hearts—important things we would like to do with our lives—but then when the Lord calls us to action, that tiny little hole located in the bottom center of our faces says, "No, not me. Do not send me, Lord. I can't do it." That seems so strange to me. Stop it! God loves the desires of your heart, and he knows the perfect time for you to stop saying no and step out in faith to accomplish his will.

What is in your heart right now? Do you want to lose fifteen pounds? Go do it! Do you want to take French lessons? Go do it! Do you want to teach a ladies' Bible study? Go do it! Do you want to be a writer? Go do it! Do you want to be a fitness trainer? Go do it! Whatever those desires are, have a great time with your Lord. Be in prayer and rejoice when he says, "Now is the time. Let's go." As he makes his way known to you, do not be afraid. If he calls you, he will equip you in every good work. Now get going!

16 And I will announce my judgments
against my people
because of their evil in turning away
from me.
They offered sacrifices to other gods
and worshiped idols they had made
with their own hands.

17 "Jeremiah, get ready. Stand up and tell
them everything I command you to say.
Don't be afraid of the people, or I will give
you good reason to be afraid of them.
18 Today I am going to make you a strong
city, an iron pillar, a bronze wall. You will be
able to stand against everyone in the land:
Judah's kings, officers, priests, and the people
of the land. 19 They will fight against you, but
they will not defeat you, because I am with
you to protect you!" says the LORD.

Israel Turns from God

2 The LORD spoke his word to me, saying:
2 "Go and speak to the people of
Jerusalem, saying: This is what the LORD says:
'I remember how faithful you were to me
when you were a young nation.
You loved me like a young bride.
You followed me through the desert,
a land that had never been planted.
3 The people of Israel were holy to the
LORD,
like the firstfruits from his harvest.
Those who tried to hurt Israel were
judged guilty.
Disasters struck them,' " says the LORD.

4 Hear the word of the LORD, family of
Jacob,
all you family groups of Israel.
5 This is what the LORD says:
"I was fair to your ancestors,
so why did they turn away from me?
Your ancestors worshiped useless idols
and became useless themselves.
6 Your ancestors didn't say,
'Where is the LORD who brought us out
of Egypt?
He led us through the desert,
through a dry and rocky land,
through a dark and dangerous land.
He led us where no one travels or lives.'
7 I brought you into a fertile land
so you could eat its fruit and produce.
But you came and made my land unclean;
you made it a hateful place.
8 The priests didn't ask,
'Where is the LORD?'
The people who know the teachings
didn't know me.
The leaders turned against me.
The prophets prophesied in the name of
Baal
and worshiped useless idols.

9 "So now I will again tell what I have
against you," says the LORD.
"And I will tell what I have against your
grandchildren.
10 Go across the sea to the island of Cyprus
and see.
Send someone to the land of Kedar to
look closely.
See if there has ever been anything like
this.
11 Has a nation ever exchanged its gods?
(Of course, its gods are not really gods
at all.)
But my people have exchanged their
glorious God
for idols worth nothing.
12 Skies, be shocked at the things that have
happened
and shake with great fear!" says the
LORD.
13 "My people have done two evils:
They have turned away from me,
the spring of living water.
And they have dug their own wells,
which are broken wells that cannot
hold water.
14 Have the people of Israel become slaves?
Have they become like someone who
was born a slave?
Why were they taken captive?
15 Enemies have roared like lions at Israel;
they have growled at Israel.
They have destroyed the land of Israel.
The cities of Israel lie in ruins,
and all the people have left.
16 The men from the cities of Memphis and
Tahpanhes
have disgraced you by shaving the top
of your head.
17 Haven't you brought this on yourselves
by turning away from the LORD your
God
when he was leading you in the right
way?
18 It did not help to go to Egypt
and drink from the Shihor River.

devotion 209

JEREMIAH 2:5, 11–12

USED BY GOD

So what is an idol? In 1 Corinthians 10:19-20, Paul says that when we worship idols, we are actually worshiping demons. Think of an idol as anything that pulls us away from God. This is exactly what the devil has tried to do from the beginning of time, right? We often think that little sins or minor idols in our lives are not a big deal. The problem is that if we give the devil a foot in the door, he will eventually push his way in completely.

Ephesians 6:11-12 describes the armor we are to use against the devil. There is nothing more our enemy would like to do than to make us useless for God by distracting us from him. Sometimes we tend to think of ourselves as lone rangers living our own little lives in our own little world, but that is far from the truth. We are part of a bigger picture, and God needs us to do our part.

We have such a glorious God. I often marvel that he uses Christians here on earth to carry out his purposes. We are inconsistent and undependable so much of the time, but God sees the best in each of us, and we need to see our potential through his eyes. Don't exchange your glorious God for idols worth nothing. You are precious in God's sight and a valuable part of the body of Christ. Be used by God today. Don't waste your time on useless idols.

It did not help to go to Assyria
and drink from the Euphrates River.
19 Your evil will bring punishment to you,
and the wrong you have done will
teach you a lesson.
Think about it and understand
that it is a terrible evil to turn away from
the LORD your God.
It is wrong not to fear me,"
says the Lord GOD All-Powerful.

20 "Long ago you refused to obey me as an
ox breaks its yoke.
You broke the ropes I used to hold you
and said, 'I will not serve you!'
In fact, on every high hill
and under every green tree
you lay down as a prostitute.
21 But I planted you as a special vine,
as a very good seed.
How then did you turn
into a wild vine that grows bad fruit?
22 Although you wash yourself with
cleanser
and use much soap,
I can still see the stain of your guilt,"
says the Lord GOD.
23 "How can you say to me, 'I am not guilty.
I have not worshiped the Baal idols'?
Look at the things you did in the valley.
Think about what you have done.
You are like a she-camel in mating season
that runs from place to place.
24 You are like a wild donkey that lives in
the desert
and sniffs the wind at mating time.
At that time who can hold her back?
Any male who chases her will easily catch
her;
at mating time, it is easy to find her.
25 Don't run until your feet are bare
or until your throat is dry.
But you say, 'It's no use!
I love those other gods,
and I must chase them!'
26 "A thief is ashamed when someone
catches him stealing.
In the same way, the family of Israel is
ashamed—

they, their kings, their officers,
their priests, and their prophets.
27 They say to things of wood, 'You are my father,'
and to idols of stone, 'You gave birth to me.'
Those people won't look at me;
they have turned their backs to me.
But when they get into trouble, they say,
'Come and save us!'
28 Where are the idols you made for yourselves?
Let them come and save you
when you are in trouble!
People of Judah, you have as many idols
as you have towns!
29 "Why do you complain to me?
All of you have turned against me," says the LORD.
30 "I punished your people, but it did not help.
They didn't come back when they were punished.
With your swords you killed your prophets
like a hungry lion.
31 "People of Judah, pay attention to the
word of the LORD:
Have I been like a desert to the people of Israel
or like a dark and dangerous land?
Why do my people say, 'We are free to wander.
We won't come to you anymore'?
32 A young woman does not forget her jewelry,
and a bride does not forget the decorations for her dress.
But my people have forgotten me
for more days than can be counted.
33 You really know how to chase after love.
Even the worst women can learn evil ways from you.
34 Even on your clothes you have the blood
of poor and innocent people,
but they weren't thieves you caught breaking in.
You do all these things,
35 but you say, 'I am innocent.
God is not angry with me.'
But I will judge you guilty of lying,
because you say, 'I have not sinned.'
36 It is so easy for you to change your mind.
Even Egypt will let you down,
as Assyria let you down.
37 You will eventually leave that place
with your hands on your head, like captives.
You trusted those countries,
but you will not be helped by them,
because the LORD has rejected them.

Judah Is Unfaithful

3 "If a man divorces his wife
and she leaves him and marries another man,
should her first husband come back to her again?
If he went back to her, wouldn't the land become completely unclean?
But you have acted like a prostitute with many lovers,
and now you want to come back to me?" says the LORD.
2 "Look up to the bare hilltops, Judah.
Is there any place where you have not been a prostitute?
You have sat by the road waiting for lovers,
like an Arab in the desert.
You made the land unclean,
because you did evil and were like a prostitute.
3 So the rain has not come,
and there have not been any spring rains.
But your face still looks like the face of a prostitute.
You refuse even to be ashamed of what you did.
4 Now you are calling to me,
'My father, you have been my friend since I was young.
5 Will you always be angry at me?
Will your anger last forever?'
Judah, you said this,
but you did as much evil as you could!"

Judah and Israel Are like Sisters

6 When King Josiah was ruling Judah, the
LORD said to me, "Did you see what
unfaithful Israel did? She was like a
prostitute with her idols on every hill and
under every green tree. 7 I said to myself,
'Israel will come back to me after she does
this evil,' but she didn't come back. And
Israel's wicked sister Judah saw what she did.

[8]Judah saw that I divorced unfaithful Israel
because of her adultery, but that didn't make
Israel's wicked sister Judah afraid. She also
went out and acted like a prostitute! [9]And
she didn't care that she was acting like a
prostitute. So she made her country unclean
and was guilty of adultery, because she
worshiped idols made of stone and wood.
[10]Israel's wicked sister didn't even come back
to me with her whole heart, but only
pretended," says the Lord.

[11]The LORD said to me, "Unfaithful Israel
had a better excuse than wicked Judah. [12]Go
and speak this message toward the north:

'Come back, unfaithful people of Israel,'
says the LORD.
'I will stop being angry at you,
because I am full of mercy,' says the LORD.
'I will not be angry with you forever.
[13]All you have to do is admit your sin—
that you turned against the LORD your
God
and worshiped gods under every green
tree
and didn't obey me,' " says the LORD.

[14]"Come back to me, you unfaithful
children," says the LORD, "because I am your
master. I will take one person from every
city and two from every family group, and I
will bring you to Jerusalem. [15]Then I will
give you new rulers who will be faithful to
me, who will lead you with knowledge and
understanding. [16]In those days there will be
many of you in the land," says the LORD. "At
that time people will no longer say, 'I
remember the Ark of the Agreement.' They
won't think about it anymore or remember
it or miss it or make another one. [17]At that
time people will call Jerusalem The Throne
of the LORD, and all nations will come
together in Jerusalem to show respect to the
LORD. They will not follow their stubborn,
evil hearts anymore. [18]In those days the
family of Judah will join the family of Israel.
They will come together from a land in the
north to the land I gave their ancestors.

[19]"I, the LORD, said,
'How happy I would be to treat you as my
own children
and give you a pleasant land,
a land more beautiful than that of any
other nation.'
I thought you would call me 'My Father'
and not turn away from me.
[20]But like a woman who is unfaithful to her
husband,
family of Israel, you have been
unfaithful to me," says the LORD.

[21]You can hear crying on the bare hilltops.
It is the people of Israel crying and
praying for mercy.
They have become very evil
and have forgotten the LORD their God.

[22]"Come back to me, you unfaithful
children,
and I will forgive you for being
unfaithful."

"Yes, we will come to you,
because you are the LORD our God.
[23]It was foolish to worship idols on the hills
and on the mountains.
Surely the salvation of Israel
comes from the LORD our God.
[24]Since our youth, shameful gods have
eaten up in sacrifice
everything our ancestors worked for—
their flocks and herds,
their sons and daughters.
[25]Let us lie down in our shame,
and let our disgrace cover us like a
blanket.
We have sinned against the LORD our God,
both we and our ancestors.
From our youth until now,
we have not obeyed the LORD our God."

4 "If you will return, Israel,
then return to me," says the LORD.
"If you will throw away your idols that I
hate,
then don't wander away from me.
[2]If you say when you make a promise,
'As surely as the LORD lives,'
and you can say it in a truthful, honest,
and right way,
then the nations will be blessed by him,
and they will praise him for what he
has done."

[3]This is what the LORD says to the people
of Judah and to Jerusalem:

"Plow your unplowed fields,
and don't plant seeds among thorns.
[4]Give yourselves to the service of the LORD,
and decide to obey him,
people of Judah and people of
Jerusalem.

If you don't, my anger will spread among
you like a fire,
and no one will be able to put it out,
because of the evil you have done.

Trouble from the North

5"Announce this message in Judah and say
it in Jerusalem:
'Blow the trumpet throughout the
country!'
Shout out loud and say,
'Come together!
Let's all escape to the strong, walled
cities!'
6Raise the signal flag toward Jerusalem!
Run for your lives, and don't wait,
because I am bringing disaster from the
north
There will be terrible destruction."

7A lion has come out of his den;
a destroyer of nations has begun to
march.
He has left his home
to destroy your land.
Your towns will be destroyed
with no one left to live in them.
8So put on rough cloth,
show how sad you are, and cry
loudly.
The terrible anger of the LORD
has not turned away from us.
9"When this happens," says the LORD,
"the king and officers will lose their
courage.
The priests will be terribly afraid,
and the prophets will be shocked!"
10Then I said, "Lord GOD, you have tricked
the people of Judah and Jerusalem. You said,
'You will have peace,' but now the sword is
pointing at our throats!"
11At that time this message will be
given to Judah and Jerusalem: "A hot wind
blows from the bare hilltops of the desert
toward the LORD's people. It is not a gentle
wind to separate grain from chaff. 12I feel a
stronger wind than that. Now even I will
announce judgments against the people of
Judah."
13Look! The enemy rises up like a cloud,
and his chariots come like a tornado.
His horses are faster than eagles.
How terrible it will be for us! We are
ruined!
14People of Jerusalem, clean the evil from
your hearts so that you can be
saved.
Don't continue making evil plans.
15A voice from Dan makes an
announcement
and brings bad news from the
mountains of Ephraim.
16"Report this to the nations.
Spread this news in Jerusalem:
'Invaders are coming from a faraway
country,
shouting words of war against the cities
of Judah.
17The enemy has surrounded Jerusalem as
men guard a field,
because Judah turned against me,' "
says the LORD.
18"The way you have lived and acted
has brought this trouble to you.
This is your punishment.
How terrible it is!
The pain stabs your heart!"

Jeremiah's Cry

19Oh, how I hurt! How I hurt!
I am bent over in pain.
Oh, the torture in my heart!
My heart is pounding inside me.
I cannot keep quiet,
because I have heard the sound of the
trumpet.
I have heard the shouts of war.
20Disaster follows disaster;
the whole country has been destroyed.
My tents are destroyed in only a
moment.
My curtains are torn down quickly.
21How long must I look at the war flag?
How long must I listen to the war
trumpet?
22The LORD says, "My people are foolish.
They do not know me.
They are stupid children;
they don't understand.
They are skillful at doing evil,
but they don't know how to do good."

Disaster Is Coming

23I looked at the earth,
and it was empty and had no shape.
I looked at the sky,
and its light was gone.

24I looked at the mountains,
and they were shaking.
All the hills were trembling.
25I looked, and there were no people.
Every bird in the sky had flown away.
26I looked, and the good, rich land had become a desert.
All its towns had been destroyed
by the LORD and his great anger.
27This is what the LORD says:
"All the land will be ruined,
but I will not completely destroy it.
28So the people in the land will cry loudly,
and the sky will grow dark,
because I have spoken and will not change my mind.
I have made a decision, and I will not change it."

29At the sound of the horsemen and the archers,
all the people in the towns run away.
They hide in the thick bushes
and climb up into the rocks.
All of the cities of Judah are empty;
no one lives in them.
30Judah, you destroyed nation, what are you doing?
Why do you put on your finest dress
and decorate yourself with gold jewelry?
Why do you put color around your eyes?
You make yourself beautiful, but it is all useless.
Your lovers hate you;
they want to kill you.

31I hear a cry like a woman having a baby,
distress like a woman having her first child.
It is the sound of Jerusalem gasping for breath.
She lifts her hands in prayer and says,
"Oh! I am about to faint
before my murderers!"

No One Is Right

5 The LORD says, "Walk up and down the streets of Jerusalem.
Look around and discover these things.
Search the public squares of the city.
If you can find one person who does honest things,
who searches for the truth,
I will forgive this city.
2Although the people say, 'As surely as the LORD lives!'
they don't really mean it."
3LORD, don't you look for truth in people?
You struck the people of Judah,
but they didn't feel any pain.
You crushed them,
but they refused to learn what is right.
They became more stubborn than a rock;
they refused to turn back to God.
4But I thought,
"These are only the poor, foolish people.
They have not learned the way of the LORD
and what their God wants them to do.
5So I will go to the leaders of Judah
and talk to them.
Surely they understand the way of the LORD
and know what God wants them to do."
But even the leaders had all joined together to break away from the LORD;
they had broken their ties with him.
6So a lion from the forest will attack them.
A wolf from the desert will kill them.
A leopard is waiting for them near their towns.
It will tear to pieces anyone who comes out of the city,
because the people of Judah have sinned greatly.
They have wandered away from the LORD many times.

7The LORD said, "Tell me why I should forgive you.
Your children have left me
and have made promises to idols that are not gods at all.
I gave your children everything they needed,
but they still were like an unfaithful wife to me.
They spent much time in houses of prostitutes.
8They are like well-fed horses filled with sexual desire;
each one wants another man's wife.
9Shouldn't I punish the people of Judah for doing these things?" says the LORD.
"Shouldn't I give a nation such as this
the punishment it deserves?

10"Go along and cut down Judah's
vineyards,
but do not completely destroy them.
Cut off all her people as if they were
branches,
because they do not belong to the LORD.
11The families of Israel and Judah
have been completely unfaithful to
me," says the LORD.

12Those people have lied about the LORD
and said, "He will not do anything to us!
Nothing bad will happen to us!
We will never see war or hunger!
13The prophets are like an empty wind;
the word of God is not in them.
Let the bad things they say happen to
them."

14So this is what the LORD God
All-Powerful says:
"The people said I would not punish
them.
So, the words I give you will be like fire,
and these people will be like wood that
it burns up.
15Listen, family of Israel," says the LORD,
"I will soon bring a nation from far
away to attack you.
It is an old nation that has lasted a long
time.
The people there speak a language you
do not know;
you cannot understand what they say.
16Their arrows bring death.
All their people are strong warriors.
17They will eat your crops and your food.
They will eat your sons and daughters.
They will eat your flocks and herds.
They will eat your grapes and figs.
They will destroy with their swords
the strong, walled cities you trust.

18"Yet even then," says the LORD, "I will not
destroy you completely. 19When the people
of Judah ask, 'Why has the LORD our God
done all these terrible things to us?' then
give them this answer: 'You have left the
LORD and served foreign idols in your own
land. So now you will serve foreigners in a
land that does not belong to you.'

20"Announce this message to the family of
Jacob,
and tell it to the nation of Judah:
21Hear this message, you foolish people
who have no sense.
They have eyes, but they don't really
see.
They have ears, but they don't really
listen.
22Surely you are afraid of me," says the
LORD.
"You should shake with fear in my
presence.
I am the one who made the beaches to be
a border for the sea,
a border the water can never go past.
The waves may pound the beach, but they
can't win over it.
They may roar, but they cannot go
beyond it.
23But the people of Judah are stubborn and
have turned against me.
They have turned aside and gone away
from me.
24They do not say to themselves,
'We should fear the LORD our God,
who gives us autumn and spring rains in
their seasons,
who makes sure we have the harvest at
the right time.'
25But your evil has kept away both rain and
harvest.
Your sins have kept you from enjoying
good things.
26There are wicked men among my people.
Like those who make nets for catching
birds,
they set their traps to catch people.
27Like cages full of birds,
their houses are full of lies.
They have become rich and powerful.
28 They have grown big and fat.
There is no end to the evil things they do.
They won't plead the case of the orphan
or help the poor be judged fairly.
29Shouldn't I punish the people of Judah
for doing these things?" says the
LORD.
"Shouldn't I give a nation such as this
the punishment it deserves?

30"A terrible and shocking thing
has happened in the land of Judah:
31The prophets speak lies,
and the priests take power into their
own hands,
and my people love it this way.
But what will you do when the end
comes?

Jerusalem Is Surrounded

6 "Run for your lives, people of Benjamin!
Run away from Jerusalem!
Blow the war trumpet in the town of
Tekoa!
Raise the warning flag over the town of
Beth Hakkerem!
Disaster is coming from the north;
terrible destruction is coming to you.
2 Jerusalem, I will destroy you,
you who are fragile and gentle.
3 Shepherds with their flocks will come
against Jerusalem.
They will set up their tents all around
her,
each shepherd taking care of his own
section."
4 They say, "Get ready to fight against
Jerusalem!
Get up! We will attack at noon!
But it is already getting late;
the evening shadows are growing long.
5 So get up! We will attack at night.
We will destroy the strong towers of
Jerusalem!"
6 This is what the LORD All-Powerful says:
"Cut down the trees around Jerusalem,
and build an attack ramp to the top of
its walls.
This city must be punished.
Inside it is nothing but slavery.
7 Jerusalem pours out her evil
as a well pours out its water.
The sounds of violence and destruction
are heard within her.
I can see the sickness and hurts of
Jerusalem.
8 Listen to this warning, Jerusalem,
or I will turn my back on you
and make your land an empty desert
where no one can live."
9 This is what the LORD All-Powerful says:
"Gather the few people of Israel who are
left alive,
as you would gather the last grapes on a
grapevine.
Check each vine again,
like someone who gathers grapes."
10 To whom can I speak? Whom can I warn?
Who will listen to me?
The people of Israel have closed ears,
so they cannot hear my warnings.
They don't like the word of the LORD;
they don't want to listen to it!
11 But I am full of the anger of the LORD,
and I am tired of holding it in.

"Pour out my anger on the children who
play in the street
and on the young men gathered
together.
A husband and his wife will both be
caught in his anger,
as will the very old.
12 Their houses will be turned over to
others,
along with their fields and wives,
because I will raise my hand
and punish the people of Judah," says
the LORD.
13 "Everyone, from the least important to the
greatest,
is greedy for money.
Even the prophets and priests
all tell lies.
14 They tried to heal my people's serious
injuries
as if they were small wounds.
They said, 'It's all right, it's all right.'
But really, it is not all right.
15 They should be ashamed of the terrible
way they act,
but they are not ashamed at all.
They don't even know how to blush
about their sins.
So they will fall, along with everyone else.
They will be thrown to the ground
when I punish them," says the
LORD.
16 This is what the LORD says:
"Stand where the roads cross and look.
Ask where the old way is,
where the good way is, and walk on it.
If you do, you will find rest for
yourselves.
But they have said, 'We will not walk
on the good way.'
17 I set watchmen over you
and told you, 'Listen for the sound of
the war trumpet!'
But they said, 'We will not listen.'
18 So listen, all you nations,
and pay attention, you witnesses.
Watch what I will do to the people of
Judah.
19 Hear this, people of the earth:

I am going to bring disaster to the
people of Judah
because of the evil they plan.
They have not listened to my messages
and have rejected my teachings.
20 Why do you bring me offerings of incense
from the land of Sheba?
Why do you bring me sweet-smelling
cane from a faraway land?
Your burnt offerings will not be accepted;
your sacrifices do not please me."
21 So this is what the LORD says:
"I will put problems in front of Judah.
Fathers and sons will stumble over
them together.
Neighbors and friends will die."
22 This is what the LORD says:
"Look, an army is coming
from the land of the north;
a great nation is coming
from the far sides of the earth.
23 The soldiers carry bows and spears.
They are cruel and show no mercy.
They sound like the roaring ocean
when they ride their horses.
That army is coming lined up for battle,
ready to attack you, Jerusalem."

24 We have heard the news about that army
and are helpless from fear.
We are gripped by our pain,
like a woman having a baby.
25 Don't go out into the fields
or walk down the roads,
because the enemy has swords.
There is terror on every side.
26 My people, put on rough cloth
and roll in the ashes to show how sad
you are.
Cry loudly for those who are dead,
as if your only son were dead,
because the destroyer
will soon come against us.

27 "Jeremiah, I have made you like a worker
who tests metal,
and my people are like the ore.
You must observe their ways
and test them.
28 All my people have turned against me and
are stubborn.
They go around telling lies about others.
They are like bronze and iron
that became covered with rust.
They all act dishonestly.
29 The fire is fanned to make it hotter,
but the lead does not melt.
The pure metal does not come out;
the evil is not removed from my people.
30 My people will be called rejected silver,
because the LORD has rejected them."

Jeremiah's Temple Message

7 This is the word that the LORD spoke to
Jeremiah: 2 "Stand at the gate of the
Temple and preach this message there:
" 'Hear the word of the LORD, all you
people of the nation of Judah! All you who
come through these gates to worship the
LORD, listen to this message! 3 This is what
the LORD All-Powerful, the God of Israel, says:
Change your lives and do what is right! Then
I will let you live in this place. 4 Don't trust
the lies of people who say, "This is the
Temple of the LORD. This is the Temple of the
LORD. This is the Temple of the LORD!" 5 You
must change your lives and do what is right.
Be fair to each other. 6 You must not be hard
on strangers, orphans, and widows. Don't kill
innocent people in this place! Don't follow
other gods, or they will ruin your lives. 7 If
you do these things, I will let you live in this
land that I gave to your ancestors to keep
forever.

8 " 'But look, you are trusting lies, which is
useless. 9 Will you steal and murder and be
guilty of adultery? Will you falsely accuse
other people? Will you burn incense to the
god Baal and follow other gods you have not
known? 10 If you do that, do you think you
can come before me and stand in this place
where I have chosen to be worshiped? Do
you think you can say, "We are safe!" when
you do all these hateful things? 11 This place
where I have chosen to be worshiped is
nothing more to you than a hideout for
robbers. I have been watching you, says the
LORD.

12 " 'You people of Judah, go now to the
town of Shiloh, where I first made a place to
be worshiped. See what I did to it because of
the evil things the people of Israel had done.
13 You people of Judah have done all these
evil things too, says the LORD. I spoke to you
again and again, but you did not listen to
me. I called you, but you did not answer. 14 So
I will destroy the place where I have chosen
to be worshiped in Jerusalem. You trust in
that place, which I gave to you and your

devotion 210

JEREMIAH 7:8–11

DO YOU THINK YOU WON'T GET CAUGHT?

It seems that throughout the Old Testament, the Lord had to constantly remind his people to turn from their wicked ways and follow him. The prophet Jeremiah asked them, "Do you think you can say, 'We are safe!' when you do all these hateful things?" (verse 10).

In some respects, we are no different than the people during Jeremiah's time. There's often a huge gap in our culture between claiming to follow God and actually doing it. Human nature can so easily take over, and the desire to follow our own way is almost overwhelming. Even though we now have the work of Jesus to look back to, we still give in to sin and believe that we can get away with it. But as we read in Jeremiah's prophecy, God watches us, just as he was watching the people who did not honor the ancient Temple. He knows our sins.

I have to admit that I can identify with the Israelites. Theirs was a long, hard road, and their walk with God was at times tumultuous, to say the least. I feel like my walk is sometimes that way, but I can tell you that when I choose to follow God, he never disappoints me. I hope you will feel motivated to not make the mistakes the Israelites made time and time again. I pray that you will choose his grace today and tomorrow and that you will give him the glory for all he has given you.

ancestors, but I will destroy it just as I
destroyed Shiloh. 15 I will push you away
from me just as I pushed away your
relatives, the people of Israel!'
16 "As for you, Jeremiah, don't pray for
these people. Don't cry out for them or ask
anything for them or beg me to help them,
because I will not listen to you. 17 Don't you
see what they are doing in the towns of
Judah and in the streets of Jerusalem? 18 The
children gather wood, and the fathers use
the wood to make a fire. The women make
the dough for cakes of bread, and they offer
them to the Queen Goddess. They pour out
drink offerings to other gods to make me
angry. 19 But I am not the one the people of
Judah are really hurting, says the LORD. They
are only hurting themselves and bringing
shame upon themselves.
20 " 'So this is what the Lord GOD says: I
will pour out my anger on this place, on
people and animals, on the trees in the field
and the crops in the ground. My anger will
be like a hot fire that no one can put out.

Obedience Is More than Sacrifice

21 " 'This is what the LORD All-Powerful, the
God of Israel, says: Offer burnt offerings
along with your other sacrifices, and eat the
meat yourselves! 22 When I brought your
ancestors out of Egypt, I did not speak to
them and give them commands only about
burnt offerings and sacrifices. 23 I also gave
them this command: Obey me, and I will be
your God and you will be my people. Do all
that I command so that good things will
happen to you. 24 But your ancestors did not
listen or pay attention to me. They were
stubborn and did whatever their evil hearts
wanted. They went backward, not forward.
25 Since the day your ancestors left Egypt, I
have sent my servants, the prophets, again
and again to you. 26 But your ancestors did
not listen or pay attention to me. They were
very stubborn and did more evil than their
ancestors.'
27 "Jeremiah, you will tell all these things
to the people of Judah, but they will not
listen to you. You will call to them, but they

will not answer you. 28 So say to them, 'This
is the nation that has not obeyed the LORD its
God. These people do nothing when I correct
them. They do not tell the truth; it has
disappeared from their lips.

The Valley of Killing

29 " 'Cut off your hair and throw it away.
Go up to the bare hilltop and cry out,
because the LORD has rejected these people.
He has turned his back on them, and in his
anger will punish them. 30 The people of
Judah have done what I said was evil, says
the LORD. They have set up their hateful
idols in the place where I have chosen to be
worshiped and have made it unclean. 31 The
people of Judah have built places of worship
at Topheth in the Valley of Ben Hinnom.
There they burned their own sons and
daughters as sacrifices, something I never
commanded. It never even entered my mind.
32 So, I warn you. The days are coming, says
the LORD, when people will not call this
place Topheth or the Valley of Ben Hinnom
anymore. They will call it the Valley of
Killing. They will bury the dead in Topheth
until there is no room to bury anyone else.
33 Then the bodies of the dead will become
food for the birds of the sky and for the wild
animals. There will be no one left alive to
chase them away. 34 I will end the happy
sounds of the bride and bridegroom. There
will be no happy sounds in the cities of
Judah or in the streets of Jerusalem, because
the land will become an empty desert!

8 " 'The LORD says: At that time they will
remove from their tombs the bones of
Judah's kings and officers, priests and
prophets, and the people of Jerusalem. 2 The
bones will be spread on the ground under
the sun, moon, and stars that the people
loved and served and went after and
searched for and worshiped. No one will
gather up the bones and bury them. So they
will be like dung thrown on the ground. 3 I
will force the people of Judah to leave their
homes and their land. Those of this evil
family who are not dead will wish they
were, says the LORD All-Powerful.'

Sin and Punishment

4 "Say to the people of Judah: 'This is what
the LORD says:

When people fall down, don't they get up
again?
And when someone goes the wrong
way, doesn't he turn back?
5 Why, then, have the people of Jerusalem
gone the wrong way
and not turned back?
They believe their own lies
and refuse to turn around and come
back.
6 I have listened to them very carefully,
but they do not say what is right.
They do not feel sorry about their wicked
ways,
saying, "What have I done?"
Each person goes his own way,
like a horse charging into a battle.
7 Even the birds in the sky
know the right times to do things.
The storks, doves, swifts, and thrushes
know when it is time to migrate.
But my people don't know
what the LORD wants them to do.

8 " 'You keep saying, "We are wise,
because we have the teachings of the
LORD."
But actually, those who explain the
Scriptures
have written lies with their pens.
9 These wise teachers refused to listen to
the word of the LORD,
so they are not really wise at all.
They will be ashamed.
They will be shocked and trapped.
10 So I will give their wives to other men
and their fields to new owners.
Everyone, from the least important to the
greatest,
is greedy for money.
Even the prophets and priests
all tell lies.
11 They tried to heal my people's serious
injuries
as if they were small wounds.
They said, "It's all right, it's all right."
But really, it is not all right.
12 They should be ashamed of the terrible
way they act,
but they are not ashamed at all.
They don't even know how to blush
about their sins.
So they will fall, along with everyone
else.

They will be thrown to the ground
when I punish them, says the
LORD.

[13]" 'I will take away their crops, says the
LORD.
There will be no grapes on the vine
and no figs on the fig tree.
Even the leaves will dry up and die.
I will take away what I gave them.' "

[14]"Why are we just sitting here?
Let's get together!
We have sinned against the LORD,
so he has given us poisoned water to
drink.
Come, let's run to the strong, walled
cities.
The LORD our God has decided that we
must die,
so let's die there.
[15]We hoped to have peace,
but nothing good has come.
We hoped for a time when he would
heal us,
but only terror has come.
[16]From the land of Dan,
the snorting of the enemy's horses is
heard.
The ground shakes from the neighing
of their large horses.
They have come and destroyed
the land and everything in it,
the city and all who live there."
[17]"Look! I am sending poisonous snakes to
attack you.
These snakes cannot be charmed,
and they will bite you," says the LORD.

Jeremiah's Sadness

[18]God, you are my comfort when I am very
sad
and when I am afraid.
[19]Listen to the sound of my people.
They cry from a faraway land:
"Isn't the LORD still in Jerusalem?
Isn't Jerusalem's king still there?"
But God says, "Why did the people make
me angry by worshiping idols,
useless foreign idols?"
[20]And the people say, "Harvest time is over;
summer has ended,
and we have not been saved."

[21]Because my people are crushed, I am
crushed.
I cry loudly and am afraid for them.
[22]Isn't there balm in the land of Gilead?
Isn't there a doctor there?
So why aren't the hurts of my people
healed?

9 I wish my head were like a spring of
water
and my eyes like a fountain of tears!
Then I could cry day and night
for my people who have been killed.
[2]I wish I had a place in the desert—
a house where travelers spend the
night—
so I could leave my people.
I could go away from them,
because they are all unfaithful to God;
they are all turning against him.

Judah's Failures

[3]"They use their tongues like a bow,
shooting lies from their mouths like
arrows.
Lies, not truth,
have grown strong in the land.
They go from one evil thing to another.
They do not know who I am," says the
LORD.
[4]"Watch out for your friends,
and don't trust your own relatives,
because every relative is a cheater,
and every friend tells lies about you.
[5]Everyone lies to his friend,
and no one speaks the truth.
The people of Judah have taught their
tongues to lie.
They have become tired from sinning.
[6]Jeremiah, you live in the middle of lies.
With their lies the people refuse to
know me," says the LORD.
[7]So this is what the LORD All-Powerful
says:
"I will test the people of Judah as a person
tests metal in a fire.
I have no other choice,
because my people have sinned.
[8]Their tongues are like sharp arrows.
Their mouths speak lies.
Everyone speaks nicely to his neighbor,
but he is secretly planning to attack
him.
[9]Shouldn't I punish the people for doing
this?" says the LORD.

"Shouldn't I give a nation like this the
punishment it deserves?"

[10]I, Jeremiah, will cry loudly for the
mountains
and sing a funeral song for the empty
fields.
They are empty, and no one passes
through.
The mooing of cattle cannot be heard.
The birds have flown away,
and the animals are gone.

[11]"I, the LORD, will make the city of
Jerusalem a heap of ruins,
a home for wild dogs.
I will destroy the cities of Judah
so no one can live there."

[12]What person is wise enough to
understand these things? Is there someone
who has been taught by the LORD who can
explain them? Why was the land ruined?
Why has it been made like an empty desert
where no one goes?

[13]The LORD answered, "It is because Judah
quit following my teachings that I gave
them. They have not obeyed me or done
what I told them to do. [14]Instead, they were
stubborn and followed the Baals, as their
ancestors taught them to do. [15]So this is
what the LORD All-Powerful, the God of
Israel, says: "I will soon make the people of
Judah eat bitter food and drink poisoned
water. [16]I will scatter them through other
nations that they and their ancestors never
knew about. I will chase the people of
Judah with the sword until they are all
killed."

[17]This is what the LORD All-Powerful says:
"Now, think about these things!
Call for the women who cry at funerals
to come.
Send for those women who are good at
that job.
[18]Let them come quickly
and cry loudly for us.
Then our eyes will fill with tears,
and streams of water will flow from our
eyelids.
[19]The sound of loud crying is heard from
Jerusalem:
'We are truly ruined!
We are truly ashamed!
We must leave our land,
because our houses are in ruins.'"

[20]Now, women of Judah, listen to the word
of the LORD;
open your ears to hear the words of his
mouth.
Teach your daughters how to cry loudly.
Teach one another a funeral song.
[21]Death has climbed in through our
windows
and has entered our strong cities.
Death has taken away our children who
play in the streets
and the young men who meet in the
city squares.

[22]Say, "This is what the LORD says:
'The dead bodies of people will lie
in the open field like dung.
They will lie like grain a farmer has cut,
but there will be no one to gather
them.'"

[23]This is what the LORD says:
"The wise must not brag about their
wisdom.
The strong must not brag about their
strength.
The rich must not brag about their
money.
[24]But if people want to brag, let them brag
that they understand and know me.
Let them brag that I am the LORD,
and that I am kind and fair,
and that I do things that are right on
earth.
This kind of bragging pleases me," says
the LORD.

[25]The LORD says, "The time is coming
when I will punish all those who are
circumcised only in the flesh: [26]the people of
Egypt, Judah, Edom, Ammon, Moab, and the
desert people who cut their hair short. The
men in all those countries are not
circumcised. And the whole family of Israel
does not give itself to serving me."

The Lord and the Idols

10 Family of Israel, listen to what the
LORD says to you. [2]This is what he says:
"Don't live like the people from other
nations,
and don't be afraid of special signs in
the sky,
even though the other nations are
afraid of them.
[3]The customs of other people are worth
nothing.

devotion 211

JEREMIAH 9:24

BRAGGING RIGHTS

To brag on God is to praise him. It is our duty and sacrifice as believers to continually praise God (Heb. 13:15). God loves it when we make a big deal out of him, when we tell people about his character, and when we point to him with our words.

When you are in awe over the glory of God, your heart is amazed by his grace, and you speak of your amazement to others. Your mind is gripped by the truth of God, and you can't help but tell others about his great truths. Your sense of right and wrong is guided by the justice of God, and you boldly tell others why you choose right. You brag on the fairness of God. Your faith rests on the assurance of God, and so your lips speak peace and security. People hear about God's faithfulness because you tell them that he has been faithful to you. Your imagination is guided by the beauty of God, and so the things you create reflect the beauty you have seen in him. When people ask about your inspiration, God is praised when you describe him as the master Creator and the source of all creativity.

Most of all, when people fall into despair, you can share hope because you have seen the glory of God, and your hope is fully anchored. God says that kind of bragging brings him such great pleasure. So never pass up an opportunity to brag on our great God!

Their idols are just wood cut from the
forest,
shaped by a worker with his chisel.
4 They decorate their idols with silver and
gold.
With hammers and nails they fasten
them down
so they won't fall over.
5 Their idols are like scarecrows in melon
fields;
they cannot talk.
Since they cannot walk,
they must be carried.
Do not be afraid of those idols,
because they can't hurt you,
and they can't help you either."
6 LORD, there is no one like you.
You are great,
and your name is great and powerful.
7 Everyone should respect you, King of the
nations;
you deserve respect.
Of all the wise people among the nations
and in all the kingdoms,
none of them is as wise as you.
8 Those wise people are stupid and
foolish.
Their teachings come from worthless
wooden idols.
9 Hammered silver is brought from
Tarshish
and gold from Uphaz,
so the idols are made by craftsmen and
goldsmiths.
They put blue and purple clothes on
the idols.
All these things are made by skilled
workers.
10 But the LORD is the only true God.
He is the only living God, the King
forever.
The earth shakes when he is angry,
and the nations cannot stand up to his
anger.

11 "Tell them this message: 'These gods did
not make heaven and earth; they will be
destroyed and disappear from heaven and
earth.' "

12God made the earth by his power.
He used his wisdom to build the world
and his understanding to stretch out the skies.
13When he thunders, the waters in the skies roar.
He makes clouds rise in the sky all over the earth.
He sends lightning with the rain
and brings out the wind from his storehouses.

14People are so stupid and know so little.
Goldsmiths are made ashamed by their idols,
because those statues are only false gods.
They have no breath in them.
15They are worth nothing; people make fun of them.
When they are judged, they will be destroyed.
16But God, who is Jacob's Portion, is not like the idols.
He made everything,
and he chose Israel to be his special people.
The LORD All-Powerful is his name.

Destruction Is Coming

17Get everything you own and prepare to leave,
you people who are trapped by your enemies.
18This is what the LORD says:
"At this time I will throw out the people who live in this land.
I will bring trouble to them
so that they may be captured."

19How terrible it will be for me because of my injury.
My wound cannot be healed.
Yet I told myself,
"This is my sickness; I must suffer through it."
20My tent is ruined,
and all its ropes are broken.
My children have gone away and left me.
No one is left to put up my tent again
or to set up a shelter for me.
21The shepherds are stupid
and don't ask the LORD for advice.
So they do not have success,
and all their flocks are scattered and lost.
22Listen! The news is coming.
A loud noise comes from the north
to make the towns of Judah an empty desert
and a home for wild dogs!

Jeremiah's Prayer

23LORD, I know that our lives don't really belong to us.
We can't control our own lives.
24LORD, correct me, but be fair.
Don't punish me in your anger,
or you will destroy me.
25Pour out your anger on other nations
that do not know you
and do not pray to you.
Those nations have destroyed the people of Jacob.
They have eaten them up completely
and destroyed their homeland.

The Agreement Is Broken

11 These are the words that the LORD
spoke to Jeremiah: 2"Listen to the
words of this agreement and tell them to
the people of Judah and those living in
Jerusalem. 3Tell them this is what the
LORD, the God of Israel, says: 'Cursed is the
person who does not obey the words of
this agreement 4that I made with your
ancestors when I brought them out of Egypt.
Egypt was like a furnace for melting iron!'
I told them, 'Obey me and do everything I
command you. Then you will be my people,
and I will be your God. 5Then I will keep the
promise I made to your ancestors to give
them a fertile land.' And you are living in
that country today."

I answered, "Amen, LORD."

6The LORD said to me, "Announce this
message in the towns of Judah and in the
streets of Jerusalem: 'Listen to the words of
this agreement and obey them. 7I warned
your ancestors to obey me when I brought
them out of Egypt. I have warned them
again and again to this very day: "Obey me!"
8But your ancestors did not listen to me.
They were stubborn and did what their own
evil hearts wanted. So I made all the curses
of this agreement come upon them. I
commanded them to obey the agreement,
but they did not.' "

9Then the LORD said to me, "I know the
people of Judah and those living in

Jerusalem have made secret plans. [10]They
have gone back to the same sins their
ancestors did. Their ancestors refused to
listen to my message and followed and
worshiped other gods instead. The families
of Israel and Judah have broken the
agreement I made with their ancestors. [11]So
this is what the LORD says: 'I will soon bring
a disaster on the people of Judah which they
will not be able to escape. They will cry to
me for help, but I will not listen to them.
[12]The people living in the towns of Judah
and the city of Jerusalem will pray to their
idols to whom they burn incense. But those
idols will not be able to help when disaster
comes. [13]Look, people of Judah, you have as
many idols as there are towns in Judah. You
have built as many altars to burn incense to
that shameful god Baal as there are streets in
Jerusalem.'

[14]"As for you, Jeremiah, don't pray for
these people or cry out for them or ask
anything for them. I will not listen when
they call to me in the time of their trouble.

[15]"What is my beloved Judah doing in my
Temple
when she makes many evil plans?
Do you think animal sacrifices will
stop your punishment?
When you do your evil, then you are
happy."
[16]The LORD called you "a leafy olive tree,
with beautiful fruit and shape."
But with the roar of a strong storm
he will set that tree on fire,
and its branches will be burned up.

[17]The LORD All-Powerful, who planted
you, has announced that disaster will come
to you. This is because the families of Israel
and Judah have done evil and have made
him angry by burning incense to Baal.

Evil Plans Against Jeremiah

[18]The LORD showed me that people were
making plans against me. Because he
showed me what they were doing, I knew
they were against me. [19]Before this, I was
like a gentle lamb waiting to be butchered. I
did not know they had made plans against
me, saying:

"Let us destroy the tree and its fruit.
Let's kill him so people will forget him."
[20]But, LORD All-Powerful, you are a fair
judge.
You know how to test peoples' hearts
and minds.
I have told you what I have against them.
So let me see you give them the
punishment they deserve.

[21]So the LORD speaks about the people
from Anathoth who plan to kill Jeremiah
and say, "Don't prophesy in the name of the
LORD, or we will kill you!" [22]So this is what
the LORD All-Powerful says: "I will soon
punish the men from Anathoth. Their
young men will die in war. Their sons and
daughters will die from hunger. [23]No one
from the city of Anathoth will be left alive,
because I will cause a disaster to happen to
them that year."

Jeremiah's First Complaint

12 LORD, when I bring my case to you,
you are always right.
But I want to ask you about the justice
you give.
Why are evil people successful?
Why do dishonest people have such
easy lives?
[2]You have put the evil people here
like plants with strong roots.
They grow and produce fruit.
With their mouths they speak well of you,
but their hearts are really far away from
you.
[3]But you know my heart, LORD.
You see me and test my thoughts about
you.
Drag the evil people away like sheep to be
butchered.
Set them aside for the day of killing.
[4]How much longer will the land stay
dried up
and the grass in every field be dead?
The animals and birds in the land have
died,
because the people are evil.
Yes, they are even saying,
"God does not see what happens to us."

The Lord's Answer to Jeremiah

[5]"If you get tired while racing against
people,
how can you race against horses?
If you stumble in a country that is safe,
what will you do in the thick
thornbushes along the Jordan
River?

6Even your own brothers and members of
your own family
are making plans against you.
They are crying out against you.
Don't trust them,
even when they say nice things to you!

7"I have left Israel;
I have left my people.
I have given the people I love
over to their enemies.
8My people have become to me
like a lion in the forest.
They roar at me,
so I hate them.
9My people have become to me
like a speckled bird attacked on all sides
by hawks.
Go, gather the wild animals.
Bring them to get something to eat.
10Many shepherds have ruined my
vineyards
and trampled the plants in my field.
They have turned my beautiful field
into an empty desert.
11They have turned my field into a desert
that is wilted and dead.
The whole country is an empty desert,
because no one who lives there cares.
12Many soldiers have marched over those
barren hills.
The LORD is using the armies to punish
that land
from one end to the other.
No one is safe.
13The people have planted wheat,
but they have harvested only thorns.
They have worked hard until they were
very tired,
but they have nothing for all their
work.
They are ashamed of their poor harvest,
because the LORD's terrible anger has
caused this."

14This is what the LORD said to me: "Here
is what I will do to all my wicked neighbors
who take the land I gave my people Israel. I
will pull them up and throw them out of
their land. And I will pull up the people of
Judah from among them. 15But after I pull
them up, I will feel sorry for them again. I
will bring each person back to his own
property and to his own land. 16I want them
to learn their lessons well. In the past they
taught my people to swear by Baal's name.
But if they will now learn to swear by my
name, saying, 'As surely as the LORD lives
. . .' I will allow them to rebuild among my
people. 17But if a nation will not listen to my
message, I will pull it up completely and
destroy it," says the LORD.

Jeremiah's Linen Belt

13 This is what the LORD said to me: "Go
and buy a linen belt and put it around
your waist. Don't let the belt get wet."

2So I bought a linen belt, just as the LORD
told me, and put it around my waist. 3Then
the LORD spoke his word to me a second
time: 4"Take the belt you bought and are
wearing, and go to Perath. Hide the belt
there in a crack in the rocks." 5So I went to
Perath and hid the belt there, just as the LORD
told me.

6Many days later the LORD said to me,
"Now go to Perath and get the belt I told you
to hide there." 7So I went to Perath and dug
up the belt and took it from where I had
hidden it. But now it was ruined; it was good
for nothing.

8Then the LORD spoke his word to me.
9This is what the LORD said: "In the same
way I will ruin the pride of the people of
Judah and the great pride of Jerusalem.
10These evil people refuse to listen to my
warnings. They stubbornly do only what
they want to do, and they follow other gods
to serve and worship them. So they will
become like this linen belt—good for
nothing. 11As a belt is wrapped tightly
around a person's waist, I wrapped the
families of Israel and Judah around me," says
the LORD. "I did that so they would be my
people and bring fame, praise, and honor to
me. But my people would not listen.

Warnings About Leather Wine Bags

12"Say to them: 'This is what the LORD, the
God of Israel, says: All leather bags for
holding wine should be filled with wine.'
People will say to you: 'Of course, we know
all wine bags should be filled with wine.'
13Then you will say to them, 'This is what
the LORD says: I will make everyone in this
land like a drunken person—the kings who
sit on David's throne, the priests and the
prophets, and all the people who live in
Jerusalem. 14I will make them smash against

one another, fathers and sons alike, says the
LORD. I will not feel sorry or have pity on
them or show mercy that would stop me
from destroying them.' "

Threat of Slavery

15 Listen and pay attention.
Don't be too proud,
because the LORD has spoken to you.
16 Give glory to the LORD your God
before he brings darkness
and before you slip and fall
on the dark hills.
You hope for light,
but he will turn it into thick darkness;
he will change it into deep gloom.
17 If you don't listen to him,
I will cry secretly
because of your pride.
I will cry painfully,
and my eyes will overflow with tears,
because the LORD's people will be
captured.
18 Tell this to the king and the queen
mother:
"Come down from your thrones,
because your beautiful crowns
have fallen from your heads."
19 The cities of southern Judah are locked up,
and no one can open them.
All Judah will be taken as captives to a
foreign land;
they will be carried away completely.
20 Jerusalem, look up and see
the people coming from the north.
Where is the flock God gave you to care
for,
the flock you bragged about?
21 What will you say when they appoint as
your heads
those you had thought were your
friends?
Won't you have much pain and trouble,
like a woman giving birth to a baby?
22 You might ask yourself,
"Why has this happened to me?"
It happened because of your many sins.
Because of your sins, your skirt was
torn off
and your body has been treated badly.
23 Can a person from Cush change the color
of his skin?
Can a leopard change his spots?
In the same way, Jerusalem, you cannot
change and do good,
because you are accustomed to doing
evil.
24 "I will scatter you like chaff that is blown
away by the desert wind.
25 This is what will happen to you;
this is your part in my plans," says the
LORD.
"Because you forgot me
and trusted in false gods,
26 I will pull your skirts up over your face
so everyone will see your shame.
27 I have seen the terrible things you have
done:
your acts of adultery and your
snorting,
your prostitution,
your hateful acts
on the hills and in the fields.
How terrible it will be for you, Jerusalem.
How long will you continue being
unclean?"

A Time Without Rain

14 These are the words that the LORD
spoke to Jeremiah about the time
when there was no rain:
2 "The nation of Judah cries as if someone
has died,
and her cities are very sad.
They are distressed over the land.
A cry goes up to God from Jerusalem.
3 The important men send their servants to
get water.
They go to the wells,
but they find no water.
So they return with empty jars.
They are ashamed and embarrassed
and cover their heads in shame.
4 The ground is dry and cracked open,
because no rain falls on the land.
The farmers are upset and sad,
so they cover their heads in shame.
5 Even the mother deer in the field
leaves her newborn fawn to die,
because there is no grass.
6 Wild donkeys stand on the bare hills
and sniff the wind like wild dogs.
But their eyes go blind,
because there is no food."
7 We know that we suffer because of our
sins.

LORD, do something to help us for the
good of your name.
We have left you many times;
we have sinned against you.
8God, the Hope of Israel,
you have saved Israel in times of
trouble.
Why are you like a stranger in the land,
or like a traveler who only stays one
night?
9Why are you like someone who has been
attacked by surprise,
like a warrior who is not able to save
anyone?
But you are among us, LORD,
and we are called by your name
so don't leave us without help!

10This is what the LORD says about the
people of Judah:
"They really love to wander from me;
they don't stop themselves from
leaving me.
So now the LORD will not accept them.
He will now remember the evil they do
and will punish them for their sins."

11Then the LORD said, "Don't pray for good
things to happen to the people of Judah.
12Even if they fast, I will not listen to their
prayers. Even if they offer burnt offerings
and grain offerings to me, I will not accept
them. Instead, I will destroy the people of
Judah with war, hunger, and terrible
diseases."

13But I said, "Oh, Lord GOD, the prophets
keep telling the people, 'You will not suffer
from an enemy's sword or from hunger. I,
the LORD, will give you peace in this land.' "

14Then the LORD said to me, "Those
prophets are prophesying lies in my name. I
did not send them or appoint them or speak
to them. They have been prophesying false
visions, idolatries, worthless magic, and
their own wishful thinking. 15So this is what
I say about the prophets who are
prophesying in my name. I did not send
them. They say, 'No enemy will attack this
country with swords. There will never be
hunger in this land.' So those prophets will
die from hunger and from an enemy's sword.
16And the people to whom the prophets
speak will be thrown into the streets of
Jerusalem. There they will die from hunger
and from an enemy's sword. And no one will
be there to bury them, or their wives, or
their sons, or their daughters. I will punish
them.

17"Jeremiah, speak this message to the
people of Judah:
'Let my eyes be filled with tears
night and day, without stopping.
My people have received a terrible blow;
they have been hurt badly.
18If I go into the country,
I see people killed by swords.
If I go into the city,
I see much sickness, because the people
have no food.
Both the priests and the prophets
have been taken to a foreign land.' "

19LORD, have you completely rejected the
nation of Judah?
Do you hate Jerusalem?
Why have you hurt us so badly
that we cannot be made well again?
We hoped for peace,
but nothing good has come.
We looked for a time of healing,
but only terror came.
20LORD, we admit that we are wicked
and that our ancestors did evil things.
We have sinned against you.
21For your sake, do not hate us.
Do not take away the honor from your
glorious throne.
Remember your agreement with us,
and do not break it.
22Do foreign idols have the power to bring
rain?
Does the sky itself have the power to
send down showers?
No, it is you, LORD our God.
You are our only hope,
because you are the one who made all
these things.

15 Then the LORD said to me: "I would
not feel sorry for the people of Judah
even if Moses and Samuel prayed for them.
Send them away from me! Tell them to go!
2When they ask you, 'Where will we go?'
tell them: 'This is what the LORD says:
Those who are meant to die
will die.
Those who are meant to die in war
will die in war.
Those who are meant to die from
hunger
will die from hunger.

Those who are meant to be taken captive
will be taken captive.'
3"I will send four kinds of destroyers
against them," says the LORD. "I will send war
to kill, dogs to drag the bodies away, and the
birds of the air and wild animals to eat and
destroy the bodies. 4I will make the people
of Judah hated by everyone on earth because
of what Manasseh did in Jerusalem.
(Manasseh son of Hezekiah was king of the
nation of Judah.)

5"Who will feel sorry for you, Jerusalem?
Who will be sad and cry for you?
Who will go out of his way to ask how
you are?
6Jerusalem, you have left me," says the
LORD.
"You keep going farther and farther
away,
so I have taken hold of you and destroyed
you.
I was tired of holding back my anger.
7I have separated the people of Judah with
my pitchfork
and scattered them at the city gates of
the land.
My people haven't changed their ways.
So I have destroyed them
and taken away their children.
8There are more widows than grains of
sand in the sea.
I brought a destroyer at noontime
against the mothers of the young men
of Judah.
I suddenly brought pain and fear
on the people of Judah.
9When the enemy attacked, a woman with
seven sons felt faint because they
would all die.
She became weak and unable to
breathe.
Her bright day became dark from sadness.
She felt shame and disgrace.
And everyone else left alive in Judah
I will hand over to the enemies, too!"
says the LORD.

Jeremiah's Second Complaint

10Mother, I am sorry that you gave birth
to me
since I must accuse and criticize the
whole land.
I have not loaned or borrowed anything,
but everyone curses me.

11The LORD said,
"I have saved you for a good reason.
I have made your enemies beg you
in times of disaster and trouble.
12No one can smash a piece of iron or
bronze
that comes from the north.
13Your wealth and treasures
I will give to others free of charge,
because the people of Judah have sinned
throughout the country.
14I will make you slaves to your enemies
in a land you have never known.
My anger is like a hot fire,
and it will burn against you."

15LORD, you understand.
Remember me and take care of me.
Punish for me those who are hurting me.
Don't destroy me while you remain
patient with them.
Think about the shame I suffer for you.
16Your words came to me, and I listened
carefully to them.
Your words made me very happy,
because I am called by your name,
LORD God All-Powerful.
17I never sat with the crowd
as they laughed and had fun.
I sat by myself, because you were there,
and you filled me with anger at the evil
around me.
18I don't understand why my pain has no
end.
I don't understand why my injury is not
cured or healed.
Will you be like a brook that goes dry?
Will you be like a spring that stops
flowing?

19So this is what the LORD says:
"If you change your heart and return to
me, I will take you back.
Then you may serve me.
And if you speak things that have worth,
not useless words,
then you may speak for me.
Let the people of Judah turn to you,
but you must not change and be like
them.
20I will make you as strong as a wall to this
people,
as strong as a wall of bronze.
They will fight against you,
but they will not defeat you,

devotion 212

JEREMIAH 15:16

LISTEN CAREFULLY

Do you realize that you are holding the very words of God right now? There are times when I take for granted my lovely leather-wrapped Bible. Anything I need is right there, not only in black and white but in Spirit. Jeremiah had one-on-one, intimate conversations with God that he shared with others, yet he never saw one single person come to know God or repent. He spent his entire ministry doing exactly what God instructed him to do, regardless of his fruitless outcome.

Once I said to my husband, "It's not fair that I do everything I am supposed to do, but it seems like I never prosper from it." In his wisdom, my husband said, "That's because you are *supposed* to do what is right!"

For some reason, that was a revelation for me. I am blessed simply because I know the truth and obey it, period! To hear from God, you have to listen to his words carefully. If you were the only person alive, he would have prepared them throughout history just for you! So if God would do all that just for you, you should listen carefully to his words of love and instruction. "All Scripture is inspired by God and is useful for teaching, for showing people what is wrong in their lives, for correcting faults, and for teaching how to live right. Using the Scriptures, the person who serves God will be capable, having all that is needed to do every good work" (2 Tim. 3:16-17).

because I am with you.
I will rescue you and save you," says the
LORD.
21"I will save you from these wicked people
and rescue you from these cruel people."

The Day of Disaster

16 Then the LORD spoke his word to me:
2"You must not get married or have
sons or daughters in this place."
3The LORD says this about the sons and
daughters born in this land and their
mothers and fathers: 4"They will die of
terrible diseases, and no one will cry for
them or bury them. Their bodies will lie on
the ground like dung. They will die in war,
or they will starve to death. Their bodies will
be food for the birds of the sky and for the
wild animals."
5So this is what the LORD says: "Jeremiah,
do not go into a house where there is a
funeral meal. Do not go there to cry for the
dead or to show your sorrow for them,
because I have taken back my blessing, my
love, and my pity from these people," says
the LORD. 6"Important people and common
people will die in the land of Judah. No one
will bury them or cry for them or cut
himself or shave his head to show sorrow for
them. 7No one will bring food to comfort
those who are crying for the dead. No one
will offer a drink to comfort someone whose
mother or father has died.
8"Do not go into a house where the people
are having a feast to sit down to eat and
drink, 9because this is what the LORD
All-Powerful, the God of Israel, says: I will
soon stop the sounds of joy and gladness and
the happy sounds of brides and bridegrooms
in this place. This will happen during your
lifetime.
10"When you tell the people of Judah
these things, they will ask you, 'Why has the
LORD said these terrible things to us? What

have we done wrong? What sin have we
done against the LORD our God?’
11“Then say to them: ‘This is because your
ancestors quit following me,’ says the LORD.
‘And they followed other gods and served
and worshiped them. Your ancestors left me
and quit obeying my teaching. 12But you
have done even more evil than your
ancestors. You are very stubborn and do only
what you want to do; you have not obeyed
me. 13So I will throw you out of this country
and send you into a land that you and your
ancestors never knew. There you can serve
other gods day and night, because I will not
help you or show you any favors.’
14“People say, ‘As surely as the LORD lives,
who brought the people of Israel out of
Egypt . . . .’ But the time is coming,” says
the LORD, “when people will not say this
anymore. 15They will say instead, ‘As surely
as the LORD lives, who brought the Israelites
from the northern land and from all the
countries where he had sent them . . . .’
And I will bring them back to the land I gave
to their ancestors.
16“I will soon send for many fishermen to
come to this land,” says the LORD. “And they
will catch the people of Judah. After that, I
will send for many hunters to come to this
land. And they will hunt the people of Judah
on every mountain and hill and in the cracks
of the rocks. 17I see everything they do. They
cannot hide from me the things they do;
their sin is not hidden from my eyes. 18I will
pay back the people of Judah twice for every
one of their sins, because they have made
my land unclean. They have filled my
country with their hateful idols.”

19LORD, you are my strength and my
protection,
my safe place in times of trouble.
The nations will come to you from all
over the world
and say, “Our ancestors had only false
gods,
useless idols that didn’t help them.
20Can people make gods for themselves?
They will not really be gods!”
21The LORD says, “So I will teach those who
make idols.
This time I will teach them
about my power and my strength.
Then they will know
that my name is the LORD.

Judah’s Guilty Heart

17 “The sin of the people of Judah is
written with an iron tool.
Their sins were cut with a hard point
into the stone that is their hearts.
Their sins were cut into the corners of
their altars.
2Even their children remember
their altars to idols and their Asherah
idols
beside the green trees
and on the high hills.
3My mountain in the open country
and your wealth and treasures
I will give away to other people.
I will give away the places of worship
in your country,
because you sinned by worshiping
there.
4You will lose the land I gave you,
and it is your own fault.
I will let your enemies take you as their
slaves
to a land you have never known.
This is because you have made my anger
burn like a hot fire,
and it will burn forever.”

Trusting in Humans or God

5This is what the LORD says:
“A curse is placed on those who trust
other people,
who depend on humans for strength,
who have stopped trusting the LORD.
6They are like a bush in a desert
that grows in a land where no one lives,
a hot and dry land with bad soil.
They don’t know about the good things
God can give.
7“But the person who trusts in the LORD
will be blessed.
The LORD will show him that he can be
trusted.
8He will be strong, like a tree planted near
water
that sends its roots by a stream.
It is not afraid when the days are hot;
its leaves are always green.
It does not worry in a year when no rain
comes;
it always produces fruit.
9“More than anything else, a person’s mind
is evil

devotion 213

JEREMIAH 17:7–8

GREEN LEAVES IN A DROUGHT

Is it a challenge for you to keep your heart focused on God and trust solely in him? I want you to understand that God is a jealous God. He desires your devotion, your attention, your heart, and most of all, the opportunity to be your provision. When the world looks at your life, God wants it to be evident to everyone that you are blessed from his hand alone. In Jeremiah 17 he refers to a person who trusts him as being a tree with green leaves that are not destroyed or fearful when the drought comes. He is not just referring to sustaining you during the droughts—he's talking about making you stand out among your peers, green with blessings. You will still be producing fruit when everyone else is dried up and fruitless. This is the Lord himself proving to you that he can be trusted.

The devil wants you to believe that humans make the difference in your personal provision. It's one of the enemy's familiar traps to make you doubt God's hand and turn to others instead. If you are unsure of your motives for keeping certain people's company, ask yourself this question: "If this person were not profiting me in some way (pay, contacts, perks, status), I would still love them and want them in my life." If the relationships you have can pass that test, they are measured by character, not personal wealth. No matter who you know, trust God as your sole provider!

and cannot be healed.
Who can understand it?
10 But I, the LORD, look into a person's heart
and test the mind.
So I can decide what each one deserves;
I can give each one the right payment
for what he does."

11 Like a bird hatching an egg it did not lay,
so are the people who get rich by
cheating.
When their lives are half finished, they
will lose their riches.
At the end of their lives, it will be clear
they were fools.

12 From the beginning, our Temple has been
honored
as a glorious throne for God.
13 LORD, hope of Israel,
those who leave you will be shamed.
People who quit following the LORD will
be like a name written in the dust,
because they have left the LORD, the
spring of living water.

Jeremiah's Third Complaint

14 LORD, heal me, and I will truly be healed.
Save me, and I will truly be saved.
You are the one I praise.
15 The people of Judah keep asking me,
"Where is the word from the LORD?
Let's see that message come true!"
16 LORD, I didn't run away from being the
shepherd you wanted.
I didn't want the terrible day to come.
You know everything I have said;
you see all that is happening.
17 Don't be a terror to me.
I run to you for safety in times of
trouble.
18 Make those who are hurting me be
ashamed,
but don't bring shame to me.
Let them be terrified,
but keep me from terror.
Bring the day of disaster on my enemies.
Destroy them, and destroy them
again.

Keeping the Sabbath Holy

19 This is what the LORD said to me: "Go
and stand at the People's Gate of Jerusalem,
where the kings of Judah go in and out. And
then go to all the other gates of Jerusalem.
20 Say to them there: 'Hear the word of the
LORD, kings of Judah, all you people of Judah,
and all who live in Jerusalem, who come
through these gates into the city. 21 This is
what the LORD says: Be careful not to carry a
load on the Sabbath day or bring it through
the gates of Jerusalem. 22 Don't take a load
out of your houses on the Sabbath or do any
work on that day. But keep the Sabbath as a
holy day, as I commanded your ancestors.
23 But your ancestors did not listen or pay
attention to me. They were very stubborn
and did not listen. I punished them, but it
didn't do any good. 24 But you must be careful
to obey me, says the LORD. You must not
bring a load through the gates of Jerusalem
on the Sabbath, but you must keep the
Sabbath as a holy day and not do any work
on that day.

25 " 'If you obey this command, kings who
sit on David's throne will come through the
gates of Jerusalem with their officers. They
will come riding in chariots and on horses,
along with the people of Judah and
Jerusalem. And the city of Jerusalem will
have people living in it forever. 26 People will
come to Jerusalem from the villages around
it, from the towns of Judah, from the land of
Benjamin, from the western hills, from the
mountains, and from southern Judah. They
will all bring to the Temple of the LORD
burnt offerings, sacrifices, grain offerings,
incense, and offerings to show thanks to
God. 27 But you must obey me and keep the
Sabbath day as a holy day. You must not
carry any loads into Jerusalem on the
Sabbath. If you don't obey me, I will start a
fire at the gates of Jerusalem, and it will burn
until it burns even the strong towers. And it
will not be put out.' "

The Potter and the Clay

18 This is the word the LORD spoke to
Jeremiah: 2 "Go down to the potter's
house, and I will give you my message
there." 3 So I went down to the potter's house
and saw him working at the potter's wheel.
4 He was using his hands to make a pot from
clay, but something went wrong with it. So
he used that clay to make another pot the
way he wanted it to be.

5 Then the LORD spoke his word to me:
6 "Family of Israel, can't I do the same thing
with you?" says the LORD. "You are in my
hands like the clay in the potter's hands.
7 There may come a time when I will speak
about a nation or a kingdom that I will pull
up by its roots or that I will pull down to
destroy it. 8 But if the people of that nation
stop doing the evil they have done, I will
change my mind and not carry out my plans
to bring disaster to them. 9 There may come
another time when I will speak about a
nation that I will build up and plant. 10 But if
I see it doing evil by not obeying me, I will
change my mind and not carry out my plans
to do good for them.

11 "So, say this to the people of Judah and
those who live in Jerusalem: 'This is what the
LORD says: I am preparing disaster for you and
making plans against you. So stop doing evil.
Change your ways and do what is right.' 12 But
the people of Judah will answer, 'It won't do
any good to try! We will continue to do what
we want. Each of us will do what his
stubborn, evil heart wants!' "

13 So this is what the LORD says:

"Ask the people in other nations this
question:
'Have you ever heard anything like
this?'
The people of Israel have done a
horrible thing.
14 The snow on the mountains of Lebanon
never melts from the rocks.
Its cool, flowing streams
do not dry up.
15 But my people have forgotten me.
They burn incense to worthless idols
and have stumbled in what they do
and in the old ways of their ancestors.
They walk along back roads
and on poor highways.
16 So Judah's country will become an empty
desert.
People will not stop making fun of it.
They will shake their heads as they
pass by;
they will be shocked at how the
country was destroyed.
17 Like a strong east wind,
I will scatter them before their enemies.

rest

Several years ago, I had a bland date with a nice guy. But I guess he had a different impression because he was in pursuit afterwards. He sent flowers, wrote letters, and sang affectionate songs on my answering machine. William Shakespeare would've been proud of this guy—he pitched some serious woo!

Amazingly, my old suitor's passion pales next to the Lover of our souls. God plants vivid panoramas of wildflowers for our pleasure. He writes living letters reminding us of his love (Rom. 15:4). He even serenades us with songs of delight and deliverance (Zeph. 3:17)! However, most women—whether single, married, or widowed—aren't very good at being romanced by God. We're prone to be performance-oriented with default settings stuck on "Go." We always think we can add one more thing to our already lengthy to-do lists. Some of us even try to wrap Bible verses around our inability to relax and insist harried is a virtue! But our perpetual motion makes lingering and listening difficult, and we're left "weak woo-ees."

As God's beloved but busy daughters, we must learn that our souls require rest. In order to really hear him, we have to be willing to abandon constant activity. A seventeenth century French Archbishop named Fe'nelon penned a similar message with great insight, long before triple espressos, instant messaging, and Blackberries exacerbated chaos in culture: "When it comes to accomplishing things for God, you will find that high aspirations, enthusiastic feelings, careful planning, and being able to express yourself well are not worth very much. The important thing is absolute surrender to God."

The concept of absolute surrender, especially surrendering our schedule, is a difficult one. But sometimes stillness is necessary in order to really connect with God.

THINK ABOUT IT: If you had to assign a "temperature" to your lifestyle, what do you think it would be? Is your heart close to overheating?
In light of David's pro-rest passage, Psalm 23, what's your most vivid "relaxing in green pastures" memory?

DIG DEEPER: Exodus 31:12–18 (Sabbath), Psalm 46:10 (stillness), Hebrews 4:9–10 (God's rest), and 1 Peter 3:3–4 (quiet spirit)

parenting

If God has blessed you with children, you know that parenting is probably the most rewarding job you'll ever have. Ephesians 4:25–32 reveals the building blocks for parenting. Let's look at them.

1. *Speak the Truth.* Our children need to see us living our lives the way we tell them they should live theirs. My four-year-old once whispered from the back of our van while my husband and I were discussing something, "I hear you." And they do hear everything!
2. *Be Angry but Don't Sin.* We all feel angry at times, but we need to teach our children how to express that anger. Allow your children to disagree with you respectfully rather than forcing them to stuff their feelings.
3. *Work Hard.* Teach your children good work ethics. Chores and responsibility are essential training tools for a child's future. We tell our children, "With responsibility comes freedom," which means if they do the things they have been asked to do, they will be able to do the things they want to do.
4. *Impart Grace.* My husband has taught me the power of grace in the lives of our children. We believe in being consistent with discipline, but there are times in the lives of each of my children that grace had a greater impact than discipline ever could. Grace is something that is undeserved, and children appreciate it more than you know.
5. *Forgive.* We need to forgive and forget when our children disobey. Don't hold their sins against them.

Our son is almost eighteen years old. Since he was fourteen, we have told him that our goal for him was to allow him to be independent by the time he was eighteen. He has proven that he is dependable and trustworthy, and I wouldn't think twice about sending him anywhere in the world. Has he blown it over the years? Yes. I just can't remember when.

THINK ABOUT IT: How do you express your anger?
How often do you tell your children that you forgive them?

DIG DEEPER: Proverbs 3:11–12 (God's discipline), Ephesians 6:1–4 (obedience), and Colossians 3:21 (parents)

fun

When was the last time you had a really good laugh? Mine was just a few weeks ago. After an overload of travel, I had a three-hour window between meetings with clients. To fill the time, someone in the group suggested bowling—yes, bowling! Not my first choice, but I relented and off we went to bowl a few games. With the lanes freshly oiled, I grabbed by ball, positioned myself like any self-respecting amateur, and made my approach. With one foot in front of another and my arm swinging back, I crossed the foul line. My feet looked like something out of a Flintstone's episode as I struggled to keep upright. I found myself totally turned around facing the crew, spread eagle, chest first on the floor.

Well, that was funny enough by itself, but the really hilarious part was when I made my next trip up, I caught a view of my perfect imprint in oil on the lane. I lost it! There was an eruption of laughter like you have never heard. I discovered something profound on that bowling lane. It had been a long time since I just laughed at myself. Somehow that part of me had been missing.

Our lives get so consumed with the needs of our families, bills, schools, schedules, and work that we simply forget to enjoy the funnier parts of life. Our life is not meant to be a pressure cooker. Solomon instructed us to enjoy life and even our work. Instead, we live like we have been confined to some sort of prison with only checklists and accomplishments. Don't be a slave to routine and external pressure, or you will find that the fun has disappeared. Round up the family, and hit the bowling alley!

THINK ABOUT IT: When was the last time you really let loose and had a great big belly laugh?
What do you need to do right now to make sure that you plan time to go out and have fun?

DIG DEEPER: Psalm 126:2 (laughter), Psalm 149:3 (praise music), Proverbs 17:22 (happiness), and Ecclesiastes 8:15 (joy)

approval

I have struggled with people pleasing all of my life. Maybe it's because I grew up as the daughter of a pastor. I spent most of my days on the grounds of Christian camps my dad ran or helping my sister and mother entertain guests at our home. Perhaps it was because I was shy, but I found myself surrounded by encouragement from peers when I excelled. I've even wondered if all the people pleasing boiled down to my own expectations of my name. Frowning just didn't seem like much of an option matched with a name like "Joy."

So I learned to bury my insecurities, to look to others for approval, and to put on a happy face in spite of myself. Even though my parents, mentors, and friends expressed on a daily basis that I was okay as I was, I still couldn't bear the thought of letting anyone down. And that pattern "worked" for almost twenty-one years.

That is, until this year. I went to a Christian counselor to tackle the plastic ways I'd invested in my life. Of course, not all of my living had been fake, but so much of my life consisted of wanting approval from people. Where was the balance? Where was the desire to honor God? To respect myself?

Fear often steals much of the vibrancy, focus, and grace God offers in this life. It is when we let the clutter of other people's expectations rule us that we become forgetful of God's generous offer to love us unconditionally. Words of fear and condemnation should never be confused with the voice of Jesus. Nor should we extend them to others. When we can fix our eyes on Christ and his boundless affection for us, we begin to encounter a gracious life free from others' expectations.

THINK ABOUT IT: What are some of your people-pleasing tendencies? How have you allowed other people to confuse your focus and identity in Christ?

DIG DEEPER: Genesis 1:27 (God's image in us), Proverbs 8:35 (God's approval), and Galatians 1:10 (pleasing people)

Play your harp well. Sing your song often.
Then people will remember you."
17After seventy years the LORD will deal
with Tyre, and it will again have trade. It will
be like a prostitute for all the nations of the
earth. 18The profits will be saved for the
LORD. Tyre will not keep the money she
earns but will give them to the people who
serve the LORD, so they will have plenty of
food and nice clothes.

The Lord Will Punish the World

24 Look! The LORD will destroy the earth
and leave it empty;
he will ruin the surface of the land and
scatter its people.
2At that time the same thing will happen
to everyone:
to common people and priests,
to slaves and masters,
to women slaves and their women
masters,
to buyers and sellers,
to those who borrow and those who
lend,
to bankers and those who owe the bank.
3The earth will be completely empty.
The wealth will all be taken,
because the LORD has commanded it.
4The earth will dry up and die;
the world will grow weak and die;
the great leaders in this land will
become weak.
5The people of the earth have ruined it,
because they do not follow God's
teachings
or obey God's laws
or keep their agreement with God that
was to last forever.
6So a curse will destroy the earth.
The people of the world are guilty,
so they will be burned up;
only a few will be left.
7The new wine will be bad, and the
grapevines will die.
People who were happy will be sad.
8The happy music of the tambourines will
end.
The happy sounds of wild parties will
stop.
The joyful music from the harps will
end.
9People will no longer sing while they
drink their wine.
The beer will taste bitter to those who
drink it.
10The ruined city will be empty,
and people will hide behind closed
doors.
11People in the streets will ask for wine,
but joy will have turned to sadness;
all the happiness will have left.
12The city will be left in ruins,
and its gates will be smashed to pieces.
13This is what will happen all over the earth
and to all the nations.
The earth will be like an olive tree after
the harvest
or like the few grapes left on a vine
after harvest.
14The people shout for joy.
From the west they praise the greatness
of the LORD.
15People in the east, praise the LORD.
People in the islands of the sea,
praise the name of the LORD, the God of
Israel.
16We hear songs from every part of the
earth
praising God, the Righteous One.

But I said, "I am dying! I am dying!
How terrible it will be for me!
Traitors turn against people;
with their dishonesty, they turn against
people."
17There are terrors, holes, and traps
for the people of the earth.
18Anyone who tries to escape from the
sound of terror
will fall into a hole.
Anyone who climbs out of the hole
will be caught in a trap.
The clouds in the sky will pour out rain,
and the foundations of the earth will
shake.
19The earth will be broken up;
the earth will split open;
the earth will shake violently.
20The earth will stumble around like
someone who is drunk;
it will shake like a hut in a storm.
Its sin is like a heavy weight on its back;
it will fall and never rise again.

21At that time the LORD will punish
the powers in the sky above
and the rulers on earth below.

[18]and roll you tightly into a ball
and throw you into another country.
There you will die,
and there your fine chariots will remain.
You are a disgrace to your master's house.
[19]I will force you out of your important job,
and you will be thrown down from your important place.'

[20]"At that time I will call for my servant
Eliakim son of Hilkiah. [21]I will take your
robe and put it on him and give him your
belt. I will hand over to him the important
job you have, and he will be like a father to
the people of Jerusalem and the family of
Judah. [22]I will put the key to the house of
David around his neck. If he opens a door, no
one will be able to close it; if he closes a door,
no one will be able to open it. [23]He will be
like an honored chair in his father's house. I
will make him strong like a peg that is
hammered into a strong board. [24]All the
honored and important things of his family
will depend on him; all the adults and little
children will depend on him. They will be
like bowls and jars hanging on him.

[25]"At that time," says the LORD All-
Powerful, "the peg hammered into the
strong board will weaken. It will break and
fall, and everything hanging on it will be
destroyed." The LORD says this.

God's Message to Lebanon

23 This is a message about Tyre:
You trading ships, cry!
The houses and harbor of Tyre are destroyed.
This news came to the ships
from the land of Cyprus.
[2]Be silent, you who live on the island of Tyre;
you merchants of Sidon, be silent.
Sailors have made you rich.
[3]They traveled the sea to bring grain from Egypt;
the sailors of Tyre brought grain from the Nile Valley
and sold it to other nations.

[4]Sidon, be ashamed.
Strong city of the sea, be ashamed,
because the sea says:
"I have not felt the pain of giving birth;
I have not reared young men or women."
[5]Egypt will hear the news about Tyre,
and it will make Egypt hurt with sorrow.

[6]You ships should return to Tarshish.
You people living near the sea should be sad.
[7]Look at your once happy city!
Look at your old, old city!
People from that city have traveled
far away to live.
[8]Who planned Tyre's destruction?
Tyre made others rich.
Its merchants were treated like princes,
and its traders were greatly respected.
[9]It was the LORD All-Powerful who planned this.
He decided to make these proud people unimportant;
he decided to disgrace those who were greatly respected.
[10]Go through your land, people of Tarshish,
like the Nile goes through Egypt.
There is no harbor for you now!
[11]The LORD has stretched his hand over the sea
and made its kingdoms tremble.
He commands that Canaan's
strong, walled cities be destroyed.
[12]He said, "Sidon, you will not rejoice any longer,
because you are destroyed.
Even if you cross the sea to Cyprus,
you will not find a place to rest."
[13]Look at the land of the Babylonians;
it is not a country now.
Assyria has made it a place for wild animals.
Assyria built towers to attack it;
the soldiers took all the treasures from its cities,
and they turned it into ruins.
[14]So be sad, you trading ships,
because your strong city is destroyed.

[15]At that time people will forget about
Tyre for seventy years, which is the length of
a king's life. After seventy years, Tyre will be
like the prostitute in this song:
[16]"Oh woman, you are forgotten.
Take your harp and walk through the city.

At that awful time they will not see me
coming to help them;
they will see me leaving."

Jeremiah's Fourth Complaint

18Then the people said, "Come, let's make
plans against Jeremiah. Surely the teaching
of the law by the priest will not be lost. We
will still have the advice from the wise
teachers and the words of the prophets. So
let's ruin him by telling lies about him. We
won't pay attention to anything he says."

19LORD, listen to me.
Listen to what my accusers are saying!
20Good should not be paid back with evil,
but they have dug a pit in order to
kill me.
Remember that I stood before you
and asked you to do good things for
these people
and to turn your anger away from
them.
21So now, let their children starve,
and let their enemies kill them with
swords.
Let their wives lose their children and
husbands.
Let the men from Judah be put to death
and the young men be killed with
swords in battle.
22Let them cry out in their houses
when you bring an enemy against them
suddenly.
Let all this happen, because my enemies
have dug
a pit to capture me and have hidden
traps for my feet.
23LORD, you know
about all their plans to kill me.
Don't forgive their crimes
or erase their sins from your mind.
Make them fall from their places;
punish them while you are angry.

Judah Is like a Broken Jar

19 This is what the LORD said to me: "Go
and buy a clay jar from a potter. 2Take
some of the elders of the people and the
priests, and go out to the Valley of Ben
Hinnom, near the front of the Potsherd Gate.
There speak the words I tell you. 3Say, 'Kings
of Judah and people of Jerusalem, listen to
this message from the LORD. This is what the
LORD All-Powerful, the God of Israel, says: I
will soon bring a disaster on this place that
will amaze and frighten everyone who hears
about it. 4The people of Judah have quit
following me. They have made this a place
for foreign gods. They have burned sacrifices
to other gods that neither they, nor their
ancestors, nor the kings of Judah had ever
known before. They filled this place with the
blood of innocent people. 5They have built
places on hilltops to worship Baal, where
they burn their children in the fire to Baal.
That is something I did not command or
speak about; it never even entered my mind.
6Now people call this place the Valley of Ben
Hinnom or Topheth, but the days are
coming, says the LORD, when people will call
it the Valley of Killing.

7" 'At this place I will ruin the plans of the
people of Judah and Jerusalem. The enemy
will chase them, and I will have them killed
with swords. I will make their dead bodies
food for the birds and wild animals. 8I will
completely destroy this city. People will
make fun of it and shake their heads when
they pass by. They will be shocked when
they see how the city was destroyed. 9An
enemy army will surround the city and will
not let anyone go out to get food. I will make
the people so hungry that they will eat the
bodies of their own sons and daughters, and
then they will begin to eat each other.'

10"While the people with you are
watching, break that jar. 11Then say this:
'The LORD All-Powerful says: I will break this
nation and this city just as someone breaks a
clay jar that cannot be put back together
again. The dead people will be buried here in
Topheth, because there is no other place for
them. 12This is what I will do to these people
and to this place, says the LORD. I will make
this city like Topheth. 13The houses in
Jerusalem and the king's palaces will
become as unclean as this place, Topheth,
because the people worshiped gods on the
roofs[n] of their houses. They worshiped the
stars and burned incense to honor them and
gave drink offerings to gods.' "

14When Jeremiah left Topheth where the

19:13 roofs In Bible times houses were built with flat roofs. The roof was used for drying things such as flax and fruit. And it was used as an extra room, as a place for worship, and as a cool place to sleep in the summer.

LORD had sent him to prophesy, he went to
the LORD's Temple, stood in the courtyard,
and said to all the people: 15"This is what the
LORD All-Powerful, the God of Israel, says: 'I
will soon bring disaster to Jerusalem and the
villages around it, as I said I would. This will
happen because the people are very stubborn
and do not listen at all to what I say.' "

Pashhur Will Be Captured

20 Pashhur son of Immer was a priest and
the highest officer in the Temple of the
LORD. When he heard Jeremiah prophesying
in the Temple courtyard, 2he had Jeremiah
the prophet beaten. And he locked Jeremiah's
hands and feet between large blocks of wood
at the Upper Gate of Benjamin of the LORD's
Temple. 3The next day when Pashhur took
Jeremiah out of the blocks of wood, Jeremiah
said to him, "The LORD's name for you is not
Pashhur. Now his name for you is Terror on
Every Side. 4This is what the LORD says: 'I will
soon make you a terror to yourself and to all
your friends. You will watch enemies killing
your friends with swords. And I will give all
the people of Judah to the king of Babylon,
who will take them away as captives to
Babylon and then will kill them with swords.
5I will give all the wealth of this city to its
enemies—its goods, its valuables, and the
treasures of the kings of Judah. The enemies
will carry all those valuables off to Babylon.
6And Pashhur, you and everyone in your
house will be taken captive. You will be
forced to go to Babylon, where you will die
and be buried, you and your friends to whom
you have prophesied lies.' "

Jeremiah's Fifth Complaint

7LORD, you tricked me, and I was fooled.
You are stronger than I am, so you won.
I have become a joke;
everyone makes fun of me all day long.
8Every time I speak, I shout.
I am always shouting about violence and destruction.
I tell the people about the message I received from the LORD,
but this only brings me insults.
The people make fun of me all day long.
9Sometimes I say to myself,
"I will forget about the LORD.
I will not speak anymore in his name."
But then his message becomes like a burning fire inside me,
deep within my bones.
I get tired of trying to hold it inside of me,
and finally, I cannot hold it in.
10I hear many people whispering about me:
"Terror on every side!
Tell on him! Let's tell the rulers about him."
My friends are all just waiting for me to make some mistake.
They are saying,
"Maybe we can trick him
so we can defeat him
and pay him back."
11But the LORD is with me like a strong warrior,
so those who are chasing me will trip and fall;
they will not defeat me.
They will be ashamed because they have failed,
and their shame will never be forgotten.

12LORD All-Powerful, you test good people;
you look deeply into the heart and mind of a person.
I have told you my arguments against these people,
so let me see you give them the punishment they deserve.

13Sing to the LORD!
Praise the LORD!
He saves the life of the poor
from the power of the wicked.

Jeremiah's Sixth Complaint

14Let there be a curse on the day I was born;
let there be no blessing on the day
when my mother gave birth to me.
15Let there be a curse on the man
who brought my father the news:
"You have a son!"
This made my father very glad.
16Let that man be like the towns
the LORD destroyed without pity.
Let him hear loud crying in the morning
and battle cries at noon,
17because he did not kill me before I was born.
Then my mother would have been my grave;

she would have stayed pregnant
forever.
18 Why did I have to come out of my
mother's body?
All I have known is trouble and sorrow,
and my life will end in shame.

God Rejects King Zedekiah's Request

21 This is the word that the LORD spoke
to Jeremiah. It came when Zedekiah
king of Judah sent Pashhur son of Malkijah
and the priest Zephaniah son of Maaseiah to
Jeremiah. 2 They said, "Ask the LORD for us
what will happen, because Nebuchadnezzar
king of Babylon is attacking us. Maybe the
LORD will do miracles for us as he did in the
past so Nebuchadnezzar will stop attacking
us and leave."
3 But Jeremiah answered them, "Tell King
Zedekiah this: 4 'Here is what the LORD, the
God of Israel, says: You have weapons of war
in your hands to defend yourselves against
the king of Babylon and the Babylonians,
who are all around the city wall. But I will
make those weapons useless. Soon I will
bring them into the center of this city. 5 In
my anger, my very great anger, I myself
will fight against you with my great power
and strength. 6 I will kill everything living
in Jerusalem—both people and animals.
They will die from terrible diseases. 7 Then,
says the LORD, I'll hand over Zedekiah
king of Judah, his officers, and the people
in Jerusalem who do not die from the
terrible diseases or battle or hunger, to
Nebuchadnezzar king of Babylon. I will let
those win who want to kill the people of
Judah, so the people of Judah and Jerusalem
will be killed in war. Nebuchadnezzar will
not show any mercy or pity or feel sorry for
them!'
8 "Also tell this to the people of Jerusalem:
'This is what the LORD says: I will let you
choose to live or die. 9 Anyone who stays in
Jerusalem will die in war or from hunger or
from a terrible disease. But anyone who goes
out of Jerusalem and surrenders to the
Babylonians who are attacking you will live.
Anyone who leaves the city will save his life
as if it were a prize won in war. 10 I have
decided to make trouble for this city and not
to help it, says the LORD. I will give it to the
king of Babylon, and he will burn it with
fire.'

11 "Say to Judah's royal family: 'Hear the
word of the LORD. 12 Family of David, this is
what the LORD says:
You must judge people fairly every
morning.
Save the person who has been robbed
from the power of his attacker.
If you don't, I will become very angry.
My anger will be like a fire that no one
can put out,
because you have done evil things.

13 " 'Jerusalem, I am against you,
you who live on top of the mountain
over this valley, says the LORD.
You say, "No one can attack us
or come into our strong city."
14 But I will give you the punishment you
deserve, says the LORD.
I will start a fire in your forests
that will burn up everything around
you!' "

Judgment Against Evil Kings

22 This is what the LORD says: "Go down
to the palace of the king of Judah and
prophesy this message there: 2 'Hear the word
of the LORD, king of Judah, who rules from
David's throne. You and your officers, and
your people who come through these gates,
listen! 3 This is what the LORD says: Do what is
fair and right. Save the one who has been
robbed from the power of his attacker. Don't
mistreat or hurt the foreigners, orphans, or
widows. Don't kill innocent people here. 4 If
you carefully obey these commands, kings
who sit on David's throne will come through
the gates of this palace with their officers and
people, riding in chariots and on horses. 5 But
if you don't obey these commands, says the
LORD, I swear by my own name that this
king's palace will become a ruin.' "
6 This is what the LORD says about the
palace where the king of Judah lives:
"You are tall like the forests of Gilead,
like the mountaintops of Lebanon.
But I will truly make you into a desert,
into towns where no one lives.
7 I will send men to destroy the palace,
each with his weapons.
They will cut up your strong, beautiful
cedar beams
and throw them into the fire.
8 "People from many nations will pass by

this city and ask each other, 'Why has the
LORD done such a terrible thing to Jerusalem,
this great city?' 9And the answer will be:
'Because the people of Judah quit following
the agreement with the LORD their God.
They worshiped and served other gods.' "

Judgment Against Jehoahaz

10Don't cry for the dead king or be sad about
him.
But cry painfully for the king who is
being taken away,
because he will never return
or see his homeland again.
11This is what the LORD says about
Jehoahaz son of Josiah who became king of
Judah after his father died and who has left
this place: "He will never return. 12He will
die where he has been taken captive, and he
will not see this land again."

Judgment Against Jehoiakim

13"How terrible it will be for one who
builds his palace by doing evil,
who cheats people so he can build its
upper rooms.
He makes his own people work for
nothing
and does not pay them.
14He says, 'I will build a great palace for
myself
with large upper rooms.'
So he builds it with large windows
and uses cedar wood for the walls,
which he paints red.

15"Does having a lot of cedar in your house
make you a great king?
Your father was satisfied to have food and
drink.
He did what was right and fair,
so everything went well for him.
16He helped those who were poor and needy,
so everything went well for him.
That is what it means to know God,"
says the LORD.
17"But you only look for and think about
what you can get dishonestly.
You are even willing to kill innocent
people to get it.
You feel free to hurt people and to steal
from them."
18So this is what the LORD says to Jehoiakim
son of Josiah king of Judah:

"The people of Judah will not cry when
Jehoiakim dies,
saying: 'Oh, my brother,' or 'Oh, my
sister.'
They will not cry for him, saying:
'Oh, master,' or 'Oh, my king.'
19They will bury him like a donkey,
dragging his body away
and throwing it outside the gates of
Jerusalem.
20"Judah, go up to Lebanon and cry out.
Let your voice be heard in Bashan.
Cry out from Abarim,
because all your friends are
destroyed!
21Judah, when you were successful, I
warned you,
but you said, 'I won't listen.'
You have acted like this since you were
young;
you have not obeyed me.
22Like a storm, my punishment will blow
all your shepherds away
and send your friends into captivity.
Then you will really be ashamed and
disgraced
because of all the wicked things you
did.
23King, you live in your palace,
cozy in your rooms of cedar.
But when your punishment comes, how
you will groan
like a woman giving birth to a baby!

Judgment upon Jehoiachin

24"As surely as I live," says the LORD,
"Jehoiachin son of Jehoiakim king of Judah,
even if you were a signet ring on my right
hand, I would still pull you off. 25I will hand
you over to Nebuchadnezzar king of Babylon
and to the Babylonians—those people you
fear because they want to kill you. 26I will
throw you and your mother into another
country. Neither of you was born there, but
both of you will die there. 27They will want
to come back, but they will never be able to
return."
28Jehoiachin is like a broken pot someone
threw away;
he is like something no one wants.
Why will Jehoiachin and his children be
thrown out
and sent into a foreign land?

[29]Land, land, land of Judah,
hear the word of the LORD!
[30]This is what the LORD says:
"Write this down in the record about
Jehoiachin:
He is a man without children,
a man who will not be successful in his
lifetime.
And none of his descendants will be
successful;
none will sit on the throne of David
or rule in Judah."

The Evil Leaders of Judah

23 "How terrible it will be for the leaders
of Judah, who are scattering and
destroying my people," says the LORD.
[2]They are responsible for the people, so
the LORD, the God of Israel, says to them:
"You have scattered my people and forced
them away and not taken care of them. So I
will punish you for the evil things you have
done," says the LORD. [3]"I sent my people to
other countries, but I will gather those who
are left alive and bring them back to their
own country. Then they will have many
children and grow in number. [4]I will place
new leaders over my people, who will take
care of them. And my people will not be
afraid or terrified again, and none of them
will be lost," says the LORD.

The Good Branch Will Come

[5]"The days are coming," says the LORD,
"when I will raise up a good branch in
David's family.
He will be a king who will rule in a wise
way;
he will do what is fair and right in the
land.
[6]In his time Judah will be saved,
and Israel will live in safety.
This will be his name:
The LORD Does What Is Right.
[7]"So the days are coming," says the LORD,
"when people will not say again: 'As surely
as the LORD lives, who brought Israel out of
Egypt . . . ' [8]But people will say something
new: 'As surely as the LORD lives, who
brought the descendants of Israel from the
land of the north and from all the countries
where he had sent them away . . . ' Then
the people of Israel will live in their own
land."

False Prophets Will Be Punished

[9]A message to the prophets:
My heart is broken.
All my bones shake.
I'm like someone who is drunk,
like someone who has been overcome
with wine.
This is because of the LORD
and his holy words.
[10]The land of Judah is full of people who are
guilty of adultery.
Because of this, the LORD cursed the land.
It has become a very sad place,
and the pastures have dried up.
The people are evil
and use their power in the wrong way.
[11]"Both the prophets and the priests live as
if there were no God.
I have found them doing evil things
even in my own Temple," says the
LORD.
[12]"So they will be in danger.
They will be forced into darkness
where they will be defeated.
I will bring disaster on them
in the year I punish them," says the
LORD.

[13]"I saw the prophets of Samaria
do something wrong.
Those prophets prophesied by Baal
and led my people Israel away.
[14]And I have seen the prophets of Jerusalem
do terrible things.
They are guilty of adultery
and live by lies.
They encourage evil people to keep on
doing evil,
so the people don't stop sinning.
All of those people are like the city of
Sodom.
The people of Jerusalem are like the
city of Gomorrah to me!"
[15]So this is what the LORD All-Powerful
says about the prophets:
"I will make those prophets eat bitter food
and drink poisoned water,
because the prophets of Jerusalem spread
wickedness
through the whole country."
[16]This is what the LORD All-Powerful says:
"Don't pay attention to what those
prophets are saying to you.
They are trying to fool you.

They talk about visions their own minds
made up,
not about visions from me.
17 They say to those who hate me:
'The LORD says: You will have peace.'
They say to all those who are stubborn
and do as they please:
'Nothing bad will happen to you.'
18 But none of these prophets has stood in
the meeting of angels
to see or hear the message of the
LORD.
None of them has paid close attention
to his message.
19 Look, the punishment from the LORD
will come like a storm.
His anger will be like a hurricane.
It will come swirling down on the
heads of those wicked people.
20 The LORD's anger will not stop
until he finishes what he plans to do.
When that day is over,
you will understand this clearly.
21 I did not send those prophets,
but they ran to tell their message.
I did not speak to them,
but they prophesied anyway.
22 But if they had stood in the meeting of
angels,
they would have told my message to
my people.
They would have turned the people from
their evil ways
and from doing evil.

23 "I am a God who is near," says the LORD.
"I am also a God who is far away.
24 No one can hide
where I cannot see him," says the LORD.
"I fill all of heaven and earth," says the
LORD.

25 "I have heard the prophets who
prophesy lies in my name. They say, 'I have
had a dream! I have had a dream!' 26 How
long will this continue in the minds of these
lying prophets? They prophesy from their
own wishful thinking. 27 They are trying to
make the people of Judah forget me by
telling each other these dreams. In the same
way, their ancestors forgot me and
worshiped Baal. 28 Is straw the same thing as
wheat?" says the LORD. "If a prophet wants to
tell about his dreams, let him! But let the
person who hears my message speak it

devotion 214

JEREMIAH 23:23–24

FINDING GOD

As a child I used to sing the song, "He's got the whole world in his hands." I remember thinking of God's hand being as big as the whole world and feeling a bit afraid of a God that big. We like to think of God as a friend who is close by when we need him. The amazing thing about God is that he is both. The Bible says that God is far *and* near. He is the God of the universe, yet he is so close to us that we cannot go anywhere that he cannot see us. This is one of the many mysteries of God.

So how can we reach a God who controls the universe with his voice? Read the story of Elijah looking for God on a mountain in 1 Kings 19. First the wind blew very hard, but God was not in the wind. Then an earthquake came, but God was not in it. After the earthquake, there was a fire, but God was not in the fire. Finally, a quiet, gentle sound like a whisper came to Elijah, and God was there. God reaches us by speaking to our spirit in that quiet place of our heart. Sometimes he speaks to us in our thoughts. Other times he speaks to us through his Word. Then there are times he uses other Christians to encourage us or help us find our way. God is a God who is near to those he loves—and he loves you.

truthfully! 29Isn't my message like a fire?"
says the LORD. "Isn't it like a hammer that
smashes a rock?
30"So I am against the false prophets," says
the LORD. "They keep stealing words from
each other and say they are from me. 31I am
against the false prophets," says the LORD.
"They use their own words and pretend it is
a message from me. 32I am against the
prophets who prophesy false dreams," says
the LORD. "They mislead my people with
their lies and false teachings! I did not send
them or command them to do anything for
me. They can't help the people of Judah at
all," says the LORD.

The Sad Message from the Lord

33"Suppose the people of Judah, a prophet,
or a priest asks you: 'Jeremiah, what is the
message from the LORD?' You will answer
them and say, 'You are a heavy load to
the LORD, and I will throw you down, says the
LORD.' 34A prophet or a priest or one of the
people might say, 'This is a message from the
LORD.' That person has lied, so I will punish
him and his whole family. 35This is what you
will say to each other: 'What did the LORD
answer?' or 'What did the LORD say?' 36But
you will never again say, 'The message of the
LORD,' because the only message you speak is
your own words. You have changed the
words of our God, the living God, the LORD
All-Powerful. 37This is how you should speak
to the prophets: 'What answer did the LORD
give you?' or 'What did the LORD say?' 38But
don't say, 'The message from the LORD.' If you
use these words, this is what the LORD says:
Because you called it a 'message from the
LORD,' though I told you not to use those
words, 39I will pick you up and throw you
away from me, along with Jerusalem, which I
gave to your ancestors and to you. 40And I
will make a disgrace of you forever; your
shame will never be forgotten."

The Good and Bad Figs

24 Nebuchadnezzar king of Babylon
captured Jehoiachin son of Jehoiakim
and king of Judah, his officers, and all the
craftsmen and metalworkers of Judah. He
took them away from Jerusalem and brought
them to Babylon. It was then that the LORD
showed me two baskets of figs arranged in
front of the Temple of the LORD. 2One of the
baskets had very good figs in it, like figs that
ripen early in the season. But the other
basket had figs too rotten to eat.
3The LORD said to me, "What do you see,
Jeremiah?"
I answered, "I see figs. The good figs are
very good, but the rotten figs are too rotten
to eat."
4Then the LORD spoke his word to me:
5"This is what the LORD, the God of Israel,
says: 'I sent the people of Judah out of their
country to live in the country of Babylon. I
think of those people as good, like these
good figs. 6I will look after them and bring
them back to the land of Judah. I will not
tear them down, but I will build them up. I
will not pull them up, but I will plant them
so they can grow. 7I will make them want to
know me, that I am the LORD. They will be
my people, and I will be their God, because
they will return to me with their whole
hearts.
8" 'But the bad figs are too rotten to eat.' So
this is what the LORD says: 'Zedekiah king of
Judah, his officers, and all the people from
Jerusalem who are left alive, even those who
live in Egypt, will be like those rotten figs. 9I
will make those people hated as an evil
people by all the kingdoms of the earth.
People will make fun of them and tell jokes
about them and point fingers at them and
curse them everywhere I scatter them. 10I
will send war, hunger, and disease against
them. I will attack them until they have all
been killed. Then they will no longer be in
the land I gave to them and their ancestors.' "

A Summary of Jeremiah's Preaching

25 This is the message that came to
Jeremiah concerning all the people of
Judah. It came in the fourth year that
Jehoiakim son of Josiah was king of Judah
and the first year Nebuchadnezzar was king
of Babylon. 2This is the message Jeremiah
the prophet spoke to all the people of Judah
and Jerusalem:
3The LORD has spoken his word to me
again and again for these past twenty-three
years. I have been a prophet since the
thirteenth year of Josiah son of Amon king
of Judah. I have spoken messages from the
LORD to you from that time until today, but
you have not listened.
4The LORD has sent all his servants the

prophets to you over and over again, but you
have not listened or paid any attention to
them. 5Those prophets have said, "Stop your
evil ways. Stop doing what is wrong so you
can stay in the land that the LORD gave to
you and your ancestors to live in forever.
6Don't follow other gods to serve them or to
worship them. Don't make me, the LORD,
angry by worshiping idols that are the work
of your own hands, or I will punish you."

7"But you people of Judah did not listen to
me," says the LORD. "You made me angry by
worshiping idols that were the work of your
own hands, so I punished you."

8So this is what the LORD All-Powerful
says: "Since you have not listened to my
messages, 9I will send for all the peoples of
the north," says the LORD, "along with my
servant Nebuchadnezzar king of Babylon. I
will bring them all against Judah, those who
live there, and all the nations around you,
too. I will completely destroy all those
countries and leave them in ruins forever.
People will be shocked when they see how
badly I have destroyed those countries. 10I
will bring an end to the sounds of joy and
happiness, the sounds of brides and
bridegrooms, and the sound of people
grinding meal. And I will take away the light
of the lamp. 11That whole area will be an
empty desert, and these nations will be slaves
of the king of Babylon for seventy years.

12"But when the seventy years have
passed, I will punish the king of Babylon and
his entire nation for their evil," says the
LORD. "I will make that land a desert forever.
13I will make happen all the terrible things I
said about Babylonia—everything Jeremiah
prophesied about all those foreign nations,
the warnings written in this book. 14Even
the Babylonians will have to serve many
nations and many great kings. I will give
them the punishment they deserve for all
their own hands have done."

Judgment on the Nations

15The LORD, the God of Israel, said this to
me: "My anger is like the wine in a cup. Take
it from my hand and make all the nations, to
whom I am sending you, drink all of my
anger from this cup. 16They will drink my
anger and stumble about and act like
madmen because of the war I am going to
send among them."

17So I took the cup from the LORD's hand
and went to those nations and made them
drink from it. 18I served this wine to the
people of Jerusalem and the towns of Judah,
and the kings and officers of Judah, so they
would become a ruin. Then people would be
shocked and would insult them and speak
evil of them. And so it has been to this day.
19I also made these people drink of the
LORD's anger: the king of Egypt, his servants,
his officers, all his people, 20and all the
foreigners there; all the kings of the land of
Uz; all the kings of the Philistines (the kings
of the cities of Ashkelon, Gaza, Ekron, and
the people left at Ashdod); 21the people of
Edom, Moab, and Ammon; 22all the kings of
Tyre and Sidon; all the kings of the coastal
countries to the west; 23the people of Dedan
and Tema and Buz; all who cut their hair
short; 24all the kings of Arabia; and the kings
of the people who live in the desert; 25all the
kings of Zimri, Elam, and Media; 26and all
the kings of the north, near and far, one after
the other. I made all the kingdoms on earth
drink from the cup of the LORD's anger, but
the king of Babylon will drink from this cup
after all the others.

27"Then say to them, 'This is what the
LORD All-Powerful, the God of Israel, says:
Drink this cup of my anger. Get drunk
from it and vomit. Fall down and don't get
up because of the war I am sending among
you!'

28"If they refuse to take the cup from your
hand and drink, say to them, 'The LORD
All-Powerful says this: You must drink from
this cup. 29Look! I am already bringing
disaster on Jerusalem, the city that is called
by my name. Do you think you will not be
punished? You will be punished! I am
sending war on all the people of the earth,
says the LORD All-Powerful.'

30"You, Jeremiah, will prophesy against
them with all these words. Say to them:

'The LORD will roar from heaven
  and will shout from his Holy Temple.
  He will roar loudly against his land.
He will shout like people who walk on
    grapes to make wine;
  he will shout against all who live on
    the earth.
31The noise will spread all over the earth,
  because the LORD will accuse all the
    nations.

He will judge and tell what is wrong with
all people,
and he will kill the evil people with a
sword,' " says the LORD.

32 This is what the LORD All-Powerful says:
"Disasters will soon spread
from nation to nation.
They will come like a powerful storm
from the faraway places on earth."

33 At that time those killed by the LORD will
reach from one end of the earth to the other.
No one will cry for them or gather up their
bodies and bury them. They will be left lying
on the ground like dung.

34 Cry, you leaders! Cry out loud!
Roll around in the dust, leaders of the
people!
It is now time for you to be killed.
You will fall and be scattered,
like pieces of a broken jar.
35 There will be no place for the leaders to
hide;
they will not escape.
36 I hear the sound of the leaders shouting.
I hear the leaders of the people crying
loudly,
because the LORD is destroying their
land.
37 Those peaceful pastures will be like an
empty desert,
because the LORD is very angry.
38 Like a lion, he has left his den.
Their land has been destroyed
because of the terrible war he brought,
because of his fierce anger.

Jeremiah's Lesson at the Temple

26 This message came from the LORD
soon after Jehoiakim son of Josiah
became king of Judah. 2 This is what the LORD
said: "Jeremiah, stand in the courtyard of the
Temple of the LORD. Give this message to all
the people of the towns of Judah who are
coming to worship at the Temple of the
LORD. Tell them everything I tell you to say;
don't leave out a word. 3 Maybe they will
listen and stop their evil ways. If they will, I
will change my mind about bringing on
them the disaster that I am planning
because of the evil they have done. 4 Say to
them: 'This is what the LORD says: You must
obey me and follow my teachings that I gave
you. 5 You must listen to what my servants
the prophets say to you. I have sent them to
you again and again, but you did not listen.
6 If you don't obey me, I will destroy my
Temple in Jerusalem as I destroyed my Holy
Tent at Shiloh. When I do, people all over
the world will curse Jerusalem.' "

7 The priests, the prophets, and all the
people heard Jeremiah speaking these words
in the Temple of the LORD. 8 When Jeremiah
finished speaking everything the LORD had
commanded him to say, the priests,
prophets, and all the people grabbed
Jeremiah. They said, "You must die! 9 How
dare you prophesy in the name of the LORD
that this Temple will be destroyed like the
one at Shiloh! How dare you say that
Jerusalem will become a desert without
anyone to live in it!" And all the people
crowded around Jeremiah in the Temple of
the LORD.

10 Now when the officers of Judah heard
about what was happening, they came out of
the king's palace and went up to the Temple
of the LORD and took their places at the
entrance of the New Gate. 11 Then the priests
and prophets said to the officers and all the
other people, "Jeremiah should be killed. He
prophesied against Jerusalem, and you heard
him yourselves."

12 Then Jeremiah spoke these words to all
the officers of Judah and all the other people:
"The LORD sent me to say everything you
have heard about this Temple and this city.
13 Now change your lives and start doing
good and obey the LORD your God. Then he
will change his mind and not bring on you
the disaster he has told you about. 14 As for
me, I am in your power. Do to me what you
think is good and right. 15 But be sure of one
thing. If you kill me, you will be guilty of
killing an innocent person. You will make
this city and everyone who lives in it guilty,
too! The LORD truly sent me to you to give
you this message."

16 Then the officers and all the people said
to the priests and the prophets, "Jeremiah
must not be killed. What he told us comes
from the LORD our God."

17 Then some of the elders of Judah stood
up and said to all the people, 18 "Micah, from
the city of Moresheth, was a prophet during
the time Hezekiah was king of Judah. Micah
said to all the people of Judah, 'This is what
the LORD All-Powerful says:
Jerusalem will be plowed like a field.

It will become a pile of rocks,
and the hill where the Temple stands
will be covered with bushes.’
19“Hezekiah king of Judah and the people
of Judah did not kill Micah. You know that
Hezekiah feared the LORD and tried to please
the LORD. So the LORD changed his mind and
did not bring on Judah the disaster he had
promised. If we hurt Jeremiah, we will bring
a terrible disaster on ourselves!”

20(Now there was another man who
prophesied in the name of the LORD. His
name was Uriah son of Shemaiah from the
city of Kiriath Jearim. He preached the same
things against Jerusalem and the land of
Judah that Jeremiah did. 21When King
Jehoiakim, all his army officers, and all the
leaders of Judah heard Uriah preach, King
Jehoiakim wanted to kill Uriah. But Uriah
heard about it and was afraid. So he escaped
to Egypt. 22Then King Jehoiakim sent
Elnathan son of Acbor and some other men
to Egypt, 23and they brought Uriah back
from Egypt. Then they took him to King
Jehoiakim, who had Uriah killed with a
sword. His body was thrown into the burial
place where poor people are buried.)

24Ahikam son of Shaphan supported
Jeremiah. So Ahikam did not hand Jeremiah
over to be killed by the people.

Nebuchadnezzar Is Made Ruler

27 The LORD spoke his word to Jeremiah
soon after Zedekiah son of Josiah was
made king of Judah. 2This is what the LORD
said to me: “Make a yoke out of straps and
poles, and put it on the back of your neck.
3Then send messages to the kings of Edom,
Moab, Ammon, Tyre, and Sidon by their
messengers who have come to Jerusalem to
see Zedekiah king of Judah. 4Tell them to
give this message to their masters: ‘The
LORD All-Powerful, the God of Israel, says:
“Tell your masters: 5I made the earth, its
people, and all its animals with my great
power and strength. I can give the earth to
anyone I want. 6Now I have given all these
lands to Nebuchadnezzar king of Babylon,
my servant. I will make even the wild
animals obey him. 7All nations will serve
Nebuchadnezzar and his son and grandson.
Then the time will come for Babylon to be
defeated, and many nations and great kings
will make Babylon their servant.

8“ ‘ “But if some nations or kingdoms
refuse to serve Nebuchadnezzar king of
Babylon and refuse to be under his control, I
will punish them with war, hunger, and
terrible diseases, says the LORD. I will use
Nebuchadnezzar to destroy them. 9So don’t
listen to your false prophets, those who use
magic to tell the future, those who explain
dreams, the mediums, or magicians. They all
tell you, ‘You will not be slaves to the king of
Babylon.’ 10They are telling you lies that will
cause you to be taken far from your
homeland. I will force you to leave your
homes, and you will die in another land.
11But the nations who put themselves under
the control of the king of Babylon and serve
him I will let stay in their own country, says
the LORD. The people from those nations will
live in their own land and farm it.” ’ ”

12I gave the same message to Zedekiah
king of Judah. I said, “Put yourself under the
control of the king of Babylon and serve
him, and you will live. 13Why should you
and your people die from war, hunger, or
disease, as the LORD said would happen to
those who do not serve the king of Babylon?
14But the false prophets are saying, ‘You will
never be slaves to the king of Babylon.’ Don’t
listen to them because they are prophesying
lies to you! 15‘I did not send them,’ says the
LORD. ‘They are prophesying lies and saying
the message is from me. So I will send you
away, Judah. And you and those prophets
who prophesy to you will die.’ ”

16Then I, Jeremiah, said to the priests and
all the people, “This is what the LORD says:
Those false prophets are saying, ‘The
Babylonians will soon return what they took
from the Temple of the LORD.’ Don’t listen to
them! They are prophesying lies to you.
17Don’t listen to those prophets. But serve
the king of Babylon, and you will live. There
is no reason for you to cause Jerusalem to
become a ruin. 18If they are prophets and
have the message from the LORD, let them
pray to the LORD All-Powerful. Let them ask
that the items which are still in the Temple
of the LORD and in the king’s palace and in
Jerusalem not be taken away to Babylon.

19“This is what the LORD All-Powerful says
about those items left in Jerusalem: the
pillars, the large bronze bowl, which is
called the Sea, the stands that can be moved,
and other things. 20Nebuchadnezzar king of

Babylon did not take these away when he
took as captives Jehoiachin son of Jehoiakim
king of Judah and all the other important
people from Judah and Jerusalem to
Babylon. 21 This is what the LORD
All-Powerful, the God of Israel, says about
the items left in the Temple of the LORD and
in the king's palace and in Jerusalem: 22 'All
of them will also be taken to Babylon. And
they will stay there until the day I go to get
them,' says the LORD. 'Then I will bring them
back and return them to this place.' "

The False Prophet Hananiah

28 It was in that same year, in the fifth
month of Zedekiah's fourth year as
king of Judah, soon after he began to rule.
The prophet Hananiah son of Azzur, from the
town of Gibeon, spoke to me in the Temple of
the LORD in front of the priests and all the
people. He said: 2 "The LORD All-Powerful, the
God of Israel, says: 'I have broken the yoke
the king of Babylon has put on Judah. 3 Before
two years are over, I will bring back
everything that Nebuchadnezzar king of
Babylon took to Babylon from the LORD's
Temple. 4 I will also bring back Jehoiachin
son of Jehoiakim king of Judah and all the
other captives from Judah who went to
Babylon,' says the LORD. 'So I will break the
yoke the king of Babylon put on Judah.' "
5 Then the prophet Jeremiah spoke to the
prophet Hananiah in front of the priests and
all the people who were standing in the
Temple of the LORD. 6 He said, "Amen! Let the
LORD really do that! May the LORD make the
message you prophesy come true. May he
bring back here everything from the LORD's
Temple and all the people who were taken as
captives to Babylon.
7 "But listen to what I am going to say to
you and all the people. 8 There were prophets
long before we became prophets, Hananiah.
They prophesied that war, hunger, and
terrible diseases would come to many
countries and great kingdoms. 9 But if a
prophet prophesies that we will have peace
and that message comes true, he can be
recognized as one truly sent by the LORD."
10 Then the prophet Hananiah took the
yoke off Jeremiah's neck and broke it.
11 Hananiah said in front of all the people,
"This is what the LORD says: 'In the same way
I will break the yoke of Nebuchadnezzar
king of Babylon. He put that yoke on all the
nations of the world, but I will break it
before two years are over.' " After Hananiah
had said that, Jeremiah left the Temple.
12 The LORD spoke his word to Jeremiah
after the prophet Hananiah had broken the
yoke off of the prophet Jeremiah's neck.
13 The LORD said, "Go and tell Hananiah, 'This
is what the LORD says: You have broken a
wooden yoke, but I will make a yoke of iron
in its place! 14 The LORD All-Powerful, the God
of Israel, says: I will put a yoke of iron on the
necks of all these nations to make them
serve Nebuchadnezzar king of Babylon, and
they will be slaves to him. I will even give
Nebuchadnezzar control over the wild
animals.' "
15 Then the prophet Jeremiah said to the
prophet Hananiah, "Listen, Hananiah! The
LORD did not send you, and you have made
the people of Judah trust in lies. 16 So this is
what the LORD says: 'Soon I will remove you
from the earth. You will die this year,
because you taught the people to turn
against the LORD.' "
17 Hananiah died in the seventh month of
that same year.

A Letter to the Captives in Babylon

29 This is the letter that Jeremiah the
prophet sent from Jerusalem to the
elders who were among the captives, the
priests, and the prophets. He sent it to all the
other people Nebuchadnezzar had taken as
captives from Jerusalem to Babylon. 2 (This
letter was sent after all these people were
taken away: Jehoiachin the king and the
queen mother; the officers and leaders of
Judah and Jerusalem; and the craftsmen and
metalworkers from Jerusalem.) 3 Zedekiah
king of Judah sent Elasah son of Shaphan
and Gemariah son of Hilkiah to Babylon to
Nebuchadnezzar king of Babylon. So
Jeremiah gave them this letter to carry to
Babylon:

> 4 This is what the LORD All-Powerful,
> the God of Israel, says to all those people
> I sent away from Jerusalem as captives
> to Babylon: 5 "Build houses and settle in
> the land. Plant gardens and eat the food
> they grow. 6 Get married and have sons
> and daughters. Find wives for your sons,
> and let your daughters be married so
> they also may have sons and daughters.
> Have many children in Babylon; don't
> become fewer in number. 7 Also do good

things for the city where I sent you as captives. Pray to the LORD for the city where you are living, because if good things happen in the city, good things will happen to you also." 8The LORD All-Powerful, the God of Israel, says: "Don't let the prophets among you and the people who do magic fool you. Don't listen to their dreams. 9They are prophesying lies to you, saying that their message is from me. But I did not send them," says the LORD.

10This is what the LORD says: "Babylon will be powerful for seventy years. After that time I will come to you, and I will keep my promise to bring you back to Jerusalem. 11I say this because I know what I am planning for you," says the LORD. "I have good plans for you, not plans to hurt you. I will give you hope and a good future. 12Then you will call my name. You will come to me and pray to me, and I will listen to you. 13You will search for me. And when you search for me with all your heart, you will find me! 14I will let you find me," says the LORD. "And I will bring you back from your captivity. I forced you to leave this place, but I will gather you from all the nations, from the places I have sent you as captives," says the LORD. "And I will bring you back to this place."

15You might say, "The LORD has given us prophets here in Babylon."

16But the LORD says this about the king who is sitting on David's throne now and all the other people still in Jerusalem, your relatives who did not go as captives to Babylon with you. 17The LORD All-Powerful says: "I will soon send war, hunger, and terrible diseases against those still in Jerusalem. I will make them like bad figs that are too rotten to eat. 18I will chase them with war, hunger, and terrible diseases. I will make them hated by all the kingdoms of the earth. People will curse them and be shocked and will use them as a shameful example wherever I make them go. 19This is because they have not listened to my message," says the LORD. "I sent my message to them again and again through my servants, the prophets, but they did not listen," says the LORD.

20You captives, whom I forced to leave Jerusalem and go to Babylon, listen to the message from the LORD. 21The LORD All-Powerful, the God of Israel, says this about Ahab son of Kolaiah and Zedekiah son of Maaseiah: "These two men have been prophesying lies to you, saying that their message is from me. But soon I will hand over those two prophets to Nebuchadnezzar king of Babylon, and he will kill them in front of you. 22Because of them, all the captives from Judah in Babylon will use this curse: 'May the LORD treat you like Zedekiah and Ahab, whom the king of Babylon burned in the fire.' 23They have done evil things among the people of Israel. They are guilty of adultery with their neighbors' wives. They have also spoken lies and said those lies were a message from me. I did not tell them to do that. I know what they have done; I am a witness to it," says the LORD.

24Also give a message to Shemaiah from the Nehelamite family. 25The LORD All-Powerful, the God of Israel, says: "Shemaiah, you sent letters in your name to all the people in Jerusalem, to the priest Zephaniah son of Maaseiah, and to all the priests. 26You said to Zephaniah, 'The LORD has made you priest in place of Jehoiada. You are to be in charge of the Temple of the LORD. You should arrest any madman who acts like a prophet. Lock his hands and feet between wooden blocks, and put iron rings around his neck. 27Now Jeremiah from Anathoth is acting like a prophet. So why haven't you arrested him? 28Jeremiah has sent this message to us in Babylon: You will be there for a long time, so build houses and settle down. Plant gardens and eat what they grow.' "

29Zephaniah the priest read the letter to Jeremiah the prophet. 30Then the LORD spoke his word to Jeremiah: 31"Send this message to all the captives in Babylon: 'This is what the LORD says about Shemaiah the Nehelamite: Shemaiah has prophesied to you, but I did not send him. He has made you believe a lie. 32So the LORD says, I will soon punish Shemaiah the Nehelamite and his family. He will not see the good things I will do for my people, says the LORD. None of his family will be left alive among the people, because he has taught the people to turn against me.' "

Promises of Hope

30 These are the words that the LORD
spoke to Jeremiah. [2]The LORD, the God
of Israel, said: "Jeremiah, write in a book all
the words I have spoken to you. [3]The days
will come when I will bring Israel and Judah
back from captivity," says the LORD. "I will
return them to the land I gave their ancestors,
and they will own it!" says the LORD.

[4]The LORD spoke this message about the
people of Israel and Judah: [5]This is what the
LORD said:

"We hear people crying from fear.
They are afraid; there is no peace.
[6]Ask this question, and consider it:
A man cannot have a baby.
So why do I see every strong man
holding his stomach in pain like a woman having a baby?
Why is everyone's face turning white
like a dead man's face?
[7]This will be a terrible day!
There will never be another time like this.
This is a time of great trouble for the people of Jacob,
but they will be saved from it."

[8]The LORD All-Powerful says, "At that time
I will break the yoke from their necks
and tear off the ropes that hold them.
Foreign people will never again make my people slaves.
[9]They will serve the LORD their God
and David their king,
whom I will send to them.
[10]"So people of Jacob, my servants, don't be afraid.
Israel, don't be frightened," says the LORD.
"I will soon save you from that faraway place where you are captives.
I will save your family from that land.
The people of Jacob will be safe and have peace again;
there will be no enemy to frighten them.
[11]I am with you and will save you,"
says the LORD.
"I will completely destroy all those nations
where I scattered you,
but I will not completely destroy you.
I will punish you fairly,
but I will still punish you."
[12]This is what the LORD said:
"You people have a wound that cannot be cured;
your injury will not heal.
[13]There is no one to argue your case
and no cure for your sores.
So you will not be healed.
[14]All those nations who were your friends have forgotten you.
They don't care about you.
I have hurt you as an enemy would.
I punished you very hard,
because your guilt was so great
and your sins were so many.
[15]Why are you crying out about your injury?
There is no cure for your pain.
I did these things to you because of your great guilt,
because of your many sins.
[16]But all those nations that destroyed you
will now be destroyed.
All your enemies will become captives in other lands.
Those who stole from you will have their own things stolen.
Those who took things from you in war
will have their own things taken.
[17]I will bring back your health
and heal your injuries," says the LORD,
"because other people forced you away.
They said about you, 'No one cares about Jerusalem!' "
[18]This is what the LORD said:
"I will soon make the tents of Jacob's people as they used to be,
and I will have pity on Israel's houses.
The city will be rebuilt on its hill of ruins,
and the king's palace will stand in its proper place.
[19]People in those places will sing songs of praise.
There will be the sound of laughter.
I will give them many children
so their number will not be small.
I will bring honor to them
so no one will look down on them.
[20]Their descendants will be as they were in the old days.
I will set them up as a strong people before me,
and I will punish the nations who have hurt them.

[21]One of their own people will lead them;
their ruler will come from among them.
He will come near to me when I invite him.
Who would dare to come to me uninvited?" says the LORD.
[22]"So you will be my people,
and I will be your God."

[23]Look! It is a storm from the LORD!
He is angry and has gone out to punish the people.
Punishment will come like a storm
crashing down on the evil people.
[24]The LORD will stay angry
until he finishes punishing the people.
He will stay angry
until he finishes the punishment he planned.
When that day comes,
you will understand this.

The New Israel

31 The LORD says, "At that time I will be God of all Israel's family groups, and they will be my people."

[2]This is what the LORD says:
"The people who were not killed by the enemy's sword
found help in the desert.
I came to give rest to Israel."
[3]And from far away the LORD appeared to
his people and said,
"I love you people
with a love that will last forever.
That is why I have continued
showing you kindness.
[4]People of Israel, I will build you up again,
and you will be rebuilt.
You will pick up your tambourines again
and dance with those who are joyful.
[5]You will plant vineyards again
on the hills around Samaria.
The farmers will plant them
and enjoy their fruit.
[6]There will be a time when watchmen in the mountains of Ephraim shout this message:
'Come, let's go up to Jerusalem to worship the LORD our God!' "
[7]This is what the LORD says:
"Be happy and sing for the people of Jacob.
Shout for Israel, the greatest of the nations.
Sing your praises and shout this:
'LORD, save your people,
those who are left alive from the nation of Israel!'
[8]Look, I will soon bring Israel from the country in the north,
and I will gather them from the faraway places on earth.
Some of the people are blind and crippled.
Some of the women are pregnant, and some are ready to give birth.
A great many people will come back.
[9]They will be crying as they come,
but they will pray as I bring them back.
I will lead those people by streams of water
on an even road where they will not stumble.
I am Israel's father,
and Israel is my firstborn son.

[10]"Nations, listen to the message from the LORD.
Tell this message in the faraway lands by the sea:
'The one who scattered the people of Israel will bring them back,
and he will watch over his people like a shepherd.'
[11]The LORD will pay for the people of Jacob
and will buy them back from people stronger than they were.
[12]The people of Israel will come to the high points of Jerusalem
and shout for joy.
Their faces will shine with happiness
about all the good things from the LORD:
the grain, new wine, oil, young sheep,
and young cows.
They will be like a garden that has plenty of water,
and they will not be troubled anymore.
[13]Then young women of Israel will be happy and dance,
the young men and old men also.
I will change their sadness into happiness;
I will give them comfort and joy
instead of sadness.
[14]The priests will have more than enough sacrifices,
and my people will be filled with the good things I give them!" says the LORD.

15This is what the LORD says:
"A voice was heard in Ramah
of painful crying and deep sadness:
Rachel crying for her children.
She refused to be comforted,
because her children are dead!"
16But this is what the LORD says:
"Stop crying;
don't let your eyes fill with tears.
You will be rewarded for your work!" says
the LORD.
"The people will return from their
enemy's land.
17So there is hope for you in the future,"
says the LORD.
"Your children will return to their own
land.
18"I have heard Israel moaning:
'LORD, you punished me, and I have
learned my lesson.
I was like a calf that had never been
trained.
Take me back so that I may come back.
You truly are the LORD my God.
19LORD, after I wandered away from you,
I changed my heart and life.
After I understood,
I beat my breast with sorrow.
I was ashamed and disgraced,
because I suffered for the foolish things
I did when I was young.'
20"You know that Israel is my dear son,
The child I love.
Yes, I often speak against Israel,
but I still remember him.
I love him very much,
and I want to comfort him," says the
LORD.
21"People of Israel, fix the road signs.
Put up signs to show you the way
home.
Watch the road.
Pay attention to the road on which you
travel.
People of Israel, come home,
come back to your towns.
22You are an unfaithful daughter.
How long will you wander before you
come home?
The LORD has made something new
happen in the land:
A woman will go seeking a man."

23The LORD All-Powerful, the God of Israel,
says: "I will again do good things for the
people of Judah. At that time the people in
the land of Judah and its towns will again
use these words: 'May the LORD bless you,
home of what is good, holy mountain.'
24People in all the towns of Judah will live
together in peace. Farmers and those who
move around with their flocks will live
together in peace. 25I will give rest and
strength to those who are weak and tired."
26After hearing that, I, Jeremiah, woke up
and looked around. My sleep had been very
pleasant.
27The LORD says, "The time is coming
when I will help the families of Israel and
Judah and their children and animals to
grow. 28In the past I watched over Israel and
Judah, to pull them up and tear them down,
to destroy them and bring them disaster. But
now I will watch over them to build them
up and make them strong," says the LORD.
29"At that time people will no longer say:
'The parents have eaten sour grapes,
and that caused the children to grind
their teeth from the sour taste.'
30Instead, each person will die for his own
sin; the person who eats sour grapes will
grind his own teeth.

The New Agreement

31"Look, the time is coming," says the
LORD,
"when I will make a new agreement
with the people of Israel
and the people of Judah.
32It will not be like the agreement
I made with their ancestors
when I took them by the hand
to bring them out of Egypt.
I was a husband to them,
but they broke that agreement," says
the LORD.
33"This is the agreement I will make
with the people of Israel at that time,"
says the LORD:
"I will put my teachings in their minds
and write them on their hearts.
I will be their God,
and they will be my people.
34People will no longer have to teach their
neighbors and relatives
to know the LORD,
because all people will know me,

devotion 215

JEREMIAH 31:33–34

WANNA GET A NEW DEAL?

God promised that one day he would make a new agreement with his people. It would be accompanied by an outpouring of God's Spirit to change the hearts of his people. In fact, under the new agreement, God's commandments would be written on the hearts of the people instead of on tablets of stone (as the original Ten Commandments were). In Jeremiah's culture, most of the people had cold hearts of stone. They didn't even put up a pretense of keeping the commandments. They were desperately in need of some kind of new arrangement.

The prophet Jeremiah was looking forward to the day when God would take away the cold hearts of stone and replace them with hearts of flesh. The fulfillment of this new agreement is found in Jesus, our great high priest (Heb. 8:6-13). Because of the work of Jesus, there are no more sacrifices, feasts, or religious rituals required. The people of God are now able to worship God in their hearts and reflect that worship in their everyday lives.

You and I live under the new agreement. God writes his will on our hearts, and by the power of the Holy Spirit who lives inside every believer, we can follow him step-by-step and moment-by-moment. We can follow God's commandments from the inside out and not be constrained by rules that only work from the outside in. The new agreement has made us free, and because of the work of Jesus Christ, we are free indeed.

from the least to the most important,"
says the LORD.
"I will forgive them for the wicked things
they did,
and I will not remember their sins
anymore."

The Lord Will Never Leave Israel

35 The LORD makes the sun shine in the day
and the moon and stars to shine at
night.
He stirs up the sea so that its waves crash
on the shore.
The LORD All-Powerful is his name.
This is what the LORD says:
36 "Only if these laws should ever fail,"
says the LORD,
"will Israel's descendants ever stop
being a nation before me."
37 This is what the LORD says:
"Only if people can measure the sky above
and learn the secrets of the earth below,
will I reject all the descendants of Israel
because of what they have done," says
the LORD.

The New Jerusalem

38 The LORD says, "The time is coming
when Jerusalem will be rebuilt for me—
everything from the Tower of Hananel to the
Corner Gate. 39 The measuring line will
stretch from the Corner Gate straight to the
hill of Gareb. Then it will turn to the place
named Goah. 40 The whole valley where dead
bodies and ashes are thrown, and all the
terraces out to the Kidron Valley on the east
as far as the corner of the Horse Gate—all
that area will be holy to the LORD. The city of
Jerusalem will never again be torn down or
destroyed."

Jeremiah Buys a Field

32 This is the word the LORD spoke to
Jeremiah in the tenth year Zedekiah

was king of Judah, which was the eighteenth
year of Nebuchadnezzar. 2At that time the
army of the king of Babylon was
surrounding Jerusalem. Jeremiah the
prophet was under arrest in the courtyard of
the guard, which was at the palace of the
king of Judah.
3Zedekiah king of Judah had put Jeremiah
in prison there. Zedekiah had asked, "Why
have you prophesied the things you have?"
(Jeremiah had said, "This is what the LORD
says: 'I will soon hand the city of Jerusalem
over to the king of Babylon, and he will
capture it. 4Zedekiah king of Judah will not
escape from the Babylonian army, but he
will surely be handed over to the king of
Babylon. And he will speak to the king of
Babylon face to face and see him with his
own eyes. 5The king will take Zedekiah to
Babylon, where he will stay until I have
punished him,' says the LORD. 'If you fight
against the Babylonians, you will not
succeed.' ")
6While Jeremiah was in prison, he said,
"The LORD spoke this word to me: 7Your
cousin Hanamel, son of your uncle Shallum,
will come to you soon. Hanamel will say to
you, 'Jeremiah, you are my nearest relative,
so buy my field near the town of Anathoth.
It is your right and your duty to buy that
field.'
8"Then it happened just as the LORD had
said. My cousin Hanamel came to me in the
courtyard of the guard and said to me, 'Buy
for yourself my field near Anathoth in the
land of Benjamin. It is your right and duty to
buy it and own it.' So I knew this was a
message from the LORD.
9"I bought the field at Anathoth from my
cousin Hanamel, weighing out seven ounces
of silver for him. 10I signed the record and
sealed it and had some people witness it. I
also weighed out the silver on the scales.
11Then I took both copies of the record of
ownership—the one that was sealed that
had the demands and limits of ownership,
and the one that was not sealed. 12And I gave
them to Baruch son of Neriah, the son of
Mahseiah. My cousin Hanamel, the other
witnesses who signed the record of
ownership, and many Jews sitting in the
courtyard of the guard saw me give the
record of ownership to Baruch.
13"With all the people watching, I told
Baruch, 14'This is what the LORD
All-Powerful, the God of Israel, says: Take
both copies of the record of ownership—the
sealed copy and the copy that was not
sealed—and put them in a clay jar so they
will last a long time. 15This is what the LORD
All-Powerful, the God of Israel, says: In the
future my people will once again buy houses
and fields for grain and vineyards in the land
of Israel.'
16"After I gave the record of ownership to
Baruch son of Neriah, I prayed to the LORD,
17Oh, Lord GOD, you made the skies and the
earth with your very great power. There is
nothing too hard for you to do. 18You show
love and kindness to thousands of people,
but you also bring punishment to children
for their parents' sins. Great and powerful
God, your name is the LORD All-Powerful.
19You plan and do great things. You see
everything that people do, and you reward
people for the way they live and for what
they do. 20You did miracles and wonderful
things in the land of Egypt. You have
continued doing them in Israel and among
the other nations even until today. So you
have become well known. 21You brought
your people, the Israelites, out of Egypt using
signs and miracles and your great power and
strength. You brought great terror on
everyone. 22You gave them this land that you
promised to their ancestors long ago, a fertile
land. 23They came into this land and took it
for their own, but they did not obey you or
follow your teachings. They did not do
everything you commanded. So you made all
these terrible things happen to them.
24"Look! The enemy has surrounded the
city and has built roads to the top of the
walls to capture it. Because of war, hunger,
and terrible diseases, the city will be handed
over to the Babylonians who are attacking it.
You said this would happen, and now you see
it is happening. 25But now, Lord GOD, you tell
me, 'Buy the field with silver and call in
witnesses.' You tell me this while the
Babylonian army is ready to capture the city."
26Then the LORD spoke this word to
Jeremiah: 27"I am the LORD, the God of every
person on the earth. Nothing is impossible
for me. 28So this is what the LORD says: I will
soon hand over the city of Jerusalem to the
Babylonian army and to Nebuchadnezzar
king of Babylon, who will capture it. 29The

Babylonian army is already attacking the
city of Jerusalem. They will soon enter it and
start a fire to burn down the city and its
houses. The people of Jerusalem offered
sacrifices to Baal on the roofs[n] of those same
houses and poured out drink offerings to
other idols to make me angry. 30From their
youth, the people of Israel and Judah have
done only the things I said were wrong.
They have made me angry by worshiping
idols made with their own hands," says the
LORD. 31"From the day Jerusalem was built
until now, this city has made me angry, so
angry that I must remove it from my sight.
32I will destroy it, because of all the evil the
people of Israel and Judah have done. The
people, their kings and officers, their priests
and prophets, all the people of Judah, and
the people of Jerusalem have made me
angry. 33They turned their backs to me, not
their faces. I tried to teach them again and
again, but they wouldn't listen or learn.
34They put their hateful idols in the place
where I have chosen to be worshiped, so
they made it unclean. 35In the Valley of Ben
Hinnom they built places to worship Baal so
they could burn their sons and daughters as
sacrifices to Molech. But I never commanded
them to do such a hateful thing. It never
entered my mind that they would do such a
thing and cause Judah to sin.

36"You are saying, 'Because of war, hunger,
and terrible diseases, the city will be handed
over to the king of Babylon.' But the LORD,
the God of Israel, says about Jerusalem: 37I
forced the people of Israel and Judah to leave
their land, because I was furious and very
angry with them. But soon I will gather
them from all the lands where I forced them
to go, and I will bring them back to this
place, where they may live in safety. 38The
people of Israel and Judah will be my people,
and I will be their God. 39I will make them
truly want to be one people with one goal.
They will truly want to worship me all their
lives, for their own good and for the good of
their children after them.

40"I will make an agreement with them
that will last forever. I will never turn away
from them; I will always do good to them. I
will make them want to respect me so they
will never turn away from me. 41I will enjoy
doing good to them. And with my whole
being I will surely plant them in this land
and make them grow."

42This is what the LORD says: "I have
brought this great disaster to the people of
Israel and Judah. In the same way I will
bring the good things that I promise to do
for them. 43You are saying, 'This land is an
empty desert, without people or animals. It
has been handed over to the Babylonians.'
But in the future, people will again buy
fields in this land. 44They will use their
money to buy fields. They will sign and seal
their agreements and call in witnesses. They
will again buy fields in the land of Benjamin,
in the area around Jerusalem, in the towns of
Judah and in the mountains, in the western
hills, and in southern Judah. I will make
everything as good for them as it once was,"
says the LORD.

The Promise of the Lord

33 While Jeremiah was still locked up in
the courtyard of the guards, the LORD
spoke his word to him a second time:
2"These are the words of the LORD, who made
the earth, shaped it, and gave it order, whose
name is the LORD: 3'Judah, pray to me, and I
will answer you. I will tell you important
secrets you have never heard before.' 4This is
what the LORD, the God of Israel, says about
the houses in Jerusalem and the royal
palaces of Judah that have been torn down to
be used in defense of the attack by the
Babylonian army: 5'Some people will come
to fight against the Babylonians. They will
fill these houses with the bodies of people I
killed in my hot anger. I have turned away
from this city because of all the evil its
people have done.

6" 'But then I will bring health and healing
to the people there. I will heal them and let
them enjoy great peace and safety. 7I will
bring Judah and Israel back from captivity
and make them strong countries as in the
past. 8They sinned against me, but I will
wash away that sin. They did evil and turned
away from me, but I will forgive them. 9Then
"Jerusalem" will be to me a name that brings
joy! And people from all nations of the earth
will praise it when they hear about the good
things I am doing there. They will be

32:29 roofs In Bible times houses were built with flat roofs. The roof was used for drying things such as flax and fruit. And it was used as an extra room, as a place for worship, and as a cool place to sleep in the summer.

surprised and shocked at all the good things
and the peace I will bring to Jerusalem.'
10"You are saying, 'Our country is an
empty desert, without people or animals.'
But this is what the LORD says: It is now quiet
in the streets of Jerusalem and in the towns
of Judah, without people or animals, but it
will be noisy there soon! 11There will be
sounds of joy and gladness and the happy
sounds of brides and bridegrooms. There
will be the sounds of people bringing to the
Temple of the LORD their offerings of thanks
to the LORD. They will say,

'Praise the LORD All-Powerful,
because the LORD is good!
His love continues forever!'

They will say this because I will again do
good things for Judah, as I did in the
beginning," says the LORD.
12This is what the LORD All-Powerful says:
"This place is empty now, without people or
animals. But there will be shepherds in all
the towns of Judah and pastures where they
let their flocks rest. 13Shepherds will again
count their sheep as the sheep walk in front
of them. They will count them in the
mountains and in the western hills, in
southern Judah and the land of Benjamin,
and around Jerusalem and the other towns
of Judah!" says the LORD.

The Good Branch

14The LORD says, "The time is coming
when I will do the good thing I promised to
the people of Israel and Judah.
15In those days and at that time,
I will make a good branch sprout from
David's family.
He will do what is fair and right in the
land.
16At that time Judah will be saved,
and the people of Jerusalem will live in
safety.
The branch will be named:
The LORD Does What Is Right."

17This is what the LORD says: "Someone
from David's family will always sit on the
throne of the family of Israel. 18And there
will always be priests from the family of
Levi. They will always stand before me to
offer burnt offerings and grain offerings and
sacrifices to me."
19The LORD spoke his word to Jeremiah,
saying: 20"This is what the LORD says: I have

devotion 216

JEREMIAH 33:11

EXPECT HIS ENDLESS LOVE

Forever love is the heart's desire of every woman I know. We want our husbands to love us completely all the days of marriage. We want our children to respect us and love us *just because they do,* not because they have to. We want our girlfriends to share all their secret passions with us and to hear ours, too.

We were created in God's image. That means we were created to give love and want love. The apostle John wrote in his first letter that the very reason we love is because God loved us first (1 John 4:7-12). Do you get that? Without him, we would not even know what love is: the unconditional sacrifice of his Son for us. I have to admit it is too great a thing for me to even get my arms around. Can you take in the enormity of the love he has for you?

Days pass, people move on, and even some marriages fail, but the love God has to pour out to you *never* changes. You never have to worry about working tirelessly to win his love or performing some act of service to get his approval. You never have to worry about crying one too many tears on his shoulder. He just loves you and wants to be part of your intimate life. God is faithful and he is consistently a lover of your soul and your tender heart! Rejoice today and know that the Lord is good. Expect his endless love!

an agreement with day and night that they
will always come at the right times. If you
could change that agreement, [21]only then
could you change my agreement with David
and Levi. Only then would my servant David
not have a descendant ruling as king on
David's throne. And only then would the
family of Levi not be priests serving me in
the Temple. [22]But I will give many
descendants to my servant David and to the
family group of Levi who serve me in the
Temple. They will be as many as the stars in
the sky that no one can count. They will be
as many as the grains of sand on the
seashore that no one can measure."

[23]The LORD spoke his word to Jeremiah,
saying: [24]"Jeremiah, have you heard what the
people are saying? They say: 'The LORD
turned away from the two families of Israel
and Judah that he chose.' Now they don't
think of my people as a nation anymore!"

[25]This is what the LORD says: "If I had not
made my agreement with day and night, and
if I had not made the laws for the sky and
earth, [26]only then would I turn away from
Jacob's descendants. And only then would I
not let the descendants of David my servant
rule over the descendants of Abraham, Isaac,
and Jacob. But I will be kind to them and
cause good things to happen to them again."

A Warning to Zedekiah

34 The LORD spoke his word to Jeremiah
when Nebuchadnezzar king of
Babylon was fighting against Jerusalem and
all the towns around it. Nebuchadnezzar had
with him all his army and the armies of all
the kingdoms and peoples he ruled. [2]This is
what the LORD, the God of Israel, said:
"Jeremiah, go to Zedekiah king of Judah and
tell him: 'This is what the LORD says: I will
soon hand the city of Jerusalem over to the
king of Babylon, and he will burn it down!
[3]You will not escape from the king of
Babylon; you will surely be captured and
handed over to him. You will see the king of
Babylon with your own eyes, and he will
talk to you face to face. And you will go to
Babylon. [4]But, Zedekiah king of Judah, listen
to the promise of the LORD. This is what the
LORD says about you: You will not be killed
with a sword. [5]You will die in a peaceful way.
As people made funeral fires to honor your
ancestors, the kings who ruled before you, so
people will make a funeral fire to honor you.
They will cry for you and sadly say, "Ah,
master!" I myself make this promise to you,
says the LORD.'"

[6]So Jeremiah the prophet gave this
message to Zedekiah in Jerusalem. [7]This was
while the army of the king of Babylon was
fighting against Jerusalem and the cities of
Judah that had not yet been taken—Lachish
and Azekah. These were the only strong,
walled cities left in the land of Judah.

Slaves Are Mistreated

[8]The LORD spoke his word to Jeremiah.
This was after King Zedekiah had made an
agreement with all the people in Jerusalem
to free all the Hebrew slaves. [9]Everyone was
supposed to free his Hebrew slaves, both
male and female. No one was to keep a
fellow Jew as a slave. [10]All the officers and all
the people accepted this agreement; they
agreed to free their male and female slaves
and no longer keep them as slaves. So all the
slaves were set free. [11]But after that, the
people who had slaves changed their minds.
So they took back the people they had set
free and made them slaves again.

[12]Then the LORD spoke his word to
Jeremiah: [13]"This is what the LORD, the God
of Israel, says: I brought your ancestors out
of Egypt where they were slaves and made
an agreement with them. [14]I said to your
ancestors: 'At the end of every seven years,
each one of you must set his Hebrew slaves
free. If a fellow Hebrew has sold himself to
you, you must let him go free after he has
served you for six years.' But your ancestors
did not listen or pay attention to me. [15]A
short time ago you changed your hearts and
did what I say is right. Each of you gave
freedom to his fellow Hebrews who were
slaves. And you even made an agreement
before me in the place where I have chosen
to be worshiped. [16]But now you have
changed your minds. You have shown you
do not honor me. Each of you has taken back
the male and female slaves you had set free,
and you have forced them to become your
slaves again.

[17]"So this is what the LORD says: You have
not obeyed me. You have not given freedom
to your fellow Hebrews, neither relatives nor
friends. But now I will give freedom, says the
LORD, to war, to terrible diseases, and to
hunger. I will make you hated by all the

kingdoms of the earth. [18]I will hand over the men who broke my agreement, who have not kept the promises they made before me. They cut a calf into two pieces before me and walked between the pieces.[n] [19]These people made the agreement before me by walking between the pieces of the calf: the leaders of Judah and Jerusalem, the officers of the court, the priests, and all the people of the land. [20]So I will hand them over to their enemies and to everyone who wants to kill them. Their bodies will become food for the birds of the air and for the wild animals of the earth. [21]I will hand Zedekiah king of Judah and his officers over to their enemies, and to everyone who wants to kill them, and to the army of the king of Babylon, even though they have left Jerusalem. [22]I will give the order, says the LORD, to bring the Babylonian army back to Jerusalem. It will fight against Jerusalem, capture it, set it on fire, and burn it down. I will destroy the towns in Judah so that they become ruins where no one lives!"

The Recabite Family Obeys God

35 When Jehoiakim son of Josiah was king of Judah, the LORD spoke his word to Jeremiah, saying: [2]"Go to the family of Recab. Invite them to come to one of the side rooms of the Temple of the LORD, and offer them wine to drink."

[3]So I went to get Jaazaniah son of Jeremiah,[n] the son of Habazziniah. And I gathered all of Jaazaniah's brothers and sons and the whole family of the Recabites together. [4]Then I brought them into the Temple of the LORD. We went into the room of the sons of Hanan son of Igdaliah, who was a man of God. The room was next to the one where the officers stay and above the room of Maaseiah son of Shallum, the doorkeeper in the Temple. [5]Then I put some bowls full of wine and some cups before the men of the Recabite family. And I said to them, "Drink some wine."

[6]But the Recabite men answered, "We never drink wine. Our ancestor Jonadab son of Recab gave us this command: 'You and your descendants must never drink wine. [7]Also you must never build houses, plant seeds, or plant vineyards, or do any of those things. You must live only in tents. Then you will live a long time in the land where you are wanderers.' [8]So we Recabites have obeyed everything Jonadab our ancestor commanded us. Neither we nor our wives, sons, or daughters ever drink wine. [9]We never build houses in which to live, or own fields or vineyards, or plant crops. [10]We have lived in tents and have obeyed everything our ancestor Jonadab commanded us. [11]But when Nebuchadnezzar king of Babylon attacked Judah, we said to each other, 'Come, we must enter Jerusalem so we can escape the Babylonian army and the Aramean army.' So we have stayed in Jerusalem."

[12]Then the LORD spoke his word to Jeremiah: [13]"This is what the LORD All-Powerful, the God of Israel, says: Jeremiah, go and tell the men of Judah and the people of Jerusalem: 'You should learn a lesson and obey my message,' says the LORD. [14]'Jonadab son of Recab ordered his descendants not to drink wine, and that command has been obeyed. Until today they have obeyed their ancestor's command; they do not drink wine. But I, the LORD, have given you messages again and again, but you did not obey me. [15]I sent all my servants the prophets to you again and again, saying, "Each of you must stop doing evil. You must change and be good. Do not follow other gods to serve them. If you obey me, you will live in the land I have given to you and your ancestors." But you have not listened to me or paid attention to my message. [16]The descendants of Jonadab son of Recab obeyed the commands their ancestor gave them, but the people of Judah have not obeyed me.'

[17]"So the LORD God All-Powerful, the God of Israel, says: 'I will soon bring every disaster I said would come to Judah and to everyone living in Jerusalem. I spoke to those people, but they refused to listen. I called out to them, but they did not answer me.' "

[18]Then Jeremiah said to the Recabites, "This is what the LORD All-Powerful, the God of Israel, says: 'You have obeyed the commands of your ancestor Jonadab and have followed all of his teachings; you have done everything he commanded.' [19]So this is

34:18 They . . . pieces. This showed that the men were willing to be killed, like this animal, if they did not keep their agreement.

35:3 Jeremiah Not the prophet Jeremiah, but a different man with the same name.

what the LORD All-Powerful, the God of
Israel, says: 'There will always be a
descendant of Jonadab son of Recab to
serve me.' "

Jehoiakim Burns Jeremiah's Scroll

36 The LORD spoke this word to Jeremiah
during the fourth year that Jehoiakim
son of Josiah was king of Judah: 2"Get a
scroll. Write on it all the words I have
spoken to you about Israel and Judah and all
the nations. Write everything from when I
first spoke to you, when Josiah was king,
until now. 3Maybe the family of Judah will
hear what disasters I am planning to bring
on them and will stop doing wicked things.
Then I would forgive them for the sins and
the evil things they have done."

4So Jeremiah called for Baruch son of
Neriah. Jeremiah spoke the messages the
LORD had given him, and Baruch wrote those
messages on the scroll. 5Then Jeremiah
commanded Baruch, "I cannot go to the
Temple of the LORD. I must stay here. 6So I
want you to go to the Temple of the LORD on
a day when the people are fasting. Read from
the scroll to all the people of Judah who
come into Jerusalem from their towns. Read
the messages from the LORD, which are the
words you wrote on the scroll as I spoke
them to you. 7Perhaps they will ask the LORD
to help them. Perhaps each one will stop
doing wicked things, because the LORD has
announced that he is very angry with them."
8So Baruch son of Neriah did everything
Jeremiah the prophet told him to do. In the
LORD's Temple he read aloud the scroll that
had the LORD's messages written on it.

9In the ninth month of the fifth year that
Jehoiakim son of Josiah was king, a fast was
announced. All the people of Jerusalem and
everyone who had come into Jerusalem from
the towns of Judah were supposed to give up
eating to honor the LORD. 10At that time
Baruch read to all the people there the scroll
containing Jeremiah's words. He read the
scroll in the Temple of the LORD in the room
of Gemariah son of Shaphan, a royal
secretary. That room was in the upper
courtyard at the entrance of the New Gate of
the Temple.

11Micaiah son of Gemariah, the son of
Shaphan, heard all the messages from the
LORD that were on the scroll. 12Micaiah went
down to the royal secretary's room in the
king's palace where all of the officers were
sitting: Elishama the royal secretary; Delaiah
son of Shemaiah; Elnathan son of Acbor;
Gemariah son of Shaphan; Zedekiah son of
Hananiah; and all the other officers.
13Micaiah told those officers everything he
had heard Baruch read to the people from
the scroll.

14Then the officers sent a man named
Jehudi son of Nethaniah to Baruch.
(Nethaniah was the son of Shelemiah, who
was the son of Cushi.) Jehudi said to Baruch,
"Bring the scroll that you read to the people
and come with me."

So Baruch son of Neriah took the scroll
and went with Jehudi to the officers. 15Then
the officers said to Baruch, "Please sit down
and read the scroll to us."

So Baruch read the scroll to them. 16When
the officers heard all the words, they became
afraid and looked at each other. They said to
Baruch, "We must certainly tell the king
about these words." 17Then the officers asked
Baruch, "Tell us, please, where did you get all
these words you wrote on the scroll? Did
you write down what Jeremiah said to you?"

18"Yes," Baruch answered. "Jeremiah spoke
them all to me, and I wrote them down with
ink on this scroll."

19Then the officers said to Baruch, "You
and Jeremiah must go and hide, and don't
tell anyone where you are."

20The officers put the scroll in the room of
Elishama the royal secretary. Then they
went to the king in the courtyard and told
him all about the scroll. 21So King Jehoiakim
sent Jehudi to get the scroll. Jehudi brought
the scroll from the room of Elishama the
royal secretary and read it to the king and to
all the officers who stood around the king.
22It was the ninth month of the year, so King
Jehoiakim was sitting in the winter
apartment. There was a fire burning in a
small firepot in front of him. 23After Jehudi
had read three or four columns, the king cut
those columns off of the scroll with a
penknife and threw them into the firepot.
Finally, the whole scroll was burned in the
fire. 24King Jehoiakim and his servants heard
everything that was said, but they were not
frightened! They did not tear their clothes to
show their sorrow. 25Elnathan, Delaiah, and
Gemariah even tried to talk King Jehoiakim

out of burning the scroll, but he would not listen to them. [26]Instead, the king ordered Jerahmeel son of the king, Seraiah son of Azriel, and Shelemiah son of Abdeel to arrest Baruch the secretary and Jeremiah the prophet. But the LORD had hidden them.

[27]So King Jehoiakim burned the scroll where Baruch had written all the words Jeremiah had spoken to him. Then the LORD spoke his word to Jeremiah: [28]"Get another scroll. Write all the words on it that were on the first scroll that Jehoiakim king of Judah burned up. [29]Also say this to Jehoiakim king of Judah: 'This is what the LORD says: You burned up that scroll and said, "Why, Jeremiah, did you write on it 'the king of Babylon will surely come and destroy this land and the people and animals in it'?" [30]So this is what the LORD says about Jehoiakim king of Judah: Jehoiakim's descendants will not sit on David's throne. When Jehoiakim dies, his body will be thrown out on the ground. It will be left out in the heat of the day and in the cold frost of the night. [31]I will punish Jehoiakim and his children and his servants, because they have done evil things. I will bring disasters upon them and upon all the people in Jerusalem and Judah—everything I promised but which they refused to hear.' "

[32]So Jeremiah took another scroll and gave it to Baruch son of Neriah, his secretary. As Jeremiah spoke, Baruch wrote on the scroll the same words that were on the scroll Jehoiakim king of Judah had burned in the fire. And many similar words were added to the second scroll.

Jeremiah in Prison

37 Nebuchadnezzar king of Babylon had appointed Zedekiah son of Josiah to be king of Judah. Zedekiah took the place of Jehoiachin son of Jehoiakim. [2]But Zedekiah, his servants, and the people of Judah did not listen to the words the LORD had spoken through Jeremiah the prophet.

[3]Now King Zedekiah sent Jehucal son of Shelemiah and the priest Zephaniah son of Maaseiah with a message to Jeremiah the prophet. This was the message: "Jeremiah, please pray to the LORD our God for us."

[4]At that time Jeremiah had not yet been put into prison. So he was free to go anywhere he wanted. [5]The army of the king of Egypt had marched from Egypt toward Judah. Now the Babylonian army had surrounded the city of Jerusalem. When they heard about the Egyptian army marching toward them, the Babylonian army left Jerusalem.

[6]The LORD spoke his word to Jeremiah the prophet: [7]"This is what the LORD, the God of Israel, says: Jehucal and Zephaniah, I know Zedekiah king of Judah sent you to seek my help. Tell this to King Zedekiah: 'The army of the king of Egypt came here to help you, but they will go back to Egypt. [8]After that, the Babylonian army will return and attack Jerusalem and capture it and burn it down.'

[9]"This is what the LORD says: People of Jerusalem, do not fool yourselves. Don't say, 'The Babylonian army will surely leave us alone.' They will not! [10]Even if you defeated all of the Babylonian army that is attacking you and there were only a few injured men left in their tents, they would come from their tents and burn down Jerusalem!"

[11]So the Babylonian army left Jerusalem to fight the army of the king of Egypt. [12]Now Jeremiah tried to travel from Jerusalem to the land of Benjamin to get his share of the property that belonged to his family. [13]When Jeremiah got to the Benjamin Gate of Jerusalem, the captain in charge of the guards arrested him. The captain's name was Irijah son of Shelemiah son of Hananiah. Irijah said, "You are leaving us to join the Babylonians!"

[14]But Jeremiah said to Irijah, "That's not true! I am not leaving to join the Babylonians." Irijah refused to listen to Jeremiah, so he arrested Jeremiah and took him to the officers of Jerusalem. [15]Those rulers were very angry with Jeremiah and beat him. Then they put him in jail in the house of Jonathan the royal secretary, which had been made into a prison. [16]So those people put Jeremiah into a cell in a dungeon, and Jeremiah was there for a long time.

[17]Then King Zedekiah sent for Jeremiah and had him brought to the palace. Zedekiah asked him in private, "Is there any message from the LORD?"

Jeremiah answered, "Yes, there is. Zedekiah, you will be handed over to the king of Babylon." [18]Then Jeremiah said to King Zedekiah, "What crime have I done against you or your officers or the people of

Jerusalem? Why have you thrown me into prison? 19Where are your prophets that prophesied this message to you: 'The king of Babylon will not attack you or this land of Judah'? 20But now, my master, king of Judah, please listen to me, and please do what I ask of you. Do not send me back to the house of Jonathan the royal secretary, or I will die there!"

21So King Zedekiah gave orders for Jeremiah to be put under guard in the courtyard of the guard and to be given bread each day from the street of the bakers until there was no more bread in the city. So he stayed under guard in the courtyard of the guard.

Jeremiah Is Thrown into a Well

38 Shephatiah son of Mattan, Gedaliah son of Pashhur, Jehucal son of Shelemiah, and Pashhur son of Malkijah heard what Jeremiah was telling all the people. He said: 2"This is what the LORD says: 'Everyone who stays in Jerusalem will die from war, or hunger, or terrible diseases. But everyone who surrenders to the Babylonian army will live; they will escape with their lives and live.' 3And this is what the LORD says: 'This city of Jerusalem will surely be handed over to the army of the king of Babylon. He will capture this city!' "

4Then the officers said to the king, "Jeremiah must be put to death! He is discouraging the soldiers who are still in the city, and all the people, by what he is saying to them. He does not want good to happen to us; he wants to ruin us."

5King Zedekiah said to them, "Jeremiah is in your control. I cannot do anything to stop you."

6So the officers took Jeremiah and put him into the well of Malkijah, the king's son, which was in the courtyard of the guards. The officers used ropes to lower Jeremiah into the well, which did not have any water in it, only mud. And Jeremiah sank down into the mud.

7But Ebed-Melech, a Cushite and a servant in the palace, heard that the officers had put Jeremiah into the well. As King Zedekiah was sitting at the Benjamin Gate, 8Ebed-Melech left the palace and went to the king. Ebed-Melech said to him, 9"My master and king, these rulers have acted in an evil way. They have treated Jeremiah the prophet badly. They have thrown him into a well and left him there to die! When there is no more bread in the city, he will starve to death."

10Then King Zedekiah commanded Ebed-Melech the Cushite, "Take thirty men from the palace and lift Jeremiah the prophet out of the well before he dies."

11So Ebed-Melech took the men with him and went to a room under the storeroom in the palace. He took some old rags and worn-out clothes from that room. Then he let those rags down with some ropes to Jeremiah in the well. 12Ebed-Melech the Cushite said to Jeremiah, "Put these old rags and worn-out clothes under your arms to be pads for the ropes." So Jeremiah did as Ebed-Melech said. 13The men pulled Jeremiah up with the ropes and lifted him out of the well. And Jeremiah stayed under guard in the courtyard of the guard.

Zedekiah Questions Jeremiah

14Then King Zedekiah sent someone to get Jeremiah the prophet and bring him to the third entrance to the Temple of the LORD. The king said to Jeremiah, "I am going to ask you something. Do not hide anything from me, but tell me everything honestly."

15Jeremiah said to Zedekiah, "If I give you an answer, you will surely kill me. And even if I give you advice, you will not listen to me."

16But King Zedekiah made a secret promise to Jeremiah, "As surely as the LORD lives who has given us breath and life, I will not kill you. And I promise not to hand you over to the officers who want to kill you."

17Then Jeremiah said to Zedekiah, "This is what the LORD God All-Powerful, the God of Israel, says: 'If you surrender to the officers of the king of Babylon, your life will be saved. Jerusalem will not be burned down, and you and your family will live. 18But if you refuse to surrender to the officers of the king of Babylon, Jerusalem will be handed over to the Babylonian army, and they will burn it down. And you yourself will not escape from them.' "

19Then King Zedekiah said to Jeremiah, "I'm afraid of some Jews who have already gone over to the side of the Babylonian army. If the Babylonians hand me over to them, they will treat me badly."

20 But Jeremiah answered, "The
Babylonians will not hand you over to the
Jews. Obey the LORD by doing what I tell you.
Then things will go well for you, and your
life will be saved. 21 But if you refuse to
surrender to the Babylonians, the LORD has
shown me what will happen. 22 All the
women left in the palace of the king of Judah
will be brought out and taken to the
important officers of the king of Babylon.
Your women will make fun of you with this
song:

'Your good friends misled you
and were stronger than you.
While your feet were stuck in the mud,
they left you.'

23 "All your wives and children will be
brought out and given to the Babylonian
army. You yourself will not even escape from
them. You will be taken prisoner by the king
of Babylon, and Jerusalem will be burned
down."

24 Then Zedekiah said to Jeremiah, "Do not
tell anyone that I have been talking to you,
or you will die. 25 If the officers find out I
talked to you, they will come to you and say,
'Tell us what you said to King Zedekiah and
what he said to you. Don't keep any secrets
from us. If you don't tell us everything, we
will kill you.' 26 If they ask you, tell them, 'I
was begging the king not to send me back to
Jonathan's house to die.'"

27 All the officers did come to question
Jeremiah. So he told them everything the
king had ordered him to say. Then the
officers said no more to Jeremiah, because no
one had heard what Jeremiah and the king
had discussed.

28 So Jeremiah stayed under guard in the
courtyard of the guard until the day
Jerusalem was captured.

The Fall of Jerusalem

39 This is how Jerusalem was captured:
Nebuchadnezzar king of Babylon
marched against Jerusalem with his whole
army and surrounded the city to attack it.
This was during the tenth month of the
ninth year Zedekiah was king of Judah. 2 This
lasted until the ninth day of the fourth
month in Zedekiah's eleventh year. Then the
city wall was broken through. 3 And all these
officers of the king of Babylon came into
Jerusalem and sat down at the Middle
Gate: Nergal-Sharezer of the district of
Samgar; Nebo-Sarsekim, a chief officer;
Nergal-Sharezer, an important leader; and
all the other important officers.

4 When Zedekiah king of Judah and all his
soldiers saw them, they ran away. They left
Jerusalem at night and went out from the
king's garden. They went through the gate
that was between the two walls and then
headed toward the Jordan Valley. 5 But the
Babylonian army chased them and caught
up with Zedekiah in the plains of Jericho.
They captured him and took him to
Nebuchadnezzar king of Babylon, who was
at the town of Riblah in the land of Hamath.
There Nebuchadnezzar passed his sentence
on Zedekiah. 6 At Riblah the king of Babylon
killed Zedekiah's sons and all the important
officers of Judah as Zedekiah watched. 7 Then
he put out Zedekiah's eyes. He put bronze
chains on Zedekiah and took him to
Babylon.

8 The Babylonians set fire to the palace
and to the houses of the people, and they
broke down the walls around Jerusalem.
9 Nebuzaradan, commander of the king's
special guards, took the people left in
Jerusalem, those captives who had
surrendered to him earlier, and the rest of
the people of Jerusalem, and he took them
all away to Babylon. 10 But Nebuzaradan,
commander of the guard, left some of the
poorest people of Judah behind. They owned
nothing, but that day he gave them
vineyards and fields.

11 Nebuchadnezzar king of Babylon had
given these orders about Jeremiah through
Nebuzaradan, commander of the guard:
12 "Find Jeremiah and take care of him. Do
not hurt him, but do for him whatever he
asks you." 13 So Nebuchadnezzar sent these
men for Jeremiah: Nebuzaradan, commander
of the guards; Nebushazban, a chief officer;
Nergal-Sharezer, an important leader; and all
the other officers of the king of Babylon.
14 They had Jeremiah taken out of the
courtyard of the guard. Then they turned
him over to Gedaliah son of Ahikam son of
Shaphan, who had orders to take Jeremiah
back home. So they took him home, and he
stayed among the people left in Judah.

15 While Jeremiah was guarded in the
courtyard, the LORD spoke his word to him:
16 "Jeremiah, go and tell Ebed-Melech the

Cushite this message: 'This is what the LORD
All-Powerful, the God of Israel, says: Very
soon I will make my words about Jerusalem
come true through disaster, not through
good times. You will see everything come
true with your own eyes. [17]But I will save
you on that day, Ebed-Melech, says the LORD.
You will not be handed over to the people
you fear. [18]I will surely save you, Ebed-
Melech. You will not die from a sword, but
you will escape and live. This will happen
because you have trusted in me, says the
LORD.' "

Jeremiah Is Set Free

40 The LORD spoke his word to Jeremiah
after Nebuzaradan, commander of the
guards, had set Jeremiah free at the city of
Ramah. He had found Jeremiah in Ramah
bound in chains with all the captives from
Jerusalem and Judah who were being taken
away to Babylon. [2]When commander
Nebuzaradan found Jeremiah, Nebuzaradan
said to him, "The LORD your God announced
this disaster would come to this place. [3]And
now the LORD has done everything he said
he would do. This disaster happened because
the people of Judah sinned against the LORD
and did not obey him. [4]But today I am
freeing you from the chains on your wrists.
If you want to, come with me to Babylon,
and I will take good care of you. But if you
don't want to come, then don't. Look, the
whole country is open to you. Go wherever
you wish." [5]Before Jeremiah turned to leave,
Nebuzaradan said, "Or go back to Gedaliah
son of Ahikam, the son of Shaphan. The
king of Babylon has chosen him to be
governor over the towns of Judah. Go and
live with Gedaliah among the people, or go
anywhere you want."

Then Nebuzaradan gave Jeremiah some
food and a present and let him go. [6]So
Jeremiah went to Gedaliah son of Ahikam at
Mizpah and stayed with him there. He lived
among the people who were left behind in
Judah.

The Short Rule of Gedaliah

[7]Some officers and their men from the
army of Judah were still out in the open
country. They heard that the king of Babylon

devotion 217

JEREMIAH 39:18

FASTEN YOUR SEAT BELT

Have you ever been on an airplane when the pilot tells you to put your seat belt on because there is some rough weather ahead? My husband and I were traveling home once when our plane ride began to get rather bumpy. And I'm not talking about a little shaky. I'm talking about twenty foot drops that leave your stomach in your throat. I have never been more fearful for my life. I grabbed my husband's hand and we started praying. As I prayed, I felt the Lord encouraging me to sing praise songs. As I began to sing, this incredible peace came over me. I stopped singing after a few minutes, and the fear immediately rose up again. I sang for the next half hour.

Proverbs 3:5-6 are verses that have carried me through many difficult situations. I think of them when I read God's promise in Jeremiah 39:18. When I was on the plane, I couldn't lean on my own understanding—I had to trust. Everything in me felt as though the plane was going to crash. But when I turned to the Lord, I had a peace that he was in control. Believe me, I'm not normally one who sings praise songs out loud in a crowd, but it was my only way of acknowledging God. I felt his presence when I sang, and I trusted the Lord to bring me home to my babies. What is it in your life that makes you fearful? Trust God to carry you through.

had put Gedaliah son of Ahikam in charge of
the people who were left in the land: the
men, women, and children who were the
poorest. They were the ones who were not
taken to Babylon as captives. [8]So these
soldiers came to Gedaliah at Mizpah:
Ishmael son of Nethaniah, Johanan and
Jonathan sons of Kareah, Seraiah son of
Tanhumeth, the sons of Ephai the
Netophathite, Jaazaniah son of the
Maacathite, and their men.

[9]Gedaliah son of Ahikam, the son of
Shaphan, made a promise to them, saying,
"Do not be afraid to serve the Babylonians.
Stay in the land and serve the king of
Babylon. Then everything will go well for
you. [10]I myself will live in Mizpah and will
speak for you before the Babylonians who
come to us here. Harvest the wine, the
summer fruit, and the oil, and put what you
harvest in your storage jars. Live in the
towns you control."

[11]The Jews in Moab, Ammon, Edom, and
other countries also heard that the king of
Babylon had left a few Jews alive in the land.
And they heard the king of Babylon had
chosen Gedaliah as governor over them.
(Gedaliah was the son of Ahikam, the son of
Shaphan.) [12]When the people of Judah heard
this news, they came back to Judah from all
the countries where they had been scattered.
They came to Gedaliah at Mizpah and
gathered a large harvest of wine and
summer fruit.

[13]Johanan son of Kareah and all the army
officers of Judah still in the open country
came to Gedaliah at Mizpah. [14]They said to
him, "Don't you know that Baalis king of the
Ammonite people wants you dead? He has
sent Ishmael son of Nethaniah to kill you."
But Gedaliah son of Ahikam did not believe
them.

[15]Then Johanan son of Kareah spoke to
Gedaliah in private at Mizpah. He said, "Let
me go and kill Ishmael son of Nethaniah. No
one will know anything about it. We should
not let Ishmael kill you. Then all the Jews
gathered around you would be scattered to
different countries again, and the few people
of Judah who are left alive would be lost."

[16]But Gedaliah son of Ahikam said to
Johanan son of Kareah, "Do not kill Ishmael!
The things you are saying about Ishmael are
not true."

41 In the seventh month Ishmael son of
Nethaniah and ten of his men came to
Gedaliah son of Ahikam at Mizpah.
(Nethaniah was the son of Elishama.) Now
Ishmael was a member of the king's family
and had been one of the officers of the king
of Judah. While they were eating a meal
with Gedaliah at Mizpah, [2]Ishmael and his
ten men got up and killed Gedaliah son of
Ahikam, the son of Shaphan, with a sword.
(Gedaliah was the man the king of Babylon
had chosen as governor over Judah.)
[3]Ishmael also killed all the Jews and the
Babylonian soldiers who were there with
Gedaliah at Mizpah.

[4]The day after Gedaliah was murdered,
before anyone knew about it, [5]eighty men
came to Mizpah bringing grain offerings and
incense to the Temple of the LORD. Those
men from Shechem, Shiloh, and Samaria
had shaved off their beards, torn their
clothes, and cut themselves.[n] [6]Ishmael son of
Nethaniah went out from Mizpah to meet
them, crying as he walked. When he met
them, he said, "Come with me to meet
Gedaliah son of Ahikam." [7]So they went into
Mizpah. Then Ishmael son of Nethaniah and
his men killed seventy of them and threw
the bodies into a deep well. [8]But the ten men
who were left alive said to Ishmael, "Don't
kill us! We have wheat and barley and oil
and honey that we have hidden in a field."
So Ishmael let them live and did not kill
them with the others. [9]Now the well where
he had thrown all the bodies had been made
by King Asa as a part of his defenses against
Baasha king of Israel. But Ishmael son of
Nethaniah put dead bodies in it until it was
full.

[10]Ishmael captured all the other people in
Mizpah: the king's daughters and all the
other people who were left there. They were
the ones whom Nebuzaradan commander of
the guard had chosen Gedaliah son of
Ahikam to take care of. So Ishmael son of
Nethaniah captured those people, and he
started to cross over to the country of the
Ammonites.

[11]Johanan son of Kareah and all his army
officers with him heard about all the evil

41:5 shaved . . . themselves The men did this to show they were sad about the Temple in Jerusalem being destroyed.

things Ishmael son of Nethaniah had done.
12So they took their men and went to fight
Ishmael son of Nethaniah and caught him
near the big pool of water at Gibeon.
13When the captives Ishmael had taken saw
Johanan and the army officers, they were
glad. 14So all the people Ishmael had taken
captive from Mizpah turned around and ran
to Johanan son of Kareah. 15But Ishmael son
of Nethaniah and eight of his men escaped
from Johanan and ran away to the
Ammonites.

16So Johanan son of Kareah and all his
army officers saved the captives that Ishmael
son of Nethaniah had taken from Mizpah
after he murdered Gedaliah son of Ahikam.
Among those left alive were soldiers,
women, children, and palace officers. And
Johanan brought them back from the town
of Gibeon.

The Escape to Egypt

17-18Johanan and the other army officers
were afraid of the Babylonians. Since the
king of Babylon had chosen Gedaliah son of
Ahikam to be governor of Judah but Ishmael
son of Nethaniah had murdered him,
Johanan was afraid that the Babylonians
would be angry. So they decided to run away
to Egypt. On the way they stayed at Geruth
Kimham, near the town of Bethlehem.

42 While there, Johanan son of Kareah
and Jezaniah son of Hoshaiah went to
Jeremiah the prophet. All the army officers
and all the people, from the least important
to the greatest, went along, too. 2They said to
him, "Jeremiah, please listen to what we ask.
Pray to the LORD your God for all the people
left alive from the family of Judah. At one
time there were many of us, but you can see
that there are few of us now. 3So pray that
the LORD your God will tell us where we
should go and what we should do."

4Then Jeremiah the prophet answered, "I
understand what you want me to do. I will
pray to the LORD your God as you have asked.
I will tell you everything he says and not
hide anything from you."

5Then the people said to Jeremiah, "May
the LORD be a true and loyal witness against
us if we don't do everything the LORD your
God sends you to tell us. 6It does not matter
if we like the message or not. We will obey
the LORD our God, to whom we are sending
you. We will obey what he says so good
things will happen to us."

7Ten days later the LORD spoke his word to
Jeremiah. 8Then Jeremiah called for Johanan
son of Kareah, the army officers with him,
and all the other people, from the least
important to the greatest. 9Jeremiah said to
them, "You sent me to ask the LORD for what
you wanted. This is what the God of Israel
says: 10'If you will stay in Judah, I will build
you up and not tear you down. I will plant
you and not pull you up, because I am sad
about the disaster I brought on you. 11Now
you fear the king of Babylon, but don't be
afraid of him. Don't be afraid of him,' says
the LORD, 'because I am with you. I will save
you and rescue you from his power. 12I will
be kind to you, and he will also treat you
with mercy and let you stay in your land.'

13"But if you say, 'We will not stay in
Judah,' you will disobey the LORD your God.
14Or you might say, 'No, we will go and live
in Egypt. There we will not see war, or hear
the trumpets of war, or be hungry.' 15If you
say that, listen to the message of the LORD,
you who are left alive from Judah. This is
what the LORD All-Powerful, the God of
Israel, says: 'If you make up your mind to go
and live in Egypt, these things will happen:
16You are afraid of war, but it will find you in
the land of Egypt. And you are worried about
hunger, but it will follow you into Egypt,
and you will die there. 17Everyone who goes
to live in Egypt will die in war or from
hunger or terrible disease. No one who goes
to Egypt will live; no one will escape the
terrible things I will bring to them.'

18"This is what the LORD All-Powerful, the
God of Israel, says: 'I showed my anger
against the people of Jerusalem. In the same
way I will show my anger against you when
you go to Egypt. Other nations will speak
evil of you. People will be shocked by what
will happen to you. You will become a curse
word, and people will insult you. And you
will never see Judah again.'

19"You who are left alive in Judah, the
LORD has told you, 'Don't go to Egypt.' Be
sure you understand this; I warn you today
20that you are making a mistake that will
cause your deaths. You sent me to the LORD
your God, saying, 'Pray to the LORD our God
for us. Tell us everything the LORD our God
says, and we will do it.' 21So today I have told

you, but you have not obeyed the LORD your
God in all that he sent me to tell you. [22]So
now be sure you understand this: You want
to go to live in Egypt, but you will die there
by war, hunger, or terrible diseases."

43 So Jeremiah finished telling the
people the message from the LORD
their God; he told them everything the LORD
their God had sent him to tell them.

[2]Azariah son of Hoshaiah, Johanan son of
Kareah, and some other men were too proud.
They said to Jeremiah, "You are lying! The
LORD our God did not send you to say, 'You
must not go to Egypt to live there.' [3]Baruch
son of Neriah is causing you to be against us.
He wants you to hand us over to the
Babylonians so they can kill us or capture us
and take us to Babylon."

[4]So Johanan, the army officers, and all the
people disobeyed the LORD's command to
stay in Judah. [5]But Johanan son of Kareah
and the army officers led away those who
were left alive from Judah. They were the
people who had run away from the
Babylonians to other countries but then had
come back to live in Judah. [6]They led away
the men, women, and children, and the
king's daughters. Nebuzaradan commander
of the guard had put Gedaliah son of
Ahikam son of Shaphan in charge of those
people. Johanan also took Jeremiah the
prophet and Baruch son of Neriah. [7]These
people did not listen to the LORD. So they all
went to Egypt to the city of Tahpanhes.

[8]In Tahpanhes the LORD spoke his word to
Jeremiah: [9]"Take some large stones. Bury
them in the clay in the brick pavement in
front of the king of Egypt's palace in
Tahpanhes. Do this while the Jews are
watching you. [10]Then say to them, 'This is
what the LORD All-Powerful, the God of
Israel, says: I will soon send for my servant,
Nebuchadnezzar king of Babylon. I will set
his throne over these stones I have buried,
and he will spread his covering for shade
above them. [11]He will come here and attack
Egypt. He will bring death to those who are
supposed to die. He will make prisoners of
those who are to be taken captive, and he
will bring war to those who are to be killed
with a sword. [12]Nebuchadnezzar will set fire
to the temples of the gods of Egypt and burn
them. And he will take the idols away as
captives. As a shepherd wraps himself in his
clothes, so Nebuchadnezzar will wrap Egypt
around him. Then he will safely leave Egypt.
[13]He will destroy the stone pillars in the
temple of the sun god in Egypt, and he will
burn down the temples of the gods of
Egypt.' "

Disaster in Egypt

44 Jeremiah received a message from
the LORD for all the Jews living in
Egypt—in the cities of Migdol, Tahpanhes,
Memphis, and in southern Egypt. This was
the message: [2]"The LORD All-Powerful, the
God of Israel, says: You saw all the terrible
things I brought on Jerusalem and the towns
of Judah, which are ruins today with no one
living in them. [3]It is because the people who
lived there did evil. They made me angry by
burning incense and worshiping other gods
that neither they nor you nor your ancestors
ever knew. [4]I sent all my servants, the
prophets, to you again and again. By them I
said to you, 'Don't do this terrible thing that
I hate.' [5]But they did not listen or pay
attention. They did not stop doing evil
things and burning incense to other gods.
[6]So I showed my great anger against them. I
poured out my anger in the towns of Judah
and the streets of Jerusalem so they are only
ruins and piles of stones today.

[7]"Now the LORD All-Powerful, the God of
Israel, says: Why are you doing such great
harm to yourselves? You are cutting off the
men and women, children and babies from
the family of Judah, leaving yourselves
without anyone from the family of Judah.
[8]Why do you want to make me angry by
making idols? Why do you burn incense to
the gods of Egypt, where you have come to
live? You will destroy yourselves. Other
nations will speak evil of you and make fun
of you. [9]Have you forgotten about the evil
things your ancestors did? And have you
forgotten the evil the kings and queens of
Judah did? Have you forgotten about the evil
you and your wives did? These things were
done in the country of Judah and in the
streets of Jerusalem. [10]Even to this day the
people of Judah are still too proud. They
have not learned to respect me or to follow
my teachings. They have not obeyed the
laws I gave you and your ancestors.

[11]"So this is what the LORD All-Powerful,
the God of Israel, says: I am determined to

bring disasters on you. I will destroy the
whole family of Judah. 12The few who were
left alive from Judah were determined to go
to Egypt and settle there, but they will all die
in Egypt. They will be killed in war or die
from hunger. From the least important to
the greatest, they will be killed in war or die
from hunger. Other nations will speak evil
about them. People will be shocked by what
has happened to them. They will become a
curse word, and people will insult them. 13I
will punish those people who have gone to
live in Egypt, just as I punished Jerusalem,
using swords, hunger, and terrible diseases.
14Of the people of Judah who were left alive
and have gone to live in Egypt, none will
escape my punishment. They want to return
to Judah and live there, but none of them
will live to return to Judah, except a few
people who will escape."

15A large group of the people of Judah
who lived in southern Egypt were meeting
together. Among them were many women
of Judah who were burning incense to other
gods, and their husbands knew it. All these
people said to Jeremiah, 16"We will not listen
to the message from the LORD that you spoke
to us. 17We promised to make sacrifices to
the Queen Goddess, and we will certainly do
everything we promised. We will burn
incense and pour out drink offerings to
worship her, just as we, our ancestors, kings,
and officers did in the past. All of us did
these things in the towns of Judah and in the
streets of Jerusalem. At that time we had
plenty of food and were successful, and
nothing bad happened to us. 18But since we
stopped making sacrifices to the Queen
Goddess and stopped pouring out drink
offerings to her, we have had great problems.
Our people have also been killed in war and
by hunger."

19The women said, "Our husbands knew
what we were doing. We had their
permission to burn incense to the Queen
Goddess and to pour out drink offerings to
her. Our husbands knew we were making
cakes that looked like her and were pouring
out drink offerings to her."

20Then Jeremiah spoke to all the people—

devotion 218

JEREMIAH 44:15–30

NOTHING BUT THE TRUTH

When you encounter sin that is evident in someone's life, you are surely responsible to speak the truth in love. Keep in mind, the Word does not say, "Cram the Bible down their throats until they choke." Nor does it say, "Tell everyone you know about that person's sin." It simply says to speak the truth with love (Eph. 4:15). Speaking the truth doesn't always mean people will listen (even for a prophet like Jeremiah), but that doesn't change our responsibility.

I manage athletes and entertainers for a living, so I get plenty of opportunity to put this principal into practice. I definitely walk in a land much like the one Jeremiah described where idols are worshiped and God is not. Early on, I learned that if I was going to make it, I'd have to make some adjustments. My heart was way too big and my patience way too small to keep up with all the drama in people's lives. One particular afternoon, after a great deal of human disappointment and a giant letdown, the Holy Spirit spoke to my heart, "Whose words do not return void?"

I answered him immediately, "Yours, Lord, not mine." In that one moment, I changed my career forever. No longer would I tire myself with judgment or disappointment. No longer would I try to fix everything. I would do the only thing that was required of me, and that was to speak the truth with love. The Holy Spirit would work out the rest.

men and women—who answered him. 21He
said to them, "The LORD remembered that
you and your ancestors, kings and officers,
and the people of the land burned incense in
the towns of Judah and in the streets of
Jerusalem. He remembered and thought
about it. 22Then he could not be patient with
you any longer. He hated the terrible things
you did. So he made your country an empty
desert, where no one lives. Other people
curse that country. And so it is today. 23All
this happened because you burned incense
to other gods. You sinned against the LORD.
You did not obey him or follow his teachings
or the laws he gave you. You did not keep
your part of the agreement with him. So this
disaster has happened to you. It is there for
you to see."

24Then Jeremiah said to all those men and
women, "People of Judah who are now in
Egypt, hear the word of the LORD: 25The LORD
All-Powerful, the God of Israel, says: You and
your wives did what you said you would do.
You said, 'We will certainly keep the
promises we made. We promised to make
sacrifices to the Queen Goddess and to pour
out drink offerings to her.' So, go ahead. Do
the things you promised, and keep your
promises. 26But hear the word of the LORD.
Listen, all you Jews living in Egypt. The LORD
says, 'I have sworn by my great name: The
people of Judah now living in Egypt will
never again use my name to make promises.
They will never again say in Egypt, "As
surely as the Lord GOD lives . . . " 27I am
watching over them, not to take care of
them, but to hurt them. The Jews who live in
Egypt will die from swords or hunger until
they are all destroyed. 28A few will escape
being killed by the sword and will come
back to Judah from Egypt. Then, of the
people of Judah who came to live in Egypt,
those who are left alive will know if my
word or their word came true. 29I will give
you a sign that I will punish you here in
Egypt,' says the LORD. 'When you see it
happen, you will know that my promises to
hurt you will really happen.' 30This is what
the LORD says: 'Hophra king of Egypt has
enemies who want to kill him. Soon I will
hand him over to his enemies just as I
handed Zedekiah king of Judah over to
Nebuchadnezzar king of Babylon, who
wanted to kill him.' "

A Message to Baruch

45 It was the fourth year that Jehoiakim
son of Josiah was king of Judah.
Jeremiah the prophet told these things to
Baruch son of Neriah, and Baruch wrote them
on a scroll: 2"This is what the LORD, the God of
Israel, says to you, Baruch: 3You have said,
'How terrible it is for me! The LORD has given
me sorrow along with my pain. I am tired
because of my suffering and cannot rest.' "

4The LORD said, "Say this to Baruch: 'This
is what the LORD says: I will soon tear down
what I have built, and I will pull up what I
have planted everywhere in Judah. 5Baruch,
you are looking for great things for yourself.
Don't look for them, because I will bring
disaster on all the people, says the LORD. You
will have to go many places, but I will let
you escape alive wherever you go.' "

Messages to the Nations

46 The LORD spoke this word to Jeremiah
the prophet about the nations:

2This message is to Egypt. It is about the
army of Neco king of Egypt, which was
defeated at the city of Carchemish on the
Euphrates River by Nebuchadnezzar king of
Babylon. This was in the fourth year that
Jehoiakim son of Josiah was king of Judah.
This is the LORD's message to Egypt:

3"Prepare your shields, large and small,
and march out for battle!
4Harness the horses
and get on them!
Go to your places for battle
and put on your helmets!
Polish your spears.
Put on your armor!
5What do I see?
That army is terrified,
and the soldiers are running away.
Their warriors are defeated.
They run away quickly
without looking back.
There is terror on every side!" says the
LORD.
6"The fast runners cannot run away;
the strong soldiers cannot escape.
They stumble and fall
in the north, by the Euphrates River.
7Who is this, rising up like the Nile
River,
like strong, fast rivers?

[8]Egypt rises up like the Nile River,
like strong, fast rivers.
Egypt says, 'I will rise up and cover the earth.
I will destroy cities and the people in them!'
[9]Horsemen, charge into battle!
Chariot drivers, drive hard!
March on, brave soldiers—
soldiers from the countries of Cush and Put who carry shields,
soldiers from Lydia who use bows.
[10]"But that day belongs to the Lord GOD All-Powerful.
At that time he will give those people the punishment they deserve.
The sword will kill until it is finished,
until it satisfies its thirst for their blood.
The Lord GOD All-Powerful will offer a sacrifice
in the land of the north, by the Euphrates River.

[11]"Go up to Gilead and get some balm,
people of Egypt!
You have prepared many medicines,
but they will not work;
you will not be healed.
[12]The nations have heard of your shame,
and your cries fill all the earth.
One warrior has run into another;
both of them have fallen down together!"

[13]This is the message the LORD spoke to
Jeremiah the prophet about Nebuchadnezzar
king of Babylon's coming to attack Egypt:

[14]"Announce this message in Egypt, and preach it in Migdol.
Preach it also in the cities of Memphis and Tahpanhes:
'Get ready for war,
because the battle is all around you.'
[15]Egypt, why were your warriors killed?
They could not stand because the LORD pushed them down.
[16]They stumbled again and again
and fell over each other.
They said, 'Get up. Let's go back
to our own people and our homeland.
We must get away from our enemy's sword!'
[17]In their homelands those soldiers called out,
'The king of Egypt is only a lot of noise.
He missed his chance for glory!' "
[18]The King's name is the LORD All-Powerful.
He says, "As surely as I live,
a powerful leader will come.
He will be like Mount Tabor among the mountains,
like Mount Carmel by the sea.
[19]People of Egypt, pack your things
to be taken away as captives,
because Memphis will be destroyed.
It will be a ruin, and no one will live there.

[20]"Egypt is like a beautiful young cow,
but a horsefly is coming
from the north to attack her.
[21]The hired soldiers in Egypt's army
are like fat calves,
because even they all turn and run away together;
they do not stand strong against the attack.
Their time of destruction is coming;
they will soon be punished.
[22]Egypt is like a hissing snake that is trying to escape.
The enemy comes closer and closer.
They come against Egypt with axes
like men who cut down trees.
[23]They will chop down Egypt's army
as if it were a great forest," says the LORD.
"There are more enemy soldiers than locusts;
there are too many to count.
[24]The people of Egypt will be ashamed.
They will be handed over to the enemy from the north."

[25]The LORD All-Powerful, the God of Israel,
says: "Very soon I will punish Amon, the god
of the city of Thebes. And I will punish
Egypt, her kings, her gods, and the people
who depend on the king. [26]I will hand those
people over to their enemies, who want to
kill them. I will give them to
Nebuchadnezzar king of Babylon and his
officers. But in the future, Egypt will live in
peace as it once did," says the LORD.

A Message to Israel

[27]"People of Jacob, my servants, don't be afraid;
don't be frightened, Israel.
I will surely save you from those faraway places

and your children from the lands where
they are captives.
The people of Jacob will have peace and
safety again,
and no one will make them afraid.
28People of Jacob, my servants, do not be
afraid,
because I am with you," says the LORD.
"I will completely destroy the many
different nations
where I scattered you.
But I will not completely destroy you.
I will punish you fairly,
but I will not let you escape your
punishment."

A Message to the Philistines

47 Before the king of Egypt attacked the
city of Gaza, the LORD spoke his word
to Jeremiah the prophet. This message is to
the Philistine people.
2This is what the LORD says:
"See, the enemy is gathering in the north
like rising waters.
They will become like an overflowing
stream
and will cover the whole country like a
flood,
even the towns and the people living in
them.
Everyone living in that country
will cry for help;
the people will cry painfully.
3They will hear the sound of the running
horses
and the noisy chariots
and the rumbling chariot wheels.
Parents will not help their children to
safety,
because they will be too weak to help.
4The time has come
to destroy all the Philistines.
It is time to destroy all who are left alive
who could help the cities of Tyre and
Sidon.
The LORD will soon destroy the Philistines,
those left alive from the island of Crete.
5The people from the city of Gaza will be
sad and shave their heads.
The people from the city of Ashkelon
will be made silent.
Those left alive from the valley,
how long will you cut yourselves?[n]

6"You cry, 'Sword of the LORD,
how long will you keep fighting?
Return to your holder.
Stop and be still.'
7But how can his sword rest
when the LORD has given it a
command?
He has ordered it
to attack Ashkelon and the seacoast."

A Message to Moab

48 This message is to the country of
Moab.
This is what the LORD All-Powerful, the
God of Israel, says:
"How terrible it will be for the city of Nebo,
because it will be ruined.
The town of Kiriathaim will be disgraced
and captured;
the strong city will be disgraced and
shattered.
2Moab will not be praised again.
Men in the town of Heshbon plan
Moab's defeat.
They say, 'Come, let us put an end to
that nation!'
Town of Madmen,[n] you will also be
silenced.
The sword will chase you.
3Listen to the cries from the town of
Horonaim,
cries of much confusion and
destruction.
4Moab will be broken up.
Her little children will cry for help.
5Moab's people go up the path to the town
of Luhith,
crying loudly as they go.
On the road down to Horonaim,
cries of pain and suffering can be heard.
6Run! Run for your lives!
Go like a bush being blown through
the desert.
7You trust in the things you do and in your
wealth,
so you also will be captured.
The god Chemosh will go into captivity
and his priests and officers with him.

47:5 sad and . . . yourselves The people did these things to show their sadness.
48:2 Madmen This name sounds like the Hebrew word for "be silenced."

8The destroyer will come against every town;
not one town will escape.
The valley will be ruined,
and the high plain will be destroyed,
as the LORD has said.
9Give wings to Moab,
because she will surely leave her land.
Moab's towns will become empty,
with no one to live in them.
10A curse will be on anyone who doesn't do what the LORD says,
and a curse will be on anyone who holds back his sword from killing.

11"The people of Moab have never known trouble.
They are like wine left to settle;
they have never been poured from one jar to another.
They have not been taken into captivity.
So they taste as they did before,
and their smell has not changed.
12A time is coming," says the LORD,
"When I will send people to pour you from your jars.
They will empty Moab's jars
and smash her jugs.
13The people of Israel trusted that god in the town of Bethel,
and they were ashamed when there was no help.
In the same way Moab will be ashamed of their god Chemosh.

14"You cannot say, 'We are warriors!
We are brave men in battle!'
15The destroyer of Moab and her towns has arrived.
Her best young men will be killed!" says the King,
whose name is the LORD All-Powerful.
16"The end of Moab is near,
and she will soon be destroyed.
17All you who live around Moab,
all you who know her, cry for her.
Say, 'The ruler's power is broken;
Moab's power and glory are gone.'

18"You people living in the town of Dibon,
come down from your place of honor
and sit on the dry ground,
because the destroyer of Moab has come against you.
And he has destroyed your strong, walled cities.
19You people living in the town of Aroer,
stand next to the road and watch.
See the man running away and the woman escaping.
Ask them, 'What happened?'
20Moab is filled with shame, because she is ruined.
Cry, Moab, cry out!
Announce at the Arnon River
that Moab is destroyed.
21People on the high plain have been punished.
Judgment has come to these towns:
Holon, Jahzah, and Mephaath;
22 Dibon, Nebo, and Beth Diblathaim;
23 Kiriathaim, Beth Gamul, and Beth Meon;
24 Kerioth and Bozrah.
Judgment has come to all the towns of Moab, far and near.
25Moab's strength has been cut off,
and its arm broken!" says the LORD.

26"The people of Moab thought they were greater than the LORD,
so punish them until they act as if they are drunk.
Moab will fall and roll around in its own vomit,
and people will even make fun of it.
27Moab, you made fun of Israel.
Israel was caught in the middle of a gang of thieves.
When you spoke about Israel,
you shook your head and acted as if you were better than it.
28People in Moab, leave your towns empty
and go live among the rocks.
Be like a dove that makes its nest
at the entrance of a cave.

29"We have heard that the people of Moab are proud,
very proud.
They are proud, very proud,
and in their hearts they think they are important."
30The LORD says,
"I know Moab's great pride, but it is useless.
Moab's bragging accomplishes nothing.
31So I cry sadly for Moab,
for everyone in Moab.

I moan for the people from the town of
Kir Hareseth.
32 I cry with the people of the town of Jazer
for you, the grapevines of the town of
Sibmah.
In the past your vines spread all the way
to the sea,
as far as the sea of Jazer.
But the destroyer has taken over
your fruit and grapes.
33 Joy and happiness are gone
from the large, rich fields of Moab.
I have stopped the flow of wine from the
winepresses.
No one walks on the grapes with shouts
of joy.
There are shouts,
but not shouts of joy.

34 "Their crying can be heard from Moabite
towns,
from Heshbon to Elealeh and Jahaz.
It can be heard from Zoar as far away as
Horonaim and Eglath Shelishiyah.
Even the waters of Nimrim are dried up.
35 I will stop Moab
from making burnt offerings at the
places of worship
and from burning incense to their
gods," says the LORD.

36 "My heart cries sadly for Moab like a flute
playing a funeral song.
It cries like a flute for the people from
Kir Hareseth.
The money they made has all been
taken away.
37 Every head has been shaved
and every beard cut off.
Everyone's hands are cut,
and everyone wears rough cloth around
his waist.[n]
38 People are crying on every roof[n] in Moab
and in every public square.
There is nothing but sadness,
because I have broken Moab
like a jar no one wants," says the LORD.
39 "Moab is shattered! The people are crying!
Moab turns away in shame!
People all around her make fun of her.
The things that happened fill them
with great fear."

40 This is what the LORD says:
"Look! Someone is coming, like an eagle
diving down from the sky
and spreading its wings over Moab.
41 The towns of Moab will be captured,
and the strong, walled cities will be
defeated.
At that time Moab's warriors will be
frightened,
like a woman who is having a baby.
42 The nation of Moab will be destroyed,
because they thought they were greater
than the LORD.
43 Fear, deep pits, and traps wait for you,
people of Moab," says the LORD.
44 "People will run from fear,
but they will fall into the pits.
Anyone who climbs out of the pits
will be caught in the traps.
I will bring the year of punishment to
Moab," says the LORD.

45 "People have run from the powerful
enemy
and have gone to Heshbon for safety.
But fire started in Heshbon;
a blaze has spread from the hometown
of Sihon king of Moab.
It burned up the leaders of Moab
and destroyed those proud people.
46 How terrible it is for you, Moab!
The people who worship Chemosh
have been destroyed.
Your sons have been taken captive,
and your daughters have been taken
away.

47 "But in days to come,
I will make good things happen again
to Moab," says the LORD.
This ends the judgment on Moab.

A Message to Ammon

49 This message is to the Ammonite
people.
This is what the LORD says:
"Do you think that Israel has no children?
Do you think there is no one to take the
land when the parents die?
If that were true, why did Molech take
Gad's land
and why did Molech's people settle in
Gad's towns?"

48:37 Every head . . . waist. The people did these things to show their sadness for those who had died.
48:38 roof In Bible times houses were built with flat roofs. The roof was used for drying things such as flax and fruit. And it was used as an extra room, as a place for worship, and as a cool place to sleep in the summer.

2The LORD says,
"The time will come when I will make Rabbah,
the capital city of the Ammonites, hear the battle cry.
It will become a hill covered with ruins,
and the towns around it will be burned.
Those people forced Israel out of that land,
but now Israel will force them out!"
says the LORD.
3"People in the town of Heshbon, cry sadly because the town of Ai is destroyed!
Those who live in Rabbah, cry out!
Put on your rough cloth to show your sadness, and cry loudly.
Run here and there for safety inside the walls,
because Molech will be taken captive
and his priests and officers with him.
4You brag about your valleys
and about the fruit in your valleys.
You are like an unfaithful child
who believes his treasures will save him.
You think, 'Who would attack me?'
5I will soon bring terror on you
from everyone around you,"
says the Lord GOD All-Powerful.
"You will all be forced to run away,
and no one will be able to gather you.
6"But the time will come
when I will make good things happen to the Ammonites again,"
says the LORD.

A Message to Edom

7This message is to Edom. This is what the LORD All-Powerful says:
"Is there no more wisdom in the town of Teman?
Can the wise men of Edom no longer give good advice?
Have they lost their wisdom?
8You people living in the town of Dedan,
run away and hide in deep caves,
because I will bring disaster on the people of Esau.
It is time for me to punish them.
9If workers came and picked the grapes from your vines,
they would leave a few grapes behind.
If robbers came at night,
they would steal only enough for themselves.
10But I will strip Edom bare.
I will find all their hiding places,
so they will not be able to hide from me.
The children, relatives, and neighbors will die,
and Edom will be no more.
11Leave the orphans, and I will take care of them.
Your widows also can trust in me."

12This is what the LORD says: "Some
people did not deserve to be punished, but
they had to drink from the cup of suffering
anyway. People of Edom, you deserve to be
punished, so you will not escape
punishment. You must certainly drink from
the cup of suffering." 13The LORD says, "I
swear by my own name that the city of
Bozrah will become a pile of ruins! People
will be shocked by what happened there.
They will insult that city and speak evil of it.
And all the towns around it will become
ruins forever."

14I have heard a message from the LORD.
A messenger has been sent among the nations, saying,
"Gather your armies to attack it!
Get ready for battle!"
15"Soon I will make you the smallest of nations,
and you will be greatly hated by everyone.
16Edom, you frightened other nations,
but your pride has fooled you.
You live in the hollow places of the cliff
and control the high places of the hills.
Even if you build your home as high as an eagle's nest,
I will bring you down from there," says the LORD.
17"Edom will be destroyed.
People who pass by will be shocked to see the destroyed cities,
and they will be amazed at all her injuries.
18Edom will be destroyed like the cities of Sodom and Gomorrah
and the towns around them," says the LORD.

"No one will live there!
No one will stay in Edom.

19"Like a lion coming up from the thick bushes near the Jordan River
to attack a strong pen for sheep,
I will suddenly chase Edom from its land.
Who is the one I have chosen to do this?
There is no one like me,
no one who can take me to court.
None of their leaders can stand up against me."

20So listen to what the LORD has planned to do against Edom.
Listen to what he has decided to do to the people in the town of Teman.
He will surely drag away the young ones of Edom.
Their hometowns will surely be shocked at what happens to them.
21At the sound of Edom's fall, the earth will shake.
Their cry will be heard all the way to the Red Sea.
22The LORD is like an eagle swooping down
and spreading its wings over the city of Bozrah.
At that time Edom's soldiers will become very frightened,
like a woman having a baby.

A Message to Damascus

23This message is to the city of Damascus:
"The towns of Hamath and Arpad are put to shame,
because they have heard bad news.
They are discouraged.
They are troubled like the tossing sea.
24The city of Damascus has become weak.
The people want to run away;
they are ready to panic.
The people feel pain and suffering,
like a woman giving birth to a baby.
25Damascus was a city of my joy.
Why have the people not left that famous city yet?
26Surely the young men will die in the city squares,
and all her soldiers will be killed at that time," says the LORD All-Powerful.
27"I will set fire to the walls of Damascus,
and it will completely burn the strong cities of King Ben-Hadad."

A Message to Kedar and Hazor

28This message is to the tribe of Kedar and
the kingdoms of Hazor, which
Nebuchadnezzar king of Babylon defeated.
This is what the LORD says:
"Go and attack the people of Kedar,
and destroy the people of the East.
29Their tents and flocks will be taken away.
Their belongings will be carried off—
their tents, all their goods, and their camels.
Men will shout to them,
'Terror on every side!'

30"Run away quickly!
People in Hazor, find a good place to hide!" says the LORD.
"Nebuchadnezzar king of Babylon has made plans against you
and wants to defeat you.
31"Get up! Attack the nation that is comfortable,
that is sure no one will defeat it," says the LORD.
"It does not have gates or fences to protect it.
Its people live alone.
32The enemy will steal their camels
and their large herds of cattle as war prizes.
I will scatter the people who cut their hair short to every part of the earth,
and I will bring disaster on them from everywhere," says the LORD.
33"The city of Hazor will become a home for wild dogs;
it will be an empty desert forever.
No one will live there,
and no one will stay in it."

A Message to Elam

34Soon after Zedekiah became king of
Judah, the LORD spoke this word to Jeremiah
the prophet. This message is to the nation of
Elam.
35This is what the LORD All-Powerful says:
"I will soon break Elam's bow,
its greatest strength.
36I will bring the four winds against Elam
from the four corners of the skies.
I will scatter its people everywhere the four winds blow;
its captives will go to every nation.

37I will terrify Elam in front of their enemies,
who want to destroy them.
I will bring disaster to Elam
and show them how angry I am!" says
the LORD.
"I will send a sword to chase Elam
until I have killed them all.
38I will set up my throne in Elam to show
that I am king,
and I will destroy its king and its
officers!" says the LORD.

39"But I will make good things happen to
Elam again
in the future," says the LORD.

A Message to Babylon

50 This is the message the LORD spoke to
Babylon and the Babylonian people
through Jeremiah the prophet.
2"Announce this to the nations.
Lift up a banner and tell them.
Speak the whole message and say:
'Babylon will be captured.
The god Bel will be put to shame,
and the god Marduk will be afraid.
Babylon's gods will be put to shame,
and her idols will be afraid!'
3A nation from the north will attack
Babylon
and make it like an empty desert.
No one will live there;
both people and animals will run
away."
4The LORD says, "At that time
the people of Israel and Judah will
come together.
They will cry and look for the LORD
their God.
5Those people will ask how to go to
Jerusalem
and will start in that direction.
They will come and join themselves to
the LORD.
They will make an agreement with him
that will last forever,
an agreement that will never be
forgotten.

6"My people have been like lost sheep.
Their leaders have led them in the
wrong way
and made them wander around in the
mountains and hills.
They forgot where their resting place
was.
7Whoever saw my people hurt them.
And those enemies said, 'We did
nothing wrong.
Those people sinned against the LORD,
their true resting place,
the God their fathers trusted.'

8"Run away from Babylon,
and leave the land of the Babylonians.
Be like the goats that lead the flock.
9I will soon bring against Babylon
many great nations from the north.
They will take their places for war
against it,
and it will be captured by people from
the north.
Their arrows are like trained soldiers
who do not return from war with
empty hands.
10The enemy will take all the wealth from
the Babylonians.
Those enemy soldiers will get all they
want," says the LORD.

11"Babylon, you are excited and happy,
because you took my land.
You dance around like a young cow in the
grain.
Your laughter is like the neighing of
male horses.
12Your mother will be very ashamed;
the woman who gave birth to you will
be disgraced.
Soon Babylonia will be the least
important of all the nations.
She will be an empty, dry desert.
13Because of the LORD's anger,
no one will live there.
She will be completely empty.
Everyone who passes by Babylon will be
shocked.
They will shake their heads when they
see all her injuries.

14"Take your positions for war against
Babylon,
all you soldiers with bows.
Shoot your arrows at Babylon! Do not
save any of them,
because Babylon has sinned against the
LORD.
15Soldiers around Babylon, shout the war
cry!

Babylon has surrendered, her towers
have fallen,
and her walls have been torn down.
The LORD is giving her people the
punishment they deserve.
You nations should give her what she
deserves;
do to her what she has done to others.
16Don't let the people from Babylon plant
their crops
or gather the harvest.
The soldiers treated their captives cruelly.
Now, let everyone go back home.
Let everyone run to his own country.

17"The people of Israel are like a flock of
sheep that are scattered
from being chased by lions.
The first lion to eat them up
was the king of Assyria.
The last lion to crush their bones
was Nebuchadnezzar king of Babylon."
18So this is what the LORD All-Powerful,
the God of Israel, says:
"I will punish the king of Babylon and his
country
as I punished the king of Assyria.
19But I will bring the people of Israel back
to their own pasture.
They will eat on Mount Carmel and in
Bashan.
They will eat and be full
on the hills of Ephraim and Gilead."
20The LORD says,
"At that time people will try to find
Israel's guilt,
but there will be no guilt.
People will try to find Judah's sins,
but no sins will be found,
because I will leave a few people alive
from Israel and Judah,
and I will forgive their sins.

21"Attack the land of Merathaim.
Attack the people who live in Pekod.
Chase them, kill them, and completely
destroy them.
Do everything I commanded you!" says
the LORD.
22"The noise of battle can be heard all over
the country;
it is the noise of much destruction.
23Babylon was the hammer of the whole
earth,
but how broken and shattered that
hammer is now.
It is truly the most ruined
of all the nations.
24Babylon, I set a trap for you,
and you were caught before you
knew it.
You fought against the LORD,
so you were found and taken prisoner.
25The LORD has opened up his storeroom
and brought out the weapons of his
anger,
because the Lord GOD All-Powerful has
work to do
in the land of the Babylonians.
26Come against Babylon from far away.
Break open her storehouses of grain.
Pile up her dead bodies like heaps of
grain.
Completely destroy Babylon
and do not leave anyone alive.
27Kill all the young men in Babylon;
let them be killed like animals.
How terrible it will be for them, because
the time has come for their defeat;
it is time for them to be punished.
28Listen to the people running to escape the
country of Babylon!
They are telling Jerusalem
how the LORD our God is punishing
Babylon as it deserves
for destroying his Temple.
29"Call for the archers
to come against Babylon.
Tell them to surround the city,
and let no one escape.
Pay her back for what she has done;
do to her what she has done to other
nations.
Babylon acted with pride against the
LORD,
the Holy One of Israel.
30So her young men will be killed in her
streets.
All her soldiers will die on that day,"
says the LORD.
31"Babylon, you are too proud, and I am
against you,"
says the Lord GOD All-Powerful.
"The time has come
for you to be punished.
32Proud Babylon will stumble and fall,
and no one will help her get up.

I will start a fire in her towns,
and it will burn up everything around her."
33This is what the LORD All-Powerful says:
"The people of Israel
and Judah are slaves.
The enemy took them as prisoners
and won't let them go.
34But God is strong and will buy them back.
His name is the LORD All-Powerful.
He will surely defend them with power
so he can give rest to their land.
But he will not give rest to those living in Babylon."
35The LORD says,
"Let a sword kill the people living in Babylon
and her officers and wise men!
36Let a sword kill her false prophets,
and they will become fools.
Let a sword kill her warriors,
and they will be full of terror.
37Let a sword kill her horses and chariots
and all the soldiers hired from other countries!
Then they will be like frightened women.
Let a sword attack her treasures,
so they will be taken away.
38Let a sword attack her waters
so they will be dried up.
She is a land of idols,
and the people go crazy with fear over them.
39"Desert animals and hyenas will live there,
and owls will live there,
but no people will ever live there again.
She will never be filled with people again.
40God completely destroyed the cities of Sodom and Gomorrah
and the towns around them," says the LORD.
"In the same way no people will live in Babylon,
and no human being will stay there.
41"Look! An army is coming from the north.
A powerful nation and many kings
are coming together from all around the world.
42Their armies have bows and spears.
The soldiers are cruel and have no mercy.
As the soldiers come riding on their horses,
the sound is loud like the roaring sea.
They stand in their places, ready for battle.
They are ready to attack you, city of Babylon.
43The king of Babylon heard about those armies,
and he became helpless with fear.
Distress has gripped him.
His pain is like that of a woman giving birth to a baby.
44"Like a lion coming up from the thick bushes near the Jordan River
to attack a strong pen for sheep,
I will suddenly chase the people of Babylon from their land.
Who is the one I have chosen to do this?
There is no one like me,
no one who can take me to court.
None of their leaders can stand up against me."
45So listen to what the LORD has planned to do against Babylon.
Listen to what he has decided to do to the people in the city of Babylon.
He will surely drag away the young ones of Babylon.
Their hometowns will surely be shocked at what happens to them.
46At the sound of Babylon's capture, the earth will shake.
People in all nations will hear Babylon's cry of distress.

51 This is what the LORD says:
"I will soon cause a destroying wind to blow
against Babylon and the Babylonian people.
2I will send foreign people to destroy Babylon
like a wind that blows chaff away.
They will destroy the land.
Armies will surround the city
when the day of disaster comes upon her.
3Don't let the Babylonian soldiers prepare their bows to shoot.
Don't even let them put on their armor.
Don't feel sorry for the young men of Babylon,
but completely destroy her army.

4They will be killed in the land of the
Babylonians
and will die in her streets.
5The Lord God All-Powerful
did not leave Israel and Judah,
even though they were completely guilty
in the presence of the Holy One of
Israel.
6"Run away from Babylon
and save your lives!
Don't stay and be killed because of
Babylon's sins.
It is time for the LORD to punish Babylon;
he will give Babylon the punishment
she deserves.
7Babylon was like a gold cup in the LORD's
hand
that made the whole earth drunk.
The nations drank Babylon's wine,
so they went crazy.
8Babylon has suddenly fallen and been
broken.
Cry for her!
Get balm for her pain,
and maybe she can be healed.

9"Foreigners in Babylon say, 'We tried to
heal Babylon,
but she cannot be healed.
So let us leave her and each go to his own
country.
Babylon's punishment is as high as the
sky;
it reaches to the clouds.'
10"The people of Judah say, 'The LORD has
shown us to be right.
Come, let us tell in Jerusalem
what the LORD our God has done.'

11"Sharpen the arrows!
Pick up your shields!
The LORD has stirred up the kings of the
Medes,
because he wants to destroy Babylon.
The LORD will punish them as they
deserve
for destroying his Temple.
12Lift up a banner against the walls of
Babylon!
Bring more guards.
Put the watchmen in their places,
and get ready for a secret attack!
The LORD will certainly do what he has
planned
and what he said he would do against
the people of Babylon.
13People of Babylon, you live near much
water
and are rich with many treasures,
but your end as a nation has come.
It is time to stop you from robbing
other nations.
14The LORD All-Powerful has promised in
his own name:
'Babylon, I will surely fill you with so
many enemy soldiers they will be
like a swarm of locusts.
They will stand over you and shout
their victory.'
15"The LORD made the earth by his power.
He used his wisdom to build the world
and his understanding to stretch out
the skies.
16When he thunders, the waters in the skies
roar.
He makes clouds rise in the sky all over
the earth.
He sends lightning with the rain
and brings out the wind from his
storehouses.

17"People are so stupid and know so little.
Goldsmiths are made ashamed by their
idols,
because those statues are only false gods.
They have no breath in them.
18They are worth nothing; people make fun
of them.
When they are judged, they will be
destroyed.
19But God, who is Jacob's Portion, is not like
the idols.
He made everything,
and he chose Israel to be his special
people.
The LORD All-Powerful is his name.

20"You are my war club,
my battle weapon.
I use you to smash nations.
I use you to destroy kingdoms.
21I use you to smash horses and riders.
I use you to smash chariots and drivers.
22I use you to smash men and women.
I use you to smash old people and
young people.
I use you to smash young men and
young women.

devotion 219

JEREMIAH 51:15-16

NEED A TASTE OF MAJESTY?

Are you spiritually dry? Is this a season of spiritual drought or distance from God? Do you feel far away from the relationship you once knew? Maybe you are unsure in your faith, even questioning the presence of the Lord you worshiped so passionately before. Maybe you need to see God's majesty with your own eyes. Ask him to remind you. Maybe you need to feel the majesty of his presence. Then cry out to him. With only a taste of his majesty, your heart will begin to thirst for more.

Once you have begun to see the holy majesty of our God Almighty, you will begin to desire again his spiritual fullness in your life. Revival happens in the soul when we have eyes to see the holiness and magnificence of God. Jeremiah saw God in his power and his authority. He saw the thundering God. He knew the One who made the earth by his power. And Jeremiah desired the Lord with all his heart.

If you are dry and without hope, get down on your knees and bow your heart before God's majesty. Speak to him in prayer. Recount his power and his authority. Remember his strength and his wisdom. Wait there in quiet as your soul remembers the splendor of God. Return over and over to seek God's holiness. Remembering the greatness of God will revive your weary soul. Revival comes from seeing God for who he is and from remembering who we are not.

23 I use you to smash shepherds and flocks.
I use you to smash farmers and oxen.
I use you to smash governors and officers.

24 "But I will pay back Babylon and all the
Babylonians for all the evil things they did to
Jerusalem in your sight," says the LORD.

25 The LORD says,
"Babylon, you are a destroying mountain,
and I am against you.
You have destroyed the whole land.
I will put my hand out against you.
I will roll you off the cliffs,
and I will make you a burned-out mountain.

26 People will not find any rocks in Babylon big enough for cornerstones.
People will not take any rocks from Babylon to use for the foundation of a building,
because your city will be just a pile of ruins forever," says the LORD.

27 "Lift up a banner in the land!
Blow the trumpet among the nations!
Get the nations ready for battle against Babylon.
Call these kingdoms of Ararat, Minni, and Ashkenaz to fight against her.
Choose a commander to lead the army against Babylon.
Send so many horses that they are like a swarm of locusts.

28 Get the nations ready for battle against Babylon—
the kings of the Medes,
their governors and all their officers,
and all the countries they rule.

29 The land shakes and moves in pain,
because the LORD will do what he has planned to Babylon.
He will make Babylon an empty desert,
where no one will live.

30 Babylon's warriors have stopped fighting.
They stay in their protected cities.
Their strength is gone,

and they have become like frightened
women.
Babylon's houses are burning.
The bars of her gates are broken.
31 One messenger follows another;
messenger follows messenger.
They announce to the king of Babylon
that his whole city has been captured.
32 The river crossings have been captured,
and the swamplands are burning.
All of Babylon's soldiers are terribly
afraid."
33 This is what the LORD All-Powerful, the
God of Israel, says:
"The city of Babylon is like a threshing
floor,
where people crush the grain at harvest
time.
The time to harvest Babylon is coming
soon."
34 "Nebuchadnezzar king of Babylon has
defeated and destroyed us.
In the past he took our people away,
and we became like an empty jar.
He was like a giant snake that
swallowed us.
He filled his stomach with our best
things.
Then he spit us out.
35 Babylon did terrible things to hurt us.
Now let those things happen to
Babylon,"
say the people of Jerusalem.
"The people of Babylon killed our people.
Now let them be punished for what
they did," says Jerusalem.
36 So this is what the LORD says:
"I will soon defend you, Judah,
and make sure that Babylon is
punished.
I will dry up Babylon's sea
and make her springs become dry.
37 Babylon will become a pile of ruins,
a home for wild dogs.
People will be shocked by what happened
there.
No one will live there anymore.
38 Babylon's people roar like young lions;
they growl like baby lions.
39 While they are stirred up,
I will give a feast for them
and make them drunk.
They will shout and laugh.
And they will sleep forever and never
wake up!" says the LORD.
40 "I will take the people of Babylon to be
killed.
They will be like lambs,
like sheep and goats waiting to be
killed.

41 "How Babylon has been defeated!
The pride of the whole earth has been
taken captive.
People from other nations are shocked at
what happened to Babylon,
and the things they see make them
afraid.
42 The sea has risen over Babylon;
its roaring waves cover her.
43 Babylon's towns are ruined and empty.
It has become a dry, desert land,
a land where no one lives.
People do not even travel through
Babylon.
44 I will punish the god Bel in Babylon.
I will make him spit out what he has
swallowed.
Nations will no longer come to Babylon;
even the wall around the city will
fall.

45 "Come out of Babylon, my people!
Run for your lives!
Run from the LORD's great anger.
46 Don't lose courage;
rumors will spread through the land,
but don't be afraid.
One rumor comes this year, and another
comes the next year.
There will be rumors of terrible
fighting in the country,
of rulers fighting against rulers.
47 The time will surely come
when I will punish the idols of
Babylon,
and the whole land will be disgraced.
There will be many dead people lying
all around.
48 Then heaven and earth and all that is in
them
will shout for joy about Babylon.
They will shout because the army comes
from the north
to destroy Babylon," says the LORD.
49 "Babylon must fall, because she killed
people from Israel.

She killed people from everywhere on
earth.
50You who have escaped being killed with
swords,
leave Babylon! Don't wait!
Remember the LORD in the faraway
land
and think about Jerusalem."

51"We people of Judah are disgraced,
because we have been insulted.
We have been shamed,
because strangers have gone into
the holy places of the LORD's Temple!"

52So the LORD says, "The time is coming
soon
when I will punish the idols of
Babylon.
Wounded people will cry with pain
all over that land.
53Even if Babylon grows until she touches
the sky,
and even if she makes her highest cities
strong,
I will send people to destroy her," says
the LORD.
54"Sounds of people crying are heard in
Babylon.
Sounds of people destroying things
are heard in the land of the
Babylonians.
55The LORD is destroying Babylon
and making the loud sounds of the city
become silent.
Enemies come roaring in like ocean
waves.
The roar of their voices is heard all
around.
56The army has come to destroy Babylon.
Her soldiers have been captured,
and their bows are broken,
because the LORD is a God who punishes
people for the evil they do.
He gives them the full punishment
they deserve.
57I will make Babylon's rulers and wise men
drunk,
and her governors, officers, and
soldiers, too.
Then they will sleep forever and never
wake up," says the King,
whose name is the LORD All-Powerful.

58This is what the LORD All-Powerful says:
"Babylon's thick wall will be completely
pulled down
and her high gates burned.
The people will work hard, but it won't
help;
their work will only become fuel for
the flames!"

A Message to Babylon

59This is the message that Jeremiah the
prophet gave to the officer Seraiah son of
Neriah, who was the son of Mahseiah.
Seraiah went to Babylon with Zedekiah king
of Judah in the fourth year Zedekiah was
king of Judah. His duty was to arrange the
king's food and housing on the trip.
60Jeremiah had written on a scroll all the
terrible things that would happen to
Babylon, all these words about Babylon.
61Jeremiah said to Seraiah, "As soon as you
come to Babylon, be sure to read this
message so all the people can hear you.
62Then say, 'LORD, you have said that you
will destroy this place so that no people or
animals will live in it. It will be an empty
ruin forever.' 63After you finish reading this
scroll, tie a stone to it and throw it into the
Euphrates River. 64Then say, 'In the same
way Babylon will sink and will not rise
again because of the terrible things I will
make happen here. Her people will
fall.' "

The words of Jeremiah end here.

The Fall of Jerusalem

52 Zedekiah was twenty-one years old
when he became king, and he was
king in Jerusalem for eleven years. His
mother's name was Hamutal daughter of
Jeremiah,[n] and she was from Libnah.
2Zedekiah did what the LORD said was
wrong, just as Jehoiakim had done. 3All this
happened in Jerusalem and Judah because
the LORD was angry with them. Finally, he
threw them out of his presence.

Zedekiah turned against the king of
Babylon. 4Then Nebuchadnezzar king of
Babylon marched against Jerusalem with his
whole army. They made a camp around the
city and built devices all around the city
walls to attack it. This happened on

52:1 Jeremiah This is not the prophet Jeremiah but a different man with the same name.

Zedekiah's ninth year, tenth month, and tenth day as king. [5]And the city was under attack until Zedekiah's eleventh year as king.

[6]By the ninth day of the fourth month, the hunger was terrible in the city; there was no food for the people to eat. [7]Then the city wall was broken through, and the whole army of Judah ran away at night. They left the city through the gate between the two walls by the king's garden. Even though the Babylonians were surrounding the city, Zedekiah and his men headed toward the Jordan Valley.

[8]But the Babylonian army chased King Zedekiah and caught him in the plains of Jericho. All of his army was scattered from him. [9]So the Babylonians captured Zedekiah and took him to the king of Babylon at the town of Riblah in the land of Hamath. There he passed sentence on Zedekiah. [10]At Riblah the king of Babylon killed Zedekiah's sons as he watched. The king also killed all the officers of Judah. [11]Then he put out Zedekiah's eyes, and put bronze chains on him, and took him to Babylon. And the king kept Zedekiah in prison there until the day he died.

[12]Nebuzaradan, commander of the king's special guards and servant of the king of Babylon, came to Jerusalem on the tenth day of the fifth month. This was in Nebuchadnezzar's nineteenth year as king of Babylon. [13]Nebuzaradan set fire to the Temple of the LORD, the palace, and all the houses of Jerusalem; every important building was burned. [14]The whole Babylonian army, led by the commander of the king's special guards, broke down all the walls around Jerusalem. [15]Nebuzaradan, the commander of the king's special guards, took captive some of the poorest people, those who were left in Jerusalem, those who had surrendered to the king of Babylon, and the skilled craftsmen who were left in Jerusalem. [16]But Nebuzaradan left behind some of the poorest people of the land to take care of the vineyards and fields.

[17]The Babylonians broke into pieces the bronze pillars, the bronze stands, and the large bronze bowl, called the Sea, which were in the Temple of the LORD. Then they carried all the bronze pieces to Babylon. [18]They also took the pots, shovels, wick trimmers, bowls, dishes, and all the bronze objects used to serve in the Temple. [19]The commander of the king's special guards took away bowls, pans for carrying hot coals, large bowls, pots, lampstands, pans, and bowls used for drink offerings. He took everything that was made of pure gold or silver.

[20]There was so much bronze that it could not be weighed: two pillars, the large bronze bowl called the Sea with the twelve bronze bulls under it, and the movable stands, which King Solomon had made for the Temple of the LORD.

[21]Each of the pillars was about twenty-seven feet high, eighteen feet around, and hollow inside. The wall of each pillar was three inches thick. [22]The bronze capital on top of the one pillar was about seven and one-half feet high. It was decorated with a net design and bronze pomegranates all around it. The other pillar also had pomegranates and was like the first pillar. [23]There were ninety-six pomegranates on the sides of the pillars. There was a total of a hundred pomegranates above the net design.

[24]The commander of the king's special guards took as prisoners Seraiah the chief priest, Zephaniah the priest next in rank, and the three doorkeepers. [25]He also took from the city the officer in charge of the soldiers, seven people who advised the king, the royal secretary who selected people for the army, and sixty other men from Judah who were in the city when it fell. [26]Nebuzaradan, the commander, took these people and brought them to the king of Babylon at the town of Riblah. [27]There at Riblah, in the land of Hamath, the king had them killed.

So the people of Judah were led away from their country as captives. [28]This is the number of the people Nebuchadnezzar took away as captives: in the seventh year, 3,023 Jews; [29]in Nebuchadnezzar's eighteenth year, 832 people from Jerusalem; [30]in Nebuchadnezzar's twenty-third year, Nebuzaradan, commander of the king's special guards, took 745 Jews as captives.

In all 4,600 people were taken captive.

Jehoiachin Is Set Free

[31]Jehoiachin king of Judah was in prison in Babylon for thirty-seven years. The year

Evil-Merodach became king of Babylon he
let Jehoiachin king of Judah out of prison.
He set Jehoiachin free on the twenty-fifth
day of the twelfth month. 32 Evil-Merodach
spoke kindly to Jehoiachin and gave him a
seat of honor above the seats of the other
kings who were with him in Babylon. 33 So
Jehoiachin put away his prison clothes, and
for the rest of his life, he ate at the king's
table. 34 Every day the king of Babylon gave
Jehoiachin an allowance. This lasted as long
as he lived, until the day Jehoiachin died.

Lamentations

From the Greek translation of the Old Testament, which means "loud cries"

Person Holding the Pen God Wrote With: It's generally agreed that the author was *Jeremiah,* although he doesn't refer to himself by name in the text.

When the Text Was Written: Jeremiah wrote this sad eyewitness account sometime during or after Jerusalem's destruction at the hands of Babylonian King Nebuchadnezzar between 586 and 583 B.C.

Spiritual Posture of the Original Recipients: God's people are shrieking in grief over the murder of their sons, the destruction of their homes, and the torching of their beloved Temple.

Storyline Synopsis: Judah was in mourning, not unlike a widow who has been forced into slavery (Lam. 1:1). The Israelites' agony is expressed in five outbursts or "laments." The first cry communicates deep sorrow over their losses and the betrayal of their political allies (chapter 1); the second lament communicates their anger at God because of his divine wrath (chapter 2); the third communicates Jeremiah's personal grief regarding Judah's destruction (chapter 3); the fourth communicates the specific details of Judah's punishment and their desire for God to punish their enemies as well (chapter 4); and finally, the last lament communicates a prayer for the restoration of God's people (chapter 5). Lamentations (with the exception of chapter 5) is actually a collection of acrostic poems that use the Hebrew alphabet in sequence (as in, "A is for Apple, B is for Ball, C is for Cat . . ."). Lamentations could also be aptly titled *A Homily on Heartache.*

A Moment Worth Discussing: As dreary as the situation in Judah gets, God's compassion still never completely leaves his people. One of the most familiar passages regarding God's faithfulness is found in Lamentations 3:22–24. It is a great rose among thorns in this Old Testament book and points to the fact that God's love will never fade or fail! The passage also serves as a catalyst for a discussion about how appropriate discipline is a part of perfect love.

Interesting (But Likely to Be Overlooked) Characters: Chapter 5 alludes to the dissolution of the *Davidic monarchy* (Lam. 5:16). The kings that were supposed to come from David's descendants are no more, and the crown does not return to David's line until Jesus, the King of Kings, is born in Bethlehem.

Jerusalem Cries over Her Loss

1 Jerusalem once was full of people,
but now the city is empty.
Jerusalem once was a great city among
the nations,
but now she[n] is like a widow.
She was like a queen of all the other cities,
but now she is a slave.

2 She cries loudly at night,
and tears are on her cheeks.
There is no one to comfort her;
all who loved her are gone.
All her friends have turned against her
and are now her enemies.

3 Judah has gone into captivity
where she suffers and works hard.
She lives among other nations,
but she has found no rest.
Those who chased her caught her
when she was in trouble.

4 The roads to Jerusalem are sad,
because no one comes for the feasts.
No one passes through her gates.
Her priests groan,
her young women are suffering,
and Jerusalem suffers terribly.

5 Her foes are now her masters.
Her enemies enjoy the wealth they
have taken.
The LORD is punishing her
for her many sins.
Her children have gone away
as captives of the enemy.

6 The beauty of Jerusalem
has gone away.
Her rulers are like deer
that cannot find food.
They are weak
and run from the hunters.

7 Jerusalem is suffering and homeless.
She remembers all the good things
from the past.
But her people were defeated by the enemy,
and there was no one to help her.
When her enemies saw her,
they laughed to see her ruined.

8 Jerusalem sinned terribly,
so she has become unclean.
Those who honored her now hate her,
because they have seen her nakedness.
She groans
and turns away.

9 She made herself dirty by her sins
and did not think about what would
happen to her.
Her defeat was surprising,
and no one could comfort her.
She says, "LORD, see how I suffer,
because the enemy has won."

10 The enemy reached out and took
all her precious things.
She even saw foreigners
enter her Temple.
The LORD had commanded foreigners
never to enter the meeting place of his
people.

11 All of Jerusalem's people groan,
looking for bread.
They are trading their precious things for
food
so they can stay alive.
The city says, "Look, LORD, and see.
I am hated."

12 Jerusalem says, "You who pass by on the
road don't seem to care.
Come, look at me and see:
Is there any pain like mine?
Is there any pain like that he has
caused me?
The LORD has punished me
on the day of his great anger.

13 "He sent fire from above
that went down into my bones.
He stretched out a net for my feet
and turned me back.
He made me so sad and lonely
that I am weak all day.

14 "He has noticed my sins;
they are tied together by his hands;
they hang around my neck.
He has turned my strength into
weakness.
The Lord has handed me over
to those who are stronger than I.

15 "The Lord has rejected
all my mighty men inside my walls.

1:1 she In this poem the city of Jerusalem is described as a woman.

He brought an army against me
to destroy my young men.
As if in a winepress, the Lord has crushed
the capital city of Judah.

16"I cry about these things;
my eyes overflow with tears.
There is no one near to comfort me,
no one who can give me strength again.
My children are left sad and lonely,
because the enemy has won."

17Jerusalem reaches out her hands,
but there is no one to comfort her.
The LORD commanded the people of Jacob
to be surrounded by their enemies.
Jerusalem is now unclean
like those around her.

18Jerusalem says, "The LORD is right,
but I refused to obey him.
Listen, all you people,
and look at my pain.
My young women and men
have gone into captivity.

19"I called out to my friends,
but they turned against me.
My priests and my elders
have died in the city
while looking for food
to stay alive.

20"Look at me, LORD. I am upset
and greatly troubled.
My heart is troubled,
because I have been so stubborn.
Out in the streets, the sword kills;
inside the houses, death destroys.

21"People have heard my groaning,
and there is no one to comfort me.
All my enemies have heard of my trouble,
and they are happy you have done this
to me.
Now bring that day you have announced
so that my enemies will be like me.

22"Look at all their evil.
Do to them what you have done to me
because of all my sins.
I groan over and over again,
and I am afraid."

The Lord Destroyed Jerusalem

2 Look how the Lord in his anger
has brought Jerusalem to shame.
He has thrown down the greatness of
Israel
from the sky to the earth;
he did not remember the Temple, his
footstool,
on the day of his anger.

2The Lord swallowed up without mercy
all the houses of the people of Jacob;
in his anger he pulled down
the strong places of Judah.
He threw her kingdom and its rulers
down to the ground in dishonor.

3In his anger he has removed
all the strength of Israel;
he took away his power from Israel
when the enemy came.
He burned against the people of Jacob like
a flaming fire
that burns up everything around it.

4Like an enemy, he prepared to shoot his
bow,
and his hand was against us.
Like an enemy, he killed
all the good-looking people;
he poured out his anger like fire
on the tents of Jerusalem.

5The Lord was like an enemy;
he swallowed up Israel.
He swallowed up all her palaces
and destroyed all her strongholds.
He has caused more moaning and
groaning
for Judah.

6He cut down his Temple like a garden;
he destroyed the meeting place.
The LORD has made Jerusalem forget
the set feasts and Sabbath days.
He has rejected the king and the priest
in his great anger.

7The Lord has rejected his altar
and abandoned his Temple.
He has handed over to the enemy
the walls of Jerusalem's palaces.
Their uproar in the LORD's Temple
was like that of a feast day.

8The LORD planned to destroy
the wall around Jerusalem.
He measured the wall
and did not stop himself from
destroying it.

He made the walls and defenses sad;
together they have fallen.

9 Jerusalem's gates have fallen to the ground;
he destroyed and smashed the bars of the gates.
Her king and her princes are among the nations.
The teaching of the LORD has stopped,
and the prophets do not have
visions from the LORD.

10 The elders of Jerusalem
sit on the ground in silence.
They throw dust on their heads
and put on rough cloth to show their sadness.
The young women of Jerusalem
bow their heads to the ground in sorrow.

11 My eyes have no more tears,
and I am sick to my stomach.
I feel empty inside,
because my people have been destroyed.
Children and babies are fainting
in the streets of the city.

12 They ask their mothers,
"Where is the grain and wine?"
They faint like wounded soldiers
in the streets of the city
and die in their mothers' arms.

13 What can I say about you, Jerusalem?
What can I compare you to?
What can I say you are like?
How can I comfort you, Jerusalem?
Your ruin is as deep as the sea.
No one can heal you.

14 Your prophets saw visions,
but they were false and worth nothing.
They did not point out your sins
to keep you from being captured.
They preached what was false
and led you wrongly.

15 All who pass by on the road
clap their hands at you;
they make fun of Jerusalem
and shake their heads.

devotion 220

LAMENTATIONS 2:19

GOOD-BYE, CHICKEN LITTLE

Are you familiar with the word "lamentations"? To lament is to cry out in grief, to regret strongly, or to complain. This is something that I am really good at. When I feel like Chicken Little, I head straight for the couch to do a little lamenting of my own. The thing that gets me about this kind of behavior is it shows up when we hit the absolute bottom of our own resources. Why do we wait so long before we turn to the Lord with the condition of our hearts? I personally do not want to be Chicken Little. I want to be a great big spiritual giant, and I do not want my couch to be a Kleenex. I would much rather sit on it and have tea with a friend.

To overcome lamenting meltdowns, we need to be women who have healthy, rich prayer lives. I know when I find myself coming unglued, I can almost certainly trace it back to several consecutive days when everyone and everything else was more important than my time with the Lord. If we want to be stable Christian women, we have to establish our prayer roots so we are not rocked every time the wind blows in an adverse direction. Paul told the early church of Corinth that through faith in Christ, we can all display God's glory and be continually changed to become more like Jesus (2 Cor. 3:18). Good-bye Chicken Little—hello spiritual giant!

They ask, "Is this the city that people
called
the most beautiful city,
the happiest place on earth?"

16 All your enemies open their mouths
to speak against you.
They make fun and grind their teeth in
anger.
They say, "We have swallowed
you up.
This is the day we were waiting for!
We have finally seen it happen."

17 The LORD has done what he planned;
he has kept his word
that he commanded long ago.
He has destroyed without mercy,
and he has let your enemies laugh at
you.
He has strengthened your enemies.

18 The people cry out to the Lord.
Wall of Jerusalem,
let your tears flow
like a river day and night.
Do not stop
or let your eyes rest.

19 Get up, cry out in the night,
even as the night begins.
Pour out your heart like water
in prayer to the Lord.
Lift up your hands in prayer to him
for the life of your children
who are fainting with hunger
on every street corner.

20 Jerusalem says: "Look, LORD, and see
to whom you have done this.
Women eat their own babies,
the children they have cared for.
Priests and prophets are killed
in the Temple of the Lord.

21 "People young and old
lie outside on the ground.
My young women and young men
have been killed by the sword.
You killed them on the day of your
anger;
you killed them without mercy.

22 "You invited terrors to come against me
on every side,
as if you were inviting them to a
feast.
No one escaped or remained alive
on the day of the LORD's anger.
My enemy has killed
those I cared for and brought up."

The Meaning of Suffering

3 I am a man who has seen the suffering
that comes from the rod of the LORD's
anger.
2 He led me
into darkness, not light.
3 He turned his hand against me
again and again, all day long.

4 He wore out my flesh and skin
and broke my bones.
5 He surrounded me with sadness
and attacked me with grief.
6 He made me sit in the dark,
like those who have been dead a long
time.

7 He shut me in so I could not get out;
he put heavy chains on me.
8 I cry out and beg for help,
but he ignores my prayer.
9 He blocked my way with a stone wall
and led me in the wrong direction.

10 He is like a bear ready to attack me,
like a lion in hiding.
11 He led me the wrong way and let me stray
and left me without help.
12 He prepared to shoot his bow
and made me the target for his
arrows.

13 He shot me in the kidneys
with the arrows from his bag.
14 I was a joke to all my people,
who make fun of me with songs all day
long.
15 The LORD filled me with misery;
he made me drunk with suffering.

16 He broke my teeth with gravel
and trampled me into the dirt.
17 I have no more peace.
I have forgotten what happiness is.
18 I said, "My strength is gone,
and I have no hope in the LORD."
19 LORD, remember my suffering and my
misery,
my sorrow and trouble.
20 Please remember me
and think about me.

21 But I have hope
when I think of this:
22 The LORD's love never ends;
his mercies never stop.
23 They are new every morning;
LORD, your loyalty is great.
24 I say to myself, "The LORD is mine,
so I hope in him."
25 The LORD is good to those who hope in him,
to those who seek him.
26 It is good to wait quietly
for the LORD to save.
27 It is good for someone to work hard
while he is young.
28 He should sit alone and be quiet;
the LORD has given him hard work to do.
29 He should bow down to the ground;
maybe there is still hope.
30 He should let anyone slap his cheek;
he should be filled with shame.
31 The Lord will not reject
his people forever.
32 Although he brings sorrow,
he also has mercy and great love.
33 He does not like to punish people
or make them sad.
34 He sees if any prisoner of the earth
is crushed under his feet;
35 he sees if someone is treated unfairly
before the Most High God;
36 the Lord sees
if someone is cheated in his case in court.
37 Nobody can speak and have it happen
unless the Lord commands it.
38 Both bad and good things
come by the command of the Most High God.
39 No one should complain
when he is punished for his sins.
40 Let us examine and see what we have done
and then return to the LORD.
41 Let us lift up our hands and pray from our hearts
to God in heaven:
42 "We have sinned and turned against you,
and you have not forgiven us.

devotion 221

LAMENTATIONS 3:22–24

MERCY THAT NEVER ENDS

God's mercies never end, but sometimes we're too distracted to see them. My friend Bertha died this week. She was a precious seventy-six-year-old woman who lived a hard, difficult life. She was born in Georgia in 1929. Her mother died when she was five years old. She never went to school and never learned to read or write. She worked most of her life as a maid in a big hotel chain and had one son who was killed in jail. She saved her money and bought her own home twenty years ago. When she had to quit working, she lived on Social Security and the occasional generosity of others.

But when you talked to Bertha, she would tell you that God's mercies never end. She loved the Lord and trusted him with her life. She would tell you that God was faithful when her electricity and water were turned off, when her refrigerator was empty, and when the heat was unbearable. She always talked of God's mercies in the midst of a difficult life. In fact, God's mercies were the only thing she knew she could depend on. Bertha understood God's faithfulness in the midst of pain. She understood God's mercy.

So the question is, do you? Is there an area of your life that's feeling a little shaky right now—a little uncertain? Try shifting your perspective to get a good look at God's never-ending love. Like Bertha, plant your hope firmly in the loyalty and rich mercies of Jesus.

43"You wrapped yourself in anger and
chased us;
you killed us without mercy.
44You wrapped yourself in a cloud,
and no prayer could get through.
45You made us like scum and trash
among the other nations.

46"All of our enemies
open their mouths and speak against us.
47We have been frightened and fearful,
ruined and destroyed."
48Streams of tears flow from my eyes,
because my people are destroyed.

49My tears flow continually,
without stopping,
50until the LORD looks down
and sees from heaven.
51I am sad when I see
what has happened to all the women of
my city.

52Those who are my enemies for no reason
hunted me like a bird.
53They tried to kill me in a pit;
they threw stones at me.
54Water came up over my head,
and I said, "I am going to die."
55I called out to you, LORD,
from the bottom of the pit.
56You heard me calling, "Do not close your
ears
and ignore my gasps and shouts."
57You came near when I called to you;
you said, "Don't be afraid."

58Lord, you have taken my case
and given me back my life.
59LORD, you have seen how I have been
wronged.
Now judge my case for me.
60You have seen how my enemies took
revenge on me
and made evil plans against me.

61LORD, you have heard their insults
and all their evil plans against me.
62The words and thoughts of my enemies
are against me all the time.
63Look! In everything they do
they make fun of me with songs.

64Pay them back, LORD,
for what they have done.
65Make them stubborn,
and put your curse on them.
66Chase them in anger, LORD,
and destroy them from under your
heavens.

The Attack on Jerusalem

4 See how the gold has lost its shine,
how the pure gold has dulled!
The stones of the Temple are scattered
at every street corner.

2The precious people of Jerusalem
were more valuable than gold,
but now they are thought of as clay jars
made by the hands of a potter.

3Even wild dogs give their milk
to feed their young,
but my people are cruel
like ostriches in the desert.

4The babies are so thirsty
their tongues stick to the roofs of their
mouths.
Children beg for bread,
but no one gives them any.

5Those who once ate fine foods
are now starving in the streets.
People who grew up wearing nice
clothes
now pick through trash piles.

6My people have been punished
more than Sodom was.
Sodom was destroyed suddenly,
and no hands reached out to help her.

7Our princes were purer than snow,
and whiter than milk.
Their bodies were redder than rubies;
they looked like sapphires.

8But now they are blacker than coal,
and no one recognizes them in the
streets.
Their skin hangs on their bones;
it is as dry as wood.

9Those who were killed in the war were
better off
than those killed by hunger.
They starve in pain and die,
because there is no food from the field.

10With their own hands kind women
cook their own children.
They became food
when my people were destroyed.

[11]The LORD turned loose all of his anger;
he poured out his strong anger.
He set fire to Jerusalem,
burning it down to the foundations.

[12]Kings of the earth and people of the world
could not believe
that enemies and foes
could enter the gates of Jerusalem.

[13]It happened because her prophets sinned
and her priests did evil.
They killed in the city
those who did what was right.

[14]They wandered in the streets
as if they were blind.
They were dirty with blood,
so no one would touch their clothes.

[15]"Go away! You are unclean," people
shouted at them.
"Get away! Get away! Don't touch us!"
So they ran away and wandered.
Even the other nations said, "Don't stay
here."

[16]The LORD himself scattered them
and did not look after them anymore.
No one respects the priests
or honors the elders.

[17]Also, our eyes grew tired,
looking for help that never came.
We kept watch from our towers
for a nation to save us.

[18]Our enemies hunted us,
so we could not even walk in the streets.
Our end is near. Our time is up.
Our end has come.

[19]Those who chased us
were faster than eagles in the sky.
They ran us into the mountains
and ambushed us in the desert.

[20]The LORD's appointed king, who was our
very breath,
was caught in their traps.
We had said about him, "We will be
protected by him
among the nations."

[21]Be happy and glad, people of Edom,
you who live in the land of Uz.
The cup of God's anger will come to you;
then you will get drunk and go naked.

devotion 222

LAMENTATIONS 5:19

COME MORNING

I sit here tonight and watch the news as another hurricane roars toward the Gulf Coast. It is an overwhelming image to see the hurricane on the radar. No one can stop it. No one can tell you exactly where it will go. It gives us a glimpse into the power of God. And yet even with all the warnings, all of the pleading by the newscasters, some people are sitting in bars drinking, unfazed by the whole event, when they could be escaping. They don't fear God *or* a hurricane. Somehow they think that they are invincible. Other people have no means to escape the fury of the storm. They just have to wait it out. They have to trust God to see them through.

Our King is all-powerful, and our King is love. He cares for those people more than you or I possibly could. I am praying for the people of the Gulf tonight with a heart of compassion. I have to ask God how this could be a good thing. So many will suffer tonight, and I have to ask why. The King doesn't have to explain himself, and yet we can trust our God. He will be in the midst of the hurricane. He will not abandon those left behind by society tonight. He will bring many people to their knees, and he will answer prayers. There will be destruction, and there will be loss. But come morning, God will still be the King of Kings.

22 Your punishment is complete, Jerusalem.
He will not send you into captivity again.
But the LORD will punish the sins of Edom;
he will uncover your evil.

A Prayer to the Lord

5 Remember, LORD, what happened to us.
Look and see our disgrace.
2 Our land has been turned over to strangers;
our houses have been given to foreigners.
3 We are like orphans with no father;
our mothers are like widows.
4 We have to buy the water we drink;
we must pay for the firewood.
5 Those who chase after us want to catch us by the neck.
We are tired and find no rest.
6 We made an agreement with Egypt
and with Assyria to get enough food.
7 Our ancestors sinned against you, but they are gone;
now we suffer because of their sins.
8 Slaves have become our rulers,
and no one can save us from them.
9 We risk our lives to get our food;
we face death in the desert.
10 Our skin is hot like an oven;
we burn with starvation.
11 The enemy abused the women of Jerusalem
and the girls in the cities of Judah.
12 Princes were hung by the hands;
they did not respect our elders.
13 The young men ground grain at the mill,
and boys stumbled under loads of wood.
14 The elders no longer sit at the city gates;
the young men no longer sing.
15 We have no more joy in our hearts;
our dancing has turned to sadness.
16 The crown has fallen from our head.
How terrible it is because we sinned.
17 Because of this we are afraid,
and now our eyes are dim.
18 Mount Zion is empty,
and wild dogs wander around it.

19 But you rule forever, LORD.
You will be King from now on.
20 Why have you forgotten us for so long?
Have you left us forever?
21 Bring us back to you, LORD, and we will return.
Make our days as they were before,
22 or have you completely rejected us?
Are you so angry with us?

Ezekiel

A Hebrew word that means "strengthened by God"

Person Holding the Pen God Wrote With: *Ezekiel,* who was both a prophet and a priest (Ezek. 1:3)

When the Text Was Written: This book was written between 597 and 572 B.C., according to various indications in the text pointing to the years of captivity in Babylon.

Spiritual Posture of the Original Recipients: In spite of the strong-arm tactics of the invading Babylonian army, many of the Jews still in Jerusalem were just going about life as usual, operating under the false security that somehow they had been spared from God's judgment. They were spiritually nearsighted.

Storyline Synopsis: Ezekiel was deported to Babylon when the second wave of Israelites were forced out of Jerusalem in 597 B.C. (the full deportation project took almost twenty years). His captivity prompted Ezekiel to jump on a soapbox to warn the rest of the Jews still residing in the Holy City that if they didn't repent, they'd soon be huddled behind the "bars" of Babylon, too! God encouraged Ezekiel by appearing to him in fantastic visions (chapters 1—5), compelling him to describe the ominous "Day of the Lord," which involved God's punishment of sin, the necessary purging, and God's provision of salvation (chapters 6—7). Ezekiel continued his prophecy by announcing the exit of God's glory (chapters 8—11) and pronouncing judgment against Jerusalem (chapters 12—24). Midway through this monologue, the prophet abruptly changes his tone: he goes from dire predictions about God's discipline to the exciting plans God has for Israel's future (chapters 25—48). After finding out that Jerusalem had indeed been completely demolished (Ezek. 33:21), his focus shifts to the restoration of their homeland and the future messianic kingdom. Ezekiel is a classic "bad news, good news" book.

A Moment Worth Discussing: Ezekiel 37:1–14 records an eye-popping prophecy. God gives Ezekiel a vivid dream regarding a bunch of skeletons scattered around in a dry, desolate valley. When this wide-eyed Jewish man obeys Jehovah's command to prophesy to the bones, they rattle across the desert floor and form a living nation! This dramatic imagery reveals that God will fulfill his promise to resurrect the Israelites. It's also a good place to discuss whether or not God is always true to his word.

Interesting (But Likely to Be Overlooked) Characters: *The Ammonites,* who often opposed Israel and were singled out as recipients of God's wrath (chapter 25), were an especially ignoble crew as they came from an incestuous relationship between Lot and his daughter (Gen. 19:30–38).

Ezekiel's Vision of Living Creatures

1 It was the thirtieth year, on the fifth day
of the fourth month of our captivity. I
was by the Kebar River among the people
who had been carried away as captives. The
sky opened, and I saw visions of God.
2 It was the fifth day of the month of the
fifth year that King Jehoiachin had been a
prisoner. 3 The LORD spoke his word to
Ezekiel son of Buzi in the land of the
Babylonians by the Kebar River. There he felt
the power of the LORD.
4 When I looked, I saw a stormy wind
coming from the north. There was a great
cloud with a bright light around it and fire
flashing out of it. Something that looked like
glowing metal was in the center of the fire.
5 Inside the cloud was what looked like four
living creatures, who were shaped like
humans, 6 but each of them had four faces
and four wings. 7 Their legs were straight.
Their feet were like a calf's hoofs and
sparkled like polished bronze. 8 The living
creatures had human hands under their
wings on their four sides. All four of them
had faces and wings, 9 and their wings
touched each other. The living creatures did
not turn when they moved, but each went
straight ahead.
10 Their faces looked like this: Each living
creature had a human face and the face of a
lion on the right side and the face of an ox
on the left side. And each one also had the
face of an eagle. 11 That was what their faces
looked like. Their wings were spread out
above. Each had two wings that touched one
of the other living creatures and two wings
that covered its body. 12 Each went straight
ahead. Wherever the spirit would go, the
living creatures would also go, without
turning. 13 The living creatures looked like
burning coals of fire or like torches. Fire
went back and forth among the living
creatures. It was bright, and lightning
flashed from it. 14 The living creatures ran
back and forth like bolts of lightning.
15 Now as I looked at the living creatures, I
saw a wheel on the ground by each of the
living creatures with its four faces. 16 The
wheels and the way they were made were
like this: They looked like sparkling
chrysolite. All four of them looked the same,
like one wheel crossways inside another
wheel. 17 When they moved, they went in
any one of the four directions, without
turning as they went. 18 The rims of the
wheels were high and frightening and were
full of eyes all around.
19 When the living creatures moved, the
wheels moved beside them. When the living
creatures were lifted up from the ground, the
wheels also were lifted up. 20 Wherever the
spirit would go, the living creatures would
go. And the wheels were lifted up beside
them, because the spirit of the living
creatures was in the wheels. 21 When the
living creatures moved, the wheels moved.
When the living creatures stopped, the
wheels stopped. And when the living
creatures were lifted from the ground, the
wheels were lifted beside them, because the
spirit of the living creatures was in the
wheels.
22 Now, over the heads of the living
creatures was something like a dome that
sparkled like ice and was frightening. 23 And
under the dome the wings of the living
creatures were stretched out straight toward
one another. Each living creature also had
two wings covering its body. 24 I heard the
sound of their wings, like the roaring sound
of the sea, as they moved. It was like the
voice of God Almighty, a roaring sound like
a noisy army. When the living creatures
stopped, they lowered their wings.
25 A voice came from above the dome over
the heads of the living creatures. When the
living creatures stopped, they lowered their
wings. 26 Now above the dome there was
something that looked like a throne. It
looked like a sapphire gem. And on the
throne was a shape like a human. 27 Then I
noticed that from the waist up the shape
looked like glowing metal with fire inside.
From the waist down it looked like fire, and
a bright light was all around. 28 The
surrounding glow looked like the rainbow
in the clouds on a rainy day. It seemed to
look like the glory of the LORD. So when I
saw it, I bowed facedown on the ground and
heard a voice speaking.

The Lord Speaks to Ezekiel

2 He said to me, "Human, stand up on your
feet so I may speak with you." 2 While he
spoke to me, the Spirit entered me and put

me on my feet. Then I heard the LORD
speaking to me.
3He said, "Human, I am sending you to the
people of Israel. That nation has turned
against me and broken away from me. They
and their ancestors have sinned against me
until this very day. 4I am sending you to
people who are stubborn and who do not
obey. You will say to them, 'This is what the
Lord GOD says.' 5They may listen, or they
may not, since they are a people who have
turned against me. But they will know that a
prophet has been among them. 6You,
human, don't be afraid of the people or their
words. Even though they may be like thorny
branches and stickers all around you, and
though you may feel like you live with
poisonous insects, don't be afraid. Don't be
afraid of their words or their looks, because
they are a people who turn against me. 7But
speak my words to them. They may listen, or
they may not, because they turn against me.
8But you, human, listen to what I say to you.
Don't turn against me as those people do.
Open your mouth and eat what I am giving
you."
9Then I looked and saw a hand stretched
out to me, and a scroll was in it. 10He opened
the scroll in front of me. Funeral songs, sad
writings, and words about troubles were
written on the front and back.

3 Then the LORD said to me, "Human, eat
what you find; eat this scroll. Then go and
speak to the people of Israel." 2So I opened
my mouth, and he gave me the scroll to eat.
3He said to me, "Human, eat this scroll
which I am giving you, and fill your
stomach with it." Then I ate it, and it was as
sweet as honey in my mouth.
4Then he said to me, "Human, go to the
people of Israel, and speak my words to
them. 5You are not being sent to people
whose speech you can't understand, whose
language is difficult. You are being sent to
Israel. 6You are not being sent to many
nations whose speech you can't understand,
whose language is difficult, whose words
you cannot understand. If I had sent you to
them, they would have listened to you. 7But
the people of Israel will not be willing to
listen to you, because they are not willing to
listen to me. Yes, all the people of Israel are

devotion 223

EZEKIEL 2:4–8

WHEN GOD SAYS, "NOW!"

When God sends you out with a passion and a purpose, you must go. Even if the people around you are stubborn and even if you feel afraid. When God sends you, there is a power attached to his sending. When God anoints you, even a woman who is timid or afraid can step out with confidence.

I promise you this: when God sends you, there will be obstacles. People will distance themselves from you. You will hear the rumors. Some will encourage you, but many will stay behind. Some days it will feel like you are all alone and that you are the only one persevering with God's message of freedom and hope. But this I also know: when God sends you, he holds you close. He makes paths for you where there have been none before. He lifts you up and over the stubborn people who harass you. He is glorified in your obedience.

Sometimes after I have spoken to a group of women, someone will say to me, "I had never heard of you before." I smile to myself and say to her, "I know. Yet God has known me all this time. It's taken years for him to get me ready to deliver his message."

God is making you ready. And when you hear him say, "Now!" then head out in a righteous confidence. Don't look around at the people who aren't listening. Don't stand still in your fear. Just go—and go for his glory.

stubborn and will not obey. 8See, I now
make you as stubborn and as hard as they
are. 9I am making you as hard as a diamond,
harder than stone. Don't be afraid of them or
be frightened by them, though they are a
people who turn against me."

10Also, he said to me, "Human, believe all
the words I will speak to you, and listen
carefully to them. 11Then go to the captives,
your own people, and say to them, 'The Lord
GOD says this.' Tell them this whether they
listen or not."

12Then the Spirit lifted me up, and I heard
a loud rumbling sound behind me, saying,
"Praise the glory of the LORD in heaven." 13I
heard the wings of the living creatures
touching each other and the sound of the
wheels by them. It was a loud rumbling
sound. 14So the Spirit lifted me up and took
me away. I was unhappy and angry, and I felt
the great power of the LORD. 15I came to the
captives from Judah, who lived by the Kebar
River at Tel Abib. I sat there seven days
where these people lived, feeling shocked.

Israel's Warning

16After seven days the LORD spoke his
word to me again. He said, 17"Human, I now
make you a watchman for Israel. Any time
you hear a word from my mouth, warn them
for me. 18When I say to the wicked, 'You will
surely die,' you must warn them so they may
live. If you don't speak out to warn the
wicked to stop their evil ways, they will die
in their sin. But I will hold you responsible
for their death. 19If you warn the wicked and
they do not turn from their wickedness or
their evil ways, they will die because of their
sin. But you will have saved your life.

20"Again, those who do right may turn
away from doing good and do evil. If I make
something bad happen to them, they will
die. Because you have not warned them, they
will die because of their sin, and the good
they did will not be remembered. But I will
hold you responsible for their deaths. 21But if
you have warned those good people not to
sin, and they do not sin, they will surely live,
because they believed the warning. And you
will have saved your life."

22Then I felt the power of the LORD there.
He said to me, "Get up and go out to the
plain. There I will speak to you." 23So I got
up and went out to the plain. I saw the glory
of the LORD standing there, like the glory I
saw by the Kebar River, and I bowed
facedown on the ground.

24Then the Spirit entered me and made
me stand on my feet. He spoke to me and
said, "Go, shut yourself up in your house.
25As for you, human, the people will tie you
up with ropes so that you will not be able to
go out among them. 26Also, I will make your
tongue stick to the roof of your mouth so
you will be silent. You will not be able to
argue with the people, even though they
turn against me. 27But when I speak to you, I
will open your mouth, and you will say to
them, 'The Lord GOD says this.' Those who
will listen, let them listen. Those who refuse,
let them refuse, because they are a people
who turn against me.

The Map of Jerusalem

4 "Now, human, get yourself a brick, put it
in front of you, and draw a map of
Jerusalem on it. 2Then surround it with an
army. Build battle works against the city and
a dirt road to the top of the city walls. Set up
camps around it, and put heavy logs in place
to break down the walls. 3Then get yourself
an iron plate and set it up like an iron wall
between you and the city. Turn your face
toward the city as if to attack it and then
attack. This is a sign to Israel.

4"Then lie down on your left side, and
take the guilt of Israel on yourself. Their
guilt will be on you for the number of days
you lie on your left side. 5I have given you
the same number of days as the years of the
people's sin. So you will have the guilt of
Israel's sin on you for three hundred ninety
days.

6"After you have finished these three
hundred ninety days, lie down a second
time, on your right side. You will then have
the guilt of Judah on you. I will give it to you
for forty days, a day for each year of their sin.
7Then you will look toward Jerusalem,
which is being attacked. With your arm
bare, you will prophesy against Jerusalem.
8I will put ropes on you so you cannot turn
from one side to the other until you have
finished the days of your attack on
Jerusalem.

9"Take wheat, barley, beans, small peas,
and millet seeds, and put them in one bowl,
and make them into bread for yourself. You

will eat it the three hundred ninety days you lie on your side. 10 You will eat eight ounces of food every day at set times. 11 You will drink about two-thirds of a quart of water every day at set times. 12 Eat your food as you would eat a barley cake, baking it over human dung where the people can see." 13 Then the LORD said, "In the same way Israel will eat unclean food among the nations where I force them to go."

14 But I said, "No, Lord GOD! I have never been made unclean. From the time I was young until now I've never eaten anything that died by itself or was torn by animals. Unclean meat has never entered my mouth."

15 "Very well," he said. "Then I will give you cow's dung instead of human dung to use for your fire to bake your bread."

16 He also said to me, "Human, I am going to cut off the supply of bread to Jerusalem. They will eat the bread that is measured out to them, and they will worry as they eat. They will drink water that is measured out to them, and they will be in shock as they drink it. 17 This is because bread and water will be hard to find. The people will be shocked at the sight of each other, and they will become weak because of their sin.

Ezekiel Cuts His Hair

5 "Now, human, take a sharp sword, and use it like a barber's razor to shave your head and beard. Then take scales and weigh and divide the hair. 2 Burn one-third with fire in the middle of the city when the days of the attack on Jerusalem are over. Then take one-third and cut it up with the knife all around the city. And scatter one-third to the wind. This is how I will chase them with a sword. 3 Also take a few of these hairs and tie them in the folds of your clothes. 4 Take a few more and throw them into the fire and burn them up. From there a fire will spread to all the people of Israel.

5 "This is what the Lord GOD says: This is Jerusalem. I have put her at the center of the nations with countries all around her. 6 But she has refused to obey my laws and has been more evil than the nations. She has refused to obey my rules, even more than nations around her. The people of Jerusalem have rejected my laws and have not lived by my rules.

7 "So this is what the Lord GOD says: You have caused more trouble than the nations around you. You have not followed my rules or obeyed my laws. You have not even obeyed the laws of the nations around you.

8 "So this is what the Lord GOD says: I myself am against you, and I will punish you as the nations watch. 9 I will do things among you that I have not done before and that I will never do anything like again, because you do the things I hate. 10 So parents among you will eat their children, and children will eat their parents. I will punish you and will scatter to the winds all who are left alive. 11 So the Lord GOD says: You have made my Temple unclean with all your evil idols and the hateful things you do. Because of this, as surely as I live, I will cut you off. I will have no pity, and I will show no mercy. 12 A third of you will die by disease or be destroyed by hunger inside your walls. A third will fall dead by the sword outside your walls. And a third I will scatter in every direction as I chase them with a sword. 13 Then my anger will come to an end. I will use it up against them, and then I will be satisfied. Then they will know that I, the LORD, have spoken. After I have carried out my anger against them, they will know how strongly I felt.

14 "I will make you a ruin and a shame among the nations around you, to be seen by all who pass by. 15 Then the nations around you will shame you and make fun of you. You will be a warning and a terror to them. This will happen when I punish you in my great anger. I, the LORD, have spoken. 16 I will send a time of hunger to destroy you, and then I will make your hunger get even worse, and I will cut off your supply of food. 17 I will send a time of hunger and wild animals against you, and they will kill your children. Disease and death will sweep through your people, and I will bring the sword against you to kill you. I, the LORD, have spoken."

Prophecies Against the Mountains

6 Again the LORD spoke his word to me, saying: 2 "Human, look toward the mountains of Israel, and prophesy against them. 3 Say, 'Mountains of Israel, listen to the word of the Lord GOD. The Lord GOD says this to the mountains, the hills, the ravines, and the valleys: I will bring a sword against

you, and I will destroy your places of idol
worship. 4Your altars will be destroyed and
your incense altars broken down. Your
people will be killed in front of your idols. 5I
will lay the dead bodies of the Israelites in
front of their idols, and I will scatter your
bones around your altars. 6In all the places
you live, cities will become empty. The
places of idol worship will be ruined; your
altars will become lonely ruins. Your idols
will be broken and brought to an end. Your
incense altars will be cut down, and the
things you made will be wiped out. 7Your
people will be killed and fall among you.
Then you will know that I am the LORD.
8" 'But I will leave some people alive; some
will not be killed by the nations when you
are scattered among the foreign lands. 9Then
those who have escaped will remember me,
as they live among the nations where they
have been taken as captives. They will
remember how I was hurt because they were
unfaithful to me and turned away from me
and desired to worship their idols. They will
hate themselves because of the evil things
they did that I hate. 10Then they will know
that I am the LORD. I did not bring this
terrible thing on them for no reason.
11" 'This is what the Lord GOD says: Clap
your hands, stamp your feet, and groan
because of all the hateful, evil things the
people of Israel have done. They will die by
war, hunger, and disease. 12The person who
is far away will die by disease. The one who
is nearby will die in war. The person who is
still alive and has escaped these will die from
hunger. So I will carry out my anger on
them. 13Their people will lie dead among
their idols around the altars, on every high
hill, on all the mountain tops, and under
every green tree and leafy oak—all the
places where they offered sweet-smelling
incense to their idols. Then you will know
that I am the LORD. 14I will use my power
against them to make the land empty and
wasted from the desert to Diblah, wherever
they live. Then they will know that I am the
LORD.' "

Ezekiel Tells of the End

7 Again the LORD spoke his word to me,
saying: 2"Human, the Lord GOD says this
to the land of Israel: An end! The end has
come on the four corners of the land. 3Now
the end has come for you, and I will send my
anger against you. I will judge you for the
way you have lived, and I will make you pay
for all your actions that I hate. 4I will have
no pity on you; I will not hold back
punishment from you. Instead, I will make
you pay for the way you have lived and for
your actions that I hate. Then you will know
that I am the LORD.
5"This is what the Lord GOD says: Disaster
on top of disaster is coming. 6The end has
come! The end has come! It has stirred itself
up against you! Look! It has come! 7Disaster
has come for you who live in the land! The
time has come; the day of confusion is near.
There will be no happy shouting on the
mountains. 8Soon I will pour out my anger
against you; I will carry out my anger against
you. I will judge you for the way you have
lived and will make you pay for everything
you have done that I hate. 9I will show no
pity, and I will not hold back punishment. I
will pay you back for the way you have lived
and the things you have done that I hate.
Then you will know that I am the LORD who
punishes.
10"Look, the day is here. It has come.
Disaster has come, violence has grown, and
there is more pride than ever. 11Violence has
grown into a weapon for punishing
wickedness. None of the people will be
left—none of that crowd, none of their
wealth, and nothing of value. 12The time has
come; the day has arrived. Don't let the
buyer be happy or the seller be sad, because
my burning anger is against the whole
crowd. 13Sellers will not return to the land
they have sold as long as they live, because
the vision against all that crowd will not be
changed. Because of their sins, they will not
save their lives. 14They have blown the
trumpet, and everything is ready. But no one
is going to the battle, because my anger is
against all that crowd.
15"The sword is outside, and disease and
hunger are inside. Whoever is in the field
will die by the sword. Hunger and disease
will destroy those in the city. 16Those who
are left alive and who escape will be on the
mountains, moaning like doves of the
valleys about their own sin. 17All hands will
hang weakly with fear, and all knees will
become weak as water. 18They will put on
rough cloth to show how sad they are.

They will tremble all over with fear. Their
faces will show their shame, and all their
heads will be shaved. 19The people will
throw their silver into the streets, and their
gold will be like trash. Their silver and gold
will not save them from the LORD's anger.
It will not satisfy their hunger or fill their
stomachs, because it caused them to fall into
sin. 20They were proud of their beautiful
jewelry and used it to make their idols and
their evil statues, which I hate. So I will turn
their wealth into trash. 21I will give it to
foreigners as loot from war and to the most
evil people in the world as treasure, and they
will dishonor it. 22I will also turn away from
the people of Israel, and they will dishonor
my treasured place. Then robbers will enter
and dishonor it.
23"Make chains for captives, because the
land is full of bloody crimes and the city is
full of violence. 24So I will bring the worst of
the nations to take over the people's houses. I
will also end the pride of the strong, and
their holy places will be dishonored. 25When
the people are suffering greatly, they will
look for peace, but there will be none.
26Disaster will come on top of disaster, and
rumor will be added to rumor. Then they
will try to get a vision from a prophet; the
teachings of God from the priest and the
advice from the elders will be lost. 27The king
will cry greatly, the prince will give up hope,
and the hands of the people who own land
will shake with fear. I will punish them for
the way they have lived. The way they have
judged others is the way I will judge them.
Then they will know that I am the LORD."

Ezekiel's Vision of Jerusalem

8 It was the sixth year, on the fifth day of
the sixth month of our captivity. I was
sitting in my house with the elders of Judah
in front of me. There I felt the power of the
Lord GOD. 2I looked and saw something that
looked like a human. From the waist down
it looked like fire, and from the waist up it
looked like bright glowing metal. 3It
stretched out the shape of a hand and caught
me by the hair on my head. The Spirit lifted
me up between the earth and the sky. He
took me in visions of God to Jerusalem, to
the entrance to the north gate of the inner

devotion 224

EZEKIEL 7:19

BUSY, BUSY, BUSY

It's so easy to get caught up in meeting the needs of all the people in our lives. You have a family to take care of, bills to be paid, friends that need help, and, if that is not enough, acts of service you volunteered for but have no idea how to finish. Sweet Christian, you are in danger if you operate in self-faith—doing everything in your own strength instead of God's. This verse says that money will not fill the hunger in our souls, but it's not just money that causes caution—it's all the people pleasing, running to and fro, and the go-go-going all the time! The minute the phone rings, do you tear out the door, or do you seek the Holy Spirit for his direction? Sometimes the Lord is trying to reveal himself to others in their circumstances, but the Spirit loses out because you rush in.

There will always be needs (and I'm not telling you to sit on the couch and eat bonbons), but there is a very real spiritual principal for seeking the Lord as your provision, which means direction, too! You will be rich in all that the Lord has for you, and you will soon see that schedules, money, and endless doing will become less of who you are as God becomes more of your strength. Your soul will be satisfied in your intimate communion with the Holy Spirit. Have a God-faith day, and remember to rely on God's strength and direction for today.

courtyard of the Temple. In the courtyard
was the idol that caused God to be jealous.
4I saw the glory of the God of Israel there, as
I had seen on the plain.
5Then he said to me, "Human, now look
toward the north." So I looked up toward the
north, and in the entrance north of the gate
of the altar was the idol that caused God to
be jealous.
6He said to me, "Human, do you see what
they are doing? Do you see how many
hateful things the people of Israel are doing
here that drive me far away from my
Temple? But you will see things more
hateful than these."
7Then he brought me to the entry of the
courtyard. When I looked, I saw a hole in the
wall. 8He said to me, "Human, dig through
the wall." So I dug through the wall and saw
an entrance.
9Then he said to me, "Go in and see the
hateful, evil things they are doing here." 10So
I entered and looked, and I saw every kind of
crawling thing and hateful beast and all the
idols of the people of Israel, carved on the
wall all around. 11Standing in front of these
carvings and idols were seventy of the elders
of Israel and Jaazaniah son of Shaphan. Each
man had his pan for burning incense in his
hand, and a sweet-smelling cloud of incense
was rising.
12Then he said to me, "Human, have you
seen what the elders of Israel are doing in
the dark? Have you seen each man in the
room of his own idol? They say, 'The LORD
doesn't see us. The LORD has left the land.' "
13He also said to me, "You will see even more
hateful things that they are doing."
14Then he brought me to the entrance of
the north gate of the Temple of the LORD,
where I saw women sitting and crying for
Tammuz.[n] 15He said to me, "Do you see,
human? You will see things even more
hateful than these."
16Then he brought me into the inner
courtyard of the Temple. There I saw about
twenty-five men at the entrance to the
Temple of the LORD, between the porch and
the altar. With their backs turned to the
Temple of the LORD, they faced east and were
worshiping the sun in the east.
17He said to me, "Do you see, human? Is it
unimportant that the people of Judah are
doing the hateful things they have done
here? They have filled the land with
violence and made me continually angry.
Look, they are insulting me every way they
can. 18So I will act in anger. I will have no
pity, nor will I show mercy. Even if they
shout in my ears, I won't listen to them."

Vision of the Angels

9 Then he shouted with a loud voice in my
ears, "You who are chosen to punish this
city, come near with your weapon in your
hand." 2Then six men came from the
direction of the upper gate, which faces
north, each with his powerful weapon in his
hand. Among them was a man dressed in
linen with a writing case at his side. The
men went in and stood by the bronze altar.
3Then the glory of the God of Israel went
up from above the creatures with wings,
where it had been, to the place in the Temple
where the door opened. He called to the man
dressed in linen who had the writing case at
his side. 4He said to the man, "Go through
Jerusalem and put a mark on the foreheads
of the people who groan and cry about all
the hateful things being done among them."
5As I listened, he said to the other men,
"Go through the city behind the man dressed
in linen and kill. Don't pity anyone, and
don't show mercy. 6Kill and destroy old men,
young men and women, little children, and
older women, but don't touch any who have
the mark on them. Start at my Temple." So
they started with the elders who were in
front of the Temple.
7Then he said to the men, "Make the
Temple unclean, and fill the courtyards with
those who have been killed. Go out!" So the
men went out and killed the people in the
city. 8While the men were killing the people,
I was left alone. I bowed facedown on the
ground and I cried out, "Oh, Lord GOD! Will
you destroy everyone left alive in Israel
when you turn loose your anger on
Jerusalem?"
9Then he said to me, "The sin of the
people of Israel and Judah is very great. The
land is filled with people who murder, and

8:14 Tammuz Tammuz was a god in Babylon. Every year people thought this god died when the plants died. After they cried for him, they believed he came back to life, and the plants lived again.

the city is full of people who are not fair. The
people say, 'The LORD has left the land, and
the LORD does not see.' 10But I will have no
pity, nor will I show mercy. I will bring their
evil back on their heads."
11Then the man dressed in linen with the
writing case at his side reported, "I have
done just as you commanded me."

The Coals of Fire

10 Then I looked and saw in the dome
above the heads of the living
creatures something like a sapphire gem
which looked like a throne. 2The LORD said
to the man dressed in linen, "Go in between
the wheels under the living creatures, fill
your hands with coals of fire from between
the living creatures, and scatter the coals
over the city."

As I watched, the man with linen clothes
went in. 3Now the living creatures were
standing on the south side of the Temple
when the man went in. And a cloud filled
the inner courtyard. 4Then the glory of the
LORD went up from the living creatures and
stood over the door of the Temple. The
Temple was filled with the cloud, and the
courtyard was full of the brightness from the
glory of the LORD. 5The sound of the wings of
the living creatures was heard all the way to
the outer courtyard. It was like the voice of
God Almighty when he speaks.
6When the LORD commanded the man
dressed in linen, "Take fire from between the
wheels, from between the living creatures,"
the man went in and stood by a wheel. 7One
living creature put out his hand to the fire
that was among them, took some of the fire,
and put it in the hands of the man dressed in
linen. Then the man took the fire and went
out.

The Wheels and the Creatures

8Something that looked like a human
hand could be seen under the wings of the
living creatures. 9I saw the four wheels by
the living creatures, one wheel by each
living creature. The wheels looked like
shining chrysolite. 10All four wheels looked
alike: Each looked like a wheel crossways
inside another wheel. 11When the wheels
moved, they went in any of the directions
that the four living creatures faced. The
wheels did not turn about, and the living
creatures did not turn their bodies as they
went. 12All their bodies, their backs, their
hands, their wings, and the wheels were full
of eyes all over. Each of the four living
creatures had a wheel. 13I heard the wheels
being called "whirling wheels." 14Each living
creature had four faces. The first face was the
face of a creature with wings. The second
face was a human face, the third was the face
of a lion, and the fourth was the face of an
eagle.
15Then the living creatures flew up. They
were the same living creatures I had seen by
the Kebar River. 16When the living creatures
moved, the wheels moved beside them.
When the living creatures lifted their wings
to fly up from the ground, the wheels did not
leave their place beside them. 17When the
living creatures stopped, the wheels stopped.
When the creatures went up, the wheels
went up also, because the spirit of the living
creatures was in the wheels.
18Then the glory of the LORD left the door
of the Temple and stood over the living
creatures. 19As I watched, the living
creatures spread their wings and flew up
from the ground, with the wheels beside
them. They stood where the east gate of the
Temple of the LORD opened, and the glory of
the God of Israel was over them.
20These were the living creatures I had
seen under the God of Israel by the Kebar
River. I knew they were called cherubim.
21Each one had four faces and four wings,
and under their wings were things that
looked like human hands. 22Their faces
looked the same as the ones I had seen by
the Kebar River. They each went straight
ahead.

Prophecies Against Evil Leaders

11 The Spirit lifted me up and brought
me to the front gate of the Temple of
the LORD, which faces east. I saw twenty-five
men where the gate opens, among them
Jaazaniah son of Azzur and Pelatiah son of
Benaiah, who were leaders of the people.
2Then the LORD said to me, "Human, these
are the men who plan evil and give wicked
advice in this city of Jerusalem. 3They say, 'It
is almost time for us to build houses. This
city is like a cooking pot, and we are like the
best meat.' 4So prophesy against them,
prophesy, human."

5Then the Spirit of the LORD entered me
and told me to say: "This is what the LORD
says: You have said these things, people of
Israel, and I know what you are thinking.
6You have killed many people in this city,
filling its streets with their bodies.
7"So this is what the Lord GOD says: Those
people you have killed and left in the middle
of the city are like the best meat, and this
city is like the cooking pot. But I will force
you out of the city. 8You have feared the
sword, but I will bring a sword against you,
says the Lord GOD. 9I will force you out of
the city and hand you over to strangers and
punish you. 10You will die by the sword. I
will punish you at the border of Israel so you
will know that I am the LORD. 11This city will
not be your cooking pot, and you will not be
the best meat in the middle of it. I will
punish you at the border of Israel. 12Then
you will know that I am the LORD. You did
not live by my rules or obey my laws.
Instead, you did the same things as the
nations around you."
13As I prophesied, Pelatiah son of Benaiah
died. Then I bowed facedown on the ground
and shouted with a loud voice, "Oh no, Lord
GOD! Will you completely destroy the
Israelites who are left alive?"

Promise to Those Remaining

14The LORD spoke his word to me, saying,
15"Human, the people still in Jerusalem have
spoken about your own relatives and all the
people of Israel who are captives with you,
saying, 'They are far from the LORD. This land
has been given to us as our property.'
16"So say, 'This is what the Lord GOD says: I
sent the people far away among the nations
and scattered them among the countries. But
for a little while I have become a Temple to
them in the countries where they have
gone.'
17"So say: 'This is what the Lord GOD says:
I will gather you from the nations and bring
you together from the countries where you
have been scattered. Then I will give you
back the land of Israel.'
18"When they come to this land, they will
remove all the evil idols and all the hateful
images. 19I will give them a desire to respect
me completely, and I will put inside them a
new way of thinking. I will take out the
stubborn heart of stone from their bodies,

devotion 225

EZEKIEL 11:16

DEPEND ON GOD

Have you ever been through the dark night of the soul? Have you experienced a season in your life when you felt isolated and alone? Even now, maybe you are feeling depressed or like you are being attacked by an unseen force. You aren't alone. We all walk that road at some point in our lives. It can come through the death of a loved one, a battle with a disease, the loss of a marriage or a career, or a disappointment that leaves you feeling hopeless or scattered. Some will tell you to pull yourself up by your bootstraps or to get over it. They have not yet walked that road, or they would offer different advice.

My husband's grandmother often says, "This too will pass." I first heard her say it after I had my first baby, and I thought I would never sleep again. Since then, I have whispered it to myself many times. This verse says "for a little while," and I think it means the same thing. Know that those difficult seasons we all go through will pass, for they are only meant for a little while. But while you are enduring the season, the Lord will be your Temple. He will hold you while you cry and encourage you to keep going with his Word. When all else fails, you can depend on God. Allow him to be your quiet sanctuary of peace when you feel scattered. He will carry you through.

and I will give them an obedient heart of
flesh. 20 Then they will live by my rules and
obey my laws and keep them. They will be
my people, and I will be their God. 21 But
those who want to serve their evil statues
and hateful idols, I will pay back for their
evil ways, says the Lord GOD."

Ezekiel's Vision Ends

22 Then the living creatures lifted their
wings with the wheels beside them, and the
glory of the God of Israel was above them.
23 The glory of the LORD went up from
inside Jerusalem and stopped on the
mountain on the east side of the city. 24 The
Spirit lifted me up and brought me to the
captives who had been taken from Judah to
Babylonia. This happened in a vision given
by the Spirit of God, and then the vision I
had seen ended. 25 And I told the captives
from Judah all the things the LORD had
shown me.

Ezekiel Moves Out

12 Again the LORD spoke his word to
me, saying: 2 "Human, you are living
among a people who refuse to obey. They
have eyes to see, but they do not see, and
they have ears to hear, but they do not hear,
because they are a people who refuse to obey.

3 "So, human, pack your things as if you
will be taken away captive, and walk away
like a captive in the daytime with the people
watching. Move from your place to another
with the people watching. Maybe they will
understand, even though they are a people
who refuse to obey. 4 During the day when
the people are watching, bring out the
things you would pack as captive. At
evening, with the people watching, leave
your place like those who are taken away as
captives from their country. 5 Dig a hole
through the wall while they watch, and
bring your things out through it. 6 Lift them
onto your shoulders with the people
watching, and carry them out in the dark.
Cover your face so you cannot see the
ground, because I have made you a sign to
the people of Israel."

7 I did these things as I was commanded.
In the daytime I brought what I had packed
as if I were being taken away captive. Then
in the evening I dug through the wall with
my hands. I brought my things out in the
dark and carried them on my shoulders as
the people watched.

8 Then in the morning the LORD spoke his
word to me, saying: 9 "Human, didn't Israel,
who refuses to obey, ask you, 'What are you
doing?'

10 "Say to them, 'This is what the Lord GOD
says: This message is about the king in
Jerusalem and all the people of Israel who
live there.' 11 Say, 'I am a sign to you.'

"The same things I have done will be done
to the people in Jerusalem. They will be
taken away from their country as captives.
12 The king among them will put his things
on his shoulder in the dark and will leave.
The people will dig a hole through the wall
to bring him out. He will cover his face so he
cannot see the ground. 13 But I will spread
my net over him, and he will be caught in
my trap. Then I will bring him to Babylon in
the land of the Babylonians. He will not see
that land, but he will die there. 14 All who are
around the king—his helpers and all his
army—I will scatter in every direction, and I
will chase them with a sword.

15 "They will know that I am the LORD
when I scatter them among the nations and
spread them among the countries. 16 But I
will save a few of them from the sword and
from hunger and disease. Then they can tell
about their hateful actions among the
nations where they go. Then they will know
that I am the LORD."

The Lesson of Ezekiel's Shaking

17 The LORD spoke his word to me, saying:
18 "Human, tremble as you eat your food, and
shake with fear as you drink your water.
19 Then say to the people of the land: 'This is
what the Lord GOD says about the people
who live in Jerusalem in the land of Israel:
They will eat their food with fear and drink
their water in shock, because their land will
be stripped bare because of the violence of
the people who live in it. 20 The cities where
people live will become ruins, and the land
will become empty. Then you will know
that I am the LORD.' "

The Visions Will Come True

21 The LORD spoke his word to me, saying:
22 "Human, what is this saying you have in
the land of Israel: 'The days go by and every
vision comes to nothing'? 23 So say to them,

'This is what the Lord GOD says: I will make
them stop saying this, and nobody in Israel
will use this saying anymore.' But tell them,
'The time is near when every vision will
come true. 24There will be no more false
visions or pleasing prophecies inside the
nation of Israel, 25but I, the LORD, will speak.
What I say will be done, and it will not be
delayed. You refuse to obey, but in your time
I will say the word and do it, says the Lord
GOD.'"

26The LORD spoke his word to me, saying:
27"Human, the people of Israel are saying,
'The vision that Ezekiel sees is for a time
many years from now. He is prophesying
about times far away.'

28"So say to them: 'The Lord GOD says this:
None of my words will be delayed anymore.
What I have said will be done, says the Lord
GOD.'"

Ezekiel Speaks Against False Prophets

13 The LORD spoke his word to me,
saying: 2"Human, prophesy against
the prophets of Israel. Say to those who
make up their own prophecies: 'Listen to the
word of the LORD. 3This is what the Lord GOD
says: How terrible it will be for the foolish
prophets who follow their own ideas and
have not seen a vision from me! 4People of
Israel, your prophets have been like wild
dogs hunting to kill and eat among ruins.
5Israel is like a house in ruins, but you have
not gone up into the broken places or
repaired the wall. So how can Israel hold
back the enemy in the battle on the LORD's
day of judging? 6Your prophets see false
visions and prophesy lies. They say, "This is
the message of the LORD," when the LORD has
not sent them. But they still hope their
words will come true. 7You said, "This is the
message of the LORD," but that is a false
vision. Your prophecies are lies, because I
have not spoken.

8" 'So this is what the Lord GOD says:
Because you prophets spoke things that are
false and saw visions that do not come true, I
am against you, says the Lord GOD. 9I will
punish the prophets who see false visions
and prophesy lies. They will have no place
among my people. Their names will not be
written on the list of the people of Israel, and
they will not enter the land of Israel. Then
you will know that I am the Lord GOD.

10" 'It is because they lead my people the
wrong way by saying, "Peace!" when there is
no peace. When the people build a weak
wall, the prophets cover it with whitewash
to make it look strong. 11So tell those who
cover a weak wall with whitewash that it
will fall down. Rain will pour down,
hailstones will fall, and a stormy wind will
break the wall down. 12When the wall has
fallen, people will ask you, "Where is the
whitewash you used on the wall?"

13" 'So this is what the Lord GOD says: I
will break the wall with a stormy wind. In
my anger rain will pour down, and
hailstones will destroy the wall. 14I will tear
down the wall on which you put whitewash.
I will level it to the ground so that people
will see the wall's foundation. And when the
wall falls, you will be destroyed under it.
Then you will know that I am the LORD. 15So
I will carry out my anger on the wall and
against those who covered it with
whitewash. Then I will tell you, "The wall is
gone, and those who covered it with
whitewash are gone. 16The prophets of Israel
who prophesy to Jerusalem and who see
visions of peace for the city, when there is no
peace, will be gone, says the Lord GOD."'

False Women Prophets

17"Now, human, look toward the women
among your people who make up their own
prophecies. Prophesy against them. 18Say,
'This is what the Lord GOD says: How terrible
it will be for women who sew magic charms
on their wrists and make veils of every
length to trap people! You ruin the lives of
my people but try to save your own lives.
19For handfuls of barley and pieces of bread,
you have dishonored me among my people.
By lying to my people, who listen to lies, you
have killed people who should not die, and
you have kept alive those who should not
live.

20" 'So this is what the Lord GOD says: I am
against your magic charms, by which you
trap people as if they were birds. I will tear
those charms off your arms, and I will free
those people you have trapped like birds.
21I will also tear off your veils and save my
people from your hands. They will no longer
be trapped by your power. Then you will
know that I am the LORD. 22By your lies you
have caused those who did right to be sad,

when I did not make them sad. And you have encouraged the wicked not to stop being wicked, which would have saved their lives. 23So you will not see false visions or prophesy anymore, and I will save my people from your power so you will know that I am the LORD.' "

Stop Worshiping Idols

14 Some of the elders of Israel came to me and sat down in front of me. 2Then the LORD spoke his word to me, saying: 3"Human, these people want to worship idols. They put up evil things that cause people to sin. Should I allow them to ask me for help? 4So speak to them and tell them, 'This is what the Lord GOD says: When any of the people of Israel want to worship idols and put up evil things that cause people to sin and then come to the prophet, I, the LORD, will answer them myself for worshiping idols. 5Then I will win back my people Israel, who have left me because of all their idols.'

6"So say to the people of Israel, 'This is what the Lord GOD says: Change your hearts and lives, and stop worshiping idols. Stop doing all the things I hate. 7Any of the Israelites or foreigners in Israel can separate themselves from me by wanting to worship idols or by putting up the things that cause people to sin. Then if they come to the prophet to ask me questions, I, the LORD, will answer them myself. 8I will reject them. I will make them a sign and an example, and I will separate them from my people. Then you will know that I am the LORD.

9" 'But if the prophet is tricked into giving a prophecy, it is because I, the LORD, have tricked that prophet to speak. Then I will use my power against him and destroy him from among my people Israel. 10The prophet will be as guilty as the one who asks him for help; both will be responsible for their guilt. 11Then the nation of Israel will not leave me anymore or make themselves unclean anymore with all their sins. They will be my people, and I will be their God, says the Lord GOD.' "

Jerusalem Will Not Be Spared

12The LORD spoke his word to me, saying: 13"Human, if the people of a country sin against me by not being loyal, I will use my power against them. I will cut off their supply of food and send a time of hunger, destroying both people and animals. 14Even if three great men like Noah, Daniel, and Job were in that country, their goodness could save only themselves, says the Lord GOD.

15"Or I might send wild animals into that land, leaving the land empty and without children. Then no one would pass through it because of the animals. 16As surely as I live, says the Lord GOD, even if Noah, Daniel, and Job were in the land, they could not save their own sons or daughters. They could save only themselves, but that country would become empty.

17"Or I might bring a war against that country. I might say, 'Let a war be fought in that land,' in this way destroying its people and its animals. 18As surely as I live, says the Lord GOD, even if those three men were in the land, they could not save their sons or daughters. They could save only themselves.

19"Or I might cause a disease to spread in that country. I might pour out my anger against it, destroying and killing people and animals. 20As surely as I live, says the Lord GOD, even if Noah, Daniel, and Job were in the land, they could not save their son or daughter. They could save only themselves because they did what was right.

21"This is what the Lord GOD says: My plans for Jerusalem are much worse! I will send my four terrible punishments against it—war, hunger, wild animals, and disease—to destroy its people and animals. 22But some people will escape; some sons and daughters will be led out. They will come out to you, and you will see what happens to people who live as they did. Then you will be comforted after the disasters I have brought against Jerusalem, after all the things I have brought against it. 23You will be comforted when you see what happens to them for living as they did, because you will know there was a good reason for what I did to Jerusalem, says the Lord GOD."

Story of the Vine

15 The LORD spoke his word to me, saying: 2"Human, is the wood of the vine better than the wood of any tree in the forest? 3Can wood be taken from the vine to make anything? Can you use it to make a peg on which to hang something? 4If the vine is thrown into the fire for fuel, and the

fire burns up both ends and starts to burn
the middle, is it useful for anything? 5When
the vine was whole, it couldn't be made into
anything. When the fire has burned it
completely, it certainly cannot be made into
anything."
6So this is what the Lord GOD says: "Out of
all the trees in the forest, I have given the
wood of the vine as fuel for fire. In the same
way I have given up the people who live in
Jerusalem 7and will turn against them.
Although they came through one fire, fire
will still destroy them. When I turn against
them, you will know that I am the LORD. 8So I
will make the land empty, because the people
have not been loyal, says the Lord GOD."

The Lord's Kindness to Jerusalem

16 The LORD spoke his word to me,
saying: 2"Human, tell Jerusalem about
her hateful actions. 3Say, 'This is what the
Lord GOD says to Jerusalem: Your beginnings
and your ancestors were in the land of the
Canaanites. Your father was an Amorite, and
your mother was a Hittite. 4On the day you
were born, your cord[n] was not cut. You were
not washed with water to clean you. You
were not rubbed with salt or wrapped in
cloths. 5No one felt sorry enough for you to
do any of these things for you. No, you were
thrown out into the open field, because you
were hated on the day you were born.
6" 'When I passed by and saw you kicking
about in your blood, I said to you, "Live!" 7I
made you grow like a plant in the field. You
grew up and became tall and became like a
beautiful jewel. Your breasts formed, and
your hair grew, but you were naked and
without clothes.
8" 'Later when I passed by you and looked
at you, I saw that you were old enough for
love. So I spread my robe over you and
covered your nakedness. I also made a
promise to you and entered into an
agreement with you so that you became
mine, says the Lord GOD.
9" 'Then I bathed you with water, washed
all the blood off of you, and put oil on you.
10I put beautiful clothes made with
needlework on you and put sandals of fine
leather on your feet. I wrapped you in fine
linen and covered you with silk. 11I put
jewelry on you: bracelets on your arms, a
necklace around your neck, 12a ring in your
nose, earrings in your ears, and a beautiful
crown on your head. 13So you wore gold and
silver. Your clothes were made of fine linen,
silk, and beautiful needlework. You ate fine
flour, honey, and olive oil. You were very
beautiful and became a queen. 14Then you
became famous among the nations, because
you were so beautiful. Your beauty was
perfect, because of the glory I gave you, says
the Lord GOD.

Jerusalem Becomes a Prostitute

15" 'But you trusted in your beauty. You
became a prostitute, because you were so
famous. You had sexual relations with
anyone who passed by. 16You took some of
your clothes and made your places of
worship colorful. There you carried on your
prostitution. These things should not
happen; they should never occur. 17You also
took your beautiful jewelry, made from my
gold and silver I had given you, and you
made for yourselves male idols so you could
be a prostitute with them. 18Then you took
your clothes with beautiful needlework and
covered the idols. You gave my oil and
incense as an offering to them. 19Also, you
took the bread I gave you, the fine flour, oil,
and honey I gave you to eat, and you offered
them before the gods as a pleasing smell.
This is what happened, says the Lord GOD.
20" 'But your sexual sins were not enough
for you. You also took your sons and
daughters who were my children, and you
sacrificed them to the idols as food. 21You
killed my children and offered them up in
fire to the idols. 22While you did all your
hateful acts and sexual sins, you did not
remember when you were young, when you
were naked and had no clothes and were left
in your blood.
23" 'How terrible! How terrible it will be
for you, says the Lord GOD. After you did all
these evil things, 24you built yourself a place
to worship gods. You made for yourself a
place of worship in every city square. 25You
built a place of worship at the beginning of
every street. You made your beauty hateful,
offering your body for sex to anyone who
passed by, so your sexual sins became worse

16:4 cord The umbilical cord that gives the unborn baby food and air from its mother.

devotion 226

EZEKIEL 16:8–14

LET GOD LOVE YOU

In Ezekiel's analogy of how much God cared for Jerusalem, he compared the nation to a lovely maiden. He said that after God found her, cleansed her, dressed her in luxurious clothing, and fed her the finest food, he made an agreement with her. And then, as we read in Ezekiel 16:14, he raised her up as perfect among the nations. Yes, God judged Jerusalem harshly for her wickedness, but this passage reminds us that he loved Jerusalem beyond what she deserved.

Perhaps your marriage has ended or a loved one has been lost. Perhaps you feel helpless and rejected by no fault of your own. Perhaps you have made a tragic and regretful decision that you know isn't what God was leading you to do. Rest assured that we will all walk a difficult journey some time in our lives, but we can find comfort in the blessed promise that he will never leave our side and that his reserves of love will never be depleted.

Turn your head toward him and accept his unfailing grace and forgiveness. Let him care for you, cleanse you, and nurture you with his unfailing love. He will never forget his agreement with those who choose to follow him. You are as beautiful to him as the day you were born. I urge you to rise up out of the depths of sorrow and let your heavenly Father love you. You are a daughter of the one true God! You are perfect in his eyes.

and worse. 26You also had sexual relations with the Egyptians, who were your neighbors and partners in sexual sin. Your sexual sins became even worse, and they caused me to be angry. 27So then, I used my power against you and took away some of your land. I let you be defeated by those who hate you, the Philistine women, who were ashamed of your evil ways. 28Also, you had sexual relations with the Assyrians, because you could not be satisfied. Even though you had sexual relations with them, you still were not satisfied. 29You did many more sexual sins in Babylonia, the land of traders, but even this did not satisfy you.

30" 'Truly your will is weak, says the Lord GOD. You do all the things a stubborn prostitute does. 31You built your place to worship gods at the beginning of every street, and you made places of worship in every city square. But you were not like a prostitute when you refused to accept payment.

32" 'You are a wife who is guilty of adultery. You desire strangers instead of your husband. 33Men pay prostitutes, but you pay all your lovers to come to you. And they come from all around for sexual relations. 34So you are different from other prostitutes. No man asks you to be a prostitute, and you pay money instead of having money paid to you. Yes, you are different.

The Prostitute Is Judged

35" 'So, prostitute, hear the word of the LORD. 36This is what the Lord GOD says: You showed your nakedness to other countries. You uncovered your body in your sexual sins with them as your lovers and with all your hateful idols. You killed your children and offered their blood to your idols. 37So I will gather all your lovers with whom you found pleasure. Yes, I will gather all those you loved and those you hated. I will gather them against you from all around, and I will strip you naked in front of them so they can

see your nakedness. 38 I will punish you as
women guilty of adultery or as murderers
are punished. I will put you to death because
I am angry and jealous. 39 I will also hand
you over to your lovers. They will tear down
your places of worship and destroy other
places where you worship gods. They will
tear off your clothes and take away your
jewelry, leaving you naked and bare. 40 They
will bring a crowd against you to throw
stones at you and to cut you into pieces with
their swords. 41 They will burn down your
houses and will punish you in front of many
women. I will put an end to your sexual sins,
and you will no longer pay your lovers.
42 Then I will rest from my anger against you,
and I will stop being jealous. I will be quiet
and not angry anymore.

43 " 'Because you didn't remember when
you were young, but have made me angry in
all these ways, I will repay you for what you
have done, says the Lord GOD. Didn't you add
sexual sins to all your other acts which I
hate?

44 " 'Everyone who uses wise sayings will
say this about you: "The daughter is like her
mother." 45 You are like your mother, who
hated her husband and children. You are also
like your sisters, who hated their husbands
and children. Your mother was a Hittite, and
your father was an Amorite. 46 Your older
sister is Samaria, who lived north of you
with her daughters; your younger sister is
Sodom, who lived south of you with her
daughters. 47 You not only followed their
ways and did the hateful things they did, but
you were soon worse than they were in all
your ways. 48 As surely as I live, says the Lord
GOD, this is true. Your sister Sodom and her
daughters never did what you and your
daughters have done.

49 " 'This was the sin of your sister Sodom:
She and her daughters were proud and had
plenty of food and lived in great comfort, but
she did not help the poor and needy. 50 So
Sodom and her daughters were proud and
did things I hate in front of me. So I got rid
of them when I saw what they did. 51 Also,
Samaria did not do half the sins you do; you
have done more hateful things than they
did. So you make your sisters look good
because of all the hateful things you have
done. 52 You will suffer disgrace, because you
have provided an excuse for your sisters.
They are better than you are. Your sins were
even more terrible than theirs. Feel ashamed
and suffer disgrace, because you made your
sisters look good.

53 " 'But I will give back to Sodom and her
daughters the good things they once had. I
will give back to Samaria and her daughters
the good things they once had. And with
them I will also give back the good things
you once had 54 so you may suffer disgrace
and feel ashamed for all the things you have
done. You even gave comfort to your sisters
in their sins. 55 Your sisters, Sodom with her
daughters and Samaria with her daughters,
will return to what they were before. You
and your daughters will also return to what
you were before. 56 You humiliated your
sister Sodom when you were proud,
57 before your evil was uncovered. And now
the Edomite women and their neighbors
humiliate you. Even the Philistine women
humiliate you. Those around you hate you.
58 This is your punishment for your terrible
sins and for actions that I hate, says the
LORD.

God Keeps His Promises

59 " 'This is what the Lord GOD says: I will
do to you what you have done. You hated
and broke the agreement you promised to
keep. 60 But I will remember my agreement I
made with you when you were young, and I
will make an agreement that will continue
forever with you. 61 Then you will remember
what you have done and feel ashamed when
you receive your sisters—both your older
and your younger sisters. I will give them to
you like daughters, but not because they
share in my agreement with you. 62 I will set
up my agreement with you, and you will
know that I am the LORD. 63 You will
remember what you did and feel ashamed.
You will not open your mouth again because
of your shame, when I forgive you for all the
things you have done, says the Lord GOD.' "

The Eagle and the Vine

17 The LORD spoke his word to me,
saying: 2 "Human, give a riddle and tell
a story to the people of Israel. 3 Say, 'This is
what the Lord GOD says: A giant eagle with
big wings and long feathers of many different
colors came to Lebanon and took hold of the
top of a cedar tree. 4 He pulled off the top

branch and brought it to a land of traders,
where he planted it in a city of traders.
5" 'The eagle took some seed from the land
and planted it in a good field near plenty of
water. He planted it to grow like a willow
tree. 6It sprouted and became a low vine that
spread over the ground. The branches turned
toward the eagle, but the roots were under
the eagle. So the seed became a vine, and its
branches grew, sending out leaves.
7" 'But there was another giant eagle with
big wings and many feathers. The vine then
bent its roots toward this eagle. It sent out its
branches from the area where it was planted
toward the eagle so he could water it. 8It had
been planted in a good field by plenty of
water so it could grow branches and give
fruit. It could have become a fine vine.'
9"Say to them, 'This is what the Lord GOD
says: The vine will not continue to grow. The
first eagle will pull up the vine's roots and
strip off its fruit. Then the vine and all its
new leaves will dry up and die. It will not
take a strong arm or many people to pull the
vine up by its roots. 10Even if it is planted
again, it will not continue to grow. It will
completely dry up and die when the east
wind hits it in the area where it grew.' "

Zedekiah Against Nebuchadnezzar

11Then the LORD spoke his word to me,
saying: 12"Say now to the people who refuse
to obey: 'Do you know what these things
mean?' Say: 'The king of Babylon came to
Jerusalem and took the king and important
men of Jerusalem and brought them to
Babylon. 13Then he took a member of the
family of the king of Judah and made an
agreement with him, forcing him to take an
oath. The king also took away the leaders of
Judah 14to make the kingdom weak so it
would not be strong again. Then the
kingdom of Judah could continue only by
keeping its agreement with the king of
Babylon. 15But the king of Judah turned
against the king of Babylon by sending his
messengers to Egypt and asking them for
horses and many soldiers. Will the king of
Judah succeed? Will the one who does such
things escape? He cannot break the
agreement and escape.
16" 'As surely as I live, says the Lord GOD,
he will die in Babylon, in the land of the
king who made him king of Judah. The king
of Judah hated his promise to the king of
Babylon and broke his agreement with him.
17The king of Egypt with his mighty army
and many people will not help the king of
Judah in the war. The Babylonians will build
devices to attack the cities and to kill many
people. 18The king of Judah showed that he
hated the promise by breaking the
agreement. He promised to support Babylon,
but he did all these things. So he will not
escape.
19" 'So this is what the Lord GOD says: As
surely as I live, this is true: I will pay back
the king of Judah for hating my promise and
breaking my agreement. 20I will spread my
net over him, and he will be caught in my
trap. Then I will bring him to Babylon,
where I will punish him for the unfaithful
acts he did against me. 21All the best of his
soldiers who escape will die by the sword,
and those who live will be scattered to every
wind. Then you will know that I, the LORD,
have spoken.
22" 'This is what the Lord GOD says: I
myself will also take a young branch from
the top of a cedar tree, and I will plant it. I
will cut off a small twig from the top of the
tree's young branches, and I will plant it on a
very high mountain. 23I will plant it on the
high mountain of Israel. Then it will grow
branches and give fruit and become a great
cedar tree. Birds of every kind will build
nests in it and live in the shelter of the tree's
branches. 24Then all the trees in the
countryside will know that I am the LORD. I
bring down the high tree and make the low
tree tall. I dry up the green tree and make the
dry tree grow. I am the LORD. I have spoken,
and I will do it.' "

God Is Fair

18 The LORD spoke his word to me,
saying: 2"What do you mean by using
this saying about the land of Israel:

'The parents have eaten sour grapes,
and that caused the children to grind
their teeth from the sour taste'?

3"As surely as I live, says the Lord GOD,
this is true: You will not use this saying in
Israel anymore. 4Every living thing belongs
to me. The life of the parent is mine, and the
life of the child is mine. The person who sins
is the one who will die.
5"Suppose a person is good and does what

is fair and right. 6He does not eat at the
mountain places of worship. He does not
look to the idols of Israel for help. He does
not have sexual relations with his
neighbor's wife or with a woman during her
time of monthly bleeding. 7He does not
mistreat anyone but returns what was given
as a promise for a loan. He does not rob
other people. He gives bread to the hungry
and clothes to those who have none. 8He
does not lend money to get too much
interest or profit. He keeps his hand from
doing wrong. He judges fairly between one
person and another. 9He lives by my rules
and obeys my laws faithfully. Whoever does
these things is good and will surely live,
says the Lord GOD.

10"But suppose this person has a wild son
who murders people and who does any of
these other things. 11(But the father himself
has not done any of these things.) This son
eats at the mountain places of worship. He
has sexual relations with his neighbor's wife.
12He mistreats the poor and needy. He steals
and refuses to return what was promised for
a loan. He looks to idols for help. He does
things which I hate. 13He lends money for
too much interest and profit. Will this son
live? No, he will not live! He has done all
these hateful things, so he will surely be put
to death. He will be responsible for his own
death.

14"Now suppose this son has a son who
has seen all his father's sins, but after seeing
them does not do those things. 15He does not
eat at the mountain places of worship. He
does not look to the idols of Israel for help.
He does not have sexual relations with his
neighbor's wife. 16He does not mistreat
anyone or keep something promised for a
loan or steal. He gives bread to the hungry
and clothes to those who have none. 17He
keeps his hand from doing wrong. He does
not take too much interest or profit when he
lends money. He obeys my laws and lives by
my rules. He will not die for his father's sin;
he will surely live. 18But his father took
other people's money unfairly and robbed
his brother and did what was wrong among
his people. So he will die for his own sin.

19"But you ask, 'Why is the son not
punished for the father's sin?' The son has
done what is fair and right. He obeys all my
rules, so he will surely live. 20The person
who sins is the one who will die. A child will
not be punished for a parent's sin, and a
parent will not be punished for a child's sin.
Those who do right will enjoy the results of
their own goodness; evil people will suffer
the results of their own evil.

21"But suppose the wicked stop doing all
the sins they have done and obey all my
rules and do what is fair and right. Then
they will surely live; they will not die.
22Their sins will be forgotten. Because they
have done what is right, they will live. 23I do
not really want the wicked to die, says the
Lord GOD. I want them to stop their bad
ways and live.

24"But suppose good people stop doing
good and do wrong and do the same hateful
things the wicked do. Will they live? All
their good acts will be forgotten, because
they became unfaithful. They have sinned,
so they will die because of their sins.

25"But you say, 'What the Lord does isn't
fair.' Listen, people of Israel. I am fair. It is
what you do that is not fair! 26When good
people stop doing good and do wrong, they
will die because of it. They will die, because
they did wrong. 27When the wicked stop
being wicked and do what is fair and right,
they will save their lives. 28Because they
thought about it and stopped doing all the
sins they had done, they will surely live;
they will not die. 29But the people of Israel
still say, 'What the Lord does isn't fair.'
People of Israel, I am fair. It is what you do
that is not fair.

30"So I will judge you, people of Israel; I
will judge each of you by what you do, says
the Lord GOD. Change your hearts and stop
all your sinning so sin will not bring your
ruin. 31Get rid of all the sins you have done,
and get for yourselves a new heart and a new
way of thinking. Why do you want to die,
people of Israel? 32I do not want anyone to
die, says the Lord GOD, so change your hearts
and lives so you may live.

A Sad Song for Israel

19 "Sing a funeral song for the leaders of
Israel. 2Say:

'Your mother was like a female lion.
She lay down among the young lions.
She had many cubs.
3When she brought up one of her cubs,
he became a strong lion.

devotion 227

EZEKIEL 18:31–32

SAYING GOOD-BYE TO WINE

When my husband and I prayed the confession of faith, we set our feet firmly on the pathway of Christ in forward motion. However, there was one consistent detour for me—drinking wine. Now I am not here to condemn anybody, and there is freedom in drinking, but for me it was a detour from righteousness. I was not an alcoholic, but while cooking dinner or at friends' intimate parties, I would partake of a glass or two of wine. Well, once one or two went down, three and four were never far behind. And before long, I would find myself drunk and sick about my behavior by morning.

Being drunk is a sin, and unfortunate events can occur when you do not have a sober mind. It didn't happen a lot, but it happened enough to convict me to the core. One fall, just after my birthday and a nice bottle of wine, the Holy Spirit asked me, "Would you lay this down for me?" I answered yes and prayed for strength. That next week the Lord called my husband into full time ministry, and I saw so clearly why the Lord wanted my heart and how awful it would be for me to cause just one of his sheep to stumble.

Is there something in your life that's causing you to detour from righteousness . . . maybe just a little bit? If so, respond resolutely when you feel the Holy Spirit nudging you. You just never know how God might reward you for answering yes.

He learned to tear the animals he hunted,
and he ate people.
4 The nations heard about him.
He was trapped in their pit,
and they brought him with hooks
to the land of Egypt.

5 " 'The mother lion waited and saw
that there was no hope for her cub.
So she took another one of her cubs
and made him a strong lion.
6 This cub roamed among the lions.
He was now a strong lion.
He learned to tear the animals he hunted,
and he ate people.
7 He tore down their strong places
and destroyed their cities.
The land and everything in it
were terrified by the sound of his roar.
8 Then the nations came against him
from areas all around,
and they spread their net over him.
He was trapped in their pit.
9 Then they put him into a cage with chains
and brought him to the king of
Babylon.
They put him into prison
so his roar could not be heard again
on the mountains of Israel.

10 " 'Your mother was like a vine in your
vineyard,
planted beside the water.
The vine had many branches and gave
much fruit,
because there was plenty of water.
11 The vine had strong branches,
good enough for a king's scepter.
The vine became tall
among the thick branches.
And it was seen, because it was tall
with many branches.
12 But it was pulled up by its roots in anger
and thrown down to the ground.
The east wind dried it up.
Its fruit was torn off.
Its strong branches were broken off
and burned up.

[13]Now the vine is planted in the desert,
in a dry and thirsty land.
[14]Fire spread from the vine's main branch,
destroying its fruit.
There is not a strong branch left on it
that could become a scepter for a king.'
This is a funeral song; it is to be used as a
funeral song."

Israel Has Refused God

20 It was the seventh year of our
captivity, in the fifth month, on the
tenth day of the month. Some of the elders
of Israel came to ask about the LORD and sat
down in front of me.
[2]The LORD spoke his word to me, saying:
[3]"Human, speak to the elders of Israel and
say to them: 'This is what the Lord GOD says:
Did you come to ask me questions? As surely
as I live, I will not let you ask me questions.'
[4]"Will you judge them? Will you judge
them, human? Let them know the hateful
things their ancestors did. [5]Say to them:
'This is what the Lord GOD says: When I
chose Israel, I made a promise to the
descendants of Jacob. I made myself known
to them in Egypt, and I promised them, "I
am the LORD your God." [6]At that time I
promised them I would bring them out of
Egypt into a land I had found for them, a
fertile land, the best land in the world. [7]I said
to them, "Each one of you must throw away
the hateful idols you have seen and liked.
Don't make yourselves unclean with the
idols of Egypt. I am the LORD your God."
[8]" 'But they turned against me and refused
to listen to me. They did not throw away the
hateful idols which they saw and liked; they
did not give up the idols of Egypt. Then I
decided to pour out my anger against them
while they were still in Egypt. [9]But I acted
for the sake of my name so it would not be
dishonored in full view of the nations where
the Israelites lived. I made myself known to
the Israelites with a promise to bring them
out of Egypt while the nations were
watching. [10]So I took them out of Egypt and
brought them into the desert. [11]I gave them
my rules and told them about my laws, by
which people will live if they obey them. [12]I
also gave them my Sabbaths to be a sign
between us so they would know that I am
the LORD who made them holy.
[13]" 'But in the desert Israel turned against
me. They did not follow my rules, and they
rejected my laws, by which people will live if
they obey them. They dishonored my
Sabbaths. Then I decided to pour out my
anger against them and destroy them in the
desert. [14]But I acted for the sake of my name
so it would not be dishonored in full view of
the nations who watched as I had brought
the Israelites out of Egypt. [15]And in the
desert I swore to the Israelites that I would
not bring them into the land I had given
them. It is a fertile land, the best land in the
world. [16]This was because they rejected my
laws and did not follow my rules. They
dishonored my Sabbaths and wanted to
worship their idols. [17]But I had pity on them.
I did not destroy them or put an end to them
in the desert. [18]I said to their children in the
desert, "Don't live by the rules of your
parents, or obey their laws. Don't make
yourselves unclean with their idols. [19]I am
the LORD your God. Live by my rules, obey
my laws, and follow them. [20]Keep my
Sabbaths holy, and they will be a sign
between me and you. Then you will know
that I am the LORD your God."
[21]" 'But the children turned against me.
They did not live by my rules, nor were they
careful to obey my laws, by which people
will live if they obey them. They dishonored
my Sabbaths. So I decided to pour out my
anger against them in the desert. [22]But I held
back my anger. I acted for the sake of my
name so it would not be dishonored in full
view of the nations who watched as I
brought the Israelites out. [23]And in the
desert I swore to the Israelites that I would
scatter them among the nations and spread
them among the countries, [24]because they
had not obeyed my laws. They had rejected
my rules and dishonored my Sabbaths and
worshiped the idols of their parents. [25]I also
allowed them to follow rules that were not
good and laws by which they could not live.
[26]I let the Israelites make themselves
unclean by the gifts they brought to their
gods when they sacrificed their first children
in the fire. I wanted to terrify them so they
would know that I am the LORD.'
[27]"So, human, speak to the people of
Israel. Say to them, 'This is what the Lord
GOD says: Your ancestors spoke against me
by being unfaithful to me in another way.
[28]When I had brought them into the land I

promised to give them, they saw every high
hill and every leafy tree. There they offered
their sacrifices to gods. They brought
offerings that made me angry and burned
their incense and poured out their drink
offerings. 29Then I said to them: What is this
high place where you go to worship?' " (It is
still called High Place today.)

30"So say to the people of Israel: 'This is
what the Lord GOD says: Are you going to
make yourselves unclean as your ancestors
did? Are you going to be unfaithful and
desire their hateful idols? 31When you offer
your children as gifts and sacrifice them in
the fire, you are making yourselves unclean
with all your idols even today. So, people of
Israel, should I let you ask me questions? As
surely as I live, says the Lord GOD, I will not
accept questions from you.

32" 'What you want will not come true. You
say, "We want to be like the other nations,
like the people in other lands. We want to
worship idols made of wood and stone." 33As
surely as I live, says the Lord GOD, I will use
my great power and strength and anger to
rule over you. 34I will bring you out from the
foreign nations. With my great power and
strength and anger I will gather you from the
lands where you are scattered. 35I will bring
you among the nations as I brought your
ancestors into the desert with Moses. There I
will judge you face to face. 36I will judge you
the same way I judged your ancestors in the
desert of the land of Egypt, says the Lord GOD.
37I will count you like sheep and will bring
you into line with my agreement. 38I will get
rid of those who refuse to obey me and who
turn against me. I will bring them out of the
land where they are now living, but they will
never enter the land of Israel. Then you will
know that I am the LORD.

39" 'This is what the Lord GOD says: People
of Israel, go serve your idols for now. But
later you will listen to me; you will not
continue to dishonor my holy name with
your gifts and gods. 40On my holy mountain,
the high mountain of Israel, all Israel will
serve me in the land, says the Lord GOD.
There I will accept you. There I will expect
your offerings, the first harvest of your
offerings, and all your holy gifts. 41I will
accept you like the pleasing smell of
sacrifices when I bring you out from the
foreign nations and gather you from the
lands where you are scattered. Then through
you I will show how holy I am so the
nations will see. 42When I bring you into the
land of Israel, the land I promised your
ancestors, you will know that I am the LORD.
43There you will remember everything you
did that made you unclean, and then you
will hate yourselves for all the evil things
you have done. 44I will deal with you for the
sake of my name, not because of your evil
ways or unclean actions. Then you will
know I am the LORD, people of Israel, says
the Lord GOD.' "

Babylon, the Lord's Sword

45Now the LORD spoke his word to me,
saying: 46"Human, look toward the south.
Prophesy against the south and against the
forest of the southern area. 47Say to that
forest: 'Hear the word of the LORD. This is
what the Lord GOD says: I am ready to start a
fire in you that will destroy all your green
trees and all your dry trees. The flames that
burn will not be put out. Every face from
south to north will feel their heat. 48Then all
the people will see that I, the LORD, have
started the fire. It will not be put out.' "

49Then I said, "Ah, Lord GOD! The people
are saying about me, 'He is only telling
stories.' "

21

Then the LORD spoke his word to me,
saying: 2"Human, look toward
Jerusalem and speak against the holy place.
Prophesy against the land of Israel. 3Say to
Israel: 'This is what the LORD says: I am
against you. I will pull my sword out of its
holder, and I will cut off from you both the
wicked and those who do right. 4Because I
am going to cut off the wicked and those
who do right, my sword will come out from
its holder and attack all people from south
to north. 5Then all people will know that I,
the LORD, have pulled my sword out from its
holder. My sword will not go back in again.'

6"So, human, groan with breaking heart
and great sadness. Groan in front of the
people. 7When they ask you, 'Why are you
groaning?' you will say, 'Because of what I
have heard is going to happen. When it
happens, every heart will melt with fear, and
all hands will become weak. Everyone will
be afraid; all knees will become weak as
water. Look, it is coming, and it will happen,
says the Lord GOD.' "

[8]The LORD spoke his word to me, saying:
[9]"Human, prophesy and say, 'This is what
the Lord says:

A sword, a sword,
made sharp and polished.
[10]It is made sharp for the killing.
It is polished to flash like lightning.

" 'You are not happy about this horrible
punishment by the sword. But my son Judah,
you did not change when you were only
beaten with a rod.

[11]The sword should be polished.
It is meant to be held in the hand.
It is made sharp and polished,
ready for the hand of a killer.
[12]Shout and yell, human,
because the sword is meant for my
people,
for all the rulers of Israel.
They will be killed by the sword,
along with my people.
So beat your chest in sadness.

[13]" 'The test will come. And Judah, who is
hated by the armies of Babylon, will not last,
says the Lord GOD.'

[14]"So, human, prophesy
and clap your hands.
Let the sword strike
two or three times.
It is a sword meant for killing,
a sword meant for much killing.
This sword surrounds the people to be
killed.
[15]Their hearts will melt with fear,
and many people will die.
I have placed the killing sword
at all their city gates.
Oh! The sword is made to flash like
lightning.
It is held, ready for killing.
[16]Sword, cut on the right side;
then cut on the left side.
Cut anywhere your blade is turned.
[17]I will also clap my hands
and use up my anger.
I, the LORD, have spoken."

Jerusalem to Be Destroyed

[18]The LORD spoke his word to me, saying:
[19]"Human, mark two roads that the king of
Babylon and his sword can follow. Both of
these roads will start from the same country.
And make signs where the road divides and
one way goes toward the city. [20]Mark one
sign to show the road he can take with his
sword to Rabbah in the land of the
Ammonites. Mark the other sign to show the
road to Judah and Jerusalem, which is
protected with strong walls. [21]The king of
Babylon has come to where the road divides,
and he is using magic. He throws lots with
arrows and asks questions of his family idols.
He looks at the liver of a sacrificed animal to
learn where he should go. [22]The lot in his
right hand tells him to go to Jerusalem. It
tells him to use logs to break down the city
gates, to shout the battle cry and give the
order to kill, and to build a dirt road to the
top of the walls and devices to attack the
walls. [23]The people of Jerusalem have made
agreements with other nations to help them
fight Babylon. So they will think this
prediction is wrong, but it is really proof of
their sin, and they will be captured.

[24]"So this is what the Lord GOD says: 'You
have shown how sinful you are by turning
against the LORD. Your sins are seen in all the
things you do. Because of this proof against
you, you will be taken captive by the enemy.

[25]" 'You unclean and evil leader of Israel,
you will be killed! The time of your final
punishment has come. [26]This is what the
Lord GOD says: Take off the royal turban,
and remove the crown. Things will change.
Those who are important now will be
made unimportant, and those who are
unimportant now will be made important.
[27]A ruin! A ruin! I will make it a ruin! This
place will not be rebuilt until the one comes
who has a right to be king. Then I will give
him that right.'

The Punishment of Ammon

[28]"And you, human, prophesy and say:
'This is what the Lord GOD says about the
people of Ammon and their insults:

A sword, a sword
is pulled out of its holder.
It is polished to kill and destroy,
to flash like lightning!
[29]Prophets see false visions about you
and prophesy lies about you.
The sword will be put on the necks
of these unclean and evil people.
Their day of judging has come;
the time of final punishment has come.
[30]Put the sword back in its holder.
I will judge you

in the place where you were created,
in the land where you were born.
31 I will pour out my anger against you
and blast you with the fire of my anger.
I will hand you over to cruel men,
experts in destruction.
32 You will be like fuel for the fire;
you will die in the land.
You will not be remembered,
because I, the LORD, have spoken.' "

The Sins of Jerusalem

22 The LORD spoke his word to me,
saying: 2 "And you, human, will you
judge? Will you judge the city of murderers?
Then tell her about all her hateful acts. 3 You
are to say: 'This is what the Lord GOD says:
You are a city that kills those who come to
live there. You make yourself unclean by
making idols. 4 You have become guilty of
murder and have become unclean by your
idols which you have made. So you have
brought your time of punishment near; you
have come to the end of your years. That is
why I have made you a shame to the nations
and why all lands laugh at you. 5 Those near
and those far away laugh at you with your
bad name, you city full of confusion.
6 " 'Jerusalem, see how each ruler of Israel
in you has been trying to kill people. 7 The
people in you hate their fathers and
mothers. They mistreat the foreigners in you
and wrong the orphans and widows in you.
8 You hate my holy things and dishonor my
Sabbaths. 9 The men in you tell lies to cause
the death of others. The people in you eat
food offered to idols at the mountain places
of worship, and they take part in sexual sins.
10 The men in you have sexual relations with
their fathers' wives and with women who
are unclean, during their time of monthly
bleeding. 11 One man in you does a hateful
act with his neighbor's wife, while another
has shamefully made his daughter-in-law
unclean sexually. And another forces his half
sister to have sexual relations with him.
12 The people in you take money to kill
others. You take unfair interest and profits
and make profits by mistreating your
neighbor. And you have forgotten me, says
the Lord GOD.
13 " 'So, Jerusalem, I will shake my fist at
you for stealing money and for murdering
people. 14 Will you still be brave and strong
when I punish you? I, the LORD, have spoken,
and I will act. 15 I will scatter you among the
nations and spread you through the
countries. That is how I will get rid of your
uncleanness. 16 But you, yourself, will be
dishonored in the sight of the nations. Then
you will know that I am the LORD.' "

Israel Is Worthless

17 The LORD spoke his word to me, saying:
18 "Human, the people of Israel have become
useless like scum to me. They are like the
copper, tin, iron, and lead left in the furnace
when silver is purified. 19 So this is what the
Lord GOD says: 'Because you have become
useless like scum, I am going to put you
together inside Jerusalem. 20 People put
silver, copper, iron, lead, and tin together
inside a furnace to melt them down in a
blazing fire. In the same way I will gather
you in my hot anger and put you together in
Jerusalem and melt you down. 21 I will put
you together and make you feel the heat of
my anger. You will be melted down inside
Jerusalem. 22 As silver is melted in a furnace,
you will be melted inside the city. Then you
will know that I, the LORD, have poured out
my anger on you.' "

Sins of the People

23 The LORD spoke his word to me, saying:
24 "Human, say to the land, 'You are a land
that has not had rain or showers when God
is angry.' 25 Like a roaring lion that tears the
animal it has caught, Israel's rulers make
evil plans. They have destroyed lives and
have taken treasure and valuable things.
They have caused many women to become
widows. 26 Israel's priests do cruel things to
my teachings and do not honor my holy
things. They make no difference between
holy and unholy things, and they teach
there is no difference between clean and
unclean things. They do not remember my
Sabbaths, so I am dishonored by them.
27 Like wolves tearing a dead animal,
Jerusalem's leaders have killed people for
profit. 28 And the prophets try to cover this
up by false visions and by lying messages.
They say, 'This is what the Lord GOD says'
when the LORD has not spoken. 29 The people
cheat others and steal. They hurt people who
are poor and needy. They cheat foreigners
and do not treat them fairly.

30“I looked for someone to build up the
walls and to stand before me where the walls
are broken to defend these people so I would
not have to destroy them. But I could not
find anyone. 31So I let them see my anger. I
destroyed them with an anger that was like
fire because of all the things they have done,
says the Lord GOD.”

Samaria and Jerusalem

23 The LORD spoke his word to me,
saying: 2“Human, a woman had two
daughters. 3While they were young, they
went to Egypt and became prostitutes. They
let men touch and hold their breasts. 4The
older girl was named Oholah, and her sister
was named Oholibah. They became my
wives and had sons and daughters. Oholah is
Samaria, and Oholibah is Jerusalem.[n]
5“While still my wife, Samaria had sexual
relations with other men. She had great
sexual desire for her lovers, men from
Assyria. The Assyrians were warriors and
6wore blue uniforms. They were all
handsome young captains and lieutenants
riding on horseback. 7Samaria became a
prostitute for all the important men in
Assyria and made herself unclean with all
the idols of everyone she desired. 8She
continued the prostitution she began in
Egypt. When she was young, she had slept
with men, and they touched her breasts and
had sexual relations with her.
9“So I handed her over to her lovers, the
Assyrians, that she wanted so badly. 10They
stripped her naked and took away her sons
and daughters. Then they killed her with a
sword. Women everywhere began talking
about how she had been punished.
11“Her sister Jerusalem saw what
happened, but she became worse than her
sister in her sexual desire and prostitution.
12She also desired the Assyrians, who were
all soldiers in beautiful uniforms—
handsome young captains and lieutenants
riding horses. 13I saw that both girls were
alike; both were prostitutes.
14“But Jerusalem went even further. She
saw carvings of Babylonian men on a wall.
They wore red 15and had belts around their
waists and turbans on their heads. They all
looked like chariot officers born in
Babylonia. 16When she saw them, she
wanted to have sexual relations with them
and sent messengers to them in Babylonia.
17So these Babylonian men came and had
sexual relations with her and made her
unclean. After that, she became sick of them.
18But she continued her prostitution so
openly that everyone knew about it. And I
finally became sick of her, as I had her sister.
19But she remembered how she was a young
prostitute in Egypt, so she took part in even
more prostitution. 20She wanted men who
behaved like animals in their sexual desire.
21In the same way you desired to do the
sinful things you had done in Egypt. There
men touched and held your young breasts.

God’s Judgment on Jerusalem

22“So, Jerusalem, this is what the Lord GOD
says: You are tired of your lovers. So now I
will make them angry with you and have
them attack you from all sides. 23Men from
Babylon and all Babylonia and men from
Pekod, Shoa, and Koa will attack you. All the
Assyrians will attack you: handsome young
captains and lieutenants, all of them
important men and all riding horses.
24Those men will attack with great armies
and with their weapons, chariots, and
wagons. They will surround you with large
and small shields and with helmets. And I
will give them the right to punish you, and
they will give you their own kind of
punishment. 25Then you will see how strong
my anger can be when they punish you in
their anger. They will cut off your noses and
ears. They will take away your sons and
daughters, and those who are left will be
burned. 26They will take off your clothes and
steal your jewelry. 27I will put a stop to the
sinful life you began when you were in
Egypt so that you will not desire it or
remember Egypt anymore.
28“This is what the Lord GOD says: You
became tired of your lovers, but I am going
to hand you over to those men you now
hate. 29They will treat you with hate and
take away everything you worked for,
leaving you empty and naked. Everyone will
know about the sinful things you did. Your
sexual sins 30have brought this on you. You
have had sexual relations with the nations

23:4 Oholah . . . Jerusalem Throughout this chapter Samaria is used in place of Oholah, and Jerusalem is used in place of Oholibah.

and made yourselves unclean by worshiping
their idols. 31 You did the same things your
sister did, so you will get the same
punishment, like a bitter cup to drink.
32 "This is what the Lord GOD says:
You will drink the same cup your sister
did,
and that cup is deep and wide.
Everyone will make fun of you,
because the cup is full.
33 It will make you miserable and drunk.
It is the cup of fear and ruin.
It is the cup of your sister Samaria.
34 You will drink everything in it,
and then you will smash it
and tear at your breasts.
I have spoken, says the Lord GOD.
35 "So this is what the Lord GOD says: You
have forgotten me and turned your back on
me. So you will be punished for your sexual
sins."

Judgment on Samaria and Jerusalem

36 The LORD said to me: "Human, will you
judge Samaria and Jerusalem, showing them
their hateful acts? 37 They are guilty of
adultery and murder. They have taken part
in adultery with their idols. They even
offered our children as sacrifices in the fire
to be food for these idols. 38 They have also
done this to me: They made my Temple
unclean at the same time they dishonored
my Sabbaths. 39 They sacrificed their
children to their idols. Then they entered my
Temple at that very time to dishonor it. That
is what they did inside my Temple!
40 "They even sent for men from far away,
who came after a messenger was sent to
them. The two sisters bathed themselves for
them, painted their eyes, and put on jewelry.
41 They sat on a fine bed with a table set
before it, on which they put my incense and
my oil.
42 "There was the noise of a reckless crowd
in the city. Common people gathered, and
drunkards were brought from the desert.
They put bracelets on the wrists of the two
sisters and beautiful crowns on their heads.
43 Then I said about the one who was worn
out by her acts of adultery, 'Let them
continue their sexual sins with her. She is
nothing but a prostitute.' 44 They kept going
to her as they would go to a prostitute. So
they continued to go to Samaria and
Jerusalem, these shameful women. 45 But
men who do right will punish them as they
punish women who take part in adultery
and who murder people, because they are
guilty of adultery and murder.
46 "This is what the Lord GOD says: Bring
together a mob against Samaria and
Jerusalem, and hand them over to be
frightened and robbed. 47 Let the mob kill
them by throwing stones at them, and
let them cut them down with their swords.
Let them kill their sons and daughters and
burn their houses down.
48 "So I will put an end to sexual sins in the
land. Then all women will be warned, and
they will not do the sexual sins you have
done. 49 You will be punished for your sexual
sins and the sin of worshiping idols. Then
you will know that I am the Lord GOD."

The Pot and the Meat

24
The LORD spoke his word to me in the
ninth year of our captivity, in the
tenth month, on the tenth day of the month.
He said: 2 "Human, write down today's date,
this very date. The king of Babylon has
surrounded Jerusalem this very day. 3 And
tell a story to the people who refuse to obey
me. Say to them: 'This is what the Lord GOD
says:
Put on the pot; put it on
and pour water in it.
4 Put in the pieces of meat,
the best pieces—the legs and the
shoulders.
Fill it with the best bones.
5 Take the best of the flock,
and pile wood under the pot.
Boil the pieces of meat
until even the bones are cooked.
6 " 'This is what the Lord GOD says:
How terrible it will be for the city of
murderers!
How terrible it will be for the rusty pot
whose rust will not come off!
Take the meat out of it, piece by piece.
Don't choose any special piece.
7 " 'The blood from her killings is still in
the city.
She poured the blood on the bare rock.
She did not pour it on the ground
where dust would cover it.
8 To stir up my anger and revenge,

I put the blood she spilled on the bare
rock
so it will not be covered.
9" 'So this is what the Lord GOD says:
How terrible it will be for the city of
murderers!
I myself will pile the wood high for
burning.
10Pile up the wood
and light the fire.
Finish cooking the meat.
Mix in the spices,
and let the bones burn.
11Then set the empty pot on the coals
so it may become hot and its copper
sides glow.
The dirty scum stuck inside it may then
melt
and its rust burn away.
12But efforts to clean the pot have failed.
Its heavy rust cannot be removed,
even in the fire.

13" 'By your sinful action you have become
unclean. I wanted to cleanse you, but you are
still unclean. You will never be cleansed
from your sin until my anger against you is
carried out.
14" 'I, the LORD, have spoken. The time has
come for me to act. I will not hold back
punishment or feel pity or change my mind.
I will judge you by your ways and actions,
says the Lord GOD.' "

The Death of Ezekiel's Wife

15Then the LORD spoke his word to me,
saying: 16"Human, I am going to take your
wife from you, the woman you look at with
love. She will die suddenly, but you must not
be sad or cry loudly for her or shed any tears.
17Groan silently; do not cry loudly for the
dead. Tie on your turban, and put your
sandals on your feet. Do not cover your face,
and do not eat the food people eat when
they are sad about a death."
18So I spoke to the people in the
morning, and my wife died in the evening.
The next morning I did as I had been
commanded.
19Then the people asked me, "Tell us, what
do the things you are doing mean for us?"
20Then I said to them, "The LORD spoke his
word to me. He said, 21'Say to the people of
Israel, This is what the Lord GOD says: I am
going to dishonor my Temple. You think it
gives you strength. You are proud of it, and
you look at it with love and tenderness. But
your sons and daughters that you left behind
in Jerusalem will fall dead by the sword.
22When that happens, you are to act as I
have: you are not to cover your face, and you
are not to eat the food people eat when they
are sad about a death. 23Your turbans must
stay on your heads, and your sandals on your
feet. You must not cry loudly, but you must
rot away in your sins and groan to each
other. 24So Ezekiel is to be an example for
you. You must do all the same things he did.
When all this happens, you will know that I
am the Lord GOD.'
25"And as for you, human, this is how it
will be. I will take away the Temple that
gives them strength and joy, that makes
them proud. They look at it with love, and it
makes them happy. And I will take away
their sons and daughters also. 26At that time
a person who escapes will come to you with
information for you to hear. 27At that very
time your mouth will be opened. You will
speak and be silent no more. So you will be a
sign for them, and they will know that I am
the LORD."

Prophecy Against Ammon

25 The LORD spoke his word to me,
saying: 2"Human, look toward the
people of Ammon and prophesy against
them. 3Say to them, 'Hear the word of the
Lord GOD. This is what the Lord GOD says: You
were glad when my Temple was dishonored,
when the land of Israel was ruined, and when
the people of Judah were taken away as
captives. 4So I am going to give you to the
people of the East to be theirs. They will set
up their camps among you and make their
homes among you. They will eat your fruit
and drink your milk. 5I will make the city of
Rabbah a pasture for camels and the land of
Ammon a resting place for sheep. Then you
will know that I am the LORD. 6This is what
the Lord GOD says: You have clapped your
hands and stamped your feet; you have
laughed about all the insults you made
against the land of Israel. 7So I will use my
power against you. I will give you to the
nations as if you were treasures taken in war.
I will wipe you out of the lands so you will no
longer be a nation, and I will destroy you.
Then you will know that I am the LORD.'

devotion 228

EZEKIEL 25:1–7

LIVING LIKE AN AMMONITE

The Ammonites suffered the wrath of God because of their unrighteousness. They had laughed at God and his people. They had lived in violation of God's authority and dishonored him with their actions. And God promised to destroy the Ammonites because of their godlessness.

The evidence of God's coming wrath is all around us. Death is an evidence of his penalty for sin. Those who die without the Savior are doomed to eternal suffering. There is also a universal misery that we watch increase as the generations continue. Our human behavior is sinking by degrees as we witness the ungodly experience God's wrath and its consequences.

But the good news is that the life and death of Jesus has the power to deliver us from the wrath of God. We have a refuge and a hope without end. Those who believe can hide themselves underneath the covering of Jesus' love and forgiveness where none will perish, but all will receive everlasting life.

We should fear the wrath of God for those who do not know Jesus as their Savior. He is serious about the consequences of an ungodly life. But we also have the great privilege of offering a safe haven from his fury. Because of his kindness, God sent Jesus to deliver us from that certain doom.

We have good news for those who live like Ammonites: the wrath of God can be averted by trusting in Jesus. He is a safe place, a strong tower, and our everlasting hope.

Prophecy Against Moab and Edom

8"This is what the Lord GOD says: 'Moab
and Edom say, "The people of Judah are like
all the other nations." 9So I am going to take
away the cities that protect Moab's borders,
the best cities in that land: Beth Jeshimoth,
Baal Meon, and Kiriathaim. 10Then I will
give Moab, along with the Ammonites, to
the people of the East as their possession.
Then, along with the Ammonites, Moab will
not be a nation anymore. 11So I will punish
the people of Moab, and they will know that
I am the LORD.'

Prophecy Against Edom

12"This is what the Lord GOD says: 'Edom
took revenge on the people of Judah, and the
Edomites became guilty because of it. 13So
this is what the Lord GOD says: I will use my
power against Edom, killing every human
and animal in it. And I will destroy Edom all
the way from Teman to Dedan as they die in
battle. 14I will use my people Israel to take
revenge on Edom. So the Israelites will do to
Edom what my hot anger demands. Then
the Edomites will know what my revenge
feels like, says the Lord GOD.'

Prophecy Against Philistia

15"This is what the Lord GOD says: 'The
Philistines have taken revenge with hateful
hearts. Because of their strong hatred, they
have tried to destroy Judah. 16So this is what
the Lord GOD says: I will use my power
against the Philistines. I will kill the
Kerethites, and I will destroy those people
still alive on the coast of the Mediterranean
Sea. 17I will punish them in my anger and do
great acts of revenge to them. They will
know that I am the LORD when I take
revenge on them.'"

Prophecy Against Tyre

26 It was the eleventh year of our
captivity, on the first day of the
month. The LORD spoke his word to me,
saying: 2“Human, the city of Tyre has spoken
against Jerusalem: ‘The city that traded with
the nations is destroyed. Now we can be the
trading center. Since the city of Jerusalem is
ruined, we can make money.’ 3So this is
what the Lord GOD says: I am against you,
Tyre. I will bring many nations against you,
like the sea beating its waves on your island
shores. 4They will destroy the walls of Tyre
and pull down her towers. I will also scrape
away her ruins and make her a bare rock.
5Tyre will be an island where fishermen dry
their nets. I have spoken, says the Lord GOD.
The nations will steal treasures from Tyre.
6Also, her villages on the shore across from
the island will be destroyed by war. Then
they will know that I am the LORD.

Nebuchadnezzar to Attack Tyre

7“This is what the Lord GOD says: I will
bring a king from the north against Tyre. He
is Nebuchadnezzar king of Babylon, the
greatest king, with his horses, chariots,
horsemen, and a great army. 8He will fight a
battle and destroy your villages on the shore
across from the island. He will set up devices
to attack you. He will build a road of earth to
the top of the walls. He will raise his shields
against you. 9He will bring logs to pound
through your city walls, and he will break
down your towers with his iron bars. 10His
horses will be so many that they will cover
you with their dust. Your walls will shake at
the noise of horsemen, wagons, and chariots.
The king of Babylon will enter your city
gates as men enter a city where the walls are
broken through. 11The hoofs of his horses
will run over your streets. He will kill your
army with the sword, and your strong pillars
will fall down to the ground. 12Also, his men
will take away your riches and will steal the
things you sell. They will break down your
walls and destroy your nice houses. They
will throw your stones, wood, and trash into
the sea. 13So I will stop your songs; the music
of your harps will not be heard anymore. 14I
will make you a bare rock, and you will be a
place for drying fishing nets. You will not be
built again, because I, the LORD, have spoken,
says the Lord GOD.

15“This is what the Lord GOD says to Tyre:
The people who live along the seacoast will
shake with fear when they hear about your
defeat. Those of you who are injured and
dying will groan. 16Then all the leaders of
the seacoast will get down from their
thrones, take off their beautiful needlework
clothes, and show how afraid they are. They
will sit on the ground and tremble all the
time. When they see you, they will be
shocked. 17They will begin singing a funeral
song about you and will say to you:

‘Tyre, you famous city, you have been
destroyed!
You have lost your sea power!
You and your people
had great power on the seas.
You made everyone around you
afraid of you.
18Now the people who live by the coast
tremble,
now that you have fallen.
The islands of the sea
are afraid because you have been
defeated.’

19“This is what the Lord GOD says: I will
make you an empty city, like cities that have
no people living in them. I will bring the
deep ocean waters over you, and the
Mediterranean Sea will cover you. 20At that
time I will send you down to the place of the
dead to join those who died long ago. I will
make you live with the dead below the earth
in places that are like old ruins. You will not
come back from there or have any place in
the world of the living again. 21Other people
will be afraid of what happened to you, and
it will be the end of you. People will look for
you, but they will never find you again, says
the Lord GOD.”

A Funeral Song for Tyre

27 The LORD spoke his word to me,
saying: 2“Human, sing a funeral song
for the city of Tyre. 3Speak to Tyre, which has
ports for the Mediterranean Sea and is a place
for trade for the people of many lands along
the seacoast. ‘This is what the Lord GOD says:

Tyre, you have said,
“I am like a beautiful ship.”
4You were at home on the high seas.
Your builders made your beauty perfect.
5They made all your boards
of fir trees from Mount Hermon.

They took a cedar tree from Lebanon
 to make a ship's mast for you.
6They made your oars
 from oak trees from Bashan.
They made your deck
 from cypress trees from the coast of
 Cyprus
 and set ivory into it.
7Your sail of linen with designs sewed on it
 came from Egypt
 and became like a flag for you.
Your cloth shades over the deck were blue
 and purple
 and came from the island of Cyprus.
8Men from Sidon and Arvad used oars to
 row you.
 Tyre, your skilled men were the sailors
 on your deck.
9Workers of Byblos were with you,
 putting caulk[n] in your ship's seams.
All the ships of the sea and their sailors
 came alongside to trade with you.

10" 'Men of Persia, Lydia, and Put
 were warriors in your navy
and hung their shields and helmets on
 your sides.
 They made you look beautiful.
11Men of Arvad and Cilicia
 guarded your city walls all around.
Men of Gammad
 were in your watchtowers
and hung their shields around your walls.
 They made your beauty perfect.

12" 'People of Tarshish became traders for
you because of your great wealth. They
traded your goods for silver, iron, tin, and
lead.
13" 'People of Greece, Tubal, and Meshech
became merchants for you. They traded your
goods for slaves and items of bronze.
14" 'People of Beth Togarmah traded your
goods for work horses, war horses, and
mules.
15" 'People of Rhodes became merchants
for you, selling your goods on many
coastlands. They brought back ivory tusks
and valuable black wood as your payment.
16" 'People of Aram became traders for
you, because you had so many good things
to sell. They traded your goods for turquoise,
purple cloth, cloth with designs sewed on,
fine linen, coral, and rubies.
17" 'People of Judah and Israel became
merchants for you. They traded your goods
for wheat from Minnith, and for honey, olive
oil, and balm.
18-19" 'People of Damascus became traders
for you because you have many good things
and great wealth. They traded your goods for
wine from Helbon, wool from Zahar, and
barrels of wine from Izal. They received
wrought iron, cassia, and sugar cane in
payment for your good things.
20" 'People of Dedan became merchants
for you, trading saddle blankets for riding.
21" 'People of Arabia and all the rulers of
Kedar became traders for you. They received
lambs, male sheep, and goats in payment for
you.
22" 'The merchants of Sheba and Raamah
became merchants for you. They traded your
goods for all the best spices, valuable gems,
and gold.
23" 'People of Haran, Canneh, Eden, and
the traders of Sheba, Asshur, and Kilmad
became merchants for you. 24They were paid
with the best clothes, blue cloth, cloth with
designs sewed on, carpets of many colors,
and tightly wound ropes.
25" 'Trading ships
 carried the things you sold.
You were like a ship full of heavy cargo
 in the middle of the sea.
26The men who rowed you
 brought you out into the high seas,
but the east wind broke you to pieces
 in the middle of the sea.
27Your wealth, your trade, your goods,
 your seamen, your sailors, your
 workers,
your traders, your warriors,
 and everyone else on board
sank into the sea
 on the day your ship was wrecked.
28The people on the shore shake with fear
 when your sailors cry out.
29All the men who row
 leave their ships;
the seamen and the sailors of other ships
 stand on the shore.
30They cry loudly about you;
 they cry very much.
They throw dust on their heads
 and roll in ashes to show they are sad.

27:9 caulk Something like tar put between the boards of a ship to make it waterproof.

31 They shave their heads for you,
and they put on rough cloth to show
they are upset.
They cry and sob for you;
they cry loudly.
32 And in their loud crying
they sing a funeral song for you:
"No one was ever destroyed like Tyre,
surrounded by the sea."
33 When the goods you traded went out over
the seas,
you met the needs of many nations.
With your great wealth and goods,
you made kings of the earth rich.
34 But now you are broken by the sea
and have sunk to the bottom.
Your goods and all the people on board
have gone down with you.
35 All those who live along the shore
are shocked by what happened to you.
Their kings are terribly afraid,
and their faces show their fear.
36 The traders among the nations hiss at
you.
You have come to a terrible end,
and you are gone forever.' "

Prophecy Against the King of Tyre

28 The LORD spoke his word to me,
saying: 2 "Human, say to the ruler of
Tyre: 'This is what the Lord GOD says:
Because you are proud,
you say, "I am a god.
I sit on the throne of a god
in the middle of the seas."
You think you are as wise as a god,
but you are a human, not a god.
3 You think you are wiser than Daniel.
You think you can find out all secrets.
4 Through your wisdom and understanding
you have made yourself rich.
You have gained gold and silver
and have saved it in your storerooms.
5 Through your great skill in trading,
you have made your riches grow.
You are too proud
because of your riches.
6 " 'So this is what the Lord GOD says:
You think you are wise
like a god,
7 but I will bring foreign people against
you,
the cruelest nation.
They will pull out their swords
and destroy all that your wisdom has
built,
and they will dishonor your greatness.
8 They will kill you;
you will die a terrible death
like those who are killed at sea.
9 While they are killing you,
you will not be able to say anymore, "I
am a god."
You will be only a human, not a god,
when your murderers kill you.
10 You will die like an unclean person;
foreigners will kill you.
I have spoken, says the Lord GOD.' "
11 The LORD spoke his word to me, saying:
12 "Human, sing a funeral song for the king of
Tyre. Say to him: 'This is what the Lord GOD
says:
You were an example of what was perfect,
full of wisdom and perfect in beauty.
13 You had a wonderful life,
as if you were in Eden, the garden of
God.
Every valuable gem was on you:
ruby, topaz, and emerald,
yellow quartz, onyx, and jasper,
sapphire, turquoise, and chrysolite.
Your jewelry was made of gold.
It was prepared on the day you were
created.
14 I appointed a living creature to guard you.
I put you on the holy mountain of God.
You walked among the gems that
shined like fire.
15 Your life was right and good
from the day you were created,
until evil was found in you.
16 Because you traded with countries far
away,
you learned to be cruel, and you sinned.
So I threw you down in disgrace from the
mountain of God.
And the living creature who guarded
you
forced you out from among the gems
that shined like fire.
17 You became too proud
because of your beauty.
You ruined your wisdom
because of your greatness.
I threw you down to the ground.
Your example taught a lesson to other
kings.
18 You dishonored your places of worship

through your many sins and dishonest
trade.
So I set on fire the place where you
lived,
and the fire burned you up.
I turned you into ashes on the ground
for all those watching to see.
19All the nations who knew you
are shocked about you.
Your punishment was so terrible,
and you are gone forever.' "

Prophecy Against Sidon

20The LORD spoke his word to me, saying:
21"Human, look toward the city of Sidon and
prophesy against her. 22Say: 'This is what the
Lord GOD says:
I am against you, Sidon,
and I will show my glory among you.
People will know that I am the LORD
when I have punished Sidon;
I will show my holiness by defeating
her.
23I will send diseases to Sidon,
and blood will flow in her streets.
Those who are wounded in Sidon will fall
dead,
attacked from all sides.
Then they will know that I am the LORD.

God Will Help Israel

24" 'No more will neighboring nations be
like thorny branches or sharp stickers to
hurt Israel. Then they will know that I am
the Lord GOD.
25" 'This is what the Lord GOD says: I will
gather the people of Israel from the nations
where they are scattered. I will show my
holiness when the nations see what I do for
my people. Then they will live in their own
land—the land I gave to my servant Jacob.
26They will live safely in the land and will
build houses and plant vineyards. They will
live in safety after I have punished all the
nations around who hate them. Then they
will know that I am the LORD their God.' "

Prophecy Against Egypt

29 It was the tenth year of our captivity,
in the tenth month, on the twelfth

devotion 229

EZEKIEL 28:22

IMPOSSIBLE ODDS ARE THE BEST POSSIBILITIES

There is no greater opportunity for the Lord to reveal himself than a person trying to overcome what seem like impossible odds. All throughout the Old Testament, you will find occurrences when the Lord told the leaders to decrease their army size. Why did he do that? Why not manifest a few thousand more? Well, because God wanted the glory. He wanted to be the deliverer.

If you are facing some impossible odds, open your mind to the possibility that the Lord wants to show you his glory. Can you recount the times you thought you were in a hopeless situation, but then at just the right moment, and in the midst of your circumstance, God delivered you? It is important for us to reflect on the moments when our faith was increased and our hearts were moved knowing that the Lord redeemed us. That remembrance brings hope and joy when we find our souls and minds under attack.

The amazing thing is not only the conquest of winning the battle but also seeing the glory of God revealed in everyday circumstances—your circumstances! He wants to defeat your enemies! He wants to be glorified! Our God is a jealous God, and he desires trust from his children. He does not want anyone or anything taking credit for the work of his hands. His hand alone claims the victory, and his hand alone brings judgment. If you are feeling trapped by the battle, stand firm and see the salvation of the Lord!

day of the month. The LORD spoke his word to
me, saying: [2]"Human, look toward the king of
Egypt, and prophesy against him and all
Egypt. [3]Say: 'This is what the Lord GOD says:
I am against you, king of Egypt.
You are like a great crocodile that lies in the Nile River.
You say, "The Nile is mine;
I made it for myself."
[4]But I will put hooks in your jaws,
and I will make the fish of the Nile stick to your sides.
I will pull you up out of your rivers,
with all the fish sticking to your sides.
[5]I will leave you in the desert,
you and all the fish from your rivers.
You will fall onto the ground;
you will not be picked up or buried.
I have given you to the wild animals
and to the birds of the sky for food.
[6]Then all the people who live in Egypt will
know that I am the LORD.

" 'Israel tried to lean on you for help, but
you were like a crutch made out of a weak
stalk of grass. [7]When their hands grabbed
you, you splintered and tore open their
shoulders. When they leaned on you, you
broke and made all their backs twist.

[8]" 'So this is what the Lord GOD says: I will
cause an enemy to attack you and kill your
people and animals. [9]Egypt will become an
empty desert. Then they will know that I am
the LORD.

" 'Because you said, "The Nile River is
mine, and I have made it," [10]I am against you
and your rivers. I will destroy the land of
Egypt and make it an empty desert from
Migdol in the north to Aswan in the south,
all the way to the border of Cush. [11]No
person or animal will walk through it, and
no one will live in Egypt for forty years. [12]I
will make the land of Egypt the most
deserted country of all. Her cities will be the
most deserted of all ruined cities for forty
years. I will scatter the Egyptians among the
nations, spreading them among the
countries.

[13]" 'This is what the Lord GOD says: After
forty years I will gather Egypt from the
nations where they have been scattered. [14]I
will bring back the Egyptian captives and
make them return to southern Egypt, to the
land they came from. They will become a
weak kingdom there. [15]It will be the weakest
kingdom, and it will never again rule other
nations. I will make it so weak it will never
again rule over the nations. [16]The Israelites
will never again depend on Egypt. Instead,
Egypt's punishment will remind the
Israelites of their sin in turning to Egypt for
help. Then they will know that I am the
Lord GOD.' "

Egypt Is Given to Babylon

[17]It was the twenty-seventh year of our
captivity, in the first month, on the first day
of the month. The LORD spoke his word to
me, saying: [18]"Human, Nebuchadnezzar king
of Babylon made his army fight hard against
Tyre. Every soldier's head was rubbed bare,
and every shoulder was rubbed raw. But
Nebuchadnezzar and his army gained
nothing from fighting Tyre. [19]So this is what
the Lord GOD says: I will give the land of
Egypt to Nebuchadnezzar king of Babylon.
He will take away Egypt's people and its
wealth and its treasures as pay for his army.
[20]I am giving Nebuchadnezzar the land of
Egypt as a reward for working hard for me,
says the Lord GOD.

[21]"At that time I will make Israel grow
strong again, and I will let you, Ezekiel,
speak to them. Then they will know that I
am the LORD."

Egypt Will Be Punished

30 The LORD spoke his word to me,
saying: [2]"Human, prophesy and say,
'This is what the Lord GOD says:
Cry and say,
"The terrible day is coming."
[3]The day is near;
the LORD's day of judging is near.
It is a cloudy day
and a time when the nations will be judged.
[4]An enemy will attack Egypt,
and Cush will tremble with fear.
When the killing begins in Egypt,
her wealth will be taken away,
and her foundations will be torn down.
[5]Cush, Put, Lydia, Arabia, Libya, and some of
my people who had made an agreement
with Egypt will fall dead in war.

[6]" 'This is what the LORD says:
Those who fight on Egypt's side will fall.
The power she is proud of will be lost.
The people in Egypt will fall dead in war

from Migdol in the north to Aswan in
the south,
says the Lord GOD.
7They will be the most deserted lands.
Egypt's cities will be the worst of cities
that lie in ruins.
8Then they will know that I am the LORD
when I set fire to Egypt
and when all those nations on her side
are crushed.
9" 'At that time I will send messengers in
ships to frighten Cush, which now feels safe.
The people of Cush will tremble with fear
when Egypt is punished. And that time is
sure to come.
10" 'This is what the Lord GOD says:
I will destroy great numbers of people in
Egypt
through the power of Nebuchadnezzar
king of Babylon.
11Nebuchadnezzar and his army,
the cruelest army of any nation,
will be brought in to destroy the land.
They will pull out their swords against
Egypt
and will fill the land with those they
kill.
12I will make the streams of the Nile River
become dry land,
and then I will sell the land to evil
people.
I will destroy the land and everything
in it
through the power of foreigners.
I, the LORD, have spoken.

Egypt's Idols Are Destroyed

13" 'This is what the Lord GOD says:
I will destroy the idols
and take away the statues of gods from
the city of Memphis.
There will no longer be a leader in Egypt,
and I will spread fear through the land
of Egypt.
14I will make southern Egypt empty
and start a fire in Zoan
and punish Thebes.
15And I will pour out my anger against
Pelusium,
the strong place of Egypt.
I will destroy great numbers of people
in Thebes.
16I will set fire to Egypt.
Pelusium will be in great pain.
The walls of Thebes will be broken open,
and Memphis will have troubles every
day.
17The young men of Heliopolis and
Bubastis
will fall dead in war,
and the people will be taken away as
captives.
18In Tahpanhes the day will be dark
when I break Egypt's power.
Then she will no longer be proud of her
power.
A cloud will cover Egypt,
and her villages will be captured and
taken away.
19So I will punish Egypt,
and they will know I am the LORD.' "

Egypt Becomes Weak

20It was in the eleventh year of our
captivity, in the first month, on the seventh
day of the month. The LORD spoke his word
to me, saying: 21"Human, I have broken the
powerful arm of the king of Egypt. It has not
been tied up, so it will not get well. It has not
been wrapped with a bandage, so it will not
be strong enough to hold a sword in war.
22So this is what the Lord GOD says: I am
against the king of Egypt. I will break his
arms, both the strong arm and the broken
arm, and I will make the sword fall from his
hand. 23I will scatter the Egyptians among
the nations, spreading them among the
countries. 24I will make the arms of the king
of Babylon strong and put my sword in his
hand. But I will break the arms of the king of
Egypt. Then when he faces the king of
Babylon, he will cry out in pain like a dying
person. 25So I will make the arms of the king
of Babylon strong, but the arms of the king
of Egypt will fall. Then people will know
that I am the LORD when I put my sword into
the hand of the king of Babylon and he uses
it in war against Egypt. 26Then I will scatter
the Egyptians among the nations, spreading
them among the countries. Then they will
know that I am the LORD."

A Cedar Tree

31 It was in the eleventh year of our
captivity, in the third month, on the
first day of the month. The LORD spoke his
word to me, saying: 2"Human, say to the
king of Egypt and his people:

'No one is like you in your greatness.
3 Assyria was once like a cedar tree in Lebanon
with beautiful branches that shaded the forest.
It was very tall;
its top was among the clouds.
4 Much water made the tree grow;
the deep springs made it tall.
Rivers flowed
around the bottom of the tree
and sent their streams
to all other trees in the countryside.
5 So the tree was taller
than all the other trees in the countryside.
Its limbs became long and big
because of so much water.
6 All the birds of the sky
made their nests in the tree's limbs.
And all the wild animals
gave birth under its branches.
All great nations
lived in the tree's shade.
7 So the tree was great and beautiful,
with its long branches,
because its roots reached down to much water.
8 The cedar trees in the garden of God
were not as great as it was.
The pine trees
did not have such great limbs.
The plane trees
did not have such branches.
No tree in the garden of God
was as beautiful as this tree.
9 I made it beautiful
with many branches,
and all the trees of Eden in the garden of God
wanted to be like it.

10 " 'So this is what the Lord GOD says: The
tree grew tall. Its top reached the clouds, and
it became proud of its height. 11 So I handed it
over to a mighty ruler of the nations for him
to punish it. Because it was evil, I got rid of it.
12 The cruelest foreign nation cut it down and
left it. The tree's branches fell on the
mountains and in all the valleys, and its
broken limbs were in all the ravines of the
land. All the nations of the earth left the
shade of that tree. 13 The birds of the sky live
on the fallen tree. The wild animals live
among the tree's fallen branches. 14 So the
trees that grow by the water will not be
proud to be tall; they will not put their tops
among the clouds. None of the trees that are
watered well will grow that tall, because they
all are meant to die and go under the ground.
They will be with people who have died and
have gone down to the place of the dead.

15 " 'This is what the Lord GOD says: On the
day when the tree went down to the place of
the dead, I made the deep springs cry loudly.
I covered them and held back their rivers,
and the great waters stopped flowing. I
dressed Lebanon in black to show her
sadness about the great tree, and all the trees
in the countryside were sad about it. 16 I
made the nations shake with fear at the
sound of the tree falling when I brought it
down to the place of the dead. It went to join
those who have gone down to the grave.
Then all the trees of Eden and the best trees
of Lebanon, all the well-watered trees, were
comforted in the place of the dead below the
earth. 17 These trees had also gone down with
the great tree to the place of the dead. They
joined those who were killed in war and
those among the nations who had lived
under the great tree's shade.

18 " 'So no tree in Eden is equal to you,
Egypt, in greatness and honor, but you will
go down to join the trees of Eden in the
place below the earth. You will lie among
unclean people, with those who were killed
in war.

" 'This is about the king of Egypt and all
his people, says the Lord GOD.' "

A Funeral Song

32 It was in the twelfth year of our
captivity, in the twelfth month, on the
first day of the month. The LORD spoke his
word to me, saying: 2 "Human, sing a funeral
song about the king of Egypt. Say to him:

'You are like a young lion among the nations.
You are like a crocodile in the seas.
You splash around in your streams
and stir up the water with your feet,
making the rivers muddy.
3 " 'This is what the Lord GOD says:
I will spread my net over you,
and I will use a large group of people
to pull you up in my net.
4 Then I will throw you on the land
dropping you onto the ground.

I will let the birds of the sky rest on you
and all the animals of the earth eat you
until they are full.
5 I will scatter your flesh on the mountains
and fill the valleys with what is left of
you.
6 I will drench the land with your flowing
blood
as far as the mountains,
and the ravines will be full of your
flesh.
7 When I make you disappear,
I will cover the sky and make the stars
dark.
I will cover the sun with a cloud,
and the moon will not shine.
8 I will make all the shining lights in the
sky
become dark over you;
I will bring darkness over your land,
says the Lord GOD.
9 I will cause many people to be afraid
when I bring you as a captive into other
nations,
to lands you have not known.
10 I will cause many people to be shocked
about you.
Their kings will tremble with fear
because of you
when I swing my sword in front of
them.
They will shake every moment
on the day you fall;
each king will be afraid for his own life.
11 " 'So this is what the Lord GOD says:
The sword of the king of Babylon
will attack you.
12 I will cause your people to fall
by the swords of mighty soldiers,
the most terrible in the world.
They will destroy the pride of Egypt
and all its people.
13 I will also destroy all Egypt's cattle
which live alongside much water.
The foot of a human will not stir the
water,
and the hoofs of cattle will not muddy
it anymore.
14 So I will let the Egyptians' water become
clear.
I will cause their rivers to run as
smoothly as olive oil,
says the Lord GOD.
15 When I make the land of Egypt empty
and take everything that is in the land,
when I destroy all those who live in
Egypt,
then they will know that I am the
LORD.'

16 "This is the funeral song people will sing
for Egypt. The women of the nations will
sing it; they will sing a funeral song for
Egypt and all its people, says the Lord GOD."

Egypt to Be Destroyed

17 It was in the twelfth year of our
captivity, on the fifteenth day of the month.
The LORD spoke his word to me, saying:
18 "Human, cry for the people of Egypt. Bring
down Egypt, together with the women of the
powerful nations; bring them down to the
place of the dead below the earth to join
those who go to the place of the dead. 19 Say
to them: 'Are you more beautiful than
others? Go lie down in death with those who
are unclean.' 20 The Egyptians will fall
among those killed in war. The sword is
ready; the enemy will drag Egypt and all her
people away. 21 From the place of the dead
the leaders of the mighty ones will speak
about the king of Egypt and the nations
which help him: 'The unclean, those killed
in war, have come down here and lie dead.'
22 "Assyria and all its army lie dead there.
The graves of their soldiers are all around.
All were killed in war, 23 and their graves
were put in the deepest parts of the place of
the dead. Assyria's army lies around its
grave. When they lived on earth, they
frightened people, but now all of them have
been killed in war.
24 "The nation of Elam is there with all its
army around its grave. All of them were
killed in war. They had frightened people on
earth and were unclean, so they went down
to the lowest parts of the place of the dead.
They must carry their shame with those who
have gone down to the place of the dead. 25 A
bed has been made for Elam with all those
killed in war. The graves of her soldiers are
all around her. All Elam's people are unclean,
killed in war. They frightened people when
they lived on earth, but now they must carry
their shame with those who have gone down
to the place of the dead. Their graves are with
the rest who were killed.
26 "Meshech and Tubal are there with the
graves of all their soldiers around them. All

of them are unclean and have been killed in
war. They also frightened people when they
lived on earth. 27But they are not buried with
the other soldiers who were killed in battle
long ago, those who went with their
weapons of war to the place of the dead.
These soldiers had their swords laid under
their heads and their shields on their bodies.
These mighty soldiers used to frighten
people when they lived on earth.
28"You, king of Egypt, will be broken and
lie among those who are unclean, who were
killed in war.
29"Edom is there also, with its kings and
all its leaders. They were mighty, but now
they lie in death with those killed in war,
with those who are unclean, with those who
have gone down to the place of the dead.
30"All the rulers of the north and all the
Sidonians are there. Their strength
frightened people, but they have gone down
in shame with those who were killed. They
are unclean, lying with those killed in war.
They carry their shame with those who have
gone down to the place of the dead.
31"The king of Egypt and his army will see
these who have been killed in war. Then he
will be comforted for all his soldiers killed in
war, says the Lord GOD. 32I made people
afraid of the king of Egypt while he lived on
earth. But he and all his people will lie
among those who are unclean, who were
killed in war, says the Lord GOD."

Ezekiel Is Watchman for Israel

33 The LORD spoke his word to me,
saying: 2"Human, speak to your
people and say to them: 'Suppose I bring a
war against a land. The people of the land
may choose one of their men and make him
their watchman. 3When he sees the enemy
coming to attack the land, he will blow the
trumpet and warn the people. 4If they hear
the sound of the trumpet but do nothing, the
enemy will come and kill them. They will be
responsible for their own deaths. 5They
heard the sound of the trumpet but didn't do
anything. So they are to blame for their own
deaths. If they had done something, they
would have saved their own lives. 6But if the
watchman sees the enemy coming to attack
and does not blow the trumpet, the people
will not be warned. Then if the enemy
comes and kills any of them, they have died
because of their own sin. But I will punish
the watchman for their deaths.'
7"You, human, are the one I have made a
watchman for Israel. If you hear a word from
my mouth, you must warn them for me.
8Suppose I say to the wicked: 'Wicked
people, you will surely die,' but you don't
speak to warn the wicked to stop doing evil.
Then they will die because they were
sinners, but I will punish you for their
deaths. 9But if you warn the wicked to stop
doing evil and they do not stop, they will die
because they were sinners. But you have
saved your life.
10"So you, human, say to Israel: 'You have
said: Surely our law-breaking and sins are
hurting us. They will kill us. What can we
do so we will live?' 11Say to them: 'The Lord
GOD says: As surely as I live, I do not want
any who are wicked to die. I want them to
stop doing evil and live. Stop! Stop your
wicked ways! You don't want to die, do you,
people of Israel?'
12"Human, say to your people: 'The
goodness of those who do right will not save
them when they sin. The evil of wicked
people will not cause them to be punished
if they stop doing it. If good people sin,
they will not be able to live by the good
they did earlier.' 13If I tell good people, 'You
will surely live,' they might think they have
done enough good and then do evil. Then
none of the good things they did will be
remembered. They will die because of the
evil they have done. 14Or, if I say to the
wicked people, 'You will surely die,' they
may stop sinning and do what is right and
honest. 15For example, they may return what
somebody gave them as a promise to repay a
loan, or pay back what they stole. If they live
by the rules that give life and do not sin,
then they will surely live, and they will not
die. 16They will not be punished for any of
their sins. They now do what is right and
fair, so they will surely live.
17"Your people say: 'The way of the Lord is
not fair.' But it is their own ways that are not
fair. 18When the good people stop doing
good and do evil, they will die for their evil.
19But when the wicked stop doing evil and
do what is right and fair, they will live. 20You
still say: 'The way of the Lord is not fair.'
Israel, I will judge all of you by your own
ways."

The Fall of Jerusalem Explained

21 It was in the twelfth year of our
captivity, on the fifth day of the tenth
month. A person who had escaped from
Jerusalem came to me and said, "Jerusalem
has been captured." 22 Now I had felt the
power of the LORD on me the evening before.
He had made me able to talk again before
this person came to me. I could speak; I was
not without speech anymore.
23 Then the LORD spoke his word to me,
saying: 24 "Human, people who live in the
ruins in the land of Israel are saying:
'Abraham was only one person, yet he was
given the land as his own. Surely the land
has been given to us, who are many, as our
very own.' 25 So say to them: 'This is what the
Lord GOD says: You eat meat with the blood
still in it, you ask your idols for help, and
you murder people. Should you then have
the land as your very own? 26 You depend on
your sword and do terrible things which I
hate. Each of you has sexual relations with
his neighbor's wife. So should you have the
land?'
27 "Say to them: 'This is what the Lord GOD
says: As surely as I live, those who are
among the city ruins in Israel will be killed
in war. I will cause those who live in the
country to be eaten by wild animals. People
hiding in the strongholds and caves will die
of disease. 28 I will make the land an empty
desert. The people's pride in the land's power
will end. The mountains of Israel will
become empty so that no one will pass
through them. 29 They will know that I am
the LORD when I make the land an empty
desert because of the things they have done
that I hate.'
30 "But as for you, human, your people are
talking about you by the walls and in the
doorways of houses. They say to each other:
'Come now, and hear the message from the
LORD.' 31 So they come to you in crowds as if
they were really ready to listen. They sit in
front of you as if they were my people and
hear your words, but they will not obey
them. With their mouths they tell me they
love me, but their hearts desire their selfish
profits. 32 To your people you are nothing
more than a singer who sings love songs and
has a beautiful voice and plays a musical

devotion 230

EZEKIEL 33:31–32

MUCK IN THE MOUTH

Why do we treat obedience like it is some infectious disease that is going to ooze over our lives like a cosmic killjoy? Hasn't obedience always been the turning point where bondage loses its grip and peace wins out? I would personally be crushed under the weight of this passage if the Lord were talking to me! Oh please, Father, do not let this be me!

I get so discouraged when I hear the things that come out of people's mouths sometimes, just talking plain smack about each other. Then I hear them yell, "I love you, see you next weekend!" from across the church parking lot. What is that? I will tell you what it is—it is the condition of a person's heart. It is revealing the muck that must be cleansed through an obedient body. Especially the mouth! That means if the Lord is quickening your heart to exercise control of your mouth, he expects you to do the physical work of keeping it closed unless you have a true praise.

A bench warmer is someone who studies the plays every week but never gets to play. I want you to be able to play and enjoy the life-changing truths that God is speaking to you through your devotional time, prayer, and pastoral feeding. But you have to get off the bench to play. "Do what God's teaching says; when you only listen and do nothing, you are fooling yourselves" (James 1:22). Could it be any clearer?

instrument well. They hear your words, but
they will not obey them.
33“When this comes true, and it surely
will happen, then the people will know that
a prophet has been among them.”

The Leaders Are Like Shepherds

34 The LORD spoke his word to me,
saying: 2“Human, prophesy against the
leaders of Israel, who are like shepherds.
Prophesy and say to them: ‘This is what the
Lord GOD says: How terrible it will be for the
shepherds of Israel who feed only themselves!
Why don't the shepherds feed the flock? 3You
eat the milk curds, and you clothe yourselves
with the wool. You kill the fat sheep, but you
do not feed the flock. 4You have not made the
weak strong. You have not healed the sick or
put bandages on those that were hurt. You
have not brought back those who strayed
away or searched for the lost. But you have
ruled the sheep with cruel force. 5The sheep
were scattered, because there was no
shepherd, and they became food for every
wild animal. 6My flock wandered over all the
mountains and on every high hill. They were
scattered all over the face of the earth, and no
one searched or looked for them.
7“ ‘So, you shepherds, hear the word of the
LORD. This is what the Lord GOD says: 8As
surely as I live, my flock has been caught
and eaten by all the wild animals, because
the flock has no shepherd. The shepherds
did not search for my flock. No, they fed
themselves instead of my flock. 9So, you
shepherds, hear the word of the LORD. 10This
is what the Lord GOD says: I am against the
shepherds. I will blame them for what has
happened to my sheep and will not let them
tend the flock anymore. Then the shepherds
will stop feeding themselves, and I will take
my flock from their mouths so they will no
longer be their food.
11“ ‘This is what the Lord GOD says: I,
myself, will search for my sheep and take
care of them. 12As a shepherd takes care of
his scattered flock when it is found, I will
take care of my sheep. I will save them from
all the places where they were scattered on a
cloudy and dark day. 13I will bring them out
from the nations and gather them from the
countries. I will bring them to their own
land and pasture them on the mountains of
Israel, in the ravines, and in all the places
where people live in the land. 14I will feed
them in a good pasture, and they will eat
grass on the high mountains of Israel. They
will lie down on good ground where they eat
grass, and they will eat in rich grassland on
the mountains of Israel. 15I will feed my
flock and lead them to rest, says the Lord
GOD. 16I will search for the lost, bring back
those that strayed away, put bandages on
those that were hurt, and make the weak
strong. But I will destroy those sheep that
are fat and strong. I will tend the sheep with
fairness.
17“ ‘This is what the Lord GOD says: As for
you, my flock, I will judge between one
sheep and another, between the male sheep
and the male goats. 18Is it not enough for
you to eat grass in the good land? Must you
crush the rest of the grass with your feet? Is
it not enough for you to drink clear water?
Must you make the rest of the water muddy
with your feet? 19Must my flock eat what
you crush, and must they drink what you
make muddy with your feet?
20“ ‘So this is what the Lord GOD says to
them: I, myself, will judge between the fat
sheep and the thin sheep. 21You push with
your side and with your shoulder, and you
knock down all the weak sheep with your
horns until you have forced them away. 22So
I will save my flock; they will not be hurt
anymore. I will judge between one sheep
and another. 23Then I will put over them one
shepherd, my servant David. He will feed
them and tend them and be their shepherd.
24Then I, the LORD, will be their God, and my
servant David will be a ruler among them. I,
the LORD, have spoken.
25“ ‘I will make an agreement of peace
with my sheep and will remove harmful
animals from the land. Then the sheep will
live safely in the desert and sleep in the
woods. 26I will bless them and let them live
around my hill. I will cause the rains to
come when it is time; there will be showers
to bless them. 27Also the trees in the
countryside will give their fruit, and the land
will give its harvest. And the sheep will be
safe on their land. Then they will know that
I am the LORD when I break the bars of their
captivity and save them from the power of
those who made them slaves. 28They will
not be led captive by the nations again. The
wild animals will not eat them, but they will

live safely, and no one will make them
afraid. 29I will give them a place famous for
its good crops, so they will no longer suffer
from hunger in the land. They will not suffer
the insults of other nations anymore. 30Then
they will know that I, the LORD their God,
am with them. The nation of Israel will
know that they are my people, says the Lord
GOD. 31You, my human sheep, are the sheep I
care for, and I am your God, says the Lord
GOD.' "

Prophecy Against Edom

35 The LORD spoke his word to me,
saying: 2"Human, look toward Edom
and prophesy against it. 3Say to it: 'This is
what the Lord GOD says: I am against you,
Edom. I will stretch out my hand against you
and make you an empty desert. 4I will destroy
your cities, and you will become empty. Then
you will know that I am the LORD.

5" 'You have always been an enemy of
Israel. You let them be defeated in war when
they were in trouble at the time of their final
punishment. 6So the Lord GOD says, as surely
as I live, I will let you be murdered. Murder
will chase you. Since you did not hate
murdering people, murder will chase you. 7I
will make Edom an empty ruin and destroy
everyone who goes in or comes out of it. 8I
will fill its mountains with those who are
killed. Those killed in war will fall on your
hills, in your valleys, and in all your ravines.
9I will make you a ruin forever; no one will
live in your cities. Then you will know that I
am the LORD.

10" 'You said, "These two nations, Israel
and Judah, and these two lands will be ours.
We will take them for our own." But the
LORD was there. 11So this is what the Lord
GOD says: As surely as I live, I will treat you
just as you treated them. You were angry and
jealous because you hated them. So I will
punish you and show the Israelites who I
am. 12Then you will know that I, the LORD,
have heard all your insults against the
mountains of Israel. You said, "They have
been ruined. They have been given to us to
eat." 13You have not stopped your proud talk
against me. I have heard you. 14This is what
the Lord GOD says: All the earth will be
happy when I make you an empty ruin.
15You were happy when the land of Israel
was ruined, but I will do the same thing to
you. Mount Seir and all Edom, you will
become an empty ruin. Then you will know
that I am the LORD.'

Israel to Come Home

36 "Human, prophesy to the mountains
of Israel and say: 'Mountains of Israel,
hear the word of the LORD. 2This is what the
Lord GOD says: The enemy has said about
you, "Now the old places to worship gods
have become ours." ' 3So prophesy and say:
'This is what the Lord GOD says: They have
made you an empty ruin and have crushed
you from all around. So you became a
possession of the other nations. People have
talked and whispered against you. 4So,
mountains of Israel, hear the word of the
Lord GOD. The Lord GOD speaks to the
mountains, hills, ravines, and valleys, to the
empty ruins and abandoned cities that have
been robbed and laughed at by the other
nations. 5This is what the Lord GOD says: I
speak in hot anger against the other nations.
I speak against the people of Edom, who
took my land for themselves with joy and
with hate in their hearts. They forced out the
people and took their pastureland.' 6So
prophesy about the land of Israel and say to
the mountains, hills, ravines, and valleys:
'This is what the Lord GOD says: I speak in
my jealous anger, because you have suffered
the insults of the nations. 7So this is what
the Lord GOD says: I promise that the nations
around you will also have to suffer insults.

8" 'But you, mountains of Israel, will grow
branches and fruit for my people, who will
soon come home. 9I am concerned about
you; I am on your side. You will be plowed,
and seed will be planted in you. 10I will
increase the number of people who live on
you, all the people of Israel. The cities will
have people living in them, and the ruins
will be rebuilt. 11I will increase the number
of people and animals living on you. They
will grow and have many young. You will
have people living on you as you did before,
and I will make you better off than at the
beginning. Then you will know that I am
the LORD. 12I will cause my people Israel to
walk on you and own you, and you will
belong to them. You will never again take
their children away from them.

13" 'This is what the Lord GOD says: People
say about you, "You eat people and take

children from your nation." 14But you will
not eat people anymore or take away the
children, says the Lord GOD. 15I will not
make you listen to insults from the nations
anymore; you will not suffer shame from
them anymore. You will not cause your
nation to fall anymore, says the Lord GOD.'"

The Lord Acts for Himself

16The LORD spoke his word to me again,
saying: 17"Human, when the nation of Israel
was living in their own land, they made it
unclean by their ways and the things they
did. Their ways were like a woman's
uncleanness in her time of monthly
bleeding. 18So I poured out my anger against
them, because they murdered in the land
and because they made the land unclean
with their idols. 19I scattered them among
the nations, and they were spread through
the countries. I punished them for how they
lived and what they did. 20They dishonored
my holy name in the nations where they
went. The nations said about them, 'These
are the people of the LORD, but they had to
leave the land which he gave them.' 21But I
had concern for my holy name, which the
nation of Israel had dishonored among the
nations where they went.

22"So say to the people of Israel, 'This is
what the Lord GOD says: Israel, I am going to
act, but not for your sake. I will do
something to help my holy name, which
you have dishonored among the nations
where you went. 23I will prove the holiness
of my great name, which has been
dishonored among the nations. You have
dishonored it among these nations, but the
nations will know that I am the LORD when I
prove myself holy before their eyes, says the
Lord GOD.

24" 'I will take you from the nations and
gather you out of all the lands and bring you
back into your own land. 25Then I will
sprinkle clean water on you, and you will be
clean. I will cleanse you from all your
uncleanness and your idols. 26Also, I will
teach you to respect me completely, and I
will put a new way of thinking inside you. I
will take out the stubborn hearts of stone
from your bodies, and I will give you
obedient hearts of flesh. 27I will put my
Spirit inside you and help you live by my
rules and carefully obey my laws. 28You will
live in the land I gave to your ancestors, and
you will be my people, and I will be your
God. 29So I will save you from all your
uncleanness. I will command the grain to
come and grow; I will not allow a time of
hunger to hurt you. 30I will increase the
harvest of the field so you will never again
suffer shame among the nations because of
hunger. 31Then you will remember your evil
ways and actions that were not good, and
you will hate yourselves because of your sins
and your terrible acts that I hate. 32I want
you to know that I am not going to do this
for your sake, says the Lord GOD. Be ashamed
and embarrassed about your ways, Israel.

33" 'This is what the Lord GOD says: This is
what will happen on the day I cleanse you
from all your sins: I will cause the cities to
have people living in them again, and the
destroyed places will be rebuilt. 34The empty
land will be plowed so it will no longer be a
ruin for everyone who passes by to see.
35They will say, "This land was ruined, but
now it has become like the garden of Eden.
The cities were destroyed, empty, and
ruined, but now they are protected and have
people living in them." 36Then those nations
still around you will know that I, the LORD,
have rebuilt what was destroyed and have
planted what was empty. I, the LORD, have
spoken, and I will do it.'

37"This is what the Lord GOD says: I will
let myself be asked by the people of Israel to
do this for them again: I will make their
people grow in number like a flock. 38They
will be as many as the flocks brought to
Jerusalem during her holy feasts. Her ruined
cities will be filled with flocks of people.
Then they will know that I am the LORD."

The Vision of Dry Bones

37 I felt the power of the LORD on me,
and he brought me out by the Spirit
of the LORD and put me down in the middle
of a valley. It was full of bones. 2He led me
around among the bones, and I saw that
there were many bones in the valley and
that they were very dry. 3Then he asked me,
"Human, can these bones live?"

I answered, "Lord GOD, only you know."

4He said to me, "Prophesy to these bones
and say to them, 'Dry bones, hear the word
of the LORD. 5This is what the Lord GOD says
to the bones: I will cause breath to enter you

devotion 231

EZEKIEL 37:1-14

JUST READ IT!

I read these verses in the summer of 2005 soon after Hurricane Katrina plowed through the Gulf Coast. I couldn't help but think of the people in New Orleans. On the news, we repeatedly heard them say that they felt helpless. Their hope was gone, and everything they owned was destroyed.

Spiritually, there are millions of people all over the world who have no hope for eternity. Their spirits have dried up, and they are going to hell . . . forever. The difference is that we are able to help them. We help by sharing the love of Christ with them. We need to encourage them, lend a helping hand when needed, and share God's plan of salvation with them. We are often afraid to share Christ with others because we feel we might offend them. What we need to be afraid of is offending Christ.

My daughter once shared the Good News with a neighbor in our front yard. She was only ten years old and he was eleven. Much to her frustration, the little boy wasn't buying the whole "born again" thing. She stormed back into our house, wrote out the sinner's prayer on a piece of paper, and went back outside. She handed the paper to the boy and said, "Just read it, you idiot!" Although she could've used a little more finesse, she obviously wasn't afraid of offending the boy, and she was definitely passionate about sharing Christ. Lovingly share him with someone today. It is their only hope.

so you will come to life. 6I will put muscles
on you and flesh on you and cover you with
skin. Then I will put breath in you so you
will come to life. Then you will know that I
am the LORD.' "
7So I prophesied as I was commanded.
While I prophesied, there was a noise and a
rattling. The bones came together, bone to
bone. 8I looked and saw muscles come on
the bones, and flesh grew, and skin covered
the bones. But there was no breath in them.
9Then he said to me, "Prophesy to the
wind.[n] Prophesy, human, and say to the
wind, 'This is what the Lord GOD says: Wind,
come from the four winds, and breathe on
these people who were killed so they can
come back to life.' " 10So I prophesied as the
LORD commanded me. And the breath came
into them, and they came to life and stood
on their feet, a very large army.
11Then he said to me, "Human, these
bones are like all the people of Israel. They
say, 'Our bones are dried up, and our hope
has gone. We are destroyed.' 12So, prophesy
and say to them, 'This is what the Lord GOD
says: My people, I will open your graves and
cause you to come up out of your graves.
Then I will bring you into the land of Israel.
13My people, you will know that I am the
LORD when I open your graves and cause you
to come up from them. 14And I will put my
Spirit inside you, and you will come to life.
Then I will put you in your own land. And
you will know that I, the LORD, have spoken
and done it, says the LORD.' "

Judah and Israel Back Together

15The LORD spoke his word to me, saying,
16"Human, take a stick and write on it, 'For
Judah and all the Israelites with him.' Then
take another stick and write on it, 'The stick
of Ephraim, for Joseph and all the Israelites

37:9 wind This Hebrew word could also mean "breath" or "spirit."

with him.' 17Then join them together into
one stick so they will be one in your hand.
18"When your people say to you, 'Explain
to us what you mean by this,' 19say to them,
'This is what the Lord GOD says: I will take
the stick for Joseph and the tribes of Israel
with him, which is in the hand of Ephraim,
and I will put it with the stick of Judah. I will
make them into one stick, and they will be
one in my hand.' 20Hold the sticks on which
you wrote these names in your hand so the
people can see them. 21Say to the people,
'This is what the Lord GOD says: I am going
to take the people of Israel from among the
nations where they have gone. I will gather
them from all around and bring them into
their own land. 22I will make them one
nation in the land, on the mountains of
Israel. One king will rule all of them. They
will never again be two nations; they will
not be divided into two kingdoms anymore.
23They will not continue to make
themselves unclean by their idols, their
statues of gods which I hate, or by their sins.
I will save them from all the ways they sin
and turn against me, and I will make them
clean. Then they will be my people, and I
will be their God.

24" 'My servant David will be their king,
and they will all have one shepherd. They
will live by my rules and obey my laws.
25They will live on the land I gave to my
servant Jacob, the land in which your
ancestors lived. They will all live on the land
forever: they, their children, and their
grandchildren. David my servant will be
their king forever. 26I will make an
agreement of peace with them, an
agreement that continues forever. I will put
them in their land and make them grow in
number. Then I will put my Temple among
them forever. 27The place where I live will be
with them. I will be their God, and they will
be my people. 28When my Temple is among
them forever, the nations will know that I,
the LORD, make Israel holy.' "

Prophecy Against Gog

38 The LORD spoke his word to me,
saying, 2"Human, look toward Gog of
the land of Magog, the chief ruler of the
nations of Meshech and Tubal. Prophesy
against him 3and say, 'The Lord GOD says this:
I am against you, Gog, chief ruler of Meshech
and Tubal. 4I will turn you around and put
hooks in your jaws. And I will bring you out
with all your army, horses, and horsemen, all
of whom will be dressed in beautiful
uniforms. They will be a large army with
large and small shields and all having swords.
5Persia, Cush, and Put will be with them, all of
them having shields and helmets. 6There will
also be Gomer with all its troops and the
nation of Togarmah from the far north with
all its troops—many nations with you.

7" 'Be prepared. Be prepared, you and all
the armies that have come together to make
you their commander. 8After a long time you
will be called for service. After those years
you will come into a land that has been
rebuilt from war. The people in the land will
have been gathered from many nations to
the mountains of Israel, which were empty
for a long time. These people were brought
out from the nations, and they will all be
living in safety. 9You will come like a storm.
You, all your troops, and the many nations
with you will be like a cloud covering the
land.

10" 'This is what the Lord GOD says: At that
time ideas will come into your mind, and
you will think up an evil plan. 11You will say,
"I will march against a land of towns
without walls. I will attack those who are at
rest and live in safety. All of them live
without city walls or gate bars or gates. 12I
will capture treasures and take loot. I will
turn my power against the rebuilt ruins that
now have people living in them. I will attack
these people who have been gathered from
the nations, who have become rich with
farm animals and property, who live at the
center of the world." 13Sheba, Dedan, and the
traders of Tarshish, with all its villages, will
say to you, "Did you come to capture
treasure? Did you bring your troops together
to take loot? Did you bring them to carry
away silver and gold and to take away farm
animals and property?" '

14"So prophesy, human, and say to Gog,
'This is what the Lord GOD says: Now that
my people Israel are living in safety, you will
know about it. 15You will come with many
people from your place in the far north. You
will have a large group with you, a mighty
army, all riding on horses. 16You will attack
my people Israel like a cloud that covers the
land. This will happen in the days to come

when I bring you against my land. Gog, then
the nations will know me when they see me
prove how holy I am in what I do through
you.

17 “ ‘This is what the Lord GOD says: You
are the one about whom I spoke in past
days. I spoke through my servants, the
prophets of Israel, who prophesied for many
years that I would bring you against them.
18 This is what will happen: On the day Gog
attacks the land of Israel, I will become very
angry, says the Lord GOD. 19 With jealousy
and great anger I tell you that at that time
there will surely be a great earthquake in
Israel. 20 The fish of the sea, the birds of the
sky, the wild animals, everything that
crawls on the ground, and all the people on
the earth will shake with fear before me.
Also the mountains will be thrown down,
the cliffs will fall, and every wall will fall to
the ground. 21 Then I will call for a war
against Gog on all my mountains, says the
Lord GOD. Everyone's sword will attack the
soldier next to him. 22 I will punish Gog
with disease and death. I will send a heavy
rain with hailstones and burning sulfur on
Gog, his army, and the many nations with
him. 23 Then I will show how great I am. I
will show my holiness, and I will make
myself known to the many nations that
watch. Then they will know that I am the
LORD.’

The Death of Gog and His Army

39 “Human, prophesy against Gog and
say, ‘This is what the Lord GOD says: I
am against you, Gog, chief ruler of Meshech
and Tubal. 2 I will turn you around and lead
you. I will bring you from the far north and
send you to attack the mountains of Israel. 3 I
will knock your bow out of your left hand
and throw down your arrows from your
right hand. 4 You, all your troops, and the
nations with you will fall dead on the
mountains of Israel. I will let you be food for
every bird that eats meat and for every wild
animal. 5 You will lie fallen on the ground,
because I have spoken, says the Lord GOD. 6 I
will send fire on Magog and those who live
in safety on the coastlands. Then they will
know that I am the LORD.

7 “ ‘I will make myself known among my
people Israel, and I will not let myself be
dishonored anymore. Then the nations will
know that I am the LORD, the Holy One in
Israel. 8 It is coming! It will happen, says the
Lord GOD. The time I talked about is coming.

9 “ ‘Then those who live in the cities of
Israel will come out and make fires with the
enemy's weapons. They will burn them,
both large and small shields, bows and
arrows, war clubs, and spears. They will use
the weapons to burn in their fires for seven
years. 10 They will not need to take wood
from the field or chop firewood from the
forests, because they will make fires with the
weapons. In this way they will take the
treasures of those who took their treasures;
they will take the loot of those who took
their loot, says the Lord GOD.

11 “ ‘At that time I will give Gog a burial
place in Israel, in the Valley of the Travelers,
east of the Dead Sea. It will block the road
for travelers. Gog and all his army will be
buried there, so people will call it The Valley
of Gog's Army.

12 “ ‘The people of Israel will be burying
them for seven months to make the land
clean again. 13 All the people in the land will
bury them, and they will be honored on the
day of my victory, says the Lord GOD.

14 “ ‘The people of Israel will choose men
to work through the land to make it clean.
Along with others, they will bury Gog's
soldiers still lying dead on the ground. After
the seven months are finished, they will still
search. 15 As they go through the land,
anyone who sees a human bone is to put a
marker by it. The sign will stay there until
the gravediggers bury the bone in The Valley
of Gog's Army. 16 A city will be there named
Hamonah. So they will make the land clean
again.’

17 “Human, this is what the Lord GOD says:
Speak to every kind of bird and wild animal:
‘Come together, come! Come together from
all around to my sacrifice, a great sacrifice
which I will prepare for you on the
mountains of Israel. Eat flesh and drink
blood! 18 You are to eat the flesh of the
mighty and drink the blood of the rulers of
the earth as if they were fat animals from
Bashan: male sheep, lambs, goats, and bulls.
19 You are to eat and drink from my sacrifice
which I have prepared for you, eating fat
until you are full and drinking blood until
you are drunk. 20 At my table you are to eat
until you are full of horses and riders,

mighty men and all kinds of soldiers,' says
the Lord GOD.
21"I will show my glory among the
nations. All the nations will see my power
when I punish them. 22From that time
onward the people of Israel will know that I
am the LORD their God. 23The nations will
know Israel was taken away captive because
they turned against me. So I turned away
from them and handed them over to their
enemies until all of them died in war.
24Because of their uncleanness and their
sins, I punished them and turned away from
them.
25"So this is what the Lord GOD says: Now I
will bring the people of Jacob back from
captivity, and I will have mercy on the whole
nation of Israel. I will not let them dishonor
me. 26The people will forget their shame and
how they rejected me when they live again in
safety on their own land with no one to make
them afraid. 27I will bring the people back
from other lands and gather them from the
lands of their enemies. So I will use my
people to show many nations that I am holy.
28Then my people will know that I am the
LORD their God, because I sent them into
captivity among the nations, but then I
brought them back to their own land, leaving
no one behind. 29I will not turn away from
them anymore, because I will put my Spirit
into the people of Israel, says the Lord GOD."

The New Temple

40 It was the twenty-fifth year of our
captivity, at the beginning of the year,
on the tenth day of the month. It was in the
fourteenth year after Jerusalem was
captured. On that same day I felt the power
of the LORD, and he brought me to Jerusalem.
2In the visions of God he brought me to the
land of Israel and put me down on a very
high mountain. On the south of the
mountain there were some buildings that
looked like a city. 3He took me closer to the
buildings, and I saw a man who looked as if
he were made of bronze, standing in the
gateway. He had a cord made of linen and a
stick in his hand, both for measuring. 4The
man said to me, "Human, look with your
eyes and hear with your ears. Pay attention
to all that I will show you, because that's
why you have been brought here. Tell the
people of Israel all that you see."

The East Gateway

5I saw a wall that surrounded the Temple
area. The measuring stick in the man's hand
was ten and one-half feet long. So the man
measured the wall, which was ten and
one-half feet thick and ten and one-half feet
high.
6Then the man went to the east gateway.
He went up its steps and measured the
opening of the gateway. It was ten and one-
half feet deep. 7The rooms for the guards
were ten and one-half feet long and ten and
one-half feet wide. The walls that came out
between the guards' rooms were about nine
feet thick. The opening of the gateway next
to the porch that faced the Temple was ten
and one-half feet deep.
8Then the man measured the porch of the
gateway. 9It was about fourteen feet deep,
and its side walls were three and one-half
feet thick. The porch of the gateway faced
the Temple.
10On each side of the east gateway were
three rooms, which measured the same on
each side. The walls between each room
were the same thickness. 11The man
measured the width of the entrance to the
gateway, which was seventeen and one-half
feet wide. The width of the gate was about
twenty-three feet. 12And there was a low wall
about twenty-one inches high in front of
each room. The rooms were ten and one-half
feet on each side. 13The man measured the
gateway from the roof of one room to the
roof of the opposite room. It was about
forty-four feet from one door to the opposite
door. 14The man also measured the porch,
which was about thirty-five feet wide. The
courtyard was around the porch. 15From the
front of the outer side of the gateway to the
front of the porch of the inner side of the
gateway was eighty-seven and one-half feet.
16The rooms and porch had small windows
on both sides. The windows were narrower
on the side facing the gateway. Carvings of
palm trees were on each side wall of the
rooms.

The Outer Courtyard

17Then the man brought me into the outer
courtyard where I saw rooms and a pavement
of stones all around the court. Thirty rooms
were along the edge of the paved walkway.
18The pavement ran alongside the gates and

was as deep as the gates were wide. This was
the lower pavement. [19]Then the man
measured from the outer wall to the inner
wall. The outer court between these two
walls was one hundred seventy-five feet on
the east and on the north.

The North Gateway

[20]The man measured the length and width
of the north gateway leading to the outer
courtyard. [21]Its three rooms on each side, its
inner walls, and its porch measured the same
as the first gateway. It was eighty-seven and
one-half feet long and forty-four feet wide.
[22]Its windows, porch, and carvings of palm
trees measured the same as the east gateway.
Seven steps went up to the gateway, and the
gateway's porch was at the inner end. [23]The
inner courtyard had a gateway across from
the northern gateway like the one on the
east. The man measured it and found it was
one hundred seventy-five feet from inner
gateway to outer gateway.

The South Gateway

[24]Then the man led me south where I saw
a gateway facing south. He measured its
inner walls and its porch, and they measured
the same as the other gateways. [25]The
gateway and its porch had windows all
around like the other gateways. It was
eighty-seven and one-half feet long and
forty-four feet wide. [26]Seven steps went up to
this gateway. Its porch was at the inner end,
and it had carvings of palm trees on its inner
walls. [27]The inner courtyard had a gateway
on its south side. The man measured from
gate to gate on the south side, which was
one hundred seventy-five feet.

The Inner Courtyard

[28]Then the man brought me through the
south gateway into the inner courtyard. The
inner south gateway measured the same as
the gateways in the outer wall. [29]The inner
south gateway's rooms, inner walls, and
porch measured the same as the gateways in
the outer wall. There were windows all
around the gateway and its porch. The
gateway was eighty-seven and one-half feet
long and forty-four feet wide. [30]Each porch
of each inner gateway was about forty-four
feet long and about nine feet wide. [31]The
inner south gateway's porch faced the outer
courtyard. Carvings of palm trees were on its
side walls, and its stairway had eight steps.

[32]The man brought me into the inner
courtyard on the east side. He measured the
inner east gateway, and it was the same as
the other gateways. [33]The inner east
gateway's rooms, inside walls, and porch
measured the same as the other gateways.
Windows were all around the gateway and
its porch. The inner east gateway was
eighty-seven and one-half feet long and
forty-four feet wide. [34]Its porch faced the
outer courtyard. Carvings of palm trees were
on its inner walls on each side, and its
stairway had eight steps.

[35]Then the man brought me to the inner
north gateway. He measured it, and it was
the same as the other gateways. [36]Its rooms,
inner walls, and porch measured the same as
the other gateways. There were windows all
around the gateway, which was eighty-seven
and one-half feet long and forty-four feet
wide. [37]Its porch faced the outer courtyard.
Carvings of palm trees were on its inner
walls on each side, and its stairway had eight
steps.

Rooms for Preparing Sacrifices

[38]There was a room with a door that
opened onto the porch of the inner north
gateway. In this room the priests washed
animals for the burnt offerings. [39]There were
two tables on each side of the porch, on
which animals for burnt offerings, sin
offerings, and penalty offerings were killed.
[40]Outside, by each side wall of the porch, at
the entrance to the north gateway, were two
more tables. [41]So there were four tables
inside the gateway, and four tables outside.
In all there were eight tables on which the
priests killed animals for sacrifices. [42]There
were four tables made of cut stone for the
burnt offering. These tables were about three
feet long, three feet wide, and about two feet
high. On these tables the priests put their
tools which they used to kill animals for
burnt offerings and the other sacrifices.
[43]Double shelves three inches wide were put
up on all the walls. The flesh for the offering
was put on the tables.

The Priests' Rooms

[44]There were two rooms in the inner
courtyard. One was beside the north

gateway and faced south. The other room
was beside the south gateway and faced
north. 45The man said to me, "The room
which faces south is for the priests who
serve in the Temple area, 46while the room
that faces north is for the priests who serve
at the altar. This second group of priests are
descendants of Zadok, the only descendants
of Levi who can come near the LORD to serve
him."
47The man measured the inner courtyard.
It was a square—one hundred seventy-five
feet long and one hundred seventy-five feet
wide. The altar was in front of the Temple.

The Temple Porch

48The man brought me to the porch of the
Temple and measured each side wall of the
porch. Each was about nine feet thick. The
doorway was twenty-four and one-half feet
wide. The side walls of the doorway were
each about five feet wide. 49The porch was
thirty-five feet long and twenty-one feet
wide, with ten steps leading up to it. Pillars
were by the side walls, one on each side of
the entrance.

The Holy Place of the Temple

41 The man brought me to the Holy
Place and measured its side walls,
which were each ten and one-half feet thick.
2The entrance was seventeen and one-half
feet wide. The walls alongside the entrance
were each about nine feet wide. The man
measured the Holy Place, which was seventy
feet long and thirty-five feet wide.
3Then the man went inside and measured
the side walls of the next doorway. Each was
three and one-half feet thick. The doorway
was ten and one-half feet wide, and the walls
next to it were each more than twelve feet
thick. 4Then the man measured the room at
the end of the Holy Place. It was thirty-five
feet long and thirty-five feet wide. The man
said to me, "This is the Most Holy Place."
5Then the man measured the wall of the
Temple, which was ten and one-half feet
thick. There were side rooms seven feet wide
all around the Temple. 6The side rooms were
on three different stories, each above the
other, with thirty rooms on each story. All
around the Temple walls there were ledges
for the side rooms. The upper rooms
rested on the ledges but were not attached
to the Temple walls. 7The side rooms around
the Temple were wider on each higher story,
so rooms were wider on the top story. A
stairway went up from the lowest story to
the highest through the middle story.
8I also saw that the Temple had a raised
base all around. Its edge was the foundation
for the side rooms, and it was ten and
one-half feet thick. 9The outer wall of the
side rooms was about nine feet thick. There
was an open area between the side rooms of
the Temple 10and some other rooms. It was
thirty-five feet wide and went all around the
Temple. 11The side rooms had doors which
led to the open area around the outside of
the Temple. One door faced north, and the
other faced south. The open area was about
nine feet wide all around.
12The building facing the private area at
the west side was one hundred twenty-two
and one-half feet wide. The wall around the
building was about nine feet thick and one
hundred fifty-seven and one-half feet long.
13Then the man measured the Temple. It
was one hundred seventy-five feet long. The
private area, including the building and its
walls, was in all one hundred seventy-five
feet long. 14Also the front of the Temple and
the private area on its east side were one
hundred seventy-five feet wide.
15The man measured the length of the
building facing the private area on the west
side, and it was one hundred seventy-five
feet from one wall to the other.
The Holy Place, the Most Holy Place, and
the outer porch 16had wood panels on the
walls. By the doorway, the Temple had wood
panels on the walls. The wood covered all
the walls from the floor up to the windows,
17up to the part of the wall above the
entrance.
All the walls inside the Most Holy Place
and the Holy Place, and on the outside, in
the porch, 18had carvings of creatures with
wings and palm trees. A palm tree was
between each carved creature, and every
creature had two faces. 19One was a human
face looking toward the palm tree on one
side. The other was a lion's face looking
toward the palm tree on the other side. They
were carved all around the Temple walls.
20From the floor to above the entrance, palm
trees and creatures with wings were carved.
The walls of the Holy Place 21had square

doorposts. In front of the Most Holy Place
was something that looked like [22]an altar of
wood. It was more than five feet high and
three feet wide. Its corners, base, and sides
were wood. The man said to me, "This is the
table that is in the presence of the LORD."
[23]Both the Holy Place and the Most Holy
Place had double doors. [24]Each of the doors
had two pieces that would swing open.
[25]Carved on the doors of the Holy Place were
palm trees and creatures with wings, like
those carved on the walls. And there was a
wood roof over the front Temple porch.
[26]There were windows and palm trees on
both side walls of the porch. The side rooms
of the Temple were also covered by a roof
over the stairway.

The Priests' Rooms

42 Then the man led me north out into
the outer courtyard and to the rooms
across from the private area and the
building. [2]These rooms on the north side
were one hundred seventy-five feet long and
eighty-seven and one-half feet wide. [3]There
was thirty-five feet of the inner courtyard
between them and the Temple. On the other
side, they faced the stone pavement of the
outer courtyard. The rooms were built in
three stories like steps and had balconies.
[4]There was a path on the north side of the
rooms, which was seventeen and one-half
feet wide and one hundred seventy-five feet
long. Doors led into the rooms from this
path. [5]The top rooms were narrower,
because the balconies took more space from
them. The rooms on the first and second
stories of the building were wider. [6]The
rooms were on three stories. They did not
have pillars like the pillars of the courtyards.
So the top rooms were farther back than
those on the first and second stories. [7]There
was a wall outside parallel to the rooms and
to the outer courtyard. It ran in front of the
rooms for eighty-seven and one-half feet.
[8]The row of rooms along the outer courtyard
was eighty-seven and one-half feet long, and
the rooms that faced the Temple were about
one hundred seventy-five feet long. [9]The
lower rooms had an entrance on the east
side so a person could enter them from the
outer courtyard, [10]at the start of the wall
beside the courtyard.

There were rooms on the south side,
which were across from the private area and
the building. [11]These rooms had a path in
front of them. They were like the rooms on
the north with the same length and width
and the same doors. [12]The doors of the south
rooms were like the doors of the north
rooms. There was an entrance at the open
end of a path beside the wall, so a person
could enter at the east end.

[13]The man said to me, "The north and
south rooms across from the private area are
holy rooms. There the priests who go near
the LORD will eat the most holy offerings.
There they will put the most holy offerings:
the grain offerings, sin offerings, and the
penalty offerings, because the place is holy.
[14]The priests who enter the Holy Place must
leave their serving clothes there before they
go into the outer courtyard, because these
clothes are holy. After they put on other
clothes, they may go to the part of the
Temple area which is for the people."

Outside the Temple Area

[15]When the man finished measuring
inside the Temple area, he brought me out
through the east gateway. He measured the
area all around. [16]The man measured the
east side with the measuring stick; it was
eight hundred seventy-five feet by the
measuring stick. [17]He measured the north
side; it was eight hundred seventy-five feet
by the measuring stick. [18]He measured the
south side; it was eight hundred seventy-five
feet by the measuring stick. [19]He went
around to the west side; it measured eight
hundred seventy-five feet by the measuring
stick. [20]So he measured the Temple area on
all four sides. The Temple area had a wall all
around it that was eight hundred
seventy-five feet long and eight hundred
seventy-five feet wide. It separated what was
holy from that which was not holy.

The Lord Among His People

43 Then the man led me to the outer east
gateway, [2]and I saw the glory of the
God of Israel coming from the east. It
sounded like the roar of rushing water, and
its brightness made the earth shine. [3]The
vision I saw was like the vision I had seen
when the LORD came to destroy the city and
also like the vision I had seen by the Kebar
River. I bowed facedown on the ground.

[4]The glory of the LORD came into the Temple area through the east gateway.

[5]Then the Spirit picked me up and brought me into the inner courtyard. There I saw the LORD's glory filling the Temple. [6]As the man stood at my side, I heard someone speaking to me from inside the Temple. [7]The voice from the Temple said to me, "Human, this is my throne and the place where my feet rest. I will live here among the Israelites forever. The people of Israel will not make my holy name unclean again. Neither the people nor their kings will make it unclean with their sexual sins or with the dead bodies of their kings. [8]The kings made my name unclean by putting their doorway next to my doorway, and their doorpost next to my doorpost so only a wall separated me from them. When they did their acts that I hate, they made my holy name unclean, and so I destroyed them in my anger. [9]Now let them stop their sexual sins and take the dead bodies of their kings far away from me. Then I will live among them forever.

[10]"Human, tell the people of Israel about the Temple so they will be ashamed of their sins. Let them think about the plan of the Temple. [11]If they are ashamed of all they have done, let them know the design of the Temple and how it is built. Show them its exits and entrances, all its designs, and also all its rules and teachings. Write the rules as they watch so they will obey all the teachings and rules about the Temple. [12]This is the teaching about the Temple: All the area around the top of the mountain is most holy. This is the teaching about the Temple.

The Altar

[13]"These are the measurements of the altar, using the measuring stick. The altar's gutter is twenty-one inches high and twenty-one inches wide, and its rim is about nine inches around its edge. And the altar is this tall: [14]From the ground up to the lower ledge, it measures three and one-half feet. It is twenty-one inches wide. It measures seven feet from the smaller ledge to the larger ledge and is twenty-one inches wide. [15]The place where the sacrifice is burned on the

devotion 232

EZEKIEL 43:5

ARE YOU IN OR OUT?

In the Old Testament Temple, the inner courtyard Ezekiel referred to was the Most Holy Place, the place where the very presence of God made a home. It was the quiet, holy place where the people ministered to the Lord. The outer courts were busier. People were there to make sacrifices for sin, to be heard by the priests, or to minister to the needs of others.

We spend most of our time with God in our equivalent of the outer courts. We run from place to place doing good things for God. We share the Good News, care for the sick, serve at church, and bring food to the needy. We teach Bible studies and Sunday school and Vacation Bible School. All good. All needed. All done in the busy outer courts. But people who minister only from their outer court strength will eventually burn out or fail miserably.

For most of us, time in the inner court is rare. But the inner court is where strength is found for outer court activities. Wisdom is given. Perspective is handed out. Only those who pursue God in the inner court will know the sustained power of his anointing. Is God's glory filling you? When he speaks, can you hear him? Step into the inner court with God today. Worship him in private with reverence and awe, then watch as his glory comes to fill your earthly temple and empower all your outer court responsibilities.

altar is seven feet high, with its four corners
shaped like horns and reaching up above it.
16 It is square, twenty-one feet long and
twenty-one feet wide. 17 The upper ledge is
also square, twenty-four and one-half feet
long and twenty-four and one-half feet wide.
The rim around the altar is ten and one-half
inches wide, and its gutter is twenty-one
inches wide all around. Its steps are on the
east side."

18 Then the man said to me, "Human, this
is what the Lord GOD says: These are the
rules for the altar. When it is built, use these
rules to offer burnt offerings and to sprinkle
blood on it. 19 You must give a young bull as
a sin offering to the priests, the Levites who
are from the family of Zadok and who come
near me to serve me, says the Lord GOD.
20 Take some of the bull's blood and put it on
the four corners of the altar, on the four
corners of the ledge, and all around the rim.
This is how you will make the altar pure and
ready for God's service. 21 Then take the bull
for the sin offering and burn it in the proper
place in the Temple area, outside the Temple
building.

22 "On the second day offer a male goat
that has nothing wrong with it for a sin
offering. The priests will make the altar pure
and ready for God's service as they did with
the young bull. 23 When you finish making
the altar pure and ready, offer a young bull
and a male sheep from the flock, which have
nothing wrong with them. 24 You must offer
them in the presence of the LORD, and the
priests are to throw salt on them and offer
them as a burnt offering to the LORD.

25 "You must prepare a goat every day for
seven days as a sin offering. Also, the priests
must prepare a young bull and male sheep
from the flock, which have nothing wrong
with them. 26 For seven days the priests are to
make the altar pure and ready for God's
service. Then they will give the altar to God.
27 After these seven days, on the eighth day,
the priests must offer your burnt offerings
and your fellowship offerings on the altar.
Then I will accept you, says the Lord GOD."

The Outer East Gate

44 Then the man brought me back to the
outer east gateway of the Temple area,
but the gate was shut. 2 The LORD said to me,
"This gate will stay shut; it will not be
opened. No one may enter through it,
because the LORD God of Israel has entered
through it. So it must stay shut. 3 Only the
ruler himself may sit in the gateway to eat a
meal in the presence of the LORD. He must
enter through the porch of the gateway and
go out the same way."

4 Then the man brought me through the
outer north gate to the front of the Temple.
As I looked, I saw the glory of the LORD
filling the Temple of the LORD, and I bowed
facedown on the ground.

5 The LORD said to me, "Human, pay
attention. Use your eyes to see, and your ears
to hear. See and hear everything I tell you
about all the rules and teachings of the
Temple of the LORD. Pay attention to the
entrance to the Temple and to all the exits
from the Temple area. 6 Then speak to those
who refuse to obey. Say to the people of
Israel, 'This is what the Lord GOD says: Stop
doing all your acts that I hate, Israel! 7 You
brought foreigners into my Holy Place who
were not circumcised in the flesh and had
not given themselves to serving me. You
dishonored my Temple when you offered me
food, fat, and blood. You broke my
agreement by all the things you did that I
hate. 8 You did not take care of my holy
things yourselves but put foreigners in
charge of my Temple. 9 This is what the Lord
GOD says: Foreigners who are not
circumcised in flesh and who do not give
themselves to serving me may not enter my
Temple. Not even a foreigner living among
the people of Israel may enter.

10 " 'But the Levites who stopped obeying
me when Israel left me and who followed
their idols must be punished for their sin.
11 These Levites are to be servants in my Holy
Place. They may guard the gates of the
Temple and serve in the Temple area. They
may kill the animals for the burnt offering
and the sacrifices for the people. They may
stand before the people to serve them. 12 But
these Levites helped the people worship
their idols and caused the people of Israel to
fall, so I make this promise: They will be
punished for their sin, says the Lord GOD.
13 They will not come near me to serve as
priests, nor will they come near any of my
holy things or the most holy offerings. But
they will be made ashamed of the things
they did that I hate. 14 I will put them in

charge of taking care of the Temple area, all
the work that must be done in it.
15“ ‘But the priests who are Levites and
descendants of Zadok took care of my Holy
Place when Israel left me, so they may come
near to serve me. They may stand in my
presence to offer me the fat and blood of the
animals they sacrifice, says the Lord GOD.
16They are the only ones who may enter my
Holy Place. Only they may come near my
table to serve me and take care of the things
I gave them to do.
17“ ‘When they enter the gates of the inner
courtyard, they must wear linen robes. They
must not wear wool to serve at the gates of
the inner courtyard or in the Temple. 18They
will wear linen turbans on their heads and
linen underclothes. They will not wear
anything that makes them perspire. 19When
they go out into the outer courtyard to the
people, they must take off their serving
clothes before they go. They must leave
these clothes in the holy rooms and put on
other clothes. Then they will not let their
holy clothes hurt the people.
20“ ‘They must not shave their heads or let
their hair grow long but must keep the hair
of their heads trimmed. 21None of the priests
may drink wine when they enter the inner
courtyard. 22The priests must not marry
widows or divorced women. They may
marry only virgins from the people of Israel
or widows of priests. 23They must teach my
people the difference between what is holy
and what is not holy. They must help my
people know what is unclean and what is
clean.
24“ ‘In court they will act as judges. When
they judge, they will follow my teachings.
They must obey my laws and my rules at all
my special feasts and keep my Sabbaths
holy.
25“ ‘They must not go near a dead person,
making themselves unclean. But they are
allowed to make themselves unclean if the
dead person is their father, mother, son,
daughter, brother, or a sister who has not
married. 26After a priest has been made clean
again, he must wait seven days. 27Then he
may go into the inner courtyard to serve in
the Temple, but he must offer a sin offering
for himself, says the Lord GOD.
28“ ‘These are the rules about the priests
and their property: They will have me
instead of property. You will not give them
any land to own in Israel; I am what they
will own. 29They will eat the grain offerings,
sin offerings, and penalty offerings.
Everything Israel gives to me will be theirs.
30The best fruits of all the first harvests and
all the special gifts offered to me will belong
to the priests. You will also give to the priests
the first part of your grain that you grind
and so bring a blessing on your family. 31The
priests must not eat any bird or animal that
died a natural death or one that has been
torn by wild animals.

The Land Is Divided

45 “ ‘When you divide the land for the
Israelite tribes by throwing lots, you
must give a part of the land to belong to the
LORD. It will be about seven miles long and
about six miles wide; all of this land will be
holy. 2From this land, an area eight hundred
seventy-five feet square will be for the
Temple. There will be an open space around
the Temple that is eighty-seven and one-half
feet wide. 3In the holy area you will measure
a part about seven miles long and three
miles wide, and in it will be the Most Holy
Place. 4This holy part of the land will be for
the priests who serve in the Temple, who
come near to the LORD to serve him. It will be
a place for the priests' houses and for the
Temple. 5Another area about seven miles
long and more than three miles wide will be
for the Levites, who serve in the Temple area.
It will belong to them so they will have cities
in which to live.
6“ ‘You must give the city an area that is
about one and one-half miles wide and
about seven miles long, along the side of the
holy area. It will belong to all the people of
Israel.
7“ ‘The ruler will have land on both sides
of the holy area and the city. On the west of
the holy area, his land will reach to the
Mediterranean Sea. On the east of the holy
area, his land will reach to the eastern
border. It will be as long as the land given to
each tribe. 8Only this land will be the ruler's
property in Israel. So my rulers will not be
cruel to my people anymore, but they will
let each tribe in the nation of Israel have its
share of the land.
9“ ‘This is what the Lord GOD says: You
have gone far enough, you rulers of Israel!

Stop being cruel and hurting people, and do what is right and fair. Stop forcing my people out of their homes, says the Lord GOD. 10You must have honest scales, an honest dry measurement and an honest liquid measurement. 11The dry measure and the liquid measure will be the same: The liquid measure will always be a tenth of a homer,[n] and the ephah will always be a tenth of a homer. The measurement they follow will be the homer. 12The shekel[n] will be worth twenty gerahs, and a mina will be worth sixty shekels.

Offerings and Holy Days

13" 'This is the gift you should offer: a sixth of an ephah from every homer of wheat, and a sixth of an ephah from every homer of barley. 14The amount of oil you are to offer is a tenth of a bath from each cor. (Ten baths make a homer and also make a cor.) 15You should give one sheep from each flock of two hundred from the watering places of Israel. All these are to be offered for the grain offerings, burnt offerings, and fellowship offerings to remove sins so you will belong to God, says the Lord GOD. 16All people in the land will give this special offering to the ruler of Israel. 17It will be the ruler's responsibility to supply the burnt offerings, grain offerings, and drink offerings. These offerings will be given at the feasts, at the New Moons, on the Sabbaths, and at all the other feasts of Israel. The ruler will supply the sin offerings, grain offerings, and fellowship offerings to pay for the sins of Israel.

18" 'This is what the Lord GOD says: On the first day of the first month take a young bull that has nothing wrong with it. Use it to make the Temple pure and ready for God's service. 19The priest will take some of the blood from this sin offering and put it on the doorposts of the Temple, on the four corners of the ledge of the altar, and on the posts of the gate to the inner courtyard. 20You will do the same thing on the seventh day of the month for anyone who has sinned by accident or without knowing it. This is how you make the Temple pure and ready for God's service.

Passover Feast Offerings

21" 'On the fourteenth day of the first month you will celebrate the Feast of Passover. It will be a feast of seven days when you eat bread made without yeast. 22On that day the ruler must offer a bull for himself and for all the people of the land as a sin offering. 23During the seven days of the feast he must offer seven bulls and seven male sheep that have nothing wrong with them. They will be burnt offerings to the LORD, which the ruler will offer every day of the seven days of the feast. He must also offer a male goat every day as a sin offering. 24The ruler must give as a grain offering one-half bushel for each bull and one-half bushel for each sheep. He must give a gallon of olive oil for each half bushel.

25" 'Beginning on the fifteenth day of the seventh month, when you celebrate the Feast of Shelters, the ruler will supply the same things for seven days: the sin offerings, burnt offerings, grain offerings, and the olive oil.

Rules for Worship

46 " 'This is what the Lord GOD says: The east gate of the inner courtyard will stay shut on the six working days, but it will be opened on the Sabbath day and on the day of the New Moon. 2The ruler will enter from outside through the porch of the gateway and stand by the gatepost, while the priests offer the ruler's burnt offering and fellowship offering. The ruler will worship at the entrance of the gateway, and then he will go out. But the gate will not be shut until evening. 3The people of the land will worship at the entrance of that gateway in the presence of the LORD on the Sabbaths and New Moons. 4This is the burnt offering the ruler will offer to the LORD on the Sabbath day: six male lambs that have nothing wrong with them and a male sheep that has nothing wrong with it. 5He must give a half-bushel grain offering with the male sheep, but he may give as much grain offering with the lambs as he pleases. He must also give a gallon of olive oil for each half bushel of grain. 6On the day of the New Moon he must offer a young bull that has

45:11 homer The Hebrew word means "donkey-load." It measured about five dry bushels or one hundred seventy-five liquid quarts. So an ephah was about one-half bushel, and a bath was about eighteen quarts. **45:12 shekel** In Ezekiel's time a shekel weighed about two-fifths of an ounce.

nothing wrong with it. He must also offer six
lambs and a male sheep that have nothing
wrong with them. 7The ruler must give a
half-bushel grain offering with the bull and
one-half bushel with the male sheep. With
the lambs, he may give as much grain as he
pleases. But he must give a gallon of olive oil
for each half bushel of grain. 8When the
ruler enters, he must go in through the
porch of the gateway, and he must go out the
same way.
9" 'When the people of the land come into
the LORD's presence at the special feasts,
those who enter through the north gate to
worship must go out through the south gate.
Those who enter through the south gate
must go out through the north gate. They
must not return the same way they entered;
everyone must go out the opposite way.
10The ruler will go in with the people when
they go in and go out with them when they
go out.
11" 'At the feasts and regular times of
worship one-half bushel of grain must be
offered with a young bull, and one-half
bushel of grain must be offered with a male
sheep. But with an offering of lambs, the ruler
may give as much grain as he pleases. He
should give a gallon of olive oil for each half
bushel of grain. 12The ruler may give an
offering as a special gift to the LORD; it may be
a burnt offering or fellowship offering. When
he gives it to the LORD, the inner east gate is to
be opened for him. He must offer his burnt
offering or his fellowship offering as he does
on the Sabbath day. Then he will go out, and
the gate will be shut after he has left.
13" 'Every day you will give a year-old
lamb that has nothing wrong with it for a
burnt offering to the LORD. Do it every
morning. 14Also, you must offer a grain
offering with the lamb every morning. For
this you will give three and one-third quarts
of grain and one and one-third quarts of
olive oil, to make the fine flour moist, as a
grain offering to the LORD. This is a rule that
must be kept from now on. 15So you must
always give the lamb, together with the
grain offering and the olive oil, every
morning as a burnt offering.

Rules for the Ruler

16" 'This is what the Lord GOD says: If the
ruler gives a gift from his land to any of his
sons, that land will belong to the son and
then to the son's children. It is their property
passed down from their family. 17But if the
ruler gives a gift from his land to any of his
servants, that land will belong to the servant
only until the year of freedom. Then the
land will go back to the ruler. Only the
ruler's sons may keep a gift of land from the
ruler. 18The ruler must not take any of the
people's land, forcing them out of their land.
He must give his sons some of his own land
so my people will not be scattered out of
their own land.' "

The Special Kitchens

19The man led me through the entrance at
the side of the gateway to the priests' holy
rooms that face north. There I saw a place at
the west end. 20The man said to me, "This is
where the priests will boil the meat of the
penalty offering and sin offering and bake
the grain offering. Then they will not need
to bring these holy offerings into the outer
courtyard, because that would hurt the
people."
21Then the man brought me out into the
outer courtyard and led me to its four
corners. In each corner of the courtyard was
a smaller courtyard. 22Small courtyards were
in the four corners of the courtyard. Each
small courtyard was the same size, seventy
feet long and fifty-two and one-half feet
wide. 23A stone wall was around each of the
four small courtyards, and places for cooking
were built in each of the stone walls. 24The
man said to me, "These are the kitchens
where those who work in the Temple will
boil the sacrifices offered by the people."

The River from the Temple

47 The man led me back to the door of
the Temple, and I saw water coming
out from under the doorway and flowing
east. (The Temple faced east.) The water
flowed down from the south side wall of the
Temple and then south of the altar. 2The
man brought me out through the outer
north gate and led me around outside to the
outer east gate. I found the water coming out
on the south side of the gate.
3The man went toward the east with a
line in his hand and measured about
one-third of a mile. Then he led me through
water that came up to my ankles. 4The man

measured about one-third of a mile again
and led me through water that came up to
my knees. Then he measured about
one-third of a mile again and led me through
water up to my waist. 5The man measured
about one-third of a mile again, but it was
now a river that I could not cross. The water
had risen too high; it was deep enough for
swimming; it was a river that no one could
cross. 6The man asked me, "Human, do you
see this?"

Then the man led me back to the bank of
the river. 7As I went back, I saw many trees
on both sides of the river. 8The man said to
me, "This water will flow toward the eastern
areas and go down into the Jordan Valley.
When it enters the Dead Sea, it will become
fresh. 9Everywhere the river goes, there will
be many fish. Wherever this water goes the
Dead Sea will become fresh, and so where
the river goes there will be many living
things. 10Fishermen will stand by the Dead
Sea. From En Gedi all the way to En Eglaim
there will be places to spread fishing nets.
There will be many kinds of fish in the Dead
Sea, as many as in the Mediterranean Sea.
11But its swamps and marshes will not
become fresh; they will be left for salt. 12All
kinds of fruit trees will grow on both banks
of the river, and their leaves will not dry and
die. The trees will have fruit every month,
because the water for them comes from the
Temple. The fruit from the trees will be used
for food, and their leaves for medicine."

Borders of the Land

13This is what the Lord GOD says: "These
are the borders of the land to be divided
among the twelve tribes of Israel. Joseph will
have two parts of land. 14You will divide the
land equally. I promised to give it to your
ancestors, so this land will belong to you as
family property.

15"This will be the border line of the land:
"On the north side it will start at the
Mediterranean Sea. It will go through
Hethlon, toward Lebo Hamath and on to the
towns of Zedad, 16Berothah, and Sibraim on
the border between Damascus and Hamath.
Then it will go on to the town of Hazer
Hatticon on the border of the country of
Hauran. 17So the border line will go from the
Mediterranean Sea east to the town of Hazar
Enan, where the land belonging to
Damascus and Hamath lies on the north
side. This will be the north side of the land.

18"On the east side the border runs south
from a point between Hauran and
Damascus. It will go along the Jordan
between Gilead and the land of Israel and
will continue to the town of Tamar on the
Dead Sea. This will be the east side of the
land.

19"On the south side the border line will
go west from Tamar all the way to the waters
of Meribah Kadesh. Then it will run along
the brook of Egypt to the Mediterranean Sea.
This will be the south side of the land.

20"On the west side the Mediterranean Sea
will be the border line up to a place across
from Lebo Hamath. This will be the west
side of your land.

21"You will divide this land among the
tribes of Israel. 22You will divide it as family
property for yourselves and for the
foreigners who live and have children
among you. You are to treat these foreigners
the same as people born in Israel; they are to
share the land with the tribes of Israel. 23In
whatever tribe the foreigner lives, you will
give him some land," says the Lord GOD.

Dividing the Land

48 "These are the areas of the tribes
named here: Dan will have one share
at the northern border. It will go from the
sea through Hethlon to Lebo Hamath, all the
way to Hazar Enan, where Damascus lies to
the north. It will stop there next to Hamath.
This will be Dan's northern border from the
east side to the Mediterranean Sea on the
west side.

2"South of Dan's border, Asher will have
one share. It will go from the east side to the
west side.

3"South of Asher's border, Naphtali will
have one share. It will go from the east side
to the west side.

4"South of Naphtali's border, Manasseh
will have one share. It will go from the east
side to the west side.

5"South of Manasseh's border, Ephraim
will have one share. It will go from the east
side to the west side.

6"South of Ephraim's border, Reuben will
have one share. It will go from the east side
to the west side.

7"South of Reuben's border, Judah will

have one share. It will go from the east side
to the west side.
[8]"South of Judah's border will be the holy
area which you are to give. It will be about
seven miles wide and as long and wide as
one of the tribes' shares. It will run from the
east side to the west side. The Temple will be
in the middle of this area.
[9]"The share which you will give the LORD
will be about seven miles long and three
miles wide. [10]The holy area will be divided
among these people. The priests will have
land about seven miles long on the north
and south sides, and three miles wide on the
west and east sides. The Temple of the LORD
will be in the middle of it. [11]This land is for
the priests who are given the holy duty of
serving the LORD. They are the descendants
of Zadok who did my work and did not leave
me when Israel and the Levites left me.
[12]They will have as their share a very holy
part of the holy portion of the land. It will be
next to the land of the Levites.
[13]"Alongside the land for the priests, the
Levites will have a share about seven miles
long and three miles wide; its full length
will be about seven miles and its full
width about three miles. [14]The Levites are
not to sell or trade any of this land. They are
not to let anyone else own any of this best
part of the land, because it belongs to the
LORD.

City Property

[15]"The rest of the area will be about one
and one-half miles wide and seven miles
long. It will not be holy but will belong to
the city and be used for homes and pastures.
The city will be in the middle of it. [16]These
are the city's measurements: the north side
will be about one mile, the south side about
one mile, the east side about one mile, and
the west side about one mile. [17]The city's
land for pastures will be about four hundred
thirty-seven feet on the north, four
hundred thirty-seven feet on the south,
four hundred thirty-seven feet on the east,
and four hundred thirty-seven feet on the
west. [18]Along the long side of the holy area
there will be left three miles on the east and
three miles on the west. It will be used to
grow food for the city workers. [19]The city

devotion 233

EZEKIEL 48:35

THE LORD IS THERE

I have a client who plays NFL football. He is a godly man that loves the Lord. You could put his name beside each and every fruit of the Spirit. Not only does he love his wife as Christ loved the church and care for his family, but he gives the teams he plays for 200 percent every season. At the start of camp this year, the rookies were responsible for putting on a skit for the veteran players. The rookies' skit depicted my client walking into the team locker room a wee bit late from a Bible study, asking them to forgive him, and then working the room asking if he could pray for the guys. There was great laughter and applause, but what struck me most was their interpretation of a man they had just met. They knew that where he was, the Lord was there.

What about you? If the people you know were to put on a skit portraying your life, what would it look like? Would the very first impression be that the Lord is there with that woman? I want to *be* that woman! And I know you do, too! When someone is hurting or in need, do others direct them to your household and say, "Go to *(insert your name)*—the Lord is there!"? Ask the Holy Spirit to help you grow in the areas where you need growth so that your life will reflect Christ to the people who are searching. And never be too busy to stop and pray.

workers from all the tribes of Israel will farm
this land. 20 This whole area will be square,
seven miles by seven miles. You shall give to
the LORD the holy share along with the city
property.

21 "Land that is left over on both sides of
the holy area and city property will belong
to the ruler. That land will extend east of the
holy area to the eastern border and west of it
to the Mediterranean Sea. Both of these areas
run the length of the lands of the tribes, and
they belong to the ruler. The holy area with
the Holy Place of the Temple will be in the
middle. 22 The Levites' land and the city
property will be in the middle of the lands
belonging to the ruler. Those lands will be
between Judah's border and Benjamin's
border.

The Other Tribes' Land

23 "Here is what the rest of the tribes will
receive: Benjamin will have one share. It will
go from the east side to the Mediterranean
Sea on the west side.

24 "South of Benjamin's land, Simeon will
have one share. It will go from the east side
to the west side.

25 "South of Simeon's land, Issachar will
have one share. It will go from the east side
to the west side.

26 "South of Issachar's land, Zebulun will
have one share. It will go from the east side
to the west side.

27 "South of Zebulun's land, Gad will have
one share. It will go from the east side to the
west side.

28 "The southern border of Gad's land will
go east from Tamar on the Dead Sea to the
waters of Meribah Kadesh. Then it will run
along the brook of Egypt to the
Mediterranean Sea.

29 "This is the land you will divide among
the tribes of Israel to be their shares," says
the Lord GOD.

The Gates of the City

30 "These will be the outside borders of the
city: The north side will measure more than
one mile. 31 There will be three gates facing
north: Reuben's Gate, Judah's Gate, and Levi's
Gate, named for the tribes of Israel.

32 "The east side will measure more than
one mile. There will be three gates facing
east: Joseph's Gate, Benjamin's Gate, and
Dan's Gate.

33 "The south side will measure more than
one mile. There will be three gates facing
south: Simeon's Gate, Issachar's Gate, and
Zebulun's Gate.

34 "The west side will measure more than
one mile. There will be three gates facing
west: Gad's Gate, Asher's Gate, and
Naphtali's Gate.

35 "The city will measure about six miles
around. From then on the name of the city
will be The LORD Is There."

Daniel

A Hebrew name that means "God is my judge"
This book is one of only two bilingual biblical texts (the other is Ezra). Both books were originally recorded in Hebrew and Aramaic, which was a universal "business" language at this time in history.

Person Holding the Pen God Wrote With: *Daniel,* who was a contemporary of the prophets Ezekiel and Jeremiah

When the Text Was Written: Between 536 and 530 B.C.

Spiritual Posture of the Original Recipients: The Jews were in exile in Babylon and no doubt needed to be reminded of God's dominion and his future plans for them.

Storyline Synopsis: The deportation of Jerusalem took place from 605 to 586 B.C. in three main stages, with the first phase involving the capture of Jewish "nobility." Daniel and his three buddies with strange names (Shadrach, Meshach, and Abednego) represented the cream of the crop of Israel's young men. These four friends persisted to trust God in spite of being exiled in the royal Babylonian court of King Nebuchadnezzar, an infamous tormentor of God's people. The description of their death-defying experience in a fiery furnace has become one of the most beloved Bible stories of all times (Dan. 3:19–30). While this book narrates literal events highlighting Daniel's unwavering faith in the face of persecution (chapters 1—6), it also includes unique apocalyptic visions of the end of this world as we know it. The three main themes of Daniel are the sovereignty of God, the misery of human pride, and the ultimate victory for those who put their hope in God.

A Moment Worth Discussing: The reason Daniel and his comrades got tossed into a blazing kiln was because of their defiance of King Nebuchadnezzar's decree to worship a golden image (Dan. 3:8–18). In light of the way God protected them, their refusal to comply with the idolatrous order was justified. It's interesting to compare this passage with the way the apostle Peter tells Christians to obey human leaders and kings in the New Testament (1 Pet. 2:13–17). Discuss when submission to ungodly government authorities is spiritually acceptable.

Interesting (But Likely to Be Overlooked) Character: The *Eternal One* (Dan. 7:9,13, and 22) is a distinctive title for God, indicating his authority over history.

Daniel Taken to Babylon

1 During the third year that Jehoiakim was
king of Judah, Nebuchadnezzar king of
Babylon came to Jerusalem and surrounded
it with his army. 2 The Lord allowed
Nebuchadnezzar to capture Jehoiakim king
of Judah. Nebuchadnezzar also took some of
the things from the Temple of God, which he
carried to Babylonia and put in the temple of
his gods.

3 Then King Nebuchadnezzar ordered
Ashpenaz, his chief officer, to bring some of
the men of Judah into his palace. He wanted
them to be from important families,
including the family of the king of Judah.
4 King Nebuchadnezzar wanted only young
Israelite men who had nothing wrong with
them. They were to be handsome and well
educated, capable of learning and
understanding, and able to serve in his
palace. Ashpenaz was to teach them the
language and writings of the Babylonians.
5 The king gave the young men a certain
amount of food and wine every day, just like
the food he ate. The young men were to be
trained for three years, and then they would
become servants of the king of Babylon.
6 Among those young men were Daniel,
Hananiah, Mishael, and Azariah from the
people of Judah.

7 Ashpenaz, the chief officer, gave them
Babylonian names. Daniel's new name was
Belteshazzar, Hananiah's was Shadrach,
Mishael's was Meshach, and Azariah's was
Abednego.

8 Daniel decided not to eat the king's food
or drink his wine because that would make
him unclean. So he asked Ashpenaz for
permission not to make himself unclean in
this way.

9 God made Ashpenaz, the chief officer,
want to be kind and merciful to Daniel,
10 but Ashpenaz said to Daniel, "I am afraid
of my master, the king. He ordered me to
give you this food and drink. If you begin to
look worse than other young men your age,
the king will see this. Then he will cut off
my head because of you."

11 Ashpenaz had ordered a guard to watch
Daniel, Hananiah, Mishael, and Azariah.
12 Daniel said to the guard, "Please give us
this test for ten days: Don't give us anything
but vegetables to eat and water to drink.
13 After ten days compare how we look with
how the other young men look who eat the
king's food. See for yourself and then decide
how you want to treat us, your servants."

14 So the guard agreed to test them for ten
days. 15 After ten days they looked healthier
and better fed than all the young men who
ate the king's food. 16 So the guard took away
the king's special food and wine, feeding
them vegetables instead.

17 God gave these four young men wisdom
and the ability to learn many things that
people had written and studied. Daniel
could also understand visions and dreams.

18 At the end of the time set for them by
the king, Ashpenaz brought all the young
men to King Nebuchadnezzar. 19 The king
talked to them and found that none of the
young men were as good as Daniel,
Hananiah, Mishael, and Azariah. So those
four young men became the king's servants.
20 Every time the king asked them about
something important, they showed much
wisdom and understanding. They were ten
times better than all the fortune-tellers and
magicians in his kingdom! 21 So Daniel
continued to be the king's servant until the
first year Cyrus was king.

Nebuchadnezzar's Dream

2 During Nebuchadnezzar's second year as
king, he had dreams that bothered him
and kept him awake at night. 2 So the king
called for his fortune-tellers, magicians,
wizards, and wise men, because he wanted
them to tell him what he had dreamed. They
came in and stood in front of the king.

3 Then the king said to them, "I had a
dream that bothers me, and I want to know
what it means."

4 The wise men answered the king in the
Aramaic language, "O king, live forever!
Please tell us, your servants, your dream.
Then we will tell you what it means."

5 King Nebuchadnezzar said to them, "I
meant what I said. You must tell me the
dream and what it means. If you don't, I will
have you torn apart, and I will turn your
houses into piles of stones. 6 But if you tell
me my dream and its meaning, I will reward
you with gifts and great honor. So tell me
the dream and what it means."

7 Again the wise men said to the king, "Tell

us, your servants, the dream, and we will tell
you what it means."
8King Nebuchadnezzar answered, "I know
you are trying to get more time, because you
know that I meant what I said. 9If you don't
tell me my dream, you will be punished. You
have all agreed to tell me lies and wicked
things, hoping things will change. Now, tell
me the dream so that I will know you can
tell me what it really means!"
10The wise men answered the king,
saying, "No one on earth can do what the
king asks! No great and powerful king has
ever asked the fortune-tellers, magicians, or
wise men to do this; 11the king is asking
something that is too hard. Only the gods
could tell the king this, but the gods do not
live among people."
12When the king heard their answer, he
became very angry. He ordered that all the
wise men of Babylon be killed. 13So King
Nebuchadnezzar's order to kill the wise men
was announced, and men were sent to look
for Daniel and his friends to kill them.
14Arioch, the commander of the king's
guards, was going to kill the wise men of
Babylon. But Daniel spoke to him with
wisdom and skill, 15saying, "Why did the
king order such a terrible punishment?"
Then Arioch explained everything to
Daniel. 16So Daniel went to King
Nebuchadnezzar and asked for an
appointment so that he could tell the king
what his dream meant.
17Then Daniel went to his house and
explained the whole story to his friends
Hananiah, Mishael, and Azariah. 18Daniel
asked his friends to pray that the God of
heaven would show them mercy and help
them understand this secret so he and his
friends would not be killed with the other
wise men of Babylon.
19During the night God explained the
secret to Daniel in a vision. Then Daniel
praised the God of heaven. 20Daniel said:

"Praise God forever and ever,
because he has wisdom and power.
21He changes the times and seasons of the
year.
He takes away the power of kings
and gives their power to new kings.
He gives wisdom to those who are wise
and knowledge to those who
understand.
22He makes known secrets that are deep
and hidden;
he knows what is hidden in darkness,
and light is all around him.
23I thank you and praise you, God of my
ancestors,
because you have given me wisdom
and power.
You told me what we asked of you;
you told us about the king's dream."

The Meaning of the Dream

24Then Daniel went to Arioch, the man
King Nebuchadnezzar had chosen to kill the
wise men of Babylon. Daniel said to him,
"Don't put the wise men of Babylon to death.
Take me to the king, and I will tell him what
his dream means."
25Very quickly Arioch took Daniel to the
king and said, "I have found a man among
the captives from Judah who can tell the
king what his dream means."
26The king asked Daniel, who was also
called Belteshazzar, "Are you able to tell me
what I dreamed and what it means?"
27Daniel answered, "No wise man,
magician, or fortune-teller can explain to
the king the secret he has asked about.
28But there is a God in heaven who explains
secret things, and he has shown King
Nebuchadnezzar what will happen at a later
time. This is your dream, the vision you saw
while lying on your bed: 29O king, as you
were lying there, you thought about things
to come. God, who can tell people about
secret things, showed you what is going to
happen. 30God also told this secret to me, not
because I have greater wisdom than any
other living person, but so that you may
know what it means. In that way you will
understand what went through your mind.
31"O king, in your dream you saw a huge,
shiny, and frightening statue in front of you.
32The head of the statue was made of pure
gold. Its chest and arms were made of silver.
Its stomach and the upper part of its legs
were made of bronze. 33The lower part of the
legs were made of iron, while its feet were
made partly of iron and partly of baked clay.
34While you were looking at the statue, you
saw a rock cut free, but no human being
touched the rock. It hit the statue on its feet
of iron and clay and smashed them. 35Then
the iron, clay, bronze, silver, and gold broke

to pieces at the same time. They became like
chaff on a threshing floor in the
summertime; the wind blew them away, and
there was nothing left. Then the rock that
hit the statue became a very large mountain
that filled the whole earth.
36"That was your dream. Now we will tell
the king what it means. 37O king, you are the
greatest king. God of heaven has given you a
kingdom, power, strength, and glory.
38Wherever people, wild animals, and birds
live, God made you ruler over them. King
Nebuchadnezzar, you are the head of gold on
that statue.
39"Another kingdom will come after you,
but it will not be as great as yours. Next a
third kingdom, the bronze part, will rule
over the earth. 40Then there will be a fourth
kingdom, strong as iron. In the same way
that iron crushes and smashes things to
pieces, the fourth kingdom will smash and
crush all the other kingdoms.
41"You saw that the statue's feet and toes
were partly baked clay and partly iron. That
means the fourth kingdom will be a divided
kingdom. It will have some of the strength of
iron in it, just as you saw iron was mixed
with clay. 42The toes of the statue were
partly iron and partly clay. So the fourth
kingdom will be partly strong like iron and
partly breakable like clay. 43You saw the iron
mixed with clay, but iron and clay do not
hold together. In the same way the people of
the fourth kingdom will be a mixture, but
they will not be united as one people.
44"During the time of those kings, the God
of heaven will set up another kingdom that
will never be destroyed or given to another
group of people. This kingdom will crush all
the other kingdoms and bring them to an
end, but it will continue forever.
45"King Nebuchadnezzar, you saw a rock
cut from a mountain, but no human being
touched it. The rock broke the iron, bronze,
clay, silver, and gold to pieces. In this way
the great God showed you what will happen.
The dream is true, and you can trust this
explanation."
46Then King Nebuchadnezzar fell
facedown on the ground in front of Daniel.
The king honored him and commanded that
an offering and incense be presented to him.
47Then the king said to Daniel, "Truly I
know your God is the greatest of all gods, the
Lord of all the kings. He tells people about
things they cannot know. I know this is true,
because you were able to tell these secret
things to me."
48Then the king gave Daniel many gifts
plus an important position in his kingdom.
Nebuchadnezzar made him ruler over the
whole area of Babylon and put him in charge
of all the wise men of Babylon. 49Daniel
asked the king to make Shadrach, Meshach,
and Abednego leaders over the area of
Babylon, so the king did as Daniel asked.
Daniel himself became one of the people
who stayed at the royal court.

The Gold Idol and Blazing Furnace

3 King Nebuchadnezzar made a gold statue
ninety feet high and nine feet wide and
set it up on the plain of Dura in the area of
Babylon. 2Then he called for the leaders: the
governors, assistant governors, captains of
the soldiers, people who advised the king,
keepers of the treasury, judges, rulers, and all
other officers in his kingdom. He wanted
them to come to the special service for the
statue he had set up. 3So they all came for
the special service and stood in front of the
statue that King Nebuchadnezzar had set up.
4Then the man who made announcements
for the king said in a loud voice, "People,
nations, and those of every language, this is
what you are commanded to do: 5When you
hear the sound of the horns, flutes, lyres,
zithers,[n] harps, pipes, and all the other
musical instruments, you must bow down
and worship the gold statue that King
Nebuchadnezzar has set up. 6Anyone who
doesn't bow down and worship will
immediately be thrown into a blazing
furnace."
7Now people, nations, and those who
spoke every language were there. When
they heard the sound of the horns, flutes,
lyres, zithers, pipes, and all the other musical
instruments, they bowed down and
worshiped the gold statue King
Nebuchadnezzar had set up.
8Then some Babylonians came up to the
king and began speaking against the men of
Judah. 9They said to King Nebuchadnezzar,
"O king, live forever! 10O king, you gave a
command that everyone who heard the

3:5 zithers Musical instruments with thirty to forty strings.

horns, lyres, zithers, harps, pipes, and all the other musical instruments would have to bow down and worship the gold statue. [11]Anyone who wouldn't do this was to be thrown into a blazing furnace. [12]O king, there are some men of Judah whom you made officers in the area of Babylon that did not pay attention to your order. Their names are Shadrach, Meshach, and Abednego. They do not serve your gods and do not worship the gold statue you have set up."

[13]Nebuchadnezzar became very angry and called for Shadrach, Meshach, and Abednego. When they were brought to the king, [14]Nebuchadnezzar said, "Shadrach, Meshach, and Abednego, is it true that you do not serve my gods nor worship the gold statue I have set up? [15]In a moment you will again hear the sound of the horns, flutes, lyres, zithers, harps, pipes, and all the other musical instruments. If you bow down and worship the statue I made, that will be good. But if you do not worship it, you will immediately be thrown into the blazing furnace. What god will be able to save you from my power then?"

[16]Shadrach, Meshach, and Abednego answered the king, saying, "Nebuchadnezzar, we do not need to defend ourselves to you. [17]If you throw us into the blazing furnace, the God we serve is able to save us from the furnace. He will save us from your power, O king. [18]But even if God does not save us, we want you, O king, to know this: We will not serve your gods or worship the gold statue you have set up."

[19]Then Nebuchadnezzar was furious with Shadrach, Meshach, and Abednego, and he changed his mind. He ordered the furnace to be heated seven times hotter than usual. [20]Then he commanded some of the strongest soldiers in his army to tie up Shadrach, Meshach, and Abednego and throw them into the blazing furnace.

[21]So Shadrach, Meshach, and Abednego were tied up and thrown into the blazing furnace while still wearing their robes, trousers, turbans, and other clothes. [22]The king's command was very strict, and the

devotion 234

DANIEL 3:16–18

AN OUTBREAK OF COURAGE

Being a Christian woman who is courageous means that you are willing to do and say the right thing, no matter what the earthly cost. A believing woman is able to make courageous choices because she trusts that God is able to help her and save her according to his promises. But because we live among so much evil, becoming a courageous woman of God seems harder than ever to attain.

Sometimes it feels like everyone around us is determined to bow down to their gods of money and power or surrender to a life of chaos and heartache. Trying to live as a righteous woman can leave you feeling like the loneliest woman on the planet. And when we believe we are alone, we can operate from our fear instead of our God-given courage.

God says that living righteously will make you courageous (Prov. 28:1). Jesus also said that we should be inspired with courage when we are forgiven for our sins (Matt. 9:2). When we have put our hope in God, we can take courage from that trust (Ps. 31:24). Over and over and in a variety of ways, God promises to add courage to our weakness.

I realize that courage feels risky sometimes, but the women of God must come out of hiding. Just like Shadrach, Meshach, and Abednego, we do not have to bow down to the cultural pressures that hinder our lives. Courage is contagious. What if God wants an outbreak of courage to begin with you?

furnace was made so hot that the flames
killed the strong soldiers who threw
Shadrach, Meshach, and Abednego into the
furnace. 23Firmly tied, Shadrach, Meshach,
and Abednego fell into the blazing furnace.
24Then King Nebuchadnezzar was so
surprised that he jumped to his feet. He
asked the men who advised him, "Didn't we
tie up only three men and throw them into
the fire?"

They answered, "Yes, O king."

25The king said, "Look! I see four men
walking around in the fire. They are not tied
up, and they are not burned. The fourth man
looks like a son of the gods."

26Then Nebuchadnezzar went to the
opening of the blazing furnace and shouted,
"Shadrach, Meshach, and Abednego, come
out! Servants of the Most High God, come
here!"

So Shadrach, Meshach, and Abednego
came out of the fire. 27When they came out,
the governors, assistant governors, captains
of the soldiers, and royal advisers crowded
around them and saw that the fire had not
harmed their bodies. Their hair was not
burned, their robes were not burned, and
they didn't even smell like smoke!

28Then Nebuchadnezzar said, "Praise the
God of Shadrach, Meshach, and Abednego.
Their God has sent his angel and saved his
servants from the fire! These three men
trusted their God and refused to obey my
command. They were willing to die rather
than serve or worship any god other than
their own. 29So I now give this command:
Anyone from any nation or language who
says anything against the God of Shadrach,
Meshach, and Abednego will be torn apart
and have his house turned into a pile of
stones. No other god can save his people like
this." 30Then the king promoted Shadrach,
Meshach, and Abednego in the area of
Babylon.

Nebuchadnezzar's Dream of a Tree

4 King Nebuchadnezzar sent this letter to
the people, nations, and those who speak
every language in all the world:

I wish you peace and great wealth!

2The Most High God has done
miracles and wonderful things for me
that I am happy to tell you about.

3His wonderful acts are great,
and his miracles are mighty.
His kingdom goes on forever,
and his rule continues from
now on.

4I, Nebuchadnezzar, was happy and
successful at my palace, 5but I had a
dream that made me afraid. As I was
lying on my bed, I saw pictures and
visions in my mind that alarmed me.
6So I ordered all the wise men of
Babylon to come to me and tell me what
my dream meant. 7The fortune-tellers,
magicians, and wise men came, and I
told them about the dream. But they
could not tell me what it meant.

8Finally, Daniel came to me. (I called
him Belteshazzar to honor my god,
because the spirit of the holy gods is in
him.) I told my dream to him. 9I said,
"Belteshazzar, you are the most
important of all the fortune-tellers. I
know that the spirit of the holy gods is
in you, so there is no secret that is too
hard for you to understand. This was
what I dreamed; tell me what it means.
10These are the visions I saw while I
was lying in my bed: I looked, and there
in front of me was a tree standing in the
middle of the earth. And it was very
tall. 11The tree grew large and strong.
The top of the tree touched the sky and
could be seen from anywhere on earth.
12The leaves of the tree were beautiful.
It had plenty of good fruit on it, enough
food for everyone. The wild animals
found shelter under the tree, and the
birds lived in its branches. Every animal
ate from it.

13"As I was looking at those things in
the vision while lying on my bed, I saw
an observer, a holy angel coming down
from heaven. 14He spoke very loudly
and said, 'Cut down the tree and cut off
its branches. Strip off its leaves and
scatter its fruit. Let the animals under
the tree run away, and let the birds in its
branches fly away. 15But leave the stump
and its roots in the ground with a band
of iron and bronze around it; let it stay
in the field with the grass around it.

" 'Let the man become wet with dew,
and let him live among the animals and
plants of the earth. 16Let him not think

like a human any longer, but let him
have the mind of an animal for seven
years.
17"'The observers gave this
command; the holy ones declared the
sentence. This is so all people may
know that the Most High God rules
over every kingdom on earth. God gives
those kingdoms to anyone he wants,
and he chooses people to rule them
who are not proud.'
18"That is what I, King
Nebuchadnezzar, dreamed. Now
Belteshazzar,[n] tell me what the dream
means. None of the wise men in my
kingdom can explain it to me, but you
can, because the spirit of the holy gods
is in you."

Daniel Explains the Dream

19Then Daniel, who was called
Belteshazzar, was very quiet for a while,
because his understanding of the dream
frightened him. So the king said,
"Belteshazzar, do not let the dream or
its meaning make you afraid."

Then Belteshazzar answered, "My
master, I wish the dream were about
your enemies, and I wish its meaning
were for those who are against you!
20You saw a tree in your dream that
grew large and strong. Its top touched
the sky, and it could be seen from all
over the earth. 21Its leaves were
beautiful, and it had plenty of fruit for
everyone to eat. It was a home for the
wild animals, and its branches were
nesting places for the birds. 22O king,
you are that tree! You have become
great and powerful, like the tall tree
that touched the sky. Your power
reaches to the far parts of the earth.
23"O king, you saw an observer, a
holy angel, coming down from heaven
who said, 'Cut down the tree and
destroy it. But leave the stump and its
roots in the ground with a band of iron
and bronze around it; leave it in the
field with the grass. Let him become
wet with dew and live like a wild
animal for seven years.'
24"This is the meaning of the dream,
O king. The Most High God has
commanded these things to happen to
my master the king: 25You will be
forced away from people to live among
the wild animals. People will feed you
grass like an ox, and dew from the sky
will make you wet. Seven years will
pass, and then you will learn this
lesson: The Most High God is ruler over
every kingdom on earth, and he gives
those kingdoms to anyone he chooses.
26"Since the stump of the tree and its
roots were left in the ground, your
kingdom will be given back to you
when you learn that one in heaven
rules your kingdom. 27So, O king,
please accept my advice. Stop sinning
and do what is right. Stop doing wicked
things and be kind to the poor. Then
you might continue to be successful."

The King's Dream Comes True

28All these things happened to King
Nebuchadnezzar. 29Twelve months
later as he was walking on the roof[n] of
his palace in Babylon, 30he said, "I have
built this great Babylon as my royal
home. I built it by my power to show
my glory and my majesty."
31The words were still in his mouth
when a voice from heaven said, "King
Nebuchadnezzar, these things will
happen to you: Your royal power has
been taken away from you. 32You will
be forced away from people. You will
live with the wild animals and will be
fed grass like an ox. Seven years will
pass before you learn this lesson: The
Most High God rules over every
kingdom on earth and gives those
kingdoms to anyone he chooses."
33Immediately the words came true.
Nebuchadnezzar was forced to go away
from people, and he began eating grass
like an ox. He became wet from dew.
His hair grew long like the feathers of
an eagle, and his nails grew like the
claws of a bird.
34At the end of that time, I,
Nebuchadnezzar, looked up toward

4:18 Belteshazzar Another name for Daniel. **4:29 roof** In Bible times houses were built with flat roofs. The roof was used for drying things such as flax and fruit. And it was used as an extra room, as a place for worship, and as a cool place to sleep in the summer.

heaven, and I could think normally
again! Then I gave praise to the Most
High God; I gave honor and glory to
him who lives forever.

God's rule is forever,
and his kingdom continues for all
time.
35 People on earth
are not truly important.
God does what he wants
with the powers of heaven
and the people on earth.
No one can stop his powerful hand
or question what he does.

36 At that time I could think normally
again, and God gave back my great
honor and power and returned the
glory to my kingdom. The people who
advised me and the royal family came
to me for help again. I became king
again and was even greater and more
powerful than before. 37 Now I,
Nebuchadnezzar, give praise and honor
and glory to the King of heaven.
Everything he does is right and fair, and
he is able to make proud people
humble.

The Writing on the Wall

5 King Belshazzar gave a big banquet for a
thousand royal guests and drank wine
with them. 2 As Belshazzar was drinking his
wine, he gave orders to bring the gold and
silver cups that his ancestor Nebuchadnezzar
had taken from the Temple in Jerusalem.
This was so the king, his royal guests, his
wives, and his slave women could drink
from those cups. 3 So they brought the gold
cups that had been taken from the Temple of
God in Jerusalem. And the king and his royal
guests, his wives, and his slave women drank
from them. 4 As they were drinking, they
praised their gods, which were made from
gold, silver, bronze, iron, wood, and stone.

5 Suddenly the fingers of a person's hand
appeared and began writing on the plaster of
the wall, near the lampstand in the royal
palace. The king watched the hand as it
wrote.

6 King Belshazzar was very frightened. His
face turned white, his knees knocked
together, and he could not stand up because
his legs were too weak. 7 The king called for
the magicians, wise men, and wizards of
Babylon and said to them, "Anyone who can
read this writing and explain it will receive
purple clothes fit for a king and a gold chain
around his neck. And I will make that
person the third highest ruler in the
kingdom."

8 Then all the king's wise men came in,
but they could not read the writing or tell
the king what it meant. 9 King Belshazzar
became even more afraid, and his face
became even whiter. His royal guests were
confused.

10 Then the king's mother, who had heard
the voices of the king and his royal guests,
came into the banquet room. She said,
"O king, live forever! Don't be afraid or let
your face be white with fear! 11 There is a
man in your kingdom who has the spirit of
the holy gods. In the days of your father, this
man showed understanding, knowledge, and
wisdom like the gods. Your father, King
Nebuchadnezzar, put this man in charge of
all the wise men, fortune-tellers, magicians,
and wizards. 12 The man I am talking about is
named Daniel, whom the king named
Belteshazzar. He was very wise and had
knowledge and understanding. He could
explain dreams and secrets and could
answer very hard problems. Call for Daniel.
He will tell you what the writing on the wall
means."

13 So they brought Daniel to the king, and
the king asked, "Is your name Daniel? Are
you one of the captives my father the king
brought from Judah? 14 I have heard that the
spirit of the gods is in you, and that you are
very wise and have knowledge and
extraordinary understanding. 15 The wise
men and magicians were brought to me to
read this writing and to explain what it
means, but they could not explain it. 16 I have
heard that you are able to explain what
things mean and can find the answers to
hard problems. Read this writing on the wall
and explain it to me. If you can, I will give
you purple clothes fit for a king and a gold
chain to wear around your neck. And you
will become the third highest ruler in the
kingdom."

17 Then Daniel answered the king, "You
may keep your gifts for yourself, or you may
give those rewards to someone else. But I
will read the writing on the wall for you and
will explain to you what it means.

18“O king, the Most High God made your
father Nebuchadnezzar a great, important,
and powerful king. 19Because God made him
important, all the people, nations, and those
who spoke every language were very
frightened of Nebuchadnezzar. If he wanted
someone to die, he killed that person. If he
wanted someone to live, he let that person
live. Those he wanted to promote, he
promoted. Those he wanted to be less
important, he made less important.
20“But Nebuchadnezzar became too proud
and stubborn, so he was taken off his royal
throne. His glory was taken away. 21He was
forced away from people, and his mind
became like the mind of an animal. He lived
with the wild donkeys and was fed grass like
an ox and became wet with dew. These
things happened to him until he learned his
lesson: The Most High God rules over every
kingdom on earth, and he sets anyone he
chooses over those kingdoms.
22“Belshazzar, you already knew these
things, because you are a descendant of
Nebuchadnezzar. Still you have not been
sorry for what you have done. 23Instead, you
have set yourself against the Lord of heaven.
You ordered the drinking cups from the
Temple of the Lord to be brought to you.
Then you and your royal guests, your wives,
and your slave women drank wine from
them. You praised the gods of silver, gold,
bronze, iron, wood, and stone that are not
really gods; they cannot see or hear or
understand anything. You did not honor
God, who has power over your life and
everything you do. 24So God sent the hand
that wrote on the wall.
25“These are the words that were written
on the wall: ‘Mene, mene, tekel, and parsin.’
26“This is what the words mean: Mene:
God has counted the days until your
kingdom will end. 27Tekel: You have been
weighed on the scales and found not good
enough. 28Parsin: Your kingdom is being
divided and will be given to the Medes and
the Persians.”
29Then Belshazzar gave an order for
Daniel to be dressed in purple clothes and to
have a gold chain put around his neck. And
it was announced that Daniel was the third
highest ruler in the kingdom. 30That very
same night Belshazzar, king of the
Babylonian people, was killed. 31So Darius
the Mede became the new king when he was
sixty-two years old.

Daniel and the Lions

6 Darius thought it would be a good idea
to choose one hundred twenty governors
who would rule his kingdom. 2He chose
three men as supervisors over those
governors, and Daniel was one of the
supervisors. The supervisors were to ensure
that the governors did not try to cheat the
king. 3Daniel showed that he could do the
work better than the other supervisors and
governors, so the king planned to put Daniel
in charge of the whole kingdom. 4Because of
this, the other supervisors and governors
tried to find reasons to accuse Daniel about
his work in the government. But they could
not find anything wrong with him or any
reason to accuse him, because he was
trustworthy and not lazy or dishonest.
5Finally these men said, “We will never find
any reason to accuse Daniel unless it is
about the law of his God.”
6So the supervisors and governors went as
a group to the king and said: “King Darius,
live forever! 7The supervisors, assistant
governors, governors, the people who advise
you, and the captains of the soldiers have all
agreed that you should make a new law for
everyone to obey: For the next thirty days no
one should pray to any god or human except
to you, O king. Anyone who doesn’t obey will
be thrown into the lions’ den. 8Now, O king,
make the law and sign your name to it so that
it cannot be changed, because then it will be a
law of the Medes and Persians and cannot be
canceled.” 9So King Darius signed the law.
10Even though Daniel knew that the new
law had been written, he went to pray in an
upstairs room in his house, which had
windows that opened toward Jerusalem.
Three times each day Daniel would kneel
down to pray and thank God, just as he
always had done.
11Then those men went as a group and
found Daniel praying and asking God for
help. 12So they went to the king and talked
to him about the law he had made. They
said, “Didn’t you sign a law that says no one
may pray to any god or human except you,
O king? Doesn’t it say that anyone who
disobeys during the next thirty days will be
thrown into the lions’ den?”

The king answered, "Yes, that is the law, and the laws of the Medes and Persians cannot be canceled."

13 Then they said to the king, "Daniel, one of the captives from Judah, is not paying attention to you, O king, or to the law you signed. Daniel still prays to his God three times every day." 14 The king became very upset when he heard this. He wanted to save Daniel, and he worked hard until sunset trying to think of a way to save him.

15 Then those men went as a group to the king. They said, "Remember, O king, the law of the Medes and Persians says that no law or command given by the king can be changed."

16 So King Darius gave the order, and Daniel was brought in and thrown into the lions' den. The king said to Daniel, "May the God you serve all the time save you!" 17 A big stone was brought and placed over the opening of the lions' den. Then the king used his signet ring and the rings of his royal officers to put special seals on the rock. This ensured that no one would move the rock and bring Daniel out. 18 Then King Darius went back to his palace. He did not eat that night, he did not have any entertainment brought to him, and he could not sleep.

19 The next morning King Darius got up at dawn and hurried to the lions' den. 20 As he came near the den, he was worried. He called out to Daniel, "Daniel, servant of the living God! Has your God that you always worship been able to save you from the lions?"

21 Daniel answered, "O king, live forever! 22 My God sent his angel to close the lions' mouths. They have not hurt me, because my God knows I am innocent. I never did anything wrong to you, O king."

23 King Darius was very happy and told his servants to lift Daniel out of the lions' den. So they lifted him out and did not find any injury on him, because Daniel had trusted in his God.

24 Then the king commanded that the men who had accused Daniel be brought to the lions' den. They, their wives, and their children were thrown into the den. The lions grabbed them before they hit the floor of the den and crushed their bones.

devotion 235

DANIEL 6:20–22

SCHEMES, LIES, AND TREACHERY

King Darius had been tricked by the governors of his kingdom. Their plot would cause Darius himself to order the death of Daniel, a man he highly respected. Darius spent his night awake, and as morning dawned, he rushed to the lions' den where just the night before he had left his favorite supervisor. "Are you there, Daniel? Did your God spare you?"

Out of the den came Daniel's exuberant voice: "O king, live forever!" There was no question that Daniel's God was mighty and supernatural. How exactly would one get a lion not to eat you, except by God's power? And who but God could move an unbelieving king's heart to be so dedicated to a man whose ultimate allegiance was for his God rather than his king?

This entire story should encourage your heart. Though it is full of schemes, lies, trickery, jealousy, and deceit, the greedy governors' scheme to cheat the king ended in their death. Not one of the attempts against Daniel went unnoticed or unpunished by God. This is an example of resting in God alone even when you know there are plots against you. The cool thing about our Lord is that he only requires us to have faith. He doesn't require that we take matters into our own hands or even defend ourselves. All throughout the Bible, there are examples of real-life men and women that were encouraged in the circumstances of their life with the sovereignty, provision, and deliverance of God.

25Then King Darius wrote a letter to all
people and all nations, to those who spoke
every language in the world:

I wish you great peace and wealth.

26I am making a new law for people in every part of my kingdom. All of you must fear and respect the God of Daniel.

Daniel's God is the living God;
he lives forever.
His kingdom will never be destroyed,
and his rule will never end.
27God rescues and saves people
and does mighty miracles
in heaven and on earth.
He is the one who saved Daniel
from the power of the lions.

28So Daniel was successful during the time Darius was king and when Cyrus the Persian was king.

Daniel's Dream About Four Animals

7 In Belshazzar's first year as king of Babylon, Daniel had a dream. He saw visions as he was lying on his bed, and he wrote down what he had dreamed.
2Daniel said: "I saw my vision at night. In
the vision the wind was blowing from all
four directions, which made the sea very
rough. 3I saw four huge animals come up
from the sea, and each animal was different
from the others.
4"The first animal looked like a lion, but
had wings like an eagle. I watched this
animal until its wings were torn off. It was
lifted from the ground so that it stood up on
two feet like a human, and it was given the
mind of a human.
5"Then I saw a second animal before me
that looked like a bear. It was raised up on
one of its sides and had three ribs in its
mouth between its teeth. It was told, 'Get up
and eat all the meat you want!'
6"After that, I looked, and there before me
was another animal. This animal looked like
a leopard with four wings on its back that
looked like a bird's wings. This animal had
four heads and was given power to rule.
7"After that, in my vision at night I saw in
front of me a fourth animal that was cruel,
terrible, and very strong. It had large iron
teeth. It crushed and ate what it killed, and
then it walked on whatever was left. This
fourth animal was different from any animal
I had seen before, and it had ten horns.
8"While I was thinking about the horns,
another horn grew up among them. It was a
little horn with eyes like a human's eyes. It
also had a mouth, and the mouth was
bragging. The little horn pulled out three of
the other horns.
9"As I looked,
thrones were put in their places,
and God, the Eternal One, sat on his throne.
His clothes were white like snow,
and the hair on his head was white like wool.
His throne was made from fire,
and the wheels of his throne were blazing with fire.
10A river of fire was flowing
from in front of him.
Many thousands of angels were serving him,
and millions of angels stood before him.
Court was ready to begin,
and the books were opened.

11"I kept on looking because the little
horn was bragging. I kept watching until
finally the fourth animal was killed. Its body
was destroyed, and it was thrown into the
burning fire. 12(The power and rule of the
other animals had been taken from them,
but they were permitted to live for a certain
period of time.)
13"In my vision at night I saw in front of
me someone who looked like a human being
coming on the clouds in the sky. He came
near God, who has been alive forever, and he
was led to God. 14He was given authority,
glory, and the strength of a king. People of
every tribe, nation, and language will serve
him. His rule will last forever, and his
kingdom will never be destroyed.

The Meaning of the Dream

15"I, Daniel, was worried. The visions that
went through my mind frightened me. 16I
came near one of those standing there and
asked what all this meant.

"So he told me and explained to me what
these things meant: 17'The four great

animals are four kingdoms that will come
from the earth. [18]But the holy people who
belong to the Most High God will receive the
power to rule and will have the power to
rule forever, from now on.'

[19]"Then I wanted to know what the fourth
animal meant, because it was different from
all the others. It was very terrible and had
iron teeth and bronze claws. It was the
animal that crushed and ate what it killed
and then walked on whatever was left. [20]I
also wanted to know about the ten horns on
its head and about the little horn that grew
there. It had pulled out three of the other ten
horns and looked greater than the others. It
had eyes and a mouth that kept bragging.
[21]As I watched, the little horn began making
war against God's holy people and was
defeating them [22]until God, who has been
alive forever, came. He judged in favor of the
holy people who belong to the Most High
God; then the time came for them to receive
the power to rule.

[23]"And he explained this to me: 'The
fourth animal is a fourth kingdom that will
come on the earth. It will be different from
all the other kingdoms and will destroy
people all over the world. It will walk on and
crush the whole earth. [24]The ten horns are
ten kings who will come from this fourth
kingdom. After those ten kings are gone,
another king will come. He will be different
from the kings who ruled before him, and he
will defeat three of the other kings. [25]This
king will speak against the Most High God,
and he will hurt and kill God's holy people.
He will try to change times and laws that
have already been set. The holy people that
belong to God will be in that king's power
for three and one-half years.

[26]" 'But the court will decide what should
happen. The power of the king will be taken
away, and his kingdom will be completely
destroyed. [27]Then the holy people who
belong to the Most High God will have the
power to rule. They will rule over all the
kingdoms under heaven with power and
greatness, and their power to rule will last
forever. People from all the other kingdoms
will respect and serve them.'

[28]"That was the end of the dream. I,
Daniel, was very afraid. My face became
white from fear, but I kept everything to
myself."

Daniel's Vision

8 During the third year of King
Belshazzar's rule, I, Daniel, saw another
vision, which was like the first one. [2]In this
vision I saw myself in the capital city of
Susa, in the area of Elam. I was standing by
the Ulai Canal [3]when I looked up and saw a
male sheep standing beside the canal. It had
two long horns, but one horn was longer and
newer than the other. [4]I watched the sheep
charge to the west, the north, and the south.
No animal could stand before him, and none
could save another animal from his power.
He did whatever he wanted and became very
powerful.

[5]While I was watching this, I saw a male
goat come from the west. This goat had one
large horn between his eyes that was easy to
see. He crossed over the whole earth so fast
that his feet hardly touched the ground.

[6]In his anger the goat charged the sheep
with the two horns that I had seen standing
by the canal. [7]I watched the angry goat
attack the sheep and break the sheep's two
horns. The sheep was not strong enough to
stop it. The goat knocked the sheep to the
ground and then walked all over him. No
one was able to save the sheep from the goat,
[8]so the male goat became very great. But
when he was strong, his big horn broke off
and four horns grew in place of the one big
horn. Those four horns pointed in four
different directions and were easy to see.

[9]Then a little horn grew from one of those
four horns, and it became very big. It grew to
the south, the east, and toward the beautiful
land of Judah. [10]That little horn grew until it
reached to the sky. It even threw some of the
army of heaven to the ground and walked on
them! [11]That little horn set itself up as equal
to God, the Commander of heaven's armies.
It stopped the daily sacrifices that were
offered to him, and the Temple, the place
where people worshiped him, was pulled
down. [12]Because there was a turning away
from God, the people stopped the daily
sacrifices. Truth was thrown down to the
ground, and the horn was successful in
everything it did.

[13]Then I heard a holy angel speaking.
Another holy angel asked the first one, "How
long will the things in this vision last—the
daily sacrifices, the turning away from God

that brings destruction, the Temple being
pulled down, and the army of heaven being
walked on?"
14 The angel said to me, "This will happen
for twenty-three hundred evenings and
mornings. Then the holy place will be
repaired."
15 I, Daniel, saw this vision and tried to
understand what it meant. In it I saw
someone who looked like a man standing
near me. 16 And I heard a man's voice calling
from the Ulai Canal: "Gabriel, explain the
vision to this man."
17 Gabriel came to where I was standing.
When he came close to me, I was very afraid
and bowed facedown on the ground. But
Gabriel said to me, "Human being,
understand that this vision is about the time
of the end."
18 While Gabriel was speaking, I fell into a
deep sleep with my face on the ground. Then
he touched me and lifted me to my feet. 19 He
said, "Now, I will explain to you what will
happen in the time of God's anger. Your
vision was about the set time of the end.
20 "You saw a male sheep with two horns,
which are the kings of Media and Persia.
21 The male goat is the king of Greece, and
the big horn between its eyes is the first
king. 22 The four horns that grew in the place
of the broken horn are four kingdoms. Those
four kingdoms will come from the nation of
the first king, but they will not be as strong
as the first king.
23 "When the end comes near for those
kingdoms, a bold and cruel king who tells
lies will come. This will happen when many
people have turned against God. 24 This king
will be very powerful, but his power will not
come from himself. He will cause terrible
destruction and will be successful in
everything he does. He will destroy powerful
people and even God's holy people. 25 This
king will succeed by using lies and force. He
will think that he is very important. He will
destroy many people without warning; he
will try to fight even the Prince of princes!
But that cruel king will be destroyed, and
not by human power.
26 "The vision that has been shown to you
about these evenings and mornings is true.
But seal up the vision, because those things
won't happen for a long time."
27 I, Daniel, became very weak and was
sick for several days after that vision. Then I
got up and went back to work for the king,
but I was very upset about the vision. I didn't
understand what it meant.

Daniel's Prayer

9 These things happened during the first
year Darius son of Xerxes was king over
Babylon. He was a descendant of the Medes.
2 During Darius' first year as king, I, Daniel,
was reading the Scriptures. I saw that the
LORD told Jeremiah that Jerusalem would be
empty ruins for seventy years.
3 Then I turned to the Lord God and
prayed and asked him for help. To show my
sadness, I fasted, put on rough cloth, and sat
in ashes. 4 I prayed to the LORD my God and
told him about all of our sins. I said, "Lord,
you are a great God who causes fear and
wonder. You keep your agreement of love
with all who love you and obey your
commands.
5 "But we have sinned and done wrong. We
have been wicked and turned against you,
your commands, and your laws. 6 We did not
listen to your servants, the prophets, who
spoke for you to our kings, our leaders, our
ancestors, and all the people of the land.
7 "Lord, you are good and right, but we are
full of shame today—the people of Judah
and Jerusalem, all the people of Israel, those
near and far whom you scattered among
many nations because they were not loyal to
you. 8 LORD, we are all ashamed. Our kings
and leaders and our fathers are ashamed,
because we have sinned against you.
9 "But, Lord our God, you show us mercy
and forgive us even though we have turned
against you. 10 We have not obeyed the LORD
our God or the teachings he gave us through
his servants, the prophets. 11 All the people of
Israel have disobeyed your teachings and
have turned away, refusing to obey you. So
you brought on us the curses and promises
of punishment written in the Teachings of
Moses, the servant of God, because we
sinned against you.
12 "You said these things would happen to
us and our leaders, and you made them
happen; you brought on us a great disaster.
Nothing has ever been done on earth like
what was done to Jerusalem. 13 All this
disaster came to us just as it is written in the
Teachings of Moses. But we have not pleaded

with the LORD our God. We have not stopped
sinning. We have not paid attention to your
truth. [14]The LORD was ready to bring the
disaster on us, and he did it because the LORD
our God is right in everything he does. But
we still did not obey him.
[15]"Lord our God, you used your power and
brought us out of Egypt. Because of that,
your name is known even today. But we
have sinned and have done wrong. [16]Lord,
you do what is right, but please do not be
angry with Jerusalem, your city on your holy
hill. Because of our sins and the evil things
done by our ancestors, people all around
insult and make fun of Jerusalem and your
people.
[17]"Now, our God, hear the prayers of your
servant. Listen to my prayer for help, and for
your sake do good things for your holy place
that is in ruins. [18]My God, pay attention and
hear me. Open your eyes and see all the
terrible things that have happened to us. See
how our lives have been ruined and what
has happened to the city that is called by
your name. We do not ask these things
because we are good; instead, we ask because
of your mercy. [19]Lord, listen! Lord, forgive!
Lord, hear us and do something! For your
sake, don't wait, because your city and your
people are called by your name."

Gabriel's Explanation

[20]While I was saying these things in my
prayer to the LORD, my God, confessing my
sins and the sins of the people of Israel and
praying for God's holy hill, [21]Gabriel came to
me. (I had seen him in my last vision.) He
came flying quickly to me about the time of
the evening sacrifice, while I was still
praying. [22]He taught me and said to me,
"Daniel, I have come to give you wisdom and
to help you understand. [23]When you first
started praying, an answer was given, and I
came to tell you, because God loves you very
much. So think about the message and
understand the vision.
[24]"God has ordered four hundred ninety
years for your people and your holy city for
these reasons: to stop people from turning
against God; to put an end to sin; to take
away evil; to bring in goodness that
continues forever; to bring about the vision
and prophecy; and to appoint a most holy
place.

devotion 236

DANIEL 9:18–19

CHRISTIANS ARE NON-EXEMPT

Sometimes when difficult things happen in your life, you may feel as though God has abandoned you. You cry as Daniel did, "Lord, listen! Lord, forgive! Lord, hear us and do something!" (Dan. 9:19). You beg God to change your situation as you fall asleep at night only to awaken in the morning with the realization that you have to face another day with the same pain that you fell asleep with. Christians are not exempt from pain and suffering. We have to walk through it like everyone else. So what makes us different from the rest of the world? How do we pass through the dark valleys of life without fear?

God tells us to come to him, and he will hear us. He teaches us perseverance, but he also gives us hope in the midst of our pain. Read Luke 18:1-8, the parable about a persistent widow who goes to her town judge asking for help. She is turned away several times, but she keeps coming back. Then Jesus says, "God will always give what is right to his people who cry to him night and day, and he will not be slow to answer them" (Luke 18:7). We have to ask God and keep on asking. We need to persevere like the widow and believe that God hears our prayers. We also have to trust God to answer our prayers in his perfect timing. God has a plan in every situation of our lives. Just don't give up.

25“Learn and understand these things. A
command will come to rebuild Jerusalem.
The time from this command until the
appointed leader comes will be forty-nine
years and four hundred thirty-four years.
Jerusalem will be rebuilt with streets and a
trench filled with water around it, but it will
be built in times of trouble. 26After the four
hundred thirty-four years the appointed
leader will be killed; he will have nothing.
The people of the leader who is to come will
destroy the city and the holy place. The end
of the city will come like a flood, and war
will continue until the end. God has ordered
that place to be completely destroyed. 27That
leader will make firm an agreement with
many people for seven years. He will stop
the offerings and sacrifices after three and
one-half years. A destroyer will do
blasphemous things until the ordered end
comes to the destroyed city.”

Daniel’s Vision of a Man

10 During Cyrus’ third year as king of
Persia, Daniel, whose name was
Belteshazzar, received a vision about a great
war. It was a true message that Daniel
understood.

2At that time I, Daniel, had been very sad
for three weeks. 3I did not eat any fancy food
or meat, or drink any wine, or use any
perfumed oil for three weeks.

4On the twenty-fourth day of the first
month, I was standing beside the great Tigris
River. 5While standing there, I looked up
and saw a man dressed in linen clothes with
a belt of fine gold wrapped around his waist.
6His body was like shiny yellow quartz. His
face was bright like lightning, and his eyes
were like fire. His arms and legs were shiny
like polished bronze, and his voice sounded
like the roar of a crowd.

7I, Daniel, was the only person who saw
the vision. The men with me did not see it,
because they were so frightened that they
ran away and hid. 8So I was left alone,
watching this great vision. I lost my strength,
my face turned white like a dead person, and
I was helpless. 9Then I heard the man in the
vision speaking. As I listened, I fell into a
deep sleep with my face on the ground.

10Then a hand touched me and set me on
my hands and knees. I was so afraid that I
was shaking. 11The man in the vision said to
me, “Daniel, God loves you very much.
Think carefully about the words I will speak
to you, and stand up, because I have been
sent to you.” When he said this, I stood up,
but I was still shaking.

12Then the man said to me, “Daniel, do
not be afraid. Some time ago you decided to
get understanding and to humble yourself
before your God. Since that time God has
listened to you, and I have come because of
your prayers. 13But the prince of Persia has
been fighting against me for twenty-one
days. Then Michael, one of the most
important angels, came to help me, because I
had been left there with the king of Persia.
14Now I have come to explain to you what
will happen to your people, because the
vision is about a time in the future.”

15While he was speaking to me, I bowed
facedown and could not speak. 16Then one
who looked like a man touched my lips, so I
opened my mouth and started to speak. I
said to the one standing in front of me,
“Master, I am upset and afraid because of
what I saw in the vision. I feel helpless.
17Master, how can I, your servant, talk with
you? My strength is gone, and it is hard for
me to breathe.”

18The one who looked like a man touched
me again and gave me strength. 19He said,
“Daniel, don’t be afraid. God loves you very
much. Peace be with you. Be strong now; be
courageous.”

When he spoke to me, I became stronger
and said, “Master, speak, since you have
given me strength.”

20Then he said, “Daniel, do you know why
I have come to you? Soon I must go back to
fight against the prince of Persia. When I go,
the prince of Greece will come, 21but I must
first tell you what is written in the Book of
Truth. No one stands with me against these
enemies except Michael, the angel ruling
over your people.

11 In the first year that Darius the Mede
was king, I stood up to support
Michael in his fight against the prince of
Persia.

Kingdoms of the South and North

2“Now then, Daniel, I tell you the truth:
Three more kings will rule in Persia, and
then a fourth king will come. He will be
much richer than all the kings of Persia

before him and will use his riches to get
power. He will stir up everyone against the
kingdom of Greece. 3Then a mighty king
will come, who will rule with great power
and will do anything he wants. 4After that
king has come, his kingdom will be broken
up and divided out toward the four parts of
the world. His kingdom will not go to his
descendants, and it will not have the power
that he had, because his kingdom will be
pulled up and given to other people.

5"The king of the South will become
strong, but one of his commanders will
become even stronger. He will begin to rule
his own kingdom with great power. 6Then
after a few years, a new friendship will
develop. The daughter of the king of the
South will marry the king of the North in
order to bring peace. But she will not keep
her power, and his family will not last. She,
her husband, her child, and those who
brought her to that country will be killed.

7"But a person from her family will
become king of the South and will attack the
armies of the king of the North. He will go
into that king's strong, walled city and will
fight and win. 8He will take their gods, their
metal idols, and their valuable things made
of silver and gold back to Egypt. Then he
will not bother the king of the North for a
few years. 9Next, the king of the North will
attack the king of the South, but he will be
beaten back to his own country.

10"The sons of the king of the North will
prepare for war. They will get a large army
together that will move through the land
very quickly, like a powerful flood. Later,
that army will come back and fight all the
way to the strong, walled city of the king of
the South. 11Then the king of the South will
become very angry and will march out to
fight against the king of the North. The king
of the North will have a large army, but he
will lose the battle, 12and the soldiers will be
carried away. The king of the South will then
be very proud and will kill thousands of
soldiers from the northern army, but he will
not continue to be successful. 13The king of
the North will gather another army, larger
than the first one. After several years he will
attack with a large army and many weapons.

14"In those times many people will be
against the king of the South. Some of your
own people who love to fight will turn
against the king of the South, thinking it is
time for God's promises to come true. But
they will fail. 15Then the king of the North
will come. He will build ramps to the tops of
the city walls and will capture a strong,
walled city. The southern army will not have
the power to fight back; even their best
soldiers will not be strong enough to stop
the northern army. 16So the king of the
North will do whatever he wants; no one
will be able to stand against him. He will
gain power and control in the beautiful land
of Israel and will have the power to destroy
it. 17The king of the North will decide to use
all his power to fight against the king of the
South, but he will make a peace agreement
with the king of the South. The king of the
North will give one of his daughters as a
wife to the king of the South so that he can
defeat him. But those plans will not succeed
or help him. 18Then the king of the North
will turn his attention to cities along the
coast of the Mediterranean Sea and will
capture them. But a commander will put an
end to the pride of the king of the North,
turning his pride back on him. 19After that
happens the king of the North will go back
to the strong, walled cities of his own
country, but he will lose his power. That will
be the end of him.

20"The next king of the North will send
out a tax collector so he will have plenty of
money. In a few years that ruler will be
killed, although he will not die in anger or in
a battle.

21"That ruler will be followed by a very
cruel and hated man, who will not have the
honor of being from a king's family. He will
attack the kingdom when the people feel
safe, and he will take power by lying to the
people. 22He will sweep away in defeat large
and powerful armies and even a prince who
made an agreement. 23Many nations will
make agreements with that cruel and hated
ruler, but he will lie to them. He will gain
much power, but only a few people will
support him. 24The richest areas will feel
safe, but that cruel and hated ruler will
attack them. He will succeed where his
ancestors did not. He will rob the countries
he defeats and will give those things to his
followers. He will plan to defeat and destroy
strong cities, but he will be successful for
only a short time.

25“That very cruel and hated ruler will
have a large army that he will use to stir up
his strength and courage. He will attack the
king of the South. The king of the South will
gather a large and very powerful army and
prepare for war. But the people who are
against him will make secret plans, and the
king of the South will be defeated. 26People
who were supposed to be his good friends
will try to destroy him. His army will be
swept away in defeat; many of his soldiers
will be killed in battle. 27Those two kings
will want to hurt each other. They will sit at
the same table and lie to each other, but it
will not do either one any good, because God
has set a time for their end to come. 28The
king of the North will go back to his own
country with much wealth. Then he will
decide to go against the holy agreement. He
will take action and then return to his own
country.
29“At the right time the king of the North
will attack the king of the South again, but
this time he will not be successful as he was
before. 30Ships from the west will come and
fight against the king of the North, so he will
be afraid. Then he will return and show his
anger against the holy agreement. He will be
good to those who have stopped obeying the
holy agreement.
31“The king of the North will send his
army to make the Temple in Jerusalem
unclean. They will stop the people from
offering the daily sacrifice, and then they
will set up a blasphemous object that brings
destruction. 32The king of the North will tell
lies and cause those who have not obeyed
God to be ruined. But those who know God
and obey him will be strong and fight back.
33“Those who are wise will help the others
understand what is happening. But they will
be killed with swords, or burned, or taken
captive, or robbed of their homes and
possessions. These things will continue for
many days. 34When the wise ones are
suffering, they will get a little help, but
many who join the wise ones will not help
them in their time of need. 35Some of the
wise ones will be killed. But the hard times
must come so they can be made stronger and
purer and without faults until the time of
the end comes. Then, at the right time, the
end will come.

The King Who Praises Himself

36“The king of the North will do whatever
he wants. He will brag about himself and
praise himself and think he is even better
than a god. He will say things against the
God of gods that no one has ever heard. And
he will be successful until all the bad things
have happened. Then what God has
planned to happen will happen. 37The king
of the North will not care about the gods his
ancestors worshiped or the god that women
worship. He won’t care about any god.
Instead, he will make himself more
important than any god. 38The king of the
North will worship power and strength,
which his ancestors did not worship. He
will honor the god of power with gold and
silver, expensive jewels and gifts. 39That
king will attack strong, walled cities with
the help of a foreign god. He will give much
honor to the people who join him, making
them rulers in charge of many other people.
And he will make them pay him for the
land they rule.
40“At the time of the end, the king of the
South will fight a battle against the king of
the North. The king of the North will attack
with chariots, soldiers on horses, and many
large ships. He will invade many countries
and sweep through their lands like a flood.
41The king of the North will attack the
beautiful land of Judah. He will defeat many
countries, but Edom, Moab, and the leaders
of Ammon will be saved from him. 42The
king of the North will show his power in
many countries; Egypt will not escape. 43The
king will get treasures of gold and silver and
all the riches of Egypt. The Libyan and
Nubian people will obey him. 44But the king
of the North will hear news from the east
and the north that will make him afraid and
angry. He will go to destroy completely
many nations. 45He will set up his royal
tents between the sea and the beautiful
mountain where the holy Temple is built.
But, finally, his end will come, and no one
will help him.

The Time of the End

12 “At that time Michael, the great prince
who protects your people, will stand
up. There will be a time of much trouble, the
worst time since nations have been on earth,

devotion 237

DANIEL 12:1–3

A NAME IN A BOOK

Daniel's prophecy says that everyone whose name is written in God's book will be saved (verse 1). I hope your name is in that book so we can meet in heaven someday. I have assurance that my name will be in it because I've asked Jesus into my heart and trusted him as my personal Savior. Even though I don't deserve his grace, I accept it because he says I *am* deserving. Is your name in that book?

Will the names of your friends be in that book? Daniel's prophecy inspires me to tell even more people the story of salvation. I admit it can sometimes be difficult to talk about Jesus face-to-face with an unbeliever, but Scripture challenges us to make sure we are teaching others. Perhaps you think you aren't a good witness, but that isn't true. For starters, living as an example to those who don't know Christ is like giving a testimony of his love to all who are watching you. You're doing the right thing when you consciously choose to live as a Christian witness.

God also wants us to teach others to live right by speaking to them. I encourage you to ask God to provide opportunities for you to share your faith and to give you the right words at the right moment. In whatever way you choose to teach others, the Lord will be pleased that you are helping him multiply the names of those who will be in heaven.

but your people will be saved. Everyone
whose name is written in God's book will be
saved. 2Many people who have already died
will live again. Some of them will wake up
to have life forever, but some will wake up to
find shame and disgrace forever. 3The wise
people will shine like the brightness of the
sky. Those who teach others to live right will
shine like stars forever and ever.

4"But you, Daniel, close up the book and
seal it. These things will happen at the time
of the end. Many people will go here and
there to find true knowledge."

5Then I, Daniel, looked, and saw two other
men. One was standing on my side of the
river, and the other was standing on the far
side. 6The man who was dressed in linen was
standing over the water in the river. One of
the two men spoke to him and asked, "How
long will it be before these amazing things
come true?"

7The man dressed in linen, who stood
over the water, raised his hands toward
heaven. And I heard him swear by the name
of God who lives forever, "It will be for three
and one-half years. The power of the holy
people will finally be broken, and then all
these things will come true."

8I heard the answer, but I did not really
understand, so I asked, "Master, what will
happen after all these things come true?"

9He answered, "Go your way, Daniel. The
message is closed up and sealed until the
time of the end. 10Many people will be made
clean, pure, and spotless, but the wicked will
continue to be wicked. Those wicked people
will not understand these things, but the
wise will understand them.

11"The daily sacrifice will be stopped.
Then, after 1,290 days from that time, a
blasphemous object that brings destruction
will be set up. 12Those who wait for the end
of the 1,335 days will be happy.

13"As for you, Daniel, go your way until
the end. You will get your rest, and at the end
you will rise to receive your reward."

Hosea

A Hebrew name that means "salvation"

Hosea is the first of the so-called "minor prophets"—not because they were petite or insignificant, but because their prophecies weren't as lengthy as those of men like Isaiah and Jeremiah.

Person Holding the Pen God Wrote With: *Hosea*, a prophet during the reigns of four successive kings of Judah authored this book. He was the last to prophecy before the northern kingdom of Israel fell to Assyria in 722 B.C.

When the Text Was Written: Based on the content, we know Hosea was written in the eighth century B.C. between 770 and 725 B.C.

Spiritual Posture of the Original Recipients: The economy in Jerusalem was thriving, and the people were experiencing relative peace with surrounding nations. But because of their newfound freedom and material excess, God's people were turning their backs on him and spending more time at the mall than at the synagogue.

Storyline Synopsis: Hosea is actually a story within a story. The primary tale is of God's disapproval at Israel's spiritual unfaithfulness, with a pronouncement of judgment and wrath to come as a consequence of their sinful rebellion. The secondary story is Hosea's marriage to Gomer. She had a very bad reputation—her phone number would have been plastered all over the boy's locker room. God orchestrates this "good guy/bad girl" setup to provide his people with a living metaphor for his redemptive relationship with them.

A Moment Worth Discussing: At the beginning of chapter 3, Gomer is in a downward spiral of sin, including adultery, abandoning her family, prostitution, and eventually selling her body to anyone who'll pay her. She's on the auction block, and in light of what history reveals about the slave trade at that time, Gomer probably stood naked so that interested buyers could examine the "merchandise." In her utter humiliation, she hears a familiar voice and looks up to see her estranged husband, Hosea, walking through the raucous crowd. He hands the required amount to the auctioneer—he has to pay for her even though she's still legally his wife—and reaches for her hand to lead her home. It's a poignant picture of a husband's forgiveness and an even more amazing image of how God redeems unfaithful people like us.

Interesting (But Likely to Be Overlooked) Character: *Ephraim* is another name God used for the kingdom of Israel after it was split into two kingdoms, most likely because the tribe of Ephraim was the largest out of the northern ten and thus considered representative (Hos. 13:1). Ephraim was Joseph's second son (Gen. 41:50–52), as well as one of Joshua's ancestors (Num. 13:8).

Gomer

HOSEA

Gomer rests from her work for a moment. Her back aches. She sold herself into slavery and works as a prostitute. Her owner keeps her busy with many men, but she dreams of being with her lover. Though she is married with children, she has had many lovers. Her husband knew her to be unfaithful when he married her. But Hosea had been kind, not treating her like some of her customers do. When Hosea asked her to come back to him, she refused. The work was humiliating, but life with her lover was exciting.

Down the street, she sees Hosea talking with her master, who accepts a pouch of money. Gomer looks weary and thin as she charges toward Hosea. "I told you once. Go away!"

Hosea speaks: "The Lord said to me . . ." She rolls her eyes, and he lifts his hand, pleading that she listen. "Go, show your love to a woman loved by someone else, who has been unfaithful to you."

She crinkles her brow, listening. Why would he want her after all she has done? Hosea explains that he has just bought her out of slavery. She shakes her head; she doesn't understand. "You must not be a prostitute," he says, "and you must not have sexual relations with any other man. I will act the same way toward you."

She leaves her work and walks home with Hosea.

Like Hosea, God loves us (his bride) and remains faithful to us. He waits for your return even now.

1 The LORD spoke his word to Hosea son of
Beeri during the time that Uzziah, Jotham,
Ahaz, and Hezekiah were kings of Judah and
Jeroboam son of Jehoash was king of Israel.

Hosea's Wife and Children

2 When the LORD began speaking through
Hosea, the LORD said to him, "Go, and marry
an unfaithful woman and have unfaithful
children, because the people in this country
have been completely unfaithful to the
LORD." 3 So Hosea married Gomer daughter of
Diblaim, and she became pregnant and gave
birth to Hosea's son.
4 The LORD said to Hosea, "Name him
Jezreel, because soon I will punish the
family of Jehu for the people they killed at
Jezreel. In the future I will put an end to the
kingdom of Israel 5 and break the power of
Israel's army in the Valley of Jezreel."
6 Gomer became pregnant again and gave
birth to a daughter. The LORD said to Hosea,
"Name her Lo-Ruhamah,[n] because I will not
pity Israel anymore, nor will I forgive them.
7 But I will show pity to the people of Judah. I
will save them, but not by using bows or
swords, horses or horsemen, or weapons of
war. I, the LORD their God, will save them."
8 After Gomer had stopped nursing Lo-
Ruhamah, she became pregnant again and
gave birth to another son. 9 The LORD said,
"Name him Lo-Ammi,[n] because you are not
my people, and I am not your God.

God's Promise to Israel

10 "But the number of the Israelites will
become like the grains of sand of the sea,
which no one can measure or count. They
were called, 'You are not my people,' but
later they will be called 'children of the
living God.' 11 The people of Judah and Israel
will join together again and will choose one
leader for themselves. They will come up
from the land, because the day of Jezreel[n]
will be truly great.

2 "You are to call your brothers, 'my
people,' and your sisters, 'you have been
shown pity.'

God Speaks About Israel

2 "Plead with your mother.[n]
Accuse her, because she is no longer my
wife,

1:6 Lo-Ruhamah This name in Hebrew means "not pitied." **1:9 Lo-Ammi** This name in Hebrew means "not my people."
1:11 Jezreel This name in Hebrew means "God plants." **2:2 mother** Refers to the nation of Israel here.

and I am no longer her husband.
Tell her to stop acting like a prostitute,
to stop behaving like an unfaithful
wife.
3 If she refuses, I will strip her naked
and leave her bare like the day she was
born.
I will make her dry like a desert,
like a land without water,
and I will kill her with thirst.
4 I will not take pity on her children,
because they are the children of a
prostitute.
5 Their mother has acted like a prostitute;
the one who became pregnant with
them has acted disgracefully.
She said, 'I will chase after my lovers,[n]
who give me my food and water,
wool and flax, wine and olive oil.'
6 So I will block her road with thornbushes;
I will build a wall around her
so she cannot find her way.
7 She will run after her lovers,
but she won't catch them.
She will look for them,
but she won't find them.
Then she will say, 'I will go back to my
first husband,[n]
because life was better then for me than
it is now.'
8 But she does not know that I was the one
who gave her grain, new wine, and oil.
I gave her much silver and gold,
but she used it for Baal.
9 "So I will come back and take away my
grain at harvest time
and my new wine when it is ready.
I will take back my wool and linen
that covered her nakedness.
10 So I will show her nakedness to her
lovers,
and no one will save her from me.
11 I will put an end to all her celebrations:
her yearly festivals, her New Moon
festivals, and her Sabbaths.
I will stop all of her special feasts.
12 I will destroy her vines and fig trees,
which she said were her pay from her
lovers.
I will turn them into a forest,
and wild animals will eat them.
13 I will punish her for all the times
she burned incense to the Baals.
She put on her rings and jewelry
and went chasing after her lovers,
but she forgot me!"
says the LORD.

14 "So I am going to attract her;
I will lead her into the desert
and speak tenderly to her.
15 There I will give her back her vineyards,
and I will make the Valley of Trouble a
door of hope.
There she will respond as when she was
young,
as when she came out of Egypt."

16 The LORD says, "In the future she will call
me 'my husband';
no longer will she call me 'my baal.'[n]
17 I will never let her say the names of Baal
again;
people won't use their names anymore.
18 At that time I will make an agreement for
them
with the wild animals, the birds, and
the crawling things.
I will smash from the land
the bow and the sword and the
weapons of war,
so my people will live in safety.
19 And I will make you my promised bride
forever.
I will be good and fair;
I will show you my love and mercy.
20 I will be true to you as my promised bride,
and you will know the LORD.

21 "At that time I will speak to you," says the
LORD.
"I will speak to the skies,
and they will give rain to the earth.
22 The earth will produce grain, new wine,
and oil;
much will grow because my people are
called Jezreel.[n]
23 I will plant my people in the land,
and I will show pity to the one I had
called 'not shown pity.'
I will say, 'You are my people'
to those I had called 'not my people.'
And they will say to me, 'You are our
God.' "

2:5 lovers Refers to the nations surrounding Israel, who led Israel to worship false gods. **2:7 husband** Refers to God here. **2:16 baal** Another Hebrew word for husband, but it was the same word as the false god Baal. **2:22 Jezreel** This name in Hebrew means "God plants."

devotion 238

HOSEA 2:14–23

A CHANCE OF RESCUE

The prophecy of Hosea includes a beautiful love song. God is singing to his unfaithful wife, Israel. By faith, we too have become children of God, and so this love song is also being sung over me and you. We have all been guilty of loving others more than we love God, yet look at these verses. God still wants us. Actually, his love is so great that he begins his song with tender romance. Like Hosea's call-girl wife, Gomer, we have wandered away from God, but he is so merciful to us. He knows that he is singing to a broken and sinful woman, but he desires her still.

In this song, God promises hope and safety. He says that no matter where we find ourselves today or how ugly or hopeless we might feel, he is able and *wants* to rescue even a sinful bunch like us. In fact, God says that when the unfaithful wife returns home, there is a paradise waiting for her.

And then, amazingly, God says we can start over with him. We can take our vows of commitment again. He will provide and love and protect like a faithful husband. Whatever has been broken between you and God, he promises to make new. This passionate love song is being sung over you this very day. God calls you his beloved, promised bride, and no matter how awful the mess you've made, he is calling you back into his arms.

Hosea Buys a Wife

3 The LORD said to me again, "Go, show
your love to a woman loved by someone
else, who has been unfaithful to you. In the
same way the LORD loves the people of Israel,
even though they worship other gods and
love to eat the raisin cakes."[n]
2So I bought her for six ounces of silver
and ten bushels of barley. 3Then I told her,
"You must wait for me for many days. You
must not be a prostitute, and you must not
have sexual relations with any other man. I
will act the same way toward you."
4In the same way Israel will live many
days without a king or leader, without
sacrifices or holy stone pillars, and without
the holy vest or an idol. 5After this, the
people of Israel will return to the LORD their
God and follow him and the king from
David's family. In the last days they will
turn in fear to the LORD, and he will bless
them.

The Lord's Word Against Israel

4 People of Israel, listen to the LORD's
message.
The LORD has this
against you who live in the land:
"The people are not true, not loyal to God,
nor do those who live in the land even
know him.
2Cursing, lying, killing, stealing and
adultery are everywhere.
One murder follows another.
3Because of this the land dries up,
and all its people are dying.
Even the wild animals and the birds of
the air
and the fish of the sea are dying.

God's Case Against the Priests

4"No one should accuse
or blame another person.
Don't blame the people, you priests,
when they quarrel with you.

3:1 raisin cakes This food was eaten in the feasts that honored false gods.

5You will be ruined in the day,
and your prophets will be ruined with you in the night.
I will also destroy your mother.[n]
6My people will be destroyed,
because they have no knowledge.
You have refused to learn,
so I will refuse to let you be priests to me.
You have forgotten the teachings of your God,
so I will forget your children.
7The more priests there are,
the more they sin against me.
I will take away their honor
and give them shame.
8Since the priests live off the sin offerings of the people,
they want the people to sin more and more.
9The priests are as wrong as the people,
and I will punish them both for what they have done.
I will repay them for the wrong they have done.

10"They will eat
but not have enough;
they will have sexual relations with the prostitutes,
but they will not have children,
because they have left the LORD
to give themselves to 11prostitution,
to old and new wine,
which take away their ability to understand.

God's Case Against the People

12"My people ask wooden idols for advice;
they ask those sticks of wood to advise them!
Like prostitutes, they have chased after other gods
and have left their own God.
13They make sacrifices on the tops of the mountains.
They burn offerings on the hills,
under oaks, poplars, and other trees,
because their shade is nice.
So your daughters become prostitutes,
and your daughters-in-law are guilty of adultery.
14"But I will not punish your daughters
for becoming prostitutes,
nor your daughters-in-law
for their sins of adultery.
I will not punish them,
because the men have sexual relations with prostitutes
and offer sacrifices with the temple prostitutes.
A foolish people will be ruined.

15"Israel, you act like a prostitute,
but do not be guilty toward the LORD.
Don't go to Gilgal
or go up to Beth Aven.[n]
Don't make promises,
saying, 'As surely as the LORD lives . . .'
16The people of Israel are stubborn
like a stubborn young cow.
Now the LORD will feed them
like lambs in the open country.
17The Israelites have chosen to worship idols,
so leave them alone.
18When they finish their drinking,
they completely give themselves to being prostitutes;
they love these disgraceful ways.
19They will be swept away as if by a whirlwind,
and their sacrifices will bring them only shame.

God's Word Against the Leaders

5 "Listen, you priests.
Pay attention, people of Israel.
Listen, royal family,
because you will all be judged.
You have been like a trap at Mizpah
and like a net spread out at Mount Tabor.
2You have done many evil things,
so I will punish you all.
3I know all about the people of Israel;
what they have done is not hidden from me.
Now that Israel acts like a prostitute,
it has made itself unclean.
4"They will not give up their deeds
and return to their God.
They are determined to be unfaithful to me;
they do not know the LORD.
5Israel's pride testifies against them.

4:5 mother Refers to the nation of Israel here. **4:15 Gilgal . . . Beth Aven** Cities in Israel where people worshiped false gods.

The people of Israel will stumble
because of their sin,
and the people of Judah will stumble
with them.
6They will come to worship the LORD,
bringing their flocks and herds,
but they will not be able to find him,
because he has left them.
7They have not been true to the LORD;
they are children who do not belong to
him.
So their false worship
will destroy them and their land.

8"Blow the horn in Gibeah
and the trumpet in Ramah.
Give the warning at Beth Aven,
and be first into battle, people of
Benjamin.
9Israel will be ruined
on the day of punishment.
To the tribes of Israel
I tell the truth.
10The leaders of Judah are like those
who steal other people's land.
I will pour my punishment over them
like a flood of water.
11Israel is crushed by the punishment,
because it decided to follow idols.
12I am like a moth to Israel,
like a rot to the people of Judah.

13"When Israel saw its illness
and Judah saw its wounds,
Israel went to Assyria for help
and sent to the great king of Assyria.
But he cannot heal you
or cure your wounds.
14I will be like a lion to Israel,
like a young lion to Judah.
I will attack them
and tear them to pieces.
I will drag them off,
and no one will be able to save them.
15Then I will go back to my place
until they suffer for their guilt and turn
back to me.
In their trouble they will look for me."

The People Are Not Faithful

6 "Come, let's go back to the LORD.
He has hurt us, but he will heal us.
He has wounded us, but he will
bandage our wounds.

devotion 239

HOSEA 6:1

EVEN PETER

If you have been away from the Lord for a while, let me be the third to say welcome back, precious woman. The Lord was the first, and the prophecy of Hosea comes in second. It gets tough at times to walk the Christian life. We battle with ourselves more than anyone or anything else. I am often curious about Jesus' follower Peter and his walk with the Lord. I am sure it was difficult as he wrestled with his passionate soul and struggled so much with the humility that Christ caused him to see in himself—one day preaching and loving the Lord and the next denying him three times in public just as Jesus predicted.

Does this sound anything like your heart? I want you to know that just as Jesus restored Peter, he is restoring you today. Our dear Peter went from a man who could not stand up under the pressure of the crowd to a man restored by Jesus and empowered in the Holy Spirit. Most of all, Peter sought after the heart of his Lord, and his Lord loved him—all of him. Have you noticed that whenever Jesus shared his most personal moments, he only pulled three from the twelve followers to experience it with him? Peter was among those three. If you have repented of your sins, Jesus has healed you, bandaged your wounds, and drawn you to himself in the same way. Don't be anxious or overwhelmed; just rest in his love for you.

[2]In two days he will put new life in us;
on the third day he will raise us up
so that we may live in his presence [3]and
know him.
Let's try to learn about the LORD;
he will come to us as surely as the
dawn comes.
He will come to us like rain,
like the spring rain that waters the
ground."

[4]The LORD says, "Israel, what should I do
with you?
Judah, what should I do with you?
Your faithfulness is like a morning mist,
like the dew that goes away early in the
day.
[5]I have warned you by my prophets
that I will kill you and destroy you.
My justice comes out like bright light.
[6]I want faithful love
more than I want animal sacrifices.
I want people to know me
more than I want burnt offerings.
[7]But they have broken the agreement as
Adam did;
they have been unfaithful to me.
[8]Gilead is a city of people who do evil;
their footprints are bloody.
[9]The priests are like robbers waiting to
attack people;
they murder people on the road to
Shechem[n]
and do wicked things.
[10]I have seen horrible things in Israel.
Look at Israel's prostitution;
Israel has become unclean.

[11]"Judah, I have set a harvest time for you
when I will make the lives of my
people good again.

7 When I heal Israel,
Israel's sin will go away,
and so will Samaria's evil.

"They cheat a lot!
Thieves break into houses,
and robbers are in the streets.
[2]It never enters their minds
that I remember all their evil deeds.
The bad things they do are all around
them;
they are right in front of me.

Israel's Evil Kings

[3]"They make the king happy with their
wickedness;
their rulers are glad with their lies.
[4]But all of them are traitors.
They are like an oven heated by a baker.
While he mixes the dough,
he does not need to stir up the fire.
[5]The kings get so drunk they get sick every
day.
The rulers become crazy with wine;
they make agreements with those who
do not know the true God.
[6]They burn like an oven;
their hearts burn inside them.
All night long their anger is low,
but when morning comes, it becomes a
roaring fire.
[7]All these people are as hot as an oven;
they burn up their rulers.
All their kings fall,
and no one calls on me.

Israel and the Other Nations

[8]"Israel mixes with other nations;
he is like a pancake cooked only on one
side.
[9]Foreign nations have eaten up his strength,
but he doesn't know it.
Israel is weak and feeble, like an old man,
but he doesn't know it.
[10]Israel's pride will cause their defeat;
they will not turn back to the LORD
their God
or look to him for help in all this.
[11]Israel has become like a pigeon—
easy to fool and stupid.
First they call to Egypt for help.
Then they run to Assyria.
[12]When they go, I will catch them in a net,
I will bring them down like birds from
the sky;
I will punish them countless times for
their evil.
[13]How terrible for them because they
left me!
They will be destroyed, because they
turned against me.
I want to save them,
but they have spoken lies against me.
[14]They do not call to me from their hearts.
They just lie on their beds and cry.

6:9 Shechem A city of safety where people could go for protection.

They come together to ask for grain and
new wine,
but they really turn away from me.
15Though I trained them and gave them
strength,
they have made evil plans against me.
16They did not turn to the Most High God.
They are like a loose bow that can't
shoot.
Because their leaders brag about their
strength,
they will be killed with swords,
and the people in Egypt
will laugh at them.

Israel Has Trusted Wrong Things

8 "Put the trumpet to your lips and give the
warning!
The enemy swoops down on the LORD's
people like an eagle.
The Israelites have broken my
agreement
and have turned against my
teachings.
2They cry out to me,
'Our God, we in Israel know you!'
3But Israel has rejected what is good,
so the enemy will chase them.
4They chose their own kings
without asking my permission.
They chose their own leaders,
people I did not know.
They made their silver and gold into idols,
and for all this they will be destroyed.
5I hate the calf-shaped idol of Israel!
I am very angry with the people.
How long will they remain unclean?
6The idol is something a craftsman made;
it is not God.
Israel's calf-shaped idol
will surely be smashed to pieces.

7"Israel's foolish plans are like planting the
wind,
but they will harvest a storm.
Like a stalk with no head of grain,
it produces nothing.
Even if it produced something,
other nations would eat it.
8Israel is eaten up;
the people are mixed among the other
nations
and have become useless to me.
9Israel is like a wild donkey all by itself.
They have run to Assyria;
They have hired other nations to
protect them.
10Although Israel is mixed among the
nations,
I will gather them together.
They will become weaker and weaker
as they suffer under the great king of
Assyria.

11"Although Israel built more altars to
remove sin,
they have become altars for sinning.
12I have written many teachings for them,
but they think the teachings are strange
and foreign.
13The Israelites offer sacrifices to me as gifts
and eat the meat,
but the LORD is not pleased with them.
He remembers the evil they have done,
and he will punish them for their sins.
They will be slaves again as they were
in Egypt.
14Israel has forgotten their Maker and has
built palaces;
Judah has built many strong, walled
cities.
But I will send fire on their cities
and destroy their strong buildings."

Israel's Punishment

9 Israel, do not rejoice;
don't shout for joy as the other
nations do.
You have been like a prostitute against
your God.
You love the pay of prostitutes on every
threshing floor.
2But the threshing floor and the winepress
will not feed the people,
and there won't be enough new wine.
3The people will not stay in the LORD's
land.
Israel will return to being captives as
they were in Egypt,
and in Assyria they will eat food that
they are not allowed to eat.
4The Israelites will not give offerings of
wine to the LORD;
they will not give him sacrifices.
Their sacrifices will be like food that is
eaten at a funeral;
it is unclean, and everyone who eats it
becomes unclean.

Their food will only satisfy their
hunger;
they cannot sacrifice it in the Temple.
5 What will you do then on the day of
feasts
and on the day of the LORD's festival?
6 Even if the people are not destroyed,
Egypt will capture them;
Memphis[n] will bury them.
Weeds will grow over their silver
treasures,
and thorns will drive them out of their
tents.
7 The time of punishment has come,
the time to pay for sins.
Let Israel know this:
You think the prophet is a fool,
and you say the spiritual person is
crazy.
You have sinned very much,
and your hatred is great.
8 Is Israel a watchman?
Are God's people prophets?
Everywhere Israel goes, traps are set for
him.
He is an enemy in God's house.
9 The people of Israel have gone deep into
sin
as the people of Gibeah[n] did.
The Lord will remember the evil things
they have done,
and he will punish their sins.

10 "When I found Israel,
it was like finding grapes in the desert.
Your ancestors were like
finding the first figs on the fig tree.
But when they came to Baal Peor,
they began worshiping an idol,
and they became as hateful as the thing
they worshiped.
11 Israel's glory will fly away like a bird;
there will be no more pregnancy, no
more births, no more getting
pregnant.
12 But even if the Israelites bring up
children,
I will take them all away.
How terrible it will be for them
when I go away from them!
13 I have seen Israel, like Tyre,
given a pleasant place.
But the people of Israel will soon bring
out
their children to be killed."
14 LORD, give them what they should have.
What will you give them?
Make their women unable to have
children;
give them dried-up breasts that cannot
feed their babies.

15 "The Israelites were very wicked in Gilgal,
so I have hated them there.
Because of the sinful things they have
done,
I will force them to leave my land.
I will no longer love them;
their leaders have turned against me.
16 Israel is beaten down;
its root is dying, and it has no fruit.
If they have more children,
I will kill the children they love."
17 God will reject them,
because they have not obeyed him;
they will wander among the nations.

Israel Will Pay for Sin

10 Israel is like a large vine
that produced plenty of fruit.
As the people became richer,
they built more altars for idols.
As their land became better,
they put up better stone pillars to
honor gods.
2 Their heart was false,
and now they must pay for their guilt.
The LORD will break down their altars;
he will destroy their holy stone
pillars.
3 Then they will say, "We have no king,
because we didn't honor the LORD.
As for the king,
he couldn't do anything for us."
4 They make many false promises
and agreements which they don't keep.
So people sue each other in court;
they are like poisonous weeds growing
in a plowed field.
5 The people from Israel are worried about
the calf-shaped idol at Beth Aven.
The people will cry about it,
and the priests will cry about it.

9:6 Memphis A city in Egypt famous for its tombs.
9:9 Gibeah The sins of the people of Gibeah caused a civil war. See Judges 19–21.

They used to shout for joy about its
glory,
6but it will be carried off to Assyria
as a gift to the great king.
Israel will be disgraced,
and the people will be ashamed for not
obeying.
7Israel will be destroyed;
its king will be like a chip of wood
floating on the water.
8The places of false worship will be
destroyed,
the places where Israel sins.
Thorns and weeds will grow up
and cover their altars.
Then they will say to the mountains,
"Cover us!"
and to the hills, "Fall on us!"
9"Israel, you have sinned since the time of
Gibeah,[n]
and the people there have continued
sinning.
But war will surely overwhelm them in
Gibeah,
because of the evil they have done
there.
10When I am ready,
I will come to punish them.
Nations will come together against them,
and they will be punished for their
double sins.
11Israel is like a well-trained young cow
that likes to thresh grain.
I will put a yoke on her neck
and make her work hard in the field.
Israel will plow,
and Judah will break up the ground.
12I said, 'Plant goodness,
harvest the fruit of loyalty,
plow the new ground of knowledge.
Look for the LORD until he comes
and pours goodness on you like water.'
13But you have plowed evil
and harvested trouble;
you have eaten the fruit of your lies.

10:9 Gibeah The sins of the people of Gibeah caused a civil war. See Judges 19–21.

devotion 240

HOSEA 10:12

CHECK THOSE SEED PACKETS

Hosea's advice to "plant goodness" is a great tool for parenting. Look at your children from that perspective, and think about what it means for you. We have to plant goodness in the lives of our children. They need to experience us being good to them, good to our parents, good to our spouses, and good to those in need. My husband and I make date night a priority in our home, and our children respect us for it. We also make serving others a priority, and I believe our children have learned how to serve the Lord through those experiences. Children are looking for an example to follow.

Another tool? "Harvest loyalty." My children need to know that outside of their father, their secrets are safe with me. I need to protect that loyalty; otherwise, I will break the trust that is so necessary for our children. When I demonstrate my trustworthiness to them, it encourages them to be trustworthy as well. The third tool is to "plow knowledge." Our children need to see us in the Word of God on a daily basis. They need to know that God is the source of all that we do.

We also need to look for the Lord until he comes. Our children need to be prepared for the Lord's return. They need to make decisions in their lives based on their eternal value. Parenting is challenging, but with the Lord at your side, it will pour goodness on you like water.

Because you have trusted in your own
power
and your many soldiers,
14your people will hear the noise of battle,
and all your strong, walled cities will be
destroyed.
It will be like the time King Shalman
destroyed Beth Arbel in battle,
when mothers and their children were
bashed to death.
15The same will happen to you, people of
Bethel,
because you did so much evil.
When the sun comes up,
the king of Israel will die.

God's Love for Israel

11 "When Israel was a child, I loved him,
and I called my son out of Egypt.
2But when I called the people of Israel,
they went away from me.
They offered sacrifices to the Baals
and burned incense to the idols.
3It was I who taught Israel to walk,
and I took them by the arms,
but they did not understand
that I had healed them.
4I led them with cords of human
kindness,
with ropes of love.
I lifted the yoke from their neck
and bent down and fed them.

5"The Israelites will become captives
again, as they were in Egypt,
and Assyria will become their king,
because they refuse to turn back to
God.
6War will sweep through their cities
and will destroy them
and kill them because of their wicked
plans.
7My people have made up their minds
to turn away from me.
The prophets call them to turn to me,
but none of them honors me at all.

8"Israel, how can I give you up?
How can I give you away, Israel?
I don't want to make you like Admah
or treat you like Zeboiim.[n]
My heart beats for you,
and my love for you stirs up my pity.
9I won't punish you in my anger,
and I won't destroy Israel again.
I am God and not a human;
I am the Holy One, and I am among you.
I will not come against you in anger.
10They will go after the LORD,
and he will roar like a lion.
When he roars,
his children will hurry to him from the
west.
11They will come swiftly
like birds from Egypt
and like doves from Assyria.
I will settle them again in their homes,"
says the LORD.

The Lord Is Against Israel

12Israel has surrounded me with lies;
the people have made evil plans.
And Judah turns against God,
the faithful Holy One.

12 What Israel does is as useless as
chasing the wind;
he chases the east wind all day.
They tell more and more lies
and do more and more violence.
They make agreements with Assyria,
and they send a gift of olive oil to
Egypt.
2The LORD also has some things against
Judah.
He will punish Israel for what they
have done;
he will give them what they deserve.
3Their ancestor Jacob held on to his
brother's heel
while the two of them were being born.
When he grew to be a man,
he wrestled with God.
4When Jacob wrestled with the angel and
won,
he cried and asked for his blessing.
Later, God met with him at Bethel
and spoke with him there.
5It was the LORD God All-Powerful;
the LORD is his great name.
6You must return to your God;
love him, do what is just,
and always trust in him as your God.

7The merchants use dishonest scales;
they like to cheat people.

11:8 Admah . . . Zeboiim Two other cities destroyed when God destroyed Sodom and Gomorrah.

[8]Israel said, "I am rich! I am someone with power!"
All their money will do them no good
because of the sins they have done.

[9]"But I am the LORD your God,
who brought you out of Egypt.
I will make you live in tents again
as you used to do on worship days.
[10]I spoke to the prophets
and gave them many visions;
through them, I taught my lessons to you."

[11]The people of Gilead are evil,
worth nothing.
Though people sacrifice bulls at Gilgal,
their altars will become like piles of stone
in a plowed field.
[12]Your ancestor Jacob fled to Northwest Mesopotamia
where he worked to get a wife;
he tended sheep to pay for her.
[13]Later the LORD used a prophet
to bring Jacob's descendants out of Egypt;
he used a prophet
to take care of the Israelites.
[14]But the Israelites made the Lord angry
when they killed other people,
and they deserve to die for their crimes.
The Lord will make them pay
for the disgraceful things they have done.

The Final Word Against Israel

13 People used to fear the tribe of Ephraim;
they were important people in Israel.
But they sinned by worshiping Baal,
so they must die.
[2]But they still keep on sinning more and more.
They make idols of their silver,
idols that are cleverly made,
the work of a craftsman.
Yet the people of Israel say to each other,
"Kiss those calf idols and sacrifice to them."
[3]So those people will be like the morning mist;
they will disappear like the morning dew.
They will be like chaff blown from the threshing floor,
like smoke going out a window.

[4]"I, the LORD, have been your God
since you were in the land of Egypt.
You should have known no other God except me.
I am the only one who saves.
[5]I cared for them in the desert
where it was hot and dry.
[6]I gave them food, and they became full and satisfied.
But then they became too proud and forgot me.
[7]That is why I will be like a lion to them,
like a leopard waiting by the road.
[8]I will attack like a bear robbed of her cubs,
ripping their bodies open.
I will devour them like a lion
and tear them apart like a wild animal.

[9]"Israel, I will destroy you.
Who will be your helper then?
[10]What good is your king?
Can he save you in any of your towns?
What good are your leaders?
You said, 'Give us a king and leaders.'
[11]So I gave you a king, but only in anger,
and I took him away in my great anger.
[12]The sins of Israel are on record,
stored away, waiting for punishment.
[13]The pain of birth will come for him,
but he is like a foolish baby
who won't come out of its mother's womb.
[14]Will I save them from the place of the dead?
Will I rescue them from death?
Where is your sickness, death?
Where is your pain, place of death?
I will show them no mercy.
[15]Israel is doing well among the nations,
but the LORD will send a wind from the east,
coming from the desert,
that will dry up his springs and wells of water.
He will destroy from their treasure houses
everything of value.
[16]The nation of Israel will be ruined,
because it fought against God.
The people of Israel will die in war;
their children will be torn to pieces,
and their pregnant women will be ripped open."

devotion 241

HOSEA 14:4–7

WHAT MAKES "GOOD ENOUGH"?

Each time I read about the children of Israel in the Bible, I am amazed at God's patience and love for his people. It's hard to fathom how God can be so forgiving to those who had abandoned their Lord, but he still showed them his favor. Sure, he still judged them, but as Hosea's prophecy tells us, he forgave and loved them—and made them prosperous. That's the way God was with Israel, and that's how he is with us, too. He forgives us of our sins and blesses us. I encourage you to renew your trust in him today. Accept God's forgiveness, choose obedience, and move on.

We know we all make mistakes, just as Israel did. But God still loves us immensely and wants to bless us. God wants us to be prosperous in our lives, whether it be in our careers, marriages, or staying home with our children. Do you ever feel unappreciated for all you do and all you give to others? Do you wonder if anyone even notices you? As women, we juggle so many things—from church involvement to personal, work, and family schedules. We are, more often than not, the primary coordinators of all things family. We do the best we can, but Satan loves to grab us when we're down and try to convince us we aren't good enough. Well, don't believe that lie. God notices everything you do, and like the Israelites, he loves to see you succeed.

Israel Returns to God

14 Israel, return to the LORD your God,
because your sins have made you fall.
2 Come back to the LORD
and say these words to him:
"Take away all our sin
and kindly receive us,
and we will keep the promises we made to you.
3 Assyria cannot save us,
nor will we trust in our horses.
We will not say again, 'Our gods,'
to the things our hands have made.
You show mercy to orphans."

4 The LORD says,
"I will forgive them for leaving me
and will love them freely,
because I am not angry with them anymore.
5 I will be like the dew to Israel,
and they will blossom like a lily.
Like the cedar trees in Lebanon,
their roots will be firm.
6 They will be like spreading branches,
like the beautiful olive trees
and the sweet-smelling cedars in Lebanon.
7 The people of Israel will again live under my protection.
They will grow like the grain,
they will bloom like a vine,
and they will be as famous as the wine of Lebanon.
8 Israel, have nothing to do with idols.
I, the LORD, am the one who answers your prayers and watches over you.
I am like a green pine tree;
your blessings come from me."

9 A wise person will know these things,
and an understanding person will take them to heart.
The LORD's ways are right.
Good people live by following them,
but those who turn against God die because of them.

Joel

A Hebrew name that means "the Lord is God"

Person Holding the Pen God Wrote With: The author identifies himself as "*Joel* son of Pethuel" (Joel 1:1).

When the Text Was Written: The text itself doesn't state a time period, but based on the parallels with other prophets, it is likely that this book was penned in the late ninth century, perhaps during the reign of Joash from 835 to 796 B.C.

Spiritual Posture of the Original Recipients: In spite of military invasions and physical hardship, God's people appear to be in a rebellious state instead of turning to him for help.

Storyline Synopsis: The theme of this minor prophet is the pending cataclysmic punishment of Israel's sins by God. Joel repeatedly employs the phrase "the Lord's day of judging" as a general reference to the coming period of divine wrath. (In fact, he uses the phrase more often than any other Old Testament writer.) Joel also uses a literal locust plague as a metaphor for how God's people will be devastated after his divine judgment (Joel 1:2–20). On the more positive side, this short prophetic book also includes an uplifting vision of the absolute (material, spiritual, and national) restoration the Lord will give to those who have trusted in him (2:18—3:21).

A Moment Worth Discussing: "Tearing your clothes is not enough to show you are sad; let your heart be broken" (Joel 2:13). The opening of this verse describes the key to godly repentance. It doesn't matter what's going on externally or how dramatic your public "penance" is. What matters is the condition of your heart. True sorrow over sin results in deep humility before God. That kind of genuine behavior pleases our heavenly Father, who thankfully, as Joel 2:13 continues, "doesn't become angry quickly, and he has great love. He can change his mind about doing harm." Discuss what *insincere* repentance looks like, as opposed to the sincere version.

Interesting (But Likely to Be Overlooked) Characters: *"Anyone who calls on the Lord"* (Joel 2:32) is a fortunate group that is mentioned again by the apostle Paul in the New Testament book of Romans (Rom. 10:13).

Locusts Destroy the Crops

1 The LORD spoke his word to Joel son of Pethuel:

2 Elders, listen to this message.
Listen to me, all you who live in the land.
Nothing like this has ever happened during your lifetime
or during your ancestors' lifetimes.
3 Tell your children about these things,
let your children tell their children,
and let your grandchildren tell their children.
4 What the cutting locusts have left,
the swarming locusts have eaten;
what the swarming locusts have left,
the hopping locusts have eaten,
and what the hopping locusts have left,
the destroying locusts[n] have eaten.

5 Drunks, wake up and cry!
All you people who drink wine, cry!
Cry because your wine
has been taken away from your mouths.
6 A powerful nation has come into my land
with too many soldiers to count.
It has teeth like a lion,
jaws like a female lion.
7 It has made my grapevine a waste
and made my fig tree a stump.
It has stripped all the bark off my trees
and left the branches white.

8 Cry as a young woman cries
when the man she was going to marry has died.
9 There will be no more grain or drink offerings
to offer in the Temple of the LORD.
Because of this, the priests,
the servants of the LORD, are sad.
10 The fields are ruined;
the ground is dried up.
The grain is destroyed,
the new wine is dried up,
and the olive oil runs out.
11 Be sad, farmers.
Cry loudly, you who grow grapes.
Cry for the wheat and the barley.
Cry because the harvest of the field is lost.
12 The vines have become dry,
and the fig trees are dried up.
The pomegranate trees, the date palm trees, the apple trees—
all the trees in the field have died.
And the happiness of the people has died, too.
13 Priests, put on your rough cloth and cry to show your sadness.
Servants of the altar, cry out loud.
Servants of my God,
keep your rough cloth on all night to show your sadness.
Cry because there will be no more grain or drink offerings
to offer in the Temple of your God.
14 Call for a day when everyone fasts!
Tell everyone to stop work!
Bring the elders
and everyone who lives in the land
to the Temple of the LORD your God,
and cry out to the LORD.
15 What a terrible day it will be!
The LORD's day of judging is near,
when punishment will come
like a destroying attack from the Almighty.

16 Our food is taken away
while we watch.
Joy and happiness are gone
from the Temple of our God.
17 Though we planted fig seeds,
they lie dry and dead in the dirt.
The barns are empty and falling down.
The storerooms for grain have been broken down,
because the grain has dried up.
18 The animals are groaning!
The herds of cattle wander around confused,
because they have no grass to eat;
even the flocks of sheep suffer.
19 LORD, I am calling to you for help,
because fire has burned up the open pastures,
and flames have burned all the trees in the field.
20 Wild animals also need your help.
The streams of water have dried up,
and fire has burned up the open pastures.

1:4 cutting . . . locusts These are different names for an insect like a large grasshopper. The locust can quickly destroy trees, plants, and crops, and in this destruction, Joel sees a warning. God will cause this type of destruction when he punishes his people.

The Coming Day of Judgment

2 Blow the trumpet in Jerusalem;
shout a warning on my holy mountain.
Let all the people who live in the land
shake with fear,
because the LORD's day of judging is
coming;
it is near.
2 It will be a dark, gloomy day,
cloudy and black.
Like the light at sunrise,
a great and powerful army will spread
over the mountains.
There has never been anything like it
before,
and there will never be anything like it
again.

3 In front of them a fire destroys;
in back of them a flame burns.
The land in front of them is like the
garden of Eden;
the land behind them is like an empty
desert.
Nothing will escape from them.
4 They look like horses,
and they run like war horses.
5 It is like the noise of chariots
rumbling over the tops of the
mountains,
like the noise of a roaring fire
burning dry stalks.
They are like a powerful army lined up
for battle.
6 When they see them, nations shake with
fear,
and everyone's face becomes pale.
7 They charge like soldiers;
they climb over the wall like warriors.
They all march straight ahead
and do not move off their path.
8 They do not run into each other,
because each walks in line.
They break through all efforts to stop
them
and keep coming.
9 They run into the city.
They run at the wall
and climb into the houses,
entering through windows like thieves.

10 Before them, earth and sky shake.
The sun and the moon become dark,
and the stars stop shining.
11 The LORD shouts out orders
to his army.
His army is very large!
Those who obey him are very strong!
The LORD's day of judging
is an overwhelming and terrible day.
No one can stand up against it!

Change Your Hearts

12 The LORD says, "Even now, come back to
me with all your heart.
Fast, cry, and be sad."

13 Tearing your clothes is not enough to
show you are sad;
let your heart be broken.
Come back to the LORD your God,
because he is kind and shows mercy.
He doesn't become angry quickly,
and he has great love.
He can change his mind about doing
harm.
14 Who knows? Maybe he will turn back to
you
and leave behind a blessing for you.
Grain and drink offerings belong to the
LORD your God.

15 Blow the trumpet in Jerusalem;
call for a day when everyone fasts.
Tell everyone to stop work.
16 Bring the people together
and make the meeting holy for the LORD.
Bring together the elders,
as well as the children,
and even babies that still feed at their
mothers' breasts.
The bridegroom should come from his
room,
the bride from her bedroom.
17 The priests, the LORD's servants, should cry
between the altar and the entrance to
the Temple.
They should say, "LORD, have mercy on
your people.
Don't let them be put to shame;
don't let other nations make fun of
them.
Don't let people in other nations ask,
'Where is their God?' "

The Lord Restores the Land

18 Then the LORD became concerned about
his land
and felt sorry for his people.

[19]He said to them:
"I will send you grain, new wine, and olive oil,
so that you will have plenty.
No more will I shame you
among the nations.
[20]I will force the army from the north to leave your land
and go into a dry, empty land.
Their soldiers in front will be forced into the Dead Sea,
and those in the rear into the Mediterranean Sea.
Their bodies will rot and stink.
The LORD has surely done a wonderful thing!"

[21]Land, don't be afraid;
be happy and full of joy,
because the LORD has done a wonderful thing.
[22]Wild animals, don't be afraid,
because the open pastures have grown grass.
The trees have given fruit;
the fig trees and the grapevines have grown much fruit.
[23]So be happy, people of Jerusalem;
be joyful in the LORD your God.
Because he does what is right,
he has brought you rain;
he has sent the fall rain
and the spring rain for you, as before.
[24]And the threshing floors will be full of grain;
the barrels will overflow with new wine and olive oil.

The Lord Speaks

[25]"Though I sent my great army against you—
those swarming locusts and hopping locusts,
the destroying locusts and the cutting locusts[n] that ate your crops—
I will pay you back
for those years of trouble.

2:25 swarming . . . locusts These are different names for an insect like a large grasshopper. The locust can quickly destroy trees, plants, and crops, and in this destruction, Joel sees a warning. God will cause this type of destruction when he punishes his people.

devotion 242

JOEL 2:25

GRASSHOPPERS FOR CONSEQUENCES

God sent locusts like an army to reprimand the people of Israel because their hearts had wandered away from God. The lives of the Israelites were dishonoring to God's faithfulness, and as a nation, they suffered the consequences of their disobedience.

Have the locusts of consequences ever swarmed into your life? Maybe you have lost years or love or even your dreams because of the devastating cost of your choices. There is always a penalty for going away from God. Blessings come from his presence, and distance always brings misery. But look at the promise of God to the people of Israel. Essentially he says, "If you return to me and turn away from your rebellious behavior, I will repay you for all the years the locusts have eaten." God's love is so great that he promises to pay you back for the trouble you've had to suffer.

Wow. God disciplines because of his love for us, and then he is so gracious to forgive and repay when we fall on our knees and return to his presence and his ways. I have seen God repay women. I've watched him give love to women who have only known heartache. I've witnessed abundant blessings for women who spent years spiritually distant and aloof. But each time, the blessings have followed the woman's soul surrender. She returned to God and then stayed. And each time, God is good on his word. He restores and even multiplies all that had been lost in life.

26Then you will have plenty to eat
and be full.
You will praise the name of the LORD your God,
who has done miracles for you.
My people will never again be shamed.
27Then you will know that I am among the people of Israel,
that I am the LORD your God,
and there is no other God.
My people will never be shamed again.

28"After this,
I will pour out my Spirit on all kinds of people.
Your sons and daughters will prophesy,
your old men will dream dreams,
and your young men will see visions.
29At that time I will pour out my Spirit
also on male slaves and female slaves.
30I will show miracles
in the sky and on the earth:
blood, fire, and thick smoke.
31The sun will become dark,
the moon red as blood,
before the overwhelming and terrible day of the LORD comes.
32Then anyone who calls on the LORD
will be saved,
because on Mount Zion and in Jerusalem
there will be people who will be saved,
just as the LORD has said.
Those left alive after the day of punishment
are the people whom the LORD called.

Punishment for Judah's Enemies

3 "In those days and at that time,
when I will make things better for Judah and Jerusalem,
2I will gather all the nations together
and bring them down into the Valley Where the LORD Judges.
There I will judge them,
because those nations scattered my own people Israel
and forced them to live in other nations.
They divided up my land
3and threw lots for my people.
They traded boys for prostitutes,
and they sold girls to buy wine to drink.

4"Tyre and Sidon and all of you regions of
Philistia! What did you have against me?
Were you punishing me for something I did,
or were you doing something to hurt me? I
will very quickly do to you what you have
done to me. 5You took my silver and gold,
and you put my precious treasures in your
temples. 6You sold the people of Judah and
Jerusalem to the Greeks so that you could
send them far from their land.
7"You sent my people to that faraway
place, but I will get them and bring them
back, and I will do to you what you have
done to them. 8I will sell your sons and
daughters to the people of Judah, and they
will sell them to the Sabean people far
away." The LORD said this.

God Judges the Nations

9Announce this among the nations:
Prepare for war!
Wake up the soldiers!
Let all the men of war come near and attack.
10Make swords from your plows,
and make spears from your hooks for trimming trees.
Let even the weak person say,
"I am a soldier."
11All of you nations, hurry,
and come together in that place.
LORD, send your soldiers
to gather the nations.

12"Wake up, nations,
and come to attack in the Valley Where the LORD Judges.
There I will sit to judge
all the nations on every side.
13Swing the cutting tool,
because the harvest is ripe.
Come, walk on them as you would walk on grapes to get their juice,
because the winepress is full
and the barrels are spilling over,
because these people are so evil!"

14There are huge numbers of people
in the Valley of Decision,[n]
because the LORD's day of judging is near
in the Valley of Decision.
15The sun and the moon will become dark,
and the stars will stop shining.

3:14 Valley of Decision This is like the name "Valley Where the LORD Judges" in 3:2 and 3:12.

16 The LORD will roar like a lion from Jerusalem;
his loud voice will thunder from that city,
and the sky and the earth will shake.
But the LORD will be a safe place for his people,
a strong place of safety for the people of Israel.

17 "Then you will know that I, the LORD your God,
live on my holy Mount Zion.
Jerusalem will be a holy place,
and strangers will never even go through it again.

A New Life Promised for Judah

18 "On that day wine will drip from the mountains,
milk will flow from the hills,
and water will run through all the ravines of Judah.
A fountain will flow from the Temple of the LORD
and give water to the valley of acacia trees.
19 But Egypt will become empty,
and Edom an empty desert,
because they were cruel to the people of Judah.
They killed innocent people in that land.
20 But there will always be people living in Judah,
and people will live in Jerusalem from now on.
21 Egypt and Edom killed my people,
so I will definitely punish them."

The LORD lives in Jerusalem!

Amos

A Hebrew name that means "burden" or "burden-bearer"

Person Holding the Pen God Wrote With: *Amos,* who was from a small village just south of Jerusalem, penned this book. Be careful not to confuse this guy with Amoz, who was Isaiah's daddy (Is. 1:1).

When the Text Was Written: In the middle of the eighth century B.C. during the reigns of Uzziah, King of Judah (790–739 B.C.), and Jeroboam II, King of Israel (793–753 B.C.)

Spiritual Posture of the Original Recipients: This Judean prophet was speaking primarily to the northern kingdom of Israel, which was experiencing a time of economic prosperity. Their material wealth, however, stood in stark contrast to their spiritual poverty.

Storyline Synopsis: Amos is the only minor prophet who reveals the job he had prior to becoming God's mouthpiece. His vocation doesn't appear interesting at first glance because he was just a shepherd (Amos 1:1). Yet his station in life becomes significant when he chastises the Israelites for their social injustice. His condemnations against his fellow Jews in the north include: the sin of irresponsibility (3:1–5), the sin of idolatry (4:1–13), and the sin of simply being morally rotten (chapters 5—6). He rebukes Israel for their greed and lack of human compassion saying, "For silver, they sell people who have done nothing wrong; they sell the poor to buy a pair of sandals" (2:6). Then he describes the horrific consequences of their spiritual and ethical shortcomings (7—9:10). But like many of the other Old Testament prophets, Amos ends on a high note, describing the eventual restoration and blessing of God's people (9:11–15).

A Moment Worth Discussing: Throughout Amos' prophesy, he champions kindness for underprivileged people. If he ever ran for political office, his platform would surely be one of social justice! Jesus also showed concern for the bottom rungs of society's ladder in the New Testament (Mark 7:24–30; Luke 17:11–19; John 4:7–26). Do you think Christians should be concerned—and involved—with social issues such as homelessness and feeding the poor?

Interesting (But Likely to Be Overlooked) Characters: Amos describes the wealthy, ungodly women of Samaria as the "*cows of Bashan*" (Amos 4:1). Since Bashan was an area known for lush pastures, it was a very direct insult against these lazy, well-fed females of Samaria!

1 These are the words of Amos, one of the shepherds from the town of Tekoa. He saw this vision about Israel two years before the earthquake. It was at the time Uzziah was king of Judah and Jeroboam son of Jehoash was king of Israel.

2 Amos said,
"The LORD will roar from Jerusalem;
he will send his voice from Jerusalem.
The pastures of the shepherds will become dry,
and even the top of Mount Carmel will dry up."

Israel's Neighbors Are Punished

The People of Aram

3 This is what the LORD says:
"For the many crimes of Damascus,
I will punish them.
They drove over the people of Gilead
with threshing boards that had iron teeth.
4 So I will send fire upon the house of Hazael
that will destroy the strong towers of Ben-Hadad.
5 I will break down the bar of the gate to Damascus
and destroy the king who is in the Valley of Aven,
as well as the leader of Beth Eden.
The people of Aram will be taken captive to the country of Kir," says the LORD.

The People of Philistia

6 This is what the LORD says:
"For the many crimes of Gaza,
I will punish them.
They sold all the people of one area
as slaves to Edom.
7 So I will send a fire on the walls of Gaza
that will destroy the city's strong buildings.
8 I will destroy the king of the city of Ashdod,
as well as the leader of Ashkelon.
Then I will turn against the people of the city of Ekron,
and the last of the Philistines will die,"
says the Lord GOD.

The People of Phoenicia

9 This is what the LORD says:
"For the many crimes of Tyre,
I will punish them.
They sold all the people of one area
as slaves to Edom,
and they forgot the agreement among relatives they had made with Israel.
10 So I will send fire on the walls of Tyre
that will destroy the city's strong buildings."

The People of Edom

11 This is what the LORD says:
"For the many crimes of Edom,
I will punish them.
They hunted down their relatives, the Israelites, with the sword,
showing them no mercy.
They were angry all the time
and kept on being very angry.
12 So I will send fire on the city of Teman
that will even destroy the strong buildings of Bozrah."[n]

The People of Ammon

13 This is what the LORD says:
"For the many crimes of Ammon,
I will punish them.
They ripped open the pregnant women in Gilead
so they could take over that land
and make their own country larger.
14 So I will send fire on the city wall of Rabbah
that will destroy its strong buildings.
It will come during a day of battle,
during a stormy day with strong winds.
15 Then their king and leaders will be taken captive;
they will all be taken away together,"
says the LORD.

The People of Moab

2 This is what the LORD says:
"For the many crimes of Moab,
I will punish them.
They burned the bones of the king of Edom into lime.
2 So I will send fire on Moab
that will destroy the strong buildings of the city of Kerioth.

1:12 Teman . . . Bozrah Since Teman was in northern Edom and Bozrah was in southern Edom, this means the whole country will be destroyed.

The people of Moab will die in a great noise,
in the middle of the sounds of war and trumpets.
3 So I will bring an end to the king of Moab,
and I will kill all its leaders with him,"
says the LORD.

The People of Judah

4 This is what the LORD says:
"For the many crimes of Judah,
I will punish them.
They rejected the teachings of the LORD
and did not keep his commands;
they followed the same gods
as their ancestors had followed.
5 So I will send fire on Judah,
and it will destroy the strong buildings of Jerusalem."

Israel Is Punished

6 This is what the LORD says:
"For the many crimes of Israel,
I will punish them.
For silver, they sell people who have done nothing wrong;
they sell the poor to buy a pair of sandals.
7 They walk on poor people as if they were dirt,
and they refuse to be fair to those who are suffering.
Fathers and sons have sexual relations with the same woman,
and so they ruin my holy name.
8 As they worship at their altars,
they lie down on clothes taken from the poor.
They fine people,
and with that money they buy wine to drink in the house of their god.

9 "But it was I who destroyed the Amorites before them,
who were tall like cedar trees and as strong as oaks—
I destroyed them completely.
10 It was I who brought you from the land of Egypt
and led you for forty years through the desert
so I could give you the land of the Amorites.
11 I made some of your children to be prophets
and some of your young people to be Nazirites.
People of Israel, isn't this true?" says the LORD.
12 "But you made the Nazirites drink wine
and told the prophets not to prophesy.
13 Now I will make you get stuck,
as a wagon loaded with grain gets stuck.
14 No one will escape, not even the fastest runner.
Strong people will not be strong enough;
warriors will not be able to save themselves.
15 Soldiers with bows and arrows will not stand and fight,
and even fast runners will not get away;
soldiers on horses will not escape alive.
16 At that time even the bravest warriors
will run away without their armor,"
says the LORD.

Warning to Israel

3 Listen to this word that the LORD has spoken against you, people of Israel, against the whole family he brought out of Egypt.

2 "I have chosen only you
out of all the families of the earth,
so I will punish you
for all your sins."

3 Two people will not walk together
unless they have agreed to do so.
4 A lion in the forest does not roar
unless it has caught an animal;
it does not growl in its den
when it has caught nothing.
5 A bird will not fall into a trap
where there is no bait;
the trap will not spring shut
if there is nothing to catch.
6 When a trumpet blows a warning in a city,
the people tremble.
When trouble comes to a city,
the LORD has caused it.
7 Before the Lord GOD does anything,
he tells his plans to his servants the prophets.
8 The lion has roared!
Who wouldn't be afraid?

The Lord GOD has spoken.
Who will not prophesy?

9 Announce this to the strong buildings of
Ashdod
and to the strong buildings of Egypt:
"Come to the mountains of Samaria,
where you will see great confusion
and people hurting others."

10 "The people don't know how to do what
is right," says the LORD.
"Their strong buildings are filled with
treasures they took by force from
others."
11 So this is what the Lord GOD says:
"An enemy will take over the land
and pull down your strongholds;
he will take the treasures out of your
strong buildings."
12 This is what the LORD says:
"A shepherd might save from a lion's
mouth
only two leg bones or a scrap of an ear
of his sheep.
In the same way only a few Israelites in
Samaria will be saved—
people who now sit on their beds
and on their couches."
13 "Listen and be witnesses against the
family of Jacob," says the Lord GOD, the God
All-Powerful.
14 "When I punish Israel for their sins,
I will also destroy the altars at
Bethel.
The corners of the altar will be cut off,
and they will fall to the ground.
15 I will tear down the winter house,
together with the summer house.
The houses decorated with ivory will be
destroyed,
and the great houses will come to an
end," says the LORD.

Israel Will Not Return

4 Listen to this message, you cows of
Bashan[n] on the Mountain of Samaria.
You take things from the poor
and crush people who are in need.

4:1 Bashan Amos compares the rich, lazy women of Samaria to well-fed cows from Bashan, a place known for its rich animal pastures.

devotion 243

AMOS 4:13

FILL 'ER UP

Are you living in an empty place right now? Is everything that you have depleted, poured out, and dried up? Are you in need of your all-powerful God to do a work in your life? Well rejoice, because today we are stopping to get filled up! Do me a favor—find a nice rug or blanket right now, spread it out, and then come back. Lay down face first, stretch out, and prepare your heart to petition and praise our loving God together. Quiet your mind as you pray these words, and be ready to receive:

Lord, I am sorry I have been so preoccupied with my own feelings and daily routines that I am here laid out before you, empty. I am asking you to refresh me with your Spirit and for your Word to grant me the wisdom to know when I am overextended. I want to be a woman that does not allow the cares and fears of this world to defeat my spirit. I want to have something to offer those who have emotional and spiritual needs. If there is any wicked way in me, please speak it to my heart. I love you and I am asking you to forgive me of my sins and allow me to take joy in our walk together. Please bring healing and strength to my physical body. I beg you to not let me get up from here and be the same. I trust you with all of me. Amen.

Then you command your husbands,
"Bring us something to drink!"
2The Lord GOD has promised this:
"Just as surely as I am a holy God,
the time will come
when you will be taken away by hooks,
and what is left of you with fishhooks.
3You will go straight out of the city
through holes in the walls,
and you will be thrown on the garbage
dump," says the LORD.

4"Come to the city of Bethel and sin;
come to Gilgal and sin even more.
Offer your sacrifices every morning,
and bring one-tenth of your crops every
three days.
5Offer bread made with yeast as a sacrifice
to show your thanks,
and brag about the special offerings
you bring,
because this is what you love to do,
Israelites," says the Lord GOD.

6"I did not give you any food in your cities,
and there was not enough to eat in any
of your towns,
but you did not come back to me," says
the LORD.
7"I held back the rain from you
three months before harvest time.
Then I let it rain on one city
but not on another.
Rain fell on one field,
but another field got none and dried up.
8People weak from thirst went from town
to town for water,
but they could not get enough to drink.
Still you did not come back to me," says
the LORD.
9"I made your crops die from disease and
mildew.
When your gardens and your vineyards
got larger,
locusts ate your fig and olive trees.
But still you did not come back to me,"
says the LORD.
10"I sent disasters against you,
as I did to Egypt.
I killed your young men with swords,
and your horses were taken from you.
I made you smell the stink from all the
dead bodies,
but still you did not come back to me,"
says the LORD.
11"I destroyed some of you
as I destroyed Sodom and Gomorrah.
You were like a burning stick pulled from
a fire,
but still you did not come back to me,"
says the LORD.
12"So this is what I will do to you, Israel;
because I will do this to you,
get ready to meet your God, Israel."
13He is the one who makes the mountains
and creates the wind
and makes his thoughts known to
people.
He changes the dawn into darkness
and walks over the mountains of the
earth.
His name is the LORD God All-Powerful.

Israel Needs to Repent

5 Listen to this funeral song that I sing
about you, people of Israel.
2"The young girl Israel has fallen,
and she will not rise up again.
She was left alone in her own land,
and there is no one to help her up."
3This is what the Lord GOD says:
"If a thousand soldiers leave a city,
only a hundred will return;
if a hundred soldiers leave a city,
only ten will return."
4This is what the LORD says to the nation
of Israel:
"Come to me and live.
5 But do not look in Bethel
or go to Gilgal,
and do not go down to Beersheba.
The people of Gilgal will be taken away as
captives,
and Bethel will become nothing."
6Come to the LORD and live,
or he will move like fire against the
descendants of Joseph.
The fire will burn Bethel,
and there will be no one to put it out.
7You turn justice upside down,
and you throw on the ground what is
right.
8God is the one who made the star groups
Pleiades and Orion;
he changes darkness into the morning
light,
and the day into dark night.

devotion 244

AMOS 5:6–8

SUPERCARPET AND BUMB PIE

My son stumbled over words when he was little and would become easily frustrated with us when we didn't understand what he was saying. His favorite word was "supercarpet" and no one knew what it meant. When he started saying it, we all just groaned because we knew he would be throwing a fit within a few minutes. One day my mother and I were driving along when he started saying "bumb pie." We tried pretending that we understood, but he wasn't buying it. Then we started guessing. "The car went over a bump?" But it still wasn't working. Finally, out of frustration, he started acting out the words by opening and closing his little fingers and humming. "Butterfly!" we exclaimed. A smile spread across his face.

Sometimes I think we have a similar lack of communication with God. Everywhere we look, God is demonstrating the promises he gives us in his Word through his creation, but are we listening? He put the stars in the heavens to confirm to us that he is out there. He brings the sun up every morning to show us his faithfulness. He waters the earth to demonstrate his love for us. God wants us to feel his presence everyday. He wants to communicate with us as we clean our house, run errands, or even as we work. Take time today to smell the roses, and then ask him what he might be showing you as you do. It will put a smile on God's face.

He calls for the waters of the sea
to pour out on the earth.
The LORD is his name.
9 He destroys the protected city;
he ruins the strong, walled city.

10 You hate those who speak in court against evil,
and you can't stand those who tell the truth.
11 You walk on poor people,
forcing them to give you grain.
You have built fancy houses of cut stone,
but you will not live in them.
You have planted beautiful vineyards,
but you will not drink the wine from them.
12 I know your many crimes,
your terrible sins.
You hurt people who do right,
you take money to do wrong,
and you keep the poor from getting justice in court.
13 In such times the wise person will keep quiet,
because it is a bad time.

14 Try to do good, not evil,
so that you will live,
and the LORD God All-Powerful will be with you
just as you say he is.
15 Hate evil and love good;
be fair in the courts.
Maybe the LORD God All-Powerful will be kind
to the people of Joseph who are left alive.
16 This is what the Lord, the LORD God All-Powerful, says:
"People will be crying in all the streets;
they will be saying, 'Oh, no!' in the public places.

They will call the farmers to come and
weep
and will pay people to cry out loud for
them.
17 People will be crying in all the vineyards,
because I will pass among you to
punish you," says the LORD.

The Lord's Day of Judging

18 How terrible it will be for you who want
the LORD's day of judging to come.
Why do you want that day to come?
It will bring darkness for you, not light.
19 It will be like someone who runs from a
lion
and meets a bear,
or like someone who goes into his house
and puts his hand on the wall,
and then is bitten by a snake.
20 So the LORD's day of judging will bring
darkness, not light;
it will be very dark, not light at all.
21 The LORD says, "I hate and reject your
feasts;
I cannot stand your religious meetings.
22 If you offer me burnt offerings and grain
offerings,
I won't accept them.
You bring your best fellowship offerings
of fattened cattle,
but I will ignore them.
23 Take the noise of your songs away
from me!
I won't listen to the music of your harps.
24 But let justice flow like a river,
and let goodness flow like a
never-ending stream.

25 "People of Israel, you did not bring me
sacrifices and offerings
while you traveled in the desert for
forty years.
26 You have carried with you
your king, the god Sakkuth,
and Kaiwan your idol,
and the star gods you have made.
27 So I will send you away as captives
beyond Damascus,"
says the LORD, whose name is the God
All-Powerful.

Israel Will Be Destroyed

6 How terrible it will be for those who have
an easy life in Jerusalem,
for those who feel safe living on Mount
Samaria.
You think you are the important people of
the best nation in the world;
the Israelites come to you for help.
2 Go look at the city of Calneh,
and from there go to the great city
Hamath;
then go down to Gath of the Philistines.
You are no better than these kingdoms.
Your land is no larger than theirs.
3 You put off the day of punishment,
but you bring near the day when you
can do evil to others.
4 You lie on beds decorated with ivory
and stretch out on your couches.
You eat tender lambs
and fattened calves.
5 You make up songs on your harps,
and, like David, you compose songs on
musical instruments.
6 You drink wine by the bowlful
and use the best perfumed lotions.
But you are not sad over the ruin of
Israel,
7 so you will be some of the first ones taken
as slaves.
Your feasting and lying around will
come to an end.

8 The Lord GOD made this promise; the
LORD God All-Powerful says:
"I hate the pride of the Israelites,
and I hate their strong buildings,
so I will let the enemy take the city
and everything in it."
9 At that time there might be only ten
people left alive in just one house, but they
will also die. 10 When the relatives come to
get the bodies to take them outside, one of
them will call to the other and ask, "Are
there any other dead bodies with you?"
That person will answer, "No."
Then the one who asked will say, "Hush!
We must not say the name of the LORD."
11 The LORD has given the command;
the large house will be broken into
pieces,
and the small house into bits.
12 Horses do not run on rocks,
and people do not plow rocks with oxen.
But you have changed fairness into
poison;
you have changed what is right into a
bitter taste.

[13]You are happy that the town of Lo Debar
was captured,
and you say, "We have taken Karnaim[n]
by our own strength."
[14]The LORD God All-Powerful says,
"Israel, I will bring a nation against you
that will make your people suffer from
Lebo Hamath in the north
to the valley south of the Dead Sea."

The Vision of Locusts

7 This is what the Lord GOD showed me: He
was forming a swarm of locusts, after the
king had taken his share of the first crop and
the second crop had just begun growing.
[2]When the locusts ate all the crops in the
country, I said, "Lord GOD, forgive us. How
could Israel live through this? It is too small
already!"
[3]So the LORD changed his mind about this.
"It will not happen," said the LORD.

The Vision of Fire

[4]This is what the Lord GOD showed me:
The Lord GOD was calling for fire to come
down like rain. It burned up the deep water
and was going to burn up the land. [5]Then I
cried out, "Lord GOD, stop! How could Israel
live through this? It is too small already."
[6]So the LORD changed his mind about this
too. "It will not happen," said the Lord GOD.

The Vision of the Plumb Line

[7]This is what he showed me: The Lord
stood by a straight wall, with a plumb line in
his hand. [8]The LORD said to me, "Amos, what
do you see?"
I said, "A plumb line."
Then the Lord said, "See, I will put a
plumb line among my people Israel to show
how crooked they are. I will not look the
other way any longer.
[9]"The places where Isaac's descendants
worship will be destroyed,
Israel's holy places will be turned into
ruins,
and I will attack King Jeroboam's
family with the sword."

Amaziah Speaks Against Amos

[10]Amaziah, a priest at Bethel, sent this
message to Jeroboam king of Israel: "Amos is
making evil plans against you with the
people of Israel. He has been speaking so
much that this land can't hold all his words.
[11]This is what Amos has said:
'Jeroboam will die by the sword,
and the people of Israel will be taken as
captives
out of their own country.' "
[12]Then Amaziah said to Amos, "Seer, go
back right now to Judah. Do your
prophesying and earn your living there,
[13]but don't prophesy anymore here at Bethel.
This is the king's holy place, and it is the
nation's temple."
[14]Then Amos answered Amaziah, "I do
not make my living as a prophet, nor am I a
member of a group of prophets. I make my
living as a shepherd, and I take care of
sycamore trees. [15]But the LORD took me away
from tending the flock and said to me, 'Go,
prophesy to my people Israel.' [16]So listen to
the LORD's word. You tell me,
'Don't prophesy against Israel,
and stop prophesying against the
descendants of Isaac.'
[17]"Because you have said this, the LORD says:
'Your wife will become a prostitute in the
city,
and your sons and daughters will be
killed with swords.
Other people will measure your land and
divide it among themselves,
and you will die in a foreign country.
The people of Israel will definitely be
taken
from their own land as captives.' "

The Vision of Ripe Fruit

8 This is what the Lord GOD showed me: a
basket of summer fruit. [2]He said to me,
"Amos, what do you see?"
I said, "A basket of summer fruit."
Then the LORD said to me, "An end[n] has
come for my people Israel, because I will not
overlook their sins anymore.
[3]"On that day the palace songs will
become funeral songs," says the Lord GOD.
"There will be dead bodies thrown
everywhere! Silence!"
[4]Listen to me, you who walk on helpless
people,

6:13 Lo Debar . . . Karnaim These were two not especially significant cities that the Israelites had captured in war.
8:2 end The Hebrew word for "end" sounds like the Hebrew word for "summer fruit."

you who are trying to destroy the poor
people of this country, saying,
5"When will the New Moon festival be over
so we can sell grain?
When will the Sabbath be over
so we can bring out wheat to sell?
We can charge them more
and give them less,
and we can change the scales to cheat
the people.
6We will buy poor people for silver,
and needy people for the price of a pair
of sandals.
We will even sell the wheat that was
swept up from the floor."
7The LORD has sworn by his name, the
Pride of Jacob, "I will never forget everything
that these people did.
8The whole land will shake because of it,
and everyone who lives in the land will
cry for those who died.
The whole land will rise like the Nile;
it will be shaken, and then it will fall
like the Nile River in Egypt."
9The Lord GOD says:
"At that time I will cause the sun to go
down at noon
and make the earth dark on a bright
day.
10I will change your festivals into days of
crying for the dead,
and all your songs will become songs of
sadness.
I will make all of you wear rough cloth to
show your sadness;
I will make you shave your heads as
well.
I will make it like a time of crying for the
death of an only son,
and its end like the end of an awful day."
11The Lord GOD says: "The days are coming
when I will cause a time of hunger in
the land.
The people will not be hungry for bread
or thirsty for water,
but they will be hungry for words from
the LORD.
12They will wander from the Mediterranean
Sea to the Dead Sea,
from the north to the east.

devotion 245

AMOS 8:11

STARVING FOR GOD

Picture in your mind the starving people in a third world country. Children are dying with swollen bellies from malnutrition. Disease is rampant. Day after day, the only task, the only important thing, is finding something to eat or drink. The people are desperate and without resources of their own.

One day the trucks from a relief organization arrive with fresh water and bags of grain. How do the people respond? Do they stand politely in line with their cup for water or grain? Do they politely ask, "May I have some water if it's not too much trouble or if there's any left?" No way. These people are desperate. They are starving. They are hopeless without supplies. And so they charge the grain truck. They climb over one another to get to the food that will save them.

God says that he is going to make us hungry and thirsty for him. But it will not be a polite "I'll take some when I can get some" kind of wanting. The hunger he desires is a desperate "I have to get to God no matter what" kind of craving.

Take a look at your starving life. Don't stand politely in line and wait for some grain to fall to the ground. Use every means necessary to go after the only thing that will save you. Let the pain of your hunger and the truth of your circumstances force you to climb over every obstacle that stands between you and God.

They will search for the word of the LORD,
but they won't find it.
13 At that time the beautiful young women
and the young men
will become weak from thirst.
14 They make promises by the idol in
Samaria
and say, 'As surely as the god of Dan
lives . . .'
and, 'As surely as the god of Beersheba[n]
lives, we promise . . .'
So they will fall
and never get up again."

Israel Will Be Destroyed

9 I saw the Lord standing by the altar, and
he said:
"Smash the top of the pillars
so that even the bottom of the doors
will shake.
Make the pillars fall on the people's
heads;
anyone left alive I will kill with a
sword.
Not one person will get away;
no one will escape.
2 If they dig down as deep as the place of
the dead,
I will pull them up from there.
If they climb up into heaven,
I will bring them down from there.
3 If they hide at the top of Mount Carmel,
I will find them and take them away.
If they try to hide from me at the bottom
of the sea,
I will command a snake to bite them.
4 If they are captured and taken away by
their enemies,
I will command the sword to kill them.
I will keep watch over them,
but I will keep watch to give them
trouble, not to do them good."

5 The Lord GOD All-Powerful touches the
land,
and the land shakes.
Then everyone who lives in the land
cries for the dead.
The whole land rises like the Nile River
and falls like the river of Egypt.
6 The LORD builds his upper rooms above
the skies;
he sets their foundations on the
earth.
He calls for the waters of the sea
and pours them out on the land.
The LORD is his name.
7 The LORD says,
"Israel, you are no different to me than
the people of Cush.
I brought Israel out of the land of Egypt,
and the Philistines from Crete,
and the Arameans from Kir.
8 I, the Lord GOD, am watching the sinful
kingdom Israel.
I will destroy it
from off the earth,
but I will not completely destroy
Jacob's descendants," says the LORD.
9 "I am giving the command
to scatter the nation of Israel among all
nations.
It will be like someone shaking grain
through a strainer,
but not even a tiny stone falls
through.
10 All the sinners among my people
will die by the sword—
those who say,
'Nothing bad will happen to us.'

The Lord Promises to Restore Israel

11 "The kingdom of David is like a fallen
tent,
but in that day I will set it up again
and mend its broken places.
I will rebuild its ruins
as it was before.
12 Then Israel will take over what is left of
Edom
and the other nations that belong
to me,"
says the LORD,
who will make it happen.

13 The LORD says, "The time is coming when
there will be all kinds of food.
People will still be harvesting crops
when it's time to plow again.
People will still be taking the juice from
grapes
when it's time to plant again.
Wine will drip from the mountains
and pour from the hills.

8:14 Dan . . . Beersheba Dan was the city farthest north in Israel, and Beersheba was the city farthest south.

[14]I will bring my people Israel back from captivity;
they will build the ruined cities again,
and they will live in them.
They will plant vineyards and drink the wine from them;
they will plant gardens and eat their fruit.
[15]I will plant my people on their land,
and they will not be pulled out again
from the land which I have given them,"
says the LORD your God.

Obadiah

A Hebrew name that means "servant of the Lord," Obadiah was a familiar name in ancient times.

Person Holding the Pen God Wrote With: Aside from his ability to be concise (his prophecy is the shortest book in the entire Old Testament), we don't know much about *Obadiah*, the minor prophet who authored this book.

When the Text Was Written: We can't be sure of the exact dates, although it was definitely before the complete destruction of Jerusalem at the hands of the Babylonians in 586 B.C.

Spiritual Posture of the Original Recipients: Obadiah's single chapter of prophecy had two intended audiences: Edom, a pagan nation who'd been especially cruel to Judah; and Judah herself, who'd been beaten up by most of her surrounding neighbors. Edom didn't recognize Jehovah as Lord, and Judah desperately needed to be reminded of God's lordship over everything that was happening in their world.

Storyline Synopsis: The Edomites were descendants of Esau, the firstborn twin son of Isaac and Rebekah, who preceded his brother Jacob into the world (Gen. 25:24–26). Esau was also called Edom, which means "red," because of his ruddy complexion and his foolish choice to sell his birthright to Jacob for some red stew (25:30). Esau broke additional covenants by marrying Canaanite women (26:34–35), along with the daughter of Ishmael (28:9). Esau's life can be summed up in five words: arrogant disregard for divine law. His offspring, sadly, were just like him. They still lived in the rugged, mountainous area near the Dead Sea where Esau settled, a region that was appropriately named "Edom" after him. Furthermore, they inherited his penchant for wild living with no regard for God's law. Obadiah's divine instructions were to summarize Edom's crimes against Jehovah and Judah (a nation made up of Jacob's descendants) and to pronounce the disastrous results of their rebellion.

A Moment Worth Discussing: Obadiah reveals the deepest of family rifts: the Edomites hated their "cousins" the Israelites so much that they had a parade when Judah was carted off into captivity by the Babylonian army (Obad. 12). What can strong family ties teach us about God's character? How does bitterness among relatives resemble rebellion against God?

Interesting (But Likely to Be Overlooked) Characters: The *"dry stalks"* of Esau (Obad. 18) refer to the total destruction of the Edomite people. It's especially interesting to remember that King Herod, who was half-Edomite, was foiled when he attempted to murder the Messiah (Matt. 2:16). Jesus survived and God's sovereignty triumphed over evil once more!

The Lord Will Punish the Edomites

[1]This is the vision of Obadiah.

This is what the Lord GOD says about Edom:[n]
We have heard a message from the LORD.
A messenger has been sent among the nations, saying,
"Attack! Let's go attack Edom!"

The Lord Speaks to the Edomites

[2]"Soon I will make you the smallest of nations.
You will be greatly hated by everyone.
[3]Your pride has fooled you,
you who live in the hollow places of the cliff.
Your home is up high,
you who say to yourself,
'No one can bring me down to the ground.'
[4]Even if you fly high like the eagle
and make your nest among the stars,
I will bring you down from there," says the LORD.
[5]"You will really be ruined!
If thieves came to you,
if robbers came by night,
they would steal only enough for themselves.
If workers came and picked the grapes from your vines,
they would leave a few behind.
[6]But you, Edom, will really lose everything!
People will find all your hidden treasures!
[7]All the people who are your friends
will force you out of the land.
The people who are at peace with you
will trick you and defeat you.
Those who eat your bread with you now
are planning a trap for you,
and you will not notice it."

[8]The LORD says, "On that day
I will surely destroy the wise people from Edom,
and those with understanding from the mountains of Edom.
[9]Then, city of Teman, your best warriors will be afraid,
and everyone from the mountains of Edom will be killed.
[10]You did violence to your relatives, the Israelites,
so you will be covered with shame
and destroyed forever.
[11]You stood aside without helping
while strangers carried Israel's treasures away.
When foreigners entered Israel's city gate
and threw lots to decide what part of Jerusalem they would take,
you were like one of them.

Commands That Edom Broke

[12]"Edom, do not laugh at your brother Israel
in his time of trouble
or be happy about the people of Judah
when they are destroyed.
Do not brag when cruel things are done to them.
[13]Do not enter the city gate of my people
in their time of trouble
or laugh at their problems
in their time of trouble.
Do not take their treasures
in their time of trouble.
[14]Do not stand at the crossroads
to destroy those who are trying to escape.
Do not capture those who escape alive
and turn them over to their enemy
in their time of trouble.

The Nations Will Be Judged

[15]"The LORD's day of judging is coming soon
to all the nations.
The same evil things you did to other people
will happen to you;
they will come back upon your own head.
[16]Because you drank in my Temple,
all the nations will drink on and on.
They will drink and drink
until they disappear.
[17]But on Mount Zion some will escape the judgment,
and it will be a holy place.
The people of Jacob will take back their land
from those who took it from them.

1 Edom The Edomites were the people who came from Esau, Jacob's twin brother. They were enemies of the Israelites.

18The people of Jacob will be like a fire
and the people of Joseph[n] like a flame.
But the people of Esau[n] will be like dry stalks.
The people of Jacob will set them on fire and burn them up.
There will be no one left of the people of Esau."
This will happen because the LORD has said it.

19Then God's people will regain southern Judah from Edom;
they will take back the mountains of Edom.
They will take back the western hills from the Philistines.
They will regain the lands of Ephraim and Samaria,
and Benjamin will take over Gilead.
20People from Israel who once were forced to leave their homes
will take the land of the Canaanites, all the way to Zarephath.
People from Judah who once were forced to leave Jerusalem and live in Sepharad
will take back the cities of southern Judah.
21Powerful warriors will go up on Mount Zion,
where they will rule the people living on Edom's mountains.
And the kingdom will belong to the LORD.

18 people of Jacob . . . Joseph The people who came from Jacob and Joseph, or the Israelites.
18 people of Esau The people who came from Esau, or the Edomites.

Jonah

A Hebrew name that means "dove"

Person Holding the Pen God Wrote With: The most likely author is *Jonah.* Although he doesn't claim authorship in the text and refers to himself in third person, that was a typical practice of authors in the Old Testament.

When the Text Was Written: Sometime during the reign of Jeroboam II from 793 to 758 B.C.

Spiritual Posture of the Original Recipients: Jonah was a prophet sent to minister mostly among the ten northern tribes of Israel, much like Amos. These tribes were enjoying a season of harmony and affluence prior to being ransacked by Assyria (722 B.C.). But their relative good times resulted in spiritual lethargy; they were basically just going through the motions with God. Jonah's narrative regarding the dramatic spiritual revival experienced by their rivals undoubtedly shook things up a bit!

Storyline Synopsis: The highlight of Jonah's story is the fantastic account of living in the belly of a sea beast for three days as punishment for going AWOL on God (Jon. 1:1–17). The story of Jonah is a true tale; Jesus referred to Jonah as a history lesson, not a parable (Matt. 12:38–41 and 16:4; Luke 11:29–32). The story reveals how a contrite, waterlogged Jonah submitted to God's orders to journey to Nineveh, which was Assyria's capital city (chapter 2). It describes how his preaching prompted a sweeping, genuine spiritual revival in that foreign land (chapter 3). Finally, the story ends with Jonah pouting that God shouldn't have been so nice to that bunch of reprobates (chapter 4).

A Moment Worth Discussing: Jonah's whiney tirade following God's display of mercy toward the people of Nineveh is a colorful example of how ugly the human heart can be (chapter 4). Although Jonah had experienced divine kindness when God poked that whale in the belly, making it burp Jonah up on the beach, he still didn't think the "trashy Gentiles" of Assyria should receive God's grace! It is interesting to compare Jonah's stinky attitude after his narrow escape to the stingy servant in Jesus' parable about compassion (Matt. 18:21–35).

Interesting (But Likely to Be Overlooked) Character: *Nimrod,* Noah's great-grandson, founded the city of Nineveh (Gen. 10:6–12). His name conjures up the image of someone wearing a dunce cap, but he probably wasn't too dim-witted since the town he started went on to become one of the largest cities in the ancient world.

God Calls and Jonah Runs

1 The LORD spoke his word to Jonah son of
Amittai: 2"Get up, go to the great city of
Nineveh, and preach against it, because I see
the evil things they do."
3But Jonah got up to run away from the
LORD by going to Tarshish. He went to the
city of Joppa, where he found a ship that was
going to the city of Tarshish. Jonah paid for
the trip and went aboard, planning to go to
Tarshish to run away from the LORD.
4But the LORD sent a great wind on the sea,
which made the sea so stormy that the ship
was in danger of breaking apart. 5The sailors
were afraid, and each man cried to his own
god. They began throwing the cargo from the
ship into the sea to make the ship lighter.
But Jonah had gone down far inside the
ship to lie down, and he fell fast asleep. 6The
captain of the ship came and said, "Why are
you sleeping? Get up and pray to your god!
Maybe your god will pay attention to us, and
we won't die!"
7Then the men said to each other, "Let's
throw lots to see who caused these troubles
to happen to us."
When they threw lots, the lot showed that
the trouble had happened because of Jonah.
8Then they said to him, "Tell us, who caused
our trouble? What is your job? Where do
you come from? What is your country? Who
are your people?"
9Then Jonah said to them, "I am a Hebrew.
I fear the LORD, the God of heaven, who
made the sea and the land."
10The men were very afraid, and they
asked Jonah, "What terrible thing did you
do?" (They knew he was running away from
the LORD because he had told them.)
11Since the wind and the waves of the sea
were becoming much stronger, they said to
him, "What should we do to you to make
the sea calm down for us?"
12Jonah said to them, "Pick me up, and
throw me into the sea, and then it will calm
down. I know it is my fault that this great
storm has come on you."
13Instead, the men tried to row the ship
back to the land, but they could not, because
the sea was becoming more stormy.

Jonah's Punishment

14So the men cried to the LORD, "LORD,
please don't let us die because of this man's
life; please don't think we are guilty of
killing an innocent person. LORD, you have
caused all this to happen; you wanted it this
way." 15So they picked up Jonah and threw
him into the sea, and the sea became calm.
16Then they began to fear the LORD very
much; they offered a sacrifice to the LORD
and made promises to him.
17The LORD caused a big fish to swallow
Jonah, and Jonah was inside the fish three
days and three nights.

2 While Jonah was inside the fish, he
prayed to the LORD his God and said,
2"When I was in danger,
I called to the LORD,
and he answered me.
I was about to die,
so I cried to you,
and you heard my voice.
3You threw me into the sea,
down, down into the deep sea.
The water was all around me,
and your powerful waves flowed
over me.
4I said, 'I was driven out of your presence,
but I hope to see your Holy Temple
again.'
5The waters of the sea closed around my
throat.
The deep sea was all around me;
seaweed was wrapped around my head.
6When I went down to where the
mountains of the sea start to rise,
I thought I was locked in this prison
forever,
but you saved me from the pit of death,
LORD my God.

7"When my life had almost gone,
I remembered the LORD.
I prayed to you,
and you heard my prayers in your Holy
Temple.
8"People who worship useless idols
give up their loyalty to you.
9But I will praise and thank you
while I give sacrifices to you,
and I will keep my promises to you.
Salvation comes from the LORD!"
10Then the LORD spoke to the fish, and the
fish threw up Jonah onto the dry land.

God Calls and Jonah Obeys

3 The LORD spoke his word to Jonah again
and said, 2"Get up, go to the great city

Nineveh, and preach to it what I tell you
to say."
3So Jonah obeyed the LORD and got up and
went to Nineveh. It was a very large city; just
to walk across it took a person three days.
4After Jonah had entered the city and walked
for one day, he preached to the people,
saying, "After forty days, Nineveh will be
destroyed!"
5The people of Nineveh believed God.
They announced that they would fast for a
while, and they put on rough cloth to show
their sadness. All the people in the city did
this, from the most important to the least
important.
6When the king of Nineveh heard this
news, he got up from his throne, took off his
robe, and covered himself with rough cloth
and sat in ashes to show how upset he was.
7He sent this announcement through
Nineveh:

By command of the king and his
important men: No person or animal,
herd or flock, will be allowed to taste
anything. Do not let them eat food or
drink water. 8But every person and
animal should be covered with rough
cloth, and people should cry loudly to
God. Everyone must turn away from
evil living and stop doing harm all the
time. 9Who knows? Maybe God will
change his mind. Maybe he will stop
being angry, and then we will not die.

10When God saw what the people did,
that they stopped doing evil, he changed his
mind and did not do what he had warned.
He did not punish them.

God's Mercy Makes Jonah Angry

4 But this made Jonah very unhappy, and
he became angry. 2He prayed to the LORD,
"When I was still in my own country this is
what I said would happen, and that is why I
quickly ran away to Tarshish. I knew that
you are a God who is kind and shows mercy.
You don't become angry quickly, and you
have great love. I knew you would choose
not to cause harm. 3So now I ask you, LORD,
please kill me. It is better for me to die than
to live."
4Then the LORD said, "Do you think it is
right for you to be angry?"
5Jonah went out and sat down east of the
city. There he made a shelter for himself and

devotion 246

JONAH 2:5–6

THE PAIN OF EVERYDAY LIFE

How did intense pain become an epidemic? Why is so much suffering replicated in the homes and hearts of believers? I don't know how or why. Actually, at this point in my life, I know so much less than I thought I knew before. I just know that life can hurt beyond words. It can feel like being taken down into the pit of death, held captive by your pain. I think God wants us to know that the only comfort that speaks stillness to the squalling soul is his supernatural comfort (Matt. 5:4). The only way out is to cry out to the One who can answer our prayers.

The things we do to comfort ourselves can be distracting, but real deliverance from the pit of overwhelming pain will only come from the hand of God. If this day finds you crying out from the deep sea that threatens your life, then lift up your head and turn in the direction of the Father. He may send someone to carry you. If he does, you must let them pick you up and hold you for a while. He may call you away for rest. If he does, you must go. He may send someone to give you your next breath. They will speak to you words of hope. Receive them as an answered prayer. Look for God. He will hear your prayers and move into your prison of pain with his glory.

devotion 247

JONAH 4:1-2

KEEP OUTTA THAT WHALE!

Jonah was a piece of work. He wanted mercy for himself, but judgment for Nineveh. Our hearts are so like that, aren't they? The minute we have done something worthy of judgment, we run to the Lord as fast as we can to repent and thank him again for not making mashed potatoes out of us. We are such peculiar people—rejoicing when judgment passes us over but secretly hoping to see judgment rendered on others. And I am not even talking about the world in general—that is our heart toward our fellow brothers and sisters in Christ! That is crazy! We need to be in a constant position of prayer for those we see struggling with their humanity.

God says the same measure you use to judge will be used against you (Matt. 7:1-2). Do you understand that scripture? In plain language, it means to stop judging, or you could find yourself in a much greater mess than Jonah, who just had a whale and a town full of degenerate people to deal with. God was looking for Jonah's heart to be obedient and to compassionately pray for the people of Nineveh to change and seek God. We can see what God wanted because he forgave the people of Nineveh when they repented (Jon. 3:10). This is what he desires of you and me—people praying for even our enemies to come to the way of repentance. I don't know about you, but I plan to stay out of the whale!

sat in the shade, waiting to see what would
happen to the city. [6]The LORD made a plant
grow quickly up over Jonah, which gave
him shade and helped him to be more
comfortable. Jonah was very pleased to have
the plant. [7]But the next day when the sun
rose, God sent a worm to attack the plant so
that it died.

[8]As the sun rose higher in the sky, God sent
a very hot east wind to blow, and the sun
became so hot on Jonah's head that he
became very weak and wished he were dead.
He said, "It is better for me to die than to live."

[9]But God said to Jonah, "Do you think it is
right for you to be angry about the plant?"

Jonah answered, "It is right for me to be
angry! I am so angry I could die!"

[10]And the LORD said, "You are so concerned
for that plant even though you did nothing
to make it grow. It appeared one day, and the
next day it died. [11]Then shouldn't I show
concern for the great city Nineveh, which
has more than one hundred twenty
thousand people who do not know right
from wrong, and many animals, too?"

Micah

A Hebrew name that literally asks the question, "Who is like the Lord?"

Person Holding the Pen God Wrote With: The authorship of *Micah* is established in the very first verse of his prophecy.

When the Text Was Written: Micah prophesied from 750 to 686 B.C. during the reigns of three Judean kings: Jotham, Ahaz, and Hezekiah. According to the text, Micah wrote this book prior to the fall of the northern kingdom in 722 B.C.

Spiritual Posture of the Original Recipients: While he directed a few of his words to the northern kingdom (Mic. 1:5–7), the majority of Micah's message was aimed at Judah, the southern kingdom. The people of God living there were hiding behind fancy masks of religiosity, hoping their money or their rituals could save them from destruction.

Storyline Synopsis: The first part of Micah's message calls the whole world to take note of God's judgment against his people (chapters 1—5). Then he employs his imagination and uses the make-believe setting of a courtroom to describe Israel as a guilty plaintiff before God, a holy judge (chapter 6). The book ends with Micah's moving personal lament over the condition of God's chosen people (Mic. 7:1–7) and includes Israel's admission of sin and hope in God's comfort (7:8–13). Micah then points to the future blessing when God forgives his people and tramples their sin under his giant feet (7:14–20). The gist of Micah's prophecy is a direct answer to the very question his name imposes: "Who is like the Lord?"

A Moment Worth Discussing: One little verse during the dramatic "courtroom scene," Micah 6:8, gives us a template for the type of behavior God wants from his people. He wants us to make a commitment to him that will supernaturally change our hearts and cause us to "do what is right," "love being kind," and "live humbly"—three basic activities that we can easily chart our growth in periodically!

Interesting (But Likely to Be Overlooked) Character: *Omri* was a cruddy and superstitious king (Mic. 6:16) who rebelled against God while presiding over Israel (1 Kin. 16:16–28).

Samaria and Israel to Be Punished

1 During the time that Jotham, Ahaz, and
Hezekiah were kings of Judah, the word
of the LORD came to Micah, who was from
Moresheth. He saw these visions about
Samaria and Jerusalem.

2 Hear this, all you nations;
listen, earth and all you who live on it.
The Lord GOD will be a witness against you,
the Lord from his Holy Temple.
3 See, the LORD is coming out of his place;
he is coming down to walk on the tops of the mountains.
4 The mountains will melt under him,
and the valleys will crack open,
like wax near a fire,
like water running down a hillside.
5 All this is because of Jacob's sin,
because of the sins of the nation of Israel.
What is the place of Jacob's sin?
Isn't it Samaria?
What is Judah's place of idol worship?
Isn't it Jerusalem?

The Lord Speaks

6 "So I will make Samaria a pile of ruins in the open country,
a place for planting vineyards.
I will pour her stones down into the valley
and strip her down to her foundations.
7 All her idols will be broken into pieces;
all the gifts to her idols will be burned with fire.
I will destroy all her idols,
and because Samaria earned her money by being unfaithful to me,
this money will be carried off by others who are not faithful to me."

Micah's Great Sadness

8 I will moan and cry because of this evil,
going around barefoot and naked.
I will cry loudly like the wild dogs
and make sad sounds like the owls do,
9 because Samaria's wound cannot be healed.
It will spread to Judah;
it will reach the city gate of my people,
all the way to Jerusalem.
10 Don't tell it in Gath.[n]
Don't cry in Acco.[n]
Roll in the dust
at Beth Ophrah.[n]
11 Pass on your way, naked and ashamed,
you who live in Shaphir.[n]
Those who live in Zaanan[n]
won't come out.
The people in Beth Ezel[n] will cry,
but they will not give you any support.
12 Those who live in Maroth[n]
will be anxious for good news to come,
because trouble will come from the LORD,
all the way to the gate of Jerusalem.
13 You people living in Lachish,[n]
harness the fastest horse to the chariot.
Jerusalem's sins started in you;
yes, Israel's sins were found in you.
14 So you must give farewell gifts
to Moresheth[n] in Gath.
The houses in Aczib[n] will be false help
to the kings of Israel.
15 I will bring against you people who will take your land,
you who live in Mareshah.[n]
The glory of Israel
will go in to Adullam.
16 Cut off your hair to show you are sad
for the children you love.
Make yourself bald like the eagle,
because your children will be taken away to a foreign land.

The Evil Plans of People

2 How terrible it will be for people who plan wickedness,
who lie on their beds and make evil plans.
When the morning light comes, they do what they planned,
because they have the power to do so.
2 They want fields, so they take them;
they want houses, so they take them away.
They cheat people to get their houses;
they rob them even of their property.

1:10 Gath This name sounds like the Hebrew word for "tell." **1:10 Acco** This name sounds like the Hebrew word for "cry." **1:10 Beth Ophrah** This name means "house of dust." **1:11 Shaphir** This name means "beautiful." **1:11 Zaanan** This name sounds like the Hebrew word for "come out." **1:11 Beth Ezel** This name means "house by the side of another," suggesting help or support. **1:12 Maroth** This name sounds like the Hebrew word for "sad" or "miserable." **1:13 Lachish** This name sounds like the Hebrew word for "horses." **1:14 Moresheth** This may be a play on the word "engaged," referring to a farewell gift to a bride. **1:14 Aczib** This name means "lie" or "trick." **1:15 Mareshah** This name sounds like the Hebrew word for a person who captures other cities and lands.

3That is why the LORD says:
"Look, I am planning trouble against such people,
and you won't be able to save yourselves.
You will no longer walk proudly,
because it will be a terrible time.
4At that time people will make fun of you
and sing this sad song about you:
'We are completely ruined;
the LORD has taken away my people's land.
Yes, he has taken it away from me
and divided our fields among our enemies!' "
5So you will have no one from the LORD's people
to throw lots to divide the land.

Micah Is Asked Not to Prophesy

6The prophets say, "Don't prophesy to us!
Don't prophesy about these things!
Nothing to make us feel bad will happen!"
7But I must say this, people of Jacob:
The LORD is becoming angry about what you have done.
My words are welcome
to the person who does what is right.
8But you are fighting against my people like an enemy.
You take the coats from people who pass by;
you rob them of their safety;
you plan war.
9You've forced the women of my people
from their nice houses;
you've taken my glory
from their children forever.
10Get up and leave.
This is not your place of rest anymore.
You have made this place unclean,
and it is doomed to destruction.
11But you people want a false prophet
who will tell you nothing but lies.
You want one who promises to prophesy good things for you
if you give him wine and beer.
He's just the prophet for you.

The Lord Promises to Rescue His People

12"Yes, people of Jacob, I will bring all of you together;
I will bring together all those left alive in Israel.
I will put them together like sheep in a pen,
like a flock in its pasture;
the place will be filled with many people.
13Someone will open the way and lead the people out.
The people will break through the gate
and leave the city where they were held captive.
Their king will go out in front of them,
and the LORD will lead them."

The Leaders of Israel Are Guilty of Evil

3 Then I said,
"Listen, leaders of the people of Jacob;
listen, you rulers of the nation of Israel.
You should know how to decide cases fairly,
2 but you hate good and love evil.
You skin my people alive
and tear the flesh off their bones.
3You eat my people's flesh
and skin them and break their bones;
you chop them up like meat for the pot,
like meat in a cooking pan.
4They will cry to the LORD,
but he won't answer them.
At that time he will hide his face from them,
because what they have done is evil."
5The LORD says this about the prophets
who teach his people the wrong way of
living:
"If these prophets are given food to eat,
they shout, 'Peace!'
But if someone doesn't give them what they ask for,
they call for a holy war against that person.
6So it will become like night for them,
without visions.
It will become dark for them, without any way to tell the future.
The sun is about to set for the prophets;
their day will become dark.
7The seers will be ashamed;
the people who see the future will be embarrassed.
Yes, all of them will cover their mouths,
because there will be no answer from God."

devotion 248

MICAH 2:13

THE SEDUCTION OF EVIL

The *Lord of the Rings* is a wonderful book, revealing such a vivid picture of how sin entices and seduces us. The ring symbolizes sin. Each time someone puts the ring on, he or she becomes self-indulgent and evil as they gain power. The ring is given to a boy named Frodo, and his mission is to take the ring to a special place to destroy it. The character Frodo battles his will throughout the story to keep from putting the ring on, but it proves to be an impossible task.

This is the plight of mankind. Sin constantly seduces us, trying to take us captive. Jesus can give us the power to resist sin, but in the same way, when we fail and give in to temptation, only Jesus can loosen us from its grasp. Jesus conquered sin when he died on the cross and set the captives free. He has opened the way for us to have a relationship with God again. He leads us to the Father once we believe in him. He is the gateway to heaven. If you have not accepted Jesus as your Lord and Savior, take time today to do so. Read John 3:16. Believe that Jesus died for you, and ask God to forgive you of your sins. Then when the power of evil tries to seduce you and hold you captive, you will be able to stand firm, knowing that your King is leading you every step of the way.

Micah Is an Honest Prophet of God

8 But I am filled with power,
with the Spirit of the LORD,
and with justice and strength,
to tell the people of Jacob how they have turned against God,
and the people of Israel how they have sinned.
9 Leaders of Jacob and rulers of Israel,
listen to me,
you who hate fairness
and twist what is right.
10 You build Jerusalem by murdering people;
you build it with evil.
11 Its judges take money
to decide who wins in court.
Its priests only teach for pay,
and its prophets only look into the future when they get paid.
But they lean on the LORD and say,
"The LORD is here with us,
so nothing bad will happen to us."
12 Because of you,
Jerusalem will be plowed like a field.
The city will become a pile of rocks,
and the hill on which the Temple stands will be covered with bushes.

The Mountain of the Lord

4 In the last days
the mountain on which the LORD's Temple stands
will become the most important of all mountains.
It will be raised above the hills,
and people from other nations will come streaming to it.
2 Many nations will come and say,
"Come, let us go up to the mountain of the LORD,
to the Temple of the God of Jacob,
so that he can teach us his ways,
and we can obey his teachings."
His teachings will go out from Jerusalem,
the word of the LORD from that city.
3 The Lord will judge many nations;
he will make decisions about strong nations that are far away.

They will hammer their swords into plow
blades
and their spears into hooks for
trimming trees.
Nations will no longer raise swords
against other nations;
they will not train for war anymore.
4 Everyone will sit under his own vine and
fig tree,
and no one will make him afraid,
because the LORD All-Powerful has
said it.
5 All other nations may follow their own
gods,
but we will follow the LORD our God
forever and ever.
6 The LORD says, "At that time,
I will gather the crippled;
I will bring together those who were
sent away,
those whom I caused to have trouble.
7 I will keep alive those who were crippled,
and I will make a strong nation of those
who were sent away.
The LORD will be their king in Mount Zion
from now on and forever.
8 And you, watchtower of the flocks,[n] hill of
Jerusalem,
to you will come the kingdom as in the
past.
Jerusalem, the right to rule will come
again to you."

Why the Israelites Must Go to Babylon

9 Now, why do you cry so loudly?
Is your king gone?
Have you lost your helper,
so that you are in pain, like a woman
trying to give birth?
10 People of Jerusalem, strain and be in pain.
Be like a woman trying to give birth,
because now you must leave the city
and live in the field.
You will go to Babylon,
but you will be saved from that place.
The LORD will go there
and buy you back from your enemies.

11 But now many nations
have come to fight against you,
saying, "Let's destroy Jerusalem.
We will look at her and be glad we have
defeated her."
12 But they don't know
what the LORD is thinking;
they don't understand his plan.
He has gathered them like bundles of
grain to the threshing floor.

13 "Get up and beat them, people of
Jerusalem.
I will make you strong as if you had
horns of iron
and hoofs of bronze.
You will beat many nations into small
pieces
and give their wealth to the LORD,
their treasure to the Lord of all the
earth."

5 So, strong city, gather your soldiers
together,
because we are surrounded and
attacked.
They will hit the leader of Israel
in the face with a club.

The Ruler to Be Born in Bethlehem

2 "But you, Bethlehem Ephrathah,
though you are too small to be among
the army groups from Judah,
from you will come one who will rule
Israel for me.
He comes from very old times,
from days long ago."

3 The LORD will give up his people
until the one who is having a baby
gives birth;
then the rest of his relatives will return
to the people of Israel.
4 At that time the ruler of Israel will stand
and take care of his people
with the LORD's strength
and with the power of the name of the
LORD his God.
The Israelites will live in safety,
because his greatness will reach all over
the earth.
5 He will bring peace.

Rescue and Punishment

Assyria will surely come into our country
and walk over our large buildings.
We will set up seven shepherds,
eight leaders of the people.

4:8 watchtower . . . flocks This probably means a part of Jerusalem. The leaders would be like shepherds in a tower watching their sheep.

6They will destroy the Assyrians with their swords;
they will conquer the land of Assyria with their swords drawn.
They will rescue us from the Assyrians when they come into our land,
when they walk over our borders.

7Then the people of Jacob who are left alive will be to other people
like dew from the LORD
or rain on the grass—
it does not wait for human beings;
it does not pause for any person.
8Those of Jacob's people who are left alive
will be scattered among many nations and peoples.
They will be like a lion among the animals of the forest,
like a young lion in a flock of sheep:
As it goes, it jumps on them
and tears them to pieces,
and no one can save them.
9So you will raise your fist in victory over your enemies,
and all your enemies will be destroyed.

10The LORD says, "At that time,
I will take your horses from you
and destroy your chariots.
11I will destroy the cities in your country
and tear down all your defenses.
12I will take away the magic charms you use
so you will have no more fortune-tellers.
13I will destroy your statues of gods
and the stone pillars you worship
so that you will no longer worship
what your hands have made.
14I will tear down Asherah idols from you
and destroy your cities.
15In my anger and rage,
I will pay back the nations that have not listened."

The Lord's Case

6 Now hear what the LORD says:
"Get up; plead your case in front of the mountains;
let the hills hear your story.
2Mountains, listen to the LORD's legal case.
Foundations of the earth, listen.
The LORD has a legal case against his people,
and he will accuse Israel."

3He says, "My people, what did I do to you?
How did I make you tired of me?
Tell me.
4I brought you from the land of Egypt
and freed you from slavery;
I sent Moses, Aaron, and Miriam to you.
5My people, remember
the evil plans of Balak king of Moab
and what Balaam son of Beor told Balak.
Remember what happened from Acacia to Gilgal
so that you will know the LORD does what is right!"

6You say, "What can I bring with me
when I come before the LORD,
when I bow before God on high?
Should I come before him with burnt offerings,
with year-old calves?
7Will the LORD be pleased with a thousand male sheep?
Will he be pleased with ten thousand rivers of oil?
Should I give my first child for the evil I have done?
Should I give my very own child for my sin?"
8The LORD has told you, human, what is good;
he has told you what he wants from you:
to do what is right to other people,
love being kind to others,
and live humbly, obeying your God.

9The voice of the LORD calls to the city,
and the wise person honors him.
So pay attention to the rod of punishment;
pay attention to the One who threatens to punish.
10Are there still in the wicked house
wicked treasures
and the cursed false measure?
11Can I forgive people who cheat others
with wrong weights and scales?
12The rich people of the city
do cruel things.
Its people tell lies;
they do not tell the truth.
13As for me, I will make you sick.

devotion 249

MICAH 6:8

A CALL TO DUTY

Many people consider Micah 6:8 a call to duty. The call "to do what is right to other people" is what inspires God's people to give to the poor, to stand up for the weak, and even to go to war. I heard a story about a soldier who, shortly after the death of his friend in Iraq, immediately enlisted in the Army and volunteered for the earliest deployment. He wanted to show honor and respect to the family of his fallen comrade by finishing the call to duty his friend had started. Without realizing it, he'd become a living testimony to what is right. In the same way, when we obediently answer a call to duty from God, we make a stand for what is right.

We don't all have to join the military, as many of our brothers and sisters in Christ choose to do, but we can still fight the good fight right in our homes and communities. All we need to do is stand up for others—stand up for what is right! Is there a charity in your community or church that needs an extra hand? Pitch in! Is there a single mom who has never connected with your women's Bible study? Invite her! Perhaps your daughter has come home asking you to buy her the latest fashion that you know is not honoring to God. Use that teachable moment! Make a point to routinely stand up for what you believe in—things that are right and just.

I will attack you, ruining you because
of your sins.
14 You will eat, but you won't become full;
you will still be hungry and empty.
You will store up, but save nothing,
and what you store up, the sword will
destroy.
15 You will plant,
but you won't harvest.
You will step on your olives,
but you won't get any oil from them.
You will crush the grapes,
but you will not drink the new wine.
16 This is because you obey the laws of King
Omri
and do all the things that Ahab's family
does;
you follow their advice.
So I will let you be destroyed.
The people in your city will be
laughed at,
and other nations will make fun of
you.

The Evil That People Do

7 Poor me! I am like a hungry man,
and all the summer fruit has been
picked—
there are no grapes left to eat,
none of the early figs I love.
2 All of the faithful people are gone;
there is not one good person left in this
country.
Everyone is waiting to kill someone;
everyone is trying to trap someone else.
3 With both hands they are doing evil.
Rulers ask for money,
and judges' decisions are bought for a
price.
Rich people tell what they want,
and they get it.
4 Even the best of them is like a thornbush;
the most honest of them is worse than
a prickly plant.
The day that your watchmen[n] warned you
about has come.
Now they will be confused.

7:4 watchmen Another name for prophets. The prophets were like guards who stood on a city's wall and watched for trouble coming from far away.

5Don't believe your neighbor
or trust a friend.
Don't say anything,
even to your wife.
6A son will not honor his father,
a daughter will turn against her mother,
and a daughter-in-law will be against her mother-in-law;
a person's enemies will be members of his own family.

The Lord's Kindness

7Israel says, "I will look to the LORD for help.
I will wait for God to save me;
my God will hear me.
8Enemy, don't laugh at me.
I have fallen, but I will get up again.
I sit in the shadow of trouble now,
but the LORD will be a light for me.
9I sinned against the LORD,
so he was angry with me,
but he will defend my case in court.
He will bring about what is right for me.
Then he will bring me out into the light,
and I will see him set things right.
10Then my enemies will see this,
and they will be ashamed,
those who said to me,
'Where is the LORD your God?'
I will look down on them.
They will get walked on, like mud in the street."

Israel Will Return

11The time will come when your walls will be built again,
when your country will grow.
12At that time your people will come back to you
from Assyria and the cities of Egypt,
and from Egypt to the Euphrates River,
and from sea to sea and mountain to mountain.
13The earth will be ruined for the people who live in it
because of their deeds.

A Prayer to God

14So shepherd your people with your stick;
tend the flock of people who belong to you.
That flock now lives alone in the forest
in the middle of a garden land.
Let them feed in Bashan and Gilead
as in days long ago.
15"As in the days when I brought you out of Egypt,
I will show them miracles."
16When the nations see those miracles,
they will no longer brag about their power.
They will put their hands over their mouths,
refusing to listen.
17They will crawl in the dust like a snake,
like insects crawling on the ground.
They will come trembling from their holes to the LORD our God
and will turn in fear before you.
18There is no God like you.
You forgive those who are guilty of sin;
you don't look at the sins of your people
who are left alive.
You will not stay angry forever,
because you enjoy being kind.
19You will have mercy on us again;
you will conquer our sins.
You will throw away all our sins
into the deepest part of the sea.
20You will be true to the people of Jacob,
and you will be kind to the people of Abraham
as you promised to our ancestors long ago.

Nahum

A shortened version of the Hebrew name Nehemiah, *which means "comfort" or "consolation"*

Person Holding the Pen God Wrote With: *Nahum,* who was an "Elkoshite," penned this book (Nah. 1:1). Elkosh might have referred to the region that would now be northern Iraq.

When the Text Was Written: This book was most likely written during the middle of the seventh century B.C. since Nahum mentions the fall of Thebes (Nah. 3:8–10), which occurred in 663 B.C., and uses futuristic terms when he brings up Nineveh's fall, which took place in 612 B.C. (3:11).

Spiritual Posture of the Original Recipients: Nineveh, Assyria's capital city, had once responded with great humility to Jonah's fire and brimstone message. But now the people have returned to their old ways of rebelling against God (Nah. 3:1–4).

Storyline Synopsis: Much like Obadiah's prophecy against Edom, this book predicts the demise of another foreign kingdom—the arrogant nation of Assyria. Nahum begins his writing by establishing the zeal and power of almighty God (Nah. 1—2:2), and then he hurls a number of choice adjectives in a graphic dialogue about the complete destruction of Nineveh (2:3–13). While Babylon represented how God's Holy Spirit can direct events in history in order to discipline his people, Nineveh illustrated how the mean spirit of man can turn against fellow human beings. In other words, Nineveh was a big, fat bully who deserved to be trounced by the Creator of the universe (chapter 3). No matter how impressive the fortress, no city can stand against the righteous fury of God.

A Moment Worth Discussing: God is often marginalized as an overly permissive Santa Claus character that spoils children with an endless supply of sweets and never enforces the rules. But that's a myth. The minor prophets make it clear that while our heavenly Father is compassionate, he will also impose punishment when necessary. Perfect love includes chastisement for wrongdoing. Now would be a good time to discuss the "soft" and "hard" sides of God's character.

Interesting (But Likely to Be Overlooked) Character: Archeologists have uncovered carvings depicting the *Assyrian king* on a lion hunt. Nahum ridicules this "great hunter" of a monarch as cowering prey (Nah. 2:11–13).

1 This is the message for the city of
Nineveh.[n] This is the book of the vision of
Nahum, who was from the town of Elkosh.

The Lord Is Angry with Nineveh

2 The LORD is a jealous God who punishes;
the LORD punishes and is filled with
anger.
The LORD punishes those who are against
him,
and he stays angry with his enemies.
3 The LORD does not become angry
quickly,
and his power is great.
The LORD will not let the guilty go
unpunished.
Where the LORD goes, there are
whirlwinds and storms,
and the clouds are the dust beneath his
feet.
4 He speaks to the sea and makes it dry;
he dries up all the rivers.
The areas of Bashan and Carmel dry up,
and the flowers of Lebanon dry up.
5 The mountains shake in front of him,
and the hills melt.
The earth trembles when he comes;
the world and all who live in it shake
with fear.
6 No one can stay alive when he is angry;
no one can survive his strong anger.
His anger is poured out like fire;
the rocks are smashed by him.

7 The LORD is good,
giving protection in times of trouble.
He knows who trusts in him.
8 But like a rushing flood,
he will completely destroy Nineveh;
he will chase his enemies until he kills
them.

9 The LORD will completely destroy
anyone making plans against him.
Trouble will not come a second time.

1:1 Nineveh The capital city of the country of Assyria. Nahum uses Nineveh to stand for all of Assyria.

devotion 250

NAHUM 1:5–7

WOULD YOU LIKE WATER WITH THAT REPENTANCE?

God is very angry about sin. And God is a good God. Both are true. But depending on where you are in your life, maybe you need to hear one more than the other. Some of us do not know the depths of God's great love. Others of us have not taken his anger seriously. He really does hate sin. And he will not tolerate continued, blatant, in-his-face disregard for the precepts and commandments he's given. He is angry when we have willfully disobeyed.

At my house, there is great mercy for a mistake, but the punishment for ongoing, obstinate disobedience is severe and extended. I want the offending child to "feel" the penalty. Sitting at home while everyone else is at the football game. Cell phone banned for months. Extra chores. My kids seem to learn a lot when they're outside mowing the yard as punishment.

In the same way, God is serious about the consequences of your sin. Be assured, his reprimand will be strong and swift when warranted. But God is also good. I'll take my suffering yard mower a glass of water, tell him I love him, and say that I'm sorry about his stinkin' punishment. When he's done, he'll apologize, I'll hold him, and then it's over.

God's goodness is even more amazing. He brings you a glass of water. He lets you say you're sorry. He forgives you and holds you close. And when it's over, he promises not to remember your sin.

[10]Those people will be like tangled thorns
or like people drunk from their wine;
they will be burned up quickly like dry weeds.
[11]Someone has come from Nineveh
who makes evil plans against the LORD
and gives wicked advice.
[12]This is what the LORD says:
"Although Assyria is strong and has many people,
it will be defeated and brought to an end.
Although I have made you suffer, Judah,
I will make you suffer no more.
[13]Now I will free you from their control
and tear away your chains."
[14]The LORD has given you this command, Nineveh:
"You will not have descendants to carry on your name.
I will destroy the idols and metal images
that are in the temple of your gods.
I will make a grave for you,
because you are wicked."

[15]Look, there on the hills,
someone is bringing good news!
He is announcing peace!
Celebrate your feasts, people of Judah,
and give your promised sacrifices to God.
The wicked will not come to attack you again;
they have been completely destroyed.

Nineveh Will Be Defeated

2 The destroyer[n] is coming to attack you, Nineveh.
Guard the defenses.
Watch the road.
Get ready.
Gather all your strength!
[2]Destroyers have destroyed God's people
and ruined their vines,
but the LORD will bring back Jacob's greatness
like Israel's greatness.
[3]The shields of his soldiers are red;
the army is dressed in red.
The metal on the chariots flashes like fire
when they are ready to attack;
their horses are excited.
[4]The chariots race through the streets
and rush back and forth through the city squares.
They look like torches;
they run like lightning.
[5]He[n] calls his officers,
but they stumble on the way.
They hurry to the city wall,
and the shield is put into place.
[6]The river gates are thrown open,
and the palace is destroyed.
[7]It has been announced that the people of Nineveh
will be captured and carried away.
The slave girls moan like doves
and beat their breasts, because they are sad.
[8]Nineveh is like a pool,
and now its water is draining away.
"Stop! Stop!" the people yell,
but no one turns back.
[9]Take the silver!
Take the gold!
There is no end to the treasure—
piles of wealth of every kind.
[10]Nineveh is robbed, ruined, and destroyed.
The people lose their courage, and their knees knock.
Stomachs ache, and everyone's face grows pale.

[11]Where is the lions'[n] den
and the place where they feed their young?
Where did the lion, lioness, and cubs go
without being afraid?
[12]The lion killed enough for his cubs,
enough for his mate.
He filled his cave with the animals he caught;
he filled his den with meat he had killed.

[13]"I am against you, Nineveh,"
says the LORD All-Powerful.
"I will burn up your chariots in smoke,
and the sword will kill your young lions.

2:1 destroyer The Babylonians, the Scythians, and the Medes destroyed Nineveh. **2:5 He** This probably means the king of Assyria. **2:11 lions'** The symbol of Assyria was the lion.

I will stop you from hunting down
others on the earth,
and your messengers' voices
will no longer be heard."

It Will Be Terrible for Nineveh

3 How terrible it will be for the city that
has killed so many.
It is full of lies
and goods stolen from other countries.
It is always killing somebody.
2 Hear the sound of whips
and the noise of the wheels.
Hear horses galloping
and chariots bouncing along!
3 Horses are charging,
swords are shining,
spears are gleaming!
Many are dead;
their bodies are piled up—
too many to count.
People stumble over the dead bodies.
4 The city was like a prostitute;
she was charming and a lover of magic.
She made nations slaves with her
prostitution
and her witchcraft.

5 "I am against you, Nineveh," says the
LORD All-Powerful.
"I will pull your dress up over your face
and show the nations your nakedness
and the kingdoms your shame.
6 I will throw filthy garbage on you
and make a fool of you.
I will make people stare at you.
7 Everyone who sees you will run away and
say,
'Nineveh is in ruins. Who will cry for
her?'
Nineveh, where will I find anyone to
comfort you?"

8 You are no better than Thebes,[n]
who sits by the Nile River
with water all around her.
The river was her defense;
the waters were like a wall around her.
9 Cush and Egypt gave her endless strength;
Put and Libya supported her.
10 But Thebes was captured
and went into captivity.
Her small children were beaten to death
at every street corner.
Lots were thrown for her important men,
and all of her leaders were put in
chains.

11 Nineveh, you will be drunk, too.
You will hide;
you will look for a place safe from the
enemy.
12 All your defenses are like fig trees with
ripe fruit.
When the tree is shaken, the figs fall
into the mouth of the eater.
13 Look at your soldiers.
They are all women!
The gates of your land
are wide open for your enemies;
fire has burned the bars of your gates.

14 Get enough water before the long war
begins.
Make your defenses strong!
Get mud,
mix clay,
make bricks!
15 There the fire will burn you up.
The sword will kill you;
like grasshoppers eating crops, the
battle will completely destroy you.
Grow in number like hopping locusts;
grow in number like swarming locusts!
16 Your traders are more than the stars in the
sky,
but like locusts, they strip the land and
then fly away.
17 Your guards are like locusts.
Your officers are like swarms of locusts
that hang on the walls on a cold day.
When the sun comes up, they fly away,
and no one knows where they have
gone.
18 King of Assyria, your rulers are asleep;
your important men lie down to rest.
Your people have been scattered on the
mountains,
and there is no one to bring them back.
19 Nothing can heal your wound;
your injury will not heal.
Everyone who hears about you applauds,
because everyone has felt your endless
cruelty.

3:8 Thebes A great city in Egypt.

Habakkuk

A name that could mean "one who embraces"

Person Holding the Pen God Wrote With: The mysterious *Habakkuk* wrote the book that bears his name. He was the prophetic peer of Jeremiah, Ezekiel, Daniel, and Zephaniah.

When the Text Was Written: This book was probably penned in the late seventh century B.C. Habakkuk's bitter lament might refer to the time period after good King Josiah's death in 609 B.C. when godly reforms were swiftly turned upside down by bad King Jehoiakim (Jer. 22:13–19).

Spiritual Posture of the Original Recipients: Habakkuk's ministry saw the final days of the Assyrian empire and Babylon's rise to world dominance. During that same period of history, Judah's king, Josiah, was killed in a battle. After his death, God's people reverted to idolatry and rebellion.

Storyline Synopsis: The ancient prophecy of Habakkuk centers around this very modern question: "If God is so good, why does he tolerate evil?" This minor prophet voices that complaint twice in this text (Hab. 1:2–4 and 1:12—2:1). God's reply to Habakkuk's earnest confusion is to explain that he will sovereignly use the Babylonian conquest for divine justice (1:5–11). Furthermore, God will judge the Babylonians for their sinfulness. The bottom line of this book is that all of history is under God's authority; history follows a divine blueprint; history submits to God's timetable; and human history precedes an eternal kingdom, which will be governed by God and inhabited by his people.

A Moment Worth Discussing: The words Habakkuk prays after he learns a lesson on God's absolute control over all the earth are the perfect response when God seems distant as we face difficult circumstances. We must remember that a lack of material wealth doesn't constitute the absence of God. Although we may have to walk through hardship, God will never abandon his people. Regardless of sickly fruit trees or dwindling farm animals, we should praise God because our hope isn't based on tangible things (Hab. 3:17–19). This prayer is an interesting precedent for Paul's motivational poster passage to the Corinthian believers (2 Cor. 4:16–18).

Interesting (But Likely to Be Overlooked) Character: Although he's not *in* this story, *Benjamin Franklin* used this divine text (particularly Habakkuk's prayer in chapter 3) to put some haughty French sophisticates in their place while he was working for the U.S. government and living in Paris. The cultured Parisians—who had mocked Mr. Franklin's admiration of the Bible—were so impressed by the fabulous "poem" he read, they asked who wrote it. They were probably speechless when he told them that it came from an Old Testament prophet.

1 This is the message Habakkuk the
prophet received.

Habakkuk Complains

2 LORD, how long must I ask for help
and you ignore me?
I cry out to you about violence,
but you do not save us!
3 Why do you make me see wrong things
and make me look at trouble?
People are destroying things and hurting
others in front of me;
they are arguing and fighting.
4 So the teachings are weak,
and justice never comes.
Evil people gain while good people lose;
the judges no longer make fair
decisions.

The Lord Answers

5 "Look at the nations!
Watch them and be amazed and
shocked.
I will do something in your lifetime
that you won't believe even when you
are told about it.
6 I will use the Babylonians,
those cruel and wild people
who march across the earth
and take lands that don't belong to
them.
7 They scare and frighten people.
They do what they want to do
and are good only to themselves.
8 Their horses are faster than leopards
and quicker than wolves at sunset.
Their horse soldiers attack quickly;
they come from places far away.
They attack quickly, like an eagle
swooping down for food.
9 They all come to fight.
Nothing can stop them.
Their prisoners are as many as the
grains of sand.
10 They laugh at kings
and make fun of rulers.
They laugh at all the strong, walled
cities
and build dirt piles to the top of the
walls to capture them.
11 Then they leave like the wind and
move on.

devotion 251

HABAKKUK 1:5

THERE GOES THE NEIGHBORHOOD

Habakkuk saw judgment coming for his people. They had been warned for generations. In the end, God used some ruthless neighbors to exact his discipline. As the prophet said, the situation was so bad you would have had to see it to believe it.

We might not battle evil neighbors like the Babylonians on a daily basis, but we do know disaster. Weather can destroy us by itself. At the time of this writing, a hurricane has just ravaged the Gulf Coast of North America. Terrorists destroy our well-being and national security. (In this sense, we may relate to Habakkuk more than ever before.) Whatever we face, we can face it knowing that it is all within God's jurisdiction. He will work through it. The Babylonians are our reminder—if he can work through a people like that, he can work through whatever troubles we face.

The key is to let our villains and hardships drive us *back to* God rather than *away from* him. It's a choice we have to make over and over again. Before whatever calamity has most recently struck, we were possibly just cruising along (spiritually speaking). It sometimes takes something bigger than our coping skills to make us look for help bigger than our own strength. Habakkuk's audience found that out when they faced national destruction born of the fact that they had failed to choose God's ways. Each day, disaster or not, you face that same choice. So what do you say?

They are guilty of worshiping their
own strength."

Habakkuk Complains Again

12 LORD, you live forever,
my God, my holy God.
We will not die.
LORD, you have chosen the Babylonians to
punish people;
our Rock, you picked them to punish.
13 Your eyes are too good to look at evil;
you cannot stand to see those who do
wrong.
So how can you put up with those evil
people?
How can you be quiet when the wicked
swallow up people who are better
than they are?
14 You treat people like fish in the sea,
like sea animals without a leader.
15 The enemy brings them in with hooks.
He catches them in his net
and drags them in his fishnet.
So he rejoices and sings for joy.
16 The enemy offers sacrifices to his net
and burns incense to worship it,
because it lets him live like the rich
and enjoy the best food.
17 Will he keep on taking riches with his net?
Will he go on destroying people
without showing mercy?

2 I will stand like a guard to watch
and place myself at the tower.
I will wait to see what he will say to me;
I will wait to learn how God will
answer my complaint.

The Lord Answers

2 The LORD answered me:
"Write down the vision;
write it clearly on clay tablets
so whoever reads it can run to tell
others.
3 It is not yet time for the message to come
true,
but that time is coming soon;
the message will come true.
It may seem like a long time,
but be patient and wait for it,
because it will surely come;
it will not be delayed.
4 The evil nation is very proud of itself;
it is not living as it should.
But those who are right with God will
live by faith.

5 "Just as wine can trick a person,
those who are too proud will not last,
because their desire is like a grave's desire
for death,
and like death they always want more.
They gather other nations for
themselves
and collect for themselves all the
countries.
6 But all the nations the Babylonians have
hurt will laugh at them.
They will make fun of the Babylonians
and say, 'How terrible it will be for the
one that steals many things.
How long will that nation get rich by
forcing others to pay them?'

7 "One day the people from whom you
have taken money will turn
against you.
They will realize what is happening
and make you shake with fear.
Then they will take everything you
have.
8 Because you have stolen from many
nations,
those who are left will take much from
you.
This is because you have killed many
people,
destroying countries and cities and
everyone in them.

9 "How terrible it will be for the nation that
becomes rich by doing wrong,
thinking they will live in a safe place
and escape harm.
10 Because you have made plans to destroy
many people,
you have made your own houses
ashamed of you.
Because of it, you will lose your lives.
11 The stones of the walls will cry out
against you,
and the boards that support the roof
will agree that you are wrong.
12 "How terrible it will be for the nation that
kills people to build a city,
that wrongs others to start a town.
13 The LORD All-Powerful will send fire
to destroy what those people have
built;

all the nations' work will be for
nothing.
14 Then, just as water covers the sea,
people everywhere will know the
LORD's glory.

15 "How terrible for the nation that makes
its neighbors drink,
pouring from the jug of wine until they
are drunk
so that it can look at their naked bodies.
16 You Babylonians will be filled with
disgrace, not respect.
It's your turn to drink and fall to the
ground like a drunk person.
The cup of anger from the LORD's right
hand is coming around to you.
You will receive disgrace, not respect.
17 You hurt many people in Lebanon,
but now you will be hurt.
You killed many animals there,
and now you must be afraid
because of what you did
to that land, those cities, and the people
who lived in them.

The Message About Idols

18 "An idol does no good, because a human
made it;
it is only a statue that teaches lies.
The one who made it expects his own
work to help him,
but he makes idols that can't even speak!
19 How terrible it will be for the one who
says to a wooden statue, 'Come to
life!'
How terrible it will be for the one who
says to a silent stone, 'Get up!'
It cannot tell you what to do.
It is only a statue covered with gold and
silver;
there is no life in it.
20 The LORD is in his Holy Temple;
all the earth should be silent in his
presence."

Habakkuk's Prayer

3 This is the prayer of Habakkuk the
prophet, on shigionoth.
2 LORD, I have heard the news about you;
I am amazed at what you have done.
LORD, do great things once again in our
time;
make those things happen again in our
own days.
Even when you are angry,
remember to be kind.

3 God is coming from Teman;
the Holy One comes from Mount
Paran.[n] *Selah*
His glory covers the skies,
and his praise fills the earth.
4 He is like a bright light.
Rays of light shine from his hand,
and there he hides his power.
5 Sickness goes before him,
and disease follows behind him.
6 He stands and shakes the earth.
He looks, and the nations shake with
fear.
The mountains, which stood for ages,
break into pieces;
the old hills fall down.
God has always done this.

7 I saw that the tents of Cushan were in
trouble
and that the tents of Midian
trembled.
8 LORD, were you angry at the rivers,
or were you angry at the streams?
Were you angry with the sea
when you rode your horses and
chariots of victory?[n]
9 You uncovered your bow
and commanded many arrows to be
brought to you. *Selah*
You split the earth with rivers.
10 The mountains saw you and shook
with fear.
The rushing water flowed.
The sea made a loud noise,
and its waves rose high.
11 The sun and moon stood still in the sky;
they stopped when they saw the flash
of your flying arrows
and the gleam of your shining spear.
12 In anger you marched on the earth;
in anger you punished the nations.
13 You came out to save your people,
to save your chosen one.

3:3 Teman . . . Paran God is seen as again coming from the direction of Mount Sinai. He came from Sinai when he rescued his people from Egypt. **3:8 sea . . . victory** This is probably talking about the Israelites crossing the Red Sea.

devotion 252

HABAKKUK 3:16–19

STRONGER NOW

The Christmas before my sister died was a difficult holiday to get through. I remember trying to think of a gift to give her that would show her how much I loved her. I went to a friend who was a musician and asked him if he could write me a song for her. Then I wrote out all the things my sister had said as she battled cancer the last couple of years, and I asked him if he could use some of them as lyrics. The song he wrote was called "Stronger Now." The theme of the song was that even though my sister was growing weaker and weaker physically, she was getting stronger and stronger spiritually. It was the most precious gift I could have given her.

The Lord is our strength. Second Corinthians 12:10 tells us, "When I am weak, then I am truly strong." Life can be like steep mountains at times. We have to be careful where we go and how we get there. God created mountain deer so that they could successfully navigate mountainous terrain. In the same way, God has prepared us to successfully navigate through life's peaks and valleys. He has a path for us to take that will keep us from stumbling, just as the deer do not stumble. So when you feel as though your own strength is at its limit, ask the Lord to give you his. For when you are weak, he is strong.

You crushed the leader of the wicked ones
and took everything he had, from head to toe. *Selah*
14 With the enemy's own spear you stabbed the leader of his army.
His soldiers rushed out like a storm to scatter us.
They were happy
as they were robbing the poor people in secret.
15 But you marched through the sea with your horses,
stirring the great waters.

16 I hear these things, and my body trembles;
my lips tremble when I hear the sound.
My bones feel weak,
and my legs shake.
But I will wait patiently for the day of disaster
that will come to the people who attack us.
17 Fig trees may not grow figs,
and there may be no grapes on the vines.
There may be no olives growing
and no food growing in the fields.
There may be no sheep in the pens
and no cattle in the barns.
18 But I will still be glad in the LORD;
I will rejoice in God my Savior.
19 The Lord GOD is my strength.
He makes me like a deer that does not stumble
so I can walk on the steep mountains.

For the director of music. On my stringed instruments.

Zephaniah

This is the last "pre-exilic" minor prophet, which refers to the books written prior to the fall of Jerusalem and Judah's exile to Babylon in 586 B.C.

Person Holding the Pen God Wrote With: The author is *Zephaniah*, and some people think he descended from royalty because he goes back four generations to include Hezekiah in the opening verse of this genealogy. (Hezekiah was the fourteenth king of Judah, 715–686 B.C.) Zephaniah is the only minor prophet to trace his ancestry back that far, which makes sense if he was trying to say, "Hey y'all, my great-great-grandfather was King Hezekiah!" However, Hezekiah was also a common name in this culture, like "Tom" or "Mike" to us. Since Zephaniah doesn't specifically refer to his forefather as *King* Hezekiah, we can't determine if he was born with a silver spoon in his mouth or not.

When the Text Was Written: Between 640 and 609 B.C. during the days of Josiah

Spiritual Posture of the Original Recipients: If they made a video about this era in Israel, it would be called *God's Kids Gone Wild!* The Israelites had wandered so far away from God that they had literally lost the Bible (2 Kin. 22:3–13). Imagine going to church and the pastor strides up to the pulpit and says, "Hey, you guys aren't going to believe what happened this week! Remember that Book we're always talking about—the Bible? Well I was cleaning out a storage room and I found one!"

Storyline Synopsis: The Book of Zephaniah is short, even among the minor prophets—only fifty-three verses long. You might assume it would be a hot topic for preachers and Bible teachers—brevity usually means fewer naps for the listening audience. But Zephaniah isn't a teacher's pet. In fact, apart from one verse (Zeph. 3:17), Zephaniah is more like the Rodney Dangerfield of the Bible—it gets no respect! Perhaps this is because it reads like the *Wrath and Destruction Diaries* (1:2–3). The gist of Zephaniah is that God will not compromise his holiness.

A Moment Worth Discussing: Zephaniah's most famous verse (Zeph. 3:17) paints the unforgettable picture of God singing over those he loves. Have you ever pondered the concept of the Creator of the universe serenading you? Jeremiah emphasizes God's posture of rejoicing, so the song would most certainly be sweet, full of God's restorative love for us—lyrics most of us are absolutely desperate for.

Interesting (But Likely to Be Overlooked) Characters: While the unrepentant pagans have been flattened like pancakes, the *remnant* (Zeph. 3:13) sought refuge in God and came out smelling like roses!

1 This is the word of the LORD that came
through Zephaniah while Josiah son of
Amon was king of Judah. Zephaniah was the
son of Cushi, who was the son of Gedaliah.
Gedaliah was the son of Amariah, who was
the son of Hezekiah.

The Lord's Judgment

2 "I will sweep away everything
from the earth," says the LORD.
3 "I will sweep away the people and
animals;
I will destroy the birds in the air
and the fish of the sea.
I will ruin the evil people,
and I will remove human beings from
the earth," says the LORD.

The Future of Judah

4 "I will punish Judah
and all the people living in Jerusalem.
I will remove from this place
all signs of Baal, the false priests, and
the other priests.
5 I will destroy those who worship
the stars from the roofs,[n]
and those who worship and make
promises
by both the LORD and the god Molech,
6 and those who turned away from the
LORD,
and those who quit following the LORD
and praying to him for direction.
7 Be silent before the Lord GOD,
because the LORD's day for judging
people is coming soon.
The LORD has prepared a sacrifice;
he has made holy his invited guests.
8 On the day of the LORD's sacrifice,
I, the LORD, will punish the princes and
the king's sons
and all those who wear foreign clothes.
9 On that day I will punish those who
worship Dagon,
those who hurt others and tell lies in
the temples of their gods.

10 "On that day," says the LORD,
"a cry will be heard at the Fish Gate.
A wail will come from the new area of
the city,
and a loud crash will echo from the hills.
11 Cry, you people living in the market area,
because all the merchants will be dead;
all the silver traders will be gone.
12 At that time I, the LORD, will search
Jerusalem with lamps.
I will punish those who are satisfied
with themselves,
who think, 'The LORD won't help us or
punish us.'
13 Their wealth will be stolen
and their houses destroyed.
They may build houses,
but they will not live in them.
They may plant vineyards,
but they will not drink any wine from
them.

The Lord's Day of Judging

14 "The LORD's day of judging is coming soon;
it is near and coming fast.
The cry will be very sad on the day of the
LORD;
even soldiers will cry.
15 That day will be a day of anger,
a day of terror and trouble,
a day of destruction and ruin,
a day of darkness and gloom,
a day of clouds and blackness,
16 a day of alarms and battle cries.
'Attack the strong, walled cities!
Attack the corner towers!'
17 I will make life hard on the people;
they will walk around like the blind,
because they have sinned against the
LORD.
Their blood will be poured out like dust,
and their insides will be dumped like
trash.
18 On the day that God will show his anger,
neither their silver nor gold will save
them.
The LORD's anger will be like a fire
that will burn up the whole world;
suddenly he will bring an end, yes, an end
to everyone on earth."

The Lord Asks People to Change

2 Gather together, gather,
you unwanted people.
2 Do it before it's too late,
before you are blown away like chaff,

1:5 roofs In Bible times houses were built with flat roofs. The roof was used for drying things such as flax and fruit. And it was used as an extra room, as a place for worship, and as a cool place to sleep in the summer.

before the LORD's terrible anger reaches
you,
before the day of the LORD's anger
comes to you.
3 Come to the LORD, all you who are not
proud,
who obey his laws.
Do what is right. Learn to be humble.
Maybe you will escape
on the day the LORD shows his anger.

Philistia Will Be Punished

4 No one will be left in the city of Gaza,
and the city of Ashkelon will be
destroyed.
Ashdod will be empty by noon,
and the people of Ekron will be chased
away.
5 How terrible it will be for you who live by
the Mediterranean Sea,
you Philistines!
The word of the LORD is against you,
Canaan, land of the Philistines.

"I will destroy you
so that no one will be left."
6 The land by the Mediterranean Sea, in
which you live,
will become pastures, fields for
shepherds, and pens for sheep.
7 It will belong to the descendants of Judah
who are left alive.
There they will let their sheep eat grass.
At night they will sleep
in the houses of Ashkelon.
The LORD their God will pay attention to
them
and will make their life good again.

Moab and Ammon Will Be Punished

8 "I have heard the insults of the country of
Moab
and the threats of the people of
Ammon.
They have insulted my people
and have taken their land."
9 So the LORD All-Powerful, the God of
Israel, says,
"As surely as I live,
Moab will be destroyed like Sodom,
and Ammon will be destroyed like
Gomorrah[n]—
a heap of weeds, a pit of salt,
and a ruin forever.
Those of my people who are left alive will
take whatever they want from
them;
those who are left from my nation will
take their land."

10 This is what Moab and Ammon get for
being proud,
because they insulted and made fun of
the people of the LORD
All-Powerful.
11 The LORD will frighten them,
because he will destroy all the gods of
the earth.
Then everyone in faraway places
will worship him wherever they are.

Cush and Assyria Will Be Destroyed

12 "You Cushites also
will be killed by my sword."
13 Then the LORD will turn against the
north
and destroy Assyria.
He will make Nineveh
a ruin as dry as a desert.
14 Flocks and herds will lie down there,
and all wild animals.
The owls and crows will sit
on the stone pillars.
The owl will hoot through the windows,
trash will be in the doorways,
and the wooden boards of the buildings
will be gone.
15 This is the happy and safe city
that thinks there is no one else as
strong as it is.
But what a ruin it will be,
a place where wild animals live.
All those who pass by will make fun
and shake their fists.

Jerusalem Will Be Punished

3 How terrible for the wicked, stubborn
city of Jerusalem,
which hurts its own people.
2 It obeys no voice;
it can't be taught to do right.
It doesn't trust the LORD;
it doesn't worship its God.
3 Its officers are like roaring lions.

2:9 Sodom . . . Gomorrah Two cities God destroyed because the people were so evil.

Its rulers are like hungry wolves that
attack in the evening,
and in the morning nothing is left of
those they attacked.
4 Its prophets are proud;
they are people who cannot be
trusted.
Its priests don't respect holy things;
they break God's teachings.
5 But the LORD is good, and he is there in
that city.
He does no wrong.
Every morning he governs the people
fairly;
every day he can be trusted.
But evil people are not ashamed of
what they do.

6 "I have destroyed nations;
their towers were ruined.
I made their streets empty
so no one goes there anymore.
Their cities are ruined;
no one lives there at all.
7 I said, 'Surely now Jerusalem will
respect me
and will accept my teaching.'
Then the place where they lived would
not be destroyed,
and I would not have to punish them.
But they were still eager
to do evil in everything they did.
8 Just wait," says the LORD.
"Someday I will stand up as a
witness.
I have decided that I will gather nations
and assemble kingdoms.
I will pour out my anger on them,
all my strong anger.
My anger will be like fire
that will burn up the whole world.

A New Day for God's People

9 "Then I will give the people of all nations
pure speech
so that all of them will speak the name
of the LORD
and worship me together.

devotion 253

ZEPHANIAH 3:17–20

TANYA'S CAFETERIA DANCE

Tanya attended public school and was in ninth grade, but due to having Downs Syndrome and a physical problem that made her walk "funny," she attended classes in the special education department. One day Tanya found herself surrounded by several teenagers during lunch. They were all smiling and telling her, "Dance for us Tanya!" Heartened by their cheering, she began to dance the little dance she did at home with her dad. She was so happy!

But then the cheering turned into laughing and the laughing into insults. Tanya, her legs hurting, sat down and cried. Suddenly her friend Mike stepped out of the crowd. He wasn't in her classes, but she knew him from her church. She jumped as his voice roared over the crowd, and she was filled with confidence when she realized he was yelling at them for making fun of her. She could tell the things he yelled made the other teens feel ashamed because one by one they lowered their heads and walked away. Mike helped Tanya to her classroom where her teacher and classmates gave her numerous hugs and told her how much they loved her.

Zephaniah's prophecy reminds me of Tanya and Mike and how God jumps to the rescue when we need to be saved. He will come down harshly on our enemies for harming us. Look for him and call out his name. He will save you and bring you home to safety where you can rest in his love.

10 People will come from where the Nile
River begins;
my scattered people will come with
gifts for me.
11 Then Jerusalem will not be ashamed
of the wrongs done against me,
because I will remove from this city
those who like to brag;
there will never be any more proud
people
on my holy mountain in Jerusalem.
12 But I will leave in the city
the humble and those who are not
proud,
and they will trust in the LORD.
13 Those who are left alive in Israel won't do
wrong or tell lies;
they won't trick people with their
words.
They will eat and lie down
with no one to make them afraid."

A Happy Song

14 Sing, Jerusalem.
Israel, shout for joy!
Jerusalem, be happy
and rejoice with all your heart.
15 The LORD has stopped punishing you;
he has sent your enemies away.
The King of Israel, the LORD, is with you;
you will never again be afraid of being
harmed.
16 On that day Jerusalem will be told,
"Don't be afraid, city of Jerusalem.
Don't give up.
17 The LORD your God is with you;
the mighty One will save you.
He will rejoice over you.
You will rest in his love;
he will sing and be joyful about you."
18 "I will take away the sadness planned for
you,
which would have made you very
ashamed.
19 At that time I will punish
all those who harmed you.
I will save my people who cannot walk
and gather my people who have been
thrown out.
I will give them praise and honor
in every place where they were shamed.
20 At that time I will gather you;
at that time I will bring you back home.
I will give you honor and praise
from people everywhere
when I make things go well again for you,
as you will see with your own eyes,"
says the LORD.

Haggai

A name that means "festal one," implying that this minor prophet was probably born on a Jewish feast day

Person Holding the Pen God Wrote With: *Haggai*, one of three prophets of the post-exilic restoration period (along with Zechariah and Malachi), penned this book. Haggai is mentioned briefly in Ezra 5:1–2 and 6:14 in connection with Zechariah.

When the Text Was Written: 520 B.C., according to Haggai 1:1, 2:1, 2:10, and 2:20

Spiritual Posture of the Original Recipients: God's people essentially have their heads buried in their hands, overwhelmed by the difficult reality of life now that they've returned to Jerusalem. Instead of putting their trust in God, they have adopted a myopic view of how impossible things seem.

Storyline Synopsis: The first wave of Israelites, about fifty thousand strong, have finally come home from exile in Babylon to find their Temple decimated. After a brief rebuilding attempt, vigorously opposed by their Samaritan neighbors, they became discouraged and quit. They started focusing on building their own homes and filling them with creature comforts rather than completing "Jehovah's house." Without the distinctive style of worship that the Temple afforded them, they experienced a faith crisis. Over the course of fifteen weeks, God initiated a revival through the prophet Haggai, giving him four unique messages to rouse the Jews from their spiritual apathy. The first emphasized a call to action (Hag. 1:1–15); next was a word of encouragement (2:1–9); third was confirmation of their heavenly Father's blessing (2:10–19); and the final message announced God's plans to restore the kingdom of David through a guy with the funny name, Zerubbabel (2:20–23).

A Moment Worth Discussing: After God used Haggai's words—"Think about what you have done" (Hag. 1:5, 7)—to shake his people awake, they repented and "feared the Lord" (1:12). God responded to their appropriate humility with the reassuring promise "I am with you" (1:13), which is the same promise God used in Joshua 1:5 to encourage his people who were struggling after the death of their beloved leader, Moses. It's interesting to talk about how the posture of contrition enables us to see God more clearly. When we demonstrate awed reverence for who God is, which is the essential meaning of biblical "fear," he graciously reminds us of his abiding presence. Although God sometimes has to discipline us, he never lets go of us while doing so.

Interesting (But Likely to Be Overlooked) Character: *Joshua*, son of Jehozadak (Hag. 1:1, 12) is not the same guy who led the Israelites into the land God had promised—that would've taken a lot of Geritol! He was one of the religious leaders in the remnant that returned to Jerusalem (1 Chr. 6:15; Ezra 3:2).

It Is Time to Build the Temple

1 The prophet Haggai spoke the word of the LORD to Zerubbabel son of Shealtiel, the governor of Judah, and to Joshua son of Jehozadak, the high priest. This message came in the second year that Darius was king, on the first day of the sixth month:

2"This is what the LORD All-Powerful says: 'The people say the right time has not come to rebuild the Temple of the LORD.' "

3Then Haggai the prophet spoke the word of the LORD: 4"Is it right for you to be living in fancy houses while the Temple is still in ruins?"

5This is what the LORD All-Powerful says: "Think about what you have done. 6You have planted much, but you harvest little. You eat, but you do not become full. You drink, but you are still thirsty. You put on clothes, but you are not warm enough. You earn money, but then you lose it all as if you had put it into a purse full of holes."

7This is what the LORD All-Powerful says: "Think about what you have done. 8Go up to the mountains, bring back wood, and build the Temple. Then I will be pleased with it and be honored," says the LORD. 9"You look for much, but you find little. When you bring it home, I destroy it. Why?" asks the LORD All-Powerful. "Because you all work hard for your own houses while my house is still in ruins! 10Because of what you have done, the sky holds back its rain and the ground holds back its crops. 11I have called for a time without rain on the land, and on the mountains, and on the grain, the new wine, the olive oil, the plants which the earth produces, the people, the farm animals, and all the work of your hands."

12Zerubbabel son of Shealtiel and Joshua son of Jehozadak, the high priest, and all the rest of the people who were left alive obeyed the LORD their God and the message from Haggai the prophet, because the LORD their God had sent him. And the people feared the LORD.

13Haggai, the LORD's messenger, gave the LORD's message to the people, saying, "The LORD says, 'I am with you.' " 14The LORD stirred up Zerubbabel son of Shealtiel, the governor of Judah, and Joshua son of Jehozadak, the high priest, and all the rest of the people who were left alive. So they came and worked on the Temple of their God, the LORD All-Powerful. 15They began on the twenty-fourth day of the sixth month in the second year Darius was king.

The Beauty of the Temple

2 On the twenty-first day of the seventh month, the LORD spoke his word through Haggai the prophet, saying, 2"Speak to Zerubbabel son of Shealtiel, governor of Judah, and to Joshua son of Jehozadak, the high priest, and to the rest of the people who are left alive. Say, 3'Do any of you remember how great the Temple was before it was destroyed? What does it look like now? Doesn't it seem like nothing to you?' 4But the LORD says, 'Zerubbabel, be brave. Also, Joshua son of Jehozadak, the high priest, be brave. And all you people who live in the land, be brave,' says the LORD. 'Work, because I am with you,' says the LORD All-Powerful. 5'I made a promise to you when you came out of Egypt, and my Spirit is still with you. So don't be afraid.'

6"This is what the LORD All-Powerful says: 'In a short time I will once again shake the heavens and the earth, the sea and the dry land. 7I will shake all the nations, and they will bring their wealth. Then I will fill this Temple with glory,' says the LORD All-Powerful. 8'The silver is mine, and the gold is mine,' says the LORD All-Powerful. 9'The new Temple will be greater than the one before,' says the LORD All-Powerful. 'And in this place I will give peace,' says the LORD All-Powerful."

10On the twenty-fourth day of the ninth month in the second year Darius was king, the LORD spoke his word to Haggai the prophet, saying, 11"This is what the LORD All-Powerful says: 'Ask the priests for a teaching. 12Suppose a person carries in the fold of his clothes some meat made holy for the LORD. If that fold touches bread, cooked food, wine, olive oil, or some other food, will that be made holy?' "

The priests answered, "No."

13Then Haggai said, "A person who touches a dead body will become unclean. If he touches any of these foods, will it become unclean, too?"

The priests answered, "Yes, it would become unclean."

14Then Haggai answered, "The LORD says, 'This is also true for the people of this

devotion 254

HAGGAI 2:4–5

FROM SCARED TO SACRED

When I am afraid in life, I play a game of hide and seek in my head. I think, "Where can I hide until this is over? Where can I go so that no one will know I'm not brave?" I get so frustrated with myself for mentally running and hiding. I hate being afraid, and I hate being a coward even more. Sometimes we're mad that we've lived like a scared wallflower, and other times, from the paralyzing fear, hiding seems like the best option.

Maybe you've felt like a wallflower ever since the first day of kindergarten. Maybe you've been noticed and then rejected, and so you've decided that hiding will spare you further pain. Maybe you've felt like a wallflower in your career or in your marriage or in a friendship. Present, but ignored. Seen, but unknown. Showing up for life, but scared to death to jump in or make a difference.

I want to tell you something. Our Father has great big arms. They are strong and able to protect you. He expects you to run to him. Hide yourself in him. Find your refuge in him. He promises to be your security and your defense. Inside the strong arms of the Lord, God takes scared women who have always been afraid and wraps them up in the shelter of his love. They know they are sacred to him, and in that knowledge, those women become brave because they have decided to believe God is for them.

nation. They are unclean, and everything
they do with their hands is unclean to me.
Whatever they offer at the altar is also
unclean.
15 "Think about this from now on! Think
about how it was before you started laying
stones on top of stones to build the Temple
of the LORD. 16 A person used to come to a pile
of grain expecting to find twenty basketfuls,
but there were only ten. And a person used
to come to the wine vat to take out fifty
jarfuls, but only twenty were there. 17 I
destroyed your work with diseases, mildew,
and hail, but you still did not come back to
me,' says the LORD. 18 'It is the twenty-fourth
day of the ninth month, the day in which
the people finished working on the
foundation of the Temple of the LORD. From
now on, think about these things: 19 Do you
have seeds for crops still in the barn? Your
vines, fig trees, pomegranates, and olive trees
have not given fruit yet. But from now on I
will bless you!' "

The Lord Makes a Promise to Zerubbabel

20 Then the LORD spoke his word a second
time to Haggai on the twenty-fourth day of
the month. He said, 21 "Tell Zerubbabel, the
governor of Judah, 'I am going to shake the
heavens and the earth. 22 I will destroy the
foreign kingdoms and take away the power
of the kingdoms of the nations. I will destroy
the chariots and their riders. The horses will
fall with their riders, as people kill each
other with swords.' 23 The LORD All-Powerful
says, 'On that day I will take you, Zerubbabel
son of Shealtiel, my servant,' says the LORD,
'and I will make you important like my
signet ring, because I have chosen you!' says
the LORD All-Powerful."

Zechariah

A name that means "the Lord remembers"

Person Holding the Pen God Wrote With: *Zechariah,* who was also a priest and possibly a member of the Great Synagogue of 120 spiritual leaders appointed by Nehemiah, authored this book that bears his name.

When the Text Was Written: Zechariah was a contemporary of Haggai, and this prophecy takes place around 520 B.C., soon after Haggai's.

Spiritual Posture of the Original Recipients: God's people were experiencing a period of spiritual indifference and selfish preoccupation.

Storyline Synopsis: As in Haggai, the Israelites had abandoned the difficult Temple rebuilding project and were fixated on constructing their own dream homes and establishing successful businesses. Thus, God anointed Zechariah to follow up Haggai's *Get Your Head Out of Your Hands and Get Back to Building God's House* revival series with one of his own. Zechariah's preaching, however, is a little more positive! Instead of focusing on the remnant's need to confess their sins and have faith, he emphasizes the fact that the Messiah will soon come to inhabit the place they're working on. The heart of Zechariah's prophetic message is, "If you build it, he will come." This inspiration helped motivate God's people to finish the Temple in a speedy four-year flurry of activity, finishing around 516 B.C.

A Moment Worth Discussing: Chapter 2 records Zechariah's vision (one of eight "night visions" in this book) of a man with a measuring line and includes this verse: "'I will be a wall of fire around it,' says the Lord. 'And I will be the glory within it'" (Zech. 2:5). The image of God inhabiting a "fence of fire" to protect his people brings to mind the flaming topiary that transfixed Moses (Ex. 3:1–2) and the big overhead bonfire that guided the Israelites on their infamous desert tour (13:21). What is the connection between God and blazing things?

Interesting (But Likely to Be Overlooked) Character: Zechariah 7:1–7 records God chastising the Israelites for fasting out of self-pity instead of true sorrow. The leader they were supposedly grieving for was *Gedaliah,* the governor who had been placed in office by King Nebuchadnezzar (2 Kin. 25:22–26; Jer. 41).

The Lord Calls His People Back

1 In the eighth month of the second year Darius was king, the LORD spoke his word to the prophet Zechariah son of Berekiah, who was the son of Iddo. The LORD said, 2“The LORD was very angry with your ancestors. 3So tell the people: This is what the LORD All-Powerful says: ‘Return to me, and I will return to you,’ says the LORD All-Powerful. 4Don’t be like your ancestors. In the past the prophets said to them: This is what the LORD All-Powerful says: ‘Stop your evil ways and evil actions.’ But they wouldn’t listen or pay attention to me, says the LORD. 5Your ancestors are dead, and those prophets didn’t live forever. 6I commanded my words and laws to my servants the prophets, and they preached to your ancestors, who returned to me. They said, ‘The LORD All-Powerful did as he said he would. He punished us for the way we lived and for what we did.’ ”

The Vision of the Horses

7It was on the twenty-fourth day of the eleventh month, which is the month of Shebat, in Darius’s second year as king. The LORD spoke his word to the prophet Zechariah son of Berekiah, who was the son of Iddo.

8During the night I had a vision. I saw a man riding a red horse. He was standing among some myrtle trees in a ravine, with red, brown, and white horses behind him.

9I asked, “What are these, sir?”

The angel who was talking with me answered, “I’ll show you what they are.”

10Then the man standing among the myrtle trees explained, “They are the ones the LORD sent through all the earth.”

11Then they spoke to the LORD’s angel, who was standing among the myrtle trees. They said, “We have gone through all the earth, and everything is calm and quiet.”

12Then the LORD’s angel asked, “LORD All-Powerful, how long will it be before you show mercy to Jerusalem and the cities of Judah? You have been angry with them for seventy years now.” 13So the LORD answered the angel who was talking with me, and his words were comforting and good.

14Then the angel who was talking to me said to me, “Announce this: This is what the LORD All-Powerful says: ‘I have a strong love for Jerusalem. 15And I am very angry with the nations that feel so safe. I was only a little angry at them, but they made things worse.’

16“So this is what the LORD says: ‘I will return to Jerusalem with mercy. My Temple will be rebuilt,’ says the LORD All-Powerful, ‘and the measuring line will be used to rebuild Jerusalem.’

17“Also announce: This is what the LORD All-Powerful says: ‘My towns will be rich again. The LORD will comfort Jerusalem again, and I will again choose Jerusalem.’ ”

The Vision of the Horns

18Then I looked up and saw four animal horns. 19I asked the angel who was talking with me, “What are these?”

He said, “These are the horns that scattered the people of Judah, Israel, and Jerusalem.”

20Then the LORD showed me four craftsmen. 21I asked, “What are they coming to do?”

He answered, “They have come to scare and throw down the horns. These horns scattered the people of Judah so that no one could even lift up his head. These horns stand for the nations that attacked the people of Judah and scattered them.”

The Vision of the Measuring Line

2 Then I looked up and saw a man holding a line for measuring things. 2I asked him, “Where are you going?”

He said to me, “I am going to measure Jerusalem, to see how wide and how long it is.”

3Then the angel who was talking with me left, and another angel came out to meet him. 4The second angel said to him, “Run and tell that young man, ‘Jerusalem will become a city without walls, because there will be so many people and cattle in it. 5I will be a wall of fire around it,’ says the LORD. ‘And I will be the glory within it.’

6“Oh no! Oh no! Run away from Babylon, because I have scattered you like the four winds of heaven,” says the LORD.

7“Oh no, Jerusalem! Escape, you who live right in Babylon.” 8This is what the LORD All-Powerful says: “After he has honored me and sent me against the nations who took your possessions—because whoever touches

you hurts what is precious to me—9I will
shake my hand against them so that their
slaves will rob them."
Then you will know that the LORD
All-Powerful sent me.
10"Shout and be glad, Jerusalem. I am
coming, and I will live among you," says the
LORD. 11"At that time people from many
nations will join with the LORD and will
become my people. Then I will live among
you, and you will know that the LORD
All-Powerful has sent me to you. 12The LORD
will take Judah as his own part of the holy
land, and Jerusalem will be his chosen city
again. 13Be silent, everyone, in the presence
of the LORD. He is coming out of the holy
place where he lives."

The Vision of the High Priest

3 Then he showed me Joshua, the high
priest, standing in front of the LORD's
angel. And Satan was standing by Joshua's
right side to accuse him. 2The LORD said to
Satan, "The LORD says no to you, Satan! The
LORD who has chosen Jerusalem says no to
you! This man was like a burning stick
pulled from the fire."
3Joshua was wearing dirty clothes and
was standing in front of the angel. 4The
angel said to those standing in front of him,
"Take off those dirty clothes."
Then the angel said to Joshua, "Look, I
have taken away your sin from you, and I am
giving you beautiful, fine clothes."
5Then I said, "Put a clean turban on his
head." So they put a clean turban on his
head and dressed him while the LORD's angel
stood there.
6Then the LORD's angel said to Joshua,
7"This is what the LORD All-Powerful says: 'If
you do as I tell you and serve me, you will be
in charge of my Temple and my courtyards.
And I will let you be with these angels who
are standing here.
8" 'Listen, Joshua, the high priest, and your
friends who are sitting in front of you. They
are symbols of what will happen. I am going
to bring my servant called the Branch.
9Look, I put this stone in front of Joshua, a
stone with seven sides. I will carve a message
on it,' says the LORD All-Powerful. 'And in one
day I will take away the sin of this land.'
10"The LORD All-Powerful says, 'In that day,
each of you will invite your neighbor to sit
under your own grapevine and under your
own fig tree.' "

The Vision of the Lampstand

4 Then the angel who was talking with me
returned and woke me up as if I had been
asleep. 2He asked me, "What do you see?"
I said, "I see a solid gold lampstand with a
bowl at the top. And there are seven lamps
and also seven places for wicks. 3There are
two olive trees by it, one on the right of the
bowl and the other on the left."
4I asked the angel who talked with me,
"Sir, what are these?"
5The angel said, "Don't you know what
they are?"
"No, sir," I said.
6Then he told me, "This is the word of the
LORD to Zerubbabel: 'You will not succeed
by your own strength or by your own
power, but by my Spirit,' says the LORD
All-Powerful.
7"Who are you, big mountain? In front of
Zerubbabel you will become flat land, and
he will bring out the topmost stone,
shouting, 'It's beautiful! It's beautiful!' "
8Then the LORD spoke his word to me
again, saying, 9"Zerubbabel has laid the
foundation of this Temple, and he will
complete it. Then you will know that the
LORD All-Powerful has sent me to you.
10"The people should not think that small
beginnings are unimportant. They will be
happy when they see Zerubbabel with tools,
building the Temple.
"(These are the seven eyes of the LORD,
which look back and forth across the earth.)"
11Then I asked the angel, "What are the
two olive trees on the right and left of the
lampstand?"
12I also asked him, "What are the two olive
branches beside the two gold pipes, from
which the olive oil flows to the lamps?"
13He answered, "Don't you know what
they are?"
"No, sir," I said.
14So he said, "They are symbols of the two
who have been appointed to serve the Lord
of all the earth."

The Vision of the Flying Scroll

5 I looked up again and saw a flying scroll.
2The angel asked me, "What do you
see?"

devotion 255

ZECHARIAH 4:6

SECRET DREAMS

Are you one of those capable women that can make things happen? I am one of those women, and it is part of my workday. I secure work, manage people's lives, and make things happen. I learned very early in my walk that the most beautiful thing about my God is that he loves to reveal his Spirit and his hand in my life. In those times, when there are no explanations, when I cannot take credit for it and couldn't have possibly made it happen in my own strength, I know that it is God's divine plan that has won out.

Managing careers for fourteen years has been full of adventure. I have traveled the globe, dined with earthly kings and queens, and visited exotic places. But I had a secret, a hidden desire that no one knew about except my Lord—I love to teach the Bible more than any of the rest of it. My desire was to be able to pen something that would one day be published.

This past year a sweet friend of mine asked me to participate in a challenging writing project. I was overtaken with emotion as I talked with her because all I heard through the phone was Jesus' sweet voice saying, "Not by your strength or your power but by my Spirit I give you this beautiful gift just because I love you." If you have a precious secret that you are keeping to yourself, I know Someone you should share it with.

I answered, "I see a flying scroll, thirty feet
long and fifteen feet wide."
3And he said to me, "This is the curse that
will go all over the land. One side says every
thief will be taken away. The other side says
everyone who makes false promises will be
taken away. 4The LORD All-Powerful says, 'I
will send it to the houses of thieves and to
those who use my name to make false
promises. The scroll will stay in that person's
house and destroy it with its wood and
stones.' "

The Vision of the Woman

5Then the angel who was talking with me
came forward and said to me, "Look up and
see what is going out."
6"What is it?" I asked.
He answered, "It is a measuring basket
going out." He also said, "It is a symbol of the
people's sins in all the land."
7Then the lid made of lead was raised, and
there was a woman sitting inside the basket.
8The angel said, "The woman stands for
wickedness." Then he pushed her back into
the basket and put the lid back down.
9Then I looked up and saw two women
going out with the wind in their wings.
Their wings were like those of a stork, and
they lifted up the basket between earth and
the sky.
10I asked the angel who was talking with
me, "Where are they taking the basket?"
11"They are going to Babylonia to build a
temple for it," he answered. "When the
temple is ready, they will set the basket there
in its place."

The Vision of the Four Chariots

6 I looked up again and saw four chariots
going out between two mountains,
mountains of bronze. 2Red horses pulled the
first chariot. Black horses pulled the second
chariot. 3White horses pulled the third
chariot, and strong, spotted horses pulled the
fourth chariot. 4I asked the angel who was
talking with me, "What are these, sir?"
5He said, "These are the four spirits of

heaven. They have just come from the
presence of the Lord of the whole world.
6 The chariot pulled by the black horses will
go to the land of the north. The white horses
will go to the land of the west, and the
spotted horses will go to the land of the
south."
7 When the powerful horses went out, they
were eager to go through all the earth. So he
said, "Go through all the earth," and they did.
8 Then he called to me, "Look, the horses
that went north have caused my spirit to rest
in the land of the north."

A Crown for Joshua

9 The LORD spoke his word to me, saying,
10 "Take silver and gold from Heldai, Tobijah,
and Jedaiah, who were captives in Babylon.
Go that same day to the house of Josiah son
of Zephaniah, who came from Babylon.
11 Make the silver and gold into a crown,
and put it on the head of Joshua son of
Jehozadak, the high priest. 12 Tell him this is
what the LORD All-Powerful says: 'A man
whose name is the Branch will branch out
from where he is, and he will build the
Temple of the LORD. 13 One man[n] will build
the Temple of the LORD, and the other[n] will
receive honor. One man will sit on his
throne and rule, and the other will be a
priest on his throne. And these two men will
work together in peace.' 14 The crown will be
kept in the Temple of the LORD to remind
Heldai, Tobijah, Jedaiah, and Josiah son of
Zephaniah. 15 People living far away will
come and build the Temple of the LORD.
Then you will know the LORD All-Powerful
has sent me to you. This will happen if you
completely obey the LORD your God."

The People Should Show Mercy

7 In the fourth year Darius was king, on
the fourth day of the ninth month,
which is called Kislev, the LORD spoke his
word to Zechariah. 2 The city of Bethel sent
Sharezer, Regem-Melech, and their men to
ask the LORD a question. 3 They went to the
prophets and priests who were at the Temple
of the LORD All-Powerful. The men said, "For
years in the fifth month of each year we
have shown our sadness and fasted. Should
we continue to do this?"

4 The LORD All-Powerful spoke his word to
me, saying, 5 "Tell the priests and the people
in the land: 'For seventy years you fasted and
cried in the fifth and seventh months, but
that was not really for me. 6 And when you
ate and drank, it was really for yourselves.
7 The LORD used the earlier prophets to say
the same thing, when Jerusalem and the
surrounding towns were at peace and
wealthy, and people lived in the southern
area and the western hills.' "
8 And the LORD spoke his word to
Zechariah again, saying, 9 "This is what the
LORD All-Powerful says: 'Do what is right and
true. Be kind and merciful to each other.
10 Don't hurt widows and orphans, foreigners
or the poor; don't even think of doing evil to
somebody else.'
11 "But they refused to pay attention; they
were stubborn and did not want to listen
anymore. 12 They made their hearts as hard
as rock and would not listen to the teachings
of the LORD All-Powerful. And they would
not hear the words he sent by his Spirit
through the earlier prophets. So the LORD
All-Powerful became very angry.
13 " 'When I called to them, they would
not listen. So when they called to me, I
would not listen,' says the LORD All-Powerful.
14 'I scattered them like a hurricane to other
countries they did not know. This good land
was left so ruined behind them that no one
could live there. They had made the desired
land a ruin.' "

The Lord Will Bless Jerusalem

8 The LORD All-Powerful spoke his
word, saying, 2 This is what the LORD
All-Powerful says: "I have a very strong love
for Jerusalem. My strong love for her is like a
fire burning in me."
3 This is what the LORD says: "I will return
to Jerusalem and live in it. Then it will be
called the City of Truth, and the mountain of
the LORD All-Powerful will be called the Holy
Mountain."
4 This is what the LORD All-Powerful says:
"Old men and old women will again sit
along Jerusalem's streets, each carrying a
cane because of age. 5 And the streets will be
filled with boys and girls playing."
6 This is what the LORD All-Powerful says:

6:13 One man This probably refers to Zerubbabel.
6:13 other This probably refers to Joshua.

devotion 256

ZECHARIAH 7:5–6

FOR *WHOSE* GLORY?

Ministry has surrounded me my whole life. I grew up in the church and attended youth group three times a week. I met my husband in ministry. I have raised my kids in the ministry, and now I serve in our church in the women's ministry. However, when I read Zechariah 7:5–6, I had to ask myself if I'm truly serving the *Lord* in ministry or just myself. To be honest, ministry can be self-serving. I think it is something that anyone who serves in ministry has to guard against. Look at the Pharisees in the New Testament. They were well-meaning priests and rabbis who had gotten caught up in their own importance rather than the importance of serving the Lord.

The people of Israel were making a show of fasting from food during the fifth and seventh months. They wanted everyone to know that they were sacrificing for the Lord. They wanted the glory and the honor that God deserved. God saw their hearts and told them they were doing this for themselves, not for him.

So how do we guard our hearts against this type of self-righteousness? Jesus gives the answer in Matthew 20:28: "In the same way, the Son of Man did not come to be served. He came to serve others and to give his life as a ransom for many people." We need to serve others without looking for the glory. Let us give all the glory to God.

"Those who are left alive then may think it
is too difficult to happen, but it is not too
difficult for me," says the LORD All-Powerful.
7This is what the LORD All-Powerful says: "I
will save my people from countries in the
east and west. 8I will bring them back, and
they will live in Jerusalem. They will be my
people, and I will be their good and loyal
God."

9This is what the LORD All-Powerful says:
"Work hard, you who are hearing these
words today. The prophets spoke these
words when the foundation was laid for the
house of the LORD All-Powerful, for the
building of the Temple. 10Before that time
there was no money to hire people or
animals. People could not safely come and
go because of the enemies; I had turned
everyone against his neighbor. 11But I will
not do to these people who are left what I
did in the past," says the LORD All-Powerful.

12"They will plant their seeds in peace,
their grapevines will have fruit, the ground
will give good crops, and the sky will send
rain. I will give all this to the people who are
left alive. 13Judah and Israel, your names
have been used as curses in other nations.
But I will save you, and you will become a
blessing. So don't be afraid; work hard."

14This is what the LORD All-Powerful says:
"When your ancestors made me angry, I
planned to punish you. I did not change my
mind," says the LORD All-Powerful. 15"But
now I will do something different. I am
planning to do good to Jerusalem and Judah.
So don't be afraid. 16These are the things you
should do: Tell each other the truth. In the
courts judge with truth and complete
fairness. 17Do not make plans to hurt your
neighbors, and don't love false promises. I
hate all these things," says the LORD.

18The LORD All-Powerful spoke his word
to me again. 19This is what the LORD
All-Powerful says: "The special days when
you fast in the fourth, fifth, seventh, and
tenth months will become good, joyful,
happy feasts in Judah. But you must love
truth and peace."

20This is what the LORD All-Powerful says:
"Many people from many cities will still
come to Jerusalem. 21People from one city
will go and say to those from another city,
'We are going to pray to the LORD and to ask
the LORD All-Powerful for help. Come and go
with us.' 22Many people and powerful
nations will come to worship the LORD
All-Powerful in Jerusalem and to pray to the
LORD for help."

23This is what the LORD All-Powerful says:
"At that time, ten men from different
countries will come and take hold of a
Judean by his coat. They will say to him, 'Let
us go with you, because we have heard that
God is with you.' "

Punishment on Israel's Enemies

9 This message is the word of the LORD.
The message is against the land of
Hadrach
and the city of Damascus.
The tribes of Israel and all people
belong to the LORD.
2The message is also against the city of
Hamath, on the border,
and against Tyre and Sidon, with their
skill.
3Tyre has built a strong wall for herself.
She has piled up silver like dust
and gold like the mud in the streets.
4But the Lord will take away all she has
and destroy her power on the sea.
That city will be destroyed by fire.
5The city of Ashkelon will see it and be
afraid.
The people of Gaza will shake with fear,
and the people of Ekron will lose hope.
No king will be left in Gaza,
and no one will live in Ashkelon
anymore.
6Foreigners will live in Ashdod,
and I will destroy the pride of the
Philistines.
7I will stop them from drinking blood
and from eating forbidden food.
Those left alive will belong to God.
They will be leaders in Judah,
and Ekron will become like the
Jebusites.
8I will protect my Temple
from armies who would come or go.
No one will hurt my people again,
because now I am watching them.

The King Is Coming

9Rejoice greatly, people of Jerusalem!
Shout for joy, people of Jerusalem!
Your king is coming to you.
He does what is right, and he saves.
He is gentle and riding on a donkey,
on the colt of a donkey.
10I will take away the chariots from
Ephraim
and the horses from Jerusalem.
The bows used in war will be broken.
The king will talk to the nations about
peace.
His kingdom will go from sea to sea,
and from the Euphrates River to the
ends of the earth.

11As for you, because of the blood of the
agreement with you
I will set your prisoners free from the
waterless pit.
12You prisoners who have hope,
return to your place of safety.
Today I am telling you
that I will give you back twice as much
as before.
13I will use Judah like a bow
and Ephraim like the arrows.
Jerusalem, I will use your men
to fight the men of Greece.
I will use you like a warrior's sword.

14Then the LORD will appear above them,
and his arrows will shoot like
lightning.
The Lord GOD will blow the trumpet,
and he will march in the storms of the
south.
15The LORD All-Powerful will protect them;
they will destroy the enemy with
slingshots.
They will drink and shout like drunks.
They will be filled like a bowl
used for sprinkling blood at the corners
of the altar.
16On that day the LORD their God will save
them
as if his people were sheep.
They will shine in his land
like jewels in a crown.
17They will be so pretty and beautiful.
The young men will grow strong on the
grain
and the young women on new wine.

devotion 257

ZECHARIAH 9:9

A SHOUT-OUT-LOUD KIND OF JOY

Zechariah is a book of promises. What God promised to the people of Israel, he has also promised to us. By faith in Christ, we become full partners in the promises made to the Israelites. Those who belong to Jesus have become the offspring of Abraham (Gal. 3:29), and we inherit these promises God made through the prophets.

What God ultimately promises is joy, a shouting-out-loud kind of joy. God's concluding plan for us is joy. In the end, beyond all the misery we have known in this world and for all eternity, you and I will live in the passionate joy God promises to Jerusalem. To seal the truth, Zechariah prophesied that our Savior would ride on a donkey when he came to save humanity. Matthew 21:1-7 confirms that Jesus rode into Jerusalem to prove that our God keeps his promises.

Do you need to hear that God promises you a rejoicing, shouting kind of joy? His kind of joy relieves heartache and heals wounds. Do you long for the brilliance of God's glory to ride in gently and release you from pain? Do you want God to deliver on his promises to restore your life and lift you up? Then hear the words of the prophet Zechariah: "Your king is coming to you" (Zech. 9:9). That's a promise you can build your life on. The King is coming. Let those words comfort your heart. The King is coming. Listen to this promise of eternal joy. Hallelujah, the King is coming!

The Lord's Promises

10 Ask the LORD for rain during the
springtime rains.
The LORD is the one who makes the
clouds.
He sends the showers
and gives everyone green fields.
2 Idols tell lies;
fortune-tellers see false visions
and tell about false dreams.
The comfort they give is worth
nothing.
So the people are like lost sheep.
They are abused, because there is no
shepherd.

3 The LORD says, "I am angry at my
shepherds,
and I will punish the leaders.
I, the LORD All-Powerful, care
for my flock, the people of Judah.
I will make them like my proud war
horses.
4 From Judah will come the cornerstone,
and the tent peg,
the battle bow,
and every ruler.
5 Together they will be like soldiers
marching to battle through muddy
streets.
The LORD is with them,
so they will fight and defeat the
horsemen.

6 "I will strengthen the people of Judah
and save the people of Joseph.
I will bring them back,
because I care about them.
It will be as though
I had never left them,
because I am the LORD their God,
and I will answer them.
7 The people of Ephraim will be strong like
soldiers;
they will be glad as when they have
drunk wine.

Their children will see it and rejoice;
they will be happy in the LORD.
8 I will call my people
and gather them together.
I will save them,
and they will grow in number as they grew in number before.
9 I have scattered them among the nations,
but in those faraway places, they will remember me.
They and their children will live and return.
10 I will bring them back from the land of Egypt
and gather them from Assyria.
I will bring them to Gilead and Lebanon
until there isn't enough room for them all.
11 They will come through the sea of trouble.
The waves of the sea will be calm,
and the Nile River will dry up.
I will defeat Assyria's pride
and destroy Egypt's power over other countries.
12 I will make my people strong,
and they will live as I say," says the LORD.

11 Lebanon, open your gates
so fire may burn your cedar trees.[n]
2 Cry, pine trees, because the cedar has fallen,
because the tall trees are ruined.
Cry, oaks in Bashan,
because the mighty forest has been cut down.
3 Listen to the shepherds crying
because their rich pastures are destroyed.
Listen to the lions roaring
because the lovely land of the Jordan River is ruined.

The Two Shepherds

4 This is what the LORD my God says: "Feed
the flock that are about to be killed. 5 Their
buyers kill them and are not punished.
Those who sell them say, 'Praise the LORD, I
am rich.' Even the shepherds don't feel sorry
for their sheep. 6 I don't feel sorry anymore
for the people of this country," says the LORD.
"I will let everyone be under the power of
his neighbor and king. They will bring
trouble to the country, and I will not save
anyone from them."
7 So I fed the flock about to be killed,
particularly the weakest ones. Then I took
two sticks; I called one Pleasant and the
other Union, and I fed the flock. 8 In one
month I got rid of three shepherds. The flock
did not pay attention to me, and I got
impatient with them. 9 I said, "I will no
longer take care of you like a shepherd. Let
those that are dying die, and let those that
are to be destroyed be destroyed. Let those
that are left eat each other."
10 Then I broke the stick named Pleasant
to break the agreement God made with all
the nations. 11 That day it was broken. The
weak ones in the flock who were watching
me knew this message was from the LORD.
12 Then I said, "If you want to pay me, pay
me. If not, then don't." So they paid me thirty
pieces of silver.
13 The LORD said to me, "Throw the money
to the potter." That is how little they
thought I was worth.[n] So I took the thirty
pieces of silver and threw them to the potter
in the Temple of the LORD.
14 Then I broke the second stick, named
Union, to break the brotherhood between
Judah and Israel.
15 Then the LORD said to me, "Get the
things used by a foolish shepherd again,
16 because I am going to get a new shepherd
for the country. He will not care for the
dying sheep, or look for the young ones, or
heal the injured ones, or feed the healthy.
But he will eat the best sheep and tear off
their hoofs.
17 "How terrible it will be for the useless shepherd
who abandoned the flock.
A sword will strike his arm and his right eye.
His arm will lose all its strength,
and his right eye will go blind."

Jerusalem Will Be Saved

12 This message is the word of the LORD
to Israel. This is what the LORD says,

11:1 trees In this poem, trees, bushes, and animals stand for leaders of countries around Judah.
11:13 worth This was a small amount. It was about the price paid for a slave.

who stretched out the skies, and laid the foundations of the earth, and put the human spirit within: 2“I will make Jerusalem like a cup of poison to the nations around her. They will come and attack Jerusalem and Judah. 3One day all the nations on earth will come together to attack Jerusalem, but I will make it like a heavy rock; anyone who tries to move it will get hurt. 4At that time I will confuse every horse and cause its rider to go crazy,” says the LORD. “I will watch over Judah, but I will blind all the horses of the enemies. 5Then the leaders of Judah will say to themselves, ‘The people of Jerusalem are strong, because the LORD All-Powerful is their God.’

6“At that time I will make the leaders of Judah like a fire burning a stack of wood or like a fire burning straw. They will destroy all the people around them left and right. But the people of Jerusalem will remain safe.

7“The LORD will save the homes of Judah first so that the honor given to David’s family and to the people of Jerusalem won’t be greater than the honor given to Judah. 8At that time the LORD will protect the people in Jerusalem. Then even the weakest of them will be strong like David. And the family of David will be like God, like an angel of the LORD in front of them. 9At that time I will go to destroy all the nations that attack Jerusalem.

Crying for the One They Stabbed

10“I will pour out on David’s family and the people in Jerusalem a spirit of kindness and mercy. They will look at me, the one they have stabbed, and they will cry like someone crying over the death of an only child. They will be as sad as someone who has lost a firstborn son. 11At that time there will be much crying in Jerusalem, like the crying for Hadad Rimmon in the plain of Megiddo. 12The land will cry, each family by itself: the family of David by itself and their wives by themselves, the family of Nathan by itself and their wives by themselves, 13the family of Levi by itself and their wives by themselves, the family of Shimei by itself and their wives by themselves, 14and all the rest of the families by themselves and their wives by themselves.

13 “At that time a fountain will be open for David’s descendants and for the people of Jerusalem to cleanse them of their sin and uncleanness.”

2The LORD All-Powerful says, “At that time I will get rid of the names of the idols from the land; no one will remember them anymore. I will also remove the prophets and unclean spirits from the land. 3If a person continues to prophesy, his own father and mother, the ones who gave birth to him, will tell him, ‘You have told lies using the LORD’s name, so you must die.’ When he prophesies, his own father and mother who gave birth to him will stab him.

4“At that time the prophets will be ashamed of their visions and prophecies. They won’t wear the prophet’s clothes made of hair to trick people. 5Each of them will say, ‘I am not a prophet. I am a farmer and have been a farmer since I was young.’ 6But someone will ask, ‘What are the deep cuts on your body?’ And each will answer, ‘I was hurt at my friend’s house.’

The Shepherd Is Killed

7“Sword, hit the shepherd.
Attack the man who is my friend,”
says the LORD All-Powerful.
“Kill the shepherd,
and the sheep will scatter,
and I will punish the little ones.”
8The LORD says, “Two-thirds of the people
through all the land will die. They will
be gone,
and one-third will be left.
9The third that is left I will test with fire,
purifying them like silver,
testing them like gold.
Then they will call on me,
and I will answer them.
I will say, ‘You are my people,’
and they will say, ‘The LORD is our
God.’ ”

The Day of Punishment

14 The LORD’s day of judging is coming when the wealth you have taken will be divided among you.

2I will bring all the nations together to fight Jerusalem. They will capture the city and rob the houses and attack the women. Half the people will be taken away as captives, but the rest of the people won’t be taken from the city.

3Then the LORD will go to war against

devotion 258

ZECHARIAH 13:9

ALL THAT GLITTERS . . .

A refining fire does not destroy or consume. Instead, it burns up what is worthless and preserves what is valuable. God says that he is a refining fire. He loves us, yet he requires a purity that only he can bring.

Have you ever known a time of spiritual refinement? I've never met a woman who hasn't been through seasons, sometimes several seasons, of refining. When God uses fire to purify our lives, there is always a pain involved. God uses the pain of affliction to take away the things that are woven into our character that are worthless and even liabilities. Impure motives are burned up. Self-importance is set ablaze. Shallow accumulation ends up in the embers of God's fire.

It is right for us to regard God's refining with fear and trembling, but even in the refinement, we have such great hope. God does not destroy us. Instead, he takes away the rubbish. Refinement makes us more valuable. It gives us character. The woman on the other side of a refining fire radiates a purity given by God's mercy.

If you have walked through a refining fire, get down on your knees and cry, "Holy!" Look for God's heart and see the beauty of his mercy even in your pain. God purifies the ones that he loves. He makes them shine like pure silver and gold. You belong to God, and he wants you to see his glory and call him Lord.

those nations; he will fight as in a day of
battle. 4On that day he will stand on the
Mount of Olives, east of Jerusalem. The
Mount of Olives will split in two, forming
a deep valley that runs east and west. Half
the mountain will move toward the north,
and half will move toward the south. 5You
will run through this mountain valley to
the other side, just as you ran from the
earthquake when Uzziah was king of Judah.
Then the LORD my God will come and all the
holy ones with him.

6On that day there will be no light, cold,
or frost. 7There will be no other day like it,
and the LORD knows when it will come.
There will be no day or night; even at
evening it will still be light.

8At that time fresh water will flow from
Jerusalem. Half of it will flow east to the
Dead Sea, and half will flow west to the
Mediterranean Sea. It will flow summer and
winter.

9Then the LORD will be king over the
whole world. At that time there will be only
one LORD, and his name will be the only
name.

10All the land south of Jerusalem from
Geba to Rimmon will be turned into a plain.
Jerusalem will be raised up, but it will stay
in the same place. The city will reach from
the Benjamin Gate and to the First Gate to
the Corner Gate, and from the Tower of
Hananel to the king's winepresses. 11People
will live there, and it will never be destroyed
again. Jerusalem will be safe.

12But the LORD will bring a terrible disease
on the nations that fought against Jerusalem.
Their flesh will rot away while they are still
standing up. Their eyes will rot in their
sockets, and their tongues will rot in their
mouths. 13At that time the LORD will cause
panic. Everybody will grab his neighbor, and
they will attack each other. 14The people of
Judah will fight in Jerusalem. And the
wealth of the nations around them will be
collected—much gold, silver, and clothes.

[15]A similar disease will strike the horses,
mules, camels, donkeys, and all the animals
in the camps.

[16]All of those left alive of the people who
came to fight Jerusalem will come back to
Jerusalem year after year to worship the
King, the LORD All-Powerful, and to celebrate
the Feast of Shelters. [17]Anyone from the
nations who does not go to Jerusalem to
worship the King, the LORD All-Powerful,
will not have rain fall on his land. [18]If the
Egyptians do not go to Jerusalem, they will
not have rain. Then the LORD will send them
the same terrible disease he sent the other
nations that did not celebrate the Feast of
Shelters. [19]This will be the punishment for
Egypt and any nation which does not go to
celebrate the Feast of Shelters.

[20]At that time the horses' bells will have
written on them: HOLY TO THE LORD. The
cooking pots in the Temple of the Lord will
be like the holy altar bowls. [21]Every pot in
Jerusalem and Judah will be holy to the LORD
All-Powerful, and everyone who offers
sacrifices will be able to take food from them
and cook in them. At that time there will not
be any buyers or sellers in the Temple of the
LORD All-Powerful.

Malachi

A Hebrew name that means "messenger of God"

Person Holding the Pen God Wrote With: As indicated in Malachi 1:1, the Jewish prophet *Malachi* authored this book.

When the Text Was Written: Most scholars agree this book was penned between 460 and 450 B.C. because of the assumption of the second Temple in chapters 2—3. Further supporting this is the fact that Malachi addresses many of the same issues that Ezra and Nehemiah did (marriage to pagans, children who can't speak Hebrew, social injustice, corruption of the priesthood, and anemic tithing). The canonical placement of the text is interesting in that Malachi is the last book in the Old Testament, marking the end of what Hebrews mentions as a time when God spoke to the Jews through prophets (Heb. 1:1–4). Almost four hundred years—the Intertestamental Period—will pass before God's voice will be recorded again in the Gospels, making this the divine drum roll before Jesus is introduced by John the Baptist.

Spiritual Posture of the Original Recipients: They're not exactly singing *Kum-Bah-Yah* and having prayer meetings. The literary style of the book—*rhetorical disputation*—essentially means that they're mad at God, arguing with him like petulant teenagers fussing about curfew with a loving, yet firm parent.

Storyline Synopsis: The first wave of Israelites was returning to Jerusalem after about fifty years of captivity in Babylon. They had been dreaming of returning to their beloved homeland all that time. But when they got there, they found Canaan wasn't quite as they remembered. The walls surrounding the city were in ruins. Squatters and wild animals were living where King David ruled. Their once-fertile fields were choked with weeds and rocks. The land of milk and honey was an absolute mess! Needless to say, they were ticked. And—big surprise—they blamed their troubles on God.

A Moment Worth Discussing: In Malachi 3:6, God explains that in spite of their incorrigible behavior, he will never abandon them. To a fickle bunch like the Israelites, that must have been quite a solace.

Interesting (But Likely to Be Overlooked) Characters: The *Israelite women*, who after sticking by their husbands through thick and thin—in captivity, on the long journey home, throughout the ensuing hand-to-mouth existence when they resettled in Jerusalem—were ditched by their faithless husbands for younger, hotter pagan babes (Mal. 2:15–16). My guess is that this group of divorcees was a force to be reckoned with!

1 This message is the word of the LORD
given to Israel through Malachi.

God Loves Israel

2The LORD said, "I have loved you."
But you ask, "How have you loved us?"
The LORD said, "Esau and Jacob were
brothers. I loved Jacob, 3but I hated Esau. I
destroyed his mountain country and left his
land to the wild dogs of the desert."
4The people of Edom might say, "We were
destroyed, but we will go back and rebuild
the ruins."
But the LORD All-Powerful says, "If they
rebuild them, I will destroy them. People
will say, 'Edom is a wicked country. The LORD
is always angry with the Edomites.' 5You will
see these things with your own eyes. And
you will say, 'The LORD is great, even outside
the borders of Israel!' "

The Priests Don't Respect God

6The LORD All-Powerful says, "A son
honors his father, and a servant honors his
master." I am a father, so why don't you
honor me? I am a master, so why don't you
respect me? You priests do not respect me.
"But you ask, 'How have we shown you
disrespect?'
7"You have shown it by bringing unclean
food to my altar.
"But you ask, 'What makes it unclean?'
"It is unclean because you don't respect
the altar of the LORD. 8When you bring blind
animals as sacrifices, that is wrong. When
you bring crippled and sick animals, that is
wrong. Try giving them to your governor.
Would he be pleased with you? He wouldn't
accept you," says the LORD All-Powerful.
9"Now ask God to be kind to you, but he
won't accept you with such offerings," says
the LORD All-Powerful.
10"I wish one of you would close the
Temple doors so that you would not light
useless fires on my altar! I am not pleased
with you and will not accept your gifts," says
the LORD All-Powerful. 11"From the east to
the west I will be honored among the
nations. Everywhere they will bring incense
and clean offerings to me, because I will be

devotion 259

MALACHI 1:7-13

BRINGING GOD THE LEFTOVERS

Malachi recorded the charges God brought against Israel with regards to their tithing, offerings, and dealing unfairly with their wives. Do you know the difference between robbing and stealing? Robbing is something you do publicly, and stealing is something you do in secret. God's charge was that they were robbing him, purposely taking from his storehouse what he required to be there. Worse than that, for the sacrifices they did make, they were bringing their throwaways, the hurt and crippled animals that they couldn't use anyway. What an affront to the very One from whom they had received everything.

Even though the people were robbing the storehouse of the tithe and laying sick animals on the altar, they were still inquiring of the Lord's blessing as if they were fulfilling his command. In all my years of ministry, I can tell you with a clear conscience that we have never had anyone who was faithful in their tithing be in need of any sort of benevolence or financial help from the church. This is a testimony to testing the truth of the Word when it says, "Bring to the storehouse a full tenth of what you earn so there will be food in my house. Test me in this . . . I will open the windows of heaven for you and pour out all the blessings you need" (Mal. 3:10). Do not withhold your generosity from the Lord—you may just miss out on the financial freedom that he has promised.

honored among the nations," says the LORD All-Powerful.

12"But you don't honor me. You say about the Lord's altar, 'It is unclean, and the food has no worth.' 13You say, 'We are tired of doing this,' and you sniff at it in disgust," says the LORD All-Powerful.

"And you bring hurt, crippled, and sick animals as gifts. You bring them as gifts, but I won't accept them from you," says the LORD. 14"The person who cheats will be cursed. He has a male animal in his flock and promises to offer it, but then he offers to the Lord an animal that has something wrong with it. I am a great king," says the LORD All-Powerful, "and I am feared by all the nations.

Rules for Priests

2 "Priests, this command is for you. 2Listen to me. Pay attention to what I say. Honor my name," says the LORD All-Powerful. "If you don't, I will send a curse on you and on your blessings. I have already cursed them, because you don't pay attention to what I say.

3"I will punish your descendants. I will smear your faces with the animal insides left from your feasts, and you will be thrown away with it. 4Then you will know that I am giving you this command so my agreement with Levi will continue," says the LORD All-Powerful. 5"My agreement for priests was with the tribe of Levi. I promised them life and peace so they would honor me. And they did honor me and fear me. 6They taught the true teachings and spoke no lies. With peace and honesty they did what I said they should do, and they kept many people from sinning.

7"A priest should teach what he knows, and people should learn the teachings from him, because he is the messenger of the LORD All-Powerful. 8But you priests have stopped obeying me. With your teachings you have caused many people to do wrong. You have broken the agreement with the tribe of Levi!" says the LORD All-Powerful. 9"You have not been careful to do what I say, but instead you take sides in court cases. So I have caused you to be hated and disgraced in front of everybody."

Judah Was Not Loyal to God

10We all have the same father; the same God made us. So why do people break their promises to each other and show no respect for the agreement our ancestors made with God? 11The people of Judah have broken their promises. They have done something God hates in Israel and Jerusalem: The people of Judah did not respect the Temple that the LORD loves, and the men of Judah married women who worship foreign gods. 12Whoever does this might bring offerings to the LORD All-Powerful, but the LORD will still cut that person off from the community of Israel.

13This is another thing you do. You cover the LORD's altar with your tears. You cry and moan, because he does not accept your offerings and is not pleased with what you bring. 14You ask, "Why?" It is because the LORD sees how you treated the wife you married when you were young. You broke your promise to her, even though she was your partner and you had an agreement with her. 15God made husbands and wives to become one body and one spirit for his purpose—so they would have children who are true to God.

So be careful, and do not break your promise to the wife you married when you were young.

16The LORD God of Israel says, "I hate divorce. And I hate people who do cruel things as easily as they put on clothes," says the LORD All-Powerful.

So be careful. And do not break your trust.

The Special Day of Judging

17You have tired the LORD with your words.

You ask, "How have we tired him?"

You did it by saying, "The LORD thinks anyone who does evil is good, and he is pleased with them." Or you asked, "Where is the God who is fair?"

3 The LORD All-Powerful says, "I will send my messenger, who will prepare the way for me. Suddenly, the Lord you are looking for will come to his Temple; the messenger of the agreement, whom you want, will come." 2No one can live through that time; no one can survive when he comes. He will be like a purifying fire and like laundry soap. 3Like someone who heats and purifies silver, he will purify the Levites and make them pure like gold and silver. Then they will bring offerings to the LORD in the right way.

devotion 260

MALACHI 3:6

GOD ALWAYS WAITS UP

The descendants of Jacob deserved to be destroyed numerous times. They turned their backs on God over and over again. I would never have put up with what God did. I guess that is why I am not God. The Lord is merciful. He is kind, full of love, and long-suffering. He is forgiving and just, but most of all, God is patient. I'm thankful for this because the reality is that I have blown it with God, just as the Israelites did. I start out with good intentions, but somehow I slip into old habits and attitudes. Yet God patiently waits for me to come back to him, asking for forgiveness and starting again.

I believe the enemy wants us to forget this truth about God. He uses our guilt to keep us from coming back to the Lord. He convinces us that somehow God has changed, that he is fed up with us and doesn't even want us back. It is a lie. God never changes, and no matter how many times we turn away from the Lord, he will be waiting to take us back. Read Luke 15:11-32, the story of the son who left home. It is such a beautiful example of our Father waiting for our return when we have turned away from him. Know that if you have turned away from God, he is waiting for your return. He loves you and he will never change or stop loving you.

[4]And the LORD will accept the offerings from
Judah and Jerusalem, as it was in the past.
[5]The LORD All-Powerful says, "Then I will
come to you and judge you. I will be quick to
testify against those who take part in evil
magic, adultery, and lying under oath, those
who cheat workers of their pay and who
cheat widows and orphans, those who are
unfair to foreigners, and those who do not
respect me.

Stealing from God

[6]"I the LORD do not change. So you
descendants of Jacob have not been
destroyed. [7]Since the time of your ancestors,
you have disobeyed my rules and have not
kept them. Return to me, and I will return to
you," says the LORD All-Powerful.
"But you ask, 'How can we return?'
[8]"Should a person rob God? But you are
robbing me.
"You ask, 'How have we robbed you?'
"You have robbed me in your offerings
and the tenth of your crops. [9]So a curse is on
you, because the whole nation has robbed
me. [10]Bring to the storehouse a full tenth of
what you earn so there will be food in my
house. Test me in this," says the LORD
All-Powerful. "I will open the windows of
heaven for you and pour out all the blessings
you need. [11]I will stop the insects so they
won't eat your crops. The grapes won't fall
from your vines before they are ready to
pick," says the LORD All-Powerful. [12]"All the
nations will call you blessed, because you
will have a pleasant country," says the LORD
All-Powerful.

The Lord's Promise of Mercy

[13]The LORD says, "You have said terrible
things about me.
"But you ask, 'What have we said about
you?'
[14]"You have said, 'It is useless to serve
God. It did no good to obey his laws and to
show the LORD All-Powerful that we were
sorry for what we did. [15]So we say that
proud people are happy. Evil people
succeed. They challenge God and get away
with it.'"

16Then those who honored the LORD
spoke with each other, and the LORD listened
and heard them. The names of those who
honored the LORD and respected him were
written in his presence in a book to be
remembered.
17The LORD All-Powerful says, "They belong
to me; on that day they will be my very own.
As a parent shows mercy to his child who
serves him, I will show mercy to my people.
18You will again see the difference between
good and evil people, between those who
serve God and those who don't.

The Day of the Lord's Judging

4 "There is a day coming that will burn
like a hot furnace, and all the proud and
evil people will be like straw. On that day
they will be completely burned up so that
not a root or branch will be left," says the
LORD All-Powerful. 2"But for you who honor
me, goodness will shine on you like the sun,
with healing in its rays. You will jump
around, like well-fed calves. 3Then you will
crush the wicked like ashes under your feet
on the day I will do this," says the LORD
All-Powerful.
4"Remember the teaching of Moses my
servant, those laws and rules I gave to him
on Mount Sinai for all the Israelites.
5"But I will send you Elijah the prophet
before that great and terrifying day of the
LORD's judging. 6Elijah will help parents love
their children and children love their
parents. Otherwise, I will come and put a
curse on the land."

New Testament

Matthew

A Hebrew name that means "gift of the Lord"

*This is the first of the three synoptic Gospels. (*Synoptic, *meaning "seeing together," commonly refers to the similarities between the first three books in the New Testament.* Gospel, *or "good news," refers to the message of Jesus Christ, who died on a cross and was resurrected to reconcile man with God.)*

Person Holding the Pen God Wrote With: *Matthew*, one of the original twelve apostles of Jesus Christ, whose "pre-ministry" name was Levi penned this book. He worked as a tax collector prior to becoming a follower of Christ.

When the Text Was Written: This book was written between 50 and 70 A.D. (definitely prior to the destruction of the second Temple in 70 A.D.).

Spiritual Posture of the Original Recipients: It's likely that Matthew's audience was primarily Jewish, based on the style and subject matter. Many weren't convinced that Jesus was the long-awaited Messiah.

Storyline Synopsis: Reading the four Gospels is like listening to four different people who are standing on four different corners of an intersection describe a parade. Even though they watched the same series of events, they all bring a unique perspective! Matthew tells the story of Jesus Christ from a decidedly Jewish perspective. Beginning with the birth narrative going all the way back to Abraham in chapter 1, it is obvious that this former taxman is intent on setting the record straight regarding the fact that Jesus is the Messianic King the Jews have yearned for. The Book of Matthew is made up of five major themes: the *revelation* of King Jesus (chapters 1—10), the *rebellion* against King Jesus (chapters 11—13), the *retirement* of King Jesus (chapters 14—20), the *rejection* of King Jesus (chapters 21—27), and the *resurrection* of King Jesus (chapter 27). Furthermore, Matthew is arranged by subject matter, not chronologically like Mark and Luke.

A Moment Worth Discussing: While the Beatitudes (chapters 5—7) are probably the most familiar section of this Gospel, offering important insights for how Christians should live, the "seven warnings" (chapter 23) also present a very compelling lesson. In this passage, Jesus chastises religious leaders for being more concerned with their external appearance than with the condition of their heart. They were much more interested in looking spiritual than with loving God—a problem that plagues the modern church today.

Interesting (But Likely to Be Overlooked) Character: *Caiaphas*, the ungodly high priest, plotted to kill Jesus for political and financial reasons (Matt. 26:3). His father-in-law was another high priest named Annas, who'd sullied his own position as a spiritual leader. Both men chose to line their pockets by embezzling from the Temple, hardening their hearts against God in the process.

Mary

MATTHEW 1

She is ordinary in every way—a girl from an obscure village where no one was known for anything special. She is engaged to Joseph who also boasts no exceptional abilities. They are, in a word, common.

Mary is preparing for bed one evening when the angel Gabriel comes to her. She jumps, hiding her face, as the angel speaks: "Don't be afraid, Mary." She turns to look at him—he knows her name! "God has shown you his grace. Listen!" Though confused, she listens without saying a word as Gabriel explains that she will give birth to a son named Jesus.

"How will this happen since I am a virgin?"

"The Holy Spirit will come upon you."

A hush falls over the room. It is an eternal moment that Mary will never forget. *God can do anything!* she thinks. She is going to carry the Son of God in her womb. Her heart is filled with fear and humility. Why has she been chosen for such a call? Why, of all the girls in the world, does the Most High God look on her with favor? Her mind races with questions, but she cannot put a voice to them. A peace that she cannot explain covers her.

"I am the servant of the Lord," she says, her heart overflowing with a sense of fear and awe. "Let this happen to me as you say!"

Mary's simple faith enabled her to believe that God could do anything. He still does the impossible today.

The Family History of Jesus

1 This is the family history of Jesus Christ. He came from the family of David, and David came from the family of Abraham.

2 Abraham was the father[n] of Isaac.
Isaac was the father of Jacob.
Jacob was the father of Judah and his brothers.
3 Judah was the father of Perez and Zerah.
(Their mother was Tamar.)
Perez was the father of Hezron.
Hezron was the father of Ram.
4 Ram was the father of Amminadab.
Amminadab was the father of Nahshon.
Nahshon was the father of Salmon.
5 Salmon was the father of Boaz.
(Boaz's mother was Rahab.)
Boaz was the father of Obed.
(Obed's mother was Ruth.)
Obed was the father of Jesse.
6 Jesse was the father of King David.
David was the father of Solomon.
(Solomon's mother had been Uriah's wife.)
7 Solomon was the father of Rehoboam.
Rehoboam was the father of Abijah.
Abijah was the father of Asa.[n]
8 Asa was the father of Jehoshaphat.
Jehoshaphat was the father of Jehoram.
Jehoram was the ancestor of Uzziah.
9 Uzziah was the father of Jotham.
Jotham was the father of Ahaz.
Ahaz was the father of Hezekiah.
10 Hezekiah was the father of Manasseh.
Manasseh was the father of Amon.
Amon was the father of Josiah.
11 Josiah was the grandfather of Jehoiachin[n] and his brothers.
(This was at the time that the people were taken to Babylon.)
12 After they were taken to Babylon:
Jehoiachin was the father of Shealtiel.
Shealtiel was the grandfather of Zerubbabel.
13 Zerubbabel was the father of Abiud.
Abiud was the father of Eliakim.
Eliakim was the father of Azor.
14 Azor was the father of Zadok.
Zadok was the father of Akim.
Akim was the father of Eliud.

1:2 father "Father" in Jewish lists of ancestors can sometimes mean grandfather or more distant relative.
1:7 Asa Some Greek copies read "Asaph," another name for Asa (see 1 Chronicles 3:10).
1:11 Jehoiachin The Greek reads "Jeconiah," another name for Jehoiachin (see 2 Kings 24:6 and 1 Chronicles 3:16).

[15]Eliud was the father of Eleazar.
Eleazar was the father of Matthan.
Matthan was the father of Jacob.
[16]Jacob was the father of Joseph.
Joseph was the husband of Mary,
and Mary was the mother of Jesus.
Jesus is called the Christ.
[17]So there were fourteen generations from
Abraham to David. And there were fourteen
generations from David until the people
were taken to Babylon. And there were
fourteen generations from the time when
the people were taken to Babylon until
Christ was born.

The Birth of Jesus Christ

[18]This is how the birth of Jesus Christ
came about. His mother Mary was engaged[n]
to marry Joseph, but before they married,
she learned she was pregnant by the power
of the Holy Spirit. [19]Because Mary's husband,
Joseph, was a good man, he did not want to
disgrace her in public, so he planned to
divorce her secretly.

[20]While Joseph thought about these
things, an angel of the Lord came to him in a
dream. The angel said, "Joseph, descendant
of David, don't be afraid to take Mary as your
wife, because the baby in her is from the
Holy Spirit. [21]She will give birth to a son,
and you will name him Jesus,[n] because he
will save his people from their sins."
[22]All this happened to bring about what
the Lord had said through the prophet:
[23]"The virgin will be pregnant. She will have
a son, and they will name him Immanuel,"[n]
which means "God is with us."
[24]When Joseph woke up, he did what the
Lord's angel had told him to do. Joseph took
Mary as his wife, [25]but he did not have
sexual relations with her until she gave birth
to the son. And Joseph named him Jesus.

Wise Men Come to Visit Jesus

2 Jesus was born in the town of Bethlehem
in Judea during the time when Herod
was king. When Jesus was born, some wise
men from the east came to Jerusalem.

1:18 engaged For the Jewish people an engagement was a lasting agreement, which could only be broken by a divorce. If a bride-to-be was unfaithful, it was considered adultery, and she could be put to death. **1:21 Jesus** The name "Jesus" means "salvation." **1:23 "The virgin . . . Immanuel"** Quotation from Isaiah 7:14.

devotion 261

MATTHEW 1:22–23

MOTHER MARY AND YOU

Do you ever wonder what it felt like to be Mary? Being called to carry God's Son in her womb must have been mind-boggling for her at first. And when Joseph initially decided not to marry her as a result of her being pregnant with a baby he knew he had not fathered, she must have been devastated. Fortunately, God told Joseph not to worry and to take Mary as his wife. We eventually see God's prophecy fulfilled when Christ is born.

While everything worked out according to prophecy, can you imagine what it was like for Mary to walk through life as the human mother of Jesus? To worship him as her Lord but to also love and worry about him as her human son must have been heart-rending at times. Her trust in God must have been great in order to stay strong. Mary's assignment from God was enormous. Even though she was a mere human, and a young one at that, she fulfilled a tremendous purpose for God.

Mary was definitely a significant woman to God, but one thing is for certain, you are too. Each of us has a purpose, and we are just as important to God as Mary was. Mary's story should not only remind us of Christ's birth but also that we each have an important assignment. Take heart from Mary and pray to the Lord that you too will know the plans he has to be glorified in your life.

[2]They asked, "Where is the baby who was born to be the king of the Jews? We saw his star in the east and have come to worship him."

[3]When King Herod heard this, he was troubled, as were all the people in Jerusalem. [4]Herod called a meeting of all the leading priests and teachers of the law and asked them where the Christ would be born. [5]They answered, "In the town of Bethlehem in Judea. The prophet wrote about this in the Scriptures:

[6]'But you, Bethlehem, in the land of Judah,
are not just an insignificant village in Judah.
A ruler will come from you
who will be like a shepherd for my people Israel.' "

Micah 5:2

[7]Then Herod had a secret meeting with the wise men and learned from them the exact time they first saw the star. [8]He sent the wise men to Bethlehem, saying, "Look carefully for the child. When you find him, come tell me so I can worship him too."

[9]After the wise men heard the king, they left. The star that they had seen in the east went before them until it stopped above the place where the child was. [10]When the wise men saw the star, they were filled with joy. [11]They came to the house where the child was and saw him with his mother, Mary, and they bowed down and worshiped him. They opened their gifts and gave him treasures of gold, frankincense, and myrrh. [12]But God warned the wise men in a dream not to go back to Herod, so they returned to their own country by a different way.

Jesus' Parents Take Him to Egypt

[13]After they left, an angel of the Lord came to Joseph in a dream and said, "Get up! Take the child and his mother and escape to Egypt, because Herod is starting to look for the child so he can kill him. Stay in Egypt until I tell you to return."

[14]So Joseph got up and left for Egypt during the night with the child and his mother. [15]And Joseph stayed in Egypt until Herod died. This happened to bring about what the Lord had said through the prophet: "I called my son out of Egypt."[n]

Herod Kills the Baby Boys

[16]When Herod saw that the wise men had tricked him, he was furious. So he gave an order to kill all the baby boys in Bethlehem and in the surrounding area who were two years old or younger. This was in keeping with the time he learned from the wise men. [17]So what God had said through the prophet Jeremiah came true:

[18]"A voice was heard in Ramah
of painful crying and deep sadness:
Rachel crying for her children.
She refused to be comforted,
because her children are dead."

Jeremiah 31:15

Joseph and Mary Return

[19]After Herod died, an angel of the Lord spoke to Joseph in a dream while he was in Egypt. [20]The angel said, "Get up! Take the child and his mother and go to the land of Israel, because the people who were trying to kill the child are now dead."

[21]So Joseph took the child and his mother and went to Israel. [22]But he heard that Archelaus was now king in Judea since his father Herod had died. So Joseph was afraid to go there. After being warned in a dream, he went to the area of Galilee, [23]to a town called Nazareth, and lived there. And so what God had said through the prophets came true: "He will be called a Nazarene."[n]

The Work of John the Baptist

3 About that time John the Baptist began preaching in the desert area of Judea. [2]John said, "Change your hearts and lives because the kingdom of heaven is near." [3]John the Baptist is the one Isaiah the prophet was talking about when he said:

"This is a voice of one
who calls out in the desert:
'Prepare the way for the Lord.
Make the road straight for him.' "

Isaiah 40:3

[4]John's clothes were made from camel's hair, and he wore a leather belt around his waist. For food, he ate locusts and wild honey. [5]Many people came from Jerusalem and Judea and all the area around the Jordan River to hear John. [6]They confessed their

2:15 "I called . . . Egypt." Quotation from Hosea 11:1. **2:23 Nazarene** A person from the town of Nazareth. Matthew may be referring to Isaiah 11:1, where the Hebrew word translated "branch" sounds like "Nazarene."

sins, and he baptized them in the Jordan
River.
7Many of the Pharisees and Sadducees
came to the place where John was baptizing
people. When John saw them, he said, “You
are snakes! Who warned you to run away
from God’s coming punishment? 8Do the
things that show you really have changed
your hearts and lives. 9And don’t think you
can say to yourselves, ‘Abraham is our father.’
I tell you that God could make children for
Abraham from these rocks. 10The ax is now
ready to cut down the trees, and every tree
that does not produce good fruit will be cut
down and thrown into the fire.[n]
11“I baptize you with water to show that
your hearts and lives have changed. But
there is one coming after me who is greater
than I am, whose sandals I am not good
enough to carry. He will baptize you with
the Holy Spirit and fire. 12He will come ready
to clean the grain, separating the good grain
from the chaff. He will put the good part of
the grain into his barn, but he will burn the
chaff with a fire that cannot be put out.”[n]

Jesus Is Baptized by John

13At that time Jesus came from Galilee to
the Jordan River and wanted John to baptize
him. 14But John tried to stop him, saying,
“Why do you come to me to be baptized? I
need to be baptized by you!”
15Jesus answered, “Let it be this way for
now. We should do all things that are God’s
will.” So John agreed to baptize Jesus.
16As soon as Jesus was baptized, he came
up out of the water. Then heaven opened,
and he saw God’s Spirit coming down on
him like a dove. 17And a voice from heaven
said, “This is my Son, whom I love, and I am
very pleased with him.”

The Temptation of Jesus

4 Then the Spirit led Jesus into the desert
to be tempted by the devil. 2Jesus fasted
for forty days and nights. After this, he was
very hungry. 3The devil came to Jesus to
tempt him, saying, “If you are the Son of
God, tell these rocks to become bread.”
4Jesus answered, “It is written in the
Scriptures, ‘A person lives not on bread
alone, but by everything God says.’ ”[n]
5Then the devil led Jesus to the holy city
of Jerusalem and put him on a high place of
the Temple. 6The devil said, “If you are the
Son of God, jump down, because it is written
in the Scriptures:

‘He has put his angels in charge of you.
They will catch you in their hands
so that you will not hit your foot on a
rock.’ ” *Psalm 91:11–12*

7Jesus answered him, “It also says in the
Scriptures, ‘Do not test the Lord your God.’ ”[n]
8Then the devil led Jesus to the top of a
very high mountain and showed him all the
kingdoms of the world and all their
splendor. 9The devil said, “If you will bow
down and worship me, I will give you all
these things.”
10Jesus said to the devil, “Go away from
me, Satan! It is written in the Scriptures, ‘You
must worship the Lord your God and serve
only him.’ ”[n]
11So the devil left Jesus, and angels came
and took care of him.

Jesus Begins Work in Galilee

12When Jesus heard that John had been
put in prison, he went back to Galilee. 13He
left Nazareth and went to live in Capernaum,
a town near Lake Galilee, in the area near
Zebulun and Naphtali. 14Jesus did this to
bring about what the prophet Isaiah had said:

15“Land of Zebulun and land of Naphtali
along the sea,
beyond the Jordan River.
This is Galilee where the non-Jewish
people live.
16These people who live in darkness
will see a great light.
They live in a place covered with the
shadows of death,
but a light will shine on them.”
Isaiah 9:1–2

Jesus Chooses Some Followers

17From that time Jesus began to preach,
saying, “Change your hearts and lives,
because the kingdom of heaven is near.”
18As Jesus was walking by Lake Galilee, he
saw two brothers, Simon (called Peter) and

3:10 The ax . . . fire. This means that God is ready to punish his people who do not obey him. **3:12 He will . . . out.** This means that Jesus will come to separate good people from bad people, saving the good and punishing the bad. **4:4 ‘A person . . . says.’** Quotation from Deuteronomy 8:3. **4:7 ‘Do . . . God.’** Quotation from Deuteronomy 6:16. **4:10 ‘You . . . him.’** Quotation from Deuteronomy 6:13.

his brother Andrew. They were throwing a
net into the lake because they were
fishermen. 19 Jesus said, "Come follow me,
and I will make you fish for people." 20 So
Simon and Andrew immediately left their
nets and followed him.
21 As Jesus continued walking by Lake
Galilee, he saw two other brothers, James
and John, the sons of Zebedee. They were in
a boat with their father Zebedee, mending
their nets. Jesus told them to come with him.
22 Immediately they left the boat and their
father, and they followed Jesus.

Jesus Teaches and Heals People

23 Jesus went everywhere in Galilee,
teaching in the synagogues, preaching the
Good News about the kingdom of heaven,
and healing all the people's diseases and
sicknesses. 24 The news about Jesus spread all
over Syria, and people brought all the sick to
him. They were suffering from different
kinds of diseases. Some were in great pain,
some had demons, some were epileptics,[n]
and some were paralyzed. Jesus healed all of
them. 25 Many people from Galilee, the Ten
Towns,[n] Jerusalem, Judea, and the land across
the Jordan River followed him.

Jesus Teaches the People

5 When Jesus saw the crowds, he went up
on a hill and sat down. His followers
came to him, 2 and he began to teach them,
saying:

3 "They are blessed who realize their
spiritual poverty,
for the kingdom of heaven belongs to
them.
4 They are blessed who grieve,
for God will comfort them.
5 They are blessed who are humble,
for the whole earth will be theirs.
6 They are blessed who hunger and thirst
after justice,
for they will be satisfied.
7 They are blessed who show mercy to
others,
for God will show mercy to them.
8 They are blessed whose thoughts are pure,
for they will see God.
9 They are blessed who work for peace,
for they will be called God's children.
10 They are blessed who are persecuted for
doing good,
for the kingdom of heaven belongs to
them.

11 "People will insult you and hurt you.
They will lie and say all kinds of evil things
about you because you follow me. But when
they do, you will be blessed. 12 Rejoice and be
glad, because you have a great reward
waiting for you in heaven. People did the
same evil things to the prophets who lived
before you.

You Are Like Salt and Light

13 "You are the salt of the earth. But if the
salt loses its salty taste, it cannot be made
salty again. It is good for nothing, except to
be thrown out and walked on.
14 "You are the light that gives light to the
world. A city that is built on a hill cannot be
hidden. 15 And people don't hide a light under
a bowl. They put it on a lampstand so the
light shines for all the people in the house.
16 In the same way, you should be a light for
other people. Live so that they will see the
good things you do and will praise your
Father in heaven.

The Importance of the Law

17 "Don't think that I have come to destroy
the law of Moses or the teaching of the
prophets. I have not come to destroy them
but to bring about what they said. 18 I tell
you the truth, nothing will disappear from
the law until heaven and earth are gone. Not
even the smallest letter or the smallest part
of a letter will be lost until everything has
happened. 19 Whoever refuses to obey any
command and teaches other people not
to obey that command will be the least
important in the kingdom of heaven. But
whoever obeys the commands and teaches
other people to obey them will be great in
the kingdom of heaven. 20 I tell you that if
you are no more obedient than the teachers
of the law and the Pharisees, you will never
enter the kingdom of heaven.

Jesus Teaches About Anger

21 "You have heard that it was said to our
people long ago, 'You must not murder

4:24 epileptics People with a disease that causes them sometimes to lose control of their bodies and maybe faint, shake strongly, or not be able to move.
4:25 Ten Towns In Greek, called "Decapolis." It was an area east of Lake Galilee that once had ten main towns.

anyone.[n] Anyone who murders another will be judged.' 22But I tell you, if you are angry with a brother or sister,[n] you will be judged. If you say bad things to a brother or sister, you will be judged by the council. And if you call someone a fool, you will be in danger of the fire of hell.

23"So when you offer your gift to God at the altar, and you remember that your brother or sister has something against you, 24leave your gift there at the altar. Go and make peace with that person, and then come and offer your gift.

25"If your enemy is taking you to court, become friends quickly, before you go to court. Otherwise, your enemy might turn you over to the judge, and the judge might give you to a guard to put you in jail. 26I tell you the truth, you will not leave there until you have paid everything you owe.

Jesus Teaches About Sexual Sin

27"You have heard that it was said, 'You must not be guilty of adultery.'[n] 28But I tell you that if anyone looks at a woman and wants to sin sexually with her, in his mind he has already done that sin with the woman. 29If your right eye causes you to sin, take it out and throw it away. It is better to lose one part of your body than to have your whole body thrown into hell. 30If your right hand causes you to sin, cut it off and throw it away. It is better to lose one part of your body than for your whole body to go into hell.

Jesus Teaches About Divorce

31"It was also said, 'Anyone who divorces his wife must give her a written divorce paper.'[n] 32But I tell you that anyone who divorces his wife forces her to be guilty of adultery. The only reason for a man to divorce his wife is if she has sexual relations with another man. And anyone who marries that divorced woman is guilty of adultery.

Make Promises Carefully

33"You have heard that it was said to our people long ago, 'Don't break your promises, but keep the promises you make to the Lord.'[n] 34But I tell you, never swear an oath. Don't swear an oath using the name of heaven, because heaven is God's throne. 35Don't swear an oath using the name of the earth, because the earth belongs to God. Don't swear an oath using the name of Jerusalem, because that is the city of the great King. 36Don't even swear by your own head, because you cannot make one hair on your head become white or black. 37Say only yes if you mean yes, and no if you mean no. If you say more than yes or no, it is from the Evil One.

Don't Fight Back

38"You have heard that it was said, 'An eye for an eye, and a tooth for a tooth.'[n] 39But I tell you, don't stand up against an evil person. If someone slaps you on the right cheek, turn to him the other cheek also. 40If someone wants to sue you in court and take your shirt, let him have your coat also. 41If someone forces you to go with him one mile, go with him two miles. 42If a person asks you for something, give it to him. Don't refuse to give to someone who wants to borrow from you.

Love All People

43"You have heard that it was said, 'Love your neighbor[n] and hate your enemies.' 44But I say to you, love your enemies. Pray for those who hurt you.[n] 45If you do this, you will be true children of your Father in heaven. He causes the sun to rise on good people and on evil people, and he sends rain to those who do right and to those who do wrong. 46If you love only the people who love you, you will get no reward. Even the tax collectors do that. 47And if you are nice only to your friends, you are no better than other people. Even those who don't know God are nice to their friends. 48So you must be perfect, just as your Father in heaven is perfect.

Jesus Teaches About Giving

6 "Be careful! When you do good things, don't do them in front of people to be

5:21 'You . . . anyone.' Quotation from Exodus 20:13; Deuteronomy 5:17. **5:22 sister** Some Greek copies continue, "without a reason." **5:27 'You . . . adultery.'** Quotation from Exodus 20:14; Deuteronomy 5:18. **5:31 'Anyone . . . divorce paper.'** Quotation from Deuteronomy 24:1. **5:33 'Don't . . . Lord.'** This refers to Leviticus 19:12; Numbers 30:2; Deuteronomy 23:21. **5:38 'An eye . . . tooth.'** Quotation from Exodus 21:24; Leviticus 24:20; Deuteronomy 19:21. **5:43 'Love your neighbor'** Quotation from Leviticus 19:18. **5:44 you** Some Greek copies continue, "Bless those who curse you, do good to those who hate you." Compare Luke 6:28.

seen by them. If you do that, you will
have no reward from your Father in
heaven.
2“When you give to the poor, don’t be
like the hypocrites. They blow trumpets in
the synagogues and on the streets so that
people will see them and honor them. I tell
you the truth, those hypocrites already have
their full reward. 3So when you give to the
poor, don’t let anyone know what you are
doing. 4Your giving should be done in secret.
Your Father can see what is done in secret,
and he will reward you.

Jesus Teaches About Prayer

5“When you pray, don’t be like the
hypocrites. They love to stand in the
synagogues and on the street corners and
pray so people will see them. I tell you the
truth, they already have their full reward.
6When you pray, you should go into your
room and close the door and pray to your
Father who cannot be seen. Your Father
can see what is done in secret, and he will
reward you.
7“And when you pray, don’t be like those
people who don’t know God. They continue
saying things that mean nothing, thinking
that God will hear them because of their
many words. 8Don’t be like them, because
your Father knows the things you need
before you ask him. 9So when you pray, you
should pray like this:
‘Our Father in heaven,
may your name always be kept holy.
10May your kingdom come
and what you want be done,
here on earth as it is in heaven.
11Give us the food we need for each day.
12Forgive us for our sins,
just as we have forgiven those who
sinned against us.
13And do not cause us to be tempted,
but save us from the Evil One.’ [The
kingdom, the power, and the glory
are yours forever. Amen.][n]
14Yes, if you forgive others for their sins,
your Father in heaven will also forgive you
for your sins. 15But if you don’t forgive
others, your Father in heaven will not
forgive your sins.

Jesus Teaches About Worship

16“When you fast,[n] don’t put on a sad face
like the hypocrites. They make their faces
look sad to show people they are fasting. I
tell you the truth, those hypocrites already
have their full reward. 17So when you fast,
comb your hair and wash your face. 18Then
people will not know that you are fasting,
but your Father, whom you cannot see, will
see you. Your Father sees what is done in
secret, and he will reward you.

God Is More Important than Money

19“Don’t store treasures for yourselves
here on earth where moths and rust will
destroy them and thieves can break in and
steal them. 20But store your treasures in
heaven where they cannot be destroyed by
moths or rust and where thieves cannot
break in and steal them. 21Your heart will be
where your treasure is.
22“The eye is a light for the body. If your
eyes are good, your whole body will be full
of light. 23But if your eyes are evil, your
whole body will be full of darkness. And if
the only light you have is really darkness,
then you have the worst darkness.
24“No one can serve two masters. The
person will hate one master and love the
other, or will follow one master and refuse to
follow the other. You cannot serve both God
and worldly riches.

Don’t Worry

25“So I tell you, don’t worry about the food
or drink you need to live, or about the clothes
you need for your body. Life is more than
food, and the body is more than clothes.
26Look at the birds in the air. They don’t
plant or harvest or store food in barns, but
your heavenly Father feeds them. And you
know that you are worth much more than
the birds. 27You cannot add any time to your
life by worrying about it.
28“And why do you worry about clothes?
Look at how the lilies in the field grow. They
don’t work or make clothes for themselves.
29But I tell you that even Solomon with his
riches was not dressed as beautifully as one of
these flowers. 30God clothes the grass in the
field, which is alive today but tomorrow is

6:13 The . . . Amen. Some Greek copies do not contain the bracketed text.
6:16 fast The people would give up eating for a special time of prayer and worship to God. It was also done to show sadness and disappointment.

thrown into the fire. So you can be even more
sure that God will clothe you. Don't have so
little faith! 31Don't worry and say, 'What will
we eat?' or 'What will we drink?' or 'What
will we wear?' 32The people who don't know
God keep trying to get these things, and your
Father in heaven knows you need them.
33Seek first God's kingdom and what God
wants. Then all your other needs will be met
as well. 34So don't worry about tomorrow,
because tomorrow will have its own worries.
Each day has enough trouble of its own.

Be Careful About Judging Others

7 "Don't judge others, or you will be
judged. 2You will be judged in the same
way that you judge others, and the amount
you give to others will be given to you.
3"Why do you notice the little piece of
dust in your friend's eye, but you don't
notice the big piece of wood in your own
eye? 4How can you say to your friend, 'Let
me take that little piece of dust out of your
eye'? Look at yourself! You still have that
big piece of wood in your own eye. 5You
hypocrite! First, take the wood out of your
own eye. Then you will see clearly to take
the dust out of your friend's eye.
6"Don't give holy things to dogs, and don't
throw your pearls before pigs. Pigs will only
trample on them, and dogs will turn to
attack you.

Ask God for What You Need

7"Ask, and God will give to you. Search,
and you will find. Knock, and the door will
open for you. 8Yes, everyone who asks will
receive. Everyone who searches will find.
And everyone who knocks will have the
door opened.
9"If your children ask for bread, which of
you would give them a stone? 10Or if your
children ask for a fish, would you give them a
snake? 11Even though you are bad, you know
how to give good gifts to your children. How
much more your heavenly Father will give
good things to those who ask him!

The Most Important Rule

12"Do to others what you want them to do
to you. This is the meaning of the law of
Moses and the teaching of the prophets.

devotion 262

MATTHEW 6:33

HOW TO GET EVERYTHING YOU NEED

I like to think things through. You know—process the options, weigh the evidence, and then come up with short directives that seem logical to me. The reason and logic of Matthew 6:33 always bring me back to spiritual center. These words from Jesus always point me toward what really matters. About twenty-five years ago, I chose this passage as my life verse because it never fails to direct my heart. It instantly realigns my priorities. I am reminded to focus on the kingdom, think about the kingdom, and work for the kingdom. And then there is the amazing promise attached to this instruction: all the other things you need will be given to you. What things? All the things you need to live. Whatever you will need for you body. Food. Clothes. Everything you will need for life and anything you are tempted to worry about.

The journey of following Jesus with our lives involves two dimensions: Christ's divinity plus us doing our part to align with his will for us. Jesus' words in Matthew 6 come with both a challenge and some instructions: focus your heart. Ask God what's next. Rearrange your priorities. Actively work with your hands and your mind for his glory. And then, at the end of everything you can do, expect God's divine provision for everything you need. Maybe God will use these very words to realign your life this day. Let him teach you to want the kingdom more than anything.

The Way to Heaven Is Hard

[13]"Enter through the narrow gate. The
gate is wide and the road is wide that leads
to hell, and many people enter through that
gate. [14]But the gate is small and the road is
narrow that leads to true life. Only a few
people find that road.

People Know You by Your Actions

[15]"Be careful of false prophets. They come
to you looking gentle like sheep, but they
are really dangerous like wolves. [16]You will
know these people by what they do. Grapes
don't come from thornbushes, and figs don't
come from thorny weeds. [17]In the same way,
every good tree produces good fruit, but a
bad tree produces bad fruit. [18]A good tree
cannot produce bad fruit, and a bad tree
cannot produce good fruit. [19]Every tree that
does not produce good fruit is cut down and
thrown into the fire. [20]In the same way, you
will know these false prophets by what
they do.

[21]"Not all those who say 'You are our Lord'
will enter the kingdom of heaven. The only
people who will enter the kingdom of heaven
are those who do what my Father in heaven
wants. [22]On the last day many people will
say to me, 'Lord, Lord, we spoke for you, and
through you we forced out demons and did
many miracles.' [23]Then I will tell them
clearly, 'Get away from me, you who do evil.
I never knew you.'

Two Kinds of People

[24]"Everyone who hears my words and
obeys them is like a wise man who built his
house on rock. [25]It rained hard, the floods
came, and the winds blew and hit that
house. But it did not fall, because it was built
on rock. [26]Everyone who hears my words
and does not obey them is like a foolish man
who built his house on sand. [27]It rained
hard, the floods came, and the winds blew
and hit that house, and it fell with a big
crash."

[28]When Jesus finished saying these
things, the people were amazed at his
teaching, [29]because he did not teach like
their teachers of the law. He taught like a
person who had authority.

Jesus Heals a Sick Man

8 When Jesus came down from the hill,
great crowds followed him. [2]Then a man
with a skin disease came to Jesus. The man
bowed down before him and said, "Lord, you
can heal me if you will."

[3]Jesus reached out his hand and touched
the man and said, "I will. Be healed!" And
immediately the man was healed from his
disease. [4]Then Jesus said to him, "Don't tell
anyone about this. But go and show yourself
to the priest[n] and offer the gift Moses
commanded[n] for people who are made well.
This will show the people what I have done."

Jesus Heals a Soldier's Servant

[5]When Jesus entered the city of
Capernaum, an army officer came to him,
begging for help. [6]The officer said, "Lord, my
servant is at home in bed. He can't move his
body and is in much pain."

[7]Jesus said to the officer, "I will go and
heal him."

[8]The officer answered, "Lord, I am not
worthy for you to come into my house. You
only need to command it, and my servant
will be healed. [9]I, too, am a man under the
authority of others, and I have soldiers under
my command. I tell one soldier, 'Go,' and he
goes. I tell another soldier, 'Come,' and he
comes. I say to my servant, 'Do this,' and my
servant does it.

[10]When Jesus heard this, he was amazed.
He said to those who were following him, "I
tell you the truth, this is the greatest faith I
have found, even in Israel. [11]Many people
will come from the east and from the west
and will sit and eat with Abraham, Isaac, and
Jacob in the kingdom of heaven. [12]But those
people who should be in the kingdom will
be thrown outside into the darkness, where
people will cry and grind their teeth with
pain."

[13]Then Jesus said to the officer, "Go home.
Your servant will be healed just as you
believed he would." And his servant was
healed that same hour.

Jesus Heals Many People

[14]When Jesus went to Peter's house, he
saw that Peter's mother-in-law was sick in

8:4 show . . . priest The Law of Moses said a priest must say when a Jewish person with a skin disease was well.
8:4 Moses commanded Read about this in Leviticus 14:1–32.

bed with a fever. [15]Jesus touched her hand,
and the fever left her. Then she stood up and
began to serve Jesus.
[16]That evening people brought to Jesus
many who had demons. Jesus spoke and the
demons left them, and he healed all the sick.
[17]He did these things to bring about what
Isaiah the prophet had said:

"He took our suffering on him
and carried our diseases." *Isaiah 53:4*

People Want to Follow Jesus

[18]When Jesus saw the crowd around him,
he told his followers to go to the other side
of the lake. [19]Then a teacher of the law came
to Jesus and said, "Teacher, I will follow you
any place you go."
[20]Jesus said to him, "The foxes have holes
to live in, and the birds have nests, but the
Son of Man has no place to rest his head."
[21]Another man, one of Jesus' followers,
said to him, "Lord, first let me go and bury
my father."
[22]But Jesus told him, "Follow me, and let
the people who are dead bury their own
dead."

Jesus Calms a Storm

[23]Jesus got into a boat, and his followers
went with him. [24]A great storm arose on the
lake so that waves covered the boat, but
Jesus was sleeping. [25]His followers went to
him and woke him, saying, "Lord, save us!
We will drown!"
[26]Jesus answered, "Why are you afraid?
You don't have enough faith." Then Jesus got
up and gave a command to the wind and the
waves, and it became completely calm.
[27]The men were amazed and said, "What
kind of man is this? Even the wind and the
waves obey him!"

Jesus Heals Two Men with Demons

[28]When Jesus arrived at the other side of
the lake in the area of the Gadarene[n] people,
two men who had demons in them met him.
These men lived in the burial caves and were
so dangerous that people could not use the
road by those caves. [29]They shouted, "What
do you want with us, Son of God? Did you
come here to torture us before the right
time?"
[30]Near that place there was a large herd of
pigs feeding. [31]The demons begged Jesus, "If
you make us leave these men, please send us
into that herd of pigs."
[32]Jesus said to them, "Go!" So the demons
left the men and went into the pigs. Then
the whole herd rushed down the hill into
the lake and were drowned. [33]The herdsmen
ran away and went into town, where they
told about all of this and what had happened
to the men who had demons. [34]Then the
whole town went out to see Jesus. When
they saw him, they begged him to leave their
area.

Jesus Heals a Paralyzed Man

9 Jesus got into a boat and went back
across the lake to his own town. [2]Some
people brought to Jesus a man who was
paralyzed and lying on a mat. When Jesus
saw the faith of these people, he said to the
paralyzed man, "Be encouraged, young man.
Your sins are forgiven."
[3]Some of the teachers of the law said to
themselves, "This man speaks as if he were
God. That is blasphemy!"[n]
[4]Knowing their thoughts, Jesus said,
"Why are you thinking evil thoughts?
[5]Which is easier: to say, 'Your sins are
forgiven,' or to tell him, 'Stand up and walk'?
[6]But I will prove to you that the Son of Man
has authority on earth to forgive sins." Then
Jesus said to the paralyzed man, "Stand up,
take your mat, and go home." [7]And the man
stood up and went home. [8]When the people
saw this, they were amazed and praised God
for giving power like this to human beings.

Jesus Chooses Matthew

[9]When Jesus was leaving, he saw a man
named Matthew sitting in the tax collector's
booth. Jesus said to him, "Follow me," and he
stood up and followed Jesus.
[10]As Jesus was having dinner at Matthew's
house, many tax collectors and "sinners"
came and ate with Jesus and his followers.
[11]When the Pharisees saw this, they asked
Jesus' followers, "Why does your teacher eat
with tax collectors and sinners?"
[12]When Jesus heard them, he said, "It is
not the healthy people who need a doctor,

8:28 Gadarene From Gadara, an area southeast of Lake Galilee. The exact location is uncertain and some Greek copies read "Gergesene"; others read "Gerasene." **9:3 blasphemy** Saying things against God or not showing respect for God.

but the sick. 13Go and learn what this means: 'I want kindness more than I want animal sacrifices.'[n] I did not come to invite good people but to invite sinners."

Jesus' Followers Are Criticized

14Then the followers of John[n] came to Jesus and said, "Why do we and the Pharisees often fast[n] for a certain time, but your followers don't?"

15Jesus answered, "The friends of the bridegroom are not sad while he is with them. But the time will come when the bridegroom will be taken from them, and then they will fast.

16"No one sews a patch of unshrunk cloth over a hole in an old coat. If he does, the patch will shrink and pull away from the coat, making the hole worse. 17Also, people never pour new wine into old leather bags. Otherwise, the bags will break, the wine will spill, and the wine bags will be ruined. But people always pour new wine into new wine bags. Then both will continue to be good."

Jesus Gives Life to a Dead Girl and Heals a Sick Woman

18While Jesus was saying these things, a leader of the synagogue came to him. He bowed down before Jesus and said, "My daughter has just died. But if you come and lay your hand on her, she will live again." 19So Jesus and his followers stood up and went with the leader.

20Then a woman who had been bleeding for twelve years came behind Jesus and touched the edge of his coat. 21She was thinking, "If I can just touch his clothes, I will be healed."

22Jesus turned and saw the woman and said, "Be encouraged, dear woman. You are made well because you believed." And the woman was healed from that moment on.

23Jesus continued along with the leader and went into his house. There he saw the funeral musicians and many people crying. 24Jesus said, "Go away. The girl is not dead, only asleep." But the people laughed at him. 25After the crowd had been thrown out of the house, Jesus went into the girl's room and took hold of her hand, and she stood up. 26The news about this spread all around the area.

Jesus Heals More People

27When Jesus was leaving there, two blind men followed him. They cried out, "Have mercy on us, Son of David!"

28After Jesus went inside, the blind men went with him. He asked the men, "Do you believe that I can make you see again?"

They answered, "Yes, Lord."

29Then Jesus touched their eyes and said, "Because you believe I can make you see again, it will happen." 30Then the men were able to see. But Jesus warned them strongly, saying, "Don't tell anyone about this." 31But the blind men left and spread the news about Jesus all around that area.

32When the two men were leaving, some people brought another man to Jesus. This man could not talk because he had a demon in him. 33After Jesus forced the demon to leave the man, he was able to speak. The crowd was amazed and said, "We have never seen anything like this in Israel."

34But the Pharisees said, "The prince of demons is the one that gives him power to force demons out."

35Jesus traveled through all the towns and villages, teaching in their synagogues, preaching the Good News about the kingdom, and healing all kinds of diseases and sicknesses. 36When he saw the crowds, he felt sorry for them because they were hurting and helpless, like sheep without a shepherd. 37Jesus said to his followers, "There are many people to harvest but only a few workers to help harvest them. 38Pray to the Lord, who owns the harvest, that he will send more workers to gather his harvest."[n]

Jesus Sends Out His Apostles

10 Jesus called his twelve followers together and gave them authority to drive out evil spirits and to heal every kind of disease and sickness. 2These are the names of the twelve apostles: Simon (also called Peter) and his brother Andrew; James son of Zebedee, and his brother John; 3Philip and Bartholomew; Thomas and Matthew, the tax

9:13 'I want . . . sacrifices.' Quotation from Hosea 6:6. **9:14 John** John the Baptist, who preached to people about Christ's coming (Matthew 3, Luke 3). **9:14 fast** The people would give up eating for a special time of prayer and worship to God. It was also done to show sadness and disappointment. **9:37–38 "There are . . . harvest."** As a farmer sends workers to harvest the grain, Jesus sends his followers to bring people to God.

devotion 263

MATTHEW 9:35–38

GET YOUR HANDS IN SOME SOIL

The words of Jesus are rich with wisdom. I never pass by a scripture without asking the Holy Spirit to show me everything that he wants me to know. Jesus wanted us to know that there were always going to be needs in the body of Christ, and there would always be a need to grow those up who have professed Christ as their Savior. As the Holy Spirit calls people and draws them to himself, they are like seedlings that have been planted and watered. They need to be trained up in the mature things of Christ by having those who have walked that same journey encourage them and build them up in the faith.

Have you asked the Lord to use you to mentor a young person or maybe spend time with someone that is searching? I want to challenge you to a really cool thing: ask the Lord to use you to encourage a total stranger today. Somewhere and somehow, in the ordinary circumstances of your day, the Lord will put that person right in front of you, and it will be clear that he is saying, "This is the one I have for you." It will be so exciting. Get out of your comfort zone and be brave. I can assure you that when you walk away, there will be a bounce in your step knowing that you worked the field just a bit to prepare for the harvest.

collector; James son of Alphaeus, and
Thaddaeus; 4Simon the Zealot and Judas
Iscariot, who turned against Jesus.
5Jesus sent out these twelve men with the
following order: "Don't go to the non-Jewish
people or to any town where the Samaritans
live. 6But go to the people of Israel, who are
like lost sheep. 7When you go, preach this:
'The kingdom of heaven is near.' 8Heal the
sick, raise the dead to life again, heal those
who have skin diseases, and force demons
out of people. I give you these powers freely,
so help other people freely. 9Don't carry any
money with you—gold or silver or copper.
10Don't carry a bag or extra clothes or
sandals or a walking stick. Workers should
be given what they need.
11"When you enter a city or town, find
some worthy person there and stay in that
home until you leave. 12When you enter
that home, say, 'Peace be with you.' 13If the
people there welcome you, let your peace
stay there. But if they don't welcome you,
take back the peace you wished for them.
14And if a home or town refuses to welcome
you or listen to you, leave that place and
shake its dust off your feet.[n] 15I tell you the
truth, on the Judgment Day it will be better
for the towns of Sodom and Gomorrah[n] than
for the people of that town.

Jesus Warns His Apostles

16"Listen, I am sending you out like sheep
among wolves. So be as clever as snakes and
as innocent as doves. 17Be careful of people,
because they will arrest you and take you to
court and whip you in their synagogues.
18Because of me you will be taken to stand
before governors and kings, and you will tell
them and the non-Jewish people about me.
19When you are arrested, don't worry about
what to say or how to say it. At that time you
will be given the things to say. 20It will not
really be you speaking but the Spirit of your
Father speaking through you.
21"Brothers will give their own brothers to

10:14 shake . . . feet A warning. It showed that they had rejected these people.
10:15 Sodom and Gomorrah Two cities that God destroyed because the people were so evil.

be killed, and fathers will give their own children to be killed. Children will fight against their own parents and have them put to death. 22 All people will hate you because you follow me, but those people who keep their faith until the end will be saved. 23 When you are treated badly in one city, run to another city. I tell you the truth, you will not finish going through all the cities of Israel before the Son of Man comes.

24 "A student is not better than his teacher, and a servant is not better than his master. 25 A student should be satisfied to become like his teacher; a servant should be satisfied to become like his master. If the head of the family is called Beelzebul, then the other members of the family will be called worse names!

Fear God, Not People

26 "So don't be afraid of those people, because everything that is hidden will be shown. Everything that is secret will be made known. 27 I tell you these things in the dark, but I want you to tell them in the light. What you hear whispered in your ear you should shout from the housetops. 28 Don't be afraid of people, who can kill the body but cannot kill the soul. The only one you should fear is the one who can destroy the soul and the body in hell. 29 Two sparrows cost only a penny, but not even one of them can die without your Father's knowing it. 30 God even knows how many hairs are on your head. 31 So don't be afraid. You are worth much more than many sparrows.

Tell People About Your Faith

32 "All those who stand before others and say they believe in me, I will say before my Father in heaven that they belong to me. 33 But all who stand before others and say they do not believe in me, I will say before my Father in heaven that they do not belong to me.

34 "Don't think that I came to bring peace to the earth. I did not come to bring peace, but a sword. 35 I have come so that

'a son will be against his father,
a daughter will be against her mother,
a daughter-in-law will be against her mother-in-law.
36 A person's enemies will be members of his own family.' *Micah 7:6*

37 "Those who love their father or mother more than they love me are not worthy to be my followers. Those who love their son or daughter more than they love me are not worthy to be my followers. 38 Whoever is not willing to carry the cross and follow me is not worthy of me. 39 Those who try to hold on to their lives will give up true life. Those who give up their lives for me will hold on to true life. 40 Whoever accepts you also accepts me, and whoever accepts me also accepts the One who sent me. 41 Whoever meets a prophet and accepts him will receive the reward of a prophet. And whoever accepts a good person because that person is good will receive the reward of a good person. 42 Those who give one of these little ones a cup of cold water because they are my followers will truly get their reward."

Jesus and John the Baptist

11 After Jesus finished telling these things to his twelve followers, he left there and went to the towns in Galilee to teach and preach.

2 John the Baptist was in prison, but he heard about what the Christ was doing. So John sent some of his followers to Jesus. 3 They asked him, "Are you the One who is to come, or should we wait for someone else?"

4 Jesus answered them, "Go tell John what you hear and see: 5 The blind can see, the crippled can walk, and people with skin diseases are healed. The deaf can hear, the dead are raised to life, and the Good News is preached to the poor. 6 Those who do not stumble in their faith because of me are blessed."

7 As John's followers were leaving, Jesus began talking to the people about John. Jesus said, "What did you go out into the desert to see? A reed[n] blown by the wind? 8 What did you go out to see? A man dressed in fine clothes? No, those who wear fine clothes live in kings' palaces. 9 So why did you go out? To see a prophet? Yes, and I tell you, John is more than a prophet. 10 This was written about him:

'I will send my messenger ahead of you,
who will prepare the way for you.' *Malachi 3:1*

11:7 reed It means that John was not ordinary or weak like grass blown by the wind.

sexual purity

I am a single woman. Some would say that I'm in the prime of my life, and I'd have to agree. These years are exciting to me. But they are not without sadness or disappointment. There is a painful loneliness that can come to the feminine soul. We were made for romantic, intimate love, and without it, our hearts become weary. Longing magnifies the emptiness until it is grief.

Some well-meaning people have said to me, "God will be your husband." To which I always want to reply, "You're a nerd," but I haven't. I realize people mean well and want to give comfort, but they don't have words for what they haven't experienced or the emptiness they've long forgotten.

Here's what I know: God made me for the arms of a man. His design. His idea. He is very aware that my heart longs for romance and physical intimacy. So here's my prayer: "Father, here's my sexuality. I lay my romantic desires at your feet—Paris in the fall and tropical island getaways. I'm entrusting my longings to you, the God that I love. Would you keep all the treasure in my heart safe until your appointed time? Would you return to me with multiplied joy all the years that I wait? And God, if it would be okay with you, I'd like to have sex with a loving husband before menopause."

I believe with my whole life that while we wait, choosing sexual purity, God can be trusted to protect and defend the treasure of the woman he loves. I also believe that the act of entrusting is an act of submission. To keep yourself in purity is to submit to God as Lord.

THINK ABOUT IT: Are you willing to entrust your sexuality to God and believe that he will be faithful?
What do you need to do or change in your life to actively entrust your purity?
Do you believe that God can multiply anything you think you've missed and give you more? How?

DIG DEEPER: Psalm 62:8 (trust), John 14:16–17 (spiritual guidance), and Ephesians 6:13 (standing strong)

distractions

I went through a mini-midlife crisis a few years ago and became the proud owner of a black and silver Harley-Davidson motorcycle. My insurance premiums shot up, along with a lot of church eyebrows. I've got just enough rebel in me to enjoy bucking convention and bending the rules! Plus, I'm learning some great lessons.

For instance, on my motorcycle, I notice little things that seem insignificant when I'm driving a car. Little things like gravel in the road, oil spots, dogs with bad attitudes, and especially large vehicles. I now smile broadly at big-car drivers hoping my friendliness will encourage them to stay in their lane—but I still watch them like a hawk. You never know when one of them is going to accidentally turn you into a hood ornament! Recently, a blue-haired elderly woman didn't stop at a red light and zoomed right in front of me in her land yacht. Fortunately, I was paying attention and slammed on my brakes before becoming another motorcycle fatality. I pulled off the road in order to collect myself and thank God for his protection. That near miss was a powerful reminder of how important it is to watch where we're going. Physically *and* spiritually.

Sometimes I find myself so distracted with the busyness of living that I neglect to pay close enough attention to my surroundings. And it's surprising how quickly sin slides into a preoccupied life. I've justified watching movies that normally would make me blush and make a beeline for the exit, I've let my mouth run ahead of my wisdom, and I've spent far too little time alone with the Lover of my soul. I'm learning that I have to be very intentional about being alert, or else I'm going to get sideswiped by a runaway case of rebellion!

THINK ABOUT IT: What are the most common things that distract you from God? What's a practical example of spiritual "caffeine"—something that can help keep us from being drowsy, drifting Christians?

DIG DEEPER: Ephesians 6:10–18 (armor), Hebrews 2:1 (pay attention), 1 Peter 5:8–9 (the devil), and 2 Peter 3:17–18 (truth)

childlessness

Most women I know have children. In fact, at this very moment I can only think of two off the top of my head that do not. With the exception of my two fur balls, Abbie and Zacky, my husband and I do not have children. The story of our inability to have children is much longer than this space will allow, but it's safe to say that short of an Immaculate Conception, we will need to be content with little black noses with soft fur to love.

It feels important to share my heart with you as a childless woman married to a pastor. Every Sunday of my life, someone new comes to the church. I introduce myself, welcome them, and without fail their first question is, "So how many children do you have?" I have mastered my response with a giant smile. I just tell them we could not have children. I am not kidding you—I have this exact conversation every single week of my life!

I planned on having children. We went through great strides to make that happen, but the Lord decided differently. There are those who feel they are less godly if their physical body has not birthed children. I am very fortunate that peace resides in my heart to accept the course the Lord planned out for us as a husband and wife. We all have the choice to either accept with trust what the Lord has for us or be consumed with bitterness and disappointment every time something does not turn out as we planned. I am in love with my Lord, and he is passionately in love with me—and he is passionately in love with you, too. Trust him as he alone decides the course of your journey.

THINK ABOUT IT: Is your heart truly free and content with where the Lord has you right now?
Is your spirit peaceful and quiet within you?

DIG DEEPER: Proverbs 16:9 (God's sovereignty), Proverbs 17:1 (strife), Matthew 6:33 (spiritual priorities), and Philippians 4:11–13 (contentment)

hope

We drove to the hospital that morning as the sun came up over the horizon. "What a beautiful day to be born," my husband said.

"Do you think it will be a boy or a girl?" I asked him as we got to the hospital to be prepped for a C-section. As we waited, I said, "I wish my sister were here today."

"She's just too weak from the cancer, honey, but I know she would be here if she could," he replied.

The next thing I knew, I was in recovery, and Stephan was standing beside me with tears in his eyes and a smile on his face. "It's a girl and she has red hair just like your sister," he whispered. Fear crept into my heart. God was giving me a replacement because he was going to take my sister.

"I don't want her," I said through my tears. "I want my sister to live." We made our way up to the room and waited for our daughter to be brought to us. They placed her in my arms, and love flooded my heart. "I think we should name her Hope," Stephan said, "because our hope is in the Lord when we're hurting."

"Yes," I agreed, "she is our Hope."

Three days later, I placed Hope in the arms of my sister, Julie. She just held her and told her how much she loved her. They lay in bed together and slept while I prayed for the redheads that I loved so much. My sister died the next day. I cradled Hope in my arms at the funeral and thanked the Lord for eternal hope. I know that one day I will walk beside the crystal sea in heaven with Julie on one side and Hope on the other and know that the Lord is good.

THINK ABOUT IT: Is the Lord your hope when you're hurting? Do you believe in eternal life?

DIG DEEPER: John 14:1–3 (heaven), 1 Peter 1:3–5 (ultimate salvation), and Revelation 21:4 (new heaven and earth)

[11]I tell you the truth, John the Baptist is
greater than any other person ever born, but
even the least important person in the
kingdom of heaven is greater than John.
[12]Since the time John the Baptist came until
now, the kingdom of heaven has been going
forward in strength, and people have been
trying to take it by force. [13]All the prophets
and the law of Moses told about what would
happen until the time John came. [14]And if
you will believe what they said, you will
believe that John is Elijah, whom they said
would come. [15]Let those with ears use them
and listen!

[16]"What can I say about the people of this
time? What are they like? They are like
children sitting in the marketplace, who call
out to each other,

[17]'We played music for you, but you did not
dance;
we sang a sad song, but you did not cry.'

[18]John came and did not eat or drink like
other people. So people say, 'He has a
demon.' [19]The Son of Man came, eating and
drinking, and people say, 'Look at him! He
eats too much and drinks too much wine,
and he is a friend of tax collectors and
sinners.' But wisdom is proved to be right by
what she does."

Jesus Warns Unbelievers

[20]Then Jesus criticized the cities where
he did most of his miracles, because the
people did not change their lives and stop
sinning. [21]He said, "How terrible for you,
Korazin! How terrible for you, Bethsaida!
If the same miracles I did in you had
happened in Tyre and Sidon,[n] those people
would have changed their lives a long time
ago. They would have worn rough cloth and
put ashes on themselves to show they had
changed. [22]But I tell you, on the Judgment
Day it will be better for Tyre and Sidon than
for you. [23]And you, Capernaum,[n] will you be
lifted up to heaven? No, you will be thrown
down to the depths. If the miracles I did in
you had happened in Sodom,[n] its people
would have stopped sinning, and it would
still be a city today. [24]But I tell you, on the
Judgment Day it will be better for Sodom
than for you."

Jesus Offers Rest to People

[25]At that time Jesus said, "I praise you,
Father, Lord of heaven and earth, because
you have hidden these things from the
people who are wise and smart. But you
have shown them to those who are like little
children. [26]Yes, Father, this is what you really
wanted.

[27]"My Father has given me all things. No
one knows the Son, except the Father. And
no one knows the Father, except the Son and
those whom the Son chooses to tell.

[28]"Come to me, all of you who are tired
and have heavy loads, and I will give you
rest. [29]Accept my teachings and learn from
me, because I am gentle and humble in
spirit, and you will find rest for your lives.
[30]The burden that I ask you to accept is easy;
the load I give you to carry is light."

Jesus Is Lord of the Sabbath

12 At that time Jesus was walking
through some fields of grain on a
Sabbath day. His followers were hungry, so
they began to pick the grain and eat it.
[2]When the Pharisees saw this, they said to
Jesus, "Look! Your followers are doing what
is unlawful to do on the Sabbath day."

[3]Jesus answered, "Have you not read what
David did when he and the people with him
were hungry? [4]He went into God's house,
and he and those with him ate the holy
bread, which was lawful only for priests to
eat. [5]And have you not read in the law of
Moses that on every Sabbath day the priests
in the Temple break this law about the
Sabbath day? But the priests are not wrong
for doing that. [6]I tell you that there is
something here that is greater than the
Temple. [7]The Scripture says, 'I want
kindness more than I want animal sacrifices.'[n]
You don't really know what those words
mean. If you understood them, you would
not judge those who have done nothing
wrong.

[8]"So the Son of Man is Lord of the Sabbath
day."

Jesus Heals a Man's Hand

[9]Jesus left there and went into their
synagogue, [10]where there was a man with a

11:21 Tyre and Sidon Towns where wicked people lived. **11:21, 23 Korazin . . . Bethsaida . . . Capernaum** Towns by Lake Galilee where Jesus preached to the people. **11:23 Sodom** A city that God destroyed because the people were so evil. **12:7 I . . . sacrifices.** Quotation from Hosea 6:6.

devotion 264

MATTHEW 11:29–30

EXHAUSTED AND OVERWHELMED

We live in a culture that is in constant motion. If you're busy and productive, then you feel important. We want those around us to think we're the best mothers, daughters, and wives on the planet. But we too often fill our lives with so many activities and responsibilities that we're overwhelmed. Years ago, I read a book called *Margins*, which changed my life. The premise of the book is that we all need margins in our lives. If you look at a typed page without margins, it is hard to read. When we fill our lives to capacity, we have no room left for the unexpected. We quickly become overwhelmed when the littlest thing is thrown to us. We also have no time to spend with God.

Jesus told his followers to find rest. We often think of rest as being lazy. If I told you I spent the day under a tree reading a good book, you might say, "Must be nice." Jesus doesn't want us to be running around exhausted and overwhelmed. He wants us to have time in our lives to listen to worship music or read a good book. He also wants us to have time to enjoy his creation, laugh with our kids, or go on an adventure with a friend. If we are in constant motion, we miss out on the most important things in life. Are you filling up your margins, carrying more than the Lord has asked of you? Find rest in him.

crippled hand. They were looking for a
reason to accuse Jesus, so they asked him, "Is
it right to heal on the Sabbath day?"[n]
11 Jesus answered, "If any of you has a
sheep, and it falls into a ditch on the Sabbath
day, you will help it out of the ditch. 12 Surely
a human being is more important than a
sheep. So it is lawful to do good things on
the Sabbath day."
13 Then Jesus said to the man with the
crippled hand, "Hold out your hand." The
man held out his hand, and it became well
again, like the other hand. 14 But the
Pharisees left and made plans to kill Jesus.

Jesus Is God's Chosen Servant

15 Jesus knew what the Pharisees were
doing, so he left that place. Many people
followed him, and he healed all who were
sick. 16 But Jesus warned the people not to tell
who he was. 17 He did these things to bring
about what Isaiah the prophet had said:

18 "Here is my servant whom I have chosen.
I love him, and I am pleased with him.
I will put my Spirit upon him,
and he will tell of my justice to all
people.
19 He will not argue or cry out;
no one will hear his voice in the
streets.
20 He will not break a crushed blade of grass
or put out even a weak flame
until he makes justice win the victory.
21 In him will the non-Jewish people find
hope." *Isaiah 42:1–4*

Jesus' Power Is from God

22 Then some people brought to Jesus a
man who was blind and could not talk,
because he had a demon. Jesus healed the
man so that he could talk and see. 23 All the
people were amazed and said, "Perhaps this
man is the Son of David!"
24 When the Pharisees heard this, they
said, "Jesus uses the power of Beelzebul, the
ruler of demons, to force demons out of
people."
25 Jesus knew what the Pharisees were

12:10 Is it right . . . day? It was against Jewish Law to work on the Sabbath day.

thinking, so he said to them, "Every kingdom that is divided against itself will be destroyed. And any city or family that is divided against itself will not continue. 26And if Satan forces out himself, then Satan is divided against himself, and his kingdom will not continue. 27You say that I use the power of Beelzebul to force out demons. If that is true, then what power do your people use to force out demons? So they will be your judges. 28But if I use the power of God's Spirit to force out demons, then the kingdom of God has come to you.

29"If anyone wants to enter a strong person's house and steal his things, he must first tie up the strong person. Then he can steal the things from the house.

30"Whoever is not with me is against me. Whoever does not work with me is working against me. 31So I tell you, people can be forgiven for every sin and everything they say against God. But whoever speaks against the Holy Spirit will not be forgiven. 32Anyone who speaks against the Son of Man can be forgiven, but anyone who speaks against the Holy Spirit will not be forgiven, now or in the future.

People Know You by Your Words

33"If you want good fruit, you must make the tree good. If your tree is not good, it will have bad fruit. A tree is known by the kind of fruit it produces. 34You snakes! You are evil people, so how can you say anything good? The mouth speaks the things that are in the heart. 35Good people have good things in their hearts, and so they say good things. But evil people have evil in their hearts, so they say evil things. 36And I tell you that on the Judgment Day people will be responsible for every careless thing they have said. 37The words you have said will be used to judge you. Some of your words will prove you right, but some of your words will prove you guilty."

The People Ask for a Miracle

38Then some of the Pharisees and teachers of the law answered Jesus, saying, "Teacher, we want to see you work a miracle as a sign."

39Jesus answered, "Evil and sinful people are the ones who want to see a miracle for a sign. But no sign will be given to them, except the sign of the prophet Jonah. 40Jonah was in the stomach of the big fish for three days and three nights. In the same way, the Son of Man will be in the grave three days and three nights. 41On the Judgment Day the people from Nineveh[n] will stand up with you people who live now, and they will show that you are guilty. When Jonah preached to them, they were sorry and changed their lives. And I tell you that someone greater than Jonah is here. 42On the Judgment Day, the Queen of the South[n] will stand up with you people who live today. She will show that you are guilty, because she came from far away to listen to Solomon's wise teaching. And I tell you that someone greater than Solomon is here.

People Today Are Full of Evil

43"When an evil spirit comes out of a person, it travels through dry places, looking for a place to rest, but it doesn't find it. 44So the spirit says, 'I will go back to the house I left.' When the spirit comes back, it finds the house still empty, swept clean, and made neat. 45Then the evil spirit goes out and brings seven other spirits even more evil than it is, and they go in and live there. So the person has even more trouble than before. It is the same way with the evil people who live today."

Jesus' True Family

46While Jesus was talking to the people, his mother and brothers stood outside, trying to find a way to talk to him. 47Someone told Jesus, "Your mother and brothers are standing outside, and they want to talk to you."[n]

48He answered, "Who is my mother? Who are my brothers?" 49Then he pointed to his followers and said, "Here are my mother and my brothers. 50My true brother and sister and mother are those who do what my Father in heaven wants."

A Story About Planting Seed

13 That same day Jesus went out of the house and sat by the lake. 2Large crowds gathered around him, so he got into

12:41 Nineveh The city where Jonah preached to warn the people. Read Jonah 3. **12:42 Queen of the South** The Queen of Sheba. She traveled a thousand miles to learn God's wisdom from Solomon. Read 1 Kings 10:1–13. **12:47 Someone . . . you."** Some Greek copies do not have verse 47.

a boat and sat down, while the people stood
on the shore. 3 Then Jesus used stories to
teach them many things. He said: "A farmer
went out to plant his seed. 4 While he was
planting, some seed fell by the road, and the
birds came and ate it all up. 5 Some seed fell
on rocky ground, where there wasn't much
dirt. That seed grew very fast, because the
ground was not deep. 6 But when the sun
rose, the plants dried up, because they did
not have deep roots. 7 Some other seed fell
among thorny weeds, which grew and
choked the good plants. 8 Some other seed
fell on good ground where it grew and
produced a crop. Some plants made a
hundred times more, some made sixty times
more, and some made thirty times more.
9 Let those with ears use them and listen."

Why Jesus Used Stories to Teach

10 The followers came to Jesus and asked,
"Why do you use stories to teach the people?"
11 Jesus answered, "You have been chosen
to know the secrets about the kingdom of
heaven, but others cannot know these
secrets. 12 Those who have understanding
will be given more, and they will have all
they need. But those who do not have
understanding, even what they have will be
taken away from them. 13 This is why I use
stories to teach the people: They see, but
they don't really see. They hear, but they
don't really hear or understand. 14 So they
show that the things Isaiah said about them
are true:

'You will listen and listen, but you will
not understand.
You will look and look, but you will not
learn.
15 For the minds of these people have
become stubborn.
They do not hear with their ears,
and they have closed their eyes.
Otherwise they might really understand
what they see with their eyes
and hear with their ears.
They might really understand in their
minds
and come back to me and be healed.'

Isaiah 6:9–10

16 But you are blessed, because you see with
your eyes and hear with your ears. 17 I tell
you the truth, many prophets and good
people wanted to see the things that you
now see, but they did not see them. And they
wanted to hear the things that you now hear,
but they did not hear them.

Jesus Explains the Seed Story

18 "So listen to the meaning of that story
about the farmer. 19 What is the seed that fell
by the road? That seed is like the person who
hears the message about the kingdom but
does not understand it. The Evil One comes
and takes away what was planted in that
person's heart. 20 And what is the seed that fell
on rocky ground? That seed is like the person
who hears the teaching and quickly accepts it
with joy. 21 But he does not let the teaching go
deep into his life, so he keeps it only a short
time. When trouble or persecution comes
because of the teaching he accepted, he
quickly gives up. 22 And what is the seed
that fell among the thorny weeds? That
seed is like the person who hears the
teaching but lets worries about this life and
the temptation of wealth stop that teaching
from growing. So the teaching does not
produce fruit[n] in that person's life. 23 But what
is the seed that fell on the good ground? That
seed is like the person who hears the
teaching and understands it. That person
grows and produces fruit, sometimes a
hundred times more, sometimes sixty times
more, and sometimes thirty times more."

A Story About Wheat and Weeds

24 Then Jesus told them another story:
"The kingdom of heaven is like a man who
planted good seed in his field. 25 That night,
when everyone was asleep, his enemy came
and planted weeds among the wheat and
then left. 26 Later, the wheat sprouted and the
heads of grain grew, but the weeds also grew.
27 Then the man's servants came to him and
said, 'You planted good seed in your field.
Where did the weeds come from?' 28 The
man answered, 'An enemy planted weeds.'
The servants asked, 'Do you want us to pull
up the weeds?' 29 The man answered, 'No,
because when you pull up the weeds, you
might also pull up the wheat. 30 Let the
weeds and the wheat grow together until the
harvest time. At harvest time I will tell the

13:22 produce fruit To produce fruit means to have in your life the good things God wants.

workers, "First gather the weeds and tie
them together to be burned. Then gather the
wheat and bring it to my barn." ' "

Stories of Mustard Seed and Yeast

31Then Jesus told another story: "The
kingdom of heaven is like a mustard seed
that a man planted in his field. 32That seed is
the smallest of all seeds, but when it grows,
it is one of the largest garden plants. It
becomes big enough for the wild birds to
come and build nests in its branches."

33Then Jesus told another story: "The
kingdom of heaven is like yeast that a
woman took and hid in a large tub of flour
until it made all the dough rise."

34Jesus used stories to tell all these things
to the people; he always used stories to teach
them. 35This is as the prophet said:

"I will speak using stories;
I will tell things that have been secret
since the world was made."

Psalm 78:2

Jesus Explains About the Weeds

36Then Jesus left the crowd and went into
the house. His followers came to him and
said, "Explain to us the meaning of the story
about the weeds in the field."

37Jesus answered, "The man who planted
the good seed in the field is the Son of Man.
38The field is the world, and the good seed
are all of God's children who belong to the
kingdom. The weeds are those people who
belong to the Evil One. 39And the enemy
who planted the bad seed is the devil. The
harvest time is the end of the age, and the
workers who gather are God's angels.

40"Just as the weeds are pulled up and
burned in the fire, so it will be at the end
of the age. 41The Son of Man will send out
his angels, and they will gather out of his
kingdom all who cause sin and all who do
evil. 42The angels will throw them into the
blazing furnace, where the people will cry
and grind their teeth with pain. 43Then the
good people will shine like the sun in the
kingdom of their Father. Let those with ears
use them and listen.

Stories of a Treasure and a Pearl

44"The kingdom of heaven is like a
treasure hidden in a field. One day a man
found the treasure, and then he hid it in the
field again. He was so happy that he went
and sold everything he owned to buy that
field.

45"Also, the kingdom of heaven is like a
man looking for fine pearls. 46When he
found a very valuable pearl, he went and
sold everything he had and bought it.

A Story of a Fishing Net

47"Also, the kingdom of heaven is like a
net that was put into the lake and caught
many different kinds of fish. 48When it was
full, the fishermen pulled the net to the
shore. They sat down and put all the good
fish in baskets and threw away the bad fish.
49It will be this way at the end of the age.
The angels will come and separate the evil
people from the good people. 50The angels
will throw the evil people into the blazing
furnace, where people will cry and grind
their teeth with pain."

51Jesus asked his followers, "Do you
understand all these things?"

They answered, "Yes, we understand."

52Then Jesus said to them, "So every
teacher of the law who has been taught
about the kingdom of heaven is like the
owner of a house. He brings out both new
things and old things he has saved."

Jesus Goes to His Hometown

53When Jesus finished teaching with these
stories, he left there. 54He went to his
hometown and taught the people in the
synagogue, and they were amazed. They said,
"Where did this man get this wisdom and
this power to do miracles? 55He is just the son
of a carpenter. His mother is Mary, and his
brothers are James, Joseph, Simon, and Judas.
56And all his sisters are here with us. Where
then does this man get all these things?" 57So
the people were upset with Jesus.

But Jesus said to them, "A prophet is
honored everywhere except in his
hometown and in his own home."

58So he did not do many miracles there
because they had no faith.

How John the Baptist Was Killed

14 At that time Herod, the ruler of
Galilee, heard the reports about Jesus.
2So he said to his servants, "Jesus is John the
Baptist, who has risen from the dead. That is
why he can work these miracles."

Herodias

MATTHEW 14

Her husband, Herod Antipas, laughs with delight as his stepdaughter dances before the dignitaries that have joined him tonight. The audience claps to the swelling music as the young girl twirls and spins in front of them. They jump to their feet as the number ends and Antipas beams. He looks at Herodias and nods.

The girl has been a tremendous success. He opens his arms to her. "Upon my oath, I shall give you anything you ask up to half my kingdom." Oohs and ahhs fill the great hall. The young girl runs to her mother's side. Whatever shall she ask? A palace of her own? A portion of the royal treasury?

But Herodias has known long before tonight what she desires. Her grudge runs deep. She wants the life of John the Baptist—the troublemaker who had dared say her marriage to Antipas was unlawful in the sight of God. (They both left their spouses to marry each other.) She'd heard enough from this uncivilized man who called everyone to repentance.

"Give me the head of John the Baptist here on a platter," the young girl says. Herod's smile fades. *What sort of uprising could this create?* he wonders. But he could not take back his public offer and agrees to the wish. Herodias smiles. She has triumphed and silenced John the Baptist and his foolish call to repentance once and for all.

Sin consumed Herodias so she missed the call to follow Christ. Have you also refused?

3 Sometime before this, Herod had arrested
John, tied him up, and put him into prison.
Herod did this because of Herodias, who had
been the wife of Philip, Herod's brother.
4 John had been telling Herod, "It is not
lawful for you to be married to Herodias."
5 Herod wanted to kill John, but he was afraid
of the people, because they believed John
was a prophet.

6 On Herod's birthday, the daughter of
Herodias danced for Herod and his guests,
and she pleased him. 7 So he promised with
an oath to give her anything she wanted.
8 Herodias told her daughter what to ask for,
so she said to Herod, "Give me the head
of John the Baptist here on a platter."
9 Although King Herod was very sad, he had
made a promise, and his dinner guests had
heard him. So Herod ordered that what she
asked for be done. 10 He sent soldiers to the
prison to cut off John's head. 11 And they
brought it on a platter and gave it to the girl,
and she took it to her mother. 12 John's
followers came and got his body and buried
it. Then they went and told Jesus.

More than Five Thousand Fed

13 When Jesus heard what had happened
to John, he left in a boat and went to a lonely
place by himself. But the crowds heard about
it and followed him on foot from the towns.
14 When he arrived, he saw a great crowd
waiting. He felt sorry for them and healed
those who were sick.

15 When it was evening, his followers
came to him and said, "No one lives in this
place, and it is already late. Send the people
away so they can go to the towns and buy
food for themselves."

16 But Jesus answered, "They don't need to
go away. You give them something to eat."

17 They said to him, "But we have only five
loaves of bread and two fish."

18 Jesus said, "Bring the bread and the fish
to me." 19 Then he told the people to sit down
on the grass. He took the five loaves and the
two fish and, looking to heaven, he thanked
God for the food. Jesus divided the bread and
gave it to his followers, who gave it to the
people. 20 All the people ate and were
satisfied. Then the followers filled twelve
baskets with the leftover pieces of food.
21 There were about five thousand men there
who ate, not counting women and children.

Jesus Walks on the Water

[22]Immediately Jesus told his followers to
get into the boat and go ahead of him across
the lake. He stayed there to send the people
home. [23]After he had sent them away, he
went by himself up into the hills to pray. It
was late, and Jesus was there alone. [24]By this
time, the boat was already far away from
land. It was being hit by waves, because the
wind was blowing against it.

[25]Between three and six o'clock in the
morning, Jesus came to them, walking on
the water. [26]When his followers saw him
walking on the water, they were afraid. They
said, "It's a ghost!" and cried out in fear.

[27]But Jesus quickly spoke to them, "Have
courage! It is I. Do not be afraid."

[28]Peter said, "Lord, if it is really you, then
command me to come to you on the water."

[29]Jesus said, "Come."

And Peter left the boat and walked on the
water to Jesus. [30]But when Peter saw the
wind and the waves, he became afraid and
began to sink. He shouted, "Lord, save me!"

[31]Immediately Jesus reached out his hand
and caught Peter. Jesus said, "Your faith is
small. Why did you doubt?"

[32]After they got into the boat, the wind
became calm. [33]Then those who were in the
boat worshiped Jesus and said, "Truly you
are the Son of God!"

[34]When they had crossed the lake, they
came to shore at Gennesaret. [35]When the
people there recognized Jesus, they told
people all around there that Jesus had come,
and they brought all their sick to him.
[36]They begged Jesus to let them touch just
the edge of his coat, and all who touched it
were healed.

Obey God's Law

15 Then some Pharisees and teachers of
the law came to Jesus from Jerusalem.
They asked him, [2]"Why don't your followers
obey the unwritten laws which have been
handed down to us? They don't wash their
hands before they eat."

[3]Jesus answered, "And why do you refuse
to obey God's command so that you can
follow your own teachings? [4]God said,

devotion 265

MATTHEW 14:25–31

WILL YOU STEP OUT OF THE BOAT?

Imagine Jesus' followers on the lake, stretched to the very limits of themselves. In the dead of night, waves crashed against the wooden frame of the boat. The thrashing winds had thrown them out into the belly of the swirling waters, tossing them like rag dolls while they tried desperately to hold on to the railing. Then, adding insult to injury, out of the angry gray they saw a frightening ghost walking toward them on the water.

Have you ever felt so overwhelmed by circumstances in your life that you couldn't possibly imagine things getting any worse? I will never forget a pastor friend of mine expressing the terror that sometimes accompanies Jesus showing up to bring change in our lives. But scarier yet, once Christ makes himself known, there are moments we must walk out to meet him—alone. Notice that none of the other followers stepped out of the boat to join Peter. But keeping his eyes fixed on Jesus, Peter was able to do the impossible. There are moments we are called to do the same thing, unaccompanied and unhindered by those around us.

It is so easy to let the circumstances of our lives engulf us, which is what happened when Peter took his gaze away from Christ. But if we keep our eyes set on the eyes of Jesus, we will be able to walk through any storm set before us. Just call his name, and Jesus will be right there to reach for you.

'Honor your father and your mother,'[n]
and 'Anyone who says cruel things to his
father or mother must be put to death.'[n]
5But you say a person can tell his father or
mother, 'I have something I could use to
help you, but I have given it to God already.'
6You teach that person not to honor his
father or his mother. You rejected what God
said for the sake of your own rules. 7You are
hypocrites! Isaiah was right when he said
about you:

8'These people show honor to me with
words,
but their hearts are far from me.
9Their worship of me is worthless.
The things they teach are nothing but
human rules.' " *Isaiah 29:13*

10After Jesus called the crowd to him, he
said, "Listen and understand what I am
saying. 11It is not what people put into their
mouths that makes them unclean. It is what
comes out of their mouths that makes them
unclean."

12Then his followers came to him and
asked, "Do you know that the Pharisees are
angry because of what you said?"

13Jesus answered, "Every plant that my
Father in heaven has not planted himself
will be pulled up by the roots. 14Stay away
from the Pharisees; they are blind leaders.[n]
And if a blind person leads a blind person,
both will fall into a ditch."

15Peter said, "Explain the example to us."

16Jesus said, "Do you still not understand?
17Surely you know that all the food that
enters the mouth goes into the stomach and
then goes out of the body. 18But what people
say with their mouths comes from the way
they think; these are the things that make
people unclean. 19Out of the mind come evil
thoughts, murder, adultery, sexual sins,
stealing, lying, and speaking evil of others.
20These things make people unclean; eating
with unwashed hands does not make them
unclean."

Jesus Helps a Non-Jewish Woman

21Jesus left that place and went to the area
of Tyre and Sidon. 22A Canaanite woman
from that area came to Jesus and cried out,
"Lord, Son of David, have mercy on me! My
daughter has a demon, and she is suffering
very much."

23But Jesus did not answer the woman. So
his followers came to Jesus and begged him,
"Tell the woman to go away. She is following
us and shouting."

24Jesus answered, "God sent me only to
the lost sheep, the people of Israel."

25Then the woman came to Jesus again
and bowed before him and said, "Lord, help
me!"

26Jesus answered, "It is not right to take
the children's bread and give it to the dogs."

27The woman said, "Yes, Lord, but even
the dogs eat the crumbs that fall from their
masters' table."

28Then Jesus answered, "Woman, you
have great faith! I will do what you asked."
And at that moment the woman's daughter
was healed.

Jesus Heals Many People

29After leaving there, Jesus went along the
shore of Lake Galilee. He went up on a hill
and sat there.

30Great crowds came to Jesus, bringing
with them the lame, the blind, the crippled,
those who could not speak, and many
others. They put them at Jesus' feet, and he
healed them. 31The crowd was amazed when
they saw that people who could not speak
before were now able to speak. The crippled
were made strong. The lame could walk, and
the blind could see. And they praised the
God of Israel for this.

More than Four Thousand Fed

32Jesus called his followers to him and
said, "I feel sorry for these people, because
they have already been with me three days,
and they have nothing to eat. I don't want to
send them away hungry. They might faint
while going home."

33His followers asked him, "How can we
get enough bread to feed all these people?
We are far away from any town."

34Jesus asked, "How many loaves of bread
do you have?"

They answered, "Seven, and a few small
fish."

35Jesus told the people to sit on the

15:4 'Honor . . . mother.' Quotation from Exodus 20:12; Deuteronomy 5:16. **15:4 'Anyone . . . death.'** Quotation from Exodus 21:17.
15:14 leaders Some Greek copies continue, "of blind people."

ground. 36 He took the seven loaves of bread
and the fish and gave thanks to God. Then
he divided the food and gave it to his
followers, and they gave it to the people.
37 All the people ate and were satisfied. Then
his followers filled seven baskets with the
leftover pieces of food. 38 There were about
four thousand men there who ate, besides
women and children. 39 After sending the
people home, Jesus got into the boat and
went to the area of Magadan.

The Leaders Ask for a Miracle

16 The Pharisees and Sadducees came to
Jesus, wanting to trick him. So they
asked him to show them a miracle from God.
2 Jesus answered,[n] "At sunset you say we
will have good weather, because the sky is
red. 3 And in the morning you say that it will
be a rainy day, because the sky is dark and
red. You see these signs in the sky and know
what they mean. In the same way, you see
the things that I am doing now, but you
don't know their meaning. 4 Evil and sinful
people ask for a miracle as a sign, but they
will not be given any sign, except the sign of
Jonah."[n] Then Jesus left them and went away.

Guard Against Wrong Teachings

5 Jesus' followers went across the lake, but
they had forgotten to bring bread. 6 Jesus said
to them, "Be careful! Beware of the yeast of
the Pharisees and the Sadducees."
7 His followers discussed the meaning of
this, saying, "He said this because we forgot
to bring bread."
8 Knowing what they were talking about,
Jesus asked them, "Why are you talking
about not having bread? Your faith is small.
9 Do you still not understand? Remember
the five loaves of bread that fed the five
thousand? And remember that you filled
many baskets with the leftovers? 10 Or the
seven loaves of bread that fed the four
thousand and the many baskets you filled
then also? 11 I was not talking to you about
bread. Why don't you understand that? I am
telling you to beware of the yeast of the
Pharisees and the Sadducees." 12 Then the
followers understood that Jesus was not
telling them to beware of the yeast used in
bread but to beware of the teaching of the
Pharisees and the Sadducees.

Peter Says Jesus Is the Christ

13 When Jesus came to the area of Caesarea
Philippi, he asked his followers, "Who do
people say the Son of Man is?"
14 They answered, "Some say you are John
the Baptist. Others say you are Elijah, and
still others say you are Jeremiah or one of
the prophets."
15 Then Jesus asked them, "And who do
you say I am?"
16 Simon Peter answered, "You are the
Christ, the Son of the living God."
17 Jesus answered, "You are blessed, Simon
son of Jonah, because no person taught you
that. My Father in heaven showed you who I
am. 18 So I tell you, you are Peter.[n] On this
rock I will build my church, and the power
of death will not be able to defeat it. 19 I will
give you the keys of the kingdom of heaven;
the things you don't allow on earth will be
the things that God does not allow, and the
things you allow on earth will be the things
that God allows." 20 Then Jesus warned his
followers not to tell anyone he was the
Christ.

Jesus Says that He Must Die

21 From that time on Jesus began telling
his followers that he must go to Jerusalem,
where the Jewish elders, the leading priests,
and the teachers of the law would make him
suffer many things. He told them he must be
killed and then be raised from the dead on
the third day.
22 Peter took Jesus aside and told him not
to talk like that. He said, "God save you from
those things, Lord! Those things will never
happen to you!"
23 Then Jesus said to Peter, "Go away from
me, Satan![n] You are not helping me! You
don't care about the things of God, but
only about the things people think are
important."
24 Then Jesus said to his followers, "If
people want to follow me, they must give up
the things they want. They must be willing

16:2–3 answered Some Greek copies do not have the rest of verse 2 and verse 3. **16:4 sign of Jonah** Jonah's three days in the fish are like Jesus' three days in the tomb. The story about Jonah is in the Book of Jonah. **16:18 Peter** The Greek name "Peter," like the Aramaic name "Cephas," means "rock." **16:23 Satan** Name for the devil, meaning "the enemy." Jesus means that Peter was talking like Satan.

devotion 266

MATTHEW 16:13–16

FULL OF HIS GLORY

Peter knew that Jesus was "Christ, the Son of the living God" (verse 16). In all likelihood, you agree with Peter. But what if the people around you don't yet know Jesus? What if they observe your life to decide just who this Christ might be? Who would they say that he is?

Would someone look at your life and believe Jesus is powerful? Would they know about divine forgiveness because you give out the forgiveness you have been given? Would they feel mercy in your presence? Would they walk away without condemnation? Are your words tender and gracious and true? Would anybody get to know the character of Jesus because they have been with you?

I believe it is the responsibility of every woman who belongs to God to carry around inside her spirit the fullness of our risen Lord. So full, in fact, that when you walk into a room, you bring the glory of God in with you. He shines through your weakness and spills out of the broken places in your humanity. This kind of divine fullness is freely available to each one of us.

Most of the time, God fills us in private. Alone in his presence. Honest. Vulnerable. Ready to follow the Spirit's promptings and his truth. From that private place of intimacy, God sends you out, full of his glory. And when you've been with God, others can't help but know that you belong to Christ, the Son of the living God.

even to give up their lives to follow me.
25Those who want to save their lives will
give up true life, and those who give up
their lives for me will have true life. 26It is
worthless to have the whole world if they
lose their souls. They could never pay
enough to buy back their souls. 27The Son of
Man will come again with his Father's glory
and with his angels. At that time, he will
reward them for what they have done. 28I
tell you the truth, some people standing here
will see the Son of Man coming with his
kingdom before they die."

Jesus Talks with Moses and Elijah

17 Six days later, Jesus took Peter, James,
and John, the brother of James, up on
a high mountain by themselves. 2While they
watched, Jesus' appearance was changed; his
face became bright like the sun, and his
clothes became white as light. 3Then Moses
and Elijah[n] appeared to them, talking with
Jesus.
4Peter said to Jesus, "Lord, it is good that
we are here. If you want, I will put up three
tents here—one for you, one for Moses, and
one for Elijah."
5While Peter was talking, a bright cloud
covered them. A voice came from the cloud
and said, "This is my Son, whom I love, and I
am very pleased with him. Listen to him!"
6When his followers heard the voice, they
were so frightened they fell to the ground.
7But Jesus went to them and touched them
and said, "Stand up. Don't be afraid." 8When
they looked up, they saw Jesus was now
alone.
9As they were coming down the
mountain, Jesus commanded them not to
tell anyone about what they had seen until
the Son of Man had risen from the dead.
10Then his followers asked him, "Why do

17:3 Moses and Elijah Two of the most important Jewish leaders in the past. God had given Moses the Law, and Elijah was an important prophet.

the teachers of the law say that Elijah must
come first?"
11 Jesus answered, "They are right to say
that Elijah is coming and that he will make
everything the way it should be. 12 But I tell
you that Elijah has already come, and they
did not recognize him. They did to him
whatever they wanted to do. It will be the
same with the Son of Man; those same
people will make the Son of Man suffer."
13 Then the followers understood that Jesus
was talking about John the Baptist.

Jesus Heals a Sick Boy

14 When Jesus and his followers came back
to the crowd, a man came to Jesus and bowed
before him. 15 The man said, "Lord, have
mercy on my son. He has epilepsy[n] and is
suffering very much, because he often falls
into the fire or into the water. 16 I brought
him to your followers, but they could not
cure him."
17 Jesus answered, "You people have no
faith, and your lives are all wrong. How long
must I put up with you? How long must I
continue to be patient with you? Bring the
boy here." 18 Jesus commanded the demon
inside the boy. Then the demon came out,
and the boy was healed from that time on.
19 The followers came to Jesus when he
was alone and asked, "Why couldn't we force
the demon out?"
20 Jesus answered, "Because your faith is
too small. I tell you the truth, if your faith is
as big as a mustard seed, you can say to this
mountain, 'Move from here to there,' and it
will move. All things will be possible for
you. [21 That kind of spirit comes out only if
you use prayer and fasting.]"[n]

Jesus Talks About His Death

22 While Jesus' followers were gathering in
Galilee, he said to them, "The Son of Man
will be handed over to people, 23 and they
will kill him. But on the third day he will be
raised from the dead." And the followers
were filled with sadness.

Jesus Talks About Paying Taxes

24 When Jesus and his followers came to
Capernaum, the men who collected the
Temple tax came to Peter. They asked, "Does
your teacher pay the Temple tax?"
25 Peter answered, "Yes, Jesus pays the tax."
Peter went into the house, but before he
could speak, Jesus said to him, "What do you
think? The kings of the earth collect
different kinds of taxes. But who pays the
taxes—the king's children or others?"
26 Peter answered, "Other people pay the
taxes."
Jesus said to Peter, "Then the children of
the king don't have to pay taxes. 27 But we
don't want to upset these tax collectors. So
go to the lake and fish. After you catch the
first fish, open its mouth and you will find a
coin. Take that coin and give it to the tax
collectors for you and me."

Who Is the Greatest?

18 At that time the followers came to
Jesus and asked, "Who is greatest in
the kingdom of heaven?"
2 Jesus called a little child to him and stood
the child before his followers. 3 Then he said,
"I tell you the truth, you must change and
become like little children. Otherwise, you
will never enter the kingdom of heaven.
4 The greatest person in the kingdom of
heaven is the one who makes himself
humble like this child.
5 "Whoever accepts a child in my name
accepts me. 6 If one of these little children
believes in me, and someone causes that
child to sin, it would be better for that
person to have a large stone tied around the
neck and be drowned in the sea. 7 How
terrible for the people of the world because
of the things that cause them to sin. Such
things will happen, but how terrible for the
one who causes them to happen! 8 If your
hand or your foot causes you to sin, cut it
off and throw it away. It is better for you to
lose part of your body and live forever than
to have two hands and two feet and be
thrown into the fire that burns forever.
9 If your eye causes you to sin, take it out
and throw it away. It is better for you to
have only one eye and live forever than to
have two eyes and be thrown into the fire
of hell.

17:15 epilepsy A disease that causes a person sometimes to lose control of his body and maybe faint, shake strongly, or not be able to move.
17:21 That . . . fasting. Some Greek copies do not contain the bracketed text.

A Lost Sheep

[10]"Be careful. Don't think these little children are worth nothing. I tell you that they have angels in heaven who are always with my Father in heaven. [[11]The Son of Man came to save lost people.][n]

[12]"If a man has a hundred sheep but one of the sheep gets lost, he will leave the other ninety-nine on the hill and go to look for the lost sheep. [13]I tell you the truth, if he finds it he is happier about that one sheep than about the ninety-nine that were never lost. [14]In the same way, your Father in heaven does not want any of these little children to be lost.

When a Person Sins Against You

[15]"If your fellow believer sins against you,[n] go and tell him in private what he did wrong. If he listens to you, you have helped that person to be your brother or sister again. [16]But if he refuses to listen, go to him again and take one or two other people with you. 'Every case may be proved by two or three witnesses.'[n] [17]If he refuses to listen to them, tell the church. If he refuses to listen to the church, then treat him like a person who does not believe in God or like a tax collector.

[18]"I tell you the truth, the things you don't allow on earth will be the things God does not allow. And the things you allow on earth will be the things that God allows.

[19]"Also, I tell you that if two of you on earth agree about something and pray for it, it will be done for you by my Father in heaven. [20]This is true because if two or three people come together in my name, I am there with them."

An Unforgiving Servant

[21]Then Peter came to Jesus and asked, "Lord, when my fellow believer sins against me, how many times must I forgive him? Should I forgive him as many as seven times?"

[22]Jesus answered, "I tell you, you must forgive him more than seven times. You must forgive him even if he wrongs you seventy times seven.

[23]"The kingdom of heaven is like a king who decided to collect the money his servants owed him. [24]When the king began to collect his money, a servant who owed him several million dollars was brought to him. [25]But the servant did not have enough money to pay his master, the king. So the master ordered that everything the servant owned should be sold, even the servant's wife and children. Then the money would be used to pay the king what the servant owed.

[26]"But the servant fell on his knees and begged, 'Be patient with me, and I will pay you everything I owe.' [27]The master felt sorry for his servant and told him he did not have to pay it back. Then he let the servant go free.

[28]"Later, that same servant found another servant who owed him a few dollars. The servant grabbed him around the neck and said, 'Pay me the money you owe me!'

[29]"The other servant fell on his knees and begged him, 'Be patient with me, and I will pay you everything I owe.'

[30]"But the first servant refused to be patient. He threw the other servant into prison until he could pay everything he owed. [31]When the other servants saw what had happened, they were very sorry. So they went and told their master all that had happened.

[32]"Then the master called his servant in and said, 'You evil servant! Because you begged me to forget what you owed, I told you that you did not have to pay anything. [33]You should have showed mercy to that other servant, just as I showed mercy to you.' [34]The master was very angry and put the servant in prison to be punished until he could pay everything he owed.

[35]"This king did what my heavenly Father will do to you if you do not forgive your brother or sister from your heart."

Jesus Teaches About Divorce

19 After Jesus said all these things, he left Galilee and went into the area of Judea on the other side of the Jordan River. [2]Large crowds followed him, and he healed them there.

[3]Some Pharisees came to Jesus and tried to trick him. They asked, "Is it right for a man

18:11 The . . . people. Some Greek copies do not contain the bracketed text. **18:15 against you** Some Greek copies do not have "against you."
18:16 'Every . . . witnesses.' Quotation from Deuteronomy 19:15.

devotion 267

MATTHEW 18:35

FORGIVEN AND FORGIVING

In Matthew 18:21-35 Peter and Jesus have a conversation about how many times to forgive someone. In answering, Jesus tells a parable about a wicked servant who wouldn't forgive. A master released the wicked servant from a huge debt, and then that same wicked servant chased down a smaller debt owed to him. In fact, this forgiven, yet wicked, servant locked his debtor in *prison* until he could pay. The principle of this parable is that God forgave us of all our sins—past, present, and even the future ones we will commit. And since he has so graciously done that for us, how much more should we extend forgiveness?

Is there someone you need to extend forgiveness to today? Believe me, there have been times when I granted forgiveness but did not feel like the Holy Spirit was telling me to continue in a personal friendship. Christian, I do not want you to confuse extending forgiveness with continuing to cultivate a relationship. These are two very different things. There have been times in my life when I have extended pure forgiveness and love from my heart but not continued a personal, intimate relationship with that person. There are those people in our lives who are like the servant who is locked up—they are still incarcerated in their own self-constructed prison because of their behavior. It's not your job to free them; that work belongs to the Holy Spirit. What is required of you is to freely forgive from your heart.

to divorce his wife for any reason he
chooses?"
4Jesus answered, "Surely you have read in
the Scriptures: When God made the world,
'he made them male and female.'[n] 5And God
said, 'So a man will leave his father and
mother and be united with his wife, and the
two will become one body.'[n] 6So there are not
two, but one. God has joined the two
together, so no one should separate them."
7The Pharisees asked, "Why then did
Moses give a command for a man to divorce
his wife by giving her divorce papers?"
8Jesus answered, "Moses allowed you to
divorce your wives because you refused to
accept God's teaching, but divorce was not
allowed in the beginning. 9I tell you that
anyone who divorces his wife and marries
another woman is guilty of adultery.[n] The
only reason for a man to divorce his wife is if
his wife has sexual relations with another
man."
10The followers said to him, "If that is the
only reason a man can divorce his wife, it is
better not to marry."
11Jesus answered, "Not everyone can
accept this teaching, but God has made some
able to accept it. 12There are different
reasons why some men cannot marry. Some
men were born without the ability to
become fathers. Others were made that way
later in life by other people. And some men
have given up marriage because of the
kingdom of heaven. But the person who can
marry should accept this teaching about
marriage."[n]

Jesus Welcomes Children

13Then the people brought their little
children to Jesus so he could put his hands

19:4 'he made . . . female' Quotation from Genesis 1:27 or 5:2. **19:5 'So . . . body.'** Quotation from Genesis 2:24.
19:9 adultery Some Greek copies continue, "And anyone who marries a divorced woman is guilty of adultery." Compare Matthew 5:32.
19:12 But . . . marriage. This may also mean, "The person who can accept this teaching about not marrying should accept it."

Salome, Mother of James and John

MATTHEW 20

When Salome's sons answered the call to follow Jesus, she was delighted. She had welcomed Jesus into their home for meals and was a follower of his teachings. He had nicknamed James and John the "Sons of Thunder." She laughed when she first heard this because it fit them so well. When they were children, they got into all sorts of mischief.

They didn't beg her to talk to Jesus for them, but it did come up in conversation one day. "He's building a kingdom," they said. "Seems like he'll need two leaders to sit at his left and his right. Perhaps you could ask Jesus to put us in those positions."

She brings James and John with her as she approaches Jesus, bowing before him. "Promise that one of my sons will sit at your right side and the other will sit at your left side in your kingdom." Jesus looks at her sons. Somehow he knows that they are behind her request.

When the others overhear, they are angry with James and John. But Jesus is not harsh in his response to her sons. He lovingly tells them that the positions they have asked for are not his to give. Indeed, he himself did not come to be served but to serve. His words endear him to Salome even more, and she follows him all the way to the cross.

God doesn't ask that we seek positions of prominence but that we seek his face.

on them[n] and pray for them. His followers
told them to stop, 14 but Jesus said, "Let the
little children come to me. Don't stop them,
because the kingdom of heaven belongs to
people who are like these children." 15 After
Jesus put his hands on the children, he left
there.

A Rich Young Man's Question

16 A man came to Jesus and asked,
"Teacher, what good thing must I do to
have life forever?"

17 Jesus answered, "Why do you ask me
about what is good? Only God is good. But
if you want to have life forever, obey the
commands."

18 The man asked, "Which commands?"
Jesus answered, " 'You must not murder
anyone; you must not be guilty of adultery;
you must not steal; you must not tell lies
about your neighbor; 19 honor your father
and mother;[n] and love your neighbor as you
love yourself.' "[n]

20 The young man said, "I have obeyed all
these things. What else do I need to do?"

21 Jesus answered, "If you want to be
perfect, then go and sell your possessions
and give the money to the poor. If you do
this, you will have treasure in heaven. Then
come and follow me."

22 But when the young man heard this, he
left sorrowfully, because he was rich.

23 Then Jesus said to his followers, "I tell
you the truth, it will be hard for a rich
person to enter the kingdom of heaven.
24 Yes, I tell you that it is easier for a camel to
go through the eye of a needle than for a rich
person to enter the kingdom of God."

25 When Jesus' followers heard this, they
were very surprised and asked, "Then who
can be saved?"

26 Jesus looked at them and said, "For
people this is impossible, but for God all
things are possible."

27 Peter said to Jesus, "Look, we have left
everything and followed you. So what will
we have?"

28 Jesus said to them, "I tell you the truth,
when the age to come has arrived, the Son of
Man will sit on his great throne. All of you
who followed me will also sit on twelve

19:13 put his hands on them Showing that Jesus gave special blessings to these children. **19:19 'You . . . mother.'** Quotation from Exodus 20:12–16; Deuteronomy 5:16–20. **19:19 'love . . . yourself'** Quotation from Leviticus 19:18.

thrones, judging the twelve tribes of Israel. 29And all those who have left houses, brothers, sisters, father, mother,[n] children, or farms to follow me will get much more than they left, and they will have life forever. 30Many who are first now will be last in the future. And many who are last now will be first in the future.

A Story About Workers

20 "The kingdom of heaven is like a person who owned some land. One morning, he went out very early to hire some people to work in his vineyard. 2The man agreed to pay the workers one coin[n] for working that day. Then he sent them into the vineyard to work. 3About nine o'clock the man went to the marketplace and saw some other people standing there, doing nothing. 4So he said to them, 'If you go and work in my vineyard, I will pay you what your work is worth.' 5So they went to work in the vineyard. The man went out again about twelve o'clock and three o'clock and did the same thing. 6About five o'clock the man went to the marketplace again and saw others standing there. He asked them, 'Why did you stand here all day doing nothing?' 7They answered, 'No one gave us a job.' The man said to them, 'Then you can go and work in my vineyard.'

8"At the end of the day, the owner of the vineyard said to the boss of all the workers, 'Call the workers and pay them. Start with the last people I hired and end with those I hired first.'

9"When the workers who were hired at five o'clock came to get their pay, each received one coin. 10When the workers who were hired first came to get their pay, they thought they would be paid more than the others. But each one of them also received one coin. 11When they got their coin, they complained to the man who owned the land. 12They said, 'Those people were hired last and worked only one hour. But you paid them the same as you paid us who worked hard all day in the hot sun.' 13But the man who owned the vineyard said to one of those workers, 'Friend, I am being fair to you. You agreed to work for one coin. 14So take your pay and go. I want to give the man who was hired last the same pay that I gave you. 15I can do what I want with my own money. Are you jealous because I am good to those people?'

16"So those who are last now will someday be first, and those who are first now will someday be last."

Jesus Talks About His Own Death

17While Jesus was going to Jerusalem, he took his twelve followers aside privately and said to them, 18"Look, we are going to Jerusalem. The Son of Man will be turned over to the leading priests and the teachers of the law, and they will say that he must die. 19They will give the Son of Man to the non-Jewish people to laugh at him and beat him with whips and crucify him. But on the third day, he will be raised to life again."

A Mother Asks Jesus a Favor

20Then the wife of Zebedee came to Jesus with her sons. She bowed before him and asked him to do something for her.

21Jesus asked, "What do you want?"

She said, "Promise that one of my sons will sit at your right side and the other will sit at your left side in your kingdom."

22But Jesus said, "You don't understand what you are asking. Can you drink the cup that I am about to drink?"[n]

The sons answered, "Yes, we can."

23Jesus said to them, "You will drink from my cup. But I cannot choose who will sit at my right or my left; those places belong to those for whom my Father has prepared them."

24When the other ten followers heard this, they were angry with the two brothers.

25Jesus called all the followers together and said, "You know that the rulers of the non-Jewish people love to show their power over the people. And their important leaders love to use all their authority. 26But it should not be that way among you. Whoever wants to become great among you must serve the rest of you like a servant. 27Whoever wants to become first among you must serve the rest of you like a slave. 28In the same way, the Son of Man did not come to be served.

19:29 mother Some Greek copies continue, "or wife." **20:2 coin** A Roman denarius. One coin was the average pay for one day's work.
20:22 drink . . . drink Jesus used the idea of drinking from a cup to ask if they could accept the same terrible things that would happen to him.

devotion 268

MATTHEW 20:25–26

WHO'S THE BOSS OF THE WORLD?

One morning on the way to preschool, my four-year-old son and I were discussing his school, his teacher, and what awaited him in his lunch box that day, when out of the blue, he asked me, "Mommy, who is the boss of our church?"

I answered, "Pastor Bob."

He thought about it for a minute, and then he said, "I know who the boss of the world is."

"Who?" I asked.

"Daddy Bill!" he said with confidence. (Daddy Bill is our name for his great-grandfather, Billy Graham.) My son just figured Daddy Bill was the most important man he knew, so he must be the boss of everyone.

We have all grown up under authority of different kinds. We first have to listen to our parents, then teachers, and eventually a boss of some kind. We work very hard to make our way up the ladder of authority. But Jesus said that we should be more interested in serving than wielding authority. How do we process this concept?

Billy Graham is probably the most humble man I know. When we bring our children to visit, he always asks them to tell him about what is going on in their lives. He has been entertaining celebrities and presidents, but he only wants to talk about them. I believe Jesus was the same way when he was on earth. He was the God of the universe, yet he came to serve man. We all need to learn how to be a great servant.

He came to serve others and to give his life
as a ransom for many people."

Jesus Heals Two Blind Men

29When Jesus and his followers were
leaving Jericho, a great many people followed
him. 30Two blind men sitting by the road
heard that Jesus was going by, so they shouted,
"Lord, Son of David, have mercy on us!"
31The people warned the blind men to be
quiet, but they shouted even more, "Lord,
Son of David, have mercy on us!"
32Jesus stopped and said to the blind men,
"What do you want me to do for you?"
33They answered, "Lord, we want to see."
34Jesus felt sorry for the blind men and
touched their eyes, and at once they could
see. Then they followed Jesus.

Jesus Enters Jerusalem as a King

21 As Jesus and his followers were
coming closer to Jerusalem, they
stopped at Bethphage at the hill called the
Mount of Olives. From there Jesus sent two
of his followers 2and said to them, "Go to the
town you can see there. When you enter it,
you will quickly find a donkey tied there
with its colt. Untie them and bring them to
me. 3If anyone asks you why you are taking
the donkeys, say that the Master needs them,
and he will send them at once."
4This was to bring about what the
prophet had said:
5"Tell the people of Jerusalem,
'Your king is coming to you.
He is gentle and riding on a donkey,
on the colt of a donkey.' "

Isaiah 62:11; Zechariah 9:9

6The followers went and did what Jesus
told them to do. 7They brought the donkey
and the colt to Jesus and laid their coats on
them, and Jesus sat on them. 8Many people
spread their coats on the road. Others cut
branches from the trees and spread them on

the road. 9The people were walking ahead of
Jesus and behind him, shouting,

"Praise[n] to the Son of David!
God bless the One who comes in the
name of the Lord! *Psalm 118:26*
Praise to God in heaven!"

10When Jesus entered Jerusalem, all the
city was filled with excitement. The people
asked, "Who is this man?"

11The crowd said, "This man is Jesus, the
prophet from the town of Nazareth in
Galilee."

Jesus Goes to the Temple

12Jesus went into the Temple and threw
out all the people who were buying and
selling there. He turned over the tables of
those who were exchanging different kinds
of money, and he upset the benches of those
who were selling doves. 13Jesus said to all the
people there, "It is written in the Scriptures,
'My Temple will be called a house for
prayer.'[n] But you are changing it into a
'hideout for robbers.' "[n]

14The blind and crippled people came to
Jesus in the Temple, and he healed them.
15The leading priests and the teachers of the
law saw that Jesus was doing wonderful
things and that the children were praising
him in the Temple, saying, "Praise[n] to the
Son of David." All these things made the
priests and the teachers of the law very
angry.

16They asked Jesus, "Do you hear the
things these children are saying?"

Jesus answered, "Yes. Haven't you read in
the Scriptures, 'You have taught children and
babies to sing praises'?"[n]

17Then Jesus left and went out of the city
to Bethany, where he spent the night.

The Power of Faith

18Early the next morning, as Jesus was
going back to the city, he became hungry.
19Seeing a fig tree beside the road, Jesus went
to it, but there were no figs on the tree, only
leaves. So Jesus said to the tree, "You will
never again have fruit." The tree
immediately dried up.

20When his followers saw this, they were
amazed. They asked, "How did the fig tree
dry up so quickly?"

21Jesus answered, "I tell you the truth, if
you have faith and do not doubt, you will be
able to do what I did to this tree and even
more. You will be able to say to this
mountain, 'Go, fall into the sea.' And if you
have faith, it will happen. 22If you believe,
you will get anything you ask for in prayer."

Leaders Doubt Jesus' Authority

23Jesus went to the Temple, and while he
was teaching there, the leading priests and
the elders of the people came to him. They
said, "What authority do you have to do
these things? Who gave you this authority?"

24Jesus answered, "I also will ask you a
question. If you answer me, then I will tell
you what authority I have to do these things.
25Tell me: When John baptized people, did
that come from God or just from other
people?"

They argued about Jesus' question, saying,
"If we answer, 'John's baptism was from
God,' Jesus will say, 'Then why didn't you
believe him?' 26But if we say, 'It was from
people,' we are afraid of what the crowd will
do because they all believe that John was a
prophet."

27So they answered Jesus, "We don't
know."

Jesus said to them, "Then I won't tell you
what authority I have to do these things.

A Story About Two Sons

28"Tell me what you think about this: A
man had two sons. He went to the first son
and said, 'Son, go and work today in my
vineyard.' 29The son answered, 'I will not go.'
But later the son changed his mind and
went. 30Then the father went to the other
son and said, 'Son, go and work today in my
vineyard.' The son answered, 'Yes, sir, I will
go and work,' but he did not go. 31Which of
the two sons obeyed his father?"

The priests and leaders answered, "The
first son."

Jesus said to them, "I tell you the truth,
the tax collectors and the prostitutes will
enter the kingdom of God before you do.
32John came to show you the right way to

21:9, 15 Praise Literally, "Hosanna," a Hebrew word used at first in praying to God for help. At this time it was probably a shout of joy used in praising God or his Messiah. **21:13 'My Temple . . . prayer.'** Quotation from Isaiah 56:7. **21:13 'hideout for robbers'** Quotation from Jeremiah 7:11. **21:16 'You . . . praises.'** Quotation from the Septuagint (Greek) version of Psalm 8:2.

live. You did not believe him, but the tax
collectors and prostitutes believed him. Even
after seeing this, you still refused to change
your ways and believe him.

A Story About God's Son

33"Listen to this story: There was a man
who owned a vineyard. He put a wall around
it and dug a hole for a winepress and built a
tower. Then he leased the land to some
farmers and left for a trip. 34When it was
time for the grapes to be picked, he sent his
servants to the farmers to get his share of
the grapes. 35But the farmers grabbed the
servants, beat one, killed another, and then
killed a third servant with stones. 36So the
man sent some other servants to the farmers,
even more than he sent the first time. But
the farmers did the same thing to the
servants that they had done before. 37So the
man decided to send his son to the farmers.
He said, 'They will respect my son.' 38But
when the farmers saw the son, they said to
each other, 'This son will inherit the
vineyard. If we kill him, it will be ours!'
39Then the farmers grabbed the son, threw
him out of the vineyard, and killed him. 40So
what will the owner of the vineyard do to
these farmers when he comes?"

41The priests and leaders said, "He will
surely kill those evil men. Then he will lease
the vineyard to some other farmers who will
give him his share of the crop at harvest
time."

42Jesus said to them, "Surely you have read
this in the Scriptures:

'The stone that the builders rejected
became the cornerstone.
The Lord did this,
and it is wonderful to us.' *Psalm 118:22–23*

43"So I tell you that the kingdom of God
will be taken away from you and given to
people who do the things God wants in his
kingdom. 44The person who falls on this
stone will be broken, and on whomever that
stone falls, that person will be crushed."[n]

45When the leading priests and the
Pharisees heard these stories, they knew
Jesus was talking about them. 46They
wanted to arrest him, but they were afraid
of the people, because the people believed
that Jesus was a prophet.

A Story About a Wedding Feast

22 Jesus again used stories to teach them.
He said, 2"The kingdom of heaven is
like a king who prepared a wedding feast for
his son. 3The king invited some people to
the feast. When the feast was ready, the king
sent his servants to tell the people, but they
refused to come.

4"Then the king sent other servants,
saying, 'Tell those who have been invited
that my feast is ready. I have killed my
best bulls and calves for the dinner, and
everything is ready. Come to the wedding
feast.'

5"But the people refused to listen to the
servants and left to do other things. One
went to work in his field, and another went
to his business. 6Some of the other people
grabbed the servants, beat them, and killed
them. 7The king was furious and sent his
army to kill the murderers and burn their
city.

8"After that, the king said to his servants,
'The wedding feast is ready. I invited those
people, but they were not worthy to come.
9So go to the street corners and invite
everyone you find to come to my feast.'
10So the servants went into the streets and
gathered all the people they could find, both
good and bad. And the wedding hall was
filled with guests.

11"When the king came in to see the
guests, he saw a man who was not dressed
for a wedding. 12The king said, 'Friend, how
were you allowed to come in here? You are
not dressed for a wedding.' But the man said
nothing. 13So the king told some servants,
'Tie this man's hands and feet. Throw him
out into the darkness, where people will cry
and grind their teeth with pain.'

14"Yes, many are invited, but only a few
are chosen."

Is It Right to Pay Taxes or Not?

15Then the Pharisees left that place
and made plans to trap Jesus in saying
something wrong. 16They sent some of their
own followers and some people from the
group called Herodians.[n] They said, "Teacher,
we know that you are an honest man and
that you teach the truth about God's way.

21:44 The . . . crushed. Some Greek copies do not have verse 44.
22:16 Herodians A political group that followed Herod and his family.

You are not afraid of what other people
think about you, because you pay no
attention to who they are. 17 So tell us what
you think. Is it right to pay taxes to Caesar or
not?"
18 But knowing that these leaders were
trying to trick him, Jesus said, "You
hypocrites! Why are you trying to trap me?
19 Show me a coin used for paying the tax."
So the men showed him a coin.[n] 20 Then Jesus
asked, "Whose image and name are on the
coin?"
21 The men answered, "Caesar's."
Then Jesus said to them, "Give to Caesar
the things that are Caesar's, and give to God
the things that are God's."
22 When the men heard what Jesus said,
they were amazed and left him and went
away.

Some Sadducees Try to Trick Jesus

23 That same day some Sadducees came to
Jesus and asked him a question. (Sadducees
believed that people would not rise from the
dead.) 24 They said, "Teacher, Moses said if a
married man dies without having children,
his brother must marry the widow and have
children for him. 25 Once there were seven
brothers among us. The first one married
and died. Since he had no children, his
brother married the widow. 26 Then the
second brother also died. The same thing
happened to the third brother and all the
other brothers. 27 Finally, the woman died.
28 Since all seven men had married her, when
people rise from the dead, whose wife will
she be?"
29 Jesus answered, "You don't understand,
because you don't know what the Scriptures
say, and you don't know about the power of
God. 30 When people rise from the dead,
they will not marry, nor will they be given
to someone to marry. They will be like the
angels in heaven. 31 Surely you have read
what God said to you about rising from
the dead. 32 God said, 'I am the God of
Abraham, the God of Isaac, and the God
of Jacob.'[n] God is the God of the living, not
the dead."
33 When the people heard this, they were
amazed at Jesus' teaching.

The Most Important Command

34 When the Pharisees learned that the
Sadducees could not argue with Jesus'
answers to them, the Pharisees met together.
35 One Pharisee, who was an expert on the
law of Moses, asked Jesus this question to
test him: 36 "Teacher, which command in the
law is the most important?"
37 Jesus answered, " 'Love the Lord your
God with all your heart, all your soul, and all
your mind.'[n] 38 This is the first and most
important command. 39 And the second
command is like the first: 'Love your
neighbor as you love yourself.'[n] 40 All the
law and the writings of the prophets depend
on these two commands."

Jesus Questions the Pharisees

41 While the Pharisees were together, Jesus
asked them, 42 "What do you think about the
Christ? Whose son is he?"
They answered, "The Christ is the Son of
David."
43 Then Jesus said to them, "Then why did
David call him 'Lord'? David, speaking by
the power of the Holy Spirit, said,
44 'The Lord said to my Lord,
"Sit by me at my right side,
until I put your enemies under your
control." ' *Psalm 110:1*
45 David calls the Christ 'Lord,' so how can
the Christ be his son?"
46 None of the Pharisees could answer
Jesus' question, and after that day no one
was brave enough to ask him any more
questions.

Jesus Accuses Some Leaders

23 Then Jesus said to the crowds and to
his followers, 2 "The teachers of the
law and the Pharisees have the authority to
tell you what the law of Moses says. 3 So you
should obey and follow whatever they tell
you, but their lives are not good examples for
you to follow. They tell you to do things, but
they themselves don't do them. 4 They make
strict rules and try to force people to obey
them, but they are unwilling to help those
who struggle under the weight of their rules.
5 "They do good things so that other
people will see them. They enlarge the little

22:19 coin A Roman denarius. One coin was the average pay for one day's work. **22:32 'I am . . . Jacob.'** Quotation from Exodus 3:6. **22:37 'Love . . . mind.'** Quotation from Deuteronomy 6:5. **22:39 'Love . . . yourself.'** Quotation from Leviticus 19:18.

boxes[n] holding Scriptures that they wear,
and they make their special prayer clothes
very long. 6Those Pharisees and teachers of
the law love to have the most important
seats at feasts and in the synagogues. 7They
love people to greet them with respect in the
marketplaces, and they love to have people
call them 'Teacher.'

8"But you must not be called 'Teacher,'
because you have only one Teacher, and you
are all brothers and sisters together. 9And
don't call any person on earth 'Father,'
because you have one Father, who is in
heaven. 10And you should not be called
'Master,' because you have only one Master,
the Christ. 11Whoever is your servant is the
greatest among you. 12Whoever makes
himself great will be made humble.
Whoever makes himself humble will be
made great.

13"How terrible for you, teachers of the
law and Pharisees! You are hypocrites! You
close the door for people to enter the
kingdom of heaven. You yourselves don't
enter, and you stop others who are trying to
enter. [14How terrible for you, teachers of the
law and Pharisees. You are hypocrites. You
take away widows' houses, and you say long
prayers so that people will notice you. So
you will have a worse punishment.][n]

15"How terrible for you, teachers of the
law and Pharisees! You are hypocrites! You
travel across land and sea to find one person
who will change to your ways. When you
find that person, you make him more fit for
hell than you are.

16"How terrible for you! You guide the
people, but you are blind. You say, 'If people
swear by the Temple when they make a
promise, that means nothing. But if they
swear by the gold that is in the Temple, they
must keep that promise.' 17You are blind
fools! Which is greater: the gold or the
Temple that makes that gold holy? 18And
you say, 'If people swear by the altar when
they make a promise, that means nothing.
But if they swear by the gift on the altar, they
must keep that promise.' 19You are blind!
Which is greater: the gift or the altar that
makes the gift holy? 20The person who
swears by the altar is really using the altar
and also everything on the altar. 21And the
person who swears by the Temple is really
using the Temple and also everything in the
Temple. 22The person who swears by heaven
is also using God's throne and the One who
sits on that throne.

23"How terrible for you, teachers of the
law and Pharisees! You are hypocrites! You
give to God one-tenth of everything you
earn—even your mint, dill, and cumin.[n]
But you don't obey the really important
teachings of the law—justice, mercy, and
being loyal. These are the things you should
do, as well as those other things. 24You guide
the people, but you are blind! You are like a
person who picks a fly out of a drink and
then swallows a camel![n]

25"How terrible for you, teachers of the
law and Pharisees! You are hypocrites! You
wash the outside of your cups and dishes,
but inside they are full of things you got
by cheating others and by pleasing only
yourselves. 26Pharisees, you are blind! First
make the inside of the cup clean, and then
the outside of the cup can be truly clean.

27"How terrible for you, teachers of the
law and Pharisees! You are hypocrites! You
are like tombs that are painted white.
Outside, those tombs look fine, but inside,
they are full of the bones of dead people and
all kinds of unclean things. 28It is the same
with you. People look at you and think you
are good, but on the inside you are full of
hypocrisy and evil.

29"How terrible for you, teachers of the
law and Pharisees! You are hypocrites! You
build tombs for the prophets, and you show
honor to the graves of those who lived good
lives. 30You say, 'If we had lived during the
time of our ancestors, we would not have
helped them kill the prophets.' 31But you
give proof that you are descendants of
those who murdered the prophets. 32And
you will complete the sin that your
ancestors started.

33"You are snakes! A family of poisonous
snakes! How are you going to escape God's
judgment? 34So I tell you this: I am sending
to you prophets and wise men and teachers.
Some of them you will kill and crucify. Some

23:5 boxes Small leather boxes containing four important Scriptures. Some Jews tied these to their foreheads and left arms, probably to show they were very religious. **23:14 How . . . punishment.** Some Greek copies do not contain the bracketed text. **23:23 mint, dill, and cumin** Small plants grown in gardens and used for spices. Only very religious people would be careful enough to give a tenth of these plants. **23:24 You . . . camel!** Meaning, "You worry about the smallest mistakes but commit the biggest sin."

devotion 269

MATTHEW 23:26

WASH YOUR CUPS

Several times in Matthew 23, Jesus referred to the Pharisees as blind. He also referred to them as hypocrites because they had set up a multitude of rules for the people—rules they didn't follow themselves. When Jesus talked about the inside of their cup being unclean, he was referring to their hearts. You can imagine how angry these self-righteous men must have been as Jesus laid all their secret sins out for the world to see. They were angry enough to want to kill him.

How often we are blind to our own mistakes. The inside of our cup is usually hiding selfishness, pride, or envy. We find ways to cover up these attitudes, but unless we deal with them, they do not go away. So how can we keep our hearts from becoming like the Pharisees? Look back at Matthew 23:23. Here Jesus tells the Pharisees the things that are the most important to the Father: justice, mercy, and loyalty. Think about those things in your own life. Is it hard to be just when your selfishness gets in the way? Is it hard to be merciful with someone you envy? Is it difficult to be loyal when you are prideful? Jesus wants us to be honest with ourselves because he already knows our true hearts. Ask the Lord to reveal to you what needs cleaned up in your cup. The cleaner you are on the inside, the more beautiful you become on the outside.

of them you will beat in your synagogues
and chase from town to town. 35So you will
be guilty for the death of all the good people
who have been killed on earth—from the
murder of that good man Abel to the murder
of Zechariah[n] son of Berakiah, whom you
murdered between the Temple and the altar.
36I tell you the truth, all of these things will
happen to you people who are living now.

Jesus Feels Sorry for Jerusalem

37"Jerusalem, Jerusalem! You kill the
prophets and stone to death those who are
sent to you. Many times I wanted to gather
your people as a hen gathers her chicks
under her wings, but you did not let me.
38Now your house will be left completely
empty. 39I tell you, you will not see me again
until that time when you will say, 'God bless
the One who comes in the name of the
Lord.' "[n]

The Temple Will Be Destroyed

24 As Jesus left the Temple and was
walking away, his followers came up
to show him the Temple's buildings. 2Jesus
asked, "Do you see all these buildings? I tell
you the truth, not one stone will be left on
another. Every stone will be thrown down to
the ground."

3Later, as Jesus was sitting on the Mount
of Olives, his followers came to be alone
with him. They said, "Tell us, when will
these things happen? And what will be the
sign that it is time for you to come again and
for this age to end?"

4Jesus answered, "Be careful that no one
fools you. 5Many will come in my name,
saying, 'I am the Christ,' and they will fool
many people. 6You will hear about wars and
stories of wars that are coming, but don't be
afraid. These things must happen before the
end comes. 7Nations will fight against other

23:35 Abel . . . Zechariah In the order of the books of the Hebrew Old Testament, the first and last men to be murdered.
23:39 'God . . . Lord.' Quotation from Psalm 118:26.

nations; kingdoms will fight against other
kingdoms. There will be times when there is
no food for people to eat, and there will be
earthquakes in different places. 8These
things are like the first pains when
something new is about to be born.
9"Then people will arrest you, hand you
over to be hurt, and kill you. They will hate
you because you believe in me. 10At that
time, many will lose their faith, and they
will turn against each other and hate each
other. 11Many false prophets will come and
cause many people to believe lies. 12There
will be more and more evil in the world, so
most people will stop showing their love for
each other. 13But those people who keep
their faith until the end will be saved. 14The
Good News about God's kingdom will be
preached in all the world, to every nation.
Then the end will come.
15"Daniel the prophet spoke about
'a blasphemous object that brings
destruction.'[n] You will see this standing in
the holy place." (You who read this should
understand what it means.) 16"At that time,
the people in Judea should run away to the
mountains. 17If people are on the roofs[n] of
their houses, they must not go down to get
anything out of their houses. 18If people are
in the fields, they must not go back to get
their coats. 19At that time, how terrible it
will be for women who are pregnant or have
nursing babies! 20Pray that it will not be
winter or a Sabbath day when these things
happen and you have to run away, 21because
at that time there will be much trouble.
There will be more trouble than there has
ever been since the beginning of the world
until now, and nothing as bad will ever
happen again. 22God has decided to make
that terrible time short. Otherwise, no one
would go on living. But God will make that
time short to help the people he has chosen.
23At that time, someone might say to you,
'Look, there is the Christ!' Or another person
might say, 'There he is!' But don't believe
them. 24False Christs and false prophets will
come and perform great wonders and
miracles. They will try to fool even the
people God has chosen, if that is possible.
25Now I have warned you about this before it
happens.
26"If people tell you, 'The Christ is in
the desert,' don't go there. If they say, 'The
Christ is in the inner room,' don't believe it.
27When the Son of Man comes, he will be
seen by everyone, like lightning flashing
from the east to the west. 28Wherever the
dead body is, there the vultures will gather.
29"Soon after the trouble of those days,
'the sun will grow dark,
and the moon will not give its light.
The stars will fall from the sky.
And the powers of the heavens will be
shaken.' *Isaiah 13:10; 34:4*
30"At that time, the sign of the Son of Man
will appear in the sky. Then all the peoples
of the world will cry. They will see the Son of
Man coming on clouds in the sky with great
power and glory. 31He will use a loud
trumpet to send his angels all around the
earth, and they will gather his chosen people
from every part of the world.
32"Learn a lesson from the fig tree: When
its branches become green and soft and new
leaves appear, you know summer is near.
33In the same way, when you see all these
things happening, you will know that the
time is near, ready to come. 34I tell you the
truth, all these things will happen while the
people of this time are still living. 35Earth
and sky will be destroyed, but the words I
have said will never be destroyed.

When Will Jesus Come Again?

36"No one knows when that day or time
will be, not the angels in heaven, not even
the Son.[n] Only the Father knows. 37When
the Son of Man comes, it will be like what
happened during Noah's time. 38In those
days before the flood, people were eating and
drinking, marrying and giving their children
to be married, until the day Noah entered
the boat. 39They knew nothing about what
was happening until the flood came and
destroyed them. It will be the same when the
Son of Man comes. 40Two men will be in the
field. One will be taken, and the other will be
left. 41Two women will be grinding grain
with a mill.[n] One will be taken, and the other
will be left.

24:15 'a blasphemous object that brings destruction' Mentioned in Daniel 9:27; 12:11 (see also Daniel 11:31).
24:17 roofs In Bible times houses were built with flat roofs. The roof was used for drying things such as flax and fruit. And it was used as an extra room, as a place for worship, and as a cool place to sleep in the summer. **24:36 not even the Son** Some Greek copies do not have this phrase.
24:41 mill Two large, round, flat rocks used for grinding grain to make flour.

42“So always be ready, because you
don’t know the day your Lord will come.
43Remember this: If the owner of the house
knew what time of night a thief was coming,
the owner would watch and not let the
thief break in. 44So you also must be ready,
because the Son of Man will come at a time
you don’t expect him.
45“Who is the wise and loyal servant that
the master trusts to give the other servants
their food at the right time? 46When the
master comes and finds the servant doing
his work, the servant will be blessed. 47I tell
you the truth, the master will choose that
servant to take care of everything he owns.
48But suppose that evil servant thinks to
himself, ‘My master will not come back
soon,’ 49and he begins to beat the other
servants and eat and get drunk with others
like him? 50The master will come when that
servant is not ready and is not expecting
him. 51Then the master will cut him in
pieces and send him away to be with the
hypocrites, where people will cry and grind
their teeth with pain.

A Story About Ten Bridesmaids

25 “At that time the kingdom of heaven
will be like ten bridesmaids who took
their lamps and went to wait for the
bridegroom. 2Five of them were foolish and
five were wise. 3The five foolish bridesmaids
took their lamps, but they did not take more
oil for the lamps to burn. 4The wise
bridesmaids took their lamps and more oil
in jars. 5Because the bridegroom was late,
they became sleepy and went to sleep.
6“At midnight someone cried out, ‘The
bridegroom is coming! Come and meet him!’
7Then all the bridesmaids woke up and got
their lamps ready. 8But the foolish ones said
to the wise, ‘Give us some of your oil,
because our lamps are going out.’ 9The wise
bridesmaids answered, ‘No, the oil we have
might not be enough for all of us. Go to the
people who sell oil and buy some for
yourselves.’
10“So while the five foolish bridesmaids
went to buy oil, the bridegroom came. The
bridesmaids who were ready went in with
the bridegroom to the wedding feast. Then
the door was closed and locked.
11“Later the others came back and said,
‘Sir, sir, open the door to let us in.’ 12But the
bridegroom answered, ‘I tell you the truth, I
don’t want to know you.’
13“So always be ready, because you don’t
know the day or the hour the Son of Man
will come.

A Story About Three Servants

14“The kingdom of heaven is like a man
who was going to another place for a visit.
Before he left, he called for his servants and
told them to take care of his things while he
was gone. 15He gave one servant five bags of
gold, another servant two bags of gold, and a
third servant one bag of gold, to each one as
much as he could handle. Then he left. 16The
servant who got five bags went quickly to
invest the money and earned five more bags.
17In the same way, the servant who had two
bags invested them and earned two more.
18But the servant who got one bag went out
and dug a hole in the ground and hid the
master’s money.
19“After a long time the master came
home and asked the servants what they did
with his money. 20The servant who was
given five bags of gold brought five more
bags to the master and said, ‘Master, you
trusted me to care for five bags of gold, so I
used your five bags to earn five more.’ 21The
master answered, ‘You did well. You are a
good and loyal servant. Because you were
loyal with small things, I will let you care for
much greater things. Come and share my joy
with me.’
22“Then the servant who had been given
two bags of gold came to the master and
said, ‘Master, you gave me two bags of gold
to care for, so I used your two bags to earn
two more.’ 23The master answered, ‘You
did well. You are a good and loyal servant.
Because you were loyal with small things, I
will let you care for much greater things.
Come and share my joy with me.’
24“Then the servant who had been given
one bag of gold came to the master and said,
‘Master, I knew that you were a hard man.
You harvest things you did not plant. You
gather crops where you did not sow any
seed. 25So I was afraid and went and hid your
money in the ground. Here is your bag of
gold.’ 26The master answered, ‘You are a
wicked and lazy servant! You say you knew
that I harvest things I did not plant and that
I gather crops where I did not sow any seed.

The Woman with Perfume

MATTHEW 26

The streets of Jerusalem are swarming with thousands of worshipers who have come to celebrate Passover. She peers out the window, watching as people are jostled about in the crowd. She has heard that Jesus will be eating with Simon. Her mind fills with the images of a day that at times feels so far away, yet on other occasions seems as if it just happened yesterday.

She had been there and watched as it happened. Lazarus had been sick for days when his sisters sent word to Jesus to come. By the time he arrived, Lazarus had been dead for four days. Tears were replaced with cries of joy when Lazarus threw off his grave clothes. But Jesus did not rejoice. As she watched him, she felt a sense of grief. What did the resurrection of Lazarus mean?

In time she would discover that this miracle was the catalyst behind the Jewish leaders' plot to kill Jesus. In her heart, she knows that Jesus will not enter Jerusalem to shouts of celebration but to insults and death. She retrieves a precious alabaster bottle of perfume and walks to Simon's house. As an act of adoration, she will lavish his head with the best she has to offer—despite what others may say. Love raised her friend from the dead, and love brings her here now.

This woman loved and worshiped Christ without considering what others would think. Are you bold in your love for Jesus?

27So you should have put my gold in the
bank. Then, when I came home, I would
have received my gold back with interest.'
28"So the master told his other servants,
'Take the bag of gold from that servant and
give it to the servant who has ten bags of
gold. 29Those who have much will get more,
and they will have much more than they
need. But those who do not have much will
have everything taken away from them.'
30Then the master said, 'Throw that useless
servant outside, into the darkness where
people will cry and grind their teeth with
pain.'

The King Will Judge All People

31"The Son of Man will come again in his
great glory, with all his angels. He will be
King and sit on his great throne. 32All the
nations of the world will be gathered before
him, and he will separate them into two
groups as a shepherd separates the sheep
from the goats. 33The Son of Man will put
the sheep on his right and the goats on his
left.
34"Then the King will say to the people on
his right, 'Come, my Father has given you his
blessing. Receive the kingdom God has
prepared for you since the world was made.
35I was hungry, and you gave me food. I was
thirsty, and you gave me something to drink.
I was alone and away from home, and you
invited me into your house. 36I was without
clothes, and you gave me something to wear.
I was sick, and you cared for me. I was in
prison, and you visited me.'
37"Then the good people will answer,
'Lord, when did we see you hungry and give
you food, or thirsty and give you something
to drink? 38When did we see you alone and
away from home and invite you into our
house? When did we see you without
clothes and give you something to wear?
39When did we see you sick or in prison and
care for you?'
40"Then the King will answer, 'I tell you
the truth, anything you did for even the least
of my people here, you also did for me.'
41"Then the King will say to those on
his left, 'Go away from me. You will be
punished. Go into the fire that burns forever
that was prepared for the devil and his
angels. 42I was hungry, and you gave me
nothing to eat. I was thirsty, and you gave

me nothing to drink. 43I was alone and away
from home, and you did not invite me into
your house. I was without clothes, and you
gave me nothing to wear. I was sick and in
prison, and you did not care for me.'
44"Then those people will answer, 'Lord,
when did we see you hungry or thirsty or
alone and away from home or without
clothes or sick or in prison? When did we
see these things and not help you?'
45"Then the King will answer, 'I tell you
the truth, anything you refused to do for
even the least of my people here, you refused
to do for me.'
46"These people will go off to be punished
forever, but the good people will go to live
forever."

The Plan to Kill Jesus

26 After Jesus finished saying all these
things, he told his followers, 2"You
know that the day after tomorrow is the day
of the Passover Feast. On that day the Son of
Man will be given to his enemies to be
crucified."
3Then the leading priests and the elders
had a meeting at the palace of the high
priest, named Caiaphas. 4At the meeting,
they planned to set a trap to arrest Jesus and
kill him. 5But they said, "We must not do it
during the feast, because the people might
cause a riot."

Perfume for Jesus' Burial

6Jesus was in Bethany at the house of
Simon, who had a skin disease. 7While Jesus
was there, a woman approached him with
an alabaster jar filled with expensive
perfume. She poured this perfume on Jesus'
head while he was eating.
8His followers were upset when they saw
the woman do this. They asked, "Why waste
that perfume? 9It could have been sold for a
great deal of money and the money given to
the poor."
10Knowing what had happened, Jesus said,
"Why are you troubling this woman? She
did an excellent thing for me. 11You will
always have the poor with you, but you will
not always have me. 12This woman poured
perfume on my body to prepare me for
burial. 13I tell you the truth, wherever the
Good News is preached in all the world,
what this woman has done will be told, and
people will remember her."

Judas Becomes an Enemy of Jesus

14Then one of the twelve apostles, Judas
Iscariot, went to talk to the leading priests.
15He said, "What will you pay me for giving
Jesus to you?" And they gave him thirty
silver coins. 16After that, Judas watched for
the best time to turn Jesus in.

Jesus Eats the Passover Meal

17On the first day of the Feast of
Unleavened Bread, the followers came to
Jesus. They said, "Where do you want us to
prepare for you to eat the Passover meal?"
18Jesus answered, "Go into the city to a
certain man and tell him, 'The Teacher says:
"The chosen time is near. I will have the
Passover with my followers at your house." ' "
19The followers did what Jesus told them to
do, and they prepared the Passover meal.
20In the evening Jesus was sitting at the
table with his twelve followers. 21As they
were eating, Jesus said, "I tell you the truth,
one of you will turn against me."
22This made the followers very sad. Each
one began to say to Jesus, "Surely, Lord, I
am not the one who will turn against you,
am I?"
23Jesus answered, "The man who has
dipped his hand with me into the bowl is the
one who will turn against me. 24The Son of
Man will die, just as the Scriptures say. But
how terrible it will be for the person who
hands the Son of Man over to be killed. It
would be better for him if he had never been
born."
25Then Judas, who would give Jesus to his
enemies, said to Jesus, "Teacher, surely I am
not the one, am I?"
Jesus answered, "Yes, it is you."

The Lord's Supper

26While they were eating, Jesus took some
bread and thanked God for it and broke it.
Then he gave it to his followers and said,
"Take this bread and eat it; this is my body."
27Then Jesus took a cup and thanked God
for it and gave it to the followers. He said,
"Every one of you drink this. 28This is my
blood which is the new[n] agreement that God

26:28 new Some Greek copies do not have this word. Compare Luke 22:20.

makes with his people. This blood is poured
out for many to forgive their sins. 29I tell you
this: I will not drink of this fruit of the vine[n]
again until that day when I drink it new
with you in my Father's kingdom."
30After singing a hymn, they went out to
the Mount of Olives.

Jesus' Followers Will Leave Him

31Jesus told his followers, "Tonight you
will all stumble in your faith on account of
me, because it is written in the Scriptures:
'I will kill the shepherd,
and the sheep will scatter.' *Zechariah 13:7*
32But after I rise from the dead, I will go
ahead of you into Galilee."
33Peter said, "Everyone else may stumble
in their faith because of you, but I will not."
34Jesus said, "I tell you the truth, tonight
before the rooster crows you will say three
times that you don't know me."
35But Peter said, "I will never say that I
don't know you! I will even die with you!"
And all the other followers said the same
thing.

Jesus Prays Alone

36Then Jesus went with his followers to a
place called Gethsemane. He said to them,
"Sit here while I go over there and pray."
37He took Peter and the two sons of Zebedee
with him, and he began to be very sad and
troubled. 38He said to them, "My heart is full
of sorrow, to the point of death. Stay here
and watch with me."
39After walking a little farther away from
them, Jesus fell to the ground and prayed,
"My Father, if it is possible, do not give me
this cup[n] of suffering. But do what you want,
not what I want." 40Then Jesus went back to
his followers and found them asleep. He said
to Peter, "You men could not stay awake with
me for one hour? 41Stay awake and pray for
strength against temptation. The spirit
wants to do what is right, but the body is
weak."
42Then Jesus went away a second time and
prayed, "My Father, if it is not possible for
this painful thing to be taken from me, and
if I must do it, I pray that what you want will
be done."
43Then he went back to his followers, and
again he found them asleep, because their
eyes were heavy. 44So Jesus left them and
went away and prayed a third time, saying
the same thing.
45Then Jesus went back to his followers
and said, "Are you still sleeping and resting?
The time has come for the Son of Man to be
handed over to sinful people. 46Get up, we
must go. Look, here comes the man who has
turned against me."

Jesus Is Arrested

47While Jesus was still speaking, Judas,
one of the twelve apostles, came up. With
him were many people carrying swords and
clubs who had been sent from the leading
priests and the Jewish elders of the people.
48Judas had planned to give them a signal,
saying, "The man I kiss is Jesus. Arrest him."
49At once Judas went to Jesus and said,
"Greetings, Teacher!" and kissed him.
50Jesus answered, "Friend, do what you
came to do."
Then the people came and grabbed Jesus
and arrested him. 51When that happened,
one of Jesus' followers reached for his sword
and pulled it out. He struck the servant of
the high priest and cut off his ear.
52Jesus said to the man, "Put your sword
back in its place. All who use swords will be
killed with swords. 53Surely you know I
could ask my Father, and he would give me
more than twelve armies of angels. 54But it
must happen this way to bring about what
the Scriptures say."
55Then Jesus said to the crowd, "You came
to get me with swords and clubs as if I were
a criminal. Every day I sat in the Temple
teaching, and you did not arrest me there.
56But all these things have happened so that
it will come about as the prophets wrote."
Then all of Jesus' followers left him and ran
away.

Jesus Before the Leaders

57Those people who arrested Jesus led him
to the house of Caiaphas, the high priest,
where the teachers of the law and the elders
were gathered. 58Peter followed far behind to
the courtyard of the high priest's house, and

26:29 fruit of the vine Product of the grapevine; this may also be translated "wine." **26:39 cup** Jesus is talking about the terrible things that will happen to him. Accepting these things will be very hard, like drinking a cup of something bitter.

he sat down with the guards to see what
would happen to Jesus.
59 The leading priests and the whole
Jewish council tried to find something false
against Jesus so they could kill him. 60 Many
people came and told lies about him, but the
council could find no real reason to kill him.
Then two people came and said, 61 "This man
said, 'I can destroy the Temple of God and
build it again in three days.' "
62 Then the high priest stood up and said to
Jesus, "Aren't you going to answer? Don't you
have something to say about their charges
against you?" 63 But Jesus said nothing.
Again the high priest said to Jesus, "I
command you by the power of the living
God: Tell us if you are the Christ, the Son of
God."
64 Jesus answered, "Those are your words.
But I tell you, in the future you will see the
Son of Man sitting at the right hand of God,
the Powerful One, and coming on clouds in
the sky."
65 When the high priest heard this, he tore
his clothes and said, "This man has said
things that are against God! We don't need
any more witnesses; you all heard him say
these things against God. 66 What do you
think?"
The people answered, "He should die."
67 Then the people there spat in Jesus' face
and beat him with their fists. Others slapped
him. 68 They said, "Prove to us that you are a
prophet, you Christ! Tell us who hit you!"

Peter Says He Doesn't Know Jesus

69 At that time, as Peter was sitting in the
courtyard, a servant girl came to him and
said, "You also were with Jesus of Galilee."
70 But Peter said to all the people there that
he was never with Jesus. He said, "I don't
know what you are talking about."
71 When he left the courtyard and was at
the gate, another girl saw him. She said to
the people there, "This man was with Jesus
of Nazareth."
72 Again, Peter said he was never with him,
saying, "I swear I don't know this man Jesus!"
73 A short time later, some people standing
there went to Peter and said, "Surely you are
one of those who followed Jesus. The way
you talk shows it."
74 Then Peter began to place a curse on
himself and swear, "I don't know the man."
At once, a rooster crowed. 75 And Peter
remembered what Jesus had told him:
"Before the rooster crows, you will say three
times that you don't know me." Then Peter
went outside and cried painfully.

Jesus Is Taken to Pilate

27 Early the next morning, all the
leading priests and elders of the
people decided that Jesus should die. 2 They
tied him, led him away, and turned him over
to Pilate, the governor.

Judas Kills Himself

3 Judas, the one who had given Jesus to his
enemies, saw that they had decided to kill
Jesus. Then he was very sorry for what he
had done. So he took the thirty silver coins
back to the priests and the leaders, 4 saying, "I
sinned; I handed over to you an innocent
man."
The leaders answered, "What is that to us?
That's your problem, not ours."
5 So Judas threw the money into the
Temple. Then he went off and hanged
himself.
6 The leading priests picked up the silver
coins in the Temple and said, "Our law does
not allow us to keep this money with the
Temple money, because it has paid for a
man's death." 7 So they decided to use the
coins to buy Potter's Field as a place to bury
strangers who died in Jerusalem. 8 That is
why that field is still called the Field of
Blood. 9 So what Jeremiah the prophet had
said came true: "They took thirty silver
coins. That is how little the Israelites
thought he was worth. 10 They used those
thirty silver coins to buy the potter's field, as
the Lord commanded me."[n]

Pilate Questions Jesus

11 Jesus stood before Pilate the governor,
and Pilate asked him, "Are you the king of
the Jews?"
Jesus answered, "Those are your words."
12 When the leading priests and the elders
accused Jesus, he said nothing.
13 So Pilate said to Jesus, "Don't you hear
them accusing you of all these things?"

27:9–10 "They . . . commanded me." See Zechariah 11:12–13 and Jeremiah 32:6–9.

14 But Jesus said nothing in answer to Pilate, and Pilate was very surprised at this.

Pilate Tries to Free Jesus

15 Every year at the time of Passover the governor would free one prisoner whom the people chose. 16 At that time there was a man in prison, named Barabbas,[n] who was known to be very bad. 17 When the people gathered at Pilate's house, Pilate said, "Whom do you want me to set free: Barabbas[n] or Jesus who is called the Christ?" 18 Pilate knew that they turned Jesus in to him because they were jealous.

19 While Pilate was sitting there on the judge's seat, his wife sent this message to him: "Don't do anything to that man, because he is innocent. Today I had a dream about him, and it troubled me very much."

20 But the leading priests and elders convinced the crowd to ask for Barabbas to be freed and for Jesus to be killed.

21 Pilate said, "I have Barabbas and Jesus. Which do you want me to set free for you?"

The people answered, "Barabbas."

22 Pilate asked, "So what should I do with Jesus, the one called the Christ?"

They all answered, "Crucify him!"

23 Pilate asked, "Why? What wrong has he done?"

But they shouted louder, "Crucify him!"

24 When Pilate saw that he could do nothing about this and that a riot was starting, he took some water and washed his hands[n] in front of the crowd. Then he said, "I am not guilty of this man's death. You are the ones who are causing it!"

25 All the people answered, "We and our children will be responsible for his death."

26 Then he set Barabbas free. But Jesus was beaten with whips and handed over to the soldiers to be crucified.

27 The governor's soldiers took Jesus into the governor's palace, and they all gathered around him. 28 They took off his clothes and put a red robe on him. 29 Using thorny branches, they made a crown, put it on his head, and put a stick in his right hand. Then the soldiers bowed before Jesus and made fun of him, saying, "Hail, King of the Jews!" 30 They spat on Jesus. Then they took his stick and began to beat him on the head. 31 After they finished, the soldiers took off the robe and put his own clothes on him again. Then they led him away to be crucified.

Jesus Is Crucified

32 As the soldiers were going out of the city with Jesus, they forced a man from Cyrene, named Simon, to carry the cross for Jesus. 33 They all came to the place called Golgotha, which means the Place of the Skull. 34 The soldiers gave Jesus wine mixed with gall[n] to drink. He tasted the wine but refused to drink it. 35 When the soldiers had crucified him, they threw lots to decide who would get his clothes.[n] 36 The soldiers sat there and continued watching him. 37 They put a sign above Jesus' head with a charge against him. It said: THIS IS JESUS, THE KING OF THE JEWS. 38 Two robbers were crucified beside Jesus, one on the right and the other on the left. 39 People walked by and insulted Jesus and shook their heads, 40 saying, "You said you could destroy the Temple and build it again in three days. So save yourself! Come down from that cross if you are really the Son of God!"

41 The leading priests, the teachers of the law, and the Jewish elders were also making fun of Jesus. 42 They said, "He saved others, but he can't save himself! He says he is the king of Israel! If he is the king, let him come down now from the cross. Then we will believe in him. 43 He trusts in God, so let God save him now, if God really wants him. He himself said, 'I am the Son of God.' " 44 And in the same way, the robbers who were being crucified beside Jesus also insulted him.

Jesus Dies

45 At noon the whole country became dark, and the darkness lasted for three hours. 46 About three o'clock Jesus cried out in a loud voice, "Eli, Eli, lama sabachthani?" This means, "My God, my God, why have you abandoned me?"

47 Some of the people standing there who heard this said, "He is calling Elijah."

48 Quickly one of them ran and got a sponge and filled it with vinegar and tied it

27:16–17 Barabbas Some Greek copies read "Jesus Barabbas." **27:24 washed his hands** He did this as a sign to show that he wanted no part in what the people did. **27:34 gall** Probably a drink of wine mixed with drugs to help a person feel less pain. **27:35 clothes** Some Greek copies continue, "So what God said through the prophet came true, 'They divided my clothes among them, and they threw lots for my clothing.' " See Psalm 22:18.

to a stick and gave it to Jesus to drink. 49But
the others said, "Don't bother him. We want
to see if Elijah will come to save him."
50But Jesus cried out again in a loud voice
and died.
51Then the curtain in the Temple[n] was
torn into two pieces, from the top to the
bottom. Also, the earth shook and rocks
broke apart. 52The graves opened, and many
of God's people who had died were raised
from the dead. 53They came out of the graves
after Jesus was raised from the dead and
went into the holy city, where they appeared
to many people.
54When the army officer and the soldiers
guarding Jesus saw this earthquake and
everything else that happened, they were
very frightened and said, "He really was the
Son of God!"
55Many women who had followed Jesus
from Galilee to help him were standing at a
distance from the cross, watching. 56Mary
Magdalene, and Mary the mother of James
and Joseph, and the mother of James and
John were there.

Jesus Is Buried

57That evening a rich man named Joseph,
a follower of Jesus from the town of
Arimathea, came to Jerusalem. 58Joseph
went to Pilate and asked to have Jesus' body.
So Pilate gave orders for the soldiers to give
it to Joseph. 59Then Joseph took the body
and wrapped it in a clean linen cloth. 60He
put Jesus' body in a new tomb that he had
cut out of a wall of rock, and he rolled a very
large stone to block the entrance of the
tomb. Then Joseph went away. 61Mary
Magdalene and the other woman named
Mary were sitting near the tomb.

The Tomb of Jesus Is Guarded

62The next day, the day after Preparation
Day, the leading priests and the Pharisees
went to Pilate. 63They said, "Sir, we remember
that while that liar was still alive he said,
'After three days I will rise from the dead.'
64So give the order for the tomb to be
guarded closely till the third day. Otherwise,
his followers might come and steal the body
and tell people that he has risen from the
dead. That lie would be even worse than the
first one."
65Pilate said, "Take some soldiers and go
guard the tomb the best way you know."
66So they all went to the tomb and made it
safe from thieves by sealing the stone in
the entrance and putting soldiers there to
guard it.

Jesus Rises from the Dead

28 The day after the Sabbath day was the
first day of the week. At dawn on the
first day, Mary Magdalene and another woman
named Mary went to look at the tomb.
2At that time there was a strong
earthquake. An angel of the Lord came down
from heaven, went to the tomb, and rolled
the stone away from the entrance. Then he
sat on the stone. 3He was shining as bright as
lightning, and his clothes were white as
snow. 4The soldiers guarding the tomb
shook with fear because of the angel, and
they became like dead men.
5The angel said to the women, "Don't be
afraid. I know that you are looking for Jesus,
who has been crucified. 6He is not here. He
has risen from the dead as he said he would.
Come and see the place where his body was.
7And go quickly and tell his followers, 'Jesus
has risen from the dead. He is going into
Galilee ahead of you, and you will see him
there.' " Then the angel said, "Now I have
told you."
8The women left the tomb quickly. They
were afraid, but they were also very happy.
They ran to tell Jesus' followers what had
happened. 9Suddenly, Jesus met them and
said, "Greetings." The women came up to
him, took hold of his feet, and worshiped
him. 10Then Jesus said to them, "Don't be
afraid. Go and tell my followers to go on to
Galilee, and they will see me there."

The Soldiers Report to the Leaders

11While the women went to tell Jesus'
followers, some of the soldiers who had been
guarding the tomb went into the city to tell
the leading priests everything that had
happened. 12Then the priests met with the
elders and made a plan. They paid the
soldiers a large amount of money 13and said
to them, "Tell the people that Jesus'

27:51 curtain in the Temple A curtain divided the Most Holy Place from the other part of the Temple. That was the special building in Jerusalem where God commanded the Jewish people to worship him.

devotion 270

MATTHEW 28:18–20

A TEACHABLE SPIRIT

Teaching the Bible is like a great adventure to discover the gems and pearls of love, wisdom, and hope that God has put there just for me to uncover. However, if I were to focus on teaching and not learning, it would all be in vain. As believers, our spirits are always directed toward heaven and into the Word to receive instruction and direction. Have you ever been in some sort of circumstance and literally all you could think about was getting to the Bible and carving out a time slot where you could pray and seek God for an answer? That is your spirit drawing you in so the Holy Spirit can show you what he wants you to know.

Jesus left behind one of the most cherished literary works ever recorded just so he would be able to teach you everything about himself and the kingdom of God. He did not leave you as someone without knowledge or hope. In Matthew, he left us instructions to share our hope, to teach people that baptism is the way to identify with his death and resurrection, and to teach others to die to their old nature and walk as a new creation in Christ.

This is my prayer for you: *My precious sister, I pray that you will seek God now with a spirit desiring to learn and then go and share what he has shown you with everyone who is seeking. Remember that God will be with you always. Amen.*

followers came during the night and stole
the body while you were asleep. [14]If the
governor hears about this, we will satisfy
him and save you from trouble." [15]So the
soldiers kept the money and did as they were
told. And that story is still spread among the
people even today.

Jesus Talks to His Followers

[16]The eleven followers went to Galilee to
the mountain where Jesus had told them to
go. [17]On the mountain they saw Jesus and
worshiped him, but some of them did not
believe it was really Jesus. [18]Then Jesus came
to them and said, "All power in heaven and
on earth is given to me. [19]So go and make
followers of all people in the world. Baptize
them in the name of the Father and the Son
and the Holy Spirit. [20]Teach them to obey
everything that I have taught you, and I will
be with you always, even until the end of
this age."

Mark

Many scholars believe this second account of the life and ministry of Jesus Christ was actually Mark's interpretation of Peter's first-hand experiences with the Messiah.

Person Holding the Pen God Wrote With: *Mark*, who is also known as John Mark (Acts 12:12, 25), penned this book. He was Barnabas's cousin (Col. 4:10) and Peter's student in the ministry (1 Pet. 5:13).

When the Text Was Written: Sometime between 50 and 70 A.D. before the destruction of the second Temple

Spiritual Posture of the Original Recipients: Mark is geared primarily toward Roman believers, who were suffering under anti-Christian leaders like Emperor Nero.

Storyline Synopsis: Whereas Matthew painted Jesus as the *King*, Mark portrays him as a *servant*. His story picks up at the beginning of Jesus' public ministry and highlights the ways Jesus met the literal and spiritual needs of people. Jesus is often shown extending compassion to those suffering painful circumstances: he heals a leper (Mark 1:40–42), restores hearing for a deaf man (7:31–35), and gives sight to a blind man at Bethsaida (8:22–25). Jesus' incarnate humanity is also more apparent in this Gospel than in the other accounts, including descriptions of him sleeping (4:38) and being hungry (11:12). Mark's perspective is very emotive and action oriented (he uses the word "immediately" a lot), and he conveys a sense of urgency.

A Moment Worth Discussing: The miraculous healing of a really sick woman epitomizes the tenderness of Christ (Mark 5:21–34). This woman had been hemorrhaging blood for twelve years, and Mark's narrative explains that she'd lost her health *and* her wealth (5:26). Plus, in light of her medical condition, she was also branded spiritually "unclean" according to Old Testament law, so other people couldn't even touch her. She was a pariah in every sense of the word. Probably a little on the grouchy side, too. But then the Messiah makes a visit. Not only does he heal her body, but he also heals her heart. Jesus delays his meeting with a very important man in the community for this ultra-compassionate detour.

Interesting (But Likely to Be Overlooked) Character: The author himself—*Mark!* Early in his walk of faith, John Mark's premature exit from a mission trip caused a rift between Paul and Barnabas (Acts 13—15). But the young man grew from his mistake and became a valuable asset to the ministry of spreading the Good News. He later reconciled with the apostle Paul (2 Tim. 4:11).

John Prepares for Jesus

1 This is the beginning of the Good News about Jesus Christ, the Son of God,[n] 2as the prophet Isaiah wrote:

"I will send my messenger ahead of you,
who will prepare your way." *Malachi 3:1*

3"This is a voice of one
who calls out in the desert:
'Prepare the way for the Lord.
Make the road straight for him.' " *Isaiah 40:3*

4John was baptizing people in the desert and preaching a baptism of changed hearts and lives for the forgiveness of sins. 5All the people from Judea and Jerusalem were going out to him. They confessed their sins and were baptized by him in the Jordan River. 6John wore clothes made from camel's hair, had a leather belt around his waist, and ate locusts and wild honey. 7This is what John preached to the people: "There is one coming after me who is greater than I; I am not good enough even to kneel down and untie his sandals. 8I baptize you with water, but he will baptize you with the Holy Spirit."

Jesus Is Baptized

9At that time Jesus came from the town of Nazareth in Galilee and was baptized by John in the Jordan River. 10Immediately, as Jesus was coming up out of the water, he saw heaven open. The Holy Spirit came down on him like a dove, 11and a voice came from heaven: "You are my Son, whom I love, and I am very pleased with you."

12Then the Spirit sent Jesus into the desert. 13He was in the desert forty days and was tempted by Satan. He was with the wild animals, and the angels came and took care of him.

Jesus Chooses Some Followers

14After John was put in prison, Jesus went into Galilee, preaching the Good News from God. 15He said, "The right time has come. The kingdom of God is near. Change your hearts and lives and believe the Good News!"

16When Jesus was walking by Lake Galilee, he saw Simon[n] and his brother Andrew throwing a net into the lake because they were fishermen. 17Jesus said to them, "Come follow me, and I will make you fish for people." 18So Simon and Andrew immediately left their nets and followed him.

19Going a little farther, Jesus saw two more brothers, James and John, the sons of Zebedee. They were in a boat, mending their nets. 20Jesus immediately called them, and they left their father in the boat with the hired workers and followed Jesus.

Jesus Forces Out an Evil Spirit

21Jesus and his followers went to Capernaum. On the Sabbath day he went to the synagogue and began to teach. 22The people were amazed at his teaching, because he taught like a person who had authority, not like their teachers of the law. 23Just then, a man was there in the synagogue who had an evil spirit in him. He shouted, 24"Jesus of Nazareth! What do you want with us? Did you come to destroy us? I know who you are—God's Holy One!"

25Jesus commanded the evil spirit, "Be quiet! Come out of the man!" 26The evil spirit shook the man violently, gave a loud cry, and then came out of him.

27The people were so amazed they asked each other, "What is happening here? This man is teaching something new, and with authority. He even gives commands to evil spirits, and they obey him." 28And the news about Jesus spread quickly everywhere in the area of Galilee.

Jesus Heals Many People

29As soon as Jesus and his followers left the synagogue, they went with James and John to the home of Simon[n] and Andrew. 30Simon's mother-in-law was sick in bed with a fever, and the people told Jesus about her. 31So Jesus went to her bed, took her hand, and helped her up. The fever left her, and she began serving them.

32That evening, after the sun went down, the people brought to Jesus all who were sick and had demons in them. 33The whole town gathered at the door. 34Jesus healed many who had different kinds of sicknesses, and he forced many demons to leave people. But he would not allow the demons to speak, because they knew who he was.

1:1 the Son of God Some Greek copies do not have this phrase.
1:16, 29 Simon Simon's other name was Peter.

[35]Early the next morning, while it was
still dark, Jesus woke and left the house. He
went to a lonely place, where he prayed.
[36]Simon and his friends went to look for
Jesus. [37]When they found him, they said,
"Everyone is looking for you!"
[38]Jesus answered, "We should go to other
towns around here so I can preach there too.
That is the reason I came." [39]So he went
everywhere in Galilee, preaching in the
synagogues and forcing out demons.

Jesus Heals a Sick Man

[40]A man with a skin disease came to Jesus.
He fell to his knees and begged Jesus, "You
can heal me if you will."
[41]Jesus felt sorry for the man, so he
reached out his hand and touched him and
said, "I will. Be healed!" [42]Immediately the
disease left the man, and he was healed.
[43]Jesus told the man to go away at once,
but he warned him strongly, [44]"Don't tell
anyone about this. But go and show yourself
to the priest. And offer the gift Moses
commanded for people who are made well.[n]
This will show the people what I have done."
[45]The man left there, but he began to tell
everyone that Jesus had healed him, and so
he spread the news about Jesus. As a result,
Jesus could not enter a town if people saw
him. He stayed in places where nobody
lived, but people came to him from
everywhere.

Jesus Heals a Paralyzed Man

2 A few days later, when Jesus came back
to Capernaum, the news spread that he
was at home. [2]Many people gathered
together so that there was no room in the
house, not even outside the door. And Jesus
was teaching them God's message. [3]Four
people came, carrying a paralyzed man.
[4]Since they could not get to Jesus because of
the crowd, they dug a hole in the roof right
above where he was speaking. When they
got through, they lowered the mat with the
paralyzed man on it. [5]When Jesus saw the
faith of these people, he said to the paralyzed
man, "Young man, your sins are forgiven."
[6]Some of the teachers of the law were

1:44 Moses . . . well Read about this in Leviticus 14:1–32.

devotion 271

MARK 2:5, 9–12

AIR RATIONS

I think most of us believe that Jesus has the power to forgive our sins. At least we initially believed that. But then somewhere along the Christian journey, we began to feel like there is a forgiveness ration and that our allowance has been depleted for a long time. I know it sounds crazy, but in truth, that's how many of us relate to God.

To say there is a forgiveness ration would be like waking up tomorrow morning, turning on the television, and hearing the newscaster say, "Local authorities are asking everyone to breathe shallow today. We are on mandatory air rations. No deep breaths until further notice." The idea of air rations is silly because we know that oxygen is being replenished every day. The air we breathe is continually being produced by nature.

In the same way, God promises that his forgiveness is without end. It is free, without a ration, to any who would call on his name. Jesus has been given the authority to forgive sins, and his authority is not limited to a per person quota.

What keeps you from new forgiveness today? Do you believe that you have used up all the forgiveness you deserve? Do you think Jesus is tired of forgiving your same old sin? It is by faith that we turn to Jesus and ask to be made clean. And every time we come in faith, God's never-ending love forgives our sin by the power of his Son.

sitting there, thinking to themselves, 7“Why
does this man say things like that? He is
speaking as if he were God. Only God can
forgive sins.”
8Jesus knew immediately what these
teachers of the law were thinking. So he said
to them, “Why are you thinking these
things? 9Which is easier: to tell this
paralyzed man, ‘Your sins are forgiven,’ or to
tell him, ‘Stand up. Take your mat and walk’?
10But I will prove to you that the Son of Man
has authority on earth to forgive sins.” So
Jesus said to the paralyzed man, 11“I tell you,
stand up, take your mat, and go home.”
12Immediately the paralyzed man stood up,
took his mat, and walked out while
everyone was watching him.
The people were amazed and praised God.
They said, “We have never seen anything
like this!”
13Jesus went to the lake again. The whole
crowd followed him there, and he taught
them. 14While he was walking along, he saw
a man named Levi son of Alphaeus, sitting
in the tax collector’s booth. Jesus said to him,
“Follow me,” and he stood up and followed
Jesus.
15Later, as Jesus was having dinner at
Levi’s house, many tax collectors and
“sinners” were eating there with Jesus and
his followers. Many people like this followed
Jesus. 16When the teachers of the law who
were Pharisees saw Jesus eating with the tax
collectors and “sinners,” they asked his
followers, “Why does he eat with tax
collectors and sinners?”
17Jesus heard this and said to them, “It is
not the healthy people who need a doctor,
but the sick. I did not come to invite good
people but to invite sinners.”

Jesus’ Followers Are Criticized

18Now the followers of John[n] and the
Pharisees often fasted[n] for a certain time.
Some people came to Jesus and said, “Why
do John’s followers and the followers of the
Pharisees often fast, but your followers
don’t?”
19Jesus answered, “The friends of the
bridegroom do not fast while the
bridegroom is still with them. As long as the
bridegroom is with them, they cannot fast.
20But the time will come when the
bridegroom will be taken from them, and
then they will fast.
21“No one sews a patch of unshrunk cloth
over a hole in an old coat. Otherwise, the
patch will shrink and pull away—the new
patch will pull away from the old coat. Then
the hole will be worse. 22Also, no one ever
pours new wine into old leather bags.
Otherwise, the new wine will break the bags,
and the wine will be ruined along with the
bags. But new wine should be put into new
leather bags.”

Jesus Is Lord of the Sabbath

23One Sabbath day, as Jesus was walking
through some fields of grain, his followers
began to pick some grain to eat. 24The
Pharisees said to Jesus, “Why are your
followers doing what is not lawful on the
Sabbath day?”
25Jesus answered, “Have you never read
what David did when he and those with him
were hungry and needed food? 26During the
time of Abiathar the high priest, David went
into God’s house and ate the holy bread,
which is lawful only for priests to eat. And
David also gave some of the bread to those
who were with him.”
27Then Jesus said to the Pharisees, “The
Sabbath day was made to help people; they
were not made to be ruled by the Sabbath
day. 28So then, the Son of Man is Lord even
of the Sabbath day.”

Jesus Heals a Man’s Hand

3 Another time when Jesus went into a
synagogue, a man with a crippled hand
was there. 2Some people watched Jesus
closely to see if he would heal the man on
the Sabbath day so they could accuse him.
3Jesus said to the man with the crippled
hand, “Stand up here in the middle of
everyone.”
4Then Jesus asked the people, “Which is
lawful on the Sabbath day: to do good or to
do evil, to save a life or to kill?” But they said
nothing to answer him.
5Jesus was angry as he looked at the
people, and he felt very sad because they

2:18 John John the Baptist, who preached to the Jewish people about Christ’s coming (Mark 1:4–8).

2:18 fasted The people would give up eating for a special time of prayer and worship to God. It was also done to show sadness and disappointment.

were stubborn. Then he said to the man,
"Hold out your hand." The man held out his
hand and it was healed. 6 Then the Pharisees
left and began making plans with the
Herodians[n] about a way to kill Jesus.

Many People Follow Jesus

7 Jesus left with his followers for the lake,
and a large crowd from Galilee followed
him. 8 Also many people came from Judea,
from Jerusalem, from Idumea, from the
lands across the Jordan River, and from the
area of Tyre and Sidon. When they heard
what Jesus was doing, many people came to
him. 9 When Jesus saw the crowds, he told
his followers to get a boat ready for him to
keep people from crowding against him.
10 He had healed many people, so all the sick
were pushing toward him to touch him.
11 When evil spirits saw Jesus, they fell down
before him and shouted, "You are the Son of
God!" 12 But Jesus strongly warned them not
to tell who he was.

Jesus Chooses His Twelve Apostles

13 Then Jesus went up on a mountain and
called to him those he wanted, and they
came to him. 14 Jesus chose twelve and called
them apostles.[n] He wanted them to be with
him, and he wanted to send them out to
preach 15 and to have the authority to force
demons out of people. 16 These are the twelve
men he chose: Simon (Jesus named him
Peter), 17 James and John, the sons of Zebedee
(Jesus named them Boanerges, which means
"Sons of Thunder"), 18 Andrew, Philip,
Bartholomew, Matthew, Thomas, James the
son of Alphaeus, Thaddaeus, Simon the
Zealot, 19 and Judas Iscariot, who later turned
against Jesus.

Some People Say Jesus Has a Devil

20 Then Jesus went home, but again a
crowd gathered. There were so many people
that Jesus and his followers could not eat.
21 When his family heard this, they went to
get him because they thought he was out of
his mind. 22 But the teachers of the law from
Jerusalem were saying, "Beelzebul is living
inside him! He uses power from the ruler of
demons to force demons out of people."

23 So Jesus called the people together and
taught them with stories. He said, "Satan
will not force himself out of people. 24 A
kingdom that is divided cannot continue,
25 and a family that is divided cannot
continue. 26 And if Satan is against himself
and fights against his own people, he cannot
continue; that is the end of Satan. 27 No one
can enter a strong person's house and steal
his things unless he first ties up the strong
person. Then he can steal things from the
house. 28 I tell you the truth, all sins that
people do and all the things people say
against God can be forgiven. 29 But anyone
who speaks against the Holy Spirit will
never be forgiven; he is guilty of a sin that
continues forever."

30 Jesus said this because the teachers of
the law said that he had an evil spirit inside
him.

Jesus' True Family

31 Then Jesus' mother and brothers arrived.
Standing outside, they sent someone in to
tell him to come out. 32 Many people were
sitting around Jesus, and they said to him,
"Your mother and brothers[n] are waiting for
you outside."

33 Jesus asked, "Who are my mother and
my brothers?" 34 Then he looked at those
sitting around him and said, "Here are my
mother and my brothers! 35 My true brother
and sister and mother are those who do
what God wants."

A Story About Planting Seed

4 Again Jesus began teaching by the lake.
A great crowd gathered around him, so
he sat down in a boat near the shore. All the
people stayed on the shore close to the
water. 2 Jesus taught them many things,
using stories. He said, 3 "Listen! A farmer
went out to plant his seed. 4 While he was
planting, some seed fell by the road, and the
birds came and ate it up. 5 Some seed fell on
rocky ground where there wasn't much dirt.
That seed grew very fast, because the ground
was not deep. 6 But when the sun rose, the
plants dried up because they did not have
deep roots. 7 Some other seed fell among
thorny weeds, which grew and choked the

3:6 Herodians A political group that followed Herod and his family. **3:14 and called them apostles** Some Greek copies do not have this phrase. **3:32 brothers** Some Greek copies continue, "and sisters."

good plants. So those plants did not produce
a crop. 8Some other seed fell on good ground
and began to grow. It got taller and produced
a crop. Some plants made thirty times more,
some made sixty times more, and some
made a hundred times more."
9Then Jesus said, "Let those with ears use
them and listen!"

Jesus Tells Why He Used Stories

10Later, when Jesus was alone, the twelve
apostles and others around him asked him
about the stories.
11Jesus said, "You can know the secret
about the kingdom of God. But to other
people I tell everything by using stories 12so
that:

'They will look and look, but they will not
learn.
They will listen and listen, but they
will not understand.
If they did learn and understand,
they would come back to me and be
forgiven.' " *Isaiah 6:9–10*

Jesus Explains the Seed Story

13Then Jesus said to his followers, "Don't
you understand this story? If you don't, how
will you understand any story? 14The farmer
is like a person who plants God's message in
people. 15Sometimes the teaching falls on the
road. This is like the people who hear the
teaching of God, but Satan quickly comes
and takes away the teaching that was planted
in them. 16Others are like the seed planted on
rocky ground. They hear the teaching and
quickly accept it with joy. 17But since they
don't allow the teaching to go deep into their
lives, they keep it only a short time. When
trouble or persecution comes because of the
teaching they accepted, they quickly give up.
18Others are like the seed planted among the
thorny weeds. They hear the teaching, 19but
the worries of this life, the temptation of
wealth, and many other evil desires keep the
teaching from growing and producing fruit[n]
in their lives. 20Others are like the seed
planted in the good ground. They hear the
teaching and accept it. Then they grow and
produce fruit—sometimes thirty times more,
sometimes sixty times more, and sometimes
a hundred times more."

Use What You Have

21Then Jesus said to them, "Do you hide a
lamp under a bowl or under a bed? No! You
put the lamp on a lampstand. 22Everything
that is hidden will be made clear and every
secret thing will be made known. 23Let those
with ears use them and listen!
24"Think carefully about what you hear.
The way you give to others is the way God
will give to you, but God will give you even
more. 25Those who have understanding will
be given more. But those who do not have
understanding, even what they have will be
taken away from them."

Jesus Uses a Story About Seed

26Then Jesus said, "The kingdom of God
is like someone who plants seed in the
ground. 27Night and day, whether the person
is asleep or awake, the seed still grows, but
the person does not know how it grows.
28By itself the earth produces grain. First the
plant grows, then the head, and then all the
grain in the head. 29When the grain is ready,
the farmer cuts it, because this is the harvest
time."

A Story About Mustard Seed

30Then Jesus said, "How can I show you
what the kingdom of God is like? What
story can I use to explain it? 31The kingdom
of God is like a mustard seed, the smallest
seed you plant in the ground. 32But when
planted, this seed grows and becomes the
largest of all garden plants. It produces large
branches, and the wild birds can make nests
in its shade."
33Jesus used many stories like these to
teach the crowd God's message—as much as
they could understand. 34He always used
stories to teach them. But when he and his
followers were alone, Jesus explained
everything to them.

Jesus Calms a Storm

35That evening, Jesus said to his followers,
"Let's go across the lake." 36Leaving the
crowd behind, they took him in the boat just
as he was. There were also other boats with
them. 37A very strong wind came up on the
lake. The waves came over the sides and into
the boat so that it was already full of water.

4:19 producing fruit To produce fruit means to have in your life the good things God wants.

38Jesus was at the back of the boat, sleeping
with his head on a cushion. His followers
woke him and said, "Teacher, don't you care
that we are drowning!"
39Jesus stood up and commanded the
wind and said to the waves, "Quiet! Be still!"
Then the wind stopped, and it became
completely calm.
40Jesus said to his followers, "Why are you
afraid? Do you still have no faith?"
41The followers were very afraid and
asked each other, "Who is this? Even the
wind and the waves obey him!"

A Man with Demons Inside Him

5 Jesus and his followers went to the other
side of the lake to the area of the
Gerasene[n] people. 2When Jesus got out of the
boat, instantly a man with an evil spirit
came to him from the burial caves. 3This
man lived in the caves, and no one could tie
him up, not even with a chain. 4Many times
people had used chains to tie the man's
hands and feet, but he always broke them
off. No one was strong enough to control
him. 5Day and night he would wander
around the burial caves and on the hills,
screaming and cutting himself with stones.
6While Jesus was still far away, the man saw
him, ran to him, and fell down before him.
7The man shouted in a loud voice, "What
do you want with me, Jesus, Son of the Most
High God? I command you in God's name
not to torture me!" 8He said this because
Jesus was saying to him, "You evil spirit,
come out of the man."
9Then Jesus asked him, "What is your
name?"
He answered, "My name is Legion,[n]
because we are many spirits." 10He begged
Jesus again and again not to send them out
of that area.
11A large herd of pigs was feeding on a hill
near there. 12The demons begged Jesus,
"Send us into the pigs; let us go into them."
13So Jesus allowed them to do this. The evil
spirits left the man and went into the pigs.
Then the herd of pigs—about two thousand
of them—rushed down the hill into the lake
and were drowned.

5:1 Gerasene From Gerasa, an area southeast of Lake Galilee. The exact location is uncertain and some Greek copies read "Gergesene"; others read "Gadarene." **5:9 Legion** Means very many. A legion was about five thousand men in the Roman army.

devotion 272

MARK 4:39

KEEP YOUR EYE ON THE CAPTAIN

My husband and I try to go on a vacation together every year. We love the Caribbean and enjoy sitting on a deserted beach with a good book. One year we boarded a boat for a one-hour ride across the ocean to a nearby island. As soon as we passed the safety of the harbor, the waves began rocking our little boat, and eventually they crashed on top of us. I was terrified and began planning how we would survive when the boat flipped over. The captain, on the other hand, was chatting away as we went. He had done this trip hundreds of times, and he was not the least bit afraid. When I focused on the waves, the fear consumed me, but when I kept my eyes on the captain, I knew we would be okay. I had faith that the captain would get us across safely.

I couldn't help but think of Jesus calming the waters. I knew how his followers must have felt when the storm hit them. The boat tosses you about, and you feel as though you will capsize at any moment. I love that Jesus was asleep in the back of the boat. When his followers finally woke him up, they didn't even ask him to help because they thought there was nothing he could do. They didn't realize that Jesus was the captain. When you feel like you are about to drown, keep your eyes on the Captain.

The Hemorrhaging Woman

MARK 5

She hovers at the edge of the crowd, looking for a way inside. The throng presses closer to Jesus, and she folds into the masses. She can see the top of his head, but there are still too many people in front of her. A man lifts his son to his shoulders, and the crowd shifts, creating an entry.

She extends her arm but can't touch him. Looking down, she notices a small hole at the feet of the men around her. Kneeling, she sees the hem of Jesus' garment. She thinks, *If I can just touch his clothes, I will be healed.* Stretching her arm through the maze of legs, the tips of her fingers brush the hem of his garment.

Her bleeding stops as a warm sensation spreads through her, flushing out the decay and easing the pain. Laughter fills her throat. She rushes through the swarm of bodies before causing a spectacle.

"Who touched my clothes?" Jesus' followers look around. It was an impossible question to answer.

The woman falls at his feet and, like a babbling brook, spills her story of suffering—twelve years of seeing physicians who could do nothing for her.

"Be encouraged," Jesus says with compassion. "You are made well because you believed." And with that, the crowd presses upon him again. But she is no longer the same—she is healed!

Many people are eager to huddle around Jesus but never actually touch him. How close are you?

14The herdsmen ran away and went to the
town and to the countryside, telling
everyone about this. So people went out to
see what had happened. 15They came to
Jesus and saw the man who used to have the
many evil spirits, sitting, clothed, and in his
right mind. And they were frightened. 16The
people who saw this told the others what
had happened to the man who had the
demons living in him, and they told about
the pigs. 17Then the people began to beg
Jesus to leave their area.

18As Jesus was getting back into the boat,
the man who was freed from the demons
begged to go with him.

19But Jesus would not let him. He said, "Go
home to your family and tell them how
much the Lord has done for you and how he
has had mercy on you." 20So the man left
and began to tell the people in the Ten
Towns[n] about what Jesus had done for him.
And everyone was amazed.

Jesus Gives Life to a Dead Girl and Heals a Sick Woman

21When Jesus went in the boat back to the
other side of the lake, a large crowd gathered
around him there. 22A leader of the
synagogue, named Jairus, came there, saw
Jesus, and fell at his feet. 23He begged Jesus,
saying again and again, "My daughter is
dying. Please come and put your hands on
her so she will be healed and will live." 24So
Jesus went with him.

A large crowd followed Jesus and pushed
very close around him. 25Among them was a
woman who had been bleeding for twelve
years. 26She had suffered very much from
many doctors and had spent all the money
she had, but instead of improving, she was
getting worse. 27When the woman heard
about Jesus, she came up behind him in the
crowd and touched his coat. 28She thought,
"If I can just touch his clothes, I will be
healed." 29Instantly her bleeding stopped,
and she felt in her body that she was healed
from her disease.

30At once Jesus felt power go out from
him. So he turned around in the crowd and
asked, "Who touched my clothes?"

31His followers said, "Look at how many

5:20 Ten Towns In Greek, called "Decapolis." It was an area east of Lake Galilee that once had ten main towns.

people are pushing against you! And you ask, 'Who touched me?' "

32But Jesus continued looking around to see who had touched him. 33The woman, knowing that she was healed, came and fell at Jesus' feet. Shaking with fear, she told him the whole truth. 34Jesus said to her, "Dear woman, you are made well because you believed. Go in peace; be healed of your disease."

35While Jesus was still speaking, some people came from the house of the synagogue leader. They said, "Your daughter is dead. There is no need to bother the teacher anymore."

36But Jesus paid no attention to what they said. He told the synagogue leader, "Don't be afraid; just believe."

37Jesus let only Peter, James, and John the brother of James go with him. 38When they came to the house of the synagogue leader, Jesus found many people there making lots of noise and crying loudly. 39Jesus entered the house and said to them, "Why are you crying and making so much noise? The child is not dead, only asleep." 40But they laughed at him. So, after throwing them out of the house, Jesus took the child's father and mother and his three followers into the room where the child was. 41Taking hold of the girl's hand, he said to her, "Talitha, koum!" (This means, "Young girl, I tell you to stand up!") 42At once the girl stood right up and began walking. (She was twelve years old.) Everyone was completely amazed. 43Jesus gave them strict orders not to tell people about this. Then he told them to give the girl something to eat.

Jesus Goes to His Hometown

6 Jesus left there and went to his hometown, and his followers went with him. 2On the Sabbath day he taught in the synagogue. Many people heard him and were amazed, saying, "Where did this man get these teachings? What is this wisdom that has been given to him? And where did he get the power to do miracles? 3He is just the carpenter, the son of Mary and the brother of James, Joseph, Judas, and Simon. And his sisters are here with us." So the people were upset with Jesus.

4Jesus said to them, "A prophet is honored everywhere except in his hometown and with his own people and in his own home." 5So Jesus was not able to work any miracles there except to heal a few sick people by putting his hands on them. 6He was amazed at how many people had no faith.

Then Jesus went to other villages in that area and taught. 7He called his twelve followers together and got ready to send them out two by two and gave them authority over evil spirits. 8This is what Jesus commanded them: "Take nothing for your trip except a walking stick. Take no bread, no bag, and no money in your pockets. 9Wear sandals, but take only the clothes you are wearing. 10When you enter a house, stay there until you leave that town. 11If the people in a certain place refuse to welcome you or listen to you, leave that place. Shake its dust off your feet[n] as a warning to them."[n]

12So the followers went out and preached that people should change their hearts and lives. 13They forced many demons out and put olive oil on many sick people and healed them.

How John the Baptist Was Killed

14King Herod heard about Jesus, because he was now well known. Some people said,[n] "He is John the Baptist, who has risen from the dead. That is why he can work these miracles."

15Others said, "He is Elijah."[n]

Other people said, "Jesus is a prophet, like the prophets who lived long ago."

16When Herod heard this, he said, "I killed John by cutting off his head. Now he has risen from the dead!"

17Herod himself had ordered his soldiers to arrest John and put him in prison in order to please his wife, Herodias. She had been the wife of Philip, Herod's brother, but then Herod had married her. 18John had been telling Herod, "It is not lawful for you to be married to your brother's wife." 19So Herodias hated John and wanted to kill him.

6:11 Shake . . . feet A warning. It showed that they were rejecting these people. **6:11 them** Some Greek copies continue, "I tell you the truth, on the Judgment Day it will be better for the towns of Sodom and Gomorrah than for the people of that town." See Matthew 10:15.

6:14 Some people said Some Greek copies read "He said."

6:15 Elijah A great prophet who spoke for God and who lived hundreds of years before Christ. See 1 Kings 17.

But she couldn't, 20because Herod was afraid
of John and protected him. He knew John
was a good and holy man. Also, though
John's preaching always bothered him, he
enjoyed listening to John.
21Then the perfect time came for Herodias
to cause John's death. On Herod's birthday,
he gave a dinner party for the most
important government leaders, the
commanders of his army, and the most
important people in Galilee. 22When the
daughter of Herodias[n] came in and danced,
she pleased Herod and the people eating
with him.
So King Herod said to the girl, "Ask me for
anything you want, and I will give it to you."
23He promised her, "Anything you ask for I
will give to you—up to half of my kingdom."
24The girl went to her mother and asked,
"What should I ask for?"
Her mother answered, "Ask for the head of
John the Baptist."
25At once the girl went back to the king
and said to him, "I want the head of John the
Baptist right now on a platter."
26Although the king was very sad, he had
made a promise, and his dinner guests had
heard it. So he did not want to refuse what
she asked. 27Immediately the king sent a
soldier to bring John's head. The soldier went
and cut off John's head in the prison 28and
brought it back on a platter. He gave it to the
girl, and the girl gave it to her mother.
29When John's followers heard this, they
came and got John's body and put it in a
tomb.

More than Five Thousand Fed

30The apostles gathered around Jesus and
told him about all the things they had done
and taught. 31Crowds of people were coming
and going so that Jesus and his followers did
not even have time to eat. He said to them,
"Come away by yourselves, and we will go to
a lonely place to get some rest."
32So they went in a boat by themselves to
a lonely place. 33But many people saw them
leave and recognized them. So from all the
towns they ran to the place where Jesus was
going, and they got there before him.
34When he arrived, he saw a great crowd
waiting. He felt sorry for them, because they

Jairus's Wife and Daughter

MARK 5

She presses a cloth to her daughter's face and the girl whimpers. The child is slipping further away. They are helpless as they watch death draw near.

In desperation, the woman looks to her husband. "Go, find this man Jesus. Beg him to come." Jairus darts from the house, and the mother picks up the limp hand of her daughter as she whispers, "Please don't let her die."

Time creeps by slowly in the tiny room. *Where is Jairus? Hasn't he found Jesus yet?* Her daughter's breath is growing shallow. Doesn't Jesus care that her child is dying? A rattle develops in the child's chest, and the mother throws herself onto the child's unresponsive body. "No!" she screams, clinging to the last shreds of life that remain in her child. With one final breath, her daughter is gone.

A mother's sobs are heard throughout the house, even into the street. Word spreads of her death, and the home is filled with mourners when Jairus arrives with Jesus and three of his followers. "The child is not dead, only asleep," he says. The mourners laugh—the child has been dead for some time now. Jesus enters the girl's room, and the mother sinks further into despair. *If only he had come sooner!* she thinks.

Jesus holds the child's hand and squeezes it. "Young girl, I tell you to stand up!" In that moment, Jesus healed a daughter's body and also a mother's heart.

Jesus still helps those who cry out to him.

6:22 When . . . Herodias Some Greek copies read "When his daughter Herodias."

were like sheep without a shepherd. So he
began to teach them many things.
35When it was late in the day, his
followers came to him and said, "No one
lives in this place, and it is already very late.
36Send the people away so they can go to the
countryside and towns around here to buy
themselves something to eat."
37But Jesus answered, "You give them
something to eat."

They said to him, "We would all have to
work a month to earn enough money to buy
that much bread!"
38Jesus asked them, "How many loaves of
bread do you have? Go and see."

When they found out, they said, "Five
loaves and two fish."
39Then Jesus told his followers to have the
people sit in groups on the green grass. 40So
they sat in groups of fifty or a hundred.
41Jesus took the five loaves and two fish and,
looking up to heaven, he thanked God for
the food. He divided the bread and gave it to
his followers for them to give to the people.
Then he divided the two fish among them
all. 42All the people ate and were satisfied.
43The followers filled twelve baskets with
the leftover pieces of bread and fish. 44There
were five thousand men who ate.

Jesus Walks on the Water

45Immediately Jesus told his followers to
get into the boat and go ahead of him to
Bethsaida across the lake. He stayed there to
send the people home. 46After sending them
away, he went into the hills to pray.
47That night, the boat was in the middle
of the lake, and Jesus was alone on the land.
48He saw his followers struggling hard to
row the boat, because the wind was blowing
against them. Between three and six o'clock
in the morning, Jesus came to them, walking
on the water, and he wanted to walk past the
boat. 49But when they saw him walking on
the water, they thought he was a ghost and
cried out. 50They all saw him and were
afraid. But quickly Jesus spoke to them and
said, "Have courage! It is I. Do not be afraid."
51Then he got into the boat with them, and
the wind became calm. The followers were
greatly amazed. 52They did not understand
about the miracle of the five loaves, because
their minds were closed.
53When they had crossed the lake, they
came to shore at Gennesaret and tied the
boat there. 54When they got out of the boat,
people immediately recognized Jesus. 55They
ran everywhere in that area and began to
bring sick people on mats wherever they
heard he was. 56And everywhere he went—
into towns, cities, or countryside—the
people brought the sick to the marketplaces.
They begged him to let them touch just the
edge of his coat, and all who touched it were
healed.

Obey God's Law

7 When some Pharisees and some teachers
of the law came from Jerusalem, they
gathered around Jesus. 2They saw that some
of Jesus' followers ate food with hands that
were not clean, that is, they hadn't washed
them. 3(The Pharisees and all the Jews never
eat before washing their hands in the way
required by their unwritten laws. 4And when
they buy something in the market, they
never eat it until they wash themselves in a
special way. They also follow many other
unwritten laws, such as the washing of cups,
pitchers, and pots.[n])
5The Pharisees and the teachers of the law
said to Jesus, "Why don't your followers obey
the unwritten laws which have been handed
down to us? Why do your followers eat their
food with hands that are not clean?"
6Jesus answered, "Isaiah was right when
he spoke about you hypocrites. He wrote,

'These people show honor to me with
words,
but their hearts are far from me.
7Their worship of me is worthless.
The things they teach are nothing but
human rules.' *Isaiah 29:13*

8You have stopped following the commands
of God, and you follow only human
teachings."[n]
9Then Jesus said to them, "You cleverly
ignore the commands of God so you can
follow your own teachings. 10Moses said,
'Honor your father and your mother,'[n] and
'Anyone who says cruel things to his father
or mother must be put to death.'[n] 11But you

7:4 pots Some Greek copies continue, "and dining couches." **7:8 teachings** Some Greek copies continue, "You wash pitchers and jugs and do many other such things." **7:10 'Honor . . . mother.'** Quotation from Exodus 20:12; Deuteronomy 5:16. **7:10 'Anyone . . . death.'** Quotation from Exodus 21:17.

The Non-Jewish Woman

MARK 7

She wraps her arms around her little girl to stop the thrashing, but it is no use. The child throws her mother off, and the small body jerks and twists on the floor, babbling nonsense in a voice her mother does not recognize. Gone is the innocent child with sweet kisses and giggles at bedtime.

The mother opens the door when she hears commotion in the streets. "He is a Jewish healer," she hears someone say. "He has been healing people in Galilee." She kneels at her daughter's side, trying to smooth the contorted features. "I'm going for help."

The child screams in agony, and the mother slams the door behind her. She sees the Jewish man ahead. "Lord, Son of David," she screams, "have mercy on me! My daughter has a demon, and she is suffering very much."

He does not respond, and she continues to shout after him, begging for help. The man's followers ask that he send the woman away. She bows before him in desperation. Her heart is breaking, but a few words fall from her lips. "Lord, help me!" He says his ministry is for the Jews, but she is unwavering in her pleas, beseeching him for the smallest crumb of relief.

"You have great faith!" he says. "I will do what you asked." At that very moment, her daughter was healed.

It was tenacious faith that compelled the mother to keep following Jesus. Don't give up. Keep following and asking!

say a person can tell his father or mother, 'I have something I could use to help you, but it is Corban—a gift to God.' 12 You no longer let that person use that money for his father or his mother. 13 By your own rules, which you teach people, you are rejecting what God said. And you do many things like that."

14 After Jesus called the crowd to him again, he said, "Every person should listen to me and understand what I am saying. 15 There is nothing people put into their bodies that makes them unclean. People are made unclean by the things that come out of them. [16 Let those with ears use them and listen.]"[n]

17 When Jesus left the people and went into the house, his followers asked him about this story. 18 Jesus said, "Do you still not understand? Surely you know that nothing that enters someone from the outside can make that person unclean. 19 It does not go into the mind, but into the stomach. Then it goes out of the body." (When Jesus said this, he meant that no longer was any food unclean for people to eat.)

20 And Jesus said, "The things that come out of people are the things that make them unclean. 21 All these evil things begin inside people, in the mind: evil thoughts, sexual sins, stealing, murder, adultery, 22 greed, evil actions, lying, doing sinful things, jealousy, speaking evil of others, pride, and foolish living. 23 All these evil things come from inside and make people unclean."

Jesus Helps a Non-Jewish Woman

24 Jesus left that place and went to the area around Tyre.[n] When he went into a house, he did not want anyone to know he was there, but he could not stay hidden. 25 A woman whose daughter had an evil spirit in her heard that he was there. So she quickly came to Jesus and fell at his feet. 26 She was Greek, born in Phoenicia, in Syria. She begged Jesus to force the demon out of her daughter.

27 Jesus told the woman, "It is not right to take the children's bread and give it to the dogs. First let the children eat all they want."

28 But she answered, "Yes, Lord, but even the dogs under the table can eat the children's crumbs."

7:16 Let . . . listen. Some Greek copies do not contain the bracketed text.
7:24 Tyre Some Greek copies continue, "and Sidon."

29 Then Jesus said, "Because of your
answer, you may go. The demon has left
your daughter."

30 The woman went home and found her
daughter lying in bed; the demon was gone.

Jesus Heals a Deaf Man

31 Then Jesus left the area around Tyre and
went through Sidon to Lake Galilee, to the
area of the Ten Towns.[n] 32 While he was
there, some people brought a man to him
who was deaf and could not talk plainly. The
people begged Jesus to put his hand on the
man to heal him.

33 Jesus led the man away from the crowd,
by himself. He put his fingers in the man's
ears and then spit and touched the man's
tongue. 34 Looking up to heaven, he sighed
and said to the man, "Ephphatha!" (This
means, "Be opened.") 35 Instantly the man
was able to hear and to use his tongue so
that he spoke clearly.

36 Jesus commanded the people not to tell
anyone about what happened. But the more
he commanded them, the more they told
about it. 37 They were completely amazed
and said, "Jesus does everything well. He
makes the deaf hear! And those who can't
talk he makes able to speak."

More than Four Thousand People Fed

8 Another time there was a great crowd
with Jesus that had nothing to eat. So
Jesus called his followers and said, 2 "I feel
sorry for these people, because they have
already been with me for three days, and
they have nothing to eat. 3 If I send them
home hungry, they will faint on the way.
Some of them live a long way from here."

4 Jesus' followers answered, "How can we
get enough bread to feed all these people?
We are far away from any town."

5 Jesus asked, "How many loaves of bread
do you have?"

They answered, "Seven."

6 Jesus told the people to sit on the ground.
Then he took the seven loaves, gave thanks
to God, and divided the bread. He gave the
pieces to his followers to give to the people,
and they did so. 7 The followers also had a
few small fish. After Jesus gave thanks for
the fish, he told his followers to give them to
the people also. 8 All the people ate and were
satisfied. Then his followers filled seven
baskets with the leftover pieces of food.
9 There were about four thousand people
who ate. After they had eaten, Jesus sent
them home. 10 Then right away he got into a
boat with his followers and went to the area
of Dalmanutha.

The Leaders Ask for a Miracle

11 The Pharisees came to Jesus and began
to ask him questions. Hoping to trap him,
they asked Jesus for a miracle from God.
12 Jesus sighed deeply and said, "Why do you
people ask for a miracle as a sign? I tell you
the truth, no sign will be given to you."
13 Then Jesus left the Pharisees and went in
the boat to the other side of the lake.

Guard Against Wrong Teachings

14 His followers had only one loaf of bread
with them in the boat; they had forgotten to
bring more. 15 Jesus warned them, "Be
careful! Beware of the yeast of the Pharisees
and the yeast of Herod."

16 His followers discussed the meaning of
this, saying, "He said this because we have
no bread."

17 Knowing what they were talking about,
Jesus asked them, "Why are you talking
about not having bread? Do you still not see
or understand? Are your minds closed?
18 You have eyes, but you don't really see. You
have ears, but you don't really listen.
Remember when 19 I divided five loaves of
bread for the five thousand? How many
baskets did you fill with leftover pieces of
food?"

They answered, "Twelve."

20 "And when I divided seven loaves of
bread for the four thousand, how many
baskets did you fill with leftover pieces of
food?"

They answered, "Seven."

21 Then Jesus said to them, "Don't you
understand yet?"

Jesus Heals a Blind Man

22 Jesus and his followers came to
Bethsaida. There some people brought a
blind man to Jesus and begged him to
touch the man. 23 So Jesus took the blind

7:31 Ten Towns In Greek, called "Decapolis." It was an area east of Lake Galilee that once had ten main towns.

man's hand and led him out of the village.
Then he spit on the man's eyes and put
his hands on the man and asked, "Can you
see now?"
24The man looked up and said, "Yes, I see
people, but they look like trees walking
around."
25Again Jesus put his hands on the man's
eyes. Then the man opened his eyes wide
and they were healed, and he was able to see
everything clearly. 26Jesus told him to go
home, saying, "Don't go into the town."[n]

Peter Says Jesus Is the Christ

27Jesus and his followers went to the
towns around Caesarea Philippi. While they
were traveling, Jesus asked them, "Who do
people say I am?"
28They answered, "Some say you are John
the Baptist. Others say you are Elijah,[n] and
others say you are one of the prophets."
29Then Jesus asked, "But who do you say I
am?"
Peter answered, "You are the Christ."
30Jesus warned his followers not to tell
anyone who he was.
31Then Jesus began to teach them that the
Son of Man must suffer many things and
that he would be rejected by the Jewish
elders, the leading priests, and the teachers
of the law. He told them that the Son of Man
must be killed and then rise from the dead
after three days. 32Jesus told them plainly
what would happen. Then Peter took Jesus
aside and began to tell him not to talk like
that. 33But Jesus turned and looked at his
followers. Then he told Peter not to talk that
way. He said, "Go away from me, Satan![n] You
don't care about the things of God, but only
about things people think are important."
34Then Jesus called the crowd to him,
along with his followers. He said, "If people
want to follow me, they must give up the
things they want. They must be willing even
to give up their lives to follow me. 35Those
who want to save their lives will give up
true life. But those who give up their lives
for me and for the Good News will have true

8:26 town Some Greek copies continue, "Don't even go and tell anyone in the town." **8:28 Elijah** A man who spoke for God and who lived hundreds of years before Christ. See 1 Kings 17. **8:33 Satan** Name for the devil meaning "the enemy." Jesus means that Peter was talking like Satan.

devotion 273

MARK 8:34–38

WHAT WOULD YOU GIVE UP?

Becoming more like Christ wasn't easy for his followers, and it isn't always easy for us either. Jesus said his followers must be willing to give up their lives to follow him. While there's nothing better than knowing Christ as our Savior, it's true that we'll be tested for our faith just as his followers were. This passage challenges me to think about what I'd do if asked to give up my life for my Christian faith. Am I willing to sacrifice the approval of others? Do I cave in to friends, co-workers, or society in general when my belief in Jesus is challenged? Do I keep quiet instead of speaking up?

I have to admit I'm not perfect, but I want to raise my voice about Jesus. If we lived in a world where everyone wanted to follow Jesus, then following him would be easy. However, it seems we're surrounded every day by messages of anti-Christianity. Missionaries and followers are dying in other countries, and even in the United States, simply for spreading the Word of God. Yet in spite of all the hostility toward my God and my salvation, I'm encouraged by these words of Jesus: "It is worthless to have the whole world if they lose their souls" (verse 36). I don't want to worry about being persecuted for my faith. I want to tell the lost about Jesus. I want to make a difference in this temporary world while I keep my eyes on eternity.

life. 36 It is worthless to have the whole world
if they lose their souls. 37 They could never
pay enough to buy back their souls. 38 The
people who live now are living in a sinful
and evil time. If people are ashamed of me
and my teaching, the Son of Man will be
ashamed of them when he comes with his
Father's glory and with the holy angels."

9 Then Jesus said to the people, "I tell you
the truth, some people standing here will
see the kingdom of God come with power
before they die."

Jesus Talks with Moses and Elijah

2 Six days later, Jesus took Peter, James, and
John up on a high mountain by themselves.
While they watched, Jesus' appearance was
changed. 3 His clothes became shining white,
whiter than any person could make them.
4 Then Elijah and Moses[n] appeared to them,
talking with Jesus.

5 Peter said to Jesus, "Teacher, it is good
that we are here. Let us make three tents—
one for you, one for Moses, and one for
Elijah." 6 Peter did not know what to say,
because he and the others were so
frightened.

7 Then a cloud came and covered them,
and a voice came from the cloud, saying,
"This is my Son, whom I love. Listen to him!"

8 Suddenly Peter, James, and John looked
around, but they saw only Jesus there alone
with them.

9 As they were coming down the
mountain, Jesus commanded them not to
tell anyone about what they had seen until
the Son of Man had risen from the dead.

10 So the followers obeyed Jesus, but they
discussed what he meant about rising from
the dead.

11 Then they asked Jesus, "Why do the
teachers of the law say that Elijah must
come first?"

12 Jesus answered, "They are right to say
that Elijah must come first and make
everything the way it should be. But why
does the Scripture say that the Son of Man
will suffer much and that people will treat
him as if he were nothing? 13 I tell you that
Elijah has already come. And people did to
him whatever they wanted to do, just as the
Scriptures said it would happen."

Jesus Heals a Sick Boy

14 When Jesus, Peter, James, and John came
back to the other followers, they saw a great
crowd around them and the teachers of the
law arguing with them. 15 But as soon as the
crowd saw Jesus, the people were surprised
and ran to welcome him.

16 Jesus asked, "What are you arguing
about?"

17 A man answered, "Teacher, I brought my
son to you. He has an evil spirit in him that
stops him from talking. 18 When the spirit
attacks him, it throws him on the ground.
Then my son foams at the mouth, grinds his
teeth, and becomes very stiff. I asked your
followers to force the evil spirit out, but they
couldn't."

19 Jesus answered, "You people have no
faith. How long must I stay with you? How
long must I put up with you? Bring the boy
to me."

20 So the followers brought him to Jesus.
As soon as the evil spirit saw Jesus, it made
the boy lose control of himself, and he fell
down and rolled on the ground, foaming at
the mouth.

21 Jesus asked the boy's father, "How long
has this been happening?"

The father answered, "Since he was very
young. 22 The spirit often throws him into a
fire or into water to kill him. If you can do
anything for him, please have pity on us and
help us."

23 Jesus said to the father, "You said, 'If you
can!' All things are possible for the one who
believes."

24 Immediately the father cried out, "I do
believe! Help me to believe more!"

25 When Jesus saw that a crowd was
quickly gathering, he ordered the evil spirit,
saying, "You spirit that makes people unable
to hear or speak, I command you to come
out of this boy and never enter him again!"

26 The evil spirit screamed and caused the
boy to fall on the ground again. Then the
spirit came out. The boy looked as if he were
dead, and many people said, "He is dead!"
27 But Jesus took hold of the boy's hand and
helped him to stand up.

28 When Jesus went into the house, his
followers began asking him privately, "Why
couldn't we force that evil spirit out?"

9:4 Elijah and Moses Two of the most important Jewish leaders in the past. God had given Moses the Law, and Elijah was an important prophet.

29 Jesus answered, "That kind of spirit can only be forced out by prayer."[n]

Jesus Talks About His Death

30 Then Jesus and his followers left that place and went through Galilee. He didn't want anyone to know where he was, 31 because he was teaching his followers. He said to them, "The Son of Man will be handed over to people, and they will kill him. After three days, he will rise from the dead." 32 But the followers did not understand what Jesus meant, and they were afraid to ask him.

Who Is the Greatest?

33 Jesus and his followers went to Capernaum. When they went into a house there, he asked them, "What were you arguing about on the road?" 34 But the followers did not answer, because their argument on the road was about which one of them was the greatest.

35 Jesus sat down and called the twelve apostles to him. He said, "Whoever wants to be the most important must be last of all and servant of all."

36 Then Jesus took a small child and had him stand among them. Taking the child in his arms, he said, 37 "Whoever accepts a child like this in my name accepts me. And whoever accepts me accepts the One who sent me."

Anyone Not Against Us Is for Us

38 Then John said, "Teacher, we saw someone using your name to force demons out of a person. We told him to stop, because he does not belong to our group."

39 But Jesus said, "Don't stop him, because anyone who uses my name to do powerful things will not easily say evil things about me. 40 Whoever is not against us is with us. 41 I tell you the truth, whoever gives you a drink of water because you belong to the Christ will truly get his reward.

42 "If one of these little children believes in me, and someone causes that child to sin, it would be better for that person to have a large stone tied around his neck and be drowned in the sea. 43 If your hand causes you to sin, cut it off. It is better for you to lose part of your body and live forever than to have two hands and go to hell, where the fire never goes out. [44 In hell the worm does not die; the fire is never put out.][n] 45 If your foot causes you to sin, cut it off. It is better for you to lose part of your body and to live forever than to have two feet and be thrown into hell. [46 In hell the worm does not die; the fire is never put out.][n] 47 If your eye causes you to sin, take it out. It is better for you to enter the kingdom of God with only one eye than to have two eyes and be thrown into hell. 48 In hell the worm does not die; the fire is never put out. 49 Every person will be salted with fire.

50 "Salt is good, but if the salt loses its salty taste, you cannot make it salty again. So, be full of salt, and have peace with each other."

Jesus Teaches About Divorce

10 Then Jesus left that place and went into the area of Judea and across the Jordan River. Again, crowds came to him, and he taught them as he usually did.

2 Some Pharisees came to Jesus and tried to trick him. They asked, "Is it right for a man to divorce his wife?"

3 Jesus answered, "What did Moses command you to do?"

4 They said, "Moses allowed a man to write out divorce papers and send her away."[n]

5 Jesus said, "Moses wrote that command for you because you were stubborn. 6 But when God made the world, 'he made them male and female.'[n] 7 'So a man will leave his father and mother and be united with his wife,[n] 8 and the two will become one body.'[n] So there are not two, but one. 9 God has joined the two together, so no one should separate them."

10 Later, in the house, his followers asked Jesus again about the question of divorce. 11 He answered, "Anyone who divorces his wife and marries another woman is guilty of adultery against her. 12 And the woman who divorces her husband and marries another man is also guilty of adultery."

Jesus Accepts Children

13 Some people brought their little children to Jesus so he could touch them,

9:29 prayer Some Greek copies continue, "and fasting." **9:44, 46 In . . . out.** Some Greek copies do not contain the bracketed text. **10:4 "Moses . . . away."** Quotation from Deuteronomy 24:1. **10:6 'he made . . . female'** Quotation from Genesis 1:27. **10:7 and . . . wife** Some Greek copies do not have this phrase. **10:7–8 'So . . . body.'** Quotation from Genesis 2:24.

but his followers told them to stop. 14When
Jesus saw this, he was upset and said to
them, "Let the little children come to me.
Don't stop them, because the kingdom of
God belongs to people who are like these
children. 15I tell you the truth, you must
accept the kingdom of God as if you were a
little child, or you will never enter it."
16Then Jesus took the children in his arms,
put his hands on them, and blessed them.

A Rich Young Man's Question

17As Jesus started to leave, a man ran to
him and fell on his knees before Jesus. The
man asked, "Good teacher, what must I do to
have life forever?"

18Jesus answered, "Why do you call me
good? Only God is good. 19You know the
commands: 'You must not murder anyone.
You must not be guilty of adultery. You must
not steal. You must not tell lies about your
neighbor. You must not cheat. Honor your
father and mother.'"[n]

20The man said, "Teacher, I have obeyed
all these things since I was a boy."

21Jesus, looking at the man, loved him and
said, "There is one more thing you need to
do. Go and sell everything you have, and
give the money to the poor, and you will
have treasure in heaven. Then come and
follow me."

22He was very sad to hear Jesus say this,
and he left sorrowfully, because he was rich.

23Then Jesus looked at his followers and
said, "How hard it will be for the rich to
enter the kingdom of God!"

24The followers were amazed at what
Jesus said. But he said again, "My children, it
is very hard[n] to enter the kingdom of God!
25It is easier for a camel to go through the
eye of a needle than for a rich person to
enter the kingdom of God."

26The followers were even more surprised
and said to each other, "Then who can be
saved?"

27Jesus looked at them and said, "For
people this is impossible, but for God all
things are possible."

28Peter said to Jesus, "Look, we have left
everything and followed you."

29Jesus said, "I tell you the truth, all those
who have left houses, brothers, sisters,
mother, father, children, or farms for me and
for the Good News 30will get more than they
left. Here in this world they will have a
hundred times more homes, brothers, sisters,
mothers, children, and fields. And with
those things, they will also suffer for their
belief. But in this age they will have life
forever. 31Many who are first now will be
last in the future. And many who are last
now will be first in the future."

Jesus Talks About His Death

32As Jesus and the people with him were
on the road to Jerusalem, he was leading the
way. His followers were amazed, but others
in the crowd who followed were afraid.
Again Jesus took the twelve apostles aside
and began to tell them what was about to
happen in Jerusalem. 33He said, "Look, we
are going to Jerusalem. The Son of Man will
be turned over to the leading priests and the
teachers of the law. They will say that he
must die, and they will turn him over to the
non-Jewish people, 34who will laugh at him
and spit on him. They will beat him with
whips and crucify him. But on the third day,
he will rise to life again."

Two Followers Ask Jesus a Favor

35Then James and John, sons of Zebedee,
came to Jesus and said, "Teacher, we want to
ask you to do something for us."

36Jesus asked, "What do you want me to
do for you?"

37They answered, "Let one of us sit at your
right side and one of us sit at your left side in
your glory in your kingdom."

38Jesus said, "You don't understand what
you are asking. Can you drink the cup that I
must drink? And can you be baptized with
the same kind of baptism that I must go
through?"[n]

39They answered, "Yes, we can."

Jesus said to them, "You will drink the
same cup that I will drink, and you will be
baptized with the same baptism that I must
go through. 40But I cannot choose who will
sit at my right or my left; those places belong
to those for whom they have been prepared."

41When the other ten followers heard

10:19 'You . . . mother.' Quotation from Exodus 20:12–16; Deuteronomy 5:16–20. **10:24 hard** Some Greek copies continue, "for those who trust in riches." **10:38 Can you . . . through?** Jesus was asking if they could suffer the same terrible things that would happen to him.

this, they began to be angry with James and
John.
42Jesus called them together and said,
"The other nations have rulers. You know
that those rulers love to show their power
over the people, and their important leaders
love to use all their authority. 43But it should
not be that way among you. Whoever wants
to become great among you must serve the
rest of you like a servant. 44Whoever wants
to become the first among you must serve all
of you like a slave. 45In the same way, the
Son of Man did not come to be served. He
came to serve others and to give his life as a
ransom for many people."

Jesus Heals a Blind Man

46Then they came to the town of Jericho.
As Jesus was leaving there with his followers
and a great many people, a blind beggar
named Bartimaeus son of Timaeus was
sitting by the road. 47When he heard that
Jesus from Nazareth was walking by, he
began to shout, "Jesus, Son of David, have
mercy on me!"
48Many people warned the blind man to
be quiet, but he shouted even more, "Son of
David, have mercy on me!"
49Jesus stopped and said, "Tell the man to
come here."

So they called the blind man, saying,
"Cheer up! Get to your feet. Jesus is calling
you." 50The blind man jumped up, left his
coat there, and went to Jesus.
51Jesus asked him, "What do you want me
to do for you?"

The blind man answered, "Teacher, I want
to see."
52Jesus said, "Go, you are healed because
you believed." At once the man could see,
and he followed Jesus on the road.

Jesus Enters Jerusalem as a King

11 As Jesus and his followers were
coming closer to Jerusalem, they came
to the towns of Bethphage and Bethany near
the Mount of Olives. From there Jesus sent
two of his followers 2and said to them, "Go
to the town you can see there. When you
enter it, you will quickly find a colt tied,
which no one has ever ridden. Untie it and
bring it here to me. 3If anyone asks you why
you are doing this, tell him its Master needs
the colt, and he will send it at once."
4The followers went into the town, found
a colt tied in the street near the door of a
house, and untied it. 5Some people were
standing there and asked, "What are you
doing? Why are you untying that colt?" 6The
followers answered the way Jesus told them
to answer, and the people let them take the
colt.
7They brought the colt to Jesus and put
their coats on it, and Jesus sat on it. 8Many
people spread their coats on the road. Others
cut branches in the fields and spread them
on the road. 9The people were walking
ahead of Jesus and behind him, shouting,

"Praise God!
God bless the One who comes in the
name of the Lord! *Psalm 118:26*
10God bless the kingdom of our father
David!
That kingdom is coming!
Praise[n] to God in heaven!"

11Jesus entered Jerusalem and went into
the Temple. After he had looked at
everything, since it was already late, he went
out to Bethany with the twelve apostles.
12The next day as Jesus was leaving
Bethany, he became hungry. 13Seeing a fig
tree in leaf from far away, he went to see if it
had any figs on it. But he found no figs, only
leaves, because it was not the right season
for figs. 14So Jesus said to the tree, "May no
one ever eat fruit from you again." And Jesus'
followers heard him say this.

Jesus Goes to the Temple

15When Jesus returned to Jerusalem, he
went into the Temple and began to throw
out those who were buying and selling
there. He turned over the tables of those who
were exchanging different kinds of money,
and he upset the benches of those who were
selling doves. 16Jesus refused to allow
anyone to carry goods through the Temple
courts. 17Then he taught the people, saying,
"It is written in the Scriptures, 'My Temple
will be called a house for prayer for people
from all nations.'[n] But you are changing
God's house into a 'hideout for robbers.' "[n]

11:10 Praise Literally, "Hosanna," a Hebrew word used at first in praying to God for help, but at this time it was probably a shout of joy used in praising God or his Messiah. **11:17 'My Temple . . . nations.'** Quotation from Isaiah 56:7. **11:17 'hideout for robbers'** Quotation from Jeremiah 7:11.

18 The leading priests and the teachers of the law heard all this and began trying to find a way to kill Jesus. They were afraid of him, because all the people were amazed at his teaching. 19 That evening, Jesus and his followers[n] left the city.

The Power of Faith

20 The next morning as Jesus was passing by with his followers, they saw the fig tree dry and dead, even to the roots. 21 Peter remembered the tree and said to Jesus, "Teacher, look! The fig tree you cursed is dry and dead!"

22 Jesus answered, "Have faith in God. 23 I tell you the truth, you can say to this mountain, 'Go, fall into the sea.' And if you have no doubts in your mind and believe that what you say will happen, God will do it for you. 24 So I tell you to believe that you have received the things you ask for in prayer, and God will give them to you. 25 When you are praying, if you are angry with someone, forgive him so that your Father in heaven will also forgive your sins. [26 But if you don't forgive other people, then your Father in heaven will not forgive your sins.]"[n]

Leaders Doubt Jesus' Authority

27 Jesus and his followers went again to Jerusalem. As Jesus was walking in the Temple, the leading priests, the teachers of the law, and the elders came to him. 28 They said to him, "What authority do you have to do these things? Who gave you this authority?"

29 Jesus answered, "I will ask you one question. If you answer me, I will tell you what authority I have to do these things. 30 Tell me: When John baptized people, was that authority from God or just from other people?"

31 They argued about Jesus' question, saying, "If we answer, 'John's baptism was from God,' Jesus will say, 'Then why didn't you believe him?' 32 But if we say, 'It was from other people,' the crowd will be against us." (These leaders were afraid of the people, because all the people believed that John was a prophet.)

33 So they answered Jesus, "We don't know."

Jesus said to them, "Then I won't tell you what authority I have to do these things."

A Story About God's Son

12 Jesus began to use stories to teach the people. He said, "A man planted a vineyard. He put a wall around it and dug a hole for a winepress and built a tower. Then he leased the land to some farmers and left for a trip. 2 When it was time for the grapes to be picked, he sent a servant to the farmers to get his share of the grapes. 3 But the farmers grabbed the servant and beat him and sent him away empty-handed. 4 Then the man sent another servant. They hit him on the head and showed no respect for him. 5 So the man sent another servant, whom they killed. The man sent many other servants; the farmers beat some of them and killed others.

6 "The man had one person left to send, his son whom he loved. He sent him last of all, saying, 'They will respect my son.'

7 "But the farmers said to each other, 'This son will inherit the vineyard. If we kill him, it will be ours.' 8 So they took the son, killed him, and threw him out of the vineyard.

9 "So what will the owner of the vineyard do? He will come and kill those farmers and will give the vineyard to other farmers. 10 Surely you have read this Scripture:

'The stone that the builders rejected
became the cornerstone.
11 The Lord did this,
and it is wonderful to us.' " *Psalm 118:22–23*

12 The Jewish leaders knew that the story was about them. So they wanted to find a way to arrest Jesus, but they were afraid of the people. So the leaders left him and went away.

Is It Right to Pay Taxes or Not?

13 Later, the Jewish leaders sent some Pharisees and Herodians[n] to Jesus to trap him in saying something wrong. 14 They came to him and said, "Teacher, we know that you are an honest man. You are not afraid of what other people think about you, because you pay no attention to who they are. And you teach the truth about God's

11:19 his followers Some Greek copies mention only Jesus here. **11:26 But . . . sins.** Some Greek copies do not contain the bracketed text. **12:13 Herodians** A political group that followed Herod and his family.

The Widow with Two Coins

MARK 12

The Temple is packed with worshipers from all over Israel who have come to celebrate the Passover. Jesus sits with his followers opposite the Temple treasury and watches as people drop their offerings in one of the thirteen cone-shaped receptacles hanging on the Temple walls. A man throws in several coins that make a racket as they go round and round before sliding through the cone's narrow cylinder. Another man throws in a handful of coins, and the sound reverberates off the walls. He is aware that the Jewish leaders are watching and listening, and he beams with pride at his offering.

A widow, slight of stature, makes her way to one of the receptacles. No one seems to take notice of her. No one except Jesus. He watches as she deposits two small coins that don't make a sound over the noise of the crowd. He recognizes the gesture of her gift and calls his followers. "This poor widow gave more than all those rich people. They gave only what they did not need. This woman is very poor, but she gave all she had; she gave all she had to live on."

The woman walks away without realizing what she has done. Her simple act of abandonment to God has encouraged Jesus. With great faith, she offered all she had to God. Soon, Jesus would offer his very life.

The size of your gift doesn't matter to God. He looks at your heart.

way. Tell us: Is it right to pay taxes to Caesar
or not? [15]Should we pay them, or not?"
But knowing what these men were really
trying to do, Jesus said to them, "Why are
you trying to trap me? Bring me a coin to
look at." [16]They gave Jesus a coin, and he
asked, "Whose image and name are on the
coin?"
They answered, "Caesar's."
[17]Then Jesus said to them, "Give to Caesar
the things that are Caesar's, and give to God
the things that are God's." The men were
amazed at what Jesus said.

Some Sadducees Try to Trick Jesus

[18]Then some Sadducees came to Jesus and
asked him a question. (Sadducees believed
that people would not rise from the dead.)
[19]They said, "Teacher, Moses wrote that if a
man's brother dies, leaving a wife but no
children, then that man must marry the
widow and have children for his brother.
[20]Once there were seven brothers. The first
brother married and died, leaving no
children. [21]So the second brother married
the widow, but he also died and had no
children. The same thing happened with the
third brother. [22]All seven brothers married
her and died, and none of the brothers had
any children. Finally the woman died too.
[23]Since all seven brothers had married her,
when people rise from the dead, whose wife
will she be?"
[24]Jesus answered, "Why don't you
understand? Don't you know what the
Scriptures say, and don't you know about the
power of God? [25]When people rise from the
dead, they will not marry, nor will they be
given to someone to marry. They will be like
the angels in heaven. [26]Surely you have read
what God said about people rising from the
dead. In the book in which Moses wrote
about the burning bush,[n] it says that God
told Moses, 'I am the God of Abraham, the
God of Isaac, and the God of Jacob.'[n] [27]God is
the God of the living, not the dead. You
Sadducees are wrong!"

The Most Important Command

[28]One of the teachers of the law came and
heard Jesus arguing with the Sadducees.
Seeing that Jesus gave good answers to their

12:26 burning bush Read Exodus 3:1–12 in the Old Testament. **12:26 'I am . . . Jacob.'** Quotation from Exodus 3:6.

questions, he asked Jesus, "Which of the
commands is most important?"
29Jesus answered, "The most important
command is this: 'Listen, people of Israel!
The Lord our God is the only Lord. 30Love
the Lord your God with all your heart, all
your soul, all your mind, and all your
strength.'[n] 31The second command is this:
'Love your neighbor as you love yourself.'[n]
There are no commands more important
than these."
32The man answered, "That was a good
answer, Teacher. You were right when you
said God is the only Lord and there is no
other God besides him. 33One must love God
with all his heart, all his mind, and all his
strength. And one must love his neighbor as
he loves himself. These commands are more
important than all the animals and sacrifices
we offer to God."
34When Jesus saw that the man answered
him wisely, Jesus said to him, "You are close
to the kingdom of God." And after that, no
one was brave enough to ask Jesus any more
questions.
35As Jesus was teaching in the Temple,
he asked, "Why do the teachers of the law
say that the Christ is the son of David?
36David himself, speaking by the Holy Spirit,
said:

'The Lord said to my Lord,
"Sit by me at my right side,
until I put your enemies under your
control."' *Psalm 110:1*

37David himself calls the Christ 'Lord,' so
how can the Christ be his son?" The large
crowd listened to Jesus with pleasure.
38Jesus continued teaching and said,
"Beware of the teachers of the law. They like
to walk around wearing fancy clothes, and
they love for people to greet them with
respect in the marketplaces. 39They love to
have the most important seats in the
synagogues and at feasts. 40But they cheat
widows and steal their houses and then try
to make themselves look good by saying

12:29–30 'Listen . . . strength.' Quotation from Deuteronomy 6:4–5.
12:31 'Love . . . yourself.' Quotation from Leviticus 19:18.

devotion 274

MARK 12:29–31

GOD FIRST AND *WHO* SECOND?

What if you asked God, "Why am I here? What do you want me to do? What was I made for? Please tell me my purpose." And he answered, "Love me with all your heart, soul, mind, and strength. And second, love your neighbor like you love yourself."

A part of me is stunned by the reminder of these words. More important than building for God or telling about God or going places for God is to love him with all that I am. Love is the verb, which sometimes results in more action. But to love him well is the absolute most important thing I can do on this earth. How many years have gone by with "accomplishments" for God pushing aside the command to love?

From the deep well of loving God, we are also supposed to love our neighbors just like we love ourselves. Do you realize what this means? We are supposed to care about their welfare, their physical bodies, their mental health, their comfort, and their joy just like we would for ourselves. This command is so radical that at this moment, I feel it cutting away at my self-centeredness. Maybe sometimes I have loved God first, but I have almost always loved myself second.

Maybe you feel the Spirit of God convicting your heart. Repent. Let your love for God be more important than anything. Then look out beyond yourself to see the ones beside you who need love.

long prayers. They will receive a greater
punishment."

True Giving

41 Jesus sat near the Temple money box
and watched the people put in their money.
Many rich people gave large sums of money.
42 Then a poor widow came and put in two
small copper coins, which were only worth a
few cents.

43 Calling his followers to him, Jesus said,
"I tell you the truth, this poor widow gave
more than all those rich people. 44 They gave
only what they did not need. This woman is
very poor, but she gave all she had; she gave
all she had to live on."

The Temple Will Be Destroyed

13 As Jesus was leaving the Temple, one
of his followers said to him, "Look,
Teacher! How beautiful the buildings are!
How big the stones are!"

2 Jesus said, "Do you see all these great
buildings? Not one stone will be left on
another. Every stone will be thrown down to
the ground."

3 Later, as Jesus was sitting on the Mount
of Olives, opposite the Temple, he was alone
with Peter, James, John, and Andrew. They
asked Jesus, 4 "Tell us, when will these things
happen? And what will be the sign that they
are going to happen?"

5 Jesus began to answer them, "Be careful
that no one fools you. 6 Many people will
come in my name, saying, 'I am the One,'
and they will fool many people. 7 When you
hear about wars and stories of wars that are
coming, don't be afraid. These things must
happen before the end comes. 8 Nations will
fight against other nations, and kingdoms
against other kingdoms. There will be
earthquakes in different places, and there
will be times when there is no food for
people to eat. These things are like the first
pains when something new is about to be
born.

9 "You must be careful. People will arrest
you and take you to court and beat you in
their synagogues. You will be forced to stand
before kings and governors, to tell them
about me. This will happen to you because
you follow me. 10 But before these things
happen, the Good News must be told to all
people. 11 When you are arrested and judged,
don't worry ahead of time about what you
should say. Say whatever is given you to say
at that time, because it will not really be you
speaking; it will be the Holy Spirit.

12 "Brothers will give their own brothers to
be killed, and fathers will give their own
children to be killed. Children will fight
against their own parents and cause them to
be put to death. 13 All people will hate you
because you follow me, but those people
who keep their faith until the end will be
saved.

14 "You will see 'a blasphemous object that
brings destruction'[n] standing where it should
not be." (You who read this should
understand what it means.) "At that time, the
people in Judea should run away to the
mountains. 15 If people are on the roofs[n] of
their houses, they must not go down or go
inside to get anything out of their houses.
16 If people are in the fields, they must not go
back to get their coats. 17 At that time, how
terrible it will be for women who are
pregnant or have nursing babies! 18 Pray that
these things will not happen in winter,
19 because those days will be full of trouble.
There will be more trouble than there has
ever been since the beginning, when God
made the world, until now, and nothing as
bad will ever happen again. 20 God has
decided to make that terrible time short.
Otherwise, no one would go on living. But
God will make that time short to help the
people he has chosen. 21 At that time,
someone might say to you, 'Look, there is
the Christ!' Or another person might say,
'There he is!' But don't believe them. 22 False
Christs and false prophets will come and
perform great wonders and miracles. They
will try to fool even the people God has
chosen, if that is possible. 23 So be careful. I
have warned you about all this before it
happens.

24 "During the days after this trouble
comes,

> 'the sun will grow dark,
> and the moon will not give its light.
> 25 The stars will fall from the sky.

13:14 'a blasphemous object that brings destruction' Mentioned in Daniel 9:27; 12:11 (cf. Daniel 11:31).
13:15 roofs In Bible times houses were built with flat roofs. The roof was used for drying things such as flax and fruit. And it was used as an extra room, as a place for worship, and as a cool place to sleep in the summer.

And the powers of the heavens will be
shaken.’ *Isaiah 13:10; 34:4*

26“Then people will see the Son of Man
coming in clouds with great power and
glory. 27Then he will send his angels all
around the earth to gather his chosen people
from every part of the earth and from every
part of heaven.

28“Learn a lesson from the fig tree: When
its branches become green and soft and new
leaves appear, you know summer is near.
29In the same way, when you see these
things happening, you will know that the
time is near, ready to come. 30I tell you the
truth, all these things will happen while the
people of this time are still living. 31Earth
and sky will be destroyed, but the words I
have said will never be destroyed.

32“No one knows when that day or time
will be, not the angels in heaven, not even
the Son. Only the Father knows. 33Be careful!
Always be ready,[n] because you don’t know
when that time will be. 34It is like a man
who goes on a trip. He leaves his house and
lets his servants take care of it, giving each
one a special job to do. The man tells the
servant guarding the door always to be
watchful. 35So always be ready, because
you don’t know when the owner of the
house will come back. It might be in the
evening, or at midnight, or in the morning
while it is still dark, or when the sun rises.
36Always be ready. Otherwise he might come
back suddenly and find you sleeping. 37I tell
you this, and I say this to everyone: ‘Be
ready!’ ”

The Plan to Kill Jesus

14 It was now only two days before the
Passover and the Feast of Unleavened
Bread. The leading priests and teachers of
the law were trying to find a trick to arrest
Jesus and kill him. 2But they said, “We must
not do it during the feast, because the people
might cause a riot.”

A Woman with Perfume for Jesus

3Jesus was in Bethany at the house of
Simon, who had a skin disease. While Jesus
was eating there, a woman approached him
with an alabaster jar filled with very
expensive perfume, made of pure nard. She
opened the jar and poured the perfume on
Jesus’ head.

4Some who were there became upset and
said to each other, “Why waste that
perfume? 5It was worth a full year’s work. It
could have been sold and the money given
to the poor.” And they got very angry with
the woman.

6Jesus said, “Leave her alone. Why are you
troubling her? She did an excellent thing for
me. 7You will always have the poor with
you, and you can help them anytime you
want. But you will not always have me.
8This woman did the only thing she could
do for me; she poured perfume on my body
to prepare me for burial. 9I tell you the truth,
wherever the Good News is preached in all
the world, what this woman has done will
be told, and people will remember her.”

Judas Becomes an Enemy of Jesus

10One of the twelve apostles, Judas
Iscariot, went to talk to the leading priests to
offer to hand Jesus over to them. 11These
priests were pleased about this and promised
to pay Judas money. So he watched for the
best time to turn Jesus in.

Jesus Eats the Passover Meal

12It was now the first day of the Feast of
Unleavened Bread when the Passover lamb
was sacrificed. Jesus’ followers said to him,
“Where do you want us to go and prepare for
you to eat the Passover meal?”

13Jesus sent two of his followers and said
to them, “Go into the city and a man
carrying a jar of water will meet you. Follow
him. 14When he goes into a house, tell the
owner of the house, ‘The Teacher says:
“Where is my guest room in which I can eat
the Passover meal with my followers?” ’
15The owner will show you a large room
upstairs that is furnished and ready. Prepare
the food for us there.”

16So the followers left and went into the
city. Everything happened as Jesus had said,
so they prepared the Passover meal.

17In the evening, Jesus went to that house
with the twelve. 18While they were all
eating, Jesus said, “I tell you the truth, one of
you will turn against me—one of you eating
with me now.”

13:33 ready Some Greek copies continue, “and pray.”

Caiaphas's Servant Girl

MARK 14

He doesn't notice, but she is watching him. *Who is he?* The courtyard has been crackling with voices since soldiers pushed Jesus into the home of her master, Caiaphas, the high priest. But this man is different from the others here tonight; he's staying outside of the fray, not involved in conversation, always glancing into the home as if trying to find someone. He moves to the fire to warm himself, and she studies his face in the fire's glow. *He's not from here,* she realizes. *He's one of them!* She walks to the fire. "You also were with Jesus, that man from Nazareth," she says.

His head snaps at the accusation, but he stretches his hands toward the fire again. "I don't know or understand what you are talking about." He walks and stands close to people gathered at the entrance. She moves toward the group, pointing at the stranger.

"This man is one of those who followed Jesus." Again, the man denies association with the rebel. She is not satisfied and buzzes around, pointing out the man who should not be in the courtyard of her master's house. He is not welcome here. If his friend Jesus is her master's enemy, this man is also an enemy. Another accusation sends the stranger fleeing, and the girl settles in for the night, pleased to be rid of filth in her master's home.

Our identity is in Christ, and we should pride ourselves in being part of his household.

19 The followers were very sad to hear this.
Each one began to say to Jesus, "I am not the
one, am I?"
20 Jesus answered, "It is one of the
twelve—the one who dips his bread into the
bowl with me. 21 The Son of Man will die,
just as the Scriptures say. But how terrible it
will be for the person who hands the Son of
Man over to be killed. It would be better for
him if he had never been born."

The Lord's Supper

22 While they were eating, Jesus took some
bread and thanked God for it and broke it.
Then he gave it to his followers and said,
"Take it; this is my body."
23 Then Jesus took a cup and thanked God
for it and gave it to the followers, and they
all drank from the cup.
24 Then Jesus said, "This is my blood which
is the new[n] agreement that God makes with
his people. This blood is poured out for
many. 25 I tell you the truth, I will not drink
of this fruit of the vine[n] again until that day
when I drink it new in the kingdom of God."
26 After singing a hymn, they went out to
the Mount of Olives.

Jesus' Followers Will Leave Him

27 Then Jesus told the followers, "You will
all stumble in your faith, because it is
written in the Scriptures:
'I will kill the shepherd,
and the sheep will scatter.' *Zechariah 13:7*
28 But after I rise from the dead, I will go
ahead of you into Galilee."
29 Peter said, "Everyone else may stumble
in their faith, but I will not."
30 Jesus answered, "I tell you the truth,
tonight before the rooster crows twice you
will say three times you don't know me."
31 But Peter insisted, "I will never say that I
don't know you! I will even die with you!"
And all the other followers said the same
thing.

Jesus Prays Alone

32 Jesus and his followers went to a place
called Gethsemane. He said to them, "Sit
here while I pray." 33 Jesus took Peter, James,
and John with him, and he began to be very

14:24 new Some Greek copies do not have this word. Compare Luke 22:20.
14:25 fruit of the vine Product of the grapevine; this may also be translated "wine."

sad and troubled. 34 He said to them, "My
heart is full of sorrow, to the point of death.
Stay here and watch."
35 After walking a little farther away from
them, Jesus fell to the ground and prayed
that, if possible, he would not have this time
of suffering. 36 He prayed, "Abba,[n] Father! You
can do all things. Take away this cup[n] of
suffering. But do what you want, not what I
want."
37 Then Jesus went back to his followers
and found them asleep. He said to Peter,
"Simon, are you sleeping? Couldn't you stay
awake with me for one hour? 38 Stay awake
and pray for strength against temptation.
The spirit wants to do what is right, but the
body is weak."
39 Again Jesus went away and prayed the
same thing. 40 Then he went back to his
followers, and again he found them asleep,
because their eyes were very heavy. And they
did not know what to say to him.
41 After Jesus prayed a third time, he went
back to his followers and said to them, "Are
you still sleeping and resting? That's
enough. The time has come for the Son of
Man to be handed over to sinful people.
42 Get up, we must go. Look, here comes the
man who has turned against me."

Jesus Is Arrested

43 At once, while Jesus was still speaking,
Judas, one of the twelve apostles, came up.
With him were many people carrying
swords and clubs who had been sent from
the leading priests, the teachers of the law,
and the Jewish elders.
44 Judas had planned a signal for them,
saying, "The man I kiss is Jesus. Arrest him
and guard him while you lead him away."
45 So Judas went straight to Jesus and said,
"Teacher!" and kissed him. 46 Then the people
grabbed Jesus and arrested him. 47 One of his
followers standing nearby pulled out his
sword and struck the servant of the high
priest and cut off his ear.
48 Then Jesus said, "You came to get me
with swords and clubs as if I were a criminal.
49 Every day I was with you teaching in the
Temple, and you did not arrest me there. But

14:36 Abba Name that a Jewish child called his father. **14:36 cup** Jesus is talking about the terrible things that will happen to him. Accepting these things will be very hard, like drinking a cup of something bitter.

devotion 275

MARK 14:34–36

A BIG GULP FULL OF SUFFERING

If suffering were associated with a drink size, then there have been times when mine must have been a Big Gulp! What is in your cup of suffering? Does your cup of suffering hold a divorce, does it hold a death, or does it just hold plain old disappointment? I know as soon as my suffering cup starts to get filled up, I always go to the Lord with a lament and ask him to take it from me. (Even Jesus himself asked his Father to take away the cup of suffering he was enduring. So if Jesus asked, certainly you can ask the Father the same.) Communication with the Father is good, and all of your requests are heard, but should he choose not to take the cup from you, then you have to draw in tight to his side and know that there is purpose in his will.

He will provide treasures for you even during the lowest and darkest of times. It will be in your suffering that compassion, training, and restoration are perfected. I am praying that whatever your cup is holding today, you will trust in him even when you cannot see the road ahead. Pour your heart and tears out to a God that will be your protection and your provision! Yes, he will take care of you, and even through great suffering, he is going to deliver you out of darkness and bring you into the light.

all these things have happened to make the Scriptures come true." 50Then all of Jesus' followers left him and ran away.

51A young man, wearing only a linen cloth, was following Jesus, and the people also grabbed him. 52But the cloth he was wearing came off, and he ran away naked.

Jesus Before the Leaders

53The people who arrested Jesus led him to the house of the high priest, where all the leading priests, the elders, and the teachers of the law were gathered. 54Peter followed far behind and entered the courtyard of the high priest's house. There he sat with the guards, warming himself by the fire.

55The leading priests and the whole Jewish council tried to find something that Jesus had done wrong so they could kill him. But the council could find no proof of anything. 56Many people came and told false things about him, but all said different things—none of them agreed.

57Then some people stood up and lied about Jesus, saying, 58"We heard this man say, 'I will destroy this Temple that people made. And three days later, I will build another Temple not made by people.'" 59But even the things these people said did not agree.

60Then the high priest stood before them and asked Jesus, "Aren't you going to answer? Don't you have something to say about their charges against you?" 61But Jesus said nothing; he did not answer.

The high priest asked Jesus another question: "Are you the Christ, the Son of the blessed God?"

62Jesus answered, "I am. And in the future you will see the Son of Man sitting at the right hand of God, the Powerful One, and coming on clouds in the sky."

63When the high priest heard this, he tore his clothes and said, "We don't need any more witnesses! 64You all heard him say these things against God. What do you think?"

They all said that Jesus was guilty and should die. 65Some of the people there began to spit at Jesus. They blindfolded him and beat him with their fists and said, "Prove you are a prophet!" Then the guards led Jesus away and beat him.

Peter Says He Doesn't Know Jesus

66While Peter was in the courtyard, a servant girl of the high priest came there. 67She saw Peter warming himself at the fire and looked closely at him.

Then she said, "You also were with Jesus, that man from Nazareth."

68But Peter said that he was never with Jesus. He said, "I don't know or understand what you are talking about." Then Peter left and went toward the entrance of the courtyard. And the rooster crowed.[n]

69The servant girl saw Peter there, and again she said to the people who were standing nearby, "This man is one of those who followed Jesus." 70Again Peter said that it was not true.

A short time later, some people were standing near Peter saying, "Surely you are one of those who followed Jesus, because you are from Galilee, too."

71Then Peter began to place a curse on himself and swear, "I don't know this man you're talking about!"

72At once, the rooster crowed the second time. Then Peter remembered what Jesus had told him: "Before the rooster crows twice, you will say three times that you don't know me." Then Peter lost control of himself and began to cry.

Pilate Questions Jesus

15 Very early in the morning, the leading priests, the elders, the teachers of the law, and all the Jewish council decided what to do with Jesus. They tied him, led him away, and turned him over to Pilate, the governor.

2Pilate asked Jesus, "Are you the king of the Jews?"

Jesus answered, "Those are your words."

3The leading priests accused Jesus of many things. 4So Pilate asked Jesus another question, "You can see that they are accusing you of many things. Aren't you going to answer?"

5But Jesus still said nothing, so Pilate was very surprised.

Pilate Tries to Free Jesus

6Every year at the time of the Passover the governor would free one prisoner whom the people chose. 7At that time, there was a man

14:68 And the rooster crowed. Some Greek copies do not have this phrase.

named Barabbas in prison who was a rebel and had committed murder during a riot. 8The crowd came to Pilate and began to ask him to free a prisoner as he always did.

9So Pilate asked them, "Do you want me to free the king of the Jews?" 10Pilate knew that the leading priests had turned Jesus in to him because they were jealous. 11But the leading priests had persuaded the people to ask Pilate to free Barabbas, not Jesus.

12Then Pilate asked the crowd again, "So what should I do with this man you call the king of the Jews?"

13They shouted, "Crucify him!"

14Pilate asked, "Why? What wrong has he done?"

But they shouted even louder, "Crucify him!"

15Pilate wanted to please the crowd, so he freed Barabbas for them. After having Jesus beaten with whips, he handed Jesus over to the soldiers to be crucified.

16The soldiers took Jesus into the governor's palace (called the Praetorium) and called all the other soldiers together. 17They put a purple robe on Jesus and used thorny branches to make a crown for his head. 18They began to call out to him, "Hail, King of the Jews!" 19The soldiers beat Jesus on the head many times with a stick. They spit on him and made fun of him by bowing on their knees and worshiping him. 20After they finished, the soldiers took off the purple robe and put his own clothes on him again. Then they led him out of the palace to be crucified.

Jesus Is Crucified

21A man named Simon from Cyrene, the father of Alexander and Rufus, was coming from the fields to the city. The soldiers forced Simon to carry the cross for Jesus. 22They led Jesus to the place called Golgotha, which means the Place of the Skull. 23The soldiers tried to give Jesus wine mixed with myrrh to drink, but he refused. 24The soldiers crucified Jesus and divided his clothes among themselves, throwing lots to decide what each soldier would get.

25It was nine o'clock in the morning when they crucified Jesus. 26There was a sign with this charge against Jesus written on it: THE KING OF THE JEWS. 27They also put two robbers on crosses beside Jesus, one on the right, and the other on the left. [28And the Scripture came true that says, "They put him with criminals."][n] 29People walked by and insulted Jesus and shook their heads, saying, "You said you could destroy the Temple and build it again in three days. 30So save yourself! Come down from that cross!"

31The leading priests and the teachers of the law were also making fun of Jesus. They said to each other, "He saved other people, but he can't save himself. 32If he is really the Christ, the king of Israel, let him come down now from the cross. When we see this, we will believe in him." The robbers who were being crucified beside Jesus also insulted him.

Jesus Dies

33At noon the whole country became dark, and the darkness lasted for three hours. 34At three o'clock Jesus cried in a loud voice, "Eloi, Eloi, lama sabachthani." This means, "My God, my God, why have you abandoned me?"

35When some of the people standing there heard this, they said, "Listen! He is calling Elijah."

36Someone there ran and got a sponge, filled it with vinegar, tied it to a stick, and gave it to Jesus to drink. He said, "We want to see if Elijah will come to take him down from the cross."

37Then Jesus cried in a loud voice and died.

38The curtain in the Temple[n] was torn into two pieces, from the top to the bottom. 39When the army officer who was standing in front of the cross saw what happened when Jesus died,[n] he said, "This man really was the Son of God!"

40Some women were standing at a distance from the cross, watching; among them were Mary Magdalene, Salome, and Mary the mother of James and Joseph. (James was her youngest son.) 41These women had followed Jesus in Galilee and helped him. Many other women were also there who had come with Jesus to Jerusalem.

15:28 And . . . criminals." Some Greek copies do not contain the bracketed text, which quotes from Isaiah 53:12.
15:38 curtain in the Temple A curtain divided the Most Holy Place from the other part of the Temple. That was the special building in Jerusalem where God commanded the Jewish people to worship him. **15:39 when Jesus died** Some Greek copies read "when Jesus cried out and died."

Jesus Is Buried

42 This was Preparation Day. (That means
the day before the Sabbath day.) That
evening, 43 Joseph from Arimathea was brave
enough to go to Pilate and ask for Jesus'
body. Joseph, an important member of the
Jewish council, was one of the people who
was waiting for the kingdom of God to
come. 44 Pilate was amazed that Jesus would
have already died, so he called the army
officer who had guarded Jesus and asked
him if Jesus had already died. 45 The officer
told Pilate that he was dead, so Pilate told
Joseph he could have the body. 46 Joseph
bought some linen cloth, took the body
down from the cross, and wrapped it in the
linen. He put the body in a tomb that was
cut out of a wall of rock. Then he rolled a
very large stone to block the entrance of the
tomb. 47 And Mary Magdalene and Mary the
mother of Joseph saw the place where Jesus
was laid.

Jesus Rises from the Dead

16 The day after the Sabbath day,
Mary Magdalene, Mary the mother
of James, and Salome bought some
sweet-smelling spices to put on Jesus'
body. 2 Very early on that day, the first day
of the week, soon after sunrise, the women
were on their way to the tomb. 3 They said
to each other, "Who will roll away for us
the stone that covers the entrance of the
tomb?"

4 Then the women looked and saw that
the stone had already been rolled away, even
though it was very large. 5 The women
entered the tomb and saw a young man
wearing a white robe and sitting on the right
side, and they were afraid.

6 But the man said, "Don't be afraid. You
are looking for Jesus from Nazareth, who has
been crucified. He has risen from the dead;
he is not here. Look, here is the place they
laid him. 7 Now go and tell his followers and
Peter, 'Jesus is going into Galilee ahead of
you, and you will see him there as he told
you before.' "

8 The women were confused and shaking
with fear, so they left the tomb and ran away.
They did not tell anyone about what
happened, because they were afraid.

devotion 276

MARK 16:6

LOST IN THE SYSTEM

I went to the hospital to have blood work done. I was having a C-section the next day, and I was a little nervous about the whole thing. While I waited for a nurse to complete my paperwork, my nervousness escalated because she couldn't find my blood or any of my personal information. The next day, I was going to put my life in their hands, and they were unable to find me in the computer!

As the tears began to well in my eyes, I prayed that the Lord would give me peace. Just then, the man who had played Jesus in our local Christmas pageant walked into the lobby. He looked at me, smiled, and continued on, but for me, Jesus had met me that day. Now, instead of focusing on the stressful situation, I was focused on Jesus. And I had peace.

I'm sure Jesus' followers felt this way. They had been holed up in a room, afraid for their lives for three days. Their beloved Teacher had been killed, and they were next on the list. Then came Mary's news. Peter and John didn't believe it was true, and they had to find out for themselves. So they took off running for the grave. When they rushed into the empty tomb, they were startled by the presence of an angel who said, "Don't be afraid. He has risen from the dead" (verse 6). Joy must have flooded their souls. He has risen from the dead. Praise the Lord!

Verses 9–20 are not included in some of the earliest surviving Greek copies of Mark.

Some Followers See Jesus

[9After Jesus rose from the dead early on
the first day of the week, he showed himself
first to Mary Magdalene. One time in the
past, he had forced seven demons out of her.
10After Mary saw Jesus, she went and told his
followers, who were very sad and were
crying. 11But Mary told them that Jesus was
alive. She said that she had seen him, but the
followers did not believe her.

12Later, Jesus showed himself to two of his
followers while they were walking in the
country, but he did not look the same as
before. 13These followers went back to the
others and told them what had happened, but
again, the followers did not believe them.

Jesus Talks to the Apostles

14Later Jesus showed himself to the eleven
apostles while they were eating, and he
criticized them because they had no faith.
They were stubborn and refused to believe
those who had seen him after he had risen
from the dead.

15Jesus said to his followers, "Go
everywhere in the world, and tell the Good
News to everyone. 16Anyone who believes
and is baptized will be saved, but anyone
who does not believe will be punished.
17And those who believe will be able to do
these things as proof: They will use my
name to force out demons. They will speak
in new languages.[n] 18They will pick up
snakes and drink poison without being hurt.
They will touch the sick, and the sick will be
healed."

19After the Lord Jesus said these things to
his followers, he was carried up into heaven,
and he sat at the right side of God. 20The
followers went everywhere in the world and
told the Good News to people, and the Lord
helped them. The Lord proved that the Good
News they told was true by giving them
power to work miracles.]

16:17 languages This can also be translated "tongues."

Luke

A Latin name that means "bringer of light," Luke is the last of the three synoptic Gospels.

Person Holding the Pen God Wrote With: *Luke*, who is most likely the only non-Jewish person to write a book in the Bible, penned this book that bears his name. He was also a medical doctor and a close friend and companion to the apostle Paul.

When the Text Was Written: Probably between 60 and 62 A.D.

Spiritual Posture of the Original Recipients: This account was addressed to Theophilus, a well-known Roman public figure. Thus, the original audience was Greek and prone to view Jesus as a *Jewish* Messiah.

Storyline Synopsis: In Luke, the genealogy of Jesus goes all the way back to the first man, Adam, underscoring God's love for *all* mankind—not just the Jews. This theme of the universality of the Good News is perpetuated in the way Luke relates affirmative stories about women, children, and Samaritans. He intentionally casts a positive light on those considered "less than" by stereotypically chauvinistic and prejudicial religious leaders. What's more, this beloved physician's concern for the sick is obvious as he gives front-page coverage to the healing ministry of Jesus. Six of the miracles Luke describes aren't found in the other Gospels. His account is also the most historically detailed, and his comprehensive rendition of the birth of Christ is the version most often shared in Christmas pageants!

A Moment Worth Discussing: Chapter 7 records the poignant story of a sinful woman washing Jesus' feet with her tears, drying them with her hair, and then anointing them with expensive perfume (Luke 7:36–50). Her actions were considered scandalous by most of those observing this overt display of adoration—especially the Pharisee at whose home this took place. But Jesus rebuked their criticism, explaining through a parable that she had shown great love (7:47). The heart of this passage is that the degree to which we comprehend God's love and sacrifice is the degree to which we will lavish love on him in response.

Interesting (But Likely to Be Overlooked) Character: *Elizabeth*, one of Mary's close relatives, was also the mother of John the Baptist (Luke 1:5–25). Not only did her miraculous—although not an "immaculate conception"—pregnancy precede Mary's but Elizabeth was also the very first human to confess that the child Mary was carrying was the long-awaited Messiah (1:39–45).

Luke Writes About Jesus' Life

1 Many have tried to report on the things that happened among us. [2]They have written the same things that we learned from others—the people who saw those things from the beginning and served God by telling people his message. [3]Since I myself have studied everything carefully from the beginning, most excellent[n] Theophilus, it seemed good for me to write it out for you. I arranged it in order, [4]to help you know that what you have been taught is true.

Zechariah and Elizabeth

[5]During the time Herod ruled Judea, there was a priest named Zechariah who belonged to Abijah's group.[n] Zechariah's wife, Elizabeth, came from the family of Aaron. [6]Zechariah and Elizabeth truly did what God said was good. They did everything the Lord commanded and were without fault in keeping his law. [7]But they had no children, because Elizabeth could not have a baby, and both of them were very old.

[8]One day Zechariah was serving as a priest before God, because his group was on duty. [9]According to the custom of the priests, he was chosen by lot to go into the Temple of the Lord and burn incense. [10]There were a great many people outside praying at the time the incense was offered. [11]Then an angel of the Lord appeared to Zechariah, standing on the right side of the incense table. [12]When he saw the angel, Zechariah was startled and frightened. [13]But the angel said to him, "Zechariah, don't be afraid. God has heard your prayer. Your wife, Elizabeth, will give birth to a son, and you will name him John. [14]He will bring you joy and gladness, and many people will be happy because of his birth. [15]John will be a great man for the Lord. He will never drink wine or beer, and even from birth, he will be filled with the Holy Spirit. [16]He will help many people of Israel return to the Lord their God. [17]He will go before the Lord in spirit and power like Elijah. He will make peace between parents and their children and will bring those who are not obeying God back to the right way of thinking, to make a people ready for the coming of the Lord."

[18]Zechariah said to the angel, "How can I know that what you say is true? I am an old man, and my wife is old, too."

[19]The angel answered him, "I am Gabriel. I stand before God, who sent me to talk to you and to tell you this good news. [20]Now, listen! You will not be able to speak until the day these things happen, because you did not believe what I told you. But they will really happen."

[21]Outside, the people were still waiting for Zechariah and were surprised that he was staying so long in the Temple. [22]When Zechariah came outside, he could not speak to them, and they knew he had seen a vision in the Temple. He could only make signs to them and remained unable to speak. [23]When his time of service at the Temple was finished, he went home.

[24]Later, Zechariah's wife, Elizabeth, became pregnant and did not go out of her house for five months. Elizabeth said, [25]"Look what the Lord has done for me! My people were ashamed[n] of me, but now the Lord has taken away that shame."

An Angel Appears to Mary

[26]During Elizabeth's sixth month of pregnancy, God sent the angel Gabriel to Nazareth, a town in Galilee, [27]to a virgin. She was engaged to marry a man named Joseph from the family of David. Her name was Mary. [28]The angel came to her and said, "Greetings! The Lord has blessed you and is with you."

[29]But Mary was very startled by what the angel said and wondered what this greeting might mean.

[30]The angel said to her, "Don't be afraid, Mary; God has shown you his grace. [31]Listen! You will become pregnant and give birth to a son, and you will name him Jesus. [32]He will be great and will be called the Son of the Most High. The Lord God will give him the throne of King David, his ancestor. [33]He will rule over the people of Jacob forever, and his kingdom will never end."

[34]Mary said to the angel, "How will this happen since I am a virgin?"

[35]The angel said to Mary, "The Holy Spirit will come upon you, and the power of the

1:3 excellent This word was used to show respect to an important person like a king or ruler. **1:5 Abijah's group** The Jewish priests were divided into twenty-four groups. See 1 Chronicles 24. **1:25 ashamed** The Jewish people thought it was a disgrace for women not to have children.

Elizabeth

LUKE 1

Elizabeth strains to see the figure on the narrow path, but it is still too far away. She places wrinkled hands on her rounded belly and smiles. Each morning she wakes to make sure her stomach is indeed still growing and that she isn't waking from some fantastical dream. And each morning she laughs. God has accomplished the impossible and placed a child inside her shriveled womb.

She peers through the window and notices the visitor is closer now. She and Zechariah have been content hiding away for the last few months. No one has bothered them until today.

The figure on the path advances quickly, and Elizabeth sees it is a girl—her own cousin Mary! She opens the door and welcomes Mary, but as she greets her, something like a strong wind blows through her. The baby she's carrying nearly lands her on the floor as it leaps and kicks the walls of her aged womb.

Elizabeth is filled with the Holy Spirit! She tries to contain her laughter, but it is no use. Her joy spills over as she clasps Mary's hands. The cousin speaks: "Why has this good thing happened to me, that the mother of my Lord comes to me?" Tears of gratitude fill their eyes as they hold on to each other. Their bonds of kinship now run deeper than flesh and blood—they are bonded by the Messiah.

Blessed is the woman who doesn't doubt that God will bring his promises to fulfillment.

Most High will cover you. For this reason the
baby will be holy and will be called the Son
of God. 36Now Elizabeth, your relative, is
also pregnant with a son though she is very
old. Everyone thought she could not have a
baby, but she has been pregnant for six
months. 37God can do anything!"
38Mary said, "I am the servant of the Lord.
Let this happen to me as you say!" Then the
angel went away.

Mary Visits Elizabeth

39Mary got up and went quickly to a
town in the hills of Judea. 40She came to
Zechariah's house and greeted Elizabeth.
41When Elizabeth heard Mary's greeting,
the unborn baby inside her jumped, and
Elizabeth was filled with the Holy Spirit.
42She cried out in a loud voice, "God has
blessed you more than any other woman,
and he has blessed the baby to which you
will give birth. 43Why has this good thing
happened to me, that the mother of my
Lord comes to me? 44When I heard your
voice, the baby inside me jumped with joy.
45You are blessed because you believed that
what the Lord said to you would really
happen."

Mary Praises God

46Then Mary said,
"My soul praises the Lord;
47 my heart rejoices in God my Savior,
48because he has shown his concern for his
humble servant girl.
From now on, all people will say that I am
blessed,
49 because the Powerful One has done
great things for me.
His name is holy.
50God will show his mercy forever and ever
to those who worship and serve him.
51He has done mighty deeds by his power.
He has scattered the people who are
proud
and think great things about themselves.
52He has brought down rulers from their
thrones
and raised up the humble.
53He has filled the hungry with good things
and sent the rich away with nothing.
54He has helped his servant, the people of
Israel,
remembering to show them mercy

55as he promised to our ancestors,
to Abraham and to his children
forever."
56Mary stayed with Elizabeth for about
three months and then returned home.

The Birth of John

57When it was time for Elizabeth to give
birth, she had a boy. 58Her neighbors and
relatives heard how good the Lord was to
her, and they rejoiced with her.
59When the baby was eight days old, they
came to circumcise him. They wanted to
name him Zechariah because this was his
father's name, 60but his mother said, "No! He
will be named John."
61The people said to Elizabeth, "But no
one in your family has this name." 62Then
they made signs to his father to find out
what he would like to name him.
63Zechariah asked for a writing tablet and
wrote, "His name is John," and everyone was
surprised. 64Immediately Zechariah could
talk again, and he began praising God. 65All
their neighbors became alarmed, and in all
the mountains of Judea people continued
talking about all these things. 66The people
who heard about them wondered, saying,
"What will this child be?" because the Lord
was with him.

Zechariah Praises God

67Then Zechariah, John's father, was filled
with the Holy Spirit and prophesied:
68"Let us praise the Lord, the God of Israel,
because he has come to help his people
and has given them freedom.
69He has given us a powerful Savior
from the family of God's servant David.
70He said that he would do this
through his holy prophets who lived
long ago:
71He promised he would save us from our
enemies
and from the power of all those who
hate us.
72He said he would give mercy to our
ancestors
and that he would remember his holy
promise.

devotion 277

LUKE 1:68–69, 78–79

DON'T DROP THE BABY!

I recall watching a Christmas play in which the little girl "Mary" tenderly cradled a baby doll "Jesus" in her arms. The crowd chuckled as Mary, mortified, dropped baby Jesus, and Joseph—losing the towel wrapped around his head—dove to catch the doll. It was not what the Sunday school teacher had planned, but later, as the children all joined together to sing "Away in a Manger" in their sweet, believing voices, we were touched nonetheless. How amazing to be reminded by those little ones that we are all living in the hope that Jesus brought to earth. While we live in a time in which Jesus has already risen, Zechariah's prophecy in Luke 1 gives us a glimpse of the excitement that must have been felt before Jesus was ever born.

Can you imagine Zechariah's enthusiasm when he learned there would not only be one new baby in the family, but two? Elizabeth's son John would be the prophet who paved the way for Mary's son Jesus, the Messiah of all the world! Elizabeth, who was too old to have children, and Mary, who was just a teenager, must have been overwhelmed by the power of the Lord upon them. And there must have been lots of rejoicing that the long-awaited Messiah was coming in their lifetime. In the words of Zechariah, "Let us praise the Lord!" (verse 68). We are living in the new day, which Zechariah proclaimed would arrive. Jesus has already risen!

Anna

LUKE 2

Anna has been a widow for eighty-four years and has spent most of her long life in the Temple fasting and praying. She was married only seven years before being widowed, but she refused to let her devotion to God die with her husband. She is relegated to the outer court—outside the Temple where the women must stay—but that restriction has not diminished her love or passion for God.

On this day she notices the old man Simeon holding a baby and declaring words that cause her heart to leap. "With my own eyes I have seen your salvation, which you prepared before all people." *He is the long-awaited One,* Anna thinks, gazing into the child's face. Simeon hands the baby back to his mother. "God has chosen this child to cause the fall and rise of many in Israel."

Anna wraps her arm around the mother. In her heart she praises God for this infant, the Messiah! More than Abraham, Jacob, or Isaac, and more than the men reciting prayers inside the Temple walls, Anna, a widow from the tribe of Asher, has felt the very presence of God in the flesh. Her eyes have beheld the promised One. It no longer matters that she is denied access to the inner Temple. God has revealed himself to her…a woman! Not inside the walls, but where she now stands is the Most Holy Place. She shares her joy with all who pass that way.

Anna's spiritual hunger was rewarded. Do you hunger for God's presence?

73 God promised Abraham, our father,
74 that he would save us from the power of our enemies
so we could serve him without fear,
75 being holy and good before God as long as we live.

76 "Now you, child, will be called a prophet of the Most High God.
You will go before the Lord to prepare his way.
77 You will make his people know that they will be saved
by having their sins forgiven.
78 With the loving mercy of our God,
a new day from heaven will dawn upon us.
79 It will shine on those who live in darkness,
in the shadow of death.
It will guide us into the path of peace."

80 And so the child grew up and became
strong in spirit. John lived in the desert until
the time when he came out to preach to
Israel.

The Birth of Jesus

2 At that time, Augustus Caesar sent an
order that all people in the countries
under Roman rule must list their names in a
register. 2 This was the first registration;[n] it
was taken while Quirinius was governor of
Syria. 3 And all went to their own towns to be
registered.

4 So Joseph left Nazareth, a town in
Galilee, and went to the town of Bethlehem
in Judea, known as the town of David.
Joseph went there because he was from the
family of David. 5 Joseph registered with
Mary, to whom he was engaged[n] and who
was now pregnant. 6 While they were in
Bethlehem, the time came for Mary to have
the baby, 7 and she gave birth to her first son.
Because there were no rooms left in the inn,
she wrapped the baby with pieces of cloth
and laid him in a feeding trough.

Shepherds Hear About Jesus

8 That night, some shepherds were in the
fields nearby watching their sheep. 9 Then an
angel of the Lord stood before them. The
glory of the Lord was shining around them,

2:2 registration Census. A counting of all the people and the things they own.
2:5 engaged For the Jewish people, an engagement was a lasting agreement. It could only be broken by divorce.

and they became very frightened. [10]The angel said to them, "Do not be afraid. I am bringing you good news that will be a great joy to all the people. [11]Today your Savior was born in the town of David. He is Christ, the Lord. [12]This is how you will know him: You will find a baby wrapped in pieces of cloth and lying in a feeding box."

[13]Then a very large group of angels from heaven joined the first angel, praising God and saying:

[14]"Give glory to God in heaven,
and on earth let there be peace among
the people who please God."[n]

[15]When the angels left them and went back to heaven, the shepherds said to each other, "Let's go to Bethlehem. Let's see this thing that has happened which the Lord has told us about."

[16]So the shepherds went quickly and found Mary and Joseph and the baby, who was lying in a feeding trough. [17]When they had seen him, they told what the angels had said about this child. [18]Everyone was amazed at what the shepherds said to them. [19]But Mary treasured these things and continued to think about them. [20]Then the shepherds went back to their sheep, praising God and thanking him for everything they had seen and heard. It had been just as the angel had told them.

[21]When the baby was eight days old, he was circumcised and was named Jesus, the name given by the angel before the baby began to grow inside Mary.

Jesus Is Presented in the Temple

[22]When the time came for Mary and Joseph to do what the law of Moses taught about being made pure,[n] they took Jesus to Jerusalem to present him to the Lord. [23](It is written in the law of the Lord: "Every firstborn male shall be given to the Lord.")[n] [24]Mary and Joseph also went to offer a sacrifice, as the law of the Lord says: "You must sacrifice two doves or two young pigeons."[n]

Simeon Sees Jesus

[25]In Jerusalem lived a man named Simeon who was a good man and godly. He was waiting for the time when God would take away Israel's sorrow, and the Holy Spirit was in him. [26]Simeon had been told by the Holy Spirit that he would not die before he saw the Christ promised by the Lord. [27]The Spirit led Simeon to the Temple. When Mary and Joseph brought the baby Jesus to the Temple to do what the law said they must do, [28]Simeon took the baby in his arms and thanked God:

[29]"Now, Lord, you can let me, your servant,
die in peace as you said.
[30]With my own eyes I have seen your
salvation,
[31] which you prepared before all people.
[32]It is a light for the non-Jewish people to see
and an honor for your people, the
Israelites."

[33]Jesus' father and mother were amazed at what Simeon had said about him. [34]Then Simeon blessed them and said to Mary, "God has chosen this child to cause the fall and rise of many in Israel. He will be a sign from God that many people will not accept [35]so that the thoughts of many will be made known. And the things that will happen will make your heart sad, too."

Anna Sees Jesus

[36]There was a prophetess, Anna, from the family of Phanuel in the tribe of Asher. Anna was very old. She had once been married for seven years. [37]Then her husband died, and she was a widow for eighty-four years. Anna never left the Temple but worshiped God, going without food and praying day and night. [38]Standing there at that time, she thanked God and spoke about Jesus to all who were waiting for God to free Jerusalem.

Joseph and Mary Return Home

[39]When Joseph and Mary had done everything the law of the Lord commanded, they went home to Nazareth, their own town in Galilee. [40]The little child grew and became strong. He was filled with wisdom, and God's goodness was upon him.

Jesus As a Boy

[41]Every year Jesus' parents went to Jerusalem for the Passover Feast. [42]When he

2:14 and . . . God Some Greek copies read "and on earth let there be peace and goodwill among people." **2:22 pure** The Law of Moses said that forty days after a Jewish woman gave birth to a son, she must be cleansed by a ceremony at the Temple. Read Leviticus 12:2–8. **2:23 "Every . . . Lord."** Quotation from Exodus 13:2. **2:24 "You . . . pigeons."** Quotation from Leviticus 12:8.

was twelve years old, they went to the feast
as they always did. 43After the feast days
were over, they started home. The boy Jesus
stayed behind in Jerusalem, but his parents
did not know it. 44Thinking that Jesus was
with them in the group, they traveled for a
whole day. Then they began to look for him
among their family and friends. 45When
they did not find him, they went back to
Jerusalem to look for him there. 46After three
days they found Jesus sitting in the Temple
with the teachers, listening to them and
asking them questions. 47All who heard him
were amazed at his understanding and
answers. 48When Jesus' parents saw him,
they were astonished. His mother said to
him, "Son, why did you do this to us? Your
father and I were very worried about you
and have been looking for you."

49Jesus said to them, "Why were you
looking for me? Didn't you know that I
must be in my Father's house?" 50But they
did not understand the meaning of what
he said.

51Jesus went with them to Nazareth and
was obedient to them. But his mother kept
in her mind all that had happened. 52Jesus
became wiser and grew physically. People
liked him, and he pleased God.

The Preaching of John

3 It was the fifteenth year of the rule of
Tiberius Caesar. These men were under
Caesar: Pontius Pilate, the ruler of Judea;
Herod, the ruler of Galilee; Philip, Herod's
brother, the ruler of Iturea and Traconitis;
and Lysanias, the ruler of Abilene. 2Annas
and Caiaphas were the high priests. At this
time, the word of God came to John son of
Zechariah in the desert. 3He went all over
the area around the Jordan River preaching a
baptism of changed hearts and lives for the
forgiveness of sins. 4As it is written in the
book of Isaiah the prophet:

"This is a voice of one
  who calls out in the desert:
'Prepare the way for the Lord.
  Make the road straight for him.
5Every valley should be filled in,
  and every mountain and hill should be
    made flat.
Roads with turns should be made straight,
  and rough roads should be made
    smooth.
6And all people will know about the
    salvation of God!'" *Isaiah 40:3–5*

7To the crowds of people who came to be
baptized by John, he said, "You are all snakes!
Who warned you to run away from God's
coming punishment? 8Do the things that
show you really have changed your hearts
and lives. Don't begin to say to yourselves,
'Abraham is our father.' I tell you that God
could make children for Abraham from
these rocks. 9The ax is now ready to cut
down the trees, and every tree that does not
produce good fruit will be cut down and
thrown into the fire."[n]

10The people asked John, "Then what
should we do?"

11John answered, "If you have two shirts,
share with the person who does not have
one. If you have food, share that also."

12Even tax collectors came to John to be
baptized. They said to him, "Teacher, what
should we do?"

13John said to them, "Don't take more
taxes from people than you have been
ordered to take."

14The soldiers asked John, "What about
us? What should we do?"

John said to them, "Don't force people to
give you money, and don't lie about them. Be
satisfied with the pay you get."

15Since the people were hoping for the
Christ to come, they wondered if John might
be the one.

16John answered everyone, "I baptize you
with water, but there is one coming who is
greater than I am. I am not good enough to
untie his sandals. He will baptize you with
the Holy Spirit and fire. 17He will come ready
to clean the grain, separating the good grain
from the chaff. He will put the good part of
the grain into his barn, but he will burn the
chaff with a fire that cannot be put out."[n]
18And John continued to preach the Good
News, saying many other things to
encourage the people.

19But John spoke against Herod, the
governor, because of his sin with Herodias,
the wife of Herod's brother, and because of

3:9 The ax . . . fire. This means that God is ready to punish his people who do not obey him.
3:17 He will . . . out. This means that Jesus will come to separate good people from bad people, saving the good and punishing the bad.

the many other evil things Herod did. 20So
Herod did something even worse: He put
John in prison.

Jesus Is Baptized by John

21When all the people were being
baptized by John, Jesus also was baptized.
While Jesus was praying, heaven opened
22and the Holy Spirit came down on him in
the form of a dove. Then a voice came from
heaven, saying, "You are my Son, whom I
love, and I am very pleased with you."

The Family History of Jesus

23When Jesus began his ministry, he was
about thirty years old. People thought that
Jesus was Joseph's son.
Joseph was the son[n] of Heli.
24Heli was the son of Matthat.
Matthat was the son of Levi.
Levi was the son of Melki.
Melki was the son of Jannai.
Jannai was the son of Joseph.
25Joseph was the son of Mattathias.
Mattathias was the son of Amos.
Amos was the son of Nahum.
Nahum was the son of Esli.
Esli was the son of Naggai.
26Naggai was the son of Maath.
Maath was the son of Mattathias.
Mattathias was the son of Semein.
Semein was the son of Josech.
Josech was the son of Joda.
27Joda was the son of Joanan.
Joanan was the son of Rhesa.
Rhesa was the son of Zerubbabel.
Zerubbabel was the grandson of Shealtiel.
Shealtiel was the son of Neri.
28Neri was the son of Melki.
Melki was the son of Addi.
Addi was the son of Cosam.
Cosam was the son of Elmadam.
Elmadam was the son of Er.
29Er was the son of Joshua.
Joshua was the son of Eliezer.
Eliezer was the son of Jorim.
Jorim was the son of Matthat.
Matthat was the son of Levi.
30Levi was the son of Simeon.
Simeon was the son of Judah.
Judah was the son of Joseph.
Joseph was the son of Jonam.
Jonam was the son of Eliakim.
31Eliakim was the son of Melea.
Melea was the son of Menna.
Menna was the son of Mattatha.
Mattatha was the son of Nathan.
Nathan was the son of David.
32David was the son of Jesse.
Jesse was the son of Obed.
Obed was the son of Boaz.
Boaz was the son of Salmon.[n]
Salmon was the son of Nahshon.
33Nahshon was the son of Amminadab.
Amminadab was the son of Admin.
Admin was the son of Arni.
Arni was the son of Hezron.
Hezron was the son of Perez.
Perez was the son of Judah.
34Judah was the son of Jacob.
Jacob was the son of Isaac.
Isaac was the son of Abraham.
Abraham was the son of Terah.
Terah was the son of Nahor.
35Nahor was the son of Serug.
Serug was the son of Reu.
Reu was the son of Peleg.
Peleg was the son of Eber.
Eber was the son of Shelah.
36Shelah was the son of Cainan.
Cainan was the son of Arphaxad.
Arphaxad was the son of Shem.
Shem was the son of Noah.
Noah was the son of Lamech.
37Lamech was the son of Methuselah.
Methuselah was the son of Enoch.
Enoch was the son of Jared.
Jared was the son of Mahalalel.
Mahalalel was the son of Kenan.
38Kenan was the son of Enosh.
Enosh was the son of Seth.
Seth was the son of Adam.
Adam was the son of God.

Jesus Is Tempted by the Devil

4 Jesus, filled with the Holy Spirit,
returned from the Jordan River. The
Spirit led Jesus into the desert 2where the
devil tempted Jesus for forty days. Jesus ate
nothing during that time, and when those
days were ended, he was very hungry.
3The devil said to Jesus, "If you are the Son
of God, tell this rock to become bread."
4Jesus answered, "It is written in the

3:23 son "Son" in Jewish lists of ancestors can sometimes mean grandson or more distant relative.
3:32 Salmon Some Greek copies read "Sala."

Scriptures: 'A person does not live on bread
alone.' "[n]

5 Then the devil took Jesus and showed
him all the kingdoms of the world in an
instant. 6 The devil said to Jesus, "I will give
you all these kingdoms and all their power
and glory. It has all been given to me, and I
can give it to anyone I wish. 7 If you worship
me, then it will all be yours."

8 Jesus answered, "It is written in the
Scriptures: 'You must worship the Lord your
God and serve only him.' "[n]

9 Then the devil led Jesus to Jerusalem and
put him on a high place of the Temple. He
said to Jesus, "If you are the Son of God,
jump down. 10 It is written in the Scriptures:

'He has put his angels in charge of you
to watch over you.' *Psalm 91:11*

11 It is also written:

'They will catch you in their hands
so that you will not hit your foot on a
rock.' " *Psalm 91:12*

12 Jesus answered, "But it also says in the
Scriptures: 'Do not test the Lord your God.' "[n]

13 After the devil had tempted Jesus in
every way, he left him to wait until a better
time.

Jesus Teaches the People

14 Jesus returned to Galilee in the power of
the Holy Spirit, and stories about him spread
all through the area. 15 He began to teach in
their synagogues, and everyone praised him.

16 Jesus traveled to Nazareth, where he had
grown up. On the Sabbath day he went to
the synagogue, as he always did, and stood
up to read. 17 The book of Isaiah the prophet
was given to him. He opened the book and
found the place where this is written:

18 "The Lord has put his Spirit in me,
because he appointed me to tell the
Good News to the poor.
He has sent me to tell the captives they
are free
and to tell the blind that they can see
again. *Isaiah 61:1*
God sent me to free those who have been
treated unfairly *Isaiah 58:6*
19 and to announce the time when the
Lord will show his kindness."
Isaiah 61:2

20 Jesus closed the book, gave it back to the
assistant, and sat down. Everyone in the
synagogue was watching Jesus closely. 21 He
began to say to them, "While you heard
these words just now, they were coming
true!"

22 All the people spoke well of Jesus and
were amazed at the words of grace he spoke.
They asked, "Isn't this Joseph's son?"

23 Jesus said to them, "I know that you will
tell me the old saying: 'Doctor, heal yourself.'
You want to say, 'We heard about the things
you did in Capernaum. Do those things here
in your own town!' " 24 Then Jesus said, "I tell
you the truth, a prophet is not accepted in
his hometown. 25 But I tell you the truth,
there were many widows in Israel during the
time of Elijah. It did not rain in Israel for
three and one-half years, and there was no
food anywhere in the whole country. 26 But
Elijah was sent to none of those widows,
only to a widow in Zarephath, a town in
Sidon. 27 And there were many with skin
diseases living in Israel during the time of
the prophet Elisha. But none of them were
healed, only Naaman, who was from the
country of Syria."

28 When all the people in the synagogue
heard these things, they became very angry.
29 They got up, forced Jesus out of town, and
took him to the edge of the cliff on which
the town was built. They planned to throw
him off the edge, 30 but Jesus walked through
the crowd and went on his way.

Jesus Forces Out an Evil Spirit

31 Jesus went to Capernaum, a city in
Galilee, and on the Sabbath day, he taught
the people. 32 They were amazed at his
teaching, because he spoke with authority.
33 In the synagogue a man who had within
him an evil spirit shouted in a loud voice,
34 "Jesus of Nazareth! What do you want with
us? Did you come to destroy us? I know who
you are—God's Holy One!"

35 Jesus commanded the evil spirit, "Be
quiet! Come out of the man!" The evil spirit
threw the man down to the ground before
all the people and then left the man without
hurting him.

36 The people were amazed and said to

4:4 'A person . . . alone.' Quotation from Deuteronomy 8:3. **4:8 'You . . . him.'** Quotation from Deuteronomy 6:13.
4:12 'Do . . . God.' Quotation from Deuteronomy 6:16.

each other, "What does this mean? With
authority and power he commands evil
spirits, and they come out." 37And so the
news about Jesus spread to every place in the
whole area.

Jesus Heals Many People

38Jesus left the synagogue and went to the
home of Simon.[n] Simon's mother-in-law was
sick with a high fever, and they asked Jesus
to help her. 39He came to her side and
commanded the fever to leave. It left her, and
immediately she got up and began serving
them.
40When the sun went down, the people
brought those who were sick to Jesus.
Putting his hands on each sick person, he
healed every one of them. 41Demons came
out of many people, shouting, "You are the
Son of God." But Jesus commanded the
demons and would not allow them to speak,
because they knew Jesus was the Christ.
42At daybreak, Jesus went to a lonely
place, but the people looked for him. When
they found him, they tried to keep him from
leaving. 43But Jesus said to them, "I must
preach about God's kingdom to other towns,
too. This is why I was sent."
44Then he kept on preaching in the
synagogues of Judea.[n]

Jesus' First Followers

5 One day while Jesus was standing beside
Lake Galilee, many people were pressing
all around him to hear the word of God.
2Jesus saw two boats at the shore of the lake.
The fishermen had left them and were
washing their nets. 3Jesus got into one of the
boats, the one that belonged to Simon,[n] and
asked him to push off a little from the land.
Then Jesus sat down and continued to teach
the people from the boat.
4When Jesus had finished speaking, he
said to Simon, "Take the boat into deep
water, and put your nets in the water to
catch some fish."
5Simon answered, "Master, we worked
hard all night trying to catch fish, and we
caught nothing. But you say to put the nets
in the water, so I will." 6When the fishermen
did as Jesus told them, they caught so many
fish that the nets began to break. 7They
called to their partners in the other boat to
come and help them. They came and filled
both boats so full that they were almost
sinking.
8When Simon Peter saw what had
happened, he bowed down before Jesus and
said, "Go away from me, Lord. I am a sinful
man!" 9He and the other fishermen were
amazed at the many fish they caught, as
were 10James and John, the sons of Zebedee,
Simon's partners.
Jesus said to Simon, "Don't be afraid.
From now on you will fish for people."
11When the men brought their boats to
the shore, they left everything and followed
Jesus.

Jesus Heals a Sick Man

12When Jesus was in one of the towns,
there was a man covered with a skin disease.
When he saw Jesus, he bowed before him
and begged him, "Lord, you can heal me if
you will."
13Jesus reached out his hand and touched
the man and said, "I will. Be healed!"
Immediately the disease disappeared. 14Then
Jesus said, "Don't tell anyone about this, but
go and show yourself to the priest[n] and offer
a gift for your healing, as Moses
commanded.[n] This will show the people
what I have done."
15But the news about Jesus spread even
more. Many people came to hear Jesus and
to be healed of their sicknesses, 16but Jesus
often slipped away to be alone so he could
pray.

Jesus Heals a Paralyzed Man

17One day as Jesus was teaching the
people, the Pharisees and teachers of the law
from every town in Galilee and Judea and
from Jerusalem were there. The Lord was
giving Jesus the power to heal people. 18Just
then, some men were carrying on a mat a
man who was paralyzed. They tried to bring
him in and put him down before Jesus. 19But
because there were so many people there,
they could not find a way in. So they went
up on the roof and lowered the man on his
mat through the ceiling into the middle of

4:38; 5:3 Simon Simon's other name was Peter. **4:44 Judea** Some Greek copies read "Galilee." **5:14 show . . . priest** The Law of Moses said a priest must say when a Jewish person with a skin disease was well. **5:14 Moses commanded** Read about this in Leviticus 14:1–32.

devotion 278

LUKE 5:15–16

LEAVING THE CHAOS

Jesus modeled the importance of getting away from the chaos to pray. He also instructed us to pray in secret where only the Father sees and hears (Matt. 6:5–6). But time alone to pray is a rare commodity these days. I don't know of anyone who has loads of *extra* time to be alone with God. That means that we have to give serious attention to this spiritual discipline. We're going to have to figure out how to be alone with God in prayer and do whatever it takes to make that happen.

Jesus very intentionally calls us to a secret prayer life with him. That doesn't preclude us from praying in public or having prayer partners or maintaining a prayer life with our families. But it is very beautiful to him when we get away from the unyielding demands to be alone in prayer.

This kind of getting-away praying has to be intentional. Some time has to be cleared in your day planner to purposefully be alone and quiet with God. You're going to have to think about it and protect the time you've blocked. And you probably already know that the enemy will do everything possible to steal this time.

The woman who maintains an intimate prayer life with her Father learns to interact with the world from the security of that relationship. In the quiet, God reminds us that we belong to him. And away from the busyness, we can commit anew to becoming women of faith and passion.

the crowd right before Jesus. 20Seeing their
faith, Jesus said, "Friend, your sins are
forgiven."
21The Jewish teachers of the law and the
Pharisees thought to themselves, "Who is
this man who is speaking as if he were God?
Only God can forgive sins."
22But Jesus knew what they were thinking
and said, "Why are you thinking these
things? 23Which is easier: to say, 'Your sins
are forgiven,' or to say, 'Stand up and walk'?
24But I will prove to you that the Son of Man
has authority on earth to forgive sins." So
Jesus said to the paralyzed man, "I tell you,
stand up, take your mat, and go home."
25At once the man stood up before them,
picked up his mat, and went home, praising
God. 26All the people were fully amazed and
began to praise God. They were filled with
much respect and said, "Today we have seen
amazing things!"

Levi Follows Jesus

27After this, Jesus went out and saw a tax
collector named Levi sitting in the tax
collector's booth. Jesus said to him, "Follow
me!" 28So Levi got up, left everything, and
followed him.
29Then Levi gave a big dinner for Jesus at
his house. Many tax collectors and other
people were eating there, too. 30But the
Pharisees and the men who taught the law
for the Pharisees began to complain to Jesus'
followers, "Why do you eat and drink with
tax collectors and sinners?"
31Jesus answered them, "It is not the
healthy people who need a doctor, but the
sick. 32I have not come to invite good people
but sinners to change their hearts and lives."

Jesus Answers a Question

33They said to Jesus, "John's followers
often fast[n] for a certain time and pray, just as

5:33 fast The people would give up eating for a special time of prayer and worship to God. It was also done to show sadness and disappointment.

the Pharisees do. But your followers eat and drink all the time."

34Jesus said to them, "You cannot make the friends of the bridegroom fast while he is still with them. 35But the time will come when the bridegroom will be taken away from them, and then they will fast."

36Jesus told them this story: "No one takes cloth off a new coat to cover a hole in an old coat. Otherwise, he ruins the new coat, and the cloth from the new coat will not be the same as the old cloth. 37Also, no one ever pours new wine into old leather bags. Otherwise, the new wine will break the bags, the wine will spill out, and the leather bags will be ruined. 38New wine must be put into new leather bags. 39No one after drinking old wine wants new wine, because he says, 'The old wine is better.' "

Jesus Is Lord over the Sabbath

6 One Sabbath day Jesus was walking through some fields of grain. His followers picked the heads of grain, rubbed them in their hands, and ate them. 2Some Pharisees said, "Why do you do what is not lawful on the Sabbath day?"

3Jesus answered, "Have you not read what David did when he and those with him were hungry? 4He went into God's house and took and ate the holy bread, which is lawful only for priests to eat. And he gave some to the people who were with him." 5Then Jesus said to the Pharisees, "The Son of Man is Lord of the Sabbath day."

Jesus Heals a Man's Hand

6On another Sabbath day Jesus went into the synagogue and was teaching, and a man with a crippled right hand was there. 7The teachers of the law and the Pharisees were watching closely to see if Jesus would heal on the Sabbath day so they could accuse him. 8But he knew what they were thinking, and he said to the man with the crippled hand, "Stand up here in the middle of everyone." The man got up and stood there. 9Then Jesus said to them, "I ask you, which is lawful on the Sabbath day: to do good or to do evil, to save a life or to destroy it?" 10Jesus looked around at all of them and said to the man, "Hold out your hand." The man held out his hand, and it was healed.

11But the Pharisees and the teachers of the law were very angry and discussed with each other what they could do to Jesus.

Jesus Chooses His Apostles

12At that time Jesus went off to a mountain to pray, and he spent the night praying to God. 13The next morning, Jesus called his followers to him and chose twelve of them, whom he named apostles: 14Simon (Jesus named him Peter), his brother Andrew, James, John, Philip, Bartholomew, 15Matthew, Thomas, James son of Alphaeus, Simon (called the Zealot), 16Judas son of James, and Judas Iscariot, who later turned Jesus over to his enemies.

Jesus Teaches and Heals

17Jesus and the apostles came down from the mountain, and he stood on level ground. A large group of his followers was there, as well as many people from all around Judea, Jerusalem, and the seacoast cities of Tyre and Sidon. 18They all came to hear Jesus teach and to be healed of their sicknesses, and he healed those who were troubled by evil spirits. 19All the people were trying to touch Jesus, because power was coming from him and healing them all.

20Jesus looked at his followers and said,
"You people who are poor are blessed,
because the kingdom of God belongs to you.
21You people who are now hungry are blessed,
because you will be satisfied.
You people who are now crying are blessed,
because you will laugh with joy.

22"People will hate you, shut you out, insult you, and say you are evil because you follow the Son of Man. But when they do, you will be blessed. 23Be full of joy at that time, because you have a great reward in heaven. Their ancestors did the same things to the prophets.

24"But how terrible it will be for you who are rich,
because you have had your easy life.
25How terrible it will be for you who are full now,
because you will be hungry.
How terrible it will be for you who are laughing now,
because you will be sad and cry.

The Widow of Nain

LUKE 7

She is a widow, and he was her only son—there is no one left to care for her as she ages. Her future is bleak; she knows she will be cast aside in society. She reaches for his body. She needs to see him—to touch him one last time—but the coffin rests on the shoulders of the men as they carry him outside the city gate. Cries of anguish fill the air as she stretches her hands toward him, but she cannot reach him. What will she do? Who can she turn to for help?

Dear friends wrap their arms around her, hoping to ease the burden. But her grief cannot be lifted. She does not see Jesus watching the funeral procession—but he sees her. When he observes her sorrow, he feels compassion for her. "Don't cry," he says. *What a foolish thing to say,* the other mourners think, walking past him. But in her anguish, the widow knows this is just another empty cliché people use to express comfort.

Jesus walks to the coffin and touches it. The mourners lean in to see what he's doing. "Young man, I tell you, get up!" Like awakening from a night's rest, the young man sits up and begins to talk. His mother screams and bolts for the coffin. In an instant, her world is transformed and her hope restored.

How dismal our future would be without the touch of Jesus in our lives.

26"How terrible when everyone says only
good things about you, because their
ancestors said the same things about the
false prophets.

Love Your Enemies

27"But I say to you who are listening, love
your enemies. Do good to those who hate
you, 28bless those who curse you, pray for
those who are cruel to you. 29If anyone slaps
you on one cheek, offer him the other cheek,
too. If someone takes your coat, do not stop
him from taking your shirt. 30Give to
everyone who asks you, and when someone
takes something that is yours, don't ask for it
back. 31Do to others what you would want
them to do to you. 32If you love only the
people who love you, what praise should
you get? Even sinners love the people who
love them. 33If you do good only to those
who do good to you, what praise should you
get? Even sinners do that! 34If you lend
things to people, always hoping to get
something back, what praise should you get?
Even sinners lend to other sinners so that
they can get back the same amount! 35But
love your enemies, do good to them, and
lend to them without hoping to get
anything back. Then you will have a great
reward, and you will be children of the Most
High God, because he is kind even to people
who are ungrateful and full of sin. 36Show
mercy, just as your Father shows mercy.

Look at Yourselves

37"Don't judge others, and you will not be
judged. Don't accuse others of being guilty,
and you will not be accused of being guilty.
Forgive, and you will be forgiven. 38Give, and
you will receive. You will be given much.
Pressed down, shaken together, and running
over, it will spill into your lap. The way you
give to others is the way God will give to
you."

39Jesus told them this story: "Can a blind
person lead another blind person? No! Both
of them will fall into a ditch. 40A student is
not better than the teacher, but the student
who has been fully trained will be like the
teacher.

41"Why do you notice the little piece of
dust in your friend's eye, but you don't
notice the big piece of wood in your own
eye? 42How can you say to your friend,

‘Friend, let me take that little piece of dust
out of your eye’ when you cannot see that
big piece of wood in your own eye! You
hypocrite! First, take the wood out of your
own eye. Then you will see clearly to take
the dust out of your friend’s eye.

Two Kinds of Fruit

43“A good tree does not produce bad fruit,
nor does a bad tree produce good fruit.
44Each tree is known by its own fruit. People
don’t gather figs from thornbushes, and they
don’t get grapes from bushes. 45Good people
bring good things out of the good they
stored in their hearts. But evil people bring
evil things out of the evil they stored in their
hearts. People speak the things that are in
their hearts.

Two Kinds of People

46“Why do you call me, ‘Lord, Lord,’ but
do not do what I say? 47I will show you what
everyone is like who comes to me and hears
my words and obeys. 48That person is like a
man building a house who dug deep and laid
the foundation on rock. When the floods
came, the water tried to wash the house
away, but it could not shake it, because the
house was built well. 49But the one who
hears my words and does not obey is like a
man who built his house on the ground
without a foundation. When the floods
came, the house quickly fell and was
completely destroyed.”

Jesus Heals a Soldier’s Servant

7 When Jesus finished saying all these
things to the people, he went to
Capernaum. 2There was an army officer who
had a servant who was very important to
him. The servant was so sick he was nearly
dead. 3When the officer heard about Jesus,
he sent some Jewish elders to him to ask
Jesus to come and heal his servant. 4The men
went to Jesus and begged him, saying, “This
officer is worthy of your help. 5He loves our
people, and he built us a synagogue.”

6So Jesus went with the men. He was
getting near the officer’s house when the
officer sent friends to say, “Lord, don’t
trouble yourself, because I am not worthy to
have you come into my house. 7That is why
I did not come to you myself. But you only
need to command it, and my servant will be
healed. 8I, too, am a man under the authority
of others, and I have soldiers under my
command. I tell one soldier, ‘Go,’ and he
goes. I tell another soldier, ‘Come,’ and he
comes. I say to my servant, ‘Do this,’ and my
servant does it.”

9When Jesus heard this, he was amazed.
Turning to the crowd that was following
him, he said, “I tell you, this is the greatest
faith I have found anywhere, even in Israel.”

10Those who had been sent to Jesus went
back to the house where they found the
servant in good health.

Jesus Brings a Man Back to Life

11Soon afterwards Jesus went to a town
called Nain, and his followers and a large
crowd traveled with him. 12When he came
near the town gate, he saw a funeral. A
mother, who was a widow, had lost her only
son. A large crowd from the town was with
the mother while her son was being carried
out. 13When the Lord saw her, he felt very
sorry for her and said, “Don’t cry.” 14He went
up and touched the coffin, and the people
who were carrying it stopped. Jesus said,
“Young man, I tell you, get up!” 15And the
son sat up and began to talk. Then Jesus gave
him back to his mother.

16All the people were amazed and began
praising God, saying, “A great prophet has
come to us! God has come to help his
people.”

17This news about Jesus spread through
all Judea and into all the places around there.

John Asks a Question

18John’s followers told him about all these
things. He called for two of his followers
19and sent them to the Lord to ask, “Are you
the One who is to come, or should we wait
for someone else?”

20When the men came to Jesus, they said,
“John the Baptist sent us to you with this
question: ‘Are you the One who is to come,
or should we wait for someone else?’ ”

21At that time, Jesus healed many people
of their sicknesses, diseases, and evil spirits,
and he gave sight to many blind people.
22Then Jesus answered John’s followers, “Go
tell John what you saw and heard here. The
blind can see, the crippled can walk, and
people with skin diseases are healed. The
deaf can hear, the dead are raised to life, and

The Woman Who Washes Jesus' Feet with Her Hair

LUKE 7

Though the men are staring and murmuring as she passes, she holds the alabaster jar tightly to her chest, making her way to where Jesus is sitting in the Pharisee's home. She trembles as she kneels at his feet. Years of sin and deception sweep over her cheeks in tears, yet a wave of gratitude and emotion fill her as she begins to kiss his feet and wash them with her tears.

The men in the room shuffle on their feet and shift in their seats, uncomfortable and embarrassed by her act. The woman opens the bottle of perfume and pours it over Jesus' feet, rubbing the sweet smell into his dirty and weary soles. The homeowner is repelled by the scene. *Jesus isn't even saying anything,* he thinks. *If Jesus were a prophet, he would know that the woman touching him is a sinner!*

The woman continues to cry as Jesus tells the Pharisee about two people whose debts have been dismissed by a banker: one owed five hundred coins and the other owed fifty. "Who had the greater debt?" Jesus asks. Simon replies, "I think it would be the one who owed him the most money."

"You are right," Jesus says, turning to the woman at his feet. "Because you believed, you are saved from your sins. Go in peace." She rises as tears of joy stream down her face. She has found life at the feet of Jesus!

Forgiveness always produces devotion.

the Good News is preached to the poor.
23 Those who do not stumble in their faith
because of me are blessed!"
24 When John's followers left, Jesus began
talking to the people about John: "What did
you go out into the desert to see? A reed[n]
blown by the wind? 25 What did you go out
to see? A man dressed in fine clothes? No,
people who have fine clothes and much
wealth live in kings' palaces. 26 But what did
you go out to see? A prophet? Yes, and I tell
you, John is more than a prophet. 27 This was
written about him:

'I will send my messenger ahead of you,
who will prepare the way for you.'
Malachi 3:1

28 I tell you, John is greater than any other
person ever born, but even the least
important person in the kingdom of God is
greater than John."
29 (When the people, including the tax
collectors, heard this, they all agreed that
God's teaching was good, because they had
been baptized by John. 30 But the Pharisees
and experts on the law refused to accept
God's plan for themselves; they did not let
John baptize them.)
31 Then Jesus said, "What shall I say about
the people of this time? What are they like?
32 They are like children sitting in the
marketplace, calling to one another and
saying,

'We played music for you, but you did not
dance;
we sang a sad song, but you did not cry.'

33 John the Baptist came and did not eat
bread or drink wine, and you say, 'He has a
demon in him.' 34 The Son of Man came
eating and drinking, and you say, 'Look at
him! He eats too much and drinks too much
wine, and he is a friend of tax collectors and
sinners!' 35 But wisdom is proved to be right
by what it does."

A Woman Washes Jesus' Feet

36 One of the Pharisees asked Jesus to eat
with him, so Jesus went into the Pharisee's
house and sat at the table. 37 A sinful woman
in the town learned that Jesus was eating at
the Pharisee's house. So she brought an
alabaster jar of perfume 38 and stood behind
Jesus at his feet, crying. She began to wash

7:24 reed It means that John was not ordinary or weak like grass blown by the wind.

his feet with her tears, and she dried them with her hair, kissing them many times and rubbing them with the perfume. 39When the Pharisee who asked Jesus to come to his house saw this, he thought to himself, "If Jesus were a prophet, he would know that the woman touching him is a sinner!"

40Jesus said to the Pharisee, "Simon, I have something to say to you."

Simon said, "Teacher, tell me."

41Jesus said, "Two people owed money to the same banker. One owed five hundred coins[n] and the other owed fifty. 42They had no money to pay what they owed, but the banker told both of them they did not have to pay him. Which person will love the banker more?"

43Simon, the Pharisee, answered, "I think it would be the one who owed him the most money."

Jesus said to Simon, "You are right." 44Then Jesus turned toward the woman and said to Simon, "Do you see this woman? When I came into your house, you gave me no water for my feet, but she washed my feet with her tears and dried them with her hair. 45You gave me no kiss of greeting, but she has been kissing my feet since I came in. 46You did not put oil on my head, but she poured perfume on my feet. 47I tell you that her many sins are forgiven, so she showed great love. But the person who is forgiven only a little will love only a little."

48Then Jesus said to her, "Your sins are forgiven."

49The people sitting at the table began to say among themselves, "Who is this who even forgives sins?"

50Jesus said to the woman, "Because you believed, you are saved from your sins. Go in peace."

The Group with Jesus

8 After this, while Jesus was traveling through some cities and small towns, he preached and told the Good News about God's kingdom. The twelve apostles were with him, 2and also some women who had been healed of sicknesses and evil spirits: Mary, called Magdalene, from whom seven demons had gone out; 3Joanna, the wife of Cuza (the manager of Herod's house); Susanna; and many others. These women used their own money to help Jesus and his apostles.

A Story About Planting Seed

4When a great crowd was gathered, and people were coming to Jesus from every town, he told them this story:

5"A farmer went out to plant his seed. While he was planting, some seed fell by the road. People walked on the seed, and the birds ate it up. 6Some seed fell on rock, and when it began to grow, it died because it had no water. 7Some seed fell among thorny weeds, but the weeds grew up with it and choked the good plants. 8And some seed fell on good ground and grew and made a hundred times more."

As Jesus finished the story, he called out, "Let those with ears use them and listen!"

9Jesus' followers asked him what this story meant.

10Jesus said, "You have been chosen to know the secrets about the kingdom of God. But I use stories to speak to other people so that:

'They will look, but they may not see.
They will listen, but they may not understand.' *Isaiah 6:9*

11"This is what the story means: The seed is God's message. 12The seed that fell beside the road is like the people who hear God's teaching, but the devil comes and takes it away from them so they cannot believe it and be saved. 13The seed that fell on rock is like those who hear God's teaching and accept it gladly, but they don't allow the teaching to go deep into their lives. They believe for a while, but when trouble comes, they give up. 14The seed that fell among the thorny weeds is like those who hear God's teaching, but they let the worries, riches, and pleasures of this life keep them from growing and producing good fruit. 15And the seed that fell on the good ground is like those who hear God's teaching with good, honest hearts and obey it and patiently produce good fruit.

Use What You Have

16"No one after lighting a lamp covers it with a bowl or hides it under a bed. Instead,

7:41 coins Roman denarii. One coin was the average pay for one day's work.

Joanna

LUKE 8

Joanna's husband, Cuza, is a very important man—the manager of Herod's house. She has everything she needs, yet she has nothing at all. She has all she wants to eat, yet she still feels hungry. She has the best physicians at her fingertips, yet she still feels sick.

She has heard the murmurings about a man who can cast out evil spirits and give able legs to the lame. She wanders about the palace grounds, recalling the words she heard on the street: "In his hands are miracles." She has seen this man Jesus with his father. They helped construct buildings close to the palace. Could there be miracles in the hands of that carpenter?

Joanna hears that Jesus is in town today, and she rushes to hear him speak of love and forgiveness and healing. *Perhaps he could heal me,* she thinks, running to his side. His eyes are different from her husband's and Herod's—filled with a grace and mercy she has never seen. He doesn't ask what's wrong but seems to know the emptiness of life in the palace, the loneliness of her marriage, and the burden of illness. He places his hand on her shoulder, and she is changed in an instant. She is rich, yet she understands she is nothing more than a beggar without him. She is still hungry, but her appetite has changed—she desires God!

Joanna offered her riches to help Christ's ministry on earth. What can you offer?

the person puts it on a lampstand so those
who come in will see the light. 17Everything
that is hidden will become clear, and every
secret thing will be made known. 18So be
careful how you listen. Those who have
understanding will be given more. But those
who do not have understanding, even what
they think they have will be taken away
from them."

Jesus' True Family

19Jesus' mother and brothers came to see
him, but there was such a crowd they could
not get to him. 20Someone said to Jesus,
"Your mother and your brothers are standing
outside, wanting to see you."
21Jesus answered them, "My mother and
my brothers are those who listen to God's
teaching and obey it!"

Jesus Calms a Storm

22One day Jesus and his followers got into
a boat, and he said to them, "Let's go across
the lake." And so they started across. 23While
they were sailing, Jesus fell asleep. A very
strong wind blew up on the lake, causing the
boat to fill with water, and they were in
danger.
24The followers went to Jesus and woke
him, saying, "Master! Master! We will
drown!"

Jesus got up and gave a command to the
wind and the waves. They stopped, and it
became calm. 25Jesus said to his followers,
"Where is your faith?"

The followers were afraid and amazed and
said to each other, "Who is this that
commands even the wind and the water, and
they obey him?"

A Man with Demons Inside Him

26Jesus and his followers sailed across the
lake from Galilee to the area of the
Gerasene[n] people. 27When Jesus got out on
the land, a man from the town who had
demons inside him came to Jesus. For a long
time he had worn no clothes and had lived
in the burial caves, not in a house. 28When
he saw Jesus, he cried out and fell down
before him. He said with a loud voice, "What
do you want with me, Jesus, Son of the Most

8:26 Gerasene From Gerasa, an area southeast of Lake Galilee. The exact location is uncertain and some Greek copies read "Gadarene"; others read "Gergesene."

devotion 279

LUKE 8:4–8, 11–15

A SOIL ANALYSIS

Patience and gardening seem to go hand in hand. You need to prepare the ground, nourish it, water it, plant the seeds, care for the seedlings as they mature, and keep the weeds from choking out the ground space. It's a lot of work! I love the final results of a beautiful garden, but I do not enjoy the process very much because I want to experience the garden now, not later! I want to enjoy the beauty of a giant bouquet centered nicely on my kitchen table. Is this you? I believe as Christians we want that instant result in our Christian walk, too. Like a Chia Pet, we want to spread a little truth on the surface, water it a little bit with church attendance, and *Poof!* have mature Christian fruit. Not!

Christian, let the Master Gardener tend your beds so that you may be a beautiful life for Christ. There was a reason why Satan tempted Jesus in the desert—there was no substance, no provision, and it was dry, infertile ground. Our gardens are alive and full because we have the Word, Jesus, and his living water. Let your walk, your home, and your life be a garden, not a desert. I pray that you become so beautiful in the Lord that your life spreads out like a rich, lush ground cover that shares the love of Christ. Jesus can bless the perseverance of an honest and obedient heart and create a life that is beyond limits.

High God? I beg you, don't torture me!" 29He
said this because Jesus was commanding the
evil spirit to come out of the man. Many
times it had taken hold of him. Though he
had been kept under guard and chained
hand and foot, he had broken his chains and
had been forced by the demon out into a
lonely place.

30Jesus asked him, "What is your name?"

He answered, "Legion,"[n] because many
demons were in him. 31The demons begged
Jesus not to send them into eternal
darkness.[n] 32A large herd of pigs was feeding
on a hill, and the demons begged Jesus to
allow them to go into the pigs. So Jesus
allowed them to do this. 33When the
demons came out of the man, they went into
the pigs, and the herd ran down the hill into
the lake and was drowned.

34When the herdsmen saw what had
happened, they ran away and told about this
in the town and the countryside. 35And
people went to see what had happened.
When they came to Jesus, they found the
man sitting at Jesus' feet, clothed and in his
right mind, because the demons were gone.
But the people were frightened. 36The people
who saw this happen told the others how
Jesus had made the man well. 37All the
people of the Gerasene country asked Jesus
to leave, because they were all very afraid. So
Jesus got into the boat and went back to
Galilee.

38The man whom Jesus had healed begged
to go with him, but Jesus sent him away,
saying, 39"Go back home and tell people how
much God has done for you." So the man
went all over town telling how much Jesus
had done for him.

Jesus Gives Life to a Dead Girl and Heals a Sick Woman

40When Jesus got back to Galilee, a crowd
welcomed him, because everyone was

8:30 Legion Means very many. A legion was about five thousand men in the Roman army.
8:31 eternal darkness Literally, "the abyss," something like a pit or a hole that has no end.

waiting for him. 41A man named Jairus, a
leader of the synagogue, came to Jesus and
fell at his feet, begging him to come to his
house. 42Jairus' only daughter, about twelve
years old, was dying.

While Jesus was on his way to Jairus'
house, the people were crowding all around
him. 43A woman was in the crowd who had
been bleeding for twelve years,[n] but no one
was able to heal her. 44She came up behind
Jesus and touched the edge of his coat, and
instantly her bleeding stopped. 45Then Jesus
said, "Who touched me?"

When all the people said they had not
touched him, Peter said, "Master, the people
are all around you and are pushing against
you."

46But Jesus said, "Someone did touch me,
because I felt power go out from me."
47When the woman saw she could not hide,
she came forward, shaking, and fell down
before Jesus. While all the people listened,
she told why she had touched him and how
she had been instantly healed. 48Jesus said to
her, "Dear woman, you are made well
because you believed. Go in peace."

49While Jesus was still speaking, someone
came from the house of the synagogue
leader and said to him, "Your daughter is
dead. Don't bother the teacher anymore."

50When Jesus heard this, he said to Jairus,
"Don't be afraid. Just believe, and your
daughter will be well."

51When Jesus went to the house, he let
only Peter, John, James, and the girl's father
and mother go inside with him. 52All the
people were crying and feeling sad because
the girl was dead, but Jesus said, "Stop
crying. She is not dead, only asleep."

53The people laughed at Jesus because
they knew the girl was dead. 54But Jesus took
hold of her hand and called to her, "My child,
stand up!" 55Her spirit came back into her,
and she stood up at once. Then Jesus ordered
that she be given something to eat. 56The
girl's parents were amazed, but Jesus told
them not to tell anyone what had happened.

Jesus Sends Out the Apostles

9 Jesus called the twelve apostles together
and gave them power and authority over
all demons and the ability to heal sicknesses.
2He sent the apostles out to tell about God's
kingdom and to heal the sick. 3He said to
them, "Take nothing for your trip, neither a
walking stick, bag, bread, money, or extra
clothes. 4When you enter a house, stay there
until it is time to leave. 5If people do not
welcome you, shake the dust off of your feet[n]
as you leave the town, as a warning to
them."

6So the apostles went out and traveled
through all the towns, preaching the Good
News and healing people everywhere.

Herod Is Confused About Jesus

7Herod, the governor, heard about all the
things that were happening and was
confused, because some people said, "John
the Baptist has risen from the dead." 8Others
said, "Elijah has come to us." And still others
said, "One of the prophets who lived long
ago has risen from the dead." 9Herod said, "I
cut off John's head, so who is this man I hear
such things about?" And Herod kept trying
to see Jesus.

More than Five Thousand Fed

10When the apostles returned, they told
Jesus everything they had done. Then Jesus
took them with him to a town called
Bethsaida where they could be alone
together. 11But the people learned where
Jesus went and followed him. He welcomed
them and talked with them about God's
kingdom and healed those who needed to be
healed.

12Late in the afternoon, the twelve
apostles came to Jesus and said, "Send the
people away. They need to go to the towns
and countryside around here and find places
to sleep and something to eat, because no
one lives in this place."

13But Jesus said to them, "You give them
something to eat."

They said, "We have only five loaves of
bread and two fish, unless we go buy food
for all these people." 14(There were about
five thousand men there.)

Jesus said to his followers, "Tell the people
to sit in groups of about fifty people."
15So the followers did this, and all the

8:43 years Some Greek copies continue, "and she had spent all the money she had on doctors."
9:5 shake . . . feet A warning. It showed that they had rejected these people.

people sat down. [16]Then Jesus took the five
loaves of bread and two fish, and looking up
to heaven, he thanked God for the food.
Then he divided the food and gave it to the
followers to give to the people. [17]They all ate
and were satisfied, and what was left over
was gathered up, filling twelve baskets.

Jesus Is the Christ

[18]One time when Jesus was praying alone,
his followers were with him, and he asked
them, "Who do the people say I am?"

[19]They answered, "Some say you are John
the Baptist. Others say you are Elijah.[n] And
others say you are one of the prophets from
long ago who has come back to life."

[20]Then Jesus asked, "But who do you say I
am?"

Peter answered, "You are the Christ from
God."

[21]Jesus warned them not to tell anyone,
saying, [22]"The Son of Man must suffer many
things. He will be rejected by the Jewish
elders, the leading priests, and the teachers
of the law. He will be killed and after three
days will be raised from the dead."

[23]Jesus said to all of them, "If people want
to follow me, they must give up the things
they want. They must be willing to give up
their lives daily to follow me. [24]Those who
want to save their lives will give up true life.
But those who give up their lives for me will
have true life. [25]It is worthless to have the
whole world if they themselves are
destroyed or lost. [26]If people are ashamed of
me and my teaching, then the Son of Man
will be ashamed of them when he comes in
his glory and with the glory of the Father
and the holy angels. [27]I tell you the truth,
some people standing here will see the
kingdom of God before they die."

Jesus Talks with Moses and Elijah

[28]About eight days after Jesus said these
things, he took Peter, John, and James and
went up on a mountain to pray. [29]While
Jesus was praying, the appearance of his face
changed, and his clothes became shining
white. [30]Then two men, Moses and Elijah,[n]
were talking with Jesus. [31]They appeared in
heavenly glory, talking about his departure
which he would soon bring about in
Jerusalem. [32]Peter and the others were very
sleepy, but when they awoke fully, they saw
the glory of Jesus and the two men standing
with him. [33]When Moses and Elijah were
about to leave, Peter said to Jesus, "Master, it
is good that we are here. Let us make three
tents—one for you, one for Moses, and one
for Elijah." (Peter did not know what he was
talking about.)

[34]While he was saying these things, a
cloud came and covered them, and they
became afraid as the cloud covered them. [35]A
voice came from the cloud, saying, "This is
my Son, whom I have chosen. Listen to
him!"

[36]When the voice finished speaking, only
Jesus was there. Peter, John, and James said
nothing and told no one at that time what
they had seen.

Jesus Heals a Sick Boy

[37]The next day, when they came down
from the mountain, a large crowd met Jesus.
[38]A man in the crowd shouted to him,
"Teacher, please come and look at my son,
because he is my only child. [39]An evil spirit
seizes my son, and suddenly he screams. It
causes him to lose control of himself and
foam at the mouth. The evil spirit keeps on
hurting him and almost never leaves him. [40]I
begged your followers to force the evil spirit
out, but they could not do it."

[41]Jesus answered, "You people have no
faith, and your lives are all wrong. How long
must I stay with you and put up with you?
Bring your son here."

[42]While the boy was coming, the demon
threw him on the ground and made him lose
control of himself. But Jesus gave a strong
command to the evil spirit and healed the
boy and gave him back to his father. [43]All the
people were amazed at the great power of
God.

Jesus Talks About His Death

While everyone was wondering about all
that Jesus did, he said to his followers,
[44]"Don't forget what I tell you now: The Son
of Man will be handed over to people." [45]But
the followers did not understand what this

9:19 Elijah A man who spoke for God and who lived hundreds of years before Christ. See 1 Kings 17. **9:30 Moses and Elijah** Two of the most important Jewish leaders in the past. God had given Moses the Law, and Elijah was an important prophet.

meant; the meaning was hidden from them
so they could not understand. But they were
afraid to ask Jesus about it.

Who Is the Greatest?

46 Jesus' followers began to have an
argument about which one of them was the
greatest. 47 Jesus knew what they were
thinking, so he took a little child and stood
the child beside him. 48 Then Jesus said,
"Whoever accepts this little child in my
name accepts me. And whoever accepts me
accepts the One who sent me, because
whoever is least among you all is really the
greatest."

Anyone Not Against Us Is for Us

49 John answered, "Master, we saw
someone using your name to force demons
out of people. We told him to stop, because
he does not belong to our group."
50 But Jesus said to him, "Don't stop him,
because whoever is not against you is for
you."

A Town Rejects Jesus

51 When the time was coming near for
Jesus to depart, he was determined to go to
Jerusalem. 52 He sent some messengers ahead
of him, who went into a town in Samaria to
make everything ready for him. 53 But the
people there would not welcome him,
because he was set on going to Jerusalem.
54 When James and John, followers of Jesus,
saw this, they said, "Lord, do you want us to
call fire down from heaven and destroy
those people?"[n]
55 But Jesus turned and scolded them. [And
Jesus said, "You don't know what kind of
spirit you belong to. 56 The Son of Man did
not come to destroy the souls of people but
to save them."][n] Then they went to another
town.

Following Jesus

57 As they were going along the road,
someone said to Jesus, "I will follow you any
place you go."
58 Jesus said to them, "The foxes have holes
to live in, and the birds have nests, but the
Son of Man has no place to rest his head."
59 Jesus said to another man, "Follow me!"
But he said, "Lord, first let me go and bury
my father."
60 But Jesus said to him, "Let the people
who are dead bury their own dead. You must
go and tell about the kingdom of God."
61 Another man said, "I will follow you,
Lord, but first let me go and say good-bye to
my family."
62 Jesus said, "Anyone who begins to plow
a field but keeps looking back is of no use in
the kingdom of God."

Jesus Sends Out the Seventy-Two

10 After this, the Lord chose seventy-
two[n] others and sent them out in
pairs ahead of him into every town and
place where he planned to go. 2 He said to
them, "There are a great many people to
harvest, but there are only a few workers. So
pray to God, who owns the harvest, that he
will send more workers to help gather his
harvest. 3 Go now, but listen! I am sending
you out like sheep among wolves. 4 Don't
carry a purse, a bag, or sandals, and don't
waste time talking with people on the road.
5 Before you go into a house, say, 'Peace be
with this house.' 6 If peace-loving people live
there, your blessing of peace will stay with
them, but if not, then your blessing will
come back to you. 7 Stay in the same house,
eating and drinking what the people there
give you. A worker should be given his pay.
Don't move from house to house. 8 If you go
into a town and the people welcome you, eat
what they give you. 9 Heal the sick who live
there, and tell them, 'The kingdom of God is
near you.' 10 But if you go into a town, and
the people don't welcome you, then go into
the streets and say, 11 'Even the dirt from your
town that sticks to our feet we wipe off
against you.[n] But remember that the
kingdom of God is near.' 12 I tell you, on the
Judgment Day it will be better for the people
of Sodom[n] than for the people of that town.

Jesus Warns Unbelievers

13 "How terrible for you, Korazin! How
terrible for you, Bethsaida! If the miracles I
did in you had happened in Tyre and Sidon,[n]
those people would have changed their lives

9:54 people Some Greek copies continue "as Elijah did." **9:55–56 And . . . them."** Some Greek copies do not contain the bracketed text.
10:1 seventy-two Some Greek copies read "seventy." **10:11 dirt . . . you** A warning. It showed that they had rejected these people.
10:12 Sodom City that God destroyed because the people were so evil. **10:13 Tyre and Sidon** Towns where wicked people lived.

long ago. They would have worn rough cloth
and put ashes on themselves to show they
had changed. 14 But on the Judgment Day it
will be better for Tyre and Sidon than for
you. 15 And you, Capernaum,[n] will you be
lifted up to heaven? No! You will be thrown
down to the depths!
16 "Whoever listens to you listens to me,
and whoever refuses to accept you refuses
to accept me. And whoever refuses to
accept me refuses to accept the One who
sent me."

Satan Falls

17 When the seventy-two[n] came back, they
were very happy and said, "Lord, even the
demons obeyed us when we used your
name!"
18 Jesus said, "I saw Satan fall like lightning
from heaven. 19 Listen, I have given you
power to walk on snakes and scorpions,
power that is greater than the enemy has.
So nothing will hurt you. 20 But you should
not be happy because the spirits obey you
but because your names are written in
heaven."

Jesus Prays to the Father

21 Then Jesus rejoiced in the Holy Spirit
and said, "I praise you, Father, Lord of heaven
and earth, because you have hidden these
things from the people who are wise and
smart. But you have shown them to those
who are like little children. Yes, Father, this
is what you really wanted.
22 "My Father has given me all things. No
one knows who the Son is, except the Father.
And no one knows who the Father is, except
the Son and those whom the Son chooses to
tell."
23 Then Jesus turned to his followers and
said privately, "You are blessed to see what
you now see. 24 I tell you, many prophets and
kings wanted to see what you now see, but
they did not, and they wanted to hear what
you now hear, but they did not."

The Good Samaritan

25 Then an expert on the law stood up to
test Jesus, saying, "Teacher, what must I do to
get life forever?"
26 Jesus said, "What is written in the law?
What do you read there?"

10:13, 15 Korazin . . . Bethsaida . . . Capernaum Towns by Lake Galilee where Jesus preached to the people.
10:17 seventy-two Some Greek copies read "seventy."

devotion 280

LUKE 10:18–20

GET YOUR NAME ON THE LIST

My parents' church has a production of *Heaven's Gates and Hell's Flames* every year. The production is made up of a dozen skits that depict people who have died and are standing at the gates of heaven to see if their names are written in the Lamb's book of life. My youngest daughter loves to go every year. And at the end of the production, she is always eager to ask Jesus into her heart again, just to be sure her name is written in the book.

We don't like to talk about hell. But we need to. Romans 6:23 tells us, "The payment for sin is death. But God gives us the free gift of life forever in Christ Jesus our Lord." Jesus' death on the cross paid for our sins. We didn't do anything to deserve or earn it; it is a gift that "Christ died for us while we were still sinners" (Rom. 5:8).

So how do you know if your name is written in heaven? John 3:16 tells us, "God loved the world so much that he gave his one and only Son so that whoever believes in him may not be lost, but have eternal life." We just need to believe that Jesus died for our sins, ask him to become our Savior, and he does. We will all stand at the gates of heaven one day. Make sure your name is written in the Lamb's book of life.

Martha

LUKE 10

Martha feels the tension in the back of her neck as she peels and washes the vegetables for dinner. *How will I ever serve all of them?* She runs to turn the meat on the fire before it burns and checks the bread in the pan. *Where did Mary get off to?*

Martha cranes her neck to spot her sister sitting at Jesus' feet, listening. *That Mary feels no sense of obligation to help at all!* In addition to the cooking, the table still needed to be set. Martha tries to get Mary's attention, but Mary isn't looking. *Or maybe she doesn't want to look,* Martha thinks.

Martha wipes her face and walks through the followers toward Jesus. She has always felt comfortable around Jesus and isn't afraid to bring a concern to him now. "Lord, don't you care that my sister has left me alone to do all the work? Tell her to help me."

But Mary doesn't jump to her feet, and Jesus' words are surprising. "Martha, Martha, you are worried and upset about many things. Only one thing is important. Mary has chosen the better thing, and it will never be taken away from her." Martha is not stung by her Lord's words—she is actually comforted. Finally, the permission she needed to let go of some of the things she constantly wrestled with and simply rest in Jesus' presence. And as she served him that evening, she did just that.

Do you allow time to sit at the feet of Jesus?

27 The man answered, "Love the Lord your
God with all your heart, all your soul, all
your strength, and all your mind."[n] Also,
"Love your neighbor as you love yourself."[n]
28 Jesus said to him, "Your answer is right.
Do this and you will live."
29 But the man, wanting to show the
importance of his question, said to Jesus,
"And who is my neighbor?"
30 Jesus answered, "As a man was going
down from Jerusalem to Jericho, some
robbers attacked him. They tore off his
clothes, beat him, and left him lying there,
almost dead. 31 It happened that a priest was
going down that road. When he saw the
man, he walked by on the other side. 32 Next,
a Levite[n] came there, and after he went over
and looked at the man, he walked by on the
other side of the road. 33 Then a Samaritan[n]
traveling down the road came to where the
hurt man was. When he saw the man, he felt
very sorry for him. 34 The Samaritan went to
him, poured olive oil and wine[n] on his
wounds, and bandaged them. Then he put
the hurt man on his own donkey and took
him to an inn where he cared for him. 35 The
next day, the Samaritan brought out two
coins,[n] gave them to the innkeeper, and said,
'Take care of this man. If you spend more
money on him, I will pay it back to you
when I come again.' "
36 Then Jesus said, "Which one of these
three men do you think was a neighbor to
the man who was attacked by the robbers?"
37 The expert on the law answered, "The
one who showed him mercy."
Jesus said to him, "Then go and do what
he did."

Mary and Martha

38 While Jesus and his followers were
traveling, Jesus went into a town. A woman
named Martha let Jesus stay at her house.
39 Martha had a sister named Mary, who was
sitting at Jesus' feet and listening to him
teach. 40 But Martha was busy with all the
work to be done. She went in and said, "Lord,
don't you care that my sister has left me
alone to do all the work? Tell her to help me."
41 But the Lord answered her, "Martha,

10:27 "Love . . . mind." Quotation from Deuteronomy 6:5. **10:27 "Love . . . yourself."** Quotation from Leviticus 19:18. **10:32 Levite** Levites were members of the tribe of Levi who helped the Jewish priests with their work in the Temple. Read 1 Chronicles 23:24–32. **10:33 Samaritan** Samaritans were people from Samaria. These people were part Jewish, but the Jews did not accept them as true Jews. Samaritans and Jews disliked each other. **10:34 olive oil and wine** Oil and wine were used like medicine to soften and clean wounds. **10:35 coins** Roman denarii. One coin was the average pay for one day's work.

Martha, you are worried and upset about many things. 42 Only one thing is important. Mary has chosen the better thing, and it will never be taken away from her."

Jesus Teaches About Prayer

11 One time Jesus was praying in a certain place. When he finished, one of his followers said to him, "Lord, teach us to pray as John taught his followers."

2 Jesus said to them, "When you pray, say:

'Father, may your name always be kept holy.
May your kingdom come.
3 Give us the food we need for each day.
4 Forgive us for our sins,
because we forgive everyone who has done wrong to us.
And do not cause us to be tempted.' "[n]

Continue to Ask

5 Then Jesus said to them, "Suppose one of you went to your friend's house at midnight and said to him, 'Friend, loan me three loaves of bread. 6 A friend of mine has come into town to visit me, but I have nothing for him to eat.' 7 Your friend inside the house answers, 'Don't bother me! The door is already locked, and my children and I are in bed. I cannot get up and give you anything.' 8 I tell you, if friendship is not enough to make him get up to give you the bread, your boldness will make him get up and give you whatever you need. 9 So I tell you, ask, and God will give to you. Search, and you will find. Knock, and the door will open for you. 10 Yes, everyone who asks will receive. The one who searches will find. And everyone who knocks will have the door opened. 11 If your children ask for[n] a fish, which of you would give them a snake instead? 12 Or, if your children ask for an egg, would you give them a scorpion? 13 Even though you are bad, you know how to give good things to your children. How much more your heavenly Father will give the Holy Spirit to those who ask him!"

Jesus' Power Is from God

14 One time Jesus was sending out a demon who could not talk. When the demon came out, the man who had been unable to speak, then spoke. The people were amazed. 15 But some of them said, "Jesus uses the power of Beelzebul, the ruler of demons, to force demons out of people."

16 Other people, wanting to test Jesus, asked him to give them a sign from heaven. 17 But knowing their thoughts, he said to them, "Every kingdom that is divided against itself will be destroyed. And a family that is divided against itself will not continue. 18 So if Satan is divided against himself, his kingdom will not continue. You say that I use the power of Beelzebul to force out demons. 19 But if I use the power of Beelzebul to force out demons, what power do your people use to force demons out? So they will be your judges. 20 But if I use the power of God to force out demons, then the kingdom of God has come to you.

21 "When a strong person with many weapons guards his own house, his possessions are safe. 22 But when someone stronger comes and defeats him, the stronger one will take away the weapons the first man trusted and will give away the possessions.

23 "Anyone who is not with me is against me, and anyone who does not work with me is working against me.

The Empty Person

24 "When an evil spirit comes out of a person, it travels through dry places, looking for a place to rest. But when it finds no place, it says, 'I will go back to the house I left.' 25 And when it comes back, it finds that house swept clean and made neat. 26 Then the evil spirit goes out and brings seven other spirits more evil than it is, and they go in and live there. So the person has even more trouble than before."

People Who Are Truly Blessed

27 As Jesus was saying these things, a woman in the crowd called out to Jesus, "Blessed is the mother who gave birth to you and nursed you."

28 But Jesus said, "No, blessed are those who hear the teaching of God and obey it."

The People Want a Miracle

29 As the crowd grew larger, Jesus said, "The people who live today are evil. They want to see a miracle for a sign, but no sign

11:2–4 'Father . . . tempted.' Some Greek copies include phrases from Matthew's version of this prayer (Matthew 6:9–13).
11:11 for Some Greek copies include the phrase "for bread, which of you would give them a stone, or if they ask for . . ."

will be given them, except the sign of Jonah.[n]
[30]As Jonah was a sign for those people who
lived in Nineveh, the Son of Man will be a
sign for the people of this time. [31]On the
Judgment Day the Queen of the South[n] will
stand up with the people who live now. She
will show they are guilty, because she came
from far away to listen to Solomon's wise
teaching. And I tell you that someone
greater than Solomon is here. [32]On the
Judgment Day the people of Nineveh will
stand up with the people who live now, and
they will show that you are guilty. When
Jonah preached to them, they were sorry and
changed their lives. And I tell you that
someone greater than Jonah is here.

Be a Light for the World

[33]"No one lights a lamp and puts it in a
secret place or under a bowl, but on a
lampstand so the people who come in can
see. [34]Your eye is a light for the body. When
your eyes are good, your whole body will be
full of light. But when your eyes are evil,
your whole body will be full of darkness.
[35]So be careful not to let the light in you
become darkness. [36]If your whole body is full
of light, and none of it is dark, then you will
shine bright, as when a lamp shines on you."

Jesus Accuses the Pharisees

[37]After Jesus had finished speaking, a
Pharisee asked Jesus to eat with him. So
Jesus went in and sat at the table. [38]But the
Pharisee was surprised when he saw that
Jesus did not wash his hands[n] before the
meal. [39]The Lord said to him, "You Pharisees
clean the outside of the cup and the dish, but
inside you are full of greed and evil. [40]You
foolish people! The same one who made
what is outside also made what is inside.
[41]So give what is in your dishes to the poor,

11:29 sign of Jonah Jonah's three days in the fish are like Jesus' three days in the tomb. See Matthew 12:40.
11:31 Queen of the South The Queen of Sheba. She traveled a thousand miles to learn God's wisdom from Solomon. Read 1 Kings 10:1–3.
11:38 wash his hands This was a Jewish religious custom that the Pharisees thought was very important.

devotion 281

LUKE 11:33

A TWENTY-WATT BULB IN A BASEMENT CLOSET

The light of Christ in you is not to be hidden. Some Sundays at my church there is so much Light in the room that I think we should be able to replace the power grid for our entire city. If that is happening at churches all over the country, then why is the light of Christ so dim in this world? Why is it dark out there? Why are people fumbling their way through empty lives, satisfied with the fleeting strike of a match, when instead they could have the radiance of the Son?

We don't see the reflections of Jesus because people take their light home and hide it. We can sing, "I'm gonna let it shine" all day long and then go right out to the car and snuff it out. What are we so afraid of? Do we fear not knowing what to say?

When Jesus tells us to be the light, we cannot settle for being a twenty-watt bulb hidden away in some useless closet in the basement. He is talking about a light as luminous as the morning sun breaking through the darkness of night. Don't worry about what to say or do or how to respond. The Light-giver will supply every need. Just go be the light!

Shine the truth of Jesus with everything you've got, and he will focus and refine and disburse your light for his glory. And when you shine instead of hide, people get to see the Father.

and then you will be fully clean. 42How
terrible for you Pharisees! You give God one-
tenth of even your mint, your rue, and every
other plant in your garden. But you fail to be
fair to others and to love God. These are the
things you should do while continuing to do
those other things. 43How terrible for you
Pharisees, because you love to have the most
important seats in the synagogues, and you
love to be greeted with respect in the
marketplaces. 44How terrible for you,
because you are like hidden graves, which
people walk on without knowing."

Jesus Talks to Experts on the Law

45One of the experts on the law said to
Jesus, "Teacher, when you say these things,
you are insulting us, too."

46Jesus answered, "How terrible for you,
you experts on the law! You make strict rules
that are very hard for people to obey, but you
yourselves don't even try to follow those
rules. 47How terrible for you, because you
build tombs for the prophets whom your
ancestors killed! 48And now you show that
you approve of what your ancestors did.
They killed the prophets, and you build
tombs for them! 49This is why in his wisdom
God said, 'I will send prophets and apostles
to them. They will kill some, and they will
treat others cruelly.' 50So you who live now
will be punished for the deaths of all the
prophets who were killed since the
beginning of the world— 51from the killing
of Abel to the killing of Zechariah,[n] who died
between the altar and the Temple. Yes, I tell
you that you who are alive now will be
punished for them all.

52"How terrible for you, you experts on
the law. You have taken away the key to
learning about God. You yourselves would
not learn, and you stopped others from
learning, too."

53When Jesus left, the teachers of the law
and the Pharisees began to give him trouble,
asking him questions about many things,
54trying to catch him saying something
wrong.

Don't Be Like the Pharisees

12 So many thousands of people had
gathered that they were stepping on
each other. Jesus spoke first to his followers,
saying, "Beware of the yeast of the Pharisees,
because they are hypocrites. 2Everything
that is hidden will be shown, and everything
that is secret will be made known. 3What
you have said in the dark will be heard in
the light, and what you have whispered in
an inner room will be shouted from the
housetops.

4"I tell you, my friends, don't be afraid of
people who can kill the body but after that
can do nothing more to hurt you. 5I will
show you the one to fear. Fear the one who
has the power to kill you and also to throw
you into hell. Yes, this is the one you should
fear.

6"Five sparrows are sold for only two
pennies, and God does not forget any of
them. 7But God even knows how many hairs
you have on your head. Don't be afraid. You
are worth much more than many sparrows.

Don't Be Ashamed of Jesus

8"I tell you, all those who stand before
others and say they believe in me, I, the Son
of Man, will say before the angels of God
that they belong to me. 9But all who stand
before others and say they do not believe in
me, I will say before the angels of God that
they do not belong to me.

10"Anyone who speaks against the Son of
Man can be forgiven, but anyone who speaks
against the Holy Spirit will not be forgiven.

11"When you are brought into the
synagogues before the leaders and other
powerful people, don't worry about how to
defend yourself or what to say. 12At that time
the Holy Spirit will teach you what you
must say."

Jesus Warns Against Selfishness

13Someone in the crowd said to Jesus,
"Teacher, tell my brother to divide with me
the property our father left us."

14But Jesus said to him, "Who said I
should judge or decide between you?"
15Then Jesus said to them, "Be careful and
guard against all kinds of greed. Life is not
measured by how much one owns."

16Then Jesus told this story: "There was a
rich man who had some land, which grew a
good crop. 17He thought to himself, 'What

11:51 Abel . . . Zechariah In the Hebrew Old Testament, the first and last men to be murdered.

will I do? I have no place to keep all my
crops.' 18Then he said, 'This is what I will
do: I will tear down my barns and build
bigger ones, and there I will store all my
grain and other goods. 19Then I can say to
myself, "I have enough good things stored
to last for many years. Rest, eat, drink, and
enjoy life!"'

20"But God said to him, 'Foolish man!
Tonight your life will be taken from you. So
who will get those things you have prepared
for yourself?'

21"This is how it will be for those who
store up things for themselves and are not
rich toward God."

Don't Worry

22Jesus said to his followers, "So I tell
you, don't worry about the food you need to
live, or about the clothes you need for your
body. 23Life is more than food, and the body
is more than clothes. 24Look at the birds.
They don't plant or harvest, they don't have
storerooms or barns, but God feeds them.
And you are worth much more than birds.
25You cannot add any time to your life by
worrying about it. 26If you cannot do even
the little things, then why worry about
the big things? 27Consider how the lilies
grow; they don't work or make clothes
for themselves. But I tell you that even
Solomon with his riches was not dressed
as beautifully as one of these flowers.
28God clothes the grass in the field, which is
alive today but tomorrow is thrown into the
fire. So how much more will God clothe
you? Don't have so little faith! 29Don't
always think about what you will eat or
what you will drink, and don't keep
worrying. 30All the people in the world are
trying to get these things, and your Father
knows you need them. 31But seek God's
kingdom, and all your other needs will be
met as well.

Don't Trust in Money

32"Don't fear, little flock, because your
Father wants to give you the kingdom. 33Sell
your possessions and give to the poor. Get
for yourselves purses that will not wear out,
the treasure in heaven that never runs out,
where thieves can't steal and moths can't
destroy. 34Your heart will be where your
treasure is.

Always Be Ready

35"Be dressed, ready for service, and have
your lamps shining. 36Be like servants who
are waiting for their master to come home
from a wedding party. When he comes and
knocks, the servants immediately open the
door for him. 37They will be blessed when
their master comes home, because he sees
that they were watching for him. I tell you
the truth, the master will dress himself to
serve and tell the servants to sit at the table,
and he will serve them. 38Those servants will
be blessed when he comes in and finds them
still waiting, even if it is midnight or later.

39"Remember this: If the owner of the
house knew what time a thief was coming,
he would not allow the thief to enter his
house. 40So you also must be ready, because
the Son of Man will come at a time when
you don't expect him!"

Who Is the Trusted Servant?

41Peter said, "Lord, did you tell this story
to us or to all people?"

42The Lord said, "Who is the wise and
trusted servant that the master trusts to give
the other servants their food at the right
time? 43When the master comes and finds
the servant doing his work, the servant will
be blessed. 44I tell you the truth, the master
will choose that servant to take care of
everything he owns. 45But suppose the
servant thinks to himself, 'My master will
not come back soon,' and he begins to beat
the other servants, men and women, and to
eat and drink and get drunk. 46The master
will come when that servant is not ready
and is not expecting him. Then the master
will cut him in pieces and send him away to
be with the others who don't obey.

47"The servant who knows what his
master wants but is not ready, or who does
not do what the master wants, will be beaten
with many blows! 48But the servant who
does not know what his master wants and
does things that should be punished will be
beaten with few blows. From everyone who
has been given much, much will be
demanded. And from the one trusted with
much, much more will be expected.

Jesus Causes Division

49"I came to set fire to the world, and I
wish it were already burning! 50I have a

baptism[n] to suffer through, and I feel very
troubled until it is over. 51Do you think I
came to give peace to the earth? No, I tell
you, I came to divide it. 52From now on, a
family with five people will be divided, three
against two, and two against three. 53They
will be divided: father against son and son
against father, mother against daughter and
daughter against mother, mother-in-law
against daughter-in-law and daughter-in-law
against mother-in-law."

Understanding the Times

54Then Jesus said to the people, "When
you see clouds coming up in the west, you
say, 'It's going to rain,' and it happens.
55When you feel the wind begin to blow
from the south, you say, 'It will be a hot day,'
and it happens. 56Hypocrites! You know how
to understand the appearance of the earth
and sky. Why don't you understand what is
happening now?

Settle Your Problems

57"Why can't you decide for yourselves
what is right? 58If your enemy is taking you
to court, try hard to settle it on the way. If
you don't, your enemy might take you to the
judge, and the judge might turn you over to
the officer, and the officer might throw you
into jail. 59I tell you, you will not get out of
there until you have paid everything you
owe."

Change Your Hearts

13 At that time some people were there
who told Jesus that Pilate[n] had killed
some people from Galilee while they were
worshiping. He mixed their blood with the
blood of the animals they were sacrificing to
God. 2Jesus answered, "Do you think this
happened to them because they were more
sinful than all others from Galilee? 3No, I tell
you. But unless you change your hearts and
lives, you will be destroyed as they were!
4What about those eighteen people who
died when the tower of Siloam fell on them?
Do you think they were more sinful than all
the others who live in Jerusalem? 5No, I tell
you. But unless you change your hearts and
lives, you will all be destroyed too!"

The Useless Tree

6Jesus told this story: "A man had a fig tree
planted in his vineyard. He came looking for
some fruit on the tree, but he found none.
7So the man said to his gardener, 'I have
been looking for fruit on this tree for three
years, but I never find any. Cut it down. Why
should it waste the ground?' 8But the servant
answered, 'Master, let the tree have one more
year to produce fruit. Let me dig up the dirt
around it and put on some fertilizer. 9If the
tree produces fruit next year, good. But if not,
you can cut it down.' "

Jesus Heals on the Sabbath

10Jesus was teaching in one of the
synagogues on the Sabbath day. 11A woman
was there who, for eighteen years, had an
evil spirit in her that made her crippled. Her
back was always bent; she could not stand
up straight. 12When Jesus saw her, he called
her over and said, "Woman, you are free
from your sickness." 13Jesus put his hands on
her, and immediately she was able to stand
up straight and began praising God.

14The synagogue leader was angry
because Jesus healed on the Sabbath day. He
said to the people, "There are six days when
one has to work. So come to be healed on
one of those days, and not on the Sabbath
day."

15The Lord answered, "You hypocrites!
Doesn't each of you untie your work animals
and lead them to drink water every day—
even on the Sabbath day? 16This woman that
I healed, a daughter of Abraham, has been
held by Satan for eighteen years. Surely it is
not wrong for her to be freed from her
sickness on a Sabbath day!" 17When Jesus
said this, all of those who were criticizing
him were ashamed, but the entire crowd
rejoiced at all the wonderful things Jesus was
doing.

Stories of Mustard Seed and Yeast

18Then Jesus said, "What is God's
kingdom like? What can I compare it with?
19It is like a mustard seed that a man plants
in his garden. The seed grows and becomes a
tree, and the wild birds build nests in its
branches."

12:50 I . . . baptism Jesus was talking about the suffering he would soon go through.
13:1 Pilate Pontius Pilate was the Roman governor of Judea from A.D. 26 to A.D. 36.

The Crippled Woman

LUKE 13

She eyes the ants that scurry across the ground below her. For eighteen years, the bugs of the earth have helped her pass the lonely hours of each day as she walks about bent over, unable to stand. Today she wanders outside the synagogue, hoping someone will take pity on her and offer her money for food. She is unaware that the Bread of Life is teaching there that day. She shuffles past a group, and the teacher stops when he sees her.

"Woman, come here," he says. Her heart sinks—she is sure that they are going to ask her to leave. Slowly she turns and walks toward the voice, stopping when she reaches his feet. "You are free from your sickness." The man places his hands on her shoulders, and for the first time in eighteen years, she stands up straight, looking directly into his eyes.

A flood of emotion fills her throat as she rejoices. But her celebration is cut short when the synagogue leader chastises the man for healing her on the Sabbath. "You hypocrites!" he says. "This woman that I healed, a daughter of Abraham, has been held by Satan for eighteen years. Surely it is not wrong for her to be freed from her sickness on a Sabbath day!" Those quick to criticize are put to shame, and the crowd rejoices with the woman who has been touched by Jesus.

When we reach out in God's grace, the law of man is put to shame.

[20]Jesus said again, "What can I compare
God's kingdom with? [21]It is like yeast that a
woman took and hid in a large tub of flour
until it made all the dough rise."

The Narrow Door

[22]Jesus was teaching in every town and
village as he traveled toward Jerusalem.
[23]Someone said to Jesus, "Lord, will only a
few people be saved?"
Jesus said, [24]"Try hard to enter through
the narrow door, because many people will
try to enter there, but they will not be able.
[25]When the owner of the house gets up and
closes the door, you can stand outside and
knock on the door and say, 'Sir, open the
door for us.' But he will answer, 'I don't know
you or where you come from.' [26]Then you
will say, 'We ate and drank with you, and
you taught in the streets of our town.' [27]But
he will say to you, 'I don't know you or
where you come from. Go away from me, all
you who do evil!' [28]You will cry and grind
your teeth with pain when you see
Abraham, Isaac, Jacob, and all the prophets
in God's kingdom, but you yourselves
thrown outside. [29]People will come from the
east, west, north, and south and will sit
down at the table in the kingdom of God.
[30]There are those who are last now who will
be first in the future. And there are those
who are first now who will be last in the
future."

Jesus Will Die in Jerusalem

[31]At that time some Pharisees came to
Jesus and said, "Go away from here! Herod
wants to kill you!"
[32]Jesus said to them, "Go tell that fox
Herod, 'Today and tomorrow I am forcing
demons out and healing people. Then, on
the third day, I will reach my goal.' [33]Yet I
must be on my way today and tomorrow and
the next day. Surely it cannot be right for a
prophet to be killed anywhere except in
Jerusalem.
[34]"Jerusalem, Jerusalem! You kill the
prophets and stone to death those who are
sent to you. Many times I wanted to gather
your people as a hen gathers her chicks
under her wings, but you would not let me.
[35]Now your house is left completely empty. I
tell you, you will not see me until that time

when you will say, 'God bless the One who
comes in the name of the Lord.'"[n]

Healing on the Sabbath

14 On a Sabbath day, when Jesus went to
eat at the home of a leading Pharisee,
the people were watching Jesus very closely.
2And in front of him was a man with
dropsy.[n] 3Jesus said to the Pharisees and
experts on the law, "Is it right or wrong to
heal on the Sabbath day?" 4But they would
not answer his question. So Jesus took the
man, healed him, and sent him away. 5Jesus
said to the Pharisees and teachers of the law,
"If your child[n] or ox falls into a well on the
Sabbath day, will you not pull him out
quickly?" 6And they could not answer him.

Don't Make Yourself Important

7When Jesus noticed that some of the
guests were choosing the best places to sit,
he told this story: 8"When someone invites
you to a wedding feast, don't take the most
important seat, because someone more
important than you may have been invited.
9The host, who invited both of you, will
come to you and say, 'Give this person your
seat.' Then you will be embarrassed and will
have to move to the last place. 10So when
you are invited, go sit in a seat that is not
important. When the host comes to you, he
may say, 'Friend, move up here to a more
important place.' Then all the other guests
will respect you. 11All who make themselves
great will be made humble, but those who
make themselves humble will be made
great."

You Will Be Rewarded

12Then Jesus said to the man who had
invited him, "When you give a lunch or a
dinner, don't invite only your friends, your
family, your other relatives, and your rich
neighbors. At another time they will invite
you to eat with them, and you will be repaid.
13Instead, when you give a feast, invite the
poor, the crippled, the lame, and the blind.
14Then you will be blessed, because they
have nothing and cannot pay you back. But
you will be repaid when the good people rise
from the dead."

A Story About a Big Banquet

15One of those at the table with Jesus
heard these things and said to him, "Blessed
are the people who will share in the meal in
God's kingdom."

16Jesus said to him, "A man gave a big
banquet and invited many people. 17When it
was time to eat, the man sent his servant to
tell the guests, 'Come. Everything is ready.'
18"But all the guests made excuses. The
first one said, 'I have just bought a field, and
I must go look at it. Please excuse me.'
19Another said, 'I have just bought five pairs
of oxen; I must go and try them. Please
excuse me.' 20A third person said, 'I just got
married; I can't come.' 21So the servant
returned and told his master what had
happened. Then the master became angry
and said, 'Go at once into the streets and
alleys of the town, and bring in the poor, the
crippled, the blind, and the lame.' 22Later the
servant said to him, 'Master, I did what you
commanded, but we still have room.' 23The
master said to the servant, 'Go out to the
roads and country lanes, and urge the people
there to come so my house will be full. 24I
tell you, none of those whom I invited first
will eat with me.'"

The Cost of Being Jesus' Follower

25Large crowds were traveling with Jesus,
and he turned and said to them, 26"If anyone
comes to me but loves his father, mother,
wife, children, brothers, or sisters—or even
life—more than me, he cannot be my
follower. 27Whoever is not willing to carry
his cross and follow me cannot be my
follower. 28If you want to build a tower,
you first sit down and decide how much
it will cost, to see if you have enough money
to finish the job. 29If you don't, you might
lay the foundation, but you would not be
able to finish. Then all who would see it
would make fun of you, 30saying, 'This
person began to build but was not able to
finish.'

31"If a king is going to fight another king,
first he will sit down and plan. He will
decide if he and his ten thousand soldiers
can defeat the other king who has twenty
thousand soldiers. 32If he can't, then while

13:35 'God . . . Lord.' Quotation from Psalm 118:26. **14:2 dropsy** A sickness that causes the body to swell larger and larger.
14:5 child Some Greek copies read "donkey."

devotion 282

LUKE 14:26–27

TO BE A GOD-FOLLOWING WOMAN

I want to follow God, but at times, I realize that I have loved my family, especially my children, more than him. Many days I carry the cross of Christ into my daily life, but other times I leave it at home, tucked inside my Bible underneath the notes from Sunday's sermon.

Jesus is calling his followers to live with a God perspective. He wants us to prioritize like he does, love with respect to his holiness, move and find our being in his purpose, and live for his glory first—over everything we value and everyone we love.

This is so hard for me, yet I have also experienced the value of living inside God's plans. Seeking God's ways. Obeying God's precepts. When I love God more than my family, I care for them like he would want me to. When I am sure that God is first in my life, I will hear myself respond to them from an unexplainable peace. My motives are made pure when I am carrying the cross of Christ. I interact with the world aware of God's presence. To love God more than anything is to live thankful, humble, and unwilling to be blown around by the demands of people or the expectations of career.

I have not always followed God with undivided attention. But as I mature in my faith, I can sense these truths going deeper into my soul. I want to be a God-following woman—God before everyone and the cross in every circumstance.

the other king is still far away, he will send
some people to speak to him and ask for
peace. 33In the same way, you must give up
everything you have to be my follower.

Don't Lose Your Influence

34"Salt is good, but if it loses its salty taste,
you cannot make it salty again. 35It is no
good for the soil or for manure; it is thrown
away.

"Let those with ears use them and listen."

A Lost Sheep, a Lost Coin

15 The tax collectors and sinners all
came to listen to Jesus. 2But the
Pharisees and the teachers of the law began
to complain: "Look, this man welcomes
sinners and even eats with them."

3Then Jesus told them this story:
4"Suppose one of you has a hundred sheep
but loses one of them. Then he will leave the
other ninety-nine sheep in the open field
and go out and look for the lost sheep until
he finds it. 5And when he finds it, he happily
puts it on his shoulders 6and goes home. He
calls to his friends and neighbors and says,
'Be happy with me because I found my lost
sheep.' 7In the same way, I tell you there
is more joy in heaven over one sinner
who changes his heart and life, than over
ninety-nine good people who don't need to
change.

8"Suppose a woman has ten silver coins,[n]
but loses one. She will light a lamp, sweep
the house, and look carefully for the coin
until she finds it. 9And when she finds it,
she will call her friends and neighbors
and say, 'Be happy with me because I have
found the coin that I lost.' 10In the same
way, there is joy in the presence of the angels
of God when one sinner changes his heart
and life."

15:8 silver coins Roman denarii. One coin was the average pay for one day's work.

The Son Who Left Home

11Then Jesus said, "A man had two sons.
12The younger son said to his father, 'Give
me my share of the property.' So the father
divided the property between his two sons.
13Then the younger son gathered up all that
was his and traveled far away to another
country. There he wasted his money in
foolish living. 14After he had spent
everything, a time came when there was no
food anywhere in the country, and the son
was poor and hungry. 15So he got a job with
one of the citizens there who sent the son
into the fields to feed pigs. 16The son was so
hungry that he wanted to eat the pods the
pigs were eating, but no one gave him
anything. 17When he realized what he was
doing, he thought, 'All of my father's
servants have plenty of food. But I am here,
almost dying with hunger. 18I will leave and
return to my father and say to him, "Father, I
have sinned against God and against you. 19I
am no longer worthy to be called your son,
but let me be like one of your servants." '
20So the son left and went to his father.

"While the son was still a long way off, his
father saw him and felt sorry for his son. So
the father ran to him and hugged and kissed
him. 21The son said, 'Father, I have sinned
against God and against you. I am no longer
worthy to be called your son.'[n] 22But the
father said to his servants, 'Hurry! Bring the
best clothes and put them on him. Also, put
a ring on his finger and sandals on his feet.
23And get our fat calf and kill it so we can
have a feast and celebrate. 24My son was
dead, but now he is alive again! He was lost,
but now he is found!' So they began to
celebrate.

25"The older son was in the field, and as he
came closer to the house, he heard the sound
of music and dancing. 26So he called to one
of the servants and asked what all this
meant. 27The servant said, 'Your brother has
come back, and your father killed the fat
calf, because your brother came home
safely.' 28The older son was angry and would
not go in to the feast. So his father went out
and begged him to come in. 29But the older
son said to his father, 'I have served you like
a slave for many years and have always
obeyed your commands. But you never gave
me even a young goat to have at a feast with
my friends. 30But your other son, who
wasted all your money on prostitutes, comes
home, and you kill the fat calf for him!'
31The father said to him, 'Son, you are
always with me, and all that I have is yours.
32We had to celebrate and be happy because
your brother was dead, but now he is alive.
He was lost, but now he is found.' "

True Wealth

16 Jesus also said to his followers, "Once
there was a rich man who had a
manager to take care of his business. This
manager was accused of cheating him. 2So he
called the manager in and said to him, 'What
is this I hear about you? Give me a report of
what you have done with my money,
because you can't be my manager any
longer.' 3The manager thought to himself,
'What will I do since my master is taking my
job away from me? I am not strong enough
to dig ditches, and I am ashamed to beg. 4I
know what I'll do so that when I lose my job
people will welcome me into their homes.'

5"So the manager called in everyone who
owed the master any money. He asked the
first one, 'How much do you owe?' 6He
answered, 'Eight hundred gallons of olive
oil.' The manager said to him, 'Take your bill,
sit down quickly, and write four hundred
gallons.' 7Then the manager asked another
one, 'How much do you owe?' He answered,
'One thousand bushels of wheat.' Then the
manager said to him, 'Take your bill and
write eight hundred bushels.' 8So, the master
praised the dishonest manager for being
clever. Yes, worldly people are more clever
with their own kind than spiritual people
are.

9"I tell you, make friends for yourselves
using worldly riches so that when those
riches are gone, you will be welcomed in
those homes that continue forever.
10Whoever can be trusted with a little can
also be trusted with a lot, and whoever is
dishonest with a little is dishonest with a lot.
11If you cannot be trusted with worldly
riches, then who will trust you with true
riches? 12And if you cannot be trusted with
things that belong to someone else, who will
give you things of your own?

15:21 son Some Greek copies continue, "but let me be like one of your servants" (see verse 19).

13“No servant can serve two masters. The servant will hate one master and love the other, or will follow one master and refuse to follow the other. You cannot serve both God and worldly riches.”

God’s Law Cannot Be Changed

14The Pharisees, who loved money, were listening to all these things and made fun of Jesus. 15He said to them, “You make yourselves look good in front of people, but God knows what is really in your hearts. What is important to people is hateful in God’s sight.

16“The law of Moses and the writings of the prophets were preached until John[n] came. Since then the Good News about the kingdom of God is being told, and everyone tries to enter it by force. 17It would be easier for heaven and earth to pass away than for the smallest part of a letter in the law to be changed.

Divorce and Remarriage

18“If a man divorces his wife and marries another woman, he is guilty of adultery, and the man who marries a divorced woman is also guilty of adultery.”

The Rich Man and Lazarus

19Jesus said, “There was a rich man who always dressed in the finest clothes and lived in luxury every day. 20And a very poor man named Lazarus, whose body was covered with sores, was laid at the rich man’s gate. 21He wanted to eat only the small pieces of food that fell from the rich man’s table. And the dogs would come and lick his sores. 22Later, Lazarus died, and the angels carried him to the arms of Abraham. The rich man died, too, and was buried. 23In the place of the dead, he was in much pain. The rich man saw Abraham far away with Lazarus at his side. 24He called, ‘Father Abraham, have mercy on me! Send Lazarus to dip his finger in water and cool my tongue, because I am suffering in this fire!’ 25But Abraham said, ‘Child, remember when you were alive you had the good things in life, but bad things happened to Lazarus. Now he is comforted here, and you are suffering. 26Besides, there is a big pit between you and us, so no one can cross over to you, and no one can leave there and come here.’ 27The rich man said, ‘Father, then please send Lazarus to my father’s house. 28I have five brothers, and Lazarus could warn them so that they will not come to this place of pain.’ 29But Abraham said, ‘They have the law of Moses and the writings of the prophets; let them learn from them.’ 30The rich man said, ‘No, father Abraham! If someone goes to them from the dead, they would believe and change their hearts and lives.’ 31But Abraham said to him, ‘If they will not listen to Moses and the prophets, they will not listen to someone who comes back from the dead.’ ”

Sin and Forgiveness

17 Jesus said to his followers, “Things that cause people to sin will happen, but how terrible for the person who causes them to happen! 2It would be better for you to be thrown into the sea with a large stone around your neck than to cause one of these little ones to sin. 3So be careful!

“If another follower sins, warn him, and if he is sorry and stops sinning, forgive him. 4If he sins against you seven times in one day and says that he is sorry each time, forgive him.”

How Big Is Your Faith?

5The apostles said to the Lord, “Give us more faith!”

6The Lord said, “If your faith were the size of a mustard seed, you could say to this mulberry tree, ‘Dig yourself up and plant yourself in the sea,’ and it would obey you.

Be Good Servants

7“Suppose one of you has a servant who has been plowing the ground or caring for the sheep. When the servant comes in from working in the field, would you say, ‘Come in and sit down to eat’? 8No, you would say to him, ‘Prepare something for me to eat. Then get yourself ready and serve me. After I finish eating and drinking, you can eat.’ 9The servant does not get any special thanks for doing what his master commanded. 10It is the same with you. When you have done everything you are told to do, you should

16:16 John John the Baptist, who preached to people about Christ’s coming (Matthew 3, Luke 3).

say, 'We are unworthy servants; we have
only done the work we should do.' "

Be Thankful

11 While Jesus was on his way to
Jerusalem, he was going through the area
between Samaria and Galilee. 12 As he came
into a small town, ten men who had a skin
disease met him there. They did not come
close to Jesus 13 but called to him, "Jesus!
Master! Have mercy on us!"

14 When Jesus saw the men, he said, "Go
and show yourselves to the priests."[n]

As the ten men were going, they were
healed. 15 When one of them saw that he was
healed, he went back to Jesus, praising God
in a loud voice. 16 Then he bowed down at
Jesus' feet and thanked him. (And this man
was a Samaritan.) 17 Jesus said, "Weren't ten
men healed? Where are the other nine? 18 Is
this Samaritan the only one who came back
to thank God?" 19 Then Jesus said to him,
"Stand up and go on your way. You were
healed because you believed."

God's Kingdom Is Within You

20 Some of the Pharisees asked Jesus,
"When will the kingdom of God come?"

Jesus answered, "God's kingdom is
coming, but not in a way that you will be
able to see with your eyes. 21 People will not
say, 'Look, here it is!' or, 'There it is!' because
God's kingdom is within[n] you."

22 Then Jesus said to his followers, "The
time will come when you will want very
much to see one of the days of the Son of
Man. But you will not see it. 23 People will say
to you, 'Look, there he is!' or, 'Look, here he
is!' Stay where you are; don't go away and
search.

When Jesus Comes Again

24 "When the Son of Man comes again, he
will shine like lightning, which flashes
across the sky and lights it up from one side
to the other. 25 But first he must suffer many
things and be rejected by the people of this
time. 26 When the Son of Man comes again, it
will be as it was when Noah lived. 27 People
were eating, drinking, marrying, and giving
their children to be married until the day
Noah entered the boat. Then the flood came
and killed them all. 28 It will be the same as
during the time of Lot. People were eating,
drinking, buying, selling, planting, and
building. 29 But the day Lot left Sodom,[n] fire
and sulfur rained down from the sky and
killed them all. 30 This is how it will be when
the Son of Man comes again.

31 "On that day, a person who is on the roof
and whose belongings are in the house
should not go inside to get them. A person
who is in the field should not go back home.
32 Remember Lot's wife.[n] 33 Those who try to
keep their lives will lose them. But those
who give up their lives will save them. 34 I
tell you, on that night two people will be
sleeping in one bed; one will be taken and
the other will be left. 35 There will be two
women grinding grain together; one will be
taken, and the other will be left. [36 Two
people will be in the field. One will be taken,
and the other will be left.]"[n]

37 The followers asked Jesus, "Where will
this be, Lord?"

Jesus answered, "Where there is a dead
body, there the vultures will gather."

God Will Answer His People

18 Then Jesus used this story to teach his
followers that they should always
pray and never lose hope. 2 "In a certain town
there was a judge who did not respect God or
care about people. 3 In that same town there
was a widow who kept coming to this judge,
saying, 'Give me my rights against my
enemy.' 4 For a while the judge refused to
help her. But afterwards, he thought to
himself, 'Even though I don't respect God or
care about people, 5 I will see that she gets
her rights. Otherwise she will continue to
bother me until I am worn out.' "

6 The Lord said, "Listen to what the unfair
judge said. 7 God will always give what is
right to his people who cry to him night
and day, and he will not be slow to answer
them. 8 I tell you, God will help his people
quickly. But when the Son of Man comes
again, will he find those on earth who
believe in him?"

17:14 show . . . priests The Law of Moses said a priest must say when a person with a skin disease became well. **17:21 within** Or "among." **17:29 Sodom** City that God destroyed because the people were so evil. **17:32 Lot's wife** A story about what happened to Lot's wife is found in Genesis 19:15–17, 26. **17:36 Two . . . left.** Some Greek copies do not contain the bracketed text.

devotion 283

LUKE 18:7

NEVER LOSE HOPE

Do you read the words in the Bible but somehow have trouble believing in their truths? Every single word laid down has power in it. It has been purposed to build you up and instruct you in the ways of your King. In your time of prayer, search the Scripture for the promises that you desperately need in order to encourage your heart. Pray those promises of the Father over your circumstances and hold on to them like a lifeline to hope. When he says he is going to answer us, he means he alone will fulfill his word. God does not pick and choose what he is going to be faithful in; he is not like humans whose faithfulness waivers. Praise the Lord!

Whatever you are hopeful for today, keep pressing on. Continue to lift your requests up to the Lord and pray his promises over your circumstances. If your mind starts to play games with your heart, take control! In 2 Corinthians 10:5, we are instructed to hold our thoughts and emotions up against the truth of the Word of God. If your thoughts fail and you know them to be a lie, cast them down. Do not believe the lies or the distorted truth that Satan tries to plant in your mind. You have the victory! If you are weary, be brave because the Father is with you. This will be a great adventure of faith just between the two of you!

Being Right with God

9Jesus told this story to some people who
thought they were very good and looked
down on everyone else: 10"A Pharisee and a
tax collector both went to the Temple to
pray. 11The Pharisee stood alone and prayed,
'God, I thank you that I am not like other
people who steal, cheat, or take part in
adultery, or even like this tax collector. 12I
fast[n] twice a week, and I give one-tenth of
everything I get!'
13"The tax collector, standing at a
distance, would not even look up to heaven.
But he beat on his chest because he was so
sad. He said, 'God, have mercy on me, a
sinner.' 14I tell you, when this man went
home, he was right with God, but the
Pharisee was not. All who make themselves
great will be made humble, but all who
make themselves humble will be made
great."

Who Will Enter God's Kingdom?

15Some people brought even their
babies to Jesus so he could touch them.
When the followers saw this, they told
them to stop. 16But Jesus called for the
children, saying, "Let the little children
come to me. Don't stop them, because the
kingdom of God belongs to people who
are like these children. 17I tell you the truth,
you must accept the kingdom of God as
if you were a child, or you will never
enter it."

A Rich Man's Question

18A certain leader asked Jesus, "Good
Teacher, what must I do to have life forever?"
19Jesus said to him, "Why do you call me
good? Only God is good. 20You know the
commands: 'You must not be guilty of
adultery. You must not murder anyone. You
must not steal. You must not tell lies about

18:12 fast The people would give up eating for a special time of prayer and worship to God. It was also done to show sadness and disappointment.

your neighbor. Honor your father and
mother.' "[n]
21But the leader said, "I have obeyed all
these commands since I was a boy."
22When Jesus heard this, he said to him,
"There is still one more thing you need to do.
Sell everything you have and give it to the
poor, and you will have treasure in heaven.
Then come and follow me." 23But when the
man heard this, he became very sad, because
he was very rich.
24Jesus looked at him and said, "It is very
hard for rich people to enter the kingdom of
God. 25It is easier for a camel to go through
the eye of a needle than for a rich person to
enter the kingdom of God."

Who Can Be Saved?

26When the people heard this, they asked,
"Then who can be saved?"
27Jesus answered, "The things impossible
for people are possible for God."
28Peter said, "Look, we have left
everything and followed you."
29Jesus said, "I tell you the truth, all those
who have left houses, wives, brothers,
parents, or children for the kingdom of God
30will get much more in this life. And in the
age that is coming, they will have life
forever."

Jesus Will Rise from the Dead

31Then Jesus took the twelve apostles
aside and said to them, "We are going to
Jerusalem. Everything the prophets wrote
about the Son of Man will happen. 32He will
be turned over to those who are evil. They
will laugh at him, insult him, spit on him,
33beat him with whips, and kill him. But on
the third day, he will rise to life again." 34The
apostles did not understand this; the
meaning was hidden from them, and they
did not realize what was said.

Jesus Heals a Blind Man

35As Jesus came near the city of Jericho, a
blind man was sitting beside the road,
begging. 36When he heard the people
coming down the road, he asked, "What is
happening?"
37They told him, "Jesus, from Nazareth, is
going by."
38The blind man cried out, "Jesus, Son of
David, have mercy on me!"
39The people leading the group warned
the blind man to be quiet. But the blind man
shouted even more, "Son of David, have
mercy on me!"
40Jesus stopped and ordered the blind man
to be brought to him. When he came near,
Jesus asked him, 41"What do you want me to
do for you?"
He said, "Lord, I want to see."
42Jesus said to him, "Then see. You are
healed because you believed."
43At once the man was able to see, and he
followed Jesus, thanking God. All the people
who saw this praised God.

Zacchaeus Meets Jesus

19 Jesus was going through the city of
Jericho. 2A man was there named
Zacchaeus, who was a very important tax
collector, and he was wealthy. 3He wanted to
see who Jesus was, but he was not able
because he was too short to see above the
crowd. 4He ran ahead to a place where Jesus
would come, and he climbed a sycamore tree
so he could see him. 5When Jesus came to
that place, he looked up and said to him,
"Zacchaeus, hurry and come down! I must
stay at your house today."
6Zacchaeus came down quickly and
welcomed him gladly. 7All the people saw
this and began to complain, "Jesus is staying
with a sinner!"
8But Zacchaeus stood and said to the Lord,
"I will give half of my possessions to the
poor. And if I have cheated anyone, I will
pay back four times more."
9Jesus said to him, "Salvation has come to
this house today, because this man also
belongs to the family of Abraham. 10The Son
of Man came to find lost people and save
them."

A Story About Three Servants

11As the people were listening to this,
Jesus told them a story because he was near
Jerusalem and they thought God's kingdom
would appear immediately. 12He said: "A
very important man went to a country far
away to be made a king and then to return
home. 13So he called ten of his servants and

18:20 'You . . . mother.' Quotation from Exodus 20:12–16; Deuteronomy 5:16–20.

gave a coin[n] to each servant. He said, 'Do
business with this money until I get back.'
14But the people in the kingdom hated the
man. So they sent a group to follow him and
say, 'We don't want this man to be our king.'
15"But the man became king. When he
returned home, he said, 'Call those servants
who have my money so I can know how
much they earned with it.'
16"The first servant came and said, 'Sir, I
earned ten coins with the one you gave me.'
17The king said to the servant, 'Excellent!
You are a good servant. Since I can trust you
with small things, I will let you rule over ten
of my cities.'
18"The second servant said, 'Sir, I earned
five coins with your one.' 19The king said to
this servant, 'You can rule over five cities.'
20"Then another servant came in and said
to the king, 'Sir, here is your coin which I
wrapped in a piece of cloth and hid. 21I was
afraid of you, because you are a hard man.
You even take money that you didn't earn
and gather food that you didn't plant.'
22Then the king said to the servant, 'I will
condemn you by your own words, you evil
servant. You knew that I am a hard man,
taking money that I didn't earn and
gathering food that I didn't plant. 23Why
then didn't you put my money in the bank?
Then when I came back, my money would
have earned some interest.'
24"The king said to the men who were
standing by, 'Take the coin away from this
servant and give it to the servant who earned
ten coins.' 25They said, 'But sir, that servant
already has ten coins.' 26The king said,
'Those who have will be given more, but
those who do not have anything will have
everything taken away from them. 27Now
where are my enemies who didn't want me
to be king? Bring them here and kill them
before me.' "

Jesus Enters Jerusalem as a King

28After Jesus said this, he went on toward
Jerusalem. 29As Jesus came near Bethphage
and Bethany, towns near the hill called the
Mount of Olives, he sent out two of his
followers. 30He said, "Go to the town you can
see there. When you enter it, you will find a
colt tied there, which no one has ever ridden.
Untie it and bring it here to me. 31If anyone
asks you why you are untying it, say that the
Master needs it."
32The two followers went into town and
found the colt just as Jesus had told them.
33As they were untying it, its owners came
out and asked the followers, "Why are you
untying our colt?"
34The followers answered, "The Master
needs it." 35So they brought it to Jesus, threw
their coats on the colt's back, and put Jesus on
it. 36As Jesus rode toward Jerusalem, others
spread their coats on the road before him.
37As he was coming close to Jerusalem, on
the way down the Mount of Olives, the
whole crowd of followers began joyfully
shouting praise to God for all the miracles
they had seen. 38They said,

"God bless the king who comes in the
name of the Lord! *Psalm 118:26*
There is peace in heaven and glory to God!"

39Some of the Pharisees in the crowd said
to Jesus, "Teacher, tell your followers not to
say these things."
40But Jesus answered, "I tell you, if my
followers didn't say these things, then the
stones would cry out."

Jesus Cries for Jerusalem

41As Jesus came near Jerusalem, he saw
the city and cried for it, 42saying, "I wish you
knew today what would bring you peace.
But now it is hidden from you. 43The time is
coming when your enemies will build a wall
around you and will hold you in on all sides.
44They will destroy you and all your people,
and not one stone will be left on another. All
this will happen because you did not
recognize the time when God came to save
you."

Jesus Goes to the Temple

45Jesus went into the Temple and began to
throw out the people who were selling
things there. 46He said, "It is written in the
Scriptures, 'My Temple will be a house for
prayer.'[n] But you have changed it into a
'hideout for robbers'!"[n]
47Jesus taught in the Temple every day.
The leading priests, the experts on the law,

19:13 coin A Greek "mina." One mina was enough money to pay a person for working three months.
19:46 'My Temple . . . prayer.' Quotation from Isaiah 56:7. **19:46 'hideout for robbers'** Quotation from Jeremiah 7:11.

and some of the leaders of the people wanted
to kill Jesus. 48But they did not know how
they could do it, because all the people were
listening closely to him.

Jewish Leaders Question Jesus

20 One day Jesus was in the Temple,
teaching the people and telling them
the Good News. The leading priests, teachers
of the law, and elders came up to talk with
him, 2saying, "Tell us what authority you
have to do these things? Who gave you this
authority?"

3Jesus answered, "I will also ask you a
question. Tell me: 4When John baptized
people, was that authority from God or just
from other people?"

5They argued about this, saying, "If we
answer, 'John's baptism was from God,' Jesus
will say, 'Then why did you not believe
him?' 6But if we say, 'It was from other
people,' all the people will stone us to death,
because they believe John was a prophet."
7So they answered that they didn't know
where it came from.

8Jesus said to them, "Then I won't tell you
what authority I have to do these things."

A Story About God's Son

9Then Jesus told the people this story: "A
man planted a vineyard and leased it to
some farmers. Then he went away for a long
time. 10When it was time for the grapes to be
picked, he sent a servant to the farmers to
get some of the grapes. But they beat the
servant and sent him away empty-handed.
11Then he sent another servant. They beat
this servant also, and showed no respect for
him, and sent him away empty-handed. 12So
the man sent a third servant. The farmers
wounded him and threw him out. 13The
owner of the vineyard said, 'What will I do
now? I will send my son whom I love.
Maybe they will respect him.' 14But when
the farmers saw the son, they said to each
other, 'This son will inherit the vineyard. If
we kill him, it will be ours.' 15So the farmers
threw the son out of the vineyard and killed
him.

"What will the owner of this vineyard do
to them? 16He will come and kill those
farmers and will give the vineyard to other
farmers."

When the people heard this story, they
said, "Let this never happen!"

17But Jesus looked at them and said, "Then
what does this verse mean:

'The stone that the builders rejected
became the cornerstone'? *Psalm 118:22*

18Everyone who falls on that stone will be
broken, and the person on whom it falls,
that person will be crushed!"

19The teachers of the law and the leading
priests wanted to arrest Jesus at once,
because they knew the story was about
them. But they were afraid of what the
people would do.

Is It Right to Pay Taxes or Not?

20So they watched Jesus and sent some
spies who acted as if they were sincere. They
wanted to trap Jesus in saying something
wrong so they could hand him over to the
authority and power of the governor. 21So
the spies asked Jesus, "Teacher, we know that
what you say and teach is true. You pay no
attention to who people are, and you always
teach the truth about God's way. 22Tell us, is
it right for us to pay taxes to Caesar or not?"

23But Jesus, knowing they were trying to
trick him, said, 24"Show me a coin. Whose
image and name are on it?"

They said, "Caesar's."

25Jesus said to them, "Then give to Caesar
the things that are Caesar's, and give to God
the things that are God's."

26So they were not able to trap Jesus in
anything he said in the presence of the
people. And being amazed at his answer,
they became silent.

Some Sadducees Try to Trick Jesus

27Some Sadducees, who believed people
would not rise from the dead, came to Jesus.
28They asked, "Teacher, Moses wrote that
if a man's brother dies and leaves a wife but
no children, then that man must marry the
widow and have children for his brother.
29Once there were seven brothers. The first
brother married and died, but had no
children. 30Then the second brother married
the widow, and he died. 31And the third
brother married the widow, and he died.
The same thing happened with all seven
brothers; they died and had no children.
32Finally, the woman died also. 33Since
all seven brothers had married her, whose

wife will she be when people rise from
the dead?"
34Jesus said to them, "On earth, people
marry and are given to someone to marry.
35But those who will be worthy to be raised
from the dead and live again will not marry,
nor will they be given to someone to marry.
36In that life they are like angels and cannot
die. They are children of God, because they
have been raised from the dead. 37Even Moses
clearly showed that the dead are raised to life.
When he wrote about the burning bush,[n] he
said that the Lord is 'the God of Abraham, the
God of Isaac, and the God of Jacob.'[n] 38God is
the God of the living, not the dead, because
all people are alive to him."
39Some of the teachers of the law said,
"Teacher, your answer was good." 40No one
was brave enough to ask him another
question.

Is the Christ the Son of David?

41Then Jesus said, "Why do people say
that the Christ is the Son of David? 42In the
book of Psalms, David himself says:

'The Lord said to my Lord,
"Sit by me at my right side,
43 until I put your enemies under your
control." '[n] *Psalm 110:1*

44David calls the Christ 'Lord,' so how can
the Christ be his son?"

Jesus Accuses Some Leaders

45While all the people were listening,
Jesus said to his followers, 46"Beware of the
teachers of the law. They like to walk around
wearing fancy clothes, and they love for
people to greet them with respect in the
marketplaces. They love to have the most
important seats in the synagogues and at
feasts. 47But they cheat widows and steal
their houses and then try to make
themselves look good by saying long
prayers. They will receive a greater
punishment."

True Giving

21 As Jesus looked up, he saw some rich
people putting their gifts into the

20:37 burning bush Read Exodus 3:1–12 in the Old Testament. **20:37 'the God of . . . Jacob'** These words are taken from Exodus 3:6. **20:43 until . . . control** Literally, "until I make your enemies a footstool for your feet."

devotion 284

LUKE 20:36–38

HEAVEN'S STAINED GLASS ARTIST

For those of us who have lost loved ones to death, these verses are so comforting. When my sister died, I wasn't prepared for the thoughts that plagued me. I didn't like to think of her in the cold ground all alone. I felt guilty if I didn't visit the grave with fresh flowers. I even had a dream that she was sitting on my bed crying because she wanted to come back to earth.

Then the Lord gave me a dream that set me free from those fears. I had the same dream again of my sister crying, and the Lord spoke to me in the dream and told me to ask her if Jesus was Lord. I asked her, "Julie, is Jesus Lord?" Immediately my sister's face was gone, and I saw a demon flee.

The truth is that death is only the beginning, and heaven is a beautiful world that we can only begin to imagine. I woke up with such a peace that next day because I knew my sister was alive in heaven, and I had nothing to fear.

These verses tell us that "God is the God of the living" (verse 38). Our loved ones who have gone to heaven are alive. They are living another life in heaven. The Bible talks about houses in heaven and jobs we will have. My sister created stained glass art when she was here on earth. I have a feeling God is using that gift in heaven in an unimaginable way.

Temple money box.[n] 2Then he saw a poor
widow putting two small copper coins into
the box. 3He said, "I tell you the truth, this
poor widow gave more than all those rich
people. 4They gave only what they did not
need. This woman is very poor, but she gave
all she had to live on."

The Temple Will Be Destroyed

5Some people were talking about the
Temple and how it was decorated with
beautiful stones and gifts offered to God.

But Jesus said, 6"As for these things you
are looking at, the time will come when not
one stone will be left on another. Every stone
will be thrown down."

7They asked Jesus, "Teacher, when will
these things happen? What will be the sign
that they are about to take place?"

8Jesus said, "Be careful so you are not
fooled. Many people will come in my name,
saying, 'I am the One' and, 'The time has
come!' But don't follow them. 9When you
hear about wars and riots, don't be afraid,
because these things must happen first, but
the end will come later."

10Then he said to them, "Nations will fight
against other nations, and kingdoms against
other kingdoms. 11In various places there
will be great earthquakes, sicknesses, and a
lack of food. Fearful events and great signs
will come from heaven.

12"But before all these things happen,
people will arrest you and treat you cruelly.
They will judge you in their synagogues and
put you in jail and force you to stand before
kings and governors, because you follow me.
13But this will give you an opportunity to
tell about me. 14Make up your minds not to
worry ahead of time about what you will
say. 15I will give you the wisdom to say
things that none of your enemies will be
able to stand against or prove wrong. 16Even
your parents, brothers, relatives, and friends
will turn against you, and they will kill some
of you. 17All people will hate you because
you follow me. 18But none of these things
can really harm you. 19By continuing to have
faith you will save your lives.

Jerusalem Will Be Destroyed

20"When you see armies all around
Jerusalem, you will know it will soon be
destroyed. 21At that time, the people in Judea
should run away to the mountains. The
people in Jerusalem must get out, and those
who are near the city should not go in.
22These are the days of punishment to bring
about all that is written in the Scriptures.
23How terrible it will be for women who are
pregnant or have nursing babies! Great
trouble will come upon this land, and God
will be angry with these people. 24They will
be killed by the sword and taken as prisoners
to all nations. Jerusalem will be crushed by
non-Jewish people until their time is over.

Don't Fear

25"There will be signs in the sun, moon,
and stars. On earth, nations will be afraid
and confused because of the roar and fury of
the sea. 26People will be so afraid they will
faint, wondering what is happening to the
world, because the powers of the heavens
will be shaken. 27Then people will see the
Son of Man coming in a cloud with power
and great glory. 28When these things begin
to happen, look up and hold your heads
high, because the time when God will free
you is near!"

Jesus' Words Will Live Forever

29Then Jesus told this story: "Look at the
fig tree and all the other trees. 30When their
leaves appear, you know that summer is
near. 31In the same way, when you see these
things happening, you will know that God's
kingdom is near.

32"I tell you the truth, all these things will
happen while the people of this time are still
living. 33Earth and sky will be destroyed, but
the words I have spoken will never be
destroyed.

Be Ready All the Time

34"Be careful not to spend your time
feasting, drinking, or worrying about worldly
things. If you do, that day might come on
you suddenly, 35like a trap on all people on
earth. 36So be ready all the time. Pray that
you will be strong enough to escape all these
things that will happen and that you will be
able to stand before the Son of Man."

37During the day, Jesus taught the people
in the Temple, and at night he went out of

21:1 money box A special box in the Jewish place of worship where people put their gifts to God.

the city and stayed on the Mount of Olives.
[38]Every morning all the people got up early
to go to the Temple to listen to him.

Judas Becomes an Enemy of Jesus

22 It was almost time for the Feast of
Unleavened Bread, called the Passover
Feast. [2]The leading priests and teachers of
the law were trying to find a way to kill
Jesus, because they were afraid of the people.
[3]Satan entered Judas Iscariot, one of Jesus'
twelve apostles. [4]Judas went to the leading
priests and some of the soldiers who guarded
the Temple and talked to them about a way
to hand Jesus over to them. [5]They were
pleased and agreed to give Judas money. [6]He
agreed and watched for the best time to
hand Jesus over to them when he was away
from the crowd.

Jesus Eats the Passover Meal

[7]The Day of Unleavened Bread came
when the Passover lambs had to be
sacrificed. [8]Jesus said to Peter and John, "Go
and prepare the Passover meal for us to eat."
[9]They asked, "Where do you want us to
prepare it?" [10]Jesus said to them, "After you
go into the city, a man carrying a jar of water
will meet you. Follow him into the house
that he enters, [11]and tell the owner of the
house, 'The Teacher says: "Where is the
guest room in which I may eat the Passover
meal with my followers?"' [12]Then he will
show you a large, furnished room upstairs.
Prepare the Passover meal there."
[13]So Peter and John left and found
everything as Jesus had said. And they
prepared the Passover meal.

The Lord's Supper

[14]When the time came, Jesus and the
apostles were sitting at the table. [15]He said to
them, "I wanted very much to eat this
Passover meal with you before I suffer. [16]I
will not eat another Passover meal until it is
given its true meaning in the kingdom of
God."
[17]Then Jesus took a cup, gave thanks, and
said, "Take this cup and share it among
yourselves. [18]I will not drink again from the
fruit of the vine[n] until God's kingdom
comes."
[19]Then Jesus took some bread, gave
thanks, broke it, and gave it to the apostles,
saying, "This is my body,[n] which I am giving
for you. Do this to remember me." [20]In the
same way, after supper, Jesus took the cup
and said, "This cup is the new agreement
that God makes with his people. This new
agreement begins with my blood which is
poured out for you.

Who Will Turn Against Jesus?

[21]"But one of you will turn against me,
and his hand is with mine on the table.
[22]What God has planned for the Son of Man
will happen, but how terrible it will be for
that one who turns against the Son of Man."
[23]Then the apostles asked each other
which one of them would do that.

Be Like a Servant

[24]The apostles also began to argue about
which one of them was the most important.
[25]But Jesus said to them, "The kings of the
non-Jewish people rule over them, and those
who have authority over others like to be
called 'friends of the people.' [26]But you must
not be like that. Instead, the greatest among
you should be like the youngest, and the
leader should be like the servant. [27]Who is
more important: the one sitting at the table
or the one serving? You think the one at the
table is more important, but I am like a
servant among you.
[28]"You have stayed with me through my
struggles. [29]Just as my Father has given me a
kingdom, I also give you a kingdom [30]so you
may eat and drink at my table in my
kingdom. And you will sit on thrones,
judging the twelve tribes of Israel.

Don't Lose Your Faith!

[31]"Simon, Simon, Satan has asked to test
all of you as a farmer sifts his wheat. [32]I have
prayed that you will not lose your faith!
Help your brothers be stronger when you
come back to me."
[33]But Peter said to Jesus, "Lord, I am ready
to go with you to prison and even to die
with you!"

22:18 fruit of the vine Product of the grapevine; this may also be translated "wine."
22:19b–20 body Some Greek copies do not have the rest of verse 19 or verse 20.

34 But Jesus said, "Peter, before the rooster
crows this day, you will say three times that
you don't know me."

Be Ready for Trouble

35 Then Jesus said to the apostles, "When I
sent you out without a purse, a bag, or
sandals, did you need anything?"

They said, "No."

36 He said to them, "But now if you have a
purse or a bag, carry that with you. If you
don't have a sword, sell your coat and buy
one. 37 The Scripture says, 'He was treated
like a criminal,'[n] and I tell you this scripture
must have its full meaning. It was written
about me, and it is happening now."

38 His followers said, "Look, Lord, here are
two swords."

He said to them, "That is enough."

Jesus Prays Alone

39 Jesus left the city and went to the Mount
of Olives, as he often did, and his followers
went with him. 40 When he reached the
place, he said to them, "Pray for strength
against temptation."

41 Then Jesus went about a stone's throw
away from them. He kneeled down and
prayed, 42 "Father, if you are willing, take
away this cup[n] of suffering. But do what you
want, not what I want." 43 Then an angel
from heaven appeared to him to strengthen
him. 44 Being full of pain, Jesus prayed even
harder. His sweat was like drops of blood
falling to the ground. 45 When he finished
praying, he went to his followers and found
them asleep because of their sadness. 46 Jesus
said to them, "Why are you sleeping? Get up
and pray for strength against temptation."

Jesus Is Arrested

47 While Jesus was speaking, a crowd came
up, and Judas, one of the twelve apostles,
was leading them. He came close to Jesus so
he could kiss him.

48 But Jesus said to him, "Judas, are you
using the kiss to give the Son of Man to his
enemies?"

49 When those who were standing around
him saw what was happening, they said,
"Lord, should we strike them with our
swords?" 50 And one of them struck the
servant of the high priest and cut off his
right ear.

51 Jesus said, "Stop! No more of this." Then
he touched the servant's ear and healed him.

52 Those who came to arrest Jesus were the
leading priests, the soldiers who guarded the
Temple, and the elders. Jesus said to them,
"You came out here with swords and clubs as
though I were a criminal. 53 I was with you
every day in the Temple, and you didn't
arrest me there. But this is your time—the
time when darkness rules."

Peter Says He Doesn't Know Jesus

54 They arrested Jesus, and led him away,
and brought him into the house of the high
priest. Peter followed far behind them.
55 After the soldiers started a fire in the
middle of the courtyard and sat together,
Peter sat with them. 56 A servant girl saw
Peter sitting there in the firelight, and
looking closely at him, she said, "This man
was also with him."

57 But Peter said this was not true; he said,
"Woman, I don't know him."

58 A short time later, another person saw
Peter and said, "You are also one of them."

But Peter said, "Man, I am not!"

59 About an hour later, another man
insisted, "Certainly this man was with him,
because he is from Galilee, too."

60 But Peter said, "Man, I don't know what
you are talking about!"

At once, while Peter was still speaking, a
rooster crowed. 61 Then the Lord turned and
looked straight at Peter. And Peter
remembered what the Lord had said: "Before
the rooster crows this day, you will say three
times that you don't know me." 62 Then Peter
went outside and cried painfully.

The People Make Fun of Jesus

63 The men who were guarding Jesus
began making fun of him and beating him.

64 They blindfolded him and said, "Prove
that you are a prophet, and tell us who hit
you." 65 They said many cruel things to Jesus.

Jesus Before the Leaders

66 When day came, the council of the
elders of the people, both the leading priests

22:37 'He . . . criminal.' Quotation from Isaiah 53:12. **22:42 cup** Jesus is talking about the painful things that will happen to him. Accepting these things will be hard, like drinking a cup of something bitter.

and the teachers of the law, came together
and led Jesus to their highest court. 67They
said, "If you are the Christ, tell us."
Jesus said to them, "If I tell you, you will
not believe me. 68And if I ask you, you will
not answer. 69But from now on, the Son of
Man will sit at the right hand of the powerful
God."
70They all said, "Then are you the Son of
God?"
Jesus said to them, "You say that I am."
71They said, "Why do we need witnesses
now? We ourselves heard him say this."

Pilate Questions Jesus

23 Then the whole group stood up and
led Jesus to Pilate.[n] 2They began to
accuse Jesus, saying, "We caught this man
telling things that mislead our people. He
says that we should not pay taxes to Caesar,
and he calls himself the Christ, a king."
3Pilate asked Jesus, "Are you the king of
the Jews?"
Jesus answered, "Those are your words."
4Pilate said to the leading priests and the
people, "I find nothing against this man."
5They were insisting, saying, "But Jesus
makes trouble with the people, teaching all
around Judea. He began in Galilee, and now
he is here."

Pilate Sends Jesus to Herod

6Pilate heard this and asked if Jesus was
from Galilee. 7Since Jesus was under Herod's
authority, Pilate sent Jesus to Herod, who
was in Jerusalem at that time. 8When Herod
saw Jesus, he was very glad, because he had
heard about Jesus and had wanted to meet
him for a long time. He was hoping to see
Jesus work a miracle. 9Herod asked Jesus
many questions, but Jesus said nothing.
10The leading priests and teachers of the law
were standing there, strongly accusing Jesus.
11After Herod and his soldiers had made fun
of Jesus, they dressed him in a kingly robe
and sent him back to Pilate. 12In the past,
Pilate and Herod had always been enemies,
but on that day they became friends.

Jesus Must Die

13Pilate called the people together with
the leading priests and the rulers. 14He said
to them, "You brought this man to me,
saying he makes trouble among the people.
But I have questioned him before you all,
and I have not found him guilty of what
you say. 15Also, Herod found nothing wrong
with him; he sent him back to us. Look, he
has done nothing for which he should die.
16So, after I punish him, I will let him go
free." [17Every year at the Passover Feast,
Pilate had to release one prisoner to the
people.][n]
18But the people shouted together, "Take
this man away! Let Barabbas go free!"
19(Barabbas was a man who was in prison for
his part in a riot in the city and for murder.)
20Pilate wanted to let Jesus go free and
told this to the crowd. 21But they shouted
again, "Crucify him! Crucify him!"
22A third time Pilate said to them, "Why?
What wrong has he done? I can find no
reason to kill him. So I will have him
punished and set him free."
23But they continued to shout, demanding
that Jesus be crucified. Their yelling became
so loud that 24Pilate decided to give them
what they wanted. 25He set free the man
who was in jail for rioting and murder, and
he handed Jesus over to them to do with him
as they wished.

Jesus Is Crucified

26As they led Jesus away, Simon, a man
from Cyrene, was coming in from the fields.
They forced him to carry Jesus' cross and to
walk behind him.
27A large crowd of people was following
Jesus, including some women who were sad
and crying for him. 28But Jesus turned and
said to them, "Women of Jerusalem, don't cry
for me. Cry for yourselves and for your
children. 29The time is coming when people
will say, 'Blessed are the women who cannot
have children and who have no babies to
nurse.' 30Then people will say to the
mountains, 'Fall on us!' And they will say to
the hills, 'Cover us!' 31If they act like this
now when life is good, what will happen
when bad times come?"[n]
32There were also two criminals led out
with Jesus to be put to death. 33When they
came to a place called the Skull, the soldiers

23:1 Pilate Pontius Pilate was the Roman governor of Judea from A.D. 26 to A.D. 36. **23:17 Every . . . people.** Some Greek copies do not contain the bracketed text. **23:31 If . . . come?** Literally, "If they do these things in the green tree, what will happen in the dry?"

crucified Jesus and the criminals—one on
his right and the other on his left. [34]Jesus
said, "Father, forgive them, because they
don't know what they are doing."[n]
The soldiers threw lots to decide who
would get his clothes. [35]The people stood
there watching. And the leaders made fun of
Jesus, saying, "He saved others. Let him save
himself if he is God's Chosen One, the
Christ."
[36]The soldiers also made fun of him,
coming to Jesus and offering him some
vinegar. [37]They said, "If you are the king of
the Jews, save yourself!" [38]At the top of the
cross these words were written: THIS IS THE
KING OF THE JEWS.
[39]One of the criminals on a cross began to
shout insults at Jesus: "Aren't you the Christ?
Then save yourself and us."
[40]But the other criminal stopped him and
said, "You should fear God! You are getting
the same punishment he is. [41]We are
punished justly, getting what we deserve for
what we did. But this man has done nothing
wrong." [42]Then he said, "Jesus, remember me
when you come into your kingdom."
[43]Jesus said to him, "I tell you the truth,
today you will be with me in paradise."[n]

Jesus Dies

[44]It was about noon, and the whole land
became dark until three o'clock in the
afternoon, [45]because the sun did not shine.
The curtain in the Temple[n] was torn in two.
[46]Jesus cried out in a loud voice, "Father, I give
you my life." After Jesus said this, he died.
[47]When the army officer there saw what
happened, he praised God, saying, "Surely
this was a good man!"
[48]When all the people who had gathered
there to watch saw what happened, they
returned home, beating their chests because
they were so sad. [49]But those who were close
friends of Jesus, including the women who
had followed him from Galilee, stood at a
distance and watched.

Joseph Takes Jesus' Body

[50]There was a good and religious man
named Joseph who was a member of the
council. [51]But he had not agreed to the other
leaders' plans and actions against Jesus. He
was from the town of Arimathea and was
waiting for the kingdom of God to come.
[52]Joseph went to Pilate to ask for the body of
Jesus. [53]He took the body down from the
cross, wrapped it in cloth, and put it in a
tomb that was cut out of a wall of rock. This
tomb had never been used before. [54]This was
late on Preparation Day, and when the sun
went down, the Sabbath day would begin.
[55]The women who had come from Galilee
with Jesus followed Joseph and saw the
tomb and how Jesus' body was laid. [56]Then
the women left to prepare spices and
perfumes.
On the Sabbath day they rested, as the law
of Moses commanded.

Jesus Rises from the Dead

24 Very early on the first day of the
week, at dawn, the women came to
the tomb, bringing the spices they had
prepared. [2]They found the stone rolled away
from the entrance of the tomb, [3]but when
they went in, they did not find the body of
the Lord Jesus. [4]While they were wondering
about this, two men in shining clothes
suddenly stood beside them. [5]The women
were very afraid and bowed their heads to
the ground. The men said to them, "Why are
you looking for a living person in this place
for the dead? [6]He is not here; he has risen
from the dead. Do you remember what he
told you in Galilee? [7]He said the Son of Man
must be handed over to sinful people, be
crucified, and rise from the dead on the third
day." [8]Then the women remembered what
Jesus had said.
[9]The women left the tomb and told all
these things to the eleven apostles and the
other followers. [10]It was Mary Magdalene,
Joanna, Mary the mother of James, and some
other women who told the apostles
everything that had happened at the tomb.
[11]But they did not believe the women,
because it sounded like nonsense. [12]But Peter
got up and ran to the tomb. Bending down
and looking in, he saw only the cloth that
Jesus' body had been wrapped in. Peter went

23:34 Jesus . . . doing." Some Greek copies do not have this first part of verse 34. **23:43 paradise** Another word for heaven.
23:45 curtain in the Temple A curtain divided the Most Holy Place from the other part of the Temple, the special building in Jerusalem where God commanded the Jewish people to worship him.

away to his home, wondering about what
had happened.

Jesus on the Road to Emmaus

[13]That same day two of Jesus' followers
were going to a town named Emmaus, about
seven miles from Jerusalem. [14]They were
talking about everything that had happened.
[15]While they were talking and discussing,
Jesus himself came near and began walking
with them, [16]but they were kept from
recognizing him. [17]Then he said, "What are
these things you are talking about while you
walk?"

The two followers stopped, looking
very sad. [18]The one named Cleopas
answered, "Are you the only visitor in
Jerusalem who does not know what just
happened there?"

[19]Jesus said to them, "What are you
talking about?"

They said, "About Jesus of Nazareth. He
was a prophet who said and did many
powerful things before God and all the
people. [20]Our leaders and the leading priests
handed him over to be sentenced to death,
and they crucified him. [21]But we were
hoping that he would free Israel. Besides
this, it is now the third day since this
happened. [22]And today some women among
us amazed us. Early this morning they went
to the tomb, [23]but they did not find his body
there. They came and told us that they had
seen a vision of angels who said that Jesus
was alive! [24]So some of our group went to
the tomb, too. They found it just as the
women said, but they did not see Jesus."

[25]Then Jesus said to them, "You are foolish
and slow to believe everything the prophets
said. [26]They said that the Christ must suffer
these things before he enters his glory."
[27]Then starting with what Moses and all the
prophets had said about him, Jesus began to
explain everything that had been written
about himself in the Scriptures.

[28]They came near the town of Emmaus,
and Jesus acted as if he were going farther.
[29]But they begged him, "Stay with us,
because it is late; it is almost night." So he
went in to stay with them.

[30]When Jesus was at the table with them,
he took some bread, gave thanks, divided it,

devotion 285

LUKE 24:32

HOW'S THE FIRE BURNING?

Have you ever been to a revival? If not, I can tell you in the words of my southern friend, "It's a hand-clapping, soul-reviving, joy-raising experience" during which many people come to the Lord or find themselves "on fire" again for Jesus. Perhaps you know what I'm talking about. Maybe you've felt it at a Christian conference or when your friend was pronounced cancer-free or when you heard a story that could only be attributed to being a miracle straight from the Lord.

Do you wish you could feel the words of Jesus "burning" inside of you today? Perhaps you would love to attend a revival or a women's retreat, but you barely have time to go to church on Sunday. Maybe your job, activities, and responsibilities make worshiping with others impossible at this time. Don't give up trying to meet with others, and don't let the absence of fellowship keep you from feeling the light of Jesus living in you. Read his Word. Do daily devotions—like you are now—and feel the Spirit of Jesus pour over you. Let his light grow bright as you turn your eyes toward God's goodness.

Do you feel him? He is your Jesus and longs for you to praise him. It only takes a spark to start a fire, so let this moment be the spark that starts his Word burning in your heart again. Let today be your personal revival. Open up your heart and praise him!

and gave it to them. 31And then, they were
allowed to recognize Jesus. But when they
saw who he was, he disappeared. 32They said
to each other, "It felt like a fire burning in us
when Jesus talked to us on the road and
explained the Scriptures to us."

33So the two followers got up at once and
went back to Jerusalem. There they found the
eleven apostles and others gathered. 34They
were saying, "The Lord really has risen from
the dead! He showed himself to Simon."

35Then the two followers told what had
happened on the road and how they
recognized Jesus when he divided the bread.

Jesus Appears to His Followers

36While the two followers were telling
this, Jesus himself stood right in the middle
of them and said, "Peace be with you."

37They were fearful and terrified and
thought they were seeing a ghost. 38But Jesus
said, "Why are you troubled? Why do you
doubt what you see? 39Look at my hands and
my feet. It is I myself! Touch me and see,
because a ghost does not have a living body
as you see I have."

40After Jesus said this, he showed them his
hands and feet. 41While they still could not
believe it because they were amazed and
happy, Jesus said to them, "Do you have any
food here?" 42They gave him a piece of
broiled fish. 43While the followers watched,
Jesus took the fish and ate it.

44He said to them, "Remember when I was
with you before? I said that everything
written about me must happen—everything
in the law of Moses, the books of the
prophets, and the Psalms."

45Then Jesus opened their minds so they
could understand the Scriptures. 46He said to
them, "It is written that the Christ would
suffer and rise from the dead on the third
day 47and that a change of hearts and lives
and forgiveness of sins would be preached in
his name to all nations, starting at Jerusalem.
48You are witnesses of these things. 49I will
send you what my Father has promised, but
you must stay in Jerusalem until you have
received that power from heaven."

Jesus Goes Back to Heaven

50Jesus led his followers as far as Bethany,
and he raised his hands and blessed them.
51While he was blessing them, he was
separated from them and carried into
heaven. 52They worshiped him and returned
to Jerusalem very happy. 53They stayed in
the Temple all the time, praising God.

John

A Hebrew name that means "God is merciful," this book is sometimes called the "Johannine" Gospel.

Person Holding the Pen God Wrote With: *John*, who often refers to himself as "the follower Jesus loved," authored this book. His older brother James was also one of the original twelve apostles.

When the Text Was Written: Between 80 and 90 A.D., approximately fifty years after he'd witnessed the earthly ministry of Jesus

Spiritual Posture of the Original Recipients: In the latter part of the first century A.D., most Christians were facing persecution because the culture they lived in was decidedly opposed to their beliefs.

Storyline Synopsis: John's account differs quite a bit from Matthew, Mark, and Luke. He relates unique stories such as: Jesus single-handedly averting a wedding-day disaster by turning ordinary tap water into wine (John 2:1–10); Jesus compassionately raising Mary and Martha's brother, Lazarus, from death to life (11:1–44); and Jesus engaging his closest friends—his twelve followers—in a lengthy conversation on the eve of Calvary to prepare them for his death (13:1—14:31). John is also the only Gospel author to refer to Jesus as both the "Word of God" and the "Lamb of God." Furthermore, John is crystal clear when communicating his purpose in recording the life and ministry of Christ: "But these are written so that you may believe that Jesus is the Christ, the Son of God. Then, by believing, you may have life through his name" (20:31). Obviously, John was an evangelist who longed for others to know the love of God that he had experienced through Jesus Christ!

A Moment Worth Discussing: Chapter 5 recounts an event that makes a compelling argument for spiritual neediness (John 5:1–9). Jesus confronts an invalid with the question, "Do you want to be well?" At first glance, this inquiry seems insensitive since this poor guy had been lying by this "healing pool," seeking a miracle, for thirty-eight years! But Jesus wasn't being tactless; he was teaching the man that he couldn't get well by himself. He needed divine help! As soon as the sick man admitted his weakness, Jesus healed him. The heart of this passage is that self-sufficiency is a spiritual liability—a theme that's atypical in our "celebrate your independence" society.

Interesting (But Likely to Be Overlooked) Character: *Joseph from Arimathea*, who's mentioned in all four Gospels (Matt. 27:57; Mark 15:42–43; Luke 23:50–51; John 19:38) was a wealthy member of the Jewish council, which was like the Jewish Supreme Court. Joseph's powerful peers despised Jesus, yet Joseph believed in him. And Joseph risked his reputation—possibly even his life—to give the Messiah a decent burial.

Christ Comes to the World

1 In the beginning there was the Word.[n]
The Word was with God, and the Word
was God. 2 He was with God in the
beginning. 3 All things were made by him,
and nothing was made without him. 4 In him
there was life, and that life was the light of
all people. 5 The Light shines in the darkness,
and the darkness has not overpowered[n] it.
6 There was a man named John[n] who was
sent by God. 7 He came to tell people the
truth about the Light so that through him
all people could hear about the Light and
believe. 8 John was not the Light, but he
came to tell people the truth about the Light.
9 The true Light that gives light to all was
coming into the world!
10 The Word was in the world, and the
world was made by him, but the world did
not know him. 11 He came to the world that
was his own, but his own people did not
accept him. 12 But to all who did accept him
and believe in him he gave the right to
become children of God. 13 They did not
become his children in any human way—by
any human parents or human desire. They
were born of God.
14 The Word became a human and lived
among us. We saw his glory—the glory
that belongs to the only Son of the Father—
and he was full of grace and truth. 15 John
tells the truth about him and cries out,
saying, "This is the One I told you about:
'The One who comes after me is greater
than I am, because he was living
before me.' "
16 Because he was full of grace and truth,
from him we all received one gift after
another. 17 The law was given through
Moses, but grace and truth came through
Jesus Christ. 18 No one has ever seen God.
But God the only Son is very close to the
Father,[n] and he has shown us what God
is like.

1:1 Word The Greek word is "logos," meaning any kind of communication; it could be translated "message." Here, it means Christ, because Christ was the way God told people about himself. **1:5 overpowered** This can also be translated, "understood." **1:6 John** John the Baptist, who preached to people about Christ's coming (Matthew 3, Luke 3). **1:18 But . . . Father** This could be translated, "But the only God is very close to the Father." Also, some Greek copies read "But the only Son is very close to the Father."

devotion 286

JOHN 1:4

NO LIGHTS ON BUT SOMEBODY'S HOME

Have you ever met an empty person? You look into their eyes and see nothing. You listen to their heart and realize they are walking in a nighttime of the soul. They make decisions that lack planning or vision because they live inside a darkness, bumping up against walls, just trying to feel their way through the days and find some way that will let them out.

Before the world ever was, God the Creator decided that life and light would come from Jesus. Nothing was made without him and nothing would live in light apart from the radiant indwelling of Christ, the Son of God. When a woman is without the fullness of Jesus inside of her, then she is destined to live in obscurity and spiritual poverty. He is the only light that can overcome that kind of darkness.

If you have an empty friend, then bring the light of Christ to her house. Send her light in e-mails and gifts. Speak light over her. She may never know the difference except that you share your light every time you can. Women who have only lived in the dark can be afraid of the light. But inside that gloomy fear is only death.

The light of Christ, while overwhelmingly bright at first, is a healing light. No one need be afraid anymore. There is hope in the light where Jesus is. The dark keeps the weak in chains, but the light sets captives free.

John Tells People About Jesus

19 Here is the truth John[n] told when the
leaders in Jerusalem sent priests and Levites
to ask him, "Who are you?"
20 John spoke freely and did not refuse to
answer. He said, "I am not the Christ."
21 So they asked him, "Then who are you?
Are you Elijah?"[n]
He answered, "No, I am not."
"Are you the Prophet?"[n] they asked.
He answered, "No."
22 Then they said, "Who are you? Give us
an answer to tell those who sent us. What do
you say about yourself?"
23 John told them in the words of the
prophet Isaiah:

"I am the voice of one
calling out in the desert:
'Make the road straight for the Lord.' "

Isaiah 40:3

24 Some Pharisees who had been sent
asked John: 25 "If you are not the Christ or
Elijah or the Prophet, why do you baptize
people?"
26 John answered, "I baptize with water,
but there is one here with you that you don't
know about. 27 He is the One who comes
after me. I am not good enough to untie the
strings of his sandals."
28 This all happened at Bethany on the
other side of the Jordan River, where John
was baptizing people.
29 The next day John saw Jesus coming
toward him. John said, "Look, the Lamb of
God,[n] who takes away the sin of the world!
30 This is the One I was talking about when
I said, 'A man will come after me, but he is
greater than I am, because he was living
before me.' 31 Even I did not know who he
was, although I came baptizing with water
so that the people of Israel would know who
he is."
32-33 Then John said, "I saw the Spirit come
down from heaven in the form of a dove and
rest on him. Until then I did not know who
the Christ was. But the God who sent me to
baptize with water told me, 'You will see the
Spirit come down and rest on a man; he is
the One who will baptize with the Holy
Spirit.' 34 I have seen this happen, and I tell
you the truth: This man is the Son of God."[n]

The First Followers of Jesus

35 The next day John[n] was there again with
two of his followers. 36 When he saw Jesus
walking by, he said, "Look, the Lamb of
God!"[n]
37 The two followers heard John say this,
so they followed Jesus. 38 When Jesus turned
and saw them following him, he asked,
"What are you looking for?"
They said, "Rabbi, where are you staying?"
("Rabbi" means "Teacher.")
39 He answered, "Come and see." So the
two men went with Jesus and saw where
he was staying and stayed there with him
that day. It was about four o'clock in the
afternoon.
40 One of the two men who followed Jesus
after they heard John speak about him was
Andrew, Simon Peter's brother. 41 The first
thing Andrew did was to find his brother
Simon and say to him, "We have found the
Messiah." ("Messiah" means "Christ.")
42 Then Andrew took Simon to Jesus. Jesus
looked at him and said, "You are Simon son
of John. You will be called Cephas."
("Cephas" means "Peter."[n])
43 The next day Jesus decided to go to
Galilee. He found Philip and said to him,
"Follow me."
44 Philip was from the town of Bethsaida,
where Andrew and Peter lived. 45 Philip
found Nathanael and told him, "We have
found the man that Moses wrote about in
the law, and the prophets also wrote about
him. He is Jesus, the son of Joseph, from
Nazareth."
46 But Nathanael said to Philip, "Can
anything good come from Nazareth?"
Philip answered, "Come and see."
47 As Jesus saw Nathanael coming toward
him, he said, "Here is truly an Israelite. There
is nothing false in him."
48 Nathanael asked, "How do you
know me?"

1:19 John John the Baptist, who preached to people about Christ's coming (Matthew 3, Luke 3). **1:21 Elijah** A prophet who spoke for God. He lived hundreds of years before Christ and was expected to return before Christ (Malachi 4:5–6). **1:21 Prophet** They probably meant the prophet that God told Moses he would send (Deuteronomy 18:15–19). **1:29 Lamb of God** Name for Jesus. Jesus is like the lambs that were offered for a sacrifice to God. **1:34 the Son of God** Some Greek copies read "God's Chosen One." **1:35 John** John the Baptist, who preached to people about Christ's coming (Matthew 3, Luke 3). **1:36 Lamb of God** Name for Jesus. Jesus is like the lambs that were offered for a sacrifice to God. **1:42 Peter** The Greek name "Peter," like the Aramaic name "Cephas," means "rock."

Jesus answered, "I saw you when you were
under the fig tree, before Philip told you
about me."
49Then Nathanael said to Jesus, "Teacher,
you are the Son of God; you are the King of
Israel."
50Jesus said to Nathanael, "Do you believe
simply because I told you I saw you under
the fig tree? You will see greater things than
that." 51And Jesus said to them, "I tell you
the truth, you will all see heaven open and
'angels of God going up and coming down'[n]
on the Son of Man."

The Wedding at Cana

2 Two days later there was a wedding
in the town of Cana in Galilee. Jesus'
mother was there, 2and Jesus and his
followers were also invited to the wedding.
3When all the wine was gone, Jesus' mother
said to him, "They have no more wine."
4Jesus answered, "Dear woman, why come
to me? My time has not yet come."
5His mother said to the servants, "Do
whatever he tells you to do."
6In that place there were six stone water
jars that the Jews used in their washing
ceremony.[n] Each jar held about twenty or
thirty gallons.
7Jesus said to the servants, "Fill the jars
with water." So they filled the jars to the top.
8Then he said to them, "Now take some
out and give it to the master of the feast."
So they took the water to the master.
9When he tasted it, the water had become
wine. He did not know where the wine came
from, but the servants who had brought the
water knew. The master of the wedding
called the bridegroom 10and said to him,
"People always serve the best wine first.
Later, after the guests have been drinking
awhile, they serve the cheaper wine. But you
have saved the best wine till now."
11So in Cana of Galilee Jesus did his first
miracle. There he showed his glory, and his
followers believed in him.

Jesus in the Temple

12After this, Jesus went to the town of
Capernaum with his mother, brothers, and
followers. They stayed there for just a few
days. 13When it was almost time for the
Jewish Passover Feast, Jesus went to
Jerusalem. 14In the Temple he found people
selling cattle, sheep, and doves. He saw
others sitting at tables, exchanging different
kinds of money. 15Jesus made a whip out of
cords and forced all of them, both the sheep
and cattle, to leave the Temple. He turned
over the tables and scattered the money of
those who were exchanging it. 16Then he
said to those who were selling pigeons,
"Take these things out of here! Don't make
my Father's house a place for buying and
selling!"
17When this happened, the followers
remembered what was written in the
Scriptures: "My strong love for your Temple
completely controls me."[n]
18Some of his people said to Jesus, "Show
us a miracle to prove you have the right to
do these things."
19Jesus answered them, "Destroy this
temple, and I will build it again in three
days."
20They answered, "It took forty-six years
to build this Temple! Do you really believe
you can build it again in three days?"
21(But the temple Jesus meant was his
own body. 22After Jesus was raised from the
dead, his followers remembered that Jesus
had said this. Then they believed the
Scripture and the words Jesus had said.)
23When Jesus was in Jerusalem for the
Passover Feast, many people believed in him
because they saw the miracles he did. 24But
Jesus did not believe in them because he
knew them all. 25He did not need anyone to
tell him about people, because he knew
what was in people's minds.

Nicodemus Comes to Jesus

3 There was a man named Nicodemus
who was one of the Pharisees and an
important Jewish leader. 2One night
Nicodemus came to Jesus and said, "Teacher,
we know you are a teacher sent from God,
because no one can do the miracles you do
unless God is with him."
3Jesus answered, "I tell you the truth,
unless you are born again, you cannot be
in God's kingdom."

1:51 'angels . . . down' These words are from Genesis 28:12. **2:6 washing ceremony** The Jewish people washed themselves in special ways before eating, before worshiping in the Temple, and at other special times. **2:17 "My . . . me."** Quotation from Psalm 69:9.

4 Nicodemus said, "But if a person is already old, how can he be born again? He cannot enter his mother's womb again. So how can a person be born a second time?"

5 But Jesus answered, "I tell you the truth, unless you are born from water and the Spirit, you cannot enter God's kingdom. 6 Human life comes from human parents, but spiritual life comes from the Spirit. 7 Don't be surprised when I tell you, 'You must all be born again.' 8 The wind blows where it wants to and you hear the sound of it, but you don't know where the wind comes from or where it is going. It is the same with every person who is born from the Spirit."

9 Nicodemus asked, "How can this happen?"

10 Jesus said, "You are an important teacher in Israel, and you don't understand these things? 11 I tell you the truth, we talk about what we know, and we tell about what we have seen, but you don't accept what we tell you. 12 I have told you about things here on earth, and you do not believe me. So you will not believe me if I tell you about things of heaven. 13 The only one who has ever gone up to heaven is the One who came down from heaven—the Son of Man.[n]

14 "Just as Moses lifted up the snake in the desert,[n] the Son of Man must also be lifted up. 15 So that everyone who believes can have eternal life in him.

16 "God loved the world so much that he gave his one and only Son so that whoever believes in him may not be lost, but have eternal life. 17 God did not send his Son into the world to judge the world guilty, but to save the world through him. 18 People who believe in God's Son are not judged guilty. Those who do not believe have already been judged guilty, because they have not believed in God's one and only Son. 19 They are judged by this fact: The Light has come into the world, but they did not want light. They wanted darkness, because they were doing evil things. 20 All who do evil hate the light and will not come to the light, because it will show all the evil things they do. 21 But those who follow the true way come to the light, and it shows that the things they do were done through God."

Jesus and John the Baptist

22 After this, Jesus and his followers went into the area of Judea, where he stayed with his followers and baptized people. 23 John was also baptizing in Aenon, near Salim, because there was plenty of water there. People were going there to be baptized. 24 (This was before John was put into prison.)

25 Some of John's followers had an argument with a Jew about religious washing.[n] 26 So they came to John and said, "Teacher, remember the man who was with you on the other side of the Jordan River, the one you spoke about so much? He is baptizing, and everyone is going to him."

27 John answered, "A man can get only what God gives him. 28 You yourselves heard me say, 'I am not the Christ, but I am the one sent to prepare the way for him.' 29 The bride belongs only to the bridegroom. But the friend who helps the bridegroom stands by and listens to him. He is thrilled that he gets to hear the bridegroom's voice. In the same way, I am really happy. 30 He must become greater, and I must become less important.

The One Who Comes from Heaven

31 "The One who comes from above is greater than all. The one who is from the earth belongs to the earth and talks about things on the earth. But the One who comes from heaven is greater than all. 32 He tells what he has seen and heard, but no one accepts what he says. 33 Whoever accepts what he says has proven that God is true. 34 The One whom God sent speaks the words of God, because God gives him the Spirit fully. 35 The Father loves the Son and has given him power over everything. 36 Those who believe in the Son have eternal life, but those who do not obey the Son will never have life. God's anger stays on them."

Jesus and a Samaritan Woman

4 The Pharisees heard that Jesus was making and baptizing more followers than John, 2 although Jesus himself did not baptize people, but his followers did. 3 Jesus knew that the Pharisees had heard about him, so he left Judea and went back to

3:13 the Son of Man Some Greek copies continue, "who is in heaven." **3:14 Moses . . . desert** When the Israelites were dying from snakebites, God told Moses to put a bronze snake on a pole. The people who looked at the snake were healed (Numbers 21:4–9). **3:25 religious washing** The Jewish people washed themselves in special ways before eating, before worshiping in the Temple, and at other special times.

Galilee. 4But on the way he had to go
through the country of Samaria.
5In Samaria Jesus came to the town called
Sychar, which is near the field Jacob gave to
his son Joseph. 6Jacob's well was there. Jesus
was tired from his long trip, so he sat down
beside the well. It was about twelve o'clock
noon. 7When a Samaritan woman came to
the well to get some water, Jesus said to her,
"Please give me a drink." 8(This happened
while Jesus' followers were in town buying
some food.)
9The woman said, "I am surprised that
you ask me for a drink, since you are a
Jewish man and I am a Samaritan woman."
(Jewish people are not friends with
Samaritans.[n])
10Jesus said, "If you only knew the free
gift of God and who it is that is asking you
for water, you would have asked him, and
he would have given you living water."
11The woman said, "Sir, where will you
get this living water? The well is very deep,
and you have nothing to get water with.
12Are you greater than Jacob, our father, who
gave us this well and drank from it himself
along with his sons and flocks?"
13Jesus answered, "Everyone who drinks
this water will be thirsty again, 14but
whoever drinks the water I give will never
be thirsty. The water I give will become a
spring of water gushing up inside that
person, giving eternal life."
15The woman said to him, "Sir, give me
this water so I will never be thirsty again
and will not have to come back here to get
more water."
16Jesus told her, "Go get your husband and
come back here."
17The woman answered, "I have no
husband."
Jesus said to her, "You are right to say
you have no husband. 18Really you have
had five husbands, and the man you live
with now is not your husband. You told the
truth."
19The woman said, "Sir, I can see that you
are a prophet. 20Our ancestors worshiped on

4:9 Jewish people . . . Samaritans. This can also be translated "Jewish people don't use things that Samaritans have used."

devotion 287

JOHN 4:13–14

GIRL, GET A DRINK!

Are you today's modern woman? Are you blessed with extraordinary abilities to move, shake, bake, and give a little love? Well, even if you are gifted with superhuman strength to accomplish your tasks, your soul knows when your spirit is dry, and your heart knows when only habit is keeping you going. A very wise woman once told me, "You cannot give what you do not have." Can a well be a well without water? Can you be a Christian without Christ?

How can you be a fountain if all you have to offer is a trickle? Take a drink today—a huge one, a big thirty-two ounce super-sized gulp of Living Water. Jesus wants you to drink in the Word. He wants your heart, your spirit, and your ministry to be a gushing fountain of his truth and love. That is the hope he offered the woman at the well: "Whoever drinks the water I give will never be thirsty" (verse 14). He promises that as long as you are diving into the Word, your spirit will be continually refreshed. That poor woman—so worn out, doing everything in her own strength, offering her body to a man that was not her husband, and operating in only the physical to complete her chores. Who wants to be dead in the daily habits of life? I want to be a fountain that leads others to the source of everlasting life. So open up the Word, drink your Big Gulp, and pour yourself out for Jesus.

The Woman at the Well

JOHN 4

The other women draw water during the morning hours, but not her. She comes when no one will be at the well—so that there will be no looks of disdain or scorn. She'd rather deal with the heat than scorching words. As she approaches, she notices a man is already there. He seems to be Jewish, and she feels relief. The Jews despise Samaritans, and for once, she is happy to be ignored.

"Please give me a drink." She stops her work and looks over her shoulder. *Surely, he's not talking to me.* But they are alone. In case he hasn't noticed, she quickly points out that she is a Samaritan woman. "Go get your husband and come back here."

"I have no husband," she replies softly. Her mind races as he tells her she has had five husbands and the man she's living with now is not her husband at all. *What kind of Jew is this?* she wonders.

She tries to change the subject, bringing up controversies between Jews and Samaritans, but he won't be diverted. "When the Messiah comes, he will explain everything to us," she says, hoping to end the conversation.

"I am he—I, the one talking to you." He has revealed himself to her? A Samaritan woman? A sinner? She does not linger but runs into town declaring her encounter with the Savior.

Jesus knows our troubled lives, yet he still invites us into a deeper relationship with him.

this mountain, but you say that Jerusalem is the place where people must worship."

21Jesus said, "Believe me, woman. The time is coming when neither in Jerusalem nor on this mountain will you actually worship the Father. 22You Samaritans worship something you don't understand. We understand what we worship, because salvation comes from the Jews. 23The time is coming when the true worshipers will worship the Father in spirit and truth, and that time is here already. You see, the Father too is actively seeking such people to worship him. 24God is spirit, and those who worship him must worship in spirit and truth."

25The woman said, "I know that the Messiah is coming." (Messiah is the One called Christ.) "When the Messiah comes, he will explain everything to us."

26Then Jesus said, "I am he—I, the one talking to you."

27Just then his followers came back from town and were surprised to see him talking with a woman. But none of them asked, "What do you want?" or "Why are you talking with her?"

28Then the woman left her water jar and went back to town. She said to the people, 29"Come and see a man who told me everything I ever did. Do you think he might be the Christ?" 30So the people left the town and went to see Jesus.

31Meanwhile, his followers were begging him, "Teacher, eat something."

32But Jesus answered, "I have food to eat that you know nothing about."

33So the followers asked themselves, "Did somebody already bring him food?"

34Jesus said, "My food is to do what the One who sent me wants me to do and to finish his work. 35You have a saying, 'Four more months till harvest.' But I tell you, open your eyes and look at the fields ready for harvest now. 36Already, the one who harvests is being paid and is gathering crops for eternal life. So the one who plants and the one who harvests celebrate at the same time. 37Here the saying is true, 'One person plants, and another harvests.' 38I sent you to harvest a crop that you did not work on. Others did the work, and you get to finish up their work."[n]

4:38 I . . . their work. As a farmer sends workers to harvest grain, Jesus sends his followers out to bring people to God.

39 Many of the Samaritans in that town
believed in Jesus because of what the
woman said: "He told me everything I ever
did." 40 When the Samaritans came to Jesus,
they begged him to stay with them, so he
stayed there two more days. 41 And many
more believed because of the things he said.
42 They said to the woman, "First we
believed in Jesus because of what you said,
but now we believe because we heard him
ourselves. We know that this man really is
the Savior of the world."

Jesus Heals an Officer's Son

43 Two days later, Jesus left and went
to Galilee. 44 (Jesus had said before that a
prophet is not respected in his own country.)
45 When Jesus arrived in Galilee, the people
there welcomed him. They had seen all
the things he did at the Passover Feast in
Jerusalem, because they had been there, too.
46 Jesus went again to visit Cana in Galilee
where he had changed the water into wine.
One of the king's important officers lived in
the city of Capernaum, and his son was sick.
47 When he heard that Jesus had come from
Judea to Galilee, he went to Jesus and begged
him to come to Capernaum and heal his son,
because his son was almost dead. 48 Jesus said
to him, "You people must see signs and
miracles before you will believe in me."
49 The officer said, "Sir, come before my
child dies."
50 Jesus answered, "Go. Your son will live."
The man believed what Jesus told him
and went home. 51 On the way the man's
servants came and met him and told him,
"Your son is alive."
52 The man asked, "What time did my son
begin to get well?"
They answered, "Yesterday at one o'clock
the fever left him."
53 The father knew that one o'clock was
the exact time that Jesus had said, "Your son
will live." So the man and all the people who
lived in his house believed in Jesus.
54 That was the second miracle Jesus did
after coming from Judea to Galilee.

Jesus Heals a Man at a Pool

5 Later Jesus went to Jerusalem for a
special feast. 2 In Jerusalem there is a pool
with five covered porches, which is called
Bethesda[n] in the Hebrew language.[n] This
pool is near the Sheep Gate. 3 Many sick
people were lying on the porches beside the
pool. Some were blind, some were crippled,
and some were paralyzed [, and they waited
for the water to move. 4 Sometimes an angel
of the Lord came down to the pool and
stirred up the water. After the angel did this,
the first person to go into the pool was
healed from any sickness he had].[n] 5 A man
was lying there who had been sick for thirty-
eight years. 6 When Jesus saw the man and
knew that he had been sick for such a long
time, Jesus asked him, "Do you want to be
well?"
7 The sick man answered, "Sir, there is no
one to help me get into the pool when the
water starts moving. While I am coming to
the water, someone else always gets in
before me."
8 Then Jesus said, "Stand up. Pick up your
mat and walk." 9 And immediately the man
was well; he picked up his mat and began to
walk.
The day this happened was a Sabbath day.
10 So the Jews said to the man who had been
healed, "Today is the Sabbath. It is against
our law for you to carry your mat on the
Sabbath day."
11 But he answered, "The man who made
me well told me, 'Pick up your mat and
walk.' "
12 Then they asked him, "Who is the man
who told you to pick up your mat and
walk?"
13 But the man who had been healed did
not know who it was, because there were
many people in that place, and Jesus had left.
14 Later, Jesus found the man at the Temple
and said to him, "See, you are well now. Stop
sinning so that something worse does not
happen to you."
15 Then the man left and told his people
that Jesus was the one who had made him
well.
16 Because Jesus was doing this on the
Sabbath day, some evil people began to
persecute him. 17 But Jesus said to them,
"My Father never stops working, and so I
keep working, too."

5:2 Bethesda Some Greek copies read "Bethzatha" or "Bethsaida," different names for the pool of Bethesda. **5:2 Hebrew language** Or Aramaic, the languages of many people in this region in the first century. **5:3–4 and . . . had** Some Greek copies do not contain all or most of the bracketed text.

[18]This made them try still harder to kill him. They said, "First Jesus was breaking the law about the Sabbath day. Now he says that God is his own Father, making himself equal with God!"

Jesus Has God's Authority

[19]But Jesus said, "I tell you the truth, the Son can do nothing alone. The Son does only what he sees the Father doing, because the Son does whatever the Father does. [20]The Father loves the Son and shows the Son all the things he himself does. But the Father will show the Son even greater things than this so that you can all be amazed. [21]Just as the Father raises the dead and gives them life, so also the Son gives life to those he wants to. [22]In fact, the Father judges no one, but he has given the Son power to do all the judging [23]so that all people will honor the Son as much as they honor the Father. Anyone who does not honor the Son does not honor the Father who sent him.

[24]"I tell you the truth, whoever hears what I say and believes in the One who sent me has eternal life. That person will not be judged guilty but has already left death and entered life. [25]I tell you the truth, the time is coming and is already here when the dead will hear the voice of the Son of God, and those who hear will have life. [26]Life comes from the Father himself, and he has allowed the Son to have life in himself as well. [27]And the Father has given the Son the approval to judge, because he is the Son of Man. [28]Don't be surprised at this: A time is coming when all who are dead and in their graves will hear his voice. [29]Then they will come out of their graves. Those who did good will rise and have life forever, but those who did evil will rise to be judged guilty.

Jesus Is God's Son

[30]"I can do nothing alone. I judge only the way I am told, so my judgment is fair. I don't try to please myself, but I try to please the One who sent me.

[31]"If only I tell people about myself, what I say is not true. [32]But there is another who tells about me, and I know that the things he says about me are true.

[33]"You have sent people to John, and he has told you the truth. [34]It is not that I need what humans say; I tell you this so you can be saved. [35]John was like a burning and shining lamp, and you were happy to enjoy his light for a while.

[36]"But I have a proof about myself that is greater than that of John. The things I do, which are the things my Father gave me to do, prove that the Father sent me. [37]And the Father himself who sent me has given proof about me. You have never heard his voice or seen what he looks like. [38]His teaching does not live in you, because you don't believe in the One the Father sent. [39]You carefully study the Scriptures because you think they give you eternal life. They do in fact tell about me, [40]but you refuse to come to me to have that life.

[41]"I don't need praise from people. [42]But I know you—I know that you don't have God's love in you. [43]I have come from my Father and speak for him, but you don't accept me. But when another person comes, speaking only for himself, you will accept him. [44]You try to get praise from each other, but you do not try to get the praise that comes from the only God. So how can you believe? [45]Don't think that I will stand before the Father and say you are wrong. The one who says you are wrong is Moses, the one you hoped would save you. [46]If you really believed Moses, you would believe me, because Moses wrote about me. [47]But if you don't believe what Moses wrote, how can you believe what I say?"

More than Five Thousand Fed

6 After this, Jesus went across Lake Galilee (or, Lake Tiberias). [2]Many people followed him because they saw the miracles he did to heal the sick. [3]Jesus went up on a hill and sat down there with his followers. [4]It was almost the time for the Jewish Passover Feast.

[5]When Jesus looked up and saw a large crowd coming toward him, he said to Philip, "Where can we buy enough bread for all these people to eat?" [6](Jesus asked Philip this question to test him, because Jesus already knew what he planned to do.)

[7]Philip answered, "Someone would have to work almost a year to buy enough bread for each person to have only a little piece."

[8]Another one of his followers, Andrew, Simon Peter's brother, said, [9]"Here is a boy

with five loaves of barley bread and two little fish, but that is not enough for so many people."

10 Jesus said, "Tell the people to sit down." There was plenty of grass there, and about five thousand men sat down there. 11 Then Jesus took the loaves of bread, thanked God for them, and gave them to the people who were sitting there. He did the same with the fish, giving as much as the people wanted.

12 When they had all had enough to eat, Jesus said to his followers, "Gather the leftover pieces of fish and bread so that nothing is wasted." 13 So they gathered up the pieces and filled twelve baskets with the pieces left from the five barley loaves.

14 When the people saw this miracle that Jesus did, they said, "He must truly be the Prophet[n] who is coming into the world."

15 Jesus knew that the people planned to come and take him by force and make him their king, so he left and went into the hills alone.

Jesus Walks on the Water

16 That evening Jesus' followers went down to Lake Galilee. 17 It was dark now, and Jesus had not yet come to them. The followers got into a boat and started across the lake to Capernaum. 18 By now a strong wind was blowing, and the waves on the lake were getting bigger. 19 When they had rowed the boat about three or four miles, they saw Jesus walking on the water, coming toward the boat. The followers were afraid, 20 but Jesus said to them, "It is I. Do not be afraid." 21 Then they were glad to take him into the boat. At once the boat came to land at the place where they wanted to go.

The People Seek Jesus

22 The next day the people who had stayed on the other side of the lake knew that Jesus had not gone in the boat with his followers but that they had left without him. And they knew that only one boat had been there. 23 But then some boats came from Tiberias and landed near the place where the people had eaten the bread after the Lord had given thanks. 24 When the people saw that Jesus and his followers were not there now, they got into boats and went to Capernaum to find Jesus.

Jesus, the Bread of Life

25 When the people found Jesus on the other side of the lake, they asked him, "Teacher, when did you come here?"

26 Jesus answered, "I tell you the truth, you aren't looking for me because you saw me do miracles. You are looking for me because you ate the bread and were satisfied. 27 Don't work for the food that spoils. Work for the food that stays good always and gives eternal life. The Son of Man will give you this food, because on him God the Father has put his power."

28 The people asked Jesus, "What are the things God wants us to do?"

29 Jesus answered, "The work God wants you to do is this: Believe the One he sent."

30 So the people asked, "What miracle will you do? If we see a miracle, we will believe you. What will you do? 31 Our ancestors ate the manna in the desert. This is written in the Scriptures: 'He gave them bread from heaven to eat.' "[n]

32 Jesus said, "I tell you the truth, it was not Moses who gave you bread from heaven; it is my Father who is giving you the true bread from heaven. 33 God's bread is the One who comes down from heaven and gives life to the world."

34 The people said, "Sir, give us this bread always."

35 Then Jesus said, "I am the bread that gives life. Whoever comes to me will never be hungry, and whoever believes in me will never be thirsty. 36 But as I told you before, you have seen me and still don't believe. 37 The Father gives me the people who are mine. Every one of them will come to me, and I will always accept them. 38 I came down from heaven to do what God wants me to do, not what I want to do. 39 Here is what the One who sent me wants me to do: I must not lose even one whom God gave me, but I must raise them all on the last day. 40 Those who see the Son and believe in him have eternal life, and I will raise them on the last day. This is what my Father wants."

41 Some people began to complain about

6:14 Prophet They probably meant the prophet that God told Moses he would send (Deuteronomy 18:15–19).

6:31 'He gave . . . eat.' Quotation from Psalm 78:24.

devotion 288

JOHN 6:28–29

DO YOU REALLY BELIEVE?

We like "to do" for God. It is easier for us to have a list of things to do so we can check them off and feel good about ourselves. Yet when Jesus was asked what people should do for God, he responded, "Believe the One he sent" (John 6:29). Just believe. Christianity is so simple, yet we somehow make it so complicated. I think this is why Jesus told his followers that they needed to come as little children. Children would climb up on Jesus' lap and simply believe everything he said.

But for most of us, believing is sometimes the most difficult thing to do. Read Mark 9:20-27, the story of a man who asked Jesus to heal his son. Jesus told him, "All things are possible for the one who believes" (Mark 9:23). I love the father's response: "I do believe! Help me to believe more!" (9:24).

We need to pray this every day. We believe that Jesus is the Son of God, but do we believe all the things he has promised us in his Word? God said he will never leave us or forsake us. Do you believe it? Jesus promised us that one day he will return to earth. Do you believe it? If we really believed these things, we would live our lives a little bit differently. As you read the Bible each day, ask God to help you believe all the truths you read. This is what God wants.

Jesus because he said, "I am the bread that
comes down from heaven." 42They said,
"This is Jesus, the son of Joseph. We know
his father and mother. How can he say, 'I
came down from heaven'?"
43But Jesus answered, "Stop complaining
to each other. 44The Father is the One who
sent me. No one can come to me unless the
Father draws him to me, and I will raise that
person up on the last day. 45It is written in
the prophets, 'They will all be taught by
God.'[n] Everyone who listens to the Father
and learns from him comes to me. 46No one
has seen the Father except the One who is
from God; only he has seen the Father. 47I
tell you the truth, whoever believes has
eternal life. 48I am the bread that gives life.
49Your ancestors ate the manna in the
desert, but still they died. 50Here is the bread
that comes down from heaven. Anyone who
eats this bread will never die. 51I am the
living bread that came down from heaven.
Anyone who eats this bread will live
forever. This bread is my flesh, which I
will give up so that the world may have
life."
52Then the evil people began to argue
among themselves, saying, "How can this
man give us his flesh to eat?"
53Jesus said, "I tell you the truth, you must
eat the flesh of the Son of Man and drink his
blood. Otherwise, you won't have real life in
you. 54Those who eat my flesh and drink my
blood have eternal life, and I will raise them
up on the last day. 55My flesh is true food,
and my blood is true drink. 56Those who eat
my flesh and drink my blood live in me, and
I live in them. 57The living Father sent me,
and I live because of the Father. So whoever
eats me will live because of me. 58I am not
like the bread your ancestors ate. They ate
that bread and still died. I am the bread that
came down from heaven, and whoever eats
this bread will live forever." 59Jesus said all
these things while he was teaching in the
synagogue in Capernaum.

6:45 'They . . . God.' Quotation from Isaiah 54:13.

The Words of Eternal Life

60 When the followers of Jesus heard this,
many of them said, "This teaching is hard.
Who can accept it?"

61 Knowing that his followers were
complaining about this, Jesus said, "Does
this teaching bother you? 62 Then will it also
bother you to see the Son of Man going back
to the place where he came from? 63 It is the
Spirit that gives life. The flesh doesn't give
life. The words I told you are spirit, and they
give life. 64 But some of you don't believe."
(Jesus knew from the beginning who did not
believe and who would turn against him.)
65 Jesus said, "That is the reason I said, 'If the
Father does not bring a person to me, that
one cannot come.' "

66 After Jesus said this, many of his
followers left him and stopped following
him.

67 Jesus asked the twelve followers, "Do
you want to leave, too?"

68 Simon Peter answered him, "Lord, who
would we go to? You have the words that
give eternal life. 69 We believe and know that
you are the Holy One from God."

70 Then Jesus answered, "I chose all twelve
of you, but one of you is a devil."

71 Jesus was talking about Judas, the son of
Simon Iscariot. Judas was one of the twelve,
but later he was going to turn against Jesus.

Jesus' Brothers Don't Believe

7 After this, Jesus traveled around Galilee.
He did not want to travel in Judea,
because some evil people there wanted to
kill him. 2 It was time for the Feast of
Shelters. 3 So Jesus' brothers said to him, "You
should leave here and go to Judea so your
followers there can see the miracles you do.
4 Anyone who wants to be well known does
not hide what he does. If you are doing these
things, show yourself to the world." 5 (Even
Jesus' brothers did not believe in him.)

6 Jesus said to his brothers, "The right time
for me has not yet come, but any time is
right for you. 7 The world cannot hate you,
but it hates me, because I tell it the evil
things it does. 8 So you go to the feast. I will
not go yet[n] to this feast, because the right
time for me has not yet come." 9 After saying
this, Jesus stayed in Galilee.

10 But after Jesus' brothers had gone to the
feast, Jesus went also. But he did not let
people see him. 11 At the feast some people
were looking for him and saying, "Where is
that man?"

12 Within the large crowd there, many
people were whispering to each other about
Jesus. Some said, "He is a good man."

Others said, "No, he fools the people."
13 But no one was brave enough to talk about
Jesus openly, because they were afraid of the
elders.

Jesus Teaches at the Feast

14 When the feast was about half over,
Jesus went to the Temple and began to teach.
15 The people were amazed and said, "This
man has never studied in school. How did he
learn so much?"

16 Jesus answered, "The things I teach are
not my own, but they come from him who
sent me. 17 If people choose to do what God
wants, they will know that my teaching
comes from God and not from me. 18 Those
who teach their own ideas are trying to get
honor for themselves. But those who try to
bring honor to the one who sent them speak
the truth, and there is nothing false in them.
19 Moses gave you the law,[n] but none of you
obeys that law. Why are you trying to
kill me?"

20 The people answered, "A demon has
come into you. We are not trying to kill
you."

21 Jesus said to them, "I did one miracle,
and you are all amazed. 22 Moses gave you
the law about circumcision. (But really
Moses did not give you circumcision; it came
from our ancestors.) And yet you circumcise
a baby boy on a Sabbath day. 23 If a baby boy
can be circumcised on a Sabbath day to obey
the law of Moses, why are you angry at me
for healing a person's whole body on the
Sabbath day? 24 Stop judging by the way
things look, but judge by what is really
right."

Is Jesus the Christ?

25 Then some of the people who lived in
Jerusalem said, "This is the man they are
trying to kill. 26 But he is teaching where
everyone can see and hear him, and no one

7:8 yet Some Greek copies do not have this word.
7:19 law Moses gave God's people the Law that God gave him on Mount Sinai (Exodus 34:29–32).

is trying to stop him. Maybe the leaders have
decided he really is the Christ. 27 But we
know where this man is from. Yet when the
real Christ comes, no one will know where
he comes from."
28 Jesus, teaching in the Temple, cried out,
"Yes, you know me, and you know where I
am from. But I have not come by my own
authority. I was sent by the One who is true,
whom you don't know. 29 But I know him,
because I am from him, and he sent me."
30 When Jesus said this, they tried to seize
him. But no one was able to touch him,
because it was not yet the right time. 31 But
many of the people believed in Jesus. They
said, "When the Christ comes, will he do
more miracles than this man has done?"

The Leaders Try to Arrest Jesus

32 The Pharisees heard the crowd
whispering these things about Jesus. So the
leading priests and the Pharisees sent some
Temple guards to arrest him. 33 Jesus said, "I
will be with you a little while longer. Then
I will go back to the One who sent me. 34 You
will look for me, but you will not find me.
And you cannot come where I am."
35 Some people said to each other, "Where
will this man go so we cannot find him?
Will he go to the Greek cities where our
people live and teach the Greek people
there? 36 What did he mean when he said,
'You will look for me, but you will not find
me,' and 'You cannot come where I am'?"

Jesus Talks About the Spirit

37 On the last and most important day of
the feast Jesus stood up and said in a loud
voice, "Let anyone who is thirsty come to me
and drink. 38 If anyone believes in me, rivers
of living water will flow out from that
person's heart, as the Scripture says." 39 Jesus
was talking about the Holy Spirit. The Spirit
had not yet been given, because Jesus had
not yet been raised to glory. But later, those
who believed in Jesus would receive the
Spirit.

The People Argue About Jesus

40 When the people heard Jesus' words,
some of them said, "This man really is the
Prophet."[n]

The Woman Caught in Adultery

JOHN 8

She is naked, covered only by a shawl she was able to grab as they dragged her from bed. She pleads for them to let her go, but they force her through the streets to the Temple steps. A small crowd is gathered listening to a man. She crumbles to the ground, averting her eyes from those staring.

A teacher of the law points at her but directs his remarks to Jesus. "This woman was caught having sexual relations with a man who is not her husband. The law of Moses commands that we stone to death every woman who does this. What do you say we should do?" Her stomach turns inside out and her hands tremble.

Jesus walks toward her. *He will throw the first stone,* she thinks, trying to catch her breath. She hears a scratching sound and quickly glances in front of her. This man is writing something in the dirt. The men continue to ask Jesus what he would do with this sinful woman, but he never stops writing.

He looks up. "Anyone here who has never sinned can throw the first stone at her." Then he writes on the ground again. She hears her heart beating. One by one, the people leave. "Has no one judged you guilty?" Jesus asks.

"No one, sir."

"I also don't judge you guilty. You may go now, but don't sin anymore."

People are quick to point out our sins, but Jesus is just as quick to forgive and redeem.

7:40 Prophet They probably meant the prophet God told Moses he would send (Deuteronomy 18:15–19).

41Others said, "He is the Christ."
Still others said, "The Christ will not come
from Galilee. 42The Scripture says that the
Christ will come from David's family and
from Bethlehem, the town where David
lived." 43So the people did not agree with
each other about Jesus. 44Some of them
wanted to arrest him, but no one was able to
touch him.

Some Leaders Won't Believe

45The Temple guards went back to the
leading priests and the Pharisees, who asked,
"Why didn't you bring Jesus?"

46The guards answered, "The words he
says are greater than the words of any other
person who has ever spoken!"

47The Pharisees answered, "So Jesus has
fooled you also! 48Have any of the leaders or
the Pharisees believed in him? No! 49But
these people, who know nothing about the
law, are under God's curse."

50Nicodemus, who had gone to see Jesus
before, was in that group.[n] He said, 51"Our
law does not judge a person without hearing
him and knowing what he has done."

52They answered, "Are you from Galilee,
too? Study the Scriptures, and you will learn
that no prophet comes from Galilee."

Some of the earliest surviving Greek copies do not contain 7:53—8:11.

[53And everyone left and went home.

The Woman Caught in Adultery

8 Jesus went to the Mount of Olives. 2But
early in the morning he went back to the
Temple, and all the people came to him, and
he sat and taught them. 3The teachers of the
law and the Pharisees brought a woman who
had been caught in adultery. They forced her
to stand before the people. 4They said to
Jesus, "Teacher, this woman was caught
having sexual relations with a man who
is not her husband. 5The law of Moses
commands that we stone to death every
woman who does this. What do you say we
should do?" 6They were asking this to trick
Jesus so that they could have some charge
against him.

But Jesus bent over and started writing
on the ground with his finger. 7When they
continued to ask Jesus their question, he
raised up and said, "Anyone here who has
never sinned can throw the first stone at
her." 8Then Jesus bent over again and wrote
on the ground.

9Those who heard Jesus began to leave
one by one, first the older men and then the
others. Jesus was left there alone with the
woman standing before him. 10Jesus raised
up again and asked her, "Woman, where are
they? Has no one judged you guilty?"

11She answered, "No one, sir."

Then Jesus said, "I also don't judge you
guilty. You may go now, but don't sin
anymore."]

Jesus Is the Light of the World

12Later, Jesus talked to the people again,
saying, "I am the light of the world. The
person who follows me will never live in
darkness but will have the light that gives
life."

13The Pharisees said to Jesus, "When you
talk about yourself, you are the only one to
say these things are true. We cannot accept
what you say."

14Jesus answered, "Yes, I am saying these
things about myself, but they are true. I
know where I came from and where I am
going. But you don't know where I came
from or where I am going. 15You judge by
human standards. I am not judging anyone.
16But when I do judge, I judge truthfully,
because I am not alone. The Father who sent
me is with me. 17Your own law says that
when two witnesses say the same thing, you
must accept what they say. 18I am one of the
witnesses who speaks about myself, and the
Father who sent me is the other witness."

19They asked, "Where is your father?"

Jesus answered, "You don't know me or
my Father. If you knew me, you would know
my Father, too." 20Jesus said these things
while he was teaching in the Temple, near
where the money is kept. But no one
arrested him, because the right time for
him had not yet come.

7:50 Nicodemus . . . group. The story about Nicodemus going and talking to Jesus is in John 3:1–21.

The People Misunderstand Jesus

21Again, Jesus said to the people, "I will
leave you, and you will look for me, but you
will die in your sins. You cannot come where
I am going."
22So the Jews asked, "Will he kill himself?
Is that why he said, 'You cannot come where
I am going'?"
23Jesus said, "You people are from here
below, but I am from above. You belong to
this world, but I don't belong to this world.
24So I told you that you would die in your
sins. Yes, you will die in your sins if you
don't believe that I am he."
25They asked, "Then who are you?"
Jesus answered, "I am what I have told
you from the beginning. 26I have many
things to say and decide about you. But I tell
people only the things I have heard from the
One who sent me, and he speaks the truth."
27The people did not understand that he
was talking to them about the Father. 28So
Jesus said to them, "When you lift up the
Son of Man, you will know that I am he. You
will know that these things I do are not by
my own authority but that I say only what
the Father has taught me. 29The One who
sent me is with me. I always do what is
pleasing to him, so he has not left me alone."
30While Jesus was saying these things, many
people believed in him.

Freedom from Sin

31So Jesus said to the Jews who believed in
him, "If you continue to obey my teaching,
you are truly my followers. 32Then you will
know the truth, and the truth will make you
free."
33They answered, "We are Abraham's
children, and we have never been anyone's
slaves. So why do you say we will be free?"
34Jesus answered, "I tell you the truth,
everyone who lives in sin is a slave to sin.
35A slave does not stay with a family forever,
but a son belongs to the family forever. 36So
if the Son makes you free, you will be truly
free. 37I know you are Abraham's children,
but you want to kill me because you don't
accept my teaching. 38I am telling you what
my Father has shown me, but you do what
your father has told you."
39They answered, "Our father is
Abraham."
Jesus said, "If you were really Abraham's

devotion 289

JOHN 8:31

TRUTH AT YOUR FINGERTIPS

I wonder if Jesus ever became frustrated as he explained his purpose for coming to earth and why people should follow him. How wearisome it must have been to be rejected by many of his own people; and how exasperating it must be for him now, when in our self-centeredness, we choose to disobey his teachings.

Today, we are fortunate to have the Holy Bible at our fingertips. Everything we need to know about Jesus' teachings is right inside. Even if we aren't fortunate enough to buy a Bible of our own, we can essentially walk through the doors of any church in the United States and someone inside will gladly hand one over. But even with his words so readily available to us, all too often we still fail to follow his teachings, even in our Christian circles. We are still guilty of going our own ways and not pausing to consider our instructions from the Lord.

I challenge you to truly live like one of Christ's followers today. You are holding a Bible in your hands right now, so dig into it. Reread today's verse, and if you really want to learn more, consider taking some extra time to read to the end of this passage in John. Make time to read the Bible often, and seek to understand and obey what you read. Then as John 8:32 says, "You will know the truth, and the truth will make you free."

children, you would do[n] the things Abraham did. 40I am a man who has told you the truth which I heard from God, but you are trying to kill me. Abraham did nothing like that. 41So you are doing the things your own father did."

But they said, "We are not like children who never knew who their father was. God is our Father; he is the only Father we have."

42Jesus said to them, "If God were really your Father, you would love me, because I came from God and now I am here. I did not come by my own authority; God sent me. 43You don't understand what I say, because you cannot accept my teaching. 44You belong to your father the devil, and you want to do what he wants. He was a murderer from the beginning and was against the truth, because there is no truth in him. When he tells a lie, he shows what he is really like, because he is a liar and the father of lies. 45But because I speak the truth, you don't believe me. 46Can any of you prove that I am guilty of sin? If I am telling the truth, why don't you believe me? 47The person who belongs to God accepts what God says. But you don't accept what God says, because you don't belong to God."

Jesus Is Greater than Abraham

48They answered, "We say you are a Samaritan and have a demon in you. Are we not right?"

49Jesus answered, "I have no demon in me. I give honor to my Father, but you dishonor me. 50I am not trying to get honor for myself. There is One who wants this honor for me, and he is the judge. 51I tell you the truth, whoever obeys my teaching will never die."

52They said to Jesus, "Now we know that you have a demon in you! Even Abraham and the prophets died. But you say, 'Whoever obeys my teaching will never die.' 53Do you think you are greater than our father Abraham, who died? And the prophets died, too. Who do you think you are?"

54Jesus answered, "If I give honor to myself, that honor is worth nothing. The One who gives me honor is my Father, and you say he is your God. 55You don't really know him, but I know him. If I said I did not know him, I would be a liar like you. But I do know him, and I obey what he says. 56Your father Abraham was very happy that he would see my day. He saw that day and was glad."

57They said to him, "You have never seen Abraham! You are not even fifty years old."

58Jesus answered, "I tell you the truth, before Abraham was even born, I am!" 59When Jesus said this, the people picked up stones to throw at him. But Jesus hid himself, and then he left the Temple.

Jesus Heals a Man Born Blind

9 As Jesus was walking along, he saw a man who had been born blind. 2His followers asked him, "Teacher, whose sin caused this man to be born blind—his own sin or his parents' sin?"

3Jesus answered, "It is not this man's sin or his parents' sin that made him blind. This man was born blind so that God's power could be shown in him. 4While it is daytime, we must continue doing the work of the One who sent me. Night is coming, when no one can work. 5While I am in the world, I am the light of the world."

6After Jesus said this, he spit on the ground and made some mud with it and put the mud on the man's eyes. 7Then he told the man, "Go and wash in the Pool of Siloam." (Siloam means Sent.) So the man went, washed, and came back seeing.

8The neighbors and some people who had earlier seen this man begging said, "Isn't this the same man who used to sit and beg?"

9Some said, "He is the one," but others said, "No, he only looks like him."

The man himself said, "I am the man."

10They asked, "How did you get your sight?"

11He answered, "The man named Jesus made some mud and put it on my eyes. Then he told me to go to Siloam and wash. So I went and washed, and then I could see."

12They asked him, "Where is this man?"

"I don't know," he answered.

Pharisees Question the Healing

13Then the people took to the Pharisees the man who had been blind. 14The day Jesus had made mud and healed his eyes was

8:39 If . . . do Some Greek copies read "If you are really Abraham's children, you will do."

a Sabbath day. 15So now the Pharisees asked
the man, "How did you get your sight?"
He answered, "He put mud on my eyes, I
washed, and now I see."
16So some of the Pharisees were saying,
"This man does not keep the Sabbath day, so
he is not from God."
But others said, "A man who is a sinner
can't do miracles like these." So they could
not agree with each other.
17They asked the man again, "What do
you say about him since it was your eyes he
opened?"
The man answered, "He is a prophet."
18These leaders did not believe that he had
been blind and could now see again. So they
sent for the man's parents 19and asked them,
"Is this your son who you say was born
blind? Then how does he now see?"
20His parents answered, "We know that
this is our son and that he was born blind.
21But we don't know how he can now see.
We don't know who opened his eyes. Ask
him. He is old enough to speak for himself."
22His parents said this because they were
afraid of the elders, who had already decided
that anyone who said Jesus was the Christ
would be avoided. 23That is why his parents
said, "He is old enough. Ask him."
24So for the second time, they called the
man who had been blind. They said, "You
should give God the glory by telling the
truth. We know that this man is a sinner."
25He answered, "I don't know if he is a
sinner. One thing I do know: I was blind, and
now I see."
26They asked, "What did he do to you?
How did he make you see again?"
27He answered, "I already told you, and
you didn't listen. Why do you want to hear it
again? Do you want to become his followers,
too?"
28Then they insulted him and said, "You
are his follower, but we are followers of
Moses. 29We know that God spoke to Moses,
but we don't even know where this man
comes from."
30The man answered, "This is a very
strange thing. You don't know where he
comes from, and yet he opened my eyes.
31We all know that God does not listen to
sinners, but he listens to anyone who
worships and obeys him. 32Nobody has ever
heard of anyone giving sight to a man born
blind. 33If this man were not from God, he
could do nothing."
34They answered, "You were born full of
sin! Are you trying to teach us?" And they
threw him out.

Spiritual Blindness

35When Jesus heard that they had thrown
him out, Jesus found him and said, "Do you
believe in the Son of Man?"
36He asked, "Who is the Son of Man, sir, so
that I can believe in him?"
37Jesus said to him, "You have seen him.
The Son of Man is the one talking with you."
38He said, "Lord, I believe!" Then the man
worshiped Jesus.
39Jesus said, "I came into this world so that
the world could be judged. I came so that the
blind[n] would see and so that those who see
will become blind."
40Some of the Pharisees who were nearby
heard Jesus say this and asked, "Are you
saying we are blind, too?"
41Jesus said, "If you were blind, you would
not be guilty of sin. But since you keep
saying you see, your guilt remains."

The Shepherd and His Sheep

10 Jesus said, "I tell you the truth, the
person who does not enter the
sheepfold by the door, but climbs in some
other way, is a thief and a robber. 2The one
who enters by the door is the shepherd of
the sheep. 3The one who guards the door
opens it for him. And the sheep listen to the
voice of the shepherd. He calls his own
sheep by name and leads them out. 4When
he brings all his sheep out, he goes ahead of
them, and they follow him because they
know his voice. 5But they will never follow
a stranger. They will run away from him
because they don't know his voice." 6Jesus
told the people this story, but they did not
understand what it meant.

Jesus Is the Good Shepherd

7So Jesus said again, "I tell you the truth, I
am the door for the sheep. 8All the people
who came before me were thieves and
robbers. The sheep did not listen to them. 9I

9:39 blind Jesus is talking about people who are spiritually blind, not physically blind.

am the door, and the person who enters
through me will be saved and will be able to
come in and go out and find pasture. [10]A
thief comes to steal and kill and destroy, but
I came to give life—life in all its fullness.
[11]"I am the good shepherd. The good
shepherd gives his life for the sheep. [12]The
worker who is paid to keep the sheep is
different from the shepherd who owns
them. When the worker sees a wolf coming,
he runs away and leaves the sheep alone.
Then the wolf attacks the sheep and scatters
them. [13]The man runs away because he is
only a paid worker and does not really care
about the sheep.
[14]"I am the good shepherd. I know my
sheep, and my sheep know me, [15]just as the
Father knows me, and I know the Father. I
give my life for the sheep. [16]I have other
sheep that are not in this flock, and I must
bring them also. They will listen to my
voice, and there will be one flock and one
shepherd. [17]The Father loves me because I
give my life so that I can take it back again.
[18]No one takes it away from me; I give my
own life freely. I have the right to give my
life, and I have the right to take it back. This
is what my Father commanded me to do."
[19]Again the leaders did not agree with
each other because of these words of Jesus.
[20]Many of them said, "A demon has come
into him and made him crazy. Why listen to
him?"
[21]But others said, "A man who is crazy
with a demon does not say things like this.
Can a demon open the eyes of the blind?"

Jesus Is Rejected

[22]The time came for the Feast of
Dedication at Jerusalem. It was winter,
[23]and Jesus was walking in the Temple in
Solomon's Porch. [24]Some people gathered
around him and said, "How long will you
make us wonder about you? If you are the
Christ, tell us plainly."
[25]Jesus answered, "I told you already, but
you did not believe. The miracles I do in my
Father's name show who I am. [26]But you
don't believe, because you are not my sheep.
[27]My sheep listen to my voice; I know them,
and they follow me. [28]I give them eternal
life, and they will never die, and no one can

devotion 290

JOHN 10:27–29

ARE YOU IN THE HANDS OF GOD?

When you are a follower of Jesus, you are guaranteed to have eternal life. Hallelujah! And from the day you give your life to Jesus until eternity, no one will be able to steal you from the hand of God. Double hallelujah!

It's not that the enemy doesn't try. He can make you think you are so far from God that there is no way home and not enough forgiveness left for a loser like you. He can send others to attack with their words and their discouragement and their guilt. He can tempt you to walk away from God and stay there. You can even make really poor choices that leave you spiritually and emotionally crippled.

But when you belong to God, no one else can have you. No circumstance can take you away from his love. No consequence can steal you from the hand of the Father. God does not turn away or give up and give you over to Satan. You might endure the punishment that comes from discipline, but you can never be taken away from God.

What would change today if you could see yourself still safe and secure inside the hand of God? Would you bow down with gratefulness? Would you love differently because of the lavish love God has given to you? Or would you just crawl up in those great big hands and rest? God has you. It's settled for now and all eternity. Let those powerful words of assurance give you peace.

Mary of Bethany

JOHN 11

Mary is surrounded in her home by mourners who have come to grieve with her, but they are unable to comfort her soul. Her brother Lazarus is dead, and her heart is broken beyond repair. Her tears have dried up, and she rocks in a chair, holding her brother's cloak in her hands.

"It is Jesus," her sister Martha says, running from the house. But Mary does not move. Even the glimpse of their trusted friend cannot bring relief. Martha enters the home and kneels before Mary, lifting her face. "The Teacher is here and he is asking for you," she whispers. Mary nods and runs to where Jesus is waiting. When she catches sight of him, her tears flow freely again. Sobs rack her body as she falls at his feet. "Lord, if you had been here, my brother would not have died."

Her loss is tremendous, and Jesus is moved by her brokenness. His voice is quiet as he bends close to her. "Where did you bury him?" She leads him to the tomb and stands at his side as Jesus weeps. Was he crying over the death of Lazarus, or was it something more?

When Lazarus walks out of the tomb, Jesus does not celebrate—and Mary's heart aches. The Light of heaven has given her brother life, but she senses that darkness will soon come for Jesus.

In times of loss and celebration, Mary looked to Jesus. Where do you turn?

steal them out of my hand. 29My Father gave
my sheep to me. He is greater than all, and
no person can steal my sheep out of my
Father's hand. 30The Father and I are one."

31Again some of the people picked up
stones to kill Jesus. 32But he said to them,
"I have done many good works from the
Father. Which of these good works are you
killing me for?"

33They answered, "We are not killing you
because of any good work you did, but
because you speak against God. You are only
a human, but you say you are the same as
God!"

34Jesus answered, "It is written in your law
that God said, 'I said, you are gods.'[n] 35This
Scripture called those people gods who
received God's message, and Scripture is
always true. 36So why do you say that I speak
against God because I said, 'I am God's Son'?
I am the one God chose and sent into the
world. 37If I don't do what my Father does,
then don't believe me. 38But if I do what my
Father does, even though you don't believe
in me, believe what I do. Then you will
know and understand that the Father is in
me and I am in the Father."

39They tried to take Jesus again, but he
escaped from them.

40Then he went back across the Jordan
River to the place where John had first
baptized. Jesus stayed there, 41and many
people came to him and said, "John never
did a miracle, but everything John said about
this man is true." 42And in that place many
believed in Jesus.

The Death of Lazarus

11 A man named Lazarus was sick. He
lived in the town of Bethany, where
Mary and her sister Martha lived. 2Mary
was the woman who later put perfume on
the Lord and wiped his feet with her hair.
Mary's brother was Lazarus, the man who
was now sick. 3So Mary and Martha sent
someone to tell Jesus, "Lord, the one you
love is sick."

4When Jesus heard this, he said, "This
sickness will not end in death. It is for the
glory of God, to bring glory to the Son of
God." 5Jesus loved Martha and her sister and
Lazarus. 6But when he heard that Lazarus

10:34 'I . . . gods.' Quotation from Psalm 82:6.

was sick, he stayed where he was for two
more days. [7]Then Jesus said to his followers,
"Let's go back to Judea."
[8]The followers said, "But Teacher, some
people there tried to stone you to death only
a short time ago. Now you want to go back
there?"
[9]Jesus answered, "Are there not twelve
hours in the day? If anyone walks in the
daylight, he will not stumble, because he can
see by this world's light. [10]But if anyone
walks at night, he stumbles because there is
no light to help him see."
[11]After Jesus said this, he added, "Our
friend Lazarus has fallen asleep, but I am
going there to wake him."
[12]The followers said, "But Lord, if he is
only asleep, he will be all right."
[13]Jesus meant that Lazarus was dead, but
his followers thought he meant Lazarus was
really sleeping. [14]So then Jesus said plainly,
"Lazarus is dead. [15]And I am glad for your
sakes I was not there so that you may
believe. But let's go to him now."
[16]Then Thomas (the one called Didymus)
said to the other followers, "Let us also go so
that we can die with him."

Jesus in Bethany

[17]When Jesus arrived, he learned that
Lazarus had already been dead and in the
tomb for four days. [18]Bethany was about two
miles from Jerusalem. [19]Many of the Jews
had come there to comfort Martha and Mary
about their brother.
[20]When Martha heard that Jesus was
coming, she went out to meet him, but Mary
stayed home. [21]Martha said to Jesus, "Lord, if
you had been here, my brother would not
have died. [22]But I know that even now God
will give you anything you ask."
[23]Jesus said, "Your brother will rise and
live again."
[24]Martha answered, "I know that he will
rise and live again in the resurrection[n] on
the last day."
[25]Jesus said to her, "I am the resurrection
and the life. Those who believe in me will
have life even if they die. [26]And everyone
who lives and believes in me will never die.
Martha, do you believe this?"
[27]Martha answered, "Yes, Lord. I believe
that you are the Christ, the Son of God, the
One coming to the world."

Jesus Cries

[28]After Martha said this, she went back
and talked to her sister Mary alone. Martha
said, "The Teacher is here and he is asking
for you." [29]When Mary heard this, she got up
quickly and went to Jesus. [30]Jesus had not
yet come into the town but was still at the
place where Martha had met him. [31]The
Jews were with Mary in the house,
comforting her. When they saw her stand
and leave quickly, they followed her,
thinking she was going to the tomb to cry
there.
[32]But Mary went to the place where Jesus
was. When she saw him, she fell at his feet
and said, "Lord, if you had been here, my
brother would not have died."
[33]When Jesus saw Mary crying and the
Jews who came with her also crying, he was
upset and was deeply troubled. [34]He asked,
"Where did you bury him?"
"Come and see, Lord," they said.
[35]Jesus cried.
[36]So the Jews said, "See how much he
loved him."
[37]But some of them said, "If Jesus opened
the eyes of the blind man, why couldn't he
keep Lazarus from dying?"

Jesus Raises Lazarus

[38]Again feeling very upset, Jesus came to
the tomb. It was a cave with a large stone
covering the entrance. [39]Jesus said, "Move
the stone away."
Martha, the sister of the dead man, said,
"But, Lord, it has been four days since he
died. There will be a bad smell."
[40]Then Jesus said to her, "Didn't I tell you
that if you believed you would see the glory
of God?"
[41]So they moved the stone away from the
entrance. Then Jesus looked up and said,
"Father, I thank you that you heard me. [42]I
know that you always hear me, but I said
these things because of the people here
around me. I want them to believe that you
sent me." [43]After Jesus said this, he cried out
in a loud voice, "Lazarus, come out!" [44]The
dead man came out, his hands and feet

11:24 resurrection Being raised from the dead to live again.

wrapped with pieces of cloth, and a cloth
around his face.

Jesus said to them, "Take the cloth off of
him and let him go."

The Plan to Kill Jesus

45Many of the people, who had come to
visit Mary and saw what Jesus did, believed
in him. 46But some of them went to the
Pharisees and told them what Jesus had
done. 47Then the leading priests and
Pharisees called a meeting of the council.
They asked, "What should we do? This man
is doing many miracles. 48If we let him
continue doing these things, everyone will
believe in him. Then the Romans will come
and take away our Temple and our nation."

49One of the men there was Caiaphas, the
high priest that year. He said, "You people
know nothing! 50You don't realize that it is
better for one man to die for the people than
for the whole nation to be destroyed."

51Caiaphas did not think of this himself.
As high priest that year, he was really
prophesying that Jesus would die for their
nation 52and for God's scattered children to
bring them all together and make them one.

53That day they started planning to kill
Jesus. 54So Jesus no longer traveled openly
among the people. He left there and went to
a place near the desert, to a town called
Ephraim and stayed there with his followers.

55It was almost time for the Passover
Feast. Many from the country went up to
Jerusalem before the Passover to do the
special things to make themselves pure.
56The people looked for Jesus and stood in
the Temple asking each other, "Is he coming
to the Feast? What do you think?" 57But the
leading priests and the Pharisees had given
orders that if anyone knew where Jesus was,
he must tell them. Then they could arrest
him.

Jesus with Friends in Bethany

12 Six days before the Passover Feast,
Jesus went to Bethany, where Lazarus
lived. (Lazarus is the man Jesus raised from
the dead.) 2There they had a dinner for
Jesus. Martha served the food, and Lazarus
was one of the people eating with Jesus.
3Mary brought in a pint of very expensive
perfume made from pure nard. She poured
the perfume on Jesus' feet, and then she
wiped his feet with her hair. And the sweet
smell from the perfume filled the whole
house.

4Judas Iscariot, one of Jesus' followers who
would later turn against him, was there.
Judas said, 5"This perfume was worth an
entire year's wages. Why wasn't it sold and
the money given to the poor?" 6But Judas
did not really care about the poor; he said
this because he was a thief. He was the one
who kept the money box, and he often stole
from it.

7Jesus answered, "Leave her alone. It was
right for her to save this perfume for today,
the day for me to be prepared for burial.
8You will always have the poor with you,
but you will not always have me."

The Plot Against Lazarus

9A large crowd of people heard that Jesus
was in Bethany. So they went there to see
not only Jesus but Lazarus, whom Jesus
raised from the dead. 10So the leading priests
made plans to kill Lazarus, too. 11Because of
Lazarus many of the Jews were leaving them
and believing in Jesus.

Jesus Enters Jerusalem

12The next day a great crowd who had
come to Jerusalem for the Passover Feast
heard that Jesus was coming there. 13So they
took branches of palm trees and went out to
meet Jesus, shouting,

"Praise[n] God!
God bless the One who comes in the
name of the Lord!
God bless the King of Israel!" *Psalm 118:25–26*

14Jesus found a colt and sat on it. This was
as the Scripture says,

15"Don't be afraid, people of Jerusalem!
Your king is coming,
sitting on the colt of a donkey."
Zechariah 9:9

16The followers of Jesus did not
understand this at first. But after Jesus was
raised to glory, they remembered that this
had been written about him and that they
had done these things to him.

12:13 Praise Literally, "Hosanna," a Hebrew word used at first in praying to God for help, but at this time it was probably a shout of joy used in praising God or his Messiah.

People Tell About Jesus

17 There had been many people with Jesus
when he raised Lazarus from the dead and
told him to come out of the tomb. Now they
were telling others about what Jesus did.
18 Many people went out to meet Jesus,
because they had heard about this miracle.
19 So the Pharisees said to each other, "You
can see that nothing is going right for us.
Look! The whole world is following him."

Jesus Talks About His Death

20 There were some Greek people, too, who
came to Jerusalem to worship at the Passover
Feast. 21 They went to Philip, who was from
Bethsaida in Galilee, and said, "Sir, we would
like to see Jesus." 22 Philip told Andrew, and
then Andrew and Philip told Jesus.
23 Jesus said to them, "The time has come
for the Son of Man to receive his glory. 24 I
tell you the truth, a grain of wheat must fall
to the ground and die to make many seeds.
But if it never dies, it remains only a single
seed. 25 Those who love their lives will lose
them, but those who hate their lives in this
world will keep true life forever. 26 Whoever
serves me must follow me. Then my servant
will be with me everywhere I am. My Father
will honor anyone who serves me.
27 "Now I am very troubled. Should I say,
'Father, save me from this time'? No, I came
to this time so I could suffer. 28 Father, bring
glory to your name!"
Then a voice came from heaven, "I have
brought glory to it, and I will do it again."
29 The crowd standing there, who heard
the voice, said it was thunder.
But others said, "An angel has spoken to
him."
30 Jesus said, "That voice was for your sake,
not mine. 31 Now is the time for the world to
be judged; now the ruler of this world will be
thrown down. 32 If I am lifted up from the
earth, I will draw all people toward me."
33 Jesus said this to show how he would die.
34 The crowd said, "We have heard from
the law that the Christ will live forever. So
why do you say, 'The Son of Man must be
lifted up'? Who is this 'Son of Man'?"
35 Then Jesus said, "The light will be
with you for a little longer, so walk while
you have the light. Then the darkness will
not catch you. If you walk in the darkness,
you will not know where you are going.
36 Believe in the light while you still have it
so that you will become children of light."
When Jesus had said this, he left and hid
himself from them.

Some People Won't Believe in Jesus

37 Though Jesus had done many miracles
in front of the people, they still did not
believe in him. 38 This was to bring about
what Isaiah the prophet had said:

"Lord, who believed what we told them?
Who saw the Lord's power in this?"
Isaiah 53:1

39 This is why the people could not believe:
Isaiah also had said,
40 "He has blinded their eyes,
and he has closed their minds.
Otherwise they would see with their
eyes
and understand in their minds
and come back to me and be healed."
Isaiah 6:10

41 Isaiah said this because he saw Jesus' glory
and spoke about him.
42 But many believed in Jesus, even many
of the leaders. But because of the Pharisees,
they did not say they believed in him for fear
they would be put out of the synagogue.
43 They loved praise from people more than
praise from God.
44 Then Jesus cried out, "Whoever believes
in me is really believing in the One who sent
me. 45 Whoever sees me sees the One who
sent me. 46 I have come as light into the
world so that whoever believes in me would
not stay in darkness.
47 "Anyone who hears my words and does
not obey them, I do not judge, because I did
not come to judge the world, but to save the
world. 48 There is a judge for those who refuse
to believe in me and do not accept my words.
The word I have taught will be their judge
on the last day. 49 The things I taught were
not from myself. The Father who sent me
told me what to say and what to teach. 50 And
I know that eternal life comes from what
the Father commands. So whatever I say is
what the Father told me to say."

Jesus Washes His Followers' Feet

13 It was almost time for the Passover
Feast. Jesus knew that it was time for

him to leave this world and go back to the Father. He had always loved those who were his own in the world, and he loved them all the way to the end.

2 Jesus and his followers were at the evening meal. The devil had already persuaded Judas Iscariot, the son of Simon, to turn against Jesus. 3 Jesus knew that the Father had given him power over everything and that he had come from God and was going back to God. 4 So during the meal Jesus stood up and took off his outer clothing. Taking a towel, he wrapped it around his waist. 5 Then he poured water into a bowl and began to wash the followers' feet, drying them with the towel that was wrapped around him.

6 Jesus came to Simon Peter, who said to him, "Lord, are you going to wash my feet?"

7 Jesus answered, "You don't understand now what I am doing, but you will understand later."

8 Peter said, "No, you will never wash my feet."

Jesus answered, "If I don't wash your feet, you are not one of my people."

9 Simon Peter answered, "Lord, then wash not only my feet, but wash my hands and my head, too!"

10 Jesus said, "After a person has had a bath, his whole body is clean. He needs only to wash his feet. And you men are clean, but not all of you." 11 Jesus knew who would turn against him, and that is why he said, "Not all of you are clean."

12 When he had finished washing their feet, he put on his clothes and sat down again. He asked, "Do you understand what I have just done for you? 13 You call me 'Teacher' and 'Lord,' and you are right, because that is what I am. 14 If I, your Lord and Teacher, have washed your feet, you also should wash each other's feet. 15 I did this as an example so that you should do as I have done for you. 16 I tell you the truth, a servant is not greater than his master. A messenger is not greater than the one who sent him. 17 If you know these things, you will be blessed if you do them.

18 "I am not talking about all of you. I know those I have chosen. But this is to bring about what the Scripture said: 'The man who ate at my table has turned against me.'[n] 19 I am telling you this now before it happens so that when it happens, you will believe that I am he. 20 I tell you the truth, whoever accepts anyone I send also accepts me. And whoever accepts me also accepts the One who sent me."

Jesus Talks About His Death

21 After Jesus said this, he was very troubled. He said openly, "I tell you the truth, one of you will turn against me."

22 The followers all looked at each other, because they did not know whom Jesus was talking about. 23 One of the followers sitting[n] next to Jesus was the follower Jesus loved. 24 Simon Peter motioned to him to ask Jesus whom he was talking about.

25 That follower leaned closer to Jesus and asked, "Lord, who is it?"

26 Jesus answered, "I will dip this bread into the dish. The man I give it to is the man who will turn against me." So Jesus took a piece of bread, dipped it, and gave it to Judas Iscariot, the son of Simon. 27 As soon as Judas took the bread, Satan entered him. Jesus said to him, "The thing that you will do—do it quickly." 28 No one at the table understood why Jesus said this to Judas. 29 Since he was the one who kept the money box, some of the followers thought Jesus was telling him to buy what was needed for the feast or to give something to the poor.

30 Judas took the bread Jesus gave him and immediately went out. It was night.

31 When Judas was gone, Jesus said, "Now the Son of Man receives his glory, and God receives glory through him. 32 If God receives glory through him,[n] then God will give glory to the Son through himself. And God will give him glory quickly."

33 Jesus said, "My children, I will be with you only a little longer. You will look for me, and what I told the Jews, I tell you now: Where I am going you cannot come.

34 "I give you a new command: Love each other. You must love each other as I have loved you. 35 All people will know that you are my followers if you love each other."

13:18 'The man . . . me.' Quotation from Psalm 41:9. **13:23 sitting** Literally, "lying." The people of that time ate lying down and leaning on one arm. **13:32 If . . . him** Some Greek copies do not have this phrase.

Peter Will Say He Doesn't Know Jesus

36 Simon Peter asked Jesus, "Lord, where
are you going?"
Jesus answered, "Where I am going you
cannot follow now, but you will follow
later."
37 Peter asked, "Lord, why can't I follow
you now? I am ready to die for you!"
38 Jesus answered, "Are you ready to die for
me? I tell you the truth, before the rooster
crows, you will say three times that you
don't know me."

Jesus Comforts His Followers

14 Jesus said, "Don't let your hearts be
troubled. Trust in God, and trust in
me. 2 There are many rooms in my Father's
house; I would not tell you this if it were not
true. I am going there to prepare a place for
you. 3 After I go and prepare a place for you, I
will come back and take you to be with me
so that you may be where I am. 4 You know
the way to the place where I am going."[n]
5 Thomas said to Jesus, "Lord, we don't
know where you are going. So how can we
know the way?"
6 Jesus answered, "I am the way, and the
truth, and the life. The only way to the
Father is through me. 7 If you really knew
me, you would know my Father, too. But
now you do know him, and you have seen
him."
8 Philip said to him, "Lord, show us the
Father. That is all we need."
9 Jesus answered, "I have been with you
a long time now. Do you still not know me,
Philip? Whoever has seen me has seen the
Father. So why do you say, 'Show us the
Father'? 10 Don't you believe that I am in
the Father and the Father is in me? The
words I say to you don't come from me, but
the Father lives in me and does his own
work. 11 Believe me when I say that I am in
the Father and the Father is in me. Or
believe because of the miracles I have
done. 12 I tell you the truth, whoever
believes in me will do the same things
that I do. Those who believe will do even
greater things than these, because I am
going to the Father. 13 And if you ask for
anything in my name, I will do it for you
so that the Father's glory will be shown
through the Son. 14 If you ask me for
anything in my name, I will do it.

14:4 You . . . going. Some Greek copies read "You know where I am going and the way to the place I am going."

devotion 291

JOHN 14:1

TRUTH IN A HEART-SHAPED BOX

John 14:1 is the beginning of one of the most promising and encouraging chapters in the Bible, so I want to encourage you to go ahead and read all of John 14. However, in case you can't right now, let me tell you that it's a message directly from Christ about his desire for us to know him and live with him in heaven. If we trust in him, as verse 1 instructs us, we can have the gifts he goes on to describe in the rest of the chapter. If we trust in Christ—if we believe he is God's Son and the only way to heaven—then we'll all be there together someday. So then, why do we worry? Why do we let our "hearts be troubled?" If we have Christ, we have no reason to worry about anything.

I know a woman who has John 14:1 nestled in a tiny heart-shaped gift box on her desk at work, and when she feels extremely tested, she takes it out and reads it to herself. She's read it so many times that she now has it memorized, but seeing the words helps her focus on their meaning, and keeping them in the box reminds her to hide his Word "in her heart" (see Ps. 119:11). We ought to borrow her idea, and while we don't have to have a heart-shaped box, we should write this verse on our own hearts and remember it when we're having a particularly demanding day.

The Promise of the Holy Spirit

15“If you love me, you will obey my
commands. 16I will ask the Father, and he
will give you another Helper[n] to be with you
forever— 17the Spirit of truth. The world
cannot accept him, because it does not see
him or know him. But you know him,
because he lives with you and he will be
in you.

18“I will not leave you all alone like
orphans; I will come back to you. 19In a little
while the world will not see me anymore,
but you will see me. Because I live, you will
live, too. 20On that day you will know that
I am in my Father, and that you are in me
and I am in you. 21Those who know my
commands and obey them are the ones who
love me, and my Father will love those who
love me. I will love them and will show
myself to them.”

22Then Judas (not Judas Iscariot) said,
“But, Lord, why do you plan to show yourself
to us and not to the rest of the world?”

23Jesus answered, “If people love me, they
will obey my teaching. My Father will love
them, and we will come to them and make
our home with them. 24Those who do not
love me do not obey my teaching. This
teaching that you hear is not really mine;
it is from my Father, who sent me.

25“I have told you all these things while I
am with you. 26But the Helper will teach you
everything and will cause you to remember
all that I told you. This Helper is the Holy
Spirit whom the Father will send in my
name.

27“I leave you peace; my peace I give you.
I do not give it to you as the world does. So
don’t let your hearts be troubled or afraid.
28You heard me say to you, ‘I am going, but I
am coming back to you.’ If you loved me,
you should be happy that I am going back
to the Father, because he is greater than I
am. 29I have told you this now, before it
happens, so that when it happens, you will
believe. 30I will not talk with you much
longer, because the ruler of this world is
coming. He has no power over me, 31but
the world must know that I love the Father,
so I do exactly what the Father told me
to do.

“Come now, let us go.

Jesus Is Like a Vine

15 “I am the true vine; my Father is the
gardener. 2He cuts off every branch of
mine that does not produce fruit. And he
trims and cleans every branch that produces
fruit so that it will produce even more fruit.
3You are already clean because of the words
I have spoken to you. 4Remain in me, and
I will remain in you. A branch cannot
produce fruit alone but must remain in the
vine. In the same way, you cannot produce
fruit alone but must remain in me.

5“I am the vine, and you are the branches.
If any remain in me and I remain in them,
they produce much fruit. But without me
they can do nothing. 6If any do not remain
in me, they are like a branch that is thrown
away and then dies. People pick up dead
branches, throw them into the fire, and burn
them. 7If you remain in me and follow my
teachings, you can ask anything you want,
and it will be given to you. 8You should
produce much fruit and show that you are
my followers, which brings glory to my
Father. 9I loved you as the Father loved me.
Now remain in my love. 10I have obeyed my
Father’s commands, and I remain in his love.
In the same way, if you obey my commands,
you will remain in my love. 11I have told you
these things so that you can have the same
joy I have and so that your joy will be the
fullest possible joy.

12“This is my command: Love each other
as I have loved you. 13The greatest love a
person can show is to die for his friends.
14You are my friends if you do what I
command you. 15I no longer call you
servants, because a servant does not know
what his master is doing. But I call you
friends, because I have made known to you
everything I heard from my Father. 16You did
not choose me; I chose you. And I gave you
this work: to go and produce fruit, fruit that
will last. Then the Father will give you
anything you ask for in my name. 17This is
my command: Love each other.

Jesus Warns His Followers

18“If the world hates you, remember that
it hated me first. 19If you belonged to the
world, it would love you as it loves its own.
But I have chosen you out of the world, so

14:16 Helper “Counselor” or “Comforter.” Jesus is talking about the Holy Spirit.

devotion 292

JOHN 15:5

RIPEN ON THE VINE

You are a tender, sweet branch that Jesus is feeding into, and if you are attached to anything other than the vine, you need a transplant—and fast! All through my walk, I have found myself attached to all sorts of things other than the vine, and it's only a matter of time before God reaches down and snips away that connection. Are you attached to your job? Is your only fulfillment coming from the attention or success you are getting through your work? What about relationships? Are you attached to someone that is not a believer, and you have slipped back into old habits that you once laid down? What about your church? Are you so consumed with *serving* at the church that you are missing out on what is going on in the pulpit—or the altar?

I know it is easy to look at everything that needs to be accomplished and think, "It's better to do it in my own strength than leave it undone." We all experience those frustrations when we throw in the towel and say, "That's it! I'll do it since no one else will." You have to realize that when Jesus guides you, he will provide a way. Sometimes that way is not through you. He wants you—all of you—not just your service. He wants to lead you with the Holy Spirit. When you follow his leading, you will see a beautiful crop of godly accomplishments that the two of you completed together.

you don't belong to it. That is why the world
hates you. 20Remember what I told you: A
servant is not greater than his master. If
people did wrong to me, they will do wrong
to you, too. And if they obeyed my teaching,
they will obey yours, too. 21They will do all
this to you on account of me, because they
do not know the One who sent me. 22If I had
not come and spoken to them, they would
not be guilty of sin, but now they have no
excuse for their sin. 23Whoever hates me
also hates my Father. 24I did works among
them that no one else has ever done. If I had
not done these works, they would not be
guilty of sin. But now they have seen what I
have done, and yet they have hated both me
and my Father. 25But this happened so that
what is written in their law would be true:
'They hated me for no reason.'[n]

26"I will send you the Helper[n] from the
Father; he is the Spirit of truth who comes
from the Father. When he comes, he will tell
about me, 27and you also must tell people
about me, because you have been with me
from the beginning.

16 "I have told you these things to keep
you from giving up. 2People will put
you out of their synagogues. Yes, the time is
coming when those who kill you will think
they are offering service to God. 3They will
do this because they have not known the
Father and they have not known me. 4I have
told you these things now so that when the
time comes you will remember that I
warned you.

The Work of the Holy Spirit

"I did not tell you these things at the
beginning, because I was with you then.
5Now I am going back to the One who sent
me. But none of you asks me, 'Where are you
going?' 6Your hearts are filled with sadness
because I have told you these things. 7But I
tell you the truth, it is better for you that I go

15:25 'They . . . reason.' These words could be from Psalm 35:19 or Psalm 69:4.
15:26 Helper "Counselor" or "Comforter." Jesus is talking about the Holy Spirit.

away. When I go away, I will send the
Helper[n] to you. If I do not go away, the
Helper will not come. 8When the Helper
comes, he will prove to the people of the
world the truth about sin, about being right
with God, and about judgment. 9He will
prove to them that sin is not believing in me.
10He will prove to them that being right
with God comes from my going to the
Father and not being seen anymore. 11And
the Helper will prove to them that judgment
happened when the ruler of this world was
judged.

12"I have many more things to say to you,
but they are too much for you now. 13But
when the Spirit of truth comes, he will lead
you into all truth. He will not speak his own
words, but he will speak only what he hears,
and he will tell you what is to come. 14The
Spirit of truth will bring glory to me,
because he will take what I have to say and
tell it to you. 15All that the Father has is
mine. That is why I said that the Spirit will
take what I have to say and tell it to you.

Sadness Will Become Happiness

16"After a little while you will not see me,
and then after a little while you will see me
again."

17Some of the followers said to each other,
"What does Jesus mean when he says, 'After
a little while you will not see me, and then
after a little while you will see me again'?
And what does he mean when he says,
'Because I am going to the Father'?" 18They
also asked, "What does he mean by 'a little
while'? We don't understand what he is
saying."

19Jesus saw that the followers wanted to
ask him about this, so he said to them, "Are
you asking each other what I meant when I
said, 'After a little while you will not see me,
and then after a little while you will see me
again'? 20I tell you the truth, you will cry and
be sad, but the world will be happy. You will
be sad, but your sadness will become joy.
21When a woman gives birth to a baby, she
has pain, because her time has come. But
when her baby is born, she forgets the pain,
because she is so happy that a child has been
born into the world. 22It is the same with
you. Now you are sad, but I will see you
again and you will be happy, and no one will
take away your joy. 23In that day you will
not ask me for anything. I tell you the truth,
my Father will give you anything you ask for
in my name. 24Until now you have not asked
for anything in my name. Ask and you will
receive, so that your joy will be the fullest
possible joy.

Victory over the World

25"I have told you these things indirectly
in stories. But the time will come when I will
not use stories like that to tell you things; I
will speak to you in plain words about the
Father. 26In that day you will ask the Father
for things in my name. I mean, I will not
need to ask the Father for you. 27The Father
himself loves you. He loves you because you
loved me and believed that I came from God.
28I came from the Father into the world.
Now I am leaving the world and going back
to the Father."

29Then the followers of Jesus said, "You
are speaking clearly to us now and are not
using stories that are hard to understand.
30We can see now that you know all things.
You can answer a person's question even
before it is asked. This makes us believe you
came from God."

31Jesus answered, "So now you believe?
32Listen to me; a time is coming when you
will be scattered, each to your own home.
That time is now here. You will leave me
alone, but I am never really alone, because
the Father is with me.

33"I told you these things so that you can
have peace in me. In this world you will
have trouble, but be brave! I have defeated
the world."

Jesus Prays for His Followers

17 After Jesus said these things, he
looked toward heaven and prayed,
"Father, the time has come. Give glory to
your Son so that the Son can give glory to
you. 2You gave the Son power over all people
so that the Son could give eternal life to all
those you gave him. 3And this is eternal life:
that people know you, the only true God,
and that they know Jesus Christ, the One
you sent. 4Having finished the work you
gave me to do, I brought you glory on earth.

16:7 Helper "Counselor" or "Comforter." Jesus is talking about the Holy Spirit.

devotion 293

JOHN 16:33

PANIC ATTACK!

When I forget whom I belong to, I begin to feel frantic on the inside. Do you know that kind of inner chaos? I'm a single mom, and I can worry about the kids and their attitudes and how much therapy they're probably going to need and how in the world we're going to pay for college. Before I know it, my heart is pounding, and I'm trying to get a deep breath. Or I can feel my singleness scream at me. Like when the guy who said he'd call doesn't call. I lose hope that there will ever be anyone to hold my hand. Or people say reckless things and my spirit nose-dives right into the pit.

And every time I feel myself lost or afraid and without peace, it's because I have forgotten whose I am. I am a daughter of God. He is wildly in love with me. I have been set apart. I don't have to live in chaos or manipulate circumstances or date a loser. In this world, there may be trouble, but I can live in confidence. Jesus has promised to come to my rescue. He will give peace. He will defeat my enemies. He will bring his love in his way and in his time.

I hate it when I forget and spend half a day whining. Then I remember, "Oh yeah, Jesus lives inside of me. He has already won the battles in my life." Remembering that truth will make every forgetful woman brave!

5And now, Father, give me glory with you;
give me the glory I had with you before the
world was made.
6"I showed what you are like to those you
gave me from the world. They belonged to
you, and you gave them to me, and they
have obeyed your teaching. 7Now they know
that everything you gave me comes from
you. 8I gave them the teachings you gave me,
and they accepted them. They knew that I
truly came from you, and they believed that
you sent me. 9I am praying for them. I am
not praying for people in the world but for
those you gave me, because they are yours.
10All I have is yours, and all you have is
mine. And my glory is shown through them.
11I am coming to you; I will not stay in the
world any longer. But they are still in the
world. Holy Father, keep them safe by the
power of your name, the name you gave me,
so that they will be one, just as you and I are
one. 12While I was with them, I kept them
safe by the power of your name, the name
you gave me. I protected them, and only one
of them, the one worthy of destruction, was
lost so that the Scripture would come true.
13"I am coming to you now. But I pray
these things while I am still in the world so
that these followers can have all of my joy in
them. 14I have given them your teaching.
And the world has hated them, because they
don't belong to the world, just as I don't
belong to the world. 15I am not asking you to
take them out of the world but to keep them
safe from the Evil One. 16They don't belong
to the world, just as I don't belong to the
world. 17Make them ready for your service
through your truth; your teaching is truth.
18I have sent them into the world, just as you
sent me into the world. 19For their sake, I am
making myself ready to serve so that they
can be ready for their service of the truth.
20"I pray for these followers, but I am also
praying for all those who will believe in me
because of their teaching. 21Father, I pray
that they can be one. As you are in me and I
am in you, I pray that they can also be one in
us. Then the world will believe that you sent

me. 22 I have given these people the glory that you gave me so that they can be one, just as you and I are one. 23 I will be in them and you will be in me so that they will be completely one. Then the world will know that you sent me and that you loved them just as much as you loved me.

24 "Father, I want these people that you gave me to be with me where I am. I want them to see my glory, which you gave me because you loved me before the world was made. 25 Father, you are the One who is good. The world does not know you, but I know you, and these people know you sent me. 26 I showed them what you are like, and I will show them again. Then they will have the same love that you have for me, and I will live in them."

Jesus Is Arrested

18 When Jesus finished praying, he went with his followers across the Kidron Valley. On the other side there was a garden, and Jesus and his followers went into it.

2 Judas knew where this place was, because Jesus met there often with his followers. Judas was the one who turned against Jesus. 3 So Judas came there with a group of soldiers and some guards from the leading priests and the Pharisees. They were carrying torches, lanterns, and weapons.

4 Knowing everything that would happen to him, Jesus went out and asked, "Who is it you are looking for?"

5 They answered, "Jesus from Nazareth."

"I am he," Jesus said. (Judas, the one who turned against Jesus, was standing there with them.) 6 When Jesus said, "I am he," they moved back and fell to the ground.

7 Jesus asked them again, "Who is it you are looking for?"

They said, "Jesus of Nazareth."

8 "I told you that I am he," Jesus said. "So if you are looking for me, let the others go." 9 This happened so that the words Jesus said before would come true: "I have not lost any of the ones you gave me."

10 Simon Peter, who had a sword, pulled it out and struck the servant of the high priest, cutting off his right ear. (The servant's name was Malchus.) 11 Jesus said to Peter, "Put your sword back. Shouldn't I drink the cup[n] the Father gave me?"

Jesus Is Brought Before Annas

12 Then the soldiers with their commander and the guards arrested Jesus. They tied him 13 and led him first to Annas, the father-in-law of Caiaphas, the high priest that year. 14 Caiaphas was the one who told the Jews that it would be better if one man died for all the people.

Peter Says He Doesn't Know Jesus

15 Simon Peter and another one of Jesus' followers went along after Jesus. This follower knew the high priest, so he went with Jesus into the high priest's courtyard. 16 But Peter waited outside near the door. The follower who knew the high priest came back outside, spoke to the girl at the door, and brought Peter inside. 17 The girl at the door said to Peter, "Aren't you also one of that man's followers?"

Peter answered, "No, I am not!"

18 It was cold, so the servants and guards had built a fire and were standing around it, warming themselves. Peter also was standing with them, warming himself.

The High Priest Questions Jesus

19 The high priest asked Jesus questions about his followers and his teaching. 20 Jesus answered, "I have spoken openly to everyone. I have always taught in synagogues and in the Temple, where all the Jews come together. I never said anything in secret. 21 So why do you question me? Ask the people who heard my teaching. They know what I said."

22 When Jesus said this, one of the guards standing there hit him. The guard said, "Is that the way you answer the high priest?"

23 Jesus answered him, "If I said something wrong, then show what it was. But if what I said is true, why do you hit me?"

24 Then Annas sent Jesus, who was still tied, to Caiaphas the high priest.

Peter Says Again He Doesn't Know Jesus

25 As Simon Peter was standing and warming himself, they said to him, "Aren't you one of that man's followers?"

18:11 cup Jesus is talking about the painful things that will happen to him. Accepting these things will be very hard, like drinking a cup of something bitter.

Peter said it was not true; he said, "No, I
am not."
26 One of the servants of the high priest
was there. This servant was a relative of the
man whose ear Peter had cut off. The servant
said, "Didn't I see you with him in the
garden?"
27 Again Peter said it wasn't true. At once a
rooster crowed.

Jesus Is Brought Before Pilate

28 Early in the morning they led Jesus
from Caiaphas's house to the Roman
governor's palace. They would not go inside
the palace, because they did not want to
make themselves unclean;[n] they wanted
to eat the Passover meal. 29 So Pilate went
outside to them and asked, "What charges
do you bring against this man?"
30 They answered, "If he were not a
criminal, we wouldn't have brought him
to you."
31 Pilate said to them, "Take him
yourselves and judge him by your own law."
"But we are not allowed to put anyone to
death," the Jews answered. 32 (This happened
so that what Jesus said about how he would
die would come true.)
33 Then Pilate went back inside the palace
and called Jesus to him and asked, "Are you
the king of the Jews?"
34 Jesus said, "Is that your own question, or
did others tell you about me?"
35 Pilate answered, "I am not one of you.
It was your own people and their leading
priests who handed you over to me. What
have you done wrong?"
36 Jesus answered, "My kingdom does not
belong to this world. If it belonged to this
world, my servants would have fought to
keep me from being given over to the Jewish
leaders. But my kingdom is from another
place."
37 Pilate said, "So you are a king!"
Jesus answered, "You are the one saying I
am a king. This is why I was born and came
into the world: to tell people the truth. And
everyone who belongs to the truth listens
to me."
38 Pilate said, "What is truth?" After he said
this, he went out to the crowd again and said
to them, "I find nothing against this man.
39 But it is your custom that I free one
prisoner to you at Passover time. Do you
want me to free the 'king of the Jews'?"
40 They shouted back, "No, not him! Let
Barabbas go free!" (Barabbas was a robber.)

19 Then Pilate ordered that Jesus be
taken away and whipped. 2 The
soldiers made a crown from some thorny
branches and put it on Jesus' head and put a
purple robe around him. 3 Then they came to
him many times and said, "Hail, King of the
Jews!" and hit him in the face.
4 Again Pilate came out and said to them,
"Look, I am bringing Jesus out to you. I want
you to know that I find nothing against
him." 5 So Jesus came out, wearing the crown
of thorns and the purple robe. Pilate said to
them, "Here is the man!"
6 When the leading priests and the guards
saw Jesus, they shouted, "Crucify him!
Crucify him!"
But Pilate answered, "Crucify him
yourselves, because I find nothing against
him."
7 The leaders answered, "We have a law
that says he should die, because he said he is
the Son of God."
8 When Pilate heard this, he was even
more afraid. 9 He went back inside the palace
and asked Jesus, "Where do you come from?"
But Jesus did not answer him. 10 Pilate said,
"You refuse to speak to me? Don't you know
I have power to set you free and power to
have you crucified?"
11 Jesus answered, "The only power you
have over me is the power given to you by
God. The man who turned me in to you is
guilty of a greater sin."
12 After this, Pilate tried to let Jesus go.
But some in the crowd cried out, "Anyone
who makes himself king is against Caesar.
If you let this man go, you are no friend of
Caesar."
13 When Pilate heard what they were
saying, he brought Jesus out and sat down
on the judge's seat at the place called The
Stone Pavement. (In the Hebrew language[n]
the name is Gabbatha.) 14 It was about noon
on Preparation Day of Passover week. Pilate
said to the crowd, "Here is your king!"

18:28 unclean Going into the Roman palace would make them unfit to eat the Passover Feast, according to their Law.
19:13 Hebrew language Or Aramaic, the languages of many people in this region in the first century.

Mary Magdalene

JOHN 20

Mary Magdalene runs through the darkened back streets, trying not to draw attention to herself. She muffles her cries as she enters the garden where Jesus has been buried. There is no one here. *Does no one care?* she wonders.

For years no one would come close to her; she had to steal or beg for food. Seven demons made her a castoff in society. Loneliness had engulfed her until he touched her. When Jesus called out the demons, she was free from the suffering and pain and humiliation. She followed him willingly and gave everything she had to help him spread his Good News.

But now Jesus is dead, and she is once again alone. She creeps to the tomb so she can draw close to him in death. She feels the wind knocked out of her—the stone has been rolled away, and her Savior is gone! *Why would they take him?* she moans. Tears stream down her face as she kneels before the gaping hole.

"Woman, why are you crying?" The voice startles her, but she is unable to contain her grief.

She assumes he's the gardener. "Did you take him away, sir?"

"Mary." The voice is gentle and strong, full of comfort and hope.

She leaps to her feet. Jesus is alive! He could have gone to the high priest or to Pilate, but instead chose her as the first witness to his resurrection.

Jesus reveals himself to the poor in spirit.

15They shouted, "Take him away! Take
him away! Crucify him!"
Pilate asked them, "Do you want me to
crucify your king?"
The leading priests answered, "The only
king we have is Caesar."
16So Pilate handed Jesus over to them to
be crucified.

Jesus Is Crucified

The soldiers took charge of Jesus.
17Carrying his own cross, Jesus went out to a
place called The Place of the Skull, which in
the Hebrew language[n] is called Golgotha.
18There they crucified Jesus. They also
crucified two other men, one on each side,
with Jesus in the middle. 19Pilate wrote a
sign and put it on the cross. It read: JESUS OF
NAZARETH, THE KING OF THE JEWS. 20The sign was
written in Hebrew, in Latin, and in Greek.
Many of the people read the sign, because the
place where Jesus was crucified was near the
city. 21The leading priests said to Pilate,
"Don't write, 'The King of the Jews.' But write,
'This man said, "I am the King of the Jews." ' "
22Pilate answered, "What I have written, I
have written."
23After the soldiers crucified Jesus, they
took his clothes and divided them into four
parts, with each soldier getting one part. They
also took his long shirt, which was all one
piece of cloth, woven from top to bottom.
24So the soldiers said to each other, "We
should not tear this into parts. Let's throw
lots to see who will get it." This happened so
that this Scripture would come true:

> "They divided my clothes among them,
> and they threw lots for my clothing."
>
> *Psalm 22:18*

So the soldiers did this.
25Standing near his cross were Jesus'
mother, his mother's sister, Mary the wife of
Clopas, and Mary Magdalene. 26When Jesus
saw his mother and the follower he loved
standing nearby, he said to his mother, "Dear
woman, here is your son." 27Then he said to
the follower, "Here is your mother." From
that time on, the follower took her to live in
his home.

Jesus Dies

28After this, Jesus knew that everything
had been done. So that the Scripture would

19:17 Hebrew language Or Aramaic, the languages of many people in this region in the first century.

come true, he said, "I am thirsty."[n] 29There was a jar full of vinegar there, so the soldiers soaked a sponge in it, put the sponge on a branch of a hyssop plant, and lifted it to Jesus' mouth. 30When Jesus tasted the vinegar, he said, "It is finished." Then he bowed his head and died.

31This day was Preparation Day, and the next day was a special Sabbath day. Since the religious leaders did not want the bodies to stay on the cross on the Sabbath day, they asked Pilate to order that the legs of the men be broken[n] and the bodies be taken away. 32So the soldiers came and broke the legs of the first man on the cross beside Jesus. Then they broke the legs of the man on the other cross beside Jesus. 33But when the soldiers came to Jesus and saw that he was already dead, they did not break his legs. 34But one of the soldiers stuck his spear into Jesus' side, and at once blood and water came out. 35(The one who saw this happen is the one who told us this, and whatever he says is true. And he knows that he tells the truth, and he tells it so that you might believe.) 36These things happened to make the Scripture come true: "Not one of his bones will be broken."[n] 37And another Scripture says, "They will look at the one they stabbed."[n]

Jesus Is Buried

38Later, Joseph from Arimathea asked Pilate if he could take the body of Jesus. (Joseph was a secret follower of Jesus, because he was afraid of some of the leaders.) Pilate gave his permission, so Joseph came and took Jesus' body away. 39Nicodemus, who earlier had come to Jesus at night, went with Joseph. He brought about seventy-five pounds of myrrh and aloes. 40These two men took Jesus' body and wrapped it with the spices in pieces of linen cloth, which is how they bury the dead. 41In the place where Jesus was crucified, there was a garden. In the garden was a new tomb that had never been used before. 42The men laid Jesus in that tomb because it was nearby, and they were preparing to start their Sabbath day.

Jesus' Tomb Is Empty

20 Early on the first day of the week, Mary Magdalene went to the tomb while it was still dark. When she saw that the large stone had been moved away from the tomb, 2she ran to Simon Peter and the follower whom Jesus loved. Mary said, "They have taken the Lord out of the tomb, and we don't know where they have put him."

3So Peter and the other follower started for the tomb. 4They were both running, but the other follower ran faster than Peter and reached the tomb first. 5He bent down and looked in and saw the strips of linen cloth lying there, but he did not go in. 6Then following him, Simon Peter arrived and went into the tomb and saw the strips of linen lying there. 7He also saw the cloth that had been around Jesus' head, which was folded up and laid in a different place from the strips of linen. 8Then the other follower, who had reached the tomb first, also went in. He saw and believed. 9(They did not yet understand from the Scriptures that Jesus must rise from the dead.)

Jesus Appears to Mary Magdalene

10Then the followers went back home. 11But Mary stood outside the tomb, crying. As she was crying, she bent down and looked inside the tomb. 12She saw two angels dressed in white, sitting where Jesus' body had been, one at the head and one at the feet.

13They asked her, "Woman, why are you crying?"

She answered, "They have taken away my Lord, and I don't know where they have put him." 14When Mary said this, she turned around and saw Jesus standing there, but she did not know it was Jesus.

15Jesus asked her, "Woman, why are you crying? Whom are you looking for?"

Thinking he was the gardener, she said to him, "Did you take him away, sir? Tell me where you put him, and I will get him."

16Jesus said to her, "Mary."

Mary turned toward Jesus and said in the Hebrew language,[n] "Rabboni." (This means "Teacher.")

17Jesus said to her, "Don't hold on to me, because I have not yet gone up to the Father. But go to my brothers and tell them, 'I am

19:28 "I am thirsty." Read Psalms 22:15; 69:21. **19:31 broken** The breaking of their bones would make them die sooner. **19:36 "Not one . . . broken."** Quotation from Psalm 34:20. The idea is from Exodus 12:46; Numbers 9:12. **19:37 "They . . . stabbed."** Quotation from Zechariah 12:10. **20:16 Hebrew language** Or Aramaic, the languages of many people in this region in the first century.

going back to my Father and your Father, to
my God and your God.' "
18Mary Magdalene went and said to the
followers, "I saw the Lord!" And she told
them what Jesus had said to her.

Jesus Appears to His Followers

19When it was evening on the first day of
the week, Jesus' followers were together. The
doors were locked, because they were afraid
of the elders. Then Jesus came and stood
right in the middle of them and said, "Peace
be with you." 20After he said this, he showed
them his hands and his side. His followers
were thrilled when they saw the Lord.
21Then Jesus said again, "Peace be with
you. As the Father sent me, I now send you."
22After he said this, he breathed on them and
said, "Receive the Holy Spirit. 23If you forgive
anyone his sins, they are forgiven. If you
don't forgive them, they are not forgiven."

Jesus Appears to Thomas

24Thomas (called Didymus), who was one
of the twelve, was not with them when Jesus
came. 25The other followers kept telling
Thomas, "We saw the Lord."
But Thomas said, "I will not believe it
until I see the nail marks in his hands and
put my finger where the nails were and put
my hand into his side."
26A week later the followers were in the
house again, and Thomas was with them.
The doors were locked, but Jesus came in
and stood right in the middle of them. He
said, "Peace be with you." 27Then he said to
Thomas, "Put your finger here, and look at
my hands. Put your hand here in my side.
Stop being an unbeliever and believe."
28Thomas said to him, "My Lord and my
God!"
29Then Jesus told him, "You believe
because you see me. Those who believe
without seeing me will be truly blessed."

Why John Wrote This Book

30Jesus did many other miracles in the
presence of his followers that are not written
in this book. 31But these are written so that
you may believe that Jesus is the Christ, the

devotion 294

JOHN 20:21

SEND ME

When we read John 20:21, we tend to think of missionaries. They are the frontline soldiers, taking the Good News to the edge of the earth. My husband was a missions pastor for five years. We have met some of the most amazing people who are serving the Lord all over the world. They have walked away from careers and families and the comforts of the United States to go where God has called them to go. They have been sent by God just as the Scriptures declare.

When we look at this verse, we have to ask ourselves if we have been sent. This verse is referring to all believers, not just missionaries. Jesus is sending us to share his love with the lost. And you will find the lost wherever you go. We need to see a mission field everywhere we go. Our neighborhoods, our grocery stores, our schools, and our unbelieving friends are all mission fields.

I woke up one day and asked the Lord to bring someone across my path that I could share the Good News with. I went about the whole day trying to find someone, a stranger I thought, to share Christ with. But sometimes he brings you someone you least expect. Much to my surprise, during a doctor's appointment as I sat on the examination table in a paper gown, my doctor asked me about my religion, and I was able to share Christ with him. If you are willing, God will send you.

Son of God. Then, by believing, you may have life through his name.

Jesus Appears to Seven Followers

21 Later, Jesus showed himself to his followers again—this time at Lake Galilee.[n] This is how he showed himself: 2 Some of the followers were together: Simon Peter, Thomas (called Didymus), Nathanael from Cana in Galilee, the two sons of Zebedee, and two other followers. 3 Simon Peter said, "I am going out to fish."

The others said, "We will go with you." So they went out and got into the boat. They fished that night but caught nothing.

4 Early the next morning Jesus stood on the shore, but the followers did not know it was Jesus. 5 Then he said to them, "Friends, did you catch any fish?"

They answered, "No."

6 He said, "Throw your net on the right side of the boat, and you will find some." So they did, and they caught so many fish they could not pull the net back into the boat.

7 The follower whom Jesus loved said to Peter, "It is the Lord!" When Peter heard him say this, he wrapped his coat around himself. (Peter had taken his clothes off.) Then he jumped into the water. 8 The other followers went to shore in the boat, dragging the net full of fish. They were not very far from shore, only about a hundred yards. 9 When the followers stepped out of the boat and onto the shore, they saw a fire of hot coals. There were fish on the fire, and there was bread.

10 Then Jesus said, "Bring some of the fish you just caught."

11 Simon Peter went into the boat and pulled the net to the shore. It was full of big fish, one hundred fifty-three in all, but even though there were so many, the net did not tear. 12 Jesus said to them, "Come and eat." None of the followers dared ask him, "Who are you?" because they knew it was the Lord. 13 Jesus came and took the bread and gave it to them, along with the fish.

14 This was now the third time Jesus showed himself to his followers after he was raised from the dead.

Jesus Talks to Peter

15 When they finished eating, Jesus said to Simon Peter, "Simon son of John, do you love me more than these?"

He answered, "Yes, Lord, you know that I love you."

Jesus said, "Feed my lambs."

16 Again Jesus said, "Simon son of John, do you love me?"

He answered, "Yes, Lord, you know that I love you."

Jesus said, "Take care of my sheep."

17 A third time he said, "Simon son of John, do you love me?"

Peter was hurt because Jesus asked him the third time, "Do you love me?" Peter said, "Lord, you know everything; you know that I love you!"

He said to him, "Feed my sheep. 18 I tell you the truth, when you were younger, you tied your own belt and went where you wanted. But when you are old, you will put out your hands and someone else will tie you and take you where you don't want to go." 19 (Jesus said this to show how Peter would die to give glory to God.) Then Jesus said to Peter, "Follow me!"

20 Peter turned and saw that the follower Jesus loved was walking behind them. (This was the follower who had leaned against Jesus at the supper and had said, "Lord, who will turn against you?") 21 When Peter saw him behind them, he asked Jesus, "Lord, what about him?"

22 Jesus answered, "If I want him to live until I come back, that is not your business. You follow me."

23 So a story spread among the followers that this one would not die. But Jesus did not say he would not die. He only said, "If I want him to live until I come back, that is not your business."

24 That follower is the one who is telling these things and who has now written them down. We know that what he says is true.

25 There are many other things Jesus did. If every one of them were written down, I suppose the whole world would not be big enough for all the books that would be written.

21:1 Lake Galilee Literally, "Sea of Tiberias."

Acts

This book is sometimes called the "Acts of the Apostles."

Person Holding the Pen God Wrote With: *Luke*, who joined Paul's missionary team in the seaport city of Troas, penned this book (Acts 16:8–10).

When the Text Was Written: Probably between 60 and 62 A.D.

Spiritual Posture of the Original Recipients: As with his Gospel account, Luke addresses this book to Theophilus, a Roman citizen. But its wider audience included the early church, which was growing like wildfire in the face of persecution.

Storyline Synopsis: Acts is basically the follow-up to Luke's Gospel. He begins with this introduction: "The first book I wrote was about everything Jesus began to do and teach until the day he was taken up into heaven" (Acts 1:1–2). Luke then proceeds with a meticulous journal of how the message of Jesus was beginning to spread throughout the ancient world. It includes significant events such as: the election of a twelfth apostle in the wake of Judas' betrayal (1:22–26); the tangible power of the Holy Spirit at Pentecost and the establishment of the church (2:1–47); the dramatic Damascus Road conversion of "Saul the persecutor" to "Paul the apostle" (9:1–31); and several of Paul's missionary journeys (chapters 13—28). Luke's record ends abruptly with Paul's imprisonment in Rome, leading most scholars to believe that Luke put away his pen before Paul was released.

A Moment Worth Discussing: Acts 4:23–31 describes a petition commonly called the "Believers' Prayer" that the early Christians exulted immediately after John and Peter bravely defended the ministry of the Good News in front of the anti-Christian Jewish council. The gist of this passage is that God planned Jesus' death from the beginning of time so that we could be reconciled into a right relationship with him. In other words, before God stretched out the heavens, he knew his only Son would have to stretch out his arms on a cross and die to save us. The crucifixion wasn't some knee-jerk reaction to rescue humanity, it was all part of God's sovereign blueprint. We've been on God's merciful mind since the beginning of time!

Interesting (But Likely to Be Overlooked) Character: The *lame beggar* who was hanging out at the Temple hoping for handouts ended up getting much more than he requested. Instead of getting the few bucks he asked Peter and John for, he received healing. He went from being crippled to doing cartwheels (Acts 3:1–10)! His miraculous experience fanned the flames of evangelism in Jerusalem (3:11–26).

Luke Writes Another Book

1 To Theophilus.
The first book I wrote was about
everything Jesus began to do and teach
2 until the day he was taken up into heaven.
Before this, with the help of the Holy Spirit,
Jesus told the apostles he had chosen what
they should do. 3 After his death, he showed
himself to them and proved in many ways
that he was alive. The apostles saw Jesus
during the forty days after he was raised
from the dead, and he spoke to them about
the kingdom of God. 4 Once when he was
eating with them, he told them not to leave
Jerusalem. He said, "Wait here to receive the
promise from the Father which I told you
about. 5 John baptized people with water, but
in a few days you will be baptized with the
Holy Spirit."

Jesus Is Taken Up into Heaven

6 When the apostles were all together,
they asked Jesus, "Lord, are you now going to
give the kingdom back to Israel?"
7 Jesus said to them, "The Father is the
only One who has the authority to decide
dates and times. These things are not for
you to know. 8 But when the Holy Spirit
comes to you, you will receive power. You
will be my witnesses—in Jerusalem, in all
of Judea, in Samaria, and in every part of
the world."
9 After he said this, as they were watching,
he was lifted up, and a cloud hid him from
their sight. 10 As he was going, they were
looking into the sky. Suddenly, two men
wearing white clothes stood beside them.
11 They said, "Men of Galilee, why are you
standing here looking into the sky? Jesus,
whom you saw taken up from you into
heaven, will come back in the same way
you saw him go."

A New Apostle Is Chosen

12 Then they went back to Jerusalem from
the Mount of Olives. (This mountain is
about half a mile from Jerusalem.) 13 When
they entered the city, they went to the
upstairs room where they were staying.
Peter, John, James, Andrew, Philip, Thomas,
Bartholomew, Matthew, James son of
Alphaeus, Simon (known as the Zealot), and
Judas son of James were there. 14 They all
continued praying together with some
women, including Mary the mother of Jesus,
and Jesus' brothers.
15 During this time there was a meeting of
the believers (about one hundred twenty of
them). Peter stood up and said, 16-17 "Brothers
and sisters, in the Scriptures the Holy Spirit
said through David something that must
happen involving Judas. He was one of our
own group and served together with us.
He led those who arrested Jesus." 18 (Judas
bought a field with the money he got for his
evil act. But he fell to his death, his body
burst open, and all his intestines poured out.
19 Everyone in Jerusalem learned about this
so they named this place Akeldama. In their
language Akeldama means "Field of Blood.")
20 "In the Book of Psalms," Peter said, "this is
written:

'May his place be empty;
leave no one to live in it.' *Psalm 69:25*

And it is also written:

'Let another man replace him as leader.'
Psalm 109:8

21-22 "So now a man must become a
witness with us of Jesus' being raised from
the dead. He must be one of the men who
were part of our group during all the time
the Lord Jesus was among us—from the time
John was baptizing people until the day
Jesus was taken up from us to heaven."
23 They put the names of two men before
the group. One was Joseph Barsabbas, who
was also called Justus. The other was
Matthias. 24-25 The apostles prayed, "Lord,
you know the thoughts of everyone. Show
us which one of these two you have chosen
to do this work. Show us who should be
an apostle in place of Judas, who turned
away and went where he belongs." 26 Then
they used lots to choose between them, and
the lots showed that Matthias was the one.
So he became an apostle with the other
eleven.

The Coming of the Holy Spirit

2 When the day of Pentecost came, they
were all together in one place. 2 Suddenly
a noise like a strong, blowing wind came
from heaven and filled the whole house
where they were sitting. 3 They saw
something like flames of fire that were
separated and stood over each person there.
4 They were all filled with the Holy Spirit, and

they began to speak different languages[n] by
the power the Holy Spirit was giving them.
5 There were some religious Jews staying
in Jerusalem who were from every country
in the world. 6 When they heard this noise,
a crowd came together. They were all
surprised, because each one heard them
speaking in his own language. 7 They were
completely amazed at this. They said, "Look!
Aren't all these people that we hear speaking
from Galilee? 8 Then how is it possible that
we each hear them in our own languages?
We are from different places: 9 Parthia,
Media, Elam, Mesopotamia, Judea,
Cappadocia, Pontus, Asia, 10 Phrygia,
Pamphylia, Egypt, the areas of Libya near
Cyrene, Rome 11 (both Jews and those who
had become Jews), Crete, and Arabia. But we
hear them telling in our own languages
about the great things God has done!" 12 They
were all amazed and confused, asking each
other, "What does this mean?"
13 But others were making fun of them,
saying, "They have had too much wine."

Peter Speaks to the People

14 But Peter stood up with the eleven
apostles, and in a loud voice he spoke to the
crowd: "My fellow Jews, and all of you who
are in Jerusalem, listen to me. Pay attention
to what I have to say. 15 These people are not
drunk, as you think; it is only nine o'clock in
the morning! 16 But Joel the prophet wrote
about what is happening here today:

17 'God says: In the last days
I will pour out my Spirit on all kinds of
people.
Your sons and daughters will prophesy.
Your young men will see visions,
and your old men will dream dreams.
18 At that time I will pour out my Spirit
also on my male slaves and female
slaves,
and they will prophesy.
19 I will show miracles
in the sky and on the earth:
blood, fire, and thick smoke.
20 The sun will become dark,
the moon red as blood,
before the overwhelming and glorious
day of the Lord will come.
21 Then anyone who calls on the Lord will
be saved.' *Joel 2:28–32*

22 "People of Israel, listen to these words:
Jesus from Nazareth was a very special man.
God clearly showed this to you by the
miracles, wonders, and signs he did through
Jesus. You all know this, because it happened
right here among you. 23 Jesus was given to
you, and with the help of those who don't
know the law, you put him to death by
nailing him to a cross. But this was God's
plan which he had made long ago; he knew
all this would happen. 24 God raised Jesus
from the dead and set him free from the pain
of death, because death could not hold him.
25 For David said this about him:

'I keep the Lord before me always.
Because he is close by my side,
I will not be hurt.
26 So I am glad, and I rejoice.
Even my body has hope,
27 because you will not leave me in the
grave.
You will not let your Holy One rot.
28 You will teach me how to live a holy life.
Being with you will fill me with joy.'
Psalm 16:8–11

29 "Brothers and sisters, I can tell you truly
that David, our ancestor, died and was
buried. His grave is still here with us today.
30 He was a prophet and knew God had
promised him that he would make a person
from David's family a king just as he was.[n]
31 Knowing this before it happened, David
talked about the Christ rising from the dead.
He said:

'He was not left in the grave.
His body did not rot.'

32 So Jesus is the One whom God raised from
the dead. And we are all witnesses to this.
33 Jesus was lifted up to heaven and is now at
God's right side. The Father has given the
Holy Spirit to Jesus as he promised. So Jesus
has poured out that Spirit, and this is what
you now see and hear. 34 David was not the
one who was lifted up to heaven, but he
said:

'The Lord said to my Lord,
"Sit by me at my right side,
35 until I put your enemies under your
control." '[n] *Psalm 110:1*

2:4 languages This can also be translated "tongues." **2:30 God . . . was** See 2 Samuel 7:13; Psalm 132:11.
2:35 until . . . control Literally, "until I make your enemies a footstool for your feet."

devotion 295

ACTS 2:24–26

A SHADOW MOVES ACROSS

The cornerstone of the Christian faith rests in the resurrection of Jesus, his victory over the power of death. There have been times in my years of ministry when I have had to dig deep to minister comfort in times of death, particularly the death of children. There is a time and a season for everything, even grieving. God understands and that's why it was so important for him to illuminate the way to heaven. He wanted to make sure you know without a doubt that the tomb was empty and death has no victory for the believer.

I once heard a pastor describe Psalm 23:4 this way: "If you were standing on a sidewalk next to a street and a huge tractor trailer passed by with nothing but the shadow passing over you, would you feel it? Of course not, it's a shadow. That is what the shadow of death must be like—no pain, no fear, just a shadow passing by as you enter into eternity."

What he shared never left me, and it was at a time when I needed encouragement because my mom had recently passed away. Although I knew there had been pain during her life here, I was confident that she was at peace with God, and I was without fear as I let her go. Jesus was raised from the dead, and so will everyone who believes in Christ as Lord. Death could not hold him in the grave—what comfort we have in Jesus!

36"So, all the people of Israel should know
this truly: God has made Jesus—the man you
nailed to the cross—both Lord and Christ."
37When the people heard this, they felt
guilty and asked Peter and the other apostles,
"What shall we do?"
38Peter said to them, "Change your hearts
and lives and be baptized, each one of you, in
the name of Jesus Christ for the forgiveness
of your sins. And you will receive the gift of
the Holy Spirit. 39This promise is for you, for
your children, and for all who are far away. It
is for everyone the Lord our God calls to
himself."
40Peter warned them with many other
words. He begged them, "Save yourselves
from the evil of today's people!" 41Then
those people who accepted what Peter said
were baptized. About three thousand people
were added to the number of believers that
day. 42They spent their time learning the
apostles' teaching, sharing, breaking bread,[n]
and praying together.

The Believers Share

43The apostles were doing many miracles
and signs, and everyone felt great respect for
God. 44All the believers were together and
shared everything. 45They would sell their
land and the things they owned and then
divide the money and give it to anyone who
needed it. 46The believers met together in
the Temple every day. They ate together in
their homes, happy to share their food with
joyful hearts. 47They praised God and were
liked by all the people. Every day the Lord
added those who were being saved to the
group of believers.

Peter Heals a Crippled Man

3 One day Peter and John went to the
Temple at three o'clock, the time set each
day for the afternoon prayer service. 2There,
at the Temple gate called Beautiful Gate, was
a man who had been crippled all his life.
Every day he was carried to this gate to beg
for money from the people going into the

2:42 breaking bread This may mean a meal as in verse 46, or the Lord's Supper, the special meal Jesus told his followers to eat to remember him (Luke 22:14–20).

Temple. 3The man saw Peter and John going
into the Temple and asked them for money.
4Peter and John looked straight at him and
said, "Look at us!" 5The man looked at them,
thinking they were going to give him some
money. 6But Peter said, "I don't have any
silver or gold, but I do have something else I
can give you. By the power of Jesus Christ
from Nazareth, stand up and walk!" 7Then
Peter took the man's right hand and lifted
him up. Immediately the man's feet and
ankles became strong. 8He jumped up, stood
on his feet, and began to walk. He went into
the Temple with them, walking and jumping
and praising God. 9-10All the people
recognized him as the crippled man who
always sat by the Beautiful Gate begging for
money. Now they saw this same man
walking and praising God, and they were
amazed. They wondered how this could
happen.

Peter Speaks to the People

11While the man was holding on to Peter
and John, all the people were amazed and
ran to them at Solomon's Porch. 12When
Peter saw this, he said to them, "People of
Israel, why are you surprised? You are
looking at us as if it were our own power or
goodness that made this man walk. 13The
God of Abraham, Isaac, and Jacob, the God
of our ancestors, gave glory to Jesus, his
servant. But you handed him over to be
killed. Pilate decided to let him go free, but
you told Pilate you did not want Jesus. 14You
did not want the One who is holy and good
but asked Pilate to give you a murderer[n]
instead. 15And so you killed the One who
gives life, but God raised him from the dead.
We are witnesses to this. 16It was faith in
Jesus that made this crippled man well. You
can see this man, and you know him. He was
made completely well because of trust in
Jesus, and you all saw it happen!

17"Brothers and sisters, I know you did
those things to Jesus because neither you
nor your leaders understood what you were
doing. 18God said through the prophets that
his Christ would suffer and die. And now
God has made these things come true in this
way. 19So you must change your hearts and
lives! Come back to God, and he will forgive
your sins. Then the Lord will send the time
of rest. 20And he will send Jesus, the One he
chose to be the Christ. 21But Jesus must stay
in heaven until the time comes when all
things will be made right again. God told
about this time long ago when he spoke
through his holy prophets. 22Moses said,
'The Lord your God will give you a prophet
like me, who is one of your own people.
You must listen to everything he tells you.
23Anyone who does not listen to that
prophet will die, cut off from God's people.'[n]
24Samuel, and all the other prophets who
spoke for God after Samuel, told about this
time now. 25You are descendants of the
prophets. You have received the agreement
God made with your ancestors. He said to
your father Abraham, 'Through your
descendants all the nations on the earth will
be blessed.'[n] 26God has raised up his servant
Jesus and sent him to you first to bless you
by turning each of you away from doing
evil."

Peter and John at the Council

4 While Peter and John were speaking to
the people, priests, the captain of the
soldiers that guarded the Temple, and
Sadducees came up to them. 2They were
upset because the two apostles were
teaching the people and were preaching that
people will rise from the dead through the
power of Jesus. 3The older leaders grabbed
Peter and John and put them in jail. Since it
was already night, they kept them in jail
until the next day. 4But many of those who
had heard Peter and John preach believed
the things they said. There were now about
five thousand in the group of believers.

5The next day the rulers, the elders, and
the teachers of the law met in Jerusalem.
6Annas the high priest, Caiaphas, John, and
Alexander were there, as well as everyone
from the high priest's family. 7They made
Peter and John stand before them and then
asked them, "By what power or authority did
you do this?"

8Then Peter, filled with the Holy Spirit,
said to them, "Rulers of the people and you
elders, 9are you questioning us about a good

3:14 murderer Barabbas, the man the crowd asked Pilate to set free instead of Jesus (Luke 23:18). **3:22–23 'The Lord . . . people.'** Quotation from Deuteronomy 18:15, 19. **3:25 'Through . . . blessed.'** Quotation from Genesis 22:18; 26:4.

thing that was done to a crippled man? Are
you asking us who made him well? [10]We
want all of you and all the people to know
that this man was made well by the power of
Jesus Christ from Nazareth. You crucified
him, but God raised him from the dead. This
man was crippled, but he is now well and
able to stand here before you because of the
power of Jesus. [11]Jesus is

'the stone[n] that you builders rejected,
which has become the cornerstone.'

Psalm 118:22

[12]Jesus is the only One who can save people.
No one else in the world is able to save us."

[13]The leaders saw that Peter and John
were not afraid to speak, and they
understood that these men had no special
training or education. So they were amazed.
Then they realized that Peter and John had
been with Jesus. [14]Because they saw the
healed man standing there beside the two
apostles, they could say nothing against
them. [15]After the leaders ordered them to
leave the meeting, they began to talk to each
other. [16]They said, "What shall we do with
these men? Everyone in Jerusalem knows
they have done a great miracle, and we
cannot say it is not true. [17]But to keep it
from spreading among the people, we must
warn them not to talk to people anymore
using that name."

[18]So they called Peter and John in again
and told them not to speak or to teach at all
in the name of Jesus. [19]But Peter and John
answered them, "You decide what God
would want. Should we obey you or God?
[20]We cannot keep quiet. We must speak
about what we have seen and heard." [21]The
leaders warned the apostles again and let
them go free. They could not find a way to
punish them, because all the people were
praising God for what had been done. [22]The
man who received the miracle of healing
was more than forty years old.

The Believers Pray

[23]After Peter and John left the meeting of
leaders, they went to their own group and
told them everything the leading priests and
the elders had said to them. [24]When the
believers heard this, they prayed to God
together, "Lord, you are the One who made
the sky, the earth, the sea, and everything in
them. [25]By the Holy Spirit, through our
father David your servant, you said:

'Why are the nations so angry?
Why are the people making useless
plans?
[26]The kings of the earth prepare to fight,
and their leaders make plans together
against the Lord
and his Christ.'

Psalm 2:1–2

[27]These things really happened when Herod,
Pontius Pilate, and some Jews and non-Jews
all came together against Jesus here in
Jerusalem. Jesus is your holy servant, the
One you made to be the Christ. [28]These
people made your plan happen because of
your power and your will. [29]And now, Lord,
listen to their threats. Lord, help us, your
servants, to speak your word without fear.
[30]Show us your power to heal. Give proofs
and make miracles happen by the power of
Jesus, your holy servant."

[31]After they had prayed, the place where
they were meeting was shaken. They were
all filled with the Holy Spirit, and they spoke
God's word without fear.

The Believers Share

[32]The group of believers were united in
their hearts and spirit. All those in the group
acted as though their private property
belonged to everyone in the group. In fact,
they shared everything. [33]With great power
the apostles were telling people that the
Lord Jesus was truly raised from the dead.
And God blessed all the believers very much.
[34]There were no needy people among them.
From time to time those who owned fields
or houses sold them, brought the money,
[35]and gave it to the apostles. Then the money
was given to anyone who needed it.

[36]One of the believers was named Joseph,
a Levite born in Cyprus. The apostles called
him Barnabas (which means "one who
encourages"). [37]Joseph owned a field, sold
it, brought the money, and gave it to the
apostles.

Ananias and Sapphira Die

5 But a man named Ananias and his wife
Sapphira sold some land. [2]He kept back
part of the money for himself; his wife knew

4:11 stone A symbol meaning Jesus.

devotion 296

ACTS 4:34–35

SHE NEEDED SO MUCH

She lived in a two-bedroom home that her son had left to her before he died. She lived alone, so after a storm blew through southern Florida, I felt like the Lord was urging me to go and check up on her. I didn't know where her home was, so I looked it up on the Internet, and my husband and I made our way to her house. It was a simple home. She had no stove or oven, no washer or dryer, her bed was falling apart, and her cupboards were bare. She lived on Social Security and food stamps, which weren't enough to cover her bills.

How do you help those whose needs are beyond your ability to help? You pray a lot and ask for help and keep on asking. We began by going to our church. They were able to help her with a stove and a new bed. We even had a carpenter who offered to build her some new kitchen cabinets. It was a start. Then I went to the Department of Social Services to see if she was eligible for more government aid. They were able to get her a washer and dryer, a doctor who came out to her house, and someone to help her grocery shop. Now, we just needed enough money to keep her electricity going each month. God provided the money. Is there someone in your life who needs assistance? Don't be afraid to help those in need. Nothing is impossible for God.

about this and agreed to it. But he brought
the rest of the money and gave it to the
apostles. 3Peter said, "Ananias, why did you
let Satan rule your thoughts to lie to the
Holy Spirit and to keep for yourself part of
the money you received for the land? 4Before
you sold the land, it belonged to you. And
even after you sold it, you could have used
the money any way you wanted. Why did
you think of doing this? You lied to God, not
to us!" 5-6When Ananias heard this, he fell
down and died. Some young men came in,
wrapped up his body, carried it out, and
buried it. And everyone who heard about
this was filled with fear.

7About three hours later his wife came in,
but she did not know what had happened.
8Peter said to her, "Tell me, was the money
you got for your field this much?"

Sapphira answered, "Yes, that was the
price."

9Peter said to her, "Why did you and your
husband agree to test the Spirit of the Lord?
Look! The men who buried your husband
are at the door, and they will carry you out."
10At that moment Sapphira fell down by his
feet and died. When the young men came in
and saw that she was dead, they carried her
out and buried her beside her husband.
11The whole church and all the others who
heard about these things were filled with
fear.

The Apostles Heal Many

12The apostles did many signs and
miracles among the people. And they would
all meet together on Solomon's Porch.
13None of the others dared to join them, but
all the people respected them. 14More and
more men and women believed in the Lord
and were added to the group of believers.
15The people placed their sick on beds and
mats in the streets, hoping that when Peter
passed by at least his shadow might fall on
them. 16Crowds came from all the towns
around Jerusalem, bringing their sick and
those who were bothered by evil spirits, and
all of them were healed.

Leaders Try to Stop the Apostles

17 The high priest and all his friends (a group called the Sadducees) became very jealous. 18 They took the apostles and put them in jail. 19 But during the night, an angel of the Lord opened the doors of the jail and led the apostles outside. The angel said, 20 "Go stand in the Temple and tell the people everything about this new life." 21 When the apostles heard this, they obeyed and went into the Temple early in the morning and continued teaching.

When the high priest and his friends arrived, they called a meeting of the leaders and all the important elders. They sent some men to the jail to bring the apostles to them. 22 But, upon arriving, the officers could not find the apostles. So they went back and reported to the leaders. 23 They said, "The jail was closed and locked, and the guards were standing at the doors. But when we opened the doors, the jail was empty!" 24 Hearing this, the captain of the Temple guards and the leading priests were confused and wondered what was happening.

25 Then someone came and told them, "Listen! The men you put in jail are standing in the Temple teaching the people." 26 Then the captain and his men went out and brought the apostles back. But the soldiers did not use force, because they were afraid the people would stone them to death.

27 The soldiers brought the apostles to the meeting and made them stand before the leaders. The high priest questioned them, 28 saying, "We gave you strict orders not to continue teaching in that name. But look, you have filled Jerusalem with your teaching and are trying to make us responsible for this man's death."

29 Peter and the other apostles answered, "We must obey God, not human authority! 30 You killed Jesus by hanging him on a cross. But God, the God of our ancestors, raised Jesus up from the dead! 31 Jesus is the One whom God raised to be on his right side, as Leader and Savior. Through him, all people could change their hearts and lives and have their sins forgiven. 32 We saw all these things happen. The Holy Spirit, whom God has given to all who obey him, also proves these things are true."

33 When the leaders heard this, they became angry and wanted to kill them. 34 But a Pharisee named Gamaliel stood up in the meeting. He was a teacher of the law, and all the people respected him. He ordered the apostles to leave the meeting for a little while. 35 Then he said, "People of Israel, be careful what you are planning to do to these men. 36 Remember when Theudas appeared? He said he was a great man, and about four hundred men joined him. But he was killed, and all his followers were scattered; they were able to do nothing. 37 Later, a man named Judas came from Galilee at the time of the registration.[n] He also led a group of followers and was killed, and all his followers were scattered. 38 And so now I tell you: Stay away from these men, and leave them alone. If their plan comes from human authority, it will fail. 39 But if it is from God, you will not be able to stop them. You might even be fighting against God himself!"

The leaders agreed with what Gamaliel said. 40 They called the apostles in, beat them, and told them not to speak in the name of Jesus again. Then they let them go free. 41 The apostles left the meeting full of joy because they were given the honor of suffering disgrace for Jesus. 42 Every day in the Temple and in people's homes they continued teaching the people and telling the Good News—that Jesus is the Christ.

Seven Leaders Are Chosen

6 The number of followers was growing. But during this same time, the Greek-speaking followers had an argument with the other followers. The Greek-speaking widows were not getting their share of the food that was given out every day. 2 The twelve apostles called the whole group of followers together and said, "It is not right for us to stop our work of teaching God's word in order to serve tables. 3 So, brothers and sisters, choose seven of your own men who are good, full of the Spirit and full of wisdom. We will put them in charge of this work. 4 Then we can continue to pray and to teach the word of God."

5 The whole group liked the idea, so they chose these seven men: Stephen (a man with great faith and full of the Holy Spirit),

5:37 registration Census. A counting of all the people and the things they own.

Philip,[n] Procorus, Nicanor, Timon, Parmenas, and Nicolas (a man from Antioch who had become a follower of the Jewish religion). 6Then they put these men before the apostles, who prayed and laid their hands[n] on them.

7The word of God was continuing to spread. The group of followers in Jerusalem increased, and a great number of the Jewish priests believed and obeyed.

Stephen Is Accused

8Stephen was richly blessed by God who gave him the power to do great miracles and signs among the people. 9But some people were against him. They belonged to the synagogue of Free Men[n] (as it was called), which included people from Cyrene, Alexandria, Cilicia, and Asia. They all came and argued with Stephen.

10But the Spirit was helping him to speak with wisdom, and his words were so strong that they could not argue with him. 11So they secretly urged some men to say, "We heard Stephen speak against Moses and against God."

12This upset the people, the elders, and the teachers of the law. They came and grabbed Stephen and brought him to a meeting of the leaders. 13They brought in some people to tell lies about Stephen, saying, "This man is always speaking against this holy place and the law of Moses. 14We heard him say that Jesus from Nazareth will destroy this place and that Jesus will change the customs Moses gave us." 15All the people in the meeting were watching Stephen closely and saw that his face looked like the face of an angel.

Stephen's Speech

7 The high priest said to Stephen, "Are these things true?"

2Stephen answered, "Brothers and fathers, listen to me. Our glorious God appeared to Abraham, our ancestor, in Mesopotamia before he lived in Haran. 3God said to Abraham, 'Leave your country and your relatives, and go to the land I will show you.'[n] 4So Abraham left the country of Chaldea and went to live in Haran. After Abraham's father died, God sent him to this place where you now live. 5God did not give Abraham any of this land, not even a foot of it. But God promised that he would give this land to him and his descendants, even before Abraham had a child. 6This is what God said to him: 'Your descendants will be strangers in a land they don't own. The people there will make them slaves and will mistreat them for four hundred years. 7But I will punish the nation where they are slaves. Then your descendants will leave that land and will worship me in this place.'[n] 8God made an agreement with Abraham, the sign of which was circumcision. And so when Abraham had his son Isaac, Abraham circumcised him when he was eight days old. Isaac also circumcised his son Jacob, and Jacob did the same for his sons, the twelve ancestors[n] of our people.

9"Jacob's sons became jealous of Joseph and sold him to be a slave in Egypt. But God was with him 10and saved him from all his troubles. The king of Egypt liked Joseph and respected him because of the wisdom God gave him. The king made him governor of Egypt and put him in charge of all the people in his palace.

11"Then all the land of Egypt and Canaan became so dry that nothing would grow, and the people suffered very much. Jacob's sons, our ancestors, could not find anything to eat. 12But when Jacob heard there was grain in Egypt, he sent his sons there. This was their first trip to Egypt. 13When they went there a second time, Joseph told his brothers who he was, and the king learned about Joseph's family. 14Then Joseph sent messengers to invite Jacob, his father, to come to Egypt along with all his relatives (seventy-five persons altogether). 15So Jacob went down to Egypt, where he and his sons died. 16Later their bodies were moved to Shechem and put in a grave there. (It was the same grave Abraham had bought for a sum of money from the sons of Hamor in Shechem.)

17"The promise God made to Abraham was soon to come true, and the number of people in Egypt grew large. 18Then a new

6:5 Philip Not the apostle named Philip. **6:6 laid their hands** The laying on of hands had many purposes, including the giving of a blessing, power, or authority. **6:9 Free Men** Jewish people who had been slaves or whose fathers had been slaves, but were now free. **7:3 'Leave . . . you.'** Quotation from Genesis 12:1. **7:6–7 'Your descendants . . . place.'** Quotation from Genesis 15:13–14 and Exodus 3:12. **7:8 twelve ancestors** Important ancestors of the people of Israel; the leaders of the twelve tribes of Israel.

king, who did not know who Joseph was, began to rule Egypt. 19This king tricked our people and was cruel to our ancestors, forcing them to leave their babies outside to die. 20At this time Moses was born, and he was very beautiful. For three months Moses was cared for in his father's house. 21When they put Moses outside, the king's daughter adopted him and raised him as if he were her own son. 22The Egyptians taught Moses everything they knew, and he was a powerful man in what he said and did.

23"When Moses was about forty years old, he thought it would be good to visit his own people, the people of Israel. 24Moses saw an Egyptian mistreating one of his people, so he defended the Israelite and punished the Egyptian by killing him. 25Moses thought his own people would understand that God was using him to save them, but they did not. 26The next day when Moses saw two men of Israel fighting, he tried to make peace between them. He said, 'Men, you are brothers. Why are you hurting each other?' 27The man who was hurting the other pushed Moses away and said, 'Who made you our ruler and judge? 28Are you going to kill me as you killed the Egyptian yesterday?'[n] 29When Moses heard him say this, he left Egypt and went to live in the land of Midian where he was a stranger. While Moses lived in Midian, he had two sons.

30"Forty years later an angel appeared to Moses in the flames of a burning bush as he was in the desert near Mount Sinai. 31When Moses saw this, he was amazed and went near to look closer. Moses heard the Lord's voice say, 32'I am the God of your ancestors, the God of Abraham, Isaac, and Jacob.'[n] Moses began to shake with fear and was afraid to look. 33The Lord said to him, 'Take off your sandals, because you are standing on holy ground. 34I have seen the troubles my people have suffered in Egypt. I have heard their cries and have come down to save them. And now, Moses, I am sending you back to Egypt.'[n]

35"This Moses was the same man the two men of Israel rejected, saying, 'Who made you a ruler and judge?'[n] Moses is the same man God sent to be a ruler and savior, with the help of the angel that Moses saw in the burning bush. 36So Moses led the people out of Egypt. He worked miracles and signs in Egypt, at the Red Sea, and then in the desert for forty years. 37This is the same Moses that said to the people of Israel, 'God will give you a prophet like me, who is one of your own people.'[n] 38This is the Moses who was with the gathering of the Israelites in the desert. He was with the angel that spoke to him at Mount Sinai, and he was with our ancestors. He received commands from God that give life, and he gave those commands to us.

39"But our ancestors did not want to obey Moses. They rejected him and wanted to go back to Egypt. 40They said to Aaron, 'Make us gods who will lead us. Moses led us out of Egypt, but we don't know what has happened to him.'[n] 41So the people made an idol that looked like a calf. Then they brought sacrifices to it and were proud of what they had made with their own hands. 42But God turned against them and did not try to stop them from worshiping the sun, moon, and stars. This is what is written in the book of the prophets: God says,

'People of Israel, you did not bring me
sacrifices and offerings
while you traveled in the desert for
forty years.
43You have carried with you
the tent to worship Molech
and the idols of the star god Rephan
that you made to worship.
So I will send you away beyond Babylon.'

Amos 5:25–27

44"The Holy Tent where God spoke to our ancestors was with them in the desert. God told Moses how to make this Tent, and he made it like the plan God showed him. 45Later, Joshua led our ancestors to capture the lands of the other nations. Our people went in, and God forced the other people out. When our people went into this new land, they took with them this same Tent they had received from their ancestors. They kept it until the time of David, 46who pleased God and asked God to let him build a house for him, the God of Jacob.[n] 47But Solomon was the one who built the Temple.

7:27–28 'Who . . . yesterday?' Quotation from Exodus 2:14. **7:32 'I am . . . Jacob.'** Quotation from Exodus 3:6. **7:33–34 'Take . . . Egypt.'** Quotation from Exodus 3:5–10. **7:35 'Who . . . judge?'** Quotation from Exodus 2:14. **7:37 'God . . . people.'** Quotation from Deuteronomy 18:15. **7:40 'Make . . . him.'** Quotation from Exodus 32:1. **7:46 Jacob** Some Greek copies read "the house of Jacob." This means the people of Israel.

48“But the Most High does not live in
houses that people build with their hands.
As the prophet says:
49‘Heaven is my throne,
and the earth is my footstool.
So do you think you can build a house for
me? says the Lord.
Do I need a place to rest?
50Remember, my hand made all these
things!’ ” *Isaiah 66:1–2*
51Stephen continued speaking: “You
stubborn people! You have not given your
hearts to God, nor will you listen to him! You
are always against what the Holy Spirit is
trying to tell you, just as your ancestors
were. 52Your ancestors tried to hurt every
prophet who ever lived. Those prophets said
long ago that the One who is good would
come, but your ancestors killed them. And
now you have turned against and killed the
One who is good. 53You received the law of
Moses, which God gave you through his
angels, but you haven’t obeyed it.”

Stephen Is Killed

54When the leaders heard this, they
became furious. They were so mad they
were grinding their teeth at Stephen. 55But
Stephen was full of the Holy Spirit. He
looked up to heaven and saw the glory of
God and Jesus standing at God’s right side.
56He said, “Look! I see heaven open and the
Son of Man standing at God’s right side.”
57Then they shouted loudly and covered
their ears and all ran at Stephen. 58They took
him out of the city and began to throw
stones at him to kill him. And those who
told lies against Stephen left their coats with
a young man named Saul. 59While they were
throwing stones, Stephen prayed, “Lord
Jesus, receive my spirit.” 60He fell on his
knees and cried in a loud voice, “Lord, do not
hold this sin against them.” After Stephen
said this, he died.

8 Saul agreed that the killing of Stephen
was good.

Troubles for the Believers

On that day the church of Jerusalem
began to be persecuted, and all the believers,
except the apostles, were scattered
throughout Judea and Samaria.
2And some religious people buried
Stephen and cried loudly for him. 3Saul was
also trying to destroy the church, going from
house to house, dragging out men and
women and putting them in jail. 4And
wherever they were scattered, they told
people the Good News.

Philip Preaches in Samaria

5Philip went to the city of Samaria and
preached about the Christ. 6When the
people there heard Philip and saw the
miracles he was doing, they all listened
carefully to what he said. 7Many of these
people had evil spirits in them, but Philip
made the evil spirits leave. The spirits made a
loud noise when they came out. Philip also
healed many weak and crippled people there.
8So the people in that city were very happy.
9But there was a man named Simon in
that city. Before Philip came there, Simon
had practiced magic and amazed all the
people of Samaria. He bragged and called
himself a great man. 10All the people—the
least important and the most important—
paid attention to Simon, saying, “This man
has the power of God, called ‘the Great
Power’!” 11Simon had amazed them with his
magic so long that the people became his
followers. 12But when Philip told them the
Good News about the kingdom of God and
the power of Jesus Christ, men and women
believed Philip and were baptized. 13Simon
himself believed, and after he was baptized,
he stayed very close to Philip. When he saw
the miracles and the powerful things Philip
did, Simon was amazed.
14When the apostles who were still in
Jerusalem heard that the people of Samaria
had accepted the word of God, they sent
Peter and John to them. 15When Peter and
John arrived, they prayed that the Samaritan
believers might receive the Holy Spirit.
16These people had been baptized in the
name of the Lord Jesus, but the Holy Spirit
had not yet come upon any of them. 17Then,
when the two apostles began laying their
hands on the people, they received the Holy
Spirit.
18Simon saw that the Spirit was given to
people when the apostles laid their hands
on them. So he offered the apostles money,
19saying, “Give me also this power so that
anyone on whom I lay my hands will receive
the Holy Spirit.”
20Peter said to him, “You and your money

should both be destroyed, because you
thought you could buy God's gift with
money. 21You cannot share with us in this
work since your heart is not right before
God. 22Change your heart! Turn away from
this evil thing you have done, and pray to
the Lord. Maybe he will forgive you for
thinking this. 23I see that you are full of
bitter jealousy and ruled by sin."
24Simon answered, "Both of you pray for
me to the Lord so the things you have said
will not happen to me."
25After Peter and John told the people
what they had seen Jesus do and after they
had spoken the message of the Lord, they
went back to Jerusalem. On the way, they
went through many Samaritan towns and
preached the Good News to the people.

Philip Teaches an Ethiopian

26An angel of the Lord said to Philip, "Get
ready and go south to the road that leads
down to Gaza from Jerusalem—the desert
road." 27So Philip got ready and went. On the
road he saw a man from Ethiopia, a eunuch.
He was an important officer in the service of
Candace, the queen of the Ethiopians; he was
responsible for taking care of all her money.
He had gone to Jerusalem to worship. 28Now,
as he was on his way home, he was sitting in
his chariot reading from the Book of Isaiah,
the prophet. 29The Spirit said to Philip, "Go
to that chariot and stay near it."
30So when Philip ran toward the chariot,
he heard the man reading from Isaiah the
prophet. Philip asked, "Do you understand
what you are reading?"
31He answered, "How can I understand
unless someone explains it to me?" Then he
invited Philip to climb in and sit with him.
32The portion of Scripture he was reading
was this:

"He was like a sheep being led to be killed.
He was quiet, as a lamb is quiet while
its wool is being cut;
he never opened his mouth.
33 He was shamed and was treated unfairly.
He died without children to continue his
family.
His life on earth has ended." *Isaiah 53:7–8*

devotion 297

ACTS 8:20–23

BITTER BETTY

Every person I know could come up with about a hundred reasons to become bitter and remain a perpetually downtrodden victim. Real life tragedies have come to all of us. Awful consequences have been suffered. Many have known more pain than one person should have to carry. I would be the first one in line to give you permission to feel grief over your circumstances, disappointment, or anger. We cannot deny the pain so many of us have known. Life turns out rotten sometimes, and to say any different would be ridiculous.

But sometimes we move beyond sadness and let our experiences become a root of bitterness that grows up inside of us. We can get some weird satisfaction in revisiting our bitter memories—reminding ourselves of the ones who hurt us, planning how to get even, brooding, and becoming even more resentful. But I don't want to become a bitter old woman. I don't want to remain inward, focused on my grievances. You and I cannot stay that way and go forward with God. When a woman has become bitter, I think it's because she has stopped believing God.

The mature follower feels pain but resists falling into bitterness because she believes God more. She trusts that he still has a plan and a purpose and that in the end, the victory will belong to those faithful to his name. Do you feel a source of bitterness inside your heart? Then ask yourself, "Where have I stopped believing God?"

Tabitha

ACTS 9

Peter enters the home, and people shuffle to the side. A man leads Peter upstairs where he sees women huddled around a bed. They hear him and step aside. Tears rim their eyes as they hold up robes and cloaks the dead woman had made for them. "She was always sewing," one of the women offers, choking on her words.

The two men who had rushed to find Peter had told him of the woman's kindness. Her name was Tabitha (her Greek name was Dorcas). "She is a follower of Christ," they had said, pulling Peter through the busy streets. As Peter approached the home and saw the number of people mourning for her, he knew that Tabitha had been well loved. When he saw the examples of her work and heard stories of her generosity, he knew why: she loved others with everything she had.

"Leave me alone with her," Peter says to the women. As the door closes, Peter kneels beside the body and prays. "Jesus, you said that anyone who has faith in you will do what you have done." He looks at the still body and addresses it. "Tabitha, stand up."

Dark brown eyes fly open with a flash of light. Peter offers her his hand and welcomes her into a life of even greater service for her Lord.

Tabitha served God in practical ways like sewing for the poor. He is glorified and lives are changed through the simplest acts of service.

34The officer said to Philip, "Please tell me,
who is the prophet talking about—himself
or someone else?" 35Philip began to speak,
and starting with this same Scripture, he
told the man the Good News about Jesus.
36While they were traveling down the
road, they came to some water. The officer
said, "Look, here is water. What is stopping
me from being baptized?" [37Philip answered,
"If you believe with all your heart, you can."
The officer said, "I believe that Jesus Christ
is the Son of God."][n] 38Then the officer
commanded the chariot to stop. Both Philip
and the officer went down into the water,
and Philip baptized him. 39When they came
up out of the water, the Spirit of the Lord
took Philip away; the officer never saw him
again. And the officer continued on his way
home, full of joy. 40But Philip appeared in a
city called Azotus and preached the Good
News in all the towns on the way from
Azotus to Caesarea.

Saul Is Converted

9 In Jerusalem Saul was still threatening
the followers of the Lord by saying he
would kill them. So he went to the high
priest 2and asked him to write letters to the
synagogues in the city of Damascus. Then if
Saul found any followers of Christ's Way,
men or women, he would arrest them and
bring them back to Jerusalem.
3So Saul headed toward Damascus. As he
came near the city, a bright light from heaven
suddenly flashed around him. 4Saul fell to the
ground and heard a voice saying to him,
"Saul, Saul! Why are you persecuting me?"
5Saul said, "Who are you, Lord?"
The voice answered, "I am Jesus, whom
you are persecuting. 6Get up now and go
into the city. Someone there will tell you
what you must do."
7The people traveling with Saul stood
there but said nothing. They heard the voice,
but they saw no one. 8Saul got up from the
ground and opened his eyes, but he could
not see. So those with Saul took his hand
and led him into Damascus. 9For three days
Saul could not see and did not eat or drink.
10There was a follower of Jesus in
Damascus named Ananias. The Lord spoke
to Ananias in a vision, "Ananias!"
Ananias answered, "Here I am, Lord."

8:37 Philip . . . God." Some Greek copies do not contain the bracketed text.

[11]The Lord said to him, "Get up and go to Straight Street. Find the house of Judas,[n] and ask for a man named Saul from the city of Tarsus. He is there now, praying. [12]Saul has seen a vision in which a man named Ananias comes to him and lays his hands on him. Then he is able to see again."

[13]But Ananias answered, "Lord, many people have told me about this man and the terrible things he did to your holy people in Jerusalem. [14]Now he has come here to Damascus, and the leading priests have given him the power to arrest everyone who worships you."

[15]But the Lord said to Ananias, "Go! I have chosen Saul for an important work. He must tell about me to those who are not Jews, to kings, and to the people of Israel. [16]I will show him how much he must suffer for my name."

[17]So Ananias went to the house of Judas. He laid his hands on Saul and said, "Brother Saul, the Lord Jesus sent me. He is the one you saw on the road on your way here. He sent me so that you can see again and be filled with the Holy Spirit." [18]Immediately, something that looked like fish scales fell from Saul's eyes, and he was able to see again! Then Saul got up and was baptized. [19]After he ate some food, his strength returned.

Saul Preaches in Damascus

Saul stayed with the followers of Jesus in Damascus for a few days. [20]Soon he began to preach about Jesus in the synagogues, saying, "Jesus is the Son of God."

[21]All the people who heard him were amazed. They said, "This is the man who was in Jerusalem trying to destroy those who trust in this name! He came here to arrest the followers of Jesus and take them back to the leading priests."

[22]But Saul grew more powerful. His proofs that Jesus is the Christ were so strong that his own people in Damascus could not argue with him.

[23]After many days, they made plans to kill Saul. [24]They were watching the city gates day and night, but Saul learned about their plan. [25]One night some followers of Saul helped him leave the city by lowering him in a basket through an opening in the city wall.

Saul Preaches in Jerusalem

[26]When Saul went to Jerusalem, he tried to join the group of followers, but they were all afraid of him. They did not believe he was really a follower. [27]But Barnabas accepted Saul and took him to the apostles. Barnabas explained to them that Saul had seen the Lord on the road and the Lord had spoken to Saul. Then he told them how boldly Saul had preached in the name of Jesus in Damascus.

[28]And so Saul stayed with the followers, going everywhere in Jerusalem, preaching boldly in the name of the Lord. [29]He would often talk and argue with the Jewish people who spoke Greek, but they were trying to kill him. [30]When the followers learned about this, they took Saul to Caesarea and from there sent him to Tarsus.

[31]The church everywhere in Judea, Galilee, and Samaria had a time of peace and became stronger. Respecting the Lord by the way they lived, and being encouraged by the Holy Spirit, the group of believers continued to grow.

Peter Heals Aeneas

[32]As Peter was traveling through all the area, he visited God's people who lived in Lydda. [33]There he met a man named Aeneas, who was paralyzed and had not been able to leave his bed for the past eight years. [34]Peter said to him, "Aeneas, Jesus Christ heals you. Stand up and make your bed." Aeneas stood up immediately. [35]All the people living in Lydda and on the Plain of Sharon saw him and turned to the Lord.

Peter Heals Tabitha

[36]In the city of Joppa there was a follower named Tabitha (whose Greek name was Dorcas). She was always doing good deeds and kind acts. [37]While Peter was in Lydda, Tabitha became sick and died. Her body was washed and put in a room upstairs. [38]Since Lydda is near Joppa and the followers in Joppa heard that Peter was in Lydda, they sent two messengers to Peter. They begged him, "Hurry, please come to us!" [39]So Peter got ready and went with them. When he arrived, they took him to the upstairs room where all the widows stood around Peter, crying. They showed him the shirts and

9:11 Judas This is not either of the apostles named Judas.

coats Tabitha had made when she was still alive. 40Peter sent everyone out of the room and kneeled and prayed. Then he turned to the body and said, "Tabitha, stand up." She opened her eyes, and when she saw Peter, she sat up. 41He gave her his hand and helped her up. Then he called the saints and the widows into the room and showed them that Tabitha was alive. 42People everywhere in Joppa learned about this, and many believed in the Lord. 43Peter stayed in Joppa for many days with a man named Simon who was a tanner.

Peter Teaches Cornelius

10 At Caesarea there was a man named Cornelius, an officer in the Italian group of the Roman army. 2Cornelius was a religious man. He and all the other people who lived in his house worshiped the true God. He gave much of his money to the poor and prayed to God often. 3One afternoon about three o'clock, Cornelius clearly saw a vision. An angel of God came to him and said, "Cornelius!"

4Cornelius stared at the angel. He became afraid and said, "What do you want, Lord?"

The angel said, "God has heard your prayers. He has seen that you give to the poor, and he remembers you. 5Send some men now to Joppa to bring back a man named Simon who is also called Peter. 6He is staying with a man, also named Simon, who is a tanner and has a house beside the sea." 7When the angel who spoke to Cornelius left, Cornelius called two of his servants and a soldier, a religious man who worked for him. 8Cornelius explained everything to them and sent them to Joppa.

9About noon the next day as they came near Joppa, Peter was going up to the roof[n] to pray. 10He was hungry and wanted to eat, but while the food was being prepared, he had a vision. 11He saw heaven opened and something coming down that looked like a big sheet being lowered to earth by its four corners. 12In it were all kinds of animals, reptiles, and birds. 13Then a voice said to Peter, "Get up, Peter; kill and eat."

14But Peter said, "No, Lord! I have never eaten food that is unholy or unclean."

15But the voice said to him again, "God has made these things clean, so don't call them 'unholy'!" 16This happened three times, and at once the sheet was taken back to heaven.

17While Peter was wondering what this vision meant, the men Cornelius sent had found Simon's house and were standing at the gate. 18They asked, "Is Simon Peter staying here?"

19While Peter was still thinking about the vision, the Spirit said to him, "Listen, three men are looking for you. 20Get up and go downstairs. Go with them without doubting, because I have sent them to you."

21So Peter went down to the men and said, "I am the one you are looking for. Why did you come here?"

22They said, "A holy angel spoke to Cornelius, an army officer and a good man; he worships God. All the people respect him. The angel told Cornelius to ask you to come to his house so that he can hear what you have to say." 23So Peter asked the men to come in and spend the night.

The next day Peter got ready and went with them, and some of the followers from Joppa joined him. 24On the following day they came to Caesarea. Cornelius was waiting for them and had called together his relatives and close friends. 25When Peter entered, Cornelius met him, fell at his feet, and worshiped him. 26But Peter helped him up, saying, "Stand up. I too am only a human." 27As he talked with Cornelius, Peter went inside where he saw many people gathered. 28He said, "You people understand that it is against our law for Jewish people to associate with or visit anyone who is not Jewish. But God has shown me that I should not call any person 'unholy' or 'unclean.' 29That is why I did not argue when I was asked to come here. Now, please tell me why you sent for me."

30Cornelius said, "Four days ago, I was praying in my house at this same time—three o'clock in the afternoon. Suddenly, there was a man standing before me wearing shining clothes. 31He said, 'Cornelius, God has heard your prayer and has seen that you give to the poor and remembers you. 32So

10:9 roof In Bible times houses were built with flat roofs. The roof was used for drying things such as flax and fruit. And it was used as an extra room, as a place for worship, and as a cool place to sleep in the summer.

send some men to Joppa and ask Simon
Peter to come. Peter is staying in the house of
a man, also named Simon, who is a tanner
and has a house beside the sea.' 33So I sent
for you immediately, and it was very good of
you to come. Now we are all here before God
to hear everything the Lord has commanded
you to tell us."

34Peter began to speak: "I really understand
now that to God every person is the same.
35In every country God accepts anyone who
worships him and does what is right. 36You
know the message that God has sent to the
people of Israel is the Good News that peace
has come through Jesus Christ. Jesus is the
Lord of all people! 37You know what has
happened all over Judea, beginning in
Galilee after John[n] preached to the people
about baptism. 38You know about Jesus from
Nazareth, that God gave him the Holy Spirit
and power. You know how Jesus went
everywhere doing good and healing those
who were ruled by the devil, because God
was with him. 39We saw what Jesus did in
Judea and in Jerusalem, but the Jews in
Jerusalem killed him by hanging him on a
cross. 40Yet, on the third day, God raised Jesus
to life and caused him to be seen, 41not by all
the people, but only by the witnesses God
had already chosen. And we are those
witnesses who ate and drank with him after
he was raised from the dead. 42He told us to
preach to the people and to tell them that he
is the one whom God chose to be the judge
of the living and the dead. 43All the prophets
say it is true that all who believe in Jesus will
be forgiven of their sins through Jesus'
name."

44While Peter was still saying this, the
Holy Spirit came down on all those who
were listening. 45The Jewish believers who
came with Peter were amazed that the gift of
the Holy Spirit had been given even to the
nations. 46These believers heard them
speaking in different languages[n] and praising
God. Then Peter said, 47"Can anyone keep
these people from being baptized with
water? They have received the Holy Spirit
just as we did!" 48So Peter ordered that they
be baptized in the name of Jesus Christ.
Then they asked Peter to stay with them for
a few days.

Peter Returns to Jerusalem

11 The apostles and the believers in
Judea heard that some who were not
Jewish had accepted God's teaching too. 2But
when Peter came to Jerusalem, some people
argued with him. 3They said, "You went
into the homes of people who are not
circumcised and ate with them!"

4So Peter explained the whole story to
them. 5He said, "I was in the city of Joppa,
and while I was praying, I had a vision. I saw
something that looked like a big sheet being
lowered from heaven by its four corners. It
came very close to me. 6I looked inside it and
saw animals, wild beasts, reptiles, and birds.
7I heard a voice say to me, 'Get up, Peter. Kill
and eat.' 8But I said, 'No, Lord! I have never
eaten anything that is unholy or unclean.'
9But the voice from heaven spoke again,
'God has made these things clean, so don't
call them unholy.' 10This happened three
times. Then the whole thing was taken back
to heaven. 11Right then three men who were
sent to me from Caesarea came to the house
where I was staying. 12The Spirit told me to
go with them without doubting. These six
believers here also went with me, and we
entered the house of Cornelius. 13He told us
about the angel he saw standing in his
house. The angel said to him, 'Send some
men to Joppa and invite Simon Peter to
come. 14By the words he will say to you, you
and all your family will be saved.' 15When I
began my speech, the Holy Spirit came on
them just as he came on us at the beginning.
16Then I remembered the words of the Lord.
He said, 'John baptized with water, but you
will be baptized with the Holy Spirit.'
17Since God gave them the same gift he gave
us who believed in the Lord Jesus Christ,
how could I stop the work of God?"

18When the believers heard this, they
stopped arguing. They praised God and said,
"So God is allowing even other nations to
turn to him and live."

The Good News Comes to Antioch

19Many of the believers were scattered
when they were persecuted after Stephen
was killed. Some of them went as far as
Phoenicia, Cyprus, and Antioch telling the
message to others, but only to Jews. 20Some

10:37 John John the Baptist, who preached to people about Christ's coming (Luke 3).
10:46 languages This can also be translated "tongues."

Rhoda

ACTS 12

"Release him, Lord," she hears someone pray. "In the name of Jesus, break down those prison walls!" Rhoda whispers her own prayers as those gathered in her master's home lift Peter in prayer. King Herod first had the apostle James killed, and when he saw that the Jews were pleased with his actions, he ordered the imprisonment of Peter. Peter wouldn't be tried until after Passover. In the meantime, he was guarded by sixteen soldiers.

"Give him strength," Rhoda hears another man say. "Prepare the way for his release, oh God." Hour after hour, the men and women pray. Rhoda wrings her hands as she passes a window. If someone hears this prayer meeting, they could all go to prison.

A knock on the door startles Rhoda, and her heart quickens. She steps lightly to the door. "Who is it?" she asks.

"It's me. I'm free," the voice says. Rhoda screams and flaps her hands, running.

"Peter is at the door!" she exclaims, jumping in the prayer warriors' midst.

Several people ignore her and continue to pray. "You are crazy!" others say, lifting their pleas once again. But Rhoda will not be dismissed. "It must be Peter's angel," a kind woman says, trying to appease the confused servant girl. A knock on the door sends a hush over the room and Rhoda smiles. The answer to their prayers is standing outside the door.

Don't be surprised when God shows up. Throw open the door and wait in anticipation of God's answer to prayer!

of these believers were people from Cyprus
and Cyrene. When they came to Antioch,
they spoke also to Greeks,[n] telling them the
Good News about the Lord Jesus. 21 The Lord
was helping the believers, and a large group
of people believed and turned to the Lord.
22 The church in Jerusalem heard about all
of this, so they sent Barnabas to Antioch.
23-24 Barnabas was a good man, full of the
Holy Spirit and full of faith. When he
reached Antioch and saw how God had
blessed the people, he was glad. He
encouraged all the believers in Antioch
always to obey the Lord with all their hearts,
and many people became followers of the
Lord.
25 Then Barnabas went to the city of Tarsus
to look for Saul, 26 and when he found Saul,
he brought him to Antioch. For a whole year
Saul and Barnabas met with the church and
taught many people there. In Antioch the
followers were called Christians for the first
time.
27 About that time some prophets came
from Jerusalem to Antioch. 28 One of them,
named Agabus, stood up and spoke with
the help of the Holy Spirit. He said, "A very
hard time is coming to the whole world.
There will be no food to eat." (This happened
when Claudius ruled.) 29 The followers all
decided to help the believers who lived in
Judea, as much as each one could. 30 They
gathered the money and gave it to Barnabas
and Saul, who brought it to the elders in
Judea.

Herod Agrippa Hurts the Church

12 During that same time King Herod
began to mistreat some who belonged
to the church. 2 He ordered James, the
brother of John, to be killed by the sword.
3 Herod saw that some of the people liked
this, so he decided to arrest Peter, too. (This
happened during the time of the Feast of
Unleavened Bread.)
4 After Herod arrested Peter, he put him
in jail and handed him over to be guarded
by sixteen soldiers. Herod planned to bring
Peter before the people for trial after the
Passover Feast. 5 So Peter was kept in jail,
but the church prayed earnestly to God for
him.

11:20 Greeks Some Greek copies read "Hellenists," non-Greeks who spoke Greek.

Peter Leaves the Jail

6The night before Herod was to bring him
to trial, Peter was sleeping between two
soldiers, bound with two chains. Other
soldiers were guarding the door of the jail.
7Suddenly, an angel of the Lord stood there,
and a light shined in the cell. The angel
struck Peter on the side and woke him up.
"Hurry! Get up!" the angel said. And the
chains fell off Peter's hands. 8Then the angel
told him, "Get dressed and put on your
sandals." And Peter did. Then the angel said,
"Put on your coat and follow me." 9So Peter
followed him out, but he did not know if
what the angel was doing was real; he
thought he might be seeing a vision. 10They
went past the first and second guards and
came to the iron gate that separated them
from the city. The gate opened by itself for
them, and they went through it. When they
had walked down one street, the angel
suddenly left him.

11Then Peter realized what had happened.
He thought, "Now I know that the Lord
really sent his angel to me. He rescued me
from Herod and from all the things the
people thought would happen."

12When he considered this, he went to the
home of Mary, the mother of John Mark.
Many people were gathered there, praying.
13Peter knocked on the outside door, and a
servant girl named Rhoda came to answer it.
14When she recognized Peter's voice, she
was so happy she forgot to open the door.
Instead, she ran inside and told the group,
"Peter is at the door!"

15They said to her, "You are crazy!" But she
kept on saying it was true, so they said, "It
must be Peter's angel."

16Peter continued to knock, and when
they opened the door, they saw him and
were amazed. 17Peter made a sign with his
hand to tell them to be quiet. He explained
how the Lord led him out of the jail, and he
said, "Tell James and the other believers
what happened." Then he left to go to
another place.

18The next day the soldiers were very
upset and wondered what had happened
to Peter. 19Herod looked everywhere for
him but could not find him. So he
questioned the guards and ordered that they
be killed.

The Death of Herod Agrippa

Later Herod moved from Judea and went
to the city of Caesarea, where he stayed.
20Herod was very angry with the people of
Tyre and Sidon, but the people of those cities
all came in a group to him. After convincing
Blastus, the king's personal servant, to be
on their side, they asked Herod for peace,
because their country got its food from his
country.

21On a chosen day Herod put on his royal
robes, sat on his throne, and made a speech
to the people. 22They shouted, "This is the
voice of a god, not a human!" 23Because
Herod did not give the glory to God, an angel
of the Lord immediately caused him to
become sick, and he was eaten by worms
and died.

24God's message continued to spread and
reach people.

25After Barnabas and Saul finished their
task in Jerusalem, they returned to Antioch,
taking John Mark with them.

Barnabas and Saul Are Chosen

13 In the church at Antioch there were
these prophets and teachers: Barnabas,
Simeon (also called Niger), Lucius (from the
city of Cyrene), Manaen (who had grown up
with Herod, the ruler), and Saul. 2They were
all worshiping the Lord and fasting[n] for a
certain time. During this time the Holy Spirit
said to them, "Set apart for me Barnabas and
Saul to do a special work for which I have
chosen them."

3So after they fasted and prayed, they laid
their hands on[n] Barnabas and Saul and sent
them out.

Barnabas and Saul in Cyprus

4Barnabas and Saul, sent out by the Holy
Spirit, went to the city of Seleucia. From
there they sailed to the island of Cyprus.
5When they came to Salamis, they preached
the Good News of God in the synagogues.
John Mark was with them to help.

6They went across the whole island to
Paphos where they met a magician named

13:2 fasting The people would give up eating for a special time of prayer and worship to God. It was also done sometimes to show sadness and disappointment. **13:3 laid their hands on** The laying on of hands had many purposes, including the giving of a blessing, power, or authority.

Bar-Jesus. He was a false prophet [7]who always stayed close to Sergius Paulus, the governor and a smart man. He asked Barnabas and Saul to come to him, because he wanted to hear the message of God. [8]But Elymas, the magician, was against them. (Elymas is the name for Bar-Jesus in the Greek language.) He tried to stop the governor from believing in Jesus. [9]But Saul, who was also called Paul, was filled with the Holy Spirit. He looked straight at Elymas [10]and said, "You son of the devil! You are an enemy of everything that is right! You are full of evil tricks and lies, always trying to change the Lord's truths into lies. [11]Now the Lord will touch you, and you will be blind. For a time you will not be able to see anything—not even the light from the sun."

Then everything became dark for Elymas, and he walked around, trying to find someone to lead him by the hand. [12]When the governor saw this, he believed because he was amazed at the teaching about the Lord.

Paul and Barnabas Leave Cyprus

[13]Paul and those with him sailed from Paphos and came to Perga, in Pamphylia. There John Mark left them to return to Jerusalem. [14]They continued their trip from Perga and went to Antioch, a city in Pisidia. On the Sabbath day they went into the synagogue and sat down. [15]After the law of Moses and the writings of the prophets were read, the leaders of the synagogue sent a message to Paul and Barnabas: "Brothers, if you have any message that will encourage the people, please speak."

[16]Paul stood up, raised his hand, and said, "You Israelites and you who worship God, please listen! [17]The God of the Israelites chose our ancestors. He made the people great during the time they lived in Egypt, and he brought them out of that country with great power. [18]And he was patient with them[n] for forty years in the desert. [19]God destroyed seven nations in the land of Canaan and gave the land to his people. [20]All this happened in about four hundred fifty years.

"After this, God gave them judges until the time of Samuel the prophet. [21]Then the people asked for a king, so God gave them Saul son of Kish. Saul was from the tribe of Benjamin and was king for forty years. [22]After God took him away, God made David their king. God said about him: 'I have found in David son of Jesse the kind of man I want. He will do all I want him to do.' [23]So God has brought Jesus, one of David's descendants, to Israel to be its Savior, as he promised. [24]Before Jesus came, John[n] preached to all the people of Israel about a baptism of changed hearts and lives. [25]When he was finishing his work, he said, 'Who do you think I am? I am not the Christ. He is coming later, and I am not worthy to untie his sandals.'

[26]"Brothers, sons of the family of Abraham, and others who worship God, listen! The news about this salvation has been sent to us. [27]Those who live in Jerusalem and their leaders did not realize that Jesus was the Savior. They did not understand the words that the prophets wrote, which are read every Sabbath day. But they made them come true when they said Jesus was guilty. [28]They could not find any real reason for Jesus to be put to death, but they asked Pilate to have him killed. [29]When they had done to him all that the Scriptures had said, they took him down from the cross and laid him in a tomb. [30]But God raised him up from the dead! [31]After this, for many days, those who had gone with Jesus from Galilee to Jerusalem saw him. They are now his witnesses to the people. [32]We tell you the Good News about the promise God made to our ancestors. [33]God has made this promise come true for us, his children, by raising Jesus from the dead. We read about this also in Psalm 2:

'You are my Son.
Today I have become your Father.'
Psalm 2:7

[34]God raised Jesus from the dead, and he will never go back to the grave and become dust. So God said:

'I will give you the holy and sure blessings
that I promised to David.' *Isaiah 55:3*

[35]But in another place God says:

'You will not let your Holy One rot.'
Psalm 16:10

13:18 And . . . them Some Greek copies read "And he cared for them."
13:24 John John the Baptist, who preached to people about Christ's coming (Luke 3).

36David did God's will during his lifetime.
Then he died and was buried beside his
ancestors, and his body did rot in the grave.
37But the One God raised from the dead did
not rot in the grave. 38-39Brothers, understand
what we are telling you: You can have
forgiveness of your sins through Jesus. The
law of Moses could not free you from your
sins. But through Jesus everyone who
believes is free from all sins. 40Be careful!
Don't let what the prophets said happen to
you:
41'Listen, you people who doubt!
You can wonder, and then die.
I will do something in your lifetime
that you won't believe even when you
are told about it!'" *Habakkuk 1:5*
42While Paul and Barnabas were leaving
the synagogue, the people asked them to tell
them more about these things on the next
Sabbath. 43When the meeting was over,
many people with those who had changed
to worship God followed Paul and Barnabas
from that place. Paul and Barnabas were
persuading them to continue trusting in
God's grace.

44On the next Sabbath day, almost
everyone in the city came to hear the word
of the Lord. 45Seeing the crowd, the Jewish
people became very jealous and said
insulting things and argued against what
Paul said. 46But Paul and Barnabas spoke
very boldly, saying, "We must speak the
message of God to you first. But you refuse
to listen. You are judging yourselves not
worthy of having eternal life! So we will now
go to the people of other nations. 47This is
what the Lord told us to do, saying:
'I have made you a light for the nations;
you will show people all over the world
the way to be saved.'" *Isaiah 49:6*
48When those who were not Jewish heard
Paul say this, they were happy and gave
honor to the message of the Lord. And the
people who were chosen to have life forever
believed the message.
49So the message of the Lord was
spreading through the whole country. 50But
the Jewish people stirred up some of the
important religious women and the leaders
of the city. They started trouble against Paul
and Barnabas and forced them out of their

devotion 298

ACTS 13:38–39

THE WOMAN AT THE WELL PLAYS MOTHER TERESA

I make the woman at the well look like Mother Teresa. I am one of those Christians who has been forgiven of so much that I am the first to extend grace to anyone who needs it. Are you familiar with Jesus' story of the two servants, one forgiven much and one forgiven little (Luke 7:41-47)? Jesus asked which one would have been more grateful. Well of course, the one who was forgiven of much was the most grateful. Have you been forgiven of much or little?

Are you withholding grace and forgiveness from someone that needs it from you? Please do not miss an opportunity to feel the amazing rush of love flow through your spirit when you extend a hand of forgiveness to someone who has sinned against you. "Most importantly, love each other deeply, because love will cause people to forgive each other for many sins" (1 Pet. 4:8). Like I said, there are plenty of times when I need that forgiveness, and I am overjoyed when I get an opportunity to show a bit of love and cover a few sins by forgiving an offense. Remember, the forgiveness of debt that Jesus was talking about was not given out of obligation, but was drawn out of love. Because this debt was forgiven, that meant that neither servant had to do anything to repay it; they just received the blessing. Do not make someone work for your forgiveness—just go and give the blessing.

area. 51So Paul and Barnabas shook the dust
off their feet[n] and went to Iconium. 52But the
followers were filled with joy and the Holy
Spirit.

Paul and Barnabas in Iconium

14 In Iconium, Paul and Barnabas went
as usual to the synagogue. They spoke
so well that a great many Jews and Greeks
believed. 2But some people who did not
believe excited the others and turned them
against the believers. 3Paul and Barnabas
stayed in Iconium a long time and spoke
bravely for the Lord. He showed that their
message about his grace was true by giving
them the power to work miracles and signs.
4But the city was divided. Some of the people
agreed with the Jews, and others believed the
apostles.

5Some who were not Jews, some Jews, and
some of their rulers wanted to mistreat Paul
and Barnabas and to stone them to death.
6When Paul and Barnabas learned about
this, they ran away to Lystra and Derbe,
cities in Lycaonia, and to the areas around
those cities. 7They announced the Good
News there, too.

Paul in Lystra and Derbe

8In Lystra there sat a man who had been
born crippled; he had never walked. 9As this
man was listening to Paul speak, Paul looked
straight at him and saw that he believed God
could heal him. 10So he cried out, "Stand up
on your feet!" The man jumped up and began
walking around. 11When the crowds saw
what Paul did, they shouted in the Lycaonian
language, "The gods have become like
humans and have come down to us!" 12Then
the people began to call Barnabas "Zeus"[n] and
Paul "Hermes,"[n] because he was the main
speaker. 13The priest in the temple of Zeus,
which was near the city, brought some bulls
and flowers to the city gates. He and the
people wanted to offer a sacrifice to Paul and
Barnabas. 14But when the apostles, Barnabas
and Paul, heard about it, they tore their
clothes. They ran in among the people,
shouting, 15"Friends, why are you doing these
things? We are only human beings like you.
We are bringing you the Good News and are
telling you to turn away from these worthless
things and turn to the living God. He is the
One who made the sky, the earth, the sea, and
everything in them. 16In the past, God let all
the nations do what they wanted. 17Yet he
proved he is real by showing kindness, by
giving you rain from heaven and crops at the
right times, by giving you food and filling
your hearts with joy." 18Even with these
words, they were barely able to keep the
crowd from offering sacrifices to them.

19Then some evil people came from
Antioch and Iconium and persuaded the
people to turn against Paul. So they threw
stones at him and dragged him out of town,
thinking they had killed him. 20But the
followers gathered around him, and he got
up and went back into the town. The next
day he and Barnabas left and went to the city
of Derbe.

The Return to Antioch in Syria

21Paul and Barnabas told the Good News
in Derbe, and many became followers. Paul
and Barnabas returned to Lystra, Iconium,
and Antioch, 22making the followers of Jesus
stronger and helping them stay in the faith.
They said, "We must suffer many things to
enter God's kingdom." 23They chose elders
for each church, by praying and fasting[n] for a
certain time. These elders had trusted the
Lord, so Paul and Barnabas put them in the
Lord's care.

24Then they went through Pisidia and
came to Pamphylia. 25When they had
preached the message in Perga, they went
down to Attalia. 26And from there they sailed
away to Antioch where the believers had put
them into God's care and had sent them out
to do this work. Now they had finished.

27When they arrived in Antioch, Paul and
Barnabas gathered the church together. They
told the church all about what God had done
with them and how God had made it
possible for those who were not Jewish to
believe. 28And they stayed there a long time
with the followers.

The Meeting at Jerusalem

15 Then some people came to Antioch
from Judea and began teaching the

13:51 shook . . . feet A warning. It showed that they had rejected these people. **14:12 "Zeus"** The Greeks believed in many false gods, of whom Zeus was most important. **14:12 "Hermes"** The Greeks believed he was a messenger for the other gods. **14:23 fasting** The people would give up eating for a special time of prayer and worship to God. It was also done sometimes to show sadness and disappointment.

non-Jewish believers: "You cannot be saved if
you are not circumcised as Moses taught us."
2Paul and Barnabas were against this
teaching and argued with them about it. So
the church decided to send Paul, Barnabas,
and some others to Jerusalem where they
could talk more about this with the apostles
and elders.
3The church helped them leave on the
trip, and they went through the countries of
Phoenicia and Samaria, telling all about how
the other nations had turned to God. This
made all the believers very happy. 4When
they arrived in Jerusalem, they were
welcomed by the apostles, the elders, and the
church. Paul, Barnabas, and the others told
about everything God had done with them.
5But some of the believers who belonged to
the Pharisee group came forward and said,
"The non-Jewish believers must be
circumcised. They must be told to obey the
law of Moses."
6The apostles and the elders gathered to
consider this problem. 7After a long debate,
Peter stood up and said to them, "Brothers,
you know that in the early days God chose
me from among you to preach the Good
News to the nations. They heard the Good
News from me, and they believed. 8God,
who knows the thoughts of everyone,
accepted them. He showed this to us by
giving them the Holy Spirit, just as he did to
us. 9To God, those people are not different
from us. When they believed, he made their
hearts pure. 10So now why are you testing
God by putting a heavy load around the
necks of the non-Jewish believers? It is a load
that neither we nor our ancestors were able
to carry. 11But we believe that we and they
too will be saved by the grace of the Lord
Jesus."
12Then the whole group became quiet.
They listened to Paul and Barnabas tell about
all the miracles and signs that God did
through them among the people. 13After
they finished speaking, James said, "Brothers,
listen to me. 14Simon has told us how God
showed his love for those people. For the
first time he is accepting from among them
a people to be his own. 15The words of the
prophets agree with this too:
16'After these things I will return.
The kingdom of David is like a fallen
tent.
But I will rebuild its ruins,
and I will set it up.
17Then those people who are left alive may
ask the Lord for help,
and the other nations that belong
to me,
says the Lord,
who will make it happen.
18And these things have been known for a
long time.' *Amos 9:11–12*
19"So I think we should not bother the
other people who are turning to God.
20Instead, we should write a letter to them
telling them these things: Stay away from
food that has been offered to idols (which
makes it unclean), any kind of sexual sin,
eating animals that have been strangled,
and blood. 21They should do these things,
because for a long time in every city the law
of Moses has been taught. And it is still read
in the synagogue every Sabbath day."

Letter to Non-Jewish Believers

22The apostles, the elders, and the whole
church decided to send some of their men
with Paul and Barnabas to Antioch. They
chose Judas Barsabbas and Silas, who were
respected by the believers. 23They sent the
following letter with them:

From the apostles and elders, your
brothers.
To all the non-Jewish believers in
Antioch, Syria, and Cilicia:
Greetings!
24We have heard that some of our
group have come to you and said things
that trouble and upset you. But we did
not tell them to do this. 25We have all
agreed to choose some messengers and
send them to you with our dear friends
Barnabas and Paul— 26people who have
given their lives to serve our Lord Jesus
Christ. 27So we are sending Judas and
Silas, who will tell you the same things.
28It has pleased the Holy Spirit that you
should not have a heavy load to carry,
and we agree. You need to do only these
things: 29Stay away from any food that
has been offered to idols, eating any
animals that have been strangled, and
blood, and any kind of sexual sin. If you
stay away from these things, you will
do well.
Good-bye.

Lydia

ACTS 16

Lydia and the other women gather at the river's edge each Sabbath to take in the beauty of the sea. She loves it here. It's so peaceful—a far cry from the heart of the city where she sells her fine purple cloth during the week. She closes her eyes, and a breeze dances across her face. A man's voice startles her.

"Do you love the Lord your God with all your soul and with all your heart and with all your strength?" The women nod. Of course they do, they say. They've gathered here so they can worship him. "You cannot really know God until you know his Son," Paul says.

Lydia leans in, eager for more. She listens as Paul tells of this man who was murdered because of his great love and then raised from the dead so that she could live with him forever. Tears stream down her face as Lydia's heart opens to the love of the Savior.

Her belief is so contagious that every member of her household wants the love of Jesus in their hearts. She extends her hospitality to Paul and Silas. She is a source of encouragement and inspiration for them and others who enter her door. Unlike her fine purple cloth, she does not have to sell the story of Jesus. It is something she freely gives away day after day.

Lydia's entire family was changed by her testimony. How precious is the example of a godly woman!

30So they left Jerusalem and went to
Antioch where they gathered the church
and gave them the letter. 31When they read
it, they were very happy because of the
encouraging message. 32Judas and Silas, who
were also prophets, said many things to
encourage the believers and make them
stronger. 33After some time Judas and Silas
were sent off in peace by the believers, and
they went back to those who had sent them
[, 34but Silas decided to remain there].[n]
35But Paul and Barnabas stayed in Antioch
and, along with many others, preached the
Good News and taught the people the
message of the Lord.

Paul and Barnabas Separate

36After some time, Paul said to Barnabas,
"We should go back to all those towns where
we preached the message of the Lord. Let's
visit the believers and see how they are
doing."
37Barnabas wanted to take John Mark
with them, 38but he had left them at
Pamphylia; he did not continue with them
in the work. So Paul did not think it was a
good idea to take him. 39Paul and Barnabas
had such a serious argument about this that
they separated and went different ways.
Barnabas took Mark and sailed to Cyprus,
40but Paul chose Silas and left. The believers
in Antioch put Paul into the Lord's care,
41and he went through Syria and Cilicia,
giving strength to the churches.

Timothy Goes with Paul

16 Paul came to Derbe and Lystra, where
a follower named Timothy lived.
Timothy's mother was Jewish and a believer,
but his father was a Greek.
2The believers in Lystra and Iconium
respected Timothy and said good things
about him. 3Paul wanted Timothy to travel
with him, but all the people living in that
area knew that Timothy's father was Greek.
So Paul circumcised Timothy to please his
mother's people. 4Paul and those with him
traveled from town to town and gave the
decisions made by the apostles and elders in
Jerusalem for the people to obey. 5So the
churches became stronger in the faith and
grew larger every day.

15:34 but . . . there Some Greek copies do not contain the bracketed text.

Paul Is Called Out of Asia

[6]Paul and those with him went through the areas of Phrygia and Galatia since the Holy Spirit did not let them preach the Good News in Asia. [7]When they came near the country of Mysia, they tried to go into Bithynia, but the Spirit of Jesus did not let them. [8]So they passed by Mysia and went to Troas. [9]That night Paul saw in a vision a man from Macedonia. The man stood and begged, "Come over to Macedonia and help us." [10]After Paul had seen the vision, we immediately prepared to leave for Macedonia, understanding that God had called us to tell the Good News to those people.

Lydia Becomes a Christian

[11]We left Troas and sailed straight to the island of Samothrace. The next day we sailed to Neapolis.[n] [12]Then we went by land to Philippi, a Roman colony[n] and the leading city in that part of Macedonia. We stayed there for several days.

[13]On the Sabbath day we went outside the city gate to the river where we thought we would find a special place for prayer. Some women had gathered there, so we sat down and talked with them. [14]One of the listeners was a woman named Lydia from the city of Thyatira whose job was selling purple cloth. She worshiped God, and he opened her mind to pay attention to what Paul was saying. [15]She and all the people in her house were baptized. Then she invited us to her home, saying, "If you think I am truly a believer in the Lord, then come stay in my house." And she persuaded us to stay with her.

Paul and Silas in Jail

[16]Once, while we were going to the place for prayer, a servant girl met us. She had a special spirit[n] in her, and she earned a lot of money for her owners by telling fortunes. [17]This girl followed Paul and us, shouting, "These men are servants of the Most High God. They are telling you how you can be saved."

[18]She kept this up for many days. This bothered Paul, so he turned and said to the spirit, "By the power of Jesus Christ, I command you to come out of her!" Immediately, the spirit came out.

[19]When the owners of the servant girl saw this, they knew that now they could not use her to make money. So they grabbed Paul and Silas and dragged them before the city rulers in the marketplace. [20]They brought Paul and Silas to the Roman rulers and said, "These men are Jews and are making trouble in our city. [21]They are teaching things that are not right for us as Romans to do."

[22]The crowd joined the attack against them. The Roman officers tore the clothes of Paul and Silas and had them beaten with rods. [23]Then Paul and Silas were thrown into jail, and the jailer was ordered to guard them carefully. [24]When he heard this order, he put them far inside the jail and pinned their feet down between large blocks of wood.

[25]About midnight Paul and Silas were praying and singing songs to God as the other prisoners listened. [26]Suddenly, there was a strong earthquake that shook the foundation of the jail. Then all the doors of the jail broke open, and all the prisoners were freed from their chains. [27]The jailer woke up and saw that the jail doors were open. Thinking that the prisoners had already escaped, he got his sword and was about to kill himself.[n] [28]But Paul shouted, "Don't hurt yourself! We are all here."

[29]The jailer told someone to bring a light. Then he ran inside and, shaking with fear, fell down before Paul and Silas. [30]He brought them outside and said, "Men, what must I do to be saved?"

[31]They said to him, "Believe in the Lord Jesus and you will be saved—you and all the people in your house." [32]So Paul and Silas told the message of the Lord to the jailer and all the people in his house. [33]At that hour of the night the jailer took Paul and Silas and washed their wounds. Then he and all his people were baptized immediately. [34]After this the jailer took Paul and Silas home and gave them food. He and his family were very happy because they now believed in God.

[35]The next morning, the Roman officers sent the police to tell the jailer, "Let these men go free."

16:11 Neapolis City in Macedonia. It was the first city Paul visited on the continent of Europe. **16:12 Roman colony** A town begun by Romans with Roman laws, customs, and privileges. **16:16 spirit** This was a spirit from the devil, which caused her to say she had special knowledge. **16:27 kill himself** He thought the leaders would kill him for letting the prisoners escape.

devotion 299

ACTS 16:25–26

AN EARTHQUAKE OF PRAISE

Paul and Silas were arrested for "teaching things that [were] not right" (Acts 16:21). (They were teaching about redemption through Jesus Christ.) They were beaten and put in jail so they would keep quiet. They were even placed in the back of the jail with their feet in wooden blocks to make sure they didn't escape. They must have been tired, hungry, and in pain from their beating, but Paul and Silas couldn't keep quiet. From the depths of a prison cell, they began to sing. It may have started as a quiet prayer from the depths of their soul, but it must have gained strength because eventually they sang loud enough for the other prisoners to hear.

We may not live in a country that puts us in jail for talking about Jesus Christ, but we can feel beaten down and silenced at times. You may feel like an outcast or you may be disappointed with the way life is going or you may even feel hopeless in your given situation. So what can we learn from Paul and Silas? Praise the Lord. There is power in our praises to God. Look at what happened to Paul and Silas when they praised the Lord. An earthquake shook the jail, and the prisoners were set free. If you feel like a prisoner today for one reason or another, respond by praising the Lord. He can and will work through those who praise him.

36The jailer said to Paul, "The officers have
sent an order to let you go free. You can leave
now. Go in peace."
37But Paul said to the police, "They beat us
in public without a trial, even though we are
Roman citizens.[n] And they threw us in jail.
Now they want to make us go away quietly.
No! Let them come themselves and bring us
out."
38The police told the Roman officers what
Paul said. When the officers heard that Paul
and Silas were Roman citizens, they were
afraid. 39So they came and told Paul and Silas
they were sorry and took them out of jail and
asked them to leave the city. 40So when they
came out of the jail, they went to Lydia's
house where they saw some of the believers
and encouraged them. Then they left.

Paul and Silas in Thessalonica

17 Paul and Silas traveled through
Amphipolis and Apollonia and came
to Thessalonica where there was a synagogue.
2Paul went into the synagogue as he always
did, and on each Sabbath day for three weeks,
he talked with his fellow Jews about the
Scriptures. 3He explained and proved that the
Christ must die and then rise from the dead.
He said, "This Jesus I am telling you about is
the Christ." 4Some of them were convinced
and joined Paul and Silas, along with many of
the Greeks who worshiped God and many of
the important women.
5But some others became jealous. So they
got some evil men from the marketplace,
formed a mob, and started a riot. They ran
to Jason's house, looking for Paul and Silas,
wanting to bring them out to the people. 6But
when they did not find them, they dragged
Jason and some other believers to the leaders
of the city. The people were yelling, "These
people have made trouble everywhere in the
world, and now they have come here too!
7Jason is keeping them in his house. All of

16:37 Roman citizens Roman law said that Roman citizens must not be beaten before they had a trial.

them do things against the laws of Caesar,
saying there is another king, called Jesus."
8 When the people and the leaders of the
city heard these things, they became very
upset. 9 They made Jason and the others put
up a sum of money. Then they let the
believers go free.

Paul and Silas Go to Berea

10 That same night the believers sent Paul
and Silas to Berea where they went to the
synagogue. 11 These people were more
willing to listen than the people in
Thessalonica. The Bereans were eager to
hear what Paul and Silas said and studied
the Scriptures every day to find out if these
things were true. 12 So, many of them
believed, as well as many important Greek
women and men. 13 But the people in
Thessalonica learned that Paul was
preaching the word of God in Berea, too.
So they came there, upsetting the people
and making trouble. 14 The believers quickly
sent Paul away to the coast, but Silas and
Timothy stayed in Berea. 15 The people
leading Paul went with him to Athens. Then
they carried a message from Paul back to
Silas and Timothy for them to come to him
as soon as they could.

Paul Preaches in Athens

16 While Paul was waiting for Silas and
Timothy in Athens, he was troubled because
he saw that the city was full of idols. 17 In the
synagogue, he talked with the Jews and the
Greeks who worshiped God. He also talked
every day with people in the marketplace.
18 Some of the Epicurean and Stoic
philosophers[n] argued with him, saying,
"This man doesn't know what he is talking
about. What is he trying to say?" Others said,
"He seems to be telling us about some other
gods," because Paul was telling them about
Jesus and his rising from the dead. 19 They
got Paul and took him to a meeting of the
Areopagus,[n] where they said, "Please explain
to us this new idea you have been teaching.
20 The things you are saying are new to us,
and we want to know what this teaching
means." 21 (All the people of Athens and
those from other countries who lived there
always used their time to talk about the
newest ideas.)
22 Then Paul stood before the meeting of
the Areopagus and said, "People of Athens, I
can see you are very religious in all things.
23 As I was going through your city, I saw the
objects you worship. I found an altar that
had these words written on it: TO A GOD WHO
IS NOT KNOWN. You worship a god that you
don't know, and this is the God I am telling
you about! 24 The God who made the whole
world and everything in it is the Lord of the
land and the sky. He does not live in temples
built by human hands. 25 This God is the One
who gives life, breath, and everything else to
people. He does not need any help from
them; he has everything he needs. 26 God
began by making one person, and from him
came all the different people who live
everywhere in the world. God decided
exactly when and where they must live.
27 God wanted them to look for him and
perhaps search all around for him and find
him, though he is not far from any of us:
28 'By his power we live and move and exist.'
Some of your own poets have said: 'For we
are his children.' 29 Since we are God's
children, you must not think that God is like
something that people imagine or make
from gold, silver, or rock. 30 In the past,
people did not understand God, and he
ignored this. But now, God tells all people in
the world to change their hearts and lives.
31 God has set a day that he will judge all the
world with fairness, by the man he chose
long ago. And God has proved this to
everyone by raising that man from the
dead!"
32 When the people heard about Jesus
being raised from the dead, some of them
laughed. But others said, "We will hear more
about this from you later." 33 So Paul went
away from them. 34 But some of the people
believed Paul and joined him. Among those
who believed was Dionysius, a member of
the Areopagus, a woman named Damaris,
and some others.

Paul in Corinth

18 Later Paul left Athens and went to
Corinth. 2 Here he met a Jew named

17:18 Epicurean and Stoic philosophers Philosophers were those who searched for truth. Epicureans believed that pleasures, especially pleasures of the mind, were the goal of life. Stoics believed that life should be without feelings of joy or grief.
17:19 Areopagus A council or group of important leaders in Athens. They were like judges.

Priscilla

ACTS 18—19

Priscilla and her husband, Aquila, had only been in Corinth a year when they met Paul, a Jewish man who was preaching the Good News wherever he traveled. He was a tentmaker, so Priscilla and Aquila invited him to stay in their home and work with them. Priscilla had no idea what that invitation would mean.

Paul preached in the synagogue and to the local non-Jewish people. His message generated a great deal of opposition from Jewish leaders. But Priscilla's prayer life grew by leaps and bounds with Paul in her home! After eighteen months, the leading Jews of Corinth called Paul before the governor of Southern Greece, accusing him of spreading an unlawful religion. Priscilla fasted and prayed on Paul's behalf. When the charges were dismissed, she and Aquila joined Paul as he set sail for Ephesus to spread the message of Jesus there.

Priscilla's heart thumped as they approached the great city. She had heard that Ephesus had constructed a temple to the goddess Artemis—a temple so enormous it was considered one of the seven wonders of the ancient world! How could they spread the Good News in an atmosphere so thick with hostility against the Truth? Despite her fears, she was determined not to turn her back on the Savior she loved. She and Aquila would risk their lives for the sake of Jesus, starting a church in their home.

You too are a valuable part of your church community, and God promises to use you.

Aquila who had been born in the country
of Pontus. But Aquila and his wife, Priscilla,
had recently moved to Corinth from Italy,
because Claudius[n] commanded that all Jews
must leave Rome. Paul went to visit Aquila
and Priscilla. 3Because they were tentmakers,
just as he was, he stayed with them and
worked with them. 4Every Sabbath day he
talked with the Jews and Greeks in the
synagogue, trying to persuade them to
believe in Jesus.

5Silas and Timothy came from Macedonia
and joined Paul in Corinth. After this, Paul
spent all his time telling people the Good
News, showing them that Jesus is the Christ.
6But they would not accept Paul's teaching
and said some evil things. So he shook off
the dust from his clothes[n] and said to them,
"If you are not saved, it will be your own
fault! I have done all I can do! After this, I
will go to other nations." 7Paul left the
synagogue and moved into the home of
Titius Justus, next to the synagogue. This
man worshiped God. 8Crispus was the leader
of that synagogue, and he and all the people
living in his house believed in the Lord.
Many others in Corinth also listened to Paul
and believed and were baptized.

9During the night, the Lord told Paul in a
vision: "Don't be afraid. Continue talking to
people and don't be quiet. 10I am with you,
and no one will hurt you because many of
my people are in this city." 11Paul stayed
there for a year and a half, teaching God's
word to the people.

Paul Is Brought Before Gallio

12When Gallio was the governor of the
country of Southern Greece, some people
came together against Paul and took him to
the court. 13They said, "This man is teaching
people to worship God in a way that is
against our law."

14Paul was about to say something, but
Gallio spoke, saying, "I would listen to you
if you were complaining about a crime or
some wrong. 15But the things you are saying
are only questions about words and
names—arguments about your own law.
So you must solve this problem yourselves.
I don't want to be a judge of these things."
16And Gallio made them leave the court.

18:2 Claudius The emperor (ruler) of Rome, A.D. 41–54.
18:6 shook . . . clothes This was a warning to show that Paul was finished talking to the people in that city.

[17]Then they all grabbed Sosthenes, the
leader of the synagogue, and beat him there
before the court. But this did not bother
Gallio.

Paul Returns to Antioch

[18]Paul stayed with the believers for many
more days. Then he left and sailed for Syria,
with Priscilla and Aquila. At Cenchrea Paul
cut off his hair,[n] because he had made a
promise to God. [19]Then they went to
Ephesus, where Paul left Priscilla and Aquila.
While Paul was there, he went into the
synagogue and talked with the people.
[20]When they asked him to stay with them
longer, he refused. [21]But as he left, he said, "I
will come back to you again if God wants me
to." And so he sailed away from Ephesus.

[22]When Paul landed at Caesarea, he
went and gave greetings to the church in
Jerusalem. After that, Paul went to Antioch.
[23]He stayed there for a while and then left
and went through the regions of Galatia and
Phrygia. He traveled from town to town in
these regions, giving strength to all the
followers.

Apollos in Ephesus and Corinth

[24]A Jew named Apollos came to Ephesus.
He was born in the city of Alexandria and
was a good speaker who knew the Scriptures
well. [25]He had been taught about the way of
the Lord and was always very excited when
he spoke and taught the truth about Jesus.
But the only baptism Apollos knew about
was the baptism that John[n] taught. [26]Apollos
began to speak very boldly in the synagogue,
and when Priscilla and Aquila heard him,
they took him to their home and helped him
better understand the way of God. [27]Now
Apollos wanted to go to the country of
Southern Greece. So the believers helped
him and wrote a letter to the followers there,
asking them to accept him. These followers
had believed in Jesus because of God's grace,
and when Apollos arrived, he helped them
very much. [28]He argued very strongly with
the Jews before all the people, clearly
proving with the Scriptures that Jesus is
the Christ.

Paul in Ephesus

19 While Apollos was in Corinth, Paul
was visiting some places on the way
to Ephesus. There he found some followers
[2]and asked them, "Did you receive the Holy
Spirit when you believed?"

They said, "We have never even heard of a
Holy Spirit."

[3]So he asked, "What kind of baptism did
you have?"

They said, "It was the baptism that John
taught."

[4]Paul said, "John's baptism was a baptism
of changed hearts and lives. He told people
to believe in the one who would come after
him, and that one is Jesus."

[5]When they heard this, they were
baptized in the name of the Lord Jesus.
[6]Then Paul laid his hands on them,[n] and
the Holy Spirit came upon them. They
began speaking different languages[n] and
prophesying. [7]There were about twelve
people in this group.

[8]Paul went into the synagogue and spoke
out boldly for three months. He talked with
the people and persuaded them to accept the
things he said about the kingdom of God.
[9]But some of them became stubborn. They
refused to believe and said evil things about
the Way of Jesus before all the people. So
Paul left them, and taking the followers with
him, he went to the school of a man named
Tyrannus. There Paul talked with people
every day [10]for two years. Because of his
work, every Jew and Greek in Asia heard the
word of the Lord.

The Sons of Sceva

[11]God used Paul to do some very special
miracles. [12]Some people took handkerchiefs
and clothes that Paul had used and put them
on the sick. When they did this, the sick
were healed and evil spirits left them.

[13]But some people also were traveling
around and making evil spirits go out of
people. They tried to use the name of the
Lord Jesus to force the evil spirits out. They
would say, "By the same Jesus that Paul talks
about, I order you to come out!" [14]Seven sons
of Sceva, a leading priest, were doing this.

18:18 cut . . . hair Jews did this to show that the time of a special promise to God was finished. **18:25 John** John the Baptist, who preached to people about Christ's coming (Luke 3). **19:6 laid his hands on them** The laying on of hands had many purposes, including the giving of a blessing, power, or authority. **19:6 languages** This can also be translated "tongues."

15 But one time an evil spirit said to them, "I know Jesus, and I know about Paul, but who are you?"

16 Then the man who had the evil spirit jumped on them. Because he was so much stronger than all of them, they ran away from the house naked and hurt. 17 All the people in Ephesus—Jews and Greeks—learned about this and were filled with fear and gave great honor to the Lord Jesus. 18 Many of the believers began to confess openly and tell all the evil things they had done. 19 Some of them who had used magic brought their magic books and burned them before everyone. Those books were worth about fifty thousand silver coins.[n]

20 So in a powerful way the word of the Lord kept spreading and growing.

21 After these things, Paul decided to go to Jerusalem, planning to go through the countries of Macedonia and Southern Greece and then on to Jerusalem. He said, "After I have been to Jerusalem, I must also visit Rome." 22 Paul sent Timothy and Erastus, two of his helpers, ahead to Macedonia, but he himself stayed in Asia for a while.

Trouble in Ephesus

23 And during that time, there was some serious trouble in Ephesus about the Way of Jesus. 24 A man named Demetrius, who worked with silver, made little silver models that looked like the temple of the goddess Artemis.[n] Those who did this work made much money. 25 Demetrius had a meeting with them and some others who did the same kind of work. He told them, "Men, you know that we make a lot of money from our business. 26 But look at what this man Paul is doing. He has convinced and turned away many people in Ephesus and in almost all of Asia! He says the gods made by human hands are not real. 27 There is a danger that our business will lose its good name, but there is also another danger: People will begin to think that the temple of the great goddess Artemis is not important. Her greatness will be destroyed, and Artemis is the goddess that everyone in Asia and the whole world worships."

28 When the others heard this, they became very angry and shouted, "Artemis, the goddess of Ephesus, is great!" 29 The whole city became confused. The people grabbed Gaius and Aristarchus, who were from Macedonia and were traveling with Paul, and ran to the theater. 30 Paul wanted to go in and talk to the crowd, but the followers did not let him. 31 Also, some leaders of Asia who were friends of Paul sent him a message, begging him not to go into the theater. 32 Some people were shouting one thing, and some were shouting another. The meeting was completely confused; most of them did not know why they had come together. 33 They put a man named Alexander in front of the people, and some of them told him what to do. Alexander waved his hand so he could explain things to the people. 34 But when they saw that Alexander was a Jew, they all shouted the same thing for two hours: "Great is Artemis of Ephesus!"

35 Then the city clerk made the crowd be quiet. He said, "People of Ephesus, everyone knows that Ephesus is the city that keeps the temple of the great goddess Artemis and her holy stone[n] that fell from heaven. 36 Since no one can say this is not true, you should be quiet. Stop and think before you do anything. 37 You brought these men here, but they have not said anything evil against our goddess or stolen anything from her temple. 38 If Demetrius and those who work with him have a charge against anyone they should go to the courts and judges where they can argue with each other. 39 If there is something else you want to talk about, it can be decided at the regular town meeting of the people. 40 I say this because some people might see this trouble today and say that we are rioting. We could not explain this, because there is no real reason for this meeting." 41 After the city clerk said these things, he told the people to go home.

Paul in Macedonia and Greece

20 When the trouble stopped, Paul sent for the followers to come to him. After he encouraged them and then told them good-bye, he left and went to the country of Macedonia. 2 He said many things to strengthen the followers in the different

19:19 fifty thousand silver coins Probably drachmas. One coin was enough to pay a worker for one day's labor. **19:24 Artemis** A Greek goddess that the people of Asia Minor worshiped. **19:35 holy stone** Probably a meteorite or stone that the people thought looked like Artemis.

places on his way through Macedonia. Then
he went to Greece, 3where he stayed for
three months. He was ready to sail for Syria,
but some evil people were planning
something against him. So Paul decided to
go back through Macedonia to Syria. 4The
men who went with him were Sopater
son of Pyrrhus, from the city of Berea;
Aristarchus and Secundus, from the city of
Thessalonica; Gaius, from Derbe; Timothy;
and Tychicus and Trophimus, two men from
Asia. 5These men went on ahead and waited
for us at Troas. 6We sailed from Philippi after
the Feast of Unleavened Bread. Five days
later we met them in Troas, where we stayed
for seven days.

Paul's Last Visit to Troas

7On the first day of the week,[n] we all met
together to break bread,[n] and Paul spoke to
the group. Because he was planning to leave
the next day, he kept on talking until
midnight. 8We were all together in a room
upstairs, and there were many lamps in the
room. 9A young man named Eutychus was
sitting in the window. As Paul continued
talking, Eutychus was falling into a deep
sleep. Finally, he went sound asleep and fell
to the ground from the third floor. When
they picked him up, he was dead. 10Paul
went down to Eutychus, knelt down, and
put his arms around him. He said, "Don't
worry. He is alive now." 11Then Paul went
upstairs again, broke bread, and ate. He
spoke to them a long time, until it was early
morning, and then he left. 12They took the
young man home alive and were greatly
comforted.

The Trip from Troas to Miletus

13We went on ahead of Paul and sailed
for the city of Assos, where he wanted to join
us on the ship. Paul planned it this way
because he wanted to go to Assos by land.
14When he met us there, we took him
aboard and went to Mitylene. 15We sailed
from Mitylene and the next day came to a
place near Kios. The following day we sailed
to Samos, and the next day we reached
Miletus. 16Paul had already decided not to
stop at Ephesus, because he did not want to
stay too long in Asia. He was hurrying to be
in Jerusalem on the day of Pentecost, if that
were possible.

The Elders from Ephesus

17Now from Miletus Paul sent to Ephesus
and called for the elders of the church.
18When they came to him, he said, "You
know about my life from the first day I came
to Asia. You know the way I lived all the
time I was with you. 19The evil people made
plans against me, which troubled me very
much. But you know I always served the
Lord unselfishly, and I often cried. 20You
know I preached to you and did not hold
back anything that would help you. You
know that I taught you in public and in your
homes. 21I warned both Jews and Greeks to
change their lives and turn to God and
believe in our Lord Jesus. 22But now I must
obey the Holy Spirit and go to Jerusalem. I
don't know what will happen to me there.
23I know only that in every city the Holy
Spirit tells me that troubles and even jail
wait for me. 24I don't care about my own life.
The most important thing is that I complete
my mission, the work that the Lord Jesus
gave me—to tell people the Good News
about God's grace.

25"And now, I know that none of you
among whom I was preaching the kingdom
of God will ever see me again. 26So today I
tell you that if any of you should be lost, I
am not responsible, 27because I have told
you everything God wants you to know. 28Be
careful for yourselves and for all the people
the Holy Spirit has given to you to oversee.
You must be like shepherds to the church of
God,[n] which he bought with the death of his
own son. 29I know that after I leave, some
people will come like wild wolves and try to
destroy the flock. 30Also, some from your
own group will rise up and twist the truth
and will lead away followers after them.
31So be careful! Always remember that for
three years, day and night, I never stopped
warning each of you, and I often cried over
you.

32"Now I am putting you in the care of
God and the message about his grace. It is
able to give you strength, and it will give you

20:7 first day of the week Sunday, which for Jews began at sunset on our Saturday. But if in this part of Asia a different system of time was used, then the meeting was on our Sunday night. **20:7 break bread** Probably the Lord's Supper, the special meal that Jesus told his followers to eat to remember him (Luke 22:14–20). **20:28 of God** Some Greek copies read "of the Lord."

devotion 300

ACTS 20:35

DEEP POCKETS

One Sunday morning, a friend's little boy rushed up and exclaimed, "Mom! I got fifty cents from my teacher for bringing my Bible!" His mom, concerned, took the Sunday school teacher aside and gently questioned her about her motive. Smiling, the teacher explained the real lesson, which was that she'd told the children they could keep the money or put it in the offering plate.

The mom nodded in understanding. The teacher had challenged the children to remember Jesus' words in Acts 20:35. Just before the church service began, the mom told her son that she was proud he'd been rewarded for bringing his Bible. He smiled proudly back at her. When the offering plate came around, she watched his inward struggle as he passed the plate on to her. Believing he'd chosen to keep his money, she started to pass the plate on. Imagine the pride she felt when he suddenly jumped up and whispered loudly as he dug into his pocket, "My teacher said, 'It's more blessed to give than to get!' "

How often do we struggle inwardly when we feel God calling us to give of ourselves, whether it is to meet a financial, practical, or emotional need in someone else's life? Do we let the offering plate pass on? Or do we dig down deep into the pockets of our own blessings and share what God has given us? Imagine how proud Jesus is when we remember his words and choose to give to others.

the blessings God has for all his holy people.
33 When I was with you, I never wanted
anyone's money or fine clothes. 34 You know I
always worked to take care of my own needs
and the needs of those who were with me.
35 I showed you in all things that you should
work as I did and help the weak. I taught you
to remember the words Jesus said: 'It is more
blessed to give than to receive.' "

36 When Paul had said this, he knelt down
with all of them and prayed. 37-38 And they
all cried because Paul had said they would
never see him again. They put their arms
around him and kissed him. Then they went
with him to the ship.

Paul Goes to Jerusalem

21 After we all said good-bye to them, we
sailed straight to the island of Cos. The
next day we reached Rhodes, and from there
we went to Patara. 2 There we found a ship
going to Phoenicia, so we went aboard and
sailed away. 3 We sailed near the island of
Cyprus, seeing it to the north, but we sailed
on to Syria. We stopped at Tyre because the
ship needed to unload its cargo there. 4 We
found some followers in Tyre and stayed with
them for seven days. Through the Holy Spirit
they warned Paul not to go to Jerusalem.
5 When we finished our visit, we left and
continued our trip. All the followers, even the
women and children, came outside the city
with us. After we all knelt on the beach and
prayed, 6 we said good-bye and got on the
ship, and the followers went back home.

7 We continued our trip from Tyre and
arrived at Ptolemais, where we greeted the
believers and stayed with them for a day.
8 The next day we left Ptolemais and went
to the city of Caesarea. There we went into
the home of Philip the preacher, one of the
seven helpers,[n] and stayed with him. 9 He had

21:8 helpers The seven men chosen for a special work described in Acts 6:1–6. Sometimes they are called "deacons."

four unmarried daughters who had the gift of prophesying. 10After we had been there for some time, a prophet named Agabus arrived from Judea. 11He came to us and borrowed Paul's belt and used it to tie his own hands and feet. He said, "The Holy Spirit says, 'This is how evil people in Jerusalem will tie up the man who wears this belt. Then they will give him to the older leaders.' "

12When we all heard this, we and the people there begged Paul not to go to Jerusalem. 13But he said, "Why are you crying and making me so sad? I am not only ready to be tied up in Jerusalem, I am ready to die for the Lord Jesus!"

14We could not persuade him to stay away from Jerusalem. So we stopped begging him and said, "We pray that what the Lord wants will be done."

15After this, we got ready and started on our way to Jerusalem. 16Some of the followers from Caesarea went with us and took us to the home of Mnason, where we would stay. He was from Cyprus and was one of the first followers.

Paul Visits James

17In Jerusalem the believers were glad to see us. 18The next day Paul went with us to visit James, and all the elders were there. 19Paul greeted them and told them everything God had done among the other nations through him. 20When they heard this, they praised God. Then they said to Paul, "Brother, you can see that many thousands of our people have become believers. And they think it is very important to obey the law of Moses. 21They have heard about your teaching, that you tell our people who live among the nations to leave the law of Moses. They have heard that you tell them not to circumcise their children and not to obey customs. 22What should we do? They will learn that you have come. 23So we will tell you what to do: Four of our men have made a promise to God. 24Take these men with you and share in their cleansing ceremony.[n] Pay their expenses so they can shave their heads.[n] Then it will prove to everyone that what they have heard about you is not true and that you follow the law of Moses in your own life. 25We have already sent a letter to the non-Jewish believers. The letter said: 'Do not eat food that has been offered to idols, or blood, or animals that have been strangled. Do not take part in sexual sin.' "

26The next day Paul took the four men and shared in the cleansing ceremony with them. Then he went to the Temple and announced the time when the days of the cleansing ceremony would be finished. On the last day an offering would be given for each of the men.

27When the seven days were almost over, some of his people from Asia saw Paul at the Temple. They caused all the people to be upset and grabbed Paul. 28They shouted, "People of Israel, help us! This is the man who goes everywhere teaching against the law of Moses, against our people, and against this Temple. Now he has brought some Greeks into the Temple and has made this holy place unclean!" 29(They said this because they had seen Trophimus, a man from Ephesus, with Paul in Jerusalem. They thought that Paul had brought him into the Temple.)

30All the people in Jerusalem became upset. Together they ran, took Paul, and dragged him out of the Temple. The Temple doors were closed immediately. 31While they were trying to kill Paul, the commander of the Roman army in Jerusalem learned that there was trouble in the whole city. 32Immediately he took some officers and soldiers and ran to the place where the crowd was gathered. When the people saw them, they stopped beating Paul. 33The commander went to Paul and arrested him. He told his soldiers to tie Paul with two chains. Then he asked who he was and what he had done wrong. 34Some in the crowd were yelling one thing, and some were yelling another. Because of all this confusion and shouting, the commander could not learn what had happened. So he ordered the soldiers to take Paul to the army building. 35When Paul came to the steps, the soldiers had to carry him because the people were ready to hurt him. 36The whole mob was following them, shouting, "Kill him!"

21:24 cleansing ceremony The special things Jews did to end the Nazirite promise.
21:24 shave their heads Jews did this to show that their promise was finished.

37 As the soldiers were about to take Paul into the army building, he spoke to the commander, "May I say something to you?"

The commander said, "Do you speak Greek? 38 I thought you were the Egyptian who started some trouble against the government not long ago and led four thousand killers out to the desert."

39 Paul said, "No, I am a Jew from Tarsus in the country of Cilicia. I am a citizen of that important city. Please, let me speak to the people."

40 The commander gave permission, so Paul stood on the steps and waved his hand to quiet the people. When there was silence, he spoke to them in the Hebrew language.

Paul Speaks to the People

22 Paul said, "Brothers and fathers, listen to my defense to you." 2 When they heard him speaking the Hebrew language,[n] they became very quiet. Paul said, 3 "I am a Jew, born in Tarsus in the country of Cilicia, but I grew up in this city. I was a student of Gamaliel,[n] who carefully taught me everything about the law of our ancestors. I was very serious about serving God, just as are all of you here today. 4 I persecuted the people who followed the Way of Jesus, and some of them were even killed. I arrested men and women and put them in jail. 5 The high priest and the whole council of elders can tell you this is true. They gave me letters to the brothers in Damascus. So I was going there to arrest these people and bring them back to Jerusalem to be punished.

6 "About noon when I came near Damascus, a bright light from heaven suddenly flashed all around me. 7 I fell to the ground and heard a voice saying, 'Saul, Saul, why are you persecuting me?' 8 I asked, 'Who are you, Lord?' The voice said, 'I am Jesus from Nazareth whom you are persecuting.' 9 Those who were with me did not understand the voice, but they saw the light. 10 I said, 'What shall I do, Lord?' The Lord answered, 'Get up and go to Damascus. There you will be told about all the things I have planned for you to do.' 11 I could not see, because the bright light had made me blind. So my companions led me into Damascus.

12 "There a man named Ananias came to me. He was a religious man; he obeyed the law of Moses, and all the Jews who lived there respected him. 13 He stood by me and said, 'Brother Saul, see again!' Immediately I was able to see him. 14 He said, 'The God of our ancestors chose you long ago to know his plan, to see the Righteous One, and to hear words from him. 15 You will be his witness to all people, telling them about what you have seen and heard. 16 Now, why wait any longer? Get up, be baptized, and wash your sins away, trusting in him to save you.'

17 "Later, when I returned to Jerusalem, I was praying in the Temple, and I saw a vision. 18 I saw the Lord saying to me, 'Hurry! Leave Jerusalem now! The people here will not accept the truth about me.' 19 But I said, 'Lord, they know that in every synagogue I put the believers in jail and beat them. 20 They also know I was there when Stephen, your witness, was killed. I stood there agreeing and holding the coats of those who were killing him!' 21 But the Lord said to me, 'Leave now. I will send you far away to the other nations.' "

22 The crowd listened to Paul until he said this. Then they began shouting, "Get rid of him! He doesn't deserve to live!" 23 They shouted, threw off their coats,[n] and threw dust into the air.[n]

24 Then the commander ordered the soldiers to take Paul into the army building and beat him. He wanted to make Paul tell why the people were shouting against him like this. 25 But as the soldiers were tying him up, preparing to beat him, Paul said to an officer nearby, "Do you have the right to beat a Roman citizen[n] who has not been proven guilty?"

26 When the officer heard this, he went to the commander and reported it. The officer said, "Do you know what you are doing? This man is a Roman citizen."

27 The commander came to Paul and said, "Tell me, are you really a Roman citizen?"

He answered, "Yes."

22:2 Hebrew language Or Aramaic, the languages of many people in this region in the first century. **22:3 Gamaliel** A very important teacher of the Pharisees, a Jewish religious group (Acts 5:34). **22:23 threw off their coats** This showed that the people were very angry with Paul. **22:23 threw dust into the air** This showed even greater anger. **22:25 Roman citizen** Roman law said that Roman citizens must not be beaten before they had a trial.

28The commander said, "I paid a lot of
money to become a Roman citizen."
But Paul said, "I was born a citizen."
29The men who were preparing to
question Paul moved away from him
immediately. The commander was
frightened because he had already tied
Paul, and Paul was a Roman citizen.

Paul Speaks to Leaders

30The next day the commander decided to
learn why the Jews were accusing Paul. So he
ordered the leading priests and the council
to meet. The commander took Paul's chains
off. Then he brought Paul out and stood him
before their meeting.
23 Paul looked at the council and said,
"Brothers, I have lived my life without
guilt feelings before God up to this day."
2Ananias,[n] the high priest, heard this and
told the men who were standing near Paul to
hit him on the mouth. 3Paul said to Ananias,
"God will hit you, too! You are like a wall
that has been painted white. You sit there
and judge me, using the law of Moses, but
you are telling them to hit me, and that is
against the law."
4The men standing near Paul said to him,
"You cannot insult God's high priest like
that!"
5Paul said, "Brothers, I did not know this
man was the high priest. It is written in the
Scriptures, 'You must not curse a leader of
your people.' "[n]
6Some of the men in the meeting were
Sadducees, and others were Pharisees.
Knowing this, Paul shouted to them, "My
brothers, I am a Pharisee, and my father was
a Pharisee. I am on trial here because I
believe that people will rise from the dead."
7When Paul said this, there was an
argument between the Pharisees and the
Sadducees, and the group was divided. 8(The
Sadducees do not believe in angels or spirits
or that people will rise from the dead. But
the Pharisees believe in them all.) 9So there
was a great uproar. Some of the teachers of
the law, who were Pharisees, stood up and
argued, "We find nothing wrong with this
man. Maybe an angel or a spirit did speak
to him."
10The argument was beginning to turn
into such a fight that the commander was
afraid some evil people would tear Paul to
pieces. So he told the soldiers to go down
and take Paul away and put him in the army
building.
11The next night the Lord came and stood
by Paul. He said, "Be brave! You have told
people in Jerusalem about me. You must do
the same in Rome."
12In the morning some evil people made a
plan to kill Paul, and they took an oath not
to eat or drink anything until they had killed
him. 13There were more than forty men who
made this plan. 14They went to the leading
priests and the elders and said, "We have
taken an oath not to eat or drink until we
have killed Paul. 15So this is what we want
you to do: Send a message to the commander
to bring Paul out to you as though you want
to ask him more questions. We will be
waiting to kill him while he is on the way
here."
16But Paul's nephew heard about this plan
and went to the army building and told Paul.
17Then Paul called one of the officers and
said, "Take this young man to the
commander. He has a message for him."
18So the officer brought Paul's nephew to
the commander and said, "The prisoner,
Paul, asked me to bring this young man to
you. He wants to tell you something."
19The commander took the young man's
hand and led him to a place where they
could be alone. He asked, "What do you
want to tell me?"
20The young man said, "The Jews have
decided to ask you to bring Paul down to
their council meeting tomorrow. They want
you to think they are going to ask him more
questions. 21But don't believe them! More
than forty men are hiding and waiting to kill
Paul. They have all taken an oath not to eat
or drink until they have killed him. Now
they are waiting for you to agree."
22The commander sent the young man
away, ordering him, "Don't tell anyone that
you have told me about their plan."

Paul Is Sent to Caesarea

23Then the commander called two officers
and said, "I need some men to go to Caesarea.
Get two hundred soldiers, seventy horsemen,

23:2 Ananias This is not the same man named Ananias in Acts 22:12.
23:5 'You . . . people.' Quotation from Exodus 22:28.

Drusilla

ACTS 24

When she was fifteen, Drusilla married King Aziz of Emesa. But when she met Felix a few years later, she married him. Felix was an ex-slave, a brutal man who loved to extort money from people he governed.

Drusilla was about twenty when a missionary named Paul was brought before Felix concerning a riot in Jerusalem. Felix didn't want to settle the case. He hoped that Paul would give him money, and then he would release him. Paul's friend Luke ran to find witnesses who could help clear up the accusations, but in the meantime, Paul was thrown back into prison.

Felix brought Paul before him on various occasions, hoping the prisoner would offer him money for his release. Instead, Paul reasoned with Felix and Drusilla, teaching them how to live right with self-control and warning them of the time that God would judge the world.

The hairs stood on the back of Drusilla's neck. *How dare this commoner tell me how to live!* She was not like her father, Herod Antipas—she hadn't murdered anyone. As far as she was concerned, she was living right and was a good person. She and Felix rejected Paul's words about forgiveness and eternal life, and Paul went back to prison.

When Mount Vesuvius erupted twenty years later while she was in Pompeii, the words of that strange prisoner rang through her ears as the burning lava covered the city.

A proud heart keeps us from hearing the Truth.

and two hundred men with spears ready to
leave at nine o'clock tonight. 24 Get some
horses for Paul to ride so he can be taken to
Governor Felix safely." 25 And he wrote a
letter that said:

26 From Claudius Lysias.
To the Most Excellent Governor Felix:
Greetings.

27 Some of the Jews had taken this
man and planned to kill him. But I
learned that he is a Roman citizen, so I
went with my soldiers and saved him.
28 I wanted to know why they were
accusing him, so I brought him before
their council meeting. 29 I learned that
these people said Paul did some things
that were wrong by their own laws, but
no charge was worthy of jail or death.
30 When I was told that some of them
were planning to kill Paul, I sent him to
you at once. I also told them to tell you
what they have against him.

31 So the soldiers did what they were told
and took Paul and brought him to the city
of Antipatris that night. 32 The next day the
horsemen went with Paul to Caesarea,
but the other soldiers went back to the
army building in Jerusalem. 33 When the
horsemen came to Caesarea and gave the
letter to the governor, they turned Paul over
to him. 34 The governor read the letter and
asked Paul, "What area are you from?" When
he learned that Paul was from Cilicia, 35 he
said, "I will hear your case when those who
are against you come here, too." Then the
governor gave orders for Paul to be kept
under guard in Herod's palace.

Paul Is Accused

24 Five days later Ananias, the high
priest, went to the city of Caesarea
with some of the elders and a lawyer named
Tertullus. They had come to make charges
against Paul before the governor. 2 Paul was
called into the meeting, and Tertullus began
to accuse him, saying, "Most Excellent Felix!
Our people enjoy much peace because of
you, and many wrong things in our country
are being made right through your wise
help. 3 We accept these things always and in
every place, and we are thankful for them.
4 But not wanting to take any more of your
time, I beg you to be kind and listen to our

few words. 5We have found this man to be
a troublemaker, stirring up his people
everywhere in the world. He is a leader of
the Nazarene group. 6Also, he was trying to
make the Temple unclean, but we stopped
him. [And we wanted to judge him by our
own law. 7But the officer Lysias came and
used much force to take him from us. 8And
Lysias commanded those who wanted to
accuse Paul to come to you.][n] By asking him
questions yourself, you can decide if all these
things are true." 9The others agreed and said
that all of this was true.

10When the governor made a sign for Paul
to speak, Paul said, "Governor Felix, I know
you have been a judge over this nation for a
long time. So I am happy to defend myself
before you. 11You can learn for yourself that
I went to worship in Jerusalem only twelve
days ago. 12Those who are accusing me did
not find me arguing with anyone in the
Temple or stirring up the people in the
synagogues or in the city. 13They cannot
prove the things they are saying against me
now. 14But I will tell you this: I worship the
God of our ancestors as a follower of the
Way of Jesus. The others say that the Way
of Jesus is not the right way. But I believe
everything that is taught in the law of Moses
and that is written in the books of the
Prophets. 15I have the same hope in God that
they have—the hope that all people, good
and bad, will surely be raised from the dead.
16This is why I always try to do what I
believe is right before God and people.

17"After being away from Jerusalem for
several years, I went back to bring money
to my people and to offer sacrifices. 18I was
doing this when they found me in the
Temple. I had finished the cleansing
ceremony and had not made any trouble;
no people were gathering around me. 19But
there were some people from Asia who
should be here, standing before you. If I have
really done anything wrong, they are the
ones who should accuse me. 20Or ask these
people here if they found any wrong in
me when I stood before the council in
Jerusalem. 21But I did shout one thing when
I stood before them: 'You are judging me
today because I believe that people will rise
from the dead!' "

22Felix already understood much about
the Way of Jesus. He stopped the trial and
said, "When commander Lysias comes here, I
will decide your case." 23Felix told the officer
to keep Paul guarded but to give him some
freedom and to let his friends bring what he
needed.

Paul Speaks to Felix and His Wife

24After some days Felix came with his
wife, Drusilla, who was Jewish, and asked for
Paul to be brought to him. He listened to
Paul talk about believing in Christ Jesus.
25But Felix became afraid when Paul spoke
about living right, self-control, and the time
when God will judge the world. He said, "Go
away now. When I have more time, I will
call for you." 26At the same time Felix hoped
that Paul would give him some money, so he
often sent for Paul and talked with him.

27But after two years, Felix was replaced
by Porcius Festus as governor. But Felix had
left Paul in prison to please the Jews.

Paul Asks to See Caesar

25 Three days after Festus became
governor, he went from Caesarea to
Jerusalem. 2There the leading priests and
the important leaders made charges against
Paul before Festus. 3They asked Festus to do
them a favor. They wanted him to send Paul
back to Jerusalem, because they had a plan
to kill him on the way. 4But Festus answered
that Paul would be kept in Caesarea and that
he himself was returning there soon. 5He
said, "Some of your leaders should go with
me. They can accuse the man there in
Caesarea, if he has really done something
wrong."

6Festus stayed in Jerusalem another eight
or ten days and then went back to Caesarea.
The next day he told the soldiers to bring
Paul before him. Festus was seated on the
judge's seat 7when Paul came into the room.
The people who had come from Jerusalem
stood around him, making serious charges
against him, which they could not prove.
8This is what Paul said to defend himself: "I
have done nothing wrong against the law,
against the Temple, or against Caesar."

9But Festus wanted to please the people.
So he asked Paul, "Do you want to go to

24:6–8 And . . . you. Some Greek copies do not contain the bracketed text.

Jerusalem for me to judge you there on these charges?"

10 Paul said, "I am standing at Caesar's judgment seat now, where I should be judged. I have done nothing wrong to them; you know this is true. 11 If I have done something wrong and the law says I must die, I do not ask to be saved from death. But if these charges are not true, then no one can give me to them. I want Caesar to hear my case!"

12 Festus talked about this with his advisers. Then he said, "You have asked to see Caesar, so you will go to Caesar!"

Paul Before King Agrippa

13 A few days later King Agrippa and Bernice came to Caesarea to visit Festus. 14 They stayed there for some time, and Festus told the king about Paul's case. Festus said, "There is a man that Felix left in prison. 15 When I went to Jerusalem, the leading priests and the elders there made charges against him, asking me to sentence him to death. 16 But I answered, 'When a man is accused of a crime, Romans do not hand him over until he has been allowed to face his accusers and defend himself against their charges.' 17 So when these people came here to Caesarea for the trial, I did not waste time. The next day I sat on the judge's seat and commanded that the man be brought in. 18 They stood up and accused him, but not of any serious crime as I thought they would. 19 The things they said were about their own religion and about a man named Jesus who died. But Paul said that he is still alive. 20 Not knowing how to find out about these questions, I asked Paul, 'Do you want to go to Jerusalem and be judged there?' 21 But he asked to be kept in Caesarea. He wants a decision from the emperor.[n] So I ordered that he be held until I could send him to Caesar."

22 Agrippa said to Festus, "I would also like to hear this man myself."

Festus said, "Tomorrow you will hear him."

23 The next day Agrippa and Bernice appeared with great show, acting like very important people. They went into the judgment room with the army leaders and the important men of Caesarea. Then Festus ordered the soldiers to bring Paul in. 24 Festus said, "King Agrippa and all who are gathered here with us, you see this man. All the people, here and in Jerusalem, have complained to me about him, shouting that he should not live any longer. 25 When I judged him, I found no reason to order his death. But since he asked to be judged by Caesar, I decided to send him. 26 But I have nothing definite to write the emperor about him. So I have brought him before all of you—especially you, King Agrippa. I hope you can question him and give me something to write. 27 I think it is foolish to send a prisoner to Caesar without telling what charges are against him."

Paul Defends Himself

26 Agrippa said to Paul, "You may now speak to defend yourself."

Then Paul raised his hand and began to speak. 2 He said, "King Agrippa, I am very blessed to stand before you and will answer all the charges the evil people make against me. 3 You know so much about all the customs and the things they argue about, so please listen to me patiently.

4 "All my people know about my whole life, how I lived from the beginning in my own country and later in Jerusalem. 5 They have known me for a long time. If they want to, they can tell you that I was a good Pharisee. And the Pharisees obey the laws of my tradition more carefully than any other group. 6 Now I am on trial because I hope for the promise that God made to our ancestors. 7 This is the promise that the twelve tribes of our people hope to receive as they serve God day and night. My king, they have accused me because I hope for this same promise! 8 Why do any of you people think it is impossible for God to raise people from the dead?

9 "I, too, thought I ought to do many things against Jesus from Nazareth. 10 And that is what I did in Jerusalem. The leading priests gave me the power to put many of God's people in jail, and when they were being killed, I agreed it was a good thing. 11 In every synagogue, I often punished them and tried to make them speak against Jesus. I

25:21 emperor The ruler of the Roman Empire, which was almost all the known world.

was so angry against them I even went to
other cities to find them and punish them.
12"One time the leading priests gave
me permission and the power to go to
Damascus. 13On the way there, at noon, I
saw a light from heaven. It was brighter than
the sun and flashed all around me and those
who were traveling with me. 14We all fell to
the ground. Then I heard a voice speaking to
me in the Hebrew language,[n] saying, 'Saul,
Saul, why are you persecuting me? You are
only hurting yourself by fighting me.' 15I
said, 'Who are you, Lord?' The Lord said,
'I am Jesus, the one you are persecuting.
16Stand up! I have chosen you to be my
servant and my witness—you will tell
people the things that you have seen and the
things that I will show you. This is why I
have come to you today. 17I will keep you
safe from your own people and also from the
others. I am sending you to them 18to open
their eyes so that they may turn away from
darkness to the light, away from the power
of Satan and to God. Then their sins can be
forgiven, and they can have a place with
those people who have been made holy by
believing in me.'
19"King Agrippa, after I had this vision
from heaven, I obeyed it. 20I began telling
people that they should change their
hearts and lives and turn to God and do
things to show they really had changed. I
told this first to those in Damascus, then in
Jerusalem, and in every part of Judea, and
also to the other people. 21This is why the
Jews took me and were trying to kill me in
the Temple. 22But God has helped me, and so
I stand here today, telling all people, small
and great, what I have seen. But I am saying
only what Moses and the prophets said
would happen— 23that the Christ would
die, and as the first to rise from the dead, he
would bring light to all people."

Paul Tries to Persuade Agrippa

24While Paul was saying these things to
defend himself, Festus said loudly, "Paul, you
are out of your mind! Too much study has
driven you crazy!"
25Paul said, "Most excellent Festus, I am

26:14 Hebrew language Or Aramaic, the languages of many people in this region in the first century.

devotion 301

ACTS 26:17-18

ONE PARTY GIRL IS DEAD AND GONE

Because of how I lived my life before Christ, I can say to anyone I meet, "Look what God has done with my life! Sit down, grab a cup of coffee, and let me share this wild story with you." Do you understand that God can use your personal story to open the eyes of those who are lost and without hope? Because of my personal pursuit of fulfilling the desires of my flesh, the Holy Spirit has taken my changed life and turned many hearts away from darkness and brought them into the light. Have you ever been sent back into old relationships after you were saved? I always find it to be an adventure, and most people are somewhat perplexed. Where did the party favor go? Where's that wild drunk woman who was so much fun? I'll tell you where she is—dead and gone.

Girls, let me tell you, take all that junk that was in your life and praise the Lord that he allowed you to live through it! Use your life to open the eyes of sinners who are dead in their transgressions and headed for pain and suffering. I cannot tell you how many young people I have been able to minister to because I can speak into their lives simply because I am sharing from first-hand experiences. The woman at the well in John 4, the one with quite a past, ran into the town to tell everyone about Jesus. Let's change the world with our lives!

not crazy. My words are true and sensible.
26King Agrippa knows about these things,
and I can speak freely to him. I know he
has heard about all of these things, because
they did not happen off in a corner. 27King
Agrippa, do you believe what the prophets
wrote? I know you believe."

28King Agrippa said to Paul, "Do you think
you can persuade me to become a Christian
in such a short time?"

29Paul said, "Whether it is a short or a long
time, I pray to God that not only you but
every person listening to me today would
be saved and be like me—except for these
chains I have."

30Then King Agrippa, Governor Festus,
Bernice, and all the people sitting with them
stood up 31and left the room. Talking to each
other, they said, "There is no reason why this
man should die or be put in jail." 32And
Agrippa said to Festus, "We could let this
man go free, but he has asked Caesar to hear
his case."

Paul Sails for Rome

27 It was decided that we would sail for
Italy. An officer named Julius, who
served in the emperor's[n] army, guarded Paul
and some other prisoners. 2We got on a ship
that was from the city of Adramyttium and
was about to sail to different ports in Asia.
Aristarchus, a man from the city of
Thessalonica in Macedonia, went with us.
3The next day we came to Sidon. Julius was
very good to Paul and gave him freedom to
go visit his friends, who took care of his
needs. 4We left Sidon and sailed close to the
island of Cyprus, because the wind was
blowing against us. 5We went across the sea
by Cilicia and Pamphylia and landed at the
city of Myra, in Lycia. 6There the officer
found a ship from Alexandria that was going
to Italy, so he put us on it.

7We sailed slowly for many days. We had
a hard time reaching Cnidus because the
wind was blowing against us, and we could
not go any farther. So we sailed by the south
side of the island of Crete near Salmone.
8Sailing past it was hard. Then we came to
a place called Fair Havens, near the city of
Lasea.

9We had lost much time, and it was now
dangerous to sail, because it was already
after the Day of Cleansing.[n] So Paul warned
them, 10"Men, I can see there will be a lot of
trouble on this trip. The ship, the cargo, and
even our lives may be lost." 11But the captain
and the owner of the ship did not agree
with Paul, and the officer believed what the
captain and owner of the ship said. 12Since
that harbor was not a good place for the ship
to stay for the winter, most of the men
decided that the ship should leave. They
hoped we could go to Phoenix and stay there
for the winter. Phoenix, a city on the island
of Crete, had a harbor which faced
southwest and northwest.

The Storm

13When a good wind began to blow from
the south, the men on the ship thought,
"This is the wind we wanted, and now we
have it." So they pulled up the anchor, and
we sailed very close to the island of Crete.
14But then a very strong wind named the
"northeaster" came from the island. 15The
ship was caught in it and could not sail
against it. So we stopped trying and let the
wind carry us. 16When we went below a
small island named Cauda, we were barely
able to bring in the lifeboat. 17After the men
took the lifeboat in, they tied ropes around
the ship to hold it together. The men were
afraid that the ship would hit the sandbanks
of Syrtis,[n] so they lowered the sail and let the
wind carry the ship. 18The next day the
storm was blowing us so hard that the men
threw out some of the cargo. 19A day later
with their own hands they threw out the
ship's equipment. 20When we could not see
the sun or the stars for many days, and the
storm was very bad, we lost all hope of being
saved.

21After the men had gone without food for
a long time, Paul stood up before them and
said, "Men, you should have listened to me.
You should not have sailed from Crete. Then
you would not have all this trouble and loss.
22But now I tell you to cheer up because
none of you will die. Only the ship will be
lost. 23Last night an angel came to me from
the God I belong to and worship. 24The angel

27:1 emperor The ruler of the Roman Empire, which was almost all the known world. **27:9 Day of Cleansing** An important Jewish holy day in the fall of the year. This was the time of year that bad storms arose on the sea. **27:17 Syrtis** Shallow area in the sea near the Libyan coast.

said, 'Paul, do not be afraid. You must stand
before Caesar. And God has promised you
that he will save the lives of everyone sailing
with you.' 25So men, have courage. I trust in
God that everything will happen as his angel
told me. 26But we will crash on an island."
27On the fourteenth night we were still
being carried around in the Adriatic Sea.[n]
About midnight the sailors thought we were
close to land, 28so they lowered a rope with a
weight on the end of it into the water. They
found that the water was one hundred
twenty feet deep. They went a little farther
and lowered the rope again. It was ninety feet
deep. 29The sailors were afraid that we would
hit the rocks, so they threw four anchors
into the water and prayed for daylight to
come. 30Some of the sailors wanted to leave
the ship, and they lowered the lifeboat,
pretending they were throwing more anchors
from the front of the ship. 31But Paul told the
officer and the other soldiers, "If these men
do not stay in the ship, your lives cannot be
saved." 32So the soldiers cut the ropes and let
the lifeboat fall into the water.
33Just before dawn Paul began persuading
all the people to eat something. He said, "For
the past fourteen days you have been
waiting and watching and not eating. 34Now
I beg you to eat something. You need it to
stay alive. None of you will lose even one
hair off your heads." 35After he said this, Paul
took some bread and thanked God for it
before all of them. He broke off a piece and
began eating. 36They all felt better and
started eating, too. 37There were two
hundred seventy-six people on the ship.
38When they had eaten all they wanted, they
began making the ship lighter by throwing
the grain into the sea.

The Ship Is Destroyed

39When daylight came, the sailors saw
land. They did not know what land it was,
but they saw a bay with a beach and wanted
to sail the ship to the beach if they could.
40So they cut the ropes to the anchors and
left the anchors in the sea. At the same time,
they untied the ropes that were holding the
rudders. Then they raised the front sail into
the wind and sailed toward the beach. 41But
the ship hit a sandbank. The front of the
ship stuck there and could not move, but the
back of the ship began to break up from the
big waves.
42The soldiers decided to kill the prisoners
so none of them could swim away and
escape. 43But Julius, the officer, wanted to
let Paul live and did not allow the soldiers
to kill the prisoners. Instead he ordered
everyone who could swim to jump into the
water first and swim to land. 44The rest were
to follow using wooden boards or pieces of
the ship. And this is how all the people made
it safely to land.

Paul on the Island of Malta

28 When we were safe on land, we
learned that the island was called
Malta. 2The people who lived there were
very good to us. Because it was raining and
very cold, they made a fire and welcomed all
of us. 3Paul gathered a pile of sticks and was
putting them on the fire when a poisonous
snake came out because of the heat and bit
him on the hand. 4The people living on the
island saw the snake hanging from Paul's
hand and said to each other, "This man must
be a murderer! He did not die in the sea, but
Justice[n] does not want him to live." 5But Paul
shook the snake off into the fire and was not
hurt. 6The people thought that Paul would
swell up or fall down dead. They waited and
watched him for a long time, but nothing
bad happened to him. So they changed their
minds and said, "He is a god!"
7There were some fields around there
owned by Publius, an important man on the
island. He welcomed us into his home and
was very good to us for three days. 8Publius'
father was sick with a fever and dysentery.[n]
Paul went to him, prayed, and put his hands
on the man and healed him. 9After this, all
the other sick people on the island came
to Paul, and he healed them, too. 10-11The
people on the island gave us many honors.
When we were ready to leave, three months
later, they gave us the things we needed.

Paul Goes to Rome

We got on a ship from Alexandria that
had stayed on the island during the winter.

27:27 Adriatic Sea The sea between Greece and Italy, including the central Mediterranean.
28:4 Justice The people thought there was a god named Justice who would punish bad people. **28:8 dysentery** A sickness like diarrhea.

On the front of the ship was the sign of the
twin gods.[n] 12We stopped at Syracuse for
three days. 13From there we sailed to
Rhegium. The next day a wind began to
blow from the south, and a day later we
came to Puteoli. 14We found some believers
there who asked us to stay with them for
a week. Finally, we came to Rome. 15The
believers in Rome heard that we were there
and came out as far as the Market of Appius[n]
and the Three Inns[n] to meet us. When Paul
saw them, he was encouraged and thanked
God.

Paul in Rome

16When we arrived at Rome, Paul was
allowed to live alone, with the soldier who
guarded him.
17Three days later Paul sent for the leaders
there. When they came together, he said,
"Brothers, I have done nothing against our
people or the customs of our ancestors. But
I was arrested in Jerusalem and given to
the Romans. 18After they asked me many
questions, they could find no reason why I
should be killed. They wanted to let me go
free, 19but the evil people there argued
against that. So I had to ask to come to Rome
to have my trial before Caesar. But I have no
charge to bring against my own people.
20That is why I wanted to see you and talk
with you. I am bound with this chain
because I believe in the hope of Israel."
21They answered Paul, "We have received
no letters from Judea about you. None of our
Jewish brothers who have come from there
brought news or told us anything bad about
you. 22But we want to hear your ideas,
because we know that people everywhere
are speaking against this religious group."
23Paul and the people chose a day for a
meeting and on that day many more of the
Jews met with Paul at the place he was
staying. He spoke to them all day long. Using
the law of Moses and the prophets' writings,
he explained the kingdom of God, and he
tried to persuade them to believe these
things about Jesus. 24Some believed what
Paul said, but others did not. 25So they
argued and began leaving after Paul said one
more thing to them: "The Holy Spirit spoke
the truth to your ancestors through Isaiah
the prophet, saying,
26'Go to this people and say:
You will listen and listen, but you will not
understand.
You will look and look, but you will not
learn,
27because these people have become
stubborn.
They don't hear with their ears,
and they have closed their eyes.
Otherwise, they might really understand
what they see with their eyes
and hear with their ears.
They might really understand in their
minds
and come back to me and be healed.'

Isaiah 6:9–10

28"I want you to know that God has also
sent his salvation to all nations, and they
will listen!" [29After Paul said this, the Jews
left. They were arguing very much with each
other.][n]
30Paul stayed two full years in his own
rented house and welcomed all people who
came to visit him. 31He boldly preached
about the kingdom of God and taught about
the Lord Jesus Christ, and no one stopped
him.

28:10–11 twin gods Statues of Castor and Pollux, gods in old Greek tales. **28:15 Market of Appius** A town about twenty-seven miles from Rome. **28:15 Three Inns** A town about thirty miles from Rome. **28:29 After . . . other.** Some Greek copies do not contain the bracketed text.

Romans

Person Holding the Pen God Wrote With: The apostle *Paul*, who authored approximately two-thirds of the New Testament

When the Text Was Written: Around 56 A.D. at the end of Paul's third missionary journey to Corinth

Spiritual Posture of the Original Recipients: The church in Rome was full of Jewish and non-Jewish converts. They not only faced persecution from their culture but were also prone to hurl insults at each other.

Storyline Synopsis: Paul had heard through the evangelical grapevine that some Christians in Rome were beginning to fancy a heretical doctrine known as *antinomianism*—which basically meant they were twisting the truth of the Good News into a license to practice immorality. Their distorted logic was, "Since our sins are covered by the blood of Christ and we're already forgiven, let's go hog wild and do whatever we want!" And because Paul couldn't get there in person to rectify the problem immediately, he picked up his pen and through the guidance of the Holy Spirit wrote this letter to set them straight. He covered three main topics in this epistle: the inherent sinfulness of all mankind (Rom. 1:18—3:20); the way God provided out of sin through Jesus (3:21—5:21); and how Christians should live after trusting in Christ (chapters 6—15). Romans is not a historical book, but rather a deeply theological and comprehensive explanation of God's amazing grace!

A Moment Worth Discussing: Many have called Romans 8 the greatest chapter in the Bible. In it, Paul explains that while the Holy Spirit may convict Christians, we don't have to deal with condemnation (Rom. 8:1–11). He tells us that we can now call the God who created the universe "Dad" (8:15–17); that suffering shouldn't surprise us because we live in a broken world (8:18–27); but that no matter what, God will work out every situation for our good and his glory (8:28). Furthermore, nothing—not even death—can separate Christians from the love of Jesus (8:31–39). The bottom line is that God's love never fails, never forgets, and never forsakes. When's the last time life threw you a curve ball and God used that circumstance to reflect his perfect love?

Interesting (But Likely to Be Overlooked) Character: *Phoebe*, a Christian woman whose name meant "bright and radiant," was given the weighty responsibility of making sure Paul's letter was delivered to the believers in Rome (Rom. 16:1–2).

1 From Paul, a servant of Christ Jesus. God called me to be an apostle and chose me to tell the Good News.

[2]God promised this Good News long ago through his prophets, as it is written in the Holy Scriptures. [3-4]The Good News is about God's Son, Jesus Christ our Lord. As a man, he was born from the family of David. But through the Spirit of holiness he was declared to be God's Son with great power by rising from the dead. [5]Through Christ, God gave me the special work of an apostle, which was to lead people of all nations to believe and obey. I do this work for him. [6]And you who are in Rome are also called to belong to Jesus Christ.

[7]To all of you in Rome whom God loves and has called to be his holy people:

Grace and peace to you from God our Father and the Lord Jesus Christ.

A Prayer of Thanks

[8]First I want to say that I thank my God through Jesus Christ for all of you, because people everywhere in the world are talking about your faith. [9]God, whom I serve with my whole heart by telling the Good News about his Son, knows that I always mention you [10]every time I pray. I pray that I will be allowed to come to you, and this will happen if God wants it. [11]I want very much to see you, to give you some spiritual gift to make you strong. [12]I mean that I want us to help each other with the faith we have. Your faith will help me, and my faith will help you. [13]Brothers and sisters, I want you to know that I planned many times to come to you, but this has not been possible. I wanted to come so that I could help you grow spiritually as I have helped the other non-Jewish people.

[14]I have a duty to all people—Greeks and those who are not Greeks, the wise and the foolish. [15]That is why I want so much to preach the Good News to you in Rome.

[16]I am not ashamed of the Good News, because it is the power God uses to save everyone who believes—to save the Jews first, and then to save non-Jews. [17]The Good News shows how God makes people right with himself—that it begins and ends with faith. As the Scripture says, "But those who are right with God will live by faith."[n]

All People Have Done Wrong

[18]God's anger is shown from heaven against all the evil and wrong things people do. By their own evil lives they hide the truth. [19]God shows his anger because some knowledge of him has been made clear to them. Yes, God has shown himself to them. [20]There are things about him that people cannot see—his eternal power and all the things that make him God. But since the beginning of the world those things have been easy to understand by what God has made. So people have no excuse for the bad things they do. [21]They knew God, but they did not give glory to God or thank him. Their thinking became useless. Their foolish minds were filled with darkness. [22]They said they were wise, but they became fools. [23]They traded the glory of God who lives forever for the worship of idols made to look like earthly people, birds, animals, and snakes.

[24]Because they did these things, God left them and let them go their sinful way, wanting only to do evil. As a result, they became full of sexual sin, using their bodies wrongly with each other. [25]They traded the truth of God for a lie. They worshiped and served what had been created instead of the God who created those things, who should be praised forever. Amen.

[26]Because people did those things, God left them and let them do the shameful things they wanted to do. Women stopped having natural sex and started having sex with other women. [27]In the same way, men stopped having natural sex and began wanting each other. Men did shameful things with other men, and in their bodies they received the punishment for those wrongs.

[28]People did not think it was important to have a true knowledge of God. So God left them and allowed them to have their own worthless thinking and to do things they should not do. [29]They are filled with every kind of sin, evil, selfishness, and hatred. They are full of jealousy, murder, fighting, lying, and thinking the worst about each

1:17 "But those . . . faith." Quotation from Habakkuk 2:4.

other. They gossip [30]and say evil things
about each other. They hate God. They
are rude and conceited and brag about
themselves. They invent ways of doing evil.
They do not obey their parents. [31]They are
foolish, they do not keep their promises, and
they show no kindness or mercy to others.
[32]They know God's law says that those who
live like this should die. But they themselves
not only continue to do these evil things,
they applaud others who do them.

You People Also Are Sinful

2 If you think you can judge others, you
are wrong. When you judge them, you
are really judging yourself guilty, because
you do the same things they do. [2]God judges
those who do wrong things, and we know
that his judging is right. [3]You judge those
who do wrong, but you do wrong yourselves.
Do you think you will be able to escape the
judgment of God? [4]He has been very kind
and patient, waiting for you to change, but
you think nothing of his kindness. Perhaps
you do not understand that God is kind
to you so you will change your hearts and
lives. [5]But you are stubborn and refuse to
change, so you are making your own
punishment even greater on the day he
shows his anger. On that day everyone
will see God's right judgments. [6]God will
reward or punish every person for what that
person has done. [7]Some people, by always
continuing to do good, live for God's glory,
for honor, and for life that has no end. God
will give them life forever. [8]But other people
are selfish. They refuse to follow truth and,
instead, follow evil. God will give them his
punishment and anger. [9]He will give trouble
and suffering to everyone who does evil—to
the Jews first and also to those who are not
Jews. [10]But he will give glory, honor, and
peace to everyone who does good—to the
Jews first and also to those who are not Jews.
[11]For God judges all people in the same way.

[12]People who do not have the law and
who are sinners will be lost, although they
do not have the law. And, in the same way,
those who have the law and are sinners will
be judged by the law. [13]Hearing the law does
not make people right with God. It is those
who obey the law who will be right with

devotion 302

ROMANS 2:7–8

WILLFULLY ENGAGED IN GOOD WORKS

If you can make some extra time, I'd like to encourage you to read the entire Book of Romans over the next two days. It's a great way to renew your heart in the Christian faith that you love so much.

You can be sure that nothing is forever in this world. We go to school and we graduate, we work and we retire, we have babies and they grow up, but in Christ we have the assurance that when we are born again, we live forever. These bodies of flesh will die, but our spirits will live on for eternity with our Lord. That is the hope we get to share with an unbelieving world.

We're not supposed to accept everlasting life and then do nothing with it. We are to be willfully engaged in good works that bring honor to our Lord. I'm sure you've met physical needs of fellow believers—making a meal for someone who is ill, secretly meeting a financial need, or being a prayer warrior. All of these acts of service bring joy, but can you imagine for a moment what kind of rejoicing there will be when the testimony of your good works in Christ keeps someone from the depths of hell? There will be one great big, giant party in heaven, and you will be appreciated more in that moment than you have ever been on earth. Each person you encouraged in word or deed will be grateful for the example you set.

him. 14(Those who are not Jews do not have the law, but when they freely do what the law commands, they are the law for themselves. This is true even though they do not have the law. 15They show that in their hearts they know what is right and wrong, just as the law commands. And they show this by their consciences. Sometimes their thoughts tell them they did wrong, and sometimes their thoughts tell them they did right.) 16All these things will happen on the day when God, through Christ Jesus, will judge people's secret thoughts. The Good News that I preach says this.

The Jews and the Law

17What about you? You call yourself a Jew. You trust in the law of Moses and brag that you are close to God. 18You know what he wants you to do and what is important, because you have learned the law. 19You think you are a guide for the blind and a light for those who are in darkness. 20You think you can show foolish people what is right and teach those who know nothing. You have the law; so you think you know everything and have all truth. 21You teach others, so why don't you teach yourself? You tell others not to steal, but you steal. 22You say that others must not take part in adultery, but you are guilty of that sin. You hate idols, but you steal from temples. 23You brag about having God's law, but you bring shame to God by breaking his law, 24just as the Scriptures say: "Those who are not Jews speak against God's name because of you."[n]

25If you follow the law, your circumcision has meaning. But if you break the law, it is as if you were never circumcised. 26People who are not Jews are not circumcised, but if they do what the law says, it is as if they were circumcised. 27You Jews have the written law and circumcision, but you break the law. So those who are not circumcised in their bodies, but still obey the law, will show that you are guilty. 28They can do this because a person is not a true Jew if he is only a Jew in his physical body; true circumcision is not only on the outside of the body. 29A person is a Jew only if he is a Jew inside; true circumcision is done in the heart by the Spirit, not by the written law. Such a person gets praise from God rather than from people.

3 So, do Jews have anything that other people do not have? Is there anything special about being circumcised? 2Yes, of course, there is in every way. The most important thing is this: God trusted the Jews with his teachings. 3If some Jews were not faithful to him, will that stop God from doing what he promised? 4No! God will continue to be true even when every person is false. As the Scriptures say:

"So you will be shown to be right when
you speak,
and you will win your case." *Psalm 51:4*

5When we do wrong, that shows more clearly that God is right. So can we say that God is wrong to punish us? (I am talking as people might talk.) 6No! If God could not punish us, he could not judge the world.

7A person might say, "When I lie, it really gives him glory, because my lie shows God's truth. So why am I judged a sinner?" 8It would be the same to say, "We should do evil so that good will come." Some people find fault with us and say we teach this, but they are wrong and deserve the punishment they will receive.

All People Are Guilty

9So are we Jews better than others? No! We have already said that Jews and those who are not Jews are all guilty of sin. 10As the Scriptures say:

"There is no one who always does what is
right,
not even one.
11There is no one who understands.
There is no one who looks to God for
help.
12All have turned away.
Together, everyone has become useless.
There is no one who does anything good;
there is not even one." *Psalm 14:1–3*
13"Their throats are like open graves;
they use their tongues for telling lies."
Psalm 5:9
"Their words are like snake poison."
Psalm 140:3

2:24 "Those . . . you." Quotation from Isaiah 52:5; Ezekiel 36:20.

14 "Their mouths are full of cursing and
hate." *Psalm 10:7*
15 "They are always ready to kill people.
16 Everywhere they go they cause ruin and
misery.
17 They don't know how to live in peace."
Isaiah 59:7–8
18 "They have no fear of God." *Psalm 36:1*
19 We know that the law's commands are
for those who have the law. This stops all
excuses and brings the whole world under
God's judgment, 20 because no one can be
made right with God by following the law.
The law only shows us our sin.

How God Makes People Right

21 But God has a way to make people right
with him without the law, and he has now
shown us that way which the law and the
prophets told us about. 22 God makes people
right with himself through their faith in
Jesus Christ. This is true for all who believe
in Christ, because all people are the same:
23 Everyone has sinned and fallen short of
God's glorious standard, 24 and all need to be
made right with God by his grace, which is a
free gift. They need to be made free from
sin through Jesus Christ. 25 God sent him to
die in our place to take away our sins. We
receive forgiveness through faith in the
blood of Jesus' death. This showed that God
always does what is right and fair, as in the
past when he was patient and did not punish
people for their sins. 26 And God gave Jesus to
show today that he does what is right. God
did this so he could judge rightly and so he
could make right any person who has faith
in Jesus.
27 So do we have a reason to brag about
ourselves? No! And why not? It is the way of
faith that stops all bragging, not the way of
trying to obey the law. 28 A person is made
right with God through faith, not through
obeying the law. 29 Is God only the God of the
Jews? Is he not also the God of those who are
not Jews? 30 Of course he is, because there is
only one God. He will make Jews right with
him by their faith, and he will also make
those who are not Jews right with him
through their faith. 31 So do we destroy the
law by following the way of faith? No! Faith
causes us to be what the law truly wants.

devotion 303

ROMANS 3:27–28

WHAT ARE YOU SO SMUG ABOUT?

As Christians, we all want to be right with God. We start our journey by believing that Jesus died on the cross for our sins. When we are first saved, we appreciate God's grace so deeply because we know the sin in our lives and how undeserving we are of God's love. Then we begin to grow in the Lord, and the sins in our lives become a little less obvious. We see how far we've come, and we begin to consider ourselves good Christians. Our thinking shifts from believing that Jesus changed us to believing that we have changed ourselves. How quickly pride roots itself in our minds if we are not careful.

Hebrews 11:6 tells us, "Without faith no one can please God." Our faith in Christ is the only thing that makes us Christians. We have nothing to brag about, only things to be thankful for. In Luke 18:9-14, Jesus tells the story of a haughty Pharisee who thought he was pleasing God because he obeyed the Ten Commandments, fasted twice a week, and tithed to the church. He looked down on those who weren't as "righteous" as him. But Jesus said that he was not right with God because of his pride.

Christian, be so careful as you grow in the Lord. We please God with our faith, not with our actions. Don't let pride convince you of how much you are accomplishing for God. Know that it is only through Christ that we are able.

The Example of Abraham

4 So what can we say that Abraham,[n] the
father of our people, learned about faith?
[2]If Abraham was made right by the things
he did, he had a reason to brag. But this is
not God's view, [3]because the Scripture says,
"Abraham believed God, and God accepted
Abraham's faith, and that faith made him
right with God."[n]

[4]When people work, their pay is not
given as a gift, but as something earned. [5]But
people cannot do any work that will make
them right with God. So they must trust in
him, who makes even evil people right in
his sight. Then God accepts their faith, and
that makes them right with him. [6]David said
the same thing. He said that people are truly
blessed when God, without paying attention
to their deeds, makes people right with
himself.

[7]"Blessed are they
whose sins are forgiven,
whose wrongs are pardoned.
[8]Blessed is the person
whom the Lord does not consider
guilty." *Psalm 32:1–2*

[9]Is this blessing only for those who are
circumcised or also for those who are not
circumcised? We have already said that God
accepted Abraham's faith and that faith
made him right with God. [10]So how did this
happen? Did God accept Abraham before or
after he was circumcised? It was before his
circumcision. [11]Abraham was circumcised to
show that he was right with God through
faith before he was circumcised. So
Abraham is the father of all those who
believe but are not circumcised; he is the
father of all believers who are accepted as
being right with God. [12]And Abraham is
also the father of those who have been
circumcised and who live following the faith
that our father Abraham had before he was
circumcised.

God Keeps His Promise

[13]Abraham[n] and his descendants received
the promise that they would get the whole
world. He did not receive that promise
through the law, but through being right
with God by his faith. [14]If people could
receive what God promised by following
the law, then faith is worthless. And God's
promise to Abraham is worthless, [15]because
the law can only bring God's anger. But if
there is no law, there is nothing to disobey.

[16]So people receive God's promise by
having faith. This happens so the promise
can be a free gift. Then all of Abraham's
children can have that promise. It is not only
for those who live under the law of Moses
but for anyone who lives with faith like that
of Abraham, who is the father of us all. [17]As
it is written in the Scriptures: "I am making
you a father of many nations."[n] This is true
before God, the God Abraham believed, the
God who gives life to the dead and who
creates something out of nothing.

[18]There was no hope that Abraham would
have children. But Abraham believed God
and continued hoping, and so he became the
father of many nations. As God told him,
"Your descendants also will be too many to
count."[n] [19]Abraham was almost a hundred
years old, much past the age for having
children, and Sarah could not have children.
Abraham thought about all this, but his
faith in God did not become weak. [20]He
never doubted that God would keep his
promise, and he never stopped believing. He
grew stronger in his faith and gave praise to
God. [21]Abraham felt sure that God was able
to do what he had promised. [22]So, "God
accepted Abraham's faith, and that faith
made him right with God."[n] [23]Those words
("God accepted Abraham's faith") were
written not only for Abraham [24]but also
for us. God will accept us also because we
believe in the One who raised Jesus our Lord
from the dead. [25]Jesus was given to die for
our sins, and he was raised from the dead to
make us right with God.

Right with God

5 Since we have been made right with God
by our faith, we have[n] peace with God.
This happened through our Lord Jesus
Christ, [2]who through our faith[n] has brought
us into that blessing of God's grace that we
now enjoy. And we are happy because of the
hope we have of sharing God's glory. [3]We

4:1, 13 Abraham Most respected ancestor of the Jews. Every Jew hoped to see Abraham. **4:3 "Abraham . . . God."** Quotation from Genesis 15:6. **4:17 "I . . . nations."** Quotation from Genesis 17:5. **4:18 "Your . . . count."** Quotation from Genesis 15:5. **4:22 "God . . . God."** Quotation from Genesis 15:6. **5:1 we have** Some Greek copies read "let us have." **5:2 through our faith** Some Greek copies do not have this phrase.

also have joy with our troubles, because we know that these troubles produce patience. 4And patience produces character, and character produces hope. 5And this hope will never disappoint us, because God has poured out his love to fill our hearts. He gave us his love through the Holy Spirit, whom God has given to us.

6When we were unable to help ourselves, at the right time, Christ died for us, although we were living against God. 7Very few people will die to save the life of someone else. Although perhaps for a good person someone might possibly die. 8But God shows his great love for us in this way: Christ died for us while we were still sinners.

9So through Christ we will surely be saved from God's anger, because we have been made right with God by the blood of Christ's death. 10While we were God's enemies, he made us his friends through the death of his Son. Surely, now that we are his friends, he will save us through his Son's life. 11And not only that, but now we are also very happy in God through our Lord Jesus Christ. Through him we are now God's friends again.

Adam and Christ Compared

12Sin came into the world because of what one man did, and with sin came death. This is why everyone must die—because everyone sinned. 13Sin was in the world before the law of Moses, but sin is not counted against us as breaking a command when there is no law. 14But from the time of Adam to the time of Moses, everyone had to die, even those who had not sinned by breaking a command, as Adam had.

Adam was like the One who was coming in the future. 15But God's free gift is not like Adam's sin. Many people died because of the sin of that one man. But the grace from God was much greater; many people received God's gift of life by the grace of the one man, Jesus Christ. 16After Adam sinned once, he was judged guilty. But the gift of God is different. God's free gift came after many sins, and it makes people right with God. 17One man sinned, and so death ruled all people because of that one man. But now those people who accept God's full grace and the great gift of being made right with him will surely have true life and rule through the one man, Jesus Christ.

devotion 304

ROMANS 6:16-18

WHO'S IN THE DRIVER'S SEAT?

Sometimes it takes a child to ask questions we might also wish we could ask, but out of fear of looking ridiculous, we stay silent. I once heard a little boy ask his teacher, "If our sins are already forgiven, then why do we need to obey?" Have you ever secretly wondered how God expects his people to obey his laws when he has told us that our sins are already forgiven because of Christ's sacrifice on the cross? Does this mean that it doesn't really matter if we run that stop sign? Perhaps it's not that big of a deal if we listen to that band. And it probably doesn't matter if we watch that television show.

Oh, but it does! It matters because if we do those things, we let sin control us. Romans 6:16 tells us that if we give into sin, then we're a slave to it. However, verses 17-18 tell us that we are free from the bondage of sin. Sin cannot control us unless we follow it and allow it to be our master. While following sinful things may seem like freedom, it's always disastrous. Even the smallest things will catch up with us.

The little boy could not yet understand, but doing whatever we want instead of obeying God is not really freedom at all. Our sin will control and ruin our lives. It is better to follow the words of verse 18 and be a slave only to goodness.

18So as one sin of Adam brought the
punishment of death to all people, one good
act that Christ did makes all people right
with God. And that brings true life for all.
19One man disobeyed God, and many
became sinners. In the same way, one man
obeyed God, and many will be made right.
20The law came to make sin worse. But when
sin grew worse, God's grace increased. 21Sin
once used death to rule us, but God gave
people more of his grace so that grace could
rule by making people right with him. And
this brings life forever through Jesus Christ
our Lord.

Dead to Sin but Alive in Christ

6 So do you think we should continue
sinning so that God will give us even
more grace? 2No! We died to our old sinful
lives, so how can we continue living with
sin? 3Did you forget that all of us became
part of Christ when we were baptized? We
shared his death in our baptism. 4When we
were baptized, we were buried with Christ
and shared his death. So, just as Christ was
raised from the dead by the wonderful
power of the Father, we also can live a new
life.

5Christ died, and we have been joined
with him by dying too. So we will also be
joined with him by rising from the dead as
he did. 6We know that our old life died with
Christ on the cross so that our sinful selves
would have no power over us and we would
not be slaves to sin. 7Anyone who has died is
made free from sin's control.

8If we died with Christ, we know we will
also live with him. 9Christ was raised from
the dead, and we know that he cannot die
again. Death has no power over him now.
10Yes, when Christ died, he died to defeat the
power of sin one time—enough for all time.
He now has a new life, and his new life is
with God. 11In the same way, you should see
yourselves as being dead to the power of sin
and alive with God through Christ Jesus.

12So, do not let sin control your life here
on earth so that you do what your sinful self
wants to do. 13Do not offer the parts of your
body to serve sin, as things to be used in
doing evil. Instead, offer yourselves to God
as people who have died and now live. Offer
the parts of your body to God to be used in
doing good. 14Sin will not be your master,
because you are not under law but under
God's grace.

Be Slaves of Righteousness

15So what should we do? Should we sin
because we are under grace and not under
law? No! 16Surely you know that when you
give yourselves like slaves to obey someone,
then you are really slaves of that person. The
person you obey is your master. You can
follow sin, which brings spiritual death, or
you can obey God, which makes you right
with him. 17In the past you were slaves to
sin—sin controlled you. But thank God,
you fully obeyed the things that you were
taught. 18You were made free from sin, and
now you are slaves to goodness. 19I use this
example because this is hard for you to
understand. In the past you offered the parts
of your body to be slaves to sin and evil; you
lived only for evil. In the same way now
you must give yourselves to be slaves of
goodness. Then you will live only for God.

20In the past you were slaves to sin, and
goodness did not control you. 21You did evil
things, and now you are ashamed of them.
Those things only bring death. 22But now
you are free from sin and have become
slaves of God. This brings you a life that is
only for God, and this gives you life forever.
23The payment for sin is death. But God
gives us the free gift of life forever in Christ
Jesus our Lord.

An Example from Marriage

7 Brothers and sisters, all of you
understand the law of Moses. So surely
you know that the law rules over people
only while they are alive. 2For example, a
woman must stay married to her husband as
long as he is alive. But if her husband dies,
she is free from the law of marriage. 3But if
she marries another man while her husband
is still alive, the law says she is guilty of
adultery. But if her husband dies, she is
free from the law of marriage. Then if she
marries another man, she is not guilty
of adultery.

4In the same way, my brothers and sisters,
your old selves died, and you became free
from the law through the body of Christ.
This happened so that you might belong to
someone else—the One who was raised
from the dead—and so that we might be

used in service to God. [5]In the past, we were
ruled by our sinful selves. The law made us
want to do sinful things that controlled our
bodies, so the things we did were bringing
us death. [6]In the past, the law held us like
prisoners, but our old selves died, and we
were made free from the law. So now we
serve God in a new way with the Spirit, and
not in the old way with written rules.

Our Fight Against Sin

[7]You might think I am saying that sin and
the law are the same thing. That is not true.
But the law was the only way I could learn
what sin meant. I would never have known
what it means to want to take something
belonging to someone else if the law had
not said, "You must not want to take your
neighbor's things."[n] [8]And sin found a way to
use that command and cause me to want
all kinds of things I should not want. But
without the law, sin has no power. [9]I was
alive before I knew the law. But when the
law's command came to me, then sin began
to live, [10]and I died. The command was
meant to bring life, but for me it brought
death. [11]Sin found a way to fool me by using
the command to make me die.

[12]So the law is holy, and the command is
holy and right and good. [13]Does this mean
that something that is good brought death to
me? No! Sin used something that is good to
bring death to me. This happened so that
I could see what sin is really like; the
command was used to show that sin is
very evil.

The War Within Us

[14]We know that the law is spiritual, but
I am not spiritual since sin rules me as if I
were its slave. [15]I do not understand the
things I do. I do not do what I want to do,
and I do the things I hate. [16]And if I do not
want to do the hated things I do, that means
I agree that the law is good. [17]But I am not
really the one who is doing these hated
things; it is sin living in me that does them.
[18]Yes, I know that nothing good lives in

7:7 "You . . . things." Quotation from Exodus 20:17.

devotion 305

ROMANS 7:22–25

A SHOPPING BUDDY

Do you ever feel like a divided woman? On one side, you know in your heart that you want to follow God and do good with your life. You have decided that you don't want anything to do with evil. And on the other side is the woman who does not do the good she desires. Instead, she allows evil to come in.

The heart that has come to know Jesus as Savior and God as Father wants to honor the holiness of God. In our minds, we desire to live beautiful lives for the glory of God. But it can be frustrating because we are confined by our humanity. We live inside these bodies that get tired and hungry. We fall asleep right in the middle of our best intentions. Physical strength wanes and spiritual power fades.

What is the weakest part of your humanity? Where can the temptation toward sin become overwhelming? That is the area in need of the greatest accountability and limitation. I have a girlfriend who has decided she can't shop by herself anymore. She overspends and has amassed a huge debt because of it. She now has a shopping buddy. She doesn't go to the mall without the accountability to stay on budget.

The next time you feel your spirit at odds, remember that your humanity is screaming for holiness. Protect yourself from the consequences of sin by doing whatever it takes to steer clear of your weakness.

me—I mean nothing good lives in the part of me that is earthly and sinful. I want to do the things that are good, but I do not do them. [19]I do not do the good things I want to do, but I do the bad things I do not want to do. [20]So if I do things I do not want to do, then I am not the one doing them. It is sin living in me that does those things.

[21]So I have learned this rule: When I want to do good, evil is there with me. [22]In my mind, I am happy with God's law. [23]But I see another law working in my body, which makes war against the law that my mind accepts. That other law working in my body is the law of sin, and it makes me its prisoner. [24]What a miserable man I am! Who will save me from this body that brings me death? [25]I thank God for saving me through Jesus Christ our Lord!

So in my mind I am a slave to God's law, but in my sinful self I am a slave to the law of sin.

Be Ruled by the Spirit

8 So now, those who are in Christ Jesus are not judged guilty.[n] [2]Through Christ Jesus the law of the Spirit that brings life made you[n] free from the law that brings sin and death. [3]The law was without power, because the law was made weak by our sinful selves. But God did what the law could not do. He sent his own Son to earth with the same human life that others use for sin. By sending his Son to be an offering for sin, God used a human life to destroy sin. [4]He did this so that we could be the kind of people the law correctly wants us to be. Now we do not live following our sinful selves, but we live following the Spirit.

[5]Those who live following their sinful selves think only about things that their sinful selves want. But those who live following the Spirit are thinking about the things the Spirit wants them to do. [6]If people's thinking is controlled by the sinful self, there is death. But if their thinking is controlled by the Spirit, there is life and peace. [7]When people's thinking is controlled by the sinful self, they are against God, because they refuse to obey God's law and really are not even able to obey God's law. [8]Those people who are ruled by their sinful selves cannot please God.

[9]But you are not ruled by your sinful selves. You are ruled by the Spirit, if that Spirit of God really lives in you. But the person who does not have the Spirit of Christ does not belong to Christ. [10]Your body will always be dead because of sin. But if Christ is in you, then the Spirit gives you life, because Christ made you right with God. [11]God raised Jesus from the dead, and if God's Spirit is living in you, he will also give life to your bodies that die. God is the One who raised Christ from the dead, and he will give life through[n] his Spirit that lives in you.

[12]So, my brothers and sisters, we must not be ruled by our sinful selves or live the way our sinful selves want. [13]If you use your lives to do the wrong things your sinful selves want, you will die spiritually. But if you use the Spirit's help to stop doing the wrong things you do with your body, you will have true life.

[14]The true children of God are those who let God's Spirit lead them. [15]The Spirit we received does not make us slaves again to fear; it makes us children of God. With that Spirit we cry out, "Father."[n] [16]And the Spirit himself joins with our spirits to say we are God's children. [17]If we are God's children, we will receive blessings from God together with Christ. But we must suffer as Christ suffered so that we will have glory as Christ has glory.

Our Future Glory

[18]The sufferings we have now are nothing compared to the great glory that will be shown to us. [19]Everything God made is waiting with excitement for God to show his children's glory completely. [20]Everything God made was changed to become useless, not by its own wish but because God wanted it and because all along there was this hope: [21]that everything God made would be set free from ruin to have the freedom and glory that belong to God's children.

[22]We know that everything God made has been waiting until now in pain, like a

8:1 guilty Some Greek copies continue, "those who do not live in the power of their sinful selves, but in the power of the Spirit."
8:2 you Some Greek copies read "me." **8:11 through** Some Greek copies read "because of."
8:15 "Father" Literally, "Abba, Father." Jewish children called their fathers "Abba."

woman ready to give birth. [23]Not only the
world, but we also have been waiting with
pain inside us. We have the Spirit as the first
part of God's promise. So we are waiting for
God to finish making us his own children,
which means our bodies will be made free.
[24]We were saved, and we have this hope.
If we see what we are waiting for, that is
not really hope. People do not hope for
something they already have. [25]But we are
hoping for something we do not have yet,
and we are waiting for it patiently.
[26]Also, the Spirit helps us with our
weakness. We do not know how to pray as
we should. But the Spirit himself speaks to
God for us, even begs God for us with deep
feelings that words cannot explain. [27]God
can see what is in people's hearts. And he
knows what is in the mind of the Spirit,
because the Spirit speaks to God for his
people in the way God wants.
[28]We know that in everything God works
for the good of those who love him.[n] They
are the people he called, because that was his
plan. [29]God knew them before he made the
world, and he chose them to be like his Son
so that Jesus would be the firstborn[n] of many
brothers and sisters. [30]God planned for them
to be like his Son; and those he planned to
be like his Son, he also called; and those he
called, he also made right with him; and
those he made right, he also glorified.

God's Love in Christ Jesus

[31]So what should we say about this? If
God is for us, no one can defeat us. [32]He did
not spare his own Son but gave him for us
all. So with Jesus, God will surely give us all
things. [33]Who can accuse the people God
has chosen? No one, because God is the One
who makes them right. [34]Who can say God's
people are guilty? No one, because Christ
Jesus died, but he was also raised from the
dead, and now he is on God's right side,
appealing to God for us. [35]Can anything
separate us from the love Christ has for us?

8:28 We . . . him. Some Greek copies read "We know that everything works together for good for those who love God."
8:29 firstborn Here this probably means that Christ was the first in God's family to share God's glory.

devotion 306

ROMANS 8:28–29

IN THE THICK OF A BIG, TANGLED MESS

A few years ago when I sold my business, I prayed earnestly before making that decision, and I know that the Lord gave me the go-ahead with numerous biblical confirmations. But several years into the deal, most of the promises the buyer made were not kept, and in an attempt to buy the business back, I found myself in a devastating financial situation. I thought I had lost my mind. Where did I go wrong?

Well, it turns out I had not been wrong after all. Within a year of regaining ownership, the value of the holding company had greatly diminished. God restored my finances and worked every detail out for my good just because he loves me! God was sparing me, and although I did not understand at the time, I held onto Romans 8:28-29 to keep my faith encouraged.

When we're in the thick of a big, tangled mess, it's hard to believe that God is going to be able to straighten it all out and be glorified. But that is exactly what he does. He takes the messes we make, and even the evil that others bring against us, and somehow turns every one of those into victories. Over the fifteen years I have walked with the Lord, I cannot think of one example when he did not come through. We have a God that works everything for our good, not because he has to, but for no other reason than his pure love for us.

Can troubles or problems or sufferings or
hunger or nakedness or danger or violent
death? 36As it is written in the Scriptures:

"For you we are in danger of death all the
time.
People think we are worth no more
than sheep to be killed." *Psalm 44:22*

37But in all these things we are completely
victorious through God who showed his
love for us. 38Yes, I am sure that neither
death, nor life, nor angels, nor ruling spirits,
nothing now, nothing in the future, no
powers, 39nothing above us, nothing below
us, nor anything else in the whole world will
ever be able to separate us from the love of
God that is in Christ Jesus our Lord.

God and the Jewish People

9 I am in Christ, and I am telling you the
truth; I do not lie. My conscience is ruled
by the Holy Spirit, and it tells me I am not
lying. 2I have great sorrow and always feel
much sadness. 3I wish I could help my
Jewish brothers and sisters, my people. I
would even wish that I were cursed and cut
off from Christ if that would help them.
4They are the people of Israel, God's chosen
children. They have seen the glory of God,
and they have the agreements that God
made between himself and his people. God
gave them the law of Moses and the right
way of worship and his promises. 5They are
the descendants of our great ancestors, and
they are the earthly family into which Christ
was born, who is God over all. Praise him
forever![n] Amen.

6It is not that God failed to keep his
promise to them. But only some of the
people of Israel are truly God's people,[n] 7and
only some of Abraham's[n] descendants are
true children of Abraham. But God said to
Abraham: "The descendants I promised you
will be from Isaac."[n] 8This means that not all
of Abraham's descendants are God's true
children. Abraham's true children are those
who become God's children because of the
promise God made to Abraham. 9God's
promise to Abraham was this: "At the right
time I will return, and Sarah will have a
son."[n] 10And that is not all. Rebekah's sons
had the same father, our father Isaac. 11-12But
before the two boys were born, God told
Rebekah, "The older will serve the younger."[n]
This was before the boys had done anything
good or bad. God said this so that the one
chosen would be chosen because of God's
own plan. He was chosen because he was
the one God wanted to call, not because of
anything he did. 13As the Scripture says, "I
loved Jacob, but I hated Esau."[n]

14So what should we say about this? Is
God unfair? In no way. 15God said to Moses,
"I will show kindness to anyone to whom
I want to show kindness, and I will show
mercy to anyone to whom I want to show
mercy."[n] 16So God will choose the one to
whom he decides to show mercy; his choice
does not depend on what people want or try
to do. 17The Scripture says to the king of
Egypt: "I made you king for this reason: to
show my power in you so that my name will
be talked about in all the earth."[n] 18So God
shows mercy where he wants to show
mercy, and he makes stubborn the people
he wants to make stubborn.

19So one of you will ask me: "Then why
does God blame us for our sins? Who can
fight his will?" 20You are only human, and
human beings have no right to question
God. An object should not ask the person
who made it, "Why did you make me like
this?" 21The potter can make anything he
wants to make. He can use the same clay to
make one thing for special use and another
thing for daily use.

22It is the same way with God. He wanted
to show his anger and to let people see his
power. But he patiently stayed with those
people he was angry with—people who
were made ready to be destroyed. 23He
waited with patience so that he could make
known his rich glory to the people who
receive his mercy. He has prepared these
people to have his glory, 24and we are those
people whom God called. He called us not
from the Jews only but also from those who

9:5 born . . . forever This can also mean "born. May God, who rules over all things, be praised forever!" **9:6 God's people** Literally, "Israel," the people God chose to bring his blessings to the world. **9:7 Abraham** Most respected ancestor of the Jews. Every Jew hoped to see Abraham. **9:7 "The descendants . . . Isaac."** Quotation from Genesis 21:12. **9:9 "At . . . son."** Quotation from Genesis 18:10, 14. **9:11–12 "The older . . . younger."** Quotation from Genesis 25:23. **9:13 "I . . . Esau."** Quotation from Malachi 1:2–3. **9:15 "I . . . mercy."** Quotation from Exodus 33:19. **9:17 "I . . . earth."** Quotation from Exodus 9:16.

devotion 307

ROMANS 8:35–37

A MOTHER LION READY TO POUNCE

It was a typical Sunday afternoon as I went from room to room to collect my children from Sunday school. As usual, they were hungry and anxious to get to our favorite restaurant for lunch. The three of them ran out the front doors of the church, my little girl trailing behind. Just as she was about to cross the street, I saw a car bearing down on her. The driver was looking down instead of watching where she was going. I ran as fast as I could, high heels clomping and Bible flying, right in front of the car, yelling at the top of my voice for the woman to stop. I had become a mother lion, ready to pounce on the one who threatened my child. I never stopped once to think about my own safety, only that of my precious little one.

That is the way Christ feels about us. He loves us more than we could possibly love our own children. He would never let anything keep us from his love. God is love and he is unable to stop loving us. It would be like a zebra trying to get rid of his stripes or a leopard his spots. Love is who God is, and nothing can change that. We don't even have to love God for him to love us. Stop and think about God's love for you today. You may realize that if God could love you that much, maybe you're worth loving.

are not Jews. 25As the Scripture says in
Hosea:
"I will say, 'You are my people'
to those I had called 'not my people.'
And I will show my love
to those people I did not love."
Hosea 2:1, 23
26"They were called,
'You are not my people,'
but later they will be called
'children of the living God.'" *Hosea 1:10*
27And Isaiah cries out about Israel:
"The people of Israel are many,
like the grains of sand by the sea.
But only a few of them will be saved,
28 because the Lord will quickly and
completely punish the people on
the earth." *Isaiah 10:22–23*
29It is as Isaiah said:
"The Lord All-Powerful
allowed a few of our descendants to live.
Otherwise we would have been
completely destroyed
like the cities of Sodom and
Gomorrah."[n] *Isaiah 1:9*
30So what does all this mean? Those who
are not Jews were not trying to make
themselves right with God, but they were
made right with God because of their faith.
31The people of Israel tried to follow a law to
make themselves right with God. But they
did not succeed, 32because they tried to
make themselves right by the things they
did instead of trusting in God to make them
right. They stumbled over the stone that
causes people to stumble. 33As it is written
in the Scripture:
"I will put in Jerusalem a stone that
causes people to stumble,
a rock that makes them fall.
Anyone who trusts in him will never be
disappointed." *Isaiah 8:14; 28:16*

10 Brothers and sisters, the thing I want
most is for all the Jews to be saved.
That is my prayer to God. 2I can say this
about them: They really try to follow God,

9:29 Sodom and Gomorrah Two cities that God destroyed because the people were so evil.

but they do not know the right way.
3Because they did not know the way that
God makes people right with him, they tried
to make themselves right in their own way.
So they did not accept God's way of making
people right. 4Christ ended the law so that
everyone who believes in him may be right
with God.

5Moses writes about being made right by
following the law. He says, "A person who
obeys these things will live because of
them."[n] 6But this is what the Scripture says
about being made right through faith: "Don't
say to yourself, 'Who will go up into
heaven?' " (That means, "Who will go up to
heaven and bring Christ down to earth?")
7"And do not say, 'Who will go down into
the world below?' " (That means, "Who
will go down and bring Christ up from the
dead?") 8This is what the Scripture says: "The
word is near you; it is in your mouth and in
your heart."[n] That is the teaching of faith
that we are telling. 9If you declare with your
mouth, "Jesus is Lord," and if you believe in
your heart that God raised Jesus from the
dead, you will be saved. 10We believe with
our hearts, and so we are made right with
God. And we declare with our mouths that
we believe, and so we are saved. 11As the
Scripture says, "Anyone who trusts in
him will never be disappointed."[n] 12That
Scripture says "anyone" because there is
no difference between those who are Jews
and those who are not. The same Lord is the
Lord of all and gives many blessings to all
who trust in him, 13as the Scripture says,
"Anyone who calls on the Lord will be
saved."[n]

14But before people can ask the Lord for
help, they must believe in him; and before
they can believe in him, they must hear
about him; and for them to hear about the
Lord, someone must tell them; 15and before
someone can go and tell them, that person
must be sent. It is written, "How beautiful is
the person who comes to bring good news."[n]
16But not all the Jews accepted the good
news. Isaiah said, "Lord, who believed what
we told them?"[n] 17So faith comes from
hearing the Good News, and people hear the
Good News when someone tells them about
Christ.

18But I ask: Didn't people hear the Good
News? Yes, they heard—as the Scripture says:

> "Their message went out through all the
> world;
> their words go everywhere on earth."
>
> *Psalm 19:4*

19Again I ask: Didn't the people of Israel
understand? Yes, they did understand. First,
Moses says:

> "I will use those who are not a nation to
> make you jealous.
> I will use a nation that does not
> understand to make you angry."
>
> *Deuteronomy 32:21*

20Then Isaiah is bold enough to say:

> "I was found by those who were not
> asking me for help.
> I made myself known to people who
> were not looking for me." *Isaiah 65:1*

21But about Israel God says,

> "All day long I stood ready to accept
> people who disobey and are stubborn."
>
> *Isaiah 65:2*

God Shows Mercy to All People

11 So I ask: Did God throw out his
people? No! I myself am an Israelite
from the family of Abraham, from the tribe
of Benjamin. 2God chose the Israelites to be
his people before they were born, and he has
not thrown his people out. Surely you know
what the Scripture says about Elijah, how he
prayed to God against the people of Israel.
3"Lord," he said, "they have killed your
prophets, and they have destroyed your
altars. I am the only prophet left, and now
they are trying to kill me, too."[n] 4But what
answer did God give Elijah? He said, "But I
have left seven thousand people in Israel
who have never bowed down before Baal."[n]
5It is the same now. There are a few people
that God has chosen by his grace. 6And if he
chose them by grace, it is not for the things
they have done. If they could be made God's
people by what they did, God's gift of grace
would not really be a gift.

7So this is what has happened: Although
the Israelites tried to be right with God, they
did not succeed, but the ones God chose did

10:5 "A person . . . them." Quotation from Leviticus 18:5. **10:6–8 But . . . heart."** Quotations from Deuteronomy 9:4; 30:12–14; Psalm 107:26. **10:11 "Anyone . . . disappointed."** Quotation from Isaiah 28:16. **10:13 "Anyone . . . saved."** Quotation from Joel 2:32. **10:15 "How . . . news."** Quotation from Isaiah 52:7. **10:16 "Lord, . . . them?"** Quotation from Isaiah 53:1. **11:3 "they . . . too"** Quotation from 1 Kings 19:10, 14. **11:4 "But . . . Baal."** Quotation from 1 Kings 19:18.

become right with him. The others were
made stubborn and refused to listen to God.
8 As it is written in the Scriptures:

"God gave the people a dull mind so they
could not understand." *Isaiah 29:10*
"He closed their eyes so they could not see
and their ears so they could not hear.
This continues until today." *Deuteronomy 29:4*

9 And David says:

"Let their own feasts trap them and cause
their ruin;
let their feasts cause them to stumble
and be paid back.
10 Let their eyes be closed so they cannot see
and their backs be forever weak from
troubles." *Psalm 69:22–23*

11 So I ask: When the Jews fell, did that fall
destroy them? No! But their failure brought
salvation to those who are not Jews, in order
to make the Jews jealous. 12 The Jews' failure
brought rich blessings for the world, and the
Jews' loss brought rich blessings for the
non-Jewish people. So surely the world will
receive much richer blessings when enough
Jews become the kind of people God wants.
13 Now I am speaking to you who are not
Jews. I am an apostle to those who are not
Jews, and since I have that work, I will make
the most of it. 14 I hope I can make my own
people jealous and, in that way, help some of
them to be saved. 15 When God turned away
from the Jews, he became friends with other
people in the world. So when God accepts
the Jews, surely that will bring them life
after death.
16 If the first piece of bread is offered to
God, then the whole loaf is made holy. If
the roots of a tree are holy, then the tree's
branches are holy too.
17 It is as if some of the branches from an
olive tree have been broken off. You non-
Jewish people are like the branch of a wild
olive tree that has been joined to that first
tree. You now share the strength and life of
the first tree, the Jews. 18 So do not brag about
those branches that were broken off. If you
brag, remember that you do not support the
root, but the root supports you. 19 You will
say, "Branches were broken off so that I
could be joined to their tree." 20 That is true.
But those branches were broken off because
they did not believe, and you continue to be
part of the tree only because you believe. Do
not be proud, but be afraid. 21 If God did not

devotion 308

ROMANS 12:1–2

WHAT DOES SHE *SEE* IN HIM?

I have a friend who married a man who isn't exactly what the world would call attractive. While he wasn't the complete opposite of handsome, there were many things about him that were imperfect, and they were the kinds of things that weren't easily masked. So when she began to date this man she eventually married, many people were thinking, and even shamefully asking, "What does she see in him?" Well, we'd soon see exactly what she saw in him. My friend saw Christ in him—plain and simple. This man displayed the fruit of the Spirit, and he shared it with everyone, most of all with her. Even though he wasn't the best-looking man in the world, she saw him through God's eyes, and she knew that he saw her the same way.

Isn't it amazing what God can do when we view the world through his eyes? I challenge you to look around at the people you live and spend time with. Do they exhibit the fruit of the Spirit? Are you surrounding yourself with beautiful people who are lovely through God's eyes? Perhaps you have been too critical of someone in your life that you need to look at in a new way. Maybe that person is you. Please remember that you are beautiful in God's eyes. I challenge you to have a new way of thinking and to begin viewing yourself and those around you not through the eyes of the world but through God's lenses.

let the natural branches of that tree stay,
then he will not let you stay if you don't
believe.
22 So you see that God is kind and also very
strict. He punishes those who stop following
him. But God is kind to you, if you continue
following in his kindness. If you do not, you
will be cut off from the tree. 23 And if the
Jews will believe in God again, he will accept
them back. God is able to put them back
where they were. 24 It is not natural for a wild
branch to be part of a good tree. And you
who are not Jews are like a branch cut from
a wild olive tree and joined to a good olive
tree. But since those Jews are like a branch
that grew from the good tree, surely they can
be joined to their own tree again.
25 I want you to understand this secret,
brothers and sisters, so you will understand
that you do not know everything: Part of
Israel has been made stubborn, but that will
change when many who are not Jews have
come to God. 26 And that is how all Israel will
be saved. It is written in the Scriptures:

"The Savior will come from Jerusalem;
he will take away all evil from the
family of Jacob.[n]
27 And I will make this agreement with
those people
when I take away their sins."

Isaiah 59:20–21; 27:9

28 The Jews refuse to accept the Good
News, so they are God's enemies. This has
happened to help you who are not Jews. But
the Jews are still God's chosen people, and
he loves them very much because of the
promises he made to their ancestors. 29 God
never changes his mind about the people he
calls and the things he gives them. 30 At one
time you refused to obey God. But now you
have received mercy, because those people
refused to obey. 31 And now the Jews refuse to
obey, because God showed mercy to you. But
this happened so that they also can[n] receive
mercy from him. 32 God has given all people
over to their stubborn ways so that he can
show mercy to all.

Praise to God

33 Yes, God's riches are very great, and his
wisdom and knowledge have no end! No
one can explain the things God decides
or understand his ways. 34 As the Scripture
says,

"Who has known the mind of the Lord,
or who has been able to give him
advice?" *Isaiah 40:13*
35 "No one has ever given God anything
that he must pay back." *Job 41:11*

36 Yes, God made all things, and everything
continues through him and for him. To him
be the glory forever! Amen.

Give Your Lives to God

12 So brothers and sisters, since God has
shown us great mercy, I beg you to
offer your lives as a living sacrifice to him.
Your offering must be only for God and
pleasing to him, which is the spiritual way
for you to worship. 2 Do not be shaped by
this world; instead be changed within by a
new way of thinking. Then you will be able
to decide what God wants for you; you will
know what is good and pleasing to him and
what is perfect. 3 Because God has given me
a special gift, I have something to say to
everyone among you. Do not think you are
better than you are. You must decide what
you really are by the amount of faith God
has given you. 4 Each one of us has a body
with many parts, and these parts all have
different uses. 5 In the same way, we are
many, but in Christ we are all one body. Each
one is a part of that body, and each part
belongs to all the other parts. 6 We all have
different gifts, each of which came because
of the grace God gave us. The person who
has the gift of prophecy should use that gift
in agreement with the faith. 7 Anyone who
has the gift of serving should serve. Anyone
who has the gift of teaching should teach.
8 Whoever has the gift of encouraging others
should encourage. Whoever has the gift of
giving to others should give freely. Anyone
who has the gift of being a leader should try
hard when he leads. Whoever has the gift of
showing mercy to others should do so with
joy.
9 Your love must be real. Hate what is evil,
and hold on to what is good. 10 Love each
other like brothers and sisters. Give each
other more honor than you want for
yourselves. 11 Do not be lazy but work hard,
serving the Lord with all your heart. 12 Be

11:26 Jacob Father of the twelve family groups of Israel, the people God chose to be his people.
11:31 can Some Greek copies read "can now."

devotion 309

ROMANS 12:9–21

HOW TO REALLY TAKE IT IN

When I read Paul's list of exhortations in Romans 12, everything inside of me wants to be that kind of person. But a weird thing happens. I read these verses, think to myself, "Yes, I want all of those," close my Bible, and forget. I don't mean to forget, but I just do. Paul wrote to remind us of the people we should be. But I am realizing that I have to be more determined in my reading and application, or else I might walk away and forget again.

As you read back through this passage, pray that God will make these words effective in your life. Tell him that you know only reading will not produce godliness. These words have to take hold down deep in your soul. You need the Holy Spirit to add power and resolve to your desire. After you have prayed, then linger. Stay with these words and meditate on them. You may even decide to journal a personal application for each instruction. Then tomorrow, go back to those things you have written. Pray over them again. Ask the Holy Spirit to make them a part of who you are.

You can't just fly over a passage and expect it to impact your life, especially one chock full of truth like this one. Stop. Look at the words. Pray each phrase into your life. Write an application. Keep remembering your commitment to godliness until your everyday life begins to line up with Paul's call to right living.

joyful because you have hope. Be patient
when trouble comes, and pray at all times.
13Share with God's people who need help.
Bring strangers in need into your homes.
14Wish good for those who harm you;
wish them well and do not curse them. 15Be
happy with those who are happy, and be sad
with those who are sad. 16Live in peace with
each other. Do not be proud, but make
friends with those who seem unimportant.
Do not think how smart you are.
17If someone does wrong to you, do not
pay him back by doing wrong to him. Try to
do what everyone thinks is right. 18Do your
best to live in peace with everyone. 19My
friends, do not try to punish others when
they wrong you, but wait for God to punish
them with his anger. It is written: "I will
punish those who do wrong; I will repay
them,"[n] says the Lord. 20But you should do
this:

"If your enemy is hungry, feed him;
if he is thirsty, give him a drink.
Doing this will be like pouring burning
coals on his head." *Proverbs 25:21–22*

21Do not let evil defeat you, but defeat evil
by doing good.

Christians Should Obey the Law

13 All of you must yield to the
government rulers. No one rules
unless God has given him the power to rule,
and no one rules now without that power
from God. 2So those who are against the
government are really against what God
has commanded. And they will bring
punishment on themselves. 3Those who do
right do not have to fear the rulers; only
those who do wrong fear them. Do you want
to be unafraid of the rulers? Then do what is
right, and they will praise you. 4The ruler
is God's servant to help you. But if you do

12:19 "I . . . them." Quotation from Deuteronomy 32:35.

wrong, then be afraid. He has the power to
punish; he is God's servant to punish those
who do wrong. 5So you must yield to the
government, not only because you might be
punished, but because you know it is right.
6This is also why you pay taxes. Rulers are
working for God and give their time to their
work. 7Pay everyone, then, what you owe. If
you owe any kind of tax, pay it. Show respect
and honor to them all.

Loving Others

8Do not owe people anything, except
always owe love to each other, because the
person who loves others has obeyed all the
law. 9The law says, "You must not be guilty
of adultery. You must not murder anyone.
You must not steal. You must not want to
take your neighbor's things."[n] All these
commands and all others are really only
one rule: "Love your neighbor as you love
yourself."[n] 10Love never hurts a neighbor,
so loving is obeying all the law.
11Do this because we live in an important
time. It is now time for you to wake up from
your sleep, because our salvation is nearer
now than when we first believed. 12The
"night"[n] is almost finished, and the "day"[n] is
almost here. So we should stop doing things
that belong to darkness and take up the
weapons used for fighting in the light. 13Let
us live in a right way, like people who
belong to the day. We should not have wild
parties or get drunk. There should be no
sexual sins of any kind, no fighting or
jealousy. 14But clothe yourselves with the
Lord Jesus Christ and forget about satisfying
your sinful self.

Do Not Criticize Other People

14 Accept into your group someone who
is weak in faith, and do not argue
about opinions. 2One person believes it is
right to eat all kinds of food.[n] But another,
who is weak, believes it is right to eat only
vegetables. 3The one who knows that it is
right to eat any kind of food must not reject
the one who eats only vegetables. And the
person who eats only vegetables must not
think that the one who eats all foods is
wrong, because God has accepted that
person. 4You cannot judge another person's
servant. The master decides if the servant is
doing well or not. And the Lord's servant
will do well because the Lord helps him do
well.
5Some think that one day is more
important than another, and others think
that every day is the same. Let all be sure in
their own mind. 6Those who think one day
is more important than other days are doing
that for the Lord. And those who eat all
kinds of food are doing that for the Lord, and
they give thanks to God. Others who refuse
to eat some foods do that for the Lord, and
they give thanks to God. 7We do not live or
die for ourselves. 8If we live, we are living for
the Lord, and if we die, we are dying for the
Lord. So living or dying, we belong to the
Lord.
9The reason Christ died and rose from the
dead to live again was so he would be Lord
over both the dead and the living. 10So why
do you judge your brothers or sisters in
Christ? And why do you think you are better
than they are? We will all stand before God
to be judged, 11because it is written in the
Scriptures:

> " 'As surely as I live,' says the Lord,
> 'Everyone will bow before me;
> everyone will say that I am God.' "
>
> *Isaiah 45:23*

12So each of us will have to answer to God.

Do Not Cause Others to Sin

13For that reason we should stop judging
each other. We must make up our minds
not to do anything that will make another
Christian sin. 14I am in the Lord Jesus, and I
know that there is no food that is wrong to
eat. But if a person believes something is
wrong, that thing is wrong for him. 15If you
hurt your brother's or sister's faith because
of something you eat, you are not really
following the way of love. Do not destroy
someone's faith by eating food he thinks is
wrong, because Christ died for him. 16Do not
allow what you think is good to become

13:9 "You . . . things." Quotation from Exodus 20:13–15, 17. **13:9 "Love . . . yourself."** Quotation from Leviticus 19:18. **13:12 "night"** This is used as a symbol of the sinful world we live in. This world will soon end. **13:12 "day"** This is used as a symbol of the good time that is coming, when we will be with God. **14:2 all . . . food** The Jewish law said there were some foods Jews should not eat. When Jews became Christians, some of them did not understand they could now eat all foods.

what others say is evil. 17 In the kingdom of God, eating and drinking are not important. The important things are living right with God, peace, and joy in the Holy Spirit. 18 Anyone who serves Christ by living this way is pleasing God and will be accepted by other people.

19 So let us try to do what makes peace and helps one another. 20 Do not let the eating of food destroy the work of God. All foods are all right to eat, but it is wrong to eat food that causes someone else to sin. 21 It is better not to eat meat or drink wine or do anything that will cause your brother or sister to sin.

22 Your beliefs about these things should be kept secret between you and God. People are happy if they can do what they think is right without feeling guilty. 23 But those who eat something without being sure it is right are wrong because they did not believe it was right. Anything that is done without believing it is right is a sin.

15 We who are strong in faith should help the weak with their weaknesses, and not please only ourselves. 2 Let each of us please our neighbors for their good, to help them be stronger in faith. 3 Even Christ did not live to please himself. It was as the Scriptures said: "When people insult you, it hurts me."[n] 4 Everything that was written in the past was written to teach us. The Scriptures give us patience and encouragement so that we can have hope. 5 May the patience and encouragement that come from God allow you to live in harmony with each other the way Christ Jesus wants. 6 Then you will all be joined together, and you will give glory to God the Father of our Lord Jesus Christ. 7 Christ accepted you, so you should accept each other, which will bring glory to God. 8 I tell you that Christ became a servant of the Jews to show that God's promises to the Jewish ancestors are true. 9 And he also did this so that those who are not Jews could give glory to God for the mercy he gives to them. It is written in the Scriptures:

"So I will praise you among the
non-Jewish people.
I will sing praises to your name."
Psalm 18:49

10 The Scripture also says,

"Be happy, you who are not Jews, together
with his people." *Deuteronomy 32:43*

11 Again the Scripture says,

"All you who are not Jews, praise the Lord.
All you people, sing praises to him."
Psalm 117:1

12 And Isaiah says,

"A new king will come from the family of
Jesse.[n]
He will come to rule over the
non-Jewish people,
and they will have hope because of him."
Isaiah 11:10

13 I pray that the God who gives hope will fill you with much joy and peace while you trust in him. Then your hope will overflow by the power of the Holy Spirit.

Paul Talks About His Work

14 My brothers and sisters, I am sure that you are full of goodness. I know that you have all the knowledge you need and that you are able to teach each other. 15 But I have written to you very openly about some things I wanted you to remember. I did this because God gave me this special gift: 16 to be a minister of Christ Jesus to those who are not Jews. I served God by teaching his Good News, so that the non-Jewish people could be an offering that God would accept—an offering made holy by the Holy Spirit.

17 So I am proud of what I have done for God in Christ Jesus. 18 I will not talk about anything except what Christ has done through me in leading those who are not Jews to obey God. They have obeyed God because of what I have said and done, 19 because of the power of miracles and the great things they saw, and because of the power of the Holy Spirit. I preached the Good News from Jerusalem all the way around to Illyricum, and so I have finished that part of my work. 20 I always want to preach the Good News in places where people have never heard of Christ, because I do not want to build on the work someone else has already started. 21 But it is written in the Scriptures:

"Those who were not told about him will
see,
and those who have not heard about
him will understand." *Isaiah 52:15*

15:3 "When . . . me." Quotation from Psalm 69:9.
15:12 Jesse Jesse was the father of David, king of Israel. Jesus was from their family.

Paul's Plan to Visit Rome

[22]This is the reason I was stopped many times from coming to you. [23]Now I have finished my work here. Since for many years I have wanted to come to you, [24]I hope to visit you on my way to Spain. After I enjoy being with you for a while, I hope you can help me on my trip. [25]Now I am going to Jerusalem to help God's people. [26]The believers in Macedonia and Southern Greece were happy to give their money to help the poor among God's people at Jerusalem. [27]They were happy to do this, and really they owe it to them. These who are not Jews have shared in the Jews' spiritual blessings, so they should use their material possessions to help the Jews. [28]After I am sure the poor in Jerusalem get the money that has been given for them, I will leave for Spain and stop and visit you. [29]I know that when I come to you I will bring Christ's full blessing.

[30]Brothers and sisters, I beg you to help me in my work by praying to God for me. Do this because of our Lord Jesus and the love that the Holy Spirit gives us. [31]Pray that I will be saved from the nonbelievers in Judea and that this help I bring to Jerusalem will please God's people there. [32]Then, if God wants me to, I will come to you with joy, and together you and I will have a time of rest. [33]The God who gives peace be with you all. Amen.

Greetings to the Christians

16 I recommend to you our sister Phoebe, who is a helper[n] in the church in Cenchrea. [2]I ask you to accept her in the Lord in the way God's people should. Help her with anything she needs, because she has helped me and many other people also.

[3]Give my greetings to Priscilla and Aquila, who work together with me in Christ Jesus [4]and who risked their own lives to save my life. I am thankful to them, and all the non-Jewish churches are thankful as well. [5]Also, greet for me the church that meets at their house.

Greetings to my dear friend Epenetus, who was the first person in Asia to follow Christ. [6]Greetings to Mary, who worked very hard for you. [7]Greetings to Andronicus and Junia, my relatives, who were in prison with me. They are very important apostles. They were believers in Christ before I was. [8]Greetings to Ampliatus, my dear friend in the Lord. [9]Greetings to Urbanus, a worker together with me for Christ. And greetings to my dear friend Stachys. [10]Greetings to Apelles, who was tested and proved that he truly loves Christ. Greetings to all those who are in the family of Aristobulus. [11]Greetings to Herodion, my fellow citizen. Greetings to all those in the family of Narcissus who belong to the Lord. [12]Greetings to Tryphena and Tryphosa, women who work very hard for the Lord. Greetings to my dear friend Persis, who also has worked very hard for the Lord. [13]Greetings to Rufus, who is a special person in the Lord, and to his mother, who has been like a mother to me also. [14]Greetings to Asyncritus, Phlegon, Hermes, Patrobas, Hermas, and all the brothers and sisters who are with them. [15]Greetings to Philologus and Julia, Nereus and his sister, and Olympas, and to all God's people with them. [16]Greet each other with a holy kiss. All of Christ's churches send greetings to you.

[17]Brothers and sisters, I ask you to look out for those who cause people to be against each other and who upset other people's faith. They are against the true teaching you learned, so stay away from them. [18]Such people are not serving our Lord Christ but are only doing what pleases themselves. They use fancy talk and fine words to fool the minds of those who do not know about evil. [19]All the believers have heard that you obey, so I am very happy because of you. But I want you to be wise in what is good and innocent in what is evil.

[20]The God who brings peace will soon defeat Satan and give you power over him.

The grace of our Lord Jesus be with you.

[21]Timothy, a worker together with me, sends greetings, as well as Lucius, Jason, and Sosipater, my relatives.

[22]I am Tertius, and I am writing this letter from Paul. I send greetings to you in the Lord.

[23]Gaius is letting me and the whole church here use his home. He also sends

16:1 helper Literally, "deaconess." This might mean the same as one of the special women helpers in 1 Timothy 3:11.

greetings to you, as do Erastus, the city
treasurer, and our brother Quartus. [[24]The
grace of our Lord Jesus Christ be with all of
you. Amen.][n]
[25]Glory to God who can make you strong
in faith by the Good News that I tell people
and by the message about Jesus Christ. The
message about Christ is the secret that was
hidden for long ages past but is now made
known. [26]It has been made clear through
the writings of the prophets. And by the
command of the eternal God it is made
known to all nations that they might believe
and obey.
[27]To the only wise God be glory forever
through Jesus Christ! Amen.

16:24 The . . . Amen. Some Greek copies do not contain the bracketed text.

1 Corinthians

Person Holding the Pen God Wrote With: *Paul,* the Bible's most prolific writer, who probably had permanent ink stains on his writing hand

When the Text Was Written: 55 A.D.

Spiritual Posture of the Original Recipients: While the church in Corinth had demonstrated a variety of spiritual gifts, they were also surrounded by all the luxury and carnal temptation a Grecian metropolis had to offer.

Storyline Synopsis: Paul founded the Corinthian church on his second missionary journey (Acts 18). Priscilla and Aquila, a Christian tent-making couple, were Paul's dear friends and partners in ministry, and they helped him start this new church plant. Their evangelistic efforts took place most often in the synagogue in town, which led to a lot of problems with local Jewish religious leaders who resented their message about some guy named Jesus being the Messiah. This particular church plant got off to a rocky start because of its infighting, gossip, cliques, and lascivious behavior. Paul wrote this first letter to the believers in Corinth soon after he departed for Ephesus in order to expose and resolve their immaturity. This book is essentially Corinth's first "spanking" from their spiritual daddy!

A Moment Worth Discussing: Chapter 13—a popular "poster passage"—has been quoted in countless wedding ceremonies, but there are many other significant lessons in 1 Corinthians. One is found scattered throughout chapters 8—10. Paul explains that while Christians have great freedoms because of God's grace, we shouldn't necessarily exercise those freedoms if they have the potential to wound other people. This is especially true if our presumptuous actions cause young believers to struggle in their faith. Paul compels us to consider the motive of our hearts, to ask ourselves why we're doing what we're doing, and to be willing to sacrifice our personal convenience and freedoms for the benefit of others.

Interesting (But Likely to Be Overlooked) Character: *Aphrodite,* the Greek "goddess of love," was worshiped by pagan Corinthians. The temple of Aphrodite was a boon to the local economy and spawned a prostitution ring that desecrated the city with the fallout of sexual immorality.

1 From Paul. God called me to be an apostle
of Christ Jesus because that is what God
wanted. Also from Sosthenes, our brother in
Christ.
2 To the church of God in Corinth, to you
who have been made holy in Christ Jesus.
You were called to be God's holy people with
all people everywhere who pray in the name
of the Lord Jesus Christ—their Lord and
ours:
3 Grace and peace to you from God our
Father and the Lord Jesus Christ.

Paul Gives Thanks to God

4 I always thank my God for you because
of the grace God has given you in Christ
Jesus. 5 I thank God because in Christ you
have been made rich in every way, in all
your speaking and in all your knowledge.
6 Just as our witness about Christ has been
guaranteed to you, 7 so you have every gift
from God while you wait for our Lord Jesus
Christ to come again. 8 Jesus will keep you
strong until the end so that there will be no
wrong in you on the day our Lord Jesus
Christ comes again. 9 God, who has called
you into fellowship with his Son, Jesus
Christ our Lord, is faithful.

Problems in the Church

10 I beg you, brothers and sisters, by the
name of our Lord Jesus Christ that all of you
agree with each other and not be split into
groups. I beg that you be completely joined
together by having the same kind of
thinking and the same purpose. 11 My
brothers and sisters, some people from
Chloe's family have told me quite plainly
that there are quarrels among you. 12 This
is what I mean: One of you says, "I follow
Paul"; another says, "I follow Apollos";
another says, "I follow Peter"; and another
says, "I follow Christ." 13 Christ has been
divided up into different groups! Did Paul
die on the cross for you? No! Were you
baptized in the name of Paul? No! 14 I thank
God I did not baptize any of you except
Crispus and Gaius 15 so that now no one can
say you were baptized in my name. 16 (I also
baptized the family of Stephanas, but I do
not remember that I baptized anyone else.)
17 Christ did not send me to baptize people

devotion 310

1 CORINTHIANS 1:8–9

AVOIDING THE LOONEY BIN

Are you feeling a bit overwhelmed today? Have the kids got you running in twenty directions and your husband is being a pill and your boss wants to know if you can put in a few extra hours? Yes, we all have those days when we feel like Sybil chained to the piano wondering which personality is going to present itself next. Then Jesus says, "Come to me and let me tell you who you are . . . you are a wife, mother, friend, taxi driver, business woman, mentor, employee, and most of all you are my daughter. And I love your crazy self!" I love it when he whispers that into my heart. When you are weak, he wants to make you strong. He didn't say it's OK to live wimpy to the end!

When Paul wrote to Timothy, he went through a list of roles that Timothy needed to be prepared to fill: a Christian, a pastor, a steward, a soldier, an athlete, a farmer, a workman, a vessel, and a servant. See girls, multi-tasking was not just designed for women! Paul was an example of Jesus providing strength through a faithful friend. Paul was a constant encourager in the way of Christ to his friends.

Ladies, love God and the people he gives you the privilege of caring for with everything you've got. Deposit the Word in your hearts and souls. If all goes well, you will avoid the looney bin and be strong to the end!

but to preach the Good News. And he sent
me to preach the Good News without using
words of human wisdom so that the cross[n] of
Christ would not lose its power.

Christ Is God's Power and Wisdom

18The teaching about the cross is
foolishness to those who are being lost, but
to us who are being saved it is the power of
God. 19It is written in the Scriptures:

"I will cause the wise to lose their
wisdom;
I will make the wise unable to
understand." *Isaiah 29:14*

20Where is the wise person? Where is the
educated person? Where is the skilled talker
of this world? God has made the wisdom of
the world foolish. 21In the wisdom of God
the world did not know God through its
own wisdom. So God chose to use the
message that sounds foolish to save those
who believe. 22The Jews ask for miracles, and
the Greeks want wisdom. 23But we preach
a crucified Christ. This causes the Jews to
stumble and is foolishness to non-Jews. 24But
Christ is the power of God and the wisdom
of God to those people God has called—Jews
and Greeks. 25Even the foolishness of God
is wiser than human wisdom, and the
weakness of God is stronger than human
strength.

26Brothers and sisters, look at what you
were when God called you. Not many of you
were wise in the way the world judges
wisdom. Not many of you had great
influence. Not many of you came from
important families. 27But God chose the
foolish things of the world to shame the
wise, and he chose the weak things of the
world to shame the strong. 28He chose what
the world thinks is unimportant and what
the world looks down on and thinks is
nothing in order to destroy what the world
thinks is important. 29God did this so that no
one can brag in his presence. 30Because of
God you are in Christ Jesus, who has become
for us wisdom from God. In Christ we are
put right with God, and have been made
holy, and have been set free from sin. 31So, as
the Scripture says, "If people want to brag,
they should brag only about the Lord."[n]

The Message of Christ's Death

2 Dear brothers and sisters, when I came
to you, I did not come preaching God's
secret[n] with fancy words or a show of
human wisdom. 2I decided that while I was
with you I would forget about everything
except Jesus Christ and his death on the
cross. 3So when I came to you, I was weak
and fearful and trembling. 4My teaching and
preaching were not with words of human
wisdom that persuade people but with proof
of the power that the Spirit gives. 5This was
so that your faith would be in God's power
and not in human wisdom.

God's Wisdom

6However, I speak a wisdom to those who
are mature. But this wisdom is not from this
world or from the rulers of this world, who
are losing their power. 7I speak God's secret
wisdom, which he has kept hidden. Before
the world began, God planned this wisdom
for our glory. 8None of the rulers of this
world understood it. If they had, they would
not have crucified the Lord of glory. 9But as
it is written in the Scriptures:

"No one has ever seen this,
and no one has ever heard about it.
No one has ever imagined
what God has prepared for those who
love him." *Isaiah 64:4*

10But God has shown us these things
through the Spirit.

The Spirit searches out all things, even
the deep secrets of God. 11Who knows the
thoughts that another person has? Only a
person's spirit that lives within him knows
his thoughts. It is the same with God. No one
knows the thoughts of God except the Spirit
of God. 12Now we did not receive the spirit
of the world, but we received the Spirit that
is from God so that we can know all that
God has given us. 13And we speak about
these things, not with words taught us by
human wisdom but with words taught us by
the Spirit. And so we explain spiritual truths
to spiritual people. 14A person who does not
have the Spirit does not accept the truths
that come from the Spirit of God. That
person thinks they are foolish and cannot
understand them, because they can only be

1:17 cross Paul uses the cross as a picture of the Good News, the story of Christ's death and rising from the dead for people's sins. The cross, or Christ's death, was God's way to save people. **1:31 "If . . . Lord."** Quotation from Jeremiah 9:24. **2:1 God's secret** Some Greek copies read "God's message."

judged to be true by the Spirit. [15]The
spiritual person is able to judge all things,
but no one can judge him. The Scripture
says:
[16]"Who has known the mind of the Lord?
Who has been able to teach him?"
Isaiah 40:13
But we have the mind of Christ.

Following People Is Wrong

3 Brothers and sisters, in the past I could
not talk to you as I talk to spiritual
people. I had to talk to you as I would to
people without the Spirit—babies in Christ.
[2]The teaching I gave you was like milk, not
solid food, because you were not able to take
solid food. And even now you are not ready.
[3]You are still not spiritual, because there is
jealousy and quarreling among you, and this
shows that you are not spiritual. You are
acting like people of the world. [4]One of you
says, "I belong to Paul," and another says, "I
belong to Apollos." When you say things
like this, you are acting like people of the
world.
[5]Is Apollos important? No! Is Paul
important? No! We are only servants of God
who helped you believe. Each one of us did
the work God gave us to do. [6]I planted the
seed, and Apollos watered it. But God is the
One who made it grow. [7]So the one who
plants is not important, and the one who
waters is not important. Only God, who
makes things grow, is important. [8]The one
who plants and the one who waters have the
same purpose, and each will be rewarded for
his own work. [9]We are God's workers,
working together; you are like God's farm,
God's house.
[10]Using the gift God gave me, I laid the
foundation of that house like an expert
builder. Others are building on that
foundation, but all people should be careful
how they build on it. [11]The foundation that
has already been laid is Jesus Christ, and no
one can lay down any other foundation.
[12]But if people build on that foundation,
using gold, silver, jewels, wood, grass, or
straw, [13]their work will be clearly seen,
because the Day of Judgment[n] will make it
visible. That Day will appear with fire, and
the fire will test everyone's work to show
what sort of work it was. [14]If the building
that has been put on the foundation still

3:13 Day of Judgment The day Christ will come to judge all people and take his people home to live with him.

devotion 311

1 CORINTHIANS 3:6

THE PLANTING'S MY JOB

I am terrified of witnessing. I have been doing it since I was in the sixth grade, but all that practice hasn't made it any easier. My first witnessing experiences were at the beach with a group of peers, along with our teacher. We would share our faith with complete strangers. I would get so nervous, jumble my words, and forget all my Bible verses. I thought I would overcome this fear as I got older, but I didn't. It has never stopped me from sharing the Good News, but I still get nervous. I think the reason is that I feel responsible for whether or not the person accepts Christ. Somehow I think that if I do a good job sharing, then the person will believe, but if I do a bad job, then I've let God down.

I know God doesn't see it this way. First Corinthians 3:6 tells me that. God just wants me to focus on planting seeds. God is the One who will make them grow. I need to stop thinking like the world, always looking for success, and let God be God. Sometimes I will plant the seed, and other times I may be the one to water a seed that someone else planted. But only God will make it grow. When I get to heaven, God isn't going to critique me on my presentation. But he will ask me if I planted and watered the seeds.

stands, the builder will get a reward. [15]But if
the building is burned up, the builder will
suffer loss. The builder will be saved, but it
will be as one who escaped from a fire.

[16]Don't you know that you are God's
temple and that God's Spirit lives in you?
[17]If anyone destroys God's temple, God will
destroy that person, because God's temple is
holy and you are that temple.

[18]Do not fool yourselves. If you think you
are wise in this world, you should become a
fool so that you can become truly wise,
[19]because the wisdom of this world is
foolishness with God. It is written in the
Scriptures, "He catches those who are wise in
their own clever traps."[n] [20]It is also written in
the Scriptures, "The Lord knows what wise
people think. He knows their thoughts are
just a puff of wind."[n] [21]So you should not
brag about human leaders. All things belong
to you: [22]Paul, Apollos, and Peter; the world,
life, death, the present, and the future—all
these belong to you. [23]And you belong to
Christ, and Christ belongs to God.

Apostles Are Servants of Christ

4 People should think of us as servants
of Christ, the ones God has trusted with
his secrets. [2]Now in this way those who are
trusted with something valuable must show
they are worthy of that trust. [3]As for myself,
I do not care if I am judged by you or by any
human court. I do not even judge myself. [4]I
know of no wrong I have done, but this does
not make me right before the Lord. The Lord
is the One who judges me. [5]So do not judge
before the right time; wait until the Lord
comes. He will bring to light things that are
now hidden in darkness, and will make
known the secret purposes of people's
hearts. Then God will praise each one of
them.

[6]Brothers and sisters, I have used Apollos
and myself as examples so you could learn
through us the meaning of the saying,
"Follow only what is written in the
Scriptures." Then you will not be more
proud of one person than another. [7]Who
says you are better than others? What do
you have that was not given to you? And if
it was given to you, why do you brag as if
you did not receive it as a gift?

[8]You think you already have everything
you need. You think you are rich. You
think you have become kings without us. I
wish you really were kings so we could be
kings together with you. [9]But it seems to me
that God has put us apostles in last place, like
those sentenced to die. We are like a show for
the whole world to see—angels and people.
[10]We are fools for Christ's sake, but you are
very wise in Christ. We are weak, but you
are strong. You receive honor, but we are
shamed. [11]Even to this very hour we do not
have enough to eat or drink or to wear. We
are often beaten, and we have no homes in
which to live. [12]We work hard with our own
hands for our food. When people curse us,
we bless them. When they hurt us, we put
up with it. [13]When they tell evil lies about
us, we speak nice words about them. Even
today, we are treated as though we were the
garbage of the world—the filth of the earth.

[14]I am not trying to make you feel
ashamed. I am writing this to give you a
warning as my own dear children. [15]For
though you may have ten thousand teachers
in Christ, you do not have many fathers.
Through the Good News I became your
father in Christ Jesus, [16]so I beg you, please
follow my example. [17]That is why I am
sending to you Timothy, my son in the Lord.
I love Timothy, and he is faithful. He will
help you remember my way of life in Christ
Jesus, just as I teach it in all the churches
everywhere.

[18]Some of you have become proud,
thinking that I will not come to you again.
[19]But I will come to you very soon if the Lord
wishes. Then I will know what the proud
ones do, not what they say, [20]because the
kingdom of God is present not in talk but in
power. [21]Which do you want: that I come to
you with punishment or with love and
gentleness?

Wickedness in the Church

5 It is actually being said that there is
sexual sin among you. And it is a kind
that does not happen even among people
who do not know God. A man there has
his father's wife. [2]And you are proud! You
should have been filled with sadness so that
the man who did this should be put out of

3:19 "He . . . traps." Quotation from Job 5:13.
3:20 "The Lord . . . wind." Quotation from Psalm 94:11.

your group. 3 I am not there with you in
person, but I am with you in spirit. And I
have already judged the man who did that
sin as if I were really there. 4 When you meet
together in the name of our Lord Jesus, and I
meet with you in spirit with the power of
our Lord Jesus, 5 then hand this man over to
Satan. So his sinful self[n] will be destroyed,
and his spirit will be saved on the day of the
Lord.

6 Your bragging is not good. You know the
saying, "Just a little yeast makes the whole
batch of dough rise." 7 Take out all the old
yeast so that you will be a new batch of
dough without yeast, which you really are.
For Christ, our Passover lamb, has been
sacrificed. 8 So let us celebrate this feast, but
not with the bread that has the old yeast—
the yeast of sin and wickedness. Let us
celebrate this feast with the bread that has
no yeast—the bread of goodness and truth.

9 I wrote you in my earlier letter not to
associate with those who sin sexually. 10 But I
did not mean you should not associate with
those of this world who sin sexually, or with
the greedy, or robbers, or those who worship
idols. To get away from them you would
have to leave this world. 11 I am writing to
tell you that you must not associate with
those who call themselves believers in
Christ but who sin sexually, or are greedy, or
worship idols, or abuse others with words, or
get drunk, or cheat people. Do not even eat
with people like that.

12-13 It is not my business to judge those
who are not part of the church. God will
judge them. But you must judge the people
who are part of the church. The Scripture
says, "You must get rid of the evil person
among you."[n]

Judging Problems Among Christians

6 When you have something against
another Christian, how can you bring
yourself to go before judges who are not
right with God? Why do you not let God's
people decide who is right? 2 Surely you
know that God's people will judge the world.
So if you are to judge the world, are you not
able to judge small cases as well? 3 You know
that in the future we will judge angels, so
surely we can judge the ordinary things of
this life. 4 If you have ordinary cases that
must be judged, are you going to appoint
people as judges who mean nothing to the
church? 5 I say this to shame you. Surely
there is someone among you wise enough to
judge a complaint between believers. 6 But
now one believer goes to court against
another believer—and you do this in front
of unbelievers!

7 The fact that you have lawsuits against
each other shows that you are already
defeated. Why not let yourselves be
wronged? Why not let yourselves be
cheated? 8 But you yourselves do wrong and
cheat, and you do this to other believers!

9-10 Surely you know that the people who
do wrong will not inherit God's kingdom.
Do not be fooled. Those who sin sexually,
worship idols, take part in adultery, those
who are male prostitutes, or men who have
sexual relations with other men, those who
steal, are greedy, get drunk, lie about others,
or rob—these people will not inherit God's
kingdom. 11 In the past, some of you were
like that, but you were washed clean. You
were made holy, and you were made right
with God in the name of the Lord Jesus
Christ and in the Spirit of our God.

Use Your Bodies for God's Glory

12 "I am allowed to do all things," but not
all things are good for me to do. "I am
allowed to do all things," but I will not let
anything make me its slave. 13 "Food is for
the stomach, and the stomach for food," but
God will destroy them both. The body is not
for sexual sin but for the Lord, and the Lord
is for the body. 14 By his power God has raised
the Lord from the dead and will also raise
us from the dead. 15 Surely you know that
your bodies are parts of Christ himself. So
I must never take the parts of Christ and join
them to a prostitute! 16 It is written in the
Scriptures, "The two will become one body."[n]
So you should know that anyone who joins
with a prostitute becomes one body with the
prostitute. 17 But the one who joins with the
Lord is one spirit with the Lord.

18 So run away from sexual sin. Every
other sin people do is outside their bodies,

5:5 sinful self Literally, "flesh." This could also mean his body. **5:12–13 "You . . . you."** Quotation from Deuteronomy 17:7; 19:19; 22:21, 24; 24:7. **6:16 "The two . . . body."** Quotation from Genesis 2:24.

but those who sin sexually sin against their
own bodies. [19]You should know that your
body is a temple for the Holy Spirit who is in
you. You have received the Holy Spirit from
God. So you do not belong to yourselves,
[20]because you were bought by God for a
price. So honor God with your bodies.

About Marriage

7 Now I will discuss the things you wrote
me about. It is good for a man not to have
sexual relations with a woman. [2]But because
sexual sin is a danger, each man should have
his own wife, and each woman should have
her own husband. [3]The husband should give
his wife all that he owes her as his wife. And
the wife should give her husband all that she
owes him as her husband. [4]The wife does
not have full rights over her own body; her
husband shares them. And the husband does
not have full rights over his own body; his
wife shares them. [5]Do not refuse to give your
bodies to each other, unless you both agree to
stay away from sexual relations for a time so
you can give your time to prayer. Then come
together again so Satan cannot tempt you
because of a lack of self-control. [6]I say this
to give you permission to stay away from
sexual relations for a time. It is not a
command to do so. [7]I wish that everyone
were like me, but each person has his own
gift from God. One has one gift, another has
another gift.

[8]Now for those who are not married and
for the widows I say this: It is good for them
to stay unmarried as I am. [9]But if they
cannot control themselves, they should
marry. It is better to marry than to burn with
sexual desire.

[10]Now I give this command for the
married people. (The command is not from
me; it is from the Lord.) A wife should not
leave her husband. [11]But if she does leave,
she must not marry again, or she should
make up with her husband. Also the
husband should not divorce his wife.

[12]For all the others I say this (I am saying
this, not the Lord): If a Christian man has a
wife who is not a believer, and she is happy
to live with him, he must not divorce her.
[13]And if a Christian woman has a husband
who is not a believer, and he is happy to live
with her, she must not divorce him. [14]The
husband who is not a believer is made holy
through his believing wife. And the wife
who is not a believer is made holy through

devotion 312

1 CORINTHIANS 6:19-20

DO YOU TRUST GOD WITH YOUR BODY?

When Christ paid the debt to set you free, he paid for your body as well as your soul to be the place where he abides. The Lord made your body, and he wants to fill his creation with his presence. You were not created to work for God. You were created to be filled by God. He promises that death will not get the last word. For eternity, you will be given the perfect and glorified version of the body you now have: no more sickness, no more back pain or deformity, no more chemical and hormonal imbalances.

When you trust God with your body, you commit to not using your body for immorality. This physical body is a temple, and impure acts blaspheme the price God paid to make you clean. God intends for your body to show off his glory. He wants you to use your body in ways that prove God can satisfy us above anything the world has to offer.

Applying and living 1 Corinthians 6:19-20 can be a huge task for most of us. But there are just as many who can testify to the power God gives to your soul when he has control of your body. For some of us, this will mean fighting addictions. For others, it will mean a righteous determination to keep the temple pure. And most of us will hear this passage reawaken the call to pursue strength in our physical bodies so that God will be glorified.

her believing husband. If this were not true,
your children would not be clean, but now
your children are holy.
15But if those who are not believers decide
to leave, let them leave. When this happens,
the Christian man or woman is free. But God
called us[n] to live in peace. 16Wife, you don't
know; maybe you will save your husband.
And husband, you don't know; maybe you
will save your wife.

Live as God Called You

17But in any case each one of you should
continue to live the way God has given you
to live—the way you were when God called
you. This is a rule I make in all the churches.
18If a man was already circumcised when
he was called, he should not undo his
circumcision. If a man was without
circumcision when he was called, he should
not be circumcised. 19It is not important if a
man is circumcised or not. The important
thing is obeying God's commands. 20Each
one of you should stay the way you were
when God called you. 21If you were a slave
when God called you, do not let that bother
you. But if you can be free, then make good
use of your freedom. 22Those who were
slaves when the Lord called them are free
persons who belong to the Lord. In the same
way, those who were free when they were
called are now Christ's slaves. 23You all were
bought at a great price, so do not become
slaves of people. 24Brothers and sisters, each
of you should stay as you were when you
were called, and stay there with God.

Questions About Getting Married

25Now I write about people who are not
married. I have no command from the Lord
about this; I give my opinion. But I can be
trusted, because the Lord has shown me
mercy. 26The present time is a time of
trouble, so I think it is good for you to stay
the way you are. 27If you have a wife, do not
try to become free from her. If you are not
married, do not try to find a wife. 28But if
you decide to marry, you have not sinned.
And if a girl who has never married decides
to marry, she has not sinned. But those who
marry will have trouble in this life, and I
want you to be free from trouble.
29Brothers and sisters, this is what I mean:
We do not have much time left. So starting
now, those who have wives should live as if
they had no wives. 30Those who are crying
should live as if they were not crying. Those
who are happy should live as if they were
not happy. Those who buy things should
live as if they own nothing. 31Those who use
the things of the world should live as if they
were not using them, because this world in
its present form will soon be gone.
32I want you to be free from worry. A man
who is not married is busy with the Lord's
work, trying to please the Lord. 33But a man
who is married is busy with things of the
world, trying to please his wife. 34He must
think about two things—pleasing his wife
and pleasing the Lord. A woman who is not
married or a girl who has never married is
busy with the Lord's work. She wants to
be holy in body and spirit. But a married
woman is busy with things of the world, as
to how she can please her husband. 35I am
saying this to help you, not to limit you. But
I want you to live in the right way, to give
yourselves fully to the Lord without concern
for other things.
36If a man thinks he is not doing the right
thing with the girl he is engaged to, if she is
almost past the best age to marry and he
feels he should marry her, he should do what
he wants. They should get married. It is no
sin. 37But if a man is sure in his mind that
there is no need for marriage, and has his
own desires under control, and has decided
not to marry the one to whom he is engaged,
he is doing the right thing. 38So the man
who marries his girl does right, but the man
who does not marry will do better.
39A woman must stay with her husband
as long as he lives. But if her husband dies,
she is free to marry any man she wants, but
she must marry another believer. 40The
woman is happier if she does not marry
again. This is my opinion, but I believe I also
have God's Spirit.

About Food Offered to Idols

8 Now I will write about meat that is
sacrificed to idols. We know that "we all
have knowledge." Knowledge puffs you up
with pride, but love builds up. 2If you think

7:15 us Some Greek copies read "you."

you know something, you do not yet know
anything as you should. 3But if any person
loves God, that person is known by God.
4So this is what I say about eating meat
sacrificed to idols: We know that an idol is
really nothing in the world, and we know
there is only one God. 5Even though there
are things called gods, in heaven or on earth
(and there are many "gods" and "lords"), 6for
us there is only one God—our Father. All
things came from him, and we live for him.
And there is only one Lord—Jesus Christ. All
things were made through him, and we also
were made through him.
7But not all people know this. Some
people are still so used to idols that when
they eat meat, they still think of it as being
sacrificed to an idol. Because their
conscience is weak, when they eat it, they
feel guilty. 8But food will not bring us closer
to God. Refusing to eat does not make us less
pleasing to God, and eating does not make
us better in God's sight.
9But be careful that your freedom does not
cause those who are weak in faith to fall
into sin. 10Suppose one of you who has
knowledge eats in an idol's temple.[n]
Someone who is weak in faith might see you
eating there and be encouraged to eat meat
sacrificed to idols while thinking it is wrong
to do so. 11This weak believer for whom
Christ died is ruined because of your
"knowledge." 12When you sin against your
brothers and sisters in Christ like this and
cause them to do what they feel is wrong,
you are also sinning against Christ. 13So if
the food I eat causes them to fall into sin, I
will never eat meat again so that I will not
cause any of them to sin.

Paul Is like the Other Apostles

9 I am a free man. I am an apostle. I have
seen Jesus our Lord. You people are all an
example of my work in the Lord. 2If others
do not accept me as an apostle, surely you
do, because you are proof that I am an
apostle in the Lord.
3This is the answer I give people who

8:10 idol's temple Building where a god is worshiped.

devotion 313

1 CORINTHIANS 9:24–25

I'M JESUS-CODEPENDENT

The other day my girlfriend said to me, "I am so codependent. All I think about is Jesus. He is always in my thoughts. I want to please him in everything. I can't do anything without him." What she said was incredibly convicting to me. She made me think, "Yes, I want to be Jesus-codependent, too."

Essentially, my friend was telling me that she is becoming like a determined athlete, focused on the prize of Jesus and glorifying him through her life. Thoughts of him are woven into every piece of her day. She's continually praying and seeking God's wisdom, exercising her body and her mind so that she is prepared for the long race ahead. She is running toward God with Olympic-sized passion and perseverance. I love that about her.

The athletes we watch on television spend their lifetimes training for the hour that they will stand on a platform and receive a medal. Multiply that reward by eternity, and you will see the value of the crown that awaits us in Christ. The goal on this earth is spiritual maturity, but that goal requires us to learn discipline in much the same way an Olympic athlete requires decades of preparation to compete. Will you take this life seriously and train yourself to depend on Jesus? Will you fight the good fight for faith? Will you run strong and self-controlled? Live a lifetime of obedience so that the message of God's love is not disqualified.

want to judge me: [4]Do we not have the right
to eat and drink? [5]Do we not have the right
to bring a believing wife with us when we
travel as do the other apostles and the Lord's
brothers and Peter? [6]Are Barnabas and I the
only ones who must work to earn our
living? [7]No soldier ever serves in the army
and pays his own salary. No one ever plants a
vineyard without eating some of the grapes.
No person takes care of a flock without
drinking some of the milk.
[8]I do not say this by human authority;
God's law also says the same thing. [9]It is
written in the law of Moses: "When an ox is
working in the grain, do not cover its mouth
to keep it from eating."[n] When God said this,
was he thinking only about oxen? No. [10]He
was really talking about us. Yes, that
Scripture was written for us, because it goes
on to say: "The one who plows and the one
who works in the grain should hope to get
some of the grain for their work." [11]Since we
planted spiritual seed among you, is it too
much if we should harvest material things?
[12]If others have the right to get something
from you, surely we have this right, too.
But we do not use it. No, we put up with
everything ourselves so that we will not
keep anyone from believing the Good News
of Christ. [13]Surely you know that those who
work at the Temple get their food from the
Temple, and those who serve at the altar get
part of what is offered at the altar. [14]In the
same way, the Lord has commanded that
those who tell the Good News should get
their living from this work.
[15]But I have not used any of these rights.
And I am not writing this now to get
anything from you. I would rather die than
to have my reason for bragging taken away.
[16]Telling the Good News does not give me
any reason for bragging. Telling the Good
News is my duty—something I must do.
And how terrible it will be for me if I do not
tell the Good News. [17]If I preach because it
is my own choice, I have a reward. But if I
preach and it is not my choice to do so, I am
only doing the duty that was given to me.
[18]So what reward do I get? This is my
reward: that when I tell the Good News I can
offer it freely. I do not use my full rights in
my work of preaching the Good News.
[19]I am free and belong to no one. But I
make myself a slave to all people to win as
many as I can. [20]To the Jews I became like a
Jew to win the Jews. I myself am not ruled by
the law. But to those who are ruled by the
law I became like a person who is ruled by
the law. I did this to win those who are ruled
by the law. [21]To those who are without the
law I became like a person who is without
the law. I did this to win those people who
are without the law. (But really, I am not
without God's law—I am ruled by Christ's
law.) [22]To those who are weak, I became
weak so I could win the weak. I have become
all things to all people so I could save some
of them in any way possible. [23]I do all this
because of the Good News and so I can share
in its blessings.
[24]You know that in a race all the runners
run, but only one gets the prize. So run to
win! [25]All those who compete in the games
use self-control so they can win a crown.
That crown is an earthly thing that lasts
only a short time, but our crown will never
be destroyed. [26]So I do not run without a
goal. I fight like a boxer who is hitting
something—not just the air. [27]I treat my
body hard and make it my slave so that I
myself will not be disqualified after I have
preached to others.

Warnings from Israel's Past

10 Brothers and sisters, I want you
to know what happened to our
ancestors who followed Moses. They were
all under the cloud and all went through the
sea. [2]They were all baptized as followers of
Moses in the cloud and in the sea. [3]They all
ate the same spiritual food, [4]and all drank
the same spiritual drink. They drank from
that spiritual rock that followed them, and
that rock was Christ. [5]But God was not
pleased with most of them, so they died in
the desert.
[6]And these things happened as examples
for us, to stop us from wanting evil things as
those people did. [7]Do not worship idols, as
some of them did. Just as it is written in the
Scriptures: "They sat down to eat and drink,
and then they got up and sinned sexually."[n]
[8]We must not take part in sexual sins, as
some of them did. In one day twenty-three

9:9 "When an ox . . . eating." Quotation from Deuteronomy 25:4.
10:7 "They . . . sexually." Quotation from Exodus 32:6.

thousand of them died because of their sins.
[9]We must not test Christ as some of them
did; they were killed by snakes. [10]Do not
complain as some of them did; they were
killed by the angel that destroys.
[11]The things that happened to those
people are examples. They were written
down to teach us, because we live in a time
when all these things of the past have
reached their goal. [12]If you think you are
strong, you should be careful not to fall.
[13]The only temptation that has come to you
is that which everyone has. But you can trust
God, who will not permit you to be tempted
more than you can stand. But when you are
tempted, he will also give you a way to
escape so that you will be able to stand it.
[14]So, my dear friends, run away from the
worship of idols. [15]I am speaking to you as
to reasonable people; judge for yourselves
what I say. [16]We give thanks for the cup of
blessing,[n] which is a sharing in the blood of
Christ. And the bread that we break is a
sharing in the body of Christ. [17]Because
there is one loaf of bread, we who are many
are one body, because we all share that one
loaf.
[18]Think about the Israelites: Do not those
who eat the sacrifices share in the altar? [19]I
do not mean that the food sacrificed to an
idol is important. I do not mean that an idol
is anything at all. [20]But I say that what is
sacrificed to idols is offered to demons, not
to God. And I do not want you to share
anything with demons. [21]You cannot drink
the cup of the Lord and the cup of demons
also. You cannot share in the Lord's table and
the table of demons. [22]Are we trying to make
the Lord jealous? We are not stronger than
he is, are we?

How to Use Christian Freedom

[23]"We are allowed to do all things," but
not all things are good for us to do. "We are
allowed to do all things," but not all things
help others grow stronger. [24]Do not look out
only for yourselves. Look out for the good of
others also.

10:16 cup of blessing The cup of the fruit of the vine that Christians thank God for and drink at the Lord's Supper.

devotion 314

1 CORINTHIANS 10:23–24

JUST A BOTTLE OF WINE

Drinking seems to be one of those stumbling blocks that Christians continue to play with. We neatly stack all our moral standards up and count them like they are brightly numbered blocks. We move them around and position them in a manner that seems to fit us best at the time. If I were to take a shot at numbering those stumbling blocks, I would number drinking as number one and sex before marriage as number two. We can save number two for another time, but both of these continue to creep up to the top of the stack of common obstacles.

I was recently discussing this very issue with a dear friend of mine. She had a sad story to tell me. She explained that a friend she had led to Lord had recently confided in her that she was struggling with drinking. This gal was not an alcoholic, but she was having enough of a struggle that she knew she needed some accountability. One weekend this woman invited a couple from the new church where she was attending over for a cookout. She was really excited because they were in leadership, and she was looking forward to getting to know them. The couple arrived at the door with a bottle of wine in hand. This was a major setback for this friend and sadly unwound many months of success for her soul. The moral of this story? Yes, all things are permissible, but not all things are beneficial.

25 Eat any meat that is sold in the meat
market. Do not ask questions about it. 26 You
may eat it, "because the earth belongs to the
Lord, and everything in it."[n]
27 Those who are not believers may invite
you to eat with them. If you want to go, eat
anything that is put before you. Do not ask
questions about it. 28 But if anyone says to
you, "That food was offered to idols," do not
eat it. Do not eat it because of that person
who told you and because eating it might be
thought to be wrong. 29 I don't mean you
think it is wrong, but the other person
might. But why, you ask, should my freedom
be judged by someone else's conscience? 30 If
I eat the meal with thankfulness, why am I
criticized because of something for which I
thank God?
31 The answer is, if you eat or drink, or if
you do anything, do it all for the glory of
God. 32 Never do anything that might hurt
others—Jews, Greeks, or God's church—
33 just as I, also, try to please everybody in
every way. I am not trying to do what is good
for me but what is good for most people so
they can be saved.

11 Follow my example, as I follow the
example of Christ.

Being Under Authority

2 I praise you because you remember me
in everything, and you follow closely the
teachings just as I gave them to you. 3 But I
want you to understand this: The head of
every man is Christ, the head of a woman is
the man,[n] and the head of Christ is God.
4 Every man who prays or prophesies with
his head covered brings shame to his head.
5 But every woman who prays or prophesies
with her head uncovered brings shame to
her head. She is the same as a woman who
has her head shaved. 6 If a woman does not
cover her head, she should have her hair cut
off. But since it is shameful for a woman to
cut off her hair or to shave her head, she
should cover her head. 7 But a man should
not cover his head, because he is the likeness
and glory of God. But woman is man's glory.
8 Man did not come from woman, but
woman came from man. 9 And man was not
made for woman, but woman was made for
man. 10 So that is why a woman should have
a symbol of authority on her head, because
of the angels.
11 But in the Lord women are not
independent of men, and men are not
independent of women. 12 This is true
because woman came from man, but also
man is born from woman. But everything
comes from God. 13 Decide this for yourselves:
Is it right for a woman to pray to God with
her head uncovered? 14 Even nature itself
teaches you that wearing long hair is
shameful for a man. 15 But long hair is a
woman's glory. Long hair is given to her as
a covering. 16 Some people may still want
to argue about this, but I would add that
neither we nor the churches of God have
any other practice.

The Lord's Supper

17 In the things I tell you now I do not
praise you, because when you come together
you do more harm than good. 18 First, I hear
that when you meet together as a church
you are divided, and I believe some of this.
19 (It is necessary to have differences among
you so that it may be clear which of you
really have God's approval.) 20 When you
come together, you are not really eating the
Lord's Supper.[n] 21 This is because when you
eat, each person eats without waiting for the
others. Some people do not get enough to
eat, while others have too much to drink.
22 You can eat and drink in your own homes!
You seem to think God's church is not
important, and you embarrass those who are
poor. What should I tell you? Should I praise
you? I do not praise you for doing this.
23 The teaching I gave you is the same
teaching I received from the Lord: On the
night when the Lord Jesus was handed over
to be killed, he took bread 24 and gave thanks
for it. Then he broke the bread and said,
"This is my body; it is[n] for you. Do this to
remember me." 25 In the same way, after they
ate, Jesus took the cup. He said, "This cup is
the new agreement that is sealed with the
blood of my death. When you drink this, do
it to remember me." 26 Every time you eat
this bread and drink this cup you are telling
others about the Lord's death until he comes.
27 So a person who eats the bread or drinks
the cup of the Lord in a way that is not

10:26 "because . . . it" Quotation from Psalms 24:1; 50:12; 89:11. **11:3 the man** This could also mean "her husband."
11:20 Lord's Supper The meal Jesus told his followers to eat to remember him (Luke 22:14–20). **11:24 it is** Some Greek copies read "it is broken."

worthy of it will be guilty of sinning against
the body and the blood of the Lord. 28Look
into your own hearts before you eat the
bread and drink the cup, 29because all who
eat the bread and drink the cup without
recognizing the body eat and drink
judgment against themselves. 30That is why
many in your group are sick and weak, and
some of you have died. 31But if we judged
ourselves in the right way, God would not
judge us. 32But when the Lord judges us,
he disciplines us so that we will not be
destroyed along with the world.
33So my brothers and sisters, when you
come together to eat, wait for each other.
34Anyone who is too hungry should eat at
home so that in meeting together you will
not bring God's judgment on yourselves. I
will tell you what to do about the other
things when I come.

Gifts from the Holy Spirit

12 Now, brothers and sisters, I want
you to understand about spiritual
gifts. 2You know the way you lived before
you were believers. You let yourselves
be influenced and led away to worship
idols—things that could not speak. 3So I
want you to understand that no one who
is speaking with the help of God's Spirit
says, "Jesus be cursed." And no one can say,
"Jesus is Lord," without the help of the Holy
Spirit.
4There are different kinds of gifts, but
they are all from the same Spirit. 5There are
different ways to serve but the same Lord to
serve. 6And there are different ways that God
works through people but the same God.
God works in all of us in everything we do.
7Something from the Spirit can be seen in
each person, for the common good. 8The
Spirit gives one person the ability to speak
with wisdom, and the same Spirit gives
another the ability to speak with knowledge.
9The same Spirit gives faith to one person.
And, to another, that one Spirit gives gifts of
healing. 10The Spirit gives to another person
the power to do miracles, to another the
ability to prophesy. And he gives to another
the ability to know the difference between
good and evil spirits. The Spirit gives one
person the ability to speak in different kinds
of languages[n] and to another the ability to
interpret those languages. 11One Spirit, the

12:10 languages This can also be translated "tongues."

devotion 315

1 CORINTHIANS 12:4–6, 16–17

I'LL BE SIMBA, YOU BE SCAR

I took my children to see the movie *The Lion King* when they were younger. As we were walking out of the movie, I asked my kids which character was their favorite character. My oldest son immediately said, "Simba." My middle daughter answered, "Nala." Then my youngest daughter, who was only four at the time, said with mischief in her voice, "Scar." And that is the way it has always been with my kids. I have three children, all one year apart, and they have three very different perspectives, personalities, gifts, and talents. I love that about them.

That is how God sees us. We are all different in his eyes. He has created us that way for a reason. Paul wrote to the Corinthians that there are different ways to serve the same Lord. Christians often assume we all need to think and act the same way. This is far from the truth. God has uniquely designed each of us to serve a purpose in the body of Christ. If we all had the same gift, there would be many needs not being met. And God is using you whether you realize it or not. Verse 6 says that "God works in all of us in everything we do." Be sensitive to the Spirit of God when you feel him nudging you to use your gifts for the kingdom of God. We are all needed to accomplish his will here on earth.

same Spirit, does all these things, and the Spirit decides what to give each person.

The Body of Christ Works Together

12A person's body is one thing, but it has many parts. Though there are many parts to a body, all those parts make only one body. Christ is like that also. 13Some of us are Jews, and some are Greeks. Some of us are slaves, and some are free. But we were all baptized into one body through one Spirit. And we were all made to share in the one Spirit.

14The human body has many parts. 15The foot might say, "Because I am not a hand, I am not part of the body." But saying this would not stop the foot from being a part of the body. 16The ear might say, "Because I am not an eye, I am not part of the body." But saying this would not stop the ear from being a part of the body. 17If the whole body were an eye, it would not be able to hear. If the whole body were an ear, it would not be able to smell. 18-19If each part of the body were the same part, there would be no body. But truly God put all the parts, each one of them, in the body as he wanted them. 20So then there are many parts, but only one body.

21The eye cannot say to the hand, "I don't need you!" And the head cannot say to the foot, "I don't need you!" 22No! Those parts of the body that seem to be the weaker are really necessary. 23And the parts of the body we think are less deserving are the parts to which we give the most honor. We give special respect to the parts we want to hide. 24The more respectable parts of our body need no special care. But God put the body together and gave more honor to the parts that need it 25so our body would not be divided. God wanted the different parts to care the same for each other. 26If one part of the body suffers, all the other parts suffer with it. Or if one part of our body is honored, all the other parts share its honor.

27Together you are the body of Christ, and each one of you is a part of that body. 28In the church God has given a place first to apostles, second to prophets, and third to teachers. Then God has given a place to those who do miracles, those who have gifts of healing, those who can help others, those who are able to govern, and those who can speak in different languages.[n] 29Not all are apostles. Not all are prophets. Not all are teachers. Not all do miracles. 30Not all have gifts of healing. Not all speak in different languages. Not all interpret those languages. 31But you should truly want to have the greater gifts.

Love Is the Greatest Gift

And now I will show you the best way of all.

13 I may speak in different languages[n] of people or even angels. But if I do not have love, I am only a noisy bell or a crashing cymbal. 2I may have the gift of prophecy. I may understand all the secret things of God and have all knowledge, and I may have faith so great I can move mountains. But even with all these things, if I do not have love, then I am nothing. 3I may give away everything I have, and I may even give my body as an offering to be burned.[n] But I gain nothing if I do not have love.

4Love is patient and kind. Love is not jealous, it does not brag, and it is not proud. 5Love is not rude, is not selfish, and does not get upset with others. Love does not count up wrongs that have been done. 6Love takes no pleasure in evil but rejoices over the truth. 7Love patiently accepts all things. It always trusts, always hopes, and always endures.

8Love never ends. There are gifts of prophecy, but they will be ended. There are gifts of speaking in different languages, but those gifts will stop. There is the gift of knowledge, but it will come to an end. 9The reason is that our knowledge and our ability to prophesy are not perfect. 10But when perfection comes, the things that are not perfect will end. 11When I was a child, I talked like a child, I thought like a child, I reasoned like a child. When I became a man, I stopped those childish ways. 12It is the same with us. Now we see a dim reflection, as if we were looking into a mirror, but then we shall see clearly. Now I know only a part, but then I will know fully, as God has

12:28; 13:1 languages This can also be translated "tongues."
13:3 give . . . burned Other Greek copies read "hand over my body in order that I may brag."

devotion 316

1 CORINTHIANS 13:4–7

SISTERHOOD AND ALL THAT JAZZ

Aren't the attributes listed in 1 Corinthians 13 the same ones you'd look for in a friend, boyfriend, or husband? Would you agree that if we all exhibited those traits, we'd all get along better with others? There's a reason why God listed those traits in the Bible. They are the exact characteristics we need to be reminded of often in order to be a good friend, wife, mother, daughter, and so on.

I'm actually fortunate enough to have a friend who exhibits all of the traits in this passage. Oh, of course she isn't perfect, but she has primarily shown me all of these attributes in her attitude throughout our lives. I have to admit that she is a rarity, at least in my generation. But because of what I like to call her "graceful spirit" in approaching our relationship, we have remained good friends.

While I hear women talk these days about how special and meaningful their relationships are to them, I also hear just as many sad stories of betrayal, jealousy, crushed hopes, and all out back-stabbing. Why is this? Is it intrinsic or is it an attitude that our culture teaches us to follow? I think it's not as true about women as we've been led to believe by today's society. I move that we all turn this stereotype upside down. We are sisters in Christ. Let's build up and encourage each other to demonstrate the attributes from 1 Corinthians 13 in all of our relationships.

known me. 13So these three things continue
forever: faith, hope, and love. And the
greatest of these is love.

Desire Spiritual Gifts

14 You should seek after love, and you
should truly want to have the
spiritual gifts, especially the gift of prophecy.
2I will explain why. Those who have the gift
of speaking in different languages[n] are not
speaking to people; they are speaking to God.
No one understands them; they are speaking
secret things through the Spirit. 3But those
who prophesy are speaking to people to give
them strength, encouragement, and comfort.
4The ones who speak in different languages
are helping only themselves, but those who
prophesy are helping the whole church. 5I
wish all of you had the gift of speaking in
different kinds of languages, but more, I
wish you would prophesy. Those who
prophesy are greater than those who can
only speak in different languages—unless
someone is there who can explain what
is said so that the whole church can be
helped.
6Brothers and sisters, will it help you
if I come to you speaking in different
languages? No! It will help you only if
I bring you a new truth or some new
knowledge, or prophecy, or teaching. 7It is
the same as with lifeless things that make
sounds—like a flute or a harp. If they do not
make clear musical notes, you will not know
what is being played. 8And in a war, if the
trumpet does not give a clear sound, who
will prepare for battle? 9It is the same with
you. Unless you speak clearly with your
tongue, no one can understand what you are
saying. You will be talking into the air! 10It
may be true that there are all kinds of
sounds in the world, and none is without

14:2 languages This can also be translated "tongues."

meaning. 11But unless I understand the
meaning of what someone says to me, we
will be like foreigners to each other. 12It is
the same with you. Since you want spiritual
gifts very much, seek most of all to have the
gifts that help the church grow stronger.
13The one who has the gift of speaking in
a different language should pray for the gift
to interpret what is spoken. 14If I pray in a
different language, my spirit is praying, but
my mind does nothing. 15So what should I
do? I will pray with my spirit, but I will also
pray with my mind. I will sing with my
spirit, but I will also sing with my mind. 16If
you praise God with your spirit, those
persons there without understanding cannot
say amen[n] to your prayer of thanks, because
they do not know what you are saying. 17You
may be thanking God in a good way, but the
other person is not helped.
18I thank God that I speak in different
kinds of languages more than all of you.
19But in the church meetings I would rather
speak five words I understand in order to
teach others than thousands of words in a
different language.
20Brothers and sisters, do not think like
children. In evil things be like babies, but in
your thinking you should be like adults. 21It
is written in the Scriptures:

"With people who use strange words and
foreign languages
I will speak to these people.
But even then they will not listen to me,"

Isaiah 28:11–12

says the Lord.
22So the gift of speaking in different kinds
of languages is a sign for those who do not
believe, not for those who do believe. And
prophecy is for people who believe, not for
those who do not believe. 23Suppose the
whole church meets together and everyone
speaks in different languages. If some people
come in who do not understand or do not
believe, they will say you are crazy. 24But
suppose everyone is prophesying and some
people come in who do not believe or do not
understand. If everyone is prophesying, their
sin will be shown to them, and they will be
judged by all that they hear. 25The secret
things in their hearts will be made known.
So they will bow down and worship God
saying, "Truly, God is with you."

Meetings Should Help the Church

26So, brothers and sisters, what should
you do? When you meet together, one
person has a song, and another has a
teaching. Another has a new truth from God.
Another speaks in a different language,[n] and
another person interprets that language. The
purpose of all these things should be to help
the church grow strong. 27When you meet
together, if anyone speaks in a different
language, it should be only two, or not
more than three, who speak. They should
speak one after the other, and someone
should interpret. 28But if there is no
interpreter, then those who speak in a
different language should be quiet in the
church meeting. They should speak only
to themselves and to God.
29Only two or three prophets should
speak, and the others should judge what
they say. 30If a message from God comes
to another person who is sitting, the first
speaker should stop. 31You can all prophesy
one after the other. In this way all the people
can be taught and encouraged. 32The spirits
of prophets are under the control of the
prophets themselves. 33God is not a God of
confusion but a God of peace.
As is true in all the churches of God's
people, 34women should keep quiet in the
church meetings. They are not allowed to
speak, but they must yield to this rule as the
law says. 35If they want to learn something,
they should ask their own husbands at
home. It is shameful for a woman to speak in
the church meeting. 36Did God's teaching
come from you? Or are you the only ones to
whom it has come?
37Those who think they are prophets or
spiritual persons should understand that
what I am writing to you is the Lord's
command. 38Those who ignore this will
be ignored by God.[n]
39So my brothers and sisters, you should
truly want to prophesy. But do not stop
people from using the gift of speaking in
different kinds of languages. 40But let
everything be done in a right and orderly
way.

14:16 amen To say amen means to agree with the things that were said. **14:26 language** This can also be translated "tongue." **14:38 Those . . . God.** Some Greek copies read "Those who are ignorant of this will stay ignorant."

The Good News About Christ

15 Now, brothers and sisters, I want you to remember the Good News I brought to you. You received this Good News and continue strong in it. [2]And you are being saved by it if you continue believing what I told you. If you do not, then you believed for nothing.

[3]I passed on to you what I received, of which this was most important: that Christ died for our sins, as the Scriptures say; [4]that he was buried and was raised to life on the third day as the Scriptures say; [5]and that he was seen by Peter and then by the twelve apostles. [6]After that, Jesus was seen by more than five hundred of the believers at the same time. Most of them are still living today, but some have died. [7]Then he was seen by James and later by all the apostles. [8]Last of all he was seen by me—as by a person not born at the normal time. [9]All the other apostles are greater than I am. I am not even good enough to be called an apostle, because I persecuted the church of God. [10]But God's grace has made me what I am, and his grace to me was not wasted. I worked harder than all the other apostles. (But it was not I really; it was God's grace that was with me.) [11]So if I preached to you or the other apostles preached to you, we all preach the same thing, and this is what you believed.

We Will Be Raised from the Dead

[12]Now since we preached that Christ was raised from the dead, why do some of you say that people will not be raised from the dead? [13]If no one is ever raised from the dead, then Christ has not been raised. [14]And if Christ has not been raised, then our preaching is worth nothing, and your faith is worth nothing. [15]And also, we are guilty of lying about God, because we testified of him that he raised Christ from the dead. But if people are not raised from the dead, then God never raised Christ. [16]If the dead are not raised, Christ has not been raised either. [17]And if Christ has not been raised, then your faith has nothing to it; you are still guilty of your sins. [18]And those in Christ who have already died are lost. [19]If our hope in Christ is for this life only, we should be pitied more than anyone else in the world.

[20]But Christ has truly been raised from the dead—the first one and proof that those who sleep in death will also be raised. [21]Death has come because of what one man did, but the rising from death also comes because of one man. [22]In Adam all of us die. In the same way, in Christ all of us will be made alive again. [23]But everyone will be raised to life in the right order. Christ was first to be raised. When Christ comes again, those who belong to him will be raised to life, [24]and then the end will come. At that time Christ will destroy all rulers, authorities, and powers, and he will hand over the kingdom to God the Father. [25]Christ must rule until he puts all enemies under his control. [26]The last enemy to be destroyed will be death. [27]The Scripture says that God put all things under his control.[n] When it says "all things" are under him, it is clear this does not include God himself. God is the One who put everything under his control. [28]After everything has been put under the Son, then he will put himself under God, who had put all things under him. Then God will be the complete ruler over everything.

[29]If the dead are never raised, what will people do who are being baptized for the dead? If the dead are not raised at all, why are people being baptized for them?

[30]And what about us? Why do we put ourselves in danger every hour? [31]I die every day. That is true, brothers and sisters, just as it is true that I brag about you in Christ Jesus our Lord. [32]If I fought wild animals in Ephesus only with human hopes, I have gained nothing. If the dead are not raised, "Let us eat and drink, because tomorrow we will die."[n]

[33]Do not be fooled: "Bad friends will ruin good habits." [34]Come back to your right way of thinking and stop sinning. Some of you do not know God—I say this to shame you.

What Kind of Body Will We Have?

[35]But someone may ask, "How are the dead raised? What kind of body will they have?" [36]Foolish person! When you sow a seed, it must die in the ground before it can live and grow. [37]And when you sow it, it does

15:27 God put . . . control. From Psalm 8:6.
15:32 "Let us . . . die." Quotation from Isaiah 22:13; 56:12.

not have the same "body" it will have later. What you sow is only a bare seed, maybe wheat or something else. 38But God gives it a body that he has planned for it, and God gives each kind of seed its own body. 39All things made of flesh are not the same: People have one kind of flesh, animals have another, birds have another, and fish have another. 40Also there are heavenly bodies and earthly bodies. But the beauty of the heavenly bodies is one kind, and the beauty of the earthly bodies is another. 41The sun has one kind of beauty, the moon has another beauty, and the stars have another. And each star is different in its beauty.

42It is the same with the dead who are raised to life. The body that is "planted" will ruin and decay, but it is raised to a life that cannot be destroyed. 43When the body is "planted," it is without honor, but it is raised in glory. When the body is "planted," it is weak, but when it is raised, it is powerful. 44The body that is "planted" is a physical body. When it is raised, it is a spiritual body.

There is a physical body, and there is also a spiritual body. 45It is written in the Scriptures: "The first man, Adam, became a living person."[n] But the last Adam became a spirit that gives life. 46The spiritual did not come first, but the physical and then the spiritual. 47The first man came from the dust of the earth. The second man came from heaven. 48People who belong to the earth are like the first man of earth. But those people who belong to heaven are like the man of heaven. 49Just as we were made like the man of earth, so we will[n] also be made like the man of heaven.

50I tell you this, brothers and sisters: Flesh and blood cannot have a part in the kingdom of God. Something that will ruin cannot have a part in something that never ruins. 51But look! I tell you this secret: We will not all sleep in death, but we will all be changed. 52It will take only a second—as quickly as an eye blinks—when the last trumpet sounds. The trumpet will sound, and those who have died will be raised to live forever, and we will all be changed. 53This body that can be destroyed must clothe itself with something that can never be destroyed. And this body that dies must clothe itself with something that can never die. 54So this body that can be destroyed will clothe itself with that which can never be destroyed, and this body that dies will clothe itself with that which can never die. When this happens, this Scripture will be made true:

"Death is destroyed forever in victory."
Isaiah 25:8

55"Death, where is your victory?
Death, where is your pain?" *Hosea 13:14*

56Death's power to hurt is sin, and the power of sin is the law. 57But we thank God! He gives us the victory through our Lord Jesus Christ.

58So my dear brothers and sisters, stand strong. Do not let anything move you. Always give yourselves fully to the work of the Lord, because you know that your work in the Lord is never wasted.

The Gift for Other Believers

16 Now I will write about the collection of money for God's people. Do the same thing I told the Galatian churches to do: 2On the first day of every week, each one of you should put aside money as you have been blessed. Save it up so you will not have to collect money after I come. 3When I arrive, I will send whomever you approve to take your gift to Jerusalem. I will send them with letters of introduction, 4and if it seems good for me to go also, they will go along with me.

Paul's Plans

5I plan to go through Macedonia, so I will come to you after I go through there. 6Perhaps I will stay with you for a time or even all winter. Then you can help me on my trip, wherever I go. 7I do not want to see you now just in passing. I hope to stay a longer time with you if the Lord allows it. 8But I will stay at Ephesus until Pentecost, 9because a good opportunity for a great and growing work has been given to me now. And there are many people working against me.

10If Timothy comes to you, see to it that he has nothing to fear with you, because he is working for the Lord just as I am. 11So none of you should treat Timothy as

15:45 "The first . . . person." Quotation from Genesis 2:7.
15:49 so we will Some Greek copies read "so let us."

unimportant, but help him on his trip in
peace so that he can come back to me. I am
expecting him to come with the brothers.
[12]Now about our brother Apollos: I
strongly encouraged him to visit you with
the other brothers. He did not at all want to
come now; he will come when he has the
opportunity.

Paul Ends His Letter

[13]Be alert. Continue strong in the faith.
Have courage, and be strong. [14]Do
everything in love.
[15]You know that the family of Stephanas
were the first believers in Southern Greece
and that they have given themselves to the
service of God's people. I ask you, brothers
and sisters, [16]to follow the leading of people
like these and anyone else who works and
serves with them.
[17]I am happy that Stephanas, Fortunatus,
and Achaicus have come. You are not
here, but they have filled your place. [18]They
have refreshed my spirit and yours. You
should recognize the value of people like
these.
[19]The churches in Asia send greetings to
you. Aquila and Priscilla greet you in the
Lord, as does the church that meets in their
house. [20]All the brothers and sisters here
send greetings. Give each other a holy kiss
when you meet.
[21]I, Paul, am writing this greeting with my
own hand.
[22]If anyone does not love the Lord, let him
be separated from God—lost forever!
Come, O Lord!
[23]The grace of the Lord Jesus be with you.
[24]My love be with all of you in Christ
Jesus.[n]

16:24 My . . . Jesus. Some Greek copies add "Amen."

2 Corinthians

Person Holding the Pen God Wrote With: Yet again, the author is *Paul.*

When the Text Was Written: 56 A.D.

Spiritual Posture of the Original Recipients: The Corinthians were continuing to be an unruly body of believers. Their church was full of quick-tempered members, including many who were quick to turn from the truth of God to the heresy of a man.

Storyline Synopsis: Paul returned to Corinth for a third visit when he found out that even more problems were popping up in the congregation. Someone (probably a false apostle) in their midst had been slandering Paul's reputation and, more importantly, doing so in order to discredit the validity of the Good News of Jesus Christ. But Paul's return to this fractious fellowship didn't go the way he had hoped. Not only did the Corinthians basically blow him off, they didn't even try to defend him or the sanctity of his message. So Paul traveled back to Ephesus, no doubt praying that the Corinthians would come to their senses through the Holy Spirit. When he got back to the ministry "offices" in Ephesus, Paul wrote the Christians in Corinth this epistle—sometimes called the "stern" letter—in order to help stir their hearts toward repentance.

A Moment Worth Discussing: Chapter 4 records Paul's straightforward and powerful "jars of clay" sermon. In light of the personal humiliation he had suffered because of the behavior of the Corinthian church, his humble metaphor is especially significant. (Clay pots were often used for toting garbage and human waste in this culture!) Instead of puffing his chest out and defending his honor, Paul was describing himself as completely dispensable. His colorful language illuminates the greatness of God and the commonality of man—even if the man is "great" by human standards. This contrast once again highlights that the Good News is based on *grace* rather than *worth.*

Interesting (But Likely to Be Overlooked) Character: "*The brothers who came from Macedonia,*" (2 Cor. 11:9) is a reference to Silas and Timothy, the two men who had brought Paul money from Christians in Macedonia. Their financial generosity enabled Paul to focus on preaching instead of fund-raising.

1 From Paul, an apostle of Christ Jesus. I am
an apostle because that is what God
wanted. Also from Timothy our brother in
Christ.

To the church of God in Corinth, and to
all of God's people everywhere in Southern
Greece:

[2]Grace and peace to you from God our
Father and the Lord Jesus Christ.

Paul Gives Thanks to God

[3]Praise be to the God and Father of our
Lord Jesus Christ. God is the Father who is
full of mercy and all comfort. [4]He comforts
us every time we have trouble, so when
others have trouble, we can comfort them
with the same comfort God gives us. [5]We
share in the many sufferings of Christ. In
the same way, much comfort comes to us
through Christ. [6]If we have troubles, it is for
your comfort and salvation, and if we have
comfort, you also have comfort. This helps
you to accept patiently the same sufferings
we have. [7]Our hope for you is strong,
knowing that you share in our sufferings
and also in the comfort we receive.

[8]Brothers and sisters, we want you to know
about the trouble we suffered in Asia. We had
great burdens there that were beyond our
own strength. We even gave up hope of
living. [9]Truly, in our own hearts we believed
we would die. But this happened so we would
not trust in ourselves but in God, who raises
people from the dead. [10]God saved us from
these great dangers of death, and he will
continue to save us. We have put our hope in
him, and he will save us again. [11]And you can
help us with your prayers. Then many people
will give thanks for us—that God blessed us
because of their many prayers.

The Change in Paul's Plans

[12]This is what we are proud of, and I can
say it with a clear conscience: In everything
we have done in the world, and especially
with you, we have had an honest[n] and

1:12 honest Some Greek copies read "holy."

devotion 317

2 CORINTHIANS 1:3–5

WHAT HAPPENED TO MY LIFE?

So many of my friends can't figure out what in the world happened to their tidy little lives. They've faced all kinds of tragedies: a husband's death, ovarian cancer, an autistic child, a messy divorce, infertility, and on and on. Our little circle has already faced so much, but a lot of strength comes from walking through heartache together, the wounded comforting the wounded. All of us have known hurt for entirely different reasons, but the weight of the pain and mourning feels the same . . . a heaviness that is overwhelming, insufferable, and suffocating.

We have learned to give one another the comfort God has already given to us. Some days, there is relief in not having to explain the waves of depression, the struggle with bitterness, or the outbursts of anger. If you have already known deep heartache, you understand. We have learned to wait together for the healing God brings over time. We have sat in darkness just to hold someone until there was enough light to see the next step to take.

When grieving is shared, there is encouragement for the soul. There are shoulders to share the burden. There is someone who has been there to remind us that God is still good. He promises to give soul healing and unimaginable hope to everyone who calls on his name. And the season of mourning really does pass away because of his faithfulness. Today, let us comfort one another with the comfort we have been given.

sincere heart from God. We did this by God's
grace, not by the kind of wisdom the world
has. 13-14We write to you only what you can
read and understand. And I hope that as you
have understood some things about us, you
may come to know everything about us.
Then you can be proud of us, as we will be
proud of you on the day our Lord Jesus
Christ comes again.
15I was so sure of all this that I made
plans to visit you first so you could be
blessed twice. 16I planned to visit you on my
way to Macedonia and again on my way
back. I wanted to get help from you for my
trip to Judea. 17Do you think that I made
these plans without really meaning it? Or
maybe you think I make plans as the world
does, so that I say yes, yes and at the same
time no, no.
18But since you can believe God, you can
believe that what we tell you is never both
yes and no. 19The Son of God, Jesus Christ,
that Silas and Timothy and I preached to
you, was not yes and no. In Christ it has
always been yes. 20The yes to all of God's
promises is in Christ, and through Christ we
say yes to the glory of God. 21Remember, God
is the One who makes you and us strong in
Christ. God made us his chosen people. 22He
put his mark on us to show that we are his,
and he put his Spirit in our hearts to be a
guarantee for all he has promised.
23I tell you this, and I ask God to be my
witness that this is true: The reason I did
not come back to Corinth was to keep you
from being punished or hurt. 24We are not
trying to control your faith. You are strong in
faith. But we are workers with you for your
own joy.

2 So I decided that my next visit to you
would not be another one to make you
sad. 2If I make you sad, who will make
me glad? Only you can make me glad—
particularly the person whom I made sad. 3I
wrote you a letter for this reason: that when
I came to you I would not be made sad by
the people who should make me happy. I felt
sure of all of you, that you would share my
joy. 4When I wrote to you before, I was very
troubled and unhappy in my heart, and I
wrote with many tears. I did not write to
make you sad, but to let you know how
much I love you.

Forgive the Sinner

5Someone there among you has caused
sadness, not to me, but to all of you. I mean
he caused sadness to all in some way. (I do
not want to make it sound worse than it
really is.) 6The punishment that most of you
gave him is enough for him. 7But now you
should forgive him and comfort him to keep
him from having too much sadness and
giving up completely. 8So I beg you to show
that you love him. 9I wrote you to test you
and to see if you obey in everything. 10If you
forgive someone, I also forgive him. And
what I have forgiven—if I had anything to
forgive—I forgave it for you, as if Christ
were with me. 11I did this so that Satan
would not win anything from us, because
we know very well what Satan's plans are.

Paul's Concern in Troas

12When I came to Troas to preach the
Good News of Christ, the Lord gave me a
good opportunity there. 13But I had no
peace, because I did not find my brother
Titus. So I said good-bye to them at Troas
and went to Macedonia.

Victory Through Christ

14But thanks be to God, who always leads
us as captives in Christ's victory parade. God
uses us to spread his knowledge everywhere
like a sweet-smelling perfume. 15Our
offering to God is this: We are the sweet
smell of Christ among those who are being
saved and among those who are being lost.
16To those who are lost, we are the smell of
death that brings death, but to those who are
being saved, we are the smell of life that
brings life. So who is able to do this work?
17We do not sell the word of God for a profit
as many other people do. But in Christ we
speak the truth before God, as messengers
of God.

Servants of the New Agreement

3 Are we starting to brag about ourselves
again? Do we need letters of introduction
to you or from you, like some other people?
2You yourselves are our letter, written on our
hearts, known and read by everyone. 3You
show that you are a letter from Christ sent
through us. This letter is not written with
ink but with the Spirit of the living God. It is

not written on stone tablets[n] but on human
hearts.
4 We can say this, because through Christ
we feel certain before God. 5 We are not
saying that we can do this work ourselves. It
is God who makes us able to do all that we
do. 6 He made us able to be servants of a new
agreement from himself to his people. This
new agreement is not a written law, but it is
of the Spirit. The written law brings death,
but the Spirit gives life.
7 The law that brought death was written
in words on stone. It came with God's glory,
which made Moses' face so bright that the
Israelites could not continue to look at it.
But that glory later disappeared. 8 So surely
the new way that brings the Spirit has even
more glory. 9 If the law that judged people
guilty of sin had glory, surely the new way
that makes people right with God has much
greater glory. 10 That old law had glory, but it
really loses its glory when it is compared to
the much greater glory of this new way. 11 If
that law which disappeared came with glory,
then this new way which continues forever
has much greater glory.
12 We have this hope, so we are very bold.
13 We are not like Moses, who put a covering
over his face so the Israelites would not see
it. The glory was disappearing, and Moses
did not want them to see it end. 14 But their
minds were closed, and even today that same
covering hides the meaning when they read
the old agreement. That covering is taken
away only through Christ. 15 Even today,
when they read the law of Moses, there is
a covering over their minds. 16 But when
a person changes and follows the Lord,
that covering is taken away. 17 The Lord is
the Spirit, and where the Spirit of the Lord
is, there is freedom. 18 Our faces, then, are
not covered. We all show the Lord's glory,
and we are being changed to be like him.
This change in us brings ever greater glory,
which comes from the Lord, who is the
Spirit.

3:3 stone tablets Meaning the Law of Moses that was written on stone tablets (Exodus 24:12; 25:16).

devotion 318

2 CORINTHIANS 4:17–18

NOT BY SIGHT

John the Baptist was a man that was wild about his job. He went from place to place, eating an occasional locust or two, and the only thing he lacked was a bit of personal hygiene. He continued his work, faithfully baptizing people after they repented of sin, and he was really excited because he knew that during his lifetime he was going to be part of the Messiah coming on the scene. John was not worried about figuring things out, manipulating the details, or fretting about timing. He was only concerned with drawing people into the water. God told John he would see the Spirit come down and rest on a man (John 1:32-33).

Just two short years after John saw the Spirit come down, he doubted what his eyes had seen. Locked in Herod's prison cell, he sent a message to inquire of Jesus, "Are you the Messiah, or should I expect someone else?" (see Matthew 11:1-6). Like John, we can become blinded in our faith because we are locked up in the prison of our own circumstances. Faith enables our precious, believing hearts to see the unseen. Jesus told his followers that they were blessed because they saw him. But he went on to tell them about his future followers who would be much more blessed because they would believe not by sight, but with their hearts. When it seems that the prison doors are locked tight and you cannot get out, look up and believe by faith.

hardships

It's been said that a woman's heart can be so connected to her mind that what she feels becomes her reality. I am often one of the unfortunate who let my emotions dictate how I process life around me. Like today, rain has been falling all afternoon, and I've been swamped for the last few . . . well, months . . . with a litany of pressure-filled checklists. In short, my soul has grown weary. But just because I feel worn or pressured does not mean that life around me is fierce or without God. On the contrary! Along this jagged journey, I've come to find something bright within the dark of the days. Christ is using the uphill climbs to make me more like him.

So what if I don't want to be in these seasons of challenge? While I cannot dictate my circumstances, I can be in charge of my response to such trials along the way. There have been days I've wanted to shake my fist at heaven, when in reality God was standing right beside me all along. I can choose to make my circumstance harder by pushing away from Christ, or I can lean into him during the times that press into me the most.

In this life, we will struggle and have pain—that's a promise. Yet Christ also promises to be with us, giving strength and peace whenever it is needed. So if you're in a place that is confusing, frustrating, or downright impossible, there is hope. God himself is aware of your struggle. He'll use each uncomfortable time to reveal his steadfast spirit in a broken world.

Let's not simply focus on why the tough situations are being thrown our way. Instead, let's look for what God wants to teach us in the process of it all.

THINK ABOUT IT: What situation is challenging you the most in this season of your life?
What do you believe God is trying to teach you through it?

DIG DEEPER: Isaiah 40:31 (renewal), Matthew 28:18–20 (our call), and James 1:2–4 (joy in trials)

mercy

We don't choose the person who sits in the cubicle beside us, the uncle we've become related to by marriage, or the neighbor who just moved in next door. We can't control the choices of wayward children or wayward parents or wayward friends. What pleases God is your mercy toward the ones you haven't chosen. They may be fallen, struggling, disappointing, or downright embarrassing. Maybe one is the stranger who rear-ended you in the parking lot. God loves it when you give to anyone the mercy he has so freely extended to you.

When your soul is being perfected by mercy, judgment fades. The rules don't matter as much, and what everyone might think becomes ridiculous. You become tender toward people in sin, the snare of addictions, and the depths of pain and suffering. On the other hand, life gets messy when you become merciful, and some people won't understand. (They didn't understand Jesus either.) Some will judge—bank on it. Someone will doubt your motives or your radical choice to extend mercy. Give on, because blessed are the merciful.

I expect that no matter how much you give, you will always receive more than you have given. God's mercy accounting is amazing. But one warning: mercy won't let you hold onto your legalism or value rules more than souls. Mercy might make you uncomfortable and blow away the box you've drawn around God. If you become merciful, things are going to change. You are going to look into the eyes of people and hurt for their pain. You are going to hear yourself offer light into their darkness. You will start to love the unlovely.

You'll be a lot more like Jesus that way.

THINK ABOUT IT: How has God come to you as mercy? How has he surprised you with grace and tenderness?
Why is it sometimes easier to choose judgment over compassion and mercy?
If the blessing of giving mercy is receiving mercy, what are the obvious implications of becoming a woman of mercy?

DIG DEEPER: Micah 7:18 (God's mercy), Matthew 5:7 (the merciful), and James 2:13 (the unmerciful)

grace

You know how some people have theme verses for their lives? Well, if I had a mascot scripture, it'd probably be 1 Corinthians 1:27—2:5 when Paul talks about being weak and foolish. I'm basically the poster girl for goobers!

One of my most colorful displays of foolishness happened when I was walking back to my office from the restroom one afternoon. I ran into a gentleman who worked in another department. I was really glad to see him because we both traveled a lot and rarely got to chat face-to-face. We stood there in the hallway for a while, talking about God's goodness, but I was also a little confused because he wouldn't look at me. Although his words were gracious, he seemed to be deliberately staring away from me. I kept trying to scoot into his line of vision so he'd have to look at me, but he kept his gaze averted. I thought, "It's really weird that he won't make eye contact while we're having this deep conversation."

Then, when he walked away, I discovered the reason for his reticence. Evidently I'd been a bit careless in the bathroom because I'd accidentally tucked my skirt into my underwear! My modest male friend had obviously been gazing at the horizon while we contemplated God's character because he was absolutely traumatized by the sight of me with my skirt wrapped around my waist!

The great news about God is that he knows we're flawed. He knows we're sometimes foolish and prone to make mistakes. That's why he sent Jesus to redeem us! God doesn't love us because we're perfect or because we made a good first impression. The King of the universe adores us because of his grace . . . it really is amazing!

THINK ABOUT IT: What's the most embarrassing thing you've ever done in a social setting?
One definition of grace is "God's unmerited favor"—what words would you use to describe his grace?

DIG DEEPER: Job 38:1–13 (God's power), Psalm 8:3–4 (God's might), 2 Corinthians 4:5–7 (humility in service), and Ephesians 2:8–9 (grace)

eternity

What would you say if you stood before God tonight and he asked you, "Why should I let you into my heaven?" The most common answer is this: "I'm a good person; I've never killed anyone or stolen anything."

The problem is that we have been separated from God by sin. The Bible says none of us are good enough for God's glorious standard (Rom. 3:23). Being a good person won't get you into heaven. But God loves you so much that he's provided a solution. God sent his only Son to die in our place and pay the penalty for our sins. After he died on the cross, he rose from the grave to bridge the separation between God and man. Christ carried our sins on the cross (1 Pet. 2:24).

So how do you get into heaven? You simply receive Christ into your life by asking him to come into your heart. The Bible says that each person who accepts Christ will become a child of God (John 1:12). You accept him by admitting that you are a sinner, repenting of your sins, and believing that Jesus Christ died on the cross for you. Once you have done this, you are a child of God. God has given you eternal life with him in heaven. Now you are ready for eternity. If you have never asked Jesus Christ into your heart as your personal Lord and Savior, pray the following prayer:

Dear Jesus, I know that I am a sinner. I ask you to forgive me of my sins. I believe that you are the Son of God and that you died on the cross for me. Come into my life, enter into all that I am, and change me. I ask you to be my Lord and Savior. In Jesus' name, Amen.

THINK ABOUT IT: What, if anything, holds you back from faith in Christ's death and resurrection?
What means the most to you about becoming a child of God?

DIG DEEPER: John 10:27–29 (salvation), 1 John 1:9 (forgiveness), and 1 John 5:12–13 (eternal life)

Preaching the Good News

4 God, with his mercy, gave us this work
to do, so we don't give up. 2But we have
turned away from secret and shameful ways.
We use no trickery, and we do not change
the teaching of God. We teach the truth
plainly, showing everyone who we are. Then
they can know in their hearts what kind of
people we are in God's sight. 3If the Good
News that we preach is hidden, it is hidden
only to those who are lost. 4The devil who
rules this world has blinded the minds of
those who do not believe. They cannot see
the light of the Good News—the Good News
about the glory of Christ, who is exactly like
God. 5We do not preach about ourselves, but
we preach that Jesus Christ is Lord and that
we are your servants for Jesus. 6God once
said, "Let the light shine out of the
darkness!" This is the same God who made
his light shine in our hearts by letting us
know the glory of God that is in the face of
Christ.

Spiritual Treasure in Clay Jars

7We have this treasure from God, but
we are like clay jars that hold the treasure.
This shows that the great power is from
God, not from us. 8We have troubles all
around us, but we are not defeated. We do
not know what to do, but we do not give up
the hope of living. 9We are persecuted, but
God does not leave us. We are hurt
sometimes, but we are not destroyed. 10We
carry the death of Jesus in our own bodies so
that the life of Jesus can also be seen in our
bodies. 11We are alive, but for Jesus we are
always in danger of death so that the life of
Jesus can be seen in our bodies that die. 12So
death is working in us, but life is working
in you.

13It is written in the Scriptures, "I
believed, so I spoke."[n] Our faith is like
this, too. We believe, and so we speak.
14God raised the Lord Jesus from the dead,
and we know that God will also raise us
with Jesus. God will bring us together with
you, and we will stand before him. 15All
these things are for you. And so the grace of
God that is being given to more and more
people will bring increasing thanks to God
for his glory.

Living by Faith

16So we do not give up. Our physical body
is becoming older and weaker, but our spirit
inside us is made new every day. 17We have
small troubles for a while now, but they are
helping us gain an eternal glory that is much
greater than the troubles. 18We set our eyes
not on what we see but on what we cannot
see. What we see will last only a short time,
but what we cannot see will last forever.

5 We know that our body—the tent we
live in here on earth—will be destroyed.
But when that happens, God will have a
house for us. It will not be a house made by
human hands; instead, it will be a home in
heaven that will last forever. 2But now we
groan in this tent. We want God to give us
our heavenly home, 3because it will clothe
us so we will not be naked. 4While we live in
this body, we have burdens, and we groan.
We do not want to be naked, but we want to
be clothed with our heavenly home. Then
this body that dies will be fully covered with
life. 5This is what God made us for, and he
has given us the Spirit to be a guarantee for
this new life.

6So we always have courage. We know
that while we live in this body, we are away
from the Lord. 7We live by what we believe,
not by what we can see. 8So I say that we
have courage. We really want to be away
from this body and be at home with the
Lord. 9Our only goal is to please God
whether we live here or there, 10because we
must all stand before Christ to be judged.
Each of us will receive what we should get—
good or bad—for the things we did in the
earthly body.

Becoming Friends with God

11Since we know what it means to fear the
Lord, we try to help people accept the truth
about us. God knows what we really are, and
I hope that in your hearts you know, too.
12We are not trying to prove ourselves to you
again, but we are telling you about ourselves
so you will be proud of us. Then you will
have an answer for those who are proud
about things that can be seen rather than
what is in the heart. 13If we are out of our
minds, it is for God. If we have our right

4:13 "I . . . spoke." Quotation from Psalm 116:10.

devotion 319

2 CORINTHIANS 5:7–9

BEFORE WE KNOW IT

One of the most difficult aspects of being a Christian is living by what we believe rather than what we see. We are continually faced with the world around us—its wars, famines, terrorists, and hurricanes. I don't know why I'm surprised by it all. Jesus warned us that these things would come. It is just so hard to have courage when we have to deal with the nightly news blaring from our televisions. Billy Graham once said, "I am learning in my own life, day by day, to keep my mind centered on Christ; the worries and anxieties and concerns for the world pass, and nothing but 'perfect peace' is left in the human heart."

My husband and I were in Israel several years ago. We stood at the top of Mount Zion, which is the place where Jesus will return, and tried to imagine that day. I placed my infant daughter on one of the many tombstones and took a picture of her with the road that Jesus will travel to the gates of Jerusalem behind her. I have that picture hanging in our house with these words below it: "Come quickly, Lord Jesus." I would love to finish raising my children in heaven. However, "our only goal is to please God whether we live here or there" (verse 9). We need to center our minds on Christ and live our lives to please our Lord, but always remember that we will be living in heaven before we know it.

minds, it is for you. 14The love of Christ controls us, because we know that One died for all, so all have died. 15Christ died for all so that those who live would not continue to live for themselves. He died for them and was raised from the dead so that they would live for him.

16From this time on we do not think of anyone as the world does. In the past we thought of Christ as the world thinks, but we no longer think of him in that way. 17If anyone belongs to Christ, there is a new creation. The old things have gone; everything is made new! 18All this is from God. Through Christ, God made peace between us and himself, and God gave us the work of telling everyone about the peace we can have with him. 19God was in Christ, making peace between the world and himself. In Christ, God did not hold the world guilty of its sins. And he gave us this message of peace. 20So we have been sent to speak for Christ. It is as if God is calling to you through us. We speak for Christ when we beg you to be at peace with God. 21Christ had no sin, but God made him become sin so that in Christ we could become right with God.

6 We are workers together with God, so we beg you: Do not let the grace that you received from God be for nothing. 2God says,

"At the right time I heard your prayers.
On the day of salvation I helped you."
Isaiah 49:8

I tell you that the "right time" is now, and the "day of salvation" is now.

3We do not want anyone to find fault with our work, so nothing we do will be a problem for anyone. 4But in every way we show we are servants of God: in accepting many hard things, in troubles, in difficulties, and in great problems. 5We are beaten and thrown into prison. We meet those who become upset with us and start riots. We work hard, and sometimes we get no sleep or food. 6We show we are servants of God by our pure lives, our understanding, patience, and kindness, by the Holy Spirit, by true love, 7by speaking the truth, and by God's

power. We use our right living to defend
ourselves against everything. 8Some people
honor us, but others blame us. Some people
say evil things about us, but others say good
things. Some people say we are liars, but we
speak the truth. 9We are not known, but we
are well known. We seem to be dying, but
we continue to live. We are punished, but
we are not killed. 10We have much sadness,
but we are always rejoicing. We are poor, but
we are making many people rich in faith.
We have nothing, but really we have
everything.

11We have spoken freely to you in Corinth
and have opened our hearts to you. 12Our
feelings of love for you have not stopped, but
you have stopped your feelings of love for
us. 13I speak to you as if you were my
children. Do to us as we have done—open
your hearts to us.

Warning About Non-Christians

14You are not the same as those who do
not believe. So do not join yourselves to
them. Good and bad do not belong together.
Light and darkness cannot share together.
15How can Christ and Belial, the devil, have
any agreement? What can a believer have
together with a nonbeliever? 16The temple
of God cannot have any agreement with
idols, and we are the temple of the living
God. As God said: "I will live with them and
walk with them. And I will be their God, and
they will be my people."[n]

17"Leave those people,
and be separate, says the Lord.
Touch nothing that is unclean,
and I will accept you."
Isaiah 52:11; Ezekiel 20:34, 41

18"I will be your father,
and you will be my sons and daughters,
says the Lord Almighty." *2 Samuel 7:14*

7 Dear friends, we have these promises
from God, so we should make ourselves
pure—free from anything that makes body or
soul unclean. We should try to become holy
in the way we live, because we respect God.

Paul's Joy

2Open your hearts to us. We have not
done wrong to anyone, we have not ruined
the faith of anyone, and we have not cheated
anyone. 3I do not say this to blame you. I
told you before that we love you so much we
would live or die with you. 4I feel very sure
of you and am very proud of you. You give
me much comfort, and in all of our troubles
I have great joy.

5When we came into Macedonia, we had
no rest. We found trouble all around us. We
had fighting on the outside and fear on the
inside. 6But God, who comforts those who
are troubled, comforted us when Titus came.
7We were comforted, not only by his coming
but also by the comfort you gave him. Titus
told us about your wish to see me and that
you are very sorry for what you did. He also
told me about your great care for me, and
when I heard this, I was much happier.

8Even if my letter made you sad, I am not
sorry I wrote it. At first I was sorry, because it
made you sad, but you were sad only for a
short time. 9Now I am happy, not because
you were made sad, but because your sorrow
made you change your lives. You became sad
in the way God wanted you to, so you were
not hurt by us in any way. 10The kind of
sorrow God wants makes people change
their hearts and lives. This leads to salvation,
and you cannot be sorry for that. But the
kind of sorrow the world has brings death.
11See what this sorrow—the sorrow God
wanted you to have—has done to you: It has
made you very serious. It made you want to
restore yourselves. It made you angry and
afraid. It made you want to see me. It made
you care. It made you want to do the right
thing. In every way you have regained your
innocence. 12I wrote that letter, not because
of the one who did the wrong or because of
the person who was hurt. I wrote the letter
so you could see, before God, the great care
you have for us. 13That is why we were
comforted.

Not only were we very comforted, we
were even happier to see that Titus was so
happy. All of you made him feel much
better. 14I bragged to Titus about you, and
you showed that I was right. Everything we
said to you was true, and you have proved
that what we bragged about to Titus is true.
15And his love for you is stronger when he
remembers that you were all ready to obey.

6:16 "I . . . people." Quotation from Leviticus 26:11–12; Jeremiah 32:38; Ezekiel 37:27.

You welcomed him with respect and fear. [16]I
am very happy that I can trust you fully.

Christian Giving

8 And now, brothers and sisters, we want
you to know about the grace God gave
the churches in Macedonia. [2]They have been
tested by great troubles, and they are very
poor. But they gave much because of their
great joy. [3]I can tell you that they gave as
much as they were able and even more than
they could afford. No one told them to do it.
[4]But they begged and pleaded with us to let
them share in this service for God's people.
[5]And they gave in a way we did not expect:
They first gave themselves to the Lord and to
us. This is what God wants. [6]So we asked
Titus to help you finish this special work of
grace since he is the one who started it. [7]You
are rich in everything—in faith, in speaking,
in knowledge, in truly wanting to help, and
in the love you learned from us.[n] In the same
way, be strong also in the grace of giving.

[8]I am not commanding you to give. But I
want to see if your love is true by comparing
you with others that really want to help.
[9]You know the grace of our Lord Jesus
Christ. You know that Christ was rich, but
for you he became poor so that by his
becoming poor you might become rich.

[10]This is what I think you should do: Last
year you were the first to want to give, and
you were the first who gave. [11]So now finish
the work you started. Then your "doing" will
be equal to your "wanting to do." Give from
what you have. [12]If you want to give, your
gift will be accepted. It will be judged by
what you have, not by what you do not have.
[13]We do not want you to have troubles while
other people are at ease, but we want
everything to be equal. [14]At this time you
have plenty. What you have can help others
who are in need. Then later, when they have
plenty, they can help you when you are in
need, and all will be equal. [15]As it is written
in the Scriptures, "The person who gathered
more did not have too much, nor did the
person who gathered less have too little."[n]

8:7 in . . . us Some Greek copies read "in your love for us."
8:15 "The person . . . little." Quotation from Exodus 16:18.

devotion 320

2 CORINTHIANS 9:7–9

WHAT CAN YOU GIVE AWAY?

I once heard about a pastor who preached a sermon on giving. His subject was actually a good and timely one. However, instead of using the Word to help people understand the spirit of giving, he used the opportunity to guilt people into putting money in the offering plate. While his heart might have been in the right place, how unfortunate that he didn't use the occasion to remind people about how much it pleases God when we give freely and joyfully to others. Paul's letter to the Corinthians warns us about our attitudes toward giving. Obligation is certainly not at the top of the list. Rather, it's out of happiness that we should give, without worrying if we will have enough left for ourselves.

Are you giving financially to God? Could you give a little bit more? Perhaps you are in a very difficult financial situation that doesn't allow you to give what you wish you could. Even if you feel you have no problem giving to God, you might still ask yourself, "Am I giving from my heart? And am I giving *myself* to him?" I can assure you there are many volunteer opportunities where you can give more than just finances to support your church and to help others. Many churches and non-profits have a shortage of volunteers, even when membership is at its highest. When you pray today, ask God what he would have you give away for him. Then listen for his answer.

Titus and His Companions Help

[16]I thank God because he gave Titus the
same love for you that I have. [17]Titus
accepted what we asked him to do. He
wanted very much to go to you, and this was
his own idea. [18]We are sending with him the
brother who is praised by all the churches
because of his service in preaching the Good
News. [19]Also, this brother was chosen by the
churches to go with us when we deliver this
gift of money. We are doing this service to
bring glory to the Lord and to show that we
really want to help.
[20]We are being careful so that no one will
criticize us for the way we are handling this
large gift. [21]We are trying hard to do what
the Lord accepts as right and also what
people think is right.
[22]Also, we are sending with them our
brother, who is always ready to help. He has
proved this to us in many ways, and he
wants to help even more now, because he
has much faith in you.
[23]Now about Titus—he is my partner who
is working with me to help you. And about
the other brothers—they are sent from the
churches, and they bring glory to Christ.
[24]So show these men the proof of your love
and the reason we are proud of you. Then all
the churches can see it.

Help for Fellow Christians

9 I really do not need to write you about
this help for God's people. [2]I know you
want to help. I have been bragging about
this to the people in Macedonia, telling them
that you in Southern Greece have been ready
to give since last year. And your desire to
give has made most of them ready to give
also. [3]But I am sending the brothers to you
so that our bragging about you in this will
not be empty words. I want you to be ready,
as I said you would be. [4]If any of the people
from Macedonia come with me and find that
you are not ready, we will be ashamed that
we were so sure of you. (And you will be
ashamed, too!) [5]So I thought I should ask
these brothers to go to you before we do.
They will finish getting in order the
generous gift you promised so it will be
ready when we come. And it will be a
generous gift—not one that you did not
want to give.
[6]Remember this: The person who plants
a little will have a small harvest, but the
person who plants a lot will have a big
harvest. [7]Each of you should give as you
have decided in your heart to give. You
should not be sad when you give, and you
should not give because you feel forced to
give. God loves the person who gives
happily. [8]And God can give you more
blessings than you need. Then you will
always have plenty of everything—enough
to give to every good work. [9]It is written in
the Scriptures:

> "He gives freely to the poor.
> The things he does are right and will
> continue forever." *Psalm 112:9*

[10]God is the One who gives seed to the
farmer and bread for food. He will give you
all the seed you need and make it grow so
there will be a great harvest from your
goodness. [11]He will make you rich in every
way so that you can always give freely. And
your giving through us will cause many to
give thanks to God. [12]This service you do not
only helps the needs of God's people, it also
brings many more thanks to God. [13]It is a
proof of your faith. Many people will praise
God because you obey the Good News of
Christ—the gospel you say you believe—
and because you freely share with them and
with all others. [14]And when they pray, they
will wish they could be with you because
of the great grace that God has given you.
[15]Thanks be to God for his gift that is too
wonderful for words.

Paul Defends His Ministry

10 I, Paul, am begging you with the
gentleness and the kindness of Christ.
Some people say that I am easy on you when
I am with you and bold when I am away.
[2]They think we live in a worldly way, and I
plan to be very bold with them when I come.
I beg you that when I come I will not need to
use that same boldness with you. [3]We do
live in the world, but we do not fight in the
same way the world fights. [4]We fight with
weapons that are different from those the
world uses. Our weapons have power from
God that can destroy the enemy's strong
places. We destroy people's arguments [5]and
every proud thing that raises itself against
the knowledge of God. We capture every
thought and make it give up and obey

devotion 321

2 CORINTHIANS 10:5

OH, BE CAREFUL LITTLE MIND WHAT YOU THINK

What kind of thoughts have already stolen too much of your life? Maybe you think, "I've got too much to do, so maybe later. I'm in too deep, and I'll never get out. I've tried and failed a million times. No one else understands. It looks like I'm just destined to live this way." If you're like me, Satan tries to paralyze you by attacking your mind. He's convincing and you can hear his defeating thoughts in your head every day. But too many years are already gone. As for me, I refuse to live the next forty years inside the prison these berating thoughts build around my heart.

Did you know that you learn to believe what you focus on, whether it's actually true or not? At times, I have focused on my own rejection to the point that I began to live like I was only worthy of rejection. That is a complete mind game formulated by Satan to steal our confidence. That kind of thinking will limit and frustrate the work God intends to do in and through his children.

In order to live as the woman God planned, you and I are going to have to capture these sinful thoughts and push them away so that we can confidently obey the truths of Christ. We must change our focus. Since we believe what we focus on, you and I must center our lives around Jesus. Thinking Jesus, believing Jesus, responding like Jesus, and loving like Jesus.

Christ. [6]We are ready to punish anyone
there who does not obey, but first we want
you to obey fully.

[7]You must look at the facts before you. If
you feel sure that you belong to Christ, you
must remember that we belong to Christ
just as you do. [8]It is true that we brag freely
about the authority the Lord gave us. But
this authority is to build you up, not to tear
you down. So I will not be ashamed. [9]I do
not want you to think I am trying to scare
you with my letters. [10]Some people say,
"Paul's letters are powerful and sound
important, but when he is with us, he is
weak. And his speaking is nothing." [11]They
should know this: We are not there with you
now, so we say these things in letters. But
when we are there with you, we will show
the same authority that we show in our
letters.

[12]We do not dare to compare ourselves
with those who think they are very
important. They use themselves to measure
themselves, and they judge themselves by
what they themselves are. This shows that
they know nothing. [13]But we will not brag
about things outside the work that was
given us to do. We will limit our bragging to
the work that God gave us, and this includes
our work with you. [14]We are not bragging
too much, as we would be if we had not
already come to you. But we have come to
you with the Good News of Christ. [15]We
limit our bragging to the work that is ours,
not what others have done. We hope that as
your faith continues to grow, you will help
our work to grow much larger. [16]We want to
tell the Good News in the areas beyond your
city. We do not want to brag about work that
has already been done in another person's
area. [17]But, "If people want to brag, they
should brag only about the Lord."[n] [18]It is not

10:17 "If . . . Lord." Quotation from Jeremiah 9:24.

those who say they are good who are
accepted but those the Lord thinks are good.

Paul and the False Apostles

11 I wish you would be patient with me
even when I am a little foolish, but
you are already doing that. 2I am jealous
over you with a jealousy that comes from
God. I promised to give you to Christ, as
your only husband. I want to give you as his
pure bride. 3But I am afraid that your minds
will be led away from your true and pure
following of Christ just as Eve was tricked by
the snake with his evil ways. 4You are very
patient with anyone who comes to you and
preaches a different Jesus from the one we
preached. You are very willing to accept a
spirit or gospel that is different from the
Spirit and Good News you received from us.

5I do not think that those "great apostles"
are any better than I am. 6I may not be a
trained speaker, but I do have knowledge.
We have shown this to you clearly in every
way.

7I preached God's Good News to you
without pay. I made myself unimportant to
make you important. Do you think that was
wrong? 8I accepted pay from other churches,
taking their money so I could serve you. 9If I
needed something when I was with you, I
did not trouble any of you. The brothers who
came from Macedonia gave me all that I
needed. I did not allow myself to depend on
you in any way, and I will never depend on
you. 10No one in Southern Greece will stop
me from bragging about that. I say this with
the truth of Christ in me. 11And why do I not
depend on you? Do you think it is because I
do not love you? God knows that I love you.

12And I will continue doing what I am
doing now, because I want to stop those
people from having a reason to brag. They
would like to say that the work they brag
about is the same as ours. 13Such men are
not true apostles but are workers who lie.
They change themselves to look like
apostles of Christ. 14This does not surprise
us. Even Satan changes himself to look like
an angel of light.[n] 15So it does not surprise us
if Satan's servants also make themselves
look like servants who work for what is
right. But in the end they will be punished
for what they do.

Paul Tells About His Sufferings

16I tell you again: No one should think I
am a fool. But if you think so, accept me as
you would accept a fool. Then I can brag a
little, too. 17When I brag because I feel sure
of myself, I am not talking as the Lord would
talk but as a fool. 18Many people are
bragging about their lives in the world. So I
will brag too. 19You are wise, so you will
gladly be patient with fools! 20You are even
patient with those who order you around, or
use you, or trick you, or think they are better
than you, or hit you in the face. 21It is
shameful to me to say this, but we were too
"weak" to do those things to you!

But if anyone else is brave enough to brag,
then I also will be brave and brag. (I am
talking as a fool.) 22Are they Hebrews?[n] So
am I. Are they Israelites? So am I. Are they
from Abraham's family? So am I. 23Are they
serving Christ? I am serving him more. (I am
crazy to talk like this.) I have worked much
harder than they. I have been in prison more
often. I have been hurt more in beatings. I
have been near death many times. 24Five
times the Jews have given me their
punishment of thirty-nine lashes with a
whip. 25Three different times I was beaten
with rods. One time I was almost stoned
to death. Three times I was in ships that
wrecked, and one of those times I spent a
night and a day in the sea. 26I have gone on
many travels and have been in danger from
rivers, thieves, my own people, the Jews,
and those who are not Jews. I have been in
danger in cities, in places where no one lives,
and on the sea. And I have been in danger
with false Christians. 27I have done hard and
tiring work, and many times I did not sleep.
I have been hungry and thirsty, and many
times I have been without food. I have been
cold and without clothes. 28Besides all this,
there is on me every day the load of my
concern for all the churches. 29I feel weak
every time someone is weak, and I feel upset
every time someone is led into sin.

30If I must brag, I will brag about the
things that show I am weak. 31God knows I

11:14 angel of light Messenger from God. The devil fools people so that they think he is from God.
11:22 Hebrews A name for the Jews that some Jews were very proud of.

am not lying. He is the God and Father of the
Lord Jesus Christ, and he is to be praised
forever. 32When I was in Damascus, the
governor under King Aretas wanted to arrest
me, so he put guards around the city. 33But
my friends lowered me in a basket through a
hole in the city wall. So I escaped from the
governor.

A Special Blessing in Paul's Life

12 I must continue to brag. It will do
no good, but I will talk now about
visions and revelations[n] from the Lord. 2I
know a man in Christ who was taken up to
the third heaven fourteen years ago. I do not
know whether the man was in his body or
out of his body, but God knows. 3-4And I
know that this man was taken up to
paradise.[n] I don't know if he was in his body
or away from his body, but God knows. He
heard things he is not able to explain, things
that no human is allowed to tell. 5I will brag
about a man like that, but I will not brag
about myself, except about my weaknesses.
6But if I wanted to brag about myself, I
would not be a fool, because I would be
telling the truth. But I will not brag about
myself. I do not want people to think more
of me than what they see me do or hear me
say.

7So that I would not become too proud of
the wonderful things that were shown to
me, a painful physical problem[n] was given
to me. This problem was a messenger from
Satan, sent to beat me and keep me from
being too proud. 8I begged the Lord three
times to take this problem away from me.
9But he said to me, "My grace is enough for
you. When you are weak, my power is made
perfect in you." So I am very happy to brag
about my weaknesses. Then Christ's power
can live in me. 10For this reason I am happy
when I have weaknesses, insults, hard times,
sufferings, and all kinds of troubles for
Christ. Because when I am weak, then I am
truly strong.

12:1 revelations Revelation is making known a truth that was hidden. **12:3–4 paradise** Another word for heaven. **12:7 painful physical problem** Literally, "thorn in the flesh."

devotion 322

2 CORINTHIANS 12:9–10

HITTING BOTTOM

Are you in your prayer closet uttering thoughts that you are simply too ashamed to say out loud? "God why are you unfair? Why are you silent? Why are you hidden?" What you are really saying to God is, "Why do the wicked prosper, and why did you reward a sluggard's efforts, and why did you pour out blessing but not on my family?" If you continue in this kind of meditation, you will find that in no time at all, there will be a purposeful and awkward separation between you and the Lord. Things are never as they appear, and before you look at someone's lot with envy, you had better make sure you would be willing to carry the cross they have carried.

It's obvious that you have been striving. You're depleted of the grace that you so desperately need to overcome this state of weakness. God doesn't want you to be empty of hope or faith—he wants you to be empty of the endless laboring that you're doing in your own strength. He wants you to submit your will to God's will. That is why Paul was so excited when things seemed hopeless because he knew that when all other resources or explanations had been exhausted, that was exactly when he would see his Lord. If you have hit bottom in your spiritual walk, lift up your hands, repent of the thoughts in your heart, and ask the Lord to allow you to boast in your weakness.

Paul's Love for the Christians

11I have been talking like a fool, but you
made me do it. You are the ones who should
say good things about me. I am worth
nothing, but those "great apostles" are not
worth any more than I am!
12When I was with you, I patiently did the
things that prove I am an apostle—signs,
wonders, and miracles. 13So you received
everything that the other churches have
received. Only one thing was different: I was
not a burden to you. Forgive me for this!
14I am now ready to visit you the third
time, and I will not be a burden to you.
I want nothing from you, except you.
Children should not have to save up to give
to their parents. Parents should save to give
to their children. 15So I am happy to give
everything I have for you, even myself. If I
love you more, will you love me less?
16It is clear I was not a burden to you, but
you think I was tricky and lied to catch
you. 17Did I cheat you by using any of the
messengers I sent to you? No, you know I did
not. 18I asked Titus to go to you, and I sent
our brother with him. Titus did not cheat
you, did he? No, you know that Titus and I
did the same thing and with the same spirit.
19Do you think we have been defending
ourselves to you all this time? We have been
speaking in Christ and before God. You are
our dear friends, and everything we do is to
make you stronger. 20I am afraid that when I
come, you will not be what I want you to be,
and I will not be what you want me to be. I
am afraid that among you there may be
arguing, jealousy, anger, selfish fighting, evil
talk, gossip, pride, and confusion. 21I am
afraid that when I come to you again, my
God will make me ashamed before you.
I may be saddened by many of those who
have sinned because they have not changed
their hearts or turned from their sexual sins
and the shameful things they have done.

Final Warnings and Greetings

13 I will come to you for the third time.
"Every case must be proved by two
or three witnesses."[n] 2When I was with you
the second time, I gave a warning to those
who had sinned. Now I am away from
you, and I give a warning to all the others.
When I come to you again, I will not be easy
with them. 3You want proof that Christ is
speaking through me. My proof is that he is
not weak among you, but he is powerful. 4It
is true that he was weak when he was killed
on the cross, but he lives now by God's
power. It is true that we are weak in Christ,
but for you we will be alive in Christ by
God's power.
5Look closely at yourselves. Test
yourselves to see if you are living in the
faith. You know that Jesus Christ is in you—
unless you fail the test. 6But I hope you will
see that we ourselves have not failed the
test. 7We pray to God that you will not do
anything wrong. It is not important to see
that we have passed the test, but it is
important that you do what is right, even
if it seems we have failed. 8We cannot do
anything against the truth, but only for the
truth. 9We are happy to be weak, if you are
strong, and we pray that you will become
complete. 10I am writing this while I am
away from you so that when I come I will
not have to be harsh in my use of authority.
The Lord gave me this authority to build you
up, not to tear you down.
11Now, brothers and sisters, I say good-bye.
Live in harmony. Do what I have asked you
to do. Agree with each other, and live in
peace. Then the God of love and peace will
be with you.
12Greet each other with a holy kiss. 13All
of God's holy people send greetings to you.
14The grace of the Lord Jesus Christ, the
love of God, and the fellowship of the Holy
Spirit be with you all.

13:1 "Every . . . witnesses." Quotation from Deuteronomy 19:15.

Galatians

This name refers to a people group that immigrated to Asia Minor from Gaul (modern-day France) in the third century B.C. as well as the two regions they inhabited. One Galatia *was a relatively small area (think: New York City). The other* Galatia *was the encompassing Roman province (think: New York state).*

Person Holding the Pen God Wrote With: *Paul*

When the Text Was Written: Most likely around 49 A.D., making it the earliest of Paul's letters

Spiritual Posture of the Original Recipients: The Galatians were being distracted by false teachers who were distorting the purity of the salvation message.

Storyline Synopsis: The Christian churches in Galatia, which Paul had planted, were being infiltrated by "Judaizers." These misguided teachers were telling the young believers that, in order to become Christians, they had to first obey Jewish customs such as circumcision. Essentially the Judaizers were preaching that you must be saved through faith in Jesus as the Messiah *and* by following every teensy part of the Old Testament Law. Paul was concerned about these fledging congregations being poisoned by this "Jesus-plus-something-equals-salvation" heresy, so he fired off a Holy Spirit-inspired message about it. Some say Galatians is the most definitive work against religious legalism in the entire Bible.

A Moment Worth Discussing: The "spiritual fruit" section in Galatians 5:22–23 has been a catalyst for hundreds of Bible studies and sermons. One key element of Paul's message is that the Greek word he uses for "fruit" is singular. In other words, the characteristics produced by the Holy Spirit don't exist in part—you don't "get" joy but "miss out" on self-control! Some Christians might *appear* to be missing one of the qualities listed, but each virtue is hiding somewhere in their hearts! Which spiritual fruit is the most evident in your life? Which seems to be on vacation?

Interesting (But Likely to Be Overlooked) Character: When Paul talks about the "*children of Abraham*" (Gal. 3:7–9), he's reiterating the extremely significant point that you don't have to be Jewish to be in God's family, but you must have faith in his Son (see Rom. 4:11–25).

1 From Paul, an apostle. I was not chosen to be an apostle by human beings, nor was I sent from human beings. I was made an apostle through Jesus Christ and God the Father who raised Jesus from the dead. 2This letter is also from all those of God's family[n] who are with me.

To the churches in Galatia:[n]

3Grace and peace to you from God our Father and the Lord Jesus Christ. 4Jesus gave himself for our sins to free us from this evil world we live in, as God the Father planned. 5The glory belongs to God forever and ever. Amen.

The Only Good News

6God, by his grace through Christ, called you to become his people. So I am amazed that you are turning away so quickly and believing something different than the Good News. 7Really, there is no other Good News. But some people are confusing you; they want to change the Good News of Christ. 8We preached to you the Good News. So if we ourselves, or even an angel from heaven, should preach to you something different, we should be judged guilty! 9I said this before, and now I say it again: You have already accepted the Good News. If anyone is preaching something different to you, let that person be judged guilty!

10Do you think I am trying to make people accept me? No, God is the One I am trying to please. Am I trying to please people? If I still wanted to please people, I would not be a servant of Christ.

Paul's Authority Is from God

11Brothers and sisters, I want you to know that the Good News I preached to you was not made up by human beings. 12I did not get it from humans, nor did anyone teach it to me, but Jesus Christ showed it to me.

13You have heard about my past life in the Jewish religion. I attacked the church of God and tried to destroy it. 14I was becoming a leader in the Jewish religion, doing better than most other Jews of my age. I tried harder than anyone else to follow the teachings handed down by our ancestors.

15But God had special plans for me and set me apart for his work even before I was born. He called me through his grace 16and showed his son to me so that I might tell the Good News about him to those who are not Jewish. When God called me, I did not get advice or help from any person. 17I did not go to Jerusalem to see those who were apostles before I was. But, without waiting, I went away to Arabia and later went back to Damascus.

18After three years I went to Jerusalem to meet Peter and stayed with him for fifteen days. 19I met no other apostles, except James, the brother of the Lord. 20God knows that these things I write are not lies. 21Later, I went to the areas of Syria and Cilicia.

22In Judea the churches in Christ had never met me. 23They had only heard it said, "This man who was attacking us is now preaching the same faith that he once tried to destroy." 24And these believers praised God because of me.

Other Apostles Accepted Paul

2 After fourteen years I went to Jerusalem again, this time with Barnabas. I also took Titus with me. 2I went because God showed me I should go. I met with the believers there, and in private I told their leaders the Good News that I preach to the non-Jewish people. I did not want my past work and the work I am now doing to be wasted. 3Titus was with me, but he was not forced to be circumcised, even though he was a Greek. 4We talked about this problem because some false believers had come into our group secretly. They came in like spies to overturn the freedom we have in Christ Jesus. They wanted to make us slaves. 5But we did not give in to those false believers for a minute. We wanted the truth of the Good News to continue for you.

6Those leaders who seemed to be important did not change the Good News that I preach. (It doesn't matter to me if they were "important" or not. To God everyone is the same.) 7But these leaders saw that I had been given the work of telling the Good News to those who are not Jewish, just as Peter had the work of telling the Jews. 8God gave Peter the power to work as an apostle

1:2 those . . . family The Greek text says "brothers." **1:2 Galatia** Probably the same country where Paul preached and began churches on his first missionary trip. Read the Book of Acts, chapters 13 and 14.

for the Jewish people. But he also gave me the power to work as an apostle for those who are not Jews. 9 James, Peter, and John, who seemed to be the leaders, understood that God had given me this special grace, so they accepted Barnabas and me. They agreed that they would go to the Jewish people and that we should go to those who are not Jewish. 10 The only thing they asked us was to remember to help the poor—something I really wanted to do.

Paul Shows that Peter Was Wrong

11 When Peter came to Antioch, I challenged him to his face, because he was wrong. 12 Peter ate with the non-Jewish people until some Jewish people sent from James came to Antioch. When they arrived, Peter stopped eating with those who weren't Jewish, and he separated himself from them. He was afraid of the Jews. 13 So Peter was a hypocrite, as were the other Jewish believers who joined with him. Even Barnabas was influenced by what these Jewish believers did. 14 When I saw they were not following the truth of the Good News, I spoke to Peter in front of them all. I said, "Peter, you are a Jew, but you are not living like a Jew. You are living like those who are not Jewish. So why do you now try to force those who are not Jewish to live like Jews?"

15 We were not born as non-Jewish "sinners," but as Jews. 16 Yet we know that a person is made right with God not by following the law, but by trusting in Jesus Christ. So we, too, have put our faith in Christ Jesus, that we might be made right with God because we trusted in Christ. It is not because we followed the law, because no one can be made right with God by following the law.

17 We Jews came to Christ, trying to be made right with God, and it became clear that we are sinners, too. Does this mean that Christ encourages sin? No! 18 But I would really be wrong to begin teaching again those things that I gave up. 19 It was the law that put me to death, and I died to the law so that I can now live for God. 20 I was put to death on the cross with Christ, and I do not live anymore—it is Christ who lives in me. I still live in my body, but I live by faith in the Son of God who loved me and gave himself to save me. 21 By saying these things I am not going against God's grace. Just the opposite, if the law could make us right with God, then Christ's death would be useless.

Blessing Comes Through Faith

3 You people in Galatia were told very clearly about the death of Jesus Christ on the cross. But you were foolish; you let someone trick you. 2 Tell me this one thing: How did you receive the Holy Spirit? Did you receive the Spirit by following the law? No, you received the Spirit because you heard the Good News and believed it. 3 You began your life in Christ by the Spirit. Now are you trying to make it complete by your own power? That is foolish. 4 Were all your experiences wasted? I hope not! 5 Does God give you the Spirit and work miracles among you because you follow the law? No, he does these things because you heard the Good News and believed it.

6 The Scriptures say the same thing about Abraham: "Abraham believed God, and God accepted Abraham's faith, and that faith made him right with God."[n] 7 So you should know that the true children of Abraham are those who have faith. 8 The Scriptures, telling what would happen in the future, said that God would make the non-Jewish people right through their faith. This Good News was told to Abraham beforehand, as the Scripture says: "All nations will be blessed through you."[n] 9 So all who believe as Abraham believed are blessed just as Abraham was. 10 But those who depend on following the law to make them right are under a curse, because the Scriptures say, "Anyone will be cursed who does not always obey what is written in the Book of the Law."[n] 11 Now it is clear that no one can be made right with God by the law, because the Scriptures say, "Those who are right with God will live by faith."[n] 12 The law is not based on faith. It says, "A person who obeys these things will live because of them."[n] 13 Christ took away the curse the law put on us. He changed places with us and put himself under that curse. It is written in the

3:6 "Abraham . . . God." Quotation from Genesis 15:6. **3:8 "All . . . you."** Quotation from Genesis 12:3 and 18:18. **3:10 "Anyone . . . Law."** Quotation from Deuteronomy 27:26. **3:11 "Those . . . faith."** Quotation from Habakkuk 2:4. **3:12 "A person . . . them."** Quotation from Leviticus 18:5.

devotion 323

GALATIANS 3:3

SPIRITUAL FOOLISHNESS

When Jesus was on earth, he told his followers that after he left, the Father would send them the Holy Spirit. He also told them that the Spirit would teach them and remind them of the things he had said. When you become a Christian, the Holy Spirit comes to live inside of you. You have then become a temple, or home, for God's Spirit. The Spirit is the one that works in your life to make you more and more like Jesus.

Watch a group of elementary school kids on the playground. Every game has a set of rules that must be followed or you are out of the game. Martin Luther put it this way: "We're all born legalists." But trying to please God by following the law is the way of the old man. When we become Christians, the Spirit begins to make us into new women. He changes our attitudes, and then our actions begin to change as well. The problem is that we tend to fall back into our old ways and try to do things in the flesh. We rely on the Spirit when we are first saved, but then as we grow, we feel stronger, so we try to change in our own strength. Galatians 3:3 says that is foolishness. Go back to your first love and allow the Spirit to work through you. Release those things that you are trying so desperately to control and trust the Spirit to finish what he started.

Scriptures, "Anyone whose body is displayed
on a tree[n] is cursed." 14Christ did this so that
God's blessing promised to Abraham might
come through Jesus Christ to those who are
not Jews. Jesus died so that by our believing
we could receive the Spirit that God
promised.

The Law and the Promise

15Brothers and sisters, let us think in
human terms: Even an agreement made
between two persons is firm. After that
agreement is accepted by both people, no
one can stop it or add anything to it. 16God
made promises both to Abraham and to his
descendant. God did not say, "and to your
descendants." That would mean many
people. But God said, "and to your
descendant." That means only one person;
that person is Christ. 17This is what I mean:
God had an agreement with Abraham and
promised to keep it. The law, which came
four hundred thirty years later, cannot
change that agreement and so destroy God's
promise to Abraham. 18If the law could give
us Abraham's blessing, then the promise
would not be necessary. But that is not
possible, because God freely gave his
blessings to Abraham through the promise
he had made.

19So what was the law for? It was given to
show that the wrong things people do are
against God's will. And it continued until
the special descendant, who had been
promised, came. The law was given through
angels who used Moses for a mediator[n] to
give the law to people. 20But a mediator is
not needed when there is only one side, and
God is only one.

The Purpose of the Law of Moses

21Does this mean that the law is against
God's promises? Never! That would be true
only if the law could make us right with
God. But God did not give a law that can
bring life. 22Instead, the Scriptures showed

3:13 displayed on a tree Deuteronomy 21:22–23 says that when a person was killed for doing wrong, the body was hung on a tree to show shame. Paul means that the cross of Jesus was like that. **3:19 mediator** A person who helps one person talk to or give something to another person.

that the whole world is bound by sin. This
was so the promise would be given through
faith to people who believe in Jesus Christ.
23 Before this faith came, we were all held
prisoners by the law. We had no freedom
until God showed us the way of faith that
was coming. 24 In other words, the law was
our guardian leading us to Christ so that we
could be made right with God through faith.
25 Now the way of faith has come, and we no
longer live under a guardian.
26-27 You were all baptized into Christ, and
so you were all clothed with Christ. This
means that you are all children of God
through faith in Christ Jesus. 28 In Christ,
there is no difference between Jew and
Greek, slave and free person, male and
female. You are all the same in Christ Jesus.
29 You belong to Christ, so you are Abraham's
descendants. You will inherit all of God's
blessings because of the promise God made
to Abraham.

4 I want to tell you this: While those who
will inherit their fathers' property are
still children, they are no different from
slaves. It does not matter that the children
own everything. 2 While they are children,
they must obey those who are chosen to care
for them. But when the children reach the
age set by their fathers, they are free. 3 It is
the same for us. We were once like children,
slaves to the useless rules of this world. 4 But
when the right time came, God sent his Son
who was born of a woman and lived under
the law. 5 God did this so he could buy
freedom for those who were under the law
and so we could become his children.
6 Since you are God's children, God sent
the Spirit of his Son into your hearts, and the
Spirit cries out, "Father."[n] 7 So now you are
not a slave; you are God's child, and God will
give you the blessing he promised, because
you are his child.

Paul's Love for the Christians

8 In the past you did not know God. You
were slaves to gods that were not real. 9 But
now you know the true God. Really, it is God
who knows you. So why do you turn back to
those weak and useless rules you followed
before? Do you want to be slaves to those
things again? 10 You still follow teachings
about special days, months, seasons, and
years. 11 I am afraid for you, that my work for
you has been wasted.
12 Brothers and sisters, I became like you,
so I beg you to become like me. You were
very good to me before. 13 You remember that
it was because of an illness that I came to
you the first time, preaching the Good News.
14 Though my sickness was a trouble for you,
you did not hate me or make me leave. But
you welcomed me as an angel from God, as if
I were Jesus Christ himself! 15 You were very
happy then, but where is that joy now? I am
ready to testify that you would have taken
out your eyes and given them to me if that
were possible. 16 Now am I your enemy
because I tell you the truth?
17 Those people[n] are working hard to
persuade you, but this is not good for you.
They want to persuade you to turn against
us and follow only them. 18 It is good for
people to show interest in you, but only if
their purpose is good. This is always true,
not just when I am with you. 19 My little
children, again I feel the pain of childbirth
for you until you truly become like Christ.
20 I wish I could be with you now and could
change the way I am talking to you, because
I do not know what to think about you.

The Example of Hagar and Sarah

21 Some of you still want to be under the
law. Tell me, do you know what the law
says? 22 The Scriptures say that Abraham had
two sons. The mother of one son was a slave
woman, and the mother of the other son was
a free woman. 23 Abraham's son from the
slave woman was born in the normal human
way. But the son from the free woman was
born because of the promise God made to
Abraham.
24 This story teaches something else: The
two women are like the two agreements
between God and his people. One agreement
is the law that God made on Mount Sinai,[n]
and the people who are under this
agreement are like slaves. The mother
named Hagar is like that agreement. 25 She is
like Mount Sinai in Arabia and is a picture of
the earthly city of Jerusalem. This city and

4:6 "Father" Literally, "Abba, Father." Jewish children called their fathers "Abba." **4:17 Those people** They are the false teachers who were bothering the believers in Galatia (Galatians 1:7). **4:24 Mount Sinai** Mountain in Arabia where God gave his Law to Moses (Exodus 19 and 20).

its people are slaves to the law. 26But the
heavenly Jerusalem, which is above, is like
the free woman. She is our mother. 27It is
written in the Scriptures:

"Be happy, Jerusalem.
You are like a woman who never gave
birth to children.
Start singing and shout for joy.
You never felt the pain of giving birth,
but you will have more children
than the woman who has a husband."
Isaiah 54:1

28My brothers and sisters, you are God's
children because of his promise, as Isaac
was then. 29The son who was born in the
normal way treated the other son badly.
It is the same today. 30But what does the
Scripture say? "Throw out the slave woman
and her son. The son of the slave woman
should not inherit anything. The son of
the free woman should receive it all."[n]
31So, my brothers and sisters, we are not
children of the slave woman, but of the free
woman.

Keep Your Freedom

5 We have freedom now, because Christ
made us free. So stand strong. Do not
change and go back into the slavery of the
law. 2Listen, I Paul tell you that if you go
back to the law by being circumcised, Christ
does you no good. 3Again, I warn every man:
If you allow yourselves to be circumcised,
you must follow all the law. 4If you try to be
made right with God through the law, your
life with Christ is over—you have left God's
grace. 5But we have the true hope that comes
from being made right with God, and by the
Spirit we wait eagerly for this hope. 6When
we are in Christ Jesus, it is not important if
we are circumcised or not. The important
thing is faith—the kind of faith that works
through love.
7You were running a good race. Who
stopped you from following the true way?
8This change did not come from the One
who chose you. 9Be careful! "Just a little
yeast makes the whole batch of dough rise."
10But I trust in the Lord that you will not

4:30 "Throw . . . all." Quotation from Genesis 21:10.

devotion 324

GALATIANS 5:16

TUG-OF-WAR WITH THE SPIRIT OF GOD?

Following the Spirit sounds easy, but I have to admit that there are many times when seeking Christ is a battle for me. During these times, I usually already have in mind exactly what I think I need to do, even though Jesus keeps whispering that it is not the direction he is leading me in. It can be a tug-of-war for a while, until he usually stops whispering and calls my name loudly. Oh, believe me, I can hear it. Maybe not in an audible voice, but I can hear it in the way my plans eventually come to a halt with an earth-shaking thud.

Through his letter to the Galatians, Paul continues to remind us to follow the Spirit of Christ. His Spirit is always there to show us the way, and only good can come from our efforts when we listen to him; because, as Paul goes on to say, the Spirit generates "the fruit of love, joy, peace, patience, kindness, goodness, faithfulness, gentleness, self-control" (Gal. 5:22-23). When we have accepted Christ as our Savior, we can enjoy this fruit through his Spirit as he moves and works in us. We are so blessed that God has sent the Spirit to comfort and to guide us.

I want to encourage you to let Paul's words inspire you to follow the Spirit today. Seek him in all of your decisions, and if you do, you won't be as vulnerable to sinful actions and thoughts—or the tug-of-war game.

believe those different ideas. Whoever is confusing you with such ideas will be punished.

11 My brothers and sisters, I do not teach that a man must be circumcised. If I teach circumcision, why am I still being attacked? If I still taught circumcision, my preaching about the cross would not be a problem. 12 I wish the people who are bothering you would castrate[n] themselves!

13 My brothers and sisters, God called you to be free, but do not use your freedom as an excuse to do what pleases your sinful self. Serve each other with love. 14 The whole law is made complete in this one command: "Love your neighbor as you love yourself."[n] 15 If you go on hurting each other and tearing each other apart, be careful, or you will completely destroy each other.

The Spirit and Human Nature

16 So I tell you: Live by following the Spirit. Then you will not do what your sinful selves want. 17 Our sinful selves want what is against the Spirit, and the Spirit wants what is against our sinful selves. The two are against each other, so you cannot do just what you please. 18 But if the Spirit is leading you, you are not under the law.

19 The wrong things the sinful self does are clear: being sexually unfaithful, not being pure, taking part in sexual sins, 20 worshiping gods, doing witchcraft, hating, making trouble, being jealous, being angry, being selfish, making people angry with each other, causing divisions among people, 21 feeling envy, being drunk, having wild and wasteful parties, and doing other things like these. I warn you now as I warned you before: Those who do these things will not inherit God's kingdom. 22 But the Spirit produces the fruit of love, joy, peace, patience, kindness, goodness, faithfulness, 23 gentleness, self-control. There is no law that says these things are wrong. 24 Those who belong to Christ Jesus have crucified their own sinful selves. They have given up their old selfish feelings and the evil things they wanted to do. 25 We get our new life from the Spirit, so we should follow the Spirit. 26 We must not be proud or make trouble with each other or be jealous of each other.

Help Each Other

6 Brothers and sisters, if someone in your group does something wrong, you who are spiritual should go to that person and gently help make him right again. But be careful, because you might be tempted to sin, too. 2 By helping each other with your troubles, you truly obey the law of Christ. 3 If anyone thinks he is important when he really is not, he is only fooling himself. 4 Each person should judge his own actions and not compare himself with others. Then he can be proud for what he himself has done. 5 Each person must be responsible for himself.

6 Anyone who is learning the teaching of God should share all the good things he has with his teacher.

Life Is like Planting a Field

7 Do not be fooled: You cannot cheat God. People harvest only what they plant. 8 If they plant to satisfy their sinful selves, their sinful selves will bring them ruin. But if they plant to please the Spirit, they will receive eternal life from the Spirit. 9 We must not become tired of doing good. We will receive our harvest of eternal life at the right time if we do not give up. 10 When we have the opportunity to help anyone, we should do it. But we should give special attention to those who are in the family of believers.

Paul Ends His Letter

11 See what large letters I use to write this myself. 12 Some people are trying to force you to be circumcised so the Jews will accept them. They are afraid they will be attacked if they follow only the cross of Christ.[n] 13 Those who are circumcised do not obey the law themselves, but they want you to be circumcised so they can brag about what they forced you to do. 14 I hope I will never brag about things like that. The cross of our Lord Jesus Christ is my only reason for bragging. Through the cross of Jesus my world was crucified, and I died to the world. 15 It is not important if a man is circumcised

5:12 castrate To cut off part of the male sex organ. Paul uses this word because it is similar to "circumcision." Paul wanted to show that he is very upset with the false teachers. **5:14 "Love . . . yourself."** Quotation from Leviticus 19:18. **6:12 cross of Christ** Paul uses the cross as a picture of the Good News, the story of Christ's death and rising from the dead to pay for our sins. The cross, or Christ's death, was God's way to save us.

devotion 325

GALATIANS 6:2

REACHING OUT INSTEAD OF REACHING IN

Jesus intended for us to live in relationship. Unfortunately, most of the time when we are hurting, we pull in, cry ourselves to sleep, and try to hide until it's over. I don't know of one person who has ever been healed crying alone on her bed in the dark. Each person I know who has found healing for her wounds or strength to battle addictions or sin has found it in the light of fellowship and love.

I know what it feels like to be nothing and want nothing and care about nothing. You just want to hide with your heartache and mourn everything you've lost. Some of that is so appropriate. It is right to grieve for a while or even a long time, but you cannot stay there and live. There is no healing in loneliness.

If your life is difficult, if your heart is broken, if your troubles seem overwhelming, then it is very important for you to continue interacting. Begin by getting yourself to church and staying there. Let the people who belong to Christ minister to you. Open up to a girlfriend. Stay connected to some healthy people so that God can work through them to help carry your burden. And then, when you have begun to know healing, look for the woman who will need you to stand alongside her. In the body of Christ, we take turns. Today it might be your day to receive. But a day will come when it will be time to give.

or uncircumcised. The important thing is
being the new people God has made. 16 Peace
and mercy to those who follow this rule—
and to all of God's people.
17 So do not give me any more trouble. I
have scars on my body that show[n] I belong
to Christ Jesus.
18 My brothers and sisters, the grace of
our Lord Jesus Christ be with your spirit.
Amen.

6:17 that show Many times Paul was beaten and whipped by people who were against him because he was teaching about Christ. The scars were from these beatings.

Ephesians

Refers to Ephesus, *the location of the church that first received this letter*

Person Holding the Pen God Wrote With: *Paul*

When the Text Was Written: Between 60 and 62 A.D. while the apostle was incarcerated in Rome (Acts 28:16–31). This book is the first—along with Philippians and Colossians—of what are commonly referred to as Paul's "prison letters."

Spiritual Posture of the Original Recipients: Like most of Paul's other new churches in Asia Minor, the congregation at Ephesus was in turmoil, mainly due to false prophets and bogus teaching.

Storyline Synopsis: The members of the church at Ephesus had started out strong, having spent three years under Paul's preaching (Acts 20:31). But after Paul left to take on other mission opportunities, putting Timothy in charge, trouble started brewing. This letter addressed not only the problems specific to Ephesus but also other issues that continued to plague other churches in Asia Minor. The first half of Paul's message is an explanation of correct Christian *doctrine* (chapters 1—3), while the second half spells out our *duty* as Christians (chapters 4—6). The gist of this written sermon is that when we fully understand the abundant blessings we have in Christ, our behavior will reflect our gratitude!

A Moment Worth Discussing: The inspirational "armor of God" description in chapter 6 is a motivating message—sort of like an athletic coach's "go out there and get 'em" lecture! But an equally challenging, yet often overlooked, exhortation is found near the end of chapter 4: "When you talk, do not say harmful things, but say what people need—words that will help others become stronger. Then what you say will do good to those who listen to you" (verse 29). In light of the fact that most women are never short of words, this verse should be posted on refrigerators all over the world!

Interesting (But Likely to Be Overlooked) Character: The "*citizens together*" that Paul mentions in Ephesians 2:19–22 describe the unity that should be evident among God's children, no matter what nationality, tongue, or color. Everyone who trusts Jesus as their Savior is part of God's family!

1 From Paul, an apostle of Christ Jesus. I am
an apostle because that is what God
wanted.
To God's holy people living in Ephesus,[n]
believers in Christ Jesus:
2 Grace and peace to you from God our
Father and the Lord Jesus Christ.

Spiritual Blessings in Christ

3 Praise be to the God and Father of our
Lord Jesus Christ. In Christ, God has given us
every spiritual blessing in the heavenly
world. 4 That is, in Christ, he chose us before
the world was made so that we would be his
holy people—people without blame before
him. 5 Because of his love, God had already
decided to make us his own children
through Jesus Christ. That was what he
wanted and what pleased him, 6 and it brings
praise to God because of his wonderful
grace. God gave that grace to us freely, in
Christ, the One he loves. 7 In Christ we are
set free by the blood of his death, and so we
have forgiveness of sins. How rich is God's
grace, 8 which he has given to us so fully and
freely. God, with full wisdom and
understanding, 9 let us know his secret
purpose. This was what God wanted, and he
planned to do it through Christ. 10 His goal
was to carry out his plan, when the right
time came, that all things in heaven and on
earth would be joined together in Christ as
the head.
11 In Christ we were chosen to be God's
people, because from the very beginning
God had decided this in keeping with his
plan. And he is the One who makes
everything agree with what he decides
and wants. 12 We are the first people who
hoped in Christ, and we were chosen so
that we would bring praise to God's glory.
13 So it is with you. When you heard the
true teaching—the Good News about your
salvation—you believed in Christ. And
in Christ, God put his special mark of
ownership on you by giving you the Holy
Spirit that he had promised. 14 That Holy
Spirit is the guarantee that we will receive
what God promised for his people until God
gives full freedom to those who are his—to
bring praise to God's glory.

Paul's Prayer

15 That is why since I heard about your
faith in the Lord Jesus and your love for all
God's people, 16 I have not stopped giving
thanks to God for you. I always remember
you in my prayers, 17 asking the God of our
Lord Jesus Christ, the glorious Father, to give
you a spirit of wisdom and revelation so
that you will know him better. 18 I pray also
that you will have greater understanding in
your heart so you will know the hope to
which he has called us and that you will
know how rich and glorious are the
blessings God has promised his holy people.
19 And you will know that God's power is
very great for us who believe. That power is
the same as the great strength 20 God used to
raise Christ from the dead and put him at his
right side in the heavenly world. 21 God has
put Christ over all rulers, authorities,
powers, and kings, not only in this world but
also in the next. 22 God put everything under
his power and made him the head over
everything for the church, 23 which is
Christ's body. The church is filled with
Christ, and Christ fills everything in every
way.

We Now Have Life

2 In the past you were spiritually dead
because of your sins and the things you
did against God. 2 Yes, in the past you lived
the way the world lives, following the ruler
of the evil powers that are above the earth.
That same spirit is now working in those
who refuse to obey God. 3 In the past all of us
lived like them, trying to please our sinful
selves and doing all the things our bodies
and minds wanted. We should have suffered
God's anger because we were sinful by
nature. We were the same as all other
people.
4 But God's mercy is great, and he loved us
very much. 5 Though we were spiritually
dead because of the things we did against
God, he gave us new life with Christ. You
have been saved by God's grace. 6 And he
raised us up with Christ and gave us a seat
with him in the heavens. He did this for
those in Christ Jesus 7 so that for all future
time he could show the very great riches of
his grace by being kind to us in Christ Jesus.

1:1 in Ephesus Some Greek copies do not have this phrase.

devotion 326

EPHESIANS 2:4–5

"DOING" LOVE RATHER THAN "BEING" LOVED

As women, we can lose our sense of "being" loved. I think about Eve in the early days of Eden, walking in the garden with God. She didn't worry about her worth; she simply knew it. She was loved and her arms were wide open to that love. She was forever in his heart and he was in hers.

How far are you from Eden? Are you out of control, "doing" love rather than "being" loved? Do you find yourself in the midst of giving love, modeling love, and keeping love alive based solely on how you perform? Oh, how you need to know you are just "being" loved by Jesus. Take in the beauty of how much richer your life is just because you know him, how he's comforted you when you've been scared, and how you belly laugh at things only the two of you know.

It's hard sometimes to really understand how his love was alive for us even when we were dead in our sin. Jeremiah 31:3 says he loves us with a love that will last, a love that takes us right into eternity without any calculation of merit pending on anything we have done. Maybe you should just spend the entire day "being" loved by the Lord. Get into the Word, pray, journal, and talk heart to heart and Spirit to spirit. Forget your lists and your "doing." Live life on the wild side—I think you'll find you have a whole lot more to offer tomorrow.

[8]I mean that you have been saved by grace
through believing. You did not save
yourselves; it was a gift from God. [9]It was
not the result of your own efforts, so you
cannot brag about it. [10]God has made us
what we are. In Christ Jesus, God made us to
do good works, which God planned in
advance for us to live our lives doing.

One in Christ

[11]You were not born Jewish. You are
the people the Jews call "uncircumcised."[n]
Those who call you "uncircumcised" call
themselves "circumcised." (Their
circumcision is only something they
themselves do on their bodies.) [12]Remember
that in the past you were without Christ.
You were not citizens of Israel, and you had
no part in the agreements[n] with the promise
that God made to his people. You had no
hope, and you did not know God. [13]But now
in Christ Jesus, you who were far away from
God are brought near through the blood of
Christ's death. [14]Christ himself is our peace.
He made both Jewish people and those who
are not Jews one people. They were
separated as if there were a wall between
them, but Christ broke down that wall of
hate by giving his own body. [15]The Jewish
law had many commands and rules, but
Christ ended that law. His purpose was to
make the two groups of people become one
new people in him and in this way make
peace. [16]It was also Christ's purpose to end
the hatred between the two groups, to make
them into one body, and to bring them back
to God. Christ did all this with his death on
the cross. [17]Christ came and preached peace
to you who were far away from God, and to
those who were near to God. [18]Yes, it is
through Christ we all have the right to come
to the Father in one Spirit.

2:11 "uncircumcised" People not having the mark of circumcision as the Jews had.
2:12 agreements The agreements that God gave to his people in the Old Testament.

19 Now you who are not Jewish are not
foreigners or strangers any longer, but are
citizens together with God's holy people.
You belong to God's family. 20 You are like a
building that was built on the foundation of
the apostles and prophets. Christ Jesus
himself is the most important stone[n] in that
building, 21 and that whole building is joined
together in Christ. He makes it grow and
become a holy temple in the Lord. 22 And in
Christ you, too, are being built together with
the Jews into a place where God lives
through the Spirit.

Paul's Work in Telling the Good News

3 So I, Paul, am a prisoner of Christ Jesus
for you who are not Jews. 2 Surely you
have heard that God gave me this work to
tell you about his grace. 3 He let me know his
secret by showing it to me. I have already
written a little about this. 4 If you read what I
wrote then, you can see that I truly
understand the secret about the Christ.
5 People who lived in other times were not
told that secret. But now, through the Spirit,
God has shown that secret to his holy
apostles and prophets. 6 This is that secret:
that through the Good News those who are
not Jews will share with the Jews in God's
blessing. They belong to the same body, and
they share together in the promise that God
made in Christ Jesus.

7 By God's special gift of grace given to me
through his power, I became a servant to tell
that Good News. 8 I am the least important of
all God's people, but God gave me this gift—
to tell those who are not Jews the Good
News about the riches of Christ, which are
too great to understand fully. 9 And God gave
me the work of telling all people about the
plan for his secret, which has been hidden in
him since the beginning of time. He is the
One who created everything. 10 His purpose
was that through the church all the rulers
and powers in the heavenly world will now
know God's wisdom, which has so many
forms. 11 This agrees with the purpose God
had since the beginning of time, and he
carried out his plan through Christ Jesus our
Lord. 12 In Christ we can come before God
with freedom and without fear. We can do
this through faith in Christ. 13 So I ask you
not to become discouraged because of the
sufferings I am having for you. My sufferings
are for your glory.

The Love of Christ

14 So I bow in prayer before the Father
15 from whom every family in heaven and on
earth gets its true name. 16 I ask the Father in
his great glory to give you the power to be
strong inwardly through his Spirit. 17 I pray
that Christ will live in your hearts by faith
and that your life will be strong in love and
be built on love. 18 And I pray that you and
all God's holy people will have the power to
understand the greatness of Christ's love—
how wide and how long and how high and
how deep that love is. 19 Christ's love is
greater than anyone can ever know, but I
pray that you will be able to know that love.
Then you can be filled with the fullness of
God.

20 With God's power working in us, God
can do much, much more than anything we
can ask or imagine. 21 To him be glory in the
church and in Christ Jesus for all time,
forever and ever. Amen.

The Unity of the Body

4 I am in prison because I belong to the
Lord. Therefore I urge you who have
been chosen by God to live up to the life to
which God called you. 2 Always be humble,
gentle, and patient, accepting each other in
love. 3 You are joined together with peace
through the Spirit, so make every effort to
continue together in this way. 4 There is one
body and one Spirit, and God called you to
have one hope. 5 There is one Lord, one faith,
and one baptism. 6 There is one God and
Father of everything. He rules everything
and is everywhere and is in everything.

7 Christ gave each one of us the special gift
of grace, showing how generous he is. 8 That
is why it says in the Scriptures,

"When he went up to the heights,
he led a parade of captives,
and he gave gifts to people." *Psalm 68:18*

9 When it says, "He went up," what does it
mean? It means that he first came down to
the earth. 10 So Jesus came down, and he is
the same One who went up above all the
heaven. Christ did that to fill everything

2:20 most important stone Literally, "cornerstone." The first and most important stone in a building.

with his presence. 11And Christ gave gifts to people—he made some to be apostles, some to be prophets, some to go and tell the Good News, and some to have the work of caring for and teaching God's people. 12Christ gave those gifts to prepare God's holy people for the work of serving, to make the body of Christ stronger. 13This work must continue until we are all joined together in the same faith and in the same knowledge of the Son of God. We must become like a mature person, growing until we become like Christ and have his perfection.

14Then we will no longer be babies. We will not be tossed about like a ship that the waves carry one way and then another. We will not be influenced by every new teaching we hear from people who are trying to fool us. They make plans and try any kind of trick to fool people into following the wrong path. 15No! Speaking the truth with love, we will grow up in every way into Christ, who is the head. 16The whole body depends on Christ, and all the parts of the body are joined and held together. Each part does its own work to make the whole body grow and be strong with love.

The Way You Should Live

17In the Lord's name, I tell you this. Do not continue living like those who do not believe. Their thoughts are worth nothing. 18They do not understand, and they know nothing, because they refuse to listen. So they cannot have the life that God gives. 19They have lost all feeling of shame, and they use their lives for doing evil. They continually want to do all kinds of evil. 20But what you learned in Christ was not like this. 21I know that you heard about him, and you are in him, so you were taught the truth that is in Jesus. 22You were taught to leave your old self—to stop living the evil way you lived before. That old self becomes worse, because people are fooled by the evil things they want to do. 23But you were taught to be made new in your hearts, 24to become a new person. That new person is made to be like God—made to be truly good and holy.

25So you must stop telling lies. Tell each other the truth, because we all belong to each other in the same body.[n] 26When you are angry, do not sin, and be sure to stop being angry before the end of the day. 27Do not give the devil a way to defeat you. 28Those who are stealing must stop stealing and start working. They should earn an honest living for themselves. Then they will have something to share with those who are poor.

29When you talk, do not say harmful things, but say what people need—words that will help others become stronger. Then what you say will do good to those who listen to you. 30And do not make the Holy Spirit sad. The Spirit is God's proof that you belong to him. God gave you the Spirit to show that God will make you free when the final day comes. 31Do not be bitter or angry or mad. Never shout angrily or say things to hurt others. Never do anything evil. 32Be kind and loving to each other, and forgive each other just as God forgave you in Christ.

Living in the Light

5 You are God's children whom he loves, so try to be like him. 2Live a life of love just as Christ loved us and gave himself for us as a sweet-smelling offering and sacrifice to God.

3But there must be no sexual sin among you, or any kind of evil or greed. Those things are not right for God's holy people. 4Also, there must be no evil talk among you, and you must not speak foolishly or tell evil jokes. These things are not right for you. Instead, you should be giving thanks to God. 5You can be sure of this: No one will have a place in the kingdom of Christ and of God who sins sexually, or does evil things, or is greedy. Anyone who is greedy is serving a false god.

6Do not let anyone fool you by telling you things that are not true, because these things will bring God's anger on those who do not obey him. 7So have nothing to do with them. 8In the past you were full of darkness, but now you are full of light in the Lord. So live like children who belong to the light. 9Light brings every kind of goodness, right living, and truth. 10Try to learn what pleases the Lord. 11Have nothing to do with the things done in darkness, which are not worth

4:25 Tell . . . body. Quotation from Zechariah 8:16.

devotion 327

EPHESIANS 5:2

HOW DOES YOUR DAY BEGIN?

When I had my third child, my first two were only one and three. My mother brought the older kids to the hospital to see their sister for the first time. When it was time for them to go, we laid all three children down on the hospital bed to change diapers. "I'm not sure I can do this," I cried. There were three of them and only one of me!

The first six months were quite chaotic. I confided in a friend at one point, "I don't even have time to take a shower, much less spend time with the Lord." She looked at me and said, "The only way you'll be able to spend time with the Lord is if you get up before the children." I knew she was right; I just didn't want to give up my sleep.

The first step in trying to be like Jesus is to spend time with him. Mark 1:35 tells us Jesus got up early and prayed. Jesus made time with God his first priority. It was the source of his strength and the foundation of his love. We need to realize that to be like Jesus, we need to start our day with him. It is the only way we can become a sweet-smelling aroma to God. I know that when I got up before my little ones to spend time with the Lord, it changed my day. Try starting your day with the Lord. It will be worth the sacrifice.

anything. But show that they are wrong.
12 It is shameful even to talk about what those people do in secret.
13 But the light makes all things easy to see,
14 and everything that is made easy to see can become light. This is why it is said:

"Wake up, sleeper!
Rise from death,
and Christ will shine on you."

15 So be very careful how you live. Do not live like those who are not wise, but live wisely.
16 Use every chance you have for doing good, because these are evil times.
17 So do not be foolish but learn what the Lord wants you to do.
18 Do not be drunk with wine, which will ruin you, but be filled with the Spirit.
19 Speak to each other with psalms, hymns, and spiritual songs, singing and making music in your hearts to the Lord.
20 Always give thanks to God the Father for everything, in the name of our Lord Jesus Christ.

Wives and Husbands

21 Yield to obey each other as you would to Christ.

22 Wives, yield to your husbands, as you do to the Lord,
23 because the husband is the head of the wife, as Christ is the head of the church. And he is the Savior of the body, which is the church.
24 As the church yields to Christ, so you wives should yield to your husbands in everything.

25 Husbands, love your wives as Christ loved the church and gave himself for it
26 to make it belong to God. Christ used the word to make the church clean by washing it with water.
27 He died so that he could give the church to himself like a bride in all her beauty. He died so that the church could be pure and without fault, with no evil or sin or any other wrong thing in it.
28 In the same way, husbands should love their wives as they love their own bodies. The man who loves his wife loves himself.
29 No one ever hates his own body, but feeds and takes care of it. And that is what Christ does for the church,
30 because we are parts of his body.
31 The Scripture says, "So a man will leave his father and mother and be united with his wife, and the two will become one body."[n]

5:31 "So . . . body." Quotation from Genesis 2:24.

32 That secret is very important—I am talking about Christ and the church. 33 But each one of you must love his wife as he loves himself, and a wife must respect her husband.

Children and Parents

6 Children, obey your parents as the Lord wants, because this is the right thing to do. 2 The command says, "Honor your father and mother."[n] This is the first command that has a promise with it— 3 "Then everything will be well with you, and you will have a long life on the earth."[n]

4 Fathers, do not make your children angry, but raise them with the training and teaching of the Lord.

Slaves and Masters

5 Slaves, obey your masters here on earth with fear and respect and from a sincere heart, just as you obey Christ. 6 You must do this not only while they are watching you, to please them. With all your heart you must do what God wants as people who are obeying Christ. 7 Do your work with enthusiasm. Work as if you were serving the Lord, not as if you were serving only men and women. 8 Remember that the Lord will give a reward to everyone, slave or free, for doing good.

9 Masters, in the same way, be good to your slaves. Do not threaten them. Remember that the One who is your Master and their Master is in heaven, and he treats everyone alike.

Wear the Full Armor of God

10 Finally, be strong in the Lord and in his great power. 11 Put on the full armor of God so that you can fight against the devil's evil tricks. 12 Our fight is not against people on earth but against the rulers and authorities and the powers of this world's darkness, against the spiritual powers of evil in the heavenly world. 13 That is why you need to put on God's full armor. Then on the day of evil you will be able to stand strong. And when you have finished the whole fight, you will still be standing. 14 So stand strong, with the belt of truth tied around your waist and the protection of right living on your chest. 15 On your feet wear the Good News of peace to help you stand strong. 16 And also use the shield of faith with which you can stop all the burning arrows of the Evil One. 17 Accept God's salvation as your helmet, and take the sword of the Spirit, which is the word of God. 18 Pray in the Spirit at all times with all kinds of prayers, asking for everything you need. To do this you must always be ready and never give up. Always pray for all God's people.

19 Also pray for me that when I speak, God will give me words so that I can tell the secret of the Good News without fear. 20 I have been sent to preach this Good News, and I am doing that now, here in prison. Pray that when I preach the Good News I will speak without fear, as I should.

Final Greetings

21 I am sending to you Tychicus, our brother whom we love and a faithful servant of the Lord's work. He will tell you everything that is happening with me. Then you will know how I am and what I am doing. 22 I am sending him to you for this reason—so that you will know how we are, and he can encourage you.

23 Peace and love with faith to you brothers and sisters from God the Father and the Lord Jesus Christ. 24 Grace to all of you who love our Lord Jesus Christ with love that never ends.

6:2 "Honor . . . mother." Quotation from Exodus 20:12; Deuteronomy 5:16.
6:3 "Then . . . earth." Quotation from Exodus 20:12; Deuteronomy 5:16.

Philippians

Written to the Roman colony in Macedonia, called Philippi, *where Paul established a church*

Person Holding the Pen God Wrote With: *Paul*

When the Text Was Written: Around 61 A.D. near the end of Paul's prison sentence

Spiritual Posture of the Original Recipients: The Philippians must have been like a balm to Paul's soul since, unlike the other Asia Minor churches, they remained steadfast in their faith and focused on Jesus!

Storyline Synopsis: Paul's purposes in writing this letter were numerous: part *gratitude*, part *explanation*, part *exhortation*, and a wee *warning* at the tail end! First of all, he thanked the Philippians for supporting him financially while he was behind bars in Rome. Second, he gave them an update on his personal circumstances and let them know why Epaphroditus—who was visiting Paul on behalf of the church in Philippi—was so tardy in returning home. Third, he attempted to wrap his arms around these faraway friends through an encouraging literary embrace! And finally, Paul wanted to make sure the Philippians kept their guard up against false prophets who would seek to destroy the church from the inside out. The emotional thread running throughout this epistle is one of joy and affection, beginning with Paul's tender greeting: "I thank my God every time I remember you, always praying with joy for all of you" (Phil. 1:3–4).

A Moment Worth Discussing: The apostle's cheer for his distant friends to burn brightly for Christ in a dim world is as compelling today as it was then: "Do everything without complaining or arguing. Then you will be innocent and without any wrong. You will be God's children without fault. But you are living with crooked and mean people all around you, among whom you shine like stars in the dark world" (Phil. 2:14–15). Would anyone in your circle of relationships accuse you of "glowing" for God?

Interesting (But Likely to Be Overlooked) Character: *King Philip*, who's not mentioned by name in this book, left his mark along with his moniker on this letter from Paul. Philippi was named for him after he conquered it in the fourth century B.C. King Philip's son made an even bigger splash in history—his name was Alexander the Great.

1 From Paul and Timothy, servants of
Christ Jesus.
To all of God's holy people in Christ Jesus
who live in Philippi, including your
overseers and deacons:
2Grace and peace to you from God our
Father and the Lord Jesus Christ.

Paul's Prayer

3I thank my God every time I remember
you, 4always praying with joy for all of you.
5I thank God for the help you gave me while
I preached the Good News—help you gave
from the first day you believed until now.
6God began doing a good work in you, and I
am sure he will continue it until it is
finished when Jesus Christ comes again.
7And I know that I am right to think like
this about all of you, because I have you in
my heart. All of you share in God's grace
with me while I am in prison and while I am
defending and proving the truth of the Good
News. 8God knows that I want to see you
very much, because I love all of you with the
love of Christ Jesus.
9This is my prayer for you: that your love
will grow more and more; that you will have
knowledge and understanding with your
love; 10that you will see the difference
between good and bad and will choose the
good; that you will be pure and without
wrong for the coming of Christ; 11that you
will be filled with the good things produced
in your life by Christ to bring glory and
praise to God.

Paul's Troubles Help the Work

12I want you brothers and sisters to know
that what has happened to me has helped to
spread the Good News. 13All the palace
guards and everyone else knows that I am in
prison because I am a believer in Christ.
14Because I am in prison, most of the
believers have become more bold in Christ
and are not afraid to speak the word of God.
15It is true that some preach about Christ

devotion 328

PHILIPPIANS 2:3–4

SAY NO TO THE "ME" MOVEMENT

While financial giving in churches continues to decline, giving to ourselves seems to be on the rise. From images seen on television to those flashed across buses, subways, and billboards, the message from marketers and retailers is clear: "It's all about you!" It can be hard to resist the desire to grow our egos, but our culture would be less selfish if we'd think more about others, just as Paul's letter to the Philippians encourages us to do. Because we are human, however, it's not always that easy.

The self-loving culture we live in today not only targets us but our children, too. I was flipping through some teen-related magazines recently and was amazed at some of the words emblazoned on the front covers. One even had a section called, "All About You." Even little girls and boys are barraged with toys and messages that promote them to think only about themselves. While I don't want to go overboard here, how are we supposed to teach children to be humble and interested in the lives of others when they're bombarded by superficiality?

I want to encourage you today to say no to the "me" movement. Let's consider seeking out volunteer opportunities in our churches and communities and setting examples for our children by reaching out to our friends and neighbors. Let's pause a few times a day to evaluate our actions. Let's pray that we'll have God's strength to resist egotism and to focus on other people in our lives instead.

because they are jealous and ambitious, but
others preach about Christ because they
want to help. 16They preach because they
have love, and they know that God gave me
the work of defending the Good News. 17But
the others preach about Christ for selfish
and wrong reasons, wanting to make trouble
for me in prison.

18But it doesn't matter. The important
thing is that in every way, whether for right
or wrong reasons, they are preaching about
Christ. So I am happy, and I will continue to
be happy. 19Because you are praying for me
and the Spirit of Jesus Christ is helping me, I
know this trouble will bring my freedom. 20I
expect and hope that I will not fail Christ in
anything but that I will have the courage
now, as always, to show the greatness of
Christ in my life here on earth, whether I
live or die. 21To me the only important thing
about living is Christ, and dying would be
profit for me. 22If I continue living in my
body, I will be able to work for the Lord. I do
not know what to choose—living or dying.
23It is hard to choose between the two. I
want to leave this life and be with Christ,
which is much better, 24but you need me
here in my body. 25Since I am sure of this, I
know I will stay with you to help you grow
and have joy in your faith. 26You will be very
happy in Christ Jesus when I am with you
again.

27Only one thing concerns me: Be sure
that you live in a way that brings honor to
the Good News of Christ. Then whether I
come and visit you or am away from you, I
will hear that you are standing strong with
one purpose, that you work together as one
for the faith of the Good News, 28and that
you are not afraid of those who are against
you. All of this is proof that your enemies
will be destroyed but that you will be saved
by God. 29God gave you the honor not
only of believing in Christ but also of
suffering for him, both of which bring
glory to Christ. 30When I was with you, you
saw the struggles I had, and you hear about
the struggles I am having now. You
yourselves are having the same kind of
struggles.

2 Does your life in Christ give you
strength? Does his love comfort you? Do
we share together in the spirit? Do you have
mercy and kindness? 2If so, make me very
happy by having the same thoughts, sharing
the same love, and having one mind and
purpose. 3When you do things, do not let
selfishness or pride be your guide. Instead,
be humble and give more honor to others
than to yourselves. 4Do not be interested
only in your own life, but be interested in
the lives of others.

Be Unselfish Like Christ

5In your lives you must think and act like
Christ Jesus.

6Christ himself was like God in
    everything.
  But he did not think that being equal
    with God was something to be
    used for his own benefit.
7But he gave up his place with God and
    made himself nothing.
  He was born as a man
  and became like a servant.
8And when he was living as a man,
  he humbled himself and was fully
    obedient to God,
  even when that caused his death—
    death on a cross.
9So God raised him to the highest place.
  God made his name greater than every
    other name
10so that every knee will bow to the name
    of Jesus—
  everyone in heaven, on earth, and
    under the earth.
11And everyone will confess that Jesus
    Christ is Lord
  and bring glory to God the Father.

Be the People God Wants You to Be

12My dear friends, you have always
obeyed God when I was with you. It is even
more important that you obey now while I
am away from you. Keep on working to
complete your salvation with fear and
trembling, 13because God is working in you
to help you want to do and be able to do
what pleases him.

14Do everything without complaining or
arguing. 15Then you will be innocent and
without any wrong. You will be God's
children without fault. But you are living
with crooked and mean people all around
you, among whom you shine like stars in
the dark world. 16You offer the teaching that

gives life. So when Christ comes again, I can be happy because my work was not wasted. I ran the race and won.

[17]Your faith makes you offer your lives as a sacrifice in serving God. If I have to offer my own blood with your sacrifice, I will be happy and full of joy with all of you. [18]You also should be happy and full of joy with me.

Timothy and Epaphroditus

[19]I hope in the Lord Jesus to send Timothy to you soon. I will be happy to learn how you are. [20]I have no one else like Timothy, who truly cares for you. [21]Other people are interested only in their own lives, not in the work of Jesus Christ. [22]You know the kind of person Timothy is. You know he has served with me in telling the Good News, as a son serves his father. [23]I plan to send him to you quickly when I know what will happen to me. [24]I am sure that the Lord will help me to come to you soon.

[25]Epaphroditus, my brother in Christ, works and serves with me in the army of Christ. When I needed help, you sent him to me. I think now that I must send him back to you, [26]because he wants very much to see all of you. He is worried because you heard that he was sick. [27]Yes, he was sick, and nearly died, but God had mercy on him and me too so that I would not have more sadness. [28]I want very much to send him to you so that when you see him you can be happy, and I can stop worrying about you. [29]Welcome him in the Lord with much joy. Give honor to people like him, [30]because he almost died for the work of Christ. He risked his life to give me the help you could not give in your service to me.

The Importance of Christ

3 My brothers and sisters, be full of joy in the Lord. It is no trouble for me to write the same things to you again, and it will help you to be more ready. [2]Watch out for those who do evil, who are like dogs, who demand to cut[n] the body. [3]We are the ones who are truly circumcised. We worship God

3:2 cut The word in Greek is like the word "circumcise," but it means "to cut completely off."

devotion 329

PHILIPPIANS 3:8–9

LOSING EVERYTHING TO GET IT ALL

I know a woman who lost everything except her physical body and her children. Through a series of poor choices, her husband gambled until one day it was all gone. Everything was sold on the courthouse steps except some clothes and a few boxes of personal belongings. The woman packed up her three kids and moved to her mom's. The husband vanished, leaving his wife to face the creditors alone at age thirty-seven, without possessions or a job and covered in debt.

But this woman knew she belonged to God. One day in the middle of her grief, she decided to live like God was more important than anything. She began to thank him for every blessing. She began to look into people's eyes and see their struggles and their kindness. The hand of God had been all around her, but she couldn't see it until everything was taken away. Step by step, God provided for my friend. We all look at her life and see the beauty of belonging to God. She lives free. She rejoices over the gifts of God, but knows they have no value without him. She walks in obedience and gives out the mercy she has been given. Her life is marked by tenderness and compassion.

She's the one who lost everything, but she knows God better than the rest of us. All of my friends secretly marvel at her spiritual transformation. May we, who have all that we need, live like Jesus is all that matters.

through his Spirit, and our pride is in Christ
Jesus. We do not put trust in ourselves or
anything we can do, 4although I might be
able to put trust in myself. If anyone thinks
he has a reason to trust in himself, he should
know that I have greater reason for trusting
in myself. 5I was circumcised eight days after
my birth. I am from the people of Israel and
the tribe of Benjamin. I am a Hebrew, and
my parents were Hebrews. I had a strict view
of the law, which is why I became a Pharisee.
6I was so enthusiastic I tried to hurt the
church. No one could find fault with the
way I obeyed the law of Moses. 7Those
things were important to me, but now I
think they are worth nothing because of
Christ. 8Not only those things, but I think
that all things are worth nothing compared
with the greatness of knowing Christ Jesus
my Lord. Because of him, I have lost all those
things, and now I know they are worthless
trash. This allows me to have Christ 9and to
belong to him. Now I am right with God, not
because I followed the law, but because I
believed in Christ. God uses my faith to
make me right with him. 10I want to know
Christ and the power that raised him from
the dead. I want to share in his sufferings
and become like him in his death. 11Then I
have hope that I myself will be raised from
the dead.

Continuing Toward Our Goal

12I do not mean that I am already as God
wants me to be. I have not yet reached that
goal, but I continue trying to reach it and to
make it mine. Christ wants me to do that,
which is the reason he made me his.
13Brothers and sisters, I know that I have not
yet reached that goal, but there is one thing I
always do. Forgetting the past and straining
toward what is ahead, 14I keep trying to
reach the goal and get the prize for which
God called me through Christ to the life
above.

15All of us who are spiritually mature
should think this way, too. And if there are
things you do not agree with, God will make
them clear to you. 16But we should continue
following the truth we already have.

17Brothers and sisters, all of you should try
to follow my example and to copy those
who live the way we showed you. 18Many
people live like enemies of the cross of
Christ. I have often told you about them, and
it makes me cry to tell you about them now.
19In the end, they will be destroyed. They do
whatever their bodies want, they are proud
of their shameful acts, and they think only
about earthly things. 20But our homeland is
in heaven, and we are waiting for our Savior,
the Lord Jesus Christ, to come from heaven.
21By his power to rule all things, he will
change our humble bodies and make them
like his own glorious body.

What the Christians Are to Do

4 My dear brothers and sisters, I love you
and want to see you. You bring me joy
and make me proud of you, so stand strong
in the Lord as I have told you.

2I ask Euodia and Syntyche to agree in the
Lord. 3And I ask you, my faithful friend, to
help these women. They served with me in
telling the Good News, together with
Clement and others who worked with me,
whose names are written in the book of life.[n]

4Be full of joy in the Lord always. I will
say again, be full of joy.

5Let everyone see that you are gentle and
kind. The Lord is coming soon. 6Do not
worry about anything, but pray and ask God
for everything you need, always giving
thanks. 7And God's peace, which is so great
we cannot understand it, will keep your
hearts and minds in Christ Jesus.

8Brothers and sisters, think about the
things that are good and worthy of praise.
Think about the things that are true and
honorable and right and pure and beautiful
and respected. 9Do what you learned and
received from me, what I told you, and what
you saw me do. And the God who gives
peace will be with you.

Paul Thanks the Christians

10I am very happy in the Lord that you
have shown your care for me again. You
continued to care about me, but there was
no way for you to show it. 11I am not telling
you this because I need anything. I have
learned to be satisfied with the things I
have and with everything that happens.
12I know how to live when I am poor, and

4:3 book of life God's book that has the names of all God's chosen people (Revelation 3:5; 21:27).

devotion 330

PHILIPPIANS 4:6–7

HOW LONG IS YOUR WORRY LIST?

Is your worry list longer than your grocery list? Have you ever wondered why worry comes so easily? Have you ever wondered how many calories worrying burns? Girls, what is it with us? Most of us worry about things that never even happen, but in our minds, we have written a full-length motion picture about them. This kind of thinking creates a stronghold that the enemy can use against us. In 2 Corinthians 10:3-6, when Paul is giving instructions on how to defeat spiritual enemies, he talks about the battleground of the mind. When we start to believe in our minds that we are left alone with nothing but fear and worry as our companions, that is exactly where we begin to lose trust and live with an attitude of defeat.

The first step of obedience and victory is surrendering your fearful mind to the Lord and trusting him with your circumstances. Today, talk heart-to-heart with Jesus: tell him everything that you need, tell him about the worries of your day, tell him that you want him to heal your heart and your mind so there is nothing between the two of you except total love, trust, and devotion. Close your eyes and recall all the joy he has brought into your life and all the encouragement he has given you along the way. Praise him for the heart he has toward you. Yes, there it is, the peace of God has just washed all over you.

I know how to live when I have plenty. I
have learned the secret of being happy at
any time in everything that happens, when
I have enough to eat and when I go hungry,
when I have more than I need and when I do
not have enough. 13I can do all things
through Christ, because he gives me
strength.
14But it was good that you helped me
when I needed it. 15You Philippians
remember when I first preached the Good
News there. When I left Macedonia, you
were the only church that gave me help.
16Several times you sent me things I needed
when I was in Thessalonica. 17Really, it is not
that I want to receive gifts from you, but I
want you to have the good that comes from
giving. 18And now I have everything, and
more. I have all I need, because Epaphroditus
brought your gift to me. It is like a
sweet-smelling sacrifice offered to God, who
accepts that sacrifice and is pleased with it.
19My God will use his wonderful riches in
Christ Jesus to give you everything you need.
20Glory to our God and Father forever and
ever! Amen.
21Greet each of God's people in Christ
Jesus. Those who are with me send greetings
to you. 22All of God's people greet you,
particularly those from the palace of Caesar.
23The grace of the Lord Jesus Christ be
with you all.

Colossians

This is the third and last of Paul's prison letters, and its name comes from the location of the church that received this letter—the city of Colosse.

Person Holding the Pen God Wrote With: The prolific New Testament author, *Paul*

When the Text Was Written: Between 60 and 62 A.D.

Spiritual Posture of the Original Recipients: The Christians in Colosse had been sidetracked by mystical false prophets masquerading as Sunday school teachers. They were turning away from the true message of Jesus as they pondered deep existential thoughts—not unlike modern coffee house muses.

Storyline Synopsis: While Paul had never visited Colosse, the church there had been enthusiastically founded by a man named Epaphras, who had become a Christian after hearing Paul preach (Acts 19:10). But the fickle believers in Colosse were being brainwashed by a bunch of charlatans teaching a dangerous blend of Judaism, philosophy, and mysticism (commonly called Dualism or Gnosticism). The basic tenants of this confused belief system were that the physical world was *bad* and the mystical/spirit world was *good*. Thus, these teachers reasoned that since Jesus came to the earth as a man, consorting with dirty people like lepers, he must not be as holy as God or even angels. When Epaphras overheard these myths, he hightailed it to Rome to ask Paul for help. Once again, God's Spirit moved through Paul's pen to clearly and irrefutably establish the supremacy of Christ!

A Moment Worth Discussing: Colossians is sometimes informally called "Christianity 101" because of its distinct "how-to-function-like-a-follower-of-Jesus" message. The behavioral guidelines in Colossians 3—4:6 offer a "What Would Jesus Do?" answer for nearly any situation! Paul's epitaph for this section sets a gold spiritual standard for daily living: "Be wise in the way you act with people who are not believers, making the most of every opportunity. When you talk, you should always be kind and pleasant so you will be able to answer everyone in the way you should" (Col. 4:5–6). Yet another convicting passage for wordy women!

Interesting (But Likely to Be Overlooked) Character: Paul's friend, *Tychicus*, was one faithful "FedEx" kind of guy. He was entrusted with delivering this letter to the Colossians (Col. 4:7–8), and he also delivered the letter to the Ephesians (Eph. 6:21).

1 From Paul, an apostle of Christ Jesus. I am
an apostle because that is what God
wanted. Also from Timothy, our brother.
2 To the holy and faithful brothers and
sisters in Christ that live in Colossae:
Grace and peace to you from God our
Father.[n]
3 In our prayers for you we always thank
God, the Father of our Lord Jesus Christ,
4 because we have heard about the faith you
have in Christ Jesus and the love you have
for all of God's people. 5 You have this faith
and love because of your hope, and what you
hope for is kept safe for you in heaven. You
learned about this hope when you heard the
message about the truth, the Good News
6 that was told to you. Everywhere in the
world that Good News is bringing blessings
and is growing. This has happened with you,
too, since you heard the Good News and
understood the truth about the grace of God.
7 You learned about God's grace from
Epaphras, whom we love. He works together
with us and is a faithful servant of Christ for
us.[n] 8 He also told us about the love you have
from the Holy Spirit.
9 Because of this, since the day we heard
about you, we have continued praying for
you, asking God that you will know fully
what he wants. We pray that you will also
have great wisdom and understanding in
spiritual things 10 so that you will live the
kind of life that honors and pleases the Lord
in every way. You will produce fruit in every
good work and grow in the knowledge of
God. 11 God will strengthen you with his
own great power so that you will not give up
when troubles come, but you will be patient.
12 And you will joyfully give thanks to the
Father who has made you[n] able to have a
share in all that he has prepared for his
people in the kingdom of light. 13 God has
freed us from the power of darkness, and he
brought us into the kingdom of his dear Son.
14 The Son paid for our sins,[n] and in him we
have forgiveness.

1:2 Father Some Greek copies continue, "and the Lord Jesus Christ." **1:7 for us** Some Greek copies read "for you." **1:12 you** Some Greek copies read "us." **1:14 sins** Some Greek copies continue, "with his blood."

devotion 331

COLOSSIANS 1:9–14

CANCER AND A CAR

They were a typical American couple, married and in their twenties. They both worked to make ends meet until she became pregnant with their first child. Then she went to a routine doctor's appointment with a minor complaint or two and found out she had cancer throughout her whole body. When we heard about their situation, our first question was, "What can we do to help?" Her greatest need was a reliable automobile to get her and the baby safely to doctor's visits. My husband knew of a family who gave away cars to those in need, so he called them. A week later, as she sat in the lobby of a dealership, my husband called her and asked, "Have you picked up the car yet?"

"Oh Stephan, isn't God good? I wake up every day and wonder what God is going to do for me today. I never would have imagined that today God was going to give me a van."

Stephan and I had a wake-up call that day. Would I have the same perspective if I were in her shoes? Would you? She was living a life that honored God—strengthened by him, bearing fruit, patiently waiting for his will to be done, and joyfully giving thanks for all that he was doing for her, even in the midst of trouble. Her life is a demonstration of what it means to live in the light. No matter what you face today, strive to make that your testimony as well.

The Importance of Christ

15No one can see God, but Jesus Christ is
exactly like him. He ranks higher than
everything that has been made. 16Through
his power all things were made—things in
heaven and on earth, things seen and
unseen, all powers, authorities, lords, and
rulers. All things were made through Christ
and for Christ. 17He was there before
anything was made, and all things continue
because of him. 18He is the head of the body,
which is the church. Everything comes from
him. He is the first one who was raised from
the dead. So in all things Jesus has first place.
19God was pleased for all of himself to live in
Christ. 20And through Christ, God has
brought all things back to himself again—
things on earth and things in heaven. God
made peace through the blood of Christ's
death on the cross.

21At one time you were separated from
God. You were his enemies in your minds,
and the evil things you did were against
God. 22But now God has made you his
friends again. He did this through Christ's
death in the body so that he might bring you
into God's presence as people who are holy,
with no wrong, and with nothing of which
God can judge you guilty. 23This will happen
if you continue strong and sure in your faith.
You must not be moved away from the hope
brought to you by the Good News that you
heard. That same Good News has been told
to everyone in the world, and I, Paul, help in
preaching that Good News.

Paul's Work for the Church

24I am happy in my sufferings for you.
There are things that Christ must still suffer
through his body, the church. I am
accepting, in my body, my part of these
things that must be suffered. 25I became a
servant of the church because God gave me a
special work to do that helps you, and that
work is to tell fully the message of God.
26This message is the secret that was hidden
from everyone since the beginning of time,
but now it is made known to God's holy
people. 27God decided to let his people know
this rich and glorious secret which he has for
all people. This secret is Christ himself, who
is in you. He is our only hope for glory. 28So
we continue to preach Christ to each person,
using all wisdom to warn and to teach
everyone, in order to bring each one into
God's presence as a mature person in Christ.
29To do this, I work and struggle, using
Christ's great strength that works so
powerfully in me.

2 I want you to know how hard I work
for you, those in Laodicea, and others
who have never seen me. 2I want them
to be strengthened and joined together
with love so that they may be rich in their
understanding. This leads to their knowing
fully God's secret, that is, Christ himself.
3In him all the treasures of wisdom and
knowledge are safely kept.

4I say this so that no one can fool you by
arguments that seem good, but are false.
5Though I am absent from you in my body,
my heart is with you, and I am happy to see
your good lives and your strong faith in
Christ.

Continue to Live in Christ

6As you received Christ Jesus the Lord, so
continue to live in him. 7Keep your roots
deep in him and have your lives built on
him. Be strong in the faith, just as you were
taught, and always be thankful.

8Be sure that no one leads you away with
false and empty teaching that is only
human, which comes from the ruling spirits
of this world, and not from Christ. 9All of
God lives fully in Christ (even when Christ
was on earth), 10and you have a full and true
life in Christ, who is ruler over all rulers and
powers.

11Also in Christ you had a different kind
of circumcision, a circumcision not done by
hands. It was through Christ's circumcision,
that is, his death, that you were made free
from the power of your sinful self. 12When
you were baptized, you were buried with
Christ, and you were raised up with him
through your faith in God's power that was
shown when he raised Christ from the dead.
13When you were spiritually dead because of
your sins and because you were not free
from the power of your sinful self, God made
you alive with Christ, and he forgave all our
sins. 14He canceled the debt, which listed all
the rules we failed to follow. He took away
that record with its rules and nailed it to the
cross. 15God stripped the spiritual rulers and
powers of their authority. With the cross, he

won the victory and showed the world that
they were powerless.

Don't Follow People's Rules

16So do not let anyone make rules for you
about eating and drinking or about a
religious feast, a New Moon Festival, or a
Sabbath day. 17These things were like a
shadow of what was to come. But what is
true and real has come and is found in
Christ. 18Do not let anyone disqualify you by
making you humiliate yourself and worship
angels. Such people enter into visions, which
fill them with foolish pride because of their
human way of thinking. 19They do not hold
tightly to Christ, the head. It is from him
that all the parts of the body are cared for
and held together. So it grows in the way
God wants it to grow.
20Since you died with Christ and were
made free from the ruling spirits of the
world, why do you act as if you still belong
to this world by following rules like these:
21"Don't handle this," "Don't taste that,"
"Don't even touch that thing"? 22These rules
refer to earthly things that are gone as soon
as they are used. They are only human
commands and teachings. 23They seem to be
wise, but they are only part of a human
religion. They make people pretend not to be
proud and make them punish their bodies,
but they do not really control the evil desires
of the sinful self.

Your New Life in Christ

3 Since you were raised from the dead
with Christ, aim at what is in heaven,
where Christ is sitting at the right hand of
God. 2Think only about the things in
heaven, not the things on earth. 3Your old
sinful self has died, and your new life is kept
with Christ in God. 4Christ is your[n] life, and
when he comes again, you will share in his
glory.
5So put all evil things out of your life:
sexual sinning, doing evil, letting evil
thoughts control you, wanting things that
are evil, and greed. This is really serving a

3:4 your Some Greek copies read "our."

devotion 332

COLOSSIANS 3:1–3

ONE BAD DECISION AWAY FROM A FALL

Sheila grew up in a Christian home, and she had never regretted her upbringing. She was even a little bit proud of her good decision making over the years. So you can imagine how humiliated she was when years later she found herself involved in a life that included a heroine addiction.

These days we hear about heroine and other addictions so often, we sometimes forget that those trapped in such horrific lifestyles are real people who are dearly loved by God. After a while, the sad, scraggly-looking people in anti-drug ads become just another face that we can't really help anyway, so we stop looking. But Jesus has never turned his back on these women—or men—at any point in their struggle. He has neither turned his back on Sheila, nor you, nor your friend who might be lost in this or some other life-draining situation.

I once heard someone say that we're all just one bad decision away from a fall. God's words in Colossians 3 remind us that our sinful selves are dead and that our new lives are in Christ. Cry out to him for yourself, for your friends, and for women you don't even know who are caught in some terrible life where our God is not glorified. We should never forget that whatever sins we have committed can be forgiven, no matter how big they might seem. If you know Christ, your new life is through him. You are clean and new.

false god. 6These things make God angry.[n] 7In your past, evil life you also did these things.

8But now also put these things out of your life: anger, bad temper, doing or saying things to hurt others, and using evil words when you talk. 9Do not lie to each other. You have left your old sinful life and the things you did before. 10You have begun to live the new life, in which you are being made new and are becoming like the One who made you. This new life brings you the true knowledge of God. 11In the new life there is no difference between Greeks and Jews, those who are circumcised and those who are not circumcised, or people who are foreigners, or Scythians.[n] There is no difference between slaves and free people. But Christ is in all believers, and Christ is all that is important.

12God has chosen you and made you his holy people. He loves you. So you should always clothe yourselves with mercy, kindness, humility, gentleness, and patience. 13Bear with each other, and forgive each other. If someone does wrong to you, forgive that person because the Lord forgave you. 14Even more than all this, clothe yourself in love. Love is what holds you all together in perfect unity. 15Let the peace that Christ gives control your thinking, because you were all called together in one body[n] to have peace. Always be thankful. 16Let the teaching of Christ live in you richly. Use all wisdom to teach and instruct each other by singing psalms, hymns, and spiritual songs with thankfulness in your hearts to God. 17Everything you do or say should be done to obey Jesus your Lord. And in all you do, give thanks to God the Father through Jesus.

Your New Life with Other People

18Wives, yield to the authority of your husbands, because this is the right thing to do in the Lord.

19Husbands, love your wives and be gentle with them.

20Children, obey your parents in all things, because this pleases the Lord.

21Fathers, do not nag your children. If you are too hard to please, they may want to stop trying.

22Slaves, obey your masters in all things. Do not obey just when they are watching you, to gain their favor, but serve them honestly, because you respect the Lord. 23In all the work you are doing, work the best you can. Work as if you were doing it for the Lord, not for people. 24Remember that you will receive your reward from the Lord, which he promised to his people. You are serving the Lord Christ. 25But remember that anyone who does wrong will be punished for that wrong, and the Lord treats everyone the same.

4 Masters, give what is good and fair to your slaves. Remember that you have a Master in heaven.

What the Christians Are to Do

2Continue praying, keeping alert, and always thanking God. 3Also pray for us that God will give us an opportunity to tell people his message. Pray that we can preach the secret that God has made known about Christ. This is why I am in prison. 4Pray that I can speak in a way that will make it clear, as I should.

5Be wise in the way you act with people who are not believers, making the most of every opportunity. 6When you talk, you should always be kind and pleasant so you will be able to answer everyone in the way you should.

News About the People with Paul

7Tychicus is my dear brother in Christ and a faithful minister and servant with me in the Lord. He will tell you all the things that are happening to me. 8This is why I am sending him: so you may know how we are[n] and he may encourage you. 9I send him with Onesimus, a faithful and dear brother in Christ, and one of your group. They will tell you all that has happened here.

10Aristarchus, a prisoner with me, and Mark, the cousin of Barnabas, greet you. (I have already told you what to do about Mark. If he comes, welcome him.) 11Jesus, who is called Justus, also greets you. These are the only Jewish believers who work with me for the kingdom of God, and they have been a comfort to me.

3:6 These . . . angry Some Greek copies continue, "against the people who do not obey God."
3:11 Scythians The Scythians were known as very wild and cruel people. **3:15 body** The spiritual body of Christ, meaning the church or his people.
4:8 so . . . are Some Greek copies read "so he may know how you are."

[12]Epaphras, a servant of Jesus Christ, from
your group, also greets you. He always prays
for you that you will grow to be spiritually
mature and have everything God wants for
you. [13]I know he has worked hard for you
and the people in Laodicea and in
Hierapolis. [14]Demas and our dear friend
Luke, the doctor, greet you.

[15]Greet the brothers and sisters in
Laodicea. And greet Nympha and the church
that meets in her house. [16]After this letter is
read to you, be sure it is also read to the
church in Laodicea. And you read the letter
that I wrote to Laodicea. [17]Tell Archippus, "Be
sure to finish the work the Lord gave you."

[18]I, Paul, greet you and write this with my
own hand. Remember me in prison. Grace be
with you.

1 Thessalonians

Refers to the church in the city of Thessalonica *that received this letter*

Person Holding the Pen God Wrote With: *Paul*

When the Text Was Written: 51 A.D., which most likely makes it the second biblical writing of Paul

Spiritual Posture of the Original Recipients: Thessalonica was a church filled with young Christians. Some were enthusiastic about their faith, but others were justifying their laziness because of an immature understanding about the return of Christ.

Storyline Synopsis: Thessalonica was a busy metropolitan city in Macedonia where Paul, Timothy, and Silas had ministered on a trip (Acts 16—18:22). Many were converted to Christ during Paul's synagogue-based teaching there, including Jews, Greeks, and some wealthy women (17:4). But Paul's message about Jesus being the Messiah made a lot of the orthodox Jews angry, so they staged a riot and ran him out of town (17:5–10). Timothy and Silas stayed behind, hooking up with Paul much later in Corinth (18:5). Paul wrote this letter after hearing Timothy's report regarding how the ministry was continuing in Thessalonica. His message was both personal and practical, warmly reminding the Thessalonians about the beginning of their walk of faith (chapters 1—3), as well as instructing them how to "walk taller" in Christian maturity (chapters 4—5).

A Moment Worth Discussing: 1 Thessalonians 2:8 records some of the sweetest words that ever came from Paul's pen: "Because we loved you, we were happy to share not only God's Good News with you, but even our own lives. You had become so dear to us!" And the verses prior to this section (1 Thess. 2:3–7) appropriately frame his affection by explaining that he and Timothy and Silas weren't trying to ingratiate themselves or manipulate people's emotions—nor were they trying to win a popularity contest. Their hearts were tender toward those they were ministering to because they were seeking to please God! It's compelling to ponder whether you "dance" before the court of other's approval more than you "dance" purely for God's applause.

Interesting (But Likely to Be Overlooked) Character: *Silvanus* is another name for "Silas" (1 Thess. 1:1), who was one of Paul's mission trip buddies (Acts 15—18), as well as a sort of secretary for Peter (1 Pet. 5:12).

1 From Paul, Silas, and Timothy.

To the church in Thessalonica, the church in God the Father and the Lord Jesus Christ:

Grace and peace to you.

The Faith of the Thessalonians

[2]We always thank God for all of you and mention you when we pray. [3]We continually recall before God our Father the things you have done because of your faith and the work you have done because of your love. And we thank him that you continue to be strong because of your hope in our Lord Jesus Christ.

[4]Brothers and sisters, God loves you, and we know he has chosen you, [5]because the Good News we brought to you came not only with words, but with power, with the Holy Spirit, and with sure knowledge that it is true. Also you know how we lived when we were with you in order to help you. [6]And you became like us and like the Lord. You suffered much, but still you accepted the teaching with the joy that comes from the Holy Spirit. [7]So you became an example to all the believers in Macedonia and Southern Greece. [8]And the Lord's teaching spread from you not only into Macedonia and Southern Greece, but now your faith in God has become known everywhere. So we do not need to say anything about it. [9]People everywhere are telling about the way you accepted us when we were there with you. They tell how you stopped worshiping idols and began serving the living and true God. [10]And you wait for God's Son, whom God raised from the dead, to come from heaven. He is Jesus, who saves us from God's angry judgment that is sure to come.

Paul's Work in Thessalonica

2 Brothers and sisters, you know our visit to you was not a failure. [2]Before we came to you, we suffered in Philippi. People there insulted us, as you know, and many people were against us. But our God helped us to be brave and to tell you his Good News. [3]Our appeal does not come from lies or wrong reasons, nor were we trying to trick you. [4]But we speak the Good News because God tested us and trusted us to do it. When we speak, we are not trying to please people, but God, who tests our hearts. [5]You know that we never tried to influence you by saying nice things about you. We were not trying to get your money; we had no selfishness to hide from you. God knows that this is true. [6]We were not looking for human praise, from you or anyone else, [7]even though as apostles of Christ we could have used our authority over you.

But we were very gentle with you,[n] like a mother caring for her little children. [8]Because we loved you, we were happy to share not only God's Good News with you, but even our own lives. You had become so dear to us! [9]Brothers and sisters, I know you remember our hard work and difficulties. We worked night and day so we would not burden any of you while we preached God's Good News to you.

[10]When we were with you, we lived in a holy and honest way, without fault. You know this is true, and so does God. [11]You know that we treated each of you as a father treats his own children. [12]We encouraged you, we urged you, and we insisted that you live good lives for God, who calls you to his glorious kingdom.

[13]Also, we always thank God because when you heard his message from us, you accepted it as the word of God, not the words of humans. And it really is God's message which works in you who believe. [14]Brothers and sisters, your experiences have been like those of God's churches in Christ that are in Judea.[n] You suffered from the people of your own country, as they suffered from the Jews [15]who killed both the Lord Jesus and the prophets and forced us to leave that country. They do not please God and are against all people. [16]They try to stop us from teaching those who are not Jews so they may be saved. By doing this, they are increasing their sins to the limit. The anger of God has come to them at last.

Paul Wants to Visit Them Again

[17]Brothers and sisters, though we were separated from you for a short time, our thoughts were still with you. We wanted

2:7 But . . . you Some Greek copies read "But we were like infants among you."
2:14 Judea The Jewish land where Jesus lived and taught and where the church first began.

devotion 333

1 THESSALONIANS 2:6

SPINNING PLATES AND CATCHING FLAMING SWORDS

Can you imagine what it would be like to be free of the need to please all the people around you and just please God? As women we can so easily find ourselves addicted to acceptance. I know it has certainly been a battle for me. Somewhere along the way, I decided that making people happy gave me energy. And so I began to order my life around caring for the ones that I love and waiting for their recognition and approval—anything to keep the troops contented.

Guess what I found out? You can never really make anybody happy. They decide in their own little hearts if they will pursue a lifetime of peace and cultivate a spirit of joy. It takes a long time to learn that. Spinning too many plates takes its toll, and trying to catch flaming swords ends up burning and wounding. A big part of me went away through the years in the effort to please.

If only I had come to apply this truth sooner. Paul said he didn't look for human praise. Instead, the only thing that mattered to him was obeying God. When we grow up in our faith, we eventually learn the value of these principles. I want you to have a twenty-year head start on me. Obey God. If it makes some people happy, then great. If they pout and turn away, then too bad for them. Train your ears to hear God's praise and learn to move toward his voice.

very much to see you and tried hard to do so.
18We wanted to come to you. I, Paul, tried to
come more than once, but Satan stopped us.
19You are our hope, our joy, and the crown
we will take pride in when our Lord Jesus
Christ comes. 20Truly you are our glory and
our joy.

3 When we could not wait any longer, we
decided it was best to stay in Athens
alone 2and send Timothy to you. Timothy,
our brother, works with us for God and helps
us tell people the Good News about Christ.
We sent him to strengthen and encourage
you in your faith 3so none of you would be
upset by these troubles. You yourselves
know that we must face these troubles.
4Even when we were with you, we told you
we all would have to suffer, and you know it
has happened. 5Because of this, when I could
wait no longer, I sent Timothy to you so I
could learn about your faith. I was afraid the
devil had tempted you, and perhaps our hard
work would have been wasted.

6But Timothy now has come back to us
from you and has brought us good news
about your faith and love. He told us that
you always remember us in a good way and
that you want to see us just as much as we
want to see you. 7So, brothers and sisters,
while we have much trouble and suffering,
we are encouraged about you because of
your faith. 8Our life is really full if you stand
strong in the Lord. 9We have so much joy
before our God because of you. We cannot
thank him enough for all the joy we feel.
10Night and day we continue praying with
all our heart that we can see you again and
give you all the things you need to make
your faith strong.

11Now may our God and Father himself
and our Lord Jesus prepare the way for us to
come to you. 12May the Lord make your love
grow more and multiply for each other and
for all people so that you will love others as
we love you. 13May your hearts be made
strong so that you will be holy and without

fault before our God and Father when our
Lord Jesus comes with all his holy ones.

A Life that Pleases God

4 Brothers and sisters, we taught you how
to live in a way that will please God, and
you are living that way. Now we ask and
encourage you in the Lord Jesus to live that
way even more. 2 You know what we told
you to do by the authority of the Lord Jesus.
3 God wants you to be holy and to stay away
from sexual sins. 4 He wants each of you to
learn to control your own body[n] in a way
that is holy and honorable. 5 Don't use your
body for sexual sin like the people who do
not know God. 6 Also, do not wrong or cheat
another Christian in this way. The Lord will
punish people who do those things as we
have already told you and warned you. 7 God
called us to be holy and does not want us to
live in sin. 8 So the person who refuses to
obey this teaching is disobeying God, not
simply a human teaching. And God is the
One who gives us his Holy Spirit.
9 We do not need to write you about
having love for your Christian family,
because God has already taught you to love
each other. 10 And truly you do love the
Christians in all of Macedonia. Brothers and
sisters, now we encourage you to love them
even more.
11 Do all you can to live a peaceful life.
Take care of your own business, and do your
own work as we have already told you. 12 If
you do, then people who are not believers
will respect you, and you will not have to
depend on others for what you need.

The Lord's Coming

13 Brothers and sisters, we want you to
know about those Christians who have died
so you will not be sad, as others who have no
hope. 14 We believe that Jesus died and that
he rose again. So, because of him, God will
raise with Jesus those who have died.
15 What we tell you now is the Lord's own
message. We who are living when the Lord
comes again will not go before those who
have already died. 16 The Lord himself will
come down from heaven with a loud
command, with the voice of the archangel,[n]
and with the trumpet call of God. And those
who have died believing in Christ will rise
first. 17 After that, we who are still alive will
be gathered up with them in the clouds to
meet the Lord in the air. And we will be with
the Lord forever. 18 So encourage each other
with these words.

Be Ready for the Lord's Coming

5 Now, brothers and sisters, we do not need
to write you about times and dates. 2 You
know very well that the day the Lord comes
again will be a surprise, like a thief that
comes in the night. 3 While people are
saying, "We have peace and we are safe,"
they will be destroyed quickly. It is like pains
that come quickly to a woman having a
baby. Those people will not escape. 4 But you,
brothers and sisters, are not living in
darkness, and so that day will not surprise
you like a thief. 5 You are all people who
belong to the light and to the day. We do not
belong to the night or to darkness. 6 So we
should not be like other people who are
sleeping, but we should be alert and have
self-control. 7 Those who sleep, sleep at night.
Those who get drunk, get drunk at night.
8 But we belong to the day, so we should
control ourselves. We should wear faith and
love to protect us, and the hope of salvation
should be our helmet. 9 God did not choose
us to suffer his anger but to have salvation
through our Lord Jesus Christ. 10 Jesus died
for us so that we can live together with him,
whether we are alive or dead when he
comes. 11 So encourage each other and give
each other strength, just as you are doing
now.

Final Instructions and Greetings

12 Now, brothers and sisters, we ask you to
appreciate those who work hard among you,
who lead you in the Lord and teach you.
13 Respect them with a very special love
because of the work they do.
Live in peace with each other. 14 We ask
you, brothers and sisters, to warn those who
do not work. Encourage the people who are
afraid. Help those who are weak. Be patient
with everyone. 15 Be sure that no one pays
back wrong for wrong, but always try to do
what is good for each other and for all
people.

4:4 learn . . . body This might also mean "learn to live with your own wife."
4:16 archangel The leader among God's angels or messengers.

devotion 334

1 THESSALONIANS 5:16–18

IN THE GOOD, THE BAD, AND EVEN THE UGLY

When God called my husband into full-time ministry as a senior pastor in Tennessee, we were beyond excited to see what the Lord had for us in this new season of our lives. On a return trip to Florida, my husband wanted to gather at the beach to pray and seek God. So off we went with a friend to beautiful Delray Beach to sit in the white sands, hold hands, and lift up our hearts together in prayer. Almost as soon as we started to pray, Rob opened the Word for the Lord to reveal 1 Thessalonians 5:16-18. As we studied it together, it was obvious that this was wisdom from the Holy Spirit to encourage us in this venture as we set out to start the church.

Over the last four years, we have held onto these verses during the adverse times and during the amazing, joyful times. They have ministered truth to us and to all those who have become part of the body of Christ in our fold. We like to paraphrase these verses this way: "Be joyful always, even when you do not feel like it. Pray continually, never stop, and keep seeking God's heart and direction. Thank him in the good, the bad, and even the ugly. Give thanks no matter what happens." God desires to see these attributes in his children. What a great motto to build a church foundation upon, and what a great motto to strengthen your Christian walk.

16Always be joyful. 17Pray continually,
18and give thanks whatever happens. That is
what God wants for you in Christ Jesus.
19Do not hold back the work of the Holy
Spirit. 20Do not treat prophecy as if it were
unimportant. 21But test everything. Keep
what is good, 22and stay away from
everything that is evil.
23Now may God himself, the God of peace,
make you pure, belonging only to him. May
your whole self—spirit, soul, and body—be
kept safe and without fault when our Lord
Jesus Christ comes. 24You can trust the One
who calls you to do that for you.
25Brothers and sisters, pray for us.
26Give each other a holy kiss when you
meet. 27I tell you by the authority of the Lord
to read this letter to all the believers.
28The grace of our Lord Jesus Christ be
with you.

2 Thessalonians

This letter is the follow-up to Paul's first message to the church at Thessalonica.

Person Holding the Pen God Wrote With: *Paul*

When the Text Was Written: Between 51 and 52 A.D., just a few months after 1 Thessalonians was written

Spiritual Posture of the Original Recipients: The church at Thessalonica had grown, but the Christians there were facing increased discrimination and were becoming disoriented by unbiblical teachers.

Storyline Synopsis: The Thessalonians had increased in faith and number, but they were beginning to struggle with persecution from outside their fellowship, bad teaching from inside their fellowship, and slothful behavior from individuals who were convinced that Christ's imminent return meant they could slack off! Those combined issues were beginning to strain the seams of the church fabric. So Paul wrote this second letter to encourage the Thessalonians about the benefit of suffering (chapter 1), to clarify the "day of the Lord" doctrine that was causing so much uncertainty (chapter 2), and to spur the lazy members on to better behavior (chapter 3). Second Thessalonians is another of Paul's "pastoral" epistles, and it further reveals his deep love and concern for the people God placed in his sphere of influence.

A Moment Worth Discussing: Church discipline is a very sticky issue, yet Paul doesn't hesitate to tackle it when it comes to the sluggards lolling around in the pews (2 Thess. 3:1–15). It is interesting to compare this passage with similar themes in other New Testament books (Matt. 18:15–20; 1 Cor. 5:1–13; Gal. 6:1–5) and then talk about what accountability should look like among Christians. How can we best confront a fellow believer's sin in an honest, yet humble way that helps restore them to God?

Interesting (But Likely to Be Overlooked) Character: In his attempt to unravel some of the mystery surrounding the end times—a subject that was not only *consuming* but also *confusing* the Thessalonians—Paul used the term "*Man of Evil*" as a pseudonym for the Antichrist (2 Thess. 2:6, 8–9). The apostle doesn't seem too worried about ruining the end of the story as he informs his friends that Satan's minion is going to be pulverized into oblivion with one holy puff from Jesus!

1 From Paul, Silas, and Timothy.
To the church in Thessalonica in God
our Father and the Lord Jesus Christ:
2 Grace and peace to you from God the
Father and the Lord Jesus Christ.

Paul Talks About God's Judgment

3 We must always thank God for you,
brothers and sisters. This is only right,
because your faith is growing more and
more, and the love that every one of you has
for each other is increasing. 4 So we brag
about you to the other churches of God. We
tell them about the way you continue to be
strong and have faith even though you are
being treated badly and are suffering many
troubles.
5 This is proof that God is right in his
judgment. He wants you to be counted
worthy of his kingdom for which you are
suffering. 6 God will do what is right. He will
give trouble to those who trouble you. 7 And
he will give rest to you who are troubled and
to us also when the Lord Jesus appears with
burning fire from heaven with his powerful
angels. 8 Then he will punish those who do
not know God and who do not obey the
Good News about our Lord Jesus Christ.
9 Those people will be punished with a
destruction that continues forever. They will
be kept away from the Lord and from his
great power. 10 This will happen on the day
when the Lord Jesus comes to receive glory
because of his holy people. And all the
people who have believed will be amazed at
Jesus. You will be in that group, because you
believed what we told you.
11 That is why we always pray for you,
asking our God to help you live the kind of
life he called you to live. We pray that with
his power God will help you do the good
things you want and perform the works that
come from your faith. 12 We pray all this so
that the name of our Lord Jesus Christ will
have glory in you, and you will have glory in
him. That glory comes from the grace of our
God and the Lord Jesus Christ.

Evil Things Will Happen

2 Brothers and sisters, we have something
to say about the coming of our Lord Jesus
Christ and the time when we will meet
together with him. 2 Do not become easily
upset in your thinking or afraid if you hear
that the day of the Lord has already come.
Someone may have said this in a prophecy
or in a message or in a letter as if it came
from us. 3 Do not let anyone fool you in any
way. That day of the Lord will not come
until the turning away[n] from God happens
and the Man of Evil,[n] who is on his way to
hell, appears. 4 He will be against and put
himself above any so-called god or anything
that people worship. And that Man of Evil
will even go into God's Temple and sit there
and say that he is God.
5 I told you when I was with you that all
this would happen. Do you not remember?
6 And now you know what is stopping that
Man of Evil so he will appear at the right
time. 7 The secret power of evil is already
working in the world, but there is one who is
stopping that power. And he will continue to
stop it until he is taken out of the way. 8 Then
that Man of Evil will appear, and the Lord
Jesus will kill him with the breath that comes
from his mouth and will destroy him with
the glory of his coming. 9 The Man of Evil will
come by the power of Satan. He will have
great power, and he will do many different
false miracles, signs, and wonders. 10 He will
use every kind of evil to trick those who are
lost. They will die, because they refused to
love the truth. (If they loved the truth, they
would be saved.) 11 For this reason God sends
them something powerful that leads them
away from the truth so they will believe a lie.
12 So all those will be judged guilty who did
not believe the truth, but enjoyed doing evil.

You Are Chosen for Salvation

13 Brothers and sisters, whom the Lord
loves, God chose you from the beginning[n] to
be saved. So we must always thank God for
you. You are saved by the Spirit that makes
you holy and by your faith in the truth.
14 God used the Good News that we preached
to call you to be saved so you can share in
the glory of our Lord Jesus Christ. 15 So,
brothers and sisters, stand strong and
continue to believe the teachings we gave
you in our speaking and in our letter.
16-17 May our Lord Jesus Christ himself and
God our Father encourage you and

2:3 turning away Or "the rebellion." **2:3 Man of Evil** Some Greek copies read "Man of Sin."
2:13 God . . . beginning Some Greek copies read "God chose you as the firstfruits of the harvest."

strengthen you in every good thing you do and say. God loved us, and through his grace he gave us a good hope and encouragement that continues forever.

Pray for Us

3 And now, brothers and sisters, pray for us that the Lord's teaching will continue to spread quickly and that people will give honor to that teaching, just as happened with you. 2And pray that we will be protected from stubborn and evil people, because not all people believe.

3But the Lord is faithful and will give you strength and will protect you from the Evil One. 4The Lord makes us feel sure that you are doing and will continue to do the things we told you. 5May the Lord lead your hearts into God's love and Christ's patience.

The Duty to Work

6Brothers and sisters, by the authority of our Lord Jesus Christ we command you to stay away from any believer who refuses to work and does not follow the teaching we gave you. 7You yourselves know that you should live as we live. We were not lazy when we were with you. 8And when we ate another person's food, we always paid for it. We worked very hard night and day so we would not be an expense to any of you. 9We had the right to ask you to help us, but we worked to take care of ourselves so we would be an example for you to follow. 10When we were with you, we gave you this rule: "Anyone who refuses to work should not eat."

11We hear that some people in your group refuse to work. They do nothing but busy themselves in other people's lives. 12We command those people and beg them in the Lord Jesus Christ to work quietly and earn their own food. 13But you, brothers and sisters, never become tired of doing good.

14If some people do not obey what we tell you in this letter, then take note of them. Have nothing to do with them so they will feel ashamed. 15But do not treat them as enemies. Warn them as fellow believers.

Final Words

16Now may the Lord of peace give you peace at all times and in every way. The Lord be with all of you.

17I, Paul, end this letter now in my own handwriting. All my letters have this to show they are from me. This is the way I write.

18The grace of our Lord Jesus Christ be with you all.

devotion 335

2 THESSALONIANS 3:16

THE DIFFERENCE BETWEEN PEACE AND QUIET

When you have a house full of children, you sometimes feel like peace is a fleeting thought. My husband is the oldest of seven, and I always wanted a large family like his. What you don't realize when your children are small is that they bring home friends as they get older, and your carefully planned number of children can multiply before your eyes. I've prayed for and even begged God for peace in my home on a regular basis. It just seems as though the dishes are unending, the laundry is never done, and the children get louder and louder all the time. "Peaceful" is not a word I would use to describe my home.

After twenty years of being a wife and mother, I have learned that peace and quiet are two different things. Peace comes from deep within your soul, but quiet is the sound level in your environment. Peace is feeling God's love and knowing that he's in control.

I recently sat in my bedroom and listened to my eighteen-year-old son yell and scream for his favorite football team with ten of his friends. I realized that I will miss these sounds when he goes off to college. I was thankful for the chaos of children in my life, and that gave me such peace. Even if your quiet moments are few, God can surround you with his peace at *all* times . . . ask him for his peace today.

1 Timothy

The first of three "pastoral" letters

Person Holding the Pen God Wrote With: *Paul,* who was a spiritual big brother to Timothy

When the Text Was Written: Probably between 62 and 64 A.D.

Spiritual Posture of the Original Recipients: The New Testament churches were struggling with issues such as proper worship and how church leadership should be organized.

Storyline Synopsis: Paul wrote this letter to Timothy after he left him behind in Ephesus to continue the work Paul had started there. The theme of this epistle is one of a mentor handing the baton to his protégé. Paul planted the church at Ephesus, and he charges Timothy in this letter to take care of it—to make sure the Good News is taught properly, to guard against false teachers, and to establish appropriate roles within the church for men and women.

A Moment Worth Discussing: Near the beginning of the letter (1 Tim. 1:12–17), Paul acknowledges that Christ came into the world to save sinners, of which he was a whopper! Paul doesn't distance himself from sin, either. In verse 15, he says that he *is* the worst sinner—not that he *was* the worst sinner. Paul's humility highlights the posture all Christians should adopt: our own sin should always loom largest in our eyes. This brings to mind Jesus' advice in Matthew about recognizing the logs in our own eyes before noticing a speck in our neighbor's eye (Matt. 7:1–5).

Interesting (But Likely to Be Overlooked) Characters: Although *widows* weren't noteworthy in this culture, Paul gives Timothy detailed instructions regarding their care (1 Tim. 5:3–16). Evidently, public assistance wasn't necessary in the early church because God's people learned how to give generously to help those in need.

1 From Paul, an apostle of Christ Jesus, by
the command of God our Savior and
Christ Jesus our hope.
[2]To Timothy, a true child to me because
you believe:
Grace, mercy, and peace from God the
Father and Christ Jesus our Lord.

Warning Against False Teaching

[3]I asked you to stay longer in Ephesus
when I went into Macedonia so you could
command some people there to stop
teaching false things. [4]Tell them not to
spend their time on stories that are not true
and on long lists of names in family
histories. These things only bring
arguments; they do not help God's work,
which is done in faith. [5]The purpose of this
command is for people to have love, a love
that comes from a pure heart and a good
conscience and a true faith. [6]Some people
have missed these things and turned to
useless talk. [7]They want to be teachers of the
law, but they do not understand either what
they are talking about or what they are sure
about.
[8]But we know that the law is good if
someone uses it lawfully. [9]We also know
that the law is not made for good people but
for those who are against the law and for
those who refuse to follow it. It is for people
who are against God and are sinful, who are
unholy and ungodly, who kill their fathers
and mothers, who murder, [10]who take part
in sexual sins, who have sexual relations
with people of the same sex, who sell slaves,
who tell lies, who speak falsely, and who do
anything against the true teaching of God.
[11]That teaching is part of the Good News of
the blessed God that he gave me to tell.

Thanks for God's Mercy

[12]I thank Christ Jesus our Lord, who gave
me strength, because he trusted me and gave
me this work of serving him. [13]In the past I
spoke against Christ and persecuted him and

devotion 336

1 TIMOTHY 1:15

ARE YOU THIS WOMAN?

Forgiveness is the greatest gift God has given us because it restores us to a right relationship with him. God offers us his love and acceptance through forgiveness, and he calls us his friend. Jeremiah 31:34 tells us, "I will forgive them for the wicked things they did, and I will not remember their sins anymore." This is complete and total forgiveness. And there is only one way to receive it—by acknowledging our sins and accepting that Jesus died on the cross for them.

Look up the story of the woman caught in adultery in John 8:1-11. The Pharisees brought her before Jesus and reminded him that the law condemned her to death for her actions. They were trying to trick Jesus into saying something that was against the law, something they could hold against him in their smear campaign. Jesus didn't answer at first, and then he said, "Anyone here who has never sinned can throw the first stone at her" (John 8:7). One by one, her accusers dropped their stones and walked away. Jesus looked at her and told her, "I also don't judge you guilty. You may go now, but don't sin anymore" (8:11).

At some time in each of our lives, we have been this woman who was brought before Jesus. We have all sinned and deserve death according to the law, but Jesus came to forgive our sins and save us from eternal death. Praise God today for the pardon and freedom from sin Christ offers!

did all kinds of things to hurt him. But God
showed me mercy, because I did not know
what I was doing. I did not believe. [14]But the
grace of our Lord was fully given to me, and
with that grace came the faith and love that
are in Christ Jesus.

[15]What I say is true, and you should fully
accept it: Christ Jesus came into the world to
save sinners, of whom I am the worst. [16]But I
was given mercy so that in me, the worst of
all sinners, Christ Jesus could show that he
has patience without limit. His patience
with me made me an example for those who
would believe in him and have life forever.
[17]To the King that rules forever, who will
never die, who cannot be seen, the only God,
be honor and glory forever and ever. Amen.

[18]Timothy, my child, I am giving you a
command that agrees with the prophecies
that were given about you in the past. I tell
you this so you can follow them and fight
the good fight. [19]Continue to have faith and
do what you know is right. Some people
have rejected this, and their faith has been
shipwrecked. [20]Hymenaeus and Alexander
have done that, and I have given them to
Satan so they will learn not to speak against
God.

Some Rules for Men and Women

2 First, I tell you to pray for all people,
asking God for what they need and being
thankful to him. [2]Pray for rulers and for all
who have authority so that we can have
quiet and peaceful lives full of worship and
respect for God. [3]This is good, and it pleases
God our Savior, [4]who wants all people to be
saved and to know the truth. [5]There is one
God and one mediator so that human beings
can reach God. That way is through Christ
Jesus, who is himself human. [6]He gave
himself as a payment to free all people. He is
proof that came at the right time. [7]That is
why I was chosen to tell the Good News and
to be an apostle. (I am telling the truth; I am
not lying.) I was chosen to teach those who
are not Jews to believe and to know the
truth.

[8]So, I want the men everywhere to pray,
lifting up their hands in a holy manner,
without anger and arguments.

[9]Also, women should wear proper clothes
that show respect and self-control, not using
braided hair or gold or pearls or expensive
clothes. [10]Instead, they should do good
deeds, which is right for women who say
they worship God.

[11]Let a woman learn by listening quietly
and being ready to cooperate in everything.
[12]But I do not allow a woman to teach or to
have authority over a man, but to listen
quietly, [13]because Adam was formed first
and then Eve. [14]And Adam was not tricked,
but the woman was tricked and became a
sinner. [15]But she will be saved through
having children if she continues in faith,
love, and holiness, with self-control.

Elders in the Church

3 What I say is true: Anyone wanting to
become an overseer desires a good work.
[2]An overseer must not give people a reason
to criticize him, and he must have only one
wife. He must be self-controlled, wise,
respected by others, ready to welcome
guests, and able to teach. [3]He must not drink
too much wine or like to fight, but rather be
gentle and peaceable, not loving money. [4]He
must be a good family leader, having
children who cooperate with full respect. [5](If
someone does not know how to lead the
family, how can that person take care of
God's church?) [6]But an elder must not be a
new believer, or he might be too proud of
himself and be judged guilty just as the devil
was. [7]An elder must also have the respect of
people who are not in the church so he will
not be criticized by others and caught in the
devil's trap.

Deacons in the Church

[8]In the same way, deacons must be
respected by others, not saying things they
do not mean. They must not drink too much
wine or try to get rich by cheating others.
[9]With a clear conscience they must follow
the secret of the faith that God made known
to us. [10]Test them first. Then let them serve
as deacons if you find nothing wrong in
them. [11]In the same way, women[n] must be
respected by others. They must not speak
evil of others. They must be self-controlled

3:11 women This might mean the wives of the deacons, or it might mean women who serve in the same way as deacons.

devotion 337

1 TIMOTHY 2:5–6

POSITION THEOLOGY

How about a little Theology 101? This lesson is called "The Theology of Position." The theology of position says this: you and I deserve punishment. We were made to glorify God, but when we chose on our own, we didn't do so hot. We came up short, sinned, made dumb mistakes, and basically failed miserably. Our humanity won more battles than obedience. God's holiness required punishment for all the failure.

But God is also perfect love. He dreamed you up before you were born and has been eternally in love with you. His love is a wild, passionate, pursuing love. He doesn't give up or go away or call it quits. He sent his Son to receive all the punishment on your behalf. I don't know if you've thought about it lately, but you don't send your only son for someone you just like a little. You send your only son for the ones you can't bear to spend eternity without. When Jesus died, God said all the punishment was paid. Done. Jesus is the way.

When a woman says, "I believe that Jesus paid for my punishment. I believe that he has saved me from the penalty I deserved," then that woman becomes a Christ-believer, a Christian. And when you believe that God loved you that much, when you believe that Jesus is the only way to be free, then God stoops down in his great big love and gives you the same position as his Son, Jesus.

and trustworthy in everything. 12Deacons
must have only one wife and be good leaders
of their children and their own families.
13Those who serve well as deacons are
making an honorable place for themselves,
and they will be very bold in their faith in
Christ Jesus.

The Secret of Our Life

14Although I hope I can come to you soon,
I am writing these things to you now.
15Then, even if I am delayed, you will know
how to live in the family of God. That family
is the church of the living God, the support
and foundation of the truth. 16Without
doubt, the secret of our life of worship is
great:

He[n] was shown to us in a human body,
proved right in spirit,
and seen by angels.
He was proclaimed to the nations,
believed in by the world,
and taken up in glory.

A Warning About False Teachers

4 Now the Holy Spirit clearly says that in
the later times some people will stop
believing the faith. They will follow spirits
that lie and teachings of demons. 2Such
teachings come from the false words of
liars whose consciences are destroyed as if
by a hot iron. 3They forbid people to marry
and tell them not to eat certain foods which
God created to be eaten with thanks by
people who believe and know the truth.
4Everything God made is good, and nothing
should be refused if it is accepted with
thanks, 5because it is made holy by what
God has said and by prayer.

Be a Good Servant of Christ

6By telling these things to the brothers
and sisters, you will be a good servant of
Christ Jesus. You will be made strong by the
words of the faith and the good teaching
which you have been following. 7But do not
follow foolish stories that disagree with

3:16 He Some Greek copies read "God."

God's truth, but train yourself to serve God.
8 Training your body helps you in some
ways, but serving God helps you in every
way by bringing you blessings in this life
and in the future life, too. 9 What I say is
true, and you should fully accept it. 10 This is
why we work and struggle:[n] We hope in the
living God who is the Savior of all people,
especially of those who believe.
11 Command and teach these things. 12 Do
not let anyone treat you as if you are
unimportant because you are young.
Instead, be an example to the believers with
your words, your actions, your love, your
faith, and your pure life. 13 Until I come,
continue to read the Scriptures to the
people, strengthen them, and teach them.
14 Use the gift you have, which was given to
you through prophecy when the group of
elders laid their hands on[n] you. 15 Continue
to do those things; give your life to doing
them so your progress may be seen by
everyone. 16 Be careful in your life and in
your teaching. If you continue to live and
teach rightly, you will save both yourself and
those who listen to you.

Rules for Living with Others

5 Do not speak angrily to an older man,
but plead with him as if he were your
father. Treat younger men like brothers,
2 older women like mothers, and younger
women like sisters. Always treat them in a
pure way.
3 Take care of widows who are truly
widows. 4 But if a widow has children or
grandchildren, let them first learn to do their
duty to their own family and to repay their
parents or grandparents. That pleases God.
5 The true widow, who is all alone, puts her
hope in God and continues to pray night and
day for God's help. 6 But the widow who uses
her life to please herself is really dead while
she is alive. 7 Tell the believers to do these
things so that no one can criticize them.
8 Whoever does not care for his own
relatives, especially his own family
members, has turned against the faith and is
worse than someone who does not believe in
God.
9 To be on the list of widows, a woman
must be at least sixty years old. She must
have been faithful to her husband. 10 She
must be known for her good works—works
such as raising her children, welcoming
strangers, washing the feet of God's people,
helping those in trouble, and giving her life
to do all kinds of good deeds.
11 But do not put younger widows on that
list. After they give themselves to Christ,
they are pulled away from him by their
physical desires, and then they want to
marry again. 12 They will be judged for not
doing what they first promised to do.
13 Besides that, they learn to waste their time,
going from house to house. And they not
only waste their time but also begin to
gossip and busy themselves with other
people's lives, saying things they should not
say. 14 So I want the younger widows to
marry, have children, and manage their
homes. Then no enemy will have any reason
to criticize them. 15 But some have already
turned away to follow Satan.
16 If any woman who is a believer has
widows in her family, she should care for
them herself. The church should not have to
care for them. Then it will be able to take
care of those who are truly widows.
17 The elders who lead the church well
should receive double honor, especially
those who work hard by speaking and
teaching, 18 because the Scripture says:
"When an ox is working in the grain, do not
cover its mouth to keep it from eating,"[n] and
"A worker should be given his pay."[n]
19 Do not listen to someone who accuses
an elder, without two or three witnesses.
20 Tell those who continue sinning that they
are wrong. Do this in front of the whole
church so that the others will have a
warning.
21 Before God and Christ Jesus and the
chosen angels, I command you to do these
things without showing favor of any kind to
anyone.
22 Think carefully before you lay your
hands on[n] anyone, and don't share in the sins
of others. Keep yourself pure.
23 Stop drinking only water, but drink a
little wine to help your stomach and your
frequent sicknesses.

4:10 struggle Some Greek copies read "suffer." **4:14 laid their hands on** The laying on of hands had many purposes, including the giving of a blessing, power, or authority. **5:18 "When . . . eating."** Quotation from Deuteronomy 25:4. **5:18 "A worker . . . pay."** Quotation from Luke 10:7. **5:22 lay your hands on** The laying on of hands had many purposes, including the giving of a blessing, power, or authority.

[24]The sins of some people are easy to see
even before they are judged, but the sins of
others are seen only later. [25]So also good
deeds are easy to see, but even those that are
not easily seen cannot stay hidden.

6 All who are slaves under a yoke should
show full respect to their masters so no
one will speak against God's name and our
teaching. [2]The slaves whose masters are
believers should not show their masters any
less respect because they are believers. They
should serve their masters even better,
because they are helping believers they love.
You must teach and preach these things.

False Teaching and True Riches

[3]Anyone who has a different teaching
does not agree with the true teaching of our
Lord Jesus Christ and the teaching that
shows the true way to serve God. [4]This
person is full of pride and understands
nothing, but is sick with a love for arguing
and fighting about words. This brings
jealousy, fighting, speaking against others,
evil mistrust, [5]and constant quarrels from
those who have evil minds and have lost the
truth. They think that serving God is a way
to get rich.
[6]Serving God does make us very rich, if
we are satisfied with what we have. [7]We
brought nothing into the world, so we can
take nothing out. [8]But, if we have food and
clothes, we will be satisfied with that.
[9]Those who want to become rich bring
temptation to themselves and are caught in
a trap. They want many foolish and harmful
things that ruin and destroy people. [10]The
love of money causes all kinds of evil. Some
people have left the faith, because they
wanted to get more money, but they have
caused themselves much sorrow.

Some Things to Remember

[11]But you, man of God, run away from all
those things. Instead, live in the right way,
serve God, have faith, love, patience, and
gentleness. [12]Fight the good fight of faith,
grabbing hold of the life that continues
forever. You were called to have that life
when you confessed the good confession

devotion 338

1 TIMOTHY 6:6–8

CONTENTMENT—A GREAT LIBERATION

Just saying the word "content" makes my heart settle down for a few moments of peace. My husband and I have often joked that when we were our poorest, we were our happiest. I'm not quite sure if we were happier, but life certainly was simpler. I understand Paul's heart in communicating this message to Timothy much more now that I am a bit older. In my twenties . . . well, let's skip over those years—in my thirties, life was about working hard to grow my business, establishing finances, and digging into the Word. In my forties, life's about being a pastor's wife, organic coffee, cooking gourmet meals, and entertaining my great friends.

I have learned that "it is better to be content with what little you have. Otherwise, you will always be struggling for more, and that is like chasing the wind" (Eccles. 4:6). As my business grew, so did the overhead. The clients were more famous and their problems even bigger. My income tripled and I just bought more stuff. One night the Lord spoke this verse in Ecclesiastes to me, and I knew he was saying, "Enough!" The next day I asked two clients to leave, and I made a commitment that I would no longer accept anyone at the office that caused confusion. Are there things in your life that you need to cut back, change, or totally give up in order to experience the great liberation and richness that God's contentment brings? True contentment is worth the courage it will take to change.

before many witnesses. [13]In the sight of God,
who gives life to everything, and of Christ
Jesus, I give you a command. Christ Jesus
made the good confession when he stood
before Pontius Pilate. [14]Do what you were
commanded to do without wrong or blame
until our Lord Jesus Christ comes again.
[15]God will make that happen at the right
time. He is the blessed and only Ruler, the
King of all kings and the Lord of all lords.
[16]He is the only One who never dies. He lives
in light so bright no one can go near it. No
one has ever seen God, or can see him. May
honor and power belong to God forever.
Amen.

[17]Command those who are rich with
things of this world not to be proud. Tell
them to hope in God, not in their uncertain
riches. God richly gives us everything to
enjoy. [18]Tell the rich people to do good, to be
rich in doing good deeds, to be generous and
ready to share. [19]By doing that, they will be
saving a treasure for themselves as a strong
foundation for the future. Then they will be
able to have the life that is true life.

[20]Timothy, guard what God has trusted to
you. Stay away from foolish, useless talk and
from the arguments of what is falsely called
"knowledge." [21]By saying they have that
"knowledge," some have missed the true
faith.

Grace be with you.

2 Timothy

Person Holding the Pen God Wrote With: *Paul*

When the Text Was Written: This is the last letter of Paul, written around 64–68 A.D. He wrote it while he was sitting in a Roman jail cell awaiting execution.

Spiritual Posture of the Original Recipients: The New Testament church was plugging along, but it was still troubled by internal strife and external persecution. Young believers were desperately seeking mature Christian role models to follow and emulate.

Storyline Synopsis: Paul's "deathbed exhortation" isn't just about correcting doctrine—it's about proper Christian conduct. It's not just about right *thinking*; it's about right *living*! He encourages Timothy to not only guard the Good News message of Jesus but to also initiate a "Good News offensive"—to be intentional about communicating the message of the living Christ at all times. Paul uses three analogies (a good soldier, a good athlete, and a good farmer) to illustrate how to live blameless Christian lives.

A Moment Worth Discussing: At the beginning of his letter, Paul lovingly affirms Timothy by calling him a "dear child" (2 Tim. 1:2) and reminds Timothy of the faithful legacy of his godly mother and grandmother (1:5). Paul then encourages Timothy to overcome his natural shyness for the sake of the Good News (1:6–14). You can almost picture timid Timothy opening this letter from his imprisoned hero with trembling hands—drinking in every single word—then taking a deep breath and squaring his shoulders as he folds it and slides it back into the envelope. Paul's reassuring voice probably echoed off the pages as if he were standing right there in the room. And young Timothy, Paul's devoted preaching protégé, longed to hear it one more time.

Interesting (But Likely to Be Overlooked) Character: *Onesiphorus* was a friend of Paul's who risked persecution—possibly even his life—to support Paul by visiting him in prison (2 Tim. 1:16–18).

1 From Paul, an apostle of Christ Jesu
the will of God. God sent me to tell a
the promise of life that is in Christ Jesus.
2 To Timothy, a dear child to me:
Grace, mercy, and peace to you from God
the Father and Christ Jesus our Lord.

Encouragement for Timothy

3 I thank God as I always mention you in
my prayers, day and night. I serve him, doing
what I know is right as my ancestors did.
4 Remembering that you cried for me, I want
very much to see you so I can be filled with
joy. 5 I remember your true faith. That faith
first lived in your grandmother Lois and in
your mother Eunice, and I know you now
have that same faith. 6 This is why I remind
you to keep using the gift God gave you
when I laid my hands on[n] you. Now let it
grow, as a small flame grows into a fire. 7 God
did not give us a spirit that makes us afraid
but a spirit of power and love and
self-control.
8 So do not be ashamed to tell people
about our Lord Jesus, and do not be ashamed
of me, in prison for the Lord. But suffer with
me for the Good News. God, who gives us
the strength to do that, 9 saved us and made
us his holy people. That was not because of
anything we did ourselves but because of
God's purpose and grace. That grace was
given to us through Christ Jesus before time
began, 10 but it is now shown to us by the
coming of our Savior Christ Jesus. He
destroyed death, and through the Good
News he showed us the way to have life that
cannot be destroyed. 11 I was chosen to tell
that Good News and to be an apostle and a
teacher. 12 I am suffering now because I tell
the Good News, but I am not ashamed,
because I know Jesus, the One in whom I
have believed. And I am sure he is able to
protect what he has trusted me with until
that day.[n] 13 Follow the pattern of true
teachings that you heard from me in faith
and love, which are in Christ Jesus. 14 Protect
the truth that you were given; protect it with
the help of the Holy Spirit who lives in us.
15 You know that everyone in Asia has left
me, even Phygelus and Hermogenes. 16 May
the Lord show mercy to the family of
Onesiphorus, who has often helped me and
was not ashamed that I was in prison.
17 When he came to Rome, he looked eagerly
for me until he found me. 18 May the Lord
llow him to find mercy from the Lord on
t day. You know how many ways he
ed me in Ephesus.

A Loy Soldier of Christ Jesus

2 You hen, Timothy, my child, be strong
in th grace we have in Christ Jesus. 2 You
should h people whom you can trust the
things you nd many others have heard me
say. Then th will be able to teach others.
3 Share in the oubles we have like a good
soldier of Chri Jesus. 4 A soldier wants to
please the enlist g officer, so no one serving
in the army waste time with everyday
matters. 5 Also an athlete who takes part in a
contest must obey all the rules in order to
win. 6 The farmer who works hard should be
the first person get some of the food that
was grown. 7 Thin about what I am saying,
because the Lord wi give you the ability to
understand everythi
8 Remember Jesus Christ, who was raised
from the dead, who is fro the family of
David. This is the Good News I preach, 9 and I
am suffering because of it to he point of
being bound with chains like criminal. But
God's teaching is not in chains. 10 So I
patiently accept all these troubles so that
those whom God has chosen can have the
salvation that is in Christ Jesus. With hat
salvation comes glory that never ends.
11 This teaching is true:

If we died with him, we will also live with
him.
12 If we accept suffering, we will also rule
with him.
If we say we don't know him, he will say
he doesn't know us.
13 If we are not faithful, he will still be
faithful,
because he must be true to who he is.

A Worker Pleasing to God

14 Continue teaching these things,
warning people in God's presence not to
argue about words. It does not help anyone,
and it ruins those who listen. 15 Make every

1:6 laid my hands on The laying on of hands had many purposes, including the giving of a blessing, power, or authority.
1:12 day The day Christ will come to judge all people and take his people to live with him.

effort to give yourself to God as the kind of
person he will approve. Be a worker who is
not ashamed and who uses the true teaching
in the right way. [16]Stay away from foolish,
useless talk, because that will lead people
further away from God. [17]Their evil teachin
will spread like a sickness inside the body
Hymenaeus and Philetus are like that.
[18]They have left the true teaching, say
that the rising from the dead has alre y
taken place, and so they are destroy g the
faith of some people. [19]But God's s ng
foundation continues to stand. Th se words
are written on the seal: "The Lor knows
those who belong to him,"[n] an Everyone
who wants to belong to the L d must stop
doing wrong."
[20]In a large house there re not only
things made of gold and lver, but also
things made of wood and clay. Some things
are used for special purposes and others are
made for ordinary jobs. [21]All who make
themselves clean from evil will be used for
special purposes. They will be made holy,
useful to the Master, ready to do any good
work.

un away from the evil desires of
[22]Try hard to live right and to have
, love, and peace, together with those
who trust in the Lord from pure hearts.
[23]Stay away from foolish and stupid
arguments, because you know they grow
into quarrels. [24]And a servant of the Lord
must not quarrel but must be kind to
everyone, a good teacher, and patient. [25]The
Lord's servant must gently teach those who
disagree. Then maybe God will let them
change their minds so they can accept the
truth. [26]And they may wake up and escape
from the trap of the devil, who catches them
to do what he wants.

The Last Days

3 Remember this! In the last days there
will be many troubles, [2]because people
will love themselves, love money, brag, and
be proud. They will say evil things against
others and will not obey their parents or be
thankful or be the kind of people God
wants. [3]They will not love others, will
refuse to forgive, will gossip, and will not
control themselves. They will be cruel,

2:19 "The Lord . . . him." Quotation from Numbers 16:5.

devotion 339

2 TIMOTHY 2:21

NO-HANDS JESUS

I once heard a story about an American soldier during World War II who was walking through the countryside and came across a statue of Jesus with his hands blown off. As the soldier sat there looking at the statue, he decided to give it a name. He wrote on a piece of paper, "I have no hands but yours," and left it at the base of the statue.

We are the hands of God. He has chosen to use us to reach the lost and hurting of this world. There is one catch, though—God can only use us if we are clean from evil. We can't allow sin to reign in our lives if we want to be used by God. The enemy loves to twist our motives and confuse us as we try to carry out God's purposes. We have to be prepared to be tempted with every kind of evil. Read James 4:7. It tells us that if we stand against the devil, he will run away. Once we have the Spirit of God living in us, we have the power to resist sin. When we draw near to God, he will draw near to us and cleanse us from all unrighteousness.

Are you ready to do good works for the kingdom of God? Will you be the hands of God in a hurting and dying world? Cleanse yourself from evil, and you will become a powerful tool in the hands of God.

will hate what is good, [4]will turn against their friends, and will do foolish things without thinking. They will be conceited, will love pleasure instead of God, [5]and will act as if they serve God but will not have his power. Stay away from those people. [6]Some of them go into homes and get control of silly women who are full of sin and are led by many evil desires. [7]These women are always learning new teachings, but they are never able to understand the truth fully. [8]Just as Jannes and Jambres were against Moses, these people are against the truth. Their thinking has been ruined, and they have failed in trying to follow the faith. [9]But they will not be successful in what they do, because as with Jannes and Jambres, everyone will see that they are foolish.

Obey the Teachings

[10]But you have followed what I teach, the way I live, my goal, faith, patience, and love. You know I never give up. [11]You know how I have been hurt and have suffered, as in Antioch, Iconium, and Lystra. I have suffered, but the Lord saved me from all those troubles. [12]Everyone who wants to live as God desires, in Christ Jesus, will be persecuted. [13]But people who are evil and cheat others will go from bad to worse. They will fool others, but they will also be fooling themselves.

[14]But you should continue following the teachings you learned. You know they are true, because you trust those who taught you. [15]Since you were a child you have known the Holy Scriptures which are able to make you wise. And that wisdom leads to salvation through faith in Christ Jesus. [16]All Scripture is inspired by God and is useful for teaching, for showing people what is wrong in their lives, for correcting faults, and for teaching how to live right. [17]Using the Scriptures, the person who serves God will be capable, having all that is needed to do every good work.

4 I give you a command in the presence of God and Christ Jesus, the One who will judge the living and the dead, and by his coming and his kingdom: [2]Preach the Good News. Be ready at all times, and tell people what they need to do. Tell them when they are wrong. Encourage them with great patience and careful teaching, [3]because the time will come when people will not listen to the true teaching but will find many more teachers who please them by saying the things they want to hear. [4]They will stop listening to the truth and will begin to follow false stories. [5]But you should control yourself at all times, accept troubles, do the work of telling the Good News, and complete all the duties of a servant of God.

[6]My life is being given as an offering to God, and the time has come for me to leave this life. [7]I have fought the good fight, I have finished the race, I have kept the faith. [8]Now, a crown is being held for me—a crown for being right with God. The Lord, the judge who judges rightly, will give the crown to me on that day[n]—not only to me but to all those who have waited with love for him to come again.

Personal Words

[9]Do your best to come to me as soon as you can, [10]because Demas, who loved this world, left me and went to Thessalonica. Crescens went to Galatia, and Titus went to Dalmatia. [11]Luke is the only one still with me. Get Mark and bring him with you when you come, because he can help me in my work here. [12]I sent Tychicus to Ephesus. [13]When I was in Troas, I left my coat there with Carpus. So when you come, bring it to me, along with my books, particularly the ones written on parchment.[n]

[14]Alexander the metalworker did many harmful things against me. The Lord will punish him for what he did. [15]You also should be careful that he does not hurt you, because he fought strongly against our teaching.

[16]The first time I defended myself, no one helped me; everyone left me. May they be forgiven. [17]But the Lord stayed with me and gave me strength so I could fully tell the Good News to all those who are not Jews. So I was saved from the lion's mouth. [18]The Lord will save me when anyone tries to hurt

4:8 day The day Christ will come to judge all people and take his people to live with him.
4:13 parchment A writing paper made from the skins of sheep.

me, and he will bring me safely to his
heavenly kingdom. Glory forever and ever
be the Lord's. Amen.

Final Greetings

19 Greet Priscilla and Aquila and the family
of Onesiphorus. 20 Erastus stayed in Corinth,
and I left Trophimus sick in Miletus. 21 Try as
hard as you can to come to me before winter.

Eubulus sends greetings to you. Also
Pudens, Linus, Claudia, and all the brothers
and sisters in Christ greet you.

22 The Lord be with your spirit. Grace be
with you.

Titus

The third and final pastoral letter written by Paul

Person Holding the Pen God Wrote With: *Paul*

When the Text Was Written: Between 63 and 65 A.D. after Paul's first release from a Roman prison (Acts 27)

Spiritual Posture of the Original Recipient: Titus was a Greek believer who came to faith in Christ through Paul's ministry (Gal. 2:3). At the time of this letter, he was pastoring a church on the island of Crete—a tough assignment because the people's hearts were as rocky as the terrain. His congregation was argumentative, deceitful, and lazy (Titus 1:10–14).

Storyline Synopsis: Since the Cretians were an unruly bunch and prone to follow false doctrines, Paul wrote these instructions to help Titus shepherd his flock more effectively. Because the people were being led astray by ignorant Christians and well-meaning Jews who blended the message of Jesus with old-fashioned legalism, Paul emphasizes the true meaning of grace in this letter. He also encourages Titus to organize a good team of elders, to recognize and affirm the various kinds of "sheep" in his congregation, and to teach them to reflect Christ in every aspect of their behavior.

A Moment Worth Discussing: In chapter 3, a terse, bullet-point admonition softens into Paul's plea for Titus to teach his followers to be humble and gentle and kind. Paul continues by reminiscing about how he used to be a jerk—probably remembering incidents when he ordered innocent believers to recant or be killed—and then goes on to describe how the miraculous love of Jesus changed him. His eyes probably welled up with tears and his voice overflowed with gratitude when he spoke of the regeneration and renewal of the Holy Spirit. This is essentially Paul's version of "Amazing Grace."

Interesting (But Likely to Be Overlooked) Character: The *senior saints* of the first century church—those older men and women who had the privilege and responsibility to model godly behavior to the "whippersnappers" among them—received specific instructions from Paul (Titus 2:2–5). It is likely that some of the believers in Crete came to faith in Christ during those colorful days of Pentecost (Acts 2), so many would be gray-headed and stooped with age by this time. Yet they also had the unique opportunity to teach others how to live for Jesus in light of their experience.

1 From Paul, a servant of God and an
apostle of Jesus Christ. I was sent to help
the faith of God's chosen people and to help
them know the truth that shows people how
to serve God. 2That faith and that knowledge
come from the hope for life forever, which
God promised to us before time began. And
God cannot lie. 3At the right time God let
the world know about that life through
preaching. He trusted me with that work,
and I preached by the command of God our
Savior.

4To Titus, my true child in the faith we
share:

Grace and peace from God the Father and
Christ Jesus our Savior.

Titus' Work in Crete

5I left you in Crete so you could finish
doing the things that still needed to be done
and so you could appoint elders in every
town, as I directed you. 6An elder must not
be guilty of doing wrong, must have only
one wife, and must have believing children.
They must not be known as children who
are wild and do not cooperate. 7As God's
managers, overseers must not be guilty of
doing wrong, being selfish, or becoming
angry quickly. They must not drink too
much wine, like to fight, or try to get rich by
cheating others. 8Overseers must be ready to
welcome guests, love what is good, be wise,
live right, and be holy and self-controlled.
9By holding on to the trustworthy word just
as we teach it, overseers can help people by
using true teaching, and they can show
those who are against the true teaching that
they are wrong.

10There are many people who refuse to
cooperate, who talk about worthless things
and lead others into the wrong way—
mainly those who insist on circumcision to
be saved. 11These people must be stopped,
because they are upsetting whole families
by teaching things they should not teach,
which they do to get rich by cheating
people. 12Even one of their own prophets
said, "Cretans are always liars, evil animals,
and lazy people who do nothing but eat."
13The words that prophet said are true. So
firmly tell those people they are wrong so
they may become strong in the faith, 14not
accepting Jewish false stories and the
commands of people who reject the truth.
15To those who are pure, all things are pure,
but to those who are full of sin and do not
believe, nothing is pure. Both their minds
and their consciences have been ruined.
16They say they know God, but their actions
show they do not accept him. They are
hateful people, they refuse to obey, and they
are useless for doing anything good.

Following the True Teaching

2 But you must tell everyone what to do to
follow the true teaching. 2Teach older
men to be self-controlled, serious, wise,
strong in faith, in love, and in patience.

3In the same way, teach older women
to be holy in their behavior, not speaking
against others or enslaved to too much wine,
but teaching what is good. 4Then they can
teach the young women to love their
husbands, to love their children, 5to be wise
and pure, to be good workers at home, to be
kind, and to yield to their husbands. Then no
one will be able to criticize the teaching God
gave us.

6In the same way, encourage young men
to be wise. 7In every way be an example of
doing good deeds. When you teach, do it
with honesty and seriousness. 8Speak the
truth so that you cannot be criticized. Then
those who are against you will be ashamed
because there is nothing bad to say about us.

9Slaves should yield to their own masters
at all times, trying to please them and not
arguing with them. 10They should not steal
from them but should show their masters
they can be fully trusted so that in
everything they do they will make the
teaching of God our Savior attractive.

11That is the way we should live, because
God's grace that can save everyone has come.
12It teaches us not to live against God nor to
do the evil things the world wants to do.
Instead, that grace teaches us to live in the
present age in a wise and right way and in a
way that shows we serve God. 13We should
live like that while we wait for our great
hope and the coming of the glory of our
great God and Savior Jesus Christ. 14He gave
himself for us so he might pay the price to
free us from all evil and to make us pure
people who belong only to him—people
who are always wanting to do good deeds.

devotion 340

TITUS 2:12–14

GRACE CHANGES EVERYTHING

A friend asked me for advice about her son. He was a good kid, but his grades had dropped. He was becoming more and more disrespectful, and now he was lying to her. "I have grounded him and taken away every privilege he's ever had. I don't know how else to punish him," she confided in me. I was at a loss for good advice, so I went to my husband.

"Tell him that you are going to forgive him and give him a fresh start," he said. "Give him back all his privileges, even though he doesn't deserve it, and set up a time each week to have fun with him." It was not the advice I would have given, but she tried it and it worked. Her son responded and really made a change.

"Grace does not excuse the sin," says Philip Yancey, "but it treasures the sinner." Grace takes people who feel unworthy and gives them a reason to feel worthy again. Paul told Titus he should live in grace. Then he went on to say that when a person does that, he becomes pure, always wanting to do good deeds. That's what happened with my friend's son. When grace was extended to him, he responded by wanting to do good. We need to remind ourselves of God's grace in our lives on a daily basis "while we wait for our great hope and the coming of . . . Jesus Christ" (verse 13). The fact is, for a Christian, grace changes everything.

15 Say these things and encourage the
people and tell them what is wrong in their
lives, with all authority. Do not let anyone
treat you as if you were unimportant.

The Right Way to Live

3 Remind the believers to yield to the
authority of rulers and government
leaders, to obey them, to be ready to do good,
2 to speak no evil about anyone, to live in
peace, and to be gentle and polite to all
people.
3 In the past we also were foolish. We did
not obey, we were wrong, and we were slaves
to many things our bodies wanted and
enjoyed. We spent our lives doing evil and
being jealous. People hated us, and we hated
each other. 4 But when the kindness and love
of God our Savior was shown, 5 he saved us
because of his mercy. It was not because of
good deeds we did to be right with him. He
saved us through the washing that made us
new people through the Holy Spirit. 6 God
poured out richly upon us that Holy Spirit
through Jesus Christ our Savior. 7 Being made
right with God by his grace, we could have
the hope of receiving the life that never
ends.
8 This teaching is true, and I want you to
be sure the people understand these things.
Then those who believe in God will be
careful to use their lives for doing good.
These things are good and will help
everyone.
9 But stay away from those who have
foolish arguments and talk about useless
family histories and argue and quarrel about
the law. Those things are worth nothing and
will not help anyone. 10 After a first and
second warning, avoid someone who causes
arguments. 11 You can know that such people
are evil and sinful; their own sins prove
them wrong.

Some Things to Remember

12 When I send Artemas or Tychicus to
you, make every effort to come to me at
Nicopolis, because I have decided to stay

there this winter. 13Do all you can to help
Zenas the lawyer and Apollos on their
journey so that they have everything they
need. 14Our people must learn to use their
lives for doing good deeds to provide what is
necessary so that their lives will not be
useless.

15All who are with me greet you. Greet
those who love us in the faith.

Grace be with you all.

Philemon

Person Holding the Pen God Wrote With: Once again, our prolific friend *Paul*

When the Text Was Written: Around 60 A.D.

Spiritual Posture of the Original Recipient: Philemon was a kind and loving Christian living in the city of Colosse. He was also a slave owner, but don't judge him too harshly—in his culture, slavery was an accepted, customary institution. From the text we can infer that Philemon was likely mad about the behavior of his runaway slave . . . at least, until he read Paul's words.

Storyline Synopsis: Onesimus (whose name means "useful") was one of Philemon's slaves (verse 16), who had betrayed Philemon by stealing and running away to Rome. Evidently, his bad deeds caught up with him there because Paul got to know Onesimus while they were both doing time in jail. According to the law, Philemon had every right to have this runaway slave put to death. But Paul intervened by writing this note that Onesimus handed his master when he made bail and returned to Colosse. Paul appealed for Philemon to extend mercy, explaining that not only had Onesimus become a Christian behind bars, he had also become a dear friend. This short letter has much to say about forgiveness and reconciliation in Christian relationships.

A Moment Worth Discussing: Toward the end of this message (verses 17–19), Paul humbly requests Philemon to receive Onesimus back as if it were Paul himself returning to him. Paul then asks Philemon to transfer Onesimus' debt into Paul's own account. By taking Onesimus' debt upon himself, Paul gave us a picture of what Christ did for us. He found us as slaves to sin, imprisoned by our old nature, and yet he had compassion on us and identified with our sin. Jesus transferred our debt into his name—a debt he ultimately paid on Calvary.

Interesting (But Likely to Be Overlooked) Character: *Epaphras*, one of Paul's cellmates, was also from the city of Colosse. He took the message Paul preached back to his hometown and started a well-known New Testament church (Col. 1:4–7; 4:12–13). No matter what situation Paul found himself in, from preaching in the synagogue to witnessing in a prison cell, he boldly preached Christ and probably accomplished more as an incarcerated prisoner that most people do as free individuals!

1From Paul, a prisoner of Christ Jesus, and
from Timothy, our brother.
To Philemon, our dear friend and worker
with us; 2to Apphia, our sister; to Archippus,
a worker with us; and to the church that
meets in your home:
3Grace and peace to you from God our
Father and the Lord Jesus Christ.

Philemon's Love and Faith

4I always thank my God when I mention
you in my prayers, 5because I hear about the
love you have for all God's holy people and
the faith you have in the Lord Jesus. 6I pray
that the faith you share may make you
understand every blessing we have in Christ.
7I have great joy and comfort, my brother,
because the love you have shown to God's
people has refreshed them.

Accept Onesimus as a Brother

8So, in Christ, I could be bold and order
you to do what is right. 9But because I love
you, I am pleading with you instead. I, Paul,
an old man now and also a prisoner for
Christ Jesus, 10am pleading with you for my
child Onesimus, who became my child
while I was in prison. 11In the past he was
useless to you, but now he has become
useful for both you and me.
12I am sending him back to you, and with
him I am sending my own heart. 13I wanted
to keep him with me so that in your place he
might help me while I am in prison for the
Good News. 14But I did not want to do
anything without asking you first so that any
good you do for me will be because you want
to do it, not because I forced you. 15Maybe
Onesimus was separated from you for a short
time so you could have him back forever—
16no longer as a slave, but better than a slave,
as a loved brother. I love him very much, but
you will love him even more, both as a
person and as a believer in the Lord.
17So if you consider me your partner,
welcome Onesimus as you would welcome
me. 18If he has done anything wrong to you
or if he owes you anything, charge that to
me. 19I, Paul, am writing this with my own
hand. I will pay it back, and I will say
nothing about what you owe me for your
own life. 20So, my brother, I ask that you do

devotion 341

PHILEMON 7

SLOSH SOME JESUS

As we become more mature in Christ, we learn to keep ourselves underneath the life-giving water of Jesus. That means we try to stay in his presence through praying and reading his Word. For encouragement and wisdom, we hang out with other people who love God. We consult God and find our comfort and hope in him. Spiritual maturity comes to us by staying on the journey with God year after year, encounter after encounter.

As we grow, this life-giving water of Jesus becomes a blessing to our souls. We may have been thirsty in the past and tried other solutions, but maturity has taught us that the only answer is Jesus. The woman who understands the source of her blessing wants to give her blessings away. If you ever meet a woman who has received the mercy of God, know that she will be the one giving out mercy. The woman who has been given God's forgiveness will be the one forgiving. The one who has tasted unconditional love from the Father is the woman who will keep loving the unlovely.

Giving away the maturity you have received will refresh everyone who comes into your presence. They will see God in you. Maybe they will feel God for the very first time. When you are full of the water of Jesus, you will eventually start spilling over. Go slosh some Jesus today, and make sure the people you love and the strangers you meet get soaking wet.

this for me in the Lord: Refresh my heart in
Christ. 21 I write this letter, knowing that you
will do what I ask you and even more.
22 One more thing—prepare a room for me
in which to stay, because I hope God will
answer your prayers and I will be able to
come to you.

Final Greetings

23 Epaphras, a prisoner with me for Christ
Jesus, sends greetings to you. 24 And also
Mark, Aristarchus, Demas, and Luke,
workers together with me, send greetings.
25 The grace of our Lord Jesus Christ be
with your spirit.

Hebrews

Written to a group of Jewish Christians

Person Holding the Pen God Wrote With: Author is unknown. Some scholars believe it was *Luke*, while feminists have argued for *Priscilla*, Aquila's wife from Acts (but since the author refers to "himself" with masculine pronouns, this is highly unlikely). While we don't know the writer's identity, it's clear that he was friendly with the apostolic circle—Timothy is called a "brother" in the author's final greetings in Hebrews 13:23. He also enjoyed a familiar, affectionate relationship with the people he was addressing. This letter might initially have been given as a sermon, in light of certain Greek phrases that denote speaking (Heb. 13:22; Acts 13:15).

When the Text Was Written: The exact date is not definitive, but historical documents and textual references to the Temple (which was destroyed in 70 A.D.), along with mentions of the sacrificial system still in practice at this time, lead scholars to believe it was written between 60 and 70 A.D. when most of the world was governed by Rome and still under the influence of Hellenistic (Greek) culture.

Spiritual Posture of the Original Recipients: Most people who lived in the first century were polytheistic—they worshiped multiple pagan gods. Archeologists tell us that there were diminutive stone deities guarding every street corner in Rome during this era. Only religious Jews and those who called themselves "Christians"—denoting their belief that Jesus was the Messiah—were monotheistic, worshiping just one God.

Storyline Synopsis: The pastor encourages his congregation of discouraged believers to hang in there. They've being maligned, persecuted, and face possible martyrdom because of their faith in Jesus—and some of them are about to throw in the proverbial towel. Much like the half-time speech of a coach whose team is getting pummeled, the writer is motivating his players to stay in the game and, more importantly, to focus on Jesus.

A Moment Worth Discussing: In Hebrews 11:32–40, the pastor uses the mistake-prone examples of Gideon (wimpy warrior, Judges 6); Barak (military hotshot who cowered behind the skirt of a woman, Judges 4); Samson (Romeo without a clue, Judges 16); and Jephthah (really dumb daddy whose rash vow cost his only daughter her life, Judges 11) to reveal how God can use imperfect people to accomplish his divine purposes.

Interesting (But Likely to Be Overlooked) Character: *Melchizedek* was an Old Testament high priest with an unusual name (Heb. 7:1–10; Gen. 14:17–20; Ps. 110:4). The writer of Hebrews used him as an allegorical example for the Messiah because he had a lot in common with Jesus: his title as a king, a timeless reign, no recorded death, and—although he was a priest—he wasn't from the tribe of Levi.

God Spoke Through His Son

1 In the past God spoke to our ancestors
through the prophets many times and in
many different ways. 2But now in these last
days God has spoken to us through his Son.
God has chosen his Son to own all things,
and through him he made the world. 3The
Son reflects the glory of God and shows
exactly what God is like. He holds everything
together with his powerful word. When the
Son made people clean from their sins, he
sat down at the right side of God, the Great
One in heaven. 4The Son became much
greater than the angels, and God gave him a
name that is much greater than theirs.
5This is because God never said to any of
the angels,

"You are my Son.
Today I have become your Father."
Psalm 2:7

Nor did God say of any angel,
"I will be his Father,
and he will be my Son." *2 Samuel 7:14*
6And when God brings his firstborn Son into
the world, he says,
"Let all God's angels worship him."[n]
Psalm 97:7
7This is what God said about the angels:
"God makes his angels become like winds.
He makes his servants become like
flames of fire." *Psalm 104:4*
8But God said this about his Son:
"God, your throne will last forever and
ever.
You will rule your kingdom with
fairness.
9You love right and hate evil,
so God has chosen you from among
your friends;
he has set you apart with much joy."
Psalm 45:6–7
10God also says,
"Lord, in the beginning you made the
earth,
and your hands made the skies.
11They will be destroyed, but you will
remain.
They will all wear out like clothes.
12You will fold them like a coat.
And, like clothes, you will change
them.
But you never change,
and your life will never end."
Psalm 102:25–27
13And God never said this to an angel:
"Sit by me at my right side
until I put your enemies under your
control."[n] *Psalm 110:1*
14All the angels are spirits who serve God
and are sent to help those who will receive
salvation.

Our Salvation Is Great

2 So we must be more careful to follow
what we were taught. Then we will not
stray away from the truth. 2The teaching
God spoke through angels was shown to be
true, and anyone who did not follow it or
obey it received the punishment that was
earned. 3So surely we also will be punished
if we ignore this great salvation. The Lord
himself first told about this salvation, and
those who heard him testified it was true.
4God also testified to the truth of the message
by using wonders, great signs, many kinds of
miracles, and by giving people gifts through
the Holy Spirit, just as he wanted.

Christ Became like Humans

5God did not choose angels to be the
rulers of the new world that was coming,
which is what we have been talking about.
6It is written in the Scriptures,
"Why are people even important to you?
Why do you take care of human
beings?
7You made them a little lower than the
angels
and crowned them with glory and
honor.[n]
8You put all things under their control."
Psalm 8:4–6
When God put everything under their
control, there was nothing left that they did
not rule. Still, we do not yet see them ruling
over everything. 9But we see Jesus, who for a
short time was made lower than the angels.
And now he is wearing a crown of glory and
honor because he suffered and died. And by
God's grace, he died for everyone.
10God is the One who made all things, and
all things are for his glory. He wanted to

1:6 "Let . . . him." These words are found in Deuteronomy 32:43 in the Septuagint, the Greek version of the Old Testament, and in a Hebrew copy among the Dead Sea Scrolls. **1:13 until . . . control** Literally, "until I make your enemies a footstool for your feet." **2:7 You . . . honor.** Some Greek copies continue, "You put them in charge of everything you made." See Psalm 8:6.

have many children share his glory, so he made the One who leads people to salvation perfect through suffering.

[11]Jesus, who makes people holy, and those who are made holy are from the same family. So he is not ashamed to call them his brothers and sisters. [12]He says,

"Then, I will tell my brothers and sisters
about you;
I will praise you in the public meeting."
Psalm 22:22

[13]He also says,

"I will trust in God." *Isaiah 8:17*

And he also says,

"I am here, and with me are the children
God has given me." *Isaiah 8:18*

[14]Since these children are people with physical bodies, Jesus himself became like them. He did this so that, by dying, he could destroy the one who has the power of death—the devil— [15]and free those who were like slaves all their lives because of their fear of death. [16]Clearly, it is not angels that Jesus helps, but the people who are from Abraham.[n] [17]For this reason Jesus had to be made like his brothers and sisters in every way so he could be their merciful and faithful high priest in service to God. Then Jesus could die in their place to take away their sins. [18]And now he can help those who are tempted, because he himself suffered and was tempted.

Jesus Is Greater than Moses

3 So all of you holy brothers and sisters, who were called by God, think about Jesus, who was sent to us and is the high priest of our faith. [2]Jesus was faithful to God as Moses was in God's family. [3]Jesus has more honor than Moses, just as the builder of a house has more honor than the house itself. [4]Every house is built by someone, but the builder of everything is God himself. [5]Moses was faithful in God's family as a servant, and he told what God would say in the future. [6]But Christ is faithful as a Son over God's house. And we are God's house if we confidently maintain our hope.

2:16 Abraham Most respected ancestor of the Jews. Every Jew hoped to see Abraham.

devotion 342

HEBREWS 2:17–18

HE KNOWS THE HUMAN CONDITION

I am so grateful that our Lord can sympathize with all the temptations that we face here on the earth. It gives me comfort to know that nothing has escaped his knowledge or understanding. Jesus being seated at the right hand of the Father in the intercessory prayer seat has become a source of confidence for us. As our high priest, he is able to understand our weaknesses. He was tempted just like we are, but he didn't sin (Heb. 4:15). It is true that he intercedes for us as a *holy* high priest, but he also has a unique perspective on our human condition.

I know what is important to me when I am struggling or even in need of some specific counsel. I seek those people that I know have walked the same path or dealt with similar issues. I want to know how someone dealt with the same set of challenges, what encouraged them, how they got through it, and what practical steps they took to overcome.

Solomon said there is nothing new under the sun. Whatever you are being tempted with today, Jesus understands your struggle, and he does not want your temptation to turn into sin in your life. Ask him to help you in every way in which you are tempted. He is there making intercession for you right now. Do not allow Satan to deceive you with his lies—Jesus is never too busy to listen, and there's nothing he hasn't already heard!

We Must Continue to Follow God

7 So it is as the Holy Spirit says:
"Today listen to what he says.
8 Do not be stubborn as in the past
when you turned against God,
when you tested God in the desert.
9 There your ancestors tried me and
tested me
and saw the things I did for forty years.
10 I was angry with them.
I said, 'They are not loyal to me
and have not understood my ways.'
11 I was angry and made a promise,
'They will never enter my rest.' "[n]

Psalm 95:7–11

12 So brothers and sisters, be careful that none of you has an evil, unbelieving heart that will turn you away from the living God. 13 But encourage each other every day while it is "today."[n] Help each other so none of you will become hardened because sin has tricked you. 14 We all share in Christ if we keep till the end the sure faith we had in the beginning. 15 This is what the Scripture says:

"Today listen to what he says.
Do not be stubborn as in the past
when you turned against God."

Psalm 95:7–8

16 Who heard God's voice and was against him? It was all those people Moses led out of Egypt. 17 And with whom was God angry for forty years? He was angry with those who sinned, who died in the desert. 18 And to whom was God talking when he promised that they would never enter his rest? He was talking to those who did not obey him. 19 So we see they were not allowed to enter and have God's rest, because they did not believe.

4 Now, since God has left us the promise that we may enter his rest, let us be very careful so none of you will fail to enter. 2 The Good News was preached to us just as it was to them. But the teaching they heard did not help them, because they heard it but did not accept it with faith.[n] 3 We who have believed are able to enter and have God's rest. As God has said,

"I was angry and made a promise,
'They will never enter my rest.' "

Psalm 95:11

But God's work was finished from the time he made the world. 4 In the Scriptures he talked about the seventh day of the week: "And on the seventh day God rested from all his works."[n] 5 And again in the Scripture God said, "They will never enter my rest."

6 It is still true that some people will enter God's rest, but those who first heard the way to be saved did not enter, because they did not obey. 7 So God planned another day, called "today." He spoke about that day through David a long time later in the same Scripture used before:

"Today listen to what he says.
Do not be stubborn." *Psalm 95:7–8*

8 We know that Joshua[n] did not lead the people into that rest, because God spoke later about another day. 9 This shows that the rest[n] for God's people is still coming. 10 Anyone who enters God's rest will rest from his work as God did. 11 Let us try as hard as we can to enter God's rest so that no one will fail by following the example of those who refused to obey.

12 God's word is alive and working and is sharper than a double-edged sword. It cuts all the way into us, where the soul and the spirit are joined, to the center of our joints and bones. And it judges the thoughts and feelings in our hearts. 13 Nothing in all the world can be hidden from God. Everything is clear and lies open before him, and to him we must explain the way we have lived.

Jesus Is Our High Priest

14 Since we have a great high priest, Jesus the Son of God, who has gone into heaven, let us hold on to the faith we have. 15 For our high priest is able to understand our weaknesses. He was tempted in every way that we are, but he did not sin. 16 Let us, then, feel very sure that we can come before God's throne where there is grace. There we can receive mercy and grace to help us when we need it.

5 Every high priest is chosen from among other people. He is given the work of going before God for them to offer gifts and sacrifices for sins. 2 Since he himself is weak, he is able to be gentle with those who do not

3:11 rest A place of rest God promised to give his people. **3:13 "today"** This word is taken from verse 7. It means that it is important to do these things now. **4:2 because . . . faith** Some Greek copies read "because they did not share the faith of those who heard it." **4:4 "And . . . works."** Quotation from Genesis 2:2. **4:8 Joshua** After Moses died, Joshua became leader of the Jewish people and led them into the land that God promised to give them. **4:9 rest** Literally, "sabbath rest," meaning a sharing in the rest that God began after he created the world.

devotion 343

HEBREWS 4:11–13

ANTISEPTIC FOR YOUR SOUL

Years ago, Billy and Ruth Graham were sitting in church one Sunday morning, and as the offering plate was being passed, Billy reached into his pocket for money. He pulled out a five-dollar bill and a fifty-dollar bill. As the plate came to him, he put the five into the offering and began to place the fifty back in his pocket. As he did, he realized he had accidentally put the fifty in the offering, and for a brief moment, he began to reach back into the plate. His wife, Ruth, gently patted his arm and said, "Don't worry dear, God only gave you credit for the five."

Nothing is hidden from God. He knows our thoughts and our feelings. However, there are times we are able to hide things from ourselves. We bury hurts, excuse attitudes, and justify behavior instead of being honest with ourselves. As this passage says, "God's Word is alive and working and is sharper than a double-edged sword" (verse 12). It will cut through all the excuses and reveal those hidden places of our hearts. God's Word is so powerful that it brings our sin to light and then shows us the way to forgiveness. It reveals our past pain and then heals us. It challenges us to be a soldier for God and then gives us the tools to do it. Applying the Word of God to our lives is like applying antiseptic; it cleanses and heals. Is God's Word active and working in you?

understand and who are doing wrong things.
3 Because he is weak, the high priest must
offer sacrifices for his own sins and also for
the sins of the people.
4 To be a high priest is an honor, but no
one chooses himself for this work. He must
be called by God as Aaron[n] was. 5 So also
Christ did not choose himself to have the
honor of being a high priest, but God chose
him. God said to him,

"You are my Son.
Today I have become your Father."
Psalm 2:7

6 And in another Scripture God says,

"You are a priest forever,
a priest like Melchizedek."[n] *Psalm 110:4*

7 While Jesus lived on earth, he prayed to
God and asked God for help. He prayed with
loud cries and tears to the One who could
save him from death, and his prayer was
heard because he trusted God. 8 Even though
Jesus was the Son of God, he learned
obedience by what he suffered. 9 And because
his obedience was perfect, he was able to
give eternal salvation to all who obey him.
10 In this way God made Jesus a high priest, a
priest like Melchizedek.

Warning Against Falling Away

11 We have much to say about this, but it is
hard to explain because you are so slow to
understand. 12 By now you should be teachers,
but you need someone to teach you again
the first lessons of God's message. You still
need the teaching that is like milk. You are
not ready for solid food. 13 Anyone who lives
on milk is still a baby and knows nothing
about right teaching. 14 But solid food is for
those who are grown up. They are mature
enough to know the difference between
good and evil.

6 So let us go on to grown-up teaching.
Let us not go back over the beginning
lessons we learned about Christ. We should

5:4 Aaron Moses' brother and the first Jewish high priest.
5:6 Melchizedek A priest and king who lived in the time of Abraham. (Read Genesis 14:17–24.)

not again start teaching about faith in God
and about turning away from those acts that
lead to death. 2We should not return to the
teaching about baptisms,[n] about laying on
of hands,[n] about the raising of the dead and
eternal judgment. 3And we will go on to
grown-up teaching if God allows.
4Some people cannot be brought back
again to a changed life. They were once in
God's light, and enjoyed heaven's gift, and
shared in the Holy Spirit. 5They found out
how good God's word is, and they received
the powers of his new world. 6But they fell
away from Christ. It is impossible to bring
them back to a changed life again, because
they are nailing the Son of God to a cross
again and are shaming him in front of others.
7Some people are like land that gets
plenty of rain. The land produces a good
crop for those who work it, and it receives
God's blessings. 8Other people are like
land that grows thorns and weeds and is
worthless. It is about to be cursed by God
and will be destroyed by fire.
9Dear friends, we are saying this to you,
but we really expect better things from you
that will lead to your salvation. 10God is fair;
he will not forget the work you did and the
love you showed for him by helping his
people. And he will remember that you are
still helping them. 11We want each of you to
go on with the same hard work all your lives
so you will surely get what you hope for.
12We do not want you to become lazy. Be
like those who through faith and patience
will receive what God has promised.
13God made a promise to Abraham. And
as there is no one greater than God, he used
himself when he swore to Abraham, 14saying,
"I will surely bless you and give you many
descendants."[n] 15Abraham waited patiently
for this to happen, and he received what God
promised.
16People always use the name of someone
greater than themselves when they swear.
The oath proves that what they say is true,
and this ends all arguing. 17God wanted to
prove that his promise was true to those who
would get what he promised. And he wanted
them to understand clearly that his purposes
never change, so he made an oath. 18These
two things cannot change: God cannot lie
when he makes a promise, and he cannot
lie when he makes an oath. These things
encourage us who came to God for safety.
They give us strength to hold on to the hope
we have been given. 19We have this hope as
an anchor for the soul, sure and strong. It
enters behind the curtain in the Most Holy
Place in heaven, 20where Jesus has gone ahead
of us and for us. He has become the high
priest forever, a priest like Melchizedek.[n]

The Priest Melchizedek

7 Melchizedek[n] was the king of Salem and
a priest for God Most High. He met
Abraham when Abraham was coming back
after defeating the kings. When they met,
Melchizedek blessed Abraham, 2and
Abraham gave him a tenth of everything
he had brought back from the battle. First,
Melchizedek's name means "king of
goodness," and he is king of Salem, which
means "king of peace." 3No one knows who
Melchizedek's father or mother was,[n] where
he came from, when he was born, or when he
died. Melchizedek is like the Son of God; he
continues being a priest forever.
4You can see how great Melchizedek was.
Abraham, the great father, gave him a tenth
of everything that he won in battle. 5Now
the law says that those in the tribe of Levi
who become priests must collect a tenth
from the people—their own people—even
though the priests and the people are from
the family of Abraham. 6Melchizedek was
not from the tribe of Levi, but he collected
a tenth from Abraham. And he blessed
Abraham, the man who had God's promises.
7Now everyone knows that the more
important person blesses the less important
person. 8Priests receive a tenth, even though
they are only men who live and then die. But
Melchizedek, who received a tenth from
Abraham, continues living, as the Scripture
says. 9We might even say that Levi, who
receives a tenth, also paid it when Abraham
paid Melchizedek a tenth. 10Levi was not yet
born, but he was in the body of his ancestor
when Melchizedek met Abraham.

6:2 baptisms The word here may refer to Christian baptism, or it may refer to the Jewish ceremonial washings. **6:2 laying on of hands** The laying on of hands had many purposes, including the giving of a blessing, power, or authority. **6:14 "I . . . descendants."** Quotation from Genesis 22:17. **6:20; 7:1 Melchizedek** A priest and king who lived in the time of Abraham. (Read Genesis 14:17–24.) **7:3 No . . . was** Literally, "Melchizedek was without father, without mother, without genealogy."

devotion 344

HEBREWS 6:18

DOUBTING THOMASINA

Do you ever doubt God? Maybe sometimes you doubt the whole thing—God, the Bible, and all the Jesus stuff. Or maybe random doubts just zing through your head from time to time. Maybe you believe in God but doubt he will really come through for you.

Hebrews says that the hope of Christ is right in front of you. You are holding a record of the promises God has made to you. He has told you the truth in every page of his Word. He has kept his promises. His vows have not changed. His character is the same yesterday, today, and forever.

You will have to make a determined decision to believe God in order to overcome doubt. You will have to decide that you believe everything God says is true. He has vowed to keep his promises. You'll have to stake your whole life on it and then live out your decision no matter what comes. Until you've made that commitment, you'll constantly struggle with doubt.

The truth of God's Word will replace your doubt, so immerse yourself in these pages. Commit to studying the Bible prayerfully. Read about how God has kept his promises. Read about the incredibly deep and powerful love he has for you. Read about his longing to know you and to be with you forever. Get these words into your heart and into your mind. Pretty soon, all your doubt will be replaced with the absolute certainty of God's existence and his truth.

[11]The people were given the law[n]
concerning the system of priests from the
tribe of Levi, but they could not be made
perfect through that system. So there was a
need for another priest to come, a priest like
Melchizedek, not Aaron. [12]And when a
different kind of priest comes, the law must
be changed, too. [13]We are saying these
things about Christ, who belonged to a
different tribe. No one from that tribe ever
served as a priest at the altar. [14]It is clear that
our Lord came from the tribe of Judah, and
Moses said nothing about priests belonging
to that tribe.

Jesus Is like Melchizedek

[15]And this becomes even more clear when
we see that another priest comes who is like
Melchizedek.[n] [16]He was not made a priest by
human rules and laws but through the
power of his life, which continues forever.
[17]It is said about him,

"You are a priest forever,
a priest like Melchizedek." *Psalm 110:4*

[18]The old rule is now set aside, because it
was weak and useless. [19]The law of Moses
could not make anything perfect. But now a
better hope has been given to us, and with
this hope we can come near to God. [20]It is
important that God did this with an oath.
Others became priests without an oath,
[21]but Christ became a priest with God's oath.
God said:

"The Lord has made a promise
and will not change his mind.
'You are a priest forever.' " *Psalm 110:4*

[22]This means that Jesus is the guarantee of a
better agreement[n] from God to his people.

7:11 The . . . law This refers to the people of Israel who were given the Law of Moses.
7:15 Melchizedek A priest and king who lived in the time of Abraham. (Read Genesis 14:17–24.)
7:22 agreement God gives a contract or agreement to his people. For the Jews, this agreement was the Law of Moses. But now God has given a better agreement to his people through Christ.

23 When one of the other priests died, he
could not continue being a priest. So there
were many priests. 24 But because Jesus lives
forever, he will never stop serving as priest.
25 So he is able always to save those who
come to God through him because he always
lives, asking God to help them.

26 Jesus is the kind of high priest we need.
He is holy, sinless, pure, not influenced by
sinners, and he is raised above the heavens.
27 He is not like the other priests who had to
offer sacrifices every day, first for their own
sins, and then for the sins of the people.
Christ offered his sacrifice only once and for
all time when he offered himself. 28 The law
chooses high priests who are people with
weaknesses, but the word of God's oath
came later than the law. It made God's Son
to be the high priest, and that Son has been
made perfect forever.

Jesus Is Our High Priest

8 Here is the point of what we are saying:
We have a high priest who sits on the
right side of God's throne in heaven. 2 Our
high priest serves in the Most Holy Place, the
true place of worship that was made by God,
not by humans.

3 Every high priest has the work of
offering gifts and sacrifices to God. So our
high priest must also offer something to
God. 4 If our high priest were now living on
earth, he would not be a priest, because there
are already priests here who follow the law
by offering gifts to God. 5 The work they do
as priests is only a copy and a shadow of
what is in heaven. This is why God warned
Moses when he was ready to build the Holy
Tent: "Be very careful to make everything by
the plan I showed you on the mountain."[n]
6 But the priestly work that has been given to
Jesus is much greater than the work that was
given to the other priests. In the same way,
the new agreement that Jesus brought from
God to his people is much greater than the
old one. And the new agreement is based on
promises of better things.

7 If there had been nothing wrong with the
first agreement,[n] there would have been no
need for a second agreement. 8 But God found
something wrong with his people. He says:[n]

"Look, the time is coming, says the Lord,
when I will make a new agreement
with the people of Israel
and the people of Judah.
9 It will not be like the agreement
I made with their ancestors
when I took them by the hand
to bring them out of Egypt.
But they broke that agreement,
and I turned away from them, says the
Lord.
10 This is the agreement I will make
with the people of Israel at that time,
says the Lord.
I will put my teachings in their minds
and write them on their hearts.
I will be their God,
and they will be my people.
11 People will no longer have to teach their
neighbors and relatives
to know the Lord,
because all people will know me,
from the least to the most important.
12 I will forgive them for the wicked things
they did,
and I will not remember their sins
anymore." *Jeremiah 31:31–34*

13 God called this a new agreement, so
he has made the first agreement old. And
anything that is old and worn out is ready
to disappear.

The Old Agreement

9 The first agreement[n] had rules for
worship and a place on earth for
worship. 2 The Holy Tent was set up for this.
The first area in the Tent was called the Holy
Place. In it were the lamp and the table with
the bread that was made holy for God.
3 Behind the second curtain was a room
called the Most Holy Place. 4 In it was a
golden altar for burning incense and the
Ark covered with gold that held the old
agreement. Inside this Ark was a golden jar
of manna, Aaron's rod that once grew leaves,
and the stone tablets of the old agreement.
5 Above the Ark were the creatures that
showed God's glory, whose wings reached
over the lid. But we cannot tell everything
about these things now.

6 When everything in the Tent was made

8:5 "Be . . . mountain." Quotation from Exodus 25:40. **8:7; 9:1 first agreement** The contract God gave the Jewish people when he gave them the Law of Moses. **8:8 But . . . says** Some Greek copies read "But God found something wrong and says to his people."

ready in this way, the priests went into the first room every day to worship. 7But only the high priest could go into the second room, and he did that only once a year. He could never enter the inner room without taking blood with him, which he offered to God for himself and for sins the people did without knowing they did them. 8The Holy Spirit uses this to show that the way into the Most Holy Place was not open while the system of the old Holy Tent was still being used. 9This is an example for the present time. It shows that the gifts and sacrifices offered cannot make the conscience of the worshiper perfect. 10These gifts and sacrifices were only about food and drink and special washings. They were rules for the body, to be followed until the time of God's new way.

The New Agreement

11But when Christ came as the high priest of the good things we now have,[n] he entered the greater and more perfect tent. It is not made by humans and does not belong to this world. 12Christ entered the Most Holy Place only once—and for all time. He did not take with him the blood of goats and calves. His sacrifice was his own blood, and by it he set us free from sin forever. 13The blood of goats and bulls and the ashes of a cow are sprinkled on the people who are unclean, and this makes their bodies clean again. 14How much more is done by the blood of Christ. He offered himself through the eternal Spirit[n] as a perfect sacrifice to God. His blood will make our consciences pure from useless acts so we may serve the living God.

15For this reason Christ brings a new agreement from God to his people. Those who are called by God can now receive the blessings he has promised, blessings that will last forever. They can have those things because Christ died so that the people who lived under the first agreement could be set free from sin.

16When there is a will,[n] it must be proven that the one who wrote that will is dead. 17A will means nothing while the person is alive; it can be used only after the person dies. 18This is why even the first agreement could not begin without blood to show death. 19First, Moses told all the people every command in the law. Next he took the blood of calves and mixed it with water. Then he used red wool and a branch of the hyssop plant to sprinkle it on the book of the law and on all the people. 20He said, "This is the blood that begins the Agreement that God commanded you to obey."[n] 21In the same way, Moses sprinkled the blood on the Holy Tent and over all the things used in worship. 22The law says that almost everything must be made clean by blood, and sins cannot be forgiven without blood to show death.

Christ's Death Takes Away Sins

23So the copies of the real things in heaven had to be made clean by animal sacrifices. But the real things in heaven need much better sacrifices. 24Christ did not go into the Most Holy Place made by humans, which is only a copy of the real one. He went into heaven itself and is there now before God to help us. 25The high priest enters the Most Holy Place once every year with blood that is not his own. But Christ did not offer himself many times. 26Then he would have had to suffer many times since the world was made. But Christ came only once and for all time at just the right time to take away all sin by sacrificing himself. 27Just as everyone must die once and then be judged, 28so Christ was offered as a sacrifice one time to take away the sins of many people. And he will come a second time, not to offer himself for sin, but to bring salvation to those who are waiting for him.

10 The law is only an unclear picture of the good things coming in the future; it is not the real thing. The people under the law offer the same sacrifices every year, but these sacrifices can never make perfect those who come near to worship God. 2If the law could make them perfect, the sacrifices would have already stopped. The worshipers would be made clean, and they would no longer have a sense of sin. 3But these sacrifices remind them of their sins every year, 4because it is impossible for the blood of bulls and goats to take away sins.

9:11 good . . . have Some Greek copies read "good things that are to come." **9:14 Spirit** This refers to the Holy Spirit, to Christ's own spirit, or to the spiritual and eternal nature of his sacrifice. **9:16 will** A legal document that shows how a person's money and property are to be distributed at the time of death. This is the same word in Greek as "agreement" in verse 15. **9:20 "This . . . obey."** Quotation from Exodus 24:8.

5So when Christ came into the world, he said:

"You do not want sacrifices and offerings,
but you have prepared a body for me.
6You do not ask for burnt offerings
and offerings to take away sins.
7Then I said, 'Look, I have come.
It is written about me in the book.
God, I have come to do what you
want.'" *Psalm 40:6–8*

8In this Scripture he first said, "You do not want sacrifices and offerings. You do not ask for burnt offerings and offerings to take away sins." (These are all sacrifices that the law commands.) 9Then he said, "Look, I have come to do what you want." God ends the first system of sacrifices so he can set up the new system. 10And because of this, we are made holy through the sacrifice Christ made in his body once and for all time.

11Every day the priests stand and do their religious service, often offering the same sacrifices. Those sacrifices can never take away sins. 12But after Christ offered one sacrifice for sins, forever, he sat down at the right side of God. 13And now Christ waits there for his enemies to be put under his power. 14With one sacrifice he made perfect forever those who are being made holy.

15The Holy Spirit also tells us about this. First he says:

16"This is the agreement[n] I will make
with them at that time, says the Lord.
I will put my teachings in their hearts
and write them on their minds."
Jeremiah 31:33

17Then he says:

"Their sins and the evil things they do—
I will not remember anymore."
Jeremiah 31:34

18Now when these have been forgiven, there is no more need for a sacrifice for sins.

Continue to Trust God

19So, brothers and sisters, we are completely free to enter the Most Holy Place without fear because of the blood of Jesus' death. 20We can enter through a new and living way that Jesus opened for us. It leads through the curtain—Christ's body. 21And since we have a great priest over God's house, 22let us come near to God with a sincere heart and a sure faith, because we have been made free from a guilty conscience, and our bodies have been washed with pure water. 23Let us hold firmly to the hope that we have confessed, because we can trust God to do what he promised.

24Let us think about each other and help each other to show love and do good deeds. 25You should not stay away from the church meetings, as some are doing, but you should meet together and encourage each other. Do this even more as you see the day[n] coming.

26If we decide to go on sinning after we have learned the truth, there is no longer any sacrifice for sins. 27There is nothing but fear in waiting for the judgment and the terrible fire that will destroy all those who live against God. 28Anyone who refused to obey the law of Moses was found guilty from the proof given by two or three witnesses. He was put to death without mercy. 29So what do you think should be done to those who do not respect the Son of God, who look at the blood of the agreement that made them holy as no different from others' blood, who insult the Spirit of God's grace? Surely they should have a much worse punishment. 30We know that God said, "I will punish those who do wrong; I will repay them."[n] And he also said, "The Lord will judge his people."[n] 31It is a terrible thing to fall into the hands of the living God.

32Remember those days in the past when you first learned the truth. You had a hard struggle with many sufferings, but you continued strong. 33Sometimes you were hurt and attacked before crowds of people, and sometimes you shared with those who were being treated that way. 34You helped the prisoners. You even had joy when all that you owned was taken from you, because you knew you had something better and more lasting.

35So do not lose the courage you had in the past, which has a great reward. 36You must hold on, so you can do what God wants and receive what he has promised. 37For in a very short time,

"The One who is coming will come
and will not be delayed.

10:16 agreement God gives a contract or agreement to his people. For the Jews, this agreement was the Law of Moses. But now God has given a better agreement to his people through Christ. **10:25 day** The day Christ will come to judge all people and take his people to live with him. **10:30 "I . . . them."** Quotation from Deuteronomy 32:35. **10:30 "The Lord . . . people."** Quotation from Deuteronomy 32:36; Psalm 135:14.

devotion 345

HEBREWS 10:25

CHURCH WOUNDS

Maybe you haven't been excited about church in a while. Maybe you were hurt at church or rejected by a church. If so, on behalf of the body of Christ, I apologize. Church should not be a dangerous place to confess your sin and find help for your brokenness. Jesus intended for church to be a safe place to encounter the living God.

If the church you attend has not been safe or healthy, then don't go back to that kind of body. Find your way into a healthy, fairly functional fellowship of believers. Be encouraged. There are great, Bible-believing, grace-filled churches all over the world. Go to a church where the pastor opens the Bible and teaches you from Scriptures. You can get topical monologues on the afternoon talk shows. But at church, you need to hear from God, so find one where the leadership is pursuing God's heart and depending on his Word for direction.

The presence of God is promised when God's people have gathered together (Matt. 18:20). And you need to get yourself into his presence every time you have the opportunity. Do everything you can. Rearrange your schedule. Make it a priority. Do whatever it takes to meet consistently with other followers of Christ.

Attending church may have been difficult for some of us in the past. Maybe you have suffered wounds from the not-so-well-intending. But do not neglect this instruction to meet with the people of God and hear consistently from his Word.

38Those who are right with me
will live by faith.
But if they turn back with fear,
I will not be pleased with them."

Habakkuk 2:3–4

39But we are not those who turn back and
are lost. We are people who have faith and
are saved.

What Is Faith?

11 Faith means being sure of the things
we hope for and knowing that
something is real even if we do not see it.
2Faith is the reason we remember great
people who lived in the past.
3It is by faith we understand that the
whole world was made by God's command
so what we see was made by something that
cannot be seen.
4It was by faith that Abel offered God a
better sacrifice than Cain did. God said he
was pleased with the gifts Abel offered and
called Abel a good man because of his faith.
Abel died, but through his faith he is still
speaking.
5It was by faith that Enoch was taken to
heaven so he would not die. He could not
be found, because God had taken him
away. Before he was taken, the Scripture
says that he was a man who truly pleased
God. 6Without faith no one can please God.
Anyone who comes to God must believe
that he is real and that he rewards those
who truly want to find him.
7It was by faith that Noah heard God's
warnings about things he could not yet see.
He obeyed God and built a large boat to save
his family. By his faith, Noah showed that
the world was wrong, and he became one of
those who are made right with God through
faith.
8It was by faith Abraham obeyed God's
call to go to another place God promised
to give him. He left his own country, not

knowing where he was to go. 9It was by
faith that he lived like a foreigner in the
country God promised to give him. He
lived in tents with Isaac and Jacob, who
had received that same promise from God.
10Abraham was waiting for the city[n] that
has real foundations
—the city planned and built by God.
11He was too old to have children, and
Sarah could not have children. It was by
faith that Abraham was made able to
become a father, because he trusted God to
do what he had promised.[n] 12This man was
so old he was almost dead, but from him
came as many descendants as there are stars
in the sky. Like the sand on the seashore,
they could not be counted.
13All these great people died in faith. They
did not get the things that God promised his
people, but they saw them coming far in the
future and were glad. They said they were
like visitors and strangers on earth. 14When
people say such things, they show they
are looking for a country that will be their
own. 15If they had been thinking about the
country they had left, they could have gone
back. 16But they were waiting for a better
country—a heavenly country. So God is not
ashamed to be called their God, because he
has prepared a city for them.
17It was by faith that Abraham, when God
tested him, offered his son Isaac as a sacrifice.
God made the promises to Abraham, but
Abraham was ready to offer his own son as a
sacrifice. 18God had said, "The descendants I
promised you will be from Isaac."[n]
19Abraham believed that God could raise the
dead, and really, it was as if Abraham got
Isaac back from death.
20It was by faith that Isaac blessed the
future of Jacob and Esau. 21It was by faith
that Jacob, as he was dying, blessed each one
of Joseph's sons. Then he worshiped as he
leaned on the top of his walking stick.
22It was by faith that Joseph, while he was
dying, spoke about the Israelites leaving
Egypt and gave instructions about what to
do with his body.
23It was by faith that Moses' parents hid
him for three months after he was born.
They saw that Moses was a beautiful baby,
and they were not afraid to disobey the
king's order.
24It was by faith that Moses, when he
grew up, refused to be called the son of the
king of Egypt's daughter. 25He chose to suffer
with God's people instead of enjoying sin for
a short time. 26He thought it was better to
suffer for the Christ than to have all the
treasures of Egypt, because he was looking
for God's reward. 27It was by faith that Moses
left Egypt and was not afraid of the king's
anger. Moses continued strong as if he could
see the God that no one can see. 28It was by
faith that Moses prepared the Passover and
spread the blood on the doors so the one
who brings death would not kill the
firstborn sons of Israel.
29It was by faith that the people crossed
the Red Sea as if it were dry land. But when
the Egyptians tried it, they were drowned.
30It was by faith that the walls of Jericho
fell after the people had marched around
them for seven days.
31It was by faith that Rahab, the prostitute,
welcomed the spies and was not killed with
those who refused to obey God.
32Do I need to give more examples? I do
not have time to tell you about Gideon,
Barak, Samson, Jephthah, David, Samuel,
and the prophets. 33Through their faith they
defeated kingdoms. They did what was right,
received God's promises, and shut the
mouths of lions. 34They stopped great fires
and were saved from being killed with
swords. They were weak, and yet were made
strong. They were powerful in battle and
defeated other armies. 35Women received
their dead relatives raised back to life. Others
were tortured and refused to accept their
freedom so they could be raised from the
dead to a better life. 36Some were laughed at
and beaten. Others were put in chains and
thrown into prison. 37They were stoned to
death, they were cut in half,[n] and they were
killed with swords. Some wore the skins of
sheep and goats. They were poor, abused,
and treated badly. 38The world was not good
enough for them! They wandered in deserts
and mountains, living in caves and holes in
the earth.
39All these people are known for their

11:10 city The spiritual "city" where God's people live with him. Also called "the heavenly Jerusalem." (See Hebrews 12:22.)
11:11 It . . . promised. Some Greek copies refer to Sarah's faith, rather than Abraham's. **11:18 "The descendants . . . Isaac."** Quotation from Genesis 21:12. **11:37 they were cut in half** Some Greek copies also include, "they were tested."

faith, but none of them received what God had promised. 40God planned to give us something better so that they would be made perfect, but only together with us.

Follow Jesus' Example

12 We are surrounded by a great cloud of people whose lives tell us what faith means. So let us run the race that is before us and never give up. We should remove from our lives anything that would get in the way and the sin that so easily holds us back. 2Let us look only to Jesus, the One who began our faith and who makes it perfect. He suffered death on the cross. But he accepted the shame as if it were nothing because of the joy that God put before him. And now he is sitting at the right side of God's throne. 3Think about Jesus' example. He held on while wicked people were doing evil things to him. So do not get tired and stop trying.

God Is like a Father

4You are struggling against sin, but your struggles have not yet caused you to be killed. 5You have forgotten the encouraging words that call you his children:

"My child, don't think the Lord's
discipline is worth nothing,
and don't stop trying when he corrects
you.
6The Lord disciplines those he loves,
and he punishes everyone he accepts as
his child." *Proverbs 3:11–12*

7So hold on through your sufferings, because they are like a father's discipline. God is treating you as children. All children are disciplined by their fathers. 8If you are never disciplined (and every child must be disciplined), you are not true children. 9We have all had fathers here on earth who disciplined us, and we respected them. So it is even more important that we accept discipline from the Father of our spirits so we will have life. 10Our fathers on earth disciplined us for a short time in the way they thought was best. But God disciplines us to help us, so we can become holy as he is. 11We do not enjoy being disciplined. It is painful at the time, but later, after we have learned from it, we have peace, because we start living in the right way.

Be Careful How You Live

12You have become weak, so make yourselves strong again. 13Keep on the right path, so the weak will not stumble but rather be strengthened.

14Try to live in peace with all people, and try to live free from sin. Anyone whose life is not holy will never see the Lord. 15Be careful that no one fails to receive God's grace and begins to cause trouble among you. A person like that can ruin many of you. 16Be careful that no one takes part in sexual sin or is like Esau and never thinks about God. As the oldest son, Esau would have received everything from his father, but he sold all that for a single meal. 17You remember that after Esau did this, he wanted to get his father's blessing, but his father refused. Esau could find no way to change what he had done, even though he wanted the blessing so much that he cried.

18You have not come to a mountain that can be touched and that is burning with fire. You have not come to darkness, sadness, and storms. 19You have not come to the noise of a trumpet or to the sound of a voice like the one the people of Israel heard and begged not to hear another word. 20They did not want to hear the command: "If anything, even an animal, touches the mountain, it must be put to death with stones."[n] 21What they saw was so terrible that Moses said, "I am shaking with fear."[n]

22But you have come to Mount Zion,[n] to the city of the living God, the heavenly Jerusalem. You have come to thousands of angels gathered together with joy. 23You have come to the meeting of God's firstborn[n] children whose names are written in heaven. You have come to God, the judge of all people, and to the spirits of good people who have been made perfect. 24You have come to Jesus, the One who brought the new agreement from God to his people, and you have come to the sprinkled blood[n] that has a better message than the blood of Abel.[n]

12:20 "If . . . stones." Quotation from Exodus 19:12–13. **12:21 "I . . . fear."** Quotation from Deuteronomy 9:19. **12:22 Mount Zion** Another name for Jerusalem, here meaning the spiritual city of God's people. **12:23 firstborn** The first son born in a Jewish family was given the most important place in the family and received special blessings. All of God's children are like that. **12:24 sprinkled blood** The blood of Jesus' death. **12:24 Abel** The son of Adam and Eve, who was killed by his brother Cain (Genesis 4:8).

[25]So be careful and do not refuse to listen
when God speaks. Others refused to listen to
him when he warned them on earth, and
they did not escape. So it will be worse for us
if we refuse to listen to God who warns us
from heaven. [26]When he spoke before, his
voice shook the earth, but now he has
promised, "Once again I will shake not only
the earth but also the heavens."[n] [27]The words
"once again" clearly show us that everything
that was made—things that can be shaken—
will be destroyed. Only the things that
cannot be shaken will remain.

[28]So let us be thankful, because we have a
kingdom that cannot be shaken. We should
worship God in a way that pleases him with
respect and fear, [29]because our God is like a
fire that burns things up.

13 Keep on loving each other as brothers
and sisters. [2]Remember to welcome
strangers, because some who have done this
have welcomed angels without knowing it.
[3]Remember those who are in prison as if you
were in prison with them. Remember those
who are suffering as if you were suffering
with them.

[4]Marriage should be honored by everyone,
and husband and wife should keep their
marriage pure. God will judge as guilty those
who take part in sexual sins. [5]Keep your
lives free from the love of money, and be
satisfied with what you have. God has said,

"I will never leave you;
I will never abandon you." *Deuteronomy 31:6*

[6]So we can be sure when we say,

"I will not be afraid, because the Lord is
my helper.
People can't do anything to me."
Psalm 118:6

[7]Remember your leaders who taught
God's message to you. Remember how they
lived and died, and copy their faith. [8]Jesus

12:26 "Once . . . heavens." Quotation from Haggai 2:6, 21.

devotion 346

HEBREWS 13:9

WHEN IT'S REAL, YOU'LL KNOW IT

Strange doctrine should be easy to avoid since you are holding all the truth of God in your hands. Believers need to understand the truth of God's Word and be ready to discuss the hope that we have in Jesus Christ at all times and with anyone who asks (1 Pet. 3:15). Studying and counseling with the Word keeps you out of trouble and sheds light on anything counterfeit that comes your way.

I once knew a man who worked for the Treasury Department. His job was to catch counterfeit currency being circulated in the United States. I asked him how many different counterfeit bills he had to learn, and his response to me was, "I never study the counterfeit, only the real thing. Then whenever counterfeit currency comes through the department, I recognize it immediately."

He was qualified to discover and determine all that was false because he truly understood what was genuine. What are you qualified to teach about? Can you teach about God's forgiveness? Maybe you are aptly qualified to teach about restoration? What about heaven? What about grace? What about tithing? We are supposed to be the teachers and the examples of the truth found in the Scriptures. Paul instructed Titus on how he should teach—with trustworthy words and true teaching that would illuminate all false teachers (Titus 1:9). Our lives should expose anything false that the world believes about Christ. When people pass by you or witness your life, they should experience the real thing.

Christ is the same yesterday, today, and
forever.
9 Do not let all kinds of strange teachings
lead you into the wrong way. Your hearts
should be strengthened by God's grace, not
by obeying rules about foods, which do not
help those who obey them.
10 We have a sacrifice, but the priests who
serve in the Holy Tent cannot eat from it.
11 The high priest carries the blood of
animals into the Most Holy Place where
he offers this blood for sins. But the bodies
of the animals are burned outside the
camp. 12 So Jesus also suffered outside the
city to make his people holy with his own
blood. 13 So let us go to Jesus outside the
camp, holding on as he did when we are
abused.
14 Here on earth we do not have a city that
lasts forever, but we are looking for the city
that we will have in the future. 15 So through
Jesus let us always offer to God our sacrifice
of praise, coming from lips that speak his
name. 16 Do not forget to do good to others,
and share with them, because such sacrifices
please God.
17 Obey your leaders and act under their
authority. They are watching over you,
because they are responsible for your souls.
Obey them so that they will do this work
with joy, not sadness. It will not help you to
make their work hard.
18 Pray for us. We are sure that we have a
clear conscience, because we always want to
do the right thing. 19 I especially beg you to
pray so that God will send me back to you
soon.
20-21 I pray that the God of peace will give
you every good thing you need so you can
do what he wants. God raised from the dead
our Lord Jesus, the Great Shepherd of the
sheep, because of the blood of his death. His
blood began the eternal agreement that God
made with his people. I pray that God will
do in us what pleases him, through Jesus
Christ, and to him be glory forever and ever.
Amen.
22 My brothers and sisters, I beg you to
listen patiently to this message I have
written to encourage you, because it is not
very long. 23 I want you to know that our
brother Timothy has been let out of prison.
If he arrives soon, we will both come to see
you.
24 Greet all your leaders and all of God's
people. Those from Italy send greetings to
you.
25 Grace be with you all.

James

Sometimes called "the Proverbs of the New Testament" because of its practicality

Person Holding the Pen God Wrote With: The common assumption is that Jesus' half-brother *James* wrote this book. Remember, they shared the same mother but had different fathers.

When the Text Was Written: This is one of the earliest New Testament writings, believed to have been penned between 40 and 50 A.D.

Spiritual Posture of the Original Recipients: James wrote this letter to Jewish Christians who, much like the Hebrews, were being persecuted for their faith. They were also in danger of getting stuck in ritualistic religion rather than truly living for the glory of Jesus Christ.

Storyline Synopsis: James is emphatic and very direct in this message about living your life under the authority of Christ. (He uses fifty-nine commands in this short book, and forty-six of those include the word "you.") James segues from preaching to almost "meddling" when he poses rhetorical questions about the authenticity of the faith of these Jewish Christians in chapter 2! The gist of this straightforward "faith quiz" is that false faith—faith without deeds to back it up—is ineffective with people and with God. Just saying, "I believe in God," without living a life that honors him and is edifying to others, doesn't mean squat.

A Moment Worth Discussing: At the beginning of his letter, James talks about the certainty of human suffering (James 1:2) and the joy that can be found in the midst of it. His theology is similar to this statement from Sheila Walsh: "Some of God's best gifts come in boxes that make your hands bleed when you open them." Discuss a time of suffering in your life that turned out to be one of God's best gifts to you.

Interesting (But Likely to Be Overlooked) Character: *Rahab* (James 2:24–25) was the plucky prostitute God sovereignly used to keep the Israelite spies safe in Jericho (Josh. 2). In spite of her sinful résumé, her bravery on behalf of God's people and trust in his absolute authority earned a divine pardon!

1 From James, a servant of God and of the
Lord Jesus Christ.
To all of God's people who are scattered
everywhere in the world:

Greetings.

Faith and Wisdom

[2]My brothers and sisters, when you have
many kinds of troubles, you should be full of
joy, [3]because you know that these troubles
test your faith, and this will give you
patience. [4]Let your patience show itself
perfectly in what you do. Then you will
be perfect and complete and will have
everything you need. [5]But if any of you
needs wisdom, you should ask God for it. He
is generous to everyone and will give you
wisdom without criticizing you. [6]But when
you ask God, you must believe and not
doubt. Anyone who doubts is like a wave in
the sea, blown up and down by the wind.
[7-8]Such doubters are thinking two different
things at the same time, and they cannot
decide about anything they do. They should
not think they will receive anything from
the Lord.

True Riches

[9]Believers who are poor should take pride
that God has made them spiritually rich.
[10]Those who are rich should take pride
that God has shown them that they are
spiritually poor. The rich will die like a wild
flower in the grass. [11]The sun rises with
burning heat and dries up the plants. The
flower falls off, and its beauty is gone. In the
same way the rich will die while they are
still taking care of business.

Temptation Is Not from God

[12]When people are tempted and still
continue strong, they should be happy. After
they have proved their faith, God will
reward them with life forever. God promised
this to all those who love him. [13]When
people are tempted, they should not say,
"God is tempting me." Evil cannot tempt
God, and God himself does not tempt
anyone. [14]But people are tempted when their

devotion 347

JAMES 1:2–4

THIRTEEN DOLLARS AND GOD'S PROVISION

My husband and I opened a retail store when we were in our early twenties. It was a surf shop, and we wanted to use it to minister to teenagers while supporting our family. The first year was lots of fun, but then a recession hit the retail industry, and our store was hit hard. Our paychecks got smaller and smaller as sales went down. My husband went to the grocery store one morning with thirteen dollars and came home with milk, cereal, bread, peanut butter, spaghetti, and tomato sauce. We were so excited because God had provided meals for a few more days.

We all go through seasons in our lives when troubles seem to overwhelm us. Verse 2 says we should be full of joy when these seasons come because they test our faith. We had no one to turn to except God, and sometimes I think God likes it that way. He wants us to come to him and watch his faithfulness unfold. The hard part is being patient while God works through each situation.

We closed our store that year and walked away with sixty thousand dollars in debt that took us ten years to repay. We had our faith tested, we learned patience, and now every time I go to the grocery store, I'm so thankful for God's faithfulness. Have you recently come through a time of testing? Are you still stuck in one? Memorize these verses and know that God has a purpose for your pain.

own evil desire leads them away and traps
them. 15This desire leads to sin, and then the
sin grows and brings death.
16My dear brothers and sisters, do not be
fooled about this. 17Every good action and
every perfect gift is from God. These good
gifts come down from the Creator of the sun,
moon, and stars, who does not change like
their shifting shadows. 18God decided to give
us life through the word of truth so we
might be the most important of all the
things he made.

Listening and Obeying

19My dear brothers and sisters, always be
willing to listen and slow to speak. Do not
become angry easily, 20because anger will
not help you live the right kind of life God
wants. 21So put out of your life every evil
thing and every kind of wrong. Then in
gentleness accept God's teaching that is
planted in your hearts, which can save you.
22Do what God's teaching says; when you
only listen and do nothing, you are fooling
yourselves. 23Those who hear God's teaching
and do nothing are like people who look at
themselves in a mirror. 24They see their faces
and then go away and quickly forget what
they looked like. 25But the truly happy
people are those who carefully study God's
perfect law that makes people free, and they
continue to study it. They do not forget what
they heard, but they obey what God's
teaching says. Those who do this will be
made happy.

The True Way to Worship God

26People who think they are religious
but say things they should not say are just
fooling themselves. Their "religion" is worth
nothing. 27Religion that God accepts as pure
and without fault is this: caring for orphans
or widows who need help, and keeping
yourself free from the world's evil influence.

Love All People

2 My dear brothers and sisters, as believers
in our glorious Lord Jesus Christ, never
think some people are more important than
others. 2Suppose someone comes into your
church meeting wearing nice clothes and a
gold ring. At the same time a poor person
comes in wearing old, dirty clothes. 3You
show special attention to the one wearing
nice clothes and say, "Please, sit here in this
good seat." But you say to the poor person,
"Stand over there," or, "Sit on the floor by my
feet." 4What are you doing? You are making
some people more important than others,
and with evil thoughts you are deciding that
one person is better.
5Listen, my dear brothers and sisters! God
chose the poor in the world to be rich with
faith and to receive the kingdom God
promised to those who love him. 6But you
show no respect to the poor. The rich are
always trying to control your lives. They are
the ones who take you to court. 7And they
are the ones who speak against Jesus, who
owns you.
8This royal law is found in the Scriptures:
"Love your neighbor as you love yourself."[n] If
you obey this law, you are doing right. 9But if
you treat one person as being more important
than another, you are sinning. You are guilty
of breaking God's law. 10A person who follows
all of God's law but fails to obey even one
command is guilty of breaking all the
commands in that law. 11The same God who
said, "You must not be guilty of adultery,"[n]
also said, "You must not murder anyone."[n] So
if you do not take part in adultery but you
murder someone, you are guilty of breaking
all of God's law. 12In everything you say and
do, remember that you will be judged by the
law that makes people free. 13So you must
show mercy to others, or God will not show
mercy to you when he judges you. But the
person who shows mercy can stand without
fear at the judgment.

Faith and Good Works

14My brothers and sisters, if people say
they have faith, but do nothing, their faith
is worth nothing. Can faith like that save
them? 15A brother or sister in Christ might
need clothes or food. 16If you say to that
person, "God be with you! I hope you stay
warm and get plenty to eat," but you do not
give what that person needs, your words are
worth nothing. 17In the same way, faith by
itself—that does nothing—is dead.

2:8 "Love . . . yourself." Quotation from Leviticus 19:18. **2:11 "You . . . adultery."** Quotation from Exodus 20:14 and Deuteronomy 5:18. **2:11 "You . . . anyone."** Quotation from Exodus 20:13 and Deuteronomy 5:17.

[18]Someone might say, "You have faith, but
I have deeds." Show me your faith without
doing anything, and I will show you my
faith by what I do. [19]You believe there is one
God. Good! But the demons believe that, too,
and they tremble with fear.
[20]You foolish person! Must you be shown
that faith that does nothing is worth nothing?
[21]Abraham, our ancestor, was made right
with God by what he did when he offered
his son Isaac on the altar. [22]So you see that
Abraham's faith and the things he did
worked together. His faith was made perfect
by what he did. [23]This shows the full
meaning of the Scripture that says:
"Abraham believed God, and God accepted
Abraham's faith, and that faith made him
right with God."[n] And Abraham was called
God's friend.[n] [24]So you see that people are
made right with God by what they do, not by
faith only.
[25]Another example is Rahab, a prostitute,
who was made right with God by something
she did. She welcomed the spies into her
home and helped them escape by a different
road.
[26]Just as a person's body that does not
have a spirit is dead, so faith that does
nothing is dead!

Controlling the Things We Say

3 My brothers and sisters, not many of you
should become teachers, because you
know that we who teach will be judged more
strictly. [2]We all make many mistakes. If
people never said anything wrong, they
would be perfect and able to control their
entire selves, too. [3]When we put bits into the
mouths of horses to make them obey us, we
can control their whole bodies. [4]Also a ship is
very big, and it is pushed by strong winds. But
a very small rudder controls that big ship,
making it go wherever the pilot wants. [5]It is
the same with the tongue. It is a small part of
the body, but it brags about great things.
A big forest fire can be started with only a
little flame. [6]And the tongue is like a fire. It
is a whole world of evil among the parts of

2:23 "Abraham . . . God." Quotation from Genesis 15:6.
2:23 God's friend These words about Abraham are found in 2 Chronicles 20:7 and Isaiah 41:8.

devotion 348

JAMES 3:5–6

DANGEROUS FLAMES

Do James's words about a tongue of fire leave you squirming in your seat? Ask yourself why. Perhaps it's because you, like most of us, feel guilty about letting your own tongue get away from you, and now you're realizing that the ramifications of doing so might be—or already are—dreadful. Or maybe, like most of us, you've been the victim of someone else's vile, insensitive gossip, and it has destroyed something that is personal and sacred to you like your reputation or even something worse. Why is it that when we know what it feels like to be the target of someone's stray tongue, we can still get trapped into letting our own mouths get away from us?

Whatever we need to do to accomplish it—hanging up the phone, leaving the room, or dismissing ourselves from the situation—we need to make certain we are controlling our tongues. Titus 3:2 tells us "to speak no evil about anyone, to live in peace, and to be gentle and polite to all people." These are good guidelines for how we can be careful not to get caught up in gossip or lash out at someone else. There's a reason James described a loose tongue as a dangerous flame that is capable of igniting a huge forest fire. We ought to stop and think before we open our mouths and remember that what we say can have far-reaching, devastating consequences.

our bodies. The tongue spreads its evil
through the whole body. The tongue is set
on fire by hell, and it starts a fire that
influences all of life. 7People can tame every
kind of wild animal, bird, reptile, and fish,
and they have tamed them, 8but no one can
tame the tongue. It is wild and evil and full
of deadly poison. 9We use our tongues to
praise our Lord and Father, but then we
curse people, whom God made like himself.
10Praises and curses come from the same
mouth! My brothers and sisters, this should
not happen. 11Do good and bad water flow
from the same spring? 12My brothers and
sisters, can a fig tree make olives, or can a
grapevine make figs? No! And a well full of
salty water cannot give good water.

True Wisdom

13Are there those among you who are
truly wise and understanding? Then they
should show it by living right and doing
good things with a gentleness that comes
from wisdom. 14But if you are selfish and
have bitter jealousy in your hearts, do not
brag. Your bragging is a lie that hides the
truth. 15That kind of "wisdom" does not
come from God but from the world. It is
not spiritual; it is from the devil. 16Where
jealousy and selfishness are, there will be
confusion and every kind of evil. 17But the
wisdom that comes from God is first of all
pure, then peaceful, gentle, and easy to
please. This wisdom is always ready to help
those who are troubled and to do good for
others. It is always fair and honest. 18People
who work for peace in a peaceful way plant
a good crop of right-living.

Give Yourselves to God

4 Do you know where your fights and
arguments come from? They come from
the selfish desires that war within you. 2You
want things, but you do not have them. So
you are ready to kill and are jealous of other
people, but you still cannot get what you
want. So you argue and fight. You do not get
what you want, because you do not ask God.
3Or when you ask, you do not receive
because the reason you ask is wrong. You
want things so you can use them for your
own pleasures.

4So, you are not loyal to God! You should
know that loving the world is the same as
hating God. Anyone who wants to be a
friend of the world becomes God's enemy.
5Do you think the Scripture means nothing
that says, "The Spirit that God made to live
in us wants us for himself alone"?[n] 6But God
gives us even more grace, as the Scripture
says,

> "God is against the proud,
> but he gives grace to the humble."
>
> *Proverbs 3:34*

7So give yourselves completely to God.
Stand against the devil, and the devil will
run from you. 8Come near to God, and God
will come near to you. You sinners, clean sin
out of your lives. You who are trying to
follow God and the world at the same time,
make your thinking pure. 9Be sad, cry, and
weep! Change your laughter into crying and
your joy into sadness. 10Humble yourself in
the Lord's presence, and he will honor you.

You Are Not the Judge

11Brothers and sisters, do not tell evil lies
about each other. If you speak against your
fellow believers or judge them, you are
judging and speaking against the law they
follow. And when you are judging the law,
you are no longer a follower of the law. You
have become a judge. 12God is the only
Lawmaker and Judge. He is the only One
who can save and destroy. So it is not right
for you to judge your neighbor.

Let God Plan Your Life

13Some of you say, "Today or tomorrow
we will go to some city. We will stay there a
year, do business, and make money." 14But
you do not know what will happen
tomorrow! Your life is like a mist. You can
see it for a short time, but then it goes away.
15So you should say, "If the Lord wants, we
will live and do this or that." 16But now you
are proud and you brag. All of this bragging
is wrong. 17Anyone who knows the right
thing to do, but does not do it, is sinning.

A Warning to the Rich

5 You rich people, listen! Cry and be very
sad because of the troubles that are
coming to you. 2Your riches have rotted, and

4:5 "The Spirit . . . alone." These words may be from Exodus 20:5.

devotion 349

JAMES 4:15

GOT A FIVE-YEAR PLAN?

They say if you want to make God laugh, tell him your five-year plan. This past weekend, I heard myself say out loud, "Everything and everyone has fallen through. I'm taking my disappointed little self, going home, and making a *ten*-year plan." Even as the words were coming out of my mouth, I realized that God was probably smiling over my need to figure everything out. I could sense him saying, "Go ahead and make your plan. But you will only go where I decide and be what I want and enjoy what I provide."

Plans are good. We are supposed to use our minds to think ahead, consider the resources, and multiply our talents. It's just that all the planning falls under the umbrella of God's will. Anything outside his divine authority will fall away.

My single girlfriends say they want God's man in God's time and in God's way. That sounds like a great prayer to me, but they have to prove they mean it. They have to wait in complete trust for God's faithfulness, even when the "perfect" man walks away, and know that nothing will come between them and God's perfect will.

Do you trust that what God wants for you will prevail? Is there an abiding peace in your heart that God has your best interests in mind? Make the best five-year plan you can, and then lay it on God's altar saying, "Lord, please take these ideas and only allow what's inside your divine will."

your clothes have been eaten by moths.
3Your gold and silver have rusted, and that
rust will be a proof that you were wrong. It
will eat your bodies like fire. You saved your
treasure for the last days. 4The pay you did
not give the workers who mowed your fields
cries out against you, and the cries of the
workers have been heard by the Lord
All-Powerful. 5Your life on earth was full
of rich living and pleasing yourselves
with everything you wanted. You made
yourselves fat, like an animal ready to be
killed. 6You have judged guilty and then
murdered innocent people, who were not
against you.

Be Patient

7Brothers and sisters, be patient until the
Lord comes again. A farmer patiently waits
for his valuable crop to grow from the earth
and for it to receive the autumn and spring
rains. 8You, too, must be patient. Do not give
up hope, because the Lord is coming soon.
9Brothers and sisters, do not complain
against each other or you will be judged
guilty. And the Judge is ready to come!
10Brothers and sisters, follow the example of
the prophets who spoke for the Lord. They
suffered many hard things, but they were
patient. 11We say they are happy because
they did not give up. You have heard about
Job's patience, and you know the Lord's
purpose for him in the end. You know the
Lord is full of mercy and is kind.

Be Careful What You Say

12My brothers and sisters, above all, do not
use an oath when you make a promise. Don't
use the name of heaven, earth, or anything
else to prove what you say. When you mean
yes, say only yes, and when you mean no,
say only no so you will not be judged guilty.

The Power of Prayer

13Anyone who is having troubles should
pray. Anyone who is happy should sing

praises. [14]Anyone who is sick should call the
church's elders. They should pray for and
pour oil on the person[n] in the name of the
Lord. [15]And the prayer that is said with faith
will make the sick person well; the Lord will
heal that person. And if the person has sinned,
the sins will be forgiven. [16]Confess your sins
to each other and pray for each other so God
can heal you. When a believing person prays,
great things happen. [17]Elijah was a human
being just like us. He prayed that it would not
rain, and it did not rain on the land for three
and a half years! [18]Then Elijah prayed again,
and the rain came down from the sky, and the
land produced crops again.

Saving a Soul

[19]My brothers and sisters, if one of you
wanders away from the truth, and someone
helps that person come back, [20]remember
this: Anyone who brings a sinner back from
the wrong way will save that sinner's soul
from death and will cause many sins to be
forgiven.

5:14 pour oil on the person Oil was used in the name of the Lord as a sign that the person was now set apart for God's special attention and care.

1 Peter

Person Holding the Pen God Wrote With: This book was penned by *Peter*—the apostle most likely to put his foot in his mouth when he was younger! This is the same guy who denied three times that he even knew Jesus prior to the crucifixion—and the very person Jesus said would be the "rock" upon whom his church would be built (Matt. 16:17–19).

When the Text Was Written: Peter wrote this letter in the mid–60s A.D.

Spiritual Posture of the Original Recipients: The Christian community in the first century struggled with persecution, religiosity, and anemic faith. They were also a nation without borders—Christians were scattered all over the world and didn't usually experience the team spirit or strength that come in numbers.

Storyline Synopsis: Peter explained to non-Jewish believers that they were the "new Israel" and their identity was secure in Christ! In other words, non-Jewish Christians have roots in all that God did for Israel in the Old Testament because of their relationship with Jesus. Peter also emphasized that suffering would galvanize them against sin; they wouldn't ever be totally immune to temptation, but they would be effectively guarded. Learning to endure difficulty and disappointment would work like spiritual sunscreen, protecting them from being burned by the devil. All five chapters read like a syllabus for *Exhibiting Holiness During Hardship 101*—a course offered at The First-Century School for Christians.

A Moment Worth Discussing: The author of this letter is the same follower who wimped out and retreated when the Messiah he had worked with and worshiped for three years was being murdered. It is a testament to God's amazing grace that a man who failed with flying colors the first time he was persecuted for his faith could mature to the point of earnestly teaching others about holiness under hardship years later. This is a perfect example of how God can transform anyone into a beautiful reflection of his glory.

Interesting (But Likely to Be Overlooked) Characters: The *mature believers* who put into practice Peter's synopsized behavioral guide for believers in trouble—*control your tongue, do good, don't fight,* and *pursue peace*—are worth noting.

1 From Peter, an apostle of Jesus Christ.
To God's chosen people who are away
from their homes and are scattered all
around Pontus, Galatia, Cappadocia, Asia,
and Bithynia. 2God planned long ago to
choose you by making you his holy people,
which is the Spirit's work. God wanted you
to obey him and to be made clean by the
blood of the death of Jesus Christ.
Grace and peace be yours more and more.

We Have a Living Hope

3Praise be to the God and Father of our
Lord Jesus Christ. In God's great mercy he
has caused us to be born again into a living
hope, because Jesus Christ rose from the
dead. 4Now we hope for the blessings God
has for his children. These blessings, which
cannot be destroyed or be spoiled or lose
their beauty, are kept in heaven for you.
5God's power protects you through your
faith until salvation is shown to you at the
end of time. 6This makes you very happy,
even though now for a short time different
kinds of troubles may make you sad. 7These
troubles come to prove that your faith is
pure. This purity of faith is worth more than
gold, which can be proved to be pure by fire
but will ruin. But the purity of your faith
will bring you praise and glory and honor
when Jesus Christ is shown to you. 8You
have not seen Christ, but still you love him.
You cannot see him now, but you believe in
him. So you are filled with a joy that cannot
be explained, a joy full of glory. 9And you are
receiving the goal of your faith—the
salvation of your souls.
10The prophets searched carefully and
tried to learn about this salvation. They
prophesied about the grace that was coming
to you. 11The Spirit of Christ was in the
prophets, telling in advance about the
sufferings of Christ and about the glory that
would follow those sufferings. The prophets
tried to learn about what the Spirit was
showing them, when those things would
happen, and what the world would be like at
that time. 12It was shown them that their
service was not for themselves but for you,
when they told about the truths you have
now heard. Those who preached the Good
News to you told you those things with the

devotion 350

1 PETER 1:3

GOD'S DEPOSIT

When we are born again of the Spirit, we have been made new by the washing and regeneration of our own hearts and spirit into the work that Christ completed on the cross. Of course, we as grown-ups cannot crawl back into our mother's womb. Even the ancient scholar Nicodemus had a tough time understanding what "born again" meant to him as a grown man. But receiving new life—spiritual life—is exactly what it means. No longer does the Spirit that God sent into the world walk alongside you, but now he has a residence inside your heart. So when you ask Jesus into your heart, the Holy Spirit is what God deposits into your physical being as a helper.

Christians do not live in an illuminated, euphoric environment where everything we say or do is proper and everyone we know is perfect in their conduct. But our lives should start to reflect the kind of living that God has given us the power to live. Paul encouraged Titus to train up the Greek believers on the island of Crete who were still living like they were spiritless. Paul's message to Titus remains an encouragement to all believers to no longer live as a critical, judgmental people. Instead, we are to live as "new people through the Holy Spirit" (Titus 3:5). We are to live like we have received God's mercy, and this mercy is the born-again Spirit. This new life is the evidence that the Holy Spirit lives in our hearts.

help of the Holy Spirit who was sent from
heaven—things into which angels desire to
look.

A Call to Holy Living

13 So prepare your minds for service and
have self-control. All your hope should be
for the gift of grace that will be yours when
Jesus Christ is shown to you. 14 Now that you
are obedient children of God do not live as
you did in the past. You did not understand,
so you did the evil things you wanted. 15 But
be holy in all you do, just as God, the One
who called you, is holy. 16 It is written in the
Scriptures: "You must be holy, because I am
holy."[n]

17 You pray to God and call him Father,
and he judges each person's work equally. So
while you are here on earth, you should live
with respect for God. 18 You know that in the
past you were living in a worthless way, a
way passed down from the people who lived
before you. But you were saved from that
useless life. You were bought, not with
something that ruins like gold or silver,
19 but with the precious blood of Christ, who
was like a pure and perfect lamb. 20 Christ
was chosen before the world was made, but
he was shown to the world in these last
times for your sake. 21 Through Christ you
believe in God, who raised Christ from the
dead and gave him glory. So your faith and
your hope are in God.

22 Now that your obedience to the truth
has purified your souls, you can have true
love for your Christian brothers and sisters.
So love each other deeply with all your
heart.[n] 23 You have been born again, and this
new life did not come from something that
dies, but from something that cannot die.
You were born again through God's living
message that continues forever. 24 The
Scripture says,

"All people are like the grass,
and all their glory is like the flowers of
the field.
The grass dies and the flowers fall,
25 but the word of the Lord will live
forever." *Isaiah 40:6–8*

And this is the word that was preached to
you.

Jesus Is the Living Stone

2 So then, rid yourselves of all evil, all
lying, hypocrisy, jealousy, and evil
speech. 2 As newborn babies want milk, you
should want the pure and simple teaching.
By it you can mature in your salvation,
3 because you have already examined and
seen how good the Lord is.

4 Come to the Lord Jesus, the "stone"[n] that
lives. The people of the world did not want
this stone, but he was the stone God chose,
and he was precious. 5 You also are like living
stones, so let yourselves be used to build a
spiritual temple—to be holy priests who
offer spiritual sacrifices to God. He will
accept those sacrifices through Jesus Christ.
6 The Scripture says:

"I will put a stone in the ground in
Jerusalem.
Everything will be built on this
important and precious rock.
Anyone who trusts in him
will never be disappointed." *Isaiah 28:16*

7 This stone is worth much to you who
believe. But to the people who do not
believe,

"the stone that the builders rejected
has become the cornerstone." *Psalm 118:22*

8 Also, he is

"a stone that causes people to stumble,
a rock that makes them fall." *Isaiah 8:14*

They stumble because they do not obey
what God says, which is what God planned
to happen to them.

9 But you are a chosen people, royal
priests, a holy nation, a people for God's
own possession. You were chosen to tell
about the wonderful acts of God, who called
you out of darkness into his wonderful light.
10 At one time you were not a people, but
now you are God's people. In the past you
had never received mercy, but now you have
received God's mercy.

Live for God

11 Dear friends, you are like foreigners and
strangers in this world. I beg you to avoid
the evil things your bodies want to do that
fight against your soul. 12 People who do not
believe are living all around you and might
say that you are doing wrong. Live such

1:16 "You must be . . . holy." Quotation from Leviticus 11:45; 19:2; 20:7. **1:22 with all your heart** Some Greek copies read "with a pure heart."
2:4 "stone" The most important stone in God's spiritual temple or house (his people).

good lives that they will see the good things
you do and will give glory to God on the day
when Christ comes again.

Yield to Every Human Authority

[13]For the Lord's sake, yield to the people
who have authority in this world: the king,
who is the highest authority, [14]and the
leaders who are sent by him to punish those
who do wrong and to praise those who do
right. [15]It is God's desire that by doing good
you should stop foolish people from saying
stupid things about you. [16]Live as free
people, but do not use your freedom as an
excuse to do evil. Live as servants of God.
[17]Show respect for all people: Love the
brothers and sisters of God's family, respect
God, honor the king.

Follow Christ's Example

[18]Slaves, yield to the authority of your
masters with all respect, not only those who
are good and kind, but also those who are
dishonest. [19]A person might have to suffer
even when it is unfair, but if he thinks of
God and can stand the pain, God is pleased.
[20]If you are beaten for doing wrong, there is
no reason to praise you for being patient in
your punishment. But if you suffer for doing
good, and you are patient, then God is
pleased. [21]This is what you were called to do,
because Christ suffered for you and gave you
an example to follow. So you should do as
he did.

[22]"He had never sinned,
and he had never lied." *Isaiah 53:9*

[23]People insulted Christ, but he did not
insult them in return. Christ suffered, but he
did not threaten. He let God, the One who
judges rightly, take care of him. [24]Christ
carried our sins in his body on the cross so
we would stop living for sin and start living
for what is right. And you are healed because
of his wounds. [25]You were like sheep that
wandered away, but now you have come
back to the Shepherd and Overseer of your
souls.

Wives and Husbands

3 In the same way, you wives should
yield to your husbands. Then, if some
husbands do not obey God's teaching,

devotion 351

1 PETER 3:3–4

GO GENTLY AND QUIETLY

When I was in high school, I was in detention twice a week. I wasn't a troublemaker—I got good grades and loved the Lord, but I also loved to talk. I still love to talk today, so when I read 1 Peter 3:3-4, I always take a deep breath and ask myself, "Do I have a gentle and quiet spirit?" Gentle and quiet are not words I would generally use to describe myself. So what is it that makes a woman precious in the eyes of God?

The dictionary definition of the word *gentle* is "kind." As women, we were designed to be nurturers, and God is looking for women who will love others selflessly. Look up 1 Corinthians 13. This is what God wants to see manifested in our lives. Another definition of *gentle* is "using little force." We may be good at loving others, but we often like to control the ones we love. God wants us to love others without forcing our expectations on them. He wants us to gently encourage, inspire, and even correct at times. Sometimes a gentle nudge will do much more in the heart of another than a shove ever could.

God is also looking for a quiet and peaceful spirit. I often think that worrying is my job as a mother. God thinks differently. He wants us to be at peace in our spirits, trusting him for all things. Spend some time today refining your beauty within. It is beauty that will last forever.

they will be persuaded to believe without
anyone's saying a word to them. They will
be persuaded by the way their wives live.
2Your husbands will see the pure lives you
live with your respect for God. 3It is not
fancy hair, gold jewelry, or fine clothes that
should make you beautiful. 4No, your beauty
should come from within you—the beauty
of a gentle and quiet spirit that will never be
destroyed and is very precious to God. 5In
this same way the holy women who lived
long ago and followed God made themselves
beautiful, yielding to their own husbands.
6Sarah obeyed Abraham, her husband, and
called him her master. And you women are
true children of Sarah if you always do what
is right and are not afraid.

7In the same way, you husbands should
live with your wives in an understanding
way, since they are weaker than you. But
show them respect, because God gives them
the same blessing he gives you—the grace
that gives true life. Do this so that nothing
will stop your prayers.

Suffering for Doing Right

8Finally, all of you should be in agreement,
understanding each other, loving each other
as family, being kind and humble. 9Do not
do wrong to repay a wrong, and do not insult
to repay an insult. But repay with a blessing,
because you yourselves were called to do
this so that you might receive a blessing.
10The Scripture says,

"A person must do these things
to enjoy life and have many happy
days.
He must not say evil things,
and he must not tell lies.
11He must stop doing evil and do good.
He must look for peace and work for it.
12The Lord sees the good people
and listens to their prayers.
But the Lord is against
those who do evil." *Psalm 34:12–16*

13If you are trying hard to do good, no one
can really hurt you. 14But even if you suffer
for doing right, you are blessed.

"Don't be afraid of what they fear;
do not dread those things." *Isaiah 8:12–13*

15But respect Christ as the holy Lord in your
hearts. Always be ready to answer everyone
who asks you to explain about the hope you
have, 16but answer in a gentle way and with
respect. Keep a clear conscience so that those
who speak evil of your good life in Christ
will be made ashamed. 17It is better to suffer
for doing good than for doing wrong if that
is what God wants. 18Christ himself suffered
for sins once. He was not guilty, but he
suffered for those who are guilty to bring
you to God. His body was killed, but he was
made alive in the spirit. 19And in the spirit
he went and preached to the spirits in prison
20who refused to obey God long ago in the
time of Noah. God was waiting patiently for
them while Noah was building the boat.
Only a few people—eight in all—were saved
by water. 21And that water is like baptism
that now saves you—not the washing of dirt
from the body, but the promise made to God
from a good conscience. And this is because
Jesus Christ was raised from the dead. 22Now
Jesus has gone into heaven and is at God's
right side ruling over angels, authorities, and
powers.

Change Your Lives

4 Since Christ suffered while he was in his
body, strengthen yourselves with the
same way of thinking Christ had. The person
who has suffered in the body is finished
with sin. 2Strengthen yourselves so that you
will live here on earth doing what God
wants, not the evil things people want. 3In
the past you wasted too much time doing
what nonbelievers enjoy. You were guilty of
sexual sins, evil desires, drunkenness, wild
and drunken parties, and hateful idol
worship. 4Nonbelievers think it is strange
that you do not do the many wild and
wasteful things they do, so they insult you.
5But they will have to explain this to God,
who is ready to judge the living and the
dead. 6For this reason the Good News was
preached to those who are now dead. Even
though they were judged like all people, the
Good News was preached to them so they
could live in the spirit as God lives.

Use God's Gifts Wisely

7The time is near when all things will end.
So think clearly and control yourselves so
you will be able to pray. 8Most importantly,
love each other deeply, because love will
cause people to forgive each other for many
sins. 9Open your homes to each other,
without complaining. 10Each of you has

received a gift to use to serve others. Be good
servants of God's various gifts of grace.
11 Anyone who speaks should speak words
from God. Anyone who serves should serve
with the strength God gives so that in
everything God will be praised through
Jesus Christ. Power and glory belong to him
forever and ever. Amen.

Suffering as a Christian

12 My friends, do not be surprised at the
terrible trouble which now comes to test
you. Do not think that something strange is
happening to you. 13 But be happy that you
are sharing in Christ's sufferings so that you
will be happy and full of joy when Christ
comes again in glory. 14 When people insult
you because you follow Christ, you are
blessed, because the glorious Spirit, the
Spirit of God, is with you. 15 Do not suffer for
murder, theft, or any other crime, nor
because you trouble other people. 16 But if
you suffer because you are a Christian, do
not be ashamed. Praise God because you
wear that name. 17 It is time for judgment to
begin with God's family. And if that judging
begins with us, what will happen to those
people who do not obey the Good News of
God?

18 "If it is very hard for a good person to be
saved,
the wicked person and the sinner will
surely be lost!"[n]

19 So those who suffer as God wants should
trust their souls to the faithful Creator as
they continue to do what is right.

The Flock of God

5 Now I have something to say to the
elders in your group. I also am an elder. I
have seen Christ's sufferings, and I will share
in the glory that will be shown to us. I beg
you to 2 shepherd God's flock, for whom you
are responsible. Watch over them because
you want to, not because you are forced.
That is how God wants it. Do it because you
are happy to serve, not because you want
money. 3 Do not be like a ruler over people

4:18 "If . . . lost!" Quotation from Proverbs 11:31 in the Septuagint, the Greek version of the Old Testament.

devotion 352

1 PETER 5:6–7

IS YOUR TANK ON EMPTY?

Before I opened my Bible this morning, I was feeling incredibly sorry for myself. I had a list of tasks I didn't think I could ever get through, and I felt exhausted and drained of creativity and enthusiasm. Where would I find the time and strength to be successful today?

As I began reading 1 Peter 5, I wondered how—in my current state of mind—I could draw any helpful conclusions at all. However, when I read the first words of verse 6, I realized I needed to change my attitude to that of humble submission. I relaxed as God reminded me of his power and that his plan for my life could not be ruined by me, a mere human being. It was as if God said, "My child, trust me. I'll lift you up when the right time comes!" I decided to give my cares to God, and he reminded me that we have a Master who is powerful and caring.

You too can hand God your worries, as the Scriptures implore you to do. Humble yourself before God, and remember it's his power that fuels your success, whether at work or at home. If you are waiting for a promotion, wondering when you will master a particular task, or seeking relief from a situation you are in, God is behind you 100 percent. Give him the credit, wait for his perfect timing, and know that he cares about your success and peace of mind.

you are responsible for, but be good
examples to them. 4Then when Christ, the
Chief Shepherd, comes, you will get a
glorious crown that will never lose its
beauty.

5In the same way, younger people should
be willing to be under older people. And all
of you should be very humble with each
other.

"God is against the proud,
but he gives grace to the humble."

Proverbs 3:34

6Be humble under God's powerful hand so
he will lift you up when the right time
comes. 7Give all your worries to him,
because he cares about you.

8Control yourselves and be careful! The
devil, your enemy, goes around like a roaring
lion looking for someone to eat. 9Refuse to
give in to him, by standing strong in your
faith. You know that your Christian family
all over the world is having the same kinds
of suffering.

10And after you suffer for a short time,
God, who gives all grace, will make
everything right. He will make you strong
and support you and keep you from falling.
He called you to share in his glory in Christ,
a glory that will continue forever. 11All
power is his forever and ever. Amen.

Final Greetings

12I wrote this short letter with the help of
Silas, who I know is a faithful brother in
Christ. I wrote to encourage you and to tell
you that this is the true grace of God. Stand
strong in that grace.

13The church in Babylon, who was chosen
like you, sends you greetings. Mark, my son
in Christ, also greets you. 14Give each other a
kiss of Christian love when you meet.

Peace to all of you who are in Christ.

2 Peter

Person Holding the Pen God Wrote With: *Peter*, the same aging follower of Christ who wrote 1 Peter, most likely authored this book.

When the Text Was Written: Peter wrote this book between 67 and 68 A.D. as he was languishing in a Roman prison not long before his death. Tradition holds that Peter died hanging upside down on a cross—a position he requested because he didn't feel worthy to be martyred the same way Jesus had been.

Spiritual Posture of the Original Recipients: Many New Testament churches were falling prey to wolfish pastors with ungodly messages. These terrible teachers sullied God's pulpit by twisting grace into a license for indulgence—and some young Christians were naïve about the poisonous lessons they were swallowing.

Storyline Synopsis: Peter's prison confinement put him in a reflective mood. As he pondered the precious sheep under his care, he felt impressed to warn them about the false prophets who would try to lure them away from the purity of the Good News. Peter was determined to protect his spiritual children from the heresies swirling around them. The storyline of 2 Peter is a cautionary tale about theologies without value. Faulty theology is similar to the imitation "Kate Spade" purses you can buy in shady New York City neighborhoods—it looks pretty good at a distance, but it falls apart under scrutiny.

A Moment Worth Discussing: In chapter 3, Peter tells his audience that there is no need to act like a jilted bride left at the altar. In other words, "Don't put away those wedding dresses or break out the Ben & Jerry's just yet!" He tenderly explains that Jesus is still coming for them. He further encourages that while their "royal wedding" is taking a bit longer than they expected, the delay is because of God's mercy. God isn't slow in keeping his promises—he is simply patient with reluctant brides.

Interesting (But Likely to Be Overlooked) Characters: Peter compared those who turn away from the truth and back toward their own disgusting habits to *dogs* or *pigs* (2 Pet. 2:22). Don't be one of those people!

1 From Simon Peter, a servant and apostle
of Jesus Christ.
To you who have received a faith as
valuable as ours, because our God and Savior
Jesus Christ does what is right.
2Grace and peace be given to you more
and more, because you truly know God and
Jesus our Lord.

God Has Given Us Blessings

3Jesus has the power of God, by which he
has given us everything we need to live and
to serve God. We have these things because
we know him. Jesus called us by his glory
and goodness. 4Through these he gave us the
very great and precious promises. With
these gifts you can share in God's nature,
and the world will not ruin you with its evil
desires.
5Because you have these blessings, do
your best to add these things to your lives:
to your faith, add goodness; and to your
goodness, add knowledge; 6and to your
knowledge, add self-control; and to your self-
control, add patience; and to your patience,
add service for God; 7and to your service for
God, add kindness for your brothers and
sisters in Christ; and to this kindness, add
love. 8If all these things are in you and are
growing, they will help you to be useful and
productive in your knowledge of our Lord
Jesus Christ. 9But anyone who does not have
these things cannot see clearly. He is blind
and has forgotten that he was made clean
from his past sins.
10My brothers and sisters, try hard to be
certain that you really are called and chosen
by God. If you do all these things, you will
never fall. 11And you will be given a very
great welcome into the eternal kingdom of
our Lord and Savior Jesus Christ.
12You know these things, and you are very
strong in the truth, but I will always help
you remember them. 13I think it is right for
me to help you remember as long as I am in
this body. 14I know I must soon leave this
body, as our Lord Jesus Christ has shown me.
15I will try my best so that you may be able
to remember these things even after I am
gone.

We Saw Christ's Glory

16When we told you about the powerful
coming of our Lord Jesus Christ, we were not

devotion 353

2 PETER 1:3–4

FAITH IS MORE THAN A TO-DO LIST

Did you know that the Christian faith means more than just praying a prayer and obeying the rules? The Christian faith is a power to be experienced! When the Holy Spirit comes to live inside of you, he brings the very power of God. As you learn to surrender to the leadership of the Holy Spirit, more and more of God's power is released in your life.

Would the people around you say that you live in power? Do they see something on the inside of you that gives an unseen strength? Are things changing in your life? Does it feel like you're being moved and guided by a divine power? Are you being shaped by God's hand? Are you looking less and less like the woman you used to be, but by his power, becoming more and more the woman he envisioned?

Someone asked me, "If the Holy Spirit left you, do you think you would know he was gone?" Would *you* know if he left you? Would you recognize that his power had been removed? What difference would it make in the way you live your everyday life?

So many of us are not living in power, yet it is freely available to each one of us. Believing God is not just believing a list of things about God. Believing God is about becoming godly, righteous women. Not because we have figured out ten steps to godliness, but because the power of God in us is able to make it so.

telling just clever stories that someone
invented. But we saw the greatness of Jesus
with our own eyes. 17Jesus heard the voice of
God, the Greatest Glory, when he received
honor and glory from God the Father. The
voice said, "This is my Son, whom I love, and
I am very pleased with him." 18We heard
that voice from heaven while we were with
Jesus on the holy mountain.
19This makes us more sure about the
message the prophets gave. It is good for you
to follow closely what they said as you
would follow a light shining in a dark place,
until the day begins and the morning star
rises in your hearts. 20Most of all, you must
understand this: No prophecy in the
Scriptures ever comes from the prophet's
own interpretation. 21No prophecy ever
came from what a person wanted to say, but
people led by the Holy Spirit spoke words
from God.

False Teachers

2 There used to be false prophets among
God's people, just as you will have some
false teachers in your group. They will
secretly teach things that are wrong—
teachings that will cause people to be lost.
They will even refuse to accept the Master,
Jesus, who bought their freedom. So they
will bring quick ruin on themselves. 2Many
will follow their evil ways and say evil
things about the way of truth. 3Those false
teachers only want your money, so they will
use you by telling you lies. Their judgment
spoken against them long ago is still
coming, and their ruin is certain.
4When angels sinned, God did not let
them go free without punishment. He sent
them to hell and put them in caves[n] of
darkness where they are being held for
judgment. 5And God punished the world
long ago when he brought a flood to the
world that was full of people who were
against him. But God saved Noah, who
preached about being right with God, and
seven other people with him. 6And God
also destroyed the evil cities of Sodom and
Gomorrah[n] by burning them until they were
ashes. He made those cities an example of
what will happen to those who are against
God. 7But he saved Lot from those cities. Lot,
a good man, was troubled because of the
filthy lives of evil people. 8(Lot was a good
man, but because he lived with evil people
every day, his good heart was hurt by the evil
things he saw and heard.) 9So the Lord
knows how to save those who serve him
when troubles come. He will hold evil
people and punish them, while waiting for
the Judgment Day. 10That punishment is
especially for those who live by doing the
evil things their sinful selves want and who
hate authority.
These false teachers are bold and do
anything they want. They are not afraid to
speak against the angels. 11But even the
angels, who are much stronger and more
powerful than false teachers, do not accuse
them with insults before[n] the Lord. 12But
these people speak against things they do
not understand. They are like animals that
act without thinking, animals born to be
caught and killed. And, like animals, these
false teachers will be destroyed. 13They have
caused many people to suffer, so they
themselves will suffer. That is their pay for
what they have done. They take pleasure in
openly doing evil, so they are like dirty spots
and stains among you. They delight in
deceiving you while eating meals with you.
14Every time they look at a woman they
want her, and their desire for sin is never
satisfied. They lead weak people into the
trap of sin, and they have taught their hearts
to be greedy. God will punish them! 15These
false teachers left the right road and lost
their way, following the way Balaam went.
Balaam was the son of Beor, who loved being
paid for doing wrong. 16But a donkey, which
cannot talk, told Balaam he was sinning. It
spoke with a man's voice and stopped the
prophet's crazy thinking.
17Those false teachers are like springs
without water and clouds blown by a storm.
A place in the blackest darkness has been
kept for them. 18They brag with words that
mean nothing. By their evil desires they lead
people into the trap of sin—people who are
just beginning to escape from others who
live in error. 19They promise them freedom,
but they themselves are not free. They are

2:4 caves Some Greek copies read "chains." **2:6 Sodom and Gomorrah** Two cities God destroyed because the people were so evil.
2:11 before Some Greek copies read "from."

slaves of things that will be destroyed. For
people are slaves of anything that controls
them. 20They were made free from the evil
in the world by knowing our Lord and
Savior Jesus Christ. But if they return to evil
things and those things control them, then it
is worse for them than it was before. 21Yes,
it would be better for them to have never
known the right way than to know it and to
turn away from the holy teaching that was
given to them. 22What they did is like this
true saying: "A dog goes back to what it has
thrown up,"[n] and, "After a pig is washed, it
goes back and rolls in the mud."

Jesus Will Come Again

3 My friends, this is the second letter I
have written you to help your honest
minds remember. 2I want you to think about
the words the holy prophets spoke in the
past, and remember the command our Lord
and Savior gave us through your apostles. 3It
is most important for you to understand
what will happen in the last days. People
will laugh at you. They will live doing the
evil things they want to do. 4They will say,
"Jesus promised to come again. Where is
he? Our fathers have died, but the world
continues the way it has been since it was
made." 5But they do not want to remember
what happened long ago. By the word of God
heaven was made, and the earth was made
from water and with water. 6Then the world
was flooded and destroyed with water. 7And
that same word of God is keeping heaven
and earth that we now have in order to be
destroyed by fire. They are being kept for the
Judgment Day and the destruction of all who
are against God.

8But do not forget this one thing, dear
friends: To the Lord one day is as a thousand
years, and a thousand years is as one day. 9The
Lord is not slow in doing what he promised—
the way some people understand slowness.
But God is being patient with you. He does
not want anyone to be lost, but he wants all
people to change their hearts and lives.

10But the day of the Lord will come like a
thief. The skies will disappear with a loud
noise. Everything in them will be destroyed
by fire, and the earth and everything in it
will be exposed.[n] 11In that way everything

2:22 "A dog . . . up." Quotation from Proverbs 26:11.
3:10 and . . . exposed Some Greek copies read "and everything in it will be burned up."

devotion 354

2 PETER 3:8–9

LEATHER PANTS ANYONE?

Do you love leather pants, yet refuse to try to shed ten pounds to get into them? Do you love chocolate chip cookies but eat Chips Ahoy so you don't have to bake? Would you look great with a few highlights but refuse to carve out three hours to be still while they process? These are all funny little examples, but when it comes to more serious decisions, it really is not much fun when we miss out on God's plan simply because we want to avoid going through a process of change. A day is like a thousand years to the Lord, but a day to us is a day, and every one we sit out is precious time lost.

Has God revealed to you a glimpse of his plan for your life? If you are afraid to jump into the process of change, would you allow me to encourage you in a plan of action? "Do it afraid!" Better to do it afraid than be stagnant in your heart when Jesus wants to rock your world. I knew my husband was going to be a pastor long before he did, you know why? Because God whispered it in my ear. Before that call came, there was a very definite process of change in both our lives. Do not miss out on these treasured adventures just because you do not want to welcome a season of change. By the way, I bet you would look great in leather pants.

will be destroyed. So what kind of people
should you be? You should live holy lives
and serve God, [12]as you wait for and look
forward to the coming of the day of God.
When that day comes, the skies will be
destroyed with fire, and everything in them
will melt with heat. [13]But God made a
promise to us, and we are waiting for a new
heaven and a new earth where goodness
lives.

[14]Dear friends, since you are waiting for
this to happen, do your best to be without
sin and without fault. Try to be at peace with
God. [15]Remember that we are saved because
our Lord is patient. Our dear brother Paul
told you the same thing when he wrote to
you with the wisdom that God gave him.
[16]He writes about this in all his letters.
Some things in Paul's letters are hard to
understand, and people who are ignorant
and weak in faith explain these things
falsely. They also falsely explain the other
Scriptures, but they are destroying
themselves by doing this.

[17]Dear friends, since you already know
about this, be careful. Do not let those evil
people lead you away by the wrong they do.
Be careful so you will not fall from your
strong faith. [18]But grow in the grace and
knowledge of our Lord and Savior Jesus
Christ. Glory be to him now and forever!
Amen.

1 John

Also known as "The First Letter of John"

Person Holding the Pen God Wrote With: *John*, the "beloved" apostle who was also the biological brother of the apostle James

When the Text Was Written: Late in John's life, in the latter half of the first century

Spiritual Posture of the Original Recipients: The church is in crisis. John describes it as the "last hour" and warns about the imminent arrival of the "enemies of Christ." He also points out the fact that some have left the faith (1 John 2:18–19).

Storyline Synopsis: The main purpose of this tender, pastoral letter is to assure these Christians in their relationship with Jesus Christ because many of them are struggling with doubt. John gives both objective grounds (as an apostle, he saw and touched a physical Messiah) and subjective grounds (if the Holy Spirit lives within us, we will display obedience to God) regarding the certainty of the Good News. He shares three tests of faith: a *moral* test—if we obey his commands, we belong to God (1 John 2:3–6); a *social* test—if we love each other, we belong to God (4:7–8); and a *theological* test—if we truly believe that Jesus is the Savior of the world, that he came in the flesh, and that he is the Son of God, we belong to God (1:5—2:6; 4:1–4; 5:5).

A Moment Worth Discussing: John refers to his congregation as "dear friends" and encourages them to love each other (1 John 4:7–21). He explains that if God lives in us, we simply must love one another. Furthermore, we don't love other people because of our own kindness or because of the warm fuzzies that human affection conjures up; we love other people because "God first loved us" (4:19). The Creator of the universe started this whole avalanche of affection, and we're supposed to follow in his compassionate footsteps!

Interesting (But Likely to Be Overlooked) Character: John makes it clear that the *false prophets* who promote anti-Christian doctrine will be obvious by their dismissal of the incarnation of Christ (1 John 4:1–6). These dubious teachers who refuse to acknowledge that Jesus Christ came to earth as a human are not from God. To say that Jesus was a good man or a good teacher, yet not acknowledge his supernatural divinity, is deceptive heresy.

1 We write you now about what has always
existed, which we have heard, we have
seen with our own eyes, we have looked at,
and we have touched with our hands. We
write to you about the Word[n] that gives life.
2 He who gives life was shown to us. We saw
him and can give proof about it. And now
we announce to you that he has life that
continues forever. He was with God the
Father and was shown to us. 3 We announce
to you what we have seen and heard,
because we want you also to have fellowship
with us. Our fellowship is with God the
Father and with his Son, Jesus Christ. 4 We
write this to you so we may be full of joy.[n]

God Forgives Our Sins

5 Here is the message we have heard from
Christ and now announce to you: God is
light,[n] and in him there is no darkness at all.
6 So if we say we have fellowship with God,
but we continue living in darkness, we are
liars and do not follow the truth. 7 But if we
live in the light, as God is in the light, we can
share fellowship with each other. Then the
blood of Jesus, God's Son, cleanses us from
every sin.
8 If we say we have no sin, we are fooling
ourselves, and the truth is not in us. 9 But if
we confess our sins, he will forgive our sins,
because we can trust God to do what is right.
He will cleanse us from all the wrongs we
have done. 10 If we say we have not sinned,
we make God a liar, and we do not accept
God's teaching.

Jesus Is Our Helper

2 My dear children, I write this letter to
you so you will not sin. But if anyone
does sin, we have a helper in the presence of
the Father—Jesus Christ, the One who does
what is right. 2 He died in our place to take
away our sins, and not only our sins but the
sins of all people.
3 We can be sure that we know God if we
obey his commands. 4 Anyone who says, "I
know God," but does not obey God's
commands is a liar, and the truth is not in

1:1 Word The Greek word is "logos," meaning any kind of communication. Here, it means Christ, who was the way God told people about himself. **1:4 so . . . joy** Some Greek copies read "so you may be full of joy." **1:5 light** Here, it is used as a symbol of God's goodness or truth.

devotion 355

1 JOHN 1:6–7

HURRICANE BABY

We called her our hurricane baby. She came to our house several hours before the hurricane hit us, simply because the shelter for foster children was overloaded with kids. She was two years old with an appetite of a teenager and a twinkle in her eye. We told people that with her in our home, we had a hurricane inside our house as well as outside. Within a very short time of her arrival, she started calling me Mom. My own children were so touched by this because they thought she wanted me to be her mom. I explained to them that we were her third foster home. She had just figured out the system; she knew that in every home, there was a mom, and I happened to be it. There was no feeling attached to the word; it was simply my name.

I believe many people do this with God. They've figured out the system. They call Jesus their Savior, but there is no personal relationship attached. They know all the right answers, and they even attend church, but Jesus has not become their Lord. Somehow the knowledge of Jesus is in their heads, but it has never reached their hearts. So how do we live in the light rather than just saying that we do? We have to spend time with God and really get to know him. Believe me, you will fall in love with him and know the privilege of calling him Daddy when you do.

that person. [5]But if someone obeys God's teaching, then in that person God's love has truly reached its goal. This is how we can be sure we are living in God: [6]Whoever says that he lives in God must live as Jesus lived.

The Command to Love Others

[7]My dear friends, I am not writing a new command to you but an old command you have had from the beginning. It is the teaching you have already heard. [8]But also I am writing a new command to you, and you can see its truth in Jesus and in you, because the darkness is passing away, and the true light is already shining.

[9]Anyone who says, "I am in the light,"[n] but hates a brother or sister, is still in the darkness. [10]Whoever loves a brother or sister lives in the light and will not cause anyone to stumble in his faith. [11]But whoever hates a brother or sister is in darkness, lives in darkness, and does not know where to go, because the darkness has made that person blind.

[12]I write to you, dear children,
because your sins are forgiven through Christ.
[13]I write to you, fathers,
because you know the One who existed from the beginning.
I write to you, young people,
because you have defeated the Evil One.
[14]I write to you, children,
because you know the Father.
I write to you, fathers,
because you know the One who existed from the beginning.
I write to you, young people,
because you are strong;
the teaching of God lives in you,
and you have defeated the Evil One.

[15]Do not love the world or the things in the world. If you love the world, the love of the Father is not in you. [16]These are the ways of the world: wanting to please our sinful selves, wanting the sinful things we see, and being too proud of what we have. None of these come from the Father, but all of them come from the world. [17]The world and everything that people want in it are passing away, but the person who does what God wants lives forever.

Reject the Enemies of Christ

[18]My dear children, these are the last days. You have heard that the enemy of Christ is coming, and now many enemies of Christ are already here. This is how we know that these are the last days. [19]These enemies of Christ were in our fellowship, but they left us. They never really belonged to us; if they had been a part of us, they would have stayed with us. But they left, and this shows that none of them really belonged to us.

[20]You have the gift[n] that the Holy One gave you, so you all know the truth.[n] [21]I do not write to you because you do not know the truth but because you do know the truth. And you know that no lie comes from the truth.

[22]Who is the liar? It is the person who does not accept Jesus as the Christ. This is the enemy of Christ: the person who does not accept the Father and his Son. [23]Whoever does not accept the Son does not have the Father. But whoever confesses the Son has the Father, too.

[24]Be sure you continue to follow the teaching you heard from the beginning. If you continue to follow what you heard from the beginning, you will stay in the Son and in the Father. [25]And this is what the Son promised to us—life forever.

[26]I am writing this letter about those people who are trying to lead you the wrong way. [27]Christ gave you a special gift that is still in you, so you do not need any other teacher. His gift teaches you about everything, and it is true, not false. So continue to live in Christ, as his gift taught you.

[28]Yes, my dear children, live in him so that when Christ comes back, we can be without fear and not be ashamed in his presence. [29]Since you know that Christ is righteous, you know that all who do right are God's children.

We Are God's Children

3 The Father has loved us so much that we are called children of God. And we really are his children. The reason the people in the world do not know us is that they have not known him. [2]Dear friends, now we are children of God, and we have not yet been

2:9 light Here, it is used as a symbol of God's goodness or truth. **2:20 gift** This might mean the Holy Spirit, or it might mean teaching or truth as in verse 24. **2:20 you . . . truth** Some Greek copies read "so you know all things."

shown what we will be in the future. But we
know that when Christ comes again, we will
be like him, because we will see him as he
really is. 3Christ is pure, and all who have
this hope in Christ keep themselves pure
like Christ.

4The person who sins breaks God's law.
Yes, sin is living against God's law. 5You
know that Christ came to take away sins and
that there is no sin in Christ. 6So anyone
who lives in Christ does not go on sinning.
Anyone who goes on sinning has never
really understood Christ and has never
known him.

7Dear children, do not let anyone lead you
the wrong way. Christ is righteous. So to be
like Christ a person must do what is right.
8The devil has been sinning since the
beginning, so anyone who continues to sin
belongs to the devil. The Son of God came
for this purpose: to destroy the devil's work.

9Those who are God's children do not
continue sinning, because the new life from
God remains in them. They are not able to
go on sinning, because they have become
children of God. 10So we can see who God's
children are and who the devil's children
are: Those who do not do what is right are
not God's children, and those who do not
love their brothers and sisters are not God's
children.

We Must Love Each Other

11This is the teaching you have heard
from the beginning: We must love each
other. 12Do not be like Cain who belonged to
the Evil One and killed his brother. And why
did he kill him? Because the things Cain did
were evil, and the things his brother did
were good.

13Brothers and sisters, do not be surprised
when the people of the world hate you. 14We
know we have left death and have come into
life because we love each other. Whoever
does not love is still dead. 15Everyone who
hates a brother or sister is a murderer,[n] and

3:15 Everyone . . . murderer If one person hates a brother or sister, then in the heart that person has killed that brother or sister. Jesus taught about this sin to his followers (Matthew 5:21–26).

devotion 356

1 JOHN 3:16

PAYING THE ULTIMATE PRICE

Our hearts break through the "Last of the Mohicans." We are stunned during "Saving Private Ryan," and we cry during "Braveheart." Paying the ultimate price for friendship, love, and honor is a phenomenon common to all of humanity; and many of us can imagine situations in which we'd sacrifice ourselves to save the life of a child, whether it be our own or another's.

Thankfully, most of us will never be called to give our physical lives. Still, we can give our lives daily as we reach out to others. As you ponder 1 John 3:16, try to think of ways others have helped you. Have your parents endured great sacrifice to help you realize a dream? Has someone stepped forward to provide a crucial financial need for you? Perhaps someone offered to pray for you. Prayer is no small gift, especially when the person praying for us takes action by helping us through our trying time.

Now think about Christ and how he literally gave his life to save you. Because he showed us what real love is, we ought to show it to others, too. Think of some ways you've given yourself to others recently. How might you make a sacrifice in the future in order to show God's love to a neighbor, friend, organization, or stranger? Pray that God will show you where you are needed, and remember that you please God when you choose to give up your money, time, or activities and give them to others.

you know that no murderers have eternal
life in them. 16 This is how we know what
real love is: Jesus gave his life for us. So we
should give our lives for our brothers and
sisters. 17 Suppose someone has enough to
live and sees a brother or sister in need, but
does not help. Then God's love is not living
in that person. 18 My children, we should
love people not only with words and talk,
but by our actions and true caring.

19-20 This is the way we know that we
belong to the way of truth. When our hearts
make us feel guilty, we can still have peace
before God. God is greater than our hearts,
and he knows everything. 21 My dear friends,
if our hearts do not make us feel guilty, we
can come without fear into God's presence.
22 And God gives us what we ask for because
we obey God's commands and do what
pleases him. 23 This is what God commands:
that we believe in his Son, Jesus Christ,
and that we love each other, just as he
commanded. 24 The people who obey God's
commands live in God, and God lives in
them. We know that God lives in us because
of the Spirit God gave us.

Warning Against False Teachers

4 My dear friends, many false prophets
have gone out into the world. So do not
believe every spirit, but test the spirits to
see if they are from God. 2 This is how you
can know God's Spirit: Every spirit who
confesses that Jesus Christ came to earth as a
human is from God. 3 And every spirit who
refuses to say this about Jesus is not from
God. It is the spirit of the enemy of Christ,
which you have heard is coming, and now
he is already in the world.

4 My dear children, you belong to God and
have defeated them; because God's Spirit,
who is in you, is greater than the devil, who
is in the world. 5 And they belong to the
world, so what they say is from the world,
and the world listens to them. 6 But we
belong to God, and those who know God
listen to us. But those who are not from God
do not listen to us. That is how we know the
Spirit that is true and the spirit that is false.

Love Comes from God

7 Dear friends, we should love each other,
because love comes from God. Everyone
who loves has become God's child and
knows God. 8 Whoever does not love does
not know God, because God is love. 9 This is
how God showed his love to us: He sent his
one and only Son into the world so that we
could have life through him. 10 This is what
real love is: It is not our love for God; it is
God's love for us. He sent his Son to die in
our place to take away our sins.

11 Dear friends, if God loved us that much
we also should love each other. 12 No one has
ever seen God, but if we love each other, God
lives in us, and his love is made perfect in us.

13 We know that we live in God and he
lives in us, because he gave us his Spirit.
14 We have seen and can testify that the
Father sent his Son to be the Savior of the
world. 15 Whoever confesses that Jesus is the
Son of God has God living inside, and that
person lives in God. 16 And so we know the
love that God has for us, and we trust that
love.

God is love. Those who live in love live in
God, and God lives in them. 17 This is how
love is made perfect in us: that we can be
without fear on the day God judges us,
because in this world we are like him.
18 Where God's love is, there is no fear,
because God's perfect love drives out fear. It
is punishment that makes a person fear, so
love is not made perfect in the person who
fears.

19 We love because God first loved us. 20 If
people say, "I love God," but hate their
brothers or sisters, they are liars. Those who
do not love their brothers and sisters, whom
they have seen, cannot love God, whom they
have never seen. 21 And God gave us this
command: Those who love God must also
love their brothers and sisters.

Faith in the Son of God

5 Everyone who believes that Jesus is the
Christ is God's child, and whoever loves
the Father also loves the Father's children.
2 This is how we know we love God's
children: when we love God and obey his
commands. 3 Loving God means obeying his
commands. And God's commands are not
too hard for us, 4 because everyone who is a
child of God conquers the world. And this is
the victory that conquers the world—our
faith. 5 So the one who conquers the world is
the person who believes that Jesus is the Son
of God.

devotion 357

1 JOHN 5:3–5

PRAYER OF THE STRUGGLING

Jesus knew exactly what the world was going to be like. That is why he sent us a Helper and a Guide so we would not be left here without hope. My dear Christian, if you believe in the birth, death, and resurrection of the Son of God, you are going to be in heaven where gold is so disregarded that it paves the streets where you will walk. Is it too hard of a thing to want to obey your Savior? He wants you to believe, but he also desires a willful, heartfelt obedience from you. “And love means living the way God commanded us to live” (2 John 6).

Is there some struggle that seems too great for you? Remember, God says he always provides a way out of temptation so that you can choose not to sin (1 Cor. 10:13). There is no other source on earth or in heaven that can provide the tools or a Spirit to help you overcome sin. Take a moment to pray this prayer:

Dear Father, I am struggling with ________________. I do not want to carry this burden and this sin any longer. It is just too great for me. Please forgive me of the sins in my life and for holding onto them. I am laying my life in your hands today because of your great love for me. I want to walk with you with a clean heart and rejoice in a victorious life. Amen.

6Jesus Christ is the One who came by
water[n] and blood.[n] He did not come by water
only, but by water and blood. And the Spirit
says that this is true, because the Spirit is the
truth. 7So there are three witnesses:[n] 8the
Spirit, the water, and the blood; and these
three witnesses agree. 9We believe people
when they say something is true. But what
God says is more important, and he has told
us the truth about his own Son. 10Anyone
who believes in the Son of God has the truth
that God told us. Anyone who does not
believe makes God a liar, because that
person does not believe what God told us
about his Son. 11This is what God told us:
God has given us eternal life, and this life is
in his Son. 12Whoever has the Son has life,
but whoever does not have the Son of God
does not have life.

We Have Eternal Life Now

13I write this letter to you who believe in
the Son of God so you will know you have
eternal life. 14And this is the boldness we
have in God’s presence: that if we ask God
for anything that agrees with what he wants,
he hears us. 15If we know he hears us every
time we ask him, we know we have what we
ask from him.

16If anyone sees a brother or sister sinning
(sin that does not lead to eternal death), that
person should pray, and God will give the
sinner life. I am talking about people whose
sin does not lead to eternal death. There is
sin that leads to death. I do not mean that a
person should pray about that sin. 17Doing
wrong is always sin, but there is sin that
does not lead to eternal death.

18We know that those who are God’s

5:6 water This probably means the water of Jesus’ baptism. **5:6 blood** This probably means the blood of Jesus’ death.
5:7–8 So . . . witnesses A few very late Greek copies and the Latin Vulgate continue, “in heaven: the Father, the Word, and the Holy Spirit, and these three witnesses agree. 8And there are three witnesses on earth:”

children do not continue to sin. The Son of
God keeps them safe, and the Evil One
cannot touch them. [19]We know that we
belong to God, but the Evil One controls the
whole world. [20]We also know that the Son
of God has come and has given us
understanding so that we can know the True
One. And our lives are in the True One and
in his Son, Jesus Christ. He is the true God
and the eternal life.

[21]So, dear children, keep yourselves away
from false gods.

2 John

Both 2 and 3 John hold the distinction of being the shortest letters in the New Testament, each containing less than three hundred Greek words!

Person Holding the Pen God Wrote With: *John* authored this letter. He refers to himself as "the Elder" to denote his seniority (2 John 1).

When the Text Was Written: Late in John's life, approximately 90–95 A.D.

Spiritual Posture of the Original Recipient: This letter was addressed to a specific Christian woman and her family (2 John 2–3). Evidently this kind woman had been tricked into extending hospitality to false prophets who were masquerading as sincere itinerant preachers. (Many prophets were nomadic, depending on the generosity of the early church as they traveled from place to place. Inns were scarce, typically dangerous, and considered immoral.) This dear woman was well-intentioned but not spiritually wise when she opened her home to these wolves dressed in sheep suits!

Storyline Synopsis: John's second letter deals with the same issue as his first: false prophets were invading the church and threatening to destroy it from the inside out. But this time, John uses the specific example of a woman unwittingly opening her home (and heart) to them. John gives a very clear warning about entertaining teachers who don't profess the pure Good News of Jesus Christ. While his admonition not to invite false prophets in for coffee or even to say hi (2 John 10) might appear harsh at first, guarded hospitality was necessary in this era of church history in order to defend the foundation of their faith.

A Moment Worth Discussing: At the end of this letter, John says, "I have many things to write to you, but I do not want to use pen and ink. Instead, I hope to come to you and talk face to face" (2 John 12). When they first met Jesus and became his followers, John and his brother James were known as the "Sons of Thunder" (Mark 3:17)—which certainly doesn't conjure up images of gentle, relational men! But the gift of love that Jesus gave John transformed his stormy reputation. He became a tender, pastoral leader in the first-century church, calling young believers "dear friends," encouraging them to live lives of love (2 John 6), and waxing emotive in his salutation, explaining that he would much rather see their faces than send his greeting through snail mail!

Interesting (But Likely to Be Overlooked) Characters: No one knows for sure who the *children of the "chosen sister"* were, but they obviously had a relationship with John because they asked him to send greetings back to the recipient of his letter (2 John 13).

1From the Elder.[n]
To the chosen lady[n] and her children:
I love all of you in the truth,[n] and all those
who know the truth love you. 2We love you
because of the truth that lives in us and will
be with us forever.

3Grace, mercy, and peace from God the
Father and his Son, Jesus Christ, will be with
us in truth and love.

4I was very happy to learn that some of
your children are following the way of truth,
as the Father commanded us. 5And now, dear
lady, this is not a new command but is the
same command we have had from the
beginning. I ask you that we all love each
other. 6And love means living the way God
commanded us to live. As you have heard
from the beginning, his command is this:
Live a life of love.

7Many false teachers are in the world now
who do not confess that Jesus Christ came to
earth as a human. Anyone who does not
confess this is a false teacher and an enemy
of Christ. 8Be careful yourselves that you do
not lose everything you[n] have worked for,
but that you receive your full reward.

9Anyone who goes beyond Christ's
teaching and does not continue to follow
only his teaching does not have God. But
whoever continues to follow the teaching of
Christ has both the Father and the Son. 10If
someone comes to you and does not bring
this teaching, do not welcome or accept that
person into your house. 11If you welcome
such a person, you share in the evil work.

12I have many things to write to you, but I
do not want to use paper and ink. Instead, I
hope to come to you and talk face to face so
we can be full of joy. 13The children of your
chosen sister[n] greet you.

1 Elder "Elder" means an older person. It can also mean a special leader in the church (as in Titus 1:5).
1 lady This might mean a woman, or in this letter it might mean a church. If it is a church, then "her children" would be the people of the church.
1 truth The truth or "Good News" about Jesus Christ that joins all believers together. **8 you** Some Greek copies read "we."
13 sister Sister of the "lady" in verse 1. This might be another woman or another church.

3 John

This is the third and final epistle bearing John's name.

Person Holding the Pen God Wrote With: *John*

When the Text Was Written: This letter was most likely written around the same time as 1 and 2 John, between 90 and 95 A.D. It is also likely that John wrote these letters while he was pastoring the church in Ephesus.

Spiritual Posture of the Original Recipient: The original recipient of John's third letter was a man named Gaius, who was a member of one of John's churches. Gaius may have struggled with poor physical health (3 John 2), but John's words point to his robust spiritual health. John calls him his "dear friend" four times (verses 1, 2, 5, and 11) and tells him that other Christians (probably traveling missionaries) speak highly of his faithfulness to the Good News and to them.

Storyline Synopsis: This letter continues to highlight the perpetual problem of false prophets eroding the Good News message and the need for discernment among Christians. John celebrates the wise grace demonstrated by Gaius, but he decries the arrogance and subversive actions of another church member, Diotrephes. John emphasizes how pettiness and pride can divide a body of believers.

A Moment Worth Discussing: In light of the overzealous and misplaced hospitality of the woman in his second letter, John prudently points to Gaius in this third correspondence as a good example of hospitality (3 John 5–8). Gaius cared for traveling Christian leaders the right way: he gave food and lodging to fellow believers because he loved them and wanted to help further their ministries. Gaius's behavior reflects the truism that while we can't all *go* as missionaries to faraway places, we can still play a part in *sending* other saints.

Interesting (But Likely to Be Overlooked) Character: *Demetrius* is the unsung hero of this letter (3 John 12). John describes him as living in such a way that he has earned the respect of other church members, implying that Demetrius lives by the "Book"—that his life is under the authority of God's Word. That's all we know about Demetrius. He is a most valuable—yet nearly invisible—player!

1From the Elder.[n]
To my dear friend Gaius, whom I love in
the truth:[n]
2My dear friend, I know your soul is doing
fine, and I pray that you are doing well in
every way and that your health is good. 3I
was very happy when some brothers and
sisters came and told me about the truth in
your life and how you are following the way
of truth. 4Nothing gives me greater joy than
to hear that my children are following the
way of truth.
5My dear friend, it is good that you help
the brothers and sisters, even those you do
not know. 6They told the church about your
love. Please help them to continue their trip
in a way worthy of God. 7They started out in
service to Christ, and they have been
accepting nothing from nonbelievers. 8So
we should help such people; when we do, we
share in their work for the truth.
9I wrote something to the church, but
Diotrephes, who loves to be their leader, will
not listen to us. 10So if I come, I will talk
about what Diotrephes is doing, about how
he lies and says evil things about us. But
more than that, he refuses to accept the
other brothers and sisters; he even stops
those who do want to accept them and puts
them out of the church.
11My dear friend, do not follow what is
bad; follow what is good. The one who does
good belongs to God. But the one who does
evil has never known God.
12Everyone says good things about
Demetrius, and the truth agrees with what
they say. We also speak well of him, and you
know what we say is true.
13I have many things I want to write
you, but I do not want to use pen and ink.
14I hope to see you soon and talk face to
face. 15Peace to you. The friends here greet
you. Please greet each friend there by
name.

1 Elder "Elder" means an older person. It can also mean a special leader in the church (as in Titus 1:5).
1 truth The truth or "Good News" about Jesus Christ that joins all believers together.

Jude

This is the last of eight general epistles, or "letters to the church at large," in the New Testament.

Person Holding the Pen God Wrote With: *Jude*, one of Jesus' four half brothers, authored this book. He is also called "Judas" in the Gospel of Mark (Mark 6:3) but should not be confused with the Judas who betrayed Jesus. Like his three brothers, Jude did not believe that Jesus was the Messiah while Jesus walked the earth in a human body (John 7:1–9). Jude became a Christian after Christ died on the cross and ascended into heaven (Acts 1:14).

When the Text Was Written: Between 68 and 70 A.D.

Spiritual Posture of the Original Recipients: Believers in the early church—to whom this letter was addressed—were being persecuted by Roman authorities from the outside and from aggressive heretics on the inside.

Storyline Synopsis: By this time in early church history, all of Jesus' original followers except for John had been martyred. Christianity as a whole appeared vulnerable to attack. So Jude, who started writing this letter as a lesson on salvation (Jude 3), altered his focus mid-message. He began to blow a literary trumpet, charging believers to battle for the purity of the faith they had in Jesus. He used multiple Old Testament examples (Israel, fallen angels, Sodom and Gomorrah, Moses, Cain, Balaam, Korah, and Enoch) to punctuate his dramatic "call to spiritual arms."

A Moment Worth Discussing: The doxology of this letter (Jude 24–25) is arguably one of the most beautiful benedictions in the whole of Scripture. In light of Jude's sobering warning about apostasy (renouncing one's faith in Christ) throughout this message, this assurance at the end that God is strong enough to keep believers from stumbling probably gave his audience a much-needed sigh of relief.

Interesting (But Likely to Be Overlooked) Character: *Balaam* (Jude 11) is a character worth remembering. His true Old Testament saga (Num. 22—24) could have inspired the "Mr. Ed" television show because Balaam conversed with a chatty four-legged animal, too!

1 From Jude, a servant of Jesus Christ and a
brother of James.
To all who have been called by God. God
the Father loves you, and you have been kept
safe in Jesus Christ:
2 Mercy, peace, and love be yours richly.

God Will Punish Sinners

3 Dear friends, I wanted very much to
write you about the salvation we all share.
But I felt the need to write you about
something else: I want to encourage you to
fight hard for the faith that was given the
holy people of God once and for all time.
4 Some people have secretly entered your
group. Long ago the prophets wrote about
these people who will be judged guilty. They
are against God and have changed the grace
of our God into a reason for sexual sin. They
also refuse to accept Jesus Christ, our only
Master and Lord.
5 I want to remind you of some things you
already know: Remember that the Lord[n]
saved his people by bringing them out of the
land of Egypt. But later he destroyed all
those who did not believe. 6 And remember
the angels who did not keep their place of
power but left their proper home. The Lord
has kept these angels in darkness, bound
with everlasting chains, to be judged on the
great day. 7 Also remember the cities of
Sodom and Gomorrah[n] and the other towns
around them. In the same way they were full
of sexual sin and people who desired sexual
relations that God does not allow. They
suffer the punishment of eternal fire, as an
example for all to see.
8 It is the same with these people who
have entered your group. They are guided by
dreams and make themselves filthy with sin.
They reject God's authority and speak
against the angels. 9 Not even the archangel[n]
Michael, when he argued with the devil
about who would have the body of Moses,
dared to judge the devil guilty. Instead, he
said, "The Lord punish you." 10 But these
people speak against things they do not
understand. And what they do know, by
feeling, as dumb animals know things, are
the very things that destroy them. 11 It will
be terrible for them. They have followed the
way of Cain, and for money they have given

5 the Lord Some Greek copies read "Jesus." **7 Sodom and Gomorrah** Two cities God destroyed because they were so evil. **9 archangel** The leader among God's angels or messengers.

devotion 358

JUDE 24–25

DON'T EVEN GO THERE

Even when you aren't strong, God promises you that he is and that he is able to prevent you from falling. If you're like most women, there are days you feel like saying, "The heck with it! I'm trying to stay strong, but I feel like I am getting crushed at every turn. *I can't take it anymore!*" Sometimes, God does allow the heat to rise a bit because he is perfecting you. Through that season of trouble, he is teaching you to depend on him and not to depend on things that please the flesh.

Even to this day, when I see a sparkling glass of wine, the enemy whispers in my ear, "Go ahead." There was a time when careful thought went into how I could manipulate any and every circumstance so I could go ahead and have that drink. I'm so glad to say that the strength of the Lord and his Word gave me victory in that area of my life. Someone once shared with me that being above reproach meant not even putting yourself in a tempting situation. I decided if I was going to continue on the path of service in ministry, I needed to be above reproach. If you have a heart that truly wants to lay some sin down, cling to this truth: God has the power to "bring you before his glory without any wrong in you" (verse 24). Go to him for the strength you need to resist falling into sin.

themselves to doing the wrong that Balaam
did. They have fought against God as Korah
did, and like Korah, they surely will be
destroyed. [12]They are like dirty spots in your
special Christian meals you share. They eat
with you and have no fear, caring only for
themselves. They are clouds without rain,
which the wind blows around. They are
autumn trees without fruit that are pulled
out of the ground. So they are twice dead.
[13]They are like wild waves of the sea, tossing
up their own shameful actions like foam.
They are like stars that wander in the sky. A
place in the blackest darkness has been kept
for them forever.

[14]Enoch, the seventh descendant from
Adam, said about these people: "Look, the
Lord is coming with many thousands of his
holy angels to [15]judge every person. He is
coming to punish all who are against God
for all the evil they have done against him.
And he will punish the sinners who are
against God for all the evil they have said
against him."

[16]These people complain and blame
others, doing the evil things they want to do.
They brag about themselves, and they flatter
others to get what they want.

A Warning and Things to Do

[17]Dear friends, remember what the
apostles of our Lord Jesus Christ said before.
[18]They said to you, "In the last times there
will be people who laugh about God,
following their own evil desires which are
against God." [19]These are the people who
divide you, people whose thoughts are only
of this world, who do not have the Spirit.

[20]But dear friends, use your most holy
faith to build yourselves up, praying in the
Holy Spirit. [21]Keep yourselves in God's love
as you wait for the Lord Jesus Christ with his
mercy to give you life forever.

[22]Show mercy to some people who have
doubts. [23]Take others out of the fire, and save
them. Show mercy mixed with fear to
others, hating even their clothes which are
dirty from sin.

Praise God

[24]God is strong and can help you not to
fall. He can bring you before his glory
without any wrong in you and can give you
great joy. [25]He is the only God, the One who
saves us. To him be glory, greatness, power,
and authority through Jesus Christ our Lord
for all time past, now, and forever. Amen.

Revelation

More specifically known as "The Revelation to John"

Person Holding the Pen God Wrote With: *John* wrote Revelation while exiled on the Greek island of Patmos, a prison colony. John was considered the "bishop" of Ephesus, and that church was the recipient of this dog-eared epistle.

When the Text Was Written: Between 95 and 96 A.D. as John neared the end of his natural life

Spiritual Posture of the Original Recipients: This revelation is a series of prophetic visions God gave John about seven actual churches in the first century A.D.—Ephesus, Smyrna, Pergamum, Thyatira, Sardis, Philadelphia, and Laodicea (Rev. 1:11)—that existed within a ninety-mile radius of each other in Asia Minor. These congregations were struggling with such issues as self-righteousness, sexual promiscuity, and indifference, and they had compromised their spiritual integrity.

Storyline Synopsis: This apocalyptic biblical caboose has confounded scholars throughout history with its complex symbolism about the last days; thus, there are many different interpretive approaches. But the basic storyline of John's dream is the apathy of the first-century church—and this book is the divine interruption of such religious sleepwalking. Jesus was knocking on the door of this lethargic spiritual community to see if anyone would wake up and commit to live zealously for God. Regardless of doctrinal nuances, this book points to God's ultimate authority—that he reigns supreme over everything. While believers will undoubtedly face battles here on earth—instigated by Satan, the father of lies—God will win the war between good and evil!

A Moment Worth Discussing: In chapter one, John paints a picture of Jesus walking among his beloved wearing a long robe with a golden sash that symbolizes dignity (Rev. 1:13); with white hair that symbolizes purity and wisdom (1:14); with eyes like blazing fire that symbolize judgment and purification (1:14); with bronze feet that symbolize a secure foundation (1:15); with a voice like the pounding surf that symbolizes power and authority (1:15); with seven stars in his hand that symbolize the churches (1:16); and with a face shining like the sun at full strength (1:16). The overall description compels shock and awe. It caused John to faint—"I fell down at his feet like a dead man" (1:17)—and it should compel us to wide-eyed wonder and worship!

Interesting (But Likely to Be Overlooked) Character: For *those who have been "sealed"* by God (chapter 7), his mark of protection ensures victory in all things!

John Tells About This Book

1 This is the revelation[n] of Jesus Christ,
which God gave to him, to show his
servants what must soon happen. And Jesus
sent his angel to show it to his servant John,
[2]who has told everything he has seen. It is
the word of God; it is the message from Jesus
Christ. [3]Blessed is the one who reads the
words of God's message, and blessed are the
people who hear this message and do what
is written in it. The time is near when all of
this will happen.

Jesus' Message to the Churches

[4]From John.
To the seven churches in Asia:
Grace and peace to you from the One who
is and was and is coming, and from the
seven spirits before his throne, [5]and from
Jesus Christ. Jesus is the faithful witness, the
first among those raised from the dead. He is
the ruler of the kings of the earth.
He is the One who loves us, who made us
free from our sins with the blood of his
death. [6]He made us to be a kingdom of
priests who serve God his Father. To Jesus
Christ be glory and power forever and ever!
Amen.
[7]Look, Jesus is coming with the clouds,
and everyone will see him, even those who
stabbed him. And all peoples of the earth
will cry loudly because of him. Yes, this will
happen! Amen.
[8]The Lord God says, "I am the Alpha and
the Omega.[n] I am the One who is and was
and is coming. I am the Almighty."
[9]I, John, am your brother. All of us share
with Christ in suffering, in the kingdom, and
in patience to continue. I was on the island
of Patmos,[n] because I had preached the word
of God and the message about Jesus. [10]On
the Lord's day I was in the Spirit, and I heard
a loud voice behind me that sounded like a
trumpet. [11]The voice said, "Write what you
see in a book and send it to the seven
churches: to Ephesus, Smyrna, Pergamum,
Thyatira, Sardis, Philadelphia, and Laodicea."
[12]I turned to see who was talking to me.
When I turned, I saw seven golden
lampstands [13]and someone among the

1:1 revelation Making known truth that has been hidden. **1:8 Alpha and the Omega** The first and last letters of the Greek alphabet. This means "the beginning and the end." **1:9 Patmos** A small island in the Aegean Sea, near the coast of Asia Minor (modern Turkey).

devotion 359

REVELATION 1:8

LESSONS FROM THE LITTLE ONES

I love being a labor coach. There is something miraculous about watching a new life come into the world. There are no words to describe watching a baby take his or her first breath. The beginning of life is so precious. This Scripture says, "I am the Alpha and Omega." This means that he is the beginning and the end. God was there before the foundation of the earth, and he will be there when the world comes to an end. He was there at your first breath, and he will be there at your last. God is with us every moment of every day, and he will bring us to heaven to live with him someday.

As a foster parent, this truth is the only thing that keeps me going at times. Before the little ones come to us, I pray for them. I have to trust God to be with them in the beginning of their lives because I know something bad happened to them to bring them to us in the first place. Then I fall in love with them and have to hand them back to God. I have to trust that God will be with them through their entire lives. If only I could learn to have this same perspective in my own life. God is the Almighty today as well as tomorrow. Carry that truth with you today, and for all of your tomorrows, trust him to figure the rest of it out.

lampstands who was "like a Son of Man."[n]
He was dressed in a long robe and had a gold
band around his chest. 14His head and hair
were white like wool, as white as snow, and
his eyes were like flames of fire. 15His feet
were like bronze that glows hot in a furnace,
and his voice was like the noise of flooding
water. 16He held seven stars in his right
hand, and a sharp double-edged sword came
out of his mouth. He looked like the sun
shining at its brightest time.

17When I saw him, I fell down at his feet
like a dead man. He put his right hand on
me and said, "Do not be afraid. I am the
First and the Last. 18I am the One who lives;
I was dead, but look, I am alive forever and
ever! And I hold the keys to death and to
the place of the dead. 19So write the things
you see, what is now and what will happen
later. 20Here is the secret of the seven stars
that you saw in my right hand and the
seven golden lampstands: The seven
lampstands are the seven churches, and the
seven stars are the angels of the seven
churches.

To the Church in Ephesus

2 "Write this to the angel of the church in
Ephesus:

"The One who holds the seven stars in his
right hand and walks among the seven
golden lampstands says this: 2I know what
you do, how you work hard and never give
up. I know you do not put up with the false
teachings of evil people. You have tested
those who say they are apostles but really
are not, and you found they are liars. 3You
have patience and have suffered troubles for
my name and have not given up.

4"But I have this against you: You have left
the love you had in the beginning. 5So
remember where you were before you fell.
Change your hearts and do what you did at
first. If you do not change, I will come to you
and will take away your lampstand from its
place. 6But there is something you do that is
right: You hate what the Nicolaitans[n] do, as
much as I.

7"Every person who has ears should listen
to what the Spirit says to the churches. To
those who win the victory I will give the
right to eat the fruit from the tree of life,
which is in the garden of God.

To the Church in Smyrna

8"Write this to the angel of the church in
Smyrna:

"The One who is the First and the Last,
who died and came to life again, says this: 9I
know your troubles and that you are poor,
but really you are rich! I know the bad
things some people say about you. They say
they are Jews, but they are not true Jews.
They are a synagogue that belongs to Satan.
10Do not be afraid of what you are about to
suffer. I tell you, the devil will put some of
you in prison to test you, and you will suffer
for ten days. But be faithful, even if you have
to die, and I will give you the crown of life.

11"Everyone who has ears should listen to
what the Spirit says to the churches. Those
who win the victory will not be hurt by the
second death.

To the Church in Pergamum

12"Write this to the angel of the church in
Pergamum:

"The One who has the sharp, double-
edged sword says this: 13I know where you
live. It is where Satan has his throne. But you
are true to me. You did not refuse to tell
about your faith in me even during the time
of Antipas, my faithful witness who was
killed in your city, where Satan lives.

14"But I have a few things against you: You
have some there who follow the teaching of
Balaam. He taught Balak how to cause the
people of Israel to sin by eating food offered
to idols and by taking part in sexual sins.
15You also have some who follow the
teaching of the Nicolaitans.[n] 16So change
your hearts and lives. If you do not, I will
come to you quickly and fight against them
with the sword that comes out of my mouth.

17"Everyone who has ears should listen to
what the Spirit says to the churches.

"I will give some of the hidden manna to
everyone who wins the victory. I will also
give to each one who wins the victory a
white stone with a new name written on it.
No one knows this new name except the one
who receives it.

1:13 "like . . . Man" "Son of Man" is a name Jesus called himself.
2:6, 15 Nicolaitans This is the name of a religious group that followed false beliefs and ideas.

To the Church in Thyatira

18“Write this to the angel of the church in
Thyatira:
“The Son of God, who has eyes that blaze
like fire and feet like shining bronze, says
this: 19I know what you do. I know about
your love, your faith, your service, and your
patience. I know that you are doing more
now than you did at first.
20“But I have this against you: You let that
woman Jezebel spread false teachings. She
says she is a prophetess, but by her teaching
she leads my people to take part in sexual
sins and to eat food that is offered to idols.
21I have given her time to change her heart
and turn away from her sin, but she does not
want to change. 22So I will throw her on a
bed of suffering. And all those who take part
in adultery with her will suffer greatly if
they do not turn away from the wrongs she
does. 23I will also kill her followers. Then all
the churches will know I am the One who
searches hearts and minds, and I will repay
each of you for what you have done.
24“But others of you in Thyatira have not
followed her teaching and have not learned
what some call Satan's deep secrets. I say to
you that I will not put any other load on you.
25Only continue in your loyalty until I come.
26“I will give power over the nations to
everyone who wins the victory and
continues to be obedient to me until the end.
27‘You will rule over them with an iron rod,
as when pottery is broken into pieces.’
Psalm 2:9
28This is the same power I received from my
Father. I will also give him the morning star.
29Everyone who has ears should listen to
what the Spirit says to the churches.

To the Church in Sardis

3 “Write this to the angel of the church in
Sardis:
“The One who has the seven spirits and
the seven stars says this: I know what you
do. People say that you are alive, but really
you are dead. 2Wake up! Strengthen what
you have left before it dies completely. I have
found that what you are doing is less than
what my God wants. 3So do not forget what
you have received and heard. Obey it, and
change your hearts and lives. So you must
wake up, or I will come like a thief, and you
will not know when I will come to you. 4But
you have a few there in Sardis who have
kept their clothes unstained, so they will
walk with me and will wear white clothes,
because they are worthy. 5Those who win
the victory will be dressed in white clothes
like them. And I will not erase their names
from the book of life, but I will say they
belong to me before my Father and before
his angels. 6Everyone who has ears should
listen to what the Spirit says to the churches.

To the Church in Philadelphia

7“Write this to the angel of the church in
Philadelphia:
“This is what the One who is holy and
true, who holds the key of David, says.
When he opens a door, no one can close it.
And when he closes it, no one can open it. 8I
know what you do. I have put an open door
before you, which no one can close. I know
you have little strength, but you have
obeyed my teaching and were not afraid to
speak my name. 9Those in the synagogue
that belongs to Satan say they are Jews, but
they are not true Jews; they are liars. I will
make them come before you and bow at
your feet, and they will know that I have
loved you. 10You have obeyed my teaching
about not giving up your faith. So I will keep
you from the time of trouble that will come
to the whole world to test those who live on
earth.
11“I am coming soon. Continue strong in
your faith so no one will take away your
crown. 12I will make those who win the
victory pillars in the temple of my God, and
they will never have to leave it. I will write
on them the name of my God and the name
of the city of my God, the new Jerusalem,[n]
that comes down out of heaven from my
God. I will also write on them my new name.
13Everyone who has ears should listen to
what the Spirit says to the churches.

To the Church in Laodicea

14“Write this to the angel of the church in
Laodicea:
“The Amen,[n] the faithful and true witness,

3:12 Jerusalem This name is used to mean the spiritual city God built for his people. See Revelation 21–22.
3:14 Amen Used here as a name for Jesus; it means to agree fully that something is true.

devotion 360

REVELATION 3:4–5

GETTING DOWN TO BUSINESS—OR BUSYNESS?

The church at Sardis was a busy place with lots of activity. It was a well-known church that probably looked and sounded like a really great place. But Jesus told this fellowship that only a few people there had kept their hearts tender toward God. A small remnant of the Sardis church devoted themselves to right living. A small number kept their white clothes unstained.

Did you know that you can show up at church every Sunday, teach in a children's class, volunteer with the mission outreach, make dinner for the sick, and still miss the heart of God? That's what was going on in Sardis. Lots of good stuff, but their hearts were not clean before the Lord. You know how the church thing can go. Without the restraint of the Holy Spirit, we can let ourselves become catty, gossipy, jealous, and bitter. Work goes on but the motives stink and God is not glorified. The hope we have is this: God promises to make you clean (1 John 1:9) and keep making you that way if you walk in relationship with him.

Before you jump into a bunch of activities or sign up for the next church committee, check your heart. Are you clean before the Lord? Are you willing to be made clean? With a pure vessel, you are prepared to jump in with both feet. God can use an imperfect woman with a white garment. The forgiveness of Jesus makes her worthy and ready to be used.

the ruler of all God has made, says this: [15]I
know what you do, that you are not hot or
cold. I wish that you were hot or cold! [16]But
because you are lukewarm—neither hot, nor
cold—I am ready to spit you out of my
mouth. [17]You say, 'I am rich, and I have
become wealthy and do not need anything.'
But you do not know that you are really
miserable, pitiful, poor, blind, and naked. [18]I
advise you to buy from me gold made pure
in fire so you can be truly rich. Buy from me
white clothes so you can be clothed and so
you can cover your shameful nakedness. Buy
from me medicine to put on your eyes so
you can truly see.
[19]"I correct and punish those whom I love.
So be eager to do right, and change your
hearts and lives. [20]Here I am! I stand at the
door and knock. If you hear my voice and
open the door, I will come in and eat with
you, and you will eat with me.
[21]"Those who win the victory will sit with
me on my throne in the same way that I
won the victory and sat down with my
Father on his throne. [22]Everyone who has
ears should listen to what the Spirit says to
the churches."

John Sees Heaven

4 After the vision of these things I looked,
and there before me was an open door in
heaven. And the same voice that spoke to
me before, that sounded like a trumpet, said,
"Come up here, and I will show you what
must happen after this." [2]Immediately I was
in the Spirit, and before me was a throne in
heaven, and someone was sitting on it. [3]The
One who sat on the throne looked like
precious stones, like jasper and carnelian. All
around the throne was a rainbow the color
of an emerald. [4]Around the throne there were
twenty-four other thrones with twenty-four
elders sitting on them. They were dressed in
white and had golden crowns on their heads.
[5]Lightning flashes and noises and thunder
came from the throne. Before the throne

seven lamps were burning, which are the
seven spirits of God. 6Also before the throne
there was something that looked like a sea of
glass, clear like crystal.
In the center and around the throne were
four living creatures with eyes all over
them, in front and in back. 7The first living
creature was like a lion. The second was like
a calf. The third had a face like a man. The
fourth was like a flying eagle. 8Each of these
four living creatures had six wings and was
covered all over with eyes, inside and out.
Day and night they never stop saying:

"Holy, holy, holy is the Lord God
Almighty.
He was, he is, and he is coming."

9These living creatures give glory, honor,
and thanks to the One who sits on the
throne, who lives forever and ever. 10Then
the twenty-four elders bow down before
the One who sits on the throne, and they
worship him who lives forever and ever.
They put their crowns down before the
throne and say:

11"You are worthy, our Lord and God,
to receive glory and honor and power,
because you made all things.
Everything existed and was made,
because you wanted it."

5 Then I saw a scroll in the right hand of
the One sitting on the throne. The scroll
had writing on both sides and was kept
closed with seven seals. 2And I saw a
powerful angel calling in a loud voice, "Who
is worthy to break the seals and open the
scroll?" 3But there was no one in heaven or
on earth or under the earth who could open
the scroll or look inside it. 4I cried bitterly
because there was no one who was worthy
to open the scroll or look inside. 5But one of
the elders said to me, "Do not cry! The Lion[n]
from the tribe of Judah, David's descendant,
has won the victory so that he is able to
open the scroll and its seven seals."
6Then I saw a Lamb standing in the center
of the throne and in the middle of the four
living creatures and the elders. The Lamb
looked as if he had been killed. He had seven
horns and seven eyes, which are the seven
spirits of God that were sent into all the
world. 7The Lamb came and took the scroll
from the right hand of the One sitting on the
throne. 8When he took the scroll, the four
living creatures and the twenty-four elders
bowed down before the Lamb. Each one of
them had a harp and golden bowls full of
incense, which are the prayers of God's holy
people. 9And they all sang a new song to the
Lamb:

"You are worthy to take the scroll
and to open its seals,
because you were killed,
and with the blood of your death you
bought people for God
from every tribe, language, people, and
nation.
10You made them to be a kingdom of priests
for our God,
and they will rule on the earth."

11Then I looked, and I heard the voices of
many angels around the throne, and the four
living creatures, and the elders. There were
thousands and thousands of angels, 12saying
in a loud voice:

"The Lamb who was killed is worthy
to receive power, wealth, wisdom, and
strength,
honor, glory, and praise!"

13Then I heard all creatures in heaven and
on earth and under the earth and in the sea
saying:

"To the One who sits on the throne
and to the Lamb
be praise and honor and glory and power
forever and ever."

14The four living creatures said, "Amen,"
and the elders bowed down and worshiped.

6 Then I watched while the Lamb opened
the first of the seven seals. I heard one of
the four living creatures say with a voice like
thunder, "Come!" 2I looked, and there before
me was a white horse. The rider on the horse
held a bow, and he was given a crown, and
he rode out, determined to win the victory.
3When the Lamb opened the second seal,
I heard the second living creature say,
"Come!" 4Then another horse came out, a red
one. Its rider was given power to take away
peace from the earth and to make people kill
each other, and he was given a big sword.
5When the Lamb opened the third seal, I
heard the third living creature say, "Come!" I
looked, and there before me was a black
horse, and its rider held a pair of scales in his

5:5 Lion Here refers to Christ.

hand. 6Then I heard something that sounded
like a voice coming from the middle of the
four living creatures. The voice said, "A quart
of wheat for a day's pay, and three quarts of
barley for a day's pay, and do not damage the
olive oil and wine!"

7When the Lamb opened the fourth seal, I
heard the voice of the fourth living creature
say, "Come!" 8I looked, and there before me
was a pale horse. Its rider was named death,
and Hades[n] was following close behind him.
They were given power over a fourth of the
earth to kill people by war, by starvation, by
disease, and by the wild animals of the earth.

9When the Lamb opened the fifth seal, I
saw under the altar the souls of those who
had been killed because they were faithful to
the word of God and to the message they had
received. 10These souls shouted in a loud
voice, "Holy and true Lord, how long until
you judge the people of the earth and punish
them for killing us?" 11Then each one of
them was given a white robe and was told to
wait a short time longer. There were still
some of their fellow servants and brothers
and sisters in the service of Christ who must
be killed as they were. They had to wait until
all of this was finished.

12Then I watched while the Lamb opened
the sixth seal, and there was a great
earthquake. The sun became black like
rough black cloth, and the whole moon
became red like blood. 13And the stars in the
sky fell to the earth like figs falling from a fig
tree when the wind blows. 14The sky
disappeared as a scroll when it is rolled up,
and every mountain and island was moved
from its place.

15Then the kings of the earth, the rulers,
the generals, the rich people, the powerful
people, the slaves, and the free people hid
themselves in caves and in the rocks on the
mountains. 16They called to the mountains
and the rocks, "Fall on us. Hide us from the
face of the One who sits on the throne and
from the anger of the Lamb! 17The great day
for their anger has come, and who can stand
against it?"

The 144,000 People of Israel

7 After the vision of these things I saw four
angels standing at the four corners of the
earth. The angels were holding the four
winds of the earth to keep them from
blowing on the land or on the sea or on any
tree. 2Then I saw another angel coming up
from the east who had the seal of the living
God. And he called out in a loud voice to the
four angels to whom God had given power
to harm the earth and the sea. 3He said to
them, "Do not harm the land or the sea or
the trees until we mark with a sign the
foreheads of the people who serve our God."
4Then I heard how many people were
marked with the sign. There were one
hundred forty-four thousand from every
tribe of the people of Israel.

5From the tribe of Judah twelve thousand
were marked with the sign,
from the tribe of Reuben twelve thousand,
from the tribe of Gad twelve thousand,
6from the tribe of Asher twelve thousand,
from the tribe of Naphtali twelve
thousand,
from the tribe of Manasseh twelve
thousand,
7from the tribe of Simeon twelve
thousand,
from the tribe of Levi twelve thousand,
from the tribe of Issachar twelve
thousand,
8from the tribe of Zebulun twelve
thousand,
from the tribe of Joseph twelve thousand,
and from the tribe of Benjamin twelve
thousand were marked with the
sign.

The Great Crowd Worships God

9After the vision of these things I looked,
and there was a great number of people, so
many that no one could count them. They
were from every nation, tribe, people, and
language of the earth. They were all standing
before the throne and before the Lamb,
wearing white robes and holding palm
branches in their hands. 10They were
shouting in a loud voice, "Salvation belongs
to our God, who sits on the throne, and to
the Lamb." 11All the angels were standing
around the throne and the elders and the
four living creatures. They all bowed down
on their faces before the throne and
worshiped God, 12saying, "Amen! Praise,

6:8 Hades The unseen world of the dead.

devotion 361

REVELATION 7:9–17

IT MAKES ALL THE DIFFERENCE

Death is a peculiar thing. We mourn the departure of our loved ones, but God welcomes the return of saints in heaven. That was not a comfort for me when my mom died because I was living like there was no hope. I didn't know the Lord. My mom was a sweet Christian woman who had her struggles in life—a husband who left her, a birth defect that left her self-conscious, and two children that she had to be both father and mother to—but her faith in the Lord alone is what got her through. When she was diagnosed with cancer, my world fell apart. Within thirty days of her diagnosis, she was gone. I was devastated! God had her and I did not!

Then came Jesus. When I asked the Lord into my heart, I devoured his words about heaven. I wanted to know where she was and what she was doing and what it was like. I wanted to know everything! After salvation, my mourning turned to peace and hope. I finally knew my mom was filled with joy and not distress and that she was not worrying about providing for us because she knew the King was taking care of it. She knew my brother and I were not thirsty because we had been led to the living water to drink and be saved. God wiped the mournful tears from my eyes that day, and I could see that the Great Shepherd was taking care of Mom.

glory, wisdom, thanks, honor, power, and
strength belong to our God forever and ever.
Amen!"
13Then one of the elders asked me, "Who
are these people dressed in white robes?
Where did they come from?"
14I answered, "You know, sir."
And the elder said to me, "These are the
people who have come out of the great
distress. They have washed their robes[n] and
made them white in the blood of the Lamb.
15Because of this, they are before the throne
of God. They worship him day and night in
his temple. And the One who sits on the
throne will be present with them. 16Those
people will never be hungry again, and they
will never be thirsty again. The sun will not
hurt them, and no heat will burn them,
17because the Lamb at the center of the
throne will be their shepherd. He will lead
them to springs of water that give life. And
God will wipe away every tear from their
eyes."

The Seventh Seal

8 When the Lamb opened the seventh seal,
there was silence in heaven for about
half an hour. 2And I saw the seven angels
who stand before God and to whom were
given seven trumpets.
3Another angel came and stood at the
altar, holding a golden pan for incense. He
was given much incense to offer with the
prayers of all God's holy people. The angel
put this offering on the golden altar before
the throne. 4The smoke from the incense
went up from the angel's hand to God with
the prayers of God's people. 5Then the angel
filled the incense pan with fire from the altar
and threw it on the earth, and there were
flashes of lightning, thunder and loud
noises, and an earthquake.

The Seven Angels and Trumpets

6Then the seven angels who had the seven
trumpets prepared to blow them.

7:14 washed their robes This means they believed in Jesus so that their sins could be forgiven by Christ's blood.

7The first angel blew his trumpet, and hail
and fire mixed with blood were poured
down on the earth. And a third of the earth,
and all the green grass, and a third of the
trees were burned up.
8Then the second angel blew his trumpet,
and something that looked like a big
mountain, burning with fire, was thrown
into the sea. And a third of the sea became
blood, 9a third of the living things in the sea
died, and a third of the ships were destroyed.
10Then the third angel blew his trumpet,
and a large star, burning like a torch, fell
from the sky. It fell on a third of the rivers
and on the springs of water. 11The name of
the star is Wormwood.[n] And a third of all the
water became bitter, and many people died
from drinking the water that was bitter.
12Then the fourth angel blew his trumpet,
and a third of the sun, and a third of the
moon, and a third of the stars were struck. So
a third of them became dark, and a third of
the day was without light, and also the
night.
13While I watched, I heard an eagle that
was flying high in the air cry out in a loud
voice, "Trouble! Trouble! Trouble for those
who live on the earth because of the
remaining sounds of the trumpets that the
other three angels are about to blow!"
9 Then the fifth angel blew his trumpet,
and I saw a star fall from the sky to the
earth. The star was given the key to the deep
hole that leads to the bottomless pit. 2Then
it opened up the hole that leads to the
bottomless pit, and smoke came up from the
hole like smoke from a big furnace. Then
the sun and sky became dark because of
the smoke from the hole. 3Then locusts
came down to the earth out of the smoke,
and they were given the power to sting like
scorpions.[n] 4They were told not to harm the
grass on the earth or any plant or tree. They
could harm only the people who did not
have the sign of God on their foreheads.
5These locusts were not given the power to
kill anyone, but to cause pain to the people
for five months. And the pain they felt was
like the pain a scorpion gives when it stings
someone. 6During those days people will
look for a way to die, but they will not find
it. They will want to die, but death will run
away from them.
7The locusts looked like horses prepared
for battle. On their heads they wore what
looked like crowns of gold, and their faces
looked like human faces. 8Their hair was
like women's hair, and their teeth were like
lions' teeth. 9Their chests looked like iron
breastplates, and the sound of their wings
was like the noise of many horses and
chariots hurrying into battle. 10The locusts
had tails with stingers like scorpions, and in
their tails was their power to hurt people for
five months. 11The locusts had a king who
was the angel of the bottomless pit. His
name in the Hebrew language is Abaddon
and in the Greek language is Apollyon.[n]
12The first trouble is past; there are still
two other troubles that will come.
13Then the sixth angel blew his trumpet,
and I heard a voice coming from the horns
on the golden altar that is before God. 14The
voice said to the sixth angel who had the
trumpet, "Free the four angels who are tied
at the great river Euphrates." 15And they let
loose the four angels who had been kept
ready for this hour and day and month and
year so they could kill a third of all people
on the earth. 16I heard how many troops on
horses were in their army—two hundred
million.
17The horses and their riders I saw in
the vision looked like this: They had
breastplates that were fiery red, dark blue,
and yellow like sulfur. The heads of the
horses looked like heads of lions, with fire,
smoke, and sulfur coming out of their
mouths. 18A third of all the people on earth
were killed by these three terrible disasters
coming out of the horses' mouths: the fire,
the smoke, and the sulfur. 19The horses'
power was in their mouths and in their tails;
their tails were like snakes with heads, and
with them they hurt people.
20The other people who were not killed by
these terrible disasters still did not change
their hearts and turn away from what they
had made with their own hands. They did
not stop worshiping demons and idols made
of gold, silver, bronze, stone, and wood—
things that cannot see or hear or walk.

8:11 Wormwood Name of a very bitter plant; used here to give the idea of bitter sorrow.
9:3 scorpions A scorpion is an insect that stings with a bad poison. **9:11 Abaddon, Apollyon** Both names mean "Destroyer."

21These people did not change their hearts
and turn away from murder or evil magic,
from their sexual sins or stealing.

The Angel and the Small Scroll

10 Then I saw another powerful angel
coming down from heaven dressed in
a cloud with a rainbow over his head. His
face was like the sun, and his legs were like
pillars of fire. 2The angel was holding a small
scroll open in his hand. He put his right foot
on the sea and his left foot on the land.
3Then he shouted loudly like the roaring of a
lion. And when he shouted, the voices of
seven thunders spoke. 4When the seven
thunders spoke, I started to write. But I heard
a voice from heaven say, "Keep hidden what
the seven thunders said, and do not write
them down."

5Then the angel I saw standing on the sea
and on the land raised his right hand to
heaven, 6and he made a promise by the
power of the One who lives forever and ever.
He is the One who made the skies and all
that is in them, the earth and all that is in it,
and the sea and all that is in it. The angel
promised, "There will be no more waiting!
7In the days when the seventh angel is ready
to blow his trumpet, God's secret will be
finished. This secret is the Good News God
told to his servants, the prophets."

8Then I heard the same voice from heaven
again, saying to me: "Go and take the open
scroll that is in the hand of the angel that is
standing on the sea and on the land."

9So I went to the angel and told him to
give me the small scroll. And he said to me,
"Take the scroll and eat it. It will be sour in
your stomach, but in your mouth it will be
sweet as honey." 10So I took the small scroll
from the angel's hand and ate it. In my
mouth it tasted sweet as honey, but after I
ate it, it was sour in my stomach. 11Then I
was told, "You must prophesy again about
many peoples, nations, languages, and
kings."

The Two Witnesses

11 I was given a measuring stick like a
rod, and I was told, "Go and measure
the temple of God and the altar, and count
the people worshiping there. 2But do not
measure the yard outside the temple. Leave
it alone, because it has been given to those
who are not God's people. And they will
trample on the holy city for forty-two
months. 3And I will give power to my two
witnesses to prophesy for one thousand two
hundred sixty days, and they will be dressed
in rough cloth to show their sadness."

4These two witnesses are the two olive
trees and the two lampstands that stand
before the Lord of the earth. 5And if anyone
tries to hurt them, fire comes from their
mouths and kills their enemies. And if
anyone tries to hurt them in whatever way,
in that same way that person will die. 6These
witnesses have the power to stop the sky
from raining during the time they are
prophesying. And they have power to make
the waters become blood, and they have
power to send every kind of trouble to the
earth as many times as they want.

7When the two witnesses have finished
telling their message, the beast that comes
up from the bottomless pit will fight a war
against them. He will defeat them and kill
them. 8The bodies of the two witnesses will
lie in the street of the great city where the
Lord was killed. This city is named Sodom[n]
and Egypt, which has a spiritual meaning.
9Those from every race of people, tribe,
language, and nation will look at the bodies
of the two witnesses for three and one-half
days, and they will refuse to bury them.
10People who live on the earth will rejoice
and be happy because these two are dead.
They will send each other gifts, because
these two prophets brought much suffering
to those who live on the earth.

11But after three and one-half days, God
put the breath of life into the two prophets
again. They stood on their feet, and everyone
who saw them became very afraid. 12Then
the two prophets heard a loud voice from
heaven saying, "Come up here!" And they
went up into heaven in a cloud as their
enemies watched.

13In the same hour there was a great
earthquake, and a tenth of the city was
destroyed. Seven thousand people were
killed in the earthquake, and those who did
not die were very afraid and gave glory to
the God of heaven.

11:8 Sodom City that God destroyed because the people were so evil.

14The second trouble is finished. Pay
attention: The third trouble is coming soon.

The Seventh Trumpet

15Then the seventh angel blew his
trumpet. And there were loud voices in
heaven, saying:
"The power to rule the world now belongs
to our Lord and his Christ,
and he will rule forever and ever."
16Then the twenty-four elders, who sit on
their thrones before God, bowed down on
their faces and worshiped God. 17They said:
"We give thanks to you, Lord God
Almighty,
who is and who was,
because you have used your great power
and have begun to rule!
18The people of the world were angry,
but your anger has come.
The time has come to judge the dead,
and to reward your servants the
prophets
and your holy people,
all who respect you, great and small.
The time has come to destroy those who
destroy the earth!"
19Then God's temple in heaven was
opened. The Ark that holds the agreement
God gave to his people could be seen in his
temple. Then there were flashes of lightning,
noises, thunder, an earthquake, and a great
hailstorm.

The Woman and the Dragon

12 And then a great wonder appeared in
heaven: A woman was clothed with
the sun, and the moon was under her feet,
and a crown of twelve stars was on her head.
2She was pregnant and cried out with pain,
because she was about to give birth. 3Then
another wonder appeared in heaven: There
was a giant red dragon with seven heads and
seven crowns on each head. He also had ten
horns. 4His tail swept a third of the stars out
of the sky and threw them down to the
earth. He stood in front of the woman who
was ready to give birth so he could eat her
baby as soon as it was born. 5Then the
woman gave birth to a son who will rule all
the nations with an iron rod. And her child
was taken up to God and to his throne. 6The
woman ran away into the desert to a place
God prepared for her where she would be
taken care of for one thousand two hundred
sixty days.
7Then there was a war in heaven.
Michael[n] and his angels fought against the
dragon, and the dragon and his angels
fought back. 8But the dragon was not strong
enough, and he and his angels lost their
place in heaven. 9The giant dragon was
thrown down out of heaven. (He is that old
snake called the devil or Satan, who tricks
the whole world.) The dragon with his
angels was thrown down to the earth.
10Then I heard a loud voice in heaven
saying:
"The salvation and the power and the
kingdom of our God
and the authority of his Christ have
now come.
The accuser of our brothers and sisters,
who accused them day and night before
our God,
has been thrown down.
11And our brothers and sisters defeated him
by the blood of the Lamb's death
and by the message they preached.
They did not love their lives so much
that they were afraid of death.
12So rejoice, you heavens
and all who live there!
But it will be terrible for the earth and the
sea,
because the devil has come down to
you!
He is filled with anger,
because he knows he does not have
much time."
13When the dragon saw he had been
thrown down to the earth, he hunted for the
woman who had given birth to the son.
14But the woman was given the two wings of
a great eagle so she could fly to the place
prepared for her in the desert. There she
would be taken care of for three and one-half
years, away from the snake. 15Then the
snake poured water out of its mouth like a
river toward the woman so the flood would
carry her away. 16But the earth helped the
woman by opening its mouth and
swallowing the river that came from the
mouth of the dragon. 17Then the dragon was

12:7 Michael The archangel—leader among God's angels or messengers (Jude 9).

very angry at the woman, and he went off to
make war against all her other children—
those who obey God's commands and who
have the message Jesus taught.
18And the dragon[n] stood on the seashore.

The Two Beasts

13 Then I saw a beast coming up out of
the sea. It had ten horns and seven
heads, and there was a crown on each horn.
A name against God was written on each
head. 2This beast looked like a leopard, with
feet like a bear's feet and a mouth like a
lion's mouth. And the dragon gave the beast
all of his power and his throne and great
authority. 3One of the heads of the beast
looked as if it had been killed by a wound,
but this death wound was healed. Then the
whole world was amazed and followed the
beast. 4People worshiped the dragon because
he had given his power to the beast. And
they also worshiped the beast, asking,
"Who is like the beast? Who can make war
against it?"
5The beast was allowed to say proud
words and words against God, and it was
allowed to use its power for forty-two
months. 6It used its mouth to speak against
God, against God's name, against the place
where God lives, and against all those who
live in heaven. 7It was given power to make
war against God's holy people and to defeat
them. It was given power over every tribe,
people, language, and nation. 8And all who
live on earth will worship the beast—all the
people since the beginning of the world
whose names are not written in the Lamb's
book of life. The Lamb is the One who was
killed.
9Anyone who has ears should listen:
10If you are to be a prisoner,
then you will be a prisoner.
If you are to be killed with the sword,
then you will be killed with the sword.
This means that God's holy people must
have patience and faith.
11Then I saw another beast coming up out
of the earth. It had two horns like a lamb,
but it spoke like a dragon. 12This beast
stands before the first beast and uses the
same power the first beast has. By this power
it makes everyone living on earth worship
the first beast, who had the death wound
that was healed. 13And the second beast does

12:18 the dragon Some Greek copies read "I."

devotion 362

REVELATION 13:9-10

WHAT FAITH REQUIRES

I have a friend who has dealt with a disease in her body since she was nine years old. It affects every aspect of her life. She's been through multiple surgeries and procedures and lives on medication. She has good days and bad days, but God has been faithful. She said to me the other day, "I've spent most of my life asking God to heal me. Now when I wake up each day, I thank God for my healing and go on with my day. When he wants to heal me is up to him." This is a demonstration of Revelation 13:9-10.

We are not exempt from the pain and suffering of this world. These verses tell us that bad things will happen in the lives of believers. We will experience disease, our children will not be perfect, and evil will come our way from time to time. So what is God's advice to us as we walk through this life? "God's holy people must have patience and faith" (verse 10). Remember, faith is believing what you do not see. It seems to me that things will be getting worse before they get better. In the end, we have to be prepared to be imprisoned and killed for being followers of Christ. Our preparation starts now. My friend is waiting patiently for her healing, even if she has to wait until heaven. Whether yours is a financial, emotional, or physical need, waiting patiently for God is what faith requires.

great miracles so that it even makes fire come down from heaven to earth while people are watching. 14It fools those who live on earth by the miracles it has been given the power to do. It does these miracles to serve the first beast. The second beast orders people to make an idol to honor the first beast, the one that was wounded by the deadly sword but sprang to life again. 15The second beast was given power to give life to the idol of the first one so that the idol could speak. And the second beast was given power to command all who will not worship the image of the beast to be killed. 16The second beast also forced all people, small and great, rich and poor, free and slave, to have a mark on their right hand or on their forehead. 17No one could buy or sell without this mark, which is the name of the beast or the number of its name. 18This takes wisdom. Let the one who has understanding find the meaning of the number, which is the number of a person. Its number is 666.[n]

The Song of the Saved

14 Then I looked, and there before me was the Lamb standing on Mount Zion.[n] With him were one hundred forty-four thousand people who had his name and his Father's name written on their foreheads. 2And I heard a sound from heaven like the noise of flooding water and like the sound of loud thunder. The sound I heard was like people playing harps. 3And they sang a new song before the throne and before the four living creatures and the elders. No one could learn the new song except the one hundred forty-four thousand who had been bought from the earth. 4These are the ones who did not do sinful things with women, because they kept themselves pure. They follow the Lamb every place he goes. These one hundred forty-four thousand were bought from among the people of the earth as people to be offered to God and the Lamb. 5They were not guilty of telling lies; they are without fault.

The Three Angels

6Then I saw another angel flying high in the air. He had the eternal Good News to preach to those who live on earth—to every nation, tribe, language, and people. 7He preached in a loud voice, "Fear God and give him praise, because the time has come for God to judge all people. So worship God who made the heavens, and the earth, and the sea, and the springs of water."

8Then the second angel followed the first angel and said, "Ruined, ruined is the great city of Babylon! She made all the nations drink the wine of the anger of her adultery."

9Then a third angel followed the first two angels, saying in a loud voice: "If anyone worships the beast and his idol and gets the beast's mark on the forehead or on the hand, 10that one also will drink the wine of God's anger, which is prepared with all its strength in the cup of his anger. And that person will be put in pain with burning sulfur before the holy angels and the Lamb. 11And the smoke from their burning pain will rise forever and ever. There will be no rest, day or night, for those who worship the beast and his idol or who get the mark of his name." 12This means God's holy people must be patient. They must obey God's commands and keep their faith in Jesus.

13Then I heard a voice from heaven saying, "Write this: Blessed are the dead who die from now on in the Lord."

The Spirit says, "Yes, they will rest from their hard work, and the reward of all they have done stays with them."

The Earth Is Harvested

14Then I looked, and there before me was a white cloud, and sitting on the white cloud was One who looked like a Son of Man.[n] He had a gold crown on his head and a sharp sickle[n] in his hand. 15Then another angel came out of the temple and called out in a loud voice to the One who was sitting on the cloud, "Take your sickle and harvest from the earth, because the time to harvest has come, and the fruit of the earth is ripe." 16So the One who was sitting on the cloud swung his sickle over the earth, and the earth was harvested.

17Then another angel came out of the temple in heaven, and he also had a sharp sickle. 18And then another angel, who has

13:18 666 Some Greek copies read "616." **14:1 Mount Zion** Another name for Jerusalem; here meaning the spiritual city of God's people.
14:14 Son of Man "Son of Man" is a name Jesus called himself.
14:14 sickle A farming tool with a curved blade. It was used to harvest grain.

power over the fire, came from the altar. This
angel called to the angel with the sharp
sickle, saying, "Take your sharp sickle and
gather the bunches of grapes from the earth's
vine, because its grapes are ripe." 19Then the
angel swung his sickle over the earth. He
gathered the earth's grapes and threw them
into the great winepress of God's anger.
20They were trampled in the winepress
outside the city, and blood flowed out of the
winepress as high as horses' bridles for a
distance of about one hundred eighty miles.

The Last Troubles

15 Then I saw another wonder in heaven
that was great and amazing. There
were seven angels bringing seven disasters.
These are the last disasters, because after
them, God's anger is finished.

2I saw what looked like a sea of glass
mixed with fire. All of those who had won
the victory over the beast and his idol and
over the number of his name were standing
by the sea of glass. They had harps that God
had given them. 3They sang the song of
Moses, the servant of God, and the song of
the Lamb:

"You do great and wonderful things,
Psalm 111:2
Lord God Almighty. *Amos 3:13*
Everything the Lord does is right and true,
Psalm 145:17
King of the nations.[n]
4Everyone will respect you, Lord,
Jeremiah 10:7
and will honor you.
Only you are holy.
All the nations will come
and worship you, *Psalm 86:9–10*
because the right things you have done
are now made known." *Deuteronomy 32:4*

5After this I saw that the temple (the Tent
of the Agreement) in heaven was opened.
6And the seven angels bringing the seven
disasters came out of the temple. They were
dressed in clean, shining linen and wore
golden bands tied around their chests. 7Then
one of the four living creatures gave to the
seven angels seven golden bowls filled with
the anger of God, who lives forever and ever.
8The temple was filled with smoke from the
glory and the power of God, and no one
could enter the temple until the seven
disasters of the seven angels were finished.

The Bowls of God's Anger

16 Then I heard a loud voice from the
temple saying to the seven angels, "Go
and pour out the seven bowls of God's anger
on the earth."

2The first angel left and poured out his
bowl on the land. Then ugly and painful
sores came upon all those who had the mark
of the beast and who worshiped his idol.

3The second angel poured out his bowl on
the sea, and it became blood like that of a
dead man, and every living thing in the sea
died.

4The third angel poured out his bowl on
the rivers and the springs of water, and they
became blood. 5Then I heard the angel of the
waters saying:

"Holy One, you are the One who is and
who was.
You are right to decide to punish these
evil people.
6They have poured out the blood of your
holy people and your prophets.
So now you have given them blood to
drink as they deserve."

7And I heard a voice coming from the altar
saying:

"Yes, Lord God Almighty,
the way you punish evil people is right
and fair."

8The fourth angel poured out his bowl on
the sun, and he was given power to burn the
people with fire. 9They were burned by the
great heat, and they cursed the name of God,
who had control over these disasters. But the
people refused to change their hearts and
lives and give glory to God.

10The fifth angel poured out his bowl on
the throne of the beast, and darkness
covered its kingdom. People gnawed their
tongues because of the pain. 11They also
cursed the God of heaven because of their
pain and the sores they had, but they refused
to change their hearts and turn away from
the evil things they did.

12The sixth angel poured out his bowl on
the great river Euphrates so that the water
in the river was dried up to prepare the way
for the kings from the east to come. 13Then I

15:3 King . . . nations Some Greek copies read "King of the ages."

saw three evil spirits that looked like frogs
coming out of the mouth of the dragon, out
of the mouth of the beast, and out of the
mouth of the false prophet. 14These evil
spirits are the spirits of demons, which have
power to do miracles. They go out to the
kings of the whole world to gather them
together for the battle on the great day of
God Almighty.
15"Listen! I will come as a thief comes!
Blessed are those who stay awake and keep
their clothes on so that they will not walk
around naked and have people see their
shame."
16Then the evil spirits gathered the kings
together to the place that is called
Armageddon in the Hebrew language.
17The seventh angel poured out his bowl
into the air. Then a loud voice came out of the
temple from the throne, saying, "It is
finished!" 18Then there were flashes of
lightning, noises, thunder, and a big
earthquake—the worst earthquake that has
ever happened since people have been on
earth. 19The great city split into three parts,
and the cities of the nations were destroyed.
And God remembered the sins of Babylon the
Great, so he gave that city the cup filled with
the wine of his terrible anger. 20Then every
island ran away, and mountains disappeared.
21Giant hailstones, each weighing about a
hundred pounds, fell from the sky upon
people. People cursed God for the disaster of
the hail, because this disaster was so terrible.

The Woman on the Animal

17 Then one of the seven angels who had
the seven bowls came and spoke to
me. He said, "Come, and I will show you the
punishment that will be given to the great
prostitute, the one sitting over many waters.
2The kings of the earth sinned sexually with
her, and the people of the earth became
drunk from the wine of her sexual sin."
3Then the angel carried me away by the
Spirit to the desert. There I saw a woman
sitting on a red beast. It was covered with
names against God written on it, and it had
seven heads and ten horns. 4The woman was
dressed in purple and red and was shining
with the gold, precious jewels, and pearls she
was wearing. She had a golden cup in her
hand, a cup filled with evil things and the
uncleanness of her sexual sin. 5On her
forehead a title was written that was secret.
This is what was written:

THE GREAT BABYLON
MOTHER OF PROSTITUTES
AND OF THE EVIL THINGS OF THE EARTH

6Then I saw that the woman was drunk
with the blood of God's holy people and
with the blood of those who were killed
because of their faith in Jesus.
When I saw the woman, I was very
amazed. 7Then the angel said to me, "Why
are you amazed? I will tell you the secret of
this woman and the beast she rides—the
one with seven heads and ten horns. 8The
beast you saw was once alive but is not alive
now. But soon it will come up out of the
bottomless pit and go away to be destroyed.
There are people who live on earth whose
names have not been written in the book of
life since the beginning of the world. They
will be amazed when they see the beast,
because he was once alive, is not alive now,
but will come again.
9"You need a wise mind to understand
this. The seven heads on the beast are seven
mountains where the woman sits. 10And
they are seven kings. Five of the kings have
already been destroyed, one of the kings
lives now, and another has not yet come.
When he comes, he must stay a short time.
11The beast that was once alive, but is not
alive now, is also an eighth king. He belongs
to the first seven kings, and he will go away
to be destroyed.
12"The ten horns you saw are ten kings
who have not yet begun to rule, but they
will receive power to rule with the beast for
one hour. 13All ten of these kings have the
same purpose, and they will give their power
and authority to the beast. 14They will make
war against the Lamb, but the Lamb will
defeat them, because he is Lord of lords and
King of kings. He will defeat them with his
called, chosen, and faithful followers."
15Then the angel said to me, "The waters
that you saw, where the prostitute sits, are
peoples, races, nations, and languages. 16The
ten horns and the beast you saw will hate
the prostitute. They will take everything she
has and leave her naked. They will eat her
body and burn her with fire. 17God made the
ten horns want to carry out his purpose by
agreeing to give the beast their power to
rule, until what God has said comes about.

devotion 363

REVELATION 17:14

THINK OF IT AS BOOT CAMP

When my son was three years old, he came downstairs one morning to find me watching CNN coverage of the Gulf War. He watched with me for a minute and then jumped off my lap and ran to the window. "Oh, Mommy," he cried as he looked into the sky. "Is Jesus coming back today? Is he coming on his white horse to take us to heaven?" I saw an earthly war, but my son saw Jesus returning for him on a white horse. The Bible says in Revelation 19:11, "Then I saw heaven opened, and there before me was a white horse. The rider on the horse is called Faithful and True, and he is right when he judges and makes war." Jesus is coming back someday on a white horse.

We struggle with day-to-day life, but often we forget how this story will end. Right here in Revelation 17:14, we are told that Jesus will defeat Satan because he is the King of kings and Lord of lords. And the amazing thing is that we will help him. We are the faithful followers. We wonder why we have to suffer through trials here on earth. Here is our answer—this is boot camp. We can't be soft or weak when we serve in the army of God. We need to be strong and full of faith. We need to believe in our Commander-in-Chief so that we can help him win the war against the Evil One once and for all.

18The woman you saw is the great city that
rules over the kings of the earth."

Babylon Is Destroyed

18 After the vision of these things, I saw
another angel coming down from
heaven. This angel had great power, and his
glory made the earth bright. 2He shouted in
a powerful voice:

"Ruined, ruined is the great city of
Babylon!
She has become a home for demons
and a prison for every evil spirit,
and a prison for every unclean bird and
unclean beast.
3She has been ruined, because all the
peoples of the earth
have drunk the wine of the desire of
her sexual sin.
She has been ruined also because the
kings of the earth
have sinned sexually with her,
and the merchants of the earth
have grown rich from the great wealth
of her luxury."

4Then I heard another voice from heaven
saying:

"Come out of that city, my people,
so that you will not share in her sins,
so that you will not receive the
disasters that will come to her.
5Her sins have piled up as high as the sky,
and God has not forgotten the wrongs
she has done.
6Give that city the same as she gave to
others.
Pay her back twice as much as she did.
Prepare wine for her that is twice as
strong
as the wine she prepared for others.
7She gave herself much glory and rich
living.
Give her that much suffering and
sadness.
She says to herself, 'I am a queen sitting
on my throne.
I am not a widow; I will never be sad.'
8So these disasters will come to her in one
day:
death, and crying, and great hunger,

and she will be destroyed by fire,
because the Lord God who judges her is powerful."

9The kings of the earth who sinned
sexually with her and shared her wealth will
see the smoke from her burning. Then they
will cry and be sad because of her death.
10They will be afraid of her suffering and
stand far away and say:

"Terrible! How terrible for you, great city,
powerful city of Babylon,
because your punishment has come in one hour!"

11And the merchants of the earth will cry
and be sad about her, because now there is
no one to buy their cargoes— 12cargoes of
gold, silver, jewels, pearls, fine linen, purple
cloth, silk, red cloth; all kinds of citron wood
and all kinds of things made from ivory,
expensive wood, bronze, iron, and marble;
13cinnamon, spice, incense, myrrh,
frankincense, wine, olive oil, fine flour,
wheat, cattle, sheep, horses, carriages, slaves,
and human lives.
14The merchants will say,

"Babylon, the good things you wanted are gone from you.
All your rich and fancy things have disappeared.
You will never have them again."

15The merchants who became rich from
selling to her will be afraid of her suffering
and will stand far away. They will cry and be
sad 16and say:

"Terrible! How terrible for the great city!
She was dressed in fine linen, purple and red cloth,
and she was shining with gold, precious jewels, and pearls!
17All these riches have been destroyed in one hour!"

Every sea captain, every passenger, the
sailors, and all those who earn their living
from the sea stood far away from Babylon.
18As they saw the smoke from her burning,
they cried out loudly, "There was never a city
like this great city!" 19And they threw dust
on their heads and cried out, weeping and
being sad. They said:

"Terrible! How terrible for the great city!
All the people who had ships on the sea
became rich because of her wealth!
But she has been destroyed in one hour!
20Be happy because of this, heaven!
Be happy, God's holy people and apostles and prophets!
God has punished her because of what she did to you."

21Then a powerful angel picked up a large
stone, like one used for grinding grain, and
threw it into the sea. He said:

"In the same way, the great city of Babylon will be thrown down,
and it will never be found again.
22The music of people playing harps and other instruments, flutes, and trumpets,
will never be heard in you again.
No workman doing any job
will ever be found in you again.
The sound of grinding grain
will never be heard in you again.
23The light of a lamp
will never shine in you again,
and the voices of a bridegroom and bride
will never be heard in you again.
Your merchants were the world's great people,
and all the nations were tricked by your magic.
24You are guilty of the death of the prophets
and God's holy people
and all who have been killed on earth."

People in Heaven Praise God

19 After this vision and announcement I
heard what sounded like a great many
people in heaven saying:

"Hallelujah![n]
Salvation, glory, and power belong to our God,
2 because his judgments are true and right.
He has punished the prostitute
who made the earth evil with her sexual sin.
He has paid her back for the death of his servants."

3Again they said:

"Hallelujah!
She is burning, and her smoke will rise forever and ever."

4Then the twenty-four elders and the four

19:1 Hallelujah This means "praise God!"

living creatures bowed down and worshiped
God, who sits on the throne. They said:
"Amen, Hallelujah!"
5 Then a voice came from the throne,
saying:
"Praise our God, all you who serve him
and all you who honor him, both small
and great!"
6 Then I heard what sounded like a great
many people, like the noise of flooding
water, and like the noise of loud thunder.
The people were saying:
"Hallelujah!
Our Lord God, the Almighty, rules.
7 Let us rejoice and be happy
and give God glory,
because the wedding of the Lamb has
come,
and the Lamb's bride has made herself
ready.
8 Fine linen, bright and clean, was given to
her to wear."
(The fine linen means the good things done
by God's holy people.)
9 And the angel said to me, "Write this:
Blessed are those who have been invited to
the wedding meal of the Lamb!" And the
angel said, "These are the true words of God."
10 Then I bowed down at the angel's feet to
worship him, but he said to me, "Do not
worship me! I am a servant like you and
your brothers and sisters who have the
message of Jesus. Worship God, because the
message about Jesus is the spirit that gives
all prophecy."

The Rider on the White Horse

11 Then I saw heaven opened, and there
before me was a white horse. The rider on
the horse is called Faithful and True, and he
is right when he judges and makes war. 12 His
eyes are like burning fire, and on his head
are many crowns. He has a name written on
him, which no one but himself knows. 13 He
is dressed in a robe dipped in blood, and his
name is the Word of God. 14 The armies of
heaven, dressed in fine linen, white and
clean, were following him on white horses.
15 Out of the rider's mouth comes a sharp
sword that he will use to defeat the nations,

devotion 364

REVELATION 19:6-9

WE WOMEN . . .

Listen to the words of this formerly single woman: "When I was a single mom, I'd go to church on Sunday with my young children in tow. After I dropped them off at their classes, I'd join the congregation—almost always late—in the sanctuary. I hated sitting by myself, but I knew I'd become invisible at the end when I got up and weaved my way through all the happy couples planning where they'd have lunch." Being single can be lonely, but I would like to encourage you to take Revelation 19:6-9 literally. These verses are a reminder that you are not alone.

While it's okay to hope that God has plans to give you an earthly husband, remember that as great as that dream is, it's still an earthly pursuit. I urge you to remember that you are the bride of Christ! Your wedding day is coming! If it's on earth, that's nice, but if you have to wait until heaven, your wedding feast will be the biggest wedding reception you've ever been to, and your groom will fulfill all your dreams.

Now, I have a message for both married and single women. It's easy to feel like we don't have anything in common with each other, but all women—single, married, moms, or not—need friendships in their lives. We might be surprised at the commonalities we can find with each other if we only shed our titles, open up, and share God's love. After all, we are the bride of Christ!

and he will rule them with a rod of iron. He
will crush out the wine in the winepress of
the terrible anger of God the Almighty. 16On
his robe and on his upper leg was written
this name: KING OF KINGS AND LORD OF LORDS.
17Then I saw an angel standing in the sun,
and he called with a loud voice to all the
birds flying in the sky: "Come and gather
together for the great feast of God 18so that
you can eat the bodies of kings, generals,
mighty people, horses and their riders, and
the bodies of all people—free, slave, small,
and great."
19Then I saw the beast and the kings of
the earth. Their armies were gathered
together to make war against the rider on
the horse and his army. 20But the beast was
captured and with him the false prophet
who did the miracles for the beast. The false
prophet had used these miracles to trick
those who had the mark of the beast and
worshiped his idol. The false prophet and
the beast were thrown alive into the lake of
fire that burns with sulfur. 21And their
armies were killed with the sword that came
out of the mouth of the rider on the horse,
and all the birds ate the bodies until they
were full.

The Thousand Years

20 I saw an angel coming down from
heaven. He had the key to the
bottomless pit and a large chain in his hand.
2The angel grabbed the dragon, that old
snake who is the devil and Satan, and tied
him up for a thousand years. 3Then he threw
him into the bottomless pit, closed it, and
locked it over him. The angel did this so he
could not trick the people of the earth
anymore until the thousand years were
ended. After a thousand years he must be set
free for a short time.
4Then I saw some thrones and people
sitting on them who had been given the
power to judge. And I saw the souls of those
who had been killed because they were
faithful to the message of Jesus and the
message from God. They had not worshiped
the beast or his idol, and they had not
received the mark of the beast on their
foreheads or on their hands. They came back
to life and ruled with Christ for a thousand
years. 5(The others that were dead did not
live again until the thousand years were
ended.) This is the first raising of the dead.
6Blessed and holy are those who share in this
first raising of the dead. The second death
has no power over them. They will be priests
for God and for Christ and will rule with
him for a thousand years.
7When the thousand years are over, Satan
will be set free from his prison. 8Then he
will go out to trick the nations in all the
earth—Gog and Magog—to gather them for
battle. There are so many people they will be
like sand on the seashore. 9And Satan's army
marched across the earth and gathered
around the camp of God's people and the
city God loves. But fire came down from
heaven and burned them up. 10And Satan,
who tricked them, was thrown into the lake
of burning sulfur with the beast and the
false prophet. There they will be punished
day and night forever and ever.

People of the World Are Judged

11Then I saw a great white throne and the
One who was sitting on it. Earth and sky ran
away from him and disappeared. 12And I saw
the dead, great and small, standing before
the throne. Then books were opened, and
the book of life was opened. The dead were
judged by what they had done, which was
written in the books. 13The sea gave up the
dead who were in it, and Death and Hades[n]
gave up the dead who were in them. Each
person was judged by what he had done.
14And Death and Hades were thrown into
the lake of fire. The lake of fire is the second
death. 15And anyone whose name was not
found written in the book of life was thrown
into the lake of fire.

The New Jerusalem

21 Then I saw a new heaven and a new
earth. The first heaven and the first
earth had disappeared, and there was no sea
anymore. 2And I saw the holy city, the new
Jerusalem,[n] coming down out of heaven
from God. It was prepared like a bride
dressed for her husband. 3And I heard a loud
voice from the throne, saying, "Now God's
presence is with people, and he will live
with them, and they will be his people. God

20:13 Hades The place of the dead.
21:2 new Jerusalem The spiritual city where God's people live with him.

himself will be with them and will be their
God.[n] 4He will wipe away every tear from
their eyes, and there will be no more death,
sadness, crying, or pain, because all the old
ways are gone."

5The One who was sitting on the throne
said, "Look! I am making everything new!"
Then he said, "Write this, because these
words are true and can be trusted."

6The One on the throne said to me, "It is
finished. I am the Alpha and the Omega,[n]
the Beginning and the End. I will give free
water from the spring of the water of life to
anyone who is thirsty. 7Those who win the
victory will receive this, and I will be their
God, and they will be my children. 8But
cowards, those who refuse to believe, who
do evil things, who kill, who sin sexually,
who do evil magic, who worship idols, and
who tell lies—all these will have a place in
the lake of burning sulfur. This is the second
death."

9Then one of the seven angels who had
the seven bowls full of the seven last
troubles came to me, saying, "Come with me,
and I will show you the bride, the wife of the
Lamb." 10And the angel carried me away by
the Spirit to a very large and high mountain.
He showed me the holy city, Jerusalem,
coming down out of heaven from God. 11It
was shining with the glory of God and was
bright like a very expensive jewel, like a
jasper, clear as crystal. 12The city had a great
high wall with twelve gates with twelve
angels at the gates, and on each gate was
written the name of one of the twelve tribes
of Israel. 13There were three gates on the
east, three on the north, three on the south,
and three on the west. 14The walls of the city
were built on twelve foundation stones, and
on the stones were written the names of the
twelve apostles of the Lamb.

15The angel who talked with me had a
measuring rod made of gold to measure the
city, its gates, and its wall. 16The city was
built in a square, and its length was equal to
its width. The angel measured the city with
the rod. The city was 1,500 miles long, 1,500

21:3 and . . . God Some Greek copies do not have this phrase.
21:6 Alpha and the Omega The first and last letters of the Greek alphabet. This means "the beginning and the end."

devotion 365

REVELATION 21:5

WANT A NEW HEART?

We are on our way home to heaven. Finally, we will be face to face with Jesus where God promises to make all things new. When you know that your future is certain, then you are free to live this life with the most radical love and grace possible. You do not have to tiptoe through each day with uncertainty. You can live as a sacrifice, operating in passion and purpose, because you know whom you belong to, and you know where you're going.

For all eternity, you will be spiritually new. No more sin or temptation to battle. There will be pure thoughts and righteous hearts and clear thinking for every mind. God is going to make our bodies new. No one will be left with a disability or pain. Our new glorified bodies will never die or hurt or cry again. He promises a new heaven and a new earth. What he seems to imply is that this earth and the heaven we see will continue, but it will be glorified. Our new earth will become a beautiful home for our perfected spirit and body. God also promises a new relationship with him. He says that we will finally behold him and see him as he is.

God can make your heart new today. He can give you new paths or new dreams or a new personality. It's amazing what God will do right here and right now, but just wait—the best is yet to come!

miles wide, and 1,500 miles high. 17The
angel also measured the wall. It was 216 feet
high, by human measurements, which the
angel was using. 18The wall was made of
jasper, and the city was made of pure gold, as
pure as glass. 19The foundation stones of the
city walls were decorated with every kind of
jewel. The first foundation was jasper, the
second was sapphire, the third was
chalcedony, the fourth was emerald, 20the
fifth was onyx, the sixth was carnelian, the
seventh was chrysolite, the eighth was beryl,
the ninth was topaz, the tenth was
chrysoprase, the eleventh was jacinth, and
the twelfth was amethyst. 21The twelve gates
were twelve pearls, each gate having been
made from a single pearl. And the street of
the city was made of pure gold as clear as
glass.

22I did not see a temple in the city, because
the Lord God Almighty and the Lamb are the
city's temple. 23The city does not need the
sun or the moon to shine on it, because the
glory of God is its light, and the Lamb is the
city's lamp. 24By its light the people of the
world will walk, and the kings of the earth
will bring their glory into it. 25The city's
gates will never be shut on any day, because
there is no night there. 26The glory and the
honor of the nations will be brought into it.
27Nothing unclean and no one who does
shameful things or tells lies will ever go into
it. Only those whose names are written in
the Lamb's book of life will enter the city.

22 Then the angel showed me the river
of the water of life. It was shining like
crystal and was flowing from the throne of
God and of the Lamb 2down the middle of
the street of the city. The tree of life was on
each side of the river. It produces fruit
twelve times a year, once each month. The
leaves of the tree are for the healing of all the
nations. 3Nothing that God judges guilty
will be in that city. The throne of God and of
the Lamb will be there, and God's servants
will worship him. 4They will see his face,
and his name will be written on their
foreheads. 5There will never be night again.
They will not need the light of a lamp or the
light of the sun, because the Lord God will
give them light. And they will rule as kings
forever and ever.

6The angel said to me, "These words can
be trusted and are true." The Lord, the God of
the spirits of the prophets, sent his angel to
show his servants the things that must
happen soon.

7"Listen! I am coming soon! Blessed is the
one who obeys the words of prophecy in this
book."

8I, John, am the one who heard and saw
these things. When I heard and saw them, I
bowed down to worship at the feet of the
angel who showed these things to me. 9But
the angel said to me, "Do not worship me! I
am a servant like you, your brothers the
prophets, and all those who obey the words
in this book. Worship God!"

10Then the angel told me, "Do not keep
secret the words of prophecy in this book,
because the time is near for all this to
happen. 11Let whoever is doing evil continue
to do evil. Let whoever is unclean continue
to be unclean. Let whoever is doing right
continue to do right. Let whoever is holy
continue to be holy."

12"Listen! I am coming soon! I will bring
my reward with me, and I will repay each
one of you for what you have done. 13I am
the Alpha and the Omega,[n] the First and the
Last, the Beginning and the End.

14"Blessed are those who wash their robes[n]
so that they will receive the right to eat the
fruit from the tree of life and may go
through the gates into the city. 15Outside the
city are the evil people, those who do evil
magic, who sin sexually, who murder, who
worship idols, and who love lies and tell lies.

16"I, Jesus, have sent my angel to tell you
these things for the churches. I am the
descendant from the family of David, and I
am the bright morning star."

17The Spirit and the bride say, "Come!" Let
the one who hears this say, "Come!" Let
whoever is thirsty come; whoever wishes
may have the water of life as a free gift.

18I warn everyone who hears the words of
the prophecy of this book: If anyone adds
anything to these words, God will add to
that person the disasters written about in

22:13 Alpha and the Omega The first and last letters of the Greek alphabet. This means "the beginning and the end." **22:14 wash their robes** This means they believed and obeyed Jesus so that their sins could be forgiven by Christ's blood. The "washing" may refer to baptism (Acts 22:16).

this book. [19]And if anyone takes away from
the words of this book of prophecy, God will
take away that one's share of the tree of life
and of the holy city, which are written about
in this book.

[20]Jesus, the One who says these things are
true, says, "Yes, I am coming soon."

Amen. Come, Lord Jesus!

[21]The grace of the Lord Jesus be with all.
Amen.

Dictionary with Topical Concordance

A

Aaron (AIR-ohn) *older brother of Moses.*
- before the king of Egypt, Exodus 4:14–16; 5:1–5; 7:1–2
- death of, Numbers 20:22–29

Abba (AB-uh) *word for "father" in Aramaic.*
- Jesus called God "Abba," Mark 14:36
- we can call God "Abba," Romans 8:15; Galatians 4:6

Abednego (a-BED-nee-go) *one of the three friends of Daniel whom God protected from the fiery furnace.*
- refused the king of Babylon's food, Daniel 1:3–17
- thrown into the fiery furnace, Daniel 3

Abel (AY-bul) *the second son of Adam and Eve.*
- born to Adam and Eve, Genesis 4:2
- approved by God, Genesis 4:3–4; Hebrews 11:4
- murdered by Cain, Genesis 4:8; 1 John 3:12

Abib (ah-BEEB) *first month of the Jewish calendar, about the time of year as our March or April; also called "Nisan"; means "young ears of grain."*
- the time the Israelites left Egypt, Exodus 13:3–4
- the time for the Feast of Unleavened Bread, Exodus 23:15; 34:18

Abigail, sister of David (AB-eh-gale) 1 Chronicles 2:13–17

Abigail, wife of Nabal
- brought food to David, 1 Samuel 25:14–35
- became David's wife, 1 Samuel 25:36–42

Abijah, king of Judah (a-BY-jah) 1 Kings 15:1–8; 2 Chronicles 13:1—14:1

Abijah, son of Jeroboam
- death of, 1 Kings 14:1–18

Abijah, son of Samuel, 1 Samuel 8:1–3

ability
- given by God, 2 Corinthians 3:5–6
- through Christ, Philippians 4:13
- differing abilities, 1 Corinthians 12:7–11

Abimelech, king of Gerar (a-BIM-eh-lek)
- tried to take Sarah as his wife, Genesis 20

Abimelech, king of the Philistines
- tried to take Rebekah as his wife, Genesis 26:6–11

Abimelech, son of Gideon
- birth of, Judges 8:29–31
- murdered his brothers, Judges 9:1–6
- defeated the people of Shechem, Judges 9:22–45
- burned the Tower of Shechem, Judges 9:46–49
- death of, Judges 9:50–55

Abishai (a-BISH-eye) *nephew of King David.*
- served in David's army, 2 Samuel 23:18–19; 1 Chronicles 18:12–13
- saved David's life, 2 Samuel 21:15–17

Abner (AB-nur) *commander of Saul's army.*
- at Goliath's defeat, 1 Samuel 17:55–57
- made Ish-Bosheth king of Israel, 2 Samuel 2:8–10
- later loyal to David, 2 Samuel 3:6–21
- killed by Joab, 2 Samuel 3:22–27

abortion
- injuring a pregnant woman, Exodus 21:22
- chosen in the womb, Jeremiah 1:5
- formed in mother, Psalm 139:13–16

Abraham (AY-bra-ham) *father of the Jewish nation.*
- called from Ur by God, Genesis 12:1–4
- lied about Sarai, Genesis 12:10–20
- separated from Lot, Genesis 13
- God's agreement with, Genesis 15; 17
- name changed, Genesis 17:3–6
- father of Isaac, Genesis 21:1–7
- offered Isaac as a sacrifice, Genesis 22:1–19
- father of the faithful, Romans 4
- God's friend, James 2:23

Absalom (AB-sah-lum) *one of David's sons.*
- turned against David, 2 Samuel 15:1—18:8
- killed by Joab, 2 Samuel 18:9–15

abstain (ab-STAIN) *to keep from doing something.*
- from food offered to idols, Acts 15:20
- from evil, 1 Thessalonians 5:22
- from lust, 1 Peter 2:11

abyss (uh-BISS) See "bottomless pit."

accept
- a prophet not accepted, Luke 4:24
- accepted by God, Acts 10:35; 15:7–8; Romans 14:3
- each other, Romans 14:1; 15:7
- Jesus, John 12:48

accuse
- Jesus accused by the Jews, Matthew 27:12–13; Mark 15:3; Luke 6:7
- Paul accused by the Jews, Acts 23:27–29; 26:7
- the devil as the accuser, Revelation 12:10

Achaia (a-KA-yuh) See "Greece."

Achan (AY-can) *an Israelite who disobeyed God during the battle of Jericho,* Joshua 7

Achish (AY-kish) *king of the Philistine city of Gath.*
- David pretends to be insane, 1 Samuel 21:10–15
- David in his army, 1 Samuel 27; 29

actions
- judged by, Proverbs 20:11; Matthew 11:19; Galatians 6:4
- of love, 1 John 3:18
- of goodness, Matthew 5:16

Adam (AD-um) *the first man.*
- created by God, Genesis 1:26—2:25
- disobeyed God, Genesis 3
- compared to Christ, 1 Corinthians 15:21–22, 45–49

adder, *a poisonous snake.* See "snake."

Adonijah (ad-oh-NY-jah) *David's fourth son.*
- son of Haggith, 2 Samuel 3:4
- tried to become king, 1 Kings 1
- killed by Solomon, 1 Kings 2:12–25

Adoni-Zedek (a-DOH-ny-ZEE-dek) *an Amorite king of Jerusalem.*
- defeated by Joshua, Joshua 10:1–28

adoption
- of Moses, Exodus 2
- God's children, Romans 8:16; Ephesians 1:5

Adullam (a-DOO-lum) *a city about thirteen miles from Bethlehem.*
- David hid in a cave there, 2 Samuel 23:13

adultery (ah-DUL-ter-ee) *breaking a marriage promise by having sexual relations with someone other than your husband or wife.*
- "You must not be guilty of adultery," Exodus 20:14
- Christ teaches about, Matthew 5:27–32; Luke 16:18
- woman caught in adultery, John 8:1–11

advice
- given by Ahithophel, 2 Samuel 15:30—17:23
- given to Rehoboam, 1 Kings 12:1–15
- teachings about, Proverbs 11:14; 12:5, 15; 19:20

Agabus (AG-uh-bus) *a Christian prophet.*
- warned the people, Acts 11:27–30
- warned Paul about going to Jerusalem, Acts 21:10–11

Agag (AY-gag) *king of the Amalekites.*
- captured by Saul, 1 Samuel 15

aging
- Moses' humility, Exodus 4
- respect for the aging, Leviticus 19:32

agreement, *a contract, promise, or covenant.*
- with Noah, Genesis 9:1–17
- with Abraham, Genesis 15; 17:1–14
- Ark of the Agreement, Exodus 25:10–22; 1 Samuel 4—5; 2 Samuel 6:1–15
- with the Israelites, Exodus 19:3–8, 24; Deuteronomy 29
- new agreement, 2 Corinthians 2:12—3:18
- difference between the old and new agreements, Hebrews 8—10

Agrippa (uh-GRIP-pah) See "Herod Agrippa."

Ahab (AY-hab) *evil king of Israel who was married to Jezebel.*
- worshiped Baal, 1 Kings 16:29–33
- had Naboth killed, 1 Kings 21
- death of, 1 Kings 22:1–40

Ahasuerus (ah-HAZ-oo-EE-rus) *Hebrew word for the Greek name Xerxes.* See "Xerxes."

Ahaz, *twelfth king of Judah,* 2 Kings 16; 2 Chronicles 28

Ahaziah, king of Judah (ay-ha-ZY-uh) 2 Chronicles 22:1–9

Ahaziah, son of Ahab
- king of Israel, 1 Kings 22:40–53

Ahijah, great-grandson of Eli (a-HY-jah) 1 Samuel 14:1–23

Ahijah, the prophet
- told Jeroboam the kingdom would be divided, 1 Kings 11:29–39
- told that Jeroboam's son would die, 1 Kings 14:1–18

Ahimelech, the high priest (a-HIM-eh-lek)
- helped David, 1 Samuel 21:1–9

Ahimelech, the Hittite warrior, 1 Samuel 26:6

Ahithophel (a-HITH-oh-fel) *gave advice to King David.*
- helped Absalom rebel against David, 2 Samuel 15:31; 16:15—17:23

Ai (AY-eye) *a city completely destroyed by the Israelites,* Joshua 7:1—8:28

Akeldama (a-KEL-dah-mah) *field bought with the money Judas received for betraying Jesus,* Matthew 27:3–10; Acts 1:18–19

alabaster (AL-a-bass-ter) *light-colored stone with streaks or stripes through it,* Matthew 26:7; Mark 14:3; Luke 7:37

alamoth (AL-a-moth) *a musical word, which may mean "like a flute" or "high-pitched,"* Psalm 46

alcohol
- given by God, Psalm 104:15
- effects of, Proverbs 23:29–35
- drunkards will not inherit, 1 Corinthians 6:9–10

alien, See "foreigner."

All-Powerful, *a name for God,* 1 Chronicles 11:9; Psalm 24:10; Isaiah 6:3–5; Malachi 3:1–17

Almighty, *a name for God.*
- "I am God Almighty," Genesis 17:1
- "I appeared to Abraham . . . by the name, God Almighty," Exodus 6:3
- "Holy, holy, holy is the Lord God Almighty," Revelation 4:8

almond
- design of the lampstands in Holy Tent, Exodus 25:31–36
- Aaron's stick produced, Numbers 17:8

aloes (AL-ohs) *oils from sweet-smelling sap of certain trees; used to make perfume and medicine and to prepare bodies for burial,* Psalm 45:8; Proverbs 7:17
- used to prepare Jesus' body for burial, John 19:39

Alpha and Omega (AL-fah and oh-MAY-guh) *the first and last letters of the Greek alphabet, like our* A *and* Z.
- used to describe Jesus, Revelation 1:8; 21:6; 22:13

altar (ALL-ter) *a place where sacrifices, gifts, or prayers were offered to a god.*
- built by Noah, Genesis 8:20
- built by Abraham, Genesis 22:9
- for burnt offerings, Exodus 27:1–8
- for incense, Exodus 30:1–10
- corners of, Exodus 27:2; 30:10; 1 Kings 1:50
- for the Temple, 2 Chronicles 4:1

Amalekites (AM-a-lah-kites) *fierce, fighting people who descended from Esau; they were enemies of Israel and were finally wiped out during the time of Hezekiah.*
- enemies of Israel, Exodus 17:8–16; 1 Samuel 15
- destroyed by King Hezekiah, 1 Chronicles 4:43

Amasa (AM-a-sa) *leader of Absalom's army when he rebelled against David,* 2 Samuel 17:25
- made leader of David's army, 2 Samuel 19:13
- killed by Joab, 2 Samuel 20:1–10

Amaziah (am-ah-ZY-uh) *the ninth king of Judah,* 2 Kings 14; 2 Chronicles 25

ambition
- of the followers, Mark 9:33–37
- interest in other lives, Philippians 2:3–4
- to do good, Titus 2:14

amen (AY-MEN or AH-MEN) *Hebrew word for "that is right,"* 1 Chronicles 16:36; Psalm 106:48; 1 Corinthians 14:16
- "Amen. Come, Lord Jesus!" Revelation 22:20

Ammonites (AM-on-ites) *descendants of Lot's son, Ben-Ammi,* Genesis 19:36–38
- enemies of Israel, Judges 10:6—11:33; 1 Samuel 11; 2 Samuel 10:1–14
- worshiped Molech, 1 Kings 11:5

Amon (AM-on) *the fifteenth king of Judah,* 2 Kings 21:18–26; 2 Chronicles 33:20–25
- an ancestor of Jesus, Matthew 1:10

Amorites (AM-or-ites) *a group of wicked people who worshiped false gods and lived in Canaan when the Israelites arrived.*
- defeated by Israel, Numbers 21:21–32; Joshua 10:1—11:14

Amos (AY-mos) *a prophet who warned Israel of God's punishment for disobedience.*
- a shepherd from Tekoa, Amos 1:1
- his visions, Amos 7:1—9:10

Anak/Anakites (A-nak/AN-uh-kites) *a group of large, fighting people who lived in Canaan when the Israelites arrived.*
- feared by the twelve spies, Numbers 13:22, 28, 33; Deuteronomy 1:26–28
- defeated by Joshua, Joshua 11:21–23

Ananias, husband of Sapphira (an-uh-NY-us)
- killed for lying to the Holy Spirit, Acts 5:1–6

Ananias, a Christian in Damascus
- helped Saul of Tarsus, Acts 9:10–19; 22:12–16

Ananias, the high priest
- at Paul's trial, Acts 23:1–5

Andrew, *a fisherman and brother of the apostle Peter.*
- chosen by Jesus to be an apostle, Mark 1:16–18; 3:13–19
- brought Peter to Jesus, John 1:40–42
- waited with the apostles in Jerusalem, Acts 1:13

angel (AIN-jel) *a heavenly being.*
- rescued Lot from Sodom, Genesis 19:1–22
- led Israel to Canaan, Exodus 23:20–23; 32:34
- announced Jesus' birth, Matthew 1:20–21; Luke 1:26–37; 2:8–15
- helped Jesus, Matthew 4:11; Luke 22:43
- helped the apostles, Acts 5:19–20; 12:6–10
- will bring judgment, Matthew 13:24–50; 24:31
- archangel, 1 Thessalonians 4:16; Jude 9
- less than Christ, Hebrews 1:4–14; 1 Peter 3:22
- rebellious angels, 2 Peter 2:4; Jude 6
- serving in heaven, Revelation 7—10

anger, *wrath.*
- of God toward people, John 3:36; Romans 1:18; 2:5–6; Colossians 3:5–6
- saved from God's anger by Christ, Romans 5:9; 1 Thessalonians 1:10; 5:9
- warnings against, Matthew 5:21–22; Ephesians 4:26, 31; James 1:19–20

animal
- created by God, Genesis 1:20–25
- to be ruled by people, Genesis 1:26
- named by Adam, Genesis 2:19–20
- saved by Noah, Genesis 6:19–20
- clean, Leviticus 11:1–3, 9; Deuteronomy 14:3–6
- unclean, Leviticus 11:4–8, 10–12, 26–44; Deuteronomy 14:7–8

Annas (AN-us) *a high priest of the Jews during Jesus' lifetime,* Luke 3:2; John 18:13
- questioned Peter and John, Acts 4:5–22

anoint (uh-NOINT) *to pour oil on.*
- to appoint a priest, Exodus 28:41; 40:13
- to appoint a king, 1 Samuel 10:1; 16:12–13; 2 Kings 9:6

- the Holy Tent, Numbers 7:1
- to heal sickness, Mark 6:13; James 5:14

Antichrist (AN-tee KRYST) See "enemy of Christ."

Antioch in Pisidia (AN-tee-ahk) *a small city in the country of Pisidia.*
- Paul preached there, Acts 13:14–15

Antioch in Syria, *third largest city in the Roman Empire.*
- Saul and Barnabas preached there, Acts 11:19–26
- followers first called "Christians" there, Acts 11:26
- Peter in Antioch, Galatians 2:11–12

anti-Semitism
- Jews persecuting Jesus, John 5:16–18
- Jews' special place with God, Romans 11:24–26
- Children of Abraham, John 8:39–44

Apollos (uh-POL-us) *an educated Jew from Alexandria.*
- taught by Aquila and Priscilla, Acts 18:24–28
- preached to the Corinthians, 1 Corinthians 1:12; 3:4–6
- friend of Paul, Titus 3:13

apostasy
- continued sinning, Hebrews 10:19–39
- "come back to me, . . . children," Jeremiah 3:14
- of Judas, Luke 22:47–53

apostle (uh-POS-'l) *someone who is sent off. Jesus chose these twelve special followers and sent them to tell the Good News about him to the whole world.*
- twelve chosen by Jesus, Mark 3:14–19
- Matthias chosen, Acts 1:12–26
- Paul chosen, 1 Corinthians 15:3–11; 2 Corinthians 12:11–12
- duties and powers of, Luke 9:1–6; Acts 5:12–16; 8:18
- leaders of the church, Acts 15; 16:4; 1 Corinthians 12:28
- false apostles, 2 Corinthians 11:13; Revelation 2:2

appearance
- not to judge by, 1 Samuel 16:7; John 7:24
- deceiving, Matthew 23:27–28
- of Jesus, Isaiah 53:2; Philippians 2:7

Aquila (AK-wi-lah) *a Jewish Christian from Rome.*
- friend of Paul, Acts 18:2–3; Romans 16:3–5
- taught Apollos, Acts 18:24–28

Arabah (AIR-uh-bah) *the Hebrew word for the Jordan Valley.* See "Jordan Valley."

Arabah, Sea of, See "Dead Sea."

Aram (AIR-um) *a country northeast of Israel,* 1 Kings 11:25; 15:18; 2 Kings 5:1; Isaiah 7:1
- known as "Syria" in the New Testament, Matthew 4:24; Acts 15:23

Aramaic (AIR-uh-MAY-ik) *the language of the people in the nation of Aram.*
- common language of the Jews, 2 Kings 18:26; John 19:13, 17, 20; Acts 21:40

Ararat (AIR-uh-rat) *a group of mountains located in what is now Turkey and the Soviet Union.*
- Noah's boat landed there, Genesis 8:3–4

Araunah (a-RAW-nah) *a Jebusite who was also called Ornan.*
- sold his threshing floor to King David, 2 Samuel 24:15–25; 1 Chronicles 21:18–28

archangel (ark-AIN-jel) *the leader of God's angels,* 1 Thessalonians 4:16; Jude 9

Areopagus (AIR-ee-OP-uh-gus) *a council or group of important leaders in Athens.*
- Paul spoke there, Acts 17:16–34

argue
- the apostles argued, Mark 9:33–37; Luke 9:46–48
- avoid arguments, Philippians 2:14; 2 Timothy 2:23–26; Titus 3:9
- Michael argued with the devil, Jude 9

Aristarchus (air-i-STAR-kus) *a man from Thessalonica who often traveled with Paul,* Acts 27:2; Colossians 4:10; Philemon 24

ark, Noah's, *the huge boat that Noah built to save his family from the flood God sent to cover the earth.* See "boat."

Ark of the Agreement, *a special box made of acacia wood and gold. Inside were the stone tablets on which the Ten Commandments were written. Later, a pot of manna and Aaron's walking stick were also put into the Ark. It was to remind the people of Israel of God's promise to be with them.*
- building of, Exodus 25:10–22; 37:1–9
- crossing the Jordan River, Joshua 3:1–17
- captured by the Philistines, 1 Samuel 4:1—7:1
- touched by Uzzah, 2 Samuel 6:1–8; 1 Chronicles 13
- placed in the Temple, 2 Chronicles 5:2–10
- contents of, Hebrews 9:4–5

Ark of the Covenant, See "Ark of the Agreement."

armor
- of Saul, 1 Samuel 17:38–39; 31:9–10
- of God, Ephesians 6:10–17

arrest
- John the Baptist arrested, Matthew 14:3; Mark 6:17
- Jesus arrested, Matthew 26:50–57; Mark 14:44–50; John 18:1–14

- Peter arrested, Acts 12:1–4
- Paul arrested, Acts 28:17–20

Artaxerxes (ar-tah-ZERK-sees) *the title or name of Persian kings,* Ezra 4:7; Nehemiah 2:1
- his letter to Ezra, Ezra 7:11–26

Artemis (AR-tuh-mis) *a goddess that many Greeks worshiped,* Acts 19:23–41

Asa (AY-sah) *the third king of Judah,* 1 Kings 15:9–24; 2 Chronicles 14—16

Asaph (AY-saf) *a leader of singers when David was king,* 1 Chronicles 16:5, 7; 25:1–2; 2 Chronicles 5:12
- songs of, Psalms 73—83

ascension (uh-SIN-shun) *lifted up; used to describe Jesus' return to heaven,* Acts 1:2–11; 2:32–33

ashamed
- of Jesus, Mark 8:38; Luke 9:26; 2 Timothy 1:8
- for suffering as a Christian, 1 Peter 4:16

Ashdod (ASH-dahd) *one of the five strong, walled cities of the Philistines; called Azotus in the New Testament.*
- Ark of the Agreement there, 1 Samuel 5:1–8
- later called "Azotus," Acts 8:40

Asherah (ah-SHIR-ah) *a Canaanite goddess thought to be the wife of the god Baal.*
- worshiped by Israelites, 1 Kings 14:14–15, 22–23; 15:13
- worship forbidden, Exodus 34:13–14; Deuteronomy 16:21–22

Ashkelon (ASH-keh-lon) *one of the five important cities of the Philistines,* Judges 1:18; Zephaniah 2:4, 7
- thirty of its men killed by Samson, Judges 14:19

Ashtoreth (ASH-toh-reth) *a goddess of the people of Assyria and Canaan. At times the Israelites forgot God and built idols to worship her.* Judges 2:13; 1 Samuel 7:3–4; 12:10
- worshiped by Solomon, 1 Kings 11:5, 33

Asia (AY-zhuh) *the western part of the country now called "Turkey."*
- Paul preached there, Acts 19:10, 26
- seven churches of, Revelation 1:4

assembly (a-SEM-blee) *a meeting; a group of people gathered for a purpose.*
- of the church, Hebrews 10:24–25
- conduct in, James 2:1–4

assurance (uh-SHURE-ans) *with confidence; without doubts.*
- about the Good News, 1 Thessalonians 1:5
- before God, Hebrews 10:22–23; 1 John 5:14–15
- faith as, Hebrews 11:1

Assyria (uh-SEER-ee-uh) *a powerful nation north and east of Israel.*
- enemy of Israel, 2 Kings 15:19–20; 17:3–6
- enemy of Judah, 2 Kings 18:13—19:36; Isaiah 36:1—37:37

Astarte (ah-STAR-tay) *another name for the goddess Ashtoreth.* See "Ashtoreth."

astrology
- God warns star-worshipers, Zephaniah 1:5
- God created the stars, Genesis 1:16
- sun stands still, Joshua 10:12–13

Athaliah (ath-uh-LY-uh) *the only woman who ruled over Judah,* 2 Kings 11; 2 Chronicles 22:10—23:21

Athens (ATH-enz) *the leading city of the country of Greece.*
- Paul preached there, Acts 17:16–34

atonement (uh-TONE-ment) *to remove or forgive sins.*
- through animal sacrifices, Exodus 30:10; Leviticus 17:11
- through faith in the blood of Jesus' death, Romans 3:25; Hebrews 2:17; 9:28; 10:11–12

Atonement, Day of, See "Cleansing, Day of."

Augustus Caesar (aw-GUS-tus SEE-zer) *or Caesar Augustus, the first Roman emperor,* Luke 2:1

authority (uh-THAR-uh-tee) *power or right to control.*
- proper use of, Matthew 20:25–26; Luke 22:24–30; Titus 2:15
- respect for, Luke 20:20–26; Romans 13:1–7; 1 Timothy 2:2; Hebrews 13:17; 1 Peter 2:13–17
- Jesus' authority, Matthew 7:29; 9:6; Mark 11:27–33; Luke 5:24; John 5:19–29

B

Baal (BAY-el) *a god of the Canaanites; "Baal" was the common word for "master, lord." He was known as the son of Dagon, or the son of El, who was known as the father of the false gods.*
- worshiped by Israelites, Judges 2:10–11; Jeremiah 11:13
- Elijah defeated prophets of Baal, 1 Kings 18:1–40
- Baal worship destroyed by Jehu, 2 Kings 10:18–28

Baal-Zebub, See "Beelzebul."

Baasha (BAY-ah-shah) *the third king of Israel,* 1 Kings 15:27—16:7; 2 Chronicles 16:1–6; Jeremiah 41:9

Babel (BAY-bel) *a tower built to reach the sky,* Genesis 11:1–9

baby
- Moses as, Exodus 2:1–10
- Solomon determined mother of, 1 Kings 3:16–28
- Elizabeth's, Luke 1:39–44
- Jesus as, Luke 2:6–21
- as a symbol of new Christians, 1 Peter 2:2

Babylon (BAB-uh-lun) *city on the Euphrates River; capital of Babylonia.*
- captives in Babylon, Psalm 137:1; Jeremiah 29:10
- destruction predicted, Jeremiah 51:36–37
- as a symbol of evil, Revelation 14:8; 17:5

Babylonians (bab-e-LONE-e-unz) *people of the country Babylonia. Also called "Chaldeans."*
- capture warned by Jeremiah, Jeremiah 21; 25
- captured the people of Judah, 2 Kings 20:12–18; 24—25; Jeremiah 39:1–10
- Daniel in Babylon, Daniel 1—4
- released Israelite captives, Ezra 2

Balaam (BAY-lum) *a prophet from Midian.*
- asked by Balak to prophesy, Numbers 22—24; 2 Peter 2:15–16; Revelation 2:14
- death of, Numbers 31:8

balm, *oil from a plant used as medicine,* Genesis 37:25; Jeremiah 8:22; 51:8; Ezekiel 27:17

Baptist, John the (BAP-tist) *someone who baptizes. John, a relative of Jesus, was called this because he baptized many people.* Matthew 3:1–6
- condemned Pharisees and Sadducees, Matthew 3:7–10
- preached about Jesus, Matthew 3:11–12
- baptized Jesus, Matthew 3:13–17
- in prison, Matthew 11:1–6; Luke 7:18–23
- described by Jesus, Matthew 11:7–12; 17:10–13; Luke 7:24–28
- death of, Matthew 14:1–12; Mark 6:14–29
- baptism of, Matthew 21:25–26; Acts 10:37; 18:25; 19:3–4
- Jesus mistaken for, Matthew 16:13–14; Mark 8:27–28; Luke 9:18–19

baptism (BAP-tiz-em) *dipping or immersing.*
- by John, Matthew 3:6; Mark 1:4; Luke 3; Acts 19:3
- of Jesus, Matthew 3:13–17
- examples of, Acts 2:38–41; 8:36–38; 16:15, 33
- with fire, Matthew 3:11; Luke 3:16
- with the Holy Spirit, Mark 1:8; Acts 1:5; 11:16

Barabbas (bah-RAB-us) *a robber who had murdered someone in Jerusalem. He was freed instead of Jesus.* Matthew 27:15–26; Mark 15:6–11

Barak (BAY-rak) *a leader of Israel's army when Deborah was judge,* Judges 4—5

Bar-Jesus, See "Elymas."

barley (BAR-lee) *a type of grain.*
- harvest of, Ruth 1:22; 2:17, 23; 2 Samuel 21:9
- loaves of, John 6:9–13

barn
- storing in, Matthew 6:26
- rich man's, Luke 12:16–20

Barnabas (BAR-nah-bus) *an encourager who helped the apostles,* Acts 4:36; 11:23
- worked with Paul, Acts 11:26; 13—15
- influenced by hypocrites, Galatians 2:13

barrenness, See "infertility."

Bartholomew (bar-THOL-oh-mew) *one of the twelve apostles of Jesus,* Matthew 10:3; Mark 3:18; Luke 6:14; Acts 1:13

Bartimaeus (bar-teh-MAY-us) *a blind man who was healed by Jesus,* Mark 10:46–52

Baruch (BAH-rook) *a friend of the prophet Jeremiah,* Jeremiah 36

Bathsheba (bath-SHE-buh) *the mother of Solomon and wife of David,* 2 Samuel 11:1—12:25; 1 Kings 1:1—2:22

beatitude (bee-A-ti-tyood) *blessed or happy; often used for Jesus' teaching in Matthew 5:3–12; Luke 6:20–22.*

Beelzebul (bee-EL-ze-bull) *false god of the Philistines; in the New Testament it often refers to the devil.*
- name for Satan, Matthew 12:24; Mark 3:22; Luke 11:15

Beersheba (beer-SHE-buh) *the town farthest south in the land of Judah,* 2 Samuel 3:10; 2 Chronicles 30:5
- Abraham made an agreement there, Genesis 21:14–34

beg
- Jesus begged by demons, Matthew 8:28–34; Mark 5:1–13; Luke 8:26–33
- Jesus begged by people, Matthew 14:36; Mark 7:24–26, 32; 8:22

beggar
- Bartimaeus, Mark 10:46–52
- Lazarus, Luke 16:19–31
- at Beautiful Gate, Acts 3:1–10
- man born blind, John 9:1–12

Behemoth (be-HEE-muth) *a large land animal, exact identity unknown,* Job 40:15

Bel, *a false god of the Babylonians,* Jeremiah 50:2; 51:44

believe
- in God, Acts 16:34; Romans 4:24
- in Jesus, Matthew 18:6; John 12:44; 14:11–12; 1 John 5:10
- in the Good News, Mark 1:15; 11:24; Acts 15:7
- rewards of believing, Matthew 21:22; John 20:31; 1 Thessalonians 2:13
- a lie, 2 Thessalonians 2:11

believers (be-LEE-vers) *the followers of Jesus,* John 3:16; Acts 4:32; 5:14; Galatians 6:10

beloved follower, the
- sitting next to Jesus, John 13:23
- writing the Book of John, John 21:20–24
- at the crucifixion, John 19:26

Belshazzar (bell-SHAZ-er) *a ruler of Babylon,* Daniel 5

Belteshazzar (BELL-teh-SHAZ-er) *the Babylonian name that Nebuchadnezzar gave to Daniel,* Daniel 4:8; 5:12

Benaiah (bee-NAY-uh) *the captain of David's bodyguard,* 2 Samuel 23:20–23
- commander of Solomon's army, 1 Kings 2:34–35

Ben-Hadad (ben-HAY-dad) *name of two or three Syrian kings who often fought against Israel,* 1 Kings 20:1–34; 2 Kings 6:24—8:15

Benjamin (BEN-jah-min) *the youngest son of Jacob and Rachel.*
- birth of, Genesis 35:16–20
- reunited with Joseph, Genesis 42—45

Bernice (bur-NY-see) *the oldest daughter of Herod Agrippa I,* Acts 25:13—26:32

Bethany (BETH-uh-nee) *a small town about two miles from Jerusalem.*
- home of Mary, Martha, and Lazarus, John 11:1; 12:1
- home of Simon, Mark 14:3

Bethel (BETH-el) *a town about twelve miles north of Jerusalem.*
- named by Jacob, Genesis 28:10–19
- Jeroboam built idols there, 1 Kings 12:26–33

Bethesda (be-THES-da) See "Bethzatha, pool of."

Bethlehem (BETH-le-hem) *a small town five miles from Jerusalem.*
- hometown of King David, 1 Samuel 16:1, 13
- birthplace of Jesus, Matthew 2:1; Luke 2:15–17

Bethsaida (beth-SAY-ih-duh) *a city in Galilee and home of Peter, Andrew, and Philip,* John 1:44; 12:21
- rejected Jesus, Matthew 11:20–21; Luke 10:13

Bethzatha, pool of (beth-ZAY-tha) *a pool in Jerusalem near the Sheep Gate.*
- Jesus healed a man there, John 5:1–18

betray (be-TRAY) *to turn against.*
- families against each other, Mark 13:12–13
- Jesus betrayed, Matthew 26:20–25; Mark 14:18–46; John 13:2–30

birds
- created by God, Genesis 1:20–21
- saved by Noah, Genesis 6:19–20; 7:1–3
- unclean, Leviticus 11:13–19
- cared for by God, Matthew 6:25–27; Luke 12:24

birth
- spiritual birth, John 1:13; 3:3–8; 1 Peter 1:23

bishop, See "elder."

bitter
- water, Exodus 15:22–25; Numbers 5:18–27; Revelation 8:11
- herbs, Exodus 12:8

bitterness (BIT-er-nes) *sorrow or pain; anger or hatred.*
- warning against, Acts 8:23; Ephesians 4:31; James 3:14

blasphemy (BLAS-feh-mee) *saying things against God or not showing respect for God.*
- examples of, 1 Timothy 1:13; Revelation 13:6
- warnings against, Matthew 12:31–32; Mark 3:28–29
- Jesus accused of, Matthew 9:3; 26:65; Mark 2:6–7; John 10:36

blessing (BLES-ing) *a gift from God; asking God's favor on.*
- promised to Abraham, Genesis 12:1–3
- Isaac blessed Jacob, Genesis 27:1–41
- from God, Acts 3:25; Romans 10:12; 15:27; Hebrews 6:7
- by Jesus, Mark 10:16; Luke 24:50; John 1:16
- by each other, Luke 6:28; 1 Corinthians 4:12; 1 Peter 3:9

blind
- the blind healed, Matthew 9:27–31; 15:30; Mark 8:22–26; John 9
- Saul struck blind, Acts 9:8–9
- spiritually blind, Matthew 23:16–26; John 9:35–41; 2 Peter 1:5–9

blood, *sometimes used to mean "death."*
- water turned into, Exodus 7:14–24
- used in the Passover, Exodus 12:13–23
- not to be eaten, Leviticus 3:17; Deuteronomy 12:16; 1 Samuel 14:31–34
- of animal sacrifices, Leviticus 1; 3; 4; Hebrews 9:12–13; 10:4
- of Christ, Matthew 26:28; Romans 5:9; Hebrews 9:14; 1 John 1:7

boasting, See "bragging."

boat, *ark.*
- built by Noah, Genesis 6:11–21
- of the apostles, Matthew 4:21–22; John 21:3–11
- used by Jesus, Matthew 8:23; 13:2; 14:13–34

body
- made of dust, Genesis 2:7; 3:19
- health of, Proverbs 3:7–8; 4:20–22; 14:30
- attitudes toward, Matthew 6:25; Romans 6:13; Ephesians 5:29
- warnings against misuse, Romans 8:13; 1 Corinthians 6:18–20; 1 Thessalonians 4:5

body of Christ, *sometimes means Jesus' human body; also a way of describing Christians.*
- Christ's physical body, John 2:19–21; 19:38; Acts 2:31; 1 Corinthians 11:24; 1 Timothy 3:16; 1 Peter 3:18

- the church as Christ's spiritual body, Romans 12:5; 1 Corinthians 12:12–31; Ephesians 1:23; 4:4; 5:23

bone
- "whose bones came from my bones," Genesis 2:23
- Ezekiel's vision of, Ezekiel 37:1–14
- none of Jesus' bones to be broken, John 19:36

book, *parchments, scroll.*
- Book of the Teachings, Deuteronomy 30:10; Joshua 1:8; 2 Chronicles 34:14–32; Nehemiah 8
- book of life, Philippians 4:3; Revelation 3:5; 13:8; 20:12; 21:27
- "Jesus did many other miracles . . . not written in this book," John 20:30
- "the whole world would not be big enough for all the books," John 21:25

bottomless pit, *the place where the devil and his demons live,* Luke 8:31; Revelation 9:1–11; 11:7; 17:8; 20:1–3

box of Scriptures, *small leather boxes that some Jews tied to their foreheads and left arms; also called "phylacteries" or "frontlets."*
- held the Law of Moses, Deuteronomy 6:6–8
- Jesus criticized misuse of, Matthew 23:5

bragging, *boasting.*
- warnings against, Proverbs 27:1; 2 Corinthians 10:12–18; James 4:16; Jude 16
- about the Lord, 1 Corinthians 1:31; 2 Corinthians 10:17; Galatians 6:14

bread, *the most important food in New Testament times; usually made of barley or wheat.*
- to feed 5,000 people, Matthew 14:13–21; Mark 6:30–44; Luke 9:10–17; John 6:1–13
- to feed 4,000 people, Matthew 15:32–39; Mark 8:1–10
- Jesus, the bread of life, John 6:25–59
- "A person does not live by eating only bread," Matthew 4:4; Luke 4:4
- "Give us the food we need for each day," Luke 11:3
- in the Lord's Supper, Luke 22:19; Acts 20:7; 1 Corinthians 10:16; 11:17–34

bread that shows we are in God's presence, *twelve loaves of bread that were kept on the table in the Holy Tent and later in the Temple; also called "Bread of the Presence" or "showbread,"* Leviticus 24:5–9
- eaten by David, Matthew 12:3–4; Mark 2:25–26; Luke 6:4

bride, Song of Songs 4:8–12
- belongs to the bridegroom, John 3:29
- of Christ, Revelation 21:2, 9

bridegroom
- sun compared to, Psalm 19:5
- Jesus compared to, Matthew 9:15; Mark 2:19–20; Luke 5:34
- Jesus' story of, Matthew 25:1–13
- at Jesus' first miracle, John 2:9

brother, *a family member; people from the same country; or Christians.*
- physical brothers, Proverbs 18:24; Matthew 19:29; Mark 12:18–23
- Jesus' brothers, Matthew 13:55; Mark 3:31; John 2:12; 7:3; Acts 1:14; 1 Corinthians 9:5
- spiritual brothers, Romans 8:29; 12:10; 1 Timothy 6:2; Hebrews 2:11; 1 Peter 2:17

burn
- sacrifices, Exodus 29:10–42; Leviticus 1—4
- incense, Exodus 30:7–8; Numbers 16:40; Jeremiah 48:35; Luke 1:9
- Jericho burned by Israelites, Joshua 6:24
- idols burned by Josiah, 2 Kings 23:4–20
- jealousy like a fire, Psalm 79:5
- chaff, Matthew 3:12; Luke 3:17
- lake of burning sulfur, Revelation 21:8

burnt offerings, *a whole animal sacrificed as a gift to God.*
- rules about, Leviticus 1; 6:8–13; Numbers 28—29
- less important than obedience, 1 Samuel 15:22; Psalm 51:16–19
- less important than love, Hosea 6:6; Mark 12:32–33

bury, Matthew 8:21–22; Luke 9:59–60
- Abraham buried Sarah, Genesis 23
- Jacob not to be buried in Egypt, Genesis 47:29–30; 50:1–14
- strangers, Matthew 27:7
- in baptism, Romans 6:4

C

Caesar (SEE-zer) *a famous Roman family; used as the title of the Roman emperors.*
- Augustus, Luke 2:1
- Tiberius, Luke 3:1; 20:22; John 19:12
- Claudius, Acts 11:28; 17:7; 18:2
- Nero, Acts 25:8; 27:24; Philippians 4:22

Caesarea (SES-uh-REE-uh) *a city on the Mediterranean Sea,* Acts 10:1; 21:8; 23:32

Caesarea Philippi (SES-uh-REE-uh fih-LIP-eye) *a city at the base of Mount Hermon,* Matthew 16:13; Mark 8:27

Caiaphas (KAY-uh-fus) *the Jewish high priest from A.D. 18 to 36.*
- plotted to kill Jesus, Matthew 26:3–5; John 11:45–54
- son-in-law to Annas, John 18:13
- at Jesus' trial, Matthew 26:57–67
- questioned Peter and John, Acts 4:5–22

Cain, *the first son of Adam and Eve.*
- killed his brother Abel, Genesis 4:1–24; 1 John 3:12

Caleb (KAY-leb) *one of the twelve men Moses sent to spy out Canaan.*

- explored Canaan, Numbers 13—14
- given the city of Hebron, Joshua 14:6–15

calf
- gold idol, Exodus 32:1–20; 1 Kings 12:26–30; 2 Kings 10:28–29
- fatted, Luke 15:23, 27, 30

camel, Genesis 37:25; 1 Samuel 30:17; 1 Kings 10:2
- Rebekah watered Abraham's camels, Genesis 24:10–20
- "easier for a camel to go through the eye of a needle," Matthew 19:24; Mark 10:25; Luke 18:25
- "swallows a camel," Matthew 23:24

Cana (KAY-nah) *a small town near the city of Nazareth in Galilee.*
- place of Jesus' first miracle, John 2:1–11

Canaan (KAY-nun) *land God promised to the Israelites,* Leviticus 25:38; Numbers 13:2; 33:51; Psalm 105:11

Capernaum (kay-PUR-nay-um) *a city on the western shore of Lake Galilee.*
- Jesus lived there, Matthew 4:12–13
- Jesus healed there, Matthew 8:5–13; Luke 4:31–41
- rejected Jesus, Matthew 11:23–24

capital, *the top of a pillar, usually decorated with beautiful carvings.*
- in the Temple, 1 Kings 7:16–20; 2 Kings 25:17

capital punishment
- punishment for killing, Genesis 9:6
- God kills Herod, Acts 12:23
- death by sword, Matthew 26:52

captive
- Israelites as captives, Deuteronomy 28:41; 2 Kings 25:21; Jeremiah 30:3

career/careerism
- Abraham's task, Genesis 12
- doing the Lord's work, John 9:4

cassia (CASH-ah) *a pleasant-smelling powder. Its odor is like the bark of the cinnamon plant.* Exodus 30:23–24; Psalm 45:8

celebration
- Feast of the Harvest, Leviticus 23:9–14
- the ark returns, 2 Samuel 6:12–23
- Feast of Purim, Esther 9:18–32

celibacy
- Jeremiah remains single, Jeremiah 16:2
- of Daniel, Daniel 1:1–21
- versus marriage, 1 Corinthians 7:1–7

census (SIN-sus) *a count of the number of people who live in an area.*
- the Israelites counted, Numbers 1:2; 26:2
- ordered by David, 1 Chronicles 21:1–2
- ordered by Augustus Caesar, Luke 2:1–3

centurion (sin-TUR-ree-un) *a Roman army officer who commanded a hundred soldiers.*
- centurion's servant healed by Jesus, Matthew 8:5–13; Luke 7:1–10
- at Jesus' death, Matthew 27:54; Mark 15:39; Luke 23:47
- Cornelius, Acts 10

Cephas (SEE-fuss) *the Aramaic word for "rock"; in Greek, "Peter." Jesus gave this name to the apostle Simon.* John 1:42

chaff (CHAF) *the husk of a head of grain. Farmers would toss the grain and chaff into the air. Since the chaff is lighter, the wind would blow it away, and the good grain would fall back to the threshing floor.*
- sinners to be destroyed like chaff, Psalms 1:4; 35:5; Matthew 3:12; Luke 3:17

Chaldeans, See "Babylonians."

change of heart and life, *repentance.*
- commanded, Matthew 3:2; Mark 1:15; Luke 13:3; Acts 3:19; 17:30
- causes of, Romans 2:4; 2 Corinthians 7:9–10
- examples of, Matthew 12:41; Luke 11:32

chariot
- Egyptians' chariots destroyed, Exodus 14:5–28
- of fire, 2 Kings 2:11; 6:17
- Ethiopian taught in a chariot, Acts 8:27–31

Chemosh (KEE-mosh) *a god of the Moabites,* Jeremiah 48:13
- worshiped by Solomon, 1 Kings 11:7

cherubim (CHAIR-uh-bim) *heavenly beings with wings and the faces of men and animals.*
- guarded the garden of Eden, Genesis 3:24
- on the Ark of the Agreement, Exodus 25:18–22; 1 Kings 6:23–28
- seen by Ezekiel, Ezekiel 10:1–20

childlessness, See "infertility."

children
- of God, John 1:12; Romans 8:14; 1 Peter 1:14; 1 John 3:1–10
- training of, Ephesians 6:4; Colossians 3:21
- obedience of, Ephesians 6:1; Colossians 3:20; 1 Timothy 3:4
- become like, Matthew 18:3–4
- "Let the little children come to me," Matthew 19:14; Mark 10:14; Luke 18:16

chosen
- Israelites chosen by God, Deuteronomy 7:7–8; 9:4–5; Isaiah 44:1
- people chosen by God, Romans 8:33; Ephesians 1:4–5; 2 Timothy 2:10; 1 Peter 1:2; 2:9
- Jesus chosen by God, Hebrews 1:2; 1 Peter 2:4

Christ (KRYST) *anointed (or chosen) one. Jesus is the Christ, chosen by God to save people from their sins.*
- active in creation, John 1:1–3; Colossians 1:15–17; Hebrews 1:2, 10
- equal with God, John 5:23; 10:30; Philippians 2:6; Colossians 2:9; Hebrews 1:3
- purpose of his death, Romans 5:6; 14:9; Hebrews 9:28; 1 Peter 3:18
- gives life, John 5:21; 6:35; 10:28; 11:25; 14:6
- as Savior, Matthew 1:21; John 12:47
- as judge, Matthew 10:32–33; 25:31–46; John 5:22; Acts 17:31
- living in Christians, John 17:23; Romans 8:10; 2 Corinthians 1:21; Ephesians 3:17
- his return, Acts 1:11; 1 Thessalonians 5:1–11; Hebrews 9:28; 2 Peter 3:10
- enemy of, 1 John 2:18, 22; 4:3; 2 John 7

Christians (KRIS-chuns) *Christ's followers,* Acts 11:26; 26:28; 1 Peter 4:16

church
- established by Christ, Matthew 16:18
- Christ as its head, Ephesians 1:22; 5:23; Colossians 1:18
- Christ died for, Ephesians 5:25
- activities of, Acts 12:5; 1 Corinthians 14:26–40; 1 Timothy 5:16; Hebrews 10:24–25

circumcision (SIR-kum-SIH-zhun) *the cutting off of the foreskin of the male sex organ; each Jewish boy was circumcised on the eighth day after he was born; this was done as a sign of the agreement God had made with his people, the Jews.*
- commanded by God, Genesis 17; Leviticus 12:1–3
- spiritual circumcision, Philippians 3:3; Colossians 2:11

citizen
- yielding to the government, Romans 13
- God is over human authority, Acts 5:29
- pray for the rulers, 1 Timothy 2:2

city
- the New Jerusalem, Revelation 21
- pray for Babylon, Jeremiah 29:4–7

city of refuge, See "safety, city of."

Claudius (CLAW-dee-us) *the fourth Roman emperor. He ruled from A.D. 41 to 54.* Acts 11:28; 17:7; 18:2

clean, *the state of a person, animal, or action that is pleasing to God. Under the Teachings of Moses, unclean animals could not be eaten. People who were considered clean could live and serve God normally.*
- clean and unclean animals, Deuteronomy 14:1–21; Mark 7:19; Acts 10
- clean and unclean people, Leviticus 13
- spiritually clean, Ephesians 5:26; Hebrews 9:14; 2 Peter 1:9

Cleansing, Day of, *the Day of Atonement; the most special day of the year for the Israelites when the high priest could go into the Most Holy Place. Animals were sacrificed for the sins of the people as a sign that people were cleansed of their sins for a year.*
- rules about, Leviticus 23:26–32; 25:9

cloud
- Israel led by pillar of cloud, Exodus 13:21
- cloud as small as a fist, 1 Kings 18:44
- Jesus leaves and will return in clouds, Luke 21:27; Acts 1:9; 1 Thessalonians 4:17; Revelation 1:7

Colossae (koh-LAH-see) *a city in the country of Turkey,* Colossians 1:1–2

comfort, *to help ease someone's pain, grief, or trouble.*
- bad comforters, Job 16:2
- by shepherd's rod, Psalm 23:4
- from God, Isaiah 49:13; Matthew 5:4; 2 Corinthians 1:3–4
- from the Holy Spirit, John 14:16–18

commands
- to be taught, Deuteronomy 6:1–7; Matthew 5:19
- to be obeyed, Deuteronomy 8:6; Proverbs 19:16; John 15:10
- a new command, John 13:34
- to love, Galatians 5:14; 1 Timothy 1:5; 2 John 6

commitment
- God promises Abraham, Galatians 3:15–17
- agreement between two people, Galatians 3:15
- agreement between kings, Ezekiel 17:11–19

communication
- why John writes, 1 John 1:1–4
- God helps Moses speak, Exodus 4:15

communion (kuh-MYU-nyun) See "Lord's Supper."

community
- in the council of churches, Acts 15
- of the early church, Acts 2:42–47
- sins with a gold calf, Exodus 32

complain
- Pharisees complained, Luke 5:30
- followers complained, John 6:61
- warnings against, Philippians 2:14

concubine (KON-kyu-bine) See "slave woman."

condemn (kun-DIM) *to judge someone guilty of doing wrong,* John 3:16–18; Romans 2:1; 8:1

coney, See "rock badger."

confess
- admitting sin, Psalm 32:5; Proverbs 28:13; James 5:16; 1 John 1:9
- admitting Christ is Lord, Romans 10:9–10; Philippians 2:11; 1 Timothy 6:12; 1 John 4:2–3

confidence (KON-fuh-dens) *a feeling of assurance; trust.*
- from the Lord, 2 Thessalonians 3:4; 2 Timothy 1:7
- in Christ, Philippians 4:13
- before God, 1 John 3:21

conflict
- at Eden, Genesis 3
- between Jews and non-Jews, Ephesians 2:14
- resolving, Matthew 18:15–17

conscience (KON-shunts) *a person's belief about what is right and wrong.*
- Paul's good conscience, Acts 23:1
- commanded to have a good conscience, 1 Timothy 3:9; Hebrews 9:14
- a troubled conscience, Hebrews 10:22; 1 John 3:20
- a corrupt conscience, 1 Timothy 4:2; Titus 1:15

contentment, *satisfaction.*
- Paul learned, Philippians 4:11
- with possessions, Luke 3:14; 1 Timothy 6:6; Hebrews 13:5

conversion (kon-VER-zhun) *a person's turning toward God and becoming a Christian.*
- examples of, Acts 9:1–22; 11:19–21; 1 Thessalonians 1:9

coral (KOR-al) *a type of limestone that forms in the ocean,* Job 28:18; Ezekiel 27:16

Corinth (KOR-inth) *a large seaport in the country of Greece.*
- Paul preached there, Acts 18:1–11
- Paul's letters to the church there, 1 and 2 Corinthians

Cornelius (kor-NEEL-yus) *a Roman army officer in charge of a hundred soldiers,* Acts 10

cornerstone, *the most important stone at the corner of the base of a building; Jesus is called the cornerstone of the new law.*
- Christ as the cornerstone, Ephesians 2:20; 1 Peter 2:4–8

council (KOWN-s'l) *or meeting; the highest Jewish court in the days of Jesus.*
- Jesus before the council, Matthew 26:57–68; Mark 14:53–65
- apostles before the council, Acts 4:1–22; 22:30—23:10
- Stephen before the council, Acts 6:8—7:60

courage
- need for, Joshua 1:6–9; Psalm 27:14; 1 Corinthians 16:13; Philippians 1:20
- examples of, Acts 4:13; 5:17–32; 20:22–24

court, courtyard, *part of a building that has walls, but no roof. The Temple had four courts:*
- the Court of the Non-Jews (Gentiles), a large open area just inside the walls of Herod's Temple, Mark 11:15–17; John 10:23; Acts 3:11
- the Court of Women, the next area, where both men and women were allowed, Mark 12:41–44
- the Court of Israel, the inner area of the Temple, where only Jewish men were allowed
- the Court of the Priests, the innermost court in the Temple, where only priests were allowed, Matthew 23:35

covenant (KUV-eh-nant) See "agreement."

covet (KUV-et) *to want strongly something that belongs to someone else.*
- forbidden by God, Exodus 20:17; Romans 13:9; Hebrews 13:5

creation
- of the world, Genesis 1—2; Job 38—41; Psalm 8; Isaiah 40:21–26; John 1:1–3; Hebrews 11:3

creation/new creation
- belongs to Christ, 2 Corinthians 5:17
- new heaven and earth, Revelation 21:1

creator, *one who makes something out of nothing.*
- God as our Maker, Deuteronomy 32:6
- "Remember your Creator," Ecclesiastes 12:1

Crete (KREET) *an island in the Mediterranean Sea.*
- Paul visited there, Acts 27:7; Titus 1:5

cross, *two rough beams of wood nailed together; criminals were killed on crosses.*
- Jesus died on a cross, Matthew 27:31–50; Mark 15:20–37; Luke 23:26–46; John 19:16–30
- importance of, 1 Corinthians 1:18; 2:2; Galatians 6:14; Ephesians 2:16; Colossians 2:13–14
- as a symbol of death to oneself, Matthew 10:38; Luke 9:23; Romans 6:6; Galatians 5:24

crown, *a special band worn around the head.*
- a king's crown, Psalm 21:2–3; Song of Songs 3:11; Revelation 12:3
- of thorns, Matthew 27:29; Mark 15:17; John 19:2
- of victory, 1 Corinthians 9:25; 2 Timothy 4:8; 1 Peter 5:4

crucifixion (kroo-suh-FIK-shun) *to be killed on a cross.* See "cross."

cubit (KU-bit) *a measurement in Bible times; about eighteen inches,* Revelation 21:17

cud, *an animal's food that is chewed slightly, swallowed, brought up, then chewed more completely a second time,* Leviticus 11; Deuteronomy 14

cults
- people turning to, Revelation 9:20
- testing authenticity of, 1 John 2:3–6
- preaching a different Jesus, Galatians 1:6–7

cultural boundaries
- defied by Jesus, Mark 2:14–17
- Ruth goes beyond, Ruth 2:11–12
- between Jew and non-Jew, Galatians 2:11–16

cup
- of the king of Egypt, Genesis 40:11
- of Joseph, Genesis 44:1–17
- of Lord's Supper, Matthew 26:27–29; Mark 14:22–25; Luke 22:17–20; 1 Corinthians 11:25–29
- of anger, Isaiah 51:17–23
- of water, Matthew 10:42; Mark 9:41

cupbearer, *the officer who tasted and served the king his wine.*
- to the king of Egypt, Genesis 40
- Nehemiah, cupbearer to Artaxerxes, Nehemiah 1:11

curse
- from God, Deuteronomy 11:26–29; John 7:49; Galatians 3:10–13
- forbidden to people, Matthew 15:4; Romans 12:14; James 3:9–10
- response to, Luke 6:28; 1 Corinthians 4:12

curtain
- of the Holy Tent, Exodus 26:1–2; 36:9
- of the Temple, Matthew 27:51; Mark 15:38; Luke 23:45

Cush, *a country in Africa,* Genesis 2:13; Psalm 68:31; Isaiah 18; 20

Cush, *grandson of Noah,* Genesis 10

Cyprus (SY-prus) *an island in the Mediterranean Sea,* Acts 11:19–20; 13:4; 15:39

Cyrene (sy-REE-nee) *a city in North Africa,* Acts 2:10; 6:9
- Simon of, Matthew 27:32; Mark 15:21; Luke 23:26

Cyrus (SY-rus) *a king of Persia,* Daniel 1:21
- sent captives home, Ezra 1; 6
- chosen by God, Isaiah 44:28—45:13

D

Dagon (DAY-gon) *a false god of the Philistines,* Judges 16:23; 1 Samuel 5:2–7; 1 Chronicles 10:10

Damascus (duh-MAS-kus) *a city forty miles east of Lake Galilee.*
- a chief city of Syria, 1 Kings 15:18; 2 Chronicles 24:23
- condemned by Amos, Amos 1:3, 5
- Paul converted there, Acts 9:1–22

Dan, a city
- Israel's most northern city, Judges 20:1; 2 Samuel 16:11

Dan, son of Jacob, Genesis 30:6; 49:16–17; Joshua 19:40–48

Daniel (DAN-yel) *a Hebrew captive taken to Babylon as a young man.*
- taken to Babylon, Daniel 1:1–6
- became king's servant, Daniel 1:7–21
- explained Nebuchadnezzar's dreams, Daniel 2; 4
- read the writing on the wall, Daniel 5
- thrown into lions' den, Daniel 6
- his visions, Daniel 7; 8; 10
- a prophet, Matthew 24:15

Darius Hystaspes (dah-RYE-us his-TAHS-peez) *a ruler of Persia who allowed the Jews to finish rebuilding the Temple,* Ezra 5—6

Darius the Mede, *the king of Persia who made Daniel an important ruler under him,* Daniel 5:31—6:28; Haggai 1:1; Zechariah 1:1

darkness, *having no light; a symbol of evil.*
- before creation, Genesis 1:2
- as a plague, Exodus 10:21–23
- at Jesus' death, Matthew 27:45; Mark 15:33; Luke 23:44–45
- spiritual, John 1:5; Romans 13:12; Colossians 1:13
- as punishment, Matthew 8:12; 2 Peter 2:17; Jude 6, 13

David (DAY-vid) *Israel's greatest king.*
- son of Jesse, 1 Samuel 16:13–23
- played harp for Saul, 1 Samuel 16:14–23
- killed Goliath, 1 Samuel 17
- friend of Jonathan, 1 Samuel 18:1–4; 19:1–7; 20
- chased by Saul, 1 Samuel 18—19; 23:7–29
- protected Saul, 1 Samuel 24; 26
- became king, 2 Samuel 2:1–7; 5:1–14
- married Bathsheba, 2 Samuel 11:1—12:25
- reign of, 2 Samuel 5—1 Kings 1
- not allowed to build the Temple, 2 Samuel 7:1–17
- death of, 1 Kings 2:1–11
- Jesus as son of David, Matthew 22:42–45; Luke 1:27; 20:41–44

Day of the Lord
- sun will become dark, Joel 2:31
- the Lord warns about, Zechariah 14
- return of Christ, 2 Thessalonians 2:2

deacon (DEE-kun) *a person chosen to serve the church in special ways,* Philippians 1:1; 1 Timothy 3:8–13

Dead Sea, *large lake at the south end of the Jordan River. Several small streams flow into it, but it has no outlet. It is so salty that nothing lives in it. It is also called the "Sea of Arabah," the "Salt Sea," and the "Eastern Sea."* Genesis 14:3; Numbers 34:3, 12; Joshua 3:16

deaf, *unable or unwilling to hear.*
- healed, Matthew 11:5; Luke 7:22
- and dumb spirit, Mark 9:25

death
- a result of sin, Genesis 2:16–17; Romans 5:12; 6:23; 1 Corinthians 15:21
- Christ's victory over, 1 Corinthians 15:24–26, 54–57; 2 Timothy 1:10; Hebrews 2:14; Revelation 1:18
- spiritual death, Ephesians 2:1; Colossians 2:13

Deborah (DEB-oh-rah) *the only woman judge over Israel,* Judges 4—5

debt
- parable of unforgiving servant, Matthew 18:21–35
- don't guarantee another's, Proverbs 22:26–27
- forgiving another's, Matthew 6:12

Decapolis (dee-KAP-oh-lis) *ten towns in an area southeast of Lake Galilee,* Matthew 4:25; Mark 5:20; 7:31

decision making/plan
- life is not yours, Jeremiah 10:23
- depends on God, Proverbs 19:21
- God controls the nations, Isaiah 40:15

Delilah (dee-LYE-luh) *an evil Philistine woman whom Samson loved,* Judges 16:4–20

Demas (DEE-mus) *a Christian who helped the apostle Paul when Paul was in prison.*
- worked with Paul, Colossians 4:14; Philemon 24
- left Paul, 2 Timothy 4:10

Demetrius (deh-MEE-tree-us) *a silver worker in Ephesus,* Acts 19:23–27, 38

demon, *an evil spirit from the devil. Sometimes demons lived in people, but Jesus could make them come out.*
- people possessed by, Matthew 8:28–32; 9:32–33; Mark 7:24–30; 9:17–29
- Jesus accused of demon possession, Mark 3:22; John 7:20; 8:48; 10:20–21
- demons recognized Jesus, Mark 1:23–26; 3:11–12; 5:7–8; Acts 19:15; James 2:19

deny (di-NY) *refusing to believe the truth.*
- denying Christ, Matthew 10:32–33; 2 Timothy 2:12; 1 John 2:22–23
- Peter denied Christ, Matthew 26:34–35, 69–75

depression
- lamenting to God about, Psalm 42
- of Elijah, 1 Kings 19
- from goals unfulfilled, Proverbs 13:12

descendants (de-SIN-dants) *family members who are born to a person or his children: grandchildren, great-grandchildren, great-great-grandchildren and so on,* Genesis 13:14–16; 15:12–16

devil (DEV-'l) *Satan; a spirit and the enemy of God and humans.*
- Jesus tempted by, Matthew 4:1–11; Luke 4:1–13
- children of, John 8:41–44; Acts 13:10; 1 John 3:7–10
- people to oppose, Ephesians 4:27; 6:11; James 4:7

Didymus (DID-ee-mus) *another name for Thomas, one of Jesus' apostles,* John 11:16; 20:24; 21:2

disciple (dih-SYE-p'l) See "follower."

disease
- a result of sin, Exodus 15:26; Deuteronomy 7:15; 28:60–61
- healed by Jesus, Matthew 4:23–24; 15:30–31; 21:14; Luke 7:21
- healed by apostles, Acts 5:12–16; 9:32–35; 14:8–10; 19:11–12; 28:8–9

dishonesty, See "lying."

disobedience
- brought sin, Romans 5:19
- to be punished, 2 Corinthians 10:6; Hebrews 4:11

divide
- heavens and earth, Genesis 1:6–8
- Red Sea, Exodus 14:16, 21
- family against itself, Matthew 12:25; Mark 3:25; Luke 11:17

divorce
- teachings about, Deuteronomy 22:13–19, 28–29; 24:1–4; Matthew 5:31–32; 19:1–12; 1 Corinthians 7:10–16

dog
- drinking water like a dog, Judges 7:5–6
- returns to its vomit, Proverbs 26:11; 2 Peter 2:22
- licked Ahab's blood, 1 Kings 22:38
- licked Lazarus's sores, Luke 16:20–21

door
- Jesus as the door, John 10:1
- "Knock, and the door will open," Luke 11:9–10
- "I stand at the door and knock." Revelation 3:20

donkey
- Balaam's, Numbers 22:21–30
- jawbone of, Judges 15:15–17
- ridden by Jesus, Matthew 21:1–7

Dorcas (DOR-kus) *Tabitha; a Christian woman known for helping the poor.*
- raised from the dead, Acts 9:36–43

doubt
- doubters will not receive, James 1:5–8
- only fools, Psalm 14:1
- Thomas doubts, John 20:24–29

dove, *a small bird similar to a pigeon; often a symbol for love, peace, and the Holy Spirit.*
- sent out by Noah, Genesis 8:8–12

- form taken by the Spirit of God, Matthew 3:16; Mark 1:10
- sellers of, John 2:14–16

dreams
- Joseph's, Genesis 37:1–11
- the king of Egypt's, Genesis 41:1–36
- Nebuchadnezzar's, Daniel 2; 4
- angel appeared to Joseph, Matthew 1:20–21; 2:13, 19
- "your old men will dream dreams," Acts 2:17

drunkenness
- Noah became drunk, Genesis 9:20–23
- warnings against, Romans 13:13; 1 Corinthians 6:10; Ephesians 5:18; 1 Peter 4:3

E

eagle
- to "rise up as an eagle," Isaiah 40:31

earth
- creation of, Genesis 1:9–10; Jeremiah 51:15
- belongs to God, Exodus 19:5; Psalm 24:1

earthquake
- experienced by Elijah, 1 Kings 19:11–12
- at the death of Jesus, Matthew 27:51–54
- at Jesus' resurrection, Matthew 28:2
- experienced by Paul and Silas, Acts 16:25–26

Ebal (EE-buhl) *a mountain in Samaria next to Mount Gerizim.*
- place to announce curses, Deuteronomy 11:29; 27:12–13; Joshua 8:30–35

Eden, garden of (EE-den) *the home God created for Adam and Eve,* Genesis 2:8—3:24; Ezekiel 36:35; Joel 2:3

Edom (EE-dum) *Esau; the land where Esau's descendants lived.*
- the land of Esau, Genesis 36:8–9
- refused to let Israelites pass through, Numbers 20:14–21; Judges 11:17–18
- broke away from Judah, 2 Kings 8:20–22
- to be punished, Jeremiah 49:7–22; Ezekiel 25:12–14; Obadiah

education
- of Moses, Acts 7:22
- of children, Deuteronomy 6:1–7
- brings wisdom, Proverbs 8:33; 22:6

Eglon (EGG-lon) *a king of Moab,* Judges 3:12–25

Egypt (EE-jipt) *a country in the northeast part of Africa.*
- Joseph there, Genesis 39—50
- Israelites there, Genesis 46:5–34; Exodus 1; Acts 7:9–38
- Israelites left, Exodus 12:31–51
- Jesus there, Matthew 2:13–15

Ehud (EE-hud) *the second judge of Israel,* Judges 3:12–30

elder (EL-der) *older men who led God's people; appointed leaders in the church.*
- leaders of the Jews, Numbers 11:16–25; Deuteronomy 19:11–12; Matthew 21:23; Acts 4:5–7
- leaders of the church, Acts 11:30; 14:23; 15:2; 16:4
- duties and qualities, Acts 20:28; 1 Timothy 3:1–7; Titus 1:6–9; 1 Peter 5:1–3

Eleazar (el-ee-A-zar) *son of Aaron.*
- birth of, Exodus 6:23–25
- Moses became angry with, Leviticus 10:16–20
- a high priest, Numbers 3:32
- divided the Promised Land, Numbers 34:17

election, *process of selecting.* See "chosen."

Eli (EE-lye) *a priest and the next-to-last judge of Israel.*
- trained Samuel, 1 Samuel 1:9–28; 2:11; 3
- didn't discipline his sons, 1 Samuel 2:12–36
- death of, 1 Samuel 4:1–18

Elihu (ee-LYE-hew) *the fourth of Job's friends to try to explain Job's troubles,* Job 32—37

Elijah (ee-LIE-juh) *a prophet who spoke for God.*
- fed by ravens, 1 Kings 17:1–6
- brought boy to life, 1 Kings 17:7–24
- against prophets of Baal, 1 Kings 18:1–40
- condemned Ahab, 1 Kings 21:17–29
- taken to heaven, 2 Kings 2:1–12
- appeared with Jesus, Matthew 17:1–13; Mark 9:2–13; Luke 9:28–36

Elisha (ee-LYE-shuh) *the prophet who took Elijah's place as God's messenger.*
- received Elijah's spirit, 2 Kings 2:9–14
- helped a Shunammite woman, 2 Kings 4:1–36
- miracles of, 2 Kings 2:19–22; 4:38–44; 6:1–7
- healed Naaman, 2 Kings 5
- death of, 2 Kings 13:14–20

Elizabeth (ee-LIZ-uh-beth) *the wife of Zechariah, a priest.*
- mother of John the Baptist, Luke 1:5–25, 57–66
- visited by Mary, Luke 1:39–45

Elkanah (el-KAY-nuh) *the father of Samuel,* 1 Samuel 1:1—2:11

Elymas (EL-ih-mus) *Bar-Jesus; a magician in the city of Paphos in Cyprus,* Acts 13:4–12

Emmaus (ee-MAY-us) *a town seven miles from Jerusalem.*
- Jesus appeared to followers near there, Luke 24:13–39

encourage
- encouragement from God, Romans 15:4–5
- Christians to encourage each other, 1 Thessalonians 5:14; 2 Timothy 4:2; Hebrews 3:13; 10:24–25

- examples of encouragement, Acts 11:23; 13:15; 15:31–32

end times/last days
- Jesus discusses, Matthew 24
- John describes, Revelation 20

endurance, See "patience."

enemy
- attitude toward, Exodus 23:4–5; Matthew 5:43–48; Luke 6:27–36; Romans 12:20
- God's enemies, Romans 5:10; Philippians 3:18–19; James 4:4

enemy of Christ, *the Antichrist,* 1 John 2:18, 22; 4:3; 2 John 7

Enoch (E-nuk) *a man who walked with God,* Genesis 5:21–24; Hebrews 11:5

enrollment, See "census."

environment
- created by God, Genesis 1:9–25
- stewardship over, Matthew 25:14–30
- making land unclean, Jeremiah 2:7

envy, See "jealousy."

Epaphras (EP-ah-fruhs) *a Christian who started the church at Colossae,* Colossians 1:7–8; 4:12–13; Philemon 23

Epaphroditus (ee-PAF-ro-DYE-tus) *a Christian in the church at Philippi,* Philippians 2:25–30; 4:18

ephah (EE-fah) *a common measurement for dry materials, about twenty quarts,* Exodus 16:36

Ephesus (EF-eh-sus) *the capital city in the Roman state of Asia.*
- Paul's work there, Acts 18:18–20; 1 Corinthians 16:8–9
- church there, Ephesians 1:1; Revelation 2:1–7

ephod (EF-ahd) See "vest, holy."

Ephraim (EE-frah-im) *Joseph's younger son,* Genesis 41:50–52; 48:8–20
- descendants of, Numbers 26:35; Joshua 16:5–10

equality (ee-KWAHL-eh-tee) *being identical in value.*
- in death, Ecclesiastes 3:19–20
- of Jewish and non-Jewish people, Romans 10:12
- in Christ, Galatians 3:26–28

Esau (EE-saw) See "Edom."

Esther (ES-ter) *a Jewish girl who became the wife of Ahasuerus, king of Persia,* Esther 1—10
- became queen, Esther 1:1—2:18
- learned of the plan to kill the Jews, Esther 3—4
- saved the Jews, Esther 5—8

eternal, See "forever."

eternal life, *the new kind of life promised to those who follow Jesus.*
- conditions for, Mark 10:17–31; John 3:14–15; 12:25; 17:3; Galatians 6:7–8
- source of, John 6:27–29; 10:28; Titus 1:2; 1 John 5:11–12

Ethiopia, *earlier called "Cush."* See "Cush."

eunuch (YOU-nuk) *a man who cannot have sexual relations. In Bible times, eunuchs were often high officers in royal palaces or armies.* 2 Kings 9:32; Esther 2:3; Isaiah 56:3–5; Acts 8:26–40

Euphrates (you-FRAY-teez) *a long, important river in Bible lands.*
- in the garden of Eden, Genesis 2:10–14
- a boundary, Genesis 15:18; 1 Kings 4:21; 2 Kings 24:7

Eutychus (YOU-ti-cus) *a young man in the city of Troas who was brought back to life,* Acts 20:7–12

evangelism
- the Great Commission, Matthew 28:16–20
- Jesus sends out seventy-two, Luke 10:1–16
- Paul preaches to the Greeks, Acts 17:16–34

evangelist (ee-VAN-juh-list) *someone who tells the Good News.*
- Philip, the evangelist, Acts 21:8
- as a gift from Christ, Ephesians 4:11

Eve (EEV) *the first woman.*
- created by God, Genesis 2:18–25
- tricked by Satan, Genesis 3; 2 Corinthians 11:3; 1 Timothy 2:13–14

everlasting, *living forever; eternal.*
- God, Genesis 21:33; Nehemiah 9:5; Isaiah 40:28
- Christ, Isaiah 9:6
- kingdom, Daniel 4:3; 2 Peter 1:11
- fire, Matthew 18:8, 25, 41
- Good News, Revelation 14:6

evil
- warnings against, Amos 5:15; Romans 12:9; 1 Thessalonians 5:22
- to be punished, Proverbs 24:20; Isaiah 13:11

evil spirit, See "demon."

Exodus, The
- out of Egypt, Exodus 12:31–51
- praising God for, Psalm 77:16–20

Exodus, New Exodus
- Isaiah's prophecy, Isaiah 40:3–5
- Christians are wanderers, Hebrews 3:7—4:13

eye
- "eye for eye," Exodus 21:23–24; Matthew 5:38
- wood in, Matthew 7:3–5; Luke 6:41–42

eyewitness, *one who sees an occurrence and reports on it.*
- of Jesus' life, Luke 1:2; 2 Peter 1:16; 1 John 1:1

Ezekiel (ee-ZEEK-yel) *a prophet during the time the Jews were captured by the Babylonians,* Ezekiel 1:3
- his vision of dry bones, Ezekiel 37:1–14

Ezra (EZ-ra) *the leader of a group of Israelites who were allowed to return to Jerusalem from Babylon,* Ezra 7—10; Nehemiah 8

F

faith (FAYTH) *belief and trust.*
- definition of, Hebrews 11:1
- sources of, Romans 1:20; 10:17
- examples of, Matthew 8:5–10; 15:21–28; Hebrews 11
- power of, Matthew 17:20–21; Ephesians 6:16
- made right with God by, Romans 4:3; 5:1; Philippians 3:9
- salvation by, Mark 16:15–16; John 5:24; 20:31; Romans 10:9; Galatians 2:16
- blessings by, Galatians 3:1–14; Ephesians 3:12; 1 Peter 1:5
- continue in, 2 Corinthians 13:5; Colossians 1:23; 1 Timothy 1:19; 2 Timothy 2:22
- lack of, Matthew 8:26; 14:31; 16:8

faithful (FAYTH-ful) *honest, loyal, true.*
- God is faithful, Deuteronomy 32:3–4; Isaiah 49:7; 2 Timothy 2:13; Hebrews 3:6; Revelation 19:11
- God's people must be faithful, Matthew 25:21; Revelation 2:10; 14:12; 17:14

fall, *sometimes used to describe the first sin.*
- Adam and Eve sinned, Genesis 3

false
- gods, Exodus 20:3; Deuteronomy 4:28; 1 Chronicles 16:26
- prophets, Deuteronomy 13:1–11; 18:22; Jeremiah 14:13–16; Matthew 7:15
- Christs, Matthew 24:24; Mark 13:22
- apostles, 2 Corinthians 11:13
- brothers, Galatians 2:4
- teachers, 2 Peter 2:1

family
- of believers, Galatians 6:10; Hebrews 2:11; 1 Peter 4:17

famine (FAM-un) *a time of hunger when there is very little food.*
- in Egypt, Genesis 41:30–31, 53–57
- in Judah, Ruth 1:1
- in Israel, 1 Kings 17:1
- in Jerusalem during Claudius's rule, Acts 11:27–28

fasting (FAST-ing) *giving up food for a while.*
- to show sorrow, 1 Samuel 1:11–12; 2 Samuel 12:15–22
- of Jesus, Matthew 4:1–2
- how to fast, Matthew 6:16–18
- combined with prayer, Ezra 8:23; Luke 5:33; Acts 13:1–3

father
- to be honored, Exodus 20:12; Ephesians 6:2
- commands to, Colossians 3:21
- God as Father, Matthew 6:9; 23:9; 2 Corinthians 6:18; Galatians 4:6; Hebrews 12:4–11

fear, *a feeling of being afraid, or one of deep respect.*
- of God, Matthew 10:26–31; Luke 23:40
- overcoming, 2 Timothy 1:7; Hebrews 13:6; 1 John 4:18
- "your salvation . . . with fear and trembling," Philippians 2:12

feast (FEEST) *a special meal and celebration for a certain purpose.*
- Feast of Dedication, an eight-day celebration for the Jews that showed they were thankful that the Temple had been cleansed again, John 10:22
- Feast of Harvest, see "Feast of Weeks."
- Feast of Purim (PURE-rim) reminded the Israelites of how they were saved from death during the time of Queen Esther, Esther 9:18–32
- Feast of Shelters, "Feast of Booths" or "Feast of Tents"; reminded the Israelites of how God had taken care of them when they left Egypt and lived in tents in the wilderness, Exodus 23:16; Deuteronomy 16:13–17
- Feast of Unleavened Bread, or "Passover"; reminded the Israelites how God brought them out of Egyptian slavery, Exodus 12:1–30; Numbers 28:16–25; Deuteronomy 16:1–8
- Feast of Weeks, or "Pentecost," the "Feast of Harvest," or the "Day of Firstfruits"; a feast of thanksgiving for the summer harvest, Exodus 34:22; Leviticus 23:15–22; Numbers 28:26–31

Felix (FEE-lix) *the Roman governor of Judea from* A.D. *52 to 54.*
- put Paul on trial, Acts 23:23–24; 24

fellowship (FEL-o-ship) *sharing friendship and love with others.*
- with Christ, Matthew 18:20; 1 Corinthians 1:9; 1 John 1:3
- with the Holy Spirit, 2 Corinthians 13:14; Philippians 2:1
- with believers, Acts 2:42; 1 John 1:7

festivals, See "feast."

Festus (FES-tus) *governor of Judea after Felix.*
- put Paul on trial, Acts 25—26

fighting
- against evil, 2 Corinthians 10:3–6; Ephesians 6:12
- "fight the good fight," 1 Timothy 1:18

- "I have fought the good fight." 2 Timothy 4:7

fire, *used by God as a sign of his presence and power.*
- the burning bush, Exodus 3:1–6
- pillar of, Exodus 13:21–22
- chariot of, 2 Kings 2:11
- wrong kind of, Numbers 26:61
- fiery furnace, Daniel 3:25
- baptism of, Matthew 3:11
- of punishment, Matthew 5:22; 13:41–42; Mark 9:43; 2 Thessalonians 1:8; Hebrews 10:27
- everything destroyed by fire, 2 Peter 3:10
- evidence of the Holy Spirit, Acts 2:3

firstborn (FIRST-born) *the oldest child in a family; the firstborn son in a Jewish family received a double share of his father's wealth and became the leader of the family when his father died.*
- Esau sold his rights, Genesis 25:27–34
- Israelites as God's firstborn, Exodus 4:22; Jeremiah 31:9
- death of, Exodus 11:1–8
- given to God, Exodus 13:1–16

firstfruits (FIRST-fruits) *the first and best crops and animals the Israelites raised and gave to God at harvest time,* Exodus 34:26; Numbers 28:26; Deuteronomy 18:3–4

fish
- clean and unclean, Deuteronomy 14:9–10
- used in miracles, Matthew 14:17; Luke 5:1–7; John 21:1–13

flax (FLAKS) *a plant used to make clothing and ropes,* Exodus 9:31; Isaiah 19:9
- used by Rahab, Joshua 2:6

flood, Genesis 6:9—8:22; Matthew 24:37–39; 2 Peter 3:5–6

follower (FAHL-o-wer) *a person who is learning from someone else; a "disciple."*
- of John, Matthew 9:14; 11:2; Mark 2:18
- of Christ, Matthew 11:1; 28:18–20; John 19:38; Acts 6:1–7; 11:26

folly, See "fool."

fool, *someone who is not wise,* Proverbs 10:8–23; 17:7–28; 26:1–12
- examples of, Matthew 7:24–27; 25:1–13
- rejects God, Psalms 14:1; 53:1; Romans 1:20–23

footwashing, *done as an act of hospitality in Bible times because people wore sandals.*
- examples of, 1 Samuel 25:41; Luke 7:44; John 13:1–17

foreigner (alien)
- believers in this world, 1 Peter 2:11; Hebrews 11:13
- being unfair to, Deuteronomy 24:14–17

forever
- God's love continues forever, 1 Chronicles 16:34; Psalm 136
- praise God forever, Psalm 44:8; Romans 9:5
- be with God forever, 1 Thessalonians 4:17; 1 John 2:17
- Jesus lives forever, Hebrews 7:24
- "word of the Lord will live forever," 1 Peter 1:25

forgiveness
- of others, Matthew 6:14–15; 18:21–35; Mark 11:25; Luke 17:3–4
- by God, Luke 24:47–48; Acts 10:43; Ephesians 1:7; 1 John 1:9
- not given, Matthew 12:31–32; Mark 3:28–29; Luke 12:10; John 20:19–23
- "Father, forgive them," Luke 23:34

fornication (for-ni-KAY-shun) *having sexual relations with someone to whom you are not married.* See "adultery."

fountain, Proverbs 10:11; 13:14; 14:27; 16:22

frankincense (FRANK-in-senz) *a very expensive, sweet-smelling perfume,* Exodus 30:34; Revelation 18:13
- given to Jesus, Matthew 2:11

freedom, *having liberty; not being a slave.*
- in Christ, 2 Corinthians 3:17; Galatians 5:1; Hebrews 2:15
- from sin, Romans 6; 8:2; Hebrews 9:15
- to be used wisely, 1 Corinthians 8:9; Galatians 5:13; 1 Peter 2:16
- "truth will make you free," John 8:32

friend
- characteristics of, Proverbs 17:17; 18:24
- of Jesus, John 15:13–15
- Abraham, as a friend of God, James 2:23

frontlet, See "box of Scriptures."

fruit, *often used to mean "result."*
- spiritual, Matthew 7:15–20; John 15:1–17; Colossians 1:10
- of the Spirit, Galatians 5:22

fulfill (full-FILL) *to give the full meaning or to cause something to come true.*
- prophecy fulfilled, Matthew 2:14–15, 17–18; Luke 4:16–21; 24:44–46; John 19:24

furnace
- Shadrach, Meshach, and Abednego thrown into, Daniel 3
- hell compared to, Matthew 13:42

G

Gabriel (GAY-bree-el) *an angel of God.*
- seen in a vision, Daniel 8:16; 9:21–27
- announced Jesus' birth, Luke 1:8–20, 26–38

Gad, a prophet
- David's seer, 1 Samuel 22:5; 2 Samuel 24:11–19

Gad, son of Jacob
- birth of, Genesis 30:9–11
- land of, Deuteronomy 33:20–21; Joshua 22:1–4
- tribe of, Numbers 26:15

Gadarenes (gad-uh-REENZ) *people who lived in Gadara, southeast of Lake Galilee,* Matthew 8:28–34

Galatia (guh-LAY-shuh) *a district of Asia,* Acts 16:6; 18:23; Galatians 1:2; 1 Corinthians 16:1

Galilee (GAL-i-lee) *the country between the Jordan River and the Mediterranean Sea,* 2 Kings 15:29; Matthew 4:23; 21:11; John 7:1

Galilee, Lake (GAL-i-lee) *or "Sea of Galilee," "Sea of Kinnereth," "Lake of Gennesaret," "Sea of Tiberias"; a lake thirteen miles long and eight miles wide.*
- Jesus preached there, Matthew 4:12–22; 8:23–27; John 6:1–2, 16–21

Gallio (GAL-ee-oh) *a Roman governor in the country of Achaia.*
- refused to punish Paul, Acts 18:12–17

Gamaliel (guh-MAY-lee-el) *a Pharisee and Jewish teacher of the Law of Moses.*
- prevented deaths of Peter and John, Acts 5:17–40
- Paul's teacher, Acts 22:1–3

gate
- Samson removed, Judges 16:3
- narrow, Matthew 7:13–14
- of heaven, Revelation 21:21

Gath, *one of the Philistines' five strong cities,* Joshua 13:3; 1 Samuel 21:10–12
- captured Ark taken there, 1 Samuel 5:1–10
- home of Goliath, 1 Samuel 17:4

Gaza (GAY-zuh) *one of the Philistines' five strong cities,* Joshua 13:3; Acts 8:26
- Samson in prison there, Judges 16

gazelle (gah-ZEL) *an animal of the antelope family; known for its beauty and speed,* Deuteronomy 12:15; 1 Chronicles 12:8

Gedaliah (ged-uh-LYE-uh) *made governor of Judah by Nebuchadnezzar after capturing Jerusalem,* 2 Kings 25:22–26; Jeremiah 39:14—41:18

Gehazi (geh-HAY-zye) *a servant of the prophet Elisha.*
- and the Shunammite woman, 2 Kings 4:8–37
- and Naaman, 2 Kings 5:1–27

Gehenna, See "Hinnom, Valley of."

genealogy (jee-nee-AHL-o-jee) *a list of the descendants in a family.*
- of Jesus, Matthew 1:1–17; Luke 3:23–38

generosity (jen-uh-RAHS-et-ee) *unselfishness.*
- shown to Ruth, Ruth 2:14–16
- to the needy, Nehemiah 8:10
- rewarded, Proverbs 11:25; Matthew 7:11

Gennesaret, Lake of, See "Galilee, Lake."

Gentiles (JEN-tiles) *anyone not Jewish.*
- received the Good News, Acts 10:44–45; 11:18; Romans 11:11–15; Ephesians 3:6–8
- conflict with the Jews, Acts 15:5–11; Galatians 2:11–14

Gerasenes (GER-uh-seenz) *or "Gadarenes."* See "Gadarenes."

Gerizim (GER-i-zim) *a mountain next to Mount Ebal about thirty miles north of Jerusalem.*
- blessings announced from there, Deuteronomy 11:29; 27:12; Joshua 8:33

Gethsemane (geth-SEM-uh-nee) *a garden of olive trees just outside Jerusalem.*
- Jesus arrested there, Matthew 26:36–56; Mark 14:32–50

Gibeah (GIB-ee-uh) *a city about three miles north of Jerusalem,* Judges 19:12—20:43; 1 Samuel 10:26

Gibeon (GIB-ee-uhn) *a town about six miles northwest of Jerusalem.*
- Joshua defeated Amorites there, Joshua 9—10

Gideon (GID-ee-uhn) *the judge who led Israel to defeat the Midianites,* Judges 6:1—8:35
- angel appeared to, Judges 6:11–24
- destroyed Baal idol, Judges 6:25–32
- defeated Midianites, Judges 6:33—8:21
- the sign of the fleece, Judges 6:36–40
- built an idol, Judges 8:22–27
- death of, Judges 8:28–32
- hero of faith, Hebrews 11:32–34

gifts, *talents or abilities.*
- spiritual, Romans 12:6–8; 1 Corinthians 7:7; 12; 14:1–25; Ephesians 4:7

Gihon (GYE-hohn) *a spring outside the walls of Jerusalem,* 1 Kings 1:38–39; 2 Chronicles 32:30; 33:14

Gilead (GIL-ee-ad) *the area that Israel owned east of the Jordan River,* Numbers 32; Deuteronomy 3:10–16

Gilgal (GIL-gal) *the first place the Israelites camped after entering the Promised Land,* Joshua 4:19—5:12

gittith (GIT-tith) *probably a musical word and a musical instrument,* Psalms 8; 81; 84

giving
- examples of generous giving, Mark 12:43; Acts 10:2; 11:29–30; 2 Corinthians 8:3–5
- proper attitude toward, Matthew 6:3–4; Romans 12:8; 1 Corinthians 13:3; 2 Corinthians 9:7

gleaning (GLEEN-ing) *to gather grain left in the field after harvest,* Ruth 2

glory, *visible sign of God's greatness.*
- appeared in a cloud, Exodus 16:10; 24:16–17
- seen by Moses, Exodus 33:18–23
- "The heavens tell the glory of God," Psalm 19:1
- seen by Ezekiel, Ezekiel 1:26–28; 3:23; 8:4
- at Jesus' birth, Luke 2:8–14
- of Jesus, Luke 9:28–32
- seen by Stephen, Acts 7:55
- in the temple in heaven, Revelation 15:8

gluttony (GLUH-tun-ee) *eating too much.*
- warnings against, Deuteronomy 21:20; Proverbs 23:20–21
- Jesus accused of, Matthew 11:19; Luke 7:34

goat
- for a sin offering, Leviticus 9:3
- divided from sheep, Matthew 25:32–33
- blood of, Hebrews 9:12–13; 10:4

God, *the One who made the world and everything in it.* See also "glory."
- the creator, Genesis 1; Acts 17:24; Romans 1:25
- nearness of, Acts 17:27–28; James 4:8
- goodness of, Matthew 19:17; Acts 14:17; Romans 2:4; 1 John 4:7–11
- eternal nature of, Psalm 102:24–28; 1 Timothy 1:17; 6:16
- images of, Exodus 33:18–23; 2 Samuel 22:7–20; Psalm 50:1–7
- names of, Exodus 3:13–14; 6:23; 1 Timothy 6:15; Hebrews 12:9; James 1:17; 5:4
- power of, Job 9:4–19; Isaiah 40:12–31; Matthew 19:26
- presence of, John 1:14; 4:21–24
- mercy of, Exodus 20:6; Numbers 14:18; Ephesians 2:4
- justice of, Psalm 67:4; Acts 17:31; Romans 2:2
- will of, Matthew 6:10; Colossians 1:9–14; Proverbs 3:5–7

golden calf, *an idol made to worship false gods.*
- made by Aaron, Exodus 32:1–24
- made by Jeroboam, 1 Kings 12:26–33

golden rule, *a name often used for Jesus' command: "Do to others what you want them to do to you,"* Matthew 7:12; Luke 6:31

Golgotha (GOL-guh-thuh) *Calvary; the hill where Jesus was crucified,* Matthew 27:33; Mark 15:22; John 19:17

Goliath (go-LYE-eth) *the giant from Gath whom David killed,* 1 Samuel 17

Gomorrah (goh-MOR-ruh) *an evil city near Sodom.*
- destroyed by God, Genesis 18:17—19:29; Matthew 10:11–15; 2 Peter 2:6

Good News, *also called the "gospel." Jesus died on the cross, was buried, and came back to life so people can be saved.* Mark 1:1; Acts 5:42; 13:26–39
- power of, Romans 1:16–17; Colossians 1:5–6; 1 Corinthians 15:2
- preached by the apostles, Luke 9:6; Acts 8:25; Philippians 1:5, 12–14

good works
- made by God to do, Ephesians 2:8–10
- faith without action, James 2:14–26
- blessing comes from faith, Galatians 3

Goshen (GO-shen) *an area in the Nile delta of Egypt.*
- home for Joseph's family, Genesis 45:9–10; 47:1–6, 27

gospel (GOS-p'l) *"good news." The first four books of the New Testament are called the Gospels because they tell the good news of what Jesus has done for us.* See "Good News."

gossip
- to be avoided, Romans 1:28–32; 2 Corinthians 12:20; 1 Timothy 5:13

government (GUV-er-ment) *group of people in charge of managing and making laws for people in a country, state, or city.*
- to be obeyed, Matthew 22:15–21; Romans 13:1–7; Titus 3:1; 1 Peter 2:13–17

governor
- Joseph, governor of Egypt, Genesis 42:6
- Nehemiah, governor of Judah, Nehemiah 5:14
- Pilate, governor of Judea, Matthew 27:2
- Felix, governor of Judea, Acts 23:26

grace, *God's kindness and love shown to us, even though we do not deserve them.*
- source of, Ephesians 3:7; Hebrews 4:14–16
- saved by, Acts 15:11; Romans 3:24; Ephesians 2:5–8; 2 Timothy 1:9
- misuse of, Romans 6; Galatians 5:4; Jude 4

grandchildren
- a blessing, Ruth 4:15; Proverbs 17:6
- inherit grandparents' wealth, Proverbs 13:22

grave, See "tomb."

Great Sea, See "Mediterranean Sea."

Greece, *once the most powerful nation in southeast Europe. Northern Greece was called "Macedonia." Southern Greece was called "Achaia."*
- Paul preached there, Acts 16:11–12; 20:1–6

greed, *selfish desire for more than one's share of something.*
- never satisfied, Proverbs 27:20
- beware of, Luke 12:15
- love of money, 1 Timothy 6:10

Greek
- the language of Greece, John 19:20; Acts 21:37; Revelation 9:11
- the people from Greece, Acts 14:1; 16:1; Colossians 3:11

grief
- of David for Absalom, 2 Samuel 18:33
- of the followers, Matthew 17:23; John 16:6

growing old
- Moses' humility, Exodus 4
- respect for the aging, Leviticus 19:32

guidance (GYD-ns) *direction.*
- by God, Exodus 13:21
- of the humble, Psalm 25:9
- of the Holy Spirit, John 16:15

guilt, *fact of having done wrong; regret, shame.*
- for improper worship, 1 Corinthians 11:27
- for breaking the Law, James 2:10
- cleansed of, Job 33:9; Isaiah 6:7; Hebrews 10:22

H

Habakkuk (ha-BAK-uk) *a prophet who wrote about the same time as Jeremiah,* Habakkuk 1—3

Hades (HAY-deez) *the world of the dead,* Revelation 6:8; 20:13–14

Hagar (HAY-gar) *Sarah's slave girl.*
- gave birth to Ishmael, Genesis 16
- sent away by Sarah, Genesis 21:8–21

Haggai (HAG-ay-eye) *a prophet in Jerusalem when the Israelites came back from Babylon,* Ezra 5:1; 6:14; Haggai 1—2

half-tribe, *one of the two parts of the tribe of Manasseh. One half-tribe settled east of the Jordan and the other settled west of the Jordan.* Joshua 1:12–15; 13:8–9; 22

Ham, *the son of Noah,* Genesis 6:10; 9:18–19; 10:6

Haman (HAY-man) *the chief officer under Ahasuerus, king of Persia.*
- planned to kill the Jews, Esther 3—6
- hanged, Esther 7

handicap, physical
- blind man healed, John 9
- care for the handicapped, Leviticus 19:14

hands, laying on, *a ceremony where a person places his hands upon another.*
- for healing, Mark 5:23; 6:5; Luke 4:40
- to receive the Holy Spirit, Acts 8:17–19; 19:6
- for blessing, Mark 10:16; Acts 13:3

Hannah (HAN-uh) *the mother of Samuel,* 1 Samuel 1:1—2:21

happiness
- of the people of God, Psalms 144:15; 146:5; Proverbs 16:20; Matthew 5:3–12
- comes from wisdom, Proverbs 3:13

Haran (HAY-ran)
- Abraham's brother, Genesis 11:26–31
- home of Abraham, Genesis 11:31—12:5

harlot, See "prostitute."

harp, *the favorite musical instrument of the Jews.*
- first played, Genesis 4:21
- played by David, 1 Samuel 16:23; 18:10–11
- to praise God, Psalms 33:2; 71:22; 150:3

harvest
- of the poor, Ruth 2
- as a symbol, Matthew 9:37–38; 13:24–30, 39; Revelation 14:14–16

hate
- seven things God hates, Proverbs 6:16–19
- a time to, Ecclesiastes 3:8
- of the world toward Jesus, John 15:18
- equal to murder, 1 John 3:15
- commands against, Galatians 5:19–21; 1 John 4:19–21

head
- a part of the body, Genesis 3:15; Psalm 23:5; Matthew 8:20; 1 Corinthians 12:21; Revelation 14:14
- a leader, Ephesians 1:22; 5:23; Colossians 1:18

heal
- a time to, Ecclesiastes 3:3
- by faith, Matthew 9:21–22; James 5:15
- "Doctor, heal yourself." Luke 4:23

heart, *the mind or feelings; not the physical heart that pumps blood,* Deuteronomy 6:5; Matthew 22:37

heaven
- the home of God, Matthew 5:34; Mark 16:19; John 3:13; Revelation 4
- angel spoke from, Genesis 21:17; 22:11
- opened, Matthew 3:16; Acts 7:56; 10:11
- fire from, 2 Kings 1:10–14; 1 Chronicles 21:26
- third heaven, 2 Corinthians 12:2
- the new heaven, Revelation 21:1–4
- kingdom of, Matthew 3:2; 5:3, 19–20

Hebrews (HEE-brooz) *another name for the Jewish people,* Exodus 7:16; 2 Corinthians 11:22; Philippians 3:5

Hebron (HEE-bron) *a city about twenty miles southwest of Jerusalem,* Genesis 13:18; Numbers 13:22; 2 Samuel 2:1–11

heir (AIR) *the person who inherits what belongs to a relative. Because through Christ we can be*

adopted children of God, Christians are heirs to God's riches.
- Abraham's heir, Genesis 15:3–4
- heir of God, Romans 8:17; Galatians 4:7

hell
- home of the devil and his angels, 2 Peter 2:4
- future home of sinners, Matthew 10:28; 23:33; Revelation 21:8
- descriptions of, Matthew 13:42; Mark 9:47–48; James 3:6; Revelation 14:11

helmet
- worn in battle, 1 Samuel 17:5; Ezekiel 23:24
- a symbol of salvation, Isaiah 59:17; Ephesians 6:17; 1 Thessalonians 5:8

help
- the stone of help, 1 Samuel 7:12
- the Holy Spirit as helper, Romans 8:26; Philippians 1:19
- from God, Psalms 46:1; 121:1–2; Isaiah 41:10
- commanded, 1 Thessalonians 5:14; Hebrews 6:10

Herod I (HEH-rud) *"Herod the Great"; king of Palestine from 40 to 4 B.C.*, Matthew 2:1; Luke 1:5

Herod Agrippa I (uh-GRIP-a) *king of Palestine from A.D. 41 to 44*, Acts 12:1

Herod Agrippa II, *king of Palestine from A.D. 52 to 70*, Acts 25:13—26:32

Herod Antipas (AN-ti-pus) *king of Palestine from 4 B.C. to about A.D. 39*, Matthew 14:1; Mark 6:14; Luke 23:7

Herodias (heh-ROW-dee-us) *the granddaughter of Herod I.*
- asked for John's head, Matthew 14:3–12; Mark 6:17–28; Luke 3:19

Hezekiah (hez-eh-KY-uh) *one of the good kings of Judah.*
- destroyed idols, 2 Kings 18:1–8; 2 Chronicles 29—31
- attacked by Assyria, 2 Kings 18:9—19:37; 2 Chronicles 32:1–23; Isaiah 36—37
- life extended by God, 2 Kings 20:1–11; Isaiah 38
- death of, 2 Kings 20:12–21; 2 Chronicles 32:24–33

higgaion (hig-GI-on) *probably a time to think quietly during a song*, Psalm 9:16

high place, *a place to worship gods*, 1 Kings 14:23; 2 Chronicles 31:1; 33:3

high priest, *the most important religious leader of the Jewish people.*
- rules for, Leviticus 21:10–15
- of the Jews, Exodus 29:30; Numbers 35:25; Matthew 26:3; Acts 23:2
- Jesus as, Hebrews 2:17; 3:1; 4:14—5:10; 8:1–6

Hilkiah (hil-KY-ah) *high priest when Josiah was king*, 2 Kings 22—23; 2 Chronicles 34

Hinnom, Valley of (HIN-num) *an area where trash was burned just outside of Jerusalem; also called "Gehenna,"* Joshua 15:8; 18:16; Nehemiah 11:30

Hiram (HY-rum) *king of Tyre when David and Solomon were kings over Israel.*
- supplied trees for Solomon's Temple, 2 Samuel 5:11; 1 Kings 5:1–18; 9:11–27; 10:22

Hittites (HIT-tites) *people who lived in what is now Turkey*, Genesis 23:1–16; Exodus 3:8; Joshua 1:4; 1 Samuel 11:3

holy (HO-lee) *pure, belonging to and willing to serve God.*
- holiness of God, Leviticus 11:45; Isaiah 6:3; Hebrews 12:10; Revelation 4:8
- holy kiss, Romans 16:16
- people to be holy, Ephesians 1:4; Colossians 1:22–23; 3:2; 1 Peter 1:15–16

Holy of Holies, See "Most Holy Place."

Holy Place, *a room in the Holy Tent and the Temple*, Exodus 26:31–35; 28:29; Leviticus 6:30; 1 Kings 8:10–11

Holy Spirit (HO-lee SPIH-rit) *one of the three persons of God. The Holy Spirit helped the apostles do miracles and led men to write God's word; he lives in Christians today.*
- in creation, Genesis 1:2
- living in Christians, John 14:15–17; 1 Corinthians 6:19; Galatians 4:6
- as a helper, John 14:25–26; 16:7–15; Romans 8:1–27; Galatians 5:22–25
- filled with, Luke 1:15; Acts 2:4; 7:55; 11:23–24
- sin against, Matthew 12:31; Acts 5:3; 1 Thessalonians 5:19; Hebrews 10:29

Holy Tent, See "Meeting Tent."

Holy War & Divine Warrior
- God as a warrior, Exodus 15:3
- laws for war, Deuteronomy 20
- spiritual battles, 2 Corinthians 10:3–6

home, See "house."

homosexuality
- Paul condemns, Romans 1:26–27
- "a hateful sin," Leviticus 18:22
- Sodom and Gomorrah, Genesis 19:1–29

honest
- heart, Luke 8:15
- people, 2 Kings 12:15
- answer, Proverbs 24:26
- commanded, Mark 10:19; Philippians 4:8

honor
- for the old, Leviticus 19:32
- from God, 1 Samuel 2:30
- comes from humility, Proverbs 15:33
- to the deserving, Romans 13:7

- shown to parents, Exodus 20:12; Matthew 15:4
- shown to God, Proverbs 3:9; John 5:23; Revelation 4:9
- not shown to a prophet in his own town, Matthew 13:57

hope, *looking forward to something you really expect to happen.*
- reason for, Romans 5:3–5; 15:4; 2 Thessalonians 2:16; 1 Peter 1:13
- nature of, Romans 8:24–25
- results of, Colossians 1:5; Hebrews 6:18

Hophni (HOF-nee) *an evil son of Eli the priest,* 1 Samuel 2:12–34; 3:11—4:18

Horeb, Mount, See "Sinai."

horses, Exodus 14:9; 1 Kings 10:26–29; Psalm 33:16–17; James 3:3

Hosanna (ho-ZAN-ah) *a shout of joy in praising God,* Matthew 21:9, 15; Mark 11:9; John 12:13

Hosea (ho-SEE-uh) *a prophet who lived about seven hundred years before Christ.*
- his unfaithful wife, Hosea 1
- his warnings to Israel, Hosea 2; 4—14

hospitality
- of Abraham, Genesis 18:1–16
- teachings about, Romans 12:13; 1 Timothy 3:2; 5:9–10; 1 Peter 4:9

hosts, *armies; God is called the "Lord of hosts."* See "Lord of hosts."

house/home
- Abram moves, Genesis 12:1
- parable of foundations, Matthew 7:24–27
- Christians as household items, 2 Timothy 2:20–21

Huldah (HUL-duh) *a woman prophet,* 2 Kings 22:14–20; 2 Chronicles 34:22–28

human
- created in God's image, Genesis 1:26–28
- "whom God made like himself," James 3:9–10

humble (HUM-bul) *not bragging or calling attention to yourself.*
- Moses as example of, Numbers 12:3
- humility commanded, Luke 14:7–11; 22:24–27; Ephesians 4:2; Philippians 2:3
- Jesus' humility, Philippians 2:5–8

hunger
- feeding the hungry, Matthew 25:34–35; Romans 12:20
- spiritual, John 6:35; 1 Peter 2:2

husband
- responsibilities of, 1 Corinthians 7:3–5; Ephesians 5:25–33; Colossians 3:19; 1 Peter 3:7

hymn (HIM) *a song that teaches us about God or praises him,* Matthew 26:30; Ephesians 5:19; Colossians 3:16
- Jesus and apostles sang, Matthew 26:30; Mark 14:26
- teachings about, Ephesians 5:19; Colossians 3:16

hypocrisy (hi-POK-ri-see) *acting as if one is good when that is not true,* Matthew 23:28; 1 Peter 2:1

hypocrite (HIP-oh-krit) *a person who acts as if he is good but isn't.*
- warnings about, Matthew 6:2, 5, 16; 7:3–5; Luke 13:15–17
- Pharisees as hypocrites, Matthew 15:1–9; 23:13–32

hyssop (HIS-op) *a small bushy plant; marjoram,* Exodus 12:22; Leviticus 14:4, 6; John 19:29

I

Iconium (eye-KOH-nee-um) *a city in Galatia where Paul preached,* Acts 14:1–7, 19–23

idol (EYE-d'l) *a statue of a false god.* See also "Baal," "Chemosh," "Molech."
- worship of, 2 Kings 17:12–17; Acts 17:16–23; 19:24; Romans 1:25
- warnings against worship of, Leviticus 19:4; Deuteronomy 6:14–15; 1 Corinthians 5:10–11; 6:9–10
- Baal, 1 Kings 18:17–40
- Chemosh, Numbers 21:29
- Molech, Jeremiah 32:35

ignorance (IG-nur-rance) *a lack of knowledge.*
- not an excuse, Leviticus 5:17

image, *likeness.*
- God's, Genesis 1:26–27
- Caesar's, Luke 20:24
- the Lord's, 2 Corinthians 3:18
- Jesus in God's image, Hebrews 1:3

immorality (IM-mor-RAL-i-tee) *evil; sinfulness.* See also "sin."
- warnings against, 1 Corinthians 5:9–11; 6:9–10; Galatians 5:19–21; Ephesians 5:5

immortality (IM-mor-TAL-i-tee) *life after death,* Job 14:1–14; Daniel 12:1–2; 1 Corinthians 15:12–58; 2 Timothy 1:10. See also "eternal life."

impossible
- people cannot do, Matthew 19:26
- for God to lie, Hebrews 6:18
- without faith to please God, Hebrews 11:6

incarnation
- "the Word became human," John 1:14
- became like a servant, Philippians 2:7
- "exactly like God," 2 Corinthians 4:4

incense (IN-sents) *a spice burned to make a sweet smell.*
- altar of, Exodus 30:1–10, 34–38; Revelation 8:3–5
- used in worship, Psalm 141:2
- as a gift, Matthew 2:11

infertility (childlessness/barrenness)
- Elizabeth was childless, Luke 1:7
- Hannah desires a child, 1 Samuel 1:11

inheritance (in-HEH-ri-tence) *something valuable that is handed down within a family.* See "land."
- of land, Numbers 36:8; Deuteronomy 3:28; Psalm 25:13

iniquity, See "sin."

inn, *a place for travelers to spend the night,* Luke 2:7; 10:34

innocence (IN-uh-sens) *not guilty of sin.*
- of Adam and Eve, Genesis 2:25
- declared by Job, Job 34:5
- declared by Pilate, Matthew 27:24

inspiration (IN-spi-RAY-shun) *"God-breathed." It is used to mean that the Bible writers wrote what God wanted them to write.* 2 Timothy 3:16; 2 Peter 1:20–21

instruction
- to Israel, Deuteronomy 6:4–9
- for children, Proverbs 22:6
- "become teachers," James 3:1

integrity
- of Job, Job 2:1–10
- guides good people, Proverbs 11:3
- of Joseph, Genesis 39:7–23

intercession
- for Jesus' followers, John 17; Romans 8:34
- Jeremiah prays for Judah, Jeremiah 42:1–6

Isaac (EYE-zak) *the son of Abraham and Sarah.*
- birth of, Genesis 21:1–4
- offered as a sacrifice, Genesis 22:1–19
- married Rebekah, Genesis 24
- tricked by Jacob, Genesis 27
- hero of faith, Hebrews 11:20

Isaiah (eye-ZAY-uh) *prophet who lived about seven hundred years before Christ.*
- became a prophet, Isaiah 6:1–8
- prophesied to Hezekiah, 2 Kings 19—20
- prophecies fulfilled, Matthew 3:3; 4:14; 13:14–15

Ish-Bosheth (ish-BOW-sheth) *son of Saul,* 2 Samuel 2:8—4:12

Ishmael (ISH-may-el) *son of Abraham and Hagar.*
- birth of, Genesis 16:2–16
- sent away from Abraham's camp, Genesis 21:8–21

Israel, kingdom of (IZ-rah-el) *the northern kingdom which had ten tribes.*
- beginning of, 1 Kings 11:27—12:33
- fall of, 2 Kings 17:1–18
- rulers of, 1 Kings 15:25—16:34; 22:51–53; 2 Kings 13; 14:23—17:6

Israel, son of Isaac, *Hebrew for "he who wrestles with God." Jacob's name was changed to Israel when he struggled with an angel at Bethel.* Genesis 32:22–28; 35:9–10. See also "Jacob."
- name given to Jacob's descendants, Genesis 49:28; Exodus 4:22; Psalm 22:23; Romans 9:3–5

Issachar (IS-uh-car) *a son of Jacob and Leah,* Genesis 30:18
- his descendants, Numbers 1:28–29; 26:23

ivory (EYE-voh-ree) *a creamy white bone that comes from elephant tusks,* 1 Kings 10:18; 22:39; Psalm 45:8; Ezekiel 27:15

J

Jabbok River (JAB-ok) *a stream about fifty miles long that runs into the Jordan River,* Numbers 21:24; Joshua 12:2; Judges 11:13

Jabesh Gilead (JAY-besh GIL-ee-ad) *a small town on the east side of the Jordan River,* Judges 21:6–14; 2 Samuel 2:4–7

Jabin, king of Hazor (JAY-bin) *led a group of kings against the Israelites,* Joshua 11:1–11

Jabin, king of Canaan, *defeated by Israel when Deborah was judge,* Judges 4

Jacob (JAY-cub) *one of the sons of Isaac.*
- cheated Esau, Genesis 25:29–34
- tricked Isaac, Genesis 27:1–29
- his dream of a ladder to heaven, Genesis 28:10–22
- tricked by his sons, Genesis 37:12–36
- moved to Egypt, Genesis 45:25—47:12
- hero of faith, Hebrews 11:20–21

Jacob's Portion (JAY-cubs POR-shun) *a name for God, meaning he cares for Jacob's people,* Jeremiah 10:16; 51:19

jailer, *a keeper of a jail.*
- of Paul and Silas, Acts 16:23

Jairus (jay-EYE-rus) *a ruler of the synagogue.*
- Jesus brought his daughter back to life, Matthew 9:18–26; Mark 5:21–43; Luke 8:40–56

James, brother of Jesus, Matthew 13:55; Acts 12:17; 21:18
- later an apostle, Galatians 1:19

James, son of Alphaeus, *an apostle,* Matthew 10:3; Mark 3:18; Luke 6:15; Acts 1:13

James, son of Zebedee, *an apostle of Jesus and a brother of the apostle John,* Matthew 10:2; Mark 10:35; Acts 12:2

Japheth (JAY-fith) *one of Noah's three sons,* Genesis 5:32; 7:13; 9:18–27; 10:1–5

Jashar, Book of, *a book mentioned in the Bible, but not part of it,* Joshua 10:12–13; 2 Samuel 1:17–27

Jason (JAY-son) *a Christian in Thessalonica,* Acts 17:5–9

jealousy
- to describe God, Exodus 20:5; 34:14; Deuteronomy 5:9
- examples of, Genesis 37:11; 1 Samuel 18:19; Matthew 27:18; Acts 5:17
- warnings against, Romans 13:13; 1 Corinthians 13:4; 1 Timothy 6:4; 1 Peter 2:1

Jebusites (JEB-you-sites) *people who lived around Jerusalem before the time of David,* Joshua 15:63; Judges 19:10–11; 2 Samuel 4:6–8

Jehoahaz, son of Jehu (jeh-HO-uh-haz) *king of Israel who lived about eight hundred years before Christ,* 2 Kings 13:1–9

Jehoahaz, son of Josiah, *king of Judah for only three months,* 2 Kings 23:31–34; 2 Chronicles 36:1–4

Jehoash (jeh-HO-ash) *a king of Israel,* 2 Kings 13:10—14:16

Jehoiachin (jeh-HO-uh-kin) *the next-to-last king of Judah.*
- surrendered to Babylon, 2 Kings 24:8–17
- in Babylon, 2 Kings 25:27–30

Jehoiada (jeh-HO-yah-duh) *the chief priest in Jerusalem during Joash's rule,* 2 Kings 11—12; 2 Chronicles 22:11–24

Jehoiakim (jeh-HO-uh-kim) *king of Judah about 600 B.C.,* 2 Kings 23:34—24:6
- tried to kill Jeremiah, Jeremiah 26:1–23
- burned Jeremiah's scroll, Jeremiah 36:1–23

Jehoram (jeh-HOR-am) *or "Joram"; the fifth king of Judah,* 2 Kings 8:16–29; 2 Chronicles 21:4–20

Jehoshaphat (jeh-HOSH-uh-fat) *one of the good kings of Judah.*
- faithful to God, 2 Chronicles 17:1–9
- appointed judges, 2 Chronicles 19:4–11
- defeated Moab and Ammon, 2 Chronicles 20

Jehovah (jeh-HOVE-uh) *a name for God; also translated "LORD,"* Exodus 3:15; 6:3; Deuteronomy 28:58; Psalm 83:18

Jehu (JEE-hew) *an army captain who became king of Israel.*
- appointed as king, 2 Kings 9:1–13
- killed Joram and Ahaziah, 2 Kings 9:14–29
- stopped Baal worship, 2 Kings 10:18–35

Jephthah (JEF-thuh) *one of the judges of Israel.*
- fought the Ammonites, Judges 11:1–29, 32–33
- his vow, Judges 11:30–31, 34–39
- fought the people of Ephraim, Judges 12:2–7

Jeremiah (jer-eh-MY-ah) *a prophet who warned the people of Judah,* Jeremiah 1—52
- became a prophet, Jeremiah 1:1–10
- songs of, 2 Chronicles 35:25
- his prophecies fulfilled, 2 Chronicles 36:21–22; Matthew 2:17; 27:9
- wrote a scroll, Jeremiah 36

Jericho (JEHR-ih-ko) *probably the oldest city in the world,* Mark 10:46; Luke 10:30; 19:1
- fall of, Joshua 2—6
- rebuilt, 1 Kings 16:34

Jeroboam, son of Jehoash (jeh-ro-BO-am) *a king of Israel,* 2 Kings 14:23–29; Amos 7:7–17

Jeroboam, son of Nebat, *first ruler of the northern kingdom of Israel.*
- given ten tribes by God, 1 Kings 11:26–40
- built idols, 1 Kings 12:26–33
- warned by God, 1 Kings 13:1–34
- death of his son, 1 Kings 14:1–20

Jerusalem (jeh-ROO-suh-lem) *"Zion" or "City of David"; the greatest city of Palestine.*
- the City of David, 2 Samuel 5:6–7
- captured by Babylonians, 2 Chronicles 36:15–23
- Jews returned to, Ezra 1—2
- the new Jerusalem, Galatians 4:26; Hebrews 12:22; Revelation 3:12; 21—22

Jesse (JEH-see) *father of King David,* 1 Samuel 16—17; 1 Chronicles 2:13–15; Luke 3:32; Romans 15:12

Jesus (JEE-zus) *"Savior"; the son of God.* See also "Christ," "Son of David," "Son of Man."
- birth and childhood of, Matthew 1—2; Luke 1—2
- temptation of, Matthew 4:1–11; Mark 1:12–13; Luke 4:1–13
- miracles of, Matthew 8—9; Mark 6:30–56; Luke 17:11; 22:50–51; John 2:1; 11
- appeared with Moses and Elijah, Matthew 17:1–13; Mark 9:2–13; Luke 9:28–36
- forced men from the Temple, Matthew 21:12–13; John 2:13–17
- the Last Supper, Matthew 26:17–30; Luke 22:1–20; John 13
- trial and death of, Matthew 26:57—27:66; Mark 15; Luke 22:66—23:56; John 18—19
- appearances after resurrection, Matthew 28; Mark 16; Luke 24; John 20—21; 1 Corinthians 15:5–8
- Son of God, Matthew 3:16–17; 26:63–64; John 1:14

Jethro (JETH-row) *father of Moses' wife,* Exodus 2:16–21
- advised Moses, Exodus 18

Jews (JOOZ) *first, the tribe of Judah; later, any of the twelve tribes,* Ezra 4:12; Esther 3—10; Acts 2:5
- against Jesus, John 5:16–18; 7:1, 32–36; 10:25–42
- Jesus, king of, Matthew 2:2; 27:11–14, 29; John 19:17–22

- and non-Jewish people, 1 Corinthians 12:13; Galatians 3:28; Colossians 3:11

Jezebel (JEZ-eh-bell) *the evil wife of King Ahab.*
- married Ahab, 1 Kings 16:31
- killed the Lord's prophets, 1 Kings 18:4–14
- killed Naboth, 1 Kings 21:1–23
- death of, 2 Kings 9:30–37

Jezreel (JEZ-reel) *the name of a town and a valley near the Jordan River,* Judges 6:33; 1 Kings 21:1; 2 Kings 8:29

Joab (JO-ab) *the commander of King David's army,* 2 Samuel 2:12—3:32; 10—11; 14; 18—20; 24; 1 Kings 1—2

Joanna (jo-ANN-uh) *a woman Jesus healed,* Luke 8:2–3; 23:55—24:11

Joash, Gideon's father (JO-ash)
- protected Gideon, Judges 6:28–32

Joash, son of Ahaziah, *became king of Judah when he was seven,* 2 Kings 11—12; 2 Chronicles 22:10—24:25

Job (JOBE) *a wealthy man who honored God.*
- ruined by Satan, Job 1:1—2:10
- wealth restored, Job 42:7
- example of patience, James 5:11

Joel (JO-el) *a prophet who wrote the Book of Joel,* Joel 1—3; Acts 2:16

Johanan (jo-HAY-nan) *a Jewish army captain,* Jeremiah 40:8—43:7

John, the apostle, *one of the sons of Zebedee.*
- called by Jesus, Mark 1:19–20
- at Jesus' transfiguration, Mark 9:2
- with Jesus in Gethsemane, Mark 14:33–42
- in the early church, Acts 3—4
- writer of Revelation, Revelation 1:1–4, 9

John the Baptist, *Jesus' relative and the son of Elizabeth and Zechariah the priest.*
- birth of, Luke 1:5–25, 57–80
- preached at the Jordan River, Matthew 3:1–12
- baptized Jesus, Matthew 3:13–17
- killed by Herod, Matthew 14:1–12

John Mark, See "Mark."

Jonah (JO-nah) *a prophet whom God told to preach to the city of Nineveh.*
- ran from God, Jonah 1:1–3
- swallowed by a fish, Jonah 1:4—2:10
- went to Nineveh, Jonah 3
- complained to God, Jonah 4
- the sign of, Matthew 12:38–41; 16:4; Luke 11:29–32

Jonathan (JAH-nah-thun) *the oldest son of King Saul.*
- David's friend, 1 Samuel 18:1–4
- saved David's life, 1 Samuel 19:1–7; 20
- death of, 1 Samuel 31:2

Joppa (JOP-uh) *a city on the coast of Palestine,* Jonah 1:3
- Peter preached there, Acts 9:36–42; 10:9–36

Joram (JO-ram) *son of Ahab; also a king of Israel,* 2 Kings 3:1–3; 8:29; 9:14–29

Jordan (JOR-d'n) *the only large river in Palestine.*
- Israelites crossed, Joshua 3
- Jesus baptized in, Matthew 3:13–17; Mark 1:9–11

Jordan Valley, *the valley along the Jordan River,* Deuteronomy 1:1; 3:17; Joshua 11:2

Joseph of Arimathea (JOZ-uf) *took the body of Jesus down from the cross and buried it in a tomb Joseph had dug for himself,* Matthew 27:57–60; Mark 15:42–46; Luke 23:50–54

Joseph of Nazareth, *husband of Mary, Jesus' mother.*
- angel appeared to, Matthew 1:18–24
- went to register in Bethlehem, Luke 2:4–7
- took Jesus to the Temple, Luke 2:21–52

Joseph, son of Jacob, *one of the twelve sons of Israel.*
- sold into slavery, Genesis 37
- put into prison, Genesis 39
- interpreted dreams, Genesis 40—41
- reunited with family, Genesis 42—50

Joshua (JAH-shoo-ah) *leader of the Israelites into the Promised Land.*
- spied out Canaan, Numbers 13
- chosen to replace Moses, Numbers 27:12–23; Deuteronomy 34:9–10
- conquered Canaan, Joshua 1; 3—12
- death of, Joshua 23—24

Josiah (jo-SY-uh) *king of Judah about 640 to 609 B.C.*
- became king, 2 Kings 22:1–2
- the lost laws of God found during his reign, 2 Kings 22:3–20
- gave the law to the people, 2 Kings 23:1–30

Jotham, youngest son of Gideon (JO-tham) Judges 9:1–21, 57

Jotham, son of Uzziah, *a king of Judah,* 2 Kings 15:32–38; 2 Chronicles 27

joy, Psalm 43:4; John 15:11; 17:13; 1 Thessalonians 1:6
- a fruit of the Holy Spirit, Galatians 5:22
- God as the source, Psalms 43:4; 45:7; Romans 15:13
- joy from the Holy Spirit, Luke 10:21; Romans 14:17; Galatians 5:22; 1 Thessalonians 1:6

Jubilee (JOO-bih-lee) *a Jewish celebration that took place once every fifty years. Israelites were to let the soil rest, to free their slaves, and to return land and houses to their first owners or their descendants.* Leviticus 25; 27:17–24; Numbers 36:4

Judah, son of Jacob (JOO-duh) Genesis 29:35
- saved Joseph, Genesis 37:26–27
- deceived by Tamar, Genesis 38
- reunited with Joseph, Genesis 43—44
- tribe of, Numbers 1:26–27; 26:20–22; Joshua 15
- Jesus, a descendant of, Matthew 1:2–3; Luke 3:33–34; Revelation 5:5

Judah, kingdom of, *the southern kingdom when Israel split in two.*
- beginning of, 1 Kings 11:27—12:20
- rulers of, 1 Kings 14:21—15:24; 22:41–50; 2 Kings 8:16–29; 11—12; 14—16; 18—24
- fall of, 2 Kings 24:18—25:22

Judas Iscariot (JOO-dus is-CARE-ee-ut) *apostle who handed Jesus over to be killed.*
- chosen by Jesus, Matthew 10:4; Mark 3:19
- apostles' treasurer, John 12:4–6; 13:27–29
- betrayed Jesus, Matthew 26:14–16, 47–50; Luke 22:1–6; John 6:70–71; 13:2, 21–30
- death of, Matthew 27:3–5

Judas, brother of Jesus, Matthew 13:55; Mark 6:3

Judas, son of James
- an apostle, Luke 6:16; Acts 1:13

Jude (JOOD) *brother of James,* Jude 1

Judea (joo-DEE-uh) *the land of the Jews,* Matthew 2:1; 3:1; Luke 1:5; 3:1; Acts 1:8

judges (JUJ-es) *leaders of Israel prior to the kings,* Judges 2:16–19; 3:7—4:24; 10—12; 1 Samuel 8:1–5

judging
- warnings against, Matthew 7:1–5; 1 Corinthians 4:5; James 4:11–12
- good kinds of judging, 1 Corinthians 5:12; 6:2; 10:15
- God's judging of people, Matthew 11:22; Acts 17:31; 2 Peter 2:9; 3:7

Judgment Day (JUJ-ment) *the day Christ will judge all people,* Matthew 11:20–24; 12:33–37; 2 Peter 2:9–10; 3:7–13

Julius (JOOL-yus) *a Roman soldier in charge of Paul while Paul was taken to Rome,* Acts 27:1–3

justice
- God discusses with Job, Job 40:8
- not found on Earth, Ecclesiastes 5:8
- proof of God's, 2 Thessalonians 1:5–7

justify (JUS-teh-fy) *to make someone right with God,* Romans 3:24; 5:1; Galatians 2:16; Titus 3:7

K

Kadesh/Kadesh Barnea (KAY-desh BAR-nee-uh) *a town in the Desert of Zin,* Numbers 20:1–21; Joshua 10:41

Kenites (KEE-nites) *a tribe of early metal workers,* Genesis 15:19; Judges 1:16; 4:11; 1 Samuel 27:10

Kerethites (KAIR-uh-thites) *King David's bodyguards,* 2 Samuel 8:18; 1 Kings 1:38

Keturah (keh-TOO-ruh) *Abraham's second wife,* Genesis 25:1–4; 1 Chronicles 1:32–33

key, *something that solves or explains.*
- to God's kingdom, Matthew 16:19
- to death, Revelation 1:18

Kidron Valley (KEH-dron) *a valley between Jerusalem and the Mount of Olives,* 2 Samuel 15:23; John 18:1
- idols burned there, 1 Kings 15:13; 2 Kings 23:4

kill
- Cain killed, Genesis 4:10–11
- laws against, Exodus 20:13
- of baby boys, Exodus 1:16; Matthew 2:16
- Jesus killed, Matthew 27:31–50; Mark 15:20–37; Luke 23:25–46; John 19:16–30

kindness
- of God, Exodus 34:6–7; Jeremiah 9:24; Romans 2:4; Ephesians 2:4–7
- commanded, 2 Corinthians 6:6; Ephesians 4:32; Colossians 3:12; 2 Peter 1:5–7

king
- King of kings, 1 Timothy 6:15; Revelation 17:14

kingdom (KING-d'm) *the kingdom of heaven is God ruling in the lives of his people.*
- the nature of, Matthew 5:19–20; 19:14; Luke 17:20–21; Romans 14:17
- parables of, Matthew 13:24–52; 18:23–35; 20:1–16; 25:1–30; Mark 4:30–33; Luke 13:18–21
- belongs to, Matthew 5:3, 10; 19:14

Kiriath Jearim (KEER-yath JEE-ah-rim) *a town in the hills about twelve miles west of Jerusalem,* 1 Samuel 6:20—7:20; 1 Chronicles 13:5–6; 2 Chronicles 1:4

Kish, *father of Saul,* 1 Samuel 9:1–2

Kishon (KY-shon) *the name of a valley and a stream,* Judges 4:13; 5:21; 1 Kings 18:40

kiss, *a greeting of friendship, love, or respect.*
- of Judas, Matthew 26:48–49; Mark 14:44–45; Luke 22:47–48
- holy kiss, Romans 16:16; 1 Corinthians 16:20; 1 Peter 5:14

Kittim (KEH-tim) *the island of Cyprus,* Genesis 10:4; Numbers 24:24; 1 Chronicles 1:7; Isaiah 23:1, 12

kneel
- Solomon kneeled before God, 1 Kings 8:54
- Daniel kneeled before God, Daniel 6:10
- everyone to kneel before Jesus, Philippians 2:10

knock
- "knock, and the door will open," Matthew 7:7
- at the door, Luke 13:25
- Peter knocked, Acts 12:13, 16
- Jesus knocks, Revelation 3:20

knowledge
- tree of, Genesis 2:9, 17
- value of, Proverbs 1:7; 8:10; 18:15; 24:5; 2 Peter 1:5–6
- lack of, Hosea 4:6; Romans 1:28
- limitations of, 1 Corinthians 8:1–2; 13:2, 8–10

Kohath (KO-hath) *a son of Levi,* Exodus 6:16–20; Numbers 3:17–19

Kohathites (KO-hath-ites) *descendants of Kohath.*
- worked in the Holy Tent and Temple, Numbers 3:27–31; 4:1–20; 1 Chronicles 9:17–32

Korah (KO-ruh) *the musician,* Psalms 42; 44—49; 84

Korah, *son of Izhar, rebelled against Moses,* Numbers 16:1–40

L

Laban (LAY-ban) *father of Leah and Rachel.*
- Jacob worked for, Genesis 29:13–30
- divided his flocks with Jacob, Genesis 30:29–43
- chased Jacob, Genesis 31:19–55

Lachish (LAY-kish) *a city about thirty miles southwest of Jerusalem.*
- Joshua defeated, Joshua 10

lake
- of Galilee, Luke 5:1–2; 8:22–23, 33
- of fire, Revelation 19:20
- of sulfur, Revelation 20:10; 21:8

lamb (LAM) *an animal that the Jews often offered as a gift to God.*
- as sacrifice, Genesis 4:4; Exodus 12:3–10; Leviticus 3:6–11; 4:32–35; 5:6; 14:24–25
- Jesus, the lamb of God, John 1:29, 36; 1 Corinthians 5:7; 1 Peter 1:19; Revelation 5—7

Lamech (LAY-mek) *a descendant of Cain,* Genesis 4:18–24

Lamech, *son of Methuselah, the father of Noah,* Genesis 5:28–31

lament, See "complain."

lamp, *a small bowl which held a wick and burned olive oil, thus giving light,* Matthew 25:1–13; Luke 8:16–18
- "Your word is like a lamp for my feet," Psalm 119:105

lampstand, *a holder for a lamp.*
- in the Holy Tent, Exodus 25:31–40; Numbers 8:1–4
- in the Temple, 1 Kings 7:49
- symbol of the church, Revelation 1:12–13, 20

land
- Promised Land, Genesis 12:1–3

language
- world spoke only one, Genesis 11:1, 6
- confused at Babel, Genesis 11:7, 9
- Aramaic, 2 Kings 18:26; Ezra 4:7; John 19:20
- Latin, John 19:20
- Greek, John 19:20; Acts 21:37

Laodicea (lay-ah-deh-SEE-uh) *a town in what is now Turkey,* Colossians 4:13–16; Revelation 3:14–22

Last Days
- "pour out my Spirit," Acts 2:17
- Israel will turn to God, Hosea 3:5
- "these are the last days," 1 John 2:18

Last Supper, *the meal Jesus ate with his followers the night before his death,* Matthew 26:17–30; Mark 14:12–26; Luke 22:7–20; 1 Corinthians 11:23–26

Latin (LAT-in) *the language spoken by the Romans during New Testament times,* John 19:20

laughter
- Sarah laughed, Genesis 18:12
- mouths filled with, Psalm 126:2
- sorrow better than, Ecclesiastes 7:3
- changed into crying, James 4:9

law
- as rules, Romans 4:15; 6:14–15; Galatians 5:18
- as God's rules or teachings, Psalm 119; Romans 7:22; 8:7; James 1:25; 1 John 3:4

Law of Moses, See "Teachings of Moses."

laying on of hands, See "hands, laying on."

Lazarus of Bethany (LAZ-uh-rus) *a brother to Mary and Martha and a friend of Jesus,* John 11:1–45; 12:1–11

Lazarus, the beggar, Luke 16:19–31

laziness
- brings poverty, Proverbs 10:4
- not to be fed, 2 Thessalonians 3:10

leadership
- blind, Matthew 15:14
- of own family, 1 Timothy 3:5
- elders worthy of honor, 1 Timothy 5:17

Leah (LEE-uh) *a wife of Jacob,* Genesis 29:15–35; 30:9–21; 49:31

leather, Leviticus 13:47–59; Matthew 3:4

leaven, See "yeast."

Lebanon (LEH-beh-nun) *a country north of Israel.*
- cedars of, 1 Kings 5:1–11; Ezra 3:7
- prophecy of Lebanon's fall, Isaiah 10:34

Legion (LEE-jun) *a man who had many evil spirits in him,* Mark 5:9; Luke 8:30

leisure
- like seed among thorns, Luke 8:14
- the uselessness of, Ecclesiastes 2:1–2
- care in living, Ephesians 5:15–20

lend
- money, Exodus 22:25
- borrower, a servant to lender, Proverbs 22:7
- sinners to sinners, Luke 6:34
- to enemies, Luke 6:35

leprosy (LEH-prah-see) *bad skin disease. A person with leprosy was called a leper and had to live outside the city.* Leviticus 13:45–46
- disease of Naaman, 2 Kings 5:1–27
- healed by Jesus, Matthew 8:2–3; Luke 7:11–19

Leviathan (lee-VI-ah-than) *a sea creature, exact identity unknown,* Job 3:8; 41:1; Psalm 74:14; Isaiah 27:1

Levites (LEE-vites) *descendants of Levi, one of Jacob's sons.*
- served as priests, Numbers 1:47–53; 8:5–26; Deuteronomy 10:8–9; 18:1–8
- towns assigned to, Joshua 21

liar
- better to be poor, Proverbs 19:22
- Satan as a, John 8:44
- Cretans as, Titus 1:12
- to be punished, Revelation 21:8

lid on the Ark of the Agreement, *the mercy seat; the gold lid on the Ark of the Agreement,* Exodus 25:17–22; Hebrews 9:5

life
- breath of, Genesis 2:7
- book of, Philippians 4:3; Revelation 3:5; 21:27
- in the blood, Leviticus 17:14
- length of, Psalm 90:10
- true life, John 12:25
- "I am the . . . life." John 14:6
- eternal, John 5:24–29; 6:35–51

light
- creation of, Genesis 1:3–4
- of the world, Matthew 5:14
- God is, 1 Timothy 6:16; 1 John 1:5
- Jesus is, John 1:4–9; 3:19–20; 8:12; 12:46
- God's word is light, Psalm 119:105
- symbol of God's presence, 2 Corinthians 4:6; Ephesians 5:8–9; 1 Peter 2:9

linen (LEH-nin) *a type of cloth made from the flax plant.*
- used for priests' clothes, Exodus 28:39–42; Leviticus 6:10
- used for royal clothes, Esther 8:15
- Jesus' body wrapped in, Matthew 27:59

lion
- killed by Samson, Judges 14:5–18
- killed by David, 1 Samuel 17:34–37
- devil like a lion, 1 Peter 5:8

lips
- touched by hot coal, Isaiah 6:5–7

loan, See "debt."

loaves
- used to feed five thousand, Matthew 14:17–19
- used to feed four thousand, Matthew 15:34–38

locust (LO-cust) *an insect that looks like a grasshopper. Locusts travel in large groups and can destroy crops.*
- as a plague, Exodus 10:3–19; Deuteronomy 28:38–42; Joel 1:1–4; Nahum 3:15–17
- food for John the Baptist, Matthew 3:4; Mark 1:6

loneliness
- of Adam, Genesis 2:18
- of Jesus, Matthew 27:46
- psalm of loneliness, Psalm 22

Lord, *master or one who is in control; ruler of all the world and universe.*
- God as Lord, Exodus 3:15; 7:16; Psalms 31:5; 106:48
- Jesus as Lord, Acts 2:36; 1 Corinthians 8:6; Philippians 2:11; 1 Peter 3:15
- Holy Spirit as Lord, 2 Corinthians 3:18

Lord of hosts, *one of the names used for God; also called "Lord All-Powerful" and "Lord Sabaoth,"* 1 Chronicles 11:9; Psalm 24:10; Isaiah 6:3–5; Malachi 3:1–17

Lord's day
- the first day of the week, Acts 20:7; Revelation 1:10
- as the Judgment Day, 1 Corinthians 5:5; 2 Corinthians 1:14; 1 Thessalonians 5:2; 2 Peter 3:10

Lord's Prayer, *the name often given to the model prayer Jesus taught his followers,* Matthew 6:9–13; Luke 11:1–4

Lord's Supper, *the meal Jesus' followers eat to remember how he died for them; also called "communion."*
- beginning of, Matthew 26:26–29; Mark 14:22–25; Luke 22:14–20
- examples of, Acts 20:7; 1 Corinthians 10:16; 11:17–34

Lot, *Abraham's nephew,* Genesis 11:27–30
- divided land with Abram, Genesis 13
- captured, Genesis 14:1–16
- escaped destruction of Sodom, Genesis 19:1–29
- death of wife, Genesis 19:15–26

lots, *sticks, stones, or pieces of bone thrown like dice to decide something. Often God controlled the result of the lots to let people know what he wanted them to do.*
- Canaan divided by, Numbers 26:55–56
- Jonah found guilty by, Jonah 1:7

- Jesus' clothes divided by, Luke 23:34
- Matthias chosen by, Acts 1:26

love, *a strong feeling of affection, loyalty, and concern for someone.*
- love of God commanded, Deuteronomy 6:5; 11:1; Matthew 22:36–38
- of God for people, Psalm 36; John 3:16; Romans 5:8; 8:39; Ephesians 1:4; 1 John 4:10–11
- of people for God, 1 Corinthians 8:3; 1 John 5:3
- of Christ for people, John 13:1; 15:9; Romans 8:35; Galatians 2:20; 1 John 3:16
- of people for Christ, Matthew 10:37; 1 Corinthians 16:22; 1 Peter 1:8
- of people for each other, Leviticus 19:18; Luke 6:27–35; John 13:34–35; 1 Corinthians 13; 1 John 4:7

Luke, *a non-Jewish doctor who often traveled with the apostle Paul,* Colossians 4:14; 2 Timothy 4:11

lust, *wanting something evil.*
- to be avoided, Proverbs 6:25; Matthew 5:28; Colossians 3:5; 1 Thessalonians 4:5
- typical of the ungodly, Romans 1:26; 1 Peter 4:3

Lydia (LID-ee-uh) *a woman from the city of Thyatira who sold purple cloth,* Acts 16:13–15, 40

lying
- warnings against, Ephesians 4:25; Colossians 3:9; Revelation 21:8
- devil as a liar, John 8:44
- to the Holy Spirit, Acts 5:1–6

lyre (LIRE) *a musical instrument with strings, similar to a harp,* 1 Chronicles 15:16; Psalms 33:2; 81:2

Lystra (LIS-tra) *a city of Lycaonia.*
- Paul preached there, Acts 14:6–20; 16:1; 2 Timothy 3:11

M

Macedonia (mas-eh-DOH-nee-uh) *the northern part of Greece.*
- Paul preached there, Acts 16:6–10; 20:1–6; 1 Corinthians 16:5–9; Philippians 4:15

Machpelah (mack-PEE-luh) *the land Abraham bought from Ephron, the Hittite.*
- Sarah buried there, Genesis 23:7–19
- Abraham buried there, Genesis 25:7–10
- Jacob buried there, Genesis 49:29–33; 50:12–13

magic (MAJ-ik) *trying to use the power of evil spirits to make unnatural things happen.*
- magicians of Egypt, Genesis 41:8; Exodus 7:11–12
- condemned, Leviticus 19:26; 20:27; Deuteronomy 18:10–12
- Simon the magician, Acts 8:9–24
- Elymas the magician, Acts 13:6–11
- Ephesian magicians burn their books, Acts 19:17–19

mahalath (mah-HAY-lath) *probably a musical word; may be the name of a tune or may mean to dance and shout,* Psalms 53; 88

Malachi (MAL-uh-ky) *a prophet who lived about the time of Nehemiah. He wrote the last book of the Old Testament.* Malachi 1:1

man, *humankind; a male.*
- created by God, Genesis 1:26–27; 2:7–23
- born of woman, Job 14:1
- important to God, Psalm 8:4–8
- woman created for, 1 Corinthians 11:9

Manasseh, son of Hezekiah (mah-NASS-uh) *a king of Judah for fifty-five years,* 2 Kings 21:1–17; 2 Chronicles 33:1–20

Manasseh, son of Joseph, *older brother of Ephraim. His descendants were the tribe of Manasseh.* Genesis 41:51; 46:20; 48:1–20
- descendants of, Numbers 1:34; 26:29–34; Joshua 13:8–13; 17
- eastern half-tribe, Joshua 1:12–17; 22
- western half-tribe, Joshua 21:5, 25; 22:7

manger (MAIN-jur) *a box where animals are fed,* Luke 2:6–17

manna (MAN-ah) *the white, sweet-tasting food God gave the people of Israel in the wilderness. It appeared on the ground during the night so they could gather it in the morning.*
- God sent to Israel, Exodus 16:11–36; Joshua 5:10–12
- kept in the Ark, Exodus 16:31–34; Hebrews 9:1–4

Manoah (mah-NO-uh) *the father of Samson,* Judges 13

Marduk (MAR-dook) *a god of the Babylonians. The Babylonians believed that people were evil because Marduk had created them from the blood of an evil god.* Jeremiah 50:2

Mark, *John Mark; a cousin to Barnabas; traveled with Paul and Barnabas and wrote the Gospel of Mark,* Acts 12:12, 25; 13:5; Colossians 4:10; 2 Timothy 4:11
- left Paul, Acts 13:13
- traveled with Barnabas, Acts 15:36–41

marketplace, *usually a large open area inside a city where people came to buy and sell goods,* Matthew 20:3; Mark 7:4; 12:38; Luke 7:32; Acts 16:19

marriage
- teachings about, Mark 10:6–9; 1 Corinthians 7:1–16; Hebrews 13:4; 1 Timothy 5:14
- authority in, Ephesians 5:21; Colossians 3:18

Mars Hill, See "Areopagus."

Martha (MAR-thuh) *the sister of Mary and Lazarus who lived in Bethany.*
- criticized Mary, Luke 10:38–42
- at death of Lazarus, John 11:17–44

martyr (MAR-ter) *"witness"; one who knows about something. Later, martyr came to mean a person who was killed for being a witness.*
- Stephen, first Christian martyr, Acts 7:54–60
- James killed, Acts 12:2
- heroes of faith killed, Hebrews 11:32–37

Mary Magdalene (MAG-duh-lun) *a follower of Jesus from the town of Magdala; the first person to see Jesus after he came back to life.*
- at Jesus' death, Matthew 27:55–56, 61
- saw Jesus after his resurrection, Matthew 28:1–10; Mark 16:1–11; John 20:10–18

Mary, mother of Jesus
- engaged to marry Joseph, Matthew 1:18–25; Luke 2:4–5
- angel appeared to, Luke 1:26–45
- birth of Jesus, Luke 2:6–21
- with Jesus in Jerusalem, Luke 2:41–52
- at wedding in Cana, John 2:1–10
- at Jesus' death, John 19:25–27
- with the apostles, Acts 1:14

Mary of Bethany, *sister of Martha and Lazarus, and a friend of Jesus.*
- sat at Jesus' feet, Luke 10:38–42
- at death of Lazarus, John 11:1–45
- poured oil on Jesus' feet, John 12:1–8

maskil (MAS-kil) *probably a description of the kind of song that some of the Psalms were,* Psalms 32; 42; 44; 45

master, *lord; ruler.*
- "No one can serve two masters." Matthew 6:24
- not to be called, Matthew 23:10
- to be obeyed, Ephesians 6:5
- how to treat slaves, Ephesians 6:9
- in heaven, Ephesians 6:9; Colossians 4:1
- Jesus as, Luke 5:5; 8:24; 17:13

materialism/possessions
- the rich leader, Luke 18:18–30
- satisfaction despite wealth, Philippians 4:10–13
- Jesus discusses selfishness, Luke 12:13–21

Matthew (MATH-you) *also called Levi; a tax collector; wrote the Gospel of Matthew,* Matthew 9:9–10; 10:3; Acts 1:13

Matthias (muh-THY-us) *chosen to be an apostle after Judas Iscariot killed himself,* Acts 1:15–26

meat
- given by God in the wilderness, Exodus 16:1–15; Numbers 11:4–34; Psalm 78:27
- eating meat sacrificed to idols, Acts 15:20; 1 Corinthians 8; 10:25–32

Medes (MEEDS) *the people who lived in Media, which is called "Iran" today,* 2 Kings 17:6; Ezra 6:2; Esther 1:3–19; Daniel 5:28; 6:8–15

mediator (MEE-dee-a-ter) *a go-between.*
- Jesus as, 1 Timothy 2:5

medicine
- happy heart as, Proverbs 17:22

meditation
- on God's rules, Psalm 119:99
- Paul's exhortation on, Philippians 4:8
- think about things in heaven, Colossians 3:1–4

Mediterranean Sea (med-ih-teh-RANE-ih-an) *a large sea west of Canaan; also called the "Great Sea" or the "Western Sea,"* Numbers 34:6–7; Joshua 1:4

medium (MEED-ee-um) *a person who tries to help living people talk to the spirits of the dead.*
- condemned, Leviticus 19:31; Deuteronomy 18:11–13; Isaiah 8:19–20
- of Endor, 1 Samuel 28
- Josiah destroyed mediums, 2 Kings 23:24

Meeting Tent, *"Tabernacle" or "Holy Tent"; a special tent where the Israelites worshiped God. It was used from the time they left Egypt until Solomon built the Temple in Jerusalem.*
- description of, Exodus 25—27
- set up, Exodus 39:32—40:36

Megiddo (meh-GID-oh) *important town in northern Israel where many battles were fought. The Book of Revelation tells about a great battle between good and evil at "Armageddon," which means "the hill of Megiddo."* Joshua 12:8–21; 2 Kings 23:29–30; Revelation 16:16

Melchizedek (mel-KIZ-ih-dek) *priest and king who worshiped God in the time of Abraham,* Genesis 14:17–24
- Christ compared to, Hebrews 5:4–10; 7

memory
- psalm of remembrance, Psalm 77
- monument to God's faithfulness, Joshua 4:7
- remember Christ, 2 Timothy 2:8

Mene, mene, tekel, parsin (MEE-nee, TEE-kul, PAR-sun) *the words written on the wall by a mysterious hand at Belshazzar's feast,* Daniel 5

mentoring, See "follower."

Mephibosheth (me-FIB-o-sheth) *crippled son of Jonathan,* 2 Samuel 4:4
- David's agreement with, 2 Samuel 9
- tricked by Ziba, 2 Samuel 16:1–4; 19:24–30

Merab (MEE-rab) *daughter of King Saul,* 1 Samuel 14:49; 18:17–19

Merarites (mee-RAY-rites) *descendants of Merari, a son of Levi; they were responsible for caring for the frame of the Holy Tent,* Numbers 3:17, 33–37; 4:29–33

mercy (MUR-see) *kindness and forgiveness.*
- God's mercy to people, Exodus 34:6; Deuteronomy 4:31; Luke 1:50; Ephesians 2:4
- people's mercy to each other, Matthew 5:7; James 2:13

mercy seat, See "lid on the Ark of the Agreement."

Mesha (MEE-shuh) *an evil king of Moab,* 2 Kings 3:4–27

Meshach (MEE-shack) *friend of Daniel who was put in the fiery furnace,* Daniel 1—3

messenger, 1 Samuel 23:27; 1 Kings 19:2
- John the Baptist as, Matthew 11:10; Mark 1:2; Luke 7:27
- of Satan, 2 Corinthians 12:7

Messiah (muh-SYE-uh) *"anointed one"; the Greek word for Messiah is "Christ." Christians believe that Jesus is the Messiah or the Christ.* John 1:40–41; 4:25–26

Methuselah (meh-THOO-zeh-lah) *lived 969 years, longer than anyone else in the Bible; the son of Enoch and the grandfather of Noah,* Genesis 5:21–27

Micah (MY-cuh) *a prophet who told the people of Israel and Judah about their sins,* Micah 1—7

Micaiah (mi-KAY-uh) *a prophet of God,* 1 Kings 22:8–28; 2 Chronicles 18

Michael (MY-kul) *the archangel of God,* Jude 9; Revelation 12:7

Michal (MY-kul) *a daughter of Saul and wife of David,* 1 Samuel 18:20–29; 19:11–17; 2 Samuel 3:13–16
- criticized David, 2 Samuel 6:16–23

Michmash (MIK-mash) *a hilly area about seven miles northeast of Jerusalem,* 1 Samuel 13:23—14:23; Isaiah 10:28

Midian (MID-ee-un) *a son of Abraham; his descendants were called "Midianites,"* Genesis 25:1–6
- Joseph sold to, Genesis 37:18–36
- Jethro, a descendant of, Exodus 2:15–21
- enemy of Israel, Judges 6—7

midnight
- when the firstborn of Egypt died, Exodus 12:29
- Paul and Silas freed from jail, Acts 16:25–26
- Paul preached until, Acts 20:7

miktam (MIK-tam) *a kind of song that may describe some of the Psalms. It may mean that it is a sad song or a song about danger.* Psalms 16; 56—60

mildew (MIL-doo) *a growth that appears on things that have been damp for a long time,* Leviticus 13:47–59; 14:33–54

milk, 1 Peter 2:2

millstones, *huge stones used for grinding grain into flour or meal,* Deuteronomy 24:6; Matthew 18:6; Luke 17:1–2
- used to kill Abimelech, Judges 9:53; 2 Samuel 11:21

minister (MIN-i-ster) *servant; one who lives serving God and others,* Romans 15:15–16; Colossians 4:7

miracle (MEER-ih-k'l) *"wonderful thing"; a great event which can be done only by God's help. Miracles are special signs to show God's power.*
- purpose of, Exodus 10:1–2; Mark 2:8–12; John 2:11; Acts 3:1–10
- over nature, Exodus 14:21–22; Joshua 10:12–13; Matthew 8:23–27; 14:22–32; 21:18–22
- of healing, Matthew 8:14–17; 9:27–31; Mark 7:31–37; Acts 14:3
- of bringing people back to life, Mark 5:21–43; John 11:1–44; Acts 9:36–43

Miriam (MEER-ee-um) *the sister of Moses and Aaron.*
- watched over Moses, Exodus 2:1–8
- song of, Exodus 15:19–21
- punished, Numbers 12:1–15
- death of, Numbers 20:1

mission
- the Great Commission, Matthew 28:16–20
- Jesus sends out the seventy-two, Luke 10:1

mistress (MISS-tres) *a female head of the household,* Proverbs 30:21–23
- Hagar as, Genesis 16:4–9

Mizpah (MIZ-pah) *the place where Jacob and Laban made a pile of stones to remind them of their agreement not to be angry with each other,* Genesis 31:44–49

Mizpah, *the city, a few miles north of Jerusalem,* Judges 11:29–34; 1 Samuel 7:5–16; 2 Kings 25:23

Moab (MO-ab) *the country on the east side of the Dead Sea.*
- fought with Israel, Numbers 22:1—25:9; Judges 3:12–30
- home of Ruth, Ruth 1:2, 4
- rebelled against Israel, 2 Kings 3:4–27

mob
- against Paul, Acts 17:5; 21:30–36

Molech (MO-lek) *a god of the Canaanite people. Those who worshiped Molech often sacrificed their own children to him by burning them on altars.* Leviticus 18:21; 20:1–5; 2 Kings 23:10; Jeremiah 32:35

money, *Many kinds of money were used in Bible days—gold, silver, and copper.*
- proper attitudes toward, Luke 16:13; Hebrews 13:5; 1 Timothy 3:3; 6:10

moneychangers, *people who traded money from other countries for Jewish money.*
- of the Temple, Matthew 21:12–13; Mark 11:15–17; Luke 19:45–46; John 2:13–16

Mordecai (MOR-deh-kye) *a man who helped Esther to save the Jews from death.*
- discovered a plot, Esther 2:19–23
- asked Esther to help, Esther 4
- honored by the king, Esther 6

Moriah (moh-RYE-uh) *the land where Abraham went to sacrifice Isaac,* Genesis 22:2
- site of the Temple, 2 Chronicles 3:1

mortar (MORE-tar) *a stone bowl where grain is ground into flour by pounding; also, the sticky material that holds bricks together,* Genesis 11:3; Exodus 1:14

Moses (MO-zez) *the man who led God's people out of the land of Egypt; the author of the first five books of the Old Testament.*
- birth of, Exodus 2:1–10
- in Midian, Exodus 2:11—4:17
- led Israel out of Egypt, Exodus 4:18—12:51; 13:17–31
- received the law, Exodus 20—31
- struck the rock, Numbers 20:1–13
- death of, Deuteronomy 31:14—34:12

Most Holy Place, *the inner and most special room in the Holy Tent and the Temple.*
- rules about, Leviticus 16:2–20
- in the Temple, 1 Kings 6:16–35
- entered by Christ, Hebrews 9:3–25

mother-in-law
- law about, Deuteronomy 27:23
- of Ruth, Ruth 1:3–4
- Peter's, Matthew 8:14–15; Luke 4:38–39
- family against, Matthew 10:35; Luke 12:53

mothers
- treatment of, Exodus 20:12; 21:15, 17; Proverbs 1:8; Matthew 15:4; 1 Timothy 5:2, 4

Mount of Olives, *a hill covered with olive trees near Jerusalem; site of the garden of Gethsemane,* Matthew 21:1; 24:3; John 8:1
- David cried there, 2 Samuel 15:30
- Jesus prayed there, Luke 22:39–53
- Jesus ascended from there, Acts 1:6–12

Mount Sinai (SYE-nye) *a mountain in the Sinai Peninsula.*
- Lord spoke with Moses there, Exodus 24:16; Acts 7:30, 38
- law given on, Exodus 31:18

Mount Zion (ZI-on) *one of the hills on which Jerusalem was built; later, it became another name for the whole city of Jerusalem; also a name for heaven.*
- hill of Jerusalem, 2 Kings 19:31; Psalm 48:2, 11; Isaiah 24:23
- as heaven, Hebrews 12:22; Revelation 14:1

mountain
- announce the Lord's blessings, Deuteronomy 11:29–30
- Israel gathers, 1 Kings 18:2–40
- vision from God, Revelation 21:10—22:7

mourning (MORN-ing) *showing sadness, especially when someone has died.*
- examples of, Genesis 50:3; Deuteronomy 34:8; 1 Samuel 31:11–13

murder
- laws against, Exodus 20:13; Deuteronomy 5:17; Matthew 5:21
- committed by Barabbas, Mark 15:7
- devil as a murderer, John 8:44
- full of, Romans 1:29

music
- to the Lord, Judges 5:3; Ephesians 5:19
- in the Temple, 1 Chronicles 25:6–7

myrrh (MUR) *sweet-smelling liquid taken from certain trees and shrubs; used as a perfume and a painkiller,* Genesis 37:25; 43:11; Proverbs 7:17
- given to Jesus, Matthew 2:11; Mark 15:23
- used in Jesus' burial, John 19:39–40

mystery (MIH-ster-ee) *a secret.*
- revealed by God, Daniel 2:28
- of the message of Christ, Romans 16:25–26; Colossians 2:2; 4:3
- of Gentiles also being saved, Ephesians 3:1–6; Colossians 1:25–27
- of life after death, 1 Corinthians 15:51

N

Naaman (NAY-uh-mun) *a commander of the Aramean army; healed by Elisha of a skin disease,* 2 Kings 5; Luke 4:27

Nabal (NAY-bal) *husband of Abigail.*
- refused to help David, 1 Samuel 25:2–13
- saved by Abigail, 1 Samuel 25:14–35
- death of, 1 Samuel 25:36–38

Naboth (NAY-both) *killed by Jezebel so she could steal his vineyard,* 1 Kings 21

Nadab (NAY-dab) *son of Aaron.*
- saw God, Exodus 24:1–11
- death of, Leviticus 10:1; Numbers 3:4; 26:61

Nahum (NAY-hum) *a prophet of God; wrote the Book of Nahum,* Nahum 1—3

naked
- Adam and Eve, Genesis 2:25
- realization of nakedness, Genesis 3:7–10
- born, Job 1:21

Naomi (nay-OH-me) *mother-in-law of Ruth,* Ruth 1:1–5
- returned to Bethlehem, Ruth 1:6–22
- encouraged Ruth, Ruth 2:19—3:4
- became a grandmother, Ruth 4:13–17

Naphtali (NAF-tuh-lye) *the sixth son of Jacob; his descendants were the tribe of Naphtali,* Genesis 30:7–8; Numbers 26:48–50; Joshua 19:32–39

nard, *an expensive perfume which was imported from India,* Song of Songs 4:13; Mark 14:3; John 12:3

Nathan (NAY-thun) *a prophet during the time of David and Solomon,* 1 Kings 1
- told David not to build the Temple, 2 Samuel 7:1–17
- told David the parable of the lamb, 2 Samuel 12:1–25

Nathanael (nuh-THAN-yul) *one of Jesus' twelve apostles; probably called "Bartholomew,"* John 1:43–51

nation
- formed and spread, Genesis 10:32
- against nation, Mark 13:8
- Good News preached to every one, Revelation 14:6

Nazarene (NAZ-uh-reen) *a person from the town of Nazareth. Jesus was called a Nazarene, so his followers sometimes were also called Nazarenes.* Matthew 2:21–23; Acts 24:5

Nazareth (NAZ-uh-reth) *the city in Galilee where Jesus grew up,* Matthew 2:21–23; Luke 4:16–30; John 1:45–46

Nazirite (NAZ-e-rite) *one who makes a special promise to God, which had rules about eating certain foods and cutting the hair.*
- rules for, Numbers 6:1–21
- made by Samson, Judges 13:2–7; 16:17

Nebo, god of the Babylonians (NEE-boh) Isaiah 46:1

Nebo, the mountain
- Moses died there, Deuteronomy 34:1–5

Nebuchadnezzar (neb-you-kud-NEZ-zur) *a Babylonian king.*
- conquered Jerusalem, 2 Kings 24—25; 2 Chronicles 36
- his dreams, Daniel 2; 4
- and fiery furnace, Daniel 3

Nebuzaradan (NEB-you-ZAR-ah-dan) *the commander of Nebuchadnezzar's army.*
- captured Jerusalem, 2 Kings 25:8–12; Jeremiah 39:8–14; 40:1–6

Neco (NECK-o) *king of Egypt from 609 to 594 B.C.*
- killed King Josiah, 2 Kings 23:29–37; 2 Chronicles 35:20–27
- captured Jehoahaz, 2 Chronicles 36:1–4
- defeated by Nebuchadnezzar, Jeremiah 46:2

Nehemiah (NEE-uh-MY-uh) *led the first group of Israelites back to Jerusalem from Babylon.*
- sent to Jerusalem, Nehemiah 2
- rebuilt walls of Jerusalem, Nehemiah 3—4; 6
- as governor, Nehemiah 8:9; 10:1

neighbor
- teachings about, Exodus 20:16–17; Leviticus 19:13–18; Proverbs 3:27–29; Matthew 19:19; Luke 10:25–37

Nephilim (NEF-eh-lim) *people who were famous for being large and strong. The ten spies who were afraid to enter Canaan had seen the Nephilim who lived there,* Genesis 6:4; Numbers 13:30–33

Ner (NUR) *father of Kish,* 1 Chronicles 8:33; 9:36, 39

net
- fishing with, Matthew 4:18; Luke 5:5–6; John 21:6–11
- kingdom of heaven like, Matthew 13:47

new
- a new song, Psalms 40:3; 98:1
- a new name, Isaiah 62:2; Revelation 2:17
- new mercies every morning, Lamentations 3:22–23
- a new heart, Ezekiel 18:31; 36:26
- a new life, Romans 6:4; Ephesians 4:23–24; Colossians 3:10; 1 Peter 1:3
- a new agreement, Jeremiah 31:31; 1 Corinthians 11:25; Hebrews 8:8; 9:15; 12:24
- a new heaven and earth, 2 Peter 3:13; Revelation 21:1

New Moon, *a Jewish feast held on the first day of the month. It was celebrated with animal sacrifices and the blowing of trumpets. It was to dedicate the month to the Lord,* Numbers 10:10; 2 Chronicles 2:4; 8:13; Psalm 81:3; Isaiah 1:11–17

Nicodemus (nick-uh-DEE-mus) *an important Jewish ruler and teacher. Jesus taught him about spiritual life,* John 3:1–21; 7:45–53; 19:38–42

night, *can refer to ordinary darkness or be a symbol of distress, judgment, or evil.*
- created by God, Genesis 1:5; Psalm 19:1–2
- time of distress, Psalms 30:5; 42:8; 77:6
- time of judgment, John 9:4
- symbol of evil, 1 Thessalonians 5:5
- no night in heaven, Revelation 21:25

Nile River, *a river in Africa more than twenty-five hundred miles long.*
- baby Moses placed there, Exodus 2:1–10
- turned to blood, Exodus 7:14–25
- produced plague of frogs, Exodus 8:1–15

Nineveh (NIN-eh-vuh) *one of the oldest and most important cities in the world. For many years it was the capital of Assyria.* Genesis 10:8–11
- Jonah preached there, Jonah 1:1–2; 3—4; Matthew 12:41
- Nahum prophesied against, Nahum 1—3

Noah (NO-uh) *saved his family and the animals from the flood.*
- built the boat, Genesis 6:8–22
- saved from the flood, Genesis 7—8
- agreement with God, Genesis 9:1–17

Nob, *a town where priests lived during the days of King Saul,* 1 Samuel 21:1

noise
- joyful, Psalm 66:1
- of many people, Isaiah 17:12
- skies will disappear with, 2 Peter 3:10

noon
- sun to go down at, Amos 8:9
- bright light at, Acts 22:6

numbers
- seven things God hates, Proverbs 6:16–19
- the number 666, Revelation 13:18

O

oath, *a promise or vow.*
- rules about, Matthew 5:33–37; 23:16–22; James 5:12
- God's oath, Hebrews 6:16–18
- examples of, 1 Samuel 14:24–28; 1 Kings 1:29–30; Psalm 132:1–12

Obadiah (oh-buh-DYE-uh) *a prophet of God who warned the Edomites they would be punished,* Obadiah 1–21

obedience
- to God, Leviticus 25:18; Deuteronomy 27:10; Acts 5:29
- to parents, Ephesians 6:1; Colossians 3:20
- to government, Romans 13:1–7; Titus 3:1–2; Matthew 22:17–21
- punishment for disobedience, Ephesians 5:6; 2 Thessalonians 1:8; 1 Timothy 1:9

offering (AW-fer-ing) *a gift or sacrifice.* See "sacrifice."
- brought by Cain, Genesis 4:3–5
- of non-Jewish people, Romans 15:16
- of Christ, Hebrews 10:5–18

Og (AHG) *the king of Bashan who was defeated by the Israelites,* Numbers 21:33–35; Deuteronomy 3:1–11

oil, *in Bible times usually means olive oil; used for cooking, medicine, burning in lamps, and anointing.* See "anoint."
- for lamps, Exodus 25:5–6; Matthew 25:1–10
- as medicine, Luke 10:34
- in offerings, Leviticus 2; 14:12–31
- in cooking, 1 Kings 17:10–16

ointment, See "perfume."

olive (OL-iv) *a small fruit; its oil was used in anointing ceremonies and as medicine.* See "oil."
- leaf, Genesis 8:11
- trees, Deuteronomy 6:11; 1 Samuel 8:14; Habakkuk 3:17; John 18:1

Omega, See "Alpha and Omega."

Omri (AHM-rih) *a strong, evil king of Israel,* 1 Kings 16:15–28

Onesimus (oh-NES-ih-mus) *the slave of a Christian named Philemon,* Colossians 4:9; Philemon

Onesiphorus (OH-nih-SIF-uh-russ) *a Christian friend of Paul who lived in Ephesus,* 2 Timothy 1:16–18; 4:19

onyx (AHN-ix) *a precious stone with layers of black and white running through it,* Genesis 2:12; Job 28:16
- used in the holy vest, Exodus 25:7; 28:9–14; 39:6–7, 13

Orpah (OR-pah) *the sister-in-law of Ruth,* Ruth 1:3–14

Ophir (OH-fur) *a land known for its gold and beautiful trees. Its location is uncertain.* Psalm 45:9; Isaiah 13:12
- Solomon traded with Ophir, 1 Kings 9:28; 10:11; 1 Chronicles 29:4

oven, *fire was built in the bottom of a clay barrel to bake bread,* Exodus 8:3; Leviticus 2:4; Hosea 7:4

oxen
- not to be coveted, Exodus 20:17
- as offering, Numbers 7:12–83
- not to be denied food, Deuteronomy 25:4; 1 Corinthians 9:9
- Elisha plowed with, 1 Kings 19:19–21
- pulled the cart containing the Ark, 1 Chronicles 13:9

P

pain
- of a woman in childbirth, Genesis 3:16; Isaiah 13:8; Romans 8:22; Galatians 4:19, 27
- not found in the new Jerusalem, Revelation 21:4

palace
- of David, 2 Samuel 5:11–12
- of Solomon, 1 Kings 7:1–12

palm tree, *a tall tree with long, fan-shaped branches growing out of the top; gives dates for food and wood for building,* Exodus 15:27; Nehemiah 8:15
- Jericho, city of, Deuteronomy 34:3; Judges 1:16; 3:13
- branches spread before Jesus, John 12:12–13

papyrus (puh-PY-rus) *a tall reed that grows in swampy places; used to make paper,* Job 8:11; 9:26

parable (PARE-uh-b'l) *a story that teaches a lesson by comparing two things.*
- of the kingdom of God, Matthew 13; 20:1–16
- of the lost sheep, coin, and son, Luke 15:1–31
- of the Judgment Day, Matthew 25

Paradise (PARE-uh-dice) *another word for heaven,* Luke 23:43; 2 Corinthians 12:3–4

Paran (PAY-ran) *a desert area between Egypt and Canaan,* Genesis 21:20; Numbers 10:12; 12:16; 13:1–26

parchment (PARCH-ment) *a kind of writing material; made from the skin of sheep or goats,* 2 Timothy 4:13

parents
- responsibilities of, Ephesians 6:4; Colossians 3:21

Passover Feast (PASS-o-ver FEEST) *an important holy day for the Jews in the spring of each year. They ate a special meal on this day to remind them that God had freed them from being slaves in Egypt.*
- first Passover, Exodus 12:1–30
- commanded, Numbers 9:1–14
- celebrated by Jesus, Matthew 26:2, 17–19

patience (PAY-shentz) *to handle pain or difficult times calmly and without complaining.*
- of God, Romans 2:4; 2 Peter 3:9
- teachings about, 1 Corinthians 13:4, 7; Hebrews 6:12
- comes from the Holy Spirit, Galatians 5:22
- commanded, Romans 12:12; Ephesians 4:2; 1 Thessalonians 5:14; James 5:7–8

Patmos (PAT-mus) *a small, rocky island in the Aegean Sea between Greece and Turkey,* Revelation 1:9

Paul, *the Roman name for "Saul." Saul was a Jew, born in the city of Tarsus. He became an apostle and a great servant of God.*
- conversion of, Acts 9:1–22
- name changed from "Saul," Acts 13:9
- healings by, Acts 14:8–10; 19:11–12; 20:7–12; 28:1–11
- imprisoned, Acts 23:35—28:31
- death of, 2 Timothy 4:6–8

peace
- from God, Psalm 29:11; John 14:27; Romans 5:1
- commanded, Romans 12:18; 14:17–19; Colossians 3:15
- Prince of Peace, Isaiah 9:6
- from the Holy Spirit, Galatians 5:22

pearl (PURL), Matthew 7:6; 1 Timothy 2:9; Revelation 21:21
- parable of, Matthew 13:45–46

Pekah (PEE-kuh) *an evil king of Israel,* 2 Kings 15:25—16:9; Isaiah 7:1–10

Pekahiah (peck-uh-HI-uh) *an evil king of Israel,* 2 Kings 15:22–26

Pelethites (PELL-eh-thites) *King David's bodyguards,* 2 Samuel 15:18; 20:6–7, 23

Peninnah (pe-NIN-uh) *a wife of Elkanah,* 1 Samuel 1:2–6

people of god, the
- a chosen people, 1 Peter 2:9–10
- God's children, 1 John 5:1–2
- defended by God, Deuteronomy 32:36–40

Pentecost (PEN-tee-cost) *a Jewish feast day celebrating the summer harvest. The apostles began telling the Good News on Pentecost after Jesus died.* Acts 2:1–41; 20:16; 1 Corinthians 16:8

perfect
- describing Jesus, Hebrews 2:10; 5:9; 7:28
- describing God, Psalm 18:30; Matthew 5:48
- God's perfect law, James 1:25
- will of God, Romans 12:2
- love, 1 John 4:18
- people made perfect, 2 Corinthians 13:11; Hebrews 10:1–14; 11:40; 12:23

perfume
- used in idol worship, Isaiah 57:9
- poured on Jesus' feet, Mark 14:3–9; Luke 7:36–39; John 12:3

Pergamum (PER-guh-mum) *a town in the Roman province of Asia in what is now Turkey,* Revelation 2:12–17

persecution (PUR-seh-CUE-shun) *trying to hurt people. Christians in the New Testament times were often persecuted by being put in jail or killed.*
- blessings with, Matthew 5:11–12; 1 Peter 3:8–17
- examples of, Acts 8:1–4; 1 Peter 3:13–15
- response to, Matthew 5:44; Romans 12:14; 1 Corinthians 4:12; 2 Corinthians 12:2
- of Christians, Matthew 13:21; 2 Timothy 3:12

perseverance
- for a heavenly reward, 2 Corinthians 5:1–5
- Israel punished for lack of, Numbers 14:26–38
- salvation for, Matthew 24:13

Persia (PUR-zhuh) *a powerful country during the last years of the Old Testament; now called "Iran."*
- defeated Babylon, 2 Chronicles 36:20–23
- let captives return to Jerusalem, Ezra 1:1–11

Peter, *a fisherman; he and his brother, Andrew, were the first two apostles Jesus chose. First called "Simon" or "Peter," Jesus changed his name to "Cephas," which means "rock."*
- called to follow Jesus, Matthew 4:18–20
- walked on water, Matthew 14:22–33
- at the Last Supper, John 13:1–11
- defended Jesus, John 18:10–11
- denied Jesus, Mark 14:66–72; Luke 22:54–62
- preached the Good News, Acts 2:14–40
- an elder in the church, 1 Peter 5:1

pharaoh (FAY-row) *the title given to the kings of Egypt.*
- made Joseph ruler of Egypt, Genesis 40—47
- made Israelites slaves, Exodus 1—14

Pharisees (FARE-ih-seez) *"the separate people"; they followed the Jewish religious laws and customs very strictly. Jesus often spoke against them for their religious teachings and traditions.*

- practices of, Matthew 9:14; 15:1–9; Mark 7:1–13; Luke 7:30
- against Jesus, Matthew 12:14; 22:15; John 8:1–6
- criticized by Jesus, Matthew 5:20; 23

Philadelphia (fill-uh-DEL-fee-uh) *a city in the country now called "Turkey,"* Revelation 3:7–13

Philemon (fih-LEE-mun) *a Christian in the city of Colossae,* Philemon 1–25

Philip, the apostle (FIL-ip) *friend of Peter and Andrew.*
- called by Jesus, John 1:43
- brought Nathanael to Jesus, John 1:44–50
- brought Greeks to Jesus, John 12:21–22

Philip, the evangelist, *a Greek-speaking Jew chosen to serve in the church in Jerusalem.*
- preached in Samaria, Acts 8:5–13
- preached to the Ethiopian, Acts 8:26–39
- his daughters prophesied, Acts 21:8–9

Philip, *the tetrarch, son of Herod I and Cleopatra.*
- ruler of Iturea and Trachonitis, Luke 3:1

Philippi (fih-LIP-eye) *a city in northeastern Greece,* Philippians 1:1; 4:15
- Paul in jail there, Acts 16:11–40

Philistines (FIL-ih-steens) *people who were Israel's enemy for many years; worshiped false gods.*
- Samson defeated, Judges 15—16
- captured the Ark of the Agreement, 1 Samuel 4—6
- David defeated, 1 Samuel 17—18; 2 Samuel 5:17–25; 21:15–22

Phinehas, son of Eleazar (FIN-ee-us) *a priest and grandson of Aaron,* Numbers 25:1–13

Phinehas, son of Eli, *an evil priest,* 1 Samuel 1:3; 2:34; 4:4–11

Phoebe (FEE-beh) *a woman in the church in Cenchrea,* Romans 16:1

Phoenicia (foh-NEE-shuh) *an early name for the land on the east coast of the Mediterranean Sea; called "Lebanon" today,* Mark 7:26; Acts 11:19; 15:3

phylactery (fil-LAK-tur-ee) See "box of Scriptures."

pigs
- considered unclean, Leviticus 11:7
- snout of, Proverbs 11:22
- "don't throw your pearls before pigs," Matthew 7:6
- demons sent into, Matthew 8:30–33; Mark 5:11–13; Luke 8:32–33
- fed by prodigal son, Luke 15:15–16

Pilate, Pontius (PIE-lut, PON-shus) *the Roman governor of Judea from* A.D. *26 to 36,* Luke 3:1; 13:1
- handed Jesus over to be killed, Matthew 27; Mark 15; Luke 23; John 18:28—19:38

pillar (PILL-ur) *a large stone that is set upright; also a tall column of stone that supports the roof of a building.*
- of Jacob, Genesis 28:18–22
- to worship false gods, 2 Kings 17:9–12
- in the Temple, 1 Kings 7:6, 15–22
- of cloud and fire, Exodus 13:21–22; 14:19–24; 33:8–10

Pisgah, Mount (PIS-guh) *one of the high spots on Mount Nebo where Moses stood to see into the Promised Land,* Numbers 23:14; Deuteronomy 3:27; 34:1

plague (PLAYG) *a disaster. God sent ten plagues on the land of Egypt so the Egyptians would set the Israelites free.*
- on the Egyptians, Exodus 7—11
- on the Israelites, Exodus 32:35; Numbers 11:31–33; 16:41–50; 25:1–9

plan, See "decision making."

pleasure
- found in the Lord, Psalm 16:11
- abuse of wealth for, James 5:1–6
- self-indulging widow, 1 Timothy 5:5–6

plumb line (PLUM LINE) *a string with a rock or other weight on one end. People used it to see if a wall was straight.*
- symbol for God's judging, 2 Kings 21:10–13; Amos 7:7–8

pomegranate (PAHM-gran-it) *a reddish fruit about the size of an apple,* Numbers 13:23; Joel 1:12
- design on priests' clothing, Exodus 28:33–34
- design of Temple decorations, 1 Kings 7:18–20

poor
- God's care for, Psalm 140:12; Proverbs 22:22–23; Matthew 11:5; James 2:5
- treatment of, Leviticus 19:9–10; Matthew 25:34–36; Luke 14:12–14

possessions
- Promised Land given to Israelites, Genesis 17:8; Numbers 32:22; Joshua 1:11
- proper attitudes toward, Ecclesiastes 5:10—6:6; Luke 12:13–21; Acts 2:45; 1 John 3:17
- danger of, Matthew 19:22
- sold by Christians, Acts 2:45

Potiphar (POT-ih-fur) *an officer for the king of Egypt. He put Joseph in charge of his household.* Genesis 39

pottage (POT-edge) *a thick vegetable soup or stew,* Genesis 25:29–34; 2 Kings 4:38–41

potter (POT-ur) *a person who makes pots and dishes out of clay.*
- as a symbol of God, Jeremiah 18:1–6

poverty, See "poor."

power
- of Jesus, Matthew 24:30; 28:18; Luke 6:19
- of the Spirit, Luke 4:14; Acts 1:8; Romans 15:19
- of Satan, Acts 26:18
- of the apostles, Luke 9:1; Acts 4:33

praetorium (pray-TORE-ee-um) *the governor's palace in New Testament times,* Matthew 27:27; Acts 23:35

praise (PRAYZ) *to say good things about someone or something. God's people can praise him by singing, praying, and by living the way he tells us to live.* 1 Chronicles 16:4–7; Psalms 103; 104; 145—150

prayer
- teachings about, Matthew 5:44–45; 21:18–22; Philippians 4:6; James 5:15–16
- Jesus' model prayer, Matthew 6:5–15

preach, *to give a talk on a religious subject; to tell the Good News.*
- Jonah preached to Nineveh, Jonah 3:2–4
- John preached, Matthew 3:1; Mark 1:4; Luke 3:3
- Jesus preached, Matthew 4:17; Mark 2:2; Luke 4:43–44
- Good News preached, Acts 8:25, 40; Galatians 2:7; 1 Thessalonians 2:9
- preaching commanded, 2 Timothy 4:2

pregnancy, crisis, See "abortion."

Preparation Day (prep-a-RAY-shun DAY) *the day before the Sabbath day. On that day the Jews prepared for the Sabbath.* Luke 23:54; John 19:14, 31

pride
- warnings against, Romans 12:3; 1 Corinthians 13:4; Philippians 2:3; James 4:6

priest (PREEST) *in the Old Testament, a servant of God who worked in the Holy Tent or Temple.* See also "high priest."
- clothes for, Exodus 28
- appointing of, Exodus 29:1–37
- rules for, Leviticus 21:1—22:16

Priscilla (prih-SIL-uh) *a friend of Paul,* Acts 18:1–4, 18–19; Romans 16:3–4
- taught Apollos, Acts 18:24–26

prison
- Joseph in prison, Genesis 39:20—41:40
- Peter in prison, Acts 5:17–20
- Paul in prison, Acts 16:23–34

prodigal (PRAH-dih-gul) *careless and wasteful.*
- the prodigal son, Luke 15:11–32

promise
- from God, Joshua 1:3; 1 Kings 8:20; Galatians 3:14; Ephesians 3:6
- first commandment with, Ephesians 6:2
- Lord is not slow in keeping, 2 Peter 2:9

prophecy (PRAH-feh-see) *a message; God speaking through chosen people called "prophets,"* Ezekiel 14:9; 1 Thessalonians 5:20; 2 Peter 1:20–21

prophesy (PRAH-fes-sy) *to speak a prophecy,* Acts 2:17–18. See "prophecy."
- a spiritual gift, 1 Corinthians 14:1–5

prophet (PRAH-fet) *a messenger; one who is able, with God's help, to tell God's message correctly. Sometimes prophets told what would happen in the future.* Matthew 11:13–14
- how to judge, Deuteronomy 13:1–5; 18:21–22
- examples of, Ezra 5:1; Jeremiah 1:1–9; Matthew 3:3
- false prophets, Deuteronomy 13:1–5

prophetess (PRAH-feh-tess) *a female prophet,* Exodus 15:20; Judges 4:4; 2 Kings 22:14; Luke 2:36. See "prophet."

prophetic symbolism
- city images from Ezekiel, Ezekiel 4
- war images from Isaiah, Isaiah 5:26–30
- belt symbol for Paul, Acts 21:11

prostitute (PRAH-sti-toot) *a person who sells his or her body for sex.*
- warnings against, 1 Corinthians 6:15
- examples of, Genesis 38:15–16; Jeremiah 3:1–3; Hosea 3:2–3; Matthew 21:32

protest, See "complain."

proverbs (PRAH-verbs) *wise sayings. The Book of Proverbs contains many wise sayings that tell how to live a good and happy life.* 1 Kings 4:32; Proverbs 1—31

psalm (SAHM) *a song. The Book of Psalms is like a songbook.* Ephesians 5:19; Colossians 3:16

publican (PUB-leh-kun) See "tax collector."

Publius (POOB-lih-us) *an important man of the island of Malta,* Acts 28:7–8

Pul, See "Tiglath-Pileser."

punishment
- of Cain, Genesis 4:13
- everlasting, Matthew 25:46; 2 Thessalonians 1:8–9
- for rejecting Jesus, Hebrews 10:29
- by government, Romans 13:4; 1 Peter 2:14

pure
- gold, Exodus 25:11–39; 37; 1 Kings 6:20–21
- heart, Psalm 51:10; Matthew 5:8
- describing Jesus, Hebrews 7:26
- describing people, Job 4:17; 15:14; Philippians 1:10; Titus 1:15
- water, Hebrews 10:22

Purim, See "Feast of Purim."

purple, *a color that, in Bible times, was worn by kings, queens, and other rich people. Purple cloth was expensive because the purple dye came from special shellfish.* Exodus 25:1–4; Judges 8:26; Mark 15:17; Acts 16:14

Q

quail (KWALE) *a brownish-white bird.*
- given by God to Israel, Exodus 16:11–13; Numbers 11:31–34; Psalm 105:40

quarrel
- Israelites quarreled with Moses, Exodus 17:1–7

Queen Goddess, *Ishtar; a goddess of the Babylonians,* Jeremiah 7:18; 44:15–29

Queen of Heaven, See "Queen Goddess."

queen of Sheba, See "Sheba, queen of."

question
- Solomon questioned by queen of Sheba, 1 Kings 10:1–3
- Jesus questioned, Mark 8:11; Luke 23:9; John 8:6
- asked by Jesus, Matthew 21:24
- apostles questioned by Jews, Acts 4:7; 5:27

quiet
- words, Ecclesiastes 9:17
- riot quieted, Acts 19:35–36
- life, 1 Thessalonians 4:11; 1 Timothy 2:2

Quirinius (kwy-RIN-ee-us) *the Roman governor of Syria when Jesus was born,* Luke 2:1–3

quiver (KWIH-vur) *a bag to hold arrows,* Psalm 127:5; Isaiah 49:2

R

Rabbah (RAB-uh) *the capital city of the Ammonites,* 2 Samuel 11:1; 12:26–29; Ezekiel 25:5

rabbi/rabboni (RAB-eye/rah-BONE-eye) *teacher. Jesus' followers often called him "rabbi" as a sign of respect.* John 1:38; 20:16

Rachel (RAY-chel) *a wife of Jacob and the mother of Benjamin and Joseph.*
- married Jacob, Genesis 29:1–30
- gave birth to Joseph, Genesis 30:22–24
- stole Laban's idols, Genesis 31:19–35
- death of, Genesis 35:16–20

racism
- Peter rejects the "unclean," Acts 10
- Jesus helps a Greek woman, Mark 7:24–30
- church council on non-Jews, Acts 15

Rahab, the dragon (RAY-hab) *In a well-known story, Rahab was defeated. Egypt was sometimes called Rahab to show that it would be defeated.* Job 9:13; Isaiah 30:7

Rahab, the prostitute, *a woman in Jericho. She hid the Israelite spies and helped them escape.*
- hid the spies, Joshua 2:1–21
- rescued from Jericho, Joshua 6:16–25
- an example of faith, Hebrews 11:31; James 2:25

rainbow
- a sign of God's agreement with people, Genesis 9:8–17

raisin, 1 Samuel 25:18; 30:12; 1 Chronicles 12:40

ram, *a male sheep.*
- offered instead of Isaac, Genesis 22:13
- used for burnt offerings, Exodus 29; Leviticus 8:18–29; Numbers 28:11—29:37
- with two horns, Daniel 8:3–22

Ramah (RAY-muh) *a town about five miles north of Jerusalem,* Jeremiah 31:15; Matthew 2:18

Rameses (RAM-eh-seez) *one of the cities built by the Israelites when they were slaves in Egypt,* Exodus 1:11; 12:37; Numbers 33:3

Ramoth Gilead (RAY-moth GIL-ee-ad) *one of the cities of safety on the east side of the Jordan River,* Joshua 20:8; 1 Kings 4:13; 2 Kings 8:28—9:14

ransom, *a payment that frees a captive.*
- Jesus as a ransom for sins, Matthew 20:28; 1 Timothy 2:6; Hebrews 9:15

Rapha (RAY-fa) *a leader of a group of people in Canaan who may have been giants. The descendants of Rapha are called "Rephaites."* 2 Samuel 21:15–22; Joshua 13:12

raven, *a large black bird similar to a crow that eats dead things.*
- sent out by Noah, Genesis 8:7
- fed Elijah, 1 Kings 17:4–6

read
- the Book of the Teachings, Joshua 8:34–35; Nehemiah 8:2–9
- reading the teachings commanded, Deuteronomy 17:18–19; 31:9–13
- brings happiness, Revelation 1:3

Rebekah (ree-BEK-uh) *the wife of Isaac and the mother of Jacob and Esau.*
- married Isaac, Genesis 24
- gave birth to Jacob and Esau, Genesis 25:19–26
- helped deceive Isaac, Genesis 27
- buried at Machpelah, Genesis 49:31

rebellion
- of the people of Israel, Numbers 14
- Pharisees' rebellion, John 8:34–47
- Samuel warns against, 1 Samuel 12:14–15

reconciliation
- by Christ, 2 Corinthians 5:18
- now a friend of God, Romans 5:9–11
- healed by his wounds, Isaiah 53:5

redeem (ree-DEEM) *to buy something back or to buy a slave's freedom.*
- property, Leviticus 25:23–34; Ruth 4:3–6
- slave, Leviticus 25:47–49
- redeemed by God, 1 Corinthians 6:20; Galatians 4:5; Titus 2:14

Red Sea, *Sea of Reeds; a large body of water between Africa and Arabia.*
- Israelites crossed, Exodus 13:17—14:31

refuge, *a place of safety or protection.*
- God as our refuge, Deuteronomy 33:27; 2 Samuel 22:3; Psalms 18:2; 31:2; 71:3; 91:2
- city of, Numbers 35:6–34; Joshua 20

Rehoboam (ree-ho-BO-um) *son of Solomon who took his place as king.*
- became king, 1 Kings 11:41–43
- Israel rebelled against, 1 Kings 12:1–24
- strengthened Judah, 2 Chronicles 11:5–17
- disobeyed God, 2 Chronicles 12

rejoice
- commanded to, Matthew 5:11–12; Romans 12:15; Philippians 4:4; 1 Peter 4:13
- examples of, 1 Samuel 6:13; Nehemiah 12:43

remission (rih-MISH-un) See "forgiveness."

remnant (REM-nant) *a small part that is left; a name used for the Jews who were left alive after their captivity in Babylon.*
- of Israelites who returned to Jerusalem, Ezra 9:15; Nehemiah 1:2; Isaiah 10:20–22

repent (ree-PENT) *being sorry for doing something wrong and not continuing to do that wrong.* See "change of heart and life."

Rephaites, See "Rapha."

reputation
- greater than wealth, Proverbs 22:1
- wives' reputations and husbands, 1 Peter 3:1
- Solomon's, 1 Kings 10:1–13

respect
- to parents, Leviticus 19:3; 1 Timothy 3:4
- between husbands and wives, Ephesians 5:33; 1 Peter 3:7
- to all people, 1 Peter 2:17; 3:16

rest
- on the seventh day, Genesis 2:2; Exodus 31:15; Hebrews 4:4
- given by the Lord, Psalm 95:11; Jeremiah 6:16; Matthew 11:28
- heaven as a place of rest, Revelation 14:13

resurrection (REZ-uh-REK-shun) *a dead person's coming back to life.*
- of Jesus, Matthew 28:1–10; Mark 16; Luke 24; John 20—21; Acts 2:24–32; Romans 1:4
- of God's people, John 6:39; Acts 24:15; 1 Corinthians 15; Philippians 3:10–11; Hebrews 11:35

Reuben (ROO-ben) *oldest of Jacob's twelve sons.*
- birth of, Genesis 29:32
- tried to save Joseph, Genesis 37:18–29
- descendants of, Exodus 6:14; Numbers 1:20; Joshua 13:15–23

revelation (rev-uh-LAY-shun) *showing plainly something that has been hidden,* 2 Corinthians 12:1; Revelation 1:1–3

revenge
- warnings against, Leviticus 19:18; Romans 12:19; 1 Thessalonians 5:15; 1 Peter 3:9

reward
- in heaven, Matthew 5:12
- for obedience, Psalm 19:11
- for what a person does, Matthew 6:1–18; 10:42; 16:27; Colossians 3:24
- children as a reward, Psalm 127:3

Rhoda (ROAD-uh) *a servant girl in the home of John Mark's mother,* Acts 12:6–17

righteousness (RY-chuss-ness) *being right with God and doing what is right.*
- explained, Romans 3:19–26; 2 Corinthians 5:21; 6:4–7; Philippians 3:8–9
- Abraham as an example of, Romans 4:3
- right living, 2 Corinthians 6:7; Ephesians 5:9; 1 Timothy 6:11; 1 Peter 2:24

road, See "way."

robber
- Temple as a hideout for, Jeremiah 7:11; Matthew 21:13
- attacked man on road to Jericho, Luke 10:30
- killed with Jesus, Matthew 27:38–44; John 18:40

Rock, *often used as a name for God. As a large rock is strong and provides a hiding place, so God is strong and protects us from our enemies.* Genesis 49:24; 2 Samuel 22:32–49; Psalm 19:14

rock badger (ROK BAD-jur) *a coney; a small, tailless animal like a rabbit that hides among the mountain gorges and rocky areas of Arabia,* Psalm 104:18; Proverbs 30:26

Rome, *the capital city of the Roman Empire at the time of Christ,* Acts 2:10; 18:2; Romans 1:7
- Paul sent there, Acts 23:11; 28:14–15

roof
- spies hid there, Joshua 2:6
- David saw Bathsheba from there, 2 Samuel 11:2
- built room for Elisha there, 2 Kings 4:8–10
- man lowered through, Mark 2:3–4
- Peter prayed there, Acts 10:9

Ruth (ROOTH) *a widow from Moab.*
- moved to Judah, Ruth 1
- worked in Boaz's field, Ruth 2
- married Boaz, Ruth 3—4
- birth of Obed, Ruth 4:13–22

S

Sabbath (SAB-uth) *means "rest"; the seventh day of the Jewish week; the Jews' day to worship God. They were not allowed to work on this day.*
- commands about, Exodus 20:8–11; 31:12–17
- Jesus is Lord of, Matthew 12:1–13; Mark 2:23–28; Luke 6:1–11

sackcloth (SAK-cloth) *a type of clothing made from rough cloth; worn by people to show their sadness,* Genesis 37:33–35; Esther 4:1; Matthew 11:21

sacrifice (SAK-rih-fice) *to give something valuable to God.*
- burnt sacrifices, Leviticus 6:8–13
- drink sacrifices, Leviticus 23:13; Numbers 15:5; 28:7
- penalty sacrifices, Leviticus 7:1–10
- fellowship sacrifices, Leviticus 3; 7:11–27
- sin sacrifices, Leviticus 4
- limits of, Hebrews 9; 10
- living sacrifice, Romans 12:1

Sadducees (SAD-you-seez) *a Jewish religious group that didn't believe in angels or resurrection; they believed only the first five books of the Old Testament were true.*
- challenged Jesus, Matthew 22:23–33
- arrested Peter and John, Acts 4:1–3
- arrested the apostles, Acts 5:17–42
- Paul spoke to the council, Acts 23:1–9

safety, city of, *city of refuge. In Bible times, someone who had accidentally killed another person could go to a city of safety for protection. As long as he was there, the dead person's relative could not punish him.*
- rules about, Numbers 35:6–34; Joshua 20

saffron (SAF-ron) *a purple flower; parts of it are used as a spice,* Song of Songs 4:14

saint, *holy person; another word for "Christian,"* Acts 9:41; Romans 1:7; 1 Corinthians 14:33

Salem (SAY-lem) *means "peace"; an old name for Jerusalem.*
- home of Melchizedek, Genesis 14:18; Hebrews 7:1–2

Salome, daughter of Herodias (sah-LO-mee)
- had John the Baptist killed, Matthew 14:3–12; Mark 6:17–29

Salome, wife of Zebedee, *the mother of the apostles James and John,* Mark 15:40; 16:1

salt
- used to preserve foods, Job 6:6; Mark 9:50
- Lot's wife turned into salt, Genesis 19:15–26
- "You are the salt of the earth," Matthew 5:13

Salt Sea, See "Dead Sea."

salvation (sal-VAY-shun) *being rescued from danger; being saved from sin and its punishment.*
- as God's gift, John 3:16; Ephesians 2:8; Titus 2:11
- through Christ, Acts 4:12; 1 Thessalonians 5:9; 1 Timothy 1:15; Hebrews 5:7–9
- as a helmet, Ephesians 6:17; 1 Thessalonians 5:8
- urgency of, 2 Corinthians 6:2; Hebrews 2:3
- rejoice in, Psalms 9:14; 13:5; 51:12; Isaiah 25:9

Samaritan (sah-MEHR-ih-ton) *a person from the area of Samaria in Palestine. These people were only partly Jewish, so the Jews hated them.* John 4:9
- Jesus taught a Samaritan woman, John 4:1–42
- story of the good Samaritan, Luke 10:25–37

Samson (SAM-son) *one of Israel's judges; he was famous for his great strength.*
- birth of, Judges 13
- married a Philistine, Judges 14—15
- tricked by Delilah, Judges 16:4–22
- death of, Judges 16:23–31
- hero of faith, Hebrews 11:32

Samuel (SAM-u-el) *the last judge in Israel.*
- birth of, 1 Samuel 1:1–20
- worked in the Temple, 1 Samuel 1:21—2:26
- became a prophet, 1 Samuel 3
- appointed Saul as king, 1 Samuel 10
- appointed David as king, 1 Samuel 16:1–13
- death of, 1 Samuel 25:1

Sanballat (san-BAL-lat) *governor of Samaria who tried to stop Nehemiah from rebuilding the walls of Jerusalem,* Nehemiah 4—6

sanctify (SANK-teh-fy) *to make holy or ready for service to God,* John 17:17–19; 1 Corinthians 6:11; 1 Peter 1:2

sanctuary (SANK-choo-air-ee) See "Holy Place."

sand
- Abraham's descendants as numerous as, Genesis 22:17; 32:12
- Job's days as numerous as, Job 29:18
- house built on, Matthew 7:26–27

Sanhedrin (san-HEE-drin) See "council."

Sapphira (sah-FY-ruh) *wife of Ananias.*
- lied to the Holy Spirit, Acts 5:1–11

Sarah (SAIR-uh) *wife of Abraham,* Genesis 11:29–30
- gave Hagar to Abraham, Genesis 16:1–6
- name changed from "Sarai," Genesis 17:15–16
- gave birth to Isaac, Genesis 21:1–7
- death of, Genesis 23

Satan (SAY-ton) *means "enemy"; the devil; the enemy of God and man.*
- encouraged David to sin, 1 Chronicles 21:1
- tested Job, Job 1:6–12; 2:1–7
- tempted Jesus, Luke 4:1–13
- a fallen angel, Luke 10:18–19
- to be thrown into lake of fire, Revelation 20:10

Satanism, See "Satan."

Saul, king of Israel
- appointed king, 1 Samuel 9—10
- disobeyed God, 1 Samuel 15
- tried to kill David, 1 Samuel 19; 23:7–29
- death of, 1 Samuel 31

Saul of Tarsus, Acts 13:9. See "Paul."

savior
- God as Savior, Psalm 25:5; Isaiah 45:21; Luke 1:47; 1 Timothy 1:1
- Christ as Savior, Luke 2:11; John 4:42; Ephesians 5:23; Titus 2:13

scarlet (SCAR-let) *a bright red color,* Exodus 26:1; Joshua 2:18; Isaiah 1:18; Matthew 27:28

scepter (SEP-tur) *a wand or a rod that the king holds; a sign of his power,* Esther 4:11; Psalm 60:7

scourge (SKURJ) *to beat someone with a whip or stick,* 1 Kings 12:11
- Jesus scourged, Matthew 27:26; Mark 15:15
- Paul scourged, Acts 21:32; 2 Corinthians 11:24

scribe, *to write, to count, and to put in order. In New Testament times scribes were men who wrote copies of the Scriptures.*
- Ezra as scribe, Nehemiah 8:1
- against Jesus, Matthew 15:1–9
- condemned by Jesus, Matthew 23:13–36

Scriptures (SCRIP-churs) *special writings of God's word for people. When the word "Scriptures" is used in the New Testament, it usually means the Old Testament. Later, it came to mean the whole Bible.*
- fulfilled, Matthew 26:52–54; John 19:24, 28, 36
- given by God, 2 Timothy 3:16

scroll, *a long roll of paper used for writing,* Deuteronomy 17:18; Jeremiah 36; Revelation 5:1–5

Scythians (SITH-ee-unz) *a group of wandering people who lived near the Black Sea,* Colossians 3:11

Sea of Galilee, See "Galilee, Lake."

Sea of Reeds, See "Red Sea."

seal, *a tool with a design or picture carved on it. Kings pressed this seal into wax and used it like a signature. Sometimes these seals were worn as rings.*
- examples of, 1 Kings 21:8; Esther 8:8

seed
- created by God, Genesis 1:11, 12, 29
- parables of, Matthew 13:1–43

seer, *another name for prophet.* See "prophet."

Selah (SEE-lah) *probably a musical direction; used in the Psalms. It may mean to pause. The word was not intended to be spoken when reading the psalm.* Psalms 3:2, 4, 8; 89:4, 37, 45, 48

self-control
- in Paul's ministry, 1 Corinthians 9:19–27
- broken walls, Proverbs 25:28
- addressed to Felix, Acts 24:25

Sennacherib (sen-AK-ur-ib) *king of Assyria from 705 to 681 B.C.*
- attacked Jerusalem, 2 Kings 18:13—19:37; 2 Chronicles 32:1–23; Isaiah 36—37

Sermon on the Mount, *a sermon Jesus preached as he was sitting on the side of a mountain near Lake Galilee,* Matthew 5—7

serpent, See "snake."

servant
- of the Lord, Deuteronomy 34:5; Joshua 2:8; 1 Kings 11:32; Luke 1:38
- Jesus as a, Philippians 2:7
- parable of, Matthew 25:14–30
- Jesus' followers to be, Matthew 20:25–27

service
- washing feet in, John 13:14
- importance of servant, Luke 22:27
- with the strength of God, 1 Peter 4:11

Seth, *the third son of Adam and Eve,* Genesis 4:25–26; 5:6–8; Luke 3:38

sexuality
- Solomon's love song, Song of Songs 1
- in marriage, 1 Corinthians 7
- created by God, Genesis 1:27

Shadrach (SHAYD-rak) *a friend of Daniel.*
- taken into captivity, Daniel 1
- became a leader, Daniel 2:49
- saved from the furnace, Daniel 3

Shallum, king of Israel (SHAL-um) *ruled for only one month in 752 B.C.,* 2 Kings 15:10–15

Shalmaneser (shal-mah-NEE-zer) *a king of Assyria,* 2 Kings 17:1–6; 18:9

shame, See "honor."

Shaphan (SHAY-fan) *an assistant to King Josiah,* 2 Kings 22:3–14; 2 Chronicles 34:8–21

sharing
- commanded, Luke 3:11; Romans 12:13; 1 Timothy 6:18
- examples of, Acts 2:42–47; 4:32; 2 Corinthians 8:1–4

Sharon (SHAIR-un) *the plain in Palestine along the coast of the Mediterranean Sea,* 1 Chronicles 5:16; 27:29; Song of Songs 2:1; Isaiah 33:9

sheaf (SHEEF) *a bundle of grain stalks that have been cut and tied together,* Genesis 37:7; Leviticus 23:10; Job 24:10

Sheba, queen of (SHE-buh) *a queen who came to visit Solomon and see his wealth,* 1 Kings 10:1–13

Shebna (SHEB-nuh) *the manager of the palace for King Hezekiah,* 2 Kings 18:17—19:4; Isaiah 36:1—37:4

sheep
- God's people compared to, Ezekiel 34; John 10:1–18; 1 Peter 2:25
- parable of, Luke 15:1–7

Shem, *Noah's oldest son,* Genesis 6:10; 7:13; 10:21–31

sheminith (SHEM-ih-nith) *a musical term in the Psalms that means an octave (eight notes); may mean to use an instrument with eight strings,* Psalms 6; 12

shepherd
- David as, 1 Samuel 17:15, 34–36
- Lord as, Psalm 23
- Jesus, the good shepherd, John 10:1–18
- elders as, 1 Peter 5:1–4

Sheshbazzar (shesh-BAZ-ur) *governor of the Jews in 538 B.C.,* Ezra 1:7–11; 5:13–16

shiggaion (shi-GY-on) *probably a musical term; used in the Psalms; may mean that the psalm is a sad song,* Psalm 7

shigionoth (shi-GY-o-noth) *probably a musical term,* Habakkuk 3:1

Shiloh (SHY-lo) *a town north of Jerusalem.*
- location of the Holy Tent, Joshua 18:1, 8; Judges 18:31; Jeremiah 7:12

Shimei (SHIM-ee-i) *a relative of King Saul.*
- cursed David, 2 Samuel 16:5–14
- asked forgiveness, 2 Samuel 19:16–23
- death of, 1 Kings 2:36–46

ship, 1 Kings 9:26–28; 22:48; Acts 27

Shishak (SHY-shak) *king of Egypt during the time of Solomon and Rehoboam.*
- attacked Jerusalem, 1 Kings 14:25–28; 2 Chronicles 12:1–9

showbread, See "bread that shows we are in God's presence."

Shunammite (SHOO-nah-mite) *a person from Shunem, a town in northern Israel.*
- Shunammite woman took care of Elisha, 2 Kings 4:8–17
- her son raised from the dead, 2 Kings 4:18–37
- given back her land, 2 Kings 8:1–6

sickle (SICK-ul) *a tool for cutting grain,* Revelation 14:14–19

sickness, See "healing."

Sidon (SY-don) *a Phoenician city on the coast of the Mediterranean Sea,* Genesis 10:19; Matthew 11:21–22; Mark 7:31; Acts 27:3–4

siege mound (SEEJ) *dirt piled against a city wall to make it easier for attackers to climb up and attack the city,* 2 Samuel 20:15; Isaiah 37:33; Jeremiah 6:6

signet ring (SIG-net RING) *a ring worn by a king or other important person. It had his seal on it.* Genesis 41:42; Esther 3:10; 8:2–10; Daniel 6:17. See "seal."

Sihon (SY-hon) *a king of the Amorites when the Israelites came out of Egypt.*
- refused to let Israelites pass, Numbers 21:21–31; Deuteronomy 2:24–37

Silas (SY-lus) *also "Silvanus"; a teacher in the church in Jerusalem who often traveled with Paul.*
- sent to the Gentiles, Acts 15:22–23; 17:16
- joined Paul in Corinth, Acts 18:5
- helped with Peter's letter, 1 Peter 5:12

Siloam, pool of (sy-LO-um) *a pool of water in Jerusalem,* John 9:1–12

Silvanus (sil-VAY-nus) See "Silas."

Simeon of Jerusalem (SIM-ee-un) *a godly man who saw baby Jesus in the Temple,* Luke 2:25–35

Simeon, son of Israel, *one of the twelve sons of Israel,* Genesis 29:33; 42:23–36
- descendants of, Numbers 1:22–23; 26:12–14

Simon, brother of Jesus (SY-mun) Matthew 13:55

Simon of Cyrene (sy-REE-ni) *carried the cross of Jesus,* Matthew 27:32; Mark 15:21; Luke 23:26

Simon Peter, See "Peter."

Simon the magician, *tried to buy the power of the Holy Spirit,* Acts 8:9–24

Simon the Zealot, *an apostle of Jesus,* Matthew 10:4; Mark 3:18; Luke 6:15; Acts 1:13

sin, *a word, thought, or act against the law of God.*
- offering for, Leviticus 4; 6:24–30; Hebrews 7:27; 10:4–12
- committed by everyone, Romans 3:23; 1 John 1:8–10
- Christ died for, Romans 4:25; 1 Corinthians 15:3; 1 Peter 2:24; 1 John 2:2; 3:5
- results of, Isaiah 59:2; Romans 6:23; Ephesians 2:1; Hebrews 12:1

Sinai (SY-ny) *a mountain in the desert between Egypt and Canaan.*
- Moses received the Ten Commandments there, Exodus 19—20

singing, *a way of praising God and teaching each other,* Judges 5:3; Psalm 30:4; Ephesians 5:19; Colossians 3:16

Sisera (SIS-er-uh) *captain of a Canaanite army,* Judges 4

slave
- rules about, Exodus 21:1–11, 16, 26–32; Ephesians 6:5–9; 1 Timothy 6:1–2

slave woman, *concubine; she bore children for her master but was not considered equal to a wife.*
- Hagar as, Genesis 16:1–3
- of Solomon, 1 Kings 11:2–3

sleep
- God never sleeps, Psalm 121:4
- danger of, Proverbs 6:10–11
- Eutychus fell asleep, Acts 20:9
- to awake from, Romans 13:11
- a gift from the Lord, Psalm 127:2

sling, *a weapon for throwing rocks,* Judges 20:16; 1 Samuel 17:39–50; 2 Kings 3:24–25

slothful (SLAWTH-ful) *lazy and undependable,* Proverbs 6:6–11; 13:4; Matthew 25:26; Hebrews 6:12

sluggard, See "slothful."

snake
- sticks became snakes, Exodus 7:8–13
- bronze snake made by Moses, Numbers 21:4–9; John 3:14
- Paul bitten by, Acts 28:1–6

Sodom (SOD-um) *a town known for its evil people.*
- destroyed, Genesis 18:17—19:29
- symbol of evil, Matthew 10:11–15; 11:20–24; Revelation 11:8

soldier
- arrested Jesus, John 18:12–13
- made fun of Jesus, Matthew 27:27–31; Luke 23:11
- at Jesus' death, Matthew 27:32–37; Luke 23:26–38, 47; John 19:1–3, 16–24, 28–35
- lied about Jesus' resurrection, Matthew 28:11–15
- Cornelius, Acts 10:1
- guarded Peter, Acts 12:6
- Christian compared to, 2 Timothy 2:3–4

Solomon (SOL-o-mon) *a son of David; famous for his wisdom.*
- became king, 1 Kings 1:28–53
- wisdom of, 1 Kings 3:1–15; 4:29–34
- made a wise decision, 1 Kings 3:16–28
- built the Temple, 1 Kings 6; 7:13–51
- visited by the queen of Sheba, 1 Kings 10:1–13; Matthew 12:42
- married many women, 1 Kings 11:1–8
- death of, 1 Kings 11:40–41

Solomon's Porch (SOL-o-mon's PORCH) *a covered courtyard on the east side of the Temple,* 1 Kings 7:6; John 10:23; Acts 3:11; 5:12

Son of David, *a name the Jews used for the Christ because the Savior was to come from the family of King David,* Matthew 1:1; 9:27; 15:22; 21:9

Son of Man, *a name Jesus called himself. It showed that he was God's Son, but he was also a human being.* Matthew 24:30; Mark 13:26; Luke 21:27; 22:69–70

son/child of God
- "the Son of the Father," John 1:14
- Israel the firstborn, Exodus 4:21–23
- a believer as, Romans 8:14–17

sorcery (SOR-sir-ee) *trying to put magical spells on people or harming them by magic,* Acts 8:9–25; 19:18–19
- warnings against, Leviticus 19:26; Deuteronomy 18:14–15; 2 Kings 17:17

soul (SOLE) *what makes a person alive. Sometimes the Bible writers used words like "heart" and "soul" to mean a person's whole being or the person himself.*
- "destroy the soul and the body," Matthew 10:28
- losing, Matthew 16:26
- "all your heart and all your soul," Matthew 22:37
- joined with the spirit, Hebrews 4:12

sower, *someone who plants seeds to grow into crops,* Matthew 13:1–43; 2 Corinthians 9:6

Spirit (SPIH-rit) See "Holy Spirit."

spirit, *the part of humans that was made to be like God because God is spirit. The New Testament also talks about evil spirits.* Isaiah 26:9; 1 Thessalonians 5:23; James 2:26
- evil spirit, Matthew 12:43; Mark 1:23; 5:2; Luke 4:33

spiritual dryness, See "spirituality."

spiritual gifts, *special talents or abilities that God gives his people,* Romans 12:6–8; 1 Corinthians 12:1–11; 14; Ephesians 4:7–13

spirituality
- spiritual growth, 1 Corinthians 3:1
- living sacrifices to God, Romans 12:1–21

spring, *a natural fountain,* Genesis 7:11; Exodus 15:27

staff, *a shepherd's walking stick,* Exodus 4:1–5; 7:8–12; Numbers 20:6–11; Psalm 23:4

steal, See also "robber."
- commands against, Exodus 20:15; Matthew 19:18; Romans 13:9; Ephesians 4:28

Stephen (STEE-ven) *one of the seven men chosen to serve the church in Jerusalem; the first martyr for Christ.*
- chosen to serve the church, Acts 6:5–6
- killed by the Jews, Acts 6:8—7:60

stewardship
- of God's secrets, 1 Corinthians 4:1
- over the earth, Genesis 1:26–28
- servants of God, Luke 12:42–48

stone
- the living "stone," 1 Peter 2:4
- "would cry out," Luke 19:40
- at Jacob and Laban's agreement, Genesis 31:43–53

stoning, *a way of killing someone by throwing rocks at him.*
- commanded, Deuteronomy 17:2–7
- Naboth stoned, 1 Kings 21:13
- Stephen stoned, Acts 7:54–60
- Paul stoned, Acts 14:19

strength
- love God with all your strength, Deuteronomy 6:5; Mark 12:30
- God as the source, Psalms 18:1; 73:26; Philippians 4:13; 1 Peter 4:11

stress
- opportunity for God's glory, James 1:2–8
- give worries to God, 1 Peter 5:7
- peace from the Lord, Matthew 14:27

stronghold, *a fortress, a well-protected place,* 1 Samuel 22:4; 2 Samuel 5:17

stubbornness
- despite Jesus' miracles, John 12:37–41
- in the king (Pharaoh), Exodus 4:21; 7:3; 10:1, 20, 27
- in Israel's continuing sin, Amos 4:6–12

success
- of God's people, Psalm 1:3
- driven by jealousy, Ecclesiastes 4:4
- Christ teaches on, Matthew 5:1–10

suffering
- proper attitude toward, 2 Corinthians 1:3–7; James 5:10
- value of, Romans 8:17–18; 1 Peter 3:8–17
- of Jesus, Isaiah 53:3–10; Luke 24:26, 46; Philippians 3:10; Hebrews 2:18

swaddling clothes, *pieces of cloth that were wrapped around a newborn baby in Jesus' time,* Luke 2:7–12

sword
- of fire, Genesis 3:24
- a weapon, Joshua 5:13; 1 Samuel 17:45; Matthew 26:51–52
- the word of God, Ephesians 6:17; Hebrews 4:12

Sychar (SY-kar) *a small town in Samaria near Jacob's well,* John 4:5–6

synagogue (SIN-uh-gog) *"a meeting." By the first century, the Jews met in synagogues to read and study the Scriptures. The building was also used as the Jewish court and as a school.*
- Jesus taught in, Matthew 4:23; Mark 1:21; Luke 4:16–17
- Paul spoke there, Acts 17:1, 10

Syria (SEER-ee-uh) *an area north of Galilee and east of the Mediterranean Sea; called "Aram" in Old Testament times.* See "Aram."
- enemy of Israel, 1 Kings 11:25; 20:1–34; 2 Kings 13:22–25
- learned about Jesus, Matthew 4:24

T

tabernacle (TAB-er-NAK-'l) See "Meeting Tent."

table fellowship, See "Lord's Supper."

tablets of the Agreement, *two flat stones on which God wrote the Ten Commandments.*
- given to Moses, Exodus 19—20; 24:12–18
- broken by Moses, Exodus 32:15–19
- the second tablets, Exodus 34:1–4
- in the Most Holy Place, Hebrews 9:4

Tabitha (TAB-eh-thuh) See "Dorcas."

Tabor, Mount (TAY-bur) *in the Valley of Jezreel about twelve miles from Lake Galilee,* Judges 4:6–16; Psalm 89:12

tambourine (tam-bah-REEN) *a musical instrument that is beaten to keep rhythm,* Exodus 15:20; 1 Samuel 18:6; Psalm 81:2

Tarshish (TAR-shish) *a city somewhere on the western side of the Mediterranean Sea,* Jonah 1:3; 4:2

Tarsus (TAR-sus) *the most important city in Cilicia, which is now the country of Turkey,* Acts 9:30; 11:25–26
- home of Paul, Acts 9:11; 21:39; 22:3

tax collector, *a Jew hired by the Romans to collect taxes,* Matthew 9:10–11
- Matthew, Matthew 10:3; Luke 5:27
- Zacchaeus, Luke 19:1–10

teacher
- Jesus called a, Matthew 8:19; Mark 10:17; John 1:38; 3:2
- in the church, Romans 12:7; Ephesians 4:11; 1 Timothy 4:13
- false, 1 Timothy 4:1–5; 2 Peter 2:1
- to be judged more strictly, James 3:1

teaching
- commanded, Deuteronomy 6:1–7; Matthew 28:20; 2 Timothy 2:2, 14–15; Titus 2

Teachings of Moses, *or the "Law of Moses,"* Deuteronomy 31:24–26; Joshua 23:6; Nehemiah 8
- purpose of, Romans 3:20; 5:20; Galatians 3:21–25
- limitations of, Romans 8:3; Galatians 2:19; Hebrews 10:1

temple (TEM-p'l) *a building where people worship. God told the Jewish people to worship him at the Temple in Jerusalem.*
- Solomon's Temple, 1 Kings 6—8; 2 Chronicles 2—7
- the Temple rebuilt, Ezra 3
- the body as a temple, John 2:19–22; 1 Corinthians 3:16–17; 6:19–20; 2 Corinthians 6:16

temptation (temp-TAY-shun) *the devil's attempt to get us to do something wrong.*
- Jesus tempted, Matthew 4:1–11; Luke 4:1–13; Hebrews 4:15–16
- a way of escape from, 1 Corinthians 10:13
- source of, James 1:13–15

Ten Commandments, *the rules God gave Moses on Mount Sinai,* Exodus 20:1–20; 31:18; 34:1–28; Deuteronomy 5:1–22

tent
- Abram's tents, Genesis 13:18
- peg, Judges 4:21–22
- makers of, Acts 18:3

Tent, See "Meeting Tent."

test, See "temptation."

Thaddaeus (THAD-ee-us) *one of the twelve apostles,* Matthew 10:3; Mark 3:18

thankfulness, Psalm 107:1; 1 Thessalonians 5:8; Hebrews 12:28

Theophilus (thee-AHF-ih-lus) *the person to whom the books of Luke and Acts were written,* Luke 1:1–4; Acts 1:1

Thessalonica (THES-ah-lah-NY-kah) *the capital of the country of Macedonia, which is now northern Greece,* 1 Thessalonians 1:1; 2 Thessalonians 1:1
- Paul preached there, Acts 17:1–9

Thomas (TOM-us) *Didymus; one of the twelve apostles,* Matthew 10:2–3
- questioned Jesus, John 14:5–7
- saw Jesus after resurrection, John 20:24–29; 21:2

thorn, *sharp points on a branch or stem of a plant.*
- as a curse on Adam, Genesis 3:17–18
- crown of, Matthew 27:29; Mark 15:17; John 19:2–5

threshing floor, *a place where farmers separated grain from chaff. This was done by beating the stalks on the hard ground, throwing them in the air, and letting the wind blow the chaff away.*
- angel visited Gideon there, Judges 6:11
- David bought, 2 Samuel 24:16–25

throne
- king's throne, 1 Kings 10:18–19
- God's throne, Matthew 5:34; Hebrews 4:16; Revelation 3:21; 4

Thummim (THUM-im) *the Urim and Thummim may have been gems. They were attached to the holy vest of the high priest and were used to learn God's will.* Exodus 28:29–30; Leviticus 8:8; Deuteronomy 33:8

Thyatira (THY-ah-TY-rah) *an important city in Asia famous for its purple cloth,* Acts 16:13–14; Revelation 1:11; 2:18–29

Tiberius Caesar (tie-BEER-ee-us SEE-zur) *Roman emperor during the last half of Jesus' life,* Luke 3:1

Tiglath-Pileser (TIG-lath-peh-LEE-zur) *king of Assyria who helped Ahaz; also called "Pul."*
- attacked Israel, 2 Kings 15:19–20
- rescued Ahaz, 2 Kings 16:7–10

Tigris (TY-gris) *a great river in the eastern part of the Bible lands,* Genesis 2:14; Daniel 10:4

time
- "a time for everything," Ecclesiastes 3:1–8
- for rest, Exodus 20:8–11
- wise use of, Ephesians 5:15–17

Timothy (TIM-oh-thee) *close friend and helper of the apostle Paul.*
- helped Paul, Acts 16:1–3; 17:13–16; 1 Corinthians 4:17
- instructed by Paul, 1 and 2 Timothy

tithe (TIETH) *"tenth." The Jews were told to give one-tenth of what they earned to God.* Leviticus 27:30–32; Deuteronomy 12:1–6; Luke 11:42; 18:12

Titus (TIE-tus) *trusted friend and helper of the apostle Paul.*
- helped Corinthians, 2 Corinthians 7:6–7, 13–15; 8:6, 16, 23
- appointed elders, Titus 1:4–5
- Paul's instructions to, Titus 1—3

Tobiah (toe-BY-uh) *tried to keep Nehemiah from rebuilding the walls of Jerusalem,* Nehemiah 2:10–20; 6:10–19; 13:4–9

tomb
- of Lazarus, John 11:38–44
- of Jesus, Matthew 27:57—28:15; Mark 15:42—16:30; Luke 23:50—24:12; John 19:38—20:9

tongue
- lying tongue hated by God, Proverbs 6:16–17
- cannot be tamed, James 3:2–12

tongues, speaking in
- as a spiritual gift, 1 Corinthians 14
- Pentecost, Acts 2
- non-Jews, Acts 10:44–48

tower of Babel, See "Babel."

transfiguration (tranz-fig-you-RAY-shun) *"to change." Jesus was transfigured in front of Peter, James, and John when his face and clothes began to shine brightly.* Matthew 17:1–9; Mark 9:2–9; Luke 9:28–36

tree
- of knowledge of good and evil, Genesis 2:9; 3:3
- of life, Genesis 2:9; Revelation 2:7; 22:2, 14
- people compared to, Psalms 1:3; 92:12; Jeremiah 17:8; Matthew 3:10; 12:33
- cross described as a tree, Galatians 3:13

trespass, See "sin."

tribe, *all descendants of a certain person. The twelve tribes of Israel were descendants of the twelve sons of Jacob, who was later named "Israel."* Numbers 1—2
- Canaan divided among, Joshua 13:7–33; 15—19

trinity
- baptizing in the name of, Matthew 28:18–20
- in Paul's salutation, 2 Corinthians 13:14
- the unity of, Ephesians 4:3–6

triumphal entry (tri-UMF-ul) *the time Jesus entered Jerusalem just before his death,* Matthew 21:1–11; Mark 11:1–19; Luke 19:28–44; John 12:12–15

Troas (TRO-az) *one of the most important cities in northwest Asia,* Acts 16:8–10; 20:5–12; 2 Corinthians 2:12

Trophimus (TROF-eh-mus) *non-Jewish Christian who traveled with Paul,* Acts 20:3–4; 21:27–29; 2 Timothy 4:20

trumpet (TRUM-pet) *in Bible times it was made from animal horns; used to call an army together or announce something important,* Numbers 10:2–10; Joshua 6:4–20; 1 Corinthians 15:52

trust
- a duty, Luke 16:11; 1 Corinthians 4:2; Titus 2:10
- in God, Psalm 20:7; Proverbs 3:5; 16:20; Romans 4:5; 10:11; 1 Peter 2:6
- in lesser things, Psalms 49:13–14; 118:9; Proverbs 11:28; Isaiah 2:22

truth
- speaking honestly, Psalm 15:2; Proverbs 16:13
- God's message, John 17:17; Romans 1:25; Ephesians 1:13; 1 John 1:6

tunic (TOO-nik) *a kind of coat,* Exodus 28:39–40; John 19:23

Tychicus (TIK-ih-kus) *Christian from Asia who did important jobs for Paul,* Acts 20:4; Ephesians 6:21–22; Colossians 4:7–9

Tyre (TIRE) *large, important city in Phoenicia, which is now part of the country of Lebanon,* Mark 7:24–31; Acts 12:20
- Hiram, king of, 2 Samuel 5:11; 1 Kings 9:10–14; 2 Chronicles 2
- a wicked city, Matthew 11:21–22; Luke 10:13–14

U

unbelief, See "faith."

uncircumcised, See "circumcision."

unclean, *the state of a person, animal, or action that was not pleasing to God. In the Old Testament God said certain animals were unclean and were not to be eaten. If a person disobeyed the rules about being clean, he was called unclean and could not serve God until he was made clean again.* See "clean."
- unclean animals, Leviticus 11; Acts 10:9–15
- unclean people, Leviticus 12—15
- God declared everyone to be clean, Acts 10

unity
- one faith, Ephesians 4:5
- of God and Christ, John 17:11, 21
- "be completely joined together," 1 Corinthians 1:10–13

unleavened bread (un-LEV-'nd BREAD) *bread made without yeast.*
- used in the Passover Feast, Exodus 12:20; Deuteronomy 16:1–4

Unleavened Bread, Day of, *the first day of the Feast of Unleavened Bread or Passover,* Matthew 26:17; Luke 22:7

upper room, *upstairs room in a house.*
- Jesus and his followers met there, Mark 14:14–15; Luke 22:9–12

Ur, *a great city thousands of years ago; today in the country of Iraq.*
- home of Abram, Genesis 11:28–31

Uriah (you-RY-uh) *a soldier in King David's army.*
- killed by David, 2 Samuel 11

Urim (YOUR-im) See "Thummim."

Uzzah (UZ-uh) *touched the Ark of the Agreement and died,* 2 Samuel 6:1–8; 1 Chronicles 13:1–14

Uzziah (uh-ZY-uh) *a king of Judah,* 2 Kings 15:13–15; 2 Chronicles 26; Isaiah 6:1

V

Vashti (VASH-ty) *the wife of Ahasuerus, king of Persia,* Esther 1:1–20

veil (VALE) *a head covering usually worn by women; also, a curtain in the Temple.*
- worn by women, Genesis 24:65; Song of Songs 4:1; Isaiah 3:19
- the Temple veil, Matthew 27:51; Mark 15:38; Luke 23:45

vest, holy, *"ephod"; a special type of clothing for the priests in the Old Testament. The holy vest for the high priest had gold and gems on it.*
- description of, Exodus 25:7; 28:6–14; 39:2–7
- one made by Micah, Judges 17:1–5; 18:14–20
- worn by David, 2 Samuel 6:14

vine
- fruit of the, Matthew 26:29; Mark 14:25; Luke 22:18
- Jesus as the, John 15:1–11

vineyard
- Naboth's, 1 Kings 21
- parables of, Matthew 20:1–16; 21:28–46; Mark 12:1–12; Luke 20:9–19

virgin (VUR-jin) *person who has not had sexual relations,* Deuteronomy 22:13–29; Isaiah 7:14; Matthew 1:23; Luke 1:34

vision (VIZ-zhun) *like a dream. God often spoke to his people in visions.*
- of Abram, Genesis 15:1
- of Daniel, Daniel 2:19
- of Peter and Cornelius, Acts 10:1–16
- of Paul, Acts 16:9

vow, *a special and serious promise often made to God.*
- rules about, Numbers 30; Deuteronomy 23:21–23
- the Nazirite, Numbers 6:1–21
- of Jephthah, Judges 11:29–40
- of Paul, Acts 18:18

W

war
- rumors of, Matthew 24:6–7; Mark 13:7–8; Luke 21:9–10
- spiritual, 2 Corinthians 10:3–4
- will end, Micah 4:1–3

warrior, divine, See "Holy War."

watchman
- examples of, 2 Samuel 18:24–27; Psalm 130:6
- prophets as watchmen, Ezekiel 3:17; Micah 7:4

water
- in creation, Genesis 1:1–2, 6–10
- bitter, Exodus 15:22–27
- from a rock, Exodus 17:1–7
- for David, 2 Samuel 23:15–17
- drink of, Matthew 10:42; Mark 9:41
- Jesus walked on, Matthew 14:22–36
- turned to wine, John 2:1–11
- living water, John 4:1–15

way
- two ways to live, Psalm 1
- Christ as the way, John 14:6
- the Way of Jesus, Acts 19:23; Acts 24:22

"Way, the," *one of the earliest names given to Christians. Jesus said he was "the way" to reach God.* Acts 9:1–2; 19:9, 23; 22:4; 24:14, 22

weapons
- the armor of God, Ephesians 6:10–18
- not of this world, 2 Corinthians 10:4
- "killed with swords," Matthew 26:52

wedding, Matthew 22:1–14; Luke 14:8; John 2:1–11

Western Sea, See "Mediterranean Sea."

widow
- examples of, Ruth 4:10; 1 Kings 17:8–24; Luke 21:2–4
- care for, Deuteronomy 24:17–22; 1 Timothy 5:3–16; James 1:27

wife
- man united with, Genesis 2:24
- the good wife, Proverbs 31:10–31
- teachings about, 1 Corinthians 7:1–16
- responsibility of, Ephesians 5:21–24, 33; Colossians 3:18; 1 Peter 3:1

wilderness, *a desert area*
- John baptizes in, Mark 1:1–8; Matthew 3:1–6, 13–17
- Israel in, Deuteronomy 8:1–5; 32:10
- will blossom, Isaiah 35

wine
- danger of, Proverbs 20:1; Ephesians 5:18
- at wedding in Cana, John 2:1–11
- for the stomach, 1 Timothy 5:23

winepress, *a pit where grapes were mashed to get the juice out. The winepress is sometimes used to describe how enemy armies will defeat people as if they were grapes crushed in a winepress.*
- examples of, Judges 6:11; Matthew 21:33
- as a symbol of punishment, Lamentations 1:15; Revelation 14:19–20; 19:15

wisdom (WIZ-d'm) *understanding what is really important in life. This wisdom comes from God.* Proverbs 1:1–2, 7; 2; 4
- Solomon asked for, 1 Kings 4:29–34
- source of, James 1:5
- a parable about, Matthew 25:1–13

wise men, *"magi"; men who studied the stars,* Genesis 41:8; Exodus 7:11; Matthew 2:1–12

witchcraft, *using the power of the devil to do magic.*
- warnings against, Deuteronomy 18:10–12; Galatians 5:19–21
- examples of, 2 Kings 9:22; 2 Chronicles 33:6

witness, Acts 1:8, 22; 2:32; 22:14–15

woman
- created by God, Genesis 2:22–23
- how to treat a, 1 Timothy 5:2, 14

word, *in the Bible often means God's message to us in the Scriptures. Jesus is called the "Word" because he shows us what God is like.*
- like a lamp, Psalm 119:105
- like a sword, Hebrews 4:12
- living in God's people, John 15:7; Colossians 3:16; 1 John 2:14
- lasts forever, Matthew 24:35; 1 Peter 1:25
- people's words, Proverbs 12:25; 25:11; Matthew 12:36–37
- as a message, 1 Peter 1:24–25; 1 John 2:14
- Jesus as the "Word," John 1:1–5, 14; 1 John 1:1–2

work
- those who won't, 2 Thessalonians 3:6–13
- of the vineyard workers, Matthew 20:1–16
- laziness, Proverbs 26:14–16

world, *the planet Earth; also the people on this earth who follow Satan.*
- as the Earth, 2 Samuel 22:16; Psalm 18:15
- as a symbol of wickedness, Romans 12:2; Ephesians 2:2

worship, *to praise and serve God.*
- commanded, Exodus 34:14; Luke 4:8; John 4:20–24

X

Xerxes (ZERK-sees) *a king of Persia; also called "Ahasuerus,"* Esther 1—10

Y

yeast (YEEST) *an ingredient used to make breads and cakes rise; used in the New Testament to stand for a person's influence over others.* See also "unleavened bread."
- as a symbol for influence, Mark 8:15; Luke 13:21

yoke, *a wooden frame that fits on the necks of animals to hold them together while working.*
- examples of, Deuteronomy 21:3; 1 Kings 19:19–21

youth
- "Remember your Creator," Ecclesiastes 12:1
- teachings about, 1 Timothy 4:12

Z

Zacchaeus (za-KEE-us) *Jewish tax collector in the city of Jericho,* Luke 19:1–8

Zadok (ZAY-dok) *priest who helped King David,* 2 Samuel 15:24–36; 17:15–21; 1 Kings 1:18–45

Zarephath (ZAIR-eh-fath) *a Canaanite town where Elijah helped a widow,* 1 Kings 17:8–24; Luke 4:25–26

Zealots (ZEL-ots) *a group of Jewish men also called "Enthusiasts." They hated the Romans for controlling their home country, and they planned to force the Romans out.*
- Simon the Zealot, Luke 6:15; Acts 1:13

Zebedee (ZEB-uh-dee) *a fisherman on Lake Galilee,* Matthew 4:21–22; Mark 1:19–20

Zechariah, father of John the Baptist (ZEK-uh-RY-uh) *a Jewish priest,* Luke 1:5–25, 57–80

Zechariah, king of Israel, *ruled for only six months; killed by Shallum,* 2 Kings 14:29; 15:8–11

Zechariah, son of Berekiah, *a prophet who wrote the next-to-the-last book in the Old Testament,* Ezra 5:1; Zechariah 1—14

Zechariah, son of Jehoiada, *a priest who taught the people to serve God,* 2 Chronicles 24:20–25

Zedekiah, son of Josiah (zed-ee-KY-uh) *the last king of Judah,* 2 Kings 24:16—25:7

Zedekiah, son of Kenaanah, *a false prophet during the time of King Ahab,* 1 Kings 22:1–24

Zedekiah, son of Maaseiah, *a false prophet in Babylon during the time of Jeremiah,* Jeremiah 29:21–23

Zephaniah (zef-uh-NY-uh) *a prophet who lived when Josiah was king of Judah; wrote the short book of Zephaniah,* Zephaniah 1:1

Zerubbabel (zeh-RUB-uh-bull) *governor of Jerusalem after the Jews had been in captivity in Babylon for seventy years.*
- returned from exile, Ezra 2:2
- built the altar of God, Ezra 3:1–6
- rebuilt the Temple, Ezra 3:7–10; 5:2

Ziba (ZY-buh) *a servant of Saul,* 2 Samuel 9:1–11; 16:1–4; 19:24–30

Zimri (ZIM-rye) *a king of Israel,* 1 Kings 16:11–20

Zion (ZY-on) *a hill inside the city of Jerusalem.* See "Mount Zion."

Ziph (ZIF) *a city about twenty-five miles south of Jerusalem,* 1 Samuel 23:14–28; 26:1–25

Zipporah (zih-PO-ruh) *the wife of Moses,* Exodus 2:15–22; 4:24–26; 18:1–3

zither (ZITH-ur) *a type of musical instrument that had about forty strings on it,* Ezekiel 3:5, 7, 10, 15